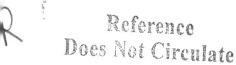

Oxford Dictionary of
National Biography

Volume 18

Oxford Dictionary of National Biography

IN ASSOCIATION WITH
The British Academy

From the earliest times to the year 2000

Edited by
H. C. G. Matthew
and
Brian Harrison

Volume 18
Ela–Fancourt

OXFORD
UNIVERSITY PRESS

OXFORD
UNIVERSITY PRESS

Great Clarendon Street, Oxford OX2 6DP

Oxford University Press is a department of the University of Oxford.
It furthers the University's objective of excellence in research, scholarship,
and education by publishing worldwide in

Oxford New York

Auckland Bangkok Buenos Aires Cape Town
Chennai Dar es Salaam Delhi Hong Kong Istanbul Karachi
Kolkata Kuala Lumpur Madrid Melbourne Mexico City Mumbai Nairobi
São Paulo Shanghai Taipei Tokyo Toronto

Oxford is a registered trade mark of Oxford University Press
in the UK and in certain other countries

Published in the United States
by Oxford University Press Inc., New York

© Oxford University Press 2004

Illustrations © individual copyright holders as listed in
'Picture credits', and reproduced with permission

Database right Oxford University Press (maker)

First published 2004

All rights reserved. No part of this material may be reproduced,
stored in a retrieval system, or transmitted, in any form or by any means,
without the prior permission in writing of Oxford University Press,
or as expressly permitted by law, or under terms agreed with the appropriate
reprographics rights organization. Enquiries concerning reproduction
outside the scope of the above should be sent to the Rights Department,
Oxford University Press, at the address above

You must not circulate this book in any other binding or cover
and you must impose this same condition on any acquirer

British Library Cataloguing in Publication Data
Data available

Library of Congress Cataloging in Publication Data
Data available: for details see volume 1, p. iv

ISBN 0-19-861368-7 (this volume)
ISBN 0-19-861411-X (set of sixty volumes)

Text captured by Alliance Phototypesetters, Pondicherry
Illustrations reproduced and archived by
Alliance Graphics Ltd, UK
Typeset in OUP Swift by Interactive Sciences Limited, Gloucester
Printed in Great Britain on acid-free paper by
Butler and Tanner Ltd,
Frome, Somerset

LIST OF ABBREVIATIONS

1 General abbreviations

AB	bachelor of arts	BCnL	bachelor of canon law
ABC	Australian Broadcasting Corporation	BCom	bachelor of commerce
ABC TV	ABC Television	BD	bachelor of divinity
act.	active	BEd	bachelor of education
A$	Australian dollar	BEng	bachelor of engineering
AD	*anno domini*	bk *pl.* bks	book(s)
AFC	Air Force Cross	BL	bachelor of law / letters / literature
AIDS	acquired immune deficiency syndrome	BLitt	bachelor of letters
AK	Alaska	BM	bachelor of medicine
AL	Alabama	BMus	bachelor of music
A level	advanced level [examination]	BP	before present
ALS	associate of the Linnean Society	BP	British Petroleum
AM	master of arts	Bros.	Brothers
AMICE	associate member of the Institution of Civil Engineers	BS	(1) bachelor of science; (2) bachelor of surgery; (3) British standard
ANZAC	Australian and New Zealand Army Corps	BSc	bachelor of science
appx *pl.* appxs	appendix(es)	BSc (Econ.)	bachelor of science (economics)
AR	Arkansas	BSc (Eng.)	bachelor of science (engineering)
ARA	associate of the Royal Academy	bt	baronet
ARCA	associate of the Royal College of Art	BTh	bachelor of theology
ARCM	associate of the Royal College of Music	*bur.*	buried
ARCO	associate of the Royal College of Organists	C.	command [identifier for published parliamentary papers]
ARIBA	associate of the Royal Institute of British Architects	*c.*	*circa*
ARP	air-raid precautions	c.	*capitulum pl. capitula:* chapter(s)
ARRC	associate of the Royal Red Cross	CA	California
ARSA	associate of the Royal Scottish Academy	Cantab.	Cantabrigiensis
art.	article / item	cap.	*capitulum pl. capitula:* chapter(s)
ASC	Army Service Corps	CB	companion of the Bath
Asch	Austrian Schilling	CBE	commander of the Order of the British Empire
ASDIC	Antisubmarine Detection Investigation Committee	CBS	Columbia Broadcasting System
ATS	Auxiliary Territorial Service	cc	cubic centimetres
ATV	Associated Television	C$	Canadian dollar
Aug	August	CD	compact disc
AZ	Arizona	Cd	command [identifier for published parliamentary papers]
b.	born	CE	Common (*or* Christian) Era
BA	bachelor of arts	cent.	century
BA (Admin.)	bachelor of arts (administration)	cf.	compare
BAFTA	British Academy of Film and Television Arts	CH	Companion of Honour
BAO	bachelor of arts in obstetrics	chap.	chapter
bap.	baptized	ChB	bachelor of surgery
BBC	British Broadcasting Corporation / Company	CI	Imperial Order of the Crown of India
BC	before Christ	CIA	Central Intelligence Agency
BCE	before the common (*or* Christian) era	CID	Criminal Investigation Department
BCE	bachelor of civil engineering	CIE	companion of the Order of the Indian Empire
BCG	bacillus of Calmette and Guérin [inoculation against tuberculosis]	Cie	Compagnie
		CLit	companion of literature
BCh	bachelor of surgery	CM	master of surgery
BChir	bachelor of surgery	cm	centimetre(s)
BCL	bachelor of civil law		

Cmd	command [identifier for published parliamentary papers]		edn	edition
CMG	companion of the Order of St Michael and St George		EEC	European Economic Community
			EFTA	European Free Trade Association
Cmnd	command [identifier for published parliamentary papers]		EICS	East India Company Service
			EMI	Electrical and Musical Industries (Ltd)
CO	Colorado		Eng.	English
Co.	company		enl.	enlarged
co.	county		ENSA	Entertainments National Service Association
col. *pl.* cols.	column(s)		ep. *pl.* epp.	*epistola(e)*
Corp.	corporation		ESP	extra-sensory perception
CSE	certificate of secondary education		esp.	especially
CSI	companion of the Order of the Star of India		esq.	esquire
CT	Connecticut		est.	estimate / estimated
CVO	commander of the Royal Victorian Order		EU	European Union
cwt	hundredweight		ex	sold by (*lit.* out of)
$	(American) dollar		excl.	excludes / excluding
d.	(1) penny (pence); (2) died		exh.	exhibited
DBE	dame commander of the Order of the British Empire		exh. cat.	exhibition catalogue
			f. *pl.* ff.	following [pages]
DCH	diploma in child health		FA	Football Association
DCh	doctor of surgery		FACP	fellow of the American College of Physicians
DCL	doctor of civil law		facs.	facsimile
DCnL	doctor of canon law		FANY	First Aid Nursing Yeomanry
DCVO	dame commander of the Royal Victorian Order		FBA	fellow of the British Academy
DD	doctor of divinity		FBI	Federation of British Industries
DE	Delaware		FCS	fellow of the Chemical Society
Dec	December		Feb	February
dem.	demolished		FEng	fellow of the Fellowship of Engineering
DEng	doctor of engineering		FFCM	fellow of the Faculty of Community Medicine
des.	destroyed		FGS	fellow of the Geological Society
DFC	Distinguished Flying Cross		fig.	figure
DipEd	diploma in education		FIMechE	fellow of the Institution of Mechanical Engineers
DipPsych	diploma in psychiatry			
diss.	dissertation		FL	Florida
DL	deputy lieutenant		*fl.*	*floruit*
DLitt	doctor of letters		FLS	fellow of the Linnean Society
DLittCelt	doctor of Celtic letters		FM	frequency modulation
DM	(1) Deutschmark; (2) doctor of medicine; (3) doctor of musical arts		fol. *pl.* fols.	folio(s)
			Fr	French francs
DMus	doctor of music		Fr.	French
DNA	dioxyribonucleic acid		FRAeS	fellow of the Royal Aeronautical Society
doc.	document		FRAI	fellow of the Royal Anthropological Institute
DOL	doctor of oriental learning		FRAM	fellow of the Royal Academy of Music
DPH	diploma in public health		FRAS	(1) fellow of the Royal Asiatic Society; (2) fellow of the Royal Astronomical Society
DPhil	doctor of philosophy			
DPM	diploma in psychological medicine		FRCM	fellow of the Royal College of Music
DSC	Distinguished Service Cross		FRCO	fellow of the Royal College of Organists
DSc	doctor of science		FRCOG	fellow of the Royal College of Obstetricians and Gynaecologists
DSc (Econ.)	doctor of science (economics)			
DSc (Eng.)	doctor of science (engineering)		FRCP(C)	fellow of the Royal College of Physicians of Canada
DSM	Distinguished Service Medal			
DSO	companion of the Distinguished Service Order		FRCP (Edin.)	fellow of the Royal College of Physicians of Edinburgh
DSocSc	doctor of social science		FRCP (Lond.)	fellow of the Royal College of Physicians of London
DTech	doctor of technology			
DTh	doctor of theology		FRCPath	fellow of the Royal College of Pathologists
DTM	diploma in tropical medicine		FRCPsych	fellow of the Royal College of Psychiatrists
DTMH	diploma in tropical medicine and hygiene		FRCS	fellow of the Royal College of Surgeons
DU	doctor of the university		FRGS	fellow of the Royal Geographical Society
DUniv	doctor of the university		FRIBA	fellow of the Royal Institute of British Architects
dwt	pennyweight		FRICS	fellow of the Royal Institute of Chartered Surveyors
EC	European Community			
ed. *pl.* eds.	edited / edited by / editor(s)		FRS	fellow of the Royal Society
Edin.	Edinburgh		FRSA	fellow of the Royal Society of Arts

FRSCM	fellow of the Royal School of Church Music	ISO	companion of the Imperial Service Order
FRSE	fellow of the Royal Society of Edinburgh	It.	Italian
FRSL	fellow of the Royal Society of Literature	ITA	Independent Television Authority
FSA	fellow of the Society of Antiquaries	ITV	Independent Television
ft	foot *pl.* feet	Jan	January
FTCL	fellow of Trinity College of Music, London	JP	justice of the peace
ft-lb per min.	foot-pounds per minute [unit of horsepower]	jun.	junior
FZS	fellow of the Zoological Society	KB	knight of the Order of the Bath
GA	Georgia	KBE	knight commander of the Order of the British Empire
GBE	knight or dame grand cross of the Order of the British Empire	KC	king's counsel
GCB	knight grand cross of the Order of the Bath	kcal	kilocalorie
GCE	general certificate of education	KCB	knight commander of the Order of the Bath
GCH	knight grand cross of the Royal Guelphic Order	KCH	knight commander of the Royal Guelphic Order
GCHQ	government communications headquarters	KCIE	knight commander of the Order of the Indian Empire
GCIE	knight grand commander of the Order of the Indian Empire	KCMG	knight commander of the Order of St Michael and St George
GCMG	knight or dame grand cross of the Order of St Michael and St George	KCSI	knight commander of the Order of the Star of India
GCSE	general certificate of secondary education	KCVO	knight commander of the Royal Victorian Order
GCSI	knight grand commander of the Order of the Star of India	keV	kilo-electron-volt
GCStJ	bailiff or dame grand cross of the order of St John of Jerusalem	KG	knight of the Order of the Garter
		KGB	[Soviet committee of state security]
GCVO	knight or dame grand cross of the Royal Victorian Order	KH	knight of the Royal Guelphic Order
		KLM	Koninklijke Luchtvaart Maatschappij (Royal Dutch Air Lines)
GEC	General Electric Company		
Ger.	German	km	kilometre(s)
GI	government (*or* general) issue	KP	knight of the Order of St Patrick
GMT	Greenwich mean time	KS	Kansas
GP	general practitioner	KT	knight of the Order of the Thistle
GPU	[Soviet special police unit]	kt	knight
GSO	general staff officer	KY	Kentucky
Heb.	Hebrew	£	pound(s) sterling
HEICS	Honourable East India Company Service	£E	Egyptian pound
HI	Hawaii	L	lira *pl.* lire
HIV	human immunodeficiency virus	l. *pl.* ll.	line(s)
HK$	Hong Kong dollar	LA	Lousiana
HM	his / her majesty('s)	LAA	light anti-aircraft
HMAS	his / her majesty's Australian ship	LAH	licentiate of the Apothecaries' Hall, Dublin
HMNZS	his / her majesty's New Zealand ship	Lat.	Latin
HMS	his / her majesty's ship	lb	pound(s), unit of weight
HMSO	His / Her Majesty's Stationery Office	LDS	licence in dental surgery
HMV	His Master's Voice	*lit.*	literally
Hon.	Honourable	LittB	bachelor of letters
hp	horsepower	LittD	doctor of letters
hr	hour(s)	LKQCPI	licentiate of the King and Queen's College of Physicians, Ireland
HRH	his / her royal highness		
HTV	Harlech Television	LLA	lady literate in arts
IA	Iowa	LLB	bachelor of laws
ibid.	*ibidem*: in the same place	LLD	doctor of laws
ICI	Imperial Chemical Industries (Ltd)	LLM	master of laws
ID	Idaho	LM	licentiate in midwifery
IL	Illinois	LP	long-playing record
illus.	illustration	LRAM	licentiate of the Royal Academy of Music
illustr.	illustrated	LRCP	licentiate of the Royal College of Physicians
IN	Indiana	LRCPS (Glasgow)	licentiate of the Royal College of Physicians and Surgeons of Glasgow
in.	inch(es)		
Inc.	Incorporated	LRCS	licentiate of the Royal College of Surgeons
incl.	includes / including	LSA	licentiate of the Society of Apothecaries
IOU	I owe you	LSD	lysergic acid diethylamide
IQ	intelligence quotient	LVO	lieutenant of the Royal Victorian Order
Ir£	Irish pound	M. *pl.* MM.	Monsieur *pl.* Messieurs
IRA	Irish Republican Army	m	metre(s)

m. *pl.* mm.	membrane(s)		ND	North Dakota
MA	(1) Massachusetts; (2) master of arts		n.d.	no date
MAI	master of engineering		NE	Nebraska
MB	bachelor of medicine		*nem. con.*	*nemine contradicente*: unanimously
MBA	master of business administration		new ser.	new series
MBE	member of the Order of the British Empire		NH	New Hampshire
MC	Military Cross		NHS	National Health Service
MCC	Marylebone Cricket Club		NJ	New Jersey
MCh	master of surgery		NKVD	[Soviet people's commissariat for internal affairs]
MChir	master of surgery		NM	New Mexico
MCom	master of commerce		nm	nanometre(s)
MD	(1) doctor of medicine; (2) Maryland		no. *pl.* nos.	number(s)
MDMA	methylenedioxymethamphetamine		Nov	November
ME	Maine		n.p.	no place [of publication]
MEd	master of education		NS	new style
MEng	master of engineering		NV	Nevada
MEP	member of the European parliament		NY	New York
MG	Morris Garages		NZBS	New Zealand Broadcasting Service
MGM	Metro-Goldwyn-Mayer		OBE	officer of the Order of the British Empire
Mgr	Monsignor		obit.	obituary
MI	(1) Michigan; (2) military intelligence		Oct	October
MI1c	[secret intelligence department]		OCTU	officer cadets training unit
MI5	[military intelligence department]		OECD	Organization for Economic Co-operation and Development
MI6	[secret intelligence department]		OEEC	Organization for European Economic Co-operation
MI9	[secret escape service]		OFM	order of Friars Minor [Franciscans]
MICE	member of the Institution of Civil Engineers		OFMCap	Ordine Frati Minori Cappucini: member of the Capuchin order
MIEE	member of the Institution of Electrical Engineers		OH	Ohio
min.	minute(s)		OK	Oklahoma
Mk	mark		O level	ordinary level [examination]
ML	(1) licentiate of medicine; (2) master of laws		OM	Order of Merit
MLitt	master of letters		OP	order of Preachers [Dominicans]
Mlle	Mademoiselle		op. *pl.* opp.	opus *pl.* opera
mm	millimetre(s)		OPEC	Organization of Petroleum Exporting Countries
Mme	Madame		OR	Oregon
MN	Minnesota		orig.	original
MO	Missouri		OS	old style
MOH	medical officer of health		OSB	Order of St Benedict
MP	member of parliament		OTC	Officers' Training Corps
m.p.h.	miles per hour		OWS	Old Watercolour Society
MPhil	master of philosophy		Oxon.	Oxoniensis
MRCP	member of the Royal College of Physicians		p. *pl.* pp.	page(s)
MRCS	member of the Royal College of Surgeons		PA	Pennsylvania
MRCVS	member of the Royal College of Veterinary Surgeons		p.a.	per annum
MRIA	member of the Royal Irish Academy		para.	paragraph
MS	(1) master of science; (2) Mississippi		PAYE	pay as you earn
MS *pl.* MSS	manuscript(s)		pbk *pl.* pbks	paperback(s)
MSc	master of science		*per.*	[during the] period
MSc (Econ.)	master of science (economics)		PhD	doctor of philosophy
MT	Montana		pl.	(1) plate(s); (2) plural
MusB	bachelor of music		priv. coll.	private collection
MusBac	bachelor of music		pt *pl.* pts	part(s)
MusD	doctor of music		pubd	published
MV	motor vessel		PVC	polyvinyl chloride
MVO	member of the Royal Victorian Order		q. *pl.* qq.	(1) question(s); (2) quire(s)
n. *pl.* nn.	note(s)		QC	queen's counsel
NAAFI	Navy, Army, and Air Force Institutes		R	rand
NASA	National Aeronautics and Space Administration		R.	Rex / Regina
NATO	North Atlantic Treaty Organization		*r*	recto
NBC	National Broadcasting Corporation		r.	reigned / ruled
NC	North Carolina		RA	Royal Academy / Royal Academician
NCO	non-commissioned officer			

RAC	Royal Automobile Club
RAF	Royal Air Force
RAFVR	Royal Air Force Volunteer Reserve
RAM	[member of the] Royal Academy of Music
RAMC	Royal Army Medical Corps
RCA	Royal College of Art
RCNC	Royal Corps of Naval Constructors
RCOG	Royal College of Obstetricians and Gynaecologists
RDI	royal designer for industry
RE	Royal Engineers
repr. *pl.* reprs.	reprint(s) / reprinted
repro.	reproduced
rev.	revised / revised by / reviser / revision
Revd	Reverend
RHA	Royal Hibernian Academy
RI	(1) Rhode Island; (2) Royal Institute of Painters in Water-Colours
RIBA	Royal Institute of British Architects
RIN	Royal Indian Navy
RM	Reichsmark
RMS	Royal Mail steamer
RN	Royal Navy
RNA	ribonucleic acid
RNAS	Royal Naval Air Service
RNR	Royal Naval Reserve
RNVR	Royal Naval Volunteer Reserve
RO	Record Office
r.p.m.	revolutions per minute
RRS	royal research ship
Rs	rupees
RSA	(1) Royal Scottish Academician; (2) Royal Society of Arts
RSPCA	Royal Society for the Prevention of Cruelty to Animals
Rt Hon.	Right Honourable
Rt Revd	Right Reverend
RUC	Royal Ulster Constabulary
Russ.	Russian
RWS	Royal Watercolour Society
S4C	Sianel Pedwar Cymru
s.	shilling(s)
s.a.	*sub anno*: under the year
SABC	South African Broadcasting Corporation
SAS	Special Air Service
SC	South Carolina
ScD	doctor of science
S$	Singapore dollar
SD	South Dakota
sec.	second(s)
sel.	selected
sen.	senior
Sept	September
ser.	series
SHAPE	supreme headquarters allied powers, Europe
SIDRO	Société Internationale d'Énergie Hydro-Électrique
sig. *pl.* sigs.	signature(s)
sing.	singular
SIS	Secret Intelligence Service
SJ	Society of Jesus

Skr	Swedish krona
Span.	Spanish
SPCK	Society for Promoting Christian Knowledge
SS	(1) Santissimi; (2) Schutzstaffel; (3) steam ship
STB	bachelor of theology
STD	doctor of theology
STM	master of theology
STP	doctor of theology
supp.	supposedly
suppl. *pl.* suppls.	supplement(s)
s.v.	*sub verbo* / *sub voce*: under the word / heading
SY	steam yacht
TA	Territorial Army
TASS	[Soviet news agency]
TB	tuberculosis (*lit.* tubercle bacillus)
TD	(1) *teachtaí dála* (member of the Dáil); (2) territorial decoration
TN	Tennessee
TNT	trinitrotoluene
trans.	translated / translated by / translation / translator
TT	tourist trophy
TUC	Trades Union Congress
TX	Texas
U-boat	*Unterseeboot*: submarine
Ufa	Universum-Film AG
UMIST	University of Manchester Institute of Science and Technology
UN	United Nations
UNESCO	United Nations Educational, Scientific, and Cultural Organization
UNICEF	United Nations International Children's Emergency Fund
unpubd	unpublished
USS	United States ship
UT	Utah
v	verso
v.	versus
VA	Virginia
VAD	Voluntary Aid Detachment
VC	Victoria Cross
VE-day	victory in Europe day
Ven.	Venerable
VJ-day	victory over Japan day
vol. *pl.* vols.	volume(s)
VT	Vermont
WA	Washington [state]
WAAC	Women's Auxiliary Army Corps
WAAF	Women's Auxiliary Air Force
WEA	Workers' Educational Association
WHO	World Health Organization
WI	Wisconsin
WRAF	Women's Royal Air Force
WRNS	Women's Royal Naval Service
WV	West Virginia
WVS	Women's Voluntary Service
WY	Wyoming
¥	yen
YMCA	Young Men's Christian Association
YWCA	Young Women's Christian Association

2 Institution abbreviations

All Souls Oxf.	All Souls College, Oxford
AM Oxf.	Ashmolean Museum, Oxford
Balliol Oxf.	Balliol College, Oxford
BBC WAC	BBC Written Archives Centre, Reading
Beds. & Luton ARS	Bedfordshire and Luton Archives and Record Service, Bedford
Berks. RO	Berkshire Record Office, Reading
BFI	British Film Institute, London
BFI NFTVA	British Film Institute, London, National Film and Television Archive
BGS	British Geological Survey, Keyworth, Nottingham
Birm. CA	Birmingham Central Library, Birmingham City Archives
Birm. CL	Birmingham Central Library
BL	British Library, London
BL NSA	British Library, London, National Sound Archive
BL OIOC	British Library, London, Oriental and India Office Collections
BLPES	London School of Economics and Political Science, British Library of Political and Economic Science
BM	British Museum, London
Bodl. Oxf.	Bodleian Library, Oxford
Bodl. RH	Bodleian Library of Commonwealth and African Studies at Rhodes House, Oxford
Borth. Inst.	Borthwick Institute of Historical Research, University of York
Boston PL	Boston Public Library, Massachusetts
Bristol RO	Bristol Record Office
Bucks. RLSS	Buckinghamshire Records and Local Studies Service, Aylesbury
CAC Cam.	Churchill College, Cambridge, Churchill Archives Centre
Cambs. AS	Cambridgeshire Archive Service
CCC Cam.	Corpus Christi College, Cambridge
CCC Oxf.	Corpus Christi College, Oxford
Ches. & Chester ALSS	Cheshire and Chester Archives and Local Studies Service
Christ Church Oxf.	Christ Church, Oxford
Christies	Christies, London
City Westm. AC	City of Westminster Archives Centre, London
CKS	Centre for Kentish Studies, Maidstone
CLRO	Corporation of London Records Office
Coll. Arms	College of Arms, London
Col. U.	Columbia University, New York
Cornwall RO	Cornwall Record Office, Truro
Courtauld Inst.	Courtauld Institute of Art, London
CUL	Cambridge University Library
Cumbria AS	Cumbria Archive Service
Derbys. RO	Derbyshire Record Office, Matlock
Devon RO	Devon Record Office, Exeter
Dorset RO	Dorset Record Office, Dorchester
Duke U.	Duke University, Durham, North Carolina
Duke U., Perkins L.	Duke University, Durham, North Carolina, William R. Perkins Library
Durham Cath. CL	Durham Cathedral, chapter library
Durham RO	Durham Record Office
DWL	Dr Williams's Library, London
Essex RO	Essex Record Office
E. Sussex RO	East Sussex Record Office, Lewes
Eton	Eton College, Berkshire
FM Cam.	Fitzwilliam Museum, Cambridge
Folger	Folger Shakespeare Library, Washington, DC
Garr. Club	Garrick Club, London
Girton Cam.	Girton College, Cambridge
GL	Guildhall Library, London
Glos. RO	Gloucestershire Record Office, Gloucester
Gon. & Caius Cam.	Gonville and Caius College, Cambridge
Gov. Art Coll.	Government Art Collection
GS Lond.	Geological Society of London
Hants. RO	Hampshire Record Office, Winchester
Harris Man. Oxf.	Harris Manchester College, Oxford
Harvard TC	Harvard Theatre Collection, Harvard University, Cambridge, Massachusetts, Nathan Marsh Pusey Library
Harvard U.	Harvard University, Cambridge, Massachusetts
Harvard U., Houghton L.	Harvard University, Cambridge, Massachusetts, Houghton Library
Herefs. RO	Herefordshire Record Office, Hereford
Herts. ALS	Hertfordshire Archives and Local Studies, Hertford
Hist. Soc. Penn.	Historical Society of Pennsylvania, Philadelphia
HLRO	House of Lords Record Office, London
Hult. Arch.	Hulton Archive, London and New York
Hunt. L.	Huntington Library, San Marino, California
ICL	Imperial College, London
Inst. CE	Institution of Civil Engineers, London
Inst. EE	Institution of Electrical Engineers, London
IWM	Imperial War Museum, London
IWM FVA	Imperial War Museum, London, Film and Video Archive
IWM SA	Imperial War Museum, London, Sound Archive
JRL	John Rylands University Library of Manchester
King's AC Cam.	King's College Archives Centre, Cambridge
King's Cam.	King's College, Cambridge
King's Lond.	King's College, London
King's Lond., Liddell Hart C.	King's College, London, Liddell Hart Centre for Military Archives
Lancs. RO	Lancashire Record Office, Preston
L. Cong.	Library of Congress, Washington, DC
Leics. RO	Leicestershire, Leicester, and Rutland Record Office, Leicester
Lincs. Arch.	Lincolnshire Archives, Lincoln
Linn. Soc.	Linnean Society of London
LMA	London Metropolitan Archives
LPL	Lambeth Palace, London
Lpool RO	Liverpool Record Office and Local Studies Service
LUL	London University Library
Magd. Cam.	Magdalene College, Cambridge
Magd. Oxf.	Magdalen College, Oxford
Man. City Gall.	Manchester City Galleries
Man. CL	Manchester Central Library
Mass. Hist. Soc.	Massachusetts Historical Society, Boston
Merton Oxf.	Merton College, Oxford
MHS Oxf.	Museum of the History of Science, Oxford
Mitchell L., Glas.	Mitchell Library, Glasgow
Mitchell L., NSW	State Library of New South Wales, Sydney, Mitchell Library
Morgan L.	Pierpont Morgan Library, New York
NA Canada	National Archives of Canada, Ottawa
NA Ire.	National Archives of Ireland, Dublin
NAM	National Army Museum, London
NA Scot.	National Archives of Scotland, Edinburgh
News Int. RO	News International Record Office, London
NG Ire.	National Gallery of Ireland, Dublin

NG Scot.	National Gallery of Scotland, Edinburgh
NHM	Natural History Museum, London
NL Aus.	National Library of Australia, Canberra
NL Ire.	National Library of Ireland, Dublin
NL NZ	National Library of New Zealand, Wellington
NL NZ, Turnbull L.	National Library of New Zealand, Wellington, Alexander Turnbull Library
NL Scot.	National Library of Scotland, Edinburgh
NL Wales	National Library of Wales, Aberystwyth
NMG Wales	National Museum and Gallery of Wales, Cardiff
NMM	National Maritime Museum, London
Norfolk RO	Norfolk Record Office, Norwich
Northants. RO	Northamptonshire Record Office, Northampton
Northumbd RO	Northumberland Record Office
Notts. Arch.	Nottinghamshire Archives, Nottingham
NPG	National Portrait Gallery, London
NRA	National Archives, London, Historical Manuscripts Commission, National Register of Archives
Nuffield Oxf.	Nuffield College, Oxford
N. Yorks. CRO	North Yorkshire County Record Office, Northallerton
NYPL	New York Public Library
Oxf. UA	Oxford University Archives
Oxf. U. Mus. NH	Oxford University Museum of Natural History
Oxon. RO	Oxfordshire Record Office, Oxford
Pembroke Cam.	Pembroke College, Cambridge
PRO	National Archives, London, Public Record Office
PRO NIre.	Public Record Office for Northern Ireland, Belfast
Pusey Oxf.	Pusey House, Oxford
RA	Royal Academy of Arts, London
Ransom HRC	Harry Ransom Humanities Research Center, University of Texas, Austin
RAS	Royal Astronomical Society, London
RBG Kew	Royal Botanic Gardens, Kew, London
RCP Lond.	Royal College of Physicians of London
RCS Eng.	Royal College of Surgeons of England, London
RGS	Royal Geographical Society, London
RIBA	Royal Institute of British Architects, London
RIBA BAL	Royal Institute of British Architects, London, British Architectural Library
Royal Arch.	Royal Archives, Windsor Castle, Berkshire [by gracious permission of her majesty the queen]
Royal Irish Acad.	Royal Irish Academy, Dublin
Royal Scot. Acad.	Royal Scottish Academy, Edinburgh
RS	Royal Society, London
RSA	Royal Society of Arts, London
RS Friends, Lond.	Religious Society of Friends, London
St Ant. Oxf.	St Antony's College, Oxford
St John Cam.	St John's College, Cambridge
S. Antiquaries, Lond.	Society of Antiquaries of London
Sci. Mus.	Science Museum, London
Scot. NPG	Scottish National Portrait Gallery, Edinburgh
Scott Polar RI	University of Cambridge, Scott Polar Research Institute
Sheff. Arch.	Sheffield Archives
Shrops. RRC	Shropshire Records and Research Centre, Shrewsbury
SOAS	School of Oriental and African Studies, London
Som. ARS	Somerset Archive and Record Service, Taunton
Staffs. RO	Staffordshire Record Office, Stafford

Suffolk RO	Suffolk Record Office
Surrey HC	Surrey History Centre, Woking
TCD	Trinity College, Dublin
Trinity Cam.	Trinity College, Cambridge
U. Aberdeen	University of Aberdeen
U. Birm.	University of Birmingham
U. Birm. L.	University of Birmingham Library
U. Cal.	University of California
U. Cam.	University of Cambridge
UCL	University College, London
U. Durham	University of Durham
U. Durham L.	University of Durham Library
U. Edin.	University of Edinburgh
U. Edin., New Coll.	University of Edinburgh, New College
U. Edin., New Coll. L.	University of Edinburgh, New College Library
U. Edin. L.	University of Edinburgh Library
U. Glas.	University of Glasgow
U. Glas. L.	University of Glasgow Library
U. Hull	University of Hull
U. Hull, Brynmor Jones L.	University of Hull, Brynmor Jones Library
U. Leeds	University of Leeds
U. Leeds, Brotherton L.	University of Leeds, Brotherton Library
U. Lond.	University of London
U. Lpool	University of Liverpool
U. Lpool L.	University of Liverpool Library
U. Mich.	University of Michigan, Ann Arbor
U. Mich., Clements L.	University of Michigan, Ann Arbor, William L. Clements Library
U. Newcastle	University of Newcastle upon Tyne
U. Newcastle, Robinson L.	University of Newcastle upon Tyne, Robinson Library
U. Nott.	University of Nottingham
U. Nott. L.	University of Nottingham Library
U. Oxf.	University of Oxford
U. Reading	University of Reading
U. Reading L.	University of Reading Library
U. St Andr.	University of St Andrews
U. St Andr. L.	University of St Andrews Library
U. Southampton	University of Southampton
U. Southampton L.	University of Southampton Library
U. Sussex	University of Sussex, Brighton
U. Texas	University of Texas, Austin
U. Wales	University of Wales
U. Warwick Mod. RC	University of Warwick, Coventry, Modern Records Centre
V&A	Victoria and Albert Museum, London
V&A NAL	Victoria and Albert Museum, London, National Art Library
Warks. CRO	Warwickshire County Record Office, Warwick
Wellcome L.	Wellcome Library for the History and Understanding of Medicine, London
Westm. DA	Westminster Diocesan Archives, London
Wilts. & Swindon RO	Wiltshire and Swindon Record Office, Trowbridge
Worcs. RO	Worcestershire Record Office, Worcester
W. Sussex RO	West Sussex Record Office, Chichester
W. Yorks. AS	West Yorkshire Archive Service
Yale U.	Yale University, New Haven, Connecticut
Yale U., Beinecke L.	Yale University, New Haven, Connecticut, Beinecke Rare Book and Manuscript Library
Yale U. CBA	Yale University, New Haven, Connecticut, Yale Center for British Art

3 Bibliographic abbreviations

Adams, *Drama*
W. D. Adams, *A dictionary of the drama*, 1: *A–G* (1904); 2: *H–Z* (1956) [vol. 2 microfilm only]

AFM
J O'Donovan, ed. and trans., *Annala rioghachta Eireann / Annals of the kingdom of Ireland by the four masters*, 7 vols. (1848–51); 2nd edn (1856); 3rd edn (1990)

Allibone, *Dict.*
S. A. Allibone, *A critical dictionary of English literature and British and American authors*, 3 vols. (1859–71); suppl. by J. F. Kirk, 2 vols. (1891)

ANB
J. A. Garraty and M. C. Carnes, eds., *American national biography*, 24 vols. (1999)

Anderson, *Scot. nat.*
W. Anderson, *The Scottish nation, or, The surnames, families, literature, honours, and biographical history of the people of Scotland*, 3 vols. (1859–63)

Ann. mon.
H. R. Luard, ed., *Annales monastici*, 5 vols., Rolls Series, 36 (1864–9)

Ann. Ulster
S. Mac Airt and G. Mac Niocaill, eds., *Annals of Ulster (to AD 1131)* (1983)

APC
Acts of the privy council of England, new ser., 46 vols. (1890–1964)

APS
The acts of the parliaments of Scotland, 12 vols. in 13 (1814–75)

Arber, *Regs. Stationers*
F. Arber, ed., *A transcript of the registers of the Company of Stationers of London, 1554–1640 AD*, 5 vols. (1875–94)

ArchR
Architectural Review

ASC
D. Whitelock, D. C. Douglas, and S. I. Tucker, ed. and trans., *The Anglo-Saxon Chronicle: a revised translation* (1961)

AS chart.
P. H. Sawyer, *Anglo-Saxon charters: an annotated list and bibliography*, Royal Historical Society Guides and Handbooks (1968)

AusDB
D. Pike and others, eds., *Australian dictionary of biography*, 16 vols. (1966–2002)

Baker, *Serjeants*
J. H. Baker, *The order of serjeants at law*, SeldS, suppl. ser., 5 (1984)

Bale, *Cat.*
J. Bale, *Scriptorum illustrium Maioris Brytannie, quam nunc Angliam et Scotiam vocant: catalogus*, 2 vols. in 1 (Basel, 1557–9); facs. edn (1971)

Bale, *Index*
J. Bale, *Index Britanniae scriptorum*, ed. R. L. Poole and M. Bateson (1902); facs. edn (1990)

BBCS
Bulletin of the Board of Celtic Studies

BDMBR
J. O. Baylen and N. J. Gossman, eds., *Biographical dictionary of modern British radicals*, 3 vols. in 4 (1979–88)

Bede, *Hist. eccl.*
Bede's Ecclesiastical history of the English people, ed. and trans. B. Colgrave and R. A. B. Mynors, OMT (1969); repr. (1991)

Bénézit, *Dict.*
E. Bénézit, *Dictionnaire critique et documentaire des peintres, sculpteurs, dessinateurs et graveurs*, 3 vols. (Paris, 1911–23); new edn, 8 vols. (1948–66), repr. (1966); 3rd edn, rev. and enl., 10 vols. (1976); 4th edn, 14 vols. (1999)

BIHR
Bulletin of the Institute of Historical Research

Birch, *Seals*
W. de Birch, *Catalogue of seals in the department of manuscripts in the British Museum*, 6 vols. (1887–1900)

Bishop Burnet's History
Bishop Burnet's History of his own time, ed. M. J. Routh, 2nd edn, 6 vols. (1833)

Blackwood
Blackwood's [Edinburgh] Magazine, 328 vols. (1817–1980)

Blain, Clements & Grundy, *Feminist comp.*
V. Blain, P. Clements, and I. Grundy, eds., *The feminist companion to literature in English* (1990)

BL cat.
The British Library general catalogue of printed books [in 360 vols. with suppls., also CD-ROM and online]

BMJ
British Medical Journal

Boase & Courtney, *Bibl. Corn.*
G. C. Boase and W. P. Courtney, *Bibliotheca Cornubiensis: a catalogue of the writings … of Cornishmen*, 3 vols. (1874–82)

Boase, *Mod. Eng. biog.*
F. Boase, *Modern English biography: containing many thousand concise memoirs of persons who have died since the year 1850*, 6 vols. (privately printed, Truro, 1892–1921); repr. (1965)

Boswell, *Life*
Boswell's Life of Johnson: together with Journal of a tour to the Hebrides and Johnson's Diary of a journey into north Wales, ed. G. B. Hill, enl. edn, rev. L. F. Powell, 6 vols. (1934–50); 2nd edn (1964); repr. (1971)

Brown & Stratton, *Brit. mus.*
J. D. Brown and S. S. Stratton, *British musical biography* (1897)

Bryan, *Painters*
M. Bryan, *A biographical and critical dictionary of painters and engravers*, 2 vols. (1816); new edn, ed. G. Stanley (1849); new edn, ed. R. E. Graves and W. Armstrong, 2 vols. (1886–9); [4th edn], ed. G. C. Williamson, 5 vols. (1903–5) [various reprs.]

Burke, *Gen. GB*
J. Burke, *A genealogical and heraldic history of the commoners of Great Britain and Ireland*, 4 vols. (1833–8); new edn as *A genealogical and heraldic dictionary of the landed gentry of Great Britain and Ireland*, 3 vols. [1843–9] [many later edns]

Burke, *Gen. Ire.*
J. B. Burke, *A genealogical and heraldic history of the landed gentry of Ireland* (1899); 2nd edn (1904); 3rd edn (1912); 4th edn (1958); 5th edn as *Burke's Irish family records* (1976)

Burke, *Peerage*
J. Burke, *A general [later edns A genealogical] and heraldic dictionary of the peerage and baronetage of the United Kingdom* [later edns *the British empire*] (1829–)

Burney, *Hist. mus.*
C. Burney, *A general history of music, from the earliest ages to the present period*, 4 vols. (1776–89)

Burtchaell & Sadleir, *Alum. Dubl.*
G. D. Burtchaell and T. U. Sadleir, *Alumni Dublinenses: a register of the students, graduates, and provosts of Trinity College* (1924); [2nd edn], with suppl., in 2 pts (1935)

Calamy rev.
A. G. Matthews, *Calamy revised* (1934); repr. (1988)

CCI
Calendar of confirmations and inventories granted and given up in the several commissariots of Scotland (1876–)

CClR
Calendar of the close rolls preserved in the Public Record Office, 47 vols. (1892–1963)

CDS
J. Bain, ed., *Calendar of documents relating to Scotland*, 4 vols., PRO (1881–8); suppl. vol. 5, ed. G. G. Simpson and J. D. Galbraith [1986]

CEPR letters
W. H. Bliss, C. Johnson, and J. Twemlow, eds., *Calendar of entries in the papal registers relating to Great Britain and Ireland: papal letters* (1893–)

CGPLA
Calendars of the grants of probate and letters of administration [in 4 ser.: England & Wales, Northern Ireland, Ireland, and Éire]

Chambers, *Scots.*
R. Chambers, ed., *A biographical dictionary of eminent Scotsmen*, 4 vols. (1832–5)

Chancery records
chancery records pubd by the PRO

Chancery records (RC)
chancery records pubd by the Record Commissions

CIPM	*Calendar of inquisitions post mortem*, [20 vols.], PRO (1904–); also *Henry VII*, 3 vols. (1898–1955)
Clarendon, *Hist. rebellion*	E. Hyde, earl of Clarendon, *The history of the rebellion and civil wars in England*, 6 vols. (1888); repr. (1958) and (1992)
Cobbett, *Parl. hist.*	W. Cobbett and J. Wright, eds., *Cobbett's Parliamentary history of England*, 36 vols. (1806–1820)
Colvin, *Archs.*	H. Colvin, *A biographical dictionary of British architects, 1600–1840*, 3rd edn (1995)
Cooper, *Ath. Cantab.*	C. H. Cooper and T. Cooper, *Athenae Cantabrigienses*, 3 vols. (1858–1913); repr. (1967)
CPR	*Calendar of the patent rolls preserved in the Public Record Office* (1891–)
Crockford	*Crockford's Clerical Directory*
CS	Camden Society
CSP	*Calendar of state papers* [in 11 ser.: *domestic, Scotland, Scottish series, Ireland, colonial, Commonwealth, foreign, Spain* [at Simancas], *Rome, Milan*, and *Venice*]
CYS	Canterbury and York Society
DAB	*Dictionary of American biography*, 21 vols. (1928–36), repr. in 11 vols. (1964); 10 suppls. (1944–96)
DBB	D. J. Jeremy, ed., *Dictionary of business biography*, 5 vols. (1984–6)
DCB	G. W. Brown and others, *Dictionary of Canadian biography*, [14 vols.] (1966–)
Debrett's Peerage	*Debrett's Peerage* (1803–) [sometimes *Debrett's Illustrated peerage*]
Desmond, *Botanists*	R. Desmond, *Dictionary of British and Irish botanists and horticulturists* (1977); rev. edn (1994)
Dir. Brit. archs.	A. Felstead, J. Franklin, and L. Pinfield, eds., *Directory of British architects, 1834–1900* (1993); 2nd edn, ed. A. Brodie and others, 2 vols. (2001)
DLB	J. M. Bellamy and J. Saville, eds., *Dictionary of labour biography*, [10 vols.] (1972–)
DLitB	Dictionary of Literary Biography
DNB	*Dictionary of national biography*, 63 vols. (1885–1900), suppl., 3 vols. (1901); repr. in 22 vols. (1908–9); 10 further suppls. (1912–96); *Missing persons* (1993)
DNZB	W. H. Oliver and C. Orange, eds., *The dictionary of New Zealand biography*, 5 vols. (1990–2000)
DSAB	W. J. de Kock and others, eds., *Dictionary of South African biography*, 5 vols. (1968–87)
DSB	C. C. Gillispie and F. L. Holmes, eds., *Dictionary of scientific biography*, 16 vols. (1970–80); repr. in 8 vols. (1981); 2 vol. suppl. (1990)
DSBB	A. Slaven and S. Checkland, eds., *Dictionary of Scottish business biography, 1860–1960*, 2 vols. (1986–90)
DSCHT	N. M. de S. Cameron and others, eds., *Dictionary of Scottish church history and theology* (1993)
Dugdale, *Monasticon*	W. Dugdale, *Monasticon Anglicanum*, 3 vols. (1655–72); 2nd edn, 3 vols. (1661–82); new edn, ed. J. Caley, J. Ellis, and B. Bandinel, 6 vols. in 8 pts (1817–30); repr. (1846) and (1970)
DWB	J. E. Lloyd and others, eds., *Dictionary of Welsh biography down to 1940* (1959) [Eng. trans. of *Y bywgraffiadur Cymreig hyd 1940*, 2nd edn (1954)]
EdinR	*Edinburgh Review, or, Critical Journal*
EETS	Early English Text Society
Emden, *Cam.*	A. B. Emden, *A biographical register of the University of Cambridge to 1500* (1963)
Emden, *Oxf.*	A. B. Emden, *A biographical register of the University of Oxford to AD 1500*, 3 vols. (1957–9); also *A biographical register of the University of Oxford, AD 1501 to 1540* (1974)
EngHR	*English Historical Review*
Engraved Brit. ports.	F. M. O'Donoghue and H. M. Hake, *Catalogue of engraved British portraits preserved in the department of prints and drawings in the British Museum*, 6 vols. (1908–25)
ER	The English Reports, 178 vols. (1900–32)
ESTC	*English short title catalogue, 1475–1800* [CD-ROM and online]
Evelyn, *Diary*	*The diary of John Evelyn*, ed. E. S. De Beer, 6 vols. (1955); repr. (2000)
Farington, *Diary*	*The diary of Joseph Farington*, ed. K. Garlick and others, 17 vols. (1978–98)
Fasti Angl. (Hardy)	J. Le Neve, *Fasti ecclesiae Anglicanae*, ed. T. D. Hardy, 3 vols. (1854)
Fasti Angl., 1066–1300	[J. Le Neve], *Fasti ecclesiae Anglicanae, 1066–1300*, ed. D. E. Greenway and J. S. Barrow, [8 vols.] (1968–)
Fasti Angl., 1300–1541	[J. Le Neve], *Fasti ecclesiae Anglicanae, 1300–1541*, 12 vols. (1962–7)
Fasti Angl., 1541–1857	[J. Le Neve], *Fasti ecclesiae Anglicanae, 1541–1857*, ed. J. M. Horn, D. M. Smith, and D. S. Bailey, [9 vols.] (1969–)
Fasti Scot.	H. Scott, *Fasti ecclesiae Scoticanae*, 3 vols. in 6 (1871); new edn, [11 vols.] (1915–)
FO List	*Foreign Office List*
Fortescue, *Brit. army*	J. W. Fortescue, *A history of the British army*, 13 vols. (1899–1930)
Foss, *Judges*	E. Foss, *The judges of England*, 9 vols. (1848–64); repr. (1966)
Foster, *Alum. Oxon.*	J. Foster, ed., *Alumni Oxonienses: the members of the University of Oxford, 1715–1886*, 4 vols. (1887–8); later edn (1891); also *Alumni Oxonienses … 1500–1714*, 4 vols. (1891–2); 8 vol. repr. (1968) and (2000)
Fuller, *Worthies*	T. Fuller, *The history of the worthies of England*, 4 pts (1662); new edn, 2 vols., ed. J. Nichols (1811); new edn, 3 vols., ed. P. A. Nuttall (1840); repr. (1965)
GEC, *Baronetage*	G. E. Cokayne, *Complete baronetage*, 6 vols. (1900–09); repr. (1983) [microprint]
GEC, *Peerage*	G. E. C. [G. E. Cokayne], *The complete peerage of England, Scotland, Ireland, Great Britain, and the United Kingdom*, 8 vols. (1887–98); new edn, ed. V. Gibbs and others, 14 vols. in 15 (1910–98); microprint repr. (1982) and (1987)
Genest, *Eng. stage*	J. Genest, *Some account of the English stage from the Restoration in 1660 to 1830*, 10 vols. (1832); repr. [New York, 1965]
Gillow, *Lit. biog. hist.*	J. Gillow, *A literary and biographical history or bibliographical dictionary of the English Catholics, from the breach with Rome, in 1534, to the present time*, 5 vols. [1885–1902]; repr. (1961); repr. with preface by C. Gillow (1999)
Gir. Camb. opera	*Giraldi Cambrensis opera*, ed. J. S. Brewer, J. F. Dimock, and G. F. Warner, 8 vols., Rolls Series, 21 (1861–91)
GJ	*Geographical Journal*

Gladstone, *Diaries* — *The Gladstone diaries: with cabinet minutes and prime-ministerial correspondence*, ed. M. R. D. Foot and H. C. G. Matthew, 14 vols. (1968–94)

GM — *Gentleman's Magazine*

Graves, *Artists* — A. Graves, ed., *A dictionary of artists who have exhibited works in the principal London exhibitions of oil paintings from 1760 to 1880* (1884); new edn (1895); 3rd edn (1901); facs. edn (1969); repr. [1970], (1973), and (1984)

Graves, *Brit. Inst.* — A. Graves, *The British Institution, 1806–1867: a complete dictionary of contributors and their work from the foundation of the institution* (1875); facs. edn (1908); repr. (1969)

Graves, *RA exhibitors* — A. Graves, *The Royal Academy of Arts: a complete dictionary of contributors and their work from its foundation in 1769 to 1904*, 8 vols. (1905–6); repr. in 4 vols. (1970) and (1972)

Graves, *Soc. Artists* — A. Graves, *The Society of Artists of Great Britain, 1760–1791, the Free Society of Artists, 1761–1783: a complete dictionary* (1907); facs. edn (1969)

Greaves & Zaller, *BDBR* — R. L. Greaves and R. Zaller, eds., *Biographical dictionary of British radicals in the seventeenth century*, 3 vols. (1982–4)

Grove, *Dict. mus.* — G. Grove, ed., *A dictionary of music and musicians*, 5 vols. (1878–90); 2nd edn, ed. J. A. Fuller Maitland (1904–10); 3rd edn, ed. H. C. Colles (1927); 4th edn with suppl. (1940); 5th edn, ed. E. Blom, 9 vols. (1954); suppl. (1961) [see also *New Grove*]

Hall, *Dramatic ports.* — L. A. Hall, *Catalogue of dramatic portraits in the theatre collection of the Harvard College library*, 4 vols. (1930–34)

Hansard — *Hansard's parliamentary debates*, ser. 1–5 (1803–)

Highfill, Burnim & Langhans, *BDA* — P. H. Highfill, K. A. Burnim, and E. A. Langhans, *A biographical dictionary of actors, actresses, musicians, dancers, managers, and other stage personnel in London, 1660–1800*, 16 vols. (1973–93)

Hist. U. Oxf. — T. H. Aston, ed., *The history of the University of Oxford*, 8 vols. (1984–2000) [1: *The early Oxford schools*, ed. J. I. Catto (1984); 2: *Late medieval Oxford*, ed. J. I. Catto and R. Evans (1992); 3: *The collegiate university*, ed. J. McConica (1986); 4: *Seventeenth-century Oxford*, ed. N. Tyacke (1997); 5: *The eighteenth century*, ed. L. S. Sutherland and L. G. Mitchell (1986); 6–7: *Nineteenth-century Oxford*, ed. M. G. Brock and M. C. Curthoys (1997–2000); 8: *The twentieth century*, ed. B. Harrison (2000)]

HJ — *Historical Journal*

HMC — Historical Manuscripts Commission

Holdsworth, *Eng. law* — W. S. Holdsworth, *A history of English law*, ed. A. L. Goodhart and H. L. Hanbury, 17 vols. (1903–72)

HoP, *Commons* — *The history of parliament: the House of Commons* [1386–1421, ed. J. S. Roskell, L. Clark, and C. Rawcliffe, 4 vols. (1992); 1509–1558, ed. S. T. Bindoff, 3 vols. (1982); 1558–1603, ed. P. W. Hasler, 3 vols. (1981); 1660–1690, ed. B. D. Henning, 3 vols. (1983); 1690–1715, ed. D. W. Hayton, E. Cruickshanks, and S. Handley, 5 vols. (2002); 1715–1754, ed. R. Sedgwick, 2 vols. (1970); 1754–1790, ed. L. Namier and J. Brooke, 3 vols. (1964), repr. (1985); 1790–1820, ed. R. G. Thorne, 5 vols. (1986); in draft (used with permission): 1422–1504, 1604–1629, 1640–1660, and 1820–1832]

IGI — *International Genealogical Index*, Church of Jesus Christ of the Latterday Saints

ILN — *Illustrated London News*

IMC — Irish Manuscripts Commission

Irving, *Scots.* — J. Irving, ed., *The book of Scotsmen eminent for achievements in arms and arts, church and state, law, legislation and literature, commerce, science, travel and philanthropy* (1881)

JCS — *Journal of the Chemical Society*

JHC — *Journals of the House of Commons*

JHL — *Journals of the House of Lords*

John of Worcester, *Chron.* — *The chronicle of John of Worcester*, ed. R. R. Darlington and P. McGurk, trans. J. Bray and P. McGurk, 3 vols., OMT (1995–) [vol. 1 forthcoming]

Keeler, *Long Parliament* — M. F. Keeler, *The Long Parliament, 1640–1641: a biographical study of its members* (1954)

Kelly, *Handbk* — *The upper ten thousand: an alphabetical list of all members of noble families*, 3 vols. (1875–7); continued as *Kelly's handbook of the upper ten thousand for 1878* [1879], 2 vols. (1878–9); continued as *Kelly's handbook to the titled, landed and official classes*, 94 vols. (1880–1973)

LondG — *London Gazette*

LP Henry VIII — J. S. Brewer, J. Gairdner, and R. H. Brodie, eds., *Letters and papers, foreign and domestic, of the reign of Henry VIII*, 23 vols. in 38 (1862–1932); repr. (1965)

Mallalieu, *Watercolour artists* — H. L. Mallalieu, *The dictionary of British watercolour artists up to 1820*, 3 vols. (1976–90); vol. 1, 2nd edn (1986)

Memoirs FRS — *Biographical Memoirs of Fellows of the Royal Society*

MGH — Monumenta Germaniae Historica

MT — *Musical Times*

Munk, *Roll* — W. Munk, *The roll of the Royal College of Physicians of London*, 2 vols. (1861); 2nd edn, 3 vols. (1878)

N&Q — *Notes and Queries*

New Grove — S. Sadie, ed., *The new Grove dictionary of music and musicians*, 20 vols. (1980); 2nd edn, 29 vols. (2001) [also online edn; see also Grove, *Dict. mus.*]

Nichols, *Illustrations* — J. Nichols and J. B. Nichols, *Illustrations of the literary history of the eighteenth century*, 8 vols. (1817–58)

Nichols, *Lit. anecdotes* — J. Nichols, *Literary anecdotes of the eighteenth century*, 9 vols. (1812–16); facs. edn (1966)

Obits. FRS — *Obituary Notices of Fellows of the Royal Society*

O'Byrne, *Naval biog. dict.* — W. R. O'Byrne, *A naval biographical dictionary* (1849); repr. (1990); [2nd edn], 2 vols. (1861)

OHS — Oxford Historical Society

Old Westminsters — *The record of Old Westminsters*, 1–2, ed. G. F. R. Barker and A. H. Stenning (1928); suppl. 1, ed. J. B. Whitmore and G. R. Y. Radcliffe [1938]; 3, ed. J. B. Whitmore, G. R. Y. Radcliffe, and D. C. Simpson (1963); suppl. 2, ed. F. E. Pagan (1978); 4, ed. F. E. Pagan and H. E. Pagan (1992)

OMT — Oxford Medieval Texts

Ordericus Vitalis, *Eccl. hist.* — *The ecclesiastical history of Orderic Vitalis*, ed. and trans. M. Chibnall, 6 vols., OMT (1969–80); repr. (1990)

Paris, *Chron.* — *Matthaei Parisiensis, monachi sancti Albani, chronica majora*, ed. H. R. Luard, Rolls Series, 7 vols. (1872–83)

Parl. papers — *Parliamentary papers* (1801–)

PBA — *Proceedings of the British Academy*

Pepys, *Diary*	*The diary of Samuel Pepys*, ed. R. Latham and W. Matthews, 11 vols. (1970–83); repr. (1995) and (2000)
Pevsner	N. Pevsner and others, Buildings of England series
PICE	*Proceedings of the Institution of Civil Engineers*
Pipe rolls	*The great roll of the pipe for . . .*, PRSoc. (1884–)
PRO	Public Record Office
PRS	*Proceedings of the Royal Society of London*
PRSoc.	Pipe Roll Society
PTRS	*Philosophical Transactions of the Royal Society*
QR	*Quarterly Review*
RC	Record Commissions
Redgrave, *Artists*	S. Redgrave, *A dictionary of artists of the English school* (1874); rev. edn (1878); repr. (1970)
Reg. Oxf.	C. W. Boase and A. Clark, eds., *Register of the University of Oxford*, 5 vols., OHS, 1, 10–12, 14 (1885–9)
Reg. PCS	J. H. Burton and others, eds., *The register of the privy council of Scotland*, 1st ser., 14 vols. (1877–98); 2nd ser., 8 vols. (1899–1908); 3rd ser., [16 vols.] (1908–70)
Reg. RAN	H. W. C. Davis and others, eds., *Regesta regum Anglo-Normannorum, 1066–1154*, 4 vols. (1913–69)
RIBA Journal	*Journal of the Royal Institute of British Architects* [later *RIBA Journal*]
RotP	J. Strachey, ed., *Rotuli parliamentorum ut et petitiones, et placita in parliamento*, 6 vols. (1767–77)
RotS	D. Macpherson, J. Caley, and W. Illingworth, eds., *Rotuli Scotiae in Turri Londinensi et in domo capitulari Westmonasteriensi asservati*, 2 vols., RC, 14 (1814–19)
RS	Record(s) Society
Rymer, *Foedera*	T. Rymer and R. Sanderson, eds., *Foedera, conventiones, literae et cuiuscunque generis acta publica inter reges Angliae et alios quosvis imperatores, reges, pontifices, principes, vel communitates*, 20 vols. (1704–35); 2nd edn, 20 vols. (1726–35); 3rd edn, 10 vols. (1739–45); facs. edn (1967); new edn, ed. A. Clarke, J. Caley, and F. Holbrooke, 4 vols., RC, 50 (1816–30)
Sainty, *Judges*	J. Sainty, ed., *The judges of England, 1272–1990*, SeldS, suppl. ser., 10 (1993)
Sainty, *King's counsel*	J. Sainty, ed., *A list of English law officers and king's counsel*, SeldS, suppl. ser., 7 (1987)
SCH	Studies in Church History
Scots peerage	J. B. Paul, ed. *The Scots peerage, founded on Wood's edition of Sir Robert Douglas's Peerage of Scotland, containing an historical and genealogical account of the nobility of that kingdom*, 9 vols. (1904–14)
SeldS	Selden Society
SHR	*Scottish Historical Review*
State trials	T. B. Howell and T. J. Howell, eds., Cobbett's *Complete collection of state trials*, 34 vols. (1809–28)
STC, 1475–1640	A. W. Pollard, G. R. Redgrave, and others, eds., *A short-title catalogue of . . . English books . . . 1475–1640* (1926); 2nd edn, ed. W. A. Jackson, F. S. Ferguson, and K. F. Pantzer, 3 vols. (1976–91) [see also Wing, *STC*]
STS	Scottish Text Society
SurtS	Surtees Society
Symeon of Durham, *Opera*	*Symeonis monachi opera omnia*, ed. T. Arnold, 2 vols., Rolls Series, 75 (1882–5); repr. (1965)
Tanner, *Bibl. Brit.-Hib.*	T. Tanner, *Bibliotheca Britannico-Hibernica*, ed. D. Wilkins (1748); repr. (1963)
Thieme & Becker, *Allgemeines Lexikon*	U. Thieme, F. Becker, and H. Vollmer, eds., *Allgemeines Lexikon der bildenden Künstler von der Antike bis zur Gegenwart*, 37 vols. (Leipzig, 1907–50); repr. (1961–5), (1983), and (1992)
Thurloe, *State papers*	*A collection of the state papers of John Thurloe*, ed. T. Birch, 7 vols. (1742)
TLS	*Times Literary Supplement*
Tout, *Admin. hist.*	T. F. Tout, *Chapters in the administrative history of mediaeval England: the wardrobe, the chamber, and the small seals*, 6 vols. (1920–33); repr. (1967)
TRHS	*Transactions of the Royal Historical Society*
VCH	H. A. Doubleday and others, eds., *The Victoria history of the counties of England*, [88 vols.] (1900–)
Venn, *Alum. Cant.*	J. Venn and J. A. Venn, *Alumni Cantabrigienses: a biographical list of all known students, graduates, and holders of office at the University of Cambridge, from the earliest times to 1900*, 10 vols. (1922–54); repr. in 2 vols. (1974–8)
Vertue, *Note books*	[G. Vertue], *Note books*, ed. K. Esdaile, earl of Ilchester, and H. M. Hake, 6 vols., Walpole Society, 18, 20, 22, 24, 26, 30 (1930–55)
VF	*Vanity Fair*
Walford, *County families*	E. Walford, *The county families of the United Kingdom, or, Royal manual of the titled and untitled aristocracy of Great Britain and Ireland* (1860)
Walker rev.	A. G. Matthews, *Walker revised: being a revision of John Walker's Sufferings of the clergy during the grand rebellion, 1642–60* (1948); repr. (1988)
Walpole, *Corr.*	*The Yale edition of Horace Walpole's correspondence*, ed. W. S. Lewis, 48 vols. (1937–83)
Ward, *Men of the reign*	T. H. Ward, ed., *Men of the reign: a biographical dictionary of eminent persons of British and colonial birth who have died during the reign of Queen Victoria* (1885); repr. (Graz, 1968)
Waterhouse, *18c painters*	E. Waterhouse, *The dictionary of 18th century painters in oils and crayons* (1981); repr. as *British 18th century painters in oils and crayons* (1991), vol. 2 of *Dictionary of British art*
Watt, *Bibl. Brit.*	R. Watt, *Bibliotheca Britannica, or, A general index to British and foreign literature*, 4 vols. (1824) [many reprs.]
Wellesley index	W. E. Houghton, ed., *The Wellesley index to Victorian periodicals, 1824–1900*, 5 vols. (1966–89); new edn (1999) [CD-ROM]
Wing, *STC*	D. Wing, ed., *Short-title catalogue of . . . English books . . . 1641–1700*, 3 vols. (1945–51); 2nd edn (1972–88); rev. and enl. edn, ed. J. J. Morrison, C. W. Nelson, and M. Seccombe, 4 vols. (1994–8) [see also *STC, 1475–1640*]
Wisden	*John Wisden's Cricketer's Almanack*
Wood, *Ath. Oxon.*	A. Wood, *Athenae Oxonienses . . . to which are added the Fasti*, 2 vols. (1691–2); 2nd edn (1721); new edn, 4 vols., ed. P. Bliss (1813–20); repr. (1967) and (1969)
Wood, *Vic. painters*	C. Wood, *Dictionary of Victorian painters* (1971); 2nd edn (1978); 3rd edn as *Victorian painters*, 2 vols. (1995), vol. 4 of *Dictionary of British art*
WW	*Who's who* (1849–)
WWBMP	M. Stenton and S. Lees, eds., *Who's who of British members of parliament*, 4 vols. (1976–81)
WWW	*Who was who* (1929–)

Ela, *suo jure* **countess of Salisbury** (*b.* in or after **1190**, *d.* **1261**), magnate and abbess, was the daughter of William, earl of Salisbury, and his wife, Eleanor de Vitré. Her father died in 1196, leaving her as his heir, and Richard I married her off in the same year to William (I) *Longespée (*d.* 1226), his illegitimate brother, who became by right of his wife earl of Salisbury. He and Ela had four sons and four daughters; two of the younger sons had notable careers: Stephen became seneschal of Gascony and justiciar of Ireland, and Nicholas bishop of Salisbury. Little is known of Ela's married life. In 1220 she and her husband laid the fifth and fourth foundation stones respectively for the new cathedral at Salisbury, and she was described in the *Register of St Osmund* as 'a woman indeed worthy of praise because she was filled with the fear of the Lord'. On the rumour in 1225 that her husband had been drowned, Hubert de Burgh's nephew sought to marry her, but she refused to consider him.

William in fact died in Salisbury Castle on 7 March 1226, and was buried in the cathedral; Ela performed homage to the king for her inheritance twelve days later, but had to surrender Salisbury Castle. However, she acted as sheriff of Wiltshire in 1227–8 and between 1231 and 1237, and accounted in person at Michaelmas 1236; this was an office which had been held at various times by her husband, father, and grandfather, although a subsequent case in the king's court made it clear that she had no hereditary right to the shrievalty.

Ela's widowhood is noted for her benefactions to the church and her religious life. Her husband founded a charterhouse at Hatherop, Gloucestershire, in 1222, but the monks found the endowments inadequate and the site unsuitable. They appealed to Ela who settled them in her park at Hinton, Somerset, and augmented the endowments. Her own foundation was a house of Augustinian canonesses at Lacock, Wiltshire, established in 1230; Ela entered this house in 1237, and became its first abbess in 1239 when the nunnery was upgraded from a priory to an abbey.

Ela resigned her position as abbess twenty years later. She died on 24 August 1261, and was buried in the abbey. She outlived her eldest son and grandson; her eldest son, Sir William (II) *Longespée, led the English crusaders on Louis IX's first crusade and died in 1250 at Mansourah in Egypt. According to Matthew Paris, Ela had a vision of her son before she received the news of his death. Her heir at her death was her great-granddaughter, Margaret Longespée, who married Henry de Lacy, earl of Lincoln.

Jennifer C. Ward

Sources *Chronica magistri Rogeri de Hovedene*, ed. W. Stubbs, 4 vols., Rolls Series, 51 (1868–71) · W. H. Rich Jones, ed., *Vetus registrum sarisberiense alias dictum registrum S. Osmundi episcopi: the register of St Osmund*, 2 vols., Rolls Series, 78 (1883–4) · H. R. Luard, ed., *Flores historiarum*, 3 vols., Rolls Series, 95 (1890) · Paris, *Chron.* · Dugdale, *Monasticon*, new edn · *Bracton's note book*, ed. F. W. Maitland, 3 vols. (1887) · Chancery records · Pipe rolls
Archives PRO

Elam, Constance Fligg. *See* Tipper, Constance Fligg (1894–1995).

Elam, Gervase (1681–1771), merchant and Quaker minister, was born on 3 October 1681 at Heath, Skircoates Moor, Halifax, the only child of John Elam (1639/40–1730), a card-maker, and his second wife, Katherine (*d.* 1682) of Kendal, daughter of Gervase Benson of Borratt, Sedbergh. Born into a devout Quaker family Elam remained a constant member of the Society of Friends throughout his life.

Little is known of Elam's early years and education aside from his having had one half-brother and a half-sister. In 1703 he moved to Leeds, where in the following year he gave notice to the Leeds meeting of the Society of Friends that he intended to set up as a clothier in Armley, where he was until at least 1750. On 26 August 1715 he married Elizabeth (1694–1777), daughter of John and Mercy Smith of Wortley, at the Meadow Lane meeting-house, Leeds. The couple had eleven children, including seven sons, six of whom went on to develop Elam's diverse trading interests during his lifetime. The success of Elam's business rested on his investment in an expanding American market previously dominated by merchants from continental Europe. Variously working alone, with family, or with other members of the Quaker merchant community he exported a range of goods, of which the most significant was cloth, and imported tobacco with the help of family members resident in the American colonies. Elam may himself have visited Virginia in 1744. Opportunities at home were also grasped with the purchase of land and a number of properties in Leeds and the surrounding area.

Throughout his life Elam was an active and conscientious member of the Leeds Friends' meeting. As a young man he accompanied 'travelling Friends' to their meetings so as to acquire the opportunity for business and social contact with fellow Quakers. He suffered frequent financial losses both in money and goods because he refused to pay tithes and other dues to the Church of England. Between 1712 and 1749 he represented the Leeds meeting on more than forty occasions at monthly meetings of the society. A generous contributor to Quaker causes and concerns, his first donation was of 15s. towards building a stable at the Quaker school at Camp Lane. In 1732 he was made an elder of the meeting; his duties, faithfully fulfilled, included vetting couples intending to marry, signing testimonies, and giving advice on the cloth trade.

Of Elam's home life little is known. His family supported him in business and religion until his death in Leeds on 14 November 1771. He was buried at the Leeds meeting burial-ground, in Meadow Lane, on 17 November and was survived by his wife and five of their children. Obituary notices appeared in 'A testament to public Friends dead' (RS Friends, Lond.), which remarked on his 'late call to the Ministry', as well as in the *Leeds Intelligencer* (19 November 1771) and the *Providence and Rhode Island Gazette* (14 March 1772). Though no will has been found his son Joseph is known to have inherited Elam's property at Armley.

Norma C. Neill

Sources U. Leeds, Brotherton L., Society of Friends Carlton Hill collection · J. Mortimer and R. Mortimer, eds., *Leeds Friends' minute book, 1692–1712*, Yorkshire Archaeological Society, 139 (1980) · N. C.

Neill, *The Elam family, Quaker merchants of England and America* (privately printed, 1995) · 'Dictionary of Quaker biography', RS Friends, Lond. [card index] · digests, Quaker London yearly meeting, RS Friends, Lond. · Yorkshire quarterly meeting marriage and burial digests, RS Friends, Lond. [John Elam and Katherine Benson; Gervase Elam]
Wealth at death property at Armley, Leeds

Elchies. For this title name *see* Grant, Patrick, Lord Elchies (1690–1754).

Elcho. For this title name *see* Wemyss, David, fourth earl of Wemyss [*formerly* Lord Elcho] (*bap.* 1678, *d.* 1720); Wemyss, David, styled sixth earl of Wemyss [*known as* Lord Elcho] (1721–1787).

Eld, George (1791–1862), antiquary, was born in Coventry, the son of George Eld, a baker in Cross Cheaping, Coventry. He was a miller until he went bankrupt in 1839; by the 1850s he was a silk dealer and dyer, associated with the silk-dyeing business of the Rotherham family. Eld owned or controlled a substantial amount of land around Coventry, and held Foleshill mill by inheritance; he had other property at Alderman's Green, Cross Cheaping, and Lammas Land at Radford. From 1815 Eld occupied the house known as Skirvyn's Moor, Hall Green, where his father had been a tenant before him; he probably took up residence after his marriage on 30 April of the same year to Mary South (*d.* 1853) of Coventry, an heiress and ward in chancery. They had five sons and one daughter.

Eld was very active in the civic life of Coventry. In 1827 he became city chamberlain, and in 1829 he was sheriff. He was a trustee of the Coventry–Stoney Stanton turnpike in 1832, of the national school, and of the freemen's seniority fund in 1843. After acting as the last mayor of Coventry (1834–5) before the Municipal Reform Act, he was an alderman of the reformed corporation until his death, and a petitioner over the management of the city charities after the reform. He laid the foundation-stone of St Peter's Church, daughter church of Holy Trinity, and was a churchwarden there. He was also editor of the *Coventry Standard* for twenty years.

Eld had keen antiquarian interests, which he manifested during his mayoralty by his restoration of the fourteenth-century interior of the mayoress's parlour at St Mary's Hall. He encouraged the preservation and public appreciation of Coventry's ancient buildings and monuments, many of which he sketched himself. A supporter of the Philographic Society, he collaborated with the antiquary Thomas Sharp in antiquarian activities. In his later years Eld lived in Hill Street in Coventry. He died in Gas Street, Coventry, on 22 May 1862.   JOANNE POTIER

Sources *GM*, 3rd ser., 13 (1862), 636 · private information (2004)
Archives Coventry Archives, collection of historical manuscripts; diaries
Wealth at death under £6000: probate, 1 Aug 1862, *CGPLA Eng. & Wales*

Eldar, Jhone. *See* Elder, John (*fl.* 1533–1565).

Elder, Charles (1821–1851), history painter, was the son of Joseph Elder of the Ordnance office, in the Tower of London. He went to St Paul's School in 1834. He first exhibited at the British Institution in 1844, to which he sent *Noli me tangere*, and at the Royal Academy in 1845, with *Sappho*. He was a frequent contributor to London exhibitions, twenty-one of his paintings being shown between 1844 and 1852. Among these works were *Florimel Imprisoned* (exh. RA, 1846), *The Death of Mark Antony* (exh. RA, 1847), *Ruth Gleaning* (exh. RA, 1848), *Rosalind* (exh. RA, 1850), and *Jael* (exh. British Institution, 1859). Elder continued to exhibit until he died on 11 December 1851, leaving a widow and three children. Two of his pictures—*On the Thames Near Twickenham* and *An Italian Fruit Girl*—were exhibited at the Royal Academy in the following year. Among his portraits were those of the marquess of Bristol and Sheriff Nicol.

L. H. CUST, *rev.* ROMITA RAY

Sources Redgrave, *Artists* · Graves, *Artists* · *GM*, 2nd ser., 37 (1852), 210, 312 · R. B. Gardiner, ed., *The admission registers of St Paul's School, from 1748 to 1876* (1884), 288

Elder, David (1784–1866). *See under* Randolph, Charles (1809–1878).

Elder, Edward (1812–1858), headmaster, the son of John William Edmund Elder, was born in Barbados on 1 October 1812. At the age of twelve he was sent to Charterhouse, where he remained until 1830, when he gained an open scholarship at Balliol College, Oxford. There he took first-class honours in classics and won the Ellerton theological essay prize. He graduated BA in 1834 and MA in 1836, was ordained in 1840, and proceeded DD in 1853. He was a tutor at Oxford until 1839, when he became headmaster of Durham Cathedral grammar school. The school was in a sorry state, but was transformed during Elder's headmastership, ultimately acquiring the standing of a public school, helped by the move to a new site in 1844. He married in 1845 Augusta, eldest daughter of H. Farley of Trinidad. So great was Elder's success as a teacher that when in 1853 he was appointed headmaster of Charterhouse, many of the Durham boys migrated to London with him. At Charterhouse he was unable to arrest the school's decline, and was increasingly subject to attacks of illness, which necessitated his absence from the school. Finally his mind gave way altogether. Elder died at Blacklands, Chelsea, on 6 April 1858 and was buried in the churchyard of Durham Cathedral. His widow survived him. Elder contributed several articles to Smith's *Dictionary of Classical Biography and Mythology*.

ALSAGER VIAN, *rev.* M. C. CURTHOYS

Sources Boase, *Mod. Eng. biog.* · A. Quick, *Charterhouse: a history of the school* (1990) · R. L. Arrowsmith, ed., *Charterhouse register, 1769–1872* (1974) · T. H. Burbidge, ed., *Durham School register*, 3rd edn (1940)
Wealth at death under £6000: probate, 27 May 1858, *CGPLA Eng. & Wales*

Elder [*née* Ure], **Isabella** (1828–1905), benefactor, was born on 15 March 1828 in Hutchesontown, Gorbals, Glasgow, the fourth and last child, and only surviving daughter, of Alexander Ure (1788–1830), writer (or solicitor), and his wife, Mary, daughter of Hector and Margaret Ross, also of Gorbals. She had one older brother, John Francis (1820–1883). Her father died when she was two years old. There is no evidence as to where she might have been educated but most likely it was privately arranged. She married on 31 March 1857 John *Elder (1824–1869) [*see under* Randolph, Charles], a brilliant marine engineer and shipbuilder.

On John Elder's death in 1869 Isabella Elder became the sole owner of his shipbuilding yard in Govan. Elder's firm had the greatest output on the Clyde, employing more than 4000 men. She ran the business successfully for nine months until partners could be found. Her brother, who was unmarried and had become a famous harbour engineer on the River Tyne, became the senior partner.

A wealthy widow with no children, Mrs Elder tried to do what she thought her philanthropic and much-loved husband would have liked done, especially for the people of Govan, and for education and health generally. In 1873 she augmented the salary of the professor of civil engineering at Glasgow University, and in 1883 created the John Elder chair of naval architecture, the first of its kind. She became involved in the struggle for the higher education of women in Glasgow, and when Queen Margaret College for Women was constituted in 1883 she purchased North Park House and grounds and gave it to the college rent free, provided £20,000 was raised as an endowment. Earlier she had given bursaries for working lads from Govan to study marine engineering at Glasgow University and instituted scholarships for girls wishing to train as teachers or governesses. In 1890 Queen Margaret College very progressively opened a medical school and Mrs Elder, sympathetic to the desire of women to study medicine, agreed to fund all the running expenses.

Mrs Elder maintained a close interest in the college, where the women students, though taught by university staff, could not graduate and obtain a degree. She realized that many women had to earn their living and that qualifications were necessary. When, in 1892, the university commissioners (Scotland) announced that women would be accepted in Scottish universities, Queen Margaret College became incorporated into the University of Glasgow. The medical course was considered satisfactory from its inception and 1894 saw the first female medical graduates, but it was 1895 before the first woman graduated in arts. Mrs Elder remained concerned lest women were given sub-standard teaching if they were taught separately from the male students and agreed to North Park House being handed over to the university for the exclusive teaching of women only on condition that the teaching provided was the equal of that for men. Despite promises she was disappointed in the lecturers, and when the principal approached her in 1899 for further largesse she refused unless the original agreement was kept. She was never associated with the suffrage movement but always with equality of educational opportunity for women. In 1901 Glasgow University at its fifth jubilee awarded her an honorary LLD.

In 1885 Mrs Elder gave Govan the 37 acre Elder Park and established and paid the expenses of a school for domestic economy, where teenage girls and young married women were taught to cook nutritious food cheaply and run a house. The US consul in Glasgow at that time commended the enterprise to the United States. She provided a district nurse to instruct women in health and hygiene and visit homes. The nurse could also assist the local general practitioners. In 1901 she provided a villa, helping to start the training home for cottage nurses in Govan, a project to help rural areas. In 1903 she built and paid the running expenses of the Elder Cottage Hospital where cottage nurses could gain experience. She built the Elder Free Library, liberally endowing it.

Mrs Elder possessed great strength of purpose and strong principles. She also had a tender and most sympathetic heart, which led to many unrecorded acts of kindness and generosity quite apart from her public benefactions (which amounted to more than £200,000 in her lifetime). Of medium height and somewhat buxom as she grew older, she had thick dark hair plaited round her head; her hazel eyes contributed a look of compassion to firm features which, in turn, reflected her self-possession and intelligence.

Isabella Elder died at her home, 6 Claremont Terrace, Glasgow, on 18 November 1905 of heart failure, gout, and bronchitis. Her death certificate was signed by Glasgow's first woman medical graduate, Dr Marion Gilchrist. She was buried on 22 November in the Elder family tomb in the Glasgow necropolis. By her will, which left more than £125,000 for charitable purposes, she established in memory of her father-in-law the David Elder lectures in astronomy at the Glasgow and West of Scotland Technical College (later Strathclyde University), and set up in memory of her husband and brother the Ure Elder Fund for Indigent Widows of Govan and Glasgow. She was described as 'a true woman, a wise benefactress of the public and of learning' (*The Bailie*, 12 Dec 1883). A statue of Mrs Elder, unveiled in 1906, stands in the Elder Park near that of her husband. The statues of husband and wife erected by public subscription are unique in Glasgow.

C. JOAN MCALPINE

Sources C. J. McAlpine, *The lady of Claremont House* (1997) · A. Craig, *The Elder Park, Govan* (1891) · A. Craig, *The statue of Mrs John Elder* (1912) · *The Bailie* (12 Dec 1883) · *The Bailie* (23 Nov 1892) · *Glasgow Herald* (20 Nov 1905) · *Glasgow Herald* (23 Nov 1905) · U. Glas., Archives and Business Records Centre, Queen Margaret College archives, DC 233 · U. Glas., Archives and Business Records Centre, Ure Elder collection, DC 122 · parish records (birth), General Register Office for Scotland, Edinburgh, 15 March 1828 · parish records (baptism), General Register Office for Scotland, Edinburgh, 27 April 1828 · parish records (marriage), General Register Office for Scotland, Edinburgh, 31 Jan 1857 · d. cert. [Scotland]
Archives U. Glas., Archives and Business Records Centre, DC 233 · U. Glas., Archives and Business Records Centre, DC 122
Likenesses J. Millais, oils, 1886, Art Gallery and Museum, Kelvingrove, Glasgow · Fergus, photograph, 1888 (after a steel engraving by J. G. Stodart), repro. in Craig, *Elder Park, Govan*, 36 · A. McF. Shannan, bronze statue, 1906, Elder Park, Govan, Glasgow · A. McF. Shannan, marble bust, 1906, Elder Free Library, Govan, Glasgow · H. Farrer, pastel, BBC Concert Hall, Queen Margaret Drive, Glasgow
Wealth at death £159,404: confirmation, 27 Dec 1905, *CCI*

Elder, John [Jhone Eldar] (*fl.* 1533–1565), cartographer and propagandist, was a native of Caithness—a 'redshank', as he styled himself. He was educated on Skye and Lewis before continuing his studies at the universities of St Andrews (where he matriculated in 1533), Aberdeen, and Glasgow. Deeply knowledgeable about highland, island, and Irish kin groups and politics, he showed himself something of a Gaelic chauvinist, trumpeting the hardiness, manliness, and sense of honour of his compatriots. But he was also a clerk, who spent time at the court of James V, and moreover converted to protestantism, with the result that by 1543 he had been forced to go into exile in England. There Elder prepared for Henry VIII the first of the four manuscripts which constitute his claim to attention, presenting the English king with what was possibly the first accurate map of Scotland, locating all the 'notable townes, castels, and abbeis', along with 'every port, loigh, creke, and haven': in its maker's words, 'the privities of Scotland' (Inglis, 11). This 'plotte' has since disappeared, but not before it was widely used and circulated. Accompanying the exercise in cartography was a guidebook, also one of Scotland's first (BL, Harley MS 289, fols. 4–9; Cotton MS Vesp. D. xviii, fol. 1350⁹). It describes all the major locations and also gives mileages.

The third work in Elder's packet of materials for the edification of Henry VIII, handsomely bound and lucidly executed in a very neat script, was his most famous pamphlet: 'To the moost Noble, Victorius and Redoubted Prynce, Henry the Eight, JHONE ELDAR Clerk a Reddshank, wisseth all wealth, all honour, and triumphant victory over all his enymies' (BL, Royal MS 18 A, fol. 38, published in *Bannatyne Miscellany*, vol. 1, 1827). The main thrust of this letter is that Prince Edward should marry the infant Queen Mary, so uniting the two kingdoms, over which Henry would be 'superiour and kynge' and fulfilling the promise contained in the legend of Brutus who had conquered the whole island. This Galfridian interpretation of British origins flew in the face of the Scottish origin-myth, which Elder found incredible. Opposing his vision stood the French, their Scottish ally, Cardinal David Beaton, and the Catholic bishops, vicious in their promotion of sedition, variance, dissension, insurrections, theft, extortion, dearth, misery, pride, hypocrisy, envy, and hatred. Against such foes and their false history Elder wished for Henry the strength and fortitude of Hercules, the manhood and chivalry of Hector, and the subtlety and wit of Achilles. He was rewarded with a pension of £20 in March 1544.

In September 1545 Elder accompanied the English army led by Edward Seymour, earl of Hertford, which ravaged the Scottish borders. On 6 October he sent Sir William Paget a lengthy report on the campaign from Newcastle, listing the devastation thus wrought, but blaming its victims for their own misfortunes, since 'the pest, hunger, fire and sword are the beginning of a punishment ordained of God for the double dealing of them of Scotland' (*LP Henry VIII*, vol. 20, pt 2, no. 533). Little is recorded of him in the next ten years, though he probably remained in England, where his pension was raised to £25 on 18 June 1547 and where he received a further £5 'reward' shortly afterwards. But by 1 January 1555 he had become tutor to Henry Stewart, Lord Darnley, and had also become a Catholic. On that day he published *The copie of a letter sent in to Scotlande, of the arivall and marryage of Philippe, prynce of Spaine to Marye quene of England, whereunto is added a brefe overture of Cardinall Poole … for reconcilement to the catholyke churche* (ESTC, 7552). Addressing his treatise to Robert Stewart, bishop of Caithness, who was Darnley's uncle, Elder refers to his pupil's parents, the fourth earl of Lennox and Countess Margaret, as his singular good patrons.

In 1559 Elder accompanied Darnley to France and apparently stayed there for more than two years. He may have taken service with Charles de Guise, cardinal of Lorraine, whom he was reported in September 1559 to be incensing against protestant heretics. But by the end of 1561 he had lost the pension he had been awarded and was planning to return to Scotland. Sir Nicholas Throckmorton suggested to Sir William Cecil that Elder might be willing to serve the English cause there, and described him as 'very skilful in drawing plats for situation of countries and declaration of the coasts' (*CSP for.*, *1561–2*, 455). The cardinal gave Elder 50 crowns at his departure. Once back in Scotland he made his peace with the reformed church, to the extent of obtaining the vicarage of Longley and Fetterangus (his presentation by William Keith, third Earl Marischal, was confirmed on 30 June 1565), a prebend in Trinity College, Edinburgh, and the parsonage of Dunnottar. None of this implies service in the reformed church, and the subsequent course of Elder's life is unrecorded.

MARCUS MERRIMAN

Sources M. Merriman, *The rough wooings: Mary queen of Scots, 1542–1551* (2000) · *LP Henry VIII*, vols. 18–21 · *CSP Scot.*, 1547–69 · *APC*, 1547–80 · *CPR*, 1547–8 · *CSP for.*, 1558–62 · H. R. G. Inglis, *Early maps of Scotland, 1524–1548* (1936) · W. Scott and D. Laing, eds., *The Bannatyne miscellany*, 1, Bannatyne Club, 19 (1827) · M. Livingstone, D. Hay Fleming, and others, eds., *Registrum secreti sigilli regum Scotorum / The register of the privy seal of Scotland*, 5 (1957) · J. Kirk, *Patterns of reform: continuity and change in the Reformation kirk* (1989) · J. M. Anderson, ed., *Early records of the University of St Andrews*, Scottish History Society, 3rd ser., 8 (1926) · M. Merriman, 'Home thoughts from abroad: national consciousness and Scottish exiles in the mid-sixteenth century', *Social and political identities in western history*, ed. C. Bjorn, A. Grant, and K. Stringer (1994), 90–117 · ESTC
Archives BL, Cotton MS Vesp. D. xviii · BL, Harley MS 289, fols. 4–9 · BL, Royal MS 18 A

Elder, John (1824–1869). *See under* Randolph, Charles (1809–1878).

Elder, Sir (William) Stewart Duke- (1898–1978), ophthalmic surgeon, was born on 22 April 1898 in Dundee, the second of three sons of Neil Stewart Elder of Tealing, a minister of the United Free Church of Scotland, and his wife, Isabella, daughter of John Duke, minister of the same church, of Campsie, Stirlingshire. After attending the Morgan Academy, Dundee, where he achieved gold medals in English, Greek, biology, and religious knowledge, he entered St Andrews University as a foundation scholar in 1915. In July 1919 he graduated MA with first-class honours in natural science and in the same year BSc with special distinction in physiology.

Elder completed his medical course at the Royal Infirmary, Dundee, and the Royal Infirmary, Edinburgh, in 1923

Sir (William) Stewart Duke-Elder (1898–1978), by Elliott & Fry, 1948

War he was consultant ophthalmic surgeon to the army, achieving the rank of brigadier in the Royal Army Medical Corps.

Duke-Elder made four important contributions to ophthalmology and of these his many writings on ophthalmology are pre-eminent. His *Recent Advances in Ophthalmology* (1927) and his *Practice of Refraction* (1928) remained in print as revised editions. Four years later appeared the first of the seven volumes of *Text-Book of Ophthalmology* (1932–54). This work, every word of which was initially written out in longhand, was known as the ophthalmologists' bible. Almost as soon as the final volume was published Duke-Elder felt that the work needed updating, so he embarked on his fifteen-volume *System of Ophthalmology* (1958–76). The first of these volumes was entirely his own work, and, though for subsequent volumes he enlisted the collaboration of his colleagues, his superb command of English and his lucidity of thought were still dominant. These books represented a distillation of the world's ophthalmic literature and were respected as the definitive work on all aspects of the subject, being very widely cited.

Duke-Elder's second achievement was the creation of the Institute of Ophthalmology in London. This was a research institute, in the founding of which Duke-Elder played a leading role and which was closely associated with Moorfields Eye Hospital. Following the amalgamation in 1947 of the three major London eye hospitals (the Central London, the Royal London, and Moorfields), the institute opened officially in 1948 with Duke-Elder as director of research, a post he held until 1965. It was largely for his research at the institute that he was elected in 1960 to a fellowship of the Royal Society, a distinction rarely awarded to a clinician.

Duke-Elder's third major contribution was the inauguration in 1945 of the faculty of ophthalmologists at the Royal College of Surgeons. It was to become the single authoritative body for the profession of ophthalmology. Duke-Elder was its first president and served for four years. His fourth interest was the hospital of St John of Jerusalem. He became a hospitaller in 1954 in succession to Lord Webb-Johnson, and as a result of his enthusiasm and hard work a new eighty-bed hospital was opened in 1960. Later he became bailiff grand cross of the order of St John. Duke-Elder was surgeon oculist to the royal family for twenty-nine years—to Edward VIII, George VI, and Elizabeth II. None of his predecessors had held this appointment for so long a period. He was appointed KCVO in 1946 and GCVO in 1958.

Despite his worldwide reputation Duke-Elder never lost his interest in and concern for young ophthalmologists, who were often referred to as Duke-Elderberries. He was a man of charm and wit, had a delightful Scottish sense of humour, was always accessible to his juniors, and was never stinting in praise and encouragement where due. At the same time if he felt that criticism was needed, it would be offered in a spirit of friendly helpfulness.

Duke-Elder received medals from sixteen universities, held nine honorary doctorates, six honorary fellowships,

graduating MB, BChir. The following year he became a fellow of the Royal College of Surgeons, London. In 1925 he was also awarded a gold medal for his MD thesis at St Andrews and the gold medal of the British Association, in addition to DSc and PhD degrees at London. While at St Andrews he found time to become president of the students' union, which he represented at council in 1921/2. He was demonstrator in physiology at St Andrews in 1918/19, university scholar in 1919, and demonstrator in anatomy at University College, Dundee, in 1920/21.

After graduation Elder settled in London and took up a number of junior appointments at St George's Hospital before being appointed honorary consulting surgeon both there and at Moorfields Eye Hospital at the age of twenty-seven. His great interest at this time was in the physiology of the eye. He was encouraged and directed by Professor E. H. Starling. He had been using the name Duke-Elder and confirmed this by deed poll in January 1928, shortly before his marriage to Phyllis Mary, daughter of William Edgar, manufacturer of gas fires and geysers, of Ealing. She was herself an ophthalmologist and played a very active part in the production of the seven volumes of *Text-Book of Ophthalmology*. They had no children.

In 1932 Duke-Elder operated on the prime minister, J. Ramsay MacDonald, for glaucoma, and the following year he received a knighthood. During the Second World and was an honorary member of twenty-eight national ophthalmological societies. He received the Howe medal of the USA in 1946, the Donders medal of Holland in 1947, the Doyne medal of the Oxford Ophthalmological Congress in 1948, and the Gullstrand medal of Sweden in 1952. He was life president of the International Council of Ophthalmology and in 1954 was presented with a Gonin medal, the highest award in international ophthalmology. Duke-Elder died on 27 March 1978 at his home, 28 Elm Tree Road, St John's Wood, London.

PHILIP AWDRY, *rev.*

Sources T. K. Lyle, S. Miller, and N. H. Ashton, *Memoirs FRS*, 26 (1980), 85–105 · *The Times* (3 April 1978) · personal knowledge (1986) · J. François, 'Sir Stewart Duke-Elder (1898–1978)', *Historia ophthalmologica internationalis*, 1 (1979–80), 111–17 · election certificate, RS · *CGPLA Eng. & Wales* (1978)
Likenesses Elliott & Fry, photograph, 1948, NPG [*see illus.*] · W. Bird, photograph, before 1961, RS · photograph, repro. in François, 'Sir Stewart Duke-Elder (1898–1978)', 115
Wealth at death £323,615: probate, 29 Sept 1978, *CGPLA Eng. & Wales*

Elder, Thomas (*bap.* 1737, *d.* 1799), politician, was baptized at Clunie, Perthshire, on 7 October 1737, the eldest son of William Elder of Loaning and Elizabeth, *née* Man. Details of his education and early life are not known. He set up as a merchant in Edinburgh, and in 1765 married Emilia, daughter of Paul Husband, also a city merchant; they had one son and four daughters.

Elder joined the town council in 1770, became master of the Merchant Company in 1779, and a member of the chamber of commerce in 1789. In the previous year he had been appointed lord provost, an office he held on three occasions (1788–90, 1792–4, and 1796–8). His reappointment may have been linked to his active suppression of radical political groups, including his breaking up of the British Convention held at Edinburgh on 5 December 1793, when ten or twelve of the principal members were taken prisoner. On the formation of the Royal Edinburgh volunteers in the summer of 1794 he became their first colonel, and on 9 September in the same year was granted a piece of plate by the town council 'for his spirited and prudent conduct while in office, and especially during the late commotions'.

Elder maintained close ties to Edinburgh University throughout his time as lord provost. The foundation stone of the new buildings was laid in the autumn of 1789 during his first term and his influence was such that he was later able to secure the appointment of his son-in-law George Husband *Baird as principal in 1793, a year after his marriage to Elder's daughter Isabella (9 August 1792). He became postmaster general of Scotland in 1795. He died at Forneth, in the parish of Clunie, on 29 May 1799, and was buried in the old church of Clunie on 2 June.

JANET SORENSEN

Sources M. Wood and T. B. Whitson, *The lord provosts of Edinburgh, 1296 to 1932* (1932) · J. Kay, *A series of original portraits and caricature etchings … with biographical sketches and illustrative anecdotes*, ed. [H. Paton and others], new edn [3rd edn], 2 vols. in 4 (1877) · A. Grant, *The story of the University of Edinburgh during its first three*

Thomas Elder (*bap.* 1737, *d.* 1799), by Sir Henry Raeburn, 1797

hundred years, 2 vols. (1884) · *Edinburgh Magazine, or, Literary Miscellany*, new ser., 14 (1799), 158–60 · *Scots Magazine*, 51 (1789), 521–8 · *Scots Magazine*, 54 (1792), 412 · *DNB*
Archives Edinburgh City Archives, letter-book | NA Scot., letters to H. Dundas
Likenesses J. Kay, etching, 1790, BM, NPG · J. Kay, etching, 1793 (with son-in-law), BM · J. Tassie, paste medallion, 1795, Scot. NPG · H. Raeburn, oils, 1797, U. Edin. [*see illus.*]

Elder, William (*fl.* 1680–1701), engraver, was born in Scotland but worked in London, principally for booksellers. He engraved a number of portraits, often copied from older engravings, many of which were used as frontispieces to contemporary publications. Among them were one of Ben Jonson, prefixed to the folio edition of his works (1692) and copied from Vaughan's engraving in the first edition (1616), and one of the naturalist John Ray, from a drawing by William Faithorne, and prefixed to his *Wisdom of God Manifested in the Creation* (1701). Other portraits include Archbishop Sancroft, John Pearson, bishop of Chester, the astrologer George Porter, the physicians Theodore de Mayerne and Richard Morton, and the writing-master Charles Snell. According to Horace Walpole, George Vertue had also found an example of engraved writing by Elder in a book dated 1681. Elder engraved his own portrait twice, once in a fur cap from a crayon drawing, and again in a wig. He also contributed some plates to John Savage's abridgement of Richard Knolles and Paul Rycaut's *The Generall Historie of the Turkes* (1701). A portrait vignette of Elder is inserted into a portrait of Robert White, engraved by A. Bannerman in Walpole's *Catalogue of Engravers* (2nd edn, 1765).

L. H. CUST, *rev.* ANNE PUETZ

most of his time to study. His *The Civil Right of Tythes* (1650), dedicated to Archbishop James Ussher, was a lengthy and learned survey, approaching the subject systematically from the laws of nature, through the donations of the Anglo-Saxon kings, the implications of the Norman conquest, and medieval and Tudor parliamentary legislation, to the writings of Christopher St German, John Selden, and Sir Henry Spelman; scriptural justifications for tithes appeared only in the last chapter. Although the subject was highly topical, the author expressly declined to engage in controversy on any other matter. He adopted an avowedly more scriptural and patristic approach to his anti-Baptist *Of Regeneration and Baptism, Hebrew and Christian*, dated 1647 but published only posthumously in 1653.

Elderfield died on 2 December 1652 at Burton Place. Although his executor, Thomas Henshaw, remarked to Sir William Goring in the dedicatory epistle to *Of Regeneration* that Elderfield had 'lived as deep in [Goring's] affections, as you lived high in his devotions' and that he 'was willing to return some considerable retributions to you, so far as he was intrusted by you, in secular affairs', Goring's expectations of a substantial legacy from his chaplain were disappointed. Dissatisfied with the modest mourning rings bequeathed to his family, Goring refused to comply with Elderfield's wish to be buried in the chancel of Burton church and had him interred instead in the nave. Other legatees were more fortunate. Faithful to his family and birthplace Elderfield left a total of £200 to his brothers and sisters and £350 for charitable purposes in the parish of Harwell, while £36 was destined for godly poor ministers. An evidently substantial collection of theological, medical, and legal books went to relatives and friends; manuscripts, including a history of Tobit in Hebrew, went to the Bodleian Library. Anthony Wood noted that Richard Baxter had described Elderfield as 'a very learned and great conformist' (Wood, 3.336).

ALSAGER VIAN, *rev.* VIVIENNE LARMINIE

Sources Wood, *Ath. Oxon.*, new edn, 3.336 • Foster, *Alum. Oxon.* • will, PRO, PROB 11/227, fols. 48*r*–50*v* • T. Henshaw, foreword, in *Of regeneration and baptism, Hebrew and Christian* (1653) • A. Fletcher, *Sussex, 1600–1660: a county community in peace and war* (1975); repr. (1980), 70, 72
Wealth at death disposed of surprisingly large sums given his apparently modest position: will, PRO, PROB 11/227, fols. 48*r*–50*v*

William Elder (*fl.* 1680–1701), by Joseph Nutting (after William Faithorne the elder)

Sources Redgrave, *Artists* • Bryan, *Painters* • J. Strutt, *A biographical dictionary, containing an historical account of all the engravers, from the earliest period of the art of engraving to the present time*, 2 vols. (1785–6) • H. Walpole, *Anecdotes of painting in England: with some account of the principal artists*, ed. R. N. Wornum, new edn, 3 vols. (1849) • Anderson, *Scot. nat.* • H. Walpole, ed., *A catalogue of engravers, who have been born, or resided in England*, 2nd edn (1765) • Vertue MSS, BL, Add. MS 23078 • Thieme & Becker, *Allgemeines Lexikon* • Engraved Brit. ports., 6.606
Likenesses A. Bannermann, vignette (inserted into engraving of Robert White), repro. in Walpole, *A catalogue of engravers*, pl. 92 • W. Elder, self-portrait, engraving • J. Nutting, line engraving (after W. Faithorne the elder), BM, NPG [*see illus.*]

Elderfield, Christopher (*bap.* 1607, *d.* 1652), Church of England clergyman, was born at Harwell, Berkshire, and baptized there on 11 April 1607, a younger son of at least three sons and three daughters of William Elderfield and his wife, Margaret. After preliminary education at a local school kept by the vicar, Hugh Lloyd, he matriculated from St Mary Hall, Oxford, on 10 November 1621, aged fifteen. He graduated BA on 22 February 1625, proceeded MA on 2 July 1627, and was ordained. He then held some minor appointments, including that of curate of Coates, Essex, before being presented by Sir William Goring in 1633 to the rectory of Burton, Sussex.

Elderfield spent the rest of his life in this tiny parish, his duties confined mainly to acting as chaplain to the Goring family at Burton Place. He never married, and devoted

Elderton, John (1755–1832), antiquary and collector of documents, was born in Salisbury, Wiltshire, son of Joseph Elderton (*d.* 1796), alderman and justice of the peace in Salisbury and register to the bishop of the diocese. A James Elderton, probably of the same family, was admitted 'an Extra-Licentiate of the College of Physicians' on 3 March 1724; he practised in Salisbury (Munk, 2.86). John Elderton matriculated at Trinity College, Oxford, on 12 July 1777, aged twenty-one. In 1781 he was collated to Aldbourne, Wiltshire, by Dr Hume, the bishop of Salisbury. In the same year he became chaplain to the earl of Cork and Orrery and was appointed vicar of Aldbourne, Wiltshire, an appointment which he held until his death.

In February 1790 he submitted the first of thirty-four contributions to the *Gentleman's Magazine*; all were sent from Bath and the last was sent in March 1794. Seven of his contributions were poems. As a poet, or versifier, he favoured octosyllabic couplets, some efforts being in a mild satiric vein, and, like many of his contemporaries, he wrote poems of occasion. He was evidently married, for he refers to a daughter, with the further information that the child's 'great ancestor' was 'Sir Edward Seymour, speaker of the House of Commons and grandfather of the present Duke of Somerset' (*GM*, 61/1, 1791, 39).

Elderton enjoyed a wide acquaintanceship and indulged in name-dropping in many of his letters to the *Gentleman's Magazine*. He writes familiarly of great personages: 'In August, 1783', he writes seven years after the events he relates,

> I paid my respects at the Grove (the Earl's [of Clarendon's] seat in Hertforshire); and although their Majesties and the Princesses had been there in the morning, and things consequently in confusion: yet all my entreaties to the contrary, could not prevent her Ladyship [the countess of Clarendon] shewing the apartments, and conversing on those subjects she had nearest at heart, *charity* and *benevolence*. (*GM*, 60/2, 1790, 1080)

He visited Sir Thomas Champneys, knew Henry Richard Vassal Fox, third Lord Holland, and wrote feelingly of that nobleman's deafness, a malady in which he showed much interest.

Elderton may be considered the prototypical contributor to the *Gentleman's Magazine*. He was a clergyman, an antiquary, a collector, and a man of varied interests. His principal interest as a collector was in old documents, especially letters, but he was also a transcriber of epitaphs and entries in parish registers, a traveller, and a collector of topographical drawings. In his first letter to the *Gentleman's Magazine* he transcribed the entry in the parish register for the birth of Edward Hyde, later earl of Clarendon, with an anecdote about Henry Hyde, Edward's father. Soon after, Elderton sent in a transcript of a letter from John Dryden to 'Lawrence Hyde, the second son of Lord Chancellor Clarendon' (*Letters of John Dryden*, 151), which he dated as '17th March, 1673–74 … from the circumstance of [a date] in another hand on the back' (*GM*, 60/2, 1790, 583); August 1683, conjectured by Edward Malone, is thought to be closer. He also transcribed a letter of Oliver Cromwell's and one by Edward VI printed in a very limited edition by Horace Walpole at the Strawberry Hill Press. Elderton's last contribution to the *Gentleman's Magazine* was a transcript and description of 'a duplicate of Mr. Russel's credentials to the Emperor to Morocco dated from Hampton-court in 1728' (*GM*, 64/1, 1794, 202). Elderton died at Gayton, Northamptonshire, on 22 November 1832. ARTHUR SHERBO

Sources Foster, *Alum. Oxon.* · *GM*, 1st ser., 61 (1791), 39 · *GM*, 1st ser., 66 (1796), 445 · *GM*, 1st ser., 102/2 (1832), 580 · *The letters of John Dryden*, ed. C. E. Ward (1942) · Munk, *Roll* · A. Sherbo, 'John Elderton, chaplain to the earl of Cork and Orrery', *Letters to Mr Urban of the Gentleman's Magazine* (1997)

Elderton, William (*d.* in or before **1592**), ballad writer, is of unknown origins. Although he and his ballads were well known in Elizabethan England—Elderton's name appears in the records of the privy council, as well as in the writings of numerous contemporary poets and dramatists—very little is known of his life, save for the fact that, as Gabriel Harvey famously put it, he had an 'ale-crammed nose' ('Foure letters', in *Works of Gabriel Harvey*, 1.201).

Attempts to reconstruct Elderton's life are fraught with difficulties. He may or may not have been the William Elderton who appears in the parish register of St Peter Cornhill, London, as the husband of a Grace Clearton and the father of a son baptized on 16 January 1548 (Rollins, *Elderton*, 200). It seems likely that Elderton the ballad writer was also the actor called Elderton whose name appears in an account of a twelfth-day entertainment performed for Edward VI in 1553, as well as the Elderton who in 1573 was in charge of the boy actors at Eton College, and who on 10 January 1574 was paid £6 13*s.* 4*d.* for a play presented before Queen Elizabeth (Kempe, 47; Rollins, *Elderton*, 216; Ritson, 197). It is unclear, however, whether Elderton the actor/ballad writer was the William Elderton recorded as having been an attorney in the London sheriff's court in 1562 and 1568.

It has also been suggested that Elderton was the inventor of a 'humourous and profitable entertainment' for taverns, which involved the performance of extemporaneous comic verse on the subject of drink, though there is no real proof of this (Collier, 3.210–12). In any event, the ballad writer is thought to have died in or before 1592, for Thomas Nash in that year made reference in his *Strange Newes* to the famous ballad writer being 'as dead as dead beere' (quoted in Rollins, *Elderton*, 233).

Given the inherently ephemeral nature of ballads and broadsheets, it is impossible to give a precise count of Elderton's works, but all the evidence suggests that his output was prolific. His first ballad, *The Panges of Love and Lovers Fttes* (sic), was printed in 1559. Other titles to which Elderton's name is attached include *The True Fourme and Shape of a Monsterous Chyld Borne in Stony Stratforde* (1565); *A Proper Newe Ballad Sheweing that Philosophers Learnynges, are Full of Good Warnynges* (1569?); and *Prepare ye to the Plowe, to the Tune, of Pepper is Blacke* (1570). Elderton was a fervent supporter of Queen Elizabeth and protestantism, a fact that is made abundantly clear in his many ballads devoted to celebrating the true faith and damning the queen's papist enemies. Ballads of this sort include the following titles: *A Ballat Intituled Northomberland Newes, wherein you maye See what Rebelles do Use* (1570); *Newes from Northumberland. This geare goythe well and better it shall, for triall will tell the treson of Ball* (1570); and *An Epytaphe uppon the Death of … I. Iuell … Bishop of Sarisburie* (1571). Many of the works attributed to Elderton in the Stationers' register have since disappeared. Other works that are extant or which are known to us through other means were never entered in the Stationers' register.

There seems little reason, however, to doubt that Elderton was well known in Elizabethan literary circles, even if his contemporaries found his capacity for alcohol more noteworthy than his poetry. Gabriel Harvey, who scornfully dismissed Elderton as a 'drunken rimester' in the second of his *Foure Letters* of 1592, none the less acknowledged him as the 'father' of Elizabethan ballad writers (Harvey, 1.233). Nash, in his *Strange Newes: Foure Letters Confuted*, playfully criticized Harvey 'for plucking *Elderton* out of the ashes of his Ale' and for 'finding fault with the brewing of his meeters' before going on to echo him by calling Elderton the father of ballad writers such as Thomas Deloney, Phillip Stubbs, and Robert Armin (quoted in Rollins, *Elderton*, 233). Harvey and Nash were not the only men to poke fun at Elderton's reputation; Elderton's legendary thirst was the subject of numerous comical and purposefully hackneyed rhymes in the years immediately following his death, and indeed well into the seventeenth century. None the less, Elderton's 'Gods of Love' (1562) may have provided Shakespeare with a song for Benedick in *Much Ado about Nothing*:

> The god of love
> That sits above,
> And knows me, and knows me,
> How pitiful I deserve.
> (*Much Ado*, V.ii)

ELIZABETH GOLDRING

Sources H. E. Rollins, *William Elderton: Elizabethan actor and ballad writer* (1920) · H. E. Rollins, *An analytical index to the ballad-entries in the registers of the Company of Stationers of London* (1924) · Arber, *Regs. Stationers*, vol. 2 · A. J. Kempe, ed., *The Loseley manuscripts* (1836) · *The works of Gabriel Harvey*, ed. A. B. Grosart, 3 vols. (1884–5) · J. P. Collier, *The history of English dramatic poetry*, 2nd edn, 3 vols. (1879) · *British Museum general catalogue of printed books … to 1955*, BM, 60 (1960) · *National union catalog, pre-1956 imprints*, Library of Congress, vol. 157 · H. Huth, ed., *Ancient ballads and broadsides published in England in the sixteenth century* (1867) · J. Ritson, *Bibliographia poetica* (1802) · J. Stow, *A survey of London* (1598)

Eldin. For this title name *see* Clerk, John, Lord Eldin (1757–1832).

Eldon. For this title name *see* Scott, John, first earl of Eldon (1751–1838).

Eldred, John (1552–1632), merchant, was born at New Buckenham, Norfolk, the son of John (*d. c.*1559) and Margaret Eldred. On moving to London he was apprenticed in the 1560s as a clothworker and lived with Edward Bates in the parish of St Michael Bassishaw. There he was well placed to take interest in the reviving Levantine trade in silks and calicoes with his distinguished near neighbours, Sir Anthony Calthorpe, of the Drapers' Company, Sir Edward Osborne, and Richard Staper.

On 12 February 1583 Osborne and Staper dispatched Eldred in the *Tiger* intending that with his experienced team he should use the queen's advance of 10,000 lb of silver to Osborne to finance a new Levantine trade especially in silks, spices, diamonds, rubies, and pearls to be found in the Persian Gulf and India. This plan also involved the London merchants John Newbery, Ralph Fitch, William Shales, Ralph Allen, and William Skinner, together with the jeweller William Leeds and a painter, James Story. Reaching Tripoli in Syria on 1 May 1583, Eldred and his companions travelled in a large caravan over the Lebanese mountains to Aleppo and thence to Bir and down the Euphrates almost to Felugia. There they had to tranship their cargo onto 100 asses for the short trip to Baghdad where Eldred lost a valuable casket. Leaving on 27 July 1583 they sailed down the Tigris to Balsora (Al Başrah). Eldred stayed six months until February 1584 trading mostly for cinnamon and nutmeg which he took back via Baghdad. He needed 14 river craft and 4000 camels to convey that cargo, arriving in Aleppo on 11 June 1584. Meanwhile Fitch, Newbery, Leeds, and Story, who had journeyed on to India, sent letters to Balsora telling of their imprisonment in Goa at the instance of rival Venetian and Portuguese traders and Jesuit missionaries. Fitch alone escaped, reaching London in 1591.

Meanwhile between 1584 and 1587 Eldred and Shales established several Middle Eastern trading bases while Eldred acted as Edward Harbourne's consular aide at Aleppo. Eldred reported:

> I made two voyages more unto Babylon and returned by the way aforesaid, over the deserts of Arabia. And afterwards, as one desirous to see other parts of the country, I went from Aleppo to Antioch, which is sixty English miles, and from thence went down to Tripoli, where, going aboard a small vessel, I arrived at Joppa, and travelled to Rama[la], Lycia, Gaza, Jerusalem, Bethlehem and to the River of Jordan, and the sea or lake of Sodom, and returned back to Joppa, and from thence by sea to Tripoli. (Hakluyt, *Principal Navigations*, 2.280)

Eldred's mission to Jerusalem features extensively in John Sanderson's diaries, including his induction as a knight of the Holy Sepulchre. On 11 November 1587 Eldred left the region only to encounter a severe storm in the *Hercules*. He had to put back to Tripoli, before reaching the Thames on 26 March 1588. Eldred's intelligence was thereupon shared with Richard Hakluyt, including his letter written from Baghdad on 14 June 1583 and other letters sent to him by Newbery and Fitch. More correspondence with Shales at Balsora survived in Harbourne's library and was printed by Samuel Purchas in *His Pilgrimes* (1625, vol. 2, bk 9, pp. 1642–6).

After a childless marriage to Jone (or Joan) Whalley (*d. c.*1581), he married in 1588 Mary Drone (1547–1613), daughter of Thomas Revett of Rishangles, Suffolk. They had five daughters and five sons baptized at St Michael Bassishaw. Emmanuel (*b.* 1590) died in infancy, but their second son, Revett (*b.* 1591), lived until 1653 and acted as John's executor in 1633, becoming a baronet in 1641. John Eldred's main asset was the manor of Great Saxham in Suffolk, acquired in 1597, where he built a large house popularly known as Nutmeg Hall. This later passed down the family of his third son, John Eldred, who was admitted as one of the free brethren of the East India Company on 7 January 1629.

When the Levant Company was merged with the Venice Company a new charter was issued in 1592 and Eldred was appointed its first treasurer. He attracted vehement criticism in this role from John Sanderson, who, in 1586, had waited in vain in Cairo for Eldred to arrive from Jerusalem. At the Levant Company meeting on 2 October its court ordered 'that Master Eldred and Master Fitch shall be in the meeting tomorrow morning to confer of the merchandise fit to be provided for the first voyage'. On 7 November 1600, in preparation 'for the discovery of the trade of the East Indies', the company minutes record:

> Mr John Eldred acquainteth this assemblie that one Thomas Eldred of Ipswich a man of good report who hath been imployed with Capten Caundish is willing to be imployed in the voyage and would go as Capten or Mr of one of the shippes, to whom answer is made that the Company will enterteyn none until they see and speak with him and have willed that Mr Eldred shall write unto them.   (BL OIOC, B1)

After its incorporation on 31 December 1600 Eldred, who had already subscribed £400, served on the East India Company's court up to 1610 and again during 1613–14. He took a close interest in how company ships were fitted out and provisioned, making a particularly important contribution with Mr Hammersley, recorded in the court minutes for 27 January 1607. By then his interest in shipping extended to ownership of some privateers lost in the West Indies, namely the *Mayflower* and three other ships fitted out jointly with Richard Hall in 1602 (two of which were captured by the Spaniards in 1603, and a third, the *Aid*, similarly captured in 1606). In 1609 he sold on his adventure of £550 in the fourth voyage to Edward Leighton. In 1610 he invested in the ill-fated voyage under Henry Hudson that attempted the north-west passage and in the subsequent return voyage of 1612 led by Thomas Button. As late as 25 May 1631 he is cited as a debtor of the Levant Company.

In 1598–1600 John Eldred joined Bevis Bulmer in an unfortunate pre-emptive purchase of Cornish tin revenues before undertaking more lucrative tax farms. In London his trading reputation was such that he was made master of the Clothworkers' Company in 1603; on 20 March 1604 he was elected alderman for the ward of Farringdon Without, but citing heavy commitments he resigned from the common council, paying the forfeit for that office of £500 on 14 June 1604. He was soon involved in Virginia Company affairs, seconding Sir Thomas Smyth for its governorship in 1606. He later supervised sales of royal lands, forging the relationships which, on 31 May 1631, led the privy council to ask him to help Colchester's poor earn sufficient to cover rising grain prices.

Eldred died on 6 December 1632 at Nutmeg Hall. His will of 8 October 1630 (PRO, PROB 11/163, fols. 5–7) was proved on 4 January 1633. He was buried at Great Saxham on 8 December 1632 as he had wished, although, should he have died in London, he had provided that he 'be buried in the church of Bassing hall in London where I have lived for many years and where my wife was buried'.

R. C. D. BALDWIN

Sources W. Foster, *The travels of John Sanderson in the Levant, 1584–1602*, Hakluyt Society, Extra Ser., 67 (1930), 53–4, 136, 143, 178, 199, 204–5, 255–6, 277, 287 · *APC*, 1630–31, no. 1062 · R. Hakluyt, *The principall navigations, voiages and discoveries of the English nation* (1589), 210, 231–3 · R. Hakluyt, *The principal navigations, voyages, traffiques and discoveries of the English nation*, 2nd edn, 3 vols. (1598–1600), 2/1, 268–80; 2/2, 245–79, esp. 248–9 · S. Purchas, *Hakluytus posthumus, or, Purchas his pilgrimes*, 2 (1625), bk 9, pp. 1642–6 · E. Arber, *An English garner*, 3 (1877); and (1903), 159–79 · A. B. Beaven, ed., *The aldermen of the City of London, temp. Henry III–[1912]*, 2 (1913), 49 · R. Cooke, *Visitation of London, 1568*, ed. H. Stanford London and S. W. Rawlins, [new edn], 2 vols. in one, Harleian Society, 109–10 (1963), 150 · A. D. Harrison, 'Thomas Eldred, merchant', *Mariner's Mirror*, 15 (1929), 54–64, 416–17 · M. Edwardes, *Ralph Fitch, Elizabethan in the Indies* (1972) · parish register, London, St Mary, Middle Street, GL · parish register, London, St Michael Bassishaw, GL · K. R. Andrews, *Trade, plunder and settlement: maritime enterprise and the genesis of the British empire, 1480–1630* (1984), 93–4, 285, 311–13 · H. N. Stevens, *The dawn of British trade to the East Indies, 1599–1603* (1886) [a transcript of manuscript court book records of the Levant and East India companies now held in BL, IOR B1/1] · P. L. Barbour, ed., *The Jamestown voyages under the first charter, 1606–1609*, 1, Hakluyt Society, 2nd ser., 136 (1969), 20, 35, 72 · first East India Company court book, BL OIOC, B1 · second East India Company court book, BL OIOC, B2, fols. 114, 132, 277, 294 · will, PRO, PROB 11/163, fols. 5–7 · London subsidy roll for 1589, Queens College, MS 72

Eldred, Thomas (1561–1624), mariner and merchant, was born in Brook Street, St Mary Quay, Ipswich, Suffolk, on 24 October 1561 and was baptized at St Mary Quay Church on 8 November following. He was the second, and eldest surviving, of the six sons of Thomas Eldred and his wife, Margery Studd. Both Eldred's father and his maternal grandfather Ralph Studd were tallow chandlers. Eldred would have been educated under John Dawes at the grammar school; on Dawes's arrival in 1567 the elder Thomas Eldred provided deal boards for new trestle tables. The elder Thomas held minor offices in the corporation and he died while his son was at sea in 1587. The younger Thomas Eldred was one of those '123 persons of all sortes' (Pretty, 290) who in July 1586 sailed from Plymouth in three ships with Thomas Cavendish. Hakluyt related how the barely fifty-strong remnant returned in September 1588 after circumnavigating the globe in the *Desire*, under its Ipswich master Thomas Fuller. The date of Eldred's father's death establishes beyond all doubt that the son, not the father, was the Thomas Eldred of this voyage.

There is no record of there being any children of Thomas Eldred's marriage to Susan (*d.* 1638), daughter of Henry Aldham (*c.*1530–1608), mariner, of St Mary Quay parish, later keeper of The Angel inn on the Quay. From Aldham in 1608 the Eldreds inherited lands in Falkenham, Trimley, and Kirton, all near Felixstowe. Thomas's sister Sara married Richard Burlingham, a fellow Ipswich mariner. From 1595 onwards Eldred was elected to various offices, but presumably because he needed his freedom to travel he paid fines to avoid them. In 1600 he was recommended by John Eldred of Great Saxham (certainly not a close relative) to his fellow directors of the East India Company for engagement in its service in the forthcoming venture for the discovery of the trade of the East Indies. Eldred was praised as 'a man of good report who hath been employed with Capt. Caundish' who was 'willing to be employed as captain or master of one of our ships' (*CSP col.*, 2.111). Whether this led to Thomas Eldred's appointment is not clear, but it was not until 1608, when he was shipping cloth to Bordeaux in other men's ships, that he accepted election as an Ipswich twenty-four-man. He was town treasurer in 1613–14. Advanced in 1620 to being one of the twelve portmen, he became eligible for the top office of bailiff (joint mayor and chief magistrate) in 1621–2. On 3 May 1624 he was buried in St Clement's Church, where on 27 December 1638 his widow was laid beside him. It has caused confusion that a nephew Thomas, son of William Eldred, merchant and mariner, was still of St Clement's parish in 1645.

Thomas Eldred's will shows him to have been a devout follower of the celebrated town preacher Samuel Ward, and a wealthy man able to leave about £500 (will, PROB 11/143, sig. 53) to his relatives and the poor of most Ipswich parishes, but there is no mention of ships or merchandise. It is probable that his nephew Thomas had already succeeded him in business. His widow, Susan, would have lived on in 99 Fore Street, in St Clement's parish, long known as Eldred's house because of three oil-painted panels showing Thomas, a ship, and a globe in the overmantel of the largest room. An inscription commemorates the voyage in the *Desire* with the lines 'He that travels the world about, Seeth God's wonders and God's works.' Although the house is demolished, the overmantel is in Christchurch Museum, Ipswich. Thomas's next younger brother was John Eldred (1565–1646) of Olivers in Stanway near Colchester, where he was an alderman. In 1620 John had copies made of the three paintings, better in quality and showing Thomas appropriately older, and in 1630 he took arms that were distinct from the bearings of the Saxham Eldreds which included globes and a merman crest to show his pride in his brother's achievement. One telling memento of Thomas Eldred remains in the Ipswich Town Library, the *Historiae animalium* of Conrad Gesner inscribed 'The guift of Thomas Eldred' (Ipswich Town Library, Ipswich School). The contemporarily hand-coloured woodcuts of animals would remind Eldred and show others some of the divine wonders that he had seen.   J. M. BLATCHLY

Sources [F. Pretty], 'The admirable and prosperous voyage of the worshipfull Master Thomas Candish', in R. Hakluyt, *The principal navigations, voyages, traffiques and discoveries of the English nation*, 11, Hakluyt Society, extra ser., 11 (1904), 290–347 · PRO, PROB 11/143, sig. 53 · A. D. Harrison, 'Thomas Eldred, merchant', *Mariner's Mirror*, 15 (1929), 54–64, 416–17 · 'East Anglian miscellany no. 5407—trade between Ipswich and France, 1608', *East Anglian Daily Times* (22 Feb 1919), 7c–d · CSP col., 2.110–11 · parish register, Ipswich, St Mary Quay, Suffolk RO, Ipswich [birth] · parish register, Ipswich, St Clement's, Suffolk RO, Ipswich [death] · Ipswich assembly and court books, 1595–1624, Suffolk RO, Ipswich · partial transcript of Henry Aldham's will, Suffolk RO, Ipswich, court rolls of the manor of Walton-cum-Trimley, HB 8/1/168, fol. 108v

Likenesses oil on board in overmantel, Christchurch Museum, Ipswich · portrait, priv. coll. · two portraits, repro. in Harrison, 'Thomas Eldred', 55

Wealth at death legacies totalling about £500; property and lands at Falkenham and Bucklesham, near Felixstowe: will, PRO, PROB 11/143, sig. 53

Eldred, William (*b.* 1562/3, *d.* in or after **1646**), master gunner, was possibly of East Anglian descent. In his youth he spent some years as a gunner in France and Germany, and about 1600 he came as a gunner to the Cinque Ports. On 11 January 1605, described as a yeoman of Dover, Eldred married at Canterbury Judith Dun (*b.* 1573), a widow, also of Dover, and in 1614 he became a freeman of Dover in right of his wife, born free of the town in right of her father, Thomas Turpin, clerk.

Eldred extended his skills as a gunner to the civilian art of surveying, and in 1616 he 'left' Dover (the roll of freemen notes beside his name 'exit ad Castr. Dovor') for Dover Castle, where he seems to have been given responsibility by Lord Zouche, the new lord warden of the Cinque Ports, for the maintenance of the fortifications and site generally. Letters from Eldred to Lord Zouche's secretary refer to the need for urgent repairs to the castle and church, as well as to insubordination on the part of a gunner. During this time Eldred made and noted down many of the practice shots described in his manual on artillery, *The Gunner's Glasse* (1646); on several occasions he fired the famous Dutch cannon which was later known as Queen Elizabeth's pocket pistol. Eldred seems to have returned briefly to Dover town in 1622, when he again took out his freedom, this time in right of a freehold in the town, but by 1624 he was back in the castle, now with the title of master gunner of Dover Castle. About 1640 he was employed by the commissioners of Dover harbour to prepare a survey of the castle, town, and harbour.

Eldred was a typical Renaissance man, skilled in both arts and sciences. A set of verses in the British Library, entitled 'William Eldred's Song', satirizes all elements of society, from the king down to a beggar, and *The Gunner's Glasse*, a practical manual in dialogue form between a gunner and a 'scholler', combines science with readability and is enlivened with occasional anecdote. Eldred had met Charles I in Dover and had been promised an opportunity to demonstrate his methods in London, 'but his Majesty never was there since, nor I was never sent for' (p. 36). *The Gunner's Glasse* is perhaps the first treatise on the subject to deal specifically with 'the naming of parts'. It concludes with an English translation of part of Diego Ufano's *Tratado dela artilleria*, published in Spanish in 1612 and shortly thereafter in several other European languages. Eldred, who knew French and Latin, may himself have translated this from the French.

The Gunner's Glasse reveals the dangers of expressing an opinion in public in the 1640s. Eldred treads a wary path between the king and parliament, praying that their differences may be resolved peacefully. He had, however, signed the Kentish petition for the reformation of the liturgy presented by Sir Edward Dering in 1641. It is possible that Eldred also had a hand in an anonymous pamphlet published in 1642, *Englands safety in navie and fortifications … conteining necessary observations concerning Dover, and other sea-towns*.

Eldred lived to be a very old man: *The Gunner's Glasse* contains a portrait of him at the age of eighty-three, though gaps in the records make it impossible to establish the date of his death. His wife had probably died by 1622, since she is not mentioned in the second application for his freedom of Dover, and he appears to have left no children.   SHIRLEY BURGOYNE BLACK

Sources W. Eldred, *The gunner's glasse, wherein the diligent practicioner may see his defects, and may from point to point reforme and amend all errours that are commonly incident to unskilfull gunners* (1646) · *CSP dom.*, 1620–24 [letters to Lord Zouche's secretary] · William Eldred to Lord Zouche's secretary, 1617, BL, Eg. 2584, fol. 7 · register of freemen of Dover, BL, Add. MS 29625 · 'William Eldred's song', BL, Add. MS 23229, fol. 20 · J. M. Cowper, ed., *Canterbury marriage licences*, 6 vols. (1892–1906), vol. 1 · W. Eldred, survey and maps of Dover castle, town, and harbour, CKS, TR/1380/1–10 and 11–19 · L. B. Larking, ed., *Proceedings principally in the county of Kent in connection with the parliaments called in 1640, and especially with the committee of religion appointed in that year*, CS, old ser., 80 (1862) · *IGI* · *Englands safety in navie and fortifications; the common interest both of king and people, conteining necessary observations concerning Dover, and other sea-towns of England* (1642) · *BL cat.* [for edns of Diego Ufano, 1700–50] · H. L. Blackmore, *The armouries of the Tower of London* (1976)
Archives CKS, TR/1380/1–10 and 11–19 · PRO
Likenesses woodcut, BM; repro. in Eldred, *The gunner's glasse*, frontispiece

Eleanor [Eleanor of Aquitaine], *suo jure* **duchess of Aquitaine** (*c.*1122–1204), queen of France, consort of Louis VII, and queen of England, consort of Henry II, was the elder daughter of Guillaume, eighth count of Poitou, and tenth duke of Aquitaine (1099–1137), and of his wife, Aliénor (*d.* before 1137), from the family of the viscounts of Châtellerault. Their only son, also Guillaume, died as a child—probably in the 1120s, not long before his mother: they were survived by Eleanor and her sister, Petronilla.

Aquitanian inheritance Uncertainties over the precise date and place of Eleanor's own birth can be explained by the fact that she was never intended to succeed to her father's duchy, since it was rumoured in Aquitaine that the duke was proposing to remarry. His sudden death at Santiago de Compostela in Easter week 1137 appears to have been unexpected and left his duchy without a direct male heir. The huge size of Eleanor's inheritance accounts for her attraction to suitors of the highest rank and for her two marriages, first to the Capetian King Louis VII (1120–1180), and then to the Angevin Count Henry (1133–1189), who became *Henry II of England. The magnificence of this inheritance does not, however, explain the important role that she played on the European political stage throughout most of her long life, and still less the fascination that she exercised over the minds of contemporaries as a 'woman without compare' (Richard of Devizes, 25).

The post-Carolingian duchy of Aquitaine, whose southern portions eventually came to form the bulk of the duchy of Guyenne of later English kings, in principle covered the lands between the River Loire and the Pyrenees, extending eastward to the Massif Central and the headwaters of the River Garonne. In practice, however, ducal authority was legally ill-defined and varied considerably in its effectiveness. To the north and east, moreover, there was apt to be conflict with the Capetians over the control of Berry and the Auvergne. Additionally, beyond the frontiers of Aquitaine Eleanor had a strong hereditary claim to the rich county of Toulouse, through the marriage of her grandfather Duke Guillaume IX, to its heir, Philippa. This claim was to have sufficient weight to induce both Eleanor's husbands (Louis in 1141, Henry in

Eleanor [of Aquitaine], *suo jure* **duchess of Aquitaine** (*c.*1122–1204), tomb effigy, early 13th cent.

1159) to besiege Toulouse in the hope of making good Eleanor's claims. Berry, Auvergne, and Toulouse would all feature prominently in peace settlements negotiated between French and English kings in the years on either side of 1200.

The dukes of Aquitaine in the early twelfth century were renowned for far more than their title to vast territories. Guillaume IX is the first named lyric poet composing in the *langue d'oc*, or Occitan—the romance speech of southern Gaul. The linguistic boundary between Occitan and the northern version of the romance tongue, or *langue d'oïl*, ran just south of Poitiers, the traditional political 'capital' of the duchy. The Poitevin duke's court became a principal focus for literary activity and patronage, and in particular for the composition of Occitan vernacular poetry. The latter, which was remarkable for its elaborate and intricate professionalism, and for the secularity of much of its subject matter, constitutes one of the main threads of the European literary tradition (as Dante appreciated). It has also been associated with the evolution of a doctrine of courtly love, which, like Eleanor's own role as literary patron and inspiration of poets, has long been the subject of controversy and debate. Scandalized monks, including the Englishman William of Malmesbury, remembered Eleanor's grandfather as having carried in battle a shield painted with his mistress's image. Although it seems likely that Malmesbury was transmitting a garbled version of one of the duke's (now lost) songs, his outrage and incomprehension underline the fact that Eleanor was the product of a very different world from that of the north European court circles into which she married.

Queen of the French In late July 1137 Eleanor was married in the city of Bordeaux to the Capetian Louis VII, who had been consecrated king during his father's lifetime by Pope Innocent II on 25 October 1131. Husband and wife were also crowned (possibly using an *ordo* devised for the occasion, declaring Louis to be the ruler of 'Franks, Burgundians, and Aquitanians'), and similar ceremonies took place in other Aquitanian cities. According to one contemporary northern chronicle Duke Guillaume had planned this match and 'left his territory to both of them according to the law of marriage' (*La chronique de Morigny*, 67), but this explanation of a marriage alliance that obviously favoured Capetian interests is not necessarily entirely trustworthy. In fact this was a time when aristocratic rules of succession were still often unclear. Resistance—such as had indeed occurred when Duke Guillaume IX tried to establish Poitevin control in Toulouse in his wife's name—might be expected when a woman succeeded to a great principality like Aquitaine; and in 1137 resistance to the imposition of Capetian rule seems to have been anticipated in the north. Louis VI (father of Eleanor's bridegroom) made important concessions to the regional bishops of Aquitaine before the French expedition set out for Bordeaux; and furthermore the adolescent bridegroom was accompanied by a papal legate, by his father's chief adviser Abbot Suger of St Denis, and by a large company of knights. The Anglo-Norman historian Orderic Vitalis wrote that after his marriage 'the boy Louis was crowned at Poitiers, and so gained possession of the kingdom of the French and the duchy of Aquitaine, which none of his forebears had held before him' (Ordericus Vitalis, *Eccl. hist.*, 6.490–91), a statement that seems to lay bare the underlying territorial aims of the Capetian dynasty. The significance of the acquisition of this great region to the Capetians is also shown by the dual title of 'king of the French and duke of the Aquitanians' ('rex Francorum et dux Aquitanorum') which was invariably attributed to King Louis during the years of his marriage to Eleanor. Indeed, the importance of that title to the French king is shown by the fact that Louis VII continued to employ it until 1154, some years after Eleanor's second marriage.

Louis and Eleanor had two daughters, Marie (*b. c.*1145) and Alice (*b. c.*1150) after their return from Jerusalem. From her marriage to Count Henri of Champagne the elder of the two is often simply referred to as Marie de Champagne, and is remembered as a patron of writers and vernacular poets; Alice was married to Count Thibault of Blois, Count Henri's brother. Despite the birth of these girls, Queen Eleanor's fertility remained an issue which would have dramatic political repercussions; and, according to one account, her first daughter was conceived only after she had suffered at least one miscarriage and as a result of saintly intervention. At a meeting between the queen and Abbot Bernard of Clairvaux at St Denis (probably in 1144), the abbot allegedly promised that, in return for Eleanor's intercession for peace with her husband, the abbot would in his turn intercede with God for the gift of a child. But Bernard did not secure her a son. Eleanor's ultimate failure to give birth to a boy who could succeed to the Capetian throne was surely the chief reason for her separation from Louis VII; but there were signs of tension within the marriage before a divorce was pronounced in the spring of 1152.

The second crusade Crisis was in fact precipitated during the course of the second crusade between 1147 and 1149. King Louis (by now in his mid-twenties) proposed an expedition to Jerusalem at the Christmas court of 1145, but an expedition was not organized until Abbot Bernard's preaching galvanized the French aristocracy into taking the cross. Queen Eleanor was present in March 1146 at the abbey of Vézelay at the most memorable of those occasions; and, after receiving a papal blessing in the church of St Denis a little over a year later (11 June 1147), both king and queen left with a great army to take the land route to Constantinople. They reached the capital of the eastern empire in early October. Statements that Eleanor raised a military company of armed and mounted ladies are based upon fanciful imaginings of the Amazons and their queen by the Byzantine writer Nicetas; it is more reliably recorded that she and the German-born Empress Bertha communicated by letter, and that the Emperor Manuel I Komnenos tried to arrange a Greek marriage for one of the ladies accompanying the French army. An expedition such as this could be used to make social and diplomatic contacts, as well as pursuing religious and military aims. But in general the crusaders' failure to agree on the expedition's strategic objectives proved to be a disaster which, at the personal level, was reflected in the deteriorating relationship between Louis VII and Eleanor.

That became apparent when, after a disastrous defeat by the Turks in Anatolia, a battered army reached Antioch in March 1148. This important principality was then ruled by Queen Eleanor's paternal uncle, Raymond, who had arrived in the crusaders' territories before his brother's death at Compostela in 1137. (His authority in Antioch derived from marriage to Constance, daughter of Prince Bohemund II.) Ever since the fall of Edessa in 1144 the territory surrounding this important city had become dangerously exposed to Muslim incursions: Prince Raymond intended to persuade the French king to go over to the offensive and join a campaign to lay siege to Aleppo. That was strategically sensible, but the king—apparently eager to discharge his pilgrim's vows in the holy city—was unwilling to participate in the proposed expedition. Eleanor's role was crucial. She was almost certainly sympathetic to her compatriots' aims; but, although aristocratic women were expected to intercede with their husbands, the frequent conversations between the prince and his niece—surely in the *langue d'oc* and perhaps not comprehensible to northerners—gave grounds for suspicion within the French court circle. Some years later John of Salisbury voiced the gossip: citing Ovid's *Heroides* he wrote allusively that 'guilt under kinship's guise could lie concealed' (John of Salisbury, *Historia pontificalis*, 53). Raymond's death in battle against Nur al-Din in the following year (June 1149) certainly justified this prince's assessment that military aid was desperately needed by the Christians in Antioch. On the other side of the Mediterranean, by contrast, royal scandal aroused far more interest: rumours from Antioch reverberated around Europe, and pursued Eleanor to the end of her life.

In any case the king's wishes prevailed and the royal party sailed for Jerusalem, putting in at Acre in June 1148. It is not known whether Eleanor was in any way involved in the disastrous siege of Damascus, which her husband joined after their arrival in Jerusalem, but it seems unlikely. On the journey home to Europe the queen was briefly held captive by a Greek naval commander after her ship was separated from her husband's; she was rescued, and in September 1149 they were reunited and magnificently received at Potenza by King Roger of Sicily. In the following month the royal couple paid a visit to Pope Eugenius III at Tusculum. By this time (as can be seen from the correspondence of Abbot Suger) news of 'discord' between Louis and Eleanor had reached the French kingdom, although that discord need not have referred exclusively to 'the Antioch affair'. Whatever the cause, the pope's chief aim (again according to John of Salisbury's recollections) was to reconcile the king and queen. Eugenius forbade discussion of the issue of their consanguinity, and rather touchingly encouraged them to sleep together in a sumptuously decorated bed which he had especially prepared for them.

Divorce and remarriage Papal mediation was for the moment effective: the return to France was followed by a long expedition to Aquitaine, as well as by the birth of the couple's second daughter. And yet a divorce was finally proclaimed during Lent 1152 at Beaugency. No official proceedings survive for that gathering but, despite the earlier papal prohibition, consanguinity was the pretext for the divorce pronounced by the assembled ecclesiastics. Some later twelfth-century writers give the more dramatic explanation that, during her first marriage, Eleanor had 'shared Louis's bed' with Count Geoffrey of Anjou—this was the charge made by Walter Map in *De nugis curialium*, probably written *c*.1181–3 (Map, 474–6). If that had been correct, incest would have been added to adultery, since Count Geoffrey was the father of Eleanor's second husband. Statements such as this have been accepted by some modern historians; but it is far more likely that these represent reflections of a prevailing clerical misogyny, court rivalries, and—when written in the late twelfth century—a more general anti-Angevin propaganda. There can be little doubt that both personal desire and dynastic need for a son were the motives underlying Louis VII's decision to obtain a divorce in 1152 (as is surely proved by the speed with which he remarried on each occasion that he lost a wife through divorce or death). In any case, even if rumours of a possibly scandalous liaison did follow Eleanor from Antioch, there was no lack of candidates willing to marry her again.

During the spring and summer of 1152 it must have become abundantly clear that there was in fact little chance that Eleanor could remain unmarried, even had she wished to do so. On her return to Aquitaine, for instance, she is portrayed by a Tours chronicler escaping from ambushes laid both by the count of Blois and by Geoffrey of Anjou (second son of the Empress *Matilda and of the Count Geoffrey le Bel who was the subject of Walter Map's later charge of adultery against Eleanor); but within a few months she was nevertheless married to Henry of Anjou, elder brother of this Geoffrey, her failed kidnapper. No information survives describing how this new match was arranged, but it seems unlikely that Eleanor's choice was made because she had already (in Map's words) 'cast incestuous eyes' on the young Count Henry. Eleanor's modern biographers have sometimes supposed that this was a love match, but, although that is not impossible, there are few signs to lend support to such speculation. For Louis VII his former wife's remarriage meant that he lost political control of Aquitaine: presumably he gambled on the chances that his own remarriage would produce a son, and that Eleanor's would not—in which case one of their daughters might eventually succeed to Eleanor's duchy.

Duchess of Normandy and queen of the English Eleanor's second marriage took place in Poitiers in May 1152 (from where she issued two charters on 26 and 27 May). Henry of Anjou was then nineteen years old, while Eleanor was about thirty, so in personal terms their union resembled that of Henry's own father, Geoffrey, who for political and dynastic reasons had been married to the older (but widowed) Empress Matilda. In 1152 Henry was duke of the Normans and had just recently succeeded to his father in Anjou (despite assertions that Count Geoffrey had intended to divide the territories between his sons). As his claims to the English throne were not yet officially recognized, marriage to Eleanor brought Henry many immediate political advantages. In particular it enabled him more easily to resist his younger brother's plots and to repel attacks on Normandy and Anjou mounted by an aristocratic coalition, backed by the Capetian king. In this context it was surely significant that Eleanor's first son by Henry was called William: 'the name proper to the counts of the Poitevins and dukes of the Aquitanians' (*Chronica Roberti de Torigneio* in *Chronicles*, ed. Howlett, 4.176). Even though William was also a name that had been borne both by dukes of Normandy and after 1066 by kings of the English, it implies acknowledgement of the importance of Aquitaine at a time when possession of the duchy could have been essential to Henry's political survival. Eleanor may have hoped that this new marriage would enable her to repair some of the effects of the maladministration of her ancestral duchy, which had suffered many financial exactions during the course of the crusade. In the long term, however, Henry's recognition as heir to King Stephen in 1153, and his succession to the English throne on Stephen's death in the following year, meant that Eleanor's duchy was once more absorbed into a larger political unit.

Eleanor was crowned queen of the English in Westminster Abbey on 19 December 1154 at the same time as her husband was consecrated king. As Henry's wife, Eleanor underwent some extraordinary reversals of fortune. By contrast with the fifteen years between 1137 and 1152, when she had experienced perhaps three pregnancies, she now had ahead of her fifteen years of regular child bearing. Before Eleanor became queen of the English she and her second husband had already had a son. Altogether Henry and Eleanor had eight children. After the short-lived William (born in August 1153, he died in December 1156) came *Henry, the Young King, born in London on 28 February 1155; *Matilda, born in 1156, who married Duke Henry the Lion of Saxony in 1168; *Richard, born at Oxford in September 1157; *Geoffrey, born on 23 September 1158; Eleanor, born at Domfront in 1161; *Joanna, born in October 1165; and *John, born probably in December 1167, possibly at Oxford. The marriages arranged for them at a young age show that the girls served their parents' political and diplomatic ends; but marriages were also arranged for the sons. It was planned that Henry, the Young King, and Richard should marry daughters of Eleanor's first husband, Louis VII; similarly, Geoffrey was actually married to Constance, heir to the duchy of Brittany—a principality whose control had long been coveted by the Norman dukes; John's proposed marriage to a daughter of the Savoyard count of Maurienne (the subject of an elaborate written agreement in 1173) never came to anything.

Queen Eleanor's involvement in the making of dynastic marriages in the years after 1189 suggests that she accepted the grounds on which such aristocratic and royal alliances were based, but it would be a mistake to suppose that this necessarily ruled out maternal or personal feelings, or (as has sometimes been claimed) that she was essentially a frivolous and selfish woman. It is difficult to assess the emotional sincerity of a twelfth-century woman but, while her children were young, the queen certainly often accompanied them during the Angevin court's peripatetic existence. In 1160 she crossed with the young Henry and Matilda to Normandy, in 1165 with Richard and Matilda, in 1167 to England with Matilda; during these same years also expenses of the queen and children are to be found quite frequently grouped together on the pipe rolls of the English exchequer.

A modern biographer of Henry II has observed that during the years of their marriage Queen Eleanor was 'almost totally eclipsed' by her husband (Warren, 121). As far as Eleanor's years of imprisonment are concerned that conclusion is obviously correct, but it surely underestimates the queen's participation in the running of the Angevin empire in the years between 1154 and 1173. During royal absences it seems that the queen's permission was needed to leave the royal court—that at least is implied in John of Salisbury's correspondence; there are also references suggesting that she had influence in at least some ecclesiastical appointments. Her presence was also specifically noted at many great ceremonial courts held throughout the territories making up the Angevin empire: at Cherbourg in 1159 and 1162, Falaise in 1160, Le Mans in 1160–61,

Poitiers in 1166, Chinon in 1172. She was almost certainly present at Clermont-Ferrand in 1173, and in the same year at Limoges. At the meetings of 1173 the political affairs of the Auvergne were considered, while the homage of Raymond of Toulouse, and the proposal to marry John to a daughter of the count of Maurienne were also negotiated. At Limoges the suspicion that a revolt was being plotted against Henry II also surfaced.

Despite her recurrent pregnancies, Eleanor played an active part in the government and administration of the English kingdom (for which documentary evidence is more abundant than for any other region); and her itinerary seems often to have been designed to complement her husband's. While Henry was campaigning in Toulouse in 1159, Eleanor intervened in England in a prolonged legal dispute between the abbot of St Albans and one of his great lay tenants; a quitclaim made before her by a Robert Flambard may be of about the same date. In late 1158 (also during the king's absence from England) her authorization for a suit brought by Richard of Anstey to be heard in *curia regis* meant that she was instrumental in initiating a long-running inheritance dispute which has become a *cause célèbre*. Evidence for the queen's administrative intervention has undoubtedly been undervalued; and even though her activity was on a limited scale compared with Henry II's, during this phase of her life she witnessed royal charters, and writs and documents embodying her mandates were issued in her own name. Although the composition of her household has never been worked out in detail, during these early years three of her officials, the steward Ralph of Hastings, and the clerks Adam of Ely and Elias, were associates or relatives of men occupying positions of importance in English ecclesiastical or royal administration; Bernard is named as her chancellor. At a later date many of those who served her apparently had Poitevin connections or origins, and her chaplains acted as her scribes, occasionally with the title of notary.

In the year 1168—thus after the birth of her last child—Queen Eleanor is found in Aquitaine together with her son Richard, and with Earl Patrick of Salisbury. The earl was fairly soon killed in a skirmish with Poitevin barons (probably members of the prominent Lusignan family) and, according to the much later vernacular life of William (I) Marshal, Eleanor herself only just avoided capture. She was rescued by the Marshal's son, whom she rewarded lavishly for his bravery; she also acted handsomely in founding a special commemoration for Earl Patrick's soul in the comital abbey church of St Hilaire in Poitiers. That venerable church was also the scene of Richard's inauguration as count of Poitou; and during the years between 1169 and 1173 this adolescent got his first taste of the exercise of authority in his mother's company, and in her ancestral territories. Regional authors writing south of the Loire lay especial emphasis on ceremonial aspects of the new regime, for in Limoges investiture with the ring of Ste Valérie seems to have symbolized the power to be wielded by the ruler of Aquitaine. On this occasion the ceremony was probably accompanied by a newly devised inauguration liturgy.

Rearrangements for the government of Aquitaine form only one facet of Henry II's political plans at this time, for the king had to pay attention to his sons' searches for spheres in which each of them could independently exercise power and patronage; but there was also an increasing threat of Capetian aggression towards Angevin territories. Both concerns are linked in the reference to a meeting at Montmirail in January 1169 at which Richard performed homage to Louis VII for the duchy of Aquitaine—an act that suggests that officially Richard had indeed been vested with authority over the whole region, but also that political concessions had to be made to the French ruler. The repeated homages of these years were a relatively novel way of attempting to solve some acute political problems arising out of the formation of Henry II's 'empire'. At the same time Richard's deep involvement in the affairs of Aquitaine, and his attraction to its language and literature, should be traced back to these years—as must be the trust which as king he later showed in his mother's political abilities. But in practice, because of Richard's youth, Eleanor must have wielded power; and that view is supported by the relatively sparse documentation available for the government of the region.

Rebel and prisoner Eleanor's return to her ancestral duchy and this phase of her life did not last very long. The political crisis apparently came to a head in the city of Limoges where, early in 1173, the count of Toulouse allegedly told Henry that his sons were plotting against him. The Young King fled to the protection of his father-in-law, Louis VII (he had been married as a child to Margaret in 1160). Contemporaries on the whole agreed that the Capetian king fomented filial disobedience, although 'it was said by some' that Queen Eleanor was among the authors of that 'deplorable betrayal' (*Gesta … Benedicti*, 1.42). Other contemporaries concealed their attitudes in the language of the prophecies of Merlin apparently made fashionable some decades earlier by Geoffrey of Monmouth. The writer known as the Norman Dragon refers directly to Merlin's prophecies and calls Eleanor 'the eagle of the broken agreement' (*Draco Normannicus*, 603), a theme further developed by the historian Richard le Poitevin. Eleanor undoubtedly did join the revolt along with Richard and Geoffrey who were then in her custody; but for a number of reasons the degree of the queen's involvement is difficult to determine.

The most basic is that her movements cannot be precisely traced: how long she evaded capture, and where she was seized by Henry's men, are unknown. It is widely held that when captured she was disguised as a man, but that seems only to be mentioned by the monastic chronicler Gervase of Canterbury, who obviously wished to discredit her for this lack of feminine modesty. More seriously, Eleanor was openly criticized by the archbishop of Rouen because, forgetting that 'man is the head of woman', she had thrown off her husband's authority. Her revolt symbolized the overturning of political and social order, strongly reinforced by religious attitudes towards the proper relationship between the sexes. Modern historians have frequently attributed the queen's encouragement of

her sons' rebellion to jealousy of Henry's mistress Rosamund Clifford, but that explanation was not advanced in the twelfth century and (apart from the problems of chronology involved) does not seem to provide an especially plausible psychological explanation for the scale of the revolt—the central political crisis of Henry II's reign. In truth Eleanor's motives are obscure: she may have been provoked by Henry's treatment of their sons, or by the terms on which she was permitted to exercise power in her duchy. More specifically she may have resented the performance of homage to her husband by Count Raymond of Toulouse in 1173, since that implied the repudiation of her own claims to the Toulouse succession, for which in 1159 Henry had been prepared to fight.

Whatever Eleanor's reasons for joining the revolt, for her its consequences were especially severe and longlasting: by early 1174 she was taken to England where she endured at least ten years' confinement. Her name is not mentioned in the settlement by which the king patched up peace with his sons (at Montlouis on 30 September 1174); and, as far as it is possible to tell from surviving records and documents, the queen never again participated in English government during the years 1174–89. An Aquitanian chronicler, Geoffroi de Vigeois, thought that Queen Eleanor was imprisoned at Salisbury, but English narrative writers are silent on this matter. A number of terse pipe roll entries record expenses allowed on her behalf (authorized either by the king's writ or by that of Ranulf de Glanville), but these do not reveal where she was held. Allegedly, one of the last requests made by the Young King on his deathbed (June 1183) was that his mother should be treated less harshly: her imprisonment does subsequently seem to have been relaxed. Notably she was allowed to meet her daughter Matilda and exiled son-in-law, Henry the Lion, duke of Saxony, when they visited England during 1184; and, since new clothes of samite and furs were then made for the queen, it presumably follows that Eleanor took part in the public ceremonies that would have been central to such a visit. In 1185 King Henry even obliged Richard formally to return power in Poitou to his mother, but that did not mean that she gained actual political control. One of Richard's first acts after his father's death was to order his mother's release; and even before he had crossed the channel the new king immediately granted Eleanor power to dispose of English affairs. He also restored to her control the lands and revenues that she had enjoyed before the revolt of 1173.

Vicereine for Richard I The last fifteen years of Eleanor's life fully reveal her extraordinary abilities as a ruler. These seem scarcely to have been recognized during the years of her first marriage; but during the years 1154–73 she was initiated into the conduct of most aspects of contemporary administration and government, even though in 1189 she had not recently exercised these in practice. Her return to government, and her control of political affairs, between the time of Richard's accession and her own death in 1204 form one of the most remarkable phases of her whole life, and were utterly uncharacteristic of any contemporary lay ruler. In 1189 Eleanor was about sixty-seven years old—therefore seventy-seven when John succeeded Richard in 1199—and energetically active at an age scarcely ever reached by any secular ruler of the eleventh or twelfth centuries or, for that matter, by any of the men of her immediate family circle. (Her two husbands died at about sixty and fifty-seven years respectively; her son King John did not quite make fifty, while Henry, the Young King, Geoffrey, and Richard did not reach forty. Her own father, too, was under forty when he died.) There were of course precedents for the conduct of government by royal or aristocratic widows, released from their husbands' control; and Richard's plans to lead an army to go to the relief of Jerusalem made it likely that, when he succeeded his father, he intended his mother to wield power during his absence on crusade. Nevertheless, although in many respects this phase of Eleanor's life can be treated as a continuum, King Richard's early death in 1199 was followed by political crises even more threatening than those which Eleanor faced with Richard's captivity and John's revolt against his brother and alliance with King Philip Augustus (1193–4). The queen's activity after John's succession should, therefore, be distinguished from her general political and governmental involvement after her husband's death, and it needs to be separately considered.

Immediately after Richard had entrusted Eleanor with power in the English kingdom she went from 'city to city and castle to castle', holding 'queenly courts', releasing prisoners and exacting oaths from all freemen to be loyal to her son as their as yet uncrowned king (*Chronica … Hovedene*, 3.4). She was especially noted among those greeting Richard at his ceremonial entry into Winchester on 14 August 1189. From this time on first Richard and then John as kings entrusted her with the direction or conduct of a number of important affairs, involving some journeys of startling length. On the first occasion, during the early stages of Richard's crusading expedition, Eleanor accompanied *Berengaria of Navarre, his prospective bride, to Messina. After a winter journey over the Alps they reached the Sicilian city in late March 1191; Eleanor almost immediately left again for England but, on her return journey through Italy in April of the same year, she became involved in negotiations at the papal curia over the appointment of Richard's bastard half-brother *Geoffrey to the archbishopric of York. Then, after King Richard's capture by the duke of Austria on his own return to Europe, and at the end of the protracted negotiations for his release, Eleanor made an extended visit to Germany. This was far more than a visit of ceremony, for it had been preceded by a stream of letters concerning the conduct of government within the kingdom and the raising of the king's ransom; moreover, there was a major political crisis produced by John's rebellion. In order to speed up the king's release Eleanor is said to have counselled Richard to do homage for his kingdom to the emperor Heinrich VI (January and February 1194); but neither the diplomatic journey, nor the collection of a huge ransom for the king, could have occurred if the queen mother had not previously succeeded in taking effective measures to suppress John's revolt. Perhaps most extraordinary of all Eleanor's

diplomatic missions was the one that she undertook soon after John's succession as king: in early 1200 she travelled to Castile to select one of her granddaughters as a bride for King Philip's heir, the future Louis VIII. The girl chosen was the future formidable Blanche of Castile, daughter of Eleanor's own daughter and namesake. That journey, too, was far more than a dynastic interlude, for these marriage proposals were central to the plans for a peace settlement between the French and English kings (enacted in the treaty of Le Goulet on 22 May 1200). On this last occasion age seems to have defeated the queen and, while Blanche travelled north under ecclesiastical protection to be married in Normandy, in Holy week Eleanor broke her return journey at Bordeaux.

Even before Richard landed in England in 1189 the queen was drawn into disputes between the monks of Christ Church, Canterbury, and their archbishop, and she was one of those eventually instrumental in ensuring that Richard's trusted ecclesiastic, Hubert Walter, was elected to the metropolitan see. Like many rulers of England since the Norman conquest Eleanor was ambivalent about papal intervention in the kingdom, and was responsible for restricting the movements of the papal legate, Giovanni da Anagni. During the early years of Richard's reign her presence was noted at many councils, in both England and Normandy during 1190, at St Albans and Westminster in 1193, at Nottingham in 1194. Eleanor took charge of improving English coastal defences after John's alliance with the French king and his plot to replace his brother became known, and she accepted custody of the royal castles of Windsor, Wallingford, and the Peak in April 1193. Her personal involvement in securing the kingdom emerges, too, from her concession that the men of the priory of Christ Church, Canterbury, would never again be obliged to work on the fortifications of the city as 'urgent necessity' had forced them to do at her request. She seems to have played an important part in the selection of hostages to be sent to Germany, and in arrangements for the dispatch of Richard's ransom. The letters sent in her name to Pope Celestine III during this crisis are written as a powerful maternal appeal, but they are surely encoded to convey a political message, drawing attention to the justice of Richard's cause as an imprisoned crusader and, although undoubtedly composed with their rhetorical impact in mind, they could perhaps represent her own political attitudes. The illegality of John's conduct underlies the struggle between her two sons—'if indeed it is a struggle', when one of them is confined in chains, and the other rampages through the kingdom 'with cruel tyranny' (Rymer, *Foedera*, 4th edn, 1.74). Eventually, after Richard's release and a second coronation, the brothers were reconciled through Eleanor's mediation, even though a date had been set for May 1194 for formal judgment to be pronounced on John. It must have been recognized that only Eleanor could make peace between them. John's reconciliation with King Richard was followed by their mother's retirement to the abbey of Fontevrault and by Richard's appointment of his nephew Otto (the future Emperor Otto IV, son of Richard's sister Matilda, duchess of Saxony) to Poitou and Aquitaine (1196–8). But Eleanor was not to be allowed a peaceful retirement.

Eleanor, King John, and the Angevin succession Richard's death at Châlus in April 1199 was immediately followed by the queen's return to the political scene: documents issued at Fontevrault during the days surrounding his funeral indicate that Eleanor was already attempting to retain the loyalty of the Poitevin aristocracy. To cite only one example: on the very day of Richard's funeral she restored lands to William de Mauzé of which he had been dispossessed by Richard. (William was a descendant of her own father's seneschal.) By late April 1199 John had joined his mother at Fontevrault and together they travelled throughout Aquitaine during the early summer, granting privileges to churches and urban communities as well as negotiating with the regional aristocracy. At this time Queen Eleanor finally ceased direct intervention in English affairs: she never again crossed the channel, and—despite the voyage to Castile in 1200—does not seem to have revisited Normandy after the winter of 1199. By contrast her involvement in the political affairs of Aquitaine persisted until the very end of her life; nevertheless, although most of her activity was directly devoted to the affairs of her ancestral duchy, she was also obliged to take measures with the most far-reaching implications to prevent the claims of her grandson *Arthur (son of John's elder brother Geoffrey and *Constance of Brittany) from undermining John's position. To that end on one occasion she directed a campaign of devastation in the area around the city of Angers (presumably the *routier* Mercadier, who accompanied her, put this policy into effect). For the first time in her life, too, she was personally drawn into the web of fealty and homages in which the Angevin and Capetian kings and their great subjects were enmeshed.

According to the Capetian apologist Rigord, at Tours in the summer of 1199 Eleanor, 'the former queen of England performed homage [to Philip Augustus] for the county of the Poitevins which was hers by hereditary right' (Rigord, 146). In itself that was a remarkable act, since women did not normally do homage in their own persons; but there can be little doubt that from the standpoint of Eleanor and John it had an ulterior political purpose. That purpose can only be grasped if it is interpreted in the light of two elaborate reciprocal agreements concluded between John and his mother at about the same time. (Neither bears a precise date, but they are entered on the charter roll for the first year of King John's reign.) These state that King John is recognized as Queen Eleanor's 'rightful heir' (*rectus heres*), while in turn he acknowledges her as lady 'of us and all our lands and possessions' and has done homage to her. As far as Eleanor was concerned, Arthur's pretensions—for Poitou-Aquitaine at least—were legalistically evaded by means of these devices. The validity of Queen Eleanor's hereditary position had been acknowledged through her personal performance of homage to the Capetian ruler, while John's claim to be her prospective successor was also affirmed. If it were indeed Eleanor who had recommended Richard to

do homage to the emperor in order to secure the immediate political end of his release, then perhaps she was also responsible for this later ingenious arrangement. On a wider political front the English record also seems to draw attention to the need for unitary control of the great Angevin 'empire', and consequently makes King Philip's acceptance of Arthur's fealty and his later promise in July 1202 that he would bestow Poitou on that prince, look extremely suspicious.

It was against this background of political double-dealing that the last events of Eleanor's life were played out. In July of 1202 in the small fortified town of Mirebeau in northern Poitou, Eleanor was trapped by Arthur and his supporters; she refused to surrender the keep, and waited for her son's arrival. After a rapid march from Le Mans, King John took the besieging force utterly by surprise on 1 August: he rescued his mother, captured the most important of his opponents, including Arthur, and was in a good position to go over to the offensive in the conflict with King Philip of France. Less than two years later, however, Eleanor was dead: under King John the Angevins' control of their great inheritance crumbled.

Ruler of Aquitaine It was entirely fitting that Eleanor's last years should have been spent in Aquitaine, both in her favoured religious house of Fontevrault, and in the cities and sites so long associated with her own ancestors. The affairs of this principality are surely a key to an understanding of Eleanor's political and social attitudes, just as problems associated with the government of Aquitaine may help to explain her actions during some of the crises of her life—especially since as a woman the conduct of affairs in the region was frequently in others' hands. The significance of her activity in Aquitaine during her last years is more comprehensible if it is placed in the context of what seem to have been lifelong aspirations to rule her ancestral territories. Already in 1139 she made a grant of 'our land' to the knights templar in La Rochelle; her annulment in 1152 of a grant of forest formerly made by King Louis to the Poitevin abbey of St Maixent draws attention both to her authority in Poitou and to the need to obtain her personal consent even to royal acts of generosity. Charters issued in her name significantly emphasize the dynastic continuity of Poitevin rule: in 1152, for instance, she confirmed the generosity of her 'great grandfather, grandfather, and father' to their Cluniac foundation of Montierneuf at Poitiers, and similar wording is to be found in her grant of 'liberties' to the city of Poitiers forty-seven years later.

Eleanor's writs employed the language of command, and like her princely forebears she made grants of immunity and issued letters of protection. Most remarkable of all are the privileges that mark the years 1199–1203 and define the communal status of cities and other sites long associated with her ancestors, most notably Poitiers, Niort, La Rochelle, Saintes, the *bourg* of St Jean d'Angély, and the island of Oléron. The citizens of Bordeaux, too, were granted extensive economic and judicial privileges. It seems likely that at this time Eleanor realized the need to provide a counterbalance to the regional aristocracy who were intent on wringing concessions from her and her sons and on exploiting the antagonism between the Angevin and Capetian kings. The political tragedy was that it was too late to reverse a movement of alienation that had been set in motion over sixty years earlier during the period of Capetian rule in Poitou and Aquitaine. She was still untiring. As an old, sick woman she wrote to John (probably in the year 1200) to tell him that she had commanded Aimery de Thouars, vicomte de Thouars, to visit her in Fontevrault to discuss her suspicions that 'without licence' the viscount and his friends were planning to seize John's Poitevin castles. As late as the year 1203, in the year before her death, documents were still being issued in her name.

Literature and courtly love Aquitaine provides the background to all the controversies that have surrounded Queen Eleanor's activity as literary patron; her mythical reputation as 'queen of the troubadours' is also substantially based on views of the nature of aristocratic courtly life in Aquitaine which often cannot be sustained. A late account in the Occitan life of one of the greatest of twelfth-century lyric poets, Bernard de Ventadour, for instance, describes him as the queen's lover who held court with her, until they were separated by her husband, King Henry of England; but this is utterly untrustworthy, and in any case could not be fitted into the complicated itinerary of Eleanor's movements which can be established from other sources. The myth owes something also to a Latin treatise in dialogue form by the puzzling figure known only as Andrew the Chaplain. It includes judgments supposedly pronounced by various noble ladies, including Eleanor, on the pleas brought before them on questions of conduct, or on the nature of love (for example, on whether love could be said to exist between a married couple). This text has often—almost certainly mistakenly—been regarded as a manual of courtly love, perhaps even written by a cleric at the court of Eleanor's daughter Marie de Champagne (but Andrew's identity is by no means certain). It does not, however, provide a reliable basis for supposing that 'courts of love' were regularly held and presided over by the queen of the English, or (as has been imagined) that Poitiers was a centre where Eleanor and her daughter held the twelfth-century equivalent of literary salons. The very existence of a system of courtly love outside the conventions of esoteric literary productions has been seriously questioned, and it is moreover virtually impossible to find traces of actual contacts between Queen Eleanor and her daughter Marie.

The more flamboyant imaginings of Eleanor's significance as a practitioner of courtly love must therefore be swept away, but she and most members of her dynasty were still important patrons of literature. Almost every type of literary production has been attributed to their patronage—Occitan lyrics and other verse, romance historical works indebted to Geoffrey of Monmouth (the *Brut*), new romances of antique or Arthurian interpretation (*Le roman de Thèbes*, for instance, and even the works of Chrétien de Troyes, who certainly did write for Marie de Champagne). Although cases where attributions to the Angevin court circle rest on intertextual references often require re-examination, there is no need to question all such attributions. On a purely literary level Bernard de Ventadour's connections with Eleanor's court are well established, as are those of a number of other troubadours, who also served or wrote for her son Richard. The Anglo-Norman court also attracted writers in the *langue d'oïl* who, like the clerk Wace, included Eleanor in his dedication of the historical *Roman de Rou*. Eleanor was surely literate (that is, she had received an education which included instruction in Latin), but elaborate and accomplished compositions, like her letters to Celestine III on behalf of her imprisoned son Richard, would have been written in her name by a clerk trained in the arts of classical rhetoric. The representation of Eleanor on her tomb effigy with its unusual iconography of a woman holding a book also surely reflects her reputation for literacy.

Death, burial, and religious patronage Eleanor died at about the age of eighty-two on 31 March 1204 (there is disagreement over whether she was then residing in the city of Poitiers, or had once more retired to Fontevrault). She was buried in the abbey church at Fontevrault, alongside her husband, King Henry, and her son King Richard; her daughter Joanna, the former queen of Sicily and countess of Toulouse, was also buried there and they would in the future be joined by Eleanor's daughter-in-law *Isabella of Angoulême, widow of her son King John. The concentration of family burials in a single chosen church was by no means common in the Romance-speaking world at the end of the twelfth century, while the creation of a group of dynastic monuments was also a relatively recent development. (The Angevin monuments, for instance, antedate the Capetian effigies at St Denis.) Eleanor was portrayed as a life-size recumbent effigy, represented as simply dressed but crowned. Unlike her husband and son who lie carrying symbols of royalty and war, she is portrayed only with an open book in her joined hands.

Eleanor's will, if she ever made one, does not survive, although on 22 July 1202 it was noted on the patent roll that the king permitted her to make 'a reasonable testament'. It might be easier to trace the pattern of Eleanor's personal piety if such a document had been preserved, for many of the charters and writs which now transmit evidence of her generosity to religious communities actually confirm benefactions made by her predecessors or other members of her dynasty. Throughout her life she made redress for encroachments of ecclesiastical privileges or for incursions onto the lands of churches. In 1199, for instance, she restored forest to the nuns of Ste Croix in Poitiers, and remitted dues exacted by comital officials on the lands of the canons of Ste Radegonde (offences that had allegedly been committed by Richard's servants, with or without his consent). It was the duty of a ruler to protect the church, and to ensure that the privileges and immunities of individual institutions were not damaged or threatened. In those respects Eleanor's acts conformed to the contemporary standards by which any ruler would be judged, regardless of gender.

There are few signs that Queen Eleanor was especially

inspired by any religious figure whom she met during her long life, or that she showed an intense personal devotion to any particular saint. She rejoiced that Gilbert of Sempringham had blessed her sons; but she was never an advocate of Thomas Becket's cause during his lifetime, and seems only to have invoked his heavenly aid about twenty years after his official canonization. Characteristically that invocation was associated with the desire to gain Richard's liberation from his German imprisonment. It is interesting, too, that—by contrast with her first husband who chose to be buried in a Cistercian church—her own early meetings with Bernard of Clairvaux were never followed by any individual display of generosity to his house or order. She showed no particular favour to other houses of more austere religious foundations either; and, even though she confirmed grants made to Grandmont, she never endowed any Carthusian establishment. Nevertheless, there can be no doubt that the queen was pious according to the lights of a twelfth-century aristocrat; and today it is impossible to tell whether she wished to have her retirement to Fontevrault as dramatically interrupted as it was by the death of her 'most beloved' son Richard. Quite possibly she may have wished to show practical and material generosity through, for instance, unbroken annual payments made via the exchequer to the 'queen's hospital' in London or (at a rather different level) through the redemption of a great gold cup which the abbey of Bury St Edmunds had been obliged to abandon to meet the financial demands of royal officials. By the terms of one of her last charters also, in return for the daily feeding of three paupers and the saying of two masses for 'the remission of our sins', she confirmed the privileges of the Poitevin abbey of St Maixent granted by her ancestors. Altogether it seems likely that her religious impulses were especially concentrated on securing intercession and commemoration for her close kin and her ancestors. That emerges with especial force from the continuous stream of benefactions enacted in favour of her chosen burial church, Fontevrault.

Historical importance and reputation The reputation of Eleanor of Aquitaine has never been easy to assess. Given the length of her life, and the range of activities in which she was involved between her marriage to Louis VII in 1137 and her death in 1204, that is understandable. The dynastic matriarch attempting to stem the tide of Capetian advance into the Angevin empire during the reigns of her sons at the turn of the twelfth and thirteenth centuries was pursuing policies that seem worlds away from the young woman whose exploits and suspected sexual indiscretions at Antioch or in French court circles have provided copy for the censorious—from monastic and clerical writers of the twelfth century to moralists and even social historians of the twentieth. Not surprisingly, historical myths have crystallized around these scandals—for instance, the legend of the queen's liaison with the poet Bernard de Ventadour, and the teasing references to judicial sentences passed on questions of courtly conduct. As early as the thirteenth century she was reported as having enjoyed an affair with Saladin (this shows a strange confusion between the second and third crusades, while Saladin would in any case have been about ten years old at the time of Eleanor's voyage to Jerusalem).

Other legends clustered round Eleanor's supposedly murderous jealousy of Fair Rosamund (Henry's young mistress Rosamund Clifford): they were elaborated in a number of later medieval chronicles and were the subject of English ballads by the sixteenth century; but even in the nineteenth century this jealousy is the central theme of the verse drama *Becket* by Alfred, Lord Tennyson. (He gave an extra twist to the tale by quite unhistorically portraying Eleanor as herself a troubadour, whose voice was silenced at the court of her second husband, in the cold lands of the north.) The same theme of jealousy, though here focused principally on Henry II's supposed liaison with the Capetian princess, Alice, helped in the twentieth century to give spice to the film *The Lion in Winter* (1968), in which Eleanor, acted with appropriate *élan* by Katherine Hepburn, spends a Christmas vacation from prison quarrelling with her husband (played by Peter O'Toole). William Shakespeare's play *King John*, by contrast, places Queen Eleanor in a more 'realistic' setting of Angevin political rivalries, and transforms her into a 'cankered grandam' who is prepared to connive at the murder of Prince Arthur following the latter's capture at Mirebeau.

On the whole historical accounts of Eleanor's life and importance can frequently be divided into those in which her literary role and emotional life are discussed to the exclusion of virtually any other topic, and those in which she appears as an often shadowy consort to her husbands and sons, the star players in an exclusively 'masculine Middle Age' (the view of Georges Duby). This dichotomy is accentuated by the tendency either to condemn the queen on grounds of her moral shortcomings, or perhaps to exaggerate her contribution to the shaping of a secularized society asserting different standards from those of an ecclesiastically dominated culture. Even in the seventeenth century the French historian F. de Mézeray wrote of her as 'an infamous and pernicious woman' (Mézeray, 1.480–81), and there were not many to 'declare that she was the most virtuous as well as the most beautiful princess in the universe' (Larrey, 3). For recent English historians Eleanor's activity in the Angevin realm has certainly been regarded as subsidiary to the political and governmental policies and achievements of her husbands and sons—a trend that has obviously been accentuated by the publication of English royal records of the twelfth and early thirteenth centuries. And yet Eleanor did play a significant part in both the government and politics of her own world. Like her husbands and sons, when called upon to do so, she harnessed—and sometimes overrode—royal bureaucratic machinery to serve her own political ends. That can be seen through the part she played in the suppression of John's revolt, the organization of Richard's release, or her attempts to restore dynastic control in Aquitaine. Political and governmental activity at the end of her life must have been based on experience gained in the late 1150s in England and Normandy, but presumably also grew out of her knowledge of the most important European secular and ecclesiastical figures—a knowledge that encompassed the worlds of northern and Mediterranean politics.

It is difficult either to gain or convey a balanced impression of Eleanor's personality and reputation, partly because even her own contemporaries were so divided in their assessments, but also because early sources do not contain essential information that might help to unravel a number of the mysteries associated with her life. There is not even any detailed account of her appearance to match Walter Map's famous description of King Henry. The impact that she made in her youth suggests that she must have been beautiful, but most writers preferred to stress her high birth and great inheritance; while much has been made of the judgement of Gervase of Canterbury that she was 'unstable'. Unfortunately, the sculpted representation of the queen on her tomb at Fontevrault must be viewed as an idealization, for it could not be the portrait of an eighty-year-old woman. The best indication of the ambivalence aroused by Eleanor's presence and actions is provided by the historian Richard of Devizes. Under an entry for the year 1190 (so when she was probably sixty-eight years old) he is still alluding to suspicions aroused by her behaviour at Antioch, but although he is condescending about what any woman could achieve in matters of government, he cannot withhold his admiration from this female ruler who was both beautiful and powerful—and, on behalf of the king her son, still indefatigably working.   JANE MARTINDALE

Sources PRINTED HISTORICAL NARRATIVES (INCLUDES COR-RESPONDENCE AND HAGIOGRAPHICAL SOURCES) *The chronicle of Jocelin of Brakelond concerning the acts of Samson abbot of the monastery of Bury St Edmund*, ed. H. Butler (1949) • W. Stubbs, ed., *Gesta regis Henrici secundi Benedicti abbatis: the chronicle of the reigns of Henry II and Richard I, AD 1169–1192*, 2 vols., Rolls Series, 49 (1867) • L. Halphen and R. Poupardin, eds., *Chroniques des comtes d'Anjou*, Collections des Textes pour Servir à l'Étude et à l'Enseignement de l'Histoire (1913) • L. Mirot, ed., *La chronique de Morigny*, Collections des Textes pour Servir à l'Étude et à l'Enseignement de l'Histoire (1912) • H. Duplès-Agier, *Chroniques de Saint-Martial de Limoges*, Société de l'Histoire de France (1874) • J. Verdon, ed., *La chronique de Saint-Maixent*, Classiques de l'Histoire de France du Moyen Age (1979) • R. H. Bautier, A.-M. Bautier, and M. Gilles, eds., *Chronique de Saint-Pierre-le-Vif de Sens, dite de Clarius* (1979) • A. Salmon, ed., *Chronicon Turonense Magnum, Recueil de chroniques de Touraine* (1854) • Stephen of Rouen, 'Draco Normannicus', ed. R. Howlett, *Chronicles of the reigns of Stephen, Henry II, and Richard I*, 2, 589–781, Rolls Series, 82 (1885) • J. B. Sheppard, ed., *Literae Cantuarienses: the letter books of the monastery of Christ Church, Canterbury*, 1, Rolls Series, 85 (1887) • Geoffrey of Vigeois, *Chronica*, ed. P. Labbe (1657), vol. 2 of *Novae bibliothecae manuscriptarum … collectio* • *The historical works of Gervase of Canterbury*, ed. W. Stubbs, 2 vols., Rolls Series, 73 (1879–80) • *Gesta abbatum monasterii Sancti Albani, a Thoma Walsingham*, ed. H. T. Riley, 3 vols., pt 4 of *Chronica monasterii S. Albani*, Rolls Series, 28 (1867–9), vol. 1 • R. Foreville and G. Keir, eds., *The book of St Gilbert* (1987) • *Gir. Camb. opera*, vol. 8 • P. Meyer, ed., *L'histoire de Guillaume le Maréchal*, 3 vols. (Paris, 1891–1901) • *The Historia pontificalis of John of Salisbury*, ed. and trans. M. Chibnall, rev. edn, OMT (1986) • *The letters of John of Salisbury*, ed. and trans. H. E. Butler and W. J. Millor, rev. C. N. L. Brooke, 2 vols., OMT (1979–86) [Lat. orig. with parallel Eng. text] • J. C. Robertson and J. B. Sheppard, eds., *Materials for the history of Thomas Becket, archbishop of Canterbury*, 7 vols., Rolls Series, 67 (1875–85) • *Nicetas Choniates Historia*, ed. I. Bekker, Corpus Scriptorum

Historiae Byzantinae, 14 (1828) • Odo of Deuil, *La croisade de Louis VII, roi de France*, ed. H. Waquet, *Documents relatifs à l'histoire des croisades* (1949) • Ordericus Vitalis, *Eccl. hist.* • *Radulphi de Coggeshall chronicon Anglicanum*, ed. J. Stevenson, Rolls Series, 66 (1875) • *Radulfi de Diceto … opera historica*, ed. W. Stubbs, 2 vols., Rolls Series, 68 (1876) • M. Bouquet and others, eds., *Recueil de historiens des Gaules et de la France / Rerum Gallicarum et Francicarum scriptores*, 24 vols. (1738–1904), vols. 11–16 [incl. correspondence of Suger, Louis VII, and others] • Richard of Devizes, *Chronicon*, ed. J. Appleby (1963) • E. Berger, *Richard le Poitevin, moine de Cluny, historien et poète*, Bibliothèque des Écoles Françaises d'Athènes et de Rome, 6 (1879) • Rigord, *Œuvres de Rigord et de Guillaume le Breton*, ed. H. F. Delaborde, 2 vols., Société de l'Histoire de France (1882–5) • *Chronica magistri Rogeri de Hovedene*, ed. W. Stubbs, 4 vols., Rolls Series, 51 (1868–71) • Suger, *Vie de Louis VI le Gros*, ed. H. Waquet, 2nd edn, Classiques de l'Histoire de France du Moyen Age (1964) • Suger, *De glorioso rege Ludovico, Ludovici filio*, ed. A. Molinier, Collections des Textes pour Servir à l'Étude et à l'Enseignement de l'Histoire (1887) • 'Vita S. Bernardi', *Patrologia Latina*, 185 (1855) • W. Map, *De nugis curialium / Courtiers' trifles*, ed. and trans. M. R. James, rev. C. N. L. Brooke and R. A. B. Mynors, OMT (1983) • *Willelmi Malmesbiriensis monachi de gestis regum Anglorum*, ed. W. Stubbs, 2 vols., Rolls Series (1887–9) • R. Howlett, ed., *Chronicles of the reigns of Stephen, Henry II, and Richard I*, 4 vols., Rolls Series, 82 (1884–9), vols. 1-2, 4 • William of Tyre, *Willelmi Tyrensis archiepiscopi chronicon*, ed. R. Huygens, 2 vols., Cahiers de Civilisation Médiévale (1986)

DOCUMENTARY AND RECORD SOURCES 'The Anstey case', *A medieval miscellany for Doris Mary Stenton*, ed. P. M. Barnes and C. F. Slade, PRSoc., new ser., 36 (1962), 1–24 • J. H. Round, ed., *Calendar of documents preserved in France, illustrative of the history of Great Britain and Ireland* (1899) • L. Landon, ed., *The cartae antiquae: rolls 1–10, printed from the original in the custody of the master of the rolls*, PRSoc., 55, new ser., 17 (1939), pt 1 • T. Grasilier, ed., *Cartulaire de l'abbaye royale de Notre-Dame de Saintes* (1871) • A. Richard, ed., *Chartes et documents pour servir à l'histoire de l'abbaye de Saint-Maixent*, Archives Historiques du Poitou, 16, 18 (1886) • L. Rédet, ed., *Documents pour l'histoire de Saint-Hilaire de Poitiers*, Mémoires de la Société des Antiquaires de l'Ouest, 14, 15 (1847–52) • Rymer, *Foedera*, new edn, vol. 4 • A. Teulet, ed., *Layettes du trésor des chartes* (1863–), vols. 1, 2 • A. Luchaire, *Études sur les actes de Louis VII* (1885) • P. Marchegay, 'Chartes de Fontevraud concernant l'Aunis et la Rochelle', *Bibliothèque de l'École des Chartes*, 19 (1858) • P. Marchegay, ed., *Cartulaires du Bas-Poitou* (1858) • *Pipe rolls* • L. Delisle and others, eds., *Recueil des actes de Henri II, roi d'Angleterre et duc de Normandie, concernant les provinces françaises et les affaires de France*, 4 vols. (Paris, 1909–27) • H. Delaborde, ed., *Recueil des actes de Philippe Auguste, roi de France*, 3 vols. (1916–) • G. Pon, ed., *Recueil des documents de l'abbaye de Fontaine-le-Comte (XIIe–XIIIe siècles)*, Archives Historiques du Poitou, 61 (1982) • F. Villard, ed., *Recueil des documents relatifs à l'abbaye de Montierneuf de Poitiers*, Archives Historiques du Poitou, 59 (1973) • *Chancery records* (RC)

'LITERARY' SOURCES (LATIN AND VERNACULAR) *Andreas Capellanus 'On Love'*, ed. P. Walsh (1982) • B. de Sainte-Maure, *Chroniques des ducs de Normandie*, ed. C. Fahlin, 3 vols. (1951) • J. Boutière and A. Schutz, eds., *Biographies des troubadours: texts provençaux des XIIIe et XIVe siècles*, 2nd edn (1964) • Cercamon, *Les poésies*, ed. A. Jeanroy, Classiques Français du Moyen Age (1922) • *Les chansons de Guillaume IX, duc d'Aquitaine*, ed. A. Jeanroy, 2nd edn, Classiques Français du Moyen Age (1972) • *Les romans de Chrétien de Troyes*, ed. M. Roques, A. Micha, and F. Lecoq, 6 vols., Classiques Français du Moyen Age (1952) • *The Historia regum Britannie of Geoffrey of Monmouth*, ed. N. Wright, 1–2 (1985–8) • L. Constans, ed., *Le roman de Thèbes*, Société des Anciens Textes Français (1890) • *Le 'Roman de Rou' de Wace*, ed. A. J. Holden, 3 vols. (Paris, 1970–73) • A. Tennyson, *Becket* (1884)

MODERN BIOGRAPHIES AND STUDIES J.-M. Bienvenu, 'Aliénor d'Aquitaine et Fontevraud', *Cahiers de Civilisation Médiévale*, 29 (1986), 15–27 • E. A. R. Brown, 'Eleanor of Aquitaine: parent, queen and duchess', *Eleanor of Aquitaine: patron and politician*, ed. W. W. Kibler (1976), 9–34 • J. Chaban-Delmas, *La dame d'Aquitaine* (1989) • G. Duby, 'Eleanor', *Women of the twelfth century* (1997), 5–20 • J. Holt,

'Aliénor d'Aquitaine, Jean sans Terre et la succession de 1199', *Cahiers de Civilisation Médiévale*, 29 (1986), 95–9 • A. Kelly, *Eleanor of Aquitaine and the four kings* (1950) • E.-R. Labande, 'Pour une image véridique d'Aliénor d'Aquitaine', *Mémoires de la Société des Antiquaires de l'Ouest*, 4th ser., 2 (1952), 174–234 • E.-R. Labande, 'Les filles d'Aliénor d'Aquitaine: étude comparative', *Cahiers de Civilisation Médiévale*, 29 (1986), 104–22 • I. de Larrey, *L'heritière de Guyenne ou Histoire d'Eleonor fille de Guillaume, dernier duc de Guyenne, femme de Louis VII, roy de France, et en-suite de Henri II roy d'Angleterre* (1691) • M. Lazar, 'Cupid, the lady, and the poet: modes of love at Eleanor of Aquitaine's court', *Eleanor of Aquitaine: patron and politician*, ed. W. W. Kibler (1976), 35–59 • M. D. Legge, 'La littérature anglo-normande au temps d'Aliénor d'Aquitaine', *Cahiers de Civilisation Médiévale*, 29 (1986), 113–18 • R. Lejeune, 'Rôle littéraire d'Aliénor d'Aquitaine et de sa famille', *Cultura Neo-Latina*, 14 (1954), 6–57 • J. McCash, 'Marie de Champagne and Eleanor of Aquitaine: a relationship re-examined', *Speculum*, 54 (1979), 698–711 • J. Markale, *La vie, la légende, l'influence d'Aliénor comtesse de Poitou, duchesse d'Aquitaine, reine de France, puis d'Angleterre, dame des troubadours et des bardes bretons* (1979) • J. Martindale, 'Eleanor of Aquitaine', *Status, authority and regional power, Aquitaine and France, 9th to 12th centuries* (1997), 11.1–23 • J. Martindale, 'Eleanor of Aquitaine, the last years', *King John: new interpretations*, ed. S. D. Church (1999) • D. D. R. Owen, *Eleanor of Aquitaine, queen and legend* (1993) • R. Pernoud, *Aliénor d'Aquitaine* (1969) • R. Pernoud, 'Les chartes de la reine Aliénor', *La femme au temps des cathédrales* (1980), 195–208 • A. Richard, 'Aliénor (1137–1204)', *Histoire des comtes de Poitou*, 2 vols. (1903), 2.60–457 • H. G. Richardson, 'The letters and charters of Eleanor of Aquitaine', *EngHR*, 74 (1959), 191–213 • R. Turner, 'Eleanor of Aquitaine and her children: an inquiry into medieval family attachment', *Journal of Medieval History*, 14 (1988), 321–35

RELATED SECONDARY SOURCES R. W. Eyton, *Court, household, and itinerary of King Henry II* (1878) • L. Landon, *The itinerary of King Richard I*, PRSoc., new ser., 13 (1935) • R. Benjamin, 'A forty years war: Toulouse and the Plantagenets, 1156–96', *Historical Research*, 61 (1988), 270–85 • J. Benton, *Culture, power and personality in medieval France*, ed. T. Bisson (1991) [valuable collected essays] • R. Bezzola, *Les origines et la formation de la littérature courtoise en occident* (500–1200), 5 vols. (1943–66) • T. Boase, 'Fontevrault and the Plantagenets', *Journal of the British Archaeological Association*, 3rd ser., 34 (1971), 1–10 • Z. N. Brooke and C. N. L. Brooke, 'Henry II, duke of Normandy and Aquitaine', *EngHR*, 61 (1946), 81–9 • P. Dronke, *The medieval lyric* (1968) • A. Erlande-Brandenbourg, 'Le "cimitière des rois" à Fontevrault', *Congrés Archaeologique*, 64 (1964), 482–92 • C. Holdsworth, 'Peacemaking in the twelfth century', *Anglo-Norman Studies*, 19 (1996), 1–17 • J. Gillingham, *Richard the Lionheart*, 2nd edn (1989) • J. Gillingham, *Richard Coeur de Lion: kingship, chivalry and war in the twelfth century* (1994) [valuable collected studies] • J. Parsons, ed., *Medieval queenship* (1993) • L. Paterson, *Troubadours and eloquence* (1975) • E. A. R. Brown, '"Franks, Burgundians and Aquitanians" and the royal coronation ceremony in France', *Transactions of the American Philosophical Society*, 82 (1992) • F. E. de Mézeray, *Histoire de France depuis Faramond jusqu'à maintenant*, 3 vols. (1685) • A. Duggan, ed., *Queens and queenship in medieval Europe* (1997) • W. Warren, *Henry II* (1973)
Likenesses tomb effigy, 1204–40, abbey of Fontevrault, Maine-et-Loire, France [*see illus.*]

Eleanor [Eleanor of Brittany], *suo jure* duchess of Brittany

(1182x4–1241), princess, was the elder daughter of *Geoffrey, duke of Brittany, and *Constance, duchess of Brittany, and sister of *Arthur, duke of Brittany. At her father's death in August 1186 she was heir to the duchy, and Philip Augustus, king of France, claimed her wardship. However, Arthur's birth on 29 March 1187 and the procrastination of Henry II temporarily reduced her diplomatic value. As part of his ransom terms from Leopold,

duke of Austria, in June 1193, *Richard I arranged for Eleanor to marry the duke's son, but her journey to join him under the care of Baldwin de Béthune in 1194 was interrupted on news of Leopold's death. In 1195 plans for marrying her to Louis, the French royal heir, were discussed but again the match was unsuccessful. Duchess Constance then pressed for her release from royal custody and by the time of Richard's death on 6 April 1199 Eleanor was living in France with her mother and brother. But further misfortune befell her in August 1202 when she was captured at Mirebeau along with Arthur by her uncle King *John.

Because of her claims on the Angevin and Breton successions and John's fear that she would transmit them by marriage, Eleanor was once again placed in protective custody from which she never emerged, despite efforts over several years by Philip Augustus and the Bretons to negotiate her release. In 1203 John had her moved to England and imprisoned in various strongholds, including the castles of Corfe (Dorset), Burgh (Westmorland), and Bowes (Yorkshire). One order for her maintenance provided for cloth, 'not however of the king's finest' (*Rotuli litterarum clausarum*, 2.168), but otherwise she was treated with consideration. She spent some time with the queen and the king of Scotland's daughters, hostages for a treaty. John also continued to use her as a diplomatic pawn: for example, in her sole surviving letter, clearly written with royal consent in 1208, she is styled 'duchess of Brittany and countess of Richmond' (*Rotuli litterarum patentium*, 91). In 1214, when John attempted to regain his continental lands, she accompanied him to Poitou, and there are occasional hints of continued support for her in Brittany. Eleanor returned to England and her latter years were spent in further comfortable confinement at various locations, including Marlborough, Gloucester, and Bristol, where she had apartments in the keep between 1224 and 1234, and again from 1238 or 1239 until her death. Her name occurs occasionally in royal accounts, and those of the constable of Bristol Castle from the 1220s furnish considerable detail on her household and lifestyle during her captivity, providing an early example of this form of documentary evidence. She was visited once or twice a week by the bailiffs and four leading citizens to ensure her welfare, while she also enjoyed the company of chaplains and serving ladies, and a typically varied, high-protein, aristocratic diet. This included many different types of freshwater and sea fish and abundant supplies of meat; the main beverages mentioned are ale and milk. Still unmarried at her death on 10 August 1241, Eleanor was first buried at St James's Priory, Bristol, but her body was later moved in accordance with her will and Henry III's instructions to Amesbury convent.   MICHAEL JONES

Sources GEC, *Peerage* • M. Sharp, ed., *Accounts of the constables of Bristol Castle*, Bristol RS, 34 (1982) • C. M. Woolgar, ed., *Household accounts from medieval England*, 1, British Academy, Records of Social and Economic History, new ser., 17 (1992), 126–50 • W. L. Warren, *King John* (1961) • T. D. Hardy, ed., *Rotuli litterarum patentium*, RC (1835) • T. D. Hardy, ed., *Rotuli litterarum clausarum*, 2 vols., RC (1833–4) • J. Everard and M. Jones, eds., *The charters of Duchess Constance of*

Brittany and her family, 1171–1221 (1999) • J. Everard, *Brittany and the Angevins: province and empire, 1158–1203* (2000)
Archives PRO, various exchequer accounts, E 101

Eleanor, countess of Pembroke and Leicester (1215?–1275), princess, daughter of King *John and *Isabella of Angoulême, was born probably in 1215, a year before the death of her father. Her brothers and sisters were the future *Henry III, *Richard (future earl of Cornwall), *Joan, and *Isabella. In 1224, at the age of nine, she was married to the powerful William (II) *Marshal, earl of Pembroke, a man about fifteen years her senior, at the behest of the king's council, after some three years of debate as to whether she should marry a foreign prince. The earl acquired a papal mandate and won both Eleanor and substantial revenues and estates in England, Wales, and Ireland. Until the marriage was consummated in 1229 Eleanor remained at her brother's court under the guardianship of Cecily of Sandford; thereafter she accompanied the Marshal on his travels in England, France, and Ireland. In 1231, however, at the marriage celebrations of Richard, earl of Cornwall, William Marshal died suddenly, and the grieving Eleanor took a vow of chastity in the presence of Edmund, archbishop of Canterbury. The king seized her estates, while her brother-in-law, Richard Marshal, earl of Pembroke, her husband's heir, took many valuable chattels. She retired to the castle of Inkberrow (Worcestershire), and in 1233 compounded with her brother and Earl Richard for £400 yearly, less than a quarter of the annual value of her estates. Their failure to meet these obligations, together with Eleanor's extravagant spending, led to substantial debts. Henry III made spasmodic payments towards some of these, and in 1237 granted her Odiham Castle (Hampshire) which became her principal residence.

In January 1238 Eleanor married Simon de *Montfort in secret. When their union became known at court, Richard, earl of Cornwall, and other councillors were greatly angered, and Archbishop Edmund appealed to the pope on the grounds that Eleanor had broken her solemn vow. Montfort visited Rome to obtain a confirmation of the union, and on 28 November 1238, shortly after his return, Eleanor gave birth to their eldest child at Kenilworth. The following spring the king confirmed the earldom of Leicester to Montfort, and ordered that Eleanor's dowry be paid to him. In August 1239, however, Henry publicly turned on him, accusing him of defiling his sister before marriage, bribing the pope, and using the crown as security for his debts; Montfort and Eleanor fled in haste from England to France. While Montfort raised funds for a crusade, and made a return visit to England, Eleanor probably remained in France. She then stayed at Brindisi in southern Italy, in a castle belonging to her brother-in-law, the emperor Frederick II, while Montfort joined Richard of Cornwall's crusade in Palestine. 1242 saw the restoration of Eleanor and Simon de Montfort to the king's favour and she accompanied her husband on campaign in Poitou. The ruinous expense of this compounded their financial problems; but the king met their debts in part and settled an annual 500 marks on Montfort as Eleanor's dower,

although the issue of her dower from her earlier marriage remained unresolved.

At the same time Henry made a formal grant of Kenilworth Castle to Eleanor, and this became her principal residence. Her eldest son, Henry de *Montfort, was followed by others: Simon de *Montfort the younger, Amaury de *Montfort, Guy de *Montfort, Richard, and a daughter, *Eleanor de Montfort. Robert Grosseteste, bishop of Lincoln, was their tutor and the Franciscan theologian Adam Marsh acted as confessor to Eleanor herself. A vivid insight into her fiery temperament emerges from letters she received from him in 1251: Marsh gently upbraids her for her language and temper, her contentiousness, and her extravagance. The last point is well borne out in her surviving household roll of 1265; yet so too is her administrative capacity. Between 1248 and 1254 Simon de Montfort, as seneschal of Gascony, spent most of his time abroad; Eleanor accompanied him in 1249–50, 1251, and 1253, and on later visits to Paris to negotiate peace with Louis IX of France over Gascony. The issue of her dowry, which remained unsettled, featured in the provisions of Oxford (1258) and complicated the settlement with Louis contained in the treaty of Paris. Eventually ratified in 1259, this included a renunciation by Eleanor and Montfort of their own hereditary rights in France, while 15,000 marks due to Henry III under the treaty were set aside to act as a pledge for his future settlement of Eleanor's claims to dower in England. But although arbitrators were appointed, no final agreement was reached, even though the French king and queen later tried to mediate.

Eleanor remained at her stronghold at Kenilworth while Montfort and their sons led the baronial coalition which defeated Henry III and Prince Edward in 1264; in 1265, as the tide turned against them, she moved south to Dover, where in August, after the battle of Evesham, she received the news of the death of her husband and her son Henry. Her next son, Simon, was holding Richard, Eleanor's brother, a prisoner at Kenilworth, and released him only on condition that he protect Eleanor's interests. This was of little effect against the king's desire to disinherit and banish Eleanor; but Prince Edward, who took Dover Castle from her in October with the help of the prisoners there, allowed her a dignified retreat into exile in France. Here she retired to the Dominican convent at Montargis, founded by her sister-in-law Amicia de Montfort. In 1267, with the help of Louis IX, she obtained an annual payment of £500 from the English exchequer provided that she remained in exile; this was confirmed in 1273 by Edward I. She died in 1275 (before 3 June) and was buried at Montargis.   ELIZABETH HALLAM

Sources J. R. Maddicott, *Simon de Montfort* (1994) • F. M. Powicke, *King Henry III and the Lord Edward: the community of the realm in the thirteenth century*, 2 vols. (1947) • *Chancery records* • 'Household roll of Countess Eleanor, AD 1265', *Manners and household expenses of England in the thirteenth and fifteenth centuries, illustrated by original records*, ed. [B. Botfield and T. H. Turner?], Roxburghe Club, 57 (1841) • 'Adae de Marisco epistolae', *Monumenta Franciscana*, ed. J. S. Brewer, 1, Rolls Series, 4 (1858), 77–489 • M. A. E. Green, *Lives of the princesses of England*, 6 vols. (1849–55) • M. W. Labarge, *A baronial*

household of the thirteenth century (1965) · C. Bémont, *Simon de Montfort, comte de Leicester* (Paris, 1884) · *CCIR*
Wealth at death £800 p.a.

Eleanor [Eleanor of Provence] (*c.*1223–1291), queen of England, consort of Henry III, was born in Provence, the second of four daughters of the count, Raymond-Berengar (V) (1209–1245), and his wife, Béatrice (*d.* 1265), the daughter of Thomas, count of Savoy. The births of two sons—probably twins—preceded the births of the four daughters, but the boys died very young. The beauty of the daughters, who all became queens, was legendary. Marguerite, the eldest, married Louis IX of France (1234), Sanchia married *Richard, first earl of Cornwall, brother of Henry III (1243), and Béatrice, the youngest, married Charles, count of Anjou (1246). Sanchia and Béatrice eventually became queens of Germany and Sicily respectively. By her marriage to *Henry III at Canterbury on 14 January 1236, and her coronation at Westminster six days later, Eleanor of Provence acquired the titles of queen of England, lady of Ireland, duchess of Normandy and Aquitaine, and countess of Anjou. The ineffectual titles to Normandy and Anjou were dropped after the treaty of Paris in 1259.

The distinctive troubadour culture of the Midi, notably secular in tone, may have prompted Eleanor's later delight in reading romances, but it was in England as a young queen that her religious sensitivity was nurtured. Her medical care and early moral guidance were entrusted to the learned and urbane Nicholas of Farnham, later bishop of Durham (*d.* 1257), and she was on terms of friendship with the reforming bishops Robert Grosseteste (*d.* 1253) and Richard Wyche (*d.* 1253), and with the scholarly Franciscan Adam Marsh (*d.* 1259). Her major religious benefactions were prompted by personal associations: the hospital of St Katharine by the Tower, which was given additional endowment by Eleanor and a new charter in 1273, in memory of her husband, and the Dominican priory at Guildford which she founded in memory of her grandson Henry. She was also patron and benefactor of the Cistercian nunnery of Tarrant (Dorset), and an enthusiastic patron of the Franciscans.

It is likely that Eleanor bore only five children, the first four before she was twenty-two: the future king, *Edward I (1239–1307); *Margaret (1240–1275), who married Alexander III of Scotland; Beatrice, who was born in 1242 at Bordeaux and who married Jean, eldest son of Jean (I), duke of Brittany; and *Edmund (1245–1296), later earl of Lancaster. Katharine (*b.* 1253) was disabled and to the grief of both her parents died in 1257. Eleanor was an attentive mother, strongly protective of her children's interests, and she spent time with them at Windsor when they were young. Later they became the vehicles of her own ambition.

Eleanor's enterprising Savoyard uncles shaped her early role in politics. William of Savoy established her in England; Thomas, count of Flanders (*r.* 1237–44), and Boniface of *Savoy, archbishop of Canterbury (1243–70), used her influence with the king; and Peter of *Savoy (*d.* 1268), who came to England in 1241 and received the honours of Richmond and Pevensey from Henry III, became her close adviser. He shrewdly encouraged Eleanor to strengthen her position at court as mother of the king's heir and to keep Edward's future appanage out of the grasp of Richard of Cornwall. More dubiously, he collaborated with the queen in securing offices and rich marriages for their Savoyard kinsfolk and dependants. This aroused criticism and brought Eleanor into political collision with the king's ambitious Lusignan half-brothers, who arrived in England in 1247 and resented the large share of royal patronage already absorbed by the Savoyards.

Eleanor accompanied Henry III on his ill-fated expedition to Poitou and Gascony in 1242–3, but when the king next left England, to suppress a serious Gascon rebellion in 1253, Eleanor remained as regent, with Richard of Cornwall as her adviser. She acquitted herself extremely well. In June 1254 she joined her husband in Gascony, and in December Henry and Eleanor were the guests of Louis IX and Queen Marguerite, in a friendly family gathering in

Eleanor [of Provence] (*c.*1223–1291), drawing [in the stern of a ship]

Paris. This proved a step towards the peace between England and France later achieved by the treaty of Paris (1259).

Eleanor's influence in this case had been constructive, but in 1254 she also became deeply committed, together with her husband, to the disastrous scheme, backed by the pope and the Savoyards, to gain the crown of Sicily for her second son, Edmund. The crippling financial conditions imposed by the papacy aggravated the rising discontent against Henry III's government in England. In 1258 discontent erupted into revolution. The queen's attitude was ambivalent. She rejoiced in the speedy eviction of the unpopular Lusignans but she deplored the severe reduction in royal power achieved by the reformers in the provisions of Oxford (1258). A significant though temporary breach between Edward and his parents added to the complex cross-currents of what became an embittered and factious struggle. From the beginning of 1260 the queen gradually came to be seen as the arch-enemy of reform. In 1261 she colluded with a small group of activists around the king to achieve a royalist *revanche*, and the pope released Henry III, Eleanor, and their sons from their oaths to uphold the provisions. In June 1263 the queen's opponents struck and her lands and those of her kinsmen and supporters were ravaged. Eleanor angrily opposed the terms imposed on the king by the rebels, now led by Simon de Montfort, and in a defiant attempt to reach her son Edward in Windsor Castle by river, she was halted at London Bridge, pelted with stones, and treated to a volley of coarse insults from an excited mob of Londoners, who had learned to hate all aliens and especially the queen. The experience hardened her resolve. She went to France, where she enlisted the sympathy of the French king and her sister Marguerite. Louis IX's judgment in favour of Henry III in an arbitration at Amiens in January 1264 was thought to owe much to Eleanor's influence. It provoked immediate civil war in England.

In adversity Eleanor of Provence was indomitable. After the defeat of the royalists at Lewes in May 1264, which left Henry virtually a captive and Edward a hostage in the hands of Simon de Montfort, she assembled a formidable invasion force in Flanders. When this plan proved abortive she made Gascony her base, pressing the diplomatic offensive against Montfort with remorseless vigour and great skill. Her network of contacts, which reached out to the papacy and the French court as well as commanding material resources from Gascony, Ireland, the Welsh march, and the English refugees and exiles on the continent, helped to bring about the royalist victory at Evesham in August 1265, and she returned to England in November. Realistic and competent in financial affairs, she persuaded the pope to allocate her £60,000 (of Tours) from the tenth imposed on the English clergy in 1266, so that she might attempt to settle the extensive debts which she had incurred abroad.

Despite her strong sense of personal obligation in money matters, Eleanor, like many of her contemporaries, was oppressive in the administration of her lands, especially those which she received from the crown in wardship. While she was consort she used the financial services of both Jews and merchants, but she dismissed all Jews from her dower towns in 1275. After Henry III's death in 1272 she had emerged as a wealthy property holder. In addition to her dower assignment, valued at £4000 a year, she enjoyed bequests from Peter of Savoy, comprising the honour of Pevensey and an annual sum of £1805 in lieu of the honour of Richmond. Even when she became a nun she retained substantial wealth in England, although surrendering her Gascon revenues. Since her lands would revert to the crown on her death she was permitted to make her will from her landed revenues, up to a sum of 10,000 marks. Eleanor was in the top band of aristocratic landowners.

To the end of her life, in political or personal matters which concerned herself or her family, Eleanor's wishes carried considerable weight with her eldest son after he became king, although she would have liked him to be even more personally attentive to her. In July 1286 she took the veil at the prestigious priory of Amesbury (Wiltshire), a house of the order of Fontevrault, having first arranged that two of her granddaughters should precede her there. Eleanor died at Amesbury Priory on 24 June 1291 and was buried there on 9 September, after the king's return from Scotland, in the presence of a large gathering of magnates. Her heart was buried in the church of the Franciscans in London in early December. No funeral monuments have survived the dissolution. Many Englishmen hated her for her political stance, but her superb courage and practical capacity, used on behalf of her family, commanded respect, and chroniclers acclaimed her as a *virago*, a warrior heroine. The many letters written during her widowhood reveal a woman quick to defend her own rights, yet capable of tact, magnanimity, and warm personal kindness. She was revered by her husband and her children.   MARGARET HOWELL

Sources Chancery records · Paris, *Chron.* · H. R. Luard, ed., *Flores historiarum*, 3 vols., Rolls Series, 95 (1890) · *Ann. mon.* · R. F. Treharne and I. J. Sanders, eds., *Documents of the baronial movement of reform and rebellion, 1258–1267* (1973) · M. Howell, *Eleanor of Provence: queenship in thirteenth-century England* (1997) · M. Howell, 'The children of King Henry III and Eleanor of Provence', *Thirteenth century England: proceedings of the Newcastle upon Tyne conference* [Newcastle upon Tyne 1991], ed. P. R. Coss and S. D. Lloyd, 4 (1992), 57–72 · M. Howell, 'The resources of Eleanor of Provence as queen consort', *EngHR*, 102 (1987), 372–93 · D. A. Carpenter, 'King Henry III's "statute" against aliens: July 1263', *EngHR*, 107 (1992), 925–44 · H. W. Ridgeway, 'Foreign favourites and Henry III's problems of patronage, 1247–58', *EngHR*, 104 (1989), 590–610 · H. W. Ridgeway, 'King Henry III and the "aliens", 1236–1272', *Thirteenth century England: proceedings of the Newcastle upon Tyne conference* [Newcastle upon Tyne 1987], ed. P. R. Coss and S. D. Lloyd, 2 (1988), 81–92 · E. L. Cox, *The eagles of Savoy: the house of Savoy in thirteenth-century Europe* (1974) · J. R. Maddicott, *Simon de Montfort* (1994)
Archives PRO, SC 1 · PRO, E 101 · PRO, E 372
Likenesses drawing, BL, Royal MS 14 C.vii, fol. 134 [*see illus.*]

Eleanor [Eleanor of Castile] (**1241–1290**), queen of England, consort of Edward I, was the daughter of Ferdinand III of Castile (1201–1252) and his second wife, Jeanne de Dammartin (*d.* 1279), heir to the French county of Ponthieu.

Eleanor [of Castile] (1241–1290), by William Torel, 1291–3 [tomb effigy]

Ancient claims to Gascony in Aquitaine, raised in 1252–3 by Eleanor's half-brother Alfonso X, were transferred to Edward [see Edward I] upon his marriage to Eleanor at the convent of Las Huelgas near Burgos on 1 November 1254. Though diplomatically advantageous the marriage was unpopular in England, as it was feared Edward's bride would bring a crowd of Castilians in her wake. Eleanor came to England in October 1255, but little is recorded of her before the barons' wars. She supported Edward's turn to the Lusignans in 1258, and was abroad with him between 1260 and 1263. When he returned from France in February 1263, mercenaries whom Eleanor obtained from Ponthieu were among the troops he installed in Windsor Castle. Contrary to general belief, she did not leave England during the crisis. She lived at Windsor after the battle of Lewes, when *Henry III ordered her to join him (17 June 1264), probably at Montfort's wishes as it was thought she might be hiring Castilian mercenaries. After the battle of Evesham she secured grants of rebels' lands and began to acquire the rich estates for which she became notorious.

In August 1270 Eleanor and Edward left England for the Holy Land. At Acre in June 1272 an assassin wounded Edward with a poisoned knife; his life was despaired of until a surgeon cut the inflamed flesh from his arm. The legend that Eleanor instead sucked poison from the wound is first found in the *Historia ecclesiastica* by the Dominican Ptolemy of Lucca (*d.* 1327?), who gave it only as a popular story. Camden first published it in England in *Britannia* (1586). Walter of Guisborough's chronicle states

merely that Eleanor, weeping and lamenting, was led from Edward's bedside before the operation.

Following Henry III's death the couple returned to England and were crowned together on 19 August 1274. With Edward's support Eleanor from 1275 expanded her estates by securing English knights' debts to Jewish moneylenders, and then taking over lands pledged for the debts. She obtained much land in this way between 1278 and 1281; thereafter she acquired more estates by purchase than through Jewish debts, but continued to collect such debts and probably exacted usury on them. Archbishop Pecham warned her in 1283 that this was causing scandal, and in 1286 wrote of continued outcry and gossip. By 1290 Eleanor's lands were worth upwards of £2500 yearly; the revenue was needed, but such economic activity was unprecedented for a queen. English reactions are seen in the Dunstable annals' description of Eleanor as 'a Spaniard by birth, who acquired many fine manors' (*Ann. mon.*, 3.362), and Guisborough's verse noting her craving for land:

> The king would like to get our gold
> The queen, our manors fair to hold.
> (*Chronicle*, 216)

Pecham's intervention in 1283 for some of Eleanor's overburdened tenants forecast her dying prayer that Edward name commissioners to assess damages for wrongs committed in her name; that inquest revealed many harsh practices by her officials, and found that she ordered them to harass or punish those who crossed her. Pecham's 1279 letter to the nuns of Castle Hedingham Priory indicates that Eleanor's ungracious behaviour when vexed was well known.

A highly cultured woman, Eleanor was a discerning patron of vernacular letters and supported the English universities. She founded several Dominican houses in England, but her liking for the friars and her dealings with the Jews distanced her from the bishops and older orders. Like Edward's parents, she arranged English marriages for many of her relatives, but discreetly enough that she incurred no criticism. None the less her liking for Castilian practices was made widely evident, and her protection of Castilian merchants irritated the men of Southampton. She was a devoted wife to Edward, with whom she had sixteen children, among them *Edward II, *Joan of Acre, and *Mary of Woodstock; he esteemed her but allowed her no part in the affairs of the realm, and restrained her from extorting money improperly. Although Eleanor was active in Anglo-Castilian relations, Alfonso X's disastrous reign left her without effective support from abroad; she succeeded her mother in Ponthieu in 1279, but the inheritance did not alter her status in England. Her political influence was in fact negligible, but her harsh administration, her traffic with the usurers, the many reminders of her foreign birth, and ironically her close relationship with Edward, none the less led some to suspect, as Pecham warned her in 1283, that she was responsible for the king's strict rule.

While with Edward in Aquitaine in 1287 Eleanor contracted a quartan fever, probably the 'low fever' of which she died at Harby near Lincoln on 28 November 1290, survived by a son and five daughters. She was buried in Westminster Abbey on 17 December with great ceremony; her viscera were interred in Lincoln Cathedral, her heart in the Dominicans' London church. Her Westminster tomb survives, its superb gilt bronze effigy cast by William Torel. Edward marked her funeral procession with twelve monumental crosses between Lincoln and Westminster; those at Geddington, Hardingstone, and Waltham survive. Camden portrayed these crosses as a bereaved king's tribute to a loved and respected queen, and embellished this view of Eleanor in *Remains* (1607). A late eulogy of her from Thomas Walsingham's *Historia Anglicana* (after 1392), first printed by Archbishop Parker in 1574, has helped to give Eleanor, a queen more controversial than politically influential, a far more attractive reputation in recent centuries than she enjoyed in her lifetime.

JOHN CARMI PARSONS

Sources J. C. Parsons, *Eleanor of Castile: queen and society in thirteenth-century England* (1995) • M. Prestwich, *Edward I* (1988) • S. L. Waugh, *The lordship of England: royal wardships and marriages in English society and politics, 1217–1327* (1988) • *The chronicle of Walter of Guisborough*, ed. H. Rothwell, CS, 3rd ser., 89 (1957) • *Ann. mon.* • G. Camdeno [W. Camden], *Britannia, sive, Florentissimorum regnorum, Angliae, Scotiae, Hiberniae* (1586) • L. A. Muratori, 'Ptolemaei Lucensis historia ecclesiastica', *Rerum Italicarum scriptores*, ed. F. Argellati, 11 (Milan, 1727) • *Registrum epistolarum fratris Johannis Peckham, archiepiscopi Cantuariensis*, ed. C. T. Martin, 3 vols., Rolls Series, 77 (1882–5) • J. C. Parsons, ed., *The court and household of Eleanor of Castile in 1290*, Pontifical Institute of Medieval Studies: Texts and Studies, 37 (1977) • *Thomae Walsingham, quondam monachi S. Albani, historia Anglicana*, ed. H. T. Riley, 2 vols., pt 1 of *Chronica monasterii S. Albani*, Rolls Series, 28 (1863–4) • W. Camden, *Remains* (1607) • J. C. Parsons, 'The year of Eleanor of Castile's birth and her children by Edward I', *Mediaeval Studies*, 46 (1984), 245–65
Likenesses W. Torel, gilt-bronze effigy, 1291–3, Westminster Abbey, London [*see illus.*] • electrotype (after an effigy by W. Torel), Westminster Abbey, London, NPG • statue (Eleanor cross), Geddington, Northamptonshire • statue (Eleanor cross), Hardingstone, Northamptonshire • statue (Eleanor cross), Waltham, Hertfordshire • wax seal, BM
Wealth at death approx. £2500—value of lands p.a.: Parsons, *Eleanor of Castile*, 84

Eleanor [Eleanor de Montfort] (*c.*1258–1282), princess of Wales, wife of Llywelyn ap Gruffudd, was the only daughter of Simon de *Montfort, earl of Leicester (*c.*1208–1265), and his wife, *Eleanor (1215?–1275). She was probably born about 1258, since she still had a nurse, but also a breviary and portiforium, and was therefore about seven, on her father's death in August 1265. By that time she had already been betrothed to *Llywelyn ap Gruffudd, prince of Wales, with whom her father had been in close and, eventually, formal alliance from 1263. She went into exile in France with her mother in October 1265. In 1275 she was married by proxy to Llywelyn and at the close of the year she set out with her brother Amaury de *Montfort for Wales, but their ship was captured in the Bristol Channel on behalf of Edward I. Eleanor was imprisoned for a week at Bristol, and afterwards at Windsor. Since Llywelyn was desperate to produce an heir, her detention was a major irritant in the fast-deteriorating relationship between the Welsh prince and Edward I in the years 1275–7. She was

released in 1278, after Llywelyn had submitted to Edward I, and was formally married to him in Edward's presence at Worcester on 13 October. In January 1281 Eleanor was at Windsor again, on a visit to the English court; on 19 June 1282 she died during the birth of a daughter, Gwenllïan. She was buried in the Franciscan house at Llanfair, Anglesey. Gwenllïan, whose father was killed in battle on 11 December 1282, was taken to England, passed her whole life as a nun at Sempringham, and died there on 7 June 1337, the last of the lines both of Llywelyn ap Gruffudd and of Simon de Montfort.

KATE NORGATE, *rev.* MARIOS COSTAMBEYS

Sources J. R. Maddicott, *Simon de Montfort* (1994) • *Florentii Wigorniensis monachi chronicon ex chronicis*, ed. B. Thorpe, 2, EHS, 10 (1849), 226

Eleanor [*née* Eleanor Cobham], **duchess of Gloucester** (*c.*1400–1452), alleged sorcerer, was the second wife of *Humphrey, duke of Gloucester, and attracted notoriety when convicted and imprisoned for treasonable necromancy in 1441. The fourth child of Sir Reginald (or Reynold) Cobham of Sterborough, Lingfield, Surrey, and his first wife, Eleanor, she became about 1422, the year of her mother's death, an attendant of Jacqueline d'Hainault, who, on divorcing John (IV), duke of Brabant, had fled to England in 1421 and in 1423 married Humphrey, duke of Gloucester (1390–1447). After unsuccessfully invading Hainault to assert his wife's claims Humphrey returned to England in March 1425 and Eleanor became his mistress. When in January 1428 his marriage with Jacqueline was pronounced invalid he married Eleanor. Though condemned as a *mésalliance*, the union proved a success. Eleanor was beautiful, intelligent, and ambitious and Humphrey was cultivated, pleasure-loving, and famous. Together they developed a manor at Greenwich into a pleasure garden, La Plesaunce, encircled by a wall with walks bordering the Thames, a tower, and a conduit. Here they gathered poets, musicians, scholars, physicians, and their friends to form a miniature court.

In the year 1435–6 when, on Bedford's death, Duke Humphrey became heir apparent and attained the height of his influence, Eleanor was accorded full recognition of her position: in November 1435 he created a jointure for her in his whole estate and in April 1436 she received the robes of a duchess for the Garter ceremony. At court she exercised some influence over the young king and became obsessed with the possibility of her husband's succeeding the unmarried and inert Henry VI. It was in this context that she began—certainly by April 1440—to consult astrologers to cast the king's horoscope and to predict her personal fortunes. This of itself was neither suspicious nor unusual. Mathematical astrology had become socially and academically respectable and other great noblemen had astrologers in their employ. Those whom Eleanor consulted were Thomas Southwell, her physician, canon of St Stephen's, Westminster, and Roger Bolingbroke, principal of St Andrew's Hall, Oxford—both men of high reputation. Unwisely, if honestly, from their reading of Henry VI's horoscope they predicted that a serious illness would endanger his life in July or August 1441. Rumours of this spread in London and reached the court. The authorities thereupon commissioned an alternative horoscope to reassure the king and took steps—on 28 and 29 June 1441—to examine Southwell, Bolingbroke, and Eleanor's chaplain, John Home, canon of Hereford. Between 10 and 12 July they were arrested and charged with necromancy and heretical practices and Eleanor fled to sanctuary in Westminster. On 23 July Bolingbroke was examined before the council and named Eleanor as the instigator. On 24 and 25 July she was examined by a panel of bishops on eighteen charges of treasonable necromancy, five of which she admitted. She was committed to Leeds Castle pending trial. After further investigations Southwell and Bolingbroke were indicted for sorcery, felony, and treason, with Eleanor as an accessory. But on her insistence it was again before an ecclesiastical tribunal that she was judged on 21 October; she denied most of the charges but admitted procuring potions from Margery Jourdemayne, the Witch of Eye (Ebury, near Westminster), in order to conceive and bear Duke Humphrey's child. On 27 July she abjured her errors and on 9 November penance was imposed on her to walk barefoot to three London churches on successive market days in November bearing a taper. She was forcibly divorced and condemned to perpetual imprisonment. Her associates suffered more harshly: Southwell died in the Tower of London, Bolingbroke was hanged, drawn, and quartered, and Margery was burnt.

Eleanor was imprisoned initially at Chester, then in 1443 moved to Kenilworth, in July 1446 to the Isle of Man, and finally in March 1449 to Beaumaris, where she died on 7 July 1452 and was buried, presumably in the parish church. How guilty was she? Although she had instigated predictions of the king's illness this fell short of devising the means to encompass his death. She admitted procuring love potions and had perhaps participated in casting spells. Such practices, common to all classes, attracted particular suspicion and alarm where women exercised influence at a high level. It is possible that her exposure was plotted by her husband's political enemies, who certainly exploited it to estrange the king from his uncle and implant suspicions which led to Humphrey's own arrest and death six years later. Finally the problem of how peeresses should be tried was resolved by a statute making them, like their husbands, judicable by the lords and judges. G. L. HARRISS

Sources R. A. Griffiths, 'The trial of Eleanor Cobham: an episode in the fall of Duke Humphrey of Gloucester', *Bulletin of the John Rylands University Library*, 51 (1968–9), 381–99; repr. in R. A. Griffiths, *King and country: England and Wales in the fifteenth century* (1991), 232–52 · H. M. Carey, *Courting disaster: astrology at the English court and university in the later middle ages* (1992), 138–53 · K. H. Vickers, *Humphrey duke of Gloucester: a biography* (1907) · Chancery rolls · J. S. Davies, ed., *An English chronicle of the reigns of Richard II, Henry IV, Henry V, and Henry VI*, CS, 64 (1856) · J. A. Giles, ed., *Incerti scriptoris chronicon Angliae de regnis trium regum Lancastrensium* (1848) · T. Wright, ed., *Political poems and songs relating to English history*, 2, Rolls Series, 14 (1861), 205–7 [lament of the duchess of Gloucester] · J. Stevenson, ed., *Letters and papers illustrative of the wars of the English in France during the reign of Henry VI, king of England*, 2, Rolls Series, 22 (1864), 762–

3 · E. M. Seaton, *Sir Richard Roos* (1961) · king's bench ancient indictments, PRO, KB 972/1–6, 9, 11, 14 [charges brought against her and her associates]
Likenesses miniature (of Cobham?; with Duke Humphrey), repro. in Vickers, *Humphrey duke of Gloucester*, appendix E

Eleanor of Brittany. *See* Eleanor, *suo jure* duchess of Brittany (1182x4–1241).

Eleanor of Brittany (1275–1342), abbess of Fontevrault, the sixth and youngest child of John (II), duke of Brittany (d. 1305), and Beatrice (d. 1275), daughter of *Henry III, took the veil at Amesbury probably at the same time as her grandmother *Eleanor of Provence, c.1286. Some time after her profession at the age of sixteen she moved, in accordance with her father's wishes, to Fontevrault where, in 1304, she was elected sixteenth abbess of the order. At her veiling Eleanor was endowed with property by her grandmother, and after her father's death she received £700 annually from his estate. Her abbatial staff of gold and silver was said to be worth £700, while her bequest to Fontevrault on her death included relics, crosses set with precious stones, vessels of gold, silver, and crystal, as well as several manuscripts and tapestries.

Eleanor maintained close links with the English houses, sending her representatives as official visitors, supervising the deployment of personnel from one house to another, and sending nuns, chaplains, and even laity from Fontevrault to live at Amesbury. At least once and possibly at other times she sent for the accounts of an English house to be brought to Fontevrault. Challenges to her authority, whether from her cousin *Mary, daughter of *Edward I, a nun at Amesbury, or from a section of the convent of Nuneaton who supported a prioress other than her appointee, were dealt with decisively and with the full measure of the means at her disposal, including appeal to the papal court. Her rule was centralized and strong at a time when the wars between England and France threatened the security of English dependencies of French orders. She died at the abbey of Fontevrault in 1342 and was buried there. BERENICE M. KERR

Sources J. Lardier, 'La saincte famille de Fontevrault', 16th cent., Archives Départmentales, Angers, Maine-et-Loire, 1 mi 74, vol. 3 [orig. in Bibliothèque Municipale de Châteaugontier, MS 12] · dons, confirmations … par les rois d'Angleterre, les seigneurs, … à Fontevrault, Archives Départmentales, Angers, Maine-et-Loire, 242 H · Prieuré d'Amesbury, Archives Départmentales, Angers, Maine-et-Loire, 243 H · Prieuré de Westwood, Archives Départmentales, Angers, Maine-et-Loire, 244 H · Prieuré d'Eton, Archives Départmentales, Angers, Maine-et-Loire, 246 H · BL, Aston MSS, Add. MSS 47380–49769; 53092–53115 · P. H. Morice, *Mémoires pour servir de preuves à l'histoire ecclésiastique et civile de Bretagne*, 1 (Paris, 1742), 1186 · H. Nicquet, *Histoire de l'ordre de Font Evraud contenant la vie et les merveilles de la sainteté de Robert d'Arbrissel et l'histoire chronologique des abbesses* (1642) · A. Jubien, *L'Abbesse Marie de Bretagne et la réforme de l'ordre de Fontevraud* (1872), 176–8
Wealth at death legacy to Fontevrault: Jubien, *L'Abbesse Marie*; Lardier, 'La saincte famille', vol. 3, fol. 513

Elen, Ernest Augustus [Gus] (1862–1940), music-hall singer, was born on 22 July 1862 at 103 Pulford Street, Pimlico, London, son of Edwin Elen, a viewer of cloth in a military store, and Mercy Elen, *née* Letherbarrow. His early life

Ernest Augustus Elen (1862–1940), by unknown photographer, c.1905

in this relatively poor working-class district contained spells as a draper's assistant, an egg-packer, and a programme seller at the Royal Aquarium. He began his entertainment career singing in London public houses and in army canteens in Aldershot. He may also have been a street singer and worked as a supernumerary at the Opera Comique in 1882. By 1884 he had developed a black-face routine and performed with a minstrel troupe in Ramsgate, and as half of a double act in provincial halls. Following the death of his partner in 1885, he turned solo and began a steady ascent to the peak of the variety profession.

Although always essentially a comic singer, Elen did not initially adopt a distinctive style, with his advertising card claiming that 'Elen is alike at home in Comic, Eccentric or Dramatic ditties … no two characters the same' (The Era, 2 May 1891). However, in April 1891 he introduced a 'coster' song, 'Never introduce your donah [sweetheart] to a pal', into his act. Coster singers, adopting the persona of the London costermonger or street fruit and vegetable vendor, had appeared on the halls from the 1860s but the huge success of Albert Chevalier's coster routine at the London Pavilion in February 1891 began a new vogue which Elen exploited. While he was to retain a mixed routine for some time, it was his coster material that made him one of music-hall's biggest stars in the 1890s and 1900s: when he was finally tempted to visit the United States in 1907, he reputedly commanded a salary of £300 a

week. Although most of his key songs and characterizations were produced in the 1890s he remained a popular turn until his retirement at the end of the First World War.

Elen's songs, performed in almost exact replica of costermonger or other London street costume, were delivered in a friendly if occasionally harsh voice and punctuated by a series of almost falsetto 'breaks' which added both emphasis and comic effect. They were mainly rather wry and sardonic commentaries on the daily life of a distinct section of the London working class and, although Elen in his personal pronouncements was firmly wedded to values of self-discipline and thrift, they sometimes contained a gentle challenge to Victorian notions of respectability. ''Arf a pint of ale', for example, in which the ''arf' eventually became 'a barrel and an 'arf', celebrated the pleasures of beer, while 'Wait until the work comes round' and ''E talks just like a picture book' hymned the joys of idleness. These mildly satirical tendencies and his avoidance of the excessive sentimentality often associated with late Victorian and Edwardian popular song (along with the size and relative availability of his recorded output) made him a particular favourite of latter-day music-hall historians and cultural commentators. In particular, he has often been compared favourably with his middle-class rival Albert Chevalier, deemed to have presented a rather generalized and less 'authentic' portrayal of London life.

Elen originally wrote some of his own material but from the early 1890s he relied largely upon professional writers, albeit cutting their songs 'about a good deal before producing them' (The Era, 23 Sept 1905). He was especially well served by lyricists Edgar Bateman, usually partnered by melodist George Le Brunn, and Harry Wright, who worked with Fred Eplett. Bateman provided the words for Elen's two best known songs, 'It's a great big shame' (1896), which charted the problems of a newly-wed friend of 'six foot free' nagged by a wife of 'four foot two', and 'If it wasn't for the 'ouses in between' (1894). This classic music-hall song dealt with a cockney's knowing pretence about the view from his back garden and featured such lines as:

if yer eyesight didn't fail yer,
yer could see right to Australia,
if it wasn't for the 'ouses in between.

As these song quotations and such song titles as 'It's a marvel 'ow 'e does it but he do' suggest, Elen made good if sometimes stylized use of London's demotic speech and idiom. Interestingly, he was extremely popular outside of the capital and 'Never introduce your donah', although first performed in London, appears to have become a major success during the course of a lengthy provincial tour in the autumn of 1891. Through his depiction of a distinct, local character, Elen both played a role in reinforcing provincial images of the Londoner and in creating a space for explorations of local and regional characterization which Scottish and northern singers were later able to exploit.

From 1898 Elen lived largely in Balham, where he bred

poultry and took up photography. He also became a keen fisherman, particularly during a spell in residence on the south coast, and enjoyed shooting. He was married, but nothing is known about his wife beyond the fact that she helped him with his extensive charitable activities. As a result of the nostalgia for music-hall's 'golden days' which was a notable feature of the 1930s, Elen made a brief comeback in 1931 and then appeared at the 1935 royal variety performance in a 'Cavalcade of Variety'. He had recorded songs as early as 1899, but he rerecorded much of his material in 1931 and 1932. After a short, final retirement, he died of liver cancer at his home, Edith Villa, 3 Thurleigh Avenue, Balham, on 17 February 1940.

DAVE RUSSELL

Sources T. Barker, 'Gus Elen', *Music Hall Records*, 5 (Feb 1979), 85–95 · *The Performer* (22 Feb 1940) · *The Performer* (31 May 1935) · *The Era* (2 May 1901) · *The Era* (23 Sept 1905) · C. MacInnes, *Sweet Saturday night* (1967) · V. Gammon and A. Hawkins, 'Noticeboard: recordings', *History Workshop Journal*, 10 (1980), 202–3 · b. cert. · d. cert.
Archives SOUND BL NSA, documentary recording · BL NSA, performance recordings
Likenesses photograph, c.1905, NPG [*see illus.*] · photograph, repro. in *The Era* (23 Sept 1905)
Wealth at death £10,755 15s.: probate, 27 March 1940, CGPLA Eng. & Wales

Elephant Man, the. *See* Merrick, Joseph Carey (1862–1890).

Elers, John Philip (1664–1738), potter and merchant, was born in Utrecht on 7 September 1664, the son of Martin Elers (*b.* 1621). His mother was a daughter of Daniel van Mildred. He had a brother, David (1656–1742), and a sister, Sarah, who married Sir William Phipps. His grandfather was Admiral Elers, commander of the fleet at Hamburg, who married a princess of the royal house of Baden. Martin Elers's brother had a shop in London where he sold pottery and porcelain imported from the East Indies, and by 1675 Martin had joined him in that enterprise. John Philip and David trained as silversmiths and chemists in Cologne; however, David Elers was in London in 1686, and it is likely that he was joined by John Philip around this date. They commenced making pottery at Fulham about 1690, manufacturing stoneware teapots.

At some date between 1691 and 1693 John Philip and David moved to Staffordshire. The Newcastle under Lyme corporation minutes for 18 August 1691 'ordered that a present be made to my Lord Chief Justice Holt at his cominge to this burroughe from Lancaster Assizes of some of Mr David Elers earthen ware to the vallew of three pounds or thereabouts'. Unfortunately this order does not include a reference to the origin of the ware.

In June 1693 the two Elers brothers were cited by John Dwight (1672–1703), the Fulham potter, for enticing from his service a workman named John Chandler and infringing his patent. Dwight's bill of complaint included the claim for his production of 'Vessells never made before in England or elsewhere and [that he had] alsoe discovered the mistery of opacous red and dark coloured porcelane or China' (Haselgrove and Murray, 83). David Elers gave

evidence that they had learned the production of stoneware in Cologne, where he had resided for a while. Furthermore he and John Philip had for three years been engaged in the production of these wares in England.

John Philip and David worked a potworks at Vauxhall, Surrey, from 1693 to 1700 and kept a shop in the Poultry, London, where they sold imported pottery and it is likely that they also sold their own products. The demand for imported oriental ceramics influenced the refined teapots the brothers manufactured. They would appear to have been operating the Staffordshire and Vauxhall works at the same time, which may have contributed to their eventual bankruptcy.

Following the lawsuit the Elerses undertook the production of red stoneware in Staffordshire under licence to Dwight until the expiry of his patent in 1698. Bradwell Farm in the parish of Wolstanton, Newcastle under Lyme, Staffordshire, was leased to John Philip. Tradition also places him at Dimsdale Hall, a nearby premises. It is possible that Dwight provided information about the rich clay seams in the area as a result of his period of service for the bishops of Chester. Part of the agreement was the supply of the red Staffordshire clay to Dwight.

The clay at this site lent itself to the Elerses' unique method of forming. Close examination of their wares and experiments using clay from the Bradwell Hall site confirms that the Elerses slip cast, lathe turned, and then applied relief designs to the fine forms. The unglazed red teapots were influenced by the fashionable, but costly, imported Yixing Chinese wares. The forming process was probably a result of their silversmith training. A limited number of their wares is known to survive, admirable for their refined quality, a factor which assisted the improvement of ceramic manufacture. Unfounded stories claim they employed local 'idiots' as workmen in order to protect the secrecy of their processes. It is also unproved that they produced salt-glazed ware at this site; excavations by Enoch Wood in 1814 revealed only a kiln used for red stoneware.

By 1698 John Philip and David Elers had left Staffordshire and 'remov'd to some other place' (Morris, 156). A lease of September 1698, for fourteen years, let the land hitherto in the possession of John Elers to a William Beech. A clause in the contract insisted upon the demolition of the potworks. At this juncture John Philip returned to the London area, possibly to Battersea.

John Philip was married on 26 August 1699 to Elizabeth Banks (*d.* c.1702) of Uttoxeter. A son, Paul, was born in 1700: among Paul's children was Maria, mother of Maria Edgeworth, the novelist. In 1700 Elers moved to Dublin where it is believed that he was set up in the merchant business by Lady Barrington. David Elers sent quantities of oriental ware purchased from the East India Company to Dublin, presumably for John Philip to sell. John Philip died in Dublin in 1738.

In 1777 Paul Elers requested that Josiah Wedgwood make a portrait medallion of his father. It was modelled by William Hackwood and impressed 'Johan Phillip Elers' on the reverse. Paul wished his father to be accredited with the transformation of the ceramic industry, but Wedgwood would only partly endorse this claim.

HELEN L. PHILLIPS

Sources C. Morris, ed., *The illustrated journeys of Celia Fiennes, 1685–1712* (1982), 56 · D. Haselgrove and J. Murray, eds., 'John Dwight's Fulham pottery, 1672–1978: a collection of documentary sources', *Journal of Ceramic History*, 11 (1979) [whole issue] · R. Edwards, 'London potters, 1570–1710', *Journal of Ceramic History* (1974) · *VCH Staffordshire*, vol. 3 · Stoke City Museum and Art Gallery, Stoke-on-Trent, Reginald Haggar MSS · W. Mankowitz and R. G. Haggar, *The concise encyclopedia of English pottery and porcelain* [1957] · G. Elliott, 'Ceramic manufacture in north Staffordshire, 1600–1760', MA diss., Keele University, 1981 · G. Elliott, 'Staffordshire red and black stonewares', *Transactions of the English Ceramic Circle*, 10 (1976–8) · F. Britton, *London delftware* (1986) · J. Ward, *The borough of Stoke upon Trent* (1843) · S. Shaw, *History of the Staffordshire potteries* (1829) · W. B. Honey, 'Elers ware', *Transactions of the English Ceramic Circle*, 1/2 (1934), 7–21
Archives City Museum and Art Gallery, Stoke-on-Trent, Reginald Haggar MSS
Likenesses W. Hackwood for J. Wedgwood, medallion, 1777 (after engraving), Brooklyn Museum, New York, Emily Winthrop Miles collection

Elfoddw (*d.* **809**), archbishop of Gwynedd, is known for three things. First, in 768, he is said by the *Annales Cambriae* to have brought about the adherence of the Britons to the Roman method of calculating Easter. He is there described as 'a man of God' which implies that the annalist perceived him as saintly, and perhaps also, though less certainly, that his reputation for holiness played some part in persuading the Britons to abandon their traditional paschal cycle. This is the last known change from the customs adopted by the Britons, probably in the fifth century, which they had spread to the Irish, and which were then handed on by the Irish to the Picts and the Northumbrians. It is not known, however, when the Bretons and Cornishmen adopted the Roman Easter. The change brought about by Elfoddw was not the first among his people. Bede says that some of the Britons conformed to the Roman Easter having been persuaded by Adomnán about 690. These were presumably the Britons of Strathclyde, with whom Iona had good relations, as shown by Adomnán's life of Columba. Bede's information also indicates that the churches of Strathclyde were not directly subject to Iona, since those that were subject apparently did not change at that date.

The second notable thing about Elfoddw is the description of him in his obit as 'archbishop of Gwynedd' (*Annales Cambriae*, s.a. 809). He is not claimed to be 'archbishop of Britannia'—that is, of Wales—as one might have expected, given some of the models for such a claim: both Kildare and Armagh had, in the seventh century, claimed to be the sees of archbishops of all Ireland. Their claims were probably modelled on the position given to Theodore of Tarsus (*d.* 690), namely archbishop of the island of Britain. As Theodore was archbishop of one island, so might Kildare, or Armagh, provide an archbishop of the other island. A British response to such claims might have taken the form of an archbishopric of Britannia (meaning Wales), yet Elfoddw was only said to be archbishop of Gwynedd. This makes it more likely that the model was the English situation after 735, when there was one archbishopric for the northern English at York and another for the southern English at Canterbury. Elfoddw's archbishopric of Gwynedd may have been the northern archbishopric of Britannia. Asser (*d.* 909) avers without any apparent sense of stating something remarkable that his kinsman Nobis of St David's was archbishop. There may thus have been a southern archbishopric of Dyfed alongside a northern archbishopric of Gwynedd.

It is usually said that these claims must have been remote from reality because no Welsh bishop could have received a pallium from Rome or had his title of archbishop conferred by the pope. This argument rests on anachronistic assumptions. Theodore's archbishopric represented an extension to the west of a position previously set out, without any reference to the papacy, by the emperor Justinian (*r.* 527–65): the archbishop or patriarch was to be the ecclesiastical head of an imperial diocese, such as Egypt or Britain, while the metropolitan bishop corresponded to an imperial province and the bishop to a city and its territory. A different, probably consciously anti-imperial, scheme is set out by Isidore of Seville (570–636) in his *Etymologiae*: patriarchs were only for apostolic sees, such as Alexandria or Rome (he carefully does not include Constantinople), while below the patriarch come archbishops, metropolitan bishops, and the ordinary bishops of cities. Neither Isidore's patriarchs nor his archbishops are said to have required papal pallia: as the register of Gregory the Great shows, pallia were given on occasion to ordinary bishops; they were not given to those metropolitan bishops in Illyricum who were traditionally known as archbishops. The link between the English metropolitan bishoprics and the papal pallium was created by the special papal sponsorship of the English mission; its link with an English archbishopric was created by the particular office conferred upon Theodore and his immediate successors. The elevation of York to an archbishopric was in substance a reversion to the earlier Gregorian scheme for Britain of two metropolitan bishoprics, but with the addition of the title of archbishop. There was no reason why an archbishop of Gwynedd should have been required to obtain a papal pallium, apart from the fact that, in the Gregorian scheme, all Britain was to be subject to his two metropolitan bishops. No doubt the claim would have been rejected at Canterbury and at Rome, but just the same problems were caused by the political impossibility of subjecting the Picts to an archbishop based at York.

The third guise in which Elfoddw appears is in the 'Nennian preface' added in the tenth century to the 'Nennian' or Cambridge recension of the *Historia Brittonum*, itself composed in 829–30. This claims that Nennius was a disciple of Elfoddw. While chronologically not impossible, this claim cannot be corroborated by evidence of ninth-century date.

T. M. CHARLES-EDWARDS

Sources E. Phillimore, ed., 'The *Annales Cambriae* and Old Welsh genealogies', *Y Cymmrodor*, 9 (1888), 141–83 [version A] · J. Williams ab Ithel, ed., *Annales Cambriae*, Rolls Series, 20 (1860) [B and C versions, with the A version] • T. Mommsen, ed., 'Historia Brittonum', *Chronica minora saec. IV. V. VI. VII.*, 3, MGH Auctores Antiquissimi, 13 (Berlin, 1898), 111–222 • *English historical documents*, 1, ed. D. Whitelock (1955), no. 191 • *Alfred the Great: Asser's Life of King Alfred and other contemporary sources*, ed. and trans. S. Keynes and M. Lapidge (1983) • Nennius, 'British history' and 'The Welsh annals', ed. and trans. J. Morris (1980)

Elford, Richard (*bap.* **1677**, *d.* **1714**), singer and composer, was baptized on 3 January 1677 at St Margaret-in-the-Close, Lincoln, the son of Thomas Elford, vicar-choral of Lincoln Cathedral, and his wife, Ann. He was a boy chorister at Lincoln Cathedral and from July 1695 a singing man at Durham. In February 1699 he was admonished 'for neglecting the Quire, & Singing in the Playhouse' and on 7 March that year was dismissed 'for his Manifest Contumacy' (Durham Cathedral, chapter minutes). He was reinstated two days later, but his salary was unclaimed at Michaelmas and on 2 November 1699 a song composed by him was published by John Walsh in London.

Elford's career as a stage singer was not a success because he was 'aukward and clumsy, and his action disgusting' (Hawkins, 4.427). Five of his thirteen surviving songs were composed for the Lincoln's Inn Fields theatre, including one for Rowe's *Tamerlane* (December 1701) and another which he sang himself. In the 1702–3 season he appeared at Drury Lane as a singing witch in Richard Leveridge's *Macbeth* music and was advertised for concerts at York Buildings.

Elford joined the choir of St Paul's Cathedral in March 1700 and was sworn a gentleman of the Chapel Royal on 2 August 1702. His flexible high tenor voice and clear, impassioned delivery of words made him London's leading church and court singer. Important solos were written for him in anthems and odes by John Blow, Jeremiah Clarke, William Croft, John Eccles, George Frideric Handel, and John Weldon, six of whose solo anthems for Elford were published as *Divine Harmony* in 1716. In 1704 he was 'sent for down by the Gentlemen of the Country' (*Diverting Post*, 18–25 Nov 1704) for a St Cecilia's day concert at Winchester and on 19 December 1706 he and Leveridge were the soloists in the D'Urfey and Eccles ode *From Glorious Toils of War* at the lord mayor's celebratory banquet for the duke of Marlborough in Vintners' Hall. Elford was granted an additional allowance of £100 annually from Christmas 1705 by Queen Anne, his 'Blessed Patroness' (Carey, 23).

Elford's brother Thomas (1674–1751) was in the choir of St George's Chapel, Windsor, from 1714 until his death; in 1722 Thomas travelled to Ireland to sing at Armagh Cathedral, carrying a letter of recommendation to Jonathan Swift in Dublin. The Mrs Elford who danced on the London stage between 1700 and 1706 cannot have been the wife of Richard or Thomas, but may have been related. In December 1706 Richard Elford 'of St James, Westminster bachelor' married Catharine London (*d.* 1715) and they had two daughters. He died on 29 October 1714 and was buried on 1 November in the west cloister of Westminster Abbey, where he had also been a member of the choir. Henry Carey's 'On the Death of the Late Famous Mr. Elford' was set by Croft, who ten years later, in his preface to *Musica sacra*, praised Elford as a 'bright Example … fit to be imitated by all that come after him'.

OLIVE BALDWIN and THELMA WILSON

Sources parish register, Lincoln, St Margaret-in-the-Close, Lincs. Arch. • chapter acts, Lincoln Cathedral, A 3.11, fol. 105v and *passim* • treasury books, Lincoln Cathedral • acts, Durham Cathedral, iv, 28, 53 • minutes, Durham Cathedral, 55 • treasurers' books, Durham Cathedral • tenor partbooks, Durham Cathedral • muniments, Westminster Abbey, London • archives, St George's Chapel, Windsor • A. Ashbee, ed., *Records of English court music*, 2 (1987) • A. Ashbee, ed., *Records of English court music*, 5 (1991) • A. Ashbee, ed., *Records of English court music*, 8 (1995) • A. Ashbee and J. Harley, eds., *The cheque books of the Chapel Royal*, 1 (2000) • J. Hawkins, *A general history of the science and practice of music*, 4 (1776) • *Post Boy* (15–17 Dec 1702) • *Post Boy* (30 Oct–2 Nov 1714) • *Daily Courant* (17 March 1703) • *Daily Courant* (7 Aug 1703) • *Diverting Post* (18–25 Nov 1704) • *Répertoire international des sources musicales*, 11 (Munich, 1986) • W. C. Smith, *A bibliography of the musical works published by John Walsh … 1695–1720* (1948); repr. (1968) • C. L. Day and E. B. Murrie, *English song-books, 1651–1702: a bibliography with a first-line index of songs* (1940) • R. Leveridge, 'The musick of Macbeth', FM Cam., MS 87 • H. Carey, *Poems on several occasions* (1720) • J. L. Chester and J. Foster, eds., *London marriage licences, 1521–1869* (1887) • Katherine Elford's will, PRO, PROB 11/549, fol. 235 • *The correspondence of Jonathan Swift*, ed. H. Williams, 2 (1963) • W. Van Lennep and others, eds., *The London stage, 1660–1800*, pt 1: *1660–1700* (1965) • E. L. Avery, ed., *The London stage, 1660–1800*, pt 2: *1700–1729* (1960)

Elford, Sir William, baronet (**1749–1837**), politician and artist, was born in August 1749 at Kingsbridge, Devon, the elder son of the Revd Lancelot Elford (*c.*1719–1782) of Bickham, near Plymouth, and his wife, Grace, daughter of Alexander Wills of Kingsbridge.

Nothing is known of Elford's early years at Bickham: in 1773, having acquired a house in Plympton, he wrote to a Plymouth friend, the painter James Northcote, that he would 'dispense Law and Justice for the benefit of the world in general' (Elford, 2.1). On election as mayor of Plympton in 1773, Joshua Reynolds looked to Elford to ensure a good position for a donated self-portrait (priv. coll.). On 20 January 1776 Elford married Mary (1753–1817), daughter of the Revd John Davies, vicar of Axmouth and former headmaster of Plympton School. A son, Jonathan (1776–1823), was born in November followed by Grace Chard (1781–1856) and Elizabeth (1782–1837).

Elford was probably a partner in the Plymouth bank (Elford, Tingcombe, and Purchase) from its formation *c.*1782. From 1786 he served in the South Devon militia and rose to the rank of lieutenant-colonel in 1798, when the regiment spent a year in Waterford during the Irish rising. In 1796 he was elected member of parliament for Plymouth, where he was recorder between 1797 and 1833. An ardent supporter of anti-sedition measures, he subscribed £20,000 to the loyalty loan of 1797. Henry Dundas encouraged his expectation of advancement and, assured of Elford's ancient west country lineage, persuaded William Pitt to bestow a baronetcy in 1800.

When Henry Addington succeeded Pitt in 1801, Elford offered his support, hoping to gain a government post for himself or his son. Among his interventions in the House of Commons, he attacked the administration of Plymouth Dockyard—making a dangerous enemy of the first lord of the Admiralty, Lord St Vincent, who ensured his replacement as member for Plymouth by Sir Charles Morice Pole in 1806. Despite the efforts of William Dacres Adams, son of the MP for Totnes and Pitt's secretary, Elford's only recompense was a seat at Rye in 1807, which he held for a year. Jonathan Elford represented Westbury briefly in 1820 but died in 1823.

With advice from Northcote, who painted the Elford family's portraits including Elford's in 1782 (Yale U. CBA), Elford became a competent artist and exhibited a Devon view at the Royal Academy most years from 1774, presenting *Landscape with a Distant Country House* in 1816 to the future George IV (Royal Collection). Another extensive but smaller Devon landscape dated 1818 is in the Royal Albert Memorial Museum, Exeter, and *Landscape with Two Artists* (1802; Plymouth Art Gallery) is notable for its finely painted tree foliage. *Pendennis Castle*, an ink and brown wash drawing (BM), confirms him as a skilled draughtsman whose works are now rare.

As in other spheres Elford worked hard for recognition, entertaining academicians including Joseph Farington, David Wilkie, and William Collins at Bickham, which he inherited in 1782. The purchase with his banking partner, now Tingcombe junior, of B. R. Haydon's *Judgment of Solomon* for 700 guineas at the watercolour exhibition in Spring Gardens in 1814 caused considerable comment but the painting failed as an attraction at Plymouth Guildhall and was resold at a loss (Plymouth Guildhall).

On 5 July 1821, four years after the death of his first wife, Elford married a widow, Elizabeth Walrond (*née* Hall). With an overdraft increased by the debts of his son and partly secured on his own properties and life insurance, Elford was left penniless when his bank failed with many others in 1825. With Bickham sold, he moved in 1831 to his son-in-law's house, The Priory, in Totnes, Devon, where he was recorder between 1832 and 1834.

Elected to the Royal Society in 1790 and the Linnean Society in 1813, this tenacious man continued to pursue his artistic, ornithological, and scientific interests, in 1836 publishing his discovery of a yeast substitute. Elford was also involved with the Plymouth and Dartmoor Railroad. A lighter side is evident in his encouraging letters to the novelist Mary Russell Mitford written between 1810 and 1836. The baronetcy became extinct at his death at Totnes on 30 November 1837, when he left only £300. He was buried at Totnes parish church.   FELICITY OWEN

Sources L. Elford, 'The Elfords', Plymouth Central Library, MSS 1972–6 • HoP, *Commons, 1790–1820*, 3.678–81 • R. Dymond, 'Seventh report of the committee on works of art in Devonshire', *Report and Transactions of the Devonshire Association*, 18 (1886), 108–41, esp. 114–20 • *The life of Mary Russell Mitford, related in a selection from her letters to her friends*, ed. A. G. K. L'Estrange, 2 vols. (1870) • Farington, *Diary*, vols. 6, 10, 13 • *GM*, 2nd ser., 9 (1838), 206–7 • B. R. Haydon, *Life and times*, ed. W. B. Pope, 5 vols. (1963) • *DNB* • O. Millar, *The later Georgian pictures in the collection of her majesty the queen*, 2 vols. (1969) • M. H. Grant, *A chronological history of the old English landscape painters*, 3 vols. (1926–47)

Archives Plymouth and West Devon RO, documents | Plymouth City Museum and Art Gallery, letters to Northcote
Likenesses J. Northcote, oils, 1782, Yale U. CBA
Wealth at death £300 post 30 Nov 1837: HoP, *Commons, 1790–1820*

Elfrith, Daniel (*fl.* 1607–1640), privateer and colonist in the West Indies, was active in the Caribbean from 1607. Nothing is known of his earlier life. He was memorialized by Alexander Brown in his *Genesis of the United States* (1890) as 'the man who carried the first rats to the Bermudas and the first negroes to Virginia' (Brown, 2.886); he is thus implicated in both the institution of slavery and the beginnings of environmental degradation in the English American colonies.

Elfrith was part of an expedition to the Amazon River led by Edward Fisher in 1613 under the royal charter issued to Robert Harcourt. He was placed in command of a captured Spanish frigate 'laden with Spanish meale', which he sailed to Bermuda in February 1614. The rats disembarked with the meal and became, as governor Nathaniel Butler wrote in his *Historye of the Bermudaes*, 'like one of Pharoath's plagues' in the islands.

In 1618–19 Elfrith was in the service of Robert Rich, the second earl of Warwick, commanding the famous privateering ship *Treasurer*, which was sailing under a commission Warwick had obtained from the duke of Savoy. After a voyage through the Caribbean he called at Virginia in consortship with a Dutch ship that carried 100 Africans captured from the Spanish, of whom about twenty were left in Virginia. The Virginia Company leadership under Sir Edwin Sandys was outraged, not by the importation of Africans, but by Warwick's attempting to use Virginia and Bermuda as privateering bases through Elfrith, thereby endangering the colonies. The remaining Africans were taken to Bermuda.

Elfrith spent much of the 1620s in Bermuda, where he was a member of the governor's council. His daughter married the island's governor, Captain Philip Bell. In 1629 two ships commanded by Elfrith and Captain Sussex Camock discovered Providence Island in the western Caribbean off the coast of Nicaragua. Leaving Camock to hold their find, Elfrith hurried to Bermuda and then to England to inform the governor of the Bermuda or Somers Islands Company, his patron the earl of Warwick. Warwick and his cousin Sir Nathaniel Rich organized the Providence Island Company, composed solely of leading puritans, and the company directed Elfrith and Bell to lead the first contingent of settlers from Bermuda to Providence Island. Bell assumed the post of governor and Elfrith became admiral of the colony and second in command.

Elfrith was frequently at odds with the puritan settlers who came directly from England. In 1631 he seized a Spanish frigate on the Central American mainland and invited a famous privateer, Diego el Mulato, to visit the colony, thereby endangering the enterprise. In order to reinstate himself in the Providence Island Company's good graces, he sent them a 'rutter', a navigation guide to the western Caribbean, claiming that he alone had the knowledge necessary to create it. Elfrith stayed on, but in their instructions of May 1632 the company defined his limits: no act of hostility without specific direction from London unless the island was attacked; and no voyages from the island 'on what pretext soever without the consent of you the Governor and Council'. The company found themselves forced again and again to deal with the friction between Elfrith and the other colonists.

The Providence Island investors came to doubt Elfrith's claims to experience-based knowledge. They felt that he had misled them in his initial report of the island's natural fruitfulness and strength. Moreover, they accepted the judgement of their fortifications expert, Captain Samuel Axe, that the island's forts were inadequately constructed because of Elfrith's 'mistakes and ignorance'. In 1640 the company rejected his demands for additional compensation for services rendered in Providence Island, asserting, 'they conceive nothing justly due him'. After this instance, he does not again appear in the historical record, leaving uncertainty as to the circumstances and time of his death.   KAREN ORDAHL KUPPERMAN

Sources 'Daniell Ellffryth's guide to the Caribbean, 1631', ed. S. Pargellis and R. L. Butler, *William and Mary Quarterly*, 1 (1944), 273–316 · [N. Butler?], *The historye of the Bermudaes or Summer Islands*, ed. J. H. Lefroy, Hakluyt Society, 1st ser., 65 (1882) · A. Brown, *The genesis of the United States*, 2 vols. (1890); repr. (1964) · W. F. Craven, *Dissolution of the Virginia Company: the failure of a colonial experiment* (1932) · W. F. Craven, 'The earl of Warwick, a speculator in piracy', *Hispanic American Historical Review*, 10 (1930) · K. O. Kupperman, *Providence Island, 1630–1641: the other puritan colony* (1993) · J. Lorimer, ed., *English and Irish settlement on the River Amazon, 1550–1646* (1989) · H. C. Wilkinson, *The adventurers of Bermuda*, 2nd edn (1958)
Archives PRO, records of the Providence Island Company, CO 124/1, 2

Elgar, Sir Edward William, baronet (1857–1934), composer and conductor,

was born on 2 June 1857 at The Firs, Broadheath, Worcestershire, the fourth of the seven children of William Henry Elgar (1821–1906), an organist and tradesman, and his wife, Ann (1821/2–1902), the daughter of Joseph Greening, a Herefordshire farmworker, and his wife, Esther. It is possible that he was the fifth of eight children, for in 1853 there may have been a daughter who died before baptism. William Elgar was born in Dover and settled in Worcester in 1841 as the owner of a shop at 10 High Street, selling sheet music and musical instruments. He was later appointed piano-tuner to Queen Adelaide (widow of William IV), who from 1844 lived at Witley Court, Worcestershire. Although a Protestant, he was appointed organist of St George's Roman Catholic Church, Worcester, in 1846. In 1848 he married Ann Greening and lived at 2 College Precincts, where their first three, possibly four, children were born. In 1856 they rented a cottage, The Firs, in the village of Broadheath, 3 miles north-west of Worcester. They lived there only until 1859 and Edward was their only child born there. Ann Elgar, but not her husband, had converted to Roman Catholicism in 1852 and Edward was baptized in St George's on 11 June 1857. Edward's lifelong Worcester friend Hubert Leicester told a Jesuit priest in 1909 that William Elgar was 'a regular terror as regards the Catholicity of his family—

Sir Edward William Elgar, baronet (1857–1934), by Charles Frederick Grindrod, *c*.1903

used to threaten to shoot his daughters if caught going to confession. Very tactful wife' (Moore, *Edward Elgar: a Creative Life*, 17).

All the Elgar children received some degree of musical instruction. Joe, born in 1859, was regarded as a prodigy (he died aged seven). Edward showed early promise as a pianist, especially as an improviser. His father, who tuned the pianos at other stately Worcestershire homes besides Queen Adelaide's, took the boy with him to display his prowess to his clients. One of Elgar's biographers, W. H. Reed, recalled that,

> when a piano had to be tuned at Croome Court or Madresfield, the boy Edward was taken for what was practically a delightful day's outing … No detail of those far-off times escaped him; he could tell me as we ambled about the lanes and passed these great houses and many others too, the names of all the people who lived in them long ago, and relate to me the sayings of the members of the household, or the yarns spun for his benefit by the groom, or the old ostler who watered his father's horse.   (Reed, 45)

From his mother Edward derived his love and knowledge of literature and his response to the beauties of the countryside. He explored Worcestershire on foot—and later on a bicycle—and knew the country lanes intimately.

Early years and education At the age of six Elgar attended a Roman Catholic dame-school in Britannia Square, Worcester, and had piano tuition and some lessons in music theory. He would also sit in the organ loft at St George's listening to his father's playing. Already he was making efforts at composition: he said in later life that he was found sitting on a river bank with pencil and music paper 'trying to fix the sounds and longing for something very great' (quoted in Kennedy, 3). Elgar himself said (in an address to the Friends of Worcester Cathedral on 18 June 1932) that 'my first music was learnt in the Cathedral … from books borrowed from the music library, when I was eight, nine or ten. They were barbarously printed in eight different clefs, all of which I learnt before I was twelve …' From 1866 to 1868 he attended a Roman Catholic school at Spetchley and then went to Littleton House School in Powick Road, Worcester. The headmaster, Francis Reeve, taught scripture and, during a lesson on Christ's disciples, remarked: 'The Apostles were young men and very poor. Perhaps, before the descent of the Holy Ghost, they were no cleverer than some of you here.' The observation caught the young Elgar's imagination, with results to be heard years later in his oratorio *The Apostles*.

The first music composed by Elgar which has survived was written in 1867 or 1869 for a play, *The Wand of Youth*, devised by the Elgar children as a protest against 'the imaginary despotic rule of my mother and father'. It was scored for piano, flute, two or three stringed instruments including a double bass they made themselves, and some improvised percussion. When he was fifty, Elgar revised and rescored the music as two orchestral suites.

When he was twelve, Elgar began to show an interest in the violin. Inspired by the aria 'O thou that tellest good tidings to Zion' in a performance of Handel's *Messiah* in Worcester Cathedral in September 1869, he was determined to be able to play it. He taught himself to some extent and had lessons from a local musician, Frederick Spray. He was now intent upon becoming a musician and left school, where he was head boy in his last year, at the age of fifteen in 1872, hoping to go to the Leipzig conservatory. But there was no money for such a venture and he became a clerk in the office of a solicitor, William Allen, who was a member of the St George's congregation. It was no life for Edward Elgar, and after less than a year he left to help his father in the shop which was now known as Elgar Bros., William having been joined in 1859 by his brother Henry. According to Hubert Leicester in a conversation with Elgar's daughter in 1935, the brothers never got on well together.

> Henry was persuaded to join W. H. E. somewhat against his will … W. H. E. always found it impossible to settle down to work in hand but could cheerfully spend hours over some perfectly unnecessary and entirely unremunerative undertaking (a trait that was very noticeable in E[dward] especially in later life …) The business should have been good if William had only given his full attention to it, as his brother was always begging him to do.   (Typewritten notes at Elgar birthplace)

But while he worked for Allen, Elgar played the organ at St George's for mass for the first time (on 14 July 1872).

In the shop Elgar had access to the scores of music by Mozart, Haydn, Beethoven, and other great composers. During his lunch break he would take a score—for example, Beethoven's 'Pastoral' symphony—and some

bread and cheese, and walk to a quiet place such as a village graveyard to study the music. In an interview he gave to the *Strand Magazine* in May 1904 he said that, when he found that

> exigencies of life would prevent me from getting any tuition, the only thing to do was to teach myself … I saw and learnt a great deal about music from the stream of music that passed through my father's establishment … I read everything, played everything, and heard everything that I possibly could. I am self-taught in the matter of harmony, counterpoint, form, and, in short, the whole of the 'mystery' of music … First was Catel [*Treatise on Harmony*], and that was followed by Cherubini [*Counterpoint*]. The first real sort of friendly leading I had, however, was from *Mozart's Thorough-Bass School*. There was something in that to go upon—something human.   (538–9)

The last-named, once thought to be by Mozart, was in a translation by Sabilla Novello; Elgar once told Bernard Shaw (according to the preface to *Music in London*, 1935) that it was 'the only document in existence of the smallest use to a student composer'.

Self-education, first posts, and engagement Elgar's musical self-education also came from the organ tutors published by Johann Rinck and W. T. Best. He played the piano music of C. P. E. Bach and listened to as much music as he could in Worcester Cathedral. He accompanied the singers of Worcester Glee Club when they met in the Crown Hotel, Broad Street, and arranged items for them. In 1875 he played in the second violins for Worcester Philharmonic Society's *Messiah* and four years later became the orchestra's leader. He earned some money by giving violin lessons and in 1877 went to London for twelve days for five violin lessons from Adolphe Pollitzer, then leader of the New Philharmonic. Pollitzer said he had the makings of a fine player, but after Elgar had heard some of the leading soloists at London concerts, he accepted that he did not command a full enough tone and abandoned his ambitions as a virtuoso. In 1878, the year of his twenty-first birthday, he played in the second violins in the orchestra for the Worcester festival. Three years later, when it was again Worcester's turn to host the Three Choirs, he was in the firsts.

Meanwhile he was developing as a composer. In May 1872 he wrote his first song, 'The Language of Flowers', for his sister Lucy's twentieth birthday. He composed motets in 1876 which were sung at St George's a few years later. He started and abandoned two string quartets and composed an overture in 1878. But his most significant compositions were the pieces he wrote for wind quintet between 1877 and 1881. The quintet comprised his brother Frank (oboe), two flautists, a clarinettist, and himself as bassoonist. They met on Sunday afternoons and Elgar composed a new piece for them each week during the sermon at St George's in the morning. The real Elgar can be detected in these miniatures and he drew on some of them in his *Severn Suite* of 1930. In 1877, too, he played in the attendants' band at the County of Worcester Lunatic Asylum, Powick. This played for staff dances, at which quadrilles were popular. Elgar arranged several of these and contributed some of his own. He became the band's conductor in 1879 (salary £32 a year) and went to Powick once a week for five years.

In 1880 Elgar went with his future brother-in-law to Paris, where he heard Saint-Saëns play the organ at the Madeleine. But this was an exotic interlude in a humdrum provincial life as teacher (an occupation he disliked), conductor of various local orchestras, shop assistant, and violinist (from 1882) in W. C. Stockley's orchestra in Birmingham, which gave a winter series of popular concerts. At last, in January 1883, Elgar visited Leipzig, not as a student but to hear operas and to attend orchestral concerts. Writing on his return from Leipzig to his Yorkshire friend Dr Charles Buck, Edward said that, at the Gewandhaus concerts, 'I got pretty well dosed with Schumann (my ideal!), Brahms, Rubinstein & Wagner, so had no cause to complain.' The reason for his visit was that Helen Weaver, 22-year-old daughter of a shoe-shop proprietor in High Street, Worcester, was a violin student at the conservatory. She and Elgar had known each other from childhood and some of his Powick quadrilles and wind quintet pieces were dedicated to her. They became engaged in the summer of 1883 but the engagement was broken off in April 1884. The reason is not known, but in 1884 Helen, who had abandoned Leipzig to care for her dying mother, developed tuberculosis and in 1885 sailed for New Zealand (where she married in 1890 and died in 1927). Elgar was deeply distressed, and it has been plausibly surmised, although without confirmatory evidence, that it was of Helen that he was really thinking in 1898 when he composed the 'Romanza' variation (no. 13) in the *Enigma Variations*, in which the engines of a liner are imitated and a clarinet quotes sadly from Mendelssohn's overture *Calm Sea and Prosperous Voyage*. She has also been advanced as a candidate for the 'soul'—said by Elgar to be feminine—enshrined in his violin concerto of 1910.

Helen had travelled to Birmingham with Elgar's mother on 13 December 1883, when his *Sérénade mauresque*, first performed in Worcester some months earlier, had been included in a Stockley concert, Elgar playing in the violins. Stockley was rewarded with the dedication of another orchestral piece, *Sevillana*, first performed in Worcester on 1 May 1884. Eleven days later, August Manns conducted it at the Crystal Palace, Sydenham, the first music by Elgar to be performed in or near London. The following year, a short piece for violin and pianoforte, *Une idylle*, became the first Elgar work to go into print when it was published by the instrument dealer John Beare. In November 1885 Elgar was appointed organist at St George's. At the age of twenty-eight, in spite of his ambitions, he seemed destined for nothing more illustrious than the life of a versatile local musician with a small gift for composition. Playing in the orchestra of the Worcester festival of 1884, Elgar took part in performances of Dvořák's *Stabat Mater* and symphony in D major (no. 6). He wrote to Charles Buck: 'I wish you could hear Dvořák's music. It is simply ravishing, so tuneful & clever & the orchestration is wonderful; no matter how few instruments he used it

never sounds thin' (quoted in Moore, *Edward Elgar: a Creative Life*, 109). It was a lesson from which he learned. Elgar wrote several more liturgical pieces for St George's in 1887 and 1888, including the exquisite *Ave verum corpus* and *Ecce sacerdos magnus*. In 1888 he composed *Three Pieces* for string orchestra, which are now lost but almost certainly were revised four years later as the *Serenade for Strings*. In July 1888 he won £5 in a publisher's competition with a song, 'The Wind at Dawn', of which the words were by Caroline Alice Roberts. She had been Elgar's pupil in Malvern for piano accompaniment since October 1886. Nearly nine years older than Elgar, she was born at Bhuj, Bombay, on 9 October 1848, the fourth and youngest child of Major-General Sir Henry Gee *Roberts of the Indian army, who died in 1860, and his wife, Julia Raikes, granddaughter of Robert Raikes, the founder of the Sunday school movement. Alice Roberts lived with her mother at Redmarley d'Abitot, Gloucester, until Lady Roberts died in 1887. She then moved into Malvern. She had studied geology and written a novel (published in 1882) and some poetry. She sang in a choir and regularly attended one of the series of orchestral concerts which Elgar conducted. In the late summer of 1888 Elgar composed a piano piece, *Salut d'amour*, which he dedicated to her. (In countless arrangements it became one of Elgar's best-selling works, but it was no profit to him, for he had sold it outright to a publisher for 2 guineas.) A few days later they became engaged. Alice's family was horrified by her intention to marry an unknown musician who worked in a shop and was a Roman Catholic. She was disinherited and one of her aunts stipulated that no money should go to any children of the union.

Marriage and move to London Alice was unmoved. She believed—no one knows how or why at that date beyond some mysterious instinct—that Elgar was a genius. (It is instructive to remember that at this date Richard Strauss, seven years younger and with whom Elgar within just over a decade was compared, had already taken Germany by storm with *Don Juan* and was second conductor of Weimar Opera.) They were married on 8 May 1889 at Brompton Oratory. Elgar's parents did not attend. After a honeymoon at Ventnor, Isle of Wight, they lived at 3 Marloes Road, West Kensington, until the lease expired, when they moved into Oakland, Fountain Road (now Drive), Upper Norwood, and later to 51 Avonmore Road, West Kensington. Alice had persuaded Elgar to give up his teaching and his organ playing and to seek fame and fortune in London, where he could attend operas and concerts. This was only a moderately successful venture: Manns conducted *Salut d'amour* and the *Suite in D* at the Crystal Palace, but otherwise no interest was shown in him beyond acceptance by two publishers, one of them Novello's, of some violin pieces, organ voluntaries, and partsongs. Meanwhile the Worcester festival committee invited him to compose a short orchestral work for the 1890 Three Choirs festival. The result was the concert overture *Froissart*, first performed in the Public Hall, Worcester, on 9 September 1890, Elgar conducting (he also played in the orchestra during the festival). Although few critics betrayed awareness of it, the work showed an originality and a mastery of the orchestra which were new in the British music of the day. Stockley conducted it in Birmingham in 1891, but it was not played in London until 1900.

Dispirited, the Elgars left London in 1891. He resumed his teaching and in June they moved into Forli, Alexandra Road, Malvern Link. A daughter, Carice, had been born on 14 August 1890. Certain facets of Elgar's personality which never left him were by now becoming apparent to close observers. He was embittered because he claimed that he was denied the opportunity to hold certain posts because of his religion; he was deeply ashamed of being the son of a shopkeeper and, after his marriage to Alice, tried to distance himself from his lowly origins. Writing in September 1900 to an editor who was preparing an article about him, Elgar said:

> Now—as to the whole *shop* episode—I don't care a d—n! I know it has ruined me & made life impossible until I what you call made a name—I only know I was kept out of everything decent 'cos 'his father keeps a shop'—I believe I'm always introduced so now, that is to say—the remark is invariably made in an undertone. (letter to F. G. Edwards, 19 Sept 1900, BL, Egerton MS 3090, fol. 39)

He dressed like a country gentleman or a retired army officer, an image accentuated by his aquiline nose and bushy moustache. He tried to avoid carrying a violin case, so as not to be identified as a musician, which was then still regarded as not a 'respectable' profession. He had a deep and lasting prejudice against 'academic' composers and those who had had a university education or held university posts. His insecurity was further compounded by his marriage to a woman of a higher social class who took him into circles where he felt ill at ease. At the same time he enjoyed playing chamber music with several of their friends, whom he immortalized in the *Enigma Variations*, and was flattered by the admiration and company of beautiful aristocratic young women. His moods fluctuated between high spirits, with a schoolboyish love of practical jokes, puns, and 'japes', and what he called 'mouldiness'.

The next eight years justified Alice's faith in Elgar. He composed a choral symphony, *The Black Knight*, which was performed in Worcester in 1893 and in London two years later. After holidays in Germany, when he and Alice heard operas including *Der Ring des Nibelungen* at Bayreuth and relaxed in the Bavarian countryside, he wrote the six choral songs *Scenes from the Bavarian Highlands* to texts provided by Alice. The organ sonata was completed in July 1895. The following year an oratorio, *The Light of Life*, was produced at the Worcester festival on 10 September 1896. Seven weeks later, on 30 October, he conducted his Longfellow cantata, *King Olaf*, at the north Staffordshire festival, Hanley. It was hailed by the critic of *The Times* as 'a work of high importance'. Manns repeated it at the Crystal Palace in April 1897 and choral conductors throughout the provinces eagerly took it up. But it was the orchestral colour in Elgar's music that appealed most strongly to percipient listeners. Orchestration was never a chore to him because he conceived his music in instrumental terms.

Dora Powell recalled how she once 'watched him orchestrating something, the 24-stave music paper held at the bottom by his left hand, the first finger at a bar on the lowest line, the right hand and pen running up to the top to do a passage for the flutes, coming down to put in something for the brass, lower for the harp, and below, a whole cascade of notes for the violins' (Powell, 150–51). Reed described Elgar as 'rather proud, and rightly so, of his prodigious skill in laying [his music] out for the orchestra. He knew unerringly what he wanted in the way of orchestral or choral tone, balance and colour' (Reed, 149). But Elgar's name was made with a wider public in 1897 with his *Imperial March* for Queen Victoria's diamond jubilee and the patriotic cantata *The Banner of St George*. He now had an ally at Novello's (who had published Elgar's major works since *Froissart*) in August Jaeger, an émigré German who was the firm's publishing office manager and who perceived that Elgar was no ordinary composer. Their published correspondence is remarkable for its demonstration of Jaeger's insight and as the outlet for Elgar's pent-up scorn and derision for so many of his contemporaries and for the organization of British musical life ('a 3-choirs festival always upsets me—the twaddle of it and mutual admiration').

International recognition The highest recognition yet accorded Elgar's music came in December 1897, when the Leeds festival asked him for a choral work. Prompted by a suggestion from his mother, he chose the subject of Caractacus, who, according to legend, made his last unsuccessful stand against the Romans in the Malvern Hills. Although the cantata dealt with a British defeat after which Caractacus was taken to Rome as a prisoner and pardoned by the emperor Claudius, it ended with a patriotic chorus in which the glory of the British empire is foreseen. Jaeger of Novello's protested to Elgar about the librettist's application of the words 'menial' and 'jealous' to foreign nations, only to be met with the response: 'I knew you wd laugh at my librettist's patriotism (& mine)—never mind: England for the English is all I say—hands off! there's nothing apologetic about me' (quoted in Moore, *Elgar and his Publishers*, 1.79). Elgar orchestrated most of *Caractacus* in the cottage Birchwood Lodge, near Storridge, which they rented for summer weekends between 1898 and 1903 and where he was at his happiest in the peaceful isolation of the countryside ('the trees are singing my music, or have I sung theirs?'). The Elgars had moved on 21 March 1898 into Craeg Lea (an anagram of C(arice), A(lice), E(dward) Elgar), Wells Road, Malvern. *Caractacus* was first performed on 5 October 1898. Elgar conducted it, and his rehearsal methods came in for criticism from the correspondent of the *Sunday Times*, who wrote (2 November 1898):

> The Malvern musician is one of those composers who understand what they want a great deal better than the art of getting it. His idea, apparently, is to worry his forces into comprehension of his intentions. He stops every third bar and calls for repeats until the band fairly lost its temper (without perhaps showing it), and there ensues a general feeling of impatience and dissatisfaction.

With more experience, Elgar eliminated these failings,

although his irritability with the choir was to be a contributory factor in 1900 to the failure of the first performance of *The Dream of Gerontius*—and Richter, not Elgar, was the conductor then. The critics were cool about *Caractacus* and Elgar was despondent. He wrote to Jaeger that he was 'never more miserable in my life … if I write a tune you all say it's commonplace—if I don't, you all say it's rot' (quoted in Moore, *Elgar and his Publishers*, 92). Nevertheless, four days later he began to sketch a set of variations for orchestra on an original theme. This theme, labelled 'Enigma', depicts Elgar himself or 'the loneliness of the creative artist', and the variations are portraits of his wife and friends, disguised by initials or pseudonyms, with the finale a defiant self-portrait. Among the friends is Jaeger ('Nimrod'), whose variation, detached from the main work, has acquired elegiac associations, especially in connection with the Remembrance day service at the Cenotaph, although its origin was the memory of a conversation about Beethoven slow movements. Elgar provided a further enigma when he wrote in the programme note for the first performance that 'through and over the whole set another and larger theme "goes" but is not played—… So the principal Theme never appears.' Whether this is a hidden melody in counterpoint, as Elgar hinted, or an abstraction such as friendship, is not certain. Many guesses at the melody have been made (from 'Auld Lang Syne' to 'Onward, Christian soldiers') but the solution will never be known. Elgar sent the score of the *Variations* to the agent of the great Austro-Hungarian conductor Hans Richter, who conducted the first performance in St James's Hall, London, on 19 June 1899. Elgar revised the finale immediately after this performance, and the work, hailed as a masterpiece, made its way into the repertory of European conductors.

Even before the success of the *Variations* Elgar had been asked (in November 1898) for a work for the 1900 Birmingham festival. One of the subjects he toyed with was St Augustine. He wrote to Joseph Bennett, the librettist and critic: 'I hope some day to do a great work—a sort of national thing that my fellow Englishmen might take to themselves and love—not a too modest ambition! I was going to write to *you* to ask if "S. Augustine" might form the basis of such a work …?' Eventually he decided to set Cardinal Newman's long poem *The Dream of Gerontius* (which he had given to Alice in 1887 when her mother had died. Alice Elgar was received into the Roman Catholic church at St George's, Worcester, on 21 July 1894). Elgar was in a state of exaltation while he composed it, and at the end of the manuscript wrote a Ruskin quotation beginning: 'This is the best of me'. Jaeger used the phrase 'the trumpet tongue of genius' in a letter to Elgar. But partly because of Elgar's lateness in correcting proofs of the score and partly because the work gave the overworked festival chorus immense difficulty, the first performance (conducted by Richter) was far from the triumph Elgar had expected. He blamed a cruel God and relapsed into depression. Yet the critics recognized the work's mastery. Two Düsseldorf performances followed in 1901 and 1902 under Julius Buths, a German conductor

who championed British music. After the second of these, Richard Strauss proposed a toast to 'the first English progressivist, Meister Edward Elgar'. When *Gerontius* was first performed at the Worcester festival in September 1902, the text was 'de-Romanized'. The first London performance was at Westminster Cathedral on 6 June 1903. Since then, the work has become as popular with British choral societies as *Messiah* and *Elijah*, although its popularity overseas did not survive 1914. Many regard it as Elgar's masterpiece, and a succession of famous singers has interpreted the solo parts of Gerontius, the Angel, the Priest, and the Angel of the Agony. It is unquestionably the greatest British work in the oratorio form, although Elgar was right in believing that it could not accurately be classified as oratorio or cantata. The quasi-operatic music for the soloists, the inspired writings for chorus, the invention of a semi-chorus, and, above all, the richly expressive orchestral scoring opened a new chapter in the English choral tradition and liberated it from its Handelian preoccupation.

After these successes at festivals, Elgar returned to Malvern to teaching, and even at times to serving in his father's shop. His mother died in 1902, awed by her son's success, his father in 1906, apparently never convinced that Edward was as good a composer as people said. In spite of Elgar's own low estimate of his status, he was by 1901, after the success of the first two *Pomp and Circumstance* marches (particularly no. 1 in D major), generally regarded as the leading English composer. Sullivan was dead, Parry and Stanford, for all their high achievements, lacked Elgar's ability to touch a chord in the national consciousness. Yet he had at this time written no symphonies, no concertos, no rhapsodies. His reputation was based on *The Dream of Gerontius*, the *Variations*, the overtures *Froissart* and *Cockaigne* (1900), the early cantatas, and smaller choral and instrumental pieces. Honours were coming his way. On 22 November 1900 Cambridge University conferred the honorary degree of doctor of music on him (followed by Durham and Leeds in 1904, Oxford and Yale in 1905, others later). He was elected to the Athenaeum, sponsored by Parry and Stanford, in 1903. In 1905 he was made an honorary freeman of the city of Worcester. With the accession of Edward VII in 1901, he moved in royal circles because of his friendship with various music-loving aristocrats and was invited to compose a *Coronation Ode*. For its finale he used the melody of the trio section of his *Pomp and Circumstance* march no. 1, which, so it is said, the king suggested should be provided with words. The text of the *Ode* was written by A. C. Benson. The finale, 'Land of Hope and Glory', was also issued as a separate song (with altered text) and rapidly became a second national anthem. In March 1904 a three-day festival of Elgar's works was given at Covent Garden, something no English composer had experienced. During it, Elgar conducted the first performance of a new large orchestral work, *In the South*, inspired by a holiday in Italy, and Richter conducted the oratorio *The Apostles* which had had its first performance at the 1903 Birmingham festival. In the summer of 1904 Elgar was knighted and on 1 July moved into an imposing new home, Plas Gwyn, in Hampton Park Road, Hereford. His thirteen-year-old daughter Carice's comment on the honour was, 'I am so glad for mother's sake that father has been knighted. You see—it puts her back where she was' (Moore, *Edward Elgar: a Creative Life*, 440).

Zenith of popularity When Elgar went on a month's Mediterranean cruise in HMS *Surprise* in 1905, his companions represented his circle of patrons: Frank Schuster, a financier at whose homes in Westminster and on the Thames at Bray Elgar was a frequent guest; Admiral Lord Charles Beresford, commander-in-chief, Mediterranean; and Lady Maud Warrender, an amateur singer who performed in Elgar's music. Another honour came to him late in 1904 when he agreed to become the first Peyton professor of music at Birmingham University. This involved giving a series of lectures. His frankness about other English composers led to controversy, which depressed him, and to a rift with Stanford which was never wholly mended. His *Introduction and Allegro for Strings* was tepidly received at its first performance in March 1905 and his spirits were not raised by his first visit to the United States. During 1905 he worked on *The Kingdom*, the second part of his projected trilogy of oratorios on the subject of the apostles. But at this period his religious views underwent a crisis. He no longer attended mass regularly. After *The Kingdom* (Birmingham festival, 3 October 1906), he wrote no large-scale religious music and never completed the trilogy. He was convinced that 'no one wants my music' and was also depressed by inadequate performances. In addition, he complained constantly about being unwell—ear trouble, eye trouble, throat trouble, all were cited at some time or other. But his spirits were lifted by the growth of one of his most important friendships. He had first met Alice Stuart Wortley (1862–1936) in 1902. She was the daughter of the artist Sir John Millais and the second wife of Charles Stuart Wortley, Conservative MP for the Hallam division of Sheffield. She was a good pianist and a devotee of Elgar's music. That he was deeply in love with her cannot be doubted, although it is unlikely that there was a physical relationship. She was his muse, something he always needed, and he confided his innermost feelings in letters to her, addressing her as 'Windflower'.

Elgar had long been urged to write a symphony and had once contemplated one on the subject of General Charles George Gordon. In the summer of 1907, as he approached his fiftieth birthday, he looked out the music from his childhood play *The Wand of Youth* and worked it up into two orchestral suites. This appears to have encouraged him and in September he played his wife what she called a 'gorgeous new tune'. This was the march theme which opens the symphony no. 1 in A♭. He continued to work on this score in Italy in 1908 and dedicated it to 'Hans Richter, true artist and true friend'. Richter conducted the first performance at a Hallé concert in Manchester on 3 December 1908 and the first London performance four days later. In both cities the public's reception was wildly enthusiastic and in just over a year the symphony received a hundred performances, in places as far apart as St Petersburg and Sydney, Australia. During a visit to Italy in 1909 he began

to compose a violin concerto and a second symphony, the latter utilizing sketches made as far back as 1903. The concerto was finished in 1910, owing much to the encouragement of Mrs Stuart Wortley when he nearly abandoned it, and was given its first performance in London by Fritz Kreisler, to whom it is dedicated, at a Philharmonic Society concert conducted by Elgar on 10 November 1910. The score contains an inscription in Spanish meaning 'Here is enshrined the soul of .....' Who was meant by the five dots is not known, but so personal and intimate is the music that the name Elgar would be as true a solution as any, even though he himself said the 'soul' was feminine. Again the work was rapturously received and taken up by violinists far and wide.

During 1910 Elgar conducted the London Symphony Orchestra on a provincial tour and in 1911 accepted their invitation to succeed Richter, who was retiring, as their principal conductor. He now had a flat in London at 58 Cavendish Street. The symphony no. 2 in E♭, dedicated to the memory of Edward VII, had its first performance in London on 24 May 1911 during celebrations preceding the coronation of George V. Perhaps because the work ends quietly and is more restless and tense in mood than its predecessor, it was received coolly and for several years had few performances. A few days before the coronation, Elgar was appointed to the Order of Merit, the first musician to be thus honoured. For some unexplained reason, and much to Lady Elgar's chagrin, he suddenly decided not to attend the coronation even though they had been to the rehearsal. At about this time, too, on receiving his annual royalty account from Novello's, he decided to terminate his agreement with the firm so that he could offer his works on the open market. In a letter to the firm's chairman, Alfred Littleton (30 June 1911, Novello archive), he wrote: 'I have never deceived myself as to my true commercial value & see that everything of mine, as I have often said, dies a natural death—if you look at the accounts you will see that a new thing of mine "lasts" about a year & then dies & is buried in the mass of English music ...' Clearly, the relative failure of the second symphony after the success of its predecessor and the violin concerto had hit him hard.

On new year's day 1912 Edward and Lady Elgar moved into a Norman Shaw house (now demolished), 42 Netherhall Gardens, Hampstead. Elgar renamed it Severn House. His principal work for this year was the choral ode *The Music Makers*, a setting of Arthur O'Shaughnessy's poem. First performed on 1 October at the Birmingham festival, it was no more than politely received. With its self-quotations and its theme of artists being 'the movers and shakers of the world for ever', it is a profoundly personal and moving work. After completing it he had written (29 August 1912) to Alice Stuart Wortley: 'I have written out my soul in the concerto, Sym. II & the Ode & you know it ... in these three works I have *shewn* myself.' During 1913 he was depressed when the LSO dispensed with his services, but he worked on a symphonic study, *Falstaff*, for the Leeds festival. Its first performance, on 2 October 1913, again aroused no enthusiasm, and the first London performance a month later was given in a half-empty hall; it is now regarded as one of his finest works.

Wartime despondency On the declaration of war on Germany in 1914, Elgar joined the special constabulary. He had a success with *Carillon*, a patriotic recitation for speaker and orchestra by Emile Cammaerts. Elgar's principal compositions during the war were two more recitations (1916, 1917); incidental music for a Barrie-like play by Algernon Blackwood, *The Starlight Express* (1915); a short ballet, *The Sanguine Fan* (1917); *The Spirit of England* (1915–17)—a setting for soloist(s), chorus, and orchestra of three poems by Laurence Binyon—and *The Fringes of the Fleet*, settings of Kipling. He was depressed by the war and by ill health in 1917 and had an operation on his tonsils in 1918. Realizing his need for the peace of the countryside, Lady Elgar found and rented an isolated cottage, Brinkwells, near Fittleworth, Sussex. There his spirits revived, and in 1918 and 1919 he composed a violin sonata, string quartet, piano quintet, and cello concerto, works which had the vigour and vitality of his heyday but with an autumnal tinge which Lady Elgar described as 'wood magic'. The concerto in particular seems like a personal requiem for a world Elgar knew had vanished with the war. Its first performance, on 27 October 1919 in Queen's Hall, London, was another failure, because of inadequate rehearsal.

Lady Elgar died from cancer on 7 April 1920 and was buried at St Wulstan's, Little Malvern, on 10 April. With her death Elgar's creative life virtually ended. 'I have gone out and I like it', he said. Without her self-sacrificing organization of his life so that he could devote himself wholly to composing, he quickly reverted to his father's time-wasting and procrastinatory habits. In a broadcast in 1957, his daughter, Mrs Carice Elgar Blake, said that Lady Elgar's small stature and soft voice concealed 'the most indomitable will … I think you might almost call her ruthless where my father was concerned … Everything had to give way to what was right for him.' Although she did not say so, Carice herself had suffered from her mother's determination that Elgar's music should always come first. For example, neither of her parents attended her confirmation because there was a rehearsal that day. Elgar's works for the next ten years comprise arrangements of J. S. Bach and Handel, incidental music to plays, some partsongs, music for the 1924 Empire Exhibition at Wembley, and, in 1930, the *Severn Suite* for brass band and a fifth *Pomp and Circumstance* march. Most of these were based on material composed years earlier. In 1924 Elgar had succeeded Sir Walter Parratt as master of the king's musick and in 1931 he composed a *Nursery Suite* for orchestra which he dedicated to the duchess of York (later Queen Elizabeth) and the princesses Elizabeth (later Queen Elizabeth II) and Margaret Rose.

Elgar left Severn House in 1921 and moved to 37 St James's Place. In 1923 he moved back to Worcestershire to Napleton Grange, Kempsey, where he could see more of his family. At the end of the year he went on a month's cruise to the Amazon. The Three Choirs festival was now the focal point of his year. He wore robes to conduct his own works and held court in a rented house in each of the cathedral cities. Since 1914 he had shown a keen interest in gramophone recording, appreciating its educational use and its importance for posterity, and he regularly visited the HMV studios to record many of his works, both in the acoustic and electric processes. As a conductor of his own music he has never been surpassed in his ability to match tempo, expressiveness, and rhythmic vitality.

Last years The 1920s saw Elgar's music go out of fashion. The extent to which this was true was even reflected by his long-time publisher, Novello's, when in 1923 they offered to issue two of his partsongs only at his own expense. Elgar told them to tear them up, but this they refused to do, eventually publishing them at half the price he had originally asked. Besides the Three Choirs festivals, his works were now heard mainly in northern cities. The first symphony had only one London performance in over three years in the early 1920s. Representative of the academic establishment's attitude to Elgar was the entry contributed by Edward J. Dent, then professor of music at Cambridge University, to the German encyclopaedia *Handbuch der Musikgeschichte* (2nd edn, 1930), in which he wrote of him as possessing 'little of the literary culture of Parry or Stanford' and added that 'for English ears Elgar's music is too emotional and not quite free from vulgarity. His orchestral works … are vivid in colour but pompous in style and with an affected nobility of expression.' This provoked a controversy in music periodicals and a letter of protest was sent to editors in England and Germany. Among the eighteen signatories were Sir Hamilton Harty, John Ireland, Augustus John, E. J. Moeran, Bernard Shaw, and William Walton. Queen's Hall was half empty for Elgar's seventieth birthday concert in 1927. Although he encouraged younger composers such as Arthur Bliss and Eugene Goossens, he had no real interest in the new directions music was taking and lacked the incentive to emulate Strauss in upholding a bygone tradition. He moved to Battenhall Manor, Worcester, in November 1927 and was at Tiddington House, Stratford upon Avon, from 1928 to December 1929. He spent much of his time being driven around Worcestershire in his car by his chauffeur, revisiting old haunts. He moved back into Worcester to a house called Marl Bank on Rainbow Hill. He was appointed KCVO in 1928, created a baronet in 1931 and GCVO in 1933. He took pride in his baronetcy, signing himself 'Edward Elgar of Broadheath', but shamelessly touted for a peerage, hoping that Lady Stuart of Wortley, as she now was, had some influence in the matter. His male friendships at this time were chiefly with the violinist W. H. Reed, the playwright Bernard Shaw, the organist Ivor Atkins, the critic Ernest Newman, and the HMV record producer Fred Gaisberg, but his two dogs probably meant as much to him. He was still susceptible to the charms of young women, and in November 1931 became infatuated with a violinist, Vera Hockman, whom he described as 'mother, child, lover and friend'. Stimulated by this passion, he began to write an opera, *The Spanish Lady*, based on Ben Jonson's play *The Devil is an Ass*. The librettist was Barry Jackson, director of Birmingham Repertory Company. Elgar discussed the work with W. H. Reed, who wrote: 'It was to be Grand Opera on the biggest scale: a tremendous work, in fact. He would explain with a wealth of detail everything that was to happen on the stage at the particular bar we were trying over. He would even draw a plan of the stage, showing all the "properties" and exactly where the characters were to stand …' (Reed, 91–2). Later that year, at the prompting of Shaw, the BBC commissioned a symphony. During 1933 Elgar worked on both projects. Meanwhile another new musical friendship was giving him great pleasure. All attempts to persuade Kreisler to record the violin concerto having failed, Gaisberg sent the score to the fifteen-year-old prodigy Yehudi Menuhin, who agreed to make the recording with Elgar conducting. They went through the concerto together with piano accompaniment. Elgar was totally satisfied and departed to Newmarket for the races. The resulting recording is a classic of the gramophone. Elgar described Menuhin to Novello's as 'the most wonderful artist I have ever heard'. In May 1933 he flew, for the first time, to Paris to conduct the concerto for Menuhin. He then visited the ailing Delius at Grez-sur-Loing. The two composers had never been close but corresponded in the 1920s; they now found they had much in common. In October Elgar underwent an operation which revealed inoperable cancer. Over the next few weeks his condition varied alarmingly. His friends visited him and he listened to new recordings of his works. On 3 January 1934 he returned to Marl Bank from the nursing home. Gaisberg suggested that he might supervise a recording session at the HMV studios in Abbey Road, Hampstead, by telephone. The General Post Office set up connecting lines on 22 January. In the morning Elgar was comatose but in the afternoon was in splendid form, talking to the conductor (Lawrance Collingwood) on the telephone and commenting on the performances. After that he declined again. He shocked Roman Catholic friends by saying he wished to be cremated and that his ashes should be scattered at the confluence of Severn and Teme. A priest administered the last rites, but Elgar was by then unconscious. He died on 23 February 1934 and was buried next to his wife on 26 February. The man who wrote *The Dream of Gerontius* had told his doctor that he had no faith in an after-life: 'I believe there is nothing but complete oblivion' (Moore, *Edward Elgar: a Creative Life*, 818). He left the opera and symphony unfinished. A performing version of *The Spanish Lady* was made by Dr Percy M. Young and staged in Cambridge in November 1994. Although Elgar on his deathbed told W. H. Reed that 'no one must tinker' with the symphony, Reed published the sketches after they had been given to the British Museum (they are now in the British Library). There they stayed for half a century, but before they came out of copyright, when anyone would be able to 'tinker' with them, the Elgar family commissioned the composer Anthony Payne, who had studied the sketches for many years, to make a full realization of the symphony. This was accomplished with admirable skill and the work was performed (and recorded) in 1998 to almost unanimous critical acclaim.

Elgar was certainly the greatest composer to arise in England since the death of Purcell in 1695. He wrote magnificently for voices and as an orchestral colourist he could stand comparison with Richard Strauss and Tchaikovsky. Parry said of him that 'he reached the hearts of the people': his ceremonial music has become part of the national heritage, while his lighter pieces appeal to a public which might not care as much for his symphonies and oratorios. But they are all a part of the whole man, tributaries feeding into the mainstream. That he was largely self-taught is miraculous, but his practical experience and retentive ear were worth more than an academic education. His genius was first fully recognized by Jaeger and then by Richter, who perceived that he belonged to the European tradition. Until 1914 his reputation was high on the continent. One can find the influences of Brahms, Wagner, Strauss, Tchaikovsky, and Bizet in Elgar, yet to many his music is the essence of 'Englishness'—it is impossible to define Englishness. Elgar said that 'there is music in the air, music all around us, and you simply take as much as you require' (Buckley, 32). He took his from the Worcestershire air, but by what process it became 'Elgarian' is both the mystery and the magic. Without resort to nationalist influences such as folk-song, he gave English music back its soul and lifted it to new heights of prestige. The foundation of his music is melody. Some of his themes are short, others broad and march-like, characterized by his use of a favourite marking, *nobilmente*. He was a master of rich and pliant string tone, but his scoring for woodwind and brass is especially assured and distinctive. Rhythmical vitality is also an essential ingredient. After his death, although never neglected, his works were unfashionable with many critics, but since the centenary of his birth they have enjoyed critical and popular esteem even greater than in his Edwardian heyday. His style is so individual and recognizable that the adjective 'Elgarian' was coined to describe it.

The complexities of Elgar's personality are reflected in his music, which is both extrovert and introvert. His music is 'autobiographical', a huge self-portrait. An outstanding example is the first movement of the second symphony, which opens with a surging outburst of exuberance but quickly relapses into self-questioning and doubt. In all his major works the music is frequently overcome by a wistful nostalgic longing, as for some idealistic land of lost content which he certainly never experienced. There is also a vein of delicate lyrical fantasy, particularly in the smaller works, such as *Chanson de matin*. The two symphonies are wayward and rhapsodical in mood but structurally are firmly braced by the interlocking of their themes. Although one may trace their origins to the best of Parry's orchestral music and to an admiration for Brahms, notably his third symphony, they tower above the music of Elgar's contemporaries by reason of their melodic content, mastery of instrumental colour, and emotional range and span. In their blending of autobiographical elements with a keen sensitivity to the spirit of the time in which they were composed, they share the ethos of Mahler's late symphonies. But Elgar did not know Mahler's music, or, in all probability, the symphonies of

Bruckner. The music 'in the air' for him while he composed them was that of Tchaikovsky, Strauss, and Puccini, whose *Tosca* he studied while scoring the first symphony. With the concert overture *In the South* (1904) and the symphonic study *Falstaff*, which form a prologue and epilogue to them, the symphonies represent Elgar's orchestral genius at its finest.

If one were to look for a literary equivalent of Elgar's blend of lyricism, grandeur, and popular appeal, it would be Tennyson. He never overcame the 'chip' on his shoulder resulting from his origins and in his last years enjoyed masquerading as an English country gentleman, roaming the lanes with his dogs and taking his recreation on the racecourse. Yet he was at his best and happiest in the company of musicians making music. There he had no 'chips' because he was the master of his art. A doctor he consulted in 1926 told one of Elgar's biographers that he considered that Elgar was 'a neurotic who most of all wanted reassurance … He told me there was only one thing he really loved in life. That was the Golden Valley of the River Teme, especially a place 500 to 800 yards below the Knightsford Bridge down the right bank, near the Ankerdine Hills. He used to sit on the banks and said he composed much of *Gerontius* there' (quoted in Moore, *Edward Elgar: a Creative Life*, 773).

A full-length statue of Elgar in ceremonial robes by Kenneth Potts, which stands facing Worcester Cathedral, was unveiled by the prince of Wales on 2 June 1981. Since 1936 Elgar's birthplace at Broadheath has been maintained as a museum containing mementoes, scores, press cuttings, and much other valuable archive material.

MICHAEL KENNEDY

Sources J. N. Moore, *Edward Elgar: a creative life* (1984) • M. Kennedy, *Portrait of Elgar*, 3rd edn (1987) [incl. complete work list and discography of Elgar's own recordings] • R. Anderson, *Elgar* (1993) • D. McVeagh, *Edward Elgar, his life and music* (1955) • P. M. Young, *Elgar OM: a study of a musician*, 2nd edn (1973) • R. Burley and F. C. Carruthers, *Edward Elgar: the record of a friendship* (1972) • W. H. Reed, *Elgar as I knew him* (1936) • D. M. Powell, *Edward Elgar: memories of a variation*, rev. edn (1994) • *Elgar and his publishers: letters of a creative life*, ed. J. N. Moore, 2 vols. (1987) • J. N. Moore, ed., *Edward Elgar: letters of a lifetime* (1990) • J. N. Moore, ed., *The Windflower letters* (1989) • P. M. Young, ed., *Letters to Nimrod* (1965) • P. M. Young, ed., *A future for English music, and other lectures by Edward Elgar* (1968) • E. W. Atkins, *The Elgar–Atkins friendship* (1984) • R. Monk, ed., *Elgar studies* (1990) • R. Monk, ed., *Edward Elgar: music and literature* (1993) • C. Redwood, ed., *An Elgar companion* (1982) • S. Craggs, *An Elgar source book* (1995) • R. J. Buckley, *Sir Edward Elgar*, 2nd edn (1912) • P. M. Young, *Alice Elgar: enigma of a Victorian lady* (1978)
Archives Birmingham Oratory • BL, music MSS • Bodl. Oxf. • Elgar Birthplace Museum, Broadheath, corresp. and papers, incl. musical manuscripts • FM Cam. • Hereford Cathedral Library • Royal Academy of Music, London, manuscripts • Royal College of Music, London • U. Birm. L., corresp. relating to University of Birmingham • U. Birm. L., diaries and corresp. • Worcs. RO, corresp. and family papers | BL, letters to Sir Hubert Leicester, Add. MS 60357 • BL, corresp. with Percy Pitt, Egerton MS 3303 • Herefs. RO, letters to Sir Percy Hull • LUL, letters to Charles Buck • LUL, letters to Charles Long • Richmond Local Studies Library, London, Sladen MSS • U. Birm. L., letters to publisher William Broome relating to 'May Song' with corrected and annotated proofs • U. Birm. L., corresp. with Ernest Newman • U. Leeds, Brotherton L., letters to Herbert Thompson • W. Sussex RO, letters to Walter Hussey •

Worcs. RO, letters to Beatrice Harrison [copies] • Worcs. RO, corresp. with De Navarro family [copies] • Worcs. RO, letters to Edward Speyer | FILM BFI NFTVA, home footage • BFI NFTVA, news footage | SOUND BL NSA, performance footage
Likenesses C. F. Grindrod, photograph, c.1903, NPG [*see illus.*] • E. T. Holding, photogravures, c.1905, NPG • T. Hughes, oils, 1905, Royal College of Music, London • W. Rothenstein, drawing, 1910, Royal Library, Windsor Castle • W. Strang, chalk drawing, 1911, Royal Collection • P. Burne-Jones, oils, 1912, Guildhall, Worcester • E. Kapp, drawings, studies, 1913–14, Barber Institute of Fine Arts, Birmingham • P. Anderson, watercolour, 1915, Elgar birthplace, Broadheath • W. Rothenstein, chalk drawing, 1917, NPG • P. Hedley, bronze bust, 1927, NPG • H. Lambert, photographs, c.1927, Elgar birthplace, Broadheath • H. Lambert, photograph, 1933, NPG • K. Potts, statue, 1981, Worcester • Rotary Co., postcard, NPG • W. Rothenstein, chalk drawing, Birmingham Museums and Art Gallery • A. Wysard, pencil and watercolour drawing, NPG • photographs • postcard, NPG
Wealth at death £13,934 6s. 9d.: probate, 9 May 1934, *CGPLA Eng. & Wales*

Elgar, Francis (1845–1909), naval architect, born at Portsmouth on 24 April 1845, was the eldest son of nine children of Francis Ancell Elgar, who was employed at Portsmouth Dockyard, and his wife, Susanna Chalkley. At fourteen, Elgar was apprenticed as a shipwright in Portsmouth Dockyard, where his general education was continued at an excellent school for apprentices maintained by the Admiralty. There he won a scholarship entitling him to advanced instruction. In 1864, when the Admiralty, with the Department of Science and Art, established the Royal School of Naval Architecture and Marine Engineering at South Kensington, Elgar was appointed, after a competitive examination among shipwright apprentices in the dockyards, one of eight students of naval architecture. After the three years' course, he graduated in May 1867 as a first-class fellow, the highest class of diploma. Of much literary ability, he long helped as an old student in the publication of the school's *Annual*. From 1867 to 1871 he was a junior officer of the shipbuilding department of the navy, and was employed at the dockyards and in private establishments.

After leaving the public service in 1871, Elgar became chief professional assistant to Sir Edward James Reed, who was practising in London as a consulting naval architect. At the same time he helped Reed in the production of the quarterly review *Naval Science*. General manager of Earle's shipbuilding and engineering company at Hull (1874–6), he practised as a naval architect in London (1876–9). From 1879 to 1881 he was in Japan as adviser on naval construction to the Japanese government, and from 1881 to 1886 resumed private practice in London, advising leading steamship companies on designs of new ships, but specially investigating the causes of loss of, or accident to, important vessels. His reports on the *Austral*, which foundered in Sydney harbour in 1881, and the *Daphne*, which capsized when being launched on the Clyde in 1883, made him a leading authority on the stability of merchant ships. He also served in 1883 on a departmental committee of the Board of Trade, whose report formed the basis of subsequent legislation and of the regulations for fixing the maximum load line for seagoing merchant ships of all classes and of most nationalities.

In 1883 Elgar was appointed to the first university professorship of naval architecture; it was founded in 1883 at Glasgow, endowed by the widow of John Elder, the marine engineer. Although permitted to continue private practice, Elgar for the next three years mainly devoted himself to the new school. His reputation secured the sympathy of shipowners and shipbuilders, and attracted many students. In 1886 Elgar on the invitation of the Admiralty re-entered the public service as director of dockyards—a newly created office. During his six years' control, work in the dockyards was done more economically and rapidly than before. This was a vital stage in the process whereby Britain met the renewed naval challenge of France and Russia, before the German threat. Elgar married in 1889 Ethel Annie Mitchell, daughter of John Howard Colls of London, who survived him; they had no children. Elgar resigned as director of dockyards in 1892, and was until 1907 consulting naval architect and director of the Fairfield shipbuilding and engineering company of Glasgow. The company, founded by John Elder and developed by Sir William Pearce, fully maintained its position during Elgar's management. The works were enlarged and improved, and their productive capacity increased. Novel types of vessels were designed and built, including torpedo-boat destroyers and cross-channel steamers of high speed. Steam turbines and water-tube boilers were employed at an early date, with satisfactory results.

In 1908, after voluntarily retiring from Fairfield with a view to rest, Elgar, at the request of friends interested in the business, undertook as chairman the reorganization of the firm of Cammell, Laird & Co. of Maryport, Cumberland, whose operations included steel and armour manufacture as well as shipbuilding and engineering. Soon after he became in addition chairman of the Fairfield company, which had close relations with Cammell, Laird & Co. Elgar's efforts proved successful, but the strain told on his health.

Elgar combined a wide range of scientific knowledge with practical and commercial capacity, and was made an honorary LLD of Glasgow University in 1885, a fellow of the Royal Society of Edinburgh soon after, and of the Royal Society of London in 1895. To the Royal Society's *Proceedings* he contributed important papers on problems of stability and strength of ships. Of the Institution of Naval Architects, of which he was a member from the outset of his career, he served on the council for twenty-six years, was treasurer for seven years, and finally was an honorary vice-president. His chief contributions to technical literature are in the *Transactions* of the institution, and include valuable papers on 'Losses of ships at sea', 'Fast ocean steamships', 'The cost and relative power of warships', and problems of strength and stability of ships. A member of the Institution of Civil Engineers for twenty-five years, Elgar sat on the council for six years, and as James Forrest lecturer in 1907 delivered an address on 'Unsolved problems in the design and propulsion of ships'. He also served on the council of the Royal Society of Arts and was a royal commissioner for the international exhibitions at Paris (1889) and Chicago (1894). His interests outside professional matters were wide. Literature always attracted him. He was elected FSA in 1896, and from 1904 he served as a member of the tariff commission. He published the well-illustrated *Ships of the Royal Navy* (1875), and as president of the London dining club called the Sette of Odd Volumes (1894–5) he privately printed an interesting paper on the earlier history of shipbuilding. Elgar's entry in the *Dictionary of National Biography* was written by W. H. White, his exact contemporary, and perhaps the only naval architect of that generation to surpass him. Although the two men had never been friends and Elgar's appointment as director of dockyards rankled with White, the article was remarkably free from personalities.

Elgar died suddenly at Monte Carlo on 17 January 1909, and was buried at Highgate cemetery. He founded a scholarship for students of naval architecture at the Institution of Naval Architects, and provided for its future maintenance by his will. He also made large bequests to the Institution of Naval Architects and the department of naval architecture in Glasgow University.

W. H. WHITE, rev. ANDREW LAMBERT

Sources D. K. Brown, *A century of naval construction: the history of the Royal Corps of Naval Constructors, 1883–1983* (1983) · W. H. W., *PRS*, 83A (1909–10), viii–xi · *PICE*, 175 (1908–9), 318–22 · J. Coutts, *A history of the University of Glasgow* (1909) · *WWW*, 1897–1915 · *CGPLA Eng. & Wales* (1909)
Archives Bodl. Oxf., letters to Sir Henry Burdett
Wealth at death £82,039 17s. 3d.: resworn probate, 18 Feb 1909, *CGPLA Eng. & Wales*

Elgin. For this title name *see* Bruce, Robert, second earl of Elgin and first earl of Ailesbury (*bap.* 1626, *d.* 1685); Bruce, Thomas, seventh earl of Elgin and eleventh earl of Kincardine (1766–1841); Bruce, James, eighth earl of Elgin and twelfth earl of Kincardine (1811–1863); Bruce, Victor Alexander, ninth earl of Elgin and thirteenth earl of Kincardine (1849–1917).

Elgood, George Samuel (1851–1943), landscape and garden painter, was born on 26 February 1851 in Oxford Street, Saint Mary, Leicester, one of the ten children of Samuel Elgood (*d.* 1874), a wool merchant, and his wife, Jane Octavia, the daughter of George Shirley of Meckworth, Derbyshire. In 1865 he was sent to Bloxham School, Banbury, but he stayed there only about a year. Although he seems to have been brought up in Suffolk, in the late 1860s, for financial reasons, the Elgood family moved back to Leicester, where Samuel Elgood ran a yarn agency. George attended the Leicester School of Art, studying under Wilmot Pilsbury; two of his brothers were also artists. Elgood sketched the Leicestershire countryside and its buildings with his brother Thomas—a topographical and landscape painter—Pilsbury, and the architectural painter John Fulleylove, who married his sister Elizabeth. His brother Richard founded the art metalwork firm of Elgood Brothers.

Elgood began a course at the South Kensington School of Art (later the Royal College of Art), specializing in architecture, but had to return to Leicester in 1874 to carry on the family business after the death of his father. Travelling about the country for the yarn agency, however, gave him the opportunity to paint landscapes in his spare time. He exhibited his work for the first time at the Walker Gallery in Liverpool in 1874, and showed again in 1878 and 1880. He also exhibited at the Dudley Gallery and at the Baillie Gallery. In 1881 he became an associate of the Institute of Painters in Water Colours, and in 1882 an associate of the Institute of Painters in Oil Colours. Most of his garden paintings were shown between 1891 and 1925 at the Fine Arts Society, where they were enormously popular and invariably sold out to affluent patrons—who included members of the royal family: Queen Victoria and Queen Mary both bought Elgood's pictures, many of which are still in the Royal Collection.

It was after his marriage about 1881 to Mary Clephan, an artist and a woman of means, that Elgood began specializing in the painting of gardens; he was to become one of the best-loved garden painters of his time. Formal, architectural gardens were his passion, and he and his wife travelled to France, Italy, Spain, and Tangier. They spent several months in Italy every year, and visited Venice, Florence, and Rome, as well as Sicily. Although Elgood painted scenes such as *Fishing Boats on the Lagoon* in Venice, it was his portrayals of the formal villa gardens of Renaissance Italy, including the Villa Borghese, the Villa D'Este, and the Villa Garzoni, which made his reputation. Among his subjects in England were many of the major gardens of the time—gardens of historic interest such as Montacute, Penshurst, Compton Winyates, and Arley Hall. In an age before gardens were taken over by the National Trust, private owners proudly showed to their house party guests at the height of the season their immaculately kept herbaceous borders, rose-clad pergolas, trim yew hedges, and topiary work. These were the scenes Elgood was commissioned to immortalize in his paintings, scenes which mirrored a slice of social history in the indulgent years before the First World War when labour was both plentiful and cheap.

Elgood's garden paintings reached a wide public after his two books were published. The first, *Some English Gardens*, was published in collaboration with Gertrude Jekyll in 1904; the second, *Italian Gardens*, appeared in 1907 and reflected his love of the formal garden in Renaissance style. He also illustrated *The Garden that I Love*, by Alfred Austen, first published in 1894. Elgood's style and the subject matter of his paintings reflected his architectural training. With his eye for detail and the contrasts of pattern and texture of building materials, he accurately depicted balustrading, finialled gate piers, flights of steps, and lichen-covered walls. The colours of his palette were mellow—soft browns, greens, and blues—as if perceived through a misty veil. No gaudy coloured flower-bedecked borders appeared in his paintings, which marked him apart from other contemporary garden painters such as Beatrice Parsons and Arthur Rowe.

In 1908 Elgood moved to Knockwood at Tenterden in Kent. The garden he made surrounding the timber-framed house, with its topiary work, mellow stone walls

and paths, pergola, and cottage garden flowers, was the subject of many paintings. Elgood's bearded, angular face, with its earnest expression, betrayed an eccentric, anti-social character. He was often critical of others, including garden designers such as Thomas Mawson. As he grew older, his idiosyncrasies became more pronounced: he lived without electric light or piped water until his death in 1943. When the council decided to cut down trees on his boundary he sat in his shed pointing a shotgun at them until they finally had to give in and the trees were saved (Eckstein). After his death, on 21 October 1943 at Knockwood, some of his antiquities and paintings went to the Maidstone Museum.　　　　DIANA BASKERVYLE-GLEGG

Sources E. Eckstein, *George Elgood: his life and work, 1851–1943* (1995) · D. Baskervyle-Glegg, 'Flower-filled canvas', *Country Life* (17 Aug 1989), 50–53 · *WWW* · b. cert. · d. cert. · G. White, 'The garden and its art with especial reference to the paintings of G. S. Elgood', *The Studio*, 5 (1895), 51–6 · T. Oldforde, 'George S. Elgood's watercolour drawings of gardens', *The Studio*, 31 (1904), 209–15
Archives NRA, priv. coll., MSS
Likenesses photographs, repro. in Eckstein, *George Elgood*
Wealth at death £21,596 3s. 1d.: probate, 15 May 1944, *CGPLA Eng. & Wales*

Elias of Dereham. *See* Dereham, Elias of (d. 1245).

Elias, John (1774–1841), Welsh Calvinistic Methodist minister, was born at Crymllwyn Bach farm in the parish of Aber-erch, Caernarvonshire, on 6 May 1774, the eldest of the six children of Elias Jones (1752–1822) and his wife, Jane Roberts (1749–1833). The most decisive influence upon his early religious development was his paternal grandfather, John Cadwaladr (c.1710–1789), a devout Anglican who served as sexton at Aber-erch church. He taught him to read Welsh, took him to hear visiting preachers, and taught him the essentials of theology. His father and grandfather were weavers as well as farmers, and when Elias was twelve years of age he began to learn their craft. From 1788 to 1790 he suffered a prolonged spiritual crisis with doubts about his own religious sincerity accompanied by intense self-loathing. Although he does not use the word 'conversion' in his autobiography, it is clear that his despondence yielded to a growing Christian conviction when, together with a group of friends, he attended the Calvinistic Methodist Association at Bala in 1792; this was followed by a vivid mystical experience of the efficacy of Christ's redemptive work. He now wished to join a Methodist society, and with that end in view he sought employment with one of the pioneers of Methodism in Caernarvonshire, Griffith Jones of Ynys-y-pandy, near Porthmadog. Jones was a member of the Methodist society that met at Hendre Hywel, near Pren-teg, and under his influence Elias was admitted into the society there in September 1793. The members encouraged him to seek recognition by the Caernarvonshire monthly meeting and it was duly granted on Christmas day 1794. That allowed him to accept invitations to preach in the county.

One difficulty was Elias's lack of education. He asked

John Elias (1774–1841), by Hugh Jones, 1838

permission to attend a school at Manchester but the Methodist distrust of higher education led the monthly meeting to refuse his request although it did allow him to spend a few months at the school conducted by Evan Richardson (1759–1824) at Caernarfon. This was all the formal education he had; otherwise Elias was an autodidact. He worked hard at his studies throughout his life, and became sufficiently familiar with Hebrew and Greek to appreciate the finer points of biblical exposition. His main field of interest, however, was the theology of Dr John Owen (1616–1683), and Owen's Calvinistic contemporaries and successors.

On 22 February 1799 Elias married Elizabeth, the eldest daughter of Richard Broadhead, Tre'r-gof, Llanbadrig, Anglesey. She kept a shop at Llanfechell; Elias joined her, and so began his lifelong association with Anglesey. She died on 2 April 1828, and of their four children, two died in infancy. The survivors were John (d. 1875) and Phoebe. On 10 February 1830, in St David's Church, Liverpool, Elias married as his second wife the widow of Sir John Bulkeley (1767–1819). Bulkeley was the squire of Presaddfed, Bodedern, Anglesey, and had married, rather romantically, one of his maids, Ann Williams (1787–1851), at Bodedern church on 10 October 1806. She was the daughter of Owen Williams, tailor, and his wife, Elizabeth, of Aberffraw. At the death of Sir John, Lady Bulkeley inherited an estate which extended over five parishes, and so her wealth provided Elias with every comfort at their new home, Y Fron, Llangefni.

In 1796 Elias had made his first preaching tour in south Wales, and that was the beginning of a tireless itinerant ministry of the kind typical of the Methodist movement, and which was to dominate his career until his death. From his first appearance as a preacher, he drew huge congregations to hear him. His early eminence made him an obvious choice for inclusion among the first group of men to be ordained in 1811 by the Calvinistic Methodists, the step that marked the formal secession of the movement from the Church of England. He preached in the fields or in the streets or in public fairs—even on one occasion at Manchester racecourse—as well as in chapels. During the first half of his career he preached with controlled passion, combining lucid exposition of his theme with a vivid oratorical imagination which transformed the sermon into an existentialist confrontation between God and the sinner. His tall, lean figure and intense seriousness conveyed to his hearers the impression of overwhelming authority: hundreds attributed their conversion to him. His preaching produced tempestuous emotional reactions expressed in weeping, shouts of joy, jumping, and even uncontrollable laughter. The result was that he became the most popular preacher of his generation; his ten published works are mostly sermons.

Elias's growing influence in the Methodist movement provided him with the authority to enforce moral discipline with unbending rigour. He condemned the theatre, horse-racing, morality plays, drunkenness, musical concerts, and the rural practice of courting in bed. In theology he insisted on strict adherence to Calvinistic orthodoxy: the one point of controversy which was to convulse the movement for several years was his adherence to the view that Christ's sufferings were precisely sufficient to atone for the sins of the elect, and that they had no reference to those outside that divinely pre-ordained group. It was in order to safeguard that orthodoxy that he advocated the formulation of the confession of faith that was adopted in 1823. His readiness to believe irresponsible accusations of deviation from orthodoxy made life unhappy for many.

In politics Elias was an unrepentant tory, who had no sympathy with democratic agitation. When members of Jewin Crescent Church in London signed a petition in 1828 advocating Catholic emancipation, he called for their immediate excommunication; so they were expelled. Similarly when a young preacher from Holyhead, William Roberts (1809–1887), spoke in support of the whig candidate, William Owen Stanley (1802–1884), in the election of 1837, Elias threatened him with excommunication, but this time his view did not prevail.

By 1830 Elias had become the dominating force in the councils of his denomination. The older generation which could check his impetuosity and autocratic temper were all dead by 1833. But a new generation of younger men was emerging. They tended to embrace the more liberal modern Calvinism associated with such thinkers as Dr Edward Williams (1750–1813). In addition, they sympathized with the growing spirit of reform that characterized contemporary society. It was these tendencies that explain the gloom with which Elias looked to the future during his closing years. But his reactionary social attitudes and his imperious spirit within his denomination did nothing to lessen public recognition of his greatness as a preacher and his utter devotion to the service of his faith. He remains a major figure in the evangelical tradition.

Elias was injured in 1832 when a gig in which he was travelling overturned, and he never fully recovered. He suffered a number of illnesses during his closing years and died at his home in Llangefni on 8 June 1841. Ten thousand mourners joined in the funeral procession when his remains were interred at Llan-faes churchyard, near Beaumaris, on 15 June.　　R. TUDUR JONES

Sources W. Pritchard, *John Elias a'i ocs* (1911) · G. P. Owen, *Hunangofiant John Elias* (1974) · J. Roberts and J. Jones, *Cofiant y Parchedig John Elias, o fôn* (1850) · E. Morgan, *A memoir of the Reverend John Elias* (1844) · E. Morgan, *Valuable letters, essays … of … John Elias* (1847) · E. Morgan, *John Elias, life, letters and essays* (1973) · R. T. Jones, *John Elias: prince amongst preachers* (1974) · O. Thomas, *Cofiant y Parch. John Jones, Talsarn* (1874), 844–71 · J. M. Jones and W. Morgan, *Y tadau Methodistaidd* (1897), chaps. 41 and 42 · G. M. Roberts, ed., *Hanes Methodistiaeth Galfinaidd Cymru*, 2 (1978) · parish register (baptism), Aber-erch, 6 May 1774
Archives NL Wales, corresp. and papers; sermons · U. Wales, Bangor | NL Wales, letters to David Ellis
Likenesses H. Hughes, oils, *c*.1812, United Theological College, Aberystwyth · H. Jones, oils, 1838, United Theological College, Aberystwyth [*see illus.*] · S. Freeman, stipple, BM, NPG; repro. in *Evangelical Magazine* (1820) · W. Roos, oils, NMG Wales · photograph, repro. in Pritchard, *John Elias a'i ocs*

Elias, Julius Salter, Viscount Southwood (1873–1946), printer and newspaper proprietor, was born in Birmingham on 5 January 1873, youngest of seven children of David Elias, a Whitby jet merchant, and his wife, Esther Jones (*d*. 1907). The failure of his father's business forced a move to London and Elias's education was truncated by family circumstances. He left St Thomas's School, Clerkenwell, at the age of thirteen and found employment as an errand- and office boy.

On his twenty-first birthday Elias joined Odhams, a family-run printing company dating from 1847, as a clerk. He spent the rest of his life with Odhams, where he rose rapidly, becoming manager within a year and, after restoring the company to profitability, a director in less than four years. He later became chairman. Recognizing magazines as an outlet for Odhams's printing presses, he persuaded the Hotel Cecil to launch a house paper, *Table Talk*, in 1896, and acquired a series of publications including *Entr'Acte*, which carried music hall bills. In May 1906 Odhams accepted the contract to print *John Bull*, a new weekly magazine run by Horatio Bottomley, a gifted populist and self-publicist. Bottomley's distaste for paying bills meant that Odhams soon acquired a share in settlement of a debt, but his genius for publicity ensured the magazine's popular success. Elias left Bottomley in charge of the perennially scurrilous, periodically libellous editorial content and attended to the business side, saying: 'My job is to keep the machines going, I don't take sides' (Wintour, 51).

John Bull attained a weekly sale of 2 million before Bottomley was exposed as a fraud in 1922, after losing a libel case in which Elias's evidence was pivotal. Sales fell to 300,000 after Bottomley was jailed, but Elias rescued the paper, recruiting new writers and introducing an insurance scheme for registered readers. Plant expansion to meet *John Bull*'s demands created surplus capacity, which Odhams filled by taking on the *Sunday People* in late 1923. Early in 1925 the *People*'s proprietor was unable to meet his print bills and Odhams acquired the paper, at that time selling around 250,000 copies, in lieu of the debt. Elias and editor Harry Ainsworth transformed its fortunes by mixing scandal—a series of 'confessions' stories—with inducements including insurance. Sales topped 2 million in April 1929 and were 4.6 million at Elias's death.

With massive print capacity devoted to a paper published once a week, acquiring a daily was the logical step. Thwarted of interest in the ultra-reactionary *Morning Post* and the Liberal *Daily Chronicle*, in 1929 Elias reached an agreement with the Trades Union Congress to publish the Labour *Daily Herald*, which had struggled for sales and survival throughout the 1920s. Elias became chair of the Daily Herald (1929) Ltd, in which Odhams had a 51 per cent holding and control of publishing and commercial activities, while the Trades Union Congress retained 49 per cent and control of editorial policy. The paper was redesigned and relaunched with a battery of sales inducements—free gifts and an insurance scheme backed by intensive door-to-door canvassing. Its arrival as a serious competitor in an already fratricidal mass market provoked one of the most intense circulation wars of the century, peaking when Odhams circumvented an agreement outlawing free gifts by using its book publishing section to produce a cut-price edition of Dickens for *Herald* readers.

The *Daily Herald* in 1933 became the first British paper to record a daily sale of 2 million—eight times its pre-Odhams sale. But it never recouped the costs of sales promotion, losing £2.1 million between 1930 and 1939, and was overtaken as the best-selling paper by the *Daily Express*. There were also tensions between Elias and journalists who felt the serious political content of the paper had been over-diluted, particularly in the late 1930s when Elias's concern to maintain good business conditions made him a strong supporter of appeasement. Conflict with Francis Williams, editor from 1937, led to Williams's departure in 1940.

Daily Herald staff who satirized the paper by singing 'We have no creed or party bias, we want a peerage for Elias' (Koss, 482), got their wish in 1937 when Elias was created Baron Southwood of Fernhurst—taking the names from his London and country homes. Although essentially apolitical, he took the Labour whip and served as a whip and, in 1945, a deputy chair in the Lords.

An unobtrusive figure in an era of ostentatious press barons, Elias was small (5 feet 4 inches), slightly built, and quietly spoken. He was described by a journalist in 1939 as 'a little ginger-faced man with sharp eyes' (Clarke, 154). A paternalistic employer, he was known to his staff as 'the little man' and took a conciliatory line on labour issues. Percy Cudlipp, editor of the *Daily Herald*, described him in 1946 as strangely but sincerely filled with humility. Yet self-effacement concealed formidable talents. Lord Beaverbrook, his antithesis in proprietorial style, pointed to a

'Remarkable personality and character. It was not visible but it was there, flowing underground' (Minney, 12). Lord Camrose wrote of him in 1947 that 'as an organiser he was outstanding and his enterprise and willingness to take risks was unusual even for Fleet Street' (Camrose, 43).

Although closely identified with an explicitly political paper, the Labour *Daily Herald*, Elias's accumulation of a press empire was driven by commercial imperatives, above all the need to keep Odhams's printing plant running at full capacity, rather than by the pursuit of political influence. Of the three publications of greatest importance in his career—*John Bull*, *The People*, and the *Daily Herald*—the first two were acquired in settlement of printing debts, the third in order to fill excess print capacity. Commercial rather than journalistic or political priorities also dictated his style as a proprietor. Odhams papers innovated in production and publicity rather than editorially: 'He was a salesman of journalism, not a journalist' (Williams, *Nothing so Strange*, 131); 'never a journalist, always a printer' (Cudlipp, 268).

Elias married Alice Louise Collard (1865–1951) in December 1906. They had no children. In 1939 he became chairman of the Hospital for Sick Children, Great Ormond Street, and presided over the raising of more than £1 million in the following seven years. He also chaired the Red Cross Penny a Week fund, raising £17.5 million, and co-ordinated the minister of supply's salvage campaign during the Second World War. He was raised to a viscountcy in the 1946 new year honours list.

Elias died at his home, Southwood Court, Highgate, Middlesex, on 10 April 1946. His ashes were buried in the Southwood memorial garden in the churchyard of St James's, Piccadilly, London. He was also commemorated by the Southwood Building of the Great Ormond Street Hospital. At his death, Odhams controlled one of the largest print and publishing empires in Britain, including two national newspapers, the *Daily Herald* and *The People*, a chain of popular magazines, and a giant printing works at Watford.   HUW RICHARDS

Sources R. J. Minney, *Viscount Southwood* (1954) · F. Williams, *Nothing so strange* (1970), 130–33 · F. Williams, *Dangerous estate: the anatomy of newspapers* (1957), 161–77 · H. Cudlipp, *At your peril* (1962), 260–91 · *Daily Herald* (11 April 1946) [esp. tribute by P. Cudlipp] · *DNB* · W. J. B. Odhams, *The business and I* (1935) · J. Symons, *Horatio Bottomley: a biography* (1955) · Viscount Camrose [W. E. Berry], *British newspapers and their controllers* (1947) · S. E. Koss, *The rise and fall of the political press in Britain*, 2 (1984) · T. Clarke, *My Lloyd George diary* (1939) · H. Richards, *The bloody circus: the Daily Herald and the left* (1997) · C. Wintour, *The rise and fall of Fleet Street* (1989), 49–61 · *Newspaper World* (13 April 1946) · *World's Press News* (11 April 1946) · *CGPLA Eng. & Wales* (1946)
Archives HLRO, corresp. with Lord Beaverbrook
Likenesses T. C. Dugdale, oils, *c.*1938, Printers' Charitable Corporation, London · A. F. Hardiman, statue, *c.*1948–1949, St James's Church, Piccadilly, London, garden of remembrance · H. Coster, photographs, NPG
Wealth at death £165,063 9s. 9d.: probate, 16 Aug 1946, *CGPLA Eng. & Wales*

Elias, Ney (1844–1897), explorer and diplomatist, was born at Widmore, Kent, on 10 February 1844, the second son of Ney Elias (*d.* 1891) of Kensington and his wife, Sophia, both from established Jewish merchant families. Elias and his four brothers and two sisters were brought up as Christians after their parents converted from Judaism. He was educated in London, Paris, and Dresden. In 1865 he was elected fellow of the Royal Geographical Society and studied geography and surveying under the society's instructors. In 1866 he went to Shanghai in the employment of his mother's family merchant house, Barnet & Co., traders between Bristol and Shanghai.

Disliking commerce, Elias turned to exploration and, after three trips in 1867, 1868, and 1869, he successfully determined the new course of the Huang He or Yellow River, following its dramatic change some fifteen years earlier, for which he earned the notice and congratulation of the Royal Geographical Society. In July 1872 he set out from Peking (Beijing) with Moses, a Chinese servant, to cross the Gobi Desert, travelling nearly 2500 miles to the Russian frontier and thence another 2300 miles to Nizhniy Novgorod, well inside European Russia. The first section of the journey was particularly remarkable: he passed through Chinese provinces overrun by Tungani rebels and was in constant fear of attack. His caravan was small, as he preferred, but therefore vulnerable; the weather was bitterly cold, the terrain was often mountainous, and communication was always difficult. Despite these difficulties, he brought back useful meteorological data and geological specimens, and, most importantly, survey measurements which allowed the construction of a remarkably accurate map. For this he received the founder's medal of the Royal Geographical Society in 1873.

Having by now formally relinquished a business career, Elias needed another position, and on the recommendation of Sir Henry Rawlinson of the Royal Geographical Society and Sir Bartle Frere he was engaged by the government of India. After accepting minor posts at Calcutta and Mandalay in 1874, he was appointed second in command of the overland mission from Burma to China to open up the area to trade. The mission failed after its interpreter, Augustus Raymond Margary, was murdered, but Elias had gone ahead by a different route, and his survey of the Shueli River was the only positive result of the ill-fated expedition. In articles in *The Times* and elsewhere Elias drew attention to the political situation in central Asia, but became increasingly frustrated at his lack of opportunity to explore and gather geographical and political intelligence to counter growing Russian influence there. His plan for an expedition to Tibet in 1876 came to nothing in the face of government indifference. In 1877 he was attached to Robert Shaw's abortive mission to Kashgar. He went in advance to Leh where, on the death of Yakub Beg, ruler of eastern Turkestan, and the abandonment of the mission, Elias remained as joint commissioner of Ladakh, reporting on events in Kashgar which had just been reoccupied by the Chinese. In 1879 Elias set out on his own initiative over the Karakoram. He sent notice to the *amban*, or Chinese resident, of Yarkand who invited him further. Without waiting for the Indian government to forbid him, he went on to Yarkand, where he gathered much useful information from Chinese and Turkic officials and secured improved trading conditions between Kashgar and India. The Indian government retrospectively approved this venture, and later approved a visit in 1880 to Kashgar with H. H. Godwin Austen, when he met the ambans of Yarkand and Kashgar, and a further visit to Kashgar in 1885. In the meantime, however, Elias had been seriously ill with a liver complaint and had spent a year on sick leave in England.

In September 1885, under orders from the Indian government, Elias left Yarkand for the Pamirs and upper Oxus, putting into effect a journey which he had planned since 1880. However, changed political conditions made his original idea of establishing a British representative in Kashgar inappropriate. None the less, he made a route survey of 600 miles from the Chinese frontier to Ishkashim in Badakshan, determined various points and altitudes in the Pamirs, and visited the confluence of the Murghab and Panjah rivers, where flow measurements suggested that the latter was the main upper course of the Oxus. The resolution of this question was politically important as the river was the accepted eastern and northern border of Afghanistan. Contrary to his conclusion, the Wakh-Jir is now thought to be the source of the Oxus, but Elias's information about the area's drainage and ethnology was none the less useful in assessing the political significance of a sensitive boundary, complementing the earlier assessment by John Wood. Elias then crossed Badakshan and Balkh, joining the Afghan boundary commission near Herat and returning to India via Balkh and Chitral. The main recommendation from his journey was that Afghanistan and China be encouraged to define a common border to cut off Russia from the Hindu Kush.

After more sick leave Elias returned to duty. In January 1888 he was made a CIE, but declined to accept such 'a damning mark of faint praise' (Morgan, 183). From November 1888 to February 1889 he was on special duty in connection with the Sikkim War, which successfully expelled the Tibetans from Sikkim, and in October 1889 he took command of a mission to report on the political geography and condition of the Shan States on the Burma–Siam frontier, being promoted first-class political agent. This work, at least temporarily, peacefully resolved the border disputes between Britain and Siam in an area politically sensitive because of increasing French influence.

On 14 December 1891 Elias was appointed agent to the governor-general at Mashhad and consul-general for Khorasan and Seitan, a posting which reflected British awareness of the importance of Persia in containing Russia. He gathered much useful intelligence and asserted British presence in an area hitherto dominated by the Russians. Forced home by ill health, he used his leave to publish with E. D. Ross an annotated translation entitled *The Tarikh-i-Rashidi of Mirza Muhamad Haidar* (1895). His notes reveal his unrivalled knowledge of central Asia's geography, history, and ethnology. He returned to his duties still weak, and in November 1896 was forced to retire. He

died suddenly, apparently from the effects of blood poisoning, in his rooms at 26a North Audley Street, London, on 31 May 1897. He was unmarried.

Elias died feeling he had achieved frustratingly little. He was a skilled linguist, a shrewd observer, a meticulous reporter; but despite his cogently argued official reports and lobbying in the British press in signed and anonymous articles, he never persuaded the Indian government to treat trans-Himalayan and central Asian matters as seriously as he thought they deserved, and thus his attempts to consolidate relations with China and exploit the Chinese antipathy for Russia were less successful than they might have been.

Although Elias was a remarkable explorer, he was soon forgotten, partly because most of his writings remained in the secret archives of the Indian government or were anonymous newspaper articles, partly because his private papers disappeared for some seventy years after his death, and partly because his mother apparently discouraged the writing of a memoir. In the estimation of Francis Younghusband he was 'the best traveller there has ever been in Central Asia' (Morgan, 285).   ELIZABETH BAIGENT

Sources E. Morgan, *Ney Elias: explorer and envoy extraordinary* (1971) · *The Times* (14 Dec 1893) · *The Times* (2 June 1897) · S. Wheeler, 'Ney Elias', *GJ*, 10 (1897) · C. E. D. Black, *A memoir on the Indian surveys, 1875–1890* (1891) · DNB

Archives RGS, corresp., journals, and papers

Likenesses C. Silvy, photograph, 1860, NPG · photograph, c.1889–1890, repro. in Morgan, *Ney Elias*, facing p. 225 · A. Elias, miniature, c.1895, repro. in Morgan, *Ney Elias*, frontispiece · portrait, repro. in Wheeler, 'Ney Elias' · wood-engraving (after photograph by Maull & Fox), NPG; repro. in *ILN* (12 June 1897)

Wealth at death £29,313 18s. 7d.: probate, 5 July 1897, CGPLA Eng. & Wales

Elias, Norbert (1897–1990), sociologist, was born on 22 June 1897 in Breslau, Germany (which later became Wrocław, Poland), the only child of Hermann Elias, businessman, and his wife, Sophie Galevski. He attended the Johannesgymnasium, Breslau, and, after service in the German army during the First World War, read philosophy and medicine at Breslau University. As a teenager and young man, Elias was a leading figure in the Zionist youth movement Blau-Weiss, a fact which—for whatever reason—he took some trouble in later life to obscure.

Elias was awarded a doctorate in philosophy at Breslau in January 1924 for a thesis entitled *Idee und Individuum*. Financial difficulties caused by the great German inflation of 1922–3 interrupted his studies, but in 1925 he went to Heidelberg to work for his *Habilitation* in sociology, at first with Alfred Weber (1868–1958). In 1930, when Karl Mannheim (1893–1947) moved to Frankfurt as professor, Elias accompanied him as academic assistant. His *Habilitation* was rushed through early in 1933, after Adolf Hitler came to power, but shortly afterwards Elias, as a Jew, sought refuge first in Paris (1933–5), and then in London (from 1935), eventually becoming a British citizen in 1952. His father died in Breslau in 1940, and his mother died in Auschwitz about 1941.

In Paris and London, Elias completed the two volumes of his *magnum opus*, *Über den Prozess der Zivilisation* (published in translation as *The Civilizing Process* in two volumes in 1978 and 1982, and in a revised, single-volume translation in 2000); they were published in Basel in 1939, and received very little notice at that unpropitious moment. In 1939 Elias was awarded a senior research fellowship at the London School of Economics, interrupted by a period of internment as an enemy alien, and 'made himself useful' to the British security services. After the Second World War he made a meagre living by extramural lecturing in London, and helped Siegmund Foulkes found the Group Analytic Society. Only in 1954, aged fifty-seven, did he obtain a post in a British university—at Leicester, from where he formally retired as reader in 1962. From 1962 to 1964 he was professor of sociology at the University of Ghana.

Elias's international reputation was gained in his long and productive old age. *Über den Prozess der Zivilisation* was republished in 1969, to acclaim in Germany, the Netherlands, and France. His later books, in their English versions, include *The Established and the Outsiders* (1965), *What is Sociology?* (1978), *The Court Society* (on the court of Louis XIV, 1983), *The Loneliness of the Dying* (1985), *Involvement and Detachment* (essays on the sociology of knowledge and the sciences, 1987), *Quest for Excitement* (essays on the sociology of sport, 1986), *The Symbol Theory* (1991), *Time: an Essay* (1992), *Mozart: Portrait of a Genius* (1993), and *The Germans* (1995). A selection of his poems, *Los der Menschen*, appeared in 1987.

Über den Prozess der Zivilisation underlies all Elias's later work. It begins by examining how the word 'civilization', derived from *civilité*, denoting the manners of courtiers, came to be used by nineteenth-century Europeans to express their sense of superiority over lower ranks or other cultures. The characteristics taken as evidence of this superiority had come to seem innate, and the Europeans were unaware that their own ancestors had acquired them through a long *process* of civilization. Through books about manners, from the middle ages to the nineteenth century, Elias traced the changing standards of good behaviour in matters such as spitting, noseblowing, undressing, the toilet, and table manners. The threshold of repugnance had advanced, the expected standard of self-constraint had become more demanding, and many matters were hidden behind the scenes of social and mental life. Elias was, however, concerned not just with outward bodily propriety, but with violence and cruelty and changing feelings towards them. This provided a link to a long discussion of state-formation processes, including the 'taming of warriors'. The monopolization of violence by the state, and longer chains of social interdependence, were associated with gradual changes in typical personality make-up.

Controversy about Elias's theory has concerned whether it is 'Eurocentric', whether twentieth-century 'permissive society' represents a reversal of the civilizing process, and whether his ideas are refuted by events such as the destruction of the Jews during the Second World War. Yet *Über den Prozess der Zivilisation* in part represents Elias's own attempt to grapple with unfolding events in Nazi Germany. The fact that his own mother died in Auschwitz was the cause of the major psychological trauma of Elias's life, and may possibly be one reason why he published little between 1939 and 1965. He could be quarrelsome, and in relation to his work was very sensitive. At the same time he was delightful company, immensely knowledgeable and stimulating, a fascinating conversationalist with a puckish interest in the trivial details of life. He was short in stature, stronger than he looked, and swam daily until his late eighties. Photographs can be found in *Human Figurations*, his Festschrift, edited by Peter Gleichmann and others (1977), and among his papers in the Deutsche Nationalliteraturarchiv at Marbach-am-Neckar, Germany. Busts of Elias by the Dutch sculptor Gerda Rubinstein can be found at the Zentrum für Interdisziplinäre Forschung, Bielefeld, at the University of Amsterdam, and in private collections. No paintings of Elias are believed to have been made.

In 1971 Elias was given the title and pension of professor emeritus of the University of Frankfurt. He was the first recipient of the Theodor W. Adorno prize, conferred by the city of Frankfurt in 1977, and had honorary doctorates from the universities of Bielefeld and Strasbourg II. He was also awarded the German Grosskreuz des Bundesdienstordens (1986) and was a commander of the order of Orange-Nassau (1987). In his adopted country of citizenship he enjoyed only a *succès d'estime*; from the mid-1970s he spent little time in Britain. Elias never married. He died peacefully in his study at J. J. Viottastraat 13, Amsterdam, on 1 August 1990. He was cremated at the Algemene Begraafplaats en Crematorium Westgaarde, Ookmeerweg, Amsterdam. STEPHEN MENNELL, *rev.*

Sources N. Elias, *Reflections on a life* (1994) · H. Korte, *Über Norbert Elias* (1988) · *The Times* (4 Aug 1990) · J. Hackeschmidt, *Von Kurt Blumenfeld zu Norbert Elias: die Erfindung einer jüdischen Nation* (1997) · R. Blomert, *Intellektuelle im Aufbruch: Karl Mannheim, Alfred Weber, Norbert Elias und die Heidelberger Sozialwissenschaften der Zwischenkriegszeit* (1999) · personal knowledge (1996)
Archives Deutsche Nationalliteraturarchiv, Marbach-am-Neckar, Germany, D-71666
Likenesses G. Rubinstein, bust, Zentrum für Interdisziplinäre Forschung, Bielefeld · G. Rubinstein, bust, University of Amsterdam · G. Rubinstein, bust, priv. coll. · photographs, Deutsche Nationalliteraturarchiv, Marbach-am-Neckar, Germany · photographs, repro. in P. Gleichmann, ed., *Human figurations* (1977)
Wealth at death left all his wealth to the Norbert Elias Stiftung; bulk of assets had been transferred to the Stiftung in the decade before his death: HF138, 562

Elibank. For this title name *see* Murray, Sir Gideon, of Elibank, Lord Elibank (*c.*1560–1621); Murray, Patrick, fifth Lord Elibank (1703–1778).

Eliezer ben Jacob. *See* Jacobs, Lazarus (1709?–1796), *under* Jacobs, Isaac (1757/8–1835).

Eliot, Sir Charles Norton Edgcumbe (1862–1931), diplomatist and university administrator, was born at Sibford Gower, Oxfordshire, on 8 January 1862, the eldest son of Edward Eliot (1827–1898), curate of Sibford Gower, who in 1863 became vicar of Norton Bavant, Wiltshire, and his wife, Elizabeth Harriet Wyatt, younger daughter of

Charles Henry Watling, rector of Tredington, Worcestershire. His father (the eldest son of Edward Eliot, archdeacon of Barbados) had a distinguished ancestry with strong Cornish links and before taking a living was a fellow of New College, Oxford. Charles was educated at home before entering Cheltenham College in 1872. In 1880 he entered Balliol College, Oxford, as a scholar. He won the Hertford, Boden, Ireland, and Craven scholarships and the Houghton Syriac prize, gained a first in *literae humaniores* in 1884, and in the same year was elected a fellow of Trinity College. He had unusual intellectual capacity with exceptional ability in classical, oriental, and modern languages. Reserved and detached, he openly scorned such popular pursuits as athletics or angling. After a chance encounter with Lord Dufferin he opted for the diplomatic service rather than a scholar's life at Trinity.

In 1887 Eliot was appointed to St Petersburg as attaché, then from 1888 as third secretary. He travelled widely in Russia and central Asia and in 1890 published the first English translation of a Finnish grammar. In 1892 he was posted to Tangier as chargé d'affaires. In 1893 he was transferred to Constantinople as second secretary. He was briefly placed in charge of the British agency in Sofia in 1895 and of the legation in Belgrade in 1897. In the latter year he also served on an international commission to Salonika. He thus had firsthand material for his book *Turkey in Europe*, published in 1900 under the pseudonym of Odysseus. Often lucid and witty, sometimes abrasively sarcastic, sometimes derivative or in error, Eliot's treatment was richly spattered with philological comment, and took the view that the Turk was not 'a sick man' but merely indolent and unlikely to benefit from an injection of western liberal practices. His chapters on Byzantium and the Orthodox church were largely based on George Finlay's *History of Greece*, while his chapters on the contemporary Balkans compared ill with William Miller's book, *Travel and Politics in the Near East* (1898), though the latter lacked Eliot's often brilliant analysis of the Ottoman situation.

In 1898 Eliot was made a CB and was posted to Washington as first secretary. He was a member of the international commission which in 1899 mediated in a dispute concerning the native kingship in Samoa. It was there that his intellectual curiosity was first drawn to the shell-less mollusc, a branch of the nudibranchs, an interest he maintained throughout his career, producing a collection of specimens and publications of value to marine biologists. In 1900 he became a KCMG and was appointed consul-general at Zanzibar and commissioner for the British East Africa Protectorate, arriving in January 1901.

The appeal of the countryside and the challenge of European settlement stimulated in Eliot a desire to spend the rest of his life in colonial administration there. He travelled widely, noting tribal customs and ecological characteristics, the problems of eradicating slavery and of improving communications, and the need for both European help and the protection of native interests. He believed that 'there is land enough for all' (C. N. E. Eliot, *The East Africa Protectorate*, 1905, 310). At the same time he learned Swahili and wrote an introduction to A. C. Hollis's book on the Maasai. He also resumed the Buddhist studies begun at school. His unusually wide range of activities and his natural reserve did not prevent contact with other administrators such as Sir Harry Johnston, and he was freely accessible to settlers of European origin already in the country such as members of the European Colonists Association of East Africa, based in Nairobi. He regarded these years as 'the happiest and most interesting' of his life (Smith, 188). However, his zeal for promoting white settlement on Maasai land brought him into conflict with the Foreign Office, and resulted in the disruption of his chosen life work. In 1904 he was ordered to cancel two land grants which he had understood to be within his terms of reference; his protest was refused a fair hearing while two of his district officers on leave in England were treated with more indulgence. He felt that resignation was his only option and he returned to England in June 1904. He expected an official inquiry to exonerate him, but none was forthcoming, and he was left to state his case in *The Times* (4 August 1904) and later in the preface to his book *The East Africa Protectorate* (1905).

Eliot had friends as well as enemies. In 1904 the University of Edinburgh awarded him an honorary doctorate. In 1905 the newly founded University of Sheffield secured him as vice-chancellor. He stayed there until 1912, spending much of the vacations travelling in the Far East. He was a shrewd and perceptive commentator on the life and traditions of Indochina, India, China, and Japan, and had mellowed since he wrote on the Turks in Europe, as is apparent from articles sent to the *Westminster Gazette* and subsequently published as *Letters from the Far East* (1907). He guided Sheffield University wisely but in 1912 moved to the more congenial environment of Hong Kong, though the university there was struggling for its very existence. It was saved by his ceaseless efforts to secure financial support, particularly from Chinese sources. Meanwhile Eliot continued his study of Asian societies, which eventually resulted in the publication of his *magnum opus*, the three-volume *Hinduism and Buddhism*, in 1921.

In August 1918 Eliot was recalled to the diplomatic service, as high commissioner and consul-general in Siberia, charged with overseeing the civilian aspects of allied military intervention in Russia. His handling of a difficult situation was widely praised, and in November 1919 he was sworn a member of the privy council. In January 1920 he was appointed ambassador to Japan, in succession to Sir Conyngham Greene; he arrived in Tokyo in April 1920. His reputation as an authority on 'the orient', and his respect and affection for the Japanese, fitted him well for this post. Nevertheless, he was unfortunate in serving at a time when Anglo-Japanese relations were increasingly strained, in particular as a result of the termination of the Anglo-Japanese alliance (which Eliot, like his hosts, regretted). Eliot himself 'helped to project an image of a Britain which had not entirely abandoned its old ally' (Smith, 196), but his views were increasingly discounted by the Foreign Office, where leading officials, most notably Victor Wellesley, successfully argued for Britain's Far

Eastern policy to be aligned with that of the United States rather than with that of Japan. When his term of office expired, in February 1926, he confidently expected its renewal, but was disappointed; his protests to the foreign secretary, Austen Chamberlain, fell on deaf ears.

Rather than return to England, Eliot stayed on in Japan, continuing his studies of Japanese Buddhism from a base at the Nara Hotel. In December 1930 he fell seriously ill with influenza, and decided to return to England to convalesce. He died while passing through the Strait of Malacca, on 16 March 1931, and was buried at sea. He was unmarried. His book *Japanese Buddhism*, revised and completed by George Sansom, was published posthumously in 1935.

G. B. SANSOM, rev. J. M. HUSSEY

Sources H. Parlett, 'In piam memoriam', in C. Eliot, *Japanese Buddhism* (1935), vii–xxxiv • B. Lewis, 'Some travellers in the East', *Middle Eastern Studies*, 4 (1968), 296–315 • Z. Marsh, *East Africa through contemporary records* (1961) • *DNB* • D. Smith, 'Sir Charles Eliot (1862–1931) and Japan', *Britain and Japan, 1859–1991: themes and personalities*, ed. H. Cortazzi and G. Daniels (1991), 187–97 • G. H. Mungeam, *British rule in Kenya, 1895–1912: the establishment of administration in the East Africa Protectorate* (1966) • G. Bennett, *Kenya, a political history: the colonial period* (1963) • M. P. K. Sorrenson, *Origins of European settlement in Kenya* (1968) • P. Lowe, *Britain in the Far East: a survey from 1819 to the present* (1981) • *CGPLA Eng. & Wales* (1931) • J. Foster, *Oxford men and their colleges* (1893)

Archives NHM, notebooks and papers • PRO, corresp., FO800 | Bodl. Oxf., letters to Lord Kimberley, MSS Eng a 2013–2014, b 2047–2049, c 3933–4514, d 2439–2492, e 2790–2797 • Bodl. RH, corresp. with Robert Arthur Chamberlain • Bodl. RH, corresp. with Sir Francis May, MSS Ind Ocns 176 • CUL, corresp. with Lord Hardinge • Mitchell L., NSW, letters to G. E. Morrison, ML MS 312 • U. Birm. L., letters to Sir Granville Bantock

Likenesses W. Stoneman, photograph, 1920, NPG

Wealth at death £12,353 18s. 8d.: probate, 3 Nov 1931, *CGPLA Eng. & Wales*

Eliot, Edward Craggs-, first Baron Eliot (1727–1804), politician, was born in the parish of St George's, Hanover Square, London, on 8 July 1727 and baptized there on 28 July. He was the eldest son of the nine children of Richard Eliot (*bap.* 1694, *d.* 1748), politician, of Port Eliot in Cornwall and his wife, Harriot (*c.*1714–1769), who was the illegitimate daughter of James *Craggs (1686–1721), MP and secretary of state under Stanhope. He was educated at Liskeard School and spent a year at St Mary Hall, Oxford, in 1742 but did not take a degree. In 1746 he set out for Europe on the grand tour, accompanying Philip Stanhope, the illegitimate son of Lord Chesterfield and recipient of his father's famous letters, and travelled through the Netherlands, Germany, Switzerland, and France. Chesterfield, whose aim was to make his son a polished gentleman, approved highly of Eliot as a companion for him, and the diplomat Sir Charles Hanbury Williams, who met him at Dresden, assured the earl in 1748 that there was 'nothing good that one may not expect' from him (*Letters of … Chesterfield*, 3.1167). Lord Charlemont, who met Eliot on his return through France, declared that his 'excellent understanding, cultivated and improved by the best education, and animated by a mind of the most pleasing cast, rendered him the most agreeable of companions' (Hardy, 1.61). His only reservation was that Eliot often seemed low-

Edward Craggs-Eliot, first Baron Eliot (1727–1804), by Sir Joshua Reynolds, *c.*1747

spirited and diffident in company, an assessment confirmed later in life by Bentham, who remarked in 1781 that he was 'a modest, civil, good kind of man … without those pretensions which one would expect to find in a man whose station in his country is so commanding, and political influence so great', but that he was despondent by nature: during the American war he said: 'he scarce ever looks into a paper … for fear of ill news' (*Works of Jeremy Bentham*, 10.96).

In 1748 Eliot's father died of consumption and Eliot inherited the family's extensive estates in Cornwall, including the control of the parliamentary boroughs of St Germans and Liskeard, to which in 1758 he added Grampound, thereby giving him six members in all whom he could return to the Commons by nomination. This made him one of the leading borough proprietors of the age and a figure of political consequence. He was courted by successive administrations, though he always divided his patronage between personal friends, particularly for the older family boroughs of St Germans and Liskeard, and nominees of the government of the day, who were accommodated at Grampound, where the electorate was financially demanding. He himself was seated for his father's former constituency of St Germans on 12 December 1748, and at the general election of 1754 he returned his former travelling companion, Philip Stanhope, and two other friends, Edmund Nugent and Anthony Champion. His earliest political connection was with Frederick, prince of

Wales, who appointed him to his father's former office of receiver-general of the duchy of Cornwall, a post worth £2000 a year, which he held for life, but on Frederick's death in 1751 he attached himself to the Pelhams. His parliamentary nominees in 1754 all supported Newcastle's administration, and he was asked by the duke to make the speech moving the address at the opening of the session, but he had to decline after setting out from Lyons because of 'a return of my spitting of blood' (BL, Add. MS 32860, fol. 408)—an ominous indication perhaps of the possible inheritance of his father's mortal illness, but one which fortunately came to nothing.

Eliot, however, found the duke an unsatisfactory patron. Ambitious to make a start on a political career, he solicited an appointment at the Board of Trade, but in Newcastle's normal dilatory manner he received only promises and assurances. In 1759 he remonstrated that he had 'waited so long, and have seen so many people ... preferred before me' (BL, Add. MS 32891, fols. 237–8) that he had 'lost some of the best years of my life' (BL, Add. MS 32895, fols. 446–7), 'a loss, in point of business, which I shall never retrieve' he pointed out on another occasion (BL, Add. MS 32900, fol. 145). When he was finally appointed in December 1759 he was so dispirited by his treatment and disillusioned by the low status of his office that he hardly ever bothered to attend board meetings, and he was also irregular in his parliamentary attendance. Not surprisingly, he never advanced further up the official ladder.

On 25 September 1756 Eliot married, at St James's, Westminster, Catherine (d. 1804), the only daughter and heir of Edward Elliston of Gestingthorpe, Essex, and his wife, Catherine Gibbon. They had four sons. His wife's mother was a cousin of the historian Edward Gibbon, with whom Eliot developed what proved to be a close but somewhat strained relationship. He made Gibbon an executor of his will and guardian of his children, and in 1774 he offered him one of his parliamentary seats at Liskeard on very favourable financial terms. It was Eliot who advised Gibbon to travel to Lausanne to reside after his conversion to Rome. Gibbon, however, had mixed feelings. In 1773, while staying at Port Eliot, he wrote that his host possessed:

> neither a pack of hounds, nor a stable of running horses, nor a large farm, nor a good library. The last only would interest me: but it is singular that a man of fortune, who chooses to pass nine months of the year in the country, should have none of them. (Portland MSS)

He also criticized Eliot's 'indolence' and fretfulness. Eliot was nevertheless a sociable man who moved in intellectual and clubland circles in London. He was a member of the Literary Club, where he associated with Burke, Fox, Sheridan, Gibbon, Garrick, and Dr Burney, among others; he was an early patron of Sir Joshua Reynolds, who described him as one of his 'most familiar and valued friends' (Leslie and Taylor, 2.431), and was also a dinner companion of Boswell and Johnson.

Eliot was a man of contradictions, who never fulfilled the political promise of his earlier years or of his potential in society. His political role was as a borough patron rather than as a participant in affairs and his allegiances fluctuated. After falling out with Newcastle by 1760, he attached himself to Bute and then to Grenville, and hovered on the fringe of the Rockingham administration, never quite committing himself, though he retained his post at the Board of Trade and appeared, Rockingham wrote, 'very well inclined' (Rockingham MSS). Nevertheless he smoothly transferred his support to Chatham's administration. At the 1768 general election he returned the usual mixture of personal friends and government candidates, but assured Rockingham that he was 'very particularly honoured' (Portland MSS) by having been solicited to take on the marquess's friends. In fact the friends he returned were left free to vote as they were inclined and they followed no common pattern of allegiance. Eliot himself neither spoke nor voted in the parliament of 1768–74 and spent most of his time in the country.

In 1775 Eliot was returned unopposed for the county of Cornwall, an unusual distinction for a borough patron normally identified with the government of the day. As a knight of the shire he was expected to devote his energies to the interests of the county at Westminster, and he resumed his parliamentary attendance, but he was now a fully-fledged supporter of the opposition. He declined to elect Gibbon again and took his nominees from Rockingham and then from Portland. In 1780 he was described as 'deeply engaged in the measures of opposition' (Gibbon, 162). In 1782, however, he sided with Shelburne against Fox and Portland, and his son Edward James *Eliot (1758–1797) took office on the Treasury board. His reward in adhering to Shelburne and later to Pitt was a peerage, conferred on 30 January 1784 during Pitt's struggle in defence of George III against the Fox–North coalition. His career in the House of Lords was unremarkable. He remained a steady adherent of Pitt and placed his borough influence at the minister's disposal. His friendship with Pitt was cemented by the marriage of his son Edward James on 24 September 1785 to Pitt's favourite sister, Harriot. In 1789 Eliot added the name of his maternal grandfather to his surname by royal licence.

A modest, indecisive, and often despondent individual, Eliot lacked the energy and the will to make a career in public life which his family, wealth, and consequence might have brought him, but he had the good opinion of many friends in artistic and intellectual circles. He died at Port Eliot on 17 February 1804, and was survived by his wife by only six days. They were buried together on 1 March 1804 at St Germans.   E. A. SMITH

Sources GEC, *Peerage* · E. Gibbon, *Memoirs of my life*, ed. G. A. Bonnard (1966) · *The letters of Philip Dormer Stanhope, fourth earl of Chesterfield*, ed. B. Dobrée, 6 vols. (1932), vol. 3 · *The last journals of Horace Walpole*, ed. Dr Doran, rev. A. F. Steuart, 2 vols. (1910) · J. Boswell, *The life of Samuel Johnson*, 2 vols. (1791) · BL, Newcastle MSS · Rockingham MSS, Sheff. Arch., Wentworth Woodhouse muniments · U. Nott. L., Portland MSS · *The works of Jeremy Bentham*, ed. J. Bowring, 11 vols. (1838–43), vol. 10 · C. R. Leslie and T. Taylor, *Life and times of Sir Joshua Reynolds*, 2 vols. (1865) · F. Hardy, *Memoirs of the political and private life of James Caulfeild, earl of Charlemont*, 2nd edn, 2 vols. (1812) · GM, 1st ser., 74 (1804), 187, 281 · DNB

Archives Cornwall RO, corresp. | BL, corresp. with duke of Newcastle, Add. MSS 32860–32934

Likenesses J. Reynolds, oils, *c.*1747, priv. coll. [*see illus.*] • J. Reynolds, oils, 1781–2, Port Eliot(?) • T. P. Harding, pen and watercolour drawing, 1805 (after J. Reynolds), NPG

Eliot, Edward Granville, third earl of St Germans (1798–1877), diplomatist and politician, was the only son of William, second earl of St Germans (*d.* 1845), and his first wife, Lady Georgiana Augusta Leveson-Gower, the fourth daughter of the first marquess of Stafford, Granville Leveson-*Gower. He was born in Plymouth on 29 August 1798, was educated at Westminster School and Christ Church, Oxford, matriculating in 1815. He was later (1843) created honorary LLD of Dublin. In 1824 Lord Eliot, as he was known until 1845, married Lady Jemima Cornwallis (1803–1856), third daughter and coheir of Charles *Cornwallis, second Marquess Cornwallis [*see under* Cornwallis, Charles, first Marquess Cornwallis], and his wife, Lady Louisa Gordon, daughter and coheir of Alexander, fourth duke of Gordon. They had three sons and one daughter.

In January 1824 Lord Eliot entered parliament for Liskeard, which he represented until the Reform Act of 1832. Canning appointed him lord of the Treasury in his brief administration of 1827, and he retained the office under Goderich and Wellington until 1830.

Eliot had been appointed secretary of legation in Madrid in 1823, and in Lisbon in 1824. In 1834 he was sent to Spain as envoy-extraordinary. The Carlist War was then raging, and Eliot concluded an agreement with the two belligerent forces, by which prisoners on both sides were to be treated according to the laws of civilized war. This treaty, known as the 'Eliot convention', effectually put an end to the sanguinary system of reprisals.

Upon his return to England in 1837 Eliot, who contested Bodmin unsuccessfully in 1835, was returned as a Conservative for East Cornwall, which he represented until 1845. England having permitted Spain to enlist soldiers within her territories, Eliot moved an address in the House of Commons in 1838, condemning the policy, which had been sanctioned by Lord Palmerston. His speech was much applauded, but the motion was defeated on a surprise division. In 1841 Eliot was appointed chief secretary for Ireland by Sir Robert Peel. He was the main proponent of an extended grant for Maynooth Seminary and the policy of Catholic incorporation which it represented. But he took a hard line against O'Connell and passed a controversial arms bill in 1843. During the Maynooth controversy of 1844–5 he was a useful line of communication to the Irish bishops.

On 21 January 1845 Eliot resigned the chief secretaryship on succeeding to the peerage as earl of St Germans. He was appointed postmaster-general by Sir Robert Peel, and held that office until the fall of Peel's administration. He was again in Ireland, as lord lieutenant, in Aberdeen's government of 1852–5, receiving the queen and the prince consort in 1853 on the opening of the Great Exhibition of Dublin. He retired shortly after Palmerston became prime

Edward Granville Eliot, third earl of St Germans (1798–1877), by Richard Rothwell

minister in 1855. After his return from Ireland, St Germans was for several years lord steward of the household (1857–8 and 1859–66). He was afterwards Queen Victoria's confidential adviser, especially on family matters. He was made CB in 1848, and GCB in 1857. He accompanied the prince of Wales on his tour through Canada and the United States in 1860.

St Germans never ceased to take a deep interest in public affairs. Although in later life he acted usually with the Liberals on political questions, his advice was frequently sought by leaders on the opposite side. He declined to join in the No Popery agitation in 1850, and published his reasons for objecting to it. He spoke seldom, but was generally respected for his fairness and ability. He was a good landlord to his tenantry in Cornwall. He was deputy lieutenant of the county (1841) and special deputy warden of the stannaries (1852). St Germans died on 7 October 1877 at Port Eliot, St Germans, Cornwall, and was buried at St Germans. He was succeeded by his son William.

G. B. SMITH, *rev.* H. C. G. MATTHEW

Sources GEC, *Peerage* • *The Times* (8 Oct 1877) • *Western Weekly News* (13 Oct 1877) • D. A. Kerr, *Peel, priests, and politics: Sir Robert Peel's administration and the Roman Catholic church in Ireland, 1841–1846* (1982) • C. K. Webster, *The foreign policy of Palmerston, 1830–1841*, 2 vols. (1951)

Archives Cornwall RO, corresp. and papers | BL, corresp. with Lord Aberdeen, Add. MSS 43207–43208 • BL, letters to George Fortescue, Add. MS 69364 • BL, corresp. with W. E. Gladstone, Add. MSS 44358–44527 • BL, corresp. with Sir Robert Peel, Add. MS 40480 • Bodl. Oxf., corresp. with Lord Kimberley • Cumbria AS,

Carlisle, corresp. with Sir James Graham · Lpool RO, letters to fourteenth earl of Derby · PRO, letters to Lord Granville, PRO30/29 · PRO, Russell MSS · U. Southampton L., corresp. with Lord Palmerston · U. Southampton L., letters to first duke of Wellington **Likenesses** W. J. Edwards, line engraving (after S. Bendixen), BM · W. Holl, stipple (after G. Richmond), BM, NPG · R. Rothwell, portrait, priv. coll. [*see illus.*] · S. C. Smith, oils, Dublin Castle · group portrait, oils (*The arrival of the lord lieutenant, Edward Granville Eliot … 1853*), NG Ire. **Wealth at death** under £50,000: probate, 21 Dec 1877, *CGPLA Eng. & Wales*

Eliot, Edward James (1758–1797), politician, was born at Port Eliot in Cornwall on 24 August 1758, the first surviving of four sons of Edward Craggs-*Eliot (1727–1804), politician, of Port Eliot, created Baron Eliot in 1784, and his wife, Catherine (*c*.1735–1804), daughter and heir of Edward Elliston of Gestingthorpe, Essex, an East India Company captain. Schooled at Liskeard, he entered Pembroke College, Cambridge, in 1775, where he became friends with the future premier, William Pitt; he proceeded MA in 1780. Eliot sat in parliament on the family interest, for St Germans, from 1780, and for Liskeard from 1784, though in 1790 he was elected for both. He had acted with the opposition to North but, supporting Shelburne, was placed at the Treasury board from July 1782 to April 1783, and again, after opposing the Fox–North coalition, from December 1783, in Pitt's ministry. That autumn, with William Wilberforce, he had accompanied Pitt to France.

Eliot was appointed king's remembrancer in the exchequer in 1785, worth £1500 a year, as a prelude to marrying, on 24 September 1785, Pitt's sister Lady Harriot (1758–1786), younger daughter of William Pitt, first earl of Chatham, and Hester Grenville. A year later she died, survived by her newborn daughter, Harriot, on 25 September 1786. In mourning, Eliot espoused religion and a virtuous life. Resident at Broomfield, Clapham, near Wilberforce's home, he participated in his philanthropic causes: the Proclamation Society, prison reform, poor relief, and abolition of the slave trade, for which he voted. He supported a Sunday observance bill in the Commons on 26 March 1795. Wilberforce taxed him with lobbying Pitt for the 'Saints', and with mediating between himself and Pitt. He had been credited with stopping succession by purchase to exchequer clerkships.

Not a ready debater, Eliot acted as a government teller in the house. His bill to stop corruption in Stockbridge elections was lost on 27 May 1793. Soon afterwards he became joint commissioner for Indian affairs, resigning for health reasons from the Treasury board. He became a captain in the Cornish fencibles in 1794. He invested in East India Company stock, and in February 1797 his friends expected him to become governor-general of Bengal. The return of a chronic stomach disorder ruled him out. Privy that summer to a plan of Pitt's to resign, he died at Port Eliot on 20 September 1797, to the dismay of Pitt and Wilberforce, the latter maintaining that Eliot's unpretentious demeanour had caused his intelligence and character to be underestimated. He was buried at St Germans on 3 October. His brother John, fellow member for Liskeard, succeeded to

the barony and was created earl of St Germans in 1815. Eliot's only child, Harriot Hester Eliot, married William Henry Pringle, later lieutenant-general, on 20 May 1806.

ROLAND THORNE

Sources L. B. Namier, 'Eliot, Hon. Edward James', HoP, *Commons, 1754–90* · R. G. Thorne, 'Eliot, Hon. Edward James', HoP, *Commons, 1790–1820* · *GM*, 1st ser., 67 (1797), 896 · R. I. Wilberforce and S. Wilberforce, *Life of William Wilberforce*, 5 vols. (1838), vols. 1–2 · Earl Stanhope [P. H. Stanhope], *Life of the Right Honourable William Pitt*, 4 vols. (1861–2), 3.63 · CKS, Stanhope papers, 731/11 · W. Cobbett, *Parliamentary debates* · GEC, *Peerage* · J. Ehrman, *The younger Pitt*, 3: *The consuming struggle* (1996), 47–9

Eliot, Francis Perceval (1756?–1818), writer on finance, entered the civil service and in 1806 became a commissioner of audit, auditing public accounts, at Somerset House. He joined the volunteer yeomanry service and became major and later colonel of the Staffordshire volunteer cavalry, writing *Six Letters on the Subject of the Armed Yeomanry* (1794).

Eliot's financial writings, mainly on currency and banking, included *Demonstration, or, Financial Remarks, with Occasional Observations on Political Occurrences* (1807), in which he discussed sinking funds; *Observations on the Fallacy of the Supposed Depreciation of the Paper Currency of the Kingdom, with Reasons for Dissenting from the Report of the Bullion Committee* (1811), in which he argued that during the war it was the gold which appreciated, and not the paper currency which depreciated; and a series of letters on the political and financial state of the nation, published in *The Pamphleteer* between 1814 and 1816, and addressed to the earl of Liverpool, under the signature Falkland.

At the time of his death Eliot was writing regularly for *Aegis*, a weekly paper. He died on 23 August 1818 at Portman Street, London. He was married, and had a large family.

FRANCIS WATT, *rev.* ANNE PIMLOTT BAKER

Sources F. Y. Edgeworth, 'Eliot, Francis Perceval', *Dictionary of political economy*, ed. H. R. I. Palgrave (1894–9) · [J. Watkins and F. Shoberl], *A biographical dictionary of the living authors of Great Britain and Ireland* (1816) · *GM*, 1st ser., 88/2 (1818), 378 **Archives** U. Birm. L., commonplace book · William Salt Library, Stafford, 5/49

Eliot, George. *See* Evans, Marian (1819–1880).

Eliot [Elliott; *née* Dalrymple], **Grace** [*nicknamed* Dally the Tall] (1754?–1823), courtesan and writer, was probably born in Edinburgh, the youngest of the three daughters of Hugh or Hew Dalrymple (*d.* 1774), lawyer, and his wife, Grisel Brown (*d. c*.1765). Her father, who claimed descent from a kinsman of the first earl of Stair, was later an author and attorney-general of Grenada. About 1758 her parents separated and Grace was probably brought up at her maternal grandfather's house. Following the death of her mother, she was sent about 1765 to a convent school in either France or Flanders. She was a tall, good-looking girl, apparently religious, but vivacious and susceptible, and fond of fashion and amusements. On 19 October 1771 she married the physician John *Eliot (1736–1786) of Cecil Street, the Strand, London, by licence at St Pancras Church in Middlesex. On 24 September 1772 she gave

Grace Eliot (1754?–1823), by Thomas Gainsborough, 1782?

birth to a son who died soon after. Unfortunately the marriage was not a success. Apparently Eliot bored his young wife, and in February 1774 she embarked on an affair with the libertine Arthur Annesley, Viscount Valentia in the Irish peerage (1744–1816). Eliot subsequently collected a mass of evidence against his wife and Lord Valentia; they were traced to a 'bawdy house' in Berkeley Row and to a bagnio in Leicester Fields; when she returned home it was noticed that her hair and clothes were dishevelled (LMA, DL/C/177), and during May the couple separated. In May or June 1774 Eliot commenced a suit for adultery against Valentia in the king's bench, and in December he applied to the London consistory court in order to divorce his wife. The libel, however, was unproved and it was only after the case had gone to appeal that the judge was given leave to proceed to judgment. On 23 February 1776 Eliot was granted his divorce. His lawyers then presented a petition to the House of Lords and on 21 March 1776 a bill was passed in parliament. The case turned Mrs Eliot into a celebrity and she was much talked about in society. 'Lord Valentia has preferred Dr Eliot's pretty wife to his own plain one', wrote Horace Walpole on 19 June 1774, 'but I do not find that there was much preference on her side, but rather on the Doctor's, for he has selected Valentia from several other lords and gentlemen who have been equally kind to the fair one' (Walpole, *Corr.*, 35.423).

In 1775 or early 1776 Mrs Eliot began an affair with the whig fourth earl of Cholmondeley (1749–1827), perhaps the most fashionable of her early admirers. Gossip intimated that she hoped to marry the libidinous earl, and month after month the newspapers chronicled her movements. In 1778 she was said to be pregnant and living with Cholmondeley at his house in Piccadilly (ibid., 33.181n.),

and he commissioned her portrait from Thomas Gainsborough. During the spring of 1779 she went to France, where she made conquests of the comte d'Artois and the Anglophile duc de Chartres, and for a while the couple were separated. She returned to London with Cholmondeley in June 1781, and so began her reign as Dally the Tall, among the most notorious of London's courtesans. Like her rival Mary Robinson (Perdita) and her friends Elizabeth Armitstead and Gertrude Mahon (the Bird of Paradise), she pursued her vocation at the highest level, counting George, prince of Wales (later George IV) among her lovers. In the summer of 1781 she briefly succeeded Mrs Armitstead as the prince's *chère amie*, and during the autumn she was again said to be pregnant. 'The Dalrymple has declared herself pregnant', reported the *Morning Herald* on 24 December, 'and taken care to have it well understood that Lord C—y cannot possibly lay claim to a single feature of the amorous produce' (Bass, 192). Contemporaries puzzled over the child's paternity—the most probable candidates were Charles William Windham, Cholmondeley, or the prince; Mrs Eliot claimed that the prince was the father. On 30 March 1782 she gave birth to a daughter, whom she had baptized with the feminine forms of the prince's names at St Marylebone Church on 30 July: Georgina Augusta Frederica Elliott. The child was brought up by Cholmondeley with his other children, at Houghton House, where she was given the surname of Seymour. Although the prince denied that the child was his, he was actively interested in her welfare. In 1808 Georgina made a splendid marriage to one of the sons of the third duke of Portland, Lord Charles William Bentinck. She died at her husband's house in Grosvenor Place on 10 December 1813, leaving one daughter, who was also named after the prince: Georgina Augusta Frederica Bentinck.

During the next few years Mrs Eliot continued to divide her time between London and France, before settling down towards the end of 1786 with the duc de Chartres (now d'Orléans) in Paris. For many years she occupied a house in the rue de Miromenil and a villa in the *arrondissement* of Versailles at Meudon. Her intimacy with Orléans and other aristocrats brought her the patronage of Marie Antoinette, and she was a close observer of the machinations of Orléans during the revolution. Her *Journal of my Life during the French Revolution* (published in 1859) is a novelized account of her conduct during these crucial years and is an important, if unreliable, source of social and political history. Some of her opinions on the revolution may have been formed with hindsight: her politics were royalist; the duke was not naturally wicked but the dupe of more clever men; and following the storming of the Bastille he should have offered Louis XVI his services. Some of Mrs Eliot's best stories have been attributed to her friend the widow Mrs Meyler, and she has frequently been accused of falsification (for example, *The Times*, 26 and 27 Jan 1859; Bleackley, 234–6). She was, however, undoubtedly brave. She apparently witnessed some of the revolution's most evocative events, such as the return of the royal family to Paris after their flight to Varennes (1791) and the public display of the princess de Lamballe's body following her atrocious murder (1792). Her concealment of the marquis de Chansenets at her house in the rue de Miromenil in 1792 was noted in London during June 1793:

> He fell out of a window on a heap of dead bodies, & continued there till every body was gone away, & then got to Mrs Elliot's who put him into her matress & laid upon the bed when [the guards] came into the room to search for him. (Earl of Bessborough and A. Aspinall, eds., *Lady Bessborough and her Family Circle*, 1940, 94)

During the terror Mrs Eliot's connection with Orléans exposed her to harassment and threats, and at some point she was imprisoned in the Recollects at Versailles and possibly in other prisons. In the Recollects she met the elderly atheist Richard Gem, who 'cried the whole time' (*Diaries and Correspondence of … Malmesbury*, 3.304). Each day she suspected would be her last, and the privations she endured until her release on 4 October 1794 were cruel and horrifying. Yet she was comforted by her religion. During the winter of 1796 she met the diplomat Sir James Harris, and was full of 'curious anecdotes' about the duc de Lauzun, the duc d'Aremberg, Louis XVI, Marie Antoinette, and Orléans. A later report says that she was followed round Paris by a 'numerous Court of Frenchmen', and that she sparked an affair with one of Napoleon's brothers—merely, she said, to have something to talk about (Granville, 1.285). She was in England in 1798, 1800, perhaps in 1803, and possibly thereafter. Her niece Lady Shelley, who met her about 1803, describes her as 'the most beautiful woman' she had ever beheld, and dressed in the 'indecent style of the French republican period' (*Diary*, 1.42). Apparently this was the only time that Mrs Eliot met her admiring niece, as family visits were not encouraged. Although Mrs Eliot received annuities from her late husband's estate and from the prince of Wales, she experienced financial difficulties during her last years. She died at the Villa d'Avray near Paris on 16 May 1823, after what appears to have been a long illness.　　　　MARTIN J. LEVY

Sources H. Bleackley, *Ladies fair and frail* (1909) · G. D. Elliott [G. Eliot], *Journal of my life during the French Revolution* (1859) · LMA, DL/C/177, 203, 279, 557, and 639; P89/MRY1/007 · LPL, Aa71/10, B18/48, D669, E41/152, and G142/28–30 · JHL, 34 (1774–6) · *Diary of Frances, Lady Shelley*, ed. R. Edgcumbe, 2 vols. (1912–13) · *Lord Granville Leveson Gower: private correspondence, 1781–1821*, ed. Castalia, Countess Granville [C. R. Leveson-Gower], 2nd edn, 2 vols. (1916) · *Diaries and correspondence of James Harris, first earl of Malmesbury*, ed. third earl of Malmesbury [J. H. Harris], 4 vols. (1844) · *The manuscripts of the earl of Carlisle*, HMC, 42 (1897) · Walpole, *Corr.* · R. D. Bass, *The green dragoon: the lives of Banastre Tarleton and Mary Robinson* (New York, 1957) · Royal Arch., GEO/30272 · *The correspondence of George, prince of Wales, 1770–1812*, ed. A. Aspinall, 8 vols. (1963–71) · *Ramblers Magazine* (1782–3) · *Ramblers Magazine* (1785) · *Town and Country Magazine*, 6 (1774) · *Town and Country Magazine*, 9–10 (1777–8) · *Town and Country Magazine*, 14–15 (1782–3)
Archives Archives Nationales, Paris · LMA, consistorial court MSS, corresp. · LPL, corresp. [copies] · Royal Arch.
Likenesses T. Gainsborough, oils, 1778, Metropolitan Museum of Art, New York · T. Gainsborough, oils, 1782?, Frick Collection, New York [*see illus.*] · J. Brown, engraving, 1859 (after R. Cosway), BM, NPG; repro. in Elliott, *Journal of my life*

Eliot, Jared (1685–1763), Congregationalist minister in America, physician, and writer on agriculture, was born on 7 November 1685 in Guilford, Connecticut, the first of four children of Joseph Eliot (1638–1694), Congregational minister, and Mary Wyllys. Eliot entered Harvard College in 1699 but studied there only a year. When Connecticut's collegiate school (from 1745 Yale College) was established only 10 miles from his home in 1702, he transferred and studied with the Revd Abraham Pierson, graduating BA in 1706. After a year of schoolteaching, Eliot replaced his mentor as the pastor of the First Church in Killingworth (now Clinton), Connecticut. He began preaching there on 1 June 1707, and was ordained on 26 October 1709, the same year he received his MA degree from Harvard. From 1707 to 1716 he received a medical training with Joshua Hobart of Southold, Long Island. He married Hannah Smithson (d. 1761) of Guilford on 26 October 1710, and together they had eleven children.

Eliot established a reputation as a learned pastor, a sociable neighbour, and an indefatigable man of business. In the towns and villages along Long Island Sound, however, he was perhaps best known as a physician with a good remedy for 'dropsy' (oedema). His great brush with public controversy came in the autumn of 1722 during what in Yale College lore is called the 'great apostasy'. Eliot, along with a college tutor and five other local ministers, including Timothy Cutler, rector of the collegiate school, and the Revd Samuel Johnson (later president of King's College in New York), indicated that they had begun to doubt the validity of Presbyterian and Congregational ordination and were veering towards the Church of England—a shocking development from the stronghold of puritan New England orthodoxy. Eliot seems to have been influenced by his father-in-law's Book of Common Prayer and a collection of books that had been recently donated to Yale's library. Unlike Cutler and Johnson, however, Eliot remained within the Congregational fold, and became a trustee of the collegiate school seven years later, an office he held until his death.

By the mid-1740s Eliot had trained enough men in medicine and no longer had to spend his weekdays riding from village to village with his medical bag. He published his first essay on field husbandry in 1748, and five more followed in the next decade. Collected in a 1761 edition, his *Essays upon Field-Husbandry in New-England* became the first important agricultural book published in North America. Between 1730 and 1760 Connecticut's population nearly doubled, and land prices rose while the acreage per family fell sharply. Eliot wrote to encourage local farmers to experiment with the intensive farming techniques that agricultural improvers across the Atlantic touted as the 'new husbandry'. He explained the theories of crop nutrition and modified the design for a drill plough found in Jethro Tull's *Horse-Hoing Husbandry* (1733). Eliot showed how to use seaweed compost to improve exhausted soil, rotate crops and plant red clover and English grasses to keep land productive, drain swamps to bring more land under cultivation, and plant mulberry trees for silk production. His essays usually ranged loosely over a number of topics, shifting from conversational reflections and anecdotes to factual, third-person observations and instructions. He culled farming hints from Bible passages, old proverbs, and classical verse. But he insisted that experience was the only true instructor, and that experimental philosophy—diligent trials, careful observation, and practical application—was the only true method for the husbandman committed to improvement.

Eliot wanted his essays to contribute to the public fund of useful knowledge but he wanted even more to promote husbandry as a respected branch of learning, and hoped to excite other pens and hands to work. He offered to publish others' observations or accounts of experiments. He kept his prose simple and his pamphlets inexpensive in order to draw common farmers as well as learned men into conversations about agricultural improvement. He corresponded with readers in Nova Scotia, New England, the mid-Atlantic colonies of British North America, and Britain. His correspondents included naturalists Peter Collinson and John Bartram, and Benjamin Franklin. Despite the enthusiasm shared by many of his readers, the practices he advocated were not widely adopted until the nineteenth century. Most mid-eighteenth-century New England farmers were more interested in cheap new land in the west than in trying to make old land more productive. Eliot also published five sermons and *An Essay on the Invention, or Art of Making Very Good, if Not the Best Iron, from Black Sea Sand* (New York, 1762). This last work earned him a medal from the London Society for the Encouragement of Arts, Manufactures, and Commerce. News of this award came to him nine days before his death on 22 April 1763 in Killingworth, Connecticut, where he was buried.

CHRISTOPHER GRASSO

Sources T. Ruggles, *The death of great, good, and useful men lamented* (New Haven, Connecticut, 1763) · R. H. True, 'Jared Eliot, minister, physician, farmer', in J. Eliot, *Essays upon field husbandry in New England, and other papers, 1748–1762*, ed. H. J. Carman and R. G. Tugwell (1934), xxiii–lvi · C. K. Shipton, *Sibley's Harvard graduates: biographical sketches of those who attended Harvard College*, 5 (1937) · C. Grasso, 'The experimental philosophy of farming: Jared Eliot and the cultivation of Connecticut', *A speaking aristocracy: transforming public discourse in eighteenth-century Connecticut* (1999), 190–229 · F. B. Dexter, *Biographical sketches of the graduates of Yale College*, 6 vols. (1885–1912), vol. 2 · W. S. Porter, *Genealogy of the Eliot family* (New Haven, Connecticut, 1854) · H. Thoms, *Jared Eliot, minister, doctor, scientist, and his Connecticut* (Hamden, Connecticut, 1967)
Archives Yale U., MSS | Yale U., Benjamin Franklin papers · Yale U., Ezra Stiles papers
Likenesses portrait, priv. coll.; repro. in W. H. E. Emerson and others, *Genealogy of the descendants of John Eliot* (New Haven, CT, 1905), 44 · woodcut, repro. in Eliot, *Essays upon field husbandry*
Wealth at death £1800: Shipton, *Sibley's Harvard graduates*, 5.203; will, Porter, *Genealogy of the Eliot family*, 155–9

Eliot, Sir John (1592–1632), politician, was born at Cuddenbeak, Cornwall, on 11 April 1592, and baptized on 20 April at St Germans, the only child of Richard Eliot (*d.* 1609) of Port Eliot and his wife, Bridget (*d.* 1618), daughter of Nicholas Carswell of Hatch Arundell, Devon. His family can be traced back to another John Eliot, who was mayor of Plymouth in 1534–5. The value of the estate was estimated in 1578 at £300 a year and seems to have slowly increased up to John's birth. His childhood produced one memorable incident. John Moyle, a neighbour, reported him to his

Sir John Eliot (1592–1632), by unknown artist, 1632

father for 'excesses', and young John replied by striking Moyle in the side with his sword. A formal apology was arranged, and Moyle was still writing him friendly letters thirty years later when he was in the Tower.

Political and historiographical significance Eliot, perhaps more than any other man, was the architect of the whig interpretation of the seventeenth century, much as John Foxe was the architect of the equivalent interpretation of the sixteenth century. Both had assistance from others, yet the reverence with which a historian of the stature of S. R. Gardiner, for example, pronounced the name of Eliot seems to show that his contribution is of peculiar importance.

Eliot, like many of the key parliamentary figures of the 1620s, grew up during the eclipse of French power after 1584 which allowed Englishmen the luxury of being anti-Spanish with a freedom never enjoyed by their fathers or their sons. Because Eliot combined this intense anti-Spanishness with an addiction to the conspiracy theory of history which shows in his medieval, as well as his seventeenth-century, history, he was unusually well placed to develop a theory of seventeenth-century politics which always tried to explain misfortune or defeat through betrayal by a single individual. His rich rhetorical talent made him exceptionally well qualified to communicate this interpretation, and the reputations of such men as the duke of Buckingham, Sir John Coke, and Sir Richard Weston (later first earl of Portland) have not yet recovered from the power of Eliot's rhetoric.

Even by the standards of seventeenth-century MPs, Eliot

was exceptionally ill equipped to understand the contemporary military revolution. His ideas of a privateering war paying for itself were, as John Pym demonstrated in one short, brilliant speech in 1626, peculiarly innocent of any grasp of figures. He was thus freer than most of his contemporaries to blame failure in military enterprise on conspiracy. Since Eliot never looked for an institutional explanation for failure, he often had no alternative.

Neither did Eliot have the countervailing pressure of day-to-day practical business which many MPs used to keep their feet on the ground. While the importance of bills in parliament has sometimes been exaggerated, there seems no parallel to the fact that, of Eliot's 172 speeches in the parliament of 1628, only one dealt with a bill. Since the bill in question related to the reversal of the attainder of Carew Ralegh, son of Sir Walter, even that did not get him away from the conspiracy view of history. It was not the popish conspiracy view of Pym or John Hampden. They both saw popery as an evil spiritual principle; they thought men might give unconscious adherence to it, and, by such things as trust in free will, might become papists without knowing it. For Eliot, unusually, a papist was a literal adherent of the Church of Rome. Moreover, as the imagery of his speeches illustrates, in the great divide of seventeenth-century culture, he was a classicist and not a biblicist: his nightmare figures were Tiberius and Sejanus. This led him into the bitter but secular conspiracy theories of Roman politics, in which the personal outweighed the religious and philosophical. When combined with an increasing pro-French bias, this led him to construct very different nightmares from those of Pym or Hampden. It may also explain why he produced in his native Cornwall political divisions which had no continuity with those of 1642. Both the Cornish royalists and Cornish parliamentarians were led by former Eliot partisans, divided by the events since Eliot's death.

Inheritance and early life On 4 December 1607 Eliot matriculated from Exeter College, Oxford, where the Calvinist John Prideaux was at that time a renowned tutor; he stayed for three years, but did not graduate. He had a short experience of wardship, for his father died in 1609, shortly after arranging a marriage for John with Radigund (d. 1628), only child of Richard Gedy or Gedye. Gedy had been a feoffee to Eliot's father since 1603. He is first known as yeoman, then as gentleman, then as esquire, and finally became sheriff before his death in 1629. Gedy succeeded in buying the wardship, and an amicable relationship between him and John Eliot lasted the rest of their lives. The family continued to reside at Cuddenbeak, while the titular home of Port Eliot was leased out. This put Eliot six miles outside Plymouth, but on the Cornish side of the Sound, and it is thus that Eliot conducted his political career as a Cornishman.

By the end of 1611 Eliot had married Radigund. The steady flow of children from then on suggests a reason why he may have failed to attend the inns of court. All except his second son, Richard (b. 1614), were baptized at St Germans: John (bap. 18 October 1612), Elizabeth (29 December 1616), Edward (9 July 1618), Bridget (26 April 1620), Radigund (11 October 1622), Susan (14 October 1624), Thomas (7 September 1626) and Nicholas (15 June 1628). In 1614 Eliot was returned as MP for St Germans, but there is no evidence that he took his seat. On 10 May 1618 he was knighted. That year his mother died, and his estate was improved by the addition of her jointure.

In 1621 Eliot became a JP for Cornwall, one of thirty-four younger gentlemen added to the commission of the peace between 1617 and 1625, of whom only six succeeded fathers or relatives. In December 1622, through the patronage of George Villiers, marquess of Buckingham, Eliot was made vice-admiral of Devon. His duties very shortly got him into trouble, over alleged collusion with a pirate called John Nutt. After a spell in prison, Eliot was released and resumed his office. The truth behind the incident is uncertain, but what is clear is that it began a rivalry with James Bagg, the Devonian vice-admiral of Cornwall, who had done Eliot's work while he was incarcerated. Bagg was a contentious man, and from 1623 Eliot had to endure a constant stream of hostile reports by Bagg to Buckingham. Increasingly, as Eliot developed into a champion of the law, Bagg developed into a champion of arbitrary power. Buckingham's patronage, because it approached monopoly, tended to set up a mechanism of internal competition between his clients, and it was in this competition that Eliot perpetually lost out, first to Bagg, and later to Sir John Coke. His hatred of these two regularly reached a note of personal bitterness it is tempting to describe as 'sibling rivalry'.

Early parliaments, 1624–1625: from Buckingham to Pembroke All this remained in the future in the parliament of 1624, where Eliot sat for Newport, Cornwall. He was possibly elected by influence of the duchy, normally exercised on Buckingham's behalf, and he operated as a loyal member of Buckingham's team. At the opening session he showed serious want of judgement in raising a privilege dispute about the imprisonments at the end of the parliament of 1621. He said that the freedom of ancient parliaments had been lost, and that some of those who had revealed the house's proceedings served the turn of others who had worse ends. John Pym, who had himself been imprisoned, realized that a successful parliament depended on avoiding such a debate, and commented in his diary that 'divers were afraid this motion would have put the House into some such heate as to disturbe the greate busines' (Northants. RO, Finch-Hatton MS, fol. 8v). Ironically, it was on this very same point, after 1629, that Eliot's parliamentary career was to end. Meanwhile, the issue can have done nothing to increase his reputation for judgement.

Eliot's support for war with Spain does not mark him out as a Buckingham client, but it was clearly enough in line with his permanent convictions, and Sir Walter Ralegh had been a family friend. His suggestion, on 1 March 1624, that 'war must be the thing that must repair us' fits with the opening reflections of his memoirs, *Negotium posterorum*, on 'the degenerate vices of a long corrupted peace' (diary of Sir Thomas Jervoise, Jervoise MSS, Hants. RO; Eliot, *Negotium*, 2.1). His proposal to finance a fleet by charging the papists showed a distinct lack of financial realism. One of his most interesting speeches is that of 7 April, on Hoby's proposal that recusants should not be allowed to be deputy lieutenants or justices of the peace. He said that the committee had decided not to put it in the petition, 'but intimate it *to the prince*' (BL, Harley MS 6383, fol. 122a: my italics). This suggests that the faith in Charles as a protestant prince which permeates the opening pages of *Negotium posterorum* is genuine. It also suggests a risky degree of commitment to the prince of Wales's interest. What really marks Eliot as a Buckingham client in 1624 is his brusque commitment to the impeachment of lord treasurer Lionel Cranfield, earl of Middlesex, a cause he had no other apparent motive for pursuing.

In 1625 Eliot was still formally a Buckingham client, but the faith was wearing a little thin. What shook him was the request for additional supply over and above the two subsidies voted at the opening of parliament. He appears to have been completely unable to see that £140,000 could not finance a fleet capable of doing honourable service against the king of Spain. He argued, correctly, that the request was unlikely to succeed, but, because he could see no need for it in the first place, recorded that the request was 'lodg'd … meerlie to be denied' (Eliot, *Negotium*, 1.113). This is a typical Eliot wording. Depending on the degree of purpose implied, it is either a statement of fact or a paranoid suggestion, and his readers are free to take it whichever way they wish. In a conspiracy-theory orator, the style is ideal. It plants a seed of suspicion, which will grow only where the soil is already fertile. It was a style Eliot perfected over the next four years.

During the months between the parliaments of 1625 and 1626, Eliot was able to contemplate the disaster of the Cadiz expedition, though it seems never to have occurred to him that if the additional supply were really needed, the failure of the expedition might rest as much on himself and his fellow MPs as it did on the lord admiral. At the same time, he was able to brood over Buckingham's preference for Sir John Coke over himself. In a letter to Buckingham of April 1625, in which he offers to be 'whollie devoted to the contemplation of your excellence', he also expresses a frustration at 'the want of opportunitie, in which I might express the character of my harte, that only takes of your impression' (PRO, SP 16/1/25). The trouble was that Buckingham clients were a drug on the market. At some stage during the winter of 1625–6, Eliot seems to have begun considering transferring his loyalty to William Herbert, third earl of Pembroke, who as lord warden of the stannaries was Buckingham's political rival in Cornwall. This may not have been mere fickleness. As he later made clear in his big speech of 3 June 1628, support for the French alliance was one of the cornerstones of his approach to foreign affairs, and his increasing hostility to Buckingham moved in tandem with Buckingham's increasing hostility to France. War with France and Spain simultaneously had been England's nightmare for a century, and even the most loyal client was entitled to the view that anyone who risked that nightmare was not safe to be left in office.

Parliament of 1626 and the impeachment of Buckingham
This attitude may account for Eliot's exceptional concentration in his attack on the duke in the parliament of 1626 on the case of the *St Peter*, a French ship seized, released, and then re-seized by the order of the duke as lord admiral. As a basis of a legal charge it was weak, but as a warning against any further moves to war with France, it was ideal. It was an issue to which Eliot returned time and time again. For good measure, he threw in charges of corruption, extortion, promotion of papists, and failure to guard the narrow seas. When faced with the point about lack of money, he replied: 'It appears and we know it too well that there was no want of monies' (Bidwell and Jansson, 2.361). He complained of excessive gifts to the duke's kin, and demanded, as had so many predecessors in medieval parliaments, an act of resumption of lands carelessly sold by the crown, leaving it unable to 'live of its own'.

Compared with the Eliot who emerged in 1628, this was a very unideological set of complaints. They were not in the first instance about religion, save in the single point of the degree of toleration extended to papists. At the very beginning of the parliament, on 10 February 1626, he proposed to consider the king's estate, 'religion being already settled' (Bidwell and Jansson, 2.17). This is not a phrase John Pym, Sir Nathaniel Rich, or Christopher Sherland could possibly have used. Eliot wanted to consider misgovernment, miscounselling, and misemployment of the king's revenues. Most strikingly, his opening proposals to restore the king's estate were designed to reduce 'the extraordinary resort to the subject for supplies' (ibid.). A programme for increasing the power of parliaments in the body politic would have had exactly the opposite objective. These are plans which would have produced less frequent, not more frequent, parliaments (ibid., 2.15).

At its beginning, Eliot's attack on Buckingham was an attack on original sin, not on arbitrary power. Original sin, of course, was no novelty in English constitutional history, which is why Eliot was able to find plenty of precedents to hand. He repeatedly claimed that in his attacks on the minister, he was making no attack on the king, but was speaking with the loyalty appropriate to a faithful counsellor. These claims have caused difficulty to modern historians, as they did to Charles I. It is easy to understand why, but when Eliot's political thought is put into its own terms of reference, some of the difficulties disappear. Eliot believed, with Sir Robert Phelips, that precedents are not more ancient than the age of which we are yet a part: he believed he was living in the same polity which had been ruled by Henry III and Richard II, and that the same political rules operated in his day as had operated in theirs. This assumption was not of course correct, but it is perhaps, in the realm of history of ideas at least, less totally incorrect than the assumption since made by historians that he was operating in 'modern times'. Eliot shared the complete commitment of his contemporaries to the doctrine of non-resistance. As he said on 3 June 1626, 'no act of the King can make him unworthy of his kingdom: it is against the tenet of our religion' (Bidwell and Jansson, 3.358).

Eliot's political thought depended on 'separating the problems of limitation and resistance' (Burgess, 36, 46). This separation was achieved through the legal fiction of ministerial responsibility, most clearly formulated by Oliver St John in the ship money case. It is this doctrine of ministerial responsibility which enabled Eliot to avoid confronting the question of his attitude to the king. In this, he was in the company of the whole of the English political class until after the drafting of the nineteen propositions in 1642. It is only the intensity with which Eliot held to standard doctrine which is worthy of any comment. What does emerge with clarity is Eliot's willingness to use the denial of supply as a weapon in demands for ministerial responsibility. This was far from an unprecedented measure, but it was a highly unusual one. It must be sharply distinguished from the denial of additional supply in 1625: it was a blanket refusal to vote any supply at all. Done in wartime, it was even more unusual, and the last use of this weapon was centuries in the past. Charles was entitled to feel at least surprise.

During the parliament of 1626, Eliot occasionally touched on other issues, but almost everything he said came under one single theme: 'the treasure, laws, persons, actions of the kingdom, the kingdom itself, suffers under the too great power of one man' (Bidwell and Jansson, 3.34). It was a familiar enough theme in medieval political thought. His reports on 24 March and 21 April from the committee on causes of causes, and his speech on 10 May summing up the articles of impeachment to the Lords, helped to bring the disorderly mass of complaints together into a whole.

It would be a mistake to see Eliot as a one-man band. The impeachment of Buckingham grew out of the most improbable of coalitions. The earl of Pembroke's men, who complained that the Spanish war was not run properly, joined with the men of the earls of Arundel and Bristol, who complained that there was a Spanish war at all. The privy council, angry at its eclipse by one man, did more than it appears to encourage the impeachment. Anti-Arminians such as Pym, Rich, and Sherland were beginning to realize they had a new crisis in the Church of England on their hands. The pro-French interest, encouraged, as the king believed, by the French ambassador, did what they could to help the impeachment forward. Eliot was not its general. He was its front man, the one always ready to step forward and risk his fortune where others waited to see who would go first. He was the ideal man for getting the cause off the ground. Whether he would have been as ready to live with the compromises towards which many others worked in vain cannot be determined. He certainly encouraged the king to get on his high horse to keep him company. When he was questioned by chief justice Randolph Crewe and attorney-general Robert Heath after his speech to the Lords of 10 May, they did not only ask whether he had had conference with any foreign ambassador. They also asked whether he had been shown any precedent concerning the deposing of kings. Eliot replied that he had been shown no such precedent 'otherwise than hath occurred in generall by readings of history' (PRO, SP 16/27/17). The notion that Eliot was planning to depose the king came from the same fantasy world as the suggestion that Buckingham was in league with Spain. Meanwhile, government had to cope with an angry dissolution without supply in time of war. In secretary Sir Edward Conway's words, 'though there be no money, yet the realm must be maintained' (Russell, 321). From that necessity followed Eliot's next round of battle.

Cornish politics and the forced loan The seat of that battle was, for once, not parliament but the county of Cornwall, where existing electoral competition between Buckingham and Pembroke, together with his deputy lord warden of the stannaries, William Coryton, intensified into political polarization. Coryton was to be Eliot's key county ally in the years 1626–8, and although in July 1626 through Buckingham's influence Eliot was removed as a JP and as vice-admiral, his knot of friends stayed loyal to him. These were rich waters for patrons who wished to go fishing for clients, and Buckingham and Pembroke were not the men to neglect such opportunities; nor were Bagg and Coryton people who would have left them in peace if they had.

Political events made it inevitable that this battle should be fought out in terms of arguments between legality and loyalty. Charles, faced with the denial of supply in wartime, decided to raise in the form of a forced loan the money parliament would have voted if he had got rid of Buckingham. It was inevitable that Eliot should be one of the numerous gentlemen who refused to pay. It was equally inevitable that his should be one of the loudest and most heard voices in protest. With Coryton, in 1627 he was imprisoned in the Gatehouse, from where he issued a petition which made a simple appeal to the rule of law. He ran through the statutes against arbitrary taxation which were later to form the basis of the petition of right—*Confirmatio cartarum, De tallagio non concedendo*, the statutes of 1340 and 1352, and the 1483 statute against benevolences—and appealed to the due process requirements for imprisonment laid down in Magna Carta. It was a powerful and emotive argument, which still retains its vitality, and the issue itself was raised to a new level of intensity that year in the *Five Knights' Case*, when, in reply to the suing of a writ of habeas corpus, the king asserted that he did not need to show any cause for imprisoning people. Eliot's petition, of which at least twenty copies survive, was found 'wandering around' in Cornwall but it faced powerful local opposition. Given their responsibility for the defence of the county, the deputy lieutenants thought that they could not attack the king when they were constantly having to appeal to him for ships, powder, and supplies, and when they themselves required power to billet soldiers before they rioted, or to impose martial law after they had done so. Bagg, his ally Lord Mohun, and others meanwhile mounted an arbitrary defence of royal authority against 'popularity'.

Parliament of 1628 None the less, having been released from prison in January 1628 under the general release which preceded the decision to summon another parliament, Eliot and Coryton obtained an overwhelming election victory which was a slap in the face for Charles. Bagg, typically, reported to Buckingham that the four or five thousand freeholders who voted them in as knights of the shire constituted an unlawful assembly. Once he had taken his seat, Eliot made no fewer than 172 speeches, yet numerous though they were, they added little to each other. Like 1626, 1628 was for him a one-issue parliament. Apart from occasional digressions like a passionate argument for putting Oxford before Cambridge in the subsidy bill, he was concerned almost exclusively with the defence of the rule of law against arbitrary power. In his first big speech of 22 March he said his case was 'for the ancient glory of the ancient laws of England' which now required defence. 'It is not for monies, or the manner how to be levied, but the propriety of goods', for the law of 'meum and tuum' had 'fallen into the chaos of a higher power' (Johnson and others, 2.57). He argued powerfully for having the cause for imprisonment expressed. If men could be imprisoned without a cause for offences such as 'speaking of things within the jurisdiction of this House', then this might be extended to 'things extrajudicial, as treason' (ibid., 3.158). In the light of his own later history, this remark was prophetic. He produced a set of notes supporting his position by the Elizabethan judge Sir Edmund Anderson, given to him by Anderson's son, a Lincolnshire loan refuser. They were instantly confirmed by Coke as being in Anderson's own hand.

Eliot showed a great fear of the power of soldiers, perhaps the natural result of living close to Plymouth, where many unpaid and defeated soldiers and sailors had disembarked. He complained of soldiers who despoiled the house of a gentleman in Cornwall, and when he remonstrated, pursued him instead. When he complained to the mayor, he was imprisoned. Perhaps this was his own case. His Cornish experience shows in a consistent hounding of deputy lieutenants who abused their power. His enthusiasm for war in 1624 had quite evaporated. 'Looking on our late disasters, I tremble to think of sending more abroad … It was ever the wisdom of our ancestors to leave foreign wars to the state and not to meddle with them' (Johnson and others, 2.247–8).

Except for those speaking to an official brief, the general outline of the case produced remarkably little dissension in the Commons. There was a wide measure of agreement that, while supply could be voted, it would not be voted until members were sure that the property from which they were paying money to the king was truly their own. There was little doubt, except perhaps in the mind of Charles, that refusal of the Commons' demands would lead to refusal of supply. Since the soldiers and sailors returned from La Rochelle were still undisbanded because they could not be paid, refusal of supply might well raise fear in administrative minds. The king's position appeared to be that he would obey the law, but he did not believe the law was what the Commons said it was, and was unwilling to create new law for their benefit. One of the first key debates to grapple with this issue of the

king's obduracy was that of 6 May, when he had offered to obey Magna Carta and the Six Statutes, but refused to allow any explanation of their meaning, and appealed to the Commons for trust. Eliot's answer was pithy and intellectually clear:

> Let us to the point of trust; upon that depends all the rest. His Majesty tells us he will admit no interpretation, so we labour in vain to prepare the way to procure that. The question is not whether we shall trust the King, yea or no, but whether in the general words we shall have the law. All the question is what the law is, and so, that not being expounded, and not explained to what that trust extends, it cannot satisfy. (Johnson and others, 3.272)

It was not good enough for the king to ask them to trust him; he had to specify in what he wanted to be trusted.

In reply, Charles equally dug in his heels. In his letter to the Lords of 12 May he objected to the idea that the cause of an imprisonment must be such as could legally be determined by the judges, since this 'would soon dissolve the very foundation and frame of our monarchy', though he promised, in the voice of executives through the centuries, that he would not extend his power 'beyond the just rule of moderation' (Johnson and others, 3.372). If he meant what he said, he was not prepared to be king if he could not imprison without showing cause. Eliot's reply was to suggest that since this letter was addressed to the Lords and not to the Commons, they should ignore it. Over the next few days he and other MPs shot down all the Lords' attempts at compromise. After long debate, the Lords agreed to join with the Commons in the original and unvarnished petition. Charles, left to face the music alone, remained unyielding. In his first answer to the petition of right, on 2 June, he affirmed his conscientious adherence 'to the laws and customs of the realm' and to the preservation of the 'rights and just liberties' of his subjects (Russell, 377), but said absolutely nothing on the key question of what their rights and just liberties were.

Eliot, having rashly claimed that words failed him, then filled the silence for much of the rest of the day with his great speech of 3 June, calling for a remonstrance of the state of the kingdom. It is hard to believe that this speech was entirely extempore. It has always been widely believed, though never proved, that there had been a tacit agreement as part of the terms on which the parliament of 1628 was called that there should be no overt attack on Buckingham. If there was such an agreement, it was now broken, first by Coke, and then, most thoroughly, by Eliot. On 5 June the speaker, Sir Heneage Finch, delivered a message from the king saying that the day of dissolution would not be altered, and interrupting Eliot's claim that Charles had been misinformed by saying no new business would be admitted. He appears to have thought Eliot was about to name Buckingham. Sir Dudley Digges, in reply, proposed the house should sit in silence, which, remarkably, it did until recalled to business by Sir Nathaniel Rich. Eliot then introduced fears of a *coup d'état* by complaining of the mercenary German horse employed by Charles as 'praetorian bands' (Russell, 381n.). The king's second answer to the petition, on 7 June, may well have been intended to stop the remonstrance, but if so, it came too late, and no such reciprocal gesture was forthcoming. It got the king his supply, and so barely saved his face, but the remonstrance went abroad as an indictment of Buckingham and all his rule. On 11 June Eliot underlined quite how much it was aimed at the duke by saying they should leave out the commission for buildings, since it was done in James's time, and did not reflect on the duke. Parliament adjourned for the summer, having achieved the petition of right and a grant of five subsidies, but leaving the question of authority for tonnage and poundage and militia unresolved. Before this happened, Eliot had gone back home because of the death of his wife on 13 June.

Hers was not the only important death of the summer of 1628. On 23 August Buckingham was murdered by Felton, who when pressed for an explanation, claimed the Commons' remonstrance as his inspiration. Since that remonstrance was Eliot's idea, largely his work, and an expression of his mind, Charles, listening to rejoicings at the death of his only real friend, was under severe temptation to hold Eliot responsible for his death: there is no reason to believe he resisted.

The 1629 session and 'tumult in the House' Charles promised each of his parliaments that if they voted a significant supply, they would be recalled for a further session in the winter. The only time Charles had occasion to keep his promise was in 1629, and he did. The one thing Charles wanted out of this session was a legal grant of tonnage and poundage, which he had been collecting without a grant ever since 1625. It was the biggest single item in his revenue, and he could not do without it. Any long-term settlement between crown and parliament would have to tackle this question. The basic struggle of 1629 was between two rival groups in the Commons, each working for a different bargain. That led by Pym and Rich wanted to vote tonnage and poundage in return for Charles's abandonment of Arminianism. In accord with Eliot's longstanding ideas on ministerial responsibility, the group led by Eliot and John Selden would vote tonnage and poundage once the king had agreed to the punishment of those who had collected it without legal authority. Their hand was greatly strengthened when the customs officers seized the goods of John Rolle, who was an MP, and so turned a general issue of liberties into a specific dispute about parliamentary privilege.

In the end, neither of these positions was negotiable: Charles was never prepared to sell his religion for money, and he was never prepared to see his servants punished for obeying his commands. Yet if fudge was to be looked for, the Pym–Rich position was distinctly more promising: theological formulae could be tailored, adapted and made ambiguous and a face-saving compromise reached. Eliot's line, because it involved the direct humiliation of the king, offered no such possibility. On 19 February the two groups had a direct confrontation in the Commons. Pym, by the immense tactical error of describing the privileges of the House as a 'mean matter', lost easily, and Eliot carried the House in resolving to undertake no more business before punishing the customs officers. They were on a collision course. On 25 February an adjournment was arranged until 2 March, in the hope that some compromise could be patched up.

When the house met on 2 March Eliot seems to have believed mistakenly that a dissolution had already been decided on, though the Venetian ambassador is more likely to be right that a majority of the privy council was still opposing it. He and his friends therefore launched a planned demonstration. When speaker Finch tried to end the sitting by rising, Denzil Holles and Benjamin Valentine, MP for St Germans, who had taken the privy councillors' seats next to the chair, held him down, Sir Miles Hobart locked the doors, while Eliot read a paper designed to appeal over the heads of the members to the country, in effect calling for a taxpayers' strike against tonnage and poundage. For good measure, he transferred to lord treasurer Richard Weston the hostility previously reserved for Buckingham. Astonishingly, he accused Weston of deliberately weakening shipping 'to make this land fit for invasion' (Russell, 416).

Imprisonment and political thought That parliament should then be dissolved on 4 March, and that simultaneously the arrest of Eliot and his allies should be ordered, is hardly surprising. Charles faced a much more difficult problem in deciding what to do with them once he had them in custody, for his legal position was weak. He had to find a way of steering round the claim for parliamentary privilege which Eliot and his fellows were bound to advance, and the new requirement of the petition of right that he should show cause for the imprisonment. Charles's determination, from the start, was that the prisoners should secure no release without a submission. He had to sell this policy to a very reluctant bench of judges.

On 7 May, Heath filed charges in the Star Chamber, which referred the privilege issue to three senior judges, who were still hearing it in June. When Charles summoned all the judges to Greenwich, he found they inclined to the arguments of the defendants by a clear majority. By the end of the summer recess, the Star Chamber case had been dropped. A habeas corpus brought by the prisoners produced rather more progress. Charles's return to the writ was that they were committed 'for notable contempt committed by them against ourself and our government, and for stirring up sedition against us' (Reeve, 123–4). These words lacked the precision needed to be brought to a legal issue. This was especially true because sedition, though a known Roman law offence, in this case became known to the common law for the first time and thus had no established definition. When by some time in June the king learned of the king's bench judges' determination to bail the prisoners, he moved them from the custody of the marshal of king's bench and thus out of the jurisdiction of the court, and had them confined in the Tower by his own warrant, in the custody of the lieutenant, Allen Apsley. On 24 June he told the judges none of them would appear in court. Charles then told the French ambassador they were 'republicans'—a charge on a level with Eliot's that Weston was preparing the country for invasion. It was only by suspending chief baron Sir John Walter on 22 October that Charles finally got a judgment against them in king's bench in February 1630. This judgment was reversed by writ of error in 1667. It also explains the two provisions in the Bill of Rights, that the judges should not question any proceeding in parliament, and that no judge can be dismissed save by an address passed by a two-thirds majority in both houses. This procedure has never yet been employed.

In the Tower, Eliot refused to submit to the king or admit his guilt and continued to write. In addition to his memoirs, *Negotium posterorum*, he produced two works of political theory, *The Monarchie of Man* and *De jure maiestatis*. These have caused some problems to his whig admirers, for they are not whig works. *The Monarchie of Man* is a straightforward great chain of being work setting forward ideas of order, harmony, and correspondence. The king is supreme in the body politic, as the head in the body, the husband in the family, and the sun in the sky, but since the whole order is God-given, headship exists only within that framework. Since the law too is part of the great chain, reverence for the king and the law are entirely compatible. Both are 'ordained of God'. *De jure maiestatis* is a different case. It is based on a work by Arnisaeus the Dutchman, which is designed to defend national sovereignty against claims of pope and emperor to supra-national jurisdiction. This leads to a standard anti-papal polemic. It takes a position closely similar to James I's 1610 speech to parliament, which is one with which most MPs could live. The defence of national sovereignty against the pope has no logical connection with any particular view on royal sovereignty against the parliament. Taken with Eliot's familiar ideas on ministerial responsibility, it is entirely consistent with his political career.

Eliot suffered from a wasting illness in the Tower for some time before he died on 27 November 1632. Charles refused to release the body for burial, writing on his son's petition 'let Sir John Eliot be buried in the church of that parish where he died' (*DNB*). His will incorporates material from that of his father-in-law Richard Gedy, for whom he was executor. In the final version he provided for four surviving sons and four daughters. His eldest son, John, was residuary legatee, while Elizabeth (who later married Nathaniel Fiennes) got a portion of £2000 and her sisters £1200 apiece. Robert Mason, an old parliamentary colleague, got a life annuity of £5 for his care in making the will. The executors were Sir Dudley Digges, John Arundell of Trerice, Bevill Grenville of Stow, Robert Mason, William Scawen 'gent of St German' and Maurice Hill.

CONRAD RUSSELL

Sources S. R. Gardiner, *History of England from the accession of James I to the outbreak of the civil war, 1603–1642*, 10 vols. (1883–4) · C. Russell, *Parliaments and English politics, 1621–1629* (1979) · H. Hulme, *The life of Sir John Eliot, 1592–1632: the struggle for parliamentary freedom* (1957) · Foster, *Alum. Oxon.* · will, PRO, PROB 11/162, fols. 473v–475v · W. B. Bidwell and M. Jansson, eds., *Proceedings in parliament, 1626*, 4 vols. (1991–6) · R. C. Johnson and others, eds., *Proceedings in parliament, 1628*, 6 vols. (1977–83) · R. P. Cust, *The forced loan and English politics, 1626–1628* (1987) · A. Duffin, *Faction and faith: politics and religion of the Cornish gentry before the civil war* (1996) · L. J. Reeve, *Charles I and the road to personal rule* (1989) · G. Burgess, *Absolute monarchy and the Stuart constitution* (New Haven, 1996) · I. H. C. Fraser, 'The agitation in the Commons, 2 March 1629', *BIHR*, 30 (1957), 86–95 · J. Eliot, *An apology for Socrates (being a vindication of Sir J. E. himself) and Negotium posterorum*, ed. A. B. Grosart, 2 vols. (1881) · J. Eliot, *The monarchie of man*, ed. A. B. Grosart, 2 vols. (1879) · J. Eliot, *De jure maiestatis, or, Political treatise of government (1628–30) and the letter book of Sir John Eliot*, ed. A. B. Grosart (1882)

Archives BL, Harley MSS, corresp., parliamentary speeches, etc. · Cornwall RO, papers · S. Antiquaries, Lond., speeches [contemporary copy] · V&A NAL, collections of his speeches in parliament; corresp. and papers

Likenesses oils, *c.*1628 (after P. van Somer), Palace of Westminster, London · portrait, 1632, priv. coll. [*see illus.*] · F. Holl, stipple (after earlier engraving), NPG

Eliot, John [*called* the Apostle to the Indians] (**1604–1690**), minister and missionary in America, was born at Widford, Hertfordshire, and baptized at St John the Baptist Church there on 5 August 1604. He was the third child and second son of seven children of Bennett Eliot and Lettese Aggar (*d.* 1620). A prosperous yeoman family with lands throughout the Lea Valley, by at least 1610 they were living at Nazing, Essex, where John spent most of his childhood and received his early education. He matriculated as a pensioner from Jesus College, Cambridge, early in 1619. His father's will, dated 5 November 1621, bequeathed £8 for his continued maintenance there and he graduated BA in 1622. Little is known of his whereabouts or activities over the next few years: although it has been asserted that he was ordained, there is no evidence for this. By 1629 Eliot was serving as usher or assistant master at Thomas Hooker's puritan academy at Little Baddow, near Chelmsford, Essex. He wrote an account of what was, in effect, a seminary; although seen later by Cotton Mather, the work does not survive. However, it is clear that, like others, Eliot made 'a great deal of spiritual, as well as intellectual, progress' (Webster, 33) in this environment. Hooker's nonconformist theology and pious life influenced Eliot's self-admitted 'dead soul' profoundly, causing him to see 'as never before the power of godliness in its lovely vigor and efficacy' (Mather 3.47). He also experienced, as he later recalled, the life of the 'voluntary community' in the surrounding parishes to whom Hooker was pastor. These pious Christians not only met privately together but also 'held publicke parochial communion so far as avoided offence, and interested themselves in all good meanes for the publicke good of the parish' (Webster, 155). However, this was not permitted to last. Hooker's flight to the Netherlands in July 1630 to avoid prosecution by the bishop of London, William Laud, closed the school and ended Eliot's employment, confirmed the bleak future that awaited dissenting clergy, and ultimately convinced him to join the puritan migration to New England.

After a ten-week voyage, on 3 November 1631 Eliot and his twenty-three barrels of books arrived in Boston aboard the *Lyon* with John Winthrop's wife and children. He was anxious to 'enjoy the holy worship of God, … according to the Word of God, without … human additions and novelties' (Cogley, 45) and immediately became the temporary pastor of the First Church at Boston while the regular minister was in England. Eliot declined the permanent position of teaching elder there, in order to become in November 1632 the 'teacher' (assistant pastor) under Thomas Weld at the new Roxbury settlement some 2 miles away. The previous month he had married Hanna Mumford (Mountford, Mountfort; d. 1687), a native of Essex and a member of the congregation at Roxbury, which also included several of Eliot's siblings and friends from Nazing. During a marriage lasting fifty-five years the couple had six children—a daughter and five sons—only two of whom outlived their parents.

Both his early arrival in the Massachusetts Bay Colony (only eighteen months after its founding) and his very long life assured Eliot a major role in many seminal events. After publicly challenging colony officials in October 1634 for negotiating an Indian treaty 'without the consent of the people' (Cogley, 48), he quickly recanted and thereafter became a bastion of conservative orthodoxy—even finding biblical condemnations of long hair for men. In 1636 he prepared a written justification for the official banishment of Roger Williams and the following year intensively interrogated the 'wayward' Anne Hutchinson before the general court. In 1640 he co-authored, with Richard Mather and Thomas Weld, the famous, metrical *Bay-Psalm Book*—the first book printed in New England. Five years later Eliot opened the Roxbury Latin School, only the second such academy in English America (after Boston's), and he later founded and funded a similar institution (now the Eliot School) in Jamaica Plain. This latter academy was notable for educating English, Indian, and African students together. In 1659 Eliot was accorded the honour of preaching the annual election sermon in Boston. He was a supporter of the half-way covenant in the 1660s and served as co-moderator of the 1679 'reform synod'.

Despite his participation in a broad range of important activities, Eliot is particularly notable for his forty years of missionary work as the 'Apostle to the Indians' of eastern Massachusetts, which included a prolific output as an author and translator of Christian texts in the Massachusett Algonquian language. Eliot was neither the first nor the only puritan missionary serving the Indians of seventeenth-century New England, and others, most notably Roger Williams, pre-dated his interest in the native Algonquian dialects. Eliot's commitment to proselytizing Indians evolved rather slowly, fifteen years after moving to Massachusetts, and his mission activities never replaced his regular clerical duties for the English congregation at Roxbury. Although the puritans of New England experienced greater missionary success among the Indians than any other seventeenth-century English colonists, they never attained the massive numbers of native converts claimed by Spanish and French Catholics, and even the ministers of New England were often ambivalent or divided about the efficacy of such a theological enterprise.

Eliot's missionary outreach was precipitated by the after-effects of the atrocity-ridden Pequot War of 1636–7

and eventually greatly curtailed by the ravages of King Philip's War in 1675–6. The Pequot War was very damaging to Indian hegemony and depleted several tribal territories, causing some native leaders in the mid-1640s to put their people under the protection of the militarily dominant English. The availability of compliant Indians for proselytizing, at a time when colony-building and military campaigning became less demanding, fortuitously coincided with growing pressure from powerful puritans in England that their co-religionists in Massachusetts should begin their promised but long-delayed conversion efforts. Spurred into action by transatlantic political concerns and their spiritual reputations, officials in Boston encouraged ministers to reach out to local Indians and begin instructing them in Christian fundamentals.

It seems that Eliot was the first to respond, commencing his missionary teachings in September 1646 with a lecture to assembled Massachusett Indians at Neponset, only 4 miles from his home church at Roxbury. Eliot was disconsolate over the audience's negative response, but his 75-minute sermon on 28 October to a completely different group of Massachusett Indians at Nonantum was considered a triumph—being commemorated as the true beginning of his missionary endeavours. Most biographers have assumed that Eliot had studied the Massachusett language as early as 1643, but contemporaries revealed that he did not commence instruction until after the revelatory events at Nonantum in 1646. His first two sermons were delivered in English and were interpreted by an Indian already proficient in speaking and reading English. Moreover, Eliot's selection by colony officials on 4 November 1646 to expand his missionary work provided the first real incentive to divert time from parish duties at Roxbury for the intensive study of a complex and strange language considered more difficult to master than Hebrew, Greek, or Latin.

Eliot's eventual proficiency in the Massachusett dialect of coastal Algonquian—both spoken and written—was the central factor in his unique style of proselytizing, for his converts were expected to become literate readers of Christian texts that he translated into their native language. Eliot's 'Indian Library' of tracts and huge volumes in Massachusett ultimately included twenty separate titles and thousands of copies, all printed in the colony between 1654 and 1688. According to one contemporary, the Indians 'love any man that can utter his mind in their words' (W. Wood, *New England's Prospect*, ed. A. T. Vaughan, 1977, 110n), and Eliot's extraordinary productivity in preparing sermons and publishing sacred texts that Indians could understand was unprecedented and never duplicated. In 1654 he published his first work in Massachusett, a catechism called *The Indian Primer*. In addition to voluminous English publications, including progress reports on missions and *Indian Dialogues* (1671), Eliot's translations published in Cambridge, Massachusetts, included the book of Genesis, metrical Psalms, a confession of faith, a New Testament (1661), and the complete 'Massachusett' Bible (1663) (the first Bible of any kind printed in North

America), versions of Richard Baxter's *A Call to the Unconverted* and Lewis Bayly's *The Practice of Pietie*, a grammar, a primer for young people, and works on prayer and dying well.

For Eliot, Indian conversion required a long process of hearing, reading, and truly comprehending the word of God, often in two languages, and like most puritans he eschewed the Catholic missionary focus on rituals and sacraments, especially baptism. Eliot also urged potential converts to live together in special 'praying towns', which provided an adequate land base for sustenance (encouraging agriculture over hunting); removed them from the influence of 'heathen' traditionalists as well as hostile whites; and made it easier to achieve 'civility'—English standards of behaviour, personal grooming, and attire, and literacy that needed to accompany religious instruction for a complete cultural, as well as religious, conversion. Eliot established the first praying town in 1650–51 at Natick, directly west of Roxbury, where several hundred Indians lived on 6000 acres, complete with framed houses, combined school and church building, and abundant fields that yielded surplus crops for profit. Thirteen other convert towns were established, all within a 25 mile radius of Boston, and at their high-water mark in 1674 Eliot could claim some 1100 praying Indians in residence, with more emphasis on the quality of converts than on the quantity. Some Indians in these enclaves never converted and none ever became fully assimilated into puritan society, but at least twenty-four praying Indians became ordained ministers and many more served as teachers in the towns' schools. That any Indians were willing and able to meet Eliot's stringent acculturative standards testifies to his powers of persuasion, but it also reflects the desperate need of some Indians to embrace Christian ministers in order to change their world view, lifestyles, and sense of identity once their traditional existence had been devastated by settlers, soldiers, and traders.

Eliot's mission programme was blessed with longevity, sincerity, and generous funding by the philanthropic Corporation for the Promoting and Propagating the Gospel among the Indians of New England, but in the end even it could not survive the divisive prejudices and cultural differences associated with King Philip's War. Although many praying Indians helped the English defeat Metacom and his Wampanoag alliance, the Natick community was removed to Deer Island in Boston harbour and endured harsh treatment during the winter of 1675–6. By underscoring the depth of the puritans' racial bias against even Christian Indians, King Philip's War signalled the end of support for Eliot's conversion efforts from colonists as well as potential converts.

In 1647 Eliot had predicted that 'in forty years more, some Indians would be all one English, and in a hundred years, all Indians here about, would be so' (Cogley, 49–50). That prediction was never realized, despite his superhuman efforts to make it so. At his death on 20 May 1690, three years after that of his wife, this dedicated apostle was fondly praised by the poorest Indians and the most powerful officials alike. Many remembered that in Eliot's case, affection was always a significant measure of success. He was buried at Roxbury.

Posthumous assessments of Eliot have revealed a broad spectrum of opinion about the man and his missionary activities, more recently dependent in particular on one's view of missionary motives in altering any native beliefs and lifestyles. The *Dictionary of National Biography* article on Eliot praised him without qualification: 'No name in the early history of New England is more revered than his. Eliot was truly of a saintly type, without fanaticism, spiritual pride, or ambition' (*DNB*). The source cited as the 'best and most complete life' at that time was Convers Francis, *Life of John Eliot, the Apostle to the Indians* (1854) which assessed him in even more hagiographic terms:

> The name of the Apostle to the Indians must always stand in distinguished brightness on that roll of the servants of the Most High, whom New England delights, and ever will delight, to honor in the records of her moral history. (Francis, 343)

A century later came the more measured conclusion that 'No man in early New England was so universally appreciated and loved', although he was intellectually undistinguished and sometimes stubborn. His 'devoted following' sprang above all 'from a single-hearted dedication to duty and service, coupled with a becoming modesty and sweetness' (A. Vaughan, *New England Frontier: Puritans and Indians, 1620–1675*, Boston, 1965, 246).

However, from the mid-1970s a succession of studies of colonial North America criticized Eliot and all puritans for the underlying racism and prejudicial Anglocentric superiority of their religious piety. He and other ministers stand accused of using missionary efforts to complete the work of military conquests and territorial dispossession, by extinguishing Indian cultural beliefs, undermining native hegemony, encouraging divisiveness between Indian Christians and traditionalists, segregating Indian converts from white people in 'praying towns' that were akin to reservations or concentration camps, and promoting acculturation while forever denying true and total cultural assimilation as equals in a biracial society. Most recently Eliot's reputation has been refurbished by closer investigation of the spiritual motivations and theological beliefs prevailing in his own lifetime, by a balanced assessment of his successes and his failures, and by separating the specific details about the man and his mission from the general anti-puritan ideology in so-called 'pro-Indian' histories. J. FREDERICK FAUSZ

Sources Venn, *Alum. Cant.* • R. W. Cogley, *John Eliot's mission to the Indians before King Philip's War* (Cambridge MA, 1999) • J. T. Copplestone, *John Eliot and the Indans, 1604–1690* (Boston MA, 1998) • E. Winslow, *John Eliot, 'Apostle to the Indians'* (Boston MA, 1968) • N. H. Salisbury, 'Red puritans: the 'praying Indians' of Massachusetts Bay and John Eliot', *William and Mary Quarterly*, 31 (1974) • J. T. Thorowgood, *Jews in America* (1660), 24 • C. Mather, *Magnalia Christi Americana*, 7 bks in 1 vol. (1702), book 3, 210 and *passim* • T. Webster, *Godly clergy in early Stuart England: the Caroline puritan movement, c.1620–1643* (1997) • C. Francis, *Life of John Eliot, the Apostle to the Indians* (NY, 1854) • J. Le Pore, *The name of war: King Philip's War and the origins of American identity* (New York, 1999), esp. 27–43 and chap. 2 • H. W.

Bowden, *American Indians and Christian missions* (Chicago, 1981), 96–133 · *DNB*
Archives DWL, corresp. with Richard Baxter · GL, letters to New England Co. · RS, letters to Robert Boyle
Likenesses oils, Museum of Fine Arts, Boston

Eliot, Sir John, baronet (1736–1786), physician, was born in Edinburgh, the only son of Thomas Eliot, agent and solicitor to Frederick, prince of Wales, and his wife, Mary, *née* Davidson. After being educated in Edinburgh, France, and the Netherlands, he was apprenticed to a surgeon in London. He later sailed as surgeon's mate, and subsequently surgeon, to a successful privateer, the prize money from which enabled him to set up in practice in London. He graduated MD at the University of St Andrews in 1759 and became a licentiate of the Royal College of Physicians in 1762. A friend and fellow Scot, Sir William Duncan, a fashionable doctor in London and physician to George III, introduced Eliot to many of his patients and on moving abroad transferred all his practice to him. On 19 October 1771 Eliot married Grace (1754?–1823) [*see* Eliot, Grace], daughter of Hew Dalrymple (*d.* 1774), attorney-general of Grenada. He divorced her in 1774, obtaining £12,000 damages, after she eloped with Viscount Valentia.

As a physician Eliot was very successful and his personal friends included many influential, artistic, and literary people of the day. He was knighted in 1776 and was appointed physician to the prince of Wales, who later took Eliot's former wife as a mistress. Despite being disliked by George III, he was created a baronet in 1778 at the request of Lord George Germain. It is recorded that to the request for the baronetcy for Eliot, the king replied, 'But if I do he shall not be my physician', to which Germain answered, 'No sire, he shall be your Majesty's baronet and my physician' (Munk, *Roll*). Eliot died from the rupture of a major blood-vessel on 7 November 1786, while on a visit to his friend Lord Melbourne at Brocket Hall, Hertfordshire, and was buried in the parish church of Bishop's Hatfield where a tablet, with lines by Edward Jerningham, was erected to his memory. Although he had no legitimate children, he had an illegitimate son and several daughters, one of whom was Elizabeth *Ogborne, who was born from his liaison with Jane Jackson.

Sir John Eliot must be distinguished from John Elliot MD (1747–1787), with whom he has frequently been confused; the latter's publications have often been attributed to Sir John Eliot, who, as far as it is known, did not publish anything. CAROLINE OVERY

Sources R. W. I. Smith, 'Sir John Eliot ... of Peebles and some of his friends', *Edinburgh Medical Journal*, 3rd ser., 40 (1933), 237–42 · J. R. Partington and D. McKie, 'Sir John Eliot, bart (1736–86), and John Elliot (1747–87)', *Annals of Science*, 6 (1948–50), 262–7 · Munk, *Roll* · *N&Q*, 3rd ser., 10 (1866), 161–2 · W. Anderson, *The Scottish nation*, 2 (1877), 136 · will, Edinburgh · will, Principal Registry of the Family Division, London
Likenesses miniature, priv. coll.
Wealth at death see will, Edinburgh; will, Principal Registry of the Family Division, London

Eliot [*formerly* Elliott], **Sir John** (1839–1908), meteorologist, was born on 25 May 1839 at Lamesley, co. Durham,

the son of Peter Elliott, a schoolmaster, and his wife, Margaret. Details of his early career are missing, but he matriculated at St John's College, Cambridge, in 1865, and graduated BA in 1869 as second wrangler and first Smith's prizeman; he was elected a fellow of his college the same year. At some time after his graduation he changed the spelling of his surname to Eliot.

His health was not robust and being advised to avoid the English climate he accepted, later in 1869, an appointment in the Indian government service as professor of mathematics at Roorkie Engineering College, in the North-Western Provinces. In 1872 he was transferred to the regular Indian educational service as professor of mathematics at the Muir Central College, Allahabad, combining the office with that of superintendent of the meteorological observatory. Two years later he moved to Calcutta as professor of physical science in the Presidency College and meteorological reporter to the government of Bengal, holding both posts for twelve years. In 1877 he married Mary, the daughter of William Nevill FGS of Godalming, Surrey; they had three sons.

In 1886 Eliot succeeded Henry Francis Blanford as meteorological reporter to the government of India and, in addition, was appointed director-general of Indian observatories in 1899. Eliot completed the organization of meteorological work which Blanford began. The number of observatories working with his department increased from 135 to 240 (including two at an elevation of over 11,000 feet) and the co-operation of the larger princely states was secured. Under Eliot's superintendence the diffusion of weather information was extended by the issue of frequent reports at various centres; methods of giving warnings of storms at sea were developed, and telegraphic intimations of impending floods to engineers on large construction works, or in charge of railway canals and bridges, were initiated, saving the state from heavy losses. Vast improvement was also effected in the mode of announcing drought warnings and the consequent danger of famine.

Eliot was elected FRS in 1895 and was made CIE in 1897. His last official step in India was to secure for his successor the increase of scientific staff of which he had himself felt the need. He retired from India in 1903 and was created KCIE. On his return to England he actively pursued his meteorological work and joined the committee of management of the solar physics observatory at South Kensington, London, under the Board of Education. He was a member of the international meteorological committee from 1896 until his death and was secretary of the solar commission that was set up following a suggestion by Sir Norman Lockyer to that committee in 1903. The purpose of the commission was to collect meteorological and solar data from all parts of the world for the purposes of comparison. Eliot also served on the Royal Society observatories committee until shortly before his death. At the British Association meeting at Cambridge in 1904 he presided over the subsection for astronomy and cosmical physics, and advocated the organization of meteorological work on an imperial basis, with provision for organized observations from areas too wide to be within the control of any single government. An accomplished musician, he played well on both the organ and the piano.

Eliot died suddenly of apoplexy on 18 March 1908 at Bon Porteau, Cavalaire, Var, in the south of France, the estate which he had acquired on account of his wife's health; he was buried within his own estate. He was survived by his wife. Eliot's contributions to meteorological science are chiefly to be found in the long and important series of Indian meteorological memoirs published by his department. Of special value is a short paper on Indian famines contributed to the congress of meteorologists at Chicago in 1893.   W. N. SHAW, *rev.* JIM BURTON

Sources *Nature*, 77 (1907–8), 490–92 · *The Times* (20 March 1908), 13 · *WW* (1906) · *WWW, 1897–1915* · RS · Meteorological Office, Bracknell, Berkshire · d. cert.
Archives Meteorological Office, Bracknell, Berkshire, corresp. · RS, corresp.
Wealth at death £12,462 9s. 4d.: probate, 25 June 1908, *CGPLA Eng. & Wales*

Eliot, Thomas Stearns (1888–1965), poet, critic, and publisher, was born on 26 September 1888 at 2635 Locust Street, St Louis, Missouri, USA, the youngest of the seven children of Henry Ware Eliot (1843–1919) and Charlotte Champe Stearns (1843–1929), into an American family that took pains to impress on him the importance of its history and achievement.

American family background Eliot's paternal grandfather, William Greenleaf Eliot (1811–1887), distantly related to illustrious figures in American life from John Adams to John Greenleaf Whittier, Nathaniel Hawthorne, and Herman Melville, was born in New England in New Bedford, Massachusetts, but moved early to the southern cities of Baltimore and Washington, DC, only to return to the Harvard divinity school as a protégé of William Ellery Channing, the doyen of American Unitarianism. After William Eliot was ordained as a Unitarian minister, a sense of duty carried him toward the frontier. He founded the Unitarian Church of the Messiah in St Louis and soon became a pillar of the south-western city's religious and civic life. He helped found the Academy of Science and Washington University (where he taught metaphysics and, after retiring from his ministry, served as chancellor), and established the Smith Academy for boys and the Mary Institute for girls. Because of William's ties to these schools the family chose to remain during T. S. Eliot's boyhood in their city house on Locust Street, long after the area ran down and their peers moved to suburbs.

William Greenleaf Eliot dearly wanted his son to enter the clergy, but Henry Ware Eliot resisted. In 1865 (after William had alienated a substantial part of his congregation by his unionist loyalties), Henry arranged for a commission as a lieutenant in the Union army, but the civil war ended before his commission arrived. He thereafter made a life in business, starting in wholesale grocery, and going bankrupt manufacturing acetic acid. By the time Thomas Eliot was born, however, he had become the prosperous president of the Hydraulic-Press Brick Company.

Thomas Stearns Eliot (1888–1965), by Sir Cecil Beaton, 1956

Charlotte Champe Stearns was also descended from a distinguished New England family; she was a distant cousin of the poet Oliver Wendell Holmes. By profession a teacher (in Henry's bankruptcy her salary kept the family going), she was also an energetic social work volunteer at the Humanity Club of St Louis, and an amateur poet with a taste for Ralph Waldo Emerson. She augmented her husband's sense of duty and industry with a humanitarianism that T. S. Eliot resisted all his life.

Early life and education T. S. Eliot, by far the youngest child, was born when his parents were financially secure in their mid-forties and his siblings were half-grown. Afflicted with a congenital double hernia, he was under the constant eye of his mother, his older sisters, or his Irish nurse, Annie Dunne (who sometimes took him with her to Catholic mass). In St Louis Eliot experienced both the city's muddy streets and its exclusive drawing-rooms. He attended Smith Academy until he was sixteen. In the year before he graduated he visited the 1904 St Louis World's Fair and was so taken with the fair's native villages that he wrote short stories about primitive life for the Smith Academy *Record*. In 1905 he left St Louis for a year at Milton Academy outside Boston before following his older brother Henry to Harvard University.

Eliot's attending Harvard seems to have been a foregone conclusion. His father and mother, jealously guarding their connection to New England's Unitarian establishment, brought the family back to the north shore of Boston every summer, and in 1896 built a substantial house at Eastern Point in Gloucester, Massachusetts. As a boy Eliot foraged for crabs and became an accomplished sailor, in the warm months trading the Mississippi for the rocky shoals of Cape Ann. But his seasonal migrations denied him regional identity and reinforced the family's sense of social alienation in St Louis. Looking back in 1928, he told Herbert Read that he had always wanted to write an essay about the point of view of an American who wasn't an American, because he was born in the South and went to school in New England as a small boy with a nigger drawl, but who wasn't a southerner in the South because his people were northerners in a border state and looked down on all southerners and Virginians, and who so was never anything anywhere and who therefore felt himself to be more a Frenchman than an American and more an Englishman than a Frenchman and yet felt that the U. S. A. up to a hundred years ago was a family extension. (Tate, 15)

Harvard and Paris Beginning at Harvard in autumn 1906, however, Eliot impressed many classmates with his social ease. Like his brother Henry before him, Eliot spent his freshman year in a fashionable private dormitory in a posh neighbourhood around Mt Auburn Street known as the Gold Coast. He joined a number of clubs, including the literary Signet, and he began a romantic attachment to Emily Hale, a refined Bostonian, who once played Mrs Elton opposite his Mr Woodhouse in an amateur production of *Emma*. Among his teachers Eliot was drawn to the forceful moralizing of the comparativist Irving Babbitt and the stylish scepticism of the philosopher-cum-literary critic George Santayana, both of whom reinforced his distaste for the reform-minded, progressive university shaped by its then president, Eliot's cousin Charles William Eliot. His attitudes, however, did not prevent him from taking advantage of the newly expansive and elective system of course offerings that President Eliot had introduced. As a freshman, Thomas Eliot's courses were so eclectic that he wound up on academic probation. He recovered and persisted, attaining a BA, in an elective programme best described as comparative literature, in three years, and an MA in English literature in the fourth.

In December 1908 a book Eliot found in the Harvard Union library changed his life. Arthur Symons's *The Symbolist Movement in Literature* introduced him to the poetry of Jules Laforgue, and Laforgue's combination of ironic elegance and psychological nuance effected what he described as a communion with the dead, convincing him that he was a poet and giving him a voice. By 1909–10 his vocation had been confirmed: he joined the board and was briefly secretary of Harvard's literary magazine, the *Harvard Advocate*, and he could recommend to his classmate William Tinckom-Fernandez the last word in French sophistication—the *vers libre* of Paul Fort and Francis Jammes. (Tinckom-Fernandez returned the favour by introducing Eliot to Francis Thompson's 'The Hound of Heaven' and John Davidson's 'Thirty Bob a Week', and these poems stayed with Eliot for the rest of his life.) On the *Advocate* Eliot started a lifelong friendship with Conrad Aiken, who remembered him as a 'dapper young man with a somewhat Lamian smile' and not a little 'waspishness' (Tambimuttu and March, 21).

In May 1910 a suspected case of scarlet fever almost prevented Eliot's graduation. By autumn, though, he was well enough to undertake a postgraduate year at the Sorbonne, Paris, where he felt alive for the first time. Lyndall Gordon notes that his handwriting even changed its shape (Gordon, *Early Years*, 38). He lived at 151bis rue St Jacques, and struck up a warm friendship with a fellow lodger, Jean

Verdenal, the medical student who later died in the Dardanelles, and to whom Eliot dedicated 'The Love Song of J. Alfred Prufrock'. With Verdenal he entered the intellectual life of France, then swirling, Eliot later recalled, around the figures of Émile Durkheim, Paul Janet, Rémy de Gourmont, Pablo Picasso, and Henri Bergson. Eliot attended Bergson's lectures at the Collège de France and was temporarily converted to Bergson's doctrine of the progressive evolution of consciousness. Characteristic of a lifetime of conflicting attitudes, Eliot also gravitated toward the politically conservative (indeed monarchistic), neo-classical, and Catholic writing of Charles Maurras. Warring opposites, these enthusiasms somehow worked together to foster a professional interest in philosophy, and propelled Eliot back to a doctoral programme at Harvard in the next year.

Early poetry In 1910 and 1911 Eliot copied into a leather notebook he entitled 'Inventions of the March Hare' the poems that were to establish his reputation: 'The Love Song of J. Alfred Prufrock', 'Portrait of a Lady', 'Preludes', and 'Rhapsody on a Windy Night'. Combining some of the robustness of Robert Browning's monologues with the incantatory elegance of symbolist verse, and compacting Laforgue's poetry of alienation with the moral earnestness of what Eliot called 'the Boston doubt', these poems explore the subtleties of the unconscious with a social wit. Above all they express Henry James's lament that Americans living within the confines of their gentility and idealism never seem to live at all. What universalizes the upper-class angst of Eliot's early poems is his ability to translate social claustrophobia into images of life and death, vitality and asphyxiation, and most interestingly into a verbal struggle for existence between fleeting moments of authentic expression and a near-universal and suffocating rhetoric. Their combined effect was unique and compelling, and their assurance staggered contemporaries privileged to read them in manuscript. Conrad Aiken marvelled at 'how sharp and complete and *sui generis* the whole thing was, from the outset. The *wholeness* is there, from the very beginning' (*Harvard Advocate*, 17).

Eliot's legacy from French and British aestheticism, however, exceeded the assurance that Aiken noted and included other interests and material to which he was unable to give form in 1910–11 but which conditioned some of the poetic and intellectual preoccupations of the next part of his life. Among these was a fascination with insanity and unmoored perspective like that in a suppressed section of 'Prufrock' called 'Prufrock's pervigilium'.

Philosophy In autumn 1911 Eliot returned from France, and as part of his graduate studies in philosophy at Harvard began to examine border states of consciousness of many kinds, from insanity in Janet's studies of hysteria to the 'primitive mind' as it had been adumbrated by Durkheim and Lucien Lévy-Bruhl, to the literature of mystic vision, both Western and Eastern. (He took almost as many courses in Sanskrit and Hindu thought as he did in Western philosophy.)

Working in a faculty that included Santayana, William James, the visiting Bertrand Russell, and Josiah Royce, Eliot eventually undertook a dissertation on Bergson's neo-idealist critic F. H. Bradley and produced a searching philosophical critique of consciousness. Acute, especially about how interpretation constitutes and constructs mental objects and discourses, Eliot's philosophical work strongly criticized the platitudes of the nascent subjects of psychology and the social sciences. Using Bradley's scepticism to question vast areas of the contemporary intellectual landscape, he finally turned it even against its source, attacking especially Bradley's suggestion that it would be possible to posit a synthesis or harmony of momentary perspectives.

Poetry, 1914–1922 It is hardly surprising, therefore, that much of Eliot's poetry from the years of his postgraduate education, and just after, has to do with madness and disconnection. In a letter to Conrad Aiken dated 25 July 1914, for example, he speaks of a long fragmentary work ('the "Descent from the Cross" or whatever I may call it') he had sent in part to Aiken that was to include, beside a 'Love song of St Sebastian', an 'Insane Section, and another love song (of a happier sort) and a recurring piece quite in the French style … Then a mystical section, and a Fool-House section' (*Letters*, 1.44). But Eliot was 'disappointed' in the verses. The stuff, he wrote to Aiken in November 1914, seemed to him 'strained and intellectual'. 'I know', he said, 'the kind of verse I want, and I know that this isn't it, and I know why' (ibid., 1.69).

'The Descent from the Cross', with its associated poems, represents an early staging of Eliot's great poems of the 1920s, also mock-serious religious quests. For Eliot and for modern poetry the important advance to be achieved lay not in the choice of his subject but in its treatment: with outrageous parody Eliot transfigured personal suffering by way of camp juxtapositions between material of wildly different tonalities. He possessed neither the private basis nor the poetic control to effect such accomplishment for another half-decade. Meanwhile he conducted formal experiments that included prose poems written in French and quatrains modelled after French satirists from Théophile Gautier to Tristan Corbière, and produced a group of acerbic and yet mercurial poems that include 'Sweeney among the Nightingales' and 'Burbank with a Baedeker: Bleistein with a Cigar' (both 1918).

Germany, Oxford, and London By 1914, when Eliot left on a travelling fellowship to Europe, he had persuaded a number of Harvard's philosophers to regard him as a potential colleague. However, his willingness to turn radical scepticism against the high-minded humanitarianism of his colleagues alienated the department and would have cost him a position in it had he wanted one. Eliot spent the early summer of 1914 at a seminar in Marburg, Germany, with plans to study in the autumn at Merton College, Oxford, with Harold Joachim, F. H. Bradley's colleague and successor. The outbreak of war speeded his departure.

Pending his September matriculation in Oxford—when he arrived he found its climate 'dreadful' and its culture 'not intellectually stimulating'—he spent August in London with Conrad Aiken. By September Aiken had shown Eliot's manuscript poems to Ezra Pound, who became, with Wallace Stevens, Eliot's only peer among his contemporaries. Pound, not easily impressed, was won over. Pound called on Eliot in late September and wrote to Harriet Monroe at *Poetry* magazine that Eliot had 'actually trained himself *and* modernized himself *on his own*' (Pound, 40). The two initiated a collaboration that changed Anglo-American poetry, but not before Eliot had put down deep English roots.

In early spring 1915 Eliot's old Milton Academy and Harvard friend Scofield Thayer, later editor of *The Dial* and then also at Oxford, introduced Eliot to Vivienne (known as Vivien) Haigh-Wood (1888–1947) [*see* Eliot, Vivienne Haigh], a friend of Thayer's sister. Eliot was drawn instantly to Vivien's exceptional frankness and charmed by what he saw as her family's Hampstead sophistication. Abandoning twenty-five years of social tentativeness, he married Vivien on 26 June 1915, on impulse at the Hampstead register office. His parents were shocked, and then, when they learned of Vivien's history of emotional and physical problems (and her associated history of taking opiates), profoundly disturbed. The marriage nearly caused a family break, but it also indelibly marked the beginning of Eliot's English life. Indeed, Eliot wrote that 'I believe that I came to persuade myself that I was in love with her simply because I wanted to burn my boats and commit myself to staying in England' (*Letters*, 1.xvii). Vivien refused to cross the Atlantic in wartime, and Eliot took his place in literary London. Bertrand Russell offered Eliot and Vivien both his London flat and his considerable social resources. Russell and Vivien, however, became briefly involved and the arrangement soured.

Meanwhile Eliot tried desperately to support himself by first teaching in schools in High Wycombe and Highgate, London, and then by a heavy load of reviewing and, through the University of London extension board, extension lecturing. To placate his worried parents he laboured on with his doctoral thesis, 'Experience and the objects of knowledge in the philosophy of F. H. Bradley'. (Eliot finished it in April 1916, but did not receive his degree because he was reluctant to undertake the trip to Massachusetts required for a thesis defence.) As yet one more stimulating but taxing activity, he became literary editor of the avant-garde magazine *The Egoist*. Then in spring 1917 he found steady employment; his languages qualified him for a job in the foreign section of Lloyds Bank at 17 Cornhill in the City of London, where his work consisted of evaluating a broad range of continental documents. The job gave him the security he needed to turn back to poetry, and in 1917 he received an enormous boost from the publication of his first book, *Prufrock and other Observations*, printed by *The Egoist* with the silent financial support of Ezra and Dorothy Pound.

For a struggling young American Eliot soon acquired extraordinary access into British intellectual life. With

Russell's help he was invited to country-house weekends where visitors ranged from political figures like H. H. Asquith to a constellation of Bloomsbury writers, artists, and philosophers. At the same time Pound facilitated his entry into the international avant-garde, where Eliot mixed with the ageing poet William Butler Yeats and the painter and novelist Wyndham Lewis. More accomplished than Pound in the manners of the drawing-room, Eliot gained a reputation as an observer who could shrewdly judge both accepted and experimental art from a platform of apparently enormous learning. It did not hurt that he calculated his interventions carefully, publishing only what was of first quality and creating around himself an aura of mystery. In 1920 he collected a second slim volume of verse (*Poems*) and a volume of criticism (*The Sacred Wood*). Both displayed a winning combination of erudition and bravura, and both built upon the understated discipline of a decade of philosophical seriousness.

The success of Eliot's essays in *The Sacred Wood* and afterwards helped to change the critical sensibilities of Britain and America. Shifting the focus of criticism from the author to the work and altering the centre of gravity of previous English writing from the Romantics to the Elizabethan dramatists and the metaphysical poets, Eliot reshaped the study of literature in and out of the academy. For almost fifty years it was nearly impossible to write about literature without acknowledging his work, one effect of which was that famous phrases of his critical shorthand ('the dissociation of sensibility' in English writing after the seventeenth century, and Shakespeare's failure to find an 'objective correlative' for the 'particular emotion' in *Hamlet*, and so on) were greatly overappreciated. Looking back in his last major essay, 'To criticize the critic' (1961) (a title also used for his last collection of criticism, 1965), Eliot acknowledged that he was 'unable to defend' these phrases 'with any forensic plausibility' (Eliot, *To Criticize the Critic*, 19). Indeed, he added, there were some statements 'the meaning of which I no longer understand' (ibid., 14), as they all had been principally a part of a programme of 'implicitly defending the sort of poetry that I and my friends wrote' (ibid., 16). Nevertheless the revolution effected by Eliot's criticism and his verse was real, part of one of those 'sudden mutation[s] of form and content in literature' that, Eliot observed in 'American literature and the American language', renders 'writing which has been practised for a generation or more' out of date, no longer able 'to respond to contemporary modes of thought, feeling, and speech' (ibid., 57). The revolutionary change that Eliot here remembers seems to have occurred to him about 1919, while he was proof-reading *The Egoist*'s serial publication of James Joyce's *Ulysses* and, with Ezra Pound's urging, starting to think of himself as part of an international movement in experimental art and literature.

The Waste Land The circumstances of Eliot's own poetic breakthrough turned out to be as private as they were professional. Eliot's father died in January 1919, producing a paroxysm of guilt in the son who had hoped he would have time to heal the bad feelings caused by his marriage and emigration. At the same time Vivien's emotional and physical health deteriorated, and the financial and emotional strain of her condition took its toll. After an extended visit in summer 1921 from his mother and sister Marian, Eliot suffered a nervous collapse and on his physician's advice took a three months' rest cure, first at the seaside in Margate and then at a sanatorium at Lausanne recommended by Bertrand Russell's friend Ottoline Morrell.

Whether because of the breakdown or the long-needed rest it imposed, Eliot broke through the limitations he had felt since 1911 and completed the long poem that he had envisioned in 1914 and had begun in earnest in 1919. Assembled out of dramatic vignettes based on Eliot's London life, *The Waste Land*'s extraordinary intensity stems from a sudden fusing of diverse materials into a rhythmic whole of great skill and daring. Though from the 1930s onwards it was forced into the mould of an academic set piece of the order of Milton's *Lycidas*, *The Waste Land* was at first perceived as an iconoclastic and provocative work of jazz-like syncopation. In a contemporary review his friend Conrad Aiken insisted that Eliot's allusive verse was important primarily for its private 'emotional value' (Tate, 200) and described the whole as 'a powerful, melancholy tone-poem' (ibid., 202).

Despite Aiken's description the literary avant-garde of post-war Britain and America took over *The Waste Land* as a programmatic rallying cry for a generation denied heroes and beliefs. Pound, who helped pare and sharpen the poem when Eliot stopped in Paris on his way to and from Lausanne, praised it, with a godparent's fervour, as a statement of the modern age. His promotion of the poem was helped immeasurably by the long-heralded publication of *Ulysses* in 1922, and by the fact that Eliot soon linked himself with Joyce and Einstein in an essay entitled '*Ulysses*, order and myth' (1923). Meteorically Eliot, Joyce, and to a lesser extent Pound were joined in a single glow—each nearly as notorious as Picasso.

Editor The masterstroke of Eliot's self-conscious attempt to put himself on the literary map was to capitalize on the international success of *The Waste Land* by means of an equally ambitious (and equally internationalist) publication of a different kind. With Jacques Rivière's *Nouvelle Revue Française* in mind, in 1922 Eliot jumped at an offer from Lady Rothermere, wife of Esmond Harmsworth, second Viscount Rothermere, publisher of the *Daily Mail*, to edit a high-profile literary journal. The first number of *The Criterion* appeared in October 1922. Like *The Waste Land*, which *The Criterion* first published, it took the whole of European culture in its sights. *The Criterion*'s editorial voice placed Eliot at the centre of first the London and then the continental literary scene.

In 1925 a lucky chance enabled Eliot to escape from his job at the bank. Geoffrey Faber, of the new publishing firm of Faber and Gwyer (later Faber and Faber), saw the advantages of Eliot's dual expertise in business and letters and recruited him as Faber's literary editor and a member of the board of directors. The arrangement was famously successful. The firm reaped the rewards of Eliot's success in cultivating and promoting younger writers (from W. H. Auden to, later, Ted Hughes), and defining the next forty years of British poetry in reference to the 'Faber poets'. For Eliot his publishing job offered a stability he found in neither marriage nor poetic composition. The firm became his support and his family, and when *The Criterion* was in financial difficulties, took over its accounts. Editing permitted Eliot to engage his wide-ranging intellectual curiosity, and his circle of colleagues (which included most prominently Herbert Read, F. S. Flint, Harold Monro, Frank Morley, Bonamy Dobrée, and Montgomery Belgion) had its parallel in various other discussion circles to which Eliot subscribed, most notably from 1937 the Moot, whose members included Karl Mannheim. But the editorial life on Russell Square was also conducted over friendly dinners that served the function of a college or a club, and Eliot seemed to thrive on such occasions, supplementing them in the 1930s with gatherings at the home of a younger friend, John Hayward, in which Geoffrey Faber, Hayward, Frank Morley, and Eliot composed mock verses under the nicknames Coot, Tarantula, Whale, and Elephant respectively.

Conversion and British citizenship At about the same time as he joined Faber and Gwyer, Eliot reached out for religious support. Having long found his family's Unitarianism unsatisfying, he turned to the Church of England. The seeds of his future faith might have already been obvious in *The Hollow Men*—concerned, as Eliot said in 'Dante' (1929) with 'the salvation of the soul' rather than for human beings 'as "personalities"' (Eliot, *Selected Essays*, 233). But Eliot's poem was read as a sequel to *The Waste Land*'s philosophical despair when it first appeared in *Poems, 1909–1925* (1925). Few followers were prepared for Eliot's baptism into the Church of England on 29 June 1927 at Finstock, Oxfordshire, and so, within five years of his avant-garde success, Eliot provoked a second storm. The furore grew in November 1927 when Eliot took British citizenship and again in 1928 when he collected a group of politically conservative essays under the title *For Lancelot Andrewes* and prefaced them with a declaration that he considered himself 'classicist in literature, royalist in politics, and anglo-catholic in religion' (Eliot, *For Lancelot Andrewes*, vii). (This was quickly recognized as an echo of a manifesto from the newspaper of Charles Maurras's rightist organization Action Française.)

After Eliot's conversion he placed religion at the centre of his life. From 1933 he lived for seven years in the Grenville Place presbytery of the Anglo-Catholic St Stephen's Church, Gloucester Road, London. He served as churchwarden, and attended the eucharist with great assiduity. As critic he joined in the contemporary controversies of the Church of England, participated in Christian discussion groups, and lectured at church meetings and conferences.

Eliot's poetry also now addressed explicitly religious situations. In the late 1920s he published a series of shorter poems in the Faber Ariel series—short pieces issued in pamphlet form within striking modern covers.

These included 'Journey of the Magi' (1927), 'A Song for Simeon' (1928), 'Animula' (1929), 'Marina' (1930), and 'Triumphal March' (1931). Steeped in Eliot's contemporary study of Dante and Shakespeare's later work, all meditate on spiritual growth and anticipate the dialogue of self and soul achieved in the longer and more celebrated *Ash-Wednesday* (1930).

Drama 'Journey of the Magi' and 'A Song for Simeon', exercises in Browningesque dramatic monologues, speak to Eliot's desire, pronounced since 1922, to exchange the symbolist fluidity of the psychological lyric for a more traditional dramatic form. Eliot spent much of the last half of his career attempting one kind of drama or another, with an idea of reaching (and bringing together) a large and varied audience. As early as 1923 he had written parts of *Sweeney Agonistes*, an experimental and striking play with jazz rhythms; it was never finished but was published in fragments in 1932 and was performed by actors in masks by London's Group Theatre in 1934.

Some critics consider Eliot's decision to pursue the writing of West End drama rather than to follow up the jazz idiom of *Sweeney Agonistes* the biggest mistake of his career. To Eliot, however, the development was a natural and inevitable part of the public duties of his new spiritual life. In early 1934, encouraged by E. Martin Browne, he composed a church pageant with accompanying choruses for the Anglican diocese of London's Forty-Five Churches Fund. As *The Rock*, it was performed in May and June 1934 at Sadler's Wells. Soon afterwards George Bell, bishop of Chichester, commissioned a church drama, *Murder in the Cathedral*, which was performed in the chapter house of Canterbury Cathedral in June 1935 as part of the Canterbury Festival. It was moved to the Mercury Theatre at Notting Hill Gate, London, in November and eventually to the Old Vic. At its best the dramatic poetry of *Murder in the Cathedral* incorporates the fraught tensions of self-examination into the rhythms of public speech.

In the plays that he wrote starting in the late 1930s Eliot attempted to conflate a drama of spiritual crisis with a treatment of social manners inspired by Noël Coward. Though Eliot based *The Family Reunion* on the plot of Aeschylus's *Eumenides*, he designed it to tell a story of Christian redemption. The play opened at the Westminster Theatre, London, in March 1939 and closed to mixed reviews five weeks later. Eliot was disheartened, but after the Second World War fashioned more popular (though less powerful) combinations of the same elements to much greater success. *The Cocktail Party*, with a cast that included Alec Guinness, opened to a warm critical reception at the Edinburgh Festival in August 1949 and enjoyed a real popular success starting in New York on Broadway in January 1950. Eliot's last two plays were more laboured and fared less well. *The Confidential Clerk* had a respectable run at the Lyric Theatre in London in September 1953, and *The Elder Statesman* premiered at the Edinburgh Festival in August 1958 and closed after a lukewarm run in London in the autumn.

Honours of middle life Eliot's reputation as a poet, critic, and man of letters, increasing from the mid-1920s, far outstripped his theatrical success. As early as 1926 he had delivered the prestigious Clark lectures at Trinity College, Cambridge (published posthumously as *The Varieties of Religious Experience*, 1993), followed in 1932–3 by the Norton lectures at Harvard (published as *The Use of Poetry and the Use of Criticism*, 1933), by the Page-Barbour lectures at the University of Virginia (*After Strange Gods: a Primer of Modern Heresy*, 1934), and the Boutwood Foundation lectures at Corpus Christi College, Cambridge (*The Idea of a Christian Society*, 1939). Thereafter he won just about every honour the academic or the literary world had to offer, including eighteen honorary degrees, honorary fellowships at Merton College, Oxford, and Magdalene College, Cambridge, and membership in the Légion d'honneur. In 1948 Eliot received both the Order of Merit and the Nobel prize for literature and took up a fellowship stay at the Princeton Institute for Advanced Study. By 1950 his authority had reached a level that seemed to make him comparable in English writing to figures like Samuel Johnson or Samuel Taylor Coleridge.

Separation and *Four Quartets* The lasting achievement of the second half of Eliot's career, however, grew not out of his successes but out of the breakdown of his marriage. After *The Waste Land* was published, his and Vivien's physical and emotional stress increased. In 1923 Vivien nearly died of colitis, and Eliot, in despair, came close to a second breakdown. The years 1924 and 1925 were almost as bad. After his conversion Eliot took a vow of celibacy in 1928, and by the early 1930s he was intent on separation. During his tenure as Norton professor at Harvard he informed Vivien of his irrevocable decision through a letter from his solicitor, and returned to live with the family of his friend Frank Morley at Pike's Farm in Surrey (Eliot was godfather to Morley's daughter Susanna), not to the Eliot flat in Clarence Gate Gardens, London. Eliot would not consider divorce because of Anglican principles. For most of the 1930s he secluded himself from Vivien's often histrionic attempts to embarrass him into a reconciliation and made an anguished attempt to order his life around his editorial duties and his work as churchwarden.

Eliot re-established communication with Emily Hale in 1927 and crossed the USA from Boston to visit her at Scripps College in Claremont, California, at the end of 1932. In 1934, when she began summering with relatives in the Cotswolds, the relationship grew more intense, though they never married. Out of an experience of 'what might have been', associated with their visit to an abandoned great house, Eliot composed 'Burnt Norton', published as the last poem in his *Collected Poems, 1909–1935*. With its combination of symbolist indirection and meditative gravity, 'Burnt Norton' gave Eliot the model for another decade of major verse. In its first movement the poem achieved dazzling brilliance, questioning the familiar through riddling negations and reaching for (and finally attaining) a hold on a mysterious reality by a semantic, syntactic, and prosodic mastery that Eliot never thereafter surpassed.

In 1938, in part on Eliot's own authority, Vivien Eliot was committed to Northumberland House, a mental hospital north of London. With the war impending in 1939 *The Criterion*, which had occupied itself with the deepening political crisis of Europe, ceased publication. During the London blitz Eliot served as an air raid warden, but spent long weekends as a guest of his friend Hope Mirrlees in Shamley Green near Guildford. In these circumstances he wrote three more poems, each more sombre than the last, patterned on the voice and five-part structure of 'Burnt Norton'. 'East Coker' was published at Easter 1940 and was named after the Somerset village from which Eliot's ancestor Andrew Eliot had departed for America in the 1660s. (Eliot had visited East Coker in 1937.) 'The Dry Salvages', published in 1941, reverted to Eliot's experience as a boy sailing on the Mississippi and on the Massachusetts coast. Its title refers to a set of dangerously hidden rocks near Cape Ann. 'Little Gidding' was published in 1942 and had a less private subject in keeping with its larger ambitions. Little Gidding, near Cambridge, had been the site of a seventeenth-century Anglican religious community that maintained a perilous existence for the first part of the English civil war. Paired with Eliot's experience as an air raid warden walking the streets of Kensington during the Second World War, the community of Little Gidding inspired an extended meditation on the subject of the individual's duties in a world of human suffering. Its centrepiece was a sustained homage to Dante written in a form of *terza rima* and dramatizing Eliot's meeting with a 'familiar compound ghost' that he associates with Yeats and with Jonathan Swift. Its effect is mesmerizing, above all in the way it suggests how poetry may be at once radically sincere and yet also surrender to the restless spirits of the dead.

Four Quartets (1943), as the suite of four poems was entitled (Eliot at one point considered calling them the 'Kensington quartets'), for a time displaced *The Waste Land* as Eliot's most celebrated work. The British public responded especially to the topical references in the wartime poems and to the tone of Eliot's public meditation on a shared disaster. Some of Eliot's academic readers, however, were more reticent. F. R. Leavis, for example, praised the philosophical suppleness of Eliot's syntax but distrusted Eliot's swerve from a rigorously private voice.

Later life Eliot wrote no more major poetry after the Second World War, turning his attention to cultural criticism such as *Notes toward a Definition of Culture* (1948), to his plays, and to literary essays. The most important of the latter (collected in *On Poetry and Poets*, 1957) revisit the French symbolists and the development of language in twentieth-century poetry. Vivien died on 22 January 1947, and from 1946 Eliot led a protected life in London as a flatmate of his old friend, the critic and editor John Hayward, in Carlyle Mansions on the Chelsea Embankment. On 10 January 1957 he unexpectedly married his secretary (Esmé) Valerie Fletcher (*b.* 1927?) and attained a degree of contentedness that had eluded him all his life.

T. S. Eliot died on 4 January 1965 of emphysema at his home, 3 Kensington Court Gardens, London. His remains were cremated, and his casket was allowed to remain for a short period in St Stephen's Church in Kensington. A family funeral preceded a memorial service in Westminster Abbey a month later. In April the ashes, following Eliot's instructions, were interred in the church of St Michael's in East Coker. A commemorative plaque on the church wall bears his chosen epitaph (lines from *Four Quartets*): 'In my beginning is my end.' 'In my end is my beginning.'

Character and reputation Eliot, elaborately gracious and, with his intimates, partial to a bonhomie of boyish pranks and popular song, possessed an intense gaze and a slow precision of speech whose manifest sincerity often produced a sobering effect on those around him. The common response to his kindly and severe mien was increased self-consciousness, expressed in its most admirable form by W. H. Auden, who wrote that 'so long as one was in Eliot's presence, one felt it was impossible to say or do anything base' (Matthews, 186). Others registered the same experience less sympathetically. Virginia Woolf, later a great friend of Eliot's, noted in her diary of 1920 Eliot's 'great driving power' and remarked, 'my word what concentration of the eye when he argues!' (*Diary of Virginia Woolf*, 77). But she complained in 1923 how difficult he was to talk to: 'One waits; sympathises, but it is dreary work. He is … infinitely scrupulous, tautologous & cautious' (ibid., 236). Ezra Pound jokingly referred to Eliot's formal exterior as 'Westminster Abbey' and affectionately called him Possum, after the American animal that affects being dead to survive. Eliot, endearingly, was conscious of his own formality, and in 'Five-Finger Exercises' (1933) acknowledged:

> How unpleasant to meet Mr. Eliot!
> With his features of clerical cut,
> and his brow so grim
> and his mouth so prim
> And his conversation, so nicely
> Restricted to What Precisely
> And If and Perhaps and But.

In middle age success softened his severity into kind enquiry, which was sometimes just as intimidating.

At the heart of Eliot's imposing presence was a lifelong moral strenuousness which was unbending. At its best it caused him, for example, to refuse to accept a patronage scheme sponsored by Ezra Pound in 1922 (that would have freed him from Lloyds Bank), because the scheme would not ensure Vivien's security in the event of his death. Moreover throughout the 1920s, when he and Vivien were frequently at daggers drawn, he nursed her through constant physical and mental distress and consistently encouraged her writing. The same rigour, however, also allowed him after their separation to justify controlling her spending allowance for her own good and (along with her brother Maurice) to sign the papers committing her to confinement against her will. More notoriously, Eliot on key occasions in his life, having long anguished about difficult decisions, carried out his resolutions swiftly and sharply. Unable to persuade Vivien in person, he informed her by solicitor's letter of their separation. He left the flat

he shared with John Hayward to marry Valerie with (the stories differ) little or no warning.

In the literary realm Eliot's passionate formality caused him, even at the start of his career, to be criticized (as he himself—just as unfairly—once criticized John Milton) for a deadening neo-classicism. At the height of his fame the assurance of his poetry and criticism surrounded him with an air of authority, at first brash, and then monumental; the former is captured in Wyndham Lewis's two portraits, the latter in the Jacob Epstein bust in the National Portrait Gallery, and in familiar photographs by Man Ray, Edward McKnight Kauffer, Angus McBean, Cecil Beaton, and Alfred Eisenstaedt. These were the images that pervaded popular culture. (As late as 1971 Simon Gray's theatrical satire of academic life, *Butley*, was presided over by an image of Eliot as pantocrator.) Eliot's sly humour and even whimsy, of the kind that pervades his nonsense poems *Old Possum's Book of Practical Cats* (1939), was appreciated more slowly. It eventually triumphed when *Old Possum* was adapted for the stage and set to music by Andrew Lloyd Webber. As the immensely popular *Cats* it swept through the West End and Broadway in the 1980s. Eliot the doting brother and uncle, the subject of the many photographs of the Eliot family archive in the Houghton Library at Harvard, has remained largely unknown.

The authority that Eliot wielded in the 1950s and 1960s could not long go unchallenged. The fortress fell after Eliot's death, and in the 1990s, combined with a leftward shift in academic politics, Eliot's reputation stood lower than at any time since 1922. Long suspicious of his conservative religious and political convictions, readers in the 1980s and 1990s reacted with increasing impatience to his assertions of transcendental authority, obvious in *Four Quartets*, implicit in the earlier poetry. This impatience, amplified by intermittent rediscovery of Eliot's occasional antisemitic rhetoric and by a feminist revulsion against the misogyny of parts of *The Waste Land* (and a sympathy for Vivien Eliot's history), has gone hand in hand with post-structuralist criticism's downward revaluation of Eliot's literary sophistication.

In a period less engaged with politics and ideology than the 1980s and 1990s, however, the lasting strengths of Eliot's poetic technique will undoubtedly reassert themselves. A master of poetic dissonance and poetic syntax, whose early verse is electric with the energies of popular speech and popular culture, and whose later verse registers the powerful focus of philosophical thought, a poet who shuddered to repeat himself, a dramatist of the horror of the inner life (and of the evasions of conscience), Eliot will retain his reputation as one of the twentieth century's major poets.   RONALD BUSH

Sources *The letters of T. S. Eliot*, ed. V. Eliot, 1 (1988) · D. Gallup, *T. S. Eliot: a bibliography*, revised and extended edn (1969) · P. Ackroyd, *T. S. Eliot: a life* (1984) · L. Gordon, *Eliot's early years* (1977) · L. Gordon, *Eliot's new life* (1988) · R. Bush, *T. S. Eliot: a study in character and style* (1984) · H. Howarth, *Notes on some figures behind T. S. Eliot* (1964) · J. J. Soldo, *The tempering of T. S. Eliot* (1983) · T. S. Eliot, *To criticize the critic: eight essays on literature and education* (1965) · *Harvard College class of 1910: third report* (1917), 108–9 · *Harvard College class of 1910: fourth* *report* (1921), 107–8 • *Harvard College class of 1910: seventh report* (1935), 219–21 • *Harvard College class of 1910: fortieth report* (1950), 78–9 • *Harvard College class of 1910: fiftieth report* (1960), 133–6 • T. S. Eliot, *Selected essays* (1932); enlarged (1960) • T. S. Eliot, *For Lancelot Andrewes: essays on style and order* (1928) • T. S. Eliot, 'A sceptical patrician', *The Athenaeum*, 4647 (23 May 1919), 361–2 • *Harvard Advocate* (Dec 1938), 5–8, 17, 47–8 [special T. S. Eliot issue] • D. Hall, 'The art of poetry, I: T. S. Eliot', *Paris Review*, 21 (spring–summer 1959), 47–70 • E. Sigg, 'Eliot as a product of America', *The Cambridge companion to T. S. Eliot*, ed. D. Moody (1994), 14–30 • T. S. Matthews, *Great Tom: notes towards the definition of T. S. Eliot* (1973) • A. Tate, ed., *T. S. Eliot: the man and his work* (1967) • E. Pound, *Selected letters, 1907–1941*, ed. D. D. Paige (1950) • T. S. Eliot, *The waste land: a facsimile and draft*, ed. V. Eliot (1971) • C. Aiken, *Ushant: an essay* (1952) • Tambimuttu and R. March, eds., *T. S. Eliot: a symposium* (1948), 20–23, 24–32 • *The diary of Virginia Woolf*, 2, ed. A. O. Bell (1978) • M. Browne, *The making of T. S. Eliot's plays* (1969) • M. Jain, *T. S. Eliot and American philosophy: the Harvard years* (1992) • J. Mayer, *T. S. Eliot's silent voices* (1989) • m. cert. • d. cert.

Archives Boston PL, MSS and letters • Cornell University, Ithaca, New York, Olin Library, MSS and letters • Harvard U., Houghton L., corresp., literary MSS, papers • Hunt. L., MSS and letters • King's AC Cam., corresp., literary MSS, and papers • Magd. Cam., papers • Merton Oxf., letters • Milton Academy Library, Massachusetts, papers • NYPL, literary MS and papers • Princeton University Library, New Jersey, MSS and letters • Ransom HRC, corresp. and literary MSS • Reed College, Oregon, Eliot family papers • State University of New York, Buffalo, E. H. Butler Library, MSS and letters • U. Lond., papers relating to the Moot • University of Bristol, corresp. relating to trial of *Lady Chatterley's Lover* • University of Chicago Library, MSS and letters • University of Maryland, papers • University of Victoria, Mcpherson Library, corresp. | Balliol Oxf., letters to A. D. Lindsay • BL, corresp. with G. K. Chesterton, Add. MS 73195, fols. 60–69 • BL, letters to S. S. Koteliansky, Add. MS 48974 • BL, letters to Margaret Nason of the Bindery tea shop, dep. 9935 • BL, letters to Sydney Schiff and Violet Schiff, Add. MS 52918 • BL, manuscript coll., letters to Tandy family • Bodl. Oxf., Vivien Eliot papers • Bodl. Oxf., letters to Helen Gardner • CAC Cam., corresp. with Monty Belgion • Georgetown University, Washington, DC, Lauinger Library, letters to Harman Grisewood relating to David Jones • Harvard U., university archives • Harvard U., Houghton L., letters to T. Bosanquet • Harvard U., Houghton L., letters to E. Martin and Henzie Browne • Hunt. L., Conrad Aiken papers • King's AC Cam., letters to John Maynard Keynes • King's AC Cam., letters to G. H. W. Rylands • McMaster University, Hamilton, Ontario, William Ready division of archives and research collections, corresp. with Bertrand Russell • NL Scot., corresp. with John Dover Wilson • NL Wales, corresp. with David Jones • NYPL, John Quinn papers • NYPL, Virginia Woolf papers • Princeton University, New Jersey, Firestone Library, Emily Hale papers • Princeton University, New Jersey, Firestone Library, Paul Elmer More papers • Princeton University, New Jersey, Firestone Library, Allen Tate papers • Rosenbach Museum, Philadelphia, Marianne Moore collection • Scripps College, California, Emily Hale papers • Tate collection, corresp. with Lord Clark • TCD, letters to Patricia Hutchins • TCD, corresp. with Thomas McGreevy • U. Sussex, corresp. mainly with Maurice Reckitt • U. Sussex, corresp. with Leonard Woolf • U. Sussex, corresp. with Virginia Woolf [copies] • University of Chicago, special collections • University of Indiana, Ezra Pound papers • Washington University, St Louis, Missouri, William Greenleaf Eliot papers • Yale U., Beinecke L., Ezra Pound papers • Yale U., Beinecke L., Osborn collection • Yale U., Beinecke L., letters to William Force Stead | FILM BBC WAC • Harvard U., Harvard film service | SOUND BL NSA, documentary recordings • BL NSA, performance recordings • Harvard U., Harvard College Library • L. Cong.

Likenesses W. Lewis, pencil drawing, 1925, U. Texas • B. Brandt, bromide print, *c.*1945, NPG • J. Gay, vintage print, 1948, NPG • W. Stoneman, photograph, 1948, NPG • P. Heron, oils, 1949, NPG •

W. Lewis, oils, 1949, Magd. Cam. • F. Man, photograph, 1949, NPG • J. Epstein, plaster cast of bust, 1951, NPG • B. Anrep, mosaic, 1952, National Gallery, London • K. B. Reynal, bromide print, 1955, NPG • C. Beaton, photograph, 1956, NPG [*see illus.*] • I. Penn, gelatine silver print, 1959, NPG • M. Gerson, group photograph, 1960 • G. Kelly, oils, 1965, U. Texas • A. Eisenstaedt, photograph • J. Epstein, bronze cast, U. Texas • E. A. Holloway, etching, NPG • E. M. Kauffer, photograph • P. W. Lewis, oils, Durban Municipal Art Gallery, South Africa; study, Eliot House, Harvard U. • W. Lewis, pen and watercolour drawing, National Gallery of Melbourne • Man Ray, photograph • A. McBean, photograph • W. Stoneman, photograph, NPG • F. Topolski, portrait, NPG • photographs, Harvard U., Horton collection

Wealth at death £105,272: probate, 8 June 1965, *CGPLA Eng. & Wales*

Eliot [*née* Haigh-Wood], **Vivienne Haigh** [Vivien] (1888–1947), writer, was born on 28 May 1888 at Knowsley Street, Bury, Lancashire, the daughter of Charles Haigh-Wood (*d.* 1927), a successful artist from a carving and gilding background, and his wife, Rose Esther Robinson (*d.* 1941). Vivienne's brother Maurice was born in 1896. He was to fight throughout the First World War—a dark, strapping, well-conducted man who was fond of his frail, intense sister.

In childhood Vivienne, known often as Vivien, suffered poor health including tuberculosis of the bone in her left arm, and some form of nervous illness alleviated by opiates. As a young woman she painted and took up ballet, and was a governess with a family in Cambridge for a short period. In 1914 she had a stormy attachment to a schoolmaster, Charles Buckle.

In spring 1915, when Vivienne was turning twenty-seven, she met the 26-year-old poet T. S. *Eliot (1888–1965), then a visiting student from America having a deadly time in an Oxford emptied by war. Repressed and shy, with a family history of puritan divines and memories of unfulfilled love for a proper Bostonian called Emily Hale, Eliot was jolted to life by the flamboyant Vivienne, her 'amusing' name (*Letters*, 97), and her daring to smoke in public. She proved a pliant dancer, keen to follow when Eliot began to 'dip' in his one-step in a style unknown in England. It appealed to him that Vivienne would never say she liked Bach or Cézanne if she didn't. She looked like an actress in her bold colours: she owned a scarf-dress in the post-war years and, in the thirties, got herself up in a cape and waistcoat, and flourished a cigarette-holder. This was not the kind of woman a gentleman could introduce to his mother. Though her parents lived comfortably in Hampstead, London, Eliot's old New England background was very much grander.

They married impulsively without waiting to tell their parents. The ceremony took place on 26 June 1915 in the presence of Vivienne's friend Lucy Ely Thayer and aunt Lillia C. Symes at the Hampstead register office near Vivienne's home at 3 Compayne Gardens. Vivienne was going to save Eliot for poetry, which meant keeping him from academe. He had been due to return to America, but rebelled against a future as a Harvard philosopher. An English marriage made it possible for him to deal that prospect an all-out blow, and Vivienne stood up for him against the disapproval of the Eliot family. 'Tom knows perfectly well that I share his feeling over the poetry. ... I look upon Tom's poetry as real genius', she told his brother. 'I provide the motive power', she added, 'I *do* shove' (*Letters*, 157). Later she was incredulous that her creative (as opposed to destructive) bond with Eliot should have been obliterated during his lifetime. During their early years together her hatred of the 'fug and slop' of sentiment (Gordon, *Eliot*, 129), her alienation from most people, and her susceptibility to horror matched and promoted the state of mind which, in Eliot's own words, 'led to *The Waste Land*' (*Letters*, introduction). Vivienne, advising on a draft of the poem, wrote 'WONDERFUL' next to the voice of the distraught wife in the second part. Later, in her copy of his *Poems, 1909–1925*, Eliot noted that only she would understand them.

On 9 July 1915, two weeks after the marriage, Vivienne told Eliot's former teacher Bertrand Russell that she had married her husband to stimulate him, but found she could not do it. She fell into a pattern of illness, convalescence, and relapse: migraines, fainting, stomach upsets, and disordered hormones which led to heavy, unpredictable menstruation. Eliot sought help from Russell, who obliged by making up to Vivienne over a long period, which culminated in a night they spent together in October 1917.

Vivienne did not care for literary society, especially the Bloomsbury group, but she befriended two of its adherents: the well-read, sophisticated Mary Hutchinson and Lady Ottoline Morrell. Vivienne also shone as an actress in private theatricals which the Eliots enjoyed with Violet and Sydney Schiff (the author Stephen Hudson) in 1919–20. Whenever she demonstrated flair as actress, dancer, or writer, Eliot liked to show her off. Katherine Mansfield observed the way he kept a wing over Vivienne when they came to dinner in summer 1920, 'admiring, listening, making the most of her' (letter to Violet Schiff, 1 May 1920, BL, quoted in C. Tomalin, *Katherine Mansfield: a Secret Life*, 197). This contrasts with the other Vivienne who could not gain her husband's love (in his poetic phantasmagoria he remained in love with an idealized memory of Emily Hale), and who increasingly took the part of an invalid. This came to a head in 1923 when Eliot wished to leave his post at Lloyds Bank in order to devote more time to writing. His wife developed colitis, and nearly died.

Vivienne did, however, show an unexpected capacity to rally. From February 1924 to July 1925 she often contributed to her husband's international journal *The Criterion*, whose name had been her choice (after a hotel where she and Buckle used to dine). Eliot thought her original, and did not hesitate to publish her stories and reviews, completing some if she were too ill to do so, or touching them up. She took on an array of pseudonyms: Fanny Marlow, Feiron Morris, Felise Morrison, FM, and Irene Fassett. Vivienne saw Fanny Marlow as the money-maker, spinning on forever like a spider. 'There is no *end* to Fanny! But Feiron will never make money. And he does not spin. He is a nasty fellow' (letter to S. Schiff [n. d.], BL, quoted in Gordon, *Eliot*, 193).

Feiron is the author of Vivienne's most ambitious story,

'The Paralysed Woman', in which the external paralysis of an immaculate wife in a perfect home holds up a mirror to the internal paralysis of a writer, Sybilla, who lives with a hypochondriacal husband in a ramshackle, carping milieu. Other sketches, of a dingy Parisian hotel and its inhabitants, a *thé dansant* in London, or a boring bohemian party where ballet dancers are shepherded by a 'macaw', are all emotionally alive and observant, with plangent minutiae, reminiscent of Katherine Mansfield. Vivienne planned an interlinked series which could appear separately but could make up a book.

Vivienne enjoyed her success, but confided to Schiff in 1924 her fear that it 'is a sort of flash in the pan—that won't *go on*'. She spoke of writing as 'this temporary aberration of mine' (letter, 2 April 1924, BL). Her diaries protest against Eliot's attempt to regulate her writing habits, which he believed might exacerbate her illness. She argued that her material came irregularly from some 'very overgrown and hidden inner spirit', which would suddenly begin to spurt:

> I think at first, until one has got the spout of this long disused fountain clear, it is better to let the water burst out when it will & so *force* away the accumulation of decayed vegetation, moss, slime & dead fish which are thick upon & around it.   (Vivienne Eliot's papers, Bodl. Oxf.)

This effort collapsed when Eliot's associates at the New York *Dial* rejected 'The Paralysed Woman'—it remained unpublished.

In a poem 'Necesse est perstare?' Vivienne (as FM) recounts a moment after a literary lunch. The wife is thankful for an end to gossip about Clive Bell, Elizabeth Bibesco, and Aldous Huxley. She longs to win her husband from his resolve to master the literary scene. But he stretches his arms above his head with the weary air of a very old monkey, impervious to her silent plea. Vivienne channelled her frustration into a diatribe against America in her 'Diary of the Rive Gauche' (under the name Fanny Marlow). The narrator repeats (mimicking the repetitive manner of Vivienne's own talk):

> that I never did understand Americans ... When I see an American coming I ought to say immediately, 'Please do not speak to me, because if you do I shall not understand you. I shall never understand you.' ... They cannot cope with European women. Ha! They can't cope with us!   (*The Criterion*, 3, Jan 1925, 292)

Vivienne was insensitive to Eliot's need for time and privacy. Eloquent, febrile, now and then on the verge of collapse, she had needs of her own, and these Eliot met with conscientious patience for seventeen years. Though Vivienne shared the snobbery, antisemitism, and virulence her husband called 'hatred of life', she did not share his moral struggle for transformation. Few could bear Vivienne for long: she was quick to fault others, and later joined Sir Oswald Mosley's British Union of Fascists. She was the sort of fascist who enjoyed wearing uniform and the excitement of a rally where public denunciations provided an outlet for fury. After Eliot left her in 1932–3 she made many attempts to intercept him. These were invariably foiled, for, aided by friends and protectors, he had put himself beyond her reach. Increasingly desperate, Vivienne had attacks of panic—as though she saw 'a goblin ghost' (Mirrlees, 50).

Vivienne rallied yet again to begin a new career in 1935–6 at the Royal College of Music, first as a pianist, then elated to discover a *huge* voice in singing lessons. Her manner, though, grew wilder as she began to fear she was the victim of some plot. As it happens, the plots of two of Eliot's plays suggest a continued, almost eerie affinity in their turn for horror: 'I knew a man once did a girl in', reports Sweeney in Eliot's first verse play, *Sweeney Agonistes* (1926); and again, in *The Family Reunion* (1939), a hero is shaken by temptation to murder. His dream-victim is his wife, a shivering painted shadow—exactly as Vivienne appeared in the thirties.

In July 1938, at the time Eliot was completing this play, Vivienne was certified insane, and was committed to a private London asylum, Northumberland House. Once, she tried to escape, but was apprehended. After some years abroad, when Maurice Haigh-Wood saw his sister in 1946 he acknowledged that she was sane. Vivienne Eliot remained in Northumberland House until she died of a heart attack on 22 January 1947.

A few years later Bertrand Russell wrote 'Mrs Ellerker', a story based on Mrs Eliot, about a woman who is too sane to lend herself to the artifice of repression. It was not, though, until the mid-seventies that Vivienne was brought out of the shadow and her talents recognized, reinforced by Valerie Eliot's inclusion of Vivienne's correspondence in her volume of Eliot's early letters (1988). The combined letters confirmed the need for a delicate biographic balance, but this was skewed by a simplistic 'biopic', *Tom and Viv* (1994), trailed by a partisan biography (2001) which sought to vindicate Vivienne by nailing Eliot. The truth is more ambiguous, and it is unlikely that the whole truth can ever be known.   LYNDALL GORDON

Sources Vivienne Eliot's papers, Bodl. Oxf. · *The letters of T. S. Eliot*, ed. V. Eliot, 1 (1988) · L. Gordon, *T. S. Eliot: an imperfect life* (1998) [incorporating *Eliot's early years* (1977), and *Eliot's new life* (1988)] · H. W. Eliot, letters to Charlotte Champe Eliot, Harvard U., Houghton L. · Harvard U., Houghton L., Eliot papers · T. S. Eliot, *The waste land: a facsimile and transcript of the original drafts*, ed. V. Eliot (1971), 10–15 · L. Gordon, 'Eliot and women', *T. S. Eliot: the modernist in history*, ed. R. Bush (1991), 9–22 · R. Monk, *Bertrand Russell: the spirit of solitude* (1996) · C. Seymour-Jones, *Painted shadow: a life of Vivienne Eliot* (2001) · C. Tomalin, *Katherine Mansfield: a secret life* (1987) · H. Mirrlees, 'The mysterious Mr Eliot', *Listener*, 85 (14 Jan 1971) · b. cert. · m. cert. · d. cert.
Archives Bodl. Oxf., corresp. and papers · Harvard U., Houghton L., family papers
Likenesses photograph, 1930, repro. in Gordon, *T. S. Eliot*, following p. 354 · photographs, repro. in Gordon, *T. S. Eliot*

Eliott, Sir Daniel (1798–1872), East India Company servant, was born on 3 March 1798 in the parish of Cavers, Roxburghshire, the fourth son of Sir William Eliot of Stobs, sixth baronet (*d.* 1812), Roxburghshire, and his wife, Mary (*d.* 1850), daughter of John Russell of Roseburne, near Edinburgh. He was educated at the Edinburgh Academy and, having been nominated to a writership in the Madras civil service, at the East India Company's college at Haileybury (1815–17). He landed at Madras in August 1817

and just over a year later, on 19 December 1818, married Georgina (*d.* 1874), daughter of General George Russell of the Bengal army, with whom he had three surviving sons and six daughters.

A competent linguist, Eliott was appointed deputy Tamil translator in 1822 and Marathi translator in 1823. In 1827 he became secretary to the Madras board of revenue, graduating to membership of the board in 1836. In January 1839 he was chosen to replace John Macleod as Madras member on the Indian law commission and subsequently wrote with C. H. Cameron two reports (1846 and 1847) defending the Indian penal code drafted by T. B. Macaulay and the original law commissioners in 1837.

On 15 February 1848 Eliott was appointed a member of the Madras council and, by virtue of this position, became president of the local revenue, marine, and college boards. In 1855 he became the first Madras representative to the new, all-India, central legislative council at Calcutta. He remained in Calcutta until 1858, when he resigned the service and returned to England. In 1867, upon the extension of the order of the Star of India, he was made KCSI.

Eliott died at his residence, 12 The Boltons, West Brompton, London, on 30 October 1872. He was survived by his wife and nine children. His youngest son, Edward Frederick (1834–1873), followed him into the Indian Civil Service.   H. M. STEPHENS, *rev.* KATHERINE PRIOR

Sources C. C. Prinsep, *Record of services of the Honourable East India Company's civil servants in the Madras presidency from 1741 to 1858* (1885) · *Madras Mail* (7 Nov 1872), 2 · Burke, *Peerage* (1967) · BL OIOC, Haileybury MSS · F. C. Danvers and others, *Memorials of old Haileybury College* (1894) · *The Times* (1 Nov 1872), 1 · *The Times* (2 Nov 1872), 5
Wealth at death under £35,000: probate, 26 Nov 1872, CGPLA Eng. & Wales

Eliott, George Augustus, first Baron Heathfield of Gibraltar (1717–1790), army officer, the seventh son of Sir Gilbert Eliott, third baronet, and his wife, Eleanor Eliott, was born in Stobs, Roxburghshire, on 25 December 1717. Educated at Leiden University, he also attended the French military college at La Fère. In 1735 and 1736 Eliott saw active service as a volunteer with the Prussian army in order to develop his military knowledge, and on his return to Britain he attended the Royal Military Academy at Woolwich. He received a commission as officer of engineers in 1739. As there was no regular corps of sappers and miners at this time Eliott also held a commission in the 2nd Horse Grenadier Guards, commanded at this time by his uncle, Colonel James Eliott. George Eliott served with his regiment as lieutenant and adjutant between 1742 and 1748, during the War of the Austrian Succession, and was wounded at the battle of Dettingen (1743). He also fought at the battle of Fontenoy (1745), and purchased a captaincy in the same year. He purchased the rank of major in 1749, and a lieutenant-colonelcy in 1754. Eliott resigned his commission as field engineer at this time, and in 1756 became aide-de-camp to George II, who greatly approved his personal conduct on campaign.

On 8 June 1748, at St Sepulchre, London, Eliott married

George Augustus Eliott, first Baron Heathfield of Gibraltar (1717–1790), by Sir Joshua Reynolds, 1787

Anne Pollexfen, only child of Sir Francis Henry Drake, fourth baronet, of Buckland Abbey in Devon. There were two children, a daughter, Anne, and a son, Francis Augustus.

George Eliott was selected to raise a regiment of light cavalry after the Prussian and Austrian hussars model, and was made colonel of the 1st light dragoons on 10 March 1759. He was known to take considerable care in the administration and training of his regiment, and for the unusually simple and spartan manner in which he lived when in the field. Eliott led his regiment with distinction throughout the campaigns in Germany during the Seven Years' War between 1759 and 1761. In June 1759 he became major-general and fought at the battle of Minden (1 August 1759) in command of a brigade of cavalry. He took a prominent part in the bold cavalry charge at the battle of Emsdorf (16 July 1760) and received the thanks of Prince Ferdinand of Brunswick for his services at this time.

In 1761 Eliott was appointed to command a brigade of cavalry intended for amphibious operations against the French coast. He was subsequently second in command to the earl of Albemarle during the arduous expedition against Cuba where his conduct attracted wide commendation. On his return to Britain in 1763 he received over £25,000 in prize money from the Havana operations, and used this money to purchase the estate of Heathfield in Sussex. At the conclusion of the Seven Years' War in 1763 George III reviewed Eliott's regiment of cavalry in Hyde Park and granted his request that they should be titled the King's Own Royal light dragoons; they subsequently

became the 15th hussars. Eliott was made lieutenant-general in 1765. His wife, Anne, died on 13 February 1772.

Late in 1774 Eliott became commander-in-chief in Ireland but in 1775 he was appointed as governor of Gibraltar. He arrived on the rock on 25 May 1777. The entry of France into the American War of Independence in 1778 made Gibraltar more vulnerable to an attack by Spain. Eliott oversaw the improvements to the fortifications in the period to 1779, executed by Gibraltar's chief engineer, William Green. In September that year Eliott pre-empted his opponents' preparations with a heavy bombardment of their lines, and the blockade of Gibraltar became an active campaign. Eliott's small garrison of less than 6000 men was subjected to continuous bombardment, to bravely conducted attacks by land and sea, and to a close and debilitating blockade designed to induce starvation. Vital supplies were first forced through to the rock by a naval squadron under Rear-Admiral Richard, fourth Viscount Howe, in January 1780, but conditions for the soldiers were often desperate. On 12 April 1781 another supply convoy reached the garrison but, among other expedients to eke out supplies, Eliott ordered his men to cease powdering their hair, as required by standing orders, in order to conserve flour. The turning point in the operations came on 13 September 1782, when the French and Spanish floating batteries off the king's bastion were ruthlessly and systematically destroyed in a tremendous counter-bombardment by Eliott's batteries, which fired more than 40,000 rounds of heated round shot in an afternoon and evening. On 11 October 1782 a third supply convoy under Howe got through to the garrison, and, following a successful conclusion to peace negotiations with Spain, the siege was lifted on 5 February 1783. Eliott's calm, competent, and firm leadership throughout the three year and seven months' siege was fundamental to the extraordinary fortitude of the hard-pressed soldiers under his command. A monument to Eliott's leadership during the siege was later erected in what became the Alameda Botanical Gardens.

George Eliott was made a knight of the Bath in 1783. He returned to Britain in May 1787 and received great popular acclaim. He was granted a pension of £1500 per annum and was created Baron Heathfield of Gibraltar on 14 June 1787. Heathfield died at Aachen in northern Germany 'of a second stroke of the palsy' (*GM*, 1st ser., 60/2, 1790, 671) shortly before a planned return to his post in Gibraltar, on 6 July 1790, and was buried in Heathfield church, Sussex. It was rumoured that he had married shortly before his death, or was about to marry, his mistress, but her name is unknown. His son, Francis Augustus, second Baron Heathfield (*d.* 1813), also followed a military career and was colonel of the 29th light dragoons (1795–7), the 20th light dragoons (1797–1810), and 1st King's dragoon guards (1810–13). Eliott's daughter, Anne, married John Trayton Fuller of Ashdown Park, Sussex, and their third son, Thomas, assumed the name Fuller-Eliott-Drake in 1813 on succeeding to the estates of the Eliotts and Drakes. He was created a baronet in 1821.

Heathfield was a bluff and dour man, with an impressive air of quiet authority. A dedicated and ambitious professional soldier, he took pains throughout his career to improve both his own military knowledge and expertise and that of the men he commanded. Having acquired a considerable reputation as a leader of light cavalry when young, he proved equally adept at the technical intricacies of positional siege warfare. His ingenuity and resourcefulness in adversity attracted wide attention and praise, most notably at the siege of Gibraltar, which is justly regarded as one of the epic episodes in eighteenth-century military history. JAMES FALKNER

Sources Army List (1739–90) · DNB · J. Drinkwater, A history of the late siege of Gibraltar (1785) · N. B. Leslie, The succession of colonels of the British army from 1660 to the present day (1974) · R. A. Savory, His Britannic majesty's army in Germany during the Seven Years' War (1966) · P. Young, The British army (1642–1970) (1967) · interactive map of Gibraltar, www.gibnet.gi/~dparody/gibmap/home.htm · GEC, Peerage · GM, 1st edn., 60 (1790), 671 · will, PRO, PROB 11/1194, sig. 330
Archives BL, day book of siege of Gibraltar, Add. MS 45188 · CKS, MSS relating to Gibraltar · Devon RO, corresp. and MSS · NMM, corresp. and MSS relating to Gibraltar | BL, letters to Lord Grantham, Add. MSS 24163–24166, 24173
Likenesses G. Carter, group portrait, gouache, 1782–7 (The siege of Gibraltar, 1782), NPG · C. de Mechel, line engraving, pubd 1784 (after G. F. Koehler), BM · J. S. Copley, oils, c.1787, NPG · J. Reynolds, oils, 1787, National Gallery, London [see illus.] · F. Bartolozzi, stipple, pubd 1788 (after A. Poggi), BM · J. C. Rossi, marble statue on monument, c.1825, St Paul's Cathedral, London · M. Brown, oils, East Sussex county council, Lewes · J. S. Copley, group portrait, oils (The siege and relief of Gibraltar, 13 September 1782), Tate collection [possibly a replica] · A. Poggi, chalk drawing, Scot. NPG · prints, BM, NPG

Elis y Cowper. See Roberts, Ellis (c.1712–1789).

Elizabeth [née Elizabeth de Burgh] (d. 1327), queen of Scots, consort of Robert I, was the second daughter and one of ten children of Richard de Burgh, earl of Ulster (d. 1326), and his wife, Margaret (d. 1304), who may also have been a de Burgh. Elizabeth was probably born in Down or Antrim. In 1302, in an alliance which conformed to a pattern of family behaviour going back at least to the later twelfth century—the earls of Carrick held lands in Ulster—she became the second wife of Robert Bruce, earl of Carrick and future king of Scots (1274–1329) [see Robert I]. From 1298 to 1300 he had been one of the guardians of Scotland for the exiled King John, but at the beginning of 1302 he had come into Edward I's peace and allegiance.

Within four years of her marriage Elizabeth de Burgh became queen of Scots when her husband led a revolt against the English occupation of Scotland and was inaugurated as king at Scone on 25 March 1306. Three months later the new king and queen were fugitives, hunted through the hills of Perthshire and Aberdeenshire. It was decided to send the queen and other women in the party to Kildrummy Castle in Strathdon, in the charge of John, earl of Atholl. Pursued there by an English force under Aymer de Valence (d. 1324), the royal party was sent on northward, perhaps with the intention of reaching Orkney. They had got only as far as St Duthac's sanctuary at Tain, Ross-shire, when they were seized by the pro-

English earl of Ross, who sent them to Edward I. King Robert's sister Mary and Isabel, countess of Buchan (who had crowned Bruce), received harsh punishment, being confined for several years in cages, but Queen Elizabeth, daughter of one of the English king's principal barons, was ordered to be confined in the manor house at Burstwick in Holderness, attended by two elderly maidservants of sober temperament. From Burstwick the queen, styling herself simply Elizabeth Bruce, sent an undated letter to Edward I or II, telling him that her warders allowed her only three changes of clothing a year, no headgear, and nothing for her bed, while her attendants had only one robe a year each, and begging him to order an improvement in her circumstances or to make her a money allowance. At various later dates she was transferred to other places, including the Tower of London and the nunnery at Shaftesbury in Dorset. It was said that she had increased her chances of leniency when at their enthronement she had jested to her husband that he might be a summer king but would never be a winter one. Fascinating as is this relatively early reference to the widespread children's custom of choosing summer kings and queens, the authenticity of the report must be regarded as doubtful. By March 1312 Elizabeth was in the Tower of London, where her situation had improved greatly: she was allowed two damsels, two esquires, and two yeomen, and 40s. a week to pay for them.

King Robert's great victory at Bannockburn in June 1314 allowed the royal prisoners still in English hands to be restored to Scotland. Queen Elizabeth and her stepdaughter Marjorie Bruce, along with Mary Bruce, the king's sister, were freed in exchange for the earl of Hereford. The daughters of Robert and Elizabeth must have been born after their mother's release from captivity. The king's only surviving brother, Edward, was declared heir presumptive to the Scottish throne in 1315 because the situation in which the realm found itself remained perilous. After Edward, however, the king's next heir was unquestionably his eldest daughter, Marjorie, whose mother, Isabel of Mar, had died young. In March 1316 Marjorie gave birth to a son, Robert Stewart, who became presumptive heir when Edward Bruce was killed at Dundalk in 1318. But at Dunfermline Abbey on 5 March 1324, a decade after her release from imprisonment, Queen Elizabeth bore a son, named David [see David II], presumably in honour of David I (d. 1153), and he at once became the heir apparent, formally recognized as such in the parliament of 1326.

Elizabeth died at the royal residence of Cullen on the Banffshire coast on 26 October 1327 and was buried in the choir of Dunfermline Abbey, resting place of Scottish kings and queens since 1093. A chaplainry was established in the church of St Mary the Virgin at Cullen to celebrate masses for the queen's soul. G. W. S. BARROW

Sources 'Ulster', GEC, Peerage, new edn, vol. 12/2 · Scots peerage, vol. 1 · A. H. Dunbar, Scottish kings, 2nd edn (1906) · National MSS of Scotland, 2, pl. 16 · CDS, vols. 2–3, 5 · G. Burnett and others, eds., The exchequer rolls of Scotland, 1 (1878) · G. W. S. Barrow, Robert Bruce and the community of the realm of Scotland, 3rd edn (1988) · F. J. H. Skene, ed., Liber pluscardensis, 1 (1877), 258 · Johannis de Fordun Scotichronicon,

cum supplementis … Walteri Boweri, ed. W. Goodall, 2 vols. (1759), 288

Elizabeth [*née* Elizabeth Woodville] (*c.*1437–1492), queen of England, consort of Edward IV, was the daughter of Richard *Woodville or Wydeville, first Earl Rivers (*d.* 1469), and his wife, Jacquetta, dowager duchess of Bedford (*d.* 1472).

Family background and first marriage Elizabeth's parents' marriage had been a *mésalliance* only slightly less shocking than Elizabeth's own match was to be with *Edward IV. Jacquetta belonged to the house of Luxemburg, one of the greatest European families that included holy Roman emperors; her brother was count of St Pol and her uncle was bishop of Thérouanne; and her first husband, Henry V's brother John (*d.* 1435), was duke of Bedford and regent of France. The Woodvilles, in contrast, were merely gentry of limited means despite the distinguished military and administrative career of Richard's father. Both father and son served Bedford, the father as chamberlain and councillor. Sir Richard was household knight to the duke at his death in 1435 and had married Duchess Jacquetta by March 1437, when he was fined £1000 for marrying without licence and for livery of her dower. His subsequent career in France and England was rewarded with his creation as Lord Rivers in 1448 and his election as a knight of the Garter in 1450. Apart from Jacquetta's substantial dower, which he held only for life, Rivers's estate in Northamptonshire and Kent was modest in extent and value, but his new status enabled him to marry three of his children to the heirs of baronies.

Woodville and Jacquetta had a large family, of whom five sons and six daughters achieved maturity. Apparently Elizabeth was the eldest, and would therefore have been born about 1437, soon after her parents' marriage. Nothing is known of her early life: two letters once thought to be addressed to her urging her marriage to Sir Hugh Johns actually relate to another lady, and identifications of her with Queen Margaret of Anjou's attendant Dame Isabella Gray are probably mistaken. Instead about 1456 she married Sir John *Grey (*c.*1432–1461) [*see under* Grey, Sir Richard], the eldest son and heir of Edward, Lord Ferrers of Groby in right of his wife Elizabeth Ferrers. Later it was claimed that Lord Rivers agreed to pay a modest portion of 200 marks in return for the settlement on the young couple and their children of a jointure worth only 100 marks, comprising the three manors of Newbottle and Brington, Northamptonshire, and Woodham Ferrers in Essex. These were conveyed to feoffees to their use in 1456. Two sons were born of the match, Thomas (later marquess of Dorset) and Richard Grey, before Sir John's death early in 1461.

In the event of Grey's death before inheriting, the jointure had been intended to provide for his widow and children, albeit at a decidedly unbaronial level, but the young widow Elizabeth had difficulty in securing it. Circumstances had changed since her marriage. Sir John's father, Lord Ferrers, had died in 1457 and his widow had married Sir John Bourchier; she was to live until 1483 and had younger sons to provide for; she also sued for 125 marks of

Elizabeth (*c.*1437–1492), by unknown artist

Elizabeth's jointure which Rivers had either not paid or for which he had no receipt. Apparently Elizabeth required the feoffees to release her jointure, but one of them refused, professing ignorance of the trust. She therefore sued for delivery of the estate in chancery, but her mother-in-law asked chancery that the lands be conveyed to her. So great were Elizabeth's difficulties that she was obliged to look for assistance to Edward IV himself.

Marriage to Edward IV Elizabeth was not best placed for favourable treatment. Although her husband escaped attainder, it had been on the Lancastrian side that he had been killed at the second battle of St Albans, and her father and brother had been on the wrong side at Towton. Although all three escaped attainder, and Lord Rivers was even restored to the royal council in 1463, his influence was apparently insufficient to help his daughter: Sir John Bourchier, on the other hand, was a younger son of Henry Bourchier, who was uncle of the king, earl of Essex, and treasurer of England (1461–2). Accordingly Elizabeth sought the intercession of her distant relative, William, Lord Hastings (*d.* 1483), chamberlain of the household, who controlled access to the king. Hastings was prepared to help only on his own terms. On 13 April 1464 Elizabeth agreed to the marriage of her son Thomas to a yet unborn daughter of Lord Hastings; she also agreed that Hastings would enjoy half the income of any inheritance from Lady Ferrers while Thomas was still under age; there were, furthermore, clauses substituting her younger son, Richard Grey, if Thomas died, and nieces if Hastings had no daughter. Hastings had this arrangement confirmed by the king on 10 August. Presumably Elizabeth's suit was indeed put to the king, apparently by her in person, with the desired effect: an inquisition post mortem found Thomas Grey to be his father's heir in the disputed manors and Elizabeth recovered possession of them. Another apparent fruit was that Elizabeth secretly married the king, traditionally on 1 May 1464.

When Elizabeth petitioned the king, according to the traditional story recorded by Sir Thomas More, he wanted to go to bed with her in return for success in her suit. When she refused, he was obliged to marry her to get his way. A secret wedding was held at her father's house at Grafton, Northamptonshire, on 1 May in the presence only of the priest, two gentlemen, and a young man to sing the responses. After going to bed, the king withdrew for several days before visiting Grafton as Lord Rivers's guest. The marriage was not revealed until the session of the great council held at Reading in September. The essence of this story is early, as it was included in Antonio Cornazzano's poem 'De mulieribus admirandis' ('Of admirable women') in 1468. Thinking herself too base to be a queen and too good to be a harlot, Elizabeth resisted Edward's advances with a dagger.

Although the story is credible, for Edward was within reach of Grafton on the relevant day, most of the details cannot be confirmed and may be fictional. 1 May, or May day, was already associated with romantic love. If the marriage did indeed occur so soon after Elizabeth's unequal agreement with Hastings, which was immediately repudiated, it indicates that the king's own chamberlain and intimate was ignorant of the betrothal, which is hardly credible, and hence that the king met Elizabeth, became infatuated with her, and married her within the three weeks from 13 April. Alternatively, did he intend marrying her at all? The precontract story reported in 1483–4, in which Edward had allegedly contracted himself to either Eleanor Butler or Elizabeth Lucy, suggests that the king may have been in the habit of luring unwilling ladies to bed by promises of matrimony. The ceremony of 1464, which was conducted by the Dominican Master Thomas Eborall, was clandestine and arguably of doubtful legality. Was Edward perhaps trapped, and obliged to honour his promise, when the validity of the marriage proved after all impossible to gainsay?

Edward revealed his marriage only when he had no choice. Pressed to proceed with plans for his marriage to Bona of Savoy, sister of the French queen, which formed part of a treaty negotiated by the earl of Warwick with Louis XI (r. 1461–83), he revealed that he was already married. There was universal disapproval. The match served no political purpose, wasted one of the new Yorkist regime's few diplomatic cards, and could potentially alienate the king of France. The bride was not a virgin, but a widow with children and numerous kindred, which, it soon emerged, the king would have to provide for. And whatever the connections of her mother, Jacquetta, her father's lineage was quite unworthy of a king. The match was considered dishonourable, as Polydore Vergil put it, because it was motivated 'by blynde affection, and not be reule of reason' (Anglica historia, 117). The sorcery suit against Elizabeth's mother, Jacquetta, in 1469–70 apparently presumed that necromancy had been necessary to secure such a marriage! However virtuous the new queen was, however romantic the story of her wooing, and however blessed the marriage was by children, political disapproval remained: the king's mother *Cecily, duchess of York (d. 1495), and his brother who was to become *Richard III were among those allegedly hostile even in the 1480s. Warwick and Clarence in 1469 and Richard III in 1483–4 took advantage of hostility to the Woodvilles.

Queen of England Despite such disapproval, the marriage had to be accepted, and the Reading great council formally received Elizabeth as queen. Her coronation, which was fully recorded by a herald, was celebrated on 26 May 1465. The first child of her marriage to the king, *Elizabeth of York, for four years Edward IV's heir apparent, was born in February 1466. Elizabeth was assigned dower from crown lands and duchy of Lancaster lands, mainly in southern England, worth £4541 in 1466/7. This was considerably less than the 10,000 marks allowed to previous queens, but her revenues were much more secure. Moreover such figures ignore the successive adjustments arranged in her favour, and the additional income provided for her wards and daughters which amounted to £866 in the 1460s. Her household was less extravagant than that of Margaret of Anjou, but it was nevertheless a princely establishment. A Hungarian visitor reported on the splendour of her churching in 1466, when the costliest food was served to her mother, her sister, and to Elizabeth herself, who is described as dining in solitary magnificence. The queen also seems to have spent much time with her husband, thereby reducing her expenses; in 1469 she accompanied him on a visit to Norwich. So large an estate and household offered Elizabeth extensive patronage, which she used to provide for her kinsfolk, both of blood and by marriage. Thus her first cousin Jacques Haute was a carver, her sister-in-law Lady Scales a damsel, and her distant cousin John Dyve her attorney-general, while her chamberlain, steward, and another damsel were chosen from among her Bourchier in-laws. Room was also found for Woodville servants, such as her solicitor-general, Robert Isham.

There were other, and more ostentatious, ways in which Elizabeth's elevation advanced her family. Her brother, Anthony *Woodville, Earl Rivers, was elected a knight of the Garter, her father became an earl, treasurer, and constable of England, and all her unmarried sisters were married to the heirs of comital or comital families, the first in October 1464. Her own son Thomas *Grey, now the king's stepson, was married in turn to Anne Holland, daughter of the king's own sister Anne, duchess of Exeter, in 1466, and then, following Anne's death, to another heiress, Cicely Bonville, in 1474. He was created earl of Huntingdon and marquess of Dorset. In 1483 parliament divided the Exeter inheritance between him and his younger brother, Richard.

Involvement in politics How far Elizabeth was active in politics is seldom clear. Following the acquittal of treason in

1468 of the London merchant Sir Thomas Cook (*d*. 1478), and his subsequent fine of 8000 marks for misprision, she showed herself personally vindictive in demanding a further 800 marks in queen's gold. In 1465 she initiated her brother's challenge to a joust sent to Antoine, count of La Roche, the Bastard of Burgundy, which was part of the Woodville-sponsored *rapprochement* of England with Burgundy. Late in the 1460s her family were prominent beneficiaries of royal patronage and in policy making at Edward IV's court. Favour to them was resented by others, in particular the Nevilles, and in 1469 Warwick's rebellion aimed in part to eliminate prominent members of the family: he succeeded in the cases of Rivers and Sir John Woodville. In October 1470, when Edward IV was driven into exile, Elizabeth took sanctuary at Westminster Abbey, where she gave birth to her son Edward, the future *Edward V. She emerged on her husband's return in April 1471, and in the following year was praised by the speaker of parliament for her 'womanly behaviour and great constancy' (Madden, 280). She pensioned the king's youngest brother Richard, duke of Gloucester, and backed him against his brother George, duke of Clarence, in the Warwick inheritance dispute in 1472–3.

Elizabeth accompanied the king to Canterbury on pilgrimage in 1471, to Oxford in 1472, and to Shrewsbury in 1473, where she assured the succession with the delivery of her second son *Richard, who became duke of York. During the 1470s she interested herself in the affairs of her sons, Edward, whose council of Wales was dominated by her family from 1473, and Richard, whose Norfolk estates were managed directly by her following his marriage to Anne Mowbray early in 1478. That wedding was synchronized with the judicial murder of her brother-in-law Clarence in parliament, which was attributed by at least some contemporaries to her jealousy and her fear that he represented an obstacle to the succession of her son. Certainly his trial was prepared with substantial Woodville involvement.

Elizabeth presented Edward with ten children from Elizabeth in 1466 to Bridget in 1480. There were three sons—Edward, Richard, and the shortlived George—and seven daughters. Two sons and five daughters outlived the king, among them *Katherine (1479–1527). Edward planned ambitious international marriages for Elizabeth and *Cecily that came to nothing: the Crowland continuator draws attention to the king's unmarried daughters at his last Christmas. However romantic Elizabeth's wooing, she did not secure King Edward's undivided attention. His reputation for lechery is difficult to substantiate, but two mistresses are identifiable and he had at least two bastards. It was his later escapades with Elizabeth Shore and Lord Hastings that exacerbated the existing hostility between the queen and her family towards Hastings.

The usurpation of Richard III On his deathbed Edward IV is reported to have sought to reconcile the Woodvilles and Hastings, unsuccessfully, and after his death, on 9 April 1483, the two factions divided the council of the new king, Edward V. The London council was apparently dominated by the queen and her son Dorset. As soon as 14 April it had

been decided to proceed at once with the coronation of the new king on 4 May, which would obviate any minority and might enable the queen's family to manage affairs, and Earl Rivers was instructed to bring the king to London at once. So early a coronation was thwarted by Gloucester's first *coup d'état* on 1 May, when he seized the person of Edward V and confined his uncle Earl Rivers and halfbrother Richard Grey. Recognizing this as a further threat to Edward V's succession, Elizabeth withdrew at once to sanctuary at Westminster with her second son Richard, her five unmarried daughters, and so much personal property that a breach was made in the walls between the palace and abbey for easier access. At this point, Archbishop Thomas Rotherham of York (*d*. 1500) allegedly assured her that he would crown her younger son Richard if Edward V was set aside, and briefly gave her custody of the great seal.

Elizabeth was not reassured by Gloucester's soothing letters, by his conveyance of Edward V to London, and the public respect that he showed him, which together allayed the alarm of Londoners and council alike. The council nominated Gloucester as lord protector and fixed a date in June for the coronation. The Woodvilles were presented as the principal enemies of the new regime. Although the council refused to sanction the execution of Rivers and Grey, they were imprisoned at Sheriff Hutton, Yorkshire, and vigorous action was taken against the fleet commanded by Elizabeth's son Dorset, which deserted him and caused him to go into exile. Negotiations by the council early in June failed to bring Elizabeth to heel. She was accused of plotting against Gloucester in his credence to York of 11 June and on 13 June of conspiring with Lord Hastings, who was executed at once, and with Elizabeth Shore. Such an alliance is unlikely and otherwise unsubstantiated. On 16 June Cardinal Thomas Bourchier (*d*. 1486), the archbishop of Canterbury, fetched her second son, Richard, from sanctuary, ostensibly to attend his brother's coronation, which was promptly postponed, and immediately afterwards doubt was cast on both the legality of her marriage and the legitimacy of her children because of the supposed betrothal that Edward IV contracted before their marriage. This was one of several justifications for Richard III's usurpation on 26 June. Rivers and Grey were executed at Pontefract on 25 June after a form of trial.

Conspiracy and submission All this time Elizabeth remained in sanctuary with her daughters, who were now potential figureheads for rebellion. Perhaps as early as July 1483 there was a plot to carry them abroad, which was thwarted by the exposure of the plotters and the blockade of the sanctuary on Richard's orders. Presumably Elizabeth supported the duke of Buckingham's rebellion in October–December 1483 in which her remaining son, Dorset, and her brothers were active participants. Originally intended to restore the two princes, the rebellion was disarmed by rumours of their death. Perhaps then, and certainly at Christmas, exiled rebels in Brittany, who included Dorset and Sir Richard and Sir Edward Woodville, witnessed Henry Tudor's vow to marry Elizabeth's eldest remaining daughter, Elizabeth of York, and recognized him as king: actions that made sense only if the princes were dead.

Meanwhile in England, in January 1484, parliament confirmed Richard's title—Elizabeth, no longer queen, had never been married to Edward IV, and was titled mere Dame Elizabeth Grey—and attainted his opponents, including Dorset and her brothers. Richard's victory appeared complete. And so, feeling that she could not remain in sanctuary indefinitely, Elizabeth agreed with the king on terms which were secured by his public and solemn promise on 1 March 1484. In return for leaving sanctuary and submitting to him, Richard agreed to support them and to find her daughters appropriate husbands. For the same reason she urged her last surviving son, Dorset, to desert Henry Tudor and return home. Her eldest daughter's presence at court at Christmas 1484 prompted suggestions that Richard intended marrying her, which he later had to deny, and which if true must have required Queen Elizabeth's consent. However that may be, Richard kept his promise to provide for her and her daughters and not to molest them.

Last years and death As Richard was overthrown at Bosworth by Henry Tudor (henceforth Henry VII), who did indeed marry Elizabeth of York, Queen Elizabeth had miscalculated, but initially there were no penalties. Indeed, she was godmother to Henry's son Prince Arthur (d. 1502). On 4–5 March 1486 she was restored to her dower lands, but no late medieval English king permitted dower to two queens simultaneously. It is scarcely credible that she had been plotting against her daughter in February 1487, when a great council deprived her of her dowerlands and transferred them to her daughter, though retribution for her having come to terms with Richard III cannot be ruled out. She withdrew to Bermondsey Abbey, where she was entitled to apartments formally reserved for the earls of Gloucester, and was awarded a pension of 400 marks (£266 13s. 4d.), increased to £400 in 1490. A proposal that she marry the widowed James III of Scotland in 1487 came to nothing. It was at Bermondsey that she made her will on 10 April 1492. As she had no worldly goods, she left the queen and her other daughters her blessing. She died there on 8 June and on 12 June was buried with little pomp beside Edward IV at St George's Chapel, Windsor, in accordance with her wishes, and in the presence of all her daughters except the queen, who was about to be confined. MICHAEL HICKS

Sources G. Smith, *The coronation of Elizabeth Wydeville* (1935) • A. R. Myers, 'The household of Queen Elizabeth Woodville, 1466–7', *Bulletin of the John Rylands University Library*, 50 (1967–8), 207–35, 443–81 • C. Fahy, 'The marriage of Edward IV and Elizabeth Woodville: a new Italian source', *EngHR*, 76 (1961), 660–72, esp. 660–63 • M. A. Hicks, 'The changing role of the Wydevilles in Yorkist politics to 1483', *Richard III and his rivals: magnates and their motives in the Wars of the Roses* (1991) • D. Mancinus, *De occupatione regni Anglie per Riccardum tercium libellus / The usurpation of Richard the third*, ed. and trans. C. A. J. Armstrong, 2nd edn (1964); pbk edn (1984) • F. Madden, 'Narratives of the arrival of Louis de Bruges, seigneur de la Gruthuyse, in England, and of his creation as earl of Winchester in 1472', *Archaeologia*, 26 (1836), 265–86 • N. Pronay and J. Cox, eds., *The Crowland chronicle continuations, 1459–1486* (1986) • J. R. Lander, 'Marriage and politics in the fifteenth century: the Nevilles and the Wydevilles', *Crown and nobility, 1450–1509* (1976), 94–126 • *The Anglica historia of Polydore Vergil, AD 1485–1537*, ed. and trans. D. Hay, CS, 3rd ser., 74 (1950) • D. MacGibbon, *Elizabeth Woodville (1437–1492): her life and times* (1938) • C. Ross, *Edward IV* (1974) • *Three books of Polydore Vergil's 'English history'*, ed. H. Ellis, CS, 29 (1844) • R. Fabyan, *The new chronicles of England and France*, ed. H. Ellis, new edn (1811) • J. Ashdown-Hill, 'Edward IV's uncrowned queen: the Lady Eleanor Talbot, Lady Butler', *The Ricardian*, 11 (1997–9), 166–90
Archives PRO, Cornwallis, SC6 and DL29
Likenesses Skinners' Company, illumination, Guild Register of Assumption • illumination, repro. in *Luton Guild Book* • manuscript illumination (*The dictes and sayings of the philosophers*), LPL, MS 265, fol. 1v • oils, Royal Collection [*see illus.*] • oils (after an oil painting, Royal Collection), Queen's College, Cambridge • portrait (version of oil painting, Royal Collection), AM Oxf. • stained glass, Canterbury Cathedral • triptych (of her marriage), Northampton Art Gallery

Elizabeth [Elizabeth of York] (**1466–1503**), queen of England, consort of Henry VII, was the eldest child of *Edward IV and his wife, *Elizabeth Woodville. She was born at Westminster on 11 February 1466 and baptized in the abbey, with the duchesses of York and Bedford and the earl of Warwick as her godparents.

Princess and dynastic pawn No son was born to Edward and Elizabeth until November 1470 and until then Elizabeth was her father's heir. In the winter of 1469–70 she was betrothed to George, the son of John Neville, Marquess Montagu, as part of Edward IV's attempts to build bridges with the Nevilles after Richard Neville's rising against him earlier in 1469. The arrangement rapidly became a dead letter, however, and was abandoned after the deaths of Montagu and Warwick in opposition to Edward at the battle of Barnet in 1471. In the will drawn up by Edward IV before his invasion of France in 1475, 10,000 marks were set aside for Elizabeth's marriage, but no candidates appear to have been under consideration. That situation was transformed by the French invasion itself. As part of the treaty of Picquigny which concluded the campaign, it was agreed that Elizabeth should marry the dauphin Charles, with a jointure of £60,000 to be provided by Louis XI. Were Elizabeth to die before reaching marriageable age, the sister next to her in age, Mary, was to take her place. In 1481 Mary was betrothed to the king of Denmark, in tacit recognition that her service as reserve was no longer needed. Elizabeth was then fifteen, old enough to marry, although the marriage had still not taken place. That it would never take place became apparent with the Franco-Burgundian treaty of Arras agreed on 23 December 1482. Under the terms of the agreement Charles was to marry the infant daughter of Maximilian of Austria and Mary of Burgundy, and although in the event this marriage, too, failed to take effect, the treaty marked the final collapse of the Picquigny settlement.

Edward IV died on 9 April 1483, his death hastened, according to some accounts, by the diplomatic débâcle. None of his daughters was then married, and their situation was transformed by the events which followed. At

Elizabeth [of York] (1466–1503), by unknown artist, *c*.1502

the end of April, Edward's brother Richard, duke of Gloucester, took possession of the young *Edward V. When news of this development reached London, Elizabeth Woodville, with her daughters and younger son *Richard, duke of York, took sanctuary at Westminster. On 16 June York was handed over to Gloucester, who immediately cancelled plans for the coronation of Edward V and on 26 June took the throne himself as Richard III. The grounds on which he justified this move were that his brother's marriage to Elizabeth Woodville had been bigamous, due to Edward's earlier betrothal to another woman, and that the children of the marriage were therefore illegitimate and barred from the succession.

Between Richard III and Henry Tudor Throughout this crisis period, and during the early months of the new reign, Elizabeth and her sisters remained in sanctuary. They were an obvious focus for political disaffection, and the Crowland chronicler believed that there were attempts to remove them from sanctuary and send them overseas. Richard took the precaution of placing a guard on the sanctuary, under the command of John Nesfield, one of his esquires of the body. This, however, could only be a short-term expedient. The presence of his sister-in-law and nieces in sanctuary was a political embarrassment as well as a potential danger for the king, and the need to find some resolution of the problem was emphasized at Christmas 1483. On that day *Henry Tudor (1457–1509),

who had emerged as the figurehead of opposition to Richard in the rebellion of the previous October, took an oath in Rennes Cathedral to marry Elizabeth of York were he to be successful in making himself king of England. This possibility had been raised earlier in the rebellion's development, and Tudor writers on the rising saw it as the fruit of negotiations between Margaret Beaufort, Tudor's mother, and Elizabeth Woodville.

From Tudor's perspective this was an extremely shrewd move. His own claims to the throne were virtually non-existent and a marriage to Elizabeth would give him credibility. More immediately, he was reliant on Yorkist support in England and associating himself with the descent of the crown through the line of Edward IV was an effective counter to the man who had disrupted that descent. Richard responded by opening negotiations with Elizabeth Woodville, aided by the completeness of the rebellion's collapse in the previous autumn. On 1 March 1484 they reached agreement. Elizabeth and her sisters were to come out of sanctuary and be placed in 'honest places of good name and fame' (Horrox and Hammond, 3.190). Richard guaranteed their safety and promised to maintain them as befitted his kinswomen. He also undertook to find suitable husbands for them, defined as 'gentlemen born', and to settle 200 marks yearly on each of them at marriage. The need to have the sisters safely married off may well have been Richard's main concern. Certainly the possibility that he would lose his chance to marry Elizabeth is said by Polydore Vergil to have 'pinched [Tudor] to the very stomach' (*Anglica historia*, 559). It is revealing, however, that the first, and, in the event, the only one of the sisters to be found a husband in Richard's reign was *Cecily—the second eldest sister after the death of Mary in 1482. Elizabeth herself remained unmarried, presumably because the risk of her transmitting a claim to the throne made the choice of husband highly sensitive. The story of Edward IV's 'bigamy' does not seem to have commanded much belief, and Tudor's promise to marry Elizabeth demonstrates the political irrelevance of Elizabeth's bastardization—as, indeed, did the murder of her brothers.

Elizabeth was at court for the Christmas festivities of 1484, where the Crowland chronicler was scandalized by the fact that she and Richard's queen wore similar clothes—although in fact this was not an uncommon assertion of closeness of rank or relationship. As queen herself Elizabeth was often to wear the same clothes as her mother-in-law on formal occasions. At Christmas 1484 the message was indeed striking, being no less than the acceptance of the bastardized daughters of Edward IV back into the royal family, and contemporaries must have been sharply aware of the shift in official thinking which that represented. Less than a year earlier Elizabeth's mother had been routinely referred to simply as 'Elizabeth, late wife of Sir John Grey'. But the chronicler's belief that it was evidence that Elizabeth was being cast as Richard's second wife is coloured by hindsight. Richard's wife, Anne Neville, died on 16 March 1485 and a search immediately began for a new wife for the childless king.

Among the names suggested was that of his niece Elizabeth, and it is likely that it was given serious consideration—serious enough for some of Richard's inner circle to become anxious about the likely political consequences. Their hostility to the proposal led Richard to make a public denial that he had ever contemplated such a marriage.

Queen of England On 22 August 1485 Richard III was defeated and killed at Bosworth by Henry Tudor, who was crowned king as Henry VII on 30 October. Elizabeth's whereabouts at the time of the battle are uncertain, but afterwards Henry had her placed in the London household of his mother, Margaret *Beaufort, along with several of her young kinsmen, including Edward Stafford and the earl of Warwick. The parliament which met on 7 November asserted the legitimacy of Henry's title and annulled the instrument embodying Richard III's title to the throne, which had included the bastardy of Edward IV's children. On 10 December the Commons, through their speaker Thomas Lovell, urged the king to act on his promise to marry 'that illustrious lady Elizabeth, daughter of King Edward IV' and so render possible 'the propagation of offspring from the stock of kings' (*RotP*, 6.278)—a formulation which suggests that, for all Henry's efforts to establish himself on the throne before his marriage, popular feeling still regarded marriage to Elizabeth as a crucial element in his title. Four days earlier Giovanni de Giglis had reported to the pope that 'it is positively asserted that the king is about to marry her, which everybody considers advantageous for the kingdom' (*CSP Venice, 1202–1509*, 1.58). The Lords endorsed the Commons' request and Henry agreed to proceed as they wished. The marriage took place on 18 January 1486. This was in advance of the papal dispensation, which was not issued until March, but had been authorized two days earlier (on 16 January) by a papal legate then present in England, an action retrospectively validated by Pope Innocent VIII in July. Plans were not set in train for Elizabeth's coronation until September 1487, and it took place on 25 November, over a year after she had given birth to Prince Arthur.

It was not until the day after her coronation that Henry made formal landed provision for his wife, although the claim by de Giglis in December 1485 that she had been declared duchess of York may imply that some provision was initially made for her from her father's duchy. The endowment then granted to her was that assigned to her mother as dower in March 1486, and it is unclear whether the transfer was in some way intended as a 'punishment' of the queen dowager (as a number of historians have claimed) or simply a negotiated reassignment of resources within the royal family. It consisted of six duchy of Lancaster manors in Essex, augmented with other land and revenues—apparently less than the provision made for her immediate predecessors. In February 1492 Elizabeth was granted the reversion of some of the duchy of York land still held by her grandmother Cecily, including Wareham, Weymouth, and Portland. Cecily died on 31 May 1495 and the parliament of the following October confirmed Elizabeth's possession of the estates, although errors in their identification meant that a corrected act had to be passed in 1497.

Public affairs Elizabeth's political role as queen has traditionally been played down, Nicolas going so far as to assert that 'from the moment in which Elizabeth of York became Queen of England her life loses its political interest' (Nicolas, lxxv). Discussion of her role is usually confined to the domestic sphere—including court ceremonial, which is well documented for the early years of Henry's reign. A number of later writers have argued that she was overshadowed by her mother-in-law, the redoubtable Margaret Beaufort, citing the claim of a contemporary Spanish observer that 'she is kept in subjection by the mother of the king' (*CSP Spain, 1485–1509*, 164). An aggrieved minor royal servant, the yeoman of the crown John Hewyk, gave a similar picture when he grumbled that he would have spoken more to the queen 'had [it] not been for that strong whore the king's mother' (Stevenson and others, 3.301). Certainly Margaret seems to have been much more about the court than had been usual for kings' mothers, and although Elizabeth is always given precedence in formal accounts it is clear that contemporaries recognized the presence of *two* powerful royal ladies rather than just one. The impact of this on the personal relationship of the two women is impossible to gauge. The rather pathetic image evoked by the Spanish commentator, who advised his correspondent that 'it would be a good thing to write to her often and show her [the queen] a little love', *might* be a perceptive glimpse behind the public persona, but foreign residents at court are far from infallible guides. The most that can be said is that in the political arena the queen's traditional role as intercessor must in practice have been shared.

'Shared', but not eclipsed. It was Elizabeth to whom a Welsh tenant appealed over an injustice involving the king's uncle Jasper Tudor, and Elizabeth responded with a firm letter to Jasper. It is likely that the relative silence about Elizabeth's political involvement means that her interventions were uncontroversial rather than nonexistent. It is usually only when queens were thought to have overstepped the mark, by intervening unilaterally in 'high' politics, that contemporaries commented on their activity. The more subtle forms of influence generally passed unremarked, but it is worth noting that Elizabeth's private expenses, with their famous payments to the humble givers of cherries and puddings, also show that she was the recipient of gifts from the eminent, who presumably thought her goodwill worth having.

Family matters and role at court Elizabeth naturally retained her links with the surviving members of the Yorkist royal family. She stayed in touch with her aunt Elizabeth, the dowager duchess of Suffolk, and was apparently responsible for arranging for the wife of her disgraced cousin Edmund de la Pole to stay with the duchess of Norfolk. It was Elizabeth who arranged the marriage between her sister Anne and the heir of the earl of Surrey in 1495, and probably that of her sister *Katherine to William Courtenay, heir to the earl of Devon, in the same year. Certainly some of the costs of Katherine Courtenay's growing family were later met by the queen, including the wages of the infants' 'rockers'. Given this concern for her sisters to marry well, it may be significant that it was Margaret Beaufort and not Elizabeth who came to the rescue when another sister, Cecily, contracted a *mésalliance* with Thomas Kyme. Beyond her immediate family, too, it is likely that Elizabeth was seen as a route to favour in the new political world. Richard III's treasurer of the chamber, Edmund Chaderton, was taken into Elizabeth's service and ended his life as her chancellor. But it is important not to see this in terms of 'rival' courts. Henry's own household and administration also had a strong Yorkist component, as did that of Margaret Beaufort. The king proved himself consistently aware of the need to win over Yorkist supporters, including former Ricardians, and his wife had an obvious role to play in that process. Indeed for contemporaries she embodied the process.

Elizabeth played a full role in courtly pursuits. In her more bookish pursuits she is again closely associated with her mother-in-law. Both women sponsored Caxton's printing of *The Fifteen Oes* in 1491, and a few years later they jointly gave a copy of Wynkyn de Worde's printing of Walter Hilton's *Scala perfectionis* to Elizabeth's lady-in-waiting Margery Roos. But if, in the sphere of literary devotion, Elizabeth can be seen as Margaret's protégé, in other areas she took a more independent line. She rewarded the court composers William Cornish and Robert Fayrfax for a Christmas carol and an anthem of Our Lady and St Elizabeth respectively. Secular court revels were a large part of her life as well, with frequent references in her accounts to minstrels and disguisings. Hunting features less often, but she kept a pack of greyhounds (presumably for coursing small game rather than as elegant pets) and a goshawk. Less predictably, she had a hand in the design of Henry's new building at Greenwich, where in 1502 Robert Vertue was working from a plan devised by the queen.

Motherhood and death For a new and shaky dynasty, ensuring the succession was crucial, and here too Elizabeth lived up to contemporary expectations. Five children survived infancy: *Arthur (1486–1502), *Margaret (*b.* 29 November 1489), *Henry (*b.* 28 June 1491), *Mary (1496–1533) and Edmund (*b.* 21–2 February 1499). Several other children died in infancy, including Elizabeth (*b.* 2 July 1492) and Katherine (her last child). But by the time of the queen's own death only Margaret, Mary, and Henry were still alive. Arthur had died on 2 April 1502, and the news reached the court at Greenwich in the early hours of Tuesday 4 April. The royal council sent the king's confessor to break the news to Henry, who asked for Elizabeth to be fetched. She comforted her husband, reminding him of their three surviving children and that 'God is where he was, and we are both young enough.' But on her return to her own chamber 'natural and motherly remembrance of that great loss smote her so sorrowful to the heart that those about her were fain to send for the king to comfort her' (Leland, 5.373–4). As numerous writers have commented, the scene gives the lie to Bacon's claim that there was little love lost between Henry and his wife, and that

'his aversion toward the house of York was so predominant in him as it found place not only in his wars and councils, but in his chamber and bed' (Bacon, 20). A similarly affectionate picture is given by the report that, upon Elizabeth's own death, Henry 'privily departed to a solitary place and would no man should resort unto him' (Chrimes, 304).

The queen's last pregnancy proved fatal. Her surgeon Master Robert was hastily summoned on 22 January, the baby Katherine was born prematurely at the Tower on 2 February 1503, and Elizabeth died nine days later on 11 February, her thirty-seventh birthday. Less than a year previously Henry's court astrologer had forecast that she would live to be at least eighty, and in humanist circles her death became a paradigm of the fallibility of astrology. She was buried at Westminster Abbey, her funeral expenses amounting to £2800. The effigy carried in her funeral procession survives, but it is carved in wood rather than based on a death mask and gives little sense of the queen's appearance. Her portrait survives only in later copies, which suggest that she may have been rather chubby-faced. The Portuguese ambassador described her in 1501 as stout and large breasted—not the image conveyed by the elegant tomb effigy by Pietro Torrigiano. Two years later the Venetian ambassador Alvise Mocenigo, sending word of her death, summed her up as a 'very handsome woman and in conduct very able' (*CSP Venice, 1202–1509*, 298). There are no dissident voices. Contemporaries were apparently united in their admiration of her, and the narrative of her funeral describes her as 'one of the most gracious and best beloved Princesses in the world' (Nicolas, xcvii).   ROSEMARY HORROX

Sources *Chancery records* · *RotP*, vol. 6 · J. Leland, *Collectanea*, ed. J. Hearne, 6 vols. (1715) · *The Anglica historia of Polydore Vergil, AD 1485–1537*, ed. and trans. D. Hay, CS, 3rd ser., 74 (1950) · N. H. Nicolas, ed., *Privy purse expenses of Elizabeth of York: wardrobe accounts of Edward the Fourth* (1830) · N. Pronay and J. Cox, eds., *The Crowland chronicle continuations, 1459–1486* (1986) · C. Ross, *Edward IV* (1974) · R. Horrox, *Richard III, a study of service*, Cambridge Studies in Medieval Life and Thought, 4th ser., 11 (1989) · S. B. Chrimes, *Henry VII* (1972) · M. K. Jones and M. G. Underwood, *The king's mother: Lady Margaret Beaufort, countess of Richmond and Derby* (1992) · F. Bacon, *The history of the reign of King Henry VII, and selected works*, ed. B. Vickers (1998) · R. Horrox and P. W. Hammond, eds., *British Library Harleian manuscript 433*, 4 vols. (1979–83) · W. H. Stevenson and others, eds., *Records of the borough of Nottingham*, 9 vols. (1882–1956) · *CSP Spain, 1485–1509* · *CSP Venice, 1202–1509* · S. Thurley, *The royal palaces of England: architecture and court life, 1460–1547* (1993)
Likenesses oils, *c.*1502, Royal Collection [*see illus.*] · Laurence, wooden funeral effigy, 1503, Westminster Abbey · P. Torrigiano, bronze effigy on monument, *c.*1512–1518, Westminster Abbey; electrotype, NPG · R. Van Leemput, group portrait, oils, 1667 (*Privy chamber group*; after H. Holbein the younger), Royal Collection · group portrait, stained-glass window (with three sisters), St Giles' Church, Little Malvern, Worcestershire · oils (after portrait, *c.*1502), NPG · portrait, Skinner's Company, London, Book of the Fraternity of Corpus Christi, MSS

Elizabeth, Princess [Elizabeth Stuart] (**1596–1662**), queen of Bohemia and electress palatine, consort of Frederick V, eldest and only surviving daughter of *James VI of Scotland (James I of England) (1566–1625) and his wife, *Anne of Denmark (1574–1619), was born at Falkland Palace in

Princess Elizabeth (1596–1662), by Gerrit van Honthorst, 1642

August 1596, on 19 August—or, according to some sources, 16 August (Oman, 1)—and was baptized on 28 November the same year.

Childhood and education As a child the Princess Elizabeth was entrusted by her father to the care of Alexander, Lord Livingstone, later earl of Linlithgow, and his wife, Helen Hay, daughter of Andrew Hay, earl of Erroll. Elizabeth grew up in Linlithgow Castle, midway between Stirling and Edinburgh, within a day's ride of each. In June 1603 Elizabeth accompanied her mother to England. Here Lady Frances Howard, who had married Henry Brooke, Lord Cobham, as her second husband, was appointed her governess. However, when Cobham's involvement in the Main and Bye plots was discovered, Lady Cobham was relieved of her charge in September 1603 and Elizabeth was removed on 19 October to the household of John, Lord Harington of Exton, and his wife, Anne. Harington was well known for his strict adherence to the Reformed faith, for his abhorrence of Catholicism, and for his belief in the virtues of learning, ideals which were to have a considerable influence on the princess. Elizabeth now lived mostly at Combe Abbey, 2½ miles north of Coventry, one of the family seats of her governor, visiting the court only on rare occasions until 1608. She received instruction in writing, French, and Italian (languages she was to master with considerable success) as well as horse riding, music, and dancing. John Bull, organist of the Chapel Royal, was one of her music instructors. At the time of the Gunpowder Plot, Harington left Combe Abbey with his charge and sought protection in Coventry as he had reason to fear that the conspirators would try to seize the princess, but otherwise Elizabeth's childhood in England was uneventful.

From the end of 1608 Elizabeth took up residence at court, where she took part in the great court festivals and danced in the masque *Tethys* in 1610. She had lodgings at Hampton Court as well as at Whitehall and in Harington's residence at Kew. During these years her elder brother *Henry, born in 1594, became her closest confidant. When they were unable to see each other, brother and sister exchanged frequent letters. The education she had received in Lord Harington's house had prepared Elizabeth for the idealistic militant protestantism which Henry cultivated. In fact one of Henry's closest companions was John Harington, son and heir of Elizabeth's preceptor. The princess clearly idolized Henry. She remained all her life true to the memory of her high-minded brother, who died prematurely in November 1612, and was later seen by contemporaries as the real inheritor of his political and religious ideals, much more so than her younger brother *Charles.

Marriage The choice of a suitable husband for the attractive princess—visitors to the court commented on the striking beauty of the golden-haired girl—was predictably a matter of great political concern. Her elder brother openly opposed a marriage with a Catholic prince, which James I and even more so his consort Queen Anne were reluctant to reject out of hand. There was certainly no lack of suitors. Among the princes asking for Elizabeth's hand were Frederick Ulrich of Brunswick, Prince Otto of Hesse, the duke of Savoy's son, and the king of Sweden's son Gustavus Adolphus, the hero of the early 1630s, all except the prince of Savoy protestants. In the end, however, **Frederick V** [Friedrich V], count palatine of the Rhine and elector of the Holy Roman empire (1596–1632), was chosen as her husband. Born on 26 August 1596 NS, he was the son of Friedrich IV (1574–1610) and Louise Juliana (1576–1644), daughter of William I of Orange (d. 1584), and had been educated in the Huguenot enclave at Sedan, under the protection of the duc de Bouillon. Having sent first Johann Albrecht, Count Solms, the lord high steward of the Palatinate, and then the steward of his household, Hans Meinhard von Schönberg (or Schomberg), to England to prepare the ground (the marriage contract itself was signed on 16 May), Frederick arrived in England himself on 16 October 1612. Although Elizabeth's mother was opposed to the marriage and warned her daughter that she was marrying beneath her station, the young princess, probably under the influence of her brother Henry, eagerly welcomed the match. On 18 December Frederick was invested with the Order of the Garter and on 27 December betrothed to Elizabeth in the banqueting house in Whitehall. The solemn wedding ceremony took place on 14 February 1613 in the chapel of Whitehall Palace, accompanied by extensive celebrations staged both at court and in the City.

The marriage was part of a wider alliance concluded in the spring of 1612 between England and the protestant union, an association of German princes and free cities under the leadership of the Palatinate. For James I this protestant alliance was to be complemented by a closer understanding with Catholic dynasties, possibly cemented by the marriage of his sons with French or Spanish princesses. Thus the palatine marriage was to be not much more than a well-calculated move in a more comprehensive dynastic policy which would allow James to play his cherished role as Europe's peacemaker. For James's son Henry, however, who died before the wedding ceremony took place, and those at court who thought like him, the marriage between his sister and the elector meant much more. The *Masque of Truth*, which was to be performed at the wedding and which had probably been commissioned by Henry, celebrated the marriage as an event of truly eschatological significance, ushering in the final battle between light and darkness in which the empire of evil, that is popery, would finally be vanquished. After Henry's death it became impossible to stage this masque, but even so numerous plays and poems written or performed in 1613 or the following year, such as *The Hector of Germanie, or, The Palsgrave, Prince Elector* by Wentworth Smith (1614), conveyed the same political message. Such sentiments were to be revived in 1619, when Frederick V accepted the crown of Bohemia, to the dismay of Elizabeth's father. In 1613 even James I had a medal struck to celebrate the wedding on which his daughter figured as 'Elizabeth altera', an allusion to James's predecessor and to the political traditions of Elizabethan England. In later years Elizabeth did not hesitate to mobilize support for the palatine cause by appealing to the almost saintlike veneration in which she was held as the heiress of the 'Name and Vertues, the Majesty and generositie of our Immortal Queene Elizabeth' (Cogswell, 96).

Electress palatine Elizabeth and her husband did not leave England until 26 April to travel slowly via Flushing, The Hague, and up the River Rhine to Heidelberg, where the new electress was solemnly welcomed on 17 June 1613. Frederick V, the prince whom Elizabeth had married, was the ruler of one of the four secular prince electorates of the Holy Roman empire, and as such a key figure in German politics before the outbreak of the Thirty Years' War. As a Calvinist he was in the forefront of the battle against the Counter-Reformation and against the house of Habsburg in Germany. Frederick V's marriage with James I's daughter seemed to be the crowning achievement of a policy which tried to give the Palatinate a central place in international politics. Moreover, the marriage with a princess of royal blood was bound to enhance the status that Frederick V enjoyed among the German princes and strengthened his own and his counsellors' political ambitions, which in retrospect were dangerously unrealistic. Indeed Elizabeth herself was later blamed for having encouraged her husband to pursue an aggressive anti-Habsburg policy and to accept the crown of Bohemia in 1619, because she thought it demeaning to be the wife of a mere German prince. There is no real proof for this supposition, but the fact that Frederick V was married to a princess who could claim precedence over him on ceremonial occasions—and did, on her father's insistence, do so—must have furthered his wish to obtain a kinglike status or indeed a royal crown for himself, which would put him on an equal footing with Europe's great monarchs or at least with his own wife.

Elizabeth's presence in Heidelberg brought an air of extravagance and refinement to the Palatinate. The princess, who had been accompanied to Heidelberg by her own numerous English household establishment, insisted on living in style. Her lack of restraint in financial matters, and her sometimes rather drastic sense of humour as well as her refusal to become 'all Dutch' (i.e. German) and indeed to learn German, however, did not make her universally popular in Heidelberg, in spite of her indisputable charm and beauty (Lemberg, 16). It took the sustained efforts of Hans Meinhard von Schönberg, who now held the office of marshall in the palatine court but acted also as James I's representative in Heidelberg, to alleviate the tensions between her servants and the elector's entourage and to reorganize Elizabeth's household, where waste and disorder reigned. But the influence which the matrimonial alliance with England had on the Heidelberg court went beyond a mere increase of expenditure and occasional conflicts of precedence. Even in earlier years the Palatinate had been more strongly influenced by the intellectual traditions of western European than other German principalities. After 1613 Heidelberg was clearly distinguished from other princely courts by an altogether grander and almost royal style at once indebted to the ideals of chivalry, humanism, and militant protestantism. This style was inspired by the dynastic alliance with the Stuarts, which also brought new artists to Heidelberg. The famous architect, engineer, and scientist Salomon de Caus, for example, who had worked for Elizabeth's brother Henry before 1613, followed her to Heidelberg and created the Hortus Palatinus, the most famous Renaissance garden in Germany.

Queen of Bohemia The marriage between Elizabeth and Frederick was a happy and affectionate one, although the elector was subject to periodic bouts of depression. On 14 January 1614 NS the couple's first child, Frederick Henry (1614–1629), was born; the birth of their second son, *Charles Lewis, followed on 1 January 1618 and that of their eldest daughter, Elizabeth, one year later (5 January 1619). By this time the political crisis in Germany had already worsened to such an extent that war was imminent. Frederick, influenced by his advisers, decided to accept the crown which the Bohemian estates, having shortly before deposed Archduke Ferdinand of Austria—soon to be elected emperor—offered him in August 1619. Elizabeth herself did not yet play a very active part in politics. She did, however, clearly identify herself with her husband's policy, and certainly did nothing to dissuade him from accepting the Bohemian crown. Personal affection and loyalty, religious enthusiasm, but probably also the encouragement she received from the archbishop of

Canterbury, George Abbott, account for her attitude. Abbott gave Elizabeth to understand that her father would be bound to support her and her husband, regardless of his reluctance to endorse the Bohemian adventure. In October Frederick and Elizabeth left the Palatinate and travelled to Prague, where they arrived on 31 October. A few days later, on 4 November, the elector was crowned king of Bohemia in St Vitus's Cathedral. This ceremony was followed by Elizabeth's own coronation three days later. However, the royal couple were not universally popular in their new capital. Elizabeth herself spoke little German, whereas the ladies of the Bohemian court hardly knew any French—a language Elizabeth spoke fluently—let alone English. Elizabeth's manners, her low-cut dresses—shameless by Bohemian standards—the irregular hours she kept, and not least the dogs and pet monkeys which surrounded her, offended the feelings of the native nobility and citizens. The strict Calvinism which Frederick and his entourage subscribed to, however, was even more offensive, and made the new king and his consort unpopular even with many non-Catholics, who preferred a more moderate form of protestantism.

On 18 December 1619 Elizabeth gave birth in Prague to her fourth child, who was christened *Rupert (Ruprecht), evoking the memory of Rupert III, elector palatine, who had been elected king of the Romans and emperor designate on the deposition of King Wenceslaus (who had ruled Bohemia as well as Germany) in the year 1400. The situation in Bohemia as well as in the Palatinate itself, however, soon became critical. In autumn 1620 Spanish troops overran large parts of the Lower Palatinate. Elizabeth, who knew that she could not really count on her father's support, entreated her brother Charles to intercede with James I for her 'that loves you more than all the world' and her husband (Elizabeth to Charles, 15 Sept 1620, Letters, 54). In October the Catholic armies advanced on Prague, and on 8 November Frederick's troops suffered a devastating defeat at the battle of the White Mountain. As Frederick's enemies had predicted, his rule in Bohemia had not lasted much longer than one winter. The Catholic pamphlets which were now published, and which satirized Frederick's short reign, often attributed the responsibility for his reckless policy to his allegedly arrogant and frivolous consort, although such criticism did nothing to diminish her popularity among the more militant protestants in Europe. The royal couple fled via Breslau, Küstrin (where her fifth child, *Maurice, was born on 16 January 1621), Berlin, and Wolfenbüttel to the Netherlands.

Elizabeth and the establishment of the palatine court in exile, 1621–1623 In The Hague Frederick and Elizabeth were received by the stadholder Maurice of Orange on 14 April 1621. The states general granted Frederick and his family financial support which was, at least initially, generous. They resided in the house Wassenaar-Duivenvoorde in The Hague, which belonged to Johan van Oldenbarnevelt's exiled son-in-law Cornelius van der Myle. In 1625 Oldenbarnevelt's own house—the owner had been executed for political reasons in 1619—also became part of their lodgings. In the Netherlands, where

Elizabeth was to spend the next decades in exile, she and her husband continued to live, at least during the 1620s, before retrenchments became inevitable, with all the trappings of royalty and little regard to the costs this entailed. Hunting, dances, and spectacles dominated life at the palatine court in exile. Elizabeth had herself and her family painted by some of the leading Dutch portrait painters of the period, in particular Gerrit van Honthorst and Michiel Jansz von Miereveldt, and sent many of the portraits to her supporters in the Netherlands and abroad. She and two of her children, Rupert and Louise Hollandine, later even took painting lessons themselves.

Politically, however, matters went from bad to worse. In 1622–3 Spain and Bavaria occupied the Upper and Lower Palatinate, where the last garrisons loyal to the elector surrendered. Frederick V had already been outlawed by the emperor in January 1621; he now lost not only his hereditary dominions but also his electoral dignity, which was transferred to Maximilian of Bavaria in February 1623. In this desperate situation Elizabeth's political role began to change. In Heidelberg and Prague she had played only a modest part in politics in spite of her elevated status as a king's daughter. In exile, however, she became much more an equal, if not in fact the stronger, partner in the marriage with Frederick V. Frederick was devoted more than ever to his wife. He relied on English diplomatic and financial support in the 1620s, the latter, apart from the Dutch subsidies which he received, his principal source of income in exile, and continued to hope for England's direct intervention in the war. Elizabeth herself had a considerable talent to inspire admiration, loyalty, and love in Germany as well as England, more so than her husband, who tended to abandon himself to despair. Her beauty and undisputed charm, her strength of character, and the high-spirited courage with which she continued to fight undismayed for the palatine cause against heavy odds, but also the fact that her upbringing and education seemed to make her the perfect protestant heroine, gave her a unique position as the symbol of militant protestantism in Europe. Seemingly sober diplomats or scholars like Sir Henry Wotton wrote sonnets in her praise or, like Sir Thomas Roe, swore to 'serve her to deathe, to poverty', adding 'if you shall ever please to command, I will be converted to dust and ashes at your Majesties feet' (Strachan, 119; Oman, 212–13). Noblemen and soldiers committed to the ideals of chivalry like Christian of Brunswick in Germany or the third earl of Essex in England took pride in fighting for her cause. A cult of the 'Queen of Hearts' (Oman, 255), in which erotic, romantic, and religious elements were combined, developed in the 1620s, and Elizabeth knew how to encourage this enthusiasm.

One of Elizabeth's most ardent admirers was Christian of Brunswick-Wolfenbüttel (1599–1626), the protestant administrator of the prince-bishopric of Halberstadt in northern Germany. Christian was a military adventurer who acquired a reputation for ruthlessness; he was not averse to acts of robbery and kidnapping to improve his financial situation. In 1621, however, he raised an army to fight for his cousin Elizabeth and Frederick V. Christian's device in his campaign was 'pour dieu et pour elle', and in serving Elizabeth he clearly modelled himself on the knightly heroes celebrated by the chivalrous novels of the time. However, in June 1622 Christian was beaten at Höchst by Tilly and, having raised a new army, again in August 1623 at Stadtlohn near the Dutch border. Nevertheless, he was made a knight of the Garter in 1624 on Elizabeth's request. He remained devoted to Elizabeth until his early death in 1626. Although Elizabeth's own feelings for the 'mad bishop of Halberstadt', as contemporaries called him, are difficult to ascertain, Christian's sister Sophie assured him in December 1625 that 'la belle' whom he so adored still had a great deal of affection for him (Opel, 317). With Christian's defeat in 1623, however, the palatine cause seemed to be desperate, and all the more so as James I was now more strongly committed than ever to a compromise with Spain. Elizabeth watched with dismay the negotiations over a Spanish marriage and the prince of Wales's journey to Madrid in 1623. She had come to distrust her father, and wrote in despair to Lord Conway in September 1623, 'yet I hope his majesty will one day see the falsehood of our enemies'; but she continued to hope for her brother's help, in particular after his return from Spain, when Charles turned to a strongly anti-Spanish policy (*Letters*, ed. Baker, 67–8).

Renewed hopes and disappointments, 1624–1632 The fact that both Charles and the king's favourite the duke of Buckingham now tried to win king and parliament for a war against Spain seemed to augur well for the palatine cause. After November 1623 Elizabeth began to wear an ornament whose centrepiece was a lock of Charles's hair as a token of the trust she put in her brother. She and her husband remained in close contact with the war party in England during the last months of 1623 and throughout 1624. However, after Charles I became king in March 1625, the war strategy soon proved to be abortive. One of Frederick's and Elizabeth's most influential and most trusted advisers, Johann Joachim von Rusdorf, who acted as their representative in England, clearly blamed the old and new favourite the duke of Buckingham for this disaster. Rusdorf was in close contact with Buckingham's opponents at court, in particular Archbishop Abbott, in 1625–6, and although it is not quite clear to what extent Frederick and Elizabeth shared Rusdorf's sentiments—they certainly could not afford to criticize the duke openly—Buckingham himself began to see the palatine court in exile as a hotbed of opposition to his policy, closely linked with his enemies at court and in the country. On the other hand, the king and queen of Bohemia were bound to react with indignation to Buckingham's plans to marry his daughter to one of their sons, possibly their heir, which he wished to promote during a visit to The Hague in November 1625. Buckingham apparently wished to silence those of his critics who still saw him as a traitor to the protestant cause by this marriage, but such an alliance would also have made his grandchild the possible heir to the English crown. The king and queen of Bohemia managed to stifle any discussion of the dubious marriage project without

openly offending the duke, but relations with the favourite remained tense. Rusdorf had to be recalled from London in January 1627 because the duke rightly suspected him of damaging his reputation abroad, in The Hague as much as in Germany and Scandinavia, by his reports. When Buckingham was assassinated in August 1628, Rusdorf on his part welcomed his death as an 'act of God' (Rusdorf, *Mémoires*, 2.606). Elizabeth was more cautious, but clearly did not regret the end of the 'great man's' influence (*Letters*, 77; Oman, 297). However, the dissolution of parliament in 1629—at about the same time as the power of the emperor and his Catholic allies in Germany had reached its apogee—and Charles's determination to abandon the war effort altogether, put paid to all hopes to regain the palatine dominions and the electoral dignity with English support. Frederick V and Elizabeth resented the treaty of Madrid, which ended the war between England and Spain in November 1630 without providing for the Palatinate. Elizabeth remained all the more popular in England, and those who were dissatisfied with Charles's policies for religious or political reasons were clearly disappointed when Queen Henrietta Maria bore Charles a son in 1630, thereby ending Elizabeth's role as Charles's heir apparent. At court Dudley Carleton, Viscount Dorchester, appointed secretary of state in December 1628, remained a close friend of the palatines—he had won Elizabeth's trust during his time as English ambassador at The Hague in the early 1620s. With the victories achieved by Sweden in 1631, there seemed to be once more a realistic chance for English intervention on the continent in the palatine dynasty's favour. Elizabeth implored her brother in a letter to enter into an alliance with Sweden (*Letters*, 81–2). Charles, though irritated by the tone of Elizabeth's letter, was not entirely unmoved by his sister's pleading, but with Dorchester's death in February 1632 the peace party nevertheless gained the upper hand at the English court.

Widowhood and political isolation, 1632–1642 The year 1632 was in many ways the most disastrous for Elizabeth since her flight from Prague. In early November Gustavus Adolphus, who was widely seen as the saviour of the German protestants, was killed in action in the battle of Lützen. Frederick V had accompanied the Swedish king on his campaign in 1632 but had later in the year left the Swedish army and visited the Palatinate, which had been liberated by the Swedes. However, while he was staying in Mainz he fell ill and died on 29 November, thirteen days after the 'lion of the north'. Elizabeth, who was deeply devoted to her husband, was shattered. Nevertheless, she declined her brother's offer to settle in England. She recognized that such a move would be tantamount to abandoning all claims to the Palatinate for herself and her children. She therefore decided to stay in the Netherlands, where she and Frederick had built a country house at Rhenen in Gelderland in 1629–30, which she now increasingly preferred to her residence at The Hague. Her younger children were educated away from her own court in Leiden. The number of her children had quickly increased during the years in exile. Louise Hollandine (*d.* 1709) was born in 1622, Louis, who died in infancy, in 1624, his brother Edward (d. 1684) one year later, and his sister Henrietta Maria (d. 1652) two years later. Four more children were to follow: Philip (1627–1650), Charlotte (1628–1631), *Sophia (1630–1714), and Gustavus (1632–1641). Elizabeth's eldest son, Frederick Henry, however, deeply mourned by his parents, fell victim to an accident on 17 January 1629. Accompanying his father on a boat trip from Haarlem to Amsterdam, he drowned when the boat capsized. In spite of the strokes of fate which Elizabeth suffered, her spirit remained unbroken. She continued to indulge her passion for horse riding and hunting, and occasionally her children and visitors even performed a play or masque at her residence, a fact which irritated the strict Dutch Calvinists and was likely to provoke the indignation of the fervent protestants in England who still considered Elizabeth their heroine.

During the 1630s Elizabeth's relations with the English court were marked by considerable political tensions. After Dorchester's death her closest confidant in her native country was Sir Thomas Roe, the former ambassador in Constantinople, who did not, however, hold any office at court, although he was employed by Charles I in diplomatic missions in the late 1630s and early 1640s. Relations with James Hay, earl of Carlisle, the king's groom of the stool (1580–1636), were also friendly, but Carlisle was neither influential nor determined enough to create a pro-palatine party at court, although men such as Sir John Coke, one of the two secretaries of state, and the earls of Holland, Northumberland, and Leicester were sympathetic to the palatines. But ardent adherents of the queen like Georg Rudolf Weckherlin, a German by birth and one of Coke's assistants, remained isolated at court, and Elizabeth's official representative in England, her former secretary Sir Francis Nethersole, lacked the tact and discretion necessary to promote the palatine cause. In December 1633 he wrote to Secretary Coke accusing Charles I of having neglected the interests of his sister. The Palatinate, Nethersole argued, had been lost through his father's and the king's own fault, and there would be no hope of regaining the principality if Charles continued to ignore his sister's interests. The king took offence, and had Nethersole, who had initially taken refuge in the Dutch embassy, arrested. His correspondence was seized and the letters he had received from Elizabeth examined by the privy council. Elizabeth had to dismiss her servant, who was banished from the court. In spite of the misgivings she clearly had about her brother's political inertia with respect to the Palatinate, she nevertheless remained opposed to a closer co-operation with France which Rusdorf, still one of her most influential advisers, advocated.

In 1635 Elizabeth sent her son Charles Lewis—who was later joined by his younger brother Rupert—to England to gain Charles's support, but he achieved very little in political terms. When King Charles sent the earl of Arundel to Vienna in 1636 in a seemingly last attempt to have the palatine problem solved by peaceful means, Elizabeth remained extremely sceptical and was as opposed as ever to any concessions to Bavarian and Habsburg interests.

The failure of the mission spared her at least the necessity of rejecting an unsatisfactory compromise between Charles and the emperor, which might have been founded on a marriage alliance between Charles Lewis and the imperial dynasty. In October 1638 Rupert, who had followed his brother Charles Lewis into the field to fight against the emperor, was taken prisoner by imperial troops. He was taken to Austria, where he remained in captivity for more than three years. Charles Lewis himself had escaped but was arrested in France in 1639, partly because the French suspected him of trying to recruit an army of his own in Germany among troops who served France, but perhaps also intending to keep him as a hostage in case England should side with Spain in the Franco-Spanish War. This incident confirmed Elizabeth in her innate distrust of French policy. Charles Lewis was released after about half a year, but he and his brothers, as well as Elizabeth herself, were now about to be confronted by difficult choices on account of the political crisis of the Stuart monarchy.

Elizabeth during the English civil war When civil war broke out in England in 1642, Rupert and his younger brother Maurice decided to fight for the king, whereas Charles Lewis showed clear sympathies for parliament and issued a manifesto in October 1642 in his own and his mother's name in which he distanced himself from his uncle (Green, 358). Elizabeth's own sympathies were apparently more with Rupert than with Charles Lewis in this matter, although she wrote to Roe in April 1643 that she had only refrained from advising Rupert and Maurice to leave England because, having once joined the king's army, their honour was now engaged in the fight for the royal cause. She certainly knew that there was a greater chance of receiving financial aid from parliament than from her brother, and she apparently accepted her eldest son's decision to go to England in 1644 to seek the support of parliament for his cause and financial relief. Elizabeth herself sent a petition to both houses in April 1643 to request their help and support on the advice of Sir Thomas Roe, who had even proposed to ask the queen of Bohemia to mediate between her brother and parliament during the earlier stages of the conflict. Parliament had hardly any money to spare for the exiled princess, but further petitions followed. Only her brother's trial and execution caused her to break off all contacts with Charles's old enemies. She came to detest Cromwell and saw him as the very Beast from the book of Revelation. Although her relations with her eldest son had always been affectionate in the past, his dubious attitude in this moment—he was present in England when his uncle was executed—was not easily forgiven. Relations further deteriorated when he refused to comply with his mother's request for generous financial support and a formal transfer to her of the lands and castles which formed her jointure according to her marriage treaty after the restoration of the palatine dynasty in the Lower Palatinate by the peace of Westphalia in 1648. In Elizabeth's eyes it was an essential precondition for an eventual return to the Palatinate that she should gain possession of these lands. As no agreement could be reached on this point between Charles Lewis and herself, she stayed at The Hague after 1648. The final success of the cause she had fought for for such a long time—the return of the Palatinate to its native dynasty—therefore brought her personally little joy or relief.

In fact, Elizabeth's financial situation in the Netherlands, which had become desperate after the outbreak of war in England, hardly improved after the Westphalian peace. In the early 1640s she had still been able to rely on the support of William, Lord Craven, one of her most ardent admirers and closest friends and a frequent visitor at her court, but the outcome of the civil war had ruined Craven, like many other real or suspected royalists. Furthermore, the Dutch states general refused to support her any longer after the end of the war with Spain in 1648 and the political eclipse of the house of Orange in 1650. The contrast between the claim to royal status which she never abandoned and the reality of life in her household, where poverty and a pronounced lack of discipline among the servants, who hardly received any regular wages, dominated, became ever more glaring and it was increasingly difficult to keep nervous creditors at bay.

Elizabeth and her children: last years and death Elizabeth's situation was not made easier by the tensions within her family. Her son Edward had gone to Paris in the 1640s, where he married Anne de Gonzague, daughter of Charles, duke of Nevers, Mantua, and Montferrat, an attractive and wealthy woman eight years his senior who played a prominent role in French aristocratic society. Before the marriage Edward converted to Catholicism, a severe shock for his mother, although Elizabeth later forgave him his apostasy. Her youngest son, Philip, caused her even more trouble. In June 1646 he killed one of her courtiers and youthful admirers, the count de l'Espinay, whom malicious tongues credited with a love affair either with the widowed queen herself or with her daughter Louise Hollandine. Philip had to leave the Netherlands, and Elizabeth broke off all contact with him. He died in 1650. Two years later another son, Maurice, also died prematurely, when his ship sank in the Caribbean during one of the privateering raids he and his brother Rupert had undertaken against the merchant fleet of the hated English Commonwealth. Of Elizabeth's daughters her namesake Elizabeth was probably the most gifted. She studied science and philosophy, and when Descartes stayed in the Netherlands a friendship between the princess and the philosopher developed. After the philosopher's death in Sweden she was disconsolate and left her mother's court, went to Brandenburg, and eventually became abbess of the protestant ecclesiastical community of Herford. Her sister Henrietta married Sigismund Rakoczi, prince of Transylvania, but died soon afterwards, in February 1652. Louise Hollandine had in many ways been closest to her mother, but life in exile and poverty proved too much of a strain for her. In December 1657 she suddenly left her mother's court in secret and went to France, where she, like her brother Edward, became a Catholic. She entered a monastery and eventually became abbess of Maubuisson in 1664. As opposed to Edward's conversion, Louise's flight

and change of religion never found Elizabeth's forgiveness. Even Sophia, her youngest daughter, who later depicted her mother in her memoirs as a somewhat distant figure who cared more for her dogs and monkeys than for her children, did not get on too well with her. Against her mother's will she left The Hague for Heidelberg in 1650, and married Ernst August of Brunswick in 1658, a younger son whom Elizabeth did not consider a suitable match for her daughter. She was unable to foresee that Ernst August was to become the first elector of Hanover and father of King *George I. Of her sons and daughters Rupert was undoubtedly closest to his mother in Elizabeth's last years. When he returned to England after the Restoration which he and his mother had so eagerly awaited, Elizabeth became reluctant to stay any longer in the Netherlands. However, the invitation by Charles II which she expected did not materialize. She therefore decided to go to England even against the king's wishes in May 1661. In London she stayed at the house her old friend the earl of Craven owned in Drury Lane. As in the past, Craven proved to be a great support in difficult times. The earl undoubtedly admired her, but rumours that they were married in secret in the 1650s, or that there was at least a secret love affair between them, seem to be unsubstantiated. In February 1662 Elizabeth decided to acquire a residence of her own and moved to Leicester House. Apparently the removal in the midst of winter was too much for her. She died shortly afterwards, on 13 February at Leicester House, in the presence of her son Prince Rupert, probably from the effects of severe bronchitis, an illness she had suffered from in its chronic form for a long time. On 17 February she was buried in Westminster Abbey next to Prince Henry.

Assessment Like few other women of the early seventeenth century Elizabeth Stuart has continued to fascinate the popular imagination in the nineteenth and twentieth centuries. Her life and character seemed in many ways to provide the ideal material for romantic novels. But even if one discards this romantic version of her life, the pertinacity and willpower she demonstrated in defending her own ideals and her family's interests for so long, with very few material resources and relying more on her charm and reputation than on political power, remain remarkable. Although sometimes considered by contemporaries as arrogant and frivolous as a young princess, she managed to adapt surprisingly well to life in exile, and later to her position as the female head of an outlawed dynasty. Political success, however, proved elusive in spite of her endeavours, and in the newly established European order, emerging from the turmoil of the Thirty Years' War, there was no longer any place for her political ideals inspired by the militant protestantism of her youth, except, possibly, in the English republic which had, however, killed her brother. At odds with most of her children she had, in the last decade before her death, become the survivor of an earlier age, isolated and without a country which she could really consider her own. RONALD G. ASCH

Sources *The letters of Elizabeth queen of Bohemia*, ed. L. M. Baker (1953) · G. Bromley, ed., *A collection of original royal letters* (1787) ·

K. Hauck, ed., *Die Briefe der Kinder des Winterkönigs*, Heidelberger Jahrbücher, 15 (1908) · J. Nichols, *The progresses, processions, and magnificent festivities of King James I, his royal consort, family and court*, 4 vols. (1828) · J. J. Rusdorf, *Mémoires et négociations secrètes*, ed. E. G. Kuhn, 2 vols. (1789) · J. J. Rusdorf, *Consilia et negotia politica* (1725) · *Memoiren der Sophie Kurfürstin von Hannover*, ed. A. Köcher (1879) · *Memoirs of Sophia, electress of Hanover*, ed. and trans. H. Forester (1888) · A. Wendland, ed., *Briefe der Elisabeth Stuart, Königin von Böhmen an ihren Sohn, den Kurfürsten Carl Ludwig von der Pfalz, 1650–1662* (Tübingen, 1902) · M. A. E. Green, *Elizabeth electress palatine and queen of Bohemia*, ed. S. C. Lomas, rev. edn (1909) [still useful being based on a wealth of sources; based on M. A. E. Green, 'Elizabeth, eldest daughter of James I', *Lives of the princesses of England*, 5 (1854), 145–573] · C. Oman, *Elizabeth of Bohemia* (1938); rev. edn (1964) · M. Lemberg, *Eine Königin ohne Reich: das Leben der Winterkönigin Elisabeth Stuart und ihre Briefe nach Hessen* (1996) · K. Hauck, *Elisabeth, Königin von Böhmen, Kurfürstin von Pfalz in ihren letzten Lebensjahren* (1905) · T. Cogswell, *The blessed revolution: English politics and the coming of war, 1621–1624* (1989) · K. Hauck, *Karl Ludwig, Kurfürst von der Pfalz* (1903) · C. M. Hibbard, *Charles I and the Popish Plot* (1983) · R. Lockyer, *Buckingham: the life and political career of George Villiers, first duke of Buckingham, 1592–1628* (1981) · *Neue deutsche Biographie*, [6 vols.] (Berlin, 1953–64) · N. Mout, 'Der Winterkönig im Exil: Friedrich V. von der Pfalz und die niederländischen Generalstaaten, 1621–31', *Zeitschrift für Historische Forschung*, 15 (1988), 259–72 · D. Norbrook, '"The masque of truth": court entertainments and international protestant politics in the early Stuart period', *Seventeenth Century*, 1 (1986), 81–110 · J. O. Opel, 'Elisabeth Stuart, Königin von Böhmen, Kurfürstin von der Pfalz', *Historische Zeitschrift*, 23 (1870), 289–328 · L. J. Reeve, *Charles I and the road to personal rule* (1989) · R. E. Schreiber, *The first Carlisle: Sir James Hay, first earl of Carlisle as courtier, diplomat and entrepreneur, 1580–1636* (1984) · F. H. Schubert, *Ludwig Camerarius, 1573–1651: eine Biographie* (1955) · F. H. Schubert, 'Die pfälzische Exilregierung im dreissigjährigen Krieg: ein Beitrag zur Geschichte des politischen Protestantismus', *Zeitschrift für Geschichte des Oberrheins*, new ser., 63 (1954), 575–680 · V. F. Snow, *Essex the rebel: the life of Robert Devereux, the third earl of Essex, 1591–1646* (1970) · M. Strachan, *Sir Thomas Roe, 1581–1644: a life* (1989) · R. C. Strong, *Henry, prince of Wales, and England's lost Renaissance* (1986) · E. Weiss, *Die Unterstützung Friedrichs V. von der Pfalz durch Jakob I. und Karl I. von England im dreissigjährigen Krieg* (1966) · J. G. Weiss, 'Die Vorgeschichte des böhmischen Abenteuers Friedrichs V. von der Pfalz', *Zeitschrift für Geschichte des Oberrheins*, new ser., 53 (1940), 383–492 · H. Werner, 'The Hector of Germanie, or, The Palsgrave, prince elector and Anglo-German relations of early Stuart England: the view from the popular stage', *The Stuart court and Europe*, ed. R. M. Smuts (1996) · S. Orgel and R. Strong, eds., *Inigo Jones and the theatre of the Stuart court*, 2 vols. (1973), vol. 1 · *Die Renaissance im deutschen Südwesten*, 2 vols. (1986), vol. 1 · H. Wotton, *Reliquiae Wottonianae*, 3rd edn (1672) · E. A. Beller, *Caricatures of the winter king of Bohemia* (1928)

Archives Alnwick Castle, corresp. · Bayerische Staatsbibliothek, Munich, collectio cameriana · Bayerisches Hauptstaatsarchiv, Munich, Geheimes Hausarchiv, Kasten Blau: Akten der pfälzischen Wittelsbacher / records of the Palatinate branch of the Wittelsbach dynasty · BL, Harley MS 7007 · BL, Add. MS 637744 · PRO, state papers foreign Germany, SP 81 · PRO, state papers foreign Netherlands, SP 84 · V&A NAL, corresp., vol. 39 | Alnwick Castle, letters of Northumberland MSS · Arundel Castle, duke of Norfolk MSS · Arundel Castle, corresp. with Lord and Lady Arundel · Berks. RO, letters to William Lenthall [transcripts] · BL, letters to Sir Edward Nicholas, Egerton MS 2548 · BL, letters to Lady Elizabeth Broughton, Add. MS 30797 · NA Scot., letters to first marquess of Montrose · priv. coll., letters to the duke of Gloucester · PRO, state papers domestic James I and Charles I, SP 14, SP 16 · TCD, corresp. of Sir Thomas Roe, MS 708

Likenesses Hilliard, miniature, *c*.1610, Royal Collection · Hilliard, miniature, *c*.1610, V&A · I. Oliver, miniature, *c*.1610, Royal Collection · I. Oliver, miniature, *c*.1610, V&A · R. Elstrack, line print,

c.1612, BM · C. de Passe, print, *c*.1612, BM, NPG · studio of M. J. van Mierevelt, oils, 1625–30, NPG · A. Van de Venne, group portrait, oils, 1626, Rijksmuseum, Amsterdam · D. Mytens, oils, *c*.1626–1627, Royal Collection · oils, 1628 (after G. van Honthorst); version, Woburn Abbey, Bedfordshire · W. J. Delff, line engraving, 1630 (after oil painting after G. van Honthorst), BM, NPG · G. van Honthorst, oils, *c*.1632, Buccleuch estates, Selkirk · attrib. F. Dieussart, marble bust, 1641, V&A · G. van Honthorst, portrait, 1642, National Gallery, London [*see illus.*] · studio of G. van Honthorst, oils, 1642, NPG · G. van Honthorst, oils, 1650, Ashdown House, Oxfordshire · B. Bolswert, line print (after M. J. van Mierevelt, 1615), BM, NPG · G. van Honthorst, group portrait (allegorical with family), Landes Museum, Hanover, Germany · studio of G. van Honthorst, oils (type of 1642), NPG · C. de Passe, group portrait, line engraving (after medal; with her husband and son), NPG · etching and woodcut, NPG · medals, BM · oils (type of *c*.1630; after G. van Honthorst), Plymouth Art Gallery; loaned by Clarendon collection

Wealth at death presumably in debt but still owned valuable moveable goods: Oman, *Elizabeth of Bohemia*; 'The last will, 8 May 1661', CS 83 (1863) 109–10

Elizabeth, Princess (1635–1650), second daughter of *Charles I (1600–1649) and *Henrietta Maria (1609–1669), was born at St James's Palace on 28 December 1635 and baptized there by William Laud on 2 January 1636. She had not reached her first birthday when her grandmother, Marie de' Medici, proposed to arrange a match between her and William, only son of Frederick Henry, prince of Orange, but King Charles at that time considered such a marriage to be beneath his daughter's rank. With the rapid collapse of the king's fortunes, in the spring of 1642 Elizabeth's sister Mary was betrothed to Prince William instead, whereupon she left England with the queen consort. Elizabeth saw neither of them again. Parliament assumed responsibility for the maintenance of the young princess and her younger brother Henry, duke of Gloucester, over whom the fourth earl of Pembroke was placed as guardian in October 1642. Subsequently it was proposed that principal members of her household be removed as unfit objects of the state's munificence. An appeal penned by the princess herself worked sufficiently on the Lords, who disdained the Commons' presumption on their privilege in so ordering the royal household, thus earning some relief in the rigour of the Reformation. But to balance this act of complaisance the children were required to hear sermons twice every Sunday, and to submit to catechism. All attempts failing, covert and overt, to have the royal children come to Oxford, they remained as virtual hostages at St James's.

In the autumn of 1643 Elizabeth broke her leg and was for a long time housebound. The following summer she and her brother were removed to the residence of Sir John Danvers at Chelsea. From about 1640 until sometime after 1644 Elizabeth was tutored by the well-known teacher and author Bathsua Makin, sister-in-law of the linguist and mathematician John Pell. She studied languages and theology and was apparently able to read and write Hebrew, Greek, Latin, French, and Italian before she was eight years old. In March 1644 'the evening star of Stepney', congregationalist preacher William Greenhill, dedicated to her his *Exposition of the First Five Chapters of Ezekiel*, extolling her 'writing out the Lord's prayer in Greek, some text of scripture in Hebrew', her 'endeavour after the exact knowledge of those holy tongues, with other languages and learned accomplishments', her 'diligent hearing of the word, careful noting of sermons, understanding answers at the catechising, and frequent questioning about holy things' (W. Greenhill, *Exposition*, 2nd edn, 1645, preface). Three years later another erudite scholar, Alexander Rowley, dedicated to the princess a vocabulary of the Hebrew and Greek words used in the Bible, with their explanation in Latin and English, entitled *The Schollers Companion*, giving as his reason the 'rare inclination of your highness to the study of the Book of books, and to its two originall languages'.

Owing to the declining health of the countess of Dorset, their governess since 1642, Elizabeth and her brother were transferred to the guardianship of the earl and countess of Northumberland in spring 1645. In September they were joined by their brother James, duke of York. Elizabeth supposedly encouraged James to escape, expressing her regret at seeing him in the hands of their father's foes, and repeatedly telling him 'that were she a boy she would not long remain a captive, however light or glittering might be the fetters that bound her' (*DNB*). If true, then she had well-developed powers of dissimulation, having apparently earned the nickname Temperance for the way she comported herself towards her parliamentarian 'protectors'. After a separation of five years, Elizabeth was permitted to meet her father at Maidenhead, Berkshire, on 16 July 1647, she and her two brothers then spending two days with him at Caversham. When Charles was removed to Hampton Court, he paid frequent visits to his children, then living at Syon House, Isleworth, Middlesex. But after the king fled to the Isle of Wight, and was confined at Carisbrooke Castle, Elizabeth supposedly once again urged the duke of York to make an escape. She has been credited with the ingenuity which enabled York to slip out of Syon House dressed as a woman on the evening of 21 April 1648. On 22 January 1649 a letter addressed from Elizabeth was written to parliament, requesting leave for the princess to join her sister in Holland. But the Commons paid it no heed until after the death of the king. The day before his execution he saw Elizabeth and the duke of Gloucester for the last time. The parting interview was an intensely emotional occasion and the conversation was recorded by Elizabeth herself.

In April 1649 the earl of Northumberland's nephew, councillor of state Philip, Lord Lisle, represented to parliament the wish of his uncle to leave off his onerous, if well-rewarded responsibility for the protection of the two young Stuarts. The house divided narrowly in rejection of Elizabeth's request to join her sister, before electing to entrust her and Henry to the care of Sir Edward Harrington. Harrington's son, Sir James, however, managed to persuade the house to settle the children elsewhere.

Elizabeth and Henry went eventually to live at Penshurst, in Kent, with the earl and countess of Leicester. MPs explicitly instructed their new hosts not to treat the princess and the duke with any more respect than was due to the children of any nobleman. Lady Leicester, while complying in the main with the parliamentary instructions, treated Elizabeth with kindness, receiving from her young ward a valuable jewel which later became the object of an unpleasant conflict between the countess and the parliamentary commissioners responsible for the husbandry of the late king and royal family's personal estate. Elizabeth's biographer has remarked that, at this time, 'her forlorn situation, combined with her reputation for learning, her profound melancholy and meek resignation interested many a heart in her fate' (Green, 377). The poet John Quarles dedicated to her in April 1649 his *Regale lectum miseriae*, praising 'that patronesse of Vertue … the sorrowfull daughter to our late martyr'd Soveraigne' (Quarles, *Regale*, 1649, A2). A more elaborate panegyric occurs in the dedication by Christopher Wase of a translation of Sophocles' *Electra*, to which an anonymous friend of the translator, one H. P., added some verses criticizing what he considered to be her unworthy treatment.

In the summer of 1650 Elizabeth's eldest brother, Charles, landed in Scotland to assume the throne. At the instance of the council of state, parliament resolved to remove Elizabeth and Henry to the Isle of Wight, on the grounds that 'if any insurrections should happen [in England], the public peace would be much the more endangered by occasion of the late king's children who are remaining here, and may be made use of to the prejudice of the public' (*CSP dom.*, 1650, 250). They were placed under the guardianship of Captain Anthony Mildmay, brother of Sir Henry, councillor of state, granted an annual allowance of £3000, and were permitted to take no more than eight servants with them. Lodged in Carisbrooke Castle, they were to await transportation 'out of the limits of the commonwealth' (ibid., 258). Despite Elizabeth's protest that her health made her move from Penshurst insupportable, in August the royal party arrived on the Isle of Wight. Having caught a cold some little time earlier, Elizabeth died on 8 September 1650. Three days before she died, the council of state had agreed to recommend that parliament grant her request to go to her sister, and to allow her £1000 annually for her maintenance 'as long as she should behave inoffensively' (ibid., 327–8). She was buried on 24 September in a small vault near the communion table in St Thomas's Church at Newport. For two centuries the initials E. S. cut in that part of the wall nearest her burial place were all that served to mark the spot. In 1856 a white marble monument by Marochetti was placed in the church to her memory by the express command of Queen Victoria.

GORDON GOODWIN, rev. SEAN KELSEY

Sources DNB · M. A. E. Green, *Lives of the princesses of England*, 6 vols. (1849–55), vol. 6, pp. 335–92 · J. Granger, *A biographical history of England, from Egbert the Great to the revolution*, 2nd edn, 4 vols. (1775)

Likenesses A. Van Dyck, group portrait, oils, 1637, Royal Collection · P. Lely, group portrait, oils, 1647 (*The youngest children of Charles I*), Petworth House, West Sussex · P. Lely, oils, *c.*1647–1650, Syon House, Brentford, Middlesex · W. Hollar, etching, 1650, BM · R. Gaywood?, etching, BM, NPG; repro. in Wase, *Electra of Sophocles* (1649)

Wealth at death see Green, *Lives of the princesses*, 383

Elizabeth [*née* Lady Elizabeth Berkeley], **margravine of Brandenburg-Ansbach-Bayreuth** [*other married name* Elizabeth Craven, Lady Craven] (**1750–1828**), travel writer and society hostess, was the youngest daughter of Augustus, fourth earl of Berkeley (1716–1755) and Elizabeth, countess of Berkeley (1719/20–1792), daughter of Henry Drax of Charlborough in Dorset. Born on 17 December 1750, she was married on 10 May 1767 to William Craven (*d.* 1791), who became the sixth Baron Craven in 1769 on the death of his uncle. They had six children before deciding to separate in 1783, following infidelities on both sides. Lady Craven had attracted scandal as early as 1773; an indiscreet liaison with the duc de Guines, the French ambassador in London, was reported in the *Town and Country Magazine* for May 1773 as a 'criminal intercourse' (p. 246), and several other such affairs were to follow. During the 1770s she led an energetic social life in London, dining with Johnson and Boswell (who described her as 'the beautiful, gay, and fascinating Lady Craven' (Boswell, *Life*, 3.22) and becoming a friend of Horace Walpole, with whom she corresponded for years afterwards and who published her earliest literary ventures. These included a translation of Pont de Vile's comedy *La somnambule* (as *The Sleep-Walker*) in 1778, and her humorous tale satirizing German snobbery, *Modern Anecdotes of the Ancient Family of the Kinkvervankotsdarsprakengotchderns* in 1779. In 1780 Walpole wrote to William Mason that he had hung her portrait (1778, by George Romney) in his 'favourite blue room' (Walpole, *Corr.*, 28.45).

In the late 1770s and early 1780s various of Lady Craven's plays were performed for the benefit of the local poor at Benham, near Newbury, where the Cravens were resident. Some of them, beginning in 1781 with *The Miniature Picture*, were then also performed in London theatres, which offered a fairly neutral response to her light farces, pantomimes, and fables. By 1783, despite having himself had a mistress for some years (with whom, a Mrs Byrne, he subsequently lived happily for the rest of his life), Lord Craven's patience with the indiscretions of his wife finally ran out. He settled £1500 a year on her. Leaving five of her children in England, Lady Craven took Keppel Richard *Craven, then aged four, to live with her in France. She settled near Versailles, wrote little plays in French for the court theatre, and soon made the acquaintance of Christian Frederick Charles Alexander (*d.* 1806), margrave of Brandenburg-Ansbach-Bayreuth, a member of the same ruling family as the king of Prussia. At this stage their relationship was apparently 'sisterly' (as she described it in a letter to her husband), since he was married to a sickly margravine who remained in Germany, and Lady Craven was carrying on an affair with Henry Vernon (great-nephew of Admiral Vernon and son of Henry and Lady Harriet Vernon); she travelled extensively with the margrave around France, Italy, Austria, Poland, Bulgaria, Russia, Greece, and Turkey between 1783 and 1786. Horace Walpole recorded in October 1785 that:

> I thought her at Paris, and was surprised to hear of her at Florence. She has, I fear, been *infinitamente* indiscreet—but what is that to you or me? She is very pretty, has parts, and is

Elizabeth, margravine of Brandenburg-Ansbach-Bayreuth (1750–1828), by George Romney, 1797

> good-natured to the greatest degree, has not a grain of malice or mischief (almost always the associates, in women, of tender hearts) and never has been an enemy but to herself. (Walpole, *Corr.*, 25.611)

In Venice she made the acquaintance of the British minister there, Sir Robert Murray Keith, with whom she began a correspondence. By March 1786 Lady Craven's affair with Vernon had become public knowledge in London and Lord Craven had successfully discouraged her children from writing to her. Her scandalous reputation was further enhanced when in March 1787 she arrived at Ansbach and there ousted the famous French actress Mademoiselle de Clairon from the margrave's favour. During the next four years, notwithstanding the continued existence of the ailing margravine, she held sway over the margrave and his court at Triersdorf.

In 1787 Walpole had suggested that Lady Craven publish an account of her travels, and *A Journey through the Crimea to Constantinople* appeared in 1789. A substantial quarto volume with plates, this is her most important work, and it exploits to the full the gossipy and self-vindicating scope of first-person travelogue. She describes manners, customs, and landscapes, pronounces Lady Mary Wortley

Montagu's favourable account of Turkey a forgery, and constructs a self-image of redoubtable British vigour as well as devoted and injured motherhood. Reviewers were critical of her arrogance, but a second, extended edition appeared in 1814 (entitled *Letters from the Right Honorable Lady Craven, to his serene highness the margrave of Anspach, during her travels through France, Germany, and Russia in 1785 and 1786*).

In December 1790 Lady Craven and the margrave visited Berlin to negotiate the sale of his principality to the king of Prussia, who paid handsomely for it. The margravine died early in 1791 and the margrave and Lady Craven left Ansbach for Portugal. Serendipitously Lord Craven also died in 1791, on 26 September, at Lausanne. Walpole related in November 1791 that 'Lady Craven received the news of her Lord's death on a Friday, went into weeds on Saturday, and into white satin and *many* diamonds on Sunday, and in that vestal trim was married to the Margrave of Anspach' (Walpole, *Corr.*, 34.132). They were married with great pomp on 13 October 1791 at Lisbon. They then returned to England and purchased a villa on the banks of the Thames at Fulham for £8500; Brandenburg House, as it became, boasted a ballroom, a chapel for the margrave, and a theatre for the new margravine. Despite influential disapproval—the margravine was not received at court, as the marriage between the margrave and the daughter of an earl was considered unequal by George III, and was cold-shouldered by leading ladies of fashion—Brandenburg House hosted many glamorous and faintly bohemian gatherings. Plays were performed, the margravine was again painted by Romney (twice, in 1794), and on 1 May 1793 she and the margrave breakfasted with the prince of Wales at Carlton House. However, although in 1793 she had been granted the title of Princess Berkeley by the Holy Roman Emperor Francis II, George III refused to acknowledge that this gave her German princely rank.

Probably in 1799 the Berkshire seat of the Cravens at Benham was purchased by the margrave, and thenceforward their life was divided between the pleasures of London and the country. The margravine took an interest in horse-racing, owning and racing several notable horses. She also intervened philanthropically in local affairs at Benham, writing in 1800 to the president of the Board of Trade to protest at the high prices which farmers were charging people for corn. On 5 January 1806 the margrave died, after an illness of only three days, leaving his widow some £150,000. She erected a large cenotaph for him on the Bath Road at Furze Hill near Benham; it was, however, removed after her own death. In 1807 she visited Ansbach to take possession of the margrave's property there, and in the years that followed she sojourned once again in France and Italy. In 1819 Ferdinand IV of Naples granted her a tract of land at Posilipo, on which she built what became known as the Villa Craven. Richard Madden, the biographer of Lady Blessington, recalls seeing the margravine 'a few years before her death, working in her garden, spade in hand, in very coarse and singular attire, a desiccated, antiquated piece of mortality, remarkable for vivacity, realising the idea of a galvanised Egyptian mummy' (Broadley and Melville, 1.cxxxiv). While at Naples she wrote her spirited, frank, and self-aggrandizing *Memoirs*, which caused a stir on their publication in 1826. She died at Villa Craven in January 1828 following a chill caught from digging in her garden on a wet day. She was buried in the British cemetery at Naples on 13 January 1828, where her loyal son Keppel, who inherited her love of travel, was later also buried in 1851.

KATHERINE TURNER

Sources *The beautiful Lady Craven: the original memoirs*, ed. A. M. Broadley and L. Melville, 2 vols. (1914) · Walpole, *Corr.* · *GM*, 1st ser., 76 (1806), 91–2 [obit. of margrave of Anspach] · Burke, *Peerage* · D. E. Baker, *Biographia dramatica, or, A companion to the playhouse*, rev. I. Reed, new edn, rev. S. Jones, 3 vols. in 4 (1812) · C. B. Hogan, ed., *The London stage, 1660–1800*, pt 5: *1776–1800* (1968) · *Town and Country Magazine*, 5 (1773), 246
Archives BL, letters to Sir Robert Murray Keith, etc., Add. MSS 35534–35542, *passim*
Likenesses H. D. Hamilton, crayon drawing, exh. Society of Artists 1775 · T. Beach, oils, exh. Society of Artists 1776, J. Paul Getty Museum, California · G. Romney, oils, 1778, Tate collection; repro. in *The Magazine of Art* (1899), 192 · O. Humphrey, oils, *c*.1780–1783, Tate collection; repro. in *Foster's Miniatures*, vol. 1, pl. 49 · J. Reynolds, oils, exh. RA 1781, Petworth House, West Sussex · G. Place, exh. RA 1797 · G. Romney, oils, 1797, priv. coll.; Christies, 16 Nov 1911, lot 11 [*see illus.*] · Ridley, miniature, 1801 · R. Cosway, drawing (as Elia), Royal Collection · attrib. T. Gainsborough, oils, priv. coll. · O. Humphrey, group portrait, oils, Berkeley Castle, Gloucestershire; repro. in *English Illustrated Magazine* (Jan 1889), 291 · H. Meyer, engraving (after J. Reynolds, 1781) · W. Ridley, stipple (after J. Reynolds), BM, NPG; repro. in *Monthly Mirror* (March 1801) · oils, priv. coll.

Elizabeth, Princess (1770–1840). *See under* George III, daughters of (*act.* 1766–1857).

Elizabeth I (1533–1603), queen of England and Ireland, was born between 3 and 4 o'clock on the afternoon of Sunday 7 September 1533 at Greenwich Palace, Kent, the only child of *Henry VIII (1491–1547), king of England and Ireland, and his second wife, *Anne (*c*.1500–1536), queen of England, the second of three children of Thomas *Boleyn, earl of Wiltshire and earl of Ormond (1476/7–1539), courtier and nobleman, of Blickling, Norfolk, and his wife, Elizabeth (*d*. 1538). Henry had married Anne in January 1533 after an untidy and protracted rupture of his first marriage to Katherine of Aragon, precipitating the constitutional and religious revolution of the Henrician reformation. On 10 September the child was baptized in the church of the Observant Franciscans at Greenwich, where her father, too, had been baptized, and named Elizabeth for her grandmother, *Elizabeth (Elizabeth of York; 1466–1503). Her godfather was Thomas Cranmer, archbishop of Canterbury, who had dissolved Henry's first marriage and blessed the second. William Shakespeare and John Fletcher in *Henry VIII* later put prophetic words into Cranmer's mouth on this occasion:

> This royal infant—heaven still move about her—
> Though in her cradle, yet now promises
> Upon this land a thousand thousand blessings,
> Which time shall bring to ripeness.
> (*Henry VIII*, V.iv)

However, at the time, Elizabeth was a bitter disappointment, for it had been confidently predicted that the child

Elizabeth I (1533–1603), by unknown artist, c.1575

would be a boy. Henry had not cast off his first wife and married a second only to acquire another daughter.

Early life, 1533–1537 As the baptism ceremony ended, Sir Thomas Wriothesley, garter king of arms, proclaimed Elizabeth to be 'the high and mighty princess of England', which was to say, heiress presumptive to the throne, displacing her seventeen-year-old half-sister *Mary (1516–1558), now deemed illegitimate. At the age of three months Elizabeth was provided with her own household, first at the royal manor of Hatfield in Hertfordshire, and then, when she was one year old, at Eltham Palace in Kent, five miles from Greenwich. Meanwhile, the household of the young woman now known only as the Lady Mary was broken up and the two sisters made to share one roof. That was not a recipe for happiness, and Mary steadfastly refused to acknowledge her baby sister as princess or to yield her precedence, although in the course of time she became reconciled to Elizabeth as a sibling, and, it seems, even grew quite fond of her. Elizabeth's earliest portraits suggest that she resembled her father in the shape of her face and her auburn hair, but had inherited her mother's coal-black eyes. Katherine died on 7 January 1536 and Henry celebrated this happy event and took delight in showing off his little daughter Elizabeth, his good mood made all the better by the new prospect of a prince. However, before the end of the month, Anne, fourteen weeks pregnant, miscarried a son. The queen's position was now

untenable, and in May she was charged with having committed adultery with no fewer than five men, one of them her own brother. On 19 May she was executed. On the following day Henry married *Jane (Jane Seymour; 1508/9–1537), who died after giving birth to *Edward VI (1537–1553), on 24 October 1537.

Elizabeth can have had few memories of her mother, and there was no anguished parting, since she was resident at another royal manor in Hertfordshire, Hunsdon, when Anne was arrested at Greenwich, which is hard to reconcile with the story that the queen held up her child to Henry as a last despairing gesture. There is no profit in speculating about the psychological damage which Anne's terrible end might have had on her daughter, although many of Elizabeth's biographers have found significance in the fact that she never in adult life invoked or otherwise referred to her mother. What is more certain is that in his later years Elizabeth seems to have been on good terms with her father, and to have made him her role model, although protocol required that relations remained formal, so that in her earliest surviving letter she wrote: 'heretofore I have not dared to write to him' (*Collected Works*, 5–6).

At Edward's baptism the four-year-old Elizabeth carried the christening robe (although she herself had to be carried), while Mary was godmother. Both daughters were now legally illegitimate, although this stigma was practically a fiction, as became clear in 1544 when they were restored by the Succession Act to their places as heirs to the throne. As pawns on the royal marriage chessboard they were too valuable not to be countenanced by their father. After Jane's death Edward was sent to live with his half-sisters, but mainly with Elizabeth, since Mary was at court for much of 1537 to 1547. It may be an unfounded legend that all three children shared a household presided over by Henry's sixth wife, *Katherine (Katherine Parr; 1512–1548), since there is no evidence that Elizabeth lived with Katherine before 1547.

Like most members of the upper class, Elizabeth was more closely bonded to her nurses and governesses than to any of her blood relations, and it was to those old servants that she showed most loyalty. At first her 'Lady Mistress' was Lady Margaret Bryan, widow of Sir Thomas Bryan and mother of one of the king's closest companions, Sir Francis Bryan. Lady Bryan had charge in turn of the three royal infants and was clearly devoted to their welfare. A letter she wrote to Sir Thomas Cromwell in the aftermath of Anne's fall gives most of what little is known about Elizabeth's infancy: she was having painful teething problems; she was short of suitable clothes, something which her mother would not have allowed to happen, for there exist the bills accounting for Anne's heavy expenditure (£40 a month) on materials for herself and her daughter. Lady Bryan also reported that the male head of the household, Sir John Shelton, insisted that Elizabeth dine and sup in state, which was not suitable for a child of her tender age, who should not be eating fruit and drinking wine. However, Lady Bryan added: 'she is as toward a child and as gentle of conditions as ever I knew any in my life' (*LP Henry VIII*, 9.90). When Lady Bryan turned her specialist attention to the rearing of the young prince in 1537, she was replaced by Lady Blanch Herbert of Troy, who remained head of Elizabeth's household until 1547. A lady from the west country, Katherine Champernowne, better known as Kate Astley, after her marriage to John Astley about 1545, became a member of Elizabeth's household in the 1540s. Astley had great influence with the young Elizabeth, not least over the first steps in her education, but at one point the close relationship was very nearly the undoing of them both.

Education, 1537–1552 The flattering memoir of Anne Boleyn composed by her chaplain, William Latimer, reports that she intended her daughter to be well trained in languages, 'that she might in after tyme be hable sufficiently to judge of all maters and embassages'. Accordingly, 'she wolde endewe her with the knowlege of all tounges, as Hebrue, Greeke, Latyne, Italian, Spanishe, Frenche' ('William Latymer's chronicklle', 63). Elizabeth, and for that matter Mary, were fortunate in being born at a time when enthusiasm for the project of educating aristocratic women was at its height, especially in Italy. In editing the works of Olympia Morata, which he later dedicated to Elizabeth, the Italian humanist and protestant Celio Secondo Curione cited no less an authority than Socrates for the opinion that women 'si diligenter instituantur' ('if they are diligently instructed') were no less 'aptas ac dociles ad literas et artes liberales' ('apt to and easily instructed in letters and liberal arts') than men (O. Morata, *Opera*, 1556, fol. A2). Among Elizabeth's contemporaries who benefited from this doctrine were Lady Jane Grey, one of only a very few people to write with affection of her tutor, John Aylmer, and whose father disapproved of all this pedagogy; and the daughters of Sir Anthony Cooke, who on the contrary vigorously promoted their education. Of these learned sisters, Mildred became the second wife of William Cecil, while Anne married Nicholas Bacon and proved herself one of the most competent translators from Latin of her generation.

Elizabeth's education began under Astley. When Astley had taught her as much as she could, she acquired as tutor William Grindal, a favourite pupil of the greatest educationist of the age, Roger Ascham, who had himself been taught by John Cheke, now tutor to Edward. These young men were all products of St John's College, Cambridge, which earlier in the century John Fisher, bishop of Rochester, had established, under the patronage of Elizabeth's great-grandmother, Margaret *Beaufort (1443–1509), as a leading centre of humanist erudition. It was more than a happy accident that, as queen, Elizabeth appointed as her principal secretary and leading counsellor, William Cecil, whose mind and rhetorical skills, the essence of his statesmanship, had been formed in the same school. Ascham himself kept a close eye on Elizabeth's lessons, for which he assumed direct responsibility after Grindal's untimely death in January 1548, and it is from the gossipy Ascham that most is known about her education.

By the age of ten Elizabeth was learning both Italian and French, which must mean that she was already well grounded in Latin. Her French tutor (shared with Edward) was Jean Belmaine, her Italian teacher Giovanni Battista Castiglione. Later, under Ascham's instruction, the mornings were spent in mastering Greek, both the Greek of the New Testament and more difficult authors such as Isocrates. Latin studies continued in the afternoon, with the orations of Cicero and the histories of Livy. Elizabeth's earliest surviving letter (31 July 1544) was written to Katherine Parr in somewhat convoluted Italian. Here is encountered for the first time the elegant italic hand which she was well on the way to mastering, and in which she was apparently schooled by the appropriately named Belmaine. In the full flowering of the Renaissance, fine penmanship was more than a mere technique of communication, and Elizabeth took great pride in it. However, later, as queen, her handwriting deteriorated, until she was often forced to apologize for 'these scribbled lines', her 'scribbling in haste'. She seems to have acquired some Spanish. Elizabeth was also a more than moderately accomplished musician, playing, in private, on the spinet and lute, and even composing.

Elizabeth would have shared the modern view that learning is a lifelong undertaking. As queen, her Greek studies with Ascham continued, and in her sixties she was still an active translator, producing her own version of Boethius's *De consolatione philosophiae*, undertaken in autumn 1593, and translations of parts of Horace's *Ars poetica* and Plutarch's *De curiositate*, in 1598. These exercises all survive, but not Elizabeth's rendering of that notoriously 'hard' author, the historian Tacitus, referred to by Henry Savile in dedicating his own translation to the queen, and by an early biographer, John Clapham. As late as 1600 she told the antiquarian William Lambarde that she was determined to be a scholar in her old age, and she spent a pleasant afternoon in the Tower of London being instructed by him in the meaning of sundry technical law terms in the ancient rolls and charters in his care.

Ascham's pedagogy was founded on the principle of double translation, both out of and back into classical and modern languages, and Elizabeth's early and precocious exercises were in this vein. Between 1545 and 1548 she regularly made translated texts her new year's gifts to her father, stepmother, and half-brother, the authors including John Calvin and the Italian reformer Bernardino Ochino. In 1545 she presented Katherine Parr with her English translation of a mystical religious poem composed by Marguerite d'Angoulême, queen of Navarre, *Miroir de l'ame pecheresse*, giving it the title *The Glasse of the Synnefull Soule*. This coincided, perhaps significantly, with thoughts of a French marriage for Elizabeth, which may have encouraged further progress in the language. The presentation copy survives in the Bodleian Library, bound and embroidered, according to tradition, by Elizabeth herself in her favourite materials, blue velvet, silks, and silver wire. As a text the choice seems strange to modern sensibilities. Was it appropriate for an eleven-year-old to ask, even if only rhetorically: 'is there any hell so profounde that is sufficient to punish the tenth parte of my synnes?' Late in 1545 Elizabeth wrote out and bound another little book as a new year's gift for her father, her rendering into Latin, French, and Italian of Katherine Parr's own *Prayers or Meditations*, a truly prodigious achievement. In the dedicatory epistle, the only known letter of Elizabeth to Henry, she seems to anticipate her future greatness, which was hardly a realistic dream in 1545: 'May I, by this means, be indebted to you not as an imitator of your virtues but indeed as an inheritor of them' (*Collected Works*, 9–10).

When Elizabeth sent her portrait to her brother, now king (traditionally in May 1549 but more probably in 1551), she wrote: 'for the face, I grant, I might well blush to offer, but the mind I shall never be ashamed to present' (*Collected Works*, 35). How good a scholar and how good a Latinist was the mature Elizabeth? There are contemporaries who complained that their knowledge had grown rusty since their schooldays when they had been required to converse in nothing but Latin. However, this was perhaps no more than a polite convention, to which Elizabeth herself may have subscribed when in 1564 she apologized to Cambridge University for her 'barbarousness' ('I would to God you had all drunk this night of the river of Lethe, that you might forget all'), and in 1566 to Oxford University for a 'speech full of barbarisms' (ibid., 87–91). She clearly had problems with the difficult Horace, although in the case of Boethius she was not so much mistranslating as altering the sense of the text into something more regal. What became a legend in Elizabeth's own time was the impromptu Latin speech she addressed to a tactless Polish ambassador in 1597, a rhetorical *tour de force*. These were the skills which Anne coveted for her daughter: learning as an accomplishment with some practical use. But Elizabeth, unlike her cousin and successor James VI and I, was never what would now be called an intellectual, not even especially bookish, and she was not noted as a patron of learned men.

Religion No single issue has more divided Elizabeth's historians and biographers than her religion. She has been accused, mainly by Catholics, of atheism, and praised by liberal sceptics as essentially 'politique', sharing their own pragmatic attitude to matters of faith; while protestants, in her own time and after, have celebrated her as godly Deborah, the only champion of their own true faith. She cannot have been all these things.

If the foundations of Elizabeth's learning were laid in her childhood, so it was with her religious faith. Her motto, *Semper eadem* ('Always the same'), is often understood as an indication that in these matters she never would change. It may also mean that she never had changed, not since her years with Katherine Parr. Katherine's own religious position, most fully articulated in her *The Lamentation of a Sinner* (1547), seems to have been of the kind often called 'evangelical', a religious fashion derived from the aristocratic Franco-Italianate piety of the circles in which Anne Boleyn grew up, but probably with some indebtedness to Cranmer, who as a senior privy councillor was in close attendance on Katherine as regent during her husband's absence on the Boulogne campaign of 1544.

This was a religion bibliocentric, Christocentric, and well expressed in an English hymn of a later century: 'nothing in my hand I bring, simply to thy cross I cling'; but, if committed to the foundational protestant doctrine (and experience) of justification by faith alone, not disposed to pursue that doctrine into its more advanced dogmatic implications, and, as a style of piety, distinctively pre-protestant. When the protestant publicist and exile John Bale published overseas the first printed edition of Elizabeth's translation of Marguerite d'Angoulême's *Miroir*, now called *A Godly Medytacyon of the Christen Sowle*, in 1548, several subtle changes were needed to turn it into a 'godly' text in the protestant sense.

Elizabeth's parentage determined that she should be, if not some kind of protestant, no kind of Catholic, since she was the product of England's breach with Rome. As queen, and not acknowledged as such in many parts of Catholic Europe, she was bound to restore the royal supremacy which Mary had repudiated. However, her religion has been characterized as either that of an 'odd sort of Protestant' (Collinson, *Elizabethan Essays*, 114) or of 'an old sort of Protestant' (Doran, 'Elizabeth I's religion', 698). It was not the mark of a 'good' protestant to employ the rich repertory of traditional Catholic oaths with which Elizabeth frequently reinforced her speech. This was a protestant who found no difficulty in her sister's reign in conforming outwardly to the religion of the mass, which makes her one of a type denounced by Calvin as 'Nicodemite', the Nicodemism of her stepmother, which she shared, among others, with Ascham, Cecil, and her favourite churchman, the first dean of her Chapel Royal, George Carew, who was Astley's cousin. To be sure, as queen she denounced the mass, but her often professed belief in some kind of real presence in the eucharist, apparently closer to Lutheran sacramental theology than to the reformed position, seems to have been more than a mere diplomatic gesture, although on occasions it was also that. Like Katherine Parr, she venerated the symbol of the cross, which set her at odds with Elizabethan protestants who regarded it as a popish idol, and demanded that she give it the same treatment as Moses' brazen serpent, which godly King Hezekiah smashed in pieces. Instead, she set up a crucifix in her chapel and for many years resisted all attempts to have it removed. Elizabeth shared with her stepmother an old-fashioned prejudice against clerical marriage, and while it is not true that she insisted on celibacy in her bishops (most were married, some twice and one three times), it is not clear how many of those bishops were chosen by her personally rather than by their courtly patrons and her privy council.

However, what made Elizabeth a particularly odd kind of protestant was her negative attitude towards preaching, which protestants regarded as the ordinary means of salvation. Her second archbishop of Canterbury, Edmund Grindal, was scandalized when she told him that three or four preachers ought to be sufficient for a shire. The official Book of Homilies, originally envisaged as a stopgap substitute for sermons, was safer, especially since Elizabeth herself carefully vetted its contents, and so far as her own consumption of sermons was concerned, although she was bound to hear a great many, it seems to have been the ritual of the procession to and from the Chapel Royal which appealed to her more than the preaching itself.

Prayers rather than sermons were at the heart of Elizabeth's personal religion: prayers which were rich in devotion and humility, but also conveyed a proper sense of a hierarchy in which she related directly, and even familiarly, to God himself. Representative of this religious style is the tiny book of prayers in five languages, enriched with miniatures by Nicholas Hilliard, prepared for her use (it is not in her hand) at the time of the Alençon courtship in the late 1570s. A publication of 1569 called *Christian Prayers and Meditations* had for its frontispiece Elizabeth on her knees at prayer, the sword of justice abandoned by her side. This came to be known as 'Queen Elizabeth's prayer book', and the same image was repeated in 1578 in a further *Booke of Christian Prayers*. On this showing, and on the evidence of the religious settlement over which she presided, it may not be altogether anachronistic to call Elizabeth the true progenitor of Anglicanism.

The threshold of adult life, 1547–1553 Elizabeth's whole life was one of artificiality, and how far her religion was one of those artifices will never be known. At fourteen, however, real life caught up with her, with consequences which may have made her for ever suspicious of aspects of it. On Henry's death on 28 January 1547 Elizabeth made her household, perhaps for the first time, with Katherine Parr, now dowager queen. But about June 1547 Katherine, with indecent haste, took for her third husband the lord admiral, Thomas Seymour, Baron Seymour of Sudeley, younger brother of Edward Seymour, duke of Somerset, lord protector and governor of Edward VI. Seymour, according to undocumented legend, had only weeks before proposed marriage to Elizabeth, who knew better than to accept him. However, not for the last time, the evidence suggests that if she was averse to marriage, she was not indifferent to men like Seymour, who was handsome and made for action. There were romps in her bedchamber in which Seymour's wife was complicit, thinking it innocent fun, and on one extraordinary occasion in the garden at Hanworth, Middlesex, Katherine held Elizabeth fast while Seymour 'cut hyr gowne yn a c [100] peces' (PRO, SP 10/6/21, fol. 55r). Elizabeth was strongly attached to Seymour. John Astley warned his wife that

> the Lady Elizabeth did bere som affection to my Lord Admirall / Ffor he did mark that when eny body did talk well of my Lord Admirall / she semyd to be well pleasid therwith / & somtyme she wold blush when he were spoken of. (Hatfield, Cecil MS 150, fol. 86r)

Kate Astley at least pretended to be shocked, and perhaps Katherine came to see that things had gone too far, for in May 1548 Elizabeth was sent away to live with Sir Anthony Denny and his wife, who was Astley's sister, at Cheshunt, Hertfordshire—or perhaps the new arrangement was her own choice. Elizabeth was not friendless at this time. She requested assistance from Cecil during the protectorate probably because he was Somerset's secretary. In an

undated letter from Astley of about 1548 she asked for his help in procuring the release of a poor man imprisoned in Scotland. Elizabeth added a postscript: 'I pray you farder this pore mans sute. Your frende, Elizabeth'. Astley noted the conventional relationship developing between her mistress and the secretary but this was strengthened by their protestantism: 'beyng so moche asured of your wellyng mynde to set forthe hyr cawses to my lord protectors grace', especially as the matter was 'so godly' (BL, Lansdowne MS 1236, fol. 41r–v).

Katherine died of puerperal fever on 5 September 1548 after giving birth, and the widower again set his sights on Elizabeth. Astley actively promoted what she now deemed to be an honourable suit, to which Elizabeth seems to have been in no way averse, although she was more cautious. However, all three, Seymour, Elizabeth, and Astley, were living dangerously. On 17 February 1549 Seymour, who was plotting against his brother in other ways, was arrested, and on 20 March he was executed for treason. Meanwhile, Astley and Thomas Parry, Elizabeth's cofferer, were clapped in the Tower and interrogated. The privy council instructed Sir Robert Tyrwhit, Katherine's former master of the horse and so possessed of an insider's knowledge, to interview Elizabeth, while Tyrwhit's wife, a distant relation of Katherine's first husband, was appointed her 'Mistress' in place of Astley. The idea was to get Elizabeth to confess to her part in what was virtually a conspiracy. However, while Astley and Parry supplied the many titillating details on which Elizabeth's biographers have feasted ever since, Elizabeth gave nothing away and stood on her royal dignity. Tyrwhit told Somerset that she was too smart to be taken in by 'policy' and commented that 'the love she sayth to Aschlay ys to be wondered at' (PRO, SP 10/6/6, fol. 17r).

David Starkey has pointed out that in a later century Elizabeth would have been regarded as the victim of child abuse and a suitable case for treatment by psychologists and social workers. Other writers have suspected that in the Seymour episode are concealed the real reasons why she never married. However, the emotional world of the sixteenth century is out of modern reach, and the most that can be said is that the experience must have provided a brutal introduction to adulthood, and soon there were other lessons to be learned from events: the fall and execution of Somerset, the death of the adolescent king, the plot (his plot it seems) to put on the throne the fifteen-year-old Lady Jane Grey (which depended for its success on returning both his sisters to the status of bastards), and Mary's successful coup and triumph.

Elizabeth marked her growing up by assuming a new persona, that of a demure and respectable young woman who dressed plainly and eschewed ostentatious jewellery. Even when the dowager queen of Scotland, Mary of Guise, visited England in October 1551, provoking a frenzy of effort to adopt the latest French fashions, Elizabeth 'kepte hir olde maydenly shamefastnes' (Aylmer, sig. M4v). However, there is no evidence Elizabeth was at court at this time. One of her servants later remembered the day when Elizabeth walked down by the river to visit his elderly and godly mother, 'who with me and our familie joied then not a little, to heare of your godlie studie and vertuous inclination' (A. Peel, ed., *The Second Parte of a Register*, 2 vols., 1915, 2.57). Yet, by the time this cameo was recorded, the disillusioned William Fuller had decided that Elizabeth had merely been acting a part.

From December 1548 the fifteen-year-old Elizabeth was the head of her own large household, numbering between 120 and 140, based mostly in the red-brick house at Hatfield originally built by John Morton, bishop of Ely, about 1480, which she acquired from Somerset and preferred to a less comfortable Hertfordshire establishment, Ashridge. She was also a woman of property. She was assured an annual income of £3000 under her father's will and (after some difficulties which were as much political as technical, but which were easily overcome after Somerset's fall in October 1549) this was turned into a portfolio of scores of manors and houses concentrated in Buckinghamshire, Hertfordshire, Huntingdonshire, Northamptonshire, Lincolnshire, and Berkshire, but with scattered estates further afield. She was one of the greatest landowners in the kingdom, with a landed estate worth £3106 13s. 1d. per annum, and when she was under investigation in her sister's reign she said that she could not remember where all her houses were. There were indications of how Elizabeth would subsequently manage the affairs of the realm in the way that she played the Tudor equivalent of the game of Monopoly and grew ever more wealthy. After its ambitious builder's fall, Somerset Place became her town house. She did not like it, partly because it was incomplete and still a building site. However, the keeper of Somerset Place was Sir Robert Dudley, fifth son of John Dudley, duke of Northumberland. She had known him since childhood and close proximity at Somerset Place might have reinforced their relationship.

Mary, and Elizabeth's 'miraculous preservation', 1553–1558
Mary's accession on 19 July 1553 soon proved bad news for Elizabeth. According to information recorded by both the martyrologist John Foxe and Giacomo Soranzo, the Venetian ambassador, the queen at first insisted on Elizabeth keeping her close company, but after her coronation on 1 October kept aloof. Besides repealing all the religious legislation of Edward's reign, the first step to the reconciliation of the realm to Rome, parliament declared Henry's marriage to Katherine of Aragon valid and Mary legitimate. Mary would have liked to remove Elizabeth from her place in the succession. Despite conforming outwardly to her religion, Elizabeth's relations with her sister deteriorated rapidly. In December she left the court for Ashridge, accompanied by a retinue of almost five hundred gentlemen. She deceived no one when, halfway there, she sent a message asking Mary to send after her copes, chasubles, and other ornaments appropriate for celebrating mass.

Darker clouds began to gather as Mary made her decision to marry her Spanish cousin, Philip of Spain. It was an unpopular choice, and by late January 1554 provoked a rebellion which, if it had been more widely co-ordinated,

would surely have toppled the regime, and which, confined as it was to the Kentish rising led by Sir Thomas Wyatt the younger, failed only when it reached Charing Cross and Ludgate. The inevitable executions followed swiftly, that of Lady Jane Grey and her husband, Lord Guildford Dudley, on 12 February, which was the very day that Elizabeth, suffering from a mysterious and perhaps psychosomatic illness, was removed from Ashridge and began a slow journey in a litter back to Whitehall Palace, which she reached on 23 February, the day when Henry Grey, duke of Suffolk, was beheaded. Elizabeth's prospects could hardly have been more bleak, for it was in her name that Wyatt rebelled, and she was part of the plot in so far as it had been intended to marry her to Edward Courtenay, earl of Devon, of the blood royal and last of the Yorkist line, who had been thought of as a suitable consort for Mary. Elizabeth was justifiably suspected of corresponding with the French ambassador, François Noailles, and there was further evidence of potentially treasonable approaches, although none that could be extracted from Wyatt and his accomplices that she had responded, at least, not in writing. The imperial ambassador, Simon Renard, to whose advice Mary leaned more readily than to her own privy councillors, was in no doubt that Elizabeth was too dangerous to be allowed to live, which was also the view of Stephen Gardiner, bishop of Winchester.

After three weeks in which Mary refused to see or hear from her sister, the decision was taken to commit Elizabeth to the Tower. Before boarding the barge which took her down the river on 18 March, she wrote Mary a letter which she must have hoped would save her life. She remembered hearing Somerset say that if his brother had been able to speak with him he would not have suffered, and her prayer was that 'evil persuasions' would not set one sister against the other. 'I humbly crave but only one word of answer from yourself' (*Collected Works*, 41–2). Yet, within hours she was lodged in the very same royal apartments in the Tower from which her mother had gone out to her trial and execution.

Both before and after Wyatt's execution on 11 April, after a scaffold speech in which he exonerated Elizabeth, she was examined by the privy council, which wanted to know why she had proposed, on the eve of Wyatt's rebellion, and apparently on his advice, to move from Ashridge to the strategically placed and defensible castle of Donnington in Berkshire. The circumstances were indeed suspicious, but Elizabeth defended herself with the same sagacity which she had shown in 1549, and the will in a divided privy council to prosecute seems to have been lacking. On 19 May she was removed from the Tower to house arrest at the Oxfordshire palace of Woodstock, where her keeper was a stolid Norfolk gentleman promoted above his merits to the privy council, Sir Henry Bedingfield. The journey to Woodstock was something like a progress, for Mary was no longer popular and royals in trouble always attracted sympathy, as Mary, queen of Scots, would find twenty years later, on her regular summer jaunts from Sheffield to Buxton.

Foxe in an appendix to his *Actes and Monuments* (editions

from 1563) turned these changes in fortune into an edifying story of near martyrdom, associating Elizabeth with
the fate of the 300 or so protestants who were burnt at the
stake by her sister's authority: 'The miraculous preservation of the Lady Elizabeth, now queen of England, from
extreme calamity and danger of life'. In successive editions the story was meant to edify not least Elizabeth herself, as Foxe grew increasingly concerned about the
strength of her commitment to the protestant cause. So in
1570 what was emphasized was not so much Elizabeth's
heroic endurance as 'God's providence' in preserving her,
but the story was in form more like a romance than history in a modern sense, which enabled Foxe to emphasize
the passivity of his heroine and what was marvellous in
her preservation. She was

> the greatest traytour in the world, clapped in the Tower, and
> againe tossed from thence, from house to house, from prison
> to prison, from post to piller, at length also prisoner in her
> own house, and guarded with a sort of cuttethrotes.   (Foxe,
> 2091)

The story became a seventeenth-century legend in
Thomas Heywood's play *If you Know not me you Know No
Bodie, or, The Troubles of Queene Elizabeth* (in two parts and
fourteen editions between 1605 and 1633).

According to Foxe, Woodstock was turned into another
Tower, and Elizabeth was guarded closely day and night by
as many as sixty soldiers. In truth, Woodstock was no dun-
geon, and Elizabeth enjoyed the company of her own
people including Parry, who installed himself in town in
the Bull Inn, where he did business with as many as forty
visitors a day and continued to administer Elizabeth's
estates, ensuring that her rents were paid and her deer not
poached. Other less innocent matters may also have been
discussed.

It is sometimes suggested that Elizabeth herself was
Foxe's source but, if so, he would hardly have presumed to
have revised her account in subsequent editions. It is
more likely that Foxe depended on several informants in
Elizabeth's entourage, both at the Tower and at Woodstock, including one of her women, Elizabeth Sandes, a
notorious protestant who later went into exile with a
group which included Lady Dorothy Stafford, who lived
close to Foxe in Basel. It is probably significant that the
account which Foxe compiled from these sources places
in a favourable light some of Elizabeth's servants, who
refused to conform to the queen's religion, while it makes
no secret of the fact (perhaps intended as critical admonition) that Elizabeth herself attended mass. However, she
also demanded repeatedly that she be allowed to have and
read an English Bible.

Elizabeth remained at Woodstock for just under a year,
twelve months during which Mary's marriage to Philip
was celebrated on 25 July 1554 and consummated and a
child confidently expected. Cardinal Reginald Pole
arrived to complete England's reconciliation to Rome.
Suddenly the obstinate Bedingfield no longer stood
between Elizabeth and her sister, and she was summoned
to Hampton Court to witness the birth of a prince who
would make her politically irrelevant. This reconciliation

was encouraged by Philip. At last she was admitted to
Mary's presence at Hampton Court, and to an uneasy
meeting on 21 May, intended to achieve reconciliation but
in which the queen still tried to secure an admission of
guilt. Events were now moving out of Mary's control. The
pregnancy was false, and her husband, who now in effect
deserted her, distracted by many other imperial designs,
began to see in Elizabeth, now almost beyond question
the heir to the throne, a means of keeping the succession
out of the hands of Mary, queen of Scots. Paradoxically,
Philip from now on kept Elizabeth, and her hopes of succeeding to the throne, alive.

In October 1555 Elizabeth settled back into her old life at
Hatfield, attended once more by Ascham, Parry, and
Astley, but soon she was at the centre of fresh plots, the
Dudley conspiracy of 1556, which once again involved
Devon, and in which she may have been more actively
involved than in 1554. However, it was Philip, now in Brussels, who gave explicit instructions, with which Mary
complied, that Elizabeth's probable guilt should not be
investigated further. As a precaution, Sir Thomas Pope, a
privy councillor, was installed at Hatfield to make sure
that she behaved herself and Astley was put back in the
Tower.

Now the worst that could happen to Elizabeth would be
marriage to some foreign prince. The candidate chosen
was Philip's cousin, Emmanuel Philibert, prince of Piedmont and duke of Savoy, a diplomatic pawn squeezed
between the Habsburg and Valois monarchs and from
Philip's point of view a perfect consort. Elizabeth's title to
succeed would be recognized, England would remain a
Habsburg dependency, and Emmanuel Philibert (who was
not Spanish) would be handsomely compensated for the
loss of his ancestral lands. However, these calculations
left out of account Elizabeth's determination not to be
coerced into an unwelcome marriage by Philip's threats,
which he pressed in person on his return to England in
March 1557. She took advice from the French ambassador,
who dissuaded her from an impulse to flee into exile.
Everything would fall into her lap if she would only be
patient.

Elizabeth was not all that patient and took nothing for
granted. She was probably now buying support, increasing the size of the retinues which always accompanied
her public appearances. As Mary's health broke down, letters were being sent to potential supporters in all parts of
the country, including Sir John Thynne, who promised to
hold the south-west for her, and Elizabeth was digging
herself into Brocket Hall, to the north of Hatfield. On 6
November 1558 Mary acknowledged Elizabeth as her heir,
and in the days which intervened before the queen's
death on 17 November Elizabeth made it clear to Philip's
envoy, Gomez Suárez de Figueroa, fifth count de Feria,
that she would not be beholden to Spain for her crown,
which she owed to her people. It may be only with hindsight that there appears to have been a smooth transition
of power. Why did Parry order a military force stationed at
Berwick upon Tweed, on a hostile frontier and in wartime,

to come with all convenient speed to Brocket Hall? However, Elizabeth held all the cards, and what was left of the Marian regime (Pole died within twenty-four hours of Mary) was bust. As Mary went through the process of dying, the road to Hatfield was clogged with traffic.

Accession, 1558 The *Annals of Queen Elizabeth* by the late Elizabethan historian Sir John Hayward opens with a dark scenario:

> Every report was greedily both inquired and received, all truthes suspected, diverse tales beleeved, many improbable conjectures hatched and nourished. Invasion of strangeres, civill dissentione, the doubtfull dispositione of the succeeding Prince, were cast in every man's conceite as present perills. (*Annals of the First Four Years of the Reign of Queen Elizabeth by Sir John Hayward*, ed. J. Bruce, CS, 7, 1840, 1)

These sentences owed as much, textually, to Tacitus and to Sir Philip Sidney's *Arcadia* as to the real circumstances of November 1558. Yet Hayward hardly exaggerated. England was still at war with France and Scotland, the treasury was exhausted, Calais lost, 'to the great dishonour of the English Nation', the queen without allies and uncomfortably dependent on her Spanish patron. So reported a better historian than Hayward, William Camden (*Historie*, trans. Norton, 14). Moreover the new queen was illegitimate, not only according to Roman law, but, until parliament ruled otherwise, by common law too.

Yet an altogether more subtle threat to Elizabeth's newly established rule was that it was represented as conditional, dependent not so much on Habsburg power as on the dispositions of her protestant subjects, and, in their perception, on the good will of God himself. John Hales, a radical survivor of the Edwardian regime, presented her 'at her first entrance to her reign' with an oration which included this warning. God, 'he only', had delivered Elizabeth from her enemies and made her queen.

> If ye fear him, and seek to do his will, then he will favour you, and preserve you to the end from all enemies, as he did king David. If ye now fall from him, or juggle with him, look for no more favour than Saul had showed to him. (Foxe, 2116-19)

It is significant that Foxe saw no occasion to put this into print until 1576.

That Elizabeth was a woman allowed, even required, such things to be said. In the ill-timed *First Blast of the Trumpet Against the Monstruous Regiment of Women* (1558), the Scottish reformer John Knox asserted that the 'imbecility' of their sex rendered women unfit to bear rule. In his riposte, ostensibly defending her title, *An Harborowe for Faithfull and Trewe Subjectes* (1559), Aylmer argued that the government of women could only be exceptional and providential, citing the precedent of the biblical figure of Deborah. He thought that there was no need for concern, since England was a mixed polity, a parliamentary monarchy, and it would not be so much government by the queen as government in her name. 'It is not she that ruleth but the laws, the executors whereof be her judges, appointed by her, her justices of the peace and such other officers' (Aylmer, sigs. H3-4r).

Elizabeth, of course, was confident that it was she who ruled, and the tension between her political ideas and those of very many of her subjects, some in the highest places, is the ground bass running through the entire history of her reign. On the very day of her accession, she is said to have warned Mary's privy councillors, who had hastily made their way to Hatfield, that she would choose for her own privy council only 'such … as in consultation I shall thinck mete, and shortlie appointe' (Harington, 2.312-14). Before she spoke, Elizabeth had appointed her old friend Cecil to be her principal secretary and the anchorman of her fledgeling government. And on 17 November Cecil was already at the desk which he would occupy for the next forty years, during the whole of which time it is often difficult to know which were his decisions and policies, which hers.

It is from Cecil's notes that it is known what was done by the first, informal, meeting of Elizabeth's privy council, gathered at Hatfield on 18 November. The privy council itself was reconstructed, excluding those who owed their positions to their personal ties with Mary and to their more than formal Catholicism. The result was a smaller and more effective privy council, with twenty former members dismissed (including all the clerics) and only ten new men admitted (none of them clerics). At the same time the royal household was reordered, with Parry knighted and made comptroller on 20 November and (the most significant of the new appointments) Dudley, once Elizabeth's fellow prisoner in the Tower, made her master of the horse. Such rapid decision making, which not all her biographers associate with Elizabeth, ran contrary to advice she had received from a political wiseacre, Sir Nicholas Throckmorton, 'to succed happilie through a discreete beginning', taking her time in making new appointments, with 'no nominacion [to] bee had or used for a time of privie councellors' (Neale, 'Sir Nicholas Throckmorton's advice', 91-8). In constructing the new regime, Elizabeth was loyal to such blood kindred as she had, promoting her Boleyn cousins, Henry *Carey (1526-1596) as first Baron Hunsdon on 13 January 1559, Sir Francis *Knollys (1511/12-1596) as vice-chamberlain on 14 January, and two generations of Sackvilles, the closest relations of all.

On 23 November 1558 Elizabeth rode up to London, accompanied by more than a thousand lords, ladies, and gentlemen. Her frequent moves around the city, bringing her to Whitehall for Christmas, with Mary decently buried, were public demonstrations of her popularity, so many dress rehearsals for her coronation. This took place on Sunday 15 January 1559, a date chosen as propitious on the astrological advice of the mysteriously learned Dr John Dee.

The sum of £16,000 was spent from Elizabeth's own purse on this splendid show, and an untold amount by the city. Nothing was lacking, except the bishops who, according to the *Liber regalis*, ought to have played the principal parts in the ceremony. They were either dead, too old and infirm, unacceptable to the queen, or unwilling to serve, and it was left to the very junior Owen Oglethorpe, bishop of Carlisle, to carry out the anointing with holy oils and the crowning itself. The day before, according to custom,

Elizabeth processed through London from the Tower to Whitehall, carried on an open litter. According to the official panegyric which celebrated the event, London was transformed into 'a stage wherin was shewed the wonderfull spectacle of a noble hearted princesse toward her most loving people, the people's excading comfort in beholding so worthy a soveraign, and hearing so princelike a voice' (Osborn, 1559, sig. A2v). At intervals there were various instructive pageants, most famously a representation of Time, which prompted Elizabeth's exclamation: 'Tyme hath brought me hether' (ibid., sig. C2v). Parts were played and explanatory lines spoken by children, and the queen repeatedly called for the 'noise' of the many musical groups to be suspended so that their piping voices should not be drowned out.

The religious settlement, 1558–1559 The most serious business confronting the new regime was the settlement of religion, which began in earnest when Elizabeth's first parliament opened on 25 January. The symbolism of the coronation tableaux suggested that London, at least, expected a protestant outcome; but in the early weeks of the reign there were many intentionally contradictory signals of the queen's intentions. She continued to hear mass in the Chapel Royal but distanced herself from its holiest mysteries. Whether she intended to recover the royal supremacy was concealed in her royal title by an 'etc.'. In religion at least she was as discreet as Throckmorton advised.

This discretion seems to have been abandoned when parliament met. All that is certainly known about the handling of religion in the very poorly documented 1559 parliament is that from it emerged a new Act of Supremacy (in its enacted form describing the queen as supreme governor rather than supreme head of the Church of England, which met the objections of some protestants as well as of Catholics, since only Christ was head of his church) and an Act of Uniformity imposing a Book of Common Prayer which was essentially the second Edwardian book of 1552 with a few significant alterations, again designed to reconcile confessional differences.

For centuries, historians assumed that that was what Elizabeth and her closest advisers, especially Cecil, intended from the outset. It was very much the programme recommended in a 'Device for alteration of religion', anonymous but just possibly composed by Cecil himself, which, with a decisiveness now known to have been in character, faced up to the internal and external dangers of such a policy, only to produce prevailing counter-arguments. However, in 1950, the most distinguished Elizabethan historian of his day, Sir John Neale, argued ingeniously that Elizabeth's original plan was to re-enact only the royal supremacy, leaving for a later occasion the reintroduction of protestantism. Among the factors which changed her mind was concerted resistance from a House of Commons dominated by returned exiles and other committed protestants. It was the beginning of a contention with her hotter protestant subjects which would develop as the reign progressed. However, the weight of historical opinion has subsequently swung back

to where it was and it is now thought that the government got what it originally wanted, and that the only significant opposition to its policy came from Catholics, lay and clerical, in the House of Lords. To overcome that, it was necessary to stage a manipulated religious disputation at Westminster Abbey (begun on 31 March), which led to the exclusion of two bishops and a mitred abbot, with a consequential change in the voting figures in the upper house. The Act of Uniformity passed by three votes. All the bishops voted against it, two lay privy councillors, and seven other peers.

It is one thing to establish that the settlement of 1559, a very conservative settlement carried further in that direction by the extraparliamentary royal injunctions of the summer of that year, was what Elizabeth wanted, quite another to argue, as some historians have done, that there was little to choose between the queen's brand of protestantism and that of those now poised to take charge of her church, and especially the returned Marian exiles who were put up to preach at court in Lent 1559, and who were now appointed to bishoprics. Prominent among these were Edmund Grindal (London), Richard Cox (Ely), Edwin Sandys (Worcester), with the non-exile Matthew Parker (Anne Boleyn's chaplain) almost the exception to prove the rule. It cannot be assumed that these appointments were what the queen personally desired, and there is no evidence of what manoeuvres at court may have preceded the making of the settlement.

What is known is that the Nicodemite queen and her émigré bishops, who carried the torch for the martyr bishops, Cranmer, Nicholas Ridley, and Hugh Latimer, did not always see eye to eye. On her state visit to Oxford in 1566, Elizabeth endured a speech by the public orator, Thomas Kingsmill, himself the brother of an exile, in which he congratulated her for recalling from Germany the friends of Pietro Martire Vermigli (Peter Martyr) and Martin Bucer. Her responses to such effusions were normally gracious, but all she is reported to have said on this occasion was 'you would have done well had you had good matter' (Nichols, 1.209). In the convocation of 1563, which otherwise approved the Thirty-Nine Articles of Religion, it was the bishops, not 'puritans' (a word not yet invented), who did their unsuccessful best to carry through a programme of further reform, and especially to remove some of the very ceremonies which were about to divide the Elizabethan church between conformists and nonconformists. When they failed in convocation, the bishops seem to have joined in a parliamentary campaign to the same end. The price of their failure was that they were obliged to enforce policies for which many of them had no taste, so provoking an anti-episcopal reaction. The queen could not be blamed. Her bishops could, and were.

The question of marriage, 1558–1581 The chorus of admiring approval for Gloriana and the Virgin Queen has often obscured the serious problem posed by Elizabeth's sex. It was not only Knox who believed a female ruler to be, if not an unnatural monstrosity, an unusual and in principle undesirable exception to the regular rule governing human affairs. Apart from any other considerations, it was not clear that a woman could exercise the oldest function of a monarch, leading her forces into battle. Nor could she, in any station or walk of life, ordinarily exercise the kind of authority associated with the mental powers of a man. Women, especially widows, might manage households, but they were excluded from all public offices. Privileged women might learn languages, but they could not study the law. On one occasion Cecil was upset when a messenger discussed with the queen an ambassadorial dispatch, it 'being too much for a woman's knowledge' (Haigh, *Elizabeth I*, 9). Elizabeth was regularly visited with unsolicited male advice, often represented as the will of God, which on Pauline principles only men were authorized to interpret.

It was universally assumed that Elizabeth would marry, and for two reasons, the less pressing of which was that she should have the support of a male consort. The major and compelling reason was to secure an orderly and, if possible, male succession to the throne. So the question of her marriage, a dynastic question which had been put in many circumstances and with different suitors in mind ever since her infancy, took on a new urgency once she became queen. On 2 February 1559 a select committee of the Commons, which included all the privy councillors in the house, presented the queen with a formal request that she should marry. Elizabeth took almost a week to respond with the first of her many answers, answerless. She first declared her disposition to remain in the same 'trade of life' in which she had lived hitherto; then professed to take the petition 'in good parte', because it placed no limit on her choice; promised that if she were to marry it would not be prejudicial to the realm, and even envisaged a time when it would 'not remayne destitute of an heire that may be a fitt governor'; but concluded with the prophecy that it would 'in the end' be sufficient that a marble stone should declare 'that a Queene, having raigned such a tyme, lived and dyed a virgin' (Hartley, 1.44–5). Despite those memorable words, the speech had more openness to the possibility of marriage than a different version provided by Camden, in which she is supposed to have chided the Commons for forgetting that she was already married to her kingdom, with a little dumbshow involving her coronation ring.

Elizabeth had no lack of suitors, including Philip II, Erik XIV of Sweden, and the archdukes Ferdinand and Karl of Austria. The more the merrier, since each proposal was an endorsement of her legitimacy. Erik was the most persistent suitor, and the most generous. A series of Swedish missions between summer 1559 and autumn 1562 came laden with 'massy bullion' and stables worth of piebald horses (Nichols, 1.79–82, 87, 104–5). Initial interest in Erik was a counterfoil to the more plausible candidature of the emperor Ferdinand's sons, Ferdinand and Charles. Charles, who symbolized an anti-French, Habsburg alliance, proved to have staying power, but religion was an almost insuperable bar, and it was one which was exploited for all that it was worth by the man whom Elizabeth would probably have chosen to marry if all things had been equal, Dudley. What kept Erik's hopes alive into

1562 was hostility to Dudley and his ambition; and it does seem that what kept all international suits at the level of diplomatic games was Elizabeth's genuine love for this man who was destined to be the longest running of her favourites, if never her spouse.

Elizabeth's 'affair' with Dudley is the stuff of which legends are made, and have been, by Sir Walter Scott and many others. Dudley was a married man, otherwise things might have been both less and more complicated. The couple were of an age, and Dudley claimed to have known Elizabeth 'familierement' from before she was eight (Doran, *Monarchy and Matrimony*, 40). While Dudley's wife, Amy, *née* Robsart, was still alive, courtiers exchanged scandalous gossip about his relationship with the queen.

Even as rumours spread, on 8 September 1560 at Cumnor Place, Oxfordshire, Amy Dudley was found dead in unusual and even suspicious circumstances. Was it suicide or murder? Modern science has found a plausible, if not conclusive, medical explanation. With Amy dead, many assumed that Elizabeth would marry her favourite. How far Dudley's chances of marrying Elizabeth were realistic depends in part upon the reading of some very complicated diplomatic transactions, relating to whether England would opt to participate in the third assembly of the Council of Trent, whether Philip could be persuaded to favour Dudley's suit as the price for a return of England to the Catholic fold, whether proposals along these lines were made to the Spanish ambassador, Alvaro de la Quadra, bishop of Aquila, and, if so, whether they were made with sincerity. While there is no historical consensus on this matter, it appears most likely that Elizabeth's and Dudley's diplomatic games with the ambassador were just that, games. For Elizabeth was unlikely to tear up her religious settlement, while Dudley later claimed, with apparent sincerity, to have been consistent in his protestantism, 'ever from my cradle brought up in it' (Collinson, *Godly People*, 95). As for Cecil, it should not be assumed that he was motivated by simple hostility to Dudley.

It is more than likely that in the months after Amy Dudley's death, Elizabeth decided that marriage with Dudley was not on. This would mean that, unlike Mary, queen of Scots, in 1565, her head and political instincts came to rule her heart. However, Dudley continued to apply what might be termed cultural pressure. Sir Thomas Smith's 'Dialogue on the queen's marriage', which circulated in manuscript, John Philip's *The Play of Patient Grissell*, and, above all, *Gorboduc*, the Senecan tragedy written by Thomas Sackville and Thomas Norton and performed in the Inner Temple at Christmas 1561, and subsequently at court, all implicitly advocated the Dudley match.

When parliament next met in January 1563, it was in the shadow of Elizabeth's close encounter with death through smallpox in October 1562. Marriage and the succession were therefore at the top of the agenda for both houses, while the dean of St Paul's Cathedral, Alexander Nowell, one of the queen's favourite divines, preached a sermon to parliament which could hardly have been more direct. If her parents had been of her mind, not to marry, where would she have been then? The Lords petitioned her to marry 'where it shall please you, with whom it shall please yow, and assone as it shall please you' (Hartley, 1.59). The Commons placed more emphasis on the need to limit the succession. More answers answerless. Elizabeth told parliament that so far as her marriage was concerned 'a silent thoght may serve', but that the idea that she would never marry was a 'heresie' they should put out of their minds (ibid., 114). Yet, that she would never marry Dudley was probably not a heresy. When she made him Baron Denbigh on 28 September 1564 and earl of Leicester on the 29th, it was to make him acceptable as a husband for Mary, a plan which misfired when the Scottish queen married Lord Henry Darnley on 29 July 1565. Thereafter Leicester remained in the wings with little prospect of gaining the prize himself. The elaborate allegories enacted in Elizabeth's presence at Leicester's castle at Kenilworth in 1575 were aimed as much at securing his release from a kind of courtly bondage (so that he could himself marry and secure an heir) as to press an ever more unattainable suit.

The Habsburg matrimonial project was now revived. It is perhaps surprising that Cecil was so much and for so long in favour of this marriage, since it was clear that the archduke Charles was not likely to change his religion, and it could only have happened on the basis of an interpretation of the religion of England which would have been unacceptable to all but the most conservative of protestants. Despite this, Elizabeth clearly signalled to Vienna in May 1565 her intention to marry, with the implication that her choice would be the archduke. When parliament met again, in September 1566, key figures were poised to assure those now inclined to press for a resolution of the succession problem that she intended to marry. At this point Elizabeth came dangerously close to committing herself to marriage in order to stave off public debate about the succession; but she had an escape route, which was to dissolve (rather than prorogue) parliament, and when Cecil and others inserted a clause in a draft of the preamble to the subsidy bill referring to the promise to marry and acknowledging the legitimacy of public concern about the succession, her indignant reaction led to its prompt removal.

When Thomas Radcliffe, third earl of Sussex, was dispatched to Vienna to resume serious negotiations, his task was to persuade Maximilian II that the religion of England was not Calvinist but consistent with the Lutheranism of the Augsburg confession (since 1555 legal in the empire), so that there would be no need for Charles to insist on the practice of his own religion, something on which, however, Vienna did insist. In order to keep the negotiations alive, Sussex went beyond his remit on these critical matters. In England both a divided privy council and Elizabeth were forced to admit that even the limited, private practice of Catholicism would be unacceptable to the protestant public. Mary's deposition on 24 July 1567 was an event still fresh in everyone's memory. In December 1567 Elizabeth called the whole thing off. It proved too divisive and politically hazardous, and its subtext was open hostility

between Sussex and Leicester, an overture to the major political crisis of 1569.

The two French marriage projects of the 1570s, to Henri, duc d'Anjou, from 1570 to 1571 and to his brother François, duc d'Alençon (himself duc d'Anjou from 1578), between 1572 and 1578, were repeat performances, insofar as both matches appeared to be diplomatically advantageous, and both were torpedoed by the same religious factor. There were, however, other impediments, including traditional anti-French sentiment, and the disparity in age between Elizabeth and the French princes. Despite these difficulties, the queen may have been in earnest in her dealings with Henri of Anjou and his mother, Catherine de' Medici, and domestically the first Anjou marriage negotiation was not an especially divisive issue. However, the later episodes in François of Alençon and Anjou's long-running suit were another matter. England in the late 1570s confronted a number of dangers, variously assessed by those in charge of its affairs. In January 1576 it was said that 'hire Majestie is troubled with these causes, which maketh hire verie malincolie; and simeth greatlie to be oute of quiate' (Lodge, 2.136). France was either the old enemy or the only 'stay' against the new enemy, Spain, its support to be secured either by marriage or a 'league'. However, England was vulnerable because of the situation in Scotland and Ireland and Anjou was unreliable, especially because of his intervention in the Dutch revolt. The Elizabethan regime was divided about whether or not to intervene in the Low Countries. Elizabeth pulled back from the brink of military intervention, the preferred policy of the would-be warlord, Leicester, and of Sir Francis Walsingham, principal secretary. Marriage to Anjou, or talk of marriage, would at least buy time.

Yet there was more to this affair than diplomacy. To the surprise and alarm of many, when Anjou sent his servant Jean de Simier, baron de Saint-Marc, to act the ardent lover in his place, the 45-year-old Elizabeth seemed to be swept off her feet. Through much of 1579, court, privy council, and country were divided by the Anjou match. In May 1578 Gilbert Talbot, Lord Talbot, told his father, George Talbot, sixth earl of Shrewsbury, that odds of three to one were offered against the marriage. Now the odds shortened. Protestant opinion was outraged. For the hot protestant Nicholas Faunt, Walsingham's secretary and clerk of the signet, writing in March 1582, the marriage would be 'but treason' (Birch, 1.20). Leicester and his friends were opposed, and not only from self-interest, for the earl was one of those who expressed what sounds like genuine concern about the medical implications of Elizabeth marrying at her age, and suspected politically motivated manipulation of her emotions. Baron Burghley (Cecil) wrote a hundred sheets of memoranda on the subject, for and against the marriage, which are preserved among the Hatfield manuscripts, and gave a speech on 6 October 1579 opposing it. However, the evidence is ambivalent and at times he seems to have supported Sussex, the principal proponent of the marriage. His judgement was perhaps swayed by the belief that England's diplomatic needs could not be secured without a marriage, the fact that this was the very last (risky) chance to secure an heir of the queen's body, and his conviction that the Anjou marriage would serve as a prophylactic against Mary, queen of Scots.

In the backlash of Elizabeth's indignant reaction to Leicester's marriage to Lettice Devereux, *née* Knollys, dowager countess of Essex, on 21 September 1578, Anjou visited the English court in person, the only one of the queen's foreign suitors to do so. He found Elizabeth either romantically interested or acting her part well. She called him her frog. Soon the proposed marriage was boldly denounced by the lawyer John Stubbe in *The Discoverie of a Gaping Gulf whereinto England is Like to be Swallowed* (1579). In what looked like a conspiracy, the book was widely disseminated. The queen suspected that greater persons than Stubbe were behind this, but historians have found in him a striking example of the existence of a public sphere in Elizabethan England, occupied and articulated by middle-ranking lawyers and politicians. Both Stubbe and the man who organized the distribution, William Page, a client of Francis Russell, second earl of Bedford, had their right hands struck off by the public hangman, which Camden recorded as a deeply unpopular sentence. Less publicly, the marriage was opposed by Sir Philip Sidney in an open letter and, obliquely, in Edmund Spenser's *The Shepheardes Calender* and in his more overt beast fable, *Mother Hubberd's Tale* (not published until 1591).

By October 1579 the conciliar argument against the marriage prevailed and Elizabeth knew that if she were to proceed it would be without the support of her privy council. In the last resort it was, after all, her decision, and for her privy councillors to say as much was not entirely a cop-out. This was effectively checkmate, although the project had an afterlife which finally petered out in the summer of 1581—as late as May 1582 Elizabeth still addressed Anjou as 'my dearest' (*Collected Works*, 237, 245, 249, 251, 253). A marriage treaty was concluded which everyone knew would never be implemented, not even when Anjou made a second and more public visit to England. As the biological clock ticked out of time, that was the end of matrimonial diplomacy. If time had been bought, reputations had been damaged, not least Elizabeth's own, and harm done, especially to Scottish policy. Walsingham wrote in 1578: 'no one thing hath procured her so much hatred as these wooing matters, as that it is conceived she dallieth therein' (Read, *Walsingham*, 2.6).

It was in the context of the Anjou courtship, and as an expression of opposition to it, that the persona of the Virgin Queen was invented, or at least perfected. On the royal progress into East Anglia in 1578, plays and masques devised by Thomas Churchyard were performed at Norwich which celebrated Elizabeth's admirable virginity, with appropriate reference to Diana and the Virgin Mary. A year later Spenser deployed similar allegorical imagery in *The Shepheardes Calender*, and a series of portraits rubbed the same point home with the symbol of a sieve held in the queen's hand, which identified her with the vestal virgin Tuccia, who had employed a sieve full of water to prove her chastity.

As with her religion, Elizabeth's emotional and sexual history is hard to disentangle from diplomacy and artifice. Was she really a virgin? Many of her subjects doubted it. Nor was the gossip confined to the alehouse and the lower orders. In an utterly scandalous letter, perhaps written in 1584, Mary, queen of Scots, enjoying the enforced hospitality of the earl and countess of Shrewsbury at Sheffield, chose to make mischief by sharing with Elizabeth what she had heard from the countess, Elizabeth Talbot: how someone to whom Elizabeth had promised herself in matrimony often slept with her (possibly Leicester); that she would never marry Anjou, since she would never forgo her freedom to make love with her favourites, including Sir Christopher Hatton. Mary, of course, believed none of this but thought that Elizabeth ought to be told. It is perhaps more intriguing still that Elizabeth's godson, Sir John Harington, chose to present her with an epigram 'Of King David', which drew a moral from David's adultery with Bathsheba. This is not evidence that Elizabeth was a nymphomaniac but an indication of what some people were prepared to believe. However, was it significant that when she faced death in the autumn of 1562, she settled the unusually generous legacy of £500 on the groom of the privy chamber, John Tamworth, keeper of the privy purse, who perhaps knew more than others what might have been going on, and named Dudley as protector of the realm? The only evidence for this comes from the often unreliable de Quadra, who affirmed that 'nothing improper had ever passed between them' (Hume, 1.263).

The succession Historians and biographers have praised Elizabeth for choosing celibacy but, leaving aside the question of how far that choice was simply hers, as long as she remained single and without heirs of her own body she gambled with the succession on the stake of her own life. As a speaker in the Commons put it in 1567: 'if God should take her Majestie, the succession being not established, I know not what shall become of my self, my wife, my children, landes, goodes, friendes or cuntrie' (Hartley, 1.138). In 1572, when the point at issue was the execution of Mary, queen of Scots, another MP demanded: 'since the Queene in respect of her owne safety is not to bee induced hereunto, let us make petition shee will doe it in respect of our safety' (ibid., 376). This was also an exclusion crisis, since to limit the succession was to exclude Mary. The pitting of the interests of subject and monarch against one another was debilitating from the royal perspective and enabling for the wider political nation.

In the absence of an heir of her body, Elizabeth's successor ought to have been the next heir presumptive, but a confused legal situation meant that the identity of such an heir could not be presumed and was likely to be contested, unless the situation could be clarified by further legislation, a course of action against which the queen consistently set her face. Henry's third and final Succession Act of 1544 provided for an orderly succession through Edward, Mary, and Elizabeth. In case none of these should have lawful issue, Henry was empowered to further limit the succession by letters patent or his will.

Henry's last will, of 30 December 1546, made the next heir his niece Frances *Grey, *née* Brandon (1517–1559), elder daughter of his younger sister, *Mary (1496–1533), widow of Louis XII of France. Frances married Henry Grey, duke of Suffolk. If she had no children, her sister Eleanor (1519–1547), who was married to Henry Clifford, second earl of Cumberland, would be heir. In fact Frances had three daughters: Jane (1537–1554) [*see* Dudley, Lady Jane], who was proclaimed queen, deposed, and executed; Katherine (1540?–1568) [*see* Seymour, Katherine]; and Mary. Henry's will by its silence on the matter excluded the Stewart descendants of his elder sister, *Margaret (1489–1541), dowager queen of Scotland, whose title passed down to *Mary, queen of Scots (Margaret's granddaughter and Elizabeth's second cousin), and to the family of Margaret's second marriage, including Darnley, who had the advantage of English birth and whose marriage to Mary made of the senior and junior Stewart lines one flesh.

With Elizabeth's accession, and for as long as she remained childless, Katherine Grey had an apparent statutory right to succeed, since Henry's will was annexed to the Succession Act. Mary Stewart had the stronger hereditary claim. However, not only Henry's will but the common law with respect to aliens was prejudicial to her position in the order of succession, which was complicated further by Henri II's refusal to acknowledge Elizabeth's legitimacy, claiming for Mary the title and arms of England, by her marriage to François II from 1558 to 1560, and, most of all and increasingly in the perception of English protestants, by the fact that she was a Catholic.

The contest was originally between the hereditary claim of the Catholic and foreign Mary and the statutory claim of the protestant native, Katherine. Katherine's chances of being recognized by Elizabeth as her successor were probably never very good, and they were blown away when, in August 1561, it was found that she was pregnant, having secretly married Edward Seymour, first earl of Hertford. The couple were sent to the Tower on 5 September 1561. Mary returned to Scotland on 19 August 1561 and began to press her claim through Sir William Maitland of Lethington. Maitland failed to extract from Elizabeth recognition of the queen of Scots as her heir presumptive but she made no secret of her preference for Mary. As for the other claimants: 'Alas! What power or force have any of them, poor souls?' (Levine, 32). Elizabeth's refusal to name a successor, another of her *semper eadems*, was in her own interest, since as the 'second person' in her sister's reign she more than anyone had experience of the double threat which that posed. It was not seen to be in the interest of her people.

So some people resorted to propaganda and agitation, both direct and indirect. *Gorboduc* (January 1562) contrived to be about the not entirely compatible claims of Dudley to marry the queen and of Katherine Grey to succeed her. Parliament met a year later, and the Commons in its petition that Elizabeth both marry and limit the succession made no secret of its opposition to the Marian claim, if only on religious grounds, and asked the queen either to

publish the terms of Henry's will if it provided the 'certainty' required, or to provide that certainty if it did not (Hartley, 1.90–93). The outlook was in fact so uncertain, and the queen so seriously ill with smallpox, that Cecil devised an extraordinary, stopgap solution to the problem, in the form of arrangements for a legalized interregnum. This constitutionally radical scheme effectively distinguished between the queen's natural body and her body politic, which could, if only temporarily, be detached from the physical life and person of the monarch and vested in a public, conciliar body. Elizabeth's own solution, a plan which was radical in a different and thoroughly inscrutable way, and dead in the water almost from the outset, was to arrange a marriage between Dudley and Mary which might sugar the pill of the Scottish succession.

Now a long-running pamphlet war began, Katherine's claims versus Mary's claims, in which John Hales, MP for Lancaster in 1563, fired the first shot, in a tract intended perhaps in its original form to sway parliament. Robert Beale and Sir Nicholas Bacon, lord keeper of the great seal and Cecil's brother-in-law, were involved. Elizabeth suspected a widespread conspiracy and steps were taken to indict Hales for presumptuously initiating a debate on 'the right, title, limitation, and succession of the Imperial Crown of England' (Levine, 72). Responses from the other side included a treatise by the eminent Catholic jurist Edmund Plowden and the *Defence* of Mary (1569) by John Leslie, bishop of Ross. These arguments hinged on whether the succession could be settled by inheritance or by statute but more potent, politically, was the growing prejudice against Mary, and not just because of her religion. Katherine's party was winning the war of words but her death on 27 January 1568 and the lack of a suitably convincing alternative snatched defeat from the jaws of victory.

Meanwhile dramatic events in Scotland blasted Mary's reputation in the eyes of the world: the murder of Darnley, her marriage to one of his murderers in a Calvinist wedding ceremony, rebellion, defeat, and enforced abdication in favour of the infant *James VI (1566–1625). Elizabeth offered Mary frank advice, following 'the abominable murder of your mad husband and my killed cousin'. Four months later she wrote:

> How could a worse choice be made for your honour than in such haste to marry such a subject [James Hepburn, fourth earl of Bothwell], who … public fame hath charged with the murder of your late husband? … This you see plainly, what we think of the marriage.

Three years later she wrote: 'Well I will overpass your hard accidents that followed for lack of following of my counsels' (*Collected Works*, 116, 118, 123).

Only when Mary escaped from captivity to take refuge in England on 16 May 1568 did she manage to persuade many Catholics of her innocence and orthodoxy. By the end of 1568, again a captive, Mary represented the alternative to the protestant ascendancy in England. Consequently, the political forces of that ascendancy were now to be concentrated on her exclusion from the succession by fair means or foul. However, protestants had no plausible candidate of their own and were stuck with a mere negation. The problem of the succession was placed on uneasy hold, for at no time, before or after Mary's execution on 8 February 1587, would Elizabeth allow it to be publicly discussed, whether in parliament or anywhere else.

The shaping and testing of the Elizabethan regime, 1558–1572
While much of the politics of the first decade of Elizabeth's reign concerned the question of what might succeed it, historians who know that her reign had forty-five years to run have enjoyed a different perspective. Aware of what the future held, they have made a teleology of the early years of uncertainty, foreign adventures, and still fragile and untested political alliances, aware that what was coming next was a major crisis at the end of the decade, the acid test of the Elizabethan regime, to be followed by relative stability in the 1570s. All these events were a mere overture to a partly invented Elizabethan golden age.

Elizabeth was credited by her earliest historians, and even on her funerary monument in Westminster Abbey, with a limited number of outstanding and historic achievements. Foremost among these was the religious settlement, and after that the reform of the currency, much abused by Henry's and Edward's financial policies, which she set in motion as early as February 1559, a process involving calling in debased coins in exchange for new, finer ones and a devaluation. It was easy on a tombstone to represent these as tidy and decisive reforms. Tidy they were not. The religious settlement could be said to have settled nothing, and to have left loose ends which remained entangled for the next two hundred years. The recoinage and devaluation took nearly two years to achieve, disturbed the markets, alarmed consumers, and failed to deal with inflationary pressures on the economy. Yet these reforms were certainly decisive, a decisiveness not always associated with Elizabeth. The question, as always, is, was the decisiveness hers or that of others?

Even more decisive and momentous was Elizabeth's intervention in Scotland in 1559–60, and here it was certainly Cecil rather than his mistress who favoured bold and swift action. The opportunity was created by the violent turn taken by the Scottish Reformation, a revolution headed by disaffected magnates who called themselves the lords of the congregation and intended to overthrow both the old religion and French domination, under the regent Mary of Guise. But it was a revolution which could succeed only with English military and financial aid, which was duly requested. This was an opportunity, wrote Cecil, which, if missed, would not come again in his lifetime. As a veteran of Somerset's aggressive Scottish policy, Cecil had the vision of a British state, Scotland either 'in a perpetuall peace with the kingdom of Ingland or to be made one Monarchie with England as they both make but one Ile devided from the rest of the world' (Alford, 223). It was all too probable that the alternative to action would not be the *status quo* but French mastery of England itself, the ambition of the dominant French faction, the

Guise family. English intervention in the maelstrom of Scottish politics and in support of a rebellion against a sovereign government which seemed likely to fail was a high risk and expensive policy towards which Cecil, by all the rhetorical forces at his command, had to convince first himself, then his fellow privy councillors, and finally a reluctant queen, whom he cajoled every foot of the way and blackmailed with threats of resignation. He wrote, in May 1560, when the English forces sent to assist the insurgency had suffered a severe setback in their assault on the French garrison in Leith: 'the Queen's Majesty never liketh this matter of Scotland' (MacCaffrey, *Shaping*, 83).

In consequence, Cecil took the greatest risk of his career when he travelled to Edinburgh with Dr Nicholas Wotton to negotiate with the Scots and the French in June 1560. A happy conjunction of accidents, including the death of Mary of Guise on 11 June, enabled him to conclude the treaty of Edinburgh on 6 July, which effectively ended the 'auld alliance' with France and looked forward to a permanent pacification, if not a political union, of the island of Britain: a truly historic moment. It was followed by the formal adoption of protestantism by the Scottish parliament.

What Elizabeth's tombstone did not record among her achievements was that she restored Calais to her dominions. This was not achieved by the somewhat humiliating peace concluded with France at Cateau Cambrésis on 3 April 1559, but it was something which she deeply desired, and for the sake of which she was prepared to place at risk the settlement of Scotland. It was in part to keep the question of Calais on the agenda that in 1562 Elizabeth, although as ever 'loath to adventure' (MacCaffrey, 'The Newhaven expedition', 9–10), sanctioned intervention in the first of the French wars of religion by sending an expeditionary force to Newhaven (Le Havre) to hold it for the Huguenots. Newhaven was to be a pledge for the return of Calais. However, a more overt reason for the intervention was to bolster the cause of French protestantism and to offset Spanish support for the contrary faction, headed by the Guise family, the French relations of Mary, queen of Scots. It no doubt helped to dispel Elizabeth's doubts that the Newhaven expedition was enthusiastically backed by Dudley, whom she appointed to her privy council in October 1562, and commanded by his brother, Ambrose Dudley, earl of Warwick; whereas it was now Cecil's turn to be all too aware of the dangers involved.

In the event, this piece of decisiveness was as unsuccessful as Cecil's Scottish war and peace had been successful. Unable to play a meaningful military role and sinking ever deeper into a diplomatic morass, the English were soon regarded as unwelcome intruders by both French sides. Finally, bubonic plague more than decimated the expeditionary force, which took the infection back to England as it withdrew. Although this had been a costly humiliation, it did not drive Elizabeth's realm into isolationism. England's participation in Europe's religious wars, and especially the unofficial part played by 'volunteers', was only just beginning. The confused diplomatic incident of

1568, which involved the English seizure of the treasure ships destined to deliver the silver bullion Fernando Álvarez de Toledo, third duke of Alba, needed to wage war in the Netherlands, was a pointer to the future, a future in which Spain rather than France would be perceived to be the enemy.

For the remainder of the decade the Elizabethan regime remained fragile, vulnerable, and lacking in direction, reactive rather than proactive. The leading political players, including Cecil, Sussex, Thomas Howard, fourth duke of Norfolk, Leicester, and his friends, were all uncertain where they stood relationally, a case of frictions if not quite of organized factions. There was no solution to the conundrum of the succession. Elizabeth herself was still learning how to be queen. In 1568 she was faced with the toughest decision of her reign, and one with which she had to live for the next eighteen years: what to do with Mary, who in that year landed on her doorstep. To restore Mary to her Scottish kingdom (Elizabeth's own preferred policy), to allow her to return to France, where she was dowager queen, or to keep her in detention in England, all were potentially dangerous options. A commission of inquiry into the issues between Mary and her half-brother, James Stewart, earl of Moray, now regent in Scotland, became, in effect, her first English trial, although it was Moray who was formally in the dock. Moray's exploitation of the casket letters between Mary and Bothwell may seem lurid but the inquiry was inconclusive and Elizabeth had no choice but to continue to accommodate her cousin as the most uncomfortable of house guests. For Catholics she was a symbol of hope. Protestants, who had no doubt as to her sexual, religious, and political guilt, soon began to demand her head on a charger.

Paradoxically, it would take a political earthquake—the events of 1569 to 1572—to invest Elizabeth's government with greater stability and confidence. It began with the idea of a marriage between Mary and England's premier nobleman, Norfolk. Mary, with Norfolk, would return to Scotland and in due course succeed Elizabeth in England. France and Spain would be neutralized. This was a plan which had much going for it, and it was supported from across the political spectrum by, among others, Leicester (albeit, in Camden's prejudiced opinion, from devious motives), but not by Cecil, who was intended to be its first victim. It was a web which began to unravel as soon as it was spun, particularly at the Scottish end, and no one dared to tell Elizabeth. When she was informed, all too late in the day, Norfolk was on the carpet. He lost his nerve and withdrew to his East Anglian estates, disobeying repeated summonses to return to court. When he did return it was to temporary custody in the Tower, while his fellow conspirators made their peace with the queen as best they could. Suddenly there could be no doubt who was in charge of Elizabethan England.

Among Norfolk's disappointed abetters were the northern earls, Thomas Percy, sixth earl of Northumberland, and Charles Neville, sixth earl of Westmorland, and in the aftermath of the Norfolk match, conspiracy lurched over the edge into outright rebellion, a rising with echoes of the Pilgrimage of Grace of 1536 and the last of its kind. Much of the far north was in the hands of the rebels from November 1569 and the symbols of protestantism were purged from Durham Cathedral on 14 November. Faced with the will of the Tudor state, an iron will in such a crisis as this, and with Mary removed beyond reach, the northern uprising was scotched, literally, as its leaders crossed into Scotland. Of the rank-and-file followers, forced to stay behind, hundreds were hanged in their own villages. There was an aftershock in the secondary rising of Leonard Dacre, which it needed a small battle to suppress, won on 20 February 1570 by Elizabeth's cousin Hunsdon, who was congratulated as 'the instrument of my glory' (*Collected Works*, 126).

Finally, in this watershed for the regime, the international dimension came into play: first a pro-Marian reaction in Scotland, following Moray's assassination on 21 January 1570 (a reaction soon reversed); and more or less simultaneously, in the early months of 1570, *Regnans in excelsis*, Pius V's bull, which impotently presumed to deprive Elizabeth of her throne and to release her subjects from their bonds of allegiance. Despite this, negotiations for Mary's restoration to her Scottish throne were going well when the first international plot against Elizabeth was uncovered, the extensive but flimsy web of conspiracy woven by the Italian Roberto di Ridolfi in 1570 and 1571, a hairbrained thing that implicated, if not Mary, her agents, the pope, the Spanish ambassador, Guerau de Spes, Alba's Spanish forces in the Netherlands, and Norfolk, who had not yet learned his lesson.

Cecil's exposure of all the ramifications of the Ridolfi plot confirmed the worst suspicions of protestant supporters of the regime while it had a transforming effect on Elizabeth's attitude towards her cousin, anatomized in verses which the queen wrote about this time as:

> The daughter of debate
> That discord aye doth sow.
> (*Collected Works*, 134)

Cecil instructed Mary's keeper, Shrewsbury, to 'tempt' her with assurances that Elizabeth could well understand why she had taken steps to secure her own liberty and to marry her son to the Spanish infanta and herself to Don John of Austria. However, Shrewsbury was also instructed to conceal Elizabeth's indignation at Mary's 'labors and devises to stirre up a new rebellion in this realme, and to have the Kynge of Spayne to asist it'. In this way Mary would be lured into confessing things which Elizabeth already knew 'by wrytyng extant' (LPL, MS 3197, fol. 33).

When parliament met in May 1572, Elizabeth allowed publication of a version of the incriminating casket letters and Norfolk was found guilty of treason, although the queen, with qualms which would never have afflicted her father, hesitated to send him to the scaffold. Parliament demanded the heads of both Mary and Norfolk. The bishops were instructed virtually to threaten Elizabeth with divine deposition if she failed to execute Mary, just as God punished Saul for his failure to kill the pagan Agag, with loss of his throne to David and his descendants. The most probable author of this ultimatum, Edwin Sandys, bishop of London, put first among measures for the public safety 'furthwith to cutte of the Scottish Quene's heade: *ipsa est nostri fundi calamitas*' ('she is the calamity of our land'; Ellis, 2nd ser., 3.25). Norfolk went to the block on 2 June 1572 but the queen resisted extreme pressure to execute Mary, preferring an act rather than an axe: that is, an act disabling the former queen of Scots from succeeding to the English throne. The Commons did not like this because a disabling act would tacitly recognize that Mary had a claim. In the end, Elizabeth put it off. As the dust settled, the leading figures in government established more stable relationships and Cecil and Leicester were not always factional rivals. With Walsingham, they formed an unusually coherent conciliar regime, which was more often divided from Elizabeth than within itself.

Court and country The Elizabeth who has become almost a historical cliché has been romanticized as a kind of queen bee at the centre of a hive populated by glittering and competing favourites. Distinctions have been drawn between on the one hand 'mere' favourites, decorative players like, above all, Leicester, Sir Christopher Hatton, who was thought to have made it to the high office of lord chancellor by his performance on the dance floor, and Sir Walter Ralegh, and, on the other, workaholic politicians, more soberly dressed, such as Burghley and Walsingham. This crude dichotomy is unhelpful. All privy councillors were, in some measure, courtiers, and if all courtiers were not privy councillors that makes the point that it was at court that politics was conducted. Leicester, the arch-courtier, was not a member of the privy council when he persuaded Elizabeth of the merits of the Newhaven expedition. It was said, by Burghley, that when the queen turned against Grindal, she listened more to her Italian doctor, Giulio Borgarucci, an interested party, than to any member of the privy council. The cliché ignores Hatton's long political apprenticeship and underestimates his considerable ability; while Leicester, thanks to his many enemies, has been unfairly dismissed and vilified, the power which he exercised, especially the power of patronage, not acknowledged for what it was, an important structural component of the regime.

This configuration of the Elizabethan court was in part the invention of Sir Robert Naunton who, writing about 1630, organized his *Fragmenta regalia, or, Observations on the Late Queen Elizabeth* as an account of favourites. Historians have been too ready to accept Naunton's claim that 'the principall note' of the reign was that the queen 'ruled much by faction and parties, which her self both made, upheld, and weakened, as her own great judgement advised' (*Sir Robert Naunton*, 16, 18). For Naunton's little book was a disguised commentary on the unsatisfactory politics of the 1620s. It is not the case that the Elizabethan court, throughout a long reign, was always clearly divided into factions and parties, still less that this divisiveness was a deliberate contrivance of Elizabeth's 'great judgement'. There is evidence that she knew how to preserve her freedom of manoeuvre by playing off one interest against another, but just as often she confronted a privy council which as a body was of a mind different from her own. Nor was Elizabeth enthroned above the frictions and factions of her court. Her variable likes, dislikes, and emotions were often more part of the destabilizing problem than of the solution.

This is not to deny that the centre of Elizabethan political activity consisted of personalities and personal relations. Elizabeth found nicknames for her leading courtiers: 'Eyes' for Leicester, for example, written as two little circles with eyebrows, 'Lids' for Hatton; and her relations with these favourites were conducted according to the codes of courtly love and mock worship. Friendship and favour (not to speak of their opposite, enmity) were the values around which court life revolved, marked and symbolized in such rituals as the exchange of new year gifts, the balance of payments somewhat unequal, the gifts carefully adjusted to the rank, standing, and wealth of donors and recipients. Over her first eleven years, the queen received gifts valued at £11,905 5s. 2d., her own gifts at £8400 11s. 1½d. From the late 1570s, as 17 November began to be almost a religious feast, there were accession day tilts at court, in which nobles and knights jousted in competition for Elizabeth's favour. Christmas was a season of misrule, which had its paradoxical function in affirming the proper order of things. In 1562 nine or ten couples of hounds were let loose to hunt a fox and a cat around the hall, with both animals 'killed beneath the fire' (Nichols, 1.139). In 1600 it was reported that over the Christmas holidays the queen had almost every night come into the presence chamber 'to see the Ladies dawnce the old and new cowntry Dawnces, with the Taber and Pipe' (Arnold, 97). There was also 'primero' and other card games, played for high stakes. The accounts for 1576 of Roger North, second Baron North, record amounts as high as £70, 'lost at play with the queen' (Nichols, 2.241).

Almost all Elizabeth's leading men were at times the victims of her extreme anger. When Leicester exceeded the terms of his commission by accepting the governor-generalship of the Netherlands in February 1586, she wrote that she could never have imagined that a man whom she had created from nothing could have so contemptibly disobeyed her commandment. However, it was Elizabeth who took steps to heal this breach, and within six months she was writing: 'Rob, I am afraid you will suppose by my wandering writings that a midsummer moon hath taken large possession of my brains this month' (*Collected Works*, 282).

Often Elizabeth's relations with her men were whimsical and playful. On one occasion she prescribed a spartan diet for Leicester, including on festival days 'the shoulder of a wren' for dinner, and for supper 'a leg of the same', but that in the case of his brother Warwick (who was fatter) the wren's leg could be 'abated' (*Collected Works*, 230–31). When the queen was embarrassed to be spotted at her window in her night attire, she later gave 'a great phyllyp [fillip] on the forehed' to the voyeur, Lord Talbot (Lodge, 2.170). The letters of condolence which had to be written so frequently to bereaved spouses and parents contain sincere sentiment. She was not above exploiting her femininity. When the Scottish ambassador, Sir James Melville, surprised her playing the virginals, she stopped, pretended to slap him, and said that 'she was not used to play before men, but when she was solitary, to shun melancholy' (Nichols, 1.293). Although depression was a chronic and recurrent condition, generally Elizabeth was affable, but she could also be irascible, and, above all, unpredictable. When on 1 February 1587 William Davison, principal secretary, came to her with papers to sign which included the warrant for Mary's execution, she congratulated him on having taken a walk in the park and said that he ought to do it more often. Yet within days she wanted him hanged.

What was the court for? It was above all a place for courtly rituals, such as the formal daily procession to the Chapel Royal; and for the physical display of majesty, the place where Elizabeth could be seen by foreign ambassadors as well as subjects, wearing the dazzling contents of her huge wardrobe, those excessively bejewelled costumes for which she served as a kind of clothes horse in the famous full-length portraits. Even though she was a late riser, not a morning person she said, it took two hours to put her together each day, and as long again to put her to bed. However, it may have been only on state occasions that the queen was displayed in the full finery of her robes of estate.

The court was, in Sir Geoffrey Elton's phrase, 'a point of contact' (Elton, 3.38–57). In a system of personal monarchy there was no substitute for access to the very person of the monarch, immediate or through a privileged intermediary. In a celebrated essay, 'The Elizabethan political scene' (1948), Sir John Neale peered beneath the Renaissance splendour to uncover the squalid, materialistic competition for place and profit which he believed to be the court's true *raison d'être*. There were simply not enough goodies to go round. Like war, life at court was mostly about boredom, as suitors waited and waited. As Spenser wrote:

> Full little knowest thou that hast not tried
> What Hell it is in suing long to bide.
> (E. Spenser, *Mother Hubberd's Tale*, ll. 895–6)

It was also about service, even servitude, before any significant office or other substantial reward was obtained; and it was about the crucial machinery of patronage and the greasing of palms. As competition grew ever fiercer, the general direction of public morality was downward and degenerative. In a refinement of Neale's argument, Wallace MacCaffrey agreed that the Elizabethan monarchy rested 'on the substantial pillars of its capacity to reward and advance its supporters', but he believed the system to have been benignly functional in cementing loyalty to the regime (Bindoff and others, 97). However, both essays had too little to say about how politics in something more like the modern sense was also transacted, and contested, at court.

Excessive attention bestowed on the greatest of the queen's men, her favourites, has distracted consideration from the many lesser men who constituted the personnel of her court, and from her women, as well as taking the place of any serious analysis of how the institution worked. At the heart of the court lay the privy lodgings, the living quarters of the monarch. Under Henry VIII, the gentlemen of the privy chamber were the companions of the king, and constituted a focal point of power, but under Mary and Elizabeth they were necessarily replaced by women. There were three or four ladies of the bedchamber, and a dozen or so ladies, gentlewomen, and maids of the privy chamber, with six maids of honour, teenagers under the supervision of the 'mother of the maids'. The most senior and long-lasting of these courtly women were Elizabeth's oldest and most constant friends: Blanche Parry, who had seen Elizabeth in her cradle and who died, still in her service, in 1590, Astley, Elizabeth Fiennes de Clinton, countess of Lincoln, Frances Seymour, countess of Hertford, Anne Dudley, countess of Warwick, and Mary Scudamore. The countess of Warwick told Walsingham in 1585 that she had 'spentt the cheffe partt of her yeares both painfully, faythfully, and servyceably' in the queen's household, and there were still many years to run (PRO, SP 12/181/77).

These women were in constant attendance on Elizabeth, dressing her and attending to her most intimate needs, eating with her in the privy chamber, sewing. This enabled them to act on behalf of suitors, and no doubt at some personal profit. Beale, the clerk of the privy council, advised that when bringing business before the queen a principal secretary should learn 'her Majesties disposicion by some in the Privie Chamber, with whom you must keepe creditt, for that will stande you in much steede', while warning him not to yield too much to their 'importuntie for sutes' (Read, *Walsingham*, 1.437). Formally, these women had no political role, but no more than Naunton is Rowland Vaughan, Parry's great-nephew, to be believed when he wrote (again, motivated by Jacobean politics) that these great ladies concerned themselves only with 'little lay matters', 'to serve their freinds turnes', and 'durst [not] intermeddle so far in matters of commonwealth' (Vaughan, sigs. Hv–H2r). It is almost inconceivable that they would not have 'intermeddled', especially in the politics of the queen's marital affairs, of which there is some hard evidence, especially from 1579. As for the maids, who slept together in a kind of dormitory, the court was a marriage market and a sexual minefield, judging by the numbers who faced disgrace and Elizabeth's anger when they were found to be pregnant or secretly married. There were many scandals between the affair of Katherine Grey in 1561 and Mary Fitton's case in the late 1590s. These liaisons and marriages were liable to involve Elizabeth's gentlemen pensioners, who were in constant attendance in the presence chamber. They were of greater social status than their predecessors under Henry and Edward because the office of gentleman of the privy chamber was no longer open to them. Many were related to the gentlewomen of the privy chamber. Appointment as a gentleman pensioner could lead to greater things. Hatton is a case in point. However, most senior courtiers remained in post throughout their careers. The countess of Lincoln was in Elizabeth's household from before 1538 until her death in 1590. One of the most remarkable features of the Elizabethan world is that almost nobody was sacked, or resigned, Davison being the most notable exception. There are verses set to music by John Dowland in 1603 which catch the spirit of the times:

> Time stands still with gazing on her face.
> Stand still and gaze, for minutes, hours and years to give her
>   place.
> All other things shall change but she remains the same,
> Till heavens changed have their course and Time hath lost
>   his name.
> (E. H. Fellowes, ed., *English Madrigal Verse, 1585–1632*, rev. F. W.
> Sternfeld and D. Greer, 1967, 479)

What of 'the people'? Posterity embellished a legend of spontaneous outpourings of love and devotion from the subjects of this paragon of a queen: the people 'running, flying, flocking to be blessed with the sight of her Gracious Countenance as oft as ever she came forth in Publicke', a monarch 'thinking it her greatest strength to be fortified with their love, and her greatest happinesse to make them happy', 'borne to possesse the hearts of her Subject'. These are the words not of the less fulsome Camden but of his translator Robert Norton, who thought it necessary to gild the former's lily, boosting Elizabeth's 'glorious Fame' (*Historie*, trans. Norton, sigs. A1r–A4r).

Elizabeth in procession may well have been a familiar sight in and around London, as she moved from one palace to another, by road or river, and displayed herself ceremonially when she returned to Whitehall to keep Christmas. There were set-piece encounters with poor subjects, especially on Maundy Thursday, when she washed the feet of as many poor women as the years of her age, and distributed clothing, loaves and fishes, claret, and purses containing the same number of silver pennies. The queen also had what might be called private friends among those who were not glittering courtiers: for example, John Lacy, a rich member of the Clothworkers' Company, who lived on the river at Putney, with whom she stayed for two or three nights at a time on at least thirteen occasions between 1578 and 1603.

The only opportunity to see Elizabeth for those living deeper into the provinces was the annual summer progress, which usually lasted ten weeks, and which never took the court further west than Bristol and Worcester or farther north than Coventry and Stafford. Even then, the greatest crowds greeting the queen were, inevitably, London crowds: estimated at 10,000 when she returned from Suffolk in 1561. Progresses were a logistical nightmare for those who had to organize them, especially since the decision where to go could be taken at almost the last moment. In July 1576 Lord Talbot reported that there was 'no certayntie' about the queen's summer itinerary, 'for these II or III dayes it hathe changed every V owers' (Lodge, 2.150). The progress was also an expensive embarrassment for the householders obliged to entertain Elizabeth and to think of a suitable present. The 1578 progress cost North £762. Yet for the ambitious, this was also an opportunity, so that some of the great prodigy houses of the age were built for the express purpose of receiving the queen. The climax of what might be called the princely kind of progress came in 1575, with the lavish entertainment laid on at Leicester's castle at Kenilworth, and celebrated in literary effusions by Robert Langham and George Gascoigne.

In so far as progresses afforded the opportunity to meet people below the rank of gentleman, these were townspeople. The ritual routine was always the same: a rich gift presented by the mayor, a speech from the recorder, something laid on by the schoolboys. When, in 1565, the mayor of Coventry presented Elizabeth with a purse containing £100 in gold, he assured her that it contained more besides: 'the hearts of all your loving subjects'. At Warwick in 1572 she told the recorder: 'Come hither, little Recorder. It was told me that youe wold be afraid to look upon me, or to speak boldly; but youe were not so fraid of me as I was of youe' (Nichols, 1.192, 315).

Papists and puritans In a speech to parliament in 1589, Hatton, the lord chancellor, said that at the beginning of her reign Elizabeth had 'placed hir Reformation as uppon a square stone to remayne constant' (Folger Shakespeare Library, MS V.b.303, pp. 183–6). The stone may have been square but it was very shaky. Even before the religious settlement of 1559 was made, the 'Device for alteration of religion' accurately forecast that it would be rejected on the one hand by 'the papist sect', and on the other by those who, dissatisfied with its moderation, would 'call the alteration *a cloaked papistry* or *a mingle-mangle*' (Gee, 196–7). Bacon opened the 1559 parliament with an inclusivist plea to eschew such divisive terms as heretic, schismatic, and papist and closed it with an even-handed warning addressed to 'those that be to swifte as those that be to slowe, those, I say, that goe before the lawe or beyond the lawe, as those that will not followe' (Hartley, 1.51). That was to draw a line in the sand which has been called the Elizabethan compromise. However, the religion of Elizabethan England and of its queen was protestant, not semi-protestant or semi-Catholic.

Nevertheless, the dynamic, interactive relation indicated by Bacon between those for whom the Elizabethan settlement was too much and those for whom it was too little worked itself out inexorably in the years to come. The stigma of 'puritan', which soon attached to the latter, was in origin, about 1565, a clever invention of exiled Catholic pamphleteers, intended as an insult to all protestants, 'hot puritans of the new clergy' (Trinterud, 6–7). It was soon adopted by conformist defenders of the settlement who deployed it, among other defamatory terms, against nonconformists, who rejected such prayer book ceremonies as vestments and the sign of the cross in baptism, refused as a matter of conscience to subscribe to the legitimacy of such things, and agitated, in parliament, in the press, and by other means, for 'further reformation'. The hot protestants for their part complained of 'papists', a category which embraced not only recusants but so-called 'church papists', closet Catholics whose outward conformity made them all the more suspect, and dangerous. So 'puritan' and 'papist' were not terms of taxonomic definition but abusive and fluid labels which progressively defined each other and fed upon each other, as well as serving both to erode and to construct the middle ground between these two extremes. Such was the basic landscape, the tectonic plates, of Elizabethan religion.

In principle, Elizabeth was even-handedly opposed to both these polarized constructions. Hatton told the 1589 parliament that it was duty bound to 'bridle' all, 'whether papists or puritanes', who were 'discontented' with the established religion (Hartley, 2.419–20). Aylmer informed his patron, Hatton, that his marching orders on elevation to the bishopric of London in 1576 had been 'to cut off … and to correct offenders on both sides which swerve from the right path of obedience' (H. Nicolas, 56). What did this mean in practice? It was Francis Bacon, not Elizabeth herself, who said that her intention was not to make windows in men's souls, but no doubt he interpreted correctly the essence of her religious policy. Outward conformity would suffice and perhaps the queen's pragmatic tolerance went beyond that. It was no secret that several members of her yeomen of the guard, including their captain, Robert Seale, charged as they were on a daily basis with Elizabeth's physical protection, were secret adherents of the Family of Love. The drawing of curtains over the soul's windows was an article of faith for Familists, so what certainty can there be that Elizabeth was not herself a secret Familist, or at least a sympathizer?

Elizabeth's relatively conservative sympathies in matters of religion have already been noticed. Provided Catholics kept their heads down and offered no threat to her regality, they were relatively safe. Despite her experiences in her sister's reign, Elizabeth would never have used the words uttered in a petition of the Commons in 1563, when there were still plenty of Catholic MPs: 'we feare a faccion of heretickes in your realme, contentious and malicious papistes … Their unkindness and cruelty we have tasted' (Hartley, 1.91–2). In the 1560s there was a considerable measure of effective toleration. In common with many of her subjects, Elizabeth counted known Catholics among her relations and constant companions, not least in the court itself, especially her favourite musicians, such as William Byrd. That lifelong trimmer Lord Henry Howard 'would come and continue at prayers when the Queene came, but otherwise would not endure them, seeming to perform the duty of a subject in attending on his prince at the one tyme, and at the other using his conscience' (*Diary of John Manningham*, 246).

Regnans in excelsis, in excommunicating and deposing Elizabeth, inevitably transformed the situation, as did the mounting of a Catholic mission in its wake dedicated to the reconversion of England. The trials and executions of seminary priests, from the mid-1570s on, fostering a cult of martyrdom, and out and out recusancy on the part of a minority of Catholics, worked as mutually exacerbatory forces. Although political Catholicism had no more determined an opponent (for it threatened her throne and perhaps her life), Elizabeth was far from heading a protestant crusade against it. When her second parliament made it treason for office-holders to refuse the oath of supremacy

on a second occasion, Elizabeth made sure that it would not be tendered twice. In 1571 parliament approved a bill (which seems to have originated with the bishops) 'concerning coming to the church and receiving of the Communion', which sharply increased the penalties for non-attendance, and for the first time proposed to enforce by statute annual reception of the sacrament (Neale, *Elizabeth I and her Parliaments, 1559–1581*, 192). This was to aim at the heart of non-recusant Catholicism, the strategy of 'church papists'. However, the queen vetoed the bill.

In 1581 parliament responded to an intensification of the perceived Catholic threat (this was in the aftermath of the mission of the Jesuits, Edmund Campion and Robert Persons) by preparing legislation which can only be called draconically anti-Catholic, a true penal code. It is a reasonable presumption that Elizabeth worked behind the scenes to mitigate the severity of what was proposed by both houses. In the terms of the bill 'to retain the Queen's majesty's subjects in their due obedience', as originally drafted, to celebrate mass would have been made a felony, carrying in principle the death penalty; to hear mass to incur penalties which would have extended to life imprisonment and the forfeiture of lands and goods. It must have been the queen who reduced the penalties for these offences to substantial fines. For all Catholics (but landowning Catholic families were meant) the penalty for refusal to go to church, the crime of recusancy, was sharply increased to £20 a month, and this was enacted. Moreover, parliament intended to make it treasonable to convert, or be converted, to Catholicism. At this point, Elizabeth appears to have been responsible for the crucial insertion in the bill of three words, 'for that intent'. Only if conversions occurred with the specific intent of withdrawing her subjects from their natural allegiance were they treasonable (Neale, *Elizabeth I and her Parliaments, 1559–1581*, 386–9). This legislation has been praised for distinguishing between being a Catholic and becoming a Catholic, and for formally reserving the death penalty for a civil rather than a religious offence. For this Elizabeth must evidently be given personal credit.

Elizabeth's religious antipathies were more naturally and instinctively expressed against 'hot Protestants'. Not only did she have a personal distaste for a religious style so different from her own, but she detected and feared in puritanism a dangerous sectarianism and a threat to her own authority more subtle than that offered by 'papists', even though puritans were always ready, on their own terms, to subscribe to the royal supremacy.

Elizabeth's religious sensibilities and prejudices were never better exposed than in a series of exchanges with bishops and other senior clergy when they appeared before her in the privy chamber at Somerset House in February 1585 to offer their clerical subsidy. Having referred to the campaign against the bishops in the Commons, currently sitting, she promised to defend them against these attacks, and that if it were shown that they were countenanced by some in the privy council she would 'uncouncil' some of them (who were probably present to hear her say so). She then complained that the bishops were allowing ministers to preach what they liked, 'some one way, some another'. It would be better if they would read the official homilies, 'for there is more learning in one of those than in twenty of some of their sermons'. She knew of evidence that Catholics were encouraged by the loose talk of some protestants, 'for I have heard that some of them of late have said that I was of no religion, neither hot [nor] cold, but such as one day would give God the vomit'. Against her Catholic enemies she could defend herself, 'but from a pretensed friend, good Lord deliver me'. When John Whitgift, archbishop of Canterbury, responded to the complaint of the hour, that there were not enough learned preachers and too many sub-standard clergy, protesting that to have a learned minister in every parish was impossible, since there were thirteen thousand parishes, the queen exploded: 'Jesus! … thirteen thousand! It is not to be looked for'—nor, apparently, desired (*Collected Works*, 177–81).

Such things would probably not have been said in a more public forum. Elizabeth was well aware that she could not afford to flaunt godly opinion. In 1582 Thomas Bentley, a member of the very well-connected Gray's Inn circle, published *The Monument of Matrones*, 1600 closely printed pages on the religion of women. This was a celebration of the queen's exemplary piety, but it was also an almost threateningly prescriptive text, in which God was made to say to Elizabeth: 'beware therefore that yee abuse not this authoritie given unto you by me, under certaine lawes and conditions … For be ye sure that I have placed you in this seate upon this condition' (Bentley, 309).

A typical tactic was to shelter behind the higher clergy, on the grounds that the state of the church was their business, under Elizabeth's more remote supreme governorship. Thus, when it was decided, in January 1565, to take a stand against creeping nonconformity and to proceed with 'all expedition' against offenders, the opening shot in the war known as the vestiarian controversy in which puritanism first became an issue took the form of a royal letter to Matthew Parker, archbishop of Canterbury. The letter was drafted by Burghley, whom Parker thought to be the true initiator of the whole business, although its language was strengthened in the queen's own hand. Once Parker received his orders, he and his episcopal colleagues were on their own. When in March 1566 Parker printed and circulated a book of articles comprising the new standard of conformity, he failed to obtain royal endorsement and was obliged to publish it under the humiliating title of *Advertisements*. His correspondence at this time is full of complaints of the lack of political back-up. The *Advertisements* campaign was successful in stirring up anti-episcopal opinion, but not in solving the problem of nonconformity, which was indeed insoluble. Similarly, when the Commons in 1576 drew up a comprehensive list of complaints about ecclesiastical abuses and presented it in the form of a petition (which may have been a tactical mistake), Elizabeth, 'considering that reformation hereof is to be principally sought in the clergy, and namely in the bishops', referred their complaints to convocation (Neale,

Elizabeth I and her Parliaments, 1559–1581, 350). Only occasionally, and under extreme provocation, was the queen persuaded of the need to confront religious dissidence head-on. The publication in 1572 of the seditious pamphlet, *An Admonition to the Parliament*, which saw puritanism enter its radical, presbyterian, phase, and the even more outrageous Marprelate tracts (1588–9) were met with royal proclamations—in the contents of which Elizabeth may, or may not, have taken a personal interest. As was apparent in the case of Stubbe, Elizabeth took particular exception to printed libels.

Elizabeth's contention with over-enthusiastic evangelical protestants was episodic rather than sustained. She reacted only when a nerve was touched, as in the 1570s, when she ordered the suppression of popular preaching rallies known as prophesyings, but it is possible that, had not Grindal chosen to make it an issue of conscience in 1576, nothing much would have happened. But since he did make it an issue, writing the most tactless, if courageous, letter Elizabeth ever received, refusing to obey her orders, Grindal's own career was destroyed and a major crisis in church and state was provoked. Noted patrons of puritans, including Leicester and Walsingham, recognized the need to avoid antagonizing the queen. The most public occasion for clashes over religion was in parliament. Some of these parliamentary movements for further reform were narrowly based, as in the drastic 'bill and book' presbyterianism of 1584–5 and 1586–7, others had strong support in both houses and sometimes, especially in 1567 and 1571, among the bishops too. Without exception, Elizabeth resisted every one of these initiatives but the 1584 parliament, where feelings reached fever pitch, found her on the defensive, maintaining that religion would be amended without the clamour of parliamentary debate, while commenting darkly about the need to depose bishops who failed to end ecclesiastical abuses. By such devices, she contrived to make her religious policy one of *semper eadem*. There were no reforms of substance, no 'further reformation'; so that James would later remark, in his own inimitable style, promising reforms on which he too was slow to deliver, that because a man had been sick of the pox for forty years that was no reason why he might not be cured.

The queen, the regime, and parliament There was an occasion, in 1583, when Mary, queen of Scots, chose to communicate with the privy council rather than Elizabeth, going over the queen's head or behind her back. She was told that Elizabeth was surprised that she should address herself to what Mary had called 'principall members of this Crowne', as if the queen were not absolute, and absolutely able to direct her own policy without conciliar assent. The queen held her privy councillors in high regard, but they were what they were by her choice, not birth, 'whose services are no longer to be used in that publike function then it shall please her Majestie to dispose of the same' (Lodge, 2.276–7).

That was constitutionally correct, and even politically realistic. On many occasions, policy initiatives favoured and even carefully constructed from within the privy council were countermanded from on high. In 1577 the English ambassador in the Low Countries, Davison, was told that Leicester was about to cross the North Sea with an expeditionary force. 'This is his full determination, but yet unknown unto her Highness, neither shall she be acquainted with it until she be fully resolved to send' (PRO, SP 15/25/35). However, Elizabeth was not 'fully resolved', and no force was sent. In 1580 Walsingham reported that the privy council had decided to shore up a crumbling Scottish policy by dispatching 1000 troops to the borders. When the queen came to hear of the proposal 'she wolde none of ytt', and proceeded to cut the force by half. Later that day, Walsingham had to add a postscript. Elizabeth had had second thoughts. No troops would be sent. Walsingham, never an optimist, wrote that Scotland was therefore 'clene lost', and with it probably Ireland as well. 'My lords here have carefully and faithfully discharged their dueties in sekinge to staye this dangerous course, but God hath thought good to dispose other wyse of thinges, in whose handes the heartes of all princes are' (Hunt. L., MSS HA 1214, 13067). The Victorian historian James Anthony Froude emerged from reading the Elizabethan state papers to conclude that 'the great results of her reign were the fruits of a policy which was not her own, and which she starved and mutilated when energy and completeness were most needed' (Froude, 12.508). Walsingham, Leicester, Burghley himself, all had the experience of rustication from both court and privy council, when their policies and actions too obviously conflicted with the royal will. When the disgraced Grindal found himself *persona non grata*, he was advised on how to conduct himself by senior politicians who had themselves been in the same boat, or might be.

And yet no privy councillor was ever sacked, and offers of resignation were never accepted, Davison excepted. If the privy council was stuck with Elizabeth, Elizabeth seems to have been stuck with her privy council. She coped with a power relationship which was often troublesome and even threatening by distancing herself from the privy council, whose meetings she hardly ever attended. In 1578, as the Anjou marriage negotiations began to turn serious, Leicester was forced to complain: 'our conference with her Majesty about affairs is both seldom and slender' (*Relations politiques des Pays-Bas et de l'Angleterre*, 10.678). The result was that Mary was not the only one to deal with the privy council as if it were the government of the realm, or even an alternative government. Foreign ambassadors on many occasions headed straight for the privy council. In January 1576 Lord Talbot told his father, Shrewsbury: 'the Counsell be all at the Couert; they site [sit] daylie, and the imbassidors cum to them' (Lodge, 2.136). It must sometimes have seemed that there were two governments, not one, in Elizabethan England.

A number of factors intersected to enhance the role of the privy council in the Elizabethan polity. One was the idea of public service, on the Roman republican model, which all these politicians had imbibed as part of their education at the hands of classical humanists. This in itself meant that Elizabeth's servants were not only subjects. They were also, in their own estimation, citizens, and part of a society which was defined as a commonwealth, a term pregnant with semi-republican resonance. Their role was to moderate the defective arbitrariness of monarchy with the salutary, if sharp, medicine of counsel. Peter Wentworth told the Commons in 1576 in a speech (which he was not allowed to finish) quoting the book of Proverbs: 'for faithfull are the wounds of a lover, … but the kisses of an enemy are deceitfull'. 'And I doubt not but that some of her Majesty's counsell have dealt plainly and faithfully with her Majestie' (Hartley, 1.428, 431). Classical republican convictions were reinforced by godly protestantism. To believe that the monarch was God's servant and instrument was to enhance monarchical authority. However, at the same time, it made that authority entirely conditional on God's approval, empty in so far as it was not exercised to godly ends, and all too many of Elizabeth's subjects, including some of her senior ministers, presumed to know what those ends were. This made Elizabeth's effective sovereignty dangerously dependent on a religious appraisal of her conduct, offered by preachers and other publicists, like Stubbe in his book *The Gaping Gulf*.

Above all, contingent circumstances strengthened the conciliar principle, and the public sphere, in Elizabethan affairs: the fact was that the monarch was a woman, unmarried, and without an heir of her own body, which left the succession a dangerously open question. In these circumstances, Burghley, a more radical thinker than he has sometimes been given credit for, envisaged a state of affairs in which the realm and its appointed leaders, the body politic, might have to take responsibility for its own preservation and perpetuation. That this was part of his political thinking is evident from as early as 1559, when he asked the Scottish lords of the congregation why they had not spoken and acted as a great council of the realm, a device often used by the commonwealth to correct errant governors. In 1563 he responded to Elizabeth's refusal to allow parliament to limit the succession by drawing up plans in the event of an interregnum for ongoing management of 'publick affayres' by the privy council, acting as 'a Counsell of estate' (PRO, SP 12/28, fols. 68r–69v).

In winter 1584–5, with Elizabeth's life apparently under threat from Catholic assassins (especially in the wake of the assassination of William of Orange), Burghley and Walsingham, and no doubt Leicester, with how much knowledgeable input from the queen herself is uncertain, devised a bond of association. This intended summary execution for anyone threatening the queen's royal person, which clearly meant Mary. It was a document to which thousands of Elizabeth's subjects were sworn, attaching their signatures and seals, and if all their names were available it would provide the best and most inclusive listing of what is sometimes called 'the political nation', albeit for the most part a confessionally defined, protestant nation. While the ostensible intent of the bond was to defend the life of the queen, its deeper purpose was to provide for the security of the body politic in the aftermath of her death. Unsatisfactory as well as unprecedented, Burghley attempted to replace the bond with a new version of the plan of 1563: interregnal government by an enlarged conciliar body, now called *magnum consilium coronae Angliae*. This idea died the death when Elizabeth ensured that it would form no part of the Act for the Surety of the Queen's Most Royal Person. Burghley had proposed. Elizabeth disposed.

The public sphere in Elizabethan England was broader than Elizabeth's relatively small privy council. Second-ranking servants of the state were evidently moved by the same public-spirited concern for the good of the body politic, conceived as a godly commonwealth. They too had internalized the Ciceronian principle that 'we are not born for ourselves alone, but our country claims a share of our being, and our friends a share' (Cicero, *De officiis*, i.7.22). Such were several of Elizabeth's diplomats, men like Davison, Thomas Randolph, and Walsingham's brother-in-law, Beale, as well as men not on the royal payroll but equally devoted to 'the public', like the London lawyer and 'parliament man', Thomas Norton. No one knew better than Beale how public business was to be communicated to the queen, even how she was to be handled. 'When her highnes is angrie or not well disposed trouble her not with anie matter which you desire to have done unles extreame necessitie urge it', and 'entertaine her with some relacion or speech whereat shee may take some pleasure' (Read, *Walsingham*, 1.423, 438). Many of these men, Beale above all, were intellectuals, sources of advice on technical matters, whether asked for or not. Such was Dee, Elizabeth's 'magus', whose immense library, which she regularly visited, was a major intellectual resource. The queen was free to seek advice from anyone, not only from her sworn privy councillors, but no one, whether privy councillor or not, had the right, as distinct from the duty, to offer it. A quite contrary doctrine was prevalent in the political culture of Elizabethan England, and especially among some members of the Commons. They believed that the Commons was an extended council, where the privilege of free speech was no privilege at all but a duty to speak on matters of public policy, including those reserved by the queen to her prerogative; and not only for themselves but on behalf of those they represented, and even for that fiction, the entire nation. When Wentworth was examined by a parliamentary committee following his inflammatory speech of 8 February 1576, he declared himself to be 'no private person; I am a publicque and a councellor to the whole state in that place' (Hartley, 1.435).

This constitutional issue was at the heart of those (to be sure exceptional) episodes of confrontation between Elizabeth and bodies of opinion in the Commons, confrontations which had to do with marriage and the succession, religious policy, Mary. Neale believed that many of these clashes were inspired by a more or less militant puritanism, whereas his critic, Elton, reidentified this puritan choir as merely men-of-business, transacting affairs on behalf of their patrons in the Lords, privy council, and

court. Elton was right to draw attention to the patronage links between such men as Norton and leading politicians, and to see in several parliamentary initiatives the displacement of issues which the queen had stonewalled in court and privy council, but wrong to play down the ideological intensity of the issues, and to have underestimated the capacity of these so-called men-of-business to be motivated by their own assessments of the needs of the commonwealth. Burghley perhaps put it best:

> I do hold and will alweis this course in such matters as I differ in opinion from hir Majesty as long as I may be allowed to gyve advise. I will not chang my opinion by affyrmyng the contrary, for that war to offend God to whom I am sworn first. But as a servant I will obey hir Majesty's commandment and no wise contrary the same, presuming that she, being Gods cheff minister heare, it shall be Gods will to have hir commandements obeyed, after that I have performed my dutye as a counsellor.   (CUL, MS Ee.3.56, no. 85)

Or when he wrote 'our parts is to counsell, and also to obey the commaunder' (*State Papers and Letters of Sir Ralph Sadler*, 2.129).

Mary, queen of Scots, 1568–1587 The conflict of policy and interest, with its considerable constitutional implications, was most dramatically demonstrated in the long-running saga of Mary, and especially in its dénouement in February 1587. The exclusion of Mary from the English throne was the lynchpin of Burghley's politics, and much desired by many. During the 1572 parliament, the bishops were particularly insistent that she should be executed, while in the Commons she was called 'the monstrous and huge dragon, and masse of the earth' and 'the most notorious whore in all the world' (Hartley, 1.312, 438). Mary was routinely identified with Jezebel, just as Elizabeth would become Jezebel in the eyes of Catholic Europe after Mary's execution. When Wentworth referred to Mary as Jezebel in his 1576 speech, he was told that she was a queen and that he ought to speak reverently of her, to which he replied: 'let him take her parte that list: I will speake the truth boldly' (ibid., 1.438).

Elizabeth's attitude to her cousin was naturally more ambivalent. She was well aware that Mary posed a constant threat, but no less aware of the risks involved in excluding her altogether from the complex equation of Scottish politics. Fundamentally, she was unreconciled to the dubious precedent of judging and executing an anointed sovereign prince, for whereas many contributors to the 1572 parliamentary debates regarded Mary as the former queen of Scots, legally and justly deposed (under the fiction of abdication) and therefore a private person, this was never Elizabeth's view. Perhaps deeper still was a justified fear for her own reputation, for if Mary were to die, international opinion would hold her accountable. Whether or not the bond of association was Elizabeth's idea, she would find it convenient to hide behind it, avoiding personal responsibility if Mary did have to die. At the time of the Throckmorton conspiracy in 1583, Elizabeth, in the opinion of Walsingham, overreacted in her angry denunciation of the French ambassador, Bertrand de Salignac de la Motte-Fénélon, who had been indirectly involved; and she was willing to throw the unfortunate double agent Dr William Parry to the wolves, perhaps to take the heat off Mary.

No such diversionary manoeuvres were possible in 1586, when the Babington conspiracy broke, with evidence of Mary's full collusion as clear as Walsingham and his code-master Thomas Phelippes could make it: a smoking gun. Under the terms of the 1584 Act for the Queen's Safety, Mary was now placed on trial before a special commission and found guilty, a sentence announced by proclamation on 4 December 1586. All that was now required was for Elizabeth to sign the death warrant. It would not be easy to obtain that signature. Three times in 1572 the queen had signed the warrant for Norfolk's execution, only three times to have second thoughts. This was why parliament was summoned, as Burghley wrote, 'to make the burden better borne and the world abroad better satisfied' (Neale, *Elizabeth I and her Parliaments, 1584–1601*, 104), but also to place pressure on Elizabeth, who distanced herself from its proceedings. At this point, another biblical phrase, and precedent, came into play: 'foolish pity'. When Mary's gaoler, Sir Amias Paulet, wrote 'others shall excuse their foolish pity as they may' (J. Morris, ed., *The Letter Books of Sir Amias Paulet*, 1874, 291), 'others' meant Elizabeth, and the reference was to the second book of Chronicles and the story of godly King Asa, who removed his idolatrous mother, Maachah, from the throne, but failed to kill her, despite Deuteronomy chapter 13, which forbade 'pity', glossed in the Geneva version as 'foolish pity', to spare even one's nearest and dearest, where idolatry was concerned.

The story of what happened next is one of the most familiar in all Elizabethan history, and yet its deeper constitutional implications have not always been explored. On 1 February 1587 Davison brought a sheaf of documents to Elizabeth for signing, including, somewhere in the pile, Mary's death warrant. According to Davison, the queen was fully aware of what she was signing, and sent him on his way to his boss, Walsingham, who was on sick leave, with a piece of black humour: she said 'the sight thereof would kill him outright' (N. H. Nicolas, 213). Davison was also to see that the warrant passed the great seal. Two days later, according to Davison, Elizabeth confirmed with an oath that the execution should be carried out, although he also said that it was his impression that she wanted nothing more to do with the matter, and favoured a hole-in-the-corner murder, which might have satisfied international opinion. However, according to Elizabeth, she signed the warrant only to be held in reserve against any new dangers and had not intended it to be dispatched to Fotheringhay Castle.

Davison, perhaps aware of the 1572 precedent, no sooner had the signed warrant in his hand than he took it to Burghley and Sir Thomas Bromley, lord chancellor, who attached the great seal at 5 o'clock on the afternoon of 1 February. On 3 February Burghley convened the entire privy council to meet in his private chamber at court, and secured their signatures to the commission under which the warrant was executed, Walsingham adding his from

his sickbed. The documents were then taken to Fotheringhay by Beale's servant, George Digby. Mary was executed on 8 February.

There followed a storm which drove Burghley out of court and parliament for weeks. Camden wrote that Elizabeth conceived 'or pretended' great grief, and anger against Davison in particular, but then he thought better of 'pretended' and removed it from an intended second edition of his *Annales* (*Camdeni annales*, ed. Hearne, 2.546). If her strategy was to exonerate herself by shifting the blame on to her privy councillors, the self-preserving concern of those privy councillors, Burghley above all, was to make Davison the scapegoat. At his trial in the court of Star Chamber, the nub of the matter was Davison's word against the queen's (whether or not she told him to delay the matter), and against Burghley's (whether or not he had told Burghley that he could safely go ahead). In these circumstances it was inevitable that Davison should be found guilty, imprisoned in the Tower and fined 10,000 marks (a sentence later remitted). What is remarkable about the trial is that almost all the speeches were favourable to Davison, and the extraordinary procedure which Burghley and the privy council had followed. Arthur Grey, fourteenth Baron Grey of Wilton, thought it was Davison's simple duty to reveal such weighty matters to the privy council, 'whom it specially concerned to know' (BL, Add. MS 48027, fol. 675r), implying that the privy council also acted properly, in the interest of the safety of the realm. Only John Lumley, Baron Lumley, took up what was surely a constitutionally more correct position. It was a contempt, *lèse-majesté*, for the privy council to have met in the queen's very house, and to have resolved a matter of such consequence without her advice, or even knowledge.

Almost the last word was left to Richard Fletcher, the dean of Peterborough, who officiated on the scaffold at Fotheringhay, and who broke the stunned silence as Mary's head fell from her shoulders with the ringing cry: 'so perish all the queen's enemies!' His 'Sermon preached before the queene immediately after the execucion of the queene of Scottes', was remarkable both for its rhetorical dexterity and for its courage. He was not afraid to compare Elizabeth with the disciples, who slept while Christ prayed and groaned in the Garden of Gethsemane, which was to apply, and more directly, the trope of the negligent prince which is found in Sidney's *Arcadia* (Walker, 122–3).

The Netherlands and the Armada, 1567–1588 England was in a state of semi-war with Spain from the late 1570s. It was also a privatized war. There was 'no peace beyond the line', where maritime operations, conducted by licensed pirates, technically 'privateers', of whom Francis Drake was only the most celebrated, preyed upon Spanish shipping and treasure. Drake's impudent circumnavigation of the world, between 1577 and 1580, defied its division between the Iberian powers under the treaty of Tordesillas of 1494. This was a venture in which Elizabeth invested, and to some advantage, and she rewarded Drake with a knighthood when he returned to the Thames with his booty. Drake's exploits decided Philip in favour of the

Armada, defence of his empire by means of a single strike. This was easier said than done. Philip's experts calculated that a fleet would be needed larger than that at Lepanto in 1571, and in 1585 there were no cannon balls available in Spain.

For the time being there was no declaration of war, and no commitment of English forces to the Low Countries, the cockpit of Europe since 1567. Leicester's hopes of a command in that theatre were dashed in 1577, but many English volunteers were active in a conflict which galvanized the aspirations of those who increasingly understood European politics in confessional terms as a universal religious war, among them Sidney. In the early 1580s events and circumstances drove Elizabeth inexorably towards the conflict which she had been so anxious to avoid. Anjou, for what he was worth, died in 1584, his brother, now Henri III, having proved unwilling to support his intervention in the Low Countries. Spain was now better placed to make trouble in France than France was in the Low Countries. William of Orange, the only credible national Dutch leader, was assassinated on 1 July 1584. Most menacing of all developments, in 1580 the Portuguese succession fell into Philip's lap, uniting two world empires, and two fleets. Now Spain, given time, could hope to deploy in Atlantic waters a fleet capable of taking on the Elizabethan navy, which made the 'Enterprise of England' no longer a pipe dream but a realizable project. If Philip were to regain undisputed control of his Dutch possessions, and Alessandro Farnese, prince of Parma, looked likely to achieve just that, it was hard to see what could save England.

By the end of 1584 the privy council accepted the need to intervene directly in the Low Countries, and in 1585 England entered into treaty obligations with the Dutch rebels. When Spain seized English shipping in Spanish harbours this was an added provocation, alienating English merchants who had been in favour of maintaining normal trading relations with the Iberian peninsula. So began a state of hostilities which was ended only in 1604, one of the longest-running wars in English history. Between 1585 and 1604 about 106,000 men out of a population of four million were conscripted for military service. The wars cost the crown £4,500,000, when its ordinary revenue was £300,000 a year. This was also the first major ideological war in English history, since the combatants, in the perception and rhetoric of the time, represented the forces of light and darkness, Christ and Antichrist. Also, it was a war with global economic consequences, as English trade began to redeploy from traditional continental markets into the wider world.

Throughout these years there was no declaration of war from either side, and for Elizabeth nothing was that simple or decisive. In her assessment of what might and should be attempted, numbers counted for more than ideology. She doubted whether she could afford the destiny which history now offered, and even after the treaty of Nonsuch with the Dutch was signed in August 1585, she tried to limit her commitment. She had no imperial ambitions, in fact some would say no ambitions at all beyond going on being queen, and in making limited war she was still seeking peace. So Elizabeth told Leicester: 'we do require you that you rather bend your cause to make a defensive than offensive war, and that you seek by all the means you may to avoid the hazard of a battle' (Haigh, *Elizabeth I*, 130).

The treaty of Nonsuch translated into an annual outlay of £126,180 10s., or a third of the ordinary expenditure of government. Elizabeth's reputation for penny-pinching parsimony, which largely derives from the Dutch adventure, is not really justified. Like other government initiatives in more recent history, the project outran its pre-estimated costs, but the queen was unwilling to foot the extra bill, or to accept that she had made an open-ended commitment. Under their treaty obligations, it was up to the Dutch to meet the shortfall. In the event, Leicester's expeditionary force of 7000, officered by his friends, many of them puritans, failed to cover itself with glory, a failure partially redeemed, in true English style, by the affecting death of Sidney on 17 October 1586.

The intervention also proved a political fiasco, when Leicester, flattered by his welcome, accepted the office of governor-general in February 1586, which implied that Elizabeth was sovereign of the Netherlands and he her viceroy. The queen let it be known:

> how highly upon just cause we are offended with his last late acceptation of the government of those provinces, being done contrary to our commandment ... which we do repute to be a very great and strange contempt least looked for at his hands, being he is a creature of our own.   (*Collected Works*, 269)

Elizabeth knew not only that she was being bounced, but that the world would assume that Leicester was following her secret orders, contrary to the war aims published in her *A Declaration of the Causes Mooving the Queene to Give Aide to the Oppressed in the Lowe Countries* (English, Latin, Dutch, and Italian editions). Leicester was commanded to resign his governorship, on pain of his allegiance—which he failed to do. Elizabeth wrote to Sir Thomas Heneage in the Netherlands: 'Jesus, what availeth wit when it fails the owner at greatest need! Do what you are bidden' (ibid., 280). Leicester was recalled in November, later given a second chance, but again recalled in November 1587, frustrated and defeated not so much by Parma, who was now keeping his powder dry against the expected arrival of the Armada, as by the complexities of Dutch politics.

Meanwhile, Drake, John Hawkins, and other privateers continued, with varying success, to prey upon Spanish shipping, coasts, and islands, a policy in the estimation of many more profitable, literally, than siege warfare in the Low Countries. In 1587, in the operation known to schoolboy history as the 'singeing of the king of Spaines beard', Drake destroyed much enemy shipping at Cadiz, together with the barrel staves intended for the Armada's water casks, so delaying the enterprise by a year; and he returned from the Azores with a booty of £140,000, of which Elizabeth, as the major investor, pocketed the lion's share, £40,000 (F. Bacon, *Considerations Touching a*

Warre with Spaine, 1629, 40). However, it was beyond English naval capacity to maintain a permanent blockade of the Iberian ports, and if the Armada was coming, the fleet would be needed in home waters. On 30 May 1588, 130 ships, carrying over 18,000 men, set sail from Lisbon. The purpose of this supposedly 'invincible' Armada was to form an escort for the main invasion force, Parma's army. Harassed along the length of the English Channel by small squadrons commanded by Charles Howard, second Baron Howard of Effingham, Drake, Hawkins, and Martin Frobisher, the Armada reached the roads of Calais on 6 August.

Elizabeth prepared to receive the Armada with more efforts to advance the peace process in the Low Countries, negotiations doomed to failure but which were still in progress when the Spanish ships appeared in the channel. The myth that the might of Spain was overcome by England's little ships is far from the true story. The English fleet was in fact the most up-to-date and formidably armed in existence. The odds were stacked against England only if the Armada succeeded in landing Parma's expeditionary force. Yet, the logistics of co-ordinating the ships of Don Alonso Pérez de Guzmán el Bueno, seventh duke of Medina Sidonia, with Parma's soldiers proved extremely problematic. With little or no prospect of success for the combined operation which was the whole point of the exercise, the advantage was seized by the English fleet on 7 August through the use of eight fireships, the existence of which was successfully hidden from the Spanish. It was a small but decisive victory, assisted by the weather. As the Spanish fleet, still more or less intact with some 112 vessels, was driven northwards, around Scotland to a series of shipwrecks in the Atlantic and on Irish coasts, Elizabeth struck the Armada medal which sounded a note of protestant providentialism rather than triumphalism. 'God breathed and they were scattered.' Sixty ships made it home to Spain, but 15,000 men perished. Henry Kamen, Philip's biographer, found little to be said in defence of the enterprise of England: 'Neither the king nor anyone else was quite sure what it was meant to achieve' (Kamen, 276).

Elizabeth paid her famous visit to the hastily assembled camp on the north side of the Thames estuary, at west Tilbury, on 8 August. Garrett Mattingly offered two alternative visions of the queen inspecting her troops, escorted by Leicester: a majestic figure clothed in white velvet on a white steed, the sun shining off her silver breastplate; or:

> a battered, rather scraggy spinster in her middle fifties perched on a fat white horse, her teeth black, her red wig slightly askew, dangling a toy sword and wearing an absurd little piece of parade-armour like something out of a theatrical property-box. (Mattingly, 195)

However, the speech which Elizabeth made the next day was pure magic. Although it exists only in versions of what was transmitted and recorded by the chaplain Lionel Sharp, who claimed 'no man hath it but myself, and such as I have given it to', there is no reason to doubt its authenticity:

> Let tyrants fear: I have so behaved myself that under God I have placed my chiefest strength and safeguard in the loyal hearts and goodwill of my subjects … I know I have the body but of a weak and feeble woman, but I have the heart and stomach of a king and of a king of England too—and take foul scorn that Parma or any other prince of Europe should dare to invade the borders of my realm. (*Collected Works*, 325–6)

After this Elizabeth was persuaded to retreat to the safety of St James's Palace. On 29 August Leicester wrote to enquire after her health, 'the chiefest thing in this world' that he prayed for. After his death at Cornbury, Oxfordshire, on 4 September, she endorsed it 'his last letter' and kept it by her until her own death (Neale, *Queen Elizabeth*, 301). Warwick followed his brother to the grave on 20 February 1590, Walsingham on 6 April, and other core members of the old regime (but not Burghley) were soon part of history: Sir Walter Mildmay, Hatton, Knollys. A page was being turned, and Elizabeth, as she approached her seventh decade, stepped into a political climate so altered that it has been called her second reign.

War and the second reign, 1588–1603 The year 1588 was by no means as decisive as a simplified and jingoistic history pretends. In 1589 Drake, as admiral, and Sir John Norreys, as military commander, headed a counter-attack. It was a complex, multi-purpose operation aimed at mopping up what was left of the Armada, attacking Lisbon, placing a pretender on the Portuguese throne, and intercepting the annual treasure fleet coming from the Indies, a kind of joint-stock enterprise in which Elizabeth sank as much as £60,000. The strategy was no better than that of Spain in 1588, and the result was a smaller-scale mirror image of the Spanish failure. In the summers which followed there were more naval ventures, concerned as much with profit as with winning a war. The lonely stand of Sir Richard Grenville and the *Revenge* on 2 September 1591 contributed to England's naval mythology, while in 1592 the queen's ships captured the great carrack *Madre di Dios*, a return of £80,000 on an investment of £3000. New Spanish armadas were sent to the waters around Britain and Ireland in 1596, 1597, and 1601.

The dagger still pointed at Elizabeth's heart was Parma and his army in the Low Countries. The emphasis now shifted to France, where the assassination in July 1589 of the last of the Valois, Henri III, saw the legitimate succession pass to the Bourbon and protestant king of Navarre as Henri IV, whose claims were contested by the remnants of the Guise faction, and by Parma, backed up by the popular politics of the Catholic league, entrenched in Paris. If Spain was not to dominate western Europe, from the Strait of Gibraltar to Friesland, England would have to engage Spanish power in France. The theatre of engagement was Normandy under the command of Sir Roger Williams and later Robert Devereux, second earl of Essex, and Brittany under Norreys. The first objective was Rouen, and beyond that, control of Paris, which Henri IV gained in 1593, not so much by conquest as by conversion to Catholicism. Elizabeth's response to this event was typically convoluted:

> And where you promise me all friendship and fidelity, I confess I have clearly merited it, and I will not repent it, provided you do not change your Father. Otherwise I will be

only a bastard sister, at least not your sister by the Father.
(*Collected Works*, 370–71)

War between Henri and Spain was concluded in 1598 and the Dutch revolt entered its final stage as the United Provinces emerged as a viable state.

Elizabeth's correspondence in these years reverberates with impotent anger at the irresponsible conduct of admirals and generals, who were so often out of touch and out of control, the impulsive and unpredictable Essex above all. This was no doubt one reason, not to speak of its expense, why she disliked war so much. As with the Low Countries in 1585–7, she limited her involvement so far as she could. After 1594 England scaled down its continental engagements, to concentrate on a naval war which was supposed to pay for itself, but which repeatedly fell victim to divided counsels and objectives: Drake's and Hawkins's last voyage to the Spanish main in 1595–6, Essex's great Cadiz expedition of 1596, when strategic opportunity fell victim to privateering greed, with a repeat performance in the Islands voyage of 1597. Whether Elizabeth liked it or not, this expansive world of *Westward Ho*, ever popular with Elizabethan historians of a romantic disposition, tends to disguise the continuing importance of events on the mainland of western Europe, and, after 1598, in Ireland, where she was obliged to sink the bulk of her treasure and the proceeds of relatively punitive taxation, direct and indirect. English troops remained in the Low Countries until the end of the reign, costing about £1,500,000. The last five years were occupied with a process which one historian has called 'shuffling towards peace' (MacCaffrey, *War and Politics*, 220–25).

By the later 1590s it had become a commonplace to speak of the 'halcyon' government of Elizabeth, but these were not halcyon years. Rather they were marked by war-weariness, high taxation, inflation, a succession of bad harvests, and recurrent plague. Real wages were at their lowest point in centuries, and there was a corresponding rise in crime and vagrancy. In reaction, a government fearful of religious, social, and political dissent and subversion became more autocratic. In 1591 the judges declared, in the context of a trial involving religious dissent, that the realm of England was 'an absolute empire and monarchy' (Guy, 11). The 'mixed polity', lauded by mid-Tudor publicists, which swung into political action in 1584–7, was giving way to an unqualified royal sovereignty.

At the same time the political system was becoming more corrupt and faction-ridden. A note survives that Burghley wanted burnt, which establishes that in the last two and a half years of his life, and in his capacity of master of the court of wards and liveries, he accepted sweeteners of £3301 when his salary was £133 a year, the crown gaining a mere £906 from these transactions. One victim of these processes was the consensuality in the protestant political nation which had characterized the 1570s and early 1580s, often, to be sure, induced by Elizabeth's own very different outlook on the issues of the day. There was a marked generational change. Those men of business, motivated by a high ideal of public service, who tended to die, if not poor, in modest circumstances, were succeeded by clever lawyers on the make, like Thomas Egerton, solicitor-general, attorney-general, lord keeper, and, eventually, lord chancellor; in his origins a Catholic and a bastard but who ended up as Baron Ellesmere and Viscount Brackley, his son and heir becoming an earl.

Elizabeth herself was part of this generational shift, markedly older and losing her grip. *Semper eadem* was now a principle of morbidity. She appointed no more privy councillors, allowing the membership of her privy council to fall to ten, and she failed to replenish her nobility. When she retired from the opening ceremonies of her last parliament, in 1601, it was noted that very few of the Commons said '"God save your Majestie" as they were wonte in all greate assemblyes', and that as she motioned with her hand to make room, one MP shouted 'yf yow would hange us wee can make noe more roume', which the queen 'seemed not to heare, thoughe she heaved upp her head and looked that waye towardes him that spake' (Hartley, 3.306). During Charles I's reign Godfrey Goodman, bishop of Gloucester, remembered that 'the people were very generally weary of an old woman's government' (J. Hurstfield, *Freedom, Corruption and Government in Elizabethan England*, 1973, 105).

Egerton said that he was 'unwilling to contend with competitors' (HoP, *Commons, 1558–1603*, 2.81). The 1590s were responsible for the Naunton-inspired legend that Elizabethan politics was dominated by factional competition. With the contest for office and other perks fiercer than ever, there was a new exclusivity in the operations of patronage. Historians have not always agreed on whether this was provoked by the Cecils, the apparently indestructible Burghley and his up-and-coming son and apprentice, Sir Robert Cecil, or by their opponents who increasingly clustered around Essex, complaining of a *regnum Cecilianum*. Either way, the Cecils were now telling their clients not to spoil their chances by relying on any other patrons, and Francis Bacon, for all that he was Burghley's nephew and Cecil's cousin, had to rely upon Essex as he made his uncertain way up the slippery political pole. It was a decade interpreted for those who lived through it in the light of the work of the Roman historian Tacitus, and expressed above all in Ben Jonson's play *Sejanus* (1603–4), itself a decidedly Tacitean drama.

Ireland Elizabeth was also queen of Ireland, although it was a foreign country which she never visited. Much of the island was 'beyond the pale'. It could be asked how interested she was in Ireland, and how well informed about it. Could she have located the Irish provinces, Leinster, Munster, Connaught, Ulster, on the map? Members of the Old English aristocracy spent long periods, voluntarily or involuntarily, in Elizabeth's presence, especially that great magnate Thomas *Butler, tenth earl of Ormond (1531–1614), Black Tom, a remote cousin of the queen and a frequent visitor. So she would not have been short of Irish advice and intelligence, however biased by corkscrew Irish politics. She also met, from time to time, the Gaelic chieftains, including Shane O'Neill, whose world the Elizabethans made little attempt to understand.

Ireland was governed indirectly, through viceroys, including Sussex, Sir Henry Sidney, Sir John Perrot, and Sir William Fitzwilliam. These men were faced with the largely thankless and near impossible task of reconciling English common law with Gaelic Brehon law and English customs with Irish customs. However, distance from the court allowed the viceroys to pursue their own programmes, distorted by local politics and pressures from England. The options available for the reduction of Ireland to the English model of civility involved varying degrees of conciliation and coercion but these measures were resisted by the Gaelic Irish, and often by the Old English too, as destructive to their way of life.

Conciliation, especially the policy of composition adopted by Sidney from 1566, was not necessarily doomed to failure: witness the ambiguous career of Ormond, who was more trusted by Elizabeth's government than not. However, in adopting this policy the viceroys, Sidney especially, bit off more than they could chew, while the violent logic of events, and the thinking of most intellectuals who addressed Irish matters, led ever more inevitably towards the simpler solution of coercion, and, ultimately, conquest, the prolepsis of which was the brutal repression undertaken by Grey from 1580 to 1582, in the aftermath of the Desmond rebellion. This was an atrocity given its prophetic chorus by the poet and Irish planter Spenser in his *A Vewe of the Present State of Ireland* (written about 1596), essaying radical social engineering, not to say genocide; and poetically and ideologically justified in his *Faerie Queene*, 'an elaborate glorification of violence whenever this was employed to promote either civil or moral goals' (Canny, *Making Ireland British*, 23).

The forces working against English success included, above all, the failure of the Irish Reformation, which left Ireland irreconcilably Catholic and a dangerous hot spot in the war against Spain. Politically, the policies of successive viceroys only succeeded in alienating almost all native political interests, even in the English pale, where efforts to make the Irish pay for their own government had mostly negative consequences. Increasingly primitive ethnology, a thoroughly racist perception of the Irish as almost subhuman, encouraged a brutality no longer to be expected in England. The colonial option, 'plantations', was used to deal with Ireland in the hope that English colonization would instil English civility. The most ambitious of these projects was undertaken in Ulster between 1573 and 1576 by Walter Devereux, first earl of Essex, with Elizabeth herself an investor, but it was a spectacular failure. All these factors were conducive to the growth of a new kind of Irish national sentiment.

Elizabeth was not indifferent to the radically unstable Irish scene. She wrote to Sidney on 17 July 1577: 'you gave us hope to diminish our charges and increase our revenue, but we find the former still to be great and the latter … is much decayed' (Brady, 152). As this suggests, her major concern was to limit the extent to which Ireland was a drain on royal revenue (how happy she would have been if Ireland had paid for its own government, as Sidney had promised). This was certainly a principal reason for the

failure of successive viceregal initiatives. So far as Ireland was concerned, the legend of Elizabeth's parsimony was no legend, although the Irish government could not support itself from its own revenues, even in peacetime. More positively, the queen's instinctive conservatism was helpful. Her way was not to destroy her over-mighty Irish subjects but to balance one interest against another, and she put up with postures and gestures of insubordination which she would never have tolerated in, for example, the north of England, implying that she acknowledged that Ireland was another place, where they did things differently. In 1580 she told Grey, her latest and most ruthless lord deputy, that she had no intention to 'root out' the Irish, since she was 'interssed [interested] alike in our subjects of both those realms', carrying a 'like affection' to them both (Canny, *Making Ireland British*, 119).

Rebellion tended to simplify the Irish problem and to resolve the mind, but not necessarily Elizabeth's mind— she always took some convincing that her Irish subjects were rebels past redemption. In the 1560s Shane, with a valid but contested claim to the O'Neill lordship of Ulster and to the earldom of Tyrone, succeeded in making himself the queen's main Irish enemy, particularly by the threat he posed to the pale. He interrupted an intriguing career with a visit to the court in 1562, where the garb of his wild Irish followers and his rhetorical Gaelic created a sensation. Back in Ulster, he reverted to type. Successive viceroys, Sussex and Sidney, wasted four campaigning seasons in vain attempts even to locate him. Elizabeth wrote to Sidney: 'you are like to enter into so great errors for the government of that realm as are not to be suffered in one that is appointed to govern as you are'; while Sidney wrote to Sir William Cecil: 'for God's sake, take me out of this world' (Brady, 233–4). Shane was killed in June 1567, by the very Scots whom English policy wanted to exclude from north-east Ireland, and this gave Sidney some shortlived relief. Other defiances followed, however, as one Irish magnate and his affinity after another declared, in effect, their unwillingness to behave according to the script written for them.

Ulster was the source of the much more serious crisis of the 1590s, the rebellion of Hugh O'Neill, second earl of Tyrone. Tyrone was a man of stature, ambition, and a kind of charisma, and he was treated with respect at court, and by the last reforming viceroy, Perrot. Yet, his resolve to establish an unchallenged power in Ulster led him into suspicious confederacies with other Gaelic leaders, and in particular with Hugh Roe O'Donnell of Tyrconnell, an old enemy who now became his son-in-law and military ally. Feelers were also put out to Spain, of which Tyrone made no secret. The Irish problem, never entirely insular, was now increasingly globalized, part of the war in which Elizabeth was engaged over large parts of the world. There was a steady drift towards organized hostilities, as the end of campaigning in Brittany released English soldiers and their commander, Norreys, for service in Ireland. In 1595 there were military setbacks, after which Tyrone was declared a traitor. However, still anxious to appease Tyrone, if possible, Elizabeth was more critical than ever of her representatives on the field and in Dublin, where second and third raters were now in charge. 'As is too apparent to the whole world there was never any realm was worse governed by all our ministers from the highest to the lowest' (*CSP Ire., July 1596–December 1597*, 266). The disastrous English defeat at the battle of the Yellow Ford on 14 August 1598 plunged most of Ireland into rebellion. Tyrone now openly expressed the doctrine of Ireland for the Gaelic, Catholic, Irish. The English counter-claim, to be defending the true interests of the Irish people against their oppressive lords, rang hollow.

This was war in a more formal sense than Ireland had known, and Elizabeth was obliged to dispatch the largest army royal sent there by the Tudors, more than 17,000 troops. They fought against an enemy who was no wild Irish savage but a sophisticated and wily commander who put professional and disciplined troops into uniform. The inevitable choice to confront Tyrone was Robert Devereux, second earl of Essex, for better or worse Elizabeth's senior general, who was now sent (most reluctantly, for his part) to a posting which he knew very well would do him and his reputation no good. He arrived in Dublin and was sworn as lord lieutenant on 15 April 1599. As things transpired, Essex had a sense of the future as well as of the present parameters of the situation (the queen was sixty-five years old), and the role he chose to play was ambivalent. While Tyrone played hard to get in Ulster, Essex undertook what was little more than a militarized progress through Munster and Leinster. In fairness to him it must be said that the Irish privy council advised against an immediate attack on Tyrone, Elizabeth gave her specific assent to the Leinster expedition, and he was not given the shipping needed to undertake amphibious operations in Lough Foyle, an essential part of the strategy, nor the heavy draught horses required to move an army into Ulster. Essex's reaction to these setbacks was more than petulant. It was paranoid, and it was met by stinging rebukes from the queen. By the time Essex set out in search of Tyrone, little enough of his grand army was left. When he met his enemy on the River Lagan on 6 September, it was to conduct a secret parley on horseback, leading to a truce, which Elizabeth immediately repudiated as dishonourable. Essex reacted by leaving his post, against her orders, and, still booted and spurred, confronted Elizabeth at Nonsuch Palace, Surrey, at 10 o'clock on the morning of 28 September, while she was still in her night attire and without make-up—conduct which not only broke all the rules of political and courtly etiquette, but implied that in the earl's perception not the queen but Sir Robert Cecil, principal secretary, and his party were now in charge. If Ireland looked to be lost, the English state was in a scarcely more stable condition.

In Essex's absence, Tyrone proclaimed a virtually independent Irish nation, inclusive of Gaelic Irish and Old English, governed, under the pope, Clement VIII, by Irishmen, respecting only a nominal English sovereignty. Essex's replacement, Charles Blount, eighth Baron Mountjoy, arrived in Ireland and, between 1600 and 1602, achieved what his predecessor was either unwilling or unable to do. Ulster was stormed, while Mountjoy's lieutenants subdued Munster. In September 1601 the anticipated Spanish intervention happened, at Kinsale in co. Cork, and the Irish war turned upon a siege and a successful onslaught on that garrison. The Irish chiefs were now picked off piecemeal. The last to surrender was Tyrone himself, who submitted, on terms, a week after Elizabeth's death, still ignorant of that fact. Elizabeth died knowing that Ireland had been reconquered at the cost of its alienation, a price to be paid by her successors and for centuries after. The historian is left with the tantalizing proposition: Elizabeth's own approach to England's Irish problem, if not to Ireland's English problem, just might have had happier results. Yet the French ambassador, André Hurault de Maisse, no doubt reported faithfully, in the winter of 1597–8, that the queen 'would wish Ireland drowned in the sea' (*Journal*, 51).

Essex, Elizabeth's last years, and her death, 1591–1603 De Maisse arrived in England in late 1597 to treat with Elizabeth and her privy councillors about matters of peace and war. Only a month before, in October, there was a new national emergency when another Spanish Armada headed for Cornwall, only to be dispersed in an autumn storm. Once again, God had blown and his enemies had been scattered. Henri IV was preparing to negotiate peace with Spain (the treaty of Vervins, 2 May 1598), and the object of the de Maisse mission was to find out whether or not Elizabeth was inclined to join in the negotiations. The interests of the Dutch estates were part of the equation, Burghley reminding the ambassador that the war was 'a game for three persons' (*Journal*, 105). However, it appeared that the Cecils favoured peace, whereas Essex, the leading military patron, was all for continuing to prosecute the war. Calais was once again an issue, the Spanish having taken the town in 1596.

De Maisse's account of his mission was modelled on the 'relations' of the Venetian ambassadors, having himself served in Venice, and the record of his audiences with the ageing Elizabeth are among the most vivid and frank of any pen portraits that there are of her. He found her face long, thin, 'and very aged', under 'a great reddish-coloured wig'; her teeth yellow with many of them missing, so that she could not be understood when she spoke quickly. Yet, the queen's tall figure was still graceful. 'So far as she may she keeps her dignity.' 'It is a strange thing to see how lively she is in body and mind and nimble in everything she does.' Evidently there was no sign of arthritis, but Elizabeth was restless and fidgety, 'for ever twisting and untwisting' her sleeves, and repeatedly opening the front of her robe down to her very navel, as if she were too hot. She fished for compliments, complaining that she was 'foolish and old'. 'See what it is to have to do with old women such as I am' (*Journal*, 25–6, 37, 58). A year later, in 1598, Elizabeth was no younger, when the German visitor Paul Hentzner described her oblong face, 'fair but wrinkled', her hooked nose and narrow lips, 'her hair ... an auburn clouir [colour], but false' (Rye, 104).

De Maisse described Burghley in 1598 as 'very old and

white' (*Journal*, 27), deaf as a post, and carried everywhere in a chair. Yet he was not allowed to retire, and in his last months he continued to attend the privy council and to take his place in parliament. His familiar letters to Cecil convey a sense of servitude, as he was forced again and again to undertake the journey from his house at Theobalds, Hertfordshire, to the court. (In 1591 Elizabeth addressed him, jocularly, as 'the eremite [hermit] of Theobalds' (*Letters*, ed. Harrison, 207–8).) He knew his queen, 'the lady', telling Cecil that 'she useth not to gyve audience in cloudy and fowle wether … but yet betwixt showers I do attend and follow hir trayne'. However, this was written to be shared with 'the lady', because he knew that it would amuse her (CUL, MS Ee.3.56, nos. 10, 14). In his final illness, with his appetite gone, Elizabeth herself sat by his bed and fed him with a spoon. The very last words from his pen, written in a quavery, arthritic hand, told his son: 'serve God by servyng of the Quene, for all other service is in dede bondage to the Devill' (ibid., no. 138). Burghley died on 4 August 1598 at Cecil House, Westminster. These affecting scenes and sentiments should not be allowed to disguise the fact that in the 1590s, after the deaths of almost all the other great Elizabethan politicians of his generation, he exercised unprecedented personal power, almost a monopoly, which he was prepared to employ ruthlessly to destroy a career like that of Perrot in Ireland; and that this hegemony was productive of destabilizing faction. Part of the problem was that the bond between Elizabeth and Burghley was so long-standing and so strong that she trusted him implicitly, favouring him above all others.

De Maisse often referred to the factional politics of these years, the tension between the Cecils and Essex, sometimes indicating that it was past and over ('formerly there was always great jealousy between them in everything, one against the other … a thing notorious to all the Court'), sometimes that it was a present factor which was likely to determine the outcome of his mission. He reveals that it suited Elizabeth to live with a faction-ridden court, that Burghley found 'these Court broils' amusing, and that his son was 'altogether immersed in them' (*Journal*, 4, 18). These were acute observations. The competition between the Cecil and Essex interests was of a fluctuating nature, of necessity balanced by the need for co-operation (Burghley, Cecil, and Essex were privy councillors), and there were many episodes of reconciliation. Burghley seems to have been anxious to save Essex from himself, and wrote letters of encouragement and support when the earl set out for the Islands voyage in 1597, almost as if Essex was still the little boy who had grown up in his household. Yet this did not prevent the Cecil interest from taking advantage of the earl's absence to make Sir Robert Cecil chancellor of the duchy of Lancaster, and Howard of Effingham, earl of Nottingham, which Essex interpreted as a personal slight, a reflection on his service at Cadiz. It was a typical Cecil gesture to compensate Essex with the office of earl marshal, which restored him to precedence over Nottingham.

Competition there was, which is evidence of insecurity on both sides of the relationship. Cecil was forced to serve a long apprenticeship before being rewarded with the office of secretary of state, and when he was appointed, on 5 July 1596, it was intended to put Essex (who was absent in Cadiz) in his place. Essex found himself unable to advance his clients, Bacon most notoriously. Patronage and clientage became more exclusive, with ambitious men forced to make difficult decisions about where they were to look for advancement, and having made their hard choices, these clients tended to become so many tails wagging the dog of patronage. In the most unedifying of all Elizabethan political episodes, Cecil and Essex jostled to reap personal advantage at the expense of the other in the affair of Elizabeth's Portuguese doctor, Roderigo Lopez, exposed (perhaps falsely) as a Spanish agent who was plotting to poison her. Above all this was a quarrel of two extreme opposites: Essex the favourite, the soldier and would-be military hero, a man made for 'virtuous' action in the pattern set by his late stepfather, Leicester, and cousin Sidney, whose widow he had married, expansionist and European in his outlook; and the Cecils, consummate, and essentially insular, politicians. It was sword versus robe. Essex's fatal mistake, which he committed repeatedly, was to suppose that he could deploy his talents, his physicality and his popularity, to command an elderly woman with whom he professed to be in love, but for whom he seems to have had scant respect. Burghley, after nearly forty years of service, still wrote of the queen, even in his private letters to his son, obsequiously and as her bondsman, grateful for every sign of favour. Elizabeth's no less fatal error, the worst she ever made, was to suppose that she could control Essex and put him in harness with Cecil as she had harnessed Leicester and Burghley.

Although in the aftermath of his father's death Cecil contributed to Essex's downfall, and was certainly willing to kick him when he was down, the earl was the architect of his own nemesis. His reaction to disappointment had always been to sulk and to absent himself from court, a risky and counter-productive strategy. When in September 1599 he returned precipitately from his Irish command to shock Elizabeth in her own bedchamber, Essex was a desperate man, knowing that he faced political extinction. There was a real chance that he would use the Irish army to coerce the court and avoid that fate. Yet at first the queen treated the affair with relative leniency, merely committing Essex to house arrest under the care of a fellow privy councillor, Egerton, on 1 October. No doubt she knew that London was full of other returnees from the Irish wars, a by now disappointed and angry Essex following. Soon Elizabeth thought that she had good grounds for a charge of treason, and had to be dissuaded from putting Essex on trial in Star Chamber. Instead, a ritual submission was arranged, before a special commission of privy councillors and others, where the earl was censured and remanded in custody. Later in the year the sun shone again, as Essex tried to woo his way back into favour, but Elizabeth remained deeply suspicious. When one of her maids, the skittish Mary Fitton, invited her to join in the dance which ended a masque at a wedding, she asked what character Mary was playing. '"Affection", she said. "Affection" said the queen, "Affection is false." Yet her Majestie rose and dawnced' (Newdegate, 35–6).

Affection was false. Essex was wading in a dangerous conspiracy which involved a plan to bring Mountjoy's army over from Ireland and some incriminating diplomacy with James in Scotland, whose English inheritance Essex promised to secure. The balance was finally tipped when Elizabeth failed to renew the customs farm on sweet wines on 22 September 1600, which was an important source of income for Essex and those who depended on him. The earl was now facing bankruptcy in more senses than one. Essex House was a cave of Adullam, full of desperate and disaffected men. The earl's popularity was orchestrated by preachers, and by the players who staged a revival of Shakespeare's all too topical *Richard II* at the Globe Theatre.

On Sunday 8 February 1601 came the dénouement, an almost farcical putsch. Summoned to appear before the privy council, Essex refused to go, and then took hostage four privy councillors, including Egerton who had come to Essex House to secure his person. With some two hundred followers, he marched on the city, declaring his loyalty to Elizabeth and announcing that there was a plot against his life. Cecil was only waiting for this, the way was blocked, and a herald appeared to denounce Essex as a traitor. By evening it was all over. Elizabeth proved as stalwart as at Tilbury in 1588, although there was some hysterical laughter. Secondary plots and rumours meant that Essex could not be spared, as Elizabeth had wanted to spare Norfolk, thirty years before. Within days he was found guilty of treason in a trial before his peers which he treated with haughty contempt, and on 25 February, at the age of thirty-four, he was executed, making a good end which was celebrated in a popular broadsheet ballad, *Essex's Last Good Night*. There was a public sense of ichabod. The glory had departed, and with it, according to Neale, the soul of Elizabethan England. Now there really was a *regnum Cecilianum*.

This was the twilight of Elizabeth's life and reign, but she had one final great performance to give, which she did, and to great effect, before her last parliament, which gathered on 27 October 1601. It was not a happy occasion, with the unhappiness crystallizing around the issue of monopoly patents on commodities, a value-added tax levied at the consumer's expense. Under the pressure of vigorous lobbying from soi-disant 'commonwealth men' outside the house, the question was, should the Commons proceed by bill or petition? Legislation would have limited the crown's prerogative, and the issue became constitutional, and heated. Then the queen, with perfect timing, gave way to all the Commons' demands. All injurious monopolies were to be revoked or suspended. The response of the Commons was a spontaneous demand that rather than receiving the thanks of a convenient number of MPs, the queen should receive them all. At such moments a parliament was pure theatre.

So the stage was set for the most celebrated of all Elizabeth's speeches, the so-called 'golden speech', which in more than one version had a life long after she was dead:

> To be a kinge and weare a crowne is a thinge moare glorious to them that see it then it is plesante to them that bear it. For my selfe, I was never so muche intized with the potent name of a kinge, or royall authoritie of a queene, as delited that God hath made mee his instrumente to maynetayne his truthe and glorie and this kingdom from dishonore, domage, tyranye, and opressione … And though you have hade, and maye have, many mightier and wiser princes sitting in this seate, yet you never had nor shall have anye that will love you bettere.   (Hartley, 3.296–7)

Later ages supposed that this was Elizabeth's last parliamentary performance, but it was not. On the last day of her last parliament (19 December 1601) she delivered her last public speech to the realm, pulling out many of the same organ stops:

> My care was ever by proceddinge justlie and uprightlie to conserve my people's love, which I accounte a gifte of God not to be marshalled in the lowest part of my mynde, but written in the deepest of my hart

and, after a lengthy review of her foreign policy and conduct of the war:

> this testimony I would have you cary hence for the world to knowe: that your soverain is more carefull of your conservation then of hir self, and will daily crave of God that they that wish you best may never wishe in vaine. (ibid., 3.278–81)

As Elizabeth approached her seventieth year she seemed in remarkably good health, still capable of riding as much as 10 miles on horseback, showing off to courtiers and ambassadors. However, in December 1602 her godson Sir John Harington came to court and reported to his wife a great change. Several contemporary accounts suggest that the death of Katherine Howard, countess of Nottingham, on 24 February 1603 precipitated the queen's final decline. What a later English statesman would call 'the black dog' had always been Elizabeth's companion, and now it dragged her into a chronic melancholy. By March she was refusing food and unable to sleep, not even going to bed, leaning against a pile of cushions, not speaking much but fetching great sighs. In this condition she died a slow death, succumbing to bronchitis and, perhaps, pneumonia. The end came in the early hours of 24 March 1603 at Richmond Palace, Surrey, her last earthly dealings having been with her 'little black husband', Archbishop Whitgift.

The final depression was partly political, induced by the knowledge that all eyes were now on the succession. The long-running Elizabethan succession crisis had been reactivated in the 1590s, as the sands of time were seen to be running out. There were at least twelve people with some kind of claim. These included the Infanta Isabella, daughter of Philip II and wife of Archduke Albert, governor of the Spanish Netherlands, the favoured candidate of Catholics, who, as in Robert Persons's *A Conference about the Next Succession* (1594), found convenient arguments against succession by simple hereditary right. There was also Lady Arabella Stuart, James VI's first cousin and granddaughter to Elizabeth Talbot, countess of Shrewsbury, whose great building projects suggested that she was not without ambitions of her own. 'Thus you see', wrote Thomas Wilson, 'this crown is not like to fall to the ground for want of heads that claim to wear it' (T. Wilson, 5).

By 1603 few doubted that the prize would go to James, who had played his cards very carefully and whose path to the throne was smoothed by Cecil, taking over from Essex as his secret friend at the English court. Whether Elizabeth actually named James as her successor is the final conundrum in a reign full of riddles. Camden reported that, while still able to speak, Elizabeth declared that she would not be succeeded by some vile person, and, being asked what she meant, replied, a king, and who else but her cousin, the king of Scots? In manuscript this passage is heavily worked over in the hand of Camden's pupil and friend, Sir Robert Cotton, who was always his guide on matters Scottish, and who was at court to observe the queen's last days (W. Camden, *Annales, tomus alter*, 1627; BL, Cotton MS Faustina F.iii, fols. 215*v*–216*r*). It was separately reported that when already speechless, Elizabeth confirmed her wishes to the privy council by a hand sign. However, another eyewitness, Sir Robert *Carey (1560–1639), confirmed only the hand signal, and alleged 'many false lies reported of the end and death of that good lady' (*Memoirs of Robert Carey*, 59–60). Carey took horse within minutes of her death to convey the news to Edinburgh, and there was general surprise and relief that the succession problem of 45 years standing was resolved so easily and peacefully.

Elizabeth's funeral took place in Westminster Abbey on 28 April. Afterwards, she was buried beside her sister. James VI and I erected the magnificent tomb for her still to be seen there today, and performed the same honour for his mother.

Representations, allegories, and images In this account of Elizabeth's life, the dichotomy of woman and queen has been constantly emphasized; but actually there is a trichotomy, the third facet being that of image and allegory. Elizabeth played many parts and enjoyed a range of mythical, symbolical, and metaphorical existences. This Elizabethan world of infinite contrivance is most familiar to readers of Spenser's *Faerie Queene*. His Elizabeth is Belphoebe and Gloriana: Belphoebe the type of virtuous and chaste beauty, Gloriana that of glorious sovereignty. Virtually every flattering female deity of classical and biblical mythology was pressed into service: from the Old Testament, the heroines, Judith and Deborah; from Greece and Rome and Renaissance Italy, Diana, Cynthia, and the Petrarchan mistress, the Platonically learned Laura. Most powerful of all these personae, replete with imperial and apocalyptic presumptions, was Virgo-Astraea, in Ovid the dying sunset of the golden age, in Virgil the promise of a golden age about to renew itself. On the magnificent engraved title-page of Christopher Saxton's *Atlas* (1579) Elizabeth sits as empress between the Pillars of Hercules, and in the portraits in the Armada series her hand rests on the globe.

Portraits of Elizabeth abound, the paintings grouped by art historians in a series of types or patterns. Sir Roy Strong counts eighty, together with another twenty-one group portraits in which Elizabeth appears, most famously in the so-called *Procession to Blackfriars* (Sherborne Castle), which has been connected to many particular and public events, such as the thanksgiving at St Paul's Cathedral for the defeat of the Armada, and to more than one wedding, although it may be simply a representation of the ageing queen on progress, carried in a litter. Strong also lists twenty-two miniature portraits, many of which were to be worn as jewellery—Elizabeth kept some of hers wrapped up. Most of these are by Hilliard (or derive from him), who is unique among Elizabethan artists in describing the circumstances in which he painted the queen from the life, chatting while he worked about the differences between his technique and that of the Italians. (Hilliard also painted a miniature of Mary, queen of Scots.) There were also any number of representations of the queen in cameos, illuminated manuscript initials (with a particularly fine example in the foundation charter of Emmanuel College, Cambridge, of 1584), engravings, and woodcuts. Strong records thirty-two engravings and twenty-three woodcuts, but there were probably more.

In 1563 it was said that 'all sortes of subjectes and people both noble and meane' wished to procure the queen's portrait for exhibition in their houses (Strong, *Portraits*, 10). Portraits were also required for diplomatic use, especially at the time of marriage negotiations, but in 1567 Sussex told the regent of the Low Countries, Margaret of Parma, that 'the picture commonly made to be solde did nothing resemble' his mistress (ibid., 25). This sheds light on a draft proclamation of 1563 which attempted to establish, one supposes with limited success, a process for vetting and licensing images of the queen which would serve as patterns for the numerous copies which the public demanded.

Whereas most portraits of Mary, queen of Scots, are instantly recognizable, few of the many representations of Elizabeth can be described as likenesses. The exception to prove the rule is the fetching portrait of the teenage Elizabeth (Windsor Castle). However, as soon as Elizabeth became queen, many portraitists abandoned all naturalistic aspirations. Strong remarks: 'the whole structure of her face is inconsistent'—together with the colour of eyes and hair (Strong, *Portraits*, 17). A person has been transformed into an icon, an image of cosmic power and divinity, an object of worship, and, it has been said, less kindly, a clothes horse, since the great portraits are as much descriptive accounts of costume and jewellery as of the woman wearing them. The question of how many of the images derive from sessions in which the queen actually sat for her portraits is not known, although it is known that she was reluctant to sit, an aspect perhaps of her somewhat inverted vanity.

The coronation portrait (NPG) is accurate in its detail, including the loose flowing hair always worn by queens for the occasion, and it stands in a tradition which goes back to the coronation portrait of Richard II (Westminster Abbey). The formal and severe Barrington Park head-and-shoulders portraits of about 1563 may reflect the aftermath of Elizabeth's brush with death months earlier. In the Pelican–Phoenix portraits of the 1570s, which bear the mark of Hilliard, there is more emblematic and heraldic symbolism, the phoenix jewel of some versions representing self-renewal, the pelican in others mystical motherhood. The Darnley portrait of the same period (NPG) is one of the finest and, in terms of continental taste, most modish, although the identity of the artist is unknown. Strong suspects that Elizabeth did not sit for an official likeness again until about 1588, and the Armada portrait. If so, this would mean that the Sieve portraits, stuffed as they are with programmatic emblems and devices, were adaptations of earlier portraits. The best of these is by Quinten Metsys the younger and was discovered in 1895, rolled up in an attic in Siena, where it still hangs.

In about 1588 an industry sprang up producing copies of a portrait in celebration of the defeat of the Spanish Armada, the original of which was probably the work of the sergeant-painter, George Gower; ten copies are listed by Strong. The climax of Elizabethan portraiture was reached in about 1592, in the full-length Ditchley portrait (NPG) by Marcus Gheeraerts the younger, so-called because of its association with a royal visit to the house of Elizabeth's champion, Sir Henry Lee, in Oxfordshire. There is no doubt that the queen's feet rest on Oxfordshire, as depicted in Saxton's map. An accompanying sonnet deciphers the codes of the picture: the sun, surpassed in radiance by Elizabeth; thunder, an image of divine power; the boundless ocean into which pour 'rivers of thankes'. It is important to note that Lee, not the queen or any official department of royal propaganda, commissioned this portrait. Strong suggests that in the Ditchley portrait Gheeraerts ventured a realistic representation of the features of the ageing queen. If so, this ran counter to a late trend towards what has been called deliberate rejuvenation, well represented in the highly idealized and emblematically obscure Rainbow portrait (Hatfield House), which dates from the very last years. This is consistent with much literary evidence, with the tragicomedy of the Essex–Elizabeth relationship, and with the observations of the foreign observers, de Maisse and Hentzner, that while complaining of old age, Elizabeth did everything she could to disguise it.

The verdict of posterity: historiography, biography, fiction, cinema, and television Several late Elizabethan observers reported that the English were tired of the reign of a woman and longed for a king. Experience of the rule of four successive Stuart monarchs overtook that prejudice and turned a legendary, not to say mythical, Elizabeth into a standard of staunchly protestant rectitude and militant patriotism, a stick with which to beat her successors and, ultimately, a whig queen. At the height of the exclusion crisis of 1679–81, a broadside proclaimed:

A Tudor! A Tudor! We've had Stuarts enough,
None ever reign'd like old Bess in her ruff.
(J. Miller, *Popery and Politics in England, 1660–1688*, 1973, 74)

The myth of Elizabeth the protestant heroine was not created by the queen's earliest historians, either because they were cool in their protestantism, or because they understood the role of the 'politic' historian, on the Tacitean model, to be a dispassionate one. John Clapham, whose 'Certain observations concerning the life and reign of Queen Elizabeth' was written very soon after her death but never published, has very little to say about religion, beyond the same kind of denunciation of the puritans that is found in Camden. As Burghley's sometime servant, Clapham's book was as much a eulogy for his old master as for Elizabeth. This was one of several more or less abortive attempts to write the history of the reign. Bacon wrote no more than a couple of pages, and Sir John Hayward, whose historical interest was in alterations in government (such as the Norman conquest), covered only the first four years in his 'Annals of Queen Elizabeth', which also remained unpublished and which conformed to the *politique* historiographical model.

Camden's *Annales* (1615, 1627; English translations 1625, 1629, 1630), more properly the result of his collaboration with Cotton, was an officially authorized and altogether more ambitious work, deeply researched and regarded as practically definitive for centuries. It owed its character to the circumstances of its gestation: first Burghley's commission, which opened the archives to Camden, and then the concern of James I that his mother should receive a better press than she was likely to receive from the great Jacques-Auguste de Thou, who had been over-reliant on George Buchanan's history of Scotland. Either because of his concern to placate James (a motive he denied), or because that was where his sympathies lay, Camden proved to be another loyal Cecilian (and Tacitean), who vilified Leicester together with his puritan friends, '*protestantes effervescentes*' (Collinson, 'One of us?', 156). He gave Mary a very fair press, with a longer and more appreciative obit than he accorded Elizabeth. It was Camden's translators, and especially Norton, who provided as it were fancy wrapping for this sober text and so helped to promote the myth of Good Queen Bess. To discover what Camden intended, as well as several interesting corrections and amendments for a second edition which never materialized, it is necessary to refer to the scholarly edition by the tory non-juror Thomas Hearne, *Guilielmi Camdeni Annales* (1717).

The eighteenth century qualified without demolishing the whig construction of Elizabeth. David Hume's *History of England* (1759) was for long the standard account of its subject. For all that he professed tory principles, Hume credited Elizabeth with vigour, constancy, magnanimity, penetration, vigilance, prudence. This was not very different from the version of Elizabeth found in the whig historians *par excellence*, Henry Hallam and Thomas Babington Macaulay (especially in his 'Burleigh' essay of 1832). For Macaulay, Elizabeth was more than a great woman. The whiggish, Victorian anatomy of her greatness lay in her identification with the nation and its destiny, her seemingly absolute power in reality dependent on the love and confidence of her subjects. This perception came to full fruition in the twentieth century in the work of A. F. Pollard and of his pupil, J. E. Neale. An altogether subtler variant on whiggish panegyrics is to be found in the great *History of England* by the Roman Catholic priest John Lingard (1819–30). As late as the mid-twentieth century, a good Catholic historian of the sixteenth century was held (by Neale) to be virtually an oxymoron, but Lingard has been called the English Ranke, the first historian to insist on the independence of history from both politics and literature, and he was a pioneer in basing his history scrupulously on the best, and often manuscript, sources. His research was at its deepest in his account of the Tudors. Here again is found an Elizabeth whose government was characterized by profound wisdom, although Lingard anticipated Froude in wondering how far it was *her* government, *her* wisdom. The hidden agenda lurking behind Lingard's scholarly impartiality was to disguise the normal prejudices of Catholic historiography in a book 'which Protestants will read' (E. Jones, *The English Nation: the Great Myth*, 1998, 175).

It was left to one of the great Victorians, the thoroughly protestant Froude, to burst the Elizabethan bubble, anticipating much twentieth-century revisionism. He created the modern study of the Tudors in his twelve volumes on the *History of England from the Fall of Wolsey to the Defeat of the Spanish Armada* (1856–70). He began with conventional admiration for what Alfred, Lord Tennyson, called 'the spacious times of great Elizabeth' ('A dream of fair women', l.7), but long before the end he had fallen out with the queen. He loathed her feminine tortuousness and artifice, to the extent that he came to share what he thought to be the privately held opinion of her privy councillors that 'she had no ability at all worth calling by the name' (Rowse, 'Queen Elizabeth', 638). Froude attributed all the achievements of the reign to Burghley, whose policies Elizabeth had done all she could to frustrate, starve, and mutilate. His Victorian vision of the Tudor age was a vision of emergent greatness, especially on the high seas, but it was a greatness achieved despite Elizabeth.

Towards the end of the century Mandell Creighton, for all his tut-tutting about Elizabeth's dubious morals, achieved a more just and balanced appreciation; which was odd, since he once wrote: 'as for the Tudors, they are awful: I really do not think that anyone ought to read the history of the sixteenth century' (L. Creighton, *Life and Letters of Mandell Creighton*, 2 vols., 1904, 1.288). He reversed Froude's harsh judgement:

> Elizabeth's imperishable claim to greatness lies in her instinctive sympathy with her people … There are many things in Elizabeth which we could have wished otherwise; but she saw what England might become, and nursed it into the knowledge of its power.   (Creighton, 197, 199)

Creighton's respect is implied in the sumptuousness of his first edition, a leather-bound folio, embossed in gold. His account was spare and exacting in its scholarship, compared with the 790 pages of Agnes Strickland's fourth volume of her *Lives of the Queens of England* (1851), which was fulsome and marred by uncritical dependence on the Italian Gregorio Leti's *Historia o vero vita di Elizabetta, regina d'Inghilterra* (1692). Leti invented some of his sources and made things up. Elizabethan historiography in the Rankeian mould came to its dry-as-dust conclusion in Edward P. Cheyney's *A History of England from the Defeat of the Armada to the Death of Elizabeth* (1914–26), continuing and completing Froude's story. The biographical element in Cheyney is reduced to the barest minimum, with no observations on Elizabeth's character or achievements.

When in 1754 Thomas Birch published his *Memoirs of the Reign of Queen Elizabeth from the Year 1581 till her Death*, mainly based on the Bacon manuscripts in Lambeth Palace Library, he was critical of Camden, but suggested that the last thing that anyone wanted was a new history of Elizabeth:

> To relate over again the same series of transactions diversified only in the method and style, and with the addition of a few particular incidents, would be no very agreeable undertaking to the historian, and certainly of little use to the Reader.   (Birch, 1.1–2)

Yet since 1890 there have been little short of a hundred books on Elizabeth of a broadly biographical character, not to speak of substantial histories of the period, like Wallace MacCaffrey's trilogy (1968–92), replacing Froude, and of aspects of the reign, such as Neale's two volumes on *Elizabeth I and her Parliaments* (1953–7), where the queen is given star billing, with all of her speeches quoted in full.

Most biographies have served a short-term purpose and can be mercifully forgotten. Neale's *Queen Elizabeth* (1934) has yet to be bettered, although it is to be regretted that his desire to reach a wide audience meant that there are no references. He continued, indeed brought to an apotheosis, the laudatory tradition which has been persistent ever since the seventeenth century, as did A. L. Rowse in his *The England of Elizabeth* (1950), dedicated 'To the glorious memory of Elizabeth queen of England', and in his many other writings. In writing about the Sealion operation of 1940, which he compared to the Armada campaign, Rowse had coined the phrase 'the new Elizabethans'. The image contributed to the upsurge of interest in Elizabeth I at the accession of Elizabeth II in 1952, and the phrase itself provided the title for Philip Gibbs's book *The New Elizabethans*, published in the new queen's coronation year, which made direct comparisons between past and present achievements. Thus Drake's circumnavigation provided a model for the conquest of Everest by Sir Edmund Hillary and Tenzing Norgay, and for the test flights of Neville Duke. Gibbs looked back to Elizabeth I's reign as 'our flowering time of genius, high adventure, and national spirit', though he was less upbeat about British imperialism, which had begun under the first Elizabeth but seemed unlikely to outlast her namesake (Gibbs, 13). In the later twentieth century, a reactive revisionism began to gather strength: in Carolly Erickson's competent and spirited *The First Elizabeth* (1983), in a debunking collection of essays edited by J. M. Walker, called *Dissing Elizabeth: Negative Representations of Gloriana* (1998), and in another edited by Susan Doran and Thomas Freeman, called *The Myth of Elizabeth* (2003). The subject of Elizabeth has also been enthusiastically gendered, where, among much dross, Helen Hackett's *Virgin Mother, Maiden Queen* (1995) and A. N. McLaren's *Political Culture in the Reign of Elizabeth I* (1999) shine forth.

There have been many fictions woven around Elizabeth's historical character but only one Elizabethan novel has achieved immortality, Sir Walter Scott's *Kenilworth* (1821). The novel is suffused with evocations of the period and many more Victorian readers will have learned a kind of Elizabethan history from Scott than from Strickland, Froude, or Creighton. However, although the book was widely researched, using available printed sources, Scott took artistic licence, played fast and loose with chronology. He conflated events, and invented some purely fictitious characters. *Kenilworth* is superficially about Elizabethan magnificence, but fundamentally about the falseness and venality that Scott discerned beneath the surface. Some passages, especially the account of the tragedy at Cumnor, read like a Gothic novel.

In the hills to the north of Los Angeles, towards Ventura, where the Hopalong Cassidy westerns were shot, there is an annual Renaissance Fayre which attracts tens of thousands of visitors. Among other attractions, an actress convincingly recreates Elizabeth, complete with tall red wig, conducted around the fairground by her courtiers attired in heavy furs, despite the scorching heat. This scene reflects not so much the historical Elizabeth as the Elizabeth of the screen, or rather the many Elizabeths, who have included Sarah Bernhardt, in a film of 1912, Lady Diana Cooper (1923), and Flora Robson cast against Laurence Olivier as Drake in Alexander Korda's *Fire over England* (1937). The Korda film was political, in the anti-fascist context of its time, and Robson's declamation of the Tilbury speech was so effective that it was recycled in wartime propaganda films. The film was denounced by Neale and F. J. C. Hearnshaw as 'second-rate melodrama' and grossly inaccurate, although these academic critics admired Robson's performance (Chapman, 17). In *The Sea Hawk*, a pro-British American film of 1940, Robson appeared as Elizabeth again, co-starring with Errol Flynn as a swashbuckling Elizabethan sea captain. Flynn was less at ease in perhaps the most famous of all Elizabethan films, *The Private Lives of Elizabeth and Essex* (1939), in which Bette Davis played Elizabeth, a role she repeated in *The Virgin Queen* (1955). In 1953 *Young Bess*, based on the Margaret Irwin novel, had Stewart Granger and his wife Jean Simmons re-enacting the scandalous Seymour story: a curious piece with which to celebrate the coronation of Elizabeth II. What all these films were about was the tension, even conflict, between Elizabeth I's private femininity and sexuality and her public, royal role, represented especially by her entrapment in the false little world of the court. How could Elizabeth resist Errol Flynn? Somehow or other she had to. Davis's Elizabeth complains: 'to be a queen is to be less than human'.

Glenda Jackson created the modern portrayal of Elizabeth in *Mary, Queen of Scots* (1971), in which Vanessa Redgrave played Mary, and then in the much-admired television series *Elizabeth R* (1971). In the 1980s and 1990s, any pretence of historical accuracy was gleefully abandoned in the TV series *Blackadder* and deliciously parodied in *Shakespeare in Love* (1998), for which Judi Dench won an Oscar for a few brief minutes on screen as Elizabeth. In the same year Shekhar Kapur won critical acclaim with his radically postmodernist *Elizabeth*, played by Cate Blanchett. As for the historians of the period, *Elizabeth* left them lost for words. It was as if the known facts of the reign, plus many hitherto unknown, were shaken up like pieces of a jigsaw and scattered on the table at random. However, with David Starkey's television series on Elizabeth, released in tandem with a two-part biography (2000), comes a return to what is perhaps more dubious: a set of images on the screen which can easily be mistaken for reality.

Achievement and legacy As the country braced itself to commemorate the fourth centenary of Elizabeth's death in 2003, her posthumous fame was never greater, Gloriana never so glorious. She was for ever on the television screens, thanks only in part to Starkey's skills as publicist and communicator. Publishers were commissioning any plausible author in sight to contribute yet another biography to the heap which already exists, confident that they would not lose their investment. It is not all that easy to explain why this should have been so. Asked why Elizabeth was great, the viewers of those programmes and the readers of those books would probably refer to her charm and affability. People would also have in mind great things that happened in Elizabeth's reign, as always, the defeat of the Armada, as ever, Shakespeare.

At the same time, professional historians have in many cases ceased to be dazzled. Paradoxically, this is one of those phases in Elizabeth's posthumous reputation when her personal stock has fallen in value. This is not because her political skills are unappreciated. On the contrary, an enriched sense of the texture of Elizabethan politics enjoyed by this generation of Elizabethan historians has if anything enhanced admiration of those skills. It is true that her instinctive reluctance to take decisive and creative action has never been so emphasized. Not even Froude called Elizabeth a do-nothing queen, which his successors have dared to do, but some biographers have decided that often it was the wisest course to do nothing, or to put off until tomorrow what need not be done today. Elizabeth has been praised not as the great achiever but as the consummate survivor, although others would say that that was not something that she could ever guarantee, and that throughout her long reign she gambled with the lives and fortunes of her subjects, above all through failing to make arrangements for their future government. However, a wave of revisionism in recent studies of the English revolution and civil wars of the mid-seventeenth century has meant that Elizabeth is no longer held culpably responsible for those in many ways calamitous events, which it is now fashionable to account for by short-term and contingent circumstances and happenings.

What has diminished Elizabeth's personal monarchy in the perception of the most recent and most academically minded of her historians is a growing realization of the limited extent to which it was in fact personal. The Elizabethan political culture was a complex organism, ceaselessly interactive at and between the many levels of society. That ancient formulation 'self-government at the king's command' proves to be a very true summary of how things were managed in England in the later sixteenth century. Elizabeth's subjects were also citizens of a commonwealth, ultra-conscious in the unstable and dangerous conditions of the time, the second phase of the Reformation, an age of religious wars and assassinations, that they were as much responsible for the safety of the state as their unmarried and heirless monarch. Elizabethan England was a monarchical republic; which is not to say that Sir Thomas Smith was wrong when he wrote in *De republica Anglorum* (1583) that his sovereign was far more absolute than any doge of Venice.

PATRICK COLLINSON

Sources PRIMARY SOURCES *Sir Robert Naunton, Fragmenta regalia*, ed. E. Arber (1870) · J. Arnold, ed., *Queen Elizabeth's wardrobe unlock'd: the inventories of the wardrobe of robes prepared in July 1600* (1988) · [J. Aylmer], *An harborowe for faithfull and trewe subjectes* [1559] · T. Bentley, *The monument of matrones* (1582) · *John Stubbs's 'gaping gulf' with letters and other relevant documents*, ed. L. E. Berry (1968) · T. Birch, *Memoirs of the reign of Queen Elizabeth, from the year 1581 till her death, from the original papers of Anthony Bacon*, 2 vols. (1754) · *The poems of Queen Elizabeth I*, ed. L. Bradner (Providence, Rhode Island, 1964) · BL, Lansdowne MSS · BL, Add. MS 48027 · CSP dom., 1547–1603 · CSP for., 1553–95 · CSP Ire., 1558–1603 · M. A. S. Hume, ed., *Calendar of letters and state papers relating to English affairs, preserved principally in the archives of Simancas*, 4 vols., PRO (1892–9) · CUL, MS Ee.3.56 · 'William Latymer's chronickle of Anne Bulleyne', ed. M. Dowling, *Camden miscellany, XXX*, CS, 4th ser., 39 (1990) · H. Ellis, ed., *Original letters illustrative of English history*, 2nd ser., 2–3 (1827); 3rd ser., 3 (1846) · T. Wilson, 'The state of England anno dom. 1600', ed. F. J. Fisher, *Camden miscellany, XVI*, CS, 3rd ser., 52 (1936) · Folger, MS V.b.303, pp. 183–6 · J. Foxe, *Actes and monuments*, 4th edn, 2 vols. (1583) · H. Gee, *The Elizabethan prayer-book and ornaments* (1902) · J. M. Green, 'Queen Elizabeth I's Latin reply to the Polish ambassador', *Sixteenth-Century Journal*, 31 (2000), 987–1008 · *The works of Edmund Spenser*, ed. E. Greenlaw and others, 11 vols. (1932–57) · *Henry VIII, or, All is true, by William Shakespeare and John Fletcher*, ed. J. L. Halio, The Oxford Shakespeare (1999) · J. Harington, *Nugae antiquae*, 2 vols. (1769–75); 2nd edn in 3 vols., ed. H. Harington (1779) · *Letters of Queen Elizabeth*, ed. G. B. Harrison (1935) · *De Maisse: a journal*, ed. G. B. Harrison and R. A. Jones (1931) · T. E. Hartley, ed., *Proceedings in the parliaments of Elizabeth I*, 3 vols. (1981–95) · *Calendar of the manuscripts of the most hon. the marquis of Salisbury*, 24 vols., HMC, 9 (1883–1976) · Hunt. L., MSS HA (Hastings MSS) · Baron Kervyn de Lettenhove [J. M. B. C. Kervyn de Lettenhove] and L. Gilliodts-van Severen, eds., *Relations politiques des Pays-Bas et de l'Angleterre sous le règne de Philippe II*, 11 vols. (Brussels, 1882–1900) · J. Knox, *The first blast of the trumpet against the monstrous regiment of women* (Geneva, 1558) · *Lettres, instructions et mémoires de Marie Stuart, reine d'Écosse*, ed. A. Labanoff, 7 vols. (1844) · LPL, MS 3197 · *LP Henry VIII*, vols. 6–21, addenda · E. Lodge, *Illustrations of British history*, 3 vols. (1791); 2nd edn (1838) · *Elizabeth I: collected works*, ed. L. S. Marcus, J. Mueller, and M. B. Rose (2000) · *The memoirs of Robert Carey*, ed. F. H. Mares (1972) · J. E. Neale, ed., 'Sir Nicholas Throckmorton's advice to Queen Elizabeth on her accession to the throne', *EngHR*, 65 (1950), 91–8 · J. Nichols, *The progresses and public processions of Queen Elizabeth*, new edn, 3 vols. (1823) · J. M. Osborn, ed., *The quenes maiesties passage through the citie of London to Westminster the day before her coronacion* (New Haven, 1960) · C. Pemberton, ed., *Queen Elizabeth's Englishings*, EETS, old ser., 113 (1899) · state papers domestic, Elizabeth I, PRO, SP 12 · state papers domestic, addenda, PRO, SP 15 · W. B. Rye, ed., *England as seen by foreigners in the days of Elizabeth and James I* (1865) · *The diary of John Manningham*, ed. R. P. Sorlien (Hanover, New Hampshire, 1976) · *The state papers and letters of Sir Ralph Sadler*, ed. A. Clifford, 2 vols. (1809) · L. J. Trinterud, ed., *Elizabethan puritanism* (1971) · R. Vaughan, *Most approved, and experienced waterworkes* (1610) · T. Wright, *Queen Elizabeth and her times*, 2 vols. (1838)

SECONDARY SOURCES S. Adams, 'Faction, clientage and party: English politics, 1550–1603', *History Today*, 32 (1982), 33–9 · S. Alford, *The early Elizabethan polity: William Cecil and the British succession crisis, 1558–1569* (1998) · S. T. Bindoff and others, eds., *Elizabethan government and society: essays presented to Sir John Neale* (1961) · J. Bossy, *The English Catholic community, 1570–1850* (1975) · C. Brady, *The chief governors: the rise and fall of reform government in Tudor Ireland, 1536–1588* (1994) · S. Brigden, *New worlds, lost worlds: the rule of the Tudors, 1485–1603* (2000) · R. Bud, 'Penicillin and the new Elizabethans', *British Journal for the History of Science*, 31 (1998), 305–33 · W. Camden, *The historie of the most renowned and victorious princesse Elizabeth*, trans. R. N. [R. Norton] (1630) · N. P. Canny, *The Elizabethan conquest of Ireland: a pattern established, 1565–76* (1976) · N. P. Canny, *Making Ireland British, 1580–1650* (2001) · J. Chapman, 'Elizabeth in film', *Bulletin of the Society for Renaissance Studies*, 17 (1999) · E. P. Cheyney, *A history of England from the defeat of the Armada to the death of Elizabeth*, 2 vols. (1914–26) · P. Collinson, *The Elizabethan puritan movement* (1967) · P. Collinson, *Godly people: essays on English protestantism and puritanism* (1983) · P. Collinson, *Elizabethan essays* (1994) · P. Collinson, 'The Elizabethan exclusion crisis and the Elizabethan polity: the Raleigh Lecture 1993', *PBA*, 84 (1994) · P. Collinson, 'One of us? William Camden and the making of history', *TRHS*, 6th ser., 8 (1998), 139–63 · M. Creighton, *Queen Elizabeth* (1896) · S. Doran, *Monarchy and matrimony: the courtships of Elizabeth I* (1996) · S. Doran, 'Elizabeth I's religion: the evidence of her letters', *Journal of Ecclesiastical History*, 51 (2000), 699–720 · S. Doran and T. Freeman, eds., *The myth of Elizabeth* (2003) · G. Elton, *Studies in Tudor and Stuart politics and government*, 4 vols. (1974–92) · C. Erickson, *The first Elizabeth* (1983) · C. Falls, *Elizabeth's Irish wars* (1950) · J. A. Froude, *History of England*, 12 vols. (1856–70) · J. Guy, ed., *The reign of Elizabeth I: court and culture in the last decade* (1995) · H. Hackett, *Virgin mother, maiden queen: Elizabeth I and the cult of the Virgin Mary* (1995) · C. Haigh, ed., *The reign of Elizabeth I* (1984) · C. Haigh, *Elizabeth I* (1988) · P. E. J. Hammer, *The polarization of Elizabethan politics: the political career of Robert Devereux, second earl of Essex, 1585–1597* (1999) · HoP, *Commons, 1558–1603* · *Guilielmi Camdeni Annales rerum Anglicarum et Hibernicarum regnante Elizabetha*, ed. T. Hearnius [T. Hearne], 3 vols. (1717) · N. L. Jones, *Faith by statute: parliament and the settlement of religion, 1559* (1982) · H. Kamen, *Philip of Spain* (1997) · M. Levine, *The early Elizabethan succession question, 1558–1568* (Stanford, Conn., 1966) · W. T. MacCaffrey, *The shaping of the Elizabethan regime: Elizabethan politics, 1558–1572* (1968) · W. Camden, *The history of the most renowned and victorious Princess Elizabeth*, [new edn], ed. W. T. MacCaffrey (1970) · W. T. MacCaffrey, *Queen Elizabeth and the making of policy, 1572–1588* (1981) · W. T. MacCaffrey, *Elizabeth I: war and politics, 1588–1603* (1992) · W. MacCaffrey, *Elizabeth I* (1993) · W. MacCaffrey, 'The New-haven expedition, 1562–1563', *HJ*, 40 (1997), 1–21 · D. MacCulloch, *Tudor church militant: Edward VI and the protestant Reformation* (1999) · P. E. McCullough, *Sermons at court: politics and religion in Elizabethan and Jacobean preaching* (1998) [incl. CD-ROM] · A. N. McLaren, *Political culture in the reign of Elizabeth I: queen and commonwealth, 1558–1585* (1999) · G. Mattingly, *The defeat of the Spanish Armada* (1959) · J. E. Neale, *Queen Elizabeth* (1934) · J. E. Neale, *Elizabeth I and her parliaments, 1559–1581* (1953) · J. E. Neale, *Elizabeth I and her parliaments,*

1584–1601 (1957) • J. E. Neale, *Elizabethan essays* (1958) • A. E. Newdegate, *Gossip from a muniment room* (1897) • N. H. Nicolas, *Life of William Davison* (1823) • H. Nicolas, *Memoirs of the life and times of Sir Christopher Hatton* (1847) • C. Read, *Mr Secretary Walsingham and the policy of Queen Elizabeth*, 3 vols. (1925) • C. Read, *Mr Secretary Cecil and Queen Elizabeth* (1955) • C. Read, *Lord Burghley and Queen Elizabeth* (1960) • A. L. Rowse, *The England of Elizabeth* (1950) • A. L. Rowse, 'Queen Elizabeth and the historians', *History Today*, 3 (1953), 630–41 • D. Starkey, *Elizabeth: apprenticeship* (2000) • R. C. Strong, *Portraits of Queen Elizabeth I* (1963) • R. Strong, *The cult of Elizabeth: Elizabethan portraiture and pageantry* (1977) • J. M. Walker, ed., *Dissing Elizabeth: negative representations of Gloriana* (1998) • R. B. Wernham, *Before the Armada: the growth of English foreign policy, 1485–1588* (1966) • R. B. Wernham, *After the Armada: Elizabethan England and the struggle for western Europe, 1588–1595* (1984) • R. B. Wernham, *The return of the armadas: the last years of the Elizabethan war against Spain, 1595–1603* (1994) • L. Wiesener, *La jeunesse d'Elizabeth d'Angleterre* (Paris, 1878); C. M. Yonge, trans., *The early life of Elizabeth of England, 1533–1558*, 2 vols. (1879) • E. C. Wilson, *England's Eliza* (1966) • F. A. Yates, *Astraea: the imperial theme in the sixteenth century* (1975)

Archives BL, autograph, MS Royal 7.D.X • BL, rolls of New Year's gifts, Add. MSS 4827, 8159, 9972; Egerton MS 3052; Harley roll v 18; Lansdowne roll 17 • BL, Sloane MSS, letters and papers • Blackburn Central Library, letter-book of diplomatic letters, incl. letters from Sir Francis Walsingham • Bodl. Oxf., autograph, MS Cherry 36 • CUL, corresp. and official papers • GL, register of letters • Hatfield House, Hertfordshire, autograph, Cecil papers 147 • Hatfield House, Hertfordshire, letters and papers • Inner Temple, London, letters and papers • LPL, letters • LPL, letters patent for disposal of monastic lands • NRA, priv. coll., letters • NYPL, transcripts of papers and letters • PRO, state papers domestic, Elizabeth, SP 12 • PRO, state papers foreign, Elizabeth, SP 15 • S. Antiquaries, Lond., papers, incl. list of offices and fees and New Year's gift rolls | Arundel Castle, West Sussex, corresp. with earls of Shrewsbury • BL, letters to James VI of Scotland, Add. MS 23240 • Carl H. Pforzheimer Library, letters to Valentine Dale • Coventry Archives, letters to mayor and aldermen of Coventry • Hunt. L., letters to earls of Huntingdon • NA Scot., letters to dukes of Hamilton • NL Scot., corresp. relating to Mary, queen of Scots • PRO, Elizabeth's translations of Boethius, Horace, Plutarch • TCD, letters to the Lord Deputy, Sir Henry Sidney • Trustees of the Berkeley Castle Muniments, letters to Sir George Carey

Likenesses oils, *c.*1542–1547, Royal Collection • group portrait, oils, before 1547 (family of Henry VIII), Royal Collection • oils, *c.*1558–1560, NPG • oils, *c.*1559 (coronation portrait), Warwick Castle; copy, NPG • J. le Boucq, drawing, 1560–99 (after a type of *c.*1560) • oils, *c.*1563, Barrington Park, south Gloucestershire • S. van Herwijck, lead medal, 1565, NPG • attrib. H. Eworth, group portrait, oils, 1569 (*Elizabeth and the three goddesses*), Royal Collection • marble bust, *c.*1570–1575, NPG • attrib. N. Hilliard, oils, 1570–79 (Pelican portrait), Walker Art Gallery, Liverpool • N. Hilliard, miniature, 1572, NPG • F. Zuccaro, drawing, 1575, BM • oils, after 1575 (Raveningham portrait), Yale U. Art Gallery • oils, after 1575 (Penshurst portrait), Penshurst Place, Kent • oils on panel, *c.*1575 (Darnley portrait), NPG [*see illus.*] • attrib. N. Hilliard, oils, *c.*1575–1580 (Phoenix portrait), NPG • oils, *c.*1575–1580 (Garter portrait), Royal Collection; version, NPG • N. Hilliard, miniature, *c.*1580, Berkeley Castle, Gloucestershire • Q. Metsys the younger, oils, *c.*1580 (Siena Sieve portrait), Pinacoteca di Siena, Italy • N. Hilliard, miniature, *c.*1580–1584, Royal Collection • oils, *c.*1580–1585 (Hampton Court portrait), Royal Collection • attrib. W. Segar, oils, 1585 (Ermine portrait), Hatfield House, Hertfordshire • oils, *c.*1585–1590, Arbury Hall, Warwickshire; version, attrib. J. Bettes junior, NPG • attrib. W. Kerwin, statue, *c.*1586, St Dunstan-in-the-West, London • attrib. G. Gower, oils, after 1588 (Armada portrait), Woburn Abbey, Bedfordshire; version, NPG • N. Hilliard, miniature, *c.*1588, Buccleuch estates, Selkirk • N. Hilliard, miniature, after 1590, V&A • oils, *c.*1590–1600 (Brocket portrait), St John Cam. • marble bust, *c.*1590–1610, NPG • M. Gheeraerts junior, oils, *c.*1592 (Ditchley portrait), NPG • oils, *c.*1594–1595, Buccleuch estates, Selkirk • oils, after 1595 (Weavers' Company portrait), Guildhall Art Gallery, London • statue, 1597, Trinity Cam. • attrib. M. Gheeraerts, *c.*1600 (Rainbow portrait), Hatfield House, Hertfordshire • attrib. R. Peake senior, group portrait, oils, *c.*1600 (*Procession to Blackfriars*), Sherborne Castle, Dorset • line engraving, pubd *c.*1600 (after I. Oliver, *c.*1588), NG Ire. • attrib. C. Anthony, gold medal, 1601, NPG • M. Colte, marble tomb effigy, *c.*1605–1607, Westminster Abbey; electrotype, NPG • R. Biagio, oils (after M. Gheeraerts junior), Audley End House, Essex • M. Gheeraerts senior, group portrait, etching (*Procession of Garter knights, 1576*), BM • attrib. F. Hogenberg, engraving, repro. in *Bishops' Bible* (1568) • I. Oliver, miniature (unfinished), V&A • C. Saxton, engraving, repro. in *Atlas of England and Wales* (1579) • C. Turner, etching and aquatint (after drawing, Royal Collection), NG Ire. • engravings, BM, NPG • medals and coins, BM • oils, NG Ire. • oils on panel (other versions of Darnley portrait), NPG, NMM • seals, BM

Elizabeth of Lancaster (1364?–1425), noblewoman, was the younger daughter of *Edward III's son *John of Gaunt, duke of Lancaster (1340–1399), and of *Blanche of Lancaster (1346?–1368) [*see under* John of Gaunt]. In September 1372 she and her sister *Philippa and younger brother Henry (the future *Henry IV) were sharing a household, and in 1376 the sisters' governess was their father's mistress, Katherine Swynford [*see* Katherine, duchess of Lancaster]. In 1380 Gaunt espoused Elizabeth to John Hastings (1372–1389), heir to the earldom of Pembroke, aged eight, giving her as a wedding present a ring with a ruby inset, and the couple £100 p.a. for the maintenance of their household. She was brought to the royal court so that she could learn courtly manners and practices, and there, probably in 1385, Sir John *Holland (*c.*1352–1400), *Richard II's half-brother, fell violently in love with her, and wooed her day and night until she succumbed. Elizabeth became pregnant and repudiated her betrothal to Hastings; with her father's approval, she married Holland at or near Plymouth on 24 June 1386. Early in July the couple embarked on Gaunt's expedition to claim the throne of Castile, Holland being constable of the army. In the spring of 1387 she accompanied the army on a brief but gruelling campaign in León: just before the retreat into Portugal, accompanied by her husband, she travelled through Castile (under safe conduct from the enemy) on the way to Gascony and England.

Elevated in her husband's right as countess of Huntingdon (1388) and duchess of Exeter (1397), Elizabeth cut a dashing figure at court. Mother of four surviving children—Richard (d. 1400), John *Holland, first duke of Exeter (1395–1447), Edward, and Constance (d. 1437)—she won the prize as the best dancer at the feast marking the prorogation of parliament at the end of September 1397. However, the banishment of her brother Henry Bolingbroke in 1398, and his usurpation of the throne in 1399, placed strains on her marriage. When she took a tearful leave of her husband in January 1400, as he set out to attempt Henry IV's overthrow and Richard's restoration, Holland reproached her bitterly for having, despite his own gloom, rejoiced and made merry when Henry had arrested Richard and himself, and when Henry was crowned.

Elizabeth, fearful for what might happen to her husband and brother, remained silent. She was to be speedily bereaved, when the fleeing Holland was beheaded by Essex peasants. Henry soon granted her his head, adorning London Bridge, and £666 13s. 4d. for her maintenance, to compensate for Holland's forfeiture. That summer Elizabeth married Sir John *Cornwall (d. 1443), of Burford, Shropshire, a vigorous and applauded practitioner of chivalry who later became Lord Fanhope. The marriage probably took place soon after Cornwall distinguished himself in jousts in Henry IV's presence at York at the end of June. The marriage was rumoured to have been made without Henry's knowledge, but the couple soon gained his favour, and had considerable success in retaining and recovering parts of the impressive comital estate that Holland had recently built up, notably in Devon. In May 1401 they received a large grant of Holland properties, in part replacement of Elizabeth's annuity, including Dartington Hall, Holland's splendid new house, and in 1404 the couple were granted her dower. In 1405 a son, John (d. 1421), was born. When Elizabeth died, on 24 November 1425, she was not buried with her husband. Her tomb, with its fine alabaster effigy, displaying her as tall and slender featured, is in Burford parish church, Shropshire.

ANTHONY GOODMAN

Sources GEC, *Peerage*, 5.195–200, 253–4 • *Chancery records* • *CIPM*, vols. 18–20 • *Calendar of inquisitions miscellaneous (chancery)*, PRO, 7 (1968) • A. Emery, *Dartington Hall* (1970) • L. C. Hector and B. F. Harvey, eds. and trans., *The Westminster chronicle, 1381–1394*, OMT (1982) • *RotP*, vol. 3 • *John of Gaunt's register*, ed. S. Armitage-Smith, 2 vols., CS, 3rd ser., 20–21 (1911) • *John of Gaunt's register, 1379–1383*, ed. E. C. Lodge and R. Somerville, 2 vols., CS, 3rd ser., 56–7 (1937) • B. Williams, ed., *Chronicque de la traïson et mort de Richart Deux, roy Dengleterre*, EHS, 9 (1846) • J. L. Kirby, *Henry IV of England* (1970)
Likenesses tomb effigy, Burford parish church, Shropshire

Elizalde, Federico [Fred] (**1907–1979**), band leader and composer, was born in Manila in the Philippines on 12 December 1907, the son of wealthy Navarro-Andalusian Spanish parents. Showing early musical talents, he was sent at the age of seven to the Madrid Royal Conservatory, where he studied under Trago and Perez Casas and won first prize in pianoforte playing when he was fourteen. In 1921 he went to England to study for two years at St Joseph's College, London. In 1923 he went, along with his brother Manuel, to California to read law at Stanford University. He was also able to study musical composition with Ernest Bloch; this convinced him of his musical vocation, and he left Stanford in 1926. He had already developed a keen interest in jazz and dance music and led the Stanford University Band for a season at the Biltmore Hotel in Los Angeles, as well as making a few recordings with his own Cinderella Roof Orchestra and giving some piano recitals.

These musical inclinations were not approved of by Elizalde's family, and in the autumn of 1926 he was sent to Cambridge University in England, where his brother Manuell was also studying and where, it was hoped, more serious interests would prevail. However, the Elizaldes soon found a few students, mainly members of the Footlights Club, who shared their jazz interests (these included

Maurice Allom, later well known as a cricketer), and they formed a group which they called the Quinquaginta Club Ramblers. They attracted sufficient attention for them to be asked to record—in March 1927 for the Brunswick label (as Fred Elizalde's 'Varsity' Band), and in June for HMV (as Fred Elizalde and his Cambridge Undergraduates). Elizalde was asked to write for *Melody Maker* and, in London, continued to record for Brunswick with a band that mainly used members of the Ambrose orchestra. His arrangements of such standards as 'Stomp your Feet' and 'Clarinet Marmalade' (both recorded for HMV and Brunswick in 1927) were considered very advanced by the commercial standards of the time. Among other works, he wrote a jazz suite called 'Heart of a Nigger' (a title later amended with only slightly less impropriety to 'Heart of a Coon'), which was performed by the Ambrose orchestra at the London Palladium in May 1927 with accompanying ballet and décor devised by Oliver Messel; but it was so experimental that he was not able to get it recorded until June 1932. Various piano pieces that he recorded in 1927 and 1933 were also of great originality, as was his symphonic poem *Bataclan*, which he performed with his own band in 1929.

At the end of 1927 Elizalde was asked to form a band to play at the Savoy Hotel. His brother (known as Lizz in music circles) went to the USA to recruit a few American musicians—including Chelsea Quealey, Fud Livingston, and Adrian and Arthur Rollini—to play alongside such British regulars as Jack Jackson and Harry Hayes. The band started its engagement at the Savoy in December 1927 opposite Reginald Batten's Savoy Orpheans and, although it received good reviews in the press, was generally criticized by the public as being too involved rhythmically, tuneless, and disinclined to play waltzes. Their recordings of 1928 included such standards as 'The Darktown Strutter's Ball', 'Somebody Stole my Girl', and 'Singapore Sorrows' (1929). The management insisted on a more popular approach and the addition of violins. In 1928 Elizalde obtained the services of the singer Al Bowlly, who came from Germany to join the band and made a number of recordings, including 'Just Imagine' and 'If I had You', with it. The proportion of dance music to jazz and the band's general style, combining 'white jazz' and 'symphonic jazz', were a reflection of the Paul Whiteman repertory in America. During July 1928 the band had a six-week engagement in Paris at the Restaurant des Ambassadeurs. On returning to the Savoy, and in spite of all the previous criticism, Elizalde was asked to provide both the Savoy bands, and in November he came top of the *Melody Maker* polls, outdoing such names as Ambrose and Jack Payne. They appeared in a film entitled *Christmas Fantasy* and in April 1929 appeared at the London Palladium with Al Bowlly as vocalist. By July 1929 the Savoy had endured the very independent Elizalde for long enough and terminated his contract. He maintained his band for a while but, after a disastrous tour in Scotland, disbanded it, and by the end of the year was leading a pit orchestra for *The Intimate Revue* at the Duchess Theatre, for which he also wrote the music.

By now Elizalde had achieved family approval for his musical ambitions, and in 1930 he returned to his homeland to become conductor of the Manila Symphony Orchestra, a duty interrupted by work in Biarritz, Paris, and Madrid and a world conducting tour in 1931. He made a return visit to England in 1932 to record 'Heart of a Nigger' and other items, including fifteen piano solos, for Decca. In France he became associated with Maurice Ravel and Darius Milhaud, conducting several premières of the latter's music. In Spain he became a close friend of Manuel de Falla, with whom he studied composition; he became a leading interpreter of Falla's works, conducting the harpsichord concerto with Falla himself at the keyboard. He wrote three symphonic poems, *Jota*, *Spiritual*, and *Moods*, and an opera, *La pajera punta*, consisting of settings of poems by Federico Garcia Lorca; and on 23 April 1936 he conducted his *Sinfonia concertante* at the festival of the International Society for Contemporary Music in Barcelona.

At the outbreak of the Spanish Civil War in July 1936 Elizalde joined the Basque regiment under General Franco, serving until 1939 when he was invalided home to Manila. He returned to France and was forced to remain on his estate near Bayonne throughout the German occupation. He made good use of the time to write an opera, *Paul Gauguin*, finished in 1943 and eventually performed on radio in 1948 to celebrate the centenary of the artist's birth. His early music, which had been strongly influenced by Falla, was distinctly Spanish and of a balletic nature; later he moved toward neo-classicism, his works including a violin concerto (1943), taken up by the celebrated violinist Ginette Neveu and recorded by the London Symphony Orchestra in 1950; a piano concerto, first performed in Paris by Leopold Querol (afterwards by the composer himself in Paris and at the Albert Hall in London); and chamber music. In 1948 he returned to Manila, where he became president of the Manila Broadcasting Corporation, continued his conducting duties, and founded the Manila Little Symphony Orchestra. He continued to travel to Europe and the USA as a conductor and composer and conducted the London Symphony Orchestra at the Royal Festival Hall during the Festival of Britain. He worked as a guest conductor in Japan, but became increasingly involved in the family's business interests in Manila and retired from the musical scene in 1974. In addition to possessing musical talents he was a marksman of international standard and led the Philippine shooting team in several competitions, winning four gold medals in the 1954 Asiad. He died in Manila on 16 January 1979.

PETER GAMMOND

Sources J. Chilton, *Who's who of British jazz* (1997) · A. Rollini, *Thirty years with the big bands* (1987) · P. Gammond, *The Oxford companion to popular music* (1991) · *New Grove*, 2nd edn

Elkan, Benno (1877–1960), sculptor, was born on 2 December 1877 at Dortmund, Westphalia, Germany, the son of Jewish parents, Salomon Elkan and his wife, Rosa Oppenheimer. He was educated at the Dortmund Gymnasium, the Château du Rosey, Rolle, Lausanne, the Munich Royal Academy, and at Karlsruhe Academy. Moving to Paris at the age of twenty-eight he came under the influence of the sculptors Auguste Rodin and Paul Bartholomé, receiving advice from the latter. By 1907 he had moved to Rome where that year he married Hedwig Einstein (d. 1959), with whom he had a son and a daughter. A highly accomplished craftsman, Elkan carved stone and marble, but chose to work principally in bronze and precious metals. His elaborate over-lifesize figure of Persephone—carved in white and coloured marbles with many semi-precious stones, including jade, jasper, onyx, and lapis lazuli—caused a sensation when exhibited in Rome in 1908. He returned to Germany in 1911 to live at Alsbach, making plaques and statuettes of allegorical subjects, and medals and portrait busts of contemporary figures. His granite figure of a sorrowing woman, completed in 1913–14 and exhibited in Cologne with the prophetic title *Germany Mourns her Heroes*, was erected in Frankfurt as a memorial to the 1914–18 war. This and several of Elkan's other monuments were removed or destroyed by the Nazis, though the Frankfurt memorial was restored in 1946.

Arriving in England as a refugee in 1933, Elkan lived in London (and Oxford during the war), exhibiting widely in Britain and on the continent, with regular showings at the Royal Academy, London, from 1934 to 1956, and a one-man show at Knoedler's Galleries in New York in 1936. He specialized in bronze portrait busts and medals, attracting the patronage of such eminent public figures as Prince Edward of Kent, Lord Beveridge, Lord Keynes, Sir Winston Churchill, Samuel Courtauld, Yehudi Menuhin, John D. Rockefeller, and Arturo Toscanini. The most distinctive aspect of Elkan's art was his large bronze candelabra, intricately scrolled and foliated like stylized espalier trees, with biblical or allegorical figures disposed about their entwining branches. The most impressive are the pair in Westminster Abbey known as *The Great Biblical Candelabra*, each 7 feet high and 6 feet wide, carrying thirty-three candles to illuminate some thirty figures. Elkan made similar candelabra for Buckfast Abbey in Devon, King's College chapel in Cambridge, New College chapel in Oxford, and a huge menorah for the Knesset in Jerusalem. Yet some of Elkan's most ambitious schemes remained unrealized, despite his attempts during the war to attract the support of Sir Kenneth Clark and the War Artists' Advisory Committee. The committee declined his offer to teach 'a number of pupils the art of the medal'—described in Elkan's imperfect English as 'the finest expression within the smallest extent in the plastic arts'—and his proposal to make a series of 'War Medals' commemorating 'leading personalities in all walks of life … military and civilian alike' and 'great events, happy and unlucky ones, as … done in old times'. Elkan also confided in Clark his plans for a 'Great Design', which he had 'kept secret for years' and which allowed him 'no rest and no peace' (Elkan, MS letter to Sir K. Clark, 11 Jan 1943, Tate collection, archives, 8812.1.1.20). The project which haunted him was conceived in the 1920s as an official national German war memorial—a vast monolithic column decorated with apocalyptic scenes of war—but this had been terminated by the Nazis.

Despite such setbacks Elkan completed many commissioned works, including a statue of Sir Walter Ralegh for a tobacco factory on Commercial Street in the City of London, a gold medal for Great Ormond Street Children's Hospital, a silver-gilt fighting cock at the Arsenal Football Club, a lead plaque on the Rudyard Kipling memorial building at Windsor, an orang-utan group at Edinburgh Zoo and Abbot Vonier's tomb at Buckfast Abbey. In addition, his work has been acquired by many German museums, as well as museums in Copenhagen, The Hague, and Rome. Apart from his work as a sculptor, Elkan was a printmaker, draughtsman, and illustrator of books, such as *Spain Seen by an Artist* (1926). Clough Williams-Ellis recalled that Elkan possessed 'an earnest forcefulness, a prophetic intensity which, with his humane sincerity, deep voice, and piercing eyes, made up an impressive personality not easily forgotten'. Elkan was naturalized in 1946, appointed OBE in 1957, and died at Central Middlesex Hospital, London, on 10 January 1960.

CLOUGH WILLIAMS-ELLIS, *rev.* ROBERT BURSTOW

Sources *The Times* (12 Jan 1960) · 'Biblical candlesticks', *Country Life*, 84 (26 Nov 1938), 538–9 · B. Elkan to Sir Kenneth Clark, 11 Jan 1943, Tate collection, 8812.1.1.20 · personal knowledge (1971) · A. Jarman and others, eds., *Royal Academy exhibitors, 1905–1970: a dictionary of artists and their work in the summer exhibitions of the Royal Academy of Arts*, 3 (1978), 14–15 · *Who's who in art* (1948), 68–9 · *CGPLA Eng. & Wales* (1960) · A. Vogt, *Den Lebenden zur Mahnung: Denkmäler und Gedenkstätten zur Traditionspflege und historischen Identität vom 19. Jahrhundert bis zur Gegenwart* (1993) · B. Elkan, 'Persephone—an over-lifesize figure in coloured stones: a sculptor's conception and manifestation', *Apollo*, 49 (June 1949), 146–8 · K. R. Towndrow, 'English portraits by Benno Elkan', *Apollo*, 50 (Nov 1949), 127
Archives Tate collection, corresp. with Kenneth Clark
Likenesses photograph, repro. in *The Times* · photograph, repro. in Towndrow, 'English portraits by Benno Elkan', 127
Wealth at death £12,580 3s. 3d.: administration with will, 27 June 1960, *CGPLA Eng. & Wales*

Elkington, George Richards (1801–1865), electroplate manufacturer, was born on 17 October 1801 at St Paul's Square, Birmingham, the son of James Elkington, gilt-toy and spectacle maker, and his wife, Lydia, *née* Richards. He was apprenticed to his uncles, Josiah Richards and George Richards, and eventually became a partner in their silversmithing and gilt-toy business. On 14 April 1825 he married Mary Augusta Balleny; they raised five sons and one daughter.

About 1824 Elkington inherited his father's manufactory at St Paul's Square, and in 1834 he filed a patent for bifocal spectacles. Until 1840 he continued in partnership with his uncle George under the name of Richards and Elkington, toy manufacturers, of Holborn, London, and St Paul's Square, Birmingham. Elkington had other concurrent partnerships: one with Joseph Taylor, a Birmingham gilt-toy maker, was dissolved in 1839; another with his cousin, **Henry Elkington** (1810–1852), began about 1836 and eventually became the firm of Elkington & Co. Henry was born in Stretton-on-Dunsmore, Princethorpe, Warwickshire, the son of John Elkington and his wife, Mary Russell. He was apprenticed to his uncle James, and on 25 May 1836 he married Emma, George Elkington's sister.

Their only son died young. After Henry entered into partnership with his cousin, the two men began experimenting with new ways of gilding base metals.

Up to 1840, silver-plated wares (known as Sheffield plate) were made by rolling or soldering thin sheets of silver upon copper. In 1836 and 1837, the Elkingtons had taken out patents for 'mercurial gilding', and by 1840—when they came to an agreement with John Wright (1808–1844), a Birmingham surgeon, who had found in cyanide of potassium the best solution for electroplating—they were ready to launch the electroplate industry in Britain. A factory was built in the late 1830s at Newhall Street in Birmingham. In 1842 further capital was injected into the business by Josiah Mason (1795–1881), the successful Birmingham manufacturer of steel pen nibs, and the firm was consequently renamed Elkington, Mason & Co. The firm originally hoped to rely on the activities of licensees to market electroplate, but Elkington's high royalties and the conservatism of the silver plate trade meant that progress was slow. Sheffield firms tried to resist Elkington's electroplating process; one—Walker and Hall—even claimed it as its own invention. However, Elkington's patents could not be breached and gradually a number of firms began using his process under licence. These included Christofle and Cie in France, William Carr Hutton in Sheffield, and Edward Barnard & Sons in London. In the 1840s, Elkington's agreement with Benjamin Smith, a London silversmith, allowed the Birmingham firm to open workshops and showrooms in London, and by 1851 another Elkington factory for cutlery had been opened at Brearley Street in Birmingham. Elkington, with Mason, established a large copper-smelting works at Pembrey, Carmarthenshire, in south Wales, to work a patent taken out by Alexander Parkes (1813–1891), the chemist and metallurgist. Henry Elkington died of heart disease on 26 October 1852 at 23 Summer Hill Terrace, Birmingham, having been influential in the artistic side of the business. He was buried at Northfield, Birmingham.

In 1861, the partnership between G. R. Elkington and Josiah Mason was terminated, the firm being renamed Elkington & Co. By the mid-1860s Elkington's employed nearly a thousand workers and was firmly established as the leading silver- and electroplate company in the world. According to the firm's historian, George Elkington's 'industry and capacity for work must have been untiring. He had half a dozen irons in the fire, any one of which might have monopolised the watchfulness of an ordinary man' (Leader, 'History of Elkington & Co.', 2).

George Elkington's whole life was spent in Birmingham. He was a governor of King Edward VI's Grammar School and was made a borough magistrate in 1856. However, he was unostentatious and retiring in his habits. He died of a stroke at his residence, Pool Park, Llanfwrog, Ruthin, Denbighshire, on 22 September 1865. The business was continued by his sons, Frederick (*d.* 1905), James Balleny (*d.* 1907), Alfred John (*d.* 1910), Howard (*d.* 1899), and Hyla (*d.* 1901).

W. J. HARRISON, *rev.* GEOFFREY TWEEDALE

Sources *Birmingham Weekly Post* (24 July 1880) • J. T. Bunce, *Josiah Mason: a biography* (1890) • J. Culme, *The directory of gold and silversmiths, jewellers, and allied traders, 1838–1914*, 2 vols. (1987) • G. Gore, *Art of electro-metallurgy* (1877) • *Journal of the Society of Arts*, 12 (1863–4), 175 • *Morning Post* (1862) • 'A day at an electroplate factory', *The Penny Magazine*, 13 (26 Oct 1844) • *The Times* (5 Dec 1865) • W. Ryland, 'The plated wares and electro-plating trades', *Birmingham and the Midland hardware district*, ed. S. Timmins (1866) • R. E. Leader, 'The early history of electro-silver plating', *Journal of the Institute of Metals*, 22 (1919) • C. G. Elkington, *Notes on the Elkington family* (1967) • S. Bury, *Victorian electroplate* (1971) • d. cert. • d. cert. [Henry Elkington] • R. E. Leader, 'History of Elkington & Co', typescript, *c.*1913, BL, 1881 a 48 • IGI

Archives V&A NAL

Wealth at death £350,000: Culme, *Directory*, 1.141

Elkington, Henry (1810–1852). *See under* Elkington, George Richards (1801–1865).

Elkington, Joseph (bap. **1740**, d. **1806**), farmer and designer of land drainage systems, was baptized on 1 January 1740, the eldest son of Joseph Elkington (1697–1758), yeoman farmer, and his wife, Mary, *née* Gallimore (d. 1750), at Stretton-on-Dunsmore, Warwickshire. He married on 26 December 1760 Sarah (bap. 1738, d. 1821), daughter of Richard and Mary Webb. Nine children survived him, and two of their grandchildren founded the famous Birmingham firm of Elkington & Co., electroplaters of gold or silver on copper.

About 1763 Elkington inherited a farm at Princethorpe, where some years later he discovered, at Long Harold Pits along a geological fault, the method of land drainage for which he is remembered. He discovered by accident, after losing more than 800 sheep to liver rot, how some strata were porous and pervious to water while others were not, and that he could locate the former with the auger used in exploring for marl and coal. In 1777 Charles Waistell reported the use of Elkington's system in Staffordshire, and John Wedge stated in 1794 that its 'mysterious manner' was introduced in Warwickshire about 1780 (Wedge, 18). Arthur Young reported on it enthusiastically when he toured the area in 1791. In 1793 William Stevens noted how 'Elkington, the self-taught drainer pretends that on viewing the face of any piece of ground he can not only ascertain whether rock is found below but exactly at what depth. There are mysteries in more trades than ours' (*Journal*, 83). Despite the mystery, from this period Elkington's services were in such demand that 'his crow bar was compared to the rod of Moses' (Lord Ernle, *English Farming*, 6th edn, 1961, 366).

A Lancashire group including the antiquary Charles Towneley (1737–1805) of Towneley and landowner Thomas Eccleston (*c.*1752–1809) of Scarisbrick, with Sir Joseph Banks, early in 1794 brought Elkington's methods to the attention of the newly founded board of agriculture. Eccleston felt that Elkington, who was epileptic, needed encouragement to 'disclose his secret … before any accident may deprive the public of so usefull a member' (Sutro Library, Banks MS F 4:80). Banks felt his 'discovery a matter of great national interest but not sufficiently known' (Sutro Library, Banks MS F 4:83) but that Elkington's rights should be those of any patentee, based

on priority of discovery. The board's president, Sir John Sinclair, was enthusiastic and late in 1794 the duke of Bedford allocated a trial site at Woburn where the board could study Elkington's methods, while in 1795 Banks started his own experiments at Revesby, Lincolnshire.

George III confirmed on 25 June 1795 that he would award a sum not exceeding £1000 as an inducement to Elkington to divulge his methods (which parliament was to repay). This was to be the 'first ever granted by Parliament for any discovery of importance to husbandry' (*Annals of Agriculture*, 24, 1795, 563), but since Elkington had worked primarily by instinct and failed to keep records of how, or where, he had worked, the board had to employ (through Sinclair's intercession) James Johnstone (d. 1838), land surveyor of Edinburgh, to study Elkington's system; he observed Elkington at work in spring 1796 and in autumn 1797 published his *Account of the Mode of Draining Land According to the System Practised by Mr Joseph Elkington* (five editions to 1841).

Despite this Elkington was felt not to have explained his techniques sufficiently clearly to obtain the grant, and payment was still being withheld in 1800. From October 1795 counter-claims of originality were submitted by James Anderson (1739–1808) that he was the system's true originator and that he had published it before Elkington, citing his *Two Letters to Sir John Sinclair* (1796), reprinted in his *Practical Treatise* (1797). Concurrently Elkington's attempt to drain Petworth Park, Sussex, for Lord Egremont was reported to have failed; this further damaged Elkington's reputation, despite support from the countess of Mansfield (for whom Elkington had drained at Kenwood), who felt his Petworth work had been misrepresented. In 1798 Elkington was taken ill and his trials at Woburn were left unfinished.

By May 1797 Elkington had been leased a 500 acre estate, 300 acres of which were bog, at Madeley in Staffordshire by John, later Lord, Crewe (1742–1829), original member of the board of agriculture. This lease must have been granted to replace in part the sum voted him by parliament. Elkington moved there (by January 1799 living at Hay House), with two of his sons, both of whom he had trained in his drainage methods: Thomas (1761–1835) and Joseph (1767–1830), who lived at newly named Bog Farm, Madeley. It was reported in May 1806 that the Elkingtons had made extraordinarily effective improvements there. Elkington died at Hay House on 17 October 1806 and was buried at Madeley on 20 October. His place in history remains complex. Donaldson noted that Elkington's 'fallacious principle has long since vanished. It is surprising that it was ever entertained at all' (J. Donaldson, *Agricultural Biography*, 1854, 81). H. S. TORRENS

Sources A. E. H. Elkington, 'Elkington records: Warwickshire branches, part 1', 1967, Society of Genealogists, London • Sutro Library, San Francisco, California, USA, Joseph Banks MSS • J. Johnstone, *An account of the mode of draining land … practised by Mr Joseph Elkington*, 2nd edn (1801) • [T. B. Bayley], *Thoughts on the necessity and advantages of care and oeconomy [sic] in collecting and preserving different substances for manure: likewise, the report of the committee of the board of* *agriculture respecting Mr Elkington's mode of draining* (1795) • 'A Warwickshire worthy', *The Times* (7 Aug 1936) • C. Waistell, 'Mr Elkington's mode of tap-draining land', *Annals of Agriculture*, 32 (1799), 629–32 • J. Farey, *General view of the agriculture and minerals of Derbyshire*, 2 (1813), 362–83 • *The journal of the Rev. William Bagshaw Stevens*, ed. G. Galbraith (1965), 83 • J. Wedge, *General view of the agriculture of the county of Warwick* (1794), 18–20 • *Memoirs of the life and works of the late Rt Hon. Sir John Sinclair*, ed. J. Sinclair, 2 vols. (1837), vol. 2, pp. 93–5 • *Staffordshire Advertiser* (3 May 1806), 3 • A. Young, *Tours in England and Wales* (1932), 262–97 • parish register, Leamington Hastings, 26 Dec 1760 [marriage] • register, 1 Jan 1740, Warks. CRO [baptism]

Archives Yale U. | Bucks. RLSS, Woburn estate records of the duke of Bedford • NL Wales, John Lloyd archive, letters • Sutro Library, California, Joseph Banks archive, letters

Likenesses portrait, repro. in *The Times*

Ella, John (1802–1888), violinist and conductor, was born at Leicester on 19 December 1802, the son of Richard Ella (*b.* 1769), a baker from Thirsk in Yorkshire. He was intended for the law, but, turning to music, studied with Fémy. He made his first professional appearance on 18 January 1821, in the orchestra at Drury Lane, and the following year moved to the King's Theatre. Having completed his musical education under Thomas Attwood, and subsequently with counterpoint lessons under F. J. Fétis in Paris in 1826, he performed with the major London orchestras, including the Philharmonic and the Ancient Concerts; he also played in the orchestra at Weber's funeral on 21 June 1826. He founded the Saltoun Club of Instrumentalists and the Società Lirica for the practice and performance of unfamiliar operatic music, was appointed to a post at the Royal Academy of Music, and became music editor of *The Athenaeum*. In 1830 he gave public concerts under the patronage of the duke of Leinster, and he wrote a *Victoria March* on the occasion of the queen's first visit to the City of London in November 1837.

During his frequent journeys abroad Ella made the acquaintance of a large number of distinguished musicians, including Meyerbeer and Wagner, and this no doubt contributed to the catholicity of his taste and the success of the Musical Union subscription chamber concerts which he ran from 1845 to 1880. These originated in a weekly meeting at his own house, and exercised a strong influence on public taste, as did the more modestly priced Musical Winter Evenings he started in 1852, and still more the Monday Popular Concerts. By the formation of an aristocratic committee, and by making the concerts to some extent social gatherings requiring a personal introduction, he secured great prestige for his Musical Union. It was to Ella's credit that under such circumstances the standard of the music performed, and that of the performances, for which he alone was responsible, remained as high as it did throughout the thirty-five years of the union's existence. The programme always contained at least two instrumental works of high quality. The performers were generally established artists, many of them appearing for the first time in England: they included Prosper Sainton, Charles Hallé, Alfredo Piatti, and Ella himself, but also Henri Vieuxtemps, Joseph Joachim,

Camillo Sivori, and Bernhard Molique. Though criticized for favouring foreign musicians, Ella held to his insistence that England should become aware of the higher standards in France and Germany; and, on his visit, Meyerbeer was full of praise. The annual series consisted of eight afternoon concerts given during the season, at first in Willis's Rooms, together with a benefit for the director, when vocal music (otherwise excluded) formed part of the programme. Two details of arrangement characterized the concerts: the placing of the artists in the middle of the room, surrounded by the audience ('en famille', Ella liked to say), and the introduction of analytical programmes (a 'synopsis analytique'), printed and sent out to the subscribers a few days before the concert. In 1855 Ella was appointed lecturer to the London Institution, and the substance of three lectures, on melody, harmony, and counterpoint, was given in the analytical programmes of the *Record of the Musical Union*.

In 1858 the Musical Union and the Winter Evenings were transferred to the Hanover Square Rooms, and in the following year to the newly opened St James's Hall; then, on the inauguration of the Monday Popular Concerts, the evening series was given up. A project for founding a Musical Union Institute was broached in September 1860, with the object of providing a library, a collection of instruments, and rooms for lectures, rehearsals, and concerts, and it was advertised as actually existing at Ella's house, 18 Hanover Square; however, the project attracted insufficient support.

Ella's published writings include *A Personal Memoir of Meyerbeer, with Analysis of 'Les Huguenots'* (1868), *Musical Sketches Abroad and at Home* (1869), consisting of anecdotes, reminiscences, and other material largely reprinted from the *Record of the Musical Union*, and a series of four lectures (1872). These lectures, originally delivered at the London Institution, put forward plans for improving public taste, including by the foundation of a National Academy. Ella also contributed to the *Morning Post*, the *Musical World*, and *The Athenaeum*, often scathingly on the subject of English musical standards. He was an honorary member of the Accademia Filarmonica Romana and of the Société Philharmonique of Paris. For the last twenty years of his life he lived at 9 Victoria Square, Pimlico, London. Towards the end of this period he became totally blind. He died at home, after several strokes, on 2 October 1888, and was buried in Brompton cemetery on the 5th.

J. A. F. MAITLAND, *rev.* JOHN WARRACK

Sources J. Ravell, 'John Ella, 1802–1888', *Music and Letters*, 34 (1953), 93–105 • *New Grove* • J. Ella, *Musical sketches abroad and at home* (1869) • *Record of the Musical Union* (1845–73) • T. L. Southgate, *Musical Standard* (6 Oct 1888) • *CGPLA Eng. & Wales* (1889) • private information (2004)

Archives U. Oxf., faculty of music | NA Scot., letters to Sir George Clerk • University of British Columbia, letters to Hugh Reginald Haweis

Likenesses C. Baugniet, lithograph, 1851 (after his portrait), NPG • portrait, repro. in *Harper's Magazine*, 60 (1880), 831

Wealth at death £6663 1s.: resworn probate, Jan 1889, *CGPLA Eng. & Wales* (1888)

Ellacombe [Ellicombe], **Henry Thomas** (1790–1885), campanologist and Church of England clergyman, son of William Ellicombe, rector of Alphington, Devon, was born on 15 May 1790. Having graduated BA from Oriel College, Oxford, in 1812 he applied himself until 1816 to the study of engineering in Chatham Dockyard, under the direction of Isambard Kingdom Brunel. In that year he graduated MA and was ordained deacon, becoming curate of Cricklade in Wiltshire. The following year, after receiving priest's orders, he moved to Bitton, Gloucestershire. He held the curacy until 1835, when he became vicar. In 1850 he became rector of Clyst St George, Devon, and was succeeded in his former benefice by his son. He was also domestic chaplain to the earl of Harrington. He died at Clyst St George on 30 July 1885, and was buried at Bitton. In the chancel of the church at Bitton, Ellacombe had erected a mural tablet recording the deaths of his three wives, Anne, Ann, and Charlotte, in 1825, 1831, and 1871. At the top his name was also inscribed, leaving a space for the date of his death and his age.

With indomitable energy and despite many difficulties Ellacombe restored the church of Bitton in 1822, and built three others in the district. After his move to Clyst St George he rebuilt the nave of the church, and in 1860 erected a schoolhouse. Ellacombe was a great authority on bells; Thomas Mozley records that one Devon clergyman, confronted by the zealous figure of Ellacombe examining his church's bells, immediately tried to exorcise him, convinced he was possessed by the devil. His church is conspicuous by its absence from Ellacombe's book *Church Bells of Devon* (1872). He invented an ingenious apparatus of chiming hammers, which enabled one man to chime all the bells in a steeple. He was also a learned antiquary, especially in ecclesiastical affairs, and a skilful botanist, having a record of 5000 different plants which he had personally grown with success, being the first in many cases to introduce them to English soil. Mozley recalls a man who cared 'for everybody and everything', and in whose company one could not be five minutes 'without learning something worth knowing, and in a distinct and positive form' (Mozley, 79). Ellacombe can fairly claim to be the first scholarly campanologist, and had a number of works on bell-ringing privately printed, including *Practical Remarks on Belfries and Ringers* (1849), a third edition of which appeared in 1871, *The Bells of the Church* (1862), and works on the church bells of Devon, Somerset, and Gloucestershire. B. H. BLACKER, *rev.* SARAH BROLLY

Sources T. Mozley, *Reminiscences, chiefly of Oriel College and the Oxford Movement*, 1 (1882), 75–81 · *Gloucestershire Notes and Queries*, 3 (1887), 230 · Allibone, *Dict.* · A. J. Horwood, *The manuscripts of H. T. Ellacombe, of Clyst St. George* (1876) · *CGPLA Eng. & Wales* (1885)
Archives BL, collections incl. grants of land and court–rolls of manors in west of England from Edward I to 1709, Add. Ch. 26417–26513 · BL, corresp. and papers relating to church bells, Add. MSS 33202–33206 · BL, sacred music collected by him, Add. MS 64886 · Bristol Reference Library, corresp., notes, and papers | Bodl. Oxf., corresp. with Sir Thomas Phillipps · U. Newcastle, Robinson L., letters to Sir Walter Trevelyan
Likenesses photograph, repro. in H. T. Ellacombe, *The church bells of Devon* (1872), frontispiece

Wealth at death £4196 0s. 4d.: probate, 25 Sept 1885, *CGPLA Eng. & Wales*

Ellenborough. For this title name *see* Law, Edward, first Baron Ellenborough (1750–1818); Law, Edward, first earl of Ellenborough (1790–1871).

Ellerker, Sir Ralph (*b.* in or before **1489**, *d.* **1546**), soldier, was the eldest son of Sir Ralph Ellerker (*d.* 1539) and Anne, daughter of Sir Thomas Gower of Stittenham, Yorkshire. On 20 February 1506 he married Joan, daughter of John Arden; they had four sons and four daughters. He married his second wife, Joan Mosely, on 20 October 1539. The Ellerkers, based at Risby in the East Riding since the early fifteenth century, were by the time of Henry VII's accession one of the county's leading families, a position reflected by the continuous service given by Ralph Ellerker the younger to the crown both in Yorkshire and the troubled regions of the Anglo-Scottish border. In company with his father and brothers he fought at Flodden in September 1513 and was knighted by the earl of Surrey in the battle's aftermath. Twice more, in 1522 and 1533, he joined the forces mustered against the Scots. Along with Thomas Wharton, Thomas Clifford, and Richard Tempest he was included in the talks that led to an Anglo-Scottish truce in July 1533. Eight years later he was again entrusted with the security of the borders. In commission with Sir Robert Bowes he was instructed to assess the numbers of light cavalry ready to serve in the east and middle marches and to estimate the expense of fortifying the area against future Scottish incursions.

When imminent hostilities did not demand his presence on the border, Ellerker's time appears to have been largely devoted to the government and administration of Yorkshire. In 1529 he was chosen as MP for Scarborough, and he may well have been reselected for the seat in 1536. In 1542 he was again elected to parliament, this time with Robert Bowes, as knight of the shire for Yorkshire. On at least four occasions he was chosen as a commissioner of the peace for the East Riding, and he was appointed sheriff of the district in 1529. At the outset of the Pilgrimage of Grace in October 1536 Ellerker and Bowes were captured, but they were later released in order to deliver the rebels' demands to the king in London. Although it has been suggested that both men were complicit in the rebellion, neither fell under lasting suspicion and indeed the following year Ellerker was appointed to the reconstituted council of the north, at least partly in recognition for his efforts in suppressing the revolt of Francis Bigod in January 1537.

Despite his close association with northern England, Ellerker spent his final years on the continent. In August 1542 he was appointed marshal of Calais. Between July and September 1544 he participated in the siege of Boulogne and was made marshal of the city upon its surrender to Henry. He was killed in a French ambush on 26 April 1546 and was buried in St Mary's Church, Boulogne. He was succeeded by his son Ralph (*d.* 1550).

LUKE MACMAHON

Sources *LP Henry VIII* · C. B. Norcliffe, ed., *The visitations of Yorkshire in the years 1563 and 1564 made by William Flower esq. Norroy king of*

arms (1881) • *VCH Yorkshire East Riding* • M. H. Dodds and R. Dodds, *The Pilgrimage of Grace, 1536–1537, and the Exeter conspiracy, 1538*, 2 vols. (1915) • HoP, *Commons, 1509–58*, 2.89–90 • M. Bush, *The Pilgrimage of Grace: a study of the rebel armies of October 1536* (1996) • B. English, *The great landowners of east Yorkshire, 1530–1910* (1990)

Archives BL, corresp. with Henry VIII and J. Heron, Add. MS 32646

Ellerker, Thomas (1738–1795), Jesuit, was born at Hart, near Hartlepool, co. Durham, on 21 September 1738. He studied at the English College, St Omer, entered the Society of Jesus in 1755, and in due course became a professed member of the order. He was ordained priest about 1762. When the order was suppressed in 1773 he accompanied his fellow Jesuits to Liège, and from there emigrated with the community in 1794 to Stonyhurst, Lancashire, where he died on 1 May 1795.

Ellerker, who was described by G. Oliver as 'one of the ablest professors of theology that the English province ever produced', was the author of *Tractatus theologicus de jure et justitiâ* (1767). His *Tractatus de incarnatione* (n.d.) was described as 'a chef d'oeuvre' (Gillow, *Lit. biog. hist.*, 2.159).

THOMPSON COOPER, *rev.* ROBERT BROWN

Sources Gillow, *Lit. biog. hist.* • H. Foley, ed., *Records of the English province of the Society of Jesus*, 7 vols. in 8 (1875–83) • G. Oliver, *Collections towards illustrating the biography of the Scotch, English and Irish members of the Society of Jesus* (1835) • G. Holt, *The English Jesuits, 1650–1829: a biographical dictionary*, Catholic RS, 70 (1984)

Ellerman, Sir John Reeves, first baronet (1862–1933), shipowner and financier, was born at 100 Anlaby Road, Kingston upon Hull, on 15 May 1862, the only son (there were also two daughters) of Johann Herman Ellerman (*d.* 1871), a Lutheran corn merchant and shipbroker, and his wife, Anne Elizabeth Reeves (*d.* 1909). His father had migrated from Hamburg to Hull in 1850; he died when his son was nine. The elder Ellerman served as Hanover's honorary consul in Hull. His mother was the daughter of a local solicitor, and outlived her husband by many years. Ellerman was nominally an Anglican, although he rarely attended a church and had little interest in religious matters.

Early career in accounting and finance After his father's death, Ellerman was taken by his mother, for unknown reasons, to live in Caen, France, where he acquired what his daughter ambiguously described as a continental view of life, as well as a keen interest in mountain climbing and swimming, and became a fluent French speaker. Returning to England, Ellerman briefly attended King Edward VI School in Birmingham. He later claimed that a public school education in a more conventional sense would have hindered his business success. Quarrelling with his mother, he lived away from home from the age of fourteen onwards, and was articled to a prominent Birmingham chartered accountant, William Smedley. At sixteen, Ellerman inherited a legacy from his maternal grandfather, part of which he lent to Smedley in return for the right to take four months' annual holiday while still serving his articles, time he spent mountain climbing in Switzerland and India. Ellerman passed his accountancy

Sir John Reeves Ellerman, first baronet (1862–1933), by unknown photographer, early 1920s [with his son, John Reeves Ellerman]

examinations with distinction and, after a brief period with a Birmingham accountancy firm, moved to London, where he worked for Quilter, Ball & Co., one of the most distinguished accountancy firms in Britain. He was offered a partnership by the firm's head, Sir Cuthbert Quilter, within two years of joining, but decided to found his own accountancy business, J. Ellerman & Co., at 10 Moorgate in 1886. Several conclusions may be drawn from Ellerman's early life. Although later Britain's largest shipowner, Ellerman had nothing whatever to do with shipping until he was twenty-nine. Unusually for a British financier, he was unrelated to any London business family or grouping and did not live there until he was an adult. Indeed, in many respects Ellerman remained a lifelong outsider in London's financial establishment. He was, however, one of the very first prominent British businessmen to have been professionally trained as an accountant, and his future success clearly owed much to this training.

In 1890 Ellerman established the first of his major financial undertakings, the Brewery and Commercial Investment Trust, which grew enormously in value, appreciating by an extraordinary 1300 per cent in nine years. Ellerman opened a branch of his accountancy business in Birmingham, and met a number of highly successful younger financial entrepreneurs who helped him at this crucial stage of his career, especially Henry Osborne O'Hagan of the City of London Contract Corporation, and

Christopher Furness (1852–1912), like Ellerman a self-made financier-turned-shipowner.

A shipping magnate In 1892 Frederick Leyland, one of the largest shipowners in Britain, collapsed and died at Blackfriars Station, London. Backed by O'Hagan, Furness and Ellerman formed a syndicate which took over and reorganized Leyland & Co., with Ellerman becoming chairman a year later. The takeover of an eminent shipping firm (itself the product of mergers with other old firms such as Bibby & Co.) by young unknowns was widely criticized in the financial press, as was the capital value of the firm they floated (£800,000), regarded as far higher than market valuation. Although nearly thirty and without any previous experience in shipping, Ellerman came to dominate the firm, which prospered under his leadership; he 'had taken to shipping like a duck to water' (Bryher, 26), his daughter observed seventy years later. Ellerman quickly eased out Furness—who went on to become a powerful shipping millionaire in his own right—with O'Hagan noting in his 1929 autobiography that 'two Napoleons could not exist' (O'Hagan, 1.384). In May 1901 Ellerman sold most of Leyland & Co. to J. P. Morgan, the American financial magnate, for a cash sum (£1.2 million) estimated to be 50 per cent higher than its actual worth. Ellerman proceeded to purchase Papyanni & Co., an old-established Liverpool shipping company, renaming it the London, Liverpool, and Ocean Shipping Company, and then expanding mightily in the shipping industry, acquiring most of the City Line (a long-established Glasgow firm), the Hall Line of Liverpool, and the smaller Westcott and Laurence of London.

All of these firms had much in common, being old-established, highly respected enterprises which had entered into a period of entrepreneurial decline following the deaths of their founders or heads. About 1902 these were united and renamed the Ellerman Lines, with a new, common uniform for its employees and a company pennant (a blue flag with the letters JRE in white) in use from October 1904. Ellerman expanded into the closely regulated Atlantic and South African routes, as well as the route to India, and became a considerable troop and war supplies carrier in the latter phases of the Second South African War. To his rapidly expanding empire in 1904–5 he added two other well-known older firms, Bucknalls and the Glen Lines, and by 1914 was also a director of Shaw, Savil, and Albion. In late 1916, with wartime shipping at its peak, Ellerman made his largest purchase in this area, buying Thomas Wilson Sons & Co. of Hull for about £4.1 million. Wilson & Co. had been the largest private shipping line in the world, but, by a familiar pattern, had fallen into entrepreneurial decline. By April 1917, Ellerman Lines owned ships to a total of 1.5 million tons, one-eighth of British shipping tonnage of over 1000 tons, and equal to the entire French merchant navy. Ellerman had served as president of the British chamber of shipping in 1907, only fifteen years after entering the trade. He was helped in his shipping (and, later, other) ventures by a small handful of close confidants, especially Miles Mattinson KC, and Val Prinsep (Frederick Leyland's son-in-law)

who unusually combined business acumen with eminence in the world of painting, being a Royal Academician; his son Thoby eventually became managing director of Ellermans.

Brewing and newspapers As his shipping empire grew, Ellerman increasingly became a significant entrepreneur in other areas, especially brewing, collieries, newspapers, and property. Indeed, while shipping continued to form the backbone of his commercial empire, his non-shipping interests increased to become perhaps as considerable as his shipping holdings. By 1902 Ellerman held shares in thirty-eight different breweries and, by 1918, more than seventy. There is no obvious reason why Ellerman branched into breweries, other than the fact that these, like the shipping firms he purchased, were often on a downward managerial path. With the proliferation of small and medium-sized local firms, Britain's breweries were probably ripe for entrepreneurial transformation, which Ellerman brought in abundance. One firm he acquired, Hoare & Co. of Tower Bridge, earned its biggest profit in 435 years within a year of Ellerman's gaining control, and then expanded rapidly. Ellerman used Hoare & Co. as a base to acquire, in 1919, the famous Red Lion Brewery (whose plant, on the future site of the Festival of Britain adjacent to Waterloo Station, was a prominent London landmark) and, in 1926, the City of London Brewery. Ellerman had also diversified into coal by 1914, in order to guarantee secure and inexpensive sources of coal for his shipping empire, providing high-quality British coal to his firms' coal bunkers around the world. By the early 1920s he held shares in at least twenty-two collieries, although he does not appear to have ever become a director of a publicly traded colliery company.

From about 1904, Ellerman also became an important shareholder in British newspapers. His Fleet Street career began in 1904, when he became the largest single shareholder in the *Financial Times*, holding this position until he sold it to the Berry brothers in 1919. Ellerman also maintained a little-known alliance with Lord Northcliffe. Before the First World War he became a major shareholder in the *Daily Mail*, and, when Northcliffe purchased *The Times* in 1911, Ellerman became its third-largest shareholder. During the First World War, Ellerman also purchased *The Sphere* and *The Tatler* magazines and the *Illustrated London News*. He was as well a major shareholder in Associated Newspapers, which owned Northcliffe's other press holdings such as the *Evening News*. Ellerman continued this largely invisible position in Fleet Street until Northcliffe's death in 1922, when he gradually sold off his press interests, selling his share in *The Times* to the Walter family.

Real estate and honours After the war, Ellerman increasingly used his wealth to acquire prime London real estate. In 1920 he purchased a portion of the Covent Garden estate, including the Drury Lane Theatre, from the duke of Bedford. In 1925 he bought 21 acres of prime Marylebone properties, including all of Great Portland Street, from Lord Howard de Walden for £3 million. Four years later, he purchased 14 acres in Chelsea, including over 500 house properties, from the Cadogan and Hans Place estates. Also in 1929, he acquired 82 acres of freehold land in South Kensington, formerly Lord Kensington's estate, from Lord Iveagh's trustees. This purchase brought Ellerman over 1150 house properties and 200 blocks of flats; and he is also known to have owned extensive properties in the City of London. By 1929 Ellerman was probably among the ten or twelve largest private London property owners, and one of the few to be actively purchasing more properties rather than selling them. As with other aspects of his investments, Ellerman primarily turned to property for the security it provided and its long-term profitability. He also owned and managed a wide variety of other trust companies; these were probably family trusts, whose precise nature is obscure.

Ellerman weathered the vicissitudes of the post-1918 world very well, compensating for the worldwide downturn in shipping by shrewd and timely investments elsewhere. He deeply mistrusted the Labour Party, freely predicting economic doom if it came to office; and his dislike of the Labour government which came to office in May 1929 caused him to rearrange his portfolio in more conservative directions. This had the unintended effect of allowing him to weather the 1929 crash and its attendant depression remarkably well, giving him, probably without reason, a reputation for having foreseen the October crash on Wall Street. Ellerman received only two official honours. In 1905 he was given a baronetcy in recognition of his role in the provision of shipping during the Second South African War. In 1921 he was made a Companion of Honour, a most unusual reward for a businessman with no ostensible record of public service. He made no efforts to obtain a peerage, although he could obviously have purchased one at this time.

Ellerman's exceptional wealth Ellerman had certainly become a multi-millionaire by the early years of the twentieth century and by the First World War was probably the richest man in Britain. In 1916 Ellerman was quoted in a newspaper as saying that he was worth £55 million (*Morning Post*, 18 July 1933). If this was accurate—and Ellerman had no reputation for personal bragging—he was not merely the richest man in Britain, but its richest man by a factor of nearly four, vastly outdistancing the duke of Westminster's £14 million fortune. In April 1917 a muckraking newspaper critic placed the value of his shipping empire alone at £35 million, and claimed that Ellerman was the largest single taxpayer in Britain, with an income in 1916 of over £3 million. At his death in early 1933—the nadir of the depression—Ellerman left an estate valued for probate at £36,685,000. This was not merely the largest estate ever left in the country, but was nearly three times the size of the second largest estate left for probate, the £13.5 million fortune left by Guinness Brewery's Lord Iveagh in 1927. Ellerman's estate represented about 30 per cent of all the wealth passing by probate in Britain in that year—that is, 30 per cent of all the wealth left by the 400,000 British adults deceased in 1933. Among modern British entrepreneurs, probably only Lord Nuffield, the automobile king, approached Ellerman's wealth; and Ellerman was probably the only British wealth-holder of his time in the same league as American industrialists such as Rockefeller and Ford. Ellerman was essentially a superlatively gifted accountant and financier whose aim was to increase his fortune through creative rather than destructive means. Having said this, however, it is not clear why Ellerman was so uniquely successful in fields such as shipping where he had hundreds of talented rivals. This mystery is only compounded by the fact that Ellerman was a self-made man who amassed in less than thirty years perhaps the greatest business fortune ever made in British history.

Cultivated secrecy, marriage, and death Ellerman deliberately shrouded his entire life in a cloak of mystery—he had an 'almost morbid passion for secrecy' (*DNB*)—and as little is known of his private life as of the precise details of his business career. An eclectic but appreciative art collector, he was depicted by his son-in-law, the American writer Robert McAlmon, as an ignorant philistine. He lived in a mansion at 1 South Audley Street, London, and a seafront house in Eastbourne. He never visited his only agricultural estate, bought in Aberdeenshire as part of a larger deal, and sold after three years. He was a keen Conservative but took no active or direct part in public life. Ellerman had few hobbies, although he visited the continent and the Mediterranean several months a year. 'He was the Silent Ford—the Invisible Rockefeller', the *Daily Mail* noted in its obituary; 'He had no public life. He had hardly ever been photographed'. In mature life Ellerman was a portly man with piercing eyes and a long white beard, and this was the feature that was highlighted in the few caricatures of him which exist.

In the early 1890s Ellerman began a lifelong companionship with Hannah (d. 1939), daughter of George Glover, with whom he had two children. The elder, Annie Winifred Glover, was born at Margate in September 1894; on her birth certificate there is a dash in the space indicating the name of the father. In October 1909, when Hannah Glover was again pregnant, Ellerman, after taking extensive legal advice, contracted a bizarre marriage with her under a little-known Scottish law, *per verba de praesenti*, under which a couple is legally regarded as married if they live together in Scotland for twenty-one successive days. They did not enter into any other form of marriage ceremony, and reference books such as *Burke's Peerage* give 14 October 1908 as the date of their marriage. The purpose of this singular proceeding was evidently to avoid the press publicity which otherwise would have attended the marriage of Britain's richest man a few months before the birth of his child; additionally it legitimized his subsequent offspring. Ellerman's move was opportunely timed, for their offspring proved to be a son and heir, John *Ellerman, born in December 1909, who could not have succeeded to Ellerman's baronetcy if he had been illegitimate. Lady Ellerman, an attractive woman, was as wholly shielded from social contact as was her husband. 'He keeps me in a glass case but I keep human', she was quoted as saying (*DNB*). Lady Ellerman died on 16 September 1939, aged seventy-one. The Ellermans' eldest child, and only daughter, Annie Winifred Glover *Ellerman (1894–1983), became known from the 1920s as a novelist and writer of some note under the pseudonym Bryher; she married the American poet Robert MacAlmon (1896–1956). Her autobiography, *The Heart to Artemis* (1963), provides one of the few intimate pictures of Ellerman.

Sir John Ellerman suffered a mild stroke in early 1933 and died at the Hotel Royale in Dieppe, France, on 16 July 1933. His wife survived him, and he was succeeded by his only son, Sir John Ellerman, second baronet.

Assessing Ellerman's place in British business is extremely difficult, for the historian must analyse a career hallmarked by both superlatives and mystery in equal measure. In essence, Ellerman was Britain's ultimate 'lone wolf' businessman, unattached to any recognizable section or social group, who existed solely to make money, something he did uniquely well although just how he did this remains thoroughly opaque. In his business activities Ellerman was at all times a constructive and creative businessman, purchasing significant, well-established firms primarily in order to improve their flagging performance. An astute financier, he was nevertheless the very opposite of an 'asset-stripper'. Ellerman's career as an entrepreneur was unique, and was certainly the greatest *tour de force* in British business history.

W. D. RUBINSTEIN

Sources J. Taylor, *Ellermans: a wealth of shipping* (1976) · W. D. Rubinstein, 'Ellerman, Sir John Reeves', *DBB* · Bryher [A. W. Ellerman], *The heart to Artemis* (1963) · R. McAlmon, *Being geniuses together* (1938) · *Daily Mail* (18 July 1933) · Burke, *Peerage* · private information (2004) [assistant registrar of baronetage, Home Office] · H. O. O'Hagan, *Leaves from my life*, 2 vols. (1929) · *Morning Post* (18 July 1933) · b. cert.
Archives U. Glas., Archives and Business Records Centre, business corresp. and notebooks, UGD 131/193 · U. Hull, Brynmor Jones L., business corresp., DEW(2)/5 | BL, corresp. with Lord Northcliffe, Add. MS 62170
Likenesses L. Fildes, oils, *c.*1920, repro. in Taylor, *Ellermans*, 19; formerly at Ellerman Lines Ltd Group, London · photograph, 1920–24 (with his son, Sir John Ellerman), repro. in Rubinstein, 'Ellerman' [*see illus.*]
Wealth at death £36,685,000; largest estate ever left in Britain at the time: PRO

Ellerman, Sir John Reeves, second baronet (1909–1973), shipowner and naturalist, was born at 5A Earls Avenue, Folkestone, Kent, on 21 December 1909, the only son and second child (Winifred *Ellerman was the eldest child) of Sir John Reeves *Ellerman, first baronet (1862–1933), the immensely wealthy shipowner and financier (probably Britain's richest ever businessman), and his wife, Hannah, *née* Glover (d. 1939). At the time of Ellerman's birth, the first Sir John Ellerman was already forty-seven; his son was therefore likely to succeed to the vast Ellerman fortune at a comparatively early age. Ellerman was educated at St Bede's preparatory school at Eastbourne and spent two years at Malvern College, before finishing his education in Switzerland. Although highly intelligent and industrious, with a rapidly growing interest in natural history, he did not attend a university but read for the bar at the Inner Temple and then was taken into the family shipping business at its Moorgate headquarters.

In July 1933 his father died suddenly, and Ellerman found himself, at the age of twenty-three, a baronet and the heir to a fortune, after death duties, of over £20 million. On 21 August, only a month after his father's death, he married Esther de Sola (d. 1984), of a prominent Montreal Jewish family, whose brother was a close friend in London. With his wife Ellerman shared a keen interest in amateur dramatics and Gilbert and Sullivan, and Lady Ellerman was a close companion to him until his death. There were no children of the marriage.

The first Sir John had built up over a long period a competent group of managers and lieutenants who ran Ellerman Lines, and the management style of the firm was based upon sound conservative principles, a product of both the proven success of this approach and the difficulties of innovation during the depression. Observers who worked with the younger Ellerman regarded him as a sound and sensible businessman. Although lacking his father's financial genius, he was a competent manager without any penchant for personal dissipation or foolish extravagance. After the Second World War, and particularly after the mid-1950s, Ellerman Lines modernized in a deliberate and rational way, placing emphasis on new shipping routes in Australia, east Asia, the United States, and the Middle East. In the mid-1960s Ellerman Lines became one of the first British shipping companies to introduce containerization, purchasing several of the earliest container vessels in Britain. Ellerman proved to be an active chairman, although the day-to-day running of the firm remained in the hands of its managerial staff.

Although extremely capable, Ellerman had little real interest in business life. From the mid-1930s he became, instead, an internationally noted student of natural history, especially of the rodent family. Between 1940 and 1961 he published five scholarly monographs and seventeen learned articles or notes on these subjects, most significantly a three-volume, 1500 page monograph on *Families and Genera of Living Rodents*, published by the British Museum (Natural History) in 1940–49. Just as his father was at home in the business world, so the younger Ellerman was renowned for his extraordinary memory and wide-ranging knowledge of natural history. He was made a fellow of the Royal Society of South Africa and was also an honorary associate of the department of zoology of the British Museum (Natural History), where he spent much of his time, and was well known around the world as an eminent authority.

For a man so blameless and retiring, Ellerman attracted a remarkable amount of press commentary, especially from the Beaverbrook press, apparently resulting from an old grudge held by the press lord against his father. He was often the subject of exposés in the *Daily Express*. Like his father, he became an active investor in the British press, in part so that he could diminish publicity of this sort. In the 1930s he owned a major share of the Odhams Press and in the early 1950s he was among the largest shareholders in the *Daily Mirror* and the *Sunday Pictorial*. He was a close friend of Lord Southwood, Odham's proprietor.

During his lifetime, Ellerman was generally regarded as Britain's richest man. During the closing years of his life estimates of his fortune ranged from £125 million to £500 million. The latter figure was given in several editions of the *Guinness Book of Records* in its entry for England's richest man. Like his father, he had a passion for privacy which was taken to extremes. He was rarely photographed and played no part in public life. He eschewed the typical lifestyle of the very rich. He divided his time between a house in Chalfont St Giles in Buckinghamshire, a suite he permanently maintained at the Dorchester Hotel, London, and frequent trips to South Africa. He helped many refugees to escape from Nazi Germany and was attacked by name by William Joyce, 'Lord Haw-Haw', in several of his broadcasts, under the mistaken but widely held belief that Ellerman, as well as his wife, was of Jewish descent. In the course of his lifetime he anonymously gave very large sums to charity, especially to assist wounded war veterans and disabled persons. In appearance (in contrast to his father) he was a tall, thin man of distinguished looks.

Ellerman died suddenly of a heart attack on 17 July 1973, in the Dorchester Hotel, London, shortly after returning from a holiday in southern France. He was later cremated. He left over £52 million, the largest estate ever left by a Briton, and the biggest fortune since his father's death forty years before. As he had no children and groomed no relatives as heirs, his shares in the family firm were reorganized into a charitable trust shortly before his death. He did not begin to rival the perhaps unique standards of business ability set by his father, but proved—unlike so many with ample means to satisfy every temptation—to be a decent and constructive human being.

W. D. RUBINSTEIN

Sources J. Taylor, *Ellermans, a wealth of shipping* (1976) • W. D. Rubinstein, 'Ellerman, Sir John Reeves', *DBB* • Burke, *Peerage* • d. cert. • b. cert. • private information (2004)
Archives U. Glas., Archives and Business Records Centre, business corresp. and papers | Bodl. Oxf., corresp. with Sir Alister Hardy
Likenesses photograph, 1920–24 (with his father, Sir John Ellerman), repro. in Rubinstein, 'Ellerman'; *see illus. in* Ellerman, Sir John Reeves, first baronet (1862–1933) • photograph, repro. in Taylor, *Ellermans*
Wealth at death £53,238,370: *Daily Mail Year Book* (1975), 274

Ellerman, (Annie) Winifred [*pseud.* Bryher] **(1894–1983)**, writer and philanthropist, was born fifteen years before her parents' marriage, on 2 September 1894 at Norfolk Villa, Harold Road, Margate, the elder child (by fifteen years) and only daughter of John Reeves *Ellerman, later first baronet (1862–1933), shipping magnate and newspaper owner, of London, formerly of Brough near Hull, and Hannah (d. 1939), daughter of George Glover. Her illegitimacy diminished her rights of inheritance when her father died in 1933 leaving one of the largest private fortunes in Britain. She showed business acumen in later life, much more so than her brother John [*see* Ellerman, Sir John Reeves (1909–1973)], who was unable to manage the money successfully (Benstock, 269).

Since Winifred's father was self made and her mother was middle-class in background, the Ellermans were never accepted as part of London high society, and Winifred and her brother experienced a sequestered upbringing in London. On the many family tours of Europe, Africa, and the Near East however, Winifred was seized by a spirit of adventure and rebellion which never left her. These excursions stimulated an interest in ancient history which informed many of her later novels. She was virtually self-educated by voracious reading, especially of history and G. A. Henty; her world was shattered when she was sent, at fifteen, to Queenwood School, Eastbourne. The experience precipitated her first novel, *Development* (1920). Childhood had bred in her 'a desire of expression, love of freedom'. School presaged future constraint:

> To possess the intellect, the hopes, the ambitions of a man, unsoftened by any feminine attribute, to have these sheathed in convention, impossible to break without hurt to those she had no wish to hurt, to feel so thoroughly unlike a girl—this was the tragedy.   (*Development*, 139–40)

It was during her school years that she visited the Isles of Scilly and was so enamoured of them that she named herself Bryher after one of the islands; she confirmed this by deed poll some years later. The genderless name was later combined with a plain and unfeminine taste in clothing and a short haircut.

After abandoning the study of archaeology Bryher planned a career in journalism, writing for *The Sphere* and *Saturday Review*, and during the First World War tried to sign up as a land worker. She persuaded her father to allow her to have her poems printed (*Region of Lutany*, 1914) and to take Arabic lessons. At nineteen she discovered imagist poetry and wrote a pamphlet championing Amy Lowell. Lowell returned the favour by fostering Bryher's reputation in America and helping her to publish three poems, 'Wakefulness', 'Rejection', and 'Waste'. Meanwhile *Development*, described as 'imagistic' and praised by Dorothy Richardson, sparked controversy in the *Daily Mail* because of its dissenting view of education. Through Lowell, Bryher became aware of *Sea Garden*, a collection of poems by the American imagist Hilda Doolittle (1886–1961), known as H.D.; Bryher was entranced, and an encounter with H.D. in Cornwall is luminously described in *Two Selves* (1923), a sequel to *Development*. Bryher also featured in many of H.D.'s prose works in the 1920s and 1930s, including *Asphodel*, where she describes Bryher as a 'hateful hard child … pedantic and so domineering'. H.D. was initially cautious of Bryher's devotion and emotional frailty, but their close personal association, which was at first sexual, lasted until H.D.'s death in 1961.

Bryher made herself indispensable to H.D., 'saving' her when H.D. became seriously ill with influenza during the 1919 epidemic while pregnant with her daughter Perdita. Bryher subsequently took charge of Perdita's upbringing, allowing H.D. to concentrate on her work. Meanwhile

H.D. nourished Bryher's talent, encouraging her to translate Callimachus. After H.D.'s recovery the women travelled to the Isles of Scilly and then to Greece in 1920 with the sexologist Havelock Ellis, with whom Bryher shared an interest in transvestism, sexual inversion, and 'colour hearing'. It was Ellis who introduced Bryher and H.D. to Freud's work, and Bryher became one of the first subscribers to the British *Journal of Psychoanalysis*; she began analysis in 1920.

In the same year the women also travelled to America to meet Amy Lowell and the poet Marianne Moore. Bryher proposed to and, on 14 February 1921 in New York's City Hall, married, a writer, Robert Menzies McAlmon (1896–1956). The New York headlines were aghast: 'Bride exploited as daughter of Sir John Ellerman, to whom Burke's peerage credits only a son' (Knoll, 147). There was some mutual regard, but principally he gained funds and access to travel while she acquired the freedom reserved for a married woman. The trip to America was fictionalized by Bryher in *West* (1925). Bryher, H.D., and McAlmon briefly returned to London where McAlmon was introduced to the Ellermans, before moving on to Paris. Here, with the Ellerman money, McAlmon founded the Contact Publishing Company which, over eight years, published Ernest Hemingway, James Joyce, Ezra Pound, William Carlos Williams, Gertrude Stein, Nathanael West, H.D., Bryher, Djuna Barnes, and Dorothy Richardson, whom Bryher greatly admired. Bryher also supported Joyce and his family with a monthly allowance, helped George Antheil, financially assisted Sylvia Beach in her running of the influential Shakespeare & Co. bookshop, and subsidized Harriet Shaw Weaver's press which published both McAlmon and H.D.

Over the next four years, with McAlmon in Paris, Bryher travelled feverishly with H.D.—from London, to Paris, to Switzerland (which she used as a tax haven), to Egypt, to Constantinople, and to Italy. She divorced McAlmon in 1927; he wrote bitterly of the Ellermans in *Being Geniuses Together* (1938). On 1 September 1927, at the Chelsea register office, London, Bryher married H.D.'s lover Kenneth Macpherson (1902/3–1971), the son of John Macpherson, an artist. The honeymoon ménage is fictionalized in H.D.'s 'Narthex'. The web of loyalties apparently worked; the marriage granted Macpherson some financial independence while it allowed H.D., who was still married to Richard Aldington, to continue her affair with Macpherson. Although Bryher and Macpherson divorced in 1947, the three remained friends for the rest of their lives.

Nurturing Macpherson's interest in cinema, Bryher started a film company, POOL Productions. Its works included *Foothills* and *Borderline*, in which Bryher appeared as a cigar-smoking innkeeper. She also founded *Close-up*, the first English-language magazine devoted to the art of film; it ran successfully until 1933, and introduced Sergey Eisenstein to a wider public. In 1929 Bryher published *Film Problems of Soviet Russia*. Her interest widened into education, and she advocated the use of film in schools. Her building in 1930–31 of a late Bauhaus home, Kenwin, above Lake Geneva, coincided with the formal adoption of

H.D.'s daughter Perdita by Bryher and Macpherson. (Bryher had no children of her own.) At this time she also supported the psychoanalytic movement in Vienna by providing the money for the publication of their *Psychoanalytic Review*, and, as well as enjoying analysis with Hanns Sachs ('the central point of my life'; Bryher, *Artemis*, 253), she also paid for H.D. to be analysed by Sigmund Freud. As war approached, she put emergency funds at Freud's disposal, and from 1933 to 1939 she risked her life to help Jewish refugees cross the border from Germany to Switzerland, and to establish them in new lives; among their number was the philosopher Walter Benjamin. She escaped to London in the nick of time.

During the war, Bryher oversaw the literary magazine *Life and Letters Today*, which she had formed in 1935 from the remnants of *Life and Letters* and the *London Mercury*, and ran it until 1950. She exercised her noteworthy business intelligence as well as literary inclinations in the international arena; and she could probably have edited it more effectively than Robert Herring. Settled in Lowndes Square with Macpherson and H.D., she learned Persian and got to know the Lowndes Square group, especially the Sitwells (she bought a house for Edith Sitwell).

This period also saw Bryher establish her own literary voice. The war made her examine her feelings towards England, expressed in *Beowulf* (1956). Between 1948 and 1972 she published twelve books including *The Fourteenth of October* (1954), *The Player's Boy* (1957), *Roman Wall* (1955), *Gate to the Sea* (1959), *The Coin of Carthage* (1964), *This January Tale* (1968), and two moving autobiographical accounts, *The Heart to Artemis: a Writer's Memoirs* (1963) and *The Days of Mars: a Memoir, 1940–1946* (1972). The novels are distinctive historical imaginings, cinematic in construction, intense but passionless, frequently using the narrative perspective of a young man, and with settings ranging from Paestum to the battle of Hastings. They are minutely researched but the detail is awkwardly assimilated.

Bryher's wealth gave her something of the freedom and independence she so envied as the especial province of men. Valuing autonomy and work so highly, she helped others to achieve it by thoughtful and responsible financial sponsorship (after the Second World War she settled £70,000 on H.D., which gave her an income for life). She said of herself: 'I have rushed to the penniless young not with bowls of soup but with typewriters'. Loyalty and friendship were a passion, as were activity and adventure, and she embraced the new ('I was completely a child of my age')—psychoanalysis, air travel, inoculation against flu, modernist fiction, experimental cinema. She died, rather lonely, in Vaud, Switzerland, on 28 January 1983.

K. S. WALWYN, *rev.* CLARE L. TAYLOR

Sources G. Hanscombe and V. L. Smyers, *Writing for their lives: the modernist women, 1910–1940* (1987) • B. Guest, *Herself defined: the poet H. D. and her world* (1984) • Bryher, *The heart to Artemis: a writer's memoirs* (1963) • S. Benstock, *Women of the left bank: Paris, 1900–40* (1986) • J. S. Robinson, *H. D.: the life and work of an American poet* (1982) • N. R. Fitch, *Sylvia Beach and the lost generation: a history of literary Paris in the twenties and thirties* (1983) • R. McAlmon and K. Boyle, *Being geniuses* *together, 1920–1930* (1984) • D. Collecott, *H. D. and Sapphic modernism* (1999) • R. E. Knoll, ed., *McAlmon and the lost generation: a self-portrait* (1962) • J. Donald, A. Friedburg, and L. Marcus, eds., *Close-up, 1927–1933: cinema and modernism* (1998) • J. Shattock, *The Oxford guide to British women writers* (1988) • Bryher, *The days of Mars: a memoir, 1940–1946* (1972) • private papers, Magd. Cam. • private information (1990) • *CGPLA Eng. & Wales* (1983)

Archives Harvard U., Houghton L., corresp. • NRA, corresp. • Yale U., Beinecke L., corresp. | Bryn Mawr College Library, letters to Mary Herr; letters to Alice Modern Alt | FILM 'Borderline'
Likenesses Man Ray, photograph
Wealth at death £462,020: administration with will, 22 July 1983, *CGPLA Eng. & Wales*

Ellerton, Edward (1771–1851), educational philanthropist, son of Richard Ellerton of Downholm, Yorkshire, was born on 30 January 1771. He attended Richmond School and matriculated at University College, Oxford, in 1787, graduating BA in 1792 and MA in 1795. He was curate of North Cerney, Gloucestershire; where, Bloxam recounts, being of strong revolutionary principles in his youth, Ellerton headed a mob and planted a tree of liberty. In later life he was a zealous Conservative. Ellerton was appointed usher of Magdalen College School in 1795, and was master from 1799 to 1810. He became fellow of that college in 1803, and was university proctor in 1804. He proceeded BD in 1805 and DD in 1815. He was appointed to the perpetual curacy of Horspath, Oxfordshire, in 1814, and to the perpetual curacy of Sevenhampton, Gloucestershire, in 1825, but resigned the latter charge early in 1851. From 1831 he acted as curate to M. J. Routh, the president of Magdalen, at Theale near Reading, a chapelry attached to the rectory of Tilehurst. He was Routh's firmest supporter among the Magdalen fellows in resisting reform of the college's statutes.

Ellerton was the founder of many scholarships and prizes. In 1825 he established at Oxford an annual prize of 20 guineas for the best English essay on some theological subject. In the earlier part of E. B. Pusey's career Ellerton was his close friend, and, in conjunction with Pusey and his brother Philip, he founded in 1832 the Pusey and Ellerton scholarships, to encourage the study of Hebrew. A staunch protestant, Ellerton published in 1845 a brief polemical treatise entitled *The Evils and Dangers of Tractarianism*. Magdalen College, at which Ellerton had for many years been sole tutor, and very frequently bursar, also shared in his benefactions. He founded a number of exhibitions, including one for boys educated at Richmond School. But perhaps his greatest legacy to his college was to have saved the old quadrangle from destruction when, in 1822, he successfully opposed a controversial scheme of architectural alteration. His comparatively humble origins and rough manners exposed him to the ridicule of his Magdalen pupils, who bribed a stonemason to represent his unrefined features on a gargoyle. Ellerton died, unmarried, at his curacy of Theale, on 26 December 1851.

G. B. SMITH, *rev.* M. C. CURTHOYS

Sources *GM*, 2nd ser., 37 (1852), 195 • J. R. Bloxam, *A register of the presidents, fellows … of Saint Mary Magdalen College*, 8 vols. (1853–85), vol. 3, pp. 24–6 • W. D. Macray, *A register of the members of St Mary*

Magdalen College, Oxford, 5 (1906), 149–51 • W. Tuckwell, *Reminiscences of Oxford*, 2nd edn (1907)
Likenesses oils, Magd. Oxf.

Ellerton, John (1826–1893), hymn writer and editor of hymnals, was born on 16 December 1826 in Clerkenwell, London, the elder son of George Ellerton, of private means, who came from an evangelical Yorkshire family, and his wife, Jemima Frances, a short-story writer. His early schooling in London was private. In 1838 his father inherited a small property in Ulverston in the Furness peninsula, Lancashire, and from there John attended King William's College, Isle of Man. In 1844 his father and younger brother died; his mother devoted her life thereafter to John, and shared his home for twenty years. After a year's study with the Revd C. Hodgson at Brathay vicarage, Ambleside, he entered Trinity College, Cambridge, in 1845, where he began a lifelong friendship with Henry Bradshaw and Dr Fenton Hort, and was influenced by the writings of F. D. Maurice. In 1848 he came second in the chancellor's medal competition with a poem 'The Death of Baldur'. Illness prevented him from sitting the honours examinations and he received an *aegrotat* in 1849, after which he spent a year in Scotland reading for holy orders.

Ellerton was ordained deacon in Chichester in 1850 and served his first curacy in Easebourne, Sussex, where he studied the writings of the Christian socialist movement, in particular those of Charles Kingsley. He was ordained priest in 1851. In 1852 Ellerton moved to become senior curate at Brighton parish church and to hold the evening lectureship at the chapel of ease, St Peter's. In 1859 he compiled *Hymns for Schools and Bible Classes*, in which a number of his own hymn texts were published.

In 1860 Ellerton became incumbent of the newly built church of St Michael and All Angels, Crewe Green, and domestic chaplain to Lord Crewe. He pursued his social concerns through his work at the London and North Western Railway Company's mechanics' institution in Crewe (of which he was vice-president). He reorganized its educational programme, and conducted classes in English and scripture history. He also organized one of the first choral associations in the midland area, which met at Nantwich. He wrote many hymns and hymn translations in these years, and in 1863 the headmaster of Shrewsbury School consulted him when compiling *Hymnologia Christiana*. In 1871 he joined the group working on *Church Hymns* with W. Walsham How.

In 1872 Ellerton was appointed rector of Hinstock, Shropshire, where he began the research for *Notes and Illustrations of Church Hymns* (1881) and to compile with W. Walsham How *Children's Hymns and School Prayers* (1874). In 1876 he was appointed rector of the large parish of Barnes, Surrey, where he participated actively in the work of the Society for Promoting Christian Knowledge (SPCK).

An attack of pleurisy in 1884 forced Ellerton's resignation from Barnes. After convalescence in Switzerland and Italy, in 1885 he became incumbent of the small parish of White Roding, Essex, and was invited to serve as consultant on a supplement to *Hymns Ancient and Modern* (1889), which contained twenty-six of his hymns. In 1888 he published a definitive edition of his own texts in *Hymns Original and Translated*.

Ellerton married in 1860 Charlotte Alicia (*d.* 1896), daughter of William Hart of Brighton. They had seven children. Following a second stroke in 1892 he retired. While lying disabled by his last illness he was nominated to a prebendal stall in St Albans Cathedral, and for the final year of his life received the honorary address of Canon Ellerton, but he was never installed. He died on 15 June 1893 at Rosemont, Torquay, while on a visit there.

While Ellerton wrote a total of eighty-six hymns his greatest contribution to hymnody was as an editor and critical assessor. In compiling *Church Hymns* for the SPCK he pleaded for the inclusion of hymns from a variety of traditions. He was also keen to provide notes and illustrations to the hymns for a general readership, believing that accessibility should be a prime feature of congregational singing. His work as an editor also taught him to appreciate the practical value of hymnals, and the diversity of local practice and theological opinion; this led him to oppose the introduction of authorized or official hymnals for particular communions. His own compositions were marked by a sensitive use of imagery and wide parish appeal; 'The day thou gavest, Lord, is ended' was chosen by Queen Victoria as one of the hymns for her diamond jubilee in 1897.   ALAN LUFF, *rev.* LEON LITVACK

Sources H. Housman, *John Ellerton* (1896) · H. Martin, 'The day thou gavest: John Ellerton (1826–93), the parish priest whose life was devoted to hymns', *They wrote our hymns* (1961), 118–25 · J. R. Watson, 'The day thou gavest', *Hymn Society Bulletin*, 158 (Sept 1983), 144–50 · D. Campbell, *Hymns and hymn makers* (1912) · A. R. Winnett, 'The Church Congress, 1875, on hymnody', *Hymn Society Bulletin*, 133 (June 1975), 109–12 · J. Julian, ed., *A dictionary of hymnology*, rev. edn (1907) · M. Frost, ed., *Historical companion to 'Hymns ancient and modern'* (1962) · E. Routley, *An English-speaking hymnal guide* (1979) · E. Routley, *A panorama of Christian hymnody* (1979) · J. I. Jones and others, *The Baptist hymn book companion*, ed. H. Martin (1962) · J. Moffatt and M. Patrick, eds., *Handbook to the church hymnary with supplement* (1935)

Likenesses photograph, Hymns Ancient and Modern Ltd, St Mary's Works, St Mary's Plain, Norwich

Wealth at death £573 0s. 3d.: probate, 23 Nov 1893, *CGPLA Eng. & Wales*

Ellerton, John Lodge (1801–1873), composer, was born on 11 January 1801 in Cheshire, the son of Adam Lodge of Liverpool, of Irish descent. He was educated at Rugby School, where, overcoming his father's opposition to music, he showed considerable skill as a pianist, and at Brasenose College, Oxford, where he graduated BA on 4 December 1821 and MA on 16 April 1828. While still at Oxford, before taking his MA degree, he published some songs and quadrilles. Their success induced him to take up music seriously, and he went to Rome to study with Pietro Terziani, during which time he wrote seven Italian operas. He also toured Germany with the earl of Scarbrough, and on 24 August 1837 married the earl's sister, Lady Harriet Barbara (1796–1864), *née* Lumley, the widow of the Revd Frederick Manners-Sutton. He made frequent visits to Germany, and his study of instrumental music there led to his writing no fewer than fifty string quartets, at a time when few English composers were interesting themselves in chamber music. His op. 100, a string quintet, was noticed in the *Neue Zeitschrift für Musik* of May 1850 as being skilfully constructed, though neither original nor attractive. His opera *Domenica* was produced at Drury Lane on 7 June 1838, but even the most favourable of his critics, while giving praise to the pure style of the music, declared that it lacked variety, vigour, effect, originality, and dramatic feeling.

On 15 June 1838 Lodge was licensed to adopt the additional surname Ellerton in commemoration of his paternal grandmother. From 1847 to 1871 he was a member of the Musical Union directed by John Ella, who testified to his culture and attainments on announcing his election to the committee for the 1851 season. Ellerton similarly held quartet meetings in his London house, with distinguished artists taking part. He was a sympathetic supporter of Wagner, who wrote to Liszt from London on 10 May 1855 that he had found a warm friend in Ellerton. Wagner also singled him out among London acquaintances in his autobiography *Mein Leben*: 'I was pleased … by a Mr Ellerton, a pleasant and dignified man, brother-in-law to Lord Brougham, who was a poet, a music-lover, and, alas, a composer'. Wagner, who took pleasure in Ellerton's resistance of the contemporary adulation of Mendelssohn, goes on to record a convivial evening at the University Club after which Ellerton had to be helped home by two men. Ellerton had some success with his oratorio *Paradise Lost* in 1856. He also wrote many glees (two of which won prizes at the Catch Club in 1836 and 1838), songs, and duets. Some of his instrumental music was performed in Germany, and he seems to have spent much time travelling abroad or in Wales. Among his other copious works are much choral and chamber music and five symphonies, of which the *Waldsymphonie* (op. 120), a work in six movements based on James Thomson's *The Seasons*, was first performed at Aix-la-Chapelle on 22 December 1857. He also published two volumes of poetry, *The Bridal of Salerno* (a romance in six cantos, with other poems, 1845) and *The Elixir of Youth* (a legend, with other poems, 1864). He died at his home, 6 Connaught Place, Hyde Park, on 3 January 1873.   JOHN WARRACK

Sources Grove, *Dict. mus.* · *New Grove* · Brown & Stratton, *Brit. mus.* · *Musical World* (1838) · *Musical World* (1839) · *Musical World* (11 Jan 1873), 28 · *Musical World* (22 March 1873), 181 · R. Wagner, *My life*, ed. M. Whittall, trans. A. Gray (1983), 521 [Ger. orig., *Mein Leben*] · Burke, *Peerage* · GM, 2nd ser., 10 (1838), 90

Wealth at death £18,000: resworn administration, Dec 1875, *CGPLA Eng. & Wales* (1873)

Ellery, Robert Lewis John (1827–1908), astronomer, was born on 14 July 1827 at Cranley, Surrey, the son of John Ellery, a surgeon, and his wife, Caroline, *née* Potter. After education at the local grammar school he was trained for the medical profession. An interest in astronomy led him to form friendships with staff at the Royal Greenwich Observatory and to become acquainted with the use of instruments there. In 1851, seeking his fortune in a new land, Ellery arrived in the Australian colony of Victoria. The discovery of gold there had led to a massive increase in shipping, with the associated urgent need for the provision of accurate time for rating chronometers. Ellery wrote to the Melbourne press urging the establishment of a small nautical observatory at nearby Williamstown. The government acted quickly, appointing Ellery superintendent of the new service in 1853; a small telescope was provided in 1854, followed by a larger one in 1857.

Ellery's early years at Williamstown were a mixture of hope and misfortune. On 17 April 1854 he married Jane, the daughter of John Shields, a builder, of Launceston, Tasmania. In the early years Jane was Ellery's only assistant at the observatory. She died on 12 May 1858 and two of their three children died in infancy. On 17 September 1859 Ellery married Jane's younger sister, Margaret. Despite personal tragedy, he consolidated his public standing in this period. The observatory was connected with Melbourne by telegraph—the first in the colony—to enable simultaneous dropping of time balls. Ellery was for a time superintendent of telegraphs, and when a geodetic survey was commenced in 1856 he served as director of that also.

A railway terminus and other developments made the Williamstown site increasingly unsatisfactory. A new Melbourne observatory was established in 1863 with Ellery as director. This incorporated the meteorological and magnetic observatory set up elsewhere in Melbourne by Dr George Neumeyer in 1858. The most prominent feature of the observatory in the nineteenth century was the Great Melbourne Telescope, one of the last of a number of large speculum reflectors which became prominent in the nineteenth century and were especially associated with Irish astronomy. The idea for this telescope was first conceived by T. R. Robinson of Armagh observatory to continue Sir John Herschel's southern hemisphere observations of nebulae. The initial scheme foundered but was revived with interest from Melbourne in 1862. Ordered from Thomas Grubb of Dublin in 1866, the Cassegrain telescope with equatorial mounting and 48 inch primary mirror was delivered and installed in 1869. Although a number of difficulties with the mirrors and other aspects of the telescope were overcome, and some fine drawings of nebulae were made by Ellery's assistants, the telescope was at best a mixed success. Adequate means were not to hand for publication of the delicate drawings, and, while some fine photographs of the moon were taken, the telescope was not sufficiently stable for the longer exposures required for stellar photography and was unsuited for spectroscopy.

Ellery regarded the series of general catalogues of meridian observations of stars published in 1869, 1874, and 1889 as much more important. These showed his mastery of meridian astronomy. For many years all meridian observations were made with a 5 inch transit circle supplied by Troughton and Simms in 1861. In 1875 Ellery obtained a year's leave to visit Europe. Soon after his return he began to consider ordering a larger transit circle. An 8 inch instrument modelled on the transit circle at Cambridge observatory was supplied by Troughton and Simms and installed in 1884. This fine instrument was used for all later meridian work, and at the closure of the observatory in 1943 it was returned to England.

The last major undertaking during Ellery's directorship was Melbourne observatory's share in the international astrographic mapping project initiated at a congress in Paris in 1887. In the early 1890s financial depression in Victoria resulted in cutbacks at the observatory. The staff was reduced and in 1895 Ellery retired, though he continued to live on the premises and was appointed to the board of visitors.

Ellery had the ideal range of skills for organizing and developing a major colonial observatory. He enjoyed the continued support of the government, worked closely with scientists at the university, and was a leading figure in Victoria's scientific community generally. His organizational skills were matched by practical talents. He devised various pieces of equipment, including a chronograph pen that foreshadowed the fountain pen and a dark-field micrometer. His skill in refiguring and polishing one of the 48 inch mirrors of the Great Melbourne Telescope made it 'undoubtedly more perfect in figure than it ever has been' (Annual report of the government astronomer [Melbourne], 1890, 6).

Besides the observatory, Ellery was associated with many official and public bodies. He headed the geodetic survey until 1874, by which time he was involved in the torpedo corps, part of Victoria's volunteer force, from which he retired as honorary lieutenant-colonel in 1889. He presided at the Intercolonial Meteorological Conferences in Melbourne in 1881 and 1888 and at the meeting of the Australasian Association for the Advancement of Science there in 1900. He joined the Royal Society of Victoria in 1856 (he served as its president from 1866 until 1885) and published numerous papers in its journal.

Ellery probably practised medicine when he first arrived in the colony, although there is no evidence to confirm this. He maintained links with the medical world as an honorary member of the Medical Society of Victoria from his election in 1866 until his death. He was a member of the committee which founded Melbourne's second general hospital, the Alfred, and he served as the hospital's second president (1886–1903). A keen apiarist, Ellery was founding president of the Victorian Beekeepers' Club and co-editor of the *Australian Bee Keepers' Journal* for some years from 1885. His achievements and services were recognized by his election as fellow of the Royal Astronomical Society (1859) and FRS (1863) and his appointment as a CMG in 1889.

Ellery was left enfeebled by an attack of paralysis a year before his death, which took place at Observatory House, The Domain, South Yarra, Melbourne, on 14 January 1908. He was buried the following day at Williamstown cemetery. He was survived by his wife, Margaret, and a daughter from his first marriage, Amy. In the words of one obituary, his 'kindly nature and fund of humour made him a universal favourite, and he passed away loved and respected by all' (*Proceedings of the Royal Society of Victoria*, 21, 1908, 553).

JULIAN HOLLAND

Sources S. C. B. Gascoigne, 'Robert L. J. Ellery, his life and times', *Proceedings of the Astronomical Society of Australia*, 10 (1992), 170–6 · S. C. B. Gascoigne, 'The great Melbourne telescope and other 19th century reflectors', *Historical Records of Australian Science*, 10 (1994–5), 223–45 · S. C. B. Gascoigne, 'Ellery, Robert Lewis John', *AusDB*, vol. 4 · *The Argus* [Melbourne] (15 Jan 1908) · *Proceedings of the Royal Society of Victoria*, 21 (1908), 553 · H. H. T., *PRS*, 82A (1909), vi–x · J. Smith, ed., *The cyclopedia of Victoria*, 1 (1903), 193 · m. certs. · d. cert. [Jane Ellery] · private information · A. M. Mitchell, *The hospital south of the Yarra* (1977)

Archives Public Record Office, Victoria, Australia, Williamstown and Melbourne Observatories MSS; Geodetic Survey MSS · RAS, letters to Royal Astronomical Society

Likenesses engraving, repro. in Gascoigne, 'Robert L. J. Ellery, his life and times' · photograph, repro. in Smith, ed., *Cyclopedia of Victoria*

Ellery, William (1727–1820), merchant and revolutionary politician in America, was born on 22 December 1727 in Newport, Rhode Island, the son of William Ellery (1701–1764), a successful merchant and politician, and Elizabeth, the daughter of a prominent Newport figure, Colonel Job Almy. Like his father Ellery attended Harvard College, graduating AB in 1747. While at Harvard he met Ann (1725–1764), daughter of Judge Jonathan Remington. When he returned to Harvard for his MA he renewed his courting of Ann and married her on 11 October 1750. They had six children before her death on 7 September 1764. To provide a mother for his young family Ellery quickly remarried. On 28 June 1767 he and his second cousin Abigail (1742–1793), the daughter of Colonel Nathaniel Carey and Elizabeth Wanton, were married. Abigail was an excellent wife, bearing five more children and maintaining the house and family during Ellery's long absences from home, and William was clearly devoted to her, but his deep love of Ann never faded.

After leaving Harvard in 1750, Ellery returned to Newport, Rhode Island, where he unenthusiastically established himself as a merchant. The inheritance gained after the death of his father in 1764 allowed him greater economic freedom and he became active in politics. In particular he became an enthusiastic leader in Newport of the Sons of Liberty, an American patriot society. Finding he enjoyed politics, Ellery in 1769 became a lawyer, an occupation that dovetailed nicely with his political activities. He became a political lieutenant of Samuel Ward, the leader of one of two factions that contested for power in pre-revolutionary Rhode Island, serving on a number of committees and working hard for the election of candidates sympathetic to the American patriot cause. When Ward, who had been representing Rhode Island in the American continental congress, died in March 1776, Ellery was chosen to replace him. Ellery took his seat in congress on 14 May 1776 and was one of the signers of the Declaration of Independence, an act he considered to be his most significant. He was re-elected repeatedly from 1777 to 1781, except in 1780 when he lost the election. Ellery remained in congress's home of Philadelphia that year, however, having been appointed to the continental board of admiralty. This appointment was recognition of the expertise Ellery had developed in maritime affairs. Coming from a state whose economy was tied to shipping and which was threatened by the British fleet, it is not surprising that Ellery had accepted membership on the marine committee, which was charged with overseeing maritime affairs. As a member of this committee he became an important advocate for the American navy. His activity on that committee and on its successor, the board of admiralty, has earned Ellery the designation 'Lord of the Admiralty' from a modern biographer (Fowler, *Ellery*, iv).

In 1782 Ellery chose not to stand for re-election. He returned to Newport and re-entered local politics, securing election to the Rhode Island general assembly. While in that body Ellery took the lead in defending his friend David Howell, a delegate to congress, against attempts by congress to censure Howell for breaching congressional secrecy in publicizing details of American diplomatic activities and attempts to raise loans in Europe. In 1783 Ellery successfully ran for congress, joining Howell as a spokesman for Rhode Island and for states' rights. He served in congress until 1785 when, having exhausted his eligibility for candidacy under America's articles of confederation, he stepped aside.

Ellery returned to Rhode Island and was elected chief justice of the superior court. He did not, however, remain in that post for long. Alarmed by the rise to power in Rhode Island of a party favouring paper money and inflation of the currency, Ellery executed a *volte-face*, abandoned his state's former position on rights, and became a champion of centralized federal power and the national government. Realizing that he would soon be removed as chief justice, he sought and received in April 1786 a federal appointment as commissioner of the loan office and receiver of continental taxes. Ellery used his position to staunchly defend the national government and to rally the conservative forces in Rhode Island. He became a leading advocate for Rhode Island's adoption of the new federal constitution. When the state finally ratified the constitution in 1790—the last to do so—Ellery was rewarded for his efforts by being named collector of customs for the Newport district, a post he held until his death, in Newport, on 15 February 1820.

One of Ellery's grandchildren was the author Richard Henry Dana, and another was the famous cleric William Ellery Channing.   DENNIS M. CONRAD

Sources W. M. Fowler, *William Ellery: a Rhode Island politico and lord of admiralty* (1973) · E. T. Channing, 'Life of William Ellery', *Library of American biography*, ed. J. S. Sparks, 9 (1836) · C. K. Shipton, *Sibley's Harvard graduates: biographical sketches of those who attended Harvard College*, 12 (1962) · P. H. Smith and others, eds., *Letters of delegates to congress, 1774–1789*, 26 vols. (1976–2000), vols. 4–23 · W. H. Munro, *Memorial encyclopedia of the state of Rhode Island* (1916) · W. M. Fowler, 'Ellery, William', *ANB* · C. C. Hubbard, 'Ellery, William', *DAB* · R. P. Brown, *Rhode Island signers of the declaration of independence* (1913) · *Biographical cyclopedia of representative men of Rhode Island*

Archives Mass. Hist. Soc., MSS · Rhode Island Historical Society, Providence, MSS

Likenesses S. B. Waugh, oils (after J. Trumbull), Independence National Historical Park

Elles, Gertrude Lilian (1872–1960), geologist and palaeontologist, was born on 8 October 1872 in Wimbledon, Surrey, one of six children of Jamison Elles, an importer of

Chinese goods, and his wife, Mary Chesney. Her father was Scottish and, when she was a child, family holidays were often spent in the Scottish highlands. She was educated at Wimbledon high school and at Newnham College, Cambridge (1891–7), where she took the natural sciences tripos (second class in part one, 1894; first class in part two, geology, 1895). From 1895 to 1897 she was a Bathurst student of Newnham, and worked for part of the time in Lund, Sweden.

The work for which Elles became known was the monumental monograph *British Graptolites* (1901–18). Brought out jointly with her friend Ethel Wood (later Shakespear), under the general editorship of Charles Lapworth, it provided reliable and detailed descriptions of this huge fossil group, critical in zonal division and correlation of Lower Palaeozoic rocks. It was perhaps the single most notable early contribution by women to British stratigraphic geology and long remained the basis of research in the area. Elles wrote the text and Wood prepared the illustrations. Also notable was Elles's 1922 paper (one of many on Lower Palaeozoic palaeontology and stratigraphy) analysing graptolite evolutionary patterns. Latterly she switched her attention to the metamorphic rocks of the Scottish highlands, her favourite part of the country.

Elles taught both men and women at Cambridge. Until 1926, when she was appointed university lecturer, she held an assistant demonstratorship in the Sedgwick Museum. In 1936 she became the university's first woman reader. At Newnham College she was successively lecturer, director of natural science, and vice-principal (1925–36). She was remembered by colleagues as an able administrator and an enthusiastic and inspiring teacher.

In her youth Elles was a striking woman, with deep blue eyes and corn-coloured hair. As a student she played on the Newnham hockey team; later she was a favourite coach. During the First World War she was Red Cross commandant of a small hospital for soldiers in Cambridge, work for which she was appointed MBE in 1920.

A fellow of the Geological Society (where she was the first woman council member, 1923–7), Elles was awarded the Murchison medal in 1919. She took a DSc at Trinity College, Dublin in 1907; in 1949, thirteen years after her retirement, Cambridge honoured her with an ScD. She moved to a nursing home in Helensburgh, Dunbartonshire, in 1960, and died there, unmarried, on 18 November of that year. Her remains were cremated at the crematorium in Cardcross, near Helensburgh, on 21 November.

MARY R. S. CREESE

Sources *Proceedings of the Geologists' Association*, 72 (1961), 168–71 · *Proceedings of the Geological Society of London* (1960–61), 143–5 · *Newnham College Roll Letter* (1961), 45–9 · [A. B. White and others], eds., *Newnham College register, 1871–1971*, 2nd edn, 1 (1979), 10 · M. R. S. Creese, *Ladies in the laboratory? American and British women in science, 1800–1900* (1998), 298–9 · J. Challinor, *History of British geology: a bibliographical study* (1971), 144–5 · Newnham College, Cambridge · M. R. S. Creese and T. M. Creese, 'British women who contributed to research in the geological sciences in the nineteenth century', *British Journal for the History of Science*, 27 (1994), 23–54, esp. 37–8 · *The Times* (21 Nov 1960)

Archives U. Cam., Sedgwick Museum of Earth Sciences, notebooks, catalogues, and papers | BGS, letters to F. L. Kitchin
Likenesses group portrait, photograph, repro. in A. Phillips, ed., *A Newnham anthology* (1979), facing p. 50 · photographs, Newnham College Archives, Cambridge

Elles, Sir Hugh Jamieson (1880–1945), army officer, was born in India on 27 April 1880, the third son of Lieutenant-General Sir Edmond Roche Elles, army officer, and his wife, Clare Gertrude (*née* Rothney). Having been educated at Clifton College, he entered the Royal Military Academy, Woolwich, in 1897 and was gazetted second lieutenant in the Royal Engineers in 1899. He experienced active service in the closing stages of the Second South African War, and was promoted lieutenant in 1901 and captain in 1908. On 9 October 1912 he married Geraldine Ada (1886/7–1922), daughter of Lieutenant-General Sir Gerald de Courcy Morton. They had two daughters. In 1913 he entered the Staff College, Camberley.

As deputy assistant quartermaster-general of the 4th division in August 1914, he was involved in the retreat from Mons to the River Marne, preceding the battles of the Aisne and First Ypres, and, in April 1915 as brigade major 10th brigade, Second Ypres, where he was wounded. Joining general headquarters as a general staff officer grade 2 (operations) in August 1915 he soon caught the eye of the commander-in-chief, General Sir John French. Promotion to major in November was followed in January 1916 by a mission from General Sir Douglas Haig, who had replaced French as commander-in-chief, to report (favourably as it happened) on 'tanks', the revolutionary weapon system designed to break the trench deadlock. In the course of his duties he saw much of these armoured, tracked fighting vehicles (AFVs) prior to their promising début on the Somme in September. So when Haig almost immediately adopted tanks as a potentially viable engine of war, Elles was the natural choice for appointment as colonel commanding what would later be called the tank corps.

Assembling a team of bright, younger officers, the level-headed, urbane, and handsome Elles chose as principal staff officer the acerbic and imaginative Major J. F. C. Fuller. Working complementarily, they led dynamically the expansion and development of the nascent corps' operational procedures, training, equipment, technology, administration, and morale to create within a year a battle-winning organization. While encouraging Fuller's sometimes brash inventiveness, Elles provided the vital diplomacy and tact required to sell the new concept of armoured warfare to sceptical senior officers. A crucial result was Haig's acceptance of a tank corps plan that brought about the victory at Cambrai on 20 November 1917, when tanks, operating in mass on ground suitable to their characteristics, and led by Elles in person, not only rapidly broke through the strongest German fortifications, but also guaranteed the future of mechanized AFVs. After receiving promotion to brigadier-general in 1917 and major-general in 1918 Elles retained command of the tank corps until the war's end.

Reduced to the substantive rank of colonel (but with a

KCMG), Elles took command of the tank corps training school at Bovington in June 1919. With Fuller he then fought for and won the permanent establishment of the tank corps: on 1 April 1923 the Royal Tank Corps (RTC) came into being, with the task of developing 'independent' tank forces. Elles was its first inspector. Yet this was to be a short-lived job for Elles, a stepping-stone on the way to stardom by a more orthodox route. He was made brigadier in command of 9th infantry brigade (1923–6), then chief general staff officer, eastern command (1926–9), and rose to substantive major-general in 1928. In the process, however, he lost some sympathy with the thinking and aims of radical RTC leaders. Moreover, for a brief period (1929–30) he was on half pay, writing a novel, *Cousins Limited*. But in May 1930 he entered the War Office as the influential director of military training (DMT), a post he held until October 1933 in a period of recession when the army was seriously starved of funds.

For six months after relinquishing his DMT post, Elles commanded a Territorial Army infantry division; and in March 1934 he joined the army council as master-general of the ordnance (MGO), with the rank of lieutenant-general. As head of the new mechanization board he was faced with the task of re-equipping the army. This included the introduction of new field and anti-aircraft artillery, virtual replacement of the horse by motor vehicles, and the introduction of new radio sets. All this was to be implemented within six years, but with totally inadequate funds. Elles tried to solve his impossible equation by sacrificing quality for quantity, purchasing cheap, 'Woolworths'-standard equipment. Among the results were the 25-pounder field gun of insufficient range; two-wheel-drive trucks which performed poorly in cross-country conditions; too many lightly armoured and armed tanks; too few medium tanks; and a slow, two-man, single-machine-gun infantry support tank. This last order Elles concealed from the tank corps in the outmoded belief that the fast, armoured formations of all arms they favoured were a 'long shot' in the face of the modern anti-tank guns. Visibly exhausted, Elles was relieved of his position of MGO in November 1937 and promoted general on his retirement in March 1938.

After his first wife's death in 1922 Elles had married on 17 September 1923 May Geraldine, widow of Lieutenant-Colonel George Franks; she died in December 1937, and on 14 July 1939 Elles married for a third time, his new wife being Blanche Laura (b. 1887/8), daughter of John Peter Hornung and widow of Lieutenant-Colonel Arthur Houssemayne du Boulay. After retiring from the army, Elles became chairman of the International Sugar Council. During the Second World War he was made a regional commissioner (1939–40), and then in April 1940 he was appointed chief-of-staff of the civil defence services, before moving in September to be regional commissioner of the south-western region; he worked tactfully in that ambivalent role until his death from cancer at 15A Great Cumberland Place, London, after the surrender of Germany, on 11 July 1945.

Elles was much decorated, being appointed DSO (1916), CB (1918), KCMG (1919), KCVO (1929), and KCB (1935). He was also a commander of the Légion d'honneur and received both the French and the Belgian Croix de Guerre, and the American DSM. His fame and reputation rest enduringly on commanding tanks so brilliantly in the First World War and leading them personally into action at Cambrai.

Sources *The Times* (13 July 1945) · B. H. Liddell Hart, *The tanks: the history of the royal tank regiment and its predecessors*, 1 (1959) · C. Williams-Ellis and A. Williams-Ellis, *The tank corps* (1919) · J. F. C. Fuller, *Memoirs of an unconventional soldier* (1936) · K. Macksey, *The tank pioneers* (1981) · K. Macksey, *A history of the royal armoured corps and its predecessors, 1914–1975* (1983) · Burke, *Peerage* · m. certs. · d. cert. · Kelly, *Handbk* (1947) · *CGPLA Eng. & Wales* (1946)
Archives Tank Museum, Bovington, MSS; medals | FILM IWM FVA, documentary footage | SOUND BL NSA, performance recordings · IWM SA, oral history interview
Likenesses W. Orpen, oils, 1918, IWM · W. Stoneman, photographs, 1919–20, NPG
Wealth at death £3978 5s. 4d.: probate, 12 Jan 1946, *CGPLA Eng. & Wales*

Ellesmere. For this title name *see* Egerton, Francis, first earl of Ellesmere (1800–1857).

Elley, Sir John (d. 1839), army officer, was, according to one statement, a native of Leeds, articled to a London solicitor, who enlisted in the Royal Horse Guards—then better known as the Oxford Blues—for his future advancement in which his father found the means. Another, seemingly better authenticated statement, given in *Biographia Leodiensis*, on the authority of the Revd John Smithson, incumbent of Headingley, near Leeds, who died in 1835, is that Elley was born in London, where his father kept an eating-house in Furnival's Inn cellars, Holborn; that he was apprenticed to John Gelderd of Meanwood tannery, near Leeds, and was engaged to Anne Gelderd, his master's daughter; and that he attended Anne's funeral at Armley Chapel in great grief. Whether the events of his apprenticeship, engagement, and the death of his fiancée took place before or after his enlistment does not appear. Like many other young soldiers, he is said to have been very anxious to get out of the army again, but to have been dissuaded by Smithson.

The regimental records show Elley enlisted in the Blues at Leeds on 5 November 1789, on 4 June 1790 as having purchased a troop quartermastership in the regiment (such warrant rank was then obtained by purchase), and on 6 June 1794 a cornetcy. He was acting adjutant of the four troops of the Blues detached to Flanders with the duke of York, with which he participated in the campaigns in Flanders and Holland of 1793–5 and distinguished himself at the cavalry action at Le Cateau on 26 April 1794. After his return from the continent he purchased a lieutenancy in the Blues on 26 June 1796 and a troop on 26 February 1801. He became major on 29 November 1804 and lieutenant-colonel on 6 March 1808, having purchased every step. He was employed on General Staveley's staff in the south of England during the Napoleonic invasion threat, and was assistant adjutant-general of cavalry in Spain in 1808–9, when he was present at the affairs of Sahagun and Benavente, among others, and in the retreat to Corunna and the ensuing battle. He was appointed to the army in Portugal in the same capacity in 1809 and fought in the subsequent campaigns of 1809–14 in the Peninsula and southern France, including the battle of Fuentes d'Oñoro, the cavalry affair at Llerena, the battle of Salamanca (where he had two horses killed under him and received a severe bayonet wound during the charge of Le Marchant's brigade), and the battles of Vitoria, Orthez, and Toulouse. As adjutant-general of cavalry, again serving under his friend whom he much admired, Lord Uxbridge (later first marquess of Anglesey), he was at the battle of Waterloo (where he was again wounded), and according to popular accounts he laid low more than one French cuirassier in single combat.

Elley was made KCB in January 1815 and KCH in 1819 and received numerous foreign decorations, including the fourth class of St George of Russia. He became major-general in 1819, governor of Galway in 1826, was employed some years on the staff in the south of Ireland, and was appointed colonel of the 17th lancers in 1829. In 1835 he was elected an MP for Windsor as a staunch supporter of Sir Robert Peel, but retired in 1837, in which year he became lieutenant-general. Elley died at his seat, Cholderton Lodge, near Amesbury, Wiltshire, on 23 January 1839 and was buried in the Chapel Royal at Windsor. By his will (personalty sworn under £25,000) he left two sums of £300 each, to be spent on mess plate for his regiment; £100, the interest on which to be distributed among decayed householders in Windsor; and six other legacies to various London charities, including the Magdalen Asylum in the London Road, the Bethnal Lunatic Asylum, and the Institution for the Cure of Cancer in the Kent Road.

H. M. CHICHESTER, rev. ROGER T. STEARN

Sources R. V. Taylor, ed., *The biographia Leodiensis, or, Biographical sketches of the worthies of Leeds* (1865) · R. V. Taylor, ed., *Supplement of the Biographia Leodiensis, or, Biographical sketches of the worthies of Leeds* (1867) · R. H. Gronow, *The reminiscences and recollections of Captain Gronow, 1810–1860*, 2 vols. (1889) · *GM*, 2nd ser., 11 (1839), 430–31 · *GM*, 2nd ser., 12 (1839), 660 · R. Cannon, ed., *Historical record of the seventeenth regiment of light dragoons, lancers* (1841) · *The dispatches of … the duke of Wellington … from 1799 to 1818*, ed. J. Gurwood, new edn, 13 vols. (1837–9) · *WWBMP*, vol. 1 · A. J. Guy, ed., *The road to Waterloo: the British army and the struggle against revolutionary and Napoleonic France, 1793–1815* (1990) · Marquess of Anglesey [G. C. H. V. Paget], *One-leg: the life and letters of Henry William Paget, first marquess of Anglesey* (1961) · T. C. W. Blanning, *The French revolutionary wars, 1787–1802* (1996) · R. Muir, *Britain and the defeat of Napoleon, 1807–1815* (1996) · J. Haydn, *The book of dignities: containing rolls of the official personages of the British empire* (1851)

Likenesses R. Trentanova, bust, *c*.1815, St George's Chapel, Windsor · J. W. Pieneman, oils, Wellington Museum, Apsley House, London · W. Salter, group portrait, oils (*Waterloo banquet at Apsley House*), Wellington Museum, Apsley House, London · W. Salter, oils (study for *Waterloo banquet*), NPG

Wealth at death under £25,000: will, 1839; *DNB*

Ellice, Sir Charles Hay (1823–1888), army officer, born at Florence on 10 May 1823, was the second son of General Robert Ellice, the brother of the Rt Hon. Edward *Ellice, secretary at war, and Eliza Courtenay. After attending Sandhurst, he was commissioned ensign and lieutenant

in the Coldstream Guards on 10 May 1839. He served in Canada in 1840–42, and became lieutenant and captain in August 1845. He exchanged to the 82nd regiment on 20 March 1846, and to the 24th regiment, of which his father was colonel, on 3 April. He went with it to India, in May, and was aide-de-camp to his father (commanding the troops in Malta) from March 1848 to March 1849. He was promoted major in December 1849, lieutenant-colonel in August 1851, and became colonel in the army in November 1854.

The 24th was at Peshawar when the Indian mutiny broke out. On 4 July 1857 Ellice was sent to Jhelum with three infantry companies, some native cavalry, and three guns to disarm the 14th Bengal native infantry and other troops. He arrived there on the 7th, and finding they had already mutinied, he, though outnumbered, attacked and routed them. He was dangerously wounded, was mentioned in dispatches, and was made CB on 1 January 1858.

In June 1858 Ellice was given the command of the 2nd battalion of the 24th, which he raised. He went with it to Mauritius in March 1860, but exchanged to half pay on 8 July 1862. In 1862 he married Louisa Caroline, daughter of William Henry Lambton, brother of the first earl of Durham. She survived him, and they had one daughter, Eliza (*d*. 1899). From 1863 to 1868 he held appointments in Ireland and England. He was promoted major-general in March 1865, lieutenant-general in September 1873, and general in October 1877, and was quartermaster-general from April 1871 to March 1876, and adjutant-general from November 1876 to March 1882. In 1877–8 he corresponded with the governors of Wellington College, alleging diversion from its original purpose. He was made KCB in May 1873 and GCB in April 1882, and became colonel of the 1st battalion, 49th (Princess Charlotte of Wales's) regiment in September 1874. He was transferred to the South Wales Borderers in April 1884, and retired on 1 April 1887. He died at his home, Brooke House, Horringer, near Bury St Edmunds, on 12 November 1888.

E. M. LLOYD, rev. JAMES FALKNER

Sources *The Times* (13 Nov 1888) · Burke, *Gen. GB* · G. Paton, F. Glennie, and W. P. Symons, eds., *Historical records of the 24th regiment, from its formation, in 1689* (1892), 318 · *Army List* · *Hart's Army List*

Wealth at death £39,866 17s. 11d.: probate, 25 Jan 1889, *CGPLA Eng. & Wales*

Ellice, Edward (1783–1863), merchant and politician, was born on 12 September 1783 in London, the third son of Alexander Ellice (*d*. 1805), merchant, and his wife, who was probably Ann Russell. The Ellices were originally an Aberdeenshire family; Edward Ellice's grandfather apparently took up business in North America and his father founded the firm of Inglis, Ellice, & Co., whose interests were mainly in New York state, Canada, and the West Indies, with representation in London. Ellice was educated at Winchester College and matriculated in 1797 at Marischal College, Aberdeen, from where he graduated MA in 1800. He started work as a clerk in London and was sent on his

Edward Ellice (1783–1863), by unknown engraver, pubd 1878

first trip to Canada and the United States in 1803. At that time Ellice's father was supplying a large share of the capital investment for the north-west fur trade. Ellice himself became connected with the fur-trading North-West Company and later with the breakaway XY Company (also known as Sir Alexander Mackenzie & Co.) and was heir to his father's business interests at the latter's death in 1805, after which date he returned to Britain.

On 30 October 1809 Ellice married Lady Hannah Althea (d. 1832), daughter of the first Earl Grey, and widow of Captain Bettesworth RN. Together they had a son, Edward *Ellice (1810–1880), later Liberal MP for St Andrews burghs from 1837 until 1880. By his marriage Ellice became brother-in-law to Charles Grey, a leading whig, and his connection to the party was cemented by his election to Brooks's Club in 1809. The prominence he achieved was, however, not just political. Ellice was part of a group, including his brother-in-law Samuel Whitbread and Lord Byron, which took on the restoration of the Drury Lane Theatre in London after its destruction by fire in 1809.

In 1818 Ellice was first elected to parliament on a whig-radical platform for Coventry, defeating Joseph Butterworth, the law publisher. With the exception of the period following his defeat in 1826 (he regained the seat in 1830) Ellice represented the town until his death. The cost of ferrying non-resident electors to the polls in Coventry meant that—especially before the passage of the first Reform Bill—his election expenses were substantial. He could afford it; Henry Brougham's characterization of

him as 'large and rich and stupid' (BL, Add. MS 52178; cited in HoP, Commons) was unjust only in its final adjective.

Ellice's experience in Canadian affairs led to a request from Lord Bathurst, the secretary for the colonies, that he try to resolve the sometimes violent and ruinous competition which had arisen between the notionally more indigenous fur-trading interests, such as the North-West Company, and the Hudson's Bay Company, which was perceived as being run from London. Agreement was reached in March 1821, by which all parties consented to trade under the charter of the Hudson's Bay Company. Ellice was very proud of his role in bringing about this union and in framing the accompanying act, which enabled the crown to grant exclusive trade licences to the company in regions beyond its original territory.

When his brother-in-law (by then the second Earl Grey), with whom Ellice's relations had not always been smooth, became prime minister in November 1830, Ellice was appointed joint secretary to the Treasury and government whip. It was in this position that he achieved greatest public recognition. In the run-up to the change in ministry he had kept Grey informed about City of London and business reaction to the political situation, and in his new role he was responsible for the management of a party used to opposition rather than government. Ellice, though not responsible for drafting the parliamentary reform proposals of the new government, was expected to deliver parliamentary support for them; he also made use of his business and provincial connections in the same cause. A view has been advanced that his radical leanings caused him to be less than forthcoming about how little chance the government's original bill had of parliamentary passage, though there appears to be no hard evidence that he actually concealed information from Grey and the cabinet. But with his knowledge of the strength of the popular reform movement, he would certainly have known that there was no going back on general principles once the original bill had held out the prospect of an enlarged franchise.

Ellice was the government's principal agent in distributing honours to those whose nomination boroughs were abolished by the Reform Act. This work apparently extended to collecting money from leading whigs—and the use of his own resources—to purchase such seats where necessary. These funds were also supposedly used to defray the expenses of government supporters hard pressed by the quick succession of the general elections of 1830 and 1831. In 1834 he was charged in the House of Commons with having used public funds for election purposes while he was secretary to the Treasury, but was saved from a committee of inquiry by a division of the house. When he left office in 1832 he was suspected of having bankrupted himself with the pledges he had made to get the Reform Bill passed. He was generally regarded as an efficient and successful patronage secretary; his fitness for the role was perhaps assisted by his freedom from the aristocratic social prejudices generally associated with the whigs. More than one claim has been advanced for

Ellice being the leading force behind the parliamentary passage of the first Reform Act.

On 28 July 1832 Ellice's wife, Hannah, died. Tired of his post, he resigned it in the following August, but was persuaded to re-enter government as secretary at war in April 1833, with a seat in the cabinet from June 1834—and is thus credited with being the first merchant to reach this level of government. He held this office until the fall of the first Melbourne ministry in December 1834. With Sir James Graham he was associated with the unsuccessful move to transfer military patronage from the commander-in-chief to the secretary at war, who was answerable to parliament. Ellice never again accepted office. Instead he earned the reputation of being the Liberal *éminence grise*, and was supposed to have been consulted on numerous ministerial appointments, especially to Melbourne's second and Russell's first administrations. In 1835 he was responsible for pacifying Daniel O'Connell, who expected an Irish office in a new Liberal administration, but whose exclusion, given the extensive prejudice against him, was necessary to its formation. Ellice was a founder of the Reform Club and was credited with helping to ensure that it was a less radical society than its original sponsors intended. Preliminary meetings were held at his house, 14 Carlton House Terrace, and he was appointed a trustee at its first formal meeting on 5 May 1836. Thereafter he was one of three guarantors of the club's building fund for new premises after those at 104 Pall Mall were found inadequate.

On 25 October 1843 Ellice married Lady Anne Amelia, *née* Keppel, widow of Thomas William Coke, first earl of Leicester, and daughter of the fourth earl of Albemarle. The marriage was short-lived as Lady Anne died on 22 July 1844, but it renewed his marital connection with the whig aristocracy. At his Scottish highland estates of Glengarry and Glenquoich he exercised famous hospitality to a great number (over 1000 in one season) and variety of guests. This behind-the-scenes role in politics was not confined to Britain. In April 1836, for example, he was in Paris pressing the French government to intervene in Spain. Over the years he had contact and correspondence with French politicians such as Prosper Mérimée and Louis Adolphe Thiers, and was supposed to have conspired to see the latter return to power in 1837. In 1840 he acted as an intermediary between the pro-French whigs around Lord Holland and, after his death, the earl of Clarendon, and the French court in urging France to resist Palmerston's policy of coercing Mehmet Ali in the Near East. In 1859 Ellice was again an intermediary, this time between the earl of Malmesbury, the foreign secretary, and the regime of Napoleon III.

The later period of Ellice's life was not free from controversy. His opposition to Palmerston's foreign policy was described by the diarist Greville as 'very vain, busy and meddling' (Fulford, 201) and when, late in 1842, Russell remonstrated with Palmerston about the tone of his criticism of the government's American policy, Palmerston went so far as to accuse Ellice of being the author of a movement against him. Ellice was, however, in sympathy with Palmerstonian reluctance to push forward with parliamentary reform: like many other pre-1832 reformers, he had by the 1850s become a defender of the constitutional status quo.

In February 1855 Ellice was appointed a member of the Roebuck committee of inquiry into the conduct of the Crimean War, although he had voted against setting it up. In 1857 he was appointed to the select committee on the Hudson's Bay Company, to which he also gave evidence, in which he sought to highlight the benefits to the indigenous population that had come from the 1821 union of fur-trading interests. He believed that the company should be allowed a temporary role in governing parts of Canada, but only until formal settlements could be established. In this respect he aligned himself with those calling for a reduction of the company's power, but he did not escape criticism when, with other shareholders, he sold his interest at a great profit to the International Finance Society in 1863. This sale and the subsequent share reissue stalled the attempts of a group connected with the government of Canada to end the company's proprietary interest and terminate its charter.

Ellice was widely known by the nickname of the (Old) Bear, which was appropriate from his connection with the fur trade of the Canadian north-west and also fitted certain aspects of his character: contemporaries wrote variously of his 'oiliness' (*Reminiscences*, 206), his 'courage and dexterity' (Le Marchant, 489), and his 'commanding stature and presence' (Watkin, 135). He was not known as an orator, but was a forcible speaker and in familiar surroundings could act the part of 'a regular showman' (Malmesbury, 1.235). Above all he was urbane and sociable, with an extensive network of contacts facilitated by his wealth and political experience. He was a deputy lieutenant of Inverness-shire and was awarded a DCL by St Andrews University in 1862, but refused a peerage. Until the last year of his life he enjoyed travel and good hospitality—despite increasingly frequent attacks of gout—and he displayed a marked taste for female company (*Letters of Prosper Mérimée to Panizzi*, 296).

Edward Ellice died in his sleep on 17 September 1863 at Ardochy, one of the residences on his Glengarry estate. He died intestate but left a memorandum requesting burial close to where he died. This took place at the west end of Loch Garry on 23 September 1863. Historically, his significance lies in his role in securing the passage of the 1832 Reform Act and in his work in unifying the fur-trading interests in Canada. He has otherwise been described as an elusive character, a reputation no doubt helped by his very regular, but almost unreadable handwriting.

GORDON F. MILLAR

Sources *The Scotsman* (18 Sept 1863); (19 Sept 1863); (21 Sept 1863); (22 Sept 1863); (26 Sept 1863) • *The Times* (21 Sept 1863); (23 Sept 1863); (26 Sept 1863) • *Inverness Courier* (24 Sept 1863) • *ILN* (26 Sept 1863); (3 Oct 1863) • *Scottish American Journal* (8 Oct 1863); (15 Oct 1863) • M. Brock, *The Great Reform Act* (1973) • D. Southgate, *The passing of the whigs, 1832–1886* (1962) • *GM*, 3rd ser., 15 (1863), 522, 778–9 • E. W. Watkin, *Canada and the States: recollections 1851 to 1886* (1887) • G. Bryce, *A short history of the Canadian people* (1914) • G. Bryce, *The remarkable story of the Hudson's Bay Co.* (1900) • *The Hudson's Bay Co.*

What is it? (1864) · 'Select committee on ... the Hudson's Bay Company', *Parl. papers* (1857), session 2, vol. 15, nos. 224, 260 · W. M. Torrens, *Memoirs of William Lamb, 2nd Viscount Melbourne* (1890) · *The Greville memoirs*, ed. R. Fulford, rev. edn (1963) · *The Greville memoirs*, ed. H. Reeve, pt 1, vol. 3 (1874); pt 2, vol. 3 (1885) · D. Le Marchant, *Memoir of John Charles, Viscount Althorp, third Earl Spencer*, ed. H. D. Le Marchant (1876) · L. J. Jennings, ed., *The Croker papers*, 2 and 3 (1885) · Earl of Malmesbury, *Memoirs of an ex-minister*, 1 and 2 (1884) · *A portion of the journal kept by Thos. Raikes, from 1831 to 1847* (1856) · *Reminiscences by Thomas Carlyle*, ed. C. Eliot, 1 (1887), 206 · Mrs Hardcastle, ed., *Life of John, Lord Campbell* (1881), 500 · L. Fagan, *The Reform Club, 1836–1886* (1887) · L. Fagan, *The life of Sir Anthony Panizzi, KCB*, 1 (1880) · P. Mérimée, *Lettres à Edward Ellice (1857–1863)* (Paris, 1963) · *Letters of Prosper Mérimée to Panizzi*, ed. L. Fagan (1881) · P. J. Anderson, ed., *Selections from the records of the Marischal College and University, 1693–1860*, 1 (1889), 508–9; 2 (1898), 381 · *Hansard 3* (1834), 25.284–303, 377–40 · 'Select committee on the army before Sebastopol', *Parl. papers* (1854–5), vol. 9, nos. 86, 156, 218, 247, 318 [reports 1–5] · *WWBMP*, vol. 1 · Burke, *Peerage* · J. Ridley, *Lord Palmerston* (1970) · L. Woodward, *The age of reform, 1815–1870* (1962) · *Inverness Courier* (17 Sept 1863) · *DNB* · R. G. Thorne, 'Ellice, Edward', HoP, *Commons, 1790–1820* · *IGI*

Archives NL Scot., corresp. and papers · NRA, priv. coll., accounts, letter-books, and estate papers · University of Toronto, Thomas Fisher Rare Book Library, family corresp. and papers | BL, corresp. with Lord Aberdeen, Add. MS 43200 · BL, corresp. with John Allen, Add. MS 52183 · BL, corresp. with W. E. Gladstone, Add. MSS 44374–44398, *passim* · BL, corresp. with J. C. Hobhouse, Add. MSS 36457–36472, *passim* · BL, corresp. with Lord and Lady Holland, Add. MSS 51587–51589, 52117 · BL, corresp. with Princess Lieven, Add. MSS 47376–47378 · Borth. Inst., corresp. with Sir Charles Wood · Derbys. RO, letters to Sir R. J. Wilmot-Horton · Lambton Park, Chester-le-Street, co. Durham, letters to the earl of Durham · Lpool RO, letters to fourteenth earl of Derby · NA Scot., letters to Sir John Dalrymple · NA Scot., letters to Lord Panmure · National Archives of Canada, corresp. with earl of Durham · NL Scot., letters to Baring family · NL Scot., letters to Sir George Brown · NL Scot., letters to John Burton · NL Scot., letters to Patrick Chalmers · NL Scot., letters to Andrew Rutherford · PRO, corresp. with Lord John Russell, PRO 30/22 · U. Durham L., letters to second Earl Grey · U. Durham L., corresp. with third Earl Grey · U. Southampton L., letters to Lord Palmerston · UCL, letters to Joseph Parkes · W. Sussex RO, letters to duke of Richmond

Likenesses engraving, pubd 1878, BM [*see illus.*] · G. Hayter, group portrait, oils (*The House of Commons, 1833*), NPG · J. Phillip, oils (*The House of Commons, 1860*), Palace of Westminster, London · portrait, Reform Club, London · woodcut, repro. in Fagan, *Reform Club*, 33

Wealth at death under £160,000 in UK: administration with will, 8 March 1864, CGPLA Eng. & Wales

Ellice, Edward (1810–1880), landowner and politician, was born in London on 19 August 1810, the only son of Edward *Ellice (1783–1863) and his first wife, Lady Hannah Althea (1785–1832), sister of Charles, second Earl Grey, and widow of Captain Bettesworth RN who was killed in action off Bergen on 25 May 1808. The Ellice family, who were English by descent, had settled in Aberdeenshire in the mid-seventeenth century. Edward Ellice was educated at Eton College (1823–6) and Trinity College, Cambridge, where he was admitted on 6 June 1828 and made MA, without previous degree, in 1831. He was made private secretary to Lord Durham during the latter's diplomatic mission to Russia in 1832, an appointment secured by his father, who was a close friend and relative of Durham (by the marriage of the latter to Louisa Elizabeth, daughter of the second Earl Grey).

On 15 July 1834 Ellice married his first wife, Katherine Jane (1813–1864) [*see* Ellice, Katherine], daughter of General Balfour of Balbirnie, Fife. At the general election of 1835 he stood as a Liberal candidate for Inverness, where he was defeated by four votes. In May 1837 he won a by-election at Huddersfield. But at the general election the same year he was returned for St Andrews burghs. In 1838, accompanied by his wife, he served as private secretary to Lord Durham during the latter's brief period as governor-in-chief of British North America. Both his wife and her sister Eglantine were captured briefly by Papineau during the Canadian uprising of 1838. Writing to Lady Durham from his father's seigneury at Beauharnois (the Ellice family owned considerable lands in Canada in addition to their financial holdings in the Hudson's Bay Company) in October 1838, he expressed support for Durham's resignation and early return to Britain. In 1839 his father purchased considerable lands at Glenquoich in Inverness-shire, formerly a part of the ancestral estate of the laird of the Macdonnell clan, for £32,000. Katherine Ellice, who was a woman of artistic and musical talents, acted as hostess to her father-in-law until his death in 1863.

The younger Ellice sat for St Andrews from 1837, often unopposed, until his death over forty years later—this longevity was typical of Scottish Liberal constituencies where landowners and their sons predominated. Of moderate whig–Liberal opinions, he remained a back-bench MP throughout his political career, concentrating in the main on Scottish questions. His political and family connections with the Grey–Halifax group in the Liberal cabinets of the 1860s gave him a wider influence among 'country house' whigs in the Commons; in 1875 he supported Lord Hartington's election as leader of the Liberal Party.

During the 1840s and 1850s Ellice took a prominent interest in reform of the Scottish poor law. He was a decided critic of the act of 1845, which established central and local machinery for the administration of relief, on the grounds that there was no power to ensure compulsory assessment by the parochial boards, who he feared would act solely in the interests of landlords. He was also critical of the act's provisions for transferring the legal remedies available to the poor from local magistrates to the central supervising board. These matters were brought to a head in 1853–4 by the tenant evictions at Knoydart, the last remnant of the bankrupt Macdonnell estate at Glenelg on the west coast of Inverness-shire. The condition of the small group of tenants who refused terms and were forcibly evicted, together with the failure of the parochial board to alleviate their distress, were used by Ellice to mount a general attack upon the whole administration of the poor law in the west highlands, published in his *Letter to the Rt. Hon. Sir George Grey, Bart., MP* in 1855. That year, as a private member, he introduced a bill to put right the failure of the central supervising board to make proper inquiry into events at Knoydart, by adopting the English practice of inspection by assistant commissioners to ensure proper local administration of relief. This was accepted and became law in 1856.

In 1860 Ellice purchased the adjacent Glengarry portion of the old Macdonnell estate from Lord Ward, for

£120,000. The combined Glenquoich and Glengarry estate was recorded in 1879 as totalling 99,500 acres, with a gross annual value of £6771. At Invergarry on Loch Oich, Ellice built a house which was renowned for its comfort. Both he and his father had a reputation as improvers and for an extravagant lifestyle; the local economy benefited to the tune of some £274,749 in estate expenditure over a period of some thirty years. After the death of his wife on 13 April 1864 he married, on 24 September 1867, Eliza Stewart, the widow of Alexander Spiers of Elderslie and daughter of Thomas Campbell Haggart (or Hagart) of Bantaskine, Stirlingshire.

As a whig landowner, he took the view that the 'clearance' of impoverished tenants, if voluntary and combined with properly funded emigration, could be beneficial, but that indiscriminate compulsory eviction was cruel and indefensible. His view on land reform was pragmatic. He argued that the effect of the land laws on the supply of land was greatly exaggerated, although he supported abolition of the law of primogeniture in cases of intestacy. With regard to landlord–tenant relations, he approved of landlord compensation to tenants for permanent improvements and took the side of the farmers in relation to the game laws. However he opposed abolition of the Scottish law of hypothec, which permitted a landlord to distrain the produce of a tenant who defaulted on rent payment, and effectively prevented the sale of crops before rent was due. He argued on grounds of expediency that this practice encouraged landlords to retain the smaller class of tenants, who had little recourse to other forms of security. To head off a long-running campaign by Scottish radical MPs for repeal he proposed assimilation with the English law of distress.

As the question of electoral reform became a ripening issue in the 1860s, with threatening implications for the role of whiggery in a more 'popular' Liberal Party led by Gladstone, Ellice worked closely with cabinet whigs such as Grey and Halifax to slow the pace of reform and secure a moderate measure. With others he lobbied successfully to ensure that franchise reform was accompanied by a redistribution of seats—the grouping of small boroughs. At various times during the passage of the second Reform Bill he supported and voted with the 'Adullamite' cave of back-bench whigs, who opposed a male household franchise. In the division of 9 May 1867 he was one of the fifty-eight Liberals who voted with Disraeli in support of a qualified ratepayer franchise. After the failure of this strategy he supported unsuccessful attempts to confine the occupation franchise in the counties to dwelling houses and other buildings with a rateable value of £15, a measure designed to prevent the creation of faggot votes by the purchase of small parcels of land by non-county residents.

Like many back-bench whigs, Ellice became increasingly uneasy with Gladstone's leadership of the Liberal Party. In November 1869 he declined Gladstone's offer of a peerage. He was strongly opposed to the government's proposals for Irish university reform in 1872–3 on the grounds of the plan's support for separate denominational colleges, which he saw as a violation of the whig anti-clerical tradition. During the 1874 general election he expressed private concerns regarding Gladstone's proposal to repeal income tax, seeing behind this scheme increased burdens on property, land, and inheritance. He was elected unopposed in 1874, when many Scottish Liberal seats fell to the Conservatives, but thereafter his health deteriorated. On 4 November 1879 he published a farewell address to his constituents and soon afterwards he retired from parliament. Following a bout of illness in June 1880 he sailed in July for a cruise in his yacht *Ita*. He died on board off Portland during the night of 2 August 1880 and was buried on 23 September at Tor-na-cairidh, near Loch Garry, Inverness-shire. He was survived by his second wife, who continued to reside at Invergarry and at Eastbury Manor, Guildford. Glenquoich was let to Lord Burton. Eliza was living in 1898, but since Ellice had no direct heirs (there were no children from either of his marriages), the estate later passed to his cousin Major Edward Charles Ellice (1858–1934), the son of his uncle Robert Ellice (1816–1858), who married Eglantine Charlotte Louisa Balfour (d. 1907), the younger sister of Ellice's first wife. Edward Charles joined the Grenadier Guards in 1876 and was made captain in 1886. He served with Lovat's scouts during the Second South African War and sat as the Liberal MP for St Andrews between 1903 and 1906. He rejoined the grenadiers in 1914 and was promoted to major in 1915. He commanded an entrenching battalion in Flanders. He retired from the army in 1918, having been appointed DSO, and died on 21 February 1934. He published *Place Names of Glengarry and Glenquoich and their Associations* (1898; 2nd edn, 1931).   JONATHAN SPAIN

Sources Burke, *Gen. GB* (1952) • Burke, *Peerage* • J. C. Lees, *A history of the county of Inverness* (1897) • *WWW*, 1929–40 • *WWBMP*, vols. 1–2 • H. E. C. Stapylton, *The Eton school lists, from 1791 to 1850*, 2nd edn (1864) • Venn, *Alum. Cant.*, 2/2 • E. C. Ellice, *Place names of Glengarry and Glenquoich* (1898); 2nd edn (1931) • J. Bateman, *The great landowners of Great Britain and Ireland*, new edn (1879) • E. Ellice, *A letter to the Rt. Hon. Sir George Grey, bart., MP, in reply to a report upon the administration of the Poor Law in the Highlands of Scotland* (1855) • E. Richards, *A history of the highland clearances: agrarian transformation and the evictions, 1746–1886*, 1 (1982) • A. A. Cormack, *Poor relief in Scotland* (1923) • T. Ferguson, *The dawn of Scottish welfare reform* (1947) • *Hansard 3* (1845), 78.1421, 1463; (1855), 138.34–48 • E. Ellice, 'Address to electors at Cupar, Fife', *The Times* (24 Jan 1873), 10b [on land reform] • *The Scotsman* (3 Aug 1880), 5a • C. W. New, *Lord Durham: a biography of John George Lambton, first earl of Durham* (1929); repr. (1968) • J. P. Parry, *Democracy and religion* (1986) • H. J. Hanham, *Elections and party management: politics in the time of Disraeli and Gladstone* (1959); repr. (1978) • M. Cowling, *1867: Disraeli, Gladstone and revolution* (1967) • T. A. Jenkins, *Gladstone, whiggery and the liberal party, 1874–1886* (1988) • *DNB*

Archives NL Scot., personal and family corresp. relating to political and public affairs and to local affairs in St Andrews and Inverness • University of Toronto, Thomas Fischer Rare Book Library, family corresp. and papers incl. Ellice junior | BL, corresp. with W. E. Gladstone, Add. MSS 44393–44786, *passim* • Borth. Inst., corresp. with Lord Halifax • NL Scot., letters to John Burton • NL Scot., letters to Andrew Rutherford • Trinity Cam., letters to Lord Houghton • U. Durham L., letters to third Earl Grey

Likenesses Richmond, oils; formerly at Invergarry, 1888

Ellice [*née* Balfour]**, Katherine Jane** [Janie] (1813–1864), diarist, was the second daughter of the four daughters and four sons of General Robert Balfour (1762–1837) of Balbirnie, Fife, and his wife, Eglantyne Katherine Fordyce (*d.* 1851). Well educated in the manner of her time and class, she spoke Italian and French, was an accomplished sketcher and watercolourist, and played the piano and guitar. On 15 July 1834 she married Edward *Ellice (1810–1880), politician and landowner, only son of Edward 'Bear' *Ellice (1783–1863), a politician with considerable land holdings in North America. Janie and Edward made their home at Glenquoich, Inverness-shire, but she also acted as hostess for her widowed father-in-law (with whom she had a close relationship) at Invergarry. There were no children of the marriage.

In April 1838 the Ellices sailed to Canada, where Edward served as private secretary to Lord Durham, the governor-general; he also used the mission to oversee his father's Canadian property. At the senior Ellice's request, Janie kept a journal (now in the Public Archives of Canada, and published in 1975) of her time in Canada. She recorded her impressions of the landscape (favourable), the wildlife (often venomous), Canadian society (comical and vulgar), the Native Americans (quaint, if embarrassingly under-dressed), and the American neighbours ('so entirely devoid of bashfulness that even awkwardness would be a relief'; *Diary*, 96). On 4 November 1838, while staying at 'Bear' Ellice's Lower Canadian property, Beauharnois, some miles from Montreal, Janie and her sister Eglantine (Tina) were taken prisoner by French Canadian insurgents, in a renewal of the troubles that had brought the Durham commission to Canada. Taken by surprise, 'alone, *en chemise*, in the middle of a group of the most "Robespierre" looking ruffians, all armed with guns, long knives & pikes' (p. 130) who proceeded to drink through the cellar, Janie appealed to her captors' sense of chivalry, and she and her sister were eventually allowed to take refuge with the Catholic priest, along with increasing numbers of prisoners. Although she was much frightened, Janie's account shows her to have retained both her courage (seeking an audience with 'one of the rebel Capts. who gave me a written permission allowing me to kill some of my *own* sheep & cattle & to get some milk from my 25 *cows*, all now in possession of the enemy'; p. 138), and her spirits (sketching the 'picturesque ruffians' guarding the house from her window; p. 140). After six days' confinement, Beauharnois was relieved by soldiers, but the village went up in flames. By 26 November the Ellices had left Canada and were sailing for England. Janie's diary ends on 26 December, back in Scotland with her mother.

Janie Ellice resumed her life as wife and hostess; this aspect of her life is commemorated in the household book of remedies, recipes, household hints, and patterns, which she kept between 1846 and 1859. Kept in an 'ordinary ruled exercise book' (*Recipes*, 11), and illustrated with pen-and-ink sketches of family and friends, the hints are attributed to various friends, and include: instructions for knitting a shawl ('very nice idle work, to be taken up in odd moments'; p. 81); recipes for fish balls, glue, and orange brandy; a cure for gout; 'How to fatten even the very leanest and scraggiest of poultry' (p. 67); and a 'Recipe for banishing Rats'—'Get a big HEELANDER with his bag-a-pipe—he blow his music—all the Rats run away' (ibid.). Janie Ellice died on 13 April 1864; her husband subsequently remarried. K. D. REYNOLDS

Sources *The diary of Jane Ellice*, ed. P. Godsell (1975) · *Jane Ellice's recipes, 1846–1859*, ed. J. A. Wentworth (1974) · Burke, *Gen. GB* (1937) · *IGI* · J. Colville, *Those Lambtons!* (1988)
Archives NA Canada
Likenesses engraving (after A. E. Chalon), repro. in *Diary*, ed. Godsell

Ellicombe, Sir Charles Grene (1783–1871), army officer, son of the Revd William Ellicombe, rector of Alphington, Devon, was born in his father's rectory on 3 August 1783. After attending the grammar school at Chudleigh, and the Royal Military Academy, Woolwich, he was commissioned first lieutenant in the Royal Engineers on 1 July 1801. He was employed for a year and a half on the military works and fortifications of Portsmouth, under Major-General Evelegh, and was then sent to Ceylon, one of the first batch of British engineers stationed there. The colony was in a very disturbed state, necessitating military operations in which Ellicombe served. He was promoted second captain on 1 July 1806, and returned to England at the end of 1807, where he was employed for a time as second engineer at Chatham, and afterwards as commanding engineer of the northern district of England.

On 1 May 1811 Ellicombe was promoted first captain, and in the October following joined the army under Wellington in the Peninsula. In January 1812 he was at the siege of Ciudad Rodrigo, where he was one of the directors of the attack, and accompanied the column of Vandeleur's brigade to the storming of the breach, left of the main breach. In March and April of the same year he was at the last siege of Badajoz. For his services at this siege he received the brevet rank of major on 27 April, having been recommended by Wellington in his dispatch of 10 April. He was present in the retreat from Burgos and the crossing of the Ebro. In 1813 he took part in the battle of Vitoria, serving on the staff as major of brigade. Throughout the siege of San Sebastian (11 July to 8 September 1813) he acted as brigade major to the Royal Engineers. For his distinguished conduct he was promoted brevet lieutenant-colonel on 21 September 1813, and received the gold medal. He fought at the passage of the Bidassoa, and at the battles of the Nivelle and Nive on 10, 11, and 12 December 1813. He also served in the campaign of 1814, particularly at the passage of the Adour, the blockade of Bayonne, and the repulse of the sortie from that fortress. At the end of hostilities he joined the headquarters of the army at Toulouse, and in July he returned to England.

On 4 June 1815 Ellicombe was one of the first people to be created CB, and for the next six years held an appointment as commanding engineer in the south of England. In 1821 he was made brigade major of the corps, and as such was on the staff of the inspector-general of fortifications at the Ordnance office in London, an appointment corresponding to the later post of deputy adjutant-general. He was selected for this duty on account of his administrative ability and knowledge of the large range of complicated details connected with the military and scientific business of the Royal Engineers. He fulfilled his duties so well that he retained the appointment for twenty-two years, until December 1842.

Ellicombe had been promoted major-general in 1841, and rose to the rank of full general (1861) and colonel-commandant of Royal Engineers (1856); on 10 November 1862 he was made KCB. He had married in 1822 a daughter of the Revd E. Peach, rector of Cheam, Surrey. She died in 1860; there were no children of the marriage. On retirement Charles Ellicombe settled at Worthing, Sussex, where he died on 7 June 1871.

R. H. VEITCH, *rev.* JAMES LUNT

Sources *Colburn's United Service Magazine*, 2 (1871) · PRO, War Office records, series WO · W. Porter, *History of the corps of royal engineers*, 2 vols. (1889) · W. F. P. Napier, *History of the war in the Peninsula and in the south of France*, 3 vols. (1878) · J. Weller, *Wellington in the Peninsula, 1808–1814*, new edn (1992) · Boase, *Mod. Eng. biog.*
Likenesses photograph, *c.*1860, Institution of Royal Engineers, Chatham
Wealth at death under £18,000: probate, 27 June 1871, *CGPLA Eng. & Wales*

Ellicott, Charles John (1819–1905), bishop of Gloucester, the only son of Charles Spencer Ellicott (1798–1880) and Ellen, daughter of John Jones, was born at Whitwell in Rutland, where his father was rector, on 25 April 1819. He was educated at grammar schools in Stamford and Oakham alongside J. W. Sheringham, a lifelong friend who was afterwards archdeacon of Gloucester. He proceeded to St John's College, Cambridge, in 1837, and gained the Bell University scholarship in 1838. He distinguished himself both at the union and on the river, which may account for his graduating second in the second class of the classical tripos. After completing his degree Ellicott engaged in tutorial work. He received his MA in 1844, and was elected to a Platt fellowship at his own college in 1845. He was made a deacon in 1846 and ordained priest in 1847. He surrendered his fellowship the following year in order to marry Constantia Anne, the daughter of Admiral Alexander Becher, on 13 August 1848; they had one son and two daughters. He was inducted to the parish of Pilton in Rutland in the same year; it was a small living which had a population of only forty-five people and an annual income of £80 in 1905. Here Ellicott embarked on what was to become a lifelong habit of academic study and writing.

Initially Ellicott pursued his mathematical interests and in 1851 he published *A Treatise on Analytical Statistics*. He also embarked on a series of commentaries on the Pauline epistles and his essay on the apocryphal gospels was included in *Cambridge Essays* (1856). Ellicott was wary of the newly emerging science of biblical criticism and his writings reflect a reverence for the traditional Catholic interpretation of scripture. His commentaries were both readable and scholarly and were widely read until J. B. Lightfoot's works began to appear. Ellicott's first commentary, on Galatians, appeared in 1854. Those on Ephesians, the pastoral epistles, Philippians, Colossians, Philemon, and Thessalonians all appeared between 1855 and 1859. The last in the series, on 1 Corinthians, appeared in 1887; commentaries on Romans and 2 Corinthians did not materialize.

In July 1851 Ellicott published a hostile review of the first volume of Henry Alford's New Testament commentary in the *Christian Remembrancer* and in July 1853 he attacked the commentary again for its open acceptance of critical biblical scholarship. Alford published a reply but his appreciation of Ellicott's *Galatians* in 1854 led to a lifelong friendship which widened his academic and religious horizons.

In 1858 Ellicott left Pilton to succeed Richard Chevenix Trench as professor of New Testament at King's College, London. In 1859 he gave the Hulsean lectures at Cambridge University, entitled 'The life of our Lord Jesus Christ', which were published in 1860 (6th edn, 1876) and were widely read. In this year he was elected to the Hulsean professorship which he held along with his chair at King's for what proved to be only a short time. He took up residence in Cambridge and it was while travelling from there to London on 19 February 1860 to lecture at King's that he was seriously injured in a train crash at Tottenham. The accident left Ellicott with a permanent limp and he was unable ever to wear episcopal gaiters. It did not, however, prevent his continuing to be a graceful skater and an active mountaineer; he joined the Alpine Club in 1871 and was still a member in 1904.

In 1861 Ellicott was made dean of Exeter, a diocese which had been for thirty years under the heavy hand of Bishop Henry Phillpotts. Here he wisely contented himself with entering into the bishop's plans for organizing a diocesan training college. In the same year he contributed to *Aids to Faith*, a series of essays aimed at counteracting the concessions to scientific discovery and biblical criticism expressed in *Essays and Reviews* (1860). His paper engaged with Benjamin Jowett's methods of interpreting scripture.

The year 1863 brought an important, and what turned out to be a final, move for Ellicott when Lord Palmerston appointed him to the united sees of Gloucester and Bristol. Although Ellicott was not an evangelical, the earl of Shaftesbury had suggested him and made clear his reasons for doing so: 'First a Cambridge man was wanted; secondly, some one in a high theological position; and thirdly, my own feeling that honour should be done to everyone (whenever occasion offered) connected with answers to *Essays and Reviews*' (Hodder, 3.199). Ellicott was consecrated in Canterbury Cathedral on 25 March 1863 and the sermon was preached by Dean Henry Alford.

Ellicott's episcopate lasted for forty-two years. He worked hard to improve the efficiency of his diocese and encouraged and motivated his clergy to higher levels of commitment and pastoral care. He devoted considerable energy to establishing the Gloucestershire Theological

College, whose student body 'goes far to supplying curates to the diocese' (*Charge*, 1874). He was keenly aware of the importance of erecting new churches, to which end he formed the Church Aid Society and actively supported the Bristol Church Extension Fund. In addition he raised £85,000 for the restoration of Bristol Cathedral.

Ellicott was a man of broad ecclesiastical sympathies but he could not abide ritualism. 'No loyal son of our mother church of England could', he declared, 'give the movement … his deliberate assent and approval' (*Ritualism: a Sermon Preached in Bristol Cathedral*, 4 Nov 1866). In 1867 he became a member of the royal commission on ritual and the rubrics. At his triennial visitation of 1873 Ellicott spoke forcibly against the reservation of the sacrament and the use of pyxes and chrismatories, and he counselled adherence 'to old truths' and 'old paths'. In 1877, he withdrew the licence of the incumbent of St Raphael's, Bristol, for his refusal to desist in ritualistic practices. Ellicott himself had no love for eucharistic vestments and wore only once those which had been presented to Bristol Cathedral. Bishop Samuel Wilberforce denounced Ellicott's attempt to have the chasuble banned as 'hot and intemperate' (R. Ashwell, *Life of Rt Revd Samuel Wilberforce*, 3.216, 1882). Ellicott was present in 1873 when a committee of the upper house of convocation drew up a report on confession. He later spoke at length on the subject. While admitting there to be a principle of confession in the Book of Common Prayer he contended that it was to be used 'only in emergency'. He warned of 'the scandal of every young priest setting himself up as a confessor' in *Some Present Dangers of the Church of England* (1878).

During his episcopate Ellicott engaged in a wide variety of academic and literary pursuits. Foremost among them, he believed, was his contribution to revision of the Bible. He termed it 'the greatest spiritual movement that has taken place since the Reformation' (*Addresses on the Revised Version*, 1901, 126). As early as 1856 he had urged the cause of revision as against a new translation in the preface to his *St Paul's Pastoral Epistles*. In the following year, together with four other clergymen, he published a revision of Romans. Corinthians followed in 1858 and other epistles in 1861. Ellicott was nominated chairman of the revision committee, which included some two dozen scholars. A total of 407 meetings were held over a ten-year period, of which he attended 405. As chairman he presented the revised edition of the New Testament to convocation in 1881, the Apocrypha in 1896, and the marginal references in 1899. A series of heated exchanges took place following the publication of the New Testament: Ellicott as chairman was accused of having gone beyond his brief and of allowing too many changes in the text. He defended himself with great grace and his *Addresses on the Revised Version of Holy Scripture* (1902) provides a very readable account of the proceedings.

The most important writing of Ellicott's later years was *The Old and New Testaments for English Readers*, for which Ellicott collected a number of able scholars, including E. H. Plumptre and W. Sanday. The New Testament appeared first in three volumes in 1878–9, and the Old Testament followed in five volumes in 1882–4. Both were subsequently reprinted. An abridged version of the New Testament for schools was also produced, and *The Complete Bible Commentary for English Readers*, in seven volumes, was published in 1897.

The publication of *Lux mundi* in 1891 stirred Ellicott to challenge the critical assumptions of some of the essayists. In his *Christus comprobator* (1891; 4th edn, 1892) he argued that Jesus's endorsement of authorship and events was a sufficient guarantee of their reliability. But Ellicott was by no means a reactionary figure: indeed his last visitation address of 1903 appears to reflect a change in his theological outlook. 'Ideas of propitiation and satisfaction to the eternal justice of God', he maintained, 'obtained a place in the past … which we cannot now feel to be holding an equally prominent place in the present' (*Doubt and its Remedy: a Charge Delivered, 1903, to the Archdeaconry of Gloucester*).

Ellicott was secretary of the first Lambeth conference in 1867, and of its successors in 1878 and 1888; he was also made registrar of the 1898 conference. On the death of Archbishop Longley he was recommended by Disraeli for the vacant see of Canterbury but Queen Victoria chose Bishop Campbell Tait. Ellicott was described by Lord Shaftesbury as a 'moderate high-churchman' (Broadlands MSS GC/SH/50). In *Some Present Dangers* (1878) Ellicott himself spoke of belonging to the party of the centre, which embraced the best spirits of both the pre-Tractarian old high-church party and the evangelical party.

Despite his scholarly work and other commitments in convocation and in the House of Lords, Ellicott did not neglect his diocese. As early as 1864 he had tabulated the state of affairs in his see (*The Times*, 16 Oct 1864). He urged his clergy to full observance of the church's festivals and seasons and he stressed the importance of baptism during the main Sunday services and of the greater frequency of holy communion. In 1872 Ellicott had an unfortunate brush with the National Agricultural Labourer's Union. In a speech at the annual Gloucestershire agricultural dinner he hinted that activists should be thrown into the village horsepond, but regretting his mistake he later did his best to make amends: in an address at Stow on the Wold in 1873 he urged his clergy to 'gentle impartiality' when dealing with the union members. In 1887 Ellicott published a volume entitled *Spiritual Needs in Country Parishes*. Among other things he advocated more restful and peaceful study of scripture, an increase of suffragan bishops, and the establishment of local clerical clubs and associations.

In 1897, with Ellicott's agreement, the united sees of Gloucester and Bristol were separated. Ellicott continued as bishop of Gloucester but his annual income was diminished by £900. As a tribute to his thirty-four years' supervision of the Bristol diocese a reredos designed by J. L. Pearson was erected in the cathedral and dedicated on 19 October. A celebration of his forty years as bishop took place in the chapter house at Gloucester Cathedral in 1903.

Ellicott was a tall man with a good sense of humour. All who knew him were struck by his simplicity of life and abstemious behaviour—he became a teetotaller to encourage those with drink problems (*Bristol Times*, 17 Oct 1905). He was remembered as an excellent preacher and a warm outgoing person, with a genuine interest in people.

Ellicott resigned from office on Lady day 1905 and died on 15 October 1905 at Trisco, Birchington, Kent, where he was buried on 21 October. He was survived by his wife.

NIGEL SCOTLAND

Sources *The Times* (16 Oct 1864) · *The Times* (16 Oct 1905) · *The Times* (24 Sept 1872) · W. A. C., *The Eagle*, 27 (1906), 84–106 · *The Eagle*, 27 (1906), 253–6 · *The Record* (7 June 1917) · *Bristol Times and Mirror* (17 Oct 1905) · *Gloucestershire Chronicle* (5 Oct 1872) · *DNB* · Venn, *Alum. Cant.* · *CGPLA Eng. & Wales* (1906) · E. Hodder, *The life and work of the seventh earl of Shaftesbury*, 3 vols. (1886)

Archives Bodl. Oxf. | BL, corresp. with W. E. Gladstone, Add. MSS 44403–44489 · Bodl. Oxf., letters to Benjamin Disraeli · Bodl. Oxf., letters to Samuel Wilberforce · Durham Cath. CL, letters to J. B. Lightfoot · Glos. RO, Estcourt MSS · LPL, corresp. with Edward Benson · LPL, corresp. with A. C. Tait · University of British Columbia, letters to Hugh Reginald Haweis

Likenesses F. Holl, oils, 1886, Bishopscourt, Gloucester · Bassano, photographs, *c.*1898, NPG · recumbent effigy, *c.*1905, Gloucester Cathedral · Barraud, photograph, NPG; repro. in *Men and Women of the Day*, 4 (1891) · J. Beattie, carte-de-visite, NPG · Cassell, Petter & Galpin, lithograph (after a photograph by London Stereoscopic Co.), NPG · M. Hanchard, photograph, Bishopscourt, Gloucester · London Stereoscopic Co., photographs, NPG · attrib. Maull & Polyblank, photograph, NPG · Spy [L. Ward], cartoon, chromolithograph, NPG; repro. in *VF* (18 July 1885) · stipple and line print, NPG

Wealth at death £73,562 15s. 4d.: probate, 1 Feb 1906, *CGPLA Eng. & Wales*

Ellicott, Edward (*c.*1733–1791). *See under* Ellicott, John (1702/3–1772).

Ellicott, John (1702/3–1772), watchmaker and scientist, was born in London, the son of John Ellicott (1674–1733), clockmaker, and his wife, Mary. John Ellicott senior, whose parents, Sampson and Elizabeth Ellicott, came from Bodmin, Cornwall, was baptized at St Anthonin's, Budge Row, on 2 September 1674. He was apprenticed in the Clockmakers' Company to John Waters on 5 September 1687, gaining his freedom on 6 July 1696. In 1726 he was living in All Hallows, London Wall, with business premises in Austin Friars. By 1728 his business was in Swithins Alley, Royal Exchange. He was elected as an assistant in the Clockmakers' Company in 1726, became junior warden in 1731, and renter warden in 1732. He died on 19 May 1733. His will, proved on 25 June 1733, granted administration to his widow.

The younger Ellicott's early life and education remain obscure but in 1719 or 1720 he was apprenticed in the Clothworkers' Company to Richard Ward, gaining his freedom in 1726. In St Anthonin's Church on 17 February 1729, at the age of twenty-six, he married Deborah Mary Saunderson (*d.* 1765), a spinster of the same age, of Mare Street, Hackney. They had five children, Edward [*see below*], John, Mary, Elizabeth, and Deborah. The daughters died unmarried, Mary in 1775, Deborah in 1789, and Elizabeth in 1790. Ellicott's sister Mary married Nicholas Crisp,

John Ellicott (1702/3–1772), by Robert Dunkarton (after Nathaniel Dance, *c.*1769)

whose father, Thomas, in his will of 1708, left his 'friend John Ellicott [senior] two guineas to buy a ring'. The Ellicotts were nonconformists and worshipped at the church of the congregation of dissenters in Mare Street, Hackney, where the Revd Samuel Palmer was pastor. Ellicott was by all accounts a keen archer and fond of a game of whist.

Ellicott began working with his father in Swithins Alley and lived in Mare Street, where his wife already owned property. He was elected to fellowship of the Royal Society on 26 October 1738, having been proposed by Sir Hans Sloane, bt, John Senex, Martin Ffolkes, and John Hadley, following presentation of a paper concerning his new pyrometer. He served on the council of the society for three years and presented a number of papers which were published in its *Philosophical Transactions*, beginning in 1738 with 'The description and manner of using an instrument for measuring the degrees of the expansion of metal by heat'. In 1744 he read 'An account of the influence which two pendulum clocks were observed to have on each other'. Papers followed on the specific gravity of diamonds, on electricity, and on the height to which rockets could be made to ascend. In 1753 his paper 'A description of two methods by which irregularities of the motion of a clock, arising from the influence of heat and cold upon the rod of the pendulum may be prevented' described and illustrated his design for a temperature-compensated clock pendulum. Its concluding paragraph referred to a 1748 model of a temperature compensating mechanism and his commissioning of a watch incorporating it.

Ellicott's pendulum was never widely adopted. Its inherent friction made its reaction to temperature change slow and erratic.

Ellicott maintained friendships with many of the leading scientists, astronomers, and instrument makers of the day, among them Peter Dollond, John Smeaton, and James Ferguson. He corresponded with Pehr Wargentin at the Swedish Royal Academy of Science in Stockholm and acted as an agent in the supply of instruments by John Bird to the Stockholm observatory. The firm of Ellicott supplied portable regulators for astronomical observations, particularly for the expeditions of Nevil Maskelyne and Charles Mason in 1761 and James Cook in 1769 to record the transits of Venus. Ellicott himself was a keen astronomer and had his own observatory in Hackney, where both he and Peter Dollond observed the 1761 transit, the results of which were published in the *Gentleman's Magazine*.

Although John Ellicott senior was a fine watchmaker, his business had been relatively small scale. When Ellicott joined the firm, however, the production of clocks and watches increased dramatically. Through the eighteenth century, under his stewardship, and from about 1754–5, that of his son Edward, with whom he went into partnership, Ellicotts became a leading supplier of clocks and watches of the highest quality. Ellicott's involvement in day-to-day production was probably minimal, as the organization of the business and cultivation of an aristocratic and wealthy clientele must have demanded his full attention. After his death the business was continued by **Edward Ellicott** (c.1733–1791) who about 1756 had married Mary, the daughter of John Lessingham, a partner in the bank of Sir George Colebrook. Following his death in Great Queen Street, London on 3 February 1791, it was under John's grandson Edward, who from about 1805 to 1818 worked in partnership with James Taylor. In the 1830s the firm became Ellicott and Smith. The fire which destroyed the Royal Exchange in 1838 precipitated the firm's move to 27 Lombard Street, where it was finally styled Ellicott and Cook before its demise in the 1840s. Between 1696 and about 1840 the Ellicotts sold almost 11,000 watches and numerous clocks, examples of which are now to be found in national museums and collections.

From 1762 until his death in 1772, John Ellicott was clockmaker to George III. He also supplied clocks and watches to the Spanish royal court and to Ferdinand VI himself. However, a letter of 3 July 1752 sent by Michael Smith, clockmaker, to the Spanish court, shows that at least one group of watches with equation of time indication supplied to the king and his entourage were actually made by Thomas Mudge.

Ellicott died at his Mare Street home in March 1772, quite suddenly, 'having dropped from his chair and instantly expired'. His will of 18 October 1771 reveals that he had been seriously ill earlier that year. It also confirms the extent of his wealth. Property left to his children consisted of six houses in West Smithfield and Cow Lane, a house held in copyhold in the manor of Hungerford Ingleford in Berkshire, his house in Mare Street, and two houses in Church Street, Hackney. His library of books, as well as his mathematical, philosophical, and scientific instruments, and all his working tools and stock were left to his son Edward. A portrait in oils by Nathaniel Dance painted in 1772 and copied in mezzotint by Robert Dunkarton shows him seated with his right arm resting on a table on which is an illustration of his compensation pendulum.   DAVID THOMPSON

Sources will, PRO, PROB 11/975, fols. 359–60 · will of Deborah Ellicot, née Saunderson, PRO, PROB 911/290 · parish register, Budge Row, St Anthonin's, GL, 10,091/69 [marriage], fol. 87, 17 Feb 1729 · 'Bibliographical notices of eminent horologists: John Ellicott', *Horological Journal*, 2 (1859–60), 152–4 · R. K. Foulkes, 'The Ellicotts', *Antiquarian Horology and the Proceedings of the Antiquarian Horological Society*, 3 (1959–62), 102–10 · G. Clifton, *Directory of British scientific instrument makers, 1550–1851*, ed. G. L'E. Turner (1995), 94 · *Cuadernos de Relojeria*, 11 (April–June 1957) · GM, 1st ser., 61 (1791), 277, 379 · J. Ellicott, 'The description and manner of using an instrument for measuring the degrees of the expansion of metals by heat', *PTRS*, 39 (1735–6), 297–9 · J. Ellicott, 'A description of two methods by which irregularities of the motion of a clock … may be prevented', *PTRS*, 47 (1753), 479–94 · C. Mason, 'Observations for proving the going of Mr Ellicott's clock at St Helena', *PTRS*, 52 (1761–2), 534–9 · J. Short, 'An account of Mr Mason's paper', *PTRS*, 52 (1761–2), 540–42 · J. V. Mallet, 'Nicholas Crisp, founding member of the Society of Arts [pts 1–3]', *Journal of the Royal Society of Arts*, 121 (1972–3), 28–32, 92–5, 170–74
Archives BL, letters relating to experiments with rockets, Add. MS 4439, fols. 101–107 · BL, letters relating to sidereal clock for George III, Kings Add. MS fol. 36 | BL, letters to T. Birch, Add. MS 4305, fols. 139–144
Likenesses N. Dance, oils, 1772 · R. Dunkarton, mezzotint (after oil painting by N. Dance, c.1769), BM [*see illus.*]
Wealth at death one copyhold and nine freehold houses; minimum £3365 money; £500 worth of annuities; plus value of business: will, PRO, PROB 11/975, fols. 359–60

Ellington, Sir Edward Leonard (1877–1967), air force officer, was born at 58 Elsham Road, Kensington, London, on 30 December 1877, the son of Edward Bayzand Ellington, a mechanical engineer, and his wife, Marion Florence (*née* Leonard). Educated at Clifton College from January 1892, he entered the Royal Military Academy, Woolwich, on 7 September 1895, being commissioned second lieutenant in the Royal Artillery on 1 September 1897. He joined the 41st battalion, Royal Field Artillery, at Lucknow, India, subsequently moving to D battalion, Royal Horse Artillery, at Ambala. Ellington advanced to lieutenant on 1 September 1900 and to captain on 27 April 1904 when joining 34th battery, Royal Field Artillery, at Meerut. Between 22 January 1907 and 21 December 1908 he attended the army Staff College, Camberley, and on 24 August 1909 he went to the War Office as a staff captain. He moved as GSO3 to the directorate of military training on 9 August 1910, later advancing to temporary GSO2 on 8 May 1913.

In 1912 Ellington took lessons at Brooklands flying school and acted also as secretary to the committee preparing plans for the separate Royal Flying Corps. In the following year he attended a course at the central flying school of the Royal Flying Corps, where he met Major H. M. Trenchard, to whose elder son he became godfather in 1921. From 17 April 1913 Ellington served as a flying officer in the Royal Flying Corps reserve, but he remained in the Royal Artillery to fight with 49th field battery during August 1914 at Mons and Le Cateau, then at the Marne and Aisne rivers, advancing to major on 30 October 1914. He became assistant adjutant and quartermaster-general as a temporary lieutenant-colonel in France on 6 March 1915. Ellington progressed to temporary lieutenant-colonel on 22 July 1915, to brevet lieutenant-colonel on 1 January 1916, and to temporary GSO1 in the directorate of military operations at the War Office on 5 February 1916. He obtained a brevet colonelcy on 1 January 1918 and became temporary brigadier-general on 14 January 1918, having been brevet colonel in the flying officers' reserve list from 17 December 1913.

Ellington was appointed deputy director-general of aeronautics at the War Office on 20 November 1917 and director-general and member of the Air Council in the new Air Ministry on 18 January 1918. At the formation of the RAF on 1 April 1918, Ellington was promoted major-general, becoming air vice-marshal when the new service adopted its own nomenclature in August 1919. Mentioned three times in dispatches during the First World War, he was made a chevalier of the Légion d'honneur (November 1914) and a member of the Russian order of St Stanislaus (1917), and was appointed CMG (1916), CB and CBE (1919), and KCB (1920). Ellington was controller-general of equipment, then director-general of supply and research, at the Air Ministry between 1919 and 1921 and air officer commanding the Middle East from 22 February 1922, India from 5 November 1923, and Iraq from 3 November 1926.

Ellington became air officer commanding-in-chief, air defence of Great Britain, on 1 January 1929 and air marshal and principal aide-de-camp to the king on 1 July 1929; he was air member for personnel on the Air Council from 26 September 1931. Promoted air chief marshal on 1 January 1933, he was unexpectedly appointed chief of the air staff from 22 May 1933, following the premature death of Sir Geoffrey Salmond. He seemed ill-suited for the post. Despite holding senior RAF staff appointments, he had never flown operationally and seen active service only in the army. Ellington was blamed for the RAF's weak state as war approached, and was criticized by contemporaries for ineffective leadership. At the Treasury, Edward Bridges believed him incapable of holding his own against the other service chiefs, and Warren Fisher, the permanent under-secretary, maintained that civil servants thus had to argue the RAF's case. However, he inherited a service well below its planned strength and, as chief of the air staff, did oversee establishment of the distinct bomber, fighter, coastal, and training commands (condemned as a dangerously divisive arrangement by those who favoured a single commander-in-chief under the chief of the air staff), besides development of radar, the eight-gun fighter, and the four-engine bomber. In 1934 he argued that occupation of the Low Countries 'would be the most effective means of mitigating the severity of German air attack on London' (Smith, 85), and during the Abyssinian crisis he devised an attack on Italy from southern France.

Ellington was appointed GCB in 1935 and promoted marshal of the Royal Air Force on 1 January 1937, and relinquished his position as chief of the air staff to become inspector-general of the RAF on 1 September 1937. He remained in that post until 4 April 1940, acquiring the nickname Uncle Ted (Probert, 14) owing to his 'kindness and absolute fairness' (*The Times*, 15 June 1967). However, his report dated 16 July 1938 about the Royal Australian Air Force's accident rate accused senior officers of failing to ensure 'a strict enforcement of regulations' (Coulthard-Clark, 307). The furious reactions included 'most regrettable', 'vicious', and 'a damnable thing … a good deal of the older school of British officer', leaving Ellington 'a surprised man' (ibid., 318–19).

Air Chief Marshal Sir Wilfrid Freeman thought Ellington 'the worst [chief of the air staff] we ever had, frightened of politicians' (Terraine, 44). When the Royal Navy regained its air arm in 1937, Trenchard reputedly told him, 'it's been decided over your head, which is well buried in the sand as usual' (Boyle, 701). But 'that distressing degree of shyness which caused Ellington to be misjudged and underrated' has been highlighted (Terraine, 44). Sir Maurice Dean, Ellington's private secretary when chief of the air staff, recognized that he 'knew little about aviation', but thought 'he had an acute mind and a remarkable memory' (Dean, 88), his administrative qualities being of paramount importance. *The Times* effusively held that he was 'a creator of the modern RAF … [which] owed much to his sagacity, sound judgement and powers of organisation and command' (15 June 1967). He remains, therefore, a controversial figure.

Ellington stayed on the active list until 1943, first as liaison officer at the directorate of ground defence, then with the north-west region civil defence commissioner. He was a member of the Windham, Marlborough, and United Service clubs. Ellington died on 13 June 1967 from coronary thrombosis at Scio House Hospital, Portsmouth Road, Putney, London.   JOHN SWEETMAN

Sources *Army List* · *Air Force List* · H. Probert, *High commanders of the Royal Air Force* (1991) · M. Smith, *British air strategy between the wars* (1984) · H. M. Hyde, *British air policy between the wars, 1918–1939* (1976) · J. Terraine, *The right of the line: the Royal Air Force in the European war, 1939–1945* (1985) · A. Boyle, *Trenchard* (1962) · U. Bialer, *The shadow of the bomber: the fear of air attack and British politics, 1932–1939* (1980) · *WWW, 1961–70* · *The Times* (15 June 1967) · Clifton College records · C. Coulthard-Clark, 'A damnable thing: the 1938 Ellington report', *Journal of Military History*, 54 (1990), 307–23 · M. Dean, *The Royal Air Force in two world wars* (1979) · b. cert. · d. cert. · *CGPLA Eng. & Wales* (1967) · Royal Military Academy records, Woolwich
Archives FILM BFI NFTVA, news footage · IWM FVA, news footage
Likenesses photograph, repro. in Dean, *The Royal Air Force in two world wars*
Wealth at death £25,279: probate, 13 Sept 1967, *CGPLA Eng. & Wales*

Ellington, Ray [*real name* Harry Pitts Brown] (**1916–1985**), drummer, singer, entertainer, and bandleader, was born on 17 March 1916 at 155 Kennington Road, Kennington, London, the second son and youngest of the four children of Harry Pitts Brown (*c*.1877–1920), a music-hall comedian and entertainer, and his wife, Eva Stenkell Rosenthal (*b.*

c.1879). His father was African American, his mother Russian. His father died when Brown was four years old and he was brought up by his Jewish mother in strict Orthodoxy. He attended St Phillip's Church of England School, Kennington, then completed his education at South London Jewish School (1924–30), before entering show business at the age of twelve, when he appeared in an acting role on the London stage. He was apprenticed to his uncle as a cabinet-maker, but an early fascination with music meant he had carved his own drumsticks before his woodwork lessons commenced. By the time he left school he was playing the drums but, still thinking of music as a sideline, he abandoned cabinet-making to follow his brother into a hairdressing apprenticeship. In 1933 he saw the Duke Ellington Orchestra and changed his name in admiration and tribute. In the same year he began his professional career. At Soho nightclubs he accompanied the charismatic American pianist Garland Wilson, eventually landing an important job at the Nest Club in Kingly Street, where, during after-hours sessions, he began to enhance his reputation by playing with the leading American jazz figures Benny Carter, Fats Waller, and Coleman Hawkins.

Ellington was not yet twenty-one when he joined the society band led by the clarinettist Harry Roy. An impressive figure, over 6 feet tall, 18 stone, and a sportsman, he cut a dashing figure behind the drums, and when Roy persuaded him to sing and act the comedian he became the band's featured artist. On a tour of South America he learned to play bongos and developed a lifelong interest in Afro-Cuban and Latin rhythms. His first experience of big-band work came with Van Phillips, and he worked with another top bandleader, Lew Stone, before war service claimed him. In the RAF he reached the rank of flight sergeant as a physical training instructor, teaching unarmed combat to officer trainees; in the later years of the war he returned to a musical role, joining the Blue Eagles dance band and playing for the Entertainments National Service Association with Don Marino Barreto.

In 1946 Ellington was influenced by bebop, the new black music of the day. This, a combination of musical formulae and attitudes arrived at in America by such figures as Charlie Parker and Dizzy Gillespie, created new artistic directions for musicians generally while representing a positive self-image for people of the African diaspora. It provided the impetus for Ellington's bandleading career. He formed a bebop group with Pete Chilver on guitar, but this failed to attract much attention and he rejoined Harry Roy. He played drums with the violinist Stephane Grappelli and sang with the accordionist Tito Burns while sowing the seeds for his new group during jam sessions with the Caribbean Club's house trio. This comprised the Trinidadian guitarist Lauderic Caton, the Jamaican double bass player Coleridge Goode, and the German pianist Dick Katz. Under the guidance of the American dance instructor Buddy Bradley the four musicians created the Ray Ellington Quartet. Launched in November 1947, the quartet provided jazz, humour, and swing in equal quantities and used intricate arrangements influenced by other popular musicians of the day, such as saxophonist/

vocalist Louis Jordan and the Nat 'King' Cole Trio. Although their repertory included musically progressive numbers, the goal of commercial success was paramount, and Bradley's influence was discernible in their choreographed 'business' routines, and their careful appearance and dress.

The Ray Ellington Quartet was one of the most successful acts of the immediate post-war period. It was voted *Melody Maker*'s top small band for two years running, and among its regular BBC radio spots was *The Goon Show*, where Ellington further developed his comedic skills and national reputation. His quartet also made a number of guest appearances in films, notably *Paper Orchid* (1949). In April 1949 Caton left, to be replaced by the equally accomplished Laurie Deniz. Appearing in variety, playing for dancers, and recording, the quartet lasted for thirty-five years, although its later editions never achieved the prominence it had enjoyed in its heyday. A certain social cohesion was an important factor in how the group was initially perceived—even with a white pianist, it was the main organized musical group to showcase black talent following the demise of Ken 'Snake Hips' Johnson. After Goode's departure in 1951, Ellington employed white musicians, with the result that the perceived cultural emphasis changed. In 1956 Ellington and a fellow bandleader, Edmundo Ros, shared the honours in the radio series *Mr Ros and Mr Ray*, written by Johnny Speight. In the same year he married the actress Ann E. D. Wuest (stage name Anita West). They had two children: Lance (b. 1957), a singer and instrumentalist, and Nina (b. 1960), but were divorced in 1963.

Ray Ellington was a black Briton respected during his lifetime for his ability and achievements. However, his contributory role in advancing British popular music has been largely overlooked, doubtless owing to his predilection for comedy. As a drummer he celebrated the modern jazz aesthetic and so knew that the irresistible progress of bebop could not be ignored. Equally he realized that, to capture public attention for radical musical ideas, these must be tempered with humour and entertainment. His quartet helped to lay the groundwork in Britain for the wider acceptance of black music and the advent of rock and roll—and the appreciation of the modern blues to come. A lifelong devotee of physical culture, Ellington set off his weightlifter's muscles with dapper tailoring, gardenia perfume, and a pencil moustache. He maintained these and his quartet into the 1980s, filling lengthy residencies at exclusive London restaurants and providing cruise-ship entertainment. He died from stomach cancer in the Royal Marsden Hospital, Chelsea, on 27 February 1985, survived by the two children of his marriage.

Val Wilmer

Sources J. Vedey, *Bandleaders* (1950) · M. Modlyn, *Jewish Chronicle* (20 July 1984) · 'Ray Ellington group under Heath banner', *The Beat*, 10 (1974), 3 · R. Ellington and B. Bradley, 'The truth about bebop!', *Accordion Times and Musical Express* (10 Sept 1948), 6 · L. Feather, 'Tempo di jazz', *Radio Times* (Jan 1937) · T. Brown, 'A rehearsal with the Ray Ellington quartet', *Melody Maker* (19 May 1951), 8 · personal knowledge (2004) · private information (2004) · b. cert. · d. cert.

Likenesses Chadel, photograph, 1948, priv. coll. · W. Hanlon, photographs, c.1948–1949, priv. coll. · Vince, photographs, 1949
Wealth at death under £40,000: probate, 17 April 1985, *CGPLA Eng. & Wales*

Elliock. For this title name *see* Veitch, James, Lord Elliock (1712–1793).

Elliot. *See also* Eliot, Elliott, Elyot.

Elliot, Adam (1645/6–1700), Church of England clergyman and slander victim, was born at Jedburgh, Roxburghshire, the son of Henry Elliot, clergyman. He matriculated at Gonville and Caius College, Cambridge, on 10 November 1664, aged eighteen, and graduated BA in 1669. Much of what is known about him appears in his memoir, *A Modest Vindication of Titus Oates* (1682). After leaving Cambridge, where Titus Oates later claimed to have known him, he travelled to France and Italy, visited Rome, and then left for Leghorn, Alicante, and Lisbon. On his return journey, in June 1670, his ship was seized by pirates and he was taken to Salé where he was sold to a rich merchant, Hamed Lucas. Despite the harsh treatment, Elliot recalled vivacious moments as he sometimes entertained his patron with English songs—'particularly I remember "Calm was the Evening", &c. in the "Mock-Astrologer"'. A few months later he escaped to the Spanish presidio of Mamoura; he returned via Cadiz and Texel to England in November 1670, never to leave his country again.

Elliot became a private tutor in Oxford to Colonel Charles Wheeler; he was ordained deacon at Ely in 1671. In May 1672 he moved to Kent, where he lived with Sir Thomas Scot. At the end of that year, as curate of Allington, Kent, he was ordained priest in London and became a private chaplain to William, Lord Grey of Warke, with whom he remained until the latter's death in 1674. Elliot left then for a church in Dublin until September 1679 when he returned to England to serve as a witness on behalf of Lord Grey's son. Lord Grey's son-in-law, Lord North, was contesting the will, and in order to undermine Elliot as a witness, he turned to Titus Oates for help. Oates, at the height of his power, accused Elliot of being a 'Circumcis'd Jesuit'—a Jesuit who had converted to Islam. But the next day, powerful friends of Elliot came to his assistance, and Oates withdrew his accusation. Elliot returned to Dublin but was soon after accused by a local protestant zealot of slandering Oates and calling him a 'Rogue'. In that anti-Catholic environment, he was fined £200. As if that suit was not enough, in May 1680 Oates brought another suit accusing Elliot of misdeeds during his Cambridge years, of conversion to Islam during his captivity, and of murdering his patron. Elliot refuted the allegations although he was eager not to be seen questioning the Popish Plot which Oates had claimed to uncover. In his memoir he showed how specious Oates's accusations against Jesuits had been, and refuted all the accusations against himself, mentioning how Hamed Lucas, who had recently visited England with the Moroccan ambassador, had confirmed that Elliot had not turned 'renegado' as Oates claimed. On 30 June 1682 Elliot brought an action of slander against Oates, who introduced a medley of witnesses to support him, including Lord North. But Elliot won his suit, having shown how Oates had lied 'most malitiously', and received £20 in damages. A year later Bartholomew Lane published a burlesque of Elliot in *A Modest Vindication of the Hermite of the Sounding Island* (1683). From 1685 Elliot was perpetual curate of St James's, Duke Place, London. He died in 1700.   NABIL MATAR

Sources A. Elliot, *A modest vindication of Titus Oates, the Salamanca doctor from perjury* (1682) · B. Lane, *A modest vindication of the hermite of the sounding island: in requital for the modest vindication of the Salamanca doctor from perjury* (1683) · G. Borlase, ed., *Cantabrigienses graduati … usque ad annum 1800* (1800), 129 · Venn, *Alum. Cant.*

Elliot, Ann (1743–1769), courtesan and actress, was born on 16 November 1743 in Tonbridge, Kent, the daughter of Richard Elliot (1706?–1771), the sexton of Tonbridge parish church, and his wife, Mary (1716–1748). She moved to London as a lady's servant, but was soon a high-class prostitute, using the name Miss Hooper. She became the protégée of the playwright Arthur Murphy (1727–1805), who trained her as an actress and wrote the part of Maria for her in his comedy *The Citizen*. She made her début in this role on 2 July 1761, during the summer season at Drury Lane Theatre managed jointly by Murphy and Samuel Foote. Murphy later dedicated the play to her, ascribing its success to her 'uncommon talents' and 'genuine comic genius'.

In a letter to Murphy dated 22 June 1761, David Garrick had criticized Elliot's pronunciation and claimed that her face was 'more form'd to create Passion, than to Express it'; he offered to give her a trial without salary in the coming season. However, she preferred to go to the Crow Street Theatre, Dublin, where Richard Cumberland remembered her playing Maria 'with admirable spirit and effect' (Cumberland, 1.232). After another summer season with Foote, she spent the rest of her career at Covent Garden under John Beard's management. For three seasons she played lively roles in comedies, such as Cherry in George Farquhar's *The Beaux' Stratagem*, Bizarre in his *The Inconstant*, and Berinthia in Sir John Vanbrugh's *The Relapse*. She was particularly successful in comic afterpieces, playing Polly in George Colman's *Polly Honeycombe*, Termagant in Murphy's *The Upholsterer*, and, above all, Maria in *The Citizen*. Her appearances were reduced by illness, particularly in the 1764–5 season. George Ann Bellamy, whose roles she had taken over, remembered that she regained her parts, 'Miss Elliot's ill health obliging her often to decline playing' (Bellamy, 4.103). In 1765–6 she performed only once, for the benefit of the actor Charles Holland at Drury Lane, and the next season at Covent Garden was to be her last. In November 1766 she took her only tragic role, Calista in Nicolas Rowe's *The Fair Penitent*; the *Court Miscellany* (November 1766, 618) thought she had 'very great merit as a tragic actress' but *Thespis* found her too 'circumscrib'd in voice' (Kelly, 43). Murphy's final gift to her was the role of Mary Ann in *The School for Guardians*, his reworking of Wycherley's *The Country Wife*. He quarrelled with Garrick ('a little sneaking rascal'; Taylor, 1.194), accusing him of forestalling the play with his own *Country*

Girl. Murphy's play was acted six times in January and February 1767, and he gave Elliot the proceeds of the two author's nights.

In his *Life of Arthur Murphy*, Jesse Foot gives a description of the 'sylphic and enchanting' Ann Elliot as she was in January 1763, when he first saw her: 'she was a good figure, somewhat above the middle stature … her complexion was very clear; her eyes were dark hazel, and her hair a beautiful brown' (Foot, 188). Her charms attracted lovers, including Augustus Hervey, later third earl of Bristol (1724–1779), who is said in the *Genuine Memoirs of the Life and Adventures of the Celebrated Miss Ann Elliot* (1769) to have removed her from the stage (possibly in 1765–6) and the king's brother, Henry Frederick, duke of Cumberland (1745–1790). Cumberland set her up in a house in Greek Street, and it was there that she died, on 30 May 1769, after a long and painful illness. She had remained in touch with Murphy and wished to bequeath him her estate, but he insisted that it should go to her poor relations and acted as one of her executors. The *Gentleman's Magazine* reported that she left £8000; her will mentions plate, jewellery, a considerable quantity of furniture, and £5000 promised her by the duke of Cumberland, of which part had been paid, £1000 being invested in the funds. Her relationship with Cumberland probably ended some months before her death, but he is said to have fulfilled her dying request and ensured that her body was buried with her mother's remains, erecting a monument in Tonbridge churchyard with memorial verses almost certainly written by Murphy.   OLIVE BALDWIN and THELMA WILSON

Sources G. W. Stone, ed., *The London stage, 1660–1800*, pt 4: 1747–1776 (1962) · J. Foot, *The life of Arthur Murphy* (1811) · J. P. Emery, *Arthur Murphy* (1946) · H. H. Dunbar, *The dramatic career of Arthur Murphy* (1946) · A. Murphy, 'Dedication', *The citizen* (1763) · A. Murphy, 'Advertisement', *The school for guardians* (1767) · J. Taylor, *Records of my life*, 1 (1832) · *Genuine memoirs of the life and adventures of the celebrated Miss Ann Elliot* (1769) · *Critical Review*, 28 (1769), 67–8 · J. G., 'Memoirs of the late celebrated Miss Anne Elliot', *Town and Country Magazine*, 1 (1769), 322–3 · *London Chronicle* (13–15 July 1769) · will, Family Records Centre, London · G. A. Bellamy, *An apology for the life of George Anne Bellamy*, ed. [A. Bicknell], 6 vols. (1785), vol. 4 · [E. Thompson], *The meretriciad*, 2nd edn (privately printed, London, 1761) · [E. Thompson], *The courtesan* (1765) · C. Churchill, 'The Rosciad', *The poetical works of Charles Churchill*, ed. W. Tooke, [2nd edn], 1 (1844) · H. Kelly, *Thespis, or, A critical examination into the merits of all the principal performers belonging to Covent-Garden Theatre* (1767) · *Smithfield Rosciad* (1763) · *Court Miscellany* (Nov 1766) · R. Cumberland, *Memoirs of Richard Cumberland written by himself*, 2 vols. (1806–7), vol. 1 · *The letters of David Garrick*, ed. D. M. Little and G. M. Kahrl, 3 vols. (1963) · *St James's Chronicle* (3–6 June 1769) · *GM*, 1st ser., 39 (1769)

Likenesses J. Saunders, engraving, pubd 1772 (as Minerva; after R. Cosway), BM · W. P. Sherlock, engraving (after T. Kettle), repro. in Foot, *The life of Arthur Murphy* · J. Watson, engraving (as Juno; after T. Kettle), BM · miniature (after T. Kettle); known to be at Garr. Club in 1936; stolen

Wealth at death £8000, according to *GM*; will, £5000 promised by duke of Cumberland; also plate, jewellery, clothes, and furniture

Elliot, Archibald (*bap.* 1761, *d.* 1823), architect, was baptized on 30 August 1761 at Ancrum, Roxburghshire, the son of Archibald Elliot, a carrier. Ancrum was a parish reputed for its building craftsmen. With his brother

James Elliot (*bap.* 1770, *d.* 1810), architect, baptized on 29 April 1770 in Ancrum, Archibald redesigned some of the largest and most imposing early nineteenth-century romantic houses in Scotland. It is not known where the brothers trained, but possibly in the expatriate community in London. Archibald was involved (possibly initially at craft level, since until the end of his life he ran a carpenter's shop beside his office in Osnaburg Street, St Pancras) in works to Douglas Castle, Lanarkshire, which James Playfair began in 1791. On Playfair's death in 1794, the year Elliot first exhibited at the Royal Academy, he took over charge of works at Douglas. Probably some time before 1799 he married Sarah Shiells, for their son Archibald, also an architect, was born that year. It is thought that the brothers had some link with George Steuart, another expatriate Scot who retired to the Isle of Man, and in particular with the construction of Steuart's Castle Mona at Douglas (1806). Certainly Steuart's clientele—the dukes of Atholl and earls of Abercorn—match with the Elliots', and may have facilitated their acceptance by aristocratic society. Any work they undertook in England has not yet been identified. In 1800 James Elliot was introduced to the second marquess of Breadalbane by Alexander Trotter of Dreghorn, for whom he was reworking and aggrandizing Dreghorn, Midlothian (dem.), as:

> a young man who has considerable talents as a draughtsman … as he is at this time quite disengaged he would be most happy to mount his poney and wait upon you at Taymouth … He is a young man of but very mean appearance but of considerable abilities as a draftsman and designer, and he proposes to join in business with a brother whom he has got in London and who has had a regular education there, and much experience with the best masters. Their good character, attention and ability has induced me to mention them (Breadalbane Muniments, NA Scot.)

and he forwarded a plan by James for Taymouth Castle, Perthshire, then being rebuilt by John Paterson. By 1805 James was appointed architect for 'the finishing' of Taymouth by the marquess (a man given to detailed design and contract interference), which appears, in essence, to symbolize the cadet house of the Campbells seeking to outclass the chief's Inveraray Castle (the residence of the dukes of Argyll). Archibald was paid a separate fee for advice whenever consulted, provided highly ornate doors for the marquess' Park Lane house, and prepared and shipped up wainscoting for Taymouth. The characteristic central tower the Elliots erected at Taymouth was used by James to denote nobility.

As architect, Archibald Elliot advertised in 1804 for contractors to rework and aggrandize Loudoun Castle, Ayrshire (now in ruins), for the earl of Moira, which implies an already substantial reputation. It was quickly followed by the Dunfermline Guildhall and Stobo House, Peeblesshire (both 1805), for Chief Baron Montgomery. The brothers were joint architects for Stobo, but James controlled the contract. Large houses such as Stobo were heavily picturesque, symmetrical, and invariably in castellated clothing in the manner of Inveraray or Monzie Castle, Perthshire. Given that his patrons were generally from the top rank of Scottish society, Archibald could liaise directly with them when he was in London for the season, living at 60 High Street and then New Road, Marylebone, and, later, at Osnaburg Street in St Pancras. The Elliots' London presence helped to prevent their clients from being tempted to commission fashionable, London-based English architects. It was William Atkinson to whom Breadalbane went, however, for advice of how to remedy water penetration in Taymouth's tower. James, meanwhile, set up as architect in Carrubber's Close, Edinburgh.

Breadalbane also appointed James Elliot, together with Allan Johnston (builder of Stirling Atheneum) to design the villa of Auchmore House, Killin (1806–7) and the delightful octagonal Glenorchy church, Dalmally (1809). In 1807 James produced a simple crow-stepped box as the new kirk in Kirkcaldy, and the following year undertook alterations to Dunkeld House. He had suffered from ill health since 1807, and died, aged forty, in October 1810, just after completing a new lodge at Taymouth.

Thereafter Archibald Elliot opened an Edinburgh base, at Calton Hill. Between 1809 and 1814 he reworked the unusual V-plan of Minto House, Hawick, into a strangely austere classical composition for Lord Elliot (with whom there may have been a connection), undertook works to Dunkeld Cathedral in 1814 (drawings at Blair Castle), and towered Lindertis House, Forfarshire (1815; dem.). The buildings of the remainder of his career veered in style between a continuation of castellated picturesque and grandly neo-classical. In the former were the prison and governor's house, Calton Hill, Edinburgh (1815–17)—'a toy castle devoid of expression and utterly meaningless', sniffed Sir Rowand Anderson (R. R. Anderson, *The Place of Architecture in the Domain of Art*, 1889, 23)—Newbyth, East Lothian (1816), the north front of Lochnell House, Barcaldine—a stylistic attribution, although General Campbell of Lochnell still owed him £113 at his death—the county and town buildings, Paisley, built with William Reid (both of 1818–20), and the diminutive Jedburgh model gaol (1820–23).

Archibald Elliot's reputation, however, rests upon his neo-classical urban designs, beginning with the momentous Regent bridge, Edinburgh (1815), which he won in competition with James Gillespie and Richard Crichton. It involved vast underbuilding, wholly obscured by the delicate columned screens visible today. While in London he entered the Edinburgh University competition of 1816 unsuccessfully and the same year was appointed for the county buildings, Edinburgh (dem.). Two years later he designed Edinburgh's Waterloo Place (and became a shareholder in the Waterloo Hotel). It is the crisp majesty of these neo-classical buildings, the use of the most up-to-date details, and the grandeur of axial conception of Waterloo Place that secured his reputation. In 1819 he designed a pantheon at the bottom of Edinburgh's Mound for the prospectus for the commissioners of the national monument, whose still outstanding fee of £200 was classed as an irrecoverable debt on his death. In 1819 he prepared a scheme building on the damlands of Rubislaw (land just west of old Aberdeen) and for Rutland Street and

Rutland Square, Edinburgh. His Broughton Place Church in Edinburgh of 1821 has an extraordinarily heavy horizontality, whereas The Haining in Selkirk was extended *c*.1818 with a delightful bow and colonnade.

In 1816 Elliot designed the ambitiously perpendicular St Paul's and St George's Episcopal Church, Edinburgh, with a superimposed lacy decoration in the manner of a Cambridge college chapel. This form was echoed at his Cockpen church tower in East Lothian (1818). Miscellaneous works include the Grecian mausoleum in Callendar Park, Falkirk (1816), unexecuted plans to restore St Giles, Edinburgh (1817), court rooms in Parliament House (1818), an extension to 35 St Andrew's Square, Edinburgh (1819), houses in Leith (1820), and Blair Atholl church (1823). To judge by the substantial debts owed to him by the duke of Atholl and John Pringle, and lesser sums by the earl of Morton, Admiral Mowbray, Sir James Montgomery, the marquess of Lothian, the earls of Eglinton and Minto, and Robert Fraser (never mind the heritors of Blair Atholl and Inveresk), he was working on a number of projects at his death. In December 1822 the directors of Inverness Academy sought a design from Elliot, expecting him to visit in the next few months, but he died at Calton Hill, Edinburgh, on 16 June 1823, aged sixty-one. He was buried in the new Calton cemetery, his wife returned to London, and the practice was carried on by his son Archibald.

CHARLES McKEAN

Sources N. Allen, ed., *Scottish pioneers of the Greek revival* (1984) • [W. Papworth], ed., *The dictionary of architecture*, 11 vols. (1853–92) • Colvin, *Archs.* • *Sheriff Court Records*, 28 June 1825, Commissariat of Edinburgh, SC 70/41/373, SC 70/31/324 • J. Macaulay, *The Gothic revival* (1975) • M. C. Davis, *The castles and mansions of Ayrshire* (1991) • *Jones' views of the seats, mansions, castles … in England, Wales, Scotland and Ireland*, Jones and Co., 4: *Series of Scottish seats* (1829) • National Monuments Record of Scotland Index • private information (2004) [Ian Fisher, Professor David Walker, Kitty Cruft and Rob Close] • *Edinburgh*, Pevsner (1984) • M. Glendinning, R. MacInnes, and A. MacKechnie, *A history of Scottish architecture* (1996) • Graves, *RA exhibitors* • J. M. Leighton, *Select views on the River Clyde* (1830) • A. J. Youngson, *The making of classical Edinburgh, 1750–1840* (1966); repr. (1975) • T. A. Markus, ed., *Order and space in society* (1982) • C. McKean, ed., *Illustrated architectural guides to Scotland* (1982–) • H. Storer, *Views in Edinburgh* (1820) • NA Scot., Breadalbane Muniments • NA Scot., Strathearn and Blair MSS • NA Scot., Lochnaw Muniments • NA Scot., Fraser Mackintosh collection, GD 128/35/5 • bap. reg. Scot. • bap. reg. Scot. [James Elliot]

Wealth at death approx. £2000—of creditors: *Sheriff Court Records*, Commissariat of Edinburgh, SC 70/41/373 • shop on Osnaburg Street; four stores in Waterloo Hotel

Elliot, Arthur Ralph Douglas (1846–1923), politician and journalist, was born at 27 Eaton Place, London, on 17 December 1846, the second son of William Hugh Elliot Murray Kynynmound, third earl of Minto (1814–1891), and his wife, Emma (d. 1882), only daughter of General Sir Thomas Hislop, first baronet. He was the younger brother of Gilbert John Elliot Murray *Kynynmound, fourth earl of Minto, governor-general of Canada and viceroy of India. At the age of four his leg had to be amputated as the result of a fall. This prevented him from going to school, but his spirit was such that he climbed, shot, rode to hounds, and learned to swim. He went to Edinburgh University in 1863, before proceeding to Trinity College, Cambridge, in 1864, as a fellow commoner, and, in spite of the loss of a year owing to a serious illness in 1866, graduated BA in 1868 as third junior optime in the mathematical tripos.

After leaving Cambridge, Elliot (the surname by which he was known) was called to the bar by the Inner Temple in 1870 and joined the northern circuit. In 1878 he published a pamphlet entitled *Criminal Procedure in England and Scotland*. At the general election of 1880 he was elected member of parliament for Roxburghshire as a Liberal. He quickly and strongly opposed home rule in 1886 and was again elected for Roxburghshire, as a Liberal Unionist, in that year, and founded the Liberal Union Club. He lost the seat in 1892 and was defeated (by one vote) in 1895 for the City of Durham, which he subsequently won at a by-election in 1898, and held until 1906. In April 1903 Elliot was appointed financial secretary to the Treasury by A. J. Balfour. Almost immediately the free-trade controversy became acute, and when C. T. Ritchie, the chancellor of the exchequer, left the government in September 1903, Elliot, who was a strong free-trader, also resigned. For some years afterwards he took part in the campaign for free trade, and he founded the Unionist Free Trade Club. But when he was defeated at Durham in the general election of 1906, he left politics, in which, as a Unionist and free-trader, he felt he had no place.

Elliot had succeeded Henry Reeve as editor of the *Edinburgh Review* in 1895, and his policy was to make the *Review* an organ of moderate and responsible opinion representing the modern developments of the old whig tradition. Under his careful management—he remained editor until 1912—the principle of anonymity was maintained, and the importance of the political side of the *Review* emphasized. For Elliot was chiefly a politician, with strong convictions coloured by the whig tradition—he was sometimes called the last of the whigs—combined with ardent patriotism. For the *Review* he wrote at least fifty-six articles. In addition, he contributed *The State and the Church* to the English Citizen series in 1882. In 1911 he published the *Life of George Joachim Goschen, First Viscount Goschen* (2 vols.), valuable for its account of the home-rule split; and in 1918 *The Traditions of British Statesmanship*.

A man of great personal charm and kindliness, and popular in the political class generally, Elliot married in 1888 Madeleine Harriet Dagmar, daughter of Sir Charles Lister Ryan, of Ascot, sometime comptroller and auditor-general; they had two sons. She died on 1 January 1906. Only the younger son survived him, and at his house, Park House, Broadlands, Romsey, Elliot died on 12 February 1923. For some years Elliot had lived at Dimbola, Freshwater, Isle of Wight, the house formerly occupied by Julia Margaret Cameron, the photographer.

MAURICE HEADLAM, rev. H. C. G. MATTHEW

Sources *The Times* (13 Feb 1923) · *EdinR*, 237 (1923), 209–14 · *Wellesley index* · A. B. Cooke and J. Vincent, *The governing passion: cabinet government and party politics in Britain, 1885–86* (1974)
Archives NL Scot., corresp., diaries, and papers; family corresp.

Likenesses B. Leighton, sketch, Grillion Club
Wealth at death £8448 15s. 7d.: probate, 21 March 1923, *CGPLA Eng. & Wales*

Elliot, Charles (1748–1790), bookseller, was born on 7 March 1748 near Selkirk, the youngest of five children of Andrew Elliot, tenant of Oakwood Miln farm, and the second child of Mary Simpson. He apparently learned bookselling in Kirkcaldy, where his sister Margaret and brother-in-law Thomas Kay were merchants. He served as an apprentice to the bookbinder Walter Smeiton of Edinburgh before buying the stock of William Sands (d. 1770) and starting as a bookseller in Parliament Square in May 1771. After five years Elliot extended his premises to two rooms with a floor below, telling John Murray in London: 'I have as good a shop as any in Fleet Street' (letter to Murray, 24 July 1777). On 5 September 1780 he married Christian Sands (1761–1832), the daughter of his predecessor. James Boswell browsed at his shop, and in May 1787 Robert Burns exchanged copies of the Edinburgh edition of his poems for the ten-volume second edition of the *Encyclopaedia Britannica*. Many other purchasers are identified in the surviving Elliot account ledgers.

Elliot resembled Bailie Gavin Hamilton in his nationalist urge to pay copy money to Scottish authors, but was more successful because he solved for a time the problem of London distribution. From the start Elliot traded with London booksellers—principally Thomas Cadell and George Robinson, though there were many others, including Murray. His strategy was to keep literary property for himself and to use one main London agent or collaborator at a time, sharing the imprint and giving a special rate. Elliot benefited his correspondents additionally by buying large quantities of books from London for sale in Edinburgh and beyond. Because of this practice, and despite his occasional importation of Irish piracies and London prosecutions against him for reprinting copyrighted works, Elliot kept up most of his London associations until starting the London firm of Elliot and Kay at 332 Strand, opposite Somerset House, in early 1787, and his friendship and a publishing venture with Robinson continued after that time. His London firm was undertaken in partnership with his brother-in-law Kay, who was in charge of the operation, and briefly with his Edinburgh manager James Mackenzie. The shop was intended for the sale of Elliot's medical copyright books, and its sign was the painted head of the physician William Cullen, his highest-paid author.

From 1779 to 1789 Elliot had a printing partnership with Colin Macfarquhar at premises in Anchor Close, Edinburgh, but he also employed other printers. He was involved with approximately 600 publications, a quarter of them medical books, and owned more than forty copyrights, including those to medical works by Alexander Monro *secundus*, the dissectors John Innes and Andrew Fyfe, Andrew Duncan, and Alexander Hamilton, the Edinburgh professor of midwifery. He paid £1200 to Cullen for *First Lines of the Practice of Physic* (1784) and £1500 for his *Materia medica* (1789), £600 to Benjamin Bell for *A System of Surgery* (1783–8), and £250 to James Gregory for *Conspectus medicinae theoreticae* (1788). The printer William Smellie was promised 1000 guineas for *The Philosophy of Natural History* (1790), and although payment was held up by Smellie's debtors, two-thirds appears to have been paid to the author in his lifetime.

In paying these enormous sums Elliot was well aware of his achievement as an Edinburgh publisher. At the beginning he said, 'the London gentlemen thought it strange that a Country Bookseller (so they are pleased to call the vendors of books in the Metropolis of Scotland) should outbid them in the purchase of Dr. Cullen's Practice of Physic' (letter to James Keir, Birmingham, 22 June 1784). Later he was proud of his enabling role in medical publishing, saying 'I am the principal Man Midwife (in the literary way) here, to Man Midwives, Physicians, Apothecaries &c' (letter to Dr H. A. Bryan, Devon, 30 April 1788). Elliot's other titles included works of science, husbandry, older Scottish poetry, history, law, and English literature, as well as songs, farces from the English stage, translations from the French, and school and self-improvement books, and he counted among his authors the agricultural economist James Anderson, the mathematicians Alexander Ewing and Robert Simson, the Gaelic writer John Smith, and the poet Christie Edwards. As a bookseller he was bold and had flair. He bought up all the remaining copies of the second edition of the *Encyclopaedia Britannica* in 1785, and when the third edition began appearing in 1788 he agreed to take at least 1850 sets. He bought large stocks of medical and general titles, and issued catalogues for their annual sale.

Elliot also traded in Scotland, the English provinces, Ireland, and Europe. His principal bookseller in Paris was Pierre-Théophile Barrois the younger, with whom he exchanged the latest books and co-operated in publishing from 1784 to 1789, often using the Paris–London coach when pressed for time. He sent books to the West Indies from 1774 and to America, starting in 1777 with a shipment to British-occupied New York. He subsequently sent shipments to booksellers, merchants, and medical men in New York, Philadelphia, Virginia, Charleston, and Boston. His greatest, and costliest, book adventures in America began in 1784. He first established his nephew William Elliot and George Millar in a book store in Petersburg, Virginia, but the business quickly fell apart because of William's bad temper and unsuspected debts, and Millar's heavy drinking. Late in 1784 he sent his friend and clerk Thomas Dobson to Philadelphia to set up a bookshop with £2000 worth of books and other goods, with more books to follow. Dobson prospered, built an expensive stone house on 2nd Street, and betrayed Elliot by failing to remit payment to Edinburgh. He owed about £4000 at the time of Elliot's death.

In 1789 Elliot was in dire straits owing to poor health and concerns about the London shop, where Kay had proved to be an inept bookseller, as well as about his copyright payments and the Dobson debt. Needing to raise cash, he wrote his final letter to Dobson: 'God knows I am at this moment going to sell my property for what it will fetch, to make good deficiencies which I for some years depended on you to relieve. I hope you will send me all assistance you can directly' (19 Sept 1789). Shortly afterwards he suffered a stroke that left him unable to speak or write. Elliot's manager, John Greig, told Dobson that Elliot still had sound understanding and every day waited for the money. It would, however, be another fifteen years before Dobson paid off the debt with interest.

Elliot died aged forty-one on 12 January 1790, at his house at 16 Queen Street, Edinburgh, and was buried in Calton burial-ground, near David Hume's tomb. According to his cousin James Sibbald, 'he was possessed of more literary property than any other in the trade' (*Edinburgh Magazine*, 11, January–June 1790, 12). Andrew Duncan said Elliot's 'spirited conduct did honour to his profession' (*Medical Commentaries for the Year MDCCXC*, vii–viii). Archibald Constable, who considered him to be the most distinguished Edinburgh bookseller of his time, wrote later that 'the encouragement which Mr. Elliot gave to literary men was the means of producing a new spirit among the printers of Scotland' (Constable, 1.533).

Elliot was survived by two sons and a daughter, Anne (1782–1845), who married the London bookseller John Murray in 1807. His estate, administered by trustees until his children came of age, grew to nearly £34,000. This included £6457 from Dobson, £8749 for Elliot's stock of books and stationery, and the proceeds from the sale of his copyrights to Edinburgh and London booksellers in 1790. The shop in Parliament Square was sold to Bell and Bradfute, and Elliot's letter-books and carefully kept business records were taken by the family to John Murray, London.

WARREN McDOUGALL

Sources John Murray, London, archives, Charles Elliot MSS, out-letter books, 1774–90; account ledgers, 1771–90; trustees' minute book, 1790–1805; factor's accounts of finances and the trust fund · W. McDougall, 'Smugglers, reprinters and hot pursuers: the Irish–Scottish book trade and copyright prosecutions in the late eighteenth century', *The Stationers' Company and the book trade, 1550–1990*, ed. R. Myers and M. Harris, St Paul's Bibliographies (1997), 151–83 · W. McDougall, 'Charles Elliot and the London booksellers in the early years', *The human face of the book trade: print culture and its creators*, ed. P. Isaac and B. McKay (1999), 81–96 · W. McDougall, 'Charles Elliot's medical publications and the international book trade', *Science and medicine in the Scottish Enlightenment*, ed. C. Withers and P. Wood [forthcoming] · W. McDougall, 'Charles Elliot's book adventure in Philadelphia: the trouble with Thomas Dobson' [forthcoming] · W. McDougall, *Charles Elliot* [forthcoming] · W. Zachs, *The first John Murray and the late eighteenth-century book trade* (1998) · P. Isaac, 'Charles Elliot and the English provincial book trade', *The human face of the book trade: print culture and its creators*, ed. P. Isaac and B. McKay (1999), 97–116 · T. Constable, *Archibald Constable and his literary correspondents*, 1 (1873), 533–5 · G. Tancred, *The annals of a border club (the Jedforest) and biographical notices of the families connected therewith*, 2nd edn (1903) · bap. reg. Scot. · bur. reg. Scot.

Archives John Murray, London, archives, out-letter books, account ledgers, trustees' minute book, factor's accounts of finances and trust fund

Wealth at death estate after death 'grew to nearly £34,000'

Elliot, Sir Charles (1801–1875), naval officer and colonial official, son of Hugh *Elliot (1752–1830) and his second wife, Margaret Lewis (1770–1819), and nephew of Gilbert Elliot, first earl of Minto, was born in 1801 at Dresden, where his father was British minister. He entered the navy in March 1815, and in 1816 was midshipman of the *Minden* (74 guns) at the bombardment of Algiers. After serving in the East Indies and on the coast of Africa, he was made lieutenant on 11 June 1822, then served in the *Hussar* on the Jamaica station. In April 1826 he was promoted commander of the hospital ship at Port Royal, and was advanced to post rank on 28 August 1828. From then he virtually retired from the navy, being actively and almost continuously employed by the foreign or Colonial Office. From 1830 to 1833 he was protector of slaves in British Guiana. In 1834, when commissioners were appointed to superintend affairs of trade in China, Elliot went as their secretary, and in June 1836 became chief superintendent and plenipotentiary. It was just at this time that the Chinese decided to stop the illegal opium trade; but the British merchants found it so lucrative that they were unwilling to abandon it, and massive smuggling continued. Elliot had from the first seen that this must lead to serious conflict, and as early as November 1837 had written home advising that a special commission should be sent out to negotiate an agreement, but the government neglected to do this or to send any special instructions. The smuggling continued; the Chinese authorities grew more determined, and at last, with threats of violence which there were no means of resisting, demanded that all the opium on the coast should be delivered up to be destroyed. To prevent a general massacre, Elliot ordered the ships to comply, and opium valued at upwards of £4 million was surrendered and burnt. All trade was meantime prohibited, and the death of a Chinese civilian, killed in a chance fight with British sailors, was made further grounds for dispute. Not only was trade prohibited, but the Chinese were forbidden to bring supplies of any kind to the resident British. This stoppage of supplies was strictly enforced by war junks, but Elliot, strengthened by the arrival of the frigate *Volage*, gave orders for these to be dispersed; at the same time he declared the port and river of Canton to be in a state of blockade. In January 1840 active hostilities began, virtually under the direction of Elliot, acting in his civil capacity and in concert with his cousin, Rear-Admiral George Elliot, and afterwards with Sir James John Gordon Bremer. The Bogue (Humen) forts, commanding the passage of the Canton River, were taken and destroyed by Bremer, and Elliot was then able to conclude a preliminary treaty with the Chinese local authorities. This treaty was disavowed by both governments. Being limited in his view to Canton, and opposing the expressed policy of the foreign secretary, Lord Palmerston, to secure trade concessions in the northern ports, Elliot had ignored his instructions. For this he was summarily superseded. The war began afresh, and the troops were on the point of storming Canton when Elliot negotiated the payment by the Chinese of £1.25 million. This was his last action as agent in China before Mr Pottinger arrived to replace him.

Elliot was afterwards chargé d'affaires in Texas from 1842 to 1846, and governor of Bermuda (1846–54), Trinidad (1854–6), and St Helena (1863–9). In 1856 he was nominated a civil KCB. His naval promotions during this time were merely honorary, on the retired list; he became rear-admiral on 2 May 1855, vice-admiral on 15 January 1862, and admiral on 12 September 1865. He was portrayed by Sir Henry Taylor as Earl Athulf in the poem 'Edwin the Fair' (1845). He died at his residence in Withecombe, near Exmouth, on 9 September 1875.

J. K. LAUGHTON, rev. ANDREW LAMBERT

Sources C. Blake, *Charles Elliot RN, 1801–1875* (1960) · G. S. Graham, *The China station: war and diplomacy, 1830–1860* (1978) · O'Byrne, *Naval biog. dict.* · *The Times* (15 Sept 1875) · Boase, *Mod. Eng. biog.* · *CGPLA Eng. & Wales* (1875)

Archives NL Scot., corresp. and papers | BL, corresp. with Lord Aberdeen, Add. MSS 43126, 43184 · BL OIOC, corresp. with Sir G. B. Robinson, MS Eur. F 142 · NL Scot., Elliot-Murray-Kynynmound MSS · NL Scot., corresp., mainly with Lady Hislop · U. Durham L., corresp. with third Earl Grey · U. Southampton L., Palmerston MSS

Likenesses photograph, repro. in Blake, *Charles Elliot RN*, frontispiece

Wealth at death under £8000: probate, 6 Oct 1875, *CGPLA Eng. & Wales*

Elliot, Lady Frances Anna Maria. See Russell, Frances Anna Maria, Countess Russell (1815–1898).

Elliot, Sir George (1784–1863), naval officer and politician, was the second son of Gilbert Elliot Murray *Kynynmound, first earl of Minto (1751–1814), and his wife, Anna Maria (1752–1829), daughter of Sir George Amyand, bt. He was born on 1 August 1784, and entered the navy in 1794 on the *St George* with Captain Foley, whom he followed to the *Britannia*, *Goliath*, and *Elephant*. He was present at Hotham's actions off Toulon, and at the battles of Cape St Vincent and the Nile. He was promoted lieutenant on 12 August 1800, and in 1801 he served in the *San Josef* and *St George*, under Nelson. In April 1802 he was promoted commander, and in May 1803 went to the Mediterranean as a volunteer with Nelson in the *Victory*. On 10 July Nelson appointed him to the sloop *Termagant* and on 1 August posted him to the frigate *Maidstone*. Elliot was shortly afterwards attached to the squadron off Cadiz, under Sir Richard Strachan; Nelson then wrote that he was one of the best officers in the navy. He married, in 1810, Eliza Cecilia, daughter of James Ness of Osgodby, Yorkshire, and they had a large family; his eldest son was Admiral Sir George Augustus *Elliot (1813–1901).

During the war Elliot continued actively employed on the home station, in the Mediterranean, and in the East Indies; he was at the capture of Java in August 1811, and the suppression of Borneo pirates in June 1813. From 1827 to 1830 he commanded the *Victory* guardship at Portsmouth, where he earned the praise of the duke of Clarence (later William IV). In September 1830 he was nominated a CB, and on 10 January 1837 he was advanced to flag rank. He was whig MP for Roxburghshire from 1832 to 1835, when he was defeated. Elliot became first political secretary of the Admiralty at the king's request from 29 November 1830 to December 1834, and a lord commissioner from April 1835. Elliot's main contribution to naval policy while serving under his brother Gilbert, second earl of Minto, first lord of the Admiralty from September 1835 to September 1841, was in ship design and construction. He opposed the system of the surveyor, Captain Sir William Symonds, and, in combination with the first naval lord, Sir Charles Adam, pressed for the limited funds available to be spent on repairs rather than new construction. The ship built to his design, the small frigate *Eurydice*, which was well regarded at the time, was lost in a squall off the Isle of Wight on 24 March 1878 with heavy loss of life while serving as a sail training ship. From September 1837 Elliot was commander-in-chief at the Cape, until February 1840, when he was sent to China as commander-in-chief and joint plenipotentiary with Captain Charles Elliot. George Elliot's handling of the Chinese negotiations struck Palmerston, the foreign secretary, as irresolute and ineffective, and Elliot admitted that he was out of his depth. His health gave way, and in November he invalided home. On the formation of Russell's ministry, Elliot and his brother Lord Minto were excluded from the Admiralty by the Lansdowne faction, which wanted to reduce the Elliot clan's influence over the prime minister. He was commander at the Nore 1848–51, and became, in course of seniority, vice-admiral on 13 May 1847, and admiral on 5 March 1853. He was transferred to the reserved half pay list in 1855. In November 1862 he was made a KCB. He died after a protracted illness on 24 June 1863, at his home, 4 Princes Terrace, Kensington. An officer of solid merits, Elliot made a notable contribution to naval policy between 1830 and 1837. His failure in China and the faction feud of 1846 ensured that he was restricted to the minor post at the Nore, and never held another seagoing command.

J. K. LAUGHTON, *rev.* ANDREW LAMBERT

Sources A. D. Lambert, *The last sailing battlefleet: maintaining naval mastery, 1815–1850* (1991) · G. S. Graham, *The China station: war and diplomacy, 1830–1860* (1978) · NL Scot., Minto MSS · NMM, Minto MSS · *CGPLA Eng. & Wales* (1863) · O'Byrne, *Naval biog. dict.* · *The dispatches and letters of Vice-Admiral Lord Viscount Nelson*, ed. N. H. Nicolas, 7 vols. (1844–6)
Archives BL, Byam Martin MSS · NL Scot., Elliot-Murray-Kynynmound MSS · NL Scot., letters to first earl of Minto; letters to second earl of Minto · NMM, letters to second earl of Minto · U. Southampton L., Broadlands MSS
Likenesses G. Hayter, oils, 1834, NPG · attrib. A. C. Sterling, salt print, 1846–9, NPG · G. Hayter, group portrait, oils (*The House of Commons, 1833*), NPG
Wealth at death under £25,000: probate, 8 July 1863, *CGPLA Eng. & Wales*

Elliot, Sir George, first baronet (1814–1893), industrialist and politician, was born in Gateshead on 18 March 1814, the son of Ralph Elliot, pitman, and his wife, Elizabeth, daughter of Henry Braithwaite, of Newcastle upon Tyne. He began work as a pit boy in 1823 at the Pensher colliery owned by Charles Stewart, third marquess of Londonderry, and was a union leader there during the strike in 1831 over the length of the working day. Elliot later recalled that it was the most violent dispute that had taken place in the coal industry, 'for it caused bloodshed and death, and men were hung in chains on the Tyneside for it' (*The Gallery of Celebrities*, 2).

At the age of seventeen Elliot was apprenticed to Thomas Sopwith, a local land surveyor and mining engineer, and was involved with the latter's investigation of coal resources in the Forest of Dean. Elliot also helped to survey the line of the proposed railway between Darlington and York. Returning to Pensher in 1837 as overman, Elliot became under-manager (1841) and then manager (1844) at Monkwearmouth pit, the deepest in Britain. In the mid-1840s he became a managing partner in Washington colliery, and then opened the Unsworth mine on his own account. Elliot was appointed Lord Londonderry's coal viewer in 1848, and two years later bought from him the Pensher colliery where he had worked as a boy.

During the next two decades Elliot became one of the most important industrialists in Britain. In the 1860s he acquired further mines in north Wales, north and south Staffordshire, and in Nova Scotia. One of his most significant investments was in the Powell Duffryn Steam Coal Company in south Wales, where he was general manager as well as the largest shareholder. Elliot's purchase of the wire-rope-making business of Kuper & Co. in 1849 was also noteworthy. He amalgamated with the Gutta Percha Company to form the Telegraph Construction and Maintenance Company, and it was this concern that laid the first permanent transatlantic telegraph cable in 1866.

Elliot was one of a new type of mining engineer, whose expertise extended to many parts of the industry. He helped to found the Institute of Mining Engineers in 1852, and was a member of its council (1852–7), vice-president (1865–8), and president (1868–9). He was in the forefront of experiments in mining technology, and an advocate of improved safety lamps, shaft detaching hooks, and coal-cutting machinery. Trials at his collieries of new ventilating methods, such as the fan and high-pressure steam jets, were widely discussed, and he made a major contribution to the most efficient method of mining coal simultaneously in adjacent seams. He argued that economy, efficiency, and safety were compatible and, unlike many of his colleagues, supported the establishment of the mines inspectorate in the 1850s.

His attitude to labour changed from that of an early nineteenth-century tory paternalist, advocating model villages provided by employers and condemning trade unions, to that of a post-Disraelian Conservative, who believed in self-help and free collective bargaining. First elected to parliament on 26 November 1868, Elliot represented the mining constituency of North Durham for a number of years: he was its MP from November 1868 to January 1874, from June 1874 to March 1880, and again from September 1881 to November 1885. He failed to be elected in February 1874 and April 1880, and was also unsuccessful at South-east Durham in December 1885, but he was MP for Monmouth from July 1886 to July 1892. His achievements were suitably recognized in 1874 when a baronetcy was bestowed on him, the first such award to a coal-industry figure. Elliot was a prominent freemason, and held high office in the movement in south Wales.

In his parliamentary work Elliot was mostly concerned with matters affecting the coal industry and the City, though he was also an early advocate of 'gas and water socialism'. He appeared as an expert witness before several government inquiries, and served on the royal commission on the coal industry (28 June 1866 to 27 July 1871). Shortly before his death he made an unsuccessful attempt to solve the coal industry's economic and labour difficulties by proposing the amalgamation of collieries into a massive semi-public enterprise monitored by the Board of Trade, which would control output, fix prices, pay fair wages, and establish a miners' welfare fund. Although the response was lukewarm, *The Times* considered that it was one of the most interesting industrial schemes of the decade (20 Sept 1893).

Elliot was a popular figure in the north-east of England. His Durham mining constituents warmly referred to him as 'Bonnie Geordie', and he never lost the unpolished manner of his lowly origins. He married Margaret Green of Rainton, Durham, in 1836, and they had two sons and four daughters. Elliot's wife died in 1880, and he never remarried, but he was involved in a well-publicized breach of promise case ten years later. He was sued by Emily Mary Hairs, a professional singer, for £5000 damages, but her claim was rejected by a jury on 18 April 1890. Elliot owned substantial estates in Monmouthshire and at Whitby, but he died at his house, 17 Portland Place, London, on 23 December 1893. His second son, George William Elliot, succeeded to the baronetcy.

COLIN GRIFFIN, rev.

Sources *The Times* (25 Dec 1893) · *Colliery Guardian* (29 Dec 1893) · 'Sir George Elliot, Bart', *The Biograph and Review*, 5 (May 1881), 414–19 · *Transactions of the North of England Institute of Mining Engineers* (1855–6) · *Transactions of the North of England Institute of Mining Engineers* (1868–9) · R. A. Church, *A history of the British coal mining industry* (1986) · H. W. Macrosty, *The trust movement in British industry* (1907), 86–7 · 'A projected coal trust', *The Times* (20 Sept 1893) · R. Galloway, *Annals of coal mining and the coal trade*, 2 vols. (1904) · 'Sir George Elliot, bart, MP', *ILN* (15 May 1875), 463, 465 · J. Junior, *VF* (29 Nov 1879), 295 · Boase, *Mod. Eng. biog.* · J. Vincent and M. Stenton, eds., *McCalmont's parliamentary poll book, 1832–1918* · *The Gallery of Celebrities*, 1/new ser. no. 1 (July 1891), 27 [short biographical note] · G. Cookson, 'The golden age of electricity', *The golden age: essays in British social and economic history, 1850–1870*, ed. I. Inkster and others (2000) · C. Griffin, introduction to pt 1, *The golden age: essays in British social and economic history, 1850–1870*, ed. I. Inkster and others (2000) · C. Griffin, 'Coalmining in mid-Victorian Britain: a golden age revisited?', *The golden age: essays in British social and economic history, 1850–1870*, ed. I. Inkster and others (2000)

Likenesses portrait, repro. in Junior, *VF* · portrait, repro. in 'Sir George Elliot, Bart, MP', *ILN*

Wealth at death £575,785 12s. 2d.: double probate, 25 May 1894, *CGPLA Eng. & Wales*

Elliot, Sir George Augustus (1813–1901), naval officer and politician, was born at Calcutta on 25 September 1813, the eldest son of Admiral Sir George *Elliot (1784–1863) and his wife, Eliza Cecilia née Ness. He entered the navy in November 1827, and was made lieutenant on 12 November 1834. For the next three years he was in the *Astraea* with Lord Edward Russell on the South American station, and on 15 January 1838 he was promoted to the command of the brig *Columbine* on the Cape and west Africa stations, under his father; he performed with notable success, and captured six slavers, two of them 60 miles up the Congo.

In February 1840 he went to China with his father, and on 3 June was promoted, on a death vacancy, captain of the *Volage*, in which in 1841 he returned to England with his invalided father as a passenger. He married on 1 August 1842 Hersey Susan Sidney, only daughter of Colonel Wauchope of Niddrie, Midlothian; they had several children.

From 1843 to 1846 Elliot commanded the frigate *Eurydice*, designed by his father, on the North American station, and in December 1849 he was appointed to the frigate *Phaeton*, which gained a reputation as one of the smartest and fastest frigates. Early in 1853 she was paid off, and in January 1854 Elliot commissioned the *James Watt*, one of the first screw battleships, which he commanded in the Baltic campaigns of 1854 and 1855, despite the poor performance of the ship, and the dissatisfaction of Vice-Admiral Napier. On 24 February 1858 Elliot became rear-admiral, and was then captain of the fleet to Sir Charles Fremantle, commanding the channel squadron. Between 1859 and 1863 he was a member of the royal commission on national defences and with Captain Cooper Key signed a report that presumed the navy would be unable to defend the British Isles. In 1861 he was considered for the post of controller of the navy, which was given to Robert Spencer Robinson. Between 1863 and 1865 he was superintendent of Portsmouth Dockyard. On 12 September 1865 he became vice-admiral, and then was repeatedly on royal commissions on naval issues. In a dissenting report appended to the 1871 committee on designs, Elliot and Alfred Ryder, who believed that the ram was the primary weapon of naval combat, pressed for increased freeboard, the retention of sailing rig, and the concentration of armour. The direct result of this report was the battleship *Temeraire*. Twenty years later Elliot's views on freeboard and armouring formed the basis of the modern battleship, but in 1871 his was a minority opinion. This radical strand of thought, revealed in his work on committees and in print, set him at odds with the mainstream, but provided an important catalyst for debate on strategy, tactics, and ship design: notably in *Flotilla, Coast and Harbour Defence: the Gunboat of the Future* (1871). In 1870 Elliot reached the rank of admiral, and in 1874 he was elected Conservative MP for Chatham; but he resigned his seat in 1875, on being appointed commander-in-chief at Portsmouth. On 2 June 1877 he was nominated a KCB, and the following year, on 26 September, he was placed on the retired list. He continued, however, to occupy himself with the study of naval questions, and published in 1885 *A Treatise on Future Naval Battles and how to Fight them*. He died in London on 13 December 1901. After a career made by his father, and reinforced by his own expertise as a sailing ship captain, Elliot went on to make a major contribution to the intelligent discussion of naval issues for forty years, and if his views were often radical and even impractical, they required consideration.

J. K. LAUGHTON, rev. ANDREW LAMBERT

Sources P. H. Colomb, *Memoirs of Admiral the Right Honble. Sir Astley Cooper Key* (1898) · 'Committee on designs for ships of war', *Parl. papers* (1872), 14.501, C. 477; 14.581, C. 477-I · A. J. Marder, *The anatomy of British sea power*, American edn (1940) · A. D. Lambert, *The*

Crimean War: British grand strategy, 1853–56 (1990) · S. Sandler, *The emergence of the modern capital ship* (1979) · R. A. Burt, *British battleships, 1889–1904* (1988) · private information (1912) · *WW* (1901) · O'Byrne, *Naval biog. dict.* · *Navy List* · *CGPLA Eng. & Wales* (1902)

Archives NMM, letter-book | NL Scot., Elliot-Murray-Kynynmound MSS · NL Scot., corresp. with third earl of Minto

Wealth at death £5719 18s. 3d.: resworn probate, July 1902, *CGPLA Eng. & Wales*

Elliot, Sir Gilbert, first baronet, Lord Minto (1650/51–1718), judge, was the younger son of Gavin Elliot (*d.* before 1678) of Midlem Mill, Roxburghshire, and his wife, Margaret Hay. After graduating MA from the University of Edinburgh in 1669 Elliot became a writer, before gaining recognition among opponents of Charles II's administration for successfully challenging the legality of treason charges brought against his friend, the covenanter William Veitch, in 1679. Having brought the case to the earl of Shaftesbury's attention, Elliot was deputed by Shaftesbury 'to go down to the Houses of Parliament with the petition, and to distribute these to the peers and members as they entered' (Elliot, 267). A royal order duly halted the proceedings against Veitch, whose sentence was commuted from death to banishment. Likewise Elliot also helped the earl of Argyll to escape from prison in 1681 by again travelling to London and obtaining advance information of the death sentence due to be pronounced against Argyll. Between these two journeys to London, Elliot married his cousin Helen (or, according to one source, Marion) Stevenson (*d.* 1689) at Edinburgh on 28 December 1680; they had one daughter, named Mary.

In 1685 Elliot joined exiled presbyterian nonconformists in the Netherlands, where he not only acted as clerk to the council of Scottish rebels involved in planning the earl of Argyll's uprising, but also travelled 'to Geneva, and to the Protestant churches of Germany, begging supply to the poor afflicted Protestants of Brittain, and thus raised a great summe', conveniently ignoring suspicions that it was 'not understood by the givers that it was to be imployed in a rebellion or invasion' (Lauder, *Historical Observes*, 191). Remaining with Argyll and his followers until the end of the failed rising in Scotland, Elliot eventually escaped, although he was subsequently convicted of treason and sentenced to forfeiture and death *in absentia* by the justiciary court on 16 July 1685. On 19 May 1687, however, he obtained a pardon from James VII, partly because of the financial losses his father had earlier incurred for the royalist cause during the mid-century civil wars. Elliot applied for membership to the Faculty of Advocates on 8 November 1687, whereupon his examiners 'stumbled to meet with him till he first shewed his remission, least it might infer converse against them' (Lauder, *Decisions*, 1.475). Despite failing the faculty's public examination on 10 December, upon re-examination on 14 July 1688 Elliot passed, and was admitted an advocate on 22 November of that year. Following the revolution of 1688 Elliot's sentence of forfeiture was rescinded on 22 July 1690 because the original process had been 'manifestly illegal and unreasonable' (*APS*, 1689–95, 212). After the revolution Elliot also visited his old friend Veitch, who was by then ministering in Dumfries. Recalling former

times, Elliot allegedly asserted that 'Ah! Willie, Willie; had it no' been for me' crows would still have been pecking at Veitch's skull in Edinburgh, to which Veitch evidently retorted 'Ah! Gibbie, Gibbie; had it no' been for me', Elliot would himself still have 'been yet writting papers' for a pittance in the same city (McCrie, 99n.).

Having been appointed a clerk to the privy council, in 1692 Elliot was knighted and on 19 April 1700 created a baronet. His first wife had been buried in Greyfriars churchyard, Edinburgh, in November 1689, and on 7 April 1692 he married again; his second wife was Jean Carre (*d.* 1751), with whom he had two sons, Gilbert *Elliot and Andrew. From 1703 he represented the county of Roxburgh in parliament and that year was permitted to plead a case before parliament despite having by then become one of its members (*APS*, 1702–7, 48). Following the death of Sir James Falconer, Lord Phesdo, Elliot was appointed a judge in the court of session on 28 June 1705, adopting Lord Minto as his title. His appointment was commended by the marquess of Annandale, who informed the English treasurer, Godolphin, that not only was Elliot 'a bred lawyer and one off [*sic*] the best in our nation … a man without a blott for his reputation and integrittie', but also that he was 'a man off [*sic*] such parts and sufficiencie and firme honestie and resolution that … no man can be so usefull in these stations to her Majestie heare' (*Laing MSS*, 1.181). In 1707 Elliot voted against the abolition of the separate Scottish parliament. He died on 1 May 1718, aged sixty-seven.

CLARE JACKSON

Sources G. F. S. Elliot, *The border Elliots and the family of Minto* (1897) · *Life and letters of Sir Gilbert Elliot, first earl of Minto, from 1751 to 1806*, ed. countess of Minto [E. E. E. Elliot-Murray-Kynynmound], 3 vols. (1874) · T. McCrie, ed., *Memoirs of Mr. William Veitch and George Brysson* (1825) · J. Lauder, *Historical observes of memorable occurrents in church and state, from October 1680 to April 1686*, ed. A. Urquhart and D. Laing, Bannatyne Club, 66 (1840) · J. Lauder, ed., *The decisions of the lords of council and session*, 2 vols. (1759–61) · J. M. Pinkerton, ed., *The minute book of the Faculty of Advocates*, 1: *1661–1712*, Stair Society, 29 (1976) · *APS*, 1670–1707 · *Report on the Laing manuscripts*, 2 vols., HMC, 72 (1914–25) · G. Brunton and D. Haig, *An historical account of the senators of the college of justice of Scotland, from its institution in 1532* (1849) · D. Laing, ed., *A catalogue of the graduates … of the University of Edinburgh*, Bannatyne Club, 106 (1858) · NL Scot., Minto MS 11030, fols. 6, 13 · H. Paton, ed., *The register of marriages for the parish of Edinburgh, 1595–1700*, Scottish RS, old ser., 27 (1905), 217 · H. Paton, ed., *Register of interments in the Greyfriars burying-ground, Edinburgh, 1658–1700*, Scottish RS, 26 (1902), 618

Archives NL Scot., MSS 11001–11349 CH. 8971–1063

Likenesses portrait, repro. in Elliot, *The border Elliots*, 263 · portrait, priv. coll.

Wealth at death see will, NL Scot., MS 11030, fol. 13

Elliot, Sir Gilbert, second baronet, Lord Minto (*bap.* 1693, *d.* 1766), judge, was baptized in Edinburgh on 30 January 1693, the elder and only surviving son of Sir Gilbert *Elliot, first baronet, Lord Minto as judge of the court of session (1650/51–1718), and his second wife, Jean Carre (Kar; *d.* 1751), daughter of Sir Andrew Carre of Cavers.

After studying civil law at the University of Utrecht, which he entered in 1712, Elliot was admitted advocate of the Scots bar in July 1715. He succeeded to his father's estate and baronetcy on 1 May 1718. From 1722 he sat as MP for Roxburghshire which gave him a taste for the cultural richesse of London, until his appointment on 4 June 1726 to the bench of the court of session, taking, as had his father, the judicial title Lord Minto. In 1733 he was appointed a lord of justiciary; having acquired for life in 1761 the office of keeper of the signet, he was in 1763 promoted lord justice clerk—the day-to-day head of the high court of justiciary—which position he held until his death. Throughout his career in the court of session, and as a criminal judge on the Jedburgh–Dumfries–Ayr circuit, he was recognized as a lawyer of great authority, keen judgement, and high integrity, whose advice and expertise were much sought. During his short time at the bar he was appointed to the committee responsible for the Faculty of Advocates library, but he did not write on the law, and is not particularly associated with any major case of importance.

Minto's enduring legacy lies in his contribution to Scotland's intellectual life and to her culture of 'improvement'. Out of court he was a significant public figure, quietly influential in civic affairs and, as an upholder of the Hanoverian *status quo*, entrusted via John Montagu, fourth earl of Sandwich, John, second duke of Argyll, and Archibald, third duke of Argyll, with certain responsibilities on a national level. An industrious committee man, he was actively involved with the administration and financial transactions of the quasi-political Society in Scotland for the Propagation of Christian Knowledge; he sat on the first board of governors of the Edinburgh Infirmary and, together with his wife, presided over the fund-raising assemblies that supported it. He is credited, though not proven, as sole or co-author of the anonymous 'Proposals for carrying on … public works in Edinburgh' presented to the town council in 1752—a persuasively argued exhortation to expand and beautify the capital city. His possible co-author, also suggested as an alternative sole author, was George Drummond, lord provost of Edinburgh. The 'Proposals' were immediately acted upon, the council appointing him to its 'Committee of Taste for the Improvement of the Town'. The eventual creation of Edinburgh's New Town was a direct result of the scheme.

Classical scholar, antiquary, and bibliophile, Minto belonged to Scotland's circle of legal literati. He was a founder member of the Edinburgh Musical Society, worked for many years on its management committee, and played the transverse flute in its orchestra. An early Scottish enthusiast for the instrument, he was regarded as an authority on it, and legend (unsubstantiated, but dating from an article by William Tytler published in 1792) credits him with introducing it to Scotland.

On 4 August 1718 at Edinburgh Minto married Helen (*d.* 1774), daughter of Sir Robert Stewart of Allanbank. Their nine surviving children included Gilbert *Elliot, subsequently third baronet, advocate, politician, and cabinet adviser, Andrew Elliot, governor of New York, John *Elliot, the admiral, and Jean (Jane) *Elliot, author of *The Flowers of the Forest*. He claimed (perhaps mischievously) that he owed his life to Jane: when the Jacobite army on its march south through Roxburghshire in 1745 halted at Minto, demanding money and supplies from his tenants, Jane held the fort, so to speak, while her father hid on Minto Craigs. Afterwards he refunded his tenants and bore the losses himself. The family divided their time between their Edinburgh residence, Minto House in Horse Wynd, which he had commissioned from William Adam, and their country house at Minto, Roxburghshire (also called Minto House), splendidly rebuilt by Adam. As an exemplary member of the Society of Improvers in Agriculture, Minto proved a progressive and caring landowner who systematically drained, planted, and enclosed his land, and rebuilt the estate village, including the school. He died suddenly at his home in Minto on 16 April 1766, and was buried at Minto kirkyard on 22 April, in an unmarked grave. That he was admired and loved is testified by the many moving tributes sent at his death, from the bench and beyond. JANE BLACKIE

Sources NL Scot., Minto MSS · J. M. Pinkerton, ed., *The minute book of the Faculty of Advocates*, 2: *1713–1750*, Stair Society, 32 (1980) · G. Brunton and D. Haig, *An historical account of the senators of the college of justice, from its institution in MDXXXII* (1832) · G. F. S. Elliot, *The border Elliots and the family of Minto* (1897) · A. J. Youngson, *The making of classical Edinburgh, 1750–1840* (1966) · W. Tytler, 'Fashionable amusements', *Transactions of the Society of Antiquaries*, 1 (1792), 509 · Edinburgh Musical Society sederunt books, 1728–60, Edinburgh Public Library, ML 28 MS · Society in Scotland for the Propagation of Christian Knowledge records, NA Scot., GD 95 · R. Maxwell, *Transactions of the Society of Improvers in Agriculture* (1743) · W. Adam, *Vitruvius Scoticus*, ed. J. Simpson (1980), pl. 59, 60 · *Scots Magazine*, 28 (1766), 223 · F. Gray, ed., *Book of the Old Edinburgh Club*, 19 (1933), 49 · 'Proposals for carrying on … public works in Edinburgh', 1752, NL Scot., Ry.1.2.90 (1) · DNB · H. Paton, ed., *The register of marriages for the parish of Edinburgh, 1701–1750*, Scottish RS, old ser., 35 (1908)
Archives NL Scot., corresp. and papers | BL, corresp. with Sir William Hamilton and Lady Hamilton, Egerton MS 2638
Likenesses A. R. Carse or D. Allan, group portrait (posthumous; *The Worthies Club*), priv. coll. · miniature (as a youth), repro. in Elliot, *The border Elliots*

Elliot, Sir Gilbert, of Minto, third baronet (1722–1777), politician and literary patron, was born at Minto, Roxburghshire, in September 1722, the eldest son of the judge Sir Gilbert *Elliot, second baronet and Lord Minto (*bap.* 1693, *d.* 1766), and Helen (*bap.* 1696, *d.* 1774), daughter of Sir Robert Stewart, first baronet, of Allanbank in Berwickshire, and Helen Lockburn. His paternal grandfather was Sir Gilbert *Elliot, first baronet and Lord Minto (1650/51–1718). One of nine children, among his siblings were the poet Jean (Jane) *Elliot (1727–1805), the naval officer John *Elliot (1732–1808), and Andrew Elliot, later governor of New York. Gilbert Elliot was educated at Dalkeith grammar school and from 1735 at Edinburgh University; a period of study at the University of Utrecht (1743) was followed by a tour of the Netherlands and the German states during 1744–5. According to Thomas Somerville, a close friend and minister from 1767 of Minto parish, Elliot was 'a distinguished classical scholar' (Somerville, 120) who claimed in a letter to another intimate companion, David Hume, to have 'read over almost all the classics, both Greek and Latin' (19 February 1751, Burton, 1.326). On 14 December 1746 at Edinburgh he married Agnes (*d.* 1778), daughter of Hugh Dalrymple-Murray-Kynynmound, of

Melgund, Forfarshire. The couple had four sons and two daughters, including Gilbert Elliot, first earl of Minto (1751–1814) [see Kynynmound, Gilbert Elliot Murray], and Hugh *Elliot (1752–1830).

Elliot qualified for the Scottish bar in December 1742, though he was never enamoured with a profession for which, as he told friends like William Mure of Caldwell, his talents left him ill-equipped:

> Nature never meant me for a lawyer: I have neither the sorts of parts, memory, or application; and yet I'm not discouraged. The same powerful habit that makes men tumblers and rope dancers may very probably mould me into a very lawyer. (letter of 28 June 1745, Mure, vol. 2, pt 1, p. 29)

At the same time the young Elliot clearly delighted in presenting a playful image to his superiors. 'I believe nobody can make anything of me … Sometimes I dress like a fop, and sometimes like a man of fashion'. Yet there were also signs of Elliot's characteristic reserve and self-restraint; as he told Mure, 'I don't avoid going to taverns, and yet I can't get drunk' (Mure, vol. 2, pt 1, p. 28). Looking back on Elliot's life, Somerville described a man of 'placid and equal' temper who was 'rigidly temperate' and who refused to 'indulge his guests in that profusion of wine which was fashionable at gentleman's tables'. To his critics such conduct, Somerville realized, was taken for 'hauteur and coldness of manner', though he believed it better explained by Elliot's caution, honesty, and preference for open, erudite conversation over the niceties of etiquette (Somerville, 123–4).

Regardless of Elliot's early efforts to succeed in the law, it was politics which became his profession. In March 1748—probably through the influence of his father, a committed whig of the 1688 stamp and associate of Scotland's political manager, Archibald, third duke of Argyll—Elliot was appointed as Roxburghshire's first sheriff-depute, one of the judges introduced in Scotland by legislation passed in the aftermath of the Jacobite rising of 1745. Cultured, civilized, and through his marriage financially independent, Elliot cut an impressive figure and came to the attention of Henry Pelham's circle. Through Argyll's influence in December 1753 he was elected MP for Selkirkshire, which he represented until May 1765.

Parliamentary career and the militia bill, 1753–1762 Elliot's first major parliamentary contribution came in February 1755 when he spoke against government proposals to determine the length of service of sheriffs-depute. In a remarkable speech which helped create his reputation for fine parliamentary performances, Elliot argued against a bill to extend the period (from seven to twenty-four years) by which sheriffs held office at the king's pleasure. Elliot's counter-argument, that the extension infringed true whig principles, was largely accepted and the measure, embarrassing and damaging for the Newcastle ministry, passed with a compromise extension of seven years. Elliot's contribution was evidently at odds with that expected from an MP of his junior status, a situation which Elliot—a keen constitutionalist—found surprising. Writing to his wife on 22 February he described his involvement as

> being a thing a little uncommon, from Scotland, for a young man, supported by none of the great, to take up a point of the constitution upon as high a key as any English Member of Parliament. (Haden-Guest, 'Elliot, Gilbert')

During the summer of 1755 there is evidence that Elliot was requested by Argyll to join William Pitt and the opposition whigs around the prince of Wales. From later that year he worked to effect a union between the supporters of Pitt and John Stuart, third earl of Bute, with whom he had recently grown friendly. Notwithstanding Argyll's support in his successful appointment as Selkirk sheriff-depute in October, Elliot's attachment to the Bute–Pitt grouping increasingly drew him away from the Argathelite interest and into opposition during the Newcastle–Fox administration. Following the formation of the Pitt–Devonshire government, in November 1756 Elliot received his first ministerial appointment as lord of the admiralty which he held until his resignation in support of Pitt in April of the following year, and to which he was reinstated in June with Pitt's return to office.

By the close of the 1750s British involvement in the Seven Years' War had come to dominate politics. For Elliot war, and the threat of invasion, also brought into sharper focus the issue of a Scottish militia for which he became a prominent spokesman in early 1760. On 4 March he gave an impressive and extremely well-prepared Commons speech for the establishment of a committee to examine the present state of Scottish militia law and to prepare a bill. Central to Elliot's argument was the obscurity of current laws, the danger Scots had faced during recent Jacobite and French invasion attempts, and, post-1745, the modernization of highland communities formerly hostile to the Hanoverian regime. A Scots militia commensurate with the English would not, he concluded, stimulate Scottish independence but rather serve to strengthen the union of 1707. The motion was passed and steps taken towards the formation of a committee with plans to call for an English-style force of 6000 men. By now, however, Elliot and his supporters, among them James Oswald, Sir Harry Erskine, and George and Charles Townshend, faced a more determined opposition from George II and the duke of Newcastle (for whom Elliot's had been 'a most pompous flaming speech'; Robertson, 109), who expressed alarm at the financial implications for the English and the possible military consequences of arming highlanders. Elliot's motion was defeated in April despite another forceful Commons performance. The result, if politically disappointing, did much to enhance his reputation as a fine parliamentarian. As David Hume told Lord Minto;

> I hope your Lordship remembers my Prophecy, that the Echo of Mr Elliot's Eloquence wou'd be as loud as a Captain's cannon … no man in the House was capable of such Exertion of Eloquence, Reason & Magnanimity; nay, that it probably never was surpassed by any one Member. (1 May 1760, Hume, *Letters*, 1.325)

Horace Walpole, unlike Hume no fan of Elliot, likewise

believed that his had been a 'masterly' argument (Walpole, *Memoirs of … George II*, 2.110), while Patrick Craufurd thought Elliot's 'one of the best speeches I ever heard, and with great freedom towards Mr Pitt, but decent and parliamentary' (to Baron Mure, 17 December 1761, in Mure, vol. 2, pt 1, p. 138). In defeat the advocates of the Scottish militia turned to satire in the shape of Adam Ferguson's *History of the Proceeding in the Case of Margaret, Commonly called Peg* (1760), in which 'Sister Peg' was left exposed to attack by her complacent brother John Bull; the essay concludes with a speech in favour of the militia from a 'parliamentarian' widely identified as Elliot. After another failed attempt in 1761 Elliot became a founder member of the Edinburgh-based *Poker Club which met from early 1762 to press the militia cause.

Since the late 1750s Elliot had moved closer to the earl of Bute, not least through personal friendships with the dramatist John Home, now the earl's secretary, and with William Mure, his Scottish manager. In March 1761, with Bute's growing pre-eminence on the accession of George III, Elliot became lord of the treasury and was soon after tipped as a future manager of Scottish affairs in the wake of Argyll's death in April. It was a role Elliot performed reluctantly, writing in June of his dislike of a position undertaken 'from a mere sense of duty … and hardly comes within the pale of what is called ambition' (to Lord Milton, Murdoch, 101). He was rescued by Bute from a career dominated by place hunters to whom Elliot's reserve was seldom encouraging or appealing. Thereafter, following Pitt's resignation from the government in October, Elliot, while expressing his gratitude to the departed minister, threw himself behind Bute and became treasurer of the chamber in May 1762, an office he held for eight years.

Later political career, 1763–1776 The mid-1760s saw Elliot's growing disillusionment with party politics following Bute's persistent secret influence which threatened a Grenville administration to which Elliot now loyally subscribed. As MP for Roxburghshire from June 1765 he abandoned party and assumed the role of a 'king's friend', which he maintained under the Rockingham ministry, stating in August 1765 that the 'partial spirit which gave so much energy to business' was now, in him, 'totally irrecoverable' (Haden-Guest, 'Elliot, Gilbert'). Elliot's independence led to political unpredictability within the chamber. Keen to prosecute John Wilkes over the *North Briton* affair, he was ambivalent towards Grenville's approach to the American colonies, being variously supportive of the right of parliamentary authority, critical of Grenville's determined prosecution of the Stamp Act in December 1765, and opposed to Pitt's attempts to have the act repealed in the new year. Generally supportive of Chatham's ministry, Elliot next came to prominence in May 1768 when he unsuccessfully pressed for Wilkes's expulsion, and again in the following February when he again spoke against Wilkes and other 'licentious men'.

In 1770 Elliot was appointed treasurer of the navy in Lord North's government. However, as might be expected from someone suspicious of party alliances, his relations with the new prime minister were not always smooth. A strong advocate of the government's handling of the Falkland Islands crisis (1770–71) and the *Printer's Case*, he was greatly offended by North's failure to appoint his son, Hugh, to an expected military rank. In American affairs Elliot maintained his moderate approach of the mid-1760s; a proponent of parliament's right to tax the colonies, he equally expected government to behave considerately once this claim was accepted. His final speech in March 1776 was, fittingly, in favour of a cause—the creation of a Scottish militia—which he had once made his own. As a politician Elliot was best remembered for performances such as that during the militia debate in 1760 which, according to Horace Walpole, placed him in an élite of a group of mid- to late-century parliamentarians who displayed 'the various powers of eloquence, art, reasoning, satire, learning, persuasion, wit, business, spirit and plain common sense' (Walpole, *Memoirs of … George II*, 2.110, 116). Thomas Somerville likewise considered Elliot one of the country's 'most accomplished speakers' (Somerville, 152), while for James Boswell, much given to worrying over his own Scotticisms, Elliot's speech—private as well as parliamentary—achieved a welcome balance between accent and a 'Good English [which] is plain, easy, and smooth' (*Boswell's Life of Johnson*, ed. R. W. Chapman, 1953, 469–70).

Patron and poet Elliot's proximity—linguistic and otherwise—to English culture was also noted by others. Writing in 1753, the duke of Argyll had attributed his belief that 'this young gentleman will be above the common run' to his having 'more of an English manner at the bar than any I see in Scotland' (Haden-Guest, 'Elliot, Gilbert'). Writing to Hume in July 1764 Elliot himself explained how a parliamentary seat gave him an 'English' identity: 'am I not a Member of Parliament with as much liberty to abuse ministers … as if I had been born in Wapping?' (ibid.). This, moreover, was an association worth defending as he sharply reminded Hume several months later when his friend appeared on the verge of abandoning Britain for France: 'Love the French as much as you will, many of the Individuals are surely the proper objects of affection, but above all continue still an Englishman' (15 September 1764, Hume, *Letters*, 1.469).

To some degree it was Elliot's involvement in English political and cultural affairs which made him the friend of so many leading men of Scottish letters, including David Hume. His London connections offered Edinburgh associates an important source of patronage, contacts, and publicity, a role similar to that played by Lord Milton and one which Elliot willingly adopted for members of the Scottish 'moderate' literati. It was probably through Elliot that the dramatist John Home met the third earl of Bute, who became his employer and leading patron; via Elliot and Home, Alexander Carlyle, Adam Ferguson, and William Robertson also came to Bute's attention. Parties at Minto House, Roxburghshire, and at his London residence in Mayfair, brought together leading Scottish and English Enlightenment figures including Robertson, Elizabeth Montagu, John Gregory, Lord Kames, and Hugh Blair.

Elliot was also an influential sponsor and critic in his own right, having a 'wide acquaintance with the works of polite literature, ancient and modern', and possessed of 'the authority of a master critic among his learned contemporaries' (Somerville, 122). In 1749 he promoted Home's first play, *Agis*, and in the autumn of 1754 read and commented on the manuscript of his controversial study *Douglas*. William Robertson later submitted to him a draft of his *History of the Reign of Charles V* (1769), for which Elliot had recommended the removal of phrases which he deemed 'peculiar to Scottish authors' (Somerville, 121).

Advice had also been sought in 1751 by David Hume during work on a provocative study on religious scepticism, his *Dialogues Concerning Natural Religion*. Elliot, an elder of the Church of Scotland and member of the general assembly, was asked to contribute to the dialogue of one of Hume's disputants, Cleanthes (a theist adhering to modern empirical philosophy), in order that Hume (who adopted the voice of the sceptic, Philo) might avoid 'that Vulgar Error … of putting nothing but Nonsense into the Mouth of the Adversary' (Mossner, 319). Aware of the work's extremely controversial nature, Elliot along with others, including Adam Smith, advised Hume against publishing a text which eventually appeared only after its author's death. Elliot's own critical response to Philo's scepticism—a stance against which he took a 'marked disapprobation' (Somerville, 122)—was published by Dugald Stewart as part of the latter's 'Dissertation: exhibiting the progress of metaphysical, ethical, and political philosophy since the revival of letters in Europe', as well as in the eighth edition of the *Encyclopaedia Britannica*.

Elliot's friendship with Hume had originated while both were students at Edinburgh University. In the following years Elliot, though critical of Hume's religious scepticism, supported his friend's unsuccessful candidacy for the Glasgow chair in logic and offered frank advice when in 1764 Hume toyed with taking French citizenship. 'I think I see you upon the very brink of a precipice', Elliot warned. 'One cannot too much clear their mind of all the little prejudices, but partiality to ones country is not a prejudice' (15 September 1764, Hume, *Letters*, 1.469). A month earlier Hume had described Elliot as a 'very ancient and intimate friend of mine … justly regarded as one of the ablest and most considerate men among us' (to the comtesse de Boufflers, ibid., 1.459), and later took responsibility for supervising the education of Elliot's sons, Hugh and Gilbert, in Paris. Towards the end of his life Hume was a regular visitor to Minto House; for Elliot to be absent on these occasions was a source of consternation spiritedly conveyed in a letter from Lady Elliot to Hume in the autumn of 1772 (see Mossner, 576).

In addition to Elliot's work as a patron and critic, he was known for his modest collection of published poetry and songs, including 'Amynta' which appeared in *The Charmer; a Choice Collection of Songs, English and Scots* (1749, incorrectly published as 'My apron dearie' in John Johnson's *Scots Musical Museum*, 6 vols., 1787–1803, and later praised by Sir Walter Scott as a 'beautiful pastoral song'). Other works include 'Twas at the hour of dark midnight', describing the death of Colonel James Gardiner (1686–1745) at Prestonpans, published in the third volume of the *Scots Musical Museum* and, on the recommendation of Sir Edward Bridges, some 'Thoughts occasioned by the funeral of the earl and countess of Sutherland in Holyrood House' which appeared anonymously in the *Scots Magazine* for October 1766. Thomas Somerville, who claimed that Elliot left an unpublished (and since untraced) volume of verse, praised his 'large portion of poetical talent' resulting in 'some beautiful verses, characterized by unaffected sensibility' (Somerville, 122). Elliot himself appears to have been content with his status as an amateur poet, warning Somerville against a professional literary career which he believed at odds with 'purity of principle … or respectability of character' (ibid., 150).

Troubled with increasing poor health, Elliot spent his final months in Marseilles where he died on 11 February 1777, the baronetcy (which he had inherited in April 1766) passing to his eldest son, Gilbert, then MP for Morpeth. He was survived by Lady Elliot who died on 30 December of the following year.   PHILIP CARTER

Sources E. Haden-Guest, 'Elliot, Gilbert', HoP, *Commons, 1754–90* • T. Somerville, *My own life and times, 1741–1814* (1861); repr. (1996) • W. Mure, ed., *Selections from the family papers preserved at Caldwell*, 2 vols. in 3 pts (1854) • H. Walpole, *Memoirs of King George II*, ed. J. Brooke, 3 vols. (1985) • *Life and letters of Sir Gilbert Elliot, first earl of Minto, from 1751 to 1806*, ed. countess of Minto [E. E. E. Elliot-Murray-Kynynmound], 3 vols. (1874) • *The letters of David Hume*, ed. J. Y. T. Greig, 2 vols. (1932) • E. C. Mossner, *The life of David Hume* (1954); 2nd edn (1980) • J. Robertson, *The Scottish Enlightenment and the militia issue* (1985) • R. B. Sher, *Church and university in the Scottish Enlightenment: the moderate literati of Edinburgh* (1985) • A. Murdoch, 'The people above': politics and administration in mid-eighteenth-century Scotland* (1980) • Walpole, *Corr.* • *DNB* • J. H. Burton, *Life and correspondence of David Hume*, 2 vols. (1846) • G. F. S. Elliot, *The border Elliots and the family of Minto* (1897)

Archives NL Scot., corresp. and papers • NL Scot., student lecture notes • NMM, corresp. and papers as treasurer of the chambers of the navy | BL, letters to first earl of Liverpool, Add. MSS 38201–38207, 38398, 38454, *passim* • NA Scot., Hepburn-Scott MSS, letters to Walter Scott of Harden • NL Scot., letters to William Mure

Elliot, Gilbert. *See* Kynynmound, Gilbert Elliot Murray, first earl of Minto (1751–1814).

Elliot, Gilbert John Murray Kynynmond. *See* Kynynmound, Gilbert John Elliot Murray, fourth earl of Minto (1845–1914).

Elliot, Sir Henry George (1817–1907), diplomatist, born at Geneva on 30 June 1817, was the second son of Gilbert Elliot Murray *Kynynmound, second earl of Minto (1782–1859), and his wife, Mary (1786–1853), eldest daughter of Patrick *Brydone of Coldstream, Berwickshire. His eldest sister, Lady Mary Elliot, married on 18 September 1838 Sir Ralph Abercromby, who was British minister at Turin and The Hague. Another sister, Lady Frances Elliot [*see* Russell, Frances Anna Maria], on 20 July 1841 became the second wife of Lord John Russell. Educated at Eton College and at Trinity College, Cambridge, where he took no degree, Elliot served as aide-de-camp and private secretary to Sir John Franklin in Tasmania from 1836 to 1839, and as précis writer to Lord Palmerston at the Foreign Office in 1840.

Having entered the diplomatic service in 1841 as attaché at St Petersburg, Elliot was promoted to be secretary of legation at The Hague in 1848, was transferred to Vienna in 1853, and in 1858 was appointed British envoy at Copenhagen. On the accession of Francis II to the throne of the Two Sicilies on 22 May 1859 the British government decided to resume diplomatic relations with the court of Naples, broken off in 1856 when Ferdinand II ignored British and French protests at his repressive rule. Elliot was in England on a short leave of absence early in 1859, and Lord Malmesbury, then foreign secretary, sent him on a special mission to congratulate King Francis on his accession, with instructions to hold out the expectation of the re-establishment of a permanent legation if a more liberal and humane policy were pursued in the new reign, and also to dissuade the king from allying himself with Victor Emmanuel in the war which had broken out between Piedmont and France on one side and Austria on the other. Elliot's brother-in-law, Lord John Russell, who succeeded Lord Malmesbury at the Foreign Office in June, instructed Elliot to remain at Naples, and eventually on 9 July appointed him permanent minister. He was instructed not to press for neutrality if the public opinion of Naples so strongly favoured alliance with Piedmont as to render that course dangerous to the dynasty. Elliot's efforts to obtain constitutional reform and abandonment of the arbitrary methods of the previous reign were approved and supported, but had no substantial result. Francis II, after some faint signs of a disposition to improve the methods of rule, returned to the old methods. Elliot's representations seem on one occasion to have been instrumental in obtaining the release of a certain number of prisoners who were being detained indefinitely without trial, but generally speaking the advice and the warnings given by him, partly on his own initiative and partly under instructions from his government, were neglected.

The result was not slow in coming. Early in 1860 Garibaldi, with a force of a thousand volunteers, seized Sicily in the name of King Victor Emmanuel. In August he advanced on Naples and handed over the fleet, which surrendered to him, to the Piedmontese admiral. The British government decided to maintain an attitude of non-intervention, despite the appeals of France to oppose Garibaldi. On 10 September Elliot, in pursuance of instructions from Russell, had an interview with Garibaldi in the cabin of Admiral Munday on board HMS *Hannibal*, which was then stationed in the Bay of Naples. Elliot stated that he was instructed to remain at Naples for the present, and tried to dissuade Garibaldi from any ulterior intention of attacking Venice. Garibaldi was not much impressed by the arguments of the British minister. Following the plebiscite of 21 October, the formal ceremony of annexation took place at Naples on 8 November. Thenceforward the British legation had no *raison d'être*, and Elliot left for England a few days later. For some time he was without active employment.

On the death of Sir Thomas Wyse, British minister at Athens, in April 1862, Elliot was sent on a special mission to Greece, where discontent against the rule of King Otho was assuming dangerous proportions and had manifested itself in a mutiny of the garrison of Nauplia. Here again his instructions were to urge the necessity of a more liberal system of administration and of the observance of the rules of constitutional government. He was also to make it clear that the British government would not countenance aggressive designs against Turkey. He returned in July. During his short residence at Athens he had been greatly impressed with the unpopularity of the king, and his forebodings were soon justified. In October a provisional government deposed the king. The British government declined the offer of the crown to Prince Alfred, but promised, if a suitable candidate were chosen, and if the constitutional form of government were preserved and all attempt at aggression against Turkey were abandoned, to cede the Ionian Islands. Elliot was sent back to Athens on a special mission to arrange matters with the provisional government on this basis. Prince William, second son of King Christian of Denmark, was on 30 March 1863 unanimously elected as King George I. Elliot returned to England in the following month.

In September 1863 Elliot succeeded Sir James Hudson as British envoy to the king of Italy, taking up his residence at Turin. The foreign secretary, Russell, was freely charged, both in private correspondence and in the press, with unjustly superseding Hudson to make a place for Elliot, his own brother-in-law. *The Times* had already suggested (13 March 1860) such an intention on Lord John's part, and a warm political controversy, which Hudson did much to fan, followed the announcement in 1863 of Elliot's appointment. But the imputation of jobbery has no justification. Hudson's retirement was quite voluntary, and he in the first instance warmly approved the choice of his successor. In May 1865 Elliot moved from Turin to Florence, now Italy's capital, and there his sister and Russell visited him in November 1866. In July 1867 he was appointed ambassador at Constantinople and sworn a privy councillor. At his new post he was almost at once engaged in the discussion over the troubles in Crete in 1868–9 and the consequent rupture of diplomatic relations between Turkey and Greece. In the winter of 1869 he was British representative at the opening of the Suez Canal, and was made GCB.

On 6 June 1870 a great fire broke out in Pera, in which the British embassy house was almost completely destroyed. Lady Elliot and her children narrowly escaped with their lives and all the ambassador's private property was destroyed, though he and the staff succeeded in saving the government archives and much of the furniture of the state rooms. Elliot was often in conflict with the Russian ambassador at Constantinople, General Ignatiev, and was held by the Russophobes in England to be no match for Russian ambition, but in the view of Lord Granville, then foreign secretary, Elliot by his 'quiet firmness' well held his own against all Russian intrigue in the sultan's court.

When in 1875 insurrections broke out in the Balkans, leading eventually to the 'Bulgarian atrocities' of 1876,

Elliot took a strong Turkophile line, his unyielding dispatch of 4 September 1876 arguing that British interests in preventing change in the Turkish empire were 'not affected by the question whether it was 10,000 or 20,000 persons who perished in the suppression' (Shannon, 23). This dispatch, quickly published, made Elliot notorious, and he became a central target of the campaign against the atrocities. However, he was not recalled and assisted Lord Salisbury at the conference at Constantinople at the end of 1876 (Salisbury had been protesting privately and in cabinet against Elliot's 'stupidity and caprices' (ibid., 19), and Disraeli kept Elliot on to shackle Salisbury). After the conference Elliot, who had been ill throughout 1876, was replaced by Sir A. H. Layard, and at the end of 1877 he was appointed ambassador at Vienna. In 1880 he reported the Austrians' protests against Gladstone's comments on them in his first Midlothian campaign, and this led to their partial retraction. Elliot retired on a pension in January 1884. In February 1888 his article in the *Fortnightly Review* on the Eastern question crisis of 1876–8 broke the traditions of the day and incensed the sultan.

On 9 December 1847 Elliot married Anne (*d.* 1899), second daughter of Sir Edmund Antrobus; they had a daughter and a son, Sir Francis Edmund Hugh Elliot, also a diplomatist. Elliot died at his home, Ardington House, Wantage, on 30 March 1907.

To have annoyed both Salisbury and Gladstone was unusual. Elliot, in fact, represented the accepted Foreign Office view of his day as to the need to maintain the Porte. His illiberal statements of 1876–7 should not mask his overall competence in maintaining whiggish objectives of liberal constitutionalism, at least in western Europe.

H. C. G. Matthew

Sources *The Times* (1 April 1907) · *FO List* (1908) · H. G. Elliot, *Some revolutions and other diplomatic experiences … edited by his daughter* (1922) · R. T. Shannon, *Gladstone and the Bulgarian agitation, 1876* (1963) · Gladstone, *Diaries* · R. W. Seton-Watson, *Disraeli, Gladstone and the eastern question: a study in diplomacy and party politics* (1935) · *The political correspondence of Mr Gladstone and Lord Granville, 1876–1886*, ed. A. Ramm, 2 vols. (1962) · *DNB*
Archives NL Scot., corresp. and papers | BL, corresp. with W. E. Gladstone, Add. MSS 44412–44453 · BL, corresp. with Sir Austen Layard, Add. MSS 38989–39134, *passim* · Bodl. Oxf., letters to earl of Clarendon · Bodl. Oxf., corresp. with Benjamin Disraeli · Lpool RO, corresp. with fifteenth earl of Derby · NL Scot., letters to Lord and Lady Minto · PRO, corresp. with Lord Cowley, FO519 · PRO, Granville MSS · PRO, letters to Lord Hammond, FO391 · PRO, corresp. with Lord John Russell, PRO30/22 · PRO, corresp. with Odo Russell, FO918 · PRO, letters to Sir William White, FO364/1 – 11
Likenesses Spy [L. Ward], caricature, chromolithograph, NPG; repro. in *VF* (17 March 1877) · wood-engraving (*The Eastern question: the conference at the admiralty, Constantinople*), NPG; repro. in *ILN* (6 Jan 1877)
Wealth at death £17,404 1s.: probate, 2 May 1907, *CGPLA Eng. & Wales*

Elliot, Sir Henry Miers (1808–1853), administrator in India and historian, was the third son, one of fifteen children, of John Elliot, colonel-commandant of the Westminster Volunteers, who had married a daughter of John

Coakley *Lettsom. Elliot attended Winchester College from the age of ten. Though destined for New College, Oxford, the East India Company's demand for civilians beyond the number usually trained at Haileybury tempted him to try for an appointment in their open examination of 1826. His excellence in oriental languages, classics, and mathematics helped him to become the first of the 'competition wallahs', twenty years ahead of his time.

Following a series of assistantships, Elliot was appointed collector, first of Moradabad, then of Meerut, where he wrote his first land settlement report and took a keen interest in Indian land revenue terms. In 1836 he was appointed secretary to Robert M. Bird's *sadr* board of revenue for the North-Western Provinces, based in Allahabad. For eleven years he aggressively supported the application of Bird's land settlement, taking on all critics, even the formidable Thomas C. Robertson who temporarily halted Bird's proceedings in 1842. Elliot argued the case for both the legality and the justice of the settlement, and persisted in his stand until he became foreign secretary under the governor-general, Lord Hardinge, in 1847, and again under Lord Dalhousie, who replaced Hardinge in 1848. Aside from his skill in diplomatic negotiations with the Punjab's rulers, Dalhousie valued his services precisely because, as an ardent annexationist, Elliot could advise the governor-general expertly on the land settlement that was to be applied to the Punjab following the annexation of 1849. Elliot had helped to organize the reports and guidelines which, in all the controversies involving the partial dispossession of the talukdars in the North-Western Provinces, became Thomason's *Directions to Settlement and Revenue Officers*. These were taken intact to the Punjab. For this and his treaty negotiations with the Sikh leaders he was made KCB in 1851.

Throughout his career Elliot devoted his leisure to Indian studies. In 1845 he produced his first edition of the *Supplement to the Glossary of Indian Terms*, which was described as 'replete with curious and valuable information' (Waller) about the Brahmans and Rajputs of the upper provinces. His most significant scholarly work was a first volume of the *Bibliographical Index to the Historians of Mohammedan India* (1849), in which he proposed to evaluate the work of 231 Arabic and Persian historians of India. Regret that his death prevented his completion of this work was not universal: Francis H. Robinson wrote in his *What Good may Come out of the India Bill* (1853) that Elliot in his evangelicalism tended to 'criminate' the great Indian historians of the past. Failing health compelled Elliot to seek a change in climate, but he died on his way to England, at Simonstown, Cape of Good Hope, on 20 December 1853, at the age of forty-five. He was survived by his wife, Rebecca, the daughter of William Wickham Cowell, formerly a judge at Bareilly, the scene of his first appointment; they had at least two surviving sons.

Other scholars saw Elliot's work through to publication. John Dowson brought out eight volumes entitled *History of India, as Told by its Own Historians* (1866–77), and E. C. Bayley brought out a *Sequel* in 1886, both using Elliot's manuscripts. In 1869 John Beames brought out a two-volume edition of Elliot's *Memoirs of the History, Folklore, and Distribution of the Races of the North-West Provinces.*

PETER PENNER

Sources *DNB* · P. Penner, *The patronage bureaucracy in north India* (1986) · E. Stokes, *The peasant and the raj: studies in agrarian society and peasant rebellion in colonial India* (1978) · C. H. Philips, ed., *Historians of India, Pakistan and Ceylon* (1961) · J. Dowson, 'Notice of Sir Henry M. Elliot', in H. M. Elliot, *The history of India, as told by its own historians: the Muhammadan period*, ed. J. Dowson, 1 (1867), xxviii–xxix · J. F. Waller, ed., *The imperial dictionary of universal biography*, 3 vols. (1857–63) · *GM*, 2nd ser., 41 (1854)

Archives BL, papers incl. notes for history of India, Add. MSS 30768–30789 · BL OIOC, letters, MS Eur. C 473 · BL OIOC, official, revenue, and misc. papers, MSS Eur. B 69, D 310–316, F 56–60 · Duke U., Perkins L., corresp. and papers · Royal Asiatic Society, London, papers

Likenesses plaque, St Paul's Cathedral, Calcutta

Wealth at death approx. £30,000–£40,000: est. from knowledge of salary rates at various levels of East India Company employment

Elliot, Hugh (1752–1830), diplomat and adventurer, was born on 6 April 1752, the second son of Sir Gilbert *Elliot, third baronet (1722–1777), MP, and Agnes Dalrymple-Murray-Kynynmound (d. 1778). Born into a family of staunch but minor government supporters, he was one of a number of Scotsmen who carved out a career in second- and third-level posts in the British diplomatic service. On several occasions his bold personality and sharp tongue carried him further than discretion would have advised, though these episodes also provided the highlights of a career lacking in substantial achievements. Unusually tall and thin, Elliot was given a cosmopolitan education along with his elder brother, Gilbert Elliot [see Kynynmound, Gilbert Elliot Murray (1751–1814)], first at home and then (1764–6), on the advice of his father's friend David Hume, at a military school at Fontainebleau where he was a classmate of Honoré Gabriel Riqueti, comte de Mirabeau (1749–1791). He returned to study first at the University of Edinburgh and then at Oxford. Travelling back to France in 1770, he studied military science at Metz and then at Strasbourg in preparation for his anticipated career in the British army. In 1762, at the age of ten, he had been commissioned into the guards as a lieutenant, subsequently becoming a captain, but a decade later the king and the ministry of the day refused to confirm his appointment. His response was characteristically bold: he sought military experience and adventure in the Russo-Turkish War (1768–74) then being waged on Europe's south-eastern rim. Travelling first to the Ottoman capital, Constantinople, he subsequently joined the Russian army under P. A. Rumyantsev and distinguished himself in the campaign of 1773.

Elliot's exploits gained him favourable attention, not least from George III whose support contributed to his first diplomatic appointment at the tender age of twenty-two. This was as envoy-extraordinary to the elector of Bavaria (1774–6), with responsibility also for the imperial diet at Regensburg (1774–7), two posts frequently combined during the second half of the eighteenth century. The diplomatic novice was not lacking in spirit or self-confidence: his brother-in-law, the under-secretary of state William Eden, referred discreetly to the widespread view that there was 'a predominancy of the Hotspur vivacity in your character' (countess of Minto, 148). A later, less sympathetic observer, the comte Roger de Damas, who encountered Elliot towards the end of his public career, declared that 'He is keenly imaginative, insincere, unscrupulous and unprincipled: in short he is as dangerous in public affairs as he is amusing in society' (Mackesy, 39).

Munich served as a springboard for the more important mission to Berlin, which hinted at a brilliant future and where Elliot served as envoy-extraordinary from 1777 until 1782. Already renowned for the mordant humour of his dispatches, he did not hesitate to exchange repartee with Frederick the Great, not always to his own disadvantage. His Prussian sojourn, however, was marred by two reprehensible escapades. In 1777 when two American agents arrived seeking support for the rebellious colonies, he recklessly encouraged his servant to steal their papers. When the theft was discovered and the envoy's culpability became clear, he was formally rebuked by his superiors in London. The second adventure was a by-product of his elopement with and marriage about 1779 to Charlotte Kraut, the young daughter of a Prussian noble family, which was opposed by her mother. When he was recalled in 1782, his young wife declined to accompany him and they were later formally divorced. Elliot blamed her cousin Knyphausen, and fought a duel with him which was for a time the talk of the diplomatic world. He himself subsequently remarried and his obituary in the *Gentleman's Magazine* claimed that he was the father of no less than nineteen children, but much about his private life remains obscure. Some time after his divorce from his first wife in 1783, but before 1796, he married Margaret Jones (1770–1819); they had nine children, including Sir Charles *Elliot (1801–1875), Sir Thomas Frederick *Elliot (1808–1880), and Emma (d. 1866), who married Sir Thomas *Hislop, first baronet (1764–1843).

In early 1783 Elliot took up his appointment as envoy-extraordinary to Denmark, a post he occupied until 1789 which indicated his failure to rise as far as might have been expected. When he arrived in Copenhagen political authority was exercised by the queen mother, Juliana Maria, and Ove Høegh Guldberg for the king, Christian VII, who was disabled by schizophrenia. In 1784 the former foreign minister Andreas Peter von Bernstorff orchestrated a constitutional coup which supplanted Guldberg and the queen mother and installed the young Crown Prince Frederik at the head of a government dominated by Bernstorff. Elliot, with his habitual enterprise— if not altogether advisedly for a foreign diplomat—had given his backing to the leading minister when the coup was taking shape. The special status this conferred upon him was evident in October 1788, during the most dramatic episode of his swashbuckling career. A new war in south-eastern Europe, between a Russo-Austrian alliance and the Ottoman empire, was on the point of spilling over into the Baltic, where in mid-summer Gustav III of Sweden attacked Catherine II's vulnerable empire. Russia's ally Denmark threatened to widen the conflict by invading Sweden. Apprised by his brother diplomat in Berlin, Joseph Ewart, that Prussia would in turn attack Denmark and so threaten a general European war, Elliot seized the moment for an unauthorized but dramatic initiative. He rushed across the Sound, finally tracking Gustav III down at Göteborg, where his persistence extracted an eight-day truce from the Swedish ruler. Back in Copenhagen he prevailed upon Bernstorff in response to the truce not to attack Sweden and to withdraw from the war, thereby averting wider hostilities. This diplomatic feat had been accomplished, however, through a private British declaration of war against Denmark, which Elliot was not authorized to issue and for which he was once more reprimanded by the government in London.

In autumn 1790 Elliot was sent unofficially to Paris, as part of shadowy British efforts to stop France aiding Madrid during the Anglo-Spanish confrontation over Nootka Sound. The mission exploited his boyhood acquaintance with Mirabeau, which had been sustained by correspondence and reinforced by the latter's visit to England in 1783. The comte was now a leading figure in the French national assembly and the secret overtures to his old friend seem to have been successful. Elliot lacked the solidity of character to secure further advancement in the diplomatic hierarchy: length of service was not accompanied by promotion. His final two postings were both appointments as envoy-extraordinary at second-rank courts: an uneventful decade in Saxony (1792–1802) and a shorter period (1803–06) in Naples. In Naples he was enchanted by that femme fatale of European monarchy, Maria Carolina, to whose defence he unwisely and unsuccessfully sought to order a British force commanded by Sir James Henry Craig.

It was one private initiative too many for the British government, and it closed Elliot's diplomatic career. Yet this was not the end of his public life. His brother, now the influential earl of Minto, secured the governorship of the Leeward Islands (1809–13) and then of Madras (1814–20) for Elliot. On his return from India he lived quietly in retirement until his death in Somerset Street, London, on 10 December 1830. His final resting place in Westminster Abbey was the closest this enterprising and ambitious but flawed personality came to the heart of Britain's political establishment.

H. M. SCOTT

Sources countess of Minto [E. E. E. Elliot-Murray-Kynynmound], *A memoir of the Right Honourable Hugh Elliot* (1868) · D. B. Horn, *The British diplomatic service, 1689–1789* (1961) · G. F. S. Elliot, *The border Elliots and the family of Minto* (1897) · J. Black, *British foreign policy in an age of revolutions, 1783–1793* (1994) · *DNB* · P. Mackesy, *The war in the Mediterranean, 1803–1810* (1957) · Walpole, *Corr.*
Archives NL Scot., corresp. and papers · NMM, corresp. and papers · PRO, corresp. and letter-books, FO 353 | Beds. & Luton ARS, corresp. with Lord Grantham · BL, corresp. with Lord Auckland and Lady Auckland, Add. MSS 34412–34460, *passim* · BL, letters to Lord Grenville, Add. MS 59031 · BL, corresp. with Lord Holland, Add. MS 51613 · BL, corresp. with Sir Robert Keith, Add. MSS 35507–35541, *passim* · BL, letters to duke of Leeds, Add. MSS 28061–28065 · BL, corresp. with Sir Hudson Lowe, Add. MSS 20107–20233, *passim* · Harrowby Manuscript Trust, Sandon Hall, Staffordshire, corresp. with Lord Harrowby · NL Scot., corresp. with Sir Robert Liston · NL Scot., letters to Lord Minto and Lady Minto · NRA, priv. coll., corresp. with Joseph Ewart · PRO, letters to Lord Granville, PRO 30/29

Elliot, James (*bap.* **1770**, *d.* **1810**). *See under* Elliot, Archibald (*bap.* 1761, *d.* 1823).

Elliot, Jean [Jane] (**1727–1805**), poet, was born in April 1727 at Minto House, near Hawick, Roxburghshire, the third daughter of Sir Gilbert *Elliot (*bap.* 1693, *d.* 1766), second baronet and (as lord justice clerk of Scotland) Lord Minto, and Helen (*bap.* 1696, *d.* 1774), daughter of Sir Robert Stuart (Stewart) of Allanbank, baronet, and Helen Cockburn. She did not marry. Miss Elliot showed herself from an early age to be a lady of bearing and determination. During the Jacobite rising of 1745 she, when only eighteen, entertained a party of Jacobites at Minto while her father took refuge among the neighbouring crags. Her claim to fame rests upon one poem, written as the result of a wager with her brother, Gilbert *Elliot, later to be the third baronet and himself the author of the 'graceful pastoral' (*DNB*) 'My Sheep I Neglected'. The brother and sister were travelling together in the family coach near Selkirk, discussing the battle of Flodden, when Gilbert wagered 'a pair of gloves or a set of ribbons' (ibid.) against his sister's ability to write a good ballad on the subject. According to tradition, of the eighty 'flowers' of Selkirk Forest who had gone to Flodden, only William Brydone, town clerk of Selkirk, had returned, bearing as trophy an English flag. It was this story that very probably formed the basis for Miss Elliot's 'The Flowers of the Forest', written in response to her brother's wager, with its powerful use of Scots contrasting markedly with Mrs Alison Cockburn's 'polite' version, which was almost certainly written earlier.

So the story goes: indeed it is sometimes said that a 'rough draft of the song' (*DNB*) was ready by the end of the journey during which the wager was made. There is, however, room to doubt the complete originality of what is indeed a highly successful version of a Flodden ballad. It has long been known that the traditional air survived, as did two lines of 'The Battle of Flodden'—'I've heard them lilting at the yowe-milking' (Elliot, 454) and 'The flowers of the forest are a' wede away' (Eyre-Todd, 1.204). In addition, the view was early voiced (by David Herd) that Miss Elliot's 'Flowers' was 'a version made up from various copies of the old ballad collated' (Henderson, 416). Current scholarship does not allow for a definitive answer, but the likelihood is that there was a significant existing framework for this most famous modern ballad composition. Although Jean Elliot remained unwilling to claim authorship of 'The Flowers of the Forest' because of her social status, the fact of it was widely known and she was called 'the Flower' in consequence (Graham, 337). It was not her only poem, and some of her other verse is printed in *The Border Elliots and the Family of Minto* (1897). 'The Flowers of

Jean Elliot (1727–1805), by unknown artist

Likenesses drawing, wash, Scot. NPG [*see illus.*] · painting (after miniature), repro. in Graham, *Scottish men of letters*, 336

the Forest' was printed in David Herd's *Scottish Songs* (1776) and by Sir Walter Scott in his *Minstrelsy of the Scottish Border* (1802–3). It should be noted that the manuscript of 'Flowers' left at Minto differs from the *Minstrelsy of the Scottish Border* text.

When her father died in 1766, Miss Elliot took a significant role in the disposition of his affairs. Subsequently she moved to Edinburgh, where she was described as 'a prodigious fund of Scottish anecdote', though it was also ungallantly said that she 'did not appear to have ever been handsome' (Elliot, 455). On the other hand (or perhaps only more politely), she was described as having 'a sensible face, and a slender, well-shaped figure' (Tytler and Watson, 1.200). From 1782 to 1804, she lived in Brown's Square in the capital; she died at Mount Teviot (or Mounteviot), Roxburghshire, the seat of her brother Admiral Elliot on 29 March 1805. In character she was elegant, fashionable, and intelligent, 'from her youth … remarkable for her discrimination, discretion, and self-control'. She was 'fond of French literature' (ibid., 200–01), though not of the French Revolution, and by her old age she was apparently the 'only lady' in Edinburgh to use a 'sedan chair' (Eyre-Todd, 1.204). MURRAY G. H. PITTOCK

Sources G. F. S. Elliot, *The border Elliots and the family of Minto* (1897) · S. Tytler and J. L. Watson, *The songstresses of Scotland*, 2 vols. (1871) · *DNB* · H. G. Graham, *Scottish men of letters in the eighteenth century* (1901) · C. Kerrigan, ed., *An anthology of Scottish women poets* (1991) · C. Craig, ed., *The history of Scottish literature*, 2: *1660–1800*, ed. A. Hook (1987) · A. Bold, *Scotland: a literary guide* (1989) · Anderson, *Scot. nat.* · G. Eyre-Todd, ed., *Scottish poetry of the eighteenth century*, 2 vols. (1896) · D. Gifford and D. McMillan, eds., *A history of Scottish women's writing* (1997) · T. F. Henderson, *Scottish vernacular literature: a succinct history*, 2nd edn (1900) · J. H. Millar, *A literary history of Scotland* (1903) · W. Donaldson, 'The Jacobite songs of eighteenth- and early nineteenth-century Scotland', PhD diss., U. Aberdeen, 1974

Elliot, John (*bap.* 1724, *d.* 1782), antiquary, was born in the parish of St Michael, Lewes, Sussex (perhaps at 91 High Street), and baptized at St Michael's on 30 October 1724, the only son of Obadiah Elliot (*d.* 1775), brewer, and his wife, Elizabeth Boarer (*d.* 1771). After attending Lewes grammar school he was articled to an attorney and built up a good practice in London, acting as agent for lawyers in his home county. He was admitted to the Society of the Inner Temple in 1779–80, having had chambers there since at latest 1771. On 22 June 1763 he married Margaret Cook (*d.* 1791) of Berwick upon Tweed; they had no children.

According to Elliot's biographer and fellow antiquary, Paul Dunvan, in his *Ancient and Modern History of Lewes and Brighthelmston* (1795), his father discouraged his antiquarian pursuits, as detracting from training for his profession, and his wife, a strict Methodist, feared for their effect on his spiritual welfare. The earliest evidence for his antiquarian research are notes of churches he visited in eastern Sussex in 1762–3. His research otherwise dates from 1770 and was confined to Lewes, the borough, the priory, and the barony, and focused on the parish of St John-sub-Castro, where his father had bought a brewery in 1743. He inherited his father's house in the parish in 1775, which he thereafter occupied. He made extracts from medieval documents in the British Museum and the public records, particularly the chartulary of Lewes Priory in the Cottonian manuscripts, though he halted his labours after transcribing the first third of the chartulary as 'it would perhaps take up the better part of one man's life to read & digest the remaining two-thirds' (Brighton and Hove Library Service, 5/8 33497, fol. 15). He drafted an account of Lewes's origin within the bounds of a Roman camp, but his only printed works were two long letters to the *Sussex Weekly Advertiser*, 3 January 1774 and 16 January 1775, on St John-sub-Castro Church. He was a competent draughtsman, and was probably the first antiquary to commission Sussex views from James Lambert.

In December 1780 Elliot was elected a fellow of the Society of Antiquaries, to which he had sent, in 1775 and 1777, two communications on antiquities relating to Lewes. He provided the Revd John Watson with information on the barony of Lewes for his *Memoirs of the Ancient Earls of Warren and Surrey* (1782, but privately circulated in draft in 1776). To Dr William Burrell, Elliot bequeathed his manuscript collections, although Burrell had already borrowed and copied from them. They did not pass with Burrell's own collections to the British Museum. Burrell's eldest son lent them to T. W. Horsfield when the latter was writing the first volume of *The History and Antiquities of Lewes and its Vicinity* (1824); and the family disposed of them in the early twentieth century. Three libraries between them hold six volumes.

Elliot died suddenly at his house at 5 Southampton Row, Bloomsbury, London, on 28 February 1782, and was buried in St Michael's churchyard in Lewes on 7 March 1782. 'In person', Dunvan said, 'he was tall, in manners unassuming and plain, in disposition gentle and disinterested, in his profession upright and candid, and in friendship liberal and sincere' (Dunvan, 344). JOHN H. FARRANT

Sources [P. Dunvan], *Ancient and modern history of Lewes and Brighthelmston* (1795), 343–5 · Sussex Archaeological Society, Barbican House, Lewes, Sussex, Elliot MSS · Eastbourne Public Library, Elliot MSS [uncatalogued] · Brighton and Hove Library Service, 5/8 33497 · will, PRO, PROB 11/1088 · parish register (baptism), Lewes, St Michael, 30 Oct 1724 · parish register (marriage), Lewes, St Anne and St Michael, 2 June 1723 · IGI · deeds, E. Sussex RO, AMS 4633, 6349 · GM, 1st ser., 52 (1782), 150 · parish register (burial), Lewes, St Michael, 7 March 1782 · F. A. Inderwick and R. A. Roberts, eds., *A calendar of the Inner Temple records*, 5 (1936) · minute book XVII, 7 Dec 1780; arts. papers, 16 Nov 1775, 8 May 1777, Society of Antiquaries
Archives Eastbourne Public Library · Hove Central Library, Brighton, Sussex, extracts from Lewes Priory cartulary made by him · Sussex Archaeological Society, Lewes, antiquarian papers | BL, papers and corresp. incl. notes on Camden's *Britannia*, Add. MSS 5703, 6351
Wealth at death see will, PRO, PROB 11/1088

Elliot, John (1732–1808), naval officer, was born in April 1732, the fourth son of Sir Gilbert *Elliot, second baronet (*bap.* 1693, *d.* 1766), lord chief justice of Scotland, who took the courtesy title Lord Minto, and Helen (*bap.* 1696, *d.* 1774), daughter of Sir Robert Stuart (Stewart) of Allanbank, Berwickshire, baronet. John's siblings included Gilbert *Elliot, third baronet, and the poet Jean (Jane) *Elliot. John Elliot appears to have entered the navy in July 1740 in the *Augusta*, and was discharged from her to the hospital ship *Princess Royal* as one of her crew. After an interlude, probably in the merchant service, as mentioned in his passing certificate, he served in the *Chesterfield* and the *Assistance*, and then for two years in the sloop *Peggy*; he went on to pass his examination on 1 May 1752, though he was not appointed lieutenant until 30 April 1756 in the *Scarborough*. After this, however, his promotion was greatly eased when his brother Gilbert entered parliament and, late in 1756, became a lord of the Admiralty. John was promoted commander on 21 January 1757 and captain on 5 April; he assumed command of the *Hussar* in the Channel Fleet, including the Rochefort reconnaissance, early in 1758.

In November 1758 Elliot commissioned the frigate *Aeolus* (32 guns), then newly launched, and on 19 March 1759, while cruising on the south coast of Brittany in company with the *Isis* (50 guns), he fell in with a squadron of four French frigates in charge of a convoy. The convoy and two of the frigates got clear away, chased by the *Isis*; the two others, the *Blonde* (36 guns) and the *Mignonne* (20 guns), interposed to prevent the *Aeolus* following. After a sharp action the *Mignonne* was captured, but the *Blonde* made good her escape. During the year the *Aeolus* continued on the coast of France, under the orders of Sir Edward Hawke, and on 27 December sailed from Quiberon Bay on a cruise, in company with the *Intrepid* (64 guns). Bad weather came on; the two ships separated; the *Aeolus*, blown off shore, was unable to work up to the Isle de Groix, the appointed rendezvous; and, her provisions running short, she put into Kinsale on 21 January 1760 in order to get a supply. Elliot intended to return to the Isle de Groix at the

earliest opportunity. However, continued bad weather prevented his sailing, so that he was still at Kinsale on 24 February, when he received a letter from the lord lieutenant addressed to the captain or commanding officer of the navy's ships at Kinsale informing him that François Thurot's squadron of three ships was in Belfast Lough, and had landed 1000 French troops at Carrickfergus. It was a circular letter, a copy of which was sent express to all the ports on the chance of finding ships of war at some of them. None was stationed on the coast; the *Aeolus* was at Kinsale solely by the accident of the weather as were two other 32-gun frigates, the *Pallas* and *Brilliant*, which had sought shelter there a few days before. Taking these two ships under his orders, Elliot immediately put to sea, and 'on the evening of the 26th made the entrance of Belfast Lough, for Carrickfergus, but could not get in, the wind being contrary and very bad weather'. Thurot, on his side, having failed in his contemplated dash at Belfast, had re-embarked his men on 25 February, but was detained by the same bad weather, and did not weigh anchor until midnight of 27 February. On the following day Elliot's squadron caught up with Thurot off the Isle of Man. The resulting engagement saw Thurot's death and the surrender of the three French ships; the action was also noteworthy for the courageous conduct of Elliot's cousin, Thomas Pasley, who was subsequently promoted lieutenant of the *Aeolus*. Thurot's presence on the coast had caused so much alarm that the news of his death prompted considerable rejoicing. The action, creditable enough in itself, was certainly magnified by popular report: over forty years later Nelson claimed that Elliot's 'action with Thurot will stand the test with any of our modern victories' (Nicolas, *Nelson Despatches*, 5.366). In fact the French force, though nominally superior, was disintegrated by disaffection, mutiny, and sickness. The ships, too, had been severely strained by the long persistent bad weather to which they had been exposed, and many of their guns had been struck below.

On 7 March 1760 the ships and their prizes, having to some extent refitted in Ramsey Bay, sailed for Plymouth; meeting with a southerly gale, they again put into Kinsale, and finally arrived at Spithead on 25 March. After a short cruise on the French coast, and the capture of a brig laden with naval stores, which was cut out from under the guns of a battery on Belle Île, the *Aeolus* returned to Spithead. She was sent to Elliot's old cruising ground in the Bay of Biscay. In the spring of 1761 Elliot again went to Spithead, bringing with him a small privateer which he had captured off Cape Finisterre. He was then appointed to the *Chichester* (70 guns), and sent out to the Mediterranean, where he remained until the peace. From 1764 to 1771 he successively commanded the *Bellona*, the *Firme*, and the *Portland* as guardships at Plymouth, and in April 1777 he commissioned the *Trident* (64 guns).

On 22 April 1777 Elliot was ordered to wear a broad pennant and to carry over to North America the commissioners appointed to negotiate with representatives of the colonies. He arrived at Sandy Hook early in June, and for two months acted as second in command of the station, under Lord Howe. He then quitted the *Trident* and returned to England. Towards the end of 1779 he commissioned the *Edgar* (74 guns), one of the fleet which sailed on 29 December, under Sir George Rodney, for the relief of Gibraltar. In the action off Cape St Vincent on 16 January 1780 the *Edgar* had a distinguished share. After Gibraltar's relief and on the departure of the fleet Elliot remained behind as senior naval officer, but he returned to England a few months later, a ship of the *Edgar*'s size being found useless under the existing circumstances.

For the next two years the *Edgar* formed part of the Channel Fleet under Francis Geary, George Darby, or Howe, and on 12 December 1781 she was one of the small squadron with which Rear-Admiral Richard Kempenfelt effected his brilliant capture of a French convoy; being the leading ship of the line as it passed the French rear, she was for a time sharply engaged with the *Triomphant*. In June 1782 Elliot was removed into the *Romney*, and was under orders to go out to the West Indies, with a broad pennant, when peace was concluded. He was MP for Cockermouth (1767–8), and colonel of marines from 1779 to 1787. For the seasons 1786 to 1788 Elliot was governor and commander-in-chief at Newfoundland, going out each year in June largely to regulate fisheries, and returning in October. He became rear-admiral on 24 September 1787 and vice-admiral on 21 September 1790, hoisting his flag in the *Barfleur* during the Spanish armament. On 16 April 1795 he became admiral, but he did not serve again, and retired to his seat, Mount Teviot in Roxburghshire, where he died on 20 September 1808. Elliot never married. He held some of the family lands in Roxburghshire, and his estates were left to his nephew, Gilbert Elliot, first earl of Minto, with bequests to various relatives. He may well have accumulated a moderate fortune, as he commanded frigates able to cruise in the more lucrative stations. Likewise he first occupied the Newfoundland station, usually a post held by a full flag-officer, while still a commodore.

J. K. LAUGHTON, rev. A. W. H. PEARSALL

Sources J. S. Corbett, *England in the Seven Years' War: a study in combined strategy*, 2 vols. (1907) · W. M. James, *The British navy in adversity* (1926) · J. K. Laughton, *Studies in naval history: biographies* (1887), 324–62 · *The Hawke papers: a selection, 1743–1771*, ed. R. F. Mackay, Navy RS, 129 (1990) · *The private papers of John, earl of Sandwich*, ed. G. R. Barnes and J. H. Owen, 4 vols , Navy RS, 69, 71, 75, 78 (1932–8) · J. Charnock, ed., *Biographia navalis*, 6 (1798), 224 · *Naval Chronicle*, 9 (1803), 425 · R. Beatson, *Naval and military memoirs of Great Britain*, 3 vols. (1790) · letters, PRO, ADM 1/472 1760 · muster books, PRO, ADM 36/183; 2619; 4812; 6124; 6310 · passing certificate, PRO, ADM 107/4 · J. Brooke, 'Elliot, John', HoP, *Commons, 1754–90* · *The dispatches and letters of Vice-Admiral Lord Viscount Nelson*, ed. N. H. Nicolas, 7 vols. (1844–6); repr. (1997–8)

Archives NL Scot., corresp. and MSS · NMM, corresp. · NRA, priv. coll., letter-book, memorandum and order book · Provincial Archives of Newfoundland and Labrador, St. John's, Newfoundland, MSS relating to Newfoundland

Wealth at death owned extensive lands as well as Mount Teviot

Elliot, John (1747–1787), natural philosopher and accused attempted murderer, was born at Chard in Somerset in December 1747, the son of John Elliott, a clothier, and his wife, Hannah. In the past he has often been completely or partly confounded with Sir John Eliot (1736–1786). After attending school at Crewkerne, Somerset, Elliot was, according to contemporary accounts, apprenticed at the age of fourteen to an apothecary in Spitalfields, London. At the expiry of his time he became assistant in the practice of John Chandler (d. 1780) in Cheapside; and according to the *Narrative of the Life and Death of John Elliot, M.D.* (1787), it was during this period that he first established a romantic attachment to Mary Boydell, niece of Alderman John Boydell (1719–1804). Miss Boydell encouraged and then rejected the clever young apothecary. By 1780 he had set up business on his own: his premises were first in Carnaby Market and then, as he prospered, in Great Marlborough Street.

Elliot's scientific significance depends on monographs and papers published between 1780 and 1786. To understand his contribution to sensory physiology it must be recalled that most eighteenth-century authors supposed that vibrations of the aether or of the air were directly communicated to the optic and auditory nerves and thence to the sensorium, where sensations were aroused. In his *Philosophical Observations on the Senses* (1780), translated as *Ueber der Sinne* (Leipzig, 1785), Elliot described simple experiments in which he mechanically stimulated his own eyes and ears; and he concluded that our senses must contain transducers, sensory receptors, each tuned to only a limited part of the spectrum of physical frequencies. In the case of the eye, each of the resonators ('vibrations') is connected with a 'fibril of the optic nerve' and 'the vibration being excited, the pulses thereof are communicated to the nervous fibril, and by that conveyed to the sensory, or mind, where it occasions, by its action, the respective colour to be perceived' (*Elements of the Branches of Natural Philosophy Connected with Medicine*, 2nd edn, 1786, 276). Elliot's hypothesis anticipates the 'doctrine of specific nerve energies' later advanced by Johannes Müller; and it was known to Müller in translation.

Having grasped that our senses contain transducers of limited bandwidth, Elliot was led to the even more important insight that there might exist optical frequencies for which we do *not* have transducers. In his anonymously published *Experiments and Observations on Light and Colours* (1786) he introduced the concept of what would now be called infra-red and ultraviolet radiation and drew, down the side of one page, a spectrum extended in both directions beyond the visible. His text develops an elaborate analogy between heat and motion, and he describes spectroscopic experiments in which he pioneered the use of a prism to judge the distribution of different colours emitted by bodies at various temperatures:

> As the body in the third experiment cooled, it was pleasant to observe how, by degrees, the violet first, and then the indigo, blue, and the other inferior colours, vanished in succession, as if the spectrum were contracting itself towards its inferior part; and how the centre of the range seemed gradually to move from orange to red, and at length beneath it, as if it sunk into the insensible part below R in the scheme, the superior part following it, till the whole range was out of sight ... (J. Elliot, *Experiments and Observations on Light and Colours*, 1786, 68)

It has sometimes been suggested that James Hutton in

1794 was the first clearly to postulate radiation of low refrangibility that had the power of heating but little power to excite the retina. The priority must go to Elliot's unambiguous statement. It has to be said, however, that the same monograph ends with the thesis that has made Elliot notorious in histories of astronomy: he postulated that the surface of the sun was inhabited and that the sun's light proceeded from 'a luminous meteor in his atmosphere' (ibid., 102). At his trial the defence was to cite this hypothesis as evidence of Elliot's insanity, but it was (as the recorder noted) ably argued; and it was not implausible in the eighteenth-century context: a decade later William Herschel also suggested that the sun was habitable.

Elliot's *Elements of the Branches of Natural Philosophy Connected with Medicine* (1782) was intended to explain those parts of physics, chemistry, and physiology that should be understood by the physician; it introduced to the English reader T. O. Bergman's table of chemical affinities. Elliot's *Medical Pocket-Book*, first published in 1781, was a novel prescribing guide that proved particularly successful: in the period 1781–1827 it went through many editions, in England, Ireland, Russia, and the United States. His other publications include *An Address to the Public, on a Subject of the Utmost Importance to Health* (n.d.), *Essays on Physiological Subjects* (1780), *An Account of … the Principal Mineral Waters of Great Britain and Ireland* (1781), *A Complete Collection of the Medical and Philosophical Works of John Fothergill* (1781), and an essay, 'Observations of the affinities of substances in spirit of wine' (*PTRS*, 76, 1786, 76, 155).

1787 found Elliot again obsessed with Miss Boydell and increasingly psychotic in behaviour. He bought two brace of pistols and loaded one pair with shot, the other with blank shot, intending to discharge the blank at Miss Boydell and then shoot himself dead at her feet—or so his attorney claimed at the trial. On 9 July 1787, in Prince's Street, Soho, he came up behind Miss Boydell, who was arm in arm with her new companion, the bookseller George Nichol. He fired at Miss Boydell, but was seized by Nichol before he could shoot himself. By 16 July he was on trial at the Old Bailey. The prosecution insisted that the pistols had been loaded and that Miss Boydell had been saved only by her whalebone stays, whereas the defence held that the pistols had not been loaded—and that in any case Elliot was of unsound mind. The jury found that the pistols were not loaded and that he should be acquitted: but the recorder nevertheless committed him to Newgate, to be tried for assault. Elliot entered on a hunger strike, but his death, on 22 July 1787, came too quickly to be attributed to this abstinence alone: some newspapers cited gaol fever, but the *Daily Universal Register* favoured 'what is commonly stiled a broken heart' (24 July 1787). He was buried at Paddington four days later.

JOHN MOLLON

Sources J. R. Partington and D. McKie, 'Sir John Eliot, bart (1736–86), and John Elliot (1747–87)', *Annals of Science*, 6 (1948–50), 262–7 · J. R. Partington and D. McKie, 'Historical studies on the phlogiston theory: III. Light and heat in combustion', *Annals of Science*, 3 (1938), 337–71 · J. D. Mollon, 'John Elliot, 1747–1787', *Nature*, 329 (1987), 19–20 · R. J. Manning, 'John Elliot and the inhabited sun', *Annals of Science*, 50 (1993), 349–64 · E. Hodgson, 'The trial of Doctor John Elliott', *The whole proceedings on the king's commission of the peace* (1786–7), 809–24 [Old Bailey sessions papers, 16 July 1787] · *Narrative of the life and death of John Elliot, M.D., containing an account of the rise, progress, and catastrophe of his unhappy passion for Miss Mary Boydell: a review of his writings, together with an apology written by himself* (1787) · A. Duncan, *Laws and order in eighteenth-century chemistry* (1996) · *Daily Universal Register* (24 July 1787) · *GM*, 1st ser., 57 (1787), 636, 645–6 · *London Chronicle* (10–12 July 1787), 39 · *London Chronicle* (14–17 July 1787), 54–5 · 'Account of the trial of Dr John Elliot', *European Magazine and London Review*, 12 (1787), 71–2 · A. C. P. Callisen, *Medicinisches Schriftsteller-Lexicon*, 6 (Copenhagen, 1831) · A. Hirsch and others, eds., *Biographisches Lexikon der hervorragenden Aerzte aller Zeiten und Völker*, 6 vols. (Vienna and Leipzig, 1884–8), vol. 2 · Suard, 'Elliot, Jean', *Biographie universelle, ancienne et moderne*, ed. L. G. Michaud and E. E. Desplaces, new edn, 12 (Paris, 1855) · D. Lysons, *The environs of London*, 3 (1795)

Wealth at death £300: *Daily Universal Register* (27 July 1787)

Elliot, Sir John [*formerly* John Elliot Blumenfeld] (1898–1988), railway manager, was born on 6 May 1898 at Albert Bridge Road, Battersea, London, the younger son and third of four children of Ralph David *Blumenfeld (1864–1948), journalist and later editor of the *Daily Express*, and his wife, Teresa (Daisie), *née* Blumfeld, a cousin. He was educated at Marlborough College and the Royal Military College, Sandhurst. In 1917 he was commissioned in the 3rd King's Own hussars and went to France in October. He took part in the battles of Cambrai, Amiens, and Selle, returning to England in autumn 1919 as an acting adjutant. Reluctant to depend upon his family for the private income he would need as a cavalry officer, he resigned his commission and went to the United States to take up his father's profession of journalism.

After three years in New York on the *New York Times*, Elliot was recruited by Lord Beaverbrook, the proprietor of the *Daily Express*, as assistant editor of the London *Evening Standard*. Knowing the disadvantage of having a German name, he had changed his name by deed poll in 1922, taking his second forename as his surname. Within two years Beaverbrook sacked him and in 1925 he was taken on by Sir Herbert Walker, general manager of the Southern Railway, to improve that railway's image, as a public relations and advertising assistant. He soon moved from public relations to the traffic department, becoming deputy general manager of the Southern Railway in 1937. As such he played a major role in the electrification of the Southern Railway, the establishment of its Second World War headquarters in Dorking, Surrey, the evacuation of the children of London, and the transport of the survivors of Dunkirk. For his work in the war he became an officer of the Légion d'honneur and received the American Medal of Freedom (1945).

After the end of the war, in 1947 Elliot became general manager of Southern Railways, and, a year later, upon nationalization, chief regional officer of the southern region of British Railways. He moved to the same position in the London midland region in 1950 and in 1951 became chairman of the railway executive, which was abolished in 1953. In that year he became chairman of London Transport, a post he held until 1959, when he had to leave after the great seven-week London bus strike in mid-1958. He was responsible for the introduction of the Routemaster bus and the construction of the Victoria line for the underground railway. He then assumed the chairmanship of Thomas Cook (1959–67) and the directorships of other organizations. Throughout this period he had travelled abroad extensively, to study other transport industries and to advise foreign governments on their transport problems. He was president of the Institute of Transport in 1953–4 and was knighted in 1954. He was also colonel (commanding) of the engineer and railway staff corps, Royal Engineers (1956–63). His last public appointment was as a director of the British Airports Authority in 1965–9, at the same time as he was campaigning against Stansted airport.

Elliot had a large circle of friends and many outside interests. He reviewed books on military history; wrote a newspaper column; shot, fished, and hunted; studied the campaigns of Napoleon, the American Civil War, and the domestic life of Victorian London; and founded a dining club. In his late seventies he succumbed to the temptation to buy a small open sports car. He wrote three books— *Where our Fathers Died* (1964), about the western front fifty years after the First World War; *On and Off the Rails*, an autobiography (1982); and, perhaps his best, *The Way of the Tumbrils* (1958), a picture of the French Revolution as seen from the streets of Paris in the 1950s, which *The Times* said should prove popular 'with every wanderer in Paris who wants, in kindred mood, to find history in stones'.

Goo Elliot (as he was known) was a short, stocky man, 5 feet 6 inches in height, and lost most of his hair by the time he was thirty. He lived in Great Easton, Essex, where he had a beautiful garden. On 30 June 1924 he married Elizabeth Marjorie (Betty) (b. 1902/3), daughter of Dr Arthur Stanbury Cobbledick, a general practitioner who later specialized in ophthalmology. He practised in a house in Bolton Street, Mayfair, London, in which Betty grew up. The Elliots had a son and a daughter. As Elliot approached the end of his life he remained always sprucely turned out, although he was physically frail. He died on 18 September 1988 at St Stephen's Hospital, Fulham.   C. S. NICHOLLS, rev.

Sources *The Times* (20 Sept 1988) · *The Independent* (21 Sept 1988) · J. Elliot, *On and off the rails* (1982) · *CGPLA Eng. & Wales* (1988) · m. cert. · d. cert.
Archives CAC Cam., corresp. with E. L. Spears · HLRO, corresp. with Lord Beaverbrook
Wealth at death £336,709: probate, 22 Dec 1988, *CGPLA Eng. & Wales*

Elliot [*née* Tennant], **Katharine**, Baroness Elliot of Harwood (1903–1994), public servant and politician, was born on 15 January 1903 at 40 Grosvenor Square, London, the third of four, and second of three surviving, daughters of Sir Charles *Tennant, first baronet (1823–1906), of The Glen, Peeblesshire, Scottish industrialist and Gladstonian Liberal politician, and his second wife, Marguerite Agaranthe (1868–1943), daughter of Colonel Charles Miles, of Malmesbury, Wiltshire. The Tennants were remarkable for their longevity. Katharine's birth in 1903 meant that

three generations of her family spanned three different centuries. Her father, Sir Charles, who was seventy-nine when she was born, had marched in support of the Reform Bill in Glasgow in 1832. His father, John Tennant, had been born in 1796—seven years after the French Revolution. From Sir Charles's first marriage, to Emma Winsloe (1821–1895), Katharine had five surviving half-brothers and three surviving half-sisters. (There were a further three half-sisters and one half-brother who died in infancy.) Sir Charles died when Katharine was only three, and in 1907 her mother married Major Geoffrey Lubbock (1873–1932), the second son of Henry James Lubbock (younger brother of the first Baron Avebury). There were two further half-brothers by her mother's second marriage.

As a child Katharine (or K, as she was invariably known) played in the nursery at 10 Downing Street, the home of her half-sister Margot [*see* Asquith, Margaret Emma Alice], who was married to the prime minister, Herbert Henry *Asquith. Aged eight, she threw a toy from the second floor nursery window onto the heads of suffragettes protesting outside. Nearly fifty years later she was one of the first life peeresses created by a Conservative prime minister, Harold Macmillan. She grew up, however, with strong Liberal ideals. Educated by governesses at home, at Abbot's Hill School in Hemel Hempstead, and finally in Paris, she was presented at the court of George V as a débutante. But, as she later said, 'I was more interested in politics than parties' (*The Scotsman*, 18 Nov 1989). She made up for her lack of formal academic training by studying at the London School of Economics under Harold Laski and William Beveridge. She was an accomplished violinist when young, and later played the organ in her local church every Sunday she was at home. She acquired fluent French, was a keen rider until the age of eighty, and a golfer of genuine skill, who reached the fourth round of the Scottish ladies' golf championship in 1931. She could boast that she had beaten two prime ministers at the game—Henry Asquith and Arthur Balfour.

She brought to a lifetime of public service a formidable combination of energy and commitment. 'I was so lucky,' she once said. 'I never had to earn my living. So I decided to work for other people' (private information from Lady Emma Tennant). On 2 April 1934 Katharine married the Rt Hon. Walter *Elliot (1888–1958), Conservative MP for Glasgow Kelvingrove, and minister for agriculture, who went on to become secretary of state for Scotland and minister of health. (This was his second marriage; his first wife, Helen Hamilton, had died in a mountaineering accident while on their honeymoon, in 1919.) From this point on, Katharine was closely involved with the affairs of the Conservative Party. As an MP's wife—like both her sisters, Margaret (Peggy) and Nancy, who also married politicians, becoming Lady Wakehurst and Lady Crathorne respectively—she worked tirelessly in the background, frequently writing speeches for her husband and attending the hustings. She campaigned, for him or for the party, in every election until well into her seventies. Among her more demanding roles was to help publicize one of her husband's innovations, the Milk Marketing Board—despite a lifelong aversion to milk. She never lost touch with her Liberal roots, however, and remained a passionate opponent of the death penalty, and closely involved in prison reform and international affairs.

The Elliot seat, at Harwood, near Bonchester Bridge in the Scottish borders, became the other focus of Katharine's life. She was keenly interested in farming, and since her husband was the son of a livestock auctioneer, she became expert in buying and selling farm animals and equipment. On her marriage, nearly every farmer in Britain subscribed 1s. towards a wedding present. With the money raised, she purchased a tractor, which she learned to drive. For sixty years at Harwood, she entertained a large circle of friends and relatives. A sturdily built woman, wearing sensible, but rarely fashionable, clothes, she was often to be found wielding a trident-shaped poker at the vast drawing-room fireplace, thumping out songs on the family piano, or rounding up guests for some expedition, with her famous rallying call: 'Come on! Come on! Come on!' (private information). The family motto, *Velis plenis* ('in full sail'), fitted her perfectly. Possessed of strong opinions, she nevertheless had the knack of disagreeing without being disagreeable. 'It takes two to quarrel and I won't be one of them' was one of her favourite expressions (Sherfield).

There were no children of the marriage. Instead, Katharine Elliot became increasingly active in public life. From 1939 to 1949 she was chairman of the National Association of Mixed Clubs and Girls' Clubs, later known as Youth Clubs UK, which promoted the policy of leisure-time activities for young people. She sat on the Home Office advisory committee on the treatment of offenders from 1946 to 1962, during which time she visited every prison in the UK. She served on the advisory committee on child care in Scotland (1956–65), and was chairman of the National Union of Conservative and Unionist Associations (1956–67). She became the first chairman of the Consumer Council in 1963. On three occasions, in 1954, 1956, and 1957, she was a member of the UK delegation to the United Nations and, in the absence of ministers during the Suez crisis in 1956, she made a powerful speech denouncing the Soviet invasion of Hungary. She was appointed CBE in 1946, and, in 1963, was awarded the grand silver cross of the Austrian order of merit.

In January 1958 Walter Elliot died following a heart attack. His widow took over as chairman of the family auctioneering firm of Lawrie and Symington, and stood in place of her husband as candidate for Kelvingrove: she lost by only a narrow margin of votes. Later that year she was made a DBE (like her sister Peggy) and was created a life peer. In 1959 she received an honorary LLD from Glasgow University. She was the first peeress to speak in the House of Lords, the first to propose the loyal address, and the first to pilot a private bill through the house; this was at the request of Margaret Thatcher, who had introduced it in the Commons: it thus became the first bill to be taken through both houses by women. In the course of ten years she made 135 speeches from the floor, tackling every subject with what she regarded as plain common sense. She was incapable of trimming, and was the despair of the whips. Her great friend Lord Home of the Hirsel, ascribed to her 'courage tempered by an acute mind and practical common sense' (*Hansard 5C*, 4 Nov 1958). She was active in local politics for thirty years, serving on the education and social work committees of Roxburghshire county council, and later as vice-convener, once claiming, modestly, that her finest achievement was to secure a new sewage works for Bonchester Bridge. There were few borders activities with which she was not involved, and she was delighted when a local newspaper group made her its 'borders man of the year'. She became a justice of the peace in 1968.

In November 1993 Baroness Elliot tripped over her parliamentary robes and fell as she left the peers' chamber, where she had attended the opening of parliament. She was taken to hospital still wearing the robes, and died at Hawick Cottage Hospital on 3 January 1994. She was buried at Hobkirk parish church, near Bonchester Bridge, on 8 January, and a service of thanksgiving was held in her memory at St Margaret's Church, Westminster Abbey, on 14 April.   MAGNUS LINKLATER

Sources WW · Burke, *Peerage* · interview, *Glasgow Herald* (14 March 1992) · *The Times* (4 Jan 1994) · *The Independent* (5 Jan 1994) · Lord Crathorne, *The House Magazine* (24 Jan 1994) · *The Scotsman* (4 Jan 1994) · J. N. and E. T., 'Baroness Elliot of Harwood', *The Scotsman* (8 Jan 1994), 10 · Lord Sherfield, memorial address delivered at St Margaret's, London, 13 April 1994 · N. Crathorne and others, *Tennant's stalk: the story of the Tennants of the glen* (1973) · E. Tennant, *Strangers: a family romance* (1998) · A. Horne, *Macmillan*, 2: *1957–1986* (1989), 82–3 · championship records, 1931, Scottish Ladies' Golfing Association · *United Nations Yearbook* (1954) · *United Nations Yearbook* (1956) · *United Nations Yearbook* (1957) · *Hansard 5C* (1958–94) · private information (2004) [Lady Emma Tennant, Lord Crathorne, Mr Andrew Lubbock, Abbot's Hill School] · *The Scotsman* (18 Nov 1989) [interview] · Crathorne MSS · 'Elliot, Walter Elliot', *DNB*

Archives priv. coll. | priv. coll., Tennant MSS · U. Glas., Walter Elliot Memorial Library | FILM 'An Extraordinary Lady', Borders TV documentary by Elinor Goodman, Oct 1993

Likenesses photograph, 1953, priv. coll.; repro. in *The Times* · N. Sinclair, bromide print, 1992, NPG · J. Barrow, oils, priv. coll. · photographs, repro. in *The Independent*

Wealth at death £702,827.93: confirmation, 29 March 1994, NA Scot., SC/CO 744/175

Elliot [*alias* Sheldon], **Nathaniel** (1705–1780), Jesuit, was born on 1 May 1705, one of at least three sons. He entered the Society of Jesus in 1723 and was admitted to the profession of the four vows in 1741. Ordained priest about 1736, he adopted the alias of Sheldon, his aunt Mary Anne, daughter of John Elliot of Gatacre Park, Shropshire, being the wife of Ralph Sheldon of Beoley, Worcestershire. In October 1748 he was appointed rector of the English College at St Omer, having been previously *socius* to the provincial, Henry Sheldon, his cousin; and from 1756 to 1762 he was rector of the English College at Rome. In 1766 he became rector of the Greater College, Bruges, and later in the same year he was nominated provincial of his order in England. While holding this office he resided in the family of Mr Nevill at Holt, Leicestershire, where he died on 10 October 1780.

The *Occasional Letters on the Affairs of the Jesuits in France* (1763) was collected and published under Elliot's direction, together with *The Judgment of the Bishops of France Concerning the Doctrine, Government, Conduct, and Usefulness of the French Jesuits* (1763). He was also the translator of F. Pinamonti's treatise *The Cross in its True Light, or, The Weight of Tribulation Lessened* (1775).

THOMPSON COOPER, *rev.* ROBERT BROWN

Sources Gillow, *Lit. biog. hist.* · G. Oliver, *Collections towards illustrating the biography of the Scotch, English and Irish members of the Society of Jesus* (1835) · G. Holt, *The English Jesuits, 1650–1829: a biographical dictionary*, Catholic RS, 70 (1984) · H. Foley, ed., *Records of the English province of the Society of Jesus*, 7 vols. in 8 (1875–83)

Elliot, Robert James (1790–1849), naval officer and topographical draughtsman, was born on 12 May 1790 in Wheldrake, Yorkshire, and baptized there on 30 May, the son of the Revd Robert Elliot (a younger brother of the governor-general of Bengal, Gilbert Elliot Murray *Kynynmound, first earl of Minto), and his wife, Mary. Elliot entered the navy as a cadet on 26 February 1802, and was promoted lieutenant in 1808 in the East Indies, where he served until his return to England in 1814. The inscription for Elliot's drawing of John Leyden MD, reproduced in J. L. Caw's *The Scott Gallery* (2 vols., 1903, vol. 1), records that it was made aboard the *Phoenix* during a voyage to Madras in 1811. In August 1814 he was promoted to the rank of commander. He was active for many years in the establishment and support of a sailors' home in London where he also supported other institutions for the benefit of sailors.

From 1822 to 1824 Elliot made a series of sketches, taken on the spot, of views in India, Canton (Guangzhou), and the Red Sea. These were worked up by Samuel Prout, Clarkson Stanfield, and others into finished drawings, and were published in parts by Fisher & Co., appearing in 2 volumes in 1833 under Elliot's name as *Views in the East, comprising India, Canton, and the Red Sea. With historical and descriptive illustrations* (and letterpress by Emma Roberts). Elliot died on 30 April 1849 at Cumming Place, Pentonville, London. Robert Elliot is sometimes confused with the marine painter William Elliot (*fl.* 1774–1794).

ANNETTE PEACH

Sources GM, 2nd ser., 32 (1849), 651 · IGI · Thieme & Becker, *Allgemeines Lexikon* · Burke, *Peerage* · *Engraved Brit. ports.*, 3.60 · DNB · Mallalieu, *Watercolour artists* · J. L. Caw, *The Scott Gallery*, 2 vols. (1903), vol. 1
Likenesses photogravure, repro. in Caw, *Scott Gallery*

Elliot, Sir Thomas Frederick (1808–1880), civil servant, was born in London in July 1808 and baptized on 29 January 1809 (*IGI*), the youngest son of the nine children of Hugh *Elliot (1752–1830), diplomat, and his second wife, Margaret Jones (1770–1819). Elliot belonged to a titled Scottish family with extensive whig connections and a long tradition of public service. His father was the second son of Sir Gilbert *Elliot, third baronet (*d.* 1777), and younger brother of Gilbert Elliot Murray *Kynynmound, first earl of Minto (1751–1814). Elliot spent six years in India following his father's appointment as governor of Madras in 1814, and considered himself fortunate to have experienced the contrasts of India and England at such a

young age, believing it had taught him 'liberality'. He was educated at Harrow School (1821–5), where he found school life tedious and complained that he learned very little.

On the strength of his family connections and traditions Elliot entered the Colonial Office as a junior clerk on 5 July 1825. His administrative ability was soon rewarded by promotion to the position of précis writer in July 1827. From June 1831 he served as secretary to the newly appointed emigration commissioners, whose brief was to assist and diffuse information to prospective emigrants to the Australian and British North American colonies. James Stephen, permanent counsel to the Colonial Office and later permanent under-secretary of state, drew attention to Elliot's aptitude and considered his advancement to be of 'national importance' (Grey MSS, GRE/B126/11). Upon the dismissal of the commissioners in August 1832 he was given sole responsibility for superintendence of emigration schemes to Australia. He worked closely with the London Emigration Committee, a philanthropic body which managed the practical arrangements of emigration on behalf of the Colonial Office. In April 1833 he achieved further promotion as senior clerk to the North American department. This relatively rapid progress displeased some of his longer-serving, less adept colleagues. On 16 May 1833 he married Jane Perry (1807–1861), daughter of James Perry (1756–1821), the former proprietor and editor of the *Morning Chronicle*. They had no children. From 1835 to 1837 he served in Quebec as secretary to the earl of Gosford's commission of inquiry into Canadian affairs, where his contribution did not go unnoticed. Elliot's private correspondence to a colleague, Henry Taylor, discussing the state of affairs in Canada was forwarded to Viscount Howick, secretary at war, who, impressed by the quality of his analysis, circulated his letters to the cabinet. Despite the failure of the Gosford commission, Elliot's reputation was undoubtedly enhanced. He published a pamphlet, *The Canadian Controversy: its Origin, Nature, and Merits* (1838), which was essentially a defence of the government's policy.

Elliot returned to England in March 1837 to take up the new post of agent-general for emigration, created to manage the bureaucratic framework for government-assisted emigration to Australia. Working with only a small staff, he had to undertake many of the more mundane duties himself, but did so with enthusiasm and commitment. In January 1840 he was appointed one of three commissioners of the newly established colonial land and emigration commission, and subsequently became its chairman. Through these areas of responsibility he achieved significant and enduring influence over emigration policies for Australia. In his attempts to rationalize and organize the process of emigration, he demonstrated a keen awareness of the diverse problems and issues surrounding colonization. He took particular satisfaction in contributing to legislation for the health and safety of ship passengers, which culminated in the Passenger Act of 1855. His paternalistic concern for the humanitarian aspects of emigration was evident, but he rarely allowed these considerations to preclude stringently applying the criteria for selecting assisted emigrants. He always acknowledged the importance of balancing British domestic needs against colonial preferences. Wherever possible he tried to adhere to free-trade doctrines, particularly in his dealings with shipowners, where he was reluctant to interfere too much in matters which might affect the cost of passages for emigrants.

Criticism of Elliot's handling of emigration was unremitting and at times severe. Colonies complained about the quality of immigrants they received; shipowners worried about the increasingly restrictive passenger regulations, and some colonial reformers, such as Edward Gibbon Wakefield, condemned Elliot as being unfit for the business of colonization. Elliot patiently but firmly defended his actions and policies. In November 1847, following the retirement of James Stephen, Elliot became one of two assistant under-secretaries of state under Stephen's successor, Herman Merivale. This new appointment allowed him to maintain his interest and influence in Australian affairs such as emigration, transportation, and self-government, and also involved him in such diverse issues as colonial military expenditure and Canadian confederation. He was a major witness before the select committee of the House of Lords on emigration from Ireland in 1848.

Family connections secured Elliot's acceptance into the exclusive circles of London society, where he met those with influence in colonial affairs. He moved within the circle of philosophical radicals, colonial reformers, celebrated writers, literati, and liberal politicians such as Lord John Russell, whose second wife, Frances, was Elliot's second cousin. His house at 13 Chesham Place, London, was described as where 'most of the persons who, in those days, were writing and reading and making speeches' met together (*Letters and Private Papers of … Thackeray*, 1.cxxvii). His lively wit and personable qualities made him a popular figure. Elliot enjoyed long-standing friendships with John Stuart Mill and Thomas Carlyle, and helped to organize the latter's series of lectures in 1837. William Makepeace Thackeray declared the Elliot home to be one of his favourite places. Following his wife's death, on 9 January 1861, Elliot moved out of Chesham Place and was seen less frequently at social gatherings.

Elliot's retirement, with a pension, from the Colonial Office on 8 December 1868 was prompted by his forthcoming second marriage, on 4 January 1869, to Elizabeth Howe Bromley (1824?–1880), daughter of Sir Robert Howe Bromley (1778–1857) and Anne Wilson (d. 1873). There were no children from this marriage. On 14 August 1869 he was appointed KCMG for his long service in colonial affairs. After his retirement he indulged his love of travel and pursued his interest in science. Michael Faraday's work, both scientific and metaphysical, held a particular fascination for him. He published privately a satirical essay entitled *A Discourse on Table Rapping* and circulated it among family and friends. He was elected vice-president of the Royal Institution of Great Britain in July 1876. He died at Shepheard's Hotel, Cairo, Egypt, on 12 February 1880, four days after the death of his second wife. Both were victims of an acute infection, diagnosed as typhoid fever, and were buried in Cairo. Elliot is representative of the 'powerful' nineteenth-century civil servant (others include Edwin Chadwick, Sir James Kay-Shuttleworth, and Sir Charles Trevelyan) who lived through the transition from a civil service characterized by jobbery and family connection to one whose progress was based on merit and ability.

MARGARET RAY

Sources NL Scot., Elliot MSS, MSS 19420–19433 · U. Durham L., archives and special collections, 3rd Earl Grey MSS · M. Ray, 'Administering emigration: Thomas Elliot and government-assisted emigration from Britain to Australia, 1831–1855', PhD diss., U. Durham, 2001 · R. F. Haines, *Emigration and the labouring poor: Australian recruitment in Britain and Ireland, 1831–1860* (1997) · O. MacDonagh, *A pattern of government growth, 1800–60: the Passenger Acts and their enforcement* (1961) · P. Buckner, 'The colonial office and British North America, 1801–50', *DCB*, vol. 8, pp. xxiii–xxxvii · R. B. Madgwick, *Immigration into eastern Australia, 1788–1851* (1969) · R. C. Mills, *The colonization of Australia, 1829–42: the Wakefield experiment in empire building* (1915) · Countess of Minto, *A memoir of the Right Honourable Hugh Elliot* (1868) · *The letters and private papers of William Makepeace Thackeray*, ed. G. N. Ray, 4 vols. (1945–6) · *The collected letters of Thomas and Jane Welsh Carlyle*, ed. C. R. Sanders and K. J. Fielding, 10 (1985); 12 (1985) · H. Taylor, *Autobiography*, 2 vols. (1885) · A. Hayden, 'Elliot, Thomas Frederick', *AusDB*, vol. 1 · *The Times* (24 Feb 1880) · IGI

Archives NL Scot., corresp., diaries, and MSS | NL Scot., letters to Lady Minto · PRO, Colonial Office records, class CO · U. Durham L., letters to third Earl Grey

Wealth at death approx. £7000: NL Scot., Elliot MSS

Elliot, Sir Walter (1803–1887), East India Company servant and archaeologist, was born on 16 January 1803, the second but eldest surviving of the eight sons and three daughters of James Elliot (1772–1855) of Wolfelee, Roxburghshire, and his wife, Caroline (1777–1824), youngest daughter of Walter Hunter, last laird of Polmood. He was educated at home and at private schools, and in 1818 he was sent to the East India College, Haileybury, having been recommended to the company by his aunt, the widow of the twelfth Lord Elphinstone, and in January 1819 was nominated to a writership in the company by his great-uncle William Fullerton Elphinstone. Leaving Haileybury with a certificate of high distinction and a name for sport, he landed in Madras on 14 June 1820. His record at the college of Fort St George (in history, law, and languages) was no less brilliant: he won an award of 1000 pagodas for proficiency in Tamil and Hindustani (Urdu).

Elliot's delight lay in languages: he became fluent in Arabic, Marathi, Persian, and Telugu. In 1823, after two years as assistant to the collector and magistrate of Salem district, he asked for a posting to a 'non-regulation' territory. Some powerful friends, including Sir Thomas Munro, governor of Madras, and Mountstuart Elphinstone, governor of Bombay, eased his transfer to the newly conquered southern Maratha districts then administered by the Madras presidency. Here, a year later, he was caught in the Kittur uprising. St John Thackeray, political agent of Dharwar, with three officers, horse artillery, and sepoys, went to maintain order, but was killed attempting to arrange a truce. Elliot, with another assistant, Stevenson, became a prisoner, and remained for six weeks in the hands of the insurgents. This experience, during which he received gentle and kind treatment and was introduced to his captors' notions of depth of kinship, caste, and pollution customs, and to their ferociousness in response to humiliation, greatly influenced his ideas and capacity to understand the Hindu population; he was long remembered in the area. When these Maratha districts were transferred to the Bombay presidency, Elliot would ordinarily have been moved to another district in Madras, but Sir John Malcolm, the governor of Bombay, asked that he be allowed to remain until he left India on furlough in 1833. By this time his reputation as an adventurer, antiquarian, historian, big-game hunter, and linguist was well established.

Elliot embarked from Bombay on 11 December 1833 with Robert Pringle of the Bombay civil service, travelling to Europe by way of the Red Sea, riding across the Egyptian desert from Quseir to Thebes, sailing down the Nile route to Cairo, and crossing further deserts to Damascus and Jerusalem. After visiting Constantinople, Athens, Corfu, and Rome, he reached England on 5 May 1835. In the autumn of 1836, on the appointment of his cousin Lord Elphinstone as governor of Madras, he solicited the post of private secretary, and the cousins sailed together on the *Prince Regent*, a yacht being presented as a royal gift to the imam of Muscat, and arrived in Madras in February 1837.

Elliot immediately plunged into the business of running Lord Elphinstone's government (which lasted until 1842), and was exceedingly active. In addition to his duties as private secretary, he became third member of the board of revenue, a college board member, Kannada translator, and acting Persian translator. In addition, he wrote from Suez in November 1838 describing the hostilities between Wahabis and Egyptians. On 15 January 1839 he married Maria Dorothea Hunter Blair (*d.* 1890), daughter of Sir David Hunter Blair, third baronet, of Blairquhan, who had come out to meet Elliot at Malta. They were to have four sons and two daughters. Later that year Elliot uncovered the Amaravati ruins on the banks of the Kistna River (pieces of which he later excavated and were placed in the entrance hall of the British Museum); and in 1840 he examined 'cromlechs and cairns' in the Nilgiri hills. When Elphinstone's term of office ended in September 1842, his successor, Lord Tweeddale, found that Elliot had been acting as 'Revenue and Judicial Secretary, and Lord Elphinstone's guide in everything'.

After Elphinstone's departure Elliot found himself employed only in the ordinary duties of the board of revenue. In 1845 he was deputed to investigate the condition of Guntur district, one of the Northern Circars. This district, even more than the other Northern Circars, had never recovered from the great famine of 1833. Elliot's enquiries into the causes of the general impoverishment and the consequent serious decline in East India Company revenues in the region uncovered a deep and systematic pattern of silent corruption and collusion between village élites, local revenue officials, and the *zamindars*, the five families who held huge landed estates in the district. Elliot concluded that a system of predatory extortion and wasteful extravagance was undermining the entire fabric of imperial control, and recommended a completely new survey and revenue assessment of all villages in the district, and a resumption of all lands and villages previously held by the debt-ridden and defaulting *zamindars*. These lands had been sold for arrears of revenue, and were now to be brought under government management. Although the terms of the acquisition were less favourable to the *zamindars* than Elliot had originally proposed, the East India Company's court of directors highly commended his work in Guntur, and appointed him commissioner of the Northern Circars. This gave him the powers of the board of revenue for the administration of the whole of those six districts. He carried this heavy responsibility until 1854, when he was appointed a member of the council of the governor of Madras. As first member of council, he was acting governor in 1857, at the time of the great mutiny in northern India. Although Madras was generally removed from the fighting, Elliot felt obliged to order Indian troops to stack their arms at morning parade. He served on the Madras council at a time when the government confronted a broad range of issues of public concern. High among these was the question of expanding education, which involved government relations with Christian missions on the one hand, and with Hindu and Muslim religious endowments on the other. Because of his fluency in several Indian languages, Elliot had always enjoyed full and friendly contacts with people from many different religious communities. In a private capacity, he had also been a generous supporter of Christian missions. He had been an early and staunch advocate of the grant-in-aid system. As the governor was ill, it fell to Elliot as senior member of council to preside over the reading at Madras of the queen's proclamation of the direct assumption of the government of India by Britain.

Beyond his work as a public servant Elliot devoted much of his private time and personal wealth to scholarly investigations. His interests ranged widely, covering disparate fields from archaeology to natural history. From his earliest years in the southern Maratha country his scholarly pursuits had been unceasing. Working in concert with a group of young Brahmans attached to his office, he mastered the calligraphy of the ancient inscriptions, and for the rest of his time in India liked to spend his leisure in deciphering and translating documents, inscriptions, and manuscripts which he found in various parts of the country. In zoology, ornithology, and botany his interests were also keen. In 1837 he published a paper entitled 'Hindu inscriptions' in the *Journal of the Asiatic Society of Bengal*; this was to be the first in a long line of contributions to scholarly journals which continued throughout his life. His observations, invariably acute and critical, were written in a clear and popular style. Most important of his works was his treatise *Coins of Southern India*. Published in 1885, this formed part 2 of the third volume of *International Numismata orientalia*. It contains a penetrating analysis of the ancient communities and dynasties of southern India, based on the hosts of inscriptions and coins which had by then been discovered. No less remarkable is the fact that all of Elliot's later works were written when, having been extremely near-sighted all his life, he was virtually blind. He had to depend on an amanuensis to commit his ideas to paper, and to relatives and friends to correct his proofs. His collection of south Indian coins, about 400 in number, was deposited, with his collection of carved marble sculptures from Amaravati, in the British Museum.

After forty years in India Elliot finally retired and returned to Britain early in 1860. In recognition of his services in India, he was created KCSI in 1866; in 1877 he was appointed a fellow of the Royal Society; and in 1878 he received the degree of LLD from the University of Edinburgh. He spent most of the rest of his life at the family home at Wolfelee, Roxburghshire, taking an active part in local affairs. He was deputy lieutenant of the county, and a magistrate. He turned his house into a veritable museum of coins, inscriptions, and memorabilia, where he welcomed many visitors and scholars. To the end of his life his intellectual vitality remained: on the very day of his death he dictated and signed a note to the renowned Tamil scholar George Pope, expressing his enthusiasm over a forthcoming edition of Pope's classic translation of the Tamil *Kural*, and observing that his own 'interest in oriental literature continues unabated'. He died at Wolfelee in the evening of 1 March 1887, survived by his wife and five of his children.

A. J. ARBUTHNOT, rev. ROBERT ERIC FRYKENBERG

Sources *Proceedings of the Asiatic Society of Bengal*, 19 (1887), 519–24 · private information (1888) · R. Sewell, *Sir Walter Elliot of Wolfelee: a sketch of his life and a few extracts from his notebooks* (1896) · R. E. Frykenberg, *Guntur district, 1788–1848: a history of local influence and central authority* (1965) · Burke, *Gen. GB* (1914)
Archives BL OIOC, MSS Eur. C 74–75, D 317–330, 336, F 46–50, G 87 | BL OIOC, letters, as private secretary to Lord Elphinstone, MSS Eur. F 87–89
Likenesses R. Sewell, portrait, 1896
Wealth at death £36,855 9s. 8d.: confirmation, 1 June 1887, CCI

Elliot, Walter Elliot (1888–1958), politician, was born on 19 September 1888 at Markgreen, Wellgate Road, Lanark, the eldest son of William Elliot (d. 1929), livestock auctioneer, and his wife, Ellen Elizabeth, *née* Shiels. In 1892 Elliot's mother died following childbirth, and he, his younger brother, and two sisters were thereafter partly brought up by their maternal grandmother in Bath Street, Glasgow, where he was influenced by the scientific interests of his uncle, Dr Shiels. In 1900 he visited relatives in the United States.

Medical officer and coalition Unionist MP Elliot received his elementary education at Lanark high school and then went on to Glasgow Academy. In 1905 he entered Glasgow University, where he studied medicine, taking a BSc in 1910, and his MB ChB in 1913. He was one of those pre-First World War students (a 'chronic') who lingered at the university and took longer over their degrees than was prescribed. This lifestyle, facilitated by his father's financial support, brought him into contact with Osborne Mavor,

later James Bridie, the playwright, and others in a spirited group of 'half-baked men of letters' (Bridie, 191) who gravitated towards the Glasgow University Union. Elliot was president in 1911–12, was editor of the *Glasgow University Magazine* in 1909–10, and was co-author of the college song, 'Ygorra'. Under the pseudonym Parvus he wrote poetry. Politically, he already showed his refusal to be bound by conventional party divisions. In the typically rumbustious rectorial election of 1908 he supported Lord Curzon, assisted the Liberal Club in running Lloyd George, and was believed by Bridie to have voted for Keir Hardie.

After graduation Elliot became a houseman at Glasgow Royal Infirmary. On the outbreak of the First World War he was mobilized as a member of the special reserve of the Royal Army Medical Corps and served as medical officer with the Royal Scots Greys on the western front from December 1914. For his part in the action at Wancourt, near Arras, in April 1917 he was awarded the Military Cross, to which was added a bar after action at Cambrai in November 1917. His younger brother, Dan, was killed at Gallipoli in 1915, and Elliot's father, who expressed incomprehension of his surviving son, was surprised by Walter's subsequent refusal to enter the family business of Lawrie and Symington, auctioneers.

Elliot was wounded in the leg in October 1918, and while recovering was asked to stand for the Lanark division of Lanarkshire as a coalition Unionist. Apocryphally he is supposed to have responded to this request by agreeing and then asking on which side he was to stand, which, if true, could have been taken as summing up his approach to party between the wars. He sat for Lanark until defeated in December 1923, and then for the Kelvingrove division of Glasgow from a by-election victory in May 1924 until his defeat in July 1945.

On 27 August 1919 Elliot married Helen Arabella Hamilton (b. 1886/7), a nurse and matron in a London hospital and the daughter of David Livingston Hamilton, a doctor. The marriage was tragically brief. Helen Elliot died on 8 September 1919 as a result of a climbing accident in the Cuillin Hills on the Isle of Skye where they were on honeymoon.

Elliot became parliamentary private secretary to the parliamentary under-secretary for health for Scotland in 1919. In this position he was involved in forming a dining club, the Alternative Government Group. Most of its members were parliamentary private secretaries, who, given the coalition's huge majority, were able to pursue an independent line. He was also a member of the New Coalition Group formed under Oscar Guest, which was promoting the notion of a centre party. Examples of Elliot's political centrism can be found in his support for devolving real powers to the Irish in the Government of Ireland Act of 1920, in his role in getting a hearing for the miners' leader Frank Hodges before a group of MPs during the miners' strike of 1921, and in his early agitation for non-traditional solutions to the Scottish housing problem, such as the prefabricated Weir steel house. He was in the minority in supporting the continuance of the coalition at the Carlton Club meeting of Conservatives on 19 October 1922.

During his first parliament Elliot formed or strengthened long-lasting friendships. One of these was with Colin Coote, then Coalition Liberal MP for the Isle of Ely, with whom he shared a house in Wilfred Street, Westminster. Coote, who later wrote a warm biography of Elliot, *A Companion of Honour*, described himself as joined by silk as strong as steel to his subject. Another friendship was with Blanche 'Baffy' Dugdale, a niece and biographer of A. J. Balfour, who brought Elliot into contact with Zionism. Elliot also continued his interest in science, accepting an invitation from John Boyd-Orr, a pre-1914 Officers' Training Corps friend, to carry out research at the Rowett Research Institute in Aberdeen during parliamentary recesses. For this work, and the resulting thesis on pig nutrition, he was awarded a DSc by Glasgow University in 1923. It also played a part in his later election as a fellow of the Royal Society in 1935.

Interventionist Conservative These two strands, political centrism and a scientific approach, run through Elliot's work in a succession of offices. Notwithstanding his vote in support of the coalition at the Carlton Club, Stanley Baldwin appointed him parliamentary under-secretary for health for Scotland in January 1923. He held the office, with the short interruption of the labour government of 1924, until July 1926, when he became parliamentary under-secretary of state for Scotland, which he remained until 1929.

The most obvious example of Elliot's interventionism during Baldwin's second government was his enthusiasm for the Empire Marketing Board. He sat on its research committee and, again together with John Boyd-Orr, was involved with the pilot scheme of 1927 for providing free milk to schoolchildren. This was extended two years later to cover the whole country. He also promoted the board's support for the documentary film, most notable in the work of John Grierson and the latter's classic *Drifters* (1929). Housing remained one of his priorities, and he continued to badger local authorities and the political representatives of the building unions to accept non-traditional construction methods. He was also involved in upgrading Scottish ministers' positions in 1926, in reorganizing Scottish central administration in 1928, and in the passage of the Local Government Act (1929). This measure, which made him much more widely known and aroused considerable opposition, consolidated Scottish local government, removing powers from smaller burghs and effectively ending the role of parish councils.

Elliot remained active beyond Scotland. There had been visits to France, Spain, and the Balkans in the early 1920s and to Prague, for example, for a conference of the League of Nations Union. In 1927 he was appointed a British delegate to the league in Geneva. In the same year he published *Toryism and the Twentieth Century*, which argued for a Conservatism that would make use of applied and social sciences and of government intervention. Out of office in 1930, these views led him to voice some support in a letter to *The Times* for the plan put forward by Oswald Mosley, then a radical Labour MP, for tackling the unemployment crisis, in particular by using protection and vigorous executive action. This was—for a rising Conservative politician—a very dangerous course, and earned a rebuke from Stanley Baldwin. Elliot apologized, and with his appointment as financial secretary to the Treasury in the National Government in summer 1931 and to the privy council early in 1932 appeared to have emerged unscathed.

The cabinet: agriculture, Scotland, and health In September 1932 Elliot was appointed to the cabinet as minister of agriculture and fisheries, which enabled him to implement more widely the ideas and policies which he had been developing over the previous decade. In the context of a slump in world agricultural demand and prices he is credited with helping to turn British agriculture round by implementing policies of modified protection. These included bilateral agreements, which limited but guaranteed entry to the British market for foreign producers, and quotas where necessary. Levies on foreign imports were used to subsidize British producers. He also used existing legislation to set up marketing boards to regulate prices and production. The best-known of these, the Milk Marketing Board, begun in 1933, helped him further promote the policy of providing low-priced milk to schools. Stimulated by the ideas of John Boyd-Orr on health and nutrition, he played a part in the moves in 1934 towards designating what came to be known as special areas, an attempt to develop a regional approach to economic depression and mass unemployment.

Physically large and craggy, Elliot had the reputation of a gallant, debonair conversationalist, whose speech was of the 'rich, unmistakeable Scots' variety (Pottinger, 64). The charm which impressed, among others, Beatrice Webb at a supper in 1930 appears to have done him no harm in the Lord North Street house of Katharine Tennant, described as 'a salon for the stimulating fringes of all parties' (Coote, *Companion of Honour*, 148). Here Elliot mixed with, among others, Alec Dunglass, Harold Macmillan, and Noel Skelton. On 2 April 1934 at North Berwick, Elliot married Katharine Tennant (1903–1994) [see Elliot, Katharine], daughter of Sir Charles *Tennant, first baronet, and his second wife, Marguerite; Katharine was half-sister of Margot *Asquith. They had no children.

In October 1936 Elliot was appointed secretary of state for Scotland. His approach in this office, which he held until Neville Chamberlain appointed him minister for health in May 1938, continued the interventionist theme. Frustrated with the lack of progress in housing by local authorities he helped set up the Scottish (Special Areas) Housing Association with central government funding. Also during his tenure the Scottish economic committee promoted industrial estates, and an act was passed making possible financial support to, for example, the Hillington industrial estate. In 1937 agricultural wage regulation for Scotland was instituted. Films of Scotland was set up in 1938, and from May to October the Empire Exhibition was held in Bellahouston Park in Glasgow, for both of which projects Elliot drew on his connections in science and the arts.

Elliot's role in the 1930s debate about British policy in Europe was controversial. On the one hand, to many outside the government his failure to resign, especially over Munich, was incomprehensible. Colin Coote and Baffy Dugdale pressed him hard. At a meeting of the Other Club in September 1938 he was savaged by Winston Churchill and Archibald Sinclair for condoning a cowardly policy. Robert Boothby thought that 'Munich broke the spring' in Elliot (Rhodes James, 184). On the other hand, he appears to have been pursuing, from within, a line of resistance to government policy. He was part of a group in cabinet, reportedly called by Chamberlain 'the Boys' Brigade' (Macleod, 159) or the 'weaker brethren' (Parker, 157), which with various degrees of intensity opposed British weakness in the face of German and Italian aggression, and from late 1938 was pressing for intensified rearmament. Loyalty to Baldwin and then Chamberlain may have prevented him from resigning. Baldwin had forgiven his past transgressions, and, although the relationship with Chamberlain was not always smooth, correspondence when Elliot lost his seat in 1923 and again when he was promoted in 1932 suggests that Chamberlain held him in some regard.

As minister for health until May 1940 Elliot helped make a major contribution to Britain's preparedness for war by initiating the organization of the permanent evacuation scheme, mainly for children and women, which was eventually put into operation in September 1939. The reorganization of hospitals under the Ministry of Health and in the Emergency Medical Service, and the compilation of registers of doctors and nurses, was completed during his tenure. He was also involved in the setting up of the Women's Voluntary Service and was able to bring his knowledge of nutrition to bear on the planning for rationing.

Out of office: public services and honours Elliot was not included in Churchill's wartime coalition government. He became deputy assistant adjutant-general at Chester with responsibility for dealing with refugees in a blitz. In October 1940 Churchill offered him the governorship of Burma, which he refused, but he agreed to become director of public relations at the War Office in January 1941. He was responsible for distributing commissions to writers such as Eric Linklater and, together with Sir Kenneth Clark, to artists working for the war effort. As a former Scottish secretary, he was invited to participate in Tom Johnston's Scottish council of state and was credited with trying to focus it on problems of wartime administration and economic development. Perhaps his most significant achievement in a period of considerable personal depression was his saving of Westminster Hall in May 1941 when, happening to be nearby, he directed firefighters to save it rather than the more recently built House of Commons chamber during a night of heavy bombing. At the end of 1941 he left the War Office and the army with the rank of colonel. In 1942, as chairman of the public accounts committee, he presided over the inquiry into the contract between the Air Ministry and the British Marconi Company, which resulted in the latter surrendering its profit.

Early in 1943 Elliot had a serious accident while trying to catch a train at Hawick station. He was effectively invalided for most of the year. Nevertheless, he still managed to publish *Long Distance*, a collection of broadcasts made during 1942, and to chair a committee on the future of the herring industry. On his recovery in early 1944 he went to west Africa, a region with which he was familiar from an official visit to Nigeria which he made in 1927, and chaired a commission on higher education which led eventually to the establishment of separate university colleges in Ghana, Sierra Leone, and Nigeria. In spring 1945 he led a parliamentary delegation to Russia, where he had an interview with Stalin.

At the general election of 1945 Elliot lost his Kelvingrove seat, but his brand of moderate, interventionist Conservatism, it has been claimed, gave the party a fund of goodwill which served it well in that otherwise disastrous election. Regarded at this time as a, if not the, Scottish Conservative leader, he returned to parliament at a by-election for the Scottish Universities seat in November 1946. In the Commons he was made opposition spokesman on the bill to set up the National Health Service and therefore faced Aneurin Bevan, whom he struggled to match in debate. Although he was a standard-bearer of progressive Conservatism between the wars, Elliot had given a cautious reception to the Beveridge report on its appearance in 1942. On housing and the effects of nationalization he was reportedly more at home.

The Scottish Universities seat was abolished at the general election of February 1950, and Elliot succeeded in recapturing Kelvingrove. Despite his work as an opposition spokesman and the efforts of Brenden Bracken to get him the Ministry of Education, Churchill offered him only minor office when the Conservatives returned to power in October 1951. This Elliot refused. Churchill claimed that he talked too much, and Elliot's biographer admits that he had come to be regarded as a conversationalist rather than as the talented administrator he really was. His unpunctuality may have reinforced this image.

Elliot travelled a great deal after the war. He regularly attended the Anglo-German parliamentarians' meetings at Koenigswinter. He was a co-founder and treasurer from 1955 of the NATO Parliamentarians' Conference, which involved trips to North America. In 1949 he visited Israel, which he strongly supported, for the *Daily Telegraph*. In 1954 he led a parliamentary delegation of inquiry into the Mau Mau uprising in Kenya. In 1955 he was a member of parliamentary delegations to Malta and to the Central African Federation; and in 1957 to west Africa, this time to study civil service conditions. He also further developed his career as a writer and broadcaster, becoming well known to audiences of the BBC's programmes *Any Questions* and *The Brains Trust*.

Elliot was made a Companion of Honour in 1952. In 1956 and 1957 he was lord high commissioner to the general assembly of the Church of Scotland. Other honours he had received included LLD degrees from the universities of Aberdeen, Leeds, Glasgow, Edinburgh, Manchester, and St Andrews, and a DSc from the University of South Africa. He was a freeman of the city of Edinburgh and of Lanark and Hawick. From 1933 to 1936 he was rector of Aberdeen University, and from 1947 to 1950 of Glasgow University. In addition to being a fellow of the Royal Society, he was a fellow of the Royal Society of Edinburgh and of the Royal College of Physicians in London and Glasgow.

At home Elliot became, after 1945, chairman of the expanding family business, Lawrie and Symington, and he farmed on a considerable scale on his estate, Harwood in Roxburghshire. He died of coronary thrombosis in the grounds of Harwood House on 8 January 1958 and was buried on 11 January in Hobkirk parish churchyard. His widow was narrowly defeated when she stood for his Kelvingrove seat at the resulting by-election in March 1958.

Elliot was described as 'at times a determined enigma' (Pottinger, 72). His mistake in career terms was his decision not to resign in the late 1930s. After 1940 he contributed in various fields, especially to the Conservative opposition between 1946 and 1951, but his career was one of failed promise and 'shameful treatment by his party' (Grimond). GORDON F. MILLAR

Sources C. Coote, *A companion of honour: the story of Walter Elliot* (1965) · DNB · *Daily Telegraph* (9 Jan 1958) · *Daily Telegraph* (13 Jan 1958) · *The Scotsman* (9 Jan 1958) · *The Scotsman* (13 Jan 1958) · *Glasgow Herald* (9 Jan 1958) · *Glasgow Herald* (13 Jan 1958) · C. Harvie, 'Elliot and the politics of adventure', *Weekend Scotsman* (9 April 1983) · *WWW*, 1951–1960; 1981–1990; 1991–1995, 343 · b. cert. · m. cert. [Helen Arabella Hamilton] · m. cert. [Katharine Tennant] · d. cert. · d. cert. [Helen Elliot, wife] · G. Pottinger, *The secretaries of state for Scotland, 1926–76* (1979), 63–73 · C. Coote, *Editorial* (1965) · *The Times* (9 Jan 1958), (11 Jan 1958), (14–15 Jan 1958), (17–18 Jan 1958), (20 Jan 1958), (29–30 Jan 1958) · J. Bridie [O. H. Mavor], *One way of living* (1939) · G. Warner, *Conquering by degrees: Glasgow University Union, a centenary history, 1885–1985* (1985) · R. Rhodes James, *Bob Boothby* (1991) · D. R. Thorpe, *Alec Douglas-Home* (1996) · C. Harvie, *No gods and precious few heroes, Scotland, 1914–1980* (1981) · I. C. G. Hutchison, *Scottish politics in the twentieth century* (2001) · I. Macleod, *Neville Chamberlain* (1961) · R. A. C. Parker, *Chamberlain and appeasement* (1993) · C. A. Oakley, *The second city: the story of Glasgow* (1990), 244–5 · *The Times* (4 Jan 1994) [obit. of Baroness Elliot, widow] · *Everyman* (24 Feb 1923) · J. Grimond, 'New roads south', *The Spectator* (30 May 1958) · CGPLA Eng. & Wales (1958)
Archives NL Scot., corresp. and papers, Acc 6721 | Bodl. Oxf., corresp. with Williams Clark · HLRO, corresp. with Lord Beaverbrook, BBKC/132 · Nuffield Oxf., corresp. with Lord Cherwell · U. Glas., Archives and Business Records Centre, letters to Donald Macmillan | FILM BFI NFTVA news footage of Elliot's second marriage (5/4/1934); appearance in promotional film for the govt on agriculture (1935); appearance in a retrospective annual review (1937); appearance in a travelogue 'Bonnie Scotland calls you' (1938); unidentified news footage (1946) | SOUND BL NSA, 1: (M4633R) interview with Baroness Elliot; 2: other short holdings (talk on society and culture and 2 discussion progs)
Likenesses photograph, 1911, repro. in Warner, *Conquering by degrees*, 70 · photograph, 1920–29, repro. in Coote, *A companion of honour*, facing p. 49 · photograph (as privy councillor), repro. in Harvie, 'Elliot and the politics of adventure'
Wealth at death no value given: confirmation, 6 June 1958, CGPLA Eng. & Wales

Elliot [Elliott], **William** (1727–1766), engraver, thought by later commentators to have been born at Hampton Court. He lived in London, but little else is known of his life except for his work. Elliot was primarily a landscape engraver who turned his hand equally to the works of old masters, such as Gaspar Poussin and Adriaen Cuyp, or contemporary artists, including Paul Sandby, the Smith brothers of Chichester, and Richard Wilson. Although he did engrave a version of Rubens's portrait of his second wife, *Helena Formans* (1766), portraiture was unusual in his *œuvre*. In general he favoured landscape engraving, where his skill, and the 'freedom of his point' (Strutt), were eminently suited to the picturesque qualities of rustic settings. This can be seen in his reproductions of Jean of Pillement's *Le retour de la pêche* (1761), a view of peasants in a woody glen, which was published simultaneously in England and France to answer the contemporary taste for a more naturalized form of rococo. Elliot was also able to exert a great deal of control when engraving architectural subjects. Signed simply 'Elliot sculp.', examples of his work can be found in William Dodsley's modest quarto publication *London and its Environs Described* (1761), which was the first guide to London to encompass the newly burgeoning suburbs.

Between 1761 and 1766 Elliot exhibited a number of landscape engravings at the Society of Artists, and in 1761 he won a premium awarded by the Society of Artists for a work after George Smith. He earned his living working for leading London publishers such as Robert Sayer, who commissioned him to engrave large-format plates for the luxury end of the print market. While Elliot's prints evince his skill, his fortunes in a competitive print market may well have been improved by his 'amiable and benevolent disposition', as Joseph Strutt recalled. After Elliot's untimely death in 1766, John Boydell reissued *Kilgarren Castle in South Wales* (1775), after Richard Wilson, ten years after the latter had first published it. LUCY PELTZ

Sources B. Adams, *London illustrated, 1604–1851* (1983) · T. Clayton, *The English print, 1688–1802* (1997) · D. Bank and A. Esposito, eds., *British biographical archive*, 2nd series (1991) [microfiche] · [R. Gough], *Anecdotes of British topography*, 2 vols. (1768) · Graves, *Soc. Artists* · J. Strutt, *A biographical dictionary, containing an historical account of all the engravers, from the earliest period of the art of engraving to the present time*, 2 vols. (1785–6) · Bryan, *Painters* (1816) · Redgrave, *Artists*

Elliot, Sir William (1896–1971), air force officer, was born in Forgan, Fife, on 3 June 1896, the elder son of Gilbert John Elliot, a schoolteacher, of Chetwynd, Shropshire, and his wife, Bessie Clark Davidson. Educated in Switzerland and at Tonbridge School, Kent (1910–14), he was commissioned in the Royal Army Service Corps in August 1914, transferred to the Royal Flying Corps in June 1917, and learned to fly in Egypt. In March 1918 he joined 142 squadron, one of seven squadrons forming the Palestine brigade. Its usual duties were the location and registration of enemy guns, tactical reconnaissance, and trench photography, but it took part in a terrible slaughter, vividly described by T. E. Lawrence, when the Turkish Seventh Army was caught in a narrow defile while retreating down the Wadi Fara from Nablus to the Jordan valley on 21 September 1918.

After the armistice, having been awarded the DFC, Elliot

volunteered for service in south Russia with 47 squadron in support of White Russian opponents of the Bolsheviks. On 30 July 1919 he was forced to land his DH9 two-seat biplane behind enemy lines after bombing and strafing barges on the Volga at Cherny Yar, some 80 miles south of Volgograd. He set fire to the aircraft while his observer kept Bolshevik horsemen at a respectful distance with bursts of machine-gun fire until a fellow pilot, Walter Anderson, landed nearby, even though his petrol tank was holed. Anderson picked up the two men, managed to get the overloaded DH9 into the air through a hail of bullets, and returned safely to base. Anderson's observer, John Mitchell, stood on the lower wing throughout the hour-long flight with his thumb sealing the hole. Anderson and Mitchell were awarded DSOs and Elliot received a second DFC for his part in this Biggles-like drama, but a broken elbow, followed by typhus, obliged him to return to England.

Elliot was granted a permanent commission as a flying officer in August 1919 and spent nearly a year from July 1920 working with W. E. Johns, the creator of Biggles, in the RAF's recruiting office at 4 Henrietta Street, Covent Garden, before joining 14 squadron in Palestine in May 1921. During the next three years Elliot qualified as a French interpreter, was promoted flight lieutenant, and developed political skills in that volatile region which led in 1924 to an appointment in the Air Ministry's directorate of operations and intelligence. He returned to the Middle East in 1928, where he served in Amman, Jerusalem, and as a liaison officer with the French in Syria.

Elliot was promoted squadron leader in February 1932, spent that year as a student at the RAF Staff College, Andover, and was then appointed to command 501 squadron (1933–4) before returning to his studies at the Army Staff College, Camberley (1935–6). In April 1937 he was promoted wing commander, and during the next four years his shrewd, discreet efficiency as assistant secretary (air) to the committee of imperial defence and to the war cabinet (1939–41), responsible for 'Air Matters, Research and Experiment, Bacteriological Warfare' (Gilbert, *Finest Hour*, 323), established his reputation in Whitehall.

In March 1941, however, Elliot was promoted group captain and briefly escaped from Whitehall. Sholto Douglas, head of Fighter Command, knew of his keen interest in night air-defence problems and asked for his services, first as commanding officer of Middle Wallop and then as head of night operations at command headquarters. Winston Churchill was 'rather cross' (Douglas, 127–8), so Douglas was told, about losing Elliot, but allowed him to go. In February 1942 Elliot returned to the Air Ministry as an air commodore and director of plans. Until February 1944 he worked closely with officers of other services in a joint planning committee that translated Anglo-American grand strategy into feasible military projects. He was then promoted air vice-marshal and appointed head of RAF Gibraltar.

As a splendid reward for all his committee work, Elliot was given command of the newly formed 'Balkan air force' in June 1944. This unique organization, with its headquarters in Bari, on Italy's south-eastern coast, eventually numbered 24 squadrons of at least eight nationalities. It also included army and navy units as well as agents of Britain's Special Operations Executive and had discreet links with both British and American political advisers. Elliot gave essential help to partisans and their British allies, who were harassing German forces throughout the Balkans, and—of equal value—evacuated by air some 10,000 wounded partisans to RAF hospitals in Italy at a time when Germans were killing any they captured. Elliot also tried to assist the Warsaw rising in August 1944, but a combination of distance, bad weather, and enemy opposition, and, above all, a total absence of Soviet co-operation obliged him to abandon the attempt in spite of pressure to continue from the Air Ministry and the British government.

Elliot was appointed assistant chief executive at the Ministry of Aircraft Production in March 1945. He returned yet again to the Air Ministry in June 1946 as an assistant chief of the air staff with special responsibility for policy. In November 1947 he was promoted air marshal and appointed head of Fighter Command, but in August 1949 he was required—much against his will—to become chief staff officer to the minister of defence, Emanuel Shinwell, and deputy secretary (military) to the cabinet. Shinwell and Churchill, though far apart politically, were entirely agreed on Elliot's intelligence and efficiency, and, better still, on his inter-service outlook and his awareness of political as well as military considerations.

Elliot was promoted air chief marshal in April 1951 and appointed chairman of the British joint services mission in Washington and British representative on the standing group of the military committee of NATO. Very few officers in any service were better qualified to handle so sensitive a position, but Elliot flourished in Washington's unique atmosphere. He came close to being appointed chief of the air staff in 1953. In Slessor's opinion he had the 'experience, brains and personality', but unfortunately he was 'physically delicate' (private information) and it was therefore decided that three more years in Whitehall might well kill him. This decision proved wise as well as humane, because Elliot suffered a coronary thrombosis in Washington in 1953 and was laid low for several months. He retired from the RAF in 1954, and later that year he was elected chairman of the council of the Royal Institute of International Affairs at Chatham House, a position he held for four years until continuing poor health obliged him to retire from public life.

Elliot married on 19 May 1931 (Elizabeth) Rosemary, the daughter of Lieutenant-Colonel Sir John Robert Chancellor, an army officer and colonial governor. Their first son died in 1938, aged only three. Fortunately, two more children—a boy and a girl—were born during years when Rosemary devoted much attention to helping very poor families in Battersea. Her 'complete absence of artifice' (*The Times*, 4 March 1971), in the words of a close friend, was a great help to her husband during his Washington years. Elliot was appointed CBE in 1942 and CB in 1944 and knighted (KBE) in 1946 and again (KCB) in 1951. He was appointed air aide-de-camp to George VI (1950–52) and then to Elizabeth II (1952–4). In the coronation honours list of 1953 he received the rare distinction of the GCVO. He died in the RAF hospital at Wroughton, Wiltshire, on 27 June 1971, less than four months after the sudden death of his dearly loved wife.　　VINCENT ORANGE

Sources J. C. Slessor, *The central blue: recollections and reflections* (1956) · M. Gilbert, *Winston S. Churchill, 6: Finest hour, 1939–1941* (1983) · M. Gilbert, *Winston S. Churchill, 7: Road to victory, 1941–1945* (1986) · H. A. Jones, *Over the Balkans and south Russia, 1917–1919* (1923) · H. A. Jones, *The war in the air*, 6 (1937) · R. Collishaw and R. V. Dodds, *Air command: a fighter pilot's story* (1973) · R. Jackson, *At war with the Bolsheviks* (1972) · L. W. Sutherland, *Aces and kings* (1929) · N. Orpen, *Airlift to Warsaw: the rising of 1944* (1984) · J. Wilson, *Lawrence of Arabia* (1989) · F. Maclean, *Eastern approaches* (1949) · S. Douglas, *Years of command* (1963) · M. Dean, *The Royal Air Force and two world wars* (1979) · P. B. Ellis and P. Williams, *By Jove, Biggles! the life of Captain W. E. Johns*, [later edn] (1985) · *The Times* (4 March 1971) · *The Times* (28 June 1971) · *The Times* (30 June 1971) · *The Times* (9 July 1971) · *WW* (1952) · *WW* (1971–80)
Archives King's Lond., Liddell Hart C., corresp. and papers | IWM, corresp. with Tizard · King's Lond., Liddell Hart C., corresp. with Sir B. H. Liddell Hart | FILM BFI NFTVA, documentary footage · IWM FVA, actuality footage
Likenesses C. Mann, portrait, priv. coll.
Wealth at death £24,449: probate, 30 Sept 1971, *CGPLA Eng. & Wales*

Elliotson, John (1791–1868), physician and mesmerist, was born on 24 October 1791 in Southwark, London, the son of John Elliotson, a prosperous apothecary and chemist, and his wife, Elizabeth. He was educated privately and (from 1805) at Edinburgh University, where he received the degree of MD in 1810; he became LRCP (London) the same year. In 1810 he went to Jesus College, Cambridge; he took his MB in 1816 and his MD in 1821. He was appointed assistant physician (1817–23) and physician (1823–34) to St Thomas's Hospital, London, and lectured at Grainger's school of anatomy (1817–23). In 1822 he became FRCP and in 1829 FRS.

During his early career Elliotson built up a high reputation as an insightful clinician, a lecturer of great verve and clarity, and an innovator in methods of treatment. In 1817 he published a translation, with extensive notes, of J. F. Blumenbach's *Institutiones physiologicae*, which he subsequently used as the basis for his own *Human Physiology* (1840). He also published monographs on the use of prussic acid in afflictions of the stomach and chest and the use of opium in diabetes (1820); on the diagnosis of heart disease (the Lumleian lectures for 1829); and on the medicinal properties of creosote (1835); he also wrote a good many articles and case reports. He was the first to use iodine in the treatment of goitre, the first to prove that glanders is communicable to humans, and the first to link atmospheric conditions with hay fever. He is also credited with the introduction of the stethoscope to England. He was the Goulstonian lecturer in 1824. Following his appointment as professor of the principles and practice of medicine at University College, London (1832), and as senior physician to University College Hospital (1834), his lectures were extensively reported in the medical press

John Elliotson (1791–1868), by James Ramsay, 1836

(they were later published as two books), and he built up perhaps the largest private practice in London. A slightly premature obituary of him in *The Times* says that during the season Conduit Street (where he lived) was daily filled with the carriages of his patients 'almost as thickly as St. James's Street on a levée day' (*The Times*, 14 April 1868).

Professional success did not bring universal professional acclaim, however. Elliotson was widely suspected, by a conservative profession, of pursuing novelty and publicity for their own sakes. He was the first British physician to abandon the traditional garb of knee-breeches and stockings, and the first to wear a beard. Rumour had it that he was overly prone to experiment on his patients with heroic doses of powerful medicines—his students said that one should let him diagnose but not treat the patient—and he was also involved with acupuncture, phrenology, and, most notoriously, mesmerism. In the 1820s phrenology was enjoying a vogue among some British medical practitioners, Elliotson included. In 1823 he founded the London Phrenological Society, and from then on was a central figure both in the phrenological movement and in the various quarrels and schisms that divided it (one phrenologist remarked that Elliotson's organs of combativeness and self-conceit were excessively developed). A particular cause of certain schisms was the view of Elliotson and his supporters that the mind is a property of the living brain. He was widely suspected of being an atheist and a materialist.

Elliotson's serious involvement with mesmerism dated from the autumn of 1837 when, after observing the work of the French mesmeric demonstrator Baron J. E. Dupotet he began to mesmerize patients in his own wards at University College Hospital. He achieved both 'excellent cures' and 'striking phenomena'. Many of the latter centred around two teenage epileptics, the Okey sisters, who, normally quiet and reserved, would, when in the 'mesmeric state', indulge in all sorts of antics and respond to 'magnetized' water, metals, and other substances. Elliotson's demonstrations were regularly reported in *The Lancet* and attracted such large audiences (including both medical and lay celebrities, and even royalty) that the venue was changed from the wards to the hospital theatre. However, in August 1838 the editor of *The Lancet*, Thomas Wakley, thought he had caught the sisters in deliberate trickery, and strongly attacked Elliotson. Elliotson responded with equal force. Further controversies ensued, and in December 1838 the hospital committee forbade the practice of mesmerism on the wards. Elliotson resigned from both the hospital and the college the following month.

His large private fortune and surviving private practice enabled Elliotson to continue his mesmeric activities and demonstrations in the teeth of a great deal of medical hostility, especially from Wakley. In 1843 he founded a periodical, *The Zoist*, devoted to mesmerism and phrenology. He was principal editor and a leading contributor. In 1849 he was instrumental in starting the London Mesmeric Infirmary, which lasted until 1866. *The Zoist* cast its net widely, and was a mine of information about not only mesmeric cures but also double consciousness, hemicerebral mesmerism, the so-called 'Reichenbach' phenomena (the lights which sensitive persons could allegedly see round the poles of a magnet), phrenomesmerism (the effect of directing 'mesmeric fluid' to particular phrenological organs), the phrenological characteristics of murderers, alleged mesmeric clairvoyance, the table-tipping craze of the early 1850s, and, above all, surgical operations with mesmeric analgesia. These last reports made a strong impression on contemporaries, and Elliotson, who had already written a pamphlet on the subject, entitled *Numerous Cases of Surgical Operations without Pain in the Mesmeric State* (1843), was the first in Britain to detail the remarkable results being published in India by James Esdaile.

The Zoist came to an end in 1856 with its thirteenth volume, and thereafter little was heard of Elliotson, though he continued to contribute articles of some substance on medical and mesmeric topics to the *Medical Times and Gazette*. In the autumn of 1863, on a visit to Dieppe, he was converted to belief in the phenomena of spiritualism by his experiences with the medium D. D. Home, and became devoutly religious. In the spring of 1865 his finances failed, owing to rash investments. He closed his house at 37 Conduit Street, and retired into the Davies Street home of Dr E. S. Symes, a former pupil. The following winter his health and his faculties began to deteriorate. He died in London on 29 July 1868 of 'natural decay' and was buried at Kensal Green cemetery.

Elliotson, who remained unmarried, was diminutive in stature with a large head and a very dark complexion. A carriage accident in 1828 left him lame but with his ferocious energy undiminished. Despite his considerable abilities, his character presents many contradictions: he was vain, irascible, and intolerant of opposition and criticism, but he was equally irascible when confronted by injustice or needless suffering. As a phrenologist he regarded capital punishment as morally indefensible; as a mesmerist he was infuriated by surgeons' neglect of mesmeric analgesia; as a human being he abhorred flogging and all similar barbarities. His kindness towards his patients won him the friendship of, among others, Dickens and Thackeray, the latter of whom founded the character of Dr Goodenough in *Pendennis* upon him. Though he somewhat naïvely attributed mesmeric cures and phenomena to the transmission of an unknown physical influence from mesmerist to patient, he was fully aware of the possible effects of imagination and suggestion, and his occasional remarks about the influence of unconscious perceptions and knowledge on action were well in advance of their time.   ALAN GAULD

Sources D. W. Forrest, *The evolution of hypnotism* (1998) • A. Winter, *Mesmerized: powers of the mind in Victorian Britain* (1998) • J. Harley Williams, *Doctors differ: five studies in contrast* (1946), 25–91 • *Men of the time* (1856) • *Medical Times and Gazette* (8 Aug 1868), 164–7 • *The Lancet* (3 Aug 1868) • *The Times* (14 April 1868) • *Morning Post* (3 Aug 1868) • J. Miller, 'A Gower Street scandal', *Journal of the Royal College of Physicians of London*, 17 (1983), 181–91 • A. Gauld, *A history of hypnotism* (1992), 194–203, 206–8 etc. • F. Podmore, *Mesmerism and Christian Science: a short history of mental healing* (1909), 126–34 • G. Rosen, 'John Elliotson, physician and hypnotist', *Bulletin of the Institute for the History of Medicine*, 4 (1936), 600–03 • *John Elliotson on mesmerism*, ed. F. Kaplan (1982) • *University College London: Proceedings of the Annual General Meeting … 1834*, 9–10 • Venn, *Alum. Cant.* • Munk, *Roll* • d. cert. • daybook of St Saviour's, Southwark, LMA

Archives RCP Lond., papers | NL Scot., corresp. with George Combe • Wisbech Museum, Wisbech, Cambridgeshire, Townshend papers, corresp.

Likenesses J. Ramsay, oils, 1836, RCP Lond. [*see illus.*] • C. Baugniet, lithographs, BM, RCP Lond. • lithograph (after J. Ramsay), Wellcome L. • lithograph, Wellcome L.

Wealth at death probably penniless: *Medical Times and Gazette*

Elliott, (Thomas) Anthony Keith (1921–1976), diplomatist, was born on 27 May 1921 at Burford, Oxfordshire, the younger son and youngest of four children of Sir Ivo D'Oyly Elliott, second baronet (1882–1961), civil servant in India, and his wife, Margery Helen (*d.* 1968), daughter of Francis Carey of Burgess Hill, Sussex. He was brought up in north Oxford, and educated first at the Dragon School, Oxford, and then at Eton College, where he was a king's scholar and won the Rosebery history prize. He went on to Balliol College, Oxford, but his studies were cut short by the war; he eventually graduated with a degree in modern history in 1946. During the Second World War he served from 1941 to 1946 with the King's Shropshire light infantry, the east African pioneers, and the east African education corps, in Ethiopia and Somaliland, reaching the rank of captain.

Elliott's career in diplomacy began when in August 1947 he joined the British foreign service. Eighteen months later, in February 1949, he was appointed third secretary in the British embassy at Belgrade, and it was during his time in Yugoslavia that he met his wife, Alethea Helen Jean Hautonville Richardson, elder daughter of Major Alistair B. H. Richardson of the King's dragoon guards. They were married on 6 October 1951 and had three daughters, Victoria Carey (b. 1952), Catherine (Katie) Frances (b. 1954), and Anne Louise (b. 1956), and a son, Thomas Anthony William (b. 1959). They remained in Belgrade until April 1952. Subsequent postings included a five-year spell in the Foreign Office, two years as first secretary in Beijing (Peking) (1957–9), and a year in Athens (1960–61). After further service in London, during which he was promoted counsellor, in 1965 Elliott was appointed political adviser to the government of Hong Kong, and in 1968 he was made CMG and became head of chancery at Washington. While there he was promoted minister.

In November 1972 Elliott was appointed British ambassador to Finland. His arrival in Helsinki was soon followed by the opening there of the multilateral preparatory talks for the Conference on Security and Cooperation in Europe (CSCE). Although originally intended to be no more than an informal gathering of ambassadors, these talks soon became a conference in their own right, and Elliott, as head of the British delegation, was able to play a key role in the diplomacy of East–West détente. He was instrumental in helping to secure agreement on an agenda and terms of reference which would ensure that full consideration was given to Western concerns with expanding human contacts and the freer dissemination of information (the so-called Basket III issues). While still in post at Helsinki, he continued to lead the British delegation during the first year of the conference's drafting stage at Geneva. His mastery of detail and sure grasp of strategy and tactics proved invaluable in complex and protracted negotiations whose subject matter ranged from divided countries to divided families; and his eloquent dispatches revealed a personal vision of détente which encompassed far more than intergovernmental accords and a simple easing of tensions between rival alliance blocs. By the summer of 1974 the communist states had acknowledged that relations between peoples, and therefore the attitudes of governments towards their citizens, could be the subject of international discourse, and Elliott urged his colleagues in Whitehall to resist American pressure for an early conclusion of the conference. The signing of the Helsinki Final Act on 1 August 1975 was seen by Elliott as, at least in part, a triumph for Finnish diplomacy. He was impressed by the way in which the CSCE had compelled the major powers to defend and justify their policies before their smaller neighbours, and he displayed genuine empathy with Finland's aspirations and interests.

A quiet and unpretentious diplomat noted for his candour and good sense of humour, Elliott readily immersed himself in the culture and history of the countries in which he served. After his appointment, in November 1975, as British ambassador in Tel Aviv, he travelled round Israel with his family, making contact with all sections of society. His mission was, however, sadly cut short when on 28 August 1976 he drowned while swimming in the sea off Caesarea. His funeral service was held on 8 September 1976 at Taynton parish church, Burford, Oxfordshire. He was survived by his wife and four children.

KEITH HAMILTON

Sources FO List · The Times (30 Aug 1976) · The Times (9 Sept 1976) · The Times (15 Sept 1976) · WWW, 1971–80 · G. Bennett and K. A. Hamilton, eds., Documents on British policy overseas, 3rd ser., 2: The conference on security and cooperation in Europe, 1972–1975 (1997) · K. Hamilton, The last cold warriors: Britain, détente and the CSCE, 1972–1975 (1999) · Burke, Peerage · college register, Balliol Oxf.
Archives PRO, FO/FCO records, FO 371 and FO 800 series
Likenesses photograph, Gov. Art Coll.; repro. in Bennett and Hamilton, eds., Conference on security, pl. 2c
Wealth at death £28,737: probate, 20 Dec 1976, CGPLA Eng. & Wales

Elliott, Charles Alfred (1822–1877). *See under* Elliott, William (1780/81–1853).

Elliott, Sir Charles Alfred (1835–1911), administrator in India, was born on 8 December 1835 at Brighton. He was the son of Henry Venn *Elliott (1792–1865), vicar of St Mary's, Brighton, and his wife, Julia, daughter of John Marshall of Hallsteads, Ullswater, MP for Leeds. Charles Elliott was educated at Brighton College, at Harrow School, and at Trinity College, Cambridge, where he won a scholarship in 1854. In 1856, the East India Company's civil service was thrown open to public competition and Elliott was among the first fifteen applicants to be appointed.

After a brief period of training, on 12 June 1857 Elliott was posted to Mirzapur district in the North-Western Provinces at the height of the Indian mutiny. His first service was spent leading military expeditions to quell disturbances. He received the mutiny medal and was mentioned in dispatches. In 1858 he was appointed an assistant commissioner in Oudh, where he remained for five years. It was here, while serving in Unao district, that Elliott made the first of what were to be several major contributions to the sociology, and ultimately literature, of British India. Believing that 'a knowledge of the popular traditions and ballads gives its possessor both influence over the people and the key to their hearts', he began a collection of genealogies, local histories, and Indian folklore. Privately published at Allahabad in 1862 under the title *Chronicles of Oonao*, his work has claims to pioneering the ethnographic study of India.

In 1863 Elliott was posted to the Central Provinces for two years, where he conducted land revenue settlement operations at Hoshangabad. He substantially reformed the previously very haphazard nature of such operations, instituting more scientific investigations of topography, economic relations, and social structure. His report on Hoshangabad was a model of its kind, which, besides increasing the revenue yield of government, helped to turn the 'settlement report' into one of the major tools of colonial sociological investigation. In 1865 he returned to the North-Western Provinces to conduct revenue settlement operations in Farrukhabad district. The following year, on 20 June, he married Louisa Jane, daughter of G. W.

Dumbell of the Isle of Man; they had three sons and a daughter before her death in 1877.

In 1870 Elliott was appointed by Sir William Muir, then the lieutenant-governor, secretary to the government of the North-Western Provinces. He served in this post until 1877, overseeing the development of revenue settlement administration, pursuing the suppression of female infanticide among Rajput communities, and implementing new legislation on municipal government. In 1877, when Sir John Strachey succeeded Muir, Elliott went briefly to Meerut as commissioner, but then left for Madras, on the orders of the viceroy, Lord Lytton, to conduct the most important work of his career. In 1876 southern and western India were struck by serious famine. Elliott was sent to direct relief operations in the princely state of Mysore, and wrote a report, graphically revealing the depth of human suffering and the shortcomings of the administration, which was published in 1878. The severity of the famine raised serious questions about the beneficence of British rule in India. A royal commission, with Elliott as its secretary, was appointed to investigate the causes of the famine and the general adequacy of relief measures. The eventual report was a landmark document in the annals of British Indian history. It put together the most comprehensive collection of materials—surveys, questionnaires, reports—ever assembled on the health, material condition, and economic relations of agrarian society, and it scrutinized them with a critical eye towards the economic theories of its day. In the light of the report, new policies emerged to combat the problem of recurrent drought, and a new famine code was designed, giving the highest priority to the saving of human life. Although famines were to continue to haunt the Indian landscape, none subsequently was to have such savage consequences.

After completing his work on famine, Elliott was briefly placed in charge of the decennial census for 1881, the first full census of British India after the perfunctory enumeration of 1871. However, in March 1881 he was appointed chief commissioner for Assam and was unable to complete this work. In 1886 he was appointed chairman of a committee to inquire into public expenditure throughout India and to recommend economies. The committee was necessitated by escalating military expenditures (particularly after the Third Anglo-Burmese War) in the context of a depreciating exchange rate. Lord Dufferin, the viceroy, urged Elliott to apply the shears which were felt most painfully by the provincial governments. On 22 September 1887 Elliott made his second marriage, to Alice Louisa, daughter of Thomas Gaussen of Guernsey, and widow of T. J. Murray of the Indian Civil Service. In the same year he was made a knight commander in the Order of the Star of India, and from 1888 to 1890 he served as a member of the executive council under lords Dufferin and Lansdowne, until appointed lieutenant-governor of Bengal on 17 December 1890.

It was a curious appointment, for Bengal was one of the few areas of British India in which Elliott had never served, and it became a turbulent one. Elliott sought to prosecute a revenue survey and record of rights in Bihar which, previously, had very much been left under the informal control of its principal *zamindars* (landlords). The *zamindars* resisted the questioning of their privileges and recruited Lord Randolph Churchill in the House of Lords to help in their defence. Sir Antony MacDonnell, a former lieutenant-governor of the North-Western Provinces, also intervened with criticism of Elliott, and the 'affair', which cut at vested interest, blew very hot until the viceroy stepped in to force a compromise. Elliott was permitted to continue with his settlement but under restrictive conditions. The second area where Elliott fell foul of Bengali custom was in his relations with the large Western-educated Indian population of Calcutta, who had developed a lively public opinion and a press often critical of British rule. Having served 'up-country' most of his life, Elliott was not used to being subject to public comment and reacted strongly. He had the manager–editor of one Indian newspaper, *Bangobasi*, arrested for sedition and planned to engage in a propaganda war, to be pursued by an official press bureau, until stopped by Lord Lansdowne.

Elliott became a patron of the Eurasian community. He also promoted sanitary and medical improvements, particularly with regard to malaria, which was a serious problem in Bengal. In foreign policy matters, he urged that pressure be applied to the Chinese to secure agreement on the borders of Sikkim and Tibet. He retired from the lieutenant-governorship and the government service in December 1895.

On returning to England, Elliott lived in London and was active in church affairs and educational charities. He served on the London school board as member for Tower Hamlets from 1897 to 1904. From 1904 to 1906 he was a co-opted member of the education committee of London county council. He was also a member of the house of laymen of the Church of England and of the Representative Church Council and, for a time, served as chairman of Toynbee Hall. He died at his home, Fernwood, Wimbledon Park, on 28 May 1911, and was survived by his second wife. The eldest son of his first marriage, Henry Venn Elliott, became the vicar of St Mark's, Brighton, near the parish of Elliott's own father, whose name he bore; the only child of his second marriage, Sir Claude Aurelius *Elliott, became headmaster and provost of Eton College.

DAVID WASHBROOK

Sources *Laborious days: leaves from the Indian record of Sir C. A. Elliott*, ed. [F. Skrine] (1892) · *The Times* (29 May 1911) · C. E. Buckland, *Bengal under the lieutenant-governors*, 2 vols. (1901) · H. Cotton, *Indian and home memories* (1911) · *CGPLA Eng. & Wales* (1911)
Archives BL, Ripon MSS · BL OIOC, letters to Arthur Godley · Bodl. Oxf., MacDonnell MSS · CUL, corresp. with Lord Mayo
Wealth at death £85,424 2s. 4d.: resworn probate, 5 July 1911, *CGPLA Eng. & Wales*

Elliott, Charlotte (1789–1871), poet and hymn writer, was the third daughter of Charles Elliott (1751–1832), a Bond Street silk merchant, and his second wife, Eling (1758–1843), daughter of the evangelical cleric Henry *Venn, author of the *Complete Duty of Man*. She was born on 18

March 1789 at Grove House, Clapham, near her uncle John Venn, vicar of Clapham, and raised among the Clapham Sect. Talented in music and drawing, she was known in youth for her wit, which sparkles in the playful satirical poems appended to *Thoughts in Verse on Sacred Subjects* (1869). After a debilitating illness in 1821 which left her permanently weak, and her meeting in 1822 with César Malan, a Reformed minister of Geneva, she turned entirely to religion. In 1823 she moved with her family to Westfield Lodge, Brighton.

Born in a year of revolution, Elliott's life was 'a hidden one' (Babington, 14). Her work was not. From 1834 to 1859 she edited and contributed to the *Christian Remembrancer Pocket Book*. Her *Hymns for a Week* (1839, 1842) sold 40,000 copies. Referring to her best-known hymn, 'Just as I am' (*Invalid's Hymn Book* and *Hours of Sorrow Cheered and Comforted*, 1836), her brother Henry admitted 'She had done more good by that hymn, than he in all his ministry' (Bateman, 207). It was widely translated: the same hymn that comforted Wordsworth's dying daughter, Dora, also inspired the Raratongans. Its role in Billy Graham's conversion is acknowledged by the title of his autobiography of 1997. It appears in *Nineteenth Century Women Poets: an Oxford Anthology* (1996). Elliott wrote a total of 150 hymns; her other widely known works, in the tradition of Anne Steele (1716–1778), include 'Christian, seek not yet repose' and 'My God, my Father, while I stray'. Most are more appropriate for private than public worship, although a letter from Edward Quillinan shows that Elliott concerned herself with their musical settings.

From 1845 to 1857 Elliott lived at Mornay Lodge, Torquay, with her sister Eleanor Babington, and afterwards at 10 Norfolk Terrace, Brighton. When well, she enjoyed travel, particularly in Switzerland. The cause of her continued ill health has not been positively identified, though she complained of rheumatism and her brother Henry mentioned 'enlargement of the heart' in 1864 (Bateman, 351).

Elliott's literary talent was shared by many of her family, including her brother Edward, author of the controversial *Horae Apocalypticae*, her niece Emily Elliott, and her cousins Leslie *Stephen and Virginia *Woolf. For 'a passing guest' on earth (Babington, 30), Elliott's visit was long. She died, unmarried, at her home in Brighton on 22 September 1871, and lies in the family vault at Hove.

BONNIE SHANNON MCMULLEN

Sources E. K. Babington, 'Memoir', in *Selections from the poems of Charlotte Elliott* (1873) · *Leaves from the unpublished journals, letters, and poems of Charlotte Elliott*, ed. E. Babington (1874) · *Christian Observer* (Nov 1871) · J. Venn, *Annals of a clerical family* (1904) · J. R. Watson, *The English hymn: a critical and historical study* (1997) · J. Bateman, *Life of the Rev. H. V. Elliott* (1868) · C. Elliott, *Words of hope and grace, with a biographical sketch of the author* (1914) · M. M. Hennell, *John Venn and the Clapham Sect* (1958) · J. Julian, ed., *A dictionary of hymnology*, rev. edn (1907); repr. in 2 vols. (1957) · E. Routley, *Hymns and human life* (1952) · E. R. Pitman, *Lady hymn writers* (1892) · L. F. Benson, *The English hymn: its development and use in worship* (1915) · DNB

Likenesses photograph, repro. in *Selections from the poems of Charlotte Elliott*

Wealth at death under £2000: probate, 21 Oct 1871, CGPLA Eng. & Wales

Elliott, Sir Claude Aurelius (1888–1973), headmaster, was born on 27 July 1888 in India, the only child of Sir Charles Alfred *Elliott (1835–1911), lieutenant-governor of Bengal, who later resided at Fernwood, Wimbledon Park, Surrey, and his second wife, Alice Louisa, daughter of Thomas Gaussen of Hauteville, Guernsey, and widow of T. J. Murray of the Bengal civil service. Sir Charles also had three sons and one daughter of a previous marriage. From Stoke Park, the notorious preparatory school, Claude Elliott was elected a king's scholar of Eton College in the 1902 election, on the strength of his history paper. His school career as a colleger was undistinguished, although he made many friends, and he left Eton a year earlier than he need have, to go up to Trinity College, Cambridge; here his promise as a historian burgeoned, and he got a first class in both parts of the history tripos, constitutional history being his forte. BA in 1909, he became a fellow of Jesus College, Cambridge, in 1910, and in 1914, tutor. He married on 17 June 1913 Gillian (d. 1966), daughter of Frederick Turner Bloxam, chief Chancery registrar, with whom he had a son.

At an early age Elliott developed an inherited love of mountaineering, which he practised in Britain, Switzerland, and France, but his ambition to tackle the Caucasus and the Himalayas was thwarted by a fall in the Lake District in 1912 which broke his kneecap and damaged his hand. These injuries did not prevent later expeditions, but they precluded active service in the First World War. After service in a Red Cross unit in Flanders in 1915 he spent the rest of the war at the Admiralty and was appointed OBE in 1920 for his services. After the war he returned to Jesus College, where his administrative skill and vigorous sense of purpose were invaluable, as they were also to the university financial board, the general board, and the council of senate.

In 1933 C. A. Alington retired from the headmastership of Eton, and Elliott was appointed to succeed him. Among the candidates he had been the darkest horse; and although the world at large may have been surprised at his selection, there was no doubt in the minds of those who knew him that he had the capacity for this formidable task. He was the first headmaster of Eton who was not in holy orders; and neither his preaching in chapel nor his teaching in school were as impressive as those of his charismatic predecessor. But he proved himself a headmaster of the highest quality; he was admired and respected by the governing body for his sound judgement and his administrative skill, by his staff for his honesty and steadfastness of purpose, and by boys for his imposing presence, his dry, almost earthy humour, his firmness in disciplinary matters, and his simple manliness; his very glance bespoke straight dealing. As an educationist he was no reformer; Alington had made several changes in the curriculum and Elliott was content to make the system work efficiently; he believed that his most important task as headmaster lay in the choice of masters, and in this he showed himself a sound judge of character.

After six years in office came the Second World War. Despite pressure in some quarters Elliott stubbornly refused

Sir Claude Aurelius Elliott (1888–1973), by Arthur Ralph Middleton Todd, exh. RA 1956

even to contemplate the removal of the school to a safer place; and, man of action that he was, he rallied his staff to cope with all the problems of a school in wartime, while ensuring that school life continued as normally as possible; two bombs which fell on the school in 1940 only hardened his rock-like resolve; he was never happier than when climbing over the rooftops at night to look for incendiaries. To have kept Eton going throughout the war was his greatest achievement.

In 1949, after sixteen arduous years as headmaster, Elliott was appointed provost, and for the next fifteen years he guided Eton's affairs with an experienced hand; a successful appeal was launched; a vast rebuilding and modernization programme was begun; and he was responsible for the replacement of the shattered glass in the chapel windows with the brilliant designs of Evie Hone and John Piper. As provost he did more for the fabric of the school than any of his predecessors for five centuries.

Throughout his life Elliott retained his passion for mountaineering. He knew all the famous climbers of his time; his own skill was universally recognized in his forty visits to the Alps, and countless other expeditions in Wales, the Lake District, and Skye; but for his injury, he must have taken part in the Everest expeditions of 1921–4. President of the Alpine Club in 1950–52, he showed the shrewdness of his judgement and his courage in the choice of John Hunt, rather than of Eric Shipton, to lead the successful 1953 Everest expedition. He was knighted in 1958.

Elliott's appearance was impressive; of well above medium height, he carried himself with dignity, and he had the strong physique of the mountaineer and oarsman (he was a member of Leander). After his retirement from Eton in 1964 he lived in Buttermere in sight of his beloved mountains, until, active to the end, he died at his home, Lower Gatesgarth, Buttermere, on 21 November 1973. His only child, John Nicholas Rede Elliott (1916–1994), worked in intelligence during and after the Second World War and was awarded the US Legion of Merit for his services to the office of strategic services.   D. H. Macindoe, *rev.*

Sources *The Times* (24 Nov 1973) · *The Times* (10 Dec 1973) · Burke, *Peerage* (1969) · private information (1986) · personal knowledge (1986) · *CGPLA Eng. & Wales* (1974)
Archives U. Birm. L., corresp. with Lord Avon | FILM BFI NFTVA, current affairs footage
Likenesses A. R. M. Todd, portrait, exh. RA 1956, Eton [*see illus.*]
Wealth at death £100,839: probate, 19 March 1974, *CGPLA Eng. & Wales*

Elliott, Denholm Mitchell (1922–1992), actor, was born on 31 May 1922 at 48 Lexham Gardens, Kensington, London, the second son of Myles Layman Farr Elliott (*d.* 1933), barrister, and his wife, Nina, *née* Mitchell (*d.* 1966), the daughter of an Ayrshire old colonial. Elliott, who had lost the tip of his right thumb in a lawnmower accident, began acting at his preparatory school, Ripley Court, Surrey. In 1933 his father was killed by terrorists while he was serving as a crown prosecutor in Palestine, and Denholm was packed off to Malvern College. Detesting public-school life, he resorted to kleptomania until a psychiatrist recommended his enrolment at the Royal Academy of Dramatic Art. Quitting after two terms, he joined the RAF as a gunner, only to be shot down off Denmark in 1942 and sent as a prisoner of war to Stalag 8B at Lansdorf, Silesia. Here he resumed his acting career as one of the No Name Players, taking roles as diverse as Macbeth and Eliza Doolittle.

Still in uniform, Elliott auditioned for Amersham repertory after his release in 1945, going on, the following year, to make both his West End bow in *The Guinea Pig* and his television début in *Mary Rose*. Great things were predicted for him after Laurence Olivier cast him in Christopher Fry's *Venus Observed* (1950), and he wowed Broadway as the twins in Jean Anouilh's *Ring Round the Moon* (1950). Yet he fell victim to the tumultuous changes occurring in British theatre in this period, not helping his situation by feuding with Binkie Beaumont of the all-powerful H. M. Tennent organization. At a time of 'angry young men', Elliott was 'tennis anyone?' (Elliott and Turner, 118), and so he sought refuge in cinema. Having made his screen début in *Dear Mr Prohack* (1949), he so impressed Sir Alexander Korda with his performance in David Lean's *The Sound Barrier* (1952) that he was offered a five-figure contract and the lead in a mooted Lawrence of Arabia biopic. But, following his excellent performance in *The Cruel Sea* (1953), he quickly became typecast as a gentleman cad in films such as *The Heart of the Matter* (1953). This professional slough was exacerbated by a personal crisis following his 1957 divorce from actress Virginia Anne McKenna (*b.* 1931), daughter of

Denholm Mitchell Elliott (1922–1992), by Anthony Buckley, 1956

Terence McKenna, an auctioneer at Christies, whom he had married on 1 March 1954. However, his fortunes revived in 1962 when his marriage, on 15 June, to American model Susan Robinson (b. 1942), daughter of Edwin Robinson, a magazine editor, was followed by his casting as 'a pompous, weak, opinionated creeper' (Elliott and Turner, 164) in *Station Six Sahara*, the first in a long line of unromantic losers that would make him one of cinema's most sought-after character actors.

Writing in *The Listener* in 1973, John Elsom described Elliott as 'one of nature's attendant lords' (Elliott and Turner, 244). Shy, sensitive, and easily discouraged, he resented authority without having the will or the anger to confront it. He considered acting a serious business, 'which I take seriously—in an amateurish sort of way' (ibid., 273), and he was quite content to remain in support, because 'as a character actor you get interesting parts and are in a good position to steal the film' (ibid., 242). Gabriel Byrne, his co-star in *Defence of the Realm* (1985), testified to this genius for shameless upstaging when he declared: 'Never act with children, animals or Denholm Elliott' (302).

Fêted for his cynical tutelage of Alan Bates in *Nothing but the Best* (1964), Elliott revealed his talent for sleaziness and corruption as the abortionist in *Alfie* (1966). Often accepting roles purely for the cash, he also delighted in rising above otherwise atrocious pictures, such as *Percy* (1969). Notable as the director reduced to filming bar mitzvahs in *The Apprenticeship of Duddy Kravitz* (1974) and as the errant father in *Brimstone and Treacle* (1982), he excelled at seedy, dishevelled types, whose ill fortune was rooted in some

private torment. However, Hollywood tended only to exploit his eccentric Englishness, with Steven Spielberg pitting him as Harrison Ford's mentor in *Raiders of the Lost Ark* (1981) and *Indiana Jones and the Last Crusade* (1989); John Landis used him as a sneering butler in *Trading Places* (1984). Yet he also possessed immaculate comic timing, as he demonstrated in *The Missionary* (1980) and *A Private Function* (1984), and he was eminently capable of the shabby gentility that brought him a best supporting actor Oscar nomination for his performance as Mr Emerson in Merchant-Ivory's *A Room with a View* (1985). In addition to his seventy-three features, Elliott was also regularly on television, particularly impressing in *School Play* (1979) and *Blade on the Feather* (1980), for which he won a BAFTA award. However, he was reluctant to return to the stage, although his work in *Hedda Gabler* (1972), *The Father* (1972), and *A Life in the Theatre* (1989) was much admired. Actively bisexual throughout his life, Elliott had already been identified as HIV positive by the time he was appointed a CBE in 1988. He died of AIDS-related tuberculosis at his long-time home of Santa Eulalia, Ibiza, Spain, on 2 October 1992. He was survived by his second wife and their two children, Jennifer (b. 1964) and Mark (b. 1967). His ashes were scattered in the garden of Santa Eulalia.

DAVID PARKINSON

Sources S. Elliott and B. Turner, *Denholm Elliott: quest for love* (1995) · *The Times* (8 Oct 1992) · *The Independent* (7 Oct 1992) · *Daily Telegraph* (7 Oct 1992) · WWW · b. cert. · m. cert. · CGPLA Eng. & Wales (1994)
Archives FILM BFI NFTVA, current affairs footage · BFI NFTVA, performance footage
Likenesses A. Buckley, photograph, 1956, NPG [see illus.] · photograph, repro. in *The Times* (7 Oct 1992) · photograph, repro. in *The Times* (8 Oct 1992) · photograph, repro. in *The Times* (14 Oct 1992) · photograph, repro. in *The Independent* (7 Oct 1992) · photograph, repro. in *The Independent* (17 Oct 1992) · portrait, Kobal Collection, London · portrait, Ronald Grant Archive, London · portrait, Huntley Film Archives, London
Wealth at death under £125,000: probate, 19 Dec 1994, CGPLA Eng. & Wales

Elliott, Ebenezer [*called* the Corn Law Rhymer] (1781–1849), poet and bar-iron merchant, was born on 17 March 1781 in the new foundry of Masbrough in the parish of Rotherham, Yorkshire, one of eleven children (of whom eight reached maturity) of Ebenezer Elliott (*fl.* 1760–1820), iron-founder. Grandson of Robert Elliott, a tinsmith of Newcastle upon Tyne, Elliott described his father's ancestors as 'neither Scotch nor English', but 'Border thieves'. His paternal grandmother was a Sheepshank, of Scottish descent. Nicknamed Devil Elliott, Elliott's father was Berean (an ultra-Calvinist), politically radical, a Jacobin convert late in life, and a partner in the foundry of Clay & Co. His mother (*fl.* 1760–1810) came from a family of prosperous freeholders in Penistone (Watkins, 4–7). Alluded to in 'The Excursion', 'To Fanny', and 'Castle Howard' (1840), Elliott's mother was a dreamer, whose sickly disposition made her life 'one long sigh' (ibid., 5). Baptized in his father's faith by Tommy Wright (presumably in Masbrough), Elliott, at the age of six, contracted smallpox, a disease which permanently disfigured and temporarily

Ebenezer Elliott (1781–1849), by unknown artist, *c.*1840

blinded him, and also activated a congenital nervous condition from which his mother also suffered. Self-described as 'intellectually poor' (ibid., 28), Elliott attended four different schools: Nanny Sykes's school, Hollis School, under Joseph Ramsbotham, Penistone grammar school (near his uncle in Thurlestone), and Dalton School, near Huddersfield and Masbrough. A truant, 'learning nothing but vagabondism' by his second year at Dalton, Elliott was removed from school and sent to work in his father's foundry (ibid., 16). Elliott continued working for his father 'as laboriously as any servant … without wages, except an occasional shilling or two, for pocket money' until twenty-three (ibid., 25).

After being introduced to Sowerby's *English Botany* by his aunt Robinson and to Thomson's *Seasons*, Elliott began collecting and sketching flowers and plants. He also resolved 'to undertake the great task of self-instruction' and stated, 'I was not in the least aware that I was learning the art of poetry, which I then hated' (Watkins, 21, 19). By the time he was seventeen he had written his first poem, 'Vernal Walk' (1801). He was 'fond of ruralities' (ibid., 9), and his earliest narrative poems—'Night, or, The Legend of Wharncliffe' (1818), and 'Tales of the Night' (1820)—were praised by Robert Southey.

In 1805 Elliott was married in Rotherham to Frances (Fanny) Gartside, who brought a small fortune to the marriage. Unfortunately, Elliott invested this in his father's business—'already bankrupt beyond redemption' (Seary, 93). The failure hastened his mother's death, and Elliott's father died soon after her. By 17 February 1818, Elliott's

foundry was bankrupt. He borrowed £150 from his wife's unmarried sisters, moved his family, then of eight children, to Sheffield, and set up in the cutlery trade. This business thrived until the 'commercial revulsion' of 1837, when he 'lost fully one-third of my savings' and 'got out … with about 6,000 pounds' (Watkins, 82).

At Sheffield, Elliott was active in literature and politics, as well as in commerce. The bust of Shakespeare in his counting-house, and the casts of Achilles, Ajax, and Napoleon in his workshop typified the fact that he had other interests besides money-making. After publishing an edition of poetic dramas consisting of 'Love', 'The Letter', 'They Met Again', and 'Withered Wild Flowers', all in 1823, Elliott's efforts came to be directed to the repeal agitation. With *The Splendid Village* (1828), *The Village Patriarch* (1829), and *The Ranter* (1830), Elliott began to infuse politics into his pastorals by denouncing the 'bread tax', the exploitation of child and adult labour, and the low wages of the working classes, and by advocating free trade. In 1830 Elliott helped to found the short-lived Sheffield Mechanics Anti-Bread Tax Society, and formed the Sheffield Anti-Corn Law Society in 1834. He briefly supported Chartism (1838–9) until Feargus O'Connor and others refused to endorse repeal of the corn laws and resorted to violence against those who opposed their Charter. Moreover, Elliott refused to endorse universal suffrage; he believed that voting privileges should be earned through economic and educational self-improvement. Elliott, twice bankrupt and parents deceased, attributed all his suffering to the corn laws of 1815.

Elliott became best-known as the Corn Law Rhymer, a title which identifies his most widely read work, the *Corn Law Rhymes* (1831, 1833, and 1834). Only a few short pieces, such as 'Song: Child is thy father dead?' (1833), 'The Death Feast' (1833), 'How Different' (1833), 'The Taxed Cake' (1834), and 'Oh Lord, how long' (1834), merit aesthetic consideration. However, the majority show Elliott as a pragmatic, propagandistic, newspaper-taught anti-religionist, especially hostile to Methodists. He tended to personalize and humanize the poverty he attributed to protectionism. Initially printed in *Tait's*, *The Athenaeum*, the *People's Journal*, the *Monthly Repository*, the *New Monthly Magazine*, the *Sheffield Independent*, the *Sheffield Iris*, and the *Rotherham Independent*, several of his pieces—'Song: Others march in freedom's van' (1831), 'Song: When the poor cease to pray' (1833), 'God of the Poor' (1838), 'Hands and Hearts, and Minds are Ours' (1839?), and 'The People's Anthem' (1847/48)—were adapted to popular and sacred tunes, and were sung frequently at the start of political rallies. Elliott also wrote 'Keronah: a Drama' (1835), and a large number of miscellaneous poems, including 'Rhymed Rambles' (1836). Still, it was his protest verse, favourably reviewed by Thomas Carlyle, Bulwer-Lytton, the Howitts, W. J. Fox, and Geraldine Jewsbury, which bolstered his reputation as poet of the poor, even after he had accumulated substantial wealth.

Elliott addressed, however, both reformist middle-class and radical lower-class audiences. Being 'self-taught' (Watkins, 26), he preached the Victorian gospel of self-help to the working class. He publicly called for a Sheffield mechanics' institute, became one of its major promoters in 1832, and was twice elected vice-president of the Sheffield Mechanics' Library (1835 and 1838). He never ceased, however, to admonish the upper and middle ranks against class indifference and inhumanity toward Britain's poor. Like other early nineteenth-century reformers, Elliott exaggerated and sensationalized the consequences of economic oppression and destitution in an attempt to awaken the Victorian bourgeois conscience. Donald Reiman remarks that Elliott's literary tastes came full circle by the end of his life. He moved from an earlier association with Crabbe and Wordsworth to an appreciation of Byron, Shelley, and Keats as socio-political issues became more pressing. In the Romantic context, though, Reiman states that Elliott's place 'may be best epitomized in his relation with James Montgomery' (Reiman, xi). Montgomery (1771–1854), another major literary figure in Sheffield, admired Elliott's passion for political reform, and his genuine interest in the well-being of individuals. Elliott, in turn, expressed fondness for Montgomery by dedicating to him his epic poem 'Spirits & Men', as a sign of his 'presumption and despair'.

In 1841 Elliott retired politically and professionally. His successors in the corn law struggle were John Bright and Richard Cobden. He bought a quiet estate on Hargate Hill at Great Houghton, near Barnsley, where he died on 1 December 1849, three years after the repeal of the corn laws; he was buried near by in Darfield churchyard. His wife survived him.

Elliott was a small, meek-looking man, essentially conservative by nature. He had thirteen children, of whom five predeceased him (William, Thomas, Charles, and two unbaptized ones). His other children included Ebenezer, a Sheffield clergyman; Benjamin Gartside, who worked in the Sheffield steel trade; Henry and Francis; George Edwin, a West Indies clergyman; and John, a Sheffield druggist. Just before his death his daughter Fanny married John Watkins (his first major biographer). He also had another daughter, named Noah.

ANGELA M. LEONARD

Sources J. Watkins, ed., *Life, poetry and letters of Ebenezer Elliott* (1850) • J. Searle [G. S. Phillips], *Memoirs of Ebenezer Elliott, the Corn Law Rhymer, with criticisms upon his writings* (1852) • A. Leonard, 'Subverting tradition: Ebenezer Elliott's Corn law rhymes', *Semiotica* (1995), 19–22 • A. Leonard, 'Reading political poetry: a discourse analysis of the antislavery poems of John Greenleaf Whittier and the corn law poems of Ebenezer Elliott', PhD diss., George Washington University, 1994 • W. Odom, *Two Sheffield poets: James Montgomery and Ebenezer Elliott* (1929) • A. A. Eaglestone [R. Datalle], *Ebenezer Elliott (the Corn Law Rhymer), 1781–1849* (1949) • E. R. Seary, 'Ebenezer Elliott: a study including an edition of his works', PhD diss., University of Sheffield, 1932 • A. Briggs, 'Ebenezer Elliott, the Corn Law Rhymer', *Cambridge Journal*, 3 (1950), 686–95 • D. Stringer and C. Grute, eds., *Ebenezer Elliott: poet of the field, of the furnace, of the poor!* (1971) • S. Brown, 'Ebenezer Elliott: the Corn Law Rhymer', PhD diss., University of Leicester, 1971 • K. C. Chandler, 'Ebenezer Elliott: a study of his poetry', MA diss., Sheffield City Polytechnic, 1984 • D. Reiman, Introduction to E. Elliott, *The village patriarch: 'Corn Law Rhymes'* (1831), repr. 1979

Archives NL Scot., corresp. and poems • Rotherham Metropolitan Borough Archives and Local Studies Section, Rotherham, business records, corresp., and papers • Sheff. Arch., corresp. and papers • U. Leeds, Brotherton L., corresp. and papers • University of Sheffield, letters

Likenesses portrait, c.1840, Rotherham Museum [*see illus.*] • N. N. Burnard, statue, 1854, Weston Park, Sheffield • photograph? (copy; Elliott's monument in the Corn Market), repro. in *The Art-Journal* (1865) • photograph? (copy; burial place of Ebenezer Elliott), repro. in *The Art-Journal* (1865) • print, repro. in *The Art-Journal* (1865) • wood-engraving, NPG; repro. in *ILN* (1849) • woodcut, NPG; repro. in *Howitt's Journal*, 1847

Elliott, Edward Bishop (1793–1875), Church of England clergyman and writer on prophecy, was born at Paddington, Middlesex, on 24 July 1793, the second son of Charles Elliott (1751–1832) and his second wife, Eling (1758–1843), daughter of Henry *Venn, and the younger brother of Henry Venn *Elliott and the hymn writer Charlotte *Elliott. Shortly afterwards the family moved to Clapham, where his uncle, John Venn, was the rector. After his early schooldays his education was entrusted to private tutors. Admitted to Trinity College, Cambridge, in 1811, he matriculated the following year, gained a scholarship in 1814, and graduated BA in 1816. From 1817 until 1824 he held a fellowship at Trinity College and won the Seatonian prize for poetry in 1821 and 1822. In 1818–19 he joined his brother Henry on his tour of Italy and Greece. Ordained deacon in 1821 and priest the following year, for a short time he undertook various curacies at the request of friends before becoming vicar of Tuxford, Nottinghamshire (1824–40), which was in the gift of Trinity College. He was prebendary of Heytesbury collegiate church in Wiltshire from 1826.

Elliott married first Mary, daughter of John King of Loxwood, Sussex, on 26 April 1826, with whom he had two sons and two daughters. From his second marriage on 1 October 1835 to Harriette, daughter of Sir Richard Steele of co. Dublin, there were a son and two daughters.

After leaving Tuxford, Elliott moved to Torquay, where he concentrated on writing the work on which his fame rests, *Horae apocalypticae* (3 vols., 1844; enlarged and revised in later editions). This massive commentary on the book of Revelation and the prophecies of Daniel generally agreed with other protestant commentators in identifying the pope as Antichrist and predicting that Christ would inaugurate his millennial reign on earth before the end of the nineteenth century. Sir James Stephen in his essay on the Clapham Sect described it as 'a book of profound learning, singular ingenuity, and almost bewitching interest' (Stephen, 581). It engendered considerable controversy and led Elliott to reply to two of his principal critics in *Vindiciae horariae* (1848), directed against the Scottish Presbyterian Alexander Keith, and *Apocalypsis Alfordiana* (1862), in refutation of the strictures of Dean Henry Alford. Most of his other writings also relate to the interpretation of prophecy, the principal exception being the *Memoir of Lord Haddo … Fifth Earl of Aberdeen*, which he edited in 1867.

In 1853 Elliott resumed parochial duties on his appointment as incumbent of St Mark's, Kemptown, Brighton, which had been built four years previously largely through the exertions of his brother Henry. There he exercised an energetic and successful ministry, establishing schools, Bible classes, and other parochial organizations. He died at his Brighton home, 11 Lewes Crescent, on 30 July 1875 from the effects of a fall and was survived by his second wife.   STEPHEN GREGORY

Sources D. M. Lewis, ed., *The Blackwell dictionary of evangelical biography, 1730–1860*, 2 vols. (1995) · Venn, *Alum. Cant.*, 2/2 · *Christian Observer* (1875), 787–93 · Crockford (1874) · E. Stock, *The history of the Church Missionary Society: its environment, its men and its work*, 1 (1899) · J. Stephen, *Essays in ecclesiastical biography*, 2 vols. (1849) · J. Bateman, *The life of the Rev. Henry Venn Elliott* (1868) · Crockford (1829) · *DNB*

Wealth at death £40,000: resworn probate, June 1876, *CGPLA Eng. & Wales*

Elliott, Edwin Bailey (1851–1937), mathematician, was born on 1 June 1851 at 35 Cornmarket Street, Oxford, the eldest son of Edwin Litchfield Elliott, shoemaker, and his wife, Matilda Bailey. He was educated at Magdalen College School, Oxford, and in 1869 went up to Magdalen College with a demyship. He graduated in 1873 after having earned first classes both in moderations (1872) and in the final school (1873). The following year, he won the senior university mathematical scholarship and was elected fellow and mathematical tutor of Queen's College. He held this post until 1892, when he was appointed the first Waynflete professor of pure mathematics, a chair that carried with it a fellowship at Magdalen College. He would hold both until his retirement as professor emeritus in 1921. From 1884 to 1893, he also served as a lecturer in mathematics at Corpus Christi College. On 29 June 1893 Charlotte Amelia Mawer (*d*. 1937), the daughter of John William Mawer, a hosier, married Elliott in an Anglican ceremony. The couple had no children and spent their married life in Oxford, principally at 4 Bardwell Road.

Elliott was an active member of the university and of the British mathematical communities. At Oxford he served as member of the hebdomadal council, visitor of the observatory, curator of the university chest, and delegate of the common university fund. His work with the last involved the influential task of appointing professors and lecturers at Oxford in fields that did not have permanent endowments. His opinion was also regularly sought on financial matters, where his strength lay more in exactness of detail than in boldness of conception. He put this talent to use in a broader civic context through his service as a trustee of the Oxford city charities and as a treasurer of the Oxford Eye Hospital. Beyond Oxford, Elliott played an active role in the London Mathematical Society, joining in 1875, serving on the organization's governing council, and assuming its presidency for the two-year term 1896–8. He was elected FRS in 1891.

Elliott's mathematical life thus circulated around the twin foci of Oxford and London. Besides his work in formal teaching and lecturing at Oxford he was one of the founders (1888) of the Oxford Mathematical Society, its first secretary, and later its president.

Elliott wrote some sixty articles and notes during his mathematical career which appeared almost exclusively in English mathematical publications. Of note among these was his paper entitled 'The interchange of the variables in certain linear differential operators' (*Philosophical Transactions of the Royal Society of London*, 181, 1890, 19–51). There he continued the algebraical research he had begun in 1886 on reciprocants, that is, differential forms which remain invariant under the action of a linear transformation of their variables. J. J. Sylvester had sparked the interest of the Oxford mathematical community in this topic in 1885 when he introduced the new theory, in the context of binary forms only, in his inaugural lecture as Savilian professor of geometry. A flurry of research ensued, including Elliott's paper of 1890 which extended Sylvester's work to forms in more than two variables. As Elliott came to recognize in 1898, however, his research on reciprocants represented but a special case of the theory of continuous groups developed on the continent by the Norwegian mathematician, Sophus Lie, and others.

Elliott's mathematical interests extended beyond differential invariant theory to the theory of elliptic functions, number theory, geometry, and the theories of convergence and integral equations. He made his most influential contribution in the theory of algebraic invariants, however, in the form of his book *An Introduction to the Algebra of Quantics* (1895; 2nd edn, 1913). Arthur Cayley, J. J. Sylvester, and others, both in Great Britain and on the continent, had developed algebraic invariant theory, that is, the study of homogeneous expressions in the coefficients of algebraic forms in n variables (or n-ary quantics) which remain essentially unchanged under the action of a linear transformation of non-zero determinant. In his book Elliott gave a readable and self-contained account of this area as it had developed, particularly in Britain. This text served to introduce a generation of English-speaking mathematicians to the subject and remains a valuable resource for penetrating the work of its late nineteenth-century British practitioners. In his presentation, Elliott largely eschewed the purely symbolic methods that characterized the continental approach to the theory, preferring instead the more direct, more immediately constructive techniques devised principally by his own countrymen.

Elliott made his final noteworthy mathematical contribution to the theory of integral equations. In his 1926 paper, 'A simple exposition of some recently proved facts as to convergency' (*Journal of the London Mathematical Society*), he gave a new, simple, and intrinsic demonstration of a key inequality in the area. His method of proof, which had eluded the efforts of such mathematicians as Issai Schur, Edmund Landau, G. H. Hardy, and J. E. Littlewood, attests to his powers as a mathematician.

Elliott's other interests lay in music, natural history, and literature. As evidence of the latter, he and a colleague founded the Addison Society, the oldest literary society at Queen's College. In 1916, Queen's acknowledged Elliott's achievements by electing him to an honorary fellowship.

In demeanour Elliott was modest and retiring, hesitant in speech, and always willing to help others. He was conservative in university as well as in national politics, deploring many of the changes that he had seen both in the city and in the university. Though he published well into the twentieth century, he persisted in doing mathematics in a largely late nineteenth-century style. As his independent discovery in 1898 of Lie's earlier and more general researches on differential invariants exemplifies, he tended to work in relative isolation at a time when mathematics was becoming increasingly international.

Elliott's wife died in May 1937. Elliott himself died of pulmonary congestion and the complications of surgery for a strangulated hernia at the Acland Nursing Home, Banbury Road, Oxford on 21 July 1937. He was buried three days later, on 24 July, at the Holywell cemetery in Oxford.

T. CHAUNDY, rev. KAREN HUNGER PARSHALL

Sources H. W. Turnbull, *Obits. FRS*, 2 (1936–8), 425–31 · *The Times* (23 July 1937) · K. H. Parshall, 'Towards a history of nineteenth-century invariant theory', *The history of modern mathematics*, ed. D. E. Rowe and J. McCleary, 1: *Ideas and their reception* (1989), 157–206 · b. cert. · m. cert. · d. cert.

Archives Magd. Oxf., MSS

Likenesses photograph, repro. in Turnbull, *Obits. FRS*

Wealth at death £25,646 17s. 1d.: probate, 19 Aug 1937, *CGPLA Eng. & Wales*

Elliott, Frederick Henry (1819–1873). *See under* Elliott, William (1780/81–1853).

Elliott, George Henry (1882–1962), black-face minstrel and music-hall entertainer, was born on 3 November 1882 at the George and Dragon inn, Blackwater Street, Rochdale, Lancashire. His publican father, Henry, was locally well known as a pianist, while his mother, Alice (*née* Gray), was an actress and accomplished contralto vocalist. From the age of three Elliott's childhood was spent in North America, to where his parents emigrated. He first appeared on stage at the age of five as a 'child soprano' and from then on continuously secured a number of theatrical parts culminating in the title-role of Frances Hodgson Burnett's *Little Lord Fauntleroy*, with which he toured Canada and the northern and southern United States. He continued a touring life with Primrose and West's minstrels, whom he joined at the age of nine as a singer and dancer. It was with this troupe that he consolidated his early stagecraft, as well as first appearing in black-face, and it was with this abundant early training that he returned to England with his family in 1894. He started in the smaller provincial halls favoured by a largely working-class clientele, and for three years in the early 1900s worked with Harry Reynolds's minstrels at such seaside resorts as Rhyl and Colwyn Bay. With Reynolds's troupe, as well as delivering his 'coon' speciality, he sang ballads and comic and eccentric songs with equal facility, performed in sketches, burlesques, and acrobatic stunts, and with another member of the troupe worked up a musical double act in which he played several instruments.

Elliott made his London début on 10 March 1902 at Sadler's Wells Theatre, and later that year was engaged at Gatti's, Westminster Bridge Road, earning £4 for the week. Big-time success came quickly after this, with his first West End engagement at the Oxford Music-Hall in October 1903, and it was then that he earned his theatrical nickname, the Chocolate-Coloured Coon. He remained in demand for the rest of his long career, on record and radio as well as on stage, though he was at the height of his powers in the first three decades of the twentieth century. He topped the bill for the first time at the Parthenon Music-Hall in Liverpool. Towards the end of the First World War, and during the subsequent armistice period, he appeared as the star of a concert party organized by the RAF. With his infectious gaiety and ability to win over an audience, regardless of the size of venue, he made a considerable impression on those he entertained. After the death of Eugene Stratton in 1918, Elliott assumed Stratton's sentimental 'coon singer' mantle and revived many of the Leslie Stuart songs that Stratton had popularized (including 'Lily of Laguna' and 'Little Dolly Daydream'), though he always meticulously acknowledged Stratton as their original singer and offered them as his personal tribute to the Dandy Coloured Coon (Stratton's own sobriquet). He did not possess the same authority of stage presence as Stratton, who was said to be able effortlessly to fill the stage with a sudden pose, and his rendition of Stratton's songs was not quite as assured, especially in his later years. None the less, Elliott was a memorable performer in his own right, having a light, tenor voice of 'flute-like clarity' (Midwinter, 105). His intense mode of singing was full of heartfelt conviction. Harry Reynolds's evaluation of him as Britain's 'leading coon exponent' and 'always a fine and conscientious artiste' (Reynolds, 238), rarely disappointing his public, is echoed in many reviews and memoirs. He assimilated ragtime material into his minstrelized routine, and also built up his own repertoire of material, written by divers hands. This included such favourites as 'I want to go to Idaho', 'Hello, Susie Green', 'The Honeysuckle and the Bee', 'If the man in the moon were a coon', 'Sue, Sue, Sue', 'I've had my fortune told', 'In Arizona', 'My Southern Maid', 'I'se a-waitin' for yer, Josie', and 'Rastus Brown'. He was known most of all for 'I used to sigh for the silv'ry moon', which he first performed at the Hackney Empire in 1908—he named his home in Saltdean, Sussex, Silvery Moon in tribute to its success. Elliott had a distinctive stage persona, always being a dapper, even snappy, dresser, appearing with aplomb in white linen suit and trilby to offset his minstrel make-up, and was adept at soft-shoe dancing, using this part of his act as a form of break between verses, or a way of suavely rounding off vocal performances. He appeared twice before royalty, first at the Alhambra in a royal variety performance on 12 February 1925 and second on 1 November 1948, when in a command performance at the London Palladium he combined with six other old music-hall performers in Don Ross's show, *Thanks for the Memory*, which had earlier enjoyed a very successful national tour.

Elliott married twice, first to Emily Hayes, singer, and then, on 28 July 1943, to Florence May Street, herself a variety artist. He had one son, Anthony. Elliott continued to give occasional performances throughout the early 1950s, coming on stage with his second wife, whom he addressed minstrel-style as his Lindy Lou. He made his farewell tour of the remaining halls in 1955. Elliott's act was developed in the long tail-end of the black-face tradition, and by the end of his life his whole métier had become rather archaic, not to say racially offensive; yet at the peak of his career he achieved as much success as Gracie Fields and Norman Evans, both also born in Rochdale, and was regarded by many as a consummate practitioner of the early twentieth-century variety stage. He died of a heart attack in a Hove nursing home at 14 New Church Road on 19 November 1962, shortly after his eightieth birthday.

MICHAEL PICKERING

Sources H. Reynolds, *Minstrel memories: the story of the burnt cork minstrelsy in Great Britain from 1836 to 1927* (1928) • C. Wilmott, 'Critical appreciation and biographical sketch', *Francis & Day's album of G. H. Elliott's popular songs* (1910) • M. Pickering, 'Mock blacks and racial mockery', in J. S. Bratton and others, *Acts of supremacy: the British empire and the stage, 1790–1930* (1991) • *The Times* (20 Nov 1962) • J. Cole, 'Chocolate-Coloured Coon was "Top of the Pops"', *Rochdale Observer* (5 Sept 1984) • M. Pickering, 'John Bull in blackface', *Popular Music*, 16 (1997), 181–201 • G. J. Mellor, *The northern music hall* (1970) • D. Farson, *Marie Lloyd and music hall* (1972) • R. Busby, *British music hall: an illustrated who's who from 1850 to the present day* (1976) • E. C. Midwinter, *Make 'em laugh: famous comedians and their worlds* (1979) • b. cert. • m. cert., 28 July 1943 • d. cert.
Archives SOUND BL NSA
Wealth at death £20,911 5s. 6d.: probate, 20 Feb 1963, *CGPLA Eng. & Wales*

Elliott, Grace. *See* Eliot, Grace (1754?–1823).

Elliott, Henry Venn (1792–1865), Church of England clergyman, was born at Paddington, Middlesex, on 17 January 1792. He was the fifth child and eldest son of Charles Elliott (1751–1832) of Clapham and his second wife, Eling (1758–1843), eldest daughter of the noted evangelical leader Henry *Venn (1725–1797). Edward Bishop *Elliott was his brother and Charlotte *Elliott, the hymn writer, his sister. His earliest years were spent among the so-called Clapham Sect, John Venn, the rector of Clapham, being his uncle. At the age of eight he was sent to school under a Mr Elwell of Hammersmith. In January 1809 he became a pupil of a well-known evangelical tutor, Henry Jowett, rector of Little Dunham, Norfolk. He went to Trinity College, Cambridge, in October 1810, became a scholar of his college the following year, and graduated as fourteenth wrangler and second chancellor's medallist in 1814. With other undergraduates he took a prominent part in the controversial formation of the Cambridge auxiliary of the British and Foreign Bible Society in 1811. He was elected to a fellowship at Trinity in October 1816.

In July 1817 Elliott with two companions embarked on an extensive tour, taking in Switzerland, Italy, Greece, Asia Minor, and Palestine, and returning to England by August 1820. He resided for a time in Cambridge, but following his ordination as deacon in November 1823 he became curate of Ampton, Suffolk, returning to Cambridge two years later. For a number of years he also took pupils, including the sons of such well-known evangelical laymen as Sir Samuel Hoare and Dudley Ryder, first earl of Harrowby. Meanwhile his father had retired to Brighton, where he built the proprietary chapel of St Mary's, consecrated in January 1827. Elliott was appointed preacher, inheriting the chapel on his father's death in 1832 and

remaining there as minister until his own death. From 1826 until 1832 he also held the mastership of St John's Hospital, Wilton, near Salisbury, a virtual sinecure.

On 31 October 1833 Elliott married Julia Anne, the fifth daughter of John Marshall of Hallsteads, Ullswater, and formerly MP for Yorkshire, with whom he had three sons and two daughters, his second son, Charles Alfred *Elliott, becoming a distinguished member of the Indian Civil Service. His wife's death from scarlet fever on 3 November 1841 affected him deeply and he never remarried.

At Brighton, which was still a fashionable watering place, Elliott was an effective evangelical preacher and pastor, successfully blending his intellectual ability with an attractive personality, and ministering to a large and wealthy congregation which often included visitors from all parts of Britain. He took a prominent role in providing for the religious and material needs of the town and was munificent in his (often anonymous) donations to many causes. In August 1836 he opened St Mary's Hall in Brighton, a school for the daughters of poor clergy modelled on that of his friend W. Carus Wilson at Casterton, Yorkshire. Elliott himself made generous financial provision for the school and during the rest of his life was closely involved in its management. He also extensively assisted in the establishment of the new church of St Mark's, Kemptown, Brighton, in 1849.

Elliott maintained an active interest in many evangelical organizations, notably the Church Missionary Society, and his congregational collections sometimes headed the society's list of subscriptions. He was a convinced but not narrow sabbatarian; however, he did publicly oppose the Sunday opening of the Crystal Palace in 1852. It appears that he did not entirely share the millennialist theology of his brother Edward. In addition to sermons he published *Psalms and Hymns for Public, Private and Social Worship* (1835), a compilation which included some of his own compositions as well as some by his wife and his sister, and which for several decades enjoyed considerable popularity among evangelicals. Elliott died at his home, 31 Brunswick Square, Brighton, on 24 January 1865.

STEPHEN GREGORY

Sources J. Bateman, *The life of the Rev. Henry Venn Elliott* (1868) • A. Pollard, 'Elliott, Henry Venn', *The Blackwell dictionary of evangelical biography, 1730–1860*, ed. D. M. Lewis (1995) • Boase, *Mod. Eng. biog.* • Venn, *Alum. Cant.*, 2/2 • *Christian Observer* (1865), 303–8 • *GM*, 3rd ser., 18 (1865), 384 • J. Julian, ed., *A dictionary of hymnology* (1892) • *DNB* • *Christian Observer* (1875), 787–93
Archives Bodl. Oxf., letters to Robert Finch
Likenesses C. Baugniet, lithograph, BM, NPG • photograph, repro. in Bateman, *Life of the Rev. Henry Venn Elliott*
Wealth at death under £40,000: probate, 7 March 1865, *CGPLA Eng. & Wales*

Elliott, John (d. 1690/91), physician and Jacobite sympathizer, is of unknown origin. He first appears in the records when he was created MD by the king's command at St Catharine's College, Cambridge, in 1681; he was incorporated MD at Oxford on 11 July 1683. Elliott was named in the new charter of the Royal College of Physicians of 30 November 1686, and duly elected as a fellow on 25 June 1687, and as censor of the society. He was presumably the Dr Elliott who was known to Bishop Cartwright of Chester in London in April–June 1687. Both men were adherents of James II.

On 13 June 1689 the House of Commons received information that Elliott (together with Sir Adam Blair, Captain Vaughan, Captain Mole, and Dr Gray) had helped to disperse a 'seditious and treasonable paper', *A Declaration of … James the Second, to All his Loving Subjects in the Kingdom of England*, which had been issued on 8 May from Dublin Castle. Elliott and his fellow distributors were ordered to be taken into custody and impeached for high treason, and the declaration to be burnt by the hangman. On 26 June the impeachment was read and delivered to the House of Lords. On 4 July, Elliott and his fellow prisoners were brought before the Lords and the articles against them read. Counsel were assigned them and they were remanded back to Newgate. On 12 July, Elliott and the others gave in their answers to the articles, Elliott pleading his innocence and arguing that the crimes he was charged with did not constitute high treason in any case. These answers were transmitted to the Commons, where debate upon them seems to have fizzled out.

Elliott took out a writ of habeas corpus on 11 February 1690, praying that he be admitted bail now that the parliament which had impeached him had been dissolved. However, the court of king's bench decided that the impeachments were still in operation and denied him bail. On 8 April, Elliott petitioned the Lords for his freedom, offering to give bail to attend whenever ordered. On the 9th he was granted bail at £5000 for himself, and £2500 each for his two sureties, Richard Morley of Petty France and John Boys of St Margaret's, Westminster, on condition that he appear before the Lords when ordered, notice of which was to be left at Mr Walton's, a grocer in the Haymarket. On 5 December 1690 Elliott again petitioned, this time to be discharged from bail, which was duly granted. Unfortunately Elliott did not enjoy his freedom for long, as Elizabeth, widow of John Elliott 'of St Martin's-in-the-Fields', was granted administration of his estate on 26 August 1691.   STUART HANDLEY

Sources Venn, *Alum. Cant.* · Munk, *Roll* · Foster, *Alum. Oxon.* · *JHC*, 10 (1688–93), 179, 191–8, 216 · *JHL*, 14 (1685–91), 254–78, 454–6, 580 · *The manuscripts of the House of Lords*, 4 vols., HMC, 17 (1887–94), vol. 2, p. 205 · N. Luttrell, *A brief historical relation of state affairs from September 1678 to April 1714*, 6 vols. (1857), vol. 1, pp. 546, 551, 555; vol. 2, pp. 13–14 · administration, PRO, PROB 6/67, fol. 135*v.* · *CSP dom., 1687–9*, 312 · *The diary of Thomas Cartwright, bishop of Chester*, ed. J. Hunter, CS, 22 (1843), 49–61
Wealth at death see administration, PRO, PROB 6/67, fol. 135*v*

Elliott, Sir John. *See* Eliot, Sir John, baronet (1736–1786).

Elliott, Leah Madeleine (1896–1955). *See under* Ritchard, Cyril Joseph (1897–1977).

Elliott, Michael Paul (1931–1984), theatre director, was born at 4 Chester Square, Westminster, London, on 26 June 1931, the second son and third child of the Revd Wallace Harold Elliott (*d.* 1957) of Brook House, Compton, near Guildford, Surrey, and his wife, Edith Evelyn Plaistowe, *née* Kilburn (1895–1988). His father, who was vicar of

St Michael's, Chester Square, chaplain to George VI and Elizabeth II, and an honorary canon of Coventry Cathedral, was a frequent broadcaster, known for many years as the Radio Parson. Elliott was educated at St Ronan's preparatory school, Worthing, Radley College, and Keble College, Oxford, where he took a third in modern history in 1954. It was at Oxford that he first met Casper Wrede and began an artistic association that lasted until Elliott's death.

Elliott entered the theatre as a television director and was staff producer with BBC television drama from 1956 to 1960. During this time he co-directed several productions with Wrede and he became his associate for the 59 Theatre Company season at the Lyric Hammersmith. He made his own stage directing début with an acclaimed production of Ibsen's *Brand* in 1959: Elliott was an Ibsen specialist and this production, with Patrick McGoohan, had 'a bleak and terrible beauty in performance and decor' (*The Times*). On 25 July 1959 he married Rosalind Marie Knight (*b.* 1933), an actress, the daughter of Esmond Pennington Knight, actor; they had two daughters.

In 1961 Elliott directed Vanessa Redgrave in *As You Like It*, a landmark in the history of the Royal Shakespeare Company, at Stratford; the play later moved to London. The next year he directed Trevor Howard in John Mortimer's *Two Stars for Comfort* in the West End. He was appointed artistic director of the Old Vic in 1962, the last year before it became the National, and directed *Peer Gynt* with Leo McKern, *The Merchant of Venice*, and *Measure for Measure*. For five years from 1963 he worked as a freelance: notable productions included *Little Eyolf* at the 1963 Edinburgh Festival, and Strindberg's *Miss Julie* (1966), with Maggie Smith and Albert Finney, at the National. This phase came to an end when, having turned down the offer to become Olivier's heir apparent at the National, as well as the posts of artistic director of the Royal Court and head of BBC drama, he opted to move to Manchester to form a group theatre, the 69 Theatre Company, with Casper Wrede, James Maxwell, Richard Negri, and Braham Murray.

Elliott first went to Manchester in 1967 to direct Tom Courtenay in *The Playboy of the Western World*, for Braham Murray's Century Theatre. In the following year he directed one of the 69 Theatre Company's opening productions there, *When we Dead Awaken*, with Wendy Hiller. Subsequently he directed *Daniel Deronda* with Vanessa Redgrave (1969); *The Tempest*; *Peer Gynt* with Tom Courtenay (1970); *The Family Reunion*; and, in Manchester Cathedral, *The Cocktail Party*.

After two extraordinary years at the small university theatre the 69 Theatre Company was invited by Manchester city council to build a new theatre. Elliott was a student of theatre form, especially through his researches into Greek theatre, and together with Negri, the designer, and Wrede, he created an extraordinary space-module theatre-in-the-round in the old Cotton Exchange in Manchester city centre. Like his colleagues he rejected the proscenium arch, the decadent Roman form, and fashioned an auditorium in direct descent from the Greek and Elizabethan forms. In his words: 'Why are we in the round?

Because we believe that theatre is a happening and that what happens among people has more effect than what happens the other side of a peep hole'.

The Royal Exchange Theatre opened in 1976, and Elliott helped to establish its traditions, with an emphasis on the actors being the magnetic point of the 250 people working in the building. He was a founding artistic director of the Royal Exchange Theatre Company and in its first season directed Albert Finney and Leo McKern in *Uncle Vanya* (1977). Three of his later productions—*The Ordeal of Gilbert Pinfold* (1977) with Michael Hordern, *The Lady from the Sea* (1978) with Vanessa Redgrave, and *The Family Reunion* (1979) with Edward Fox—transferred to London, while *Crime and Punishment* (1978) was seen in Germany, and *The Dresser* went on to New York in 1981 after its West End success the previous year. His final productions were *Philoctetes* (1982); Ronald Harwood's *After the Lions* (1982); and at Christmas 1983 his own adaptation of *Moby Dick*.

Elliott also produced two operas, both world premières by Gordon Crosse: *The Story of Vasco* for the English National Opera at the London Coliseum, and *Potter Thompson* at the Aldeburgh Festival. He was responsible for more than fifty major television productions in Britain, and several in Norway and Sweden, and directed the CBS coast-to-coast spectacular of *The Glass Menagerie* in New York in 1964. His memorable BBC plays included *Antigone* with Dorothy Tutin, *Time Remembered* with Edith Evans, *The Lower Depths*, *The Cherry Orchard* with John Gielgud and Peggy Ashcroft, and *Ghosts* with Tom Courtenay, Celia Johnson, and Donald Wolfit. His last television production was the award-winning *King Lear* with Laurence Olivier for Granada Television.

Elliott was a member of the Arts Council drama panel from 1963 to 1970, and a member of the Arts Council from 1972 to 1975. He served on the advisory council of the BBC, was a member of the board of governors for the Central School of Speech and Drama, and from 1963 to 1966 sat on the building committee for the National Theatre, where he was 'perhaps the coolest mind … very practical and impatient with dogma' (Elsom and Tomalin, 174). He was appointed OBE in 1980. He died on 30 May 1984 at the Royal Infirmary, Manchester, and was buried on 5 June at the southern cemetery, Barlow Moor Road, Manchester. He was survived by his wife and two daughters.

Michael Elliott was one of the most admired directors of his day. He combined a daunting intelligence and passionate intensity with breathtaking natural stagecraft. One leading critic said that he was the only director for whom nobody had a bad word. His fierce integrity led him into a counter-movement against the pessimism and nihilism of the established theatre. By selflessly leaving a glittering career in London to break the old pattern of assumption that first-rate theatre could not be created in the provinces, he pioneered the concept of regional theatres of national standards which would later be taken for granted. His legacy lived on with all those who worked with him, and with the new artistic directors at the Royal Exchange, who included his daughter Marianne.

BRAHAM MURRAY

Sources *The Times* (1 June 1984) · www.royalexchange.co.uk [Royal Exchange Theatre] · *WWW* · J. Elsom and N. Tomalin, *The history of the National Theatre* (1978) · B. St G. Drennan, *Keble College centenary register, 1870–1970* (1970) · b. cert. · m. cert. · d. cert. · U. Oxf., archives · *CGPLA Eng. & Wales* (1984)

Wealth at death £148,482: administration, 29 Aug 1984, *CGPLA Eng. & Wales*

Elliott, Thomas Renton (1877–1961), physician and physiologist, was born at Willington, co. Durham, on 11 October 1877, the eldest son of Archibald William Elliott, retailer, and his wife, Anne, daughter of Thomas Renton, of Otley, Yorkshire. He went to Durham School where he was head boy, played rugby and cricket for the school, and won the fives challenge cup. He obtained a leaving exhibition to Cambridge, where his father's two elder brothers, Sir John *Eliot and Thomas Armstrong Elliott, in their time had been second and eighth wrangler respectively. Elliott himself entered Trinity College, Cambridge, to read natural sciences as a prelude to a career in medicine. He obtained first-class honours in both parts of the tripos (1900–01) and would certainly have obtained a fellowship of his college had not a misunderstanding caused him to apply too late, a severe attack of typhoid fever having delayed his graduation. His abilities and maturity had, however, already marked him out, and scholarships were forthcoming to allow him to proceed to research. A fellowship of Clare College followed.

Elliott's interests as a physiologist focused on the autonomic nervous system and in six short years he produced a sequence of papers which, in the words of his near contemporary, Sir Henry Dale, 'were of well-nigh incomparable brilliance and authority for a worker so young in years and experience'. Elliott had grasped the significance of the similarity between the action of the sympathetic nerves and that of adrenaline; and, on this basis, he put forward the concept of the chemical transmission of nerve impulses. But Elliott was a quarter of a century in advance of his time: his work was received with scepticism, not least by some to whom he was bound by strong ties of personal loyalty and esteem. This was a severe blow and it was probably for this reason that in 1906 he left Cambridge for London and resumed his medical studies at University College Hospital. He obtained his MD in 1908, and in 1910 was appointed an assistant physician on the hospital staff. A Beit fellowship followed and in 1913 he was elected FRS and in 1915 FRCP.

Before Elliott could do more than pick up the threads of his interrupted research, war broke out. Within a month he was in France and for the next four years he drove himself relentlessly. He was twice mentioned in dispatches and appointed DSO (1918) and CBE (1919). In 1918 he married Martha, daughter of A. K. McCosh of Airdrie; they had three sons and two daughters.

After the war, Elliott returned to University College Hospital as a consultant physician. His aptitude for imaginative administration was by now apparent and he also became, under the cloak of his seniors, a member of the committee which later became the Medical Research Council. The Haldane commission in 1913 had severely criticized clinical education in London: it found that the academic structure was scarcely more than the apprenticeship system under another name, and that clinical professorships were in general simply titles of seniority. The radical solution proposed was the creation of academic departments in clinical subjects with whole-time professors at their head. Elliott was an obvious choice for such a post at his old hospital and he remained professor of medicine there until 1939.

Elliott's new task was formidable. Not only had he to translate an idea into a living and operative organization but he had to overcome the opposition of colleagues whose traditional standards had been so summarily displaced. He succeeded and made his department a prototype. But, after a few abortive attempts, he abandoned personal research. From then on he acted vicariously. His constructive criticisms of research proposals and his perceptive appreciation of scientific intent brought out the best in young colleagues. It was no accident that Elliott was perhaps the only person ever to serve three terms on the Medical Research Council. He was always in demand when major policy was at issue and his ability to identify potential talent was uncanny. Increasingly, as the years passed, he came to be quietly consulted by those who had the responsibility for large decisions not only in research but in academic and medical policy at the highest levels. He was a Beit and a Wellcome trustee and served on the Goodenough committee on medical education in 1942–4. Throughout his professional career and beyond into his retirement he contributed substantially to many constructive achievements, with most of which his name was never connected.

By ordinary standards Elliott's should have been thought a successful life. But despite the robust appearance and genial laugh with which Elliott moved in the background of power, it seemed that this organizational role was no lasting satisfaction to him. In his early research career he had glimpsed what to him were the real heights and it was by this measure that he judged the worth of his later life. Elliott died on 4 March 1961 at his home, Broughton Place, Peeblesshire, his wife surviving him. HAROLD HIMSWORTH, *rev.*

Sources H. H. Dale, *Memoirs FRS*, 7 (1961), 53–74 • *BMJ* (11 March 1961), 752–4 • *The Lancet* (11 March 1961) • personal knowledge (1981) • private information (1981)
Archives Wellcome L., corresp. and papers | CAC Cam., corresp. with A. V. Hill • Wellcome L., letters to Sir Thomas Lewis
Likenesses H. Lamb, oils, UCL, medical school

Elliott, William. *See* Elliot, William (1727–1766).

Elliott, William (*fl.* 1774–1794), naval officer and marine painter, was renowned for his paintings of naval actions of the 1780s. Of the two William Elliotts listed in the Royal Navy, it is believed that the William Elliott who entered the merchant service as master's mate of the *Roebuck*, before being promoted lieutenant in 1782, commander in 1790, and subsequently captain in 1810, was the painter. This William Elliott died in 1838. However, it should be noted that the painter Elliott ceased to exhibit in 1791 and his last known work, *Victory off Bastia*, is recorded in Archibald as dated 1794 (Archibald). The *Gentleman's Magazine* records the death, on 21 September 1792, 'at Leeds [of] Captain William Elliott, of the Royal Navy' (*GM*, 866).

William Elliott first exhibited at the Free Society of Artists in 1774, showing *A Perspective View of the European Factory at Canton in China* and *A View of the Green, etc. at Calcutta in Bengal*. At the Royal Academy he appeared as an honorary exhibitor in 1784 with *A Frigate and Cutter in Chase*, a large-scale naval scene in oils, typical of his work. He exhibited at the Royal Academy from 1784 to 1789, focusing on three themes: ships in conflict, at anchor, or caught in foul weather. He was also a fellow of the Incorporated Society of Artists and contributed thirteen pictures to their exhibitions in 1790 and 1791. In 1791 he was elected president of the society and exhibited one of his most famous paintings, *George III Reviewing the English Fleet at Spithead* (National Maritime Museum, Greenwich, London), which he signed 'Lieutenant W. Elliott'. His last dated work is *Victory off Bastia* (1794), after which date little is known of his activities. During his lifetime several of his pictures were engraved by such notable men as Valentine Green, and Elliott himself experimented in aquatint, engraving *The Dreadful Situation of the 'Halsewell', East Indiaman, 6 Jan. 1786* (British Museum, London). Other examples of his work are in the United States Naval Academy Museum, Annapolis, Maryland.

L. H. CUST, *rev.* NATASHA EATON

Sources E. H. H. Archibald, *Dictionary of sea painters* (1980) • Waterhouse, *18c painters* • Redgrave, *Artists*, 2nd edn • Bryan, *Painters* (1816) • Graves, *RA exhibitors*, vol. 2 • G. K. Nagler, *Allgemeines Künstler-Lexikon*, ed. J. Meyer, rev. edn, 3 vols. (Leipzig, 1872–85) • *GM*, 1st ser., 62 (1792), 866
Archives BM, department of prints and drawings, MSS • Courtauld Inst., Witt Library, MSS • NMM, MSS • United States Naval Museum, Annapolis, MSS

Elliott, William (1780/81–1853), maker of scientific instruments, was born in 1780 or 1781 in the parish of St Andrew, High Holborn, London, the son of William Elliott, yeoman, of Tash Court, Gray's Inn Lane in the county of Middlesex. On 14 April 1795 he was bound apprentice for seven years to William Backwell, compass and drawing instrument maker, of Tash Street, Gray's Inn Lane. He was re-bound in May 1795 in the Coach and Coach Harness Makers' Company; in 1804 he became a freeman and bound his own first apprentice. This was probably the year when he commenced his own business.

Between 1804 and 1814 Elliott took five apprentices and between 1832 and 1839 another four, thus usually having two or three apprentices at a time. All these were bound in the Coach and Coach Harness Makers' Company; there may have been others between those years. He was, very probably, the William Elliott living at 26 Wilderness Row, Goswell Street, from 1808 to 1816 and his addresses are known with certainty thereafter. From 1817 to 1827 his business was at 21 Great Newport Street, and from then until 1833 at 227 High Holborn. His home and business were at 268 High Holborn from 1835 to 1849 and at 56 Strand from 1850 until his death.

In 1804 Elliott married Elizabeth Thrale, or Thrah, at St Martin-in-the-Fields. Their son, William (*b.* 1804), studied at Queens' College, Cambridge, and entered the Church of England. As the Revd William Elliott he wrote *A Treatise on the Slide Rule* which was advertised in the catalogues of the family's company. From Elliott's second marriage, to Anne Berner, there was a daughter, Anne. His third wife was Emma Paget, the widow of a Captain Kelly. Their children were Frederick Henry (*b.* 1819) [*see below*], George Augustus (*b.* 1821), Charles Alfred (*b.* 1822) [*see below*], Eliza (*b.* 1829), and possibly others. In Elliott's will there was provision for a married daughter Mary, whose birth record is untraced.

The absence of advertisements and catalogues prior to 1850 suggests that Elliott supplied his products mostly to the trade and was well known within it. No record has been found of his gaining prizes or awards for his products. He was not active in guild matters. He did not seek membership of learned societies or the protection of patents, again suggesting that he worked within the trade and its requirements, as he did with J. W. Woolgar on his new plotting scale. Elliott was one of the first to use German silver, a new alloy with good resistance to corrosion, in his drawing instruments. Many examples of these, and of scales, survive from his early places of work. Later he described himself as a mathematical, optical, and philosophical instrument maker and other products from these years include a theodolite and a vacuum pump. In 1850, under a deed of partnership, his sons Frederick Henry and Charles Alfred were taken into their father's business which then carried on as William Elliott & Sons at 56 Strand, London.

Elliott died in 1853; in his will he left his share in the partnership to provide his wife with an annuity. His passing went largely unrecorded but years later he was referred to in his son Frederick's obituary as 'the well-known mathematical instrument-maker, Mr. W. Elliott in Holborn'.

Frederick Henry Elliott (1819–1873) was privately educated at Baldock and Edmonton, then obtained his master's degree at Christ's College, Cambridge in 1848. He practised as a surveying engineer before joining his father and brother in business in 1850. The new partnership began to make itself more widely known, advertising in textbooks, issuing catalogues, and taking part in exhibitions. Two medals were won in the 1851 Great Exhibition, beginning a series of successes in exhibitions in Britain and abroad.

Frederick Elliott became a fellow of the Royal Society of Arts in 1850 and in 1859 a fellow of the Royal Astronomical Society. Jointly, Frederick and Charles obtained patents for improvements in drawing boards, barometers, and telescopes. The company worked willingly with academics and others to realize their inventions; instruments for the new applications of electricity were produced and became an important part of the firm's activity. Customers included J. C. Maxwell, Charles Wheatstone, J. W. Strutt, and other leading scientists. The company prospered, its success attributed to Frederick's business ability. Details of his marriage, to Susan Pearse, are unknown. He died of a stroke in his office at 449 Strand, London on 18 January 1873.

Charles Alfred Elliott (1822–1877) was apprenticed to his father as mathematical instrument maker on 27 October 1837 for seven years and became a partner in 1850. He was married; his wife's name was probably Maria Sarors; there was a daughter Gertrude. He retired before 1873 and died at Teddington, Middlesex on 9 October 1877.

When William Elliott's career began London's thriving scientific instrument trade was the province of individual craftsmen. By widening his activities he remained a significant and respected supplier through its transition to large-scale manufacture and application. The creation of a partnership with his sons ensured the continuity and expansion of a business which became one of the largest producers of scientific instruments, remaining so until 1967 when it was taken over by English Electric, which itself became part of GEC soon afterwards.

H. R. BRISTOW

Sources apprenticeship indenture of William Elliott, GEC Marconi Avionics Ltd, Airport Works, Rochester, Kent, Elliott Archive and Collection · G. C. Clifton, 'An introduction to the history of Elliott Brothers up to 1900', *Bulletin of the Scientific Instrument Society*, 36 (1993) · Marwick MSS, Elliott Archive and Collection, Ref 4.8/1 · census returns, 1841, PRO, HO 107/673/5; 1851, HO 107/1481/289/*r*, fol. 19*v* · Last will and testament of William Elliott, 12 Feb 1851, PRO, PROB 11/2177 · Venn, *Alum. Cant.* · Deed of Partnership, 24 Oct 1850 [cited in reference 5 (last will and testament); original not found] · Rate Books for Wilderness Row, Clerkenwell, Finsbury Library, 245 St John's Street, Local History Dept. · *Monthly Notices of the Royal Astronomical Society*, 34 (1873–4), 139–40 [obit. of Frederick Henry Elliott] · patents, nos. 2789 of 1859; 2641 and 2631 of 1860; 889 of 1868 · d. certs · IGI

Archives GEC Marconi Avionics Ltd, Airport Works, Rochester, Kent, archives, MSS · MHS Oxf., instruments · NMM, instruments · priv. coll., instruments and catalogues [copies] · Sci. Mus., catalogues and instruments · Whipple Museum, Cambridge, instruments and Maxwell ledgers, etc.

Likenesses photographs (Frederick Henry Elliott; Charles Alfred Elliott), GEC Marconi Avionics Ltd, Airport Works, Rochester, Kent, Elliott Archive and Collection

Wealth at death business of William Elliott incorporated in partnership with two sons (who continued to operate it after his death in accordance with will); sons required to provide from it an annuity of £200 p.a. for William's widow: will, PRO, PROB 11/2177

Elliott, Sir William Henry (1792–1874), army officer, was born at Elliott House, near Ripon, the son of Captain John Elliott RN, who sailed with Captain Cook on his second and third voyages. Elliott was commissioned ensign in the 51st King's Own light infantry on 6 December 1809. In January 1811 the 51st joined Wellington's army at Torres Vedras, and Elliott's first battle was at Fuentes de Oñoro. He was present at the capture of Ciudad Rodrigo and of Badajoz, and at the battle of Salamanca, and was promoted lieutenant on 13 August 1812. During the retreat from Burgos he acted as aide-de-camp to Colonel Hugh Henry Mitchell, and was wounded while carrying dispatches under fire. In June 1813 he was appointed acting aide-de-camp to Major-General William Inglis, and served with him at the battles of the Pyrenees, when he was again wounded, and at the battles of the Nivelle and of Orthez. He was then appointed brigade major to the 1st brigade, 7th division, in which capacity he served until 1814. He was present with the 51st at Waterloo, and he had charge of the scaling ladders at the siege of Cambrai.

From 1821 to 1834 Elliott, who was promoted captain on 9 November 1820, served with the 51st in the Ionian Islands. He was promoted major on 12 July 1831 and made KH in 1837. On 27 June 1838 he was promoted lieutenant-colonel, and commanded the 51st in Australia, Van Diemen's Land, New Zealand, and at Bangalore, until 1852. On 11 November 1851 he was promoted colonel.

In 1852 Elliott's regiment was ordered for service in the Second Anglo-Burmese War. Elliott was detailed to command the Madras brigade, which led the way in the fierce fighting of 10, 11, and 12 April 1852, in which Rangoon was captured, and in the storming of the Shwedagon pagoda on 14 April. In the second campaign, which began in September 1852, Elliott again had command of a brigade, consisting of his own regiment and two battalions of Madras native infantry, and he co-operated successfully in the capture of Danubyu, the stronghold of Myat-Tun, who had a short time before defeated Captain Loch. He was made a CB and commandant at Rangoon. While there he discovered and suppressed on 20 November 1853 an attempted rising against the British in Rangoon. In 1855 he gave up the colonelcy of the regiment which he had so long commanded.

On 20 January 1857 Elliott was promoted major-general. He never again went on active service, but he was made KCB in 1862. He became colonel of the 55th foot on 15 November 1861, and of his old regiment, the 51st, on 1 June 1862; he was promoted lieutenant-general on 27 July 1863, made a GCB in 1870, and became a general on 25 October 1871. He died at his house, 20 Cambridge Square, Hyde Park, London, on 27 March 1874, leaving a widow, Jane.   H. M. STEPHENS, *rev.* ALEX MAY

Sources Army List · *The Times* (3 April 1874) · W. Wheater, *A record of the services of the 51st regiment* (1870) · C. P. Deedes, *History of the king's own Yorkshire light infantry*, 4 vols. (1947) · W. F. P. Napier, *History of the war in the Peninsula and in the south of France*, rev. edn, 6 vols. (1876) · C. W. C. Oman, *A history of the Peninsular War*, 7 vols. (1902–30) · W. F. B. Laurie, *Our Burmese wars and relations with Burma: being an abstract of military and political operations* (1880) · G. Bruce, *The Burma Wars, 1824–1886* (1973) · B. Bond, ed., *Victorian military campaigns* (1967) · Boase, *Mod. Eng. biog.* · *CGPLA Eng. & Wales* (1874)
Wealth at death under £300: probate, 1 June 1874, *CGPLA Eng. & Wales*

Ellis. *See also* Ellys.

Ellis [*formerly* Sharpe], **Alexander John** (1814–1890), phonetician and mathematician, was born Alexander John Sharpe in Hoxton, London, on 14 June 1814, the elder of the two sons of James Birch Sharpe (*bap.* 1789) and his wife, Ann Ellis. They first sent him to a private boarding-school at Walthamstow, London. While there he was offered, at the age of eleven, the opportunity of a future lifetime of study and research 'unhampered by pecuniary cares' on condition that he adopted his mother's maiden

Alexander John Ellis (1814–1890), by Naudin & Co., 1886

name of Ellis. The change of name, by royal licence, was gazetted on 24 November 1825. A relative of his mother, William Ellis, a schoolmaster, provided the finance which was to pay for the young man's later schooling, as well as to give him opportunities as an adult for travel, residence abroad, and the undertaking of publishing ventures, and to invest in scientific and cultural activities close to his heart. He never had to earn a living.

After Walthamstow, Ellis attended Shrewsbury School where, with his brother, James Birch Sharpe, he spent three relatively happy years, from August 1826 to December 1829. There then followed four relatively joyless ones at Eton College. In 1833 he entered Trinity College, Cambridge, to study mathematics; his curriculum also included classical languages, together with some German and French. In 1835 he was elected to a college scholarship. He graduated BA in 1837, being placed sixth wrangler in mathematics and first in the second class of the classical tripos.

Ellis retained a connection with Cambridge for some time before setting off on a fifteen-month period of travel and study in Italy and Sicily. One consequence was the large collection of daguerreotypes that he made of Italy. Although they were never published—they are now in the National Museum of Science and Industry—they constitute the earliest topographic photographs of Italy, including the first of the leaning tower of Pisa. While in Italy, Ellis also took a particular interest in the pronunciation of languages, and this led to his devising a phonetic notation to reflect the variation in pronunciation to be heard across the Italian dialects.

On 31 August 1840, in Naples, he married Ann Chaytor (1814–1888) of Spennithorne Hall, near Leyburn, North Riding of Yorkshire, the daughter of John Clervaux Chaytor and his wife, Anne Carter. They later settled at Colamandene Lodge, a spacious country house in Dorking, Surrey. Their first son, Edwin John, was born in Nottingham in 1841. He later became known as a painter, particularly of marine scenes; he died on 19 April 1895. Twins were born in Great Malvern in 1844: Tristie (Tristram) James (d. 25 July 1922) and Miriam Anne. Like Edwin, Tristie later achieved fame as a painter. Because of Ellis's wife's health following the birth of the twins, the family spent some time in Dresden, Germany. In November 1847 they moved to Bath, and in 1853 to Bristol. From 1869 until their deaths Ellis and his wife lived in Kensington, London.

Spelling and pronunciation In August 1843 Ellis began a sixteen-year association with Isaac Pitman, the inventor of stenography, later known as Pitman's shorthand. Both were deeply committed to the view that the condition of the bulk of the working classes in Britain could be improved by education, with particular emphasis on literacy. Encouraged and supported by Ellis, Pitman perceived that an obstacle to literacy for many people was the spelling system of English. Thus, they argued, a reformed spelling system of English (phonotypy), based on the sounds of the language, could be created from the phonetic system inherent in Pitman's shorthand (phonography). Ellis generously founded production of the type founts for the new symbols. A variety of phonotypic alphabets were produced—not always by mutual agreement—with the aim of providing a more logical, and therefore more quickly acquired, method of learning to read English. Their work attracted considerable attention and a degree of support among the Victorian public. Weekly journals were published to further the aims of phonography and phonotypy; books, especially extracts from the Bible or the literary classics, were published in a phonotypic alphabet. Ultimately, however, both men had to admit that a completely new alphabet for English, even if it visually resembled the traditional one, was impracticable. A compromise, namely an orthography which was not fully 'scientific', but which acted as a transition to traditional orthography, had a greater chance of success. Ellis's *Alphabet of Nature* (1845) is an exposition of the logical structure of the alphabet devised by him and Pitman. (The alphabet devised and popularized in the 1970s by Sir James Pitman, Isaac's grandson, the Initial Teaching Alphabet, is a further development of this principle.)

Ellis was at the same time refining concepts in phonetics which made him one of the significant British phoneticians of the nineteenth century. Even though, as he put it in 1843, he had never mingled with any but well-educated people at Eton and Cambridge, he was well aware of the wide differences of pronunciation between speakers in London, Shrewsbury, and Cambridge. From his schooldays he knew that different styles of pronunciation of classical Latin and Greek also existed. Later, from his travels in Europe, he discovered that an Italian pronunciation of classical Latin differed in several respects from an English one. His first major publications in phonetics were *Phonetics* (1844) and *Essentials of Phonetics* (1848), which present an analysis of English pronunciation with a specific emphasis on questions of sound notation.

His experiments with various phonotypic alphabets led Ellis in time to the creation of a series of phonetic alphabets—that is, systems of notation capable of symbolizing nuances of pronunciation, rather than providing simply a more logical method of printing or writing English. His most sophisticated phonetic alphabet was Palaeotype (that is, 'old type'), first published in 1867 and subjected to regular revision over the following years. By using only roman symbols, but by altering their position on the printed page (for example, by reversing or tilting them), as well as by associating small diacritical marks with them, Ellis achieved a total inventory of more than 250 characters many years before the creation of the International Phonetic Alphabet in the 1880s.

By the mid- to late 1860s Ellis was increasingly interested in not only the current state of English pronunciation within the British Isles, the colonies, and former colonies, but also in the forms of pronunciation at earlier stages in the language's history. His monumental five-volume *On Early English Pronunciation* (1869–89) reflected an intensive, systematic study which, for the pre-nineteenth century periods, involved analysing printed and manuscript materials from the time of Chaucer onwards. For the contemporary period Ellis and a team of phonetician–dialectologists collected data on pronunciation, where possible at first hand, throughout the British Isles, and sometimes further afield. *On Early English Pronunciation* was the first major study of the history and current state of English pronunciation ever published. Additionally, Ellis was the driving force behind the creation of the English Dialect Society in 1873, which published monographs, and later a dictionary and grammar, on mainly the vocabulary and grammar of regional forms of English.

Acoustics and mathematics In 1862 the German physicist Hermann Helmholtz published *Die Lehre von den Tonempfindungen als physiologische Grundlage für die Theorie der Musik*, a major contribution to the study of acoustics and music. Ellis later undertook to translate the work into English, using the third German edition of 1870. To this he added more than 150 pages of notes and an extra appendix. (The latter is mostly the contents of lectures Ellis read before the Royal Society in 1864 and 1874.) The translation appeared in 1875 under the title *On the Sensations of Tone as a Physiological Basis for the Theory of Music*. A further edition followed in 1885, based on the revised, fourth German edition of 1877.

Ellis's interest in musical acoustics was not merely academic. With the help of numerous friends and supporters, but especially the piano-tuner and scholar Alfred Hipkins (1826–1903), he made detailed calculations of the pitch of several hundred musical instruments, particularly organs, throughout Great Britain and parts of Europe. Calculations were also made of the pitch ranges of several London choirs, and Ellis interested himself in general questions to do with the tuning of orchestral instruments.

The result of these investigations was a significant paper, entitled 'On the history of musical pitch', published in March 1880. In it Ellis showed that the pitch of concert A has varied by as much as a fifth through time and across different countries, and that different styles of tuning (for example, just, equal) had been, and were still, in use. Ellis himself played but one instrument—the concertina. After his death the Ellis collection of musical instruments was presented by Hipkins to the Royal Institution.

There is no evidence that Ellis was interested in the aesthetics of music; the scientific basis of music was his only concern. This included the concept of pitch and pitches in non-Western cultures, namely Indian, Chinese, and Japanese, and for this he has rightly been described as 'the true founder of comparative scientific musicology'. His *Pronunciation for Singers* (1877) and *Speech in Song* (1877) provide valuable insights from phonetics and acoustics about the appropriate pronunciation of foreign words in cantatas, oratorios, lieder, and opera.

After his undergraduate career at Cambridge, Ellis maintained his interest in mathematics, and between 1843 and 1883 he published a variety of papers and short books on mathematical topics. Some were intended, in the spirit of educational progress which he and Pitman had espoused in the 1840s and 1850s, as popular works. Two examples were his *Self-Proving Examples in the Four First Rules of Arithmetic* (1855), which he had 'especially adapted for self-practice as well as school or family use', and *The Spirit of Mathematical Analysis* (1843), a translation of Martin Ohm's *Der Geist der mathematischen Analyse und ihr Verhältniss zur Schule*. Ellis's most significant work, however, was *Algebra Identified with Geometry* (1874), the result of twenty years' work. His aim was to 'present the arsenal of mathematics with a new arm of precision', for which he had earlier (1863) coined the term 'stigmatics'. Algebra, he argued, should be regarded as a measure of quantity—in short, as a form of analytic geometry. Ellis's ideas were received courteously by fellow mathematicians, though hardly enthusiastically.

Further interest in mathematics is evidenced by Ellis's being asked by the British government's meteorological department to undertake a complex set of barometric computations. A paper he read to the Royal Society in the early 1860s showed how it was possible to simplify Friedrich Wilhelm Hessel's formula for measuring heights from barometric observations. And the world of mathematics was reminded in 1877 and 1878 that in Robert Flower's *The Radix* (1771) there lay a simplified version of John Napier's concept of logarithms. After nearly forty years' active involvement in mathematics, Ellis made the decision, in 1882, to give up work in this area, solely because of the pressures being created by his massive

study of the history and present state of English, *On Early English Pronunciation*.

Ellis was a member of numerous scientific, scholarly, and cultural organizations, reflecting the diversity of his interests; he also held executive positions in some of them. They included the Philological Society, the Early English Text Society, the College of Preceptors, the London Dialectal Society, the Mathematical Society of London, the Association for the Improvement of Geometrical Teaching, the Royal Institution, the Society of Arts, the Tonic Solfa College, and the London Musical Association. He was elected a fellow of the Cambridge Philosophical Society (1837), of the Royal Society (1865), of the Society of Antiquaries (1870), and of the College of Preceptors (1873). He was made a life governor of University College, London, in 1886, and in June 1890, just a few months before his death, he received the honorary degree of LLD from Cambridge University.

Personal characteristics In matters of religion Ellis's views changed. His undergraduate adherence to Anglicanism later gave way to a particular interest in the positivism of Auguste Comte. Several of Ellis's publications testify to this, based on sermons he delivered in 1875 and 1876 at the South Place Chapel in London, on the subjects of salvation, truth, and duty.

By any criterion Ellis was an individualist to the point of idiosyncrasy. According to Alfred Hipkins's daughter, he was in later life a portly man, who wore a greatcoat (except in summer) which he called Dreadnought. It contained twenty-eight pockets, into which he stuffed manuscripts and 'articles for an emergency'. He carried with him a large bag containing a variety of tuning forks, together with two sets of nail scissors—one for each hand—a corkscrew, string, and a knife sharpener. His furled umbrella ('bumbershoot'), monocle (for formal occasions), and shoes 3 inches too large for him ('barges') were further distinguishing characteristics. A strict teetotaller, he allowed himself only a limited intake of food and drink—the latter being 'warm water and a little milk'. He weighed himself daily, with and without clothes. Ellis died of cardiac failure, aged seventy-six, on 28 October 1890 at his home, 21 Auriol Road, West Kensington. He was buried in Kensal Green cemetery, in plot 140. His wife died in July 1888, aged seventy-three.

Despite his outward appearance, Ellis was a thoughtful, sociable, and affable person, and modest about his considerable erudition. He was driven by a genuine love of learning and the desire to put that learning at the service of others, especially the economically less advantaged members of society. His activities and published work, voluminous (about 300 publications) and crossing several disciplines, attracted the attention and approval of scholars in Britain, Europe, and North America.

M. K. C. MacMahon

Sources R. A. Sanders, 'Alexander John Ellis: a study of a Victorian philologist', PhD diss., Memorial University of Newfoundland, St John's, Newfoundland, 1977 • J. Kelly, 'The 1847 alphabet: an episode of phonotypy', *Towards a history of phonetics*, ed. R. E. Asher and E. J. A. Henderson (1981), 248–64 • I. Darreg, 'A kind word or two about Alexander John Ellis on the occasion of the centennial 1885–1985 of the second English edition of his translation of and appendix to Helmholtz's *Sensations of Tone*', *Xenharmonikon*, 9 (1986), 1–8 · R. K. Engen, *Dictionary of Victorian wood engravers* (1985) · A. J. Hipkins, 'Ellis (formerly Sharpe), Alexander John', Grove, *Dict. mus.* (1904–10), 776 · J. Kelly, '"This Great Reform": Mr Pitman & Mr Ellis at Bath', 1978 [paper read to the British Association meeting in Bath, September 1978] · M. K. C. MacMahon, 'Alexander John Ellis', *The encyclopedia of language & linguistics*, ed. R. E. Asher and J. M. Y. Simpson (1994), 1106 · W. P. W. Phillimore and E. A. Fry, eds., *An index to changes of name, 1760–1901* (1905), entry 2165 · D. W. Scully, 'Ellis, Alexander, J.', *Biographical dictionary of the phonetic sciences*, ed. A. J. Bronstein and others (New York, 1977), 53–4 · G. Shorrocks, 'A. J. Ellis as dialectologist: a re-assessment', *Historiographia Linguistica*, 18/2–3 (1991), 321–34 · R. T., *Proceedings of the London Mathematical Society*, 1st ser., 21 (1889–90), 457–61 · W. R. Thomas and J. J. K. Rhodes, 'Ellis [Sharpe], Alexander J(ohn)', *New Grove*, online edn · Venn, *Alum. Cant.* · *WWW* [Alexander John Ellis and Tristram Ellis, son] · P. Wright, 'Alexander J. Ellis, *On early English pronunciation, part V*: key dialect tool or forgotten antique?', *Journal of the Lancashire Dialect Society*, 34 (1985), 3–10 · CGPLA Eng. & Wales (1890) · private information (2004) [secretary, Friends of Kensal Green cemetery]

Archives BL, letters to A. J. Hipkins, etc., Add. MSS 41636–41668 · CUL, letters to Sir George Stokes

Likenesses Naudin & Co., carte-de-visite, 1886, NPG [*see illus.*] · photograph, Bodl. Oxf., Hallam-Ellis papers, d.13, fol. 492 · photograph, BL, Hipkins papers, Add. MS 41638

Wealth at death £5139 4s. 3d.: probate, *CGPLA Eng. & Wales*

Ellis, Alfred Burdon (1852–1894), army officer and writer, the son of Lieutenant-General Sir Samuel Burdon *Ellis KCB (1787–1865) and his wife, Louisa, née Drayson, was born at Bowater House, Woolwich, on 10 January 1852. He was educated at the Royal Naval School, New Cross, London, and entered the army as sub-lieutenant in the 34th foot on 2 November 1872, having married, on 5 June 1871, Emma, the daughter of Philip King, with whom he had four children, though he later seems to have started a second family. He became lieutenant in the 1st West India regiment on 12 November 1873. He went with the regiment to the Second Anglo-Asante War, arriving at the Gold Coast (the coastlands of modern Ghana) in December 1873.

This was the beginning of a long connection with west Africa. During the early part of 1874 Ellis was temporarily employed as civil commandant at Sekondi on the Gold Coast, being recalled to military duty in May 1874. After periods in England on leave, and in the West Indies, he returned to west Africa where his regiment was based in Sierra Leone. In October 1877 he was seconded for service with the Gold Coast constabulary. He was sent to survey the country around Mankesim, the traditional capital of the Fante country. In January 1878 he went to act as district commissioner at Keta, and in October and November of that year he conducted constabulary operations against Anlo, being wounded in the fighting. He claimed the operations did much to check smuggling, and objected bitterly to his removal to Accra in December 1878.

On 2 July 1879 Ellis was promoted captain in the 1st West India regiment and returned to military duty, being sent on special service to South Africa where he was attached to army intelligence during the Anglo-Zulu War. However, his absence from west Africa did not last long. He left

South Africa on 10 October, and towards the close of 1879 visited Ouidah, the seaport of Dahomey, which led him to advocate the annexation of the Slave Coast. In the spring of 1880 he visited Lagos, Bonny, and Old Calabar, returning to Sierra Leone in January 1881 in time to be ordered to the Gold Coast with his regiment when there was a threat of war with the Asante. On 8 February he was sent to garrison Anoumabu with a force of 100 men. However, the threat of war passed, and he left Anoumabu on 20 March, though he remained for some time at Cape Coast in command of the troops.

During the period 1871–82 Ellis made use of various opportunities to visit most of the islands off the western coast of the African continent, including St Helena and Ascension Island as well as those nearer to the British west African colonies.

Ellis was promoted major on 13 February 1884. In 1886–9 he was again in command of the troops on the Gold Coast. In 1889 he went with part of his regiment to the Bahamas and commanded the troops in that colony until his promotion to lieutenant-colonel (4 February 1891). He then returned to west Africa, where he was placed in command of all the troops on the west coast, being based at Freetown, Sierra Leone. On 2 March 1892 he was given the local rank of colonel. In April and May 1892 Ellis proceeded on a punitive expedition to the Tambaka country in the Sierra Leone protectorate, where he captured Tambi. Almost immediately afterwards he was in command of military operations in the Gambia where, consequent upon the Anglo-French convention of 1889, the British authorities were endeavouring to end the Soninke–Marabout wars. At the end of 1893, back in Sierra Leone again, he conducted a major expedition against Sofa soldiers of Samori who had avoided French efforts to defeat them by moving into British territory. On 23 December his force was involved in a brush with French troops at Waima which cost in all the lives of four European officers and fifteen African soldiers. Shortly after this, struck down with fever, Ellis went to Tenerife to recuperate, but he did not recover and died there on 5 March 1894. Ellis had been appointed CB in August 1892, and in a gazette of 17 July 1894 it was announced that, had he lived, he would have been recommended for KCB.

Ellis was an able and ambitious soldier, always keen to promote his own or his regiment's interests. But of some sixteen years spent in west Africa, hardly more than six months were occupied in active service in the interior. Most of his time was spent at Cape Coast, Freetown, and other coastal stations. Here he organized himself to enlarge his own restricted first-hand knowledge by systematically collecting information—from local informants and newspapers and from books—about the African countries he had seen, and the ethnology, history, and languages of their inhabitants. This information was used for the writing of ten books published in London between 1881 and 1894, which also serve as the best historical sources for his life. Despite the continual expression in them of his personal dislikes and prejudices, for thirty or forty years after Ellis's death these were regarded as standard works.

Ellis, although he had married young in England, cannot have seen much of his English family, especially during his last seven years, when he is not known to have made any visits to Britain; he apparently had a second, Fante, wife and family at Cape Coast.

C. A. HARRIS, rev. J. D. FAGE

Sources R. Jenkins, 'Confrontations with A. B. Ellis, a participant in the scramble for Gold Coast Africana, 1874–1894', *Paideuma*, 33 (1987), 313–35 · C. Fyfe, *A history of Sierra Leone* (1962) · *The Times* (8 March 1894) · Colonial Office records · *Army List* · A. B. Ellis, *West African sketches* (1881) · A. B. Ellis, *The land of fetish* (1883) · A. B. Ellis, *The history of the first West India regiment* (1885) · A. B. Ellis, *West African islands* (1885) · A. B. Ellis, *South African sketches* (1887) · A. B. Ellis, *The Tschi-speaking peoples of the Gold Coast* (1887) · A. B. Ellis, *West African stories* (1890) · A. B. Ellis, *The Ewe-speaking peoples of the Slave Coast* (1890) · A. B. Ellis, *A history of the Gold Coast* (1893) · A. B. Ellis, *The Yoruba-speaking peoples of the Slave Coast* (1894)

Ellis, Arthur Ayres (1830–1887), biblical scholar, was the son of Charles Ellis of Birmingham. He was born in Birmingham and educated at King Edward VI's Grammar School, there under James Prince Lee. He matriculated at Trinity College, Cambridge, as a sub-sizar in 1848 and graduated BA, with a first class in the classical tripos, in 1852. He was elected a fellow of Trinity in 1854, and proceeded to the degree of MA in 1855. From 1853 to 1857 he acted as senior classical master at the Liverpool Collegiate Institution. He was ordained a priest and then took the posts of junior dean of Trinity College and, in 1859, divinity lecturer at Christ's College, Cambridge. In 1860 he was presented by Trinity College to the vicarage of Stotfold in Bedfordshire, where he remained for the rest of his life. He died there on 22 March 1887.

While resident in college Ellis worked on Richard Bentley's preparations for an edition of the Greek New Testament. In 1862 he published at Cambridge the volume entitled *Bentleii critica sacra*, which contains a large number of Bentley's notes taken from his manuscripts in Trinity College Library, together with the Abbé Rulotta's collation of the Vatican codex (B), an edition of the epistle to the Galatians, as an example of Bentley's research, and an account of his editorial work.

H. R. LUARD, rev. JOANNA HAWKE

Sources personal knowledge (1888) · Boase, *Mod. Eng. biog.*
Wealth at death £2082 18s.: probate, 18 April 1887, CGPLA Eng. & Wales

Ellis, Arthur Edward (1914–1999), football referee, was born on 8 July 1914 at 6 New Street, Pellon, Halifax, the elder of two sons of William Ellis (1888–1965), picture frame maker, and his wife, Zylpha Binns (1888–1976). He received his only formal education at Christ Church School, Pellon, from the age of six until he left in 1928 to work in a local textile mill. His passion was football and this led, with his father's encouragement, to refereeing. At the age of sixteen he officiated at his first match. He made a rapid rise in junior and amateur football and was placed on the Football League list of referees and linesmen at the age of twenty-two. He remained on it until, as

league rules required, he retired at the age of forty-seven in 1961.

On 7 August 1937 Ellis married Kathleen Robertshaw (1914–1986) of Newstead, Halifax, and they continued to live in the area throughout their married life. They had two sons. During the war Ellis joined the RAF as a physical training instructor, spending most of his time in Yorkshire and continuing to referee in regional football. On returning to civilian life he resumed work as a warehouseman in the textile industry until, in 1952, he was appointed a representative of a local brewery company, Thomas Ramsden, subsequently part of Allied Breweries.

From 1946, when he was chosen as linesman for an international fixture, Ellis rose within a few years to the highest level of refereeing. His first major domestic match was the Football Association (FA) cup semi-final of 1948, and in 1950 he was appointed by the Fédération Internationale de Football Associations (FIFA) as a referee for the world cup finals in Brazil, the first of three such competitions in which he officiated. He was awarded the FA cup final in 1952, but the match for which Ellis was most remembered was that between Hungary and Brazil played at Bern, Switzerland, in the world cup finals of 1954. What should have been an outstanding match between two excellent teams quickly degenerated into an ill-tempered contest described by the British press as 'the battle of Berne'. 'Never in my life', observed the *Times* correspondent, 'have I seen such cruel tackling' (*The Times*, 28 June 1954). In attempting to control players determined to do violence to each other Ellis was forced to dismiss three from the field, a decision that drew criticism from some sections of the foreign press. The fact that the match was completed and that Ellis continued to be offered FIFA matches for the remainder of the decade nevertheless testifies to the confidence that the football authorities had in him, reflected later in FIFA's awarding him its gold badge and certificate in 1967. Indeed, together with a group of his contemporaries which included George Reader, Ken Aston, and Mervyn Griffiths, he brought to refereeing a skill which has rarely been surpassed and made an important contribution to the development of the modern game. The respect in which Ellis was held by both players and spectators resulted from his combining good humour and unequivocal authority. Players knew that it was pointless to argue with Ellis, yet his relations with them were jovial. He knew how to defuse confrontations, and to the delight of spectators he took every opportunity within reason to keep the game flowing.

Ellis's renown, enhanced by two books of reminiscences (*Refereeing Round the World*, 1954, and *The Final Whistle*, 1962) ensured that he remained in the public eye after his refereeing days. He joined the pools panel, a body formed by the football pools promoters in 1963 to predict the results of matches postponed through bad weather, and remained a member until 1995. An invitation from the BBC in 1966 to join its commentary team in the world cup finals led to Ellis taking the role of referee in the BBC's innovative and popular competition *It's a Knockout*, launched in that year. He remained with the programme until it was wound up in 1982, when he also retired from brewery work.

In retirement Arthur Ellis lived in Brighouse, playing golf and bowls and maintaining a close interest in football. His wife, Kathleen, died in 1986, and in his last years he enjoyed the companionship of Vera Culpan. Having enjoyed excellent health throughout his life, he died of prostate cancer at Halifax General Hospital on 23 May 1999, aged eighty-four.   JEFFREY HILL

Sources private information (2004) [Ian Ellis] · A. Ellis, *Refereeing round the world* (1954) · A. Ellis, *The final whistle* (1962) · b. cert. · m. cert. · d. cert. · *The Guardian* (5 June 1999) · *Halifax Courier* (24 May 1999) · *Halifax Evening Courier* (24 May 1999) · *The Independent* (8 June 1999) · *The Times* (28 June 1954) · *The Times* (2 June 1999) · G. Green, *Soccer in the fifties* (1974) · A. H. Fabian and G. Green, eds., *Association football*, 4 (1960)
Archives priv. coll., private papers
Likenesses photograph, 1951, Hult. Arch. · group portraits, photographs, 1966, Hult. Arch. · photograph, repro. in *The Guardian* · photograph, repro. in *The Independent* · photograph, repro. in *The Times* (2 June 1999) · photographs, repro. in Ellis, *Refereeing round the world* · photographs, repro. in Ellis, *Final whistle*, facing p. 85

Ellis, Sir **Arthur William Mickle** (1883–1966), physician and university professor, was born in Toronto, Canada, on 4 May 1883, the eldest son of William Hodgson Ellis, professor of chemistry in the university there, and his wife, Ellen Maude Mickle. Ellis was educated at Upper Canada College and the University of Toronto, where he graduated BA with honours in natural science (1906), MB with honours (1908), and MD. After a short period of clinical training he was appointed resident in pathology at Lakeside Hospital, Cleveland, Ohio, and demonstrator in pathology at Western Reserve University medical school (1909–10). This was followed by an appointment as assistant resident physician at the hospital of the Rockefeller Institute, New York (1911–14). There he made contact with a group of young physicians and pathologists, including Homer Fordyce Swift, Tom Rivers, and many others, who had been drawn to the institute by their interest in medical research. Their friendship and professional contacts provided a valuable link with American medicine and they were responsible for the warm hospitality which Ellis's pupils later enjoyed in many American medical schools. In New York he engaged in serious clinical research and published a number of papers with Swift on the intensive treatment of neurosyphilis (the 'Swift–Ellis' treatment).

At the outbreak of war, Ellis came to England with the Canadian Army Medical Corps in which he rose to the rank of major. In 1915–17 he commanded no. 5 Canadian laboratory with the British expeditionary force in France and then served as assistant adviser in pathology with the Fourth Army. He was four times mentioned in dispatches and was appointed OBE in 1917. During this period he was befriended by Sir William Osler, a fellow Canadian and then regius professor of medicine in Oxford, and it was undoubtedly Osler's influence which led Ellis to take up clinical medicine in England after demobilization. He worked for a time at Guy's Hospital with a grant from the Medical Research Council and in 1920 was appointed assistant director of the newly formed medical unit at the London Hospital. A chair in medicine was established there in 1924 and, after a controversial passage between the medical college and the university, Ellis was appointed as the first professor of medicine at the London Hospital.

During his twenty years' tenure of the chair, Ellis's outstanding contribution was to foster, by his example and by his shrewd selection of colleagues, the growth and influence of full-time university departments of medicine, particularly in the metropolis. The appointment of university professors in charge of full-time clinical units in the London medical schools had been recommended by the Haldane commission in 1913, in order to improve medical teaching and research which hitherto had been carried out by honorary part-time consultants. Ellis was particularly qualified for such a post by his training in pathology and his research work at the Rockefeller Hospital. He was elected MRCP in 1920 and FRCP in 1929. His clinical experience was at first limited and on appointment his main objective was to train himself and his staff to be no less proficient in clinical diagnosis and treatment than his colleagues, many of whom practised with great distinction in Harley Street. In this aim he was eminently successful, so that students and qualified doctors alike were attracted to his unit where daily attendance and teaching in the wards were supplemented by a lively interest in clinical research. Ellis was an indifferent lecturer and had little use for the examination coaching in which some more popular teachers took part. He excelled in instruction at the bedside and in the personal training he gave to the members of his staff. He repeatedly emphasized that errors of diagnosis more frequently arose from faulty observation than from misinterpretation, and he abhorred intellectual dishonesty and authoritarianism in the teaching and practice of medicine. He was a man of great humanity and humility, who believed that the academic physician must be first and foremost a good doctor. His success as a teacher was by example rather than by precept; he had a deep personal regard for his patients who throughout his career held him in great respect and affection.

During the 1920s, largely owing to wartime discoveries and the growth of more critical attitudes, the discipline of clinical science began to make an impact on the traditional practice of medicine, and post-war travelling fellowships to the United States produced a generation of young physicians who returned to question the dogmas and oracular pronouncements of some of their teachers. Ellis developed a remarkable faculty for selecting and attracting people of promise from his own hospital and elsewhere, and of guiding them into careers of great diversity and distinction. Lord Brain, Lord Evans, Sir Robert Aitken, and a large group of professors and specialists had graduated from his unit and were largely responsible for the high reputation which the London Hospital enjoyed as a medical centre. Ellis's research activities, as with most of the clinical professors at this time, were cramped by his administrative and teaching duties and by a shortage of trained staff. Over the years, however, he made a number of contributions in the field of metabolism and endocrinology. Most notable was his correlation of the clinical and pathological features of renal disease, which he summarized in his Croonian lectures of 1941 on the natural history of Bright's disease (*Lancet*, 3, 10, and 17 January 1942). Ellis was strongly influenced by the work of the German nephrologists Volhard and Fahr, whom he visited after the war, and the experimental work of his associates on renal hypertension greatly clarified the relationship between high blood pressure and kidney disease.

At the outbreak of war in 1939 Ellis became an adviser in medicine to the Ministry of Health, and later he was director of research in industrial medicine under the Medical Research Council. In 1943 he was appointed regius professor of medicine in Oxford and he held this post until he reached the age of retirement in 1948. The post-war years brought difficult problems in medical organization, particularly in Oxford where there was a sharp controversy over the formation of an undergraduate clinical school. Ellis had little skill as a committee chairman and his health began to suffer. Nevertheless he carried on his clinical work and teaching with great patience and enthusiasm, and enhanced his reputation for professional integrity and for unstinting helpfulness to patients and pupils alike. He was awarded the Moxon medal of the Royal College of Physicians in 1951 for his distinguished contributions to the knowledge of diseases of the kidney, and he was knighted in 1953.

On 25 September 1922 Ellis had married Winifred Hadley Rose, *née* Mitchell (1887/8–1965), a widow, daughter of William Foot Mitchell, member of parliament for Saffron Walden, and his wife, Elizabeth Hannah, *née* Hadley. Their marriage brought him a rich family life—they had a son (Timothy) and two stepdaughters—and friendships within a wide social circle far outside the field of medicine. Two activities he particularly enjoyed were duck shooting in Essex and salmon fishing in Iceland. This social background, together with his own not inconsiderable wealth and Canadian forthrightness, made him an excellent host to his friends, pupils, and colleagues, and the annual parties after the Oxford and Cambridge boat race, at his London home, Bedford House, Chiswick Mall, were a major social event. On retirement from Oxford he returned to his house in Chiswick Mall, which had been the scene of so many happy occasions in the past, but his last years were clouded by his wife's prolonged and serious illness until her death in 1965. He died in London on 20 May 1966.   CLIFFORD WILSON, rev.

Sources The Lancet (4 June 1966) · BMJ (4 June 1966), 1426–7 · personal knowledge (1981) · m. cert.

Wealth at death £295,446: probate, 3 Nov 1966, CGPLA Eng. & Wales

Ellis, Sir Barrow Helbert (1823–1887), East India Company servant, was born in London on 24 January 1823, the son of S. Helbert Ellis, treasurer of the Great Synagogue, Duke's Place, London, and his wife, Fanny, daughter of

Samuel Lyons de Symons. The family name was originally Israel; as a young man his father had taken the name of Ellis.

Ellis was educated at University College School, London, and matriculated in 1839 at University College, London. In 1841 he entered the East India Company's college at Haileybury, graduating two years later as the college's senior student, with numerous prizes in law, classics, Persian, and Hindustani to his credit. In July 1843 he was appointed to the Bombay civil service. At Haileybury he had been excused from attending Sunday service, and upon his graduation London's *Voice of Jacob* triumphantly wrote up his achievements as proof that a Jewish boy could retain his religious integrity while courting employment in the protestant establishment.

Ellis arrived in Bombay in December 1843 and was posted to Ratnagiri as third assistant collector. In 1848 he was appointed to investigate certain claims against the government of Hyderabad and in 1851 was made deputy commissioner of Sind. In Sind, Ellis was able to indulge fully his linguistic talents and interest in Indian education. In 1852 he chaired a committee charged by the court of directors with devising a script for the Sindhi language and subsequently supervised the preparation of the first educational texts in the new script. In 1855 he edited George Stack's *Dictionary of Sindhi and English* and in 1856 published a report on education in Sind.

In 1855, in Sir Bartle Frere's absence on furlough, Ellis was appointed officiating chief commissioner of Sind. From 1857 to 1859 he variously filled the offices of revenue commissioner for the southern division of the Bombay presidency, special commissioner for *jagirs* (alienated lands) in Sind, secretary to the government of Bombay in the revenue, finance, and general departments, and, briefly, collector and magistrate of Broach. In April 1860 he was appointed chief secretary to the government of Bombay. In 1862 he was made an additional member, and in 1865 an ordinary member, of the Bombay legislative council.

Ellis's term on the Bombay council expired in 1870, whereupon he was promoted to the executive council. He had been a popular and accessible figure in Bombay and upon his departure for Calcutta more than Rs7000 were collected in public subscriptions and an annual scholarship established in his name at Bombay University for the best BA candidate in English literature. In 1875 he retired from the executive council and returned to London, where he was made a KCSI and appointed to the Council of India. He retired finally from public office in 1885.

In London, Ellis was vice-president of the Anglo-Jewish Association, chairman and vice-president of the Council of Jews' College, president of the Jews' Deaf and Dumb Home, and first warden of the New West End Synagogue in St Petersburg Place. Ironically, he was not always the most active of community members because, as the *Jewish Chronicle* noted ruefully, he had acquired 'an almost insurmountable objection to Sunday meetings' (24 June 1887, 8). He was also a member of the Royal Asiatic Society and served on its council from 1878 until his death.

Ellis died, on 20 June 1887, at Evian-les-Bains, Savoy, Switzerland, and was buried in the Jewish cemetery at Willesden. Unmarried, he was renowned for his hospitality and support of charitable causes. On his death he left £2500 in trust for the benefit of the poor of Ratnagiri, the first posting of his career.   KATHERINE PRIOR

Sources *Jewish Chronicle* (24 June 1887) · *Jewish Chronicle* (1 July 1887) · *The Times* (24 June 1887) · *Journal of the Royal Asiatic Society of Great Britain and Ireland*, new ser., 19 (1887), 688–90 · S. Z. Lari, *A history of Sindh* (1994) · *DNB* · T. Orme, *University College School, London, alphabetical and chronological register for 1831–1891* (1892)
Archives Bodl. Oxf., corresp. with Lord Kimberley | BL OIOC, Salisbury MSS · Bodl. Oxf., corresp. with Lord Kimberley · CUL, corresp. with Lord Mayo
Likenesses photograph, BL OIOC · portrait, Jews' College, London
Wealth at death £53,658 14s.: resworn probate, Feb 1888, *CGPLA Eng. & Wales* (1887)

Ellis, Charles Augustus, sixth Baron Howard de Walden and second Baron Seaford (1799–1868), diplomatist, elder son of Charles Rose *Ellis MP, and his wife, Elizabeth Catherine Hervey, only daughter of John Augustus, eldest son of Frederick Augustus Hervey, earl of Bristol and bishop of Derry, was born in London on 5 June 1799. On 8 July 1803 he succeeded his great-grandfather, the bishop of Derry, as Baron Howard de Walden. His right to the title, which involved a complex pedigree, was confirmed, after petition, in February 1807 (see his entry in GEC).

Lord Howard de Walden was educated at Eton College, and on 4 April 1817 he entered the army as an ensign and lieutenant in the Grenadier Guards. During the reductions in the size of the army after 1815, on 25 December 1818 he was placed on half pay. He again entered the Grenadier Guards on 6 January 1820, but on 3 October 1822 he was promoted captain in the 8th regiment and once more placed on half pay. In 1820 he took his seat in the House of Lords, and was, like his father, a follower of Canning. In July 1824 Canning appointed him under-secretary of state for foreign affairs, and in January 1826 sent him as attaché to Lord Stuart de Rothesay in his famous special mission to Rio de Janeiro. After his return from Brazil, Howard de Walden married, on 8 November 1828, Lady Lucy Joan Cavendish-Scott-Bentinck (d. 29 July 1899), fourth daughter of William Henry Cavendish-Scott-Bentinck, fourth duke of Portland.

On 2 October 1832 Howard de Walden was appointed minister-plenipotentiary and envoy-extraordinary to the court of Stockholm, and on 22 November 1833 he was transferred in the same capacity to Lisbon. During the thirteen years in which he held this appointment he made his reputation as a diplomatist. He took up his duties while the civil war between the Miguelites and the Pedroites was still raging, and he remained to see more than one *pronunciamiento* in the streets of Lisbon and Oporto. Howard de Walden, in Sir Charles Webster's view, 'did well enough', though 'he sometimes found the strain of dealing with the corrupt and emotional Portuguese politicians more than he could bear' (Webster, 69, 479). Portugal twice asked for his recall, but Palmerston stood by him, though refusing to commit British troops as he

requested. Howard de Walden assisted in negotiating the treaties ending the Portuguese slave trade. He was made GCB on 22 July 1838 and received the highest Portuguese order, the Tower and the Sword, in 1841. In 1845 he succeeded his father as second Baron Seaford and on 10 December 1846 he was appointed minister-plenipotentiary at Brussels, which post he held until his death, enjoying the friendship of both Leopold I and Leopold II of Belgium. He died on 29 August 1868 at his country château of Lesve, near Namur, leaving a family of six sons and two daughters.

H. M. STEPHENS, *rev.* H. C. G. MATTHEW

Sources *FO List* (1868) · *The Times* (12 Sept 1868) · *ILN* (12 Sept 1868) · C. K. Webster, *The foreign policy of Palmerston, 1830–1841*, 2 vols. (1951) · GEC, *Peerage*
Archives PRO, corresp. and MSS, FO 360 | BL, corresp. with Lord Aberdeen, Add. MSS 43148–43150, 43173–43174 · BL, corresp. with Sir William A'Court, Add. MSS 41547–41556 · BL, corresp. with William Huskisson, Add. MSS 38749–38753 · BL, letters to Sir Austen Layard, Add. MSS 38989–39120 · Bodl. Oxf., letters to Lord Kimberley · NMM, corresp. with Sir William Parker · Norfolk RO, letters to Sir Henry Bulwer · PRO, corresp. with Stratford Canning, FO 352 · PRO, corresp. with earls Granville, 030/29 · PRO, Russell MSS · U. Southampton L., corresp. with Lord Palmerston · U. Southampton L., letters to first duke of Wellington · W. Sussex RO, letters to duke of Richmond · W. Yorks. AS, Leeds, corresp. with Lord Canning
Wealth at death under £2000: probate, 16 Jan 1869, *CGPLA Eng. & Wales*

Ellis, Sir Charles Drummond (1895–1980), physicist and scientific administrator, was born on 11 August 1895 in Hampstead, London, the son of Abraham Charles Ellis, a general manager of the Metropolitan Railway, London, and his wife, Isabelle Flockart Carswell. From Peterborough Lodge Preparatory School in Hampstead he won a scholarship to Harrow School, where from 1909 to 1913 he enjoyed considerable intellectual and sporting success. In 1913 he passed third in order of merit into the Royal Military Academy, Woolwich, as a cadet in preparation for his chosen career in the Royal Engineers. A model student, he passed out first of his class in 1914.

Holidaying in Germany that summer Ellis was trapped by a sudden internment order on the outbreak of war and detained at Ruhleben camp, near Spandau. Among the other prisoners at Ruhleben was James Chadwick, a Manchester physicist who had been working with Hans Geiger in Berlin. Chadwick fostered Ellis's interest in physics and they undertook some scientific work together, including a study of photochemical processes. Another significant meeting for Ellis was with Paula Warzcewska, a librarian in the nearby town and daughter of Paul Warzcewska (Dantziger), a Polish shipbuilder. Her marriage to H. S. Hatfield, an inventor-physicist also interned at Ruhleben, subsequently brought her to England as a British citizen. On dissolution of that marriage she married Ellis in 1925 and, as the colourful and unconventional Polly Ellis, she lived happily with him until her sudden death in 1966. There were no children, although a daughter from her first marriage was adopted.

On his release from internment, enthused for physics

and recognizing that a military career would now be difficult, in 1919 Ellis entered Trinity College, Cambridge, to study natural sciences. He graduated with a first in physics in 1920 and was awarded a college scholarship allowing him to undertake research work at the Cavendish Laboratory. Sir Ernest Rutherford had become director of the Cavendish in 1919, and had brought Chadwick (also recently released from Ruhleben) with him from Manchester. Rutherford and Chadwick established a programme of radioactivity research at the Cavendish; while they concentrated principally on alpha radioactivity and alpha particles for nuclear disintegration experiments they set Ellis to work in the complementary but more complex field of beta and gamma radiation. In 1921 Ellis published a paper in the *Proceedings of the Royal Society* on the 'Magnetic spectrum of the β-rays excited by γ-rays', the first of many publications over the next fifteen years in the field in which he rapidly became a leading authority. In the same year he was elected to a fellowship at Trinity and was appointed assistant lecturer in natural science, laying the foundation of his academic career.

Over the following years, in addition to his teaching at Trinity and the Cavendish, Ellis made important contributions to research on the energetics and mechanism of beta and gamma ray emission from nuclei. A skilled and versatile experimentalist, he also contributed to the development of technique, including improvements to the photographic method of measuring the energies and intensities of groups of subatomic particles. In this work he supervised a number of Cavendish research students with whom he co-authored numerous papers, among them H. W. B. Skinner, W. A. Wooster, and G. H. Aston. While his work formed an integral part of the research programme of the Cavendish, however, for much of this period Ellis was in dispute with Lise Meitner of the Kaiser Wilhelm Institute for Chemistry, Berlin, over the nature and interpretation of the beta ray spectrum. Out of this controversy emerged a new understanding of nuclear structure. Ellis's experiments in 1926–7, a technical tour de force, helped to establish the existence of energy levels in the nucleus and the main features of the energy level distribution for both natural and artificial radioactive nuclei. He was elected a fellow of the Royal Society in 1929. The following year he co-authored with Rutherford and Chadwick the classic monograph *Radiations from Radioactive Substances* (1930).

In the early 1930s Ellis and N. F. Mott developed the earlier work on the energetics of nuclear processes to explore the energy relations in beta decay in the light of the new wave mechanics. This work was important in developing Pauli's theory of the neutrino. Indeed, Mott considered later that Ellis had 'practically discovered the neutrino' (Hutchinson, Gray, and Massey, 204). In 1934, with W. J. Henderson, Ellis turned his attention to the energy distribution of positrons in artificial radioactivity, which had just been discovered by the Joliot-Curies. In 1936, a year after Chadwick's departure from the Cavendish for a professorship at Liverpool, Ellis accepted the Wheatstone chair of physics at King's College, London, and continued

his nuclear research while also faced with increased demands of teaching and administration. Before he could extend his existing research and establish new lines of investigation, however, mobilization for war diverted scientific effort elsewhere. When, in 1939, the physics department at King's was moved to Bristol, he was granted leave of absence for war work.

In 1940, as a leading member of Britain's nuclear establishment, Ellis became a member of MAUD, the committee charged by the government with evaluating the feasibility of using nuclear fission to develop new weapons. Convinced of such a possibility Ellis lobbied for the expansion and acceleration of the nuclear weapon programme. After a period in charge of work on proximity fuses at the Air Defence Research and Development Establishment, Christchurch, he was scientific adviser to the army council from 1943 to 1946. He used this position to bring together a group of outstanding colleagues who contributed to the solution of a wide variety of operational research problems. Chairman of the joint technical warfare committee and a member of the Ministry of Supply's Advisory Council on Scientific Research and Technical Development and various other high-level wartime committees, he was knighted in 1946 for his war service.

In 1945 Ellis was appointed a director of the Finance Corporation for Industry. When the National Coal Board (NCB) was established the following year, Ellis, with his wartime experience of managing applied science and operational research, was a natural choice as the member responsible for the scientific service within the industry. For nine years until its reorganization in 1955 he was responsible for initiating many valuable activities in its research and development, and encouraged liaison with university research groups. He was president of the British Coal Utilization Research Association from 1946 to 1955, and a member of the advisory council to the minister of fuel and power from 1947 to 1955. In the wake of political criticism of the NCB in the early 1950s it was reconstituted in 1955. In order to facilitate this reorganization its board members offered their resignations. To his surprise and bitter disappointment Ellis was not reappointed. Instead, he accepted posts as scientific adviser to the British American Tobacco Company (BAT) and as part-time scientific adviser to the Gas Council, in addition to a number of other advisory positions he already held.

At BAT, Ellis oversaw a reorganization and expansion of research activity at the time when a statistical association between smoking and various diseases was being put forward. Ellis initiated fundamental research into the physical, physiological, and psychological processes involved in smoking and encouraged dialogue between the industry and the medical profession. At the Gas Council he oversaw the rationalization of research at a time of revolutionary technical change in the gas industry, strongly advocating a long-term strategy. In both posts Ellis's insistence on high standards in research made significant contributions to technical and industrial development and earned him the respect and admiration of those who worked under him. He retired from the Gas Council in 1966, and, faced with increasing ill health, from BAT in 1972.

A regular swimmer and golfer until his later years, Ellis continued to take an interest in research activities at BAT as long as he was physically able. He died in a nursing home, Glenore, Berries Road, Cookham, on 10 January 1980 after a short illness.   JEFFREY A. HUGHES

Sources R. W. Clark, *Tizard* (1965) · G. Hartcup and T. E. Allibone, *Cockcroft and the atom* (1984) · K. Hutchinson, J. A. Gray, and H. Massey, *Memoirs FRS*, 27 (1981), 199–233 · C. Jensen, 'A history of the beta spectrum and its interpretation', PhD diss., University of Copenhagen, 1990 · A. R. Mackintosh, 'The third man: Charles Drummond Ellis', *Notes and Records of the Royal Society*, 49 (1995), 277–93 · CAC Cam., Meitner MSS · S. Zuckerman, *From apes to warlords* (1978) · d. cert.
Archives Bohr Institute, Copenhagen, N. Bohr MSS · CAC Cam., L. Meitner MSS · U. Texas, O. W. Richardson MSS
Likenesses photograph, 1920–29, Trinity Cam. · photograph, RS; repro. in Hutchinson, Gray, and Massey, *Memoirs FRS*
Wealth at death £120,257: probate, 21 March 1980, *CGPLA Eng. & Wales*

Ellis, Charles Rose, **first Baron Seaford** (1771–1845), politician, was the second son of John Ellis, of an old Jamaican family, and his wife, Elizabeth, daughter of John Pallmer, also of Jamaica. He was born on 19 December 1771, and, having inherited a large West Indian property worth £20,000 p.a. on his father's death (at sea) in 1782, was educated at Christ Church, Oxford, for a year from 1789 but took no degree. He was there a favourite of Dean Jackson and the friend of C. J. Canning. He entered the House of Commons in March 1793, when barely of age, as MP for Heytesbury, paying £3500 to W. P. A'Court for the seat (HoP, *Commons*). He was not a brilliant speaker, being content to support Pitt unobtrusively and without expectation of office. In 1796 he bought both the Wareham and the Seaford constituencies, but chose to sit for the latter. On 2 August 1798 Ellis married Elizabeth Catherine Caroline Clifton, only daughter and heir of John, Lord Hervey. About the same period he purchased the estate of Claremont in Surrey, where he entertained lavishly, and he was re-elected for Seaford in 1802. His wife died of consumption at Nice on 21 January 1803, and on 8 July of that year his infant son, Charles Augustus *Ellis, succeeded his maternal great-grandfather, Frederick Hervey, earl of Bristol and bishop of Derry, in the ancient barony of Howard de Walden.

Ellis, absent in Jamaica in 1805, lost his seat in 1806, but was elected for East Grinstead in 1807. He was re-elected for Seaford in 1812, which he represented until he gained his peerage in 1826. In the Commons he was a leader and co-ordinator of the 'friends of Canning'. He supported moral improvement of West Indian slaves, and certain other reforms, but he was never an abolitionist. He came to be regarded as 'perpetual chairman of the West Indian body' in the Commons (HoP, *Commons*). He sold Claremont in 1815 and purchased Woodend, near Chichester. In 1826 his close friend Canning (Ellis was his second in his duel with Castlereagh) was allowed to nominate a friend for a peerage, and he nominated Ellis, to the surprise of everyone, according to Greville. Ellis was consequently created

Lord Seaford on 16 July 1826. On 2 October 1840 he married Anne Louisa Emily, widow of Vice-Admiral Sir Thomas Masterman and daughter of Sir George Berkeley and his wife, Emily Charlotte Lennox. She died aged eighty-nine in 1877. Seaford died on 1 July 1845 at Woodend, and was succeeded by his elder son, C. A. Ellis, sixth Baron Howard de Walden.   H. M. STEPHENS, *rev.* H. C. G. MATTHEW

Sources HoP, *Commons* · GEC, *Peerage* · *GM*, 2nd ser., 24 (1845) · J. Bagot, ed., *George Canning and his friends*, 2 vols. (1909) · W. Hine, *George Canning* (1973)
Archives BL, corresp. with Lord Holland and Lady Holland, Add. MS 51818 · BL, corresp. with William Huskisson, Add. MSS 38573, 38739–38744, 38749, 38752, 38754–38755 · BL, corresp. with Lord Liverpool, Add. MSS 38241, 38246, 38248, 38252, 38292, 38296–38297, 38301 · Derbys. RO, letters to Sir R. J. Wilmot-Horton · PRO, letters to Lord Granville, 030/29
Likenesses T. Lawrence, oils, *c.*1829, Ickworth House, Park and Garden, Suffolk
Wealth at death under £20,000: GEC, *Peerage*

Ellis, Clement (1633–1700), Church of England clergyman, was born in the episcopal palace of Rose Castle, Carlisle, Cumberland, where his father, Philip, was steward to Bishop Barnaby Potter, who acted as godfather to Clement. In the anonymous biography prefixed to his *Three Discourses* (published posthumously by his son Thomas in Sheffield in 1704) Ellis is said to have been born in 1633. At the start of the civil war Philip Ellis held Rose Castle for the king, for which he was imprisoned and his estate sequestered by the parliamentarian authorities. In 1650 Clement matriculated as servitor at his godfather's and his father's old college, Queen's, Oxford; to help him complete his studies he received secret support, possibly from Jeremy Taylor and Henry Hammond, who had been entrusted with funds to help distressed loyalists, or possibly through the kindness of two fellows of the college, Thomas Barlow and Thomas Tully. Ellis became a tabardar, graduated BA on 2 February 1654, and proceeded MA on 9 July 1656; six months later, in December 1656, he was secretly ordained by Robert Skinner, the ejected bishop of Oxford, at his retreat at Launton. In 1657 Ellis was elected a fellow of Queen's, and until the Restoration he preached regularly in Oxford and Abingdon.

In 1660 Ellis published (in London) *To the king's most excellent majesty: on his happie and miraculous return to the government of his three (now) flourishing kingdoms*, verses which proved (in his own words) that he was 'much a better subject than a poet' (p. 6). In 1661 he was appointed domestic chaplain to William Cavendish, marquess (later duke) of Newcastle, who presented him to the rectory of Kirkby in Ashfield, a large parish in Nottinghamshire that Ellis served until his death, in 1700. By 1665 he had married Elizabeth, the daughter of a Yorkshire knight, Sir Thomas Remington. They raised five children—four sons and one daughter, baptized between February 1666 and March 1675—for whom Ellis compiled a Latin grammar, *Magnum in parvo: the English Guide to the Latin Tongue* (published in 1675). His wife died in July 1691. In 1693 Ellis, held 'in great repute for his religion and learning' (Wood, *Ath. Oxon.*, 4.516), was given a prebend at Southwell by Archbishop John Sharp but remained the conscientious, courteous, hard-working, abstemious parish priest that he had always been. He died on 28 June 1700. There is a fine portrait of him 'aged 68', in wig and clerical garb, prefixed to *Three Discourses*.

Over two dozen works by Ellis were published, mostly during his lifetime. Some of the early ones reflect his education and background, others the challenges thrown up by his ministry. As a corpus they demonstrate his willingness to embrace a variety of genres and to target different readerships through print. There was the florid epitaph to a former fellow of Queen's, published with other verses in *Memoriae sacrum Lancelot Dawes* ([1654]). There was the loyalism evident in his congratulatory verse of 1660; in his *Sermon* [on Psalm 118: 22–4] *preached on the 29th of May 1661. The day of his majestie's birth, and happy restauration* (2 editions in Oxford, 1661) delivered in his patron's household at Welbeck; and (to the post-1688 regime) in *Religion* [*and*] *Loyalty Inseperable* (1691), an assize sermon (on Proverbs 24: 21) given at Nottingham in September 1690. There was also his concern that the educated élite should live truly Christian lives, as in *Piae juventuti sacrum* (1658), an elegy on the pious example set by 'the most vertuous and hopefull young Gentleman, George Pitt esquire', who had died recently (title-page); in *The Gentile Sinner* (1660), in which Ellis used the form of an open letter to complain that too few gentlemen were sincere Christians—a little work dashed off in a fortnight but which passed through several editions during his lifetime; and in *The Vanity of Scoffing* (1674), another open letter, trying to persuade 'a witty gentleman' descended from 'noble and Christian parents' to stop scoffing at Christian doctrine (title-page, and p. 1).

Ellis occasionally attacked protestant nonconformists, as in some sections of *The Right Foundation of Quietness, Obedience, and Concord* (1674), which was republished in 1704 as *Study to be Quiet*. In 1687–8 he became briefly embroiled in anti-Catholic polemic when he joined the debate between Edward Stillingfleet, dean of St Paul's, on the protestant side and Peter Gooden and John Sergeant on the Catholic on the infallibility claimed by the church of Rome. Posing as an informed layman Ellis published anonymously *A letter to a friend, reflecting on some passages in 'A letter'* (by John Sergeant) *to the d[ean] of P[aul's]* [Stillingfleet] (1687) and then defended himself against Sergeant's reply in *The Reflecter's Defence of his Letter to a Friend* (1688), which covered much the same ground in the form of four dialogues. Ellis's tone was more conciliatory, though his stance was firm, in a work licensed shortly afterwards: *The protestant resolved, or, A discourse shewing the unreasonableness of his turning Roman Catholick for salvation* (1688). This was sufficiently respected to be reprinted in the first volume of the collection of anti-Catholic pamphlets issued by Bishop Gibson in 1738 as *A Preservative Against Popery* at a time of renewed fear of Catholicism.

But the great majority of Ellis's writings from the 1670s were 'practical tracts' that reflected his efforts as a pastor. The biographical account of 1704, embellished by John Veneer in 1738, described Ellis's extraordinary labour in preaching, catechizing, holding monthly communions, visiting the sick, charitable works, teaching local gentlemen's sons, and encouraging young divines. He was said to have found his Nottinghamshire parish in miserable disorder, with a number of former parliamentarian soldiers infected with antinomian principles and hostile to both crown and church, but by his prudent and timely interventions and gentle manner he apparently soon reconciled nearly all of his parishioners to the established church.

Ellis was still not satisfied that his parishioners fully understood and practised their Christian faith, and bombarded them with advice and information, by word of mouth and in print. He composed three different catechetical works, all with strong scriptural content: *A catechism wherein the learner is at once taught to rehearse and prove all the main points of the Christian religion* (2 editions, 1674, 1679); *The Lambs of Christ Fed with the Sincere Milk of the Word* (1692 and 1700); and *The Scripture Catechist*, written in the year that he died and published posthumously by John Veneer in 1738. Between 1682 and 1699 four official editions of *Christianity in Short, or, The Way to be a Good Christian* were published in London and Nottingham for those of his neighbours who lacked the 'time or capacity to read longer and learneder discourses'; it was also published in New England in 1723 (though by then it had also been 'pirated and vilely printed on tobacco paper ... "for the benefit of the poor"' by Henry Hills in London *c.*1701) (Granger, 3.299–300). In 1685 Ellis published *The Communicant's Guide*, to help the 'poorer and weaker sort of Christians' among his flock prepare for worthy reception of the sacrament; in 1686 *Rest for the Heavy-Laden* (reprinted in 1756); in 1691 *The Necessity of Serious Consideration, and Speedy Repentance*; and in 1692 *The Folly of Atheism*, aimed at 'the most unlearned reader'. In 1694 he issued *The Christian Hearer's First Lesson*, a lecture on what it took to be a good minister and how the laity should support him, and in 1696 he produced the first of the editions of *The Summe of Christianity*, a handbook that combined instruction, prayers, and a form of engagement to keep one's baptismal covenant. Described in 1704 and 1738 as 'one of the best of its kind' this work, together with *The Lambs of Christ*, was 'distributed in great numbers among the poorer sort of people in his own and other counties' (Ellis, *Three Discourses*, sig. A6r; *Scripture Catechist*, p. xxxvii). Posthumous publications included not only the *Three Discourses* (reprinted in London in 1705) and *The Scripture Catechist*, noted above, but also *The Self-Deceiver Plainly Discover'd*, in a 'conference' between a minister and a parishioner (1731), and *The Duty of Parents and Masters of Families* (to educate their children and servants properly, 1734).   IAN GREEN

Sources C. Ellis, *Three discourses* (1704); repr. (1705) · C. Ellis, *The self-deceiver plainly discover'd* (1731) · C. Ellis, *The duty of parents and masters of families* (1734) · C. Ellis, *The scripture catechist* (1738) · *CSP dom.*, 1656–7, 23, 51, 242; 1657–8, 201, 216; 1660–61, 502; 1661–2, 362, 621 · Foster, *Alum. Oxon.* · Wood, *Ath. Oxon.*, new edn, 4.516–17 · C. Wordsworth, *Ecclesiastical biography*, 4th edn, 4 vols. (1853), vol. 4, p. 358n. · *ESTC* · J. Granger, *A biographical history of England, from Egbert the Great to the revolution*, 2nd edn, 4 vols. (1775), vol. 3, pp. 299–300 · *DNB* · *IGI*

Likenesses line engraving, BM, NPG; repro. in Ellis, *Three discourses*

Ellis, Clifford Wilson (1907–1985), designer and art teacher, and promoter of education through art, was born on 1 March 1907, at Bognor, the eldest in the family of two sons and two daughters of John Wilson Ellis, a designer who was trained in cabinet-making, and his wife, Annie Harriet Westley. His grandfather, William Blackman Ellis, artist, naturalist, and taxidermist, who took him as a child for walks in Arundel Park, taught him much about the flora and fauna of the area, and this background of a love of nature and of skill in craftsmanship doubtless sowed the seed in him of a passion to perfect such love and skills in himself and, through teaching, to develop them in others. At a slightly later stage when the family moved to Highbury he fostered his knowledge of natural history by keeping stick insects, lizards, toads, and frogs in his bedroom and by frequent sketching visits to the London Zoo.

Ellis was educated first in small rural schools, and from 1918 to 1923 at Dame Alice Owen's Boys' School, Islington, to which he gained the scholarship. He then won a place at the Regent Street Polytechnic School of Art, qualified, and through the University of London took the Board of Education's art teachers' diploma, studying under Marion Richardson. He was invited to join the polytechnic staff in 1928 and became head of department for teaching first-year students.

In 1931 he married (Dorothy) Rosemary Collinson, herself an artist, daughter of the designer Frank Graham Collinson, who shared his work and ideals throughout his life. They had two daughters. Their joint signature, C and RE, on book jackets, posters, and other designs indicated work of a highly original and imaginative order based on a close knowledge of form and structure. The series of jackets for Collins's *The New Naturalist* was begun in 1943. Over ninety were produced. In the 1930s they collaborated in poster designs for London Transport (in 1938 London buses carried their 'Summer is flying' poster), the Empire Marketing Board, the General Post Office, and Shell-Mex ('Antiquaries prefer Shell' was one of the most admired in the Shell Professions series which Ellis initiated), and they designed a mosaic floor for the entrance to the British pavilion at the Paris Exhibition of 1937. In 1947 they were among the group of distinguished artists invited by J. Lyons & Co. to cheer up the post-war public with lithographs for the Corner Houses.

In 1936 Ellis was appointed assistant master at the Bath School of Art; he became headmaster in 1938. At this time the school was attached to the technical college but after the bombing of the city in 1942 when the rooms of the art school were destroyed it moved to new premises in Sydney Place. This was the beginning of what proved to be a long-term and almost visionary scheme which culminated in 1946 in a change of status from school to academy (teachers' training college as well as art school) and the removal from Sydney Place to Corsham Court, the home of Lord Methuen RA, some 8 miles away in Wiltshire. In this year Ellis was offered, but refused, the chair of fine art in the University of Durham.

Ellis was a man of great enthusiasm, determination, and vigour, and he conveyed a sense of urgency, importance, and delight to all who worked with him. Early on in the Bath days he attracted the friendship of Walter Sickert, who came voluntarily once a week to talk to the students. Similarly he found a firm ally in Lord Methuen who was glad to see a large part of his house and grounds used by the academy, and put the fine Capability Brown picture gallery and the collection at its disposal. Among the staff were Isabelle Symons, Kenneth Armitage, and William Scott who moved out from Bath and, later, Peter Potworowski and Peter Lanyon. Sir Kenneth Clark and John Piper were on the board of governors as co-opted members, the overall responsibility remaining with the city of Bath education authority. Corsham was a great experiment and was unique. Students were taught to understand the making of everything from the elaborate plaster-work ceilings and the finely chased door locks in the state rooms at the court to the glazing bars of terraced houses in Bath, from the culture of orchids to drawing from wild nature, from music and dance on the lawns to music and dance in painting and sculpture, from history to art history. The production of an idiosyncratic but enchanting adaptation of Gluck's *Orfeo ed Euridice* was memorable. All this was due to the inspiration of Ellis and his conviction that the arts are the staple of the fulfilled life. His approach to all these matters was essentially realist. Ellis retired from the Bath academy in 1972.

Ellis's activities were ceaseless and multifarious. He saved fine railings in Bath from being sent for scrap metal. He advised the authorities on camouflage and devised apparatus for the visual training of tank commanders and gunners. He served on advisory committees of the Arts Council and UNESCO, and formed a link between Corsham and the new University of Bath by establishing a research centre in art and education. Ellis died at Urchfont, Wiltshire, on 19 March 1985.

KENNETH GARLICK, *rev.*

Sources *The Times* (19 March 1985) · C. Ellis, 'Preparing art educators', *Education and art* [Paris, 1953], ed. E. Ziegfeld [1953] · private information (1996) · personal knowledge (1996) · D. Pope, ed., *A celebration of Bath Academy of Art at Corsham* (1997) · CGPLA Eng. & Wales (1985)
Likenesses photograph, 1966, repro. in Pope, ed., *Celebration of Bath Academy*
Wealth at death £32,226: probate, 24 June 1985, CGPLA Eng. & Wales

Ellis, Sir (Bertram) Clough Williams- (1883–1978), architect, was born in his father's rectory at Gayton, Northamptonshire, on 28 May 1883, the fourth of the six sons (there were no daughters) of the Revd John Clough Williams-Ellis (1833–1913), formerly fellow and tutor of Sidney Sussex College, Cambridge, and his wife, Ellen Mabel (May), daughter of John Whitehead Greves JP and DL, of Bericote House, Warwickshire. On his father's side he descended from the Ellises of Glasfryn, Caernarvonshire, and from the Williamses of Plas Brondanw in Merioneth, while his

Sir (Bertram) Clough Williams-Ellis (1883–1978), by John Hedgecoe, 1969

mother's family owned slate quarries at Blaenau Ffestiniog. In 1887, when he was four, his father gave up his Cambridge University living to move back to Glasfryn on its bleak and boggy plateau in the Llŷn peninsula. Here Clough learned to build and sail small boats and with his mother's help to draw and dream (for lack of the reality) of architecture. A 'born' architect, it surprised him that his playful baroque taste should have emerged from this austere environment.

Williams-Ellis was sent to Oundle School, where the headmaster was F. W. Sanderson, whose 'modern' outlook his father admired. Inevitably, he went up to Cambridge to read science at Trinity College, which he had selected himself because of its Great Court and blue gowns. Determined to be an architect, he soon abandoned Cambridge and science; to support himself in London, he took a job in electrical engineering. From this too he soon escaped, looking up 'architecture' in the telephone directory, and enrolling as a student at the Architectural Association (AA). In the intervening vacation he worked as an assistant to a country builder and got his first commission (through 'family jobbery') for a fee of £10. On the strength of this, he left the AA within three months and set up a practice, which his family connections and his appetite for dining and dancing rapidly expanded. His most important pre-war building was the romantic Tudoresque Llangoed Castle on the upper Wye (designed in 1912 and completed

in 1915), but to him the most exciting event was the handing over to him by his father of Plas Brondanw, then a quarry-workers' tenement. Its classically conceived garden was wholly his creation, and his delight.

Physically tough and ingenious, Williams-Ellis had an adventurous war, first in the Welsh Guards and later as an intelligence officer in the tank corps, in which he won the MC and bar and was mentioned in dispatches. He collaborated on a history of the corps with his young wife, (Mary) Amabel (Nassau; *b.* 1893/4), daughter of John St Loe *Strachey (1860–1927), the owner and editor of *The Spectator*; they had married on 31 July 1915. Her influence and the experience of war developed in him a determination to campaign for effective town and country planning in Britain. He had met the influential biologist, sociologist, and town planner Patrick Geddes in Edinburgh; he soon formed a working alliance with other disciples such as Frederic Osborn, Charles Reilly, and L. Patrick Abercrombie, and was the most effective, because the wittiest, propagandist of this lively group, with a distinctive writing style. His Cautionary Guides to supposedly beautiful cities, illustrating the 'horrors' being perpetrated in them, and his books (mostly written with his wife), such as *England and the Octopus* (1928) and, as editor, *Britain and the Beast* (1937), were both enjoyable and disturbing. He was among the founders of the councils for the preservation of rural England and of Wales and an enthusiast for the National Trust and for the creation of national parks. *The Pleasures of Architecture* (1924), on which he worked with his wife, was reissued in 1954, and he wrote two autobiographies; he also contributed the notice of Benno Elkan to the *Dictionary of National Biography*.

Williams-Ellis's practice, mainly domestic in character, flourished between the wars: it included the adaptation of and additions to Stowe (1924), a handsome baroque chapel at Bishop's Stortford (1920)—the first building by a living architect to be 'listed'—and neo-Georgian country-house work and cottages at Cornwell, Oxfordshire (1934) and Oare, Wiltshire. Later he designed the Lloyd George memorial at Llanystumdwy (1948). The romantic holiday village of Portmeirion, his most celebrated work, was begun in 1925, mainly for fun, but also as a demonstration of enlightened exploitation. In it he showed an almost Chinese sensitivity to the relation between buildings and landscape. Striding the Peninsula in yellow stockings and cravat, he cut a dashing figure, powerful and elegant, his strong features an expression of his zest for life.

After 1945 his wife's close connection with the Attlee government, not least through her brother John Strachey, involved Williams-Ellis in the problems of post-war planning and reconstruction, in particular in the new towns, and led to his accepting the chairmanship of the Stevenage New Town Development Corporation. But he had by then little time or patience for London committee work and soon resigned the appointment. His politics were dutifully left of centre, but did not command his emotions; architecture always dominated them, as his wife recognized. It pleased him that left-wing friends of hers, such as Arthur Koestler and Patrick Blackett, came to live on or near his mountain territory and that Bertrand Russell, always wonderful company, spent his last years on the Peninsula. But he was equally content when Portmeirion ceased to be the resort of a social élite and became a popular tourist attraction.

Williams-Ellis was vice-president of the Institute of Landscape Architects, an honorary LLD of the University of Wales (1971), and FRIBA (1929). He was appointed CBE in 1958 and knighted in 1972.

Williams-Ellis had two daughters and a son, who was killed in 1944. He died at his home, Plas Brondanw, Llanfrothen, on 8 April 1978 at the age of ninety-four, still full of physical and mental energy, and was buried at Llanfrothen. His wife survived him. He had lived to see postwar modernism (with which he was never at ease) come and go, and to be admired by a new generation for the light-heartedness of his approach to architecture, for the pleasures of his and his wife's company, and for his lifelong battle against those whom he regarded as the philistines.   Lionel Esher

Sources C. Williams-Ellis, *Architect errant* (1971) · C. Williams-Ellis, *Around the world in ninety years* (1978) · R. Haslam, *Clough Williams-Ellis* (1996) · personal knowledge (2004) · m. cert. · d. cert. · Venn, *Alum. Cant.*
Archives NL Wales, corresp. and MSS · RIBA, corresp. and articles relating to Wales, in particular Snowdonia national park | HLRO, corresp. relating to Lloyd George's house · JRL, letters to the *Manchester Guardian* · Welwyn Garden City Central Library, Hertfordshire, corresp. with Sir Frederic Osborn
Likenesses O. Birley, oils, 1930, Portmeirion · H. Coster, photograph, 1936, NPG · B. De Hamel, photograph, c.1969, NPG · J. Hedgecoe, photograph, 1969, NPG [*see illus.*] · K. Pollak, photograph, NPG
Wealth at death £86,942: probate, 14 Aug 1978, *CGPLA Eng. & Wales*

Ellis, Edwin Joseph (1844–1878), violinist and composer, received his professional training from his father, and appeared as a solo violinist at Cremorne Gardens, London, when he was only seven years old. He joined the orchestras of the Princess's and Adelphi theatres, and about 1867 became general musical director and conductor at the Adelphi. He composed a great quantity of music suitable for the dramas given there; his published works consist of selections for small orchestra from Flotow's *Alessandro Stradella*, Ambrose Thomas's *Le caïd*, and Offenbach's *La belle Hélène*, besides a few songs to words by E. L. Blanchard and others, all of which date from 1877.

Ellis remained at the Adelphi for eleven years before moving to Liverpool, where he was sent for a change of air to improve his health. While there he undertook some successful work with the band of the Queen's Theatre, but his health did not improve, and he died aged thirty-five on 20 October 1878 at St Thomas's Hospital. In a letter to *The Era* of 10 November the same year, Charles Reade paid a cordial tribute to the memory of a 'dramatic musician and amiable man', describing the 'vigilant delicacy' with which he accompanied a mixed scene of action and dialogue. On 30 November *The Athenaeum* published notice of a 'mixed musical and dramatic entertainment to be given on the 4th of Dec, in St. James's Hall … in aid of the fund

now being raised for the widow, nine children, and two aged relatives of Mr Edwin Ellis', which was to involve 'the leading vocalists, instrumentalists, actors, actresses, managers, &c.'   L. M. Middleton, *rev.* David J. Golby

Sources *The Athenaeum* (30 Nov 1878), 697 · *The Era* (10 Nov 1878) · private information (1888) · d. cert.

Ellis, Francis Whyte (1777–1819), orientalist, grew up in Compton, Bedfordshire, and was schooled at The Academy, Burlington Street, London. He became a writer in the East India Company's service at Madras in 1796. He was promoted to the offices of assistant under-secretary, deputy secretary, and secretary to the board of revenue in 1798, 1801, and 1802 respectively. In 1806 he was appointed judge in Tanjore, but was transferred the same year to the zillah (district) of Masulipatam, when he offended the raja, having incarcerated one of his servants for extorting rents by force. In 1809 he became collector of land customs in the Madras presidency, and in 1810 collector of Madras. He was largely responsible for planning the college of Fort St George to teach the languages of south India to the junior civil servants posted to Madras, and was senior member of the board of superintendence from its inception in 1812 until his death. He was a leading light of the Madras Literary Society, also begun in 1812. He died unmarried at Ramnad, Madras, of accidental poisoning on 10 March 1819 while on sick leave. His mother, Elizabeth Hubbard, was the main beneficiary of the will he made on his deathbed.

Ellis was a brilliant scholar of the south Indian languages, especially Tamil, and vowed not to publish before the age of forty; because of his untimely death, he published little in his lifetime. Moreover, his private papers were all lost or destroyed; it was said they ended up in the kitchen of the collector of Madura, and were used by his cook 'to kindle his fire and singe fowls'.

Ellis's most important accomplishment was the discovery of the Dravidian language family, a proof of which appeared in 1816, thirty years before Robert Caldwell's *A Comparative Grammar of the Dravidian or South-Indian Family of Languages* (1856), which consolidated Ellis's finding, and forty years after Sir William Jones proposed the concept of the Indo-European language family. The proof appears in an introduction to A. D. Campbell's *A Grammar of the Teloogoo Language*, published by the college of Fort St George for the use of its students. In it Ellis demonstrated that the Tamil, Telugu, and Kannada languages, although containing abundant loanwords from Sanskrit, are not descended from it, as are the languages of north India, but constitute a separate language family. He showed that the three languages have many cognate words that have no roots in Sanskrit, comprising a common core vocabulary of related words. He further asserted, correctly, that the south Indian languages now called Malayalam, Tulu, and Codagu, and Malto (a tribal language in north India) belong to the same family, but that Marathi and Sinhalese, though influenced by it, belong to the Sanskritic language family.

The published proof began as a separate *Dissertation on*

Telugu printed for the use of students, and Ellis intended to do the same for Malayalam and Tamil. The *Dissertation on Malayalam* was published after his death (1878), but the 'Dissertation on Tamil' probably was never printed, because his plans for it grew ever larger, judging from manuscript remains that include a very long treatise on Tamil prosody. Towards the end of his life the college press was printing his translation of the *Tirukkural* of Tiruvalluvar (*c*.1819), a Tamil classic, but he did not finish it. His contributions to the study of Tamil, had he lived, would have been considerable.

Two other works are of special importance. A treatise on *mirasi* (freehold) right was written when he was collector of Madras and in collaboration with his *sheristadar* (chief clerk), B. Sancaraya, to explain the system of land tenure prevailing there through ancient legends and historical inscriptions, in response to a request for information from the board of revenue. It is notable for its attack upon the belief that oriental despotism (the ownership of all land by the sovereign) was the original constitution of India, arguing that private property in land was ancient in this region. It was first published by the government of Madras in 1818. Second, he wrote a long article dealing with the purported Veda called the Ezour Vedam, which had become famous in Europe through Voltaire, who, relying on its authenticity and antiquity, had used it as evidence that deism was the original and universal religion of mankind, against the claims of Christianity. Ellis's article, published in the *Asiatic Researches* in 1822, proved that the Ezour Vedam had been composed by Jesuit missionaries in India. THOMAS R. TRAUTMANN

Sources C. C. Prinsep, *Record of services of the Honourable East India Company's civil servants in the Madras presidency from 1741 to 1858* (1885) · W. Elliot, 'Mr F. W. Ellis', *The Athenaeum* (10 April 1875), 489 · T. R. Trautmann, *Aryans and British India* (1997) · Bodl. Oxf., MSS F. W. Ellis · will, BL OIOC, L/AG/34/29/219, fols. 44–5

Archives Bodl. Oxf., MSS | BL OIOC, Walter Elliot collection · BL OIOC, William Erskine collection · BL OIOC, writer's petitions, J/1/16 [fols. 514–17] · NL Scot., William Erskine collection · Tamil Nadu State Archives, Madras public proceedings · Tamil Nadu State Archives, Madras district records

Wealth at death over Rs.200,000: BL OIOC, L/AG/34/29/219, fols. 44–5

Ellis, Frederick Startridge (1830–1901), bookseller and author, the sixth son of Joseph Ellis, keeper of the famous Star and Garter Hotel in Richmond, Surrey, was born in Richmond on 7 June 1830. At the age of sixteen, he entered the house of Edward Lumley of Chancery Lane, London, and afterwards became assistant to C. J. Stewart, the well-known bookseller of King William Street, Strand, from whom he acquired his knowledge of books. In 1860 he went into business for himself at 33 King Street, Covent Garden, and on 8 January 1861 he married Caroline Augusta Flora, the daughter of William Moates of Epsom. They had two sons and a daughter, Phillis M. Ellis, who was to share her father's love of rare books and calligraphic manuscripts.

In 1871, Ellis took into partnership G. M. Green (1841–1872), who had had a similar specialist training to his own. After the death of Green in 1872 Ellis took the premises, 29

New Bond Street, previously occupied by T. and W. Boone, and carried on a large and successful business, chiefly in old books and manuscripts. These premises became a gathering place for the literati of the day. His next partner was David White, who retired in 1884. For many years Ellis was official buyer for the British Museum, which brought him into rivalry with trade opponents in the auction rooms. He was also commissioned to edit the catalogue of Henry Huth's famous library, which was printed in 1880 in five volumes. The English books were catalogued by W. C. Hazlitt, those in other languages by Ellis. Another excellent catalogue compiled by Ellis was the privately printed *Descriptive catalogue of a collection of drawings and etchings by Charles Meryon, formed by the Rev. J. J. Heywood* (1880). He also produced *Horae Pembrochianae: some account of an illuminated MS. of the hours of the B. V. M., written for William Herbert, first earl of Pembroke, about 1440* (1880), and a biographical notice appended to *The Hours of Albert of Brandenburg*, by W. H. J. Weale (1883). In 1885 he retired from business because of incipient tuberculosis, and his stock of rare books and manuscripts was sold by Sothebys for about £16,000. He was succeeded in business by his nephew, G. I. Ellis.

Ellis was a publisher on a limited scale, and brought out the works of William Morris and Dante Gabriel Rossetti, with whom he was on terms of close friendship. It was Rossetti who composed the well-known limerick at the time Ellis was making his first overtures:

> There's a publishing party named Ellis
> Who's addicted to poets with bellies:
> He has at least two—
> One in fact, one in view—
> And God knows what will happen to Ellis.
> (L. M. Packer, *Christina Rossetti*, 1963, 273)

Among other friends were A. C. Swinburne, Sir Edward Burne-Jones, and John Ruskin, whose *Stray Letters to a London Bibliopole* were addressed to Ellis and republished by him in 1892. Ruskin called him Papa Ellis (E. T. Cook, *Life of John Ruskin*, 1911, 1.371). It was in 1864 that William Morris was first introduced by Swinburne to Ellis, who later took over from Dante Gabriel Rossetti the joint tenancy, with Morris, of Kelmscott Manor in Oxfordshire. They shared an enthusiasm for fishing. Ellis advised Morris on his purchases of manuscripts. In Morris's last illness in 1896 he was with him every day, discussing a projected edition of the *Border Ballads*, and Ellis was one of the poet's executors (J. W. Mackail, *Life of W. Morris*, 1899, 1.193).

After his retirement from business Ellis pursued a second career as textual critic and editor. The first fruits of his labours on Shelley was *An Alphabetical Table of Contents to Shelley's Poetical Works*, drawn up for the Shelley Society in 1888. He devoted six years to compiling *A Lexical Concordance to the Poetical Works of P. B. Shelley* (1892), an excellent piece of work which remains Ellis's main claim to fame. He was an enthusiastic supporter of Morris's Kelmscott Press, and read the proofs of the folio edition of Chaucer's *Works* (1896), Morris's masterpiece of printing, and edited many other Kelmscott productions, including Cavendish's *Life of Wolsey* (1893) and Caxton's *Golden Legend* (1892), which also appeared in the Temple Classics (1899 and 1900). He went on to edit Guillaume de Lorris's *Romance of the Rose*, in an 'englished' version (1900, Temple Classics), and *H. Pengelly's Memoir*, with a preface (1897), and contributed some memoirs to his rival Bernard Quaritch's *Dictionary of English Book Collectors*. Ellis's surviving verses suggest that his criticism was less rigorous when applied to his own work.

Ellis died at the Bedford Hotel, Sidmouth, on 26 February 1901, after a short illness following pneumonia; his wife survived him. He was a widely read and accomplished man, conservative in his outlook and tastes, tall, rubicund and handsome, warm-hearted and emotional, with the ebullience that prompted Philip Webb to describe him as 'a kind of Falstaff' (letter to S. C. Cockerell, 28 Feb 1901, BL, Add. MS 52715). He was loyal to a wide circle of literary and artistic friends.

H. R. Tedder, *rev.* Fiona MacCarthy

Sources *The Times* (1 March 1901) · *The Athenaeum* (2 March 1901) · *The Athenaeum* (9 March 1901) · *The Athenaeum* (16 March 1901) · *The Bookseller* (7 March 1901) · *A note by William Morris on his aims in founding the Kelmscott Press* (1898) · F. S. Ellis, 'The life-work of William Morris', *Journal of the Society of Arts*, 46 (1897–8), 618–28 · *The letters of Dante Gabriel Rossetti to his publisher, F. S. Ellis*, ed. O. Doughty (1928) · *The collected letters of William Morris*, ed. N. Kelvin, 4 vols. (1984–96) · *CGPLA Eng. & Wales* (1901) · *IGI*
Archives BL, corresp. and papers, Add. MS 41130 · FM Cam., family MSS | BL, corresp. with Sir Sydney Cockerell, Add. MS 52715
Likenesses Window & Grove, photograph, 1895–6, NPG · E. Walker, photograph, NPG
Wealth at death £44,709 1s. 5d.: probate, 14 March 1901, *CGPLA Eng. & Wales*

Ellis, George (1753–1815), writer, was the only and posthumous son of George Ellis (*d.* 1753), member of the house of assembly of St George, Grenada, West Indies, and of Susanna Charlotte, daughter of Samuel Long, member of the council of Jamaica. He was educated at Westminster School and then at Trinity College, Cambridge. He made his début in literature as the author of some mock heroic couplets on Bath, its beauties, and amusements, published anonymously in 1776. In 1778 *Poetical Tales by Sir Gregory Gander* appeared, and was at once attributed to Ellis and had much vogue. Horace Walpole called the tales 'pretty verses' (letter to the earl of Strafford, 24 June 1783). Gilbert Elliot, first earl of Minto, had 'never read anything so clever, so lively, and so light'. Years afterwards Walter Scott referred to them in the introduction to the fifth canto of *Marmion*, which is addressed to Ellis. In 1783 Horace Walpole noted as a sign of the anglomania prevailing in France that Ellis was 'a favourite' at Versailles.

Ellis was one of the contributors to the rebellious journal *The Rolliad*, and in particular is said to have written severe attacks on Pitt and his administration. In December 1784 he accompanied Sir James Harris, afterwards Lord Malmesbury, on his mission to The Hague, and was employed by him in diplomatic business. He thus gained an insight into the secret springs of the Dutch revolution of 1785–7, which he recorded in the *History of the Dutch Revolution*, published anonymously in 1789, and translated

into French by 'Monsieur', afterwards Louis XVIII. A *Memoir of a Map of the Countries Comprehended between the Black Sea and the Caspian*, published anonymously in 1788, is almost certainly by Ellis; the British Library's copy, a gift from Ellis's wife to her niece, has a note from the latter confirming this, and stating that it was written after his return from a visit to the British ambassador to Russia. In 1790 Ellis published one of his most valuable literary contributions, entitled *Specimens of the Early English Poets*, which went through six editions between 1801 and 1851.

In 1791 Ellis made a tour in Germany and Italy with Lord and Lady Malmesbury. He entered parliament in 1796 as junior member for Seaford, one of the Cinque Ports, his cousin, Charles Rose Ellis, afterwards Baron Seaford, being the senior member. He never spoke in the house, and did not stand for re-election. He accompanied Lord Malmesbury to the conference at Lille in 1797, and wrote a long letter to George Canning defending the English plenipotentiary's conduct of the negotiations. Shortly after his return to England he became a fervent tory, and in concert with Canning and William Gifford founded *The Anti-Jacobin*. Ellis appears to have been a constant contributor to *The Anti-Jacobin* in the 1790s. He also edited in 1796, with a preface, notes, and appendix, Gregory Lewis Way's translations of select *Fabliaux* of the twelfth and thirteenth centuries, taken from the collection of Legrand d'Aussy; a second edition appeared in 1800, and a third in 1815 in three volumes.

On 10 September 1801 Ellis married Anne, daughter of Sir Peter Parker, first baronet, of Basingbourn, admiral of the fleet. They remained childless. Also in 1801 Ellis made the acquaintance of Walter Scott, and this soon ripened into a friendship terminated only by death. A portion of the voluminous correspondence which passed between them can be found in Lockhart's *Life of Scott*, which also relates that on his visits to London, Scott was accustomed to stay with Ellis at his house, Connaught Place, Sunninghill, near Ascot. 'Mr. Ellis', says Scott, 'was the first converser I ever knew; his patience and good breeding made me often ashamed of myself going off at score upon some favourite topic' (*Diary*, 29 Aug 1826). In 1805 Ellis published *Specimens of Early English Metrical Romances*, a second edition of which appeared in 1811; a third edition, edited by J. O. Halliwell FRS, was published in 1848. Ellis wrote the review of the *Lady of the Lake* in the *Quarterly Review* in May 1811. He began, but did not live to finish, an edition of the diary of his friend William Windham. The introductory sketch of Windham, however, was complete, and can be found in Mrs Henry Baring's edition of the diary, published in 1866. Ellis was a fellow of the Royal Society and of the Society of Antiquaries. His work on early English dramatic literature meant that he was often compared to his European scholarly contemporaries, men such as Jean-Baptiste de la Curne de Sainte-Palaye, author of *Projet d'un glossaire de l'ancienne langue française* (1756). In his 1803 review of Ellis's *Specimens of the Early English Poets*, Scott made an extensive comparison between the work of Ellis and that of the Count de Tressan. Such comparisons meant that Ellis was often called the Tressan and the Sainte-Palaye of England. He died on 10 April 1815 at Connaught Place.   J. M. RIGG, rev. REBECCA MILLS

Sources S. J. Kunitz and H. Haycraft, eds., *British authors before 1800: a biographical dictionary* (1952), 174–5 · *GM*, 1st ser., 85/1 (1815), 371–2 · *Diaries and correspondence of James Harris, first earl of Malmesbury*, ed. third earl of Malmesbury [J. H. Harris], 3 (1844), 429–34 · *Life and letters of Sir Gilbert Elliot, first earl of Minto, from 1751 to 1806*, ed. countess of Minto [E. E. E. Elliot-Murray-Kynynmound], 1 (1874), 189–90, 388–402 · Watt, *Bibl. Brit.*, 1.334 · Burke, *Peerage* · *GM*, 1st ser., 71 (1801), 1052
Archives BL, corresp., Add. MS 28099 | BL, letters to H. Legge, Add. MS 37907 · Bodl. Oxf., corresp. with Frances Douce · NL Scot., letters to Sir Walter Scott

Ellis, George James Welbore Agar-, first Baron Dover (1797–1833), politician and patron of art, was the only son of Henry Welbore Agar-Ellis, second Viscount Clifden, and his wife, Lady Caroline Spencer, eldest daughter of George *Spencer, fourth duke of Marlborough. He was born in Upper Brook Street, London, on 14 January 1797, and was sent as a town boy to Westminster School in 1811, but did not remain there long. He afterwards went to Christ Church, Oxford, where he graduated BA in 1816, and proceeded MA in 1819. While at Christ Church, he hoped to visit Elba to collect materials for a life of Napoleon, but the latter's escape frustrated him.

At the general election in June 1818 Agar-Ellis, then just twenty-one, was returned by the A'Court interest as one of the tory members for the borough of Heytesbury. In March 1820 he purchased the seat of Seaford, and on 30 April 1822 he seconded Canning's motion for leave to bring in a bill to relieve the Roman Catholic peers from the disabilities then imposed upon them with regard to the right of sitting and voting in the House of Lords.

In March 1822 he married, at Chiswick, Lady Georgiana Howard, second daughter of the sixth earl of Carlisle, George *Howard; they had four sons and three daughters.

In a discussion on the estimates for the grant to the British Museum in July 1823 Agar-Ellis stated his intention of moving for a grant in the next session to be applied to the purchase of the Angerstein collection of pictures, and towards the formation of a national gallery. The government, however, adopted his suggestion, and in the following year the collection was purchased for £60,000. These pictures were selected chiefly by Sir Thomas Lawrence, and, together with those which had been presented by Sir George Beaumont, formed the nucleus of the National Gallery collection.

At the general election in June 1826 Agar-Ellis was returned for Ludgershall, and in March 1827 spoke in favour of the petition of the Roman Catholic bishops of Ireland. In July 1830 he was elected for Okehampton. Upon Grey's becoming prime minister, Agar-Ellis was sworn a member of the privy council on 22 November 1830, and was appointed chief commissioner of woods and forests by a patent dated 13 December 1830. He was, however, compelled by ill health to resign this office within two months of his appointment.

Agar-Ellis was created Baron Dover in the peerage of the United Kingdom on 20 June 1831. He died at Dover House, Whitehall, on 10 July 1833, in his thirty-seventh year, and was buried in the family vault in St Mary's Church, Twickenham, on 17 July. His widow died on 17 March 1860, aged fifty-five.

Although he did not take much part in the debates on the great political questions of the day, Agar-Ellis was a consistent supporter of liberal principles, as well as an earnest advocate of everything which tended to the improvement of the people. He was a generous patron of the fine arts, and formed a valuable collection of paintings by English artists. In his review of Dover's edition of *Letters of Horace Walpole … to Sir Horace Mann* (3 vols., 1833), Macaulay wrote: 'The editing of these volumes was the last of the useful and modest services rendered to literature by a nobleman of amiable manners, of untarnished public and private character, and of cultivated mind' (*Edinburgh Review*, 58, 1833–4, 227). He was a trustee of the British Museum and of the National Gallery, a commissioner of the public records, and a member of several learned societies. In 1832, on the resignation of Thomas Burgess, the bishop of Salisbury, he was elected president of the Royal Society of Literature. He published various works on art and history and edited *The Ellis Correspondence* (2 vols., 1829).   G. F. R. BARKER, rev. H. C. G. MATTHEW

Sources GEC, *Peerage* · G. Agar-Ellis, ed., *The Ellis correspondence: letters written during the years 1686, 1687, 1688, and addressed to John Ellis*, 2 vols. (1829), vol. 1, p. 23 · C. Holmes and C. H. C. Baker, *The making of the National Gallery* (1924) · HoP, *Commons*
Archives Northants. RO, diaries, corresp., and papers · UCL, letters to Society for the Diffusion of Useful Knowledge | BL, corresp. with Lord Holland, Add. MS 51590 · Chatsworth House, Derbyshire, letters to duke of Devonshire · W. Sussex RO, letters to duke of Richmond
Likenesses B. Thorvaldsen, plaster bust, 1818, Thorvaldsen Museum, Copenhagen, Denmark · W. Ward, mezzotint, pubd 1823 (after J. Jackson), BM, NPG · T. Lawrence, oils, 1833, Yale U. CBA · J. Burnet, line print (after G. Sanders), BM, NPG · G. Hayter, group portrait, oils (*The trial of Queen Caroline, 1820*), NPG · J. Jackson, portrait · T. Phillips, portrait · E. Scriven, stipple (after T. Phillips), repro. in W. Jerdan, *National portrait gallery of illustrious and eminent personages* (1834) · J. Slater, portrait, repro. in J. Slater and G. Richmond, *Portraits of members of Grillion's Club, from 1813 to 1863*, 1 (privately printed, 1864) · P. C. Wonder, group portrait (*Patrons and lovers of art, 1826*), NPG

Ellis, (Henry) Havelock (1859–1939), writer and sexologist, was born on 2 February 1859 at 1 St John's Grove, Croydon, Surrey, the eldest child and only son of Edward Peppern Ellis (1827–1914), a sea captain, and his wife, Susannah Mary (1829–1888), whose father, John Wheatley, was also a seaman. Both parents were of Suffolk stock and Ellis was later to devote a great deal of time to exploring his East Anglian ancestry, but he spent most of his early life with his four sisters in various homes in the Surrey suburbs of London. The boy was named after a distant ancestor, Sir Henry Havelock, a general during the Indian mutiny, and when young he was known as Henry or Harry. He adopted the name Havelock Ellis when he began his literary career.

Influences and education His father was rarely home, and Ellis was to pay little attention to him in his posthumously this state of mind that he read, for the second time, a book entitled *Life in Nature* (1862) by James Hinton, an aural surgeon and a writer on political, social, religious, and sexual matters. The book sparked a spiritual transformation:

> The clash in my inner life was due to what had come to seem to me the hopeless discrepancy of two different conceptions of the universe … The great revelation brought to me by Hinton … was that these two conflicting attitudes are really but harmonious though different aspects of the same unity. (Ellis, 130–31)

Each person, Ellis believed, constructed a personal pattern of meaning, the shaping of which was an art—and much of his philosophical work was concerned with the depiction of this 'Art of Life'. The dance for Ellis most perfectly represented the form of life: a unity of pattern, rhythm, feeling, and intellect. But balancing this spiritual outlook was a conviction that science, guided by a humanist outlook, could lay bare the truths of human nature. In particular, for the young Ellis the belief that sexual freedom could bring in a new age of happiness helped direct him towards the scientific study of sex. To prepare him for this he resolved to train as a doctor, and with his new inner self-confidence and ambitions he returned to London in April 1879. Ellis soon embarked on his medical training, supported financially by his mother and the Hinton circle, eventually becoming a medical student at St Thomas's Hospital, London. His training took a long eight years (1881–9) and, having failed to achieve more prestigious qualifications, he ended up as a licentiate of the Society of Apothecaries, which nevertheless qualified him to practise. Thereafter, however, his actual work as a doctor was spasmodic. During his training and in the years that followed his real preoccupation was with his literary and scientific studies. The London of the 1880s was a focus of intense intellectual and political ferment, and Ellis immersed himself in this new culture. Through his work on the radical journal *Today*, his secretaryship of the Progressive Association, and membership of the Fellowship of the New Life (a loose gathering of radicals exploring new ways of living from which the Fabian Society later developed after an acrimonious split), he met many of the radical luminaries of the time, including H. M. Hyndman, Eleanor Marx, George Bernard Shaw, and Edward Carpenter. He began publishing essays on religion, philosophy, travel, and politics. He briefly edited a pioneering series of unexpurgated editions of English plays, the Mermaid series, and started editing the highly influential Contemporary Science series of books, which was to provide a major source of his income for the next thirty years. In 1890 he published his own first book, *The New Spirit*, which described what he saw as the spiritual awakening of the age. The chief elements of this were the growth of science, the rise of women, and the march of democracy, all of which demanded education and a reasonable organization of life.

Character and private life Ellis described himself throughout his life as a socialist, but despite his association with various radical groups he was never a political activist.

(Henry) **Havelock Ellis** (1859–1939), by Emil Otto Hoppé, 1922

published memoirs. Ellis's mother was the dominant influence in his early life. As an ardent evangelical Christian, who had experienced a conversion at the age of seventeen, she had vowed never to visit a theatre in her life. Despite this she was a warm influence on the young Ellis, who early on slipped away from the more rigid aspects of her faith. He was provided with a basic education at Mrs Granville's school in south London, the French and German College, Merton (1868–71), and The Poplars, Mitcham (1871–4). His schooling was interrupted by a year-long sea voyage with his father at the age of seven. His main education, however, derived from wide reading, including in his adolescence J. E. Renan, A. C. Swinburne, and Percy Bysshe Shelley. But the crucial formative influence was his stay in Australia for four years from the age of sixteen. Occasioned by health worries, this second trip with his father was intended as a journey round the world, but he stopped off in Australia, becoming a very young, and not over-competent, teacher and, at the age of nineteen, briefly a headmaster, at schools in the outback. Here, in almost total isolation, he began to experience conflicts in his awakening sexual life and in his spiritual outlook. The turning point, as he ever after saw it, came when he was teaching at a small school in Sparkes Creek in New South Wales. Born in the year of the first publication of Charles Darwin's *On the Origin of Species*, Ellis was a child of a new scientific optimism, unattracted to a religious world outlook which he saw as dying, but repelled by the absorption of science into a chilly utilitarianism. It was in

Even as a well-known writer in later life, giving his formal support to campaigns for sex reform, eugenics, abortion, and voluntary euthanasia, he was extremely reluctant to become involved in public controversy. Although physically a handsome and commanding figure with a flowing beard which, as he grew older, increasingly confirmed his reputation as a sage, he was diffident in manner, generally finding excuses to avoid high profile events or even social engagements. Despite frequent foreign travel, often with his close friend Arthur Symons, he regularly described himself as a recluse. It was in private involvements, through a vast daily correspondence, and by his voluminous writings that he exercised his influence. Even in his publications his manner was often indirect, preferring, as he put it, 'to express the shocking things in a quiet, suave, matter-of-course way, sugar coating the pill' (Grosskurth, 384). Yet both his private life and his public writings had the potentiality to shock his contemporaries.

It was in these early years of incessant intellectual activity that Ellis began the two most important emotional involvements of his early life. The first was with the South African author Olive *Schreiner (1855–1920), already famous for her novel *The Story of an African Farm* (1883) when they met early in 1884 through their mutual friend Eleanor Marx. Olive was a forceful and passionate woman, though prone to ill health, and the two writers quickly established a fervent relationship. It is not clear whether it was conventionally consummated. Ellis himself appears not to have been strongly drawn to heterosexual intercourse, and had a lifelong interest in urolagnia, a delight in seeing women urinate. The sexual ardour of the relationship, certainly on Schreiner's part, appears to have soon cooled, though the emotional intensity remained. It survived Schreiner's return to South Africa in 1889, continuing until her death via an almost daily correspondence and occasional meetings.

Ellis's relationship with the woman who was to become his wife, Edith Mary Oldham Lees (1861–1916), daughter of Samuel Oldham Lees, a landowner, began the year after Schreiner's departure, and was consolidated by a common interest in the work of Hinton and with the Fellowship of the New Life. Edith Lees had become secretary of the fellowship house in London (an experience which was to convince her that 'fellowship was hell'), though she gave this up when she and Ellis married on 19 December 1891. She too was a passionate woman who, despite an intense mutual involvement with Ellis (he was to devote almost half of his autobiography to their relationship), pursued an independent life as a lecturer and writer. By Victorian standards the partnership was highly unconventional. They maintained separate incomes (neither of which was high or secure) and, for large parts of the year, separate dwellings. Both were devoted to their homes in Carbis Bay, Cornwall (here Ellis began his lifelong practice of writing in the open air), and in Surrey, but Ellis also used rooms in the Temple, Chelsea, Brixton, West Drayton, and the Chilterns. Edith's emotional and sexual passions were primarily lesbian, and both she and Ellis were to have a series of close emotional involvements with other women, certainly sexual in Edith's case, more ambiguously erotic in Ellis's case.

Studies in the Psychology of Sex By the early 1890s Ellis was ready to embark on what he regarded as his crowning achievement, *Studies in the Psychology of Sex* (1897–1910, with a seventh, supplementary, volume in 1928). The series began with *Sexual Inversion*, the first serious study of homosexuality published in Britain. It was conceived as a collaboration with the poet and critic John Addington Symonds, himself homosexual, and anxious to promote a more tolerant climate towards homosexuality. The co-authors (who never in fact met, both preferring correspondence) were in many ways ill-matched, but Ellis was strongly committed to the project, partly as a result of his awareness of the homosexuality of his wife and friends such as Edward Carpenter, whose own accounts appeared as slightly disguised case studies in the book. He completed the book after Symonds's death in 1893, the first print appearing in German, then in English in 1897 under their joint names. Ellis now became embroiled in an unfortunate series of events. First of all, Ellis was forced by Symonds's family to withdraw his co-author's name from the book. The aftermath of the trials of Oscar Wilde was not the best time to publish a major text on homosexuality that might sully another aesthete's reputation. Then Ellis found himself caught in the web of a dubious publisher and in a subsequent trial of the secretary of the sexually progressive Legitimation League, George Bedborough, for selling the book. In the 1898 trial, which did not directly involve Ellis, the book was labelled a 'certain lewd, wicked, bawdy, scandalous libel', and was subsequently withdrawn from sale. Ellis was confirmed in his caution about getting involved in public controversy. More crucially, he determined thereafter that the *Studies* should be published in the USA.

Despite this unfortunate beginning the *Studies* were to prove enormously influential. The first volume set the tone. By collating all the available evidence, historical, anthropological, social, and scientific, Ellis's aim was to demonstrate that homosexuality (or inversion, his preferred term) was not a product of peculiar national vices, or periods of social decay, but a common and recurrent part of human sexuality, a quirk of nature, a congenital anomaly. In line with what was then considered advanced thinking, his conviction of the biological origins of human behaviour was to colour much of his thought. His book *The Criminal* (1890) had already argued that criminal behaviour was innate. The various volumes of the *Studies* explored this biological emphasis across the range of sexual behaviours. First, he sought to establish the natural basis of human sexuality in all its forms; nothing that was based in nature could be seen as inherently wrong. But second, he attempted to reconcile these variations to what he regarded as the supreme biological origin and function of sex, the man wooing a woman for the purpose of reproduction. Though an advanced advocate of a woman's right to sexual fulfilment, his view of an essential female passivity in sexual matters subsequently attracted sharp criticism, particularly as it appeared to subordinate female sexuality to male. His biological determinism led him to give support throughout his life to eugenics, the planned breeding of the best, and to differentiate him from his great contemporary Sigmund Freud, with whom he had a mutually respectful but somewhat fractious relationship (conducted entirely through correspondence and print). Yet despite his biological preoccupations Ellis was no empirical scientist. His method was that of the naturalist, collecting facts from a vast variety of sources and presenting them in an ordered, but essentially descriptive, fashion. As a result, unlike Freud, he never established a scientific school, nor is it possible to see an intellectual master plan in his work. But for his progressive contemporaries he seemed a prophet of a more humane attitude to sex. Through the *Studies*, probably read about more than read, he became internationally famous as a sexologist, and a magnet for other would-be sex reformers. Many, like the American birth control pioneer Margaret Sanger, became lifelong friends. Thousands of lesser known people wrote to him about sexual issues, and for advice.

Later works On completing the sixth volume of the *Studies* Ellis wrote, 'The work that I was born to do is done'. In fact, many years of productive writing and growing fame lay ahead. He continued writing on sexual matters, including a textbook, *The Psychology of Sex* (1933). His various other interests were reflected in a number of collections of essays, and the publication of *The Dance of Life* (1923) made him a best-selling author for the first time. From the 1920s he also contributed short articles to American newspapers and journals, which did little for his intellectual reputation, but contributed significantly to his finances. Edith Lees had died in 1916, after some years of growing ill health, accentuated by then untreatable diabetes. In the last months she had secured a legal separation from Ellis, but her death left him emotionally bereft, and facing substantial debts left by his wife. Though legally no longer liable, he struggled to pay these off, and also to pay her a debt of honour by editing for publication her study of their common inspiration, *James Hinton: a Sketch* (1918).

Ellis's emotional life was not, however, over. From 1918 he shared his life with an acquaintance of Edith's, Françoise Lafitte-Cyon, also known as Delisle (1886–1974), separated wife of a Russian journalist, and mother of two boys. As he had with Edith, for many years Ellis retained his own home, and each of them continued to cultivate strong relationships outside their partnership. From 1928, however, as a result of the generosity of Margaret Sanger, Ellis, Françoise, and her sons shared a house in south London, 24 Holmdene Avenue, Herne Hill—which Ellis seems to have regarded as a mixed blessing. Eventually, again thanks to Sanger, Ellis found a cottage in Wivelsfield Green, Sussex, where he spent a substantial part of each year, indulging his new taste for nude bathing. In 1937 the two found a new home, Cherry Ground, Hintlesham, near Ipswich, Suffolk, the county of his ancestors. The last

years of Ellis's life were shadowed by ill health—largely caused by an undiagnosed dysphagia, a pouch in his throat which caught all the food he ate—as well as continuing poverty. He died at Cherry Ground on 8 July 1939. His ashes were scattered at Golders Green crematorium, Middlesex. Ellis had intended that his autobiography, *My Life*, published in 1940, would provide an income for his companion, but wartime conditions led to poor sales; little else was left. He was survived by Françoise and her sons. He had no children of his own.　　　J. WEEKS

Sources H. H. Ellis, *My life* (1940) · P. Grosskurth, *Havelock Ellis: a biography* (1980) · V. Brome, *Havelock Ellis, philosopher of sex: a biography* (1979) · S. Rowbotham and J. Weeks, *Socialism and the new life* (1977) · F. Delisle, *Friendship's odyssey* (1964) · R. First and A. Scott, *Olive Schreiner: a biography* (1980) · m. cert. · d. cert.

Archives BL, corresp. and MSS, Add. MSS 70524–70589 · Boston PL, letters · Col. U., corresp. · Harris Man. Oxf., MSS · Harvard U., Houghton L., MSS · Indiana University, Bloomington, Lilly Library, MSS · Meninger Foundation, Topeka, Kansas, division of museums and archives, letters and literary MSS · Ransom HRC, corresp. and MSS · Yale U., Beinecke L., letters and literary MSS | Birm. CA, letters to Bernard Sleigh · BL, corresp. with George Bernard Shaw, Add. MSS 50533, 61891 · BL, corresp. with Society of Authors, Add. MSS 56701–56702 · BL, corresp. with Marie Stopes, Add. MS 58564 · BLPES, letters to Bronislaw Manilowski · Indiana University, Bloomington, Lilly Library, letters to Josephine Walter · Internationaal Instituut voor Sociale Geschiedenis, Amsterdam, corresp. with Emma Goldman · JRL, letters to Andre Raffalovich · Mitchell L., NSW, corresp. with William Chidley · Sheff. Arch., letters to Edward Carpenter · Smith College, Northampton, Massachusetts, corresp. with Jane Burr · U. Reading L., letters to the Bodley Head · UCL, letters to Francis Galton · UCL, corresp. with Karl Pearson · University of Bristol, corresp. with J. A. Symonds · University of Toronto, Thomas Fisher Rare Book Library, letters to James Mavor

Likenesses Man Ray, photograph, 1920–30, NPG · E. O. Hoppé, bromide print, 1922, NPG [*see illus.*] · H. Bishop, oils, 1924–5, RCP Lond. · W. Rothenstein, chalk drawing, 1931, NPG · B. Sleigh, drawing, 1931, Birmingham Museums and Art Gallery · H. Coster, photograph, 1934, NPG · H. Coster, seven negatives, 1934, NPG · E. Kapp, sketch, 1937, NPG · H. Channing Stephens, portrait, RCP Lond. · A. G. Walker, bronze bust, Ipswich Museum · bust, Book Trust, London · photographs, repro. in Grosskurth, *Havelock Ellis*

Wealth at death £5662 5s. 1d.: probate, 12 Dec 1939, *CGPLA Eng. & Wales*

Ellis, Henry (1721–1806), explorer and colonial governor, was born in Monaghan town, co. Monaghan, Ireland, the eighth but second surviving child of Francis Ellis (1683–1773), landowner, and Joan Maxwell. Descended from Sir Thomas Ellis of Wyham, England, his paternal grandfather had become an Ulster planter during the reign of Charles II. Baptized into the Church of Ireland, Ellis was locally educated and although he never married he legally adopted John Joyner in the 1760s. John Joyner Ellis became a major-general and member of parliament for Worcester. His son was Colonel Sir Henry Walton Ellis (1783–1815), who was killed at Waterloo. Francis Ellis disinherited his elder son, James, and following Francis's death in June 1773, Henry Ellis inherited the family estate spread throughout the barony of Monaghan. By prudent management Ellis became one of the largest landowners in the county.

In 1741 Ellis ran away to sea and little is known of him

until he returned to London from Italy in 1746. He became a subscriber to a privately funded expedition to discover the north-west passage and was appointed by Arthur Dobbs, the expedition's major sponsor, a family friend, and later the governor of North Carolina, to be the voyage's hydrographer, or scientific officer. Dobbs had sponsored the voyage of Christopher Middleton in 1742 but had been disappointed with its finding that Hudson Bay had no navigable western outlet. The new expedition left England on 20 May 1746 and in August the *Dobbs*, a galley of 180 tons, and the *California* (150 tons) passed through the Hudson Strait. Having wintered near the mouth of the Hayes River, the expedition attempted to locate a passage through Wagner Bay in the summer of 1747. Although Dobbs was convinced that this would lead to the western ocean, their exhaustive searches suggested otherwise and led them to conclude that the only western outlet from Hudson Bay could be via Roe's Welcome Sound. By August 1747 increasing ice made further exploration impossible and the captain decided to return home to England. They had travelled farther north than any other expedition, although the north-west passage still proved elusive. Later expeditions under William Back and John Franklin followed the same route with the same results and, although the 1746–7 voyage failed to bring back the desired answer, Ellis's role in it greatly enhanced his reputation in London. Introduced to Frederick, prince of Wales, Ellis quickly became associated with his political followers at Leicester House. In 1748 Ellis published his *Voyage to Hudson's Bay*, a popular book and the main account of the expedition to have been published. He followed it with a call for further exploration in *Considerations on the great advantage which would arise from the discovery of the north west passage* (1750). Following his election as a fellow of the Royal Society in November 1749, Ellis became associated with George Montague Dunk, second earl of Halifax.

Appointed to the presidency of the Board of Trade in 1748 Halifax secured for Ellis his first government sinecure as deputy commissary-general to His Majesty's stores as well as the command of the *Earl of Halifax*. Ellis took the ship on two scientific expeditions to the west coast of Africa in 1750 and 1754 to test the possible use of ventilators to improve conditions below deck, a matter of considerable concern on slave ships. He also undertook experiments to determine the effect depth had upon sea water temperature. These experiments were designed by the Revd Dr Stephen Hales FRS, who later presented Ellis's findings to the Royal Society. On these voyages the *Earl of Halifax* also acted as a slaver and Ellis was responsible for enslaving more than 600 Africans who were later sold in Jamaica. In 1756 Halifax appointed Ellis the successor to Captain John Reynolds, the unpopular governor of Georgia.

Ellis arrived in Savannah in February 1757 and proved a successful administrator. A popular governor, he placated the factious colonial legislature, helped secure the southern frontier during the Seven Years' War, and laid the foundations for later treaties with the increasingly hostile Cherokee and Creek nations. Claiming ill health, Ellis resigned his post in November 1760 and in March 1761 was appointed by Halifax to the governorship of Nova Scotia. As was common at the time he did not take up his duties himself or return to America, but became the colonial policy adviser to Charles, Lord Egremont, who served as the southern secretary of state in the administrations of Lord Bute and George Grenville.

Between November 1761 and Egremont's sudden death in August 1763 Ellis was an important voice in London, advocating a more energetic and systematic approach to colonial policy. He supported the establishment of a regular army in America, securing the southern frontier by the acquisition of Florida, the imperial regulation of the Indian trade, and the protection of Indian tribal lands by erecting a geographical limit to colonial westward expansion. Ellis shared many of the attitudes common among British officials regarding the administration of the American colonies. He was unquestionably a formative influence upon the proclamation of 1763 and supported Lord North's attempted coercion of Massachusetts in 1774. His actual influence on later British policy is, however, difficult to establish for he resigned his governorship of Nova Scotia in 1763 and refused an appointment as under-secretary to the new American department in 1767. Returning to private life after 1763 he nevertheless continued to receive a large income from a collection of minor, yet lucrative, colonial offices, secured for him by Egremont.

Away from public life Ellis enjoyed wide respect and popularity as a generous host. Abstemious in his personal habits, he none the less became a renowned figure on the European social scene, following the season from Bath, to the south of France, and on to Italy. While resident in Naples he suffered a paralytic stroke in 1805 and died there on 21 January 1806. Ellis had become a wealthy man, and in his will made generous bequests to friends, servants, and charities. Henry Walton Ellis inherited some of his Nova Scotian lands, but the bulk of his estate, including his Irish lands, was left to his nephew Francis Ellis. An important colonial expert in the period of the treaty of Paris, 1763, his correspondence and papers are scattered among the Egremont, Knox, and William Whenwell manuscripts. His burial place remains unknown.

RORY T. CORNISH

Sources L. J. Bellot, *William Knox: the life and thought of an eighteenth-century imperialist* (1977) • E. J. Cashin, *Governor Henry Ellis and the transformation of British North America* (1994) • J. Shy, *A people numerous and armed: reflections on the military struggle for American independence*, rev. edn (1990) • F. B. Wickwire, *British subministers and colonial America, 1763–1783* (1966) • D. Clarke, *Arthur Dobbs, esquire, 1689–1765* (1957)
Archives Trinity Cam., corresp. and papers | BL, letters to Charles Jenkinson, and others • PRO, memoranda to Lord Egremont, PRO 30/47/14–15 • U. Mich., letters to William Knox • U. Mich., corresp. with William Knox
Likenesses T. Lawrence, portrait, c.1768
Wealth at death £20,000 in cash; also extensive Irish estates: Cashin, *Governor Henry Ellis*, 278

Ellis, Sir Henry (1777–1869), librarian, was born in the parish of St Botolph without Bishopsgate, London, on 29

Sir Henry Ellis (1777–1869), by Henry Corbould, 1836

November 1777, the son of John Ellis (1744–1812), master of the free school, Primrose Street, and Sarah Ellis, *née* Belknap. He was educated at the Mercers' School, Budge Row, until 1788, when he gained a scholarship to Merchant Taylors' School. In 1796 he gained a Merchant Taylors' exhibition at St John's College, Oxford; he graduated BCL in 1802 and obtained a law fellowship at St John's, which he vacated on his marriage in 1805. In 1798, through the influence of John Price, Bodley's librarian, he was appointed one of the two assistants in the Bodleian Library, the other being his subsequent museum colleague, the Revd H. H. Baber. In August 1800 he was appointed extra assistant in the British Museum printed books department, and succeeded Samuel Ayscough as assistant keeper on 27 March 1805. He was also regularly employed as a sub-commissioner on the public records. On 5 December 1805 he married Frances Jane (*d.* 12 Oct 1854), daughter of John and Elizabeth Frost. They had four sons and two daughters. In 1806 he was appointed keeper of printed books in the place of the Revd William Beloe, dismissed for negligence following the theft of prints by Robert Dighton. In March 1807 he began, with his assistant Baber, the revision of the 1787 printed books catalogue, then in two volumes with manuscript additions, inadequate, inaccurate and the source of much complaint. He continued work on his portion, the letters A–F and P–R, after his transfer to the manuscripts department as keeper in 1812. The new catalogue, published in seven volumes (1813–19), was later severely criticized by Sir Anthony Panizzi for its slapdash

method and want of scholarship; strictures rather unfair, given the lack of any systematic cataloguing rules at the time (they had to await Panizzi's keepership) and the urgency of the task. His *Catalogue of the Lansdowne Manuscripts* (1819) produced with Francis Douce, was a great improvement on the earlier catalogues of the Cotton and Harley manuscripts.

Ellis was never a profound scholar, but he was a methodical and industrious antiquary. He published a history of the parish of St Leonard, Shoreditch (1798), and produced numerous works on antiquarian and historical subjects during the following half-century; his publications fill four columns of the museum's printed books catalogue. His indexes, additions, and introduction to Domesday Book (1816) were of great value. The text of Domesday published by the government in 1783 was remarkably accurate but without note or comment of any kind; Ellis's work made it usable by scholars for the first time. With J. Caley and B. Bandinel, he edited Dugdale's *Monasticon* in eight enormous and prodigiously expensive volumes (1817–30). The edition was extravagantly praised at the time, but is now seen to be, in the words of D. C. Douglas, 'something of a literary imposture … which … added nothing to that which it was supposed to improve' (*English Scholars*, 1939, 44). Ellis's industry is well exemplified in his still valuable *Original Letters, Illustrative of English History*, published in three series in twelve volumes (1824–46; materials for a projected fourth series are in a priv. coll.). He was elected fellow of the Society of Antiquaries (1807), became its senior secretary (1814), and held this post for forty years before becoming director (1853–7). He wrote biographies of early fellows of the society, published a catalogue of its manuscripts (1816), and made numerous contributions to its journal, *Archaeologia*. His depletion of the society's funds in the publication of early literary and historical texts, however, upset archaeological interests and led to the establishment in 1843 of the British Archaeological Association.

In 1814 Ellis was appointed secretary to the trustees of the British Museum, in which capacity he eventually did much of the work of the principal librarian, Joseph Planta. He expected to succeed Planta after his death on 3 December 1827, but the archbishop of Canterbury, the principal trustee, who regarded the office as his to bestow, favoured his protégé the antiquary Henry Fynes Clinton. Warned by Lord Farnborough, a trustee, that the king inclined to Clinton, and that the royal favourite Lady Conyngham might also interest herself in the appointment, Ellis persuaded his patron Lord Aberdeen to induce Lord Lansdowne, the home secretary, to speak to the king on his behalf. He is also said to have chased on foot the carriage of the influential Sir William Knighton, the king's physician, to beg his support. His lobbying was successful, and although the trustees placed his name second to Clinton's in their submission to the king, he was nevertheless appointed; the only known occasion in the history of the museum when the sovereign passed over the trustees' first choice.

Ellis would have been an unexceptionable head of the

old museum. Short and plump, with a broad, open face and full lips, he exuded Pickwickian bonhomie. He was industrious, learned, and helpful to scholars; genial, kind-hearted, and unfailingly calm and good-humoured. He was affable and approachable to his subordinates, the more junior of whom he was fond of entertaining with racy stories. It was his, or rather the museum's, misfortune that he took office at a time when public expectations of that institution were changing fast. Unfriendly eyes were being turned on its management, staffing, and procedures. The radical MP and essayist William Cobbett denounced it as 'a place intended only for the amusement of the curious and the rich', officered by 'clergymen, who employed poor curates to perform their duty ... whilst they were living in indolence and affluence here in London' (Miller, 136, 138). An agitation got up by John Millard, a museum employee dismissed for incompetence, and supported by the radical MP Benjamin Hawes, occasioned the appointment of a House of Commons select committee in 1835, ostensibly to investigate his grievance. Its real agenda, however, was a broad attack on the museum, particularly on the exclusively aristocratic composition of the trustee body, and the museum's reluctance to address the needs of a wider public. The committee found no evidence of the gross misgovernment, nepotism, and corruption of which rumours were rife, but it got from Ellis only bland assurances that the museum's administration fell scarcely short of perfection. In his view literary and scientific men were quite unsuitable to be trustees. Making the museum more accessible through longer opening hours would attract people 'of a very low description', which would offend 'the more important class of the population'. He observed that 'the mere gazing at our curiosities is not one of the ... objects of the Museum'. In his opinion 'the Museum library is rather too much used than too little used'. Evening opening would simply attract 'lawyers' clerks, and persons who would read ... novels, and light literatures' (Miller, 139–42). It was very evident that he was quite unfitted by character and temperament to manage the changes that public opinion was forcing on the museum. The select committee recommended nothing very drastic, but in order to strengthen the museum's central administration, it proposed that the office of secretary should be a full-time post and no longer combined with the headship of a department.

This proved to be a disastrous proposal because of the personalities involved. Josiah Forshall, keeper of manuscripts and secretary, gave up his keepership to be the full-time secretary in 1837. In that office he virtually supplanted the amiable but ineffectual Ellis in the government of the museum. He was able to exclude him from board meetings, whose composition he tailored to his own requirements by deciding whom to summon to them. He controlled the flow of information to and from the trustees; minutes of meetings, if communicated to the keepers at all, were sometimes so garbled as to be unintelligible. Ellis was quite unable to control Forshall and his other imperious and quarrelsome subordinates, Sir Anthony Panizzi, keeper of printed books, and the latter's arch-enemy Sir Frederic Madden, who had succeeded Forshall as keeper of manuscripts. The situation was intolerable, complaints multiplied, and after protests by the British Association at the continued absence of scientists from the trustee body, a royal commission was appointed in 1848 to investigate the museum. Ellis confronted the commissioners as he had confronted the select committee, coolly imperturbable and seemingly quite unaware of any personal responsibility for the anarchic situation uncovered by their questioning. The commission's report (1850) regretted the 'want of harmony' between the principal officers and ascribed much that was amiss to the usurping of Ellis's authority by Forshall, who fulfilled its recommendation that the secretaryship should be abolished by retiring through ill health in the same year.

It was, however, too late for Ellis to establish any real authority, even if he had been disposed to do so. Panizzi's bravura performance at the royal commission hearings marked him out as the coming man; his dynamic energy and domineering personality quite overwhelmed the principal librarian, who was, in Madden's view, no more than his enemy's 'slave'. His casual attitude to his responsibilities was well exemplified in the inglorious part he played in the great Chartist scare of 1848, when the museum was thought to be in danger of pillage by the marchers assembling in Russell Square; a groundless fear, as it happened, but a very real one at the time, with memories of the Gordon riots and the sacking of Lord Eldon's house in Bedford Square in 1815 still strong. The museum was very vulnerable, as it was protected only by a wooden palisade on its east side because of the building works in progress. Ellis simply abandoned the organization of its defence to Panizzi and Madden, who wrote that he 'behaved like a child from the first, taking no responsibility, giving no orders, except such as were positively injurious, and finally shutting himself up in his own home' (Miller, 167).

Armoured against any consciousness of his own failings by urbane good temper and sublime indifference to criticism, Ellis continued in office for six years after the royal commission reported in 1850, though Panizzi was head in all but name. He was in fact irremovable; he enjoyed excellent health and there was no compulsory retirement. He was eventually induced to retire in 1856, aged seventy-nine, by the promise of the continuance of his full salary. He was made KH in 1832 and KB in 1833. He died at his house at 24 Bedford Square on 15 January 1869 and was buried with his wife at Woking.   MICHAEL BORRIE

Sources E. Miller, *That noble cabinet: a history of the British Museum* (1973) · A. Esdaile, *The British Museum Library: a short history and survey* (1946) · 'Royal commission to inquire into ... the British Museum', *Parl. papers* (1850), vol. 24, no. 1170 · J. Evans, *A history of the Society of Antiquaries* (1956) · DNB · Biographical memoranda, BL

Archives BL, corresp. and papers, Add. MSS 6306, 6335, 6363, 6518, 6525, 36298, 36653, 36658, 37034–37041, 37938, 38514–38515, 38626, 38650, 41312–41319, 42137, 42506, 4684C, 48340, 52184, 57521–57522, 57557–57558, 64065–64171, 65155, 70842–70844 · Bodl. Oxf., corresp. and papers incl. historical collections relating to Oxford · CUL, notes and papers, incl. observations on Anglo–Saxon literature · E. Sussex RO, corresp. relating to Ashburnham Library · Harvard U., Houghton L., papers relating to early English history and literature · Hunt. L., letters · S. Antiquaries, Lond., papers incl. biographical collections relating to early members of the Society of Antiquaries · UCL, letters to Society for the Diffusion of Useful Knowledge | BL, letters to P. Bliss, Add. MSS 34567–34579 · BL, corresp. with Sir Austen Layard, Add. MSS 38942–38943, 38978–38981 · BL, letters to Richard Gough and the Nichols family, Add. MS 36987 · BL, corresp. with Sir Frederic Madden, Egerton MSS 2837–2845 · BL, letters to J. B. Nichols and J. G. Nichols, Add. MS 57850 · BL, letters to Sir Robert Peel, Add. MSS 40345–40603 · BL, letters to T. J. Pettigrew, Add. MS 56229 · Bodl. Oxf., letters to Sir Thomas Phillipps · CKS, corresp. with Lord Stanhope · Lpool RO, letters to Matthew Gregson · U. Edin. L., letters to James Halliwell–Phillipps · U. Edin. L., letters to David Laing · U. Newcastle, Robinson L., letters to Sir Walter Trevelyan · Yale U., Beinecke L., letters to T. J. Pettigrew

Likenesses E. H. Corbould, drawing, 1836, BL · H. Corbould, lithograph, 1836, BM, NPG [*see illus.*] · M. S. Carpenter, portrait, BM

Wealth at death under £20,000: resworn probate, Aug 1870, *CGPLA Eng. & Wales* (1869)

Ellis, Sir Henry (1788–1855), diplomatist, was born on 1 September 1788, the illegitimate son of Robert *Hobart, fourth earl of Buckinghamshire (1760–1816). The identity of his mother is unknown, but the boy was brought up in his father's household. He was educated at Harrow School (1799–1803) and at William Nicholson's private academy in Soho (1804–5). He joined the East India Company in 1805 and in 1808 became an assistant to Sir John Malcolm. In 1809 Malcolm obliged Lord Minto by sending Ellis to join his second mission to Sind. On his return, Ellis wrote a damning account of the Talpura emirs, which formed the basis of British attitudes to the territory until it was annexed in 1843.

In 1810 Ellis joined Malcolm's third mission to Persia. From 1812 to 1814 he served as private secretary to his father when the latter was president of the Board of Control. In 1814 he returned to Persia on a secret mission to obtain revisions of the 1809 treaty of Tehran. He was successful, and the revised treaty provided the basis of Anglo-Persian relations until 1838. In 1815 he advised Castlereagh on the best way to deal with the perceived Russian threat to India. Castlereagh, following Ellis's advice, persuaded the Russians to return Qarabagh and Talesh to Persia. In the summer of 1815 Ellis acted as a secretary during the Anglo-American negotiations.

In 1816 Ellis accompanied Earl Amherst on his mission to China, and he recorded his experiences in *A Journal of the Proceedings of the Late Embassy to China* (1817). The mission, to negotiate a new trade agreement, was unsuccessful. Ellis was not impressed by the Chinese, whom he considered xenophobic, ultra-traditional, and 'uninteresting' (Ellis). On the return voyage, Ellis and his companions were wrecked in the Strait of Gaspar and only reached Batavia after a perilous journey of several hundred miles in an open boat. Later they called at St Helena, where Ellis met Napoleon. Napoleon later hotly disputed Ellis's account of the meeting.

Ellis unsuccessfully contested Boston at a by-election in 1818; he was helped in his campaign by Frederick Robinson (later Viscount Goderich and earl of Ripon). Robinson had married Lord Buckinghamshire's only legitimate child, Sarah, who inherited her father's considerable wealth, and, after the earl's death in 1816, Robinson accepted her illegitimate brother as 'a sort of charge upon the estate' (Jones, 124) and acted as his patron. Ellis was elected for Boston in 1820 but, in the meantime, had accepted the posts of deputy colonial secretary and commissioner of stamps in Cape Town, and was unseated on the grounds that he held an office of profit under the crown. On 10 June 1820 at Cape Town he married Louisa Amelia Wilson of Leominster. They had three sons. Ellis returned to Britain and was made commissioner of customs (1824–5), clerk of the pells (1825–34), and commissioner of the Board of Control (1830–35). In 1830 he published *A Series of Letters on the East India Question*, addressed to members of parliament, in which he defended the role of the East India Company.

Ellis was sworn of the privy council and made a knight of the Royal Guelphic Order in 1832. He was briefly ambassador in Persia (1835–6), but advised that Afghanistan was now more important to Britain than Persia. He unsuccessfully contested Lincoln in the 1837 general election. In 1842 Lord Aberdeen, at Ripon's request, asked Ellis to head a special trade mission to Brazil. The mission failed, partly because of the offence caused by Britain's unilateral action to suppress the Brazilian slave trade. In 1848 Ellis was named as a delegate for the abortive Brussels conference on the affairs of Italy; the same year he was made a knight commander in the Order of the Bath. Sir Henry Ellis died at Marine Parade, Brighton, on 28 September 1855.   R. M. HEALEY

Sources W. D. Jones, *'Prosperity' Robinson* (1967) · E. Ingram, *Britain's Persian connection, 1798–1828* (1992) · M. E. Yapp, *Strategies of British India: Britain, Iran and Afghanistan, 1798–1850* (1980) · H. Ellis, *Journal of the proceedings of the late embassy to China* (1817) · A. K. Manchester, *British preeminence in Brazil* (1933) · B. E. O'Meara, *Napoleon in exile, or, A voice from St Helena*, 2 vols. (1822) · B. D. Mirchandani, 'Sind in 1809: extracts from Henry Ellis's account', *Journal of the Sind Historical Society*, 7 (1943), 254 · *Annual Register* (1855) · *GM*, 2nd ser., 44 (1855), 648 · P. Philip, *British residents at the Cape* (1981) · d. cert. · PRO, PROB 2/2220/834 · BL OIOC, J/1/19 f. 224

Archives BL OIOC, MSS · PRO, MSS | Auckland Public Library, letters to Sir George Grey · BL, corresp. with Lord Aberdeen, Add. MSS 43124, 43160 · Derbys. RO, letters to Sir R. J. Wilmot-Horton · NL Scot., letters to J. G. Lockhart · U. Southampton L., corresp. with Lord Palmerston

Ellis, Sir Henry Walton (1783–1815), army officer, born at Worcester, was the son of Major-General John Joyner Ellis and grandson of J. Joyner of Berkeley, Gloucestershire. Joyner Ellis took the name Ellis in consequence of his adoption by 'Governor' Henry Ellis, lieutenant-governor of Georgia, in 1758, who resided for some time at Lansdowne Place, Bath, and died at Naples in 1806. Joyner Ellis served successively in the 18th (Royal Irish), old 89th, and 41st (Welsh) regiments, became lieutenant-colonel 23rd foot (Royal Welch Fusiliers) in 1793, major-general in 1798, and died in 1804. He and his wife, whose maiden name was

Walton, had several children, the eldest of whom was Henry Walton Ellis.

Immediately upon his birth Ellis was appointed to an ensigncy in the 89th foot, of which his father was major. The regiment, which had been chiefly recruited in the area of Worcester, was disbanded at the peace of Versailles a few months later, and the infant was put on half pay. He was brought on full pay again as an ensign, at the age of five, in the 41st foot, of which his father had been appointed major on its reorganization in 1787. Young Ellis became a lieutenant 41st foot in 1792 and captain 23rd foot on 20 January 1796. As a boy-captain of barely fourteen, he served with the 23rd foot in the descent on Ostend in 1798, and then in the northern Netherlands in 1799 (where he was wounded), in the channel, at El Ferrol and in the Mediterranean in 1800, in Egypt in 1801 (where he was wounded, received a gold medal, and promoted major), in Hanover in 1805, and at Copenhagen in 1807. A youthful veteran at the age of twenty-five, he succeeded to the command of the 1st battalion of his regiment, without purchase, in Nova Scotia in 1808 and commanded it in the expedition against Martinique in 1809, where at the siege of Fort Bourbon he offered to take the flints out of his men's firelocks and carry the works with his fusiliers at the point of the bayonet, a daring enterprise which the commander-in-chief, Sir George Beckwith, refused to sanction.

Ellis went with his battalion to Portugal in 1810 and commanded it through the campaigns in the Peninsula and southern France, during which he repeatedly distinguished himself, particularly at Albuera in 1811 in the historic charge of the fusilier brigade, at the siege of Badajoz in 1812 (when he was wounded), and in the desperate fighting at the pass of Roncesvalles, in the Pyrenees, on 28 July 1813. For his Peninsular services he was promoted colonel and made a KCB, on 2 January 1815. Under his command the Royal Welch Fusiliers joined the duke of Wellington's army on the field of Waterloo the night before the battle, having made a forced march from Grammont. They were in reserve during the greater part of 18 June, but were brought up into the front line on the left later in the day and received several French charges in square. There Ellis was wounded in his right breast by a musket-ball. Feeling faint, he rode out of the square towards the rear, but in getting over a small ditch he fell from his horse and sustained further injuries. He was carried to a neighbouring hovel, where his wounds were dressed. On the evening of the 19th, after the army had moved on, the hut caught fire. Ellis was rescued with great difficulty by Assistant Surgeon Munro of his regiment, but not before he had received severe burns, from which he died on the morning of 20 June 1815. He was buried at Waterloo. In his memory the officers and men of the Royal Welch Fusiliers placed a monument, costing £1200, in Worcester Cathedral.

Ellis never married, but he left two illegitimate sons, to whom Wellington gave commissions. The younger, Henry Ellis, died young on his passage home from India. The elder, Francis Joyner Ellis, died a major in the 62nd foot at Moulmein in 1840. On his death the name of Ellis was assumed by William Joyner, who was for many years coroner of Gloucestershire and was a surviving brother of Major-General John Joyner Ellis.

H. M. CHICHESTER, rev. ROGER T. STEARN

Sources W. S. Ellis, *Notices of the Ellises of England and France* (privately printed, 1855–66) · *Army List* · R. Cannon, ed., *Historical record of the seventh regiment, or the royal fusiliers* (1847) · W. F. P. Napier, *History of the war in the Peninsula and in the south of France*, 6 vols. (1828–40) · *GM*, 1st ser., 85/1 (1815) · *LondG* · A. J. Guy, ed., *The road to Waterloo: the British army and the struggle against revolutionary and Napoleonic France, 1793–1815* (1990) · T. C. W. Blanning, *The French revolutionary wars, 1787–1802* (1996) · R. Muir, *Britain and the defeat of Napoleon, 1807–1815* (1996) · J. Haydn, *The book of dignities: containing rolls of the official personages of the British empire* (1851)
Likenesses miniature, Regimental Museum, Caernarvon Castle?; repro. in *The royal Welch fusiliers* (1974) · stipple, NPG

Ellis, Humphrey. *See* Waring, Humphrey (*bap.* 1605, *d.* 1676).

Ellis, Humphry Francis (1907–2000), humorous writer, was born on 17 July 1907 in Metheringham, Lincolnshire, one of the five children of John Constable Ellis, a country doctor, and his wife, Alice Marion Elizabeth Raven. During the First World War the family lived in Hampshire. Ellis was educated at Tonbridge School and Magdalen College, Oxford, where John Betjeman was a contemporary. 'You think you're funny', the future poet laureate told him. 'Well, you are' (personal knowledge). Ellis was a keen cricketer, and played rugby for the University Greyhounds and later for Richmond. Between school and Oxford he had taught at his old prep school near Liphook, and after leaving Oxford in 1930 with a first in *literae humaniores* he taught for a term at Marlborough College. But he found the work uncongenial, and gave up teaching for the more perilous life of a writer. A cheque from *Punch* for £3 4*s.* 6*d.*, as payment for his first article, arrived just as he was about to propose to Barbara Pauline Hasseldine (1908/9–1997). This was enough encouragement and they were married on 21 December 1933; they had a son and a daughter. Sir Owen Seaman, the editor of *Punch*, encouraged Ellis to become a regular contributor, and Seaman's successor E. V. Knox appointed him assistant editor in 1933, at a salary of £100 a year. He was in charge of an editorial staff of four, and the Ellis family's home in Roehampton became a rendezvous for *Punch* contributors such as A. P. Herbert, Bernard Partridge, E. H. Shepherd, and A. A. Milne; other pleasant ingredients of *Punch* life included long lunches at the Garrick Club and country house weekends with the added attraction of a cricket match.

Ellis's creation, A. J. Wentworth, a self-important, accident-prone, and alarmingly incompetent prep school-master, made his first appearance in *Punch* in November 1938 in 'The algebra case'. 'I never wake up sleeping boys by throwing books at them, as hundreds of old Burgrove boys will be able to testify', Wentworth explained, after he had inadvertently stunned a slumbering pupil with a copy of Hall and Knight's algebra textbook. *The Papers of A. J. Wentworth, BA* was published in 1949; it was followed by *A. J. Wentworth BA (Ret'd)* (1962)—in which the great man endures Women's Institute members and jovial vicars—and by *The Swansong of A. J. Wentworth* (1982), widely regarded as an inferior work. Ellis was clearly influenced by George Grossmith's Mr Pooter—Ellis, like Grossmith, delighted in the pathos as well as the comedy of the pompous, bustling 'little man'—and he was sometimes annoyed by the comparison. Wentworth, however, has nothing to fear from it. Ellis thought Arthur Lowe perfectly cast in the television adaptation in 1982, though neither the script nor the production passed muster.

After serving in the Royal Artillery during the Second World War, Ellis returned to *Punch* under the editorship of Bernard Hollowood and Malcolm Muggeridge, acting as both literary and deputy editor. He took an instant dislike to the editorship of William Davis, and severed all connection with the magazine in 1968. By this time however he was a regular contributor to the *New Yorker*. Whereas Wentworth had a chequered publishing career, surging back into print when an eager publisher came his way before lapsing into oblivion once more, Ellis's account of rugby football's rules, *Why the Whistle Went* (1947), was endlessly reprinted and translated. Other books included two collections of pieces, *Twenty-Five Years Hard* (1960) and *A Bee in the Kitchen* (1983), and *Mediatrics* (1961), a guide to the hazards of middle age. Ellis edited the *Royal Artillery Commemoration Handbook* (1950), and co-edited *The Manual of Rugby Football* (1952).

Ellis was a lean, fit-looking man with fine, aquiline features; he had red hair when young, earning him the nickname of Copper. A Penguin reprint of Wentworth once carried an author photograph of a moon-faced individual, later identified as an eminent child psychologist: this led to some confusion among those meeting Ellis for the first time. H. F. Ellis was appointed MBE in 1945. He spent his later years in Somerset, and died in Musgrove Park Hospital, Taunton, on 8 December 2000. His wife predeceased him in 1997.　　　　　　　　　　　　　　　　JEREMY LEWIS

Sources H. F. Ellis, *The papers of A. J. Wentworth* (2000) • H. F. Ellis, *A. J. Wentworth BA (ret'd)* (1962) • J. Lewis, *Oldie* (22 Jan 1993) [profile of H. F. Ellis] • J. Lewis, *Daily Telegraph* (12 Dec 2000) • *The Times* (23 Dec 2000) • M. Kington, *The Independent* (9 Dec 2000) • *WW* • personal knowledge (2004) • b. cert. • m. cert. • d. cert.
Likenesses photograph, repro. in *Daily Telegraph*
Wealth at death £993,863—gross; £988,657—net: probate, 15 March 2001, *CGPLA Eng. & Wales*

Ellis, James (1763–1830), antiquary, was born in Hexham, Northumberland, where he was baptized on 30 July 1763, the son of William Ellis, a glover and town sergeant of Hexham, and his wife, Jane Charlton. He was at school near Haltwhistle. He was apprenticed first in Hexham and then from 1783 to John and Thomas Davidson, solicitors of Newcastle upon Tyne, where his contemporaries were Thomas Bedingfeld and George Pickering (he collected their verses, with some slight pieces of his own, for publication under his anonymous editorship in 1814). He thereafter practised as a solicitor briefly at Hexham and then at Newcastle. In 1795 he married Rachel (d. 17 Jan 1830), the daughter of John Gallon of High Shaws, Elsdon; their only child died young.

In 1796 Ellis and John Davidson acquired the Otterburn estate (which Ellis spelt 'Otterbourne' in his letters), Davidson taking the larger portion west of the burn and Ellis 1200 acres including the tower, manor, and demesne. In 1819 he reported to Walter Scott having discovered near this house a brick pavement apparently of Roman date. It was his Otterburn connection that gave him an introduction to Scott, to whom he wrote in February 1812 about a passage in *The Minstrelsy of the Scottish Border* (2nd edn, 1.29), correcting the location of the Scottish encampment at the battle of Otterburn: it lay on his own rather than on Davidson's portion of the estate. 'Being somewhat fond of Border history', he then and for some years afterwards provided Scott with lists of addenda and errata to his writings, all of which display much familiarity with border terrain and documents. Scott reacted appreciatively to this punctilious attention to his texts, and with his family first visited him at Otterburn in 1814. John Hodgson, the historian of Northumberland, likewise acknowledges his helpfulness, and he was a patron of Robert White. Ellis was an early member of the Society of Antiquaries of Newcastle upon Tyne, of which Scott was elected an honorary member. He wrote verses, and prepared a full index to Froissart (which, however, Scott could not recommend for publication). A proposal by Scott that he should re-edit the border laws came to nothing. He died on 25 March 1830, and was buried with his wife's family in Elsdon churchyard.　　　　　　　　　　　　　　　ALAN BELL

Sources R. Welford, *History of the Berwickshire Naturalists' Club*, 22 (1913), 118–21 • M. A. Richardson, ed., *The local historian's table book ... historical division*, 5 vols. (1841–6), vol. 4, pp. 52–4 • *The letters of Sir Walter Scott*, ed. H. J. C. Grierson and others, centenary edn, 12 vols. (1932–79), vols. 3–4 • J. Hodgson, *A history of Northumberland*, 3 pts in 7 vols. (1820–58), pt 2, vol. 1 • letters to Sir Walter Scott, NL Scot.
Archives NL Scot., letters to Sir Walter Scott

Ellis, John (1598/9–1665), Church of England clergyman and religious writer, was born at Gwylan, Maentwrog, in Merioneth, the only son of Elis John and Lowry ferch Ieuan (1567?–1647). He matriculated at Oxford as a student of Hart Hall in 1617; in the matriculation register he is described as being eighteen years old and a resident of Llandecwyn, Merioneth. He was ordained deacon on 23 September 1621, graduated BA on 27 February 1622, and was ordained priest on 22 September 1622; he proceeded MA on 29 April 1625 and became a fellow of Jesus College in 1628. On 3 August 1629 he was instituted to the rectory of Whitfield (later Wheatfield), Oxfordshire, and held that benefice for about seventeen years. He married Rebekah, daughter of John Petty of Stoke Talmage on 24 August 1631 at Thame in the same county. He received his BD at Oxford on 12 May 1632 and his DD at St Andrews in August 1634; he was incorporated DD at Oxford on 21 October 1634 and at Cambridge in 1635.

Ellis's first two books were published before the civil wars. *Bellum in idumaeos* (1641), dedicated to Thomas Tipping of Wheatfield, is a commentary on the Old Testament Book of Obadiah, chapters 1–21. *Clavis fidei* (1642;

reprinted 1643) dedicated to John Lisle, the future regicide, is an exposition of the apostles' creed, based on lectures Ellis had delivered to students of Hart Hall. He refers to the creed as 'Zodiacus Christiani' (p. 3) because it has twelve articles. It was translated into English by William Flower in 1668 and by H. Handley in 1842.

Following the sequestration of Nathaniel Gyles in 1644, Ellis acquired, probably in 1646, the rectory of Chinnor, Oxfordshire. That year he was also made rector of Dolgellau, Merioneth, by nomination of the commissioners of the great seal, and held that position until his death. In 1648 he had an income of more than £200 from the rectories of Dolgellau and Towyn, and the prebend of Y Faenol, Caernarvonshire; he was 'the best paid minister in Wales' (Richards, *Religious*, 143). Ellis was named one of the twenty-five approvers under the Act for the Better Propagation of the Gospel in Wales (1650). In a 1657 letter to John Lewis of Glasgrug, Cardiganshire, Ellis argued for the establishment of a national college in Wales and volunteered 'to reade at the first, till wee could procure assistants in the several sciences' (Nuttall, 132). Although Lewis forwarded the letter to Richard Baxter, then vicar of Kidderminster, nothing seems to have come of Ellis's offer or his specific suggestions.

Ellis conformed following the Restoration and published *Defensio fidei*, a defence of the Thirty-Nine Articles, in September 1660. This book was reprinted several times in London and Amsterdam and was translated into English by 'J. L.' in 1700. Ellis was 'weake in body' when he made his will on 4 December 1665, and died before 11 December, when an inventory was taken. Although he requested burial in the church or churchyard at Dolgellau, there is no record of the burial. Legacies went to his sisters Katherine and Dorothy, his brother-in-law Robert Owen of Llanfrothen and other relatives; there is no mention of a wife or children. He left the income from a tenement called Penrhyn in Llanaber parish for the employment of a schoolmaster for Dolgellau; this endowment led to the establishment of the Dolgellau grammar school. Ellis was succeeded as the rector of Dolgellau by his kinsman Thomas Ellis. EDWARD A. MALONE

Sources J. Lloyd, ed., 'The will of Dr John Ellis, rector of Dolgelley (1647–1665)', *Journal of the Merioneth Historical and Record Society*, 2 (1954), 228–31 · A. M. Rees, '"Dr John Elis" school", Dolgellau, and its successors, 1665–1965', *Journal of the Merioneth Historical and Record Society*, 5/2 (1966), 112–15 · Wood, *Ath. Oxon.*, new edn, 3.709–10 · *DWB* · G. F. Nuttall, 'The correspondence of John Lewis, Glasrug, with Richard Baxter and with Dr. John Ellis, Dolgelley', *Journal of the Merioneth Historical and Record Society*, 2/2 (1954), 120–34 · Foster, *Alum. Oxon.* · Venn, *Alum. Cant.* · *Reg. Oxf.*, vol. 2/3 · W. J. Oldfield, 'Index to the clergy whose ordination, institution, resignation, licence or death is recorded in the diocesan registers of the diocese of Oxford … 1542–1908', 1915, Bodl. Oxf., MS Top. Oxon. c. 250 · *STC, 1475–1640* · T. Richards, *Religious developments in Wales, 1654–1662* (1923) · private information (2004) [Robert Evans, cataloguing assistant, department of manuscripts and records, NL Wales; Chris Gilliam, archivist, Oxon. RO; Mark Lawrence, senior librarian at the Centre for Oxfordshire Studies, Westgate; Einion Wyn Thomas, head archivist at Merioneth RO, Dolgellau] · *Walker rev.*, 74

Archives DWL, MSS 59.2.124, 59.1.128 · LPL, autograph letters, MS 989, fols. 190–199

Wealth at death £40 0s. 6d. at Dolgellau and £53 2s. 6d. at Perhyn and Ryddalld; inventory goods worth £40 0s. 6d. but bequests imply a significantly larger estate: NL Wales, B 1665/59; Lloyd, ed., 'The will of Dr John Ellis', 230–31

Ellis, John (d. **1681**), Church of England clergyman and religious controversialist, was born in Yorkshire, the son of John Ellis (d. 1643?). He matriculated as a pensioner at St Catharine's College, Cambridge, in 1630. He graduated BA in 1634 and was elected to the fellowship of the college, proceeding MA in 1638. Ellis stayed at Cambridge, becoming a university proctor, but must have resigned his fellowship by the time he married, on 3 May 1641 at St Edward's, Susannah (1624/5–1700), daughter of William Welbore.

Ellis sided with parliament when the civil war broke out. He gained notoriety at the university for preaching in June 1642 against the royalist casuistry of Henry Ferne's *The Resolving of Conscience*. It is likely that this dissection of Ferne's work reached the attention of parliament, and Ellis was invited to preach before the House of Commons on 22 February 1643. In dedicating *The Sole Path to a Sound Peace* (1643) to the house, Ellis, who is described as preacher in Cambridge, says that he had been mourning the recent loss of his father and so had only had ten days to prepare, but he managed to preach a rousing sermon on the need for reformation in church and state, taking his text from Micah 5: 5.

Ellis soon moved to London and became of the Independent persuasion. In 1643 he discussed with Thomas Gataker and Alexander Henderson whether taking the solemn league and covenant would compel him to support the presbyterian position on church government; they convinced him that it would not, but he later felt cheated by them. The dominance of presbyterian ecclesiology led Ellis in 1647 to publish a book entitled *Vindiciae Catholicae*, which defended Independency and criticized the views of theologians who believed in a single visible universal church order. In particular, Ellis singled out Samuel Hudson and the London presbyterian ministers for reproach. Hudson replied with a long vindication against Ellis in 1650. The latter's flirtation with Independency was, however, brief. It appears that he was a member of a congregation but found his 'expectation of the beauty of holiness' in the gathered church to be frustrated by the 'confusion, breaches, doting about endless questions' and 'time vainly spent' as he later explained in *St Austin Imitated* (1661) (Ellis, *St Austin Imitated*, 14–15). Ellis became concerned that the people who remained in parish churches were neglected by the Independents and 'look'd upon as people of another world'; he was also disturbed by the Independents' reliance on the military. As a result of these difficulties he left his congregation in October 1648.

As the autumn progressed, Ellis became dismayed at the revolutionary turn of events and later claimed to have gone to the village of Caversham, near Reading, to try to reason with the army leaders. He said that he had conference with Lord General Fairfax and Oliver Cromwell about the army's plans, but that the meeting broke down after he argued with Cromwell. The subsequent execution of the king and the purge of parliament deeply disturbed Ellis; he stated in 1661 that the former caused such a crisis of conscience in him that he was paralysed with sickness and fear. At about this time he became a public lecturer at Aylesbury, Buckinghamshire, and took up some kind of position in the parish of Waddesdon in the same county, where his son Samuel was baptized on 28 November 1649. Ellis refused the oath of engagement to the new republic, publicly preaching against it at Aylesbury. By 1659 Ellis had been appointed to a third portion of the rectory at Waddesdon. That year he published *The Pastor and the Clerk*, a defence of infant baptism, which included a short recantation of his former position. He prepared a longer recantation in 1660, but was prevented from publishing it until 1661 because he was struck down with 'a whole squadron of diseases' for three months. Ellis was treated by Thomas Coxe, the famous doctor and an old friend from Cambridge.

Ellis's conformity was rewarded by the restored royalist regime when on 24 October and 8 November 1661 he was confirmed in his third at Waddesdon and granted the other two-thirds of the living to become its sole rector. However, he was criticized by his former Independent brethren and by Henry Hickman who attacked Ellis in his *Apologia pro ministris in Anglia (vulgo) Non-Conformists* (1664). Ellis died on 3 November 1681 at Waddesdon and was buried in the chancel of his church with a monumental inscription. He was survived by his wife (who died on 29 April 1700) and nine of their eleven children, including John *Ellis (1642x6–1738), William *Ellis (1641x7–1732), Welbore *Ellis (1661/2–1734), and Philip *Ellis (1652–1726).   E. C. VERNON

Sources J. Ellis, *St Austin imitated* (1661) • J. Ellis, *The pastor and the clerk* (1659) • J. Ellis, *Vindiciae Catholicae* (1647) • Venn, *Alum. Cant.*, 1/2.96 • letters to children and Dr Oldys, 1673–1680, BL, Add. MS 28930, fols. 32, 34, 52, 153 • Wood, *Ath. Oxon.*, new edn, 3.710; 4.371–2

Ellis, John (1642x6–1738), government official, was the eldest son of John *Ellis (d. 1681), clergyman, and his wife, Susannah (d. 1700), daughter of William Welbore of Cambridge, and brother of the Jacobite Sir William *Ellis, of Philip (Michael) *Ellis, vicar apostolic, and of Welbore *Ellis, bishop of Meath. He was educated at Westminster School, which he entered in 1660 aged fourteen, and at Christ Church, Oxford, whence he matriculated on 22 July 1664 aged eighteen. He was recommended by the dean of Christ Church, Bishop Fell, to Sir Joseph Williamson, then under-secretary of state and a well-known patron of promising young men. Williamson sent Ellis to France to further his education and, although this sojourn abroad was not a success, by 1672 he was working under Williamson at the paper office. However, when Williamson was promoted to secretary of state in 1674 Ellis found himself unemployed and contemplated a career as a civil lawyer. Another Oxford luminary, Sir Leoline Jenkins, principal of Jesus College, rescued him from that fate by appointing

Ellis as his secretary during the peace negotiations at Nijmegen in 1675–7, and Ellis left England in December 1675. During this time he made the acquaintance of the prince of Orange, whom he attended at the siege of Maastricht in 1676 and the battle of Mons in 1678. Upon his return Ellis took up employment as secretary to Thomas Butler, earl of Ossory, heir to the dukedom of Ormond, which included a trip to the states general of the United Provinces to promote Ossory's claims to a military commission granted by Prince William. Following Ossory's death in August 1680 Ellis seems to have become employed by Ormond himself, although his friend Humphrey Prideaux referred to Ellis's being kept with the lord lieutenant of Ireland 'to your [Ellis's] disadvantage' (*Letters*, 82). By April 1681 Ellis was in London with a letter for Jenkins, and Ormond himself wrote to the recently appointed secretary of state, the earl of Conway, recommending Ellis as 'a very honest man and very well qualified for service at home or abroad. If I had room for him I would not have been without him' (*Ormonde MSS*, new ser., 6.43).

Ellis continued to look for official advancement and in February 1682 seems to have been marked out for a secretarial role to the embassy in France. However, his connection with Butler secured him employment following the appointment as lord deputy in Ireland of Richard Butler, earl of Arran, a younger brother of Ossory: with the combined patronage of Ormond, Jenkins, and the earl of Arlington, who described him as 'a very ingenious and well deserving man' (*Ormonde MSS*, new ser., 6.424), Ellis was named as secretary to the Irish revenue commissioners, a post worth £300 per annum plus £200 per annum from wool licensing. Despite a desire to return to England, and the possibilities opened up by the favour shown to his brother Philip by James II, Ellis continued in this post until the revolution of 1688. He then returned to England, no doubt prompted by the hope of furthering his career and perhaps in order to avoid accusations of Jacobitism given the allegiance of several of his brothers to James II. In the event he became secretary to the young second duke of Ormond (Ossory's son) until his appointment as a commissioner of transports in 1691. He remained in that post until he became under-secretary to the secretary of state Sir William Trumbull in May 1695. James Vernon described him at this time as having the reputation of an 'ingenious man and a good scholar' (BL, Add. MS 46527, fol. 89). The office of under-secretary was a post of some burden, as Trumbull was often absent and Ellis had himself to wait on the king. This no doubt led to the comment reported by James Vernon in May 1697 that 'there are two little fellows in Sir William Trumbull's office (I suppose she means Ellis and Tucker) who are pretending to all places' (Vernon to duke of Shrewsbury, 18 May 1697, Northants. RO, Montagu (Boughton) MSS, 46/103). Ellis survived Trumbull's fall, being taken on by his successor, none other than James Vernon, in December 1697. Indeed, by now he had earned a reputation for hard work and loyalty. He claimed never to have made even £500 per annum from his office, but he was well placed to solicit and be granted in 1699 the forfeited Irish estates of his brother William in repayment of a loan to the government. He had little difficulty in securing parliamentary confirmation of the grant in an act passed in May 1702. Meanwhile, Sir Charles Hedges had succeeded Vernon in November 1700 and retained the services of Ellis as his under-secretary. Ellis added to his offices in May 1701 when he was appointed comptroller of the Royal Mint. Again he survived the vicissitudes of political change when the duke of Manchester was named as secretary in January 1702, and again when Hedges returned to office in the following May.

After a four-year search for a parliamentary seat Ellis was returned for Harwich at the election following the accession of Queen Anne. However, he made a minimal impact on the house, although he worked hard behind the scenes on behalf of his constituents. He did, of course, loyally support the ministry of the day. Unfortunately, owing to a dispute with Hedges over some passes which Ellis had issued, he was dismissed from his post in the secretary's office in May 1705. This did not alter his support for the ministry in the 1705–8 parliament—indeed, contemporaries found it impossible to agree on his party affiliation. However, without ministerial backing he could not cling on to his seat in the Commons at the 1708 election, and despite several attempts to return to the house he never succeeded. After his final attempt was rebuffed by the Commons' committee of elections in February 1711, he lost his place as comptroller of the mint in the following June.

By now Ellis was a man of independent means. Although he petitioned George I for a return to his place in the mint he was never reappointed to central office. He was active in 1718 as a Middlesex JP in the suppression of Jacobite meetings. He died 'immensely rich' (GM) at his house in Pall Mall on 8 July 1738, reputedly aged ninety-five, having been cared for in his declining years by Samuel Seddon. He left his Irish estates in trust to his nephew, Welbore Ellis. Although a John Ellis of Westminster married a Jane Holloway in 1697, this would seem to have been a namesake because in July 1703 Adam de Cardonnel mentioned to Ellis the second marriage of Sir Stephen Fox with the comment that 'you and I must plead for old people's marrying, for neither of us can do it young' (BL, Add. MS 28918, fol. 192). Although Ellis was reputed to have been a lover of the duchess of Cleveland there does not seem to have been much evidence of this beyond a few allusions in the work of Alexander Pope. Ellis left a voluminous correspondence and other papers, many of which were subsequently purchased by the British Museum, and selections from which were published in the nineteenth century.

STUART HANDLEY

Sources HoP, *Commons, 1690–1715* [draft] · BL, Add. MSS 28875–28956 · G. Agar-Ellis, ed., *The Ellis correspondence: letters written during the years 1686, 1687, 1688, and addressed to John Ellis*, 2 vols. (1829) · *Letters of Humphrey Prideaux … to John Ellis*, ed. E. M. Thompson, CS, new ser., 15 (1875) · *Calendar of the manuscripts of the marquess of Ormonde*, new ser., 8 vols., HMC, 36 (1902–20), vol. 6 · CSP dom., 1671–1700 · W. A. Shaw, ed., *Calendar of treasury books*, 9–25, PRO (1931–61) · J. C. Sainty, ed., *Officials of the secretaries of state, 1660–1782* (1973), 77 · BL, Egerton MS 929, fol. 148 · BL, Add. MS 46527, fol. 89 · *GM*, 1st ser., 8 (1738), 380 · will, PRO, PROB 11/690, sig. 173

Archives BL, corresp., Add. MS 4194 · BL, corresp., official and private corresp. and MSS, Add. MSS 28875–28956 | BL, letters to Lord Lexington, Add. MS 46525 · CKS, letters to Alexander Stanhope · Longleat House, Warminster, corresp. with Matthew Prior

Wealth at death unknown but 'immensely rich': GM

Ellis, John (1698–1791), scrivener and poet, was born on 22 March 1698 in the parish of St Clement Danes, London, one of four known children of James Ellis and Susannah Philpot. His mother was a 'fanatical dissenter' (*DNB*) and his upbringing turned him against nonconformity. His restless, eccentric father worked on the fringes of the legal profession. James Ellis was employed as a clerk to his uncle and guardian, Sergeant Denn, the recorder of Canterbury, and then at the post office in Deal, followed by work as a searcher of the customs. He left this last employment and went to London, where he was employed at the trial of Henry Sacheverell, to take down evidence. Isaac Reed, in his obituary of John Ellis, accurately described the father's qualifications as 'not those which lead to riches' (Reed, 3). John's meagre education comprised attendance at a day school in Dogwell Court, White Friars, London, along with his three siblings, followed by a school in Wine Office Court, Fleet Street, London, where he learned the rudiments of grammar. Reed reported that Ellis translated Payne Fisher's *Marston Moor*, originally published in 1650, while still a schoolboy. No trace of his original translation has been found but it was an intimation of his future preoccupations. He was probably apprenticed to John Taverner, an eminent scrivener of Threadneedle Street and cousin to the playwright and lawyer William Taverner. The profession of scrivener was in decline at this period; customarily scriveners drew up legal documents, but they were also involved in money-lending and arranging property transactions. Taverner taught Ellis Latin alongside his own son Charles and his other apprentices.

In 1715 Ellis was admitted a freeman of the Scriveners' Company and began to develop friendships in the literary world. His company was sought by Nicholas Fayting, a schoolfellow of Charles Taverner at Merchant Taylors' who later became rector of St Martin Outwich, and their friendship was to last until Fayting's death in 1789, an event marked by a bequest of £100 to Ellis in his will. He was encouraged to write by William King, principal of St Mary Hall, Oxford, and by John Boyle, Lord Broghill, later fifth earl of Orrery, who supposedly met Ellis while Charles Taverner was at St John's College, Oxford, although Ellis does not appear in the matriculation lists. His first published work was *The South Sea Dream* (1720). He continued to work as a clerk to John Taverner until the latter's death in 1736. He then entered into partnership with Charles Taverner; this was not a good business relationship, and Ellis 'was a considerable sufferer both in his peace of mind and his purse' (Reed, 4). He continued to

John Ellis (1698–1791), by William Pether, 1781 (after Thomas Frye, 1761)

play a part in the Scriveners' Company, acting as master on four occasions between 1735 and 1784.

Ellis's literary work, mainly satirical in nature, continued unabated, although he was reluctant to publish. Among those works that did appear were a verse transcription of King's *Templum libertatis* in 1742–3 and *The Canto Added by Maphaeus, to Virgil's Twelve Books of Aeneas* in 1758. Several small poems were published in Dodsley's collection in 1763. Moses Mendes, a London stockbroker, effusively described Ellis's attendance at the Cock tavern, Threadneedle Street, every Friday night, in verse. Perhaps the most famous reference to him was made by Samuel Johnson, who commented to James Boswell: 'The most literary conversation I ever enjoyed was at the table of Jack Ellis, a money-scrivener behind the Royal Exchange, with whom I at one period used to dine generally once a week' (Bate).

Ellis settled in the Broad Street ward of the City of London and lived for a time at Black Swan Court and then at Capel Court. As a freeman of the City and a householder he was elected to the common council of Broad Street ward in 1750 and made a deputy to the alderman in 1771. In 1765 he failed to be elected chamberlain of London. He was of small build, with hard features. Reed described him as a man 'whose genius, manners, urbanity, wit, good-humour, and social qualifications endeared him to friends of three generations' (Reed, 3). On a visit to Johnson in 1784 Ellis told him of a sudden change in his eyesight that had occurred on a visit to Margate in 1778, and later detailed the event in a letter. Boswell visited Ellis in

October 1790 and described his capacity to recite poetry, his alert mind, and his ability to walk up to 20 miles a day.

Ellis remained a bachelor, probably as a result of his parents' turbulent relationship, and his family background remains obscure. In his will, made on 4 December 1788, three years before his death, he named two grand-nephews, Robert and John Over, as recipients of his watch and his red morocco Bible, respectively. Their unnamed sister was to receive his copybooks, teaching writing and arithmetic, and his housewifery books. The profits from the sale of his goods were to go to his nephew James Over or to be divided equally between Over's two children. He also left his housekeeper £200 to buy an annuity. His legal papers were left to his long-standing friend William Wheatley Hussey, clerk of the Scriveners' Company. His numerous poetical manuscripts and printed works, and their copyright, were left to his friend John Sewell, a Cornhill bookseller; Sewell passed some of these on to their mutual friend Isaac Reed. Ellis's edition of Aesop's fables fetched £6 when sold as part of Reed's library in 1807.

Ellis asked to be buried adjacent to his 'late deceased friend' Miss Arabella Taverner (will) in the church of St Bartholomew by the Exchange. His own burial was to be in 'as frugal a manner as consistent with decency without shew by daylight' (ibid.). He died in the City of London on 31 December 1791 and, according to Isaac Reed, most of the council of Broad Street ward were in attendance when he was laid to rest alongside Arabella in the south aisle of St Bartholomew by the Exchange on 5 January 1792.

ANNE TARVER

Sources I. Reed, 'An account of Mr John Ellis', *European Magazine and London Review*, 21 (1792), 1–5, 125–30 · will, PRO, PROB 11/1223, sig. 508 · Scriveners' Company wardens' accounts, 1732–1894, GL, MS 8720 · lists of freemen of the Company of Scriveners, GL, MS 8721/1 · parish register, St Bartholomew by the Exchange, GL, microfilm 4375 · London, Broad Street ward minute book, 1754–1813, GL, MS 1228/1 · F. W. Steer, *A history of the Worshipful Company of Scriveners of London*, 1 (1973) · *Burlington Magazine*, 124 (1982), 624 · *DNB* · W. J. Bate, *Samuel Johnson* (1977); repr. (1984), 212 · C. W. Brooks, R. H. Helmholz, and P. J. Stein, *Notaries public in England since the Reformation* (1991)

Likenesses W. Pether, mezzotint, 1781 (after T. Frye, 1761), AM Oxf., NPG [*see illus.*] · T. Frye, portrait, repro. in Steer, *A history of the Worshipful Company of Scriveners* · B. Reading, line engraving (after Frye), BM, NPG; repro. in *European Magazine and London Review*

Wealth at death see will, PRO, PROB 11/1223, sig. 508

Ellis, John (*c.*1710–1776), zoologist, was probably born in Ireland to a middle-class English family, but his childhood home is unknown. His father, also named John, was probably a cutler, some time in Dublin, the son-in-law of a public notary there; his mother was Martha, *née* Sissons. Ellis was apprenticed in his youth to a London clothworker. He later acquired the freedom of the City, and remained in London, save for three years in Surrey, for the rest of his life. By the time he was forty his business in Irish linen had made him affluent, giving him leisure for natural history. His zoology was academic but his botany and microbiology were mainly 'applied'. He typically researched, albeit skilfully, topics then under debate and the suggestions or specimens of others rather than breaking entirely new ground. He avoided subjects requiring great learning such as British botany, choosing to study invertebrates, particularly unfamiliar marine animals such as the zoophytes. He championed their animal nature, and argued that they did not link animals and plants as had been suspected. With the Swede Daniel Solander (1733–1782) he discovered that sponges are animals.

Ellis's zoophyte descriptions and professionally drawn engravings, and his scientific approach, were outstanding. His two longest books, *Natural History of the Corallines* (1755; French and Dutch edns, 1756; pirated German edn, 1767) and the posthumous *Natural History of Zoophytes* (1786, partly written by Solander), were seminal. In the 1750s he was one of the British Museum's first noteworthy scientific visitors. He became a fellow of the Royal Society in 1754 and was its Copley medallist in 1768.

In 1754 Ellis married Carolina Elizabeth Peers, who died 'of a consumption' on 15 June 1758. Their sole surviving child, Martha (1754–1795), who married Alexander Watt of Northaw, Hertfordshire, in July 1781, was raised by her aunt Martha Peers. In 1782 Martha Watt enlisted Sir Joseph Banks's help to retrieve the manuscript of the *Natural History of Zoophytes* from Solander's effects at the Swedish embassy. Her industry ensured its publication.

After being widowed in 1758, and bankrupted in the following year, Ellis spent three years (1760–63) as head gardener to P. C. Webb, MP for Haslemere, at Busbridge, near Godalming. He returned to London to a career of administration and science. Through the Royal Society for the Encouragement of Arts, Commerce and Science (founded 1754) he promoted the use of newly discovered tropical plants in colonial agriculture, by introductions from overseas. He produced lists of suitable plants, and wrote *Directions for Bringing over Seeds and Plants* (1770) during slow tropical journeys. His other books were *Coffee* (1774), and *Mangosteen and Breadfruit* (1775). The last emphasized that the Tahitian breadfruit tree, locally a staple and noted by Dampier, Cook, Banks, Solander, and others, might enable Caribbean plantation owners to feed their slaves more cheaply. After his death breadfruit translocation was attempted by William Bligh on the ill-fated HMS *Bounty* expedition (1787).

In later life Ellis made trips in most years to the southeast coast of England studying invertebrates: he was one of the earliest marine zoologists. His two dozen biological papers appeared mainly in the *Philosophical Transactions of the Royal Society* (1754–76). His skill with microscopes—to the development of which he made a minor contribution, the 'Ellis microscope'—led Linnaeus to suggest he might investigate certain motile fungal spores. Simultaneously he followed up work by Spallanzani. He concluded that micro-organisms caused putrefaction—some eighty years before Pasteur, to whom the discovery is usually attributed. His microscopes could not resolve bacteria, and he assumed that protists (protozoans) were the cause. He published his findings but poor health prevented further experiments. He and James Badenach MD concurred that micro-organisms might also cause disease: they were perhaps the first in the world to reach this conclusion but their ideas were unpublished and overlooked.

Ellis received salaries as representative of the Irish linen board (1760–76); as king's agent for the colony of West Florida, disbursing government funds (1763–76), and as agent in London (1770–76) for the government of Dominica, for whom he wrote his book *Coffee*. He died in Hampstead, probably on 5 October 1776, and was buried on 12 October at St Leonard's, Bromley by Bow. His surviving specimen collections were mostly destroyed in the blitz during the Second World War.

PAUL F. S. CORNELIUS and PATRICIA A. CORNELIUS

Sources J. Groner and P. F. S. Cornelius, *John Ellis* (1996) · P. F. S. Cornelius and J. W. Wells, 'Ellis and Solander's *The natural history of many curious and uncommon zoophytes ...*, 1786: unpublished plates and other aspects', *Bulletin of the British Museum (Natural History)* [Historical Series], 16 (1988), 17–87 · *Calendar of the Ellis manuscripts (The correspondence and miscellaneous papers of John Ellis, F.R.S.)*, ed. S. Savage (1948), pt 4 of *Catalogue of the manuscripts in the library of the Linnean Society of London* (1934–48) · S. Savage, 'John Ellis (?1705–1776) and his manuscripts', *Proceedings of the Linnean Society of London*, 146th session (1933–4), 58–62 · *A selection of the correspondence of Linnaeus, and other naturalists, from the original manuscripts*, ed. J. E. Smith, 2 vols. (1821) · A. Rees and others, *The cyclopaedia, or, Universal dictionary of arts, sciences, and literature*, 45 vols. (1819–20), vol. 12 · J. Groner, 'Some aspects of the life and work of John Ellis, King's Agent for West Florida, 1763 to 1776', Doctoral thesis, Loyola University, Chicago, 1987 · R. R. Rea, 'The King's Agent for West Florida', *Alabama Review*, 16 (1963), 141–53 · R. A. Rauschenberg, 'John Ellis, FRS: eighteenth century naturalist and royal agent to West Florida', *Notes and Records of the Royal Society*, 32 (1977–8), 149–64 · R. A. Rauschenberg, 'John Ellis, naturalist: an early member of the society', *Journal of the Royal Society of Arts*, 126 (1977–8), 577–81 · R. A. Rauschenberg, 'John Ellis, Royal Agent for West Florida', *Florida Historical Quarterly*, 62/1 (1983), 1–24 · W. Carruthers, 'The president's address', *Journal of the Royal Microscopical Society* (1901), 113–22 · P. S. Dixon, 'The herbarium of John Ellis (?1705–1776)', *British Phycological Bulletin*, 2 (1960), 28–31 · E. C. Nelson, '*Dionaea* D. Solander ex J. Ellis (Droseraceae): notes on the nomenclature and typification of Venus's Fly-trap', *Botanical Journal of the Linnean Society*, 99 (1989), 249–54 · E. C. Nelson, *Aphrodite's mousetrap: a biography of Venus's flytrap with facsimiles of an original pamphlet and the manuscripts of John Ellis* (1990) · J. Robson, *Auction of the library of Solomon Dayrolles ... also of John Ellis* (1786) · R. J. Rowbury, 'The naturalist John Ellis and the development of the botanical microscope', *Microscopy* [*The Journal of the Quekett Microscopical Club*], 34 (1982), 419–21 · J. Young, 'Corals in the Hunterian Museum figured by Ellis and Solander', *Annals and Magazine of Natural History*, 4th ser., 19 (1877), 116 · L. J. Pitt, 'An account of the work on Polyzoa', *Proceedings of the Geologists' Association*, 72 (1961), 171–86 · parish register (burial), St Leonards, Bromley by Bow, Middlesex, 12 Oct 1776

Archives Linn. Soc., corresp. and papers · RCS Eng. · RS, papers | BL, letters to Thomas Birch, Add. MSS 4305, 4439 · BL, letters to Daniel Solander, Add. MS 29533 · U. Aberdeen, letters to David Skene

Wealth at death recovered from bankruptcy of late 1759; then supported by modest family annuity and later by emoluments as London representative for Irish linen board, 1760–76; king's agent for erstwhile colony of West Florida, 1763–76; agent in London for government of Dominica, 1770–76; may not have regained substantial pre-bankruptcy wealth; perhaps concealed resources from creditors; subsequent letters imply only enough to live on comfortably

Ellis, John (1789–1862), railway promoter and politician, was born on 3 August 1789 at Sharman's Lodge, near

Leicester, the eldest of six children of Joseph Ellis (1755–1810), farmer, and his wife, Rebekah, *née* Burgess (1760–1826), who was Joseph's second cousin. Both parents were Quakers.

Ellis was married twice: first, on 8 February 1816, to Martha (1787–1817), daughter of John and Ann Shipley of Uttoxeter, who died on 2 February 1817, after giving birth to their only child, a son; and second on 18 October 1820, to Priscilla (1798–1872), daughter of Daniel and Hannah Evans of Alveston; they had ten children, three boys and seven girls.

From 1806 to 1846 Ellis was a successful farmer at Beaumont Leys, near Leicester, and had extensive business interests in the Leicester area, dealing in coal, lime, and corn. In 1829 he joined forces with William Stenson, a Leicestershire mining engineer, to promote a railway to link the undeveloped coalfield around Swanwick in north-west Leicestershire with the county town. He induced George Stephenson to join them in the venture. Stephenson's son Robert was engineer for the line, which was completed in 1833, despite unforeseen engineering problems. The Leicester and Swannington Railway Company purchased a locomotive engine, the *Comet*, which was the first to run south of Manchester.

A compassionate man, despite occasional irascibility, Ellis was actively involved in the anti-slavery movement; and he gave important evidence before a select committee of the House of Commons on agricultural distress in 1836.

In 1846 Ellis moved to the village of Belgrave, which was then on the outskirts of Leicester, because of his increasing business commitments. On the formation of the Midland Railway Company in 1844 he became its vice-chairman, succeeding George Hudson as chairman in 1849, a post he held until 1858 when he resigned. A man of great personal integrity, and widely respected, Ellis was an ideal chairman in the financially difficult years that followed the departure of Hudson. He instituted retrenchment at a time of falling revenues, and put an end to the construction of expensive branch lines. However, he authorized the Erewash valley line from Nottingham, in order to allow it to carry the rich coal reserves being mined in the Derbyshire coalfield; and by 1860 the Midland Railway carried more than 12 per cent of the country's minerals.

Ellis successfully, and largely on his own initiative, took over the Bristol and Birmingham Railway in 1845, against strong opposition from the Great Western Railway (GWR). 'I had better run the risk of losing a few thousand pounds than admit the plague of the broad gauge to Birmingham', he wrote (Williams, 43). This transformed the midland from a purely provincial line into a national railway, linking the manufacturing districts with their markets, and with trunk routes running north to south, and west to north. Ellis laid the groundwork for the acquisition of a London terminal (St Pancras) before his retirement, and more than anyone else was responsible for the transformation of a near-bankrupt provincial line into a prosperous and vigorous 'premier line'.

Throughout his life Ellis was a Liberal in politics. He was elected to the Leicester borough council as a councillor in 1837, becoming an alderman the following year and continuing in that office until his death in 1862. He was also a county magistrate. He was a member of parliament for the borough from 1848 to 1852. Not surprisingly, he supported Cobden and Hume in measures like proposed reductions in the army and navy estimates, calculated to discourage a bellicose foreign policy. Also, despite his affinity with the agricultural interest, he believed that the 1850 campaign for the reintroduction of a duty on corn stood no chance of success, and that those who supported it deceived themselves.

After a prolonged illness in which cystitis was a leading symptom, Ellis died at his Belgrave home on 26 October 1862, and was buried in Leicester public cemetery on 1 November 1862. He was survived by his second wife.

MILLER CHRISTY, rev. ALAN R. GRIFFIN

Sources DNB · typed register extracts file, RS Friends, Lond. · 'Dictionary of Quaker biography', RS Friends, Lond. [card index] · A. T. Bassett, *Life of John Edward Ellis* (1914) · I. C. Ellis, ed., *Records of nineteenth century Leicester* (privately printed, St Peter Port, 1935) · *Leicester Chronicle* (1 Nov 1862) · trade directories · *CGPLA Eng. & Wales* (1862) · *Biographical catalogue: being an account of the lives of Friends and others whose portraits are in the London Friends' Institute*, Society of Friends (1888) [on Bowker-Saur British biographical microfiche] · R. Williams, *The Midland railway: a new history* (1988) · E. G. Barnes, *The rise of the Midland railway, 1844–1874* (1966) · d. cert.

Archives Leics. RO, MSS

Likenesses J. Lucas, oils, 1858, Museum of British Transport, York · B. R. Haydon, group portrait, oils (*The Anti-Slavery Society convention, 1840*), NPG · oils, Leicester Museum and Art Gallery

Wealth at death under £40,000: probate, 28 Nov 1862, *CGPLA Eng. & Wales*

Ellis, John (1874–1932), executioner, was born on 4 October 1874 at Buersil, Rochdale, the eldest child of Joseph James Ellis, a hairdresser, and his wife, Sarah Ann, *née* Dawson. He left school to work for the local Eagle Spinning Company. When he was twenty, he married Annie Beaton Whitworth, aged twenty-two, a cotton operative at the Eagle Mill. The wedding took place at Middleton on 20 April 1895.

The couple settled down to a normal family life until events took an unexpected turn. Ellis requested a reference from his foreman at the Eagle Mill, who was startled to learn that the young man wanted to become an executioner. He advised Ellis to discuss it with his family and come back after a week if he had not changed his mind. Ellis duly returned, and soon sent off his application. The Home Office sought a confidential report from local police, who said that the applicant seemed a man of good character. Summoned to Strangeways prison for an interview with the governor, he was recommended for training in May 1901. Ellis was among the last executioners trained at Newgate before its demolition. He said afterwards that he had applied for the job when a friend had contended that he would never have the nerve to hang a man. Ellis had discussed his ambition with his wife, but

John Ellis (1874–1932), by unknown photographer

concerned. Mrs Thompson, in a state of collapse, had to be carried to the scaffold and held over the trapdoors while Ellis prepared her for the drop. A year later Ellis resigned. He had been an executioner for twenty-three years, and told a reporter later that he had carried out 203 hangings at £10 a time (*Daily Express*). One morning in August 1924 Annie Ellis was woken by a loud bang and found her husband lying on the floor downstairs with blood pouring from his neck. When a policeman arrived, he found Ellis heavily bandaged. 'I have shot myself,' he said, 'I am sorry' (*News of the World*). Charged with attempting to commit suicide, Ellis was discharged after promising not to repeat the attempt and to give up intoxicating drink.

Ellis wrote his reminiscences for Thomson's *Weekly News*, commencing 5 April 1924, under the heading 'Secrets of my Life Revealed'. 'Conversations cease suddenly when I am about', he wrote,

> and I can feel people eyeing me as if I am some exhibit in the chamber of horrors. They will avoid shaking hands with me when they are introduced—they shudder at the idea of grasping the hand that has pinioned murderers and worked the gallows lever. (Ellis)

He caused a sensation in 1927 by appearing on stage as a hangman in a melodrama. He also toured seaside resorts and fairgrounds giving lectures about his experiences. On 20 September 1932, suffering from neuritis, and reduced by the depression to selling counter cloths to public houses, Ellis suddenly snatched a razor from a shelf in the kitchen at his home in Kitchen Lane, and after threatening his wife and daughter, slashed his own throat. He was fifty-seven. The inquest verdict was suicide while of unsound mind. He was buried on 24 September in Rochdale cemetery.

Speculation has often homed in on the Thompson execution as a cause of Ellis's mental condition, but he strongly denied it. He was always a nervous character, however, and admitted to 'stage fright' before every execution. Billington once remarked that he wondered how Ellis had stuck it so long, 'being so nervous and anxious about everything going OK' (*Empire News*). It seems likely that the cumulative effect of more than 200 executions had taken its toll in the disillusionment of harsh reality following youthful bravado. As the consultant psychiatrist A. Hyatt Williams later wrote, 'the long-term ill effects upon the character balance of those who participate in legal homicide are not to be underestimated' (Blom-Cooper, 98).   BRIAN BAILEY

not his parents. When Joseph Ellis heard of it, he raised the roof. A respected businessman in the neighbourhood, he owned 'a tidy number of houses' (private information). A strict disciplinarian, his response to his son's action was to cut him off without the proverbial farthing.

Ellis's first job was to assist William Billington, one of a dynasty of Lancashire hangmen, in a double execution at Newcastle, later in 1901. He received his first commission as senior hangman when he executed a murderer named Davis at Warwick on new year's day 1907, recording proudly that death was instantaneous, and 'there was not even a quiver of the rope' (Ellis, May 1924). On 23 November 1910 Ellis executed Dr Crippen at Pentonville prison. He adopted a new procedure on this occasion, which he used invariably thenceforth. It had been the practice for the hangman to head the ritual procession from condemned cell to execution chamber. Ellis, however, walked quickly to the gallows and awaited the arrival of the others there. He considered this less distressing for the prisoner. Several other notorious murderers crossed Ellis's fatal threshold, including George Joseph Smith and Herbert Rouse Armstrong. But his most famous victim was not a murderer at all. On 3 August 1916, at Pentonville, Ellis hanged Roger Casement, recalling later: 'Casement may have been a traitor, but he died like a soldier' (*Empire News*).

Ellis had gone into the hairdressing business. He and his wife had a son and three daughters, and lived at 3 Kitchen Lane, Balderstone, Rochdale. Slightly built, with pale complexion and pale blue eyes, Ellis sported a bushy auburn moustache. He collected press cuttings about himself, but one evening he fell asleep by the fire and his records fell into the flames.

On 9 January 1923 Ellis executed Edith Thompson at Holloway prison. She had been controversially sentenced with her lover, Frederick Bywaters, for the murder of her husband, and the execution was distressing for everyone

Sources J. Ellis, 'Secrets of my life revealed', *Weekly News* (5 April 1924–Feb 1925) · B. Bailey, *Hangmen of England* (1989) · S. J. Coe, *Down Murder Lane* (1945) · C. Duff, *A new handbook on hanging* (1954) · L. Blom-Cooper, ed., *The hanging question* (1969) · private information (2004) · *Empire News* (25 Sept 1932) · *Daily Express* (13 Dec 1927) · *News of the World* (31 Aug 1924) · b. cert. · m. cert. · d. cert. · *CGPLA Eng. & Wales* (1933)

Likenesses photograph, Press Association Photo Library, London [*see illus.*] · portrait, repro. in Bailey, *Hangmen of England*, facing p. 118

Wealth at death £294 9s. 9d.: probate, 13 June 1933, *CGPLA Eng. & Wales*

Ellis, John Devonshire (1824–1906), steel manufacturer, was born on 20 April 1824, at Handsworth, one of the several children of Charles Ellis, a Birmingham brass manufacturer. Educated at King Edward VI School, Birmingham, he subsequently joined the family firm and became a partner aged twenty-four. For seven years he superintended the manufacturing and engineering departments of Charles Ellis & Sons. Ellis married, on 5 December 1848, Elizabeth Parsons, daughter of Edward Bourne, a Shropshire farmer; they had a daughter and five sons.

In 1854 the Sheffield steelmaker John Brown invited Ellis to join him and William Bragge in the partnership that founded a new steelworks in Sheffield's Brightside district. This was the Atlas works of John Brown & Co., which had a capital of £14,000, about 200 workers, and a turnover in the first year of about £3000. While Bragge concentrated on sales, and Brown became a public figure, Ellis managed the works, achieving prominence and respect both for his engineering abilities and the fact that he was such an 'indefatigable and perservering worker' (John Brown & Co. Ltd archives, London, minute book no. 1, 14 June 1866). When the Atlas works became a public limited company in 1864, Ellis became managing director and he added the chairmanship to his duties when Sir John Brown left the company in 1871. Henceforth, 'The history of the firm … [was] … the history of John Devonshire Ellis' (*Sheffield Daily Independent*, 12 Nov 1906).

Ellis's contribution to John Brown & Co. was in three main areas: armour-plate, the bulk steelmaking technologies, and overall business strategy. For several years Ellis was occupied in devising methods for the manufacture of a superior armour-plate. Steel was tried, but was not found to have the necessary toughness under the impact of shot. After many experiments, by 1879 Ellis had perfected a process for uniting a hard steel face with a wrought-iron backing, producing so-called compound armour, which was subsequently in great demand. As early as 1871, Ellis also turned his attention to the process of cementing (carburizing) armour-plate to improve its defensive capabilities; while another engineer at the Atlas works, Captain T. J. Tressider, developed a chilling process by high-pressure water sprinklers. The two processes were combined and the first Ellis–Tressider chilled compound plate was tried with success at Shoeburyness in 1891. American and especially German innovations surpassed those of British makers in the 1890s, but Ellis ensured that Browns remained a leading armour-plate maker by acquiring licences and continuing to make improvements.

Ellis was instrumental in promoting the success of the Bessemer converter, which was first demonstrated in Sheffield by its inventor in 1858. John Brown & Co., virtually next door to Bessemer's plant, was the first Sheffield firm to take out a licence in 1860. Sir Henry Bessemer later recalled that Ellis was the first man in Sheffield to reach the conclusion that the new process had promise. The Bessemer converter was soon utilized for rail production, allowing the Atlas works to become the leading rail maker in the world in the 1860s.

Under Ellis's (and Sir John Brown's) direction John Brown & Co. became more than simply a Sheffield-based steel firm. It became a company of national importance, with a world-wide reputation for mechanical engineering of all kinds. By the 1890s it produced a wide range of specialities, particularly for the railways (axles, springs, and buffers) and shipping (armour-plate, flues, engine shafting, and general forgings). Many products and ideas, such as ribbed boiler flues and the Ellis–Eaves system of smoke control, reflected Ellis's technical influence. Under his leadership the company, like Vickers and Cammell, pursued a policy of vertical integration, seeking control of raw materials and shipbuilding outlets. Hence, the company's acquisition of the Aldwarke Main and Car House collieries in 1874 and the Clydebank engineering and shipbuilding works in 1899. An informal merger with Sheffield neighbours Thos. Firth & Sons followed in 1903. Ellis's strategy was to develop Browns as a heavy special steelmaker, with a key position in naval ordnance. In this he was broadly successful: when he retired the company's nominal capital had risen to £2.6 million and it employed about 16,000 men.

Ellis retired from the managing directorship in June 1904, when he had turned eighty, though he remained chairman until his death. For over fifty years he had devoted himself to the company, habitually starting work at 9 o'clock after a train journey from his home at Worksop. He admitted to taking only two days' holiday each year and took little part in public life. An Anglican and Conservative, he took on few outside appointments, apart from a term as a JP and as chairman of the South Yorkshire Coal Owners' Association, and was never honoured (a contrast with his two sons, Charles and William *Ellis (1860–1945), who both joined the management of the company and were both knighted). Even in the professional world, Ellis avoided publicity. He received the Bessemer gold medal of the Iron and Steel Institute in 1889 and was its vice-president in 1901; but his only other professional involvement was his election as a member of the Institution of Civil Engineers in 1884. He died on 11 November 1906 at his residence, Sparken House, at Worksop, Nottinghamshire, and was buried at Carlton in Lindrick.

GEOFFREY TWEEDALE

Sources P. Nunn, 'Ellis, John Devonshire', *DBB* · *Sheffield Daily Independent* (12 Nov 1906) · A. J. Grant, *Steel and ships: the history of John Brown's* (1950) · *Men of the period* (1896) · J. H. Stainton, *The making of Sheffield, 1865–1914* (1924) · C. J. Erickson, *British industrialists: steel and hosiery, 1850–1950* (1959) · E. Mensforth, *Family engineers* (1981) · G. Tweedale, *Steel city: entrepreneurship, strategy, and technology in Sheffield, 1743–1993* (1995) · minute book no. 1, John Brown & Co. Ltd archives, London, 14 June 1866 · d. cert. · m. cert. · *DNB*
Archives John Brown plc, 20 Eastbourne Terrace, London, John Brown & Co. Ltd archives
Likenesses A. S. Cope, oils, repro. in Grant, *Steel and ships*; formerly at Atlas works, Sheffield, 1912
Wealth at death £60,752 18s. 9d.: probate, 9 April 1907, *CGPLA Eng. & Wales*

Ellis, John Edward (1841–1910), colliery owner and politician, was born on 15 October 1841 at Castle View, The Newarke, Leicester, the eldest of the five children of Edward

Shipley Ellis (1817–1879), railway chairman and social reformer, and his wife, Emma Burgess (1809–1899), both of whom came from Quaker families.

Educated at Friends' schools at Hertford and Kendal, in 1857 Ellis accompanied his father (by that time chairman of the Midland Railway Company) on a trip to the USA to study the American railway system. From 1858 to 1861 he served an apprenticeship with Kitson and Hewitson, railway and general engineers, of Leeds. In 1861 he was appointed to a management position at the Hucknall colliery then being sunk by a partnership in which his father and uncle were initially joined by two others, and Ellis soon assumed overall managerial control. This was the first mine to be sunk in Nottinghamshire's Leen valley, which was to become Britain's most prosperous coalfield. A paternalistic employer, Ellis was concerned to provide fair wages and good working conditions, as well as decent housing and social infrastructure. He was largely responsible for the establishment of a local board in the Leen valley in 1866, a school board in 1871 (he served as chairman of both bodies for some years), a town water supply, and adult schools (in which he himself lectured for a time).

In 1867 Ellis married Maria (1845–1941), the fifth child of John and Jane Rowntree of Scarborough, whom he met at the Quaker meeting there. They lived at The Park, Nottingham, and had three sons (two of whom died in early adulthood), and twin daughters, one of whom, Marian *Ellis, became a philanthropist and political activist. In Nottingham, Ellis again became involved in educational work and was a member of the city's school board. Between 1882 and 1886 he was also chairman of the Nottingham Joint Stock Bank.

Ellis promoted the formation of a Liberal association in north Nottinghamshire in 1880, and in 1885 he became MP for the newly created seat of Rushcliffe, which then included Hucknall. He held this seat until shortly before his death in 1910. A highly principled man, as befits a Quaker, Ellis campaigned against Irish injustices and for home rule; supported the temperance movement; opposed the arms trade and the Second South African War; and supported free trade. In 1902 he welcomed the emergence of labour representation in parliament. He chaired many standing and select committees of the house; in 1895 he became temporary chairman of ways and means, but subsequently declined nomination as speaker. From December 1905 to December 1906 he was under-secretary for India under John Morley, and he was sworn of the privy council in 1905.

Because of his early belief in classical economic doctrine Ellis was unsympathetic to trade unions in the 1860s and 1870s, but he gradually came to recognize their value; soon after the formation of the Nottinghamshire Miners' Association in 1881, he gave it encouragement and support. He formed a particularly close relationship with the association's second agent, William Bailey (appointed 1886), and the good relationship then established with the association continued after Bailey's untimely death in 1896. Ellis, assisted by two other Nottinghamshire colliery owners who were Liberal politicians, induced the Leen valley colliery proprietors to break the owners' lock-out by their men in 1893 by re-opening their pits on the pre-stoppage conditions and by forming a breakaway owners' association. This split in the coal owners' ranks was subsequently exploited by the union.

Ellis was asthmatic and it was partly for this reason that he bought a country estate near Scarborough (Wrea Head, Scalby) in 1883. On his election to parliament in 1885, he also bought a London residence, 40 Pont Street; in 1906 he moved from there to 37 Prince's Gate, Knightsbridge. He died from acute bronchitis at his London home on 1 December 1910, and was buried in the churchyard at Scalby on 6 December. ALAN R. GRIFFIN

Sources A. T. Bassett, *The life of John Edward Ellis* (1914) · typed register extracts file, RS Friends, Lond. · 'Dictionary of Quaker biography', RS Friends, Lond. [card index] · D. Gilbert, *Class, community and collective action* (1992) · A. R. Grffin, *Mining in the east midlands, 1550–1947* (1971) · A. R. Griffin, *The miners of Nottinghamshire, 1881–1914* (1956) · *Hucknall Dispatch* (8 Dec 1910)
Archives BL, corresp. with Henry Campbell-Bannerman, Add. MS 41214 · BL, letters to Gladstone, Add. MSS 46057–46068 · Sheff. Arch., letters to H. J. Wilson
Likenesses photograph, repro. in Bassett, *Life of John Edward Ellis*
Wealth at death £101,382 7s. 0d.: resworn probate, 11 Feb 1911, CGPLA Eng. & Wales

Ellis, Marian Emily [married name Marian Emily Cripps, Lady Parmoor] (1878–1952), philanthropist and political activist, was born at The Park, Standard Hill, Nottingham, on 6 January 1878, one of the twin daughters of the colliery owner and Liberal MP John Edward *Ellis (1841–1910) and his wife, Maria Rowntree (1845–1941), philanthropist, both of whom were Quakers and radicals. She was educated at home and became her politician father's secretary at the time of the Jameson raid (1895). At the close of the subsequent Second South African War she was involved in Ruth Fry's Quaker relief projects for women victims of that war.

When the First World War rallied young men on both sides to massacre one another for righteousness's sake, Marian Ellis was a steadfast voice against that madness. Not only did she and her twin sister Edith give huge sums of money to relieve the suffering of families of conscientious objectors and finance the No-Conscription Fellowship, but they also gave tirelessly of their moral and intellectual energy. Edith Ellis was imprisoned in Holloway under the Defence of the Realm Act in 1918 for joining with other Quakers to print a leaflet, *A Challenge to Militarism*, without first submitting it to the government censor. Meanwhile Marian Ellis had made a major contribution to Quaker thinking on the issue of 'just war'. The collaborative, anonymous Quaker pamphlet *Looking towards Peace* (1915), which she had helped to draft, stated:

> War, tyranny and revolt have produced tyranny, revolt and war throughout time … We maintain that the moral law is binding upon States as upon individuals … We hold that the fundamental interests of humanity are one … The time for absolute isolated sovereignty is gone by … Our aim should be a very loose international federation … the reasoned worship of force [is] the real devil-worship … We therefore keep alight the hope that, late or soon, the intercourse of nations will be carried on without armed force.

In 1917 Marian Ellis wrote:

> At the end of this war the world will have to decide which way it desires to go, towards disarmament or destruction ... Disarmament is not merely scrapping our guns and our battleships. It is the working out of a national policy, which, being inspired by love for all men, cannot be antagonistic ... it is the problem of India, of Ireland, of our relations with Russia and Persia, Germany and Belgium as God would have them to be. (M. Ellis, 'Disarmament', *Friends' Quarterly Examiner*, 1917, 182–3)

She testified to her unweaponed faith for the rest of her life.

In 1919 Marian Ellis helped Kate, Lady Courtney of Penwith, to establish the Fight the Famine Committee. Lady Courtney later wrote of Marian Ellis: 'what a splendid worker she is—capable and selfless—a volunteer who does all the grind and most of the paying too' (Courtney, 177). On 14 July 1919, she married, as his second wife, Charles Alfred *Cripps, first Baron Parmoor (d. 1941), politician; she became the respected sister-in-law of Beatrice Webb. There were no children of the marriage; Marian was, however, an influence upon the youngest son of her husband's first marriage, (Richard) Stafford Cripps.

From 1924 to 1928 Lady Parmoor was president of the World YWCA and she helped found the Fellowship of Reconciliation. A founder member of the Women's International League for Peace and Freedom, she became president of its British section in 1950; she was treasurer of the Friends' Peace Committee and an active vice-president of the National Peace Council. But none of her official committee responsibilities adequately reveals the quality of her spirit. At every depressing turn of world politics she would follow the direction of her idealistic conscience and struggle for the implementation of those ideals in international relations. Thus she advocated the admission of communist China to the United Nations, she urged an end by negotiation to the Korean War, and at the age of seventy she began a serious study of nuclear fission in order to speak with some authority about the uses and dangers of atomic energy. Her last political act, two days before her death, was to help draft a Quaker message to the prime minister protesting against the aerial bombardment of North Korea.

Marian Ellis was a gifted cellist and an attractive and eloquent speaker, whose 'obstinate optimism made her one of the most lovable of a notable generation of women' (*The Times*, 18 July 1952). She died at her home, 1 Endsleigh Street, London, on 6 July 1952 and was cremated at Golders Green; her ashes were taken to Frieth, Buckinghamshire. SYBIL OLDFIELD

Sources *The Times* (7 July 1952) · *The Times* (10 July 1952) · *The Times* (18 July 1952) · *Manchester Guardian* (8 July 1952) · S. Oldfield, 'England's Cassandras in World War One', *This working-day world*, ed. S. Oldfield (1994) · K. Courtney, *Extracts from a diary during the war* (privately printed, London, 1927) · Burke, *Peerage* (1967) · b. cert. · m. cert. · d. cert. · *CGPLA Eng. & Wales* (1952)
Likenesses photograph, c.1920, priv. coll.
Wealth at death £145,680 5s. 0d.: probate, 4 Sept 1952, *CGPLA Eng. & Wales*

Ellis, Mary Baxter (1892–1968), commanding officer of the FANY, was born on 12 November 1892 at North Ashfield, Newcastle upon Tyne, the elder daughter in the family of four children of Joseph Baxter Ellis, grocer and miller, and his second wife, Mary Sharp Taylor. Her father, later knighted, was three times mayor of Newcastle and its first lord mayor on creation of the title by Edward VII in 1906.

Baxter Ellis, known as Dick, was educated at Newcastle Central high school and University College, London. At the outbreak of the First World War, determined to serve her country and in the face of fierce parental opposition, she enrolled on a chauffeur's course, gaining a first-class certificate at the Motor Supply Company School of Motoring. In August 1915 she joined the First Aid Nursing Yeomanry (FANY) corps. This organization had been founded in 1907 by a sometime cavalry sergeant-major, Edward Baker, as an all-female mounted ambulance unit. By the outbreak of war the FANY had moved to mechanized transport and was the first uniformed women's organization to go to France on 27 October 1914 where, first driving for the Belgian and French, in 1916 they became the first women to drive officially for the British army. They were an entirely voluntary unit. Baxter Ellis arrived in France in December 1915, and served with the British Calais convoy and the corps de transport armée Belge. She was personally decorated by the queen of the Belgians in 1918.

At the end of the First World War official policy was to disband all the women's services. The FANYs, highly decorated for gallantry by Britain, France, and Belgium, survived because of their voluntary status and financial independence, but the 1920s saw a dramatic decline in recruitment. Disarmament and appeasement were the prevailing sentiments. That the FANY continued to grow in competence and numbers was due largely to the inspirational leadership of Mary Baxter Ellis. Convinced by her experiences in the war that women had an important contribution to make, and that the FANY, based on the two great essentials of self-discipline and spirit of service, had a particular contribution, she determined to build the corps up again. She became the officer commanding the Northumberland section in 1928 and corps commander in 1932. A historian of the FANY has written that Mary Baxter Ellis was 'in the true sense of the word a leader. She had a great capacity for enthusing others, both collectively and individually ... a creative brain and a gift for public speaking ... for spreading a knowledge of [the Corps'] traditions' (Ward, 96). Although these traditions were born before the First World War, they were crystallized during that war and strengthened, augmented, and established on a high ethical and regimental standard by Mary Baxter Ellis, in the period from 1932 to 1939.

In 1937 the name of the corps was changed to Women's Transport Service (FANY) to reflect their specialization. In 1938 the War Office created a new women's force, the Auxiliary Territorial Service (ATS). Mary Baxter Ellis was asked to lead it but declined to leave the FANY to do so. Instead she negotiated that, in return for administrative independence within the new organization, the corps would

Mary Baxter Ellis (1892–1968), by Bassano, c.1939

provide 1500 trained driver/mechanics for the ATS transport wing. Dame Helen Gwynne-Vaughan, subsequently appointed director, was fiercely hostile to the idea of the FANY as a self-governing entity within the ATS, and in breach of the 1938 agreement forced Baxter Ellis to accept absorption in December 1939. Baxter Ellis understood quite clearly that service entailed sacrifice and that self has no place in leadership (Ward, 314). She relinquished her command and took a substantial part of the corps into the ATS. The only condition she demanded was that the FANYs should be allowed to wear their FANY shoulder flashes. The remainder of the corps, under Marion Gamwell, became known as the Free FANYs and saw war service with the Special Operations Executive, the Polish army, and the British Red Cross Society.

Baxter Ellis was commandant of the ATS motor companies no. 1 training centre at Camberley until December 1940, then GSO1 (military training) at the War Office. She became deputy director of the ATS in 1943, and was appointed CBE (military) in 1942. At the end of the war she returned to FANY headquarters as corps commander, but beset by increasingly severe arthritis retired in 1947. Her medals were subsequently put on display at FANY (Princess Royal's Volunteer Corps) headquarters at the duke of York's headquarters in Chelsea, London.

A tall, slender woman with dark hair always swept back into a bun, Mary Baxter Ellis loved Northumberland, where she spent much of her life. She lived in a cottage on the moors near Bellingham with her fellow Northumbrian and close friend Marjorie (Tony) Kingston Walker,

also a distinguished FANY and a gifted artist, and later at West Woodburn, nearby. In addition, she was a member of the Northumberland county council. Her interests were wide-ranging, from dog-breeding to local archaeology. She was also a writer of fiction, and a regular contributor to several magazines.

Mary Baxter Ellis never married. She died on 12 April 1968 in the Charlotte Straker Cottage Hospital, Corbridge, Northumberland, from pneumonia, and was cremated at All Saints, Newcastle, on 16 April.

LYNETTE BEARDWOOD

Sources *FANY Gazette* (1918) [available at FANY archives, Duke of York's HQ, London] · *FANY Gazette* (1932) [available at FANY archives, Duke of York's HQ, London] · *FANY Gazette* (1968) [available at FANY archives, Duke of York's HQ, London] · Duke of York's HQ, London, FANY archives · I. Ward, *FANY invicta* (1955) · H. Popham, *FANY* (1984) · private information (2004) [niece, Mrs Dorothy Wattsford] · b. cert. · d. cert. · *WWW*
Archives Women's Transport Service (FANY), London, Duke of York's Headquarters
Likenesses Bassano, photograph, *c.*1939, NPG [*see illus.*] · M. Kingston Walker, oils, 1948, Duke of York's HQ, London, FANY archives
Wealth at death £22,398: probate, 20 June 1968, *CGPLA Eng. & Wales*

Ellis, Philip [*name in religion* Michael] (**1652–1726**), vicar apostolic of the western district, was born on 8 September 1652 in Stratford, London, and was baptized on 12 September. He was the third son of the Revd John *Ellis (d. 1681) of Kiddall Hall in the West Riding, rector of Waddesdon, Buckinghamshire, and his wife, Susannah (d. 1700), daughter of William Welbore of Cambridge. His brothers were John *Ellis (1642x6–1738), under-secretary of state to William III, Sir William *Ellis (1641x7–1732), secretary of state to James II, and Welbore *Ellis (1661/2–1734), Church of Ireland bishop of Killala and afterwards of Meath. These brothers were all to benefit from Ellis's later attachment to James II. Philip Ellis was admitted into Westminster School on its foundation in 1667. He was converted to Catholicism in 1668 while at school, where he was reputed to speak 'ex cathedra like an angel' (Agar-Ellis, 1.68). It was this eloquence which later attracted the notice of James II. He entered the Benedictine priory of St Gregory at Douai, where he was professed on 30 November 1670, taking the name in religion Michael, and he studied at the University of Douai. For many years he was not heard of by his family, and perhaps he might never have been discovered but for the circumstance of his being called Jolly Phil at Douai, as he had been at Westminster (Agar-Ellis, 1.xviii–xxi). He was appointed the first official annalist of the English Benedictines in 1681, and wrote his 'Chronology', which contained biographies of Benedictine luminaries and martyrs and set forth the privileges of the English Benedictine congregation. His poor health forced him to employ a secretary, who was responsible for some errors and drafting a second copy. This chronology was used by Dom Benet Weldon in compiling his 'Memorials'.

After being ordained priest Ellis was appointed preacher-general in 1685 and sent to work in England. His abilities recommended him to the notice of James II, who appointed him one of his chaplains-in-ordinary and preachers. He was attached to the chapels royal at Whitehall, St James's, Somerset House, and Windsor, where he became known as 'the great pulpit man' of the Catholics, and a number of his sermons delivered between 1685 and 1687 were published, notably one delivered on 13 November 1686 reassuring landowners that he had been authorized to declare that the monks renounced all claim to the old 'abbey lands', 'his method, stile, and delivery being far above the common, and very much admired even by Protestants' (*Dodd's Church History*, 3.467). He helped persuade the king to appoint his friend John Massey to the deanery of Christ Church, Oxford, in October 1686.

In 1687 Innocent XI divided England into four ecclesiastical districts, and allowed James to nominate persons to govern them. Ellis, reckoned to pull the king's sleeve and one of a triumvirate of favourite chaplains, although 'outshot by many bar-lengths by the High-Priest', Edward Petre SJ (Agar-Ellis, 1.224), was accordingly appointed by letters apostolic dated 30 January 1688, the first vicar apostolic of the western district, and was consecrated on 6 May 1688 by Ferdinand d'Adda, archbishop of Amasia *in partibus*, at the Chapel Royal in St James's, where the king had founded a monastery of fourteen Benedictine monks. A delay in choosing him had been occasioned by his being an 'ex-heretic' in his early life. He received the see of Aureliopolis *in partibus* for his title. Like the other vicars apostolic he had a salary of £1000 p.a. out of the royal exchequer, and £500 when he entered on his office. In the second week of July 1688 he confirmed a number of youths, some of whom were converts, in the new chapel of the Jesuits attached to their Savoy College. He was said to have reconciled the earls of Sunderland and Melfort to the Catholic church on 30 August 1688 and was present at the baptism of James Stuart, the prince of Wales, in October, when he represented Louis XIV. His name is subscribed to the 'Pastoral letter of the four Catholic bishops to the lay-Catholics of England', issued in 1688, and some opponents believed he was already acting as titular archbishop of Canterbury. There are doubts that he ever visited his district, although he may have gone to Wales some time in 1688.

On the breaking out of the revolution in November 1688 Ellis was betrayed by a serving maid, arrested, and imprisoned in Newgate, where he was visited by Gilbert Burnet, representing William III, who ordered that he be well treated. He was free, however, by early January 1689, and repaired to the court of St Germain, becoming chaplain to the queen and a correspondent of Bossuet. In France he was known as the bishop of Ely. By early 1693 he was settled in Rome, being commended to the pope by James II in March. There he became secretary to Philip Thomas, Cardinal Howard, who appreciated his acquaintance with English affairs. It seems he was granted a benefice in Brittany by Innocent XII at the behest of Queen Mary Beatrice and then tried repeatedly to obtain Roman preferment. This may explain his transfer to the Italian Benedictines and his profession in the abbey of Subiaco

on 13 November 1703. At some point he became life abbot of the College of St Gregory the Great *de Urbe* in Rome. He asked to become James II's official agent in Rome, preferring that role to returning to England, although the king wished he would return home to his district. In Rome he also served as a procurator for the English Benedictines, for whom he gained in October 1699 papal permission for an extension of the Benedictine privileges in the bull *Plantata* (1633) to all Benedictine chapels in England.

Cardinal Howard left 500 ecus and effects, including his coach and horses, to Ellis, in his will of 1694, and after the cardinal's death Ellis took a house of his own in Rome, the English College being reluctant to provide accommodation for him. In the 1695 dispute concerning the jurisdiction of the vicars apostolic over the regular clergy in England, he sided with the vicars, but was prepared to safeguard Benedictine rights. In 1696 he was appointed assistant prelate to the pontifical throne, a lowlier position than he would have liked, but he continued to enjoy papal favour, being appointed to the legation of Bologna in 1706. He was by now a familiar figure in Roman circles, witnessed by his singing of high mass in the French church in the city on the feast of St Louis in August 1699, where he was welcomed by the Cardinal de Bouillon.

Despite some disingenuous protestations, Ellis seems always to have been reluctant to return to England to take charge of his vicariate, but continued to support the candidature of a Benedictine to succeed him there. In 1705 he was eventually forced, after protests, to resign his vicariate into the hands of Clement XI, who, on 3 October 1708, appointed him to the insignificant see of Segni in the Campagna within the Papal States. By his own admission it was not a wealthy see and he tried unsuccessfully to resist accepting it. Once installed, however, and known as 'My Lord Ellis of Wales', he had his first pastoral letter published, began regular visitations and went on to found a much needed diocesan seminary in the disused monastery of St Clare, and substantially repaired and embellished the episcopal palace. The acts of a synod attended by about seventy of his clergy, held in the choir of the cathedral in November 1710, were highly approved by Clement XI, who ordered them to be published. Segni thus became a model for other Italian sees implementing the Tridentine reforms, and Ellis achieved some fame as reformer, preacher, and pastor. He continued to enjoy favour at the Jacobite court, and in December 1720 he was present at the birth of Charles Edward Stuart, the prince of Wales. He remained close to the English Benedictines, who recognized him as a confrater and in 1725 allowed him chapter rights.

Ellis died at the episcopal palace, Segni, from dropsy of the chest on 16 November 1726, and was buried in the centre of his seminary church, to which he bequeathed his mitre and vestments, the bulk of his property being left to his seminary. He was remembered as a great benefactor of the poor. Leo XII gave Ellis's library and ring to Bishop Augustine Baines for the use of his successors in the western district.   GEOFFREY SCOTT

Sources B. Navarra, *Filippo Michele Ellis* (1973) · G. Agar-Ellis, ed., *The Ellis correspondence: letters written during the years 1686, 1687, 1688, and addressed to John Ellis*, 2 vols. (1829) · Gillow, *Lit. biog. hist.* · J. A. Williams, 'Bishops Giffard and Ellis and the western vicariate, 1688–1715', *Journal of Ecclesiastical History*, 15 (1964), 218–28 · B. Hemphill, *The early vicars apostolic of England, 1685–1750* (1954) · F. A. Gasquet, 'Segni', *Downside Review*, 16 (1897), 231–40 · 'Memoirs of the vicars apostolic of the western district', *Catholic Gentleman's Magazine* (Nov 1818), 707–8 · J. B. Gavin, 'An Englishman in exile', *Recusant History*, 15 (1979–81), 11–14 · G. Hay, 'An English bishop in the Volscians', *The Venerabile* (Nov 1959) · G. Dolan, 'Gleanings in Italy', *Downside Review*, 19 (1900) · *The life and times of Anthony Wood*, ed. A. Clark, 5 vols., OHS, 19, 21, 26, 30, 40 (1891–1900) · J. Flint, 'James II and the English Benedictines', *American Benedictine Review*, 39 (1988), 113–32 · *Sainte Fare et Faremoutiers: treize siècles de vie monastique*, Abbaye de Faremoutiers (1956) · *A rare a show, or, England's betrayers expos'd* (1688) [Bod. Pamph. A179 (81)] · B. Weldon, 'Memorials', Douai Abbey, Woolhampton, Berkshire, English Benedictine Congregation Archives · A. Allanson, *Biography of the English Benedictines* (1999) · *Dodd's Church history of England*, ed. M. A. Tierney, 5 vols. (1839–43), vol. 3, p. 295

Archives Royal Arch., corresp. | Ampleforth Abbey, York, Allanson MSS · Archivio Vaticano, Vatican City · BL, corresp. of Cardinal Gualterio · Bodl. Oxf., Carte MSS · Douai Abbey, Woolhampton, Berkshire, B. Weldon, 'Memorials' · Episcopal Archives, Segni · Royal Arch. · Westm. DA, Main Series XXXVI, XXXVIII

Likenesses H. Meyer, stipple, 1828 (after portrait), BM, NPG; repro. in Agar-Ellis, ed., *The Ellis correspondence*, vol. 1, frontispiece; priv. coll. · oils (after H. Meyer), Downside Abbey, near Bath · oils (after H. Meyer), Ambrose House, Bristol

Ellis, (Esyllt) Priscilla [Pip] Scott- (1916–1983), diarist, was born at Seaford House, Belgrave Square, London, on 15 November 1916, fourth of the six children of Thomas Evelyn *Ellis, eighth Baron Howard de Walden and fourth Baron Seaford (1880–1946), and his wife, Margherita (Margot; 1890–1974), elder daughter of Charles van Raalte, a wealthy banker of Dutch origins. Thomas Evelyn Ellis, who changed his name to Scott-Ellis by royal licence on 21 April 1917, served in the Second South African War and the First World War. The children were brought up in the splendour of Seagrave House, Belgrave Square; at Chirk Castle, Llangollen, north Wales; and at Brownsea Island, in Poole harbour. Priscilla Scott-Ellis, known to family and friends as Pip, was a pretty, blue-eyed, fair-haired child, 'cheerful and jolly' (Preston, 20). She attended a London day school, Queen's College, and when at Chirk was taught by governesses. Her parents were sparing in the time and affection that they bestowed on their children and Pip grew up insecure and eager to please. In 1932 she was sent to Benenden School and in autumn 1933 to a finishing school in Paris.

Pip came out in 1934 and settled in to the gilded routine of the London season. She worried about her weight and appearance, and her mother thought her frivolous even by the standards of the débutante. Her love of travel was kindled by visits to Kenya, the West Indies, and New York with her father. In New York in 1936, and on the boat home, she had her first sexual experiences, their liberating effect 'incredible for the erstwhile priggish me' (Preston, 27). These liaisons, however, only intensified her love for Prince Ataúlfo de Orleans (or Touffles as he was known), the youngest of the three sons of her mother's close friends Prince Alfonso de Orleans, a cousin of

Alfonso XIII of Spain, and his wife, Princess Beatrice of Saxe-Coburg and Gotha, a granddaughter of Queen Victoria. Pip's indefatigable optimism made it harder for her to comprehend the coded messages of Ataúlfo's mother that he would never marry, and only late in life was his homosexuality openly recognized.

After the outbreak of the Spanish Civil War in July 1936 Prince Alfonso became a commander in the nationalist air force. His sons all became airmen, and Ataúlfo joined the condor legion of the Luftwaffe, which was sent to Spain by Hitler in November 1936. In March 1937 Pip learned that her near-contemporary, Gabriel Herbert, the daughter of Aubrey Herbert, the diplomat, had volunteered to nurse for the nationalist side. Pip determined to follow her example. Her motivation was not primarily ideological, although she shared the monarchist and anti-communist sentiments of her Spanish friends. Nor did she have any profound religious conviction, unlike the militantly Catholic Gabriel Herbert. She sought instead adventure, a sense of purpose, and above all to be near Ataúlfo.

Pip prepared for Spain by taking courses in first-aid and Spanish, and by reading pro-nationalist accounts of the war. Politically naïve, she accepted Francoist mythology unquestioningly and became callous to the atrocities perpetrated against 'the reds'. She left England on 21 September 1937 in the care of Princess Beatrice, who ran the nationalist nursing-service Frentes y Hospitales. After a luxurious stay at the Orleans' palace at Sanlúcar de Barrameda, Pip began a nursing course at Jérez on 18 October. She wrote in her diary: 'I did not feel sick at all, but afterwards when I left the hospital I kept seeing wounds all the time and hearing the screams of agony … I understand now why nurses are so often hard and inhuman' (Carr, 6). Almost every night, however tired, she kept a detailed diary. It shows a schizophrenic world of extreme hardship at the front juxtaposed with relative normality elsewhere.

After Pip passed her qualifying exam she was sent to a clearing station (*equipo*) at Burgos de Osma, where she was joined by Consuelo Osorio de Moscoso, the daughter of a Spanish aristocrat and a friend throughout her stay in Spain. On 28 January 1938 the pair managed, despite their youth and inexperience, to be sent to Cella in Aragon, 8 kilometres from the front. They nursed casualties from the final engagements of the battle for Teruel. From March until July 1938 her unit followed the nationalist Aragon offensive. On 11 March the *equipo* reached Belchite, where eighty-five prisoners of the International Brigades awaited their fate: 'They will all be shot', Pip noted dispassionately, 'as the foreigners always are' (Carr, 52). Her diary reveals intense frustration at the petty jealousies of her colleagues, resentment at their prudishness, a lack of confidence in her own nursing ability, but also her resilience: she functioned best in adversity and was unfazed when the *equipo* came under heavy artillery fire at Escatrón.

By July Pip was severely run down and after contracting paratyphoid she returned to England to convalesce. She rejoined her *equipo* at Calaceite in late September. It was not long before her health and morale were again strained by the demands of nursing heavy casualties, this time from the final stages of the battle of the River Ebro. Her twenty-second birthday dawned without a letter or telegram from home: 'I can't say on the whole it has been a vastly successful year', she wrote, 'although it has been adventurous' (Carr, 149). The failure of the republican offensive on the Ebro ensured a nationalist victory in the civil war. She entered Madrid with Princess Beatrice on 28 March 1939, her elation tempered by the grim spectacle of the emaciated civilian population. She spent several weeks working in hospitals in the city. In May she was decorated by the nationalist government for her bravery under fire at Escatrón. After Frentes y Hospitales was disbanded she reluctantly returned to England, arriving in London on 9 June. Her sister Gaenor Heathcote Amory likened her experience to that of a soldier returning from the western front: she felt displaced, exhausted, and depressed.

Pip soon began editing her civil-war diary for publication, but the project was abandoned with the outbreak of hostilities in September 1939. The war meant a confusion of emotions; she feared losing her Germanophile Spanish friends, but finally reconciled herself to having lost Ataúlfo, and drank heavily in her despair. In January 1940 she joined a field hospital in northern France, which was evacuated to England in June. She later helped to organize a hospital for Polish troops in Scotland. In December 1940 she was given the title of honorary colonel in the Polish army and in 1943 she was awarded the Polish golden cross of merit. After several approaches from British intelligence she returned to Spain in 1943 and was based at the consulate in Barcelona, where she was probably involved in arranging the safe passage of escaped allied airmen to Lisbon.

Pip was thrilled to be back in Spain, and to renew her friendship with Prince Alfonso and Princess Beatrice. They nevertheless had grave misgivings about her plans to marry José Luis de Vilallonga, 'the handsome and dissolute playboy son of a rich Catalan aristocrat' (Preston, 102), whom she probably first met in January 1944. The marriage went ahead at Sanlúcar on 20 September 1945; none of Pip's family could attend. The couple reached England, penniless, in April 1946, and her father, recognizing the predatory instincts of his son-in-law, altered his will in a vain effort to protect Pip financially. She and Vilallonga had a son and daughter, and lived in Argentina and France before separating in 1958.

After a Spanish court granted her a divorce in 1972 she married Ian Hanson, a young opera singer, whom she met in London in 1966. They settled in Los Angeles, where a disastrous land investment wiped out her savings. She died there of lung cancer on 8 March 1983. She was devotedly nursed during a long illness by Ian Hanson, who died two years later, an early casualty of the AIDS epidemic in the city. She was survived by her two children. Her ashes were scattered on the hills above Chirk. Towards the end of her life she planned to re-edit her Spanish diary. It was eventually published in 1995 as *The Chances of Death*, edited by Sir

Raymond Carr, and has been recognized as a remarkable addition to the original literature on the Spanish Civil War, written from the perspective of one of only two British women known to have volunteered for the Francoist cause.   MARK POTTLE

Sources R. Carr, ed., *The chances of death: a diary of the Spanish Civil War* (1995) [with foreword by G. Heathcote Amory] · P. Preston, *Doves of war: four women of Spain* (2002) · Baron Howard de Walden, *Earls have peacocks* (1992) · Burke, *Peerage* · *CGPLA Eng. & Wales* (1986) · b. cert.
Likenesses photographs, repro. in Preston, *Doves of war*
Wealth at death £8607—in England and Wales: administration with will, 22 Jan 1986, *CGPLA Eng. & Wales*

Ellis, Robert [*pseud.* Cynddelw] (1812–1875), Baptist minister and poet, was born on 3 February 1812 in Ty'n-y-meini, near Pen-y-bont-fawr, Montgomeryshire, the son of Robert Ellis (1776–1816), and his wife, Elizabeth Thomas. He went to school for two months at Llanwyddelan, and for one month at Llanarmon. His only other education was at Sunday school, and from his mother and neighbours. Particularly strong influences included the turner Richard Morris, the tailor James Jones, and Humphrey Bromley, a Unitarian preacher. Ellis later studied under John Williams of Llansilin, whose biography he afterwards wrote (1871). An avid reader and collector of books, his library ultimately became perhaps one of the largest and most valuable private libraries in the principality.

On 5 October 1834 Ellis began preaching, and in May 1837 he became minister of Llanelian and Llanddulas, moving to Glynceiriog, Denbighshire, in 1838. He also served as a minister in Sirhowy, Monmouthshire, from 1847, concluding his ministry at Caernarfon (1862–75). As a preacher Ellis is said to have been learned and doctrinal rather than popular. As a public lecturer, he wore his learning more lightly, bringing the history of Wales to life with remarkable wit. Contemporary scholars, such as Thomas Stephens, had researched antiquarian subjects more fully, but Ellis showed a greater flair in popularizing them. Among subjects of his lectures were ancient Welsh wisdom, Welsh proverbs, and Welsh law. From 1849 his reputation as a poet developed, as well as that of adjudicator, and editor, of other poetic work. He served briefly as editor of *Y Tyst* (1851) and *Y Greal* (1852–3), and later edited the poetry column in *Seren Gomer* (1854–9). Among his most important poetical works were 'Cywydd y berwyn' and 'Awdl y distawrwydd', both published posthumously in *Barddoniaeth Cynddelw* in 1877. Of equal significance were his studies into Welsh poetic heritage, notably *Tafol y beirdd* (1853), *Gorchestion beirdd Cymru* (1853), an edition of the poetry of Rhys Jones (1861), and an edition of the medieval poet Dafydd ap Gwilym, *Barddoniaeth Dafydd ab Gwilym* (1875?). He also wrote on antiquarian subjects, publishing *Manion hynafiaethol* (1873), and contributing chapters to Gweirydd ap Rhys's *Hanes y Brytaniaid a'r Cymry*.

Ellis died at Gartheryr, in the parish of Llanrhaeadr-ym-Mochnant, Denbighshire, on 19 August 1875, while on a preaching tour.   R. M. J. JONES, *rev.* ROBERT V. SMITH

Sources D. Williams, *Cofiant Robert Ellis* (1935) · *DWB* · H. E. Hughes, *Eminent men of Denbighshire* [1946] · J. S. Jones, *Cynddelw:*

Graethawd bywgraffiadol a beirniadol (1877) · *Y Geninen*, 8 (1890), 127 ·
CGPLA Eng. & Wales (1875)
Archives NL Wales, corresp. and papers; papers
Wealth at death under £600: administration, 24 Sept 1875,
CGPLA Eng. & Wales

Ellis, Robert (1819/20–1885), classical scholar, was the son
of John Ellis of Peckham, Surrey and was born there. He
entered St John's College, Cambridge, in 1836, was elected
a scholar in 1839, and graduated BA as fifth wrangler in
1840, obtaining a fellowship in 1841. He took his MA
degree in 1843, and was ordained deacon in 1845 and
priest in 1846. In 1850 he commenced BD. He vacated his
fellowship by his marriage on 2 April 1872 to Jane, daughter of Francis France of Nobold, Shropshire. He died on 20
December 1885, at 3 Higher Summerland Place, Exeter,
aged sixty-five.

Ellis is chiefly known for his fierce controversy with William John Law, which raged from 1854 to 1856, on the
route followed by Hannibal in his passage of the Alps. Ellis
had investigated the subject during excursions in the Alps
in July 1852 and in April and May 1853. He wrote *A treatise
on Hannibal's passage of the Alps, in which his route is traced over
the Little Mount Cenis* (1853), and two lengthy articles in
answer to Law in December 1855 and in March 1856 in the
Journal of Classical and Sacred Philology (2, 308–29; 3, 1–34). In
1867 he produced a further work on the ancient routes
between Italy and Gaul. The arguments of Ellis and Law
are not cited in most recent discussions of Hannibal's
route. Ellis also wrote various works on primitive
languages.   GORDON GOODWIN, *rev.* RICHARD SMAIL

Sources Venn, *Alum. Cant.* · *The Eagle*, 14 (1887), 108 · *CGPLA Eng. &
Wales* (1886)
Wealth at death £12,186 2s. 4d.: probate, 11 Jan 1886, *CGPLA Eng.
& Wales*

Ellis, Robert Leslie (1817–1859), mathematician and classical scholar, was born on 25 August 1817 in Bath, the
youngest of the six children of Francis Ellis of Bath. His
father was fond of speculative inquiry and spent much
time with him from an early age. He was educated at home
by two private tutors, one in classics and another in mathematics. At the age of ten he read Virgil and Xenophon, as
well as Cuvier's *Theory of the Earth* and the *Edinburgh Review*.
He soon got involved with mechanics and made rapid progress in the calculus. Accustomed to conversing with his
seniors, he picked up an elderly sobriety of manner which
distinguished him from his contemporaries.

Ellis is said to have inherited his lifelong predisposition
to depression and sickliness from his mother. In 1834 he
became a private pupil of the Revd James Challis at Papworth Everard, near Cambridge, but due to ill health he
was soon compelled to disrupt his studies and to delay his
entrance to Cambridge University. In 1836 he matriculated at Trinity College as a pupil of George Peacock, who
discovered with amazement that on his arrival Ellis had
commenced reading Robert Woodhouse's *Isoperimetrical
Problems* (1810). Ellis's intellect was much admired, even by
his rivals.

Ellis studied mathematics on his own, but in his last
years he had the advantage of the direction of William

Hopkins, a well-known private tutor of tripos candidates.
As his sight was weak he regularly employed someone to
read for him; in this way he mastered J. H. Pratt's *Mechanical Philosophy* (1836), the first Cambridge treatise to present Laplace's analytical treatment of the earth's shape.
Ellis deliberately evaded intimacy and his seclusion added
to the depression to which he was predisposed. Nevertheless, he was highly respected, and his suggestions, when
disputes arose in the Cambridge Union Society, were readily adopted. Ellis graduated as senior wrangler in 1840
(having been examined in private at his special request)
and was first Smith's prizeman, and was elected fellow of
Trinity several months later. He remained in Cambridge
until 1849, when he ceased to be a fellow. He was admitted
to the Inner Temple in 1838 and duly called to the bar in
1840, but as his elder brothers and father successively died
he became heir to considerable property and thus lacked
the inducement to work as a lawyer. Still, he devoted
much time to the study of the civil law, leaving behind
him several volumes of notes, but his ultimate ambition
to be appointed professor of civil law remained unfulfilled. Ellis had further intended to enter political life in
Bath; he was attached to Sir William Napier (1785–1860),
and professed himself a whig.

During his residence at Cambridge, Ellis undertook, in
conjunction with D. D. Heath and J. Spedding, the edition
of Francis Bacon's works published between 1857 and
1874. His wide reading and intellectual labour are
nowhere as evident as in the general prefaces to Bacon's
philosophical writings, which were allotted to him. The
deterioration of his health in 1847 prevented him from
completing his project, a fact that caused him great
sorrow.

Ellis had many intellectual interests but it is mathematics which features in forty out of the fifty papers which
were edited after his death (by W. Walton) in a volume
entitled *The Mathematical and other Writings of R. L. Ellis*
(1863). His significant contributions date from 1837, when,
together with D. F. Gregory, he founded the *Cambridge
Mathematical Journal*. In 1843, a year before Gregory died,
Ellis undertook the edition of the last two volumes, in the
latter of which he inserted a memoir of his deceased
friend (1845). By that time, he had furnished the journal
with several papers on functional and differential equations, which revealed his skill in Laplace's and J. Fourier's
analyses. Motivated by Gaskin's symbolical solution of
the equation for the ellipticity of the earth, which
appeared in J. Hymers's *Differential Equations* (1839), Ellis
devoted his paper 'On the integration of certain differential equations' (1841) to a general treatment of second-
order equations important in physics. This paper helped
inspire George Boole's masterpiece 'On a general method
in analysis' (*PTRS*, 134, 1844, 225–82). Ellis was particularly
drawn towards subjects that involved philosophical
thinking, as illustrated in his paper 'On the foundations of
the theory of probabilities' (1849). Together with Boole he
is regarded as a notable critic of the subjective aspects of
the classical interpretation of probability theory.

Ellis expressed no desire to be appointed professor of

mathematics; he occasionally gave college lectures on higher mathematics, but he never had a private pupil. After receiving his MA in 1843 he was moderator of the tripos examination in the following year, producing, together with Matthew O'Brien, a collection of the problems proposed, with their solutions. At the request of the British Association in 1845, he contributed a masterly report upon the recent progress of analysis (1846). Soon after this his health gave way altogether.

In an attempt to improve his health Ellis removed to the south of France, but after an attack of rheumatic fever at San Remo in Italy in 1849 he returned to England an invalid. He continued to travel, seeking medical help, eventually settling at Anstey Hall, Trumpington, near Cambridge, in 1853. Despite his worsening health he continued to dictate on a variety of subjects, ranging from bees' cells and Roman money to the formation of a Chinese dictionary and Boole's *Laws of Thought* (1854). Moreover, he read the New Testament in Swedish, translated Danish ballads, and rediscovered J. Napier's conception of logarithms. He was noted for his excellent conversational powers, the accuracy and historical framework of his speech, and his retentive memory. In his last years he lost his sight altogether. After years of acute suffering, he died on 12 May 1859 at Anstey Hall, and was buried in Trumpington churchyard. He was unmarried.

MARIA PANTEKI

Sources H. Goodwin, 'Biographical memoir of R. L. Ellis', *The mathematical and other writings of R. L. Ellis*, ed. W. Walton (1863), ix–xxxvi • M. Panteki, 'Relationships between algebra, differential equations, and logic in England, 1800–1860', PhD diss., Middlesex University (CNAA), 1992 • *The Athenaeum* (11 Feb 1860) • J. P. Norris, 'Notes, privately printed', 1853–9, Cambridge MSS, Cam.c. 859.18 • J. P. Norris, 'Review of a biographical memoir of R. L. Ellis by H. Goodwin', 1863–4, Cambridge MSS, Cam.c. 864.25 • L. Daston, *Classical probability in the Enlightenment* (1988) • Venn, *Alum. Cant.* • *DNB* • d. cert.

Archives Trinity Cam., diaries and notebooks | Bodl. Oxf., letters to Sir William Napier • CUL, letters to Lord Kelvin • Trinity Cam., A. De Morgan, Kelvin, W. F. P. Napier, J. P. Norris, J. Spedding MSS • U. Nott., letters to C. B. Marlay • U. St Andr., corresp. with James Forbes

Likenesses T. C. Wageman, watercolour drawing, 1844, Trinity Cam. • S. Lawrence, crayon drawing, 1849, Trinity Cam. • T. Woolner, marble bust, 1867, Trinity Cam. • S. Lawrence, portrait, priv. coll. • engraving (after portrait by S. Lawrence), repro. in R. L. Ellis, *The mathematical and other writings of R. L. Ellis*, ed. W. Walton (1863)

Wealth at death under £140,000: probate, 25 June 1859, *CGPLA Eng. & Wales*

Ellis, Robinson (1834–1913), classical scholar, was born at Barming, near Maidstone, Kent, on 5 September 1834, the third son of James Ellis, wealthy landowner and hopgrower, and his third wife, a Miss Robinson, who was described, disparagingly, by Keats in his first letter about her friend Fanny Brawne. Educated at Elizabeth College, Guernsey, and from August 1850 at Rugby School, where he owed much to George Granville Bradley, in 1852 Ellis won a scholarship at Balliol College, Oxford. He matriculated in November 1852, and obtained a first class in classical moderations in 1854, the Ireland scholarship and the

chancellor's Latin verse prize in 1855, a first in *literae humaniores* in 1856 (BA 1857, MA 1859), and the Boden (Sanskrit) scholarship in 1858. In 1858 he was elected fellow of Trinity College, Oxford, where he resided, save for partial absence from 1870 to 1876, the rest of his life. All his life Ellis was very short-sighted. He refused to wear glasses, which he said gave him headaches. As his eyes were very weak, he could read only for short periods. He was also absent-minded. In later life he was often lame and walked with difficulty, leaning on the arm of a companion. He was influenced by Benjamin Jowett and John Conington, and was for a time interested in ritualism and mesmerism. In later life he was attracted, but possibly only aesthetically, by the Church of Rome, since, apart from pure scholarship and literature, he apparently cared only for music. He enjoyed listening to Latin chants. His attitudes to religion seemed enigmatic: some called him a pagan, but in his younger days he passed through a high-church phase. After twelve years of college teaching, mostly in composition and Latin authors, varied by reading parties, he was elected in 1870 professor of Latin at University College, London; but he was not successful with the larger and less advanced classes there, and in 1876 returned to Oxford.

By this time Ellis's position as a Latinist was well established. He was elected reader in Latin in 1883, and professor (on the death of Henry Nettleship) in 1893, thereby becoming a fellow of Corpus Christi College. Vice-president of Trinity from 1879 to 1893, he was made honorary fellow in 1894 and allowed to retain his college rooms. When nearly blind and otherwise infirm, he finally consented unwillingly to the appointment of a deputy a few months before he died. He was honorary LLD of Dublin (1882), FBA (1902), and a corresponding associate of the Accademia Virgiliana of Mantua.

Ellis was well read in standard English poetry, essays, and translations and took great interest, as an occasional contributor—especially from sixteenth-century translators from Greek and Latin—in the *New English Dictionary* (later the *Oxford English Dictionary*). In Greek he published emendations to Herodas and other fragmentary works, but his *forte* was in Latin. He was a fine composer of verse and some of his best pieces, mostly in hendecasyllables, are in *Nova anthologia Oxoniensis*, which he edited with A. D. Godley in 1899. His work on Catullus began in 1859; he published a plain text, with conjectures based on study of manuscripts, in 1866, and a larger edition in 1867 (2nd edn, 1878; revised text, 1904). In 1871 he published an unexpurgated translation in the original metres, very ingenious but barely intelligible without the Latin, and dedicated to Tennyson. His great *Commentary on Catullus* appeared in 1876 (2nd edn, 1889). His erudition is shown rather by his wide knowledge of the early Italian commentators—whose achievement he claimed was underestimated—than by skill in dealing with the codices, and he was severely criticized, notably by E. Baehrens and H. A. J. Munro; but his mastery of the subject was unmistakable. In later life he devoted more attention to palaeography, but, probably owing to his defective eyesight, never became really proficient.

Ellis's next work was an elaborate edition of the *Ibis* of Ovid in 1881; then, considering that it would be 'too marked to edit another amatory poet', he devoted himself to minor authors. His principal recensions were of Avianus (1887), Orientius (1888), the *Opuscula Virgiliana* (1895, 1907), Velleius Paterculus (1898), and the *Aetna* (1901). He dealt exhaustively, though less formally, with other authors in his *Noctes Manilianae* (1886–91)—on the work of Manilius, the astrological poet—and in the glosses on Apollinaris Sidonius (1885), and published a dozen of the public lectures which from time to time were read for him in the hall of Corpus Christi College. He published articles at frequent intervals in journals including the Cambridge and the American journals of philology, and *Hermathena*, *Hermes* and *Philologus*. His professorial lectures to undergraduates were usually on Catullus, Propertius, Lucan, or Statius, on Latin verse composition, position, and (later) on Latin palaeography with specimen pages selected by himself from Bodleian manuscripts. He was assiduous in maintaining friendly, though cautious, relations with foreign scholars—'not Baehrens', however; and he visited distant libraries in search of codices. He repeatedly urged that 'the study of MSS. is indispensable for any one who aspires to do original work' (Clark, 524). His work both as commentator and as textual critic was characterized by vast erudition and minute investigation, but was perhaps deficient in decision and logical exactness. He was, however, under no illusions about the art of emendation; in Catullus he believed that he had 'divined the truth' in one, or perhaps two, passages only (Ellis, 'Preface' to *Commentary*, 2nd edn, xiv).

Ellis led a simple, frugal—and latterly penurious—ascetic, and reclusive life; his gentleness, his simplicity, his dependence on physical help, his unconventional but frequent hospitality, and not least his impressive devotion to scholarship, attracted the interest not only of his colleagues but also of many of the undergraduates, especially the rising scholars of about 1880 to 1900. He was influenced by the attitudes of the early humanists, and some of his chosen subjects and his annotations on Latin poets were considered indelicate, and led some people to misunderstand him. The naïvety, possibly not always unintentional—some thought he expressed ironic humour—of his remarks about his acquaintances and himself, and his casual familiarity with the improprieties of his favourite authors, made him somewhat embarrassing in social life, and led to the circulation of numerous stories about him. New material could be obtained by artful questions; and eventually there was a considerable body of *anecdota*, some of which have been printed in Oxford reminiscences. His manner and dress were peculiar: he wore an old tall hat set on the back of his head, very large boots, and outdoors always an overcoat. He was frequently caricatured. He took little interest in national or academic politics, but generally voted on the Liberal side; he claimed, 'I have been a lifelong Liberal' (Clark, 524).

Ellis died of exhaustion and pulmonary trouble after an operation at Acland House, Banbury Road, Oxford, on 9 October 1913, and was buried in St Sepulchre's cemetery, Jericho, Oxford, leaving distant relations a much larger sum than expected.

H. E. D. Blakiston, *rev.* Roger T. Stearn

Sources *Encyclopaedia Britannica*, 11th edn (1910–11) • *The Times* (14 Oct 1913) • A. C. Clark, 'Ellis Robinson, 1834–1913', *PBA*, [6] (1913–14), 517–24 • Foster, *Alum. Oxon.* • *WWW* • *Hist. U. Oxf.* 6: *19th-cent. Oxf.*

Archives Bodl. Oxf., corresp. and papers, MSS Lat misc d 39–44, Lat misc e 54–73, Lat misc f 22–29, Gr misc d 3–4 | LPL, letters to Claude Jenkins, MS 1630

Likenesses G. P. Jacomb-Hood, oils, 1889, Trinity College, Oxford • M. Beerbohm, caricature, *c*.1893, Merton Oxf. • A. Broadbent, bronze bust, exh. RA 1918, Bodl. Oxf. • Spy [L. Ward], chromolithograph caricature, NPG; repro. in *VF* (24 May 1894)

Wealth at death £31,494 14*s.* 11*d.*: probate, 26 Nov 1913, *CGPLA Eng. & Wales*

Ellis, Roger Henry (1910–1998), archivist, was born on 9 June 1910 at Garsdale, Mansfield Woodhouse, Nottinghamshire, eldest of the four children of Francis Henry Ellis (1882–1953), managing director and chairman of the Sherwood Colliery Company, and his wife, Sybil Mary (1881/1882–1969), daughter of Adrian Roger Chicken of Nottingham. From Sedbergh School (1923–9) he went to King's College, Cambridge (1929–33), where he took firsts in both parts of the classical tripos and was awarded an Augustus Austen Leigh studentship. After a brief spell of research on Greek vase painting, and in default of any vacancies in a gallery or museum, he joined the staff of the Public Record Office on 1 January 1934. He soon absorbed the scholarly traditions of the office and became a disciple of Hilary Jenkinson, the most dynamic of the assistant keepers and a major influence on his subsequent professional career. His interest in seals and in conservation arose at this time.

On 20 November 1939 Ellis married Audrey Honor (1912–1993), only daughter of Herbert Arthur Baker of London and Tilford, Surrey. They had two daughters. War interrupted his career: he enlisted as a private in 1939 and rose to captain in the 5th fusiliers. In May 1944 he was assigned to the monuments, fine arts, and archives subcommission of the Allied Control Commission, where Jenkinson was archives adviser. From May to November 1944 he visited and reported on Italian archives in the wake of the allied advance, incidentally developing an enduring love of Italy. In November he was transferred to the German sector and promoted major.

Ellis returned to the Public Record Office in 1945, and was soon involved in the post-war expansion of archival work, notably the establishment of an intermediate repository for non-current records, for which he appropriated the term 'limbo'. He was one of the first lecturers (1947–57) on the diploma course in archive administration at University College, London, and also taught document repair at the London School of Printing. In technical matters he was a pioneer, stressing that the first duty of the archivist was to preserve records, and only secondarily to make them available for study. He formulated five principles of archive repair which have remained basic despite changes in materials and techniques. He was later chairman of the British Standards Institution committee that drafted BS 5454, *Recommendations for the Storage and Exhibition of Archival Documents* (1977). His close involvement with the British Records Association also dated from this period; he was the founder editor (1947–57) of its journal *Archives*.

In 1957 Ellis became the first full-time secretary of the Royal Commission on Historical Manuscripts, established in 1869 to report on non-governmental records. During his fifteen years as secretary he transformed its role and widened the scope of its activities and influence, laying a solid foundation for subsequent developments. His first priorities were to move the commission out of the Public Record Office into separate offices in Chancery Lane and to secure a revised and extended royal warrant. Its publications were both pruned and expanded. The expensive calendars were gradually discontinued but new series were inaugurated: the papers of nineteenth-century prime ministers and joint publications with local record-publishing societies. The revised warrant ensured the permanence of the National Register of Archives, whose importance as a tool for historical research had become clear by 1957. During his secretaryship its scope and use increased greatly, and a first step was taken to computerize its indexes.

Ellis had for some time been concerned about the probable loss of the working papers of British scientists. A joint committee of the commission and the Royal Society (1966) resulted in a published guide, *The Manuscript Papers of British Scientists, 1600–1940*, and the establishment of the Contemporary Scientific Archives Centre in Oxford, though slow progress meant that both postdated his secretaryship.

The commission's centenary exhibition at the National Portrait Gallery in 1969 allowed Ellis to combine a succinct and entertaining history with a wide selection of documents illustrated by appropriate portraits and artefacts, drawing on his own interests and knowledge.

Ellis retired in 1972 but soon returned to the Public Record Office to catalogue medieval seals. Between 1978 and 1986 three illustrated volumes of a seal catalogue were published. After his wife's death in 1993 he began cataloguing the Fuller collection of seals in the University of London Library, and was still engaged in this at his death. Retirement afforded him time for travel and his many other interests. He diffidently published two slim volumes of poetry, *Ode on St Crispin's Day* (1979) and *Walking Backwards* (1986).

Ellis was a distinctive figure, tall, debonair, with expressive eyebrows and no time for pomposity. His precision of mind was matched by his elegant handwriting and literary style. He came across as an amused and tolerant observer of men—and of himself. His visual sense was strong; as well as the fine arts, he derived pleasure from fine printing and binding, the pattern of poetry on a page, the bounty of the garden in autumn. He lovingly tended his collections of furniture, silver, paintings, books, and the family archives in his beautiful Hampstead house. A long-time member of the Athenaeum and fellow of the Society

of Antiquaries, he epitomized the connoisseur. Strong beliefs and high standards informed everything he did. His writings, mostly in professional journals, give an inadequate idea of the wise and quiet influence he exerted in the development of archive services after the war. He died at home at 7 Straffan Lodge, 1 Belsize Grove, London, on 19 March 1998 of heart failure and was cremated at Golders Green on 26 March.   FELICITY STRONG

Sources personal knowledge (2004) · private information (2004) [daughter] · R. H. Ellis, 'The British archivist and his society', *Journal of the Society of Archivists*, 3 (1965–9), 43–8 · *The Times* (9 April 1998) · *The Independent* (24 March 1998) · b. cert. · m. cert. · d. cert. · D. M. Owen and A. Owen, 'Roger Henry Ellis (1910–1998)', *Archives*, 23 (1998), 97–8 · F. Strong, 'Roger Henry Ellis', *Journal of the Society of Archivists*, 19 (1998), 235–8 · Burke, *Gen. GB* (1969) · *WW* · Sedbergh School register · register of admissions, 1919–58, King's Cam.
Archives PRO, papers | PRO, letters to Sir Henry Jenkinson, PRO 30/75/2, 42, 53, 58 | SOUND BBC Sound Archives, 'Dear Martyn Skinner: a poetical friendship', first broadcast 29/4/1992
Wealth at death £776,404: probate, 23 Sept 1998, *CGPLA Eng. & Wales*

Ellis [*née* Neilson], **Ruth** (1926–1955), nightclub hostess and convicted murderer, was born on 9 October 1926 at 74 West Parade, Rhyl, north Wales, the fourth of six children of Arthur Neilson (formerly Hornby), musician, and his wife, Elisaberta Goodall, a seamstress.

Born into poverty, Ruth determined very early that she would not live a life like her parents. 'She wasn't like my other children' her mother recalled, 'she was so very ambitious for herself. She used to say "Mum, I'm going to make something of my life"' (Hancock, 16). When her father's work as a jobbing musician on the ocean liners and in the cinemas evaporated with the advent of the 'talkies', the family moved to Basingstoke, and Ruth attended the local Fairfields Senior Girls' School. It was soon obvious that she intended her passport to a better life to be not education but rather her charm, prettiness, and opportunistic energy. Marriage seemed the first and most obvious means of escape, but the Canadian serviceman on whom she pinned her hopes, and with whom she had become pregnant, proved to have a wife and two children back home. It was 1944 and Ruth Neilson was just eighteen. This common betrayal destroyed what little confidence Ruth had in human relations. 'I did not feel that anything could hurt me any more and I had become emotionally rather cold and rather spent … somehow in my association with men nothing touched me' (ibid., 19) was how she described herself then. Her son, Clare Andrea Neilson, was born on 15 September 1944 and given his father's forenames.

From being a factory hand, waitress, and shop worker, Ruth turned to more lucrative and risky pursuits: photographer's model at an amateur camera club, and then hostess for a notorious vice boss with a string of clubs and brothels in Mayfair. The Court Club in Duke Street and the Hollywood in Welbeck Street were the first two clubs where Ruth worked in 1946, taking home £20 a week, almost ten times what she had been earning in Woolworths in Brixton.

Ruth Ellis (1926–1955), by unknown photographer, 1955

Ruth Neilson became Ruth Ellis when she married, on 8 November 1950, George Johnston Ellis (1909–1958), a divorced and alcoholic dentist for whom she felt vaguely sorry and with whom she hoped to gain some financial security. But the drinking, continual arguments over money, and Ruth's suspicions and violent jealousy meant the marriage was bitterly over by the time their daughter, Georgina, was born on 2 October 1951.

Short of money again and now with two children to support, Ruth returned to the vice boss: she continued her work as a hostess and call-girl. She then met in 1953 David Moffatt Drummond Blakely (1926–1955), a racing car enthusiast and the youngest child of a Sheffield doctor. Blakely was a reckless and feckless young man who frequented the Little Club, a disreputable drinking club in Knightsbridge where Ellis had become manager. Although he was engaged to another woman, and Ellis was still seeing her clients, the two became lovers. Quite soon, however, his drinking and possessiveness caused trouble in the club and Ellis found herself a second man friend, sharing her favours between them.

Desmond Edward Cussen had been a bomber pilot during the war and then became a director of the family firm of tobacconists. Well-off and bored, he belonged to the same circle of motor racing enthusiasts as Blakely. Alcohol was the most important currency between them and Ruth Ellis, Blakely, and Cussen all drank excessively. Resentments, jealousies, and violent drunken fights between Blakely and Ellis were commonplace. Cussen wanted to extract Ellis from the explosive relationship with his younger rival and had offered to marry her himself. But Ellis was infatuated with Blakely, and became obsessively and morbidly so when he decided to end the relationship at the beginning of the 1955 Easter holiday.

By Easter Sunday, 10 April, Ruth Ellis had endured three days of sleeplessness, panic, and pathological jealousy, fuelled by quantities of Pernod and a reckless consumption of tranquillizers. It appears that in this state she was given a 38 Smith & Wesson revolver by Cussen, who had oiled and loaded it and shown her how to use it. He then drove her to the Magdala public house in Hampstead where they expected David Blakely to be. Cussen waited in the car while Ellis set off to find her former lover. She caught Blakely as he left the pub with a friend: oblivious to everything else she pumped four bullets into his fleeing body. Hysteria broke out around her: 'Arrest me—I have just shot this man—and fetch an ambulance' (Hancock, 10) she said with icy calm to the first available policeman.

It seemed to the witnesses to be a cold-blooded murder, and nothing Ruth Ellis said in court in her defence altered the opinion that it was premeditated. She refused to plead insanity and the jury would not accept her defence of provocation. For her own reasons, Ellis had shielded Cussen's crucial involvement in the tragedy. Only the day before her execution did she admit his complicity to her lawyer, Victor Mishcon, afterwards Lord Mishcon. However, Desmond Cussen could not be found in time to corroborate her story and the home secretary, Gwilym Lloyd George, later Viscount Tenby, refused to reprieve her.

Ruth Ellis was hanged on the morning of 13 July 1955 at Holloway prison, north London. She was twenty-eight years old. She impressed everyone with her control and courage; the prospect of being executed for a crime she never denied was marginally less unpleasant to her than that of growing old in prison, as unprivileged and deprived of hope and opportunity as she had been as a child. She was buried first in Holloway prison, and later reburied in Amersham, Buckinghamshire.

The circumstances of her death assured Ruth Ellis the fame and significance she had failed to find in life. The natural public interest in her case was intensified by her startling platinum-blonde looks, glacial manner, and life in the seedier reaches of Mayfair's clubland. The guilty verdict and the death sentence ensured the trial became a *cause célèbre*, the verdict still debated today. As it turned out, Ruth Ellis was the last woman to be judicially hanged in Britain: the widespread and international revulsion against her punishment expedited the establishment of a law of 'diminished responsibility' in the Homicide Act of 1957.

Following her death some campaigned for Ruth Ellis's verdict of murder to be commuted to one of manslaughter, on the grounds of provocation and diminished responsibility; judgment was reserved after a hearing at the Court of Appeal in September 2003. But she will remain memorialized as the last woman to be hanged, the glamorous blonde, guilty of a classic *crime passionnel*, whose execution hastened the abolition of the death penalty in Great Britain. Circumstances, timing, and the fact that she was so young, good-looking, and a woman had combined to award Ruth Ellis her small, brave place in history. It seems likely she would have been happy enough with that. Miranda Richardson played the part of Ruth Ellis in Mike Newell's film of her life, *Dance with a Stranger* (1985).   JANE DUNN

Sources R. Hancock, *Ruth Ellis: the last woman to be hanged* (1963) • J. Goodman and P. Pringle, *The trial of Ruth Ellis* (1974) • G. Ellis, *Ruth Ellis, my mother* (1996) • b. cert. • m. cert. • A. Travis, 'Ruth Ellis: the other confession', *The Guardian* (19 Jan 1999)
Archives PRO, MSS relating to her case, incl. medical details and letters, PCOM 9 [letters: copies]
Likenesses photographs, *c*.1955, Hult. Arch. [*see illus.*] • photograph, repro. in Hancock, *Ruth Ellis* • photograph, repro. in Goodman and Pringle, *Trial of Ruth Ellis* • photograph, repro. in Ellis, *Ruth Ellis*

Ellis, Sir Samuel Burdon (1787–1865), Royal Marines officer, was the son of Captain Charles Ellis RN. His father intended him for the legal profession, and on leaving school he was articled to a Yarmouth lawyer. Disliking this, he left after about one year, and entered the Royal Marine light infantry as a second lieutenant on 1 January 1804. He was at once sent on board ship, and, after first seeing service in Sir Robert Calder's action off Cape Finisterre, was present at the battle of Trafalgar, and was promoted lieutenant in 1806. He was on the Walcheren expedition in 1809 and at the capture of Guadeloupe in 1810. On board the *Nymphe* he was employed off the coasts of Spain and of southern France during the latter years of the Peninsular War. He specially distinguished himself in the operations which the navy took in helping to form the siege of Bayonne, after Wellington's victory of the Nive and Soult's retreat on Toulouse. His ship, the frigate *Pomona*, was then ordered to the North American coast, where she captured the US frigate *President* after a fierce fight, during which Ellis particularly distinguished himself, being the first man to board the enemy.

On the conclusion of peace Ellis had no further opportunity of active service. In 1817 he joined the Portsmouth division. In November 1820, when recruiting in Salisbury, he, with his armed party, suppressed a riot occasioned by the trial of Queen Caroline, and was thanked by the mayor and justices. On 15 November 1826, after more than twenty years in the marines, he was promoted captain. It was not until many years later, during which Ellis served on many different ships, that he again saw active service in the capture of Fort Manora, at the entrance to the harbour of Karachi in Sind, in 1839. On the *Wellesley*, seventy-four guns, he next commanded the marines in the Persian Gulf, and was mentioned in dispatches for, in March 1839, despite Persian fire, bringing off the political resident at Bushehr, Captain Samuel Hennell.

When the First Opium War broke out Ellis was still on the *Wellesley*, at the China station; for his services in command of a battalion of marines at the capture of Chusan (Zhoushan) on 5 July 1840, and at the battle of Chuenpe (Chuanbi) on 7 January 1841, he was mentioned in dispatches, and was promoted brevet major on 6 May 1841. He further distinguished himself with his marines in the bombardment of the Bogue (Humen) forts; he commanded the advance on Canton (Guangzhou), and the services of his men were so great at the storming of the Canton forts on 26 May 1841 that he was promoted brevet lieutenant-colonel, antedated to that day, and made a CB (1842). He commanded a battalion of marines at Ningpo (Ningbo) and Chusan until the end of the war, when he returned to England.

From his return until 1847 Ellis was with the Plymouth division. During this period he was 'induced by some speculators' (*Memoirs*, 325) to become a director of the Direct Exeter and Plymouth Railway Company. It failed in 1852, and he lost his savings and, for many years, a substantial part of his income. From 1847 he served with the Chatham division, except for a short interval at Pembroke. He lost the sight of one eye from an accidental blow by a driver's whip. He married, about 1852, Louisa, *née* Drayson; they had two sons, one of whom was Alfred Burdon *Ellis. He was promoted colonel on 3 November 1851, and commanded the Chatham division of the Royal Marines until he became major-general on 20 June 1855. He was promoted lieutenant-general in 1857, made a KCB in May 1860, and promoted general in 1862. He died, aged seventy-eight, at his residence, Old Charlton, Kent, on 10 March 1865, having been an officer of marines for more than sixty years, and was buried in Charlton cemetery. His widow, 'in comparative poverty', unpensioned and aggrieved, edited his memoirs; published in 1866, they are largely about the Second Opium War.

H. M. STEPHENS, *rev.* ROGER T. STEARN

Sources *Memoirs and services of the late Lieutenant-General Sir S. B. Ellis, KCB, Royal Marines*, ed. Lady Ellis (1866) • *Hart's Army List* • *GM*, 3rd ser., 18 (1865) • Royal Marines records • J. B. Kelly, *Britain and the Persian Gulf, 1795–1880* (1968) • Boase, *Mod. Eng. biog.*
Wealth at death under £1500: probate, 16 May 1865, *CGPLA Eng. & Wales*

Ellis [*née* Stickney]**, Sarah** (1799–1872), writer and educationist, was born at Ridgmont, in Holderness, Yorkshire, the youngest of the five children of William Stickney (*d*. 1848), a Quaker farmer, and his wife, Esther, *née* Richardson (*d*. 1803). By his second wife, 'a lady from Norfolk', whom he married in 1808, William Stickney had a further four children. No detailed account of Sarah Stickney's life remains apart from a memoir entitled *The Home Life and Letters of Mrs. Ellis Compiled by her Nieces* (1893). The unnamed nieces may be tentatively identified as Rachel Binns (daughter of Sarah Stickney's sister Rachel, who married Jonathan Binns of Lancaster about 1808) and Mary Backhouse (daughter of Sarah Stickney's sister Hannah, who married Thomas Backhouse of York in 1826). Her other sister, Dorothy, married Abraham Sewell of Great Yarmouth, and through this connection Sarah Stickney became related by marriage to the future authors Mary Wright Sewell and Anna Sewell, wife and daughter respectively of Abraham Sewell's brother Isaac. Mary Sewell and Sarah Stickney became close friends and appreciated each other's status as popular authors.

Sarah Stickney's family were in comfortable circumstances during her girlhood, and, apart from attending the Quaker school at Ackworth between 1813 and 1816, she was educated mainly at home. As well as receiving a thorough training in practical housewifery, and helping to bring up her younger siblings, she was encouraged to read widely in literature by her father, a man of scientific interests and patriarchal authority. Sarah Stickney also learned to ride and train her own horses and developed a love for animals, natural beauty, and art; in many ways her upbringing, much more free and easy than that of many nineteenth-century girls, fostered her considerable resilience of physique and independence of mind. The latter quality, clearly present in the letters quoted in her nieces' memoir, cannot have made it easy for her to submit to the subordinate position her writings later encouraged women both to accept and to alleviate by their moral influence. Sarah Stickney also became proficient in drawing, water-colour, and oil-painting, and was briefly taught drawing by John Sell Cotman, as she recalled, to the painter's gratification, in *The Poetry of Life* (2 vols., 1835). However, Sarah Stickney always considered the loss of her mother when she was four as having had the most profound influence on her later life. Certainly her experience of maternal bereavement influenced her later writings on the importance of a mother's role within the middle-class family.

William Stickney's financial position worsened during the agricultural depression of the 1820s, and Sarah Stickney determined to earn money herself, first by painting portraits in oils and by selling illustrations to Ackermann, who published her *Contrasts*, a series of drawings with a moral theme, in 1832; no further published illustrations by her are recorded. Working as an artist was not sufficiently remunerative, and in 1830 Sarah Stickney published the anti-slavery tale *The Negro Slave: a Tale Addressed to the Women of Great Britain*, and was at work on a series of short stories, *Pictures of Private Life* (3 series, 1833–7) remarking in a letter to a friend in 1831 'I have some feelings left, though I have taken to writing little books and painting for money' (letter to M. Crossfield, *Home Life*, 43). Her early literary career relied on Quaker links with established writers such as Mary Howitt, and on help provided by Thomas Pringle, secretary of the Anti-Slavery Society, but although she intended to write for the market, she always determined that her fiction should have a moral theme and a domestic setting. Her theoretical defence of moral fiction and of what would later be called domestic realism, in the 'Apology for fiction' prefaced to *Pictures of Private Life*, is a significant critical contribution that may have influenced George Eliot's discussion of the same question in chapter 17 of *Adam Bede* (1859). In *The Poetry of Life* Sarah Stickney also wrote on art and aesthetics, and in 1836 she published her first three-volume novel, *Home, or, The Iron Rule*, typically emphasizing the importance of female self-sacrifice and moral example within the family.

By now an established author, Sarah Stickney married the widowed William *Ellis (1794–1872), Congregational minister, missionary, and author, on 23 May 1837 at Burstwick parish church, near Ridgmont. With his first wife

William Ellis had four children, John, Mary, Elizabeth, and Annie; Mary died soon after her father married Sarah Stickney, but both Elizabeth and Annie later taught at Rawdon House School. Influenced by her future husband, Sarah Stickney became a Congregationalist and also a convinced teetotaller and temperance supporter; the marriage lasted thirty-five years and seems to have been remarkably happy. In 1841, on returning from a trip to Pau undertaken for Mr Ellis's health, the Ellises rented Rose Hill, a substantial house with large grounds in Hoddesdon, Essex, where they remained until their deaths in 1872. The only detailed account of Sarah Ellis's appearance and personality was written retrospectively by a former pupil of Rawdon House School, who recalls her generous build, commanding personality, attractive features, blue eyes, and curling black hair. A frontispiece to volume 1 of *The Morning Call* is roughly contemporary with this account.

After her marriage, Sarah Ellis always used her married name (Mrs William Ellis, or Mrs Ellis) for professional purposes. As well as acting as her husband's amanuensis, she continued to develop a varied literary career and for over thirty years produced moral and didactic fiction, conduct-books, works on moral education and in support of temperance, a considerable body of verse, accounts of travel and of missionary work, and a book on cookery and household management. She also edited *Fisher's Drawing-Room Scrap-Book* between 1843 and 1845, *Fisher's Juvenile Scrap-Book* between 1840 and 1848, and *The Morning Call: a Table-Book of Literature and Art*, volumes 1–4, between 1850 and 1852. All these involved not only editing, but also writing major contributions, and from letters quoted in *The Home Life and Letters of Mrs. Ellis* it seems that she also contributed to several other periodicals. All her verse, much of which appears in the various journals she edited, is on pious, didactic, or aesthetic themes, and is unremarkable. Although Sarah Ellis wrote almost always with a moral or educational purpose it is clear that she also had a keen eye for her niche in the literary market place and intended her works to make money. In this she was successful: in 1870, two years before they died, the Ellises were able to buy their home, Rose Hill, for £2250; a good proportion of this amount must have derived from her own writings as well as from her husband's popular accounts of his missionary travels. Of all her works, her conduct-books, particularly *The Women of England*, were the most successful, and both these and her temperance fiction were widely reprinted in the United States.

In 1844 Sarah Ellis went into partnership with a friend, Isabella Hurry, and opened a non-denominational school for girls, Rawdon House School, in a Jacobean mansion close to Rose Hill at Hoddesdon, Essex. It was unusual both because of its non-denominational policy and because its curriculum included practical instruction in cookery and household management. In her writings on education, Sarah Ellis had stressed the need for middle-class girls to be taught practical skills as well as accomplishments, and she put her theories into practice at Rawdon House. In 1847, when she was well known for her conduct-books and her temperance writings, her school also attracted attention. Thackeray contributed to a series of jokes at her expense that ran in *Punch* from 1843 to 1847, suggesting that her conduct-books encouraged women to manipulate men, and both Douglas Jerrold's series 'Mrs. Caudle's Curtain Lectures' (*Punch*, 8–9, 1845–6) and his following series 'Capsicum House' (*Punch*, 12–13, 1847) are part of these running jokes, the latter series being modelled on Rawdon House School with its distinctive part-domestic curriculum.

Although Sarah Ellis continued publishing on a number of topics until 1869, her most influential works were those that focused on the role of women in the middle-class family, and emphasized the moral influence a Christian woman, particularly as wife and mother, should bring to bear on the men of that family. Her first conduct-book, *The Women of England, their Social Duties and Domestic Habits* (1839) was an instant success and was followed by three others: *The Daughters of England, their Position in Society, Character and Responsibilities* (1842); *The Wives of England, their Relative Duties, Domestic Influence, and Social Obligations* (1843); and *The Mothers of England, their Influence and Responsibility* (1843). In many ways a conservative writer, Sarah Ellis accepted that women were socially and legally subordinate to men, but she endorsed the concept of 'separate spheres' in order to claim considerable autonomy for women within the domestic sphere. She also believed in the inherent moral equality of the sexes, but argued that women's seclusion in the home protected them from many of the temptations to which men succumbed; domestic seclusion could therefore give the moral advantage to women, which it was their duty to exploit. Her endorsement of 'separate spheres' thus becomes an argument for the empowerment of women through moral influence, albeit an influence exerted covertly, lest the ostensibly superior status of father or husband be compromised. The inherent tensions within this view of women's domestic role that surface particularly in *The Wives of England* are never directly dealt with by Sarah Ellis, but both her conduct-books and her fiction can appear to license manipulation of men by women, albeit for the general good as perceived by the woman, and some of the clearest examples of such covert manipulation appear as late as 1860 in a collection of short stories, *Chapters on Wives* (1860).

Although Sarah Ellis was generally reviewed as an admirably moral writer, dislike of such covert manoeuvring for power led to Geraldine Jewsbury's objections to her writing, expressed in letters to Jane Carlyle (1845), in the novel *The Half-Sisters* (1848), and in her *Athenaeum* review, on 14 July 1860, of *Chapters on Wives*. In book 1 of *Aurora Leigh* (1857), Barrett Browning's account of the limited education Aurora's middle-class aunt considered suitable for her niece is clearly intended to recall Sarah Ellis's conduct-book view of women as existing in relation to men and hence 'relative creatures', although in *The Daughters of England*, as elsewhere in her writings, Sarah Ellis does suggest that middle-class girls should be taught

to earn a living, or even help in the family business, without this being regarded as a loss of status. The 'Sketch of the literary career of Mrs. Ellis' also suggests that she was criticized for promoting a domestic role for others while devoting herself to writing, a charge that is there unconvincingly rebutted by the statement that 'her books are but as an accident of her experience' ('Sketch of the literary career of Mrs. Ellis', viii). A writer of limited range and ability, Sarah Ellis nevertheless acted as a catalyst for discussion of middle-class women's role in the family and society, and she thus made a significant contribution to the 'woman question', particularly in the 1840s and 1850s, when her influence was at its height. In her own terms she was dignifying women by giving them moral work to do within their domestic setting, to balance the active role undertaken by men outside the home, and she was thus redressing to some extent the imbalance of power between middle-class men and women. A review of the whole body of her work, however, leads to the inescapable impression that as a Christian moralist Sarah Ellis had in general a higher opinion of women than of men, and therefore believed women's influence to be vital for the health of society. A similar view of gender relationships appears in *Family Secrets, or, Hints to those who would Make Home Happy* (3 vols., 1842), a collection of short stories advocating temperance that apparently brought their author considerable notoriety. These stories have a middle-class setting, and depict comfortably-off families disrupted by the violence and loss of caste caused by alcoholism. Although not exclusively male, most of the alcoholics concerned are middle-class fathers or husbands, whose addiction leads them to inflict severe physical or mental suffering on their families. Typically such men are saved by the devoted attention of wives or daughters, who on occasion not only emerge in possession of the moral high ground but also in effective control of the man. Her graphic presentation of alcoholism within comfortable middle-class families is without parallel in the early 1840s, and may well have influenced both Ann Brontë's *The Tenant of Wildfell Hall* (1848) and George Eliot's 'Janet's Repentance' (in *Scenes of Clerical Life*, 1858).

Sarah Ellis's other fiction divides into that written for children, found mainly in *Fisher's Juvenile Scrap-Book*, and that written for adults, whether short stories or full-length novels; a middle-class audience is always assumed. Her children's fiction inculcates simple moral lessons applicable to either sex, whereas her adult fiction has a female focus and emphasizes moral obligation and duty, acceptance of which leads to happiness and empowerment, while dereliction of duty and attention to 'self' leads to the opposite. Although non-denominational, many of her writings place strong emphasis on her belief that a Christian woman should depend for her security on her faith in God, rather than on father or husband.

By the 1860s Sarah Ellis's significance was effectively over, but she continued to write on her usual themes, publishing her last novel in 1868 and her last educational tract in 1869; she and her husband died within a week of each other in 1872, William Ellis having succumbed on 9 June to a cold which he passed to his wife, who died on 16 June. Sarah Ellis was buried in the Quaker burial-ground at Hoddesdon. H. S. TWYCROSS-MARTIN

Sources *The home life and letters of Mrs. Ellis compiled by her nieces* (1893) · J. E. Ellis, *Life of William Ellis: missionary to the south seas and to Madagascar* (1873) · 'Sketch of the literary career of Mrs. Ellis', S. Ellis, *The mother's mistake: a tale* (1856) [preface] · Mrs Bayly, *The life and letters of Mrs Sewell* (1889) · Allibone, *Dict.* · J. Smith, ed., *A descriptive catalogue of Friends' books*, 2 vols. (1867); suppl. (1893) · A. G. Hay, *Afterglow memories* (1905) · S. D. Kitson, *The life of John Sell Cotman* (1937); repr. (1982) · *Punch*, 5–13 (1843–7)
Archives NL Scot., corresp. with George Combe
Likenesses Dalziel, woodcut, BM · P. Greatbach, stipple and line engraving (after W. Gush), NPG · W. Holl, stipple and line engraving (after P. A. Gaugain), NPG · etching, repro. in *The Morning Call, a Table-Book of Literature and Art*, 1 (1850), frontispiece · portrait, repro. in *The women of England*, frontispiece [cited in Smith, *Descriptive catalogue*] · portrait, repro. in *Home life and letters*, frontispiece
Wealth at death under £5000: probate, 10 Aug 1872, *CGPLA Eng. & Wales*

Ellis, Thomas (1625–1673), antiquary and Church of England clergyman, was born at Ystumllyn, near Cricieth, Caernarvonshire, the son of Griffith Ellis, a landowner. Having matriculated at Jesus College, Oxford, in June 1640, he graduated BA in 1644. That year, according to Anthony Wood, he bore arms for the king in the Oxford garrison; although a namesake published in July 1644 *The Exact and Full Relation of the Last Fight between the King's Forces and Sir William Waller*, describing the battle at Cropredy Bridge, that writer was in the parliamentarian army.

Ellis proceeded MA on 23 January 1646. Having initially held out against the parliamentary visitors who came to Jesus College in 1648, like several other college members he then submitted. In 1649 he became a fellow, and continuing to reside there as a tutor, became a persistent critic of the new principal, Michael Roberts. At the Restoration Ellis retained his fellowship and became vice-principal under the reinstated principal Francis Mansell. When Mansell retired in 1661 Ellis's expectations of succeeding him were disappointed, and relinquishing his tutorial work, he lived in Oxford in seclusion. However, having proceeded BD on 17 June 1661, he was one of the university Lent preachers appointed to officiate on Easter Tuesday 1662.

While at Oxford, Ellis had devoted himself largely to the study of Welsh antiquity, for which he had gained a reputation. At the request of Robert Vaughan of Hengwrt whose intention to publish a revised and enlarged edition of David Powel's *The Historie of Cambria* (1584) had been thwarted for lack of time, Ellis undertook to continue it, incorporating his own notes with Vaughan's additions and corrections. One hundred and twenty-eight sheets of the book had been printed by Hall of Oxford, when Ellis refused to proceed, alleging that all the materials with which he had been supplied by Vaughan had been already utilized by Percie Enderbie in his *Cambria triumphans*. As the latter work was published in 1661 and the sheets of Ellis's book are dated 1663, it is curious that he did not make the discovery earlier. Persisting in the belief that he had been anticipated in his researches, Ellis published nothing further. *Memoirs of Owen Glendowr*, published in

1775 with H. Rowlands's *A History of the Island of Anglesey*, was attributed to Ellis, but the historian Sir John Edward Lloyd has shown that the work was written by Robert Vaughan; Ellis was a mere copyist.

Ellis's fortunes revived when the king, court, and parliament moved to Oxford in 1665 to escape the plague raging in London. On 15 January 1666 he became rector of St Mary's, Dolgellau, Merioneth, succeeding John Ellis, often referred to as his kinsman. Ellis died in April 1673 at his birthplace, where he was buried.

ALSAGER VIAN, *rev.* D. BEN REES

Sources DWB · T. Richards, 'The puritan visitation of Jesus College, Oxford, and the principalship of Dr Michael Roberts (1648–1657)', *Transactions of the Honourable Society of Cymmrodorion* (1922–3), 1–111 · J. E. Lloyd, *Owen Glendower* (1931) · BL cat.
Archives Jesus College, Oxford, MSS | All Souls Oxf., Wynne MSS 239 (578), 240 (512–16)

Ellis, Thomas Edward [Tom] (1859–1899), politician and Welsh nationalist, was born at Cynlas Farm, Cefnddwysarn, near Bala, Merioneth, on 16 February 1859, the third of six surviving children and only son of Thomas Ellis, tenant farmer, and his wife, Elizabeth Williams. That same year one of Ellis's relatives was evicted from his holding by the local landlord for voting Liberal in the general election. A Calvinistic Methodist, Ellis was educated at the British School, Llandderfel, and then at the grammar school in Bala. In 1875 he entered the newly established University College of Wales, Aberystwyth, where his contemporaries included many other nationally minded young Welshmen. He left Aberystwyth in 1879 and spent a year in Oxford on a non-collegiate basis. Entering New College as an undergraduate in October 1880, he became deeply stirred by the social and imperialist ideas current in Oxford at the time. He graduated in 1884 with a second-class honours degree in modern history, taking his BA in 1885 and his MA in 1897. After a short period as a private tutor, he became private secretary to the Liberal industrialist MP Sir John Brunner. A political career was now inevitable and in the July 1886 general election he was elected MP for his native county of Merioneth.

In the next six years, he emerged as an ardent champion of the nonconformist causes of Welsh church disestablishment and tithe reform, the Welsh tenant farmers' campaign for land reform, and Irish home rule. He was also much involved in the passage of the Welsh Intermediate Education Act in 1889 and the movement for a national University of Wales. He became close to other young Welsh Liberal members, including David Lloyd George. In September 1890 Ellis's declaration at Bala on behalf of a Welsh legislative assembly made a strong, though transient, impression: he seemed the very embodiment of 'Young Wales'. However, he suffered from indifferent health, and a visit to Egypt led to his becoming seriously ill from typhoid. To help himself recover, he travelled to South Africa in the winter of 1890–91, where he met Cecil Rhodes, who greatly impressed him.

When the Liberals returned to power in 1892, it was generally assumed that Ellis would receive government office. But it was a surprise when Gladstone offered him the post of deputy whip, an offer which he decided to accept. This was to drive something of a wedge between him and Lloyd George and other former Welsh allies. Ellis could still work on behalf of Wales, notably in the appointment of a Welsh land commission, and the foundation of a University of Wales, both in 1893; but he disapproved of Lloyd George's efforts to turn Welsh Liberalism into a nationalist movement somewhat on the lines of the Irish one. Ellis became chief whip in March 1894 when Lord Rosebery succeeded Gladstone as prime minister, and found life exceptionally difficult since the Liberals had only the narrowest of majorities. He was blamed for being too lax a disciplinarian, and indeed for the defeat on the snap 'cordite' vote on 21 June 1895, which saw the government resign. After his party's heavy defeat in the subsequent general election, Ellis stayed on as chief whip. In addition to his close involvement in Welsh affairs, he was active in trying to recruit more Labour candidates for the Liberals. He was broadly in the Liberal imperialist camp, and played a somewhat curious role in the manoeuvres that followed the Jameson raid in South Africa.

Tom Ellis was a deeply cultured man, of much personal charm, with a strong interest in Welsh art and literature: he edited the works of the seventeenth-century puritan mystic Morgan Llwyd. He was active in the movement for a national library and became warden of the University Guild of Graduates in 1896. His politics and cultural interests combined to make him a nationalist of an unusually rounded kind. Some saw him as a prophet, a Welsh Kossuth or Mazzini, a 'lost leader'. He would hardly have risen as high as his colleague Lloyd George but, had he lived, would surely have been a major figure in the Liberal government of 1905–15.

In 1898 Ellis married Annie, the daughter of Robert Joseph Davies, freehold farmer and a leading Calvinistic Methodist, of Cwrt-Mawr, Llangeitho, Cardiganshire. They had one son, born after Ellis's death. His health continued to be uncertain and on 5 April 1899, aged only forty, he died at the Hôtel Métropole, Cannes, during a brief holiday on the French riviera.

KENNETH O. MORGAN, rev.

Sources A. J. Ellis, ed., *Speeches and addresses of the late T. E. Ellis, MP* (1912) · T. I. Ellis, *Thomas Edward Ellis: cofiant*, 2 vols. (1944–8) · N. Masterman, *The forerunner* (1972) · K. O. Morgan, *Wales in British politics, 1868–1922*, 3rd edn (1980)
Archives Meirionnydd RO, papers relating to parliamentary work as chief whip · NL Wales, corresp. and papers · NL Wales, notes and papers relating to editing of works of Morgan Llwyd | BL, corresp. with Lord Gladstone, Add. MS 45022 · Bodl. Oxf., corresp. with Sir William Harcourt · NL Scot., corresp. incl. to Lord Rosebery · NL Wales, letters to Sir Ellis Ellis-Griffith · NL Wales, letters to Thomas Jones · NL Wales, letters to David Lloyd George · NL Wales, corresp. with Sir John Herbert Lewis and papers · U. Wales, Bangor, letters to W. J. Parry
Likenesses J. F. R. Wood, U. Wales, Aberystwyth · bust, U. Wales, Aberystwyth · statue, U. Wales, Aberystwyth · statue, Bala
Wealth at death £12,423

Ellis, Thomas Evelyn Scott-, **eighth Baron Howard de Walden** (1880–1946), writer, sportsman, and patron of the arts, was born in London on 9 May 1880, the only son of Frederick George Ellis, seventh Baron Howard de Walden (1830–1899), and his wife, Blanche (d. 1911), daughter of William Holden of Palace House, Lancashire, and grandson of the sixth baron, Charles Augustus *Ellis. In 1917 he assumed the additional name and arms of Scott on succeeding to the Dean Castle estate in Kilmarnock. He was educated at Eton College and the Royal Military College, Sandhurst, and was commissioned in the 10th hussars in time to see two years' service in South Africa. After retiring from the regular army, he became a zealous and efficient territorial; in the First World War he served in the Westminster dragoons (of which he later became honorary colonel) and in the 9th battalion of the Royal Welch Fusiliers both in Gallipoli and in France.

On coming of age in 1901 Lord Howard de Walden succeeded to the control of his great estates in London and elsewhere. To this rich inheritance he brought great generosity and a rare variety of talents. In 1906, within the space of a few days, he distinguished himself as spare man of the British Olympic fencing team at Athens and one of his horses won a good race at Newmarket. He was a consistent supporter of the turf, and a member of the Jockey Club from 1905 until 1924; perhaps his best season was in 1933, when he won a total of seventeen races. He was also a lover of sailing, a member of the Royal Yacht Squadron, and an early exponent (with the second duke of Westminster) of motor-boat racing.

But if he paid these tributes to the contemporary world, Howard de Walden had also strong antiquarian tastes, which included genealogy, heraldry, and armour. Of the last-named he formed an important collection at his Scottish home, including a number of classical specimens. In 1904 he produced the three volumes of the De Walden Library, of which perhaps *Some Feudal Lords and their Seals* is the most interesting. Furthermore, he played an important part in the production of *The Complete Peerage*: in addition to acting as one of the editors of volumes 6–10 and 13, he was a financial benefactor to the extent of at least £10,000. Throughout his life he was a keen medievalist, finding most interest perhaps in the fourteenth century, but often linking his scholarship to active life. Not only was he a good swordsman with either hand, but an exponent of falconry and hawking. Indeed it was probably his love of medieval history and architecture that led him to give up in 1912 Audley End, Essex (the Tudor seat of the first Lord Howard de Walden), which for the preceding seven years he had rented from Lord Braybrooke, in favour of Chirk Castle, Denbighshire, which he leased and made his home for thirty-four years.

In London, Howard de Walden bought Seaford House in Belgrave Square, but the important urban property, which he had inherited through his grandmother from the Bentinck and Cavendish families, lay farther north in Marylebone and St John's Wood. In this area he led the way as an enlightened landlord. Before he came of age there had been friction between his trustees and John Lewis, the founder of the well-known retail business. As a result of this, Lewis, who had already been to prison for contempt of court, in March 1911 goaded Howard de Walden into bringing a libel action, having for the past eighteen months posted placards abusing his landlord. Sir Edward Carson and F. E. Smith appeared for the defence; Howard de Walden was represented by H. E. Duke (later Lord Merrivale), and after a three-day hearing was awarded damages of 1 farthing. Reinforced in his earlier plans by the moral of this verdict, he announced in the autumn of that year that he was offering a new type of 999-year lease to his tenants, which made them virtually independent. Lewis, who had remained throughout on good terms with his landlord, acknowledged the virtue of this arrangement in a letter to *The Times* (14 November 1911) and also admitted that his litigiousness had cost him over £40,000.

Lord Howard de Walden desired to spread his interests more widely and to take a share in colonial development. Accordingly in 1914 he sold 60 acres near Regent's Park for about £500,000, and in 1925 40 acres of land north-east of Oxford Circus were sold to the Audley Trust. Meanwhile the General Real Estates Investment and Trust Ltd (of which he himself was chairman) had acquired in 1922 a large portion of his West End estate for a sum which was reported to exceed £4 million. He extended his interests by buying property and forest land on a large scale in Kenya, and also in Wales, whence the Ellis family originally stemmed. His concern in Cymric affairs was strong; he bred the native ponies, learned Welsh, and fostered the study of that language.

Throughout his life Howard de Walden was keenly interested in the stage. He was himself the author of both dramas and librettos. With the composer Josef Holbrooke he produced (as T. E. Ellis) an operatic trilogy, *The Cauldron of Annwn*. The first opera, *The Children of Don*, was presented by Oscar Hammerstein at the London Opera House in 1912; *Dylan* was conducted by Thomas Beecham at Drury Lane in 1914 and marked the first use of cinematographic effects on the stage, which was another of Lord Howard de Walden's pursuits. The third opera, *Bronwen*, was played by the Carl Rosa Company at Huddersfield in 1929. Neither the unfamiliar Welsh mythological plots nor the music of Holbrooke attracted the favourable notice of the critics. Using Byzantine themes, Howard de Walden was also the author of several plays, including *Heraclius* (performed at the Holborn Empire in the autumn of 1924). He wrote in addition a charming series of pantomimes for children which were successively produced by his own family and their friends at Chirk.

Howard de Walden married on 19 February 1912 Margherita Dorothy, daughter of Charles van Raalte JP of Brownsea Island and Grosvenor Square. They had one son, John Osmael (b. 1912), who succeeded to the titles, and five daughters, including (Esyllt) Priscilla Scott-*Ellis. To the Tate Gallery, of which he was a trustee from 1938, he presented the bust of himself by Rodin, which is his best likeness. He was also a collector of modern paintings. In 1930 he embarked on a new field with his expedition to Uganda and the eastern Belgian Congo, the valuable botanical and zoological fruits of which were presented to the Natural History Museum.

The diverse talents of this versatile man were matched by his generosity to many branches of art and charity; hospitals, orchestras, and numerous individual artists, including the poet Dylan Thomas, benefited by his munificence and taste. In the breadth of his patronage and in his own widespread activity, Howard de Walden epitomized a splendid tradition of the English aristocracy, practising as well as stimulating the arts, sports, and learning which he loved. He died in London on 5 November 1946 at the London Clinic, Devonshire Place, and was buried in the family vault at Dean Castle.

MICHAEL MACLAGAN, rev. H. C. G. MATTHEW

Sources *The Times* (6 Nov 1946) · private information (1959) · *CGPLA Eng. & Wales* (1947)

Archives City Westm. AC, Marylebone Estate MSS | NL Wales, letters to John Glyn Davies | FILM BFI NFTVA, sports footage

Likenesses A. Rodin, bronze bust, 1905–6, Tate collection · W. Stoneman, photograph, 1930, NPG · Lenare, photograph, 1940, NPG · M. Beerbohm, drawing, caricature, U. Texas · Spy [L. Ward], lithograph, NPG; repro. in *VF* (17 May 1906)

Wealth at death nil—trust property only: probate limited, 4 Feb 1947, *CGPLA Eng. & Wales* · £1,248,489 16s. 9d.—save and except settled land: probate, 20 March 1947, *CGPLA Eng. & Wales*

Ellis, Thomas Flower (1796–1861), law reporter, was born at Walthamstow in Essex, the son of Thomas Flower Ellis. After being educated at Hackney by Dr Heathcote, he matriculated at Trinity College, Cambridge, in Michaelmas term 1814, graduating BA in 1818 and becoming a fellow in the following year. He graduated MA in 1821, and relinquished his fellowship in the same year on his marriage. With his wife, Susan, he had five sons and two daughters. At Cambridge, Ellis was a brilliant classical scholar, although only a senior optime in the mathematical tripos. He was admitted to Lincoln's Inn on 8 April 1816, and shared rooms as a law student with his Cambridge contemporary Benjamin Heath Malkin. He was called to the bar on 5 February 1824, whereupon he joined the northern circuit.

Ellis played an active role in public affairs throughout his life, and was a member of a number of royal commissions. In 1831 he was appointed a commissioner under the Reform Bill to determine the boundaries of parliamentary boroughs in Wales; and in July 1833 he joined the royal commission on municipal corporations, looking at the south-eastern circuit. He was also one of the two commissioners appointed to examine the state of the criminal law of Jersey, and reported on this in 1847; and in 1853 he was appointed to the commission on the reform of judicial establishments, judicial procedure, and the laws of India. In 1847, he briefly considered a political career, but gave up the idea when he found himself unable to get sufficient support in a constituency. Throughout this time, Ellis built up a successful professional practice. He became attorney-general for the duchy of Lancaster in 1839 (a post which he held until his death) and a QC within the county palatine of Lancaster. In 1851 he was counsel for the plaintiff in the libel case brought by G. G. Achilli against John Henry Newman, and in 1857 he acted as counsel to Lord Talbot in his claim to the title of earl of Shrewsbury, which was that year brought before the committee of privileges in the House of Lords. He was also counsel for the Royal Mint for many years. In 1839, he became recorder of Leeds, and in 1859 he turned down the offer of the county court judgeship of Northumberland. Although his professional career was a success, the judgeship of the common pleas, to which he also aspired, remained beyond his grasp; and he was said by many lawyers to be the ablest man in his profession not to have risen high. His greatest legacies to lawyers are the reports of cases in the queen's bench which he published between 1834 and 1852 with his close friend John Leycester Adolphus, Colin Blackburn, and his son Francis Ellis.

Outside his professional pursuits, Ellis had a deep interest in literature and scholarship, and besides his classical studies he also studied Italian, Spanish, German, and Hebrew. He was for many years one of the most active members of the Society for the Diffusion of Useful Knowledge, both as an editor and as a contributor. He agreed in 1827 to write the work published as *An Outline of General History*, which was designed to accompany the histories published by the society. The first part appeared in 1828, and the second part in 1830; but professional engagements hindered Ellis from completing the project, and he finally abandoned it in 1838. However, he continued in the 1830s to read and revise works for the society on a wide range of subjects, and was made an honorary life member of the society. He also contributed a number of articles to the *Edinburgh Review*, including a critique of Whewell.

Ellis is perhaps best known for his friendship with T. B. Macaulay. The two men, who had been contemporaries at Trinity, struck up a friendship when Macaulay joined the northern circuit, and Ellis remained Macaulay's closest friend throughout his life. They shared many literary interests, and Macaulay wrote of Ellis that 'a large part of the literary success which I have obtained I owe to the minute attention which he has bestowed on my writings, and to the kind severity of his criticism' (*Letters of Thomas Babington Macaulay*, 5.206). Macaulay took a strong interest in the welfare of Ellis's family, as well as his career, particularly after the death of Ellis's wife on 18 March 1839. The two men also travelled widely together: Ellis accompanied Macaulay on the latter's travels to the Netherlands and France in the late 1840s while researching his *History*, and in later life they visited the continent together every autumn. Ellis was the executor of Macaulay's will, and he prepared a posthumous edition of Macaulay's unpublished essays. Ellis died at his house, 15 Bedford Place, Russell Square, London, on 5 April 1861.

MICHAEL LOBBAN

Sources *The letters of Thomas Babington Macaulay*, ed. T. Pinney, 6 vols. (1974–81) · *The Times* (8 April 1861) · *Law Times* (27 April 1861) · *GM*, 3rd ser., 10 (1861), 588 · Venn, *Alum. Cant.* · J. M. Collinge, *Officials of royal commissions of enquiry, 1815–70* (1984) · *Wellesley index* · W. P. Baildon, ed., *The records of the Honorable Society of Lincoln's Inn: admissions*, 2 (1896) · d. cert.
Archives UCL, letters to Society for the Diffusion of Useful Knowledge | Trinity Cam., corresp. with Macaulay · Trinity Cam., letters to W. Whewell · Trinity Cam., MS memoir by his daughter [Marian or Louisa] · UCL, corresp. with Brougham
Likenesses W. Behnes, plaster bust, 1842?, Trinity Cam.

Wealth at death under £6000: probate, 4 May 1861, *CGPLA Eng. & Wales*

Ellis, Thomas Peter (1873–1936), lawyer and historian, was born on 4 June 1873 at Berse Cottage, near Wrexham, Denbighshire, the second son of Peter Ellis, a grocer, and his wife, Mary, *née* Lewis. After the early death of his father Ellis's family resided at his maternal grandmother's home at Chester St Oswald, Cheshire, and then lived at Rhosddu, Wrexham. From Oswestry high school he went in 1891 to Lincoln College, Oxford, and after gaining a second class in modern history in 1895 entered the Indian Civil Service to serve in the Punjab from 1898. In India he married Rosetta McAlister, and they had a son and a daughter; his wife died in 1912 and he married Hilda Lilian Broadway in 1915.

As a district judge (from 1909) and a sessions judge (from 1913) in the Punjab, Ellis acquired a detailed knowledge of the customary law of the province, a custom which still awaited codification, and his *Judge's Note-Book* (1913) addressed the practical difficulties that arose in the course of judicial administration. In a greatly enlarged version, published as *Notes on Punjab Custom* (1918), he commented on the anthropological interest of the evidence that he assembled, notably the respective functions of tribe and family and the place of the agnatic principle in the practice of kinship groups. He drew a contrast between the 'ancient, certain and invariable' usage of custom in England and the variability of custom in the Punjab, where legal sanctions were based on the current practice of diverse social groups and localities. His discussion of matters such as succession and alienation provided a detailed record of the infinitely varied practices of the province, and he also wrote a major study, *The Law of Pre-Emption in the Punjab* (1918).

Ellis was appointed legal remembrancer (attorney-general) to the Punjab government in 1917 and secretary to the legislative council for the province in 1918. Civil disturbances in the Punjab led to a massacre at Amritsar on 13 April 1919 and when martial law was imposed Ellis drafted the ordinances for the guidance of the civil and military authorities. According to the testimony of Sir Michael O'Dwyer, then lieutenant-general of the Punjab, Ellis was troubled by what he regarded as the premature amnesty granted to persons convicted of grave offences and declined to serve as a judge of the high court at Lahore. During this period Ellis was closely associated with an administration that incurred considerable criticism for its handling of the political problems of the Punjab and, after twenty-five years' service in the province, he retired in 1923. He returned to Wales, setting up his home at Llys Mynach, Dolgellau, Merioneth.

Ellis's interests in retirement are reflected in a range of published works. In *Welsh Tribal Law and Custom in the Middle Ages* (1926) he offered a major synoptic study based on the law texts and the fiscal surveys, one of which he published as *The First Extent of Bromfield and Yale* (1924). In a perceptive discussion of kinship groups Ellis, though he made no reference to earlier suggestions in the work of

F. W. Maitland, recognized in the single term *cenedl* two differing institutions. One was a broad cognatic group that would be assembled to make and receive compensation for homicide, the other a narrower agnatic group with specific functions particularly in land inheritance. He argued, against the view of Frederic Seebohm, that the practice of partible succession did not create a new inheritance group, or *gwely*, in each generation, but that partition continued to be made within the single enduring *gwely*. Ellis's work was impaired by his reliance on printed texts of the laws and his view of the sources as the outcome of a single early codification rather than the several distinct products of a prolonged period of redaction. His inability to take account of the extent of social change in the medieval period is instanced in his attribution of semi-nomadic conditions to the upland areas of fifteenth-century Merioneth. None the less, bringing to the study of Welsh law the benefit of his experience of the study of custom gained in the Punjab, Ellis provided an informed study more comprehensive than anything previously attempted, and established a basis for further investigation.

In the following years Ellis published a number of historical studies as well as more occasional writings. He could write engagingly about the Welsh fairy tales that gave some relief from 'the rationalism, theological vagaries and commercialism' of contemporary life (T. P. Ellis, *Dreams and Memories*, 1936, 68), and he wrote a volume of local history, *The Story of Two Parishes, Dolgelley and Llanelltyd*. In 1929 Ellis was received into the Roman Catholic faith and, reacting to the modernist views of those in the Anglican and nonconformist churches who, in his view, denied the incarnation, he pronounced his belief that the growth in Catholic numbers might prove enough 'to leaven the whole of Wales' (*Western Mail*, 11 Sept 1933). He wrote extensively on the history of the Welsh church, envisaging a tradition of saintly witness extending from St Illtud in the sixth century to John Roberts, the seventeenth-century Benedictine martyr with whom he felt a close spiritual affinity, men who were 'united in one True Faith and in common surrender to its service' (dedication to *Welsh Benedictines of the Terror*, 1936). His patriotic instinct, expressed in essays on Welsh nationality, brought him into close contact with the Welsh Nationalist Party. Writing to John Saunders Lewis from his hospital bed, he urged that a great march be arranged, in which he would take part, to oppose the government's intention to set up a bombing range in the Llŷn peninsula. A few days later, on 7 July 1936, Ellis died of heart failure at the Royal Southern Hospital, Liverpool, and he was buried on 10 July at Dolgellau. J. B. SMITH

Sources NL Wales · BL OIOC · *The Times* (14 July 1936) · *DWB* · *The India office list for 1936*, 631 · *Welsh Catholic Times* (17 July 1936), ii · *Welsh Catholic Times* (24 July 1936), ii · T. P. Ellis, 'A constructive policy for Wales', *Welsh Outlook*, 14 (1927) · M. O'Dwyer, *India as I knew it, 1885–1925* (1925) · b. cert. · d. cert. · census returns, 1881
Archives NL Wales, MSS 9324–9326
Likenesses photograph, NL Wales

Wealth at death £10,613 9s. 5d.: probate, 1936, *CGPLA Eng. & Wales*

Ellis, Vivian John Herman (1903–1996), composer and lyricist, was born on 29 October 1903 at 207 Goldhurst Terrace, Hampstead, London, the only son of Henry Herman Ellis (*c*.1868–1909), tailor, and his wife, Maud Alexandrina Isaacson (1870–1961). He inherited musical talent from his mother, a violin pupil of Ysaÿe and daughter of the composer and pianist Julia Woolf. He was educated at Cheltenham College, then studied the piano with Myra Hess and composition at the Royal Academy of Music. His father having died when he was five, he was set to work in the family business, but found more congenial employment as a song-plugger for Francis, Day, and Hunter. He began composing songs for musical comedy and revue, and in 1928 was given a song-writing contract by Chappell & Co. His first big success came when he supplemented songs by Richard Myers for the show *Mr Cinders* (1928). This featured Bobby Howes and Binnie Hale, and Ellis's contributions included the enduringly popular 'Spread a Little Happiness'. He became perhaps the most prolific British musical theatre composer of the 1930s, forging a reputation alongside that of Ivor Novello and Noël Coward and creating rewarding material for dance bands. Particular successes included the song-and-dance musical comedy *Jill Darling* (1933), in which John Mills and Louise Browne sang 'I'm on a See-Saw' (the title of Ellis's 1953 autobiography), and the revue *Streamline* (1934), to which Ellis contributed with A. P. Herbert, and which produced 'Other People's Babies'. Later came *Hide and Seek* (1937), with 'She's my Lovely' for Bobby Howes, and films and stage shows for Jack Hulbert and Cicely Courtneidge.

During the war, Ellis served in the Royal Naval Volunteer Reserve in Plymouth, becoming entertainments officer and attaining the rank of lieutenant-commander. Afterwards his collaboration with A. P. Herbert was renewed in a series of 'light operas' for C. B. Cochran at the Adelphi Theatre. *Big Ben* (1946) was only a moderate success; but *Bless the Bride* (1947), with romantic idol George Guétary, fed post-war optimism and captured the mood of celebration over the wedding of Princess Elizabeth to Prince Philip. Consciously a period piece, it retained its appeal through songs such as 'This is My Lovely Day', 'Ma belle Marguerite', and 'I Was Never Kissed Before'. The third Cochran light opera, *Tough at the Top* (1949), with Giorgio Tozzi as a boxer, was less successful, and brought the end of the series. Ellis was then both composer and lyricist for *And So to Bed* (1951), which had Leslie Henson as Samuel Pepys and for which he contributed effective period music. He likewise wrote both lyrics and music for the children's piece *Listen to the Wind* (1954), before collaborating for the last time with A. P. Herbert on *The Water Gypsies* (1955), with Peter Graves, Jerry Verno, and Dora Bryan.

The Water Gypsies was Ellis's last significant new show, as the fashion for the American musical took hold in Britain. He remained active in a variety of ways. A musical adaptation of *The Importance of being Earnest* was produced in America, and he wrote a number of novels and humorous volumes on favourite topics such as gardening and investing, as well as being a frequent contributor to the correspondence columns of *The Times*. He never married, and he lived with his sister at The Kennels, Holnicote, near Minehead, and in Kensington, from where he frequented the Garrick Club. It was a train journey between London and Somerset that inspired 'Coronation Scot' (1948), which attained the status of light music classic after being used as the signature tune for the BBC's *Paul Temple* radio detective series. Another light music composition, 'Alpine Echoes' (1955), became hardly less familiar as the signature tune for the radio series *My Word*. Ellis was a council member of the Performing Right Society, becoming deputy president (1975–83) and president (1983–96). In 1984 he was appointed CBE and gave his name to an annual prize for young British composers of musicals.

Mr Cinders and *Bless the Bride* remained part of the repertory of amateur operatic societies; but in 1982 a revival of interest in Ellis's work began when 'Spread a Little Happiness' entered the pop charts after being sung by Sting in the film *Brimstone and Treacle*. In 1983 Dan Crawford revived *Mr Cinders* at the tiny King's Head Theatre in Islington, with Denis Lawson in the title role. When it transferred to the West End, Ellis collaborated by telephone with original lyricist Greatrex Newman on a new song, 'Please, Mr Cinders', over fifty-four years after the show's original creation. *Bless the Bride* was revived at the Northcott Theatre, Exeter, in 1985 and at Sadler's Wells Theatre in 1987. The King's Head also produced a revue of Ellis's songs in 1992, and in 1996 revived *Listen to the Wind*, for which Ellis provided some revisions and new songs. He died at Beaumont House, Beaumont Street, Westminster, on 19 June 1996, and was survived by his sister.

ANDREW LAMB

Sources V. Ellis, *I'm on a see-saw* (1953) · *Who's who in the theatre* · personal knowledge (2004) · private information (2004) · *The Independent* (21 June 1996) · *Daily Telegraph* (21 June 1996) · *The Times* (21 June 1996) · b. cert. · d. cert. · birth and death indexes, Family Records Centre, London

Likenesses photographs, 1933–40, Hult. Arch. · photograph, 1936, repro. in *The Times* · photograph, 1962, repro. in *Daily Telegraph* · M. Gerson, photograph, priv. coll. · photograph, repro. in *The Independent*

Wealth at death £1,477,604: probate, 20 Aug 1996, *CGPLA Eng. & Wales*

Ellis, Welbore (1661/2–1734), Church of Ireland bishop of Meath, was the fourth son of John *Ellis (d. 1681), rector of Waddesdon, Buckinghamshire, and Susanna (d. 1700), daughter of William Welbore of Cambridge. Descended from an ancient family at Kiddall Hall, Yorkshire, he was one of eleven children and the brother of John *Ellis (1642x6–1738), Sir William *Ellis (1641x7–1732), and Philip *Ellis (1652–1726). He was educated at Westminster School and at Christ Church, Oxford, where he matriculated on 17 December 1680, aged eighteen, graduating BA in 1684, MA in 1687, and BD and DD by diploma in 1697. He also received in 1732 the *ad eundem* degree of DD from Trinity College, Dublin.

Ellis became a chaplain to the duke of Ormond in 1693, was appointed a prebendary of Winchester in 1696, and

became rector of St Peter's, Northampton, in 1702. He was promoted in 1705, by patent dated 22 September, to the bishopric of Kildare, with the deanery of Christ Church, Dublin, *in commendam*, and was consecrated in Christ Church Cathedral by the archbishop of Armagh on 11 November 1705. As dean, he staunchly defended the privileges of the cathedral against the archbishop of Dublin, William King. He was translated on 13 March 1732 to the premier bishopric of Meath, and was sworn of the Irish privy council on 28 June. He married, on 30 July 1706, Diana (d. 1739), daughter of Sir John Briscoe of Boughton, Northamptonshire, and Amberley Castle, Sussex, and had two daughters, Anne and Diana, and six sons, John (1709–1711), William, John (d. 1712), Philip, Charles, and Welbore *Ellis, later first Baron Mendip. He died on 1 January 1734, and was buried on 3 January with great ceremony in the vault of Christ Church, Dublin, where a monument, originally on the south side of the nave and now in the crypt, was erected by his only surviving son, Welbore. The funeral procession included the boys of the Blue Coat Hospital, to which he had bequeathed £100 and the bishop's crozier and mitre, the only recorded instance of their use in the diocese since the Reformation. Ellis wrote two publications: *The dean of Dublin, plaintiff, archbishop of Dublin, defendant, upon a writ of error—the defendant's case* (1724) and *The lord bishop of Kildare, dean of the church of the Holy Trinity of Dublin, plaintiff in error. The lord archbishop of Dublin defendant in error. The plaintiff in error's case* (1724).

B. H. BLACKER, rev. RAYMOND REFAUSSÉ

Sources G. Agar-Ellis, ed., *The Ellis correspondence: letters written during the years 1686, 1687, 1688, and addressed to John Ellis*, 2 vols. (1829) · H. Cotton, *Fasti ecclesiae Hibernicae*, 6 vols. (1845–78) · J. B. Leslie, 'Unpublished biographical succession list of Irish clergy', Representative Church Body Library, Dublin, MS 61 · R. Mant, *History of the Church of Ireland*, 2 vols. (1840) · J. Finlayson, *Inscription … in Christ Church Cathedral, Dublin* (1878) · R. Refaussé and C. Lennon, eds., *The registers of Christ Church Cathedral, Dublin* (1998) · K. Milne, ed., *Christ Church Cathedral: a history* (2000) · A. Vicars, ed., *Index to the prerogative wills of Ireland, 1536–1810* (1897) · T. F. O'Rahilly, 'Irish poets, historians and judges in English historical documents, 1538–1615', *Proceedings of the Royal Irish Academy*, 36C (1921–4), 86–120 · Mrs R. Lane Poole, ed., *Catalogue of portraits in the possession of the university, colleges, city and county of Oxford*, 3, OHS, 82 (1926) · Foster, *Alum. Oxon.*

Archives BL, letters to John Ellis, Add. MSS 28931–28936

Likenesses W. Sonmans, oils, before 1721, Christ Church Oxf.

Ellis, Welbore, first Baron Mendip (1713–1802), politician, was born at Kildare, Ireland, on 15 December 1713, the sixth and youngest but only surviving son of Dr Welbore *Ellis (1661/2–1734), bishop of Kildare and from 1732 of Meath, and his wife, Diana Briscoe (d. 1739), the daughter of Sir John Briscoe of Boughton, Northamptonshire, and Amberley Castle, Sussex. He was educated at Westminster School (1727–32) and proceeded to Christ Church, Oxford, where he graduated in 1736. In 1738 he succeeded his uncle John Ellis, a former under-secretary of state to William III and member of parliament, to an estate augmented by the Irish property of another uncle, Sir William Ellis, secretary of state to the exiled James II. Statesmanship was the diminutive Ellis's ambition. He had no

Welbore Ellis, first Baron Mendip (1713–1802), by Thomas Gainsborough, 1763

electoral influence of his own, but his return to the Commons for Cricklade on 24 December 1741, when the house decided a double return at the general election contest there in his favour, was a prelude to over fifty-two years' membership. He attached himself principally to Henry Fox, using his friend Lord Hartington as intermediary, and supported the government. A speech defending the deployment of Hanoverian troops in British pay, on 6 December 1743, led to his being chosen to second the address in 1744 and 1745, and in the ensuing two years he made two keynote speeches on behalf of the ministry. In 1747, on Henry Pelham's recommendation, he was returned for Weymouth and Melcombe Regis, which he retained until 1761. He at once obtained a seat at the Admiralty board, and on 18 November 1747, 'against consent of her friends', according to Mrs Delany, he married the 'very plain, quiet' Elizabeth Stanhope (d. 1761), the only daughter of Sir William Stanhope, 'a vast fortune': he himself had 'a good estate, and is a pretty sort of man' (*Autobiography … Mrs Delany*, 2.554). The couple lived at Tylney Hall, Hampshire, and at Pope's Villa, Twickenham, which Elizabeth had acquired from her father. The villa attracted a procession of dinner guests, but subjected Ellis to the merciless barbs of a critical neighbour, Horace Walpole, who dismissed him as an incorrigible placeman. The couple had no children; Elizabeth Ellis died on 1 August 1761.

Ellis was the leading Admiralty spokesman in the Commons in the 1747 parliament. When his patron Fox became secretary of state in 1755 he tried to obtain the war office for Ellis, and, failing that, a seat at the Treasury board. Ellis, however, preferred a joint Irish vice-treasurership, for which he kissed hands in December that year and which he held for seven years. In the house he managed the Minorca inquiry for Fox in 1757, and was not dropped, as expected, when William Pitt joined the ministry that year. The duke of Newcastle secured his appointment as a privy councillor on 20 March 1760. Even so, he was nearly turned out of office later that year: Fox, who prevented this, recalled 'Ellis had by my friendship and accident got into a place much above his pretensions, and he was the only man in England who did not think so' (*Life and Letters of Lady Sarah Lennox*, 1.15). Displaced from his constituency in 1761, he spent £3000 to secure his return for Aylesbury, where his father-in-law had some influence, with government support. He then made a succession of bids for higher office—as peace plenipotentiary in 1761, as chancellor of the exchequer in 1762, as a cabinet minister in 1763—and was rumoured to be in line for ambassadorial appointments to The Hague or Vienna in 1762. In December 1762 he became secretary at war and was required to disband the troops engaged in the Seven Years' War. His speech on the army estimates on 4 March 1763 was well received. Although he pressed George Grenville to make him first lord of the Admiralty in August 1763, he remained at the war office until July 1765, and that year deployed troops to suppress the riotous Spitalfields weavers in London. When dismissed by Rockingham he commended himself, for the second time the same year, to George III as 'only yours; I have carefully avoided every other connexion and support' (*Correspondence of George III*, 1.151).

Anxious to be restored to office, Ellis thought the joint paymastership of the forces beneath him. He would have been content with the joint vice-treasurership again, but even that eluded him. On 20 July 1765, after falling in love with Lady Jane Stuart the year before, he married, second, Anne Stanley (1725–1803), the eldest daughter of the late George Stanley and his wife, Sarah Sloane, of Paultons, Hampshire, and the sister and coheir of Hans Stanley (1721–1780), politician. The king, noting Ellis's hostility to the American colonists' cause, tried to induce Pitt to place him in his ministry in September 1766, but failed. Ellis, in turn, opposed Pitt's East Indian inquiry on 9 December, but later supported the administration. In the 1768 parliament he sat for Petersfield. Despite his criticisms of the North ministry's concessions to American grievances, he returned to office on 21 April 1770, again as joint Irish vice-treasurer. In 1771 he had Lord Mayor Crosby and Alderman Oliver of London committed to the Tower for obstructing the house's orders, and thereafter gave further proof of his hostility to popular agitation and constitutional reform. He was therefore satirized by Junius as 'Grildrig', 'little mannikin', and 'the most contemptible little piece of machinery in the whole Kingdom' (*Letters of Junius*, 190–91, 244–5, 481); Philip Francis, the supposed author of *The Letters of Junius*, had held a war office appointment under Ellis. Ellis criticized the house's appetite for debating matters of state and opposed the publication of debates, as well as electoral and parliamentary reform. He had opposed the repeal of the Townshend duties, which he regarded as a signal for American colonial intransigence, on 5 March 1770, and set his face against further concessions by North, who glossed over Ellis's friendly opposition in his reports of parliamentary proceedings to George III, even when Ellis led the opposition on 20 February 1775 to North's conciliatory proposals. On 20 February 1776 he advocated crushing the rebellious Americans.

As MP once more for Weymouth from 1774 until 1790, in June 1777 Ellis substituted the treasurership of the navy for his Irish Treasury post. He reached his apogee as secretary of state for America from February to March 1782, in the last month of North's administration. 'Ellis', reported George Selwyn, 'has added another footman to his chariot, and is a Minister in form and fact and pomp and everything' (*Carlisle MSS*, 580). He had time for one bellicose speech—though he denied its being so—which he delivered on 22 February. Out of office again, he voted against Shelburne's peace preliminaries on 18 February 1783, and remained attached to Lord North. On taking office in 1782 he had hinted at his wish for a peerage, with remainder to a nephew, as he had no children of his own. In 1783, when North coalesced in government with the Foxites, Ellis solicited a peerage from the king, but North procrastinated. Ellis had assured George III that in forty-two years in parliament he had never joined any opposition faction. Denied his ambition, however, he regularly opposed Pitt the younger's government from 1784 to 1790 as a Northite, by vote and speech. The disconsolate nature of this opposition was remarked upon in 1787, and in 1790 he had to give up Weymouth and purchase his return for Petersfield on 29 April 1791, from its patron William Jolliffe. This time he was silent in debate. He voted with the opposition on 1 March 1792, acting after North's death with the duke of Portland's adherents: he dissented from Charles James Fox's support of the French Revolution. On 14 May 1794 he was named to the secret committee on sedition. After the Portland whigs joined Pitt's administration, Ellis obtained the barony of Mendip, on 13 August 1794. But the 'Nestor' of the Commons played no role in the Lords.

Ellis had become a fellow of the Society of Antiquaries in 1745, doctor of civil laws at Oxford in 1773, and a trustee of the British Museum in 1780. He assembled a valuable library. From 1780 his country seat was Paultons, Hampshire; his town house was latterly at Brook Street, Westminster. He died on 2 February 1802 in Brook Street, and was buried in Westminster Abbey on 7 February. His wife survived him and died on 7 December 1803. His title passed to his great-nephew and heir, Henry Welbore Agar, second Viscount Clifden, who assumed the surname Ellis.   ROLAND THORNE

Sources HoP, *Commons, 1715–54*, 2.10 · HoP, *Commons, 1754–90*, 2.397–400 · HoP, *Commons, 1790–1820*, 3.701–2 · *DNB* · Walpole, *Corr.* · *The letters of Junius*, ed. J. Cannon (1978), 190–1, 244–5, 481 · *The autobiography and correspondence of Mary Granville, Mrs Delany*, ed. Lady Llanover, 1st ser., 2 (1861), 554 · Earl of Ilchester [G. S. Holland Fox-Strangways], *Henry Fox, first Lord Holland, his family and relations*, 1 (1920), 271, 297; 2 (1920), 125 · *The life and letters of Lady Sarah Lennox*, ed. M. E. A. Dawson, countess of Ilchester and Lord Stavordale, 1 (1901), 15 · *The correspondence of King George the Third from 1760 to December 1783*, ed. J. Fortescue, 1 (1927), 151 · T. Hayter, *The army and the crowd in mid-Georgian England* (1978), 67, 130–35 · Cobbett, *Parl. hist.* · J. Almon, ed., *The debates and proceedings of the British House of Commons*, 11 vols. (1766–75) · *The Grenville papers: being the correspondence of Richard Grenville … and … George Grenville*, ed. W. J. Smith, 2 (1852), 112–14 · *The manuscripts of the earl of Carlisle*, HMC, 42 (1897), 580 · *Life and letters of Sir Gilbert Elliot*, ed. Lady Minto, new edn (1913), 1.134 · GEC, *Peerage*

Archives University of Chicago Library, corresp. | BL, letters to Frederick Haldimand, Add. MS 21705 · BL, corresp. with first and second earls of Hardwicke, Add. MSS 35593–35620, *passim* · BL, corresp. with Lord Holland, Add. MS 51386 · BL, Holland House MSS · BL, corresp. with Lord Liverpool, Add. MSS 38198–38209, 38306–38309, *passim* · BL, corresp. with Lord Loudon, Add. MSS 44078–44084 · BL, letters to duke of Newcastle, Add. MSS 32699–32939, *passim* · BL, Newcastle MSS · BL OIOC, corresp. with Philip Francis, MSS Eur. C 8, D 18, E 12–22, F 5–6 · Chatsworth House, Derbyshire, letters to duke of Devonshire · CKS, corresp. with Sir Jeffrey Amherst · Hants. RO, corresp. with first earl of Normanton · Hunt. L., letters to Lord Pery · PRO NIre., letters to Lord Townshend · Royal Arch., Grenville MSS · U. Mich., Clements L., corresp. with Thomas Gage

Likenesses G. Townshend, engraving, caricature, 1757, priv. coll. · T. Gainsborough, oils, 1763, Christ Church Oxf. [*see illus.*] · J. Whessell, line engraving, 1763 (after T. Gainsborough), BL, BM · plaster medallion, 1780, Scot. NPG · C. Watson, stipple, pubd 1791 (after J. Meyer), BM, NPG · K. A. Hickel, oils, 1793, NPG · K. Hickel, group portrait, oils (*The House of Commons, 1793*), NPG

Ellis, Sir William (1609–1680), judge and politician, was born in Lincoln and baptized on 19 July 1609 at Grantham, Lincolnshire, the second son of Sir Thomas Ellis, or Ellys (*d.* 1627), of Grantham, barrister, and his wife, Jane Armstrong of Wysall, Nottinghamshire. After beginning his schooling in Lincoln under a Mr Phipps he was admitted as a pensioner to Christ's College, Cambridge, in 1623, graduating BA in 1627. On 9 November 1627 he was admitted to Gray's Inn and was called to the bar on 9 February 1635.

Ellis was elected to represent Boston, Lincolnshire, in both the Short and Long parliaments, and in 1641 he was named to chair a Commons committee of fens (*CSP dom.*, *1640–41*, 264). Remaining at Westminster during the civil war, in December 1645 he was one of the Commons' members appointed to a committee of both houses who were to plan together for a 'vigorous prosecution of the enemy and speedy ending of the war' (*CSP dom.*, *1645–7*, 264). In September 1646 he was placed on a committee to hear complaints from the Levant Company regarding a takeover of their property in Constantinople by agents of the king. Despite his support for parliament Ellis was one of the members arrested by the army at Pride's Purge, and as a likely presbyterian he may well have supported the motion for further negotiations with the king. However, he was probably one of 'those others from the Inns of Court' who 'had liberty granted to go to their chambers on their parole' on 12 December 1648 (Rushworth, 7.1361).

Ellis was readmitted to the Commons on 4 June 1649 and five years later he was evidently fully reconciled with the Cromwellian regime, as on 24 May 1654 he was appointed to serve 'during pleasure' as solicitor-general. Six days later he was called to serve as one of the governing body of benchers (or ancients) of his inn. In June 1654, as solicitor-general, he took part in the prosecution of Gerhard,

Vowell, and Somerset Fox on a charge of corresponding with Charles Stuart and conspiring to assassinate the lord protector; both Gerhard and Vowell were convicted and executed. That same year he was again returned to parliament for Boston, and in 1656 for Grantham. In March 1656 he served on the committee appointed to frame statutes for Durham College and in June 1658 he was engaged in the prosecution of Dr Hewet and John Mordant, charged with levying war against the protector. Hewet was found guilty and Mordant acquitted. One of Oliver Cromwell's last acts was to sign a patent creating Ellis a baronet, but apparently it never passed the great seal. Nevertheless, he continued in the office of solicitor-general under Richard Cromwell and retained his seat for Grantham in the January 1659 election. In the protracted debate on the competency of the Scottish members to be seated in the house he spoke at length in support of their claims on 18 March 1659, observing that 'the argument that the act of Union is no good law, this argument makes way for Charles Stuart' (*The Diary of Thomas Burton*, ed. J. T. Rutt, 4 vols., 1824, 4.181).

Re-elected for Grantham in 1660, Ellis was excluded from the Commons because of his radical views. However, in 1657 he had been elected as treasurer of Gray's Inn, in which capacity he served until 1666, and he also served the inn as one of their two readers for 1663–4. In the 1669 Michaelmas term he was made a serjeant-at-law, and moved first into the Serjeants' Inn in Chancery Lane and later into the one in Fleet Street. In 1671 he was made a king's serjeant and knighted, and on 18 December 1672 he was appointed a justice of the court of common pleas. The most interesting case to come before him in that capacity was that of *Barnardiston v. Soame*, concerning a disputed parliamentary election in the county of Suffolk. Originating in the court of king's bench, the case was appealed, in 1676, to the court of exchequer chamber, where Ellis was joined only by Sir Robert Atkyns in finding in favour of Barnardiston, who had been denied his seat in the Commons by a falsified return. That decision was probably the main reason for his replacement on the common pleas bench, in October 1676, by Sir William Scroggs, a political ally of Lord Treasurer Danby, the reigning favourite at Charles II's court.

In February 1679 Ellis was elected to the Commons once again by the borough of Boston, where his political career had first begun. On 30 April of that year, in the context of the Popish Plot, the exclusion crisis, and Danby's forced resignation from office a month earlier, he was reappointed to the common pleas bench. He died on 11 December 1680, aged seventy-one, at his chamber in Serjeants' Inn, Fleet Street, and was buried on 17 December at Nocton in Lincolnshire. Nothing is known of any wife or children.   J. M. RIGG, *rev.* MICHAEL DE L. LANDON

Sources J. Foster, *The register of admissions to Gray's Inn, 1521–1889, together with the register of marriages in Gray's Inn chapel, 1695–1754* (privately printed, London, 1889) · Baker, *Serjeants* · Sainty, *King's counsel* · Sainty, *Judges* · Foss, *Judges* · *State trials* · A. Pulling, *The order of the coif* (1884) · *CSP dom.*, 1640–41; 1645–7 · IGI · Venn, *Alum. Cant.* · D. Underdown, *Pride's Purge: politics in the puritan revolution* (1971) · J. Rushworth, *Historical collections*, 2nd edn, 7 (1701)

Likenesses J. M. Wright, oils, 1650–60, GL

Ellis, Sir William (1641x7–1732), Jacobite politician, was the second son of the eleven children of the Revd John *Ellis (d. 1681) and Susanna, *née* Welbore (d. 1700). John *Ellis (1642x6–1738), Philip *Ellis (1652–1726), and Welbore *Ellis (1661/2–1734) were his brothers. He was educated at Westminster School and Christ Church, Oxford, where he matriculated on 14 July 1665. He was awarded a BA degree in 1669, an MA at Cambridge (*per literas regias*) in 1671, and was admitted to the Middle Temple on 27 November 1673.

In 1678 Ellis was, together with his brother Welbore, customer, comptroller, and searcher for the provinces of Leinster and Munster, after which he acquired considerable property in Ireland. His success was such that when Tyrconnell was sworn in as the lord deputy of Ireland on 12 February 1686, his first act was to appoint Ellis as his secretary. 'I know him to be a great knave and a villain', said Tyrconnell, 'but yet he is a useful knave and being a protestant can do me good, but no hurt' (*Stuart Papers*, 6.19). Within a few days of being appointed, Ellis took Thomas Sheridan, Tyrconnell's chief secretary, aside and told him how he could earn them each an extra £1500 a year by 'engrossing the agency of the army and by joining his interest to get the reversion of the Custom House employments' (ibid., 20), which accounted at least in part for Ellis's fortune from earlier administrations. Within a month Ellis had succeeded in squeezing Sheridan out of Tyrconnell's confidence and, to the annoyance of the council members, Tyrconnell had Ellis stand behind him during meetings of the privy council. Ellis gathered evidence against Sheridan which resulted in Sheridan's being charged with corruption and replaced as a commissioner of the revenue.

At the time of the revolution of 1688 in England, when Ireland was on the brink of civil war and the protestants of Dublin were scrambling to get across the sea to England, Ellis increased his fortune by selling passes to leave the country. He was instrumental in buying time for Tyrconnell by letting John Temple, William III's new secretary of state, know that Tyrconnell would surrender rather than risk a war. This view was reinforced by the Irish general Richard Hamilton who was released to negotiate terms with the Dublin government. When Hamilton arrived in Ireland in January 1689 he greeted Ellis with the title 'Brother Sham', and said: 'The Kingdom of Ireland is beholden to you and I for diverting this storm off from them; else you had had ere this an enemy in the bowels of the Kingdom' (*House of Lords MSS*, 189). John Temple committed suicide when he discovered the true nature of affairs.

Ellis was knighted in 1689 and in the following year was commissioner of the revenue in Ireland, assessor of the city and county of Dublin, and chamberlain and treasurer of the city. After the defeat of the Jacobites in Ireland, he fled to France where he became secretary to the exiled King James at St Germain-en-Laye. The fortune in land

Ellis had acquired in Ireland was forfeited by the new government, and in 1702 it was by an act of parliament transferred to his brother John Ellis in settlement of the debts he supposedly owed him.

Ellis was in 1695 commissioned by James to be controller-general of the revenue from prizes taken by royal privateers, and after he exposed the fraudulent practices of the king's agent, he became in 1697 the 'agent, consul and commissary in all matters concerning the king and his subjects in any of the ports of France'.

From 1698 Ellis was one of the commissioners of the royal household in St Germain-en-Laye, and after James's death in 1702, he was appointed one of the two clerk controllers of the green cloth to James Francis Edward Stuart, the Pretender. He was later appointed treasurer and had charge of the finances of the Jacobite court for the next twenty years. He was disapproved of by the Pretender's half-brother, the duke of Berwick, who in 1712 wanted him sent away from court because 'he is alwayse full of politick and will be medling in affaires he ought not' (*Stuart Papers*, 1.253), and in 1713 Berwick advised the Pretender to warn Ellis not to write to England about his own concerns. Ellis nevertheless proved to be indispensable to the Jacobite exiles.

Despite his unshaken political allegiance, Ellis remained a protestant until his death in Rome in the autumn of 1732, aged between eighty-five and ninety.

PIERS WAUCHOPE

Sources *DNB* · Foster, *Alum. Oxon.*, *1500–1714* · *Old Westminsters*, vols. 1–2 · *Calendar of the Stuart papers belonging to his majesty the king, preserved at Windsor Castle*, 7 vols., HMC, 56 (1902–23), vols. 1, 5–7 · *The manuscripts of the House of Lords*, new ser., 12 vols. (1900–77), vols. 4–5 · *Calendar of the manuscripts of the marquess of Ormonde*, new ser., 8 vols., HMC, 36 (1902–20), vol. 7 · G. Agar-Ellis, ed., *The Ellis correspondence: letters written during the years 1686, 1687, 1688, and addressed to John Ellis*, 2 vols. (1829) · W. King, *The state of the protestants of Ireland under the late King James's government* (1691) · *GM*, 1st ser., 39 (1769), 328
Archives BL, letters to his brother and others; papers relating to Irish properties, Add. MSS 28930–28946 · BL, letters to Cardinal Gualterio, Add. MSS 20310, 31267

Ellis, William (*c*.1700–1758), agriculturist and writer, began employment as a customs officer. He then worked in the brewing industry in London until he bought Church Farm, Little Gaddesden, near Hemel Hempstead, Hertfordshire, with money from his second wife, and he began to write about farming, describing improvements made by himself and others.

Ellis's early works made his name, and farmers in all parts of the country asked him to visit and report on their farms. He travelled over the country giving advice and observing different farming methods. He added to his income by travelling as an agent for seeds and farming implements. From the early 1740s Ellis was employed by a bookseller to write in monthly instalments, but he began padding out the pages with anecdotes, and his reputation waned.

Many farmers visited Ellis's farm at Little Gaddesden, but they found that he did not practise what he advocated in print, that his implements were old-fashioned, and that his land was neglected and in bad condition. For example, in 1748 Pehr Kalm, a pupil of Linnaeus, was sent to Little Gaddesden by Baron Bielke, a Swedish nobleman who wanted more information on the new farming methods advocated by Ellis, but Kalm formed a poor opinion of Ellis.

Ellis's most important work was *The Modern Husbandman* (8 vols.), which came out in instalments, ending in 1744. His many other publications include *Chiltern and Vale Farming Explained* (1733); *A Complete System of Experienced Improvements Made on Sheep, etc.* (1749), the first book to be published on sheep and in which Ellis stressed the value of turnips to the sheep farmer; *The Timber Tree Improved* (1738); and *The Complete Cyderman* (1754). *Ellis's Husbandry Abridged and Methodized*, a compendium of all his works on agriculture, appeared in 1772 in two volumes, and the editor defended Ellis, claiming that many of his observations were valuable. Ellis is mentioned in Arthur Young's *General View of the Agriculture of Hertfordshire* (1804). Ellis was twice married, but nothing else is known about his personal life. He died in 1758. ANNE PIMLOTT BAKER

Sources J. Thirsk, ed., *The agrarian history of England and Wales*, 5/1 (1984), 263–5 · J. Donaldson, *Agricultural biography* (1854), 50–52 · V. Bell, *Little Gaddesden* (1949), ch. 6 · preface, *Ellis's husbandry, abridged and methodized: comprehending the most useful articles of practical agriculture*, 1 (1772)

Ellis, William (1747–1810), printmaker, the son of Joseph Ellis (*d.* 1793), writing engraver, was born in London in 1747 and apprenticed in 1760 to Joseph Ellis, Stationers' Company. From about 1770 he was working in William Woollett's studio. A drawing of Blythburgh church, Suffolk, dated 1770, was almost certainly a product of one of the regular sketching tours in that region to which Woollett took his pupils. In 1778 Ellis was acknowledged jointly with Woollett as the engraver of *Solitude* after Richard Wilson. He contributed to Thomas Hearne and William Byrne's *Antiquities of Great Britain* (1778–). In March 1780, from Clerkenwell, Ellis published a pair of plates from *The Vicar of Wakefield* after drawings by Hearne with figures engraved by Woollett. By November he was established in a long-term home at 9 Gwyn's Buildings, Islington. From this address he published further beautiful interpretations of landscape drawings by Hearne, another artist trained by Woollett.

In 1785 Ellis married Elizabeth Smith who was conceivably related to Samuel Smith, who lived with Woollett as a pupil from 1772 to 1776. She too was a printmaker. Two large etchings published in 1785 of a pair of Suffolk drawings by Woollett are signed in the first state 'Elizabeth Smith' and in the second 'Elizabeth Ellis'. In 1786 the couple published a pair of large views of London from Wandsworth and from Greenwich Park after Hearne and Charles Tomkins. They also worked in aquatint, publishing in 1788 a series of thirty-two views on the Rhine and the Maas after drawings by the Revd Gardnor. A set of aquatints of villages round London, *The Campagna of London*, accompanied by text, was launched in 1792. In 1799 Ellis aquatinted the set *The Memorable Victory of the Nile* after William Anderson and engraved by Francis

Chesham. The Ellises contributed illustrations to a number of books including J. Aikin's *Description of the Country Round Manchester* (1795), G. Staunton's *Embassy to the Emperor of China*, and A. Bertrand de Molevill's *Costumes of Austria* (1804). Ellis died in 1810. On 24 November 1810 *A South View of the City of Exeter* engraved after a drawing 'by the late Mr William Ellis' was published in aid of his five orphan children.   TIMOTHY CLAYTON

Sources L. A. Fagan, *A catalogue raisonné of the engraved works of William Woollett* (1885) · T. Clayton, *The English print, 1688–1802* (1997) · D. Morris, *Thomas Hearne and his landscape* (1989) · L. Lambourne and J. Hamilton, eds., *British watercolours in the Victoria and Albert Museum* (1980), 122 · *DNB* · apprenticeship registers, PRO

Ellis, William (1794–1872), missionary, was born in London, on 29 August 1794, in humble circumstances; details of his parents are not known. At an early age he left the family home to work as a gardener. Inspired by the preaching of John Campbell on the work of Christian evangelists in southern Africa, he offered himself as a candidate to the London Missionary Society (LMS) in November 1814. During a probationary period of three months he studied scripture, the rudiments of medicine, and printing. On 6 November 1815 he was ordained as an Independent (Congregational) minister and missionary. Three days later he married Mary Mercy Moor (d. 1835), who had previously been a teacher at an institution for the feebleminded. At the beginning of 1816 they sailed for the Society Islands (later French Polynesia) in the south Pacific. Ellis's principal contribution to the Tahitian mission was the installation of the printing press on Moorea Island, where for the first time readers, grammars, and catechisms were printed in the Tahitian language. The stimulating missionary environment enabled him to transcend the deficiencies of his rudimentary childhood education. In 1818 he moved to the island of Huahine, where he gave his first sermon in Tahitian and transformed himself into a skilled linguist and a chronicler of Polynesian life and natural history.

In 1822 Ellis accompanied nine Tahitian evangelists to the Hawaiian Islands, where he was enthusiastically welcomed by the newly arrived missionaries of the American board of commissioners for foreign missions (ABCFM), who had not yet mastered the local language. With their encouragement he convinced the secretaries of the LMS to sponsor an operation, under his direction, complementary to the American effort. During three years of work he helped standardize the orthography of the Hawaiian language and collected a great deal of information on island life. He also gained admission to court circles and baptized the mother of King Kamehameha II.

In 1825 his wife's ill health compelled Ellis to return with her to England. They travelled eastwards via Boston, where Ellis was warmly received by members of the ABCFM and made those contacts from which sprang his lasting friendship with Rufus Anderson (ABCFM foreign secretary, 1832–66). At home, the secretaries of the LMS employed him to promote awareness of their operations in the Pacific. He was particularly useful in the campaign

William Ellis (1794–1872), by C. Taylor, pubd 1826 (after Derby)

to refute Lord Byron's criticisms of Hawaiian missionaries, a battle largely fought out in the columns of the *Quarterly Review*. The publication of *Polynesian Researches* (1833) established Ellis's reputation as a keen scientific and ethnographic observer. In 1830 he succeeded William Orme as LMS secretary in charge of foreign relations. His growing reputation as an author brought him a large circle of friends in pious literary circles and the editorship of a periodical, the *Christian Keepsake*. After years of intense physical suffering, his wife died in 1835. Two years later Ellis married Sarah Stickney [see Ellis, Sarah (1799–1872)], a talented artist and prolific writer on women's affairs and Christian morality. Their partnership flourished in shared passions for literature, foreign missions, and temperance. Periodic bouts of depression, which Ellis had suffered since 1838, led him to resign as LMS foreign secretary in 1844, although he remained a member of its governing body for the rest of his life.

Ellis's attention was first drawn to Madagascar by Queen Ranavalona's suppression of Christianity in 1835. In his *History of Madagascar* (1838) he aimed to vindicate the work of LMS missionaries on the island and to arouse opposition to the persecution of their converts. Although he did not succeed, the plight of Christian converts remained a source of intense concern. In 1852 he was commissioned by the LMS to visit the island with the aim of negotiating an amelioration of their condition. In *Three Visits to Madagascar* (1858) he combined an account of the failure of his mission with a wealth of information on the island and its inhabitants. He collected botanical samples for the Royal Botanic Gardens at Kew, displayed an impressive command of the new art of photography, and engaged in some prescient speculations on the structural affinities of the Malagasy, Malay, and Polynesian language groups.

Following Queen Ranavalona's death in 1861 the passionately pro-European new king, Radama II, granted liberty of conscience to all his subjects. Although sixty-seven years of age, Ellis readily agreed to oversee the rehabilitation of LMS missions on the island. Reaching the capital in May 1862 he fearlessly—perhaps rashly—plunged into the court intrigues which swirled around the new monarch. Confounding the popular image of missionary prudishness, he was known to have had public meetings with the king's concubine, whose position, he insisted, was not unusual in that society. This earned him a disapproving dispatch from the British consul, Thomas Pakenham, which the foreign secretary, Lord John Russell, forwarded to the LMS directors. Just as Ellis thought he might be on the brink of converting the king to the Christian faith, Radama was attacked and apparently killed by his own troops. French Catholic missionaries believed Ellis had plotted to bring about the coup and the report was relayed to London, again by the British consul, leading Lord Russell to write privately that 'Mr. Ellis the missionary seems to have behaved very ill' (Delaval). Not long after Radama's widow was installed as queen, the capital was shaken by the rumour that the king had survived the attempted assassination and was hiding in the countryside. Despite initial scepticism, Ellis was drawn into an attempt to make contact with the king, an act which laid him open to further charges of political meddling. At this point he sagely withdrew from court circles, content to accept the queen's confirmation, on 27 June 1865, of the repeal of all anti-Christian decrees.

Ellis's public account of his mission, *Madagascar Revisited* (1867), led to his election as a fellow of the Royal Geographical Society and a busy life as a lecturer until, after a brief illness, he succumbed to a respiratory ailment and died on 9 June 1872 at his home, Rose Hill, Hoddesdon, in Hertfordshire, where he had served as pastor of an Independent congregation since 1847. His career exemplified the main features of British protestant missionary effort in the first half of the nineteenth century, when most agents were drawn from the artisan and labouring classes rather than from the educated élite. Beyond the frontiers of European political influence their success depended on their ability to sustain their own health, to provide for most of their own practical needs, to master unfamiliar languages, and to gain the confidence of local rulers. In all these respects Ellis was exceptionally successful. To have had personal dealings with Pomare of Tahiti, Kamehameha II of Hawaii, and Radama of Madagascar was truly remarkable. Throughout his life he championed the prevailing policy of self-supporting, self-governing, self-propagating native churches. His troubled last mission to Madagascar demonstrated that the era of straightforward dealings between missionaries and indigenous rulers was giving way to a world dominated by Europe's imperial rivalries.   NORMAN ETHERINGTON

Sources J. Ellis, *Memoir of Rev. William Ellis* (1873) • C. Newbury, 'Preface', in W. Ellis, *À la recherche de la Polynésie d'autrefois*, 2 vols. (1972) • R. Delaval, *Radama II, prince de la renaissance malgache* (1972) • R. Lovett, *The history of the London Missionary Society, 1795–1895*, 2 vols. (1899) • J. Garrett, *To live among the stars* (1982) • G. Campbell, 'Missionaries: Fanompoana and the Menalamba revolt in late 19th century Madagascar', *Journal of Southern African Studies* (1988), 5–73 • *CGPLA Eng. & Wales* (1872) • *DNB*
Archives SOAS, letters | DWL, corresp. with Joseph Ketley • Harvard U., Houghton L., American board of commissioners for foreign missions, archives
Likenesses C. Taylor, stipple, pubd 1826 (after Derby), BM, NPG [*see illus.*] • engraving, repro. in W. Ellis, *Polynesian researches* (1833), frontispiece • photographs, SOAS, London Missionary Society Archives
Wealth at death under £6000: probate, 21 Aug 1872, *CGPLA Eng. & Wales*

Ellis, William (1800–1881), economist and educational reformer, was born in London on 27 January 1800, the fourth child of a naturalized Frenchman of Huguenot extraction, Andrew Ellis de Vezian (who took the name Andrew Ellis Ellis during the Napoleonic wars), and an Italian, Maria Sophia Fazio. Aged fourteen, Ellis left school at Bromley to work with his father, a Lloyd's underwriter. In 1824 he was offered the assistant managership of the Indemnity Mutual Marine Assurance Company (IMMAC), and after saving the firm from ruin he rose to be chief underwriter in 1826. He became renowned in the City as a hard-working and brilliant businessman; for thirty years he never took a holiday. The IMMAC under his control became the most successful and profitable firm of its type.

Ellis married Mary, daughter of Sharon *Turner, a solicitor and historian, at Ewell church in Surrey on 14 May 1825, and the couple moved to Croydon soon after. The marriage was very happy and brought four children: William Henry (d. 1844), Edward (d. 16 Feb 1865), Lucy, and Mary (who both survived him). Mary Ellis died in January 1870.

An introduction to Jeremy Bentham, James Mill, and their circle inaugurated Ellis's first intellectual career. In 1822 he joined John Stuart Mill's Utilitarian Society and attended its twice-weekly discussions. 'An original thinker in the field of political economy' (Mill, 83), Ellis contributed six articles on economic subjects to the *Westminster Review* (1824–6), in which he displayed both his debt to the two Mills and his own Ricardian economics and radical utilitarianism.

From 1832 to 1835 Ellis and his wife wrote and produced a series of elementary didactic and amusing works for children, entitled *The Parent's Cabinet of Amusement and Instruction*. Ellis was also actively involved with the London Mechanics' Institute and allowed Lord Brougham to disseminate a popular series of his lectures on political economy in 1835. These projects reflected Ellis's growing belief that only through the inculcation of correct moral lessons, at the earliest age, and the teaching of useful subjects could a more self-dependent citizenry be moulded. All Ellis's subsequent works concerned this twin-faceted philosophy of education.

Ellis's claim to originality in his practical attempts to bring this philosophy to bear lies in his focus on the working classes and in his methods. As his biographer states,

Ellis sought to inculcate useful knowledge by 'investigation and well-directed research', rather than rote learning, always with a view to the most important knowledge of all: 'the knowledge of the laws of conduct which affect human well-being and the obedience to which only can the welfare of the individual and the community be obtained' (Blyth, 72). This approach was first encapsulated in Ellis's *Outlines of Social Economy* (1846), but was reiterated in a series of works aimed at teachers: *Outlines of the History and Formation of the Understanding* (1847), *Questions and Answers* (1848), *Introduction to the Study of the Social Sciences* (1849), and *Progressive Lessons in Social Science* (1850).

Use of the Socratic teaching method, the absence of corporal punishment, and the emphasis on useful, secular knowledge characterized the series of schools which Ellis founded. The first 'Birkbeck school', established in the Southampton Buildings, Chancery Lane, in 1848 and named in honour of George Birkbeck, was so successful that Ellis erected a number of others: at Finsbury (1849), Westminster (1850), Bethnal Green (1851), Peckham (1852), Kingsland (1852), and Gospel Oak (1862, renamed the William Ellis School and still in existence at the end of the twentieth century). Ellis funded these institutions out of his £2000 salary and the £10,000 annual bonus he derived from the success of the IMMAC, but was supported by a number of other advocates of popular and secular education, most notably George Combe, Dr William Hodgson, and the three Rüntz brothers, John, George, and James.

An extremely modest man, Ellis only published his first signed work (*Education as a Means of Preventing Destitution*) in 1851. His second, entitled *Lessons on the Phenomena of Industrial Life* (1854), edited by Richard Dawes, a treatise on the delivery of oral lessons, proved to be his most popular, selling 10,000 copies by 1871. In 1855 Ellis delivered a series of lessons to young members of the royal family, published as *Religion in Common Life* (1857), and the following year was invited to air his views before the royal commission on popular education. Between 1861 and 1864 Ellis published, in eight parts, his *Philo-Socrates*, intended as a complete system of ethics.

In 1865 Ellis wrote a series of reading lessons, later adopted by the London board schools, and in 1866 he published his *Thoughts on the Future of the Human Race*, which led to an invitation to give evidence before the schools inquiry commission and the royal commission on scientific instruction and the advancement of science. Outside education, Ellis was a vigorous proponent of free trade, a supporter of the movement for Italian freedom, and an active neo-Malthusian and supporter of women's suffrage. However, two crippling sciatica attacks in 1867 and 1868, coupled with fading eyesight, dramatically reduced the sphere of his capabilities. As a consequence, towards the end of his life Ellis published only minor articles and pamphlets, offering no further theoretical advances. Ellis resigned his duties at the IMMAC on 1 January 1877 but continued to advise the board. He died on 18 February 1881 at 6 Lancaster Terrace, Regent's Park, London.

MATTHEW LEE

Sources E. K. Blyth, *Life of William Ellis* (1889) · W. D. Sockwell, *Popularizing classical economics: Henry Brougham and William Ellis* (1994) · E. E. Ellis, *Memoir of William Ellis* (1888) · T. D. Wickenden, *William Ellis School, 1862–1962* (1962) · W. A. C. Stewart and W. P. McCann, *The educational innovators*, 2 vols. (1967–8) · *The collected works of John Stuart Mill*, 1: *Autobiography and literary essays*, ed. J. M. Robson and J. Stillinger (1981) · F. F. Miller, 'William Ellis and his work as an educationist', *Fraser's Magazine*, new ser., 25 (1882), 233–52 · G. R. Searle, *Entrepreneurial politics in mid-Victorian Britain* (1993) · R. T. Van Arsdel, 'Ellis, William', *BDMBR*, vol. 2 · *DNB*
Archives NL Scot., corresp. with George Combe
Likenesses A. E. Durham, photograph, repro. in Ellis, *Memoir of William Ellis* · A. V. Swan, photogravure, repro. in Blyth, *Life of William Ellis*
Wealth at death under £160,000: probate, 16 March 1881, *CGPLA Eng. & Wales*

Ellis, William (1828–1916), astronomer, was born on 20 February 1828 in Greenwich, the son of Thomas Ellis, an assistant to John Pond, the sixth astronomer royal. After attending local schools he was appointed at the age of thirteen to the temporary computing staff at the Royal Greenwich Observatory. He was one of a group that George Airy, the seventh astronomer royal, had assembled to reduce lunar observations made at Greenwich between 1750 and 1830. He was also involved in work on establishing British standards of length. When the lunar computations ended in 1848, Ellis was transferred to observational work. In 1852 the post of observer at Durham University observatory became vacant, and Airy recommended Ellis for the post. At Durham he continued the series of observations of comets and minor planets that had already been started, but his stay there proved to be short. In 1853 he was asked to return to Greenwich as a member of the permanent staff, and became one of the small team of observers that Airy relied on for continuing the observatory's fundamental positional measurements.

One of the first projects on which Ellis was engaged required his return to the north of England where, in 1854, he assisted in a series of pendulum experiments at Harton colliery. Small differences in the period of oscillation of a pendulum at the top and bottom of a pit shaft would, it was hoped, provide information on the earth's density, but in the event local geology made the results unreliable. In the following year Ellis took charge of the telegraph system at Greenwich. This both provided regular time signals throughout the country and acted as a means of measuring longitudes relative to Greenwich. Soon afterwards he took over the task of rating the Royal Navy chronometers brought to the observatory. In consequence he came to be involved in all the time measurement activities at Greenwich. Ellis assisted in the reduction of longitude and latitude data obtained elsewhere, not least from expeditions. Perhaps the best known of these was his reduction of data gathered in Africa by Livingstone. Ellis married Sarah Elizabeth Campion of Bellingham, Northumberland, in 1869. She died in 1906, and two years later he married a distant cousin, Margaret Anne Ellis of Settle, Yorkshire, who survived him. There were no children from either marriage. In 1874 James Glaisher resigned as superintendent of the magnetic and meteorological department at Greenwich. At Ellis's request, Airy appointed him to the position thus left vacant, and it is for his work on the topics covered by this department that Ellis is best remembered. Airy was initially opposed to the idea, proposed by Sir Edward Sabine, that changes in sunspot numbers and terrestrial magnetism are linked. Ellis reduced the Greenwich magnetic data for the years 1841–77 (and thereafter for other years) and convinced Airy that he was wrong, showing that a significant correlation did, indeed, exist. He was equally assiduous in his reduction of the Greenwich meteorology data, becoming, in the process, a leading authority on barometers and their history. He served on the council of the Royal Meteorological Society for thirty years (1878–1908), and was president in 1886–7. He was elected a fellow of the Royal Society in 1893, a few months before his retirement from the Greenwich observatory. Ellis was a well-known figure in Greenwich, who spent much of his spare time on local church affairs. He retained his interest in astronomy and meteorology to the end. His last publication—on sunspots and terrestrial magnetism—appeared only a few months before his death at Greenwich on 11 December 1916.

A. J. MEADOWS

Sources *Monthly Notices of the Royal Astronomical Society*, 77 (1916–17), 295–9 · G. B. Airy, *Autobiography of Sir George Biddell Airy*, ed. W. Airy (1896) · A. J. Meadows, *Greenwich observatory: the story of Britain's oldest scientific institution*, 2: *Recent history (1836–1975)* (1975) · *CGPLA Eng. & Wales* (1917)

Archives CUL, Royal Greenwich Observatory archives · CUL, papers · RAS, letters to Royal Astronomical Society

Likenesses photograph, Sci. Mus.

Wealth at death £3152 1s. 5d.: probate, 2 Feb 1917, *CGPLA Eng. & Wales*

Ellis, Sir William Charles (1780–1839), physician and asylum superintendent, was born on 10 March 1780 at Alford, Lincolnshire, the son of William Ellis, rector of All Hallows Staining in the City of London, and his wife, Sarah Francis Ellis. He received a classical education before being apprenticed to a surgeon–apothecary in Hull, going on to become a member of the Royal College of Surgeons. On 14 February 1806 he married Mildred Wood, daughter of John Wood, at Louth in Lincolnshire. Although brought up in the Church of England it was only after his marriage that Ellis acquired strong religious convictions. While living in Hull, and suffering from poor health, he became a Methodist and went on to become a lay preacher. Strong religious convictions exercised a profound influence on his subsequent career. He became widely regarded as a kind man, paternalistic in his approach towards his patients, an image enhanced by his rather stout appearance.

Ellis's interest in the treatment of mental disorders developed during his practice as an apothecary in Hull. By 1814 he had acquired an interest in Sculcoates Refuge, a private lunatic asylum whose treatment principles were modelled on those of the Quaker inspired York Retreat. Ellis's approach to the treatment and management of mentally disordered people owed much to the methods developed at the retreat. At this time public interest in the plight of Yorkshire's insane had been heightened by exposures in the 1815 report of the select committee on the state of madhouses of scandalous conditions at the York Lunatic Asylum, a charitable institution. In response the West Riding magistrates agreed to adopt legislation passed in 1808 and to erect a county pauper lunatic asylum, thus providing William Ellis with a fortuitous opportunity to consolidate his career.

Ellis published a lengthy pamphlet in response to the findings of the select committee and the plans for the county asylum. In *A Letter to Thomas Thompson, Esq. M. P.* (1815), though acknowledging his own limited experience in the field, he summarized his ideas on the nature of madness and put forward detailed proposals for the operation of the new asylum. His plan was based on the principle that the asylum should operate on a curative rather than a custodial philosophy, with the productive employment of patients as a central tenet. The leading county magistrate, Godfrey Higgins, was evidently impressed. Ellis was appointed as director of the West Riding Asylum at Wakefield and took up the post in December 1817, with his wife, Mildred, as its matron. By the time the asylum opened to receive patients in November 1818 Ellis had obtained the degree of MD, the only county asylum superintendent thus qualified.

According to his daughter Harriet, Ellis regarded the appointment at Wakefield as a call from God. He regarded each of his patients as a man and a brother, entitled to every effort to bring about either recovery or at least alleviation. The Ellises' regime at the asylum was permeated by the practical expression of faith. Religious instruction was provided every morning both to staff and to the more sensible patients. Each Sunday the patients attended divine service, which always included a sermon from Dr Ellis.

It was, however, in the promotion of work as an essential therapeutic tool that Ellis built his reputation. He and Mrs Ellis developed sophisticated arrangements at Wakefield whereby most physically capable patients worked in some way. The men were employed in agricultural and horticultural work, as well as in trades like baking, brewing, shoemaking, bricklaying, painting, spinning, and weaving. Female patients undertook domestic tasks such as kitchen work, cleaning, and laundry.

Ellis remained at the West Riding Asylum for thirteen years. His considerable reputation led the Middlesex magistrates to ask him to superintend their prestigious new asylum which opened at Hanwell in 1831. At this, the largest asylum in the country, he and Mrs Ellis sought to further advance the system they had implemented at Wakefield. An elaborate programme of work was set in place with patients employed in a wide range of occupations. Harriet Martineau, visiting the asylum in 1834, described large numbers of apparently contented people engaged in all sorts of outdoor and indoor occupations. William and Mildred Ellis created something akin to a large working religious community at Hanwell, an achievement recognized by the award of a knighthood to Ellis.

Ellis's book, *A Treatise on the Nature, Symptoms, Causes, and Treatment of Insanity*, was published in 1838, having been in preparation since before he left Wakefield. In this substantial volume Ellis demonstrated his continued adherence to established ideas on the origins and practical management of mental disorders. His analysis of causation comprised all the accepted genetic, physical, social, and psychological factors. The treatment methods he outlined included a range of medicines, as well as other physical treatments like bleeding and warm and cold baths, though he recognized their therapeutic limitations. He continued to advocate strongly the more progressive moral treatment techniques, with work retaining its central place in his treatment system.

Ellis retired from the Hanwell post in summer 1838, having taken exception to some decisions which followed political changes among the Middlesex magistracy. His pursuit of a policy of strict economy in the asylum's management was increasingly viewed as penny-pinching at the expense of vulnerable people. After leaving Hanwell, Ellis established a private lunatic asylum at nearby Southall Park. However, he did not long enjoy the benefits of a less pressured existence. The poor health that had dogged his career culminated in his untimely death from dropsy at Southall Park on 24 October 1839.

Ellis earned a prominent place among the great pioneers of psychological medicine, primarily for promoting work as a key instrument of therapeutic change. By successfully implementing moral treatment methods and adapting them to the circumstances of a large pauper institution he paved the way for further liberalization in treating the insane which accompanied the dissemination of the non-restraint system in the 1840s.

LEONARD D. SMITH

Sources H. W. Ellis, 'Our doctor': memorials of Sir William Charles Ellis, M.D., of Southall Park, Middlesex (1868) · W. C. Ellis, A letter to Thomas Thompson, Esq. M.P., containing considerations on the necessity for proper places being provided by the legislature for the reception of all insane persons (1815) · A. Halliday, A general view of the present state of lunatics and lunatic asylums in Great Britain and Ireland (1828) · H. Martineau, 'The Hanwell Lunatic Asylum', Tait's Edinburgh Magazine (1834), 305–10 · A. Suzuki, 'The politics and ideology of non-restraint: the case of the Hanwell asylum', Medical History, 39 (1995), 1–17 · L. D. Smith, 'Cure, comfort and safe custody': public lunatic asylums in early nineteenth-century England (1999) · C. Crowther, Some observations respecting the management of the pauper lunatic asylum at Wakefield (1830) · L. Ashworth and J. Todd, 'The House': Wakefield asylum (1993) · IGI · d. cert.

Archives LMA, Middlesex County Lunatic Asylum visiting justices' minutes, reports of the resident physicians · West Riding County RO, West Riding Lunatic Asylum, annual reports of director, case books

Likenesses photograph (after an engraving), repro. in Ashworth and Todd, 'The House' · portraits, Stanley Royd Hospital, Wakefield

Ellis, Sir William Henry (1860–1945), civil engineer and iron and steel manufacturer, was born at Thurnscoe Hall, near Rotherham, Yorkshire, on 20 August 1860. He was fourth of five sons and one daughter of John Devonshire *Ellis (1824–1906), a founding partner of John Brown & Co. in 1854, and his wife, Elizabeth (*née* Bourne).

Educated at Uppingham School, and at Leeds College of

Sir William Henry Ellis (1860–1945), by Ernest Moore

Science, Ellis was in November 1878 apprenticed to Tannett, Walker & Co. of Leeds. In 1882 he oversaw transport and erection of a vertical blowing engine at copper smelting works in Serbia, and then worked for two years as erecting shop foreman in the works at Leeds. He set up a 4000 ton hydraulic forging press, two hydraulic pumping engines, and two overhead cranes at John Brown & Co. Ltd, before joining his father's forge department as under-manager in 1887. In 1889 he married Lucy Rimington (d. 1938), daughter of Francis William Tetley, a director of Joshua Tetley & Son (brewers) of Leeds. They had two sons and two daughters.

An elder brother, Charles (d. 1937), who had qualified as a barrister, specializing in legal and commercial problems, had joined the board of John Brown & Co. Ltd in 1884. However, Ellis became a director only twenty-two years later, after the death of their father in 1906; and in the period down to 1914 Ellis's technical and commercial energies were concentrated on the Atlas works in Carlisle Street, Sheffield, heart of one of Britain's three largest steel and engineering enterprises. In 1904, 2600 men were employed on a 34 acre site, plus 5400 men in Rotherham collieries, with weekly wage bills of £10,000. Some 43 furnaces consumed 400 tons of coal and 100 tons of coke a day; and with 10 hydraulic presses, 33 steam hammers, 94 travelling cranes, and 307 machine tools, the works produced 100,000 tons of output and £3 million turnover per annum.

From 1906 to 1914 Ellis extended facilities, adding a 6000 ton forging press in 1911. He supervised the decommissioning of all the outmoded Bessemer steel plants, and during this time the Atlas works ceased to produce steel rails. The shipyards of John Brown & Co. Ltd benefited from the arms race, and large battleships and liners for Cunard were conspicuously launched at Clydebank. In 1908 a joint research and development laboratory with the neighbouring firm of Thomas Firth & Co. (associated by exchange of shares since 1902) was the first in Sheffield. Effective innovations confounded sceptics, including stainless steel for cutlery and aero-engine valves in the First World War. After three profitable years, John Brown & Co. Ltd was valued at £5 million in 1914, employing 55,000 employees nationally. As master cutler (1914–18) Ellis oversaw scrutiny of 200,000 export licences for goods containing tungsten or molybdenum intended for neutrals, after the hasty controls of July 1915, a function resumed during 1939–45. Manufacture of 4 million cutthroat razors for conscript armies and fund-raising for the wounded were other tasks.

In 1915 East Forge was erected at the Atlas works. In addition, a new rolling mill and electric arc steel smelting furnaces were installed. Operating from September 1915, these were enlarged versions of those in use at Thomas Firth & Co. since 1907. After 1917 the capacity of the Atlas works was further increased, foundry work was moved to Scunthorpe, and the Carnforth Iron Company was bought to secure haematite ore. William Ellis chaired the Sheffield management of John Brown & Co., with others responsible elsewhere. Charles Ellis was seconded to the Ministry of Munitions and Lord Pirie of Harland and Woolf was a member of the board from July 1915 to November 1918, while the Sheffield and Clydebank works were government controlled. Charles Ellis, knighted in 1918, returned to the board in 1919, resulting in a triumvirate with William and Sir Thomas Bell.

A leading Sheffield notable, Ellis was a JP as well as a town trustee and a church burgess. He served as a trustee of the savings bank, and was a member of Sheffield University council and also of the infirmaries board. A trustee of Uppingham School, he donated an organ in 1930. He also undertook a number of professional appointments, serving as president of the Iron and Steel Institute (1924–5), and of the Institution of Civil Engineers (1925–6); he was chairman of the engineering section of the British Association meeting held at Glasgow in 1928. A member of the privy council committee of the Department of Scientific and Industrial Research (1925–6), he also served on the executive board of the National Physical Laboratory and on the University of Cambridge appointments board, and was a governor of Imperial College. In 1920 he joined the disposals board and overseas committee of the Board of Trade. Appointed GBE and Commander of the Crown of Italy in 1918, he was awarded an honorary DEng by Sheffield University.

While managing director of John Brown & Co. Ltd in Sheffield from 1919 to 1931, Ellis's difficulties included strikes by miners, moulders, and railwaymen in 1919, escalating costs, and an end to armaments work, as well as contracting markets in shipbuilding. A link with the Craven Railway Carriage and Waggon Company of Darnall in

1918–21 provided markets for machine shops installed to produce tyres, axles, and springs. The Coventry ordnance works for naval guns was also sold off at this time to the new English Electrical Company. Dividends held at 5 per cent until 1921–2, when competition intensified, battleship orders were cancelled, and reduced output and employment followed. There was a modest recovery in the company's situation in 1924–5, but matters were made worse by the shortages of fuel and the disruption of the general strike.

Mounting losses culminated in reorganization in August 1930, after debenture holders refused renewal after two dividendless years. With advice from two eminent chartered accountants, Sir Gilbert Garnsey and William MacKinnon, capital was reduced to £2.375 million in 1930. The scheme also involved a sinking fund, which promised debenture redemption by 1965. Further substantial rationalization was also necessary, and in 1930 Thomas Firth & Sons and John Brown & Co. Ltd merged. This involved the transfer of the Atlas and Scunthorpe works to Firths, for which John Brown & Co. Ltd received a significant number of shares in that firm. 'It was a merger between complementary enterprises with differing specialisms' (Nunn, 287). Thereafter, John Brown produced heavy forgings and armour plate, while Firths made projectiles, special steel products, high class tools, and forgings. John Brown & Co. Ltd continued with shipbuilding and the mining of coal, and it also became the parent company of a new steelmaking firm, Thomas Firth and John Brown Ltd, which entered the growth market of large hollow forged boiler drums for electrical power stations in 1931. Ellis retired 'early', aged seventy-one, in 1931.

'Apart from business activities, what may well have been nearest to Ellis's heart were mountains and hills' (Alpine Journal, 208–10). An Alpine Club member from 1905, Ellis attended the fiftieth jubilee celebrations in 1907. An incessant world traveller, in summer often he climbed in Switzerland, in the Engadin and Oberland with Josef Kuster of Engelberg. Small and light, he ran daily near his home at Weetwood in Ecclesall and at weekends enjoyed long walks in the Peak District and Lakes. In later life he climbed Helvellyn every year, the Matterhorn when aged seventy, and the Jungfrau on his seventy-fifth birthday with Sir Leonard Pearce, his daughter, a friend, and guides. About the time of his wife's death in 1938 he established a fund of £4000 in Switzerland to help sick or disabled guides and their families, and became an honorary member of the Swiss Alpine Club.

Ellis was an Anglican; he played the organ before work, for friends, and in church. A politically inactive Conservative, he was a member of the Carlton Club. Friends recalled an original thinker and keen critic, forceful and restless in personality, yet a pleasant and interesting companion. He died on 4 July 1945 at the Royal Infirmary in Sheffield. J. F. BRIDGE, *rev.* PAUL JAMES NUNN

Sources A. J. Grant, *Steel and ships: the history of John Brown's* (1950) • *DNB* • P. Nunn, 'Ellis, Sir William Henry', *DBB* • C. J. Erickson, *British*

industrialists: steel and hosiery, 1850–1950 (1959) • D. L. Burn, *The economic history of steelmaking, 1867–1939* (1940) • L. du Garde Peach, *The Company of Cutlers in Hallamshire in the county of York, 1906–56* (1960) • S. Pollard and P. Robertson, *The British shipbuilding industry, 1870–1914* (1979) • *Alpine Journal*, 55 (1945), 208–10 • *The Engineer* (13 July 1945) • *Engineering* (13 July 1945)
Archives Sheff. Arch., newspaper cuttings relating to Sheffield
Likenesses A. Hackor, portrait, Sheffield Hallamshire Hospital; copy, Inst. CE • E. Moore, oils, NPG [*see illus.*] • photograph, repro. in *Alpine Journal*
Wealth at death £149,301 10s. 2d.: probate, 22 Sept 1945, *CGPLA Eng. & Wales*

Ellis, William Webb (1807–1872), Church of England clergyman and supposed originator of rugby, was born in Manchester in November 1807, the younger of two sons of James Ellis (*d.* 1811), soldier, who had married Ann Webb at St Peter's, Exeter, in 1804. His father, an ensign in the 1st dragoon guards, served in Ireland in 1807, moved to the regimental depot in Manchester in 1808, then proceeded to the Peninsular War in 1809. On 14 September 1809, he bought a commission in the 3rd dragoon guards for £735. He was killed in the battle of Albuera on 16 May 1811, and was commended for gallantry.

William Webb Ellis himself would probably have been forgotten were it not for the claim that, in 1823, 'with a fine disregard for the rules of football as played in his time [he] first took the ball in his arms and ran with it'. A stone, which was set in a wall at Rugby School in February 1900, thus commemorates this act. It is because of this supposed action that any details of Ellis's life are known.

Ellis was at Rugby School from 1816 to 1825. All the indications are that, if not unpopular, he was at least an 'outsider'. He was a 'town-boy' and a foundationer and, as such, received free education at Rugby, his mother having been left 'totally unprovided for' by his father's death. She applied for a pension and was granted £10 for each child. His father did not attain any great rank and was of limited means. The purchase of his commission probably used up most of his capital. The fathers of most of the boys at Rugby in Ellis's time were members of the clergy, gentry, and aristocracy. It seems highly improbable that they would have been influenced by the actions of a social inferior, either on the football field or elsewhere.

On leaving school, aged eighteen, Ellis was admitted at Brasenose College, Oxford, in 1825, his expenses being partly met by scholarships and, from 1828, a Hulme exhibition. He won a cricket 'blue'—although this term was not used then—in 1827, batting number 3 against Cambridge and scoring 12 runs. He also, 'in the best traditions of Rugby football', wrote a poem on beer ('Brasenose Ale', 1828), although no copies of this appear to have survived. He graduated BA in 1829 and proceeded MA in 1831. After leaving Oxford, he entered the church, and was minister of St George's, Albemarle Street, London, from 1836 until 1855. He was rector of St Clement Danes (1836–1855), where the Royal Air Force Rugby Football Union later erected a tablet to his memory. During the last seventeen years of his life he was rector of Laver Magdalen (now Magdalen Laver) in Essex. He never married.

William Webb Ellis (1807–1872), by unknown engraver, pubd 1854 (after Richard Beard)

The only known portrait of Ellis is a daguerreotype published in the *Illustrated London News* (24, 1854, 400) following a sermon he preached during the Crimean War. He had established something of a reputation for himself in London as an evangelical clergyman, bolstered by such publications as *A Concise View of Prophecy which Relates to the Messiah* (1832), *Sermons at St. George's* (1838), and *Dangerous Errors of Romanism* (1853), and he was classified in 1844 as one of the low-church clergy in London who 'abhor[red] the Tractarian heresy' (Bodl. Oxf., MS Add C.290, fol. 17). This reputation probably explains the interest taken in his Crimean War sermon.

Ellis apparently lived a comfortable life and on his death at Menton, Alpes Maritimes, France, on 24 January 1872, left £9000, subsequently divided among a variety of charitable causes, including the Society for the Rescue of Young Women and Children. The residue went to the widow of his brother Thomas. Little was known about his death until October 1959, when his grave was traced to a cemetery in Menton. The French rugby union, apparently delighted that the 'founder' of the game was buried in France, renovated the grave, at le cimetière du vieux château at Menton, which was visited by their president, the French captain, and a brass band.

Many people argue that the story of Ellis's act in 1823 is a myth, although Macrory, in 1991, remained convinced that Ellis picked up the ball and ran with it. However, it hardly matters whether he did or not, for this practice was not immediately adopted in 1823 but was gradually institutionalized over the following thirty years. Furthermore, it was also in the second quarter of the nineteenth century that rugby acquired such distinctive features as an oval ball, H-shaped goals, scoring above the cross bar, and points for 'tries' as well as 'goals'. Thus, in focusing solely on the development of carrying, the Ellis story fails to explain all aspects of the emerging uniqueness of the game.

Significantly, Ellis was never interviewed about his claimed role in the development of rugby football and died in 1872 apparently unaware of his 'fame'. The story was first advanced in 1876 by the antiquarian Matthew Holbeche Bloxam, who was responding to a series of letters in the London *Standard* newspaper by Old Rugbeians reminiscing about their game, which was gaining in popularity at the time. One correspondent had suggested that the Rugby game was simply a refinement of the ancient game of English football, seemingly implying—correctly—that the transition from traditional folk-football had been a gradual development over the years and not the reaction to a particular revolutionary event. Bloxam objected to this version of events, claiming that the distinctive Rugby game was not played at the school when he was there from 1813 to 1821. Shortly afterwards, in a letter to the Rugby School magazine, *Meteor* (10 Oct 1876, 528), Bloxam 'ascertained' that 'in the second half of 1824' Ellis had caught the ball and run with it. In 1880 Bloxam, again writing in *Meteor* (22 Dec 1880, 155–6), but this time responding to a recent leader in *The Times* about differences between the rules of the rugby union and association football games, changed this date to 1823 and provided further biographical information about Ellis which helped consolidate the story. Nevertheless, the supposed contribution of William Webb Ellis to rugby football remained little known outside Rugby School and indeed a history of football, co-authored by J. E. Vincent and Montague Shearman in 1885, made no mention of him, and nor did Shearman's book in the popular Badminton Library series *Athletics and Football* (1889) or the Revd Frank Marshall's book *Football: the Rugby Union Game* (1892).

Bloxam's account would probably have faded into obscurity but for circumstances affecting the game's development in the 1890s. By then, rugby union had spread to northern England and begun to emerge as a commercial spectacle, with players and spectators drawn principally from the working class. This process was conducive to conflict and led, in 1895, to a split between the Rugby Football Union and the Northern Union, which later became the Rugby League. The year 1895 also saw the appointment of a subcommittee of the Old Rugbeian Society to inquire into the origins of the game. It published its report in 1897 and accredited the emergence of a distinctive game to William Webb Ellis, resurrecting Bloxam's account as supporting 'evidence'. Revealingly, the commemorative stone was ordered from a local stonemason before all the evidence had been gathered in or the report completed. By giving pride of place in their report to the Ellis story, which correctly located the beginnings of rugby football in their school, the Old Rugbeians were attempting, it has been suggested, to reassert their proprietorship of the rugby game at a time when it was escaping their control and changing in ways of which they disapproved. As Baker put it: 'The mythological explanation of the origins of Rugby football provides historians with a valuable clue to the mind and spirit of late-Victorian England, not to the early nineteenth century beginnings of the game. The two should not be confused' (Baker, 130).

K. G. Sheard

Sources K. G. Sheard, 'Rugby football: a study in developmental sociology', MPhil diss., University of Leicester, 1972 • E. Dunning and K. Sheard, *Barbarians, gentlemen and players: a sociological study of the development of rugby football* (1979) • U. A. Titley and R. McWhirter, *Centenary history of the Rugby Football Union* (1970), 27– 38 • J. Macrory, *Running with the ball: the birth of rugby football* (1991) • Old Rugbeians' Society, *Report of the subcommittee on the origin of rugby football* (1897) • W. J. Baker, 'William Webb Ellis and the origins of rugby football: the life and death of a Victorian myth', *Albion*, 13 (1981), 117–30 • Boase, *Mod. Eng. biog.* • Foster, *Alum. Oxon.* • [C. B. Heberden], ed., *Brasenose College register, 1509–1909*, 2 vols., OHS, 55 (1909)

Archives Rugby School, Warwickshire

Likenesses engraving (after daguerreotype by R. Beard), NPG; repro. in *ILN* (29 April 1854), 400 [*see illus.*]

Wealth at death under £9000: probate, 10 Feb 1872, *CGPLA Eng. & Wales*

Ellis, Wynne (1790–1875), haberdasher and art collector, was born at Oundle, Northamptonshire, in July 1790, the son of Thomas Ellis, who traced his ancestry to the Ellises of mid-Wales, and his wife, Elizabeth, *née* Ordway. He received a good education, then went to London, where in 1812 he became a haberdasher, hosier, and mercer, at 16 Ludgate Street, in the City of London. Here he gradually took over other firms to create the largest silk business in London, moving to wholesale trade as Everington, Ellis & Co., warehousemen, from about 1830. He retired from business in 1871. He also purchased the leases of numerous residential and commercial properties in the most fashionable parts of the West End. He married in 1814 Mary Maria (*d.* 1872), daughter of John and Mary Smith of Lincoln.

In 1831 Ellis contested the parliamentary seat of Leicester, holding it as an advanced Liberal from 4 May 1831 to 29 December 1834, and again from 22 March 1839 to 23 July 1847. He wielded considerable influence in the House of Commons committees, advocating total repeal of the corn laws, and supporting free trade, reform of the bankruptcy laws, and greater freedom in the laws of partnership. He purchased the manor of Ponsbourne Park, Hertfordshire, in 1836, but sold it in May 1875. In the same county, he restored the Brocket family chapel of St Etheldreda in Bishop's Hatfield. He was a JP for Hertfordshire, where he also served as sheriff in 1851–2, and for Kent, where he was selected for sheriff but excused from having to serve a second time.

Although fond of sports, Ellis had an intense dislike of betting, horseracing, and gambling. He was a passionate collector of pictures, with an extensive collection of furniture and other fine art. The pictures were variable in quality, as Ellis did not rely on his own judgement and was sometimes badly advised. Otherwise moderate and simple in his habits, his preferred method of dispensing charity during his lifetime was to employ needy people rather than simply handing out cash. He was a fluent talker and a good listener, a man of vigorous intellect, strong-willed and of determined character.

Ellis's wife died in 1872 and was buried in a mausoleum designed by E. M. Barry and built in Whitstable churchyard. Near this, Ellis erected almshouses in her memory. He died at his London house, 30 Cadogan Place, Knightsbridge, on 20 November 1875, and was buried with his wife at Whitstable. By his will, Ellis left numerous legacies to schools, hospitals, and homes for the sick, also £50,000 to the Simeon fund for church patronage. He offered his pictures to the nation, from which ninety-four, principally those by Dutch and Flemish masters, were selected for the National Gallery, London. In April 1876 the sale of his leases, worth some £5000 per annum and disposed of in twenty-five lots, attracted a large gathering. The remainder of his pictures, together with the drawings, porcelain, decorative furniture, and marbles, were sold by auction at Christies in May, June, and July 1876, fetching over £56,000.   G. C. BOASE, rev. ANITA MCCONNELL

Sources *Warehousemen and Drapers' Trade Journal* (27 Nov 1875), 618 · *Warehousemen and Drapers' Trade Journal* (11 Dec 1875), 641 · *Warehousemen and Drapers' Trade Journal* (25 Dec 1875), 660 · *The Athenaeum* (4 Dec 1875), 756–7 · *Annual Register* (1875), 150–51 · *Annual Register* (1876), 402–3 · *ILN* (8 Jan 1876), 35, 37–8 · *ILN* (13 May 1876), 475 · *ILN* (20 May 1876), 500 · *ILN* (3 June 1876), 500 · *The Times* (25 Nov 1875), 11f · *The Times* (27 April 1876), 11d · J. E. Cussans, *History of Hertfordshire*, 2/3 (1874); facs. repr. (1972), 270, 276 · Burke, *Gen. GB* · *CGPLA Eng. & Wales* (1875)
Likenesses J. E. Boehm, marble bust, Tate collection · bust, Tate collection · wood-engraving, repro. in *ILN* (8 Jan 1876), 38
Wealth at death under £600,000: probate, 31 Dec 1875, *CGPLA Eng. & Wales*

Ellison, Gerald Alexander (1910–1992), bishop of London, was born on 19 August 1910 at the vicarage, 9 Park Street, New Windsor, Berkshire, in the family of three sons and two daughters of the Revd John Henry Joshua Ellison (1855–1944), Church of England clergyman, and his second wife, Sara Dorothy Graham, daughter of Walter Ewing Crum. He was named Gerald Crum Ellison at birth, but shortly afterwards the middle name Alexander was substituted for Crum. He had a half-brother by his father's first marriage, to a daughter of Archbishop Tait. At the time of his birth his father was, and had been since 1894, vicar of Windsor (as his father, Canon Ellison, founder of the Church of England Temperance Society, had been), but from 1913 he was rector of St Michael Cornhill. He was at various times chaplain to Queen Victoria, King Edward VII, archbishops Tait and Davidson, the London stock exchange, and the lord mayor of London.

Ellison was educated at St George's choir school, Windsor, where the foundations were laid of his lifelong love of music and his very considerable expertise, and he always retained his love of the chapel. From there he went to Westminster School, where he learned to row. At New College, Oxford, he was soon a member of the Oxford boat. He rowed in the university races of 1932 and 1933, but stood down in 1934, when he was president, due to lack of form. He retained his lifelong association with rowing and on occasion umpired the boat race and judged at Henley regatta. He graduated with a third-class degree in politics, philosophy, and economics in 1932. He then went to Westcott House, Cambridge, and was ordained deacon in 1935 and priest in 1936.

From 1935 to 1937 Ellison was curate at Sherborne Abbey. From there he went to be chaplain to Cyril Garbett, bishop of Winchester. On the outbreak of the Second World War he volunteered at once for the navy and left Winchester at Christmas 1939, as Garbett recorded in his diary: 'he has been a first-rate chaplain … and will go a long way if life and health are spared. I shall miss him terribly' (Garbett diaries, York Minster Library, COLL/82/5). In the navy he was chaplain to the battleship *Barham* in the Mediterranean, but after a disagreement with the captain over some alterations to divine service, he was posted to the cruiser *Orion*, on which he took part in the battle of Cape Matapan, and was mentioned in dispatches. His firmness over the incident on *Barham* probably saved his life, for she was subsequently sunk with great loss of life, including that of his successor.

In 1943 Garbett, who by then had become archbishop of York, obtained Ellison's release from the navy, and he went to Bishopthorpe as chaplain. Although he spent only three years there, they were very important, one might say seminal, in his development, and years later when bishop of London he could introduce himself in the vestry of St Paul's to Archbishop Runcie's chaplain with: 'I am the life-president of the Slope club' (a reference to the Revd Obadiah Slope, chaplain to Dr Proudie, Trollopian bishop of Barchester). It was not an easy appointment, as Garbett was a very different bishop from his predecessor, William Temple, and Ellison had to use all his tact in interpreting the new archbishop to a bewildered and sometimes unhappy diocese. The courage which he had displayed in standing up to the captain of *Barham* was also called for in standing up to the archbishop, who could sometimes be somewhat overbearing.

From Bishopthorpe Ellison went in 1946 to St Mark's, Portsea. While there he married, on 18 June 1947, Jane Elizabeth, the daughter of Brigadier John Houghton Gibbon, army officer. She became one of the pillars of his life. They had two daughters and a son. St Mark's was at that time almost the next step to a bishopric, and it was no surprise when in 1950 he was appointed suffragan of Willesden in the diocese of London, and after five years there became bishop of Chester in 1955. Many thought that he would proceed to Lambeth, but preferment at all levels in the Church of England is very much a matter of luck and politics, and he remained at Chester for the next eighteen years.

While bishop of Chester, Ellison played a leading role in the church assembly during the debates on the Paul report (drawn up by the distinguished sociologist Leslie Paul), which he saw as destroying the parochial system in the Church of England. He was largely responsible for its rejection. It was soon a moot point whether he was right, for within twenty years the situation had changed out of all recognition, and it is not clear to what extent Paul's suggested reforms would have been of any great help. While bishop of Chester, Ellison also chaired the Archbishop's Commission on Women and Holy Orders (1963–6), and although women had nearly thirty years to wait before they could be ordained in the Church of England, he was convinced that it was right, a view from which he never wavered.

In 1973 Ellison moved to London as its bishop, remaining there until his retirement in 1981. He was concurrently dean of the chapels royal, prelate of the Order of the British Empire, and episcopal canon of Jerusalem. As bishop of London he made a series of appointments which proved that he was not the arch-conservative that he was so often believed to be. Two of his suffragans were committed socialists, and all three of his appointments subsequently became diocesans. His lasting memorial in London was the area system, which he started to work on almost as soon as he arrived; with, at that time, more than five hundred parishes, the diocese was too large for one bishop, so he devolved a substantial amount of power to the five suffragans, and was scrupulous in not interfering with their decisions. He played a key role at the church commissioners, where he usually took the chair when the archbishop was not able to be present. He also became the spokesman for all church legislative matters in the House of Lords, where his meticulous preparation and grasp of detail made a great contribution. He was a uniquely respected figure there, and there was some talk of a life peerage when he retired, but lack of precedent was too strong; instead he was appointed KCVO. In the synod he became a more and more important figure, and his magisterial speeches, delivered in his strong firm voice, and not without humour, carried great weight; he played a particularly important role in the passage of the Worship and Doctrine Measure, 1975, paving the way for liturgical reform. With all this he also had a deep pastoral side to his character; as Lady Du Cann noted, 'he practised the Good Samaritan' (*The Times*, 6 Nov 1992).

After Ellison's retirement in 1981 the archbishop of Canterbury asked him to go to Bermuda as vicar-general, to set up a new constitution for the diocese. This he did with his usual efficiency and dispatch. He retired to Cerne Abbas, Dorset, and took an active part in local affairs until the onset of his final illness, which dragged on for several years. He died of cancer at his home, Billeys House, 16 Long Street, Cerne Abbas, Dorchester, Dorset, on 18 October 1992. He was survived by his wife and their three children. A memorial service was held at St Paul's Cathedral on 8 December 1992. DEREK HAYWARD

Sources *The Independent* (20 Oct 1992) · *The Times* (22 Oct 1992) · *The Times* (6 Nov 1992) · *The Times* (9 Dec 1992) · *WWW*, 1991–5 · personal knowledge (2004) · private information (2004) · b. cert. · m. cert. · d. cert.
Archives LPL, corresp. and papers · St George's Chapel, Windsor, papers | SOUND BL NSA, Bow dialogues, 12 Nov 1974, C812/41 C8
Likenesses photograph, 1973, repro. in *The Independent* · photograph, repro. in *The Times* (22 Oct 1992) · photograph, Hult. Arch.
Wealth at death £60,665: probate, 18 Dec 1992, *CGPLA Eng. & Wales*

Ellison, Sir Gerald Francis (1861–1947), army officer, was born on 18 August 1861, the second son of Canon Henry John Ellison (1813–1899) and his wife, Mary Dorothy (*née* Jebb). He was educated at Marlborough College and entered the army in 1882. He passed out from the Staff College, Camberley, in 1889, thereafter holding a series of staff appointments at the War Office and at Aldershot. On 3 January 1894 he married Lilian Amy (1861/2–1949?), only child of Colonel Robert Bruce. They had a son and a daughter. For his services in South Africa during the Second South African War, Ellison was mentioned in dispatches

and awarded the queen's medal with four clasps. He had earlier advertised his status as an outstanding 'thinking' soldier by the publication of a book, *Home Defence* (1896), which in the previous year had won the gold medal of the Royal United Services Institution.

The defeats and disappointments of the British army at the hands of the Boers prompted a long-overdue radical examination of the army and a series of recommendations for its reform. Ellison played an important part in this exercise, demonstrating outstanding gifts as an administrator. A three-man committee comprising Lord Esher, Admiral Fisher, and Sir George Clarke (later Lord Sydenham) was constituted in November 1903 and given the task of reorganizing the War Office. Ellison was appointed the committee's secretary. In four months the committee produced a whole series of far-reaching recommendations. Clarke, who was later to criticize Ellison, acknowledged the secretary's outstanding contribution to the committee's report. Even more interestingly, R. B. Haldane was to write that 'he recognized [Ellison's] hand in much of the Report' (Haldane, 184). When Haldane was appointed secretary of state for war in the Liberal government in December 1905, Esher counted it 'a great stroke' (*Journals and Letters*, 2.126) that they had 'nobbled' the minister by persuading him to appoint Ellison as his principal private secretary. Ellison held the post until 1908.

Historians have speculated and disagreed about the precise degree of influence that Ellison exercised over Haldane, and how much he was responsible for the form and content of Haldane's army reforms of 1906–7. Haldane stated in *An Autobiography* (1929) that when first he became minister for war, he was 'instructed' by Ellison. Also, that Ellison was 'one of those who co-operated in advising me' in fashioning the reforms (Haldane, 184, 189). But neither Ellison in his memoirs nor Haldane suggested that the reforms were based upon ideas supplied by Ellison. This claim was made by Clarke in a letter to Esher: 'the whole scheme is from Ellison's book' (21 March 1906, Esher MSS). Haldane, in a letter to his mother, had described his exact working method. Ellison, he stated, was 'an enthusiastic convert to my scheme of reform' and was 'working out the details' from notes supplied by Haldane (29 Jan 1906, Haldane MS 5875, fol. 37). On the available evidence, the fairest conclusion would seem to be that Haldane emphasized the political primacy of economy in his reform measures, which Ellison acknowledges, but 'undoubtedly, in a two-way flow of opinions, both men were influenced by each other' (Spiers, 77).

After leaving Haldane, for the next three years (1908–11) Ellison served as director of army organization at the War Office. Then he was appointed to the staff of General Sir Ian Hamilton, the inspector general of overseas forces, a position Ellison held until the outbreak of the First World War. Hamilton commented with obvious satisfaction on how the two men 'worked hand in glove … our qualities usefully complement one another' (Hamilton, 1.7). It was natural that, when Hamilton was given the command of the Dardanelles expedition, he should have asked for the services of Ellison. He needed 'an organizer of outstanding calibre' and 'a real business man at the head of our mission' (ibid., 1.280, 2.6). Typically, Kitchener insisted that Ellison could not be spared from staff work at home, but later relented.

The failure of the Dardanelles campaign did not hinder Ellison's career as an outstanding staff officer. With the substantive rank of major-general he served first at Aldershot from 1916 to 1917 and later at the War Office as deputy quartermaster general and inspector of general communications. In 1923 he was promoted lieutenant-general. His service was recognized by a series of decorations: CB (1904), CMG (1916), KCMG (1919), and KCB (1922). He retired from the army in 1925, shortly thereafter publishing a second book, *The Perils of Amateur Strategy* (1926). His costive and discreet 'Reminiscences' appeared in thirty parts over an eight-year period in the *Lancashire Lad* (1931–9), the journal of the Loyal regiment (North Lancashire), of which he was appointed colonel in 1926.

Ellison, who had been a Royal United Services Institution trustee since 1920, made his home at Canons House, Canon Street, Taunton, where, on 28 October 1947 he died of cerebral thrombosis, at the age of eighty-six. Ellison was no flamboyant character. It was his professional competence that inspired the respect and affection of his peers. The importance of the contribution he made to the improvement of the British army in the decade before the First World War deserves to be acknowledged.

A. J. A. MORRIS

Sources 'Reminiscences of Lt. Gen. Sir Gerald Ellison KCB, KCMG', *Lancashire Lad* (1931–99) [in 30 pts] · WWW · E. M. Spiers, *Haldane: an army reformer* (1980) · m. cert. · d. cert. · R. B. Haldane, *An autobiography* (1929) · *Journals and letters of Reginald, Viscount Esher*, ed. M. V. Brett and Oliver, Viscount Esher, 4 vols. (1934–8) · I. Hamilton, *Gallipoli diary*, 2 vols. (1920) · Venn, *Alum. Cant.* · CAC Cam., Esher MSS · NL Scot., Haldane MSS · Kelly, *Handbk* · CGPLA Eng. & Wales (1948)
Archives NAM, corresp. and papers | CAC Cam., Esher MSS · NL Scot., Haldane MSS | FILM IWM FVA, documentary footage
Likenesses F. A. Swaine, photograph, repro. in Hamilton, *Gallipoli diary*, 2.6 · photograph, repro. in *The Times history of the War*, 22 vols. (1914–21), 6.89
Wealth at death £7893 1s. 5d.: probate, 10 Jan 1948, CGPLA Eng. & Wales

Ellison, Thomas (1833–1904), historian and statistician of the cotton trade, was born in Liverpool, possibly the son of Joseph Ellison, bookkeeper. He left school at sixteen and was apprenticed to Maurice Williams (1825–1878), who had himself just begun business as a cotton broker. Ellison's first task was to meet the incoming mailboat from America, and to help in compiling the summaries of the market reports and crop advices. He also drew up much of the reports themselves, which formed the core of the weekly cotton circulars issued by the firm to its clients in the inland spinning towns. Thus was he introduced to what became his life's work. He worked thirteen hours a day for six days a week, and devoted his leisure to a systematic investigation of the production and consumption

of cotton in the world, acquiring an incomparable knowledge of the trade. In 1854 he became a salesman, remaining with the firm for a further ten years.

Handbooks of the cotton trade From 1858 Ellison began to publish studies of the cotton trade. The immediate stimulus was supplied by the close of a long period of declining prices and the onset of a new trend of rising prices, which doubled between 1848 and 1857. The cotton dearth of 1857 threatened to curtail further expansion in the staple trade of Liverpool and inspired Ellison's detailed investigation of possible sources of supply. His *Handbook of the Cotton Trade* (1858), comprising sections on cotton cultivation and cotton consumption, was a pioneer work of reference for a trade whose growth had been 'the most extraordinary phenomenon of modern industry', and whose prosperity was 'unparalleled in the history of the world's industry' (Ellison, vii, 149). Ellison's achievement was given immediate recognition: he was elected a fellow of the Statistical Society in 1859. The second section of the book included a study of the industry in eleven states of continental Europe. In brevity and comprehension it constituted a virtual 'handbook to the cotton trade of the world' (*The Times*, 7 Oct 1858). It was freely used in the *Dictionnaire du commerce* (1859) and was translated into German by Bernhard Noest for publication in 1860, with four later editions by 1884. No other British writer on the subject secured such extensive and prolonged recognition in Europe. Ellison emphasized the pernicious influence of slavery upon the progress of the southern states and, for Lancashire, the essential insecurity of a slave-produced supply of cotton. In two of his predictions, however, he was mistaken. He believed that India rather than Egypt offered the sole source of immediate relief from the threat of a cotton dearth and that India would replace the USA as the main source of supply. During the cotton famine of 1861–5 Egypt surprised Lancashire as much as India disappointed it. Ellison also assumed that the cotton industry would progress indefinitely at the rate of increase manifest before the 1840s, whereas ever since the 1840s it had been expanding faster in the world outside Lancashire.

Study of slavery In 1861 Ellison published *Slavery and Secession in America*, a more remarkable work than his handbook. Appearing seven weeks after the outbreak of hostilities in the United States, it undertook a detailed study of the history of slavery, the history of the secession movement and the social and economic structures of the two warring sections. Ellison sympathized with the cause of the north and blamed the revolt of the southern states solely upon the institution of slavery. As a moderate abolitionist, he recommended the gradual emancipation of the slaves and their transformation into free labourers, hired by contract and paid at piece-rates on the Lancashire pattern. Above all, he examined the prospects which the civil war would open up for the cotton trade. He recognized that the loss of the American crop would entail serious consequences to 'Manchester'. But he believed that the effect upon Britain would be temporary, and soon remedied by the increase in supplies from other quarters, especially Africa. On the other hand the effect upon the USA would, he thought, be permanent because once the cotton trade was lost it would never again be restored to the influential position it had obtained in 1860. That prophecy proved to be fundamentally mistaken on both counts, as Ellison himself later recognized. During the cotton famine in Lancashire other producers failed to fill the gap left by the USA, making up by 1864 less than half of the deficit. The average price attained by raw cotton in 1860 was not touched again until 1876. Not merely did the USA re-establish its position as the world's leading producer and exporter, but it also enhanced and extended its supremacy for a further thirty years by incorporating Texas into the cotton kingdom of the south. *The Times* afforded the book a three-column review, approving Ellison's facts but declining to endorse 'his liberal vaticinations' (*The Times*, 16 Aug 1861). The author's strong literary tastes predisposed him to journalism. He founded his own periodical, characteristically entitled *The Exchange*, which survived for eleven monthly issues from April 1862 until February 1863. He became a valued contributor to the local press, writing in succession for the *Liverpool Journal* (1862–4), the *Liverpool Daily Albion* (1866–75), and the *Liverpool Daily Post* (1875–1904). From 1862 he compiled the statistics of cotton afloat for the weekly circular of the associated cotton brokers and his cotton trade circulars were first cited by Board of Trade officials ('Half-yearly report of Alexander Redgrave esq. inspector of factories, for the six months ended the 31st October 1863', 98–9, *Parl. papers*, 1864, 22.555–769). From 1864 the cotton brokers issued a weekly circular in a form settled by Ellison. From 1874, two years after the Atlantic telegraph cable was restored, they issued an official daily circular.

Brokerage operations The year 1864 marked the end of the era of rising prices and ushered in a new trend of declining prices, lasting until 1898. In the same year Ellison declined the offer of a partnership because he disliked the speculation to which Maurice Williams had become addicted. He established his own firm, and resolved to confine his operations to brokerage. He also began to issue his own monthly cotton report, which was precise and comprehensive. Time after time his estimates proved remarkably accurate. His circulars achieved the premier status in the trade of those published successively from 1805 by Samuel Hope, George Holt, Thomas Littledale, Daniel Buchanan, and, in 1861–4, Maurice Williams. From 1868 they were regularly quoted by *The Economist*, especially in its annual commercial review. They were supplemented from 1872 by regular monthly statistics relating to the continent. They were used by Isaac Watts in his article on 'Cotton' in the ninth edition (1877) of the *Encyclopaedia Britannica*. From 1875 Ellison undertook to continue the report issued at the end of each cotton season by Caspar Ott Trumpler (1802–1880) of Zürich, who had since 1842 been the cotton statistician of the world. His reports were based upon returns made in French and German as well as English from correspondents whose number increased to

some three to four hundred. Such a wide range of sources and close continuous contact with the largest cotton market in the world made his reports precise, accurate, and authoritative. They bore down the competition of all rivals and remained the premier reports upon the market for nearly forty years. They enhanced the status of the market and helped to reduce the mistrust of its reports engendered during the speculation of the 1860s, which had led to the passage of the Cotton Statistics Act 1868, at the insistence of Hugh Mason. Thus Ellison elaborated and perfected the statistical machinery of the cotton trade and catered to the interest of a wider public, becoming a consultant to foreign governments, and a contributor to the trade press of New York. In 1870 he became a 'country member' of the Manchester Royal Exchange.

In the 1880s Ellison wrote another series of statistical and biographical essays on the history and economy of the cotton trade. They were collected in *The Cotton Trade of Great Britain* (1886), which immediately became a standard work wherever cotton was spun. The book concentrated on Britain but set its subject in a broad comparative perspective. During the 1890s he wrote seven more essays on the history of the cotton industry in Egypt, Europe, the USA, India, and Japan. Therein he identified India as the most dangerous competitor of Lancashire, as he had in 1886, but he failed in 1895 to recognize the full potential capacity of Japan. Together those essays formed a study of the cotton trade of the world, broadly comparable in rigour of method and in insight to the work of 1886. The longest piece, a centennial history of the American cotton trade printed in 1892, was translated into German and published in 1895. He also contemplated but never produced a series of articles upon the cotton trade of each separate country on the continent, which he envisaged as a companion volume to that on Great Britain. Such national histories had already been included in the valuable series of articles on 'Cotton' which he wrote and regularly updated for six successive editions of *Chambers' Encyclopaedia* (1862–1908).

Final years and death A Liberal in politics and an Anglican in religion, Ellison set the seal on his success in business by transferring his residence in 1888 across the Mersey to West Kirby in the Wirral. During his business career of fifty-five years (1849–1904) the consumption of cotton in the world quintupled but only trebled in Britain, reflecting the slower growth of Lancashire. His lifetime coincided with the golden age of his native city: Liverpool became the seat of one of the most highly developed commodity markets in the world. Its municipal area quadrupled and its trade quintupled. It was the second most populous city and the country's leading port of export. That saga of progress was faithfully chronicled in Ellison's posthumously published reminiscences, which made a notable contribution to the topographical and biographical history of the city and included a study of the corners of 1879–83 in the cotton market. On the completion of fifty years in the cotton market in 1899 he was presented with his portrait painted by R. E. Morrison, amid scenes of boisterous enthusiasm on the exchange (*Liverpool Daily*

Post, 3 Feb 1899). His sudden death at Hoscote Park, West Kirby, on 30 May 1904, at the age of seventy-two, caused considerable grief on the exchange, where the flag was hoisted at half-mast. He was buried on 1 June at West Kirby parish church. His estate amounted to £16,278 while Maurice Williams made and lost a fortune of £100,000, leaving on his death in 1878 under £200. Ellison's work has retained its value, unimpaired by the passage of time and unsullied by criticism. His 1886 book was reprinted in 1968 and 1999. His true intellectual heir was R. Robson, director of statistics for the Cotton Board established in 1940, whose *Cotton Industry in Britain* (1957) studied the British industry from an international perspective, and paid explicit homage to the work of his predecessor.

D. A. FARNIE

Sources D. A. Farnie, 'Three historians of the cotton industry', *Textile History*, 9 (1978), 75–9 · *Liverpool Daily Post* (31 May 1904) · T. Ellison, *Gleanings and reminiscences* (1905) · *Cotton Movement and Fluctuations*, 13–31 (1885–1903) · *CGPLA Eng. & Wales* (1904) · d. cert.
Likenesses portrait, repro. in W. W. Carson, *Sketches of life ... in Liverpool* (1875) · portrait, repro. in Ellison, *Gleanings and reminiscences*, frontispiece
Wealth at death £16,278 10s. 5d.: probate, 30 Aug 1904, *CGPLA Eng. & Wales*

Elliston, Henry Twissleton (*c.*1801–1864), organist, was the second son of the actor and theatre manager Robert William *Elliston (1774–1831) and his wife, Elizabeth Rundall (1774/5–1821). He spent most of his life at Leamington Spa, Warwickshire, where his father had previously leased the theatre. Having decided on music as his profession, he received a careful training and became a highly competent theoretical musician and an able performer on the organ and several other instruments. His father presented an organ to Leamington parish church, and Elliston was elected organist, a post he held until his death. He demonstrated considerable mechanical ingenuity in enlarging the organ, and also later invented a successful transposing piano. He was an early and active member of the choral society of Leamington Spa, during which time the society produced *Messiah* and similar works during a music festival lasting three days. Elliston was also responsible for the construction of the music-hall in Bath Street, and with his brother William Gore Elliston, who later emigrated to Australia, he established the later county library, which began on the site of Copp's Hotel before moving to the music-hall. While he and his brother were in partnership they produced many large-scale concerts. Elliston later became lessee of the Royal Assembly Rooms. Other than some popular church services, he composed little. In September 1863 he was appointed librarian of the free public library at Leamington Spa.

Elliston never married; he died from oedema and dropsy at Leamington Spa on 19 April 1864, and was buried in the town's cemetery.

GORDON GOODWIN, rev. DAVID J. GOLBY

Sources *GM*, 3rd ser., 16 (1864), 807–8 · *CGPLA Eng. & Wales* (1864)
Wealth at death under £200: administration, 8 Dec 1864, *CGPLA Eng. & Wales*

Elliston, Robert William (1774–1831), actor and theatre manager, was born on 7 April 1774 in Orange Street, London, the only child of Robert Elliston (*d.* 1799), a watchmaker, and his wife, *née* Martyn (*d.* 1798). Since his father was an alcoholic, Elliston was cared for by two uncles, Dr William Elliston, master of Sidney Sussex College, Cambridge, and Dr Thomas *Martyn, professor of botany, of the same college. Under their supervision he was educated at St Paul's School, London, where he took a special interest in oratory. It would appear that his uncles planned for him a career as a clergyman, and a critic was later to say that a capital parson was spoilt when Elliston turned player. But turn player he did, in the romantic style which also at this time made boys run away to sea. Having begun to take part in amateur theatricals in 1790, Elliston became stage-struck and early in 1791 ran away to Bath, where he made his first appearance at the Orchard Street Theatre on 14 April in the minor role of Tressel, in Cibber's version of *Richard III*. A recommendation followed to the well-known manager Tate Wilkinson, who had a touring company in Yorkshire, and on 30 May 1791 Elliston began a two-year apprenticeship during which he played forty-four roles in a repertory system calling for a nightly change of programme. He then returned to Bath and established himself as a versatile actor of the new romantic school, in both tragedy and comedy. At this time the theatre at Bath (joined up with Bristol) was justly famous. Jane Austen, who admired Elliston as actor, has left several indications in her novels of how important diversion and entertainment were in this elegant resort. Here Elliston settled and thrived until 1804. On 1 June 1796 he married Elizabeth Rundall (*b.* 1774/5), a dancing instructor, with whom he had ten children before she died in 1821. Through her dancing academy she helped Elliston's productions when he later became a theatre manager.

A leading actor in London On 20 September 1804 Elliston began as leading actor at Drury Lane. He had played successfully in London during the summers of 1796 and 1797, mainly at the Haymarket Theatre, run by the playwright George Colman, but wisely waited until his reputation was ripe before making a complete break with Bath and Bristol. Although he was versatile, Elliston's appearance was against him for the playing of tragedy, for his face was described as

> the very Mirror of Comedy. His countenance was round and open, his features small, yet highly expressive; laughter lay cradled in his eye, and there was a muscular play of lip, so pregnant of meaning, as frequently to leave the words that followed but little to explain.   (Raymond, *Memoirs*, 1.8)

He seems to have been best in the Charles Surface sort of role (Sheridan's *The School for Scandal*), rakish but generous and warm-hearted, versions of which were available by the score in the comedies of this era. He was known as a great lover on stage, just as he was a notorious womanizer off stage. Leigh Hunt has left an interesting analysis of Elliston's skill in this area, as displayed in James Kenney's now forgotten farce *Matrimony*, in which Elliston played opposite Dorothy Jordan in 1805: 'altogether the most

Robert William Elliston (1774–1831), by George Henry Harlow, in or before 1808

complete scene of amorous quarrel that I have witnessed' (Hunt, 190). In 1805 Elliston also played in his own adaptation of a French melodrama, *The Venetian Outlaw*, which revealed his skill in rapidly shifting from one role to another within the same play. Unfortunately for Elliston, 'Monk' Lewis brought out a more successful version of the same play at the rival Covent Garden; otherwise, he might have had a lasting hit.

When Drury Lane was destroyed by fire in 1809, Elliston looked around for new worlds to conquer and hit upon theatre management. Eventually known as 'the Great Lessee' and 'the Napoleon of the Theatre' for his interest in acquiring new property, he began with the Royal Circus in St George's Fields, which he transformed and managed for five years. At the same time he leased the Manchester Theatre Royal (1809–10), purchased Croydon (1810; it was seized by creditors in 1826), leased Birmingham (1813–18), to which he added Worcester and Shrewsbury (1815) to make up a circuit, purchased the Olympic Pavilion in London (1813), and leased Lynn (1817–18), Leicester, and Northampton (1818), Leamington (where he also had a lending library and assembly rooms, 1817; renegotiated 1819), and Coventry (1821). When he became the magisterial manager of Drury Lane in 1819 Elliston was king indeed, and was soon to play that role in his magnificent coronation spectacle of 1821. It was in the Leamington Library that Charles Lamb first met Elliston, who inspired two delightful essays of Elia. Lamb captured with loving precision Elliston's mixture of eccentricity and histrionic lordliness when he described meeting him in London in the autumn of 1819.

Grasping my hand with a look of significance, he only uttered, 'Have you heard the news?' Then with another look following up the blow, he subjoined, 'I am the future Manager of Drury Lane Theatre'. Breathless as he saw me, he stayed not for congratulation or reply, but mutely stalked away, leaving me to chew upon his new-blown dignities at leisure. In fact, nothing could be said to it. Expressive silence alone could muse his praise. This was in his *great* style. (Lamb, 'Ellistoniana', 110)

The monopoly question In undertaking management of the Royal Circus, which he renamed the Surrey Theatre, and subsequently undertaking the Olympic, Elliston was entering into a battle with the theatrical establishment over the so-called monopoly question. By law, only theatres with a royal patent were allowed to present drama as such on stage; all other theatres were confined to producing either mimes and ballets or else burlettas (rhymed comic pieces accompanied by music). It was not until 1843 that the laws conferring this monopoly on only three London theatres, Drury Lane, Covent Garden, and (for the summer months only) the Haymarket, were repealed, and free competitition was allowed. Then the bigger houses became homes of musical comedy, pantomime, and opera, while the smaller venues developed into either music-halls, centres for melodrama, or havens where Shakespeare's plays could be painstakingly staged. In Elliston's day all was in transition. His achievement as manager of 'minor' theatres was to show the absurdity of the monopoly laws and to prove how a minor theatre could actually achieve high standards of entertainment. Among his first productions at the Royal Circus, for example, in 1809, was an adaptation of *Macbeth* which kept to the strict letter of the law by containing only 326 lines of rhymed verse accompanied by music. Yet almost 50 per cent of Elliston's repertory at the Royal Circus between 1809 and 1814 consisted of adaptations of 'legitimate' plays. As manager of the Olympic Theatre in 1818 he effectively answered a series of charges made against him by Drury Lane and Covent Garden in *Copy of a Memorial Presented to the Lord Chamberlain* (1818). He then starred in a so-called burletta in three acts by Thomas Moncrieff, actually a fully fledged comedy in prose, *Rochester, or, King Charles the Second's Merry Days*, a very good example of Regency drama at its effervescent best. Although Elliston went rapidly into reverse on this question once he became manager of Drury Lane himself in 1819, and reminded smaller theatres of his monopoly, he ran the place in much the same way as he had managed the Surrey or the Olympic, with copious helpings of light opera, melodramas, farces, spectacular shows, and pantomimes, together with occasional Shakespearian productions, much 'puffed' (hyped) in characteristic style. When all failed and he was declared bankrupt in December 1826, Elliston again leased the Surrey Theatre, and from 1827 until his death in 1831 once again bent the monopoly laws in his own favour. It can be claimed that the select committee of the House of Commons which in 1832 sat to enquire into the state of English theatre might have learned from Elliston's experiments the folly of continuing the old restrictions. To be sure, Elliston as a true-blue tory was no reformer and belongs firmly rather to the old Georgian era than to the new age of reform; yet in spite of his naked opportunism, he proved that the old theatrical arrangements were in mutation towards more spectacular and at the same time more democratic cultural forms.

Performing Shakespeare and Byron While manager of Drury Lane, Elliston came close to showing that Shakespeare spelt bankruptcy and Byron ruin. At first, he thought he could make a contribution by providing historically correct costumes and settings for *Richard III*, *Coriolanus*, and *King Lear* in 1819 and 1820. But this proved a thankless undertaking, even with the great Edmund Kean at his disposal. Kean was, however, successful in *Lear*, now allowed for the first time following the death of mad King George III, but even Kean soon felt the need of the risqué afterpiece *Giovanni in London* in support. Shakespeare's plays were no draw unless there was a brilliant farce or spectacular melodrama or pantomime as backup. Moreover, the famous writers of the day were unable or unwilling to write for the stage. Elliston, who had played in Coleridge's *Remorse* at Drury Lane in 1813, tried in vain to coax scripts from Walter Scott and Thomas Moore, the most popular novelist and poet at the time, and had to turn away the unsuitable submissions of Keats and Shelley. Byron was perhaps the most promising playwright among the romantic poets after Coleridge, but he did not want his works staged. On 25 April 1821, nevertheless, Elliston presented Byron's *Marino Falieri* at Drury Lane by a characteristic piece of sharp practice. Some days before publication, he obtained a copy from the publisher's office and with feverish haste, because Covent Garden was also interested, 'got up' a production, obtained the necessary licence from the lord chamberlain's office, and rushed the play on stage, Byron's injunction notwithstanding. Had Kean been available to play the lead *Marino Falieri* might have been a hit—for this was an age of the actor, not the playwright—but since he was not, the play lasted only seven nights and drew poor houses each time. The critics agreed with Byron's preface that the play was unsuited to the stage, but the real explanation was that the current taste for spectacular action was romantic where Byron's style was classical. As Byron himself put it, in words which clearly explain the impossibility of Elliston's general task:

It is too regular—the time, twenty-four hours—the change of place not frequent—nothing melodramatic—no surprises, no starts, nor trapdoors, nor opportunities, 'for tossing their heads and kicking their heels'—and no *love*—the grand ingredient of a modern play. (*Letters and Journals of Lord Byron*, ed. T. Moore, 3 vols., 1833, 3.102–3)

During his reign at Drury Lane Elliston had many successes with spectacular melodramas, operas, and pantomimes (complete with the latest invention, the diorama), but with not a single new 'legitimate' play of any significance. Theatre, not drama, and novelty of every kind were what the public now demanded, and Elliston was caught on the horns of this dilemma.

Last years Following a severe stroke in August 1825, by which time the alcoholic Elliston was but a shadow of his former self, his place as manager was taken by his eldest son, William Gore Elliston, who formed a successful partnership with his brother, Henry Twissleton *Elliston. He returned to the stage, however, to create his last original role, Falstaff in *The First Part of King Henry IV*, in May 1826. As sometimes happens, he was brilliant in the final rehearsal but unable to reproduce that quality in public. Having lost Drury Lane but partially regained his health, Elliston finished his days as manager of the Surrey, where he trod the boards as of yore. There he acted Falstaff again with supreme effect.

We fear that few, very few, critics crossed the bridge to see the fat knight, which, it is our faith, was the highest triumph of Elliston as an actor, inasmuch as it combined, heightened, and enriched all the qualities which he severally displayed in other parts,

enthused the *New Monthly Magazine* in 1836. At the Surrey, too, Elliston had a major hit with Douglas Jerrold's nautical melodrama *Black-Eyed Susan* (1829), which ran for 208 performances in just over a year. His last appearance was as Sheva in Cumberland's *The Jew*, one of his most popular characters, on 24 June 1831. Two weeks later, on 8 July 1831, Elliston died of 'apoplexy', presumably a cerebral haemorrhage, and was buried at St John's Church, Waterloo Road.

CHRISTOPHER MURRAY

Sources G. Raymond, *Memoirs of Robert William Elliston, comedian*, 2 vols. (1844–5) · C. Lamb, 'To the shade of Elliston', *The dramatic essays of Charles Lamb*, ed. B. Matthews (1891) · C. Lamb, 'Ellistoniana', *The dramatic essays of Charles Lamb*, ed. B. Matthews (1891) · C. Murray, *Robert William Elliston, manager* (1975) · L. Hunt, *Critical essays on the performers of the London theatres* (1807) · E. B. Watson, *Sheridan to Robertson* (1926) · W. Nicholson, *The struggle for a free stage in London* (1906) · G. Raymond, *The life and enterprises of Robert William Elliston, comedian* (1857) · W. C. Russell, *Representative actors* [1888] · *Drury Lane journal: selections from James Winston's diaries, 1819–1827*, ed. A. L. Nelson and G. B. Cross (1974) · M. J. Wood, *The descendants of Robert William Elliston* (1996) · *Oxberry's Dramatic Biography*, 3/37 (1825), 73–90

Archives BL, MSS · Harvard TC, MSS | BL, Drury Lane memoranda

Likenesses G. H. Harlow, oils, in or before 1808, NPG [*see illus.*] · C. Turner, mezzotint, pubd 1808 (after G. H. Harlow), BM, NPG · A. Cardon, stipple, pubd 1810 (after W. M. Bennett), BM, NPG · West, 1821 (as George IV), V&A, Enthoven collection · W. Sheldrick, lithograph, pubd 1823 (after E. H. Lambert), NPG · T. Wageman, 1826 (as Falstaff) · S. De Wilde, oils (as Duke Aranza in *The honey moon*), Garr. Club · J. W. Gear, lithograph (after his portrait), NPG · G. H. Harlow, oils, second version, Garr. Club · G. H. Harlow, pencil and sanguine drawing, Garr. Club · W. Ridley, stipple (after S. Drummond), BM, NPG; repro. in *Monthly Mirror* (1796) · H. Singleton, oils (as Octavian in *The mountaineers*), Garr. Club

Ellman, John (1753–1832), agriculturist, was born at Hartfield, Sussex, on 17 October 1753, son of Richard and Elizabeth Ellman. His father, who was an established grazier at Hartfield, removed to Place Farm, Glynde, in 1761. Ellman was educated at the village school in Hartfield and by the vicar of Glynde. On his father's death in 1780 Ellman succeeded to the tenancy of this farm. He was twice married: first on 27 January 1783 to Elizabeth Spencer—they had one son, John, also a very successful farmer—and second to Constantia Davies, daughter of the vicar of Glynde, with whom he had a number of children.

Place Farm was a large downland occupation of 580 acres, later increased to 700 acres. It was conveniently situated on a tributary of the Ouse, a few miles from Lewes, and well placed for the sale of stock and crops in London and nearer markets. Ellman had 150 acres of arable and hill pastures for cattle and horses, but his land was ideally suited to the development of the Southdown breed of sheep, on which he concentrated. By careful choice of rams and ewes he rapidly achieved success, and his stock was widely sought by leading agricultural figures.

Ellman generously gave advice to anyone who cared to ask for it. As a result his assistance was eagerly sought, and among those who frequently visited his farm or corresponded with him were the duke of Bedford, the earl of Albemarle, Lord Somerville, who introduced him to George III, and lords Egremont, Sligo, Darnley, Londonderry, Sheffield, and Chichester. In 1786 he founded, together with Lord Sheffield, the Lewes wool fair, and it was at his suggestion that Lord Egremont formed the Sussex Agricultural Society, which served as a means of publicizing the Southdown breed. He also took a leading part in the founding of the Smithfield Club, and on the death of Richard Astley was made 'father' of the show, an office he held for many years.

Ellman was a frequent prizewinner in both London and Sussex, and won with such ease that he soon decided to refrain from exhibiting, or to withdraw his sheep while the judging was in progress, so that his animals would not detract from the appearance of the others. In 1798 he sold two of his rams to the emperor of Russia for 300 guineas, a price fixed as fair by the duke of Bedford. Ellman was also successful with his cattle, and in 1819 the board of agriculture awarded him the gold medal for the best cultivated farm in Sussex. In 1800 a silver cup was presented to him by the landowners of Sussex, and five years later the duke of Bedford gave him a silver vase as a mark of his personal esteem.

Ellman wrote on a variety of agricultural subjects. He contributed to the *Transactions* of the first board of agriculture, to Arthur Young's *Annals of Agriculture*, and also to the *Farmer's Journal*. Some of his correspondence with an agricultural society at Rouen was published by the Société d'Amélioration des Laines. He wrote the article entitled 'Sheep' in *Baxter's Library of Agricultural and Horticultural Knowledge* (1834) and revised other entries in the same work.

Ellman served as steward of the Trevor estates in Sussex from 1792 to 1829, a period of considerable extension and reorganization. Outside agriculture Ellman interested himself largely in county affairs. He was a commissioner of taxes, and as expenditor of Lewes and Laughton levels he carried out a difficult scheme for the improvement of navigation on the Ouse. The reconstruction of Newhaven harbour also owed a great deal to his energy. A generous and paternalistic employer, in his own village of Glynde he maintained a school for labourers' children. While he refused to allow the licensing of any public house there, he realized the vital importance of beer to farm labourers,

and afforded facilities for home brewing. Unmarried labourers were provided with lodgings, as well as a plot of grass for a cow and pig, and a certain amount of arable land on their marriage. However, he was opposed to any allotment system on a larger scale.

In 1829 Ellman retired from active work, and his celebrated flock was sold by auction. The rest of his life he resided alternately at High Cross, his small estate at Uckfield, in Sussex, and in Albion Street, Lewes, where he died on 22 November 1832. He was survived by his second wife.

Ellman's achievement was in helping to transform the Southdown sheep from a light and long-legged animal into one that was solid and compact, excellent for mutton, and still very good for wool. The Southdown, as improved by Ellman and Jonas Webb, led to the development of new breeds of downland shortwool sheep—the Hampshire, the Oxford Down, and the Suffolk. Ellman was fortunate in having an ideal sheep-corn farm for the purpose, on the light lands to which the Southdown was well suited, at a time (until 1818) of high farming prosperity. He was a persuasive promoter of the breed, and successful in attracting the notice of the leading agricultural authorities of the age. ALSAGER VIAN, rev. G. E. MINGAY

Sources S. Farrant, 'John Ellman of Glynde in Sussex', *Agricultural History Review*, 26 (1978), 77–88 · R. J. Moore-Colyer, 'Sheep', *The agrarian history of England and Wales*, ed. J. Thirsk, 6, ed. G. E. Mingay (1989) · R. Trow-Smith, *A history of British livestock husbandry, 1700–1900*, 2 vols. (1957–9) · J. G. Gazley, *The life of Arthur Young, 1741–1820* (1973) · J. Ellman, 'An account of the expense and produce of a flock of 560 Southdown ewes, stating the average of the last seven years', *Annals of Agriculture*, 11 (1789), 345–55 · J. Baxter, *Baxter's library of practical agriculture*, 4th edn (1851), vol. 2 [memoir of Ellman]

Likenesses E. Scriven, stipple, pubd 1830 (after J. Lonsdale), BM, NPG · Lonsdale, portrait; formerly in possession of the family, 1888

Ellmann, Richard David (1918–1987), literary scholar and biographer, was born on 15 March 1918 in Highland Park, Detroit, Michigan, the second of the three sons (there were no daughters) of James Isaac Ellmann, lawyer, a Jewish Romanian immigrant, and his wife, Jeanette Barsook, an immigrant from Kiev in Ukraine. He attended local schools before going to Yale University, where he graduated with exceptional distinction in English in 1939 and completed an MA dissertation in 1941.

On the entry of the United States into the Second World War in 1942 Ellmann joined the office of strategic services (OSS), but that August he began his academic career as an instructor at Harvard University. This was interrupted in 1943 when he enlisted in the American navy and was posted to a construction battalion. Although he disliked military service, he was to turn it to account in 1945 when he unexpectedly found himself seconded to the OSS in London. That September he visited the widow of William Butler Yeats in Dublin. Impressed by his knowledge of her husband's work, she gave him access to her immense archive. He returned to Ireland immediately on his discharge from the navy in May 1946 and wrote a LittB at Trinity College, Dublin, while simultaneously undertaking a Yale PhD on Yeats's life and writings. This, the first Yale

Richard David Ellmann (1918–1987), by Seán O'Mordha

doctorate on a twentieth-century writer, was published in 1949 as *Yeats: the Man and the Masks* and remains one of the best introductions to the poet's work.

In 1947 Ellmann returned to teach at Harvard, where he met, and in August 1949 married, a talented Irish-American feminist critic, Mary Donahue, the daughter of William Henry Donahue, baker, of Newburyport, Massachusetts. Two years later he was appointed professor of English at Northwestern University, Evanston, Illinois. He had already begun research for his biography of James Joyce, but his next book was a sophisticated critical study of Yeats's poetry, *The Identity of Yeats* (1954). His magisterial *James Joyce* appeared in 1959 and immediately confirmed his reputation as the outstanding literary biographer of his generation, its research, narrative control, and wit setting new standards in the genre. His growing distinction was reflected in a series of academic honours, fellowships, and visiting professorships, and in 1963 by his promotion to the Franklin Bliss Snyder chair at Northwestern, which he held until 1968. Deeply involved in editing Joyce's writings and letters, he also found time to co-edit *The Modern Tradition* (1965), a collection of key modernist texts, as well as anthologies of modern poetry. In 1967 he published *Eminent Domain*, a series of elegant essays on Yeats's various literary relationships. The following year he moved to Yale as professor of English, and it was supposed that he would see out his career at his old alma mater. But after only two years he was invited to apply for the Goldsmiths' chair of English literature at Oxford and was duly elected (1970), with a fellowship at New College.

The move to Oxford was partly prompted by Ellmann's proposed biography of Oscar Wilde, but was also because, established at Yale, he could predict exactly which meetings he would be attending on any given day in the foreseeable future; Oxford offered no such predictability. The move was marred when his wife suffered a cerebral haemorrhage that permanently confined her to a wheelchair. Of their three children, the eldest, Stephen, remained in the United States while their two daughters, Maud and Lucy, settled in England with their parents. Ellmann delivered his inaugural lecture, 'Literary biography', on 4 May 1971, and in 1972 he published *Ulysses on the Liffey*, which examined the principles of construction of Joyce's novel. A book of essays in the following year, *Golden Codgers*, ranged from George Eliot to T. S. Eliot, and *The Consciousness of Joyce* appeared in 1977. Ellmann was at once bemused and delighted by Oxford; his forte was the seminar rather than the lecture, and he excelled in his supervision of graduate students.

In 1984 Ellmann retired as Goldsmiths' professor and took up the Woodruff chair at Emory University in Georgia. But he remained resident in Oxford, holding both an honorary fellowship at New College (1987) and an extraordinary fellowship at Wolfson College (1984), and he and his wife continued to keep open house at 39 St Giles' to a wide circle of friends. During this time he had been working on his biography of Oscar Wilde, garnering new information and drafting and redrafting the book. He was elected a fellow of the British Academy in 1979, and had honorary degrees from several American universities and from Göteborg, Sweden.

Ellmann was a tall man, balding and bespectacled, and tending to plumpness, with a warm smile and an infectious laugh. It was in the summer of 1986 that his friends began to notice a slight slurring of speech and an awkwardness of posture. These symptoms became more pronounced and motor neurone disease was diagnosed. With typical fortitude he refused to be intimidated by this terrible illness, and when his speech finally failed he communicated through a ticker-tape machine, the messages showing that he had lost nothing of his intellectual edge and personal kindness. His final days were occupied with preparing *Oscar Wilde* (1987) for the press; he was able to read the proofs shortly before he died in Oxford on 13 May 1987.   JOHN KELLY, *rev.*

Sources S. Dick and others, eds., *Omnium gatherum: essays for Richard Ellmann* (1989) · personal knowledge (1996) · private information (1996) · *The Times* (15–19 May 1987)
Likenesses S. O'Mordha, photograph, NPG [*see illus.*]
Wealth at death £182,441 in England and Wales: administration with will, 9 Sept 1988, *CGPLA Eng. & Wales*

Ellsworth, Oliver (1745–1807), revolutionary politician and jurist in the United States of America, was born on 29 April 1745 in Windsor, Connecticut, the second son of Captain David Ellsworth (1709–1782), farmer and militia officer, and Jemima Leavitt (1721–1790). His father intended him for the ministry and after preparing for college with the noted New Light clergyman Joseph Bellamy, he entered Yale College in 1762. In 1764 with his parents' approval he transferred to the College of New Jersey, graduating with the class of 1766. After studying theology for another year, he was apprenticed with two eminent legal counsellors, Matthew Griswold and Jesse Root. In 1772 he married Abigail Wolcott (1755–1818) of East Windsor. Shortly afterwards he was elected to represent Windsor in the Connecticut general assembly.

In 1775 Ellsworth moved to neighbouring Hartford, which became the revolutionary capital of the state. For the next eight years he served in various state offices including state's attorney for Hartford county, member of the council of safety, which directed Connecticut's war effort, and, beginning in 1779, as one of the twelve assistants who constituted the upper house of the state legislature. In 1777 he was also appointed delegate to the continental congress, where he served intermittently until 1783. His sojourn in congress convinced him that a stronger national government alone could solve the problems of small states like Connecticut just when many of his fellow citizens had reached the opposite conclusion. Although a populist attempt to purge him as assistant failed in 1783–4, Ellsworth accepted appointment to the state's newly constituted supreme court in 1785 partially to insulate himself from electoral pressures.

Connecticut's delegation to the Philadelphia constitutional convention in 1787 included Roger Sherman, William S. Johnson, and Ellsworth. Collectively they are credited with fashioning the key compromise of the convention, often referred to as the 'Connecticut compromise', which matched a house of representatives that proportionately represented the population with a senate in which each state had equal representation. Ellsworth also served on the committee of detail, which produced the first draft of the constitution, and vigorously supported its acceptance in the public prints and at Connecticut's ratifying convention. Chosen by Connecticut's legislature to serve in the senate of the first congress, he was the principal draftsman of the Judiciary Act of 1789 which established the structure and defined the jurisdiction of the federal judiciary.

Ellsworth was critical of the French Revolution almost from its inception and after 1792, as the war in Europe threatened United States neutrality, favoured an accommodation with Britain. In 1794 he with other like-minded congressmen urged Washington to appoint a special envoy to negotiate the outstanding differences between the two countries. When the resulting Jay treaty proved controversial, Ellsworth did everything in his power to secure its ratification and implementation.

In 1796 Ellsworth accepted appointment as the second chief justice of the United States supreme court. During his brief tenure the court affirmed the supremacy of federal treaties over state laws and defined rules and procedures that would govern appeals from state to federal courts as well as within the federal judicial system. Ellsworth also wrote advisory opinions supporting the executive's privilege to deny congress access to diplomatic correspondence and the constitutionality of the Sedition Act.

In 1799 Ellsworth accepted President John Adams's appointment as one of three commissioners to negotiate an end to the limited naval war the United States had been waging against French armed vessels since 1798. While the convention of Môrtefontaine failed to resolve many of the differences between the two countries, it did restore friendly diplomatic relations with France. Ellsworth's health, already compromised by gout and kidney problems, collapsed on the journey to Paris, leading him to resign as chief justice after concluding the convention of 1800. When he returned to the United States in 1801, he retired to his native Windsor where he remained active in Connecticut's public life until his death, in Windsor, on 26 November 1807. He was buried in Windsor burial-ground.   RICHARD BUEL JUN.

Sources W. Craven, 'Oliver Ellsworth', *Princetonians: a biographical dictionary, 1748–1768*, ed. J. McLachlan (1976), vol. 1 · W. G. Brown, *The life of Oliver Ellsworth* (1905) · D. J. Lettieri, *Connecticut's young man of the revolution: Oliver Ellsworth* (1978) · W. R. Casto, 'Ellsworth, Oliver', *ANB* · W. R. Casto, *The supreme court in the early republic: the chief justiceships of John Jay and Oliver Ellsworth* (1996) · W. R. Casto, 'Oliver Ellsworth, "I have sought the felicity and glory of your administration"', *Seriatim: the supreme court before John Marshall*, ed. S. D. Gerber (1998) · A. DeConde, *The quasi-war: the politics and diplomacy of the undeclared war with France, 1797–1801* (1966) · M. Farrand, ed., *The records of the federal convention of 1787*, rev. edn, 4 vols. (1937); repr. (1966) · J. H. Hutson, ed., *Supplement to Max Farrand's 'The records of the federal convention of 1787'* (1987) · H. R. Stiles, *The history and genealogy of ancient Windsor, Connecticut*, 2 (1892)
Archives Connecticut Historical Society, Hartford, MSS · L. Cong., papers of the continental Congress
Likenesses R. Earle, oils, Wadsworth Atheneum, Hartford, Connecticut · D. C. Hinman, engraving (after a miniature by Trumbull), repro. in *Analectic Magazine*, 3 (1814), 382

Ellwood, Thomas (1639–1713), religious controversialist, was born at Crowell, Oxfordshire, in October 1639, and baptized there on the 15th of the month, the son of Walter Ellwood (d. c.1684), a JP and local magistrate, and Elizabeth Potman (d. c.1658), 'both well descended, but of declining families' (*Life*, ed. Crump, 1900, 1–2). He had a brother and two sisters, all older than himself. Ellwood's family lived in London during the first civil war (1642–6), as his father supported parliament's cause and was 'a constant hearer' of puritan preachers (ibid., 39). At seven Ellwood, who had 'a natural propensity to learning' (ibid., 3), was sent to the Thame Free School in Oxfordshire, which provided a classical education, though (to save expenses) his father removed him from the school before he was able to settle into his studies. In 1659 he and his father visited Isaac and Mary Penington (having known them in London) at Chalfont St Peter, Buckinghamshire, and found them Friends; on a second visit they attended a Quaker meeting in a nearby farmhouse where they met the itinerant preachers Edward Burrough and James Nayler. There Ellwood 'drank in [Burrough's] words with desire', though those of Nayler struck Ellwood with a 'greater force' when that charismatic Quaker leader made the case for 'the universal free grace of God to all mankind' (ibid., 12–13). Soon after, Ellwood underwent a profound religious conversion: he began to believe in the primacy of an inner light and to repudiate (in the manner of early Friends) traditional customs of dress, speech, and social deference. He was one of the handful of gentlemen, including Isaac Penington the younger and William Penn, to join the early Friends. His unconventional behaviour provoked anger and grief in his father, who tried to confine him at home, and the young Friend soon fled to the Peningtons, with whom he lived for about two years.

Quaker and friend of Milton The Restoration brought severe persecution of dissenters (especially after Thomas

Venner's insurrection in January 1661, 'that mad prank of those infatuated fifth-monarchy men' (*Life*, ed. Crump, 1900, 55) in Ellwood's own words), and Ellwood, refusing to take the oaths of allegiance and supremacy, was imprisoned for some months in Oxford and later arrested at a Quaker meeting at Chalfont, and again at Beaconsfield as a rogue and vagabond. During this period of persecution he also visited Aylesbury gaol to see Isaac Penington and other imprisoned Friends there. Early in 1662 Ellwood suffered a bout of smallpox, though his 'countenance was not much altered by it' (ibid., 87). As soon as he recovered he went to London to resume his studies, and through the mediation of Penington and Penington's friend Dr Nathan Paget, Ellwood was employed as a reader to the now blind John Milton (then living a private and retired life), with whom he studied classical Latin and learned the continental pronunciation. Ellwood pursued learning under Milton with 'earnest desire', but this period of study of about six weeks was interrupted by ill health owing to the 'sulphurous air' of the city (ibid., 90); when Ellwood returned to London in October 1662 after a spell in the country, he continued as a reader to Milton. A further interruption occurred when he was arrested in London on 26 October at a Quaker meeting-house at the Bull and Mouth in Aldersgate Street; he was imprisoned with thirty-one other Friends in Bridewell, where he made night-waistcoats to avoid accepting aid. Put on trial at the Old Bailey in late December, he refused to take the oath of allegiance and was sent to Newgate ('a type of hell upon earth') and then to Bridewell again, where, feeling the 'horrid impieties of the age', he composed verses called 'Speculum seculi, or, A looking-glass for the times', which bewailed England's 'sad estate' and envisioned the Lord's vengeance on persecutors of the suffering Friends (ibid., 114, 116, 120). Allowed to visit Friends in Newgate, he was soon deeply distraught by the death of Edward Burrough, 'the immediate instrument' of Ellwood's 'convincement' (ibid., 129), as a result of protracted confinement; Ellwood composed verses lamenting the young Quaker leader's untimely death.

After his discharge from Bridewell in January 1663 Ellwood returned to the Peningtons, who engaged him as a tutor to their children in Latin (though this diverted him from further studies with Milton). Ellwood carried on as tutor until 1669, and also acted as a companion to Mary Penington's daughter, Gulielma Springett. Under the first Conventicle Act of May 1664, Ellwood was arrested along with Isaac Penington and other Friends at the funeral of Edward Perrot at Amersham, on 1 July 1665, and committed to Aylesbury gaol for one month. Prior to his arrest, and in response to the great plague, he had taken a nearby cottage—'a pretty box' (*Life*, ed. Crump, 1900, 144) at Chalfont St Giles—for Milton and his family; this house is the only one of Milton's still standing. On his release from prison Ellwood visited Milton there. Ellwood famously reports that the poet invited him to read *Paradise Lost*, which he did 'with the best attention'. Milton asked him what he thought of the poem, to which Ellwood replied: 'Thou hast said much here of "Paradise Lost", but what

hast thou to say of "Paradise Found"?' At this point Milton made Ellwood 'no answer, but sat some time in a muse'; however, when Ellwood later visited him in London (after the plague abated) the poet showed him a partial or perhaps a complete version of the sequel, *Paradise Regained*, and observed: 'This is owing to you, for you put it into my head by the question you put me at Chalfont, which before I had not thought of' (ibid., 145). This attractive anecdote (whether or not it is altogether accurate) reminds us that Milton's contentious religious epic about an inward-looking Jesus led by the Holy Spirit and tempted in the wilderness of the world owes something to his connections with the persecuted Friends, including Ellwood. At the end of his life Milton entrusted his collection of Cromwell's personal and state papers to Ellwood, after whose death they were published.

Marriage and writings In March 1666 Ellwood was convicted again under the Conventicle Act and illegally committed to the Wycombe house of correction for twelve weeks. He was required on 7 June to find sureties for his appearance at the next assize and refusing to do so was kept in prison until 25 June. After his discharge he was temporarily led astray by the Quaker schismatic John Perrot (who opposed the removal of hats during prayer); Ellwood confessed his error to the Friends in London and he soon thereafter travelled with Guli Springett to the west of England to meet George Fox (and where he also publicly avowed his error). Meanwhile, his passion for Guli Springett remaining unrequited, Ellwood courted and then married Mary Ellis (1623–1708) on 28 October 1669; she was sixteen years older than he, and they had no children. Though less well-known as a Quaker controversialist than her husband, Mary later published (with Margery Clipsham) a diatribe against the female visionary Susanna Aldridge for publicly attacking Friends and engaging in disorderly preaching: *The Spirit that Works Abomination* (1685).

Ellwood himself wrote much controversial prose, beginning with a fiery denunciation of hireling priests, *An Alarm to the Priests* (1660), and ending with *The Glorious Brightness of the Gospel-Day* (1707), which repudiated outward ceremonies, especially the practice of water baptism since 'the true Baptism', he believed, must 'begin Inward' (*Life*, ed. Crump, 1900, 13). With William Penn, George Whitehead, and other Quaker writers, he engaged in animadversions and heated debate with Baptists including Thomas Hicks, Jeremiah Ives, and Thomas Plant in *A Fresh Pursuit* and *Forgery No Christianity* (both 1674). In *Truth Prevailing, and Detecting Error* (1674) and *The Foundation of Tythes Shaken* (1678), the latter work exceeding 500 pages, he engaged in controversy with two unnamed priests who defended tithes (which Ellwood considered oppressive and unchristian) while viciously maligning him and the Friends. In 1683 he published several tracts protesting against Charles II's final wave of religious persecution (the 1670 Conventicle Act still being in force), while comparing Quaker constancy to that of the apostles: *A Caution to Constables*, *A Discourse Concerning Riots*, and *A Seasonable Disswasive from Persecution*. As a result of the Rye House plot

(1683), Ellwood was examined by two justices for his 'seditious book' *A Caution to Constables* (ibid., 198); Ellwood challenged them and they did not prosecute him. Strife and separatism within the Quaker sect itself—'an intestine war' (ibid., 195) beginning in 1675 and severely testing the movement's unity—fuelled more polemical writings. Some of Ellwood's most heated tracts were written to combat Quaker schismatics, including the followers of John Wilkinson and John Story, who opposed George Fox and were discontented over church discipline and government: the separatist William Rogers (Ellwood's *Antidote Against the Infection*, 1682; and *Rogero-Mastix*, 1685, written in satirical verse), as well as John Raunce, Charles Harris, and Leonard Key (five tracts or broadsides written by Ellwood between 1690 and 1693). Ellwood also wrote a series of lengthy tracts against the divisive and contentious George Keith: *An Epistle to Friends* and *A Further Discovery*, 1694; *Truth Defended*, 1695; and *An Answer to George Keith's Narrative*, 1696. In addition, Ellwood attacked petitions against the sect associated with the bitter former Friend, Francis Bugg (Ellwood's *A Sober Reply* in 1699).

Ellwood wrote a variety of shorter poems: these included satire, pastoral verses, love lyrics, anagrams, verse epistles to Friends, hymns and religious verses, verses on the origins and rise of maypoles, poems praising Edmund Waller the poet (while chastising Rochester's lascivious poetry), elegies commemorating Burrough and Isaac and Mary Penington, and an epitaph on Milton:

> Invention never higher rose
> in Poetic strayns, or Prose.
> (Ellwood, 'Rhapsodia', 145–6)

He began a 300-page, five-book biblical epic, *Davideis: the Life of David*, in 1688 (before he read Cowley's *Davideis*), but did not complete and publish it until 1712; written 'for common Readers' in 'a Stile familiar' and espousing a government 'Where none, by Pow'r, can be oppress'd' (T. Ellwood, *Davideis*, 1712, XI.81), the sacred poem was frequently reprinted (most recently in 1936). Ellwood's well-known autobiography, *The History of the Life of Thomas Ellwood*, first published in 1714, provides a vivid account of his conversion to Quakerism (and the varied, sometimes hostile responses it provoked), memorable portraits of notable early Friends (including Isaac and Mary Penington, Edward Burrough, James Nayler, George Fox, and William Penn), and a narrative of his active role in the sect during the stormy years of persecution against dissenters at the time of the Restoration. The first edition of his *Life* included a supplement by Ellwood's friend Joseph Wyeth; this continued the narrative from 1683 (where the original left off) until Ellwood's death in 1713, quoted extensively from his later writings, and provided accounts of the fierce polemical controversies associated with some of them. After Fox's death, Ellwood was entrusted to transcribe and edit for the press the manuscript of Fox's *Journal* (1694). Ellwood's edition gave it a more coherent, polished form, which softened its millenarian rhetoric and rustic language, and omitted many cures which Fox

claimed to have performed; this edition also included miscellaneous papers and epistles as well as Fox's dictated narratives.

In his last years Ellwood digested and paraphrased the entire biblical story in two dense folio volumes, *Sacred History … of the Old Testament* (1705) and *Sacred History … of the New Testament* (1709; both works were subsequently reprinted together). These intended to show more continuously providence delivering God's servants and people out of the greatest hardships and sufferings, as well as offering both 'godly Instruction and virtuous Pleasure', especially for youthful readers who indulge in romances, 'lewd Novels, lascivious Poems, and Vice-promoting Play-Books' (T. Ellwood, *Old Testament*, 1705, preface).

Later years Possessing 'a Peculiar Gift for Government in the Church' (Ellwood, *Life*, 1714, 474), Ellwood was active and prominent in Quaker life and worship. Over a period of about forty years, regular meetings for worship gathered at his home—at Hunger Hill, in Amersham—where he had moved after marrying Mary Ellis. Quaker meetings at Ellwood's house, which stood in an outlying area, were relatively safe from the interference of Hertfordshire and Buckinghamshire authorities. For several decades Ellwood served as the first clerk of the monthly meeting, variously named Hunger Hill and Upperside of Buckinghamshire. He served on the national meeting for sufferings, monthly from 1675, and from 1674 (when he was able) on the weekly morning meeting in London which oversaw Quaker publications. In 1707 and 1708 Ellwood, who wrote extensively against tithes, was prosecuted for non-payment. His wife, Mary, died on 5 April 1708 and Ellwood himself died on 1 May 1713, aged seventy-four, at his home in Amersham. He was buried three days later beside his wife in the Quaker burial-ground (near the Peningtons and William Penn's family) at Jordans meeting-house, near Chalfont St Giles.   DAVID LOEWENSTEIN

Sources T. Ellwood, *The history of the life of Thomas Ellwood* (1714) • T. Ellwood, *The history of the life of Thomas Ellwood*, ed. C. G. Crump (1900) • *A journal or historical account of … George Fox*, ed. [T. Ellwood], 1 (1694) • T. Ellwood, 'Rhapsodia: a collection of some few poems', RS Friends, Lond., MS vol. S.80 • L. M. Wright, *The literary life of the early Friends, 1658–1725* (1932) • B. S. Snell, 'The making of Thomas Ellwood', *Journal of the Friends' Historical Society*, 36 (1939), 21–47 • W. C. Braithwaite, *The second period of Quakerism*, ed. H. J. Cadbury, 2nd edn (1961) • R. M. Crane, 'Thomas Ellwood: Quaker writer, 1639–1713', MA diss., University of Illinois, 1963 • E. T. McLaughlin, 'Milton and Ellwood', *Milton Newsletter*, 1 (1967), 17–28 • R. T. Vann, *The social development of English Quakerism, 1655–1755* (1969) • H. Barbour, 'Ellwood, Thomas', Greaves & Zaller, *BDBR*, 1.252–3 • B. Reay, *The Quakers and the English revolution* (1985) • T. Corns and D. Loewenstein, eds., *The emergence of Quaker writing: dissenting literature in seventeenth-century England* (1995) • A. Davies, *The Quakers in English society, 1655–1725* (2000) • 'Dictionary of Quaker biography', RS Friends, Lond. [card index] • *DNB* • will, PRO, PROB 11/533, fols. 50*v*–52*r* • parish register, Cromwell, Oxfordshire, 15 Oct 1639 [baptism]

Archives RS Friends, Lond., letters and misc. material • RS Friends, Lond., Buckinghamshire sufferings

Ellys, Anthony (*bap.* **1690**, *d.* **1761**), bishop of St David's, was born at Great Yarmouth, Norfolk, the son of Anthony

Ellys (d. 1736) and his wife, Judith and was baptized at St Nicholas's, Great Yarmouth, on 8 June 1690. His father and grandfather were both merchants in the borough and also served as aldermen and as mayor, his father holding the latter office twice, in 1705 and 1719. A great-uncle, Sir John Ellys, was master of Gonville and Caius College, Cambridge, and left Ellys a legacy in his will of 1716.

Ellys was educated at Clare College, Cambridge, where he was admitted pensioner on 7 June 1709. He graduated BA in 1713, MA in 1716, and DD in 1728, on the occasion of a royal visit to the university. He was a fellow of the college from 1714 to 1722, having been ordained deacon (22 September 1717) and priest (21 September 1718). In 1719, during his father's mayoralty, Yarmouth corporation appointed him minister of St George's Chapel in the town (founded 1714) with a salary double the normal rate. Ellys quickly found London preferment. In 1721 he became a chaplain to Lord Chancellor Macclesfield and was named rector of St Michael, Wood Street. He exchanged these places in 1724 for the vicarage of St Olave Jewry and a canonry at Gloucester (presented 27 August). He retained these last two appointments after receiving the vicarage of Great Marlow, Buckinghamshire, in 1729 from the dean and chapter of Gloucester. Ellys was also named a fellow of the Royal Society in 1723.

Ellys was a moderate whig and a defender of the ecclesiastical establishment; he looked to Martin Benson, bishop of Gloucester, as his main patron after Macclesfield's disgrace. In 1736, at a moment when the Church of England was trying to resist the Walpole government's various schemes for its further reform, he published anonymously *A plea for the sacramental test as best security for the church established, and very conductive to the welfare of the state*. This tract offered a historical review of the test and contended that the act's abolition was likely to inspire dissenters to increase their political power. Ellys warned that those who in the past had objected to vestments and bowing 'have made no scruple to swallow her Revenues, and lay waste her sanctuaries' (132). He was popular with Archbishop Herring, who secured his appointment as bishop of St David's in October 1752 (consecrated 28 January 1753) on Bishop Trevor's translation to Durham. Herring told Newcastle that 'the City of London has not, in all respects, a more valuable Clergyman, in point of scholarship, as a Preacher, & a writer, or of steady loyalty to the king' (19 June 1752, Nottingham University, Newcastle of Clumber MSS, NeC 1463/1). Newcastle was less enthusiastic and told Lord Hardwicke that he had been 'buffeted in the closet for Dr Ellis' because of George II's ignorance of the candidate (18 Oct 1752, BL, Newcastle MS 126). This promotion was by some attributed to the reputation which Ellys had gained as being engaged on a great work in defence of the protestant reformation. Others objected to the nomination of an upholder of the Test Act as 'detrimental to liberty'. Archbishop Herring, however, insisted that the 'stick had been bent rather too far on the side of liberty' and that it was time to 'give it now a bent to the contrary side' (Nichols, *Lit. anecdotes*, 2.720).

After appointment to his bishopric Ellys retained his prebend and his city living to supplement the see's meagre income (there were no further *commendam* appointments for him as there had been for previous bishops) and he preached most Sundays at St Olave. In the St David's diocese he did little to raise the church's depressed state and he discountenanced the scheme of John Jones of Welwyn for establishing a seminary for clerical education; the books offered by Jones to the bishop went to the presbyterian academy at Carmarthen. Meanwhile his defence of the Reformation failed to appear from the press, a sign of limited energy or confidence which disappointed Ellys's friends and patrons; as bishop his only publications were sermons preached on special occasions. These he used to express his support for the established order in church and state and propose measures for their defence. A sermon preached before the Incorporated Society for the Propagation of the Gospel in Foreign Parts (1759) argued that Native Americans and African slaves in Britain's North American colonies should be converted to protestantism, both on the grounds that in failing to do so the British would be neglecting their duty as Christians, and that if they left the task to Catholic missionaries this would only serve the interests of the French.

Ellys died at Gloucester on 16 January 1761 and was buried in the south aisle of the cathedral. He had married, on 20 March 1732, Anne (b. c.1713), eldest daughter of Sir Stephen Anderson, second baronet, of Eyworth, Bedfordshire. She had heard him preaching in London, and the match was based on mutual admiration. She brought a fortune of £4000, and £3000 in annuities. There was one surviving daughter, who married unhappily and died insane. Anne Ellys left a manuscript volume of poems mostly lamenting her husband's death. Friends posthumously published Ellys's *The Spiritual and Temporal Liberty of Subjects in England in Two Parts* (1765), a portion of the long expected *magnum opus* and the most complete collection of his writings. The first part was mainly a sophisticated anti-Catholic broadside; the second was a treatise on constitutional liberty, which displayed great zeal for the revolution settlement and considerable historical knowledge. Those who knew Ellys echoed Archbishop Herring's view of him as 'a scholar & a good man—of integrity, I know, & always courteous' (to William Herring, 27 Oct 1752, Nottingham University, Portland MSS, PwV 121). And as the preface to his posthumous tract on liberty noted, 'he always thought a person, though on the right side of the question, with principles of persecution, to be a worse man than he that was on the wrong' (*Spiritual and Temporal Liberty*, viii).   NIGEL ASTON

Sources Venn, *Alum. Cant.*, 1/2.95 • *GM*, 1st ser., 31 (1761), 44 • *GM*, 1st ser., 66 (1796), 737, 1012 • *Great Yarmouth baptism transcripts*, 1, pt 2 (1995), 274 • *A calendar of the freemen of Great Yarmouth, 1429–1800* (1910), 149 • C. J. Palmer, *The perlustration of Great Yarmouth*, 1 (1872), 330–32 • Nichols, *Lit. anecdotes*, 1.625, 631; 2.414, 720, 725; 4.481 • *Monthly Review*, 29 (1763), 117–34 • GEC, *Baronetage*, 3.294–5 • G. Lipscomb, *The history and antiquities of the county of Buckingham*, 4 vols. (1831–47), vol. 3, p. 601 • *Fasti Angl., 1541–1857*, [Bristol], 60 • E. Saunders, *A view of the state of religion in the diocese of St David's about the beginning of the eighteenth century* (1721) • E. Pyle, *Memoirs of a royal* *chaplain, 1729–1763*, ed. A. Hartshorne (1905), 190 · private information (2004) [B. W. Young]

Archives BL, Newcastle MSS, Add. MS 32730, fols. 126, 129, 130, 132, 140, 159–160, 171 · Norfolk RO, letters to his father · U. Nott., Newcastle of Clumber MSS, ecclesiastical preferments, NeC 1463–9

Ellys, John (1701–1757), portrait painter, born (according to Vertue) in March 1701, is probably the John, son of John and Sarah Ellis, baptized in St Paul's, Covent Garden, on 21 March 1701. He studied briefly under Sir James Thornhill (reputedly assisting him in decorative painting at Greenwich Hospital) and under the Swiss-born portraitist Johann Rudolf Schmutz (*d.* 1715). By the age of sixteen Ellys is listed among students at the academy in Great Queen Street, Lincoln's Inn Fields, where Thornhill succeeded Kneller as governor. From 1720 he attended the academy conducted in 1720–24 by Louis Chéron and John Vanderbank in St Martin's Lane. There Hogarth, his fellow student, became his firm friend. When this academy closed, Thornhill allowed his own house to be used by students as a 'free academy', leaving its management to Ellys and Hogarth. In 1735 Ellys and Hogarth together established a second academy in St Martin's Lane, welcoming artists such as Gravelot, Hayman, Rysbrack, and Roubiliac as teachers; of this highly influential academy (which flourished until 1768), Ellys was a director from 1735 to 1747. In 1755 he was among the signatories to the plan for a royal academy, but did not live to see its establishment.

While much involved with artists, Ellys himself was neither single-minded nor prolific as a painter. He was a worldly and energetic man, and his commitments extended beyond the orbit of St Martin's Lane. In or about 1729 Ellys bought, from Moses Vanderbank, the Soho Tapestry Manufactory in Great Queen Street, and with it the office of yeoman arras worker to the (royal) wardrobe. Ellys already enjoyed court favour, having secured permission by the mid-1720s to copy pictures in the Royal Collection (his studio sale, conducted by Mr Langford on 27 February 1760, was to include many copies after Van Dyck, Lely, and Kneller). From 1733 until at least the mid-1740s, Ellys was variously employed by Frederick, prince of Wales, officially replacing Philip Mercier as serjeant-painter to the prince on 7 October 1736. His half-length portrait of the prince of Wales was engraved by John Faber junior *c.*1733. He also painted two 'Pastroll Pictures … of figures as big as life' for the gallery of Kew Palace; these, described by William Chambers as 'grotesque paintings, and children in theatrical dresses' (Croft-Murray, 2.205), sound Haymanesque, but were destroyed in subsequent rebuilding. Ellys advised Sir Robert Walpole over the formation of the collection at Houghton Hall, Norfolk, acting as his agent, for instance, in the purchase at Rotterdam (late 1730s?) of Van Dyck's magnificent *Holy Family* (*Rest on the Flight into Egypt*) (Hermitage Museum, St Petersburg). Walpole rewarded him with the office of master keeper of the lions in the Tower of London, a sinecure worth nine shillings a day (with an apartment in the Tower) which Ellys enjoyed for some twenty years before his death.

Ellys's own portraiture was based on that of Kneller, whose sound technique he defended against that of the rising star, Joshua Reynolds. Ellys reputedly remarked, on seeing Reynolds's paintings in 1753: 'Ah! Reynolds, this will never answer. Why, you don't paint in the least like Kneller' (Leslie and Taylor, 1.101). Many of Ellys's portraits are now known only through engravings (chiefly by John Faber junior). His early portraits were of sober worthies (including *George Stanhope, Dean of Canterbury*, painted in 1717 and engraved in 1722, and *Edmund Gibson, Lord Bishop of London*, engraved by Vertue in 1727). Increasing financial independence allowed him to choose livelier sitters. Ellys particularly frequented the theatre and the boxing ring. His portraits of the actresses *Lavinia Fenton* (the original Polly in *The Beggar's Opera*) and *Kitty Clive*, as a shepherdess, were both engraved *c.*1728; and he appears to have enjoyed a particular rapport with Hester Booth, dancer, actress, Drury Lane shareholder, and collector, whom he painted several times *c.*1720–25, both in and out of character, most notably in *Hester Booth as a Harlequin Woman* (V&A; Theatre Museum, London; version in priv. coll.). Ellys was closely associated with Robert Wilks, actor-manager of Drury Lane Theatre and the subject of one of his most spirited portraits (engraved by Faber, 1732). On Wilks's death in 1732, Ellys managed his widow's one-third share in the theatre. Hogarth included a sketch of Ellys, paint-pot at his feet, ready to take up the cudgels for Mrs Wilks, among the crowded details of *Southwark Fair* (engraved 1733). Ellys's portraits of the pugilists *Jack Broughton* and *James Figg, the Mighty Combatant* (who was to appear in several of Hogarth's scenes), were both engraved by Faber *c.*1730.

Ellys's portraits are invariably direct and confrontational; among the most remarkable of them is a forthright, wholly uncondescending portrait of *Fulke Howard, the Gardener at Houghton Hall*, painted (by 1744) for Sir Robert Walpole (priv. coll.). Ebullient and gregarious, Jack Ellys, as he was sometimes known, belonged to the Rose and Crown dining club of artists and to the same freemasons' lodge as Hogarth. His circle of friends included the journalist James Ralph and (reputedly) Henry Fielding. Ellys also enjoys the peculiar distinction of having sat to Rysbrack, as Vertue noted, for the 'thighs … and leggs' of *Hercules* (Stourhead), modelled in 1744, as Walpole observed, from 'the strongest and best-made men in London, chiefly the bruisers' (Walpole, 4.98). Ellys lived chiefly in or near Covent Garden Piazza, but owned property in Orford, Suffolk. He died on 14 September 1757, and was survived by his son Charles and daughter Agnes.

JUDY EGERTON

Sources Vertue, *Note books*, 3.30, 38, 47, 89, 95, 121–2 · I. Bignamini, 'George Vertue, art historian, and art institutions in London, 1689–1768', *Walpole Society*, 54 (1988), 1–148, esp. 53, 57 (n. 28), 74, 79 (n. 37), 115, 119 (n. 21) · H. Walpole, *Anecdotes of painting in England: with some account of the principal artists*, ed. J. Dallaway, [rev. and enl. edn], 4 (1827), 98 · R. Paulson, *Hogarth: his life, art and times*, 1 (1971), 322, 342, 346–7, 352–5, 369–70, 425, 455, 553 n. 7, 540 n. 34, 546 n. 18, n. 20, 55 n. 85 · E. Croft-Murray, *Decorative painting in England, 1537–1837*, 2 (1970), 204–5 · A. Moore, ed., *Houghton Hall: the prime minister, the empress and the Hermitage* (1996), 52, 56–7, 88–9 [exhibition catalogue, Norwich Castle Museum and The Iveagh

Bequest, Kenwood, 12 Oct 1996 – 20 April 1997] • O. Millar, *The Tudor, Stuart and early Georgian pictures in the collection of her majesty the queen*, 2 vols. (1963), vol. 1, p. 176, cat. no. 530; 196, cat. no. 619 • J. C. Smith, *British mezzotinto portraits*, 4 vols. in 5 (1878–84) • *Mr Ellys's collection* [sale catalogue, Mr Langford, Great Piazza, Covent Garden, London, 27 Feb 1760] • W. H. Hunt, ed., *The registers of St Paul's Church, Covent Garden, London*, 1, Harleian Society, register section, 33 (1906), 115 • *GM*, 1st ser., 27 (1757), 436 • C. R. Leslie and T. Taylor, *Life and times of Sir Joshua Reynolds*, 1 (1865), 101

Likenesses S. Hogarth, group portrait, engraving (*Southwark Fair*)

Ellys, Sir Richard, third baronet (1682–1742), book collector and biblical scholar, was born on 23 December 1682, the second, but eldest surviving, son of Sir William Ellys, second baronet (*c*.1654–1727), landowner and MP, of Nocton in Lincolnshire and Isabella Hampden (*d*. 1686), granddaughter of John Hampden. Sir William served as an influential country whig MP for Grantham from 1679 to 1710, excepting the years 1685 to 1689; he voted for exclusion and developed Presbyterian sympathies. Nothing is known about Richard Ellys's education, although nineteenth-century historians claimed that his tutor was Ludolf Kuster, the German classical-Greek philologist. He was twice married, first in 1714, to Elizabeth (1687/8–1724), daughter and coheir of Sir Thomas Hussey, second baronet, of Doddington Hall, Lincolnshire, and his second wife, Sarah Langham. Following his first wife's death on 11 August 1724, on 1 December 1726 Ellys married Sarah (*d*. 1769), daughter and coheir of Thomas Gould of Iver, Buckinghamshire.

Ellys was in close touch with continental scholars. He created libraries at Nocton, and in his London home in Bolton Street, and possibly also at his third property, Place House, Ealing, Middlesex, that were extraordinarily rich in biblical and classical texts. He possessed forty-four different bibles, including six in Hebrew, seven in Greek, and seventeen in Latin. The product of Ellys's own scholarship was *Fortuita sacra* (Rotterdam, 1727), a detailed philological and theological analysis in Latin of a range of disputed New Testament texts. He associated with the mathematician and theologian Charles Hayes, who disliked the 'modern criticks' such as 'the learned Scaliger' (C. Hayes, *A Vindication of the History of the Septuagint from the Misrepresentation of the Learned Scaliger, Dupin, Dr Hody, Dr Prideaux, and other Modern Critics*, 1736). Ellys used his own learning to support theological positions such as anti-Arianism rather than as part of an objective or enlightened academic stance.

Ellys was a keen patron of learning who encouraged William Stukeley, the pioneer archaeologist who made field drawings for him in Lincolnshire, and supported Thomas Boston, the Scottish Hebrew scholar and minister, in his attempts to publish his theories on the significance of the Hebrew system of points. Ellys was the dedicatee of *Britannia Romana* (1732) by the Morpeth Presbyterian minister John Horsley, and of the translations of Horace's sixth satire by the minor Augustan poet Edward Walpole. When Francis Peck, the Stamford antiquarian, published his *Memoirs of the Life and Actions of Oliver Cromwell* (1740) he acknowledged the gift of a portrait of John

Hampden from Ellys. Ellys subscribed to fifty books published between 1720 and 1742, and in the late 1740s his secretary, Dr John Mitchell, listed twenty further books that Ellys had subscribed to before his death, including Stukeley's *Abury* (1743).

Ellys's social position and wealth gave him a role to play in public life. Sitting alongside his father, who was determined 'to spare neither charge nor trouble' to bring his son into parliament (Weston), Ellys was MP for Grantham from 1701 to 1705. When whig political exigencies led to his seat being demanded for the marquess of Granby he retired from national politics for a time. He returned to the House of Commons at a by-election in 1719, winning the second seat for the borough of Boston by defeating the deceased MP's tory nephew. He upheld the whig interest in Boston until 1734, maintaining an independent position against the Boston tory corporation. As the heir to a rich baronetcy, to which he succeeded on 6 October 1727, he never needed to look for a paid place in government. He was a member of the Commons committee investigating overseers of the poor but he voted against Walpole's plans for an increase in the civil list for the crown in 1729 and took the opposition paper, *The Craftsman*, judging from papers sorted by Dr Mitchell in the 1740s. These papers included copies of broadsheets: *Case for the Dissenters* and *Reasons for the Repeal of the Test Act*.

In his later years Ellys was known for his strong Calvinist theological position. While residing in London he was the leading member and financial supporter of the nonconformist Princes Street 'Religious Society, or Congregation of Protestant Dissenters in Westminster' (Cozens-Hardy, 83), where Dr Edmund Calamy the younger was minister. As many Presbyterian societies fell away from their rigid positions of Christological theology some ministers felt unable to subscribe to Calvinistic confessions of faith, preferring to leave unsaid their increasingly liberal views on theology. This displeased Ellys, who was referred to by a fellow London Presbyterian in 1734 as 'a gentleman of Learning & Piety. His learning mostly in the classical and critical way. His notions in Religion are strict Calvanisms [*sic*]. He greatly affects the books of the old Puritans' (ibid., 87).

Ellys inherited from his father not only his puritan sympathies but also his library of over 1200 volumes. About 200 of these were moved to London, where his library concentrated on works concerned with the law and governance of England and antiquities. His particular interest was in versions and translations of the Bible; to complement these he had commentaries on the Bible and its text. His collection was wide-ranging, including histories of the ancient world, scientific and medical works, topography, and travellers' tales. Of seventeenth-century theological writings he favoured those of William Prynne and Gilbert Burnet. His eye for excellence is demonstrated by finely bound, elegant editions of the classics from the Aldine Press at Venice. John Mitchell and agents such as Robert Trevor, Ellys's second cousin, aided his collecting. Ellys was active at many of the great sales of the 1720s and 1730s, both in England and on the continent. In November

1741 Robert Trevor, by then minister-plenipotentiary to the British legation at The Hague, reported Ellys's success at the Uilenbroek auction to Mitchell, enclosing with his letter a catalogue for the forthcoming sales of Edward Harley, earl of Oxford. Unfortunately Ellys's death on 14 February 1742 prevented him from bidding. He was buried at Nocton. Since he had no children his property passed to his widow, who on 19 December 1745 married Francis *Dashwood, eleventh Baron Le Despencer (1708–1781). Following this marriage the Hobart family, Ellys's eventual heirs by his will proved on 23 February 1742, removed his famous library to their ancestral home at Blickling Hall in Norfolk, where it is today in the care of the National Trust.

MICHAEL HONEYBONE and YVONNE LEWIS

Sources Bodl. Oxf., MS D.D. Dashwood c.6 · PRO, PROB 11/716, sig. 50 · B. Cozens-Hardy, 'Letters incidental to Samuel Say's call to Westminster, 1734', *Transactions of the Congregational Historical Society*, 19 (1960–64), 81–90, 129–37 · MSS catalogue, Blickling Hall Library, Norfolk · *Blickling Hall*, National Trust, new edn (1989), 50–55 · J. Cannon and F. J. G. Robinson, *Biography database, 1680–1830* (1995–) [CD-ROM] · A. Weston, 'Lincolnshire politics in the reign of Queen Anne', *Lincolnshire History and Archaeology*, 6 (1971), 86 · GEC, *Baronetage* · *Reports and Papers of the Architectural and Archaeological Societies of the Counties of Lincoln and Northampton*, 24 (1898), 365–6 · parish register, St Martin-in-the-Fields, City Westm. AC [baptism] · C. Bennett, 'E. J. Willson and the architectural history of Nocton Old Hall', *Lincolnshire people and places: essays in memory of Terence R. Leach*, ed. C. Sturman (1996), 26–42 · P. Watson, 'Ellys, Richard', HoP, *Commons, 1690–1715*
Archives Bodl. Oxf., Dashwood MSS
Wealth at death £4000 p.a.: *GM* (February 1742)

Elmer [Æthelmaer, Herlewin] (*d.* **1137**), prior of Christ Church, Canterbury, and theologian, may have come to England from Bec but certainly became a monk at the Benedictine monastery of Christ Church, Canterbury. The first abbot of Bec was called Herluin, and Elmer's use of this name may support the view that he spent some time at Bec. But his baptismal name, which is Old English in origin, may indicate that he was English by birth. He was one of the younger monks at Christ Church in the time of Archbishop Anselm (*d.* 1109), who greeted him in a letter while he was himself still at Bec and Elmer was already at Canterbury.

Elmer became prior of Christ Church, Canterbury, at a date between 1128 and 1130. He was in office at the dedication of the cathedral church on 4 May 1130. Gervase of Canterbury records that in 1136 there was a dispute between the cathedral priory monks and Archbishop William de Corbeil, who died in November of that year, about the church of St Martin at Dover, in which Elmer seems to have felt that honour required him to side with William. He attested a charter of Archbishop William between 1128 and 1136 and, with his monks, confirmed that they had witnessed a charter of Archbishop William between 1130 and 1136. Elmer died on 11 May 1137, according to his obit in BL, Arundel MS 68, folio 27.

In writing his own letters and meditations Elmer achieved a style not wholly unworthy of a pupil of Anselm of Canterbury, although he is master of a monastic spirituality rather than a theologian. Gervase of Canterbury calls him 'a man of great simplicity and excellent religion' (*Works of Gervase of Canterbury*, 1.98). He is the author of more than a dozen letters, several meditations, and a sermon, on whose subject matter and approach the Anselmian stamp is clear. One letter survives in Bodleian Library, Oxford, MS Digby 30, folios 99–100. Letter S is also in Oxford, Magdalen College, MS 60, folios 222–6. BL, Cotton MS Otho A.xii, contained fifteen letters; this was burnt in the fire of 1731 and only fragments survive, but there is a seventeenth- or eighteenth-century copy, probably of this manuscript, now Cambridge, Trinity College, MS 1468 (0.10.16), 410–16, containing mainly letter collections, among them letters of Elmer to an abbot called Andrew, to Henry, to Nicholas of Gloucester, to Willermus, and to seven others. The Cambridge manuscript has meditations *De cordis munditia* ('Of pureness of heart'), *De bono vitae claustralis* ('Of the good of the monastic life'), and *Excitatio mentis in inquisitionem Dei* ('The arousal of the mind in the search for God'), along with a *Sermo Elmeri* (*Beatus venter*; 'Blessed is the womb'), and a sermon on the gospel proper to masses of the Blessed Virgin Mary. The first of the meditations (*Excitatio mentis*) was edited by Gerberon among the *Meditationes Anselmi*. A third is found with the second (*Querimonia de absentia vultus Dei*; 'Complaint of the absence of God's countenance') in various collections of Anselm's meditations, but it is not found in the Cambridge manuscript. The meditations are mentioned in letter 6 to Nicholas, a monk of St Peter's Abbey, Gloucester, and they follow it in the manuscript. The letters themselves include elements of 'spiritual writing', notably in the meditative material *De cordis munditia* which Elmer included in letter 3 to Abbot Turstanus (Thurstan).

G. R. EVANS

Sources R. W. Southern, *Saint Anselm: a portrait in a landscape* (1990), 368–9 · R. W. Southern and F. S. Schmitt, eds., *Memorials of Saint Anselm* (1969), 161n. · *Epistolae*, ed. A. R. Anstruther (1846) [using the Cambridge maunuscript] · J. Leclercq, 'Écrits spirituels d'Elmer de Canterbury', *Studia Anselmiana*, 31 (1953), 45–118 · F. R. H. du Boulay, 'Bexley church: some early documents', *Archaeologia Cantiana*, 72 (1958), 41–53 · *The historical works of Gervase of Canterbury*, ed. W. Stubbs, 1: *The chronicle of the reigns of Stephen, Henry II, and Richard I*, Rolls Series, 73 (1879), 98 · *The letters of Osbert of Clare*, ed. E. W. Williamson (1929) · A. Wilmart, *Auteurs spirituels et textes dévots du moyen âge latin* (Paris, 1932)
Archives BL, corresp., Cotton MS Otho A.xii [fragments] · Bodl. Oxf., letter, MS Digby 30, fols. 99–100 · Magd. Oxf., letter, MS 60, fols. 222–6 · Trinity Cam., corresp., MS 1468 (0.10.16), 410–16 [copy]

Elmer, Stephen (*bap.* **1715**, *d.* **1796**), still-life painter, was baptized on 1 April 1715 at Farnham in Surrey, the son of Stephen Elmer. His father painted murals for St Andrew's Church, Farnham, and Elmer trained in his studio, depicting dead game, and in time became a successful painter of still lifes. He was a member of the Free Society of Artists in 1768, and exhibited 113 pictures up to 1772. In that year he was elected associate of the Royal Academy and contributed 117 paintings to its exhibitions over the next twenty-five years. His works, which were very popular, were painted in a bold, free manner, showing the influence of French and Dutch artists such as Jan Fyt. Elmer's subjects included birds, dogs, fish, flowers, and fruit. He received many commissions from aristocratic patrons to paint prize game and was compared favourably to Stubbs. He also painted portraits including one of a local florist and gardener, John Cartwright, which was engraved by J. M. Ardell (1748). He occasionally painted genre pictures, such as *The Miser* (engraved by B. Granger), but by far his most ambitious picture is *The Last Supper*, formerly over the altar, now in the vestry of Farnham church. By 1781 he owned two houses in West Street, Farnham, and acted as landlord to a local brewhouse. A collection of his paintings is kept in his former home in West Street, Willmer House, now the Museum of Farnham, Surrey, which in 1996 acquired a portrait of Thomas Ashburne, aged eleven, signed and dated by Elmer in 1735. Elmer died, unmarried, at Willmer House, and was buried at Farnham in 1796. He left his property to his niece Caroline, and a large collection of his paintings and his painting equipment to his nephew, William [see below]. The paintings were exhibited at the great room at 28 Haymarket, London, in 1799, under the title 'Elmer's sportsman's exhibition', when it was noted in the catalogue that:

> this modest, unassuming and admirable artist, retained for half a century the first rank in that branch of the arts which he professed and practised. In laborious and high-finishing he may have been equalled by some of the Flemish and Dutch painters; but, in accuracy of drawing, character of species, and spirit he excelled them all. (Sumner)

Many paintings sold well and the remainder were removed to Gerrard Street, Soho, London, where they were accidentally destroyed by fire on 6 February 1801. William Elmer's claim for £3000 in insurance is an indication of how highly his uncle's work was valued in the eighteenth century.

William Elmer (*b. c.*1761), still-life painter, was the nephew of Stephen Elmer. About 1788 he was induced 'by some sporting gentlemen to try the effects of his genius' (Strickland, 1.323), in Ireland, where he lived at 76 Grafton Street, Dublin, and was successful as a painter of still lifes, landscapes, and portraits. On the death of his uncle in 1796 he returned to Farnham. He exhibited at the Royal Academy between 1783 and 1799. A portrait by Stephen Elmer in the Museum of Farnham is thought to represent William Elmer at the age of eleven. A small mezzotint portrait of him as a schoolboy, of 26 June 1772, was engraved by Butler Clowes.   L. H. CUST, *rev.* NATASHA EATON

Sources A. Sumner, *Stephen Elmer* (Museum of Farnham publications, [1993]) · W. Gilbey, *Animal painters of England*, 3 vols. (1900–11) · S. Deuchar, *Sporting artists in 18th century England* (1988) · J. C. Wood, *A dictionary of British animal painters* (1973) · Waterhouse, *18c painters* · W. G. Strickland, *A dictionary of Irish artists*, 2 vols. (1913) · Redgrave, *Artists*, 2nd edn · E. Edwards, *Anecdotes of painters* (1808); facs. edn (1970) · Graves, *RA exhibitors*, vol. 2 · IGI · F. Lewis, *A dictionary of British bird painters* (1974) · inscription, B. Clowes, *William Elmer as a schoolboy*, 1772 [engraving]

Archives Courtauld Inst., Witt Library · NPG, Heinz archives

Likenesses B. Clowes, mezzotint, 1772 (William Elmer as a schoolboy; after S. Elmer) · S. Elmer, oils (William Elmer aged eleven?), Museum of Farnham, Surrey

Elmer, William (*b. c.*1761). *See under* Elmer, Stephen (*bap.* 1715, *d.* 1796).

Elmes, Harvey Lonsdale (1814–1847), architect, was born on 10 February 1814 in Oving, near Chichester, Sussex, where he was also baptized on 26 May 1814. He was the only son of James *Elmes (1782–1862), an architect and a prolific writer on art and architecture, and his wife, Mary Anne. A pupil of his father, he was also trained by his uncle Henry John Elmes and by John Elger (1802–1888), who were both London builders. His father was a friend of the architects John Soane (1753–1837), C. R. Cockerell (1788–1863), and Joseph Gwilt (1784–1863), as well as of the painter Benjamin Robert Haydon (1786–1846), so that he was brought up in an atmosphere where aesthetic discussion was taken seriously.

Education and training In 1831 Elmes was admitted as a student at the Royal Academy Schools, following in the footsteps of his father, who had entered the schools in 1804 and had subsequently attended Soane's lectures there. When Elmes was a pupil at the schools in the 1830s, he would have heard Soane's lectures read for him by Henry Howard. Soane was a powerful influence on both James and Harvey Lonsdale Elmes, and the latter's masterpiece, St George's Hall, Liverpool, was hailed as a building which 'represents the goal of Soane's teaching in the sphere of monumental, as distinct from domestic, architecture' (A. T. Bolton, *The Portrait of Sir John Soane, R.A.*, 1927, 143).

In 1834 Elmes entered the office in Bath of Henry Edmund Goodridge (1797–1864), a highly inventive and eclectic architect who was in touch with Soane. Elmes remained with him for three years, during which time Goodridge was at work on remodelling 19 Lansdown Crescent, for William Beckford (1769–1840), and on designing the Roman Catholic pro-cathedral in Clifton. The latter, though not completed to Goodridge's designs, was a striking classical building which was to be influential on Elmes's designs for St George's Hall, Liverpool.

Major work In 1837 Elmes returned to London, where he assisted his father in designing houses in Park Street (now Queen Anne's Gate), Westminster, in one of which, no. 11, he set up his office. In July 1839 he won the competition for St George's Hall, a grandiose concert hall in Liverpool which it was intended would be built by public subscription. Associated with the city's recently founded triennial music festival, it was to contain a main hall to seat 3000 and a concert hall to seat 1000. Being inexperienced and uncertain of the wisdom of entering the competition, Elmes sought the advice of his father's friend Haydon, who replied, 'By all means, my dear boy. They are noble fellows at Liverpool. Send in a design, and mind, let it combine grandeur with simplicity. None of your broken-up and frittered abortions, but something *grand*' (*Art Union*, 1 Feb 1848, 52). It was good advice, for it helped Elmes win the first premium of 250 guineas in a competition in which no fewer than seventy-five architects submitted designs. It was a remarkable achievement for a young man of twenty-five with no independent building to his credit.

The corporation of Liverpool then decided to build new assize courts. Eighty-nine architects submitted designs in

Harvey Lonsdale Elmes (1814–1847), by Thomas Oldham Barlow, pubd 1849 (after Thomas Crane)

the ensuing competition, for which the premium was £300. Once again, to everyone's surprise, the youthful Elmes was the winner in April 1840. The civic grandeur represented by these joint commissions was in direct emulation of the city of Birmingham, which had just built an imposing new town hall. Moreover, the population of Liverpool had grown from 80,000 inhabitants in 1800 to over 286,000 in 1840, during which time it had become the country's principal Atlantic port as well as the central distribution point for the cotton produced by the Lancashire cotton mills. In an indication of the importance to the city of this project the foundation-stone of the concert hall was laid, prematurely, on the day of Queen Victoria's coronation in 1838.

In Elmes's grandiose project the two buildings, concert hall and law courts, were grouped at right angles to each other in an imposing civic forum approached through propylaeum-like gateways. He presented the corporation with five different designs for the layout of this forum, in which he may have been influenced by his father, whose interest in urban improvements was represented by the text he contributed to T. H. Shepherd's *Metropolitan Improvements: London in the Nineteenth Century* (1827–9). The terms of the competition, like that of 1839, had stipulated that the new buildings should be in the Greek or Roman styles of architecture. Elmes therefore designed the assize courts in a powerful Greek Doric style and St George's Hall in a weaker Roman Ionic. These early designs were strongly influenced by the Fitzwilliam Museum, Cambridge (1834–5), by George Basevi (1794–1845), and by

Cockerell's unexecuted design of 1829–30 for Cambridge University Library.

Subscriptions for the concert hall were not raised as easily as had been expected. As a result, the corporation decided to take it over in 1840 and to unite it and the assize courts in a single building serving both functions. The city architect, Joseph Franklin (c.1785–1855), was thus instructed to produce a design combining elements from both of those by Elmes. However, following protests from Elmes, Franklin generously chose not to stand in the young man's way. Elmes accordingly produced a third design, which the corporation accepted on 27 October 1840. Like Goodridge's Catholic cathedral at Clifton, Elmes's building is on a sloping site and features largely windowless walls set off by a great Corinthian entrance portico with a sculptured pediment. At the other, north, end of the building, the elliptical concert hall is expressed externally by a powerful apse with engaged columns. It is all so much more mature than his initial designs that it is tempting to assume that C. R. Cockerell may have given the young architect some guidance.

In the centre of the building is a vast civic hall inspired by the tepidarium of the baths of Caracalla in Rome, as restored in a drawing by Cockerell and in another by Guillaume-Abel Blouet published in his book *Restauration des thermes d'Antonin Caracalla à Rome* (1828). The vault at Liverpool is actually slightly larger than its antique original. The hall below it is flanked on one side by the crown court and on the other by the civil court. Long corridors connect these on the north and south sides of the building. Elmes originally wanted a grand vista through the heart of this building, but this was subsequently blocked when a great organ was inserted at the north end of the central hall.

Unlike Sir Robert Smirke (1780–1867), whose identical colonnades at the British Museum (1823–46) give no sense of the variety of interiors which lie within, Elmes did not shrink from creating a succession of varied façades. The articulation of the east and west façades in a grid form with massive square pilasters and a screen of detached piers is a disposition which may be derived from Grange Park, Hampshire (1809), by William Wilkins (1778–1839), rather than from the work of Karl Friedrich Schinkel (1781–1841), as has sometimes been thought. The handling of these square piers, partly engaged in the wall, has a certain Egyptian flavour which influenced the slightly later work of the Glasgow architect Alexander (Greek) Thomson (1817–1875). For Thomson, the trabeated architecture of the ancient Near East was a fundamental principle from which we should never deviate as the Romans and the Goths had done. Thomson praised the Royal High School, Edinburgh (1825–9), by Thomas Hamilton (1754–1858), and Elmes's St George's Hall, Liverpool, as the 'two finest buildings in the kingdom' (*The Builder*, 9 May 1866, 369).

Illness and early death   The task of producing drawings for so vast a project with little assistance proved too much for an architect whose lungs were already suffering from the tuberculosis from which he was to die prematurely. Elmes was frequently found in an exhausted state, having worked throughout the night. Moreover, his wife's health was also poor and he found the frequent journeys to Liverpool from London difficult and tiring. He was therefore advised to go abroad in 1842, leaving work in the able hands of his friend the engineer Sir Robert Rawlinson (1810–1898). Travelling with his friend William Earle in 1842, Elmes visited Belgium and made an extensive tour of southern Germany. In the course of this, he made drawings of the sixteenth-century Jesuit church of St Michael in Munich. He admired this for its solution of vaulting the kind of large space with which he was confronted at St George's Hall. Illustrations of the work of Schinkel, as well as the buildings of Leo von Klenze (1784–1864), which he will have seen in Munich, may already have influenced his designs for St George's Hall. The north entrance hall is as striking as any interior by Schinkel, with its semicircular ceiling, Doric columns screening the staircase, and casts of the Parthenon frieze.

On his return to Britain, Elmes continued work on St George's Hall, directing his attention in particular to the problem of vaulting the 74-foot span of the great hall. However, his health failing, he left Britain for a second time. He first went to Ventnor on the Isle of Wight, but when his condition failed to improve he undertook an unpleasantly stormy sea voyage to Jamaica in October 1847. Here he died in Spanish Town on 26 November at the age of thirty-three. He was accompanied by his young wife and child, whom he left without financial provision, though a subscription of £1400 was subsequently raised for them. Doomed never to see the completion of his masterpiece, he was also financially handicapped by the fact that his fee of five per cent on St George's Hall was based on the original estimate of £92,000, not on the £145,000 that had been spent on it by the time of his death.

Completion of St George's Hall; other works by Elmes Robert Rawlinson completed the structural work of St George's Hall between 1847 and 1851, providing the hall with a lightweight, fireproof vault of hollow, wedge-shaped bricks. John Weightman, city surveyor, was appointed architect in 1848, while C. R. Cockerell completed the interior, largely to his own designs, in 1851–4. The courts were ready for use in 1852, the great hall in 1854, and the concert hall in 1855. The building is a remarkably successful attempt to recapture the grandeur of imperial Rome by an architect who, like Sir Christopher Wren, had never visited Italy or Greece. It can only be paralleled by the work of Beaux-Arts architects in France such as Jakob Ignaz Hittorff (1792–1867) and Pierre-François-Henri Labrouste (1801–1875), and in America such as McKim, Mead, and White, whose masterpiece, Pennsylvania station, New York (1906–10), was, like St George's Hall, a masterly restatement of the theme of the baths of Caracalla for a non-thermal function.

Not surprisingly, in view of the magnitude of his principal commission and his premature death, Elmes designed few buildings other than St George's Hall. The principal is

the Liverpool Collegiate Institution, Shaw Street, Liverpool (1840–43), the commission for which he won in a competition held in 1840, in which the Tudor style was stipulated. His imposing eleven-bay façade in a late Perpendicular Gothic style was closely modelled on that of King Edward VI's Grammar School, Birmingham, built in 1833–7 from designs by Sir Charles Barry (1795–1860). The description of the institution in Liverpool as 'collegiate' rather than as a school indicates the essentially middle-class outlook of the promoters of this new foundation. It was divided into upper, middle, and lower schools to house boys drawn from different social classes. They were not allowed to meet, so that the long corridors were divided by iron gateways into three parts.

Unfortunately, Elmes had a disagreement with his clients at the collegiate institution which reflects an interesting light on the establishment of the professional status and responsibility of the architect in early Victorian Britain. His clients ignored what was becoming the accepted five per cent charge made by architects for preparing the specification and working drawings, and superintending their execution. Instead, they decided to economize by handing over this task to Edward Argent, a local surveyor. As a result, Elmes had only partial control over the appearance and execution of the building, the only payment he received being the competition premium of 100 guineas, plus an additional fee of the same amount, supposedly as an extra mark of the respect of his clients.

Elmes's other works in Liverpool included two classical mansions, Allerton Tower, Allerton (1846; dem. 1937), and Druid's Cross, Woolton (1846–7; dem. 1977), as well as the county lunatic asylum, Rainhill, executed after his death by William Moseley in 1847–51. His few surviving domestic works include Redcliffe, a villa of 1845 in the Tudor style at New Brighton, Wallasey, Cheshire, and the dull Italianate façades of houses in Ennismore Gardens and Prince's Gate, Kensington (c.1843–6), for the speculative builder John Elger.

Assessment of Elmes's work No personal reminiscences of Elmes survive, but there is a large collection of his architectural drawings in the RIBA drawings collection. Given the brevity of his career, these show his intense aptitude for work, for they include unexecuted designs for the town hall and market place at Bedford; two banks, an assembly room, and a church at Biggleswade; a church for blind people at Liverpool; and a court house at Worsley, Lancashire. He exhibited drawings at the Royal Academy in his lifetime.

There are a number of obvious impracticalities in the planning of St George's Hall, particularly its inadequate entrances and vestibules, which were partly consequent on the curious amalgam of concert halls and law courts in the same building. Elmes's father defended the building from these criticisms in an article in *The Builder* in 1855, but it had been all but universally admired as a masterpiece, even before its completion. The prince consort visited work in progress in 1846 and presented Elmes with a gold medal. It was described two years later as 'one of the finest architectural buildings in Europe' (*Art Union*, 1 Feb 1848, 52), and in 1875 as 'one of the greatest triumphs of the art [of architecture] in modern times' (J. A. Picton, *Memorials of Liverpool*, 1875).

The architect Richard Norman Shaw (1831–1912) was also one of its passionate admirers. In 1904, when he was one of those who chose Giles Gilbert Scott (1880–1960) as the architect for the new Anglican cathedral in Liverpool, he noted that, since Scott was only twenty-four, this was an example of history repeating itself in Liverpool. Praise from a more unexpected quarter came from the influential German architect and architectural writer Hermann Muthesius, who hailed Elmes as a master of the Greek revival (*Das englische Haus*, 1904–5, 1.54). In another epoch-making book of 1914, Sir Albert Richardson claimed of St George's Hall that 'The whole building fulfils the highest canons of the academic style, and is unsurpassed by any other modern building in Europe' (*Monumental Classic Architecture in Great Britain and Ireland during the Eighteenth and Nineteenth Centuries*, 1914, 86). He was followed by H. S. Goodhart-Rendel, who described it as 'the grandest Neo-classical building in England' (*English Architecture since the Regency*, 1953, 75), and by Nikolaus Pevsner, for whom it was 'the freest neo-Grecian building in England and one of the finest in the world' (Pevsner, *South Lancashire*, 155).

Elmes will also be remembered as the tragic genius whose death at the age of thirty-three, following that of Basevi at the age of fifty-one two years before, and combined with the rising tide of the Gothic revival, helped bring to an end the dominance which the classical tradition had enjoyed in British architecture since the seventeenth century.   DAVID WATKIN

Sources J. Elmes, 'The architect of St George's Hall', *The Builder*, 13 (1855), 53–5 · *Art Union*, 10 (1848), 51–2 · *The Builder*, 6 (1848), 24 · *The Builder*, 6 (1848), 71–2 · J. Olley, 'St George's Hall, Liverpool', *Architects' Journal* (18 June 1986), 36–57 · J. Olley, 'St George's Hall, Liverpool', *Architects' Journal* (25 June 1986), 36–61 · D. Wainwright, 'Elmes', *ArchR*, 125 (1959), 349–50 · R. P. Jones, 'The life and work of Harvey Lonsdale Elmes', *ArchR*, 15 (1904), 230–45 · J. A. Tanner, 'A contemporary account of St George's Hall', *ArchR*, 41 (1917), 122–5 · G. Hemm, *St George's Hall, Liverpool* (1949) · *Catalogue of the drawings collection of the Royal Institute of British Architects: C–F* (1972), 103–9 · Q. Hughes, 'Neo-classical ideas and practice: St George's Hall, Liverpool, by Harvey Lonsdale Elmes', *Architectural Association Quarterly*, 5 (1973), 36–44 · S. Bayley, 'A British Schinkel', *Architectural Association Quarterly*, 7 (1975), 28–32 · *IGI* · Colvin, *Archs*.
Archives Lpool RO, corresp. relating to St George's Hall, Liverpool · RIBA BAL, memoir of Elmes by his father and papers
Likenesses T. O. Barlow, engraving, pubd 1849 (after T. Crane), NPG [*see illus.*] · T. O. Barlow, engraving (after J. Lonsdale)

Elmes, James (1782–1862), writer on architecture, was born in London on 15 October 1782, the son of Samuel Elmes, builder, and his wife, Mary. He was educated at the Merchant Taylors' School from April 1796, and later became a pupil of George Gibson RA. He was admitted to the Royal Academy Schools in 1805, where, in the same year, he won the silver medal for an architectural design. He exhibited thirty-six designs at the Royal Academy

James Elmes (1782–1862), by James Lonsdale, 1810?

between 1801 and 1842. He built up an architectural practice in London and Sussex, and was vice-president of the Royal Architectural Society and surveyor to the Port of London from 1809 to 1848, when failing eyesight forced him to resign. Elmes and his wife, Mary Anne, were the parents of the architect Harvey Lonsdale *Elmes (1814–1847), who was born at Oving, near Chichester, Sussex, on 10 February 1814. They also had one daughter. James Elmes's buildings include: Oakwood House, Chichester (1809–12); the new gaol, Bedford (1819–20); and the house of correction, Waterford, Ireland (1820). He also rebuilt the upper part of the spire of Chichester Cathedral (1812–13).

It was as a writer that Elmes was best-known. In 1816 he launched the *Annals of Fine Arts*, which he edited until 1820. The *Annals* included many articles by Elmes's friend Benjamin Robert Haydon. Through Haydon, Elmes met John Keats, and several of Keats's poems first appeared in the *Annals*, including his 'Ode to a Nightingale', 'Ode on a Grecian Urn', and 'On Seeing the Elgin Marbles'. Elmes also drew the attention of his readers to the Elgin marbles, which were not well known. He was the author of *Memoirs of the Life and Works of Sir Christopher Wren* (1823), the first life of Wren to be written, and after he had finished it he sold a manuscript volume of Wren's papers, known as 'Court orders', to Sir John Soane. His most celebrated work was his *Metropolitan Improvements* (1827–9), illustrated by T. H. Shepherd. Other works included *Hints on the Improvement of Prisons* (1817), *The Arts and Artists* (3 vols., 1825), and *A Practical Treatise on Ecclesiastical and Civil Dilapidations* (1829). At the end of his life Elmes turned to theology, writing about medieval Hebrew poetry. He also published *Thomas Clarkson: a contribution towards the history and abolition of the slave trade and slavery* (1854). His last work was *The Gospel, Blended into one Narrative* (1856).

Elmes died at his home, 4 Alfred Place, Greenwich, on 2 April 1862 and was buried at Charlton three days later.

C. J. ROBINSON, *rev.* ANNE PIMLOTT BAKER

Sources Colvin, *Archs.* · *Dir. Brit. archs.* · E. B. Chancellor, 'James Elmes: architect and author', *The Builder*, 149 (1935), 1139 · *Wren Society*, 18 (1941) · *The autobiography and memoirs of Benjamin Robert Haydon (1786–1846)*, ed. T. Taylor, new edn, 1 (1926) · *IGI* · Graves, *Artists* · S. C. Hutchison, 'The Royal Academy Schools, 1768–1830', *Walpole Society*, 38 (1960–62), 123–91 · *The Builder*, 20 (1862), 275 · [W. Papworth], ed., *The dictionary of architecture*, 11 vols. (1853–92) · *GM*, 3rd ser., 12 (1862), 784 · *CGPLA Eng. & Wales* (1862)

Archives RA, corresp. · RIBA, scrapbook and memoir of his son H. L. Elmes | BL, letters to Sir Robert Peel, Add. MSS 40356, 40368, 40370, 40380, 40612

Likenesses J. Lonsdale, oils, 1810?, RIBA [*see illus.*]

Wealth at death under £100: probate, 14 May 1862, *CGPLA Eng. & Wales*

Elmham, Thomas (*b.* 1364, *d.* in or after 1427), historian and prior of Lenton, was born on 8 April 1364, and made his profession as a monk in 1379, according to entries in his unprinted *Cronica regum nobilium Angliae* (BL, Cotton MS Claudius E.iv, fol. 32*v*). His early career is obscure, but by 1407 he was treasurer of St Augustine's Abbey in Canterbury, in which capacity he was briefly arrested in a dispute over rents from a London church. A St Augustine's computus roll from 1407–8 (BL, Harley Roll Z.19) states that he was a scholar at Oxford. On 11 June 1414 he was made prior of the Cluniac house at Lenton in Nottinghamshire. A letter of Henry V to the abbot of Cluny, dated 24 November 1414, refers to Elmham as *capellanus noster*, perhaps indicating that he was at some stage in his career a royal chaplain. Within a year of his appointment to Lenton, Elmham was acting as vicar-general of the Cluniac houses in England and Scotland, a position officially confirmed by the abbot of Cluny on 26 October 1417. Almost ten years later, on 18 February 1427, he resigned as prior of Lenton and probably died soon afterwards.

Three major works by Elmham are known, all of them apparently belonging to the period between *c.*1414 and 1418; in each the author identifies himself in an acrostic. The earliest, probably representing several years' labour, is the ambitious and incomplete history of St Augustine's Abbey which Elmham himself appears to have referred to as the *Speculum Augustinianum*. This is extant in a single magnificent manuscript, which may be a fair copy in the author's own hand (Cambridge, Trinity Hall, MS 1); it contains two celebrated illustrations, perhaps Elmham's own work, the first a depiction of the principal altars in the abbey church, and the second a map of the abbey's lands in Thanet. The complex chronological table prefacing the *Speculum* shows that Elmham intended to cover the whole period from 597 to 1414 (a later hand has extended the table to 1418), but in the event the history proper breaks off in 806; the remainder of the text is merely a preparatory collection of documents from 1066 to 1191. Elmham may have abandoned the project when he was appointed to Lenton. His intelligent handling of his documentary

sources, particularly Anglo-Saxon charters, has impressed modern scholars: he compared the originals to the cartulary texts and adduced reasons to prefer the readings of the former; he used the evidence of charters to establish the dates of early Kentish kings; and he reproduced in facsimile four of the earliest documents in the archive, supposedly relating to the seventh-century foundation, but actually eleventh-century forgeries. In his approach to this material Elmham relied heavily on earlier research by generations of St Augustine's scholars, particularly Thomas Sprott (*fl.* 1272); in places this scholarly activity had led to modification of the dates and beneficiaries of the muniments, and even to the production of imitative pseudo-originals. Many of Elmham's historical observations are in fact vitiated by his use of contaminated documents.

Nothing Elmham wrote after leaving Canterbury reached the standard of the *Speculum*. In 1416 he produced the *Cronica regum nobilium Angliae*, an undistinguished compilation on the kings of England from Brutus to Richard II, based to an uncomfortable degree on Geoffrey of Monmouth. He later turned his attention to writing Latin prose and verse lives of Henry V; only the *Liber metricus* survives, a work notable for little more than its cryptic style and word play. In the past the lost Latin life has been identified with the *Gesta Henrici quinti*, written by an anonymous royal chaplain; but it has now been established that Elmham was not the author of that work, although he evidently used it as the basis for the *Liber metricus* (and presumably the prose life).

S. E. KELLY

Sources Thomas of Elmham, *Historia monasterii S. Augustini Cantuariensis*, ed. C. Hardwick, Rolls Series, 8 (1858) · Thomas Elmham, 'Cronica regum nobilium Angliae', BL, Cotton MS Claudius E.iv · *Elmhami 'Liber metricus de Henrico Quinto'*, ed. C. A. Cole, Rolls Series, 11 (1858) · BL, Harley Roll Z.19 · G. F. Duckett, ed., *Charters and records from the ancient abbey of Cluni*, 2 vols. (1888). 2.15–22 · F. Taylor, 'A note on Rolls Series 8', *Bulletin of the John Rylands University Library*, 20 (1936), 379–82 · J. S. Roskell and F. Taylor, 'The authorship and purpose of the *Gesta Henrici quinti*', *Bulletin of the John Rylands University Library*, 53 (1970–71), 428–64 · A. Gransden, 'Antiquarian studies in fifteenth-century England', *Antiquaries Journal*, 60 (1980), 75–97, esp. 79–81 · A. Gransden, *Historical writing in England*, 2 (1982), 206–10, 345–55 · S. E. Kelly, ed., *Charters of St Augustine's Abbey, Canterbury, and Minster-in-Thanet*, Anglo-Saxon Charters, 4 (1995), xcvi–cvi · J. H. Wylie and W. T. Waugh, eds., *The reign of Henry the Fifth*, 2 (1919), 81–8 · R. A. Skelton and P. D. A. Harvey, eds., *Local maps and plans from medieval England* (1986), 107–26

Archives BL, Cotton MS Claudius E.iv, fol. 32*v* · Trinity Hall, Cambridge, MS 1

Elmhirst [*née* Whitney], **Dorothy Payne** (1887–1968), patron of education and the arts, was born at 1731 I Street, in Washington, DC, United States of America, on 23 January 1887, the fifth and youngest child of William Collins Whitney (1841–1904), statesman and company promoter, and his first wife, Flora (1842–1893), daughter of the attorney and businessman Henry B. Payne and his wife, Mary.

Early years Dorothy Whitney started life in the 'public eye'. Born when her father held the post of secretary of the United States navy, her baptism at St John's Church, Lafayette Square, Washington, on 11 April 1887, necessitated a grand social gathering. Her childhood was spent

Dorothy Payne Elmhirst (1887–1968), by unknown photographer, 1930s

predominantly in New York—once her father had given up politics to focus on making money. Dorothy's three surviving siblings were all more than ten years her senior and at boarding-school before her birth. She saw little of her parents at home on West 57th Street where, with a handful of children she was educated at Mr Roser's private school, within the family mansion. She developed close friendships with among others Gladys Vanderbilt, who lived in a 'french chateau' next door, near enough for the two girls to attach a rope between their bedroom windows. Her forceful, party-loving mother died of a heart attack while planning Dorothy's sixth birthday celebrations. Whitney married the widowed Mrs Edith Randolph in 1896; but the new extended family life was short-lived. When Dorothy and Edith were out riding in Aiken, South Carolina, Edith fell and broke her cervical vertebra, and after months as an invalid, she died in 1899. From the age of twelve to twenty-four Dorothy's closest companion was her governess Beatrice Bend. Beatrice sent Dorothy to Miss Spence's school for a year, where learning passages of Shakespeare by heart sparked a lifelong interest in the theatre. Dorothy also became increasingly involved in her father's cultural life: his latest grand New York house had been refurbished for his new wife although she never lived to see the transformation. In 1904 her father died of peritonitis and blood poisoning.

From 1904 to 1911 Dorothy was based at her eldest brother Harry's New York home. His wife, Gertrude, was a sculptor who later founded the Whitney Museum of American Art. Dorothy made her official social début in

January 1906, in Harry's ballroom. Contemporary photographs show her quiet sideways smile and hands-on-hips jaunty posture. Taking her independence seriously, she felt compassion for those experiencing loss and an obligation to make amends for the money she would inherit, which was increasingly seen to have been gained through dubious means. Scandals broke in 1908, the year Dorothy came of age, regarding Whitney's trading activities during his lifetime. She wanted to assist those with a vision of social reform who lacked her financial means, and devised a work schedule for herself, visiting the slums and the settlement housing schemes, working in a children's court and with the women's suffrage movement.

Travels abroad and marriage Dorothy Whitney travelled abroad extensively, chaperoned by Beatrice Bend. In Peking (Beijing) they spent a captivating fortnight in the company of Willard Dickerman Straight (1880–1918), a young banker and diplomat with whom Dorothy formed an understanding. After rejecting his first proposals, Dorothy married him in Geneva on 7 September 1911 and lived for six months in Peking, where Willard was working. An uprising against the Manchu dynasty saw them return to New York. In 1912 a son, Whitney Willard *Straight, was born, in 1914 a daughter, Beatrice, and in 1916, a year after they moved into their newly built permanent home on Fifth Avenue, a second son, Michael, arrived. Willard, too, was an orphan and Dorothy inspired him with radical ideas for social reform. They founded the non-partisan magazine the *New Republic*, first published in 1914, which President Theodore Roosevelt denounced as 'parlor bolshevism' (MS letter to Willard Straight, 14 July 1918, Dorothy Whitney Straight Elmhirst MSS, Cornell University). Later they revamped *Asia*, a magazine for the American Asiatic Association. Dorothy praised Willard for his 'wonderful power of sympathy' (MS letter to Katherine Barnes, 18 Nov 1909, Dorothy Whitney Straight Elmhirst MSS, Cornell University). Straight enlisted in 1917, and in 1918 was based with the United States army in Europe. He died unexpectedly on 1 December 1918 when influenza turned to pneumonia and was buried at the American military cemetery at Suresnes, Paris.

Social reform projects Dorothy threw herself into voluntary work at New York's YMCA and became increasingly active in the women's trade union movement with her long-time friend Eleanor Roosevelt. She helped the socialist leader Kate Richard O'Hare organize the children's crusade for amnesty for political prisoners gaoled during the war. Acquainted with the educationist John Dewey (1859–1952), she was also a founder of New York's New School for Social Research, which studied contemporary international education practices. Cecil Beaton's portrait of her from this period, with bobbed hair, graceful in a chaste black dress, is a far cry from his usual 1920s society portraits. Willard Straight's bequest had allocated money to make his own college, Cornell, a more welcoming place for students. Dorothy became involved in plans for a student union building, Willard Straight Hall, completed in 1924 at the university campus in Ithaca, New York state.

Through her attentive concern for Cornell, Dorothy Straight first met Leonard Knight *Elmhirst (1893–1974), a graduate student from England studying agriculture, who fell in love with her at once. He graduated in 1921 and established a rural reconstruction institute, with the poet Rabindranath Tagore (1861–1941), at Santiniketan in West Bengal. The aim was to lessen starvation in the area through successful cultivation of the land. Leonard and Dorothy, who was financing the research at Santiniketan, were regular correspondents during these years. In 1923 Leonard returned to the United States, embarrassed by their disparity in wealth but unwavering in his devotion to her. In April 1925 they had a quiet wedding at Westbury, Long Island. Photographs taken during the forty years of their marriage show her laughing again, head thrown back, elegant in well-cut skirts and jackets, the occasional necklace and broad brimmed hats.

In 1925 Dorothy and Leonard discovered a ruined fourteenth-century manor, Dartington Hall, in the hills of south Devon, near Totnes. The buildings and accompanying estate were to become the couple's own working experiment in education and rural regeneration—an attempt to resolve the problems of successful rural living in an industrial age. That year Dorothy's fortune was worth $35 million. For the rest of her life Dartington was her home and the focus of her financial investment, although she was still loyal to funding various commitments in the United States. In 1932 the Dartington Hall Charitable Trust was established to administer the land, buildings, school, and research, with Leonard and Dorothy as two of the four trustees. The couple had two children, a daughter, Ruth, born in 1926, and a son, Bill, born in 1929. Dorothy's three eldest children moved to England and partly for their benefit a small co-educational boarding-school opened at Dartington in September 1926 with a manifesto inspired by Tagore, Dewey, and Jean Jacques Rousseau's novel Émile (1762). In the first five years the school was strongly integrated into the activities of the Dartington estate—metalwork, forestry, work in the dairy, rearing poultry, cider making, textile production, and decorating all played a large part in the curriculum and Dorothy and Leonard were both involved with teaching small groups. In 1931 William B. Curry was appointed the first headmaster. The school became one of the most renowned progressive institutions of the twentieth century, and continued to educate children at primary and secondary levels until its closure in 1987.

Dorothy Elmhirst's primary interest at Dartington was patronage of the arts. She showed foresight in backing R. C. Sheriff's play Journey's End, which opened in London in 1928 with Laurence Olivier playing Captain Stanhope. The Elmhirsts became financially involved in the ownership of the Globe Theatre and Queen's Theatre, London.

The next decade saw Dartington's most celebrated period of cultural involvement. The artists Mark Tobey, Cecil Collins, Ben and Winifred Nicholson, sculptor Henry Moore and the potter Bernard Leach were all involved with Dartington and their work was collected by the Elmhirsts. In 1933 Walter Gropius visited, hoping to create a design studio after Nazi persecution had led to the closure of the Bauhaus. This did not materialize, but he was commissioned as architect for the last stages of conversion of Dartington's Barn Theatre. Another refugee from Nazi persecution, the internationally acclaimed ballet dancer Kurt Joos, settled at Dartington for several years and formed a successful avant-garde dance troupe.

Mikhail Chekhov, the Russian director and nephew of playwright Anton Chekhov, also established a theatre group. He inspired Dorothy to act on the stage in a professional production for the first time. She travelled to New York to rehearse the role of Mrs Stavrogin in Chekhov's Broadway production of Dostoyevsky's The Possessed, scheduled to open in the autumn of 1939. The outbreak of war between Britain and Germany threatened that Dorothy could be cut off from Britain, and so she returned to Dartington, leaving the play to open without her.

The war forced various foreign visitors to leave Dartington under threat of internment, and Dorothy began to develop Dartington's 38 acre garden, inspired by English models—both scented cottage gardens and the landscaped parks of a country house. She secretly compiled My Favourite Anthology, a collection of poetry with a strongly religious emphasis, which was posthumously published in a limited edition. Although she took up no orthodox religious practice in adult life she placed great emphasis on the spiritual life and psychoanalysis, especially the works of Carl Gustav Jung. After the war Dartington expanded its programme of further education and Dorothy took a particular interest in art and music as developed by Peter Cox and Imogen Holst respectively. She gave weekly Shakespeare classes at Dartington arts department from 1945 to 1961, and when at home never missed a production at the Barn Theatre. She also continued her regular visits to London shows: Waiting for Godot she learned to like but the violence of Look Back in Anger she abhorred.

At Dartington Dorothy was the guiding force. Yet her position showed up an irony inherent in this 'experiment': her position as benefactor reinforced the very hierarchy Dartington had hoped to break. She died at Dartington on 14 December 1968. Her funeral took place at the local Anglican church and her ashes were scattered over Dartington Hall Garden. Leonard's ashes were also scattered there when he died in 1974. LOTTIE HOARE

Sources W. A. Swanberg, *Whitney father, Whitney heiress* (New York, 1980) · M. Young, *The Elmhirsts of Dartington: the creation of an utopian community* (1982) · private information (2004) [Maurice Ash, son-in-law] · private information (2004) [M. Bride Nicholson] · H. Croly, *Willard Straight* (New York, 1925) · R. Snell, *From the bare stem: making Dorothy Elmhirst's garden at Dartington Hall* (1989) · WWW, 1971–80

Archives Cornell University, Ithaca, New York, Dorothy Whitney Straight Elmhirst project, interview [transcripts] · Cornell University, Ithaca, New York, MSS · Dartington Hall, near Totnes, Devon, archive, MSS | King's Lond., papers of Capt Sir Basil Henry Liddell Hart · Ransom HRC, Nancy Wilson Ross collection | SOUND Col. U., Oral History Collection

Likenesses W. Straight, pastel drawing, 1912, Cornell University · C. Beaton, photograph, 1918–25 · photograph, 1930–39, Dartington Hall, Devon [see illus.] · W. D. Goldberg, portrait, Dartington Hall, Devon

Wealth at death £96,495: probate, 12 Dec 1969, CGPLA Eng. & Wales

Elmhirst, Leonard Knight (1893–1974), agricultural economist and philanthropist, was born on 6 June 1893 at Laxton, Yorkshire, the second of eight sons and nine children of the Revd William Heaton Elmhirst, clergyman, of Laxton, subsequently owner of the Elmhirst estate, Worsbrough Dale, Yorkshire, and his wife, Mary, second daughter of the Revd William Knight, clergyman, of Hemsworth, Yorkshire. He was educated at Repton School, at Trinity College, Cambridge, where he obtained third classes in both parts of the historical tripos (1914 and 1915) and, from 1919 to 1921, at New York State College of Agriculture, Cornell University (where he obtained a BSc in agriculture in 1921).

Countryman by upbringing, philanthropist and internationalist by conviction, and friend to all sorts and conditions of men, Elmhirst was committed to improving the quality of life in rural communities. In the First World War YMCA work took him to India, where he learned of that country's rural problems. From 1921 to 1925 he worked with Rabindranath Tagore, the Indian educationist, poet, and social reformer. Elmhirst was the first director of the Institute of Rural Reconstruction at Santiniketan, Bengal. In 1925 he married Dorothy Payne *Elmhirst, née Whitney (1887–1968), daughter of William Collins Whitney, lawyer, politician, and millionaire businessman, of New York. She had been married previously to Willard Dickerman Straight (1880–1918), American diplomat and financier, and had two young sons and a daughter from that marriage—Beatrice, Michael, and Whitney Willard Straight. The Elmhirsts had one son and one daughter.

In 1925 the Elmhirsts bought the Dartington estate near Totnes, Devon. They started a progressive school, restored the medieval buildings, and did much new construction. Forestry was conducted as both commercial venture and research undertaking, as was farming in association with the estate's laboratory and agricultural economics research department. In 1943 Elmhirst helped establish privately the Dartington Cattle Breeding Centre. There were experiments with small enterprises: orchards, cider, sawmilling, woodworking, and poultry. The building department, with its quarries, became Staverton Builders. Joinery, textile mill, and craft shops also lasted. Alongside regeneration of a depressed rural economy went the provision of welfare benefits for employees. There were opportunities for all for further education and enjoyment of the arts, of which the Elmhirsts were eclectic patrons. In particular, from 1953 Dartington became renowned for its international summer music school. They also created Dartington's fine gardens. While remaining fully involved, they relinquished personal ownership and control of the enterprise in 1931–2 to the Dartington Hall Trust, a charitable trust of which Elmhirst was chairman until 1972.

As active outside as inside Dartington, and an inveterate traveller, Elmhirst was a founder member of the international conference of agricultural economists in 1930, its first president until 1958, and founder president until his death. Elmhirst's Second World War contribution arose from his international connections and agricultural interests. He was a member of a Board of Trade mission to the USA. At the US department of agriculture's invitation he toured the USA for discussions on wartime agriculture. He was a member of an agricultural mission from the Ministry of War Transport to advise the Middle East Supply Centre. In 1944 and 1945 he was agricultural adviser to the governor of famine-stricken Bengal. He visited India regularly from 1949 to 1961 as honorary consultant on land use to the Damodar Valley Corporation and member of the council of Visva-Bharati University, Santiniketan. In 1954 and 1955 he served on the Indian government's committee on higher education in rural areas.

At home, Elmhirst and his wife supported the research organization Political and Economic Planning from its inception in 1931; Elmhirst was chairman from 1939 to 1953. From 1950 to 1960 they supported the Withymead Clinic, Exeter, which helped people under psychological stress. Elmhirst was on the national parks committee from 1945 to 1947 and a development commissioner from 1949 to 1965. He was president of the Agricultural Economics Society from 1949 to 1950. He served on the committee on the provincial agricultural economics service from 1954 to 1969. Close to his heart was his championship of private forestry. He was president of the Royal Forestry Society from 1946 to 1948 and an architect of the dedication scheme introduced in the Forestry Acts of 1947 and 1951. A favourite occupation was working in the Dartington woodlands. He was involved in local affairs as Devon county councillor, Dartington parish councillor, governor and manager of schools in Totnes and Dartington, and member of the council of first the University College of the South West and then Exeter University.

Elmhirst's indefatigable and unostentatious service, which went with unfailing optimism and zest for life, was recognized by honorary degrees: DPolSci, Freiburg, 1953; DLitt, Visva-Bharati, 1960; DCL, Durham, 1962; DCL, Oxford, 1970; and DCL, Exeter, 1972. Widowed in 1968, in 1972 Elmhirst married Susanna Isaacs, daughter of Hubert Foss, music publisher of Oxford University Press.

Elmhirst appeared unmistakably an English country gentleman, well groomed and dressed with unobtrusive good taste, with an erect although not an imposing figure, a trim moustache, and an eagle eye for detail. His manner combined impeccable courtesy with lively and sympathetic interest in people and places. Elmhirst died on 16 April 1974 in Beverly Hills, California.

ANTHEA WILLIAMS, rev.

Sources The Times (18 April 1974) · M. Young, The Elmhirsts of Dartington: the creation of an utopian community (1982) · private information (1986) · V. Bonham-Carter, 'Dartington Hall 1925–56, a report', Dartington Hall RO, Devon · V. Bonham-Carter, 'The enterprise of

Dartington Hall, a first supplement, 1956–65', Dartington Hall RO, Devon · *WWW* · *CGPLA Eng. & Wales* (1974)
Archives Dartington Hall, near Totnes, Devon | Derbys. RO, corresp. with J. L. S. Vidler · King's Lond., Liddell Hart C., corresp. with Sir B. H. Liddell Hart · Rice University, Houston, Texas, Woodson Research Center, corresp. with Sir Julian Huxley
Likenesses photographs, Dartington Hall Trust, Totnes, Devon
Wealth at death £56,770: probate, 14 Oct 1974, *CGPLA Eng. & Wales*

Elmhirst, Sir Thomas Walker (1895–1982), air force officer, was born on 15 December 1895 in Laxton, Yorkshire, the fourth of the eight sons and nine children of the Revd William Heaton Elmhirst and his wife, Mary, the daughter of the Revd William Knight, of Hemsworth, Yorkshire. He was a younger brother of Leonard Knight *Elmhirst. In 1899 his parson father became head of a small estate which had been in the family since 1340. From the age of six Elmhirst intended to become a sailor, and in 1908, at the age of twelve, he entered the Royal Naval College at Osborne. He then went to Dartmouth. He saw naval action at the Dogger Bank under Admiral Sir David Beatty in January 1915, and in March 1915 he was one of twenty young officers selected by Admiral Lord Fisher to start a new naval airship service to combat the German submarine threat. After qualifying as a balloon pilot he captained airships on anti-submarine patrols over the North and Irish seas. From April 1918 until the end of the First World War he commanded, at the age of twenty-two, the airship stations on Anglesey and at Malahide in Ireland. He was awarded the Air Force Cross (1918).

In 1919 Elmhirst transferred to the RAF and flew seaplanes and flying boats. On graduating from the staff college in 1925 he served for three years in intelligence on the staff of Sir Hugh Trenchard in the Air Ministry before returning to flying duties at RAF Leuchars. After further staff appointments he was sent to form and command 15 bomber squadron at Abingdon (1935–7). He then went to Ankara as air attaché to Turkey (1937–9).

Elmhirst was a good all-round sportsman, excelling at rugby football and playing at scrum half for the RAF against the Royal Navy and the army in 1921. He later became honorary secretary of the RAF rugby union.

In 1939 Elmhirst returned to England to command RAF Leconfield in the rank of group captain, and on 3 September he prepared to dispatch the first bombers detailed to attack Germany—though at the last moment the bombs were off-loaded and replaced with leaflets. On promotion to air commodore in January 1940 he was posted to the Air Ministry as director of intelligence before going to Fighter Command headquarters as duty air commodore during the crucial months of August and September in the battle of Britain. In December his experience in intelligence and his service in Turkey led to his selection, together with an admiral and a general, for a mission for conversations with the Turkish general staff. He was retained in Cairo after the talks and was appointed in April 1941 to command no. 202 group, which was responsible for the air defence of Egypt. His ability for senior command was demonstrated in the build-up of an efficient organization modelled on that in Britain.

Sir Thomas Walker Elmhirst (1895–1982), by Vandyk, 1958

In February 1942 Elmhirst was asked by his commander-in-chief, Sir Arthur Tedder, to go to the desert air force as chief administrative officer to its recently arrived commander, Sir Arthur Coningham. Although he was reluctant to give up his command in Egypt, he recognized the importance of the desert campaign and went cheerfully to begin a partnership with Coningham that continued through Libya, Tunisia, Sicily, Italy, Normandy, and Brussels to final victory in Germany. In this operational administrative role he planned and organized mobile air forces which enabled the development of Coningham's concept of tactical air forces for operations with armies, an idea which was subsequently adopted in other theatres of war. He regarded this as his greatest single achievement in his service career, and it was marked by the award of the US Legion of Merit and the CB (1945).

After returning to England early in 1944 to prepare (for the invasion of Europe) the 2nd Tactical Air Force, which Coningham was to command, Elmhirst was promoted air vice-marshal. The achievements of 2nd Tactical Air Force from the invasion of Normandy onwards owed much to his preparatory work. In 1945 his service was recognized when he was appointed KBE (he was made CBE in 1943).

Elmhirst's first peacetime post was as assistant chief of the air staff (intelligence) in the Air Ministry, but within two years he was pressed to go to India as chief of administration on the staff of Field Marshal Sir Claude Auchinleck and was promoted air marshal. When India achieved independence in 1947 he was asked by Jawaharlal Nehru and

Earl Mountbatten of Burma to remain and become the first commander-in-chief of the new Indian Air Force. In 1950 ill health forced his resignation, but as a tribute he was made an honorary air marshal for life in the Indian Air Force.

On his retirement to Scotland Elmhirst served as deputy lieutenant (1960–70) and county councillor for Fife and controller of civil defence for east Scotland. In 1953 he was called to join the Ministry of Supply responsible to Sir William Penney for the organization of his atom bomb team and its transportation to Australia for the first British atom bomb to be exploded on land. On completion of this task that same year he was appointed lieutenant-governor of Guernsey, where he served until 1958. He then retired for the second time to Fife.

Elmhirst was a small man, always impeccably dressed in his uniform. His outstanding physical feature was his large bushy eyebrows, which rose perceptibly when he saw anything that displeased him. He married on 16 September 1930 Katharine Gordon, the daughter of William Black, a chartered accountant, of Chapel, Fife. They had a son and a daughter. She died in 1965 and in 1968 he married Marian Louisa, the widow of Colonel Andrew Ferguson and the daughter of Lieutenant-Colonel Lord Herbert Montagu-Douglas-Scott. Elmhirst died on 6 November 1982 at Basingstoke, Hampshire.

KENNETH CROSS, rev.

Sources private information (1990) · personal knowledge (1990) · *The Times* (10 Nov 1982) · *WWW* · Burke, *Gen. GB* (1937) **Archives** CAC Cam., corresp. and papers | FILM IWM FVA, home footage | SOUND IWM SA, 'British group captain served with Royal Navy Air Force …', IWM Air Operations, 20 Dec 1977, 998 **Likenesses** Vandyk, photograph, 1958, NPG [*see illus.*] **Wealth at death** £12,256: probate, 7 Feb 1983, *CGPLA Eng. & Wales*

Elmore, Alfred (1815–1881), history and genre painter, was born in Clonakilty, co. Cork, on 18 June 1815, son of a retired surgeon of the 5th dragoon guards. At the age of twelve he moved with his family to London and, after practising drawing from the antique at the British Museum, he entered the Royal Academy Schools in 1832. He first exhibited at the Royal Academy in 1834; during the next few years he visited Paris to copy in the Louvre and study in private ateliers. Probably about this time he executed a group of watercolours depicting knights, ladies, troubadours, and other medieval subjects, as well as landscapes, executed in bold washes of brilliant colour in a style reminiscent of Richard Parkes Bonington. Neither signed nor dated, the sheets remained in Elmore's family until their sale in 1933, when they entered the Victoria and Albert Museum and the British Museum in London, and other public and private collections.

In 1839 Elmore's *Crucifixion* gained a favourable spot at the British Institution and the following year he exhibited at the Royal Academy *The Martyrdom of Thomas à Becket*, which was purchased by the politician Daniel O'Connell and subsequently hung in St Andrew's Roman Catholic Church in Dublin. After a three-month stay in Munich in 1840, Elmore travelled to Italy to study the works of the old masters, visiting Venice, Bologna, and Florence before settling in Rome, where he remained for two years; one of his Italian sketchbooks is now in the Victoria and Albert Museum.

Following his return to London in 1844, Elmore exhibited frequently at the Royal Academy, chiefly richly costumed and elaborately staged historical-literary subjects which, though resembling traditional history paintings in their large scale and complex compositions, also incorporate the anecdotal narratives, individualized characterizations, and painstaking brushwork of the domestic genre mode. Among his many Italian subjects are *Rienzi in the Forum* (exh. RA, 1844; ex Sothebys, London, 16 March 1988), drawn from Byron, the success of which helped win his election to associate of the Royal Academy the following year; and *The Fainting of Hero* (exh. RA, 1846; priv. coll., USA), from *Much Ado about Nothing*, one of his many Shakespearian canvases. Elected to full membership in the academy in 1857, he presented as his diploma work a scene from *The Two Gentlemen of Verona* (exh. RA, 1858; Royal Academy, London). By 1858 he was living at 1 St Alban's Road, Kensington, where he remained until his death. Attracted to royal subjects, Elmore painted scenes from the lives of such beleaguered heroines as Marie Antoinette and Mary, queen of Scots; his male monarchs were most often French but also included the Holy Roman emperor, as in *The Emperor Charles V at Yuste* (exh. RA, 1856; Royal Holloway and Bedford New College, University of London, Egham). Other works were inspired by eighteenth-century English literature and early American history. Two of his pictures represent precursors of the industrial revolution: *The Invention of the Stocking Loom* (exh. RA, 1847), which was engraved for the Art Union of London; and *Invention of the Combing Machine* (exh. RA, 1862; Nottingham Castle Museum).

Elmore is now best-known for *On the Brink* (exh. RA, 1865; Fitzwilliam Museum, Cambridge), a morality tale on the theme of the 'fallen woman' cast in the guise of a contemporary genre scene in much the same vein as William Holman Hunt's *Awakening Conscience* (exh. RA, 1854) and Augustus Egg's *Past and Present* (exh. RA, 1858; both Tate collection). Evidently set in the fashionable resort of Homburg in Hesse-Nassau, Germany, *On the Brink* depicts a despondent young woman seated in the cold moonlight outside the gaming-rooms, which are teeming with gamblers and suffused with a lurid red glow. Leaning out toward her through an open window is a young man cast in shadow, most likely a potential seducer. In the vegetation framing her at the right are pure white lilies and purple passion flowers, which represent the two poles of her dilemma.

From 1868 Elmore exhibited a number of Old Testament figures and Arabic scenes, including several set in Algiers. He was elected an honorary member of the Royal Hibernian Academy, Dublin, in 1878. One of his last exhibited pictures, *A Greek Ode* (exh. RA, 1879; Roy Miles Gallery, London), set in the ancient world in the mode of Sir Lawrence Alma-Tadema, shows a young poet reading to his sweetheart. Late in life Elmore was severely injured in a fall from his horse which left him lame. He died of cancer at his home, 1 St Alban's Road, on 24 January 1881 and was buried in Kensal Green cemetery in London. Among his executors was the painter William Powell Frith, who was presumably a close friend.   LUCY OAKLEY

Sources *L'Art* (1881), 240 · *Art Journal*, new ser., 1 (1881), 95 · *Magazine of Art*, 4 (1880–81), xvii · *The Portfolio*, 12 (1881), 54 · 'British artists, their style and character: no. XXIII, Alfred Elmore', *Art Journal*, 19 (1857), 113–15 · W. Sandby, *The history of the Royal Academy of Arts*, 2 vols. (1862) · L. Nead, 'Seduction, prostitution, suicide: *On the brink* by Alfred Elmore', *Art History*, 5 (1982), 309–22 · M. Hardie, *Water-colour painting in Britain*, ed. D. Snelgrove, J. Mayne, and B. Taylor, 2: *The Romantic period* (1967) · J. W. Goodison, *Catalogue of paintings in the Fitzwilliam Museum, Cambridge*, 3: *British school* (1977) · J. Chapel, *Victorian taste: the complete catalogue of paintings at the Royal Holloway College* (1982) · G. Ashton, *Shakespeare's heroines in the nineteenth century* (1980) [exhibition catalogue, Buxton Museum and Art Gallery, 22 July – 17 Aug 1980] · G. Reynolds, *Victorian painting* (1966) · W. G. Strickland, *A dictionary of Irish artists*, 2 vols. (1913) · C. Wood, *Olympian dreamers* (1983) · L. Oakley, 'Words into pictures: Shakespeare in British art, 1760–1900', in L. Oakley and C. Mazer, *A brush with Shakespeare: the bard in painting, 1780–1910* (1985), 3–22 [exhibition catalogue, Montgomery Museum of Fine Arts, 11 Dec – 14 June 1986] · *CGPLA Eng. & Wales* (1881) · Graves, *RA exhibitors* · Graves, *Brit. Inst.*
Likenesses C. Baugniet, lithograph, pubd 1857, BM · H. N. O'Neil, group portrait, oils, 1869 (*The billiard room of the Garrick Club*), Garr. Club · Caldesi, Blanford & Co., carte-de-visite, NPG · Lock & Whitfield, woodburytype photograph, NPG; repro. in T. Cooper, *Men of mark: a gallery of contemporary portraits* (1881) · Maull & Polyblank, carte-de-visite, NPG
Wealth at death under £80,000: probate, 21 March 1881, *CGPLA Eng. & Wales*

Elmpt. For this title name *see* Anrep, Boris Vasileyich, Count Elmpt in the nobility of the Holy Roman empire (1883–1969).

Elmsley, Peter (1735/6–1802), bookseller, was born in Aberdeenshire. For a time he was a partner with the bookseller Paul Vaillant, whose family had conducted a foreign bookselling business in the Strand, London, opposite Southampton Street, since 1686, but from 1768 Elmsley was trading there alone (from 1778 his address was 87 Strand). He was principally involved in importing foreign books and was often described as a French bookseller. Later in his career he invested in works with others of his trade in London, and despite losing his warehouse to a fire on 2 March 1776 he became one of London's best-known booksellers. According to John Nichols, a friend of both Elmsley and his wife, Isabella (*d*. 1819), his 'consummate ability and the strictest integrity' earned him the 'regard and respect' of the duke of Grafton, Topham Beauclerk, Clayton Mordaunt Cracherode, John Wilkes, and Edward Gibbon (*GM*, 72/1). He was also 'beloved and regarded' by 'his more immediate friends and patrons', such as Earl Spencer, Earl Stanhope, Sir Joseph Banks, Thomas Rennell (later dean of Winchester), and Louis Dutens (Nichols, *Lit. anecdotes*, 6.441). Nichols praised Elmsley's fund of general knowledge and suggests that his 'uncommonly accurate … discrimination of language', both in English and in French, would have secured him 'a permanent niche in the Temple of Fame', had he chosen to be a writer (*GM*, 72/1).

Elmsley served as bookseller and shipping agent for Gibbon, assisting in the management of his affairs in London when Gibbon was in Lausanne. In a letter of 31 July 1783 Gibbon wrote to Georges Deyverdun: 'je trouve dans le libraire Elmsley un conseiller sage, instruit et discret' ('I find in the bookseller Elmsley a wise, informed and discreet counsellor'; *Letters of Edward Gibbon*, 2.348). Some years later, on 28 February 1789, Gibbon wrote to Elmsley:

> whatsoever modesty you may feel or affect I sincerely assure you that I set the highest value on the observations of a cool, intelligent, impartial man who converses every day with all ranks of people from a duke to a printer's devil. Therefore write on public as well as private business, and be persuaded that on all subjects your correspondence will be acceptable to a person who has long considered you not only as a bookseller but as a friend. (ibid., 3.144–5)

Elmsley was also friends with John Wilkes, a great book collector. On Wilkes's death, in 1797, his books remained in his house in Grosvenor Square until the death of his daughter Mary Wilkes, who directed her executors 'to deliver all her honoured Father's Library, according to the Catalogue, to Mr. Elmsly of Sloane Square' (Nichols, *Lit. anecdotes*, 9.478–9). Elmsley, however, died before her.

Elmsley was a member of the club of major booksellers that met monthly at the Shakespeare tavern, where, according to Nichols, 'the germ of many a valuable publication' originated, including the ideas that led to the publication in 1779 of *The Works of the English Poets with Prefaces, Biographical, and Critical, by Samuel Johnson* (Nichols, *Lit. anecdotes*, 5.325). His name first appears with those of his fellow club members and others in the imprint of the second edition (1781) of *The Lives of the Poets* and continues through to the edition of 1801. His name also appears with much the same group in the imprint of the first collected edition of Johnson's works (1787), compiled by Sir John Hawkins, and in the editions of Johnson's works, compiled by Arthur Murphy, published between 1792 and 1801.

In 1797 Elmsley gave up his business to his shopman, David Bremmer, who died a few years later and was succeeded in 1802 by J. Mackinlay, one of Elmsley's assistants, and James Payne, a younger son of Thomas Payne, of the Mews-gate, a fellow club member. Elmsley died at Brighthelmstone (Brighton) on 3 May 1802, in his sixty-seventh year. His remains were brought to his house in Sloane Street, and on 10 May were taken to Marylebone and deposited in the family vault. According to John Nichols's obituary 'For strength of mind, soundness of judgment, and unaffected friendship, he has left not many equals' (*GM*, 72/1). Much of Elmsley's large fortune went to his nephew the clergyman and classical scholar Peter *Elmsley. In December 1819 Isabella Elmsley died; she was described in her obituary as the widow of the 'well-known and justly-respected bookseller in the Strand' (ibid., 89/2).

O. M. BRACK

Sources J. D. Fleeman, *A bibliography of the works of Samuel Johnson*, 2 vols. (2000) · *The letters of Edward Gibbon*, ed. J. E. Norton (1956), vols. 2–3 · I. Maxted, *The London book trades, 1775–1800: a preliminary checklist of members* (1977) · Nichols, *Lit. anecdotes*, 3.310; 5.325; 6.440–41; 8.558–9; 9.478–9 · *GM*, 1st ser., 72 (1802), 477 · *GM*, 1st ser.,

89/2 (1819), 640 [obit. of Isabella Elmsley] · J. Nichols, 'Peter Elmsley', *Minor lives: a collection of biographies*, ed. E. L. Hart (1971), 259–64 · H. R. Plomer and others, *A dictionary of the printers and booksellers who were at work in England, Scotland, and Ireland from 1726 to 1775* (1932) · C. H. Timperley, *Encyclopaedia of literary and typographical anecdote*, 2nd edn (1842), 811 · *DNB*

Elmsley, Peter (1774–1825), classical scholar, was born on 5 February 1774 in Hampstead, Middlesex, the younger son of Alexander Elmsley of St Clement's, Westminster, of Scottish ancestry. His uncle was the famous London bookseller Peter *Elmsley, who in 1802 bequeathed him a considerable fortune. He was educated at Westminster School and Christ Church, Oxford, where he graduated BA in 1794, MA in 1797, BD and DD in 1823.

Elmsley was apparently promised a studentship at Christ Church, but this did not materialize. He failed to win a fellowship at Merton College, despite his reputation for learning; it was said that jealousy, or dislike of his frequent levity, thwarted him. He quickly took holy orders and in 1798 was presented to the living of Little Horkesley, Essex, where he lived until his uncle's death gave him independent means, allowing him to relinquish both duties and income to his curate, although he kept the title until 1816. He moved then for a time to Edinburgh, and was associated with the founders of the *Edinburgh Review*, to which he contributed his earliest articles, chiefly on Greek literature. After a year or two in London, from 1807 to 1816 he lived with his mother at St Mary Cray in Kent. From there he published the greater part of his learned papers, almost all on Greek tragedy, in the *Quarterly Review*, *Classical Journal*, and *Museum Criticum*, and his first editions of individual plays: Aristophanes, *Acharnians* (1809); Sophocles, *Oedipus tyrannus* (1811); and Euripides, *Heraclidae* (1813). While at Cray in 1815 he is said to have misled his neighbour, G. Grote, into believing that he was engaged to Harriet Lewis, so deferring Grote's marriage to her and provoking that family's lasting disgust.

At the end of this period Elmsley began lengthy travels on the continent, especially to Italian libraries, to examine manuscripts of Sophocles and Euripides. Some of his meticulous collations survive, together with all manner of working papers and letters, in the Bodleian Library in Oxford, where he returned to live in 1818. His fame as a collator brought him in 1819 a commission, funded largely by the prince regent, to join the chemist Sir Humphrey Davy in attempting new methods of unrolling and transcribing the carbonized papyri at Herculaneum; a mixture of physical problems and Italian jealousies frustrated everything, as Elmsley described resignedly in surviving letters. In 1822 he was proposed for the Oxford regius chair of divinity but blocked by the prime minister, Lord Liverpool, as 'not an able divine' (indeed he took his BD and DD only in 1823), but in the same year declined the see of Calcutta, later accepted by Reginald Heber: a rare instance of a recusant 'Greek play bishop'. In 1823, however, he was made Camden professor of ancient history and principal of St Alban Hall at Oxford, holding these offices for only the two years until his death.

According to contemporaries Elmsley was 'the fattest undergraduate' of his day, while a friend of Grote described him in 1818 as 'a monster … that weighs about 20 stone'. Always sedentary and self-indulgent, he was as genial as he was obese, and his company prized. His friend the poet Southey, for whose studies at Oxford he in part paid, compared him with Keble in his attempts 'to bridge the gap between undergraduates and dons' (*Selections from the Letters*, 3.511)—throughout Oxford he was known familiarly as Peter Elmsley. He died, unmarried, at Oxford of heart disease on 8 March 1825 and was buried in Christ Church Cathedral. A memorial tablet (advertising on marble scrolls the Greek titles of the plays he edited) was erected by the politician Sir Charles W. W. Wynn, his friend since Westminster days.

Elmsley's learning and curiosity were famously wide, extending particularly to church history and to legal and political history. He was elected FRS in 1814. As a Greek scholar he was pre-eminent in Britain after the death of Richard Porson in 1808, coming to be rated more highly than C. J. Blomfield and J. H. Monk; his fame diminished only when the extensive critical notes of his contemporary P. P. Dobree were posthumously published in the 1830s. These last three saw in him a unique Oxford rival for the reputation of their Cambridge master, Porson, Dobree in particular making much of Porson's own reported suspicion that Elmsley had appropriated some of his unpublished conjectures. The truth of this is not clear: Elmsley defended himself privately, and letters between Monk, Blomfield, and himself were amicable enough (Horsfall, 452–61); Dobree himself later acknowledged Elmsley's 'sovreignty' in Greek drama. Scholars admired Elmsley's meticulous accuracy, exact observation of idiom, and wealth of illustrative matter. His conservative critical method was contested by his great German contemporary Gottfried Hermann, who nevertheless wrote generously of his penetrating and disinterested learning. Modern judgements confirm his great merit as systematic student of manuscripts and text, and as subtle interpreter rather than as cautious emender; he lacked Porson's brilliance or Dobree's shrewdness. His best and fullest editions were those of Euripides, *Heraclidae* (1813; 2nd edn, 1821) and *Medea* (1818), both reprinted in Germany in 1828 with Hermann's reviews and notes, and Sophocles, *Oedipus coloneus* (1823). His important collation of Sophoclean scholia from the famous Florence manuscript was brought out a few months after his death by Gaisford (1825). CHRISTOPHER COLLARD

Sources W. Gray, *GM*, 1st ser., 95/1 (1825), 374–7 · *British Critic, Quarterly Theological Review, and Ecclesiastical Record*, 1 (1827), 281–99 · *Selections from the letters of Robert Southey*, ed. J. W. Warter, 4 vols. (1856) · G. Hermann, *Opuscula*, 6 (1821), 295–6 · G. Hermann, 'Annotationes', in *Euripidis Heraclidae et Medea*, ed. P. Elmsley (1828), 483–555 · J. E. B. Mayor, *Twelve Cambridge sermons*, ed. H. F. Stewart (1911), 203, 220 · N. M. Horsfall, 'Classical studies in England, 1810–1825', *Greek, Roman and Byzantine Studies*, 15 (1974), 449–77 · D. L. Page, *Richard Porson* (1959), 9–11 · M. L. Clarke, *George Grote* (1962), 10–12 · C. O. Brink, *English classical scholarship: historical reflections on Bentley, Porson, and Housman* (1986), 88–9, 113 · J. E. B. Mayor, *Bibliography of Porson, Elmsley etc.* (1867) · P. G. Naiditch, 'Classical studies in nineteenth-century Great Britain as background to the "Cambridge ritualists"', *The Cambridge ritualists reconsidered: First*

Oldfather Conference [Urbana-Champaign, IL 1989], ed. W. M. Calder (1991), 123–52, esp. 126 n.11
Archives Bodl. Oxf., notes and papers · Westminster School, London, John Murray archive, letters | NL Wales, corresp. with C. W. W. Wynn · Trinity Cam., Wren Library, Sanford papers · U. Edin., letters to W. Laing
Likenesses N. Whittock, lithograph (*The Geological lecture room, Oxford, 1823*), AM Oxf.

Elizabeth Clarke Wolstenholme Elmy (1833–1918), by A. & G. Taylor, c.1907

Elmy, Elizabeth Clarke Wolstenholme (1833–1918), campaigner for women's rights, was born on 30 November 1833, in the Manchester area, daughter of Joseph Wolstenholme, a Methodist minister, and his first wife, Elizabeth Clarke, the daughter of a cotton spinner; Elizabeth died shortly after her daughter's birth. Doubly orphaned by the age of fourteen, Elizabeth Wolstenholme then enjoyed her only two years of formal education, at the Moravian School, Fulneck, near Leeds. After a period of further self-education, she took over a private girls' school at Boothstown, near Worsley, of which she became headmistress. Her philosophy of education was set out in her contribution to Josephine Butler's collection of essays *Woman's Work and Woman's Culture* (1869). It was an enlightened one for its time, especially in emphasizing the need to prepare girls for economic independence.

In 1865 Elizabeth Wolstenholme joined the Kensington Society as a corresponding member. This women's debating group had grown out of the Langham Place circle, a socially disparate group of women's rights advocates that had gathered around the Unitarian radicals Barbara Leigh Smith and Bessie Rayner Parkes in the late 1850s. Reform of the laws governing marriage, improved educational provision for girls, and an expansion of economic opportunities for women were among the chief concerns of this circle.

So began a lifetime career campaigning for women's rights. Sylvia Pankhurst recalled Elizabeth Wolstenholme Elmy in her later years as a 'tiny Jenny-wren of a woman, with bright, bird-like eyes, and a little face, child-like in its merriment and its pathos, which even in extreme old age retained the winning graces of youth' (Pankhurst, 31). Another suffragist colleague, Dora Montefiore, claimed: 'The work of Mrs Elmy has never been sufficiently recognised, because she was frowned upon by the official suffragists, though she had quite the most able mind and memory of any nineteenth-century woman' (Montefiore, 113). More conventional colleagues were alienated by Elizabeth Wolstenholme's ultra-radical views, notably on marriage. She expected from others, especially the well-to-do, the same unstinting dedication that she herself gave to the women's movement. She was always antagonistic to party-political loyalties where these impinged on campaigns for women's rights. There was, too, a certain prickliness, springing largely from her relative poverty and consequent dependence on positions financed by other, more wealthy, leaders of the movement. Altogether, those more cautious, pragmatic, and conformist, or less generous-spirited and courageous than herself, sometimes found her a difficult colleague with whom to work.

For the larger part of her career Elizabeth Wolstenholme Elmy concentrated her efforts on behalf of women's rights in her own region. In the early 1860s, for example, she established the Manchester Board of Schoolmistresses to advance educational provision for women and provide collegial support among women teachers. She was also active in the North of England Council for the Promotion of the Education of Women, which grew out of this and similar bodies. She was among those who successfully pressed for the establishment of the Cambridge higher examinations for women, and for the programme of advanced lectures for women that eventually led to the foundation of Newnham College, Cambridge. In 1866 she gave evidence concerning existing provision for female education to the schools inquiry commission, among the first four women whose opinion was sought by a royal commission.

In the mid-1860s advanced women's rights activists also began to pursue the enfranchisement of women. A new Reform Act was anticipated, and John Stuart Mill offered support for women's suffrage during his successful election campaign for the seat of Westminster in 1865. Her attendance at one of his election meetings was among Elizabeth Wolstenholme Elmy's fondest memories in old age. Once elected, Mill undertook to pursue the question of women's suffrage in parliament, on the condition that a petition was raised in support of this demand. To this end, Elizabeth Wolstenholme established a women's suffrage committee in Manchester with the support of local radical Liberals, including Ursula and Jacob Bright and a young lawyer, Richard Pankhurst. Similar committees were established in London and in major provincial centres, leading within a few years to the formation of a permanent national network of women's suffrage societies.

In 1867 Elizabeth Wolstenholme moved out of Manchester and established a new school at Moody Hall, Congleton, in Cheshire. She also relinquished the honorary secretaryship of the Manchester Society for Women's Suffrage to Lydia Becker, whom she had recruited to its founding committee. Now she pursued a number of other reforms that reflected her radical approach to women's emancipation. The first of these reforms was pursued by the Married Women's Property Committee (MWPC), of which she became honorary secretary after it was formed in Manchester in 1867, a cause closely linked to that of women's suffrage. Eligibility for the parliamentary franchise still rested on the ownership of property of a certain value or above. Most married women were deprived of the ability to hold property by the common law doctrine of coverture, which subsumed their legal personality under that of their husbands. Hence married women were effectively, though not expressly, excluded from any formulation of the suffrage demand in terms of sexual equality. The goal of the MWPC was to enable married women to retain their property and put an end to coverture, thus also advancing the eligibility of married women to the vote once equal rights were secured. It met with only limited success in the passage of the Married Women's Property Act of 1870. Married women's rights over property, especially in the form of earnings, were extended, but the bill had been so comprehensively amended as it went through parliament as to leave intact the doctrine of coverture.

At the conference of the National Association for the Promotion of Social Science in Bristol in 1869 Elizabeth Wolstenholme first learnt of the passage, over the previous few years, of the Contagious Diseases Acts. This legislation aimed to control the extent of venereal disease among the armed forces. It provided for the enforced medical supervision of all women deemed prostitutes by the police in designated military and naval towns. Those women who refused to comply with the acts might receive a prison sentence with hard labour. Elizabeth Wolstenholme contacted her old friend Josephine Butler, a matron of impeccable reputation and some standing in philanthropic work among prostitutes, and urged on her the need to resist the continuance of such legislation. The formation of the Ladies National Association for Repeal of the Contagious Diseases Acts followed consultation with others of the more intrepid among women's rights activists. Its campaigns resulted in the suspension of these acts in 1884, and their repeal in 1886.

In 1871 Elizabeth Wolstenholme joined with Josephine Butler and other reformers in forming the Committee for Amending the Law in Points Injurious to Women. Its goals were more extensive than either women's suffrage or married women's property rights, and encompassed any aspect of legislation that treated women unequally with men. The same concerns and leadership were evident in the subsequent formation of the Vigilance Association for the Defence of Personal Rights. In 1872 Elizabeth Wolstenholme gave up her school and moved to London to become the paid secretary of this new organization, an appointment that recognized her now extensive knowledge of parliamentary procedure and her skills as a lobbyist.

By the mid-1870s Elizabeth Wolstenholme, like other radical Liberals, was increasingly at odds with the leadership of the suffrage movement, in which Lydia Becker had moved to the fore. In the changed parliamentary context that followed the election of a Conservative government, Lydia Becker and other pragmatists, such as Millicent Garrett Fawcett, were prepared to narrow the programme of the women's movement. They advocated limiting the suffrage demand to single and widowed women, and sought the suspension of the campaign for still further reform of the Married Women's Property Acts. Most of the radicals in the northern leadership of the women's movement rejected such a restriction of their original goals.

Elizabeth Wolstenholme's private life now became a matter for further discord. Some years earlier she had joined the secularist movement. Freethinkers found much to criticize in the existing institution of marriage, and Elizabeth Wolstenholme was by now well-versed in the legal disabilities of married women. So, with some deliberation, she entered a free union with one of her former neighbours in Congleton, Ben Elmy (1838–1906), a teacher turned silk crape manufacturer and sometime vice-president of the National Secular Society. Though there appears to have been some kind of informal wedding ceremony, probably early in 1874, theirs was a marriage not recognized under English law. When, some months later, Elizabeth Wolstenholme's pregnancy became evident the couple were urged, in the interests of the women's movement, to formalize their union. They did so on 12 October 1874, a few months before the birth of their son.

When Elizabeth Wolstenholme Elmy sought to return to public life in the autumn of 1875, she met with opposition from some among the leadership of the women's movement, notably Lydia Becker and Millicent Garrett Fawcett. With the support of Josephine Butler and Ursula Bright she resisted exclusion from the offices to which she sought reappointment, but with only limited success. She did not return to the secretaryship of the Vigilance Association, but her work for the Married Women's Property Committee, of which her wealthy friend Ursula Bright was treasurer, appears to have continued anonymously prior to her gradual reacceptance into public life in the early 1880s. The eventual passage of the 1882 Married Women's Property Act has often been credited almost entirely to the campaigning of these two women. Once again, however, the original bill was so amended as to leave the doctrine of coverture in place. But it so extended the capacity of married women to hold property that in the years that followed they became increasingly eligible for local government franchises and offices.

For the next two decades Elizabeth Wolstenholme Elmy concentrated on securing civil equality for wives. Her views are set out in numerous contributions to the *Personal Rights Journal* in the 1880s and the *Westminster Review* in the 1890s (where she wrote under her pseudonym, Ignota). She is said virtually single-handedly to have secured the passage of the 1886 Infant Custody Act, whereby women's custodial rights over their children were extended. Thereafter, she returned to the campaign for women's suffrage, but concentrated on defending and advancing the claims of married women to inclusion in the demand, a question that had by this stage split the national leadership. To such ends she helped form two successive splinter organizations, again largely with the support of northern radicals such as Richard and Emmeline Pankhurst.

The Women's Franchise League was formed in 1889, with Elizabeth Wolstenholme Elmy appointed its paid secretary. The league promoted a formulation of the suffrage demand that included married women, alongside reform of the divorce and other laws that left women unequal rights in marriage. Within a year, however, internal tensions led Elizabeth Wolstenholme Elmy to resign her post. In 1892 she formed the Women's Emancipation Union (WEU). The programme of this body was similar to that of the league, but put particular emphasis on the injustices arising from coverture, including the legality of marital rape. It also promoted the greater participation of women in local government, an area where women were receiving steadily growing voting rights and expanding eligibility for office. Some of Ben Elmy's writings on sex education, under the pseudonym Ellis Ethelmer, were also published under its auspices.

The enfranchisement of married women under the Municipal Corporations Act of 1894 eased the way for the reunification of the suffrage movement. The National Union of Women's Suffrage Societies (NUWSS) was formed in 1897, under the leadership of Millicent Garrett Fawcett, out of the largest of the pre-existing suffrage societies. The league and the WEU were gradually wound down in the years that followed.

Elizabeth Wolstenholme Elmy was never at ease with the national leadership of the suffrage movement, however, after the bitter controversy that had surrounded her marriage. She remained, also, a northern radical, suspicious of metropolitan ways and influences. For the next few years, she worked most closely with the North of England Society of the NUWSS, becoming an enthusiastic supporter of the campaign it waged, at the turn of the century, among the women textile workers of the region. She was also among the earliest supporters of the new 'militant' society formed by Emmeline and Christabel Pankhurst in 1903, the Women's Social and Political Union (WSPU), eventually joining its national committee. She soon also joined the Independent Labour Party, with which the WSPU still had close links and which published her pamphlet *Women's Franchise: the Need of the Hour* (1907). In her seventy-fifth year she walked at the head of the main procession to Hyde Park, where one of the WSPU's most impressive popular demonstrations was staged in 1908. By now, though, she found regular travel between London and her home increasingly taxing, and gradually her public life became largely limited to letters to the press.

The financial plight of Elizabeth Wolstenholme Elmy was a cause for increasing concern among her friends in the 1890s, after the failure of Ben Elmy's silk mill. A 'grateful fund' was established to acknowledge her services to women, and provided her with a small annuity in the years that followed. She died at 231 Upper Brook Street, Chorlton upon Medlock, on 12 March 1918, shortly after the enactment of women's suffrage, but before she herself could cast a parliamentary vote.

SANDRA STANLEY HOLTON

Sources E. Ethelmer [B. Elmy], 'A woman emancipator: a biographical sketch', *Westminster Review*, 145 (1894), 424–8 · E. S. Pankhurst, *The suffragette movement: an intimate account of persons and ideals* (1931) · D. B. Montefiore, *From a Victorian to a modern* (1927) · S. S. Holton, *Suffrage days: stories from the women's suffrage movement* (1996) · M. L. Shanley, *Marriage, feminism and the law in Victorian England, 1850–1895* (1989) · *Manchester Guardian* (13 March 1918) · Ignota [E. W. Elmy], 'Pioneers! Oh Pioneers!', *Westminster Review*, 165 (1906), 415–17 · B. Stephen, *Emily Davies and Girton College* (1927) · 'Wolstenholme, Joseph', *DNB* · d. cert. · *Common Cause* (22 March 1918), 655

Archives Women's Library, London, MSS | BL, letters to Harriet McIlquham, Add. MSS 47449–47455 · Internationaal Instituut voor Sociale Geschiedenis, Amsterdam, letters to Sylvia Pankhurst

Likenesses A. & G. Taylor, photograph, *c*.1907, Women's Library, London [*see illus.*] · photograph (in middle age), Women's Library, London · photograph (in old age), repro. in *Common Cause* (15 March 1918), 649

Elmy [*née* Morse], **Mary** (1712–1792), actress, perhaps began her career in a provincial company and may have acted at the Haymarket in 1732 and in early 1733. On 18 October 1733 a Miss Morse is listed as playing Charlotte in Thomas Southerne's *Oroonoko* at Drury Lane. She made two more appearances at Drury Lane as Miss Morse—as Chloe in *Timon of Athens* on 23 November and as Lucy in Edward Phillips's *The Livery Rake* on 8 January 1734—then some time between 14 and 31 January she became Mrs Elmy: probably Mrs William, perhaps Mrs James Elmy. Nothing more is known of her husband. The remainder of the 1730s suggests occasional appearances in London at Drury Lane, the Haymarket, and Covent Garden, where she made her début as Florinda in Aphra Behn's *The Rover* on 11 April 1737. She may well have had regular employment in small and unadvertised parts at these and other houses. Whatever the case, in 1738 she left London for Dublin, and made her first appearance there as Mrs Sullen in George Farquhar's *The Beaux' Stratagem* at the Aungier Street Theatre in October, when she was advertised as from Drury Lane. She made her début at the Smock Alley Theatre on 11 December 1739 and stayed in that company through to the season of 1743–4.

In autumn 1744 Mrs Elmy returned to London and the roles of Phyllis in Richard Steele's *The Conscious Lovers* at the Haymarket with Theophilus Cibber's 'Academy' and Lady Dainty in Colley Cibber's *The Double Gallant* at Drury Lane. In 1745–6 she appeared again in Dublin and remained for the season at the Aungier Street Theatre and at Smock Alley, where she was part of the supporting company for Garrick's engagement. She then appeared as Lady Grace in Sir John Vanbrugh's *The Provoked Husband* at Drury Lane (3 January 1747) and stayed in Garrick's company until the end of the 1740s, appearing in a range of increasingly high-profile roles.

On 16 October 1750 Mrs Elmy was Belinda in Vanbrugh's *The Provoked Wife* at Covent Garden, and she remained with that company until her retirement in 1762. Her roles included Lady Touchwood in William Congreve's *The Double Dealer*, Lady Brute in *The Provoked Wife*, Regan in *King Lear*, and, throughout the 1750s, Gertrude in *Hamlet*: she was greatly praised for her portrayal of Gertrude to Spranger Barry's Hamlet. The *European Magazine* lists her death on 1 April 1792 at the age of eighty at Knightsbridge, London.

Mary Elmy made a will on 12 October 1780 and added a codicil on 28 April 1789; it was proved on 19 April 1792. In the will she noted herself to be a widow. She left £100 each to four cousins in Norwich and £20 to another cousin in London. In addition four children of a cousin were each to receive £10. One Anne Williams received a diamond ring, and the rest of her estate—including £1000 in stock—was left to her cousin Sarah Smith, also of Norwich. The codicil left £50 to Anne Crawford, Spranger Barry's widow.

Mary Elmy was never of the first rank of performer but became a solid and reliable company member, though she occasionally excelled in the right part. For example, in the 1753 season her Desdemona was greatly praised. Her fellow actress George Anne Bellamy considered her a 'good humorist and possessed of a great good sense, but by her want of powers was prevented from making a conspicuous figure upon the stage'. *The Thespian Dictionary* (1802) adds that Elmy was 'respectable both in tragedy and comedy … [and] had a tolerable share of wit and good sense'. Chetwood's *A General History of the Stage* (1749) was surprised that 'She seems to have more Spirits *off* the Stage, in a Chamber, than she has *in* the public Theatre', and in *The Actor* (1750) Hill saw her as 'an actress of great judgement, endowed with a sweet voice and a pleasing deportment' (*BDA*).   ADRIENNE SCULLION

Sources Highfill, Burnim & Langhans, *BDA* · *The thespian dictionary, or, Dramatic biography of the eighteenth century* (1802) · G. A. Bellamy, *An apology for the life of George Anne Bellamy*, ed. [A. Bicknell], 3rd edn, 6 vols. (1785) · S. D'Amico, ed., *Enciclopedia dello spettacolo*, 11 vols. (Rome, 1954–68)

Likenesses F. Hayman, portrait (of Elmy? as Gertrude in *Hamlet*), Garr. Club

Wealth at death £1500; plus diamond ring: Highfill, Burnim & Langhans, *BDA*, 5.70–74

Elphinston, James (1721–1809), educationist and advocate of spelling reform, was born on 6 December 1721 in Edinburgh, the son of William Elphinston, an Episcopalian minister, and his wife, Rachel Honeyman (d. 1750), niece of the bishop of Orkney. He was educated at the high school and at the university in Edinburgh, but left the latter at the age of seventeen to become tutor to Lord Blantyre. At twenty-one he was introduced to the historian Thomas Carte, whom he accompanied on a tour through the Netherlands that ended in Paris, where he stayed long enough to become proficient in both spoken and written French. On his return to Edinburgh he became tutor to the eldest son of James Moray of Abercairney, Perthshire. In 1750 he began producing an edition of *The Rambler* in Edinburgh, with Johnson's Latin epigrams translated into English by Elphinston himself. This opportunity may have presented itself because Elphinston's sister was married to William Strachan, Johnson's publisher. Johnson was

James Elphinston (1721–1809), by James Caldwall (after John Graham)

evidently pleased with Elphinston's work and became his correspondent, sending a letter of condolence when he heard from Mrs Strachan of the death of Elphinston's mother in 1750.

In 1751, Elphinston married Miss Gordon (d. 1778), a niece of General Gordon of Auchintoul, and two years later moved to London, where he set up a school in Brompton and then moved to Kensington ten years later. Elphinston's educational philosophy and methods are outlined in an undated publication entitled *The Plan of Education at Mr. Elphinston's Academy*. The teaching of English was clearly a priority: '*Language*, being the expression of reason and the vehicle of knowledge, becomes Education's first object in the culture of the mind' (p. 3). This interest in language is reflected in his first dated publication, *The Analysis of the French and English Languages* (1756), and in *The Principles of the English Language Digested, or, Grammar Reduced to Analogy* (1766), later published in an abridged edition as *The Principles of the English Language Digested for the Use of Schools* (1766). As a Scot residing in London, Elphinston took it upon himself to correct the 'Scotticisms' of his countrymen. His *Animadversions upon Elements of Criticism* (1771) was a critique of Lord Kames's *Elements of Criticism* (1761) and focused on Kames's style, in particular his use of Scotticisms. Elphinston added to this work an 'Appendix on Scotticism', which had already been published with David Hume's *Political Discourses* and reproduced, with Elphinston's commentary, in the *Scots Magazine* (1760 and 1764).

Elphinston's school closed in 1776, apparently because

of a lack of pupils. Contemporary accounts of his ability as a schoolmaster are very varied. Johnson, whose friendship with him had continued after the latter's move to London, remarked: 'I would not put a boy to him whom I intended for a man of learning; but for the sons of citizens who are to learn a little, get good morals, and then go to trade, he may do very well' (Boswell, *Life*, 2.171). Elphinston's teaching certainly inspired devotion in at least one of his pupils, R. C. Dallas, who wrote: 'No man was ever more faithful, competent or indefatigable in the trust he had undertaken' (Dallas, 1060).

Following his wife's death in 1778 Elphinston left Kensington and returned to Scotland. In the same year he published *An Universal History*, translated from the French of Bossuet, and *A Specimen of the Translations of Epigrams of Martial*. In the preface to the latter he solicited subscriptions for a complete translation of Martial, which was published in 1782 but was received very badly. Elphinston replied to his numerous critics, who included David Garrick and Robert Burns, in *The Hypercritic* (1783).

A group of Elphinston's Scottish friends tried to establish a chair of modern languages at the University of Edinburgh, with the intention that he himself should occupy it, but nothing came of this. In 1779 he gave a course of lectures on the English language in Edinburgh and in the public hall of the University of Glasgow before returning to London. In 1785 his brother-in-law Strachan died, leaving him £100 a year plus £100 cash and 20 guineas for mourning. Strachan's widow died about a month later, leaving him a further £200 a year. This upturn in his fortunes allowed him to marry, on 6 October 1785 at St Marylebone, Mary Clementina Charlotte, daughter of the Revd James Falconer and niece of Bishop Falconer. Elphinston paid another visit to Scotland in 1787 and returned to live in Islington.

From 1786 Elphinston's efforts were devoted to devising and advocating the system of reformed spelling that brought him to the attention of twentieth-century philologists such as Jespersen, Müller, Wyld, and Rohlfing. This scheme was first set out in *Propriety Ascertained in her Picture, or, Inglish Speech and Spelling Rendered Mutual Guides* (2 vols., 1786–7) but Elphinston must have been advocating reformed spelling earlier than this, for Dallas reports disagreement on this matter between Elphinston and Strachan before the latter's death in 1785. After 1787 all Elphinston's publications were written in his reformed orthography: *Inglish Orthography Epittomized: and Propriety's Pocket-Diccionary* (1790); *A Miniature ov Inglish Orthoggraphy* (1795), and *A Dialogue, Contrasting … Dhe Practice and Propriety ov Inglish Speech and Spelling* (1797). He also published his correspondence in his reformed spelling: six volumes were published in 1791 as *Forty Years' Correspondence between Geniusses ov Boath Sexes and James Elphinston*; a second edition, with a further two volumes added and entitled *Fifty Years' Correspondence, Inglish, French, and Lattin, in Proze and Verse*, appeared in 1794, as did *Dhe Sentencious Poets … Arranged and Translated into Correspondent English Mezzure*.

Elphinston was convinced that reformed spelling was necessary if those living in the provinces were to learn how to pronounce English 'correctly', in other words, as spoken in London. In *Propriety Ascertained in her Picture* he argued that, with regard to the acquisition of 'correct' pronunciation, 'the distant hav no possibel chance, unles from repprezentacion' (p. xiii). His efforts were not well received, even by his friends, who considered this obsession with spelling reform an unfortunate aberration. Dallas wrote: 'Mr. Elphinston's works were numerous: a critical investigation of them would lead to great length: most of them possess sterling merit, which, however, has been veiled by the orthographical clothing he perseveringly gave to all he wrote' (Dallas, 106). John Walker, in his highly influential *Critical Pronouncing Dictionary*, recognized that Elphinston's work was worthwhile but could not see any merit in his reformed spelling:

> Among those writers who deserve the first praise on this subject, is Mr. Elphinstone … who, in his Principles of the English Language, has reduced the chaos to a system, and laid the foundation of a just and regular pronunciation. But this gentleman, by treating his subject with an affected obscurity, and by absurdly endeavouring to alter the whole orthography of the language, has unfortunately lost his credit with the public for that part of his labours which entitles him to the highest applause. (Walker, iii)

Elphinston's only supporter seems to have been Benjamin Franklin, whose illegitimate grandson, William Temple Franklin, had been employed by William Strachan. Although Benjamin Franklin's *Scheme for a New Alphabet and Reformed Mode of Spelling* had appeared in 1779 Elphinston appears to have been unaware of it until 1785, when William Temple Franklin sent him a specimen of his grandfather's scheme. Elphinston felt that Franklin's scheme departed too radically from conventional orthography in introducing six new symbols, while his own scheme used only characters already present in the English alphabet. Though Elphinston's ideas attracted ridicule in his lifetime they have come to be valued as primary evidence for the pronunciation of English in the late eighteenth century.

Elphinston moved to Elstree in 1792 and, finally, to Hammersmith in 1806, where he died on 8 October 1809, after the amputation of a swollen leg. He was buried in Kensington, according to his wishes. He was survived by his wife.   JOAN C. BEAL

Sources R. C. Dallas, 'Biographical memoir', *GM*, 1st ser., 79 (1809), 1057–63 · H. Rohlfing, *Die Werke James Elphinstons (1721–1809) als Quellen der englischen Lautgeschichte* (1984) · J. Walker, *Critical pronouncing dictionary* (1791) · E. Müller, *Englische Lautlehre nach James Elphinston (1765, 1787, 1790)* (1914) · H. C. Wyld, *A history of modern colloquial English* (1920) · O. Jespersen, *A modern English grammar on historical principles, part 1: sounds and spellings* (1909) · DNB · IGI

Likenesses J. Caldwall, line engraving (after J. Graham), BM, NPG [see illus.]

Elphinston, John (1722–1785), naval officer in the Russian service, was the son of Captain John Elphinston RN and Anne Williams. He may have been born at Lopness in the Orkney Islands, from where his family, with its history of seafaring, was descended. Elphinston went to sea in 1739 at seventeen and was made lieutenant in July 1745. On 23

October 1750 he married Amelia (*d.* 1786), daughter of John Warburton.

During the Seven Years' War Elphinston advanced rapidly. He commanded the fireship *Salamander* in May 1757, and served under Lord Howe in expeditions against St Malo, Cherbourg, and St Cas. Although taken prisoner at St Cas, he was exchanged and then advanced to captain of the frigate *Eurus*, in which he served under Sir Charles Saunders and took part in the capture of Quebec in 1760. The next year in the *Richmond* he destroyed the French frigate *Félicité* near The Hague. The following spring he carried instructions to the West Indies concerning the expedition against Havana. Elphinston played a vital role when he surveyed the Old Bahama passage, a channel previously thought impassable by the British, and so allowed the invasion fleet to surprise the Spanish. He then assisted Admiral Pocock during the successful siege. Recognizing Elphinston's experience in combined operations, Pocock put him in charge of the transports and afterwards rewarded him with command of the Spanish prize *Infante*. After the peace he commanded the *Firme* for three years, until he was placed on half pay.

Although he had established himself as a bold officer with exceptional experience in joint operations Elphinston's career had stalled; but the moment was propitious, for Russia was then aggressively recruiting seasoned British combat officers for its war against Turkey. In May 1769 he accepted a commission as a rear-admiral. Elphinston took charge of a pitiful Baltic squadron and was then ordered to join Vice-Admiral Grigory Spiridov, who was already headed for the Mediterranean with a larger force. Count Aleksey Orlov, a royal favourite, who freely admitted his ignorance of naval matters, was named admiral as Russia launched a campaign in Turkey's home waters.

A fiery and forthright combat veteran, Elphinston was shocked by the state of the Russian navy and did not conceal his disdain for it, alienating himself from superiors and subordinates. Though his difficulties began in Kronstadt, they grew worse at Copenhagen, where he was delayed by the misconduct of his officers, which obliged him to make a damaging late season voyage across the North Sea. At Portsmouth most of the ships underwent repairs before they could proceed. The following spring the various elements of the fleet reached Leghorn (Livorno) where Orlov took command. By then Spiridov and Elphinston had become implacable rivals. Heeding the advice of his flag-captain, the ever-politic Commodore Samuel Greig, Orlov separated his two commanders and assigned Elphinston to an independent squadron.

On reaching the eastern Mediterranean the Russians terrorized Turkish ports and captured Navarino. In mid-May Elphinston learned that fourteen Turkish warships with a large number of transport and supply vessels were off Nauplia preparing for an operation to retake Navarino. He set sail immediately and encountered the Turkish fleet on 27 May. According to his own *Authentic Narrative* his subordinate commanders disobeyed his order to engage and he fired on them to force compliance. The *Ne Tron Menya*

and the *Saratov* then put three Turkish vessels out of action but found themselves in jeopardy when the wind changed and threatened to expose them to attack from the Turkish galleys. Aboard the *Svyatoslav* Elphinston closed immediately, firing explosive shells, which caused great confusion. Intimidated, the Turks retreated into Nauplia harbour. In his narrative Elphinston applauded the bravery of the Russian sailors, writing 'they fought at their guns like lions'. The next morning Elphinston entered the harbour, exchanged fire with the fortress and then withdrew to a safer distance, where his ships anchored and began a long-range bombardment of the Turkish fleet at its anchorage. After several hours he feared that another unfavourable wind might again expose his ships to a galley attack and he withdrew. Finally realizing their numerical superiority, the Turks left Nauplia and Elphinston joined the Russian fleet. Elphinston had shown himself a daring commander but his squadron was too small to gain a victory. None the less, the action at Nauplia panicked and intimidated the Turks on the eve of Chesma, where they made similar blunders that proved fatal.

On 1 July 1769 the Russians learned that the Turkish fleet was anchored between the island of Chios and the Anatolian coast. The nine Russian warships were opposed by fourteen Turkish ships of the line, several frigates and a host of smaller transports and store ships, totalling nearly 200 vessels. At a war council Elphinston and Spiridov disagreed on tactics and vented their hostility for each other. Elphinston argued that a fresh on-shore breeze would permit him to bring the fleet to attack the weathermost enemy ships, where they could anchor with springs on their cables in order to gain a local superiority. He later wrote that

> our nine line of battle ships would have been engaged against only five or six of the enemy, and the rest of their numerous fleet would have been rendered useless, as they could neither come to the assistance of those ships engaged nor attempt to get out of the situation they were in without the greatest danger of running ashore. (Elphinston, *Authentic Narrative*, 56)

Orlov supported Spiridov's argument for a line attack, which he led, but the tactics he employed resembled those advocated by Elphinston.

The Turks were so situated that only five vessels were able to engage the Russian line as it approached. Leading the way in the *Evstafi* Spiridov took most of the original fire and was quickly disabled, causing the ship to drift alongside the Turkish flagship *Real Mustsafa*. After fierce hand-to-hand combat both vessels caught fire and the *Evstafi*'s powder magazine blew up. Although he lost his ship and most of his crew, Spiridov escaped. Elphinston engaged as he had at Nauplia; the panicked Turks blundered once more when they cut their cables and fled into the cramped harbour at Chesma.

After hours of wrangling, the Russians attacked again after midnight with fireships and explosive shells. Commodore Greig brought four ships of the line, three frigates, a bomb-ketch, and four fireships into action.

Elphinston, commanding the rest of the fleet, sealed off the harbour. At 1.30 a.m. on 7 July incendiary shells from the *Grom* ignited the topsails of a Turkish battleship, which exploded and then set two more ships afire. Greig then ordered his fireships to attack and unleashed a conflagration that spread throughout the Turkish fleet. Explosion after explosion destroyed eleven men of war, six frigates, and forty-six other vessels. Only one Turkish warship and a few galleys avoided the terrible inferno. On the second day the Turks lost 8000–11,000 men, while the Russians lost only thirteen men and sustained no damage of consequence. The victory was total.

Chesma is often described as Russia's greatest naval battle, a 'Russian Lepanto', but it did not provide victory, which was won on land four years later. Although he acknowledged that he had done nothing himself, Orlov was showered with honours; and Spiridov, despite the loss of his ship, was rewarded and honoured and retired soon after the peace. The discreet Greig won promotion to rear-admiral, remained attached to Orlov, and prospered in Russian service, while Elphinston complained indignantly of the depreciation of his role in the victory.

After Chesma, Russia enjoyed a naval superiority in the Aegean which it did not exploit. As an expert in combined operations, Elphinston stridently advocated immediate attack on the Dardanelles to win the straits and then to liberate Constantinople. Savouring the Chesma victory, his cautious superiors chose instead to blockade the Dardanelles and Turkish ports and regarded Elphinston as an annoyance. When his ship ran aground at Lemnos they launched an admiralty inquiry, which cleared him of responsibility. None the less, when Britain withdrew its support for the Russian war effort in 1771 Elphinston left Russian service. After his return from Russia he wrote his *Authentic Narrative of the Russian Expedition Against the Turks by Sea and Land* (published anonymously). The study, described by Anthony Cross as the 'Elphinstone version' of the campaign, has been the subject of argument ever since, as nationalistic Russian historians continue to depreciate his contributions at Chesma and British historians accept his narrative uncritically.

Elphinston was reinstated in the British navy and commanded several ships during the American War of Independence, serving first with Joshua Rowley in the West Indies and then with George Rodney in three actions against France. On conclusion of the war Elphinston's career suffered partly as a result of his outspoken support of the North ministry and the conflict with the American revolutionaries.

Captain Elphinston died on 28 April 1785 and was survived by his wife, six sons, and three daughters. The eldest son, Samuel, rose to captain in the Russian navy, married the daughter of Admiral Cruys, and died in 1789. The second, Thomas, became a captain in the Royal Navy and died in 1812. The third, Howard, distinguished himself as Wellington's commander of engineers during the Peninsular War, was made first baronet Elphinstone of Sowerby in 1816, and was promoted major-general.

RICHARD H. WARNER

Sources DNB · M. S. Anderson, 'Great Britain and the Russo-Turkish war of 1768–74', *EngHR*, 69 (1954), 39–58 · A. Cross, 'The Elphinstones in Catherine the Great's navy', *Mariner's Mirror*, 48 (1998), 268–77 · L. G. Beskrovnyi, *Russkaia armiia i flot v xviii veke* (1958) [the Russ. army and the fleet in the eighteenth century] · K. V. Elphinston, *The Elphinstones of Blytheswood and Lopness* (1925) · [J. Elphinston], *An authentic narrative of the Russian expedition against the Turks by sea and land* (1772) · V. F. Golovachev, *Chesma* (1944) · F. S. Krinitsyn, *Chesmenskoe srazhenie* (1962) [The battle of Chesma] · E. V. Tarle, *Chesmenskii boi i pervaia russkaia ekspeditsiia v Arkhipelag, 1769–1774* (1945) [the battle of Chesma and the first Russ. expedition to the Archipelago] · D. Syrett, *The Royal Navy in American waters, 1775–1783* (1989) · D. Syrett, *The Royal Navy in European waters during the American revolutionary war* (1998) · D. Syrett, ed., *The siege and capture of Havana, 1762*, Navy RS, 114 (1970) · *Osmankaia imperiia: problemy vneshnei otnoshenenii s Rossiei, sbornik statei* (1996) [The Ottoman empire: problems of foreign relations with Russia, a collection of articles] · M. S. Anderson, 'Great Britain and the Russian fleet, 1769–70', *Slavonic and East European Review*, 31 (1952–3), 148–63
Archives NA Scot., letter-book, 6D 156/69

Elphinstone, Alexander, fourth Lord Elphinstone (1552–1638), administrator, was born on 28 May 1552, the eldest of ten children of Robert Elphinstone, third Lord Elphinstone (1530–1602), and his wife, Margaret Drummond. His father was incapable of managing his own affairs, and in 1577 resigned his lands to Alexander, then master of Elphinstone. The lands were scattered through Stirlingshire (with his main residence, Elphinstone), Perthshire, and Aberdeenshire, where they included the great castle and barony of Kildrummy. His relations with some of the greater lords of central and north-east Scotland were to be important throughout his career, with the Gordons, earls of Huntly, who dominated Aberdeenshire, and above all with the Erskines (from 1565 earls of Mar), who disputed Elphinstone's rights in Kildrummy, granted to his great-grandfather by James IV.

Elphinstone was appointed a gentleman of the king's chamber by the royal favourite, Esmé Stewart, earl of Lennox, on 15 October 1580, although 'misliked greatly' by King James (*CSP Scot.*, 5.531). Between 1587 and 1593 he was loosely associated with the earl of Huntly, then challenging the court's pro-English orientation. Although in April 1589 he accompanied a royal army that suppressed Huntly's rebellion, he interceded on Huntly's behalf in May 1590 and March 1592. After Huntly's eclipse in 1594 Elphinstone's influence grew along with that of his brother James *Elphinstone, the future Lord Balmerino, one of the Octavians (eight powerful exchequer auditors between 1596 and 1598). The Octavians opposed the influence of the king's chamber, but Elphinstone had good relations with both. Along with Lord Livingstone, his brother-in-law, he was hostile to the earl of Mar.

On 18 April 1599 Elphinstone was appointed treasurer. The parlous royal finances had caused past treasurers to leave office greatly superexpended—that is, with the crown heavily in their debt—and Elphinstone insisted that he would not 'pay old debts' (*CSP Scot.*, 13.447). He also became a privy councillor and lord of session. The English agent described the new treasurer as 'a very stout and a wise man, as the Chamber are much stronger by him' (*CSP Scot.*, 13.450). On 5 February 1600 Elphinstone's daughters

Anna and Jane married the earl of Sutherland and the master of Forbes respectively, strengthening his connections among the nobility. But the royal finances went from bad to worse, and Elphinstone ran into debt. Disputes arose with other financial officials, and the king was dissatisfied. In July 1600:

> the king came over in great anger against his officers of state, especially the Treasurer and Collector, for that they give him not money enough, swearing ere he came, for that the Treasurer had made up his account and therein made the king 40,000*l*. Scots [£4000 sterling] in his debt, he should check his accounts and would not be so used, but do many things. Yet when he was here among them he calmed … The Treasurer would have given up his office and is every day offering it almost.   (*CSP Scot.*, 13.673)

Elphinstone would not resign, however, without settlement of his debts.

Elphinstone eventually left office on 22 September 1601, superexpended by £45,899 Scots. He received £14,899, and probably another £26,000, promised during 1602 from a drastic coinage debasement; no further payments are recorded. His chamber position lapsed in 1603 on King James's departure for England. On 18 May 1602 he had succeeded his father as fourth Lord Elphinstone, and in March 1605 his son Alexander, master of Elphinstone, joined him on the privy council. But Elphinstone himself faded from public life, leaving the council in 1610.

Elphinstone's religious stance now became more prominent. He had associated with the openly Catholic Huntly, and his brother James was a closet Catholic, but Elphinstone himself was a protestant. In July 1605 the banned presbyterian minister Robert Bruce preached a special sermon for him, marking him as an opponent of royal religious policies. In 1621 Elphinstone voted in parliament against ratification of the five articles of Perth (which introduced new ceremonies into church worship), incurring lasting royal displeasure as a 'puritain'. This came at a crucial time, for his rival the earl of Mar brought a lawsuit against Elphinstone over the latter's Kildrummy estates. In 1626 an arbitration finally awarded the lands to Mar in return for 48,000 merks (£2666 sterling). Lord Elphinstone died at Elphinstone on 14 January 1638. In April 1575 he had married Jane (*d.* 1621), daughter of William Livingstone, sixth Lord Livingstone; ten of their nineteen children reached adulthood.   JULIAN GOODARE

Sources *CSP Scot.*, 1574–1603 · *Reg. PCS*, 1st ser. · *Reg. PCS*, 2nd ser. · W. Fraser, ed., *The Elphinstone family book of the lords Elphinstone, Balmerino and Coupar*, 2 vols. (1897) · J. Goodare, 'The Scottish parliament of 1621', *HJ*, 38 (1995), 29–51 · treasurer's accounts, 1599–1600, NA Scot., E21/73 · D. Calderwood, *The history of the Kirk of Scotland*, ed. T. Thomson and D. Laing, 8 vols., Wodrow Society, 7 (1842–9)
Archives NA Scot., family MSS, GD 156 | NL Scot., letters to Sir Robert Gordon
Likenesses portrait, repro. in Fraser, *The Elphinstone family book*, vol. 1, p. 107

Elphinstone, Arthur, sixth Lord Balmerino and fifth Lord Coupar (1688–1746), Jacobite army officer, son of John *Elphinstone, fourth Lord Balmerino and third Lord Coupar (1652–1736) [see under Elphinstone, John, second Lord Balmerino], and his second wife, Anne (*d.* 1712),

daughter of Arthur Ross, archbishop of St Andrews, was born in Scotland. He married Margaret (1710–1765), daughter of Captain Chalmers; they had no children. A member of a family with a tradition of 'fierce Episcopalian nationalism' (Szechi, *Jacobitism*, 86) (his father was an opponent of the Union), he none the less accepted (as did other Jacobites such as Lord George Murray and George Keith, Earl Marischal) a commission under Queen Anne, commanding a company of foot in Lord Shannon's regiment, while being apparently convinced that 'she had no more Right to the *Crown* than the *Prince of Orange*, whom I always looked upon as a *vile, unnatural Usurper*' (*True Copies*). Thus, although he fought as a Hanoverian officer at the battle of Sheriffmuir 'against his conscience', as he said, Elphinstone subsequently deserted to the Jacobites. On the defeat of the rising of 1715 he had to fly to the continent, where his name appears as a lieutenant-colonel among the list of refugees at Avignon on 2 April 1716. He arrived in exile in France unable to speak a word of the language, and remained on the continent until 1734, when his father, anxious for his return after the death of his brother Alexander, obtained a pardon for him from the government without his knowledge or consent. After asking James's permission, and receiving it together with travelling expenses, he returned home from Switzerland.

Elphinstone joined the prince, Charles Edward, in mid-October 1745. He captained (with the honorary rank of colonel) a troop of forty horse in the Life Guards originally intended for Viscount Kenmure, who had abandoned the Jacobites almost immediately after joining them. Present on the march south, he was affected by the proclamation of 'King James' at Lancaster, where his generous nature was shown by his socializing with Henry Bracken, a surgeon whom he had met abroad, who was in fact acting for the duke of Newcastle in supplying him with the names of all the Jacobites in the town. On 4 December, Elphinstone was the first Jacobite commander to take his troops into Derby. Following the death of his half-brother John, fifth Lord Balmerino and fourth Lord Coupar, on 5 January 1746, Elphinstone succeeded him in both titles. Three months later, as the cannonballs fell round the Stuart standard at Culloden, he helped the prince away from his post.

After the defeat Balmerino, 'against Elcho's advice', gave himself up the following day (Tomasson and Buist, 198). As a nobleman who had been active in the risings of both 1715 (and that as a deserter) and 1745, he could expect little clemency from government, and was brought to trial with the earls of Kilmarnock and Cromarty at Westminster Hall on 29 July on a charge of high treason. He pleaded not guilty, alleging that he was not present at Carlisle at the time specified in the indictment. Removed to the Tower, he was brought up for trial the next day, conducting his own defence with a futile determination before at length resigning it by saying that 'he was sorry he had given their lordships so much trouble and that he had nothing more to say' (*DNB*). Horace Walpole, who was an eyewitness, described Balmerino as 'the most natural brave old fellow he had ever seen', who 'behaved himself like a soldier and a man' (Walpole to H. Mann, 1 Aug 1746, Walpole, *Corr.*, 19.281). Unlike Kilmarnock and Cromarty, Balmerino declined to sue for mercy. A kinsman of Clementine Walkinshaw cared for Balmerino in his final days and later looked after his wife. Balmerino staged a public interview with the earl of Kilmarnock (whose son had served in Balmerino's troop) before their execution, partly at least to refute charges of Jacobite barbarity towards government prisoners and the claim that a 'no quarter' battle order (withholding the provision of quarter) had been given at Culloden by the prince's army. This allegation in particular stung him, and he denied it again publicly from the scaffold on 18 August, whither he marched in 'full ... [Jacobite] regimental uniform' as a statement of his continuing fidelity (Szechi, 'Jacobite theatre of death', 67, 73). He also wore a plaid cap under his wig to signify his loyalty to Scotland. As one song written shortly afterwards put it

> brave Balmerrony ... in the midst of all his foes
> Claps Tartan on his eyes ...
> A Scots Man I livd ...
> A Scots Man now I die ...
> May all the Scots my footsteps trace.
> (Aberdeen University Library, MS 2222)

Calmly requesting his friends to drink him 'ain degrae ta haiven', Balmerino gave the executioner a fee of 3 guineas, but none the less three blows were required to sever his head. In his speech on the scaffold he said that he had been brought up in 'true, loyal, and ANTI-REVOLUTION Principles'. His last words were 'God preserve my *Friends*, forgive my *Enemies*, restore the *KING*, and have Mercy upon my *Soul*!' His description of Charles Edward from the scaffold as a man of 'incomparable Sweetness ... Affability ... Compassion ... Justice ... Temperance ... Patience ... Courage' differs somewhat from other accounts of the prince's character, which, then as now, widely diverge (*True Copies*). What this demonstrates, however, is the quality of Balmerino's own character in judgement on the man whose call on his loyalty had cost him his life. He was buried at the chapel of St Peter ad Vincula on Tower Hill. With his death the male branch of the Elphinstone family and the Balmerino peerage became extinct. He was survived by his wife, who died 'in poverty' at Restalrig on 24 August 1765 (GEC, *Peerage*, 1.392).

The dignity of Balmerino's death 'evoked universal admiration' (Tomasson and Buist, 206). The 'gallant Arthur' who 'goes to Death as others go to Sleep' was contrasted in Jacobite martyrology with the treacherous Murray of Broughton as the true type of the patriot Scot, and the continuing popularity of relics of Balmerino is shown by Burns's 'great veneration' for what he believed had once been his dirk (R. Burns to J. Johnson, Feb 1794, *Letters*, 2.280). Balmerino was described as 'very plain, his shape clumsy, but his make strong, and had no marks about him of the polite gentleman, tho' his seeming sincerity recompensed all these defects' (*Daily Advertiser*, cited in *DNB*). It is this integrity, rather than any act or work of his life, which earned him both his contemporary and lasting reputation.   MURRAY G. H. PITTOCK

Sources *DNB* · *True copies of the papers wrote by Arthur, Lord Balmerino &c.* (1746) · U. Aberdeen, MS 2222 [printed in *Studies on Voltaire*, 267 (1989), 1–75] · F. J. McLynn, *The Jacobite army in England, 1745: the final campaign* (1983) · F. J. McLynn, *Charles Edward Stuart: a tragedy in many acts* (1988) · *The letters of Robert Burns*, ed. J. de Lancey Ferguson, 2nd edn, ed. G. Ross Roy, 2 vols. (1985) · A. Tayler and H. Tayler, *1715: the story of the rising* (1936) · summary description of Society of Antiquaries papers, NA Scot., GD103 · C. Humphreys, *A letter sent to the late Lord Balmerino* (1746) · D. Szechi, *Jacobitism and tory politics, 1710–14* (1984) · D. Szechi, '"Cam ye o'er frae France?" Exile and the mind of Scottish Jacobitism', *Journal of British Studies*, 37 (1998), 357–90 · K. Tomasson and F. Buist, *Battles of the '45* (1962) · D. Szechi, 'The Jacobite theatre of death', *The Jacobite challenge*, ed. E. Cruickshanks and J. Black (1988), 57–73 · A. Livingstone, C. W. H. Aikman, and B. S. Hart, eds., *Muster roll of Prince Charles Edward Stuart's army, 1745–46* (1984) · A. M. Smith, *Jacobite estates of the Forty-Five* (1982) · GEC, *Peerage*, new edn, vol. 1 · R. Sharp, *The engraved record of the Jacobite movement* (1996) · D. Daiches, *Scotland and the Union* (1977) · Walpole, *Corr.*

Archives NL Scot., engraving of execution, a copy of last speech, RH 1/2/504/5 · NL Scot., muniments, GD 156 | NA Scot., Episcopal Church records, Jolly Kist, CH 12/13/35 · NA Scot., Society of Antiquaries MSS, petition of Lady Balmerino, GD 103/2/385 · U. Aberdeen L., MacBean collection, forfeited estates MSS, E 740

Likenesses J. Basire, engraving, NPG · line print, vignette (of his execution; with Lord Kilmarnock), BM · mezzotint, Scot. NPG; repro. in J. C. Smith, *British mezzotinto portraits*, 4 vols. in 5 (1878–84) · mezzotint, U. Aberdeen, MacBean collection · mezzotint, BM · portrait, repro. in K. Thomson, *Memoirs of the Jacobites of 1715 and 1745*, 3 (1846) · print, repro. in Humphreys, *A letter sent to the late Lord Balmerino*, frontispiece · print (of his execution), repro. in photocopy, NA Scot., Register House, RH 1/2/504-5

Wealth at death estate sold 1752: Smith, *Jacobite estates*

Elphinstone, George Keith, Viscount Keith (1746–1823), naval officer and politician, was born on 7 January 1746 at Elphinstone Tower, Airth, near Stirling, the fourth son and seventh child of the eight children of Charles Elphinstone, tenth Lord Elphinstone (1711–1781), and Lady Clementina Fleming (1719–1799); she was the daughter and heir of the sixth earl of Wigtown and also heir to her uncle, George Keith, the last Earl Marischal. The eldest son joined the army; the second, Charles, also in the army, was killed on passage to join his regiment when the *Prince George* (90 guns) caught fire and sank in the Bay of Biscay in 1758; the third, William, after a short period in the Royal Navy transferred to the marine service of the East India Company of which he eventually became a director.

Apprenticeship for command, 1761–1775 On 4 November 1761 George Elphinstone joined the *Royal Sovereign* (100 guns) at Portsmouth but transferred on 1 January 1762 to the *Gosport* (44 guns), commanded by Captain John Jervis, later earl of St Vincent, whom he impressed. In her he saw action in September when the French were driven out of Newfoundland and Halifax, Nova Scotia, which they had briefly occupied; he returned home in her at the end of the year and in March 1763 transferred to the frigate *Juno*. Two months later he joined the frigate *Lively*, commanded by another Scot, the Hon. Keith Stewart, and served in the Mediterranean from July 1763 to January 1765.

After a period at home Elphinstone joined the frigate *Emerald*, commanded by his fellow countryman Charles Douglas, in August 1766, but left her at his own request in

George Keith Elphinstone, Viscount Keith (1746–1823), by John Hoppner, c.1799

December to embark as third mate in his elder brother's East Indiaman, the *Tryton*. Their great-uncle the Earl Marischal is said to have lent them £2000 each for a voyage to China, thus laying the foundation of their financial independence.

On his return home Elphinstone rejoined the *Emerald* at Leith in August 1768, serving mostly in northern waters until he moved in September 1769 to the frigate *Stag*, flagship of Commodore Sir John Lindsay. On passage to Madras, Elphinstone was promoted to acting lieutenant on 21 December 1769, a promotion which was confirmed on 28 June 1770. Taken ill, he was landed at Madras in October and returned home the following March. Two months later he joined the *Trident* (64 guns) as second lieutenant, sailing in August to the Mediterranean with the flag of the commander-in-chief, Rear-Admiral Sir Peter Denis. In April 1772 he was appointed first lieutenant, and on 18 September was promoted to commander with command of the sloop *Scorpion*, serving in the western Mediterranean for two years. In April 1774 he was deputed by Sir Peter Denis to conduct delicate negotiations with the dey of Algiers about his treatment of the British consul, and on their successful conclusion was sent home overland with Denis's dispatches reporting the outcome. After seven months in Scottish waters, during which he took part in his first parliamentary campaign standing unsuccessfully for Dunbartonshire in November 1774, Elphinstone transferred in March 1775 from the *Scorpion* to the *Romney* (50 guns) in the acting rank of captain which was confirmed on 11 May 1775.

Early commands, 1775–1782 In the *Romney* Elphinstone escorted a troop convoy to Newfoundland and gave passage to Rear-Admiral Robert Duff, governor-designate of the colony. He returned home the following February and in March took command of the frigate *Perseus* (20 guns), sailing in July 1776 with a convoy to New York soon after the American Declaration of Independence, and capturing an American privateer on the way. Off New York he was actively employed in cruising against the enemy's privateers and blockade runners, capturing some twelve small vessels. At Antigua in February 1777 he transferred to the larger *Pearl* (32 guns) on the death of her captain, returning to the *Perseus* off Delaware in May. Her task of harassing the privateers and co-operating with the army ashore in North America continued for much of the next three years, broken by four months in the West Indies in early 1779, when she survived two hurricanes on the passage south, and was then employed cruising among the islands to frustrate French attempts against the sugar plantations. In November, off Charlestown harbour, *Perseus* captured the French *Thérèse*, also 20 guns, in a brisk action in which *Perseus* suffered considerable damage to her rigging. In spring 1780 Elphinstone was put in charge of the landing of General George Clinton's army near Charlestown, with all the transport ships under his control; he then led the naval brigade at the capture of the town. Clinton wrote of Elphinstone that his 'unremitted attention to us from his so ably and successfully conducting the transports … with the great benefit I have derived from his knowledge of the Inland Navigation of this part of the coast, merit my warmest thanks' (Clinton to Germain, colonial secretary, 9 March 1780, *London Gazette*, 25 April 1780). After the capitulation of Charlestown (7 May), Elphinstone returned home with the dispatches of Vice-Admiral Marriot Arbuthnot, the naval commander-in-chief.

Elphinstone was immediately given command of the *Warwick* (50 guns) in home waters and on 14 February 1781, after an acrimonious contest against the Argyll interest, he was elected as whig member of parliament for Dunbartonshire, a seat which he held until 1790. Meanwhile on 5 January, cruising in the English Channel, he captured the Dutch *Rotterdam* of equal force without losing a man. In March, with a large convoy, he sailed again to North America where he embarked Midshipman Prince William Henry (the future William IV), who was anxious to see some action. In September, Elphinstone's squadron, after a long chase, captured the large French frigate *Aigle* (44 guns) and all but one of her convoy off Delaware (though the prince was ill and confined to his bunk). Elphinstone transferred to the frigate *Carysfort* in November 1782 and returned to England, himself in poor health.

For the next ten years Elphinstone was on half pay. He took his seat in the House of Commons but seldom spoke, and divided his time between London and his family estates in Scotland. He acted as unpaid treasurer and comptroller of the household to his former midshipman, Prince William, from 1785 to 1789, when the king objected to his further employment as he was politically in opposition to the government. He also acted as a secretary to the prince of Wales. On 10 April 1787 he married Jane, daughter and coheir of Colonel William Mercer of Aldie, Perthshire, but she died two years later (12 December 1789) in Yorkshire on the way to Scotland. Margaret [see Flahault de la Billardrie, Margaret de], the only child of the marriage, was born in London on 12 June 1788. In November 1790 Elphinstone travelled to Nice, Venice, and Florence for his health but returned home in May 1791 after reading reports in the newspapers that the naval force was about to be increased.

War with France and the capture of Toulon, 1793 In fact it was not until January 1793, on the outbreak of war, that Elphinstone received orders to take command of the *Robust* (74 guns); in May he sailed to the Mediterranean in Lord Hood's squadron, which in August took possession of Toulon at the request of the French royalists. Elphinstone, who had been put in command of the troops by Hood, landed on the 28th with 1500 men to capture Fort La Malgue (of which he was appointed governor by Hood) and to protect the eastern side of the harbour. To secure his base he then led a force of 600 British and Spanish troops and seamen, and successfully drove the French from the Ollioules Gorge, capturing all their ordnance, horses, and ammunition. Elphinstone held his position as military governor of La Malgue until December when the arrival of a French republican army, its siege guns commanded by a youthful Major Bonaparte, forced Hood to abandon Toulon. The evacuation by the fleet of more than 14,000 troops and royalist fugitives was entrusted to Elphinstone: 'I have infinite pleasure in acknowledging my very great obligation to Captain Elphinstone for his unremitting zeal and exertions, who saw the last man off' wrote Hood to Henry Dundas, secretary of state, on 20 December (*London Gazette*, 17 Jan 1794). The *Robust*, with at one stage 500 royalist refugees and some 2000 troops on board, was the last ship to leave on 27 December. All refugees were landed in Hyères and *Robust* returned to Gibraltar and thence to England, escorting a convoy of 130 ships. Elphinstone's experience of fighting on shore at Charlestown thirteen years earlier had proved invaluable. He was created a knight of the Bath for his services and on 12 April 1794 was promoted to rear-admiral of the blue.

Capture of Cape Colony, 1795 On 30 July 1794 Elphinstone hoisted his flag in the *Barfleur* (90 guns) for service in the Channel Fleet until the following March when he transferred to the *Monarch* (74 guns). The Netherlands had been occupied by the French in January 1795 and in April Elphinstone sailed with a small squadron to south Africa to prevent the Dutch Cape Colony from falling into French hands. It was hoped that the name of the prince of Orange, who had found refuge in England, would prevent any opposition. On arrival off Cape Town on 10 June Elphinstone, who had been promoted to vice-admiral on 1 June 1795, was joined by Commodore John Blankett and his four ships; meanwhile 3000 troops sailed to Bahia, Brazil, to await orders. The fleet sailed round to False Bay from

where Elphinstone endeavoured to negotiate with the Dutch governor and council. When an American ship arrived from Amsterdam with a Dutch newspaper reporting that all persons were absolved from their allegiance to the prince of Orange the governor determined to take a stronger line with Elphinstone. On 7 August, therefore, Elphinstone's ships bombarded the Dutch camp at Muizenberg in False Bay, and a landing force of 1000 seamen and marines persuaded the Dutch to abandon their camp. On 4 September the reinforcements from Bahia arrived. Bad weather delayed their landing for ten days but on the 16th Cape Town capitulated. Although Elphinstone had little part in the final action, his ability and energy leading to the occupation of Muizenberg won for him the acknowledgements of both his army colleagues and the government. Lord Spencer, the first lord, for example, wrote to express his 'very sincere congratulations on the very valuable acquisition which you have obtained for this country at so little expense of lives or money' (29 Dec 1795, Allardyce, 103).

In November, Elphinstone with his squadron sailed east for Madras with the intention of seizing the Dutch settlements in India and Ceylon but found that Rear-Admiral Peter Rainier, commander-in-chief in the East Indies, had anticipated him. On receiving intelligence of a Dutch expedition sent to recapture the Cape, Elphinstone returned to Simon's Bay in May 1796, but it was August before a Dutch squadron of eight ships, mostly small, and a transport arrived and was discovered at anchor in Saldanha Bay, 100 miles north of Cape Town. Elphinstone's force, with seven ships of the line and several frigates, was so overwhelming in gunpower that the Dutch were persuaded to surrender without a shot being fired, the ships' companies becoming prisoners of war and their ships taken into the Royal Navy. Elphinstone sailed home in the *Monarch* with 500 passengers, suffering severe gales for thirty-six days before arriving at Spithead on 3 January 1797, when he struck his flag. For his successes in south Africa he was created an Irish baron (7 March 1797) with the title of Baron Keith of Stonehaven Marischal and with remainder to his daughter. It was another three months before Jervis, the captain under whom he had served as a midshipman, was created a peer.

Meanwhile Elphinstone had been returned unanimously as MP for Stirlingshire in June 1796 though, as he wrote in 1804, he 'made it an invariable rule since the year 1792 not to engage in any political career whilst employed on service, thinking it my duty to execute the commands of my superiors faithfully without entering into their motives' (19 June 1804 to Lord Melville, Lloyd, 3.213).

On 1 June 1797 Lord Keith was sent to the Nore to assist in putting down the mutiny which had recently broken out. Accused by the mutineers' delegates of withholding their Cape prize money, he was able to assure them that he had not as yet received any himself. In an open letter on 6 June he explained the reason for the delay, adding: 'For God's sake reflect on the happy times in which we served together, and on the advantages we brought to our country. Be not misled by designing men, but return to your old friends' (Allardyce, 144–5). By the 15th all the ships had surrendered. Keith was then sent to Plymouth with his flag in the *Queen Charlotte* (100 guns), where the mutiny, quelled in May, had broken out again. His tact and firmness as a negotiator with the mutineers' leaders was instrumental in finally ending the mutiny in July.

The Mediterranean, 1798–1800 After a few months off Ushant, Keith struck his flag in November and went on leave for a year. In December 1798 he sailed in the *Foudroyant* (80 guns), transferring in February 1799 to the *Barfleur* (98 guns), to command the blockading squadron off Cadiz and as second in command in the Mediterranean to Jervis, now earl of St Vincent. In April 1799 a French fleet of twenty-six ships under Admiral Bruix sailed from Brest and, assisted by a gale off Cadiz, evaded Keith's squadron of only fifteen ships, entered the Mediterranean, and (unknown to the British) reached Toulon on 14 May. Meanwhile Keith followed them to Gibraltar where he joined St Vincent, who was in poor health. Delayed by bad weather it was 12 May before the British fleet, with St Vincent in command, could leave Gibraltar to search for the French. At Minorca they learned that a Spanish fleet of twenty-two ships from Cadiz had also passed through the strait and entered Cartagena, and that the French were in Toulon harbour. On 1 June St Vincent retired sick to Minorca and on the 16th temporarily relinquished command of the Mediterranean Fleet to Keith. Meanwhile, again unknown to the British, the French had left Toulon on 27 May. After searching for them there and off Genoa, Keith learned that they had joined the Spaniards in Cartagena. Fearing a combined attack on Minorca, the only British base in the western Mediterranean, he returned there on 6 July, where he was joined by twelve ships which had just arrived from England. On the 8th he learned that the combined fleets had left Cartagena, apparently for the Strait of Gibraltar. He was, however, still concerned for Minorca, undefended because of Nelson's refusal of his orders to send ships from Sicily for its defence, and felt obliged to remain there for three more days before sailing in chase of the French. On 14 August he arrived off Brest with thirty-one of the line to find that the French and Spanish fleets had found safety there a week before. The only consolation in this unhappy episode was the capture of five French frigates off Toulon in June. Keith has been criticized for failing to find the enemy fleet and bringing it to action, but to quote the *Dictionary of National Biography* 'he seems to have been in a great measure the victim of circumstances; and the divided command and St Vincent's ill health had enormously increased the inherent difficulties of the problem'. C. Lloyd, the editor of the second volume of *The Keith Papers* (Navy Records Society, 1950), described the search in great detail and came to the same conclusion.

After three months in England, Keith was appointed commander-in-chief of the Mediterranean Fleet in succession to St Vincent. He arrived at Gibraltar in the *Queen Charlotte* in December 1799 and resumed the command from Nelson, who had acted as commander-in-chief during the continued illness of St Vincent. Nelson, himself in poor health, was deeply hurt that the command had not gone to him and, after visiting Keith at Leghorn and accompanying him to Palermo and Malta, retired to Sicily and its royal family, proving of little use as a second in command.

For Keith's fleet Minorca was available as a base but the French fleet in Toulon had to be watched, Malta was still in French hands until September 1800, a French army was still in Egypt, and the Austrian army in northern Italy needed support from the sea in its endeavours to drive the French out of Tuscany and Piedmont. On 17 March 1800, while Keith was on shore in Leghorn with some of his staff, his flagship, the *Queen Charlotte*, caught fire and was utterly destroyed with the loss of about 690 lives. The accidental burning of some hay stored under the half-deck was thought to have been the cause.

Keith, having lost all his papers, signal books, and belongings, transferred first to the *Audacious* and then to the *Minotaur* (both 74 guns). His squadron supported the Austrians by bombarding the French army near Genoa, and in enforcing a tight blockade which in nine weeks was broken by only one small ship (carrying sacks of flour and chestnuts). On 5 June the French evacuated Genoa, but nine days later the position was reversed by Napoleon's victory at Marengo and the armistice with Austria. Keith was obliged to withdraw his squadron to Leghorn where he saw Nelson off on the latter's return overland to England.

In August 1800 Keith shifted his flag to the *Foudroyant* to prepare, in concert with Lieutenant-General Sir Ralph Abercromby, for a descent on Cadiz with 20,000 troops carried in thirty-six transports. On arrival at Cadiz on 4 October with seven ships of the line, sixteen smaller vessels, and the transports it was learned that yellow fever was rampant in the town. Moreover there were neither suitable landing places nor safe anchorages in bad weather. Keith did not perform well. He could not decide whether a landing should be attempted, and Abercromby found him a difficult colleague. Major-General Sir John Moore, the second in command, wrote that Keith was 'all confusion, blaming everybody and everything, but attempting to remedy nothing … repeating much more incoherent nonsense' (*Diary of Sir John Moore*, ed. J. F. Maurice, 2 vols., 1904, 1.378). On the 7th the attempt was called off and the fleet and transports returned to Gibraltar. Spencer, the first lord of the Admiralty, endorsed the decision.

Egypt, 1801 After touching at Malta (which the French had surrendered in September) Keith's fleet and Abercromby's army sailed east to deal with the French army which Napoleon had left behind in Egypt, and to prevent any risk of France obtaining possession of the Red Sea and advancing on India. On 1 January 1801, the day Keith's promotion to admiral was gazetted, the fleet anchored in the sheltered harbour of Marmorice Bay in south-west Turkey—five of the line, two frigates, twelve smaller vessels, 100 troopships carrying 16,150 soldiers, and fifty-seven Turkish vessels. For seven weeks the landing of the army in ships' boats was rehearsed and equipment repaired and improved. The fleet arrived off Abu Qir on 2 March and after a week of gales the army, including its horses and artillery, was successfully landed on the beaches of Abu Qir Bay against strong opposition and heavy fire. Throughout the campaign Keith was responsible for feeding the army; he had also to guard against any interference by the French navy whose squadrons twice approached the Egyptian coast. Unlike his performance at Cadiz he co-operated well with Abercromby until the latter was killed, meeting on terms of intimacy every day as he told his sister in February, but he found Abercromby's successor, General Hely Hutchinson, indolent and needing constant urging to hasten the campaign.

Keith's relationships with his own captains, particularly Alexander Cochrane and Benjamin Hallowell, were also much strained. Cochrane, whom Keith later described as a 'crackhanded, unsafe man' (to Markham, 23 Feb 1804, *Selections from the Correspondence of … Markham*, 153), went so far as to tell Keith that he and his fellow captains 'consider your Lordship much more inclined to take merit to yourself than to bestow it on others, and that the laurels gained by many deserving officers have been allowed to fade in silence' (29 Aug 1801, Lloyd, 2.350).

After the fall of Cairo on 28 June and of Alexandria on 2 September the French capitulated, leaving Keith responsible, under the terms of the surrender, for returning more than 24,000 Frenchmen and their baggage to France. 'It fell to the lot of the army to fight and of the navy to labour', said Nelson in seconding the vote of thanks in the House of Lords; 'they had equally performed their duty and were equally entitled to thanks' (*GM*, 71, December 1801, 1133). It was indeed a successful example of combined operations with 6000 seamen labouring to assist the army in all weathers. Throughout the operation Keith's administrative ability and his long experience were paramount; he was his own controller, victualler, contract and purchase agent, director of transports, and director of works, as well as having the responsibility for the general command of the Mediterranean Fleet. For his services Keith received the freedom of the City of London with a sword of the value of 100 guineas, the order of the Crescent from the sultan of Turkey, and on 5 December was created a baron of Great Britain and Ireland which necessitated his giving up his seat in the Commons. He was further ennobled on 10 September 1803 when he became Baron Keith of Banheath of county Dumbarton, with remainder to his daughter.

Commander-in-chief, North Sea, 1803–1807 After some months in Malta, Keith returned to England in July 1802. With the resumption of war in May 1803 he was appointed commander-in-chief in the North Sea. When offered the appointment by St Vincent, the first lord, he wrote that he was deeply hurt that a junior officer, Nelson, was being sent to the command he had himself so recently held. Nevertheless his new command, which stretched from Selsey Bill in Sussex to the Shetland Islands, gave him the heavy responsibility of preparing the defence of the coast against a likely invasion from across the channel. He hoisted his flag at the Nore and set up his headquarters in

East Cliff Lodge, near Ramsgate; his letters to Rear-Admiral John Markham, one of St Vincent's sea lords, show that he soon realized both the importance and interest of his new command and quickly found much scope for his administrative skills. In addition to controlling operations in the channel and the North Sea, and protecting trade, he was responsible for organizing the sea fencibles from Hampshire to the Forth, the signalling and telegraph systems on shore, the extension of the chain of Martello towers, and liaising with the army. French ports had to be blockaded, and all movements of the enemy, real or pretended, had to be watched since a feint might always be converted into an actual attempt at invasion, and this might come from either Boulogne or the Texel. By 1805 he had six flag officers and nearly 150 ships of all sizes under his command. After Napoleon had transferred his interests to Austria in 1805 and the threat of invasion was therefore much reduced, Keith was more concerned with the continental blockade, with his ships stationed off nearly every port in northern Europe.

Keith struck his flag in May 1807 and retired to his estates at Purbrook Park, near Portsmouth, and Kincardine in the Firth of Forth. On 10 January 1808, at the house of his friend Henry Hoare in York Place, London, he was married by the duke of Clarence's chaplain to Hester Maria Thrale (1764–1857) [*see* Elphinstone, Hester Maria], eldest daughter and heir of Henry Thrale, brewer and MP for Southwark, and Hester Thrale (later Piozzi; 1741–1821). Lady Keith, known as Queeney, made for her husband an excellent companion in his declining years (at their marriage she was forty-three and he sixty-four). They had one child, Georgiana, who married first the Hon. Augustus Villiers, second son of the fifth earl of Jersey, and second Lord William Osborne, brother of the eighth duke of Leeds, but had no children.

Final years and assessment On 24 February 1812, after five years ashore, aged sixty-six, and an admiral of the red since July 1810, Keith was appointed commander-in-chief of the Channel Fleet on the death of Sir Charles Cotton. He hoisted his flag in the *San Josef* (114 guns) but in practice spent much of his time ashore in Plymouth to preserve his health. His command extended from Portsmouth to the north coast of Spain and his prime duty was the close blockade of Brest and Rochefort, but he also conducted a remote control over his ships supporting Wellington in northern Spain. He periodically cruised off Brest but the successful command of the blockading squadrons was normally exercised by his subordinate rear-admirals. In April 1814, with Napoleon on his way to Elba, Keith was at La Rochelle supervising the embarkation of Wellington's army for its return to England. He was back at Plymouth on 29 July and hauled down his flag. His time at Plymouth was also marked by his encouragement of the building of the breakwater in the sound. He had been created a viscount on 14 May and received the GCB on 2 January 1815.

However, at the end of April 1815, as soon as it was known that Napoleon had escaped from Elba, Keith returned to his command with his flag in the *Ville de Paris* (110 guns) at Plymouth. His instructions were to resume the blockade of the western ports of France and to assist the royalists in the Vendée. After Napoleon's defeat at Waterloo (18 June) Keith sent out over thirty ships to search enemy vessels between Ushant and Finisterre in order to prevent an escape to America. As a result Napoleon offered himself to the *Bellerophon* (74 guns, Captain Maitland) at Rochefort on 15 July and was taken to Plymouth Sound. To Keith fell the tasks of informing him that the government had decided that he was to be exiled to St Helena, of receiving the full force of Napoleon's objections, of refusing (on the government's instructions) his demands to be treated as an emperor but informing him that he was to be known as General Bonaparte, and of reducing the number of people who could accompany him in his exile. When the time came for Bonaparte to transfer to the *Northumberland*, which was to take him to St Helena, he is said to have kept the seventy-year-old admiral waiting for two hours in his barge. Admiral Cockburn of the *Northumberland* remonstrated, but Keith replied: 'Much greater men than either you or I have waited longer for him before now; let him take his time' (G. Home, *Memoirs of an Aristocrat*, 1838, 251). Bonaparte sailed that day, 7 August, and Keith received both the gratitude of the government for handling the matter with such skill and judgement and the respect of Bonaparte.

On 19 August, Keith struck his flag and terminated his long naval career. He had accumulated a handsome fortune from prize money, more perhaps than any other naval officer, thanks mainly to his long years as a commander-in-chief which entitled him to a large share of the prize money awarded for ships captured within his command. For example, his service in south Africa and India brought him £64,000 and during the years 1803 to 1806 he received £177,000. He devoted his remaining years to improving and adorning his two estates, Purbrook Park in Hampshire, and Tulliallan, near Kincardine, on the north bank of the Forth, where he reclaimed land and built piers, embankments, and a castle—used by the Polish General Sikorski in the Second World War. His great sadness during these years was that his elder daughter and heir, having wisely declined the hand of the duke of Clarence in 1811, should choose to marry, in 1817, Napoleon's former aide-de-camp, the comte de Flahault. Flahault was later to be the French ambassador to Italy, Austria, and, in 1860, to Great Britain. In 1822 Keith received his last honour, the grand cross of the order of St Maurice and St Lazarus, from the king of Sardinia for his services at the siege of Genoa in 1800. On 10 March 1823 he died in his castle at Tulliallan, aged seventy-seven, and was buried at Overtown church, Kincardine, where he had constructed a mausoleum. His title of a baron of Great Britain and Ireland descended to his elder daughter but expired on her death in 1867.

Though he commanded all three main fleets, the channel, the North Sea, and the Mediterranean, Keith never (unlike many of his contemporaries) commanded nor fought in a fleet battle which might have brought him greater fame. But he was unrivalled in his day in his experience and skill in combined operations—Charlestown, Toulon, south Africa, Abu Qir—and he was both a consummate seaman and a meticulous administrator. This, and his success in dealing with the several problems he had to face, give his career a particular interest. Steady, persevering, and cautious, he made few mistakes. He was a good, though not quite a great, commander, but a difficult colleague, quick to take offence, and slow to forget a grievance or forgive an error. Yet he had his admirers—St Vincent for example, who openly scorned Scots, wrote that 'Lord Keith is by far the best [Scot] I ever met with by land or sea' (to Nepean, 22 Sept 1800, Richmond, 4.4). And again, many years later: 'I have esteemed you from the hour you embarked with me in the *Gosport*' (W. M. James, *Old Oak: Life of Earl St Vincent*, 1950, 203; about 1807). Successive first lords of the Admiralty, in addition to St Vincent, seem to have had no less confidence in him.

C. H. H. Owen

Sources DNB · PRO, Admiralty papers, ADM 1/159, ADM 1/399–1/402, ADM 1/1761–1765, ADM 36, ADM 52 · *The Keith papers*, 1, ed. W. G. Perrin, Navy RS, 62 (1927) · *The Keith papers*, 2–3, ed. C. Lloyd, Navy RS, 90, 96 (1950–55) · NMM, Keith papers · A. Allardyce, *Memoir of G. K. Elphinstone, Viscount Keith* (1882) · *Private papers of George, second Earl Spencer*, ed. J. S. Corbett and H. W. Richmond, 3–4, Navy RS, 58–9 (1924) · *Selections from the correspondence of Admiral John Markham*, ed. C. Markham, Navy RS, 28 (1904) · *Letters and papers of Charles, Lord Barham*, ed. J. K. Laughton, 3, Navy RS, 39 (1911) · B. Lavery, 'George Keith Elphinstone, Lord Keith', *Precursors of Nelson: British admirals of the eighteenth century*, ed. P. Le Fevre and R. Harding (2000), 377–99 · J. Holland Rose, *Lord Hood and the defence of Toulon* (1922) · 'Biographical memoir of the Right Hon. Lord Keith', *Naval Chronicle*, 10 (1803), 1–23 · J. Marshall, *Royal naval biography*, 1 (1823), 43–56 · *The dispatches and letters of Vice-Admiral Lord Viscount Nelson*, ed. N. H. Nicolas, 7 vols. (1844–6) · *The later correspondence of George III*, ed. A. Aspinall, 5 vols. (1962–70) · *The correspondence of George, prince of Wales, 1770–1812*, ed. A. Aspinall, 8 vols. (1963–71) · F. L. Maitland, *Narrative of the surrender of Buonaparte* (1826) · *Thraliana: the diary of Mrs. Hester Lynch Thrale (later Mrs. Piozzi), 1776–1809*, ed. K. C. Balderston, 2nd edn, 2 vols. (1951) · E. Haden-Guest, 'Elphinstone, George', HoP, *Commons, 1754–90*, 2.400–01 [see also 1.476–8] · D. G. Henry, 'Elphinstone, George', HoP, *Commons, 1790–1820*, 3.705 · GEC, *Peerage* · death duty registers, PRO, IR 26/965, fol. 761

Archives NA Scot., letters · NL Scot., corresp., MS 3420 · NMM, corresp. and papers | BL, letters to Lord Bridport, Add. MS 35197 · BL, corresp. with first and second lords Melville, Add. MSS 41081–41082 · BL, letters to Lord Nelson, Add. MSS 34906–34932, *passim* · Bucks. RLSS, letters to Lord Hobart · Falkirk Museums History Research Centre, letters to W. Forbes · Hunt. L., letters to Grenville family · NL Scot., corresp. with Sir Alexander Cochrane, MSS 2569, 3022 · NL Scot., corresp. with Lord Lynedoch, MSS 3595–3625, *passim* · NL Scot., corresp. with first and second Lords Melville · NMM, corresp. with Lord Barham · NMM, letters to Lord Nelson · NRA Scotland, priv. coll., letters to William Adam · priv. coll., corresp. with Lord Elgin · PRO NIre., corresp. with Lord Castlereagh · U. Durham L., letters to Lord Grey · U. Hull, Brynmor Jones L., letters to Sir Henry Hotham · U. Nott. L., letters to Lord William Bentinck

Likenesses G. Stuart, oils, *c*.1794, priv. coll. · H. P. Danloux, oils, 1798, NG Scot. · J. Hoppner, oils, 1799, NG Scot. · J. Hoppner, oils, *c*.1799, Royal Collection [see illus.] · W. Owen, oils, *c*.1799, NMM · P. Audinet, line engraving, pubd 1801 (after H. P. Danloux, 1798), BM · G. L. Sanders, oils, *c*.1816, NMM · marble bust, exh. RA 1883 · Ridley & Hall, stipple (after M. Brown), BM, NPG; repro. in *European*

Magazine (1806) • W. Staveley, oils (after oil painting by G. L. Sanders, *c*.1816), Scot. NPG • plaster medal (after J. G. Hancock, 1801), Scot. NPG

Wealth at death under £60,000: PRO, death duty registers, IR 26/965, fol. 761

Elphinstone [*née* Thrale], **Hester Maria**, Viscountess Keith (1764–1857), protégée of Samuel Johnson, the eldest daughter of Henry *Thrale (1728–1781), brewer, and his wife, Hester, afterwards Mrs *Piozzi (1741–1821), was born on 17 September 1764 at Southwark, London. Dr Johnson, a friend of the family from 1765, called her 'Queeney', wrote childish rhymes for her, played horses with her, wrote to her, and directed her education. The death of her only surviving brother in 1776 made her a rich heiress. In 1778 Fanny Burney described her as 'cold and reserved, though full of knowledge and intelligence'; a depiction amplified in Beryl Bainbridge's fictional account of her childhood, *According to Queeney* (2001). In 1781 her father died, and her mother's subsequent marriage in 1784 to Gabriel Piozzi caused her acute mortification. Although her father's heir, she was still a minor and had no access to her fortune. She retired to her father's Brighton house, where she saw no company, and studied Hebrew and mathematics, of which she became a considerable scholar. In 1784, when her mother and Piozzi were in Italy, she took a house in London for herself and her sisters. Her hostility to her mother's remarriage continued, although they remained on civil terms. The unusual education bestowed on 'Queeney' had little beneficial effect on her temperament; her mother lamented that she was 'reserved and shy with a considerable Share of Obstinacy, & I think a Heart void of all Affection for any Person in the World' (Clifford, 79).

Determined to marry a lord, Hester Thrale declined a proposal of marriage from the poet Samuel Rogers, and on 10 January 1808, in London, she married Admiral George Keith *Elphinstone, Baron Keith (1746–1823), who had then been a widower some years. Her new homes were Tulliallan, on the Firth of Forth, and Purbrook Park, near Portsmouth; and on 12 December 1809, at the age of forty-five, in Harley Street, London, she gave birth to her only child, a daughter, Georgiana Augusta Henrietta.

Lady Keith was one of the original patrons of Almack's. She became viscountess in 1814, on the elevation of the admiral to the United Kingdom peerage, and, together with her stepdaughter, the Hon. Margaret Mercer Elphinstone [*see* Flahault de la Billardrie, Margaret de], she was prominent in society during the regency and the next two or three decades in London and Edinburgh. In 1823 she was left a widow. Towards the end of her life, she retired from company and devoted herself to works of charity. She died on 31 March 1857 at her house, 110 Piccadilly, London.   JENNETT HUMPHREYS, *rev.* K. D. REYNOLDS

Sources *GM*, 3rd ser., 2 (1857), 615–16 • J. L. Clifford, *Hester Lynch Piozzi (Mrs Thrale)* (1941) • *Diary and letters of Madame D'Arblay*, ed. [C. Barrett], 7 vols. (1842–6) • J. Boswell, *The life of Samuel Johnson*, 2 vols. (1791) • Lord Lansdowne [H. W. E. P. F. Lansdowne], *The Queeney letters* (1934) • GEC, *Peerage* • Ward, *Men of the reign*

Likenesses J. Zoffany, oils, 1786 (as a child), repro. in Clifford, *Hester Lynch Piozzi* • J. Marchi, mezzotint (as a child; after J. Zoffany), BM

Elphinstone, Sir Howard, first baronet (1773–1846), military engineer, born on 4 March 1773, was of Scottish descent and was the sixth son of Captain John Elphinstone RN (1722–1785), later lieutenant-general and vice-admiral in the Russian service, who commanded the Russian fleet in the Baltic in 1769 and won the battle of Chesma. His mother was Amelia Warburton (*d.* February 1786), only daughter of John Warburton (*d.* 11 May 1759), Somerset herald of arms from 1720. He entered the army as second lieutenant, Royal Engineers, on 17 October 1793 and first saw service in the capture of the Cape of Good Hope in 1795. He was promoted first lieutenant on 5 February 1796, and went to India, where he became captain-lieutenant on 1 July 1800. In 1801 he accompanied the division sent from India to Egypt, under Sir David Baird, as commanding royal engineer. He married, on 14 February 1803, his first cousin, Frances Warburton (*d.* 24 Aug 1858), eldest daughter of John Warburton of Parliament Street, Westminster, London; they had one son (who succeeded to the baronetcy) and three daughters.

In 1806 Elphinstone was attached to the special mission to Portugal of Lord Rosslyn and General Simcoe, to advise the Portuguese government on the defence of Lisbon, and in the latter part of 1806 he accompanied Major-General Whitelocke to South America as commanding royal engineer. In 1808 he went in the same capacity to the Peninsula with the force under Sir Arthur Wellesley (later duke of Wellington). He was severely wounded at the battle of Roliça, and for his services there he received the gold medal. Promoted captain on 1 March 1805, he was promoted major by brevet on 1 January 1812 and in that year ordered to the Peninsula again. While Sir Richard Fletcher was the commanding royal engineer in the Peninsula, Major Elphinstone (Lieutenant-Colonel Elphinstone, as he became on 21 July 1813) remained in Portugal, but when Fletcher was killed before San Sebastian, Elphinstone, as senior Royal Engineers officer, asserted his right to be present at headquarters. Wellington would have preferred to keep, as senior to Elphinstone, Lieutenant-Colonel John Fox Burgoyne, who had long been with him and whose ways as commanding royal engineer he knew (especially as Burgoyne was in the army, though not in the Royal Engineers), but he had to yield to Elphinstone's demand and summon him to the front. Elphinstone therefore superintended the passage of the Adour as commanding royal engineer and held that post at the battles of the Nivelle and the Nive. Wellington then left him with Sir John Hope to besiege Bayonne, while Burgoyne accompanied the headquarters of the army in the pursuit after Maréchal Soult.

At the end of the war, when honours were freely bestowed on the leaders of the Peninsular army, Elphinstone was rewarded as commanding royal engineer with a baronetcy, on 25 May 1816, and he was made a CB. He did not again see service; he was promoted colonel on 2

December 1824, major-general on 10 January 1837, and colonel-commandant of the Royal Engineers in 1834. He died at Ore Place, near Hastings, Sussex, on 28 April 1846.

H. M. STEPHENS, rev. ROGER T. STEARN

Sources GM, 2nd ser., 26 (1846) · J. Philippart, ed., The royal military calendar, 3 vols. (1815–16) · Burke, Peerage (1959) · S. G. P. Ward, Wellington's headquarters: a study of the administrative problems in the Peninsula, 1809–14 (1957) · A. J. Guy, ed., The road to Waterloo: the British army and the struggle against revolutionary and Napoleonic France, 1793–1815 (1990) · R. Muir, Britain and the defeat of Napoleon, 1807–1815 (1996)

Elphinstone, Sir Howard Craufurd (1829–1890), army officer, fourth son of Captain Alexander Francis Elphinstone RN, a noble in Livonia, and his wife, Amelia Anne, daughter of A. Lobach of Cumenhoff, near Riga, was born on 12 December 1829 at Wattram in Livonia. His family were Scottish, and his great-grandfather, Captain John Elphinstone RN, also an admiral in the Russian navy, commanded the Russian fleet in 1770 at the battle of Chesma Bay. He was named Howard after his uncle, Major-General Sir Howard Elphinstone. Educated largely abroad, he passed out of the Royal Military Academy, Woolwich, at the head of his batch, and was commissioned in the Royal Engineers as second lieutenant on 18 December 1847. His promotions included: lieutenant, November 1851; second captain, April 1856; brevet major, December 1856; first captain, April 1862; major, July 1872; lieutenant-colonel, May 1873; colonel, May 1884; and major-general, January 1887.

Elphinstone officially attended military reviews in Prussia in 1853, then worked in the Ordnance Survey in Scotland until March 1854. In 1854 and 1855 he served in the Crimea, and he was awarded the Victoria Cross on 18 June 1855 for bravery on the night of the unsuccessful attack on the Redan. At the final assault on Sevastopol on 8 September he was wounded and lost an eye. He was mentioned in dispatches, and received a brevet majority, the Légion d'honneur (fifth class), the Mejidieh (fifth class), and a wound pension.

In March 1856 Elphinstone went on an official mission to the Netherlands, and in September reported on the Koblentz siege operations. He was employed from 5 September 1857 in the topographical department of the War Office on an official history of the Royal Engineers in the Crimea. He afterwards served in the North British military district.

In January 1859 Elphinstone was selected by the prince consort as governor to Prince Arthur, then eight years old; when the prince came of age, he was appointed in May 1871 treasurer and comptroller of his household, an office he held until his death. He attended the prince in England and overseas.

In 1858 Elphinstone arranged for Prince Albert his gift of the Prince Consort's Library at Aldershot. He was made CB (civil division) in August 1865, CB (military division) in May 1871, CMG in July 1870, and KCB in July 1871. He commanded the Royal Engineers units at Aldershot from August 1873 to December 1881. He was appointed aide-de-camp to the queen on 1 October 1877, and was colonel on

the staff and commanding royal engineer at Aldershot from 31 December 1881 to 30 December 1886. In 1884–5 he acted temporarily as military attaché at Berlin. On 1 April 1889 he was appointed to command the western military district.

Elphinstone married, on 5 December 1876, Annie Frances, second daughter of W. H. Cole of West Woodhay, Berkshire, and afterwards of Giffords Hall, Suffolk. They had four daughters. On 8 March 1890 Elphinstone left Plymouth for Tenerife in the steamer Tongariro on leave for his health, accompanied by his wife. That evening, off Ushant, he accidentally fell overboard and was drowned. His body was not found. By the queen's command a memorial service was held in Exeter Cathedral on 20 March.

R. H. VETCH, rev. JAMES FALKNER

Sources War Office records, PRO · Royal Engineers records, Royal Engineers Institute, Chatham · The Times (14 March 1890) · The Times (19 March 1890) · The Times (21 March 1890) · The Times (26 March 1890) · Army List · Hart's Army List · Royal Engineers Journal (April 1890) · Royal Engineers Journal (May 1890) · Royal Engineers Journal (Aug 1890) · dispatches, LondG (21 June 1855) · dispatches, LondG (21 Dec 1855) · A. W. Kinglake, The invasion of the Crimea, 8 vols. (1863–87) · W. H. Russell, The British expedition to the Crimea (1858)

Likenesses Maull & Fox, photograph, 1895 (Heroes of the Victoria cross) · L. W. Desanges, portrait, Royal Engineers, Aldershot · H. Schmeichen, oils, Royal Engineers mess room, Aldershot, 1901; replica given to Lady Elphinstone · photograph, Royal Library, Duke of Connaught's Album · wood-engraving (after a photograph by Reichard and Lindner of Berlin), NPG; repro. in ILN (22 March 1890)

Wealth at death £13,487 16s. 10d.: administration, 20 May 1890, CGPLA Eng. & Wales

Elphinstone, James, first Lord Balmerino (1557–1612), administrator and judge, was born on 19 August 1557, the third son of Robert, third Lord Elphinstone (1530–1602), and Margaret, daughter of Sir John Drummond of Innerpeffray. He studied at the University of Angers in 1582 and graduated MA from the University of Poitiers in 1584, apparently reading law.

Upon returning to Scotland Elphinstone was introduced to court and quickly came to the attention of James VI, with whom he became a great favourite. On 4 March 1586 he was appointed an ordinary lord of the court of session, the highest civil court in Scotland, under the designation of Lord Invernochty; this gave him a seat on the temporal side of the bench, which he exchanged in 1593 for a judgeship on the spiritual side, from which all lord presidents were drawn. During the 1580s he was sometimes designated as Mr James Elphinstone of Eaglesham or parson of Eaglesham, from an ecclesiastical office in the patronage of his family. In November 1589 he remained in Scotland as secretary with remit of correspondence in Latin and French during the king's absence in Norway to marry Anne of Denmark. He subsequently became one of the financial advisers in the queen's household. He attended a handful of privy council meetings in 1589 and again in 1593. So successful was his administration of the queen's finances that in 1596 Elphinstone became one of the treasury commissioners known as the Octavians, with the office of collector, while his attendance at privy council meetings increased dramatically. However, his conduct as an Octavian was particularly denounced by the Edinburgh mob in the riot of December 1596 which hastened the ending of the Octavian experiment.

In 1598 Elphinstone became secretary of state, being one of the best-qualified holders of this office during James VI's majority, and for the next five years he was a member of all the more important privy council commissions. From 1592 he was sometimes designated Mr James Elphinstone of Barnton, after one of a number of estates he had acquired: others included Ballumby and Innerpeffer (1597), Restalrig (1605), Balgregie (1603), Kirknewton (1607), Delny (1608), Dingwall (1608), and extensive lands in Ross-shire, including baronies with land in Glenelg, Lewis, and Skye (1597); he subsequently sold several of these lands. In April 1599 he brought his brother Alexander *Elphinstone, later fourth Lord Elphinstone, into the government as treasurer, and by 9 August that year he had himself been knighted.

In 1603 Elphinstone accompanied James VI to London, and on 20 February 1604 he was created a peer with the title of Lord Balmerino, the estates of the Cistercian abbey of Balmerino in Fife having been converted into a temporal lordship for him and his heirs male. In the latter year he was nominated one of the Scottish commissioners to treat for a union with England, and when the negotiations ended he was chosen by the privy council of Scotland to convey its thanks to James. In March 1605 he was made president of the court of session. In that office he often successfully opposed the earl of Dunbar, the lord treasurer, who was the antithesis of Elphinstone's cultured and urbane style of crown service, although their different yet complementary skills made each essential to James's administration of Scotland.

By religion Elphinstone was an undisguised Roman Catholic. This caused some concern among Scottish courtiers and was noted in English diplomatic correspondence in the 1590s. James Melville records that Elphinstone used his influence to persecute the more extreme presbyterian ministers, but this conformed with the king's plans to bring the kirk to heel, particularly after 1603. However, Elphinstone also opposed a complete re-establishment of episcopal power, fearing the consequences of a restoration of ecclesiastical lands—such properties formed the core of his own estate. The embodiment of King James's tolerant attitude toward Scottish Catholics, Elphinstone was at the same time an exemplary crown official who put national interests before those of his own religion. His undisputed administrative skills and knowledge of law, combined with the king's personal friendship, insulated him from any repercussions in Scotland arising from his personal faith.

During the late 1590s, however, Elphinstone's self-confidence led him to make a mistake that ultimately caused his disgrace. In 1599 a letter signed by James was sent to Pope Clement VIII requesting him to give a cardinal's hat to William Chisholm, bishop of Vaison (a kinsman of Elphinstone), and expressing high regard for the pope and the Catholic faith. The master of Gray sent a copy of this letter to Elizabeth, who asked James for an explanation. James asserted that the letter must be a forgery, and Elphinstone, as secretary of state, also repudiated its authorship. When James published his *Triplici nodo triplex cuneus* in 1607, however, Cardinal Robert Bellarmine's reply quoted the letter of 1599 as a proof of James's former favour to Catholicism, causing James to question Elphinstone anew on the subject during an interview in October 1608 concerning the condition of the Scottish Catholics. Elphinstone now confessed that he had written the letter and surreptitiously passed it in among papers awaiting the king's signature; he fully acknowledged that the king had not known what he was about when he signed it (surely an extraordinary oversight for an otherwise careful and shrewd monarch who monitored state affairs with particular attention to detail). Put on trial at St Andrews in March 1609, he acquitted the king of any knowledge of the letter written to the pope, which he said had been sent by himself as a matter of policy. The jury convicted him and the king confirmed the verdict, whereupon Elphinstone was sentenced to be beheaded, quartered, and attainted as a traitor.

The death sentence was not carried out because, according to a detailed account of the affair now drawn up by Elphinstone, James was aware of the contents of the letter, and had signed it without hesitation. Severe pressure was exerted on Elphinstone by Dunbar and Cecil to take full responsibility, and on the promise that his life and estates should be secured to him if he once more exculpated the king. However, James's duplicity in the matter seems clear; it would appear that Elphinstone was sacrificed in a show trial once the affair became sufficiently public to become a cause of political embarrassment in England. Elphinstone remained imprisoned at Falkland until October 1609, when having found security in £40,000, he was allowed free ward in the town and 1 mile round. Afterwards he was permitted to retire to his own estate at Balmerino, where he died on 21 June 1612, a broken man.

Elphinstone married, first, on 21 March 1588, Sarah, daughter of Sir John Menteith, with whom he had one son, John *Elphinstone, who became second Lord Balmerino; and second, by the end of 1597, Marjory, daughter of Hugh Maxwell of Tealing, with whom he had a son, James, created Lord Coupar in 1607, and three daughters, Margaret, married to Andrew, second Lord Fraser; Barbara, married to John Hamilton of Blair; and Marjory, married to Francis Fraser of Kinmundie, second son of the first Lord Fraser.

R. R. ZULAGER

Sources J. Durkan, 'The French connection in the sixteenth and early seventeenth centuries', *Scotland and Europe*, ed. T. C. Smout (1986), 19–44 · G. Plattard, 'Scottish masters and students at Poitiers', *SHR*, 21 (1923–4), 82–6, 168 · W. Fraser, ed., *The Elphinstone family book of the lords Elphinstone, Balmerino and Coupar*, 2 vols. (1897) · *Scots peerage*, 1.555–62 · *CSP Scot.*, 1585–1603 · S. Gardiner, *History of England from the accession of James I to the disgrace of Chief Justice Coke, 1603–1616*, 2 vols. (1863) · G. Brunton and D. Haig, *An historical account of the senators of the college of justice, from its institution in MDXXXII* (1832) · J. H. Burton and D. Masson, eds., *The register of the privy council of Scotland*, 1st ser., 14 vols. (1877–98), vols. 8–10 · J. M.

Thomson and others, eds., *Registrum magni sigilli regum Scotorum / The register of the great seal of Scotland*, 11 vols. (1882–1914), 1580–1620 · *The autobiography and diary of Mr James Melvill*, ed. R. Pitcairn, Wodrow Society (1842) · GEC, *Peerage*, 1.389–90

Archives NRA, priv. coll., corresp. and papers as secretary of state for Scotland

Elphinstone, John, **second Lord Balmerino** (d. 1649), nobleman and politician, was the son of James *Elphinstone, first Lord Balmerino (1557–1612), and his first wife, Sarah (d. 1592x7), daughter of Sir John Menteith of Carse, whom he married on 21 March 1588. Nothing is known of his early life or education. In 1609, following the revelation of compromising correspondence with Pope Clement VIII undertaken before 1603 with the object of winning Catholic support for James's accession to the English throne, Elphinstone's father was deprived of his estates and condemned to death, although the sentence was not carried out. Lord Balmerino's disgrace must have deeply affected his eldest son, and it may explain John Elphinstone's later hostility to the 'popish' policies of James's son Charles I. He was perhaps determined to avoid his father's mistakes of flirting with Rome and trusting too much in kings. Because his father had died under forfeiture, Elphinstone did not succeed to the title in 1612, but he was restored to the peerage on 4 August 1613 as the second Lord Balmerino. Shortly after 30 August the same year he married Anne Ker (d. 1650), daughter of Sir Thomas *Ker of Ferniehirst and sister of Robert Ker (or Carr), Viscount Rochester and from 3 November earl of Somerset, the king's favourite. In 1614 Balmerino was granted his father's estates. In 1617, during the king's visit to Scotland, Balmerino and his wife petitioned James to reinstate Robert Carr after his disgrace in the Overbury scandal.

During the 1620s Balmerino took a more prominent role in public life. At the parliament of 1621 he was among those who voted against ratifying the articles of Perth. In the convention of estates of 1625 he sat on a select committee charged with advising the king on dealing with the problems of the Scottish currency. In August 1627 Balmerino and the lord treasurer, Sir John Stewart of Traquair, visited the court at London on a deputation representing titulars and lay patrons who were potential teind-sellers (tithe-sellers); the two nobles had failed to instigate voluntary negotiations with the commission for surrenders and teinds established to carry out the king's controversial revocation scheme, and Charles made sure they knew of his displeasure and his determination to push through a wholesale redistribution of teinds. Although the revocation scheme proved impossible to carry through, Charles did insist on a strict line against nonconforming clergy. In the convention of estates of 1630 Balmerino protested that the oath of conformity (being demanded of all new clergy by the bishops) lacked parliamentary approval.

When Charles I visited Scotland in 1633 there were heated exchanges in parliament over his religious policies, particularly over an act requiring the clergy to wear vestments. The disaffected employed a lawyer, William

Haig, to draw up a petition airing their grievances. Balmerino and the sixth earl of Rothes were involved in revising the petition, but Charles refused to read it when Rothes tried to present it to him at Dalkeith. Balmerino kept a copy of the petition, with his own interlinings, and in 1634 he showed it to John Dunmure, who was visiting Balmerino at his home in Barnton, near Edinburgh. Without Balmerino's knowledge Dunmure made a copy of the document, and showed it to Peter Hay of Naughton in Fife. Hay was a firm episcopalian, and wasted no time in taking the petition to the archbishop of St Andrews, who in his turn took the petition to the king in London.

The council in Edinburgh decided to make an example of Balmerino. He was summoned to appear before it in June 1634. Before going to the council he met Haig and warned him of what was happening. Haig immediately fled to the Netherlands via Harwich. Balmerino was then examined by the council and placed in close confinement until his trial, 'so that his ladie got no accesse to him' (Row, 383). The trial began on 3 December and lasted until 20 March 1635. Balmerino was accused of 'penning and setting down of a scandalous libel, and divulging and dispersing it amongst his Majesty's lieges; at the least of concealing and not revealing of Mr William Haig' (Hargrave, 1.593). The prosecution referred to an act of the tenth parliament of James VI against speaking or writing reproach or slander to the king's person 'under the Pain of Death'. The defence argued that Balmerino had not promulgated or disclosed the petition, but merely shown it to a lawyer for his private opinion, and they pointed out that his own interlineations softened the terms of a petition which was intended to be respectful and conciliatory. They also maintained that there was no precedent for such a trial. The assessors, however, sustained the verdict and referred it to the jury. The jury was split down the middle, and only the casting vote of its foreman, the treasurer Sir John Stewart, now earl of Traquair, ensured a guilty verdict. Balmerino was sentenced to death, and accepted his sentence 'with a smyle … and with a low curtsie' (Row, 378). The sentence was suspended until the king's will was declared, and Balmerino was returned to Edinburgh Castle.

The trial and sentence scandalized many contemporaries. Throughout the trial, according to Row:

> the commone people avowedlie, with loud and high lifted up voices, were praying for my Lord Balmerino, and for all those that loved him and his cause, and prayed for a plague to come upon them that had the blame of his trouble; and from doing this the Magistrates could not possiblie get them stayed.   (Row, 384)

More significantly, the Scottish nobility were appalled that one of their number could be sentenced to death for the mere possession of a petition critical of royal ecclesiastical policy. According to one historian the trial inflicted 'crucial damage … on the personal rule of Charles I' and 'marked a decisive shift from reform towards revolution' (Macinnes, 140–41). The disaffected nobility blamed the trial on the bishops, and edged closer to an alliance with the nonconformist clergy. Well aware of public opinion,

Traquair advised the king not to carry out the death sentence. In July 1635, after thirteen months incarceration, Balmerino was freed from Edinburgh Castle, and allowed to return to his estates in Fife on condition that he remained within 6 miles of his house at Balmerino. In November, he was finally granted his full liberty.

Royalists later condemned Balmerino's ingratitude for the king's gracious pardon. According to Henry Guthry, Balmerino had received the king's remission 'before the Council Table ... upon his Knees, with ample acknowledgements of the Kings Mercy to him, and solemn Promises of Exemplary Loyalty thereafter, which how he perform'd his actings in the Troubles that ensued do testifie' (*Memoirs of Henry Guthry*, 12). Guthry believed that Balmerino was one of those who met dissident presbyterian ministers in April 1637 to plan protests against the new prayer book. His estates were located in an area renowned for conventicling and certainly, in the wake of the prayer book riot at St Giles's Cathedral in July, Balmerino emerged as one of the leading figures in the protest movement. When the disaffected met in October, Balmerino and Alexander Henderson were commissioned to draw up a formal complaint against the prayer book and the bishops. Baillie reported that 'the whole nobilitie' had 'supper in Balmerino's lodgeing' in Edinburgh, and then resolved to reassemble on 15 November to hear the government's response. 'In this meeting', wrote Baillie, 'Loudon and Balmerinoch were moderators; both of them, bot especially Balmerinoch, drew me to admiration. I thought them the best spoken men that I ever heard open a mouth' (*Letters and Journals of Robert Baillie*, 1.38–9). In the climactic month of February 1638 Balmerino helped to revise Archibald Johnston of Wariston's drafts of the national covenant, and was present at the signing of the covenant in Greyfriars Kirk on 28 February. At the Glasgow general assembly in November and December Balmerino 'resolved to be well near mute' (*Letters and Journals of Robert Baillie*, 1.125), but he was active in several committees. In February 1639 he worked with Henderson and Sir Thomas Hope to write a paper setting forth reasons for the lawfulness and necessity of a defensive war. On 22 March he was present when the covenanters took over the king's house at Dalkeith, and carried the royal ensigns back to Edinburgh Castle. During the first bishops' war he wrote from the castle to update General Leslie on the military supplies being gathered for the covenanter army. In July the king accused Balmerino of using an armed force to prevent 'our good subjects from coming to us', when they had tried to obey the king's summons to Berwick (*Historical Works of Balfour*, 2.336, 339). Balmerino rejected the charge, but it was little wonder that he was bitterly denounced by the royalists as 'one of the chief contrivers and most malicious prosecutors of this wicked covenant made against us and our authority' (Balcanquall, 13–15). In October 1640 Sir Patrick Drummond alleged that Balmerino 'carried himself now as a king' (*CSP dom.*, 1640–41, 136).

When Charles I visited Scotland in 1641 his visit was in stark contrast to that of 1633. At the parliament in August,

Charles yielded to the covenanters' agenda, and Balmerino was unanimously elected president of the parliament. When the covenanters debated the controversial actions of James Graham, earl of Montrose, Balmerino 'spake very patheticklie' on behalf of the man who was soon to inflict such damage on the covenanter cause (*Letters and Journals of Robert Baillie*, 1.374–5). In September he was made a privy councillor, and in November he became an extraordinary lord of session and a commissioner for the committee of both kingdoms. In a speech to parliament on 4 November, published as *The Lord Balmerino's Speech* (1641), he pointed to the Irish rising as evidence of a popish conspiracy against protestants in the three kingdoms. 'Let us not procrastinate this businesse', he urged, 'lest in the deferment thereof, God himselfe be angry with us, whose cause wee ought to maintaine: What fears can be conceived to oppose us, when Almighty omnipotence will fight for us? Therefore let us raise a sufficient army against them, for no better cause can ever offer it selfe unto us, then the maintenance of true Religion' (sigs. A3r–A4).

From 1639 onwards Balmerino worked energetically to raise money for the covenanter armies, and contributed at least 40,000 merks of his own to the cause; he later lamented the damage caused to his private finances. In 1643 he accompanied the Scottish army on its march into England to assist the English parliament in its war with the king. His attempts to raise revenue by levying an excise tax on various consumer goods provoked a riot in Edinburgh in January 1644. The rioters surrounded the council chamber, and warned 'that unless it were repealed, they would tear Balmerino in pieces', but the measure was still approved (*Memoirs of Henry Guthry*, 125–6).

In summer 1644 parliament appointed Balmerino one of the Scottish commissioners to London, and he sat regularly on the committee of both kingdoms, assisting its efforts to win the war. However, he was also the most active of the Scottish commissioners in pursuing negotiations with the French peace envoy, Jean de Montereul, who went to London in July 1645. Along with other covenanters Balmerino had become increasingly concerned that the English parliamentarians would not establish presbyterianism on the Scottish model, nor reform the union of the crowns, and a deal with the king seemed a promising option. The Scottish commissioners made positive noises, and in March 1646 Montereul visited Oxford to assure the king that his interests would be safe with them. However, when Montereul visited the Scottish army in April, Balmerino and his fellow covenanters took a hard line on the establishment of presbyterianism and the prosecution of Montrose. The king was furious, declaring that 'the Scots are abominable relapsed rogues, they have retracted almost everything' (Stevenson, 64). The covenanters hoped that the king would nevertheless choose to surrender to their army, and Balmerino returned to Edinburgh on 2 May predicting that this would happen. Charles did indeed join the Scottish army, and Balmerino travelled south and 'kissed the King's Hand' (*Memoirs of*

Henry Guthry, 176). Shortly afterwards Balmerino and Argyll returned to London to negotiate with the English parliament. In early 1647 the covenanter army withdrew from England and surrendered Charles I to the parliamentarians. In the same year Balmerino was one of the commissioners appointed by the general assembly to conclude a treaty of religious uniformity with the English parliament and the Westminster assembly of divines.

In 1648 Balmerino took a firm stand against the engagers, and supported the militant covenanters of the west of Scotland. After the defeat of the engagers he became one of only fourteen nobles to sit in the kirk party parliament of 1649. He was aligned with 'the Argilian faction' (*Memoirs of Henry Guthry*, 252), and had not death intervened he would have led the Scottish commissioners in their negotiations with Charles II in the Netherlands in 1649. His willingness to make peace with the new king disturbed hardliners such as Wariston, who later recorded in his diary that 'God's humbling hand' had been placed on the families of Balmerino and Loudoun as judgement for the two men's 'great imployments, and loosness of conversation, and unfaythfulnesse to the publick weal' (*Diary*, 2.204–5).

On the evening of 27 February 1649 Balmerino dined with Argyll in Edinburgh and retired to bed in good spirits, but awoke feeling sick about three in the morning of 28 February, and died suddenly of an apoplexy. He was buried next to the old church of Restalrig. His wife survived him a year, dying on 15 February 1650.

Balmerino's heir was his son **John Elphinstone**, third Lord Balmerino and second Lord Coupar (1623–1704), nobleman, who was born on 18 February 1623 in Edinburgh. He married, on 30 October 1649, Lady Margaret, daughter of John *Campbell, first earl of Loudoun (1598–1662), in a ceremony at the palace of Holyroodhouse, Edinburgh. In 1650 he received Charles II at his mansion in Leith on the king's visit to Scotland. However, because of his father's heavy debts and several lawsuits, Balmerino was eventually forced to sell almost all his estate. In 1662 he was fined £6000 Scots by parliament for compliance with the Cromwellian regime. His wife died in 1665. His fortunes revived on the death of his uncle James Elphinstone, Lord Coupar, in 1669. Balmerino succeeded to the title of Lord Coupar, and to the Coupar estate in Forfarshire. In 1674 he was brought before the privy council after being charged with attending conventicles at Cramond; he denied the charge, and was dismissed after kneeling to take the oath of allegiance. He lived until his eighty-second year, dying on 10 June 1704.

The third Lord Balmerino's heir, **John Elphinstone**, fourth Lord Balmerino and third Lord Coupar (1652–1736), lawyer, was born in Edinburgh on 26 December 1652. Despite his father's problems, he rose to become one of Scotland's leading lawyers. On 16 February 1672 he married Lady Christian, daughter of Hugh *Montgomery, seventh earl of Eglinton (1613–1669), and after her death he married, on 7 June 1687, Anne (d. 1712), daughter of Arthur *Ross (1634–1704), the last archbishop of St Andrews (a match that would no doubt have grieved his grandfather).

In the same year he was appointed a privy councillor. Although he firmly opposed the Act of Union, he was elected one of the sixteen representative peers of Scotland in the British parliament in 1710 and again in 1713. He was appointed general of the mint in 1710, and a commissioner of the office of lord chamberlain in 1711, but removed from all his offices for political reasons on the accession of George I, probably because of his tory principles. However, he remained loyal to the Hanoverians during the Jacobite rising of 1715. He died aged eighty-four, in his house in Leith, on 13 May 1736, and four days later was buried at Restalrig.   JOHN COFFEY

Sources F. Hargrave, ed., *A complete collection of state-trials*, 4th edn, 11 vols. (1776–81), vol. 1 • J. Row, *The history of the Kirk of Scotland, from the year 1558 to August 1637*, ed. D. Laing, Wodrow Society, 4 (1842) • *The letters and journals of Robert Baillie*, ed. D. Laing, 3 vols. (1841–2) • *The historical works of Sir James Balfour*, ed. J. Haig, 4 vols. (1824–5) • *Memoirs of Henry Guthry, late bishop* (1702) • *Scots peerage* • GEC, *Peerage* • *Diary of Sir Archibald Johnston of Wariston*, 1, ed. G. M. Paul, Scottish History Society, 61 (1911) • *Diary of Sir Archibald Johnston of Wariston*, 2, ed. D. H. Fleming, Scottish History Society, 2nd ser., 18 (1919) • *CSP dom.* • J. Spalding, *Memorialls of the trubles in Scotland and in England, AD 1624 – AD 1645*, ed. J. Stuart, 2 vols., Spalding Club, [21, 23] (1850–51) • *Reg. PCS*, 1st ser. • *Correspondence of Sir Robert Kerr, first earl of Ancram, and his son William, third earl of Lothian*, ed. D. Laing, 2 vols., Roxburghe Club, 100 (1875) • A. I. Macinnes, *Charles I and the making of the covenanting movement, 1625–1641* (1991) • W. Balcanquall, *A large declaration concerning the late tumults in Scotland* (1639) • D. Stevenson, *Revolution and counter-revolution in Scotland, 1644–1651*, Royal Historical Society Studies in History, 4 (1977)

Archives Hunt. L., letters to earl of Loudon • NL Scot., advocates MSS • NL Scot., Wodrow MSS, documents relating to his trial, Wodrow Octavo XXVII. FF. 8–13*v* [copies]

Wealth at death substantial debts: *Scots peerage*

Elphinstone, John, third Lord Balmerino and second Lord Coupar (1623–1704). *See under* Elphinstone, John, second Lord Balmerino (d. 1649).

Elphinstone, John, fourth Lord Balmerino and third Lord Coupar (1652–1736). *See under* Elphinstone, John, second Lord Balmerino (d. 1649).

Elphinstone, John, thirteenth Lord Elphinstone and first Baron Elphinstone (1807–1860), administrator in India, was born on 23 June 1807, the only son of John, twelfth Lord Elphinstone in the peerage of Scotland (1764–1813), a lieutenant-general in the army and colonel of the 26th regiment, and Janet Hyndford (d. 1825), widow of Sir John Gibson-Carmichael and youngest daughter of Cornelius Elliot, of Woolflee, Roxburghshire. He succeeded his father as Lord Elphinstone on 2 May 1813, and entered the army in 1826 as a cornet in the Royal Horse Guards. He was promoted lieutenant in that regiment in 1828, and captain in 1832. He was a lord-in-waiting to William IV from 1835 to 1837; in 1836 he was made a GCH and was sworn of the privy council.

In 1837 Elphinstone left the guards on being appointed governor of Madras by Lord Melbourne. It was said at the time that his appointment was made in order to dispel a rumour that the young Queen Victoria had fallen in love with him. The only notable fact of his administration was his building a house at Kaiti, in the Nilgiri hills, and his efforts to bring those hills into use as a hot-weather residence for Europeans. On resigning his governorship in 1842 he travelled for some years in the East, and he was one of the first Britons to explore Kashmir. He returned to England in 1845, and from 1847 to 1852, and again in 1853, was lord-in-waiting to the queen.

In October 1853 Elphinstone was appointed governor of Bombay and was in office during the Indian mutiny of 1857. He promptly checked the few disturbances in his presidency, and put down the insurrection of the raja of Sholapur. He also discovered a serious conspiracy in Bombay itself, which, by arresting the ringleaders, he prevented from becoming a threat. He quickly sent every soldier he could spare to the more troubled localities, almost stripping his presidency of European troops. For these services he was made a GCB in 1859, and on 21 May 1859, on his return to England, was created a peer of the United Kingdom as Baron Elphinstone of Elphinstone, Stirlingshire, on the personal urging of Queen Victoria. He was a Scottish representative peer in 1832–4 and 1847–59. He died unmarried at his home in King Street, St James's, London, on 19 July 1860, when his United Kingdom peerage became extinct; his Scottish title went to his first cousin John.   H. M. STEPHENS, *rev.* ELIZABETH BAIGENT

Sources Burke, *Peerage* · *CGPLA Eng. & Wales* (1860) · *GM*, 3rd ser., 9 (1860), 190 · J. W. Kaye, *A history of the Sepoy War in India, 1857–1858*, 9th edn, 3 vols. (1880) · G. B. Malleson, *The Indian mutiny of 1857*, 4th edn (1892) · *The letters of Queen Victoria*, ed. A. C. Benson and Lord Esher [R. B. Brett], 3 vols., 1st ser. (1907), vol. 3

Archives BL OIOC, corresp. and papers, MS Eur. F 87–89 · Royal Artillery Institution, Woolwich, London, papers · U. Nott. L., department of manuscripts and special collections, papers relating to India | BL OIOC, corresp. with J. C. Hobhouse, MS Eur. F 213 · BL OIOC, letters to John Jacob, MS Eur. F 75 · BL OIOC, letters to John Lawrence, MS Eur. F 90 · BL OIOC, corresp. with Lord Tweeddale, MS Eur. F 96 · Lpool RO, corresp. with fifteenth earl of Derby · NA Scot., corresp. with Sir Charles Augustus Murray · NAM, letters to Melvill · NAM, letters to Sir James Outram · PRO, letters to Lord Ellenborough, PRO 30/12 · W. Yorks. AS, Leeds, letters to Lord Canning

Likenesses J. H. Foley, statue, 1864, Bombay, India · Count D'Orsay, lithograph, BM, NPG · M. Noble, statue on monument, St Peter's Church, Limpsfield, Surrey · watercolour drawing, Scot. NPG

Wealth at death under £16,000: probate, 31 July 1860, *CGPLA Eng. & Wales*

Elphinstone, Sir (George) Keith Buller (1865–1941), electrical engineer, was born at 11 Melville Street, Edinburgh, on 11 May 1865, the second son of Captain Edward Charles Buller Elphinstone, of the 92nd highlanders, brother of the fifteenth Lord Elphinstone. His mother was Elizabeth Harriet Clerk, daughter of Sir George *Clerk of Penicuik, sixth baronet. Elphinstone was educated at Charterhouse School, followed during 1884 by a year's pupillage with Woodhouse and Rawson, electric light engineers of London, before working for two years with Lord Elphinstone's company, the Elphinstone-Vincent Electro Dynamo Machine Company at 79½ Gracechurch Street, London. He became a student member of the Society of Telegraph Engineers and Electricians in May 1886, his business address given as Corrie Castle, Dunfermline.

From 1887 to 1891 there were two more pupillages, the first with the new London Electric Company (formerly Grosvenor Gallery) and the second with Professor Alexander Kennedy at University College, followed by an apprenticeship at the Brush Electrical Engineering Company, Leicester.

In 1891 Elphinstone purchased Theiler & Sons, electrical instrument makers, at 86 Cannonbury Road, London, and when the instrument makers Elliott Brothers acquired Theiler in 1893, Elphinstone became a partner in that firm, with his office at 36 Leicester Square. He became a member of the Institution of Electrical Engineers in April 1896, his business address given as 101 St Martin's Lane, and over the next two decades was personally involved with patenting and developing various electrical and mechanical instruments, many for road, rail, and aviation use. He invented motor car speedometers, installed the original electric speed recording equipment at Brooklands, and jointly with H. E. Wimperis in 1909 designed a very popular accelerometer for testing road and rail transport, which measured acceleration irrespective of the gradient or curvature of the track. Also, in the years preceding the First World War, he jointly patented with Wimperis several early aircraft instruments and bombsights, and, although these were never produced commercially, the relationship resulted in Elliott Brothers manufacturing all Wimperis bombsights and navigation instruments after the war.

However, Elphinstone is most remembered for his development work in the field of naval fire control equipment. He had been responsible for licensing the Anschütz naval gyrocompass from Germany and was involved with the gunnery calculator of Prince Louis of Battenberg and then in 1902 with that of Captain John S. Dumaresq. However, as the speed of warships increased and target ranges changed rapidly, these early calculators became obsolete and were replaced by large complex fire control equipment and plotting tables, specifically that designed by Frederick Charles Dreyer in 1911, in which the integrating mechanism, or clock, stretched contemporary electromechanical technology to its limits. The Elliott equipment with its Dreyer-Elphinstone clock was selected in preference to the Argo equipment of A. J. H. Pollen for early installations and was used on many warships throughout the war. Elphinstone's service to the Admiralty was recognized by his OBE in 1917 and his KBE in 1920, and Pollen received a substantial award in 1925 for those ideas of his that were also incorporated. Elphinstone remained keenly interested in naval fire control equipment after the war, an interest which led to close friendship with several senior naval officers. He remained with Elliott Brothers until 1931 and was chairman of the company for some years.

On 25 April 1899 Elphinstone married Katherine Amy (b. 1868/9), daughter of Colonel Alfred James Wake RA, of Blackheath, and they had one daughter. After Katherine died in 1925 he married, on 16 February 1926, Isobel Penrose (b. 1876/7), daughter of Sir Theodore Fry, first baronet.

Elphinstone was a man of great charm and integrity and the artist in him found expression in watercolours, woodcuts, and the construction of furniture and clocks. His life was one of personal courage and endurance to overcome the severe handicap of partially paralysed legs caused by polio. He died at his home, 5 Kingston House South, Ennismore Gardens, London, on 6 July 1941 following a long illness aggravated by an earlier fall, which completely incapacitated him. He was survived by his second wife.

H. G. PETERKIN, *rev.* JOHN K. BRADLEY

Sources *WWW* · *The Times* (8 July 1941), 9c · *The Times* (5 Aug 1941), 6e · J. T. Sumida, *In defence of naval supremacy: finance, technology and British naval policy, 1889–1914* (1989) · J. K. Bradley, 'The history and development of aircraft instruments, 1909 to 1919', PhD diss., ICL, 1994 · private information (2004) · *DNB* · b. cert. · d. cert. · m. cert.

Likenesses W. Stoneman, photograph, 1930, NPG · E. I. Halliday, priv. coll.

Wealth at death £31,574 19s. 0d.: probate, 9 Oct 1941, *CGPLA Eng. & Wales*

Elphinstone, Mountstuart (1779–1859), administrator in India, fourth son of John Elphinstone, eleventh Lord Elphinstone (1737–1794), and his wife, the Hon. Anne (1737–1801), daughter of Lord Ruthven, was born on 6 October 1779, at Cumbernauld House, Dunbartonshire, where he spent his early years. His father was governor of Edinburgh Castle and Mountstuart was educated at Edinburgh high school (1791–2), before being moved to Kensington, where he studied at Dr Thompson's school.

Early years in India Elphinstone obtained an appointment in East India Company service through an uncle who was member of the court of directors, and arrived in Calcutta on 26 February 1796. Since his brother was in Benares, he was posted to that city on the instructions of the governor-general, Sir John Shore. He served there under Samuel Davis, judge and magistrate of the district, who was one of the several British officers at this centre of ancient learning to profess an interest in Indian literature and philosophy. Elphinstone quickly learned Persian and began a lifelong interest in oriental studies which had been foreshadowed by his attainments in the Latin and Greek classics. Elphinstone's knowledge of the intricacies of Indian politics also expanded rapidly because Benares was a key centre of British intelligence gathering in northern India. This, however, brought him into danger in January 1799, when he narrowly escaped assassination by Wazir Ali, the deposed nawab of Oudh, who killed his older mentor, George Cherry, a judge in the city.

After briefly attending Lord Wellesley's newly established Fort William College for the instruction of young civil servants in 1801, Elphinstone was appointed assistant to the governor-general's political agent at the court of the Maratha peshwa, effective head of this military coalition, in Poona. To reach the capital he made a long land journey along the east coast of India to Madras, and then cut across the upland Deccan to the Maratha territories. His journal on this journey demonstrates an eye for ethnographic and geographical detail which was later so apparent in his accounts of the Deccan and of north-western

Mountstuart Elphinstone (1779–1859), by Charles Turner (after Sir Thomas Lawrence, begun 1829)

India and Afghanistan. He arrived in Poona early in 1802 at a critical point in the history of British expansion in India. Wellesley, who intended to create a new balance of power in which the British were totally dominant, drew the peshwa into a subsidiary alliance through the treaty of Bassein of December 1802. This alliance effectively put the head of the Maratha 'confederacy' under British control by establishing a British military force in the Poona area, at the peshwa's expense. Two of the major Maratha princes, Madhav Rao Shinde (Sindhia), whose lands stretched up into the Ganges valley and adjoined British territories, and the raja of Berar, whose territory abutted the Bengal presidency, perceived this as an imminent threat to their own independence and mobilized their armies. British forces under Sir Arthur Wellesley moved against the alliance, and Elphinstone, who was attached to Wellesley's staff, took part in the fateful battle of Assaye on 23 September 1803 which effectively crushed the Maratha threat to British supremacy. Elphinstone later participated in the storming of Shinde's powerful fortress at Gwalior which was regarded as the key to central India. Though Arthur Wellesley praised Elphinstone's military acumen, the young man was destined for a civil career and in early 1804 was appointed resident minister to the court of another Maratha, the defeated Bhonsla ruler of Berar. He spent the next four and a half years in this post at the capital city, Nagpur, where he perfected his knowledge of Indian politics and continued to read the Persian classics.

Mission to Afghanistan, 1808 As the global struggle between Britain and Napoleonic France came to a climax, the Indian authorities under the governor-general, Lord Minto, became increasingly concerned that a hostile alliance of Persia, Afghanistan, and the newly powerful Punjab, under the Sikh ruler Ranjit Singh, might coalesce on the northern frontiers of British India. A French embassy was already in the Persian capital, and so in 1808 Elphinstone was sent to treat with Afghan ruler Shah Shuja, and Charles Metcalfe was dispatched to make a defensive alliance with Ranjit Singh. Elphinstone's mission to Kabul was formally a failure. Suspicious of the British, the Afghan court refused to allow the embassy to proceed beyond the border town of Peshawar. Shah Shuja was only prepared to make an alliance in return for substantial British aid which the envoy was unable to offer. Meanwhile, a revolt in Kashmir had made the shah's tenure of power increasingly precarious. Elphinstone did, however, return to India with a mass of new information about the Punjab and the north-west. He and his aides delineated the tension in the Afghan polity between the Kabul monarchy and the tribal societies of the periphery in which the mullahs played an important role. He created route plans for the lands through which he was allowed to travel and skilfully drew on the knowledge of the mercantile communities of Peshawar, professional runners, and well-connected Islamic teachers to create a skeleton geography of the lands to the north and west. He even drew upon information provided by the Indian physicians who travelled constantly between Peshawar, Kabul, and central Asia. In its depiction of climate, diseases, agriculture, and manufactures, Elphinstone's *Report* was a typical product of the statistical methods of the later Scottish Enlightenment. But the literary and historical materials he accumulated during this journey also contributed to the foundations of his later *History of India* (1841). Elphinstone's subsequent *Account of the Kingdom of Caubul* (published 1815) continued to inform British policy on the north-western frontier until the 1840s. He himself was unable to offer much to the rulers of the region, but he did sketch out a plan by which he hoped an extension of the British alliance could stabilize the whole tract beyond the River Jumna and up the Indus valley. Ironically, the foundering of this plan in the disastrous British campaign in Afghanistan of 1839–42 was to encompass an attempt to put back this same Shah Shuja on the Kabul throne.

Resident at Poona Following his return to India, in 1811 Elphinstone was appointed resident at Poona. During the years 1811–17 British relations with Peshwa Baji Rao gradually deteriorated. The heavy subsidiary tribute demanded by the company in payment of the troops quartered on Maratha territory caused interminable financial wrangles. The exploitative fiscal system which the peshwa was forced to introduce in order to maintain his revenues precipitated revolts which the British ascribed to 'misgovernment'. The residencies at the different Maratha courts tried to make themselves the only channel of communication between the rulers, thus violating the spirit of diplomacy within the Indian system of states. Meanwhile, Elphinstone in particular gradually increased his clout in the factional conflicts which were slowly pulling apart the peshwa's state. A rare 'diary of intelligence' of Elphinstone's which has survived from 1816 shows him manipulating a widespread network of intelligence, with agents among commercial people, at the major religious centres, and even stationed with the headmen of the villages around Poona. When the confrontation finally came, at the end of 1817, the British understanding of Maratha politics, as much as their military advantages, ensured victory.

The ostensible cause of the breakdown in relations between the peshwa and the British was the murder of a princely envoy to Poona by Trimbakji Denglia, the peshwa's minister. The underlying cause was British fears of instability in the Maratha states. This was matched by Maratha alarm at the appearance in central India of a large British force ostensibly bent on extirpation of the pindaris (bodies of irregular horse) who had been cashiered by Indian armies under pressure from the British, but who now threatened commerce and revenue in British India with their predatory raids. In June 1817 Elphinstone had managed to coerce the peshwa into another unequal treaty, but the absence of part of the British subsidiary force from the capital persuaded the Maratha ruler to risk one final bid for independence. Just before the crisis, Elphinstone's authority was subordinated to that of Sir Thomas Hislop, the commanding general in the sector, and that of his old comrade Sir John Malcolm. But his cool behaviour when the peshwa drove the British out of the residency and at the consequent sharp engagement near Kirkee on 5 November 1817, in which the Marathas were defeated, persuaded the governor-general to invest him with plenipotentiary powers with orders to annex the peshwa's territories. Elphinstone, who continued to favour indirect rule, was unable to protect the peshwa, who was retired on a pension to Bithur near Cawnpore in north India. He was, however, able to maintain the partial independence of the raja of Satara, who was a descendant of the most senior line of Maratha kingship, and he worked to maintain other indigenous institutions.

Governor of Bombay Between 1817 and 1818 Elphinstone was responsible for the British pacification and settlement of the newly conquered Deccan. In December 1819 he became governor of the whole Bombay presidency; this included both the commercial coast, long dominated by Bombay city, and other newly conquered areas on the Konkan coast to the south, and the cotton-growing plains of Gujarat to the north. This was a critical time, when the debate between Westernizers and those who saw virtue in Indian institutions was at its height. Experience of the settlement of the Deccan made Elphinstone cautious, inclined neither to put all his faith in the indigenous landed élite, as in the earlier Bengal system, nor to succumb to the new Benthamite ideals of efficient, European-style government. For instance, he was among those who deprecated the complex system of regulations which Lord Cornwallis had introduced into Bengal and eastern India. He displayed an almost romantic attachment to what he thought of as the 'genius' of Maratha administration, particularly the self-governing village judicial body (*panchayat*), and the corps of village officers gathered under the headmen (*patels*). Yet he was less inclined to disregard supra-village authorities and the landlords than his contemporaries Sir Thomas Munro and Sir John Malcolm, who argued for a radical ryotwari settlement of the revenue with village leaders. Thus, for instance, he supported indigenous kingships and the old Maratha revenue officers (*mamlatdars*) wherever he could. In a classic statement of his policy he wrote:

> I am not democratic enough to insist on a ryotwar system: I think that the aristocracy of the country whether it consists of head of villages or heads of zemindarees [landed estates] should be kept up, but I also think its rights and the opposite rights of the ryots should be clearly defined and the latter especially effectually defended.   (Ballhatchet, 32)

This moderate conservatism went with the grain of Indian society better than either the regulators of the Cornwallis generation or the radical utilitarians of the 1830s and 1840s. Above all, selective reliance on indigenous agency made it possible to save money in a period of financial stringency; the British simply did not have the manpower and resources to regulate the vast new territories they had conquered. On the other hand, the relentless pressure for revenues to finance India's internal and external wars meant that, even under Elphinstone's relatively benign rule, the revenue demand was pushed up very high, and parts of the peasant economy, especially in the drier, upland areas of the Deccan, were seriously undermined.

Those members of the Maratha aristocracy of *jagirdars* and *patwardhans* who had not joined the war against the British were generally maintained under Elphinstone's rule. He tried to preserve the position of the *patels* and the *mamlatdars*, but did not go so far as to reinstate the older level of hereditary officers (*deshpandes* and *desais*) who had once held power in the countryside. Where possible he and his officers maintained the influence of Brahmans and left the revenue free grants for temples and mosques undisturbed. The policy pursued by his subordinate John Briggs towards the tribal Bhil peoples of the hills and forests was less conciliatory. Attempts were made to settle them to agriculture and to recruit them into a regular Bhil corps which was to serve in the company's army. However, the periodic Bhil raids into the cultivated area, which under the old regime had been virtually sanctioned by custom, were severely punished. Aspects of the Maratha system which were deemed hostile to the stability of landed property could not be countenanced.

Elphinstone remained broadly consistent in this policy of reforming conservatism when he became governor of the whole presidency. In the northern Konkan (the coastal region), where a local gentry did not really exist, he favoured a village-level revenue settlement and opposed the creation of a landlord class, as initially recommended by the collector, Saville Marriot. By contrast, in the southern Konkan he cautioned against the abrupt removal of the existing landed notable class, the *khots*, whom some officials thought were exploiting the peasantry. Elphinstone generally urged the need for a village survey in order to create a basis of knowledge on which a reasoned agrarian policy could be based. His caution was further illustrated by his determination to spare the old ruling class from the more vigorous imposition of judicial regulations by district magistrates and by his continuing support for the role of village *panchayats* as the basic judicial form.

Cultural projects Reforming conservatism revealed itself also in Elphinstone's cultural projects. Under his rule colleges were established at Poona and Nasik but, against the wishes of several of the Anglicist directors of the East India Company, these continued to teach classical Indian sciences and literature even though the organization of the institutions was influenced by European models. Like other members of the moderate orientalist party, Elphinstone believed that Western learning could only slowly be grafted onto Indian knowledge, and that the Indian learned classes—pandits and *maulavis*—and Indian languages, including Sanskrit and Persian, had to be the vehicles of change. Elphinstone opposed the general introduction of English. He also opposed the direct Christian teaching which was being urged by missionaries and some of their supporters among civil servants. This was partly because he feared indigenous resistance to anything which smacked of proselytization. His own religious beliefs were at best lukewarm; he seems to have been a lapsed Unitarian, more at home in the works of his beloved pagan classical poets and the broad-church Islam of Hafiz and Saʿdi, the classical Persian poets, than he was with the new generation of Christian evangelicals. This freethinking was perhaps the only remnant in his mentality of the radicalism which had briefly inspired him at Edinburgh Castle immediately after the French Revolution.

Retirement, writing, and death Elphinstone resigned from the company's service at the end of 1827; despite offers of the governor-generalship of British North America and other important offices in Britain and abroad, he spent the remainder of his life as a gentleman scholar. He rejected a baronetcy, always being very conscious of his own aristocratic lineage. Between November 1827 and May 1829 he travelled in Greece, now on the verge of independence, and in Italy and France. On his return to Britain he lived in chambers in the Albany in London, regularly visiting friends in the country. He made occasional interventions in public debates about India, and gave evidence before the Lords' committee on Indian affairs. Consistently upholding his official views, he argued strongly against Lord Dalhousie's policy of annexing Indian states in the later 1840s and early 1850s.

Most of Elphinstone's remaining time was devoted to historical and literary work, notably his *History of India: the*

Hindu and Mohametan Periods (1841) and a posthumously published volume on the British conquest; the former was probably the most popular work of its sort among the early Victorian public. The book was a learned refutation of James Mill's *History*, which Elphinstone mildly considered 'left some room for doubt and discussion' in its savage attack on Indian civilization. Elphinstone felt that Indian civilization had indeed declined since the classical era, and subscribed to a less favourable view of Islam and its 'false prophet' than many eighteenth-century commentators. He also accepted Mill's charge of the 'want of veracity' among Hindus. On the other hand, he asserted the antiquity of Indian astronomical calculations, which contemporary evangelicals tended to disparage, praised basic institutions such as the *panchayat*, and felt that Indian despotism had at least been tempered by the 'lack of scruple' with which rulers were assassinated. Elphinstone's work, which was based on a wide range of Indian sources from Manu through Ferishta to the sixteenth-century authorities Abu'l-Fazl and Faizi, consolidated the periodization of Indian history into the Vedic, medieval, Islamic, and British periods with which historians are still contending. Yet he dissented from the common contemporary view that Brahmans and other high caste people were Aryans from outside India, on the ground that early Indian texts mention no such external homeland. He thus anticipated modern Hindu supremacists who also reject the theory of Aryan expansion and insist that, Muslims excepted, all Indian peoples have always lived in India.

In 1847 Elphinstone took a house at Hookwood, Limpsfield, near Godstone, Surrey, and it was there that he died, of apoplexy, on 20 November 1859. He was buried in the churchyard at Limpsfield. A passionate, but rather shy and angular man, Elphinstone never married. Though he declared himself fond of 'nautching' with Indian dancing girls and 'philandering' with Calcutta society ladies in his youth, there is no record of the children of Indian and European descent that so many of his contemporaries fathered. C. A. BAYLY

Sources T. E. Colebrooke, *Life of the Honourable Mountstuart Elphinstone*, 2 vols. (1884) · *Selections from the minutes and official writings of the Honourable Mountstuart Elphinstone*, ed. G. W. Forrest (1884) · J. Sarkar and others, eds., *English records of Maratha history: Poona residency correspondence*, 12–13: *Poona affairs: Elphinstone's embassy*, ed. G. S. Sardesai (1950–53) · K. Ballhatchet, *Social policy and social change in western India, 1817–1830* (1957) · J. C. G. Duff, *A history of the Mahrattas*, rev. S. M. Edwardes, rev. edn, 2 vols. (1921) · S. N. Sen, *Administrative history of the Marathas* (1923) · S. Gordon, *The Marathas, 1600–1818* (1993) · S. Guha, *The Bombay Deccan, 1818–1939* (1988) · d. cert. · *CGPLA Eng. & Wales* (1859)
Archives BL OIOC, Home misc. series, corresp. and papers relating to India · BL OIOC, corresp. and papers, MS Eur. F 87–89 · Maharashtra State Archives, Bombay · NL Scot., family corresp. and papers · U. Edin. L., special collections division, report on territories conquered by the Paishwa | BL, letters to Lord Wellesley and N. B. Edmondstone, Add. MS 13590 · BL OIOC, letters to Sir T. Munro, MS Eur. F 151 · BL OIOC, letters to members of Strachey family, MS Eur. F 128 · BL OIOC, letters to H. H. Wilson, MS Eur. E 301 · NL Scot., corresp. with Anne Elizabeth Bontine · NL Scot., corresp. with his sister and niece · NL Scot., letters to William Erskine · NRA Scotland, priv. coll., corresp. with John Adam · NRA Scotland, priv. coll., letters to Archibald Robertson · PRO, corresp.
with Lord Ellenborough, PRO 30/12 · PRO, letters to Henry Pottinger, FO 705 · U. Southampton L., corresp. with Arthur Wellesley
Likenesses Edridge, portrait, c.1794, repro. in Colebrooke, *Life* · T. Lawrence, oils, 1829 (finished by Simpson), Elphinstone College, Bombay, India · M. Noble, statue, 1832, St Paul's Cathedral, London · F. Chantrey, statue, exh. 1833, Bombay, India; version, model, AM Oxf. · plaster medal, 1833 (after W. Wyon), Scot. NPG · F. Chantrey, bust, AM Oxf. · H. W. Pickersgill, oils, Oriental Club, London · G. J. Stodart, stipple, NPG · C. Turner, engraving (after T. Lawrence, begun 1829), AM Oxf. [*see illus.*] · C. E. Wagstaff, engraving (after oil painting by H. W. Pickersgill), BL OIOC
Wealth at death under £30,000: probate, 12 Dec 1859, *CGPLA Eng. & Wales*

Elphinstone, William (1431–1514), administrator, bishop of Aberdeen, and founder of the University of Aberdeen, was probably born in Glasgow. His father, also named William, was a younger son of Sir William Elphinstone of Pittendreich, Stirlingshire, but by 1430 had embarked upon an ecclesiastical career and had thereby committed his son to the illegitimate state. The Elphinstone muniments do not give the name of his mother, but contemporary records in the Vatican Archives state that she was an unmarried lady belonging to a baronial family. The eighteenth-century writer George Mackenzie, following an early but now lost Elphinstone genealogy, names her as Margaret Douglas, daughter of Sir William Douglas of Drumlanrig, a statement which commands support from other early records. The young boy cannot have remained long in his mother's care, since by 1437 his father was rector of Ashkirk and a prebendary canon of Glasgow, and is recorded as having brought up his son from an early age in his own household near the cathedral, whose grammar school he attended; he quickly became a favourite of Bishop John Cameron and sometimes read to him at supper. By the age of twenty-one the young Elphinstone had resolved to become a priest himself and, being dispensed from his illegitimacy by the church on 26 February 1454, he was ordained the following year. He entered the University of Glasgow on 24 October 1457 and graduated MA on 3 July 1462.

About this time, with the backing and patronage of the third laird of Drumlanrig, Elphinstone also received his first benefice, as rector of Kirkmichael in Nithsdale. He proceeded to the study of canon law at the university, but before graduating was persuaded by his uncle Laurence, at the latter's expense, to continue his studies in canon law at the University of Paris; he enlisted in its law faculty in the autumn of 1465. He was to spend the next five years there, graduating as bachelor by 1468, and then, as their first reading bachelor, lecturing on set texts from the *Decretals* of Gregory IX, the *Liber sextus* of Boniface VIII, the *Constitutiones* of Clement V, and commentaries on them. He left Paris in the autumn of 1470 to study civil law at the University of Orléans. While there he was exposed to some of the most contentious jurisprudential problems of the day, including the nature of sovereignty and the relationship between statutory and customary law: intractable issues which also required definition in his own country, and to which, as a senior judge, he was later to give much attention. His time in Orléans was to prove much shorter than he anticipated, for a few months after his arrival he was urged to supplicate for the post of official, the chief legal officer of the diocese of Glasgow, then about to become vacant, and to which he was appointed following a public examination on his return to Glasgow in the spring of 1471. His studies in France were crucial to his legal formation, the skills he acquired there and as official of Glasgow being evident in his surviving judgments and in the copious notes still to be seen in the marginalia of his legal manuscripts.

During the years which followed Elphinstone was also active in Glasgow University affairs: he was dean of the faculty of arts in 1472, awarded an honorary licentiate in canon law in 1473, and elected rector for 1474–5. In 1478 he was transferred to Edinburgh as official of Lothian, and by 1 June that year was sitting as a lord of council in parliament, having already represented the clergy there in judicial matters since 1471. His entry into the political arena first came when James III included him in an embassy to Louis XI in 1479 to reassure the French king that, although James was now committed to a peace treaty with Edward IV, Scotland's ties of friendship and alliance with France were to remain as close and binding as ever. An Anglo-Scottish peace treaty, however, was the last thing Louis XI desired, since his own policy of national aggrandizement depended on keeping the Scots and English permanently hostile to each other. By skilfully playing on the disloyalty of those Scottish magnates who disapproved of James III's pro-English policies, Louis was able to wreck the Anglo-Scottish treaty of 1474—a broken fence which Elphinstone, as the chief negotiator commissioned to draw up fresh peace treaties with Richard III in 1484 and Henry VII in 1486, spent much of his time trying to mend. For these labours James III had persuaded Sixtus IV to provide Elphinstone to the bishopric of Ross on 3 August 1481, but since he could not pay the common services of his predecessor to the apostolic camera, he was never consecrated. He was transferred to the see of Aberdeen on 19 March 1483, and for similar reasons was unable to be consecrated until April or May 1488.

During the whole of this period Elphinstone was a firm supporter of the policies of James III. As a leading member of the king's council, a senior appeal judge, an auditor of the exchequer, and finally in February 1488 as chancellor of Scotland, he was in the best possible position to understand the real weaknesses of the country's fiscal, legal, and administrative structures, and how they could be strengthened. Consequently he chose to persevere with the crown's long-term aim of a permanent peace treaty with England, rather than to hark back to the broken truces and border warfare preferred by disparate groups of the king's enemies who had by then won over the king's fifteen-year-old son and heir to their cause. The slaughter of James III by a rebel army at Sauchieburn on 11 June 1488 put an end to Elphinstone's efforts as peacemaker and, being relieved of his chancellorship, he retired to Aberdeen to concentrate on his pastoral duties. There was a great deal to reform in his diocese, and it says much for his tenacity that from 1488 until his death in

1514 Elphinstone strove tirelessly to carry through a programme of reform, some of which extended to the whole of the Scottish church. His constitutions of 1506 completely reorganized the division of his chapter's funds and laid down the canons' corporate responsibilities and duties. He leaded the roof of his cathedral, completed its central tower, added its steeple, and extended its choir eastwards. He initiated the erection of a permanent stone bridge over the River Dee and funded most of it himself. His Aberdeen breviary, printed in 1510, introduced the feasts and historical lessons of a selection of Scottish saints proper to every diocese, and became the first official use of the Scottish church.

Elphinstone's most lasting contribution to the well-being of his diocese and the nation itself was his foundation of the University of Aberdeen, which he saw as essential for the educational needs of the people of the northeast, the highlands, and the islands. For this reason he had gone to Rome to inform Alexander VI in person of the remoteness of his area from centres of higher learning, with the result that both his diocese and the nation suffered from a serious shortage of lay administrators, doctors of medicine, civil lawyers, and schoolmasters; he added that his proposed foundation was financially viable and had the king's full support. The pope confirmed the supplication in a bull of foundation dated 10 February 1495. Teaching began in October 1497, and by 17 September 1505, when King's College received its charter, Elphinstone had collected sufficient funds to support an academic community of thirty-six masters and students, increased to forty-two by 1514, within the faculties of theology, canon and civil law, medicine, and the liberal arts; the medical chair (the first in the country) had been funded by James IV on 22 May 1497. Moreover, Elphinstone's single college university accepted all that was best in the humanist movement of the day, its first principal, Hector Boece, being a friend of Erasmus.

Despite all this local activity, Elphinstone had been drawn back into the service of the young James IV as early as October 1488, and had soon become deeply involved in hearing those civil causes which had foundered in the franchisal courts, besides touring the country with James on justice ayres. This enabled him to recognize the weaknesses still inherent in the country's civil and criminal administrative procedures, and to help frame the legislation required to improve them. James IV also made good use of Elphinstone's experience as a commissioner of crown lands by appointing him as keeper of the privy seal in 1492, whereby he was able, with the introduction of the country's first land register, to control crown patronage. In the realm of foreign policy, however, Elphinstone's last years were clouded with failure. A permanent peace treaty with England had finally been achieved in 1502, but by joining the Holy League against France in 1511, Henry VIII placed an intolerable strain on Anglo-Scottish relations, and by 1512 Louis XII had manoeuvred James IV into agreeing to invade England if Henry VIII invaded France: a commitment which James was not obliged to give, and which specifically broke the terms of the Anglo-Scottish peace treaty of 1502. Although strongly opposed by Elphinstone, James IV nevertheless believed that such an agreement was required of him to uphold his country's honour. The result was the death of the Scottish king and most of his nobility at Flodden on 9 September 1513. In the subsequent months Elphinstone was appointed guardian of the infant James V and nominated to the metropolitan see of St Andrews, though Leo X refused to confirm this, and he died in Edinburgh on 25 October 1514, working to the last on the restoration of the country's political and legal stability following the disaster of Flodden. He was buried at the foot of the sanctuary in his chapel at King's College, Aberdeen.

A genuine patriot, Elphinstone had striven constantly to make the community of the realm a workable reality. He could understand the crown's aims; indeed, to a considerable extent he helped to formulate them. But he could also understand with rare compassion the fears of those whose patriotism was still limited to the frontiers of their own local jurisdictions, interests, and habits. It was his country's good fortune that he had been able to use his great legal and administrative gifts where and when they were most needed, for as a constructive lawyer and administrator he had no equal in fifteenth-century Scotland; and as a man there was about him an indefinable goodness which many from all walks of life found warm and attractive. He was a man of peace, and all peace lovers were his friends.   LESLIE J. MACFARLANE

William George Keith Elphinstone (1782–1842), by William Salter, 1836–9

Sources L. J. Macfarlane, *William Elphinstone and the kingdom of Scotland, 1431–1514: the struggle for order*, quincentenary edn (1995) · *Hectoris Boetii murthlacensium et aberdonensium episcoporum vitae*, ed. and trans. J. Moir, New Spalding Club, 12 (1894) · C. Innes, ed., *Registrum episcopatus Aberdonensis*, 2 vols., Spalding Club, 13–14 (1845) · W. Blew, ed., *Breviarium Aberdonense*, 2 vols., Bannatyne Club, 96 (1854) · C. Innes, ed., *Fasti Aberdonenses … 1494–1854*, Spalding Club, 26 (1854) · *APS*, 1424–1567 · [T. Thomson], ed., *The acts of the lords of council in civil causes, 1478–1495*, 1, RC, 41 (1839) · R. K. Hannay, ed., *Acts of the lords of council in public affairs, 1501–1554* (1932) · M. Wood, ed., *Flodden papers: diplomatic correspondence between the courts of France and Scotland, 1507–1517*, Scottish History Society, 3rd ser., 20 (1923) · C. Innes, ed., *Munimenta alme Universitatis Glasguensis / Records of the University of Glasgow from its foundation till 1727*, 2, Maitland Club, 72 (1854) · L. J. Macfarlane, 'William Elphinstone's library revisited', *The Renaissance in Scotland: studies in literature, religion, history, and culture offered to John Durkan*, ed. A. A. Macdonald and others (1994), 66–81 · G. Mackenzie, *The lives and characters of the most eminent writers of the Scots nation*, 2 (1711) · L. Campbell, 'Scottish patrons and Nederlandish painters in the fifteenth and early sixteenth centuries', *Scotland and the Low Countries, 1124–1994*, ed. G. G. Simpson (1996), 89–103
Archives Mitchell L., Glas., MS BIO.1.4 · NA Scot., muniments, boxes 1–3, 5, 9
Likenesses oil on wood, c.1505, U. Aberdeen; repro. in Macfarlane, *William Elphinstone*, frontispiece · D. S. Erskine, pencil and chalk drawing (after unknown artist), Scot. NPG

Elphinstone, William George Keith (1782–1842), army officer, was the elder son of the Hon. William Fullarton Elphinstone and his wife, Elizabeth (d. 1834), eldest daughter of William Fullerton of Carstairs, Lanarkshire. W. F. Elphinstone was a director of the East India Company and formerly captain of one of the company's ships, and was himself third son of Charles, tenth Lord Elphinstone, and

elder brother of Admiral Lord Keith. Elphinstone entered the army as an ensign in the 41st foot on 24 March 1804, and was promoted lieutenant on 4 August 1804 and captain into the 93rd foot on 18 June 1806. He exchanged into the 1st (Grenadier) guards on 6 August 1807 and into the 15th light dragoons on 18 January 1810, and was promoted major into the 8th West India regiment on 2 May 1811. On 30 September 1813 he purchased the lieutenant-colonelcy of the 33rd foot, with which he served under Sir Thomas Graham in Holland, and which he commanded with such distinction at Waterloo that he was made a CB and a knight of the order of William of Holland and of the order of St Anne of Russia. He continued to command the 33rd in England and Ireland until 1821, when he exchanged into the 16th light dragoons (lancers) in command, going on half pay in April 1822. On 27 May 1825 Elphinstone was promoted colonel, and appointed aide-de-camp to the king, and on 10 January 1837 he was promoted major-general. In 1839 he was appointed to command the Benares division of the Bengal army; although he was already a sick man he went out to India to take up his command. From a comfortable situation in Bengal, he was uprooted by the governor-general, Lord Auckland, to succeed General Willoughby Cotton in command of the British troops in Kabul. Despite his protest that he was unfit physically for such an active command, he was overruled; suffering from gout, he had to make most of the journey from Calcutta to Kabul in a palanquin.

By late 1840 the war in Afghanistan was apparently over. Dost Muhammad had surrendered and abandoned the throne to Shah Shuja, the British nominee. The major part of the British invasion army had returned to India, leaving only garrisons in Kabul and Kandahar to support Shah Shuja, and the British resident, Sir William Macnaghten. When Elphinstone arrived in Kabul the situation seemed calm enough for wives and children to come from India to Kabul, where the garrison was enjoying as normal a peacetime existence as in an Indian cantonment.

However Sir William Macnaghten and his principal assistant, Sir Alexander Burnes, had misjudged the political situation. The Afghan chiefs were opposed to Shah Shuja and resented the British occupation. Even Elphinstone, who reached Kabul exhausted, mentally and physically, queried the defensibility of the British cantonment at Sherpur, outside Kabul, but any attempt at improvement was turned down on the grounds of expense. 'Unfit for it, done up body and mind' (Macrory, 47) is how Elphinstone described himself to Major George Broadfoot in October 1841. He intended to ask for relief on medical grounds. Incapable through pain and debility of making up his mind, he held repeated conferences, soliciting the opinion of even the most junior of those attending, but never reaching a conclusion. He was little helped to do so by his second in command, Brigadier John Shelton of the 44th foot, who openly despised him.

Elphinstone was utterly unfitted to cope with the increasingly grave situation following the Kabul insurrection of 2 November and the assassination of Sir William Macnaghten by Akbar Khan, a son of Dost Muhammad, on 23 December 1841. The Afghans closed communication with Kabul and besieged the cantonment. Against his better judgement Major Eldred Pottinger, himself wounded, as the senior remaining political officer, was ordered to negotiate with Akbar Khan for the safe return of the Kabul garrison to India at the height of the Afghan winter. The terms were humiliating, the Afghan guarantees worthless, and subsequently almost the entire garrison was destroyed in the passes between 6 and 13 January 1842.

Some nineteen officers and ten wives with their children were taken into Afghan captivity, some as hostages, Elphinstone among them. He was wounded at Jagdalak during the retreat on 12 January. The prisoners were mostly not treated badly, but Elphinstone, racked with dysentery, had lost the will to live. He died unmarried, on the night of 23 April at Zanduk, near Tezin. Akbar Khan arranged for the body to be taken to Jalalabad, then British-held, and there Elphinstone was buried with military honours on 30 April; his grave is unmarked. Colin Mackenzie and other Anglo-Afghan war survivors later paid tribute to his personal qualities: he was well-meaning and kindly—though inadequate for command.

In the immediate aftermath of the Afghanistan disaster Elphinstone was much blamed, but the true blame lay with Lord Auckland and his adviser Sir William Macnaghten for undertaking the invasion of Afghanistan and for choosing a sick, disabled, and prematurely aged general, who had not served in battle since Waterloo, to command in Kabul. H. M. STEPHENS, *rev.* JAMES LUNT

Sources Hart's Army List (1841) · G. R. Gleig, Sale's brigade in Afghanistan: with an account of the seisure and defence of Jellalabad (1846) · J. W. Kaye, *History of the war in Afghanistan*, 3rd edn, 3 vols. (1874) · P. Macrory, *Signal catastrophe: the story of a disastrous retreat from Kabul, 1842* (1966) · J. A. Norris, *The First Afghan War, 1838–1842* (1967) · H. Havelock, *Narrative of the war in Afghanistan in 1838–39*, 2 vols. (1840) · J. C. Pollock, *Way to glory: the life of Havelock of Lucknow* (1957) · V. Eyre, *The military operations at Cabul, which ended in the retreat and destruction of the British army, January 1842* (1843); repr. with an introduction by J. Lunt as *Journal of an Afghanistan prisoner* (1976) · G. Pottinger, *The Afghan connection* (1983) · Lady Sale, *A journal of the disasters in Affghanistan* (1843) · A. Forbes, *The Afghan wars, 1839–42 and 1878–80* (1892) · Fortescue, *Brit. army*, vol. 12 · *GM*, 2nd ser., 18 (1842), 322 · Burke, *Peerage*
Archives BL OIOC, papers and corresp., MS Eur. F 87–89
Likenesses W. Salter, oils, 1836–9, NPG [*see illus.*] · W. Salter, group portrait, oils (*Waterloo banquet at Apsley House*), Wellington Museum, London

Elrington, Charles Richard (1787–1850), Church of Ireland clergyman and university professor, was born in Molesworth Street, Dublin, on 25 March 1787, the elder of the two sons of Thomas *Elrington (1760–1835), bishop of Leighlin and Ferns, and Charlotte, the daughter of Plunket Preston, rector of Duntryleague, co. Limerick; he also had several sisters. He was initially educated at home by a private tutor and then entered Trinity College, Dublin, on 3 November 1800, under the tutorship of the Revd Dr Davenport. He gained all the honours of his class and was awarded the gold medal in 1805. In the same year he won the Law mathematical premium, and in 1806 the Law Hebrew prize. He graduated BA in 1805, MA in 1811, BD in 1816, and DD in 1820. In 1810 he was elected a fellow of Trinity College, Dublin, having obtained the Madden premium in the three preceding years. He was ordained a deacon on 28 October 1810, and became a priest on 23 February 1812. In December 1814 he married Letitia Anne (*d.* 1827), the daughter of David Babington, of Rutland Square, Dublin. They had two sons and three daughters.

In 1819 Elrington was elected Donnellan lecturer at the university, but his lectures were not published. In 1825 he was appointed vicar of St Mark's, Dublin, which was in the gift of the Irish lord chancellor; he kept this benefice until 1831. On 31 January 1832 he became rector and prebend of Edermine in the diocese of Ferns, and three months later chancellor of Ferns. In 1829, having resigned his fellowship, he was elected regius professor of divinity at Trinity College. During his twenty years as regius professor he undertook a number of important reforms, which included a broadening of the curriculum and making attendance at lectures and exams compulsory. In 1840 he resigned the chancellorship of Ferns when, on 14 December, he was sent to be rector of Loughgilly, in the diocese of Armagh. On 22 September 1841 he was moved from Loughgilly to become rector of the union of Armagh.

Elrington had a keen interest in education and served as secretary to the Association for Discountenancing Vice and as treasurer to the board of governors of the schools founded by Erasmus Smith. He also took a prominent part in the formation and management of the Church Education Society for Ireland, which helped to support parochial schools when government subsidies were removed from church schools. In Elrington's view many of the initial objections of the clergy to the national schools were met by successive managerial reforms of the state system. In 1847 he retired from his official position in the Church Education Society, and publicly declared that the clergy ought to accept the amended terms offered by the board of national education.

In 1847 Elrington began to edit a collection of the works of the Anglican divine Archbishop James Ussher (1581–1656), to which he prefixed a full biography. He did not live to complete the task, but several volumes were published posthumously, one of them containing an index to the seventeen volumes by William Reeves, later bishop of Down, Connor, and Dromore. Besides theological contributions to periodicals, Elrington published several sermons and a few pamphlets upon the education question. He died at Armagh on 18 January 1850, and was buried in St Mark's churchyard in that city, where there is a brief Latin inscription to his memory.

B. H. BLACKER, rev. DAVID HUDDLESTON

Sources A. J. Stephens, introduction, *The Book of Common Prayer*, ed. A. J. Stephens, 3 (1850), iii–xvi · *Irish Ecclesiastical Journal*, 6 (1 Feb 1850), 17–18 · J. B. Leslie, *Armagh clergy and parishes* (1911), 115–16 · H. Cotton, *Fasti ecclesiae Hibernicae*, 2 (1848), 357–8, 371 · H. Cotton, *Fasti ecclesiae Hibernicae*, 5 (1860), 180 · D. Bowen, *The protestant crusade in Ireland, 1800–70* (1978) · [J. H. Todd], ed., *A catalogue of graduates who have proceeded to degrees in the University of Dublin, from the earliest recorded commencements to … December 16, 1868* (1869), 179 · Burtchaell & Sadleir, *Alum. Dubl.* · *GM*, 2nd ser., 33 (1850), 678

Archives TCD, corresp. and papers | BL, corresp. with J. W. Croker, Add. MS 52466 · BL, corresp. with Sir Robert Peel, Add. MSS 40423, 40569 · TCD, corresp. with Beresford · TCD, letters to J. H. Todd

Elrington, Thomas (1688–1732), theatre manager and actor, was born in London in June 1688 near Golden Square. His father is thought to have served the duke of Montagu in some capacity. Nothing is known about his mother, but Thomas had three brothers, Francis (1692–1746), Joseph (d. 1715), and Ralph (d. 1761). He was apprenticed by his father to a French upholsterer but showed an early interest in the theatre, acting in numerous amateur productions in London. Around 1708 the actor Theophilus Keene saw Elrington in one of these and introduced him at Drury Lane theatre, where Elrington made his professional acting début on 2 December 1709 as Oroonoko. Clearly he had arrived at Drury Lane well prepared, and within the next two months he played no fewer than seven major roles. In the summer of 1710 he appeared at Pinkethman's theatre in Greenwich. He continued at Drury Lane for the 1710–11 and 1711–12 seasons, learning many new roles in both tragedy and comedy. His friend W. R. Chetwood recalled that the young Elrington was tall and well proportioned and possessed a strong, sweet voice (Chetwood, 135).

In the spring of 1712 Elrington was seen by Thomas Griffith, one of the sharers in Dublin's Smock Alley Theatre, who invited him to perform there for the 1712–13 season. Impressed with Elrington's talent, the manager, Joseph Ashbury, invited him to become one of the theatre's four directors, and in 1713 Elrington married Ashbury's daughter, Frances; the couple had a daughter and three sons: all but one son went on the stage. The same year, Elrington and the Smock Alley managers established the first professional theatres in the cities of Cork and Waterford. Elrington was to become the most important theatre manager in Ireland between the death of Ashbury in 1720 and the ascendancy of Thomas Sheridan from 1745, and is considered to have been 'one of the most important actors alive during the transitional period between Betterton and Garrick' (Highfill, Burnim & Langhans, *BDA*).

Elrington confined his exertions to the Irish theatres as sharer and chief tragic actor until January 1715, but for the next four seasons he travelled between London and Dublin: he was at Drury Lane from February to May 1715; at Smock Alley from May to the autumn of 1716; at Rich's new theatre in Lincoln's Inn Fields for the entire 1716–17 season, playing such major roles as Hamlet, Essex in John Banks's *The Unhappy Favourite*, and Alexander in Nathaniel Lee's *The Rival Queens*; at Smock Alley for the 1717–18 season; and then again at Drury Lane for the 1718–19 season.

Upon the death of Joseph Ashbury in the summer of 1720 Elrington assumed the managership of the Smock Alley Theatre and also became deputy master of the revels in Ireland, a post that customarily accompanied the proprietorship of the Theatre Royal. Other sinecures that Elrington held at this time and later were steward of the king's inns of court, gunner to the train of artillery, and a post in the quit-rent office. During most of his career he and his family lived in a house in Drumcondra Lane, Dublin.

Elrington evidently shared the duties of management with two others, confining himself to acting and directing the company of actors. Between 1720–21 and his death in 1732 he played a wide variety of principal parts, including Othello, Bajazet, the title role in Aphra Behn's *The Rover*, Macbeth, Archer in Farquhar's *The Beaux' Stratagem*, Myrtle in Richard Steele's *The Conscious Lovers*, Brutus in *Julius Caesar*, Hotspur, Cato, Dumont in Nicholas Rowe's *Jane Shore*, and Barnwell in George Lillo's *The London Merchant*.

Virtually nothing is known about Elrington's personal character. That he was an actor of great merit is illustrated by the fact that he was enlisted by the Drury Lane management for the 1728–9 season to fill in for the ailing star Barton Booth. When Elrington played the role of Zanga in *The Revenge*, its author, Edward Young, observed that he had never seen the part so well done. The Drury Lane managers asked Elrington to engage with them on a permanent basis, but he refused because of his many attachments in Ireland.

By 1730 the Smock Alley Theatre had been used for plays for nearly seventy years and was badly in need of repair. With an eye to building a new theatre in Dublin (and perhaps also in Cork), Elrington engaged the architect Sir Edward Pearce and began planning. He was not to see his new playhouse, however, for he died, suddenly, of a malignant fever attended with violent convulsions, on 22 July 1732; he was buried in St Michan's churchyard, Dublin.

After his death Elrington was hailed as 'the most celebrated Tragedian' and 'the ornament and delight of the

Irish Stage'. Isaac Reed, in his manuscript 'Notitia dramatica', said of him that:

> Nature certainly formed him as an actor, and to his amazing genius for representing such a variety of grand characters gave him a voice and person scarce ever equalled and never excelled by any of his contemporaries or predecessors of the Stage.

W. R. Chetwood observed that Elrington 'was a true copy of Mr. Verbruggen', the great tragic actor of the previous generation, but also observed that he had 'an infinite Fund of (what is called Low) humour upon the Stage' (Chetwood, 135).   JOHN C. GREENE

Sources Highfill, Burnim & Langhans, *BDA* · J. C. Greene and G. L. H. Clark, *The Dublin stage, 1720–1745: a calendar of plays, entertainments, and afterpieces* (1993) · W. S. Clark, *The early Irish stage: the beginnings to 1720* (1955) · W. S. Clark, *The Irish stage in the county towns, 1720–1800* (1965) · E. K. Sheldon, *Thomas Sheridan of Smock-Alley: recording his life as actor and theater manager in both Dublin and London* (1967) · W. R. Chetwood, *A general history of the stage, from its origin in Greece to the present time* (1749) · *DNB* · I. Reed, 'Notitia dramatica: being notes of performances on the English stage', 3 vols., BL, Add. MSS 25390–25392
Likenesses engraving (as Pembroke in *Lady Jane Grey*), Harvard TC; repro. in A. Daly, *Woffington: a tribute to the actress and the woman*, 2nd edn (New York, 1891), 14

Elrington, Thomas (1760–1835), Church of Ireland bishop of Leighlin and Ferns, was the only child of Richard and Catherine Elrington of Dublin and was born in co. Dublin on 18 December 1760. He entered Trinity College, Dublin, on 1 May 1775, under the tutorship of the Revd Dr Drought and Mr Butler. He was elected a scholar in 1778 and excelled as an undergraduate, especially in mathematics. He graduated BA in 1780, MA in 1785, BD in 1790, and DD in 1795. In 1781 he was elected a fellow of Trinity College. About 1786 he married Charlotte, daughter of the Revd Plunket Preston, rector of Duntryleague, co. Limerick. They had two sons, the elder of whom was Charles Richard *Elrington, and one daughter.

Elrington was the Donegal lecturer in 1790 and in 1794 was the first to hold the office of Donnellan divinity lecturer at Trinity College. He delivered a series of sermons, which were published in 1796, on proofs of Christianity from the miracles of the New Testament. In 1795 he was appointed professor of mathematics and succeeded to a senior fellowship. He served as Archbishop King's lecturer in 1795 and 1798. He exchanged his professorship of mathematics for that of natural philosophy in 1799. On resigning his fellowship in 1806 he was presented by his college to the rectory of Ardtrea, in the diocese of Armagh. He resigned this post in December 1811, having been appointed provost of Trinity College by the duke of Richmond, lord lieutenant of Ireland, by letters patent dated the 15th of the preceding month. As provost of Trinity he was the acting manager of almost every public board, and a generous supporter of many charitable institutions. On 25 September 1820 he was promoted to the bishopric of Limerick. During his short period as bishop he made an extensive tour of the diocese and was actively involved in famine relief.

On 21 December 1822 Elrington was moved to Leighlin

and Ferns. He was outspoken in his attacks against the Roman Catholic church and it was his diocese which became one of the chief areas of controversy over the influx of Roman Catholic converts into the Church of Ireland. Although much of this renewed activity within the Church of Ireland stemmed from the evangelical party, Elrington forbade the evangelical Established Church Home Mission from sending agents into his diocese. While on his way to attend his parliamentary duties in London, Elrington died of a paralytic stroke at Liverpool on 12 July 1835. He was buried under the chapel of Trinity College, Dublin, where a marble tablet with a Latin inscription to his memory was placed. Another inscribed monument was presented by his clergy and placed in the cathedral church of Ferns. The Elrington theological essay prize was instituted in Trinity College in 1837.

Elrington was an active member of the Royal Irish Academy, and of other literary and scientific societies. He wrote widely on controversial church matters of the day. His published works include: *Thoughts on the Principles of Civil Government, and their Foundation in the Law of Nature* (1793), *Reflections on the Appointment of Dr Milner as the Political Agent of the Roman Catholic Clergy of Ireland* (1809), *An Inquiry whether the Disturbances in Ireland have Originated in Tythes* (1822), and *Miscellaneous Observations on a Letter of J. K. L. [Dr Doyle, Roman Catholic Bishop of Leighlin]* (1824). He also published many individual sermons and charges and edited, for the use of Trinity College, *Euclid's Elements, the First Six Books* (1788) and *Locke on Government, with Notes* (1798).   B. H. BLACKER, *rev.* DAVID HUDDLESTON

Sources *British Magazine*, 8 (1835), 507–10 · *British Magazine*, 9 (1836), 57 · H. Cotton, *Fasti ecclesiae Hibernicae*, 2 (1848), 344–7 · *GM*, 2nd ser., 4 (1835), 316–17 · J. B. Leslie, *Ossory clergy and parishes* (1933) · W. A. Phillips, ed., *History of the Church of Ireland*, 3 (1933) · [J. H. Todd], ed., *A catalogue of graduates who have proceeded to degrees in the University of Dublin, from the earliest recorded commencements to … December 16, 1868* (1869) · Burtchaell & Sadleir, *Alum. Dubl.*
Archives TCD, corresp. and papers, mainly as provost | BL, corresp. with Sir Robert Peel, Add. MSS 40223–40386
Likenesses T. Foster, oils, 1820, TCD · W. J. Ward, mezzotints, pubd 1836 (after oil painting by T. Foster, 1820), NG Ire. · attrib. T. Kirk, marble bust, TCD

Elsdale, Robinson (*bap.* 1744, *d.* 1783), author and privateer, the son of Samuel and Mary Elsdale, was baptized on 25 December 1744 at Surfleet, Lincolnshire, where his family had long maintained an estate. He entered the navy as a midshipman, but left soon afterwards on account of the slowness of promotion. From 1762 he served in various privateers cruising against the French, chiefly off the coast of Hispaniola and the west coast of Africa, until his retirement in 1779.

On 31 March 1779 Elsdale married Mary Gibbins, with whom he settled in Surfleet. For her benefit he wrote a lively account of some of the most exciting adventures and experiences he had had during his life at sea. The manuscript fell into the hands of the naval officer and novelist Frederick Marryat, who used it freely in the early chapters of *The Privateer's-man One Hundred Years Ago* (1846). Elsdale died, probably at Surfleet, in 1783, and was survived by his two sons.

Elsdale's elder son, **Samuel Elsdale** (1779/80–1827), schoolmaster and poet, matriculated, aged nineteen, at Lincoln College, Oxford, on 9 April 1799. He graduated BA in 1803, proceeded MA in 1809, took holy orders, and became a fellow of Lincoln College. Later he was appointed the master of Moulton grammar school, Lincolnshire. A frequent contributor to magazines, Elsdale also published, for the benefit of Lincoln Lunatic Asylum, a volume of sacred poetry, *Death, Judgment, Heaven, and Hell; a Poem, with Hymns and other Poems* (1812). He died on 13 July 1827.

Robinson Elsdale's second son, also Robinson (*bap.* 1783, *d.* 1850), was educated at Corpus Christi College, Oxford, and later became headmaster of the free school, Manchester. J. M. RIGG, *rev.* PHILIP CARTER

Sources F. Marryat, *The privateer's-man one hundred years ago*, 2 vols. (1846) · Foster, *Alum. Oxon.* · [J. Watkins and F. Shoberl], *A biographical dictionary of the living authors of Great Britain and Ireland* (1816)

Elsdale, Samuel (1779/80–1827). *See under* Elsdale, Robinson (*bap.* 1744, *d.* 1783).

Elsie, Lily [*real name* Elsie Cotton; *married name* Lily Elsie Bullough] (1886?–1962), actress and singer, was apparently born at Wortley, near Leeds, on 8 April 1886, and was brought up as the daughter of William Thomas Cotton, a theatre proprietor. Her mother, Elsie, later kept a lodging-house. When the young Elsie became celebrated, it was whispered that her roots were not so prosaic, but that she was in fact the illegitimate daughter of Lord Buchan, whose mistress it was said Mrs Cotton had become. As a child performer she worked in variety, doing imitations under the name Little Elsie. She played in pantomime from the age of ten and was seen in London for the first time at Sara Lane's Britannia Theatre at Christmas 1898 as the Spirit of the Air in *King Klondike* ('she is quite the fairy of childish fancy … she is a clever little girl and should make her mark', reported *The Era* in December 1898). Her first appearances in musical comedy were made while touring in Edwin Garth's reprise of the American farce comedy *McKenna's Flirtation*, in *The Silver Slipper* (1901–2), and in *Three Little Maids* (1903). Lily Elsie was first seen in the West End in 1903, when she took over from Beatrice Edwards the *ingénue* role of Princess Soo-Soo in Frank Curzon's long-running production of *A Chinese Honeymoon*.

Thereafter the actress worked exclusively for George Edwardes, rising swiftly and surely up the playbill in roles which ranged from the perky to the serenely ingenuous. She succeeded to Delia Mason's *soubrette* role of Gwenny Holden in *Lady Madcap*, toured in the distinctly soprano role (which had been created by and for the Savoy's Isabel Jay) of Lady Patricia Vereker in *The Cingalee*, and took the tiny part of Madame du Tertre in the Daly's Theatre production of *Les p'tites Michu* (1905). In 1906 she teamed up with Zena Dare and Gabrielle Ray as Willie Edouin's would-be actress daughters in *The Little Cherub* (in the part of Lady Agnes Congress), until the family of daughters

was reduced to just two when Edwardes attempted to save the show by getting it rewritten; although it was reported she had been fined, then sacked, for endless unprofessional giggling, she was moved on to appear in the supporting role of Humming Bird in the same management's *See See* (1906).

Owing to the unavailability of Gertie Millar, Lily Elsie created the title role of Lally in *The New Aladdin* (1906) at the Gaiety, but she was removed when Miss Millar was ready to come back to 'her' theatre. Edwardes more than made it up to the young singer, however, when he made her the heroine of *The Merry Widow* (8 June 1907), a part which made her into a major star and proved that she was altogether more at home when cast in a ladylike role than in the *soubrette* character she had taken in *Lady Madcap*. She soon found herself at the centre of a craze as the show became the fashionable entertainment of its time. Approximations of her picture appeared in advertisements and on wrappings for everything from hats to stays to cosmetics and chocolates, and—since this was the height of the picture-postcard age—she became the heroine of a million posted photographs.

Having made his star, Edwardes hastened to confirm her, and as the passion for Viennese operetta reached its peak in London, she followed up by starring as Alice in his successful Anglicization of Leo Fall's *The Dollar Princess* (1909), in succession to Gertie Millar as the lively but love-lorn Franzi in the producer's second attempt to make a success out of *A Waltz Dream* (1911), and as the glamorous heroine, Angèle Didier, of Lehár's *The Count of Luxembourg* (1911). During the run of this last piece she quit the cast in order to marry, on 7 November 1911, John (Ian) Bullough (1885/6–1936), the well-heeled son of a textile manufacturer with a castle in Perthshire.

Although life in the highlands, interleaved with the occasional appearance at social and theatrical occasions in London, at which she was fabulously dressed, apparently suited her 'retiring' temperament, Elsie languished, and finally, it is said, in 1917, her husband preferred to have her return to the stage. The vehicle chosen was a made-to-measure piece called *Pamela*. Owen Nares was her leading man, Gerald Du Maurier the director, Arthur Wimperis the author, and Frederic Norton, red-hot from his success with *Chu Chin Chow*, the songwriter. *Pamela*, however, was routine stuff, and the languid star, chiding 'Cupid, Cupid, don't be stupid' or reminiscently singing, in waltz time, 'I loved you so', did nothing to lift it. After 172 performances it was gone, and Lily Elsie with it. However, she was to be seen one more time in the West End. Ten years later she took on the leading lady's role in an adaptation of the German musical comedy *Mädi*, produced in Britain as *The Blue Train*. Even an on-stage toboggan slide couldn't persuade the public to patronize this piece for more than 116 nights, and although the press reacted kindly to a star who had once, briefly, been of the brightest, Elsie failed to relight the success of her four years as Edwardes's star of Daly's Theatre.

Elsie later appeared on the non-musical stage in Ivor

Novello's *The Truth Game* (1928). However, she was increasingly subject to spells of the real or imagined illness and ill temper (caused, it has been suggested, by an early and difficult menopause) which had so long bedevilled her life, and her marriage ended in divorce in 1930. Thereafter she spent much of her time in sanatoria and nursing homes. She died at St Andrew's Hospital, Dollis Hill, Middlesex, on 16 December 1962.   KURT GÄNZL

Sources K. Gänzl, *The encyclopedia of the musical theatre*, 2 vols. (1994) · K. Gänzl, *The British musical theatre*, 2 vols. (1986) · *DNB* · *The Era* (1898–1929) · *The Times* (18 Dec 1962) · C. Beaton, 'Lovely Lily Elsie', *The rise and fall of the matinée idol*, ed. A. Curtis (1974), 3–19 · m. cert. · d. cert.
Likenesses R. Martin, photograph, 1907, NPG · J. J. Shannon, oils, 1916, NPG · C. Beaton, photograph, NPG · Mrs A. Broom, photograph, NPG · H. van Dusen and Hassall, lithograph, NPG · Rotary Photo, photograph, NPG · photographs, Hult. Arch.
Wealth at death £32,545 19*s*.: probate, 9 May 1963, *CGPLA Eng. & Wales*

Elsmie, George Robert (1838–1909), administrator in India and author, was born at Aberdeen on 31 October 1838, the only child of George Elsmie (*c*.1801–1860), steamship builder of Aberdeen and, from 1843, superintendent of steamship construction at Southampton for the Royal Mail Steam Packet Company, and his wife, Anne (1804–1879), daughter of Robert Shepherd, parish minister of Daviot, Aberdeenshire. Elsmie was educated at private schools at Southampton and from 1852 to 1855 attended Marischal College, Aberdeen. In the summer of 1855 he was studying German at Canstatt, near Stuttgart, when his mother's brother, John Shepherd (1796–1859), a director and thrice chairman of the East India Company, prevailed upon him to accept the last nomination within his patronage to the Bengal civil service. Elsmie returned to Britain and, at the close of 1855, took his place among the last batch of students to enter East India College, Haileybury.

Arriving in India in February 1858, Elsmie was appointed assistant commissioner in the Punjab, initially in Ludhiana. He returned to Britain in 1861, shortly after his father's death, and while there married, on 29 October, Elizabeth, youngest daughter of Thomas Spears of Kirkcaldy, and a friend since childhood. The couple travelled to India at the end of 1861 and Elsmie resumed his post of assistant commissioner, this time at Lahore. In 1863 he became acting judge of the small causes court at Lahore, and afterwards at Delhi and then at Simla. Meanwhile, he compiled for the government's use *An Epitome of Correspondence Regarding our Relations with Afghanistan and Herat, 1854–63* (1863). In March 1865 he became deputy commissioner of Jullundur and embarked upon his first stint as an independent district officer—a job he found exhilarating but exhausting. In his autobiography, *Thirty-Five Years in the Punjab, 1858–1893* (1908), Elsmie chronicles the difficulties and embarrassments as a civilian in these early years with wit and engaging candour. Composed largely of extracts from letters to his mother, the book relates Elsmie's fears that he was not up to the work, could not master one strange language after another, and would never earn

enough to support his burgeoning family. Elsmie's wife, 'E.', who bore ten surviving children, rarely features explicitly in *Thirty-Five Years*, but her pragmatic and uncomplaining presence is implicit throughout as, year after year, she packed up their large household and settled down anew wherever her husband had been posted.

In the spring of 1869, after six months as acting under secretary to the government of India in the home department, Elsmie took furlough. Back in England, he entered Lincoln's Inn and was called to the bar on 26 January 1871. On his return to India he was appointed additional commissioner (in effect, acting civil and sessions judge) of Amritsar and Jullundur divisions, the beginning of fourteen years of judicial work. In November 1872 he was transferred to Peshawar with instructions to overhaul that division's judicial administration so as to effect a reduction in murder and violent crime. Elsmie remained at Peshawar until February 1878, when he was appointed acting judge of the chief court of Lahore for a year. On furlough for most of 1879 and 1880, Elsmie was appointed commissioner of Lahore in December 1880. In April 1882 he was appointed permanently to the chief court and in October of the same year served on the Punjab reorganization committee. In spite of his judicial experience, Elsmie was keen to return to executive work and in February 1885 he took a pay cut in order to become the first commissioner of the new enlarged division of Lahore. From 1885 to 1887 he was also vice-chancellor of Punjab University.

In 1884 Elsmie had published *Crime and Criminals on the Peshawur Frontier*, a compilation of all the heavy criminal cases he had tried during his five years at Peshawar. In 1886, as a result of this publication, he was appointed to preside over a committee of inquiry into the criminal administration of the frontier division and helped draft the new frontier criminal regulations of 1887. These were designed to enhance the authority and disciplinary powers of the Pathans' traditional councils of elders.

Elsmie was made second financial commissioner of the Punjab in April 1887, a member of the central legislative council in May 1888 and again in June 1892, and first financial commissioner in March 1889. In January 1893, on the eve of his retirement, he was made a CSI.

Modest and good-humoured, Elsmie had no sympathy for party politics and was renowned throughout his career for his independence of opinion. In retirement he co-authored (with General Sir Peter Lumsden) Sir Harry Lumsden's biography, *Lumsden of the Guides* (1899), and wrote the authorized life of Sir Donald Stewart (1903). In 1904 he published a selection of his mother's correspondence, *Anne Shepherd or Elsmie: a character sketch of a Scottish lady of the nineteenth century as disclosed by her letters*. The letters, thoughtful and witty, reveal much about the shaping of Elsmie's own character—mother and son shared a love of literature and a dislike of dogma and entrenched attitudes. Both were devout but eclectic protestants, willing to entertain any preacher of eloquence and intelligence.

Elsmie died at Drayton, Torquay, on 26 May 1909 and was buried at Deeside cemetery, Aberdeen. His wife and ten children survived him. Two of their three sons joined the Indian army, four daughters married Indian civil servants, and two more married officers in the army.

F. H. BROWN, *rev.* KATHERINE PRIOR

Sources G. R. Elsmie, *Thirty-five years in the Punjab, 1858–1893* (1908) · G. R. Elsmie, ed., *Anne Shepherd or Elsmie: a character sketch of a Scottish lady of the nineteenth century as disclosed by her letters* (1904) · BL OIOC, Haileybury MSS · *The Times* (28 May 1909), 11 · *The Times* (29 May 1909), 1
Likenesses photograph, 1891, repro. in Elsmie, *Thirty-five years*
Wealth at death £7531 19*s*. 11*d*.: probate, 24 June 1909, *CGPLA Eng. & Wales*

Elssler, Fransiska [Fanny] **(1810–1884)**, dancer, was born in a suburb of Vienna, Austria, on 23 June 1810, the seventh of the nine children of Johann Florian Elssler (1769–1843), valet and copyist to Haydn, and his wife, Theresia Prinster (1779–1832), an embroideress. Many stories circulated about her youth, the veracity of which cannot be established, among them that Fanny and her sister Therese were the natural daughters of Prince Esterházy, in whose service their grandfather had worked, and that they had begun their studies at the scandal-ridden Kinderballet at the Theater an der Wien. Fanny's name appeared on the playbill of the Kärntnertortheater on 20 April 1818, and she was also on stage at the same theatre on 10 June 1822, when her future rival Marie Taglioni made her début. By 1825 the impresario Barbaja was sufficiently impressed with her progress to introduce the blue-eyed, auburn-haired dancer to audiences in Naples. There she had a liaison with the elderly Leopold, prince of Salerno, whose son, Franz Robert, she bore in 1827, thereby earning an annuity of 3000 ducats.

Elssler rapidly became one of the stars of European ballet under the patronage of Friedrich von Gentz, a friend of Metternich. Her career was not impeded by a series of affairs with prominent men and the births of two further children; indeed, she had danced at the King's Theatre, London, in *Flore et Zéphyr* with Taglioni on 27 April 1833 while pregnant with her third child. She took up residence in London in 1834 with her sister Therese; Count D'Orsay squired them about the town. The two women made their début in *Faust* on 9 March 1834, but were soon engaged by Louis Véron of the Paris Opéra, where Fanny first appeared in *La tempête* on 15 September. Charles Maurice of *Le Courrier* described her 'astonishing strength … rich *pointes* … abundance of *entrechats* … [and] much suppleness' (quoted in Guest, *Fanny Elssler*, 63).

Elssler's position as a serious rival to Taglioni was established in 1836 when she enjoyed a sensational success in *Le diable boiteux*, introducing her celebrated dance, the chachuca. The performance earned her ecstatic reviews from Théophile Gautier, who described her somewhat hermaphrodite beauty and spectacular technique. In *La tarentule* and *La Gypsy* she revealed great pantomimic ability, although her appearance in Taglioni's favourite role, *La sylphide*, was less successful. Gautier compared the two dancers, finding Taglioni a Christian, religious dancer, appreciated by women, and Elssler a pagan dancer, full of the pleasures of life, and appealing most strongly to men.

Fransiska Elssler (1810–1884), by John Hayter, 1843

He did, however, suggest that she paint her nails a less vivid shade of pink. Both Elssler and Taglioni were in London for the brilliant season of the coronation year, 1838, and in 1840 Elssler danced at her own benefit before Queen Adelaide, Queen Victoria, Prince Albert, and Louis Napoleon.

In 1840 Elssler set off on a tour of the United States, arranged by her current lover, the marquis de la Valette, and a future one, the American Henry Wikoff. She left her daughter, Therese, in the care of George and Harriet Grote, who had befriended her. Her tour, which included New York, Richmond, Charleston, and Boston, was a great success. The enthusiasm of her reception, and the size of the fees she commanded, caused her to overstay her leave of absence from the Paris Opéra and embroiled her in a prolonged and acrimonious dispute: she never danced in Paris again. She remained in America with Wikoff until July 1842, when she returned to London and peremptorily removed her daughter from the Grotes (although she was soon to be abandoned with them again). Elssler broke off with Wikoff, claiming that he had stolen from her; rumour had it that he had also beaten her. She took up instead with the wealthy Count Samuel Klostrowicki, who offered her marriage, which she refused. Despite her two-year absence and the arrival of a new star, Fanny Cerito, Elssler was rapturously received on her return to the London stage, in *Giselle* at Her Majesty's Theatre.

Elssler spent some four years in Italy, where she danced one of her most celebrated roles, *La Esmerelda*, to great applause, and in 1848 went to Russia, where she was also triumphant, despite the initial hostility of the Russian ballet establishment. She announced her retirement at St Petersburg in 1850, and at her final performance of *La Esmeralda* took forty-two curtain calls.

With a collection of caged birds and her devoted cousin and companion, Katti Prinster, Elssler proceeded to enjoy her retirement, first in Hamburg and then in Vienna. The rift with the Grotes was eventually healed, and all were pleased with the marriage in 1859 of Elssler's daughter Therese, whose own daughter was named after her grandmother. The death of Therese in 1870, the suicide of Elssler's son in 1875, and the death of her sister Therese (who had become the morganatic wife of Prince Adalbert of Prussia) in 1878 saddened her last years. Elssler died at her home in Seilerstätte, Vienna, on 27 November 1884 and was buried in the Heitzing cemetery.

According to her *New York Times* obituary (28 November 1884), Elssler had been long forgotten by the time of her death; if this was ever so, her eclipse was soon over. A stream of biographies memorialized her life and talents, as did an operetta (1936), a ballet (1934), and a film by Paul Martin (1936).   J. GILLILAND

Sources I. Guest, *Fanny Elssler* (1970) [incl. bibliography] · C. W. Beaumont, *Fanny Elssler, 1810–1884* (1931) · E. Pirchan, *Fanny Elssler: eine Wienerin tanzt um die Welt* (1940) · A. Ehrhard, *Une vie de danseuse: Fanny Elssler* (1909) · S. D'Amico, ed., *Enciclopedia dello spettacolo*, 11 vols. (Rome, 1954–68) · J. Weissenbock, *Fanny Elssler: materialen* (1984) · H. Wikoff, *Reminiscences of an idler* (1880) · H. Koegler, *The concise Oxford dictionary of ballet* (1977) · B. Grun, *Fanny beloved* (1960) · *New York Times* (28 Nov 1884), 3 · *Figaro* (19 Oct 1837) · *La Presse* (24 Sept 1838) · I. Guest, *Gautier on dance* (1986)

Archives FILM *Fanny Elssler* [1936, Paul Martin]

Likenesses J. Hayter, drawing, 1843, BM [*see illus.*] · porcelain statuettes · portraits, repro. in Guest, *Fanny Elssler* · portraits, Harvard TC · portraits, repro. in Pirchan, *Fanny Elssler* · portraits, repro. in Guest, *Gautier on dance*

Elstob, Elizabeth (1683–1756), Anglo-Saxon scholar, was born on 29 September 1683 at Newcastle upon Tyne, the youngest of eight children of Ralph Elstob (1647–1688), merchant, and his wife, Jane Hall (*d.* 1692). After her mother's death Elizabeth was brought up in the household of her father's younger brother Charles Elstob, prebendary of Canterbury Cathedral, and his wife, Matilda. There, having overcome her uncle's initial hostility to learning in women, she was able to continue her private education (which she had begun under her mother's tutelage), and acquire a knowledge of several ancient and modern languages. In the late 1690s, while apparently still living in Canterbury and through the agency of her elder brother William *Elstob (1674?–1715), a fellow of University College, Oxford, she was introduced to the scholarly concerns of the Oxford Saxonists, a group of Oxford scholars who, under the intellectual leadership of George Hickes, pursued the study of Old English and other northern languages and literatures, and of Anglo-Saxon history and culture. She apparently had no difficulty in gaining access to this circle and, in addition to the encouragement and tutelage of her brother William, George Hickes

Elizabeth Elstob (1683–1756), by Simon Gribelin, pubd 1709

became her mentor and actively supported her scholarly undertakings until his death, in 1715.

In 1702, after William had been appointed rector of the parishes of St Swithin London Stone and St Mary Bothaw, Elizabeth Elstob set up house with him in Bush Lane, London, where they lived together until William's premature death, in 1715. In 1708 she published an English translation of Madeleine de Scudery's *Discours de la gloire* (1671), reflecting her early enthusiasm for the study of French. That year also saw the publication of her first edition of an Anglo-Saxon text, namely a transcript that she had made of the Latin text and its Old English interlinear gloss of the Athanasian creed appended to the Salisbury psalter (Salisbury Cathedral, 150). At Hickes's instigation this text was included in William Wotton's *Conspectus brevis*, a pocket-sized version of Hickes's *Thesaurus* that was designed to boost the sales figures of that monumental work. The addition of Elizabeth's text to the extracts drawn from the *Thesaurus* reveals the encouraging confidence that the doyen of Anglo-Saxon studies placed in the philological skill and accuracy of a newcomer in the field.

In 1709 Elizabeth Elstob's first major publication appeared: an edition of the Old English life of Pope Gregory the Great by the late tenth-century grammarian and homilist Ælfric. Her edition, *An English-Saxon Homily on the Birthday of St. Gregory*, is a lavishly produced book equipped with copious text-critical and explanatory notes, with a modern English translation facing the Old English text on each page and a lengthy introduction and appendix dealing *inter alia* with the role and enduring importance of Gregory in the English church. The historiated initial of the modern English translation of Ælfric's text (p. 1) contains Elizabeth Elstob's portrait engraved by Simon Gribelin; this initial was reused in her *Rudiments of Grammar* (1715).

Between 1709 and 1712 Elizabeth Elstob assisted her brother William in his projected edition of the Anglo-Saxon laws, as she had done with his projected edition of the Old English Orosius. During this time she continued on a monumental scale the project that she had begun with her *English-Saxon Homily*, which was a complete edition of Ælfric's *Catholic Homilies*. This is a collection of sermons and saints' lives that is of paramount importance for the study of Old English language and literature. Furthermore Ælfric's sermons had strong political and doctrinal implications for the seventeenth and early eighteenth centuries inasmuch as the representatives of the Church of England sought to validate their claims to priority over the Roman Catholic church by pointing to the anticipation of distinctive Anglican doctrines such as that of transubstantiation in these sermons. These aspects of Ælfric's works had already been emphasized in Elizabeth Elstob's edition of his Gregory homily. Publication of her edition of the *Catholic Homilies* was scheduled for Michaelmas 1715 but only thirty-six pages were printed; they survive in proof stage in the British Library (BL, 695.1.8.; 224.e.17). The manuscripts of the projected edition, preserved in the British Library (Lansdowne MSS 370–374 and Egerton MS 838), make it clear that the edition was still some way from being completed. It is also clear, however, that it was planned in the same encyclopaedic format as the edition of the Gregory homily. Had Elizabeth Elstob been able to complete this massive project her edition of the *Catholic Homilies* would have antedated the first critical and annotated edition of that important text by almost three centuries.

In 1715 Elizabeth Elstob published her last book, *The Rudiments of Grammar for the English-Saxon Tongue*—the first grammar of Old English to be published in English. It is based, principally but not exclusively, on Hickes's authoritative grammar in the first volume of his *Linguarum veterum septentrionalium thesaurus grammatico-criticus et archaeologicus* (1703) and on the abridged version extracted from it by Edward Thwaites (1711), both of which are written in Latin. She prefaced *The Rudiments* with a passionate but well-documented apologia for Anglo-Saxon studies, directing her remarks against the indifference towards the subject as evidenced in the writings of Jonathan Swift, who sought to establish a language academy in England on the model of the Académie Française.

Though small in size and only partly available in print Elizabeth Elstob's scholarly œuvre is on a par with the best work produced in Anglo-Saxon studies at the beginning of the eighteenth century. Moreover, her concept of writing her Old English grammar in English, and of providing her editions with a critical apparatus, introductions, and translations—all in English—at a time when scholarly publications in the field were almost invariably written throughout in Latin, clearly pointed to the future. The evidence of her works and letters does not permit the conclusion—often drawn—that her books were written in English to cater for the demands and abilities of the women of the leisured classes. No doubt she aimed to include women among the readership of her books but her primary concern was with Anglo-Saxon studies. By the early eighteenth century scholarship in that domain (culminating in the publication of Hickes's *Thesaurus*) had attained a level that was not to be surpassed for more than a century; but the future of the subject was threatened, nevertheless, by public neglect and lack of financial security for scholars working in the field. This is the context in which

to judge Elizabeth Elstob's attempts to arouse genuine interest in the Anglo-Saxon past in a wider—both male and female—public than had hitherto been reached. Her learned contemporaries (men such as George Hickes, Humfrey Wanley, John Hudson, Richard Rawlinson, Ralph Thoresby, and Edward Rowe Mores) and scholars in the early nineteenth century appear to have appreciated her aims and scholarly standing more perceptively than twentieth-century critics, who have often judged her by the criteria of the moving details of her biography and her role as a woman in a male-dominated society.

Elizabeth Elstob's scholarly career came to an abrupt end with William's death, which left her without an income and with considerable debts, apparently incurred by funding their publishing projects. The only financial support that she seems to have received during the first years after William's death came from George Smalridge (1663–1719), who was at that time bishop of Bristol. Upon his death, or shortly before it, Elizabeth Elstob disappeared from London, presumably because she felt unable to repay her debts. She had to abandon her books and manuscripts, and never recovered them. She took refuge in Evesham, Worcestershire, where to earn a modest living she established a humble elementary school for girls. Her whereabouts apparently remained unknown to most of the scholarly world until 1735. From that year dates her acquaintance with the amateur antiquary George Ballard, with whom she kept up correspondence until 1753 and for whom, in 1738 or thereabouts, she wrote a brief autobiographical note. In the mid-1730s, through Ballard, she was introduced to Mrs Chapone, the wife of a clergyman and herself a schoolmistress, who possibly wrote or initiated a circular letter to be distributed among ladies more affluent than herself with the aim of raising some money, or perhaps an annuity, for Elizabeth.

The last major change in Elizabeth Elstob's life—a change that provided her with a home and financial security for the remaining seventeen years of her life—occurred in 1739, when she became governess in the household of the duke and duchess of Portland. This post appears to have resulted from Mrs Chapone's initiative on Elizabeth's behalf. The duchess, wife to the second duke, was Margaret Harley, granddaughter of Robert Harley, who seems to have supported Elizabeth and William Elstob's projects many years earlier. Thus the outward course of Elizabeth Elstob's life came to a tranquil close in the household of a descendant of one of her early benefactors. Ever since she had had to leave London she had suffered from frequent attacks of what in her letters she called 'nervous fever', and during her last years she seems almost constantly to have been in poor health. She died, in the duchess's service, on 30 May 1756 and was buried on 3 June at St Margaret's, Westminster.

MECHTHILD GRETSCH

Sources E. Elstob, *An English-Saxon homily on the birthday of St. Gregory; anciently used in the English-Saxon church; giving an account of the conversion of the English from paganism to Christianity. Translated into modern English, with notes etc.* (1709) • E. Elstob, *The rudiments of grammar for the English-Saxon tongue, first given in English with an apology for*

*the study of northern antiquities. Being very useful towards the under-
standing of our ancient English poets, and other writers* (1715) · Elizabeth
Elstob's edition of Ælfric's *Catholic homilies*, BL, Lansdowne MSS
370–374; Egerton MS 838 · E. Elstob, letters to George Ballard,
Bodl. Oxf., MS Ballard 43, fols. 3r–98r [incl. her autobiographical
note, fols. 59r–60v] · Elstob family tree, BL, Harley MS 1397, fols.
237–9 [drawn up by Elizabeth Elstob in 1710] · Nichols, *Lit. anecdotes*, 4.112–40 · M. Gretsch, 'Elizabeth Elstob: a scholar's fight for
Anglo-Saxon studies', *Anglia*, 117 (1999), 163–300, 481–524 · S. H.
Collins, 'Elizabeth Elstob: a biography', PhD diss., Indiana University, 1970 · S. H. Collins, 'The Elstobs and the end of the Saxon
revival', *Anglo-Saxon scholarship: the first three centuries*, ed. C. T.
Berkhout and M. McC. Gatch (Boston, 1982), 107–18 · M. Ashdown,
'Elizabeth Elstob: the learned Saxonist', *Modern Language Review*, 20
(1925), 125–46 · K. Sutherland, 'Elizabeth Elstob', *Medieval scholarship: biographical studies on the formation of a discipline*, ed. H. Damico,
vol. 2 (New York, 1998), 59–73 · K. Sutherland, 'Editing for a new
century: Elizabeth Elstob's Anglo-Saxon manifesto and Ælfric's St
Gregory homily', *The editing of Old English: papers from the 1990 Manchester Conference*, ed. D. G. Scragg and P. E. Szarmach (1994), 213–
37 · parish register, 3 June 1756, St Margaret's, Westminster
[burial]

Archives BL, part of a collection of Anglo-Saxon homilies transcribed and translated by her, Egerton MS 838 · BL, collections,
copies, and extracts taken from Anglo-Saxon MSS made together
with her brother, Stowe MSS 940, 985 · BL, Elstob family tree, Harley MS 1397 · BL, Saxon homilies transcribed and translated by her
and her brother, Lansdowne MSS 370–374 · Bodl. Oxf., collections
for an edition of Anglo-Saxon laws, made together with her
brother · Bodl. Oxf., transcripts of Latin and English testimonies
concerning Aelfric Abbot of Eynsham, copies of some of her MSS,
and essays · CUL, transcript of liturgical pieces, incl. the 'Athana-
sian Creed', from Salisbury Cathedral, 150 | Bodl. Oxf., letters to
George Ballard and papers, Ballard MS 43, fols. 3r–98r [incl. her
autobiographical note (fols. 59r–60v) and a brief biography of William Elstob (fols. 14r–16v)]

Likenesses S. Gribelin, line engraving (in historiated initial G),
BM; repro. in Elstob, *An English-Saxon homily*, 1 [*see illus.*] · B. Reading,
line engraving, NPG; repro. in Elstob, *Rudiments*

Elstob, William (1674?–1715), Anglo-Saxon scholar and
Church of England clergyman, was probably born on 1
January 1674 and baptized on 15 January at All Saints'
Church, Newcastle upon Tyne, the son of Jane Hall (*d.*
1692) and Ralph Elstob (1647–1688). His parents had married on 20 October 1672 at All Saints' in Newcastle and his
father was a merchant 'who descended from a very
ancient Family at Foxton in the Bishoprick of Durham'
(Elstob), according to his younger sister Elizabeth *Elstob
(1683–1756). He was first educated at the Royal Free Grammar School, Newcastle, and from there went to Eton,
where he was a colleger from 1687 to 1690. On the advice
of his uncle Charles Elstob DD, prebendary of Canterbury
(1685–1721), who had assumed the guardianship of William and Elizabeth after the premature deaths of both parents, Elstob matriculated at Cambridge in 1691 and was
admitted sizar at St Catharine's College on 23 June of that
year. He was unhappy there for two reasons, being placed
'in a Station below his Birth and Fortune … and the air not
agreeing with his Constitution, which was Consumptive'
(ibid.), so he migrated to Oxford, where he matriculated as
a commoner of the Queen's College on 15 December 1691.
He graduated BA in 1694 and was elected fellow of University College on 23 July 1696, proceeded MA on 8 June 1697

and was incorporated at Cambridge in 1698, and DD in
1705. He was rector of the united parishes of St Swithin
London Stone and St Mary Bothaw, Cannon Street, Lon-
don, from 2 January 1702 to his death, 'by the procure-
ment, no doubt, of his uncle the prebendary' (Pegge, 12),
for the dean and chapter of Canterbury were patrons of St
Mary Bothaw. Elstob was also titular chaplain to William
Nicolson, bishop of Carlisle (consecrated 14 June 1702).
Friends and patrons tried to obtain other positions for
Elstob that would assist his research, but in vain.

Elstob's sister described him as a man of sweet temper
and a loving disposition. He supported her education and
made it possible for her, as well as for himself, to become
one of the most proficient Anglo-Saxon scholars of the
age. When he went up to Queen's, he joined a college
which was the centre of the emerging discipline of Anglo-
Saxon studies, led by George Hickes, Edward Thwaites,
and Humfrey Wanley. Elstob soon became a member of
this group and shared its objectives, which were to publish reliable editions of the major Old English texts, particularly historical and legal works and, above all, the
writings ascribed to King Alfred, the supposed founder of
both the university and University College. Most of the
Oxford Saxonists were also inspired by Anglican religious
principles, and were eager to prove the continuity of
church doctrine and English institutions from Anglo-
Saxon times to their own.

Elstob would probably have published more than he
actually did if he had had adequate financial backing. His
first scholarly project was an edition of the Anglo-Saxon
version of Orosius's *Historiarum adversum paganos*, ascribed
to King Alfred. This was part of the effort by Hickes and his
group to publish all of Alfred's scholarly work, as Wanley
wrote to Hickes on 18 February 1698: 'an honest Gentleman of this College [Elstob], may publish Orosius, and so
compleat our Royal Founders works' (Harris, 199). A specimen of this edition was published at the Sheldonian Theatre in 1699 (a copy of it is extant as BL, MS Lansdowne 373,
fols. 86–7). The project failed for lack of subscribers.
Elstob's transcript of the Old English Orosius text from
Bodleian MS Junius 15 is extant as Trinity College, Oxford,
MS 92. His work on the edition eventually served as the
basis for Daines Barrington's *The Anglo-Saxon Version, from
the Historian Orosius, by Ælfred the Great* (1773).

Elstob undertook an edition and translation of Archbishop Wulfstan's *Sermo Lupi ad Anglos*, and this was published at the Sheldonian Theatre in 1701, though it seems
that he had already finished it in 1698. Hickes incorporated it at pages 98–106 of the *Dissertatio epistolaris* in his
Thesaurus (1703–5). Elstob helped Sir Andrew Fountaine
with his dissertation on Anglo-Saxon coins, also published
in Hickes's *Thesaurus*. Among Elstob's other publications
were a new, enlarged edition of Roger Ascham's letters
(1703), two sermons on current political events (both published in 1704), a translation from the Latin of Sir John
Cheke's 'A treatise of superstition', appended to John
Strype's *The Life of the Learned Sir John Cheke* (1705), and a
Latin version of the Abbot Ælfric's Anglo-Saxon homily on

the nativity of St Gregory, edited and translated into modern English by his sister Elizabeth (1709). He also published in 1713 *An Essay on the Great Affinity and Mutual Agreement of the Two Professions of Divinity and Law*, to which Hickes contributed a preface, and himself contributed 'A publick office of daily and nightly devotion for the seven canonical hours of prayer, used in the Anglo-Saxon church, with a translation and notes' to Hickes's *Several Letters which Passed between Dr. George Hickes and a Popish Priest* (1715). Some poetry by Elstob is also extant, and his 'An essay concerning the Latin tongue and upon grammar' is in the Bodleian (MS Ballard 63).

Elstob died on 3 March 1715 'after a long and lingering illness' (Elstob), and was buried in the chancel of St Swithin London Stone, under the communion table. He was unmarried. At his death he left a major project in Anglo-Saxon studies unfinished. This was an edition of the Anglo-Saxon laws, intended to correct the mistakes of earlier editors and to collate their notes, add new material, particularly from the Textus Roffensis, and prepare a new translation of the texts, with glossaries, indices, and contextual information. Some of his and his sister's notes and collations towards this edition are extant. Elstob refers to the project in his 1713 essay on divinity and law, and it is also mentioned by Sir John Fortescue-Aland in the preface to his *Difference between an Absolute and Limited Monarchy* (1714) and in the preface to David Wilkins's 1721 edition of the Anglo-Saxon laws, which was indebted to Elstob's work.   MARGARET CLUNIES ROSS

Sources E. Elstob, 'A short account of the life of the Reverend Mr William Elstob, M. A. and rector of St Swithins and St Mary Bothaw, London', Bodl. Oxf., MS Ballard 63, fols. vii–xi [with annotations by G. Ballard] · S. Pegge, 'An historical account of that venerable monument of antiquity the *Textus Roffensis; including memoirs of the learned Saxonists Mr. William Elstob and his sister*', *Bibliotheca topographica Britannica*, ed. J. Nichols, 25 (1784), 1–32 · Nichols, *Lit. anecdotes*, 1.16–18; 4.112–40 · G. B. R. [George Bouchier Richardson], 'William and Elizabeth Elstob, the learned Saxonists', *Reprints of rare tracts & imprints of antient manuscripts, chiefly illustrative of the history of the northern counties; and printed at the press of M. A. Richardson*, 1 (1847) · BL, MS Harley 1397, fols. 237r–238v [pedigree of the Elstob family on both paternal and maternal sides, drawn up by Elizabeth Elstob in 1710, and sent to Humfrey Wanley] · Venn, *Alum. Cant.* · Foster, *Alum. Oxon.* · *A chorus of grammars: the correspondence of George Hickes and his collaborators on the 'Thesaurus linguarum septentrionalium'*, ed. R. L. Harris (1992) · G. Hickes and others, *Linguarum vett. septentrionalium thesaurus grammatico-criticus et archaeologicus*, 3 vols. (1703–5); facs. edn in 1 vol. (Hildesheim and New York, 1970) · 'Chartaceus in 4to pp.167 e legatis Jacobi Ingram STP coll. Trin, præsidentis 1850, hormesta Pauli Orosii ex interpretatione Alfredi Regis. Liber ex apographo Juniano manu Gulielmi Elstob descriptus. Præmissæ sunt pp iv in quibus Samuel Pegge cujus olim liber fuit de eo commentus est', Trinity College, Oxford, MS 92 [on deposit in Bod.] · 'A collection of Saxon homilies in four volumes, transcribed by the Rev. Mr. Elstob, rector of St. Swithin's at Londonstone, and his sister Elizabeth, and in part translated by them, with a view to their publication', BL, MSS Lansdowne 370–373 · *Letters of Humfrey Wanley: palaeographer, Anglo-Saxonist, librarian, 1672–1726*, ed. P. L. Heyworth (1989) · *Remarks and collections of Thomas Hearne*, ed. C. E. Doble and others, 2, OHS, 7 (1886), 107–9 · D. Barrington, *The Anglo-Saxon version, from the historian Orosius, by Ælfred the Great* (1773) · M. Murphy, 'The Elstobs, scholars of Old English and Anglican apologists', *Durham University Journal*, 58 (1965–6), 131–8 · S. H. Collins, 'The Elstobs

and the end of the Saxon revival', *Anglo-Saxon scholarship: the first three centuries*, ed. C. T. Berkhout and M. McC. Gatch (1982), 107–18 · J. A. W. Bennett, 'The history of Old English and Old Norse studies in England from the time of Francis Junius till the end of the eighteenth century', DPhil diss., U. Oxf., 1938, Bodl. Oxf., MS D. Phil. d. 287, 154–9 · D. Fairer, 'Anglo-Saxon studies', *Hist. U. Oxf.* 5: *18th-cent. Oxf.*, 807–29 · S. Keynes, 'The cult of King Alfred the Great', *Anglo-Saxon England*, 28 (1999), 225–356 · M. Gretsch, 'Elizabeth Elstob: a scholar's fight for Anglo-Saxon studies', *Anglia*, 117 (1999), 163–300, 481–524 [incl. references to William Elstob's work] · *IGI*
Archives BL, letters to Humfrey Wanley, Add. MS 70478

Elston [Elstow], **Henry** (*fl.* 1517–1559), Observant Franciscan friar, is of obscure origins. The name Elstow, by which he is sometimes referred to, is without contemporary justification. He first appears at Peterhouse, Cambridge, where he was elected fellow in April 1517. But by 1520 he had joined the Observants at Richmond, Surrey, and in early 1532 he was warden of the friary attached to the palace at Greenwich.

On Easter Sunday 1532 the provincial minister, William Peto, gave a powerful sermon before the king in the Greenwich friary chapel to dissuade him from putting away Katherine of Aragon and marrying Anne Boleyn. Elston achieved notoriety when, on the following Sunday, he heckled, from the rood-loft, a sermon by the king's chaplain, Dr Richard Curwen, who had been put up to contradict Peto. Subsequently Peto refused the king's command to deprive Elston of office, and both men were imprisoned at Lambeth Palace, and examined before the bishops and the Canterbury convocation. Later, to isolate them from other partisans of Katherine, they were moved to the house of the Conventual Franciscans at Bedford, where they were still detained in September.

By June 1533 Peto and Elston were living, with other English friars, in the friary at Antwerp. Here Elston was engaged in posting books and letters across the channel. In October 1533 he forwarded letters from Rome to Peto's replacement as provincial minister in England, and in April 1534 was alleged to be predicting a Spanish invasion of England. In 1538 Peto joined Cardinal Reginald Pole at Rome, but Elston stayed in Antwerp, where he was known as Pole's factotum, and remained active in forwarding letters to and from England, Scotland, Padua, and Rome. He was warden of the Antwerp Franciscans in 1545, twice visitor of the Observant province of Lower Germany, and provincial minister in 1549.

Elston returned to England as warden when the Greenwich friary (suppressed in 1534) was refounded by Queen Mary in 1555. But in July 1559 the friary was again suppressed, following Elizabeth's accession, and Elston died in exile at an unknown date.   KEITH BROWN

Sources N. Harpsfield, *A treatise on the pretended divorce between Henry VIII and Catharine of Aragon*, ed. N. Pocock, CS, new ser., 21 (1878), 202–5 · *LP Henry VIII*, vols. 5–7, 12/2, 13/1, 16, 22/1, *addenda* 1/1 · *CSP Spain*, 1531–3, 934 · T. A. Walker, *A biographical register of Peterhouse men*, 1 (1927), 114 · register of Bishop Fitzjames, GL, MS 9531/11, fols. 190r–v, 192r · *APC*, 1554–6, 169 · Franciscus à Sancta Clara [C. Davenport], *Manuale missionariorum regularium*, 2nd edn (1661), 204–5 · Angelus à Sancto Francisco [R. Mason], *Certamen* *seraphicum provinciae Angliae pro sancta Dei ecclesia*, 2nd edn (Quaracchi, 1885), 15 · D. Knowles [M. C. Knowles], *The religious orders in England*, 3 (1959) · 'Peto, William', *DNB*

Elstrack [Elstracke], **Renold** (*b.* 1570, *d.* in or after 1625), engraver, was the foremost English engraver of his time and the greatest successor to William Rogers, of whom he was most probably a pupil. His father, 'Joselphe Elstrage of Lukeland' (that is, the province of Liège), was a glazier and was recorded as a member of the Dutch Reformed church in London in 1582–3. He arrived in England in 1552 and had two sons, one of whom, 'Reginold', was ten months old in 1571.

Elstrack's first dated plates, five maps used in a translation of Jan Huygen von Linschoten's *Voyages into ye Easte and West Indies*, for which Rogers engraved the title-plate, were made in 1598. At this time he was aged twenty-eight, and it is possible that this late start can be explained by his having first trained as a glazier. No documents survive to record his later career, and information can only be deduced from his engraved plates. Of these Hind catalogued ninety-nine, which are of very uneven quality. The last dated plates are from 1620, and the latest dateable is a map used in Samuel Purchas's *Hakluytus posthumus* in 1625.

Apart from maps, Elstrack's subjects were mostly portraits. The best of these are of members of the royal family; they are the only parallel in print-making to the great full-length Jacobean costume paintings and are their equal in grandeur. Their design bears no relation to any known painting, and it has always been assumed that Elstrack was himself responsible for the compositions. Their beauty and rarity made them in the early nineteenth century among the most sought after of all prints, and in the Sykes sale of 1824 they fetched higher prices than any etching by Rembrandt. At that time Elstrack's plate of the chimney sweep and thief John Cottingham, titled *Mull'd Sake*, was regarded as one of the most desirable of all rarities for the print collector.

Elstrack seems never to have published himself, but to have worked for the main London publishers, initially mostly for the partnership of John Sudbury and George Humble, and from 1616 for the newly established Compton Holland. It was for Holland that he engraved most of the plates in the *Basiliologia* of 1618, a book whose fame among book collectors has always been far greater than its quality merits. By this time, however, his work was rapidly becoming outdated, as the recently arrived Simon de Passe and Francis Delaram had introduced new patterns and styles from abroad.

Among Elstrack's plates are a few non-portraits of great interest. The most famous of these is a two-plate engraving of James I in parliament, first published in 1604 by John Speed, and regularly updated thereafter for later openings of parliament. Another, *Bulchin and Thingut*, although recorded in the nineteenth century, was only rediscovered in America and published in 1998. Bulchin is a fat monster that only eats good men, while Thingut, who can only eat good women, starves. Elstrack was last recorded in 1625.   ANTONY GRIFFITHS

Sources A. M. Hind, *Engraving in England in the sixteenth and seventeenth centuries*, 2 (1955), 163–214 · R. E. G. Kirk and E. F. Kirk, eds., *Returns of aliens dwelling in the city and suburbs of London, from the reign of Henry VIII to that of James I*, Huguenot Society of London, 10/2 (1902), 113 · S. O'Connell, 'The Peel collection in New York', *Print Quarterly*, 15 (1998), 66–7 · A. Griffiths and R. A. Gerard, *The print in Stuart Britain, 1603–1689* (1998), 45–52 [exhibition catalogue, BM, 8 May – 20 Sept 1998]

Elsum, John (*fl.* 1700–1703), writer on painting, wrote two books: *Epigrams on the Paintings of the most Eminent Masters, Ancient and Modern* (1700; 2nd edn, 1705) and *The Art of Painting after the Italian Manner* (1703; reprinted in 1703 and 1704); both books argued painting's status as a liberal art. Drawing on Alberti, Giovanni Pietro Bellori, and C. A. Du Fresnoy, Elsum stressed painting's ability to refine natural beauty, suggesting in *The Art of Painting* that the rules of colour and proportion were 'the very soul and spirit of painting', which reveal the ideas in historical subjects. He also attacked fashion and the abuse of patronage in Britain, and advised on the appropriate display of different genres of painting. Nothing definite is known about his life. It is possible that this is the same person as the John Elsum who matriculated at Queen's College, Oxford, in 1667 aged sixteen, was bar-at-law at the Inner Temple, London, in 1673, and who died in London in 1714, bequeathing property and inherited estate to a nephew and a cousin.

NICHOLAS GRINDLE

Sources Foster, *Alum. Oxon.* · will, Family Record Centre, London, PROB 11/557.58 · C. A. Du Fresnoy, *De arte graphica / The art of painting*, trans. J. Dryden (1695)
Wealth at death title 'J. E. esq.' suggests property: *Epigrams on the paintings* (1700)

Elsynge, Henry (*bap.* 1577, *d.* 1635), parliamentary official, belonged to a family that came originally from Duxworth in Cambridgeshire and was baptized on 21 August 1577 at St Dunstan-in-the-West, London. He was the eldest of the three sons and second of the four children of another Henry Elsynge (*d.* 1582), merchant tailor of the same parish, and his wife, Frances, the daughter of Edmund Browne, also a merchant tailor of St Dunstan's. In 1584 Frances married Henry Knyvett (*d.* 1601), an elder half-brother of Robert *Bowyer, later clerk of the parliaments.

Elsynge was educated at St Alban's School. He entered Gonville and Caius College, Cambridge, as a pensioner on 14 October 1597 but did not graduate. He was admitted a student at the Middle Temple on 19 February 1597 and was called to the bar on 19 April 1605. In 1604 he was appointed, jointly with Robert Bowyer, keeper of the records in the Tower of London, an office that they held until 1612. On 27 November 1609 Bowyer succeeded to the office of clerk of the parliaments and shortly afterwards brought Elsynge to assist him in the House of Lords. On 1 September 1613 Elsynge was granted the reversion of the office of clerk of the parliaments, to which he succeeded on Bowyer's death on 15 March 1621. He held the office until his death, although he ceased to officiate in the House of Lords at the dissolution of parliament in March 1629. Thereafter he lived principally at his manor of Cornwell in Oxfordshire.

Elsynge played an important part in the codification of the procedure of the House of Lords and in the development and preservation of its records. His principal claim to recognition is as a scholar and historian of parliament, using the original documents to which his official positions at the Tower and at Westminster gave him access. His studies formed the basis of his treatise on parliament entitled *The Manner of Holding Parliaments in England, or, Modus tenendi parliamentum apud Anglos*, which remained unfinished at his death. Subsequently various parts have been published. Book 1 first appeared in 1660. A chapter on judicature, formerly attributed in error to John Selden, appeared in an imperfect form in 1681 and in a corrected version in 1990. A further chapter, *Expedicio billarum antiquitus*, was published in 1954, edited by Catherine S. Sims. A tract entitled *The Manner of Passing Bills in Parliament*, published in 1685, may have formed part of the same work. Elsynge's notes of debates in the House of Lords between 1621 and 1628 were published in 1870, 1879, and 1929.

Elsynge married on 12 July 1600 Blanche, or Alse (d. 1612), daughter of Richard Hyett and niece of Robert Bowyer. They had two sons of whom the elder, Henry *Elsynge (bap. 1606, d. 1656), was clerk of the House of Commons from 1639 to 1649. With his second wife, Jane, daughter of Richard Hardy of Dorset, Elsynge had a further four sons and one daughter. He died in 1635, probably in the month of November, as his will was dated 13 October 1635 and his successor was appointed on 1 December that year.

J. C. SAINTY

Sources M. F. Bond, 'The formation of the archives of parliament, 1497–1691', *Journal of the Society of Archivists*, 1 (1955–9), 151–8 · F. R. Foster, *The painful labour of Mr. Elsyng* (1972) · *Miscellanea genealogica et heraldica*, 4th ser., 5 (1904), 142 · *Collectanea Topographica et Genealogica*, 4 (1837), 103 · A. M. Burke, ed., *Memorials of St Margaret's Church, Westminster* (1914) · Venn, *Alum. Cant.*, 1/2.100 · H. A. C. Sturgess, ed., *Register of admissions to the Honourable Society of the Middle Temple, from the fifteenth century to the year 1944*, 3 vols. (1949), vol. 1, p. 372; vol. 2, p. 453 · PRO, PROB 11/170, fol. 28; C 66/2693 · parish register, London, St Dunstan-in-the-West, 21 Aug 1577 [baptism]
Archives BL, minute books of the House of Lords, Add. MSS 40085–40090 · BL, 'Modus tenendi parliamentum apud Anglos', Harley MS 1342; Add. MSS 26642–26643; Lansdowne MSS 489 (3), 492; Hg MSS 228, 255 (1) · CUL, treatise on judicature in parliament · HLRO, parliamentary papers, papers relating to parliamentary procedures · Inner Temple, London, corresp., annotated parliamentary journals, notes, and drafts mainly for 'Modus tenendi parliamentum apud Anglos' · NL Wales, 'Modus tenendi parliamentum apud Anglos', minutes of the House of Commons

Elsynge [Elsyng], **Henry** (*bap.* 1606, *d.* 1656), clerk of the House of Commons, was baptized on 2 March 1606 at St Dunstan-in-the-West, London, the elder of the two surviving sons of Henry *Elsynge (*bap.* 1577, *d.* 1635), clerk of the parliaments, and his wife, Blanche (*d.* 1612), daughter of Richard Hyett of Cornwell, Oxfordshire. Having been educated at Westminster School he matriculated at Christ Church, Oxford, on 24 July 1624, graduating BA on 22 June 1625. He was admitted a student at the Middle Temple on 24 November 1628 but was not called to the bar. He continued his education by spending seven years abroad acquiring proficiency in several languages. He married on 8 November 1636 Margaret Tyas (*d.* 1650), with whom he had at least two sons and three daughters.

For a time Elsynge acted as his father's assistant in the House of Lords and after his death in 1635 unsuccessfully petitioned the crown for the reversion of the office of clerk of the parliaments. Instead he obtained, through the influence of Archbishop Laud, the office of clerk of the House of Commons, his patent being dated 21 December 1639. He officiated first at the Short Parliament which met in April and May 1640 and then for the first eight years of the Long Parliament which began the following November, remaining at Westminster after the final break between the king and parliament in 1642. In this unprecedented situation Elsynge was required to exercise exceptional procedural and administrative skills. He numbered John Selden and Bulstrode Whitelocke among his intimate friends. Whitelocke described him as 'the most excellent Clerk, both to make and express the sense of the House that I believe ever sat there' (Whitelocke, 364).

Elsynge resigned his office in December 1648 ostensibly on grounds of poor health but in reality because he wanted no part in the proceedings against the king. He retired to Hounslow in Middlesex where he died; he was buried on 30 September 1656 at St Margaret's, Westminster. At the Restoration the House of Commons authorized a payment of £500 for the upkeep of his impoverished children.

The various parts of the treatise entitled *The Manner of Holding Parliaments in England, or, Modus tenendi parliamentum apud Anglos*, sometimes attributed to Elsynge, were in fact the work of his father and namesake.

J. C. SAINTY

Sources Wood, *Ath. Oxon.*, new edn, 3.363–5 · *JHC*, 6 (1648–51), 107, 111; 8 (1660–67), 231 · *Collectanea Topographica et Genealogica*, 4 (1837), 103 · *Miscellanea Genealogica et Heraldica*, 4th ser., 5 (1912–13), 142 · A. M. Burke, ed., *Memorials of St Margaret's Church, Westminster* (1914) · W. P. W. Phillimore and R. J. Fynmore, eds., *Kent parish registers: marriages*, 2 (1910), 109 · *Old Westminsters*, 1.311 · Foster, *Alum. Oxon.* · H. A. C. Sturgess, ed., *Register of admissions to the Honourable Society of the Middle Temple, from the fifteenth century to the year 1944*, 1 (1949), 121 · B. Whitelocke, *Memorials of the English affairs*, new edn (1732), 364
Archives BL, minute book of the House of Lords, Add. MS 40091 · BL, notes on parliamentary procedures, Harley MS 6585; Add. MSS 26644–26645 · NL Wales, notes, drafts, and papers relating to parliamentary history and procedures
Wealth at death died in relative poverty; House of Commons made provisions for his children in 1660; unemployed since 1649 resignation

Elton, Sir Arthur Hallam Rice, tenth baronet (1906–1973), film producer and director, was born in London on 10 February 1906, the elder son (there were no daughters) of Sir Ambrose Elton, ninth baronet (1869–1951), barrister, of Clevedon, and his wife, Dorothy Wynne (*d.* 1957), daughter of Arthur Robert Wiggin, of Oddington estate, Ceylon. He was educated at Marlborough College. From there, together with John Betjeman, he would cycle to Swindon to haunt the Great Western Railway yards and

Sir Arthur Hallam Rice Elton, tenth baronet (1906–1973), by Wolfgang Suschitzky, 1963

buy the first items in his collection of books on locomotives and industrial machinery. At Jesus College, Cambridge, he took third classes in the English tripos (1926) and the second part of the moral sciences tripos (1927), and acquired his other major passion, the cinema, as a film critic for *Granta*.

In 1927 Elton became a scriptwriter for Gainsborough Pictures Ltd, working in London and Germany. Four years later he was recruited by John Grierson for the Empire Marketing Board film unit (which was absorbed by the General Post Office film unit in 1933), and joined the group of enthusiasts who created the British documentary film movement. He was associated with many of their outstanding achievements, as an assistant director for the coalmining sequences of Robert J. Flaherty's *Industrial Britain* (1931), as director of films such as *Shadow on the Mountain* (1931), dealing with the study of grassland in the Welsh hills, and *Housing Problems* (1935), and after 1935 as a producer organizing the work of others for the General Post Office, the Gas Council, and the Ministry of Labour, which financed the innovatory work of the group. Elton's *Voice of the World* (1932), sponsored by His Master's Voice Gramophone Company, was the first instance of industrial sponsorship for the documentary film movement. Elton moved easily from his privileged landowning and Cambridge background into the factories and slums of the depression. He pioneered the use of direct film interviews on location in *Workers and Jobs* (1935) and won the confidence of working men and women. He carried his passion for machinery into the cinema in films such as *Aero Engine* (1933), which portrayed technology and industrial processes as vividly as other documentaries portrayed social conditions. In 1938 Grierson, Elton, and Basil Wright formed Film Centre Ltd to offer a consultative and managerial service for the producers and sponsors of documentary films.

During the war the government became responsible for most non-fictional film-making. In April 1940 the Ministry of Information asked Elton to become a supervisor of films. He soon brought order into a confusion of competing interests and personalities. He inspired the work of

creative directors and writers, while retaining the confidence of the civil servants, who feared that irresponsible film-makers might evade their budgetary controls. A steady stream of impressive propaganda films appeared from Elton's studios. In 1946 he was sent as film adviser to the Danish government and subsequently (1947) to the Allied Control Commission for Germany (British element). During the years 1943–5 he was chairman of the Scientific Films Association.

In 1947 Elton returned to Film Centre Ltd and became adviser to the Shell Petroleum Company for a number of years before being appointed production head of Shell Films in 1957. He made for Shell an outstanding group of short films on the history, achievement, and worldwide impact of British technology. Elton, together with Edgar Anstey at British Transport Films and for a few years Paul Rotha at the BBC, kept alive the spirit of the British documentary movement. Elton sent Shell cameramen to Egypt, India, Iraq, and Venezuela. He combined his enthusiasm for art and technology in works such as *The Flintknappers*, *The Chairbodgers*, *How an Aeroplane Flies*, and *Prospecting for Oil*. Future generations of historians will be grateful for his work in recording, as only moving pictures can, aspects of mid-twentieth-century British life and industry, with a combination of poetry and scientific insight that was essentially Elton. He will also be remembered for recognizing the importance of film as historical evidence in his address 'The film as source material for history' in 1955 (Association of Special Libraries and Information Bureaus, *Proceedings*, 7/4, 1955). Elton was a tireless advocate of the need to preserve film as carefully as literary source materials and he served as a governor of the British Film Institute, 1948–9.

In 1948 Elton married Margaret Ann Bjornson (1915–1995), a historian, daughter of Dr Olafur Bjornson, professor of obstetrics at the University of Manitoba. They had two daughters and a son. After inheriting the family title and estates when his father died in 1951, Elton devoted himself to local affairs at Clevedon, Somerset, and returned to roots markedly different from his life in industry. He restored Clevedon Court, dating from 1320 and occupied by Eltons from 1709, and handed the house over to the National Trust in 1960. As chairman of the Clevedon Printing Company, he helped to run the *North Somerset Mercury*. The technical skill that he had devoted to the house was next dedicated to the project to rebuild Clevedon pier, an outstanding Victorian iron structure that collapsed in 1970. It is unlikely that any other small community has contained architectural features as different as Clevedon Court and the pier, together with a local squire with the knowledge and energy to care for both.

Elton was a lifelong collector of industrial art, artefacts, and literature. Edgar Anstey said that 'a constant theme in his life was a love of order' and he reduced to order his unique collection of pictures, prints, books, and objects recording British industrial development. After his death the collection, valued at over £250,000, was passed to the Ironbridge Museum in Shropshire. Elton had sponsored exhibitions in industrial art and archaeology before they became fashionable in the 1970s. In 1968 he revised and reissued *Art and the Industrial Revolution*, written by his friend Francis Klingender and first published in 1947. Elton was the outstanding builder of bridges between 'the two cultures' of the arts and the sciences.

Elton's appearance was as impressive as his personality. He stood well over 6 feet tall, with a broad frame, usually dressed informally even in the City, surmounted by blond hair and beard. He carried himself like a viking, and made a strong impression even before he began to pour out his enthusiasms. The powerful exterior concealed a basic shyness: he did not make friends easily and could sometimes appear obstinate and overbearing when he tried to overcome this reserve. He would rather wound a susceptibility than lose a cause. But he was unfailingly kind and generous to those he trusted. Elton was a remarkably gifted man, who believed that his good fortune in being born with these talents in a comfortable home carried with it an obligation to serve his fellow men. He was a pioneer whose work in non-fictional film, in 'the aesthetics of technology', and in film and history, was developed extensively in the decade after his death.

Elton died in Bristol on 1 January 1973. His only son, Charles Abraham Grierson (*b.* 1953), succeeded to the baronetcy. D. J. WENDEN, *rev.* SARAH STREET

Sources I. Aitken, *Film and reform: John Grierson and the documentary film movement* (1990) · private information (1986) · *The Times* (2 Jan 1973) · WWW · Burke, *Peerage*
Archives General Post Office Archive, London · Ironbridge Gorge Museum Library and Archives, Telford, collections relating to transport and industrial revolution · University of Stirling, corresp. with John Grierson | FILM BFI NFTVA
Likenesses W. Suschitzky, photograph, 1963, NPG [*see illus.*] · E. Disher, portrait, Clevedon Court, Somerset · J. M. Heaton, portrait, Clevedon Court, Somerset · C. Morris, portrait, Clevedon Court, Somerset

Elton, Sir Charles Abraham, sixth baronet (1778–1853), poet and theologian, was born in Bristol on 31 October 1778, the eldest of three sons of the Revd Sir Abraham Elton (1755–1842), fifth baronet and heir to a large Bristol mercantile fortune, and his first wife, Elizabeth (*d.* 1822), daughter of Sir John Durbin, a Bristol merchant. Charles Elton's only sister, Julia Maria (1807–1840), married Henry Hallam (1777–1859), the historian. On leaving Eton College in 1793 Elton was commissioned in the 48th regiment of foot, rising to the rank of captain; he was later colonel of the Somerset militia. On 27 February 1804 he married Sarah (*d.* 1830), daughter of Joseph Smith, a Bristol merchant; they had five sons and eight daughters; the two eldest sons were drowned while bathing near Weston-super-Mare in 1819. The youngest daughter, Jane [*see* Brookfield, Jane Octavia], became a successful literary hostess and writer.

In the same year as his marriage Charles Elton brought out a volume of poems; his literary output over the next two decades included *The Brothers, a Monody* (1820), following the death of his sons, and translations from classical authors, among them Hesiod and Propertius. His most important publication was a critically acclaimed anthology of Latin and Greek verse, *Specimens of the Classic Poets* (3 vols., 1814).

In 1818 Elton published *An Appeal to Scripture and Tradition in Defence of the Unitarian Faith*. His forebears, powerful figures in Bristol politics, had been dissenters and leading members of the Presbyterian (later Unitarian) congregation that met in Bridge Street and subsequently in Lewin's Mead. He dedicated the *Appeal* to the Revd Lant Carpenter (1780–1840), minister at Lewin's Mead, and explained in letters to him how respect for his father's feelings led to hesitancy in acknowledging his changed views by public worship with the Unitarians, but conscience obliged him to concede the correctness of their views. The Unitarians had welcomed his accession and were correspondingly outraged when in 1827 he published *Deuterai phrontides: Second Thoughts on the Person of Christ, on Human Sin, and on the Atonement*. Lant Carpenter was deeply disturbed by what Harriet Martineau (1802–1876) called Elton's 'shameless book' (letter to James Martineau, 14 May 1827, Martineau papers). The long rebuttal, 'Elton vs. Elton' by the Revd Robert Aspland (1782–1845), published over several numbers of the *Christian Reformer* in 1827, pointed out that Elton continued to distance himself from certain points of church doctrine, but did not hide disappointment and even contempt at the desertion. Elton attributed his recantation to his having read works on philosophical necessity and (as he had explained his earlier adoption of Unitarianism) to close study of the Bible. His rejection of necessitarian views of evil must have been affected by the accidental deaths of his sons, although other publications between 1819 and 1827 show a continuity in his Unitarian opinions.

Following his wife's death in 1830, Elton published no more, living a largely secluded life. In 1842 he succeeded to the baronetcy and to the picturesque family house, Clevedon Court, Somerset. He died in Bath on 1 June 1853; the funeral took place on 7 June at Clevedon church, where he was buried. R. K. WEBB

Sources Burke, *Peerage* (1970) · C. A. Elton, letters to L. Carpenter, Harris Man. Oxf., Carpenter papers [one undated, one dated 8 Sept 1818] · Harris Man. Oxf., Martineau papers · [R. Aspland], *Elton versus Elton* (1828) · GM, 2nd ser., 3 (1835), 359–60 · GM, 2nd ser., 17 (1842), 665 · GM, 2nd ser., 40 (1853), 88–9 · S. R. Matthews, 'Elton, Abraham', HoP, Commons, 1715–54
Archives Harris Man. Oxf., letters to Lant Carpenter
Likenesses miniature, *c.*1804, Clevedon Court, Somerset · T. Barker, oils (in youth), Clevedon Court, Somerset · E. Bird, oils, Clevedon Court, Somerset
Wealth at death under £10,000: PRO

Elton, Charles Isaac (1839–1900), lawyer and antiquary, was born on 6 December 1839 at Southampton, the eldest son of Frederick Bayard Elton of Clifton, Gloucestershire, magistrate and collector in India, and Mary Elizabeth, daughter of Sir Charles Abraham *Elton of Clevedon, Somerset, sixth baronet, poet. His parents were members of the same old west country landed family. He was educated at Cheltenham College under the headship of William Dobson, and at Balliol College, Oxford, where he matriculated as a commoner in 1857. He took a first class in classical moderations in 1859, a second class in *literae humaniores*, and a first class in law and history in 1861. He graduated BA in 1862, and the same year won the Vinerian law scholarship and was elected to an open fellowship at Queen's (1862–4). He entered Lincoln's Inn on 7 June 1862. On 6 August 1863 he married Mary Augusta, daughter of Richard Strachey of Ashwick Grove, Somerset; they had no children.

Elton was called to the bar on 17 November 1865 and went on to practise at the Chancery bar. Early in his career he attracted the attention of Sir George Jessel by his quick application of a passage of Henry de Bracton's treatise on English law to a case in which Jessel was employed. Elton did not have to wait for briefs long. He had been a rigorous student of black-letter law, and his great powers of concentration and tenacious memory combined to gain him a reputation as one of the most erudite lawyers of his generation. It was largely due to his acumen and research, presented in letters to *The Times*, that the chapter of Christ Church, Oxford, was induced (in February 1865) to carry out a moral obligation imposed upon them by a conveyance from Henry VIII to endow the chair of the regius professor of Greek. Elton rapidly acquired a large conveyancing and equity practice, and was largely employed in court work in real property cases. In 1885 he was made a queen's counsel, and in 1887 he became a bencher of his inn. He then practised as a 'special'.

Elton was a man of many interests. In 1869 he succeeded somewhat unexpectedly under the will of his uncle, R. J. Elton, to the Whitestaunton estate near Chard in Somerset. As lord of the manor, owner of a house ranging in date from Edward IV to Elizabeth I, and with the remains of a Roman villa in his grounds, he had ample opportunities to satisfy his exceptionally varied tastes. He wrote a paper on the Roman villa which was published by *The Academy*, 1 September 1883. He was a big, burly man, his appearance giving the impression of a west country yeoman. He was fond of all field sports, and took a practical interest in farming. In a by-election on 15 February 1884 he was elected MP for Somerset. He was defeated by Sir Thomas Acland for the Wellington division in 1885, but secured re-election in 1886, retiring in 1892. A Conservative, he seldom spoke in parliament except on legal subjects, but served on several important committees and royal commissions.

Elton read omnivorously and spent much time in writing on historical, archaeological, legal, and literary topics. He was an original member of the Selden Society (29 January 1887), and an FSA (7 June 1883). His large and wide-ranging library contained many rare books and some fine specimens of sixteenth- to eighteenth-century binding. In 1891, in conjunction with his wife, he privately printed a catalogue of a portion of his library, and in 1893 he wrote *Great Book Collectors* in collaboration with his wife. He was an enthusiastic collector and a good judge of *objets d'art*. On 26 March 1901 his collection of old Damascus, Rhodian, Persian, and Anatolian Faience was sold at Christies for about £2000.

Elton died at Whitestaunton of pneumonia, after a short illness, on 23 April 1900. He was survived by his wife. Elton wrote eleven books. His first, *Norway, the Road and the Fell* (1864), was published before he was called to the bar. His fourth book, *The Law of Copyholds* (1874), gave him the reputation of being one of the first English jurists of the historical school, and his sixth volume, *Origins of English History* (1882), was judged 'a brilliant and trustworthy work' by the *Spectator*. Other books dealt with various aspects of tenure; there was one on Christopher Columbus (1892) and his last, published posthumously in 1904, was on Shakespeare.   J. B. ATLAY, rev. BETH F. WOOD

Sources A. Lang, in C. Elton, *Shakespeare, his family and friends* (1904), 1–18 · *The Times* (24 April 1900), 6 · *Solicitors' Journal*, 44 (1899–1900), 405–6 · *ILN* (1 March 1884), 200–05 · L. C. Sanders, *Celebrities of the century: being a dictionary of men and women of the nineteenth century* (1887) · Boase, *Mod. Eng. biog.* · *WWBMP* · J. Foster, *Men-at-the-bar: a biographical hand-list of the members of the various inns of court*, 2nd edn (1885) · Foster, *Alum. Oxon.* · E. Abbott and L. Campbell, *The life and letters of Benjamin Jowett*, 1 (1897), 319 · C. Elton, letter, *The Times* (25 Nov 1864), 5 · C. Elton, letter, *The Times* (16 Jan 1865), 5
Archives BL, corresp., Add. MS 60635
Likenesses Spy [L. Ward], caricature, chromolithograph, NPG; repro. in *VF* (6 Aug 1877) · portrait (after a photograph by W. C. Waldron), repro. in *ILN*
Wealth at death £4466 0s. 9d.: probate, 6 Dec 1900, *CGPLA Eng. & Wales*

Elton, Charles Sutherland (1900–1991), animal ecologist, was born on 29 March 1900 at Withington, Manchester, the youngest of the three children, all sons, of Oliver *Elton (1861–1945), literary scholar and translator, and his wife, Letitia Maynard (1865–1948), writer, daughter of the Revd Dugald MacColl of Glasgow and his wife, Janet Mathieson. The Elton forebears were from Cheshire, and later from near Ledbury, Herefordshire. His maternal great-grandmother, Janet Sutherland, from the east coast of Sutherland, was the source (via his uncle, Dugald Sutherland MacColl, the watercolour artist) of his middle name.

Education and early ecological research Elton's youthful zest for natural history was actively encouraged and directed by his eldest brother, Geoffrey, seven years his senior, who was to die suddenly in 1927, aged thirty-four, and to whom he dedicated his first and most famous book, *Animal Ecology* (1927). Eight long summer family holidays spent on the Eastnor estate in the Malvern hills also had a huge influence on his outlook.

Military training dominated Elton's schooldays at Liverpool College (1913–18), but he immersed himself in Darwin's *Origin of Species* and in the complete works of Alfred Russel Wallace. On leaving school he was called up briefly into the Royal Engineers, signal training service, before going up to New College, Oxford, in 1919, to read zoology under E. S. Goodrich. Elton and others rebelled against the continuing emphasis, in zoology then, on comparative anatomy and descriptive embryology. In any spare time he studied the behaviour and life histories of living animals in a large number of ponds near his Liverpool home and also in the Lake District and near Oxford. He used his windowsill in New College for early experiments on the warning colours of water mites.

Charles Sutherland Elton (1900–1991), self-portrait, 1968

balanced treatment of a subject with copious references to both sides of an argument. (Macfadyen, 500)

'It was when he dropped his voice and became least audible that he made his most profound and original remarks' (Crowcroft, 142).

Soon after the last Spitsbergen expedition, Elton produced his first book, *Animal Ecology* (1927), about general principles regulating animal communities. 'Elton ... set out to turn natural history into science, and that, of course, is what ecology is: the quantitative and experimental study of living organisms in relation to their environments' (Hardy, 'Influence', 3). Great clarity and deceptive simplicity of language and style mark out this classic work, which had a major influence on generations of young biologists the world over. Reprinted nine times (and republished with a new preface and 'selected later reading' in 1966) it was still in print more than fifty years later, and was translated into Russian, Polish, Spanish, and Japanese. It was republished in North America in 2001.

Investigating population fluctuations The second main line of research which engaged Elton and colleagues for many years was into fluctuations in numbers, and at times plagues, of animals and the importance of movements of their populations. His participation in the 1930 Oxford University expedition to Lapland fuelled his interest in this problem. These fluctuations can be of serious economic and epidemiological importance, so Elton and his colleagues carried out intensive investigations into the population dynamics of mice and voles in Bagley Wood, near Oxford, from 1923 to 1931. About the same time he had begun extensive research into the roughly ten yearly and three to four yearly cycles of Canadian wildlife, notably those of the fur bearing mammals. They all hit the bottom of their cycles in 1931. Elton, in his broad survey *Voles, Mice and Lemmings: Problems in Population Dynamics* (1942), described the poverty this caused in northern Labrador. Added to the trough of the worldwide depression, this hit projects like the Oxford work. Elton had been the Hudson Bay Company's biological consultant since 1925, and now took part in an international conference on biological cycles called at the remote fishing village of Matamek, on the north shore of the Gulf of St Lawrence. One result was that the New York Zoological Society gave financial support to the Oxford work. To this the Royal Society added a large sum for research on vole populations, and in 1932 Elton, as director, was able to start his Bureau of Animal Population; it was primarily to act as a clearing house for information on population changes in Canadian wildlife, but also to be a centre for the study of mammalian populations (mainly rodents at first). However, despite many decades of research on both sides of the Atlantic on the problems of cycling / fluctuating mammalian populations, the mechanism was still not satisfactorily resolved within Elton's lifetime.

On the outbreak of the Second World War in 1939 the bureau (with its expertise in the study of mice and voles) was switched to research, under the Agricultural Research Council, into effective control of rodents and

Fired with enthusiasm for polar exploration after the reports and films of Scott's and Shackleton's pre- and mid-war expeditions, a group of young biologists and geologists, most of them from Oxford University, set up the Oxford University expedition to Spitsbergen (Svalbard) in 1921. Invited by his tutor, Julian Huxley, to join it as his assistant, Elton, then a second-year undergraduate, was in fact given a free hand to do his own work. This expedition, followed by two more in 1923 and 1924, was to have the most profound influence on Elton's thinking and ideas about animal communities and interactions within them, in this high latitude, isolated land that was 'heavily glaciated, ice-bound for most of the year and some parts even in summer' (Elton MSS, A47, 1). He worked closely with V. S. Summerhayes, a botanist from University College, London, and veteran of the battle of the Somme. Summerhayes and Elton, publishing in the *Journal of Ecology* in 1923 and 1928, found that the effect on climate of the Gulf Stream meeting the polar ice-pack in Spitsbergen was reflected in four life zones for both the plant and animal communities. In 1927 Elton was a founding member of the Oxford University Exploration Club. In 1929 he was awarded the Royal Geographical Society's Murchison grant for his three seasons' study of the distribution of life in Spitsbergen.

After taking first-class honours in zoology in 1922 Elton was appointed departmental demonstrator in 1923, university demonstrator in 1929, and finally university reader in animal ecology and senior research fellow of Corpus Christi College in 1936, posts he held until his retirement in 1967. In his statutory lectures to undergraduates his scholarly teaching was, much later, considered to be

marked by a complete lack of dogmatism. ... One felt that to tell his audience what to think would have appeared to him to be insulting. ... He always gave a carefully researched and rabbits to protect the nation's foodstuffs. 'The Bureau team, under Elton's low-key but powerful leadership, introduced some novel ideas into British rodent control' (Crowcroft, 29). A most generous anonymous donor (much later revealed, by Crowcroft, as Sir John Ellerman, second baronet) enabled the results of the bureau's war work to be published in 1954 as *The Control of Rats and Mice*, in three volumes (the first two, on *Rats*, edited by D. H. Chitty, and the third, on *House Mice*, edited by H. N. Southern). Elton provided a masterly introduction and overview to this work.

During the war Elton and other ecologists were also looking forward to the post-war reconstruction period and planning the practical aspects of future national nature reserves. With A. G. Tansley and Captain C. Diver he played a major part in the report of the Wildlife Conservation Special Committee (1947), chaired by J. S. Huxley. Much of its advice was accepted by the government, and the Nature Conservancy was established in 1949, under the privy council. Elton was a member of its scientific policy committee from 1949 to 1956, and was closely involved with the Nature Conservancy throughout its sixteen-year existence.

In the light of his long-standing interest in zoogeography (on which he lectured to undergraduates, as well as on animal ecology), Elton outlined his own ideas on conservation and invasion biology in *The Ecology of Invasions by Animals and Plants* (1958, republished in North America in 2000). He showed how Wallace's realms had been broken down over the previous 200 years following the huge increase in, and speed of, man's mobility all over the world, with many animal and plant species becoming pests in their new homes and new food chains replacing old ones. He maintained that ecological principles had to be applied to practical conservation (and gave three BBC broadcasts about this in 1957): 'Conservation', he believed, 'should mean the keeping or putting in the landscape of the greatest possible ecological variety—in the world, in every continent or island, and so far as practicable in every district … provided the native species have their place' (*Ecology of Invasions*, 155).

Studying complex communities Fresh opportunities arose after the war for Elton to develop research into more complex animal communities, since Oxford University had just acquired the nearby Wytham estate, with roughly 1000 acres of deciduous woodland and grassland and small freshwater bodies. In 1949 Elton, as president of the British Ecological Society, gave an inspired address, 'Population interspersion: an essay on animal community patterns' (published in the *Journal of Ecology* in 1949), in which he envisaged a continuing ecological survey which was to study all groups of animals and all kinds of habitat, involving plant ecologists as well. He thought that the newly founded Nature Conservancy might set up active research centres where ecologists' data and notes on communities and species could be accumulated and used scientifically. The computerized Biological Records Centre at Monks Wood, near Huntingdon, later did just that, though its primary task was the mapping of species' distribution.

At first Elton's ecological survey covered Oxfordshire, Berkshire, and Buckinghamshire, but later it concentrated on the Wytham area, contributions to the whole picture being made by some of his staff, visiting scientists, and graduate students. With R. S. Miller, an American postgraduate from Colorado, Elton developed for ecological survey a practical system of habitat classification by structural characters (published in the *Journal of Ecology* in 1954). In his *magnum opus*, *The Pattern of Animal Communities* (1966), Elton set out to assess all that had been revealed using these methods over the previous twenty years. Besides bird and mammal populations (using the whole wood), communities in many kinds of minor habitats had thrown light on the larger canvas of interactions, which he referred to as a 'girder system' of partly interlocking community units which might show 'ecological resistance'.

Just before and after retirement Elton went on several expeditions to tropical South America and to Montserrat in the West Indies to experience and study, though very briefly, the complexity and diversity of tropical rain forest—at the opposite extreme from his Spitsbergen tundra communities. The results of his studies were published in articles in the *Journal of Animal Ecology* in 1973, and in *Biological Conservation* in 1975.

Elton had founded the *Journal of Animal Ecology* in 1932, continuing as editor until 1951. In his honour, after his retirement, the British Ecological Society published the February 1968 issue of the journal as a Festschrift, consisting entirely of papers (all, as usual, rigorously refereed) by members and ex-members of the Bureau of Animal Population. The bureau had become a world centre for research in terrestrial animal ecology, attracting younger research workers 'who carried the Elton tradition to distant places' (Hardy, 'Elton, Charles'). It had been properly established in 1947 as part of the administrative department of zoological field studies, under the sympathetic chairmanship of the newly appointed Linacre professor of zoology and comparative anatomy, Alister Clavering Hardy (of plankton recorder fame). The essence of the bureau was bound up with Elton's genius as a field naturalist and observer, with his breadth of scholarship, his worldwide appreciation of the nature of learning, and with his insight as a scientist, and it ceased to exist when he retired. (An insect physiologist, J. W. S. Pringle, was by then the Linacre professor.)

Besides the books already noted, Elton published *Animal Ecology and Evolution* (1930, from three lectures at University College, London), *Ecology of Animals* (1933), and *Exploring the Animal World* (1933, BBC talks for amateur naturalists), and some book reviews which were, at times, hard hitting. All but one of his books were translated into several languages. He also wrote ninety-eight articles (most published in scientific journals), of which twenty-eight were either co-authored or edited by him. There are thirty-four unpublished natural history notebooks in the Bodleian Library. He was honoured by eight American scientific bodies, including the New York Zoological Society, of which he became an honorary member in 1931, and the

Ecological Society of America (life member and eminent ecologist award, 1961); he also received the John and Alice Tyler ecology award (1976) and the Edward W. Browning award (1977) for conserving the environment. Honours from British scientific societies included honorary membership of the British Ecological Society (1960), fellowship of the Royal Society (1953) and its Darwin medal (1970), and the Linnean Society's gold medal (1967).

Elton's first marriage, in 1928, was to Rose Montague (1906–1997); this marriage, without issue, was dissolved amicably in 1937. On 1 December of the same year he married (Edith) Joy *Scovell (1907–1999), the poet, and daughter of the Revd Frederick George Scovell, vicar of St Andrew's Church, Sharrow, Sheffield. They had a daughter, Catherine Ingrid (b. 1940), a nurse, and a son, Robert Andrew (b. 1943), a medical statistician.

Character and memorials Of medium height and build Elton had, by middle age, lost much of the hair from 'his heavy thoughtful head'—as his wife put it in her poem *A Naturalist* (E. J. Scovell, *Collected Poems*, 1988, 87). Fair skinned, blue-eyed, and clean-shaven, and usually a very serious man, he 'was never an easy person to know' (*The Times*, 7 May 1991). His mild manner and quiet voice belied his underlying toughness, and he came to be known, in a friendly way, as 'The Boss' by staff and students in the post-war bureau. He could not abide crowds and, even in his fifties, refused to attend meetings with more than thirty people present, so in 1976 had to receive the munificent Tyler award in Los Angeles by proxy. He hated unauthorized photography and in the early 1970s refused to sit for his portrait to be painted with three other eminent former colleagues for a set piece commissioned for the new zoology building—'I don't intend to adorn the walls of the Sistine Chapel!' (private information). However, Denys Kempson's portrait photographs of him were hung in Oxford University's department of zoology and Corpus Christi College.

Having lived all his adult life in Oxford, Elton died at St Luke's Nursing Home, Latimer Road, Oxford, on 1 May 1991, following a stroke. His funeral service took place at Oxford crematorium on 4 May 1991. He was survived by his wife and two children.

Four animals bear Elton's name: *Camptocladius eltoni*, a small chironomid fly (with aquatic larvae), collected by Elton on Bear Island in 1921 and described by Edwards in 1922; *Micaria eltoni*, a male spider, collected by Elton at Klaas Billen Bay, Spitsbergen, in 1921 and described by Jackson in 1922; *Enchytraeus eltoni*, a small, white enchytraeid worm, collected by Elton at Liefde Bay, Spitsbergen, in 1923 and described by Stephenson in 1924; and *Eutrombicula* (S. G. *Eltonella*) *eltoni*, a tropical forest trombiculid mite (ectoparasitic on a scorpion in Malaya), described by Audy in 1956. The last was

> named for Charles Elton F.R.S. to whom ecologists and epidemiologists must be grateful for ideas and guiding principles in the sphere of animal ecology, and to whom the present writer is indebted in many ways, not the least being the example set of lucidity in writing on ecological subjects without a trace of the jargon and monstrous Greek

> derivatives which have ministered by cryptology and neologism to an esoteric obfuscation of ecological neoconcepts. (Audy, *Bulletin of the Raffles Museum*, 28, 1956, 36)

Two ecological concepts, from Elton's first book, have also had his name appended to them by later writers: the 'Eltonian Pyramid of Numbers', and the 'Eltonian concept of Niche' (as an animal's role in a community, contrasting with the habitat-niche used by the American ecologist J. Grinnell and others). The Elton Library, situated in the Bodleian's zoology library, houses the Bureau of Animal Population library, its research photographs and archives, and Elton's and the bureau's publications. Elton's Spitsbergen material and Wytham ecological survey material are now in the Hope collections in the Oxford University Museum of Natural History.   KITTY PAVIOUR-SMITH

Sources Bodl. Oxf., MSS Elton · *WWW*, 1991–5 · *The Times* (7 May 1991) · *The Independent* (13 May 1991) · *The Guardian* (13 May 1991) · *Daily Telegraph* (26 Oct 1999) · A. Macfadyen, 'Obituary: Charles Sutherland Elton', *Journal of Animal Ecology*, 61 (1992), 499–502 · A. Hardy, 'Charles Elton's influence in ecology', *Journal of Animal Ecology*, 37 (1968), 3–8 · A. C. H. [A. C. Hardy], 'Elton, Charles', *Encyclopaedia Britannica*, 15th edn · 'Charles S. Elton: eminent ecologist', *Bulletin of the Ecological Society of America*, 42/4 (1961), 124–8 · B. Campbell, 'Elton: modest ecomaster', *The Countryman*, 88/2 (1983–4), 65–70 · E. Dunn, 'On top of the pyramid', *The Countryman*, 97/1 (1992), 116–17 · J. Sheail, *Seventy-five years in ecology: the British Ecological Society* (1987) · P. Crowcroft, *Elton's ecologists: a history of the Bureau of Animal Population* (1991) · C. Elton, *Voles, mice and lemmings* (1942) · R. Southwood and J. R. Clarke, *Memoirs FRS*, 45 (1999), 129–46 · D. Simberloff, 'Foreword', in C. S. Elton, *The ecology of invasions by animals and plants* (2000), vii–xiv · private information (2004) · personal knowledge (2004) · b. cert. · d. cert. · autobiographical notes, Bodl. Oxf., CE Archive A33

Archives Bodl. Oxf., corresp. and papers | ICL, corresp. with J. W. Munro · Oxf. U. Mus. NH, Hope, Spitsbergen and Wytham ecological survey material · Rice University, Houston, Texas, Woodson Research Center, corresp. with Sir Julian S. Huxley

Likenesses D. A. Kempson, photographs, 1926–53, repro. in Crowcroft, *Elton's ecologists*, 7, 64, 146 · D. A. Kempson, photograph, 1948, repro. in Hardy, 'Charles Elton's influence', frontispiece · D. A. Kempson, photographs, c.1960, U. Oxf., zoology department · C. S. Elton, self-portrait, photograph, 1968, repro. in *The Times* [see illus.] · C. S. Elton, self-portrait, photograph, 1968, repro. in *The Independent* · W. Vandivert, photograph, c.1973–1974, repro. in *The Guardian* · W. Vandivert, photograph, c.1973–1974, repro. in *The Smithsonian*, 5 (May 1974) · photographs, Bodl. Oxf., MSS Elton

Wealth at death £145,822: probate, 1 July 1991, *CGPLA Eng. & Wales*

Elton, Edward (c.1569–1624), Church of England clergyman, was born in Shropshire or Herefordshire into a family of at least four sons, possibly the son of John Elton (d. 1613). He attended the same, but unidentified, grammar school as John Brinsley senior, and matriculated at Christ's College, Cambridge, as a pensioner in 1585, taking his BA in 1589 and MA in 1592, proceeding to BD at Magdalene College, Cambridge, in 1599. His first preferment was to the depopulated parish of Thorpe-le-Glebe, Nottinghamshire, in August 1601, which he resigned in 1606, having been appointed to the rectory of St Mary Magdalen, Bermondsey, Surrey, in January 1605. His ministry in this crowded and poverty-stricken suburb became his life's work although, as several fulsome prefaces to his books indicate, he was not of robust health and his exertions in preaching and pastoral work took their toll. At least three curates are known to have assisted as lecturers during Elton's ministry, but Elton was continuously resident, marrying there Mrs Katherine Ryther (d. 1619) on 24 September 1605, their ten children being baptized in the parish church. Of these only Edward, the eldest (1606–1623), and a daughter, Elizabeth, survived infancy.

Elton's publications were all founded on courses of sermons and catechetical exercises at Bermondsey. These works were to earn him the admiration of Richard Baxter, who in 1667 placed Elton as one of the major figures from the great age of English puritan writing, alongside such as William Perkins, Richard Greenham, and John Dod: one of those whose 'solid, grave and pious labours … are by the most neglected, as if we were quite above their parts' (N. H. Keeble and G. F. Nuttall, eds., *Calendar of the Correspondence of Richard Baxter*, 1991, 2.57). First to appear was *An Exposition of the Epistle of St Paule to the Colossians* (1615), dedicated to Rowland Traps, the owner of the living, where he already mentions his 'knowne debilitie of body' and sets out his stylistic and didactic approach. The same year also saw the first appearance of Elton's most popular work, *A Forme of Catechizing* (1616), running to ten editions up to 1634, in which he takes a firmly puritan position. A similar work followed in 1619, *A Plaine and Easie Exposition of Six of the Commandements*, expanded to cover all ten commandments in a new edition of 1623, in which he reiterates his fervent opposition to maypoles, which was still recalled in 1660 (Hall, 27). This particular strictness met opposition from more traditional parishioners, and when in 1617 Elton preached repeatedly against their new pole, which they had agreed to erect for only a fortnight, and gathered a band to cut it down and carry it to his yard, he and his followers were brought before Star Chamber. In 1618 appeared the first of Elton's detailed commentaries upon the epistle to the Romans, chapters 7–9, *The Complaint of a Sanctified Sinner Answered*, followed by *The Triumph of a True Christian Described* (1623) and posthumously by *The Great Mystery of Godliness Opened* (1653). Elton's puritanism was again evident in his preface to a new edition of James Balmford's *A Modest Reply to Certain Answeres* (1623), where Balmford continued a long-running debate with Thomas Gataker on the morality of casting lots, which Balmford supported, but Elton, while describing both these neighbour ministers as dear friends, opposed.

Elton's strict interpretation of the commandments pursued him beyond the grave, when in 1624 Daniel Featley was called to account for licensing the posthumous *Gods Holy Minde Touching Matters Morall* and its associated work *A Plaine and Easie Exposition upon the Lords Prayer* (1624). The accounts of J. Featley and his printer Robert Milbourne (*Featley Revived*, 1–9, 39–41) report that Featley had looked only at the text set up before Elton's death, and had seen nothing objectionable, but the king had questioned Featley on the work, and they claimed that, for its views of the sabbath and deathbed communion, more than 800 copies were burned at Paul's Cross on 13 February 1625. The work was republished, unamended, in 1647.

Elton died at the rectory, Bermondsey, Surrey, in September 1624 and was buried at the church of St Mary Magdalen, Bermondsey, on 6 September, sharing a grave and a monumental inscription with Jeremiah Whitaker, the puritan who replaced Elton's Laudian successor Thomas Paske. His will shows regard for his college and parish, and modest riches in the ownership of a house, and, in two bequests to his 'nursekeepers', considerable frailty.

R. A. CHRISTOPHERS

Sources Venn, *Alum. Cant.*, 1/1 · will, PRO, 73 Byrde, PROB 11/144, fols. 58–9 · parish registers, Bermondsey, 1548–1609, LMA, P71/MMG/3; pubd. in *The Genealogist*, new ser., 6–9 (1906) · Bermondsey churchwardens' and overseers' accounts, Southwark public library, MS 1678 · complaint against Elton and others for cutting down maypole, 1617, PRO, STAC 8/21/12 · D. Featley, *Cygnea cantio* (1629) · J. Featley, *Featlaei … or, Doctor Daniel Featley revived* (1660) [Thomason tract E1937/2] · T. Hall, *Funebria floriæ* (1660) · S. B. Lewicowicz, 'Elton's "An exposition of the ten commandements of God" (1623): a burnt book ?', *Proceedings of the Bibliographical Society of America*, 71 (1977), 201–8 · W. Rendle, *Old Southwark and its people* (1878) · E. T. Clarke, *Bermondsey: its history, memories and associations* (1902) · J. Brinsley, *The third part of the true watch* (1622) · J. Balmford, *A modest reply to certaine answeres* (1623) · Arber, *Regs. Stationers* · I. Green, *The Christian's ABC: catechisms and catechising in England, c.1530–1740* (1996)

Wealth at death over £500—house(s) in Bermondsey; residuary estate left to daughter: will, PRO, PROB 11/144, fols. 58–9

Elton, Edward William [*real name* Edward William Elt] (1794–1843), actor, whose real name was Elt, was born in August 1794 in London, in the parish of Lambeth. He was trained for the law in the office of a solicitor named Springhall in Verulam Buildings, Gray's Inn. His father, who was a schoolmaster in the neighbourhood of Tottenham Court Road, organized plays among his scholars, and as a youth Elton acted in these, first at the Sans Souci Theatre in Leicester Place, and then at Pym's private theatre, Wilson Street, Gray's Inn Lane. After joining a strolling company he appeared in 1823 as utility actor at the Olympic in Joseph Lunn's *A Fish out of Water*, where he made the acquaintance of Tyrone Power. At Christmas he went to the Liverpool Amphitheatre, where the following year, after a summer engagement at Birmingham, under Alfred Bunn, he played Napoleon in the spectacle of *The Battle of Waterloo*. He then played Cominius in *Coriolanus* at the Theatre Royal, Liverpool. After starring in Chester, Worcester, Shrewsbury, and elsewhere, he attracted in Manchester the favourable notice of Charles Mayne Young, with whom he appeared in Norwich and Cambridge.

In 1831 Elton's career was established by his appearance at the Garrick Theatre in Whitechapel, where he opened under Conquest and Wynn in *Richard III*. He enjoyed great popularity from 1832 to 1836 in the East End at both the Strand and the Surrey theatres. An unsuccessful engagement at the Haymarket in 1833, under David Morris, came to a speedy termination. Elton then returned to the minor theatres, and in the spring of 1836 was at the Adelphi. In January 1837 he took the title role of *Walter Tyrell*, at Covent Garden, under Osbaldiston's management, to considerable acclaim. On the production, on 26 June 1837, at the Haymarket of *The Bridal*, adapted by Sheridan Knowles from *The Maid's Tragedy* of Beaumont and Fletcher, he gained much credit as Amintor. He was then engaged at Covent Garden, where he created the original Beauseant in Bulwer-Lytton's *The Lady of Lyons*, one of several original parts. From 1839 he was a member of W. C. Macready's company at Drury Lane, where he played Romeo and Rolla, and was the original Rizzio in Haynes's *Mary Stuart*. After some work in the minor theatres, he returned in 1841–2 with Macready to Drury Lane. He also fulfilled a month's engagement at William Murray's Edinburgh Theatre. It was on his return journey to London on board the *Pegasus*, bound from Leith to Hull, that he was drowned on 18 July 1843, the ship having struck a rock near Holy Island and sunk. His death drew considerable public sympathy. Successful benefits for his seven children took place at many theatres. The chair at a preliminary meeting in London for the purpose was taken by Charles Dickens.

Elton was unfortunate in marriage: his first marriage ended in separation, and his second wife, a Miss Pratt, the mother of five of his seven children, went mad. Elton contributed a little to periodical literature, and gave lectures on drama at the National Hall (later the Royal Music Hall), Holborn. He was one of the original promoters of the General Theatrical Fund Association.

JOSEPH KNIGHT, *rev.* KATHARINE COCKIN

Sources Adams, *Drama* · Hall, *Dramatic ports.* · *GM*, 2nd ser., 20 (1843), 325 · *The Era* (30 July 1843) · *The Owl* (30 July 1831)
Archives NL Aus., letters to his family
Likenesses W. H. V., pencil drawing, NPG · portrait (as Sir Giles Overreach), repro. in *The Owl* · prints, Harvard TC

Elton, (James) Frederic (1840–1877), explorer of Africa, born on 3 August 1840, probably at Dedham, Essex, was the second son of Lieutenant-Colonel Roberts W. Elton of the 59th regiment, Bengal army, and the grandson of Jacob Elton of Dedham. When the Indian mutiny broke out in 1857 he entered the Bengal army and saw much active service. Having been with the relieving armies at Delhi and Lucknow he was placed on the staff of the commander-in-chief, Sir Hugh Rose (Lord Strathnairn), to whom he was aide-de-camp for some years. His services obtained for him the Indian medal with two clasps. In 1860 he volunteered for service in China, and was present at the taking of Peking (Beijing) and other engagements; after the campaign he received the China medal. Soon after gaining his captaincy (98th regiment) he left the English service, and in 1866 joined the staff of the French army in Mexico during the 'reign' of Emperor Maximilian. On his return to England at the end of the war he published a graphic account of his adventures entitled *With the French in Mexico* (1867).

In 1868 Elton went to Natal in pursuit of adventure and sport. His journey from the Tati goldfields to the mouth of the Limpopo River was recounted in an article for the *Journal* of the Royal Geographical Society. For the remainder of his life he was more or less continuously employed in government service. In 1871 he made a general survey of potential mineral resources and undertook the first in a series of diplomatic missions aimed at delimiting the

(James) Frederic Elton (1840–1877), by unknown engraver, pubd 1879

boundaries between British and Portuguese spheres of influence in southern Africa. In 1872 he joined the staff of Natal's department of native affairs as a border agent on the Zulu frontier. This led to his appointment to the colony's executive and legislative councils, in the capacity of protector of immigrant African labourers. He was a tireless advocate of promoting Natal's development through increased labour migration from the north-east, an object connected in his mind with the diminution of Portuguese influence.

In 1873 Elton was commissioned by the Natal government to promote these objectives along the east African coast by conferring with the governor-general of Mozambique and with Sir Bartle Frere, who was in the process of concluding an anti-slavery treaty between Britain and the sultan of Zanzibar. Although Elton's primary objective was to arrange for the passage of freed slaves as contract labourers in Natal, Frere convinced him to assist the suppression of the east African slave trade by remaining in Zanzibar as assistant political agent and vice-consul. In this capacity he explored portions of the coast between Dar es Salaam and Kilwa. Following promotion to the post of consul in Portuguese territory in 1875, Elton expanded the scope of his expeditions. His articles for the *Journal* of the Royal Geographical Society concentrated on features of the social and physical landscape, while his dispatches to the foreign secretary argued that the Portuguese presence in Mozambique was obstructing economic development and efforts to suppress the slave trade. He recommended that the British government attempt to purchase the territory or at the very least to push the boundaries of Portuguese dominion closer to the Indian Ocean littoral.

His survey of the slave trade took him on numerous journeys by sea and land, to the south as far as Delagoa Bay, and over the Indian Ocean to the Seychelles Islands and Madagascar.

Late in 1876 Elton advised the Foreign Office against entering into the scheme of the Belgian king, Leopold, for an 'international' consortium to develop central Africa. Instead, he encouraged the rival consortium headed by William Mackinnnon, which attempted unsuccessfully to secure the lease of the sultan of Zanzibar's territories on the African mainland as a base for commercial penetration and anti-slavery action. The following year Elton undertook his last major expedition, the objects of which were to assess the validity of Portuguese claims to the Nyasa region, to determine the extent of the slave trade in its southern reaches, and to promote British commercial access to central Africa by finding a suitable route circumventing Portuguese territory from Lake Nyasa to the Zanzibar coast. Among his companions in the enterprise were the gold-seeker Herbert Rhodes (elder brother of Cecil Rhodes) and the anti-slavery activist H. B. Cotterill, who was acting to promote the work of the Presbyterian Livingstonia mission. Before accomplishing his aims Elton succumbed to the ravages of malaria and dysentery, and died on 19 December 1877 near the town of Iseke in central Tanzania. He was buried about 2 miles from his last camp, under a baobab tree. His companions marked the spot by a large wooden cross, and carved his initials on the tree which overshadowed his grave.

At the time of his death Elton was known chiefly as an intrepid explorer who had taken up David Livingstone's challenge to crush the east African slave trade by opening routes for the advent of legitimate commerce and Christianity. Access to Foreign Office records in the twentieth century revealed his central role as an agent of expansive British interests in south and east Africa. Elton nurtured visions of British dominion from the Cape to Cairo, which contributed directly to the development of the colonial territories later carved out by Cecil Rhodes's British South Africa Company and Sir William Mackinnon's British East Africa Company. His journals were edited and completed by Cotterill as *Travels and Researches among the Lakes and Mountains of Eastern and Central Africa* (1879); a preface, by Horace Waller, contained a brief memoir of Elton.

NORMAN ETHERINGTON

Sources N. Etherington, 'Frederic Elton and the South African factor in the making of Britain's east African empire', *Journal of Imperial and Commonwealth History*, 9 (1980–81), 255–74 · R. Coupland, *The exploitation of east Africa, 1856–1890* (1939) · E. Axelson, *Portugal and the scramble for Africa* (1967) · A. J. Hanna, *The beginnings of Nyasaland and north-eastern Rhodesia, 1859–95* (1956) · S. Miers, *Britain and the ending of the slave trade* (1975) · J. S. Galbraith, *Mackinnon and east Africa, 1878–1895: a study in the new imperialism* (1972) · J. F. Elton, *Travels and researches among the lakes and mountains of eastern and central Africa*, ed. H. B. Cotterill (1879)
Archives PRO, Foreign Office papers · PRO, Colonial Office papers | Natal Archives, Pietermaritzburg, South Africa
Likenesses engraving, NPG; repro. in Elton, *Travels and researches*, facing p. 1 [see illus.]
Wealth at death under £200: administration, 19 April 1880, *CGPLA Eng. & Wales*

Elton, Sir Geoffrey Rudolph [*formerly* Gottfried Rudolph Otto Ehrenberg] (1921–1994), historian, was born at Tübingen, Germany, on 21 August 1921. His father was Victor Leopold Ehrenberg (1891–1976), a distinguished classicist and ancient historian who was the son of a banker, Otto Ehrenberg, but came from a long line of teachers and scholars: his uncles included Richard Ehrenberg, an economic historian and an authority on the Fuggers. Victor Ehrenberg had trained as an architect, partly in London, but had moved on to studies in ancient history in Berlin under Eduard Meyer. His career took him to a chair of classics in the German university in Prague, where Gottfried and his brother Ludwig (Professor Lewis Elton) spent their late childhood and early adolescence. After the family moved to England in 1939, Victor Ehrenberg held a number of temporary posts before becoming a reader in ancient history at Bedford College in the University of London. Elton's mother was Eva Dorothea Sommer (*d.* 1973), daughter of Siegfried Sommer, a judge of the court of appeal, who had married Helene Edinger, daughter of a wealthy merchant family of Worms and a talented portrait painter. Eva Sommer was a poet, and a lifelong critic of the work of her son Gottfried. Both families were Jewish, but scarcely aware of their Jewishness, certainly not as something which separated or even distinguished them from their fellow Germans. Eva was named after Eva in Wagner's *Die Meistersinger*. The equally Wagnerian Siegfried Sommer was educated at Kassel in the same class as the future Kaiser Wilhelm II, who became his greatest friend at school, and later made sure that Sommer's career was not blocked by antisemitism.

Education and British naturalization In the winter of 1938–9 arrangements were made by the Society for the Protection of Science and Learning to bring Victor Ehrenberg to England, but it was not clear what could be done, financially, for the rest of the family. It was a chance encounter on a train in Wales that enabled a childhood friend of Eva to renew contact with a governess they had shared years before, and led to a correspondence between the governess and Eva, and the offer of scholarships at Rydal School in Colwyn Bay. When Eva and her sons arrived at Dover on 14 February 1939, the boys knew scarcely a word of English. And yet within a few months they had passed their school certificate examinations in all subjects, and Gottfried had won the school English essay prize. In the following winter he narrowly failed to gain a place at New College, Oxford, having been interviewed by H. A. L. Fisher in the last weeks of the latter's life. He remained at Rydal, teaching German, studying for an external London degree, and discovering an enthusiasm for the English game of cricket, while finding his newly adopted country 'absolutely strange'. Elton's last book, *The English* (1992), would be an expression of gratitude for St Valentine's day 1939, and for his reception by that strange land. He took first-class honours, and won the coveted Derby scholarship, tenable at the University of London. Up to this point it may have been thought that Gottfried would follow in his father's footsteps, and indeed Victor coached him for a

Sir Geoffrey Rudolph Elton (1921–1994), by unknown photographer

special subject in Roman history, which led to his earliest publication, 'The terminal date of Caesar's Gallic proconsulate' (*Journal of Roman Studies*, 36, 1946). But the presence of the University College history department a few miles along the coast from Colwyn Bay at Bangor led to a meeting with Professor John Neale, the Tudor historian, and an understanding that Gottfried would work under Neale's supervision when (Elton later wondered whether Neale had said 'if') he came back from the war.

First came the army, and before that the question of which army: Czech or British? It was a momentous decision, for British naturalization might compromise any future the family might hope to have in Prague. But, as it happened, the decision to join the British army was the right one, since the Ehrenbergs were defined as Czechoslovak citizens of German nationality, which would probably have made them victims of ethnic cleansing in postwar Czechoslovakia. On joining the army, Gottfried was given twenty-four hours to change his name 'by Army Council Instructions'. The name he chose, Elton, would later be adopted by his brother Ludwig when, after the war, the remainder of the family were naturalized as British subjects, and is therefore shared by Lewis Elton's son Ben Elton, a popular writer and entertainer. Geoffrey Elton saw action, briefly, at Anzio, but was then assigned, as a native German speaker, to field intelligence at Graz in Austria. His rank was sergeant and his function the debriefing of suspected Nazis. According to Lewis Elton, it

was the army which turned his brother into an Englishman, even a 'super Englishman', who, unlike Lewis, henceforth took little interest in his ethnic background and ancestry.

Cambridge lecturer When Elton reappeared before Neale in 1946 there was another critical choice to be made. Should he work in Neale's shadow, on Elizabethan parliamentary history? Neale's other students advised against this. Neale's own teacher and the founder of historical studies in University College and the Institute of Historical Research, A. F. Pollard, was nearing the end of his life, and this had the effect of releasing the reign of Henry VIII, which Pollard had been careful to keep to himself for many years. So Elton told Neale that he would 'do Henry VIII, sir', whereupon Neale advised him to immerse himself in the *Letters and Papers of the Reign of Henry VIII*, which he duly did. Elton and Neale later fell out, and Elton was to pursue an almost obsessional vendetta against Neale's reputation as a historian and as a man for many years after the older man's death. Often he would say of this or that gesture that it was 'the only generous thing he ever did', and he claimed that the advice about *Letters and Papers* was the only good advice he ever received from his supervisor.

Unlike Pollard, Elton went behind *Letters and Papers* to the original documents in the Public Record Office, where he worked steadily, almost every day, for a couple of years, for a daily five hours, before emerging to travel up to Lord's, where Denis Compton was playing cricket. He finished his doctoral thesis, 'Thomas Cromwell: aspects of his administrative work', in record time, in September 1948. His career moved forward with equal rapidity: first, and with the thesis yet to be examined, to an assistant lectureship at Glasgow and then, in October 1949, to Cambridge, where Elton would spend the rest of his life, the next forty-five years. Again a fortunate chance had played into his hands. Kenneth Pickthorn of Corpus Christi College had taught Tudor history while sitting as the MP for Cambridge. When the Attlee government abolished university seats, Pickthorn went off in search of pastures new, which created the vacancy that Elton filled. But Neale can only have been helpful in securing both the Glasgow and the Cambridge posts.

On 30 August 1952 Elton married Sheila (*b.* 1926), daughter of John William Lambert, a joiner, of Hartlepool. She was a contemporary at the Institute of Historical Research, later an assistant to Lord Beaverbrook, and an authority on parliament, the press, and press censorship in a period a little later than Elton's own.

Within a few years Elton had established himself as the most pungent, opinionated, and therefore, at first, popular lecturer in the Cambridge history faculty. He began to teach for Clare College but was not elected a fellow until 1954, against some internal opposition. It was in the same year that Walter Ullmann, another émigré historian, was elected at Trinity, after six years in Cambridge. Evidently there was some apprehension about admitting to common rooms two such formidable and combative personalities. At first Elton had few postgraduate pupils, and as late as 1960 those who had worked under his supervision could still be counted on the fingers of one hand. But in the 1960s and 1970s all that changed, especially with the recruitment of many North American graduate students. In all, Elton supervised more than seventy doctoral theses, most of which proved successful, and for many years he presided over a postgraduate seminar that was the principal powerhouse of Tudor studies, taking over from the London seminar of first Pollard and then Neale. His exemplary supervision practice included open house hospitality on Sunday evenings at the Elton home in Millington Road.

The Tudor revolution Out of the mine that is the Henrician state papers in the Public Record Office, Elton had extracted the key involvement in the hectic public affairs of the 1530s—a decade that contained the Henrician reformation and seismic constitutional and administrative change—of Henry VIII's minister Thomas Cromwell. Pollard, with his exaggerated veneration of the king, had dismissed Cromwell as a mere functionary, not to be compared with Cardinal Wolsey, who had dominated the 1520s; while the American scholar R. B. Merriman, who in 1902 had published what was thought to be the definitive account of Cromwell, had taken a somewhat negative view of his qualities. Elton would later claim that, far from going into the archives in search of a Cromwell who was a kind of *alter ego* of himself, something often suggested, in the manner of Croce and Collingwood, Cromwell had reached out from the past to pluck Elton's sleeve and bring to his attention his true greatness. Cromwell would occupy the centre ground of Elton's attention for forty-five years, and was the subject of one of his very last publications. He never attempted a historical biography, a pursuit he considered, for the sixteenth century, undesirable and perhaps even unattainable. The nature of his interest was revealed in his first and in some ways most famous, not to say notorious, book, *The Tudor Revolution in Government*. This monograph had a pointed shape, even an audacity, not to be found in the thesis out of which it grew. The preface stated that changes had been made 'in response to criticisms of Professor J. E. Neale …; my debt to him is very great'. It would be ironical, but not wholly surprising, if Neale was in some measure responsible for the essential 'whiggishness' of the argument now advanced. This was that in the 1530s, Cromwell's decade, the English state parted company with the middle ages and entered a recognizably modern world. It attained full sovereignty, the sovereignty of the king in parliament, almost unchallenged authority within its own borders and marches, a potential hegemony in the British Isles, and a set of institutions which replaced the personal government and financial management of the royal household with a Westminster bureaucracy. Moreover, that bureaucracy had at its heart that progenitor of modern cabinet government, the privy council, and the king's principal secretary, no longer a clerkly body servant of the monarch but 'the chief national executive'.

It was the foundation-stone of Elton's conception of the historian's function that the past, and especially past politics, has a substantial reality which the skilled historian can and must establish, not telling partial and contestable stories but recovering the essential truth about the past. But the stories he told about the 1530s were hotly contested, first by critics in Oxford, writing in the journal *Past and Present*, and later, in the 1970s, by some of his own erstwhile pupils. First the medievalists fought back, against the notion that the 1530s constituted a watershed of cosmic proportions. Then a new generation of Tudor historians parted company with Elton on the nature and significance of what was done in the 1530s, and carried beyond Elton the identification of the human agencies by which it was done. In particular, study of the royal court called in question Elton's claims for the new bureaucracy and renewed interest in the personal and contingent nature of early modern politics. In 1955 Elton published *England under the Tudors*, which may have been the most popular and influential history textbook ever published. Naturally it enshrined his original vision of the significance of the Tudor age for the English state, and the primacy within, in principle, any historical period of the state and its politics and administration. But by the 1970s Elton was fighting a rearguard action against his younger critics, and in his second textbook, *Reform and Reformation*, a volume in the Edward Arnold series the New History of England, as well as in a series of presidential addresses to the Royal Historical Society, he made many concessions to new perceptions. Nevertheless, to the very end he continued to insist that Cromwell had been 'a principled reformer of everything that came within his purview'.

As for the idea that Elton found, or even invented, Thomas Cromwell in his own image, the truth is that he identified not with Cromwell but with the great Cambridge legal historian F. W. Maitland, a scholar whose work was done 'well, conscientiously, circumspectly, methodically' (G. R. Elton, *F. W. Maitland*, 1985, 100), and a historian who in his working methods was everything that Pollard, and Neale, in Elton's perception, were not. In 1985 he published a book on Maitland which, or so he alleged, had taken only a month to write.

Long before that, the Public Record Office mine had yielded much more ore, and smelted and finished metal: most notably Elton's Ford lectures, published in 1972 as *Policy and Police*, an account of the enforcement of the Henrician reformation and of the England that Cromwell saw from across his desk, and the accompanying Wiles lectures, published as *Reform and Renewal: Thomas Cromwell and the Common Weal* (1973). The Cromwell who was the hero of these books was a great parliamentarian, and a strong believer in the rule of and by law, not the unprincipled Machiavellian politician as seen by Merriman. In addition, Elton continued to publish a steady stream of articles and essays, the majority concerned with the same narrow segment of English history, and republished in (eventually) four volumes of *Studies in Tudor and Stuart Politics and Government*. But Elton was not a merely insular historian. Commissioned by G. N. Clark to edit the second volume of the *New Cambridge Modern History* (1958; extensively revised in 1975), he also wrote a beautifully crafted general history of sixteenth-century Europe in the Fontana series, *Reformation Europe, 1517–1559* (1963). He was an active member of the Verein für Reformationsgeschichte and addressed German audiences on the subject of Martin Luther. By contrast, he took little interest in French history and had less sympathy for French historians, a difficulty of both language and temperament.

By now Elton's English historical interests were diversifying, while still confined for the most part to the sixteenth century. The advent of the Yale edition of the *Works* of Thomas More suggested a Cambridge special subject on the subject of More, and more than one provocative, debunking essay, but nothing more considerable. It seems unlikely that More and Elton would have ever have hit it off, while Elton found it hard to deal with religious ardour of the kind which More exemplified, unless he could subject it to a more human and less worthy reductionism. Even Cromwell was somewhat reduced in his estimation when it began to appear that he was one of the evangelically inclined 'Christian brethren', and had 'got religion'. More significant was a growing interest in Elizabethan parliamentary history, a subject that Elton believed Neale, with his whiggish fascination for the 'constitutional' conflicts of queen and Commons, and neglect of what Elton believed to be the fundamental record of the business of an English parliament, had seriously misrepresented. Elizabethan parliaments were about legislation, not politics. *The Parliament of England, 1559–1581* was the last of Elton's substantial, research-based publications. It contained the most technically competent account of the workings of parliament in any period of its long history, but was marred by the extremity of its reaction against Neale's books on the subject. And, having written it, Elton confessed that he was 'perhaps exceptionally relieved to be done with the Parliaments of Elizabeth', since altogether too much had been made of what was only one of the crown's instruments of government. Ambivalences of this kind were very typical of Elton in his late maturity. For example, he could denounce women's history, while lending invaluable support to those feminist historians of whom he happened to approve. Only the immense generosity of his spirit will explain some of these contradictions.

The practice of history All Elton's writings were strongly indicative of his philosophy of history; however, the formulation of any such philosophy was anathema to Elton, who would have associated it with the subversion of history by theorists, mainly French, who had never known what it was to be a working historian and were therefore disqualified from uttering on the subject. It was above all necessary to get on with it. The subject had its own rules and protocols, which only historians understand. His own theoretical and practical utterances were contained in four books, of which the most widely read and influential was *The Practice of History* (1967), usually read as a response to the Trevelyan lectures of E. H. Carr published as *What is History?*, but in fact directed at more than one Cambridge

colleague of the time. This was followed by *Political History: Principles and Practice* (1970), in which traditional history fought back against the trendy 'new ways in history' of the 1960s. If the historian was tired of past politics he was, like Dr Johnson's disillusioned Londoner, tired of life. The positive value of these books lies in a no-nonsense account of what the best historians are good at, and of how all apprentice historians should learn their trade. Their weakness lies in a shaky and perhaps even untenable epistemology, which refuses to face the fact that no historian can tell the whole truth about all of the past, and that he therefore has to select, shape, and even in some sense invent his material. At his most reasonable, as in a published dialogue with a historian of a very different tendency, R. W. Fogel, published as *Which Road to the Past?* (1983), Elton could acknowledge the existence of an almost limitless variety of 'ways' in history: 'We are all historians, differing only in what questions interest us, and what methods we find useful in answering them' (p. 109). At his most unreasonable, he merely lashed out at a range of dangerous heretics, whigs, Marxists, Weberians, postmodernists, in tones and terms that suggested that he thought them unworthy of engagement in serious conversation. It would have been better if the Cambridge University Press had not thought itself bound by an old association to publish his swansong, *Return to Essentials: some Reflections on the Present State of Historical Study* (1991), which, in addition to his two Cambridge inaugural lectures, contained some lectures delivered in an American university which had found them an embarrassment.

Cambridge chair The Cambridge in which Elton had at first found himself a marginal and somewhat alien figure he eventually came to dominate. In 1967 he was promoted to a personal chair and chose the unfashionable title professor of English constitutional history (Pollard's title of 1903). This was a consolation prize for the disappointment which had occurred in 1963, when Elton and J. H. Plumb were leading candidates for the chair of modern history, vacated by Sir Herbert Butterfield on his appointment to the regius chair. In the event, the prize had gone to Charles Wilson, who had been favoured for the chair of economic history. Again in 1968 Elton and Plumb were passed over when the crown appointed Owen Chadwick to the regius chair, which he would occupy for fifteen years, until 1983. Chadwick remembered that Elton never conveyed any resentment or hostility: quite the contrary.

Elton's commitment to the faculty of history was very great. Those foolish enough to wager that he would not speak to every item on the agenda of a board meeting could expect to lose their stake. Usually he spoke first. These were years in which the cyclically recurrent exercise of tripos reform became lively, and political. There was pressure for an expansion of the scope of the Cambridge syllabus from new emphases and methodologies, and relatively new areas of historical study—American, Asian, and African. Elton was sceptical about exotic and relatively untried new sub-disciplines of history, and hostile to what threatened to become a reduction in the rigour of the subject. Differences in the faculty brought the issue into the open forum of the Senate House in 1965–6, when Elton, while insisting that he was not opposed to change as such, spoke with passion against a new tripos 'directed against any proper standard of scholarship … which proposes to reduce the study of history in this University below the proper level of university attainment' (*Cambridge University Reporter*, 96, 2 Feb 1966, 1018). When a new report was discussed in 1970, Elton appeared to have shifted his position, even, in the perception of some medievalists, to have changed sides, impressed by what he had seen of the strength of the student desire for change that had been expressed in the events of the late 1960s. His altered position found him pitted against Professor Walter Ullmann, who would later refer to Elton as his oldest and closest friend in the faculty, but who for a time was not on speaking terms. Fourteen years on again, in his inaugural lecture as regius, Elton made no bones about his disillusionment with what had by then been done to history at Cambridge. 'Our historical tripos now lacks all cohesion and with it any real understanding of what it is trying to do' (*Return to Essentials: some Reflections on the Present State of Historical Study*, 1991, 108).

Elton was heavily involved in the provision of a purpose-built home for the history faculty, Sir James Stirling's controversial glass house, which today houses the Seeley Library, the largest single-subject history library in the world, and rooms for teaching and administration. Perhaps this building has done more to shape the character of the history faculty and the experience of its students even than tripos reform itself, and in ways not always beneficial. Elton played a central role in the committee which awarded the contract to Stirling and which worked closely with his firm between 1963 and 1968, when the building was ready for occupation. The Seeley is still admired by students of architecture, but it incorporated some very serious design faults, and has cost large sums of money to make it habitable. In 1984 the university came close to a decision to demolish the building, while the original plan to complement the Seeley with another structure containing lecture-rooms of various sizes fell by the wayside. Yet Elton remained deaf to criticism of the house that Stirling built.

Elton's participation in the life of his college, Clare, was less intense. He was a very loyal college man, and loved to entertain a ceaseless flow of visitors to lunch, but his attitude to decision making was one of affectionate detachment. He was in favour of the controversial plan to build the Forbes Mellon Library, which now blocks the vista through Memorial Court to the university library, and which he intended to be the eventual resting place of his own library, but his role was not as proactive as it had been in the case of the Seeley.

The Eltonian legacy Geoffrey Elton's creative contribution to the subject and profession of history beyond his own university was greater than that of any of his peers and contemporaries. He was one of the greatest presidents of the Royal Historical Society of all time, and brought the society into a new age of usefulness, especially to younger members of the historical profession. The monograph series Studies in History was his brainchild, created to enable talented PhDs to publish their dissertations. He was the very active editor of this series to the end of his life. The Royal Historical Society's *Annual Bibliography of British and Irish History*, which was launched in 1976, was not merely dreamed up by Elton. For many years he edited it, on his own typewriter. Elton bequeathed his royalties to the society, which also, under the terms of his will, had the disposition of his library, choosing to deposit the bulk of it in the Borthwick Institute of the University of York. So it would be possible to regard as ungrateful a Royal Historical Society conference, 'The Eltonian legacy', in which most of the papers, printed in the *Transactions* of the society (1997), concentrated on the defects and deficiencies of a historian nevertheless acknowledged to have had the quality of greatness. As an act of dismemberment, it was reminiscent of the last scene of Marlowe's *Doctor Faustus*, or of the Orpheus legend.

That Geoffrey Elton served as president of both the Selden Society (1983–5) and the Ecclesiastical History Society (1983–4) testifies to a more catholic breadth of interest and sympathy than he was sometimes credited with. He founded and presided over the List and Index Society, which from 1965 made widely available a long series of essential guides to the public records. For twenty years he was at the centre of the annual gatherings of so-called 'senior historians' at Cumberland Lodge. From 1981 to 1990 he served as publications secretary of the British Academy. He had a close connection with the Wiles lectures in Belfast, which he himself gave in 1972. His frequent visits to universities in the United States and, on one occasion, to New Zealand and Australia, were celebrity progresses.

In 1983, with Sir Owen Chadwick about to retire from the regius chair, there were widespread fears that Margaret Thatcher would overlook Elton's claim to the succession in favour of a nakedly political appointment. Three professors of history in a university in the north-west of England even took the unusual step of writing to 10 Downing Street to say that the entire historical profession would feel a sense of affront if Elton were not appointed. They need not have worried. The prime minister did the proper thing, and there was immense relief and pleasure at Elton's elevation, even among those whose approach to history was very different from his. Elton's inaugural, which for once was delivered from a written script, can have pleased very few of those who heard it for its content, for it was a pugnacious affirmation of the primacy that ought to be accorded by the University of Cambridge to the history of England. But, especially since the regius had risen from a hospital bed to deliver it, the lecture caused much delight by the manner of it. A colleague remembered: 'God was in his heaven, Geoffrey was still himself, and all was right with the world'.

Did Geoffrey remain himself in the final five years of his career and the six years of retirement that were to follow, and was all right with the world as he saw it? His undergraduate lectures, more than ever, consisted of an exaggerated version of what it was to be himself, and failed to attract an audience. His interventions in meetings were fewer than they had once been, and less constructive. As for the world, Elton was no friend of the Wilson and Callaghan governments, still less of militant trade unionism and radical student insurgency, and the Thatcher years, with their scant regard for scholarship and the best features of the British university system, were a disappointment. Some suspected that the immigrant who had fallen in love with his adoptive country had almost fallen out of love with it, while *The English* stopped short of recent times. He was also suffering severely from ill health, something he did his best to conceal from others, until a progressive lack of mobility made it obvious. In this respect he was by no means any longer his original self.

So much for Elton's view of the world. What the world saw of Elton were the crowning glories of a splendid career. Elton was the recipient of no fewer than five Festschriften, including one from his American friends, another from Australia and New Zealand, and others reflecting his interests in parliamentary and European history. Honorary degrees were conferred by the universities of Glasgow, Newcastle, Bristol, London, Göttingen, and Cambridge. The last was a particular cause of pleasure, for, since Elton was already a LittD of the university, the degree awarded *honoris causa* was the LLD, Maitland's degree. In 1986 came a knighthood.

Famously, Elton told his pupils, and readers of *The Practice of History*, that they must devote themselves to the subject with single-mindedness, almost to the exclusion of any distractions. Consequently, it may be, a myth grew up about his own indifference to anything outside his work. It is not true that the Eltons never took a holiday, and they were active gardeners. There was cricket as a spectator sport, and, as a participant, squash, which Elton played into his sixties. Among his recreations he listed joinery and beer drinking, although his hosts were more familiar with a penchant for malt and rye whiskies. He was not fond of music—indeed he was tone-deaf—but he appreciated poetry, wrote some comic verse himself, and was interested in and very knowledgeable about art. Geoffrey Elton died at his home, 30 Millington Road, Cambridge, on 4 December 1994, survived by his wife. There were no children of the marriage.   PATRICK COLLINSON

Sources P. Collinson, 'Geoffrey Rudolph Elton, 1921–1994', *PBA*, 94 (1997), 429–55 · private information (2004) [O. Chadwick, R. Matthews, L. Elton, and correspondence in the possession of Lady Elton] · personal knowledge (2004) · R. M. Cooper, ed., *Refugee scholars: conversations with Tess Simpson* (1992) · J. C. G. Röhl, *Wilhelm II: die Jugend des Kaisers, 1859–1880* (1993) · 'Bibliography', *Law and government under the Tudors: essays presented to Sir Geoffrey Elton*, ed. C. Cross, D. Loades, and J. J. Scarisbrick (1988) · *Cambridge University Reporter* (1965–6) · *Cambridge University Reporter* (1969–70) · U. Cam., faculty of history, archives, bay 3, boxes 1, 2 · m. cert. · *CGPLA Eng. & Wales* (1995) · b. cert. [Sheila Lambert, wife]

Archives priv. coll., MSS | SOUND BL NSA, recorded talk

Likenesses photograph, News International Syndication, London [*see illus.*] · portrait, repro. in Cross, Loades, and Scarisbrick, eds., *Law and government under the Tudors*, frontispiece

Wealth at death £737,494: probate, 9 Feb 1995, *CGPLA Eng. & Wales*

Elton, Godfrey, first Baron Elton (1892–1973), historian, was born at Sherington rectory, Newport Pagnell, Buckinghamshire, on 29 March 1892, the elder son and eldest of the three children of Edward Fiennes Elton, of Burleigh Court, Gloucestershire, and Ovington Park, Hampshire, and his wife, Violet Hylda, daughter of the Revd Carteret John Halford Fletcher, rector of Carfax church, Oxford. He was educated at Rugby School and at Balliol College, Oxford, which he entered with a classical scholarship in 1911. He obtained a first class in classical honour moderations in 1913 and then turned from classics to history. But although his tutors thought extremely highly of him, he never took his finals, for in September 1914 he was commissioned in the 4th Hampshire regiment and saw service in Mesopotamia. During the siege of Kut al-Amara he was wounded, and was then taken into captivity in Turkey when Kut surrendered in April 1916. His interest in history was maintained so far as conditions allowed, and soon after the war ended Queen's College, Oxford, elected him in 1919 to a fellowship and praelectorship in modern history. In 1921 he married Dedi (d. 1977), daughter of Gustav Hartmann of Oslo, Norway. They had two daughters and a son.

Elton was dean of Queen's College from 1921 to 1923 and tutor from 1927 to 1934. With his wife, he was exceptionally generous in entertaining colleagues and undergraduates. As a tutor he was painstaking and interesting, though his only strictly historical publication was *The Revolutionary Idea in France, 1789–1878* (1923), which went to many impressions. He was devoted to his college, but it cannot be said that in college and university affairs his attitude changed much as the years went on. He believed strongly not only in customs but in rules: the dean of Queen's in the 1930s remembers being urged by Elton to conduct a close investigation into the reasons why a young lady, in a gown, had been seen descending an undergraduate staircase at 11 a.m. Yet his career was paradoxical. Soon after the war he had joined the Labour Party, and he was their (unsuccessful) candidate for Thornbury, Gloucestershire, in 1924 and 1929. He looked back, as did many of those demobilized in 1918, to pre-war social and economic conditions which he found distasteful; he greatly disliked militarism, and he was dissatisfied with the efforts of the allies to prevent war recurring. Whether he ever absorbed deeply the principles or details of Labour policy is doubtful, and when the government broke up in 1931 he followed Ramsay MacDonald into the National Labour Party. He was a strong admirer of the prime minister, whose son Malcolm had been his pupil at Queen's, and in 1939 he published the first volume of his biography. He wrote the notice of MacDonald for the *Dictionary of National Biography* as well as that of Philip Guedalla. In 1934 Elton was made a baron.

L. B. Namier commented that 'whereas in the 18th century the tutors of peers were made Under-Secretaries, in the 20th the tutors of Under-Secretaries are made peers'. But if this was intended as a criticism of Elton, it was quite unfair. By 1935, it is true, he had lost much interest in the questions which excited most people at that time, but he

Godfrey Elton, first Baron Elton (1892–1973), by Bassano, 1939

spoke often and ably in the Lords on such subjects as the environment, agriculture, broadcasting, and ecclesiastical affairs (he was a devout Anglican). He also served on a wide range of governmental and semi-public committees. He wrote several books, including novels and, in 1938, an autobiographical volume, *Among Others*.

In 1939 Elton gave up his teaching fellowship at Queen's and became a supernumerary fellow. To his younger colleagues in recent years he had undeniably seemed to be a reactionary. But they were pleased when they could agree with his advice, which could often be helpful; and when they disagreed they were never apprehensive that either discourtesy or unpleasantness would result. He was a man without malice. In later years he served above all as secretary to the Rhodes Trust (1939–59), but he continued much other work on committees. His academic life was perhaps disappointing in the light of his early promise. But he was a man of energy and wide interests, and in these later years he performed widely and well.

Elton died at his home, the Dower House, Sutton Bonington, Nottinghamshire, on 18 April 1973, and was succeeded in the barony by his son Rodney.

G. E. F. CHILVER, rev.

Sources G. Elton, *Among others* (1938) · *The Times* (19 April 1973) · *CGPLA Eng. & Wales* (1973)
Archives Bodl. Oxf., corresp. with Gilbert Murray
Likenesses W. Stoneman, photograph, 1934, NPG · Bassano, photograph, 1939, NPG [*see illus.*]
Wealth at death £12,148: probate, 7 Nov 1973, *CGPLA Eng. & Wales*

Elton, John (*d.* 1751), merchant and adventurer, is of unknown origins. He arrived in Russia in 1732 to present to the Russian government a memorandum for finding a northern sea passage to Japan. In 1735 the Russian government sent him with an official expedition, with V. N. Tatishchev, to explore and reinforce Russia's eastern borders in the region of Orenburg. This gave Elton the idea of trading with the khanates of central Asia via the Caspian Sea and Persia. In 1739 he set off down the Volga and across the Caspian with a Scot, Mungo Graeme, to investigate the possibilities, proceeding down the Volga from Nizhniy Novgorod to Astrakhan and across the Caspian to Karagansk. Tribal unrest around the eastern shores made trade impracticable, however, and Elton instead based himself at Resht, in the south-western corner of the Caspian, where he won permission to trade from Reza Quli Khan, eldest son of the Persian ruler, Nadir Shah.

Elton then returned north and presented an enthusiastic petition to the (British) Russia Company to promote the trade. This was sanctioned in 1741 by act of parliament and also by the Russian government. In 1742 Elton commissioned the construction of two vessels at Kazan on the Volga to carry his goods downriver to Astrakhan and across the Caspian to Resht; one of them was commanded by Captain Woodroofe, flying the English flag for the first time since Anthony Jenkinson in the mid-sixteenth century. Elton and Woodroofe also surveyed the Persian Caspian shore. Other British merchants followed Elton to Resht, including the traveller and scholar James Brown. In 1743 Nadir Shah, in need of a fleet to keep his armies supplied during campaigns in the east against the Turkomans and in the west against rebellious Lesghians in the Caucasus, appointed Elton his chief shipbuilder; as such he oversaw the construction of a 20-gun vessel, the most powerful war vessel ever seen on the Caspian. Nadir Shah also appointed Elton admiral of the Caspian, with authority to oblige all Russian vessels on those waters to salute the Persian flag. Elton thus made enemies of the Russians, whose shipping had previously monopolized traffic on the Caspian.

In 1744 the Russia Company ordered Elton to return to England but he replied by sending a copy of a decree by Nadir Shah, dated November 1745, forbidding him to leave Persia. Offers of an annual pension of £400 from the Russia Company or a post in the British navy were equally ineffectual. Despite the damage he was inflicting on the Russia Company Elton argued that a British subject may serve with any foreign ruler on friendly terms with Britain and that he was under no obligation to Russia.

The chief authority for Elton's activities is Jonas Hanway, who, noting St Petersburg's fury at Elton's activities (stimulated by Armenian merchants who had previously acted as middlemen), offered to investigate the situation. Hanway found Elton living beyond his means and beginning to realize the damage to British trans-Caspian trade caused by his employment by Nadir Shah. At the same time he also pointed to the relative success of the trade in the four years of direct trading: between 1742 and 1746 English cloth and goods to the value of £174,398 had been exported across the Caspian. In 1746 the Empress Elizabeth of Russia forbade all direct trade by British merchants across the Caspian. In 1747 Nadir Shah was assassinated and an attempt was also made on Elton's life. He survived the ensuing anarchy in the country for a while but in 1751 rival factions besieged his house in Resht and he was forced to surrender on condition that his life and his possessions were spared. The promise proved ineffectual and he was executed on the road, near Resht, before he could be rescued. Much of Elton's journal of his first expedition to Persia in 1739 is printed in Hanway's *Historical Account of the British Trade over the Caspian Sea* (1754). E. I. CARLYLE, *rev.* S. SEARIGHT

Sources J. Hanway, *An historical account of the British trade over the Caspian Sea*, 2nd edn, 2 vols. (1754) · *GM*, 1st ser., 12 (1742), 18–29 · L. Lockhart, *Nadir Shah* (1938) · D. Reading, *The Anglo-Russian commercial treaty of 1734* (1938) · W. E. Minchinton, *English overseas trade* (1969) · J. G. Garrard, *The eighteenth century in Russia* (1973) · S. Searight, *The British in the Middle East* (1969) · J. B. Fraser, *Travels and adventures in Persia* (1826)

Elton, Oliver (1861–1945), literary scholar and translator, was born on 3 June 1861 at Gresham grammar school, Holt, Norfolk, the only child of the Revd Charles Allen Elton (1820–1887), headmaster of the school, and his wife, Sarah Amelia (*b.* 1833), daughter of John Ransom, solicitor, of Holt, and his wife, Augusta. Educated by his father until he went to Marlborough College in 1873, Elton entered Corpus Christi College, Oxford, as a classical scholar in 1880, and was awarded a second class in classical moderations in 1881 and a first in *literae humaniores* in 1884. Some of his notable friends from Oxford included Arthur Sidgwick, Michael Sadler, Charles Eliot, Leonard Huxley, and Dugald Sutherland MacColl. Elton was closely associated with the newly founded *Oxford Magazine*, and contributed to it his first verse translations. On leaving Oxford he engaged in private tutoring in London (1884–90), gave extension lectures, and began reviewing. He edited for schools two of Shakespeare's plays (*1 Henry IV*, 1889, and *King John*, 1890), as well as the early poems of Milton (1890–93), and he published, on the suggestion of Frederick York Powell, *The Life of Laurence Bishop of Hólar in Iceland* (1890), a translation from the Icelandic. In 1888 he married Letitia Maynard MacColl (1865–1948), daughter of the Revd Dugald MacColl and Janet Matheson of Glasgow, and sister of his friend D. S. MacColl. They had three sons: Geoffrey York (*d.* 1927), Leonard Sidgwick, and Charles Sutherland *Elton (1900–1991).

Elton's first university appointment came in 1890, when he was made independent lecturer in English literature at the University of Manchester (1890–1900). His friendship with C. E. Montague, W. T. Arnold, and Arthur Johnstone, the music critic, brought him into connection with the *Manchester Guardian*, for which he wrote reviews and dramatic criticism—six articles of which were reprinted in *The Manchester Stage, 1880–1900* (1900). During his ten years in Manchester he published three books: his *Danish History*, a translation of the first nine books of the *Gesta Danorum* of Saxo Grammaticus, with an introduction by F. York Powell (1894); an *Introduction to Michael Drayton*

Oliver Elton (1861–1945), by Augustus John

(Spenser Society, 1895, largely rewritten as *Michael Drayton, a Critical Study*, 1905); and *The Augustan Ages* in Saintsbury's Periods of European Literature. With the publication in 1899 of this last volume, which covers the period roughly from 1650 to 1730 and contains his fullest treatment of French literature, he won his place among the academic critics.

Elton was invited to Liverpool to be King Alfred professor of English literature, in succession to Walter Raleigh, and entered on his new duties in January 1901. When the college at Liverpool (hitherto in the federal Victoria University) was raised to the status of an independent university in 1903, he played a tireless part in dealing with the problems connected with its development.

The first book which Elton published while at Liverpool was *Frederick York Powell: a Life, and a Selection from his Letters and Occasional Writings* (1906), a tribute to the encourager of his early days. In *Modern Studies* (1907) he included four articles contributed to the *Quarterly Review* ('Giordano Bruno in England', 'The meaning of literary history', 'Recent Shakespeare criticism', and 'The novels of Mr. Henry James') as well as his inaugural lecture at Liverpool, on Tennyson, in which he had surprised his audience by his qualifications of the then accepted view. But he was now beginning to think of what was to prove his main work, his surveys of English literature during three periods of fifty years. *A Survey of English Literature, 1780–1830* (2 vols.)

appeared in 1912; *Survey, 1830–1880* (2 vols.) followed in 1920, and *Survey, 1730–1780* (2 vols.) in 1928. Each, as he said in the preface to the first, was not so much a history as 'a direct criticism of everything I can find in the literature of fifty years that speaks to me with any sound of living voice'. His gift of concise yet clear expression is nowhere seen better than in his *Surveys*.

In 1908 Elton was asked by the English Association to give its centenary address on Milton and took as his subject 'Milton and party'; and in 1932, as its president, he spoke on 'Robert Bridges and *The Testament of Beauty*'. Between these two dates he contributed three essays ('English prose numbers', 'Reason and enthusiasm in the eighteenth century', and 'The poet's dictionary') to the association's *Essays and Studies*, and edited two volumes in the series (1914, 1925). He gave two lectures to the British Academy: 'Poetic romancers after 1850', the Warton lecture, 1914, and 'Style in Shakespeare', the Shakespeare lecture, 1936. He gave the Taylorian lecture at Oxford in 1929 on Chekhov. The earlier of these lectures are included in *A Sheaf of Papers* (1922), the last collection of his lectures or essays which he published while at Liverpool.

On retiring from his professorship in 1925 Elton made his home in Oxford. He had paid his first visit to America in 1892 when he lectured at Johns Hopkins University, Baltimore, Maryland, and he had been in India at the Punjab University in 1917–18. He now began his retirement by spending several months in America in 1926 as visiting professor at Harvard, and as Lowell lecturer. He gave courses at Bedford College for Women, London, in 1927–8, and at Gresham College, London, in 1929–30. He was again visiting professor at Harvard in 1930–31. Thereafter he remained at home.

At Oxford, Elton completed his third *Survey*, and then wrote another tribute to a great friendship, *C. E. Montague: a Memoir* (1929). But the chief work of his later years was *The English Muse: a Sketch* (1933), an account of English poetry in its whole range from Anglo-Saxon times to the First World War. He described it as 'a companion to an imaginary, and most imperfect, anthology'. Though independent of the *Surveys*, even when it covers the same ground, it is like them in the vigour and sureness of its criticism and the lucid conciseness of its style. In the same year he edited as literary executor a collection of Saintsbury's *Prefaces and Essays* (1933), and wrote the obituary of Saintsbury for the British Academy. *Essays and Addresses* (1939), largely composed of pieces mentioned above, was his last collection of his own writings. It included 'The nature of literary criticism', his Ludwig Mond lecture at Manchester in 1935, and 'Alexander Pushkin', delivered at the Royal Institution in 1938.

Elton had a wide command of languages. In his early days he had translated from Icelandic and from Old English. During the First World War he learned Russian, and in his retirement he found happy occupation in making verse renderings of poems in Russian, Polish, and Serbo-Croat. They were contributed to the *Slavonic Review* and *Slavonic Year-Book*, and formed two independent volumes,

Verse from Pushkin and Others (1935) and *Evgeny Onegin* (1937). On the latter, his reputation as a translator rests securely.

Among the last things which Elton published were the obituary of Lascelles Abercrombie for the British Academy (1939), translations from Mickiewicz's *Pan Tadeusz* (1940), and the preface to J. B. Yeats's *Letters to his Son W. B. Yeats and Others* (1944).

Elton died in Oxford on 4 June 1945, at 293 Woodstock Road, Oxford. He had hurt his heart by cycling against a head wind in 1933, and in his final years his handsome frame—he was well over 6 feet—had put an increasing strain on it.

Elton received honorary degrees from the universities of Durham (1912), Manchester (1919), Edinburgh (1922), Oxford (1925), Liverpool (1928), and Reading (1935). He was elected FBA (1924), and honorary fellow of Corpus Christi College, Oxford (1930).

D. N. SMITH, *rev.* REBECCA MILLS

Sources L. C. Martin, 'Oliver Elton, 1861–1945', *PBA*, 31 (1945), 317–34 · *The Times* (7 June 1945) · *Manchester Guardian* (6 June 1945) · D. Bank and A. Esposito, eds., *British biographical index*, 4 vols. (1990) · *WWW* · A. Treneer, *Cornish years* (1949) · private information (1959) · personal knowledge (1959) · Venn, *Alum. Cant.* · *CGPLA Eng. & Wales* (1945) · *IGI*
Archives JRL, letters to the *Manchester Guardian* | JRL, letters to Allan Monkhouse · NL Ire., letters to John Butler Yeats · NL Scot., corresp. with David Nicholl Smith · NL Wales, letters and postcards to John Glyn Davies · U. Glas. L., letters to D. S. MacColl
Likenesses A. Lipczinski, group portrait, oils, 1915 (with staff), U. Lpool · H. Carr, oils, *c*.1925, U. Lpool · W. Stoneman, photograph, 1930, NPG · F. Dodd, etching, repro. in Martin, *PBA* · A. John, oils, University of Liverpool Art Gallery [*see illus.*]
Wealth at death £4956 16*s.* 2*d.*: probate, 22 Aug 1945, *CGPLA Eng. & Wales*

Elton, Richard (*b.* *c*.1610), army officer and author, was born in Bristol. He was active in the prestigious military company of the City of Westminster and in the smaller volunteer association the Loving Gentlemen of Town-Ditch before the civil war. The former was a voluntary association of responsible citizens formed by Henry, prince of Wales, in 1611 to provide a similar pattern of training in Westminster to that provided in London by the Society of the Artillery Garden (later the Honourable Artillery Company). Members of the company (like their London counterparts) were trained in Dutch military practice and were expected to provide a pool from which officers could be drawn for the Westminster trained bands. Elton records the debt he owed to the tuition provided by Henry Tillier, a professional soldier who was captain of the military company and later a royalist major-general. The Westminster militia generally was always suspected of royalist sympathies, though Elton was a supporter of the parliament.

He does not seem to have seen any active service during the first or second civil wars, as his military writing does not include any personal examples or anecdotes. He had been appointed sergeant-major (major) of a militia regiment, the White auxiliaries of the City of London, by September 1646, when he was named among the city militia officers appearing in the funeral procession of the parliament general, the earl of Essex, but by this time the London militia regiments were no longer involved in campaigning outside London. His appointment, to a technically demanding post, was unusual, as most officers in the London militia regiments were drawn from the Society of the Artillery Garden, and this is an indication that his military ability was respected among the amateur officers in London. Following the occupation of London by the New Model Army in August 1647, he became acquainted with the New Model Army officer Captain Thomas Walker through their common interest in the more complex points of military practice, and thereby gained further advice on current military practice.

Elton's background colours the style and format of the influential military manual *The Compleat Body of the Art Military* (1650, 1659, 1668), for which he is best known. Previously the most popular training manual had been *Military Discipline* (first published 1635) by William Barriffe, a member of the Society of the Artillery Garden. Barriffe's work had combined training instructions for an infantry company for purely military exercises with the more elaborate variations favoured by militia officers for military displays in London. After Barriffe's death in 1643 Elton built upon his work by expanding his own ideas into a manual which included regimental formations for infantry and army deployments, making it a more complete guide. This still included some formations better suited to the parade ground than the battlefield, but was also a usable practical manual. The signatories to his application for permission to print the manual represented leading figures of the city's militia establishment, including General Philip Skippon, providing further evidence of the respect in which he and his work were held. The second and third editions include some additions, the most notable being the inclusion in the third of sections on cavalry and artillery. His work remained influential among English military writers until the early 1670s.

At some time after 1650 Elton transferred from the militia to service in the army. By May 1654 he was deputy governor of Kingston upon Hull, with the rank of major and effective responsibility for the garrison, and by mid-1657 had been promoted to lieutenant-colonel and city governor. His son, also Richard Elton, is recorded as an ensign in the Hull garrison regiment. The elder Elton retained his association with the voluntary military associations, and was one of several army officers with similar connections associated with a petition on behalf of the Society of the Artillery Garden in June 1658. In 1659 he was given command at Carlisle, and in October opposed George Monck's plans to secure that garrison. By January 1660, however, the Carlisle troops had declared for Monck's restoration of parliament, deposing their officers. The facts of Elton's later life are unknown.   KEITH ROBERTS

Sources DNB · *CSP dom.*, 1653–60 · J. Turner, *Pallas armata: military essayes of the ancient Grecian, Roman and modern art of war, written in the years 1670 and 1671* (1683), 217 · *The true mannor and forme of the proceeding to the funerall of Robert earle of Essex* (1646) [Thomason tract E 360(1)] · K. Roberts, '"Citizen soldiers": the military power of the City of London', *London and the civil war*, ed. S. Porter (1996), 89–116, esp. 114 · K. Roberts, *London and liberty: ensigns of the London trained bands* (1987), 52 and 75 · K. Roberts, 'Lessons in revolution: the impact of the London military companies', *Cromwelliana* (1992) · T. Venn, *Military and maritime discipline in three books* (1672), 30, 31, 33, 80, 168 · C. H. Firth and G. Davies, *The regimental history of Cromwell's army*, 2 vols. (1940) · R. Elton, *The compleat body of the art military* (1650)
Likenesses J. Droeshout, line engraving, BM, NPG; repro. in Elton, *Compleat body of the art military*

Elveden, Walter (*d.* in or before **1360**), ecclesiastic and astrologer, is first recorded as a scholar at Cambridge, probably of Gonville Hall. As a student Elveden had an inclination toward astrology, drafting a table of planetary 'lords of the month' for the period 1332–57. He also compiled an almanac, his *Kalendarium*, for the years 1330–86. Ironically, Elveden's astrological efforts were better received in Oxford than in Cambridge—William Rede (*d.* 1385) and John Ashenden (*d.* in or before 1368?), both fellows of Merton College, consulted his astrological tables and almanac, and the late fourteenth-century Oxford Carmelite Nicholas Lynn published a famous continuation of the *Kalendarium*. Elveden had graduated MA by 1348, and, turning to more remunerative legal studies, was made DCL by 1350. His interest in canon law is demonstrated by his having compiled a *Tabula sexti libri decretalium super diversis signifacionibus verborum*, an index to papal decrees. He came to hold a number of benefices in the 1340s and 1350s, mostly in the diocese of Norwich.

A close associate of William Bateman, bishop of Norwich (*d.* 1355), Elveden doubtless took part in Bateman's litigious assertion of his episcopal prerogatives, notably against the monks of Bury St Edmunds; he also accompanied the bishop on a diplomatic mission to the continent in March 1349. He became Bateman's vicar-general in 1351 and keeper of the spiritualities of Norwich at the bishop's death; but despite his education and experience, Elveden does not seem to have been considered as a candidate to succeed Bateman. At his death, which took place no later than 1360, Elveden left his books, and perhaps an astrolabe, to Gonville Hall; nine of his books, including legal and medical texts as well as a biblical concordance, remain in the Gonville and Caius College Library. One of these (Gonville and Caius, MS 483 fol. 275r–v) preserves a legal *quaestio disputata* between Elveden and John Acton (*d.* 1350).   KEITH SNEDEGAR

Sources Emden, *Cam.* · H. M. Carey, *Courting disaster: astrology at the English court and university in the later middle ages* (1992)
Archives Gon. & Caius Cam., MSS 54, 78, 95, 115, 147, 242, 254, 468, 483

Elvey, Sir George Job (1816–1893), organist and composer, born in Union Street, Canterbury, on 27 March 1816, was the younger son of John Elvey and Abigail Hardiman. For several generations his family had been connected with the musical life of the city. At an early age he was admitted as a chorister of Canterbury Cathedral, under the organist Highmore Skeats, where his brother, Stephen *Elvey, was master of the boys. In 1830 Stephen Elvey was appointed organist of New College, Oxford, and George went to live with him. He completed his musical education under his brother's guidance. Before he was seventeen he had become a very expert organist, and took temporary duty at Christ Church, Magdalen, and New College. In 1834 he gained the Gresham gold medal for his anthem 'Bow down thine ear, O Lord'. In 1835 he succeeded Skeats as organist of St George's Chapel, Windsor. Among his earliest pupils were Prince George (duke of Cambridge) and Prince Edward of Saxe-Weimar, for whose confirmation he composed his well-known anthem 'Wherewithal shall a young man cleanse his way?' He matriculated from New College in May 1838, and graduated BMus in June 1838, his exercise being an oratorio, *The Resurrection and Ascension*, which was performed by the Sacred Harmonic Society at Exeter Hall later that year, and subsequently in the USA at Boston, and also at Glasgow. On 19 June 1838, he married Harriette Skeats, the daughter of Highmore Skeats. They had one son, George Highmore Elvey, born in 1851. Meanwhile in July 1840, by a special dispensation of the chancellor of the university, Elvey graduated DMus two years earlier than was allowed by the statutes. His exercise on this occasion was the anthem 'The ways of Zion do mourn'. He wrote two anthems with orchestral accompaniments, 'The Lord is king' and 'Sing, o heavens', respectively for the Gloucester festival of 1853 and the Worcester festival of 1857.

On 22 August 1854 Elvey married Georgiana Nichols, the daughter of John Bowyer *Nichols (1779–1863) [*see under* Nichols family (*per. c.*1760–1939)], a printer and antiquary, and the granddaughter of John Nichols (1745–1826), also a printer and antiquary. They had three sons and a daughter. Following her death on 22 December 1863, Elvey married, on 20 April 1865, Eleanora Grace Jarvis, the daughter of Richard Jarvis.

Of Elvey's best-known works—produced chiefly between 1856 and 1860—many were composed for special services at St George's Chapel. With the death of the prince consort in 1861 Elvey lost one of his most sympathetic patrons. The funeral anthems 'The souls of the righteous' and 'Blessed are the dead' were both written for anniversary services in memory of the prince. For the marriage of Edward VII, when prince of Wales (1863), Elvey composed a special anthem with organ and orchestral accompaniment, 'Sing unto God', and for the marriage of Princess Louise (duchess of Argyll) in 1871 a festal march. He was knighted on 24 March 1871. The last important public event in which he took part was the marriage of the duke of Albany at St George's Chapel on 6 May 1882. In June of that year he resigned his post as organist. On 20 June, his third wife having died on 23 January 1879, he married, for the fourth and last time; his new wife was Mary Savory, the daughter of Sir Joseph Savory of Buckhurst Park, lord mayor of London in 1890–91. After some years spent in retirement Elvey died, at The Towers, Windlesham, Surrey, on 9 December 1893, and was buried in the catacombs of St George's Chapel on 14 December. He was survived by his wife.

Elvey was a prolific writer of church music. Besides the anthems already mentioned, his chants, his *Cantate domino*, a *Deus misereatur* in D, and the tune to the harvest hymn 'Come, ye thankful people, come' were among his most popular compositions. He also wrote fifteen part songs, an introduction and gavotte for piano and violin, and four piano pieces.

Elvey was a staunch admirer of old English church music, and the school of the restoration was fully represented in his services at St George's Chapel. He was also famous for his rendering of Handel's music. In the words of E. H. Thorne, a former pupil: 'Elvey's style of organ playing was pre-eminently a grand church style. He was particularly fine in the anthems of Purcell, Greene, Croft, and Boyce, and knew how to bring out all the devotional and dramatic qualities of these composers'.

R. H. NEWMARCH, *rev.* NILANJANA BANERJI

Sources M. Elvey, ed., *Life and reminiscences of George J. Elvey* (1894) · Grove, *Dict. mus.* · W. Cowan and J. Love, *The music of the church hymnary and the psalter in metre* (1901) · Brown & Stratton, *Brit. mus.* · Foster, *Alum. Oxon.* · D. Baptie, *Sketches of the English glee composers: historical, biographical and critical (from about 1735–1866)* [1896] · J. D. Brown, *Biographical dictionary of musicians: with a bibliography of English writings on music* (1886) · D. Baptie, *A handbook of musical biography* (1883)
Archives Bodl. Oxf., corresp. · St George's Chapel, Windsor, corresp. and papers
Likenesses Lock & Whitfield, woodburytype photograph, NPG; repro. in T. Cooper, *Men of mark: a gallery of contemporary portraits* (1882) · portrait, repro. in Elvey, ed., *Life and reminiscences*
Wealth at death £1335 5s. 7d.: probate, 9 Jan 1894, *CGPLA Eng. & Wales*

Elvey, Maurice [*real name* William Seward Folkard] (**1887–1967**), film director, was born on 11 November 1887 at 14 Park Road, Stockton-on-Tees, the eldest son of William Clarence Folkard, an inspecting engineer, and his wife, Sarah Anna Seward Pearce. Little is known about his childhood but it is believed his father had travelled north from Southsea, in search of engineering work; the family moved lodgings frequently. By the age of eleven he was in London, surviving on odd jobs, before getting work in the theatre in the early 1900s. Between 1908 and 1911 he undertook small roles in popular romantic dramas mounted by the Fred Terry and Julia Neilson company. On 31 December 1910, by which time he had assumed the name Maurice Elvey, he married Adeline Maud Charlton Preston (*b.* 1889/90), an actress and journalist, known as Philippa Preston. A member of the Fabian Society, Elvey read voraciously, and developed a lifelong appreciation of music, opera, and ballet. In pursuit of a more adventurous repertoire he formed the Adelphi Play Society (July 1911), and produced and acted in plays by Ibsen, Strindberg, Schnitzler, and Chekhov, including the first English performance of *The Seagull* (1912).

It was while taking *Fanny's First Play* to New York in 1912 at the behest of Harley Granville Barker that Elvey saw his first film, a four-minute version of *The Flying Dutchman*. The sight of 'a real ocean with a ghost ship' converted him to cinema as a 'new and magical world' of which he wanted to be a part. Following an introduction to a small London-based company, Elvey directed his first film, *The Fallen Idol*

Maurice Elvey (1887–1967), by Howard Coster, 1935

(1913). He quickly grasped the techniques and potentialities of the new medium, and at the London Film Company encountered the more systematic methods of American film-makers. He also built up a company of established theatre actors, including his leading lady, Elisabeth Risdon, who was to feature in his divorce in January 1915. On 2 February 1916 he remarried; his new wife was Florence Hill Clarke (b. 1890), a sculptor.

Elvey was soon recognized as a rising talent. His 1914 adaptation of Robert Louis Stevenson's *The Suicide Club* was declared to be a 'marked advance of work from this studio in every detail' (*The Bioscope*, 9 July 1914). As well as introducing up-to-date techniques, he brought a new seriousness about the medium as an artistic undertaking. Overcoming British and Colonial's doubts about costume drama, he pioneered film biography with *Florence Nightingale* (1915), which was followed in 1917 by the highly successful *Nelson* for British Instructional. He then made for the Ideal Film Company *The Life Story of David Lloyd George* (1919), which for political reasons was never screened and, until recently, was assumed lost. Shortly afterwards Elvey became chief director for Stoll, then the largest film production company in Britain, for whom he undertook an ambitious programme of adaptations from classic and popular authors, including Charles Dickens, A. E. W. Mason, H. G. Wells, Arthur Conan Doyle, Ethel M. Dell, and Marie Corelli.

Elvey consolidated his reputation with films such as *Comradeship* (1919), one of the first to tackle issues of social change raised by the war, *Mr Wu* (1919), and *The Passionate*

Friends (1922). His films were praised for their 'painstaking detail' of setting, furnishing, and costume, their emotionally and pictorially effective photography and lighting, their strong performances and ensemble playing, their creation of an involving story world and atmospheric pictures, their combination of 'melodramatic punch' with tasteful restraint, and their feeling for English social types and settings, and the English countryside in particular. Above all Elvey was seen to challenge the dominance of Hollywood. *At the Villa Rose* (1920), an intricate tale of spiritualism and detection, was for the reviewer in the *Kinematograph Weekly* 'a magnificent day's work for the reputation of British film' (*Kinematograph Weekly*, 6 May 1920) and justified Elvey's claim to be among the best directors in Britain. It was characteristic that he prefixed to the credits his own portrait—depicting an aesthetic looking thinker in pince-nez.

Motion Picture Studio described Elvey on set as 'spruce and dapper', always impeccably dressed, even while 'darting here and there' among his technicians and actors, 'polish-[ing] off scene after scene with smooth celerity, but no trace of haste' (*Motion Picture Studio*, 24 March 1923). A noted ladies' man, he divorced for a second time, marrying on 13 January 1923 his then leading lady, Isobel Elsom (b. 1895); her real name was Isabella Reed. In 1924 Elvey escaped the slump in the British film industry by going to Hollywood, where he made five films. However, apparently unable to adapt, he returned the following year. During this difficult period his marriage to Isobel Elsom was dissolved. Aptly perhaps, their last film together, *Human Law*, made independently in Germany in 1926 and influenced by expressionism, was about a nasty divorce, and featured a psychotically jealous husband; *The Bioscope* found it 'sombre to the point of being sordid' (*The Bioscope*, 3 June 1926).

Following two successful independent productions in 1926, *The Flag Lieutenant* and *Mademoiselle d'Armentieres*, another First World War drama which mixed espionage and romance in the trenches, Elvey's career reached a creative peak. *Mademoiselle* brought together Elvey, Victor Saville, and V. Gareth Gundrey (scriptwriter) in a 'winning team' that was to flourish at Gaumont-British, 1927–9. They made the remarkable *Palais de danse* (1927), a Cinderella tale set within the emerging dance-hall sex industry; and also produced *Hindle Wakes* (1927). Elvey's first talking picture for Gaumont was the futuristic *High Treason* (1929), only just beaten as England's first sound film by Hitchcock's *Blackmail*. Elvey's brother, Fred Merrick, joined him on this film as assistant director, a position he was to occupy sporadically until the Second World War.

Victor Saville praised Elvey's 'authoritative technical know-how … and sensitive feeling for the emotional' (Saville). This was combined with a capacity to work quickly and efficiently within budget and schedule, an ability to weld a team of actors and crew, and a shrewd grasp of the popular imagination. In 1930 Elvey secured a contract to make a number of films for Basil Dean, including Gracie Fields's first film, *Sally in our Alley* (1931). He then remade *The Lodger* (1932) and adapted *I Lived With You* (1933), both with Ivor Novello. A second period with Gaumont (1933–5), devoted largely to musical comedies, peaked with the spectacular and sinister *The Clairvoyant* (1935). The financial failure of the high-budget *The Tunnel* (1935) and further industrial crisis returned Elvey to freelance work. Throughout the depressed years of the 1930s he was involved in struggles to establish and gain recognition for the Association of Cinematograph Technicians (1933), and later, as chair of the directors' section, he fought to secure minimum pay and working conditions for the now vast army of film workers (1939).

Elvey's first wartime film was *For Freedom* (1940), a characteristic mix of social document and romance, which he repeated in *The Lamp Still Burns* (1943), about the struggle between a nurse's call to duty and obedience and the new wartime independence of women. It recalled his earlier fascination with Florence Nightingale. In the brief golden age of British cinema after the war, Elvey adapted Stephan Zweig's *Beware of Pity* (1947), often considered his best film.

During the 1950s Elvey directed a series of low-budget but popular comedies. However, his film career came to a halt when an insurance medical revealed blindness in one eye. Ever resourceful, he turned to broadcasting, with a radio series, *Opera Alphabet*, and a television series, *Picture Parade* (1956–62). He also directed an episode in an Independent Television thriller series, *White Hunter* (1960). In 1953 he was described as still being 'an immensely vital and vigorous man, with a small white beard and soft speaking voice of an enfant terrible who has not necessarily been tamed but has mellowed' (*Radio Times*, 23 Dec 1953). Despite earlier prosperity, Elvey died impoverished in Raylands Nursing Home at 54 Marine Parade, Brighton, on 28 August 1967.

The only British director to continue making successful films for four generations, separated by two world wars, Elvey has been consistently praised for his work. Throughout the 1920s and 1930s he was consistently named 'one of our best directors' alongside Alfred Hitchcock and Herbert Wilcox, and in 1947 *The Cine-Technician* introduced him as 'doyen of British directors' (May–June 1947). Despite such achievement, Elvey has not been accorded the critical attention his interesting career deserves because his films do not fulfil the criteria for the film *auteur* largely established in relation to European or Hollywood directors. Thus later attention to his work has characterized him as a craftsman rather than artist. Yet his films brilliantly convey a peculiarly English sensibility.

CHRISTINE GLEDHILL

Sources L. Wood, *The commercial imperative in the British film industry: Maurice Elvey, a case study* (1987) · R. Low, *The history of the British film*, 3: *1914–1918* (1950) · R. Low, *The history of the British film*, 4: *1918–1929* (1971) · R. Low, *The history of the British film*, 7: *1929–1939: film making in 1930s Britain* (1985) · D. Gifford, 'The early memoirs of Maurice Elvey', *Griffithiana*, 60–61 (Oct 1997), 77–124 · V. Saville, 'Shadows on the screen', unpublished memoirs, BFI, 32–7 · D. Quinlan, *Illustrated guide to film directors* (1983), 87–8 · R. W. Pohle and D. C. Hart, *Sherlock Holmes on the screen* (1977), 73, 77–9, 167 · K. Brownlow, *David Lean* (1996), 26, 49, 54–5, 57–60, 679 · *Radio Times* (23 Dec 1953) · B. Dean, *Mind's eye: an autobiography, 1927–1972*

(1973), 108 · *The Bioscope* (16 Oct 1913) · *The Bioscope* (9 July 1914) · *The Bioscope* (3 June 1926) · *The Bioscope* (10 Feb 1927) · *The Bioscope* (5 Jan 1928) · *Kinematograph Weekly* (Aug 1919) · *Kinematograph Weekly* (6 May 1920) · *Kinematograph Weekly* (22 April 1920) · *Kinematograph Weekly* (9 Feb 1922) · *Kinematograph Weekly* (19 June 1924) · *Kinematograph Weekly* (10 Feb 1927) · *Kinematograph Weekly* (11 Jan 1934) · *Kinematograph Weekly* (20 June 1935) · *Kinematograph Weekly* (9 Nov 1939) · *Motion Picture Studio* (24 March 1923) · *Pictures and Picturegoer* (Jan 1924) · *The Picturegoer* (Sept 1927) · private information (2004) · b. cert. · m. certs. [Adeline Preston, Florence Clarke, Isabella Reed] · d. cert. · CGPLA Eng. & Wales (1967) · *The Era* (19 March 1910) · *The Times* (29 Aug 1967) · *North East Daily Gazette* (12 Jan 1915)
Archives BFI, letter to the British Film Institute | FILM BFI NFTVA, performance footage | SOUND BBC WAC
Likenesses H. Coster, photographs, *c.*1935–1936, NPG [*see illus.*] · photographs, priv. colls. · photographs, Green Dragon Museum, Stockton-on-Tees
Wealth at death £376: probate, 10 Nov 1967, CGPLA Eng. & Wales

Elvey, Stephen (1805–1860), organist and composer, was the son of John Elvey and Abigail Hardiman, and the elder brother and for some time the music instructor of Sir George *Elvey (1816–1893). Stephen was born on 27 June 1805, at Canterbury, and received his training as chorister of the cathedral under Highmore Skeats. At the age of seventeen he was accidentally shot in the leg by a friend, whose sister, Louisa, he later married. The loss of a leg did not deter him from following his chosen career, and he learned to operate the pedals of the organ with a wooden substitute. In 1830 he succeeded Alfred Bennett as organist of New College, Oxford, where he established a reputation for his skilful playing. He took the MusB degree in 1831 and the MusD in 1838. Following the establishment of a glee club at New College in 1839, Elvey suggested modifications of the rules to ensure high standards, which were much appreciated. He was organist of St Mary the Virgin, the university church, in 1845, and from 1846 organist of St John's College. While William Crotch held simultaneously the offices of professor of music and choragus at Oxford, Elvey acted as his deputy in all professorial matters for some years (Crotch died at the end of 1847). In 1848 the offices were divided, Sir Henry Bishop becoming professor, and Elvey choragus. He retained his appointments until his death.

Elvey made a few but not unimportant contributions to sacred music. The *Evening Service in Continuation of Croft's Morning Service in A*, subsequently re-edited by Dr Martin, was composed about 1825, when Elvey was lay clerk at Canterbury Cathedral. The *Oxford Psalm Book* (1852), containing six original tunes, *The Psalter, or, Canticles and Psalms of David, Pointed for Chanting upon a New Principle* (1856) and *The Canticles* (1858) were his most important publications, and helped in improving the conduct of the services of the established church. Elvey died at Oxford on 6 October 1860, in the parish of St Peter-in-the-East, and was survived by his wife. He was succeeded as organist of New College by George Benjamin Arnold.

L. M. MIDDLETON, *rev.* NILANJANA BANERJI

Sources Grove, *Dict. mus.* · Brown & Stratton, *Brit. mus.* · W. Cowan and J. Love, *The music of the church hymnary and the psalter in metre* (1901) · Foster, *Alum. Oxon.* · H. W. Shaw, *The succession of organists of the Chapel Royal and the cathedrals of England and Wales from c.1538* (1991) · J. Buxton and P. Williams, eds., *New College,*

Oxford, 1379–1979 (1979) • *GM*, 3rd ser., 9 (1860), 557 • *Jackson's Oxford Journal* (12 Feb 1848) • *CGPLA Eng. & Wales* (1860)

Wealth at death under £6000: probate, 23 Nov 1860, *CGPLA Eng. & Wales*

Elviden, Edmund (*fl.* 1569–1570), poet, was the author of three works. He first published, in 1569, *The closet of counsels, conteining the advice of diverse wise phylosophers, touchinge sundrie moral matters, in poesies, precepts, proverbs, and parables, translated and collected out of divers authours into English verse*. *The most Excellent … Historie of Pesistratus and Catanea* was probably published in 1570, along with his *Neweyeres Gift to the Rebellious Persons in the North Partes of England*. All three books are extremely rare—in the case of the last work, this might be owing to the destruction of such politically and religiously charged material (Huth, xix–xx). Nothing concrete is known of Elviden's personal history, though it would seem, based upon the closing lines of his *Neweyeres Gift*, that he may have been a north-countryman:

> This wrote your frende, a wyshyng frende
> Unto his *natyve soyle*.

ALSAGER VIAN, *rev.* ELIZABETH GOLDRING

Sources H. Huth, ed., *Fugitive tracts written in verse which illustrate the condition of religious and political feeling in England* (1875) • T. Corser, *Collectanea Anglo-poetica, or, A … catalogue of a … collection of early English poetry*, 6, Chetham Society, 100 (1877) • W. T. Lowndes, *The bibliographer's manual of English literature*, ed. H. G. Bohn, [new edn], 6 vols. (1869)

Elvin, Sir Arthur James (1899–1957), sports promoter, was born in Norwich on 5 July 1899, the son of John Elvin, a police officer who died while his son was still at school, and his wife, Charlotte Elizabeth, *née* Holley. Arthur (as he was always known) left his local school at fourteen and after a variety of jobs joined the Royal Flying Corps as soon as he was seventeen. He was sent to France as an observer, and was taken prisoner after being shot down. He escaped, possibly on two occasions, but was recaptured because he knew neither French nor German and could not swim. This experience, he later said, had given him the determination to build a public swimming-pool.

After the war Elvin was employed by a scrap merchant who was salvaging the metal from shells. He returned to London at a time of depression and obtained a job which took him as a cigarette salesman to the British Empire Exhibition at Wembley in 1924. From this lowly viewpoint he realized how profitable the kiosks and exhibits were. The following year he borrowed money and opened his own shops there, and did extremely well. Also in 1925 he met and married Jennie (*née* Harding), the widow of William Heathcote Dolphin, who was then the manageress of the jewellery section of the Palace of Industry there. They did not have any children.

Having closely inspected the exhibition site in 1925, Elvin was encouraged to bid for certain of the smaller buildings when the entire Wembley site was sold to James White in 1926. Other contractors asked to be paid for the task; Elvin made an offer to pay, retaining the demolished materials, and got the contract.

While occupied in the demolition, Elvin became interested in greyhound racing, already successfully established at Manchester and the White City, and was advised by Sir Owen Williams that it would be possible to adapt the Wembley stadium which was then being used for football once a year and was consequently rapidly deteriorating. Elvin purchased the stadium, floated it as a private company, became managing director, and the first greyhound meeting was held in December 1927.

Elvin was not concerned with money-making as an end in itself, but liked to spend money, and he had moreover an ambition to make Wembley more than a racing track. Attached to the stadium was a considerable area of land and a lake and he first had ideas of a great amusement park, but finally decided to realize his early ambition and built the Empire pool. Indoor swimming-pools were not financially very successful, so the bath was covered over with a removable floor in order to stage skating, ice hockey, ice spectacles, and boxing. This, together with greyhound racing and dirt-track cycle racing, involved Elvin in attending every day and night except Sundays. He was a great party giver and he had a restaurant for his parties on the balcony of the Empire pool. He was inclined to asthma, however, and the smoky atmosphere of these entertainments did not help his health.

During the Second World War, Elvin carried on as best he could at Wembley, where he generously entertained servicemen and women. The pool was at this time occupied as a hostel for Gibraltarians. As far back as 1936 and earlier he yearned to have the Olympic Games in Wembley and he had visited the games when they were opened in Berlin by Hitler. The war over, he returned to his ambition which he achieved in 1948, believed to be the only occasion when the Olympic Games, without a government subsidy, made a small surplus. This, of course, increased his entertaining and his work. Ever the perfectionist, Elvin was hardly ever out of Wembley, where he was a stern disciplinarian; yet he could unbend when people went sick or were in trouble, when he proved their greatest friend. He was made an honorary freeman of the borough of Wembley in 1945, appointed MBE in the same year, and knighted in 1946.

Elvin's health deteriorated and he took a sea voyage to South Africa to recuperate, but died on the voyage and was buried at sea on 4 February 1957. He was survived by his wife.

OWEN WILLIAMS, *rev.* ANITA McCONNELL

Sources *The Times* (8 Feb 1957), 11b • A. M. Low, *Wonderful Wembley* (1953) • private information (1971) • *WWW* • m. cert. • *CGPLA Eng. & Wales* (1957)

Likenesses T. Hopkins, photograph, 19 Sept 1953, Hult. Arch. • A. J. Banks, bronze bust, Wembley Stadium, London • photograph, repro. in Low, *Wonderful Wembley*

Wealth at death £69,522 11*s*. 10*d*.: probate, 9 April 1957, *CGPLA Eng. & Wales*

Elvin, Joe [*real name* Joseph Peter Keegan] (1862–1935), music-hall entertainer, was born on 29 November 1862 at 3 Rose Street, Soho, central London, the son of Joseph Peter Keegan (1840–1901), actor and music-hall artiste, and his wife, Annie Delaney. He was educated at a Catholic school in Tottenham Court Road while simultaneously receiving tuition in dancing and other performance skills. He made his début in pantomime at Brighton Theatre Royal in 1871 and began his music-hall career the following year as a juvenile comic and clog dancer at Crowder's, Greenwich. About this time he began appearing with his father in the short, dramatic, and comic sketches then in their infancy on the music-hall stage. Appearing as Joe Keegan and Little Elvin, their first real success was the sentimental *Poor Jo* based on Dickens's *Bleak House*. During a season for the vaudeville entrepreneur Tony Pastor in New York in 1882 they turned increasingly to comic material. It was within this genre that Elvin established himself as one of the most gifted and successful among late Victorian and Edwardian music-hall performers, while at the same time playing a major role in expanding the potential of the music-hall sketch and making it a central element of the variety stage.

Working closely with the influential sketch writer Wal Pink (1862–1922), Elvin developed the character of the loud, lovable, and pleasingly irreverent cockney working man having a good time. This figure reached maturity in Tom Tweedlam in 'The Tinker's Holiday' (1886), the sketch that really established father and son as a major act. Keegan senior, a brilliant 'feed', retired in 1894 but Elvin adjusted easily to working with new partners. Among the other 100 or more sketches that made up his career were 'I ain't Barmy', which provided the catch-phrase shouted by the gallery whenever he appeared, and a string of pieces relating to sport in general and horse-racing in particular. These often involved extremely large casts and dramatic special effects and features; 'Over the Sticks', performed at the Oxford in 1895, included a hurdle race with live horses. Other major successes included ''Appy 'Ampstead, the Bookie' and 'Riding to Orders'. Although the music-hall was never in any sense politically or socially radical, some commentators have seen his work (especially with Pink) as mildly challenging dominant contemporary attitudes. His characters invariably failed to be impressed by social superiors and by displays of social pretension. In 'Under Cross Examination' (1912) his character, William Nutt, manages to win out over the legal system despite a degree of complicity in a minor theft, while 'Who Ses So?' (1912) contained something of a critique of middle-class philanthropy. Elvin certainly produced a rather tougher and edgier cockney working man than more sentimental performers of the period such as Albert Chevalier.

Above all, however, Elvin's popularity was based on his comic timing, his gregariousness, and his ebullience. Initially not a major earner, he became one of the best-paid Edwardian performers on the variety stage, although this undoubtedly involved a punishing schedule. In February 1903, for example, he was appearing six nights a week in three different sketches in three different London halls within less than three hours. It was perhaps this type of experience, coupled with what most contemporaries agreed to be a kindly and thoughtful disposition, which made Elvin such a key figure within the industry's philanthropic and benevolent organizations. In December 1907

he helped found and became first president of the Variety Artistes' Benevolent Fund, a body set up by performers to replace a previous society (founded by Elvin's father) which had been controlled largely by agents and managers. In 1909 Elvin was the prime mover in a scheme that eventually caused Brinsworth Home to be built for retired music-hall performers. Unsurprisingly, he strongly supported the variety artistes' strike in 1907. Perhaps his most significant contribution, however, came through his role as a founder of the theatrical charity the Grand Order of Water Rats in 1889. It began life when a betting syndicate that had grown up around a trotting pony owned by Elvin agreed to donate any winnings to charity, gaining its name when someone referred to the pony during a rainy trip to the Derby as looking more like a water rat. Elvin served as King Rat in 1894.

Elvin married his wife, Lottie, probably in the late 1880s; there is no evidence of their having children. They lived for much of his career in Brixton and their house in Effra Road was a popular port of call for variety artistes on Sundays. His main hobbies comprised his extensive charitable and benevolent work and a lifelong interest in horse-racing, as owner, spectator, and enthusiastic gambler. He appears to have retired in the early 1920s and a benefit concert held for him at the Palladium in March 1923 guaranteed him a weekly income of £5 for the rest of his life. After his wife's death he moved to live with a lifelong variety colleague and friend, Joe O'Gorman, whose wife nursed Elvin in the poor health that dogged his final years. He died in St Columba's Hospital, Swiss Cottage, on 3 March 1935 and was buried at Bandon Hill cemetery, Wallington, Croydon, on 7 March. DAVE RUSSELL

Sources *The Performer* (7 March 1935) • *The Era* (6 March 1935) • *The Era* (12 Oct 1901) • R. Busby, *British music hall: an illustrated who's who from 1850 to the present day* (1976) • L. Rutherford, '"Harmless nonsense": the comic sketch and the development of music-hall entertainment', *Music hall: performance and style*, ed. J. S. Bratton (1986), 131–51 • b. cert. • d. cert. • *The Performer* (14 March 1935)

Elwall, Edward (*bap.* 1676, *d.* 1744), Seventh Day Baptist and religious controversialist, was baptized on 9 November 1676 at Ettingshall in the parish of Sedgley, Staffordshire, the son of Thomas Elwall, yeoman and ironmonger, and his wife, Elizabeth Gibbins. He claimed his family had been settled in the neighbourhood of Wolverhampton 'above eleven hundred Years, ever since the Saxons conquer'd the Britons' (Elwall, *Supernatural Incarnation*, 27). Elwall began business as an ironmonger, becoming later a mercer and grocer in Wolverhampton, attending the Bristol and Chester fairs, and making 'an easy fortune, insomuch that he built a little town' of eighteen brick houses, about half a mile from Wolverhampton, on the Dudley Road (J. T., 283). He married Jane Woodward about 1698. He served as constable of the town in 1709–10. Elwall was originally a member of the Presbyterian meeting in Wolverhampton, registering his house there for worship at the county quarter sessions in 1704.

During the meeting-house riots of June and July 1715 Elwall led a small party who successfully fought off the high-church mob which was attempting to pull down the meeting-house in Wolverhampton. Because of his vigorous defence of the Hanoverian accession in public, Elwall was particularly odious to the mob. 'They often, yea, very often, threatened to kill me', and on one occasion as he was riding down Bilston Street someone fired at him from a window, 'whether with a Ball or not, I can't say' (Elwall, *Declaration*, 46; Elwall, *Supernatural Incarnation*, 28–9). Another occasion about 'three-score of 'em' threatened his house, and 'continued roaring, *Down with the House*, a long time'; eventually, 'by the Intreaties of some Neighbours, and throwing some Money to 'em out at the Windows', they left, but before they went 'some of 'em to spite me and my Wife' knelt at his door and drank the Pretender's health (Elwall, *Declaration*, 46).

Elwall's visits to Bristol seem to have brought about his first religious change. A Baptist minister immersed him and his wife in the Severn, though he did not then cease attending the presbyterian meeting. According to the account given by his wife to John Byrom, 'notions about the Trinity' were first put into his head by John Hays of Stafford, and he became a Unitarian. After John Stubbs, the presbyterian minister at Wolverhampton, preached against him, Elwall became 'a churchman' (*Private Journal*, 321). He wrote six letters to the archbishop of Canterbury, William Wake, on the subject of the Trinity and received four in reply, but they did not settle his doubts. He was probably drawn towards the Quakers through sympathy with Penn's views on the Trinity, and he adopted some of their modes of thought and expression; but his scripture studies may have led him to a close, if unconscious, reproduction of Ebionite views.

Holding the perpetual obligation of the Jewish sabbath, Elwall closed shop on Saturday and opened it on Sunday. He discarded his wig and grew long hair and a flowing beard. This he followed up with some eccentricities of dress, wearing 'a cap or turban' instead of a hat (*Private Journal*, 323). By following 'the Patriarchs and Prophets, and Christ and his Apostles, in wearing my Beard and my own hair … as they did', he had been 'a thousand times mocked and scorned at' and indeed subjected to 'the most bitter Curses, opprobrious Names, and malicious words; often throwing stones and other things after me, and crying, damn him, stop him, a Jew, a Turk, the Devil, … cut off his Beard &c' (Elwall, *Grand Question*, 28–9). The different stages in the development of his opinions are difficult to date, but it was reported in the minutes of the Seventh-Day General Baptist church at Mill Yard, Goodman's Fields, London, that on 6 December 1719 'Mr Elwaar' of Wolverhampton was 'newly come to the observation of the seventh day Sabbath'. On 1 May 1720 he was admitted 'as a transient member' (Mill Yard minutes).

In 1724 Elwall published his *True Testimony* arguing for the unity of God. This was answered locally by James Barter, a miller and former Baptist preacher, to which Elwall replied with *Dagon Fallen*, which went through various revisions and at least two editions (1725 or 1726; 1732) with slightly altered titles. The publication of *True Testimony* at the insistence of some clergymen eventually led to his prosecution for blasphemy. The trial took place at the summer assize at Stafford in 1726, and caused a great sensation locally. Elwall thought about a thousand people attended the trial. The only account is Elwall's own narrative, which is not very clear. The case did not go to jury, and was probably quashed on the grounds that Elwall had not been served with a copy of the indictment, which he described as 'near as big as half a door'. John Martin, who was present at the trial, told Priestley in 1788 that the figure of Elwall, 'a tall man, with white hair [though he was only in his fiftieth year], a large beard and flowing garments, … struck everybody with respect' (*Theological and Miscellaneous Works of Joseph Priestley*, 2.417). The judge, Alexander Denton, proposed to defer the case to the next assize if Elwall would give bail for his appearance. This he refused to do, and asked to be permitted to plead to the indictment in person. Denton allowed him to enter on a long and enthusiastic argument in defence of 'the unitarian doctrine', at the close of which Rupert Humpatch, a justice who had been his next-door neighbour for three years, spoke of his honesty and sincerity. The testimony was corroborated by another justice. There was some sensation in court when Elwall disclosed that the archbishop of Canterbury was aware of his opinions. After consulting the prosecutors, and making a fruitless attempt to get Elwall to promise to write no more, Denton discharged him. Fortunate in his judge, Elwall himself thought the justices disliked the indictment because 'the priests had done it' (Elwall, *Grand Question*, 55), and a number when entertaining him after the trial expressed pleasure at his acquittal. A clergyman present, however, said bitterly that 'He ought to have been hanged' (ibid., 60). The same year he disturbed a meeting at Pinner's Hall after a sermon by Samuel Wright, when he tried to address the congregation in Quaker fashion.

During the early 1730s Elwall moved to London, where he published *A Declaration Against George, King of Great Britain*, in which he denied the civil powers had any authority in spiritual matters. The work went through four editions (1732, 1734, and 1741) and a partial change of title. While taking the opportunity to record his loyalty and sufferings on behalf of the Hanoverians, the work included an extraordinary challenge to George II to meet him in St James's Park for a discussion, if necessary with his 'Black-guards' and 'Red-guards': 'name the Day, How and Place, as thou thyself pleaseth' (Elwall, *Declaration*, 3). Dr Johnson has been accused of misquoting Elwall, but 'black-coats' (clergy) and 'red-coats' (soldiers) were substituted for the former terms in subsequent editions. The second edition included a defence of sabbatarianism which was answered by Daniel Dobel in *The Seventh-Day Sabbath not Obligatory on Christians* (1739). Elwall also wrote against tithes (1738). His main works, however, were either in support of sabbatarianism or questioned the Trinity and the incarnation of Christ: notably his *The Supernatural Incarnation of Jesus Christ Proved to be False* (1742; 2nd edn, 1743) and *Idolatry Discovered and Detested* (1744). Later publications also included accounts of his trial, which were discovered in the late eighteenth century by Joseph Priestley. Priestley, loaned a copy at Leeds by a Quaker friend, was responsible for a new popular edition which went through at least ten imprints between 1771 and 1794, including two published in Philadelphia. There were a further four abridgements issued between 1788 and 1791. Priestley's reprint encouraged J. W. Fletcher, Wesley's intended successor, to prepare an answer, but it was never completed. Theophilus Lindsey included an account of the trial in his *Sequel to the Apology* (1776). Further editions were issued during the early nineteenth century by the Unitarian Tract Society and in America.

Elwall was a colourful and eccentric figure who does not fit comfortably within any of the conventional doctrinal descriptions of the period. He was ready to defend both unitarianism and sabbatarianism; he underwent adult baptism, and followed many of the customs of contemporary Quakers. Dr Johnson, who once dined in his company, saw Elwall as a self-publicist who 'had a mind to make himself famous, by being the founder of a new sect, which he wished much should be called *Elwallians*' (Boswell, *Life*, 2.164). Elwall's challenge to George II in his *Declaration Against George* was 'to try to make himself distinguished' and 'had something of the impudence of Junius to our present King' (ibid.). To Boswell's suggestion that Elwall might have been sincere, Johnson replied that he 'should have been put in the stocks; a proper pulpit for him; … We are not providing for mad people' (ibid., 251). Priestley, however, believed 'such firmness in the cause of truth, and such presence of mind in asserting and vindicating it, as appear in his trial, are truly apostolical, and have had but few examples since the first promulgation of Christianity' (Priestley, *Triumph of Truth*, 3). He had seven sons and seven daughters, of whom only one son, Sion, and three daughters survived to adulthood. Elwall's religious opinions appear not to have been shared by the rest of his family. His wife remained a presbyterian and, according to Byrom, his son showed little interest in his father's writings and went to church. He died in London in 1744 and was buried in the graveyard of the General Baptist Church, Mill Yard, Goodman's Fields, London, on 29 November 1744.   DAVID L. WYKES

Sources J. T. [Joshua Toulmin], 'Biography: memoir of Mr Edward Elwall', *Universal Theological Magazine and Impartial Review*, 1 (1804), 283–7 • [R. B. Aspland], 'Some account of Edward Elwall and his writings', *Christian Reformer*, 11 (1855), 329–45 • *The private journal and literary remains of John Byrom*, ed. R. Parkinson, 2 vols. in 4 pts, Chetham Society, 32, 34, 40, 44 (1854–7) • E. Elwall, *A declaration against George, king of Great Britain and Irel … and all other kings and states whatsoever under heaven* (1732) • E. Elwall, *The grand question in religion consider'd. Whether we shall obey God, or man; Christ, or the Pope; the prophets and apostles, or prelates and priests: with an account of the author's tryal or prosecution at Stafford-Assizes. Before Judge Denton* [1736] • E. Elwall, *The supernatural incarnation of Jesus Christ proved to be false; having no foundation in the prophets, … And that our Lord Jesus Christ was the real son of Joseph and Mary* (1742) • The Mill Yard minutes, the church book of the Seventh Day General Baptist congregation meeting at Mill Yard, Goodman's Fields, 1673–1840, DWL [microfilm copy] • Boswell, *Life*, 2.164–5, 251 • [J. Priestley], *The triumph of truth; being an account of the trial of Mr. E. Elwall, for heresy and blasphemy, at Stafford assizes, … To which are added, extracts from William Penn's Sandy foundation shaken*, 2nd edn (1775?) • *The theological and miscellaneous works of Joseph Priestley*, ed. J. T. Rutt, 25 vols. (1817–35) • C. J. L. Elwell, *The iron Elwells: a family social history* (1964), 24–32 • B. W. Ball, *The Seventh-Day men: sabbatarians and sabbatarianism in England and Wales, 1600–1800* (1994) • parish register, Sedgley, 9 Nov 1676, Staffs. RO [baptism] • burial register, DWL, microfilm 533.B.1 • *IGI*

Elwell [*née* Glass], **Ann Catherine** (1922–1996), intelligence officer and diplomat, was born on 16 June 1922 at 12 Leinster Gardens, Bayswater, London, the only child of Robert Lionel Glass, a general practitioner and former surgeon-lieutenant in the Royal Navy, of 106 Inverness Terrace, Bayswater, and his wife, Eileen Ann, daughter of the Revd W. H. Smartt, Irish scholar and honorary canon of Manchester Cathedral. She was educated at Miss Faunce's day school in Queens Gardens, Bayswater, learning French and German from a governess, and having passed her school certificate at fifteen she was sent in 1938 to Miss Lestrange's finishing school in Florence, where she spent a year learning Italian, acquired a love of Italian opera, and became skilled in bookbinding. Back in London she learned typing, domestic science, and deportment at the Monkey Club, in Pont Street, came out as a débutante in May 1939, and began to train as an actress at the Webber-Douglas School of Dramatic Art.

In May 1940, because of her fluency in languages, Ann Glass was recruited onto the temporary wartime staff of MI5 by the deputy director-general, Brigadier Harker, whom she had met at a party. When MI5 was evacuated from its temporary quarters at Wormwood Scrubs prison to Blenheim Palace in October 1940 she moved to Oxford, where she led a hectic and exhausting social life while working on Italian translations for MI5. In November 1941 she left MI5 to work on its behalf as a secretary, and later a scriptwriter, for the film company making *In which we Serve*, 'minding' the Italian film director Filippo del Giudice, who had been released from an internment camp at Noel Coward's insistence in order to act as art director. She returned to the London office of MI5, now in St James Street, in September 1942, for the rest of the war, and continued her endless round of parties, mixing with literary figures such as Henry Yorke, who wrote novels under the pseudonym Henry Green (1905–1974), and Cyril Connolly (1903–1974), and her American friends Charles Collingwood, one of the CBS correspondents in London, and Dorsey Fisher, press attaché at the American embassy—following the advice of her friend William Saroyan (1908–1981) to 'live while you live'. In November 1945 she was sent to Rome to take over the work of Anthony Blunt (1907–1983), and spent the next ten months looking at the secret papers that had been captured with Mussolini and going through the Italian official archives, searching for documents of interest to MI5. From the end of 1946 until 1950 she worked at the head office of MI5 in Curzon Street, investigating Russian spies, and in April 1948 was sent to Egypt to lecture on double agents to security intelligence officers in the canal zone; on this trip she contracted dengue fever, and she continued to suffer bouts of ill health all her life.

On 24 June 1950 Ann Glass married Charles John Lister

Ann Catherine Elwell (1922–1996), by unknown photographer

Elwell, a former naval officer newly recruited to MI5; they had two sons and two daughters. He was posted in 1950 to Singapore to a position with SIFE (security intelligence Far East), but because the head of SIFE did not like to employ women Ann had no job. She was later able to work for a branch of the commission-general for south-east Asia, engaged in countering communist propaganda, a job that she loved.

After five years in Singapore, where three of their children were born (the fourth was born in 1958), the Elwells returned to England in 1955. Ann became a first secretary at the information research department (IRD) of the Foreign Office, set up in 1948 to counter communism. As head of the Middle East section she travelled extensively, especially to Iran, Pakistan, and Turkey, and also to Washington, collaborating closely with colleagues in the Central Treaty Organization (CENTO), who were also attempting to expose the aims of the USSR and China in the Middle East. In the belief that communist propaganda would best be countered by bringing the people of these countries into contact with representatives of the best in British life she sent distinguished Englishmen, including the footballer Sir Stanley Matthews and Vic Feather, general secretary of the TUC, on missions to the Middle East. She entertained constantly, and her ability to make friends easily contributed greatly to the effectiveness of her work for the IRD. She was appointed OBE in 1970, and on her retirement in 1971 the Ariel Foundation, an organization dedicated to Anglo-Arab understanding, gave a lunch in her honour.

Ann Elwell combined a diplomatic career with running the family home—a large house in Chalfont St Giles, Buckinghamshire, which she and her husband bought in 1964. Beautiful and witty, with a deep, husky voice, she was also an excellent cook with a large collection of cookbooks, although she maintained that she did not enjoy cooking but just loved good food. She died, of cancer, on 12 January 1996 at the London Clinic, Westminster.

ANNE PIMLOTT BAKER

Sources C. Elwell, *Ann Catherine Elwell: a memoir* (1997) · *The Times* (17 Jan 1996) · *The Independent* (26 Jan 1996) · b. cert. · m. cert. · d. cert.
Likenesses photograph, 1939, repro. in *The Independent* · photograph, repro. in *The Times* [*see illus.*]

Elwes [Helwys], **Sir Gervase** (*bap.* 1561, *d.* 1615), court official and convicted accessory to the murder of Sir Thomas Overbury, was baptized at Askham, Nottinghamshire, on 1 September 1561, the eldest son of John Elwes (*d.* 1581) of Worlaby, Lincolnshire, and his wife, Mary, daughter of Thomas Blagden of Thames Ditton. His grandfather was William Elwes of Askham (*d.* 1557). His uncle, Geoffrey Elwes (1541–1616), a merchant tailor and alderman, was sheriff of London in 1607. Gervase Elwes married Mary Brooke of Norfolk, with whom he had fourteen children. Four died in infancy, and at least two others predeceased their parents. In the early seventeenth century, the family name was spelt in numerous ways (including Elvis, Helwisse), but the spelling eventually stabilized as Elwes.

Elwes had a conventional gentleman's education. University records show that he matriculated at Easter 1573 as a pensioner of St John's College, Cambridge, but took no degree. In May 1579, after a period at New Inn, he was admitted to the Middle Temple. His contemporary Nicholas Overbury (Thomas's father) remembered Elwes as 'a dexterous and witty man' who was chosen as the Temple's Christmas lord of misrule and 'acted his part very gallantly' (BL, Add. MS 15476, fol. 93*v*). He later travelled in France, where he became a friend of John Chamberlain, the political intelligencer. Elwes presumably succeeded to his father's Lincolnshire estates in 1581 and was residing in the county at the birth of his daughters Bridget and Jane, who were baptized in Gainsborough in 1595 and 1602 respectively. Elwes was knighted by James I at Theobalds on 7 May 1603, and some time later, probably in 1612, he settled in London and began to follow the court. He was described by John More in May 1613 as 'an esquire of the body and a creature of my Lord Chamberlain' (the earl of Suffolk) (*Downshire MSS*, 4.105).

Elwes's appointment as lieutenant of the Tower on 6 May 1613 surprised Chamberlain, who noted that his friend was 'somewhat an unknown man' and of 'too mild and gentle a disposition for such an office' (*Letters of John Chamberlain*, 1.452). The appointment was engineered by Henry Howard, earl of Northampton and lord privy seal. Using his uncle Geoffrey either as an intermediary or as a source of money Elwes paid £1400 for the office to a fellow Lincolnshire man, Sir Thomas Monson, master of the armoury in the Tower and Northampton's client.

At this point, Elwes became unwittingly complicit in the plot to murder the courtier Sir Thomas Overbury, who had been committed to the Tower two weeks earlier. Given the tainted nature of much of the surviving evidence, the precise workings of the plot are difficult to establish with certainty. It was in part a political man-oeuvre, designed to cement a court alliance between the Howard family (led by Northampton and Thomas How-ard, earl of Suffolk) and the king's favourite, Robert Carr, Viscount Rochester, later earl of Somerset. The glue cementing the alliance was Frances Howard—Suffolk's daughter and Northampton's great-niece—who was attempting to have her marriage to the third earl of Essex nullified in order to marry Carr. Overbury, Carr's friend and adviser, opposed Carr's romantic relationship with Frances and the concomitant political relationship with the crypto-Catholic Howard faction. Overbury's commit-ment to the Tower, which removed him from the factional arena, had been arranged by his political and personal enemies. Some or all of those same enemies were also resolved on a more permanent solution to Overbury's intransigence.

Elwes's role in Overbury's death can be reconstructed with some certainty from his later confessions. On Mon-son's recommendation, the day after assuming his new office, Elwes appointed Richard Weston as Overbury's keeper. According to Elwes, Monson told him that West-on's job was to regulate the flow of messages between Overbury and the outside. But shortly after Weston's appointment, Elwes discovered the keeper bringing poison to the imprisoned courtier. Elwes claimed he had terrified Weston into throwing away the poison and had helped intercept poisoned tarts and jellies sent to Over-bury later on. In his initial confessions, Elwes asserted that at the time he believed he had thwarted the poison plot, only to discover after the fact that Weston and his employers had evaded his precautions by bribing an apothecary to give Overbury a poisoned enema. Even after his trial and conviction as an accessory before the fact, Elwes insisted he had never had a 'felonious intent' to murder Overbury and had been guilty only of not report-ing what he had discovered. His silence, he admitted, was the result of his cowardice and ambition, his obeisance to 'worldly report of greatness or great men's favour' (PRO, SP 14/83/49–51). He had realized that Northampton and the countess of Essex were behind the plot but had kept quiet lest he lose their patronage. As his self-styled apol-ogy, penned in 1615, reveals, Elwes soothed his conscience by cobbling together a variety of casuistical rationaliza-tions for his silence.

Overbury's death in September 1613 was much noted, but foul play was not widely suspected. The eventual 'dis-covery' of Overbury's murder two years later was largely Elwes's doing. In June 1615 Gilbert Talbot, earl of Shrews-bury, who had known Elwes for many years, attempted to broker a closer relationship between Elwes and the king's secretary, Sir Ralph Winwood. Though the source of his suspicions is unclear, Winwood informed Shrewsbury that he baulked at committing himself to one suspected of complicity in Overbury's death. In order to clear his name, Elwes agreed to meet Winwood and Shrewsbury at Whitehall. At this point Elwes revealed only that he had known of a plot to poison Overbury, that Weston was involved in it, and that he himself had attempted to

thwart it. Presumably waiting to see which way the polit-ical winds would blow, Shrewsbury and Winwood con-cealed this information over the summer while the king and court were on progress. Eventually informed of the lieutenant's information early in September, James ordered Winwood to get Elwes's story in writing. This written statement, dated 10 September 1615, triggered the investigation and legal proceedings that eventually took four lives, destroyed the fortunes of Somerset, the royal favourite, and supplied the Jacobean public with a disturb-ing parade of scandalous revelations implicating the court in moral and political transgressions ranging from ambition, adultery, and sartorial excess to murder, witch-craft, and popery. On Elwes's information, Weston was examined. Weston confirmed much of Elwes's version of events and then implicated several others in the plot, including the earl of Somerset and his wife. Although he, too, was repeatedly questioned, Elwes was not dismissed as lieutenant or placed under arrest until 26 October, three days after Weston's conviction as principal in Over-bury's murder.

On 16 November 1615 Elwes was tried at the Guildhall in London for the 'malicious aiding, comforting, and abet-ting of Weston in the poisoning and murdering of Over-bury' (State trials, 2.935). The most damaging evidence against him was a series of suspicious phrases, plucked from the recently deceased earl of Northampton's corres-pondence, that implied Elwes's active participation in the poison plot. Elwes defended himself vigorously and with some skill, offering plausible alternative readings of the incriminating phrases. He was unable, however, to explain away the confession of the poison-supplier James Franklin, who earlier that morning had told investigators that he had seen a letter from Elwes to Frances Howard in which the lieutenant had said of Overbury that 'this scab is like the fox, who the more he is cursed the better he fareth'. In his report to the king, Lord Chief Justice Edward Coke, the lead investigator and prosecutor of the case, recorded that upon hearing this testimony Elwes stood amazed and 'striking his hand on his breast, said to him-self', but in the hearing of the foreman of the jury, 'then Lord have mercy on me' (PRO, SP 14/83/49–51).

The jury found Elwes guilty and he was sentenced to death. With the consent of the king, who also remitted the condemned man's forfeited estate back to his wife and children, Elwes was hanged on 20 November 1615 at Tower Hill, instead of the more infamous Tyburn, out of respect for his former office. Encouraged by clerics sent by the authorities, Elwes made an exemplary end on the scaf-fold. He acknowledged and fully repented his guilt in fail-ing to expose the plot against Overbury, and he warned his audience away from the vices to which he had been addict-ed—swearing, gambling, vanity, and ambition. He died thankful for the chance to repent his sins and, mouthing orthodox Calvinist doctrine, appeared fully confident of his salvation. At least three editions of a moralizing pamphlet describing Elwes's gallows repentance were published by Nathaniel Butter in 1615–16. A broadsheet with a crude woodcut and verses also commemorated the event, as did a now-lost ballad. Many of these publications' themes were reworked in the section on Elwes in Richard Niccols's lengthy 1616 poem on Overbury. Copies of Elwes's last speech and transcripts of his trial were also circulated in manuscript and collected by scandal-hungry gentlemen across the country. ALASTAIR BELLANY

Sources letters, statements, and interrogations from the Overbury investigation, PRO, SP 14 (reign of James I) 14/81/86, 117–18; 14/82/20, 105, 107; 14/83/42, 49–51 · report on the star chamber case against Sir John Holles, 1615, Hunt. L., MS HM 41952, fol. 104v · 'Sir Gervase Ellowis, Lieutenant of the Tower, his Apologie, touching his knowledge of the Death of Sir Thomas Overbury', 1615, Bodl. Oxf., MS Tanner 299, fols. 194r–196r · *State trials*, 2.935–41 · *The lieutenant of the Tower his speech and repentance* (1615) · J. J. Howard, ed., *Miscellanea genealogica et heraldica*, 1 (1868), 68–75 · G. W. Marshall, ed., *The visitations of the county of Nottingham in the years 1569 and 1614*, Harleian Society, 4 (1871), 29–30 · A. R. Maddison, ed., *Lincolnshire pedigrees*, 1, Harleian Society, 50 (1902), 328–9 · *The letters of John Chamberlain*, ed. N. E. McClure, 1 (1939), 452 [letter to Dudley Carleton, 13 May 1613] · N. Oldisworth, 'A Booke Touching Sir Thomas Overbury', 1637, BL, Add MS 15476, fol. 93v [section dictated by Sir Nicholas Overbury] · J. Venn and J. A. Venn, eds., *The book of matriculations and degrees … in the University of Cambridge from 1544 to 1659* (1913), 234 · H. A. C. Sturgess, ed., *Register of admissions to the Honourable Society of the Middle Temple, from the fifteenth century to the year 1944*, 1 (1949), 44 · W. A. Shaw, *The knights of England*, 2 (1906), 104 · W. H. Overall and H. C. Overall, eds., *Analytical index to the series of records known as the Remembrancia* (1878), 82 · R. Niccols, *Sir Thomas Overburies vision* (1616) · *The picture of the unfortunate gentleman, Sir Gervis Elvies* (1615) · Arber, *Regs. Stationers*, 3.580 · *Report on the manuscripts of the marquis of Downshire*, 6 vols. in 7, HMC, 75 (1924–95)
Archives PRO, SP 14
Likenesses line engraving, 1813 (after woodcut), BM, NPG; repro. in R. S. Kirby, *The wonderful and scientific museum*

Elwes, Gervase Henry (1866–1921), singer, was born on 15 November 1866 at Billing Hall, Northamptonshire, the eldest son of Valentine Dudley Henry Cary-Elwes (*d.* 1909), landowner, and his second wife, Alice Ward (*d.* 1907). His parents converted to Roman Catholicism when Elwes was a child, and he attended two Catholic schools, The Oratory, Edgbaston (1877–81), and Woburn Park (1881–5), where he studied the violin and the piano as well as singing in school choirs until his voice broke. From 1885 to 1888 he read law at Christ Church, Oxford.

On 11 May 1889 Elwes married Winefride Mary Elizabeth Feilding (1868/9–1959), daughter of the earl of Denbigh, and the couple had eight children between 1890 and 1905. The sixth child was the portrait painter Simon *Elwes (1902–1975). In the same year as his marriage Elwes decided to enter the diplomatic service, and although he moved to Munich to study for the Foreign Office examination, he did not actually sit the examination. He accepted a post as an honorary attaché in Vienna in 1891, followed in 1892 by a post in Brussels. In both cities he continued to study music, learning harmony with Mandyczewski in Vienna and singing with Demest in Brussels.

In 1895 Elwes returned to England to live at the family estate, Brigg Manor in Lincolnshire, where he managed the shooting and served as a local magistrate. He continued to study singing, taking lessons in London with Henry Russell, and musical performance became the driving passion of his otherwise somewhat aimless life. Over the next few years he appeared as an amateur singer at public concerts in London and elsewhere, and, together with Winefride and her brother Everard Feilding, he initiated the North Lincolnshire Musical Competition Festival, which encouraged choral singing and the preservation of local folk-song.

In 1901 Elwes went to Paris to study with Jules Bouhy and started singing as a tenor rather than a baritone. He also decided to turn professional. This was a bold step for a man of his class, and one which his father strongly opposed. But, supported by Winefride, Elwes eventually obtained his father's approval, and in Paris in December 1902 he undertook his first professional engagement. He continued to take lessons, studying in London with Victor Beigel, the man he always regarded as his most important teacher.

Elwes became one of Britain's most popular singers, much in demand for song recitals (often with the accompanist Frederick Kiddle), ballad concerts, and oratorio performances. Critics were quick to praise his sensitive and intelligent interpretation of composers such as Brahms and J. S. Bach, a quality regarded as being closely linked to his class and breeding. They were less impressed with his vocal tone and general technique. Elwes gave enthusiastic support to British composers, notably by means of the 'jamborees' he organized with Everard Feilding, at which composers met in an informal atmosphere with singers and instrumentalists to try out their works. He also gave important public performances of new British music. In 1904 he first sang the title role in Elgar's *The Dream of Gerontius* (1900), and he was soon established as the ideal interpreter of this deeply Catholic work. He also gave the first performance of Vaughan Williams's song cycle *On Wenlock Edge* (1909), a setting of A. E. Housman's *Shropshire Lad* poems. Elwes was particularly associated with the songs of Roger Quilter.

While always continuing to be involved with upper-class music-making, such as the soirées of the patron Frank Schuster, Elwes also worked with charitable organizations such as the People's Concert Society. During the First World War he sang for numerous military charities and on three occasions visited the front to entertain the troops. Although best-known in England, he toured in continental Europe and the United States on several occasions, including a highly successful tour of Germany with the pianist Fanny Davies in 1907. It was while on tour in the United States, on 13 January 1921, that Elwes fell between the train and the platform at Boston Back Bay station, Boston, Massachusetts. He died a few hours later that day and was buried at Billing, Northamptonshire; he was survived by his wife. His family, friends, and colleagues established the Gervase Elwes Memorial Fund for Musicians, later to become the Musicians' Benevolent Fund.

SOPHIE FULLER

Sources W. Elwes and G. Elwes, *Gervase Elwes: the story of his life* (1935) · 'Gervase Elwes', *MT*, 53 (1912), 197–9 · 'Gervase Elwes', *MT*, 62 (1921), 81–2 · *The Times* (14 Jan 1921) · J. Bird, *Percy Grainger* (1976) · M. Kennedy, *Adrian Boult* (1987) · m. cert. · *CGPLA Eng. & Wales* (1921)

Archives Northants. RO, diaries │ SOUND BL NSA, performance recordings

Likenesses F. Müller, photograph, 1889, NPG · J. Russell & Sons, photograph, before 1917, NPG · photographs, repro. in Elwes and Elwes, *Gervase Elwes*

Wealth at death £168,027 8s. 5d.: probate, 16 April 1921, CGPLA Eng. & Wales

Elwes, Henry John (1846–1922), natural historian and traveller, was born on 16 May 1846, the eldest child of the four sons and four daughters born to John Henry Elwes (1815–1891) of Colesbourne, Gloucestershire, and his wife, Mary (d. 1913), fourth daughter of Admiral Sir Robert Howe Bromley, third baronet, of Stoke Hall, Newark. His sister Caroline Susan (d. 1865) was the first wife of Sir Michael Edward Hicks Beach, ninth baronet and first Earl St Aldwyn; another sister, Edith Mary, was the first wife of Frederick du Cane Godman FRS, a close friend and colleague of Elwes. He was great-great-grandson of the eccentric miser John *Elwes (1714–1789) of Marcham, Berkshire, on whose Marylebone property Portman Square and Portland Place were built. His great-grandfather, John Elwes, bought the Colesbourne estate.

Elwes was educated at Eton College between 1858 and 1861, went in 1862 to Brussels and Dresden to learn French and German, and entered the Scots guards in 1865, retiring with the rank of captain five years later. In 1871 he married Margaret Susan, second daughter of William Charles Lowndes-Stone, of Brightwell Park, Oxfordshire; they had one son, Henry Cecil (b. 1874), and one daughter, Susan Margaret, who married Major-General Sir Frederick Carrington. Elwes devoted his life to natural history and travel. His original interest was in ornithology and it was in the *Proceedings of the Zoological Society* (1873) that his paper on 'The geographical distribution of Asiatic birds' was published. This was the result of a visit in 1871 to Sikkim and, illegally, to Tibet, and was important in establishing that the Himalayan region was part of the same biogeographical region as China. Elwes attributed his election in 1897 to the Royal Society to this paper. In 1880 he produced his folio *Monograph of the Genus Lilium*, which remains an authoritative work on that subject; although the work was issued under Elwes's name, the strictly botanical parts of the work were done by J. G. Baker. He then turned to entomology, collecting butterflies and moths wherever he travelled; he discovered fifteen new species and gave 15,000 specimens to the British Museum (Natural History). After his marriage and particularly after inheriting Colesbourne, he turned to the collecting of plants. He was unusually adept at growing new and rare plants: ninety-eight species, mostly collected by Elwes and first flowered by him, were described in the *Botanical Magazine*. Several bear his name, of which the first— *Galanthus elwesii*, the snowdrop which he gathered near Smyrna in 1874—is the most familiar. The most important work of Elwes's life was begun in 1903 when, with his friend Augustine Henry, he undertook the production of *Trees of Great Britain and Ireland* (7 vols., 1906–13). Henry wrote the strictly botanical parts and Elwes contributed

Henry John Elwes (1846–1922), by Elliott & Fry

sections on the distribution, history, and cultivation of species, drawing on his knowledge of an immense number of species in their native habitat.

Elwes travelled, sometimes with his wife, in Turkey, Asia Minor, India (four times), and Tibet; in Mexico and North America (three times); in Chile; in Russia and Siberia (three times); and in Formosa (Taiwan), China, and Japan (twice). In the manner of his time he thought hunting a complement to natural history and made regular hunting trips to Austria, Norway, and France. In his expedition to central Asia in 1898 he secured specimens of *Ovis ammon*, the great sheep of the Altai. Elwes was the British official representative at the botanical and horticultural congresses held at Amsterdam in 1877 and St Petersburg in 1884. In 1886 he was appointed scientific member of the embassy to Tibet which, however, never crossed the frontier. His frequent and ambitious journeys were made possible by his ample means and good health, and successful by his love of adventure, keen eye, and facility with languages.

At home Elwes lived the life of a Gloucestershire squire. He was a keen huntsman, a congenial host, and a good steward of his estate and plantations. Unfortunately, the oolitic soil of the Cotswolds hindered the creation of a first-rate arboretum, which he planned at Colesbourne. He was active and generous in the establishment and maintenance of the school of forestry at the University of Cambridge. In 1912 and 1913 he published papers on primitive breeds of sheep, of which he kept small flocks for their fine wool and hardiness.

Elwes was president, council member, and fellow of many scientific societies including the Royal Society, the Linnean Society, and the Royal Horticultural Society, of whose Victoria medal of honour he was the first recipient. He died at Colesbourne on 26 November 1922, survived by his wife and his son.

Elwes is remembered not primarily as a scientist—he had no formal scientific training and relied on co-authors for the strictly botanical sections of his writings—but as a traveller, collector, and particularly as a plantsman. He knew what to collect, was determined in his travels to find it, was highly observant in describing the geographical distribution of what he found, and was particularly skilled in propagating specimens he brought back.

F. R. S. Balfour, *rev.* Elizabeth Baigent

John Elwes (1714–1789), by unknown engraver

Sources *PRS*, 95B (1923–4), xlviii–liii · Burke, *Gen. GB* · *CGPLA Eng. & Wales* (1923) · *Nature*, 110 (1922), 780–81 · H. H. Stevenson, *Who's who in science* (1913) · G. W. E. Loder, *Proceedings of the Linnean Society of London*, 135th session (1922–3), 41–3 · *The Eton register*, 2 (privately printed, Eton, 1905)
Archives RBG Kew, journals and notebooks | BL OIOC, corresp. with Frederick Bailey, MSS Eur. F 157
Likenesses Elliott & Fry, photograph, Royal Horticultural Society, London [*see illus.*] · Maull & Fox, carte-de-visite, RBG Kew · photograph (in old age), RBG Kew
Wealth at death £66,318 2s. 5d.: probate, 19 May 1923, *CGPLA Eng. & Wales*

Elwes [*formerly* Meggott], **John** (1714–1789), landowner and eccentric, was born on 7 April 1714 in the parish of St James, Westminster, the son of Robert Meggott (*d.* 1718), landowner and brewer, and his wife, Amee (Amy; *d.* 1754), daughter of Gervase Elwes. His sister, Amy (*d.* 1743), married John Timms and died leaving a son, John. Robert Meggott owned three houses in Great Marlborough Street, Westminster; Theydon Hall, Essex; and an estate at Marcham, Berkshire. At his death in 1718, his widow inherited property said to be worth nearly £100,000; she, however, carried thrift to excess, and was said to have starved herself to death.

John Meggott entered Westminster School in 1722 where he remained for ten or twelve years, becoming an excellent classical scholar and the best runner in the school. But in later life he was never seen to read any books, and he had no knowledge of accounts. From school he went to Geneva for two or three years, and learned riding, earning a reputation for his skill and daring. He was introduced to Voltaire, whom he somewhat resembled in looks, but whose character failed to impress him.

On his return to England, Meggott was introduced to his uncle, Sir Hervey Elwes, second baronet, of Stoke College, near Clare, Suffolk. Sir Hervey was also a noted miser, who had inherited an encumbered estate which he cleared and thereafter zealously guarded his considerable wealth. Meggott fell in with his uncle's humour and, when visiting him, called at a little inn at Chelmsford where he changed into old clothes. Having a large appetite, he also took the precaution of dining beforehand with a neighbour, for at his uncle's table it was said that they shared one glass of wine, and warmed themselves at a fire fuelled by one stick at a time. They then repaired to bed when it got dark, to save the cost of a candle. Sir Hervey, despite fragile health, lived to be over eighty, but Meggott was rewarded by inheriting his uncle's estate when he died, on 22 October 1763, one of the conditions being that he took the name of Elwes.

Under his uncle's influence, Elwes became himself a miser and his name became a byword for penury. An excessive reluctance to spend anything on himself led him to wear for a fortnight a wig which he had found lying in a muddy lane, and he would not have his shoes cleaned lest that helped to wear them out. He moved to Stoke College and acquired good horses and a pack of hounds, which were well cared for. He allowed the rain to come through the house at Marcham, but was not a hard landlord. He had bought the freehold of the Marlborough Street houses in 1751, and he built other houses in Marylebone, while living in town in his unlet houses, with only an old woman to look after his needs. His friends knew him as a connoisseur of good wines and French cookery, but he never entered a theatre. He was, however, addicted to cards; he was a member of Arthur's, and would often play through the night, on one occasion sitting at the table for two days and a night. After a night at cards, he would often walk to Smithfield and see his cattle brought down from Theydon Hall, haggling with the buyers for 1s. more. Elwes lost a great deal of his money at cards. He was also a foolish speculator and was easily taken in, on one occasion losing £25,000 on an ironworks project in America which was no more than imagination.

Having sat as a magistrate in Berkshire, Elwes was put forward by Lord Craven as MP for Berkshire. He moved back to Marcham with his hounds, but soon gave the pack away. He sat in three successive parliaments from December 1772 until 1784. He paid nothing for his elections but, being ready to lend money to other members, he parted with considerable sums which were never repaid. He did not join the opposition under Charles James Fox, as had been expected, but sat indiscriminately on either side of the house, in which he never spoke.

Elwes never married, but Elizabeth Moran, his housekeeper at Marcham, bore him two sons, John (*d.* 1817) and George, to whose welfare he was devoted. It was said, however, that he would not educate them, on the novel principle that putting things into people's heads was the sure way to take money out of their pockets. Many examples of Elwes's personal kindness, and his pathological miserliness, were published after his demise. In later life his memory declined, and it was said that one of his maidservants endeavoured to persuade him into marriage. By 1789 his memory had completely gone and he was taken into care by his son George, who was then living at Marcham with his wife and daughter. Elwes died at Marcham on 26 November 1789. In the following year Edward Topham published his *Life of John Elwes* in which Elwes's reputation for self-denial was firmly established.

The entailed Stoke estate could not be left to illegitimate children and so passed to John Timms, son of his deceased sister, Amy; in 1793 he took the name of Hervey-Elwes, and rose to the rank of lieutenant-general. The Marlborough Street houses were shared between George, who also had Marcham, and John, who also inherited Theydon Hall. He became a lieutenant in the Horse Guards, bought the estate of Colesbourne, Gloucestershire, married, and had two children.

ALEXANDER GORDON, *rev.* ANITA MCCONNELL

Sources E. Topham, *Life of John Elwes* (1790) · H. Lemoine and J. Caulfield, *The eccentric magazine, or, Lives and portraits of remarkable persons*, 2 vols. (1812–13) · W. Granger and others, *The new wonderful museum, and extraordinary magazine*, 2 (1804), 951–74 · Burke, *Gen. GB* (1965–72) · *Old Westminsters*, 1.312 · *VCH Essex*, 4.252 · *VCH Berkshire*, vol. 4 · R. Malcolm, ed., *Curiosities of biography, or, Memoirs of wonderful and extraordinary characters* (1855), 271–87 · *The parish of St James, Westminster*, 2/1, Survey of London, 31 (1963), 119, 257, 259 · will of Robert Meggott, PRO, PROB 11/564, sig. 148 · will of John Elwes, PRO, PROB 11/1185, sig. 540 · parish register, St James, Piccadilly, City Westm. AC · L. B. Namier, 'Elwes, John', HoP, *Commons, 1754–90* · A. Barnes, *Essex eccentrics* (1975)

Likenesses W. Austin, etching, pubd 1790 (after portrait), BM · G. Scott, stipple, pubd 1805, NPG · engraving, repro. in Topham, *Life of John Elwes* · mezzotint, repro. in *Country Life*, 92 (1943), 610 [*see illus.*]

Elwes, Simon Vincent Edmund Paul (1902–1975), portrait painter, was born on 29 June 1902 at Hothorpe Hall, Northamptonshire, the sixth and youngest son (two daughters were born later) of the singer Gervase Henry *Elwes (1866–1921), a famous Gerontius, and his wife, Lady Winefride Mary Elizabeth (*d.* 1959), fourth daughter of Rudolph William Basil Feilding, eighth earl of Denbigh. The boy went to Catholic schools—Lady Cross School, Seaford, Sussex, and The Oratory, Edgbaston. In 1918, at the age of sixteen, he entered the Slade School of Fine Art, London, when Henry Tonks was the austerely demanding professor there, and soldiers of the First World War, such as Gilbert and Stanley Spencer, A. R. Middleton Todd, and Allan Gwynne-Jones, were taking up their studies again. Courteous, handsome, and a devout Catholic, Elwes might have come out of Brideshead.

Finding the teaching regime at the Slade uncongenial, however, Elwes was asked by Tonks to leave after barely a year there. He then went to Paris where he lived for some seven years, studying first at the École de l'Écluse and then at the Académie des Beaux Arts, and also visiting the galleries in Germany, Holland, and Italy. He came back to England in 1926 and that year married Gloria Elinor, daughter of James Rennell *Rodd, first Baron Rennell, diplomat and scholar. They had four sons, one of whom died in infancy, and one of whom, Dominic, died in the same year as his father. The next year Elwes showed a portrait at the Royal Academy of Lady Lettice Lygon. She was the first of his many noble sitters, who included the duke and duchess of York (later George VI and Queen Elizabeth), the princess royal, Prince George and Princess Marina, Queen Mary, Prince Henry, duke of Gloucester, Princess Margaret, and Elizabeth II. His portraits hung in the summer exhibition of the Royal Academy every year. In 1929 he was created a knight of Malta and in 1933 he was elected a member of the Royal Society of Portrait Painters.

Elwes joined the Welsh Guards at the outbreak of the Second World War, to be transferred later to the tenth Royal Hussars in Egypt. After fighting in the battles of Benghazi, Mersa Matruh, and Knightsbridge, he was made an official war artist. In Cairo he painted King Farouk and Queen Farida, in South Africa the king and queen of the Hellenes as well as J. C. Smuts, and in India the viceroy Archibald Wavell, first Earl Wavell, the maharaja of Patiala, Lord Louis Mountbatten, and Indian army soldiers who had won the VC. The journeys, the heat, and the astonishing activity must all have helped to bring about the stroke he suffered when he came back to England after the Japanese surrender. He spent two years in hospital. He never used his right hand for painting again, but as soon as he could stand, he taught himself to paint with his left. Until then, his portraits owed much to Sir William Orpen, not only with the light reflected on the side of the face, the folds of the curtain radiating from the sitter's waist, the chair which brought the hands high up in the composition, but also with the fluent and continuous surface of paint.

There is not much in the way of manual skill that a painter needs; but he wants to be able to control the direction of his brush. In default of that precision of movement, Elwes now broke his surface with separate touches, which, instead of weakening his pictures, gave them a new vivacity. He surmounted his disability enough to become president of the Guild of Catholic Artists, vice-president of the Royal Society of Portrait Painters from 1953, an associate of the Royal Academy in 1956, and Royal Academician in 1967. To read through a list of his sitters is like turning over the pages not only of *Who's Who* but of

Debrett and the *Almanach de Gotha*. No other painter since Philip de Laszlo had painted such eminences, not even Frank Salisbury. Like de Laszlo and Salisbury, Elwes was sustained by a craft which ensured that his portraits went ahead as he intended; they owed their virtue to their confidence. Elwes endowed his subjects with a good nature and a joy of life which, enhanced by brilliant colour, expressed his own character and appearance. He had none of the guilt that seems to afflict some portrait painters, either from talent unfulfilled or taxes unpaid.

Nothing could be stronger than the contrast at a council meeting of the Royal Academy between Elwes and the rest of the members, teachers to a man. Handsome, fresh of complexion, finely dressed, with a scarlet flower in his buttonhole, he enriched the proceedings with his smile, no less than with his air of being a visitor from a world more carefree and elegant than the one in which deficits and disappointments were certain to be discussed. When he used the old ballroom in Burlington House to paint a portrait, a beautiful girl brought him his brushes and set up his paintbox, for that was his own exhilarating way of making light of his useless right arm and dragging leg. It was natural that he should have been at ease painting Cardinal Hinsley, richly robed in a red cassock, yet benign, and Sir Thomas Beecham in a white dressing gown, and mischievous. It is no surprise that his paintings of roses, peonies, and lilies are not in the least like the hedgerow flowers of his contemporary Allan Gwynne-Jones, but are blithe and sumptuous. His *Dictionary of National Biography* memoir of Frederick Lonsdale, the playwright, is equally light-hearted.

In his last months Elwes had to be pushed about in a chair, hardly able to speak, no longer spotless in his dress; but his face, thinner and paler, had a look of the greatest nobility—wistful, unearthly; not old. He could have been the embodiment of the dying Gerontius. He died on 6 August 1975, at his home, Blakedene, Lyminster, Sussex, and his wife died two months later.

PETER GREENHAM, *rev.*

Sources private information (1986) · private information (2004) [N. Usherwood] · personal knowledge (1986) · *The Times* (9 Aug 1975) · G. Popp and H. Valentine, *Royal Academy of Arts directory of membership: from the foundation in 1768 to 1995, including honorary members* (1996) · S. King, *The Times* (31 May 1971) · d. cert. · b. cert.
Archives Lincs. Arch., papers
Likenesses photograph, 1929, Hult. Arch. · Baron, photograph, c.1950, Hult. Arch. · B. Bosshart, photograph, repro. in *The Times*

Elwin, (Harry) Verrier Holman (1902–1964), missionary and anthropologist, was born on 29 August 1902 at Pemole House, Castle Avenue, Dover, the eldest of the three children of Edmund Henry Elwin (1871–1909), bishop of Sierra Leone, and Minnie Ornsby, daughter of William Laban Holman, an engineer in India. His parents were English, with Scottish and Irish connections on his mother's side.

After preparatory schools in London, Reigate, and Eastbourne, Elwin attended Dean Close School, Cheltenham, from 1915 to 1921, both school and home being devoutly evangelical. From there he went to Merton College, Oxford, where he obtained a double first in English and

(Harry) **Verrier Holman Elwin** (1902–1964), by unknown photographer, 1926

theology, developed a lifelong love of English literature, evident in both his later academic studies and his poetry, and was attracted to Anglo-Catholicism and the English mystical tradition. From 1926 to 1927 he was vice-principal of the Oxford theological college, Wycliffe Hall, during which time he was ordained to the Anglican priesthood.

He then went to join J. C. Winslow's religious community, the Christa Seva Sangha, a pioneer Christian *ashram* at Poona in western India, arriving there in November 1927. India was his home thereafter (he took Indian citizenship in 1954). During his first four years in India, Elwin pursued his interest in mysticism, publishing a series of books and articles, adventurous at that time, seeking to relate such Christian texts as *The Cloud of Unknowing* and the writings of Richard Rolle and St Francis to the Indian mystical tradition.

An early encounter and ensuing friendship with M. K. Gandhi, and encouragement from some of his *ashram* colleagues and from C. F. Andrews, led to a brief involvement in the Indian national movement, including a risky escapade in the North-West Frontier Province, amusingly recounted in his autobiographical *The Tribal World of Verrier Elwin* (1964), and a number of books and articles on Gandhi and Indian nationalism. Pressure, however, from the imperial authorities helped persuade him to abandon politics.

At the prompting of Gandhi and others Elwin decided to devote his life to the welfare of India's tribal peoples, and in 1932 he and an Indian colleague, Shamrao Hivale, established their St Francis Ashram among the Gonds, at Karanjia, in central India, making it the centre of a network of schools and clinics, including a home for leprosy patients. Elwin's work at this stage earned him among the Gandhians the title of Din-Sevak (Servant of the Poor), and from Romain Rolland the remark, 'In Africa, Albert Schweitzer, the philosopher; in India, Verrier Elwin, the poet' (foreword to V. Elwin, *Leaves from the Jungle*, 1936, 7), while his association with the nationalists earned the disapproval of his diocesan, Alex Wood, the bishop of Nagpur. In 1935 he left the church, with 'the utmost sorrow' (V. Elwin to Sorella Minore, 30 Nov 1935, Elwin MSS, BL OIOC), though later he spoke of this as 'a liberation' (Hivale, 112).

From 1932 to 1953 Elwin and Hivale lived at various places, mostly in tribal central India, much of the time in considerable poverty but with irrepressible good humour. A first marriage, to Kosi, a Gond, took place on 4 April 1940, and ended in divorce in 1949; there was one son. His first publication (with Hivale) on a tribal theme, *Songs from the Forest* (1935), marked a shift from personal poetry, at its best in his *Twenty-Eight Poems* (n.d.), to the poetry that he was to make thereafter out of his translations of many hundreds of tribal songs. This was followed by the much weightier study, *The Baiga* (1939), with which Elwin achieved full recognition as a leading authority on India's tribal peoples, his work deriving a unique quality from his life in close and continuous contact with his subjects. There followed a dozen monographs on ethnography, folk poetry, and art, described variously as 'a *tour de force* in anthropological literature' (Pradhan and others, 8), and 'a landmark in the history of our knowledge of the human mind' (review in the *American Anthropologist*). There followed also much campaigning in pamphlets and articles on behalf of the tribals, in which Elwin's controversial and often controverted shift, from 'improver' to 'defender of the aboriginal' against the values of both Hindu and Western civilization, is evident. In 1944 he became honorary anthropologist to the government of Orissa, and was awarded the degree of DSc from his old university, Oxford, while from 1946 to 1949 he was deputy director of the Anthropological Survey of India. On 23 September 1953 he married Lila, from the Pardhan tribe; they had three sons.

In 1954 he was invited by the prime minister, Jawaharlal Nehru, to become adviser for tribal affairs to the North-East Frontier Agency, and he and the family moved to Shillong, which became their home for the rest of his life. This appointment involved much arduous travel in north-east India, and afforded the opportunity to train a body of officials aware of the needs of the tribals. Though increasingly discouraged by the relentless destruction of the tribal world he was able with Nehru's support to influence public policy at the highest level, for example in the Scheduled Tribes Commission, and had the fullest possible scope for what he called his 'philanthropology'. He was awarded the national honour, the Padma Bhushan, in

1961. Verrier Elwin died of a heart attack at Shillong on 22 February 1964, and was cremated at Shillong two days later. DANIEL O'CONNOR

Sources *The tribal world of Verrier Elwin* (1964) · BL OIOC, Elwin MSS · D. O'Connor, *Din-Sevak: Verrier Elwin's life of service in tribal India* (1993) · BL OIOC, W. G. Archer MSS · R. Guha, review of D. O'Connor, *Din-Sevak*, *Seminar* (Dec 1993) · S. Hivale, *Scholar Gipsy: a study of Verrier Elwin* (1964) · N. Rustomji, 'Verrier Elwin Memorial Lectures I–IV', typescript, [n.d.] · M. C. Pradhan, R. D. Singh, P. K. Misra, and D. B. Sastry, eds., *Anthropology and archaeology: essays in commemoration of Verrier Elwin, 1902–64* (1969) · W. W. Emilsen, *Violence and atonement: the missionary experience of Mohandas Gandhi, Samuel Stokes and Verrier Elwin in India before 1935* (1994) · b. cert. · R. Guha, *Savaging the civilized: Verrier Elwin, his tribals, and India* (1999)

Archives BL OIOC, corresp. and papers, Eur. MS D 950 · National Archives of India, Delhi, MSS · National Museum of India, New Delhi, collection of tribal art and artefacts · Nehru Museum, New Delhi, MSS · Society of St Francis, Hilfield, Dorset, file | Bishop's College, Calcutta, Christa Seva Sangha MSS · Bishop's College, Calcutta, corresp. with Bishop Wood and Bishop Foss Westcott · BL OIOC, W. G. Archer MSS · Christa Prema Seva Sangha Record Room, Poona · Society of St Francis, Hilfield, Dorset, Christa Seva Sangha MSS · U. Cam., Centre of South Asian Studies, E. S. Hyde MSS | SOUND BL NSA, oral history interview

Likenesses photograph, 1926, Wycliffe Hall Seminary, Oxford [*see illus.*] · photographs, priv. coll. · photographs, BL OIOC, Elwin MSS · photographs, repro. in *The tribal world of Verrier Elwin* · photographs, repro. in Guha, *Savaging the civilized*

Wealth at death not at all well off; sold art and artefacts to assist widow

Elwin, Whitwell (1816–1900), Church of England clergyman and journal editor, was the third son of Marsham Elwin of Thurning, Norfolk, and his wife, Emma Louisa Whitwell. He was born at Thurning on 26 February 1816, and, after education at Paston grammar school, North Walsham, was admitted at Gonville and Caius College, Cambridge, on 26 June 1834; he graduated BA in 1839. He married, on 18 June 1838, Frances, daughter of Lieutenant-Colonel Fountain Elwin; they had four sons and a daughter. He was ordained deacon at Wells in 1839, and priest in 1840, and became curate of Hardington, Somerset. There he wrote an article, which J. G. Lockhart accepted for the *Quarterly Review*, on the *Histoire du chien* of Elzéar Blaze. It was published in September 1843, and his connection with the review continued until 1885. He succeeded Caleb Elwin, his kinsman, as rector of Booton, Norfolk, in 1849, built a rectory, and resided there until his death, earning a reputation as a devoted and scholarly cleric.

Elwin became editor of the *Quarterly Review* in 1853 and continued in that post until 1860, living at his rectory and going to London each quarter to bring out the journal. He wrote many articles himself—in all forty-two—a number of which were collected in *Some XVIII-Century Men of Letters* (2 vols., 1902); these reflected his best work and central interest. He also maintained a good body of contributors, including Lord Robert Cecil and W. E. Gladstone. But the review's moderate and uncertain Conservatism reflected the more general weakness of that creed in the 1850s, and the *Quarterly* lost much of its influence. Elwin lacked the tact and discipline required of an effective editor, and his ultimate loyalty was to his parish.

Whitwell Elwin (1816–1900), by Henry Weigall, exh. RA 1876

After resigning the editorship, Elwin undertook to produce the edition of Pope that John Wilson Croker had long projected but had not begun. Elwin published five volumes, in 1871–2, two of poetry and three of letters, but he then became dissatisfied with the work, and the edition was completed in five more volumes by W. J. Courthope (1881–9). In 1852 he prepared for John Murray a volume of selections from the poems and letters of Byron, which appeared without his name. Other minor works of interest were two amusing and forceful pamphlets, published in 1869, in defence of an undergraduate who had been treated with injustice by the authorities of his college, entitled *A Narrative* and *A Reply to the Remarks of Mr. Carr*. He also wrote the *Life of John Forster* prefixed to the catalogue of the Dyce and Forster Library (1888).

Elwin's second son, Hastings Philip Elwin, a man of great promise, died in 1874, and his only daughter in 1875, and feeling the need of a new occupation in these sorrows he rebuilt his parish church. His wife rarely left the house, and shared his absolute indifference to money and to every kind of distinction; she died on 22 February 1898. After taking a service in his church on 31 December 1899, Elwin died suddenly while dressing the following morning. He was buried beside his wife in the churchyard of Booton; they were survived by two sons, both clergymen.

NORMAN MOORE, *rev.* H. C. G. MATTHEW

Sources W. Elwin, *Some XVIII century men of letters*, ed. W. Elwin, 2 vols. (1902) · *Wellesley index* · Crockford · Venn, *Alum. Cant.*
Archives Hunt. L., letters · NL Scot., corresp. · Norfolk RO, family corresp. and MSS | BL, corresp. with W. E. Gladstone, Add. MS 44152 · BL, letters to Sir Austen Layard, Add. MSS 38982–39040 · Bodl. Oxf., letters to Sir William Napier · CKS, corresp. with countess of Westmorland · Herts. ALS, corresp. with first and second lords Lytton · Hunt. L., letters to Frederick Locker-Lampson · NRA, priv. coll., letters to Sir Norman Moore · U. St Andr., corresp. with James Forbes · UCL, corresp. with Edwin Chadwick
Likenesses H. Weigall, portrait, exh. RA 1876, NPG [*see illus.*] · H. Weigall, oils, 1902, Booton
Wealth at death £33,002 19s. 5d.: probate, 30 March 1900, *CGPLA Eng. & Wales*

Elwood [*née* Curteis], **Anne Katharine** (1796–1873), traveller and writer, was the seventh of the ten children of Edward Jeremiah Curteis and his wife, Mary Barrett, of Windmill Hill, near Battle, in Sussex. Her father was a classical scholar, became an independent member of parliament for Sussex (1820–30), and was a frequent contributor to the *Gentleman's Magazine*. On 9 January 1824 she married Major (later Lieutenant-Colonel) Charles William Elwood (1781/2–1860) of the East India Company. He had served in India in the army and as a political agent for some dozen years. In 1825 she set out with him for India: 'the first and only female who has hitherto ventured over-land from England to India' (Elwood, *Narrative*, 1.vi). (In fact Eliza Fay had preceded her, via Suez, in 1779.) She published her letters written over the next three years as *Narrative of a Journey Overland from England to India*, illustrated by herself and her husband, in 1830.

The Elwoods travelled slowly south through Europe, viewing all the sights, landing in Egypt in April 1826, and sailed up the Nile to Cairo and Luxor. She wrote vivid, if somewhat romantic, descriptions of the social life, the surroundings of Cairo and its people, and the often comical happenings along the Nile. At Luxor they met Joseph Bonomi and Robert Hay, who, according to Hay's diary, admired her good looks. Her observations on how she was treated as a European woman are of particular interest. The Elwoods' journey from Luxor to Bombay by land and sea took over two months. From the Nile they travelled across the desert, with Mrs Elwood in a traditional litter slung between two camels. Although along the way her imagination conjured up 'Bedouins and Arabs, wolves, jackals, and hyaenas' (Elwood, *Narrative*, 1.244) out of the wind, the journey was 'performed with utmost ease' (ibid., 1.261). They sailed down the Red Sea to Jiddah, where they picked up a ship for Bombay. At al-Hudaydah she visited an Arab harem.

Mrs Elwood's observations of life in India are vivid and irreverent, particularly concerning the lifestyle of the expatriates. She wrote also about plant and animal life, and Indian religions and languages. In 1826–7, when her husband was given command of a regiment, they moved north to the province of Cutch. Mrs Elwood was again in her element, writing about everything around, including her visit to a zenana. In 1828 the Elwoods sailed for England by way of Ceylon, the Cape of Good Hope, and St Helena.

Later, unable to find any published biography of literary females, Mrs Elwood decided to write her own. *Memoirs of the Literary Ladies of England from the Commencement of the Last Century* appeared in 1841. It covered the lives of twenty-nine women, including Lady Mary Wortley Montagu, Hannah More, Mary Wollstonecraft, Mrs Radcliffe,

Jane Austen, Jane Taylor, Mrs Hemans, and others now less well known. The articles are more personal reports and chronologies than literary critiques, and repeat scandals and gossip alongside achievements. Some of the women or their relatives were almost certainly known personally to Mrs Elwood, who had access to many personal documents. Her work was used as a reference for the *Dictionary of National Biography* articles. Her assessments can be somewhat subjective. Of some of Jane Austen's characters she commented 'though one is occasionally annoyed with the underbred personages of Miss Austen's novels, that annoyance is only such as we would feel if we were actually in their company' (Elwood, *Memoirs*, 2.186). She criticized Emma Roberts, who also went overland to India, for the speed of her journey—a mere two months in all.

Until Charles Elwood's death in 1860 the Elwoods lived at Clayton Priory, Sussex. They had no children. Anne Elwood died there on 24 February 1873, aged seventy-seven. Her gravestone records that she was religious and charitable and 'her literary values were of a very high class'.   DEBORAH MANLEY

Sources A. K. Elwood, *Narrative of a journey overland from England to India etc.*, 1825–8 (1830) · A. K. Elwood, *Memoirs of the literary ladies of England from the commencement of the last century* (1841) · *GM*, 2nd ser., 3 (1835) · *GM*, 2nd ser., 16 (1841) · Allibone, *Dict.* · Burke, *Gen. GB* · *GM*, 1st ser., 94/1 (1824), 176 · *GM*, 3rd ser., 8 (1860), 310 [Charles William Elwood] · gravestone, Clayton churchyard, Sussex
Archives BM, Hay MSS

Elworthy, Frederick Thomas (1830–1907), philologist and antiquary, eldest son of Thomas Elworthy of Wellington, Somerset, woollen manufacturer, and his wife, Jane, daughter of William Chorley of Quarm, near Dunster, Somerset, was born at Wellington on 10 January 1830, and was educated at a private school at Denmark Hill, London. Although studious from boyhood, Elworthy was middle-aged when he began to pursue his interest in the dialect and antiquities of west Somerset and east Devon. His paper 'The dialect of west Somerset' was read before the Philological Society in 1875, and two further papers, with a contribution by James A. H. *Murray, were published in 1877 as *The Grammar of the Dialect of West Somerset*: Murray described the latter as 'the first grammar of an English dialect of any scientific value' (*Wellington Weekly News*).

A close friendship between Elworthy and Murray was established in the spring of 1877 when Murray went to Wellington to clarify points of dialect pronunciation; the visit was the first of many. Although Elworthy was no more than a gifted amateur of philology, Murray valued him greatly for his cheerful good sense, sympathetic encouragement, and practical help during the long years in which Murray's *New English Dictionary* was in preparation. Elworthy became one of Murray's 'most zealous volunteer lieutenants' (*Wellington Weekly News*), and together with his wife and daughters contributed over 15,000 quotations for the dictionary. His most substantial contribution to dialect philology, however, was *The West Somerset Word-Book* (1886), a glossary of dialect words which extended to some 900 pages and the preparation of which occupied him for more than ten years. Extensive travels in Spain, Italy, and elsewhere provided him with the materials for his studies of folk magic and popular superstition, published as *The Evil Eye* (1895) and *Horns of Honour and other Studies in the Byways of Archaeology* (1900).

Elworthy was a member of the council of the Philological Society, and from 1891 to 1895 served as editor for the Somersetshire Archaeological and Natural History Society, to whose *Proceedings*, as well as to those of the Devonshire Association, he contributed papers on archaeological and historical subjects. He was elected FSA on 14 June 1900.

Elworthy was a good linguist and an able draughtsman, engraver, and artist in watercolours. He was also a prominent churchman—the building of All Saints' Church, Wellington, owed much to his generosity and encouragement—and a magistrate, a churchwarden, an active member of the Wellington school board, and a prominent freemason. He married Maria, daughter of James Kershaw MP, on 17 August 1854. They had three sons, who all predeceased him, and three daughters, two of whom survived him, as did his wife. His daughter Florence was the second wife of Sir Alexander Christison, second baronet, and the mother of General Sir (Alexander Frank) Philip Christison, fourth baronet. After an illness which began in the summer of 1906 Elworthy died at his home, Foxdown, Wellington, on 13 December 1907, and was buried on 18 December in the churchyard of St John's parish church.

T. W. MAYBERRY

Sources *Wellington Weekly News* (18 Dec 1907) · *Somerset County Gazette* (21 Dec 1907) · C. Tite, *Proceedings of the Somersetshire Archaeological and Natural History Society*, 53/2 (1907), 188–91 · K. M. E. Murray, *Caught in the web of words: James A. H. Murray and the 'Oxford English dictionary'* (1977) [pbk edn (1979)] · CGPLA Eng. & Wales (1908)
Likenesses photograph, repro. in Murray, *Caught in the web of words*, 78
Wealth at death £31,180 9s. 1d.: probate, 21 Jan 1908, CGPLA Eng. & Wales

Elworthy, Samuel Charles, Baron Elworthy (1911–1993), air force officer, was born on 23 March 1911 at Gordon's valley, Timaru, New Zealand, the second of five children and the elder son of Percy Ashton Elworthy, a sheep farmer, and his wife, Bertha Victoria, née Julius. The family later moved to England. Elworthy attended Marlborough College and subsequently read law at Trinity College, Cambridge, where he was captain of the boat club and twice a trial cap. He graduated in 1933, was called to the bar at Lincoln's Inn in 1935, and on 5 June 1936 married Audrey (1910–1986), the daughter of Arthur Joseph Hutchinson, a company director; they had three sons and one daughter.

An enthusiastic pilot in the Auxiliary Air Force, Elworthy changed career in 1936 and took a permanent commission in the RAF. A year flying Hawker Harts and Hinds with 15 squadron at Abingdon was followed in November 1937 by appointment as aide-de-camp to Sir Edgar Ludlow-Hewitt, commander-in-chief of Bomber Command—a remarkable acknowledgement in one so young of the talents that would eventually take him to the top. He was thus able to observe the strengths and weaknesses of one of the RAF's most senior commanders, to appreciate the huge problems facing the bomber force as war approached, and to gain an inside view of the events of the time, notably the Munich crisis.

In January 1939 Elworthy returned to flying, building up a new operational training unit for the Blenheim bomber (for which he received the Air Force Cross) and then commanding 82 (Blenheim) squadron operating over northwest Europe during late 1940 and early 1941; this earned him the DFC and DSO, whose citation stated that, 'by his magnificent leadership and complete disregard of danger, he brought his squadron to the highest peak of war efficiency'. Now it was back to the headquarters of Bomber Command, where in 1942, as group captain operations, he won the trust of the new commander-in-chief, Sir Arthur Harris. There followed a year in charge of one of the command's most important stations, Waddington, after which Harris chose Elworthy as his representative with the headquarters of General Eisenhower for operation Overlord. Elworthy finished his war as senior air staff officer (SASO) at 5 group.

Elworthy remained in the bomber world for two more years, now at the central bombing establishment at Marham, leading the development of bombing tactics, before going to India as SASO of 2 (Indian) group. After independence he was seconded to the new Pakistan Air Force. In 1949 he attended the Staff College at Camberley and went on to serve on the personnel staff in the Air Ministry. In 1951 he entered the fighter world, first commanding the Meteor station at Tangmere, next Odiham, at the time of the queen's coronation review, and finally the metropolitan sector of Fighter Command at North Weald. In 1957 he became commandant of the Bracknell Staff College, which provided a good opportunity for bringing himself up to date on the major issues of RAF policy arising from the Sandys defence review and led to his appointment to the Air Council as deputy chief of air staff in November 1959.

Elworthy did not stay long. In July 1960—at the specific instance of Lord Mountbatten, chief of defence staff—he became commander-in-chief of the first post-war integrated command, British forces Arabian peninsula, soon to be retitled Middle East command. In due course, despite considerable single-service resistance, a remarkable degree of co-operation was achieved between the three services and the civilian administration. The contingency planning which Elworthy had also set in train paid off in July 1961 after Iraq had renewed its long-standing claim to Kuwait and massed a large armoured force on the frontier. In operation Vantage, Elworthy quickly moved major reinforcements in from Aden and elsewhere, and the Iraqi army stayed put. It was an object lesson in deterrence. By the time Elworthy departed in 1963 the unified command had been severely tested, both operationally and administratively, and its efficiency gave proof of his talents for achieving harmony between the three services and handling the political intricacies.

It was another story in Whitehall, where Elworthy returned in September 1963 as chief of air staff. Here he encountered entrenched attitudes and constant controversy, though he and Denis Healey, the Labour government's defence secretary for most of his time there, had great respect for each other and generally got on well together. Much time was devoted to future aircraft purchases, and a major issue that came to a head in 1964, soon after the Labour Party's election victory, was the future of the tactical strike and reconnaissance aircraft (TSR2) by which the RAF had hitherto set great store. Elworthy was becoming increasingly worried that its costs seemed to be running out of control and at risk of draining dry the RAF budget, and he agreed to its cancellation on the firm understanding that the American F111 strike aircraft would be ordered instead. The HS 681 transport aircraft he also saw as ambitious and over-extravagant, and this was dropped in favour of the American C130, the future Hercules. Thus ended the peacetime policy of always buying British military aircraft; here was the realist at work. One major British project that did survive was the Harrier, destined to fill a long-term place in Britain's armoury.

Another of Elworthy's preoccupations was Britain's worldwide role, especially east of Suez. The confrontation with Indonesia demanded much attention; it provided a stern reminder of how far all three services were now stretched and caused much debate on how far such distant commitments should be retained and by what means. Among such issues was the aircraft-carrier controversy, which led to the resignation in 1966 of Sir David Luce, the first sea lord; Elworthy, though not opposed to large carriers *per se*, thought it no longer practicable to provide sufficient of these and was convinced that the job must be done in other ways. Other major matters were the evacuation from Aden and the possibility of military intervention in Rhodesia, which he strongly opposed. More domestic concerns included the withdrawal of Britain's first V-bomber, the Valiant, the planned reorganization of the RAF's home command structure, and the decision to end the cadet entry at the RAF College, Cranwell, in favour of graduate entrants, a switch he thought essential in the light of changing patterns of national education.

In April 1967 Elworthy became chief of defence staff, where over the next few years he exercised much influence on defence policy under both Denis Healey and Lord Carrington. This was in his view a period of great and alarming Soviet expansion, marked particularly by the Czechoslovak crisis of 1968, and he accompanied Healey to many of the NATO meetings where the new policy of flexible response was being worked out. Several times he visited Northern Ireland, where the emergency was beginning to cause severe problems, particularly for the army and its garrison in Germany. In 1968 the order for the F111 was cancelled against the advice of the air staff; this flew in the face of the assurances Elworthy had previously received when the TSR2 was abandoned, and both he and Healey seriously considered resignation. On more positive notes, however, the nuclear deterrent was successfully transferred from the V-bomber force to the Polaris submarines, planning was started for the multi-role combat aircraft, the future Tornado, the military salary was introduced, and the position of the chief of defence staff was gradually strengthened.

Elworthy departed the national scene in 1971, after eight years at the heart of military affairs. He had been much criticized for not having made a firmer stand over some of the cutbacks being demanded by the politicians, but in retrospect hard choices were unavoidable. The political and economic circumstances of the 1960s had compelled strong measures to contain Britain's defence spending and commitments, and Elworthy had never hesitated to take on the politicians and civil servants in the attempt to secure the best deal he could. For him 'the art of the possible' was always the final guideline.

Ennobled in 1972 as Baron Elworthy of Timaru, the first RAF officer to be thus honoured since the high wartime commanders, Elworthy spent the next seven years as constable and governor of Windsor Castle. He became knight of the Garter in 1977, and he also served as lord lieutenant of Greater London and held several academic and business appointments. In 1978 he returned to Gordon's valley, in his native New Zealand, where he spent the rest of his life, visiting Britain annually to attend the Garter ceremony and perform duties as a steward at Henley Royal Regatta. Elworthy died at Christchurch, New Zealand, on 4 April 1993. He was cremated and his ashes were returned to Gordon's valley. He was one of the most distinguished of the RAF's chiefs, a man who, as both chief of air staff and chief of defence staff, was held in the highest regard and respect by service colleagues and politicians alike during the years when the United Kingdom came to accept that she was no longer a world power.

HENRY A. PROBERT

Sources H. Probert, *High commanders of the RAF* (1991) · H. Probert, *Bomber Harris: his life and times* (2001) · official RAF records · *The Times* (6 April 1993) · *The Times* (14 April 1993) · *The Independent* (6 April 1993) · *WWW* · personal knowledge (2004) · private information (2004) · m. cert.
Archives SOUND RAF, taped interview held by the Air Historical Branch
Likenesses photograph, 1971, repro. in *The Independent* · photograph, repro. in *The Times* (6 April 1993)

Elwyn-Jones. For this title name *see* Jones, (Frederick) Elwyn, Baron Elwyn-Jones (1909–1989).

Ely. For this title name *see* O'Carroll, Tadhg, baron of Ely (d. 1553) [*see under* O'Carroll, Mulroney (c.1470–1532)]; Loftus, Jane, marchioness of Ely (1821–1890).

Ely [*alias* Havard, Howard], **Humphrey** (1539?–1604), Roman Catholic priest, was the brother of William *Ely, and was born in Herefordshire—according to John Pitts. Probably it was he who entered Brasenose College, Oxford (William's first college), in 1552 and was *lector bibliae* in 1553. Humphrey certainly became a scholar of William's new college, St John's, in 1563 and a fellow in 1566; shortly after, William asked the college to let Humphrey live with him, possibly in London. If identical with the Brasenose student, this would indicate rather protracted study for one with no recorded first degree; however, it may be that

he had already progressed to the postgraduate legal study which he was to take up later. He survived at St John's (although was apparently non-resident from 1569 to 1571) at least until the academic year 1571/2, presumably being less notoriously Catholic than William, though he later assigned the change in his religious views to the influence of Nicholas Sander's *Image of Christ* (1567). So the erased entry in the Douai diaries to the effect that he entered the seminary there in 1570 is probably incorrect. He is definitely described as a doctor teaching canon and civil law there in 1576, before he was formally incorporated in the English College. Probably, like other Catholic exiles, he acquired this doctorate in Italy or Rome; when visiting the latter, he was still described by Robert Persons as a licentiate. A later entry in the Douai diaries could be construed as implying that he had taken his LLD actually at Douai, but this seems less likely. Later Ely was to reproach the Jesuits especially with obtaining 'a strang and extraordinary bull' to prevent English exiles getting doctorates outside their control (Ely, 87).

In July 1577 Ely and others rented a house in Douai, apparently as a form of legal academic hall. Flemish suspicions of the English College were considerable. Ely was abused as a traitor in the streets, and his house was searched. He accompanied William Allen on visits preparatory to the college's migration to Rheims and, in Allen's absence, seconded Richard Bristow in negotiations with the Douai authorities. In 1579–80 Ely accompanied Allen to Rome, where he stayed at the English College and (even in retrospect) approved of the transfer of its governance from Morris Clynog to the Jesuits. Ely may already have accompanied Allen there in 1576 if, as Robert Persons later recalled, he was 'threatened greatly' by Thomas Stukeley (d. 1578). Persons was, however, inaccurate in describing Ely as 'an ancient man', 'some littel tyme before come from England' (*Miscellanea II*, 2.161–2).

In June 1580 Ely—under the name of Havard, Harvard, or Howard—sailed for England with the priests Thomas Cottam, Edward Rishton, and John Hart. A spy had warned of their coming, describing Ely as 'about 38 yeares of adge, of a reasonable stature, well timbred, bige of speache' and brown-bearded (Talbot, 207). Cottam was arrested at Dover, but Ely's cover story remained convincing, which led to the townsmen (saving expenses, for which they nevertheless claimed reimbursement) entrusting him with the prisoner to take to London. Ely naturally let Cottam go, though the latter sought spiritual counsel as to whether he might let Ely run this risk; but in the course of this, a Dover man appeared in London and had Ely arrested, which confirmed Cottam in his resolution to give himself up to death. Ely spent some time in the Marshalsea, appearing on a list usually dated 1581. None the less, still being a layman, he was released in time to appear in Spain in November 1580 and convey to the nuncio, Filippo Sega, a proposal allegedly from 'certain nobles' in England to plot Elizabeth's death if Rome could guarantee its moral justification. Sega seemed sure of it himself, given Pius V's bull of deposition; Ely proposed, if an authoritative answer could be provided, 'that he would take the reply to them personally' (Hughes, 213). He returned to Rheims in April 1581. He was ordained subdeacon and deacon in March 1582 and priest the following month, and was said to have paid another visit to England in May, of which (and of any pursuit of his proposals to Sega) nothing is known. Between his visits, he had been indicted (*in absentia*) for high treason, after Allen and Nicholas Morton but ahead of Persons and Edmund Campion, and outlawed—apparently not because of his actual Spanish dealings but for a general 'plot' with those seminary priests captured by the government, hatched 'at Rome and at Rheims', to 'imagine, contrive, and compass' the queen's death by 'bringing strangers into the realm to make war' (PRO, KB 27/1279).

In 1586 the duke of Lorraine made Ely professor of both laws at the University of Pont-à-Mousson, a post that removed him from further dangers in the English mission but brought with it a running feud with Jesuits in the divinity faculty. This had its influence on Ely's entry into print (for the first time, although he seems to have collected materials for John Gibbons's *Concertatio ecclesiae catholicae* and organized their translation into Latin) with *Certaine Briefe Notes* (1602), directed against Robert Persons and other supporters of the appointment of the archpriest George Blackwell. Although involving as collaborators the more partial Christopher Bagshaw and William Bishop—not to mention the widely distrusted Charles Paget—it claimed in its subtitle to be the work of 'an unpassionate secular prieste, friend to both partyes, but more frend to the truth'; but Ely's later elaboration seems accurate that 'I mislike with the … [appellants] for one thing, with the Jesuites for two thinges' (in the epistle of the author). Ely had connections on both sides—his brother William favoured the arch-priest, while his nephew Anthony Major had gone so far the other way as to conform to the Church of England (though Ely tried to woo him back).

The conclusion of the most exhaustive historian of the controversy is that Ely's book was the only one 'to proceed from an impartial and independent hand' (Law, *Historical Sketch*, 5). None the less, both the book and his hospitality in Lorraine to Robert Charnock (condemned by Rome) make clear his rejection of the Jesuit model of authority even when backed by the pope, making him an honorary, if not an actual, appellant. Writing probably to Cecil (also in 1602), he drew a thoroughly appellant distinction between the Jesuits as 'unnaturall bastards th[at] doo attend to nought els but conquests and invasions' and 'naturall children' of England such as himself (Law, *Archpriest Controversy*, 2.196–7). He overlooked his former discussions with Sega and also his intercepted letter of 1587 to Gibbons—'God send us a Catholicke kinge quickly. For my part I care not of what country and nation he be, so that religion were restored, and so many of our poor frends that goe to perdition might be saved' (Pollen, 141–2). Ely had, however, little time to respond to the arrival of James: he died on 15 March 1604 and was buried in the church of the Poor Clares at Pont-à-Mousson.

JULIAN LOCK

Sources G. Anstruther, *The seminary priests*, 1 (1969) • T. F. Knox and others, eds., *The first and second diaries of the English College, Douay* (1878) • H. Ely, *Certaine briefe notes upon 'A briefe apologie'*, facs. of 1602 edn, English Recusant Literature, 171 (1973) • T. G. Law, ed., *A historical sketch of the conflicts between Jesuits and seculars in the reign of Queen Elizabeth* (1889) • T. G. Law, ed., *The archpriest controversy: documents relating to the dissensions of the Roman Catholic clergy, 1597–1602*, 2, CS, new ser., 58 (1898), 195–201 • C. Talbot, ed., *Miscellanea: recusant records*, Catholic RS, 53 (1961), 207, 231 • 'The memoirs of Father Robert Persons', ed. J. H. Pollen, *Miscellanea, II*, Catholic RS, 2 (1906), 12–218, esp. 161–2 • J. H. Pollen, ed., 'Official lists of Catholic prisoners during the reign of Queen Elizabeth', *Miscellanea, II*, Catholic RS, 2 (1906), 219–88, esp. 219–20 • *Miscellanea VII*, Catholic RS, 9 (1911) • H. Foley, ed., *Records of the English province of the Society of Jesus*, 7 vols. in 8 (1875–83) • P. Hughes, *Rome and the Counter-Reformation in England* (1942) • A. O. Meyer, *England and the Catholic church under Queen Elizabeth*, trans. J. R. McKee (1916); repr. with introduction by J. Bossy (1967) • M. H. South, *The Jesuits and the joint mission to England during 1580–1581* (1999) • Gillow, *Lit. biog. hist.* • J. H. Pollen, ed., *Unpublished documents relating to the English martyrs*, 1, Catholic RS, 5 (1908) • *Letters of William Allen and Richard Barret, 1572–1598*, ed. P. Renold, Catholic RS, 58 (1967) • P. Renold, ed., *The Wisbech stirs, 1595–1598*, Catholic RS, 51 (1958), 184, 276 • *The letters and memorials of William, Cardinal Allen (1532–1594)*, ed. T. F. Knox (1882), vol. 2 of *Records of the English Catholics under the penal laws* (1878–82) • W. H. Stevenson and H. E. Salter, *The early history of St John's College, Oxford*, OHS, new ser., 1 (1939) • [C. B. Heberden], ed., *Brasenose College register, 1509–1909*, 1, OHS, 55 (1909), 16 • J. Pitts, *De illustribus Angliae scriptoribus* (1619), 803–4 • A. Pritchard, *Catholic loyalism in Elizabethan England* (1979) • P. Holmes, *Resistance and compromise: the political thought of the Elizabethan Catholics* (1982), 188, 200 • A. Bellesheim, *Wilhelm Cardinal Allen (1532–1594) und die englischen Seminare auf dem Festlande* (1885) • E. H. Burton and T. L. Williams, eds., *The Douay College diaries, third, fourth and fifth, 1598–1654*, 1, Catholic RS, 10 (1911), 198–9 • chief justice's roll, queen's bench, PRO, KB 27/1279

Archives BL, Lansdowne MSS, corresp. with John Gibbons • Inner Temple, London, Petyt MSS, 'narrative', MS 538/54 • Stonyhurst College, Lancashire, MS on English persecution, Anglia I, n. 23

Ely, Nicholas of (*d.* 1280), administrator and bishop of Winchester, was of unknown origins. He is first clearly identified in record on 6 August 1249, officiating as archdeacon of Ely, and described as 'magister Nicholas'. He remained archdeacon of Ely, which may account for his name, until his election as bishop of Worcester in 1266. On 31 October 1252 he was given a papal indult to hold two additional benefices in England, and two papal letters of July 1257 describe him as papal chaplain as well as archdeacon.

Nicholas of Ely was projected into the centre of politics by the circumstances of the barons' wars. A close roll memorandum records that on 18 October 1260 the chancellor, Wingham, handed in the old and new seals, that the old seal was broken and the king gave Ely the new seal with his own hand, and the council's agreement, Ely taking the oath. About six months later Henry III complained that whereas he himself had nominated good and useful persons to be justiciar, treasurer, and chancellor, the councillors had appointed less suitable persons against his wish. The council responded that the ministers were chosen by a council-appointed committee of five, sworn to secrecy. On 12 July 1261 the king, having secured papal dispensation from his oath to the baronial provisions, dismissed Ely from the chancery, but two days later recorded that he held him in special commendation for his good service. In September 1262 Ely was favoured with a gift of three bucks from the forest of Wabridge, Huntingdonshire.

By 6 May 1263, following an upsurge in the baronial position, Ely was in post as treasurer, and remained in office until 19 July 1263, when he was reappointed chancellor. He received the seal in Montfort's presence, and remained in office until the end of November 1263. Latterly Ely was faced with an awkward situation. A patent roll memorandum records that the king, going overseas, left Westminster on 18 September, that the great seal remained in Ely's keeping, and that nothing was sealed with the great seal while the king was abroad except cursory writs to which Hugh Despenser, the justiciar, was witness, with certain listed exceptions. Although the king returned on 8 October, the great seal seems only to have come back into regular use on 2 November. At Windsor writs sealed between 17 and 28 October were sealed with the lesser seal, and the great seal was not used in this period in London to authenticate writs on the baronial government's behalf. It has been suggested that Ely simply withheld the great seal until it became clear which side was in control. The tide was flowing in the king's favour and within the month Ely had been dismissed again.

It is clear from these events that Ely was a nominee of the baronial provisional government, and removed whenever the royalists recovered power, although clearly he managed to remain personally acceptable to the king. An innovation of his first period as chancellor was the introduction of an allowance of 400 marks per annum, paid quarterly, to maintain the chancellor and his clerks. This was the beginning of a practice destined to lead to regular allowance.

On 9 May 1266 Ely was formally elected to the bishopric of Worcester, the royal assent was given on 8 June, and the order to restore temporalities on 18 June. He was consecrated by Archbishop Boniface on 19 September, and enthroned in his cathedral on 26 September. During the course of these events, on 31 August 1266, he was appointed one of the six dictors of Kenilworth, chosen to elect another six and proceed as twelve makers of the peace following the barons' wars. Their award was published at Kenilworth on 31 October. On 2 March 1268, following the death of John Gervais, bishop of Winchester, at the papal curia, Ely was translated to Winchester by the pope. The order to restore temporalities was given on 2 May, and Ely was enthroned on 27 May. Unusually, he made a second profession of obedience to Canterbury.

For the remainder of his life Ely was above all a conscientious bishop, visible on diocesan visitation, participating in other episcopal consecrations, joining with the bishop of Exeter to confer the pallium on Archbishop Kilwardby (d. 1279), receiving the archbishop on visitation, receiving the king and queen, and supervising ecclesiastical tax collection in the diocese. In 1269 he obtained an eight-day extension to the St Giles fair at Winchester. He seems to have had particular affection for the Cistercian abbey of Waverley, Surrey, which lay close to Odiham, and

was a house of Montfortian sympathies. It was at Waverley that Ely consecrated John Breton (d. 1275) as bishop of Hereford on 2 June 1269, in the presence of seven other bishops. He consecrated chrism at Waverley in 1274, eating with the convent in the refectory, according to the Worcester annals at his own expense. On 21 September 1278 he dedicated the abbey church on its completion, granting copious indulgences and remissions, and feasting those present splendidly at his own expense. After his death on 12 February 1280 Ely was buried at Waverley on 16 February; his heart was taken to the cathedral at Winchester. The abbot and convent of Waverley established a perpetual chantry for his soul in 1310. A daily mass and anniversary commemorations were established, paid for from rents from a manor (Curridge, Berkshire) given to the monastery for the bishop's soul by his executor Master Hugh Tripacy. The executors also erected a brass candlestick at the bishop's tomb, and a marble cross at Froyle, Hampshire.

Ely's relations with the monks of St Swithun's were less amicable, though dissension between the cathedral priory and the bishops of Winchester existed before Ely took office. The related annals of Waverley, Winchester, and Worcester, and the register of Ely's successor John de Pontoise (d. 1304), tell of a protracted struggle in Ely's episcopate, during which the successive interventions of the legate, royal justices itinerant, the abbots of Reading and Glastonbury, the provincial prior of the Dominicans, Bishop Antony (I) Bek, and Edward I brought only temporary respites. However, in 1299 St Swithun's undertook to celebrate daily masses for Ely as a benefactor.

From the episcopal bench Ely took an occasional part in secular affairs. In 1270 he was the first listed witness to Edward's consigning of his children to the care of Richard, earl of Cornwall, before departing on crusade. In 1272 he was third signatory, after the archbishop of York and bishop of Rochester, to the letter to Edward I announcing his father's death, and according to the Winchester annals he went with the bishops of Worcester and Exeter to meet Edward in Paris on his return from the Holy Land. In 1278 he headed the list of those present when Alexander III, king of Scots, performed homage to Edward at Westminster. Excluding the dissension with St Swithun's, which was probably more institutional than personal, there is evidence of long and useful public life, and the chronicler Wykes's comment at the time of Ely's election to Worcester that he was 'a man of knowledge and prudence' (Ann. mon., 4.180) may not be far from the truth.

Helen M. Jewell

Sources Emden, *Oxf.* · *Fasti Angl., 1066–1300,* [Monastic cathedrals] · *Fasti Angl., 1066–1300,* [St Paul's, London] · *Ann. mon.,* vols. 2, 4 · *Registrum Johannis de Pontissara, episcopi wyntoniensis AD MCCLXXXII–MCCCIV,* ed. C. Deedes, 1 vol. in 9 pts, Surrey RS, 6 (1916) · *Chancery records* · *CEPR letters,* 1.280, 349 · Rymer, *Foedera,* new edn, 1.433, 484, 497 · *Registrum epistolarum fratris Johannis Peckham, archiepiscopi Cantuariensis,* ed. C. T. Martin, 1, Rolls Series, 77 (1882), 36–7, 118–19, 255–6 · L. B. Dibben, 'Chancellor and keeper of the seal under Henry III', *EngHR,* 27 (1912), 39–51 · R. F. Treharne, *The baronial plan of reform, 1258–1263* (1932) · *Registrum Henrici Woodlock, diocesis wintoniensis, AD 1305–1316,* ed. A. W. Goodman, 1, CYS, 43

(1940), 470–1 • M. Richter, ed., *Canterbury professions*, CYS, 67 (1973), 78–79 • W. Stubbs, *Registrum sacrum Anglicanum*, 2nd edn (1897), 63

Ely, Reginald (d. **1471**). *See under* Wastell, John (d. *c.*1518).

Ely, Richard of (*fl.* **1177–1189**), prior of Ely and historian, was a monk of Ely Cathedral priory from boyhood. Little is known of the details of his life and death, but he is commonly identified with the Richard who was sub-prior of Ely in the early 1170s and prior from 1177 until at least 1189. Richard is usually regarded as having been the author of the *Liber Eliensis*, a work in three books covering the main phases of the history of Ely. However, authorship has also been claimed for one **Thomas** (*fl. c.*1177), also a monk at Ely, on the basis of a miraculous cure recorded in the *Liber* as wrought by St Æthelthryth 'in me myself, Thomas by name', a cure whose authenticity could not be doubted on the grounds that 'I Thomas have had it inserted on this page' (*Liber Eliensis*, ed. Blake, 312, 314). The 'I myself', it is argued, was the compiler of the *Liber*, whose name was thus Thomas, and whose reference to Richard as prior shows that he was writing no earlier than 1177. Although this story has its own interest, as showing a monastic writer attempting to shame the writers of his day into making greater efforts to spread the merits of their saints by introducing an exemplary story of his own, the likelihood is that the whole episode, containing the Thomas miracle and the 'I Thomas' passages, was derived from an earlier collection, one that had no connection with the compiler of the *Liber*. But even if Thomas's authorship be conceded, this would only affect the first two books, from Æthelthryth's foundation to the creation of the bishopric in 1109, and book 3, dealing with the acts of the first two bishops of Ely, down to 1169, is substantially Richard's work.

As far as his training for the writing of history was concerned, Richard probably benefited from the teaching at Ely from about 1138 by the rhetorician Julian, who had taught liberal arts (his grammar being preferable to that of some of the Latin writers), philosophy, and theology in his own home town of London. Later Richard seems to have performed the duties of a cellarer, being praised for his prudent provision for the needs of each individual monk from the abbey's common substance. This probably explains why he 'alone of all' refused to accept the alienation of the manor of Stetchworth assigned to the monks' food and clothing. Conducting the subsequent appeal to Rome in 1150 with the newfangled procedure of papal judges-delegate, Richard so impressed Pope Eugenius III with his eloquence that he earned a much fuller access and colloquy than the others, which he used to air the grievances of the priory. This papal audience must have been the high point of his career, second only to his other achievement as the priory historian.

The quality of books 1 and 2, and of the approximately 140 documents in book 3, is bound to be uneven, varying with the value of each component part, the accuracy of its transmission, and its placing in an appropriate chronological and historical context. This last was successfully achieved with the incorporation of the *Libellus* of Bishop

Æthelwold (d. 984) into book 2, but not with the divers sources of the Norman conquest. The contemporary history of book 3 evoked some lively historical narrative—including the use of Sallust's *Bellum Catilinae*, as in the description of King Stephen's 'anarchy'—such that the later redactor of the *Liber* was able to admire Richard 'as a man most zealous in the business of histories [*historiarum studiosissimus*], accomplished and most eloquent in discourse' (*Liber Eliensis*, ed. Blake, 284). Yet he could be guilty of quite atrocious bias. The professional administrators installed by Bishop Nigel (d. 1169) to administer the see of Ely during his own absences in the 1130s are pictured as a bunch of 'malefactors' bent on looting the abbey's treasures. Oppressed, however, by the sufferings (including seven deaths) inflicted by the avenging St Æthelthryth, he would have deferred a promise to name them and their punishments, but for a fear of being called a liar. But eventually, fatigued by the burden of his zeal, Richard arranged to enjoy his retirement 'thinking that, long buffeted by the waves of this great labour, he had been released from the demands of this prolix work and reached the harbour of perpetual idleness' (*Liber Eliensis*, ed. Blake, 391). E. O. BLAKE

Sources E. O. Blake, ed., *Liber Eliensis*, CS, 3rd ser., 92 (1962) • E. O. Blake, 'The *Historia Eliensis* as a source for twelfth-century history', *Bulletin of the John Rylands University Library*, 41 (1958–9), 304–27 • E. O. Blake, '*Historia Eliensis*', PhD diss., U. Cam., 1952 • D. J. Stewart, ed., *Liber Eliensis* (1848) • [H. Wharton], ed., *Anglia sacra*, 2 vols. (1691) • W. Holtzmann, ed., *Papsturkunden in England*, 3 vols., Abhandlung der Gesellschaft der Wissenschaften zu Göttingen, new ser., 25; 3rd ser., 14–15, 33 (Berlin, 1930–52) • T. Gale, ed., *Historiae Britannicae, Saxonicae, Anglo-Danicae scriptores XV* (1691) • *Acta sanctorum: Junius*, 4, vol. 4 • E. Miller, *The abbey and bishopric of Ely*, Cambridge Studies in Medieval Life and Thought, new ser., 1 (1951)

Ely, William (d. **1609**), Roman Catholic priest, was born in Herefordshire; he was the brother of Humphrey *Ely. He received his BA at Brasenose College, Oxford, in 1547 and his MA two years later. In 1552 the university appointed him one of the clerks of Oxford market. Edwardian religion drove him in March 1553 to seek the college's permission to study medicine; but on Mary's accession he reverted to divinity, promptly becoming vice-principal of Brasenose and in 1557 BTh. Ely (like Nicholas Morton) was made priest at Edmund Bonner's first Marian ordination in London. He was noted in Foxe's *Acts and Monuments* as refusing to give his hand to Thomas Cranmer who was going to the stake in March 1556, Cranmer having relapsed into heresy. Although expelled from Brasenose for disobedience in August 1556, Ely was specified by Sir Thomas White in 1558 as one of the original graduate students in his new foundation of St John's College, Oxford; the award of Ely's university preaching licence on 25 November was awkwardly timed. He was presented by Maurice Griffith, bishop of Rochester (whose chaplain he may have been), to Norton rectory in Kent, and by Sir Thomas White to Freckenham, Suffolk, but it was probably another man provided to Crick, Northamptonshire, in 1560.

White chose Ely in 1559 as the second president of St

John's, after Alexander Belsyre was deprived (for faults in his accounts rather than in his religion). However, by early 1561 (perhaps late 1560) Ely had resigned in the face of the oath of supremacy, and he was deprived of his livings in the course of the next year and a half. In a list of popish priests, possibly dating to 1561 and certainly no later than 1564, he is described as 'lurking secretly' in Herefordshire (PRO, SP 15/11/45)—maintained by John Scudamore of Kentchurch and others, as Bishop Scory's letter of 1564 to the privy council also noted. Once the periodic recusancy panics of that period had subsided, Ely presumably resurfaced. He witnessed White's second will in September 1564 and his last one in November 1566, possibly by now acting as his private chaplain. In 1566 White wrote to St John's, asking that Humphrey, although a fellow, be permitted to reside with his brother.

While William Ely was believed by Wood to have retired, like Humphrey, to the continent, this is unconfirmed—and William had no need to attend a seminary. He took no part in written controversy, though he is said to have been more favourable than Humphrey towards the appointment of George Blackwell as arch-priest. Certainly he resumed underground activities in Herefordshire as a missioner, but was eventually confined to Hereford gaol, at least in principle. The sheriff complained to the privy council in 1605 that Ely set forward 'desperate designs with all his might, having such liberty as that he rideth up and down the country as he listes' (Foley, 4.370), a circumstance which the Catholic riots of that year in the county rendered sinister. Natural infirmity may, however, have been some check; he had attained a venerable age and reputation when he died in 1609, possibly in Hereford. Yet a testimony to his continued activity was the recent nineteen-year-old convert of his who arrived at Valladolid from Hereford in 1610. One of the last surviving Marian priests and guardian of the relics of St Thomas of Hereford, Ely had found a receptive area in which to maintain Catholic continuity across the Reformation, but was as willing as the graduates of continental seminaries to enlarge the faith in a missionary role. JULIAN LOCK

Sources W. H. Stevenson and H. E. Salter, The early history of St John's College, Oxford, OHS, new ser., 1 (1939) • Gillow, Lit. biog. hist. • [C. B. Heberden], ed., Brasenose College register, 1509–1909, 1, OHS, 55 (1909), 12 • H. Foley, ed., Records of the English province of the Society of Jesus, 4 (1878), 453–4 • R. W. Jeffery, 'History of the college, 1547–1603', Brasenose quatercentenary monographs, ed. F. Maden, 2/1, 7, OHS, 53 (1909), 7 • The acts and monuments of John Foxe, ed. J. Pratt, [new edn], 8 (1877), 89 • Registrum Matthei Parker, diocesis Cantuariensis, AD 1559–1575, ed. W. H. Frere and E. M. Thompson, 3 vols., CYS, 35–6, 39 (1928–33), 700, 783, 788 • list of recusant priests, PRO, SP 15/11/45 • M. Bateson, ed., 'A collection of original letters from the bishops to the privy council, 1564', Camden miscellany, IX, CS, new ser., 53 (1893), 19 • W. R. Trimble, The Catholic laity in Elizabethan England, 1558–1603 (1964), 10, 15, 33 • Wood, Ath. Oxon.: Fasti • R. Mathias, Whitsun riot: an account of a commotion amongst Catholics in Herefordshire and Monmouthshire in 1605 (1963), 17–20 • register of Edmund Bonner, bishop of London, GL, MS 9531/12, fols. 14, 18–20 • E. Henson, ed., The registers of the English College at Valladolid, 1589–1862, Catholic RS, 30 (1930), 108

Elyot, Sir Richard (d. 1522), judge, was son of Simon Elyot, who may have been mayor of Shaftesbury, Dorset, and grandson of Michael Elyot. The Elyot family was closely associated with Coker, near Yeovil, Somerset, and its twentieth-century American descendant Thomas Stearns Eliot celebrated his family's English roots in Four Quartets, one of which bears the title 'East Coker'. Richard Elyot's mother was Joan, daughter of John Bryce, also known as Basset. His own estates came to be based upon Chalk and Winterslaw in Wiltshire.

A practising advocate by 1492, Richard Elyot was a member of the Middle Temple, where he served as autumn reader in 1503; in the same year he became a serjeant-at-law, being promoted to king's serjeant in 1506. He was a JP for Wiltshire from 1494, for Essex between 1501 and 1508, for Oxfordshire from 1509, and for Berkshire from 1514. MP for Salisbury in 1495, he held the very lucrative office of attorney-general to Queen Elizabeth, and also served as a commissioner in Wiltshire for the collection of the aid of 1504 for the marriage of the king's eldest son, Arthur, and for the marriage of his daughter Margaret. Elyot acted as judge of the assize on the western circuit from 1507, before being appointed a judge of the court of common pleas on 26 April 1513. By 1517 he had been knighted. With Wolsey and others he acted as arbitrator in the long-running dispute between the corporation and cathedral priory of Norwich, and in 1521 he took part in the preliminary investigations into charges of treason against Edward Stafford, duke of Buckingham.

Elyot married twice. His first wife was Alice, daughter of Sir Thomas Delamere. The widow of Thomas Daubridgecourt of Strathfieldsaye, Hampshire, she was the cousin, and ultimately the heir, of Sir William Findern of Carlton, Cambridgeshire. They had two children: the famous humanist and educational theorist Sir Thomas *Elyot, and Marjory, wife of Robert Puttenham, son of Sir George Puttenham of Sherfield, near Basingstoke, Hampshire. Some time after 1510 Elyot married again; his new wife was Elizabeth, widow of Richard Fetiplace of East Shefford, Berkshire, and daughter and heir of William Besilles of Besselsleigh, Berkshire, through whom he acquired property in Berkshire and Oxfordshire.

Richard Elyot died between February and 26 May 1522, when his will (drawn up on 9 October 1520) was proved. It directed that his body and his wife's be buried in the cathedral church of Salisbury, 'in the place there prepared for me and my wife' (PRO, PROB 11/20, fols. 189–90v), but it is not known whether this direction was carried out. He provided that all his English books were to go to his daughter, and his Latin and French books to his son. He also made many bequests to religious foundations.

R. J. SCHOECK

Sources LP Henry VIII, 1.940 • J. B. Williamson, ed., The Middle Temple bench book, 2nd edn, 1 (1937), 52 • W. Dugdale, Origines juridiciales, or, Historical memorials of the English laws (1666), 47, 113, 215 • Baker, Serjeants • E. Foss, Biographia juridica: a biographical dictionary of the judges of England … 1066–1870 (1870) • T. Elyot, The governour, ed. H. H. Croft, 2 vols. (1883) • J. Hutchinson, ed., A catalogue of notable Middle Templars: with brief biographical notices (1902) • E. W. Ives, The common lawyers of pre-Reformation England (1983) • will, PRO, PROB 11/20, sig. 24
Wealth at death see will, PRO, PROB 11/20, sig. 24

Elyot, Sir Thomas (*c*.1490–1546), humanist and diplomat, was the only son of Sir Richard *Elyot (*d.* 1522) and his first wife, Alice Delamere, a descendant of the Finderns of Derbyshire. Alice died about 1510 and Sir Richard subsequently married Elizabeth Besilles, whose father, William, held the manor of Besselsleigh, Berkshire. Sir Richard Elyot was a king's serjeant-at-law, justice of assize for the western circuit, and judge of the court of common pleas. He inherited the manors of Chalk and Winterslow, near Salisbury, and acquired land at Long Combe, Oxfordshire, where Thomas lived during his youth.

Early life and education In the preface to the first edition of his Latin-English dictionary (1538) Thomas Elyot wrote that he was educated at his father's house 'and not instructed by any other teacher from his twelfth year, but led by himself into liberal studies and both sorts of philosophy'. This would seem to indicate that he did not attend a university. However, the registers of Oxford University include four references to a Thomas Eliett, Eyllyett, Elyett, or Elyott, who was admitted in 1516, took his BA degree in 1519, and received a bachelor of civil law degree in 1524. These entries may refer to the present subject, although it has been argued that the name is common and another man may be meant. If it was another Thomas Elyot nothing is known about him. It is not known which college Thomas Elyot (whoever he was) attended, but there is a tradition that he was a member of St Mary Hall, a small house associated with Oriel College. It is possible that Elyot was largely self-taught, as his preface states, but that he was allowed to take Oxford degrees at a somewhat older age than usual, perhaps because of his intellectual abilities, his father's prominence, or his residence near Oxford. The university curriculum would not in any case have included the humanist studies that interested Elyot. Cambridge has also claimed Elyot. C. H. Cooper wrote that he was educated at Jesus College, Cambridge, proceeding BA in 1507, but he did not cite his evidence.

The comment in the dictionary would also appear to suggest that Elyot did not attend an inn of court, but the records of the Middle Temple indicate that he was admitted to clerk's commons in November 1510. His father had long been associated with that inn. There is no evidence that Thomas was called to the bar or ever practised law, but from 1510 to 1526 he served as clerk to the justices of assize for the western circuit, assisting his father and continuing for four years after Sir Richard's death. About 1510 he married Margaret à Barrow (*d.* 1560), daughter of Sir Maurice Barrow or Abarough, who held land in Hampshire and Wiltshire, where he was a neighbour of Sir Richard Elyot.

Although the evidence is slight—the source is More's later biographer Thomas Stapleton—it appears that both Thomas and Margaret Elyot were members of the scholarly circle centred on Sir Thomas More. Following More's execution Elyot went to some pains to dissociate himself from the former chancellor; he asked Thomas Cromwell to

lay apart the remembrance of the amity betweene me and Sir Thomas More, which was but usque ad aras, as is the

Sir Thomas Elyot (*c*.1490–1546), by Hans Holbein the younger

proverb, consydering that I was never so moche adict unto him as I was unto truthe and fidelity towards my soveraigne lord. (BL, Cotton MS Cleopatra E. IV, fol. 260)

The Latin phrase 'usque ad aram' appears in Erasmus's *Adages*, where it is glossed to mean that one should not give false evidence, even for a friend. Through More Elyot may have known Erasmus, and it is likely that he studied medicine with Thomas Linacre; the preface to Elyot's book *The Castel of Helth* states that when he was twenty years old 'a worshypfull phisition, and one of the most renoumed at that tyme in England, perceyving me by nature inclyned to knowledge, radde unto me the workes of Galene' and Hippocrates (Elyot, *Castel of Helth*, sig. A4). More was probably also responsible for introducing Elyot to Hans Holbein the younger, whose drawings of both Thomas Elyot and his wife survive in the Royal Collection at Windsor Castle.

Upon the death of his father in 1522 Thomas inherited most of his lands and a large library that included French and Latin books and some fine manuscript primers. The manor of Long Combe was left to Thomas Elyot's relative Thomas Findern of Carleton, Cambridgeshire; following Findern's death in 1523 both Long Combe and Carleton came to Elyot. Elyot later complained to Cromwell that he was troubled with costly lawsuits for possession of these lands, instituted by those 'which made title withoute ryght or goode consyderation' (BL, Cotton MS Titus B. I, fols. 376–7). Between 1515 and 1529 Elyot served as a JP for Oxfordshire and Wiltshire; in 1527 and 1529 he was named sheriff of the two counties. After 1530 he made Carleton his principal residence, and he was named a JP for Cambridgeshire. In 1528 Elyot purchased the wardship of a cousin, Erasmus Pym, who was an ancestor of the seventeenth-century parliamentarian John Pym. The families were related, for Erasmus's father Reginald Pym had married Sir Richard Elyot's stepdaughter Mary Daubridgecourt.

Government service and *The Boke Named the Governour* Late in 1523 Elyot was appointed senior clerk of the king's council. He later wrote that he owed his advancement to Cardinal Wolsey, who encouraged him to resign his lucrative post with the justices of assize but never gave him a patent for the office in the council or paid him the fee of 40 marks a year. Elyot served for more than six years, handling Star Chamber affairs as well as those proper to the council itself. After Wolsey's fall Elyot lost the office; he later complained to Cromwell that he had never been properly compensated for his services. In June 1530 Elyot was knighted, probably in recognition of his work with the council.

Elyot's reputation as a humanist scholar rests primarily on his treatise *The Boke Named the Governour*. First published in 1531 and dedicated to Henry VIII, it is divided into three books and deals with a variety of topics. The first few chapters advance a monarchical political theory, with Elyot arguing that a 'publike weale' is made up of a hierarchic order of degrees of men. At the top of the hierarchy there must be a single ruler, the king. Monarchy, therefore, is the only natural and proper form of government; Elyot says that the king within his realm is like God within His, thus implying that the king's power is unlimited. This view of government can be traced back to Plato, Aristotle, Aquinas, and Castiglione, whose book *The Courtier* may have been given to Elyot by Thomas Cromwell.

The remainder of book 1 describes the form of education appropriate for young men who are destined to be members of the governing class. Here Elyot prescribes the classical works to be read in the original Greek and Latin and deals also with physical education, dancing, and music. The second and third books are of less importance. They are concerned with setting out the virtues that governors should display; the definitions are often trite, but there is considerable interest in the anecdotes drawn from ancient history that Elyot uses as examples of virtuous behaviour. The *Governour* demonstrates the considerable breadth of Elyot's knowledge of classical and Renaissance literature; it became very popular, running through eight editions during the sixteenth century, and was very influential in disseminating new humanist ideas on the role of the gentleman in England. It is likely that Elyot in publishing the *Governour* was deliberately courting the king's favour, and it is possible that the section praising monarchy was added at the request of Thomas Cromwell. Like Elyot's other writings the treatise was brought out by the king's printer Thomas Berthelet.

Ambassador to Charles V Elyot's next appointment probably came as a mark of the king's favour. In September 1531 he was named ambassador to the emperor Charles V. Ostensibly he was to represent Henry VIII at a chapter of the order of the Golden Fleece, but in fact his principal charge was to sound out Charles regarding the king's divorce from Katherine of Aragon, who was the emperor's aunt. Since Elyot's own sympathies lay with Katherine, and since it was in any case unlikely that Charles would abandon her cause, the embassy was unpleasant and fruitless, and it did not last long; in January 1532 Elyot was recalled, and Thomas Cranmer, the future archbishop of Canterbury, was sent to take his place.

Instead of returning to England directly, Elyot remained on the continent until June, travelling with Cranmer to visit the towns of Worms, Speier, and Nuremberg. In Nuremberg, although he approved of the married priests, he joined the French ambassador in walking out of a church service in order to avoid taking communion according to the Lutheran rite. He also spent some time in the Netherlands, following the king's order to try to apprehend William Tyndale, whose radical writings offended the English court. It was probably following Elyot's recall that Charles V made his famous comment that he 'wold rather have lost the best city of our dominions than have lost such a worthy councellour' (Roper, 103). Upon his return it was evident that the king's opinion of him was diminished. He had also lost money; as he complained to Cromwell, his allowances had not covered his expenses. Although he sought further preferment, he was never again to hold a prominent office.

Henry's divorce, granted by Cranmer in 1533 after parliament had rejected papal jurisdiction in England, and his subsequent marriage to Anne Boleyn seriously distressed Elyot. He expressed his views in a letter sent to John Hackett, English ambassador in the Netherlands, in April, at exactly the time of the passage of the Act in Restraint of Appeals. 'We have hanging over us a grete kloude', he wrote, 'which is likely to be a grete storm whan it fallith' (PRO, SP 1/75/81). Elyot hoped that he would die in the true faith, but he would not abuse the sovereign to whose loyalty he was sworn.

The dictionary and the *Castel of Helth* No longer in favour at court, Elyot retired to his Cambridgeshire estates and spent the rest of his life in scholarly activities. His most important contribution was his Latin–English dictionary, first published in 1538 and like the *Governour* dedicated to Henry VIII. It would have appeared sooner, Elyot wrote in the preface, had not the king expressed an interest in it and sent additional books for him to study. The printer had already worked through the letter M; the later portions of the dictionary are fuller, and an appendix contains additional entries beginning with the letters A–M. An enlarged second edition appeared in 1542 and was reprinted without significant changes in 1545, shortly before Elyot's death. As Elyot said, he had given English equivalents for virtually all the words found in classical texts, and had also provided tables of ancient weights and measures. His was not the earliest Latin dictionary, but it was the first based on classical sources and applying humanist principles.

Together with the *Governour* and the dictionary, Elyot's *Castel of Helth* completes the trilogy of his major works. It is an attempt to summarize the teachings of the ancient Greek and Roman physicians, especially Galen, so that English men and women may understand and regulate their health accordingly. It popularized the theory of the four humours and complexions, which became a basic part of the intellectual make-up of Renaissance Britain, and suggested medicines and treatments for a variety of ailments. Probably based on Elyot's studies with Linacre, it differed from Linacre's own writings, for Linacre translated the works of Galen from Greek to Latin, hoping to make them accessible to doctors but not wishing to allow ordinary men and women to diagnose their own complaints. It was Elyot who provided an accessible handbook in the vernacular.

Later writings A number of Elyot's late writings are thinly veiled comments on Henrician politics. *The Defence of Good Women* (1540) purports to be an account of the life of Queen Zenobia of Palmyra but in fact is intended as a eulogy of Katherine of Aragon. *Pasquil the Playne* (1533) is a dialogue set in ancient Rome; it castigates the flatterers who have come to surround the ruler. A translation from Isocrates, *The Doctrinal of Princes* (1533?) directs monarchs how they should govern their realms and cities. 'Th'office of a good counsellour', Elyot wrote, 'with magnanimity or good courage in tyme of adversity, may be apparantly founden in my boke called, *Of the Knolege Beloning to a Wise Man*' (preface to the dictionary, 1538). The book is based on Diogenes Laertius' account of Plato's experiences at the court of Dionysius of Sicily; it shows that Plato acted fittingly when he warned Dionysius about tyranny. Some other writings are unrelated to contemporary events. *The Education or Bringinge up of Children* (1533?) is a translation from Plutarch, dedicated to Elyot's sister Margery (or Marjory) Puttenham. More personal, spiritual works include translations of a sermon by St Cyprian and the *Rules of a Christen Life* by Pico della Mirandola (1534) and *A Preservative Agaynste Deth* (1545). Roger Ascham wrote that he was once in Elyot's company and asked him if he knew when the longbow was first used in England. Elyot replied that he was writing a history of England, *De rebus memorabilibus Angliae*, which would soon be published; it included an account of the use of bows and shafts by King Vortigern, at the time the Saxons first came into the realm. The work, if ever completed, was almost certainly never printed and no manuscript is known to have survived.

Elyot was a member of the parliament of 1539, having been elected a knight of the shire for Cambridgeshire. The official returns do not survive, but Elyot's preface to the 1539 edition of the *Castel of Helth* apologizes for errors in the text resulting from his 'attendance on the Parlyament, I being a member of the lower house'. There is no record of his activities there. The eighteenth-century antiquarian Browne Willis believed that Elyot sat again for Cambridgeshire in the parliament of 1542, but the returns show that he was wrong. It is possible that Elyot represented the borough of Guildford in the parliament of 1545; the return names 'Thomas Elyatt, gent., of Shalford', which may refer to Sir Thomas, who held land at Shelford, Cambridgeshire, but it is also possible that another Thomas Elyot who was a servant of Sir Anthony Browne's at Cowdray is meant.

Death and burial Elyot was one of the gentlemen appointed to receive Anne of Cleves in 1540. He was ordered to provide ten men for the army in France in 1543 and twenty in 1544. He had made a will in 1531, before going on his embassy to Charles V, and he confirmed its provisions on 23 March 1546. He died three days later and was buried in the parish church at Carleton, Cambridgeshire; a commemorative brass has disappeared. As he had no offspring, he left his property to his wife Margaret for her lifetime and then to his nephew Richard Puttenham, elder brother of George *Puttenham, author of *The Arte of English Poesie*. Perhaps because he did not think that his library would be appreciated by either heir, he directed that his books be sold and the proceeds be distributed to poor scholars.

Elyot's public services, while significant, were not of the highest importance, and his writings lack originality. His great contribution was as a popularizer of the culture of classical antiquity; no one did more to bring the ideas of the ancient Greeks and Romans to Tudor England.

STANFORD LEHMBERG

Sources S. E. Lehmberg, *Sir Thomas Elyot, Tudor humanist* (1960) · J. M. Major, *Sir Thomas Elyot and Renaissance humanism* (1964) · P. Hogrefe, *Life and times of Sir Thomas Elyot, Englishman* (1967) · T. Elyot, *The boke named 'The governour'*, ed. H. H. S. Croft, 2 vols. (1880) [ed. from 1st edn of 1531] · T. Elyot, *The book named the governor*, ed. S. E. Lehmberg (1962) · T. Elyot, *The castel of helth* (1541) · M. Dowling, *Humanism in the age of Henry VIII* (1986) · S. E. Lehmberg, *The later parliaments of Henry VIII, 1536–1547* (1977) · HoP, *Commons, 1509–58* · will, PRO, PROB 11/31, sig. 14 · Wood, *Ath. Oxon.*, new edn · Cooper, *Ath. Cantab.*, vol. 1 · B. Willis, *Notitia parliamentaria*, 3 vols. (1715–50) · R. Ascham, *Toxophilus* (1571), sig. 28v · 'Registrum H, Registrum congregationis', 1518–36, Oxf. UA · letter from Elyot to Cromwell, BL, Cotton MS Cleopatra E. IV, fol. 260 · letter from Elyot to Cromwell, BL, Cotton MS Titus B. I, fols. 376–7 · letter from Elyot to Hackett, PRO, SP 1/75/81 · W. Roper, *The life of Sir Thomas Moore*, ed. E. V. Hitchcock (1934)

Likenesses H. Holbein the younger, chalk drawings, Royal Collection [*see illus.*]

Wealth at death manors: will, PRO, PROB 11/31, sig. 14

Elys, Edmund (1633x5–1708), nonjuring Church of England clergyman and writer, was the son of Edmund Elys (1603/4–1659), rector of East Allington, Devon, and his wife, Ursula (c.1606–1678), daughter of John Carew. He was born at Haccombe, the parish of his mother's family. His date of birth is derived from his age on a portrait of him engraved in 1662 by William Faithorne as an illustration for one of his collections of poetry ('aet 28', either aged twenty-eight or in his twenty-eighth year) and from his age in 1707, seventy-two. He was prepared for university at Exeter under William Hayter. He was admitted a commoner of Balliol College, Oxford, in Lent term 1651; however, his matriculation is recorded at Wadham College on 24 June 1653. He graduated BA on 16 October 1655 and was admitted a fellow of Balliol the following month, following the precedent set by his father a generation earlier. He proceeded MA on 11 June 1658.

In July 1659 Elys was ordained by the deprived bishop of Oxford, and three weeks after the death of his father took unchallenged possession of the rectory of East Allington on 1 November. In the same year or early in the next he was imprisoned by the authorities at Exeter on suspicion of being an 'enemy to the Common Wealth' (*DNB*). Elys's time at East Allington continued somewhat fraught. In 1677 the living was sequestrated for reasons that are unclear, but which are presumably linked to the financial difficulties which saw him absconding to London between 1677 and 1680, finding himself in the debtor's prison of king's bench, and writing begging letters to Archbishop Sancroft. In 1688 Elys read James II's declaration of indulgence from his pulpit and published a letter justifying his actions. After the revolution he refused the oaths of allegiance to William and Mary, and was deprived of his living as a nonjuror. He moved to Totnes, Devon, where he was buried on 6 April 1708.

Elys's prolific writings show the workings of a spirited but eccentric mind. His poetry is inferior, and he records the mockery made of it when he declaimed some verses from his *Divine Poems* (1658) in hall at Balliol. Other collections of verse include *Dia poemata* (1655), and *Miscellanea* (1658). Elys was also a keen if somewhat superficial participant in several of the theological and ecclesiastical controversies of his day. Surprisingly for a clergyman of the established church, he was well disposed towards the Quakers throughout his life and published several pamphlets in their defence. Among others are the self-explanatory *Vindiciae Roberti Barclaii* and *A Letter … in Vindication of the Quakers from the Charge of being Socinians*, both of which appeared in 1693, while *A Vindication of the Doctrine Concerning the Light within* was published in 1699. A full list can be found in Joseph Smith's *A Descriptive Catalogue of Friends' Books* (2 vols., 1867).

Elys's concern with Socinianism (a radical anti-trinitarian theology of continental origin) was not limited to his defences of the Quakers from such accusations. As the controversies concerning the doctrine of the Trinity grew more acute in the 1690s, Elys was one of many seeking to defend the traditional orthodoxy. *Dominus est Deus* (1690) was an attack on the Racovian catechism, a compendium of Socinian teaching. *Dei incarnati vindiciae* (1693) which was dedicated to John Wallis, one of the leaders of the trinitarian party, continued this line of thought. In his *Letters on Several Subjects* (1694) Elys turned his fire on William Sherlock, who had attempted a defence of the doctrine of the Trinity along Cartesian lines, describing the three persons as three infinite minds. Another letter from the same period attacked the author of *The Brief Notes on the Athanasian Creed*, Stephen Nye, whose *Brief History of the Unitarians* had ignited the controversies in the first place. In 1701 Elys published *Socinianismus purus putus Antichristianismus*, a further repudiation of Socinian theology. Elys continued to produce pamphlets touching on other theological issues of his day, commenting unfavourably on Limburg's *Dogmata* in 1702, and the works of Cornelius Jansen and other authors in 1706. This last re-echoed an earlier work, *Animadversions upon the Nature of a Gospel Church* (1690) in which he had sought to refute certain Calvinistic doctrines he found in the work of Jansen and John Owen. The extent of Elys's peripatetic scholarship is probably best illustrated by the fact that in 1660 he republished *The Opinion of Mr. Perkins and Mr. Bolton and Others Concerning the Sport of Cock-Fighting* which condemned the practice as thoroughly unchristian.

PHILIP DIXON

Sources Wood, *Ath. Oxon.*, new edn, 4.470–75 · A. Chalmers, ed., *The general biographical dictionary*, new edn, 32 vols. (1812–17) · Wood, *Ath. Oxon.: Fasti* (1820) · E. Evans, *Catalogue of a collection of engraved portraits*, 1 [1836], 112 · F. Madan, *Oxford books: a bibliography of printed works*, 3 vols. (1895–1931); repr. (1964), vol. 3 · H. W. C. Davis, *A history of Balliol College*, rev. R. H. C. Davis and R. Hunt (1963) · *DNB* · *Walker rev.* · J. L. Vivian, ed., *The visitations of the county of Devon, comprising the herald's visitations of 1531, 1564, and 1620* (privately printed, Exeter, [1895]), 144 · R. B. Gardiner, ed., *The registers of Wadham College, Oxford*, 1 (1889), 200
Archives Bodl. Oxf., corresp. mostly with J. Wallis relating to trinitarian orthodoxy, MS Eng.th.e.22
Likenesses W. Faithorne, line engraving, BM, NPG; repro. in E. Elys, *Miscellanea*, 2nd edn (1662)

Emanuel, Barrow (1842–1904). *See under* Davis, Henry David (1839–1915).

Emberton, Joseph (1889–1956), architect, was born on 23 December 1889 at Shraley House, Audley, Staffordshire, the eldest of the three sons and four children of Samuel Emberton, draper, and his wife, Annie Amelia, daughter of John Hodgkins, farmer and miller. He was educated at the Orme Boys' School, Newcastle under Lyme, then articled to the local architects Chapman and Snape. By studying in the evenings at Burslem Art School, Emberton won a scholarship to the Royal College of Art in 1911; he worked for the London architects Trehearne and Norman from 1913 to 1914. He served during the First World War in the Honourable Artillery Company, first as a gunner in Egypt and later as a trajectory officer in France, and was badly wounded in October 1918.

On recovery, in 1918 Emberton joined Sir John Burnet and T. S. Tait, until he established a practice with P. J. Westwood, from 1922 to 1926. They designed kiosks for the British Empire Exhibition, Wembley (1924), using simple shapes with colourful decoration. Summit House, Holborn (1925), for Austin Reed Ltd, whose Regent Street shop interiors Westwood and Emberton designed in 1926, shows Burnet and Tait's influence. Emberton continued to design shops in the fashionable art deco style, for Lotus and Delta shoes and others. He was selected by Sir Lawrence Weaver to design the advertising exhibition, Olympia, West Kensington (1927), the first such exhibition with a unified style.

Emberton showed the influence of Dutch modern architecture in the façade added to New Empire Hall, Olympia (1930). The Royal Corinthian yacht club, Burnham-on-Crouch, Essex (1931), established his modernist reputation, and was the only British building included in the exhibition 'The international style' at the Museum of Modern Art, New York, in 1932. The functionalist design owed much to Emberton's assistant George Fairweather (1906–1986). With Universal House, London (1933; dem.),

Emberton enveloped a framed structure in glass curtain-walling, intended to rise higher than the original three storeys. Simpson's shop in Piccadilly, London (1936), was structurally innovative, although the welded plate girders designed by the consulting engineer, Felix Samuely, had to be modified to meet London county council regulations. The simple façade was enlivened at night by thin coloured neon lights and the interior had elegant shopfittings and modern furnishings. It demonstrated the maturity of English modernism and its commercial advantages.

Apart from the HMV shop in Oxford Street, London (1939), and the temporary Soleil pavilion at the Paris 1937 exhibition, Emberton's other main work is the circular casino at the Blackpool pleasure beach, Lancashire (1939), where he had already designed the fun house and grand national (1935), showing the adaptability of modernism to popular entertainment. The casino, containing restaurants and a flat for the owners, was given holiday spirit with a viewing platform reached by a spiral stair adjoining the entrance.

During the Second World War Emberton was housing officer to the Ministry of Aircraft Production, architectural adviser on hostels to the Ministry of Works, and consultant to the Ministry of Supply on the design of steel houses. After 1945 he designed mostly flats in London and developed planning ideas influenced by Le Corbusier.

Emberton's approach was practical rather than theoretical, and enabled him to make elegant and workable buildings for commercial clients. He was fair-haired and blue-eyed, with great charm of manner. He loved horses, the birds in his outdoor aviary, and his 1934 Bentley. On 23 June 1926 he married Kathleen Marie (b. 1906/7), daughter of William Herbert Chantrey, a chartered accountant; they had two daughters. Emberton died at Charing Cross Hospital, London, on 20 November 1956. His wife survived him.   ALAN POWERS

Sources R. Ind, *Emberton* (1983) • b. cert. • m. cert. • d. cert. • *CGPLA Eng. & Wales* (1956) • private information (1993) • *The Times* (22 Nov 1956)
Wealth at death £60,860 10s. 10d.: probate, 24 Dec 1956, *CGPLA Eng. & Wales*

Embleton, Clifford (1931–1994), geomorphologist and geographer, was born on 11 May 1931 at Highfield, 11 Fairacres Road, Bebington-cum-Bromborough, Chester, the only son of Arthur Thomas Embleton (1895–1954), shipping clerk, and his wife, Constance Fitzgerald (1896–1948). He was educated at Birkenhead School and then won an open exhibition to St John's College, Cambridge, from where he graduated in geography in 1952, winning the Philip Lake prize. He remained at Cambridge to undertake doctoral research on the glacial landforms of north Wales, and he graduated PhD in 1956. The same year, on 19 May at St Mary-the-Less, Cambridge, he married Davina Caroline (b. 1932/3), daughter of Ernest Harry Cherry, grocer. They had three sons.

In the 1950s Cambridge was a major centre for geomorphological research and had an especially strong reputation in glacial geomorphology, largely because of the influence of the Antarctic geologist Professor Frank Debenham and of Vaughan Lewis. A number of gifted graduate students emerged, of whom Embleton was one. Besides undertaking fieldwork in Wales, he took part in glaciological research expeditions to Norway (in 1951, 1952, and 1955) and to Iceland (in 1953). On these expeditions he gained invaluable experience of modern cold climate processes, including those operating in and beneath glaciers. His research led to a series of innovative papers published during the 1960s on the geomorphology of north Wales and culminated in his classic text, written with Cuchlaine King, *Glacial and Periglacial Geomorphology* (1968). This was long the standard work on the matter, and a substantially revised two-volume second edition appeared in 1975.

Embleton was a lecturer and then senior lecturer at Birkbeck College and King's College in the University of London and was appointed to a chair at King's in 1982. His inaugural address was entitled 'Glaciology in the service of man'. He was a good lecturer and an assiduous leader of student field trips, and served on a wide range of college committees. He collaborated with Professor John Thornes, Professor Denys Brunsden, and Professor David Jones, all notable geomorphologists within the joint school of geography of King's and the London School of Economics. The four played a very significant role in creating a major international reputation for British geomorphology which led, in due course, to the establishment of the International Association of Geomorphologists. Embleton uniquely brought to this role a profound knowledge of the German literature as well as a deep understanding of the Anglo-American and French traditions.

Embleton wrote some seventy-five scientific papers in all. In these he demonstrated his power as a fieldworker, his commitment to international collaboration, his early appreciation that process studies in geomorphology were important, and his recognition that geomorphology enhances the understanding of human activities. His work was soundly empirical and meticulous in execution. However, Embleton's interests extended beyond the study of icy mountains. For example, with Alan Mountjoy, he produced *Africa: a Geographical Study* (1965). Moreover, during the 1970s and 1980s he developed a great interest in geomorphological hazards, mapping, and techniques, and this involved liaison with a large number of European scholars in Poland and elsewhere. Notable results of this activity were *The Geomorphology of Europe* (1984), an edited compendium, and *Geomorphological Hazards in Europe* (1997), which was edited with his second wife, Christine Embleton-Hamann, and published posthumously.

Embleton was secretary, then chairman, of the International Geographical Union's working group on geomorphological survey and mapping and president of its study group on rapid geomorphological hazards (1988–92). He made editorial work his forte, and edited the *Transactions of the Institute of British Geographers* from 1967 to 1974, achieving notably high standards of presentation and content.

Outside geography, Embleton was a gifted organist. He was elected fellow of the Royal College of Organists in 1949, when only eighteen years old. During his final illness he devoted himself to the restoration of the organ in Hanworth parish church, and his last paper (in 1994) was a history of that organ. He had a strong Christian faith. His first marriage having been dissolved, he married on 27 February 1991 at the Middlesex Hospital Christine (*b.* 1951/1952), daughter of Herbert Hamann, retired civil servant. She was a university lecturer and geomorphologist of the University of Vienna.

Embleton died, after a fight against cholangiocarcinoma, on 4 July 1994, at the Middlesex Hospital, Westminster. His funeral took place on 14 July in Feltham, Middlesex, where he had lived at 18 Sycamore Close. He was survived by his second wife.

ANDREW S. GOUDIE

Sources *The Times* (21 July 1994) · *Zeitschrift für Geomorphologie*, 39/2 (1995), 265 · C. L. Rosenfeld, 'Dedication to Professor Clifford Embleton', *Geomorphological hazards in high mountain areas*, ed. J. Kalvoda and C. L. Rosenfeld · *College Newsletter* (1994), vol. 80, p. 11 [King's College, London] · personal knowledge (2004) · private information (2004) [Christine Embleton-Hamann, widow] · b. cert. · m. certs. · d. cert.

Likenesses photograph, repro. in *The Times*

Wealth at death £215,990: probate, 16 Feb 1995, *CGPLA Eng. & Wales*

Embleton, Richard (*c.*1273–1333), merchant and mayor of Newcastle, is believed to have come from Embleton near Dunstanburgh, a barony given to Edmund, earl of Lancaster, after its forfeiture by Simon de Montfort. His parents are unknown, but he may have been related to the Richard of Sweethope who in 1296 had the highest assessment in the liberty of Embleton, where he was one of the assessors. By 1296 Embleton was in business in Newcastle, where he was assessed in the parish of St Nicholas, listed next to Sampson Cutiller, the wealthiest merchant in the town, for whom, with Sampson's wife, Agnes, Embleton endowed two chantries in 1332. This suggests a family relationship, probably matrimonial. Embleton married three times: first, before 1305, Alice, and second Isabel (their surnames are unknown); his third wife, who survived him, was Christian, daughter of John (I), Lord Mowbray.

Embleton appears in the Newcastle customs accounts for 1295–7 as shipping wool, wool-fells, and hides; and in the detailed customs of 1308 he is the leading shipper of wool. Entries in the royal wardrobe books show him supplying Edward II with stores, including grains, malt, and wine (1311/12), and oxen and sheep (1312/13). He was still shipping wool in 1325. In December 1330 he was granted a personal freedom from all tolls throughout the realm, in consideration of his losses during the wars with Scotland, while in October 1332 he was granted a safe conduct for two years to buy wine in Gascony.

In 1301 Embleton was one of the four town bailiffs, who served under the mayor, and he represented Newcastle in the convention of burgesses held at York in 1303. Many times mayor between 1306 and 1333, often for several years in succession, he was also one of Newcastle's representatives in parliament in 1311, 1314, 1324, 1325, 1328 (twice), and 1332. In 1314 and 1315 he was ordered to supervise the sheriff of Northumberland in garrisoning Newcastle Castle. He was responsible for maintaining order in Northumberland in 1317, following the plot to seize the cardinal legates on embassy to secure peace between England and Scotland (and the subsequent insurrection led by Gilbert Middleton), and was authorized to receive into the king's peace such rebels as submitted. In 1322, immediately before the final rebellion of Thomas, earl of Lancaster, Embleton was made joint custodian of the town of Newcastle with the mayor, and, after the earl's defeat, was made keeper of the lands of the earl and his followers within Northumberland, with responsibility for their management. This included the garrisoning of Dunstanburgh Castle with forty men-at-arms and forty hobelars. In June 1323 he was granted for his services interim possession of two parts of the manor of Silksworth in co. Durham, forfeited by Robert Holland, subsequently confirmed with the remaining third in March 1324. At the same time he was appointed, with Ralph Neville of Raby, a keeper of the truce with Scotland. His responsibilities in maintaining the king's peace in Northumberland and Durham were renewed in June 1324, and widened to include reconciling men who had joined the Scots and rebels through poverty and now wished to return to their first allegiance. In June 1333 he brought eleven men-at-arms and twenty-one hobelars from Newcastle to serve Edward III at Berwick against the Scots. He was then ordered back to Newcastle on royal business, but later returned with seventeen men-at-arms and thirty hobelars and other armed men, and was killed at the battle of Halidon Hill outside Berwick on 19 July 1333.

By then Embleton held the manor of Silksworth in co. Durham and lands throughout Northumberland, from Jesmond by Newcastle to Newton on the Moor, Embleton, and Mindrum, some of them acquired by purchase. He was commemorated in the chantries which in 1332 he was licensed to found at St Nicholas's, Newcastle, and at Embleton, to be served by two priests each. He used two seals. One was an antique gem. The other showed a sleeping lion with the motto 'Ci dort le [lio]n fort'. Embleton was unusual in the frequency and lengths of his tenures of office as mayor of Newcastle, and also in the use which successive kings made of his services to supervise the maintenance of law and order in Northumberland and Durham. This strongly suggests his origins were in a landowning family of administrators, a conclusion supported by his final marriage alliance with Christian Mowbray. Although his failure to produce a male heir frustrated any hopes of founding a local dynasty, the thirds of his estate which passed to daughters formed an important element in the capital of later merchant grandees of Newcastle—Bertram Anderson (*c.*1520–1570), Richard Hodgson (*c.*1516–1585), and, through Sir Reginald Carnaby, William Cavendish, first earl of Ogle and duke of Newcastle (1593–1676).

C. M. FRASER

Sources *Chancery records* · PRO, Exchequer queen's remembrancer, customs accounts, E 122/105/3, 4, 6, 9 · PRO, Exchequer queen's remembrancer, accounts various, E 101/373/26, fol. 90 [wardrobe account] · BL, Nero C VIII, fols. 71, 157v, 164v, 176v · Exchequer queen's remembrancer, memoranda rolls, 93, mm 21r–d, 148:97, mm 275d, 284d:100, mm 66d, 135, 195d · *CIPM*, 7, no. 536 · *RotS*, 1.180b · A. M. Oliver, ed., *Early deeds relating to Newcastle upon Tyne*, SurtS, 137 (1924), 209–12 · *Liber Cartarum*, Tyne and Wear Archives Service, Newcastle upon Tyne, TWAS 574/95, 121–3 · C. H. H. Blair, 'Members of parliament for the boroughs of Northumberland, 1295–1377', *Archaeologia Aeliana*, 4th ser., 13 (1936), 59–94, esp. 70 · C. H. H. Blair, 'The mayors and lord mayors of Newcastle upon Tyne', *Archaeologia Aeliana*, 4th ser., 18 (1940), 1–14, esp. 3 · C. M. Fraser, ed. and trans., *The Northumberland lay subsidy roll of 1296*, Society of Antiquaries of Newcastle upon Tyne, Record Series, 1 (1968), 115
Wealth at death lands: *CIPM*

Embry, Sir Basil Edward (1902–1977), air force officer, was born in Longford, Gloucestershire, on 28 February 1902, the youngest of the three children and the second son of James Embry, an Anglican clergyman, and his wife, Florence Ada Troughton. In conversation he always claimed to be Irish, though only his paternal grandfather is traceable to Ireland.

Embry's early years were uneventful, and he attended Bromsgrove School without scholastic distinction, though he showed athletic prowess coupled with a precocious longing, from his tenth year onwards, to fly aeroplanes. The main part of his schooling coincided with the First World War, and when it ended he thought that his chance of flying was gone. However, in spite of strong opposition from his parents, who wanted him to go to Cambridge, he managed to join the Royal Air Force as a short service officer, and he was commissioned on 29 March 1921.

After flying training Embry joined 4 bomber squadron, but found the immediately post-war home service scene too tame for his taste, and applied for service in Iraq. This was the first of his many initiatives to 'march towards the sound of the guns'. In Iraq he was able to pioneer the air-mail route across the desert and join in the development of new techniques of 'air control', devised by Sir Hugh Trenchard, to keep the peace in the Kurdish border districts. This, and his work with the first air ambulance service, won him an AFC in 1926 and the award of a permanent commission. In 1927 he returned to England, and the following year he married (Margaret Mildred Norfolk) Hope, the daughter of Captain Charles Sinclair Elliott RN, with whom he had three sons and one daughter. Meanwhile he qualified as a flying instructor, commanded a training flight, and specialized in the development of instrument flying. He remained an instructor until he took the RAF Staff College course in 1933.

For Embry this was more than enough of training and home service, so he applied for a posting to India. He arrived there in 1934, and after suffering staff and training appointments was promoted to squadron leader in 1936 and given his first command, 20 squadron at Peshawar. This was far more to his taste, and in the hazardous flying on the north-west frontier, during the various campaigns of 1937 and 1938, he was appointed to the DSO (1938) and established a lifelong reputation for courage and leadership.

Embry was therefore discontented to find himself, at the outbreak of war in 1939, in the directorate of operations in Whitehall. It took him eight days to get out, to the command of 107 day bomber squadron, and to the opportunity to continue to apply his principles of leadership in operational practice. The air service's greatest morale problem had always been the confinement of commanders to the ground, usually on account of their age and lack of flying practice, so that while their men endured the greatest dangers of any combatant they themselves were safer than many civilians. It might have been deplorable, but it was accepted. Embry would have none of this. His own Blenheim was riddled with bullets on his first sortie over Germany, but he continued to lead the squadron on missions of great danger, bringing home a damaged aircraft fifteen times and even flying in the air-gunner's position, the better to understand his problems. It would be hard to exaggerate the affection he inspired in the members of his squadron. His extreme personal recklessness made them feel protective towards him.

His luck could not last. On the day he was promoted and posted from his squadron Embry was wounded and shot down over France. He was captured, and while marching towards a prison he passed a signpost labelled Embry; taking this as a portent, he slipped away from the column and hid in a French farm. Although he was recaptured, he escaped again by belabouring his guards with an iron bar, and finally arrived safely in Gibraltar.

Back in England Embry was promoted to group captain and commanded a night fighter wing and a fighter sector. During this period at home he was received into the Roman Catholic faith. He was sent to north Africa in 1941, at the request of Sir A. W. Tedder, to advise on tactics. He then had two staff appointments in England until, in May 1943, he was given command of 2 bomber group, with the rank of air vice-marshal. His task was to prepare this tactical group for the Overlord invasion, and thereafter to support the allied armies in continental Europe. In these operations he continued to use his individual style of personal leadership, flying with his crews and carrying forged identity documents, for fear of execution if captured. He was awarded the DFC (1945) for these operations, a most unusual decoration for a man of his rank. In 1945 he was awarded a third bar to his DSO, appointed CB and KBE, and received a number of foreign honours—thus becoming one of the most highly decorated officers in the three fighting services.

But the end of the war brought him to Whitehall again as assistant chief of air staff (training). Although Embry liked training he hated Whitehall; yet through this appointment he was able to supervise the complete overhaul of RAF training that followed the war. In April 1949 he was promoted air marshal and made commander-in-chief, Fighter Command, and though there was now nobody to fight he used all his explosive energy to bring the command to a new peak of efficiency. In 1953 he was appointed KCB and, in December, air chief marshal. In

July 1953 he was posted to France as commander of allied air forces central Europe, in the new NATO organization. This ponderous multinational organization was little suited to his qualities. Although he was buttressed by his great reputation, he spoke little French, distrusted politicians, suspected diplomats, and was unenthusiastic about foreigners generally. It was not the best use of an outstanding fighting leader, and this miscasting contributed to his early retirement in September 1956, at the age of fifty-four, when he was appointed GCB.

Embry had long planned to take his whole family to start life anew in New Zealand, and he now put this scheme into practice, though shortly after arriving he moved on to Western Australia. There he bought a tract of bush and worked, helped by his wife and eldest children, to create a farming estate out of the wild. As the years went by the Embry family, now naturalized Australians, gradually conquered all obstacles. Embry built a house with his own hands, and by 1972 he was president of the Farmers' Union of Western Australia and founder and first chairman of the Rural Traders' Co-operative. He was made first chairman of the worldwide RAF Escaping Society, a freeman of the City of London and of the cinque port of Dover, and a liveryman of the Worshipful Company of Glass-sellers. He died at Boyup Brook, Western Australia, on 7 December 1977. He bequeathed to the Royal Air Force an example of personal leadership which became an enduring tradition of the service.

Embry was a small, spare man, wiry and strong, Celtic in colouring, with extremely piercing blue eyes under fierce eyebrows. He had a puckish face, by no means handsome, which could express a wide variety of emotions from demonic rage to delight, laughter, and goodwill, often within a few seconds. He had a trick of speaking to people from such close range, and with so fixed a blue glare, that even those whom he meant only to please were disconcerted. While he was not particularly witty, he had a strong sense of fun and a great capacity to inspire and charm most people, coupled with a talent to dismay and antagonize some others.   PETER WYKEHAM, *rev.*

Sources B. E. Embry, *Mission completed* (1956) · personal knowledge (1986) · private information (1986) · *The Times* (9 Dec 1977) **Archives** FILM BFI NFTVA, documentary footage · IWM FVA, actuality footage | SOUND IWM SA, oral history interview **Likenesses** J. A. Hampton, photograph, 10 June 1949, Hult. Arch. · E. Kennington, portrait, priv. coll. · E. Kennington, portrait, Gov. Art Coll.

Emden, Alfred Brotherston (1888–1979), historian, was born on 22 October 1888 in West Ealing, Middlesex, the elder son of Alfred Charles Emden (1849–1911), barrister and later county court judge, and his wife, Lizzie Whitfield (d. 1955). He was a scholar at both the King's School, Canterbury (1903–7), and Lincoln College, Oxford (1907–11), though he obtained only a second class in modern history (1911).

His future career then seemed uncertain: he qualified for the bar at the Inner Temple, ran a hostel in London for disadvantaged boys, Edghill House, Sydenham (1913–15),

and then began schoolmastering at Strand School, Brixton, London. The war intervened, and from 1915 he was an able seaman (Royal Naval Volunteer Reserve) in a destroyer leader, HMS *Parker*. In January 1919, while still an able seaman, he accepted an almost chance offer of a tutorship in modern history at St Edmund Hall, Oxford. He was appointed bursar in the same year and vice-principal in 1920.

Emden now immersed himself in university life and history, and remained at St Edmund Hall for the next thirty years. In 1920 he published his first article, on the hall's history, in the first issue of its magazine, which he had launched, and in 1927 he produced a pioneering, scholarly study, *An Oxford Hall in Medieval Times*. Two years later he was appointed principal of the hall. It was then a small society, unendowed but relatively inexpensive for undergraduates; its principal had virtually complete control over it, choosing both undergraduates and tutors. Emden entered his role with infectious enthusiasm, increasing the number of students and greatly enhancing the hall's prestige in the university. He successfully ran it as what he wished it to remain, the last of the medieval halls; he never wanted it to have full collegiate status. In 1937 the reorganization of the hall's constitution was in some respects amended by congregation before it was enacted by a statute of the university. Another statute made special trustee arrangements for the site and the buildings, the freehold of which had belonged to Queen's College since 1557. However, an uneasy relationship with the tutors (now called fellows) subsequently developed. An enlightened paternalist, he was happier in his relations with the students and shaped the careers of many of them. Until 1939 he continued to teach medieval history, giving tutorials that often lasted for a couple of hours. He was also responsible for the restoration of the hall's old buildings, the near-completion of the south side of its quadrangle in 1934, and the beginnings of an endowment.

During the Second World War Emden remained in charge of St Edmund Hall, while also being lieutenant-commander in charge of the Oxford University naval division (1942–4): he had persuaded a reluctant Admiralty to raise such divisions in several universities. He was, besides, still very active in public school and Church of England affairs, being much consulted over appointments. The strain of all this told, especially when he did such things as going on a submarine foray to the Bay of Biscay while the French coast was still in German hands. His health broke down, and in 1951 he resigned the principalship, going to live with his mother in Headington.

Emden was now sixty-two. He had already written one book, and revised another—H. Rashdall's *Universities of Europe in the Middle Ages*, edited with F. M. Powicke, in 1936—but it is on the prosopographical works of his years of retirement that his scholarly reputation depends. Combing the collegiate and university records of Oxford, and going through all the medieval episcopal registers, as well as a vast range of other English sources, he compiled three substantial volumes of *A Biographical Register of the*

University of Oxford to A.D. *1500* (1957–9). He made such thorough notes that it was then no great labour to produce a similar *Biographical Register* for Cambridge (1963)—in 1958 he estimated that such a work could be completed within eighteen months—and a more summary *Survey of Dominicans in England, based on the ordination lists in episcopal registers (1268–1538)* (1967). He forestalled any criticism of the supplementary *Biographical Register of the University of Oxford,* A.D. *1501 to 1540* (1974) by the comment that 'octogenarians, like young men, are apt to be in a hurry'.

Emden was unconcerned that his chosen areas of research were not then fashionable. He had a gift for friendship, and a wide range of acquaintances, but his close friends were few and in his later years were drawn from a small circle who shared his interest in the lives and books of medieval scholars. His lifestyle was comfortable but simple; he had strong Christian convictions. His manner was normally gracious and unperturbed, although he was a man of powerful emotions and could on occasion explode violently. He delighted in the careful observation of birds, wild flowers and grasses, and medieval floor tiles.

He was elected an honorary fellow of Lincoln College (1939) and of St Edmund Hall (1951), FBA (1959), FSA (1969), and corresponding fellow of the Medieval Academy of America (1968); he received honorary doctorates from both Oxford (1959) and Cambridge (1964). He was a trustee of the Oxford Preservation Trust (1932–67), and he served on the governing bodies of the King's School, Canterbury (1933–62), St Edward's School, Oxford (1933–57), and two other schools, while he was a member of Oxford University's hebdomadal council from 1935 to 1947. He died at his home, Dunstan Cottage, Old Headington, Oxford, on 8 January 1979, a bachelor. His ashes were buried in the ante-chapel at St Edmund Hall. The bulk of his estate, over £400,000, was left to St Edmund Hall.

NIGEL RAMSAY, *rev.*

Sources R. B. Pugh, 'Alfred Brotherton Emden, 1888–1979', *PBA*, 65 (1979), 641–52 · J. N. D. Kelly, *St Edmund Hall Magazine*, 11/6 (1979) · J. N. D. Kelly, *St Edmund Hall: almost seven hundred years* (1989) · Bodl. Oxf., MSS Emden · St Edmund Hall, Oxford, Emden MSS · personal knowledge (1993) · private information (1993) · *CGPLA Eng. & Wales* (1979)

Archives Bodl. Oxf., corresp. and papers relating to his *Biographical register of the University of Oxford* · St Edmund Hall, Oxford, documents relating to St Edmund Hall or its members [transcripts] | Bodl. Oxf., corresp. with L. G. Curtis · Bodl. Oxf., corresp. with Graham Pollard

Likenesses F. W. Elwell, oils, *c.*1935–1936, St Edmund Hall, Oxford · H. A. Freeth, watercolour, *c.*1953, St Edmund Hall, Oxford

Wealth at death £419,115: probate, 16 July 1979, *CGPLA Eng. & Wales*

Emeléus, Harry Julius (1903–1993), inorganic chemist, was born on 22 June 1903 in Poplar, London, the second of three sons and the second of the five children of Karl Henry Eméleus (1869–1948), pharmacist, and his wife, Ellen, *née* Biggs (1873–1965), a secretary at the Scandinavian Sailors' Home near the West India docks in London. His father, a Swedish speaking Finn, was born in

Harry Julius Eméleus (1903–1993), by unknown photographer, *c.*1958

Vaasä, Finland, but eventually settled in England at the turn of the century. His mother was the daughter of George Biggs, an engineer in charge of the dock gates. Three months after Eméleus was born the family moved to the Old Pharmacy in Battle, Sussex, and this was to remain the family home. Eméleus's older brother, Karl George (1901–1989), later became professor of physics at the Queen's University of Belfast.

Eméleus attended St Leonards Collegiate School, Hastings, and Hastings grammar school (1914–21) before going up to the Royal College of Science, Imperial College, London, graduating ARCS with first-class honours in chemistry in 1923. At that time this did not automatically qualify for the University of London BSc, so he took the London External BSc with a different syllabus later in the same year, again obtaining first-class honours. He was awarded his PhD (London) for work on the luminescent oxidation of phosphorus in 1926 and DSc three years later. An Exhibition of 1851 senior studentship in 1927 enabled him to spend some time in Karlsruhe with Alfred Stock, one of the world's greatest exponents of preparative inorganic chemistry, and this had a profound influence on his subsequent research. He also became fluent in German and an expert glassblower. Then as a Commonwealth Fund fellow (1929–31) he spent two highly productive years at Princeton University working on various aspects of photochemistry with Professor Hugh Stott Taylor. It was also at Princeton that he met his future wife, (Mary) Catherine

Horton (1906–1991) of Richmond, Virginia, who was working in the university library, and who shared Emeléus's interest in folk dancing. They married in New York on 26 May 1931. The marriage was a long and happy one and they had four children: George Cowling (1934), Sidney Carlstrum (1938), Frances Virginia (1943) and Martha Ann (1950).

Returning to England, Emeléus was appointed as a junior demonstrator / assistant lecturer in the chemistry department at Imperial College, where he set up an active research group studying the chemistry of several main group elements. He also collaborated with his colleague J. S. Anderson in writing a renowned textbook, *Modern Aspects of Inorganic Chemistry* (1938), which ran through several editions and was to change the perception of the subject throughout the world. Defence related studies at Imperial College occupied most of 1939–45, except for a short period at Oak Ridge, Tennessee, as part of the British contingent working on the atomic bomb project. Emeléus also held a commission in the Home Guard, as battalion gas officer, and, with Ewart Jones, was senior gas adviser for London. Fortunately gas was never used, and his responsibilities were limited to lecturing to gas officers.

In October 1945 Emeléus took up a permanent appointment at Cambridge, first as reader and then, after a few months, as a personal professor in inorganic chemistry and fellow of Sidney Sussex College. He remained in Cambridge for the rest of his life. At the old university chemical laboratory in Pembroke Street there was virtually no research in inorganic chemistry. Alexander Todd had recently been appointed as head of the department and had already begun a drastic reorganization of the labs, which were still lit by gas and were very poorly serviced. By mutual agreement Emeléus was able to concentrate on teaching and research without being greatly burdened by matters of finance and administration. He always acknowledged his good fortune in this respect and it undoubtedly contributed to his happiness and productivity in Cambridge.

Several research groups on preparative inorganic chemistry were set up under Emeléus's general leadership to study new volatile compounds of silicon and the preparation of novel metal fluorides. He also opened up a fertile new field which exploited the use of highly reactive halogen fluorides as non-aqueous solvents. His most extensive series of investigations was the development over some twenty-five years of the chemistry of the extraordinarily versatile trifluoromethyl group. This resulted in more than sixty papers (one third of his total output) and involved some thirty-seven co-workers, more than half of them from a dozen different countries overseas. With these and other similar studies he succeeded in building up an internationally acclaimed school of inorganic chemistry at Cambridge, which dominated the subject for several decades. Indeed, an astonishing number of his research students and collaborators went on to distinguished careers and to senior academic positions both in Britain and abroad.

Emeléus was closely involved with the Ministry of Defence's Chemical Defence Advisory Board during the Second World War, and for several years after served as its chairman. He was a member of the technical committee concerned with the development of the first British nuclear power plant at Windscale, and was a consultant for many years to several major chemical firms. He was particularly active in the learned societies and served as president both of the Chemical Society (1958–60) and of the Royal Institute of Chemistry (1963–5); he was also president of the inorganic chemistry division of the International Union of Pure and Applied Chemistry (1955–60). He served as a trustee of the British Museum (1963–72) and was chairman of its committee for the research laboratory, whose work included the development of conservation treatments and techniques.

After his retirement in 1970 Emeléus continued to do experimental work until he was over eighty. Throughout his long career he was awarded many scholarships and prizes and received a remarkable number of international honours and awards. These included the Harrison memorial prize (1932), Tilden lectureship (1942) and Liversidge lectureship (1954) of the Chemical Society; fellowship of the Royal Society (1946); CBE (1958); the Davy medal of the Royal Society (1962); the Henri Moissan prize for fluorine chemistry, Germany (1991); the Lavoisier medal of the French Chemical Society; Alfred Stock memorial prize and medal of the Gesellschaft Deutscher Chemiker; honorary doctorates from seven universities; honorary membership of six chemical societies worldwide; and honorary membership of eight overseas academies of science. Despite this panoply of honours Emeléus remained a quiet, modest man, always appearing at ease with himself. His kindly manner, abiding courtesy and gentle sense of humour endeared him to colleagues and students alike. He had a passion for fly-fishing and it was said that he did much of his chemical thinking with a rod in his hand. His legacy was a rejuvenated academic discipline in the UK and a worldwide network of disciples who were enriched both by him and by the southern charm and generous hospitality of his wife who kept open house for them in Cambridge. He died peacefully of heart failure at Addenbrooke's Hospital, Cambridge, on 2 December 1993. The funeral was held in Trumpington church, Cambridge, a week later, followed by cremation. His ashes were interred in Battle churchyard. A memorial service was held in Sidney Sussex chapel on 30 April 1994. He was survived by his four children, his wife having died in January 1991.

NORMAN N. GREENWOOD

Sources N. N. Greenwood, *Memoirs FRS*, 42 (1996), 123–50 · RS · Royal Society of Chemistry Archives · U. Lond., archives · 'Professor H. J. Emeleus 90th birthday presentation volume', 1993, RS, MS/824 · *The Times* (9 Dec 1993) · *The Independent* (23 Dec 1993) · *The Sidney Sussex College Annual* (1994), 64–5 · *WWW*, 1991–5 · personal knowledge (2004) · private information (2004) · b. cert. · *CGPLA Eng. & Wales* (1994) · d. cert.

Archives Royal Society of Chemistry, London, MSS · RS · U. Lond., MSS | SOUND RS, interview recording, 1 March 1989 [also in Royal Society of Chemistry and priv. coll.]

Likenesses photograph, *c.*1958, Royal Society of Chemistry, Burlington House, London [*see illus.*] · photograph, repro. in *The Times* ·

portraits, RS · portraits, Royal Society of Chemistry, Burlington House, London · portraits, U. Lond. · portraits, university chemical laboratory, Lensfield Road, Cambridge

Wealth at death under £125,000: probate, 15 Feb 1994, *CGPLA Eng. & Wales*

Emerson, Sir Herbert William (1881–1962), administrator in India, was born at Hilbre Lodge, West Kirby, Cheshire, on 1 June 1881, the son of Stephen Samuel Emerson and his wife, Amelia Susan, *née* Norman. He was educated at Calday Grange grammar school and Magdalene College, Cambridge, where he was later made an honorary fellow.

Emerson joined the Indian Civil Service in 1905, and was posted to the the Punjab, where he was to spend the most significant part of his career in India. He was married in 1906 to Anne Evelyn, only daughter of Edwin Bellars of Wisbech. They had three sons, of whom one was killed in action in 1943. Emerson went through the entire hierarchy of the Indian Civil Service in the Punjab, starting as manager of a Himalayan hill station and eventually reaching the pinnacle as governor of the province. In the course of his early career in the Punjab, when he was assistant commissioner and settlement officer, Emerson was brought into close contact with rural people. There he developed a keen appreciation of the special conditions, customs, and folklore, as well as the problems, of the Punjab countryside. In 1926 Emerson served as financial secretary to the Punjab government, and in the following year he became chief secretary of the province.

In 1930 Emerson was appointed to New Delhi as the home secretary of the government of India, and was immediately thrust into the maelstrom of the Gandhi-led civil disobedience movement. He was to play a key role in the negotiations that led to the conclusion of the 'pact' between Gandhi and the viceroy, Lord Irwin, in March 1931, which brought about a temporary cessation of the civil disobedience campaigns and Gandhi's participation in the London round-table conference on constitutional reform. Emerson's skilful handling of the many contentious issues during the negotiations won him the approbation of both his adversary and his superior. Gandhi had such confidence in Emerson as to entrust to him willingly the drafting of the Gandhi–Irwin settlement, while Lord Irwin acknowledged that he was 'tremendously helped [by Emerson] in what had hitherto been a single-handed contest' (Low, 123). In summer 1931, with the resumption of non-violent resistance to the British raj, Emerson was once again engaged in a series of talks with Gandhi. Irwin's successor as viceroy, Lord Willingdon, also found it necessary to entrust Emerson with key discussions with 'much the most astute political operator the British Raj ever faced' (ibid., 133). His careful and considered handling of the situation—in his dealings with his provincial subordinates as well as the Congress—contributed in no small measure to the effective management of the crisis.

In April 1933 Emerson returned to the Punjab as governor, a post he was to occupy for the next five years. During his term at the helm of the province that he now knew intimately, he persisted with his predecessor's policy of cultivating cross-communal co-operation by leaders of Muslim, Hindu, and Sikh landed interests. He supported the intercommunal Punjab Unionist Party, and maintained close relations with its chiefs, particularly the Muslim leader Fazl-i Husain and his successor, Sikandar Hayat Khan. It was largely due to his working relationship with them that he was able to manage the communal conflicts arising in the main during the controversy over the Shahidganj mosque, a contested place of worship between the Sikhs and Muslims of the Punjab. His adroit handling of the communal problems enabled him skilfully to steer the Punjab from 'dyarchy' (the more limited form of provincial self-government in existence after 1919) into autonomous government provided for by the Government of India Act of 1935. His considerable ability as governor earned him an appointment for a further two years when his initial five-year term ended in 1937. However, he had to resign in 1938 owing to a prolonged spell of illness.

Emerson did not end his public career with his retirement from the Punjab. A year after he ended his tenure as governor, he was appointed to the League of Nations for five years as high commissioner for refugees. Following the outbreak of the Second World War, which added enormously to the 'complexities and anxieties' of the organization, Emerson was given the additional appointment of director of the Inter-Governmental Committee for Refugees. In 1941 the British foreign secretary, Anthony Eden, appointed him chairman of the Advisory Council on Aliens. By 1943 'he was concerned with the repatriation of some 20 million people of different nationalities scattered over Europe' (*The Times*, 14 April 1962). In 1947, after nine years of devoted humanitarian work on the relief, resettlement, and repatriation of war refugees at the League of Nations and later the United Nations, he retired. He died on 12 April 1962 at Orpington Hospital, Kent. Over 6 feet tall, broad-shouldered, and robust, he has been described as the 'archetypical member of the Indian Civil Service' (Low, 133). To his admirers, he was 'an admirable type of Indian civilian, perfectly straightforward with plenty of character' (ibid., 123).   TAI-YONG TAN

Sources D. A. Low, *Britain and Indian nationalism: the imprint of ambiguity, 1929–1942* (1997) · C. Dewey, *The settlement literature of the Greater Punjab: a handbook* (1991) · *The Times* (14 April 1962) · C. Dewey, *Anglo-Indian attitudes: the mind of the Indian civil service* (1993) · S. N. Ahmad, *From martial law to martial law: politics in the Punjab, 1919–1958*, ed. C. Baxter, trans. M. Ali (1985) · D. Gilmartin, *Islam and empire: Punjab and the making of Pakistan* (Berkeley, CA, 1988) · d. cert.

Likenesses W. Stoneman, three photographs, 1933–44, NPG

Wealth at death £49,121 16s. 6d.: probate, 21 June 1962, *CGPLA Eng. & Wales*

Emerson, Peter Henry (1856–1936), photographer and writer, was born on 3 May 1856 in Casa Grande, La Palma, Cuba, the first of the three children of Henry Ezekiel Emerson and his wife, Jane, *née* Billing Harris. Both parents were of English extraction, his mother directly (she

Peter Henry Emerson (1856–1936), by J. Havard Thomas, 1925

came from Cornwall) and his father through descent. Among his relatives were the Americans Samuel Morse and Ralph Waldo Emerson. Emerson, who was baptized Pedro Enrique, spent his early childhood in Cuba. Following a brief period in the United States (1864–9) the family went to England, where Peter, as he now called himself, was sent to Cranleigh, a public school in Surrey. After a short time at King's College, London, in 1874, he opted for a career in medicine and studied at Clare College, Cambridge (1874–9), where his athletic skills in football and rowing were allied to his interests in science. To the amazement of his contemporaries he won the Leathes prize in theology. His father had a highly successful sugar plantation in Cuba, and Emerson always enjoyed a private income.

Emerson practised medicine only briefly before turning to notions of art and to playing billiards. Typically, he excelled at both. He was a naturalist and an ornithologist, and his first book, a novel entitled *Paul Ray at the Hospital* (privately published, 1882), reputedly took him only two weeks to write. He was on honeymoon at the time, but Emerson managed to balance maverick tendencies: eccentricity and idiosyncrasy were combined with a fine sense for art, science, and sport (particularly rowing). He had married Edith Amy (*b*. 1853/4), the daughter of Joseph Ainsworth, a cotton spinner, on 22 June 1881, and the couple had five children: Leonard (1882), Sylvia (1884), Gladys (1885), Zoë (1893), and Ralf (1897).

Emerson began working in photography in 1882, and his major published works were photographic, both visual and theoretical. Of these, *Life and Landscape on the Norfolk Broads* (1886) and *Naturalistic Photography for Students of the Art* (1889) are the most significant—the former for its evocative pastoral scenes and its depictions of East Anglian life, which epitomized his strong and poetic work, and the latter for its polemical discourse which

countered much contemporary thinking. His approach was typified by his attitude to the retouching of photographs, which he described as 'the process by which a good, bad or indifferent photograph is converted into a bad drawing or painting' (Leggat). Among his realist contentions was that the photographer should seek to imitate human vision by blurring the periphery of the image. This brought him into conflict with the eminent photographer Henry Peach Robinson; in the course of an ill-tempered debate, Emerson memorably described Robinson's seminal *Pictorial Effect in Photography* as 'the quintessence of literary fallacies and art anachronisms' (ibid.). In all, Emerson was the author of twenty-four books and portfolios, some of which ran to several editions. His original work is now held by, among others, the National Museum of Photography, Film and Television, Bradford (Royal Photographic Society collection), the Getty Museum in Los Angeles, and the George Eastman House in Rochester, New York. Emerson was also a prolific writer of magazine articles and letters.

With his scientific background, Emerson initially favoured the platinum process for printmaking. It had an exceptional tonal scale and was archivally as stable as the paper base would allow. It was, however, time-consuming, and he changed to using photogravure, invented by a Czech, Károly Klics, in the 1850s. This means of reproducing images, which combined photographic techniques with those of etching, was less subtle than platinum but still allowed for a great deal of tonal control by the artist.

Emerson was a naturalistic photographer at a time when reality had fallen from favour. He eventually decided he had been wrong to claim photographs as 'great works of art' (in *The Death of Naturalistic Photography*, a privately published pamphlet of 1891). Yet he did not abandon photography immediately, and in 1895 he was awarded the Royal Photographic Society's progress medal; later, in the 1920s, he began to issue his own merit awards. As if to accentuate his freedom from conformity, in 1908 he compiled and issued a rule book for billiards. He died of heart trouble on 12 May 1936 at his home, 3 Avenue Road, Falmouth, Cornwall, and was buried in the town. His wife survived him.

Emerson was a photographic revolutionary who set the tenor for the method of picture making which evolved into pictorialism and later into modernism. He was also a magniloquent writer and a fighter for photography as fine art. That he was so influential can be traced to several causes: first, to his implicit self-belief, which some found insufferable; second, to his iron self-discipline and ability to succeed in everything to which he applied himself; and third, to his recognition of the place which photography held within the broader sphere of visual art and how, too, it related to science. He was a protean person; a mover and shaker—Victorian in the manner that made fortunes, empires, and discoveries. Born to a life of privilege, he used his inheritance wisely, albeit with flashes of bravura. He preached and practised at the same rate, with no quarter given, which is why some found him difficult. Others found Emerson's lack of capacity for compromise admirable. He had resolve and resolution and was a scholar, an athlete, and an intellectual.   PETER TURNER

Sources P. H. Emerson and T. F. Goodall, *Life and landscape on the Norfolk Broads* (1886) • P. H. Emerson, *Naturalistic photography for students of the art* (1889) • P. Turner and R. Wood, *P. H. Emerson, photographer of Norfolk* (1974) • N. Newhall, *P. H. Emerson* (1975) [incl. extensive bibliography] • M. Weaver, ed., *British photography in the nineteenth century: the fine art tradition* (1989) • R. Leggat, 'Emerson, Dr Peter Henry', www.rleggat.com/photohistory/history/emerson.htm • m. cert. • d. cert. • private information (2004)
Archives BM, MSS • Courtauld Inst., MSS • National Museum of Photography, Film and Television, Bradford, Royal Photographic Society collection • Norfolk RO, corresp., papers, and photographs • Norwich Central Library, MSS • V&A, MSS | priv. coll.
Likenesses portrait, 1908, BM; repro. in Turner and Wood, *P. H. Emerson* • J. H. Thomas, medal, 1925, BM [*see illus.*]
Wealth at death £6080 17s. 0d.: resworn probate, 14 July 1936, CGPLA Eng. & Wales

Emerson, William (1701–1782), mathematician, was the son of Dudley Emerson, a schoolmaster. He was first educated by his father and a curate who boarded in the house at Hurworth, near Darlington, co. Durham, and was afterwards sent to school in Newcastle and in York. After returning to Hurworth he opened a school of his own in 1730. Having little patience and no gift for teaching, Emerson soon lost his pupils, and his school closed in 1733. After this he determined to live on the income of between £70 and £80 left to him by his father. Though by no means studious as a boy, he devoted himself entirely to the study of mathematics, and in 1743 published the first of his textbooks, *The Doctrine of Fluxions*. About 1735 he married Elizabeth, a niece of the Revd Dr John Johnson, then rector of Hurworth. The couple had no children.

In 1763 Emerson arranged with the publisher John Nourse to write a series of mathematical manuals for young students, which were published in rapid succession. His books were successful, for though Emerson was not a creative mathematician he had a comprehensive grasp of existing knowledge in the various branches of his subject. With the profit from his writing he could settle some debts that burdened his heritage, and spend his life at Hurworth, living as an eccentric. He wrote textbooks on trigonometry, mechanics, arithmetic, geometry, finite differences, algebra, optics, astronomy, geography, and surveying, most of which were best-sellers. For instance, his *The Principles of Mechanics*, first published in 1754, ran to six editions, a revised and corrected issue of the sixth appearing in 1836. In 1770 he published *A Short Comment on Sir Isaac Newton's 'Principia'*. It is interesting to note that Emerson did not contribute papers to the *Philosophical Transactions* but rather to mathematical periodicals such as the *Ladies' Diary*. It seems that he declined to become a member of the Royal Society. His scientific production was addressed to a public composed of people interested in science and mathematics (amateurs, instrument makers, land surveyors, and so on) rather than academics or researchers.

In addition to writing for the *Ladies' Diary*, Emerson was

William Emerson (1701–1782), by Charles Turner, pubd 1812 (after Sikes)

a frequent contributor to *The Palladium*, the *Miscellanea Curiosa Mathematica*, and other periodicals. His contributions appeared under various signatures, including Merones, Nichol Dixon, and Philofluentimechanalgegeomastrolongo. In 1746–7 Robert Heath, editor of the *Ladies' Diary*, backed him in a controversy with Thomas Simpson. He also carried on a long controversy in the *Gentleman's Magazine* with an anonymous correspondent who had attacked his views on astronomy.

While staying in London Emerson lived with a watchmaker so that he might learn his trade, in which, in common with all branches of practical mechanics, he took a keen interest. He was accustomed to make for himself all instruments required for the illustration of his studies, and he constructed for his wife an elaborate spinning-wheel, a drawing of which is inserted in his *Mechanics* of 1754 (fig. 191). His knowledge extended to the theory of music, and though he was a poor performer, his services were much in request for the tuning of harpsichords, as also for the cleaning of clocks. It seems that he was one of the late opponents of equal temperament and he added to his virginals some half-tones so as to avoid the small imperfections in tuning required by equal temperament. His favourite amusement was fishing, and he would frequently stand up to his waist in water for hours together. The studied eccentricity of his dress produced a belief that he dealt in magic, and he professed to be much annoyed at the frequency with which his advice was sought for the discovery of secrets. His manner and address were extremely uncouth, and though he could talk well on almost any subject, he was very positive and impatient of contradiction. Towards the end of his life he suffered much from stones, from which he eventually died in May 1782, probably on the 20th. He was buried at Hurworth.

ALSAGER VIAN, rev. NICCOLÒ GUICCIARDINI

Sources W. Bowe, 'Some account of the life and writings of the author', in W. Emerson, *Tracts* (1793) • R. V. Wallis and P. J. Wallis, eds., *Biobibliography of British mathematics and its applications*, 2 (1986) • J. M. Wheeler, *A biographical dictionary of freethinkers of all ages and nations* (1889) • J. Aikin and others, *General biography, or, Lives, critical and historical of the most eminent persons*, 10 vols. (1799–1815) • A. Chalmers, ed., *The general biographical dictionary*, new edn, 32 vols. (1812–17) • *GM*, 1st ser., 63 (1793), 610 • C. Hutton, *A philosophical and mathematical dictionary*, new edn, 1 (1815), 471 • C. Knight, ed., *The English cyclopaedia: biography*, 6 vols. (1856–8)
Archives UCL, Graves MSS
Likenesses C. Turner, mezzotint, pubd 1812 (after Sikes), BM, NPG [*see illus.*]
Wealth at death left library to bookseller at York

Emerson, Sir William (1843–1924), architect, was born on 3 December 1843 at 28 Spital Square, Whitechapel, London, the son of William Emerson, silk manufacturer, and his wife, Jane Robinson. He was educated at King's College School in London and began his architectural training about 1861, with Habershon and Pite of Bloomsbury Square, before moving in 1865 to the practice of William Burges, the most scholarly and visionary of the Gothic revivalists. In his first year with Burges he assisted with the designs for a new school of art in Bombay, and in 1866 was dispatched to Bombay with the plans, but they were never realized, owing to a disagreement over fees. Emerson, who had family connections in India, stayed in Bombay, however. His first major commission there was the Crawford market (1865–71), in which Burges's influence was strongly evident, both in its style and structure, and in the fantastical character of its decorative ironwork and fountain, sculpted by John Lockwood Kipling (1837–1911), the father of Rudyard Kipling.

In 1869 Emerson returned to London and established offices in Westminster. For a few years he exhibited designs annually at the Royal Academy. He was married on 27 July 1872 to Jenny (*b.* 1852), daughter of the architect Coutts Stone and his wife, Mary, of Bayswater, and built a house for his family, Little Sutton, at Chiswick (1879). His relatively few buildings in England also included the church of St Mary and St James, Brighton (1877–9), and the Clarence Wing of St Mary's Hospital, Paddington, London (1896). Some of his best schemes were not built. His competition designs for the parliament in Berlin (1872) and the South Kensington Museum (1892) were not successful, and his entry in the limited competition for Liverpool Cathedral (1885), which was selected, was never started as the site and scheme were abandoned.

Emerson's Indian work continued to flourish, however. For churches—Girgaum church, near Bombay (*c.*1870–73), and All Saints' Cathedral, Allahabad (*c.*1869–93)—he preferred Gothic forms, but for secular buildings he championed the eclectic combination of neo-Gothic planning and construction with Eastern, so-called Indo-Saracenic, details. He did not believe that purely European buildings worked satisfactorily in the East. In the case of his Muir College, Allahabad (1872–8), his most startling and thoroughly eclectic work, he drew on Egyptian, as well as Indian and European, models. Other works included a hospital (*c.*1879–83) and huge new maharaja's palace (1894–5) at Bhaunagar. His final and most prestigious Indian work was the Victoria Memorial, Calcutta (1903–21), a museum of British rule in India commissioned by the viceroy, Lord Curzon, which dominates the centre of Calcutta.

Emerson was active on the council and committees of the Royal Institute of British Architects from 1885, and served as its honorary secretary (1893–9) and president (1899–1902). During his presidency he advised the government on the competition for improvements to Buckingham Palace and St James's Park. He was also president of the Royal Architectural Museum and oversaw its amalgamation with the Architectural Association in 1902. He was knighted that year. As well as achieving public eminence, the sociable Emerson also maintained a wide circle of friends in the profession. On his retirement, Emerson's son William Ernest continued his practice. Emerson died at his home, Eastcliffe, Shanklin, on the Isle of Wight on 26 December 1924, aged eighty-one.

CHRISTOPHER MARSDEN

Sources *The Builder*, 128 (1925), 2, 5 • *The Times* (30 Dec 1924), 15 • *RIBA Journal*, 32 (1924–5), 191–2 • *Architectural Association Journal*, 40 (1925), 152 • T. R. Metcalf, *An imperial vision: Indian architecture and Britain's raj* (1989) • J. Mordaunt Crook, *William Burges and the High Victorian dream* (1981) • P. Davies, *Splendours of the raj: British architecture in India, 1660–1947* (1985) • P. Davies, *The Penguin guide to the monuments of India*, 2 (1989) • B. Dinesen, 'Emerson, William', *The dictionary of art*, ed. J. S. Turner (1996) • G. H. R. Tillotson, 'A visible monument: architectural policies and the Victoria Memorial Hall', *Marg*, 49/2 (1997), 8–23 • G. H. R. Tillotson, 'Orientalizing the raj: Indo-Saracenic fantasies', *Marg*, 46/1 (1994), 15–34 • *WWW*, 1929–40, 329–30 • b. cert. • m. cert. • d. cert. • *CGPLA Eng. & Wales* (1925)
Likenesses J. J. Shannon, oils, *c.*1903, RIBA; repro. in Davies, *Splendours of the raj*, 185 • photograph, repro. in *The Builder*, 5
Wealth at death £31,530 5s. 3d.: probate, 25 Feb 1925, *CGPLA Eng. & Wales*

Emery, (Walter) Bryan (1903–1971), Egyptologist, was born on 2 July 1903 at Liverpool, the second son of Walter Thomas Emery, principal of the technical college at Liverpool, and his wife, Beatrice Mary Benbow, also of Liverpool. He was educated at St Francis Xavier's College, Liverpool, and early became fascinated with Egyptology, which, after a brief apprenticeship to a firm of marine engineers, he studied from 1921 to 1923 under T. E. Peet at the Institute of Archaeology of Liverpool University. In 1923–4 he worked on the Egypt Exploration Society's excavations at al-Amarna under F. G. Newton and F. L. Griffith. In 1924 he was appointed by Robert Mond to direct the Liverpool expedition to clear and restore the tomb of the vizier Ramose and other new kingdom nobles' tombs in the Theban necropolis. While accomplishing this, Emery saw the tomb of Tutankhamun during excavation, and discovered the burial place of the Buchis bulls at Armant, which he helped the Egypt Exploration Society to excavate in 1927–8.

On 18 July 1928 Emery married Mary (Molly; 1902/3–

1974), daughter of James Joseph Cowhey, head postmaster of Liverpool; he returned with his bride to Thebes. They had no children. He was then appointed by the Egyptian government antiquities service to direct the second archaeological survey of Nubia. From 1929 to 1934 the Emerys and their assistants traversed the southern part of Egyptian Nubia by boat and on foot, excavating each site discovered. At Ballana near the Sudanese frontier Emery discovered and excavated rich royal burial mounds (fourth to sixth century AD), the treasure from which came to grace the Cairo Museum. *The Excavations and Survey between Wadi es-Sebua and Adindan*, with L. P. Kirwan (Cairo, 1935), *The Royal Tombs of Ballana and Qustul*, with L. P. Kirwan (2 vols., Cairo, 1938), and *Nubian Treasure* (London, 1948) resulted.

From 1935 Emery excavated at Saqqara for the Egyptian government, uncovering a series of rich tombs of the first to third dynasties illuminating the beginnings of Egyptian history. He enlisted in 1939, and was employed at the headquarters of the British troops in Egypt with the long range desert patrol before serving with the Eighth Army. He was mentioned in dispatches in 1942 and appointed MBE (military) in 1943. He ended the war as director of military intelligence in Egypt as a lieutenant-colonel. In 1945–6 he returned to Saqqara, but, owing to financial difficulties, accepted a post in the British embassy at Cairo, where he rose to the rank of first secretary (1950–51).

In 1951 Emery was elected to the Edwards chair of Egyptology at University College, London. He returned to Saqqara as field director of the Egypt Exploration Society in 1952, and completed excavation of the first dynasty tombs in 1956 (*Great Tombs of the First Dynasty*, vol. 1, Cairo, 1949; vol. 2, London 1954; vol. 3, London, 1958). After the Suez crisis of 1956 he led the Egypt Exploration Society to Sudan to excavate the magnificent middle kingdom brick fortress town of Buhen, built about 1970 BC. His work there was published posthumously in *The Fortress of Buhen* (2 vols., London, 1974–9). He advised both the Egyptian and the Sudanese antiquities services throughout the UNESCO campaign to save the monuments of Nubia (1959–64); he arranged for the temple of Buhen to be moved to Khartoum, organized the third archaeological survey of Egyptian Nubia, and excavated the cemeteries of Qasr Ibrim, a Meroïtic city which later became a fortress of the medieval Nubians.

In 1964 Emery returned to Saqqara, where he discovered the sacred animal necropolis of Memphis, comprising the catacombs of mummified cows, baboons, ibises, and falcons. The associated temple site yielded rich hoards of bronze figurines and temple furniture, and valuable documents of the sixth to first centuries BC in Egyptian, Aramaic, Greek, and Carian. Late in 1967 he underwent major lung surgery, but he returned immediately to Saqqara to make further spectacular discoveries. He retired as professor in 1970. He died in Cairo on 11 March 1971, after collapsing on the excavations at Saqqara, and was buried in the British cemetery in Cairo. His Saqqara work was published posthumously by the Egypt Exploration Society.

Emery's direct approach and knowledge of terrain were the basis of his flair for finding major sites. His outstanding contributions were undoubtedly his magnificent architectural reconstructions of ancient buildings. He loved Egypt and Sudan and their peoples, and his infectious enthusiasm and absolute integrity led them to love and respect him. His versatility and attractive personality earned him friends everywhere, whom he regaled with his delightful stories of archaeology and archaeologists. His academic distinction was recognized by many awards, of which the principal included an honorary MA degree (Liverpool University, 1939) and DLitt degree (London University, 1959); he was appointed FBA (1959), and CBE (1969). H. S. SMITH, *rev.*

Sources A. Klasens, *PBA*, 58 (1972) · personal knowledge (1981) · m. cert. · *The Times* (13 March 1971) · *CGPLA Eng. & Wales* (1921)
Archives Egypt Exploration Society, London, papers
Wealth at death £21,807: probate, 20 July 1971, *CGPLA Eng. & Wales*

Emery, Edward (1801/2?–1851?), numismatist, under whose direction the notorious imitations of coins known as 'Emery's forgeries' were produced, was a coin collector and coin dealer living in London. He was probably the same Edward Emery who maintained premises as a plate-glass grinder and factor at 7 Kirby Street, Hatton Garden, and at 16 Henrietta Street, Covent Garden, between 1833 and 1843. He is said to have belonged to 'a respectable family', and to have been well off. He probably engaged an engraver, who may have been William Joseph Taylor (1802–1885), to manufacture dies of rare English, Scottish, and Irish coins, and some of the specimens struck from these dies sold for large sums. The forgeries were in the market during the summer of 1842, and some were exposed in *The Times* and in the *Numismatic Chronicle* shortly after their appearance. Before the end of that year, Emery (or his engraver) was obliged to surrender the dies, which were then cut through the centre and thus rendered useless. Over 100 probable Emery forgeries have been identified, particularly in the fields of Anglo-Saxon, Norman, and Tudor coins; Scottish coins, especially of Mary; and Roman coins of Carausius and Allectus. The forgeries are clever, though the lettering is not always successful. After 1842 Emery was thought to have left London in debt, and to have died at Hastings about 1850. However, no such death certificate survives, and he is probably to be associated with the Edward Emery, looking-glass silverer and plate-glass factor, who died on 6 June 1851 at 96 High Holborn, aged forty-nine, leaving a widow, Martha.

W. W. WROTH, *rev.* N. J. MAYHEW

Sources H. E. Pagan, 'Mr. Emery's mint', *British Numismatic Journal*, 40 (1971), 139–70 · *The Times* (19 July 1842)
Archives BL
Wealth at death see Pagan, 'Mr. Emery's mint', 147

Emery, John (1777–1822), actor, was born in Sunderland, co. Durham, on 22 September 1777, and obtained a rudimentary education at Ecclesfield in the West Riding of Yorkshire. His father, Mackle Emery (1740–1825), was a provincial actor, and his mother, as Mrs Emery senior, appeared, in July 1802, at the Haymarket as Dame Ashfield in Thomas Morton's *Speed the Plough* and later played at

Covent Garden. Emery was brought up to be a musician, and when he was twelve years of age was in the orchestra at the Brighton theatre. It was here that he made his first acting appearance, as Old Crazy in the farce *Peeping Tom*. In the summer of 1792 he was with John Bernard at Teignmouth and at Dover, where he played country boys; the following year he appeared at Plymouth. After a short engagement in Yorkshire with Tate Wilkinson, who predicted his success, he was engaged to replace Thomas Knight at Covent Garden, where he was first seen, on 21 September 1798, as Frank Oatland in Morton's *A Cure for the Heartache*, and where, in the next two years, he went on to play many other parts. In June 1800 he appeared for the first time at the Haymarket, as Zekiel Homespun in George Colman's *The Heir-at-Law*. At Covent Garden, in February 1801, he was the original Stephen Harrowby in Colman's *The Poor Gentleman*, and later in the same year, at the Haymarket, he played Clod in John O'Keeffe's *The Young Quaker*, Farmer Ashfield in *Speed the Plough*, and other parts. From this time until his death he remained at Covent Garden, with an interruption in August 1821 when he played at the English Opera House in a comic opera. In May 1802 Emery married Anne Thompson, the daughter of a tradesman. They had seven surviving children, one of whom, Samuel Anderson *Emery, became a professional actor.

Emery's reputation as an actor had been established by his representation of country characters, parts he continued to play with great success. He was the original Dan in Colman's *John Bull* (1803), Tyke in Morton's *The School of Reform* (1805), Dandie Dinmont in Daniel Terry's *Guy Mannering* (1816), and Ratcliff in Terry's *The Heart of Midlothian* (1819). He was successful in Shakespearian parts as well, such as Barnadine in *Measure for Measure*, Caliban in *The Tempest*, Silence in *Henry IV, Part 2*, and Williams in *Henry V*.

Emery was about 5 feet 9 inches tall, robustly built, with a light complexion and light blue eyes; he looked like one of his own farmers. He sang well with a low tenor voice, composed the music and words of a few songs, and wrote comic effusions, one of which, a song entitled 'York, you're Wanted', enjoyed a long reputation. In addition he had considerable powers of painting, and exhibited between 1801 and 1817 nineteen pictures, chiefly sea pieces, at the Royal Academy. He drank to excess and was said to seek the society of jockeys and pugilists. He was a keen sportsman, a shrewd observer, and an amusing companion. He died of inflammation of the lungs on 25 July 1822 at his home in Hyde Street, Bloomsbury, London, and was buried on 1 August in a vault at St Andrew's, Holborn. A benefit performance was given at Covent Garden for his parents, widow, and children.

JOSEPH KNIGHT, rev. NILANJANA BANERJI

Sources *Oxberry's Dramatic Biography*, 2/29 (1825) • T. Gilliland, *The dramatic mirror, containing the history of the stage from the earliest period, to the present time*, 2 vols. (1808) • Adams, *Drama* • *The thespian dictionary, or, Dramatic biography of the eighteenth century* (1802) • P. Hartnoll, ed., *The Oxford companion to the theatre*, 3rd edn (1967) • P. Hartnoll, ed., *The concise Oxford companion to the theatre* (1972) • Hall, *Dramatic ports.* • Genest, *Eng. stage* • *Drama, or, Theatrical Pocket Magazine*, 1 (1821), 203, 292 • Graves, *Artists*, 1st edn • T. Dibdin, *The reminiscences of Thomas Dibdin*, 2 (1827)

Likenesses C. Linsell, drawing, 1815, Garr. Club • J. Varley, pencil drawing, 1816, Garr. Club • G. Clint, group portrait, oils, exh. RA 1830, Garr. Club • S. De Wilde, drawing, Garr. Club • S. De Wilde, three oils, Garr. Club • S. Raven, miniature, NPG • J. Turmeau, watercolour drawing, Garr. Club • portrait, repro. in *Monthly Mirror* (1803) • portrait, repro. in *The Cabinet* (1808) • portrait, repro. in *Theatrical Inquisitor* (1814) • portrait, repro. in *The Drama* (1822) • portrait, repro. in Oxberry, *New English Drama* (1822) • portrait, repro. in *Mirror of the stage* (1822) • portrait, repro. in *Oxberry's Dramatic Biography* • prints, Harvard TC • theatrical prints, BM, NPG

Emery, Josiah (*bap.* **1725**, *d.* **1794**), watchmaker, was baptized on 11 November 1725 at Etagnières, north-west of Lausanne in the pays de Vaud, Switzerland, the son of Jacques and Suzanne-Marie Gammeter-Emery, one of nine children (three boys and six girls). He was probably trained in Geneva and by the time he was in his thirties he had emigrated to London; on 22 April 1762 he was appointed one of the elders of the consistory of the new Swiss church in Endell Street, London (led by watchmaker Justin Vulliamy) and he remained active in that church for the rest of his life.

On 4 July 1762 Emery married, at St Martin-in-the-Fields, Charing Cross, Ann (*d.* 1769), daughter of John Jacob and his wife, Ann, a member of the great Courtauld family of goldsmiths (and later textile manufacturers). They had four daughters. In February 1769 Ann died and on 24 January 1771 Emery married the 25-year-old Susannah Smith at St George's, Hanover Square. There were four daughters and two sons from this marriage, including John Claudius, who also became a watchmaker.

Emery's home and business was at 2 Cockspur Street (his trade card described it as opposite Hedge Lane), Charing Cross, and in the course of his career he gained a reputation as one of the top makers in London (and thus worldwide), supplying the nobility and, at least on one occasion, the king. The great French chronometer maker Louis Berthoud wrote that Emery's work contained:

> a profound understanding of the causes of regularity and irregularity in watches; a highly finished execution in the essential parts; nothing luxurious that is extraneous to the main objective; but every care that absolute precision demands—all this, I think, we find in the products of Emery, which should make them precious to those well informed people who own them. (Clutton, 399)

Ostensibly a watchmaker—his total production during the course of his career was about 1400 watches—Emery did also sell clocks and regulators, and one turret clock is known, dated 1787 and signed by him although made to order by Thwaites of Clerkenwell. In 1772 he made a precision timekeeper, no. 615 (now preserved in the Musée des Arts et Métiers in Paris) which had similarities to John Harrison's mould-breaking 'H4' and was clearly influenced by it. In 1788 an Emery watch answering this exact description (almost certainly the same watch) was tested by Count F. S. van Bylandt in longitude experiments. In the mid-1770s Emery was asked by Count von Brühl, ambassador to Britain for the court of Saxony and a close friend and champion of the great watchmaker Thomas Mudge, to make parts of the temperature compensation mechanism for Mudge's timekeepers 'Green' and 'Blue' and in these very special parts Emery incorporated a new alloy of his own invention.

Emery was one of a large group of watchmakers, all working outside the city boundaries, who met as an informal professional group at the Devil tavern. On 15 September 1780, they met to discuss the increasing problem of cheap, foreign imports (somewhat ironically, as a number of them were, like Emery, first generation immigrants themselves) and to organize a petition to the Worshipful Company of Clockmakers. In their petition they offered to join the company and pay quarterage if the company would take positive steps to curb illegal imports of clocks and watches to London. Fifty-four makers signed the original petition, and, in 1781, many, including Emery, were made honorary freemen of the company. Some then continued paying quarterage and formally took part in the company, but Emery appears to have lost interest immediately and failed to pay any quarterage thereafter.

Since the mid-1770s Count von Brühl had been trying to persuade Emery to make copies of Thomas Mudge's precision watch, with Mudge's new lever escapement, made for George III and given to Queen Charlotte (1769); Mudge himself had begun work on his marine timekeepers (those of 1774 and 1777) of a different construction and had no time to develop this very important element of watchwork. For several years Emery resisted von Brühl's proposals, saying Mudge was the best person to make his own designs, besides which, he complained, they were very difficult to construct on a small scale (watch no. 661 made by Emery c.1775 with an early, crude lever escapement is extant and suggests Emery secretly tried out the ideas von Brühl had described to him). However, in 1780 he finally agreed to make some copies and was given by von Brühl a large model made by Mudge of his escapement. The series of watches which resulted were the first to incorporate Mudge's lever escapement, and they proved to be of immense historical significance; Mudge's escapement was to be the central feature of the majority of all watches made up to the introduction of quartz technology in the early 1970s. Emery did not really know Mudge (he said that in his life he only ever spoke three words to him) and did not see Mudge's original watch until some years later, during an audience he had with the king. Therefore he applied this escapement to a watch of his own design, using a number of his own features and incorporating the 'Double S' compensation balance patented by John Arnold in 1782, presumably with Arnold's permission. It was the combination of Mudge's escapement with Arnold's balance which was the secret of the design's success and Emery can take the credit for this. About thirty-five of these watches were signed and sold by him, costing between 100 and 150 guineas. They were thus very expensive and were chiefly bought by the nobility and the scientifically minded. (No doubt their high quality explains the relatively high survival rate; at least twenty-two are extant.) According to Thomas Mudge junior, the majority were constructed for Emery by Richard Pendleton of Pentonville, but this probably refers to the escapements of the watches only. In 1792, the Spanish watchmaker Cayetano Sanchez was sent by the Spanish government to Emery for training (Sanchez having previously spent three years with Ferdinand Berthoud in Paris). Within a year his training was complete and Emery was given £200 for his trouble, along with an undertaking that Sanchez would not set up a manufactory in France. Nevertheless, Emery's lever watches were soon imported into France and makers such as Robert Robin and Abraham Louis Breguet in Paris began to make watches based on their design. In the same year, when Thomas Mudge junior was petitioning the board of longitude and parliament for reward for his father's achievements, Emery was one of a number of specialists who gave evidence at the parliamentary select committee. In contrast to some of the answers given by others, his replies to the questions of the board were both modest and very fair.

About 1785 Emery decided to compete for reward from the board of longitude by designing a new marine timekeeper. By March 1791 two such timekeepers were ready and, after a trial with von Brühl and George Gilpin, the board agreed to have them tried at Greenwich. The trial lasted from 8 July 1793 to 27 February 1794 but the timekeepers unfortunately did not excel. (One of them, marked 'no. 1', is now preserved in the collection of the Clockmakers' Company at the Guildhall in London.) On 7 June 1794, Emery asked the board to try two more of his timekeepers at Greenwich, to which it consented; these promised a much better performance. (Of these, the 'no. 4' is now preserved in the collection of the Mariners' Museum, Newport News, Virginia.) However, on 2 July 1794 Emery suddenly fell ill and, on his deathbed in Chelsea (probably at the house of his friend Francis David Pittonet), wrote his will (in French), leaving everything to his wife, Susannah, save £10 to his 'eldest daughter', Elizabeth. Emery died later the same day. A notice in the *Gentleman's Magazine* gives the cause as 'a mortification in his bowels' (probably bowel cancer) and remarks 'a man much respected'. He was buried at St Martin-in-the-Fields on 7 July and the will was proved on 16 July.

Emery's brother Salomon, who had been employed by him and who lived at Cockspur Street, appears to have continued the business as an employee of Josiah's widow, but he too died less than a year later. From his will we learn that he and Josiah had shares in the family's Swiss estate which had recently been sold. In 1795 Susannah Emery sold the Cockspur Street business to Louis Recordon and William Dupont. On 1 May 1796 she petitioned the board of longitude for financial reward for her husband's efforts in making timekeepers, complaining that she had incurred heavy losses in 'extricating herself from the business' and 'with a family of six children' was now 'in very limited circumstances' (CUL, Board of Longitude MSS, RGO 14/11, 171), but the board was unable to help.

JONATHAN BETTS

Sources J. Betts, 'Josiah Emery: watchmaker of Charing Cross', *Antiquarian Horology and the Proceedings of the Antiquarian Horological*

Society, 22 (1995–6) [5 pts] • N. Maskelyne, *An answer to a narrative of facts…* (1792) • 'Report of the select committee of the House of Commons to whom it was referred to consider of the report which was made from the committee to whom the petition of Thomas Mudge, watch-maker, was referred', *JHC*, 48 (1792–3), 877–920 • A. Roehrich and C. Reverdin, *L'église Suisse de Londres* (1932) • P. Chamberlain, *It's about time* (1941) • L. Berthoud, *Entretiens sur l'horlogerie* (1812) • C. Allix and R. Foulkes, 'A precision bracket clock', *Horological Journal*, 93 (1951), 224–5 • J. L. Evans, 'A precision clock by Josiah Emery', *Antiquarian Horology and the Proceedings of the Antiquarian Horological Society*, 12 (1979–81), 197–200 • *GM*, 1st ser., 64 (1794), 676 • C. Clutton, 'Philosophy of Louis Berthoud', *Antiquarian Horology and the Proceedings of the Antiquarian Horological Society*, 8 (1972–4), 399–401 • Archives Cantonales Vaudoises, Switzerland, Eb 6/2, 226 • parish register (burials), St Martin-in-the-Fields, London, 7 July 1794 • CUL, Board of Longitude MSS, RGO 14/11, 171 • parish register (marriages), St Martin-in-the-Fields, London, 4 July 1762 • parish register (marriages), St George, Hanover Square, London, 24 Jan 1771
Archives Clockmakers' Company Museum, London • Mariners' Museum, Newport News, Virginia • NMM | CUL, board of longitude MSS

Richard Gilbert Emery (1915–1983), by unknown photographer, 1979

Emery, Richard Gilbert [Dick] (1915–1983), comedian, was born on 19 February 1915 at University College Hospital in St Pancras, London, the only child of Laurence Cuthbert Emery, an actor, and his wife, Bertha Gilbert Callen, a former Gaiety girl. During most of Dick Emery's childhood his mother and father performed as a music-hall act, Callen and Emery, and young Emery had little formal education as his parents were in a different town each week appearing at the theatre while Emery attended the local school. The marriage broke up in 1926 and Emery, offered the choice, opted to stay with his mother. She was a dominating influence on him, and Emery later recounted how he both adored and feared her. After her divorce Emery's mother gave up show business but was determined that her son should be a star. For Emery performing was a nightmare and he was always apprehensive and often physically sick before a performance. He possessed, from childhood, a good singing voice—when he was small his mother always insisted he sang to visitors, an early taste of what became for Emery in later life the torture of performing in public. He is quoted as saying that he would have preferred a career in opera, but family background and natural accomplishments directed him towards comedy. His first big chance came during the war, when serving in the RAF. In 1942 he joined one of the RAF gang shows organized by Ralph Reader, where he made his first appearance as a female impersonator—the forerunner of roles which later made him famous. After demobilization he spent some time fruitlessly auditioning for various agents and managers but at last, like many ex-service performers, he became a mainstay of the Windmill Theatre in London, where he worked for nine months in 1948. It was on radio that Emery began to develop the characters that gave him lasting popularity. He performed in such series as *Pertwee's Progress* (1955), which starred Jon Pertwee, *We're in Business* (1960), with Peter Jones, Harry Worth, and Irene Handl, and *Educating Archie* (1958), where he created the character of the elderly, grumbling odd-job man Lampwick.

On television Emery appeared with Michael Bentine in *It's a Square World* (1962), and in Granada TV's *The Army Game* (1960). In 1963 came *The Dick Emery Show*, in which for the first time he was the star. Its success with the public, if not always with the critics, lasted until his death in 1983. For nearly twenty years his loyal public laughed at Emery's characterizations which included, among others, a vicar, a homosexual, a traffic warden, a frustrated spinster called Hettie, a leather-clad motor cyclist, the aged Lampwick, the bovver boy, College the tramp, and, best remembered and certainly the most popular with the audience, the ageing sex kitten Mandy with her inevitable catchphrase, 'Ooh, you are awful—but I like you'. His shows were among the most popular on British television, and frequently featured in the top ten audience ratings. Emery's work in the cinema was mainly limited to minor roles. In 1968 he appeared in the X-certificate *Baby Love* with Diana Dors and Keith Barron, and in 1970 he appeared as Bateman in the film of *Loot*, the play by Joe Orton. In 1972 he starred in *Ooh, you are awful*.

But if Emery's professional life prospered, his private life appears to have been a series of crises. In 1952 his self-confidence was at such a low ebb that he resorted to hypnosis and subsequently psychoanalysis to pull him out of a deep depression which lasted for five years. His continual insecurity as a performer perhaps prevented his comic abilities from ever developing fully. Contemporaries thought that despite his great popularity his talent remained unfulfilled. In his last years he also suffered from a range of medical problems. Emery was married five times. He and his first wife, Zelda, had a son; but she left him after five years. His second marriage, to Irene Dorothy Ansell (*b.* 1920/21), an actress, on 13 August 1946, lasted only a few months and there was no child. Emery's third wife, Iris, with whom he had a son, died from a brain tumour; her father was William Paulk Tully, butcher. His fourth wife, Victoria, was eighteen when they married, *c.*1958, and Emery was then forty-three. She was the daughter of Harold Booth Chambers, a musical director. They had two children. His fifth wife was a singer and actress, Josephine Sheila Blake (*b.* 1936/7). They married on 1 November 1969 and had no children. When Emery died he had by then left Josephine and was living with a dancer, Fay Hillier. Dick Emery died on 2 January 1983 at King's College Hospital, London, and was cremated at Mortlake, London, on 13 January.   BARRY TOOK, rev.

Sources *The Times* (4 Jan 1983) · *The Times* (15 Jan 1983) · *Who's who on television* (1980) · personal knowledge (1990) · T. Vahimagi, ed., *British television: an illustrated guide*, 2nd edn (1996) · *CGPLA Eng. & Wales* (1983) · b. cert. · m. cert. [Irene Ansell] · m. cert. [Josephine Sheila Blake]
Archives FILM BFI NFTVA, 'Dick Emery: a life on the box', BBC1 20 Aug 1997
Likenesses photograph, 1979, Camera Press, London [*see illus.*] · photograph, repro. in *Who's who on television* · photographs, Hult. Arch.
Wealth at death £311,437: probate, 12 May 1983, *CGPLA Eng. & Wales*

Emery, Samuel Anderson (1817–1881), actor, the son of the actor John *Emery (1777–1822), and his wife, Anne Thompson, was born in Hyde Street, Bloomsbury, on 10 September 1817. He was educated at Bridport Hall, Edmonton, under W. Fitch, a schoolmaster and lessee of the City Theatre, Milton Street. On leaving school he was placed with his uncle, John Thompson, an Irish provision dealer, and became also clerk, first to a stockbroker and then to a jeweller and goldsmith.

In May 1834 Emery appeared at the Queen's Theatre, Tottenham Street (then known as the Fitzroy), in his father's character of Dan in Colman's *John Bull*. This led to an engagement, and under the name of Anderson he played at the same house as Robin Roughhead, among other parts. He was then engaged at Hull by Downe, the manager of the York circuit; he proceeded in 1835 to Edinburgh under William Murray, and played in various small Scottish houses. He then became established in Liverpool, and for several years performed there, as well as at Manchester, Chester, and neighbouring towns.

Emery's London début was as Giles in *The Miller's Maid* and Lovegold in *The Miser*, in April 1843 at the Lyceum. He was engaged by Henry Wallack for Covent Garden, and appeared there on 19 October 1843 as Fixture in Thomas Morton's *A Roland for an Oliver*. Here, through the intended vengeance of a stage carpenter whose schemes he frustrated, an attempt is said to have been made on his life. In 1844 Emery was at the Lyceum under the Keeleys, and he established his reputation in such parts as Jonas Chuzzlewit, Will Fern in *The Chimes*, Peerybingle in *The Cricket on the Hearth*, and Antony Latour in *The Creole* of Shirley Brooks. He then joined Leigh Murray at the Olympic, was stage-manager for Charles Shepherd at the Surrey, and went in 1850 to Drury Lane, then under Anderson. He played at various country houses during the summer, and at Drury Lane was seen in many parts, chiefly in his father's line of rustic, older characters, such as Dandie Dinmont, Silky, Baillie Nicol Jarvie, Autolycus, Touchstone, the Gravedigger, Miramont in Fletcher's *The Elder Brother*, Sam in *Raising the Wind*, Gibbie in *The Wonder*, and Harrop in *Mary the Maid of the Inn*. He then joined Benjamin Webster of the Haymarket and Adelphi. At the Olympic in 1853 under Alfred Wigan he was the original Fouché in

Tom Taylor's *Plot and Passion*, and was subsequently Mr Potter in *Still Waters Run Deep* by the same author. In 1857 he managed the Marylebone Theatre briefly. Emery married Emma King, with whom he had a daughter, Maud [see Emery, Winifred].

In March 1863 Emery made his American début at Barnum's Old Theatre, New York, in *The Shadow on the Wall*, but he returned to England in September following disagreements with his managers. He was seldom long at any theatre. At various houses accordingly he played Simon Legree in *Uncle Tom's Cabin*, McClosky in *The Octoroon*, Dan'l Peggotty in *Little Em'ly*, and Captain Cuttle in *Heart's Delight*, A. Halliday's version of *Dombey and Son*. This last character, played at the Globe on 17 December 1873, served for his return to the theatre on 20 July 1878. Emery toured Australia in 1880–81, without much success. Six weeks after his return, on 19 July 1881, he died of erysipelas at King William Street, Strand. He was a striking actor whose success was greatest in his father's line of characters.   JOSEPH KNIGHT, rev. KATHARINE COCKIN

Sources T. A. Brown, *History of the American stage* (1870) · C. E. Pascoe, ed., *The dramatic list*, 2nd edn (1880) · Adams, *Drama* · Hall, *Dramatic ports.* · *The Era* (23 July 1881) · *The Theatre*, 4th ser., 3 (1884), 70–2 · Boase, *Mod. Eng. biog.* · personal knowledge (1888)
Likenesses A. Beau, cartes-de-visite, NPG · G. Greatbach, stipple and line engraving (as Robin Roughhead in *Fortune's frolics*; after a daguerreotype by Mayall), BM, NPG; repro. in *Tallis's drawing room table book* (1851) · carte-de-visite, NPG · theatrical prints, Harvard TC

Emery, William (1825–1910), Church of England clergyman, born on 2 February 1825 in St Martin's Lane, London, was the only son of William Emery (1798–1867), a lighterman who became master of the Feltmakers' Company in 1848, and his first wife, Mary Ann, née Thomson (d. 1847). From an early age Emery's father encouraged an interest in religion, and Emery often referred affectionately to him when addressing audiences of working men. He was one of the first intake at the new City of London School in 1837, where he was a favourite of G. F. W. Mortimer, headmaster from 1840, and became the first holder of the *Times* scholarship. Admitted at Corpus Christi College, Cambridge, on 29 March 1843, he was elected Mawson scholar in May 1844; he graduated BA as fifth wrangler in 1847, and proceeded MA in 1850 and BD in 1858. From 1847 to 1865 he was fellow of Corpus, and was ordained deacon in 1849 and priest in 1853. At Corpus he served as dean (1853–6), introducing weekly sermons in chapel, bursar (1855–60), and tutor (1855–65), and in 1905 was made an honorary fellow. In 1861 he was senior proctor of the university. On 6 July 1865 he married Fanny Maria (1840–1916), daughter of Sir Antonio *Brady, with whom he had six children.

Emery never confined himself to college concerns. He was chairman of the managing committee of the Cambridge School of Art, a regular visitor of the sick at Addenbrooke's Hospital, and worked for numerous church and philanthropic causes. In 1859 his rooms saw the inauguration of both the Universities Central Africa Mission and the volunteer movement in the city, Emery becoming honorary chaplain to the university rifle corps in 1861. Emery achieved national prominence as an organizer of assemblies in which clergy and churchgoing laity could work together to promote church unity and defence. He worked with Henry Hoare for the revival of convocation, and helped establish a Cambridge branch of the Church Defence Institution in 1859. In 1861 this committee invited churchmen and secretaries of church defence associations to a conference in King's College hall. From this assembly originated the annual church congress, which at its height attracted several thousand clergy and laity to its extensive programme of debates and meetings. This was largely Emery's achievement, and he served as permanent secretary of the congress from 1869 to 1907, attending all but one meeting over this period and becoming known as the 'father of Church Congress'.

In 1864 Lord Palmerston appointed Emery archdeacon of Ely. Here, in close co-operation with his friend Bishop Harold Browne, he helped establish the first diocesan conference. After consultative meetings in 1864 and 1865 the conference met annually from 1866, the clerical and lay sections being fully integrated from 1868. In 1881 he helped organize a central council to co-ordinate the work of other conferences which had, by then, been founded throughout the country, and remained its honorary secretary until 1906. Emery further promoted the co-ordination of church work in his own diocese by establishing both the *Ely Diocesan Calendar* and in 1885 the *Ely Diocesan Remembrancer* (which he edited until 1906), inaugurating conferences as part of his archidiaconal visitations, developing ruridecanal meetings of clergy and laity, and encouraging choral festivals and diocesan associations. Emery was instrumental in founding the Hunstanton Convalescent Home (of which he was chairman 1872–1908), which accommodated more than a thousand patients a year, and in promoting a clean water supply for Ely. He was also a central figure in the creation of the Church Schools Company, which he chaired from 1883 to 1903, created to promote distinctively Anglican middle-class secondary education, although Emery was a convinced advocate of a conscience clause. By 1897 the company had established some twenty-four schools. Emery frequently addressed both convocation and the church congress on a wide range of issues, including temperance, the desirability of the offertory and free seating, and, above all, lay involvement in church defence.

In 1868 Emery was made a minor canon of Ely, and was a residentiary from 1870 until his death at The College, Ely, on 14 December 1910. He was buried in the precincts of the cathedral.

Emery's charges and sermons discussed practical rather than theological questions, and he rarely spoke on contentious doctrinal issues. He was above all an organizer: 'Set a committee to work, and I maintain that generally some good comes from it' (*Report of Church Congress: Liverpool*, 1869, 181) he told the congress of 1869. Behind all his efforts lay a desire to bring men of all classes within the fold of the 'grand old national church of England' (*Report of Church Congress: Portsmouth*, 1885, 479), 'the most tolerant church in the world' founded on 'the sound and broad basis of Scriptural truth and primitive tradition' (W. Emery, *Church Union and Church Progress*, 1867, 14; W. Emery, *Church Organization and Efficient Ministry*, 1866, 23). He thus abhorred church party, although personally inclined to orthodox high-churchmanship. In politics he was a Conservative. ARTHUR BURNS

Sources Reports of Church Congress: Portsmouth · Reports of Church Congress: Liverpool · Report of Church Congress: Cambridge, 1910, xix–xx [memoir] · F.G.V., 'Memoir', *Ely Diocesan Remembrancer* (Jan 1911), 5–8 · *The Times* (15 Dec 1910) · *The Guardian* (16 Dec 1910) · *Cambridge Chronicle* (11 June 1864)
Archives GL, papers, MS 21463 · LPL, church congress MSS, 1782 · LPL, corresp. and papers on central council of diocesan conferences, 2, fols. 1–51; 33, fols. 276–90 · LPL, minutes of consultative committee, church congress, MS 1781 | CUL, letters to Sir George Stokes
Likenesses S. Walker, photograph, 1877, LPL, MS 2154 fol. 11 · A. E. Fradelle, photograph, LPL, MS 2944 fol. 30v · J. Russell & Sons, photograph, repro. in *The Church Schools Company, 1883–1933* (1934)
Wealth at death £15,108 12s. 8d.: probate, 23 Dec 1910, CGPLA Eng. & Wales

Emery, Winifred [*real name* Maud Isabel Emery; *married name* Maud Isabel Maude] (**1861–1924**), actress, was born on 1 August 1861 at 3 Chatham Street, Manchester, and given the names Maud Isabel. She was the daughter of Samuel Anderson *Emery (1817–1881), an actor, and his wife, Emma, née King (d. 1886). She came from a well-established theatrical family and, taking the name Winifred Emery, made her first stage appearance in 1870, as Geraldine in J. B. Buckstone's *The Green Bushes* at Liverpool's Alexandra Theatre. She first performed in London on 23 December 1874 as Happy New Year in the pantomime *Beauty and the Beast* at the Princess's Theatre. Her adult career began in a period of innovation and expansion, at the Aquarium Theatre, London, in 1879, with Marie Litton's company; she then joined Wilson Barrett, first at the recently opened Leeds Grand Theatre, then in October of that year at London's Court Theatre, where she later claimed to have 'really started' (*The Sketch*, 7 Dec 1911), playing Minnie Heritage in H. A. Jones's one-act piece *A Clerical Error*.

After appearing at the Haymarket Theatre in August 1880, as Rosie Laborde in *A Bridal Tour*, and again at the Court Theatre, Emery played at the St James's Theatre under Sir John Hare and W. H. and Madge Kendal. In July 1881 she joined Henry Irving's company at the Lyceum, where she was seen, *inter alia*, as Annette in *The Bells* and Nerissa in *The Merchant of Venice*. Engagements followed at the Vaudeville, under Thomas Thorne, where she was particularly successful as Lydia Languish in *The Rivals*, and at Toole's Theatre. In 1884 she returned to the Lyceum to understudy Ellen Terry and to join Irving's tour of the United States, where she appeared as Olivia in *Twelfth Night*, Hero in *Much Ado about Nothing*, and Jessica in *The Merchant of Venice*. She remained with Irving, starred in October 1885 as W. G. Wills's eponymous Olivia, and went again to America in 1887–8.

Typically characterized for her 'personal beauty and

Winifred Emery (1861–1924), by Barraud, pubd 1890

womanly charm' (Reid and Compton, 77) and her 'sympathy and fidelity' both on and off the stage (Maxwell, 12), Emery gave some of her most memorable performances as Mrs Errol in *The Real Little Lord Fauntleroy* at Terry's Theatre, London, in May 1888. Shortly before this, on 28 April 1888, she married at Kensington register office Cyril Francis *Maude (1862–1951), an actor. For reasons which remain obscure, she married him again at the Chapel Royal, Savoy, on 2 June 1888. They had two daughters and a son.

Further engagements followed at the Vaudeville Theatre and at Drury Lane, where, under Augustus Harris, Emery had leading parts, including that of Mildred in *The Royal Oak*. She proved an impressive Clarissa, with a 'virginal air of sweetness' (*The Times*, 7 Feb 1890) in Robert Buchanan's version of Richardson's novel at the Vaudeville Theatre in February 1890. There, later that year, she played Lady Teazle in *The School for Scandal*, Kate in *She Stoops to Conquer*, and Fanny Hoyden in Robert Buchanan's *Miss Tomboy*.

After starring as Vashti Dethic in H. A. Jones's *Judah* at the Shaftesbury Theatre in September 1890, Emery rejoined Wilson Barrett at the newly rebuilt Olympic Theatre that December. She returned to the Shaftesbury in May 1891, and in February 1892 took the title role in the first production of Oscar Wilde's *Lady Windermere's Fan* at the St James's Theatre. She was the leading lady at the Comedy Theatre under Comyns Carr between 1893 and 1895 in Sydney Grundy's *The New Woman* and *Sowing the*

Wind and A. W. Pinero's *The Benefit of the Doubt*, and returned to the Lyceum, then taken by Sir Johnston Forbes-Robertson, in February 1896.

When Cyril Maude entered management, at the Haymarket Theatre in 1896, Winifred Emery was his leading lady. Following childbirth and illness between 1898 and 1905, when she appeared only as Muriel in Robert Marshall's *The Second in Command* in July 1901, her career resumed in February 1905, when she played Beatrice in *Much Ado about Nothing* at His Majesty's under Beerbohm Tree. In January 1906 she appeared at the Waldorf Theatre as Mrs Pellender in *The Superior Miss Pellender*. She then formed her own company to tour provincial theatres, and starred in *Olivia* and *Her Son*, a new play by Horace Annesley Vachell, in which she appeared as Dorothy Fairfax and Cyril Maude as Richard Gascoyne. This opened at Cyril Maude's newly rebuilt Playhouse in March 1907.

For the next fourteen years Emery continued to play leading, albeit more mature, roles in London's West End, not only under her husband's management at the Playhouse, but also at His Majesty's (Mistress Ford in *The Merry Wives of Windsor*), the Theatre Royal, Drury Lane (Betty Gordon in *The Bunking of Betty*), the St James's (Esther in *Caste*), the Lyric (Queen Elizabeth in *Sir Walter Ralegh*), the Vaudeville (Miss Dyott in *The Schoolmistress*), the Apollo (Hon. Mrs Stevenson in *Never Say Die*), the Gaiety (Fairy Berylune in *The Betrothal*), and the Duke of York's (Mrs Smallwood in *The Enchanted Cottage*, 1922). At the command performance at Drury Lane during the state visit of the German emperor, Wilhelm II, in May 1911, she played Lady Franklin in an excerpt from *Money*, and at the coronation gala performance at His Majesty's Theatre on 27 June, under the direction of Sir Squire Bancroft, she was Queen Elizabeth in Sheridan's *The Critic*. Her last performance was at His Majesty's Theatre on 26 February 1923, as Nicole in a charity production of *The Ballad Monger*.

Winifred Emery died of stomach cancer at the family home, The Corner, Little Common, Bexhill, Sussex, on 15 July 1924, and was buried at St Mark's Church, Bexhill, on 18 July.   C. M. P. TAYLOR

Sources J. Parker, ed., *Who's who in the theatre*, 4th edn (1922) · E. Reid and H. Compton, eds., *The dramatic peerage*, rev. edn [1892] · *The Era* (23 July 1924) · *The Stage* (17 July 1924) · *Bexhill Chronicle* (19 July 1924) · *The Times* (16 July 1924) · *The Times* (21 Feb 1951) · W. Emery, 'My first appearance', *The Sketch* (7 Dec 1911) · W. Macqueen-Pope, *Gaiety: theatre of enchantment* (1949), 90, 360, 452 · A. E. Wilson, *Edwardian theatre* (1951), 97, 120 · A. E. Wilson, *The Lyceum* (1952), 116 · W. Macqueen-Pope, *Pillars of Drury Lane* (1955), 202–3 · W. Macqueen-Pope, *St James's: theatre of distinction* (1958), 103, 127 · W. B. Maxwell, *The Times* (18 July 1924) · b. cert. · m. cert. · d. cert.

Archives Theatre Museum, London

Likenesses Barraud, photograph, pubd 1890, NPG [see illus.] · St Etienne, pen-and-ink drawing, NPG · photographs, Theatre Museum, London

Wealth at death £12,955 16s. 2d.: probate, 26 Aug 1924, CGPLA Eng. & Wales

Emes, John (1762–1808), engraver and goldsmith, was born on 30 December 1762, one of the family of five sons and three daughters of William *Emes (1729/30–1803), landscape gardener, of Bowbridge Fields, Mackworth,

Derbyshire, and his wife, Mary (d. 1789), a servant, daughter of John Innocent, tailor. He was apprenticed to the engraver William Woollett in 1778, and was admitted to the Royal Academy Schools on 6 October 1780. His best-known engraving is *The Destruction of the Spanish Batteries before Gibraltar* (1786), after a painting by James Jefferys. As it was published in October 1789 by Emes and Elizabeth Woollett, the engraver's widow, it may have been begun by William Woollett. Emes was also a watercolour painter, and some of his tinted drawings of views in the Lake District and elsewhere were exhibited at the Royal Academy in 1790 and 1791. There are two watercolour drawings by Emes in the British Museum, *Greenwich Park* and *Wynnstay Park*, which show the influence of Thomas Hearne, also a former apprentice of William Woollett. A set of sixteen views of the Lake District, drawn by Emes and J. Smith, was engraved in aquatint by S. Alken and included in Thomas West's *Guide to the Lakes* (1778; 11th edn, 1821), and his engravings of Dorset appear in *Vitruvius Dorsettiensis* (1816). His collection of prints was sold on 22 March 1810.

John Emes was better known as a goldsmith, although he was not apprenticed through the Goldsmith's Company, and was never a freeman of the company. He entered his first mark as a plateworker (a supplier to the retail trade) on 27 August 1796 in partnership with Henry Chawner at Amen Corner, on the corner of Paternoster Row and Ave Maria Lane, London. The firm at this address can be traced back at least to the end of the seventeenth century, when Anthony Nelme registered his mark. After the retirement of Henry Chawner, Emes registered his second and third marks alone, on 10 January 1798, and his fourth mark on 21 July 1802. Emes specialized in silver tea and coffee services, and there is a silver cheese toaster (1802–3) at Temple Newsam House, Leeds. Emes died in 1808, before 30 June, leaving a widow, Rebecca.

Rebecca Emes (d. 1828?), businesswoman, took over the business on her husband John's death, entering her mark on 30 June 1808 in partnership with William Emes, who may have been her brother-in-law or her son, 'virtue of a power of attorney'. This partnership was short-lived, as on 14 October 1808 she went into partnership with Edward Barnard (d. 1855), who had served his apprenticeship with Thomas Chawner, father of Henry Chawner, becoming the manager of John Emes's workshop on the retirement of Henry Chawner. Rebecca Emes and Edward Barnard entered three further marks on 29 April 1818, 20 February 1821, and 29 October 1825. This partnership was very successful, especially after the end of the Napoleonic wars, and became one of the largest silver workshops of the day, supplying leading retailers including Rundell, Bridge, and Rundell in London, and selling all over the country, from Portsmouth to Manchester, Newcastle, and Scotland, while through their overseas agents they exported silver to Charleston, South Carolina, and Calcutta. As well as domestic silver, including coffee and tea services, goblets, cruets, soup and sauce tureens, inkstands, and brandy saucepans, the firm specialized in presentational plate: their Weymouth regatta cup is in the Victoria and Albert Museum. They made all the Doncaster gold cups from 1821

to 1829, including the famous 1828 cup, an exact replica of the antique marble Buckingham Vase, with serpent handles, engraved by Piranesi in 1778 for his *Vasi*. They used this design again for a series of wine coolers. They were inspired by other antique forms, and surviving pieces include sauce tureens derived from Roman sarcophagi. Another special piece was the silver vase made in 1824 for presentation to the earl of Clancarty, twice ambassador to The Hague, which incorporated two diplomatic box covers on the sides. When the rococo style became popular, Emes and Barnard used abundant decoration on their silverware, and they kept in touch with changing demand: for example, when toast became part of the buffet breakfast, they began to make silver toast racks.

On 25 February 1829 a new mark was entered, that of Edward Barnard and three of his sons, and the firm was renamed Edward Barnard & Sons, indicating that Rebecca had either died or retired.   ANNE PIMLOTT BAKER

Sources A. G. Grimwade, *London goldsmiths, 1697–1837*, rev. edn (1990) · P. Glanville and J. F. Goldsborough, *Women silversmiths, 1685–1845* (1990) · J. P. Fallon, *The marks of the London goldsmiths and silversmiths* (1972) · J. Banister, 'Identity parade: the Barnard ledgers', *Proceedings of the Society of Silver Collectors*, 2 (1980), 165–9 · J. Lomax, *British silver at Temple Newsam and Lotherton Hall* (1992) · J. Culme, *The directory of gold and silversmiths* (1987), vol. 1, pp. 29–30 · L. Lambourne and J. Hamilton, eds., *British watercolours in the Victoria and Albert Museum* (1980) · I. O. Williams, *Early English watercolours and some cognate drawings by artists born not later than 1785* (1952) · D. Gaze, ed., *Dictionary of women artists* (1997) · Graves, *RA exhibitors* · S. C. Hutchison, 'The Royal Academy Schools, 1768–1830', *Walpole Society*, 38 (1960–62), 123–91 · IGI

Emes, Rebecca (d. 1828?). *See under* Emes, John (1762–1808).

Emes, Thomas (d. 1707), medical practitioner and millenarian, is of unknown origin, and details of his early life are obscure; he described himself in 1698 as 'chirurgo-medicus' (*Dialogue*). In 1694 Emes was expelled from the Baptist church in Cripplegate, London, for denying the divinity of Christ and the doctrine of the Trinity. Three years later Emes's wife, Mary, suffered the same fate, 'being infected with the same damnable heresy' as her husband (Cripplegate Baptist Congregation Church Book, 10 Jan 1698). In 1698 Emes published *The Atheist Turn'd Deist, and the Deist Turned Christian* and *A Dialogue between Alkali and Acid*, the latter of which argued the case for the medicinal properties of alkalis and the harmful effects of acids. A response to this in the anonymous *Letter to a Physician* (1700) prompted Emes to defend his remarks in *A Letter to a Gentleman Concerning Alkali and Acid* (1700).

Emes became one of the British adherents of a millenarian group known as the French Prophets, soon after they arrived in London in 1706. At some time around 4 December 1707 he was taken ill 'with a most violent head ache or meagrim' (Aikin, 26). As Emes was dying John Lacy, a Prophet who had already gained notoriety with his *Prophetical Warnings* (1707), predicted that Emes could expect to be raised from the dead. Emes died at his home in Old Street Square, London, on 22 December 1707 but 'instead of being laid out as is usual for a dead corpse, he was kept hot in bed, till he stunk so as there was scarce any enduring it, several imagining that he would come to life again' (Aikin, 27). Emes was buried on 25 December 1707 at Bunhill Fields, London. However, another Prophet, John Potter, promised that Lacy would raise Emes from his grave between noon and 6 p.m. on 25 May 1708. Great store was placed by the Prophets on Emes's resurrection, and news of the prophecy was spread by Lacy in his pamphlet *The Mighty Miracle* (1708) in which he confirmed that 'about the twelfth hour of the day, behold the wonderful doctor fairly rise; and in two minutes time the earth over his coffin will crack, and spread from the coffin, and he will instantly bounce out and slip off his shroud' (Lacy, *Mighty Miracle*, 63). The authorities, fearing disturbances from the crowds gathered to witness the event, placed two regiments of trained bands around the cemetery three days before the resurrection was due to take place. Emes's failure to reappear severely damaged the credibility of the Prophets. Emes's fame rests not so much on any activity during his lifetime but on the absence of it following his death. MICHAEL BEVAN

Sources M. Aikin, *Memoirs of religious imposters, from the seventh to the nineteenth century* (1821) · J. Lacy, *Predictions concerning the raising of the dead body of Mr Thomas Emes* (1708) · J. Lacy, 'The mighty miracle', *The Harleian miscellany*, ed. W. Oldys and T. Park, 11 (1810), 62–4 · H. Schwartz, *The French prophets: the history of a millenarian group in eighteenth-century England* (1980) · T. Emes, *A dialogue between alkali and acid* (1698) · N. Luttrell, *A brief historical relation of state affairs from September 1678 to April 1714*, 6 (1857) · Cripplegate (London) Baptist Congregation Church Book, 1693–1723, Regent's Park College, Oxford, Angus Library · *GM*, 3rd ser., 1 (1856), 398 · N. Spinckes, 'The new pretenders to prophecy examined', in G. Hickes, *The spirit of enthusiasm exorcised* (1709), 353–530, 372, 373, 508, 509–30

Emes, William (1729/30–1803), landscape designer and gardener, whose early life is obscure, took up the post of head gardener to Sir Nathaniel Curzon at Kedleston, Derbyshire, on 8 September 1756. He remained there until 1760, perhaps leaving his post because the appointment of Robert Adam with 'the intire manadgement of his Grounds' left Emes with little scope. While at Kedleston he had already started altering the earlier, formal landscape and had made the upper lake. On 17 December 1758 Emes, then twenty-eight, married his servant Mary (d. 1789), the daughter of John Innocent, a tailor. They had five sons and three daughters. One son, John *Emes (1762–1808), was an artist and engraver, but later became better known, with his wife, Rebecca, as a goldsmith.

Emes moved to Bowbridge Fields, Mackworth, a farmhouse about 2 miles from Kedleston. He developed an extensive practice as a landscape designer (ninety commissions are known), largely in the north midlands and Wales. His style is similar to that of Lancelot 'Capability' Brown, although there is no evidence that he ever worked with Brown, and at Eaton Hall, Cheshire, in 1763, Lord Grosvenor called Emes in to replace Brown. The elegant plans, in indian ink on vellum, which he presented to his clients showed his proposed alterations to the landscape—often with serpentine lakes whose ends were concealed in woodland, with single trees and clumps set in

parkland and with tree belts around the boundary, often with a 'ride round the Improvements' winding through them. It was said that 'Mr Eame excells in the laying out Water' and he was called in to introduce it into landscapes where it was lacking, as at Hawkstone Park, Shropshire, where in 1786 he made the River Hawk into a lake 1½ miles long. He anticipated the work of Humphry Repton by creating flower gardens adjacent to the house, as at Sandon Hall, Staffordshire, in 1781, where he laid out a garden under the windows of the drawing-room, planted with flowers and flowering shrubs and with a central basin of water with goldfish. Some of his commissions continued for many years; at both Chirk Castle and Erddig, Denbighshire, he supervised the landscaping for twenty-four years.

Although Emes designed a few minor buildings, such as a lodge at Attingham Hall, Shropshire, and a greenhouse at Penrice Castle, Glamorgan, his role as an architect is not significant. At a number of places his landscaping was contemporaneous with work on the house by Samuel or James Wyatt, a professional association that may have started at Kedleston. After his wife died in 1789, Emes moved to Hampshire and took a lease of Elvetham Park from Sir Henry Gough-Calthorpe. A number of commissions in the south of England date from this period, some of which were carried out in partnership with John Webb (1754–1828), who had earlier been his foreman and continued the practice after Emes's death. Emes moved to London and died on 13 March 1803 at Vicarage House, St Giles Cripplegate, the home of his daughter Sarah, wife of the Revd William Holmes. He was buried at the church of St Giles Cripplegate. KEITH GOODWAY, *rev.*

Sources Kedleston Hall, Derbyshire · Eaton Hall, Cheshire · Sandon Hall, Staffordshire · Hants. RO, Elvetham archives · bishop's transcripts, Mugginton, Derbyshire, Lichfield Joint RO · bishop's transcripts, Mackworth, Derbyshire, Lichfield Joint RO · marriage bond, Lichfield Joint RO · parish register, St Giles Cripplegate, GL [burial] · will, PRO, PROB 11/1398, fol. 767
Archives Eaton Hall, Cheshire · Kedleston Hall, Debyshire · Sandon Hall, Staffordshire | Hants. RO, archives

Emett, (Frederick) Rowland (1906–1990), cartoonist and inventor of whimsical creations, was born on 22 October 1906 at Eskdale, Natal Road, New Southgate, London, the elder son (there were no daughters) of Arthur Emett, businessman, and his wife, Alice, *née* Veale. His father, the proprietor of a small advertising business, was a perpetually optimistic, always disappointed, spare-time inventor. Rowland's birth certificate registered him as Frederick Roland. Emett did not achieve fame until his late thirties, although from his youngest days his future was well signposted. He was educated at Waverley grammar school, Birmingham. Described as a lazy pupil, he invariably came top of the school in drawing and caricatured not only his masters but also, prophetically, machinery and vehicles. At the age of eleven he wrote publishable poems; at fourteen he took out a world patent on a pneumatic volume control for the acoustic gramophone. While studying briefly at Birmingham School of Arts and Crafts he aspired to become a landscape painter, and in 1931 his *Cornish Harbour* was hung on the line at the Royal Academy. During the depression he worked for an advertising agency, failed as a freelance commercial artist, then returned to agency work until his career was interrupted by the Second World War, throughout which he worked as a draughtsman for the Air Ministry. At the same time he discovered and perfected his gift for drawing cartoons.

On 12 April 1941 Emett married Mary, daughter of Albert Evans, silversmith, at King's Norton church, Birmingham. They had one daughter, Claire. Mary Emett, a formidable personality who was methodical and firm in business matters, was shocked by her husband's insouciant attitude towards bookkeeping. Her offer to disentangle his business affairs was gratefully accepted, and from then until the end of his life she successfully propelled and managed his business interests.

Emett first contributed to *Punch* in 1939; there the originality of his humour was quickly recognized by the art editor, Kenneth Bird (Fougasse). Soon his strange, bumbling, increasingly attenuated trains, called Nellie, or Bard of Avon, or Humphrey, unsteadily rode branch lines through the pages of *Punch* from Paddlecombe to Prawnmouth, from Friars Ambling to Little Figment. There was warmth in these endearing creations, which generally appeared as half-page drawings, some of them packed with gossamer-fine cross-hatching, others bathed in subtle washes. His occasional full-page colour work displayed a mastery of watercolour and gouache. Seeking a resident cartoonist, Arthur Christiansen, the editor of the then hugely successful *Daily Express*, favoured Emett for the post, but the artist realized that his work, in which delicacy of line and thought played a major part, would suffer under the rigours of daily newspaper journalism, and sensibly refused the offer. Among Emett's publications were *Engines, Aunties, and Others* (1943), *Sidings and suchlike* (1946), *Saturday Slow* (1948), *The Early Morning Milk Train* (1976), and *Emett's Ministry of Transport* (1981).

In 1951 *Nellie*, Emett's most famous steam engine (the first of three—the others were *Neptune* and *Wild Goose*) was created in beaten copper and mahogany and rode the rails from Far Twittering to Oyster Creek to become one of the most popular attractions in the Festival of Britain. Following the publication of a twelve-page spread in *Life* magazine (5 July 1954) Emett's name spread from Britain to the United States, where his work was much in demand, and beyond. *Punch* failed to grasp how far his reputation had increased, and was unhappy at the encroachment upon his time and energy. In 1944 he had signed a contract to draw exclusively for the magazine, but in 1951, after several polite disagreements, financial and editorial, they parted company. Soon afterwards the artist also parted from what was arguably the most endearing of his work— the trains.

Although Emett never entirely gave up drawing, he lost interest in drawing cartoons, and devoted his energies to designing and naming the inventions which he called his 'things'. The reality of Nellie led to commissions for the astro terremare (for Shell Oil), the Hogmuddle rotatory

niggler and fidgeter, the Featherstone openwork basket-weave gentleman's flying machine, and many others. In 1968 Emett designed machines for the film *Chitty Chitty Bang Bang*. Emett's work—Emettland—travelled around the world, leaving behind trails of laughter. These large creations were later housed in numerous museums and galleries, among them the Smithsonian Institution in Washington, DC, the Ontario Science Centre, and the Museum of Science and Industry, Chicago. Nottingham's Victoria Centre has his rhythmical time fountain (1974).

Comparisons, often erroneous, were sometimes made between Emett's 'things' and the contraptions of W. Heath Robinson. They differed fundamentally in that Heath Robinson's devices worked better as drawings. Contrary to popular belief, Heath Robinson's contraptions did not always translate into working models. While broadly obeying the principles of engineering, they often ignored the laws of physics. In contrast, Emett's constructions, with few exceptions, were built with motion in mind. A more pertinent comparison can be made between Emett and the artist Jean Tinguely, whose 1960s constructions were an 'assemblage of industrial detritus springing to life, use[ing] movement to burlesque effect' (*Force Fields: Phases of the Kinetic*, 2000, exhibition catalogue, Hayward Gallery, London). Emett, when not manufacturing his own bits and pieces, assembled industrial detritus, using movement to similar effect, but with less rust and more humour.

In his cartoon world Emett worked in that English tradition of wildly exaggerated humour which encompassed the young (pre-teetotal) George Cruikshank's burlesques of high fashion, Ernest Griset's animal creations, and, although more literary, the fantasy worlds of Edward Lear and Lewis Carroll. His *jeu d'esprit* escapism was welcomed by a public fed up with the harsh years of war and postwar austerity, at a time, before mass television, when the cartoon was still a major form of light entertainment. The 'things', those contraptual offspring of his cartoons, extended the welcome.

Devising, designing, and ultimately making the 'things' devoured Emett's time and energy. He rose at 5.15 each morning. In summer he might bicycle the 3 miles to the forge at Streat, where several talented assistants—fifteen of them when he was at his busiest—helped to shape his creations into their daft reality. Otherwise he would draw or paint in the studio-cum-guesthouse behind Wild Goose Cottage at Ditchling, Sussex, the home he had bought on the proceeds of his spread in *Life* magazine. His religion was hazy Church of England. A conventional man who dressed formally for formal occasions, he wore an artist's smock when painting, or more usually, shirt, tie, sweater, old corduroys, and expensive, comfortable leather shoes—typical informal wear of the period. He kept in trim all year round by swimming in the heated pool in his garden. He rarely took holidays (he claimed that his work was a holiday), and then only when a 'thing' had been completed. Drained of energy and sometimes speechless with exhaustion, he would rest and recuperate in France or at a health farm for a week or two with Mary.

A naturally shy, charming, mild-mannered person, Emett was occasionally mistaken for the actor–comedian Danny Kaye, to whom he bore a strong physical resemblance. Fair-haired and fresh-faced, even in old age, he looked much younger than his years. He enjoyed classical music, and sometimes whistled with exceptional clarity excerpts from Beethoven and Mozart. In 1978 he was appointed OBE. He died in a nursing home in Hassocks, Sussex, on 13 November 1990. His body was cremated. He was survived by his wife and daughter. His ashes, with those of his wife, were scattered on the South Downs in 1998.   JOHN JENSEN

Sources *Punch* archive, Punch Library, 3 Hans Crescent, London, SW1X 0LN · A. Kitching and M. Lee, *Rowland Emett: from Punch to 'Chitty-Chitty-Bang-Bang' and beyond* (1988) [exhibition catalogue, Chris Beetles Gallery, London, 1988] · M. Bryant, *Dictionary of twentieth-century British cartoonists and caricaturists* (2000) · *British comic art, 1750 to 1980* [n.d.] [exhibition catalogue] · *The early morning milk train* (1976) · B. Hillier, *Cartoons and caricatures* (1970) · personal knowledge (2004) · private information (1996) · b. cert.
Archives BFI, newspaper articles · Punch Library, 3 Hans Crescent, London SW1X 0LN
Likenesses photograph, repro. in *The Times* (16 Nov 1990) · photographs, Chris Beetles Ltd, 8 and 10 Ryder Street, London · photographs, priv. coll. · photographs, Hult. Arch. · portraits, repro. in Kitching and Lee, *Rowland Emett*, 15–16
Wealth at death under £115,000: probate, 3 April 1991, *CGPLA Eng. & Wales*

Emidy, Joseph Antonia (*c*.1770–1835), violinist and composer, was born in Guinea, west Africa. Only two sources suggest a date, although neither is definitive. The muster books for the frigate *Indefatigable* after 1 September 1795 state that he was then twenty-five years old whereas his gravestone records his age at death in April 1835 as sixty; it is probable that, due to his chequered origins, Emidy himself did not know his exact age. The gravestone, which, together with the burial record, are the only records of his second forename, describes him as 'a native of Portugal' but James Silk Buckingham, who knew Emidy in the period 1805–7, reports in his *Autobiography* (1855) that he had been taken in childhood from Guinea into slavery by Portuguese traders, first to Brazil and subsequently to Lisbon.

By 1795 Emidy was playing second violin in a Lisbon opera house orchestra when he came unwillingly into contact with the British navy. On 10 May 1795 the frigate *Indefatigable*, captained by Sir Edward Pellew—later Lord Exmouth—put into the Tagus for major repairs. Due to the crowded conditions aboard ship Pellew required a violinist to play for the sailors' recreation and ordered the kidnapping of the young black violinist whom he had noticed playing energetically in the theatre. Josh Emede, described as a volunteer, first appears in the muster taken on 24 June. The *Indefatigable* sailed on 8 July to resume duties on the western approaches with Emidy, now categorized as a landsman, among the crew. He was to remain aboard, messing alone and in close confinement, until March 1799 when Pellew changed command in his home port of Falmouth.

Cornwall became Emidy's home for the remainder of his life. From a house near the market square in Falmouth he developed a career as a teacher and violinist, appearing as soloist and leader with amateur harmonic societies in many Cornish towns. His professional duties are recorded in newspaper advertisements, reports, and—occasionally—personal memoirs. An anonymous watercolour, dated Truro, 8 November 1808, showing a black violinist leading a group of orchestral musicians, is the only visual record of his career. Emidy married Jane Hutchins (1778–1842), the daughter of a local mariner, on 16 September 1802 at Falmouth parish church. Eight children were born to the couple. In 1815 the family moved to Truro, where they lived at 4 Charles Street, a modest address close to the assembly rooms, theatre, and fashionable town houses where many of Emidy's professional activities were centred. Contemporary accounts speak highly of his ability as a violinist; Buckingham describes him 'playing to a degree of perfection never before heard in Cornwall' (Buckingham, 1.169), and Tuck, remarking that Emidy's fingers 'were not much larger than a goose quill', regarded him as 'the most finished musician I ever heard of'; the source of his 'great talent ... was always a mystery to me, and to all who came in contact with him' (Tuck, 19).

That a slave and victim of the press-gang should play an instrument professionally at all is remarkable, but more surprising is Emidy's flair for composition. The earliest reference to this occurs in advertisements for a concert in Falmouth in 1802 which included a violin concerto, composed and performed by Emidy. His compositions were of sufficient quality for Buckingham to attempt in 1807 to interest the impresario Salomon in furthering Emidy's career in London. A selection of orchestral and chamber scores was privately performed, but, although they were well regarded, nothing came of Buckingham's venture. It is impossible to judge any of Emidy's music today as no works were published and no manuscripts have been found. Joseph Emidy died at his home in Truro on 23 April 1835 and was buried in the churchyard of Kenwyn parish church, Truro, on 26 April. Both local newspapers carried brief obituaries, that of the *Royal Cornwall Gazette* being the most informative.   RICHARD McGRADY

Sources R. McGrady, *Music and musicians in early nineteenth-century Cornwall: the world of Joseph Emidy; slave, violinist and composer* (1991) · J. S. Buckingham, *Autobiography of James Silk Buckingham*, 2 vols. (1855) · W. R. Tuck, *Reminiscences of Cornwall* [n.d.] · muster books, the *Indefatigable*, PRO, ADM 36 13142–13146 · *Royal Cornwall Gazette* (25 April 1835) · *West Briton* (1 May 1835) · M. A. Emidy, *The Emidy family: Joseph Antonio Emidy and Jane (Jenefer) Huthcens of Cornwall England and some descendants* (privately printed, Viroqua, WI, 2000) [copies donated to BL, NMM, Royal Institution of Cornwall] · parish register (burials), Kenwyn, Truro, Cornwall
Likenesses watercolour, 1808, Royal Institution of Cornwall, Truro; repro. in McGrady, *Music and musicians*

Emily, Edward (*bap.* 1617, *d.* 1657), physician, was baptized on 20 April 1617 at Helmdon, Northamptonshire, third son of the four sons and five daughters of Maximilian Emily (1583–1636) of Helmdon, and his wife, Elizabeth (*d.* 1657), daughter and coheir of John Waleston of Ruislip, Middlesex. He matriculated at St Mary Hall, Oxford, on 13 December 1633, graduated BA in 1636, and proceeded MA in 1639. He was entered on the books at the University of

Leiden, in the Low Countries, on 8 November 1640, and received the degree of MD there on 10 November the same year with a thesis 'De melancholia humore', which won the praise of his professors and was complimented in the acts of the university senate.

Emily was back in London by June 1641, when he was admitted a licentiate of the College of Physicians, and having meanwhile been incorporated MD at Oxford was elected a fellow of the college in May 1647. (Wood, *Ath. Oxon.: Fasti*, 1.736, refers to him as 'of Christchurch' but this is not confirmed by surviving records.) As a candidate for the college Emily's political and religious views led him to support the parliamentarians during the civil war. In 1644 he was among the forces of the earl of Manchester besieging York, from where he wrote at length to his royalist colleague Baldwin Hamey junior about the terms for royalist surrender. Hamey retained his loyalty to the king and the episcopal church, but this did not damage their lifelong friendship.

In 1646 Emily was lodging with Nicholas Rodesby, pharmacist, at Lincoln, prior to his marriage in 1648 or 1649 to Elizabeth, which brought them one child, John (*bap.* 1651, *d.* 1711). In 1649 his Goulstonian lectures in London were well received, Hamey describing them in his 'Bustorum aliquot reliquiae' as 'treating no less learnedly of atoms than of anatomy' (Munk, 243). On 23 January 1651 he was appointed senior physician at St Thomas's Hospital at a fee of £40 p.a. for appearing there on Monday and Thursday mornings. Hamey described him as 'a sagacious investigator of diseases, careful in prognosis, and successful in treatment' (ibid.), a performance which presumably satisfied the governors as he retained his post until his death. In 1653 Emily and others petitioned the admiralty for payment for attending to sick and wounded seamen, as naval battles were bringing many such men to St Thomas's door. The petition was not granted, and ultimately the hospital governors met the bills. Emily rose in the estimation of the college, and Wood's unsourced statement that he was charged at Oxford with counterfeit coining is difficult to square with his status as head physician in a famous hospital and a responsible official (at that time censor) of the College of Physicians.

It is not clear why Emily was chosen to give the first Harveian oration, founded by William Harvey in 1656, nor why he chose to give offence by speaking out against the army and Commonwealth, for which in earlier days he had taken up arms. It was a touchy topic in 1656, and one on which the members of the College of Physicians, as elsewhere, were divided. In the college *comitia* Emily was accused of 'having declaimed more bitterly than was proper against military matters, and also of disparaging the present role of the Commonwealth'. Emily responded that 'he had said nothing in bad spirit' ('Harveian memorials'). But the remainder of his oration was found to have merit and nothing further was done, although a rule was passed requiring all future Harveian orators to submit their papers beforehand for the scrutiny of the president and censors.

Emily also practised in the neighbourhood of the City parish of St Olave, Silver Street, where he died on 12 or 14 November 1657. His burial at St Olave's is recorded in the parish register without date. His death may have been somewhat unexpected, for although his wife and child were alive, he left no will. According to Hamey, Emily was an uncompromising supporter of the army to the end of his days; whatever his true sentiments, Emily was followed to his grave by the whole college in procession, in company with the displaced royalist bishop of Chichester, Henry King.   ANITA MCCONNELL

Sources Wood, *Ath. Oxon.: Fasti* (1815) · Munk, *Roll*, 1.244–5 · G. Baker, *The history and antiquities of the county of Northampton*, 1 (1822–30), 628–9 · R. W. Innes Smith, *English-speaking students of medicine at the University of Leyden* (1932), 79 · *CSP dom.*, 1653 · H. S. Robinson, 'The first Harveian orator: Edward Emily', *Medical Life*, 34 (1927), 30–36 · 'Harveian memorials', *Journal of the Royal College of Physicians of London*, 19 (1985), 98 · administration, PRO, PROB 6/34, fol. 99*v* · parish register, London, St Olave, Silver Street, GL [burial; no burial date]

Emin, Emin Joseph (1726–1809), army officer in the East India Company and Armenian nationalist, was born in Hamadan, Persia, the son of Hovsep (also known as Joseph; *d.* 1777), merchant. During Emin's youth internecine wars killed his mother (in 1734) and next youngest brother, scattering his family. about 1735 Hovsep emigrated with a new wife, Thekghi (*d.* 1758), to Calcutta; Emin and his paternal grandfather, Michael, joined them in 1745. Emin studied under a Mr Parrent at the English School in the Old Court-House. Rejecting a merchant's life, Emin worked his passage to England on the East India Company ship *Walpole* (14 February to 14 September 1751).

In London the Armenian Stephanus Coggigian of the London Royal Exchange employed Emin to represent Armenian interests at the king's bench and advanced Emin money for tuition at Mr Middleton's Academy for Boys in Bishopsgate. When Stephanus converted to Roman Catholicism, he demanded repayment from Emin, who left school in debt.

For three years Emin laboured for a bricklayer in Drury Lane, signed (then broke) indentures for a West India plantation, and briefly rejoined Middleton's academy as a servant–student until Middleton went bankrupt. Destitute, Emin served Mr Roberts in the City as grocer's porter and then Mr Webster in Cheapside as a law clerk. Emin also briefly studied military drill with Colonel Dingley. In 1755, while strolling in St James's Park, Emin met Edmund Burke, who guided Emin's education, employed him as a copyist, and presented him with maps of Armenia. That year Emin also gained the patronage of the duke of Northumberland, who elicited his story of his militant Armenian nationalist ambitions and encouraged him to compose an autobiographical epistle, which he then circulated among 300 members of the British elite. William, duke of Cumberland, subsequently sponsored him as a cadet officer in the Royal Military Academy, Woolwich, where he studied mathematics and fortification under John Muller. He also received patronage and exchanged correspondence with, among others, the literary patron Elizabeth Montagu, the physician Messenger Monsey,

Amelia, Lady Yarmouth, George, Lord Lyttelton, and William Pitt the elder.

After thirteen months at Woolwich Emin campaigned (from May 1757) on the continent as a gentleman officer attached to the British and Prussian armies during the Seven Years' War, including at the battle of Hastenbeck (26 July 1757). He briefly accompanied the Prussian army under Frederick the Great against Russia, but his English patrons withdrew him on the eve of the battle of Zorndorf (25 August 1758). He joined the British St Malo raid (June 1758). Between 1759 and 1761 he travelled to rouse Armenians living under Ottoman rule. After a brief return to England he went via Russia to serve Heraclius II, prince of Georgia. For eight years he used his European-style military training, limited Russian support, and financial subsidies from Lord Northumberland in vain attempts to achieve Armenian liberation from the Turkish and Persian empires. He returned from these futile guerrilla actions to Calcutta in 1770.

Despite his impressive credentials, the East India Company's Bengal army classed Emin as non-British, which barred him from the regular officers' corps. Instead the company appointed him (27 October 1770) only as the most junior brevet ensign (risaldar) of the first troop of Turksowars (irregular cavalry) in the 1st brigade, at Rs 300 (including *batta*, or extra pay) per month. Not even the dukes of Northumberland and Cumberland could arrange his nationalization or full commission from London. He served two frustrating years in the Bengal army, garrisoned at Dinapore, advancing (1771–2) under General Sir Robert Barker to the assistance of Nawab Shuja ud-Daula of Oudh, then returning via Benares to Calcutta.

When Governor-General Warren Hastings disbanded the Bengal army's irregular cavalry in 1772, Emin perforce retired to half pay. Seeking advancement of the Armenian cause, he took leave and journeyed via Madras and Bombay. Settling in Jolfa, Persia, in 1776, he married Thangoom Khatoon (1748–1843), daughter of Aga David. Emin subsequently returned to India in 1782, taking his eldest son, Arshak (1777–1792), but leaving behind in Persia for a decade his wife, second son, Joseph (1781–1868), and two daughters, Begoom (b. 1778/9) and Ismeen (1780/82–1831). Resettling in Calcutta in 1784, Emin managed a posting in 1786 to the Bengal army's 3rd European Invalid regiment. Owing to his irregular status, he had repeatedly to petition the company for his back pay and monthly pension of Rs 91, granted only in February 1797. Emin's 640-page memoir *Life and Adventures of Joseph Emin, an Armenian, Written in English by himself* was published in London in 1792. Thereafter he lived among the struggling Armenian community in Bengal, dying in Calcutta on 2 August 1809.

MICHAEL H. FISHER

Sources J. Emin, *Life and adventures of Joseph Emin* (1792) · E. J. Emin, *Life and adventures of Emin Joseph Emin*, ed. A. Apcar, rev. 2nd edn (1918) · *The correspondence of Edmund Burke*, ed. T. W. Copeland and others, 10 vols. (1958–78) · General Return of the Troops under the Command of the Presidency of Fort William, 1770–1800, National Archives of India, New Delhi · *Elizabeth Montagu, the queen of the blue-stockings: her correspondence from 1720 to 1761*, ed. E. J. Climenson, 2 vols. (1906) · *Memoirs of the life, writings and correspondence of Sir William Jones*, ed. Lord Teignmouth [J. Shore, first Baron Teignmouth] (1804) · *Mrs Montagu, 'Queen of the Blues': her letters and friendships from 1762 to 1800*, ed. R. Blunt, 2 vols. (1923) · M. J. Seth, *History of Armenians in India* (1897)

Likenesses E. J. Emin, self-portrait, repro. in Emin, *Life and adventures of Emin Joseph Emin*, frontispiece

Emly. For this title name *see* Monsell, William, first Baron Emly (1812–1894).

Emlyn, Henry (1728/9–1815), architect, was baptized on 19 September 1729 in the parish of Cookham, Berkshire, the son of Henry Emblin (d. 1782), builder, and his first wife, Anne Edwards (d. 1730). His father, a bricklayer by trade, was four times mayor of the borough of Maidenhead, Berkshire, and apparently the first of a family of building craftsmen which was active in the area until the mid-nineteenth century. In 1744 Emlyn was apprenticed to a carpenter, William May of Windsor. Of his early career little is known, except that he remained in Windsor after his apprenticeship. On 8 November 1751 he married Mary Gregory of Windsor at St George's Chapel, Mayfair, London, and their four daughters and one son were baptized in Windsor over the next ten years.

From 1761 Emlyn was employed by the office of works as a carpenter at Windsor Castle, and from 1773 he also worked for the dean and chapter of St George's Chapel there; he served as official chapter carpenter from 1784 until 1791, when he was succeeded by his half-brother James. His duties for the chapter were often mundane, including building repairs and the management of timber on the chapter estate, yet he was a more than competent draughtsman and designer, as he demonstrated by his 1781 publication *Proposition for a New Order in Architecture*. Emlyn's was not the first attempt to produce a 'British order' of classical architecture, but it was perhaps the most imaginative, a somewhat bizarre combination of classical forms with chivalric motifs such as the feathers and badge of the knights of the Garter. Each column of the order was split awkwardly into two shafts part way up, the point of division being decently draped in a wolf's skin bearing a Garter knight's shield and armour; the idea was inspired by the twin trees of Windsor Forest. He incorporated the new order in the portico of his own house in Windsor, in a large scheme (1786; unexecuted) to replace the Lower Ward of Windsor Castle, and at Beaumont Lodge, Old Windsor (c.1790), which still stands. There was no very general enthusiasm among architects for Emlyn's idea, but he nevertheless published expanded second and third editions of the *Proposition* in 1784 and 1797.

Emlyn seems to have enjoyed rising social as well as professional status in his middle years. His daughter Anne (d. 1801) made an advantageous marriage in 1778 to the writer Capel Lofft and in 1785 came Emlyn's most prestigious commission when he was put in charge of the restoration, at George III's expense, of St George's Chapel, Windsor. His achievements there included the design of the richly decorated Gothic organ screen in Coade's artificial stone, complete with fan vaulting, and a particularly successful repair and extension of the choir stalls, where his new work, incorporating carved incidents from the life of George III, imitated the spirit of the medieval woodwork with considerable skill. During the restoration the tomb of Edward IV was opened and Emlyn's illustrated account of the discovery was published by the Society of Antiquaries, of which he was elected fellow in 1795 (*Vetusta monumenta*, 3, 1796, 1–4 and pls. 7–9). Emlyn died at Windsor on 10 December 1815, aged eighty-six, and was buried on 19 December in St George's Chapel.

CHRISTOPHER MARSDEN

Sources S. M. Bond, 'Henry Emlyn of Windsor: a craftsman of skill and invention', *Report of the Society of the Friends of St. George's*, 4 (1962), 99–103; repr. without footnotes in *Country Life* (13 Sept 1962), 607–9 • Colvin, *Archs.* • E. Harris and N. Savage, *British architectural books and writers, 1556–1785* (1990), 186–8 • J. Roberts, 'Henry Emlyn's restoration of St. George's Chapel', *Report of the Society of the Friends of St. George's*, 5 (1976–7), 331–8 • *GM*, 1st ser., 85/2 (1815), 573 • J. W. Walker, *History of Maidenhead* (1931), 74–5 • will, 1782, PRO, PROB 11/1087, fol. 206 [Henry Emblin, father] • will, PRO, PROB 11/1576, fol. 127–30 • parish registers, Bray, Cookham, and Windsor, Berks. RO • register, St George's Chapel, Mayfair, 8 Nov 1751, City Westm. AC [marriage]
Archives St George's Chapel, Windsor, sketchbook, annotated copies of plans, designs, etc.
Likenesses R. Livesey, oils, repro. in Bond, 'Henry Emlyn of Windsor', 607; priv. coll.
Wealth at death £9188: PRO, death duty registers, IR 26/672, fol. 2 (1815)

Emlyn, Sollom (1697–1754), legal writer, was born in Dublin on 27 December 1697, the only surviving son of Thomas *Emlyn (1663–1741), minister of the nonconformist congregation in Wood Street, Dublin, and subsequently a Unitarian minister, and his wife, Esther or Hester (1671/2–1701), daughter of David Sollom of co. Meath, and widow of Richard Cromleholme Bury of co. Limerick.

Emlyn was admitted to Lincoln's Inn on 27 July 1714, and, as was not uncommon among dissenters, entered the University of Leiden on 17 September of the same year. He was called to the bar on 29 April 1721, and on 10 November 1729 married Mary (1707–1764), daughter of the Revd William Woodhouse of Rearsby, Leicestershire. They had two sons, Sollom (d. 1744), and Thomas (d. 1797), a chancery barrister, bencher of Lincoln's Inn, and fellow of the Royal Society.

Emlyn practised successfully as a chamber counsel, and became a commissioner in bankruptcy and in the lead office, but his chief fame was as a writer. In 1730 there appeared in six volumes his *A complete collection of state-trials and proceedings for high treason, and other crimes and misdemeanours; from the reign of King Richard II to the end of the reign of King George I*. This was the second edition of the collection of state trials first edited by Thomas Salmon from material collected by the printer John Darby the younger, which had appeared in four volumes in 1719. Emlyn's edition made considerable improvements on its predecessor: the trials were arranged in chronological order, and the names of judges and counsel, dates, and notes and references were added. Emlyn included an appendix of records and wrote a preface assessing the merits of English law in comparison with other systems. He was critical of both the civil and the ecclesiastical aspects of English law and their delays, technicalities, and costs, but suggested that despite room for improvement, in their criminal law the English had 'by far the better' of their neighbours and were 'deservedly their admiration and envy' (S. Emlyn, preface, iii), principally through the public nature of English prosecutions and the use of trial by jury. Two further, supplementary, volumes appeared in 1735. A third edition of the work, without the supplementary volumes, appeared in 1742. Further editions, with additional material, by Francis Hargrave and by Thomas Bayley Howell and Thomas Jones Howell appeared after Emlyn's death. Also in 1730 appeared a statement by Emlyn and Sir Philip Yorke, subsequently first earl of Hardwicke, lord chancellor, of the appellants' case in the appeal to the House of Lords from Lord Chancellor King's decision in *Poulson v. Wellington* (1729).

In 1736 appeared Emlyn's edition of Sir Matthew Hale's important though unfinished textbook on the criminal law, *Historia placitorum coronae: the History of the Pleas of the Crown*, dedicated to Sir Joseph Jekyll, master of the rolls, who had instigated Emlyn's preparation of the work for the press. After his death in 1676 the House of Commons had appointed a committee in 1680 to supervise the publication of Hale's writings on the pleas of the crown, but nothing was done until Emlyn's edition appeared. Dr Johnson reflected on how 'Hale would have borne the mutilations which his *Pleas of the Crown* have suffered from the editor' (*The Idler*), but the charge was unfounded: Hale's manuscript draft and its transcript show that Emlyn edited the work with care, comparing the transcript with the draft, incorporating Hale's revisions and additions, and checking quotations and references. Himself a dissenter and the 'very worthy Christian friend' (Whiston, 318) of the Arian William Whiston, whose society for promoting primitive Christianity his father had chaired, Emlyn published his father's sermons in 1742, and in 1746 contributed a memoir of his father to an edition of his father's works. His last published work, *Queries Relating to E[lizabeth] C[anning]'s Case*, appeared in 1754, one of the numerous pamphlets stimulated by the alleged abduction of the London domestic servant Elizabeth Canning. Emlyn died of 'gout in his stomach' at his house in Bell Yard, London, on 28 June 1754, and was buried on 8 July in Bunhill Fields burial-ground, London.

N. G. JONES

Sources W. P. Baildon, ed., *The records of the Honorable Society of Lincoln's Inn: admissions*, 1 (1896) • W. P. Baildon, ed., *The records of the Honorable Society of Lincoln's Inn: the black books*, 3 (1899) • Holdsworth, *Eng. law*, vols. 6, 11, 12 • P. R. Glazebrook, introduction, in M. Hale, *Historia placitorum coronae*, ed. P. R. Glazebrook (1971) • S. Emlyn, ed., *A complete collection of state-trials*, 2nd edn, 6 vols. (1730) • J. W. Wallace, *The reporters*, 4th edn (1882) • *The works of Mr Thomas Emlyn*, 4th edn, 3 vols. (1746) • W. Whiston, *Memoirs of the life and writings of Mr William Whiston: containing memoirs of several of his friends also*, 2nd edn, 2 vols. (1753), vol. 1 • W. Prest, 'Law, lawyers and rational dissent', *Enlightenment and religion: rational dissent in eighteenth-century Britain*, ed. K. Haakonssen (1998), 169–92 • G. du Rieu, ed., *Album studiosorum academiae Lugduno Batavae, MDLXXV–MDCCCLXXV: accedunt nomina curatorum et professorum per eadem* *secula* (The Hague, 1875) · *GM*, 1st ser., 24 (1754) · Bunhill Fields burial registers, PRO, RG4/3981, vol. 8, RG4/3983, vol. 10 · *Public Advertiser* (1754) · *Read's Weekly Journal* (1754) · *The Idler*, 65 (1759) · *IGI*

Archives DWL, MSS

Emlyn, Thomas (1663–1741), dissenting minister, was born at Stamford, Lincolnshire, on 27 May 1663, the son of Silvester Emlyn (*d.* 1693), shopkeeper, and his third wife, Mildred Dering. His father became a Stamford municipal councillor on 26 August 1652, but was removed for non-conformity on 29 August 1662. Though a nonconformist he was a churchman in practice, and intimate with Richard Cumberland, then (1667–91) beneficed in Stamford. His second wife, Agnes, was the sister of the poet John Dryden. Silvester became a prosperous shopkeeper and acquired a small estate.

Thomas, the only son who reached manhood, was sent in August 1674 to a boarding-school at Walcot, Lincolnshire, kept by an ejected minister of foreign birth, George Boheme, younger brother of Mauritius Bohemus. Here he attended the ministry of Richard Brocklesby (1636–1714) at the neighbouring church of Folkingham. Emlyn was placed in 1678 at the academy of another ejected minister, John Shuttlewood, then held in secret at Sulby, near Welford, Northamptonshire. He was dissatisfied with the few opportunities for reading presented by his tutor's scanty library, however, and paid a visit to Cambridge, where on 20 May 1679 he was entered (as Thomas Emlin) at Emmanuel College; but he never came into residence, and remained with Shuttlewood until 1682. In August of that year he was transferred to the academy of Thomas Doolittle at Islington. In London he acquired a distaste for precise and dogmatic theology and preached his first sermon in Doolittle's meeting-house on 19 December 1682.

On 15 May 1683 Emlyn became domestic chaplain to the widowed countess of Donegal (Letitia, daughter of Sir William Hicks), a presbyterian, who had a London house in Lincoln's Inn Fields. He accompanied his patron to Belfast in 1684 and continued as her chaplain after her marriage to Sir William Franklin. The presbyterian congregation of Belfast, of Scottish origin, had displeased the countess by the removal of an English minister and the appointment of Patrick Adair. However, Emlyn had no involvement with this body and attended the parish church twice a day; when he preached at the castle in the evening the vicar, Claudius Gilbert, came to hear him. Bishop Hackett gave him, without ordination or subscription, a preaching licence; he wore a clergyman's habit and often officiated in the parish church. Franklin offered him a living on his estate in the west of England, but he did not wish to conform to the established church. His engagement lasted until 1688, when the household was broken up by domestic differences, as well as by the troubles which caused many protestant families to hurry from Ireland. In May Emlyn declined an offer to minister to the presbyterian congregation of Wood Street, Dublin.

In the autumn of 1688 Emlyn left Belfast for London. Passing through Liverpool, he preached at St Nicholas's and, *en route*, at other churches, arriving in London in

THOMAS EMLYN. V.D.M.
Nat. 27. Maij. 1663. Obiit. 30. Iulij. 1741.
Ante leves ergo pascentur in æthere cervi
Et freta destituent nudos in littore pisces
Quàm nostro illius labatur pectore vultus Virg

Thomas Emlyn (1663–1741), by Gerard Vandergucht, pubd 1742 (after Joseph Highmore)

December. In May 1689 he became chaplain to Sir Robert Rich at Rose Hall, near Beccles, Suffolk. Rich, a lord of the Admiralty, was a leading member of a presbyterian congregation meeting in a barn in Blue Anchor Lane, Lowestoft. Emlyn ministered there for about a year and a half, without accepting any pastoral charge. He was on good terms with John Hudson, the vicar, and took his people to charity sermons in the parish church. He was friendly with an elderly Independent minister, William Manning, ejected from Middleton, Suffolk, who subsequently preached at his own licensed house in Peasenhall. The two of them read and discussed William Sherlock's *Vindication of the Trinity* (1690), and Manning became a Socinian (a form of Unitarianism). He tried to convert Emlyn, keeping up a correspondence with him until his death in 1711. Manning's influence brought him to a semi-Arian position, but no further. At what date Emlyn broke with established views is not clear; probably not until 1697, for on 18 January 1698 he wrote to Manning that he could not hope to retain his charge, and was waiting for 'a fair occasion' to speak out.

The invitation to Wood Street, Dublin, was renewed on 23 September 1690, and this time Emlyn accepted. In May 1691 he was ordained in Dublin as a colleague of Joseph Boyse. His preaching was popular, avoiding controversial subjects, but puritanical in tone. On 4 October 1698 he delivered a discourse before the societies for the reformation of manners, in which, while refusing to condemn differences of religious opinion, he strongly advocated severe measures against vice and profanity, including sabbath-breaking.

Among those attracted to Emlyn's ministry was Hester (1671/2–1701), younger daughter and coheir of David Sollom, a converted Jewish merchant, who had purchased (16 May 1678) the estate of Syddan and Woodstown in the barony of Slane, co. Meath. She had become, in her twentieth year, the widow of Richard Cromleholme Bury, a landed proprietor near Limerick, who left her a good income at his death in 1691. Emlyn married her in 1694 (the licence was dated 10 July). On 13 October 1701 Hester died, aged twenty-nine.

The 'fair occasion' for disclosing Emlyn's views was brought about by the suspicions of Duncan Cumyng, an elder in his congregation who had been educated for the ministry. Cumyng noticed omissions in Emlyn's preaching, and interviewed him with Boyse in June 1702. Emlyn at once owned his heresy and wished to resign his charge. Boyse thought the matter should be laid before the Dublin presbytery, a body formed out of a coalition of presbyterians and Independents. The ministers immediately resolved to dismiss and silence Emlyn. However, the congregation resolved that he should withdraw to England for a time, but not preach. This condition Emlyn declined to accept. Next day he left for London, where he found friends, in spite of angry letters from Dublin. His erstwhile colleagues in Dublin then engaged John Howe to interview him, but without effect. At this time Emlyn published a statement in his defence, to which Boyse drafted a reply. A well-meaning private letter from Boyse (3 September 1702), however, advised Emlyn to seek some other engagement. On 16 September, at Cork, the Munster presbytery testified against his errors.

After ten weeks' absence Emlyn returned to Dublin to settle his affairs, sold his books, and prepared to depart. Before doing so he put to press *An Humble Inquiry into the Scripture Account of Jesus Christ* (1702). This was intended to inform the public of the true grounds of his opinion: that God was the supreme being or spirit, and the man Jesus was inspired by and united with Him, but not one and the same person. His nonconformist colleagues were anxious to hinder it from getting abroad, however, as alarm had been excited by an anonymous Socinian tract, *The Scandal and Folly of the Cross Removed* (1699), with which Emlyn had nothing to do, though it seems to have been reprinted in Dublin. Caleb Thomas, a Baptist deacon on the grand jury, got a warrant against Emlyn from Chief-Justice Sir Richard Pine: Emlyn was arrested, but released on bail.

At the end of Easter term 1703 the grand jury found a true bill against Emlyn for publishing a blasphemous libel 'that the blessed Jesus has declared himself not to be the supreme God or equal to the Father' (Wiles, 137). The trial came on in the queen's bench on 14 June. Publication was not proved, and there was nothing to support the charge of blasphemy. But the two Irish primates and a number of bishops had seats on the bench; Emlyn's counsel were browbeaten, and he was not permitted to speak for himself. In the event, the jury brought in a verdict of guilty. Emlyn again declined to retract, and although Boyse pressed for clemency Emlyn was sentenced to a year's imprisonment, to be extended until he had paid a fine of £1000 and found security for good behaviour during life. Emlyn was then forced to walk around the Four Courts with a placard on his breast specifying his offence. Bishop B. Hoadly summed up the judgment: 'The nonconformists accused him, the conformists condemned him, the secular power was called in, and the cause ended in an imprisonment and a very great fine, two methods of conviction of which the gospel is silent' (*Works*, 1773, 1.537).

Emlyn was at first allowed to remain a prisoner in the sub-sheriff's house at his own expense. After five weeks in the common gaol he was transferred to the Marshalsea debtor's prison. Here he hired a large room and preached on Sundays to the debtors and a few of 'the lower sort' of his Wood Street flock. He employed himself in writing a couple of treatises and publishing the funeral sermon which he had preached on the death of his wife in 1701. None of his dissenting brethren came near him except Boyse, who made repeated attempts to obtain a reduction of his fine. On the other hand, there was a clerical petition for a grant of it, to rebuild a parish church, and a petition from Trinity College, Dublin, to apply it in additions and repairs. At length one of his friends, Thomas Medlicote, got the ear of Ormond, the lord lieutenant, and the fine was reduced to £70. Yet the primate of Armagh (Narcissus Marsh) demanded, as queen's almoner, a shilling in the pound of the original fine. Emlyn was released on Saturday 21 July 1705. Next day he preached a farewell sermon to the debtors discharged with him by an act of grace. Immediately before his release the Ulster general synod (June 1705) for the first time made subscription to the Westminster confession imperative upon all entrants to the ministry.

Emlyn settled in London, and a small congregation of his sympathizers met at Cutlers' Hall. In 1706 Emlyn published anonymously *A Vindication of the Worship of the Lord Jesus Christ on Unitarian Principles* (written in 1704). Charles Leslie, the nonjuror, protested vehemently against the toleration of this new sect: in response Emlyn wrote several tracts attacking Leslie in 1708, and in the first one he called himself 'a true scriptural trinitarian' (*Remarks on Mr Charles Leslie's First Dialogue*). Francis Higgins, a Dublin clergyman, complained to Archbishop Tenison, who nevertheless refused to interfere. In June 1711 the lower house of convocation complained to the queen that weekly sermons were preached in defence of Unitarian principles. After a few years the congregation died out, and Emlyn found all pulpits closed against him except at the General Baptist church in the Barbican (Paul's Alley); he preached once or twice for its ministers, James Foster and Joseph

Burroughs. Their liberality is the more remarkable, as Emlyn in his *Previous Question* (1710) had made a radical onslaught on the sacrament of baptism. At length, in 1726, on the death of James Peirce, a nonconformist minister of Arian views at Exeter, his congregation sought Emlyn as his successor, but he declined on the grounds of old age.

With the possible exception of John Cooper (*d.* 1682) at Cheltenham Emlyn was the first preacher who described himself as a Unitarian, a term introduced by Henry Healworth, a friend of Thomas Firmin. He maintained, however, that he never once preached Unitarianism, advocating his theology only through his published works. Although he wrote that his treatises were 'dry speculations', he engaged in a notable controversy with David Martin of Utrecht on the authenticity of 1 John 5: 7. William Whiston, the natural philosopher, revered him as 'the first and principal confessor' of primitive Christianity, and it was Emlyn who chaired the weekly meetings of Whiston's Society for Promoting Primitive Christianity (started 1715) from 4 January to 28 June 1717 (the final meeting). Robert Cannon introduced him to the radical Cambridge Socinian thinker Samuel Clarke (1675–1729), with whom he became friendly. In 1731 Emlyn wrote some memoirs of Clarke which later appeared in his collected *Works*.

Emlyn's unpublished manuscripts convey the impression of strong domestic affections and unaffected piety. He lived at Islington, and was admitted to the communion at the parish church until excluded by the rector. He wrote to the bishop of London desiring readmission, but without effect. After 1739 he moved to Hackney. Gradually disabled by annual attacks of gout, Emlyn succumbed to a fever and died in London on 30 July 1741. He was buried on 8 August in Bunhill Fields. At his funeral on 16 August the sermon was preached by James Foster. He left the residue of his small estate to his sole surviving son, Sollom *Emlyn (1697–1754). Emlyn's collected *Works* was published by his son in 1746.

The case of Thomas Emlyn is of historical interest not merely because he was a pioneer of Unitarian Christianity but also because his trial and punishment illustrate the treatment of heresy by the clerical and lay authorities in Ireland and England. It also throws light upon the limits of toleration and of human rights at this date. Unitarianism was illegal until the Trinity Act of 1813.

ALEXANDER GORDON, rev. H. J. McLACHLAN

Sources M. Wiles, *Archetypal heresy: Arianism through the centuries* (1996) • *The works of Benjamin Hoadly*, ed. J. Hoadly, 3 vols. (1773) • *The case of Mr E. in relation to the difference between him and some dissenting ministers of the city of Dublin* (1702–3) • *The suppression of public vice* (1698) • *A true narrative of the proceedings ... against Mr Thomas Emlyn, and of his prosecution*, new edn (1719); new edn (1829) • T. Emlyn, *Memoirs* • 'Two letters from Mr Emlyn to Mr William Manning', *Monthly Repository*, 12 (1817), 387–9 • 'Original letter of Mr Emlyn's to Mr Manning', *Monthly Repository*, 20 (1825), 705–8 • 'Mr Emlyn to Mr Manning', *Monthly Repository*, 21 (1826), 33–9, 87–91, 203–6, 333–7 • 'Portions of Emlyn's correspondence with Manning (1703–1710)', *Unitarian Magazine and Chronicle* (1834), 276–7 [reprinted from *Monthly Repository* (1817, 1825, 1826).] • R. Wallace, *Antitrinitarian biography*, 2 (1850), 503–38 • parish register, birth and baptism (27/5/1663; 11/6/1663), St Michael's, Stamford, Lincolnshire •

Calamy rev. • H. McLachlan, *English education under the Test Acts: being the history of the nonconformist academies, 1662–1820* (1931) • H. J. McLachlan, *Socinianism in seventeenth-century England* (1951)
Archives DWL
Likenesses J. Highmore, portrait (now lost) • J. Hopwood, stipple (after J. Highmore), BM, NPG • G. Vandergucht, line engraving (after J. Highmore), BM, NPG; repro. in T. Emlyn, *Sermons* (1742) [*see illus.*]

Emma [Ælfgifu] (*d.* 1052), queen of England, second consort of Æthelred II, and second consort of King Cnut, was the daughter of Richard (I), count of Rouen (*d.* 996), and of Richard's second wife, Gunnor (*d.* 1031), herself of Norman stock and Danish origin; she was thus the sister of Richard (II), duke of Normandy (*d.* 1026), and of Robert, archbishop of Rouen from 989 to 1037. Emma was born probably in the early 980s, but nothing is known of her upbringing. It would appear that marauding vikings were able to use Normandy as a base at this time, precipitating a dispute between King *Æthelred and Count Richard, and prompting the pope to broker a peace treaty between them in 990–91. The viking army which went to England in 991 seems initially to have confined its activities to the British Isles; but in the summer of 1000 it went across to 'Richard's kingdom', returning to England in 1001. This turn of events seems to have prompted a new arrangement between England and Normandy, symbolized by the marriage between Æthelred and Emma. She went to England in the spring of 1002, and was known as Ælfgifu in her new country. Little is recorded of her activities as Æthelred's wife, and one can but register William of Malmesbury's remarks in his *Gesta regum Anglorum* to the effect that they were never on good terms with each other. She was certainly more visible at court than the king's first wife, Ælfgifu, had been, in the sense that she was immediately accorded a prominent place in the witness-lists of the king's charters; but it is apparent that she did not gain preferential treatment for her sons *Edward (later known as the Confessor), and *Alfred over the king's sons from his first marriage. In 1012 King Æthelred gave Emma a plot of land on the north side of the High Street in Winchester, which seems to have served as her main base in England for the next forty years. In 1013 Emma and her children were sent to Normandy, and were presently joined there by King Æthelred himself; but following the death of Swein Forkbeard, in February 1014, the family was able to return to England, for the two years that remained of Æthelred's unfortunate life.

It has long been assumed that following Æthelred's death, on 23 April 1016, Emma accompanied her sons Edward and Alfred back to her brother's court in Normandy, and that *Cnut sought to marry her, as his second wife, soon after his own accession, so that she might serve his interests as a symbol of continuity from the previous regime and in order to discourage Duke Richard from interfering in England on behalf of her sons. It is conceivable, however, that Emma had in fact been unable or disinclined to escape from England in 1016, and that Cnut made her his wife in order to draw her away from the cause of her exiled sons in Normandy, with the prospect of a return to power and a promise that the succession

Emma (*d.* 1052), drawing [seated, with her sons Edward and Harthacnut behind her]

After Cnut's death, in 1035, Emma assumed a major political role in her own right, as one committed (with the support of Earl Godwine) to uphold the interests of the Anglo-Danish political establishment, in the person of her son *Harthacnut, against the competing ambitions of Ælfgifu of Northampton (Cnut's first wife), Harold Harefoot [*see* Harold I], and entrenched interests north of the River Thames. The cause of Emma and Harthacnut was, however, undermined by Harthacnut's prolonged absence from England; and when Earl Godwine defected to Harold's side, in 1036, the need to preserve her position gave Emma little option but to make overtures to her sons Edward and Alfred in Normandy, leading the former to the ignominy of an aborted invasion and the latter to capture, blinding, and death. The notional joint rule of Harthacnut and Harold (1035-7) now gave way to the sole rule of Harold (1037-40). In 1037 Emma was 'driven out without any mercy to face the raging winter' (*ASC*, s.a. 1037, Texts C, D); and it is significant that this time she should have taken refuge not with her family in Normandy, but with Baudouin (V), count of Flanders. From Flanders she turned to Edward for help, without result, and soon afterwards she was joined by Harthacnut. Following the death of Harold Harefoot in 1040, Emma returned to England, and was able to preside over the kingdom with Harthacnut; but the new regime was not popular, and it was presumably she who engineered Edward's return from Normandy to England in 1041, in an attempt to strengthen her own position. It was at this stage during the reign of Harthacnut (1040-42) that Emma commissioned a monk of St Bertin (in St Omer, Flanders) to produce the *Encomium Emmae Reginae*, which must rate as one of the most remarkable political biographies of the middle ages. Although presented to the reader quite simply as a tract in praise of Queen Emma, it is the product of an attempt to exonerate herself from criticism for alleged complicity in the death of her son Alfred, and to generate support for the new regime, as much for the intended benefit of those in positions of power and influence at the Anglo-Danish court, as for the intended benefit of posterity. The *Encomium* survives in one mid-eleventh-century manuscript (BL, Add. MS 33241), notable for its inclusion of a prefatory image depicting the enthroned queen receiving the book from the encomiast, with her sons Harthacnut and Edward the Confessor confined to a subsidiary position.

When Harthacnut died, in June 1042, he was succeeded by his half-brother Edward the Confessor, who was consecrated king at Winchester in April 1043. The king's feelings would appear to have been turning against his mother, for in November 1043 he came unexpectedly to Winchester and deprived Emma of her treasures, 'because she had formerly been very hard to the king, her son, in that she did less for him than he wished both before he became king and afterwards as well' (*ASC*, s.a. 1043, Text D). In effect, the event marked the eclipse of Winchester as a centre of political power, at least for the duration of Edward's reign; and although Emma herself was allowed to remain there for the rest of her life, and

would belong to the child of them both. This alternative view makes some sense of the remark that Cnut 'ordered the widow of King Æthelred … to be fetched as his wife' (*ASC*, s.a. 1017), which might seem high-handed if Emma had been 'fetched' from Normandy and if the marriage were actually a reaffirmation of the Anglo-Norman alliance; and since the author of the *Encomium Emmae Reginae* (written in 1041-2) states explicitly that Cnut sought out Emma in Normandy, the alternative view would also add to the evidence that the said author took considerable liberties with the truth. Emma evidently enjoyed high status at the Anglo-Danish court; indeed, she was of far greater importance to Cnut than she had ever been to Æthelred, and it is striking how often in surviving records she and Cnut are mentioned or addressed as a pair, as if contemporaries fully realized that each gave the other support. The double act is symbolized in the famous image which serves as a frontispiece to the *Liber vitae* of the New Minster, Winchester: Cnut and Ælfgifu (Emma) are shown together, placing a great cross on the altar. Emma is also known to have extended her patronage towards numerous religious houses, including Bury St Edmunds, Ely, and Christ Church and St Augustine's at Canterbury, and the Old Minster and the New Minster at Winchester.

although she even recovered her position at court, the event also reflected the removal of the political establishment away from the heartland of Wessex and back to the environs of London on the River Thames. A later Winchester chronicler, evidently intrigued by the story of Emma's discomfiture, told how she had had an improper affair with Ælfwine, bishop of Winchester from 1032 to 1047, and how (with some help from St Swithun) she cleared herself and the bishop by undergoing the ordeal of the hot ploughshares (*Annales monasterii de Wintonia*, s.a. 1043). Emma died on 7 March 1052, and was buried, appropriately enough, beside her second husband and her son Harthacnut in the Old Minster at Winchester.

The marriage of Emma to King Æthelred the Unready has long been regarded as the event which led inexorably to the Norman conquest of England. William of Malmesbury took the view that after the death of Edward the Exile in 1057, Edward the Confessor gave the succession to Duke William, because he was the nearest blood relative, tracing a line back from his father Robert I to his grandfather Richard II, across to Richard's sister, Emma, and so down to Edward. Henry of Huntingdon began the sixth book of his *Historia Anglorum*, 'On the Coming of the Normans', with an account of the marriage, stating that 'from this union … the Normans were justified according to the law of peoples, in both claiming and gaining possession of England' (*Historia Anglorum*, 6.1). It was more to the point, however, that Emma's marriage to Æthelred created the circumstances in which the athelings Edward and Alfred took refuge in Normandy in 1016; that her marriage to Cnut helped to create the highly charged political situation which prevailed in the period from Cnut's death in 1035 to Edward's accession in 1042, and which led thereafter to the extraordinary events of 1051–2; and that it was in this brief period of political freedom that Edward made an approach to Duke William which was construed as a promise of the succession to the throne. There was far more to it, in other words, than the distant ties of blood, just as there is more to Emma than the tale of her political career. It may be that she stands above all other queens of the English, before the conquest, because she can be seen to have played a significant role for a period of fifty years; but she also stands for other queens as one who played out her role in ways which illustrate how much may always have depended on tensions and competing interests within the royal family. SIMON KEYNES

Sources A. Campbell, ed. and trans., *Encomium Emmae reginae*, CS, 3rd ser., 72 (1949); repr. with introduction by S. Keynes, CS, Classic Reprints, 4 (1998) · S. Keynes, ed., *The Liber vitae of the New Minster and Hyde Abbey, Winchester* (Copenhagen, 1996) · *ASC* · William of Malmesbury, *Gesta regum Anglorum | The history of the English kings*, ed. and trans. R. A. B. Mynors, R. M. Thomson, and M. Winterbottom, 2 vols., OMT (1998–9), vol. 1, pp. 276, 322, 350 · Henry, archdeacon of Huntingdon, *Historia Anglorum*, ed. D. E. Greenway, OMT (1996), 338–40 · *Ann. mon.*, vol. 2 · *AS chart.*, S 925 · *English historical documents*, 1, ed. D. Whitelock (1955) · *English historical documents*, 2, ed. D. C. Douglas and G. W. Greenaway (1953) · P. Stafford, *Queen Emma and Queen Edith: queenship and women's power in eleventh-century England* (1997) · S. Keynes, 'Queen Emma and the *Encomium Emmae reginae*', *Encomium Emmae reginae*, ed. and trans. A. Campbell, CS, Classic Reprints, 4 (1998), xiii–lxxxvii

Likenesses drawing (with her sons Edward and Harthacnut), BL, 'Encomium Emmae reginae', Add. MS 33241, fol. 1v, frontispiece [*see illus.*] · drawing (with King Cnut), BL, MS Stowe 944, fol. 6r

Emmanuel, Edward (*fl.* 1900–1930). *See under* Sabini, (Charles) Darby (1889–1950).

Emmerson, Sir Harold Corti (1896–1984), civil servant, was born in Warrington, Lancashire, on 7 April 1896, the son of Henry Emmerson. His father worked in a wire mill and, owing to limited family resources, he was unable to accept the university scholarship which he was awarded while at Warrington secondary school. Instead he joined the civil service as a second-division clerk before serving in the Royal Marine Artillery during the First World War. After the war Horace Wilson secured his appointment to the fledgeling Ministry of Labour. He was to remain there for most of his career, rising steadily through its ranks. He was appointed a principal in 1931 and so he could at last afford to marry. With his wife, Lucy Kathleen Humphreys (*b.* 1900/01), whom he married on 23 December 1931, he had two sons and three daughters. His career peaked as permanent secretary while Iain Macleod was minister of labour between 1956 and 1959.

Emmerson was a generalist in the best traditions of the British civil service. He served a varied apprenticeship. Most notably, he was secretary to a government mission to North America on industrial conditions (1926–7), of which Ernest Bevin was a member, and to the important royal commission on unemployment insurance (1930–32). He also served as private secretary to senior officials and two ministers (1933–5). He was then responsible for juvenile employment and special areas policy, before becoming chief industrial commissioner (1942–4) and director-general of manpower (1944–6). In this last post, he was responsible for demobilization. He left the ministry between 1939 and 1942 to take control of civil defence in the northern region and then to join the Ministry of Home Security. Between 1946 and 1956 he also left to be permanent secretary at the Ministry of Works, where he was responsible for the detailed arrangements of the coronation in 1953.

Emmerson was a powerfully built man with eyebrows to rival Dennis Healey. He was affable and had a good sense of humour which, together with his sheer administrative ability, enabled him to defuse many crises. His childhood and his later work for Toynbee Hall gave him a commitment, like many of his junior colleagues, to help those in need. In particular he sought to explain to them their rights and the services which the ministry could provide. He used the considerable latitude ministry officials were allowed to draft a series of guides which gained wide circulation, including one to the unemployment insurance acts in the late 1920s and the *Industrial Relations Handbook* (1st edn, 1944). He was also a committed defender of voluntarism in industrial relations and was behind Macleod's repeated rebuffs of demands from within the Conservative Party for greater legalistic intervention. His summary of the impossibility of imprisoning a thousand striking Kent coalminers in 1941 made a powerful impression on the 1965–8 Donovan commission on trade unions and employers' associations.

Emmerson's affability led Horace Wilson to attempt to entice him into his widespread network of informants throughout Whitehall, first as secretary to the new Economic Advisory Council in 1930 and then as secretary to Sir Thomas Phillips at the ministry. The Treasury in 1956 sought, through his appointment as permanent secretary, to effect finally the scaling down of the ministry which had been stoutly resisted by his predecessor, Sir Godfrey Ince. Emmerson, however, was too much a man of principle to be used in this way. He was knighted (KCB) in 1947, and was made KCVO in 1953 and GCB in 1956.

After his retirement in 1959, Emmerson served on a variety of official committees, most importantly the Council on Prices, Productivity and Incomes (1960–62) and the Portland spy security inquiry (1963–5). He died on 2 August 1984 at his home, Littlebourne House, Littlebourne, Kent.

RODNEY LOWE

Sources *The Times* (8 Aug 1984) · H. Emmerson, 'Masters and servants', unpublished autobiography, priv. coll. · E. Wigham, *Strikes and the government, 1893–1974* (1976) · *Lancashire and Whitehall: the diary of Sir Raymond Streat*, ed. M. Dupree, 2 vols. (1987) · private information (2004) · Burke, *Peerage* (1967) · m. cert. · d. cert. · *CGPLA Eng. & Wales* (1984) · WWW

Archives priv. coll., MSS autobiography

Likenesses portrait, repro. in *London Evening News* (23 Dec 1944)

Wealth at death £12,607: probate, 6 Dec 1984, *CGPLA Eng. & Wales*

Emmet, Dorothy Mary (1904–2000), philosopher, was born on 29 September 1904 at 14 St Ann's Villas, Kensington, London, the elder daughter and eldest of the three children of the Revd Cyril William Emmet (1875–1923), Church of England clergyman and theologian, and his wife, Gertrude Julia, daughter of James Weir. At the time of her birth her father was curate of St James's, Norlands, but in 1906 the family left London when he became vicar of West Hendred, near Wantage, Oxfordshire, and her childhood was spent in an Edwardian country vicarage: cold rooms, country chores and pleasures, and high standards in the schoolroom. In 1918 the Revd Emmet published *Conscience, Creeds and Critics: a Plea for Liberty of Criticism within the Church of England*; its title could serve as a motto for his daughter's lifelong, anti-dogmatic Christian faith. In the following year he became vice-principal of Ripon Hall and fellow of University College, Oxford, and the family moved to Oxford.

Dorothy Emmet attended school at St Mary's Hall, Brighton (1918–23), and went on to Lady Margaret Hall, Oxford (1923–7), as a classical exhibitioner. She was awarded firsts in both parts of *literae humaniores*. She attended lectures by H. Joachim, H. A. Prichard (who 'always seemed to be in a state of agonised worry'; Emmet, *Philosophers and Friends*, 4), W. D. Ross, author of *The Right and the Good* (1930; undergraduates, she said, dubbed his daughters 'the Right' and 'the Good': ibid., 7), and R. G. Collingwood. Her tutor was A. D. Lindsay, master of Balliol; his interests in democracy, in Christian ideals, and in an undogmatic rethinking of Plato and of Kant were

Dorothy Mary Emmet (1904–2000), by Elliott & Fry, 1958

recurring themes in her work. Firsts in both parts of her degree, however, were no passport to academic employment in the 1920s, and both as an undergraduate and later she worked as a WEA tutor at Maes-yr-haf Settlement, in the Rhondda valley. George Thomas, later speaker of the Commons, was one of her youngest students and became a lifelong friend. Her work in the mining communities of the Rhondda during the depression formed her political sentiments and sympathies.

From 1928 to 1930 Emmet studied at Radcliffe College, the women's college at Harvard, supported by a Commonwealth scholarship. There she worked with A. N. Whitehead, co-author with Bertrand Russell of *Principia mathematica* (1910–13), and became a leading expositor of his work with the publication of *Whitehead's Philosophy of Organism* (1932). From 1930 to 1932 she was a research fellow at Somerville College. After further teaching in the Rhondda she began her academic career as lecturer at Armstrong College, Newcastle upon Tyne (later the University of Newcastle), in 1932. In 1938 she moved to the University of Manchester, initially as lecturer in the philosophy of religion. *The Nature of Metaphysical Thinking* (1945)—written in part during nights of wartime firewatching—established her reputation, and in 1946 she was appointed professor of philosophy and head of department (having been appointed reader in the previous year). In post-war Manchester she was part of a group of distinguished philosophers and social scientists including Max Gluckman, Michael Polanyi, and Arthur Prior. During these productive years she worked increasingly on social explanation, action, and ethics, and wrote a number of books, of which *Rules, Roles and Relations* (1966) was probably the most widely known.

In 1966 Emmet retired to Cambridge, where she shared a house with Richard Braithwaite and Margaret Masterman. All three were active members of the Epiphany Philosophers, a group of religiously inclined philosophers who held that philosophy should investigate rather than marginalize religious experience and phenomena. From 1966 to 1981 she edited the group's journal, *Theoria to Theory*. During these years she also taught philosophy in west Africa (principally at the University of Ife, Nigeria) and became a fellow of Lucy Cavendish Society. She continued an energetic pattern of writing throughout her nineties, publishing *The Role of the Unrealisable* (1994) and a volume of reworked essays in social and religious philosophy, *Outward Forms and Inner Springs* (1998).

Dorothy Emmet's life spanned almost the entire twentieth century, and her philosophical activity extended for over seventy of those years. She was educated in the older and broader climate of Oxford philosophy of the 1920s and was already professor of philosophy at Manchester before the analytic movement transformed philosophy in Britain. Her numerous writings in the second half of the twentieth century shared the movement's aspirations to rigour and clarity but deplored its loss of contact with a wider public. She wrote extensively on then unfashionable themes in metaphysics and the philosophy of religion, and linked philosophy to anthropology and sociology. Her engaging *Philosophers and Friends: Reminiscences of Seventy Years in Philosophy* (1996) charted this philosophical journey and depicted friends and colleagues, conversations and disputes, across an exceptionally long, varied, and active philosophical life. Only failing sight ended her writing; with her many friends she discussed philosophy up to the time of her death, at the Hope residential and nursing care home, Brooklands Avenue, Cambridge, on 20 September 2000. She was unmarried.

ONORA O'NEILL

Sources papers, Lucy Cavendish College, Cambridge · D. Emmet, *Philosophers and friends: reminiscences of seventy years in philosophy* (1996) · *The Independent* (22 Sept 2000) · *The Guardian* (25 Sept 2000) · *The Times* (6 Oct 2000) · D. Emmet, 'An interview with Dorothy Emmet', *Cogito*, 8 (1994), 115–22 · WWW · personal knowledge (2004) · private information (2004) · b. cert. · d. cert.
Archives Lucy Cavendish College, Cambridge, corresp. and papers | JRL, letters to the *Manchester Guardian*
Likenesses Elliott & Fry, photograph, 1958, NPG [*see illus.*] · R. Muspratt, photograph, repro. in *The Guardian*
Wealth at death £537,839—gross; £532,424—net: probate, 15 Dec 2000, CGPLA Eng. & Wales

Emmet [*née* Rodd]**, Evelyn Violet Elizabeth**, Baroness Emmet of Amberley (1899–1980), politician, was born on 18 March 1899 at Qasr al-Dubara, Cairo, Egypt, the elder daughter in the family of four sons and two daughters of James Rennell *Rodd, first Baron Rennell of Rodd (1858–1941), diplomatist, and his wife, Lilias Georgina Guthrie (*d.*

1951). Francis James Rennell *Rodd was her elder brother. She was educated at St Margaret's School, Bushey, in Hertfordshire, and at Lady Margaret Hall, Oxford (1917–20), where she read *literae humaniores* and took a third in 1920. She received further education in Sweden, Germany, France, Switzerland, and Italy, and she spoke fluent Italian, French, and German. On 9 June 1923, at St James's Roman Catholic church, Marylebone, she married Thomas Addis Emmet, an artist, who later joined the Royal Navy, of Amberley Castle, Sussex, son of Robert Emmet, of independent means. They had four children, two boys and two girls. Her husband died on 3 June 1934, and she never married again.

Evelyn Emmet's political career began in local government. In 1925 she was elected as a Conservative to the London county council for North Hackney, and during the succeeding years she chaired numerous committees. She lost her seat in the 1934 election, but subsequently became a co-opted member. Despite being a widow with four young children to bring up, her energy was boundless. After her husband's death she bred cattle and worked on the restoration of Amberley Castle. In 1936 she was made a JP. From 1938 to 1945 she was the county organizer for the WVS in Sussex. She served as chair of the children's court and matrimonial court in the county from 1935 to 1944, and from 1945 she was chair of the Sussex county probation advisory committee. For over twenty years (1946–67), she was a member of West Sussex county council. Nationally, she was a member of the Home Office probation advisory committee and of the Home Office special commission on cinema and the child in 1950. In 1952 and 1953 she was a delegate for the United Kingdom to the United Nations general assembly—one of the few women who were not members of parliament to hold such a position.

Since 1945, Emmet had sought a seat in parliament. In a letter to one constituency committee, she tried to make a virtue of her sex:

> One of the principal reasons I am offering you my services is that I am a Woman. I know this may sound a strange reason to those who still object to women Members of Parliament. … On the Socialist side there are 19 women, on our side two only. These two gallant ladies are being killed by the work that is being put upon them and it is no secret that the Leaders of the party are very seriously concerned and desperately anxious to get a few more well qualified women in the House to relieve the pressure.   (Emmet MSS)

She did not immediately succeed in her aim, and devoted her energies to the Conservative Party women's organization, chairing the party's women's national advisory committee from 1951 to 1954. In 1955 she reached a pinnacle in the party hierarchy, becoming chair of the national union and, as such, chaired the party's annual conference at Bournemouth in October 1955. At the May 1955 general election she finally entered parliament for the safe Conservative seat of East Grinstead, Sussex. She became one of the few women to have become MPs without first having contested another seat or without the influence of relatives.

During her parliamentary career Evelyn Emmet was

influential behind the scenes but was not known as a good speaker. Politically, she was to the left in the Conservative Party. She strongly supported British membership in the European Community and voted in favour of legalizing homosexuality. She is probably best remembered, however, for her interest in women's issues. In 1949 she produced, under the auspices of the Conservative Political Centre, *The Women's Point of View: some Subjects for Discussion by Women's Meetings and Groups* (1949). Particularly within the Conservative Party, she worked tirelessly for equal rights. She supported equal pay between men and women, improvements in widows' pensions, separate taxation of married women, and the admission of women peers to the House of Lords. She constantly pushed the party to include issues of interest to women in the party manifesto, and to increase the number of Conservative women in parliament. Thanks to her firsthand knowledge of international affairs, she became the first woman elected vice-chairman of the Conservative back-bench foreign affairs committee in 1963.

After the dissolution of 1964, Emmet was elevated to the House of Lords with a life peerage as Baroness Emmet of Amberley. She served as chair of the lord chancellor's legal aid advisory committee from 1966 to 1972 and was a member of Lady Tweedsmuir's select committee on the European Community from 1974 to 1977. As a deputy speaker and deputy chair of committees in the House of Lords from 1968 to 1977, she became the first Conservative woman to sit on the woolsack. Baroness Emmet died at Amberley Castle on 10 October 1980.   G. E. Maguire

Sources Bodl. Oxf., MSS Evelyn Emmet · *The Times* (11 Oct 1980) · b. cert. · m. cert. · *WWW* · Burke, *Peerage* (1967), ('Emmet of Amberley') · G. E. Maguire, *Conservative women* (1998) · P. Brookes, *Women at Westminster: an account of women in the British parliament, 1918–1966* (1967) · S. McCowan, *Widening horizons: women and the conservative party* (1975)

Archives Bodl. Oxf., corresp. and papers | Nuffield Oxf., corresp. with Lord Cherwell | FILM BFI NFTVA, news footage

Wealth at death £66,700: probate, 10 Nov 1980, *CGPLA Eng. & Wales*

Emmet, Robert (1778–1803), Irish nationalist, was the youngest son of Robert Emmet (1729–1802), state physician, and his wife, Elizabeth Mason (1740–1803). He was born in Dublin on 4 March 1778, and baptized in St Peter's Church there on 10 March. There were three other children in the family, two sons and a daughter, Mary Anne. The sons, (Christopher) Temple *Emmet (1761–1788) and Thomas Addis *Emmet (1764–1827), became barristers. The family was well-connected and comfortably off, with a town house at 109–10 St Stephen's Green and a country residence at Casino, on the outskirts of Dublin, near Milltown. The Emmets were at the centre of the advanced reformism which was fashionable among Dublin's professional class in the 1780s and early 1790s, and, among the friends of his elder brother Thomas Addis Emmet, Robert would have grown up in an environment where the early leaders of the United Irishmen discussed their views. He was only three or four when Theobald Wolfe Tone became a regular visitor to his home.

Robert Emmet (1778–1803), by John Comerford

After being privately educated at a number of schools in Dublin, latterly at that of the Revd Mr Lewis in Camden Street, Robert Emmet entered Trinity College, Dublin, in October 1793, at fifteen. He was an able student, securing eight premiums at his exams, only two fewer than his brilliant brother Temple. In December 1797 he was admitted as a member of the College Historical Society, the first college debating society in the British Isles, where most of Ireland's political class received their early training. Here he was remembered by his friend and fellow member Thomas Moore as a brilliant orator. But his time at Trinity saw the political climate turn to one of rebellion and repression, in which his brother Thomas and family friends became deeply involved. Emmet became secretary to one of the four United Irish societies in college, and was therefore expelled in April 1798 when the college was purged of republican sympathizers in a visitation by its vice-chancellor, the lord chancellor of Ireland, John Fitz-Gibbon, earl of Clare.

Emmet became active in reorganizing the United Irish Society after its defeat in the 1798 rising. He was one of a small group that acted under orders from the main leaders in prison (who included his brother). The secretive military structure which he helped devise provided the basis for 'Emmet's rebellion' of 1803. In April 1799 a warrant was issued for his arrest. But he escaped, and the following summer he and the Kildare leader, Malachy Delaney, travelled to the continent to commence negotiations for French military assistance. On the strength of their memorial sent to Napoleon in September 1800, they were invited to Paris for further negotiations in January 1801. They impressed France's powerful foreign minister,

Talleyrand, and were encouraged in their plans by France's republican generals. But Napoleon probably used the implied threat of another French invasion of Ireland to strengthen his hand in peace negotiations with Britain, further deepening the United Irishmen's disillusionment with the new regime in France.

In August 1802 Emmet travelled to Amsterdam to join his brother Thomas and some of the other recently released state prisoners, including old friends such as Thomas Russell. At that time he considered settling either on the continent or in America with his brother and family. However, rumblings of renewed war and informal French overtures to the United Irish exiles revived hopes that France might again assist another rising in Ireland. Emmet returned to Ireland in October 1802, not, it seems, to begin preparations for another rising, and he lived quite openly in Ireland until the following March. However, that winter soundings taken of the situation in Ireland convinced the United Irish exiles that Ireland could stage another rising, and in March 1803 Emmet began preparations.

Emmet had long shown an interest in scientific experiments and latterly in military tactics. In Paris he had befriended the American engineer Robert Fulton, then developing the idea of the torpedo, and in 1803 Emmet was carrying out trials of rockets on the beach at Irishtown for use in the forthcoming rising. He and three other United Irish exiles recently returned from France masterminded the military preparations from their headquarters at Butterfield Lane, south of the city. The plan was to seize the main government buildings in Dublin, mobilize adjacent counties such as Kildare and Wicklow, and use former United Irish leaders, who had escaped to Dublin after the collapse of the 1798 rising, to bring out their home counties. Houses were bought at strategic points in Dublin and turned into military depots, where weapons were amassed and hidden behind false walls. The fact that such preparations could progress under the very noses of the authorities testified to the collapse of government intelligence channels. The rebel leaders still expected French support, and those in Paris had embarked on new negotiations to bring this about. But their mistrust of Napoleon was such that they were simultaneously trying to ensure success without the French, and were forced into premature action by a series of mishaps at the Dublin depots which alerted the authorities.

The rising was set for 23 July 1803, and Emmet and the other leaders planned to attack Dublin Castle from their Thomas Street depot. But at such short notice the confusion which resulted was predictable. As troops began to fill the streets surrounding Emmet's depot, he and the others abandoned their plans. He took refuge in the Wicklow hills, but was arrested at Harold's Cross in Dublin on 25 August, having returned apparently to take leave of Sarah Curran (1780?–1808). She was the daughter of the Emmet family friend and celebrated radical barrister John Philpot Curran (1750–1817), and Emmet had been conducting a love affair with her since his return to Ireland. In consequence Curran refused to defend him at his trial, though he had defended almost every other prominent United Irishman before then.

Emmet's trial, conviction, and sentencing took place on 19 September 1803, at which point the making of the extraordinary Emmet legend began. The fact that he was represented by the main government informer of the period, Leonard McNally, was prosecuted with unusual vindictiveness by Lord Norbury and W. C. Plunket, the former friend of Tone, was ill-treated in prison, and had his execution conducted with unseemly haste the following day threw into startling relief his speech from the dock. The speech was dominated by Emmet's repudiation of the idea that he was a French puppet, but it was the following lines which passed into Irish nationalist tradition:

> Let no man write my epitaph … and when I am prevented from vindicating myself, let no man dare to calumniate me. Let my character and my motives repose in obscurity and peace, till other times and other men can do them justice; *Then* shall my character be vindicated. *Then* may my epitaph be written. (*State trials*, 1177)

Other versions (and those usually cited) added the line: 'When my country takes her place among the nations of the earth, then, and not till then, let my epitaph be written. I have done' (Madden, *United Irishmen*, 246). There has been much debate over whether the speech was embroidered by later nationalist propagandists. But Emmet was acclaimed as a public speaker and it is likely that the original was as dramatic as the one which has passed into tradition. His tragic love affair with Sarah Curran (later Mrs Sturgeon), the sufferings in prison of his young housekeeper, Anne Devlin, his youthfulness and good breeding, and perhaps most of all his personal friendship with the poet Thomas Moore made him the epitome of the romantic and tragic hero. Moore's writings and melodies 'Breathe not his name' and 'She is far from the land' brought Emmet to the attention of the Romantic movement, a number of leading figures devoting works to him. R. R. Madden's impassioned accounts of Emmet, the hugely popular *Speeches from the Dock* by A. B. Sullivan and A. D. Sullivan (1867), and Patrick Pearse's elevation of Emmet to pride of place in the 'blood sacrifice' tradition of Irish republican nationalism ensured Emmet his central position in Irish nationalist tradition.

Emmet's body was buried on the day of his execution, 20 September, in Bully's Acre, Kilmainham. Tradition has it that it was later reburied, possibly in St Michan's churchyard in Dublin. But later investigations disproved this and the location of his grave remains a mystery.

MARIANNE ELLIOTT

Sources 'Journal of the Historical Society', 1796–8, TCD, MUN Soc/Hist. 12 · college muniments, TCD, MUN V/23/4, V/25/3 · college visitation, 19–21 April 1798, TCD, MS 1203 · TCD, Sirr MSS, MSS 868–869 · TCD, Madden MS 873 · NA Ire., Rebellion MSS, 620/11–14 · Hants. RO, Wickham papers, MS 38M49 · R. R. Madden, *The United Irishmen: their lives and times*, 3rd ser., vol. 3 (1846) · R. R. Madden, *The life and times of Robert Emmet* (1856) · M. MacDonagh, *The viceroy's post-bag* (1904) · *Memoirs and correspondence of Viscount Castlereagh, second marquess of Londonderry*, ed. C. Vane, marquess of Londonderry, 12 vols. (1848–53), vol. 4 · M. Elliott, *Partners in revolution: the United Irishmen and France* (1982) · *Memoirs of Miles Byrne*, ed.

F. Byrne, 3 vols. (1863), vol. 1 • N. C. Vance, 'Text and tradition: Robert Emmet's speech from the dock', *Studies: an Irish Quarterly Review*, 71 (1982), 185–91 • *State trials*, vol. 28 • J. Maxwell, 'Sources in Trinity College Library Dublin, for researching the 1798 rebellion', *Irish Archives*, 5/1 (1998), 3–22 • private information (2004)

Archives NA Ire., state of the country papers, 1025 • NA Ire., rebellion papers, 620/11–14 • PRO, Home Office papers, 100/113–15
Likenesses English school, lithograph with watercolour, 19th cent. (after portrait by English school, 19th cent.), NG Ire. • Irish school, stipple and line engraving, 19th cent. (after J. Petrie), NG Ire. • Irish school, watercolour on paper, 19th cent., NG Ire. • Irish school, stipple, pubd 1808 (after J. Petrie), NG Ire. • English school, mezzotint, pubd 1846 (after daguerreotype of death mask, 1803; after A. F. J. Claudet), NG Ire. • English school, two stipples, pubd 1846 (after J. Petrie), NG Ire. • J. Comerford, watercolour on ivory miniature, NG Ire. [*see illus.*] • H. Doyle, watercolour on paper (after J. Comerford), NG Ire. • J. Heath, stipple (after J. Petrie), BM, NPG; repro. in J. Barrington, *Historic memoirs of Ireland* (1812) • Irish school, group portrait, line engraving (after J. Petrie; *The speech from the dock by Robert Emmet, patriot, at his trial on 19th September 1803*), NG Ire. • attrib. P. Lightfoot, engraving, repro. in W. H. Maxwell, *History of the Irish rebellion in 1798* (1845), p. 398 • G. Petrie, engraving, repro. in Madden, *United Irishmen*, frontispiece • J. Petrie, pencil on paper, NG Ire. • J. Petrie, two plaster casts of death mask, NG Ire. • W. Read, stipple and line engraving (after portrait by English school, 19th cent.), BM, NPG • J. Sleator, oils, Abbey Theatre, Dublin • group portrait, coloured lithograph (*The united Irish patriots of 1798*), NPG

Emmet, (Christopher) Temple (1761–1788), barrister, was born probably in Dublin, the eldest child of Dr Robert Emmet (1729–1802), subsequently state physician and physician to the viceregal household, and Elizabeth (1740–1803), daughter of James Mason of Ballydowney, co. Kerry. He was baptized in St Peter's parish church, Cork, on 28 October 1761; the forename Temple, by which he was invariably known, was derived from the family name of his paternal grandmother, Rebecca. Emmet was thus related to the Irish Temple family headed by Viscount Palmerston, and more remotely to George Nugent-Temple-Grenville, first marquess of Buckingham, twice lord lieutenant of Ireland in Emmet's time. He was the elder brother of Robert *Emmet and Thomas Addis *Emmet.

Emmet matriculated at Trinity College, Dublin, on 1 May 1775 and was awarded a scholarship in 1778. His performance as an undergraduate at Trinity was brilliant. Henry Grattan the younger recalled:

> Temple Emmet, before he came to the Bar, knew more law than any of the judges on the bench; and if he had been placed on one side and the whole bench opposed to him, he could have been examined against them, and would have surpassed them all; he would have answered better both in law and divinity than any judge or bishop in the land. (Emmet, 2.192)

It was also said that his performance before the examiners was so impressive that they changed the usual approbation of 'valde bene' to the laudatory 'o quam bene'. He graduated BA in 1780. He had been admitted to the Middle Temple on 5 January 1779 (Irish barristers being then required to belong to an English inn of court) and was called to the Irish bar in Trinity Term 1781. His immense natural abilities and unstinting labour, which had served him so well at Trinity, also brought him rapid success at the bar. Allied to his tremendous gifts of memory and reasoning, and to the vast corpus of legal knowledge that he had acquired, was a fine oratorical style. His oratory was certainly flamboyant and had in fact been criticized by some of his college contemporaries, who complained that he could not speak prose, but only poetry. Peter Burrowes, for instance, opined that his mode of address was altogether too 'flowery and eloquent … it was full of talent, but it was a speech of blank verse' (Emmet, 2.194). These criticisms notwithstanding, Emmet's eloquence was well received at the bar and served to add to the reputation that he acquired through his learning and industry. Another significant event in his life to take place in 1781 was his marriage to his second cousin Anne Western Temple (d. 1788), daughter of Robert Temple, an American loyalist formerly from Massachusetts who had settled in Ireland.

Within a few years of his call Emmet had come to be recognized as one of the foremost practitioners at the Irish bar, and in 1787 he took silk at the remarkably early age of twenty-five. His high professional standing is further attested by his membership of the Monks of the Screw, a social club founded by Barry Yelverton, first Viscount Avonmore, whose membership was restricted to some of the leading figures in Irish professional society, including John Philpot Curran, Henry Grattan, and Henry Flood. In February 1788 Emmet went on the Munster circuit, where he was suddenly taken ill and died within two days. The Emmet family have traditionally ascribed his death to overwork. He was buried on 9 March 1788 in St Peter's, Dublin.

Emmet's meteoric rise within the legal profession was perhaps unparalleled, and the reputation that he acquired during a mere seven years of practice gives some idea of what he might have achieved had he survived. So strong was the impression created by him during his brief professional life that his attainments continued to be referred to at the Irish bar for twenty years after his death; thus at the trial of Robert Emmet in 1803 the presiding judge, John Toler, Baron Norbury, recalled: 'You had an elder brother whom death snatched away and who when living was one of the greatest ornaments of the bar' (Emmet, 2.225). Politically he lived and died a loyal subject of the crown, although he gave evidence in his poem 'The Decree' of valuing Ireland's freedom from undue external interference. This poem is one of the few known to have been written by him, and evidences a pleasant literary style and some ability.

Emmet was survived by his wife and their daughter Catherine. Anne Emmet had a delicate constitution, and died in November 1788, only a few months after her husband. Catherine apparently spent much of her life as a semi-invalid, and died unmarried.   NATHAN WELLS

Sources T. A. Emmet, *Memoir of Thomas Addis and Robert Emmet, with their ancestors and immediate family*, 2 vols. (1915) • L. Ó Broin, *The unfortunate Mr Robert Emmet* (1958) • Burtchaell & Sadleir, *Alum. Dubl.* • R. W. Postgate, *Robert Emmet* (1931) • D. J. O'Donoghue, *Life of Robert Emmet* (1902) • E. Keane, P. Beryl Phair, and T. U. Sadleir, eds., *King's Inns admission papers, 1607–1867*, IMC (1982) • H. A. C. Sturgess,

ed., *Register of admissions to the Honourable Society of the Middle Temple, from the fifteenth century to the year 1944*, 1 (1949)
Likenesses miniature, repro. in Emmet, *Memoir*

Emmet, Thomas Addis (1764–1827), barrister and Irish nationalist, was born on 24 April 1764 in Cork, the second of the four children of Dr Robert Emmet (1729–1802), state physician, and his wife, Elizabeth Mason (1740–1803). His younger brother was Robert *Emmet (1778–1803), fellow United Irishman. The family moved to Dublin and in the 1770s were residing at 109 St Stephen's Green; they also acquired a country residence at Casino, on the outskirts of Dublin at Milltown. Emmet was educated at Mr Kerr's school in Dublin and entered Trinity College, Dublin, in July 1778 at the age of fourteen. He graduated in 1783 and entered Edinburgh University to study medicine, and graduated in 1786. There he befriended a number of future luminaries, including James Mackintosh and Dugald Stuart, and appears to have taken a leading role in the literary and debating societies for which the university was famous. Reacting to the premature death in 1788 of his elder brother, Christopher Temple *Emmet (1761–1788), a brilliant young lawyer, Thomas renounced medicine for law, attended Lincoln's Inn in London, and was called to the Irish bar in 1790. He married Jane Patten that year.

Also in 1790, Emmet became involved in a political club, organized by Theobald Wolfe Tone, a forerunner to the Society of United Irishmen. He became Tone's close friend and confidant, second only to Thomas Russell. He was prominent in the Dublin Society of United Irishmen from its foundation in 1791, during its so-called constitutional phase. It was then that he (a protestant) began his lifelong campaign for Catholic emancipation. After the outbreak of war between Britain and revolutionary France brought about the United Irish Society's suppression in 1794, he remained one of an inner group seeking, with French military assistance, full separation from Britain. The society was later reconstituted as an underground military organization preparing for this event, and late in 1796 Emmet became a member of its national executive. In February 1797 he was one of only three chosen to appoint a secret agent to France. But he was considered one of the more moderate among the leaders, and resisted pressures to organize a rising before the French arrived. The leadership became badly split over this issue and when Emmet (along with most of the main Leinster leaders) was arrested at Oliver Bond's house in Dublin on 12 March 1798, preparations for such a rebellion went ahead, only to be crushed before a French fleet arrived.

In order to stop the executions—and in return for permission to exile themselves to America—the chief United Irish prisoners, including Emmet, offered to make a full confession to government. This became the Kilmainham treaty of August 1798. It was one of a number of statements in which 'moderates' such as Emmet sought to distance themselves from the bloodshed of 1798 by implying that it had been provoked by the British government

Thomas Addis Emmet (1764–1827), by T. W. Huffam, pubd 1843 (after Louis François Aubry, 1803)

rather than planned by themselves. However, the agreement to release the prisoners to another country foundered on the refusal of the American minister in London, Rufus King, to grant entry to such dangerous radicals. Emmet and the other main prisoners were accordingly sent to an open prison in Scotland, Fort George, where they remained until the Peace of Amiens in 1802. Jane Emmet was allowed to join her husband, and one of their children was born there.

In June 1802 Emmet and most of the other Fort George prisoners were released to the Netherlands, and by February 1803 he and his family had arrived in Paris. Despite his growing disillusionment with France, particularly with the advent of Napoleon, Emmet re-involved himself in new negotiations to secure French military help. He became nominal president of a revamped United Irish committee in Paris and knew of the early stages of the plans of his younger brother Robert for his ill-fated rebellion of July 1803. But signs that the French government preferred to deal with the other main United Irish leader in France, Arthur O'Connor—a talented, though vainglorious, aristocrat, with whom Emmet had been in dispute since 1798—determined him to withdraw entirely. In October 1804 he sailed for America.

Though often criticized by some United Irishmen for an excess of caution, Emmet was recognized even by his enemies as a man of courage, honour, and ability. In America he was taken up by the Jeffersonian republicans (notably the Clintons of New York) and went on to have a distinguished legal career there. His bitterness at being denied entry to America in 1799 underpinned his campaigns against Rufus King, the man whom he held responsible, and he helped engineer King's defeat in elections in 1807 and again in 1816. The former campaign produced his only major publication. Though published under the authorship of his friend and co-prisoner at Fort George, William James MacNeven, *Pieces of Irish History* was substantially Emmet's work. It is the fullest surviving contemporary history of the United Irish movement until 1795. But by stopping in that year, Emmet avoided having to confront many of the less savoury aspects of the militant underground movement which developed thereafter. The book was the key document supporting the claim of early leaders such as Emmet that they were at heart simply reformers, who were forced to more extreme measures by arbitrary government and then denounced by the likes of Rufus King for following in the steps of the American founding fathers.

The former United Irishmen remained close in America, their families intermarrying, and Emmet was involved with a number of Irish–American societies and causes. He died in New York on 15 November 1827, following a seizure while pleading a case in the United States circuit court. He was buried on 16 November in St Paul's churchyard, Broadway, and the funeral procession included most of the leading dignatories of New York, the governor, judges, district attorney, members of the bar, and professors of the medical school. Two years later a monument to him was raised in the cemetery, much of the funding supplied by the American Catholic Association in recognition of his commitment to Catholic emancipation. He was survived by his wife and nine of their ten children.

MARIANNE ELLIOTT

Sources NA Ire., Rebellion MSS · TCD, Madden MS 873 · entrance book, 1769–1825, TCD, MUN V/23/4 · M. Elliott, *Partners in revolution: the United Irishmen and France* (1982) · R. R. Madden, *The United Irishmen: their lives and times*, 2nd ser., 2 (1843) · W. T. W. Tone, *Life of Theobald Wolfe Tone*, 2 vols. (1826) · W. J. MacNeven, ed., *Pieces of Irish history* (1807) · N. J. Curtin, *The United Irishmen: popular politics in Ulster and Dublin, 1791–1798* (1994) · D. A. Wilson, *United Irishmen, United States: immigrant radicals in the early republic* (1998)
Archives TCD, papers | TCD, corresp., mainly with Martha Bradstreet
Likenesses Irish school, pastel drawing, 1775–9, NG Ire. · T. W. Huffam, mezzotint, pubd 1843 (after L. F. Aubry, 1803), NG Ire. [*see illus.*] · T. W. Huffam, mezzotint, pubd 1843 (after drawing by J. D. Herbert, 1798), NG Ire. · group portrait, lithograph (*The United Irish Patriots of 1798*), NPG · pastel drawing, NG Ire. · portrait, repro. in Madden, *United Irishmen*, frontispiece

Emmett, Anthony (1790–1872), army officer, attended the Royal Military Academy, Woolwich, and was commissioned second lieutenant in the Royal Engineers on 16 February 1808. He joined the army in the Peninsula early in 1809, and remained with it until the summer of 1812, when he was severely wounded at the siege of Badajoz. He returned to the army in October of the following year at his own request, and remained with it to the close of the war.

During his service in the Peninsula Emmett was constantly in action: in Abrantes and skirmishes near it, while the French were in front of the lines at Lisbon; at both the sieges of Badajoz in 1811, at the cavalry affair of El Bodon, and in the trenches before Ciudad Rodrigo; and at the siege of Badajoz in 1812, when he led the Portuguese column of the 4th division to the assault of the breach of the curtain, and was severely wounded. He was sent to England to recover his health. Prior to the siege he was occupied in improving the navigation of the Upper Douro to facilitate the transfer of supplies for the operations in Badajoz.

On rejoining the army as a captain in 1813 Emmett investigated the fords of the Nive, held by the enemy's posts prior to the successful passage of the river. During the following campaign he was attached to the 2nd division, and was present at the battle of St Pierre, near Bayonne, at the attack on the heights of Garres St Palais at Tarbes, and at the battles of Orthez and Toulouse. Soon after his return to England he was sent, in 1815, with General Keane, on the expedition against New Orleans; he landed with the advance, and was present at the American attack, at the assault made on the enemy's lines, and at the siege of Fort Bowyer.

Emmett was next appointed commanding royal engineer at St Helena, where he went with Sir Hudson Lowe, and held the command until after the death of Napoleon. He held various commands at home, at Bermuda, and in the Mediterranean, until he was compelled in May 1855 to retire as a major-general on account of bad health caused by the wounds received in the Peninsula. He died at his home, 17 Marine Square, Brighton, on 27 March 1872.

R. H. VEITCH, rev. JAMES LUNT

Sources Corps papers (Royal Engineers) · Boase, *Mod. Eng. biog.*
Wealth at death under £2000: probate, 1 May 1872, *CGPLA Eng. & Wales*

Emmison, Frederick George [Derick] (1907–1995), archivist, was born at 35 Sandhurst Road, Bedford, on 28 May 1907, son of George Emmison, a telegraph clerk with the London, Midland, and Scottish Railway, and his wife, Kate Ann, *née* Field (d. 1967). A bright boy, inspired by his father with a love of history, he gained a scholarly reputation at Bedford modern school with every expectation of a place at Cambridge University to follow. Unhappily, family circumstances prevented this progression and in 1925 he started work, entering the employ of Bedfordshire county council. Here what must have been disappointment was promptly replaced by opportunity. Appointed the county's first clerk of the records, the young Emmison acquired as his mentor and profited from the experienced guidance of Dr G. H. Fowler, chairman of the county records committee and justifiably acknowledged as the 'father of local archives'.

Under this tutelage Emmison gained a thorough grounding in archive administration and absorbed the crucial concept of the broad-based county record office. 'It was my singular fortune', he reminisced later in life, 'to be trained in the late 1920s as the first local archivist' (personal knowledge). He soon gained a reputation for his imaginative and energetic approach to his pioneering endeavours. The Bedford years saw many initiatives, not least his wholehearted policies of record survey. That he was from the first a doer as well as a thinker is evidenced in his report of conducting the pursuit of a survey of Bedfordshire parish records by visiting, mainly by bicycle, 'over one hundred churches on forty-five Saturdays as a voluntary scheme' (ibid.). In 1935 he married Margaret, daughter of Dr Hamilton Langwill, with whom he had a son and a daughter.

The defining event in Derick Emmison's career came in August 1938 with his appointment as the first county archivist of Essex. His opportunities to lead, to influence, to proselytize, became more fully realizable and he set himself to make Essex Record Office pre-eminent in its field and an inspiration to and model for county record offices to come. He remained in post until he retired in 1969, creating in due time the largest English county record office in terms of staffing, size and range of collections, accommodation, and of always steady and at times spectacular increases in user numbers. Meantime his seemingly boundless energy generated a ceaseless flow of often influential initiatives, especially in the related fields of education and publication. He achieved the appointment of the first full-time education officer to an archives service and the lease of part of Ingatestone Hall for major annual exhibitions and facilities for school classes and group visits. Characteristically Derick and Margaret endowed an annual prize for a study based on historical research in original sources by Essex schoolchildren. The Essex Record Office publications programme, begun in 1946, has often been emulated but never yet surpassed, constituting another key legacy in the provision of archive services and the furtherance of local studies.

Far from content with leading by example, Emmison involved himself in the work of numerous organizations, national and local, pertinent to archives and local studies. He was a founder member in 1932 of the British Records Association and in 1947 of the Society of Local Archivists, and was for many years prominent in the British Records Society, the Historical Association, and the Society of Genealogists, being honoured by office in these and many local bodies. It is, indeed, arguable that his most important contribution to the cause of local archives lay in his talent as a publicist and his instinctive ability to enthuse a wider than specialist audience. No one did more to establish in the public mind an awareness of what the local record office could and should be. The quiet post-war revolution in the availability of and access to the 'nation's memory' would assuredly have been quieter and less profound without him.

For Emmison, busy as he was with professional concerns, the professional and the scholarly always marched hand in hand. His work as researcher and writer began as early as 1927 and ceased only with his death. His most substantial publications are his *Guide to the Essex Record Office*, parts 1 and 2 (1946–8); *Catalogue of Maps in the Essex Record Office* and supplements thereto (1947, 1952, 1964, 1968); *Elizabethan Life* (5 vols., 1970–80)—all in the Essex Record Office Publications series; *Wills at Chelmsford, 1620–1720* and *1721–1858* (British Records Society, 79 and 84; 1959,

1969); *Tudor Secretary: Sir William Petre at Court and at Home* (1961); *Archives and Local History* (1966); and *Essex Wills* (from 1558), of which ten of the projected twelve volumes were published by the New England Historical Genealogical Society, Boston, USA, between 1982 and 1995.

Emmison's achievements were duly honoured. He was a fellow of the Society of Antiquaries and of the Royal Historical Society. In 1966 he was made an MBE and in 1970 an honorary doctorate was conferred on him by the University of Essex. He was awarded in 1974 the Julian Bickersteth medal of the Institute of Heraldic and Genealogical Studies, and the Historical Association gave him in 1987 its Medlicott medal 'for outstanding service to history, both in the record office field and as a local historian'. Derick Emmison died from pancreatic cancer in Broomfield Hospital, Chelmsford, on 9 November 1995 and was buried at Chelmsford following cremation. BILL SERJEANT

Sources K. Neale, ed., *An Essex tribute: essays presented to Frederick G. Emmison as a tribute to his life and work for Essex history and archives* (1987) · 'F. G. Emmison: a bibliography', *Journal of the Society of Archivists*, 5 (1974–7), 527–34 · *Archives*, 22/95 (1996) · S. Tyacke, *Journal of the Society of Archivists*, 18 (1997), 103–4 · b. cert. · d. cert. · personal knowledge (2004) · private information (2004) [Martin Emmison, son]

Archives Essex RO, Chelmsford, papers · Essex RO, Chelmsford, antiquarian notes and corresp., semi-official papers

Wealth at death £201,935: probate, 18 April 1996, *CGPLA Eng. & Wales*

Emmott, Alfred, Baron Emmott (1858–1926), politician and cotton manufacturer, was born at Chadderton, near Oldham, on 8 May 1858, the third son of Thomas Emmott, cotton manufacturer, of Oldham, and his wife, Hannah, daughter of John Barlow, of Chorley, Lancashire. Educated at the Friends' school, Kendal, Westmorland, where he was a good cricketer, and at Grove House, Tottenham, he graduated BA from London University in 1880. In 1881 he and his brother John were given partnerships in the family spinning business, Emmotts and Walkshaw, and Alfred was eventually appointed managing director. The firm employed 800 operatives in the 1920s, and was of a middling size within the industry. Emmott, who was known as a considerate employer, maintained an active interest in this business throughout his life, but it was not the main focus of his career. He married Mary Gertrude, daughter of John William Lees, of Oldham, in 1887. They had two daughters, Mary Gwendolen and Dorothy. Besides becoming president of the Oldham chamber of commerce, and the powerful Oldham Master Cotton Spinners' Association, he was elected to Oldham council as a Liberal in 1881, becoming mayor in 1891. He was a grandee of Oldham society and the local cotton industry. In appearance he was tall, with a receding hairline, largish nose, moustache, and somewhat pointed ears.

Emmott decided to enter national politics: at Oldham in 1899 he and Walter Runciman, the Liberal candidates, defeated their Conservative rivals, Winston Churchill (contesting his first election) and James Mawdsley, the leader of the spinners' trade union. Emmott, unlike the more flighty Churchill, remained committed to Oldham. Campbell-Bannerman, the Liberal premier, made

Alfred Emmott,
Baron Emmott
(1858–1926), by
unknown
photographer,
c.1899

Emmott (an Anglican) chairman of committees in the House of Commons in 1906, a post he held until 1911, through a period marked by some very heated controversies including disputes over religious education, Lloyd George's 'people's budget', and the prolonged battle between the government and the tory peers. Emmott performed his trying duties in an exemplary fashion. He was sworn of the privy council in 1908. The government's social reforms, such as the introduction of old age pensions, were welcomed by Emmott, who thought that they added to the liberties of the people, a criterion by which he always set great store. But social reforms had to be paid for, and Lloyd George was determined that the rich should contribute their share. Speaking in 1910 and, presumably in jest, Emmott remarked that he:

> was astonished that more of the rich and well-to-do in this world did not leave the [liberal] party … It might almost be said to be easier for a camel to pass through the eye of a needle than for a rich man to remain in the Liberal party. (Clarke, 405)

By 1911 Emmott was quite worn out by his exertions and welcomed elevation to the House of Lords as a baron and a move to the relatively balmy atmosphere of the Colonial Office, where he served as undersecretary of state. He led a delegation of the Empire Parliamentary Association to Australia, Canada, New Zealand, and South Africa in 1913. His time at the Colonial Office was one of the happiest of his life, and in 1914 he was created GCMG. He became a supporter of imperial preference, which suggests that he was not dogmatically committed to the Manchester school.

Emmott joined H. H. Asquith's cabinet in 1914 as first commissioner of works. He was one of those wartime ministers who believed in business as usual, opposing the establishment of a rigid blockade in the North Sea, so as to avoid offending the neutral countries. Cabinet meetings were frustrating for him and he complained in his diary of the 'difficulty of obtaining a hearing' (French, 'Rise and fall', 26), and the way in which important topics were rushed through without proper debate. He did not impress his superiors and, in a letter to Venetia Stanley, Asquith made it clear that he was regarded as a tail-ender

within the cabinet. Charles Hobhouse, another cabinet colleague, described Emmott as 'honest, slow, laborious … [with] a whining mechanical voice which detracts from a good and sober judgement and hard work' (David, 229). The pinnacle of Emmott's career was reached on 14 January 1915, when Asquith for a fleeting moment considered him as a possible viceroy of India; he then thought better of it. In August 1915 Emmott attempted to put another spoke into Churchill's wheel. There were rumours at that time that Churchill might be given the Colonial Office. Emmott sent a strongly worded protest to Asquith: 'I do implore you for the sake of the Dominions not to put Churchill [at the colonial office] … He has neither the temperament nor manners to fit him for the post' (Gilbert, 460). He alleged that the staff at the Colonial Office would be unable to work with a man such as Churchill. Andrew Bonar Law rather than Churchill went to the Colonial Office in 1915, although there is no reason to believe that Emmott's rather pompous intervention had any effect on the outcome.

With the formation of a coalition government in 1915 Emmott left the cabinet to become director of the war trade department, the official body responsible for regulating British exports for the duration of the war. Export industries such as cotton were expected to continue their activities, although at a more modest level due to the disruption of European markets, the competing demands for personnel of the services and war industries, and the increasingly chronic shortages of coal and shipping. Earnings from British exports would help to pay for imports of munitions, especially from the United States. The department's most urgent task was the oversight of trade with continental countries, such as the Netherlands and Switzerland, through which it was feared that the enemy could obtain succour from Britain in the form of coal for their industries, food for their troops, and even cotton yarn for the manufacture of Zeppelins. Emmott's job was a tricky one, requiring immense tact and good humour, and in this sense it was similar to the work he had done before the war in the management of parliamentary business. It was a matter of striking a balance between the interests of exporters, who were earning foreign exchange, neutrals, who saw no reason why their imports should be disrupted, and the armed forces, who were anxious to maintain an effective blockade of the enemy. A system of rationing was introduced. Neutral countries were supplied with sufficient imports from Britain to meet their legitimate domestic needs, but without any surplus that could be re-exported to Germany. Estimates of the effectiveness of this system have varied, and some supplies continued to get through to Germany, no doubt as a result of the tergiversations of neutrals. A Zeppelin shot down near Potters Bar in 1916 was found to have been constructed using yarn exported from Lancashire to Switzerland.

Could Emmott have been too sympathetic towards the claims of British exporters? While the military struggle was escalating in France and Belgium in the summer of 1916 he was engaged in a rearguard action in Whitehall against the supporters of total war, who wanted to cut trade with the neutrals to the bone. Further restrictions on the export industries would have reduced contraband trade and freed productive resources for use in the munitions industries. But Emmott, the Liberal businessman, was quite unable to transform his way of thinking into that of an economic warlord and guardian of empire. State interference with trade should be kept to a minimum, he argued, because freedom to conduct one's business was one of the principles for which Britain was fighting. Despite his protests the screws were tightened on the neutrals during this phase of the war. Emmott's opposition to draconian restrictions on trade was not entirely anachronistic. There were pragmatic grounds for wanting to keep up a brisk export trade, to safeguard traditional markets for the post-war period. Moreover, during 1917 a growing body of opinion began to doubt whether a military solution was possible in Europe, for the German defences appeared to be impregnable. There was a danger that military stalemate would be followed by an economic war, in which British and German exporters competed for the domination of world markets. No doubt the victors in this economic struggle would be enriched, refreshed, and eager for the resumption of the real war, which they could prosecute from a position of strength. Although plausible, this argument had a serious drawback: undue protection of the export industries would have reduced deliveries of munitions and troops to the front in the short term, thereby increasing the probability that stalemate, or even defeat, would be the outcome in France and Belgium. In the event Germany collapsed at the end of 1918, suggesting that the believers in stalemate had been excessively pessimistic. Emmott's contribution to the war effort, while not crucial, was significant: controls over exporters were tighter than he would have liked, but they would have been even tighter in his absence.

Emmott was created GBE in 1917 in recognition of his contribution to the war. He supported Asquith rather than Lloyd George and did not figure very strongly in post-war politics. His activities were those of a semi-retired politician of middle rank. He wrote a substantial tract against the doctrine of nationalization and in defence of private property, calling instead for partnership and understanding in industry. In 1920 he chaired a commission of investigation into conditions in Russia and in particular the ill treatment of British subjects by the Bolsheviks. He chaired further commissions, on decimal coinage and teachers' superannuation, and in 1921 chaired the World Cotton Congress. Emmott was a member of the court of governors of Manchester University; president of the Royal Statistical Society between 1922 and 1924; and president of the National Association of Building Societies. He took an active role in the management of the Lancashire and Cheshire YMCA and was a founder of the Anglo-Belgian Union. In 1923 he laid the foundation-stone of the memorial for those who had died in the raid on Zeebrugge.

During the 1920s Emmott had time to take more of an interest in business and in the direction of Emmotts and Walkshaw. Platt Brothers, Britain's largest textile machinery producer and one of Oldham's leading firms, appointed him chairman in 1924. The firm had been experiencing difficulties in the depressed economic climate of the 1920s, and it is uncertain what assistance they expected from Emmott, by no means an aggressive business tycoon and now well into his sixties. His other business interests included directorships of the Yorkshire Bank, the National Boiler General Insurance Company, Manchester Liners, and the Calico Printers Association. On 10 December 1926 Emmott presided at a dinner at the Manchester Reform Club, where the chief guest was his old running mate from the 1899 Oldham election, Walter Runciman. This was his last public engagement: on 13 December he died suddenly of angina pectoris at his home at 39 Ennismore Gardens, Kensington, London, and was buried two days later at Kensington Hanwell cemetery, Ealing. Lord Balfour, paying tribute to him in the Lords, described Emmott as a man of 'clear common sense' (*The Times*, 14 Dec 1926, 8b). Lord Grey said that he was a man who could be trusted with any confidence (ibid., 16b). Emmott was survived by his wife and daughters, the barony being extinct.

JOHN SINGLETON

Sources J. McDermott, 'Total war and the merchant state: aspects of British economic warfare against Germany, 1914–16', *Canadian Journal of History*, 21/1 (1986), 61–76 · DNB · *The Times* (14 Dec 1926) · *The Times* (16 Dec 1926) · *The Times* (8 Feb 1927) · H. H. Asquith: *letters to Venetia Stanley*, ed. M. Brock and E. Brock (1982) · P. F. Clarke, *Lancashire and the new liberalism* (1971) · *Inside Asquith's cabinet: from the diaries of Charles Hobhouse*, ed. E. David (1977) · A. Emmott, *Nationalization of industries: a criticism* (1920) · D. A. Farnie, 'The marketing strategies of Platt Bros & Co. Ltd of Oldham, 1906–1940', *Textile History*, 24 (1993), 147–61 · D. French, *British economic and strategic planning, 1905–1915* (1982) · D. French, 'The rise and fall of "business as usual"', *War and the state: the transformation of British government, 1914–1919*, ed. K. Burk (1982), 7–31 · M. Gilbert, *Winston S. Churchill*, 3: *1914–1916* (1971) · R. Jenkins, *Asquith*, 3rd edn (1986) · J. Singleton, 'The cotton industry and the British war effort, 1914–1918', *Economic History Review*, 2nd ser., 47 (1994), 601–18 · CGPLA Eng. & Wales (1927)

Archives HLRO, papers · Nuffield Oxf., corresp. and papers incl. diaries | BL, letters to Lord Gladstone, Add. MSS 46052–46805 · BLPES, corresp. with E. D. Morel · Bodl. Oxf., corresp. with L. Harcourt · Bodl. Oxf., letters to Herbert Asquith · HLRO, letters to David Lloyd George · U. Newcastle, Robinson L., letters to Walter Runciman · Women's Library, London, corresp. with Herbert Asquith relating to honours for women

Likenesses photograph, c.1899, NPG [*see illus.*] · Who, caricature, Hentschel-colourtype, NPG; repro. in *VF* (19 Oct 1910) · photograph, repro. in *The Times* (14 Dec 1926), 18

Wealth at death £91,756 16s. 5d.: probate, 3 Feb 1927, CGPLA Eng. & Wales

Emmwood. *See* Wood, John Bertram Musgrave- (1915–1999).

Empson, Hester Henrietta, Lady Empson (1915–1996). *See under* Empson, Sir William (1906–1984).

Empson, Sir Richard (c.1450–1510), administrator, was the son of Peter Empson (d. 1473) and his wife, Elizabeth Joseph. The story that he was the son of a sieve maker, first recorded by John Stow, was adopted by Francis Bacon but has no known factual basis—Peter Empson was of local consequence in Northamptonshire, holding property at Towcester and in nearby Easton Neston.

Servant of the crown Richard Empson trained as a lawyer, entering the Middle Temple, and on 1 July 1477 was granted the reversion of the office of attorney-general of the duchy of Lancaster in succession to Thomas Tremayle. Fees were paid from August that year, and although the infrequent duchy minutes record Tremayle as attorney still in the summer of 1478, Empson was certainly in full possession by 12 November, holding the position during good behaviour. He was removed from office by Richard III, possibly on account of his association with Anthony Woodville, Lord Rivers, executed in 1483, who had retained Empson as steward for his lands in Northamptonshire. But as an apprentice-at-law he continued to be employed by the duchy as counsel and on other business, and to attend council sessions. He even succeeded to Rivers's farm of Passenham, Northamptonshire. Restored as attorney-general for life on 13 September 1485, shortly after the accession of Henry VII, Empson surrendered the office on being appointed chancellor of the duchy, with a salary of 100 marks per annum, on 3 October 1505. He had acted as keeper of the duchy seal in the vacancy following the death in 1504 of Sir John Mordaunt, who had himself succeeded Sir Reynold Bray in 1503 after a vacancy during which Empson exercised many of Bray's responsibilities by the king's command, but was then passed over for the chancellorship itself. The king took personal custody of the indenture by which Empson undertook the office.

In the meantime Empson had been building up a position in the government of his native county and its surrounding shires. He was first appointed a JP for Northamptonshire on 10 November 1475, and remained a member of the county bench for the rest of his life. He was added to the Warwickshire commission from November 1490, being joined by his eldest son, Thomas, from November 1507, and to the Buckinghamshire bench from 1494. He was also recorder of Northampton by February 1490 and of Coventry by late 1491. He represented Northampton in parliament from 1489 to 1495, and in 1491 was chosen speaker; he probably sat in the parliaments of 1497 and 1504 also. He was regularly appointed to commissions with a wide range of administrative and judicial responsibilities in Northamptonshire from 1476 onwards, and took in a wider range of counties under Henry VII. He was included in the treason commissions in the midland counties in 1493, and in the west after the uprisings of 1497; during the latter Perkin Warbeck's proclamation named Empson as one of the king's 'low-born and evil counsellors'. Of the king's council by 1494, and of the council learned from its inception about 1498, by 1499 he was one of a small group of councillors, mostly lawyers, taking bonds in the king's name, or entering in feoffments on lands mortgaged to the king's use.

By 1501 Empson had become a councillor to Henry, duke of York, presumably by the king's appointment, and on 18 February 1504 he was one of many to be made a knight of the Bath when the duke's becoming prince of Wales was celebrated; in the process he secured release from an exchequer action for distraint of knighthood. He was appointed high steward of Cambridge University in the same year. Henry VII included him among his executors, having appointed him a trustee in 1504 for the lands enfeoffed to the use of his will; he also included Empson among the executors appointed to act after the king's death to hear and redress wrongs done by Henry or in his name. Those who gave fees to him as a lawyer included Queen Elizabeth of York, for whom he was a justice on eyre for her forests in 1489; Edward Stafford, third duke of Buckingham; Edward, Lord Hastings; Sir Walter Mantell, for whom he was also an executor; and the priors of Durham and of the houses of St James and St Andrew, Northampton. After Empson's death the prior of St James complained that he had retained him in order to secure the appropriation of Cold Norton Priory, but that Empson took the lease of the priory for himself. However, since Edmund Dudley gave Henry VII 750 marks in cash and bonds for Cold Norton's appropriation to St Stephen's, Westminster, from whom Empson obtained the lease, this charge may not represent the clear-cut abuse of position that it at first sight appears, especially as Empson's son, who held the annuity jointly with his father, later successfully sued for payment of arrears. Empson also had a long association, dating from the 1470s, with Luffield Priory; moreover he was steward of the liberty of Peterborough by 1490, and high steward of the abbey by 1505.

Gathering an estate From the 1470s lands in which Empson stood feoffee to the use of others are numerous and suggest a network of beneficial relationships centred on south Northamptonshire and its adjacent counties. His relationship with Sir Reynold Bray, one of Henry VII's chief ministers, was especially important in this respect. In February 1488 the bishop of Lincoln appointed the two men jointly constable and steward in Banbury, where Empson held property. With Bray he was appointed king's steward of Kenilworth, Warwickshire, in 1492, and of Ascot and Deddington, Oxfordshire, in March 1493, in each case for life, and he later succeeded Bray as steward of Sutton and Potton, Northamptonshire. A feoffee of Bray's by 1486, Empson was in 1503 an executor of his will, though his marriage of his own son John to Agnes Lovell, the niece of Bray's wife, may represent a breach of that trust. Other royal grants boosted Empson's local interests. On 9 September 1507 he was appointed steward of Higham Ferrers, Northamptonshire, and in the same year steward of Hanslope, Buckinghamshire, and Cosgrove, Northamptonshire. By the end of his life he had accumulated an estate worth between £200 and £300 per annum, in addition to a perhaps equivalent income from fees. Further income derived from a number of monastic properties which were held on long leases and realized a small profit above the rate of the farm, from properties held in wardship, and from lands and revenues farmed from the crown.

Empson's principal estates lay in Northamptonshire, centred on Towcester and Easton Neston, where he gradually acquired property from the mid-1470s, enlarging a minimal inheritance into a coherent landholding. The process, which was complemented after 1485 by his accumulation of local stewardships and other estate offices, was a protracted one. It was only in 1507 that he finally gained the lay manor of Towcester by an agreement with John Hussey and Edmund Dudley, through a collusive action against the earl of Kent (who retained a life annuity and compensated Hussey with other lands at Empson's expense); he had acquired the 'priors manor' within Towcester in 1502, in a hostile suit which later gave rise to a charge of forcible disseisin followed by a legal settlement under compulsion, although he appears to have paid the vendor the full market rate. Greenscourt manor in Easton Neston was similarly acquired in 1499 after litigation against Maud Green, whose son Sir Thomas Green was then under suspicion of treason, appearing both before Empson (at common law) and the council. He also purchased lands in Oxfordshire and Warwickshire, and in 1507 the Hampshire manor of Upclatford. Interests in other counties were acquired by lease or wardship, for instance the Gloucestershire manor of Sezincote, leased from John Greville, which he passed in his lifetime to his sons. Empson retained chambers in the Middle Temple, London, until at least 1503, by when he was a senior member of the inn. But from 1507 he was leasing a house in St Bride's from Westminster Abbey, and lands in Bridewell from Sir Thomas Docwra, the prior of the hospitallers. Empson invested heavily in these properties, intending them for his son Thomas.

Empson's moveable wealth is difficult to estimate. In 1491, before the significant expansion of his estates, he had contributed the relatively modest sum of £40 to the king's benevolence (admittedly this amounted to two years of his salary as attorney-general), and even in 1497 he advanced only £20 by way of loan for the wars in Scotland; he was in debt in 1509. However, by the late 1490s he was building substantially at Easton, and in 1499 obtained licence to impark, wall, and crenellate there, building gatehouses (which were said to obstruct the local highways) and a major range of buildings; he entertained the king there between 20 and 22 August 1507. He also spent considerable sums at St Bride's, although the precise location within the parish of the 'new council chamber of the duchy' remains unclear. After his death Empson's interests in St Bride's passed first to Thomas Wolsey and then to Henry VIII.

The intended beneficiaries of much of Empson's accumulation of wealth and property were his children, and it was partly on their behalf that from 1491 he acquired a number of wardships from the crown. The family of his wife, Jane, is unrecorded, though on the tenuous evidence of an entail she may have had lands in Buckinghamshire. With her he had at least two sons and four daughters. Empson arranged the marriage of Thomas, his eldest son, to Audrey or Etheldreda, daughter of Sir Guy Wolston, and that of his younger son, John, to Agnes Lovell, a coheiress whose wardship had been obtained by Edmund Dudley. His daughter Elizabeth married George Catesby (the son of Richard III's henchman), part of whose lands Empson

held at farm, in 1496, the year of her husband's restoration; her second husband, in August 1509, was Sir Thomas Lucy. Joan married first Henry Sotehill (d. 1504) and afterwards her father's client Sir William Pierrepoint, while Anne married her father's ward Robert Ingleton; she was widowed in 1503 and her second marriage, to John Higford, was made under compulsion, since in 1504 Higford was pardoned for her rape, burglary, and other offences. But Empson did secure the marriage of Ingleton's baby heir, afterwards married to Humphrey Tyrell. His daughter Mary was married to Edward, son of Richard Bulstrode, and his ward Richard Druell may also have become a son-in-law.

The king's hatchet man Behind the acquisition of status and riches lay the activities that have given Empson his unenviable reputation in history. These derived largely from his position as chancellor of the duchy of Lancaster and, associated with it, as the leading member after 1504 (along with the no less notorious Edmund Dudley) of the council learned in the law. As chancellor, Empson continued Bray's efforts to increase revenue, authorizing the raising of rents or disallowance of rebates, and directing surveys and audits, enclosures of commons, and investigations of feudal incidents. The drive to maximize feudal revenues, to pursue old bonds, and to manipulate the penal laws in the king's interests was centred on the council learned, even in those cases where parallel actions were sued at common law. Indictments brought against Empson in 1509, which can be backed by the independent evidence of the administrative record, usefully summarize his services to Henry VII in the latter's final years, and help to account for the opprobrium into which they brought both. The methods he used included the use of promoters for prosecution; imprisonment to facilitate settlement by fine or composition; and summonses issued (as in other council courts) by privy seal, but on Empson's fiat for appearance before him at St Bride's and elsewhere. His particular responsibilities were the authorization of pardons, countersigned by the king; the finding and traverse of intrusions and the issue of commissions of concealments; pardons and forfeitures on outlawry; wards and liveries of lands. Most actions or grants of grace resulted in fines to the king, in amounts and by methods which led Polydore Vergil and others to characterize both Empson and Dudley as extortioners.

Ruthless though he was, Empson acted by the king's command and was occasionally subject to his check, although Henry VII's frequent incapacity between 1507 and 1509 undoubtedly increased his influence. But he was also active at law on his own account, and on occasions used the power of his position to pervert the course of justice. The best-known example of this is his manipulation of assize commissions from 1501 to 1503 to disinherit Sir Robert Plumpton in the interests of Empson's daughter Joan Sotehill and her husband, the son of one of the heirs general of Sir William Plumpton, Robert's father. Charges of maintenance and embracery (corrupting the jury) in this suit seem to be well founded, despite the anachronism of Plumpton's allegation that Empson appeared at York in 1502 with an armed retinue of mounted gentlemen and liveried yeomen, and with footmen at his stirrup 'more liker the degree of a duke then a batchelor knight' (Kirby, 186): Empson was then still unbelted. He was the subject of a lampoon by the court composer and dramatist William Cornysshe, who was imprisoned for his pains. The poem has not survived, but its existence receives circumstantial confirmation from a bond given by Empson in July 1504 to keep the peace towards Cornysshe, and from a further oblique reference from Cornysshe's own pen, written in the same month.

Henry VII died on 21 April 1509, and Empson was arrested just three days later. He was indicted in both his private and public capacities before oyer and terminer commissions appointed later that year. Treason was read into his summons (for his own protection) of armed men to London as and after the king lay dying: for this he was charged before a special commission which met at Northampton on 8 August 1509. Taken from the Tower of London to Northampton Castle, Empson pleaded his own case at the bar of the court on 1 October, but was convicted and sentenced to the death of a traitor. He was attainted in the parliament of January–February 1510, and beheaded, along with Dudley, on Tower Hill on 17 August following. He was buried in the London Whitefriars; his wife survived him. His eldest son, Thomas, was restored in blood in 1512: one of his first acts was to grant a life annuity to Richard Trust, the servant who had had custody under Richard Empson of bonds taken on behalf of the crown, and who, along with Thomas himself, had shared his imprisonment in the Tower. **M. M. CONDON**

Sources Chancery records • R. Somerville, *History of the duchy of Lancaster, 1265–1603* (1953) • M. R. Horowitz, 'Richard Empson, minister of Henry VII', *BIHR*, 55 (1982), 35–49 • duchy of Lancaster, entry books of decrees and orders, PRO, DL 5/1–4 • duchy of Lancaster, accounts various, receivers-generals' accounts, PRO, DL 28/5–6 • duchy of Lancaster, chancery rolls, PRO, DL 37/62 • duchy of Lancaster, ministers' accounts, PRO, DL 29 • chancery, inquisitions post mortem, series II, PRO, C 142 • exchequer, inquisitions post mortem, series II, PRO, E 150 • court of king's bench, ancient indictments, PRO, KB 9 • court of king's bench, baga de secretis, PRO, KB 8/4 • court of king's bench, plea rolls, PRO, KB 27 • court of common pleas, plea rolls, PRO, CP 40 • court of common pleas, feet of fines, PRO, CP 25/1 • exchequer, treasury of receipt, miscellaneous books, PRO, E 36/14, 160, 174, 212, 214, 285 • exchequer, king's remembrancer, memoranda rolls, PRO, E 159/277 • exchequer, king's remembrancer, memoranda rolls, PRO, E 368 • chancery, warrants for the great seal, PRO, C 82 • special collections, ministers' accounts, PRO, SC 6 • state papers, Henry VIII, general series, PRO, SP 1/1, 3 • exchequer, treasury of receipt, ancient deeds, PRO, E 40 • wills, PRO, PROB 11/8, sig. 8 [Sir Walter Mantell]; PROB 11/13, sig. 26 [Sir Reynold Bray] • chancery: equity petitions, early, PRO, C 1 • muniments, Westminster Abbey • muniments of title, Northants. RO, Fermour–Heskith papers • BL, Add. MSS 21480, 59899; Lansdowne MS 127 • E. W. Ives, *The common lawyers of pre-Reformation England* (1983) • G. R. Elvey, ed., *Luffield Priory charters 2*, Buckinghamshire RS, 18 (1975) • W. T. Mellows, ed., *Peterborough local administration: the last days of Peterborough monastery*, Northamptonshire RS, 12 (1947) • M. D. Harris, ed., *The Coventry leet book*, 4 vols., EETS, 134, 135, 138, 146 (1907–13) • *The Plumpton letters and papers*, ed. J. Kirby, CS, 5th ser., 8 (1996) • R. Horrox and P. W. Hammond, eds., *British Library Harleian manuscript 433*, 4 vols. (1979–83) • *The Anglica historia of Polydore Vergil, AD 1485–1537*, ed. and trans. D. Hay, CS, 3rd ser., 74 (1950) • A. H. Thomas and I. D. Thornley, eds.,

The great chronicle of London (1938) • *Reports from the lost notebooks of Sir James Dyer*, ed. J. H. Baker, 1, SeldS, 109 (1994) • Baker, *Serjeants*, 267 • J. C. Wedgwood and A. D. Holt, *History of parliament*, 1: *Biographies of the members of the Commons house, 1439–1509* (1936) • *DNB*

Archives Westminster Abbey, muniments | Northants. RO, Fermour–Heskith MSS, muniments to title • PRO, Fermour and Lucy MSS

Likenesses group portrait, oils, Belvoir Castle, Leicestershire; repro. in N. Williams, *The life and times of Henry VII* (1973), p. 61

Wealth at death approx. £200–£300 in lands; £100 in goods: PRO, E 150; PRO, E 36/160; PRO, KB 8/4

Empson, William (1791–1852), lawyer and literary reviewer, was possibly the son of the Revd Amaziah Empson (1755–1798) and his wife, Ann, *née* Kelk, of Brigg. He was educated at Winchester College and then at Trinity College, Cambridge, where he graduated BA in 1812 and MA in 1815. He was called to the bar in 1819 and as a member of Lincoln's Inn practised until 1824 when he was appointed professor of law (of 'general polity and the laws of England') at the East India College, Haileybury, in succession to the philosopher and historian Sir James Mackintosh.

Empson began to write for the *Edinburgh Review* in 1823 during the last years of Francis *Jeffrey's editorship, and on Jeffrey's departure in 1829 was persuaded to support the appointment of Macvey Napier as his successor. Napier was based in Edinburgh and Empson, in London, acted as a *de facto* sub-editor, keeping the peace between Napier and his two most powerful contributors, Henry Brougham, who was bent on using the *Edinburgh* for his own political ends, and Macaulay, the review's rising star, whose brilliant essays helped to sustain its circulation during the early years of Napier's editorship. Empson was a prolific and versatile reviewer, writing on history, biography, literature, law, and politics over a period of nearly thirty years, often contributing two articles to a single number. Jeffrey found him a sympathetic and intellectually congenial colleague. Their relationship was further cemented in 1838 when Empson married his only daughter, Charlotte. For the more provincial Napier, Empson was the *Edinburgh Review*'s crucial London representative, channelling political and literary gossip and acting as a sounding board for metropolitan contributors. In the latter role Carlyle found him a welcome presence, exuding sanity, tolerance, and a gentlemanly demeanour, when he visited him in his lodgings in the Temple. Empson, he recalled, was clad in a flannel nightgown, reading a newspaper, 'a tall, broad thin man with wrinkled face, baldish head and large mild melancholy dreamy blue-eyes under bushy brows … in the threshold of mysticism' (*Collected Letters*, 5.378–9). His appearance suggested vagueness and other-worldliness, which was the case, but it cloaked a shrewdness and intelligence which served both Jeffrey and Napier well.

Following Napier's death in 1847, Empson assumed the editorship of the *Edinburgh Review*. Consequently the periodical moved its centre of operations to London, making it for the first time in its history 'Edinburgh' in name only. Harriet Martineau waspishly repeated the rumour that both Empson and Napier before him had routinely inserted all articles sent to the review by whig ministers and their associates, even when the articles contradicted each other (*Harriet Martineau's Autobiography*, 1.213). She also alleged that Empson did not have sufficient grip on the literary reviewing so that the *Edinburgh*'s reputation declined. Others took a more kindly view of his editorship, but it was undoubtedly the case that the influence of the review was waning. Empson's health was also failing. For the next five years he combined his career as a professor at the East India College with the responsibilities of editor. He died suddenly of influenza at Haileybury on 10 December 1852, and was survived by his wife.

JOANNE SHATTOCK

Sources J. Shattock, *Politics and reviewers: The Edinburgh and The Quarterly in the early Victorian age* (1989) · *Selections from the correspondence of … Macvey Napier*, ed. M. Napier (1879) · *Wellesley index* · H. Cockburn, *Life of Lord Jeffrey, with a selection from his correspondence*, 2 vols. (1852) · *Harriet Martineau's autobiography*, ed. M. W. Chapman, 3 vols. (1877) · *The collected letters of Thomas and Jane Welsh Carlyle*, ed. C. R. Sanders, K. J. Fielding, and others, [30 vols.] (1970–) · Venn, *Alum. Cant.*, 2/2 · *GM*, 2nd ser., 39 (1853), 99–100 · Boase, *Mod. Eng. biog.*, vol. 1
Archives BL, letters to Macvey Napier, Add. MSS 34616–34626 · Herts. ALS, letters to E. B. Lytton · NL Ire., letters to Thomas Spring-Rice · NL Scot., letters to John Burton · NL Scot., corresp. with Lord Rutherford · RS, corresp. with Sir John Herschel · U. St Andr., corresp. with James Forbes
Likenesses W. Walker, mezzotint (after J. Linnell), BM

Empson, Sir William (1906–1984), poet and literary critic, was born at Yokefleet Hall, Howden, near Goole, Yorkshire, on 27 September 1906, the youngest of five children of Arthur Reginald Empson (1853–1916), landowner, squire, and magistrate, of Yokefleet Hall, and his wife, Laura Micklethwait (1865–1944), daughter of Richard Micklethwait, of Ardsley House, near Barnsley, Yorkshire.

Early years, education, and expulsion, 1906–1929 After attending a preparatory school, Praetoria House, in Folkestone, Kent, where mathematics became his forte, in 1920 William was awarded a scholarship to Winchester College. At school he won an English literature prize even while specializing in mathematics and science; and in 1924 the Richardson prize for mathematics. 'I must never deny', he wrote later, 'what I felt at the time, that the other children (not the teachers at all) were giving me such a ripping education that it equipped a man to go anywhere in the world alone, from leaving school on' (letter to Desmond Lee, *c*.1955, Empson papers). When myopia prevented him from taking up the naval career his family wished for him, in 1925 he won a Milner scholarship in mathematics to Magdalene College, Cambridge, where he was tutored by A. S. Ramsey (father of the legendary mathematical prodigy Frank Ramsey and the future archbishop of Canterbury, Michael Ramsey). Though he gained the expected first class in part one of the mathematical tripos in 1926, he achieved only senior optime (upper second) in part two in 1928. He then registered for the recently established English tripos, under the tutelage of I. A. Richards, author of *Principles of Literary Criticism* (1924) and *Science and Poetry* (1926), and in June 1929 he won

Sir William Empson (1906–1984), by Rupert Shephard, *c*.1944

a first-class result, with 'special distinction', in the first part of the English tripos (a feat also achieved that year by Muriel Bradbook, future mistress of Girton College, Cambridge). As a prized student he was elected to a Charles Kingsley bye-fellowship for 1929–30.

Within a month, however, the master of Magdalene chose to make an example of an Empson inadvertence. When Empson was discovered by porters to be in possession of contraceptives, and was reported also to have entertained a woman in his rooms at a late hour, an extraordinary meeting of the governing body of the college resolved to deprive him of his junior fellowship and to remove his name from the books (since sexual misconduct was deemed to be a university offence). For the next two years he lived in London, where he established himself as a writer and was cultivated by literary figures including T. S. Eliot, Virginia Woolf, and Harold Monro.

Precocious publications, 1929–1930 At Cambridge Empson had written numerous reviews of books, film, and theatre for the *Cambridge Review* and for *The Granta* (for which he also served, while still a student of mathematics, as 'Skipper' or literary editor); and in 1928 he launched an avant-garde magazine, *Experiment*, co-edited with Jacob Bronowski, Humphrey Jennings, and Hugh Sykes Davies. In that year he also became president of a humanist discussion society, the Heretics.

It was at Cambridge, too, that Empson made his reputation as one of the outstanding poets of his generation, a 'rival' to W. H. Auden, who was emerging as leader of the Oxford Group (though Empson always called himself a minor poet in comparison to Auden). Many of the poems collected in his *Poems* (1935) first appeared in periodicals published in Cambridge, and his modest output was strongly represented in *Cambridge Poetry, 1929* (published by Leonard and Virginia Woolf at the Hogarth Press). The metaphysical density and emotional passion of his poetry met with astonishment and applause, such that the critic F. R. Leavis in the *Cambridge Review* (1 March 1929) hailed him as a true successor to John Donne (whom Empson took as his model). (A second volume, *The Gathering Storm*, appeared in 1940; the two collections were brought together in *Collected Poems*, 1949, and in an enlarged edition, 1955.) The poetry has a wide range of themes, from metaphysics to melancholy, from social climbing to political satire, and from love to loss, all of which are treated with stoic dignity. Though intellectually spry to a high degree, the poems give ample evidence of being inspired by much 'isolation and suffering', as Empson claimed in a letter to A. Alvarez (29 Aug 1956, BL). Above all, however, Empson was stimulated by the findings of modern science, which he once called 'the only fertile part of the contemporary mind' (letter to Qien Xuexi, 7 Sept 1947, priv. coll.). At Cambridge, where the Nobel prize-winning physicist Ernest Rutherford was director of the Cavendish Laboratory, and Sir Arthur Eddington professor of astronomy, Empson was enthralled by the latest advances in scientific knowledge, especially in physics and astronomy, so that the moral and philosophical implications of the new science became central to his work. The argumentative wit of his compacted and riddling poetry thus puzzles about, as well as suffers from, the 'strangeness of the world' (Duval Smith, BBC broadcast) and the conflicting problems of conduct and belief.

Yet Empson made his name outside Cambridge not so much through his poetry but with his precocious work of literary criticism, *Seven Types of Ambiguity*, which he began as an undergraduate in 1928 and published in November 1930 (when he was twenty-four), just sixteen months after being expelled from Magdalene. Provoked by the aesthetic theories of I. A. Richards, who claimed that the point of poetry is to balance 'impulses' so that a satisfying 'equilibrium' might be attained, Empson believed to the contrary that poetic utterance is fundamentally a function of conflict. He defined ambiguity as 'any verbal nuance, however slight, which gives room for alternative reactions to the same piece of language' (*Ambiguity*, rev. edn, 1953, 1). Taking from the run of English literature a plethora of passages (though not always complete poems, which formalist critics have felt to be a weakness of his approach), ranging from Spenser and Shakespeare through Herbert's 'The Sacrifice' to Hopkins's 'The Windhover', he traced the complexities of the ambiguous behaviour of poetic language through seven stages of 'advancing logical disorder'. The most extreme case, the seventh type, accordingly expresses, or betrays, a total contradiction in the writer's mind—whereby 'the two meanings of the word, the two values of the ambiguity, are the two opposite meanings defined by their context, so that the total effect is to show a fundamental division in

the writer's mind' (ibid., 192)—a state which Richards, with his sheer regard for the supposedly harmonizing powers of poetry, had refused to allow. Focusing principally on semantics and syntax, Empson aimed primarily to demonstrate, by means of analyses that are more lively, ingenious, and detailed than had ever been accomplished before in English literary criticism, just how the 'machine' that is a poem does its work. Though often claimed or criticized as a pioneer of the 'new criticism', a school which insisted upon the autonomy of the poem and discounted authorial intention and historical context, Empson eschewed any such affinity. The historical moment and the consciousness of the author were always to the fore in his thinking, he insisted (albeit he sometimes omitted to take account of them in his early work). All the same, no literary historian has disputed the fact that Empson's first book raised the standards of English literary–critical analysis.

Teaching and writing in the Far East, 1931–1939 From August 1931 to July 1934 Empson was a professor of English at Tokyo University of Literature and Science (Bunrika Daigaku), where he was appalled by the ethos of perniciously developing nationalism. 'Of course,' he wrote to a friend in November 1932, 'one feels the jingoism and official militarism like a weight on the back of the neck' (letter to Michael Roberts, 12 Nov 1932, priv. coll.). However, he enjoyed the company of his students, one of whom later remarked of him: 'What I liked most about him was his childlike naiveté, his forthrightness, his unwillingness to compromise on his opinions, and the way he would read books at every possible spare moment' (Sato Nabuo, 'Remembering Mr Empson', *Eibungaku-Fukai*, 2/1, 1934). He also went to exhausting lengths to comprehend the culture of the Far East. In particular he took every opportunity to study Buddhist religion and art; and throughout the 1930s he worked on a monograph entitled 'The faces of Buddha' (the sole copy of his text was lost by a friend in the 1940s). In addition he supported the interests of Basic English, a simplified form of the English language, with a rudimentary grammar and a vocabulary of only 850 words, devised by C. K. Ogden (1889–1957) and promoted by Richards. But Empson found Basic English less vital as what Ogden hoped it would become (an international 'auxiliary' language, for the benefit of science and peace), than as an excellent pedagogical device, a demonstrably practical 'first step in the direction of full English which gives the right feeling about the words'. Furthermore, he discovered, the system was just as instructive 'as a test of a bit of writing for the Englishman himself … For myself at least it has become a fixed process on reading something deeply true to see if it is still good sense in Basic' (Empson, *Argufying: Essays on Literature and Culture*, ed. J. Haffenden, 1987, 230).

Empson's second book, *Some Versions of Pastoral* (1935), took shape in Japan; and 'Proletarian literature' (the introductory essay) is a substantial document of the period and a permanently valid analysis. In the face of what Japan's rulers considered to be the dangerous flood of international communism, Empson judged that 'bourgeois' art would assuredly survive even in a proletarian state. While a 'pure' proletarian art might slip into propaganda, the social conflicts of which the pastoral is evidence would continue to produce a genuine art of implicit resistance. The 'trick' of the old pastoral, as Empson revalued it, was

> to imply a beautiful relation between rich and poor [and] to make simple people express strong feelings … The effect was in some degree to combine in the reader the merits of the two sorts; he was made to mirror in himself more completely the effective elements of the society he lived in.
> (*Some Versions of Pastoral*, 1966, 17)

Pastoral thus puts the 'complex into the simple', and works to conciliate the received social order (ibid., 49). The unorthodoxy of Empson's approach to pastoral as a mode inheres in the texts he chose to analyse, for they range from Milton's *Paradise Lost* to Gay's *The Beggar's Opera* and Carroll's *Alice*. Yet the idea of what the 'swain' represents in such texts, whether it is the rogue or the child, is the crux of Empson's thesis. At once insider and outsider, the quasi-divine (exemplary and exceptional) hero of pastoral, spokesperson for both the many and the one, is the type of the 'Christ and scapegoat': hero and anti-hero, redeemer and victim, reconciler and critic. By so assimilating and assuaging areas of potential and actual conflict in society, the pastoral hero ultimately stands for a secret freedom from the doctrines of both church and state. Empson's exploration of his theme thus goes to the heart of the very purpose of art. As he summed up his great and enduring argument, 'literature is a social process, and also an attempt to reconcile the conflicts of an individual in whom those of society will be mirrored' (ibid., 22).

In 1937 Empson went east again, to teach at the Peking National University. But as ill luck would have it he arrived at his post on a Japanese troop train: he found himself in the thick of the Sino-Japanese War, forced to flee from the advancing Japanese with the northern Chinese universities and enduring two years of what he called 'the savage life and the fleas and the bombs' (Empson papers). There is a splendid pen-portrait of Empson in China by Victor Purcell in *Chinese Evergreen* (1938), in which Empson is scarcely disguised as Dudley. He was in fact the only European to share the academic exodus with the Chinese intellectuals, and stoically survived a poor diet, primitive living quarters, and even a personal assault by bandits. To begin with, from November 1937 to February 1938, he worked with the temporary university at a monastic site on a sacred mountain called Nan-Yueh, near Changsha in Hunan province (where he wrote one of his most richly meditative poems, 'Autumn on Nan-Yueh'). Thereafter, in 1938–9, he was with the National Southwest Associated University, first in the primitive town of Mengtzu and then in Kunming, the capital of Yunnan province, near the Indo-China (later Vietnam) border. Since there were no books to study, he managed the extraordinary feat of teaching his courses almost entirely from memory. Moreover, he gained well-deserved status in the Chinese classical tradition of venerably inebriated poets.

The war years, marriage, and after, 1940–1952 Back in England during the Second World War Empson joined the BBC, working first as a sub-editor for the monitoring service at Wood Norton Hall, Worcestershire. Upon transferring to the overseas service in London in 1941, he became a talks assistant and then Chinese editor, organizing broadcasts to China as well as propaganda programmes for the Home Service (including drama-documentaries such as 'Japan wants the earth' and 'The Battle of the Yangtze'). One of his colleagues and friends was the restless and prickly Indian services editor, George Orwell, who continually chafed at the knowledge that his broken health prevented him from being a war correspondent. According to the BBC's own monitoring service, the biting effectiveness of Empson's work for the BBC provoked the Nazi propagandist Hans Fritzsche to call him a 'curly-headed Jew'—a charge which gave him enormous satisfaction.

At the BBC Empson met a South African artist, Hester Henrietta (Hetta) Crouse [Hester Henrietta Empson] (1915–1996) [*see below*], a handsome and forthright woman who was working for the Afrikaans service. They were married in London on 2 December 1941 at St Stephen's Church, Hampstead, and had two sons. In 1947 he returned with his family to the Peking National University, where he found himself caught up in the communist siege of the city at the close of 1948—he crossed the fighting lines to deliver a weekly lecture on Shakespeare at a university outside the walls—and witnessed Mao Zedong's triumphant entry in 1949. 'I was there for the honeymoon between the universities and the communists,' he recalled; 'we were being kept up to the mark rather firmly' (*The Strengths of Shakespeare's Shrew: Essays, Memoirs and Reviews*, ed. J. Haffenden, 1996, 216). In 1948 and 1950 he travelled to teach at the Kenyon College summer school in Ohio, USA. The second of those trips he thought especially 'plucky', for he relished the comic irony of his situation: 'My position here really seems to me very dramatic; there can be few other people in the world who are receiving pay simultaneously and without secrecy from the Chinese Communists, the British Socialists, and the capitalist Rockefeller machine' (letter to Hetta Empson, undated, priv. coll.).

From the late 1930s to the 1940s Empson drafted a series of interrelated critical essays, many of them incited by the ideas of his mentor Richards, which were collected in *The Structure of Complex Words* (1951). Richards postulated a distinction between emotive language (the 'pseudo-statements' of poetry) and cognitive or referential language (the stuff of science). Empson in *Complex Words* argues back that it is wrong to split the atom of sense-and-feeling in poetic utterance. Through a sequence of compellingly detailed analyses he proceeds to demonstrate how key words, such as 'wit' in Pope's *Essay on Criticism*, 'fool' in *King Lear*, and 'sense' in *The Prelude*, coalesce emotions, senses, and even doctrines. 'Roughly,' he wrote in 1955, 'the moral is that a developing society decides practical questions more by the way it interprets words it thinks obvious and traditional than by its official statements of current dogma' (Kunitz and Colby, 308). His comprehension of the complex historical freight of language validates his method in the volume, and the theory of poetic value he adduces; the work is marred only by the rather eccentric quasi-mathematical 'machinery' he erects as a scaffolding round the headily perceptive analyses of the individual essays.

Later years and controversies, 1952–1984 In 1952, when the British Council withdrew its subsidy for his post in Peking (where he learned about the initial stages of 'the dragooning of independent thought and the hysteria of the confession meetings,' as he put it), Empson returned to England. From 1953 to 1971 he held the chair of English literature at the University of Sheffield, where he engaged more vigorously than ever before in public controversy, spurred on by a desire to correct what he believed to be the wrong-headed orthodoxies of modern literary criticism—most notably the influence of what he designated 'neo-Christianity'. 'I was considered a bold appointment,' he acknowledged on his retirement (*Argufying*, 1987, 641).

Empson acquired massive publicity for his view of the wickedness of Christianity when he published *Milton's God* in 1961. The snag in his approach, which gave some reviewers the opportunity to criticize the book, lay in the fact that he confronted the Christian God through a work of literary imagination, on the perilous assumption that Milton's version of God could be identified with the 'truth' of the gospel. While C. S. Lewis, in *A Preface to 'Paradise Lost'* (1942), had demonstrated the orthodoxy of Milton's theology, other critics found poem and doctrine incommensurable. By arguing that Christianity was morally ugly, Empson praised Milton's integrity in outstaring the myth in poetry that was all the more brilliant because unblinking. 'The poem is wonderful because it is an awful warning,' he wrote in an unpublished blurb. 'The effort of reconsidering Milton's God, who makes the poem so good just because he is so sickeningly bad, is a basic one for the European mind.' In *Ambiguity* he had not perceived himself as a polemicist; he had simply practised the close reading of literature in terms of 'depth psychology'. In his later years he resolved to reconstruct any and every kind of literary student—the mass of misreaders—for 'the intentions of the authors [they read]', he insisted in a letter, 'were very unlikely to be so nasty as those of your many-legged neo-Christian torture-worshippers' (letter to Mr Montague, undated, Empson papers).

The customary critical verdict on the post-war Empson is that he became virulently obsessed with exploding the myths of Christianity. But he had studied the ethics of what he called 'the other half of Christian theology, let alone the other half of the old world—India and China and their satellites', and thought it a sickening symptom of the very habit of mind he opposed that so many critics interpreted his anti-Christianity as a blind assault on the One God. 'What is heartening about people,' he wrote in 1940, 'is the appalling stubbornness and the strong roots of their various cultures, rather than the ease with which you can convert them' (*Argufying*, 1987, 373). A number of readers see only the one facet of Empson, the supposed bigot who assailed Christianity. The side they neglect, the equally important aspect of his revisionary campaign, is the Empson who laboured to recover a hopeful and humane view of ethics and literary interpretation, as in his writings on Marlowe's *Dr Faustus*, on Donne and Marvell, and on Coleridge's *The Ancient Mariner* (in a controversial edition, *Coleridge's Verse*, edited with David Pirie, 1972).

'It is of great importance now,' Empson wrote in the 1950s,

> that writers and other artists should try to keep a certain world-mindedness ... Without the literatures you cannot have a sense of history, and history is like the balancing-pole of the tightrope-walker (it looks only a nuisance, but without it he would fall off); and nowadays we very much need the longer balancing-pole of not national but world history.

Despite some interpretative excesses, the world-mindedness of Empson's work, with its passion for a rational, humanistic standard of debate and ethical incisiveness, has secured his place as one of the giants of twentieth-century literature and criticism.

A shy and essentially solitary (though sociable) man, with a rapid, shuffling gait, tense, impatient movements, and a childlike gentleness, Empson left some with an impression of slightly arrogant courtesy. 'I am a proud man, but, good heavens,' he once remarked, 'I'm not a vain man—vanity is silly.' In his later years, as Graham Hough remarked in an obituary, he looked like 'something between a slightly batty retired colonel and a Taoist sage' (Hough, 16–17). His literary acumen, his oblivious eccentricity, and his personal generosity won him great esteem and affection among his colleagues and students; and so did his conversational wit.

Empson held visiting appointments at the University of Ghana (1964), the State University of New York at Buffalo (1968), York University, Toronto (1973), Pennsylvania State University (1974–5), and the University of Miami (1982). He received honorary doctorates from East Anglia (1968), Bristol (1971), Sheffield (1974), and Cambridge (1977); and he was knighted in 1979. He died at his home, Studio House, 1 Hampstead Hill Gardens, London, on 15 April 1984 from cirrhosis of the liver. He was cremated at Golders Green and his ashes were scattered at the cottage of his son Jacob at Harwood Dale, Yorkshire. Posthumous publications include *Essays on Shakespeare* (1986), *Argufying: Essays on Literature and Culture* (1987), *Faustus and the Censor* (1987), *Essays on Renaissance Literature* (2 vols., 1993–4), *The Strengths of Shakespeare's Shrew* (1996), and *Complete Poems* (2000).

Hester Henrietta [Hetta] **Empson** [*née* Crouse], Lady Empson (1915–1996), sculptor and political activist, was born on 18 September 1915 in Kroonstad, a small town in the Orange Free State, South Africa, the daughter of Johannes Jacobus Crouse, a fierce and powerful cattle dealer. Her family traced its ancestry back to David Sénécal (Senechal), a Huguenot refugee, who arrived in South Africa in the 1690s, married a Parisienne, and fathered eleven children. Brought up strictly as a member of the Dutch Reformed church (she said later that she was a lapsed Lutheran), Hetta studied humanities for two years at Bloemfontein University. In Cape Town she worked as an apprentice to Midford Barbiton, a well-known South

African sculptor; her works of the time include a bas-relief cornucopia for the façade of the post office at Stellenbosch. She went on to study art in Munich, and on returning to South Africa she earned her living as publicity manager for a communist-orientated weekly paper, *The Guardian*. She read the Marxist classics, and while living in Johannesburg became actively involved in the African situation, organizing the laundry workers' union. She later said that she was inspired by 'saint-like' communists in Johannesburg and Cape Town to 'help the blacks to recognise their worth'. When posted to an uninviting small town in the northern Transvaal, she got to know many Jewish farmers, and convinced them to give financial aid to combat the prevalent brown shirt movement.

But as a passionate artist Hetta Crouse also wished to visit the galleries of Europe. Together with a fellow artist, René Graetz, they did a 'dirty thing' to raise money: they cashed in on the centenary of the great trek of 1836 by designing and printing anniversary ties. Once they had accumulated £40 each, they travelled by steamer to Europe, and after a period in France and Switzerland Hetta took poorly paid jobs in London; she even claimed to have modelled for Vanessa Bell. In the early years of the Second World War she drove an ambulance for the ARP, which she continued to do, courageously, throughout the blitz. Because of her pro-Soviet allegiances she felt unable to take a more active part in the war effort, but Hitler's betrayal of the Russo-German pact changed all that. Answering a BBC advertisement for a speaker of Afrikaans, she was involved with a woman's magazine programme, and as Soekie Trottle she broadcast a laconic propaganda piece, calculated to combat the German propaganda aimed at South Africa.

At the BBC's training unit Hetta Crouse met William Empson, and they were engaged soon afterwards. When Empson warned her that if she married him she would have to accompany him to China, she told him she was eager to go. With her tall and slim good looks, her exuberance and strength of character, he felt that she could provide him with the 'backing and stiffening' he needed from a wife. She was attracted to his intelligence and wit. George Orwell, their colleague at the BBC, refused to come to the wedding: he had at one time proposed to Hetta. Ominously he sent the couple a carving knife and fork as a wedding present. Hetta enjoyed discussing politics with Orwell (though 'I was a Marxist, and he was a Trot'), and she found him 'enchanting, very imaginative and very sweet; child-like in a way': he taught her to construct a hay-box, a device that kept porridge hot. But she had no interest in developing a closer relationship. Orwell's jealousy soon passed, and the Empsons remained on good terms with him. The Empsons had two sons, William Hendrik Mogador and Jacobus Arthur Calais, each given an English name, an Afrikaans name, and the name of a town captured by the allies on the day of their birth. Jacob recalled that he was almost called Dago Island, but 'fortunately for me news came in at the last minute of the siege of Calais' (private information).

While in China with her husband Hetta supported the communist cause in the civil war, and she helped persecuted students escape the purges of Guomindang, the nationalist government. 'She saved lives', Empson related with pride. In 1948 she made an expedition through the war zone into Inner Mongolia, and her account of that extraordinary journey, together with observations on life in Peking during the first year after the liberation, is included in *Contemporary Chinese Woodcuts* (1950). At the end of 1948, during the six-week siege of Peking, Hetta was accredited as a correspondent for *The Observer*. After witnessing the inauguration of the People's Republic of China she continued to put faith in the communist government throughout the early years of the new regime. David Hawkes, a close friend in China, who later held the chair of Chinese at Oxford, remembered that Hetta spoke Chinese in an idiosyncratic way ('incantatory, ululatory, full of despairing cadences'), and that she was 'a free spirit, the first really free spirit I had ever met'. Her most notable work of art from that period was a bronze bust of Sardar Pannikar, the Indian ambassador and doyen of the diplomatic corps.

In later years, while Empson worked at Sheffield, Hetta lived in London, cultivating and supporting artists, writers, and politicians ranging from Tambimuttu and Semakula Mulumba to Louis MacNeice and Elizabeth Smart. She posed nude for Felix Topolski, who remembered that Hetta, not having done it before, 'trembled all over reclination at first, thus implanting flesh-awareness on to her remarkable South African-moulded monumentality. With the years she developed her innate dominance—an impressive stomping far from motherly personage.' Admired for her flamboyant conviviality and sense of drama, Hetta was the cynosure of a large circle. Among the hand-picked lodgers at Studio House in Hampstead were the anarchist and writer A. G. (Dinah) Stock, the puppeteer John Wright, the broadcaster Bob Harris, and the biologist Lewis Wolpert. Fay Weldon remembered her as brave, beautiful, and wild, 'so powerful and extraordinary a personality … She always knew things nobody else did.' She openly took a number of lovers, including the journalist and BBC producer Peter Duval Smith (they had a son, Simon), and a former sailor Michael Avery (Josh) who was the hero of Nigel Richardson's fictionalized biography *Dog Days in Soho* (2000).

In her later years Hetta continued to relish adventurous travel, and in her late seventies visited the Galápagos Islands. Her grandson recalled that when they travelled on camels through the Sahara desert, looking for neolithic cave paintings, Hetta taught him to make Afghan butter (with hashish), and to mix cocktails based on surgical spirit. Hetta Empson died at the Royal Free Hospital, Camden, on 22 December 1996, and was cremated in London. Her last words were: 'Get me a strong Scotch'.

JOHN HAFFENDEN

Sources Harvard U., Houghton L., Empson papers · Magd. Cam., I. A. Richards collection · W. Empson, *The royal beasts and other works*, ed. J. Haffenden (1986) · P. Gardner and A. Gardner, *The god approached: a commentary on the poems of William Empson* (1978) · R. Gill, ed., *William Empson: the man and his work* (1974) · R. Luckett and R. Hyam, 'Empson and the engines of love: the governing body decision of 1929', *Magdalene College Magazine and Record*, new ser., 35 (1990–91), 33–40 · S. J. Kunitz and V. Colby, eds., *Twentieth-century authors: a biographical dictionary of modern literature, first supplement* (1955), 307 · F. Day, *Sir William Empson: an annotated bibliography* (1984) · P. Duval Smith, ed., 'The poems of William Empson' [BBC Third Programme, 15 Dec 1952] · BBC WAC · F. R. Leavis, 'Cambridge poetry', *Cambridge Review*, 50 (1 March 1929), 317–18 · 'Graham Hough thinks about William Empson and his work', *London Review of Books* (21 June–4 July 1984), 16–17 · BL, A. Alvarez papers · d. cert. · private information (2004) [Hetta Empson] · d. cert. [Hester Henrietta Empson]

Archives BBC WAC · Harvard U., Houghton L., papers · NL Scot., letters · U. Reading L., corresp. and literary papers | King's AC Cam., letters to John Hayward · Magd. Cam., I. A. Richards collection · U. Hull, Brynmor Jones L., Hetta Empson collection | SOUND BL NSA

Likenesses R. Shephard, oils, *c.*1944, NPG [*see illus.*] · K. Hutton, photograph, 1946, Hult. Arch. · K. Hutton, R. K. Ieboe, B. Brandt, H. Magee, F. Reiss and M. Severn, photograph, 1946, Hult. Arch. · S. Barker, photograph · F. Godwin, photograph

Wealth at death £193,666: probate, 17 Sept 1984, *CGPLA Eng. & Wales* · £660,201—Hester Henrietta Empson: probate, 9 April 1997, *CGPLA Eng. & Wales*

Emrys ap Iwan. *See* Jones, Robert Ambrose (1848–1906).

Emu. *See* Dyson, William Henry (1880–1938).

Ena, princess of Battenberg (1887–1969), queen of Spain, consort of Alfonso XIII, was born Victoria Eugénie Julie Ena at Balmoral on 24 September 1887, the second child and only daughter of Princess *Beatrice (1857–1944) and Prince *Henry of Battenberg (1858–1896) [*see under* Beatrice, Princess]. She was the youngest grandchild of Queen *Victoria; her last name, Ena, by which she was invariably known in England and by her own family, was especially chosen for her by her grandmother as 'a Gaelic Highland name' (Noel, 4) to mark the first royal birth to take place in Scotland since that of Charles I.

Ena was educated privately and spent her childhood largely at the royal residences of Windsor, Osborne, and Balmoral; her father, governor of the Isle of Wight, died when she was only nine. She developed into a tall, blonde, slender beauty and on 31 May 1906 was married to the nineteen-year-old King Alfonso XIII of Spain (1886–1941), then widely regarded as Europe's most eligible bachelor. Ena—known variously thereafter as Queen Ena, Queen Victoria, and Queen Victoria Eugénie—had been first received into the Roman Catholic church, which led to some resentment at the match in Great Britain, while in Spain there was opposition from ultra-conservative elements in church, aristocracy, and court. Her unpopularity among these elements increased when it became known that she carried the blood disease haemophilia, which she had inherited from Queen Victoria. It was alleged at the time in Spain—and the charge has endured—that because of the British desire for a Spanish royal match, no warning was ever extended about this to the Spanish government or royal family. A clear warning had in fact been given through the Spanish ambassador in London, the marqués de Villa-Urrutia, while King Alfonso's aunt, the infanta Eulalia, had counselled him against the union on this ground (Noel, 54–8).

In the event two of the four surviving sons of Alfonso and Ena were haemophiliacs; the eldest son, Alfonso, prince of the Asturias (1907–1938), was a chronic invalid from his youngest days, and like his younger brother Gonzalo (1914–1934) he died as an indirect result of the disease, in a car accident. Jaime (1908–1975) was deaf from the age of four and later renounced all claim to the Spanish throne; and only Juan Carlos (1913–1993) enjoyed perfect good health. There were also two daughters, Beatriz (1909–1986) and Maria Christina (1911–1996). King Alfonso was deeply affected by this series of family tragedies and, though he had known about the risks of their union, he turned bitterly against Ena after about five years of marriage. Thereafter he became increasingly unfaithful, taking numerous mistresses and fathering several illegitimate children.

Alfonso's reign was beset increasingly by political unrest. A grim foretaste of this, particularly to Ena as a newcomer to Spain, came when an anarchist's bomb was hurled at their carriage on their wedding day. Several bystanders and members of the royal staff were killed and many others injured; the newly married couple only narrowly escaped death.

The First World War was a difficult time for Ena, as many in the Spanish court, including her mother-in-law, were sympathetic to the German cause. Her fondness for Parisian fashions, too, did little to endear her to conservative elements in the court, who regarded some of her dresses as 'indecent'. She achieved great popularity in the country at large, however, thanks to her extensive charitable and philanthropic work. She reorganized the Spanish Red Cross, which came to be of vital international importance during the war; established a lottery to fund improvements in medical services and new hospitals; and was founder and president of both the Anti-Tuberculosis League and the Anti-Cancer League. She was the founder, too, of a needlework guild, the Ropero de Santa Victoria, and she did much to encourage the reform of education at a time when illiteracy was widespread in Spain.

In the elections of 1931 there were heavy reverses for the monarchist party, as King Alfonso had become fatally identified with the rule of Primo de Rivera and thereby lost the favour of the Spanish people. He did not abdicate immediately but left the country on 14 April in order to avoid civil war. Ena followed the next day with their children, having been escorted to the French frontier by the troops of Spain's nascent second republic. The republican government was popular to begin with, but was subverted by ultra-conservative forces and was eventually overturned after a bloody civil war whose victor, General Francisco Franco, would not then countenance the restoration of the Bourbon monarchy.

Ena and Alfonso separated almost immediately upon their arrival in France, never to be reconciled. The king abdicated on 15 January 1941 and died soon afterwards in Rome on 28 February. Ena, then also living in Rome, returned briefly to England and for some years lived in London at 34 Porchester Terrace. After the Second World War she settled at Lausanne in Switzerland, though she continued to pay regular visits to England. Her third son, Juan Carlos, count of Barcelona, was by this time the claimant to the Spanish throne, but because of his liberal views he was strongly opposed by Franco. Ena was likewise antipathetic towards the Caudillo, who found himself outmanoeuvred in 1968 when she visited Spain for the baptism of her great-grandson Felipe. Franco received her and tried to play down the event, but her rapturous public reception was certainly a factor in the awakening of popular feeling in Spain for a restored monarchy.

Ena died at Vieille Fontaine, her home in Lausanne, on 15 April 1969 and was buried initially at the church of the Sacred Heart, Ouchy, Lausanne; she was later reinterred in the Spanish royal mausoleum at the Escorial. On 22 July 1969 Franco selected her grandson Juan Carlos (b. 1938) to be his successor-designate as head of state, with the title prince of Spain. He had always had a close bond with his grandmother, who—mindful of her own experiences as a foreigner at the Spanish court—had set him phonetic exercises to teach him the correct pronunciation of Castilian Spanish. Soon after his proclamation as king of Spain on 22 November 1975, Juan Carlos led his country back to democracy, thus undoing many of the injustices of the Franco years that had so dismayed his father and grandmother.   GERARD NOEL

Sources Royal Arch. · G. Noel, *Ena, Spain's English queen* (1984) · Royal Archives, Madrid · J. M. Potts and W. T. W. Potts, *Queen Victoria's gene* (1995) · *Burke's guide to the royal family* (1973) · DNB
Archives Archivo General de Palacio, Madrid, corresp., etc. · Royal Arch., corresp., etc.
Likenesses photographs, c.1890–1924, Hult. Arch.

Énda mac Conaill (*fl.* 6th cent.?). *See under* Munster, saints of (*act. c.*450–*c.*700).

Endecott, John (d. 1665), colonial governor, is of unknown parentage and first appears in the historical record when he was sent by the New England Company to take charge of its settlements near Cape Anne in 1628. The most recent genealogical research casts doubts on earlier claims that he was born in Devon, perhaps as early as 1588. There is no reliable record of his life, education, or activities before 1628. Nevertheless his correspondence shows him to have been well read and thoughtful, and a Jesuit priest who visited Massachusetts in 1651 reported that he conversed 'with Sieur Indicott, who speaks and understands French well' (*Jesuit Relations*, 36.94–5), which, along with the trust reposed in him by the colonial authorities, suggests that he was well educated.

A Devon background would explain his involvement with the Dorchester Adventurers, a company that had sought to develop a fishing enterprise off the coast of New England and had placed colonists on Cape Anne as early as 1623. When the venture faltered, the Revd John White of Dorchester, along with John Humfry and other members of the company, worked to transform the settlements into a refuge for puritans. The assets of the company were transferred and a new grant sought from the Council for New England. Endecott was one of the patentees of the newly formed New England Company for a plantation in Massachusetts Bay and a 1628 list of forty-one adventurers indicates that like most of his fellow investors he pledged £50. On 20 June of that year he sailed on the *Abigail* to take charge of the existing settlements.

The inhabitants of the original Cape Anne settlements had moved to Naumkeag, a location on the coast of the mainland, and it was there that Endecott arrived on 6 September to assume the governance of the colony. The New England Company primarily consisted of investors from the English west country but during 1628 began to reach out to broaden its base. The new members, even more puritan in background than those they joined, sought a reorganization and a royal charter to secure their investment, receiving patent as the Massachusetts Bay Company in March 1629. Endecott, who was probably aware of these manoeuvres before he left England, was listed as an officer of the new company and continued his efforts at Naumkeag in their name. In fact, Matthew Craddock, the first governor of the Massachusetts Bay Company, referred to Endecott's wife, Anne Gower, who died in 1629, as his 'cousin'. Endecott married again on 18 August 1630; his second wife was Elizabeth Gibson (b. c.1609), probably the daughter of Philobert Cogan. It is possible that he married yet a third time. He had at least three sons, two of whom were with Gibson.

Endecott demonstrated a quick temper and strong religious zeal in his early years in the colony. His management of Naumkeag, which he renamed Salem, proved to be controversial. In the autumn he visited the nearby settlement called Merrymount, where Thomas Morton's trade with the American Indians had recently been stopped by Plymouth Colony's Captain Miles Standish. Morton had been sent back to England but some of his supporters remained. Endecott cut down the maypole which had been the centre of revelry at the site, and warned the settlers against further disorder and illegal trade. He established positive relations with the pilgrim colonists at Plymouth, drawing on that colony's experience and material support to advance the survival of Salem. He supported the revds Samuel Skelton and Francis Higginson in establishing a Congregational church at Salem, and defended them against attacks from English puritans such as John Cotton, who accused the colonists of turning towards separatism. When two prominent settlers, John and Samuel Browne, criticized those church forms, he had them expelled and shipped back to England.

With the arrival of the *Arbella* in 1630, Endecott turned over the reins of government to John Winthrop, the recently elected governor of the company whose arrival in the bay signalled the merger of colony and company government. Winthrop and his fellow emigrants carried the charter with them, relocating the government to the colony and thereby gaining a large degree of autonomy. In addition, Winthrop soon moved the seat of administration from Salem to Boston. Endecott became an assistant under the new regime, with the powers of justice of the peace. As the foremost magistrate in Salem he played an important role in the colony's dealings with Roger Williams. Endecott initially defended the Salem church's

1633 decision to call Williams to be its teacher, but gradually dissociated himself from Williams when the latter's more extreme views emerged. Endecott again became the centre of a storm when he cut the red cross from the English ensign during a muster of the Salem train band in 1634. Winthrop and others agreed with him that the cross was a popish item, and quietly eliminated further use of the ensign. But it was feared that Endecott's action might provoke royal action against the colony, and so the court of assistants censured the Salem leader and disabled him from holding office for a year for having shown improper zeal and having acted on his own without consulting his fellow magistrates. He was returned to office as soon as his deprivation expired.

In 1636 Endecott commanded the bay colony's expedition to punish the Pequot Indians for the deaths of John Oldham and other English settlers in the area that would become Connecticut. Rather than settling the dispute, Endecott's destruction of American Indian villages only exacerbated the rift, which resulted in the Pequot War of 1637 and the almost complete extermination of the tribe. After the 1636 division of the colony into four districts, later renamed counties, he headed the Essex district bench. In 1640 he was one of the bay commissioners who reached an amicable agreement settling the border between Massachusetts and Plymouth. When the colony briefly experimented with a standing council, he was one of those chosen to life terms. Endecott was also regularly chosen as a colony assistant, and in 1644 he was elected to a term as governor, distinguishing himself for a new, more conciliatory style. The following year he was chosen the colony's sergeant-major-general, second only to the governor as commander of the colony's military forces.

When John Winthrop died in 1649 the colonists again chose Endecott governor, returning him to that post in thirteen of the next fifteen years. Bowing to his new responsibilities he soon moved from Salem to Boston. The Endecott era saw the colony coping with the consequences of England's civil wars. As governor he was forced to deal in the 1650s with the influx of what the colonists viewed as heresies that had emerged in England during the turmoil of the interregnum. Baptists were imprisoned, confuted to the satisfaction of the orthodox, and banished or, on occasion, whipped. But such tested methods of dealing with dissent were not sufficient to discourage Quakers, who began to arrive and spread their message in the summer of 1656, and proved eager to return to the colony after being sentenced to banishment. The aggressiveness of the sect triggered an escalation of legislative sanctions, calling for physical mutilation and then, when this failed, a new law in 1658 prescribing banishment on pain of death. Under the terms of this law, in October 1659, Endecott approved the execution of three Quakers, though providing a last-minute reprieve to one of them, Mary Dyer. But when Dyer returned to the colony yet again in the following year, she too was executed. Popular uneasiness at these harsh measures led to modifications in the law in 1661, but before the changes could take effect persecution of all Quakers was brought to a halt by order of Charles II.

The Restoration had presented Endecott with another serious challenge to the colony. Like most New Englanders he had supported the parliamentary cause, though he had been reluctant to do anything that would acknowledge too great a subjection of the colony to any English government. It had been under his leadership that the colony in 1652 established a mint and began to coin its own currency. In 1654 he approved the raising of up to 500 volunteers to join an expedition dispatched by Oliver Cromwell to aid New Haven and Connecticut in an attack on the Dutch New Netherland colony. When peace with the Dutch terminated that plan, the expedition was redirected to the conquest of Acadia. With the fall of the protectorate, Endecott was one of those helping the fleeing regicides Edward Whalley and William Goffe to find refuge in New England, and as governor misled the royal agents empowered to track down the two fugitives. He was responsible for delaying the colony's recognition of the Restoration, but finally acquiesced in the tardy proclamation of the new king's authority in August 1661. Endecott worked hard to fend off efforts of the English government to undermine the New England way, seeking to preserve the purposes of the colony in defiance of new imperial realities. Under his leadership Massachusetts appointed agents to represent their cause before the Council for Foreign Relations and developed new ties with English friends in a position to lobby for the colony.

Endecott died in Boston on 15 March 1665 and was buried at Boston's Granary burial-ground. While chronically short of currency, he had acquired a substantial estate, most of which consisted of real estate in Salem and the surrounding area. Endecott has generally been overshadowed by John Winthrop in accounts of the colony, and his zeal in persecuting Baptists and Quakers is often contrasted with Winthrop's more moderate character. But the two men were generally allied in the disputes of the 1630s and 1640s, and Endecott's selection to replace Winthrop suggests that the colonists saw him as likely to carry on Winthrop's policies. Faced with the new circumstances ushered in by the Restoration, he struggled to continue the course the colony had taken from its founding. The diarist John Hull captured the contemporary judgement when he called him 'a man of pious and zealous spirit' who had 'died poor, as most of our rulers do, having more attended the public than their own private interests'.

FRANCIS J. BREMER

Sources L. S. Mayo, *John Endecott* (1936) · *The journal of John Winthrop, 1630–1649*, ed. R. S. Dunn, J. Savage, and L. Yeandle (1996) · W. Bradford, *History of Plymouth plantation*, ed. C. Deane (1856) · R. C. Anderson, ed., *The great migration begins: immigrants to New England, 1620–1633*, 1 (Boston, MA, 1995) · W. C. Endicott, *John Endecott and John Winthrop* (1930) · *The Jesuit relations and allied documents*, 36 (1899) · C. L. Cohen, 'Winthrop, John', *ANB* · *New England Historical and Genealogical Register*, 1 (1847), 201–24
Archives Mass. Hist. Soc., MSS
Likenesses D. L. Glover, stipple, NPG · oils; known to be in family possession, in 1888 · oils (after portrait, 1665?), Mass. Hist. Soc.;

repro. in A. Oliver, A. M. Huff, and E. W. Hanson, *Portraits in the Massachusetts Historical Society* (Boston, 1988)

Wealth at death £1031 8s. 7d., of which £731 was in real estate, incl. home farm in Salem, valued at £551; also a 150 acre farm on Ipswich river, and house 'at the town' with 3 acres: inventories taken in Salem (27 April 1665) and Boston (31 July 1665)

Enderby family (*per. c.*1750–1876), whale and seal oil merchants and promoters of Antarctic exploration, came to prominence in the early 1750s, when the firm of Samuel Enderby & Sons is recorded as oil merchants trading from Paul's Wharf, Thames Street, in the City of London. The founder was **Samuel Enderby** (1717x20–1797), son of Daniel Enderby (1681–1766), tanner, of Bermondsey, and his wife, Mary, *née* Cook. Little is recorded of Samuel's early life. He married Mary Buxton, possibly related to a business acquaintance, John Buxton. They reared seven children: Charles (1753–1819), Daniel (*b.* 1756), Samuel (1756–1829) [*see below*], Mary (*b.* 1757), Hannah (*b.* 1759), Elizabeth (*b.* 1761), and George (*b.* 1762). As early as 2 January 1742 the elder Samuel Enderby's name appears among the freedom admissions to the Coopers' Company. By 1773 or 1774 he had become concerned with the northern whale fishery in Arctic waters. More significant was the firm's involvement with the American whalers of Massachusetts and Nantucket Island, suppliers of sperm whale oil and the spermaceti wax essential at that period for industrial and domestic use, but this lucrative trade ceased with the outbreak of the American War of Independence in 1775 in which Enderby ships came to prominence, being those in which the famous shipment of tea rached Boston in 1777. Enderby reacted by sending whaling vessels, manned largely by experienced Nantucketers, to the newly developing southern whale fishery south of lat. 44° N, where sperm whales were to be found in abundance. The confirmation by the College of Arms in 1778 of the Enderby armorial ensigns was perhaps a reflection of the family's growing prosperity and influence in the City of London and in government circles.

In subsequent years the elder Samuel Enderby appeared as a frequent and persuasive petitioner before the committee for trade, seeking, along with other leading merchants, an extension to the fishery limits imposed by the East India Company. These views tended to coincide with those of government, whose policy was to achieve British supremacy in the southern whale fishery. A measure of the firm's success was the rounding of Cape Horn in 1788–9 by the Enderby vessel *Emilia*, the first British whaler to enter the Pacific, returning in 1790 with a highly profitable catch of oil. The colonization of New South Wales in 1788 gave the firm further opportunities to expand its business in whale and seal oil and to compete fairly with foreign competitors. By 1791 Enderby had opened an office in Port Jackson (Sydney), and his whalers were transporting convicts on their outward voyages to the whaling grounds. In his latter years he continued to lobby government for legislation beneficial to the whaling industry. As the boundaries of the fisheries expanded so did the need for more favourable premiums for British whalers, for permission to revictual in certain foreign ports, and for

the freedom for the whaling crews from arbitrary impressment by the navy.

The elder Samuel Enderby died on 12 September 1797 and was succeeded as senior partner by the younger **Samuel Enderby** (1756–1829), partnered by his brothers Charles and George, all three of whom were freemen of the Coopers' Company. (The younger Samuel was indentured with the company in 1771 and became a freeman on 1 April 1783.) Samuel was seemingly his father's natural successor; as early as 1783, at the time of the peace treaty concluded with the former American colonies, he had been deputed to visit Boston, Massachusetts, for the purpose of gathering information on the state of the whale fishery and to engage Nantucket whalers to serve on Enderby vessels. Under his leadership the firm continued to pursue the expansionist policies of his father, the founder. In 1802 an act of parliament permitted fishing without licence throughout the Pacific, and a whale fishery with New Zealand was established. Enderby vessels were to find themselves engaged in discovery as well as hunting. In 1806 the sub-Antarctic Auckland Islands were discovered by their vessel the *Ocean*, and in 1808 Bouvet Island (Bouvet-øya) was rediscovered by the *Swan* and *Otter* and rediscovered again in 1825 by the *Sprightly* and *Lively* when it was claimed for the crown.

Enderby died in 1829 at Crooms Hill House, Crooms Hill, Blackheath, Kent, and was survived by his widow, Mary Enderby *née* Goodwyn (*d.* 1846), and nine children. One of their daughters, Elizabeth (1794–1873), married Lieutenant-General Henry William Gordon (1785/6–1865) and became the mother of Charles George *Gordon RA (1833–1885), the hero of Khartoum. The firm continued to trade under the name of Enderby Bros., headed by the younger Samuel Enderby's second son, Charles [*see below*], and partnered by two of his brothers, Henry and George. After 1832 the office was moved from Paul's Wharf, Thames Street, to 15 Great St Helen's, Bishopsgate Street, London.

Charles Enderby (1797–1876), born on 21 November 1797, was admitted a freeman of the Coopers' Company on 23 November 1819. He was a founder fellow of the Royal Geographical Society and fellow of both the Royal Society and the Linnean Society. An enthusiastic promoter of trade with New Zealand, whose colonization he advocated, he also encouraged the commercial and scientific exploration of Antarctic waters. To this latter purpose he dispatched Captain John Biscoe on a voyage of discovery (1830–32), which resulted in Biscoe's circumnavigation of the Antarctic continent and made history with the discovery of Enderby Land and Graham Land, the latter being claimed for the crown. In 1836–9 another Enderby captain, John Balleny, discovered the eponymous Antarctic islands as well as land to the east of Sabrina Coast. These voyages, though commercially unrewarding, earned Charles Enderby considerable kudos. In 1847, at the suggestion of certain London merchants, Enderby published a plan for the reinvigoration of the British whaling industry by establishing a whaling station and colony on the Auckland Islands. The Enderby brothers' grant to the islands was subsequently transferred to the British Southern Whale Fishery Company, a royal charter was secured, and Charles Enderby was appointed as lieutenant-governor. In 1849 the settlement was established and whaling commenced. Few whales were caught, however, and as governor Charles Enderby proved a failure. The company was subsequently declared bankrupt and in 1852 the colony was abandoned.

Commenting on this final phase of the Enderby history the historian Hugh Robert Mill wrote: 'There is, perhaps, no other instance of a private mercantile firm undertaking so extensive a series of voyages of discovery without much encouragement in the way of pecuniary returns' (H. R. Mill, *Siege of the South Pole*, 1905, 146). Charles Enderby died intestate on 31 August 1876, aged seventy-eight, at his sister's house, 12 Neville Terrace, West Brompton, London.   H. G. R. KING

Sources C. H. Gordon, 'The vigorous Enderbys: their connection with New Zealand', *New Zealand Railways Magazine* (Dec 1938); (Jan 1939) · G. Jackson, *The British whaling trade* (1978) · T. Beale, *The natural history of the sperm whale* (1839) · E. K. Chatterton, *Whales and whaling* (1925) · W. J. Dakin, *Whalemen adventurers* (1934) · E. A. Stackpole, *Whales and destiny* (1972) · H. Melville, *Moby Dick, or, The white whale* (1851) · C. Enderby, *Proposal for re-establishing the British southern whale fishery through the medium of a chartered company* (1847) · F. B. McLaren, *The Auckland Islands: their eventful history* (1948) · G. Enderby, 'The Enderby family etc.', Mitchell L., NSW, MS 315 [copy of a dictated letter addressed to his great-nephews and nieces relating to the colonisation of Australia and Norfolk Islands] · family tree, Scott Polar RI · d. cert. [Charles Enderby] · *GM*, 1st ser., 68 (1798) · *Journal of the Royal Geographical Society*, 47 (1877), cliii

Archives Mitchell L., NSW, MS material · Scott Polar RI, archives | Mitchell L., NSW, Chalmers collection · PRO, Board of Trade papers

Likenesses R. G. Rees, engraving, pubd 1838 (Charles Enderby), BM · F. C. Turner, portrait (Charles Enderby) · carte-de-visite (Charles Enderby), RGS

Enderby, Charles (1797–1876). *See under* Enderby family (*per. c.*1750–1876).

Enderby, Samuel (1717x20–1797). *See under* Enderby family (*per. c.*1750–1876).

Enderby, Samuel (1756–1829). *See under* Enderby family (*per. c.*1750–1876).

Endeus. *See* Énda mac Conaill (*fl.* 6th cent.?) *under* Munster, saints of (*act. c.*450–*c.*700).

Enfield, David of (*d. c.*1260). *See under* Moneyers (*act. c.*1180–*c.*1500).

Enfield, Edward (1811–1880), philanthropist, was born on 15 May 1811 at Nottingham, the third son of Henry (1775?–1845) and Frances Enfield (1778?–1844). His father was town clerk of Nottingham from 1815, and his grandfather was William Enfield (1741–1797), minister at Liverpool, Warrington, and Norwich. He was a lay student at Manchester College, York, in 1826–9.

Through the influence of Lord Holland, Enfield was appointed one of the moneyers of the mint and continued as one of the most active members of that corporation

until, on its reorganization in 1851, he retired with a pension. Thereafter he gave his time and energy to education and philanthropy. He was a member of the council and committee of management of University College, London, and served as president of the senate from 1878; he was also a member of the council of University Hall, a residence for Unitarian students in Gordon Square. From 1867 he acted as treasurer, and was the guiding spirit, of the University College Hospital, supervising most of the sanitary and structural improvements in the hospital. He took a large share in the conduct of the London Domestic Mission Society for the elevation of the poor in east London. In 1857 he was elected a trustee of the nonconformist endowments under Dr Williams's Trust, and became a member of the estates and audit committees. At the time of his death he was president of Manchester New College, London.

Enfield was twice married: first, to Honora (d. 1849), daughter of John Taylor FRS; and second, in 1854, to Harriet (1835?–1919), daughter of Henry Roscoe of Liverpool (d. 1836), barrister and legal writer and at his death judge of the court of passage in Liverpool. He had one son with his first wife. He died at his residence, 19 Chester Terrace, Regent's Park, London, on 21 April 1880, and was buried at Brookwood cemetery, Woking, on 26 April.

     R. K. WEBB

Sources *In memoriam Edward Enfield* (1880) [repr. obits from *Daily News* (23 April 1880); *The Inquirer* (24 April 1880); *The Times* (27 April 1880)] · *Christian Reformer, or, Unitarian Magazine and Review*, 11 (1844), 1004 [death notice of Frances Enfield] · *Christian Reformer, or, Unitarian Magazine and Review*, new ser., 1 (1845), 332, 458–9 · *Christian Reformer, or, Unitarian Magazine and Review*, new ser., 6 (1850), 63 [death notice of Honora Enfield] · *The Inquirer* (1919), 43, 68 · d. cert.

Archives DWL, corresp. and papers as secretary of Free Christian Union

Likenesses photograph, DWL

Wealth at death under £45,000: probate, 28 May 1880, *CGPLA Eng. & Wales*

Enfield, William (1741–1797), Unitarian minister, was born on 29 March 1741 at Sudbury, Suffolk, son of William Enfield (Infield) and his wife, Ann Leaver, both poor members of the Little or Lower Meeting of the Independent congregation in Friars' Street. Encouraged and educated by his minister, William Hextal (or Hextall; 1711?–1766), in 1758 he entered Daventry Academy. In 1763 he became sole minister at Benn's Garden Chapel, Liverpool, which drew many members from the merchant aristocracy. In 1767 he married Mary Holland (d. 1830), daughter of a Liverpool draper; they had three daughters and two sons, Richard and Henry, both of whom served as town clerk of Nottingham. The degree of doctor of laws was conferred on him by the University of Edinburgh in 1774.

In 1770 Enfield became minister to the Cairo Street Chapel in Warrington, tutor in *belles-lettres* at Warrington Academy, and *rector academiae*, with oversight of student discipline, a responsibility for which he was entirely unsuited. When the academy closed in 1783 he remained at Cairo Street until 1785, when he became minister of the distinguished congregation at the Octagon Chapel, Norwich, remaining there until his sudden death from an intestinal obstruction on 3 November 1797.

Like many Unitarians of his generation Enfield retained an admiration for the established church and gave presumptive credit to government. In *Remarks on Several Late Publications … in a Letter to Dr Priestley* (1770) he attacked his friend Joseph Priestley over three recent works aggressively advocating the dissenting cause. Priestley's vehemence and naïvety, Enfield insisted, could endanger the gains dissenters had made through improved laws and their mild administration. Priestley's dismissive response did not weaken Enfield's admiration for him on other grounds, and in time he grew deeply disappointed by the slow progress of religious and civil freedom, about which he had been so hopeful in the 1770s. He could still draw comfort from events abroad, and as late as 1792 could write to his close friend Nicholas Clayton that French liberty having been won, all else must follow, including self-government throughout the world and the establishment of universal equality.

As a preacher, Enfield was a sober and imposing mediator of ethical instruction, to which speculative theology was subordinate. He published many sermons (some of them collected in *Sermons on Practical Subject*, 3 vols., 1798) and periodical essays, compiled a hymnal, and was active in the general literary world. He contributed regularly to the *Monthly Magazine* and at the time of his death was collaborating with his old Warrington friend John Aikin on a general biographical dictionary. *An Essay toward the History of Liverpool* (1774) drew on papers collected by George Perry, a Liverpool antiquary. When his teaching duties required attention to natural philosophy, Enfield learned mathematics in a summer, with help from Clayton, and in 1783 published *Institutes of Natural Philosophy, Theoretical and Experimental*, a successful textbook dedicated to Priestley. His two-volume abridgement and translation made more accessible the five-volume *Historia critica philosophiae* by Johann Jakob Brucker (1696–1770) and won praise on both sides of the Atlantic. His greatest publishing success was *The Speaker* (1774), an anthology of extracts from classical and English literature intended for practice in the art of elocution, which a prefatory essay explained; a sequel, *Exercises in Elocution*, appeared in 1780. *The Speaker* went through many editions in Britain and America and remained in print well after the middle of the nineteenth century.

Cultivated, eirenic, and humane, Enfield was widely admired, but by none more than the friends made in his Warrington days—Clayton (to whom he wrote some surviving letters of great interest), the physician John Aikin, and Aikin's sister Anna Laetitia Barbauld, whom he inspired to two poems, one urging him to discipline youth by the example of his candour and moral qualities rather than by precept, the other a wistful celebration of a vanished Warrington on the occasion of Enfield's revisiting the town in 1789.   R. K. WEBB

Sources J. Aikin, 'Biographical account of the author of these volumes', in W. Enfield, *Sermons on practical subjects*, 3 vols. (1798), iii–xxvii • A. Holt, *Walking together: a study in Liverpool nonconformity, 1688–1938* (1938) • R. K. Webb, 'And the greatest of these is liberty: the Manchester College motto in its setting', *Faith and Freedom*, 40 (1987), 4–20 • *Monthly Repository*, 10 (1815), 612 • *The poems of Anna Laetitia Barbauld*, ed. W. McCarthy and E. Kraft (1994), nos. 46, 47, 85 • correspondence, JRL • correspondence, Liverpool City Libraries • correspondence, DWL • register of births and baptisms, Friars' Street Chapel, 1707–1903

Archives JRL, Unitarian College MSS • Norfolk RO, corresp. | Bodl. Oxf., letters to Ralph Griffiths • Lpool RO, Nicholson MSS

Likenesses A. Smith, line print, silhouette, pubd 1798, BM, NPG • portrait, repro. in Holt, *Walking together*, 168; formerly in possession of Charles Booth, 1938

Engelbach, Charles Richard Fox (1876–1943), motor engineer, was born on 20 May 1876 in Kensington, London, son of Lewis William Engelbach, a clerk in the War Office, and his wife, Jessie Bryan. He left Sandringham School at Southport, Lancashire, when he was sixteen and was apprenticed at the great armaments manufacturer Armstrong Whitworth at Newcastle upon Tyne. After several years of working on naval gun-turrets, in 1906 he was given the task of reviewing the faltering production of Wilson–Pilcher motor cars, a sideline recently purchased by Armstrongs to provide alternative peacetime work. His lucid analysis highlighted problems common to the fledgeling motor industry in Britain, and became the basis for his career as one of the key figures in developing the industry into an effective producer.

Engelbach found no specialized motor department and little planning and organization devoted to Wilson–Pilcher. Parts were produced in six or seven different shops, depending on what other work was available. As a result an erratic mix of components arrived at the assembly department. Of thirty-two cars, only ten had been delivered without being returned with complaints. Engelbach's plans for organized large-scale production were rejected but he was given charge of a new plant to build limited numbers of the larger 30 hp Armstrong Whitworth cars, which he did successfully.

On the outbreak of war in 1914, Engelbach, a keen reserve naval officer, was called up, but after a year his skills were recognized and he was put in charge of the howitzer department of the Coventry ordnance works. He was made an OBE for his work. After the armistice he worked briefly for a components supplier before being called in by the team restructuring the Austin Motor Company which was in the hands of the official receiver in the post-war slump. The Austin works at Longbridge in Birmingham had grown hugely during the war but had required expensive re-engineering for peacetime production and lacked popular models.

Engelbach was appointed works director. On the back of the success of the Austin 7 small car, introduced in 1922, he reorganized production systematically, drawing on his experience and people from Coventry. Principal components were made and assembled in the same shop and then delivered to the appropriate position for assembly on a track. Bodies were built in series and carried on an overhead runway to a mounting shop where they met the chassis from the assembly line. It was a pattern familiar in the USA, but much less so in Britain.

Engelbach's reforms, spelt out in a lecture to the Institution of Automobile Engineers, whose president he became, meant that between 1922 and 1927 the number of man-weeks required to build a car fell from fifty-five to ten. Labour relations benefited from carefully worked out wage rates which increased output and earnings, and the firm later pioneered sick pay and pension schemes in line with Engelbach's belief that secure work at a good wage produced the best results.

The changes, though much copied, helped Austin meet the challenge of Ford's new factory, opened on a green-field site at Dagenham in 1931. But by 1938 Engelbach's eyesight had deteriorated so much that he had to be guided round the factory, and he retired. He was, nevertheless, an obvious choice for the committee which planned the government's pre-war 'shadow' factory programme to construct ready-equipped plants for possible wartime production by existing manufacturers.

A sympathetic man, witty, with a range of interests, Engelbach had once turned down a professional singing career with the D'Oyly Carte company. His wife, Florence Ada, *née* Neumegen, whom he married on 4 October 1902, painted, exhibiting at the Royal Academy. They had two sons. He also enjoyed the conventional activities of the motor manufacturers—golf and yachting—and was an active freemason and office bearer in local and national employers' associations. He died on 19 February 1943 at his home, Quarry Farm, Quarry Lane, Northfield, Birmingham. MARTIN ADENEY

Sources R. J. Wyatt, *The Austin, 1905–52* (1981) · K. Richardson and C. N. O'Gallagher, *The British motor industry, 1896–1939* (1977) · C. Engelbach, 'Some notes on reorganising a works to increase production', *Proceedings of the Institution of Automobile Engineers*, 23 (1927–8), 496–544 · C. Engelbach, 'Problems in manufacture', *Proceedings of the Institution of Automobile Engineers*, 28 (1933–4), 5–21 · C. Engelbach, 'Engineering', *The Listener* (1 Feb 1933), 181 · d. cert. · m. cert. · R. J. Wyatt, 'Engelbach, Charles Richard Fox', *DBB*
Archives U. Warwick Mod. RC, papers | SOUND broadcasts c.1933 with Sir Herbert Austin
Likenesses photographs, British Motor Industry Heritage Trust, Gaydon, near Banbury
Wealth at death £110,733 15s. 3d.: probate, 1943, *CGPLA Eng. & Wales*

Engels, Friedrich [Frederick] (1820–1895), businessman and revolutionary leader, was born on 28 November 1820 in Barmen, Westphalia, the son of Friedrich Engels (1796–1860), a textile manufacturer, and Elizabeth, *née* van Haar (1797–1873), the daughter of a schoolmaster of Dutch origin. Frederick (as he came to be known in England later in life) was the eldest of three brothers and four sisters. Brought up in a strongly Calvinist protestant household, Engels attended the Elberfeld Gymnasium, before being sent to Bremen to be trained in the merchant's profession. From school onwards, however, Engels developed radical literary ambitions which first drew him towards the literary movement Young Germany and then in 1841 brought him into contact with the Young Hegelian circle in Berlin, where he served one year's military service. During these

Friedrich Engels (1820–1895), by unknown photographer

years in Bremen and Berlin Engels abandoned his family faith and developed a double life, which he was to maintain through most of his life. While preparing himself for work in the family business he wrote prolifically for the liberal and radical press under the pen-name Friedrich Oswald.

Manchester and *The Condition of the Working Class in England* In November 1842 Engels left for England to work in his father's Manchester textile firm, Ermen and Engels. Already a revolutionary republican and an admirer of Jacobinism from his days in the Young Hegelian circle in Berlin, Engels was converted on his way to England by Moses Hess to a belief in 'communism'. Convinced also by Hess's book of 1841, *Die europäische Triarchie*, of the imminence of social revolution in England, Engels used his two-year stay to study the conditions which would bring it about. From this visit came two pieces of writing which were to establish his lasting importance. The first, an essay entitled 'Umrisse zu einer Kritik der Nationalökonomie' ('Outlines of a critique of national economy') published in the *Deutsche-Französische Jahrbücher* in 1844, was the earliest Young Hegelian attempt at economic criticism and exerted a decisive influence upon Marx's identification of socialism with the critique of political economy. The second, *Die Lage der arbeitenden Klasse in England nach eigner Anschauung und authentischen Quellen*, was published in Leipzig in 1845 (Eng. trans. as *The Condition of the Working Class in England*, New York, 1887). It established his fame in Germany and has remained famous as a classic account of urban conditions during the period of the industrial revolution. Together these works attest to the importance of what Engels accomplished before his collaboration with Karl Marx and indicate that Marxist socialism was as much the creation of Engels as of Marx.

Early relations with Marx Returning home through Paris in the summer of 1844, Engels had his first serious meeting with Marx. Their lifelong collaboration dated from this point with an agreement to produce a joint work, *Die heilige Familie, oder, Kritik der kritischen Kritik* (1845; Eng. trans. as *The Holy Family*, 1956), setting out their disagreements with other tendencies within Young Hegelianism. This was followed by a second and unfinished joint enterprise, *Die deutsche Ideologie* (*German Ideology*) written in 1845–6, in which their 'materialist conception of history' was expounded systematically for the first time. In both these works, however, Engels's contribution was marginal.

After residing with his family in Barmen, while writing *The Condition of the Working Class in England*, Engels left for Brussels in April 1845. Ostensibly travelling for purposes of research and continuing to rely upon an uncertain allowance from his father, he spent the years between 1845 and 1848 engaged in political activity among German artisan and communist groupings in Paris and Brussels. The political strategy of the Communist Correspondence Committee, of which he was part, was to encourage international discussion of 'scientific questions' among communists and socialists and to win supporters in German workers' educational societies for open democratic and communist agitation. It was for one of these groups, The League of the Just (subsequently the Communist League), that Engels wrote the first draft of the *Communist Manifesto* in 1847.

During the 1848 revolution, Engels joined Marx in Cologne to work as a collaborator on the *Neue Rheinische Zeitung*. Until the spring of 1849 the strategy of the paper was to act as the democratic wing of a middle-class liberal movement against absolutism. Only after the bourgeoisie had failed to play its allotted role in the revolution did the paper openly espouse independent social revolutionary action on the part of workers and peasants. Engels wrote on international and central European affairs until September 1848, but after a warrant was issued for his arrest he fled to Belgium and then France. During the rest of the autumn of 1848 he followed the wine harvest and its pleasures through the Loire and Burgundy to Switzerland, where he remained until he judged it safe to return to Cologne in January 1849. He continued to work on the paper until May 1849, when Elberfeld and other towns rose in revolt against the rejection by the German princes of the Frankfurt liberal constitution. Engels participated in the defence of Elberfeld until expelled as a communist. He then travelled to Baden and the Palatinate, where in June and July he took part in the last phase of armed resistance to the counter-revolution. He then crossed over into Switzerland, made his way to Genoa, and from there travelled by sea to England, where he arrived in November 1849.

During the following year Engels and Marx attempted to resume their previous political and journalistic activity in London. They re-established the *Neue Rheinische Zeitung* as a bi-monthly review aimed at the democratic and communist diaspora. It was for this journal that Engels composed his long essay 'The peasant war in Germany', aimed at strengthening awareness of German traditions of revolutionary resistance. Engels also wrote extensively on developments in France and Germany for Harney's Chartist monthly, the *Democratic Review*. When the *Neue Rheinische Zeitung* folded Engels decided in November 1850 to return to work for the family firm in Manchester. But he continued journalistic activity over the next few years, both as a way of remaining prepared for the next revolutionary upheaval and as a means of supporting Marx in London while he elaborated the critique of political economy upon which he had been engaged since the mid-1840s. Thus, it was initially to combat the firebrand insurrectionism of remnants of the Communist League that Engels developed a journalistic expertise in military affairs and it was to assist Marx that he wrote a series of articles under Marx's name, later published as *Revolution and Counter-Revolution, or, Germany in 1848* (an account of the revolutions of 1848) reprinted from the *New York Daily Tribune* and edited by Eleanor Marx Aveling (1896).

Manufacturing and marriage: the ambiguities of a bourgeois From November 1850 to July 1869 Engels worked—first as an employee and then (from 1861) as a partner—in the firm of Ermen and Engels, manufacturers of cotton twist in Manchester. His income rose from around £100 per annum in the early 1850s to around £3000 in 1869. Throughout this period Engels led an elaborate double life. As English representative of the family firm he maintained lodgings in the centre of Manchester and participated in the lifestyle of the city's business élite. He was a member of the Albert Club and the Manchester Athenaeum, rode in the Cheshire hunt, and patronized the Schiller Institute. His personal and political life, on the other hand, was lived in a separate household in suburban Ardwick, where he maintained a relationship with Mary Burns (*c.*1823–1863) and subsequently with her sister, Lizzie (Lydia Burns; 1827–1878).

Engels apparently first met Mary, an Irish-born worker employed in the Ermen and Engels Victoria Mills, while collecting material for his book during his stay in England between 1842 and 1844, and she accompanied him to Brussels in 1845. But there is no indication of her being with him in Paris or Cologne, and some evidence of his involvement with other women during these years. In the 1850s Engels and Mary were registered in Ardwick as Mr and Mrs Boardman, with Lizzie keeping house. In 1863, after Mary's death of heart disease, Engels transferred his affections to Lizzie. After his move to London in 1870 he lived with her openly, and he married her on her deathbed on 12 September 1878. The status of these relationships has been the object of controversy. In Brussels in 1847, for example, one eyewitness noted that Mary was not acknowledged by Mrs Marx; similarly in 1851, in his correspondence with Marx, Engels was still referring to himself as a bachelor. Nor is there any indication that either of the Burns sisters was ever introduced to the Engels family. On the other hand, Engels was deeply hurt when Marx expressed only cursory regret about Mary's death in a letter begging funds for his family. Thereafter relations appear to have become more relaxed; Marx's daughter, Eleanor, paid visits to the Engels household, and Lizzie appears to have enjoyed friendly relations with Mrs Marx once the couple moved to Regent's Park Road, around the corner from the Marx family. Nevertheless, in the whole of his correspondence there is little detail about his relationship with Lizzie and virtually nothing beyond his reproachful letter to Marx about his feelings for Mary. Despite his theoretical commitment to female emancipation as part of the transcendence of class society (stated in *Der Ursprung der Familie, des Privateigentums und des Staates*, *The Origin of the Family, Private Property and the State*, 1884), it seems clear that in his personal life Engels's views on a woman's role were quite conventional and that he avoided relationships with women who might challenge him as equals.

The ambiguity surrounding Engels's personal relationships formed part of a larger tension between his life as businessman and his commitment to revolutionary politics. Although Engels openly espoused the communist cause even in his native Barmen from 1844 onwards, he never broke with his family. During the 1850s, before the time when he became comparatively wealthy, it is estimated that he sometimes diverted as much as half his annual income to the Marx family. Yet Engels appears also to have remained a diligent member of the family firm and a dutiful son, escorting his parents on a tour of Scotland in 1859, regularly meeting up with his mother during summer holidays at Ostend or Ramsgate into the 1870s, and keeping up with his brothers and sisters until his death. It is clear also that his tastes remained unapologetically bourgeois. He once confessed that his idea of paradise was a bottle of Château Margaux 1848.

Popularizing and supporting Marx During the 1850s and 1860s Engels wrote little of substance. But among his numerous journalistic contributions were a series of attempts to publicize Marx's *Zur Kritik der politischen Ökonomie* in 1859 and volume 1 of *Das Kapital* in 1867. These contributions are perhaps most noteworthy in highlighting the extent to which Engels's outlook and his interpretation of Marx's work still derived from his Young Hegelian formation. 'Marx was, and is', he wrote in 1859, 'the only one who could undertake the work of extracting from Hegelian Logic the kernel which comprised Hegel's real discoveries … and to construct the dialectical method divested of its idealistic trappings' (*Selected Works*, 1.513). They also indicate Engels's growing interest in the philosophy of science and the philosophy of nature, and his ambition to situate what he called Marx's 'materialist conception of history' within an overall schema which would also reconcile his revised version of Hegelian dialectics with evolutionary biology, embryology, and other sciences of nature. Engels's interest in the development of science was already apparent in his 'Umrisse' of 1844, in which he supported his argument by reference to the work of Davy and Liebig. The idea of supporting Marx's discoveries with a general cosmology buttressed by reference to the latest scientific findings may also have originated in his first stay in Manchester. It was an approach employed by the Owenites and, in particular, by his friend the Owenite lecturer John Watts (1818–1887), who in his 1843 lectures 'The philosophy of socialism' at the Manchester Hall of Science used the chemical discoveries of Davy and Liebig to discredit the Malthusian notion of static agricultural productivity. Engels's writings on dialectics and the development of the natural sciences were published posthumously as *Dialektik der Natur* in 1925. But contemporaries were given some indications of his position in *Anti-Dühring* (1877) and *Ludwig Feuerbach und der Ausgang der klassischen deutschen Philosophie* (1886).

In 1869 Engels retired from the firm with a settlement of £12,500 and resumed his political life. As Marx's health declined in the 1870s Engels took over his work during the last years of the International Working Men's Association (1864–72) and shouldered increasing responsibility for corresponding with infant socialist parties, most notably the newly founded German Social Democratic Party. Engels's most important work during this period was his polemic against the German positivist socialist Eugen Dühring. *Anti-Dühring* was the first comprehensive exposition of Marxian socialism in the realms of philosophy, history, and political economy. The success of this work, and in particular extracts from it such as *Socialisme utopique et socialisme scientifique* (1879), published in English as *Socialism, Utopian and Scientific* in 1892, represented the decisive turning point in the international diffusion of Marxism and shaped its understanding as a theory in the period before 1914.

After Marx's death in 1883, when he delivered a lapidary funeral oration, Engels devoted most of his own last years to the editing and publishing of the remaining volumes of *Das Kapital* from Marx's manuscripts. Volume 2 appeared in 1885 and volume 3 in 1894. He also hoped to prepare a related volume dealing with the history of political economy, but failing eyesight and the formidable difficulties of editing the preceding volumes forced him to hand over this task to Karl Kautsky, who subsequently published the work under the title *Theories of Surplus Value*.

When Engels retired in 1869 he settled an annual allowance upon the Marx family, and in 1870 he and Lizzie, together with her niece, Mary Ellen (known as Pumps), and a maid moved to London. After Lizzie's death in 1878 Pumps briefly took over as housekeeper, followed in 1883 after Marx's death by the Marx family servant, Helene (Lenchen) Demuth. After her death in 1890 the house was managed by Louise, *née* Strasser (1860–1950), the recently divorced wife of Karl Kautsky, and, from 1893, Mrs Louise Freyberger. Engels died of cancer of the throat at his house, 41 Regent's Park Road, London, on 5 August 1895. He was cremated at Woking, Surrey, on 10 August 1895, and his ashes were scattered off Beachy Head in accordance with his wishes.

In 1962 a document surfaced, purportedly a letter from Louise Freyberger to August Bebel, dated 2–4 September 1898. It claimed that on his deathbed Engels, writing on a slate, had revealed that the father of Lenchen Demuth's illegitimate son, Henry Frederick (born on 23 June 1851), had been Marx himself, and that he was making this known lest it be thought that he was the father and had acted shabbily towards the child. This letter was apparently corroborated by the correspondence between the Marx daughters in which allusions were made to feelings of guilt towards Frederick and to Engels's irritation. But there are a number of unlikely elements in the story, most obviously the absence of any evidence of strain in the relations between Lenchen and Mrs Marx. The guilt towards Frederick may simply have been the result of his being sent out to care. The circumstances in which this letter became public are slightly suspicious, and there is no other evidence either direct or circumstantial linking Frederick Demuth with either Marx or Engels. Most probably the letter was a forgery.

Engels and the British context: an assessment Three aspects of Engels's life and work deserve particular attention in a British context. The first concerns his 'Umrisse zu einer Kritik der Nationalökonomie', written for the *Deutsche-Französische Jahrbücher* in Paris in 1844. As noted above, this essay has generally been regarded as important because of its impact upon Marx, who acknowledged it in his own *Zur Kritik der politischen Ökonomie* of 1859 as a 'brilliant sketch'. The core of Engels's case was that all the categories of political economy presupposed competition, which in turn presupposed private property. For Marx, the Engels critique suggested an alternative to Proudhon's approach (*Qu'est-ce que la propriété?*, 1840), which led to a notion of equal wages and of society conceived as 'abstract capital'. If Engels's essay did mark the beginning of Marx's ambition to reach a 'scientific' notion of socialism through the critique of political economy, it suggests a far higher degree of continuity between Marxian and British Owenite socialism than has generally been assumed. For Engels was probably stimulated to write his 'Umrisse' by the appearance in 1843 of *Facts and Fictions of Political Economists* by his friend John Watts. Watts, drawing upon the work of previous radical and socialist critics, Thomas Hodgskin, William Thompson, and John Bray, condemned the split between moral and political economy, condemning the latter for its exclusive focus upon wealth and its acceptance of the 'competitive system' as a starting point. Although restating the argument in historical and Young Hegelian terms, Engels relied heavily upon Watts both for the basis of his argument and for many of its points of detail.

Secondly, and most obviously, Engels's British reputation rests on his account *The Condition of the Working Class in England*. Engels's book is important in several respects. Not only was it written from an unusual perspective—that of a German philosophical communist dedicated to the cause of the working classes—and not only was it based on extensive reading of government inquiries and press reports, it was also the product of Engels's extensive contacts with local labour activists. In particular, Engels relied upon information supplied by the Chartist leader and factory campaigner James Leach (*b*. 1806), whose *Stubborn Facts from the Factories by a Manchester Operative* appeared in 1844. Engels's acquaintance with local leaders makes his account of Chartism of particular interest.

In addition, in his eyewitness description of the vivid contrast between suburban and proletarian Manchester, Engels produced what many have regarded as a classic account of the nineteenth-century industrial town, fit to stand comparison with Dickens's *Hard Times* or Disraeli's *Sybil*. In particular his description of the spatial configuration of Manchester, constructed in such a way that its affluent burghers need never confront the squalor and misery upon which their wealth was based, has been seen as a decisive symbol for the invisibility of the conditions in which wealth under capitalism was produced.

It is important, however, to realize that Engels's description was not simply the product of raw and unprecedented experience. It was not his first visit to Britain (he had been in Manchester in 1838) and he had arrived in 1842 fully convinced by Hess's *Die europäische Triarchie* that England was heading for social revolution. In other respects, too, he came to his material with formed views: acquaintance with Hegel's work predisposed him towards contrasts of 'appearance' and 'essence'; agreement with the views of Feuerbach and Marx on the alienation of labour predisposed him to associate the condition of the proletariat with degradation; and a reversion to animality and an admiration for Thomas Carlyle reinforced his conviction of the inhumanity of the 'cash nexus'. Nevertheless, the result was a particularly powerful and memorable portrait of urban and industrial England, and a classic account of the industrial revolution and the development of the working class. This was to form the basis of Marx's account of industrial capitalism. Engels, following Hess, believed himself only to be tracing the destiny of England. Marx, however, in the *Communist Manifesto* turned Engels's account into a universal picture of modern industry and proletarian revolt.

The third point concerns Engels's political and intellectual legacy. Engels's political conception of British society was ultimately quite uncomplicated and remained remarkably constant: communism (or socialism) was the modern form of democracy. Modern capitalism had brought to power a new bourgeois class who controlled the state and exploited the proletariat—the great majority of the people. The aim, therefore, was to establish rule by a party representing the proletarian majority and to abolish private ownership of the means of production, the main cause of the poverty of the people. This democratic-communist transformation was to be accomplished, if necessary, by force. In the first half of his life the legacy of the French Revolution, an upbringing under Prussian absolutism, and his experiences of 1848 all led him to associate this change with violent revolution. But in his later years, as the condition of British workers improved and their political rights increased, as a result, Engels thought, of Britain's supremacy in the world market, Engels turned increasingly away from the romantic insurrectionism of his youth. Unlike Marx he was happy to acknowledge the improvements which had occurred since his book of 1845 and to adjust his theory to the changing political situation. He believed that British workers would again turn to socialism once economic supremacy was lost, and thought this to be happening the 1880s. In consequence he was generally opposed to revolutionary or 'Marxist' sects and favoured mass constitutional working-class parties. Towards the end of his life he warmly welcomed the new unskilled trade unionism of 1889 and the formation of the Independent Labour Party in 1892. Engels's pragmatism, his ecumenical stance towards parties of labour, and his economistic approach to political change left a lasting impact upon British radicals, socialists, and communists, and his picture of the development of the nineteenth-century British labour movement has remained and will continue to be an important influence upon the work of social and labour historians.   GARETH STEDMAN JONES

Sources *Karl Marx and Frederick Engels: selected works*, ed. Institute of Marxism-Leninism, 3 vols. (1969–70) · G. Mayer, *Friedrich Engels: eine Biographie*, 2 vols. (1971) · W. O. Henderson, *The life of Friedrich Engels*, 2 vols. (1976) · D. Rjazanov, *Marx and Engels* (1927) · T. Carver, *Friedrich Engels: his life and thought* (1989) · H. Schmidtgall, *Friedrich Engels' Manchester-Aufenthalt 1842–1844* (Trier, 1981) · G. S. Jones, 'Engels and the history of Marxism', *The history of Marxism*, ed. E. J. Hobsbawn, 1 (1982), 290–326 · G. Claeys, 'The political ideas of the young Engels, 1842–1845: Owenism, Chartism and the question of violent revolution', *History of Political Thought*, 6 (1985), 455–78 · *Die Herkunft des Friedrich Engels: Briefe aus der Verwandtschaft, 1791–1847*, ed. M. Knieriem and others (Trier, 1991) · G. S. Jones, 'Voir sans entendre: Engels, Manchester et l'observation sociale en 1844', *Genèses* (March 1996), 4–17 · D. McLellan, *Karl Marx: his life and thought* (1973) · M. Rubel, *Bibliographie des oeuvres de Karl Marx avec un appendice, un répertoire des oeuvres de Friedrich Engels* (1956)
Archives Internationaal Instituut voor Sociale Geschiedenis, Amsterdam, corresp. and papers
Likenesses photograph, repro. in G. Mayer, *Friedrich Engels*, 2 vols. (1934), frontispiece [*see illus.*]
Wealth at death £25,267 13s. 11d.: resworn probate, Jan 1896, CGPLA Eng. & Wales

England, George (*fl.* 1733–1737), author and Church of England clergyman, of whose upbringing details are uncertain, was a member of the England family who were prominent in the politics of Great Yarmouth during the sixteenth and seventeenth centuries. The *Dictionary of National Biography* suggested that his grandfather may have been Sir George England, knighted by Charles II in 1672; however, it is more likely that Sir George was his great-grandfather, making George England the son of George England (1679–1725), MP for Great Yarmouth, and of Alice, *née* Jermy. George and Alice England had four sons and one daughter; parish registers record the baptism at Great Yarmouth of a son, George, in January 1707, who may be the subject in question.

George England was chaplain to Lord Hobart, by whom

he was presented in 1733 to the living of Hanworth, Norfolk. Four years later he resigned Hanworth to become rector of Wolterton and Wickmere, a consolidated living in the same county. He was the author of *An Enquiry into the Morals of the Ancients* (1737), a work based on the belief that Greek and Roman societies were superior to Christians in the practice of morality. The date of England's death is unknown.   ALSAGER VIAN, *rev.* PHILIP CARTER

Sources F. Blomefield and C. Parkin, *An essay towards a topographical history of the county of Norfolk*, [2nd edn], 11 vols. (1805–10), vol. 6, pp. 452, 462; vol. 8, p. 132 · P. Gauci, *Politics and society in Great Yarmouth, 1660–1722* (1996)

England, George (*fl.* 1740–1788), organ builder, built a considerable number of organs, principally in London, including those of St Mildred Poultry, the German Lutheran church, Goodman's Fields, and the chapel of Dulwich College. That of St Stephen Walbrook (1760) was repaired in 1825, rebuilt in 1872, and later considerably enlarged by Hill & Son. He also built some organs in partnership with Hugh Russell. On 21 November 1757, at St James's, Clerkenwell, he married Sarah, daughter of Richard Bridge, organ builder. Their son, **George Pyke England** (1765?–1814), also an organ builder, left an account book of the organs he built, including those of Gainsborough church, Lincolnshire (1793), St Martin's, Birmingham (1805), and St Mary's, Islington (1812). According to J. W. Warman, the organ of Durham Cathedral (1815) was ascribed to G. P. England and W. A. Nicholls. George Pyke England married Ann Wilson at St Pancras Old Church on 13 October 1789; the baptisms of two sons and a daughter took place at the same church between 1795 and 1801.

L. M. MIDDLETON, *rev.* K. D. REYNOLDS

Sources 'England, George', Grove, *Dict. mus.* (1927) · E. J. Hopkins and E. F. Rimbault, *The organ: its history and construction* (1855) · J. W. Warman, *The organ: its compass, tablature, and short and incomplete octaves* (1884) · *IGI*

England, George (1811/12–1878), engineer and locomotive builder, was born in Newcastle upon Tyne. He was probably the George England baptized on 28 July 1811 in Newcastle, son of George England and Mary Whinney. Both were presumably English. George England trained at John Penn's Deptford boilerworks and shipyards. He patented the traversing screw jack (patent no. 8058, 1839), which enabled a derailed locomotive not only to be lifted but also to be moved laterally so that it could be lowered back onto the rails.

About 1839 England established Hatcham Iron Works in Pomeroy Street, New Cross, London. Here he manufactured patent jacks and other tools, and towards the end of the 1840s he started to build locomotives, specializing in light locomotives of the type originated by W. Bridges Adams. George England's locomotive *Little England* was awarded a prize medal at the Great Exhibition of 1851, and his works then became busy constructing locomotives for railways in Britain—for collieries and contractors—and for export to India and Australia. He is best-known for having built in 1863 the first locomotives for the Ffestiniog Railway (FR), with its exceptionally narrow gauge of under 2 ft. These two tiny machines were very successful:

with them C. E. Spooner, the railway's engineer, was able to replace horses by locomotives and then to introduce passenger trains—the first in Britain—on a gauge substantially less than the standard 4 ft 8½ in.

England built four more similar locomotives for the FR, two of them to an enlarged design. Then in 1868 he commenced construction for the FR of a double-bogie, double-boiler locomotive of the type patented by Robert Fairlie. This locomotive, *Little Wonder*, was the first wholly successful 'double Fairlie': warranted by England to be as powerful as two of the small locomotives, it proved almost as powerful as three. Demonstrations of it as it hauled immensely long trains up grade through sinuous curves were a vital influence in worldwide adoption of economical narrow gauges.

England was elected a member of the Institution of Mechanical Engineers in 1853, and he became a director of the Crystal Palace Company about 1857. He was twice married: to whom and when for the first time is not known, but by 1843 he was living with Sarah Hannar, whom he eventually married after his first wife died. On 6 July 1843 he and Sarah Hannar had a daughter, Eliza Ann; there was an older daughter, Mary, and subsequently a son, George.

In appearance, England was tubby, even jovial; in character, he became increasingly irascible and contentious as he grew older. In 1858 he was fined for assaulting and beating an apprentice. In 1862 he indicted Robert Fairlie, who had eloped with Eliza Ann, for perjury, on the grounds that Fairlie had not, as claimed, received her father's consent to their marriage. When England was obliged to reveal his own marital history the case collapsed. The next general meeting of the Crystal Palace Company consisted largely of uproar as England, following these revelations, was forced to resign his directorship.

Increasingly tyrannical behaviour towards employees at Hatcham led in 1865 to a disastrous strike. Much business was lost. England himself retired from ill health in 1869; the works was taken on lease by Fairlie, George England junior, and J. S. Fraser, under whom *Little Wonder* was completed. England junior died a few months later and locomotive building ceased.

George England died at Cannes, France, on 2 March 1878; his estate was left to George William Linghorn, born 17 July 1871, who adopted and became known by the name of George England. Five locomotives built by George England survive: *Shannon*, on long-term loan to Didcot Railway Centre from the National Railway Museum, and *Princess*, *Prince*, *Palmerston*, and *Welsh Pony*, on the Ffestiniog Railway.   P. J. G. RANSOM

Sources P. J. G. Ransom, *Narrow gauge steam: its origins and worldwide development* (1996) · private information (2004) · *The Times* (8 April 1862) · *The Times* (10 April 1862) · *The Times* (11 June 1862) · *The Times* (21 June 1862) · D. Perrett and O. James, 'The Hatcham Ironworks, New Cross', *London's Industrial Archaeology*, 3 (1984) · C. H. Dickson, 'Locomotive builders of the past (VI)', *Stephenson Locomotive Society Journal* (May 1961), 138–43 · A. R. Bennett, 'Locomotive building in London', *Railway Magazine* (Nov 1907), 382–90 · *Festiniog Railway Magazine*, 99/winter (1982–3), 3 · *Festiniog Railway Magazine*, 100 (1983), 18–29 · *Festiniog Railway Magazine*, 133 (1991), 20–21 · IGI · d. cert. · census returns, 1861 · CGPLA Eng. & Wales (1878)

Archives Ffestiniog railway, locomotives *Prince*, *Princess*, *Palmerston*, *Welsh Pony* · National Railway Museum, York, locomotive *Shannon*
Likenesses photograph, Sci. Mus.
Wealth at death under £3000: probate, 29 March 1878, *CGPLA Eng. & Wales*

England, George Pyke (1765?–1814). *See under* England, George (*fl.* 1740–1788).

England, John (1786–1842), Roman Catholic bishop of Charleston, was born at Cork on 23 September 1786, the son of Thomas England and his wife, Honora Lordan. The Revd Thomas *England was his younger brother. John attended school at Cork and was briefly apprenticed to a barrister there before entering St Patrick's College, Carlow, in 1802 to train for the priesthood. In 1808 he returned to Cork to be ordained at the exceptionally early age of twenty-two, under a dispensation obtained by his bishop, John Moylan. In addition to his official duties as lecturer in philosophy at the newly established seminary of St Mary's (of which he was president from 1814 to 1817) and as a convent chaplain, he devoted his energies to schemes of social, pastoral, and political reform. In June 1813 he was appointed trustee of the *Cork Mercantile Chronicle*, recently acquired by the Catholic interest as an organ of opposition to the proposed right of veto by the government on the appointment of Catholic bishops. As editor from 1813 to 1818 he vigorously championed civil and religious liberties and advocated the separation of church and state. He was also founder (1809) and editor of a pioneering popular monthly, the *Religious Repertory*. As chaplain to the Cork gaol he ministered to convicts awaiting transportation to Australia, and was instrumental in persuading the government to allow priests to be sent out to the convict settlements. He was inspector of schools for the Catholic poor, and in 1814 founded a school at the Mardyke which, though attended mainly by Catholic children, was open to all denominations, religious education being voluntary.

In 1818 England helped to manage the electoral campaign at Cork of the pro-emancipationist candidate Christopher Hely-Hutchinson. His use of the mass meeting as an instrument of political agitation anticipated the methods later successfully adopted by Daniel O'Connell. The vehemence of his editorials in the *Cork Mercantile Chronicle* and his growing success as a political activist alarmed Moylan's successor as bishop of Cork, John Murphy. Frustrated in his efforts, England petitioned Rome for permission to go on the American mission, and after three years as parish priest of Bandon, co. Cork (1817–20), he was appointed the first bishop of Charleston in the ecclesiastical province of Baltimore, being consecrated at Cork on 21 September 1820.

The diocese of Charleston comprised the states of North and South Carolina and Georgia—a total area of more than 140,000 square miles, with a Catholic population of little more than 5000 and only four priests. England's Irish experience of democratic politics, popular journalism, and educational reform served him well in his new tasks. The Catholic community in the United States was beset by internal divisions, partly due to the tensions between a largely French and English hierarchy and increasing numbers of Irish clergy and laity. While attempting to heal these divisions England supported Irish claims to greater representation. He had also to contend with the trustee system, whereby parishes were controlled by lay vestries which in some places usurped the right to appoint or dismiss pastors. However, in his *Constitution of the Catholic Church of North Carolina, South Carolina and Georgia* (1823) England set out proposals for a series of consultative councils at state, diocesan, and provincial levels which would allow for participation in decision making by clergy and laity. Though this constitutionalism disarmed 'nativist' critics who viewed the Roman Catholic church as an alien, absolutist, and un-American institution incompatible with republican principles, it was regarded with suspicion by his fellow bishops, and his reputation as a democrat probably prevented his promotion to a more important see. The series of provincial councils held in Baltimore at his instigation between 1829 and 1849 led paradoxically to the emergence of a monarchical model of the episcopate which was to be the norm in the American church until the Second Vatican Council.

As in Cork, so in Charleston, England was particularly concerned with education and the formation of the laity. He established a diocesan college and seminary in 1825, and founded a religious congregation of sisters to catechize poor children and to care for orphans and the sick. He published a popular missal and simple catechism, and from 1822 edited the weekly *United States Catholic Miscellany*, the first American Catholic newspaper, for which he himself wrote most of the articles. He championed the rights of other religious minorities, including Jews, but although he opened a school for black children soon after arriving in Charleston, he was later forced to close it as a result of pressure from the slave owners. Though personally opposed to slavery he maintained a careful balance on the issue of abolition, and argued that the condemnatory letter of Gregory XVI (1839) did not apply to domestic slavery, which was sanctioned by scripture and tradition.

In January 1826 England became the first Roman Catholic prelate to address Congress, at the invitation of President John Quincy Adams. He became an American citizen the same year. In 1832 he paid an *ad limina* visit to Rome, where his energy had earned him the sobriquet *il vescovo a vapore*—'the steam bishop'. There he was appointed by Gregory XVI as a special legate to the government of Haiti, which had been in schism since acquiring independence in 1804. Previous overtures had failed, and England's attempts to negotiate with the government in the course of his visit in 1833 were equally unsuccessful, a concordat not being reached until 1860. He made two more journeys to Europe in 1836 and 1841 and continued to take a keen interest in the affairs of Ireland, where he promoted a greater awareness of the mission field. He died at Charleston on 11 April 1842. His works, collected and edited by Dr Ignatius Reynolds, his successor, were published in five volumes at Baltimore in 1849. England was a decidedly radical churchman and although he played an important role in raising the consciousness of the Catholic community in the United States and establishing its civic credentials, his vision of a collegial church was not realized in his lifetime.   G. MARTIN MURPHY

Sources P. Guilday, *Life and times of John England*, 2 vols. (1927) · P. Carey, *An immigrant bishop: John England's adaptation of Irish Catholicism to American republicanism* (1982) · E. Bolster, *A history of the diocese of Cork*, 3: *From the penal era to the famine* (1989) · P. Clark, 'John England: missionary to America', *Patterns of episcopal leadership*, ed. G. P. Fogarty (1989), 68–88 · T. Corcoran, 'John England, 1786–1842: educator, journalist and first bishop of Charleston', *Studies*, 17 (March 1928) · T. T. McAvoy, *A history of the Catholic church in the United States* (1969) · S. Ahlstrom, *A religious history of the American people* (1972), 538 · R. T. Handy, *A history of the churches in the United States and Canada* (1977), 215–16, 218, 220 · *Catholic Miscellany*, 2 (1823), 56–60
Likenesses J. Peterkin, engraving, repro. in *Irish Catholic Directory* (1843) · J. Sartain, engraving, repro. in J. England, *Collected works*, 1 (1849), frontispiece

England, Sir Richard (1793–1883), army officer, was born at Detroit, Upper Canada, the son of Lieutenant-General Richard England of Lifford, co. Clare, and Anne, daughter of James O'Brien of Ennistyen, a cadet of the family of the marquess of Thomond. His father was a veteran of the War of American Independence, colonel of the 5th foot, lieutenant-governor of Plymouth, and one of the first colonists of western Upper Canada.

After education at Winchester College, England entered the army as an ensign in the 14th foot on 25 February 1808, and in that year served in the expedition to Walcheren and in the attack on Flushing; he became lieutenant on 1 June 1809. He served in the adjutant-general's department in Sicily in 1810 and 1811; on his way there he participated as a volunteer in the defence of Tarifa in Spain. On 11 July 1811 he was promoted captain in the 60th foot, exchanging into the 12th foot on 1 January 1812. In that year he went on leave to Canada to join his father, returning in 1815 to rejoin his regiment after the battle of Waterloo. He served in France in the army of occupation until its withdrawal in 1818. He was then aide-de-camp to Major-General Sir Colquhoun Grant, commanding at Dublin, from 1821 to 1823, and on 4 September 1823 he was promoted major in the 75th foot. On 29 October 1825 he was promoted lieutenant-colonel to succeed the duke of Cleveland in command of the 75th foot. He commanded that regiment for many years and took it to the Cape of Good Hope in 1833. There Lieutenant-General Sir Lowry Cole, the governor, on the outbreak of the Cape Frontier War, chose him to command on the eastern frontier in the appointment of brigadier-general, which rank he held in the campaigns of 1836 and 1837. He was promoted colonel on 28 June 1838.

In 1839 England was transferred to the 41st foot and appointed to command the Belgaum district in the Bombay presidency with the rank of brigadier-general. His wife, Anna Maria, sister of Sir James Caleb Anderson, whom he had married in 1814, died almost immediately on their arrival in India. The First Anglo-Afghan War (1838–42) was then in progress and England was appointed to command the Bombay brigade dispatched to the relief of Colonel Palmer at Ghazni and General Nott at

Kandahar. It marched from Quetta on 26 March 1842 with only two, incomplete, infantry battalions and small detachments of cavalry and horse artillery, England having decided not to wait for the rest of the brigade to catch up with him. On 28 March he met serious opposition at Haikalzai where the Afghans held the heights, forcing England to retire with about a hundred killed and wounded. This unnecessary rebuff annoyed General Nott at Kandahar, not the most even-tempered of men, and he instructed England not to advance again until a brigade had been sent from Kandahar to meet him roughly half way. This was done and England entered Kandahar on 10 May. He acted as second in command to Nott in the defeat of Akbar Khan outside Kandahar on 29 May 1842, but relations between the two men were never good. When Nott marched out of Kandahar on 7 August 1842 with upward of 6000 of his best troops to join forces at Kabul with General Pollock, who was *en route* for India, England marched with his brigade for India via Quetta and the Bolan Pass. Both going and coming he had suffered at the hands of the Baluchi tribesmen and he had not added to his reputation by his service in Afghanistan—but then very few generals had. This did not prevent England's being made KCB on 27 September 1843, after which he resigned his appointment in India, returned home, and settled at Bath.

England was unemployed until 1849, when he was appointed to command the Curragh brigade in Ireland. He was promoted major-general on 11 November 1851. When war was declared on Russia by Britain, France, and Turkey on 28 March 1854, and it was decided to send an expeditionary force to the aid of Turkey, he was given command of the 3rd division. He was aged sixty-one. Neither at the battle of the Alma (20 September 1854) nor at Inkerman (5 November 1854) was the 3rd division deeply engaged, although at the Alma England sent his artillery forward in support of the 1st division. At Inkerman he did not hesitate to take ground to the east to cover the movement forward of Cathcart's 4th division. However, England does not seem to have been highly regarded by some of his officers. 'He never knows his own mind', wrote one of them, 'and it takes him an age to get his division into position' (Hibbert, 126). It was during the trying winter of 1854–5 that England chiefly distinguished himself. He suffered the greatest privations with his troops, but he never applied to come home, and was the last of the original general officers who had accompanied the army to the Crimea to leave it. Before he did return his division was involved in the attack on the Redan at Sevastopol on 18 June 1855, and it was not his fault, nor that of his troops, that the result of that day's hard fighting was unsuccessful. England has been described as a man of meagre talent and reputation but he certainly displayed more staying power than some of his colleagues, remaining at his post until ordered home by his doctor in August 1855.

England was promoted lieutenant-general on 4 June 1856 and made GCB. He was also a grand officer of the Légion d'honneur, a knight of the first class of the Mejidiye, and a knight of the Royal Guelphic Order of Hanover. He never again saw service but was appointed colonel of the 41st foot on 20 April 1861. Promoted general on 6 July 1863, he was placed on the retired list in 1877. He died at St Margaret's, Titchfield, near Fareham, on 19 January 1883. H. M. STEPHENS, *rev.* JAMES LUNT

Sources *The Times* (23 Jan 1883) · Hart's *Army List* · E. H. Nolan, *The illustrated history of the war against Russia*, 2 vols. (1855–7) · A. W. Kinglake, *The invasion of the Crimea*, [new edn], 5 (1877) · J. W. Kaye, *History of the war in Afghanistan*, 3rd edn, 3 (1874) · J. H. Stocqueler, *Memoirs and correspondence of Major-General Sir William Nott*, 2 vols. (1854) · P. Macrory, *Signal catastrophe: the story of a disastrous retreat from Kabul, 1842* (1966) · C. Hibbert, *The destruction of Lord Raglan* [1961] · Fortescue, *Brit. army*, vols. 12–13 · J. A. Norris, *The First Afghan War, 1838–1842* (1967) · CGPLA *Eng. & Wales* (1883)
Archives Bodl. Oxf., letters to Sir C. H. Doyle and Col. Doyle MP
Likenesses C. Holl, stipple (after miniature), NPG
Wealth at death £31,938 10s. 10d.: probate, 17 Feb 1883, CGPLA *Eng. & Wales*

England, Thomas Richard (1790–1847), Roman Catholic priest and biographer, the younger son of Thomas England and his wife, Honora Lordan, and brother of John *England, bishop of Charleston, was born at Cork. After taking holy orders in the Roman Catholic church he was appointed curate of the church of St Peter and St Paul in his native city. He became parish priest of Glanmire, and afterwards of Passage West, co. Cork, where he died on 18 March 1847.

Besides occasional pamphlets, England published three books, including *Letters from the Abbé Edgeworth to his Friends, with Memoirs of his Life* (1818) and *The Life of the Reverend Arthur O'Leary* (1822), a work which reflected the author's own belief in religious toleration and liberty of conscience. Both publications were inspired by papers in the collection of Bishop Moylan of Cork, whose will had named John England as executor. Thomas England hoped to publish an account of eighteenth-century Irish Roman Catholicism based on these documents, but apparently this work was never written. J. Windele praised England's publications as exhibiting 'ability, extensive and varied reading, research and industry' (Windele, 127), qualities which failed, however, to win a lasting reputation for either the works or their author.

THOMPSON COOPER, *rev.* ROSEMARY MITCHELL

Sources J. S. Crone, *A concise dictionary of Irish biography*, rev. edn (1937), 63 · J. Windele, *Historical and descriptive notices of the city of Cork and its vicinity* (1839), 127 · private information (1888) · T. R. England, 'Introductory epistle', *The life of the Reverend Arthur O'Leary* (1822)

Engledow, Sir Frank Leonard (1890–1985), plant scientist and agriculturist, was born on 20 August 1890 at Dartford, Kent, the fifth and youngest child of Henry Engledow of Norfolk, and Elizabeth Prentice from Essex. Henry Engledow was police station sergeant at Bexleyheath, Kent, and on retirement became agent to a brewery. Engledow attended Dartford grammar school from 1904 to 1909, and then entered University College, London, with a one-year scholarship to study pure and applied mathematics with physics. He obtained a London BSc and in 1910 entered St John's College, Cambridge, on an exhibition to read for the mathematical tripos. At half-term he transferred to the natural sciences tripos and he obtained a first in part one (1912). St John's made him a scholar and awarded him a Slater studentship. He also received a Ministry of Agriculture research scholarship and entered the school of agriculture for the two-year diploma course organized by Rowland Biffen. The fruits of the first two years of Engledow's research career were three papers published in 1914 (two written in collaboration). They dealt with the statistical analysis of acquired data, the genetics of wheat, and the quality of wool.

Anticipating the outbreak of the First World War in 1914 Engledow enlisted in the 5th battalion of the Queen's Own Royal West Kent regiment. He had a distinguished war career, and later rose to the rank of lieutenant-colonel in the Territorial Army (1921). He was mentioned in dispatches and awarded the Croix de Guerre (1918) while serving in the Middle East and India. He also had a short spell as assistant director of agriculture in Mesopotamia.

On his return to Cambridge in 1919 Engledow continued his researches on the genetics and yield of wheat, and the use of statistical methods in data analysis and field experimentation. He published this work in a series of important papers over ten years. Later he bred new wheat varieties, the most important of which was Holdfast, a top-class bread wheat. Engledow was also a very effective lecturer. His most important contribution was at the school of agriculture, where he taught at graduate level for the diploma courses, designed for the training of officers for the colonial service and for the Empire Cotton Growing Corporation. The rapid expansion of the biological sciences, combined with the receptive state of agriculture, were then stimulating both research and teaching. Engledow seized the opportunity with great effect, thus fulfilling the expectations of his college, which had elected him to a founders' fellowship in 1919. On 17 March 1921 he married botanist Mildred Emmeline (d. 1956), daughter of Frederick Edward Roper, merchant, of Cape Town. They had four daughters.

In 1930 Engledow was elected Drapers' professor of agriculture and head of the department of agriculture at Cambridge. An expansive period followed as his reputation as an academic agriculturist grew, and the school of agriculture's reputation became international. With the threat and advent of the Second World War he became increasingly involved with policy in food production, not only in this country but on a world scale. He served on many official bodies, including the Agricultural Research Council and the Agricultural Improvement Council, and produced an official memorandum on food and agriculture.

Engledow was closely involved in scientific and agricultural problems of the tropical empire. For thirty years from 1927 he travelled extensively in the tropics, reporting to some fifteen royal commissions and inquiries. He was concerned with major tropical crops, particularly tea, cotton, and rubber, and their associated industries. His concern with agricultural policy was widely based, and his last publication, in 1980, was *Britain's Future in Farming*, written with Leonard Amey and other collaborators. Engledow retired from his chair in 1957. He was appointed

CMG in 1935 and knighted in 1944. In 1946 he was elected a fellow of the Royal Society, on whose council he served in 1948–9.

Engledow was a deeply religious practising Christian and a considerable student of the Bible. He and his family were regular churchgoers and he was a churchwarden. He believed in self-discipline and practised it physically as well as mentally by exercise, games, horse-riding, and carpentry. He died on 3 July 1985 in the Hope Nursing Home, Brooklands, Cambridge, and was buried at St Andrew's Church, Girton, on 3 August. A memorial service was held at St John's College chapel on 12 October 1985.

G. D. H. BELL, *rev.*

Sources G. D. H. Bell, *Memoirs FRS*, 32 (1986), 187–219 · personal knowledge (1990) · A. W. F. Edwards, 'The early history of the statistical estimation of linkage', *Annals of Human Genetics*, 60 (1996), 237–49

Archives Bodl. RH, journals of tours; letters to his wife from Kenya · Cambs. AS, Cambridge, papers relating to history of Girton College · St John Cam., papers · U. Cam., Centre of South Asian Studies | ICL, corresp. with J. W. Munro

Wealth at death £169,129: probate, 6 Sept 1985, *CGPLA Eng. & Wales*

Englefield, Sir Francis (1522–1596), courtier and Roman Catholic exile, was the eldest son of Sir Thomas Englefield (1488–1537) of Englefield, Berkshire, and Elizabeth Throckmorton (d. 1543) of Coughton, Warwickshire. His grandfather Sir Thomas Englefield (1455–1514) was an adviser to the young Henry VIII and speaker of the House of Commons in 1497 and 1510. His father was appointed sheriff of Oxfordshire and Berkshire in 1519. Privately educated, Francis inherited his father's estate in November 1543. At a similar date he married Katherine Fettiplace (d. 1579/80), heir of Compton Beauchamp, Berkshire, as his father had requested him to do before his death.

In the last year of Henry VIII's reign John Dudley, the future duke of Northumberland, selected Englefield for his retinue in two visits to France to negotiate the treaty of 7 June 1546 with Francis I. At the coronation of the young Edward VI he was knighted, and in November 1547 he followed in his father's footsteps as sheriff of Oxfordshire and Berkshire. Early in 1549 Princess Mary appointed him to her household as a 'servant', probably with a higher status unofficially, for on three occasions he was among those summoned before the king's council about her Catholic rites. In July 1549 Englefield, together with her comptroller, Robert Rochester, and her chaplain, was summoned before the council by Edward Seymour and ordered to inform the princess that the Roman ritual used in her residences was prohibited. However, her resolute defiance, and Somerset's prudent preoccupation with his own political survival, left the matter unresolved for two years.

On 9 August 1551, when John Dudley dominated the council's agenda, Englefield, Rochester, and Edward Waldegrave were summoned and ordered to convey to Mary another strong prohibition of her Catholic rites. On 22 August they returned to report that she had forbidden them to repeat this order on pain of dismissal. Since Englefield and the two others refused to repeat again the council's order to her all three were committed to the Tower on 29 August 1551 and not released until 18 March 1552, 'for reasons of health'. Later, after he had returned to Mary's household, in which her Catholic rites had continued privately, Englefield alone was summoned by the exasperated Northumberland to hear a third order of the council on 21 February 1553. However, as the health of the young king was declining and Mary delayed her response, nothing further was done. This series of confrontations between Northumberland and Englefield continued into June 1553, when the duke imprisoned him during his own unsuccessful coup on behalf of Lady Jane Grey.

Once Mary Tudor had vindicated her claim to the throne the career of Englefield prospered visibly, for the queen welcomed him into her entourage at Ipswich and he was sworn as a privy councillor on 25 July 1553. Other influential offices awaited him as well. On 1 May 1554 he became master of the court of wards and liveries, where, under his careful leadership, the crown's revenues rose to £20,020 annually, in comparison with less than half that return under the inefficient earlier regime. At the same time he was elected a knight of his home shire of Berkshire in four of the five sessions of the House of Commons; he did not stand for election in April 1554. The journal for these parliaments, relatively short by later standards, shows that he was not a leading debater but was entrusted with two bills in November and December 1555. The privy council needed more of his attention, not so much at its ordinary meetings, but in the twelve major commissions, such as those for heresy or Irish affairs, on which he served between June 1554 and June 1557.

At the court of Mary, together with his earlier colleagues from her household, Waldegrave and Rochester, Englefield's opinions were more in line with Stephen Gardiner's. Accordingly he was said to be opposed to the queen's marriage with Philip of Spain, but supported the plans of Gardiner for the Catholic restoration. He was suspicious of Roger Ascham's unorthodox religious views but on this occasion both Gardiner and Mary were firm in protecting a gifted humanist. In general, since he held crown offices without previous experience and had begun his career at the age of twenty-seven, he had to defer to many senior courtiers around him. Mary rewarded him with the manor and park of Fulbroke, Warwickshire, which had once belonged to Northumberland, and other lands at £330 a year. King Philip granted him a pension of £150 a year, which, together with his patrimony and the perquisites attached to several minor crown offices, such as constable of Windsor Castle and keeper of the park there, gave him an income which he would never equal again. On the accession of Elizabeth he was asked to resign his various crown appointments and sought instead a licence, which was granted on 12 April 1559, to travel for his health for two years, on condition that he avoid the queen's enemies and return when summoned. After assigning his wife's revenues on 8 May 1559, he left England for Flanders with 600 ounces of plate, 100 marks in coins, eight servants and horses, plus other necessities, but quite unaware that he was leaving for good.

In 1562, after his licence had expired and a summons to return had arrived, Englefield thought it more prudent to remain in Flanders after he heard that some of his Marian courtier contemporaries were being mistreated. Accordingly, Elizabeth ordered a survey of his properties under lease from the crown for later distribution to others. Vainly he appealed in 1564 to Cecil and the privy council to intervene on his behalf, and denied the 'malicious insinuations' against his name (CSP dom., 1547–80, 238). As a last resort he made the hazardous journey to Madrid to ask Philip II to intercede with Elizabeth through his ambassador in London, but the queen politely refused to change her mind. Therefore, as a favour to his former pensioner, Philip wrote on 30 October 1568 to the duke of Alva that Englefield had been appointed one of the duke's advisers at 1000 florins a year until he recovered his property.

After Englefield's return to Flanders a more severe calamity occurred, since he suffered the loss of his eyesight, so that he could no longer write or read. He required a special secretary for his correspondence and, for personal safety, was forced to travel by coach. Meanwhile, the queen bestowed more of his properties on her favourite, Leicester. In August 1574 a protocol was signed in Bristol whereby England and Spain agreed to expel the 'rebels' of each kingdom from their territories. Englefield had to depart from Flanders, despite his poor health, in the spring of 1575 and find sanctuary in Liège. Since the English College at Douai was also forced to find a new home in France, Englefield and his close friend, the president of Douai, William Allen, decided to go to Rome early in 1576 to appeal to Pope Gregory XIII to finance a 'holy enterprise', in which 5000 armed men were to invade England to enforce the previous excommunication of Elizabeth by Pius V in February 1570. The Spanish ambassador in Rome, who described this naïve plan to Madrid, did not report that the two Englishmen had prepared it, but that they were its keen advocates. However, they were unsuccessful since Philip was on friendly terms with Elizabeth and close to bankruptcy, and the pope was without the resources to finance it. Before leaving Rome in 1576 Englefield signed before witnesses a conveyance of his rights to his estates to his nephew in England, 'to the use of himself for life' (Loomie, 23), which could revert to their original owner only after the presentation of a gold ring to the nephew.

In 1580, following the death of his wife in England, Englefield had his pension as an adviser on English affairs transferred to Madrid. It is well known that Philip II had already organized a network of councils to advise on the numerous problems of his empire, but documents from Englefield in the file of the council of state contain his comments about the pensions requested by English strangers, his opinions of suspected spies, and newsletters about events in England. He was a strong advocate for the needs of Mary, queen of Scots, and, together with Jane Dormer, dowager duchess of Feria, was anxious in 1589 to secure approval for St Alban's College, the first English seminary in Castile. Meanwhile, the final assault on his estates began after the revelations of the Throckmorton plot in London, after which he was indicted for treason and outlawed in 1584. In 1587 he was named in an act of attainder (29 Eliz. c. 1), which had to be supplemented by an act in 1593 (35 Eliz. c. 5) directed at his 'golden ring' conveyance. In any case his properties had already been judged by a disappointed courtier in 1587 to have 'little of any value' in them (*Salisbury MS*, 13.273, 287).

For Englefield and other leading exiles a graver incident by far was the failure of King Philip's advisers to consult them before the Armada of 1588. In the aftermath of that débâcle Englefield renewed his study of the succession to the throne after Elizabeth. In 1595 he was one of a small group of pro-Spanish exiles who petitioned Philip II to promote the candidacy for the throne of his daughter, the Infanta Isabella. However, Philip had already formed other dynastic plans for her. It is certain that Englefield provided genealogical information about possible claimants to Robert Persons, who was in Spain at that time, which was included in the famous *Conference about the Next Succession* published in English and Latin in 1595.

The last months of Englefield's life were spent at St Alban's College in Valladolid, where he wrote his last will, in which from his Castilian sources he gave legacies to three Spanish servants and three English secretaries and his executor. There is no evidence to support a later rumour that he was admitted to the Jesuit order at this time. He died at St Alban's College on 13 September 1596 and was buried in the college chapel.   A. J. LOOMIE

Sources T. F. T. Baker, 'Englefield, Sir Francis (1521/22–1596)', HoP, *Commons, 1509–58* · A. J. Loomie, *The Spanish Elizabethans* (1963), 14–51 · D. M. Loades, *The reign of Mary Tudor: politics, government and religion in England, 1553–58* (1979) · J. Hurstfield, *The queen's wards: wardship and marriage under Elizabeth I* (1958) · A. Weikel, 'The Marian council revisited', *The mid-Tudor polity, c.1540–1560*, ed. J. Loach and R. Tittler (1980), 52–73 · *Letters of William Allen and Richard Barret, 1572–1598*, ed. P. Renold, Catholic RS, 58 (1967) · E. Duffy, *The stripping of the altars: traditional religion in England, c.1400–c.1580* (1992) · G. Parker, *The grand strategy of Philip II* (1998) · *Calendar of the manuscripts of the most hon. the marquis of Salisbury*, 3, HMC, 9 (1889); 13 (1915) · *VCH Berkshire*, vols. 3–4 · *CSP dom.*, 1547–80, 238, 507, 524

Archives Archivo General de Simancas, Valladolid, Spain, Sección de Estado, MSS · Bucks. RLSS, an account certifying his will [translation] · PRO, state papers, domestic and foreign, intercepted letters · St Alban's College, Valladolid, Spain, MSS · Westminster Cathedral Archive, London, MSS

Wealth at death modest gifts to servants; English estate forfeited by attainder: 29 Eliz. c. 1, 1587 (35 Eliz. c. 5, 1593); will, Westminster Cathedral Archives Series A; inquisition post mortem, Bodl. Oxf., Eng. Hist. MS B172

Englefield, Sir Henry Charles, seventh baronet (*c*.1752–1822), antiquary and writer on science, was the eldest of the five children of Sir Henry Englefield, sixth baronet (1715–1780), landowner, and his second wife, Catharine Buck (1725–1805), daughter of Sir Charles Buck, third baronet. A member of a long-established family of Catholic gentry, he is said to have been educated at one of the English Catholic colleges abroad. He succeeded his father as the seventh baronet in 1780, but moved from the family home at White Knights, Sonning, Berkshire, allegedly because of the prejudices of the neighbouring gentry. He lived at 5 Tilney Street, Mayfair, until his death. He never

Sir Henry Charles Englefield, seventh baronet (*c*.1752–1822), by Thomas Phillips, 1815

married but had a mistress, Milburgh Allpress, Mrs Crewe (1764/5–1803), from at least 1794 until her death and was cited in a divorce case successfully brought by her husband, Major-General Richard Crewe, before Doctors' Commons in 1800. The previous year he had to pay the husband damages as a result of a civil action of criminal conversation. Their son, Henry, born within a year, was illegitimate and was unable to succeed to the baronetcy. Although William Cole told Horace Walpole that Sir Henry was indifferent about his religion, Englefield was a prominent member of the Catholic Committee, 1782–92, a founder member of the Catholic Cisalpine Club, 1792, and sent his son to the Catholic Oscott College, Oscott, Warwickshire, in 1814.

Englefield's scholarship in several branches of knowledge earned him election to most of the learned societies in London, namely, the Royal Society in 1778, the Society of Antiquaries of London in 1779, the Linnean Society in 1807, the Geological Society in 1811, the Astronomical Society in 1820, and as antiquary to the Royal Academy in 1821. He was a member of the Society of Dilettanti from 1781 and its secretary from 1808 until his death. He was also elected fellow of the Royal Society of Edinburgh in 1796. Among his numerous scientific publications, the most substantial was *On the Determination of the Orbit of Comets* (1793), on which subject he corresponded with William Herschel. He had a particular interest in improving scientific instruments so as to make them suitable for use by travellers, giving his name to the Englefield mountain barometer, which he first described in *Nicholson's Magazine* (1806). He devised a portable telescope for astronomers, details of which he published in Tilloch's *Philosophical Magazine* (1814).

As an antiquary, Englefield made numerous contributions to *Archaeologia*, starting with his first paper read to the Society of Antiquaries in 1779, on Reading Abbey, which was near his childhood home at White Knights. With Richard Gough he fostered the society's major Cathedral Series, in an attempt partly to match the Society of Dilettanti's publications on classical architecture with an equivalent for Gothic. He wrote the descriptive notes for six of the volumes. He was a controversial figure in the society, making many enemies when he took the side of John Carter against James Wyatt over the latter's work at Durham Cathedral. As senior vice-president, he was chosen president by the society's council in August 1811 on the death of the earl of Leicester, but he was rejected in favour of Lord Aberdeen at the closely fought election held in April 1812. Both were satirized in George Cruikshank's cartoon, *The Antiquarian Society*, published five months later in his monthly magazine *The Scourge*. He rarely attended subsequent meetings.

Englefield had a strong interest in the visual arts from an early age. Some of his sketches survive for tours in England and Wales around 1781–3, and he exhibited at the Royal Academy in 1787–9. His chief topographical work, *Picturesque Beauties of the Isle of Wight* (1816), was the result of observations made between 1799 and 1801 and is illustrated with several of his drawings. He was friend or patron to artists such as Dr Monro, John Carter, and J. S. Cotman, who dedicated his first portfolio of etchings to Englefield (1811). His development of a durable red colour from madder earned him the Society of Arts gold medal, and was published in their *Transactions* for 1804. Several portraits of him were drawn and painted, of which the most notable is that by Sir Thomas Lawrence in 1812 for the Society of Dilettanti. Sir Francis Chantrey completed a marble bust of him in 1820. He owned an important collection of Greek and Etruscan vases, which was sold after his death.

He had engaged in hazardous optical experiments with the surgeon Sir Everard Home and the instrument maker Jesse Ramsden, and by 1814 his sight was beginning to fail. He was nearly blind by 1819 when he undertook the operation of couching, and is said by his friend the writer William Sotheby to have made a partial recovery shortly before his death. Sotheby paid tribute to the vivacity of his conversation, his eloquence, judgement, and remarkable memory. He quoted Charles Fox as claiming that he never left his company uninstructed. Englefield died at his home, 5 Tilney Street, on 21 March 1822, and was buried on 28 March with his ancestors and his mistress in the parish church of Englefield, Berkshire. His son, who was still at school, was the chief beneficiary of his will of 1819 and the family trust, but the baronetcy became extinct. His collections were sold at Christies, on 6–8 March 1823.

BERNARD NURSE

Sources *GM*, 1st ser., 92/1 (1822), 293–4 · W. Sotheby, *To the members of the Society of Dilettanti* (1822); repr. in *GM*, 92/1 (1822), 418–20 · Gillow, *Lit. biog. hist.*, vol. 2 · 'Civil action, *Richard Crewe esq. v. Sir Henry Inglefield*', *The Times* (26 June 1799), 3 · 'Divorce court proceedings, *Crewe v. Crewe and Englefield*', *The Times* (6 May 1800), 3 · 'Divorce court proceedings, *Crewe v. Crewe and Englefield*', *The Times* (14 July 1800), 3 · E. B. Nurse, 'George Cruikshank's *The Antiquarian Society*, 1812, and Sir Henry Charles Englefield', *Antiquaries Journal*, 80 (2000), 316–20 · J. Evans, *A history of the Society of Antiquaries* (1956) · E. G. R. Taylor, *The mathematical practitioners of Hanoverian England, 1714–1840* (1966) · will of 27 April 1819, proved 21 June 1822, PRO, PROB 11/1658, sig. 312 · Sir Henry Englefield, private estate acts, 1818–19, 59 G3 c92 · Sir Henry Englefield, private estate acts (Wharram Percy Estate), 1834, 3–4 W4 c3 · students' register, 1814–23, Oscott College, Sutton Coldfield · R. E. Scantlebury, 'The Catholic registers of Reading, 1780–1840', *Catholic Record Society*, 32 (1932), 117–31 · B. Ward, *The dawn of the Catholic revival in England, 1781–1803*, 2 vols. (1909) · Farington, *Diary* · Mallalieu, *Watercolour artists*, vol. 1 · Walpole, *Corr.*, vol. 2 · L. Cust and S. Colvin, eds., *History of the Society of Dilettanti* (1898); repr. with suppl. chaps. (1914) · J. M. Crook, *John Carter and the mind of the Gothic revival*, Society of Antiquaries of London Occasional Papers, 17 (1995) · A. McConnell, 'Features of portable, travelling and mountain barometers', *Antique Collecting*, 24/10 (1990), 5–9 · GEC, *Baronetage* · *DNB* · IGI

Archives Bodl. Oxf., 'Description of the Isle of Wight', copy with MS additions by Thomas Webster · Bodl. Oxf., corresp. · Exeter Central Library, Westcountry Studies Library, observations on Charles Lyttelton's account of Exeter Cathedral · Exeter Central Library, notes · priv. coll. · priv. coll., journal of Welsh tour with Lady Palmerston [copy] · S. Antiquaries, Lond., observations on Exeter Cathedral · U. Southampton L., notes · U. Southampton L., MS additions to 'A walk through Southampton' and letters to the printer for second edition | Bodl. Oxf., letters to F. Douce, T. Percy, J. Buchler, M. Noble · RAS, letters to William Herschel

Likenesses J. Reynolds, oils, 1787, priv. coll. · G. Dance, pencil drawing, 1794, NPG · J. S. Cotman, pencil drawing, 1804, BM · T. Lawrence, oils, 1812, Brooks's Club, London, Society of Dilettanti · C. Picart, stipple, 1812 (after H. Edridge), BM, NPG; repro. in *Contemporary portraits* (1812) · J. S. Cotman, pencil drawing, 1814, V&A · T. Phillips, oils, 1815, NPG [*see illus.*] · F. Chantrey, drawing, 1817, V&A · medal, 1817, NPG · G. Mills, medals, 1817–19, BM · F. Chantrey, bust, 1818, AM Oxf. · H. Moses, etching, pubd 1819, NPG · F. Chantrey, marble bust, 1820, Cleveland Museum of Art, Ohio · C. Turner, mezzotint, pubd 1821 (after T. Phillips), BM, NPG · G. Cruikshank, cartoon, BM; repro. in G. Cruikshank, *The Antiquarian Society* (1812) · Evans, engraving (after Scott), repro. in H. C. Englefield, *Description of the Isle of Wight* (1816)

Wealth at death will, PRO, PROB 12/214 · property held in trust: Englefield, private estate acts, 1818–19, 59 G3 c 92

Engleheart, Francis (1775–1849), engraver, was born on 28 July 1775 in London, the son of Thomas *Engleheart (*bap.* 1745, *d.* 1809), a sculptor, and his wife, Ann Wade (1753–1779), whom he married on 8 October 1774. He was educated in Hertford and London at Christ's Hospital, where he was admitted on 12 May 1784 from Richmond, his father being described as a needlemaker. On 7 December 1790, for a fee of £52, he was apprenticed to the engraver Joseph Collyer (1748–1827), and later he assisted James Heath, a former Collyer apprentice. On 22 May 1799 he married Jane Diana (*b.* 1771), the daughter of Joseph Le Petit, at St Marylebone, Marylebone Road; the couple had a daughter, Sarah Jane (*bap.* 3 Sept 1800) and two sons, Timothy Stansfeld and Jonathan Henry [*see below*].

Engleheart worked mainly in line. Among his earliest plates was *General Fairfax*, after Bowers (1808). Between 1810 and 1812 he engraved part of *The Canterbury Pilgrims*, after Thomas Stothard, begun by Luigi Schiavonetti (d. 1810), finished by James Heath, and published in 1817. He achieved notice by engraving some of Richard Cook's designs for several publications, notably Homer's *Iliad* and *Odyssey* and *The Castle* for Walter Scott's *The Lady of the Lake*. Cadell and Davies commissioned Robert Smirke to produce designs for their publications, after which Engleheart engraved, for example, three for Le Sage's *Gil Blas*, first published in 1809, and about thirty for Cervantes' *Don Quixote* in 1818. Eleven subjects from *Don Quixote* were exhibited at W. B. Cooke's exhibition of engravings in 1821, together with *A Gentleman*, after William Owen, and three plates from Scott's *Poems*, after Richard Westall and Stothard. Engleheart was then living at 2 Bayham Street, Camden Town. His work on steel began with the annuals, for example, the *Literary Souvenir* (1826–32), *The Keepsake* (1829–34), *The Amulet* (1827), *The Gem*, and *Wreath of Friendship*. Engleheart's engraving after a self-portrait by Hans Holbein was reproduced in Horace Walpole's *Anecdotes of Painting* (1827), and a vignette of a lute player after Parmigiano was engraved for Samuel Rogers's *Poems* in 1834. Engleheart etched plates for the *Description of the Collection of Ancient Marbles in the British Museum* (1812–45), as did his son Timothy. F. G. Moon published Engleheart's engravings of David Wilkie's *Duncan Gray* and *The Only Daughter* (c.1835–1839). His last and most important production was *Serena Rescued by the Red-Cross Knight*, after William Hilton, which appeared in the *Art Union* in 1846. His plates were signed 'F. Engleheart'. The number of plates produced was not great, but their regular appearance over a period of time indicated some popularity with the publishers. Engleheart died after a short illness on 15 February 1849 in his seventy-fourth year.

His elder son, **Timothy Stansfeld Engleheart** (1803–1879), engraver, was probably his father's pupil. In 1818 he was awarded the silver Isis medal of the Society of Arts for an outline drawing of the Farnese Hercules; his address was then Bayham Street, Camden Town. He and his wife, Ann, had two sons, Stansfeld (*bap.* 14 Nov 1833) and Francis James (*bap.* 8 Aug 1834), and one daughter, Lucy Mary (*bap.* 27 April 1837). He worked for annuals such as *The Casket*, *Forget-me-Not*, and the *Literary Souvenir*. Two plates were done for William Hogarth's *Works* (1833), and *The Black Linn of Linklater*, after Alexander Chisholm, for G. N. Wright's *Landscape-Historical Illustrations of Scotland* (1836–8). Engleheart moved to Germany as a portrait engraver and about 1840 engraved *Ecce homo*, after G. Reni, at Darmstadt. Six steel-engravings after German artists were done for *Rheinisches Taschenbuch*, published at Frankfurt by Sauerlander (1842), and in J. J. Sievers's *A Russian Statesman* his engraved portrait of Prince Besborodko was signed with his name and 'sc. Darmstadt'. His plates were signed 'T. S. Engleheart'. He later returned to London, where he died in 1879 aged seventy-six.

Francis Engleheart's younger son, **Jonathan Henry Engleheart** (*bap.* 1808, *d.* after 1841), engraver, was baptized at St Marylebone on 20 January 1808, and was also probably his father's pupil. His landscape work came to the fore with *Cardiff Castle*, after Henry Gastineau, in the latter's *Wales Illustrated* (1830), and in T. Rose's *Westmorland* (1832) he did two plates after George Pickering. *Col. Maxwell's Last Charge at Assaye*, after Abraham Cooper, engraved for W. H. Maxwell's *Life of the Duke of Wellington* (1839–41), was signed 'J^no H. Engleheart', though most of his work was signed 'J. Engleheart', or occasionally 'J. H. Engleheart'. From 1839 he engraved plates for the *Sporting Review*.   B. HUNNISETT

Sources *Art Journal*, 11 (1849), 206 · D. F. McKenzie, ed., *Stationers' Company apprentices*, [3]: 1701–1800 (1978) · [W. B. Cooke], *Exhibition of engravings* (1822), 3, 6, 18, 19 [exhibition catalogue, 9 Soho Square, London, 1822] · Thieme & Becker, *Allgemeines Lexikon* · J. Heath, *The Heath family engravers, 1779–1878*, 1 (1993), 26 · IGI · indexes of births, marriages, and deaths, Family Records Centre, London · GL, Christ's Hospital MSS, MS 12818/11

Engleheart, George (1750–1829), miniature painter, was born on 26 October 1750 at Kew, Surrey, the third surviving son of Francis Engelhardt or Engleheart (1713/14–1773), a plaster modeller who had emigrated from Germany in his childhood, and his wife, Ann Dawney (*bap.* 1713, *d.* 1780), daughter of Thomas Dawney, parish clerk of Kew, and his wife, Anne. Engleheart's formal training as an artist began when he enrolled as a student at the Royal Academy Schools on 3 November 1769 and gave his age, incorrectly, as sixteen. However, some early landscape and animal sketches in watercolour survive (priv. coll.), which reflect the additional instruction Engleheart gained in the studio of the landscape artist George Barret. Barret's bankruptcy may have been the reason for Engleheart's transferring to the studio of Sir Joshua Reynolds, where he served an apprenticeship perhaps intermittently between 1773 and 1776. A series of miniature copies on ivory of paintings by Reynolds, some painted by Engleheart as late as 1793, was kept by him and left as treasured bequests to his children, showing the longstanding high regard in which he held his master. Reynolds's influence is evident in certain examples of Engleheart's work in miniature, such as his *Mrs Lesley* (1778; ex Sothebys, 4 December 1985, lot 238), a three-quarter-length composition with an extensive landscape background. What is certain is that during or soon after the completion of this apprenticeship Engleheart became established with remarkable swiftness and success as a miniaturist. He worked initially in premises owned by his late father in Shepherd Street, Mayfair, and from 1776 at a studio in Princes Street, near Hanover Square, London. The first entry in Engleheart's fee-book dates from January 1775 but he had been exhibiting portrait miniatures at the Royal Academy since 1773 and it may have been there that he first attracted the custom of the eminent clientele who were immediately drawn to him. His preferred medium was watercolour on ivory but he also produced the occasional full-length coloured drawing, such as *The Loftus Children* (c.1800; ex Phillips, 17 March 1998, lot 135A). It seems that he also experimented with enamels but barely a handful of examples have survived, in contrast to the 4853 ivory miniatures that this prolific artist painted in the course of a career of almost forty years.

Engleheart was a quick worker; in May 1782 alone he

George Engleheart (1750–1829), self-portrait, c.1803

these traits are illustrated in his miniature of *Maria Tryphena Blunt, Lady Cockerell* (c.1789; Fitzwilliam Museum, Cambridge). Graham Reynolds identifies a 'chapeau de paille phase' within this period, during which Engleheart portrayed many of his female sitters wearing the jaunty, beribboned straw hats so popular at the time (Reynolds, *English Portrait Miniatures*, 141). His *Portrait of a Woman* of about 1790 (Metropolitan Museum of Art, New York) shows the impact of high fashion on his female portraits of this era. His later work (c.1790–1813) is marked by his use of larger ivory plaques (usually 3–3½ inches in height) but there was no diminution in the quality of his work as he reached the end of his professional life.

Engleheart was a frequent exhibitor at the Royal Academy between 1773 and 1822, the only long interruption perhaps being accounted for by the death of his first wife, Elizabeth Brown (1753–1779), daughter of Nathaniel and Elizabeth Brown of Marylebone Street, Golden Square, London, whom he had married in 1776. With his first wife's sister Ursula Sarah Brown (1760–1817), whom he married on 27 May 1781, he had four children: George (d. 1833), Nathaniel (d. 1869), Henry (d. 1885), and Emma (d. 1863). Family life was based at 4 Hertford Street, Mayfair, where Engleheart worked from 1783, and at their country home at Bedfont, near Hounslow in Middlesex. It was to Bedfont that Engleheart retired quite suddenly in July 1813, painting only portraits of family and friends thereafter. His closest circle included the group of artists and poets who had met for many years at the home of the poet William Hayley at Felpham in Sussex, and he numbered George Romney, William Blake, John Flaxman, and Jeremiah Meyer among them. One of Engleheart's miniatures of his friend William Hayley (1809) is now in the Fitzwilliam Museum, Cambridge. In 1827 Engleheart moved to Blackheath, Kent, to live with his son Nathaniel, and he died there on 21 March 1829; he was buried in the family vault at Kew church.

Engleheart trained two pupils who continued to work in his style after his death: a distant cousin, the miniaturist Thomas Richmond, and a nephew, **John Cox Dillman Engleheart** (1784–1862), miniature painter. Born in Kew on 2 January 1784 and baptized there on 29 January, he was the eighth child of George Engleheart's elder brother John Dillman Engleheart (1735–1810) and his wife, Jane Parker. He worked as an assistant to George Engleheart, contributing to backgrounds and making copies of his miniatures, before entering the Royal Academy Schools on 21 June 1800. His earliest recorded miniature dates from 1799 and by 1801 he was exhibiting his work at the Royal Academy, but he probably did not set up his own independent practice until about 1807. In that year he took a studio at 88 Newman Street, London, from which he worked for many years, although he appears also to have worked in Birmingham about 1810, and in 1811 he married Mary Barker (d. 1878) of Edgbaston, Birmingham. He contributed to exhibitions at the British Institution (1808–9) as well as continuing to exhibit at the Royal Academy until 1828, the year in which his health finally broke down, compelling him to retire and travel abroad. On his

painted twenty-seven miniatures. His rapid rate of work would have been assisted by his method of working straight from the life without making preliminary sketches, and the numerous tracings of his work which survive were probably made after the completion of each miniature as a record to assist in the production of copies, should they be required. Fortunately the existence of Engleheart's fee-book (priv. coll.) charts comprehensively the progress of his career and documents the astonishingly consistent level of his success. By 1776, within only two years of the start of his career, he had already had three sittings from George III; the fee-book records that he painted the king no fewer than twenty-five times. His popularity with the monarch was eventually recognized by his appointment as miniature painter to the king (1789), on the death of Jeremiah Meyer. The title formalized his role as court miniaturist in contrast with his main competitor, Richard Cosway, whose patrons included the prince of Wales and members of his glamorous coterie. Unlike Cosway's flamboyant, dashing style Engleheart's work was characterized by the dignity and sobriety of its presentation, by his realistic observation of his sitters, and by his excellent draughtsmanship. Three distinctive phases have been recognized in the development of his work: his early miniatures (c.1773–1780) were on a relatively small scale and were somewhat muted in feel in comparison with the confident handling and bolder brushwork of his middle period (c.1780–1795). At this point his characteristic heavy emphasis on the eyes of his sitters, his linear treatment of the hair, and his generous highlighting of the costume of his sitters with zigzag touches of opaque white became more noticeable; all return from Switzerland and southern Italy in 1834 he returned to the home in East Acton, Middlesex, which he had occupied since 1816. In 1852 he moved to Beech Holm, Tunbridge Wells, Kent, where he died on 29 October 1862; he was buried at Woodbury Park cemetery, Tunbridge Wells. An able miniaturist, his capacities are well illustrated by his miniatures *Unknown Officer* (1814; Glynn Vivian Art Gallery, Swansea) and *Richard Brinsley Sheridan* (repr. Williamson, 73; version in the National Museum, Stockholm). Initially his style resembled a weaker version of his uncle's but after about 1810 his work became finer and more distinctive. He signed his work with the monogram JCDE on the front and back and also in full on the reverse. Perhaps in response to his nephew's establishment in the same trade George Engleheart adapted his own early form of signature, a cursive GE or E on the front, to a full signature and date on the reverse.

Self-portraits of both uncle and nephew are in the National Portrait Gallery, London; significant collections of the work of George Engleheart are in the Victoria and Albert Museum, London (together with his paintbox and palettes) and the Fitzwilliam Museum, Cambridge. Important holdings in the United States include those in the Huntington Library and Art Gallery, San Marino, California, and the William Rockhill Nelson Gallery and Mary Atkins Museum, Kansas City. George Engleheart's reputation, high enough to ensure a constant demand for his work throughout his professional career, remained undiminished under the scrutiny of the art historian G. C. Williamson, writing in collaboration with H. L. D. Engleheart, in 1902. In recent times Graham Reynolds has reaffirmed the consensus of critics in placing Engleheart among the group of 'late eighteenth-century miniaturists of the first rank', together with Richard Cosway, John Smart, and Ozias Humphry (Reynolds, *English Portrait Miniatures*, 138).   V. REMINGTON

Sources private information (2004) [H. Engleheart] · G. C. Williamson and H. L. D. Engleheart, *George Engleheart* (1902) · 'Kew, Surrey: baptisms 1714–91, marriages 1714–83, burials 1714–85', transcribed by J. Challoner-Smith, 1989, Society of Genealogists Library, London [typescript] · S. C. Hutchison, 'The Royal Academy Schools, 1768–1830', *Walpole Society*, 38 (1960–62), 123–91, esp. 134, 159 · B. S. Long, *British miniaturists* (1929), 141–4 · D. Foskett, *Miniatures: dictionary and guide* (1987), 369–73, 535–6 · L. R. Schidlof, *The miniature in Europe in the 16th, 17th, 18th, and 19th centuries*, 1 (1964), 237–9 · G. Reynolds, *English portrait miniatures* (1952); rev. edn (1988) · R. Ormond, *Early Victorian portraits*, 1 (1973), 161–2 · G. Hall and others, *Summary catalogue of miniatures in the Victoria and Albert Museum* (1981), 17–19 · R. Bayne-Powell, ed., *Catalogue of portrait miniatures in the Fitzwilliam Museum, Cambridge* (1985), 72–9 · G. Reynolds, *The Starr Collection of miniatures in the William Rockhill Nelson Gallery* (1971), 27 · Graves, *RA exhibitors* · CGPLA Eng. & Wales (1862) [John Cox Dillman Engleheart]
Archives priv. coll., fee-book and tracings book
Likenesses G. Engleheart, pencil and wash drawing, c.1796 (John Cox Dillman Engleheart), priv. coll. · G. Engleheart, self-portrait, watercolour, c.1803, NPG [see illus.] · J. C. D. Engleheart, self-portrait, watercolour on ivory, c.1810 (John Cox Dillman Engleheart), NPG; version, priv. coll. · J. C. D. Engleheart, drawing, watercolour on ivory, 1814, priv. coll. · J. C. D. Engleheart, self-portrait, watercolour on ivory, 1821 (John Cox Dillman Engleheart), priv. coll.; version, priv. coll. · G. Engleheart, self-

portrait, V&A · G. Engleheart, self-portrait, watercolour, two versions, priv. coll. · portraits, repro. in Williamson and Engleheart, *George Engleheart*
Wealth at death under £16,000—John Cox Dillman Engleheart: probate, 26 Nov 1862, *CGPLA Eng. & Wales*

Engleheart, John Cox Dillman (1784–1862). *See under* Engleheart, George (1750–1829).

Engleheart, Jonathan Henry (*bap.* 1808, *d.* after 1841). *See under* Engleheart, Francis (1775–1849).

Engleheart, Thomas (*bap.* 1745, *d.* 1809), modeller and carver, was born in Kew, Surrey, and baptized on 15 April 1745 at St Anne's Church, Kew Green. He was the third surviving son of Francis Engelheart or Engleheart (1713/14–1773), an ornamental plasterer who had emigrated from Germany c.1721 and settled at Kew, and his wife, Ann Dawney (*bap.* 1713, *d.* 1780). Thomas's younger brother was the miniaturist George *Engleheart (1750–1829). After serving an apprenticeship (1760–67) to Sefferin Alkin, a carver of St James's, Westminster, Engleheart was admitted as a student at the Royal Academy Schools in 1769. In 1772 he was in competition with John Flaxman for the Schools' highest honour, the gold medal awarded that year for the best bas-relief of *Ulysses and Nausicaa*. Engleheart's unequivocal success in the competition was a bitter disappointment for Flaxman. Between 1773 and 1786 Engleheart exhibited models in wax and busts at the Royal Academy, and in 1777 gained a premium from the Society of Arts for a lifesize model in clay, or cast in plaster, *John the Baptist in the Desert*. His wax portraits of Queen Charlotte and George III remain in the Royal Collection. His last attested work is as a carver of capitals for Dodington, ancestral home of the Codrington family, between 1804 and 1809.

Engleheart married, on 8 October 1774, Ann Wade (1753–1779); their son, Francis *Engleheart (1775–1849), was an engraver. Following Ann's death in April 1779 he married, on 9 October 1780, Mary King (1756–1831). They had at least two daughters and a son. In 1784 Engleheart was made a freeman of the Needlemakers' Company. According to family records he died on 20 March 1809, possibly at Dodington: a payment to Francis Engleheart 'on Acct of his Father's Carving', recorded in the Dodington estate account books for 25 March 1809, would seem to confirm this date. Engleheart's will was proved on 15 December 1809.   MICHAEL J. FOGG

Sources A. Cunningham, *The lives of the most eminent British painters, sculptors, and architects*, 3 (1830) · J. T. Smith, *Nollekens and his times*, 2nd edn, 2 (1829) · R. Dossie, *Memoirs of agriculture, and other oeconomical arts*, 3 (1782) · *Premiums offered by the society instituted at London for the encouragement of arts, manufactures and commerce* (1776) · general assembly minutes, vol. 1, 1768–96, RA · E. J. Pyke, *A biographical dictionary of wax modellers* (1973) · R. Gunnis, *Dictionary of British sculptors, 1660–1851* (1953); new edn (1968) · Glos. RO, Codrington MSS, D1610; A77; A97 · Henry Moore Institute, Leeds, Centre for the Study of Sculpture, Gunnis MSS · Graves, *RA exhibitors* · S. C. Hutchison, 'The Royal Academy Schools, 1768–1830', *Walpole Society*, 38 (1960–62), 123–91 · private information (2004) [Henry F. A. Engleheart] · will, PRO, PROB 11/1506, fols. 235r–235v · B. Hunnisett, 'Engleheart', *The dictionary of art*, ed. J. Turner (1996) · parish register, Kew, St Anne's Church, 15 April 1745 [baptism] · apprenticeship books, PRO, IR 1/22 · parish register, St George, Hanover

Square, 8 Oct 1774 [marriage] • parish register, St George, Hanover Square, 9 Oct 1780 [marriage]
Likenesses G. Engleheart, drawing, priv. coll.
Wealth at death £600 of lawful money; bequests to children of £700: will, PRO, PROB 11/1506, fols. 235r–235v

Engleheart, Timothy Stansfeld (1803–1879). *See under* Engleheart, Francis (1775–1849).

English, Sir David (1930–1998), journalist, was born on 26 May 1930 in Combe, near Woodstock, Oxfordshire, the only child of Alfred Joseph English (1901–1930), a bank clerk and innkeeper, and his wife, Kathleen Victoria (Kitty) Brazenor (1899–1964). Alfred English died when his son was less than three months old. English's mother earned a living working as a secretary for the Post Office, then running a boarding-house in Broadstairs, and her parents helped bring up the small boy. The influence of English's grandfather upon him seems to have been profound. A devout Methodist, by his beliefs and actions he instilled in his grandson a regard for the values of family life. He had been a district manager of the Transport and General Workers' Union, and read three newspapers a day. His grandson therefore grew up in a household of acute political awareness, where the press was keenly read and discussed. While English was still a child his mother and her parents bought a hotel in Bournemouth, and this was where he spent his formative years, being educated at Bournemouth grammar school.

Early career As soon as English left school in 1946 he became a cub reporter on a local paper, the *Christchurch Times*. Fiercely ambitious, he was also thrilled by the romance of newspapers, and his own life story—moving from the bottom rung of the trade to being a multi-millionaire newspaper executive on the back of success he had largely created for himself—was the stuff of that romance. Although remarkably healthy throughout his life he managed to fail the medical for national service, so his career continued uninterrupted. In 1949 he moved to the *Portsmouth Evening News* and in 1951, aged still only twenty-one, he made it to Fleet Street as a reporter on the *Daily Mirror*. Once established in the national press he was determined not to allow the grass to grow under him. On 30 August 1952 he married Irene (*b*. 1931), an actress and dancer, and daughter of William Mainwood, a licensed victualler. They had a son and two daughters. In 1953 English left the *Mirror* for a stint on *Reynolds' News*, a Sunday newspaper. Then in 1956 he changed tack to become features editor of the *Daily Sketch*, and learned something of the trade of the newspaper executive.

English did not enjoy being tied to a desk. He had an unfulfilled ambition to travel, and was able to satisfy it in 1959 when he joined the *Sunday Dispatch*, then near the end of its life, as New York correspondent. It was with this widening of his experience that the English legend really began to take shape. It was a legend he played an assiduous part in creating. In New York he boasted that he was the youngest foreign correspondent in the city, though he was silenced on discovering that the *Daily Telegraph*'s man was five years younger. When he qualified for a *Who's Who*

Sir David English (1930–1998), by Nikki English, *c*.1995

entry he altered the date of his birth from 1930 to 1931, and that of his marriage from 1952 to 1954, for reasons that were never entirely clear but which were dismissed by colleagues as vanity. He sent a stream of front-page exclusives back to London, not suffering from the fact that when other journalists tried to follow many of them up for Monday's daily papers the basis on which they had been written was found to have been flimsy. One colleague, Alan Watkins, arriving to take up a post in New York, was warned from all sides that English was 'a sharp fellow, very sharp. He would readily pull a fast one and might even, if he thought it necessary, practise deception' (*Daily Telegraph*, 12 June 1998). As far as Watkins was concerned the warning turned out to be unfounded, but English never quite threw off a reputation for sharpness, and indeed later seemed to revel in it. He was always ruthless, and saw no reason to be ashamed of that trait. Watkins wrote of the young English that he 'looked a decade younger than his 29 years and had about him something of the Artful Dodger. He fizzed' (ibid.).

There was no faulting English's competence or professionalism, and when the *Dispatch* closed in 1960 he fell on his feet. He was hired by Lord Beaverbrook—who had been warned that English sometimes 'chanced his arm' (*The Independent*, 12 June 1998)—to be the *Daily Express*'s Washington correspondent. In 1963, after two successful years in Washington, he was promoted to the post of the *Express*'s chief American correspondent, retaining his base in the capital. He was not with the press party that accompanied John F. Kennedy to Dallas in November 1963, though he made his way there swiftly from New York once he heard the news of the president's death. This did not prevent him, as part of his later reminiscences about the event, from gilding the personal legend by implying that he had been present at the assassination.

In 1965 English returned to England to serve as foreign editor of the *Express*. After two years in the post he became an associate editor of the paper, and harboured legitimate expectations of succeeding as editor. He asked Max Aitken, who had succeeded his father Lord Beaverbrook as proprietor, to make him editor, only to be told that the *Express* already had one. He disregarded hints from Aitken that he was the heir apparent and accepted, in 1969, the editorship of the *Daily Sketch*. He was still only thirty-nine.

The Daily Mail The *Sketch* was not in the best of health, with a declining readership and set in a contracting market. There was nothing that even someone of English's talent could do to save it by conventional journalistic means. However—and this was typical of the shrewd operator he was—he sought to devise a means that would benefit the paper's owners, Associated Newspapers, and, naturally enough, himself. Early in 1971 secret talks began with Vere Harmsworth (later Lord Rothermere), the deputy chairman of Associated, to merge the paper into a new-style *Daily Mail*, the flagship of the Harmsworth empire. English would edit the new *Mail* and it would give the *Express*—then selling 3.5 million copies a day, twice the *Mail*'s circulation—a run for its money. Harmsworth agreed, even though the plan involved the radical step of changing the *Mail* from a broadsheet to a tabloid—or compact paper, as it was then called—as well as closing the *Sketch*. Harmsworth's condition was that the new paper should look like the London *Evening Standard* (which he later came to own), then a successful and popular tabloid. English had been thinking along the same lines, and the deal was done. Harmsworth, though, deserved credit for being astute enough to realize that English's entrepreneurial skills could be put to good use in the necessary modernization of his own newspapers. He also had a vision, which English grasped, of a paper aimed at modern women.

The operation, in May 1971, involved substantial casualties. The combined editorial staffs of the *Sketch* and the *Mail* were cut from 830 to just 320 on the new *Mail*. English did the sacking on what became known as 'the night of the long envelopes'. He thrived on the challenge, but the struggle to establish the new-style paper was hard. 'It seems like only yesterday we were all working 19 hours a day trying to give birth to a new *Daily Mail*', English wrote to his news editor two months after the change. 'Now we're working only 14 hours a day. I told you it would get better' (*Daily Telegraph*, 12 June 1998). He believed that 'in a competitive world working in a winning environment makes people happy' (*The Independent*, 12 June 1998). He would win in the end, but happiness was not always inevitable. He would not hesitate to humiliate those who did not reach his own high standards. Loyal to those who served him well, he could bear deep grudges against those who did not.

Despite all English's efforts, however, the circulation of the *Mail* fell from 1.814 million to 1.754 million immediately after the change. In fact, things were worse than that. The 764,000 buyers of the *Sketch*, who were supposed to move over to the *Mail*, had vanished from Associated Newspapers and been picked up by the *Sun*. By August 1971 matters had become so bad that the paper was down to just twenty-four pages, but English refused to be cowed. To reverse this trend he embarked on more, and further-reaching, changes to the nature of his product. Most of his ideas proved highly successful in maintaining and then increasing his readership. He and Harmsworth were, however, helped by the entry of the *Express* into a long period of steep decline, and by that title's failure to modernize in response to what its main competitor had done. By the time of his retirement from the editorship in 1992 English had taken the *Mail*, from being so far behind the *Express*, to overhauling that paper's circulation—though the *Mail*'s had, at 1.69 million, remained fairly static, while the *Express*'s had collapsed to 1.54 million.

Whereas Harmsworth's and English's idea had been to boost the *Mail*'s circulation significantly by making it far more attractive to women, what they in fact did was prevent sales being eroded at a time when the middle market in newspapers was rapidly contracting. English also had the great journalistic talent of sheer opportunism—spotting at long range either a promotional opportunity or a story (or best of all a combination of the two) that would pull in more readers. He introduced the *Mail*'s Femail section not just as a magnet for the largely untapped market of women readers, but ensured it had a modern edge that was a far cry from the knitting patterns and recipes of most other Fleet Street women's pages. In the paper's news and features coverage he highlighted, and campaigned on, stories that reflected the concerns of his middle-class readers—about family matters, the welfare of their children, the value of their property, and the decline of the country.

It was in relation to the last point that English threw his paper firmly behind Margaret Thatcher even before she had become leader of the Conservative Party in 1975. It was not just in the election campaign of 1979, but in the years leading up to it, that English acted as one of her cheerleaders and, eventually, confidants. However, in this, as in much of his management of the *Mail* brand, he learned valuable lessons from the formidable editor of the *Sun*, Albert (Larry) Lamb, who led the way in conviction and flair when it came to editing a tabloid paper. Ironically, given the effect the *Mail* had on the *Express*, English also applied at his paper lessons of populism and immediacy learned from the *Express* in happier days. The key to his success was that he identified his market precisely and then ensured that his paper appealed to it.

Such a brazen approach to news and the selling of newspapers as English had brought with it risks. As Saigon was about to fall in 1975 he had the *Mail* sponsor an airlift of ninety-nine small children to Britain. It was a fabulous coup, typical both of English's showmanship and of his opportunism. However, it later attracted criticism because while many of the children flourished in their new environment, others did not. The low point of English's career came in 1977. He published in the *Mail* a letter alleging that Lord Ryder, the chairman of the National Enterprise Board, knew of a slush fund for British Leyland, whose contents were used to pay bribes to secure overseas orders. The letter was a forgery and the fund did not exist. English offered his resignation after 123 MPs called for it, but Harmsworth did not accept it. One Labour MP even called for English to be tried for sedition, claiming the story was a deliberate attempt to bring down the government. Later, the Press Council criticized the *Mail* for hampering the police investigation into the case of the Yorkshire Ripper, and rebuked English for refusing to attend a hearing on the matter.

Success There were, though, conspicuous successes that made English indispensable to his masters. Not only did the *Mail* attract favourable publicity and more readers by a long-running campaign against the influence of the Moonies, it also won the long libel trial brought against the paper in 1981 by the Unification Church after a story headlined 'The church that breaks up families'. In addition, once Margaret Thatcher became prime minister in 1979, the paper grew in influence, as did its editor. His own conspicuous contribution to the Conservative success was rewarded with a knighthood in 1982. By the late 1980s he had, it appeared, achieved his main ambition: the *Mail* had overtaken the circulation of the once mighty *Express*. Soon the *Mail on Sunday* accomplished a similar feat over the *Sunday Express*. The part the *Mail* played in Thatcher's three election victories was significant, English's own version of the Thatcherite vision being broadcast to a growing readership with unerring certainty throughout her eleven years in power.

English was not only, by this time, a formidable figure in his own newspaper, but an increasingly towering one in the industry. He had more than an element of Machiavelli, and was regarded with ambivalence by many who worked with him. Much of this can be attributed to the envy of less original and less successful men; but English was a willing practitioner of the double standard when it suited him. He terrified some journalists who were of a mind to be terrified by him, but he also at times manipulated them rather than handled them. He was thought to have learned the technique of 'creative tension' while in America. This would involve commissioning two journalists to write the same story, and then publishing the better result. It represented an almost Darwinian approach to man management, for only the fittest survived. He hoped for his own high personal standards to be emulated by his staff, though in this he was somewhat optimistic. He once withdrew a bureau chief from New York when he learned that the man had been conducting an extramarital affair, and later tried to prevent a reporter joining the *Mail* after it had been reported that he had been caught engaging in indecent acts in a public lavatory.

English's ruthlessness was masked, most of the time, by a carapace of charm. He had a distinctive high-pitched laugh, a slightly rasping voice, and a talent for bonhomie that grew the longer he spent in company with the rich, powerful, and famous. He was a sophisticated gossip, hugely enjoying any tales about colleagues, which he would wait to retail (with appropriate amplifications) until the moment when the effect would be most devastating. He could switch from charm to ferocity in an instant, and it was by such caprices and unpredictability that he kept all about him wary and on their toes. He was a small figure, always immaculately dressed, who in his later years relished playing the part of a Fleet Street elder statesman, and revelled in the influence he knew he had had on the rest of British journalism.

Editorial style For all his occasional faults as a man manager English commanded immense loyalty, not least because under him the *Mail* became a newspaper that generally paid its staff well, and sacked people only rarely. The key to the respect in which he was held was that everyone who worked for him knew he could do any task he asked of them. Once his trust was won—and winning it was an exacting process—it was rarely withdrawn. He had a tremendous talent for turning poorly written raw copy into a compelling news story or feature, and as such he shaped the voice of the *Daily Mail*. He was also a brilliant talent spotter. As well as bringing on his eventual successor, Paul Dacre, he also filled the *Mail* with the most popular and authoritative columnists available, such as Nigel Dempster, Ian Wooldridge, and Lynda Lee-Potter. By the early 1990s, shortly before he handed over to Dacre, the *Mail* had become a byword for the middle market, which it dominated. Other newspapers, and not just in the *Mail*'s own market, strove to imitate wherever possible the style, tone, and approach that English had forged at his paper. Few succeeded in any measure, not least because English had usually cornered the market in the high-calibre journalists needed to maintain such a product.

Although he himself was not above the occasional lapse in taste, English deplored what he saw as the sleaziness of the 'red top' tabloid newspapers such as the *Sun*, the *Star*, and the *Mirror*. When he felt he noticed, in the mid-1990s, attempts by those papers to move towards the middle of the market, he thought he deserved some credit for it. Explaining his philosophy, he once said:

> It's simple, and very complex. The core is attention to detail. My view is that no story, no headline, no design, no subbing, nothing, is perfect. It can always be improved. That's what I mean by quality, keeping at it, never giving up. We've never wavered from that. Call it mainstream journalism, call it quality journalism, call it whatever you like. It's what makes the *Mail* titles special. (*The Guardian*, 11 June 1998)

With the growth of his eminence came wider responsibilities. English had helped launch the *Mail on Sunday* in 1982, and even edited it for a while during early teething troubles. He became vice-chairman of Associated Newspapers in 1986, then joint deputy chairman and editor-in-chief in 1989, and finally chairman in 1992, when he ceased editing the *Daily Mail* after twenty-one years. He and Rothermere maintained a formidable double act at the helm of the group until their sudden deaths, within months of each other, in 1998. From 1988 English was chairman both of New Era TV and of Burlington Magazines. In 1993 he became chairman of the cable television company Channel One, a rare unsuccessful business venture for him, and in 1997 he became chairman of ITN. He became president of the Commonwealth Press Union in 1994 and was active on the National Council for the Training of Journalists.

English sat on the Press Complaints Commission (PCC) from 1993, though it was his appointment as chairman of the editors' code committee of the commission that caused controversy over accusations of hypocrisy. The

Mail had been accused of various intrusions of privacy, not least concerning Diana, princess of Wales. The chief shareholder of the Telegraph group, Conrad Black, said that in that light putting English in charge of a standards committee was 'like having appointed Al Capone as head of a commission to investigate organised crime in Chicago in the 1920s' (*Daily Telegraph*, 12 June 1998). English did, however, preside over a committee that eventually produced a code with greatly strengthened provisions. He was also responsible for appointing Lord Wakeham as head of the PCC, which was regarded as means of toughening up self-regulation—something English knew would be necessary if a privacy law were to be avoided.

Towards the end of his life English became deeply disillusioned with the Conservative Party, and wrote in a mischievous diary in the *Spectator* magazine soon after Tony Blair's rise to the Labour leadership that he could foresee the day when the *Mail* would back 'new' Labour. Lord Rothermere, as if to emphasize the point, signalled that he would sit on the Labour benches in the House of Lords. Whether English wrote what he did just to make waves or to curry favour is not clear, but it was revealed at the time of his death that he was to have been created a life peer in the 1998 birthday honours list.

English had a full life outside journalism. He had bought, and successfully ran, a chain of launderettes and a chain of free newspapers. Both ventures gave him the financial independence that allowed him to back his own judgement as a newspaper editor. They also made him, as an entrepreneur, a natural soulmate of Margaret Thatcher. He was devoted to his family, and especially to his wife, who was seriously ill for several years towards the end of his life. He enjoyed skiing and, especially, sailing his 40-foot motor cruiser.

It was his wide combination of talents that in the end made English the success he was. These included his journalist's nose for a good story, and his carefully honed skill in presenting a story in the most arresting way possible. Crucial to his success were his self-confidence, his determination, his ambition, his political judgement, his entrepreneurialism, and above all his ability to manipulate, exploit, and extract the best from others. His legacy was not just a newspaper that continued to grow mightily after he moved on, but a template for a compact newspaper that was copied and used around the world.

English suffered a stroke at his home in Westminster on 10 June 1998, and died shortly afterwards at St Thomas's Hospital, Lambeth. After a funeral service at St Bride's, Fleet Street, the journalists' church, he was buried on 18 June at Villars-sur-Ollon, Switzerland, where he and his family had enjoyed many skiing holidays. He was survived by his wife and their three children. SIMON HEFFER

Sources *The Times* (11 June 1998) · *The Guardian* (11 June 1998) · *Daily Telegraph* (12 June 1998) · *The Independent* (12 June 1998) · *WWW* · personal knowledge (2004) · private information (2004) · b. cert. · m. cert. · d. cert. · *CGPLA Eng. & Wales* (1999)
Archives Associated Newspapers Ltd, London, business papers · priv. coll., papers

Likenesses photograph, 1988, repro. in *Daily Telegraph* · N. English, photograph, *c*.1995, priv. coll. [*see illus.*] · D. Sillitoe, photograph, repro. in *The Guardian* · photograph, repro. in *The Times* · photograph, repro. in *The Independent*
Wealth at death £1,252,581—gross; £796,346—net: probate, 17 June 1999, *CGPLA Eng. & Wales*

English, Isobel. *See* Braybrooke, June Guesdon (1920–1994).

English, Sir John Hawker (*bap.* **1786**, *d.* **1840**), army surgeon, the son of John and Elizabeth English, was baptized at Fareham, Hampshire, on 2 November 1786. He served as second assistant surgeon in the ordnance medical department of the British army from August 1806 to July 1811. English entered the employment of the king of Sweden as a surgeon, and became surgeon-in-chief to the Swedish army. In recognition of his services he was decorated with the order of Gustavus Vasa in 1814, and, having received permission to accept it, was knighted by the prince regent in 1815. On 7 Jaunary 1817 he married Elizabeth Wigglesworth Bogle of Manchester Square, London.

On leaving Sweden, English graduated MD at both Göttingen, on 3 March 1814, and Aberdeen, on 26 May 1823. He became a licentiate of the Royal College of Physicians on 25 June 1823.

English lived at Warley House, Essex, but died on 29 June 1840 at St Leonards, Sussex.

ALSAGER VIAN, *rev.* CLAIRE E. J. HERRICK

Sources *GM*, 2nd ser., 14 (1840), 221–2 · A. Peterkin and W. Johnston, *Commissioned officers in the medical services of the British army, 1660–1960*, 1 (1968), 177 · Munk, *Roll* · *IGI* · *GM*, 1st ser., 87/1 (1817), 82

English, Josias (*d.* **1705**), etcher, was one of the group of etchers at the end of the 1640s who were associated with the publisher Thomas Rowlett. He was closely linked with Francis Clein and the tapestry manufacture at Mortlake, Surrey, and most of his etchings are after Clein's drawings. The main source of information on his life is George Vertue, who noted that:

> Mr Josias English painter at Mortlack died about 1718 [*sic*]. Of this English a small print etched disciples at Emaus after the design of Titian. He had a picture of Mr Cleyn & his wife & many more of the Dutch tapestry workers. These pictures & his goods were left to Mr Crawley at Hempsted in Hartfordshire. (Vertue, *Note books*, 1.59)

No paintings or drawings by English are known, and his only surviving work is a small number of high-quality etchings, all very rare, made between 1649 and 1656. The earliest (which cannot be later than 1649, but might be as early as 1646) is after a self-portrait by William Dobson which was published by Thomas Rowlett. The print after Titian to which Vertue refers is signed 'Josias English fecit de Mortlake', and in his will, proved on 9 June 1705, the painting was bequeathed to a Mr Richardson. Following her death on 21 March 1680, English's first wife, Mary, was buried in the church at Barnes, near Mortlake. In 1690 he married Phebe Bunn. There is nothing to explain what he was doing in the half-century between 1656 and his death in 1705 in Barnes.

English's etchings have been listed by Thieme and

Becker. He made two extensive sets after drawings by Clein: *Severall Borders of Grotesco Work* (1654) contains a title and thirteen plates, and the title and eleven plates (of possibly a longer sequence) of *Variae deorum ethnicorum effigies* (1653/4) survive. These are the earliest known British prints of figures from classical mythology or history. Also after Clein is a portrait of a toper, dated 1656, which has been thought to be a self-portrait. The attribution to English of a mezzotint of a smoker after a design by Adriaen Brouwer relies on an old pencil annotation which there is no reason to believe. His prints are held in the British Museum, London. ANTONY GRIFFITHS

Sources A. Griffiths and R. A. Gerard, *The print in Stuart Britain, 1603–1689* (1998), 123–4, 172–3 [exhibition catalogue, BM, 8 May – 20 Sept 1998] · Thieme & Becker, *Allgemeines Lexikon*, 10.554-5 · O. Manning and W. Bray, *The history and antiquities of the county of Surrey*, 3 (1814), 322 · Vertue, *Note books*, 1.59 · will, proved 9/6/1705, PRO, PROB 11/483, fol. 137

English, William (*fl.* 1219–1231), physician and astronomer, is known only through references in his own works or in the manuscripts in which those works are found. He says of himself that he was born in England and settled at Marseilles, and describes himself as a practising physician, learned in astronomy. There is a question as to whether he knew Arabic. Among the works doubtfully attributed to him is the translation, from Arabic, of a short treatise in the tradition of Kiranides, as *De virtute aquile* ('On the virtue of the eagle'). The manuscript in which it is found (Oxford, Merton College, MS 324, fol. 14*r*) gives the translator as 'magister Willelmus Anglicus'. It is true that in his genuine astronomical works William English introduced new Arabic material, but most probably he gathered his information through hearsay, perhaps through Jewish scholars.

Four works can be attributed to English with confidence. *De urina non visa* ('On unseen urine') is found in numerous manuscripts and consists of a short treatise on astrological medicine. It first deals with the general principles of astrology applied to the parts of human body and their diseases; then follow some medical details about the liver (supposed to 'cook' urine) and some rules governing the evolution of diseases. The aim of this work, which influenced a few other treatises of the same kind, was to offer a method, founded on astrology, of making diagnosis and prognosis without examining the urine of the patient. In one anecdote English says that he predicted exactly, during the year 1219, that a patient would continue to live two months and eight days. According to the given astral positions, this event took place at the very end of 1219, thus placing the redaction of the treatise after this time. A French version of *De urina non visa* was transcribed in 1463 by Johannes de Boorles (Turin, Biblioteca Nazionale, MS M IV 11, fols. 125–131*v*).

The second work, *Astrologia*, is found in four manuscripts, one of which (Seville, Biblioteca Capitular y Colombina, MS 5-1-25, fols. 1–33) gives 1220 as the date of composition and the author as 'magister Werbellinus, civis Massiliensis, qui anglicus est natione' ('Master Werbellinus, citizen of Marseilles, who is English by birth'). It

presents the theory of planets according to Ptolemy's *Almagest*, focusing on the principles ruling the construction of astrolabes and the establishing of astronomical tables. Without explicitly mentioning them, English relied on the Toledan tables.

Astrolabium Arzachelis is dated 1231 in some manuscripts and appears as the first introduction (actually rather clumsy) into the Latin West of the universal astrolabe known as the *saphea [Arzachelis]*, that is, 'Arzachel's plate'. The astrolabe is universal in the sense that it is not restricted to a particular geographical latitude; Arzachel (Ibn al-Zarqali) was an eleventh-century Toledan astronomer. Contrary to what has sometimes been stated, the work by English is not an abridgement of that of Arzachel (which was translated into Latin in 1263 by Profatius) and English declares that he worked for six years on this topic. Both sections of the *Astrolabium Arzachelis* have been edited: the first, on the construction of the *saphea*, by L. A. Sédillot (*Mémoire sur les instruments astronomiques des Arabes*, Mémoires Présentés par Divers Savants à l'Académie des Inscriptions et Belles-lettres, 1st ser., 1, 1841, 185–8; reprinted in R. T. Gunther, *The Astrolabes of the World*, 1, 1932, 259–62) and the second, on the uses of the *saphea*, by P. Tannery ('Le traité du quadrant de maître Robert Anglès', *Notices et extraits des manuscrits de la Bibliothèque Nationale*, 35, 1897, 75–80; reprinted in P. Tannery, *Mémoires scientifiques*, 5, 1922, 190–97). At the end of the treatise is appended a table of the stars (*De stellis fixis*), which has sometimes been wrongly considered as an independent work.

The fourth work by English is *Tractatus de metheoris*. The only manuscript in which this is found (Paris, Bibliothèque Nationale, MS Lat. 6552, fols. 39*v*–41*v*) gives 1230 as the date of composition. Contrary to what is stated in the rubric title (which has been repeated by all scholars), it is a summary of the four books of Aristotle's *Meteorologics*, not of the fourth book only, even though it begins with this— English ordered his matter according to where the phenomena take place: in the earth, in the air, or in the ether. The interest of this *Tractatus* lies in its early date.

The attribution of other works to William English is very doubtful. The *Scripta Marsiliensis* cannot have been written, on the evidence of their content, before the end of the thirteenth century. The supposed translation of Canamusali's treatise on ophthalmology is actually a compilation by a twelfth-century Salernitan physician, David Armenicus. Other works also should be rejected: *De quadratura circuli*, *Questio de scientia*, *Utrum in maiori quantitate …*, *De qualitatibus et proprietatibus signorum*. The identification of William English with William of Aragon, author of a commentary on Pseudo-Ptolemy's *Centiloquium* and of a treatise on dreams, is not firmly grounded.

William English was during the sixteenth century confused with **William Grisaunt** (*supp. fl.* 1350) in the writings of the controversialist John Bale. Grisaunt was the name which Bale, in his *Acta pontificum Romanorum* (1558), gave to the father of Pope Urban V (*r.* 1362–70) and he described him as a physician born in England. In the second edition of his *Scriptorum illustrium maioris Brytanniae* *catalogus* (1557–9), Bale added that the pope's father had studied philosophy at Merton College, Oxford, and medicine at the University of Montpellier and he attributed to him the works which he had entered in his notebook (*Index*), without any date, under the name of William English. In fact Urban V's father, named Guillelmus, was lord of Grisac (hence the derivation 'Grisaunt'), near Mende in the southern Auvergne. He was not born in England, nor was he a physician. The confusion may have arisen from the fact of Pope Urban's brother having been named Anglic ('Anglicus'). While he was bishop of Avignon, and later of Albano, Anglic contributed to the papal foundation of colleges in Montpellier, among them the college of Mende (also called the 'college of the twelve physicians') for students of medicine. Modern authorities have rejected Bale's statements concerning the father of Urban V, but have continued to refer to a William Grisaunt (*fl.* 1350), a physician supposed to have studied at Oxford and Montpellier. This physician probably never existed.

DANIELLE JACQUART

Sources L. Thorndike, *A history of magic and experimental science*, 8 vols. (1923–58), vol. 2, pp. 485–7 · E. Poulle, 'William the Englishman', *DSB*, 14.399–402 · L. Thorndike and P. Kibre, *A catalogue of incipits of mediaeval scientific writings in Latin*, rev. edn (1963), 388, 439, 508, 906, 1261, 1349 · P. Duhem, *Le système du monde: histoire des doctrines cosmologiques de Platon à Copernic*, 10 vols. (Paris, 1913–59); repr. (Paris, 1958–76), vol. 3, pp. 287–91 · D. C. Lindberg, *A catalogue of medieval and Renaissance optical manuscripts* (1975), 100–01 · J. M. Millás Vallicrosa, *Estudios sobre Azarquiel* (1943–50), 438–47 · E. Poulle, 'Un instrument astronomique dans l'Occident latin, la saphea', *Studi Medievali*, 3rd ser., 10 (1969), 491–510 · L. A. Sédillot, 'Mémoire sur les instruments astronomiques des Arabes', *The astrolabes of the world*, ed. R. T. Gunther, 2 vols. (1932), 259–62 · P. Tannery, 'Le traité du quadrant de maître Robert Anglès', *Mémoires scientifiques*, 5 (1922), 190–97 · J. Bale, *Acta pontificum Romanorum* (1558), 273 · Bale, *Cat.*, 446 · Bale, *Index*, 114–15, 137 · Emden, *Oxf.*, 2.827 [William Grisaunt] · G. Mollat, 'Grimoard, Anglic', *Dictionnaire d'histoire et de géographie ecclésiastiques*, ed. A. Baudrillart and others, 22 (Paris, 1988), 279–81 [William Grisaunt] · Merton Oxf., MS 324, fol. 14*r* · Biblioteca Capitular y Columbina, Seville, MS 5-1-25, fols. 1–33
Archives Biblioteca Capitular y Colombina, Seville, MS 5-1-25, fols. 1–33 · Biblioteca Nazionale, Turin, MS M IV 11, fols. 125–131*v* · Bibliothèque Nationale, Paris, MS Lat. 6552, fols. 39*v*–41*v* · Merton Oxf., MS 324, fol. 14*r*

English, William (1708x15–1778), priest and Gaelic poet, may have been a native of Newcastlewest, co. Limerick, or of co. Tipperary. His date of birth has been given variously as 1708–9 and 1715 but is not known for certain. He moved to co. Cork as a young man and lived in the east and north of the county, where he became part of the Munster literary circle which included the poets Liam Rua Mac Coitir, Éadbhard de Nógla, Seán na Ráithíneach Ó Murchadha, and priest-poets Seán Lluyd, Seán Ó Briain, and Domhnall Ó Briain. His earliest work includes laments for members of well-known Cork families and he is among those mentioned in a literary summons, composed about 1733, by Father Seán Ó Briain to the court of poetry run by Mac Coitir in Castlelyons, co. Cork. Tradition records that he served as tutor to the young Edmund Burke (1729–1797) some time during the period from 1735 to 1741 when Burke was living with his mother's family, the Nagles of Ballyduff.

According to the evidence of the poetry, English entered the Dominican convent in Old Friary Lane, Cork, but was expelled nine months later because he and the prior of the convent—probably Father John O'Brien, who was elected prior in 1741 and who was known for his strict views on novices—did not agree on the meaning of the vow of poverty. English subsequently joined the small Augustinian community in Fishamble Lane, Cork, from which he travelled to the Irish Augustinian convent of San Matteo in Rome, where he was subsequently ordained. He returned in 1749 to Fishamble Lane. English is recorded as prior of the Cork community between the years 1754 and 1758; vicar-prior in 1764–6 and again in 1769–70; prior again from 1770 to 1774; and vicar-prior once again from 1774 to 1776.

Upwards of thirty poetic compositions are ascribed to English in manuscript sources. These include a body of political verse where strong Jacobite sentiments are presented through well-informed though highly selective reportage of contemporary international military and political events. He is most famous for his political poetry of the late 1750s, especially his comic poem 'Cré agus cill go bhfaghaidh gach bráthair' (popularly known as 'The Friar's Firkin'), where military rivalry between the Prussian–British alliance and Austria and her allies France and Russia at the outset of the Seven Years' War (1756–63) is likened to the squabble over the division of a friar's keg of multi-coloured butter at the Cork butter market. The poem ends on a conciliatory note, where the poet implores God to settle the matter by providing enough for everyone.

As the war progressed, however, greater partiality enters into English's account of events and his Jacobitism becomes more overt. A poem addressed to Éadbhard de Nógla after the execution of the British admiral John Byng for his failure as leader of the British fleet against French forces in the battle of Minorca in May 1756 uses the example of the ill-fated Byng to raise hopes of a Stuart reinstatement. Military successes in Europe during the summer of 1757 are acknowledged in a series of poems where commanders such as the Austrian marshal Leopold J. von Daun—whose army relieved Prague from Prussian control in June 1757—are presented as heroes in the Jacobite cause. When there is nothing favourable to report from the European theatre of war, English moves to comment on the British–French conflict in North America, and in particular to report major set-backs for the British forces.

One of his best-loved non-political works is a light-hearted poem on the subject of alms and may have been composed while he was absent from the Cork convent for a period of seven months in 1764. English's association with Gaelic literary culture is illustrated by the fact that no fewer than fourteen poems are extant in which he is named or addressed by various fellow poets. He died at the priory in Fishamble Lane in January 1778 and was buried in St John's churchyard, Douglas Street, Cork.

MÁIRÍN NIC EOIN

Sources R. Ó Foghludha, ed., *Cois na bríde: Liam Inglis O.S.A., 1709–1778* (1937) · D. Ó Catháin, 'Augustinian friars and literature in Irish, 1600–1900', *Analecta Augustiniana*, 58 (1995), 101–52 · W. D. O'Connell, 'Augustiniana Corcagiae, 1746–1834', *Analecta Hibernica*, 12 (1943), 165–74 · C. G. Buttimer, 'Gaelic literature and contemporary life in Cork, 1700–1840', *Cork: history and society—interdisciplinary essays on the history of an Irish county*, ed. P. O'Flanagan and C. G. Buttimer (1993), 585–653 · H. Fenning, *The undoing of the friars of Ireland* (1974), 249–50 · H. Fenning, *The Irish Dominican province, 1698–1797* (1990), 134–40 · H. Fenning, ed., 'Clerical recruitment, 1735–83: documents from Windsor and Rome', *Archivium Hibernicum*, 30 (1972), 1–20 · W. D. O'Connell, 'The regulars in the post-Reformation period', *Journal of the Cork Historical and Archaeological Society*, 2nd ser., 48 (1943), 19–25 · É. Ó Ciardha, 'A voice from the Jacobite underground: Liam Inglis (1709–1778)', *Radical Irish priests, 1660–1970*, ed. G. Moran (Dublin, 1998), 16–38
Archives Royal Irish Acad., MSS, R/A Cat. Ire. MSS, p. 3542

Ennals, David Hedley, Baron Ennals (1922–1995), politician, was born at Walden, Mellish Road, Walsall, Staffordshire, on 19 August 1922, the second of the three sons of Arthur Ford Ennals, master draper and subsequently funeral director, and his wife, Jessie Edith, *née* Taylor. He was brought up in a devoutly Baptist family and all three brothers were to fill significant public roles: all were concerned with the plight of the less privileged, and each had a strong interest in international affairs. Like his two brothers, Ennals was educated at Queen Mary's Grammar School, Walsall. He did not attend a British university, being seventeen when the Second World War began. He served in north Africa, Italy, and on the Rhine, ending the war as a captain in the Royal Armoured Corps. He then spent a year in the United States, as a student at the Loomis Institute, Windsor, Connecticut.

Ennals returned to England in 1947 to become secretary of the Council for Education in World Citizenship. He stood as a Liberal candidate for Richmond but failed to get elected in 1950 and 1951. On 10 June 1950 he married Eleanor Maud Caddick (*b.* 1924/5), secretary, daughter of Reginald Victor Caddick, company director; there were three sons and a daughter of the marriage. In 1952 Ennals became secretary of the United Nations Association (1952–7). In this post he showed great energy and raised its profile at a time when there were few competing internationally focused pressure groups. It was his work there that helped him gain his next position, as secretary to the international department of the Labour Party's head office at Transport House, in 1957. This was almost a one-man band, so limited were the party's resources at that time. It was also a period when the great debate about nuclear disarmament nearly tore the party asunder. Labour was in opposition throughout this period, so Ennals was its main source of professional advice on British foreign policy. He managed to chart a difficult path between the entrenched party groups. He wrote the chapters in the briefing book for Labour candidates before the 1964 general election, *Twelve Wasted Years* (1963). It was characteristic that he devoted a whole chapter in the brief space allotted to international affairs to the United Nations. 'It has thus been the Party's policy constantly to urge an "increase in the authority of the United Nations"—not as

David Hedley Ennals, Baron Ennals (1922–1995), by unknown photographer

an end in itself but as a step toward eventual world government' (*Twelve Wasted Years*, 369). This probably captured Ennals's central, driving utopian dream.

Ennals became Labour MP for Dover in October 1964, a victory that reflected a prodigious amount of constituency work. Both his own majority and that of Labour nationally were tiny. In March 1966 the Labour prime minister, Harold Wilson, won a much larger majority. Ennals was one of the few new MPs to be given a junior ministerial post in the new government, being made parliamentary under-secretary of state for the army (1966–7). He was well fitted for this post. He was then moved to a similar position in the Home Office (1967–8), where he was deputy to James Callaghan and had to take responsibility for the Commonwealth Immigrants Act (1968) limiting the entry of east African Asians. It caused Ennals considerable personal and family discomfort. His younger brother, Martin, fought the measure. His next post was that of minister of state (1968–70) at the new Department of Health and Social Security. The secretary of state, Richard Crossman, saw Ennals as extremely hard working and loyal. Then came the June 1970 election, Labour's defeat, and the loss of Ennals's own seat. He went back to a campaigning job, this time as campaigning director of the National Association for Mental Health (later renamed MIND).

In February 1974 Ennals was elected Labour MP for Norwich North. He returned to his old interests as minister of state at the Foreign and Commonwealth Office (1974–6). There he dealt with a wide range of issues and showed himself assured and informed. This was the nearest he was to get to what must have been his ultimate ambition—to be foreign secretary. He had risen steadily and was now just one rung below that coveted position. It was not to be. Wilson resigned as prime minister in April 1976 and James Callaghan took his place. Ennals had supported Callaghan in his leadership bid but he was not rewarded with the Foreign and Commonwealth Office. Instead he went to the Department of Health and Social Security, as secretary of state (1976–9). This was the peak of his career but it was also a painful and difficult period. The economic crisis, and the International Monetary Fund visit and its aftermath, left the Labour government with little choice but to constrain severely public spending. Ennals was a surprise replacement for Barbara Castle, who had carried through some major reforms—to pensions, to the National Health Service, and to the benefits system, introducing a cash benefit for all children paid to the mother (child benefit). This was at a period when the government was seeking to impose strict limits on wage increases. The chancellor (Denis Healey) and the prime minister became convinced that the loss of child tax allowances and the reduction in take-home pay this involved would fatally undermine the pay policy. They had been told as much by trade union leaders, they claimed. The cabinet decided to limit drastically the new child benefit scheme. Ennals's first major announcement as secretary of state was the backtracking on this major reform, which was the pride of Barbara Castle. She put on one of her most devastating performances in the House of Commons, attacking his announcement as 'an abandonment of one of this Party's major reforms' (*Hansard 5C*, 912, 1975–6, 287). The contents of the cabinet discussion were leaked and published in *New Society*. This provoked a furious row within the Labour Party, with Barbara Castle leading the attack, and with the opposition able to quote freely from attacks by the Child Poverty Action Group. Ennals also conspicuously failed to implement Castle's policy restricting the number of private pay beds in the National Health Service. Meanwhile, the limits on public-sector pay were increasingly opposed by health service unions. Ennals personally intervened to try to stop ambulance workers ceasing even to meet emergency calls. An agreement was reached with union leaders, but it was rejected by local branches. He himself was ill during much of this period. In March 1979, before he was to meet the unions again, he was taken into Westminster Hospital with leg thrombosis. He was refused tea, mail, and other services by the ancillary workers' union. Only a few weeks later the Labour Party lost the general election called as a result of the no-confidence vote largely prompted by the 'winter of discontent'. It was a sad end to such a promising and idealistic ministerial career. Just before leaving office, however, Ennals did appoint the Black committee, whose report on health inequalities was to become a landmark.

Ennals's first marriage ended in divorce in 1977, and on 4 July the same year he married (Katherine) Gene Tranoy (*b.* 1926/7), a divorced schoolteacher, and daughter of Walter Eugene Wilkins, consultant surgeon. Following the 1979 general election Ennals remained on the backbenches. He lost his seat in the June 1983 election, whereupon he was made a life peer, as Baron Ennals of Norwich. He was for many years his party's health spokesman in the House of Lords, and was a prominent supporter of a wide range of liberal causes. He was chairman of the Gandhi Foundation (1984–95) and of the Children's Medical Charity (1984–95), and president of the Tibet Society (1988–95) and of MIND (1989–95). He died of pancreatic cancer at his home, the Garden Flat, 6 Glenloch Road, Belsize Park, London, on 17 June 1995. He was survived by his second wife and the four children of his first marriage. Phuoc Ky Ennals, a Vietnamese orphan whom Ennals had informally adopted in 1975, predeceased him in 1993, as a result of an accident on an army firing range.

Ennals's elder brother, **John Arthur Ford Ennals** (1918–1988), human rights activist, was born in Walsall on 21 July 1918. He was educated at Queen Mary's Grammar School, Walsall, and St John's College, Cambridge, graduating in history and psychology; he was president of the British Universities League of Nations Society in 1938–9. In 1939–40 he was a lecturer for the British Council in Romania and Yugoslavia, and subsequently was a war correspondent in the Balkans. In 1941 he joined the Foreign Office, serving in Madrid and London, and then from 1943 to 1945 he served with British forces in Egypt, Italy, and Yugoslavia. He was secretary-general of the World Federation of United Nations Associations from 1946 to 1956 (honorary president from 1977), tutor in international relations at Ruskin College, Oxford, from 1956 to 1966, director-general of the United Nations Association from 1966 to 1970 (vice-president from 1978), chairman of the Anti-Apartheid Movement from 1968 to 1976 (following his brother David, who was chairman from 1960 to 1964), and director of the United Kingdom Immigrants Advisory Service from 1970 to 1983. He unsuccessfully contested Walsall South for the Labour Party in 1955 and 1959, and the European parliament constituency of Thames Valley in 1979; for many years he was a parish councillor for Kidlington, Oxfordshire, and then for Hedgerley, Buckinghamshire. He died on 14 September 1988.

Ennals's younger brother, **Martin Francis Antony Ennals** (1927–1991), human rights activist, was born in Walsall on 27 July 1927. He was educated at Queen Mary's Grammar School, Walsall, and the London School of Economics, graduating in international relations. He then worked briefly for the National Union of Students as assistant secretary. On 11 May 1951 he married Jacqueline Betty Morris (*b.* 1927/8), shorthand typist, daughter of David Morris, schoolteacher; there were one son and one daughter of the marriage. Later in the year he took up a post with UNESCO in Paris, where he was president of the staff association. He returned to England in 1960 to become general secretary of the National Council for Civil Liberties (later renamed Liberty). From 1966 to 1968 he was information officer for the National Committee for Commonwealth Immigrants, in which post he came into direct conflict with the government of which his brother David was a member. He was then secretary-general of Amnesty International from 1968 to 1980, overseeing a period of rapid growth during which the staff of the secretariat grew from nine to 150 and its annual budget from £20,000 to more than £1.6 million. Characteristically, when Amnesty received the Nobel peace prize in 1977, he insisted that a released 'prisoner of conscience' should actually accept the award. After leaving Amnesty he was head of the Greater London council's police committee support unit, from 1982 to 1985, but in the latter year he reverted to his interest in international human rights issues by becoming secretary-general of International Alert. He remained with this organization until 1991, when he became Ariel F. Sallows professor of human rights at the University of Saskatchewan, Canada. He died of lung cancer in Saskatoon, Canada, on 5 October 1991, survived by his wife, from whom he was separated, and his two children.   HOWARD GLENNERSTER

Sources C. Webster, *The health services since the war*, 2 (1996) • R. H. S. Crossman, *The diaries of a cabinet minister*, 3 (1977) • N. Timmins, *The five giants: a biography of the welfare state* (1995) • P. Whitehead, *The writing on the wall* (1985) • B. Pimlott, *Harold Wilson* (1992) • *The Times* (19 June 1995) • *The Independent* (19 June 1995) • *WWW* • b. cert. • m. certs. • d. cert. • *CGPLA Eng. & Wales* (1995) • *CGPLA Eng. & Wales* (1991) [M. F. A. Ennals] • m. cert. [M. F. A. Ennals] • *The Times* (7–15 Oct 1991) [M. F. A. Ennals] • *The Independent* (7 Oct 1991) [M. F. A. Ennals] • *The Independent* (9 Nov 1991) [M. F. A. Ennals]
Archives SOUND BL NSA, news recording • BL NSA, party political recording
Likenesses photograph, repro. in *The Times* (19 June 1995) • photograph, repro. in *The Independent* (19 June 1995) • photograph, Press Association Photo Library, London [*see illus.*] • photographs, Hult. Arch.
Wealth at death under £145,000: probate, 9 Oct 1995, *CGPLA Eng. & Wales* • under £125,000—M. F. A. Ennals: probate, 22 May 1992, *CGPLA Eng. & Wales*

Ennals, John Arthur Ford (1918–1988). *See under* Ennals, David Hedley, Baron Ennals (1922–1995).

Ennals, Martin Francis Antony (1927–1991). *See under* Ennals, David Hedley, Baron Ennals (1922–1995).

Enniskillen. For this title name *see* Maguire, Connor, second baron of Enniskillen (*c*.1612–1645).

Eno, James Crossley (1827/8–1915), manufacturer of patent medicine, was born in Newcastle, the son of James Eno (*c*.1793–1829), a general shopkeeper, and his wife, Elizabeth (1792/3–1874), daughter of John Jackson. After leaving school, he was apprenticed to a Newcastle retail chemist, and in 1846 became a dispenser at the infirmary there at £60 a year. In his spare time, he practised as a dentist. In 1852 he was able to buy a local chemist's business. He continued his dentistry work and sold some of his own products, among them a hair restorer. That year on 20 June he married Elizabeth Ann (*d.* 1907), daughter of John Edward Cooke, gardener, of Winlaton, co. Durham. They had two daughters and also a son, Crossley, who died of typhoid before reaching adulthood.

Eno was one of several Newcastle chemists, such as Joseph Wilson Swan, who at that time were striving to break out of the dull dispensing routine. Using a by-product of the area's burgeoning alkali industry, he began, probably in the late 1850s, to make a saline preparation comprising a mixture of tartaric and citric acid with sodium bicarbonate, which created an effervescent drink when water was added. As this proved a palatable remedy for hangovers and digestive troubles, Eno advertised it by giving free samples to the captains of vessels in Newcastle docks. Consequently overseas sales soon outstripped those at home, the ranks of dyspeptic seafaring customers being joined by British expatriates, especially in the tropics. As Eno's advertisements constantly stressed, excessive drinking could lead only to biliousness and attacks of dysentery; while advocating moderation in food and drink, plentiful exercise, and so on, he urged the use of his preparation to help secrete healthy bile and hence purify the blood.

In the early 1870s demand began to soar. According to his own testimony, Eno invented the title of Eno's Fruit Salt in 1873; it was later registered under the Trade Marks Registration Act of 1875, but it was never patented, as he was wont to claim. When his elder daughter married in 1874, her husband, John Nicholson Fleming MD (*d.* 1889), joined the firm as manager. That year Eno published a puffing *Treatise on the Stomach and its Trials*. In 1876 the firm was transferred to London, where a factory was opened at New Cross. Eno acquired Wood Hall, a mansion with large grounds, in nearby Dulwich.

Eno sold only to wholesalers, in quantities not under a gross, charged them outward carriage, and required cash with orders. The firm grew on a tide of change in tastes among digestive sufferers. Although sales of old-fashioned pills, such as those of Thomas Beecham, remained buoyant, demand was mounting for remedies that were more palatable. Eno exploited the trend with plentiful advertising, on which he was spending between £14,000 and £16,000 annually by the early 1890s; in 1914 profits were £128,000 on £260,000 turnover. So far from emulating the Beechams with catchy and amusing advertisements, he preferred to disseminate his views on many topics: in half-page spreads inserted in prestige weeklies such as the *Illustrated London News* he would cram up to a thousand words, headed by barely penetrable aphorisms such as 'contemplation is the only lasting pleasure'. At one stage he ran a campaign about the poor sanitary condition of Britain's inner cities.

While Eno's wordy offerings must have been the despair of his London advertising agents, Gordon and Gotch, few people were put off his rather agreeable product. With branches in Australia and South Africa, the agency doubtless helped to make the business truly international. At home, Eno's claim that the product was a fruit salt was challenged in several high-profile legal cases. After the second, in 1889, which was fought up to the House of Lords, the description 'fruit salt' was struck from the register, not to be restored until an amending act of 1907.

In 1897 J. C. Eno was registered as a private limited company, with a capital of £100,000 and Eno as governing director. He continued to take an active part until 1905, thereafter dividing his time between his home and the National Liberal Club. He was generous to his old infirmary in Newcastle, donating over £10,000 in 1899 and a further £40,000 in his will. He also left £50,000 to Guy's Hospital, London. Tall and of singularly handsome appearance when young, in old age he kept his spare frame, with a shock of white hair and a white beard. He was afflicted with total deafness and was entirely indifferent to everything at his club except the newspapers; the club secretary could recall no member who had ever had the slightest contact with him. Eno died of pneumonia at his home, Wood Hall, College Road, Dulwich, on 11 May 1915 and was cremated at Golders Green four days later. A granddaughter was Dame Isobel Cripps, wife of Sir Stafford Cripps who wrote a legal opinion on how to retain exclusive rights to the words 'fruit salt' by playing down the name of Eno; this remained a doctrine of the Eno company even after it was taken over by Beechams in 1938.

T. A. B. CORLEY

Sources J. C. Eno, estate valuation, 1915, PRO, IR 59/457 · W. A. Campbell, 'Eno, James Crossley', *DBB* · D. Hindley and G. Hindley, *Advertising in Victorian England, 1837–1901* (1972), 97–100 · *Beecham Group Journal*, 1/4 (winter 1961) · H. G. Lazell, *From pills to penicillin: the Beecham story* (1975) · J. J. Howard and F. A. Crisp, eds., *Visitation of England and Wales*, 21 vols. (privately printed, London, 1893–1921), vol. 20, p. 204 · *Chemist and Druggist* (22 May 1915) · *Newcastle Weekly Chronicle* (22 May 1915) · m. cert. · d. cert.
Wealth at death £1,611,607 6s. 7d.: probate, 27 July 1915, *CGPLA Eng. & Wales*

Enoch ap Evan (*c*.1599–1633), murderer, was born at Clun, Shropshire, the elder son of Edward ap Evan (*d*. 1633), yeoman, and his wife, Joan (*c*.1561–1633). Enoch and his brother John (*c*.1602–1633) helped their father farm his holding, and Enoch served in the trained bands in 1631. The family, including Enoch's five sisters, was pious, reading the Book of Common Prayer twice daily. He purchased a Bible, which he carried with him, attended weekday lectures, and sometimes rode three or four miles to hear sermons. About 1631 he became dissatisfied with episcopal polity, kneeling at communion, and the sign of the cross in baptism, probably owing to his exposure to the network of puritan ministers centred around Julines Herring, a protégé of Arthur Hildersham and lecturer at St Alkmund, Shrewsbury, from 1618 to 1635. A year later he ceased to kneel at communion, believing this posture 'thrust the heeles and legges behind the bodie' and thus impeded the flow of spiritual nourishment. 'By inspiration' he came to the conclusion that the Lord's supper should be received while sitting or standing and bowing (PRO, SP 16/244/67). Convinced that he was one of the elect, he believed the Holy Spirit guided him.

Enoch's mother and brother attempted to dissuade him from such views, and during a discussion about kneeling on 30 June 1633 she reputedly told him he was 'a very sorry fellow' (Studley, *Looking-Glasse*, 36–7). After being jilted on the night of 4 July by the woman he expected to marry he got little sleep. About one o'clock the next afternoon, feeling called to 'vindicate the cause of God … by effusion of his owne brothers blood' (ibid., 35), he hit John in the head with the blunt end of a hatchet as the latter napped with his head on the kitchen table, knocking him to the floor, and then decapitated him with two more blows. When his mother entered the room, shrieked, and rebuked him, he hit her in the face, though he had not planned to harm her. In the ensuing struggle he struck her with the hatchet between the left shoulder and the neck, slicing into her breast and pushing her to the floor, and then decapitated her. After knocking a hole in the wall to create the impression of a break-in, he carried the heads, wrapped in linen and a jerkin, into a meadow and secreted them under a pile of ferns to be burnt. He then went to his cousin's house, read Isaiah 1, and borrowed a copy of Lewis Bayly's *The Practise of Pietie*. As the two men walked toward Enoch's house two maids and some neighbours apprehended him and turned him over to a local magistrate, Sir Robert Howard.

At first Enoch professed his innocence, but he finally confessed to Erasmus Powell, vicar of Clun, who had baptized him. According to the record of his examination, 'the divill being strong with him at that instan[t] tempted him to doe this' (PRO, SP 16/242/39). As he was transported to the county gaol at Shrewsbury his sister confronted him, asking why he had committed the murders. 'Peace foole', he reportedly replied, 'hold thy tongue, wee live in a false Church, and thou shalt see a change shortly' (Studley, *Looking-Glasse*, 53). At his trial he manifested neither 'distraction' nor a remorseful countenance, though he expressed sorrow for the crimes (PRO, SP 16/244/67). Numerous ministers visited him in prison, hoping to obtain his repentance, and the puritans also wanted him to blame his actions on something other than the family argument over kneeling, which he had cited. Mental illness would have been a better explanation in their judgement, and there were unsubstantiated rumours that he was an Anabaptist. Determined to use the murders to tarnish puritans, Peter Studley, Arminian-inclined minister of St Chad's, Shrewsbury, visited him eighteen times, concluding that he was not insane, that he continued to hold Calvinist tenets, and that he believed Satan could not prevail over God's children. However, he told Gervase Needham, vicar of Bishop's Castle, Shropshire, that he had experienced visions of a dove.

Prior to his execution, on 20 August, ap Evan allegedly told other prisoners that killing the hangman would not be sinful. In order to take communion before his execution he received it kneeling, and on the gallows at Bishop's Castle he cried to God for mercy and exhorted the audience to heed his example. Bound in chains, his corpse remained on the gibbet for more than two weeks before unknown persons secretly buried it.

Accounts of the murders appeared in several penny dreadful pamphlets, *A True Relation of a Barbarous and most Cruel Murder* (1633) and *A Mirror for Murders* (1633), as well as Studley's tract, *The Looking-Glasse of Schisme* (1634), which Archbishop William Laud's chaplain licensed. Although he refused to approve a rival account by another local magistrate, Richard More, *A True Relation of the Murders*, which deemed ap Evan insane, it circulated in manuscript and was rebutted by Studley in *A Refutation of such Calumnies* (1635). In 1636 the puritan Henry Burton cited Studley's book as evidence of a Jesuit conspiracy to defame puritans, and its publication was noted in a list of grievances presented to the Short Parliament by Sir Robert Harley. The refusal of Laud's chaplain to license More's account, eventually published in 1641, was the subject of a complaint to the Long Parliament. Robert Wright, bishop of Coventry and Lichfield, was interested in the case, and Augustine Lindsell, bishop of Hereford, responded to the affair by restricting the combination lecture at Bishop's

Castle to conformist ministers. The author of *The Ranters Ranting* (1650) retold the story with gross inaccuracies to conclude his sensationalist pamphlet.

RICHARD L. GREAVES

Sources PRO, 16/242/39; 16/243/66; 16/244/67 · P. Studley, *The looking-glasse of schisme*, 2nd edn (1635) · P. Lake, 'Puritanism, Arminianism and a Shropshire axe-murder', *Midland History*, 15 (1990), 37–64 · P. Studley, *A refutation of such calumnies* (1635) · *The Ranters ranting* (1650), 6 · P. Lake, '"A charitable Christian hatred": the godly and their enemies in the 1630s', *The culture of English puritanism, 1560–1700*, ed. C. Durston and J. Eales (1996), 174–8

Ensom, William (*bap.* 1796, *d.* 1832), engraver, was baptized on 6 November 1796 at St Pancras, London, the son of John and Elizabeth Ensom. After his father's death his mother married James Burnham (*d.* before 1832). In 1815, when he was living at Swinton Street, off Gray's Inn Road, Ensom was awarded a silver medal by the Society of Arts for a pen and ink drawing of William Blake's head, and in 1816 he was given a similar award for another pen and ink drawing of one of Le Brun's battles. In W. B. Cooke's 1821 exhibition of engravings—by which time he had moved the short distance to Chapel Street, Pentonville—Ensom was represented by two portraits after J. Thurston of the poets William Whitehead and Richard Glover. Eight plates were engraved for J. P. Neale's *Views of the Seats of Noblemen and Gentlemen* (1818–24), and between 1825 and 1831 he exhibited six engravings at the Suffolk Street Gallery, signing as W. Ensom. His work on steel for the annuals began with *The Amulet*, 1827 and 1828. For *The Bijou*, 1829–30, he engraved portraits of George IV and Lady Elizabeth Wallscourt after Sir Thomas Lawrence, thought to be some of his best work. The *Literary Souvenir* of 1828, 1832, and 1834 each carried one of his engravings; that in the last volume was *The Oriental Love-Letter* after Destouches, engraved by Ensom when the original engraver died. He also contributed to *Friendship's Offering* (1833). He engraved portraits after Sir Thomas Lawrence of Mrs Harriet Arbuthnot (1829), Master Charles William Lambton, and Frances, marchioness of Salisbury, with some biblical plates which included *Christ Appearing to Mary Magdalene* after Titian, *Christ Blessing the Bread* after Carlo Dolci, and *St John in the Wilderness* after Carlo Cignani. Most of Ensom's work was in line, mostly on steel, with some on copper. Ensom also worked in watercolour, and probably met R. P. Bonington through Cooke and Barnett who were Bonington's hosts during his visits to England from France from 1825 to 1828.

For some years Ensom lodged with Mrs Evatt at East Hill, Wandsworth, where he died on 13 September 1832. Among the friends remembered in his will were the 'much esteemed' William John Cooke the engraver, his 'worthy' John Barnett, printer (both being executors), and the engravers Joseph Phelps and John Bishop. His mother was the main beneficiary, and his brother Joseph received his clothes and linen, his tools being distributed to his friends. His collection of engravings, drawings and so on was auctioned on 12 December 1832. B. HUNNISETT

Sources Redgrave, *Artists*, 2nd edn · Graves, *Artists*, 3rd edn · *GM*, 1st ser., 102/2 (1832), 284 · will, PRO, PROB 11/1811, fol. 233r–v · parish register, London, St Pancras, LMA, 6 Nov 1796 [baptism] · *Literary Souvenir* (1834), vii · *Transactions of the Society of Arts*, 33 (1815), 22 · *Transactions of the Society of Arts*, 34 (1816), 29 · M. Cormack, *Bonington* (1989), 152 · *Engraved Brit. ports.*, 6.607
Archives BM, department of prints and drawings

Ensor, George (1769–1843), political writer, was born in Dublin, although his father, George Ensor, was English. He was educated at Trinity College, Dublin, and graduated BA in 1790. He was admitted to the King's Inns in 1792 and wrote extensively on politics and religion. His pamphlets were widely read, and were written in a powerful and sarcastic, though sometimes inflated, style. His attacks were especially directed against the English government of Ireland after the union.

Ensor never belonged to any political grouping. He was considered able, but reviewers thought him erratic and too apt to attribute all political problems to virtual representation. Bentham, while admiring his good intentions and learning, believed him to be inconsistent, and James Mill thought him impractical. Most of his life was spent at Ardress, co. Armagh, where he died on 3 December 1843. His first publication, in 1801, was a treatise on *The Principles of Morality*. It was followed by many books and pamphlets on Irish politics, the poor laws, Catholic emancipation, and education. His *Defects of the English Laws and Tribunals* (1812) was described by a legal reviewer as 'a rambling, desultory, fault-finding, ill-digested volume' (Allibone, *Dict.*).

FRANCIS WATT, rev. MARIE-LOUISE LEGG

Sources D. J. Hickey and J. E. Doherty, *A dictionary of Irish history* (1980); pbk edn (1987) · D. J. O'Donoghue, *The poets of Ireland: a biographical and bibliographical dictionary* (1912) · *The works of Jeremy Bentham*, ed. J. Bowring, [new edn], 11 vols. (1843–59) · review, *QR*, 22 (1819–20), 102–7 · W. J. Fitzpatrick, *The life, times and correspondence of the Right Rev. Dr Doyle, bishop of Kildare and Leighlin*, new edn, 2 vols. (1880) · E. Keane, P. Beryl Phair, and T. U. Sadleir, eds., *King's Inns admission papers, 1607–1867*, IMC (1982) · Allibone, *Dict.*
Likenesses H. Meyer, stipple (after drawing by J. Comerford), BM, NG Ire., NPG

Ensor, Sir Robert Charles Kirkwood (1877–1958), journalist and historian, was born on 16 October 1877 at The Knap, Milborne Port, Somerset, the third child and only son to survive infancy of Robert Henry Ensor, master glover, and his wife, Olivia Priscilla, daughter of Charles Curme, banker, of Dorchester. A scholar of Winchester College and of Balliol College, Oxford, he obtained firsts in classical moderations (1898) and *literae humaniores* (1900) and in 1899 the chancellor's Latin verse prize and a Craven scholarship. He was elected president of the Oxford Union for Hilary term 1900 a few weeks before winning his Craven scholarship.

Ensor was urged by his Oxford tutors and by M. J. Rendall of Winchester towards the bar and public life. 'You have too much vigour and force to be a don', Rendall wrote in August 1900, 'although I think you would make a good one.' This was perilous advice. As a result of disastrous speculation by his father some years earlier Ensor was short of money. His family was kept going by a finishing school which his mother and sisters ran in Brussels. He was not elected to the Oxford prize fellowships, which would have given him some financial security. To overcome the drawback of poverty and succeed at the bar he would have needed a fine physique, patient devotion to the main chance, and acceptable views. He possessed none of these attributes. He was a small man, not notably robust, who blinked constantly. He was apt to disperse his energies: he might have had a fellowship of Merton or St John's in September 1900 had he not been helping C. P. Scott in the election campaign at Leigh, Lancashire, until just before the examination. He was not willing to wait indefinitely for an income: he married within six years of leaving Oxford. He had become an ardent socialist and was soon editing the collection of speeches and writings published in 1904 as *Modern Socialism*.

Ensor joined the *Manchester Guardian* at the end of 1901, succeeding L. T. Hobhouse as a leader writer. Three years later he moved to London, and in 1905 he was called to the bar by the Inner Temple. He contributed to a number of journals at this time, notably *The Speaker*, *The Nation*, and the short-lived daily *Tribune*. He lived in Poplar and was soon active in Labour politics. In 1909 he served on the national administrative council of the Independent Labour Party. He was on the executive committee of the Fabian Society in 1907–11 and 1912–19 and a member of the London county council from 1910 to 1913.

In 1909 Ensor abandoned the bar and became a leader writer on the *Daily News*. He lost this post two years later when the paper was planning to amalgamate with the *Morning Leader*. In February 1912 he was appointed by Robert Donald to a similar post on the *Daily Chronicle*, and he remained there as chief leader writer until the paper was amalgamated in 1930 with the *Daily News* to become the *News Chronicle*. During Ensor's early years with it the *Daily Chronicle* was a powerful paper. Most of its pronouncements came from his pen, and Liberal politicians treated them with respect. He wrote, for instance, the leader of 29 November 1916 which called for an improved prime minister's secretariat, and for a war council reduced to four members and given 'the widest powers of prompt action'.

Although Ensor had moved in 1910 to High Wycombe, where he was able to indulge his hobbies of gardening and bird-watching, he remained for some years near the centre of affairs. He was the secretary of the foreign policy committee which a group of Liberals established early in 1912, in the hope of checking Sir Edward Grey and promoting 'a friendly approach to the German government'. Ensor now became the leading Fabian authority on foreign policy. He was far more realistic about it than were most of his fellow socialists. He argued, for instance, that objections to tsarist despotism should not affect British statesmen: there was 'a strong case for the entente with Russia' (*New Statesman*, 25 April 1914). He knew, according to his own later statements (*England, 1870–1914*, 1936), more about German war preparations than he was allowed to write in the *Daily Chronicle*.

None the less, the German invasion of Belgium seems to have surprised him. He had long been at home in that country: the assault on it affected him deeply and drove him politically to the right. On 1 August 1914 the *Daily Chronicle* was still taking the traditional Liberal view: a leader warned that Russia should not be supported 'so far as to win for her an unbalanced hegemony'. A leader by Ensor on 4 August announced a complete change; and to the *Chronicle* three days later the German invasion of Belgium represented 'a survival of immoral and barbarous forces which in the long run Europe must inevitably have had to subdue'. On 3 May 1915 Beatrice Webb recorded in her diary in a survey of Fabian views on the war: 'Ensor, one of the most accomplished of the middle-aged members, is complacently convinced of the imperative need not only of beating Germany but of dismembering the German Empire' (*The Diary of Beatrice Webb, 1905–1924*, ed. N. Mackenzie and J. Mackenzie, 1984, 226).

Writing for the *Daily Chronicle* suited Ensor. He refused a proposal that he should become Berlin correspondent of *The Times*. But he suffered by the sale of the *Chronicle* to the Lloyd George group and by the Liberal decline in the twenties. When the amalgamation of 1930 brought his retirement he seemed a brilliant failure. He had attracted the attention, however, of George Clark, the editor of the Oxford History of England; and in November 1930, although he had written nothing substantial except a short book on Belgium in the Home University Library (1915), he was chosen to write the most recent volume of the history. This bold choice proved to be inspired. Ensor's gifts and experience gave him a unique equipment as the historian of his own times. The range of his information was formidable, and he had a wide acquaintance among public men. He was used to working quickly through masses of material. He had preserved in a career of journalism high standards of scholarship. He had himself published several volumes of verse and wrote with discernment on literature, music, and the other arts. *England, 1870–1914* appeared in 1936 and was acclaimed at once as a masterpiece. Authoritative and just in judgement, it was never heavy. A crisp style and delightful touches of idiosyncrasy made every chapter marvellously readable. His account of the events leading up to the outbreak of war in 1914 was particularly notable. He had already guessed when he wrote it that German policy would produce a crisis in 1938. In an article in *The Spectator* (7 October 1938) he explained that to someone who had studied *Mein Kampf* German methods, in both conscription and the purchase of raw materials, had pointed to this date.

Ensor had maintained his income meanwhile by freelance journalism and by some university work. He lectured at the London School of Economics in 1931–2 and was deputy for the Gladstone professor of political theory and institutions at Oxford in 1933. He even found time to write a comparison of the British, French, and German judicial systems (*Courts and Judges*, 1933). Once the history was published, recognition from his university came quickly. He was a senior research fellow of Corpus Christi College, Oxford, from 1937 to 1946. He was made a faculty fellow of Nuffield College in 1939 and deputized again for the Gladstone professor from 1940 to 1944. In Oxford as elsewhere he was handicapped by his inability ever to admit that he was wrong. But he became a renowned common-room conversationalist and an influential figure in the faculty of social studies, where he joined in devising the degree of bachelor of philosophy. The first in his long series of 'Scrutator' articles in the *Sunday Times* appeared on 9 February 1941, and he contributed a number of notices to the *Dictionary of National Biography*. He served on the royal commissions on population (1944–9) and the press (1947–9). He became an honorary fellow of Balliol and Corpus Christi colleges in 1953 and was knighted in 1955.

Ensor was happy in his private life. He married on 31 May 1906 Helen (*d.* 1960), daughter of William Henry Fisher, of Manchester; they had two sons and three daughters. He died in St Joseph's Nursing Home, Beaconsfield, Buckinghamshire, on 4 December 1958.

MICHAEL BROCK, *rev.*

Sources CCC Oxf., Ensor MSS · personal knowledge (1971) · private information (1971) · *CGPLA Eng. & Wales* (1959) · b. cert. · m. cert. · d. cert.
Archives Bodl. Oxf., corresp., diaries, MSS, and notebooks | BLPES, corresp. with the Independent Labour Party · Bodl. Oxf., letters to Sir Alfred Zimmern · JRL, letters to the *Manchester Guardian*
Likenesses photograph, CCC Oxf.
Wealth at death £27,446 4s. 6d.: probate, 12 Feb 1959, *CGPLA Eng. & Wales*

Ent, Sir George (1604–1689), physician, was born on 6 November 1604 at Sandwich, Kent, the son of Josias Ent, a merchant and probable religious refugee from Flanders. He attended school in Wallachia and Rotterdam, after which he entered Sidney Sussex College, Cambridge, on 8 July 1624, where he earned the rank of scholar (1628); he graduated BA (1627) and MA (1631), following which he travelled to Padua, where he took an MD on 28 April 1636 (incorporated at Oxford on 9 November 1638). Upon his graduation at Padua under the tutelage of J. D. Sala he was presented with a volume of congratulatory verses (*Laurae Apollinari*) by his friends, who included P. M. Slegel, J. Rhode, and J. Greaves. In 1636 Ent also chanced to meet William Harvey in Venice, while Harvey was travelling in the delegation of the earl of Arundel; Harvey was also from Kent, Cambridge, and Padua, and the two developed a close bond. In the autumn Ent and Greaves accompanied Harvey to Rome and perhaps even to Naples.

After returning to England, Ent settled in London, where in December 1638 the College of Physicians instructed him to conform to their authority; he duly took their examinations for membership and became a candidate and fellow (in April and June 1639, respectively). Ent's first book, *Apologia pro circulatione sanguinis* (1641), dedicated to Harvey, counter-attacked the anti-Harveian Emilio Parigiano and emphasized the importance of experiment. It also contained remarks on respiration that spoke of the importance of a nitre in air and water, which inspired later work among English physiologists. The following year Ent gave the annual Goulstonian lecture on pathology at the College of Physicians. He was among the London experimentalists (the '1645 Group') that is often

taken to be a precursor of the Royal Society. Ent was also an active participant in the experimental investigations carried on at the College of Physicians during the interregnum. Perhaps most importantly, probably around Christmas 1647, Ent obtained from Harvey his manuscript on generation, which Ent edited, prefaced, and saw through the press (published as *De generatione*, 1651). Harvey's will charged Ent with dispersing his library to the College of Physicians, and left £5 to him for a ring in his remembrance. Ent also joined the founding membership of the Royal Society, and in October 1664 he sponsored the first meeting of the society's anatomical committee at his house. He helped Hooke dissect lungs of a viper to further study respiration in the same year. With Charles II in attendance he gave the College of Physicians' anatomy lecture in 1665, following which he was knighted.

Ent had risen rapidly in the esteem of his colleagues, serving as a censor of the college (1645–69 except for 1650, 1652, and 1658), registrar (1655–70), elect (1657 until he resigned in 1689), consiliarius (1667–9 and 1676–86), and president (1670–75, 1682, and 1684). His rise may have been helped by his marriage (on 10 February 1646) to Sarah, daughter of Othowell *Meverell, recently president of the college. The marriage took place at St Olave Jewry (where in 1644 a merchant, Peter Ent, probably a brother, was listed as a vestryman), although in 1640 Ent had been listed as a member of the Dutch church at Austin Friars. Ent also apparently prospered as a physician, subscribing £170 in September 1670—the second greatest contribution—to help rebuild the college following the fire of 1666.

While in his later years Ent's responsibilities to patients and colleagues received most of his attention, he continued to advance the new philosophy. Some of his anatomical studies (probably done in the 1650s) appeared in 1677 in the second edition of Walter Charleton's *Onomasticon zoicum*; in 1678 he published posthumously in the *Philosophical Transactions* John Greaves's memoir on the Egyptian method of hatching eggs in incubating ovens; in 1679 (with editions of 1681 and 1685) his *Antidiatribē, sive, Animadversiones in Malachiae Thurstoni, M.D.* corrected Thurston's account of Ent's views on respiration, and a much revised edition of his *Apologia* appeared in 1685. The 1687 Leiden edition of his *Opera omnia* also contains an essay on tides. In his will, dated 25 November 1687, he left the manor and rectory of East Langton, Lincolnshire, and property at Sandwich, Kent, to his son Josias, and money bequests in all amounting to over £4000 to his son Edward, his daughter Dame Sarah Barrett and her children, and to Josias's wife Katherine. His wife was the residuary legatee but he also left £10 to Mrs Dorothy Lamplugh (probably a nurse) 'who now lives with me'. Ent died at his house in St Giles-in-the-Fields on 13 October 1689, and was buried in St Lawrence Jewry. His wife Sarah survived him, but she died on or before 10 April 1690.

HAROLD J. COOK

Sources annals, RCP Lond. · W. Birken, 'Dr John King (1614–1681) and Dr Assuerus Regemorter (1615–1650)', *Medical History*, 20 (1976),

276–95 • Foster, *Alum. Oxon.* • R. G. Frank, *Harvey and the Oxford physiologists* (1980) • M. Hunter, *The Royal Society and its fellows, 1660–1700: the morphology of an early scientific institution* (1982) • Munk, *Roll* • Venn, *Alum. Cant.* • C. Webster, 'Ent, George', *DSB* • will of Sir George Ent, 25 Nov 1687, PRO, PROB 11/396, sig. 136, and PROB 11/397, sig. 139

Archives BL, Add. MSS; Sloane MSS • RCP Lond., 'Apologia pro circulatione sanguinis', anatomical lectures

Likenesses R. White, line engraving, 1679, BM, NPG; repro. in G. Ent, *Antidiatrib, sive, Animadversiones … (1679)*

Wealth at death £4487—in bequests and land: will, PRO, PROB 11/396, sig. 136; PRO, PROB 11/397, sig. 139

Entick, John (*c.*1703–1773), author, lived as an adult in St Dunstan and All Saints' parish, Stepney. According to the address prefixed to his *New Latin and English Dictionary* (1771) he was ten years at 'college'. His first publication, the *Speculum Latinum* (1728) was designed 'to make Latin neither tedious nor obscure', on a system he had successfully tried when it was his 'lot to be perplexed with a very dull boy'. A Greek sequel followed in 1729. In the same year Entick described himself on the title-page of *The Evidence of Christianity Asserted and Proved from Facts*, as a student of divinity. In 1736 he issued an (unrealized) proposal to print 'Chaucer' in two folio volumes, with explanatory notes: from this proposal onwards he styled himself MA, although there is no evidence for where he obtained his degree. Nothing appeared under his name for the next eighteen years. In 1754 he published a school edition of the fables of Phaedrus, and in the same year edited a pocket companion to freemasonry. From 1755 he was paid £200 a year to write for Jonathan Scott and John Shebbeare on a weekly anti-government periodical *The Monitor, or, The British Freeholder*, the first issue appearing on Saturday 9 August 1755 and the last on 30 March 1765. His attacks on the government (in numbers 357, 358, 360, 373, 376, 378, and 380) caused his house to be entered and his papers seized on 11 November 1762 under a general warrant issued by Lord Halifax. Entick sued the authorities for illegal seizure, and Lord Camden gave judgment in his favour (for £300 damages) in *Entick v. Carrington* in 1765.

In 1757 Entick produced *A New Naval History*, dedicated to Admiral Vernon. On 7 January 1760 he married a widow, Elizabeth Fisher, at St Dunstan's; she died in the same year. In 1763–4 (now as 'the Rev. John Entick, M.A.') he published *The General History of the Late War*, in five volumes. He issued a *New Spelling Dictionary* in 1764 and a *New Latin and English Dictionary* in 1771. In 1766 he published an edition of William Maitland's *History and Survey of London, Westminster, Southwark and their Environs*, also issued in weekly numbers in 1771. He is credited also with a *Ready Reckoner*, and a share in the new *Week's Preparation* and the new *Whole Duty of Man*, as well as with a grammar contributed to John Gignoux's *Child's Best Instructor* (1773).

Entick died on 22 May 1773 at Stepney, where he was buried on 28 May. He left nearly ready for the press a collaborative work in four volumes, *The Present State of the British Empire*, published posthumously in 1774. A portrait of Entick in clerical dress, from a picture by Burgess, appears as frontispiece to *The General History of the Late War*

and later works. Kept in constant employment by booksellers during most of his life, his dictionaries repeatedly edited through the first half of the nineteenth century, he is now remembered chiefly for the trial of 1765, which has acquired textbook status for establishing the right to possession of home and property free from state interference.

JENNETT HUMPHREYS, rev. PENELOPE WILSON

Sources *State trials*, 19.1029ff. • J. Entick, *New Latin and English dictionary* (1771) • D. Lysons, *The environs of London*, 3 (1795), 437, 457 • Watt, *Bibl. Brit.* • Nichols, *Illustrations*, 5.803 • *Lady's Magazine*, 4 (1773) • H. Bromley, *A catalogue of engraved British portraits* (1793), 360 • *Engraved Brit. ports.*, 2.166 • IGI

Likenesses W. Benoist, line engraving (after Burgess), BM, NPG; repro. in J. Entick, *The general history of the late war*, 5 vols. (1763–4)

Entwisle, Joseph (1767–1841), Wesleyan Methodist minister, the second son of William Entwisle and his wife, Ellen Makin, who were members of a Presbyterian church in Manchester, was born in the city on 15 April 1767. He was taught at the free school connected with the old Presbyterian chapel, Manchester. At the age of fourteen Entwisle joined the Methodists, and made good use of the library at the preacher's house in Oldham Street. When almost sixteen he began to preach, and was known as 'the boy preacher'. Wesley called him out to itinerant work, and in 1787 sent him to the Oxfordshire circuit. At the Manchester conference he was received into full connexion while stationed in Halifax. In May 1792 he married Mary Pawson, second daughter of Marmaduke Pawson, farmer, of Thorner, near Leeds. They had six children, two of whom, Joseph and William, became Methodist ministers. During the next few years Entwisle served in Leeds, Wakefield, Hull, Macclesfield, Manchester, Liverpool, and London, winning popularity by his preaching power and judicious management. While he was in Macclesfield (1802–4) his wife died, and when stationed in London (1804–6) he married his second wife, Lucy Hine, of Kingsland Crescent, in October 1805. In 1804 Entwisle became secretary of the first missionary committee established. The conference of 1812 was held in Leeds, and Entwisle was elected president. The busy public life he led left him little time for literary work, but in 1820 he published his *Essay on Secret Prayer*, which was translated into French. He also contributed biographical and practical articles to the *Methodist Magazine*. His reflections of 1797 that form 'The present state of Methodism', published in his memoir, are an important contribution to Methodist historiography.

The later years of Entwisle's ministry were spent in Bath, Bristol, Birmingham, Sheffield, and London, where he was several times reappointed. In 1825 he was elected president of the conference for a second time. In 1834 he was appointed house governor of the new Wesleyan Theological Institution opened at Hoxton for the education and training of candidates for the ministry. His seniority, saintliness, and the position of respect he held allowed the institution to survive despite widespread opposition to its formation. He resigned the office four years later because of ill health and retired to Tadcaster, where his only daughter lived. He preached occasionally until within a few days of his death, which occurred on Saturday 6 November 1841 at Thorner, near Leeds.

W. B. LOWTHER, *rev.* TIM MACQUIBAN

Sources W. Hill, *An alphabetical arrangement of all the Wesleyan-Methodist ministers, missionaries, and preachers*, rev. J. P. Haswell, 9th edn (1862) · *Minutes of the Methodist conferences, from the first, held in London by the late Rev. John Wesley …*, 20 vols. (1812–79) [1842 conference] · R. E. Davies, A. R. George, and G. Rupp, eds., *A history of the Methodist church in Great Britain*, 1 (1965) · N. B. Harmon, ed., *The encyclopedia of world Methodism*, 2 vols. (1974) · W. Entwisle, *Memoir of the Rev. J. Entwisle* (1848) · K. D. Brown, *A social history of the nonconformist ministry in England and Wales, 1800–1930* (1988)
Archives JRL, corresp., journals | Wesley College, Bristol, letters, mainly to George Morley · Wesley's Chapel, London, letters
Likenesses W. Ridley, stipple, BM, NPG; repro. in *Arminian Magazine*

Entwistle, William James (1895–1952), Spanish scholar, was born on 7 December 1895 at Cheng Yang Kuan, the eldest of the four children of William Edmund Entwistle and his wife, Jessie Ann Buchan, both missionaries in China. Entwistle was taught by his father and at the China Inland Mission's school at Chefoo (Yantai) until 1910, and acquired a working knowledge of Chinese which he never lost. To the circumstances of his boyhood he must have owed something of his sobriety of taste and manner, and his marked inclination, as a scholar, to walk alone. After a year at Robert Gordon's College, Aberdeen, he entered the University of Aberdeen with a bursary and in 1916 obtained a first class in classics, with distinctions in Greek history and comparative philology, and was awarded the Simpson and Jenkyns prizes and the Seafield and the town's gold medals. He then joined the Royal Field Artillery, later transferring to the Scottish Rifles, and was seriously wounded in 1917.

In the following year Entwistle was awarded the Fullerton classical scholarship at Aberdeen and an academic career in classics seemed the natural sequel. Already, however, the natural sweep of his mind, his voracious curiosity, and his restless explorer's instinct urged him to seek less well-mapped territory, and he turned to Spanish. In 1920, with a Carnegie grant, he went for a year to Madrid. His prodigious assimilative powers enabled him, in that time, to acquaint himself with most aspects of the subject and also to accumulate a quantity of research material which kept him supplied for years. He learnt Spanish thoroughly, also Catalan and Portuguese, although he always spoke his languages with a pronounced Scots accent. Either then, or soon afterwards, he acquired some knowledge of Arabic and Basque. He formed no emotional attachment to Spain and his subsequent visits to the country were rare.

Entwistle married in 1921 Jeanie Drysdale, daughter of John Buchanan, a Kirkcaldy businessman, with whom he had one son, and who provided him with the happy, unpretentious, and secure home life which his highly strung temperament needed. Although he had the speech

William James Entwistle (1895–1952), by Elliott & Fry

and religion of Scotland, and his dark hair, high cheekbones, and slight physical ungainliness suggested a characteristic Scots type, his parents in fact came from Manchester and Sheffield. But his marriage completed the process of making him a Scot by adoption.

In 1921 Entwistle became lecturer in charge of Spanish at Manchester, where he wrote his first book, *The Arthurian Legend in the Literatures of the Spanish Peninsula* (1925), a pioneer effort which showed his flair for ordering and relating a mass of facts, and some of those suggestive intuitions, at times bold to the point of rashness, which prevented his works from becoming mere tools for purveying erudition. In this year he became first Stevenson professor of Spanish at Glasgow, where, as always, he eagerly undertook whatever administrative duties came his way. He now embarked on the immense scholarly output which characterized his academic career. When in 1932 he became King Alfonso XIII professor of Spanish studies at Oxford, with a fellowship at Exeter College, at the early age of thirty-six he had two major works and thirty learned articles to his credit. His edition of the second part of the *Chronicle of John I of Portugal* was, however, never published. The proofs were deposited in the Taylor Institution.

Entwistle's previous experience and avowed belief in the professoriate as 'a sacred priesthood' did not make it easy for him to accept the marginal, undepartmentalized status of an Oxford arts professor, or many other Oxford attitudes to learning and teaching. For a time he seemed more anxious to introduce into Oxford the ways of the universities he knew than to adapt himself. There was in him, however, nothing intolerant or fanatical; while he always practised what he preached, he gradually reconciled himself with wry good humour to the fact that many of his opinions were not acceptable in Oxford. By dint of continuous pressure, he did succeed in getting an honour school of Portuguese established and himself became director of Portuguese studies (1933). He also succeeded in getting Catalan and Spanish-American literature put on the syllabus. Some felt this to be an empire-building gesture, but it would seem to have been justified by the increase in numbers reading Spanish to about a hundred by the end of his career.

Entwistle's first major work at Oxford was *The Spanish Language* (1936), a descriptive account of the languages of the Iberian peninsula which broke entirely new ground by the weight it gave to historical and social interpretations of linguistic fact. *European Balladry* (1939), his most important work on a literary subject, went for the first time beyond Iberian themes. He studied about a dozen more European languages, remarking apologetically in his preface that he had not read with his own eyes the Finnish and Estonian ballads. The book marked an epoch in ballad criticism and despite the density of its material and the rigour of its method is humane and readable. In 1949 Entwistle published, in collaboration with W. A. Morison, *Russian and the Slavonic Languages*, which he approached in the pioneer manner of his book on Spanish. Although he had taken up Slavonic only a few years previously, this book, and several articles, established him as an authority.

While preparing his major works Entwistle wrote, or collaborated in, various other books, including an attempt to reassess Cervantes as a literary craftsman (1940) and a history of English literature (1943). His output of learned articles while at Oxford seems to have exceeded sixty, to say nothing of endless reviews. His articles deal with a great variety of Spanish, Portuguese, and South American literary, linguistic, and historical themes, with Slavonic language and literature, with Scandinavian material, with general linguistics, and much else besides. His attitude to his articles was peculiar. Whenever new ideas occurred to him, as they ceaselessly did, he at once worked them out in article form, but after they had been proof-corrected he often seemed to have no further interest in them. Sometimes they were so rapidly composed that his meaning is not easy to follow, but all contain a new point of view or a new contribution to knowledge. On the other hand, with his books he took endless pains, sometimes rewriting them as many as ten times before sending to the publishers a manuscript bare of any corrections.

Entwistle's other activities were immense. He was joint editor of the *Modern Language Review* (1934–48), general editor of the *Year's Work in Modern Language Studies* (1931–7), and of the Great Languages Series (1940–52). He was also general editor of the linguistic contributions to the new edition of *Chambers's Encyclopaedia*, to which he himself contributed an important article on language. He served on several editorial boards including *Medium Ævum*, the *Bulletin of Hispanic Studies*, and the *Romanistisches Jahrbuch*. He was always ready to attend congresses or lecture abroad, visiting South America, Spain and Portugal, and Scandinavia. From 1942 to 1943 he was educational director of the British Council. Outside Oxford, academic honours, which he received with an unexpected degree of satisfaction, were frequent. He was an honorary LLD of Aberdeen (1940) and Glasgow (1951) and LittD of Coimbra and Pennsylvania, as well as a corresponding member of the Spanish and Portuguese academies of history, the Norwegian Academy, and other foreign learned societies. In 1950 he was elected FBA and in 1952 he was president of the Modern Humanities Research Association.

A major operation, coupled with his extreme conscientiousness while visiting professor at Philadelphia and California in 1948–9, overstrained Entwistle beyond repair. Soon after his return home he was taken seriously ill and, until his death, he was stricken but undaunted. His daemon seemed to drive him harder than ever. He began to write two new books. One, on Calderón, was never finished. The other, *Aspects of Language* (published posthumously in 1953), a synthesis, is his greatest book and contains the fruits of his thinking based on a knowledge of many of the languages of the world. Its exploration of the non-Indo-European linguistic world is remarkable. Empirical, eschewing techniques and doctrines, and characterized by an optimism and dry humour difficult to associate with the circumstances in which it was written, it is largely free from the disconcerting whimsicalities of vocabulary and style which, in his determination not to be dull, he had sometimes used in earlier books.

The two men to whom Entwistle most wished to be compared were Wilhelm von Humboldt and Gaston Paris. The choice was characteristic, for he regarded much contemporary scholarship as narrow, and both arrogant and timid; his own work had the quality of genius. In private he was not formidable, conducting himself with a courtesy, loyalty, good humour, and absence of showmanship which caused the sophisticated to underestimate him. On the surface it seemed that he possessed a natural orderliness of habit and mind, probably the result of the rigid disciplining of a naturally romantic temperament. Even in his later work his emotions were so implacably controlled that only some of the warmth which was in the man emerged. He died suddenly in St Edmund Hall, Oxford, on 13 June 1952, and was survived by his wife.

P. E. L. R. RUSSELL, *rev.*

Sources A. Ewert, *PBA*, 38 (1952), 333–43 · private information (2004) · personal knowledge (2004) · P. E. R., *Oxford Magazine* (16 Oct 1952), 6–8
Likenesses W. Stoneman, photograph, 1950, NPG · Elliott & Fry, photograph, NPG [*see illus.*]
Wealth at death £7017 1s. 11d.: probate, 1952

Enty, John (1675?–1743), Presbyterian minister, was the son of John Enty, a travelling tailor in Cornwall. According to John Fox (1693–1763), the biographer of Devon dissent, Enty was working with his father at Tregothnan when he attracted the attention of a Mrs Fortescue, 'a great friend to the Dissenting interest' who paid for the 'intelligent and towardly' boy to attend a grammar school and subsequently the Taunton Academy, under Matthew Warren ('Memoirs', 325). Fortified by a recommendation from Warren, Enty went to preach at Plymouth, some time after the death on 15 May 1696 of Nicholas Sherwill, pastor of one of the two Presbyterian congregations. Sherwill's place was briefly filled by his assistant, Byfield, 'who had the best sense and parts of any Dissenter that ever lived there', but he was passed over in favour of Enty, 'a bright and serious young man' ('Memoirs', 326). Enty was ordained at Plymouth on 11 May 1698. The 500-strong congregation continued to meet at the Marshalsea, the Dominican house in Southside Street (often referred to as Black Friars), until the completion of the Batter Street Chapel in 1708. This also became known as the Scotch Kirk because of the attendance of Scottish soldiers stationed in the city. The other Presbyterian congregation, led by Nicholas Harding (d. 1744), numbered 760 hearers, and the two ministers enjoyed considerable local prominence.

On 7 December 1704 Enty married Mary Gilberd (d. 1712), at Kingsbridge, Devon. An 'agreeable woman', 'of a good fortune', she wed him 'contrary to the advice of her relations'. They remained childless, and on 4 March 1712 she was buried at St Andrew, Plymouth. 'His grief seemed immoderate for about three weeks; for on the least mention of her he always broke into tears' ('Memoirs', 327). Very soon afterwards his old friend Mrs Vincent, whose house at Plymouth was 'the great inn for all Dissenting ministers' ('Memoirs', 135) proposed a new match with Anne Savery (bap. 1694, d. 1776), the eldest daughter of Servington *Savery and Elizabeth Hale of Shilston, near Modbury, Devon. Anne was initially averse to Enty, but was ultimately won over, 'and in less than a month his tears for his first love were dried up and forgot, and he was in high and eager pursuit' ('Memoirs', 327) of his new bride. The marriage was concluded on 24 February 1713 at Ugborough, Devon: 'now he had more money, and a reputable alliance, and in his way began to make a figure' (ibid.). However, he never concerned himself much with domestic affairs.

Enty actively promoted the interest of the Assembly of the United Ministers of Devon and Cornwall, which met half-yearly at Exeter. On 10 September 1707 he preached a sermon before them on Paul's advice to Timothy, 'Let no man despise thee'. This successfully stimulated their self-esteem and they encouraged him to publish it as *The Ministry Secur'd from Contempt* (1707). A sermon preached in Plymouth on 30 January 1717 was also printed as *The innocence of protestant dissenters clear'd and vindicated in reference to the transactions of '41 and the death of King Charles I* (1717).

Fox, who came to have strong personal reasons for disliking Enty, none the less concedes that he 'was generally much liked as a preacher, for he had a strong, musical voice, a lively imagination, and a great command and flow of words' ('Memoirs', 326) and conversed 'with great freedom among his friends' (ibid., 326). However, Fox also delights in recalling that Mr Kellow of Fowey depicted

Enty in a satirical print 'in all his natural pride and ambition, and very nimbly mounting a ladder, part of which was out of view, in full assurance of getting to the top of it' (ibid., 327). In Fox's view Enty's pride was rooted in a firm belief of 'his divine commission' (ibid., 326) and caused him to behave with a haughtiness at odds with his humble background. Enty quarrelled with Fox over his insistence that candidates for public preaching should be examined by the assembly. In the Exeter controversy Enty took the lead on the orthodox side against the supposed Arians, and in September 1718 the moderator, John Cox of Kingsbridge, accused him of departing from the usual method of speaking in the assembly. Fearing that both their authority and the credit of nonconformity were at stake, Enty and his supporters secured a vote in favour of all ministers proclaiming their faith in the Trinity. This led to the exclusion of James Pierce and Joseph Pierce and their followers from James's Meeting, and the establishment of a new, specially constructed chapel at the Mint in 1719, with some 300 worshippers. The schism saw Enty publish a number of pamphlets in a prolonged battle with Pierce, including *An Answer to Mr. Pierce's Western Inquisition, etc.* (1721), a very able narrative connecting a series of first-hand statements by people concerned in the controversy.

To Fox's lasting disgust a schism born of 'unaccountable, destructive bigotry' ('Memoirs', 200) was Enty's opportunity to enhance his already strong position at the head of 'a spiritual tyranny ... under cover of three words—*agreement*, *order* and *decency*' ('Memoirs', 326), while a number of ministers found their 'reputation, interest and usefulness ... absolutely ruined by the rage, aspersions and violence' ('Memoirs', 200) that he had unleashed. Enty and Walter Furze of Bristol now became pastors of the congregation at James's Meeting. For more than twenty years all church affairs were directed by Enty, who acted as scribe to the assembly. To ensure orthodoxy a declaration of faith was required from candidates for ordination. In 1738 Aaron Pitts of Topsham only received a grant from the Congregational Fund following a declaration of his orthodoxy by Enty, John Ball of Honiton, and John Walrond. Enty published his sermon at the ordination of Peter Jilleard as 'St Paul's love to souls considered and recommended' in the same volume as John Withers's *A Stated Ministry and Presbyterian Ordination Vindicated* (1725). He also published two sermons preached at Exeter, one on the coronation of George II (1727) and the other originally delivered on Guy Fawkes night 1737. Enty's supporters held him in high regard: he was left legacies by John Osmond and his son Samuel, both tallow chandlers of St Sidwell's, Exeter, in 1725 and 1730, and by the widowed Sarah Gibbs of Exeter, who left £1 1s. to each of the four local Presbyterian ministers, including Enty. Enty was succeeded at Plymouth by Peter Baron, his assistant since 1700, yet municipal accounts show that Enty retained a house near the Batter Street meeting-house as late as 1731–2.

Enty had enjoyed very good health until May 1743, when he fell victim to an 'epidemical disorder' which 'quite broke him' ('Memoirs', 327). He declined in the following months, dying, probably at Exeter, on 26 November 1743 'with great decency, having taken a distinct and solemn leave of his family' (ibid.). On 1 December 1743 Enty, described as 'of Holy Trinity, Exeter', was buried at Ugborough. His father-in-law, Servington Savery, was also buried there, on 6 March 1744, near his wife, who had been buried there on 8 November 1725. Savery's will, dated 17 December 1743, reveals that he was then residing in Exeter with his daughter, Anne Enty, an arrangement that may have been of long standing given his advanced years. Anne Enty was buried at Ugborough on 7 February 1776. Although there is no reference to any children from this second marriage, a family headed by another John Enty is recorded at Exeter in the 1770s at both St Thomas's parish church and, suggestively, at the Bow Meeting.

PATRICK WOODLAND

Sources 'Memoirs of himself, by Mr John Fox … with biographical sketches of some of his contemporaries; and some unpublished letters [pt 5]', *Monthly Repository*, 16 (1821), 325–31, esp. 325–7 [memoir of J. Enty] · 'Memoirs of himself, by Mr John Fox … with biographical sketches of some of his contemporaries; and some unpublished letters [pts 1–2]', *Monthly Repository*, 16 (1821), 129–35, 193–200, esp. 134–5, 196–200 · IGI · C. Worthy, *Devonshire wills: a collection of annotated testamentary abstracts* (1896), 44, 153, 230–31 · O. Moger, *Copies of transcripts and extracts from wills and other records*, typescript, 1921–41, West Country Studies Library, Exeter, 18.6468–9 · Devon and Cornwall Record Society parish register transcripts: Exeter, Holy Trinity; Modbury; Plymouth, St Andrew; Ugborough, West Country Studies Library, Exeter · Boase & Courtney, *Bibl. Corn.*, 1.142–3 · A. Brockett, *Nonconformity in Exeter, 1650–1875* (1962) · J. Murch, *A history of the Presbyterian and General Baptist churches in the west of England* (1835) · M. Towgood, letter to Philip Doddridge, 20 Dec 1743, DWL · receivers' book, 1731–2, Plymouth and West Devon Record Office, Plymouth, Plymouth borough collection, W133 [reference to John Enty's house 'near the meeting house' (Batter Street)] · S. Griffin, 'A history of the Batter Street Congregational Church, 1704–1921', *Transactions of the Plymouth Institution and the Devon and Cornwall Natural History Society*, 19 (1943–4), 70–75 · R. N. Worth, *History of Plymouth from the earliest period to the present time* (1890), 253–4 · C. W. Bracken, *A history of Plymouth and her neighbours* (1934), 146 · C. G. Bolam and others, *The English presbyterians: from Elizabethan puritanism to modern Unitarianism* (1968), 206 · T. G. Crippen, 'The story of nonconformity in Somerset', *Somerset County Express* (25 Oct 1913–11 July 1914) [ser. of articles] · N&Q, 4th ser., 7 (1871), 55 · DNB

Enzinas, Francisco de [*known as* Francis Dryander] (1518?–1552), humanist scholar, was born in the parish of San Gil, Burgos, Spain, the son of Juan de Enzinas (d. 1556?), a prosperous wool merchant. According to one of his contemporaries he was born on 1 November 1518 (Herminjard, *Correspondance des réformateurs*, 1897, 9.462). His mother was probably Ana de Sandoval (d. 1527?); his stepmother was Beatriz de Santa Cruz (c.1495–c.1573), a member of an influential Burgos family, whom his father married about 1528. His family's commercial activities drew Enzinas to the Low Countries where in 1539 he enrolled at the Collegium Trilingue, Louvain, a centre of humanist learning. There he came under evangelical influences, Hellenized his surname, becoming known as Francis Dryander, and began a career of biblical and classical scholarship. During this period he formed an acquaintance with the Oxford bookseller Garbrand Harkes and with Edmund Crispin of Oriel College, and perhaps visited Oxford. On 22 September 1541 he wrote to Crispin from Louvain describing a confrontation between Stephen Gardiner and the Louvain theologians in which Gardiner defended Henry VIII's supremacy over the English church.

On 27 October 1541 Dryander matriculated at the University of Wittenberg, drawn by admiration for Melanchthon, with whom he was to enjoy a lifelong friendship. There he completed the first modern Spanish translation of the New Testament, printed at Antwerp in October 1543 by Steven Mierdman. Strict controls on printing, and the opposition to vernacular scripture shown by some Spaniards at the imperial court, led to Dryander's seeking an imprimatur by unusual means: he gained an audience with Charles V and requested the emperor's personal protection for the work. However, Charles turned the matter over to his confessor Pedro de Soto, who arranged for Dryander's arrest and the confiscation of the printed copies. Imprisoned at Brussels on suspicion of heresy, Dryander escaped in February 1545, thus becoming an imperial outlaw. He describes these events in his *De statu Belgico et religione Hispanica* (written in 1545), a work used in manuscript by several protestant martyrologists, including Foxe. In 1546 at Basel he published *Historia de morte sancti viri Ioannis Diazii*, also excerpted by Foxe. Early in 1547 he matriculated at the University of Basel, but found the teaching not to his liking. In March 1548 at Strasbourg he married Marguerite d'Elter (d. 1553), a religious exile from Gueldres.

Urged by Martin Bucer to take refuge in England from imperial spies, Dryander arrived at Lambeth in July 1548 carrying a letter of introduction from Melanchthon. It is possible that soon afterwards he provided Cranmer with a copy of Spain's ancient Mozarabic liturgy, to which the blessing of the baptismal font in the 1549 Book of Common Prayer can be traced. In his reports to Heinrich Bullinger and Joachim Vadianus on the state of English reform in 1549 Dryander showed keen insight into the issues, while characteristically revealing little confessional bias of his own. The duchess of Suffolk (whose mother was Spanish) offered him a place in her household but he chose to teach Greek at Cambridge, where he and Marguerite resided from October 1548 to November 1549 and where their first child, Margarita, was born. Dryander never held a professorship but was paid from Cranmer's treasury as Greek reader. It is doubtful that he had a college connection, but probably adhered to a small group of married university men which Bucer himself joined in 1549. He also corresponded with the Oxford men James Haddon and Pietro Martire Vermigli during this period.

At Cambridge, Dryander continued his vocation of translating ancient texts into Spanish. He corresponded with the London printers Reyner Wolfe and Steven Mierdman, and also with the bookseller Johannes Birckmann, who kept him in touch with the continent. In a letter of 1549 Birckmann urged him to fix a selling price for copies of the Spanish New Testament then at Antwerp; clearly the imperial order had failed to suppress it completely. But ultimately Dryander expressed disappointment with the state of English printing, and he disapproved of

Bucer's choice of the Strasbourg printer Rémy Guédon for setting up a press at Cambridge. In December 1549 he took his manuscripts to Basel, leaving his wife and daughter in Bucer's care; his decision to abandon his family and the cause of English reform elicited sharp words from John Hooper. By June 1550 Dryander had decided not to return to Cambridge. His family rejoined him in Strasbourg, where he set up a Spanish publishing house from which came at least nine Old Testament and classical translations over the next two years. A second child, Beatriz, was born about 1551. Dryander died on 30 December 1552 during a plague at Strasbourg and was buried the next day; his wife died about 1 February 1553.

JONATHAN L. NELSON

Sources J. L. Nelson, 'Francisco de Enzinas and Spanish evangelical humanism before the Council of Trent', PhD diss., University of Manchester, 1999 · *Francisco de Enzinas: Epistolario*, ed. I. J. Garcia Pinilla (Geneva, 1995) · E. Boehmer, *Bibliotheca Wiffeniana: Spanish reformers of two centuries* (1874–1904), 1.133–84 · C. Gilly, *Spanien und der Basler Buchdruck bis 1600* (Basel, 1985), 326–53, 458, 510–12 · CCC Cam., MS 119 · C.-A. Campan, ed., *Mémoires de Francisco de Enzinas*, 2 vols. (Brussels, 1862–3) · Burgos diocesan archives, San Gil 1, 46 · notarial protocols of Asensio de la Torre and Celedón de Torroba, Burgos provincial historical archives · H. Robinson, ed. and trans., *Original letters relative to the English Reformation*, 1 vol. in 2, Parker Society, [26] (1846–7) · *Historia de statu Belgico deque religione Hispanica*, ed. F. Socas (1991) · J. L. Nelson, '"Solo Salvador": printing the 1543 New Testament of Francisco de Enzinas (Dryander)', *Journal of Ecclesiastical History*, 50 (1999), 94–116 · I. J. García Pinilla and J. L. Nelson, 'Una carta de Francisco de Enzinas (Dryander) en el martirologio de John Foxe', *Bibliothèque d'Humanisme et Renaissance*, 61 (1999), 515–28
Archives Archives Municipales de Strasbourg, Archives de Saint Thomas, letters

Eochaid (*d.* 697). *See under* Dál Riata, kings of (*act. c.*500–*c.*850).

Eochaid Buide (*d. c.*629). *See under* Dál Riata, kings of (*act. c.*500–*c.*850).

Eochaid ua Flannucáin [Eochaid ua Flainn] (*c.*936–1004), poet and historian, was guestmaster in the monastery of Armagh, and superior of the church of Clonfeacle, near Dungannon. He was born about 936 and his father, Cellach, belonged to the Clann Shínaich, a branch of the Uí Echdach dynasty which supplied several of the rulers of the kingdom of Airthir, in which Armagh was situated. At the close of the eighth century the Clann Shínaich unsuccessfully attempted to secure hereditary control of the abbacy of Armagh; the next member of the family to become abbot was Eochaid's brother Dub dá Leithe (*d.* 998). Dub dá Leithe's successor was replaced in 1001 by Eochaid's son Máel Muire (*d.* 1020); thereafter, until the accession in 1134 of the reforming abbot Máel Máedóc Ó Morgair (St Malachy), all of the abbots were Eochaid's descendants. Eochaid was a young man at the time of Dub dá Leithe's accession in 965 and presumably owed his various offices to his brother's position; it was probably through his own influence that his son became abbot a few years after Dub dá Leithe's death, decisively establishing the Clann Shínaich as hereditary rulers of the monastery.

Eochaid died in 1004 and the obituary notices in the Irish annals style him *suí filidechta ocus senchasa* ('sage of poetry and history'; annals of Ulster) and *suí senchasa Gaídel* ('sage of the history of the Gaels'; annals of the four masters). His reputation for scholarship is further reflected in the statement of a medieval colophon that the antiquarian poets Flann Mainistrech and Eochaid Éolach ua Céirín gathered information 'from the books of Eochaid ua Flannucáin in Armagh'; and in the seventeenth-century *Annals of Clonmacnoise*, where he is cited as an authority. Two quatrains of verse with explicit attributions to Eochaid survive: one on the origins of St Secundinus (Sechnall), traditionally held to have been the second bishop of Armagh; and one commemorating the death while visiting Armagh of Dúnchad ua Broín, abbot of Clonmacnoise (*d.* 989). These pieces may be interpreted as reflecting respectively a concern with the Armagh succession and Eochaid's responsibilities as guestmaster.

Interest in Eochaid ua Flannucáin centres primarily on his presumed identification (first proposed in 1913 by Rudolf Thurneysen and generally accepted since) with Eochaid ua Flainn, author of a series of poems which form an essential part, and probably supplied much of the basis, of the pseudohistorical treatise *Lebor gabála Érenn* ('the book of the settlement of Ireland'; perhaps of late eleventh-century date). Explicit statements of authorship by Eochaid occur in 'A chóemu cláir Chuinn choímfhinn', on the original settlements of Ireland by Cesair and Partholón; 'Ériu co n-uaill, co n-idnaib', on the island's conquest by the supernatural Tuatha Dé Danann; 'Éistet, áes ecnai oíbinn', tracing Ireland's history from the creation down to the reign of the prehistoric king Óengus Olmuccaid; 'A Emain idnach oíbinn', on the origins of Emain Macha (modern Navan Fort), ancient capital of Ulster and a site immediately adjacent to Armagh; and 'Úgaine uallach amra', on the division of Ireland between the children of the legendary Úgaine Már. Other poems which bear plausible scribal attributions to Eochaid deal with the mythical settler Nemed, with the fortress of Dunseverick, and with the ancestry of the three principal Irish dynasties. With the exception of 'A Emain', all of these compositions appear in R. A. S. Macalister's edition of *Lebor gabála Érenn*.

Thurneysen based his identification of the two Eochaids on the similarity of their names, probably also on the fact that both are referred to as *in suí senchasa* ('the sage of history'). His suggestion gains further force from the consideration that Eochaid ua Flainn's two poems about specific places deal with sites in Ulster, one of them closely connected with Armagh; when, in 'A Emain', he calls himself 'a support for the progeny of Eochaid', he alludes to the lineage of Uí Echdach to which Eochaid ua Flannucáin belonged.

JOHN CAREY

Sources T. Ó Fiaich, 'The church of Armagh under lay control', *Seanchas Ardmhacha*, 5 (1969–70), 75–127 · R. Thurneysen, 'Zu irischen Handschriften und Literaturdenkmälern; zweite Serie', *Abhandlungen der königlichen Gesellschaft der Wissenschaften zu Göttingen* [Philologisch-historische Klasse, neue Folge], 14/3 (1913), 5 · *Ann. Ulster* · *AFM*, 2nd edn · T. O'Rahilly and others, *Catalogue of Irish manuscripts in the Royal Irish Academy*, 30 vols. (Dublin, 1926–70) ·

T. Abbott and E. Gwynn, eds., *Catalogue of the Irish manuscripts in the library of Trinity College, Dublin* (1921) • J. Carey, introduction, in R. Macalister, *Lebor gabála Érenn*, Irish Texts Society, 34 (1993) [5] • T. Ó Concheanainn, '"Aided Nath Í" and the scribes of Leabhar na hUidhre', *Éigse*, 16 (1975–6), 146–62 • D. Murphy, ed., *The annals of Clonmacnoise*, trans. C. Mageoghagan (1896); facs. edn (1993) • J. H. Bernard and R. Atkinson, eds. and trans., *The Irish Liber hymnorum*, 2 vols., HBS, 13–14 (1898), vol. 1, pp. 4, 6 • R. Macalister, ed. and trans., *Lebor gabála Érenn*, 5 parts, Irish Texts Society (1938–56)

Éogan mac Dega (*fl.* late 6th cent.). *See under* Ulster, saints of (*act. c.*400–*c.*650).

Eoganán (*d.* 839). *See under* Picts, kings of the (*act. c.*300–*c.*900).

Eorcenberht (*d.* 664), king of Kent, was the son of his predecessor *Eadbald (*d.* 640) and Ymmae, or Emma (*d.* 642), who may have been the daughter of a powerful Frankish aristocrat named Erchinoald. The first element of Eorcenberht's name is Frankish (it is identical to that of Erchinoald), and he gave Frankish names to his second son *Hlothhere, and to his daughters, Eormenhild and Eorcengota (he sent the latter across the channel to be a nun in the monastery of Faremoutiers, near Meaux). Eorcenberht succeeded his father in 640 and was the first English king to order the destruction of pagan idols in his kingdom; he also used his royal authority to enforce the keeping of the Lenten fast in Kent. Little is known of the secular events of the reign, apart from a series of marriage alliances with other royal families. Eorcenberht himself married *Seaxburh (*d. c.*700), the eldest daughter of King *Anna of the East Angles, and their daughter Eormenhild became the wife of King *Wulfhere of Mercia. In addition, the powerful King Oswiu of Northumbria married Eorcenberht's first cousin, *Eanflæd, who had been brought up in Kent and with whom he was on good terms. This network of alliances may have afforded Kent some protection against aggressors. Eorcenberht died on 14 July 664, the same day as Deusdedit, archbishop of Canterbury; it is possible that both were victims of the great plague which swept Britain and Ireland in that year. Eorcenberht was probably buried alongside his father in St Mary's Church in the monastery of St Peter's and St Paul's (later St Augustine's), Canterbury. His widow, Seaxburh, eventually became abbess of the monastery at Ely, founded by her sister Æthelthryth; Kentish tradition also connects her with the foundation of Minster in Sheppey.

Eorcenberht's successor was his son **Ecgberht I** (*d.* 673). Later hagiographical texts, which may preserve some genuine historical information, mention that Eorcenberht had a brother named Eormenred (another Frankish name) and describe him as king; he may have ruled jointly with Eorcenberht (although Bede does not mention him), or he may perhaps have acted as an underking. Eormenred is said to have died before Eorcenberht, leaving to his brother's care his two sons, Æthelberht and Æthelred. After Eorcenberht's own death, Ecgberht arranged for the murder of his cousins, presumably to secure his own position. Later, as compensation for his blood-guilt, he gave land to their sister Æbba (or Domneva), which she used to found a monastery in

Thanet. In 669 the minster at Reculver was established by Ecgberht's mass priest Bassa on land granted to him by the king. Ecgberht also seems to have been involved in the foundation of the minster at Chertsey in Surrey, which is an indication that his power extended, at least for a short time, beyond the frontiers of Kent. Ecgberht died in July 673. Although his two sons, *Eadric (*d.* 686) [*see under* Hlothhere] and *Wihtred (*d.* 725), were passed over initially and his brother *Hlothhere (*d.* 685) succeeded him, they did become kings later.   S. E. KELLY

Sources Bede, *Hist. eccl.*, 3.8, 29; 4.1, 19, 26; 5.19, 24 • N. Brooks, *The early history of the church of Canterbury: Christ Church from 597 to 1066* (1984), 69–70 • D. W. Rollason, *The Mildrith legend: a study in early medieval hagiography in England* (1982) • I. Wood, *The Merovingian kingdoms, 450–751* (1994), 177 • *ASC*, s.a. 669 • *AS chart.*, S 1165 • K. H. Krüger, *Königsgrabkirchen der Franken, Angelsachsen, und Langobarden* (Munich, 1971), 264–87

Eormenric (*fl.* 550×600). *See under* Kent, kings of (*act. c.*450–*c.*590).

Eos Ceiriog. *See* Morys, Huw (1622–1709).

Epine, Francesca Margherita de l'. *See* L'Epine, Francesca Margherita de (*d.* 1746).

Eppillus (*fl.* c.AD 5–*c.*10). *See under* Roman Britain, British leaders in (*act.* 55 BC–AD 84).

Epps, George Napoleon (1815–1874), homoeopathic practitioner, was born on 22 July 1815, at Bessels Green, Sevenoaks, Kent, the second son of John Epps, a butcher, and his second wife, Elizabeth Schneider. The physician John *Epps (1805–1869) was his half-brother. After being educated at a dissenters' grammar school and at Mill Hill School he became his brother's pupil, and later he assisted him with his lectures on chemistry, botany, and materia medica. He became a member of the Royal College of Surgeons, London, in 1845, and from then onwards he practised in accordance with the homoeopathic system. Also in 1845 he was appointed surgeon at the homoeopathic dispensary in Hanover Square, and later he joined his brother at the Royal Jennerian Vaccine Institution, where he was appointed surgeon.

Epps quickly demonstrated an aptitude for the treatment of spinal curvatures and deformities, and in 1847 he was elected surgeon to Harrison's Spinal Institution. His mechanical skill was demonstrated by his invention of an efficient device for the reduction of dislocations. He published several volumes on orthopaedics, including *Spinal Curvature, its Theory and Cure* (1849), and *On Deformities of the Spine and on Club Foot* (1859). He added a fourth part to Pulte's *Homoeopathic Physician*, brought out by his brother in 1852, entitled 'Treatment of accidents'. He also published revised editions of Walter Williamson's *Diseases of Infants and Children* (1857) and *Diseases of Women and their Homoeopathic Treatment* (1857). Epps had a large practice, to which he was devoted. He never took a holiday and used to boast that he had not slept away from home for twenty years.

Epps was married to Charlotte Bacon in 1833. Their daughter Ellen (1850–1929) married the scholar Sir

Edmund William Gosse (1849–1928), and another daughter, Laura Teresa (d. 1909) was the wife of the painter Sir Lawrence Alma-Tadema (1836–1912). Epps died at 20 Devonshire Street, London, on 28 May 1874 and was buried at Kensal Green cemetery. He was survived by his wife and their large family.   BERNARD LEARY

Sources Diary of the late John Epps, ed. Mrs Epps [1875] · British Journal of Homoeopathy, 32 (1874), 574–5 · London Medical Directory (1847) · London and Provincial Medical Directory (1855) · CGPLA Eng. & Wales (1874) · DNB

Wealth at death under £200: administration, 14 July 1874, CGPLA Eng. & Wales

Epps, John (1805–1869), physician and phrenologist, was born at Blackheath, Kent, on 15 February 1805, the son of John Epps, a wealthy pork butcher of Sevenoaks, Kent, and his first wife (d. c.1810). He had two sisters, and George Napoleon *Epps (1815–1874) was his half-brother. His father was a strict Calvinist and he felt the 'depressing' influence of the doctrine of predestination throughout his life (Diary, 44). After being educated at home by a governess he left home at the age of nine to attend a dissenters' grammar school, which he left two years later for Mill Hill School. At the age of sixteen Epps was apprenticed to a Dr Durie, a medical practitioner in London. During this apprenticeship he was introduced to phrenology by William Sleigh, a lecturer who taught him anatomy.

In 1823 Epps went to Edinburgh University to continue his medical studies. Because his father had run into financial difficulties he had to support himself by teaching classics and chemistry, which enabled him to hire a room and feed himself on an unvarying diet of bread, coffee, haddock, and oatmeal. About 1821 he became interested in phrenology; he joined the Phrenological Society in Edinburgh and met George Combe and other leading exponents of the subject. He graduated MD in 1826 and in 1827 opened a practice in Edgware Road, London. He joined the London Phrenological Society, and met J. C. Spurzheim, the leader of the movement in Britain. Epps had joined the Scottish Baptists during his time in Edinburgh, approving of their democratic congregational organization. During the late 1820s he combined Combe's ideas about the 'organs' of the mind with his own religious beliefs to produce:

> a form of phrenological Christianity [which] was solidly Calvinistic. Indeed, Epps never wavered in his Calvinistic belief that man was 'necessarily evil' and could do nothing to save himself. But to be 'born again' man had only to believe the testimony of God, and phrenology for Epps showed that the faculties of Benevolence, Veneration, and Conscientiousness were 'busily engaged' in every person in bringing about this end. (Desmond, 168)

In addition to publishing widely on phrenology Epps lectured on chemistry, botany, and materia medica at the Hunterian School of Medicine in Great Windmill Street, London, and, when that closed, at the Westminster medical school. He became editor of the London Medical and Surgical Journal and later of the Anthropological Journal and the Journal of Health and Disease. In 1831 he was appointed director of the Royal Jennerian Vaccine Institution, which he supported all his life. During the same year he married Ellen (1809–1876), an author, daughter of John Ford Elliott, but could not resist the chance to take the clergyman to task because, although a dissenter, he had to marry in the established church. Ellen Epps had some success as a novelist. After his death she published the Diary of the Late J. Epps, an unsatisfactory book, which failed to give a connected account of his life.

In 1837, after reading a work by Dr Paul Curie, Epps became interested in homoeopathy. This interest was confirmed in 1844 by a favourable phrenological examination of Jacques-Louis David's bust of C. F. S. Hahnemann, the founder of homoeopathy. Epps's independence of mind soon led him into conflict with Frederic Quin, the first British homoeopathic practitioner. In 1844 Quin held a party to celebrate Hahnemann's birthday. After Epps had left, the remaining guests held a foundation meeting of the British Homoeopathic Society. Epps was unable to accept the proposed rules which made those at the party foundation members while all other doctors, some more senior in homoeopathy, would have to submit to election by them. He did not join the society but worked with Curie in the rival English Homoeopathic Association. After Curie's death in 1853, unlike the other members of that association, he still held himself aloof from the British Homoeopathic Society. He was loyal to Curie in 1845 when the latter was accused by Thomas Wakley, coroner of Middlesex and editor of The Lancet, of causing the death of a patient. At that time the members of the British Homoeopathic Society publicly dissociated themselves from Curie's ideas of pathology.

Epps had already come into conflict with Wakley who, until Epps became a homoeopath, had been a personal friend. Wakley published some early cases of Epps in The Lancet in 1844, but these caused such a torrent of correspondence that he refused further cases. This allowed Epps to publish 'Rejected cases', including a letter attacking Wakley's attitude. However, these events did not prevent him from being an active exponent of homoeopathy. He lectured extensively on the subject and wrote many books and pamphlets, notably Domestic Homoeopathy (1842), Homoeopathy and its Principles Explained (1950), and editions of Pulte's Homoeopathic Domestic Physician (1852). Epps built up a successful practice, most of his former patients remaining with him when he adopted the new system.

Epps remained a dissenter all his life, in conflict with the establishment in the church and in politics. After leaving the Scottish Baptists he became a member of the Plymouth Brethren. In London he then became associated with Dock Head Church in Bermondsey, where he gave a series of orations, in one of which he attempted to prove that the devil did not exist; his arguments were published in a pamphlet in 1842. Epps supported many radical causes: the Anti-Corn Law League, disestablishment, Catholic emancipation, anti-slavery, parliamentary reform, and Italian independence. In 1847 he stood unsuccessfully as a radical for election as member of parliament for Northampton, with Chartist backing.

Epps was of short stature and possessed a beaming self-confidence. He was an able and incessant lecturer on any subject that interested him. He was regarded as a healer and a prophet in medicine by many of the working classes, though this was doubted by some of his colleagues. However, few argued against his being a man who desired to benefit humanity and that he was kind-hearted and pious. At the beginning of 1869 he began to suffer from congestion of the lungs, and he died following a stroke on 12 February at his home, 89 Great Russell Street, London. He was buried at Kensal Green cemetery later the same month.   BERNARD LEARY

Sources *Diary of the late John Epps*, ed. Mrs Epps [1875] · *British Journal of Homoeopathy*, 27 (1869), 350–51 · *British Journal of Homoeopathy*, 33 (1875), 290–97 · *Homoeopathic World*, 4 (1869), 66–8 · J. Epps, *Homoeopathy and its principles explained* (1850) · A. Desmond, *The politics of evolution: morphology, medicine and reform in radical London* (1989) · R. Cooter, *Phrenology in the British Isles: an annotated historical biobibliography and index* (1989) · D. de Giustino, 'Epps, Dr John', *BDMBR*, vol. 2 · d. cert. · *DNB*

Likenesses W. B. Scott, etching (after his portrait), BM, Wellcome L. · W. B. Scott, print, etching, BM

Wealth at death under £3000: probate, 15 April 1869, *CGPLA Eng. & Wales*

Epstein, Arnold Leonard [Bill] **(1924–1999)**, social anthropologist, was born on 13 September 1924 at 152 Bedford Street, Liverpool, the son of Maurice Epstein (1898–1965), a travelling draper, from Liverpool, and his wife, Ethel Esther (1897–1989). Epstein, whose family came from Austrian Poland, was himself brought up in Belfast and attended the Royal Belfast Academical Institution (1938–41). He read law at the Queen's University, graduating with an LLB in 1944 before war service with the Royal Navy as a communications rating.

His father hoped that after demobilization (1947) Epstein would practise as a barrister. As an undergraduate, however, he had become aware of anthropology, read whatever he could, and even wrote to Bronisław Malinowski at the London School of Economics (LSE) seeking advice. Although he returned to Queen's and qualified for the bar, within a year he secured a Colonial Office social science research council fellowship, joining a group of budding anthropologists who 'converted' to the discipline under Raymond Firth at the LSE.

Epstein combined his interest in law and anthropology by conducting research (1950) in Northern Rhodesia into the operation of the urban African courts, adopting the case study approach employed in legal training in the USA. He attracted the attention of Max Gluckman, professor at Manchester, also writing about African legal systems, who encouraged Epstein to register for a doctorate. He completed this in 1955, and became a key figure in the so-called 'Manchester school'.

Although Epstein undertook fieldwork among the rural Bemba, it was the copperbelt which caught his attention, and his study focused on mine workers. This was a crucial moment in the struggle for African independence, and his research did not meet with official approval; indeed he was excluded from the mine compounds. The resulting monograph (*Politics in an Urban African Community*, 1958) compellingly described the intersection of race, class, and ethnicity in the penultimate period of colonial rule. The copperbelt also figured in *Urbanization and Kinship* (1981), and in many papers, including those brought together in *Scenes from African Urban Life* (1992).

On 16 August 1957 Epstein married Trude Scarlett Trent, *née* Grünwald (*b.* 1922), an expert in the anthropology of development in India. Together they went to the Australian National University at Canberra whence Epstein undertook fieldwork among the Tolai of the Gazelle peninsula, the subject of *Matupit: Land, Politics and Change among the Tolai of New Britain* (1969). The 1960s were spent teaching at Manchester (1961–6), and then Canberra, where he was professorial fellow and later chair of anthropology at the Research School in Pacific Studies (1970). In 1972 he returned to Britain as professor at the University of Sussex, and was elected chair of the Association of Social Anthropologists. His period of office (1977–81) was difficult, coinciding as it did with severe cuts in university funding. Epstein encouraged the association to bring together other bodies concerned with anthropology in the UK (Royal Anthropological Institute, Group for Anthropology in Policy and Practice, department heads) for a conference in 1980, from which emerged a strategy for defending the subject from the most damaging features of the decade ahead.

Epstein took early retirement in 1983. Although beset by poor health, he revisited Melanesia and continued to be a prolific writer and researcher. He was preparing a book on Freud when he died of a heart attack in the Royal Sussex County Hospital, Brighton, on 9 November 1999. He was survived by his wife; they had two daughters and three grandchildren to whom he was devoted. He was buried in the Jewish cemetery at Hove.

Politics in an Urban African Community, which was welcomed by Zambian nationalists, remains an outstanding text of urban and industrial anthropology. His insistence that rural and urban formed a 'single social field' continued to have resonance in later writing about transnational migration, as did his advocacy of the case-study method and situational analysis (in the edited collection *The Craft of Social Anthropology*, 1967). He also made a decisive contribution to the anthropology of ethnicity. Reworking fieldwork data, and reflecting on his Jewish heritage, led him to write *Ethos and Identity* (1978), which established him as one of the foremost thinkers on the subject. Against instrumentalist views, Epstein emphasized the affective component: identity, he argued, is 'always psychosocial' (A. L. Epstein, *Ethos and Identity*, 1978, xiii). This approach reflected his concern with the interface between anthropology and psychoanalysis. Training with Anna Freud (1971) led him to develop what he called the anthropology of the emotions or of affect (in *The Experience of Shame in Melanesia*, 1984, and two books about the Tolai, *In the Midst of Life*, 1992, and *Gunantuna*, 1999). But he was writing against the grain of much contemporary British anthropology, and the project never attained the success he hoped. A Festschrift (*Identity and Affect*, 1999), edited by former students John Campbell and Alan Rew, paid tribute to his work in this field. Throughout his life

Epstein was held in the highest esteem by colleagues and students, for his intellect, his modesty, and his ultimate faith in ordinary humanity.   R. D. GRILLO

Sources A. L. Epstein, *Scenes from African urban life* (1992), introduction and chap. 1 · K. Yelvington, 'An interview with A. L. Epstein', *Current Anthropology*, 38/2 (1997), 289–99 · R. D. Grillo, 'Bill Epstein', *Anthropology Today*, 16/1 (Feb 2000), 22 · L. Shumaker, *Africanizing anthropology: fieldwork, networks, and the making of cultural knowledge in central Africa* (2001) · *The Independent* (19 Nov 1999) · *The Guardian* (11 Feb 2000) · b. cert. · m. cert. · d. cert. · private information (2004) [Trude Epstein]

Wealth at death £77,965: probate, 17 Jan 2000, *CGPLA Eng. & Wales*

Epstein, Brian Samuel (1934–1967), popular music entrepreneur and retailer, was born on 19 September 1934 at a private nursing home at 4 Rodney Street, Liverpool, the first of two children of Harold (Harry) Epstein (1901–1967) furniture retailer, and his wife, Malka (Queenie), *née* Hyman (d. 1996). Both parents were of the Jewish faith. Harry's father, Isaac, was a penniless Polish immigrant who opened a furniture store, I. Epstein & Sons, in Walton Road, Liverpool, in 1901. Queenie's family owned the Sheffield Cabinet Company. The family house at 197 Queens Drive, Childwall, Liverpool, was given to the couple as Queenie's dowry. The family moved to Prestatyn, north Wales, for a short time in 1939, at the onset of the Second World War, and then lived for three years in Southport, where Brian attended Southport College. The young Epstein was also educated at Croxton preparatory school and, at the age of ten, entered Liverpool College. He was unhappy there and left after twelve months to attend Wellesley School in Aigburth, Liverpool. Following a further period of insecurity he was dispatched to a Jewish boarding-school, Beaconsfield School in Frant, Sussex. He spent two undistinguished and disconsolate years there, followed by a brief period at Clayesmore, near Taunton, and then Wrekin College (where his younger brother, Clive, excelled). He left Wrekin in the summer of 1950 to begin work in the prospering family business.

At the age of eighteen Epstein was conscripted for national service. Having been rejected by the RAF, he began a two-year stint in the Royal Army Service Corps at Aldershot. He was, however, discharged after ten months, deemed mentally and emotionally unfit for service. Upon returning to the family business he was placed in charge of a subsidiary branch, Clarendon Furnishing, in Hoylake, Wirral, where he proved to be a highly successful retailer and manager ('Brian was a great hit on the Wirral ... he could sell snow to the Eskimos', Joe Flannery commented in 1996). Along with his close friend Flannery, Epstein had a great interest in theatre and became friendly with actors and actresses from the Liverpool Playhouse. He passed an audition for the Royal Academy of Dramatic Art (RADA), on 19 September 1956, but left and returned to Liverpool, and the family business, in 1957.

When Epstein's father decided to expand his business into the centre of Liverpool, he opened a branch in Great Charlotte Street. The North End Music Stores (NEMS) was originally the name of an annexe to this Epstein furniture store selling pianos and sheet music. Brian and his

Brian Samuel Epstein (1934–1967), by Robert Whitaker, 1964

brother, Clive (1936–1988), were placed in charge of this new outlet. Brian handled the ground-floor record section, while Clive ran the white goods and furniture-based electrical goods department on the first floor. Following the success of the record department, the family then opened a larger record store at 12–14 Whitechapel, and Brian was placed in charge while his friend Peter Brown took over the record section at Great Charlotte Street.

Despite his retailing success, Epstein's personal life was constantly in a fragile condition. He was homosexual at a time when it was still illegal, and he was constantly searching for other artistic outlets after his deficiencies at RADA. Joe Flannery recalled:

> Brian informed me he was gay—not an expression we used then, of course—before his family ... I felt sorry for him, I realised that his sense of (Jewish) family honour had placed him in an invidious position ... open to blackmail and beatings ... which happened, of course. But his confessions to me also made me realise just what a 'lost soul' he really was ... a 'lost soul' with great attention to detail! (Flannery and Brocken)

Enchanted by a unique local popular music publication in July 1961 (*Mersey Beat*), Epstein became absorbed by the local rock 'n' roll scene and, in particular, by a group which featured prominently in the paper, the Beatles. At lunchtime on 9 December 1961 Brian arranged to see the Beatles play at the Cavern cellar club, only a short walk away from his office in Whitechapel. He became their manager the next day. Epstein's commission as manager was to be 10 per cent of all income up to £1500 p. a. and 15 per cent above that figure. The deal was for five years. By 1963 Epstein's commission had increased to 25 per cent.

The Beatles were already good musically, but Epstein further reconstructed them into a thoroughly professional outfit. Paul McCartney was later to admit:

> we were getting good. But we needed someone to push us … it became obvious that Brian was that person. He had a theatrical flair, having gone to RADA … It is always helpful having someone theatrical out front … It's a director, that's really what he was.   (Savage)

Relying on the advice of several local experts such as the Cavern disc jockey Bob Wooler and his old friend Joe Flannery, Epstein began promoting not only the Beatles but also large dances and concerts at such venues as the Tower Ballroom, New Brighton, the Empire Theatre, Liverpool, and the Queen's Hall, Widnes, in order to have the Beatles support such rock luminaries as Little Richard, Bruce Channel, and Joe Brown.

A record contract for the group was also arranged with the smallest EMI imprint Parlophone (after many refusals from other labels) and the Beatles' first disc, 'Love Me Do', was issued on 5 October 1962. One anecdote persisted in Liverpool that Epstein had purchased 100,000 copies of the disc to 'hype' this first Parlophone single into the charts. Whatever truth lies behind this rumour (and it was ceaselessly denied by Epstein), its minor chart success signalled the group's emergence on the national scene.

In the mean time, and taking his cue from that other famous pop entrepreneur Larry Parnes, Epstein built up his own stable of 'personally managed' artists. Following the signing of the Beatles he signed Gerry and the Pacemakers, Billy J. Kramer, Cilla Black, the Fourmost, the Big Three, the Remo Four, and Tommy Quickley—all popular artists in Liverpool. During 1963 (the year of 'Beatlemania') and 1964 most of these 'Merseybeat' artists achieved some degree of success. The Beatles, of course, went on to become the most celebrated artists in the history of popular music. Brian Epstein was at the helm, guiding them all.

Epstein's NEMS Enterprises outgrew Liverpool and moved to a prestigious suite of offices in London. He also signed more (non-Liverpudlian) artists such as Sounds Incorporated and the Silkie as well as promoting his own shows. In 1964, after the Beatles had conquered the United States, he published his autobiography, *A Cellarful of Noise*. His business dealings with the American music industry, however, were criticized as rather naïve and, despite considerable personal financial backing, his later signings did not prove successful. Furthermore, his venture to establish the Savile Theatre in London's West End as a major rock and theatre venue was an expensive failure. His personal life also remained precarious and he had developed a passion for gambling. He made a suicide attempt in the autumn of 1966.

Certainly by 1967 Epstein appeared to be losing confidence. He was heavily dependent on a combination of narcotics (some of which were prescription drugs that he had been taking since the late 1950s) and he expressed fears that the Beatles would not re-sign with him when their contract lapsed ('there was no question in our minds that we would stay with Brian. We didn't want another manager', Paul McCartney told Jon Savage in 1998). He unquestionably had less of a role in their day-to-day affairs after they ceased touring in 1966, and was subsequently seldom seen at his offices.

On Sunday 27 August 1967 Brian Epstein was found dead at his home, 24 Chapel Street, Belgravia, London. The coroner's verdict was that he had died, probably on 25 August, of an accidental overdose of Carbitol. Despite the finding—and because of his profile and sexuality—some publications have perpetuated myths about suicide and even murder, but it appears that it was simply a tragic mistake made by a depressed and fragile character. Epstein's body was buried at the Jewish cemetery in Long Lane, Aintree, Liverpool (section A, grave H12). John Lennon was to admit to *Rolling Stone*'s Jann Wenner in 1970:

> The Beatles broke up after Brian died … it was just me and a backing group, Paul and a backing group … And I enjoyed it, but we broke up then … I knew that we were in trouble then. I didn't really have any misconceptions about our ability to do anything other than play music and I was scared. I thought 'we've fuckin' had it'.   (Wenner)

Brian Epstein was undoubtedly a deeply troubled man, but also someone who found his true vocation. His crucial musical judgements in the early 1960s heavily influenced the development of popular music. His often compassionate managerial approach attempted to take his artists *and* their fans seriously, and he helped to change, immutably, the face of popular music performance, appreciation, and consumption. He was clearly one of the first pop managers who considered himself an artist, an approach far removed from that of the majority of managers of the day, who were primarily interested in money. Much criticism and dismissal of Epstein circulated after his death, generated and complicated by the mythologizing of the Beatles phenomenon. But his importance as a mould-breaking manager should not be underestimated, and Paul McCartney was to comment in 1998: 'If anyone was the fifth Beatle, it was Brian' (Savage).

MICHAEL BROCKEN

Sources B. Harry, *The ultimate Beatles encyclopedia* (1992) · J. Flannery and M. Brocken, *Standing in the wings* [forthcoming] · B. Epstein, *A cellarful of noise* (1964) · private information (2004) [J. Flannery] · J. Wenner, *Lennon remembers* (1972) · J. Savage, *The Guardian* (18 Dec 1998) · CGPLA Eng. & Wales (1967)
Archives U. Lpool, Institute of Popular Music, MSS | FILM BFI NFTVA, *Arena*, BBC2, 25 Dec 1998 · BFI NFTVA, documentary footage | SOUND BL NSA, documentary recordings · BL NSA, oral history interviews · U. Lpool, Institute of Popular Music, Robert Shelton archive
Likenesses R. Whitaker, photograph, 1964, NPG [*see illus.*] · photographs, 1964–7, Hult. Arch. · four photographs, repro. in *The Guardian*
Wealth at death £486,032: administration, 19 Dec 1967, CGPLA Eng. & Wales

Epstein, Sir Jacob (1880–1959), sculptor, was born on 10 November 1880 at 102 Hester Street, New York city, the second son and third of eight surviving children of Max Epstein (1859–1941), businessman, and his wife, Mary, *née* Solomon (*c*.1859–1913). Both parents were from Orthodox

Sir Jacob Epstein (1880–1959), self-portrait, *c.*1901

Jewish families and had immigrated to the United States from Augustów, Poland, his father changing his name from Jarogenski or Jarudzinski to Epstein.

Early years and education Epstein's formal education at the free local school, PS Seven, was interrupted by a two-year illness and ended when he was thirteen, but he attended classes and events organized by the settlement house movement at the nearby Neighbourhood Guild and Education Alliance. There he was influenced by the literature and ideas introduced by James Kirk Paulding, and mixed in socialist–anarchist political and literary circles. During 1893–8 he attended classes at the Art Students' League. Increasingly he rejected the rigorous Orthodox observance of his upbringing. His early drawings were inspired by the lively multi-ethnic communities round him in the Lower East Side, especially the Jewish community. He organized a local artists' exhibition at the Hebrew Institute during 1898 and was emerging as the leading figure in a nascent group of Jewish New York artists. The journalist Hutchins Hapgood commissioned him to carry out most of the illustrations for his pioneering book about the Lower East Side, *The Spirit of the Ghetto* (1902). However, about 1899–1900, following a winter spent with his Russian artist friend, Bernard Gussow, in an isolated community at Greenwood Lake, New Jersey, when they worked at ice cutting, he turned to sculpture. During 1901–2 he got a job in a bronze foundry and attended an Art Students' League class for sculptors' assistants run by

George Grey Barnard, before leaving to study in Paris in September 1902.

Epstein attended the École des Beaux-Arts between October 1902 and March 1903 and the Académie Julian from April 1903 to 1904, initially sharing a studio in Montparnasse with Bernard Gussow. Impatient of academic traditionalism, he then worked independently, studying pre-classical and non-European sculpture in the Louvre, Musée Cernuschi, Musée Guimet, and Musée de Trocadéro, and making clay studies for Rodinesque figures and groups which he subsequently destroyed.

London before the war In 1905 Epstein moved to London, encouraged by his experience of the London museums during a short visit in 1904, and by a Scotswoman, Margaret Dunlop (1873–1947), at that time Mrs Thomas Williams, whom he married in November 1906. They lived first at 219 Stanhope Street, Regent's Park, then at Stamford Street Studios in Fulham where they remained until 1908. The early years were extremely difficult but a brief visit to New York in 1905 failed to lure him home. In December 1910 he became a naturalized British citizen.

A letter of introduction from Rodin to George Bernard Shaw led to contacts within the New English Art Club circle, and thence to portrait commissions which quickly established Epstein's reputation as a penetrating observer and brilliant modeller. His *Lamb* (bronze, 1908, Tate collection, and Birmingham Museum and Art Gallery) paid homage to idealized early Renaissance prototypes but *Romilly John* (bronze, 1907, Fitzwilliam Museum, Cambridge), *Bust of Nan* (bronze, 1909, Tate collection), and *Lady Gregory* (bronze, 1910, Hugh Lane Municipal Gallery of Modern Art, Dublin, and Leeds City Art Gallery) fused searching realism with spontaneous expression. From 1911 he exhibited at the National Portrait Society and his portraits were the first and, for years, the only works to enter public collections.

Epstein leapt to public prominence in 1908 through the controversy, fomented by an anonymous article in the *Evening Standard* (19 June 1908), over his carvings on the façade of Charles Holden's British Medical Association building in the Strand in London. In the eighteen figures representing the ages of man and woman he fulfilled the architect's hopes for 'a programme as wide in scope as Whitman' (Holden MS); austerely classical-realist in style, they nevertheless challenged public taste by frank depictions of nudity and pregnancy. At about this time Epstein was proposed by Havard Thomas for membership of the Royal Society of British Sculptors, but was rejected. His second public commission, the tomb of Oscar Wilde (1909–12) for Père Lachaise cemetery, Paris, was a radical departure in style and technique; he abandoned the conventional standing figure he had prepared in favour of a directly carved, winged male figure inspired by Assyrian sculpture in the British Museum.

Epstein's new-found enthusiasms for non-European art forms and for direct carving were shared by Eric Gill, with whom he developed a close relationship between 1910 and 1912. They worked collaboratively and on parallel themes; carvings in Hoptonwood stone, such as *Rom* (1910,

National Museum and Gallery of Wales, Cardiff) and the voluptuous Indian-inspired *Maternity* (1910, Leeds City Art Gallery), constituted a primitivistic alternative to the classical traditions still dominant in British sculpture. His friendship with Gill ended acrimoniously after the failure of their attempt to set up at Asheham House, Sussex, an artistic commune where they planned to create and place sculptures which would express the primitive life-force in humanity, in a sort of modern Stonehenge.

The critical success enjoyed by the Oscar Wilde tomb when it was exhibited in Epstein's Cheyne Walk studio in June 1912 contrasted with the official opposition to its explicit nudity once installation began in Paris. There he came into contact with the Parisian avant-garde and especially with Modigliani and Brancusi, whose sculpture, also directly carved, epitomized a far more radical approach to form. He also discovered a lifelong passion for African and Oceanic sculpture, becoming one of the first British-based artists to collect 'primitive art'.

During the First World War During 1913–15 Epstein became more closely involved with the avant-garde circle around Wyndham Lewis, whom he had met during the decoration in 1912 of Madame Strindberg's cabaret theatre club, the Cave of the Golden Calf, in London. Working from a secluded cottage at Pett Level, near Hastings, Sussex, and in a garage in Lamb's Conduit Street, London, he produced a series of drawings and carvings which combined formal lucidity with sexually explicit themes of procreation, pregnancy, and birth. His *Flenite Figures* in serpentine (1913, Tate collection, and Minneapolis Institute of Arts), copulating *Doves* (marble, 1913–15, Hirshhorn Museum and Sculpture Garden, Washington, DC; Israel Museum, Jerusalem; and Tate collection), and versions of *Venus* (marble, 1913–15, Baltimore Museum of Art, and Yale University Art Gallery, New Haven, Connecticut) established him as the leading British avant-garde sculptor. His first one-man show took place at the Twenty-One Gallery, London, in December 1913 and in 1914 he was a founder member of the London Group, widely credited with suggesting its name. A number of his portraits and carvings were purchased by the American collector John Quinn.

Despite his close friendship with the philosopher T. E. Hulme, who saw in his increasingly precise abstracted forms the first signs of a distinctively modern art, and his association with Ezra Pound, Wyndham Lewis, and Henri Gaudier-Brzeska, Epstein resisted affiliation with the vorticist group [see Vorticists]. Ironically, his most experimental work, *Rock Drill* (1913–14, des.; reconstruction, Birmingham Museum and Art Gallery), which comprised a plaster figure astride a real rock drill, could be seen as the embodiment of the vorticist passion for dynamism and of their virile aesthetic. Exhibited once in 1915, it was dismantled and reduced to a truncated *Torso from Rock Drill* (gunmetal, National Gallery of Canada, Ottawa; bronze casts: Tate collection, City Art Gallery, Auckland, New Zealand, and Museum of Modern Art, New York).

In 1916, under suspicion at Pett Level because of their foreign surname, accents, and bohemian lifestyle, the Epsteins returned to London, moving to 23 Guilford Street, Bloomsbury. Epstein campaigned unsuccessfully to be appointed a war artist, producing several distinguished portraits, including *Admiral Lord Fisher* (bronze, 1915), *The Tin Hat* (bronze, 1916), and *Sergeant Hunter V. C.* (1918–19)—all in the Imperial War Museum, London—characterized by the broken, impasted surface which was to become a hallmark of his style. He was finally conscripted in autumn 1917 as a private in the Jewish 38th battalion of the Royal Fusiliers just as his second one-man show, at the Leicester Galleries in London (henceforth his principal dealers), brought fame and a measure of critical and financial success. He was discharged in 1918 without leaving England, having suffered a breakdown, which probably accounts for the surprising dearth of war memorial commissions.

Between the wars After the war Epstein retained his position as the leading modernist sculptor while becoming more isolated as a result of the deaths of Hulme and Gaudier-Brzeska, the dissolution of several pre-war groupings and friendships, notably with Augustus John, and of his own renewed commitment to modelled sculpture in the Western tradition. His notoriety led to his rejection as a candidate for the professorship of sculpture at the Royal College of Art in 1924, while a damaging attack on his modelled portraiture by the influential Roger Fry, published in the *New Statesman* in 1924, weakened his reputation within the critical establishment.

During a visit to Italy in 1920 Epstein visited the Carrara quarries and considered working there, but he did not return to free-standing carved figures until 1929. His two architectural commissions during the 1920s—*Rima* (1924–5), the carved relief memorial to the naturalist and author W. H. Hudson, for the bird sanctuary in Hyde Park, and two monumental figure groups, *Night* and *Day* (1928–9), for Charles Holden's London Underground headquarters at St James's Park—were both surrounded by public controversy. Such was Epstein's reputation that it was only with difficulty that Muirhead Bone and R. B. Cunninghame Graham secured him the commission of the former and that Holden persuaded Frank Pick to agree to his working on the latter project. Once unveiled, praise for the design and architectural qualities of the carvings was almost drowned out by public and media criticisms of their ugliness and primitivism. Throughout the 1920s and 1930s Epstein and his large carvings became a frequent butt of cartoons and popular rhymes, some of which were blatantly antisemitic, and the works were vandalized.

Epstein exhibited life-size bronzes and portraits in regular exhibitions at the Leicester Galleries. With the exception of *Risen Christ* (bronze, 1917–19, Scottish National Gallery of Modern Art, Edinburgh), which was bitterly attacked for its austere and unsentimental depiction of Christ, these were generally much better received, *Visitation* (1926) being promptly presented to the Tate Gallery by the Contemporary Arts Society. Despite Fry's criticism his portraits were widely acclaimed and he attracted numerous commissions. During a visit to the United States in 1927 to coincide with his one-man show at the Ferargil Gallery, New York, he received several portrait commissions, notably that of Paul Robeson (1928, Usher Gallery, Lincoln; York City Art Gallery; and National Portrait Gallery, Washington, DC). It became fashionable for wealthy foreign visitors to visit his studio and commission a portrait. His sitters ranged from the eminent—R. B. Cunninghame Graham (1923), Elsa Lanchester (1924), Joseph Conrad (1924), Sibyl Thorndyke (1925), Rabindranath Tagore (1926), Ramsay MacDonald (1926 and 1934), Albert Einstein (1933), Chaim Weizmann (1933), George Bernard Shaw (1934), Haile Selassie (1936)—to the outsiders and fringe figures whom he invited to sit. A number of bronze portraits and nude drawings, and his life-size bronze *Mother and Child* (1926, Riverside Church, Riverside Drive, New York) were based on a Kashmiri model, Amina Patel (known as Sunita), her son, and her sister. Performers from the 'Blackbirds' revue, and Chinese, Russian, Ethiopian, Senegalese, and Arab women were among his chosen models. Epstein made numerous portraits of his family—his daughter Peggy Jean (*b*. 1918) and son Jackie (*b*. 1934). Epstein and his wife remained childless but brought up as their own his children by liaisons with Dorothy (Meum) Lindsell-Stewart (1895–1957), and Isabel Nicholas (1912–1992). Another frequent model was Kathleen Esther Garman (1900/01–1979), daughter of Walter Chancellor Garman, surgeon; they met in 1921 and formed a lasting relationship, eventually having three children—Theo (1924–1954), Kitty (*b*. 1926), and Esther (1929–1954).

Epstein's increasing income enabled him to rent a cottage in Loughton, Essex, as a secluded place to work and, in 1928, to move from Guilford Street to 18 Hyde Park Gate, Kensington, which remained his home for the rest of his life and which housed the ever expanding mass of his own works and of his sculpture collection. At his 'Sunday teas' a wide cross-section of friends, sitters, models, musicians, and visitors could be encountered. These included Matthew Smith, who became a lifelong friend; the ballet critic Arnold Haskell, whose *The Sculptor Speaks* (1931) was based on numerous visits and interviews; and the young Henry Moore, whose early work Epstein supported, and for whose one-man show at the Leicester Galleries in 1931 the older artist wrote the catalogue introduction.

During the 1930s, probably stimulated by the renewed interest of Moore and his contemporaries in direct carving and increasingly stung by critics who not only considered carving superior to modelling but also considered him a modeller rather than a carver, Epstein embarked on a succession of large free-standing sculptures on symbolic themes: *Genesis* (marble, 1929–30, Whitworth Art Gallery, Manchester), *Primeval Gods*, carved on the reverse of his 1910 *Sun God* relief (Hoptonwood stone, 1931–3, Metropolitan Museum of Art, New York), *Behold the Man* (Subiaco stone, 1934–5, Coventry Cathedral ruins), *Consummatum est* (alabaster, 1936, Scottish National Gallery of Modern Art, Edinburgh), *Adam* (alabaster, 1938–9, Harewood House, Yorkshire), and *Jacob and the Angel* (alabaster, 1940–41, Tate collection). These uncommissioned works, on the one hand perpetuating the nineteenth-century monumental tradition and on the other challenging traditional

interpretations of religious and sexually charged themes, were increasingly at odds with the more abstract modernist mainstream while attracting sensationalized press treatment. *Genesis* and *Adam* were toured extensively by their owners to raise money, ventures which owed their success to the nationwide curiosity aroused by the regular press 'sensation' which followed each début at the Leicester Galleries. Other pieces remained unsold; *Genesis*, *Adam*, *Consummatum est*, and *Jacob and the Angel* eventually ended up on permanent exhibition at Louis Toussaud's in Blackpool before being purchased in 1960 by Lord Harewood and Jack Lyons shortly before the artist's memorial exhibition. Epstein's carving was supported by the continuing success of his portraits and by the ready market for his watercolours of flowers and landscapes. Two other watercolour projects, Old Testament subjects exhibited in 1932, and illustrations for Baudelaire's *Fleurs du mal* in 1938, were less well received. A further blow was his failure to prevent the mutilation, ostensibly on the grounds of public safety, of his British Medical Association sculptures in 1937 at the instigation of the building's new owners, the high commission for Southern Rhodesia.

Epstein never became directly engaged in politics but he supported the Artists' International Association's efforts on behalf of the Spanish Republican cause, and he acted as spokesperson for the London Group in urging artists to refuse co-operation with a Nazi attempt to organize an exhibition of British art (excluding Jewish artists) in Berlin in 1937. During the Second World War he carried out portrait commissions for the War Artists' Advisory Committee, including likenesses of Charles Portal (bronze, 1942, Imperial War Museum, London), Ernest Bevin (bronze, 1946, Tate collection, and Transport and General Workers' Union, London), and Winston Churchill (bronze, 1946, various locations).

Last decade—an Indian summer After the Second World War Epstein finally began to receive the public recognition he craved; his last major carving, *Lazarus* (Hoptonwood stone, 1948) was exhibited at Battersea Park as part of the Festival of Britain (1951) and was purchased for the chapel of New College, Oxford, and *Madonna and Child* (lead, 1950–52) for the convent of the Holy Child Jesus, Cavendish Square, London, received unprecedented critical and public acclaim. He had ceased to be an *enfant terrible* and had become a grand old man trusted to handle religious and symbolic themes with dignity and conviction. Ignoring his failing health and pushing aside grief at the tragic deaths of two of his children, he completed eight large public commissions during his last decade, as well as many commissioned portraits: *Jan Christian Smuts* for Parliament Square, London (bronze, 1953–5); *Christ in Majesty* at Llandaff Cathedral (aluminium, 1954–5); *Liverpool Resurgent* (1954) for Lewis's department store, Liverpool; the Trades Union Congress war memorial (Roman stone, 1956–7) in Great Russell Street, London; *St Michael and the Devil* for the new Coventry Cathedral (bronze, 1956–8); and the Bowater House group, Edinburgh Gate, Knightsbridge, London (bronze, 1958–9), completed on the day he died. In addition to these six, he received two commissions from the United States: a huge group, *Social Consciousness*, for Philadelphia (bronze, 1951–3) and the 1956 Franklin medal presented to Winston Churchill and Eleanor Roosevelt.

Apart from an honorary doctorate from Aberdeen in 1938, Epstein had received no public honours until, in 1953, he was made an honorary DCL at Oxford, and in 1954 was knighted. He became a founder member of the Society of Portrait Sculptors in 1953, but rejected as coming much too late the membership of the Royal Society of British Sculptors finally offered in 1954. He and Kathleen Garman married on 27 June 1955.

Death Epstein continued working to the last and died of a heart attack at his home at Hyde Park Gate on 19 August 1959. He was survived by his second wife. On the 24th he was buried at Putney Vale cemetery, London, in a ceremony conducted by Dr Hewlett Johnson, dean of Canterbury. A memorial service took place at St Paul's Cathedral on 10 November and a huge memorial exhibition was held at the Edinburgh festival, and subsequently at the Tate Gallery in 1961. His collection of primitive sculpture, the best in Britain, was exhibited by the Arts Council in 1960 before being dispersed to public and private collections.

Early portraits, such as the etchings by Augustus John and Francis Dodd, and Epstein's own self-portrait in red chalk (c.1901, Walsall, Garman Ryan collection), show an attractively Romantic bohemian figure. His later bronze self-portraits (1917, National Portrait Gallery, London; 1920, Hull University, and Castle Museum, Nottingham), and numerous photographic studies by Geoffrey Ireland, Yousuf Karsh, and others show a sturdy, powerful figure and a face marked by tribulation and intense concentration. Despite his formidable presence and occasional outbursts, his usual manner was quiet and courteous and his conversation wide-ranging and knowledgeable, though he had little patience with art pretence of any kind and expressed decisive, often derisive, views on the contemporary art scene. He never lost his New York accent nor did he ever entirely relinquish a bohemian approach, especially in financial matters which caused him frequent anxiety. As a sculptor he worked alone; his only assistants were plaster moulders and he never had the opportunity to teach. Although he had no immediate followers, his modelling technique has influenced later portrait sculptors. At times he seemed to relish and court his position as an outsider—Henry Moore's tribute was that 'Epstein took the brickbats for modern art' (*Sunday Times*, 23 Aug 1959)—but under a show of resilience manifest in his work, he was deeply wounded by critical marginalization and attacks on his work. In recent years his reputation as a pioneer modernist, direct carver, and collector—one of the leading British sculptors of the twentieth century—has been more widely recognized. The furore about his work often generated more heat than light, but it succeeded in bringing debate about modernist sculpture into the public arena.　　　　　　　EVELYN SILBER

Sources J. Epstein, *Let there be sculpture: an autobiography* (1940); rev. edn as *Epstein: an autobiography* (1955) • A. Haskell, *The sculptor speaks: Jacob Epstein to Arnold Haskell: a series of conversations on art* (1931) • E. Silber, *The sculpture of Epstein* (1986) • J. Rose, *Daemons and angels: a life of Jacob Epstein* (2002) • S. Gardiner, *Epstein: artist against the establishment* (1992) • E. Silber and T. Friedman, eds., *Jacob Epstein: sculpture and drawings* (1987) • J. F. Babson, *The Epsteins: a family album* (1984) • H. Hapgood, *The spirit of the ghetto* (1902) • B. van Dieren, *Epstein* (1920) • R. Buckle, *Jacob Epstein: sculptor* (1963) • L. B. Powell, *Jacob Epstein* (1932) • C. Holden, 'Memoir', 3 Dec 1940, RIBA BAL [unpublished MS] • D. Wilcox, 'British art, Nazi Germany and the London Group: a "friendship" exhibition as propaganda', *Apollo*, 142 (Oct 1995), 14–16 • R. Cork, *Art beyond the gallery* (1985) • m. certs. • d. cert. • *DNB* • H. Moore, *Sunday Times* (23 Aug 1959) • d. cert. [Margaret Epstein] • private information (2004) [Martin Evans, nephew]

Archives Henry Moore Institute, Leeds, photographs, corresp., cuttings, MSS, naturalization papers • Ransom HRC, letters • Tate collection, letters • U. Hull, corresp., MSS | JRL, letters to the *Manchester Guardian* • NRA, priv. coll., corresp. with Sir Robert Sainsbury and Lady Sainsbury • NYPL, Quinn and Ordway corresp. • Tate collection, letters to Mr and Mrs S. Samuels | SOUND BL NSA, BBC transcripts, interviews

Likenesses A. John, chalk drawing, c.1900, NPG • J. Epstein, self-portrait, red chalk, c.1901, Walsall New Art Gallery, Garman Ryan collection [*see illus.*] • A. John, etching, c.1905–1906, NPG • A. John, drawing, c.1906, NPG • A. John, etching, c.1906, NPG • F. Dodd, drypoint etching, 1909, U. Hull • E. Hoppé, photograph, c.1911–1912, U. Reading, department of English • A. L. Coburn, photogravure, 1914, NPG • J. Epstein, self-portrait, bronze head, 1917, NPG • G. C. Beresford, photographs, 1917–24, NPG • J. Epstein, self-portrait, bronze, 1920, Castle Museum, Nottingham • P. Evans, pen-and-ink drawing, c.1925, NPG • H. Coster, photographs, 1930–39, NPG • G. Ireland, photographs, 1950–59, NPG • A. John, etching, Auckland Art Gallery

Wealth at death £55,972 10s. 11d.: probate, 14 July 1960, CGPLA Eng. & Wales

Equiano, Olaudah [Gustavus Vassa] (c.1745–1797), author and slavery abolitionist, was in his own words born 'in a charming vale, named Essaka', most likely in present-day Nigeria. He later described his father as a local Igbo eminence and slave owner. Kidnapped about the age of eleven, along with his sister, by slave raiders Equiano was sold and resold on the journey to the coast, travelling for months before finally being sold onto an Atlantic slave ship. His account, written more than thirty years later, of enslavement and of the Atlantic crossing, forms perhaps the classic account of the experience which was the fate of millions of Africans in the era of Atlantic slavery. Equiano made landfall in Barbados, but was quickly moved on to Virginia, before being sold again to an English sailor, Michael Pascal. Renamed Gustavus Vassa (the name he used throughout most of his life), Equiano travelled to England in 1757. For five years he served on British ships as a slave. Fellow sailors taught him to read and write and to understand mathematics. He was also converted to Christianity, reading the Bible regularly on board ship. Baptized at St Margaret's Church, Westminster, in February 1759, he struggled with his faith until finally opting for Methodism.

Despite thinking he had been freed by Pascal, Equiano found himself re-enslaved in London in 1762 and shipped to the West Indies. For four years he worked for a Montserrat-based Quaker, sailing between the islands and North America, but also trading to his own advantage as he did so. Ever alert to commercial openings, Equiano accumulated cash and in 1766 bought his own freedom.

Olaudah Equiano (c.1745–1797), by Daniel Orme, pubd 1789 (after W. Denton)

He returned to London as a free man, working as a hairdresser before returning to sea on voyages to the Mediterranean, Turkey, and, in 1772, on Constantine Phibb's expedition to the Arctic (along with the young Horatio Nelson). In 1776–7 he was employed in an abortive plantation settlement on the Mosquito Coast. His account of those adventures and other maritime experiences (shipwrecked in the Bahamas in 1767, for example) became part picaresque travel account. Tired of the sea and wary of the dangers posed to Africans in an Atlantic world dominated by slavery, Equiano again settled in London between 1777 and 1784, working as a servant. He considered returning to Africa as a missionary but was rebuffed by the Church of England. In 1784 he went back to sea, when his visits to Philadelphia proved a turning point. There he visited recently established 'African' schools and churches, and made contact with local Quakers. He was now known to Quakers on both sides of the Atlantic. When, in the mid-1780s, the problems of London's black poor became acute (they were mainly free black people who had retreated from North America with the defeated British in 1783), Equiano was ideally placed to act as go-between. Appointed commissary to the ill-fated Sierra Leone scheme (to encourage resettlement there), Equiano proved an unrepentant defender of black interests among settlers on the ships. He was dismissed from his post (a move which almost certainly saved his life), and the expedition sailed to a disastrous fate. Arguments in the press about Equiano's role in the Sierra Leone scheme brought his name to the public's attention.

Equiano was naturally attracted to the parallel campaign against the slave trade. On 21 March 1788 he took the remarkable step of sending a petition, or personal letter, 'on behalf of my African brethren' to Queen Charlotte (Walvin, 156). In the following year he added to a rising level of abolitionist propaganda with the publication of his autobiography, *The Interesting Narrative of the Life of Olaudah Equiano*. It proved a remarkable success and went through numerous editions during his lifetime. Thanks to Equiano's energetic promotional efforts the *Narrative* sold well, helping to provide the author with a modest estate. This was also helped by his marriage on 7 April 1792 to Susanna Cullen (1761/2–1796) of Cambridgeshire. They had two daughters, Ann Mary (Maria) and Joanna, but by 1797 Joanna was the sole family survivor. She inherited her father's estate, valued at almost £1000, on her majority in 1816.

In the early 1790s Equiano moved in popular radical circles. But reaction against revolutionary excess in France and the slave uprising in Haiti undermined popular politics. Equiano continued to promote his book via friends and sympathizers. It was a fitting example of his lifelong industry and money-making interests.

After Equiano's death in London on 31 March 1797, his book was anthologized by abolitionists (especially before the American Civil War). Thereafter, however, Equiano was virtually forgotten for a century. In the 1960s his autobiography was rediscovered and reissued by Africanist scholars; various editions of his *Narrative* have since sold in large numbers in Britain, North America, and Africa.

Equiano's autobiography remains a classic text of an African's experiences in the era of Atlantic slavery. It is a book which operates on a number of levels: it is the diary of a soul, the story of an autodidact, and a personal attack on slavery and the slave trade. It is also the foundation-stone of the subsequent genre of black writing; a personal testimony which, however mediated by his transformation into an educated Christian, remains the classic statement of African remembrance in the years of Atlantic slavery.　　JAMES WALVIN

Sources *The interesting narrative of the life of Olaudah Equiano, or Gustavus Vassa, the African*, 2 vols. (1789) · O. Equiano, *The interesting narrative and other writings*, ed. V. Carretta (1995) · J. Walvin, *An African's life: the life and times of Olaudah Equiano, 1745–1797* (1998) · P. Edwards, 'Introduction', *The life of Olaudah Equiano* (1988)

Likenesses D. Orme, stipple, pubd 1789 (after W. Denton), NPG [see illus.]

Wealth at death approx. £1000: Walvin, *An African's life*, 161

Erard. *See* Erhard (d. before 784).

Erasmus, Desiderius (c.1467–1536), humanist scholar and reformer, was born in Rotterdam during the night of 27–28 October in the late 1460s—a year about 1467 seems plausible. He was illegitimate, a circumstance that doubtless contributed to the uncertainty attending all record of his origins, family name, and early life. The source of much information is the *Compendium vitae*, ostensibly written by Erasmus and clearly tendentious, and in any case known only from the seventeenth century. Earlier accounts, likewise tendentious in stressing both his youth

Desiderius Erasmus (*c.*1467–1536), by Hans Holbein the younger, 1523

and reluctance to enter a religious order, include the versions he wrote to popes Julius II and Leo X to gain the dispensations he needed to earn his own living while still in religious vows. With the assistance of his correspondence and other contemporary evidence, one may aim at reasonable conjecture. His father, who came from near Gouda, was Gerard Helye; his mother was one Margareta, possibly the daughter of a physician of Zevenbergen near Breda. In the address of a papal brief he is called Erasmus Rogerii, suggesting either that his father's full name was Roger Gerard Helye, or that his mother's surname was Roger. He had a brother, Pieter, older by three years, and possibly a half-brother from his mother's earlier marriage; Erasmus was in touch with Pieter until the latter's death in 1527. Their father, who had earned his living in Italy as a scribe, was lettered in classical Latin and Greek, the aspiration of all those—later known as 'humanists'—who sought in the civic life of antiquity the models for a revitalized political and religious culture in their own day. At some point he became a priest. Erasmus owned books from his library, and Greek manuscripts copied by him in Italy.

Education and early career   The boys were provided with a good education. The young Erasmus was sent to the school of Pieter Winckel attached to the church of St John at Gouda and later, about 1475, to the school of the chapter of St Lebuin in Deventer, which rose to great prominence under its headmaster Alexander Hegius. Seemingly, his

mother accompanied him to Deventer and fell a victim of the plague in 1483; his father died shortly afterwards. The two boys were then placed under the protection of three guardians, one of whom was Pieter Winckel. In 1484 they were sent to the school at 's-Hertogenbosch where they stayed at a hostel run by the Brethren of the Common Life. According to Erasmus, Winckel and the guardians pressed both boys to enter the religious life, although Erasmus longed to attend university. His account of the brethren is bitter and resentful, insisting that their main aim was to serve as recruiting sergeants for religious orders. At any rate, Pieter had already joined the canons regular of St Augustine at Sion near Delft when Erasmus joined the same congregation at Steyn, near Gouda, in 1487. He was by then about twenty years old, not sixteen as he later claimed. His earliest letters reveal that his life there was by no means unhappy, and that the Augustinian cloister was not at all inhospitable to humanistic studies. They also reveal his considerable mastery of the style and conventions of classical rhetoric, and his prominence within a literary circle of young Augustinians devoted to the cultivation of good letters.

Erasmus was ordained priest on 25 April 1492 by the bishop of Utrecht, and shortly afterwards, with the permission of his superiors, entered the service of the bishop of Cambrai, Hendrick van Bergen, as his secretary. While so employed he revised his first important work, *Antibarbari*, composed during his monastic years but unpublished until 1518. It is a manifesto defending classical learning as an indispensable adjunct to Christian revelation, and testifies strikingly to its author's literary gifts and already remarkable erudition. By September 1495 Hendrick had released Erasmus to take up theological studies at Paris, with some promise of continuing financial support. Their relationship continued until 1501 after which the bishop's subsidy—never found sufficient—was withdrawn. While studying at Paris (initially residing at the Collège de Montaigu) he took pupils to supplement his income, among them the young William Blount, fourth Lord Mountjoy. In the summer of 1499 he accompanied Mountjoy to England. This was his début in a courtly and scholarly world which would be of lasting importance to him, a world as well on which he would leave a lasting mark.

Early periods of English residence, 1499–1506   In the course of this first, brief visit Mountjoy's connections enabled Erasmus to befriend people who would later provide powerful support and congenial society, prominent among them Thomas More, who introduced him to the eight-year-old Prince Henry. Until January 1500 he stayed in Oxford at St Mary's College, the house of the Augustinian canons, where the prior, Richard Charnock, was a kindred spirit. In the company of such others as John *Colet, William Grocyn, William Latimer, and Thomas Linacre, his resolve to devote himself to sacred studies was confirmed. Erasmus, whose literary reputation evidently had preceded him, had been recommended to Colet by Richard Charnock as a truly virtuous man. The two were near in age, and they formed a relationship which was close and enduring. Colet's lectures on the epistles of St Paul impressed Erasmus deeply. Since Erasmus was already convinced that theology should concern itself with conversion of life and the fostering of individual devotion through the study of the scriptures, rather than with the speculative sciences dear to the scholastics, their influence may well have been less decisive than was once claimed; it was probably Colet's non-scholastic approach to scripture that chiefly attracted the Dutch humanist. Certainly, Erasmus's confidence in the providential role of pagan wisdom and the importance of understanding classical antiquity to repristinate Christian evangelism—convictions asserted in his as yet unpublished *Antibarbari*—far exceeded that of Colet.

A second English friend of great importance, close also to Colet, was Thomas More. With Mountjoy, More and Colet were doubtless responsible for introducing Erasmus to his wide circle of influential friends and followers in Oxford, London, and Cambridge. In addition to those already mentioned, Cuthbert Tunstall, John Fisher, William Warham, Richard Fox, Christopher Urswick, Richard Pace, and John Clerk are notable. Erasmus's closer involvement with these would await his return. He left England for Paris in January 1500, deeply impressed with what he had found and praising his English associates to his friends. His overriding aim now was to acquire Greek before venturing further into sacred studies.

Subsequently Colet probably helped to finance Erasmus's return to England in 1505–6, and the transcriptions of Erasmus's translation of the epistles and gospels made by Pieter Meghen (BL, Royal MS 1 E.v, 2 vols., and CUL, MS Dd 7. 3) are associated with Colet, whose pupil Thomas Lupset helped Erasmus to collate the New Testament. Colet's support continued through the years, but the most striking evidence of their friendship was Erasmus's involvement in St Paul's School, founded by Colet with his own patrimony: revision of William Lily's advanced Latin syntax, the *De octo orationis partium constructione libellus*, first published anonymously in 1513; various Latin poems; the *Concio de puero Jesu*; and his treatise on rhetorical variation *De copia* (see below). Erasmus's *De ratione studii* was also written for St Paul's School. His admiration for Colet was evinced repeatedly throughout his lifetime, and he left an indelible portrait of him in a memorial letter written to Justus Jonas in June 1521.

The *Adagiorum chiliades* and *Enchiridion* A stepping-stone towards the mastery of Greek was Erasmus's first published book, the *Adagiorum collectanea*, printed in Paris in the summer of 1500 and dedicated to Mountjoy. It was a small quarto of 818 adages culled from Greek sources and printed in humanistic format, a new presence in the Paris book trade. It was also the harbinger of one of Erasmus's greatest achievements, the *Adagiorum chiliades* ('ordered in thousands'). In successive editions it grew, along with Erasmus's command of Greek authors, to become an invaluable quarry for the revived classical culture of Europe: in the *Chiliades* of 1508 the number of adages rose from 818 to 3260. This edition also revealed the potential of classical proverbs to serve as pegs on which to display

curious byways of erudition or inspire reflections on the issues of the day. In successive editions the enrichment continued, providing 4151 adages in that of 1536, the year of his death.

In his Greek studies Erasmus turned further to editing the works of Jerome, a pathway also to his ultimate goal, revision of the Vulgate text of the New Testament, and he resumed his study of pagan Greek authors: Euripides, Lucian, Plutarch, and Libanius, along with the popular grammar of Theodore of Gaza. In the spring of 1501, driven by plague first from Paris, then from Orléans, he settled in Flanders where he met the Observant Franciscan reformer Jean Vitrier, who encouraged his study of St Paul and fostered his appreciation of Origen. In this atmosphere, while preparing to write his own commentary on the epistle to the Romans, he composed the *Enchiridion militis Christiani* ('Handbook of the Christian knight'), his first great pastoral essay, infused with citations from Origen's *Homilies*. It appeared in a collection of *Lucubratiunculae* from Antwerp in February 1503. This first edition attracted little attention, but in 1515 it was printed independently for the first time, and underwent seven more printings before that of 1518 by Froben, after which it swept Europe, so that by the end of the century there were seventy editions of the Latin text, and innumerable vernacular translations. The remarkable impact of this brief treatise, not obvious today, derived from its endorsement, with a strong Pauline emphasis, of the lay vocation to holiness in the Christian life as lived in the world. Erasmus's advocacy of life well led in the community—'the city as a monastery'—directed the faithful towards the renewal of the entire Christian polity rather than more monastic ideals. Additionally, with its broad undercurrent of mystical theology, it served as a spur to the contemplative revival in sixteenth-century Spain. A key addition to the 1518 version was the introductory letter to a reforming Benedictine abbot, Paul Volz, which was effectively an epitome of Erasmus's doctrine of personal piety and the Christian mission.

In Flanders, Erasmus continued his studies on the epistle to the Romans, made a brief attempt at Hebrew, and in 1504 discovered a manuscript of Lorenzo Valla's notes on the text of the Vulgate New Testament in the Premonstratensian abbey of Parc near Louvain. In 1505 he returned to England as the guest of Thomas More at Bucklersbury, where together they translated dialogues of Lucian, and Erasmus made a translation of Euripides' *Iphigeneia in Aulis* and *Hecuba* (dedicated to Archbishop Warham). That April, Josse Bade in Paris published Erasmus's edition of Valla's notes. Although his own approach would be more complex, Valla's was a further incentive to Erasmus in his driving ambition to revise the legacy of St Jerome in the Latin Vulgate. In April 1506 he apparently visited Cambridge during a royal progress to Walsingham, staying at Queens' College, of which John Fisher was president. Acquainted with Fisher through mutual friends, Erasmus was nominated for the degree of DTh, which however he did not take.

In May 1506 Erasmus left for Italy, professedly further to

improve his knowledge of Greek, but this is the most obscure period of his adult life since no letters survive from his pen between December 1508 and April 1511. He took a doctorate in theology from the University of Turin by oral examination, witnessed the entry of the victorious Julius II into Bologna, and stayed with Aldus in Venice to prepare editions of Plautus, Seneca, and Terence's tragedies, and to complete the greatly enlarged *Adagiorum chiliades* of 1508. From Venice he travelled to Padua, Siena, and Rome, and visited the cave of the Sibyl at Cumae accompanied by his pupil Alexander Stewart, the illegitimate son of James IV of Scotland; in Naples, Alexander presented his tutor with a gem supposedly bearing the image of the boundary god Terminus, which Erasmus subsequently adopted as his personal symbol with the motto *Cedo nulli* ('I yield to no one').

The *Praise of Folly* and the Cambridge years On the accession of Henry VIII to the English throne in April 1509, and at the urging of Mountjoy and Warham, Erasmus returned to England for the longest and most productive of his visits. He arrived in August that year at the home of Thomas More, where he completed his most famous literary work, the *Moriae encomium* ('Praise of folly'). This complex satire, a distillation of his critique of contemporary Christendom, did not appear until 1511, but by Erasmus's death in 1536 there were thirty-six Latin editions, with translations into Czech, French, and German. An Italian version followed in 1539, and Thomas Chaloner's English version in 1549. It was famous—and notorious—in his lifetime, and is the only product of his pen to survive intact into the modern era.

Like many other of Erasmus's works the *Folly* derived from classical antecedents: it is a mock encomium, a praise of folly by Folly herself with a punning allusion in the title to the author's English friend. It grew in time to be the centrepiece of Erasmus's tireless, satirical moralizing about the world as he found it and the professed ideals of those responsible for it. He himself insisted that it be understood as an essay in evangelical humanism, one entirely consistent with the purpose of the *Enchiridion*. Bantering and playful in tone for the most part, it is suffused with ambiguity and paradox to capture the interest of those who might otherwise have shunned the radicalism of its impudent assault on the established order of the day, assailing everything from the uncritical acceptance of conventional pieties to real abuses of power and responsibility. None was spared, from princes to schoolmasters, from lawyers to monks, from philosophers and theologians to poets and grammarians like Erasmus himself. While the mask of Folly is always in place, the deeper purpose of the piece emerges with increasing clarity in the later pages: to contrast the Christendom of his own day with the ideals of the New Testament, especially as they were voiced by St Paul.

The years immediately following Erasmus's return to England are again obscure, but in 1511 he went to Paris to supervise the printing of the *Moriae encomium*, and on his return repaired to Cambridge at the invitation of John

Fisher, now chancellor, where he stayed until 1514. He lectured in theology (on St Jerome) and on Greek—the first person known to have done so at either university—from the grammars of Manuel Chrysoloras and Theodore of Gaza. He edited the letters of St Jerome, completed his Latin translation of the epistles and gospels, the *Novum instrumentum*, and, among other like tasks, translated St Basil's commentary on Isaiah for presentation to Fisher. In early 1512 he finished his *De copia verborum ac rerum* ('Foundations of the abundant style'), his letters suggesting that he was by now quite at home in England. *De copia* was dedicated to Colet, and a revised and amplified edition of his Lucian translations was dedicated to Archbishop Warham, who in March appointed him rector of Aldington in Kent. The income from Aldington he commuted to a pension worth some £20 a year, an amount matched by Mountjoy. For a time it appeared that he would accompany John Fisher to the Fifth Lateran Council as his theologian, but Fisher reconsidered, and in the end England was represented only by Silvestro Gigli, bishop of Worcester. In the summer of 1512 Erasmus joined the Cambridge scholar Robert Aldridge on a pilgrimage to the shrine of Our Lady of Walsingham, commemorated in his colloquy *Peregrinatio religionis ergo* (1526), and also went on a pilgrimage to Canterbury with John Colet. In July there was published in Paris the first authorized edition of the *De ratione studii*, the foundation of the curriculum at St Paul's School and, along with *De copia*, a widely influential treatise on the foundations of learning. At some point he also composed the epitaph on the tomb of Lady Margaret Beaufort in Henry VII's chapel in Westminster Abbey, for which he was paid £20 in December.

During the following year, 1513, Erasmus continued his various undertakings, most notably further revision of the *Adagia*, along with a by-product of that revision, a compilation of aphorisms called the *Parabolae* ('Parallels'), the collation of the New Testament, and his edition of Jerome. In the latter tasks he enjoyed the assistance of Colet's protégé, Thomas Lupset, whom he praised in the same letter of 11 July 1513 in which he reminded Colet of a promise to provide the sum of 15 angels in return for dedicating the *De copia* to St Paul's School rather than to Prince Henry.

In January 1514, writing from Cambridge, Erasmus inscribed his translation of Plutarch's *De utilitate capienda ex inimicis* ('On profiting from one's enemies') as a new year's gift to Thomas Wolsey. At the same time the worsening relations between England and France disturbed him. He wrote to Warham of an acute attack of the stone, which he attributed to the Cambridge beer and scarcity of French wine owing to the prospect of war, and in March told Antoon van Bergen of rising prices, the threat to his income, the scarcity of French wine, and England's growing isolation from the continent. Accordingly, he looked to the Netherlands—to Prince Charles and the emperor Maximilian—for new support. The argument of this important letter was the basis of his adage *Dulce bellum inexpertis* ('War is sweet to those who know it not'), one of those published in the Froben edition of 1515 and destined to have an independent life, with fifteen separate printings before 1540. By early June he was staying in London at the house of Andrea Ammonio, and after making his farewells to the king, to Wolsey, Warham, Ruthall, and Fisher, he crossed the channel in early July, arriving at the castle of Hammes near Calais on the 8th, to stay with his patron Mountjoy. Here he composed a letter for Servatius Roger, prior of Steyn, excusing himself for his failure to return to his home monastery, one of a series of such *apologiae* from which the variable details of his early life must be construed.

Basel and the New Testament By July 1514 Erasmus was undoubtedly ready to make for the Froben press with the fruits of his studies in the previous decade. These included a greatly revised and expanded version of the *Adagia*, his revision of the letters of Jerome, his revised text of Seneca, a number of translations from Plutarch, the *Parabolae*, and his accumulated work on the New Testament, a substantial part of which had been done in England. From this last grew Froben's historic undertaking: the printing of the Greek text of the New Testament with Erasmus's new Latin translation and annotations. He proceeded up the Rhine to Basel, a journey that took him to Mainz and Strasbourg especially; there he was fêted by societies of German humanists, among whom he met Ulrich von Hutten, Jakob Wimpheling, Sebastian Brant, and the educator Jakob Sturm. His reception in Basel by Johannes Froben, Beatus Rhenanus, and many others was no less warm.

In September 1514 Erasmus for the first time stated that what was to be published of the New Testament was his Latin translation 'with the Greek facing' and his notes (*Opus epistolarum*, ep. 305). In the first edition (*Novum instrumentum*, 1516) the Greek was printed with Erasmus's Latin rendering in parallel, while his annotations, keyed to the established Vulgate and unprecedented in their scope and references to Greek texts, were printed separately. Erasmus's constant purpose was to provide a reasoned revision of the Vulgate in his annotations. But it was the Greek text—a late addition possibly suggested to Froben by the annotations themselves—combined with his Latin translation that made the widest and most enduring impression. The work was reprinted 229 times in the course of the sixteenth century, and fostered allied treatises. These included the *Paraclesis* ('Exhortation'), an impassioned plea for a life informed by the word incarnate which introduced the *Novum instrumentum* and acquired independent celebrity, and Erasmus's *Paraphrases* on the books of the New Testament, intended to make the text accessible to the lay reader.

The year 1516 also saw the appearance of Froben's great edition of the works of Jerome in nine volumes, for the first four of which—containing chiefly the letters and dedicated to Archbishop Warham—Erasmus had special responsibility. And finally, Thomas More's *Utopia*, whose publication More had entrusted to Erasmus, appeared that December at Louvain. From this time Erasmus was increasingly taken up with activities on the continent, but contacts with his English friends continued for many years, and it will be expedient to deal briefly with the rest of his career before returning to the more complex question of his influence in England.

Except for trips to Froben in Basel and occasional visits to England, Erasmus spent the years from 1514 to 1521 chiefly in Brabant, moving about between Louvain, Bruges, and Antwerp. He was closely involved in the project for a trilingual college at Louvain, initiated in 1517, and his appointment as an imperial councillor early in 1516 kept him close to Brussels. His *Institutio principis Christiani* ('Education of a Christian prince'), published in 1516, had been completed in recognition of this appointment, and in October 1520 he attended the coronation of Charles V as king of the Romans at Aachen. There were occasional forays to England, chiefly on business concerning his pension, and the obtaining of a papal dispensation from Leo X which would allow him to earn his own living while still retaining his religious vows. The growing tumult around Luther worried him lest he be indirectly discredited by it, and he employed every rhetorical means at his disposal to distance his own proposals from Luther's, while urging that Luther himself 'be put right rather than put down'. In November 1521 Erasmus left Brabant for good, and returned to Basel.

Controversy and the Basel years, 1522–1529 From this point onwards controversy was a constant preoccupation for Erasmus. It had begun already in 1517 with conservative critics of his great editorial projects, the Jerome edition and New Testament. Among the first of these was the English Franciscan Henry Standish, an Oxford theologian and provincial of his order. Another vexed issue was Erasmus's ardent advocacy of 'trilingualism', a doctrine shared within the humanist circle that mastery of Latin, Greek, and Hebrew was essential for the renewal of learning, more especially of theology. It was one of the reasons why Erasmus's scholarly base in those years was Louvain, where the project for a trilingual college was finally realized within the university in 1520. Yet one of his chief opponents on this issue also resided at Louvain, Jacobus Latomus (Jacques Masson). The *Novum instrumentum* in turn brought a new wave of critics, first among them another Englishman, Edward Lee, a Cambridge divine and prebendary of Lincoln. Lee was soon joined by several friars, among them the Carmelite prior at Louvain, Nicolaus Baechem, and several Louvain Dominicans. In the same years Erasmus collaborated with Johannes Faber, prior of the Dominican house, in a project for mediation in the dispute with Luther. This was the *Consilium cuiusdam*, published in Cologne in 1521, a companion piece to the eirenic *Axiomata Erasmi pro causa Lutheri* written at the request of the elector of Saxony, which contained twenty-two short axioms on which to base a settlement of the whole affair.

Luther's manifest intransigence and the propagation of his own *Colloquia* were the dominant preoccupation of Erasmus's years in Basel, although he continued tirelessly to publish: successive revisions of the *Adagia*, paraphrases on the New Testament (Hebrews, Matthew, Luke, John, Mark, Acts), editions of such fathers as Arnobius, Hilary,

Irenaeus, and Augustine, classical texts (Cicero, Pliny, Seneca), and other humanistic and pedagogical works in abundance (*De conscribendis epistolis*, *Lingua*, *De civilitate morum puerilium*, *Christiani matrimonii institutio*, *Ciceronianus*, *De recta Latini Graecique sermonis pronuntiatione dialogus*, *De pueris instituendis*).

If the *Adagia* and the New Testament represent the scholarly cornerstones of Erasmus's literary and theological enterprises, then the *Colloquia* were the summation of his satirical campaign against the follies of the day and misuse of power, ecclesiastical and secular. Derived from his own teaching experience and rooted in the rhetorical handbooks of the later middle ages, the *Colloquia* were first adumbrated in the unauthorized *Familiarium colloquiorum formulae* from the Froben press in Basel in November 1518, apparently printed from a text belonging to a friend of Erasmus's Paris years, Augustinus Vincentius Caminadus, a fellow tutor and sometime roommate. Erasmus made corrections in the Froben edition of 1519, and the book was reprinted at least thirty times before March 1522. In 1522 Froben published a much enhanced version, after which the work appeared at regular intervals, new colloquies being added sporadically, until the final edition of Erasmus's lifetime in 1533. In successive revisions the constantly amplified *Colloquia* became a running, often trenchant, commentary on the affairs of the day. As the fully developed dialogues they now were, they experienced countless reprintings throughout Europe, both authorized and pirated, virtually initiating a new literary genre. They also reflect frequently their author's experience of England, dealing with such subject matter as St Paul's School, Thomas More, John Colet, and pilgrimages to Walsingham and to Canterbury.

Controversy with Martin Luther Erasmus's collision with Martin Luther marked a divergence within the community of reformers that was of lasting import. Luther was one of those in the generation after Erasmus who could not but be a pupil of the pre-eminent northern humanist's achievement as a pioneering editor of the fathers and of the New Testament, as well as an educational propagandist and master of satire: the *Adagia*, the *Enchiridion*, and the *Moria* were all a part of Luther's formation, but important above all was Erasmus's Greek New Testament. Luther's earlier training was scholastic, not humanistic, and his attitude to Erasmus was from the first ambivalent. After Luther's open break with Rome in his publications of 1520 Erasmus was seen by him increasingly as, at best, a half-hearted ally, if not indeed an obstacle to the kind of revolution Luther thought essential, while Erasmus was more and more concerned by Luther's apparent indifference to the unity of the church. Under pressure from Rome, from Duke Georg of Saxony, and from many other quarters including the English court, Erasmus finally took up his pen in public opposition to Luther on an issue that was central not only to the latter's doctrine, but to the humanist's reform programme: the issue of the freedom of the will.

The *De libero arbitrio diatribe* (literally, a 'discussion' of free will), issued by Froben in September 1524 (an advance copy had been sent to Henry VIII in March) was a measured response to Luther's *Assertio omnium articulorum per bullam Leonis X*. In the *Assertio* Luther had replied, article by article, to the bull of Leo X condemning his views, *Exsurge domine* (15 June 1520). Article 36 of *Exsurge domine* proclaimed free will, and in his reply Luther repudiated the orthodox Catholic teaching that by their own freely willed good deeds, performed in a proper relationship to divine grace, human beings might contribute to their own salvation. This was Erasmus's chosen ground of debate. He upheld the traditional view, drawing heavily upon scripture, on the fathers, and on the consensus of belief throughout earlier centuries. Luther's reply *De servo arbitrio* ('On the enslaved will'), which appeared in December 1525, was an aggressive rebuttal, section by section, point by point, to *De libero arbitrio*. Stung by his tone and belligerence Erasmus, convinced now that Luther was resolved to disrupt Christendom, denounced his reckless arrogance and insolence, and turned to a lengthy response. This was *Hyperaspistes diatribae adversus servum arbitrium Martini Lutheri* ('A warrior shielding a discussion of free will against the enslaved will of Martin Luther'), the first part of which appeared in March 1526. The second, three times as long as the first, appeared in September of the following year.

The exchange between the two men, arguing over the same scriptural texts, reflected their contrasting intellectual formations. Where Erasmus's approach was inductive and consensual, Luther's was deductive and systematic, from the outset placing the biblical texts in a doctrinal framework. Where Erasmus accepted diversity in the understanding of the Bible, appealing to the larger context of Christian practice and tradition, Luther's hermeneutic was impelled by his central conviction that human collaboration could contribute nothing to salvation, which proceeds from God's grace alone. Behind these differences lay contrasting anthropologies. Luther saw man as determined by his being wholly a sinner; Erasmus emphasized his vocation as a 'new creation' capable of serving God. At base, Erasmus thought that within the unfathomable mystery posed by God's omnipotence over against the fate of individuals, the human experience of freedom could not be dismissed, that Luther's doctrine of human unfreedom could not be proved in scripture, and that in any case to proclaim it publicly could have only disastrous consequences for the mass of believers already lethargic about their Christian calling. His concern was, as usual, more pastoral than doctrinal, so that what was all-important to Luther was of secondary interest only to Erasmus.

The argument with Luther was not Erasmus's only concern, however, and his involvement with neighbouring reformers—Huldrych Zwingli in Zürich, Johannes Oecolampadius in Basel, and Martin Bucer in Strasbourg—impinged more directly on his personal fortunes. These were men who found Erasmus's humanist approaches much more congenial than did Luther, and who could appeal to the Dutch reformer's utterances in support of their own more radical opinions. Within a few months of his arrival in Basel, Erasmus intervened with eirenic intentions in a local row over compulsory fasting with a treatise *De esu carnium* ('On the eating of meat'), which questioned the entire status of man-made ecclesiastical laws (including celibacy). His many earlier attacks on such rules as a 'legalism' opposed to 'evangelical freedom' were now hostages to fate, since reformers like Zwingli were prepared to cite him in support of their views, and to demand the entire abolition of such practices in the name of the gospel. Erasmus disagreed, seeing in such demands only a new legalism. *De esu carnium* appealed to the bishops, on the one hand, to show pastoral prudence and openness, and to the reformers to act with moderation within the established church. His stand pleased neither side. His personal view of the church as an evolving community of faith under the perpetual tuition of the Holy Spirit put preservation of its unity and spiritual harmony above all other imperatives, but for those of a more doctrinaire turn of mind this was incomprehensible. Protestant and Catholic critics alike rejected or simply failed to comprehend his pneumatic ecclesiology and hermeneutic theology. The former envisaged the church almost entirely under the aspect of the Holy Spirit through the ages, while the latter shunned scholastic definitions of doctrine in favour of a core of belief drawn simply from the New Testament and the teachings of the early fathers. A subsequent row over the eucharist, provoked by Oecolampadius, exposed Erasmus's profound sympathy with a view that was not in accord with the *consensus ecclesiae*, to which nevertheless Erasmus loyally adhered. The theologians of Louvain and Paris took up the cry, and in 1526 the *Colloquia* were condemned, the first censures to be passed against his writings. As Catholic critics from Spain as well as France took up their pens, his *Apologia adversus monachos quosdam Hispanos* (1528) addressed their dangerous accusation that he questioned the very doctrine of the Trinity. His vulnerability to the scrutiny of systematic theologians was again demonstrated, as it had been with Luther.

The final years, 1529–1536 In April 1529, driven from Basel by the radical party's successful campaign of iconoclasm and the replacement of the mass by compulsory celebration of communion in the protestant rite, Erasmus saw his independence imperilled and removed his household to Freiburg im Breisgau, a Catholic city within the territories of the Archduke Ferdinand. His *Epistola in pseudevangelicos* later that year stated his position, without withdrawing his familiar objections to the church of the day. Although editions and revisions continued to pour from his study, his most substantial new achievement in the last years was the final version of *Ecclesiastes* (1535), an extensive treatise on preaching which is also rich in theological reflection. His *De sarcienda ecclesiae concordia* of 1533 ('On repairing the unity of the church'), a long reflection on Psalm 83 (84), was an eirenic résumé of his position on the need both for appropriate reforms and for diversity of observance within a unified church. It gave satisfaction neither in Rome nor in Wittenberg and, like other of Erasmus's late works, reflected both a less sanguine view of

the prospects for reform through education and a more cautious attitude to what mere human powers could achieve.

Debilitated by failing health, in 1534 Erasmus returned to Basel where a more accommodating religious policy now prevailed, and where he was sought by his old friend and influential associate, Bonifacius Amerbach, who became his heir and executor. He died at Zum Luft, Basel, the house of Hieronymus Froben, son of the printer Johann, of dysentery during the night of 11 July 1536 and was buried on the 18th in the cathedral. The most important component of his estate was the so-called 'Legatum Erasmianum', a sum of 5000 florins invested at 5 per cent with the duke of Württemburg and the city of Geneva to provide support for students and the poor.

Influence in England Erasmus's influence on the generation that came of age under Henry VIII was immense, especially in education. Episcopal and aristocratic patrons of his project included Edward Fox of Winchester, John Fisher of Rochester, and Lady Margaret Beaufort, all connected to Erasmus and key figures in the establishment of humanism in the universities. The names of Roger Ascham, Sir John Cheke, Leonard Cox, Richard Croke, Sir Thomas Elyot, Thomas Lupset, Thomas Paynell, Thomas Ruthall, Cuthbert Tunstall, Nicholas Udall, and Christopher Urswick must be added to those just mentioned as instrumental in the promotion of the Erasmian agenda directly or indirectly. There was also a notable translation industry involving predictably the *Paraclesis* (1529), *Enchiridion* (1533), and *Praise of Folly* (1549), but including works of devotion and, most prominently, the *Paraphrases* on the New Testament on the initiative of Queen Katherine Parr. By royal injunction of 1547 the latter were to be made accessible in every parish in the realm along with the Great Bible.

To the list of adherents the name of Thomas Cranmer should be added, but direct citations of Erasmus in Cranmer's reforms of the liturgy are conspicuously absent. While it is tempting to think that the patristic orientation and ecclesiologically conservative character of the later Anglican settlement reflected the views of Erasmus, it is impossible to document such a continuing influence. Nevertheless in England he was generally regarded as an honorary protestant. Bishop Edward Stillingfleet (1635–1699) saw him as the father of Anglican moderation, while Alexander Pope, who had been brought up a Catholic, hailed Erasmus as 'that great, injur'd name', and praised him as the man who revived the study of letters after they had been corrupted by superstitious monks, 'those holy Vandals' (*Essay on Criticism*, ll. 693–6). The first English biographer of Erasmus, Samuel Knight (1677/8–1746), saw him chiefly as a scholar and writer. John Jortin (1698–1770), whose two-volume study was more influential, acknowledged Erasmus's sincere adherence to the Roman church despite his criticisms, and provided a sympathetic estimate of his religion with influential extracts from Erasmus's works. His reputation as an eirenicist and advocate of peace was already clear, as it would be on the continent.

The first English Catholic to compose a biography was Charles Butler (1750–1832), of old recusant stock, who was also a student of Grotius. Relying heavily on the earlier biographies, Butler admired Erasmus for his contributions to learning, sacred and profane, and criticized him chiefly for presenting abuses in the church as universal when they were not. Arthur Lionel Smith (1850–1924), a liberal protestant admirer, saw Erasmus as the most representative proponent of the Renaissance, anti-ecclesiastical and anti-dogmatic. In his admiration of Erasmus's moderation and partiality to gradual reform as opposed to Luther's violence, he fairly sums up the congenial attitude of most English authors to the Dutch reformer. It should be added, however, that it was Charles Reade's *The Cloister and the Hearth* (1861), a romantic reconstruction of Erasmus's origins, based largely on the *Compendium vitae*, that fixed Erasmus's story in the minds of most readers in later generations.

The modern critical study began with the monumental life's work of Percy Stafford Allen (1869–1933), the assembly and ordering of Erasmus's vast correspondence. This established for the first time a reliable framework within which the works could be located, and the development of Erasmus's thought explored. Its consummation is the new critical edition from Amsterdam along with the wealth of scholarship developed in the wake of the Second World War and the Second Vatican Council, after which Erasmus's eirenicism, advocacy of a European polity, and insistence that Christians agree to concentrate on the essentials of the gospel message acquired new relevance and urgency. He remains one of the architects of modern scholarship as a paradigm of critical intelligence and unflagging industry, and as an admired advocate of international peace and concord.   JAMES McCONICA

Sources *Desiderii Erasmi Roterodami opera omnia*, ed. J. Leclerc, 10 vols. (Leiden, 1703–6) · *Opus epistolarum Des. Erasmi Roterodami*, ed. P. S. Allen and others, 12 vols. (1906–58) [incl. *Compendium vitae*] · *Collected works of Erasmus*, ed. W. K. Ferguson and others, [86 vols.] (1974–) · J.-C. Margolin, *Quatorze années de bibliographie érasmienne, 1936–1949* (Paris, 1969) · J.-C. Margolin, *Douze années de bibliographie érasmienne, 1950–1961* (Paris, 1963) · J.-C. Margolin, *Neuf années de bibliographie érasmienne, 1962–1970* (Paris, 1977) · J. McConica, *Erasmus* (1991) · M. M. Phillips, *Erasmus and the northern Renaissance* (1949) · R. J. Schoeck, *Erasmus of Europe*, 2 vols. (1990–93) · J. Chomarat, *Grammaire et rhétorique chez Érasme*, 2 vols. (1981) · J. D. Tracy, *Erasmus: the growth of a mind* (1972) · C. Augustijn, *Erasmus, his life, works and influence* (1991) · E. J. Devereux, *Renaissance English translations of Erasmus: a bibliography to 1700* (1983) · J. K. McConica, *English humanists and Reformation politics under Henry VIII and Edward VI* (1965) · J. K. McConica, 'Erasmus and the grammar of consent', *Scrinium Erasmianum*, ed. J. Coppens, 2 (Leiden, 1969), 77–99 · M. M. Phillips, *The 'Adages' of Erasmus: a study with translations* (1964) · J. Ijsewijn, 'The coming of humanism to the Low Countries', *Itinerarium Italicum*, ed. H. A. Oberman and T. A. Brady (1975), 193–301 · A. Rabil, *Erasmus and the New Testament* (San Antonio, 1972) · A. Brown, 'The date of Erasmus' Latin translations of the New Testament', *Transactions of the Cambridge Bibliographical Society*, 8 (1981–5) · B. Mansfield, *Phoenix of his age: interpretations of Erasmus, c. 1550–1750* (1979) · B. Mansfield, *Man on his own: interpretations of Erasmus, c. 1750–1920* (1992) · J. K. McConica, 'Erasmus in Amsterdam and Toronto', *Editing texts from the age of Erasmus*, ed. E. Rummel (Toronto, 1996), 81–100 · J. Étienne, *Spiritualisme érasmien et*

théologiens louvanistes (Louvain, 1956) · D. MacCulloch, *Thomas Cranmer: a life* (1996) · G. Marc'hadour, *L'univers de Thomas More: chronologie critique de More, Érasme, et leur époque, 1477–1536* (1963) · tombstone, Basel Cathedral, Switzerland
Archives BL, Egerton MS 1651 · BL, letters to E. Schets, etc., Add. MS 38512 · Katholieke Universiteit Brabant, Tilburg, D 141 · Municipal Library, Gouda, Librije coll. 1323, 1324 · Public Library, Rotterdam, Codex Horawitzianus
Likenesses H. Holbein the younger, pen caricatures, *c.*1515, Kupferstichkabinett, Basel · Q. Metsijs, oils, 1517, Royal Collection · Q. Metsijs, bronze statue, 1519, Historischesmuseum, Basel · Q. Metsijs, medal recto, 1519, Royal Library of Belgium, Brussels · A. Dürer, charcoal drawing, 1520, Louvre, Paris · H. Holbein the younger, portrait, 1523, priv. coll. [*see illus.*] · H. Holbein the younger, tempera, 1523, Louvre, Paris · H. Holbein the younger, tempera, 1523, Öffentliche Kunstsammlung, Basel · H. Holbein the younger, tempera, 1523, Radnor Collection, Longford Castle · A. Dürer, wood-engraving, 1526, Royal Library of Belgium, Brussels · H. Holbein the younger, miniature tempera, *c.*1530, Öffentliche Kunstsammlung, Basel · H. Holbein the younger, wood-engraving, 1535, Kupferstichkabinett, Basel
Wealth at death 8000 florins; 5000 florins invested at 5 per cent forming the 'Legatum Erasmianum' in support of scholars and the poor; 1960 florins in property in Brabant; 1100 in bequests; plus valuable personal possessions: C. Roth, 'Das Legatum Erasmianum', *Gedenksschrift zum 400. Todestage des Erasmus von Rotterdam* (Basel, 1936), 283; *Opus epistolarum*, ed. Allen and others, 362–3

Erbery, Dorcas (*fl.* 1656–1659), Quaker preacher, possibly born in Cardiff, was the daughter of William *Erbery (1604/5–1654), puritan minister, and his wife, Mary (d. 1667×70), who also became a Quaker preacher. Young female preachers often followed the missionary tradition practised by their mothers. Thus Quaker daughters, it has been suggested, acted as female 'apprentices' and this is indicated in the actions of Dorcas Erbery, who undertook missionary journeys with her mother and suffered with her for her Quaker beliefs. In June 1656, when accompanied by Tobias (Toby) Hodge, she was arrested and imprisoned in Cardiff gaol for disturbing a local clergyman in the market place. In the following month she was again arrested and imprisoned in Exeter, along with her mother and many other Friends, 'among Felons and lay generally in straw by reason of which, and the filth of the place, many of them fell sick' (Besse, 1.149). It is possible that Dorcas could have contracted a disease while in prison but was able to survive it—unlike her fellow Quaker missionary Jane Ingram.

Dorcas Erbery, is, however, best known for her involvement on 24 October 1656 as one of the Quaker women who accompanied James Nayler, the leading Quaker preacher, during his symbolic entry into Bristol. She took a leading part in the re-enactment by Nayler of Christ's entry into Jerusalem. During her appearance before the local magistrates on 27 October Erbery told the magistrates that Nayler had earlier raised her from the dead while imprisoned in Exeter between July and August 1656: a claim which Nayler strenuously denied, commenting that only God had the power of life and death. During Nayler's court case for blasphemy at Bristol (5–16 December 1656) Erbery argued that Nayler 'shall sit at the right hand of the Father and shall Judge the world' (Farmer, 19) and claimed further that Nayler was 'the only begotten son of God ... I know of no other Saviour but him' (ibid., 18). Erbery's words led to suspicions that she was either mad or bewitched. Such sentiments were given greater credence when she joined Martha Simmonds and Hannah Stranger near the pilloried Nayler in emulation of the women who had assembled at the crucifixion of Christ.

The Nayler episode nevertheless divided the Quakers, who were now split between those expressing the ecstasy of God's word in ranting behaviour and those who used more conventional Quaker means of proclaiming their message. In 1657 George Fox specifically admonished those Cardiff Quakers who 'had run out with James Naylor' (*Journal of George Fox*, 292), notably Dorcas Erbery, who 'seems not to have expressed any remorse for what occurred. Indeed she may well have been among those who continued to be a disruptive influence among Quakers of the "mainstream" for some months after their release' (Trevett, 'William Erbery and his daughter Dorcas', 37).

Undaunted by her experience of imprisonment and the ridicule heaped upon her, Erbery remained committed to the Quaker cause. It has been suggested further that 'the country-wide disapproval among Friends of James Nayler's followers had done nothing to dampen the ardour of Dorcas Erbery or her enthusiasm for public ministry' (Trevett, 'William Erbery and his daughter Dorcas', 35). Along with her widowed mother Dorcas Erbery, as an unmarried preacher, had time to devote to the Quaker cause and remained unmarried until at least 1658. She returned to Cardiff, where she and Toby Hodge were imprisoned in the summer of 1658 for berating the local presbyterian minister, Benjamin Flower, at St John's Church. The 'Great book of sufferings' compiled by Friends recorded that, although both Quakers were briefly released, they were nevertheless 'brought in againe by order of Reece Davis bailiffe' ('Great book of sufferings', vol. 2, fol. 3). The protector's council called upon the keeper of Cardiff gaol for an account of their 'commitment and detention' as they had not been brought to trial (*CSP dom.*, *1658*, 165). The reply from the keeper stated that both Quakers were detained for their disruption of divine service on 19 July, and as no general sessions court had been held since their apprehension they were being held over until the next assize. It is likely that Dorcas had interrupted Flower on a later occasion as her mittimus was not signed until 31 August. Even after these inquiries, which seem to indicate that the Quakers had acted illegally, they were released and 'neverr brought to tyrall' ('Great book of sufferings', vol. 2, fol. 3).

A further record in 1658 noted that Dorcas Erbery was again arrested and imprisoned in Bristol gaol with many other Friends for 'preaching and declaring the truth to the people in the public places of resort and concourse' (Besse, 1.365). She was again imprisoned in London in 1659 along with her mother and Esther Biddle, another female Quaker missionary, for public preaching. After this date, however, she disappears from the Quaker records and to date there has been little evidence as to her whereabouts

thereafter. It is known that in 1658 she was unmarried, but in the will of her mother, proven in 1670, there is a reference to the unnamed children of Dorcas. No provision was made for Dorcas, which would suggest that she had died in the 1660s. Christine Trevett has suggested that, like many of her co-religionists, she may have emigrated to America or the West Indies. Indeed her sister Lydia Erbery had married Henry *Fell, a Quaker missionary in the West Indies, and many other Friends Dorcas associated with had made their way there. What became of Dorcas Erbery is difficult to tell and it can only be conjectured that she 'married, embraced sobriety and died' or 'remained a troublesome woman in the eyes of society, and a nonconformist one even in Quaker circles, so that she was sidelined quietly in Quaker records' (Trevett, 'William Erbery and his daughter Dorcas', 43).

RICHARD C. ALLEN

Sources 'Great book of sufferings', RS Friends, Lond., vol. 2, fol. 3 · T. Holme, letter to M. Fell, 4 April 1656, RS Friends, Lond., Swarthmore MS 1.205 · *CSP dom.*, *1658*, 165 [mittimus for Dorcas Erbery, dated 31 Aug] · F. Gawler, *A record of some persecutions ... in south Wales* (1659), 16 · R. Farmer, *Sathan inthron'd in his chair of pestilence, or, Quakerism in its exaltation. Being a narrative of James Nailer's entrance into Bristoll, 24 October, together with blasphemous letters about him* (1656), 18–20 · J. Besse, *A collection of the sufferings of the people called Quakers*, 1 (1753), 149, 365, 740 · *JHC*, 7 (1651–9), 470 · will, proved 4 Feb 1670, NL Wales [Mary Erbery of Cardiff] · *Mercurius Politicus* (22 Feb 1658) · J. Miller, *Anti-Christ in man: the Quakers idol* (1655) · J. Miles, *An antidote against the infection of the times. A faithfull watchword from Mount Sion, to prevent the ruine of soules* (1656) · C. Trevett, 'The women around James Nayler, Quaker: a matter of emphasis', *Religion*, 20 (1990), 249–73 · C. Trevett, *Women and Quakerism in the 17th century* (1991), 32, 36, 38, 141 n. 99 · C. Trevett, 'William Erbery and his daughter Dorcas: dissenter and resurrected radical', *Journal of Welsh Religious History*, 4 (1996), 23–50 · M. F. Williams, 'The Society of Friends in Glamorgan, 1654–1900', MA diss., U. Wales, Aberystwyth, 1950, chap. 1, esp. pp. 33–5, 38, 48–9 · M. F. Williams, 'Glamorgan Quakers, 1654–1900', *Morgannwg*, 5 (1961), 49–75, esp. 53–4, 56 · B. L. James, 'The evolution of a radical: the life and career of William Erbery', *Journal of Welsh Ecclesiastical History*, 3 (1986), 31–48, esp. 46–8 · T. M. Rees, *A history of the Quakers in Wales* (1925), 32–3, 80 · M. R. Brailsford, *A Quaker from Cromwell's army: James Naylor* (1927), 110, 122, 154, 157 · *The journal of George Fox*, rev. edn, ed. J. L. Nickalls (1952), 292 · W. C. Braithwaite, *The beginnings of Quakerism*, ed. H. J. Cadbury, 2nd edn (1955), 247, 252–3, 256, 266, 347 · E. Fogelklou, *James Nayler, the rebel saint, 1618–1660*, trans. L. Yapp (1931), 175, 185, 194 · R. C. Allen, 'The Society of Friends in Wales: the case of Monmouthshire, c.1654–1836', PhD diss., U. Wales, Aberystwyth, 1999, 203, 417–8, 434 n. 111 · G. H. Jenkins, *Protestant dissenters in Wales* (1992), chap. 4, esp. p. 37 · C. R. Simpson, 'William Erbery: a forerunner of Quakerism', *Friends' Quarterly Examiner*, 54 (1920), 21–31, 117–25 · W. G. Bittle, *James Nayler, 1618–1660: the Quaker indicted by parliament* (1986), 95, 104, 110, 116, 131, 133, 142, 172 · L. Damrosch, *The sorrows of the Quaker Jesus: James Nayler and the puritan crackdown on the free spirit* (1996), 156–7, 163, 173–4, 178, 188–90, 223–4 · G. F. Nuttall, *The Welsh saints, 1640–1660* (1957), chap. 4 · P. Crawford, *Women and religion in England, 1500–1720* (1993), 166–72 · T. Richards, *A history of the puritan movement in Wales* (1920), 180 · T. Richards, *Religious developments in Wales, 1654–1662* (1923), 253, 262

Erbery [Erbury], **William** (1604/5–1654), clergyman, was probably born at Roath Dagfield, east of Cardiff, and certainly lived there for some time in the 1650s. His father, Thomas Erbery, was a businessman with interests in the iron industry at Merthyr Tudful, but was settled in Cardiff by 1635. The Erburys were not a Welsh family, the name being common in Somerset and Wiltshire, but William's mother (whose name was possibly Elizabeth David) certainly was Welsh. This parentage helps explain Erbery's capacity to understand the Welsh language, but not to speak it. Admitted to Brasenose College, Oxford, at the age of fifteen in February 1620, he matriculated there in November 1621 and graduated BA in 1623, moving thence to Queens' College, Cambridge, where he was incorporated BA in 1624 and proceeded MA in 1626. On 26 December 1626 he subscribed for deacon's orders in the diocese of Bristol, but no further record of his ordination is extant.

Erbery's first clerical appointment was at Newport, Monmouthshire, probably as curate, and it was here that he must have come under the influence of William Wroth, founder of the Independent church at Llanfaches. It is possible that a link between Erbery and Wroth was the Lewis family of Y Fan near Caerphilly, patrons of Wroth and business associates of Erbery's father. It is likely that he consciously adopted the tenets of radical protestantism in a decisive experience of spiritual conversion at Newport. On 7 August 1633 he became vicar of Cardiff, on the presentation of Sir Thomas Lewis of Pen-marc, a scion of the family of Y Fan. Erbery's ministry at Cardiff was influential; about this time he converted Christopher Love, later executed by the Commonwealth government for treason. Soon after his presentation to Cardiff, Erbery and his curate, Walter Cradock, were reported to Archbishop William Laud for refusing to read the Book of Sports; they 'preached very schismatically and dangerously to the people' (*Works of … Laud*, 5.329). Cradock left Cardiff soon after, but Erbery persisted in his opposition to the church hierarchy, and citation in the court of high commission inevitably followed. By 1637 Erbery had written his first book, although it was not until 1639 that a work by him was published. By July 1638 he had resigned as vicar of Cardiff, and spent the next few years in close contact with the church at Llanfaches, although he was never a member of it. In the autumn of 1640 he was preaching to large crowds in Burrington and Chew Stoke, Somerset, and there is some evidence that he preached elsewhere in south Wales and the borders as an itinerant. His message on church government was an undisguised promotion of Independency. He started his own short-lived Independent church at Cardiff, before the civil war scattered the nonconformist cells in different directions in England.

Erbery's own property was plundered by the royalists in 1642; in dire poverty he visited Christopher Love, by now a presbyterian minister at Windsor, who helped him to a post as chaplain in the regiment of the earl of Essex. It was during his war service, and through his contacts with a range of people in London, the midlands, and East Anglia, that Erbery's theology developed in radical directions. He became a regular contender in theological disputations, and transferred his service from Essex's army to the New Model regiments of Ingoldsby and Lambert. He was still an army chaplain in 1647 when at Oxford his preaching appearances offended the presbyterian visitors of the university, delighted ordinary soldiers, and provoked General Sir Thomas Fairfax to remove him from the city. As a participant in the Whitehall army debates of January 1649 Erbery cogently argued that the role of the army was to remove oppressions complained of by the people, and asserted that 'a dozen or twenty-four may in a short time do the kingdom as much good as four hundred that sit in the Parliament in seven years' (A. S. P. Woodhouse, *Puritanism and Liberty*, 2nd edn, 1974, 173).

Under the terms of the Act for the Propagation of the Gospel in Wales of February 1650, Erbery was named as an itinerant minister, and received £200 for his services in 1650 and 1651. In the spring of 1652, however, he became convinced, after at least four years of doubt about the matter, that tithes were oppressive, and severed his links with the lay commissioners. From this point his main work was as a polemicist, writing a large number of tracts from a radical perspective, on social and religious topics. In Glamorgan during 1652 he engaged in disputations with former 'Propagator' colleagues, and he was haled before the Rump Parliament's committee for plundered ministers in March 1653. Charged with preaching blasphemously and contumaciously against lawful churches and ordinances, Erbery mounted a characteristically robust self-defence. It is doubtful whether he ever returned to Wales after this hearing in London, and in October 1653 he attended the committee for tithes, under the Barebone's Parliament, doubtless to argue against a ministry dependent on state sponsorship.

Erbery's earliest publication, of 1639, was in its theology a statement of orthodox Calvinism, but by 1646 at the latest he had become highly unorthodox in his views. According to the hostile commentator Thomas Edwards, Erbery had by this time espoused the doctrine of universal redemption, and become a Seeker. Other unsympathetic observers reported his preaching against the ordained ministry and the visible church, and his promotion of millenarian ideas. Certainly, by 1647 he had developed antinomian ideas on the meaning of sainthood. Running through his theology, from his interventions in the Whitehall debates to his stream of polemical writings in 1652 and 1653, is an acute reading of historical change, which he naturally interpreted as the hand of God. He held the millenarian vision of divinely inspired historical change measured in the broad sweep of the rise and fall of kingdoms and armies, and thus went beyond the orthodox protestant belief in providence as God's often unfathomable interventions in daily life. He shared this millenarian outlook with Morgan Llwyd, minister at Wrexham, with whom he maintained a friendly correspondence, much of it published as it proceeded. He considered the armies in which he had served to have been a more effective instrument of God's will than parliament. Erbery commented often on how king, parliament, and army had been successive rulers, and pursued the logic that the people of God would prevail over all. He analysed recent history to link forms of secular authority with ecclesiastical dispensations: Anglicanism and monarchy, presbyterianism and 'aristocracy' (by which Erbery meant parliament), Independency and 'democracy' (rule by the Rump). This perception of a logically unfolding divine plan for state power made him more optimistic about the potentialities of the protectorate of Oliver Cromwell than some of his Welsh radical contemporaries, notably Vavasor Powell, although Erbery's death only months after the inauguration of that regime cut off any possible disillusionment that might have set in later.

This reading of history brought Erbery to a social outlook that was fiercely egalitarian, and he preached systematically in the interests of minority groups he identified in successive sermons: the poor, the oppressed, and prisoners. After an uncomfortable flirtation with state power in the Welsh experiment, he was moved to argue for an ending of what he called the oppressions against the common people of tithes. He was prepared to concede that lay impropriators could and would defend their rights to tithes as a form of private property, but denied that tithing provided a lawful basis on which to finance the worship of God. In his views on the churches Erbery berated the various sects and groups with equal vigour. By the time of his break with the commissioners for the propagation of the gospel, Baptists, Independents, and presbyterians, let alone the proponents of submerged Anglicanism, had all received short shrift in print and in the disputations which he evidently relished. Believing that no organized, institutionalized church was valid, he advocated meetings of believers, without membership rituals or ordinances of any kind, in private houses.

Erbery maintained links with various of the 'Welsh saints', who observed his disputations in London with a mixture of admiration and a reluctance to endorse his increasingly individualistic theological line. More like Morgan Llwyd than any other of the Welsh radicals, Erbery expressed developed views on Wales and its significance. Again employing his personal reading of history, Erbery pronounced optimistically on the role of the Welsh: as prelacy fell by the Scots, and presbyterianism by the English, so Independents and Baptists would be felled by the Welsh. His vision was broader than a merely British one, however, and Erbery's protestantism, however unorthodox, was never less than internationalist in scope. His belief that Wales had a divinely ordained part to play in the building of the kingdom of God was not maintained in his publications after his disillusionment over tithes set in. But he and Llwyd seem to have maintained their friendship, not to say mutual admiration, and, like Llwyd, Erbery moved away from political activism, despite his fierce language. He concluded that 'the people of God should not meddle with state matters' (*Testimony*, 184–5). After 1652, living at least as much in London as in Wales, Erbery concentrated on exposing the formalism of gathered churches, on one occasion interrupting even the Fifth Monarchists Feake and Simpson at one of their meetings. In his own defence before the committee for plundered ministers, in March 1653 while under house arrest,

he claimed the 'freedom intended to all persons of this nation, to search and try all things' (ibid., 311) and denied that he was one of the 'profane people called Ranters' (ibid., 312).

Erbery died in 1654, a few days after the publication of his *Jack Pudding, or, A Minister Made a Black Pudding* (of which George Thomason's copy is dated 17 March), and certainly before 20 April. The place of his burial is uncertain, although Anthony Wood suggests it was the churchyard of Christ Church Greyfriars. His antiformalism might well have brought him to positions adopted by the Quakers, had he lived longer; indeed, his wife and daughter are known to have become Quakers. By October 1655 Erbery's widow, Mary (*d.* 1667×70), was prominent in the Cardiff Friends' meeting, and in the summer of 1656, both she and her daughter, Dorcas *Erbery, accompanied James Nayler to Devon and Exeter, where both were imprisoned. Both were also participants in Nayler's notorious ride into Bristol after the manner of Christ's entry to Jerusalem, provoking the wrath of members of the second protectorate parliament. Imprisoned for further periods in Cardiff and London for Quaker activities, mother and daughter thus completed the spiritual journey that William Erbery had begun. In 1667 Mary Erbery gave land in Cardiff for a Quaker burial-ground, and what little is known of others bearing the name in the Cardiff area suggests that the wider family was drawn into the Quaker movement. In 1693 the Quaker leader William Penn recommended William Erbery's works to those seeking to understand the origins of their movement. The contemporary perception that William Erbery was deranged at the end of his life, a view accepted by later historians made uncomfortable by the sheer volume and vociferous radical tone of his published work, is not one shared by modern commentators.

STEPHEN K. ROBERTS

Sources *The testimony of William Erbery left upon record for the saints of succeeding ages*, ed. J. Webster (1658) · B. L. James, 'The evolution of a radical: the life and career of William Erbery', *Journal of Welsh Ecclesiastical History*, 3 (1986), 31–48 · W. Erbery, *The mad man's plea* (1653) · *A cleare and necessary vindication ... of Christopher Love* (1651) · W. Erbery, *Apocrypha* (1652) · W. Erbery, *The general epistle to the Hebrews* (1652) · W. Erbery, *The Welsh curate* (1652) · C. Hill, *The experience of defeat: Milton and some contemporaries* (1984) · A. Laurence, *Parliamentary army chaplains, 1642–1651*, Royal Historical Society Studies in History, 59 (1990) · T. Richards, *A history of the puritan movement in Wales* (1920) · Wood, *Ath. Oxon.*, new edn, 3.360 · *The works of the most reverend father in God, William Laud*, 5, ed. J. Bliss (1853) · Foster, *Alum. Oxon.* · Venn, *Alum. Cant.* · [C. B. Heberden], ed., *Brasenose College register, 1509–1909*, 2 vols., OHS, 55 (1909) · J. H. Matthews, ed., *Cardiff records: being materials for a history of the county borough from the earliest times*, 6 vols. (1898–1911) · Glamorgan RO, D/D SF 28 · will, 4 Feb 1670, NL Wales, Llandaff probate records [Mary Erbury] · PRO, PROB 6/29, fol. 519 · R. Farmer, *The imposter dethron'd* (1658), 54

Erc mac Dega (*d.* 513). *See under* Meath, saints of (*act. c.*400–*c.*900).

Erceldoune, Thomas of. *See* Thomas of Erceldoune (*fl.* late 13th cent.).

Ercnat ingen Dáire (*fl.* 5th–6th cent.). *See under* Ulster, saints of (*act. c.*400–*c.*650).

Ercolani, Lucian Randolph (1888–1976), furniture designer and manufacturer, was born on 8 May 1888 at Sant' Angelo in Vado, in the Marche, Italy, the eldest son of Abdon Ercolani, a picture framer, and his wife, a dressmaker. He was left in the care of his grandmother when his parents moved to Florence for his father's employment, being reunited with them in 1895. Ercolani's father was a protestant evangelist, and sent his son to a Baptist school in Florence; however in 1898 local Salvation Army representatives encouraged the father to migrate to London, from where he was shortly able to send for his wife and family and settle at Walthamstow. After a brief schooling, Ercolani began work as a messenger boy for the Salvation Army. He was encouraged by his father to attend night school, and in 1902 enrolled at Shoreditch Technical Institute where he studied drawing and design, followed by the construction of furniture. About 1906 he transferred to the Salvation Army joinery department, where he remained several years. Ercolani took every opportunity to familiarize himself with furniture of all historical periods, by visiting museums and great houses open to the public. On Sundays he played the trombone in the Salvation Army band but he did not have enough free time for rehearsals, and in 1909 the bandmaster asked him to resign. Ercolani then began attending services at his local Baptist church, where he met his future wife, Eva Mary (1886/7–1971), daughter of George Brett, a retired policeman.

At about this time Ercolani left his course at Shoreditch. He began to earn money as a freelance artist and designer and after leaving the joinery he was hired as a furniture designer by Frederick Parker of High Wycombe, the firm which later became Parker-Knoll. Ercolani began teaching in the evenings and it was as his pupil that he first met Edward Gomme, son of a chairmaker and later famous for his G-plan furniture. The two men became lifelong friends and professional colleagues. On the outbreak of the First World War Ercolani volunteered to enlist in the British army, but before he could be directed into active service he was placed on the reserve list and sent to Gomme's factory, which was already fully engaged on war work, principally on aircraft components and propellors. He and Eva Brett were married on 1 June 1915; they had two sons, Lucian and Barry, and a daughter, Roma.

The opportunity of independence came when a consortium of people connected with the furniture trade invited Ercolani to join them in the construction and operation of a new manufactory in High Wycombe. These were Rich and Peters, twine merchants, and Harding and Ironmonger, merchant bankers; they were willing to put up the money, and when Ercolani, who was to be managing director and in charge of the factory, explained that he could not afford to invest, they gave him shares worth £1000. A site was acquired, the factory built and equipped, and production commenced in a modest way in 1920, trading as Furniture Industries.

After surmounting the inevitable problems associated with running a factory during the depression, Ercolani's backers encouraged him to visit the USA. A month in New York brought him many new insights and a glimpse of different business methods, but the most important inspiration came on his last afternoon when he discovered at the back of the Metropolitan Museum a room full of Shaker furniture which greatly impressed him with its simple practicality and beauty of form.

Ercolani's takeover of the respected, but then loss-making, furniture business of Skull, in 1931, was totally unexpected, the offer and acceptance taking only twenty-five minutes. He sold off the unprofitable Skull properties and expanded the joint business. Much of Ercolani's custom came in the form of large outfitting contracts for government or commercial organizations, rather than from the retail trade. His sons were already involved in the business when the Second World War broke out, but they joined the Royal Air Force, returning with rank and decorations at the end of the war. Ercolani, who had taken British nationality in 1923, turned his factory over to war work, beginning with an order for 6 million tent pegs, and ultimately producing 36 million, made from small and malformed timber rejected as useless for more important products.

Towards the end of the war the Board of Trade was seeking to place a large order for cheap windsor-type chairs. The price offered ruled out the use of expensive beech wood, and demanded some inexpensive process of manufacture. Ercolani met the specification by making the chairs of elm, a wood previously considered unsuitable for furniture because of its long-term liability to warp, a problem which he cured by designing a kiln to dry it more effectively. He was the British Furniture Manufacturers' representative on the 'Britain can make it' exhibition, which spurred him to design a suite of sideboard, table, and chairs based on the windsor style. Somewhat to his surprise, these items later appeared at the 1951 Festival of Britain.

From these beginnings Ercolani and his sons developed the successful Ercol range, which became a household name. He was one of the few British furniture manufacturers who succeeded in putting an individual stamp on a mass-market product and, in the face of denials that it was possible, he succeeded in combining machine production with true craftsmanship. Ercolani died at Wycombe General Hospital, High Wycombe, on 9 June 1976.

ANITA MCCONNELL

Sources L. R. Ercolani, *A furniture maker* (1975) • H. Reid, 'Ercolani, Lucian Randolph', *DBB* • *The Times* (12 June 1976) • L. J. Mayes, *The history of chair making in High Wycombe* (1960) • d. cert. • m. cert.
Likenesses R. Spear, portrait, repro. in Ercolani, *A furniture maker*, frontispiece
Wealth at death £99,558: probate, 10 June 1977, *CGPLA Eng. & Wales*

Erdélyi [formerly Diamand], **Arthur** (1908–1977), mathematician, was born on 2 October 1908 in Budapest, the eldest of the five children (three sons and two daughters) of Ignác József Ármin Diamand, a shoe merchant, and his wife, Frederike (Frieda) Roth. After his father's death his mother married Paul Erdélyi, who subsequently adopted Arthur. His secondary school education was at Madách

Arthur Erdélyi (1908–1977), by I. N. Sneddon, 1973

Imre Fögimnázium in Budapest (1918–26). He started his university education in 1926, studying electrical engineering in the Deutsche Technische Hochschule at Brno, Czechoslovakia. He passed the first examination with distinction in 1928 but left, without completing the course, for employment as a mathematician. He acquired the degree of *doctor rerum naturalium* from the German University of Prague in 1938 having submitted a collection of his published papers in lieu of a thesis. He was awarded his doctorate at the last degree ceremony before the university was taken over by the Nazis.

To escape the Nazi persecution of Jews, Erdélyi emigrated to Britain and arrived at Edinburgh in February 1939. At first he was supported by a research grant from the university and financial aid from the Academic Assistance Council (later the Society for the Protection of Science and Learning Limited). This state of affairs continued, despite the award of the degree of DSc by Edinburgh in 1940, until 1941 when he was appointed assistant lecturer. He was promoted to a lectureship in 1942. At this time he was also a consultant to the Admiralty and, with others, was responsible for the proposal to create a national mathematical laboratory which eventually became part of the National Physical Laboratory.

Erdélyi married, on 4 November 1942, Eva Griffel, daughter of Frederic Neuburg, of Litoměřice, Czechoslovakia, and Helene (*née* Feitis), second cousin of Max Perutz. They had no children, but there was a stepson who came to know Erdélyi well when he was a teenager. Erdélyi became a naturalized British citizen in 1947 and was promoted to a senior lectureship in 1948, having been elected a fellow of the Royal Society of Edinburgh in 1945. His two brothers and one of his sisters died in a concentration camp during the war.

In 1949 Erdélyi was appointed as full professor by the California Institute of Technology, one of his duties being the direction of the Bateman project, the task of editing the mass of notes left by Harry Bateman on his death in 1946. With the assistance of W. Magnus, F. Oberhettinger, and F. G. Tricomi three volumes of *Higher Transcendental Functions* and two volumes of *Tables of Integral Transforms* were ready by 1951. Erdélyi carried out the mammoth job of seeing the five volumes through the press while fulfilling a normal teaching load at the institute, supervising two research students, and looking after his wife who had contracted tuberculosis. These books have been used and referred to by so many scientists that their impact on science is immeasurable and the scientific community is indebted to Erdélyi for his devotion to this project. He was elected a foreign member of the Academy of Sciences of Turin in 1953.

Erdélyi returned to Edinburgh as head of department and professor of mathematics in 1964 at considerable personal sacrifice because he felt that his alma mater (as he regarded it) needed his help. Here, as a talented violinist and violist, he participated in chamber music and, as a keen walker, explored the Scottish highlands, awakening a deep interest in geology (and a passion for deserts when he was abroad).

Erdélyi contributed nearly 200 papers to learned journals and his quality was recognized by election as FRS in 1975. In 1977 he had the rare distinction of being awarded the Gunning Victoria jubilee prize of the Royal Society of Edinburgh. He was also president of the Edinburgh Mathematical Society (1971–2). A special issue of *Applicable Analysis* and the *Proceedings* of the 1978 Dundee conference on differential equations were dedicated to him. He was a superb expositor and lecturer, who received ovations at international colloquia. One reason for this was his mastery of special functions, for he unveiled the beauty of the underlying patterns with typical elegance. Another area in which he was a major figure was asymptotics; his systematic exploitation of asymptotic scale and Volterra singular integral equations provided a general theory for differential equations and subsequently for the asymptotic evaluation of integrals. Later he was involved in laying the foundations of matched asymptotic expansions. Another field for which he forged the fundamental tools was that of fractional integration—the Erdélyi–Kober operations, leading to many applications in integral and partial differential equations, are now basic. Erdélyi's innovation and exposition initiated a considerable amount of modern research.

As a head of department Erdélyi displayed courtesy and faultless manners to all. Level-headed and tolerant, he was always in command and his natural authority was immediately recognizable. His dress was dapper, with spotless white shirts and bow tie. His cheerful disposition was unaffected by ill health in later years. He remarked, on appearing in the department not long after major surgery: 'My doctor forbade me to teach; he did not forbid me to learn' (Jones, 276). Erdélyi died suddenly of heart failure on 12 December 1977, at his home, 26 Gilmour Road, Edinburgh. He was survived by his wife.   D. S. JONES, rev.

Sources D. S. Jones, *Memoirs FRS*, 25 (1979), 267–86 · *WWW* · d. cert.
Archives Bodl. Oxf., Society for the Protection of Science and Learning; Home Office files
Likenesses I. N. Sneddon, photograph, 1973, repro. in *Memoirs FRS* [facing p. 267] [*see illus.*] · photographs, RS
Wealth at death £52,667.30—in UK: confirmation, 10 April 1978, *CCI* · £132,650.75—outside UK: confirmation, 10 April 1978, *CCI*

Erdeswick [Erdeswicke], **Sampson** (c.1538–1603), historian, was the son of Hugh Erdeswick of Sandon, Staffordshire (1520/21–1596), and Mary, daughter of Roger Leigh of Ridge in Sutton Downe, Cheshire. He was born probably in the later 1530s: his parents were married by 1537 and he entered Brasenose College, Oxford, in 1553. The Erdeswick family took their name from their estate of that name in Minshull Vernon, Cheshire; they exchanged it in 1311–12 for half the manor of Leighton, also in Cheshire, having acquired the other half in the mid-1280s. They acquired Sandon by marriage in 1338.

In 1555 Sampson Erdeswick was admitted to the Inner Temple, but he seems to have played little part in the life of the inn. He was one of a group of Roman Catholic recusants there and was remembered as such in 1577, although none was then still in residence. By 1575 he was living in Staffordshire, at Sandon, and along with his father was in constant trouble for recusancy. In August that year, immediately after Elizabeth I's progress through Staffordshire, they were both before the privy council at Worcester with several other Staffordshire gentry for failing to attend the parish church. All admitted the charge, 'alleging their consciences and examples of their forefathers who taught them so' (*APC*, 1575–7, 15). Hugh and Sampson were committed to the bishop of Worcester to be persuaded into conformity, although Sampson was allowed to fetch his books and notes from home. In November they were transferred to the bishop-elect of Norwich (Edmund Freake) and a Dr Busshe, but without success. In December Sampson was sent to close confinement in the Marshalsea in London with one servant; Hugh was sent to the Gatehouse in Westminster. They were released temporarily in April 1576. In June they were given a further respite on condition of reporting every month to the bishop of Coventry and Lichfield 'to make offer unto him of conference in religion to be resolved in those points that they stand in doubt of'. They were not to 'suffer any unnecessary repair of people' to their home, nor were they to journey away from home to meet 'such persons as be noted to be of the contrary religion' (ibid., 145–6).

In 1580 Hugh and Sampson Erdeswick were again summoned before the privy council. In May 1582 there was a fracas during a meeting of justices in Sandon churchyard when Hugh struck one of them with his staff. The council sent a pursuivant for him and in June ordered Sandon Hall to be searched for a massing priest, other suspect persons, and popish trumpery. Sampson, described as one of the most obstinate and dangerous Staffordshire recusants, was then in trouble with the council for having been married during a mass, and his name begins to appear in the exchequer records as a convicted recusant. Father and son had their armour confiscated in 1585. Early in 1588, under the impending threat of the Armada, the earl of Shrewsbury, as lord lieutenant of Staffordshire, ordered the sheriff and deputy lieutenants to arrest Sampson along with other Catholic gentry and to commit him to the rector of Stoke-on-Trent; he had, however, retired to the family estate at Leighton, having perhaps been forewarned. Later the same year he was committed to the bishop's palace at Ely. He was back at Sandon by 1592 when he was committed to the custody of the firmly protestant Richard Bagot of Blithfield. In 1597 he was one of a large group of Staffordshire recusants summoned to appear at the next assizes.

Sampson Erdeswick played a prominent part in the running of the Sandon estate even before succeeding his father, figuring in most of the feet of fines relating to Sandon and its neighbourhood from 1580. Both men are described as lords of Sandon manor in a petition from the inhabitants, accusing them of inclosing much of the land and converting arable to pasture. It was Sampson who contributed in 1592 to the rebuilding of the shire hall in Stafford. By the 1590s Hugh seems to have been a sick man and living at Leighton.

Sampson Erdeswick's main activity was that of an antiquary, at least in his later years. To his friend William Camden he was 'venerandae antiquitatis cultor maximus' ('a very great reverencer of venerable antiquity'; Camden, 518). In 1586, at Sampson's request, Robert Glover, Somerset herald, wrote and emblazoned the Erdeswick pedigree. Sampson had two trees bearing his ancestors' shields painted in the chancel of Sandon church. He had further ancestral shields depicted in the east window and had two windows painted on the chancel walls containing more arms. In the gallery of Sandon Hall he set up the names and arms of Staffordshire gentry. According to his antiquarian friend William Burton he claimed to be the real author of *The True Use of Armorie*, published in 1592 under the name of his assistant William Wyrley. By 1598 he was a member of the Society of Antiquaries, which had been meeting in London since about 1586; he was probably admitted through Camden's influence.

About 1593 Erdeswick began work on what he called a 'View' of Staffordshire and Cheshire. By his death he had finished a draft of Staffordshire but had written little of the Cheshire section. Sir William Dugdale described it as 'a brief but elaborate work ... compiled from public records and ancient evidences' (Dugdale, *Antient Usage*, 4n). It perambulated the county place by place along the rivers—a method used by Camden in his *Britannia*—starting in the north at the source of the Trent and recording whatever was worthy of note. That meant primarily genealogy and heraldry, but the work also includes natural features, place names, and archaeological remains. Buildings are noted, especially castles and manor houses. Churches are mentioned mainly for their monuments, but there is a description of the close and cathedral at Lichfield; Erdeswick considered the cathedral 'one of the fairest and best repaired in England (being thoroughly builded and finished, which few are)' (Erdeswick, 281). There follows a list of the bishops, but for the city of Lichfield there is mention only of its topography and its government. Towns in fact are only briefly noted, mainly as market centres. For Stafford mention is made of its government, its custom of borough English, its walls, its castles, and its two friaries, but most of the section is taken up by the history of the Stafford family and a description of their arms. The account of Staffordshire ends with a discussion of early landholding, with particular reference to Domesday Book.

Erdeswick's personality often comes through: he enjoys a good story and local gossip; he dislikes the parvenu. In view of his staunch recusancy it is surprising that there is no mention of religious changes, apart from a laconic mention of the fate of Calwich Abbey: 'now a Lancashire gentleman is owner thereof; who, as I have heard, hath made a parlour of the chancel, a hall of the church, and a kitchen of the steeple' (Erdeswick, 489–90). When Erdeswick speaks of 'the iniquity of this age' (ibid., 250) it is because the copper has been removed from a monument at Caverswall. The work is addressed to an unnamed recipient, probably Camden, and the author likes to buttonhole his reader, particularly in his discussion of his sources. The frequent inclusion of sources, documentary, heraldic, monumental, and oral, is a notable advance on earlier topographical writing. In all, the 'View' is a learned but attractively informal work, pointing the way towards the fuller achievement of Dugdale over half a century later.

Erdeswick married twice, each time taking a wife from within the recusant community. His first was Elizabeth, daughter and coheir of Humphrey Dixwell of Churchover, Warwickshire, and they had five daughters. In 1593 he married Mary, daughter of Francis Neale of Prestwold in Keythorpe, Leicestershire, and widow of Thomas Digby of Tugby, Leicestershire. She had fourteen children from her first marriage, and she and Erdeswick had two sons and a daughter.

Erdeswick died at Sandon on 28 June 1603. According to Anthony Wood, writing some ninety years later, Sampson had been 'oftentimes crazed, especially in his last days, and fit then for no kind of serious business … as 'tis very well known at this day among the chief of the College of Arms' (Wood, *Ath. Oxon.*, 2.217–18). In 1601 he erected his own tomb in Sandon church, with a more than life-size recumbent effigy of himself and the figures of his two wives kneeling in niches above. He adorned it with coats of arms and the Erdeswick pedigree from 1086.

William Burton, who regarded the 'View' as 'opus grande, doctissimum, laboratissime que navatum' ('a

great work, very learned, and most painstakingly accomplished'; Nichols, 3/1, xv), stated that Erdeswick had intended to publish it when completed. A version in the author's own hand was copied by Dugdale but subsequently lost. In the epistle dedicatory to his own *Antiquities of Warwickshire* (1656), Dugdale stated that Erdeswick's memory was 'very precious' in Staffordshire 'for his great knowledge in antiquities'. By 1842 the existence of twenty-five copies of the 'View' had been traced; the whereabouts of another fifteen were unknown. An unsatisfactory edition was published in 1717 under the title *A Survey of Staffordshire* and reissued in 1723. Thomas Harwood of Lichfield produced a scholarly edition in 1820, and his further revised edition of what was still called *A Survey* appeared posthumously in 1844.

M. W. GREENSLADE

Sources M. W. Greenslade, *The Staffordshire historians*, Staffordshire RS, 4th ser., 11 (1982), chap. 3 · S. Erdeswick, *A survey of Staffordshire*, ed. T. Harwood, new edn (1844) · G. Camdeno [W. Camden], *Britannia, sive, Florentissimorum regnorum, Angliae, Scotiae, Hiberniae*, new edn (1600), 518 · W. Dugdale, *The antient usage in bearing of … arms* (1682), 4n · Wood, *Ath. Oxon.*, new edn, 2.217–18 · *APC*, 1575–7 · will, PRO, PROB 11/102, sig. 82 · inquisition post mortem, 10 Sept 1603, PRO, C142/281, no. 91 · J. Nichols, *The history and antiquities of the county of Leicester*, 3/1 (1800); repr. (1971) · W. Dugdale, *The antiquities of Warwickshire illustrated* (1656) · M. McKisack, *Medieval history in the Tudor age* (1971)

Archives BL, extracts from heraldic and antiquarian collections, Harley MSS 338, 471, 473, 506, 814, 1990 · Bodl. Oxf., account of Staffordshire with MS additions and annotations; collections · CUL, survey of Staffordshire [copy] · S. Antiquaries, Lond., MS 99 · Staffs. RO, pedigrees, notes and papers, D.649/1/1

Likenesses effigy on monument, 1601, Sandon church, Staffordshire · W. Dugdale, drawing, 1640, repro. in Greenslade, *Staffordshire historians*

Wealth at death grain and moveable goods: will, PRO, PROB 11/102, sig. 82 · settled Sandon on second wife in 1593 and Leighton to father, both with reversion to self and male heirs: inquisition post mortem, 10 Sept 1603, PRO, chancery, C 142/281, no. 91

Ergome, John (*fl.* 1385–1386). *See under* John of Bridlington (*c*.1320–1379).

Erhard [St Erhard, Erard] (*d.* before **784**), bishop of Regensburg, bears an alternative name of Erard or Erhart. He is associated with the cult of St Odile in the Vosges, as well as with Regensburg, where he is supposed to have continued the evangelizing work of St Emmeranus. He is commemorated, as a bishop, in the confraternity book of the abbey of St Peter at Salzburg, composed in 784. The calendars of the monasteries of Einsiedeln and Niedermünster at Regensburg, written in the tenth and eleventh centuries respectively, give his feast day as 8 January, but there is no reliable indication of the year of his death. He was buried in the Niedermünsterkirche, Regensburg, and was canonized by Pope Leo IX in 1052.

It is almost certain that Erhard did not come from the British Isles, despite the fact that shortly after 1152 monks at the Irish abbey at Regensburg wrote a life of Albart, another saint of obscure origin, which claimed that both he and Erhard, or Erard, as they called him, were of Irish birth and had found their way to Regensburg, where Erard had died, after a pilgrimage to Rome and Jerusalem. There is no earlier corroboration of this story and the life of Erhard written in Germany between 1053 and 1074 gives an entirely different account of the saint's origin, making him a native of the Narbonne region. Even by that time, a number of divergent stories about Erhard were in circulation. It is likely that the Irish monks had attempted to give this popular saint an Irish pedigree because of the similarity between the German Erhard and the well-attested Irish name Erard. In the thirteenth century the German and Irish traditions blended at Regensburg to make Erhard, Albart, and Hildulf, the founder of Moyenmoutier, companions in the effort to evangelize Germany in the eighth century. This story, in its fourteenth-century version, is reproduced in the *Dictionary of National Biography*.

MARIOS COSTAMBEYS

Sources Paul, 'Vita Erhardi episcopi Bavarici', *Passiones vitaeque sanctorum aevi Merovingici*, ed. B. Krusch and W. Levison, MGH Scriptores Rerum Merovingicarum, 6 (Hanover, 1913) · S. Herzberg-Fränkel, ed., *Dioecesis Salisburgensis*, MGH Necrologia Germaniae, 2 (Berlin, 1890–1904) · 'Kalendarium Einsieldense', *Acta sanctorum: November*, 2/1 (Brussels, 1894) · M. Gerbert, ed., *Monumenta inferioris Ratisbonense*, Monumenta Veteris Liturgiae Alemannicae, 1 (1777), 492 · A. Dürrwaechter, *Die Gesta Caroli Magni der Regensburger Schottenlegende* (1897) · P. Morsbach, 'Der heilige Erhard', *Ratisbona sacra* (1989) · *Lexikon des Mittelalters*, 3 (1986), 2138–9

Erichsen, Sir John Eric, baronet (1818–1896), surgeon, born at Copenhagen on 19 July 1818, was the eldest son of Eric Erichsen, banker, of Copenhagen, and his wife, who belonged to the Govett family of Somerset. Erichsen received his early education at the Mansion House, Hammersmith. He obtained his medical education at University College, London, and was admitted a member of the Royal College of Surgeons on 11 January 1839. Next he visited Paris, and then he served as house surgeon at University College Hospital. In 1842 Erichsen married Mary Elizabeth (d. 1893), the eldest daughter of Captain Thomas Cole RN. They had no children.

In 1844 Erichsen was appointed joint lecturer on anatomy and physiology at the Westminster Hospital and between 1846 and 1848 he was joint lecturer on anatomy. Also in 1844 he acted as secretary of the physiological section of the British Association for the Advancement of Science, and he was afterwards a member of the committee appointed both to inquire into the mechanism and effects of asphyxia and to suggest methods for its prevention and cure. He drew up a report, published in 1845 under the title *An Essay on Asphyxia*, which won the Fothergillian gold medal of the Royal Humane Society.

In 1848 Erichsen was appointed assistant surgeon to University College Hospital, in succession to John Phillips Potter. Two years later he became full surgeon to the hospital, and professor of surgery at University College; his rapid promotion was due to the various quarrels and resignations which followed the death of Robert Liston. Erichsen retained the chair of surgery until 1866, when he was appointed Holme professor of clinical surgery. He resigned the office of surgeon in 1875, and was immediately appointed consulting surgeon.

Erichsen became a fellow of the Royal College of Surgeons on 17 April 1845, and was a member of its council from 1869 to 1885; he was a member of its court of examiners (1875–9), vice-president (1878–9), and president (1880). He was president of the Royal Medical and Chirurgical Society (1879–81), and in 1881 he was president at the surgical section at the meeting in London of the International Medical Congress.

As a Liberal, Erichsen contested (unsuccessfully) the parliamentary seat of the universities of Edinburgh and St Andrews in 1885. He was elected a fellow of the Royal Society in 1876, and in 1884 the honorary degree of LLD was conferred upon him by the University of Edinburgh. In 1877 he was appointed the first inspector under the 1876 Cruelty to Animals Act, and he was made surgeon-extraordinary to the queen in the same year. He was created a baronet in January 1895. But the honour which he regarded as most important was his election in 1887 to the post of president of the council of University College, an office he occupied until his death.

Erichsen's reputation rests mainly on his authorship of a widely read textbook, which claimed that surgery was a science to be studied rather than an art to be displayed. He had studied the subject of aneurysm from early in his career and he contributed several articles dealing with its pathology and treatment. Later in life he turned his attention to the effects of railway accidents on the nervous system and wrote on the so-called 'railway spine'. In 1853 he published the first edition of the *Science and Art of Surgery*. A pirated edition was issued by the American government to every medical officer in the Federal army during the American Civil War. It was translated into German by Dr Thudichum of Halle; into Italian by Dr Longhi of Milan; and into Spanish by Dr Benavente and Dr Ribera.

Erichsen died on 23 September 1896 at Folkestone, Kent, and was buried in London, in Hampstead cemetery. His estate was valued at nearly £90,000. The baronetcy ceased on his death.

D'A. POWER, rev. B. A. BRYAN

Sources E. A. S., *PRS*, 61 (1897), i–iii · *The Lancet* (3 Oct 1896), 962–3 · *BMJ* (3 Oct 1896), 885–7 · *The Times* (24 Sept 1896) · *The Times* (28 Sept 1896) · Boase, *Mod. Eng. biog.*
Likenesses C. Baugniet, lithograph, 1853, BM, Wellcome L. · Claudet Studio, cabinet photograph, 1880, NPG · G. Yerrard, photograph, 1881, Wellcome L. · W. H. Thornycroft, marble bust, exh. RA 1883, UCL · replica, RCS Eng. · R. Burgess, group portrait, 1973 (of doctors and residents in the Wellcome Institute, London) · Barraud, photograph, Wellcome L. · Beguon Co., coloured lithograph
Wealth at death £89,633 10s. 6d.: probate, 17 Oct 1896, *CGPLA Eng. & Wales*

Erik Bloodaxe [Eiríkr Blóðöx, Eiríkr Haraldsson] (d. 954), viking leader and king of Northumbria, was the son of Harald Haarfagre ('Harald Fairhair'), king of Norway (*fl.* 872?–*c*.930). The identity of his father can be inferred from the report of version E of the Anglo-Saxon Chronicle, which describes him as 'Harold's son' (*Haroldes sunu*, *ASC*, s.a. 952, text E). Few facts about Erik are as reliably attested. Although the various extant versions of the

Anglo-Saxon Chronicle are the most contemporary and dependable written sources for Erik, they nevertheless differ in their narratives of his career in Britain. The faint image of Erik in the near contemporary evidence contrasts with the strongly drawn portrayal of a warrior king in the Icelandic sagas of the twelfth and thirteenth centuries. Although the saga writers' information is often demonstrably defective, it offers an attractive richness of detail that has led to attempts to vindicate some, at least, of their stories about Erik, in order to construct a coherent narrative of his life. The motivation for such attempts is, above all, the prominence that Erik has in the saga literature, in which his profile is uniquely high for a tenth-century Scandinavian king in the British Isles. Why he attained this status in Scandinavian culture, typified by the epithet Bloodaxe (Blóðöx), which was first coined by *Egils saga* of the late twelfth century, is an enduring puzzle.

Slotting together the annals in the two principal versions of the Anglo-Saxon Chronicle for this period, texts D and E, produces a continuous narrative for Erik's career in Britain. His first appearance, in an annal for 948, records his selection as their king by the Northumbrians, meaning the inhabitants of the kingdom centred on York, formerly known as Deira. By this act the Northumbrians reneged on a pledge that they had made shortly before to King Eadred (r. 946–55), whose response was to invade and ravage Northumbria, burning down St Wilfrid's minster at Ripon. As the English army returned southward, the army of York overtook its rearguard at Castleford, and 'made a great slaughter there'. When an enraged Eadred threatened to return to Northumbria and 'destroy it utterly', however, the Northumbrians abandoned Erik and paid reparations to the English king (*ASC*, s.a. 948, text D). If text E of the chronicle is correct, the Northumbrians' loyalty once again proved fickle, for its annal for 949 records the arrival in Northumbria, for the second time, of Óláf Sihtricson. According to text E, in 952 Óláf in turn was driven out, and the Northumbrians again received Erik as their king. Both versions agree that Erik was expelled for the final time in 954, 'and Eadred succeeded to the kingdom of the Northumbrians' (*ASC*, s.a. 954, texts D, E). A twelfth-century Durham tradition records that after his expulsion Erik was killed by a certain Maccus, son of Óláf. The *Flores historiarum* of Roger of Wendover (d. 1236), which includes material drawn from an earlier lost set of northern annals, adds that Erik was betrayed, with his son Henricus (Hæric, Erik) and his brother Reginaldus (Ragnall), by Earl Oswulf of Bamburgh, and was treacherously killed by Maccus on Steinmor—that is, Stainmore, across which runs the Roman road (the modern A66) from York to Cumbria. Oswulf then became earl of all Northumbria.

While this narrative is coherent as far as it goes, others are possible, for the chronology of the Anglo-Saxon Chronicle for this period is extremely confused. In particular, version E's annals dated 949 and 952 may be as awry as that entered under 948, which records the death of Edmund and accession of Eadred, the true date of which is 946. The sixth section of the *Historia regum* attributed to Symeon of Durham (*fl. c.*1090–*c.*1128), which preserves from an earlier northern source annals covering some of these events, often under different dates, only complicates matters further. The evidence of southern English charters suggests that Eadred did not claim to rule over the Northumbrians from 947/8 to 948/9 and from 950/51 to 951/2, leaving room for the sequence of short reigns at York that the standard narrative envisages, that is, Erik–Eadred–Óláf–Erik. Taking account of the severe dislocation of the annals' dates, however, suggests a different sequence, giving Erik only one reign at York. The two different coin types inscribed with Erik's name may correspond to his two supposed reigns, or may represent two issues in a single reign. The contemporary and near contemporary sources offer little certainty as to Erik's status in Northumbria: his influence appears to have been less important than that of Wulfstan, archbishop of York, whose attitude towards him remains frustratingly unclear. Such sources also record a Scottish raid as far as the Tees in 948 or 949, which may have been directed against, or mounted in favour of, Erik, though the protagonist could just as easily have been Óláf Sihtricson. Similarly, it is not certain that, as sometimes suggested, Erik was the leader of the Scandinavian force that the Irish annals attest as defeating a combined army of Scots, Strathclyde Britons, and Bamburgh English in the battle that they date to 952.

Erik appears in a brighter light in the sagas written in Iceland in the late twelfth and thirteenth centuries, principally the sagas of Hákon the Good (*Hákonar saga Góða*) and of Harald Finehair (*Haralds saga ins Hárfagra*) in *Heimskringla* by Snorri Sturluson (d. 1241), *Orkneyinga Saga*, *Egils saga*, and the longer saga of Óláf Tryggvason (*Óláfs saga Tryggvasonar en mesta*). These allege that Erik's mother was Ragnhild, the daughter of a Danish king. Erik is said to have begun his viking career at the age of twelve. On an expedition to the White Sea he discovered his wife, Gunnhild, the daughter either of one Özurr Tóti, or of Gorm inn Gamli (Gorm the Old), king of Denmark. She is said to have practised witchcraft. Erik became king in Norway after the death of his father, Harald, and slew several of his brothers and rivals, before being ousted by his younger brother Hákon, who had been brought up at the court of King Æthelstan (d. 939) in England. Erik made his way to Orkney, where he immediately commanded the loyalty of the joint earls, Arnkel and Erlend, sons of Einarr (*fl.* 900). He was then placed in charge of the Northumbrian kingdom by Æthelstan, and fixed his residence at York. Having been displaced by Óláf Sihtricson during Edmund's reign, he undertook plundering expeditions in the neighbouring lands, but was eventually killed in battle against Óláf, along with the Orkney earls and five other princes. The sagas record the names of two of his children: Ragnhild, whom the thirteenth-century *Orkneyinga Saga* portrays as a power-hungry schemer who married three earls of Orkney in succession, and Harald Gráfeld

(Harald Greycloak) (*d. c*.970), who became king of Norway.

A funeral lay for Erik, *Eiríksmál*, reputedly written at Gunnhild's instigation soon after he was killed, is included in the saga *Fagrskinna*. Only the opening fragment, in which the god Odin welcomes Erik into Valhalla, survives. Erik also appears in *Egils saga*, as the enemy of the famous psychopath and poet Egill Skallagrímsson. When he came before Erik at York, Egill was allowed to redeem his head after he eulogized the king in the praise poem *Höfudlausn* ('The head-saver'). Notwithstanding this kingly act of clemency, the Icelandic texts generally give Erik a bad press, probably because of their antipathy towards centralized royal authority rather than through any reliance on genuine historical tradition. They are largely responsible for his enduring reputation for ferocious barbarism, cataloguing as they do a career of plunder and homicide remarkable even among tenth-century vikings. The contemporary evidence suggests that in fact Erik was no more violent than other kings and warlords of the time.

Lacking a historical basis, the saga's stories add no reliable information to Erik's biography, but there are hints that not all of them are entirely fictional. Although it receives no support from the annals, a link between Erik and the famous Æthelstan became current relatively early. The life of St Catroe, written *c*.1000 by a monk who apparently knew the saint, recounts Catroe's journey, to be dated apparently to 939–40, from his native Strathclyde to the continent, visiting on the way a King Erich in York and King Edmund in England. The dating indicates that King Erich could have been appointed by Æthelstan, and his presence at York would fill a gap in the sources for Northumbria between the battle of 'Brunanburh' in 937 and the advent of Olaf Guthfrithson in 940; there is, however, no explicit statement that this Erich is identical with Erik Bloodaxe. Tales of Erik's plundering Strathclyde, Scotland, Wales, and Ireland may be less fanciful, since it is likely, as the sagas report, that he did not dare to deprive the Northumbrians of their land in order to reward his followers, and had to turn to viking raids instead. It should be noted, however, that no Irish source reports raiders answering to the description of Erik and his men at this period.

Erik Bloodaxe embodies the contrasts that characterize the modern perception of the viking world, and it is in this that his true significance lies. He was a warrior chieftain in fact and, even more so, in fable. He was a viking leader from the Norwegian royal dynasty, apparently opposed equally to the Dublin–York dynasty of Scandinavian rulers, represented by Óláf Sihtricson, and to the West Saxon kings. The range of his activity, straddling the North Sea and the entire north British mainland, would only be enhanced if he can be identified with the 'Éiric, king of the Isles' mentioned in the twelfth-century Irish saga *Caithréim Chellacháin Chaisil*. Despite the decided heathenism of *Eiríksmál*, he was clearly not antipathetic towards Christianity: he is said to have given Catroe a favourable reception, and his name appears, as 'Eiric rex Danorum' ('Erik, king of the Danes')—probably indicating the origin of many of his subjects—in the contemporary commemoration book (*Liber vitae*) of the church of Durham. This is a surprising memorial for one whose funeral lay has Odin praise him 'because he has reddened his sword in many a land … and carried a bloodstained blade' (*Eiríksmál*, 97). MARIOS COSTAMBEYS

Sources A. P. Smyth, *Scandinavian York and Dublin*, 2 (1979) • F. M. Stenton, *Anglo-Saxon England*, 3rd edn (1971) • B. E. Crawford, *Scandinavian Scotland* (1987) • P. Sawyer, 'The last Scandinavian kings of York', *Northern History*, 31 (1995), 39–43 • N. Lund, 'Scandinavia, *c.* 700–1066', *The new Cambridge medieval history*, 2, ed. R. McKitterick (1995), 202–27 • C. P. Wormald, 'Viking studies: whence and whither?', *The Vikings*, ed. R. T. Farrell (1982), 128–53 • *ASC*, s.a. 948, 954 [text D]; s.a. 949, 952, 954 [text E] • John of Worcester, *Chron.* • 'Historia regum', Symeon of Durham, *Opera*, vol. 2 • *Rogeri de Wendover liber qui dicitur flores historiarum*, ed. H. G. Hewlett, 3 vols., Rolls Series, [84] (1886–9) • Snorri Sturluson, *Heimskringla: sagas of the Norse kings*, ed. P. Foote, trans. S. Laing (1961) • *Eiríksmál, Anglo-Saxon and Norse poems*, ed. and trans. N. Kershaw (1922) • H. Pálsson and P. Edwards, eds., *Egils saga* (1976) • H. Pálsson and P. Edwards, eds. and trans., *The Orkneyinga saga: the history of the earls of Orkney* (1978) • Ó. Halldórsson, ed., *Óláfs saga Tryggvasonar en mesta* (1958) • [A. H. Thompson], ed., *Liber vitae ecclesiae Dunelmensis*, SurtS, 136 (1923) • A. O. Anderson, ed. and trans., 'Vita Kaddroae', *Early sources of Scottish history, AD 500 to 1286*, 1 (1922), 431–43 [based on edn in *Acta Sanctorum: Martius*, 1 (Antwerp, 1688), 468–81] • A. Bugge, *Caithréim Cellacháin Caisil* (1905) • S. Keynes, *An atlas of attestations in Anglo-Saxon charters, c.670–1066* (privately printed, Cambridge, 1993) • S. Kelly, *Royal styles in Anglo-Saxon diplomas* (1993)

Erik of Hlathir [Eiríkr af Hlaðir, Eiríkr Hákonarson], **earl of Northumbria** (*fl.* 995–1023), magnate, was the son of Hákon Sigurdson, earl (*jarl*) of Hlathir, or Lade (now part of Trondheim), in Norway. He married Gytha, daughter of *Swein Forkbeard, king of the Danes, and was thus a brother-in-law of King Cnut.

After the death of Harald Gráfeld (Harald Greycloak; *c*.970) the earls of Hlathir were the most powerful chieftains in Norway. Their court was a centre for the production of skaldic verse; Erik, poorly documented in England, was a famed warrior in northern Europe. In the Scandinavian power struggles of the late tenth century Hákon and his sons, Erik and Swein, often allied with the Danes. By the 990s these struggles involved the prestige and profit of raids on England. In 995 the successful adventurer, Óláf Tryggvason, backed by the English king, Æthelred, returned from England to take the Norwegian throne. Hákon was killed and Erik and his brother went into exile, Erik taking refuge with Swein of Denmark. Now if not before he raided widely around the Baltic, until in 999 he joined the Swedish–Danish alliance that defeated and removed Óláf at the battle of Svold. He and his brother then ruled western Norway, acknowledging some Danish lordship. This military and political background made him an obvious companion to his brother-in-law Cnut in the conquest of England in 1015–16. English and Scandinavian sources agree on his significance in the important siege and fighting around London in these years. His involvement in the famous battle at Ringmere in 1010 is found in Scandinavian sources alone and is debatable.

Erik was one of Cnut's most important followers in England after 1016. After the murder of Uhtred of Bamburgh, earl of Northumbria, he was made earl 'as Uhtred was' according to the Anglo-Saxon Chronicle, although Durham sources record Eadulf's succeeding his brother Uhtred. Northumbria was often divided along the Tees in the later tenth century, though Erik may have had overall lordship with Eadulf holding of him. Erik was frequently at court from 1018 to 1023, and is alleged to have been instrumental in the death of Eadric Streona, ealdorman of Mercia, in 1017. He may have been Cnut's trusted companion, but he did not become the most important earl until Thorkell's outlawry in 1021. Erik had lost power in Norway to Óláf Haraldsson during the English campaign, whereas Thorkell remained an independent force. Raids on England had meshed with and been driven by Scandinavian politics. The sparse sources contain no hint of the likely cross-currents and tensions among men like Erik, Thorkell, and Cnut in these years. Erik disappeared in 1023, by which date he must have been forty, if not considerably older. William of Malmesbury has him driven back to Scandinavia into exile. Cnut's subsequent favour to his son Hákon argues against his father's disgrace; Hákon was an earl in the west midlands and Cnut's regent in Norway between 1028 and 1030, and may have been married to Cnut's niece. But the king's favour could equally have been an attempt to limit the repercussions of Erik's fall. Scandinavian sources contain no hint of Erik's exile; they place his death in England, due to loss of blood after an operation.

PAULINE STAFFORD

Sources A. Campbell, ed. and trans., *Encomium Emmae reginae*, CS, 3rd ser., 72 (1949), 66–73 · S. Keynes, 'Cnut's earls', *The reign of Cnut*, ed. A. R. Rumble (1994), 43–88 · P. Sawyer, 'Cnut's Scandinavian empire', *The reign of Cnut*, ed. A. R. Rumble (1994), 10–22 · R. Poole, 'Skaldic verse and Anglo-Saxon history: some aspects of the period 1009–1016', *Speculum*, 62 (1987), 265–98 · William of Malmesbury, *Gesta regum Anglorum / The history of the English kings*, ed. and trans. R. A. B. Mynors, R. M. Thomson, and M. Winterbottom, 2 vols., OMT (1998–9), vol. 1 · M. K. Lawson, *Cnut: the Danes in England in the early eleventh century* (1993) · W. E. Kapelle, *The Norman conquest of the north: the region and its transformation, 1000–1135* (1979)

Erith, Raymond Charles (1904–1973), architect, was born on 7 August 1904 at 50 Filey Avenue, Upper Clapton, London, the second child and eldest of three sons in the family of five children of Henry Charles Erith, mechanical engineer, and his wife, Florence May Laubenberg. In the year after his birth the Eriths moved from Clapton to Sutton, Surrey, where Raymond was brought up. At four he contracted tuberculosis and this led to twelve years of intermittent illness (he attended school for only two terms), which left him permanently lame in his left leg. During these long periods of enforced idleness, Erith discovered an interest in drawing, to which his father's work gave a technical twist, leading him to architecture. At fifteen he received an honourable mention in a competition for model houses, conducted by the *Daily Express*. In 1921 his mother took him and his two sisters to Italy. Later that year he entered the Architectural Association School of Architecture.

The school was then in a phase of enthusiastic reaction to influences from abroad, especially those of the more avant-garde kind. These had no appeal for Erith, an incipient classicist, but he nevertheless enjoyed the course and won several awards, including the Henry Florence travelling studentship (1924). To obtain the practical office experience requisite for professional qualification he served for a period in the office of Percy Morley Horder. He was elected ARIBA in 1927.

In 1928, on the strength of a modest legacy from his grandfather, Erith opened an office of his own in Westminster but the following year he moved to Warwick Street, where he formed a partnership with Bertram Hume (1901–1977) which was to last until 1939. On 18 August 1934 he married Pamela Dorothy (b. 1909/10), younger daughter of Arthur Spencer Jackson, solicitor; they were to have four daughters. Two years later Jackson became a client, commissioning him to build a house in the main street of Dedham, Essex. In the design of this house, the Great House, Erith adopted the idiom of the most refined and reserved domestic architecture of about 1800, thus defining the route he was to follow, with variations, for the remainder of his career. He adopted the same style when in 1939, on the recommendation of the president of the Royal Institute of British Architects, H. S. Goodhart-Rendel, he was appointed to design lodges at the approach to the Royal Lodge, Windsor Great Park, for George VI. Unluckily these were damaged by a bomb soon after completion and the design was altered in the course of reconstruction by another hand. With Hilda Mason (1880–1955) he designed the church of St Andrew, Felixstowe (1931); this intriguing early work combined a Perpendicular plan with a concrete frame and brick panels.

With the outbreak of war the practice was wound up and in 1940 Erith bought a farm with 150 acres of arable land at Little Bromley, Essex. He farmed successfully until 1945, but in 1946 architecture reclaimed him and he opened an office in Ipswich; he became FRIBA in the same year. Now forty-two, he found himself with few opportunities measuring up to his abilities. He possessed no flair whatever for self-advertisement but in 1949 started, to please himself and perhaps others, to send drawings to the Royal Academy exhibitions. These combined his idiosyncratic quality as a designer with draughtsmanly execution of exceptional beauty. To some they seemed the work of a brilliantly eccentric deviationist but they deeply impressed those who were sceptical about the universal validity of the modern manner. The first worthwhile commission to come his way was a terrace of three houses, 15–19 Aubrey Walk, Kensington (for the misses Alexander, 1951). In 1955 he was invited to design new lodgings for the provost of the Queen's College, Oxford (1959–60). This, though not a large work, is notable for an ingeniously simple plan and for the subtle handling of rustication on the front towards Queen's Lane. It was followed immediately by a commission for a new library at Lady Margaret Hall, Oxford. This was to run parallel with a block by Sir Reginald Blomfield so as to form a new quadrangle which would be closed by another new block, the Wolfson residential building. Erith designed both: the library was completed in 1961 and the Wolfson building, providing a new entrance to the college, in 1966.

In 1958 Erith received the most exacting commission of his career, the reconstruction of 10 and 11 Downing Street and the rebuilding of no. 12 (1959–63). The rationalization of this intricate complex of Georgian buildings, involving the preservation of historic rooms, was a task to which he was ideally suited. The progress of the work, however, was bedevilled by disputes in the building trade and extravagant delays, causing him great anxiety and distress before its ultimate completion. Erith's later work included: The Pediment, Aynho, Northamptonshire (for Elizabeth Watt, 1956–7); the Folly, Gatley Park, Herefordshire (for Mrs Victor Willis, 1961–4), a fortress-like tower on an elliptical plan; the rebuilding of Jack Straw's Castle, the famous Hampstead tavern (for Charrington & Co., 1963–4), where he adapted an eighteenth-century weather-boarded vernacular to a modern function; Wivenhoe New Park, Essex (for Charles Gooch, 1962–4), a study in Palladian villa design; King's Walden Bury, Hertfordshire (for Sir Thomas Pilkington, 1969–71), where Palladianism is combined with evocations of Queen Anne; and the common-room building at Gray's Inn (1971–2).

Erith was unique among the architects of his generation for his resistance to the influence of functionalism and his consistent adherence to what he conceived to be the true nature of architecture, a fluent and thoughtful classicism. This he believed to have been at the heart of a tradition which had disintegrated in the middle of the nineteenth century, and from whose ruins it could be retrieved. He admired Sir John Soane and sometimes, but rarely, imitated him. Later influences in his work include Italian mannerism, Swedish neo-classicism (the original as well as the revived varieties), and the vernacular of the Essex countryside, for which he had a deep affection. His unpublished writings show a rooted conviction that it is the purpose of architecture not merely to serve practical purposes efficiently but to bring positive delight and spiritual comfort to mankind.

From 1958 Erith conducted his practice from Dedham but took an active part in professional affairs, notably in architectural education. Quinlan Terry, the prominent neo-classical architect, was his assistant from 1962 and his partner from 1967. He was elected ARA in 1959 and RA in 1964. From 1960 to 1973 he served on the Royal Fine Arts Commission. He was a shy man, of singular modesty and charm, marked but not embittered by physical suffering, happy at his drawing-board, in his married life, and with his daughters. He died in the London Hospital, Stepney, on 30 November 1973.   JOHN SUMMERSON, *rev.*

Sources L. Archer, *Raymond Erith: architect* (1985) · b. cert. · m. cert. · d. cert. · A. Powers, 'Erith, Raymond (Charles)', *The dictionary of art*, ed. J. Turner (1996) · *The Times* (3 Dec 1973) · *The Times* (5 Dec 1973)
Archives RIBA, job files | RIBA, corresp. with Marshall Sisson
Wealth at death £168,615: probate, 18 March 1974, *CGPLA Eng. & Wales*

Erkenwald. *See* Earconwald (*d.* 693).

Erle, Thomas (1649/50–1720), army officer, was the second son of Thomas Erle (*d.* 1650), of Bindon House, Axmouth, Devon, and his wife, Susanna, fourth daughter of William *Fiennes, first Viscount Saye and Sele. Despite the impeccable parliamentary credentials of his father, Thomas Erle was brought up in a royalist household following his mother's second marriage, to Robert Hawley, younger brother of Francis, first Baron Hawley, although his grandfather Saye and Sele persisted in attempts to influence his upbringing. He matriculated from Trinity College, Oxford, on 12 July 1667 and entered the Middle Temple in 1669. In 1675 he married Elizabeth, daughter of Sir William Wyndham, first baronet, of Orchard Wyndham, Somerset (1633–1683). On the death of his paternal grandfather the parliamentarian Sir Walter *Erle in 1665, he succeeded to the family estates and established himself in the house at Charborough. A deputy lieutenant for Dorset from 1674, he sat as a whig MP for Wareham in every parliament from March 1679 until 1718, when he resigned his seat in return for a pension of £1200 p.a., except for the general elections of 1698 and 1701, during which he exerted his military influence to be returned for Portsmouth. In addition he sat in the Irish parliament for Cork from 1703 until 1713.

During Monmouth's rebellion in 1685, Erle served as the major of the Red regiment of the Dorset militia, fighting as a volunteer at Sedgemoor. Afterwards John, Lord Churchill presented him to James II at an unpropitious time for those who had voted for the Exclusion Bill in 1679, as he had done, and he received a predictably chilly reception. His great-grandson, Henry Drax, caused an inscription to be placed above the icehouse at Charborough stating that 'under this roof in the year 1686 a set of patriotic gentlemen of this neighbourhood concerted the great plan of the Glorious Revolution' (Hutchins, 3.128). There is no extant corroboration for this claim, and recent historiography has argued that plans for the invasion of William of Orange were fomented during the spring of 1688, at the earliest. However, it is not impossible that Erle held informal gatherings of actual and potential malcontents at Charborough from 1686 as he had developed a strong antipathy towards James long before 1688. He answered adversely the three questions in 1687 and was duly purged from the deputy lieutenancy and the commission of peace in May–June 1688 although reinstated in October. There is every suggestion, although no proof, that he was actively involved in the conspiracy that smoothed the path of William of Orange into England during November 1688: as a satellite of John Churchill, he certainly knew of the conspiracy, its aims, and its intended methods. He received a pass on 21 June 1688 to travel overseas and may well have visited the Low Countries on some conspiratorial business; he was back in England by mid-August. Soon after the Dutch landing on 5 November 1688 he declared himself for William and began raising troops in Dorset. For his services, he was rewarded on 8 March 1689 with the colonelcy of a newly raised regiment of infantry, and for the rest of his life he followed the military profession.

Erle's new battalion went to Ireland with the duke of Schomberg's expeditionary force in August 1689, but he fell ill soon after arrival and his command deteriorated badly during its sojourn at the camp near Dundalk. He and his soldiers fought at the Boyne in 1690 and Aughrim in 1691, where he was twice captured but rescued on each occasion by his own men. Already gaining a reputation as a reliable and competent soldier, he was described by General Hugh Mackay as of 'very good sense, a hearty man for his country, brave, and loves his bottle' (H. Mackay, *Memoirs of the War Carried on in Scotland and Ireland*, 1833, 104). On 1 January 1691 he succeeded Francis Luttrell as colonel of the 19th foot. After the treaty of Limerick, Erle's battalion was transferred to the confederate army in the Spanish Netherlands, where it took part in the battle of Steenkerke on 24 July 1692. During the debate on the employment of foreign officers (21 November 1692) he made his only recorded speech in the House of Commons, a self-effacing contribution in support of the king: military preferment had converted the active whig into a trimmer and loyal placeman. Promoted brigadier-general on 22 March 1693, he rose from his sickbed in Malines to lead his brigade at the battle of Landen on 18 July 1693 only to be severely wounded in the struggle for the village of Rumsdorp. His battalion took part in the unsuccessful Brest expedition commanded by Thomas Tollemache in June 1694, although there is no record that Erle was present, and in the following year formed part of the covering army during the great siege of Namur. Taking passage for the Netherlands in readiness for the 1695 campaign, Erle and a number of his regimental officers were captured by a Dunkirk privateer but promptly released in exchange for a payment of 4000 crowns each. In 1694 he was appointed governor of Portsmouth, a position held until 1712 and again from 1714 to 1720.

On 1 June 1696 Erle was promoted to major-general. Posted as second-in-command to the earl of Galway in Ireland in 1699, he became an Irish privy counsellor in 1701 prior to succeeding Galway as commander-in-chief on the accession of Queen Anne in 1702. A lord justice in Ireland between 1702 and 1703, on 11 February 1703 he was promoted to lieutenant-general. When he was raised to membership of the English privy council on 3 May 1705 and appointed lieutenant-general of the ordnance in the same year, it appeared that his campaigning days were over and he would end his career in senior administrative positions within the home establishment. However, in 1706 his patron, Marlborough, ordered him to take a senior command in Earl Rivers's expeditionary force bound for Seville during the War of the Spanish Succession, apologizing for 'calling you away from so agreeable a retirement, which I should not have done if I had not thought it absolutely necessary to the service that a person of your experience and authority should be joined with Lord Rivers in his expedition' (*Letters and Dispatches*, 1.612). Erle sailed to Spain in January 1707 and commanded the infantry of the allied centre at the battle of Almanza on 14 April. He

returned to England in March 1708 to take command of an expeditionary force earmarked for an amphibious assault on Abbeville in order to distract French attention from Flanders during Marlborough's siege of Lille. Nothing came of the attempt, and the eleven battalions were eventually landed at Ostend. His health undermined by gout, he returned to England at the end of the year, and in 1709 sold the colonelcy of his foot regiment to George Freke, the lieutenant-colonel. In 1711 he was advanced to full general and given command of the foot in Flanders but never assumed his responsibilities. On the fall of Marlborough, Erle was removed from the lieutenant-generalcy of the ordnance but resumed this position on the accession of George I in 1714. During the Jacobite rising of 1715 he was ordered to put Portsmouth into a state of defence. He died at Charborough on 23 July 1720 and was interred beside his wife in the family vault within the parish church. Thomas and Elizabeth Erle had one daughter, who married Sir Edward Ernle, third baronet, of Maddington, Wiltshire. Erle's second granddaughter married Henry Drax of Ellerton Abbey, Yorkshire, sometime secretary to Frederick, prince of Wales, who thus succeeded to the Charborough properties. JOHN CHILDS

Sources Churchill College, Cambridge, Plunkett-Ernle-Erle-Drax MSS · *The manuscripts of his grace the duke of Portland*, 10 vols., HMC, 29 (1891–1931), vol. 3 · *Calendar of the manuscripts of the marquis of Bath preserved at Longleat, Wiltshire*, 5 vols., HMC, 58 (1904–80), vol. 1 · *Eighth report*, 1, HMC, 7 (1907–9) · C. Dalton, ed., *English army lists and commission registers, 1661–1714*, 6 vols. (1892–1904) · *The letters and dispatches of John Churchill, first duke of Marlborough, from 1702 to 1712*, ed. G. Murray, 5 vols. (1845) · J. Hutchins, *The history and antiquities of the county of Dorset*, 3rd edn, ed. W. Shipp and J. W. Hodson, 4 vols. (1861–74) · J. P. Ferris, 'Erle, Thomas', HoP, *Commons, 1660–90* · *The parliamentary diary of Narcissus Luttrell, 1691–1693*, ed. H. Horwitz (1972)
Archives BL, letter-book as Lord Justice of Ireland, Add. MS 37531 · CAC Cam., corresp. and papers | Yale U., Beinecke L., letters to William Blathwayt
Likenesses J. Simon, mezzotint, *c.*1710 (after G. Kneller), BM, NPG; repro. in J. C. Smith, *British mezzotinto portraits*, 4 vols. in 5 (1878–84), no. 56

Erle [Earle], **Sir Walter** (1586–1665), politician, was born on 22 November 1586, the eldest son of Thomas Erle, esquire (*d.* 1597), of Charborough, Dorset, and his wife, Dorothy, daughter of William Pole of Shute, Devon. Walter was aged ten when his father died and his mother's second husband, Sir Walter Vaughan of Fallersden, Wiltshire, became his guardian. He was educated at Queen's College, Oxford, where he matriculated in 1602, and at the Middle Temple, London, where he was admitted in 1604, but he neither graduated nor completed his studies. He was knighted on 4 May 1616, three days before his marriage to Anne (*d.* 1654), a wealthy heiress, daughter of Francis Dymoke of Erdington, Warwickshire. They had one son, Thomas, who died before them in 1650, and two daughters. Sir Walter sat as MP for Poole in 1614, 1621, 1624, and 1660; for Dorset in 1625, 1628, 1654, and 1659; for Lyme Regis in 1626 and the Short Parliament; and for Weymouth and Melcombe Regis in the Long Parliament.

Up to the mid-1620s Erle made his mark chiefly in local affairs. His family came originally from Devon and had settled at Charborough in 1549 when his grandfather married the heir of Richard Wikes to acquire this and the neighbouring manors of East and West Morden. Charborough became Sir Walter's principal residence, though he also owned Bindon House and extensive landholdings in the area around Axmouth, Devon. He had taken charge of his estates by 1609 when he was reprimanded by Lord Ellesmere, the lord chancellor, for his 'hard conscience' in evicting one of his tenants at Axmouth (*DNB*). He became a JP for Dorset in 1615 and remained so for most of the period up to the outbreak of civil war. He also served as sheriff for the county in 1618–19 and as deputy lieutenant during the 1620s.

Throughout his career Sir Walter Erle was renowned for his staunchly Calvinist religious views; these were probably formed, at least in part, while he was a student at Queen's College which was notably godly. He became a close ally of John White, the puritan patriarch of Dorchester, and between 1624 and 1627 he served as the governor of the Dorchester New England Company, set up by White as a puritan colonizing venture. Erle first came to public notoriety in the 1621 parliament when, after promoting a bill for sabbath observance, he was attacked as a puritan by the MP Thomas Shepherd.

From 1625 onwards Erle emerged as an important spokesman in the Commons and a vociferous critic of crown policy. His principal concern was with defending the Calvinist religion against the threats from popery and Arminianism. In the 1624 parliament he had denounced the Arminian Richard Montagu as a promoter of the ancient heresy of Arianism; in 1625 he led complaints over a letter of pardon which Secretary Conway had issued to a Jesuit priest; and in 1628 he expressed alarm over the prospect of Irish Catholic troops billeted in Kent assisting an invasion from Flanders.

If religion was Erle's priority, however, he was even more active in defending the liberties of the subject. In the 1625 parliament he proposed that the king should be granted tonnage and poundage for one year only instead of for life, ostensibly because he was failing to guard the seas against pirates, but also in the hope of getting it established that customs duties could only be levied with the consent of parliament. In 1626 his attacks on Buckingham and Richard Montagu during the parliament resulted in his removal from the commission of the peace, and when the king levied the forced loan in late 1626 and early 1627 he was one of the ringleaders of the resistance. His refusal to pay in Dorset led to imprisonment in London, where he and other opponents agitated to have their cause heard in the courts. This resulted in their trial—the five knights' case—which eventually led to the safeguards against the crown's imprisoning without showing cause enshrined in the petition of right.

In an important speech in the 1629 parliament Erle made a characteristic connection between the defence of Calvinist doctrine and the liberties of the subject. Both were under threat from 'popery and Arminianism joining hand in hand … to bring in a Spanish tyranny amongst us'. He warned:

> Take away my religion and you take away my life, and not only mine but the life of the whole state and kingdom. For I may boldly say never was there a more near conjunction between matter of religion and matter of state in any kingdom in the world than there is in this kingdom at this day.   (Notestein and Relf, 18–19)

This summed up his political priorities.

During the 1630s Erle consolidated his links with the leaders of the opposition to Charles's regime. He had been identified as a close ally of Lord Saye and Sele when he was involved with the attempted impeachment of Buckingham in 1626, and the connection was reinforced in May 1639 when his son, Thomas, contracted to marry Saye's daughter, Susanna. In the aftermath of the Short Parliament Sir Walter was threatened with arrest for colluding with the Scots, and in November 1640 he was working closely with John Pym on preparations for the Long Parliament. Erle also continued his opposition to prerogative taxation, resisting payment of the 1636 levy of ship money in Dorset. In 1630 he travelled to the Netherlands and served briefly as a volunteer, under the command of Lord Vere. Thereafter he liked to present himself as an expert in military affairs, claiming in 1641 that he was a 'sword man rather than a gown man' (Keeler, *Long Parliament*, 166) and building scale models in his back garden of the sieges he had witnessed.

During the Long Parliament Erle was regarded as something of an elder statesman among those opposed to the crown. He remained vigilant against the threat from popery and Arminianism, taking a prominent role on committees to prepare charges against the Laudian bishops and purge the royal army of Catholics. He was particularly concerned about the dangers posed by the Irish army and in the impeachment proceedings against Strafford took charge of the twenty-fourth article which accused him of intending to bring an army over from Ireland to deal with opposition in England. When the first army plot was discovered in May 1641 he took a prominent role in the investigations and was then sent down to Dorset to organize local defence. He returned to parliament in October, just as news of the Irish rising was breaking and immediately became involved in parliament's efforts to counter this. During November 1641 he helped to draft the grand remonstrance and the following January he urged his Dorset friend William Strode to go into hiding when the house learned of the king's attempt to arrest the five members.

During the early stages of the civil war Erle divided his energies between Dorset and Westminster. In July 1642 he was sent down to the county to execute the militia ordinance. He raised his own troop of horse and supported the earl of Bedford's siege of Sherborne Castle in August. He returned to Westminster in January 1643 and during the negotiations over the treaty of Oxford allied himself with the more hawkish elements who opposed a lenient peace with the king. Back in Dorset in April he became commander of the county's parliamentarian forces. At Corfe Castle in June he organized an elaborate siege, trying out various experimental siege engines before being reduced to making a frontal assault which failed, with heavy casualties. Royalist accounts made much of the fact that, in spite of his boasting about his military prowess, he panicked at the first exposure to gunfire. The siege was abandoned in August, as a large royalist force entered the county, and Erle faced an inquest at Westminster which resulted in his being deprived of his command.

Back in the Commons Erle aligned himself with Pym, St John, and what has become known as the middle group in opposition to the earl of Essex. In February 1644 he was entrusted with the office of lieutenant of the ordnance which gave him control over the provision of artillery and weapons for the parliamentarian forces. He used this, in part, to cut off supplies to Essex's army. He was also closely involved in the setting up of the New Model Army, but lost his lieutenancy in April 1645 under the terms of the self-denying ordinance.

During 1645, while remaining on good terms with Saye personally, Erle drifted away from the Independent leadership and generally sided with the Presbyterians. The main reason for this appears to have been his alarm over the increase in sectaries in the New Model Army. He worked closely with the Scots, took an increasing interest in Presbyterian schemes for reform of the church, and voted with Denzil Holles and his allies. He co-operated with the Scots commissioners over the peace negotiations of 1646 and 1647, supporting a Presbyterian church settlement and acting as one of the four MPs chosen to present the propositions of Newcastle to Charles. He also backed Holles's efforts to disband the New Model Army in 1647, but avoided impeachment in the summer, probably because of his links with Saye. In August 1647, as part of an effort to conciliate moderate Presbyterians, he was restored to the office of lieutenant of the ordnance, and during early 1648 he was gradually drawn back into working with the army. By the start of the second civil war, however, he was once more siding with the Presbyterians over religious matters and became a vigorous supporter of continuing negotiations with the king. At the time of Pride's Purge he was secluded from the house, briefly imprisoned, and stripped of his lieutenancy.

Erle was shut out from further involvement in politics until the first protectorate parliament when he served as MP for Dorset. He made little impact on proceedings, but soon after began to recover his local offices. He returned to the Dorset commission of the peace in 1657, remaining active until his death and becoming a strong opponent of the Quakers. He sat once more as knight of the shire in Richard Cromwell's parliament, but by this stage he was getting a reputation for being a parliamentary bore—one observer noting that he 'took a liberty to stand up twenty times a day' (J. P. Ferris and P. Little, HoP, *Commons, 1604–29, 1640–60*). At the age of seventy-three he represented Poole in the Convention Parliament of 1660. As father of the house, he argued vigorously for a moderate religious settlement and warned of the dangers of the Militia Bill, as well as sitting on fifty-eight committees.

A staunch Calvinist, an unremitting opponent of popery, and a strong defender of the subject's liberties, Erle was in many respects the archetype of the 'patriots' and 'public men' who acted as spokesmen for 'the country' in the years up to and during the civil war. He died in 1665 and was buried on 1 September at Charborough; his grandson, Thomas *Erle, succeeded to his estate.

RICHARD CUST

Sources J. P. Ferris, 'Erle, Sir Walter', HoP, *Commons, 1604–29*; P. Little, 'Erle, Sir Walter', HoP, *Commons, 1640–60* [drafts] · Keeler, *Long Parliament*, 165–7 · M. W. Helms and J. P. Ferris, 'Erle, Walter', HoP, *Commons, 1660–90* · W. Notestein and F. H. Relf, eds., *Commons debates for 1629* (1921), 18–19 · J. Hutchins, *The history and antiquities of the county of Dorset*, 3rd edn, ed. W. Shipp and J. W. Hodson, 3 (1868), 498–9 · *N&Q*, 4th ser., 10 (1872), 326 [notes by Sir James Bagg on the parliament of 1626] · C. Russell, *Parliaments and English politics, 1621–1629* (1979) · R. P. Cust, *The forced loan and English politics, 1626–1628* (1987) · D. Underdown, *Fire from heaven: the life of an English town in the seventeenth century* (1992) · D. Underdown, *Pride's Purge: politics in the puritan revolution* (1971) · A. R. Bayley, *The great civil war in Dorset, 1642–1660* (1910)

Erle, Sir William (1793–1880), judge, was born on 1 October 1793 at Fifehead-Magdalen, Dorset, the third son in the family of four sons and two daughters of the Revd Christopher Erle (1761–1817) and his wife, Margaret, *née* Bowles. Peter Erle (1796–1877), chief charity commissioner, was his younger brother. He was educated between 1804 and 1811 at Winchester College and afterwards at New College, Oxford, where he graduated BCL in 1818 and was a fellow until 1834, when he married Amelia, daughter of David Williams, warden of New College. He was admitted as a member of the Middle Temple on 9 November 1813 and called to the bar on 26 November 1819. In 1822 he was admitted *ad eundem* to membership of the Inner Temple. He joined the western circuit, where his progress was steady rather than brilliant. He also gained experience by purchasing a place as one of the counsel of the palace court, which had jurisdiction over all personal actions arising within 12 miles of Whitehall.

In 1834 Erle was appointed king's counsel and became a bencher of the Inner Temple, where he was later treasurer (1844). In the general election of July 1837 he stood as a whig candidate and entered parliament as one of the members for the city of Oxford. In parliament he voted regularly with his party but never spoke, nor did he seek re-election in 1841.

In November 1844 Erle was promoted by a Conservative lord chancellor, Lyndhurst, to a puisne judgeship in the court of common pleas and received a knighthood (23 April 1845). He was transferred to the court of queen's bench in 1846, where he sat until June 1859, when he returned to the court of common pleas as chief justice and was sworn a member of the privy council.

As a judge Erle had a reputation for being accurate, painstaking, upright, and conscientious; but he found it difficult to balance opposing views or to change his mind once he had made it up. In trying a case, however, he was swayed by merits and had nothing but contempt for the technicalities favoured by Baron Parke. The latter once boasted to Erle that he had helped to build up sixteen volumes of Meeson and Welsby's exchequer reports. 'It's a lucky thing', retorted Erle, 'that there was not a seventeenth volume, for if there had been, the Common Law itself would have disappeared altogether, amidst the jeers and hisses of mankind' (Coleridge, 801).

Erle decided a large number of important cases, mainly in contract law. The decision of most general interest, however, was probably that in *Kennedy* v. *Broun* (1863). His judgment in this case, in which it was held that there could be no contract of hiring and service for advocacy in litigation, eloquently displayed Erle's high opinion of the advocate's calling.

In 1857 Oxford University awarded Erle the degree of DCL by decree of convocation, and in 1860 he was elected a fellow of the Royal Society. He retired from the bench in November 1866. From 1867 until 1869 he headed a royal commission on trade unions, and was a signatory to the majority report. His memorandum to the commission on the law was published in 1869 as *The Law Relating to Trade Unions*. In 1870 he became an honorary fellow of New College.

After retirement Erle lived the life of a country gentleman on his estate, Bramshott Grange, near Liphook, Hampshire. According to one obituary, he was often to be seen in the lanes about his neighbourhood, dressed in a loose country coat, knee-breeches, and gaiters, fondling his dogs and caressing his carthorses, which, for their part, seemed quite at home with him. He was not a sportsman and it was said that he would not allow birds or animals to be killed on his estate. He contributed much to charitable works, especially to those of a religious or educational nature. Erle died at Bramshott on 28 January 1880, and was survived by his wife; there were no children.   C. J. W. ALLEN

Sources *The Times* (30 Jan 1880), 10 · *Law Times* (7 Feb 1880), 268 · Holdsworth, *Eng. law*, 15.454–8 · T. F. Kirby, *Winchester scholars: a list of the wardens, fellows, and scholars of … Winchester College* (1888) · Foster, *Alum. Oxon.* · E. Foss, *Biographia juridica: a biographical dictionary of the judges of England … 1066–1870* (1870) · Boase, *Mod. Eng. biog.* · J. E. Martin, ed., *Masters of the bench of the Hon. Society of the Inner Temple, 1450–1883, and masters of the Temple, 1540–1883* (1883) · J. D. Coleridge, 'The law in 1847 and the law in 1889', *Contemporary Review*, 57 (1890), 797–807 · *CGPLA Eng. & Wales* (1880)

Archives Bodl. Oxf., corresp.

Likenesses F. Grant, drawing, exh. RA 1851, New College, Oxford · F. A. Tilt, watercolour drawing, 1868, NPG · T. Woolner, marble bust, exh. 1883, Temple Library, London

Wealth at death under £100,000: probate, 19 March 1880, *CGPLA Eng. & Wales*

Erlend [Erlendr þorfinnsson], **earl of Orkney** (*d.* **1098/9**). *See under* Paul (*d.* 1098/9).

Ermengarde [Ermengarde de Beaumont] (*d.* **1233**), queen of Scots, consort of William I, was a daughter of Richard, vicomte de Beaumont-sur-Sarthe, who was the son of Constance, an illegitimate daughter of King Henry I of England. She thus had (somewhat thin) royal blood to commend her when Henry II of England proposed her, in May 1186, as a bride for *William I (William the Lion), king of Scots. The bride's social rank meant that the king was disparaged by the match, but he and his advisers reluctantly accepted it. The marriage took place at Woodstock on 5

September 1186; Henry II paid for the four days of festivities and returned Edinburgh Castle (in his hands since 1174) to the king of Scots as part of the bride's tocher (dowry). King William was to provide £100 of rents and forty knights feus in Scotland for Ermengarde; he probably honoured the first part of this, as she later had her own household, and dwellings and lands at Crail and Haddington.

At the time of her marriage Ermengarde, whose date of birth is unknown, was called 'a girl' (*puella*) by a contemporary; possibly she was just at (or even below) the canonical age of twelve years for marriage and that this was another reason for the king's reluctance to accept her. After the wedding she was escorted back to Scotland by Jocelin, bishop of Glasgow, and other Scottish nobles; the two kings went off to Marlborough, perhaps for some hunting.

Whatever her age, the queen's duty was to bear a legitimate and preferably male heir. During the years between 1187 and 1195 her eldest child, *Margaret, was born, and probably also another daughter, Isabella. Then, on 24 August 1198, a boy, the future king *Alexander II was born at Haddington. He was the first surviving legitimate son born to a reigning king of Scots for some seventy years and, not surprisingly, a contemporary noted that 'many rejoiced at his birth' (Anderson, 2.348). Later, there was a third daughter, Marjorie.

In July–August 1209 a diplomatic crisis between England and Scotland led to the treaty of Norham. By it the marriages of Ermengarde's two eldest daughters into the English royal house were proposed, and a few days later both girls were delivered at Carlisle, along with other hostages, to the justiciar of England. Whether their mother had art or part in the treaty is unknown; probably she did not. But in further negotiations at Durham in early 1212, when her husband was absent, she mediated actively between the two sides. A contemporary observer calls her 'an extraordinary woman, gifted with a charming and witty eloquence' (Bower, 4.469). She may have charmed King John; no more Scottish hostages were handed over and Alexander was to be knighted and, later, married to an English princess. The Scottish representatives had ensured that he would succeed to a still separate kingdom of the Scots.

After her husband's death, on 4 December 1214, Ermengarde remained grieving at Stirling, while the inauguration of Alexander II took place at Scone. The royal Christmas feast for 1214 was held at Forfar and the king and his mother were back at Stirling in January 1215; afterwards they went together to Arbroath to see the tomb of King William. Ermengarde probably played a part in Scottish politics, especially with regard to relations with England in 1215 and later; with other Scottish leaders she was excommunicated and then absolved in 1217. In 1225 she and Alexander II began to assemble property for their foundation of the Cistercian abbey of Balmerino, and by 1229 the first members of the house were in place. Unusually for Scotland, it was dedicated to St Edward the Confessor, for whom the queen seems to have had a special veneration; her only other known religious gift was to the hospital of St Edward at Berwick. Ermengarde died on 11 February 1233 and was buried at Balmerino.

Ermengarde's eldest daughter, Margaret, was married at London on 3 October 1221 to Hubert de *Burgh, justiciar of England and later earl of Kent. Her second daughter, Isabella, still single, returned to Scotland in 1223. In May 1225 she was married at Alnwick to Roger (III) *Bigod, earl of Norfolk, a minor and probably some twenty years her junior. Custody of Roger was given to Alexander II, but the earl probably returned to England after 1233. The couple were childless; Bigod repudiated his wife in 1245 but was compelled to take her back in 1253. She was still alive in October 1263, but her date of death is unknown. She was buried at Blackfriars in London. In 1227 Marjorie was sought as a bride by Henry III's brother, Richard of Cornwall, who came to Scotland to speak to Ermengarde about the match. But his proposals pleased neither the Scots nor Henry III, and negotiations were broken off. She was married on 1 August 1235 at Berwick to Gilbert *Marshal, earl of Pembroke [see under Marshal, William (II)], who died in 1241. They, too, were childless. Marjorie died on 17 November 1244 and was also buried at Blackfriars in London.

W. W. SCOTT

Sources A. O. Anderson, ed. and trans., *Early sources of Scottish history, AD 500 to 1286*, 2 (1922) · A. C. Lawrie, ed., *Annals of the reigns of Malcolm and William, kings of Scotland* (1910) · W. Bower, *Scotichronicon*, ed. D. E. R. Watt and others, new edn, 9 vols. (1987–98), vols. 4–5 · [W. B. D. D. Turnbull], ed., *Liber sancte Marie de Balmorinach*, Abbotsford Club, 22 (1841) · C. C. H. Harvey and L. MacLeod, eds., *Calendar of writs preserved at Yester House, 1166–1625*, Scottish RS, 55 (1930) · GEC, *Peerage*, new edn, vols. 9–10

Ernest (1830–1904), by Frederick Richard Say, 1856–7 [right, with his cousin Victor, prince of Hohenlohe-Langenburg, Count Gleichen]

Ernest (1830–1904), prince of Leiningen and naval officer, was born Ernst Leopold Victor Karl August Joseph Emich at Amorbach, Bavaria, on 9 November 1830. He was the elder son of Charles, reigning prince of Leiningen (1804–1856), and his wife, Marie, countess of Klebelsberg. His father was the only son of Princess Victoria of Saxe-Coburg-Saalfeld, by her first husband, Emich Charles, reigning prince of Leiningen; the princess's second husband was the duke of Kent, and she was mother of Queen Victoria, who was thus a half-sister of the admiral's father. The duchess of Kent took much interest in her grandson Prince Ernest as a boy, and through the influence of his step-aunt, Queen Victoria, he entered the British navy on 14 March 1849.

Ernest served during the Second Anglo-Burmese War of 1851–2, being present at the capture of Prome. At the end of 1853 he was appointed to the *Britannia*, flagship of Vice-Admiral Sir James Whitley Deans Dundas in the Mediterranean, and in June 1854 was sent up the Danube, with a small party from the *Britannia* under Lieutenant Glyn, to man river gunboats at Rustchuk, then the headquarters of Omar Pasha, the Turkish commander-in-chief, arriving on 10 July. Three days earlier a small Turkish force had seized Giurgevo on the north bank of the Danube. Prince Gorchakov with 70,000 men was moving on this Turkish force to drive it south across the Danube, and Omar, immediately turning the gun-boats over to Glyn, directed him to hold a creek which separated the Turkish position from the Russian advance. The Russians were checked, and the British and Turks meanwhile succeeded in throwing a bridge of boats across the river. Gorchakov then withdrew to Bucharest, leaving the Turks masters of the lower Danube. Prince Ernest received a gold medal from the Turkish government for distinguished service in the field, and on passing his examination was promoted lieutenant on 2 April 1855. He was appointed to the *Duke of Wellington*, the flagship of Vice-Admiral Richard Dundas in the Baltic, and later to the *Cossack*, in which he was present at the bombardment of Sveaborg. He served as lieutenant in the paddle-frigate *Magicienne*, on the Mediterranean station, and in the royal yacht, from which he was promoted commander on 1 February 1858. Ernest married at Karlsruhe, on 11 September 1858, Princess Marie Amalie of Baden, daughter of Leopold, grand duke of Baden; she died on 21 November 1899. From 1858 onwards Ernest was employed almost continuously in the yacht, first as commander, then as captain, his only foreign service being in 1862–3, when he commanded the *Magicienne* in the Mediterranean. His promotion to captain was dated 25 October 1860, and he was still serving in the yacht when he reached flag rank on 31 December 1876. On 18 August 1875 the yacht *Alberta*, with Queen Victoria on board, was crossing from Cowes to Portsmouth when, in Stokes Bay, she ran down the schooner yacht *Mistletoe*, which sank with the loss of four lives. The accident caused much excitement, especially locally, the tendency being to lay the blame on the royal yacht and her captain. A court of inquiry was held at Portsmouth, and exonerated the prince and his officers; however, the Admiralty voluntarily paid compensation for the loss of the yacht, without in any way suggesting that it accepted blame.

Early in 1880 the prince was selected for the post of second in command of the channel squadron; but in April, after the appointment had been gazetted, the Gladstone government came into office, and rescinded the appointment. This chain of events was closely linked to the Conservative Party, and the queen's preference for Disraeli. During that government's period of office Ernest was not employed, though he was promoted vice-admiral on 1 December 1881. When Lord Salisbury's government was formed in 1885 he was appointed commander-in-chief at the Nore on 1 July, a post which he held until his promotion to admiral on 7 July 1887. This was his last service, and on 9 November 1895 he reached retirement age. He was made GCB in 1866 and GCVO in 1898. After hauling down his flag he resided chiefly at Amorbach, where he died on 5 April 1904. His only son, Prince Emich Edward Carl, succeeded him as reigning prince; his only daughter, Princess Albertine, died in 1901.

Ernest's career was made by royal patronage. He was a brave junior officer, but thereafter spent two decades on the royal yacht, which removed him from active service.

L. G. C. LAUGHTON, rev. ANDREW LAMBERT

Sources *CGPLA Eng. & Wales* (1904) · *The Times* (6 April 1904) · Kelly, *Handbk* (1893) · E. Longford, *Victoria RI* (1964)
Likenesses F. D'A. Durade, portrait, 1847, Royal Collection · F. D'A. Durade, oils, 1848, Osborne House, Isle of Wight · F. R. Say, portrait, 1856–7, Royal Collection [*see illus.*] · Victor, prince of Hohenlohe-Langenburg, marble bust; at Wald Leiningen in 1912
Wealth at death £22,951 7s. 9d.: probate, 24 June 1904, *CGPLA Eng. & Wales*

Ernest Augustus, Prince, duke of York and Albany (1674–1728), bishop of Osnabrück, was born in Osnabrück on 7 / 17 September 1674 and named, in German, Ernst August. He was the sixth son and seventh and youngest child of *Sophia (1630–1714), later designated heir presumptive to the English throne by the Act of Settlement of 1701, and her husband, Ernst August of Brunswick-Lüneburg (1629–1698), ruling bishop of Osnabrück since 1661. In 1714 his elder brother, George Lewis, elector of Hanover, acceded to the British throne as *George I. The young Ernest Augustus spent the early years of his life in Osnabrück and after 1679 in Hanover, where his parents moved after his father inherited the duchy. His upbringing followed the pattern of that of other German princes, learning European diplomacy by visiting other courts before undertaking military service. In July 1687 he and his brother Christian travelled to Versailles via Amsterdam; they remained in France for several months, where they became favourites of their Orléans cousins. Ernest Augustus subsequently fought against the French in the Nine Years' War, being present at the battle of Neerwinden in 1693, and again in the War of Spanish Succession, where he fought at Lille. In 1703 he began his lengthy correspondence with fellow officer Johann Franz Diedrich von Wendt, which some commentators have seen as revealing a homosexual relationship; the correspondence was published by Erich, Graf Kielmansegg, in 1902.

Ernest Augustus had played no part in the dynastic quarrels over the introduction of primogeniture into the Hanoverian succession. It was perhaps as a result of this as much as his apparent lack of ambition in other respects that he became the most trusted sibling of his older brother George Lewis, elector from 1698. He played his part in the social and political life of the court at Herrenhausen, receiving diplomatic visitors and corresponding with several royal and princely cousins. Some commentators have seen Ernest Augustus in the role of guardian of cultural interests in his brother's court. This takes for granted the traditional assumption that George Lewis was uninterested in the arts, which was not the case. However, Ernest Augustus revived his father's connection with Venetian opera, through which he was the first of his family to make contact with George Frideric Handel, probably in 1707. Although it seems unlikely that a formal offer was made, it may have been at a later meeting in 1709 that Ernest Augustus suggested that Handel could find a post at the electoral court.

The situation of Ernest Augustus changed dramatically in 1714 with the accession of George Lewis to the British throne. It was decided that Ernest Augustus should remain in Germany as the senior adult representative of the family and effective regent. As such he was the guardian of his seven-year-old great-nephew Frederick Lewis. The future prince of Wales had been left in Hanover as a symbol of the continued commitment of the ruling family to their electorate.

The connection of Ernest Augustus to the administration at Hanover was weakened in 1715 when the bishopric of Osnabrück became vacant. The bishopric had been held by the Catholic Prince Charles Joseph of Lorraine, archbishop and elector of Trier, following the death of Elector Ernest Augustus in 1698; the see reverted to the house of Hanover, and George I nominated his remaining protestant brother to the bishopric. Ernest Augustus became possessed of the substantial revenues attached to the principality and henceforth divided his time between Schloss Osnabrück and Hanover.

Perhaps in order further to emphasize dynastic unity and the identification of the family with Great Britain, on 29 June 1716 George I created Ernest Augustus duke of York and Albany and earl of Ulster. These titles had previously been held by James II during the reign of his brother Charles II. The new duke of York was also made a knight of the Garter on 3 July, shortly before George I left to visit his continental possessions.

It was rumoured in the London press in late July 1716 that the granting of British and Irish peerages to Ernest Augustus foreshadowed a marriage between the duke of York and the princess dowager of Nassau-Friesland, mother of the infant prince of Orange, but the story failed to be substantiated and no marriage took place. The anticipated court ceremony in Hanover to install the duke and his great-nephew Frederick as knights was intended for August 1716 but was delayed until December. Their official installation by proxy at Windsor did not take place until 30 April 1718, when the duke of York was represented by the whig MP and former aide-de-camp to the duke of Marlborough, Adolphus Oughton, who was rewarded with a baronetcy.

Ernest Augustus continued to divide his time between Osnabrück and Hanover until his death at Osnabrück on 3 / 14 August 1728. He was unmarried and his British and Irish peerages became extinct at his death. The *London Journal* of 24 August 1728 reported his encouragement of the salt industry and that he had begun construction of a new episcopal residence at Osnabrück, Augustusburg, left uncompleted at the time of his death. He was buried in Osnabrück.   MATTHEW KILBURN

Sources R. Hatton, *George I: elector and king* (1978) · E. Kielmansegg, ed., *Briefe des Herzogs Ernst August zu Braunschweig-Lüneburg an Johann Franz Diedrich von Wendt* (1902) · D. Burrows, *Handel* (1994) · P. H. Lang, *George Frideric Handel* (1967) · *St James's Evening Post*, 180 (24 July 1716), 3 · *LondG* (30 June 1716), 4 · *Weekly Journal, or, British Gazetteer* (5 Jan 1717) · *Weekly Journal, or, British Gazetteer* (3 May 1718) · M. Kroll, *Sophie—electress of Hanover* (1973) · *London Journal* (17 Aug 1728) · *London Journal* (24 Aug 1728) · H. Schmidt, 'Ernst-August II, Herzog von Braunschweig-Lüneburg', *Neue deutsche Biographie*, ed. Otto, Graf zu Stolberg-Wernigerode (Berlin, 1953), 617–18

Likenesses J. Simon, mezzotint, 1718, BM · group portrait, oils, 1725 (*Royal hunting party at Göhrde*), Royal Collection · engraving, repro. in Kielmansegg, ed., *Briefe des Herzogs Ernst August*, frontispiece · print (after J. Simon?), Royal Collection

Ernest Augustus (1771–1851), king of Hanover, fifth son of *George III and Queen *Charlotte, was born on 5 June 1771 at Buckingham House (later Palace), St James's Park, London. His boyhood was spent at Kew, in a cottage set aside by George III for his sons Ernest, *Augustus, duke of Sussex, and *Adolphus, duke of Cambridge, and their tutors. The three princes were invested as knights of the Garter on 2 June 1786 and a few weeks later sailed from Gravesend to begin four years of study at the University of Göttingen, even though when they left England they knew no German.

Prince Ernest—slim, tall, and handsome in his youth—wished to follow a military career and in June 1790 sought permission to train with the Prussian army. But George III insisted he should serve with the 9th Hanoverian hussars, later transferring him to the less dashing heavy dragoons, a move the prince bitterly resented. He fought with courage in Flanders and the Netherlands against the French, and at Tournai (10 May 1794) he lost his left eye and was wounded in the arm. Even so, six months later he distinguished himself outside Nijmegen by lifting a French dragoon bodily off his horse and carrying him captive to the allied lines. When the prince returned finally to England in February 1796, his face was scarred for life and his sharp wit became cruelly sardonic and malicious.

The prince was created duke of Cumberland and Teviotdale, and earl of Armagh, in April 1799, parliament approving an allowance of £12,000 a year. By conviction Cumberland was a strong tory, staunchly protestant (especially over Irish affairs) and critical of his eldest brother's passing attachment to the Foxite whigs. Most of his

Ernest Augustus (1771–1851), by George Dawe, *c.*1828

speeches in the House of Lords expressed reactionary principles with fearless defiance, prompting concern over his influence at court. There were unsavoury rumours of private vices, which were magnified by his political enemies smarting from the lash of his vituperative tongue. *George, the prince of Wales, uneasy at his brother's conduct, complained to Queen Charlotte in February 1807 of 'some very sarcastick remarks which the Duke made, for you know that HsRl Hnss is very comical though very imprudent sometimes' (*Correspondence of George, Prince of Wales*, 6.131); and he was so alarmed by Cumberland's behaviour that he warned his sisters not to be left alone in any room with him.

In the small hours of 31 May 1810 Cumberland's valet, Joseph Sellis, was found with his throat cut in the duke's apartments at St James's Palace. Cumberland, who had a deep wound in the head, maintained he had been awakened by blows struck by Sellis, whom he forced to flee to his own bedroom, where the valet committed suicide. At the inquest on Sellis this account was accepted by a jury whose foreman was the radical, Francis Place. The motive for Sellis's assault on the duke remains unclear; it is probable that, as a Corsican and a Roman Catholic, he was goaded by taunts and insults from his ultra-protestant and anti-French master. But so deep was the abhorrence felt towards Cumberland that it was widely believed he had murdered Sellis to prevent him from revealing scandalous details of the duke's private life.

Cumberland regarded himself as a professional soldier, but after 1796 he never again held command in the field, despite his wish to serve in the Peninsular campaign. He was, however, sent as 'observer' to allied headquarters in

Germany in 1813 and was present at the battle of Leipzig. As the only member of the royal family then on the continent, he showed enterprise in returning to Hanover on 4 November 1813, a few days after the French left the city. He was bitterly disappointed when, a month later, his youngest brother, Adolphus, duke of Cambridge, arrived as designated governor-general of the electorate.

While in Germany, Cumberland became deeply attached to his twice-widowed cousin, Friederike Caroline Sophia Alexandrina of Solms-Braunfels (1778–1841), born a princess of Mecklenburgh-Strelitz. A Lutheran marriage at Neu Strelitz on 29 May 1815 was solemnized again at Carlton House, London, three months later; Queen Charlotte refused ever to receive the duchess, who, seventeen years earlier, had jilted the duke of Cambridge. The marriage, like most of Cumberland's undertakings, remained unpopular and the Commons declined to increase his allowance. A campaign of calumny, including accusations of murder and incest, against both the duke and his wife continued in London society and in the press, and from 1818 to 1828 the Cumberlands lived in voluntary exile, mostly in Berlin, where their son, *George, later second duke of Cumberland, was born in May 1819. An affectionate mutual tolerance sustained the marriage happily until Friederike's death in Hanover in June 1841.

In the summer of 1828 Cumberland spent several months at Windsor, seeking to stiffen George IV's resistance to proposals for removing the civil disabilities of Roman Catholics. When the tory ministers, Wellington and Peel, moved towards Catholic emancipation, Cumberland was prepared to intrigue with Grey and the whig opposition, even though he deplored Grey's advocacy of reform. But British parliamentarians shunned contact with Cumberland: 'No government can last that has him either for a friend or an enemy' (Stanhope, *Conversations*, 25 April 1840), said Grey, coining an epigram which Wellington was to quote with approval. With *William IV's accession, Cumberland lost political influence; the brothers had scant regard for each other. During the early 1830s Cumberland was actively involved in the ultra-tory, ultra-protestant Orange order, of which he had been Irish grand master since 1817. Increasing sectarian violence and allegations of a plot to replace William IV with the duke forced Cumberland to preside over the dissolution of the lodges in 1836. There was, moreover, a recurrent popular fear that Cumberland would in some way rob the heir-presumptive, Princess Victoria, of her 'youthful life'. Tales of an alleged 'Cumberland plot' persisted well into the following reign, although condemned by the queen herself in later years as 'utterly false' and 'quite an invention' (Woodham-Smith, 434–5).

As Victoria's eldest surviving uncle the duke was certain of accession in Hanover where, unlike the United Kingdom, the Salic law prevailed. On 28 June 1837 King Ernest made a triumphant entry into the city. He gave early proof of his authoritarian convictions by abrogating the parliamentary constitution granted by William IV in 1833. When seven distinguished liberal professors at Göttingen protested at the king's absolutism, they were dismissed.

Yet, at a time of economic growth in Hanover, the king's benevolent autocracy suited the majority of his subjects. He won a popular respect which was in striking contrast to the mistrust his reputation perpetuated in Britain. Relations with his niece, Queen Victoria, remained strained; he complained that she held crown jewels belonging rightly to Hanover; and he did not approve her choice of husband, for to him the Coburgs were ambitious upstarts. During a visit to London in 1843 he was again pilloried in the newspapers. Yet when revolution shook Germany in 1848 he found he could count on his subjects' loyalty; only one life was lost that year in demonstrations in Hanover.

'Cumberland (alias the Black Sheep)' (*Correspondence of George, Prince of Wales*, 6.125), as Queen Victoria's father once called him, outlived his eight brothers, finally succumbing 'to a chill' at the Altes Palais in Hanover on 18 November 1851. His son, accidentally blinded when he was thirteen, acceded to the Hanoverian throne as George V. Cumberland was buried in the mausoleum at Herrenhausen, Hanover. Voluntary contributions paid for an equestrian statue, erected outside Hanover's Hauptbahnhof. It was inscribed, 'To the Father of His Country from a Faithful People'.

ALAN PALMER

Sources G. M. Willis, *Ernest Augustus, duke of Cumberland and king of Hanover* (1954) · H. van Thal, *Ernest Augustus, duke of Cumberland and king of Hanover* (1936) · *The correspondence of George, prince of Wales, 1770–1812*, ed. A. Aspinall, 8 vols. (1963–71) · *The letters of King George IV, 1812–1830*, ed. A. Aspinall, 3 vols. (1938) · C. Woodham-Smith, *Queen Victoria: her life and times*, 1: 1819–1861 (1972) · P. H. Stanhope, *Notes of conversations with the duke of Wellington, 1831–1851* (1888) · *GM*, 2nd ser., 37 (1852) · *Punch*, 4 (1843) · A. Palmer, *Crowned cousins: the Anglo-German royal connection* (1985) · J. Wolffe, *The protestant crusade in Great Britain, 1829–1860* (1991) · J. Wardroper, *Wicked Ernest* (2002)
Archives Königinvilla, Gmünden, Austria, MSS · Niedersächsisches Hauptstaatsarchiv, Hanover, MSS · Royal Arch., MSS · Schloss Marienburg, Hanover, MSS | BL, corresp. with Princess Lieven, Add. MSS 47350–47354 · Bucks. RLSS, corresp. with Richard Vyse · Harrowby Manuscript Trust, Sandon Hall, Staffordshire, corresp. with Richard Ryder · LPL, letters to Archbishop Howley · Northumbd RO, letters to Lord Wallace · NRA, priv. coll., letters to Lord Eldon · NRA, priv. coll., corresp. with Spencer Perceval, etc. · Royal Arch., letters to George III · U. Southampton L., letters to first duke of Wellington · W. Sussex RO, letters to duchess of Richmond · Warks. CRO, letters to Sir J. A. Waller
Likenesses J. Zoffany, oils, 1772, Royal Collection · B. West, group portrait, oils, 1776, Royal Collection · B. West, group portrait, oils, 1779 (*Queen Charlotte with her children*), Royal Collection · T. Gainsborough, oils, 1782, Royal Collection · B. West, group portrait, oils, 1782 (*Queen Charlotte with her children*), Royal Collection · J. C. Lochée, Wedgwood medallion, 1787, Royal Collection · W. Beechey, oils, exh. RA 1802, Royal Collection · H. Edridge, drawing, 1802, Royal Collection · P. Turnerelli, marble bust, 1809, TCD · J. Nollekens, marble bust, 1814, Royal Collection · W. Owen, oils, exh. RA 1814, Gov. Art Coll.; on loan · J. G. P. Fischer, miniature, *c*.1823, Royal Collection · W. Behnes, marble bust, 1828, Royal Collection · G. Dawe, oils, *c*.1828, NPG [*see illus.*] · J. P. Danton, caricature, plaster statue, 1834, NPG · D. Wilkie, group portrait, oils, 1837 (*The first council of Queen Victoria*), Royal Collection · A. Woolf, bronze equestrian statue, 1860–61, Ernst-August-Platz, Hanover · J. Doyle, caricatures, drawings, BM

Ernle. For this title name *see* Prothero, Rowland Edmund, first Baron Ernle (1851–1937).

Ernley, Sir John (*c.*1464–1520), lawyer, was the son of John Ernley (*d.* 1465), landowner of Sidlesham near Chichester, Sussex, and his wife, Margaret (*d.* in or before 1485), daughter of Nicholas Morley (1410–1472x4) and Joan Waleys, both of Glynde, near Lewes, Sussex. The family had been lords of the manor of Earnley near Chichester since the thirteenth century, and Ernley rose from local to national prominence in the administration of justice and finance under Henry VII and Henry VIII.

Ernley probably owed his upbringing, and certainly his marriage, to John Wood of Chichester, who may have been his stepfather—having possibly married Margaret Ernley at some point after 1465. After a preliminary legal education at an inn of chancery (*c.*1478–80) he was admitted to Gray's Inn. In 1485 Wood left Ernley extensive property in St Olave Old Jewry which had belonged to his brother, Sir John Wood, treasurer of the exchequer and speaker of the House of Commons in 1483, on condition that he marry Wood's great-niece Margaret Dawtry (*c.*1470–1518); they married shortly after 1485. Ernley secured this inheritance only after litigation to oust the treasurer's widow Margery. By 1490 he was established in London, noticed by his students as an increasingly conspicuous member of the Sussex circle gathered around Edmund Dudley at Gray's Inn.

In his county Ernley sustained a substantial legal practice as feoffee, arbitrator, commissioner, and justice, joining the home assize circuit as an associate in 1496 and 1497 and the county bench the following year. He acquired ecclesiastical patronage in the same decade, acting as steward of a Battle Abbey manor in the west of the county, taking a place among Edward Story, bishop of Chichester's council, and beginning the family's tenure of the episcopal manor house at Cakeham, Sussex, to which he may have added its innovative brick tower.

During these years Ernley had, at least as counsel, an unremarkable practice in the central courts. But in the first decade of the new century his horizons expanded. He began to act as one of Dudley's feoffees, and it was almost certainly to Henry VII's minister that he owed his unheralded appointment as attorney-general, replacing the out of favour James Hobart on 12 July 1507. Having paid a premium of £100 for his office Ernley readily joined Sir Richard Empson and Dudley in the financial exactions for which they alone became notorious. The association also paid dividends in Sussex, where Ernley may have involved Dudley in his local affairs to enable his cousin Agnes Morley's foundation of Lewes grammar school in December 1507.

Henry VIII reappointed him on 28 April 1509 and, though Empson and Dudley went to the block, Ernley prospered. Within a year he devised a scheme to thwart the claim of Edward Stafford, third duke of Buckingham, to the office of constable of England, despite secretly admitting that he had a strong right to the title. His adroit handling of such issues soon brought him additional responsibilities. One of the most frequent attenders among the judicial members of the king's council he was assiduous in enforcing royal rights to feudal revenues and took an active role in parliament: forty-nine bills were committed to the attorney- or solicitor-general in the assemblies of 1510, 1512, and 1515. His disqualification by office from the order of serjeants-at-law was no handicap to advancement: he remained at Gray's Inn, probably as senior bencher, and in 1510 began to ride the northern assize circuit. He took the home circuit for a year in 1516–17, the western circuit until 1519, and the Norfolk circuit for the rest of his life, almost invariably paired with another Gray's Inn man. Increasingly in demand as a feoffee Ernley was 'especial good master and friend' (BL, Add. MS 5813, fol. 116*r*) to the University of Cambridge, on whose behalf he obstructed a writ of *praemunire*.

Ernley invested his growing wealth in Sussex, not always scrupulously. There is more than a suspicion that he exploited Dudley's fall to gain outright possession of the manor of Sheffield in Fletching near Lewes, which Roger Lewknor had ceded to Dudley's feoffees in 1508 in a successful bargain to escape conviction for murder. While in the Tower of London, Dudley made provision in his will to defeat Ernley's ambitions; the title remained in dispute in chancery and on the latter's conscience until the end of his life, when he compensated Lewknor's family in his will 'not of duty … but of my charity' (PRO, PROB 11/20, sig. 3).

When Robert Rede, the chief justice of the court of common pleas, died on 8 January 1519 corners were cut to put Ernley in his place. Having spent a single day as a serjeant-at-law he replaced Rede on 27 January in the first documented instance of a private call. As well as three puisne judges, Ernley's elevation *per saltum* passed over the entire order of the coif. He was knighted that spring but the hopes vested in him came to a premature end when, after only five terms in his new court, he died on 22 April 1520, still in his mid-fifties, having requested burial at Sidlesham, near Chichester. His wife had predeceased him in August 1518. Although his son William Ernley (1501–1546) enjoyed an ample inheritance, followed him at Gray's Inn, and sat for Chichester in the parliament of 1542, he failed to achieve his father's eminence. The family's fortunes were to be carried on by its Wiltshire branch, descended (to the subsequent confusion of genealogists) from Ernley's elder brother, John Ernley (*b.* 1461/2) of Fosbury and Bishops Cannings.   **CHRISTOPHER WHITTICK**

Sources *VCH Sussex*, vol. 4 · A. S. Bevan, 'The role of the judiciary in Tudor government, 1509–1547', PhD diss., U. Cam., 1985 · Baker, *Serjeants*, 269, 536 · J. H. Baker, *Readers and readings in the inns of court and chancery*, SeldS, suppl. ser., 13 (2000), 27 · Sainty, *King's counsel*, 44 · Sainty, *Judges*, 48 · *The notebook of Sir John Port*, ed. J. H. Baker, SeldS, 102 (1986), 96 · *Reports of cases by John Caryll*, ed. J. H. Baker, 2 vols., SeldS, 115–16 (1999–2000), 647–8 · J. H. Baker, ed., *Readings and moots at the Inns of Court in the fifteenth century*, 2, SeldS, 105 (1989) · escheators' inquisitions, PRO, E150/1274, E150/1067 · BL, Lansdowne MS 127, fol. 217*r*. · PRO, C1/305/42–52, C1/330/38 · *The book of John Rowe*, ed. W. H. Godfrey, Sussex RS, 34 (1928), 156–8 · BL, Add. MS 5813, fol. 116*r*.; 40013, E7 · *CIPM*, 1, no. 657 [Henry VII] · will, PRO, PROB 11/5 [John Ernley, *d.* 1465] · R. F. Dell, ed., *The Glynde Place archives* (1964) · PRO, CP 40/841, rot. 399 · W. D. Peckham, ed., *The acts of the dean and chapter of the cathedral church of Chichester, 1472–1544*, Sussex RS, 52 (1952), 101 · will, PRO, PROB 11/20, sig. 3

Ernulf [Arnulf] (**1039/40–1124**), bishop of Rochester, was of French birth, according to William of Malmesbury, and probably from the region of Beauvais, where he was later a monk. His reported age at death indicates that he was born in 1039 or 1040. He entered the abbey of Bec in Normandy early in the 1060s, and made his profession soon afterwards. Here he would have been instructed by Lanfranc (*d.* 1089) in the liberal arts, and perhaps in the study of the fathers, elements that appear in his surviving work. After some years at Bec, he moved to the Benedictine house of St Symphorien in Beauvais. Here Ernulf was occupied as schoolmaster, apparently in a school for external pupils attached to the monastery. At a time after 1070 and before 1077, distracted by some 'insolent business' (*Patrologia Latina*, 162.100) beyond his control—no doubt the bitter conflict between bishop and citizens in Beauvais—Ernulf, invited by Lanfranc (now archbishop), and encouraged by Anselm (*d.* 1109) to abandon teaching for a more enclosed monastic life, left for Christ Church, Canterbury. He is known to have taught grammar there, but in 1096, or shortly after, Anselm, now himself archbishop, made Ernulf his prior. The letters Anselm wrote from exile in the period that followed express deep confidence in Ernulf's judgement, but the strain created by the primate's absence shows through when Ernulf, in a letter printed with Anselm's letters, and incorporated anonymously by Eadmer in his *Historia novorum*, reproaches Anselm for abandoning his pastoral duty by failing to agree terms with the king and return to England. None of this prevented Ernulf from pulling down Lanfranc's choir at Christ Church, and beginning the building of a new choir (its glass, marble paving, and its paintings were admired by William of Malmesbury) and a new crypt. He also did much to stimulate the development of the monastic scriptorium at Canterbury.

It was at Canterbury, probably in 1097 or 1098, that Ernulf wrote his letter *De incestis coniugiis*, which continues in his written discussion with Walkelin, bishop of Winchester (*d.* 1098), on a case of incest between stepmother and stepson. In giving his reasons for disagreeing with Walkelin's judgment, Ernulf, with elaborate rhetoric, unfolds his argument from the axiom that no biblical statement, correctly handled, will conflict with subsequent pronouncements of the historical church. For the construction of the argument Ernulf used as his reference book one of the recently made, systematic, collections of canon law. It is unidentified, but must have been near in structure to the *Decretum* of the great canonist Ivo of Chartres, who had also been at Beauvais in the early 1070s, and may have known Ernulf before this at Bec.

Ernulf's obvious familiarity with a collection of this type, as well as the attention he gives to legal method, makes him witness to the earliest development in England of the new canon law which would achieve its accomplished form in the *Decretum* of Gratian (*c.*1140), but was to have little impact in England until the 1150s. Another letter, written in or after 1095, answers questions put to Ernulf by Lambert, abbot of St Bertin, arising chiefly from the recent controversy over the eucharist. It offers a loyal defence of Lanfranc's teaching on the change in the *substantia* of bread and wine into the body and blood of Christ. In an interesting passage, the division of the host into three parts by the priest is explained by association with the three orders of society: nobility, priesthood, and married laity, the implication being that the presence of Christ in the sacrament has a political dimension. These two letters are printed by d'Achery, *Spicilegium*, 3.464–70 (to Walkelin), and 470–74 (to Lambert).

In 1107 Ernulf succeeded to the abbacy of Peterborough. The abbey had been held vacant for four years, but under Ernulf numbers swelled and new buildings were begun. The monks 'wept tears and then more tears' (*Hugh Candidus*, 96), when in 1114 Henry I, overriding the custom that allowed the archbishop of Canterbury to make appointments to Rochester without royal consultation, 'forced on [Ernulf] the bishopric of Rochester, and the archbishops and bishops, and the nobility that was in England, supported the king; and he long withstood, but it did him no good' (*ASC*, s.a. 1113-15). He was invested by Archbishop Ralph on 28 September 1114, installed at Rochester on 10 October, and consecrated on 26 December. At Rochester he built again—a refectory, a cloister, and a dorter. A series of disputes with Ralph the Clerk, that ended only when Ralph surrendered lands that had apparently once formed part of the episcopal estate, also shows Ernulf protecting his own position as bishop. But his most lasting monuments were the Textus Roffensis, and the organization of the library.

The Textus Roffensis, which can be dated to the end of Ernulf's episcopate (1122 or 1123), was originally in two parts, the first a collection mainly of Anglo-Saxon law codes, running from the Kentish laws of the seventh century (extant only here) to the coronation charter of Henry I, the second a cartulary of the church at Rochester. It was attributed to Ernulf by an entry on the flyleaf in the late thirteenth century, and although he was not its author in the modern sense, his hand in it can be guessed at. The collecting and ordering of the laws of the Anglo-Saxons recall his methodical approach in ecclesiastical law; and the care with which the old English laws were set down, and in their own language, is marked by the appearance in another field of law of the stress on *usus et antiquitas* ('ancient usage and long standing') in the letter to Walkelin, in other words on the idea that a ruling in law accumulates authority with reiteration through time.

The contents of the library at Rochester, much of which was copied during Ernulf's residence there, show a taste for the historical, and included, besides volumes of ecclesiastical history, the *History of the Britons* attributed to Nennius, and the lives of the English saints Aelfheah (*d.* 1012) and Dunstan (*d.* 988). Ernulf's interest in the Anglo-Saxon past, perhaps more natural in a Frenchman than a Norman, was no backwater antiquarianism. The notion that law was custom—and therefore historical in content—which was embedded in both the letter to Walkelin and the Textus Roffensis, was an important aspect of the attempt made by the Normans to rule at least partly through the instruments of government taken over from those they had supplanted. All this helps explain why King Henry sent his writ to Ernulf in 1114 and made him bishop. Although at first glance a figure difficult to discern from the shadow of his friend Archbishop Anselm, Ernulf is on scrutiny a man 'of probity and prudence' (*De gestis pontificum*, 138), whose high reputation in his own day was by no means mere eulogy. He died at Rochester on 15 March 1124, at the age of eighty-four.   PETER CRAMER

Sources 'Epistolae Anselmi', ed. F. S. Schmitt, *S. Anselmi Cantuariensis archiepiscopi opera omnia*, 3–5 (1938–61), esp. *epp.* 38, 64, 74, 310 (from Ernulf), 311 · *Willelmi Malmesbiriensis monachi de gestis pontificum Anglorum libri quinque*, ed. N. E. S. A. Hamilton, Rolls Series, 52 (1870), 137–8 · P. Sawyer, ed., *Textus Roffensis: Rochester Cathedral Library manuscript A.3.5*, 2 vols. (1957–62) · *ASC*, s.a. 1113–15 [texts E, H]; s.a. 1124–5 [text E] · *Eadmeri Historia novorum in Anglia*, ed. M. Rule, Rolls Series, 81 (1884), 197, 225–6, 236 · 'Epistolae', *Patrologia Latina*, 162 (1854), 100 [letter 78] · *The chronicle of Hugh Candidus, a monk of Peterborough*, ed. W. T. Mellows (1949), 90, 96 · F. Liebermann, 'Raginald von Canterbury', *Neues Archiv*, 13 (1888), 537–40 [repr. as *Raginald von Canterbury* (Hannover, 1888)] · *The historical works of Gervase of Canterbury*, ed. W. Stubbs, 2 vols., Rolls Series, 73 (1879–80) · P. Cramer, 'Ernulf of Rochester and early Anglo-Norman canon law', *Journal of Ecclesiastical History*, 40 (1989), 483–510 · M. P. Richards, *Texts and their traditions in the medieval library of Rochester Cathedral priory* (1988), 1–60 · K. Waller, 'Rochester Cathedral Library: an English book collection based on Norman models', *Les mutations socio-culturelles au tournant des XIᵉ–XIIᵉ siècles: études anselmiennes* [Le Bec-Hellouin 1982], ed. R. Foreville (Paris, 1984), 237–50 · Ernulf, 'Ernulfi Rossens. episcopi, qua variis Lamberti quaestionibus respondet', in L. d'Achery, *Spicilegium, sive, Collectio veterum aliquot scriptorum qui in Galliae bibliothecis detiluerant*, 3 (1723), 470–74 · Ernulf, 'Tomellus, sive, epistola Ernulfi ex monacho benedictino episcopi Roffensis, de incestis conjugiis', in L. d'Achery, *Spicilegium, sive, Collectio veterum aliquot scriptorum qui in Galliae bibliothecis detiluerant*, 3 (1723), 464–70 · M. Brett, *The English church under Henry I* (1975) · P. Collinson, P. N. Ramsay, and M. Sparks, eds., *A history of Canterbury Cathedral* (1995)

Erpingham, Sir Thomas (*c.*1355–1428), soldier, was the son of Sir John Erpingham of Erpingham and Wickmere, Norfolk, the head of an established East Anglian gentry family. His early career was a military one. In September 1368 he accompanied his father to Aquitaine in the service of Edward, prince of Wales. By 1372 he was a knight, and in that year he served with William Ufford, earl of Suffolk, on the abortive naval expedition of the summer; in the following year he served in France, again in Ufford's company. By February 1379, however, he was associated with a group of the duke of Lancaster's knights, who were being sent to reinforce the garrison at Calais, and, the following year, he was formally retained by John of Gaunt, duke of Lancaster, at a fee of £20 p.a. in peace and 50 marks in war. It was the start of a connection that was to dominate, and eventually to transform, his career. Erpingham was with the duke of Lancaster on the king's expedition to Scotland in 1385 and he followed his lord to Castile in the following year, apparently remaining in Gaunt's company until the duke's arrival back in England in November 1389. Soon afterwards Erpingham was attached to the household of Henry, earl of Derby, Gaunt's eldest son; he accompanied the earl on his expedition to Prussia and Lithuania between July 1390 and April 1391 and on his second journey, from Prussia to Palestine, between April 1392 and July

Sir Thomas Erpingham (*c.*1355–1428), effigy

1393. Sir Thomas seems to have remained chiefly in Derby's service thereafter: he received a new year's gift from the earl in January 1394 and was closely involved in the preparations for his master's trial by combat in the summer of 1398.

The condemnation and exile of Henry in July 1398 created a crisis in the lives of his servants and ushered in the most decisive years of Erpingham's career. Sir Thomas went into exile with his master in October 1398 and remained abroad with him until Henry's invasion attempt the following July. Erpingham played a conspicuous role in the ensuing Lancastrian revolution. Immediately after landing, he was dispatched to raise funds from the ducal estates, returning to the main army in time to accompany Henry Percy, earl of Northumberland, to the crucial interview with King Richard at Conwy. His part in the formal proceedings that led to the king's deposition was no less prominent: he carried Henry's sword before him as he processed into Westminster Hall and, on behalf of 'all the bachelors and commons of this land of the South' (*RotP*, 3.424), formally renounced allegiance to Richard.

The new king rewarded this consistent loyalty by granting Sir Thomas several positions of confidence and trust which he, in turn, discharged with characteristic reliability. Appointed as constable of Dover Castle and warden of the Cinque Ports, a strategically vital command, as early as 21 August 1399, Erpingham was made chamberlain of the royal household following Henry's accession. In January 1400 he commanded a division of the royal army that put down the 'Epiphany rising' and, in the summer, served on the king's expedition against the Scots. He was appointed a knight of the Garter in the same year. In October 1401 Sir Thomas was appointed a guardian in England of the king's second son, Thomas of Lancaster, and in November he was the only commoner considered by the council for the post of master of Henry, prince of Wales. Erpingham was frequently at court during the early years of Henry IV's reign but an apparent distaste for administrative business meant that he attended the council only occasionally. In February 1404 Sir Thomas relinquished the chamberlainship and was immediately appointed as steward of the royal household. He became acting marshal of England in October 1404 and his services to the king and the kingdom were specifically commended by the Commons in the Coventry parliament, as they were to be again during the Long Parliament (March–December 1406). Following his resignation from the stewardship of the household in November 1404, however, Erpingham seems to have withdrawn from active involvement in court life. His subsequent royal employments were chiefly diplomatic: as an ambassador to treat for peace with the French, and one of the prince of Wales's proxies to negotiate a marriage to a French princess (June–December 1407); and as a conservator of the truce with Brittany (July 1408 and 1409).

Such a record of service brought Sir Thomas considerable rewards. By 1399 he was already in receipt of an annuity of 70 marks, supplemented by a grant of the hundreds of North and South Erpingham, from the duke of Lancaster, but such sums were dwarfed by the avalanche of grants and annuities, such as the £300 p.a. he enjoyed as constable of Dover, made to him after the usurpation. At the peak of his career under Henry IV, between 1402 and 1409, Erpingham enjoyed a fee income of over £600 p.a., quite apart from the emoluments he received for his service in the royal household and the escheats and wardships he held by royal grant. In February 1409, however, Sir Thomas was persuaded to surrender the constableship of Dover, in favour of the prince of Wales, who compensated him with a life annuity of £100 p.a. This exchange seems to mark a shift in the focus of Erpingham's political loyalties, away from the king and towards the prince of Wales, which, though it led to a temporary loss of royal favour, stood him in good stead once Prince Henry succeeded his father.

On Henry V's accession Sir Thomas was immediately appointed to his old post of steward of the royal household. He joined the king's expedition to France in 1415, serving as a banneret with a company of twenty men-at-arms and sixty archers, and took a prominent part in the campaign. At Harfleur, Erpingham was one of the negotiators who secured the surrender of the town, while at Agincourt he was responsible for deploying the archers into their battle positions. Sir Thomas returned to France in 1416, travelling to Beauvais in July in order to treat with the French envoys and, in his capacity as steward of the household, he was one of the party who welcomed the duke of Burgundy to Calais in October. In May 1417, however, Erpingham resigned as steward of the household and he did not join the king's second expedition to France. Thereafter, he seems once again to have retired from life at court, though he still retained privileged access to the king and attended occasional council meetings as late as July 1421.

Erpingham's withdrawal from court did not, however, mark the end of his career, or his influence. A distinctive feature of his service to the Lancastrian dynasty is the sway Sir Thomas exercised in his native East Anglia after Henry IV's accession. A series of crown grants gave him custody of the two most important concentrations of magnate estates in the region, the Mowbray and Mortimer inheritances, between 1399 and 1409, held either solely or in joint custody with the prince of Wales. Together with his extensive circle of kinsmen and associates and his ready access to the court, these grants made Erpingham a considerable figure in East Anglia and enabled him to exercise what amounted, in the absence of any resident magnate, to a regional dominance. This was first demonstrated in 1401, by his orchestration of a bill of impeachment against Henry Despenser, bishop of Norwich—and Erpingham's only real rival for regional pre-eminence—for his alleged participation in the 'Epiphany rising'. His importance was quickly recognized by the citizens of Norwich, who paid Sir Thomas 20 marks 'for bearing his good word to the king for the honour of the city' (Hudson and Tingey, 2.53) in the year after Henry IV's accession. Erpingham returned the favour by helping the city to secure the status of a shire incorporate in 1404 and by successfully arbitrating a long-standing dispute over city government in 1414. It was as an arbitrator and umpire in such local quarrels that Sir Thomas was most useful to the king and council: his influence is indicated by his request to several correspondents to await a final resolution of their disputes 'until my arrival in the country' (Legge, 429) while, as late as 1425, he was still powerful enough to impose a settlement upon an unwilling William Paston.

Sir Thomas Erpingham died on 27 June 1428. In his will he made extensive bequests to the religious houses and recluses of East Anglia and asked to be buried in Norwich Cathedral. He was a generous public benefactor, paying for the construction of the 'Erpingham gate' at the entrance to the cathedral precinct in Norwich and for the rebuilding of the Dominican friars' church in the city, as well as financing the west tower at Erpingham parish church. Sir Thomas also gave a new east window to the church of the Augustinian friars at Norwich, commemorating the many East Anglian lords and knights who had died without a male heir since the coronation of Edward III; his own arms were among those depicted, for though he married twice—to Joan, daughter of Sir William Clopton, and to Joan, daughter of Sir Richard Walton and widow of Sir John Howard—both marriages were childless.

Erpingham was one of the most characteristic figures of the early Lancastrian regime, a representative member of the small group of knights and esquires whose loyalty to Henry IV took them to positions of unusual eminence during his reign. What especially distinguishes his career is the facility with which he converted royal favour into local influence; his consistent popularity, which meant that his intimacy with the king never attracted resentment; and his ability to maintain this prominence and influence at court well into the reign of Henry's son and successor. SIMON WALKER

Sources Chancery records, esp. Duchy of Lancaster, various accounts, PRO, PRO DL 28 · T. John, 'Sir Thomas Erpingham, East Anglian society and the dynastic revolution of 1399', Norfolk Archaeology, 35 (1970–73), 96–108 · W. Hudson and J. C. Tingey, eds., The records of the city of Norwich, 2 vols. (1906–10) · E. F. Jacob, ed., The register of Henry Chichele, archbishop of Canterbury, 1414–1443, 2, CYS, 42 (1937) · F. Blomefield and C. Parkin, An essay towards a topographical history of the county of Norfolk, [2nd edn], 11 vols. (1805–10) · N. H. Nicolas, ed., Proceedings and ordinances of the privy council of England, 7 vols., RC, 26 (1834–7) · Rymer, Foedera, 3rd edn · L. T. Smith, ed., Expeditions to Prussia and the Holy Land made by Henry, earl of Derby, CS, new ser., 52 (1894) · N. H. Nicolas, ed., The Scrope and Grosvenor controversy, 2 vols. (privately printed, London, 1832) · M. D. Legge, ed., Anglo-Norman letters and petitions from All Souls MS 182, Anglo-Norman Texts, 3 (1941) · CIPM, 4, no. 116
Likenesses line engraving, pubd 1793 (after window, Norwich Cathedral), BM, NPG · effigy, Norwich Cathedral precinct, Erpingham gate [see illus.] · line engraving, BM, NPG; repro. in S. Harding, Shakespeare illustrated (1793) · window; formerly in Norwich Cathedral · window, Great Snoring church, Norfolk; repro. in Blomefield and Parkin, An essay, [2nd edn], vol. 9, p. 257
Wealth at death lands: CIPM, 4, no. 116

Errington, Anthony (d. 1719x24), Roman Catholic priest, was a member of a Northumbrian family. His name appears in a list of Douai writers, but he may have been educated at Lisbon and Paris. He wrote Catechistical Discourses (1654), dedicated to the 'Princesse Henrietta Maria, daughter of England', presumably Charles I's fifth daughter, Henrietta or Henrietta Anne, being raised a Catholic in France. He may also have written Missionarium, sive, Opusculum practicum, pro fide propaganda et conservanda, published at Rome in 1672. He is said to have died between 1719 and 1724. THOMPSON COOPER, rev. RUTH JORDAN

Sources Dodd's Church history of England, ed. M. A. Tierney, 5 vols. (1839–43), vol. 3, p. 295 · Gillow, Lit. biog. hist., 2.176 · Catholic Magazine, 2 (1832), 257 · D. A. Bellenger, ed., English and Welsh priests, 1558–1800 (1984)

Errington, George (1804–1886), Roman Catholic archbishop, was born on 14 September 1804 at Clints Hall, Richmond, Yorkshire, the second of three children of Thomas Errington and his wife, Katherine, daughter of Walter Dowdall. He had one brother, Michael, and one sister, Isabel. He was educated at St Cuthbert's College, Ushaw, between 1814 and 1821, entering the English College at Rome on 2 November 1821 as an ecclesiastical student. Between 1824 and 1826 he received three prizes in scholastic and moral theology. In September 1827 he graduated DD and on 22 December he was ordained priest.

In December 1828 Nicholas Wiseman was appointed to the rectorship of the college, and Errington became his vice-rector until 1831, when he resigned owing to ill health. He then spent several years travelling in Europe and developing his interest in natural history, geology, and archaeology. Restored to better health, he returned to England in 1843 to work once again with Wiseman, who had been appointed president of St Mary's College, Oscott. Errington became prefect of studies at St Mary's, remaining there until August 1847. Shortly after this date he volunteered for the mission of St Nicholas, Liverpool, disregarding the dangers posed by a typhus epidemic in the city. His name first appears in the registers of St Nicholas in April 1848. Early in 1849 he was engaged as rector of the new mission of St John's in Salford, with a commission to reduce debts caused by the extravagance of its building. His success in this endeavour was attributed partly to his 'extreme parsimony in his private and household expenditure' (Powell, 8). On the restoration of the Catholic hierarchy Errington was raised to the episcopate, and consecrated as first bishop of Plymouth on 25 July 1851 by Wiseman, now cardinal-archbishop of Westminster. Plymouth, one of the poorest of the new dioceses, proved to be a difficult charge since it lacked both staff and money. Yet Errington organized the diocese sufficiently well for his successor to reap the benefits. When he left Plymouth to become coadjutor-archbishop of Westminster he handed over a diocese which was free from debt and beginning to show signs of growth.

In May 1855 Errington was created archbishop of Trebizond in partibus infidelium and translated to Westminster as coadjutor to Cardinal Wiseman, with right of succession to the archdiocese. Errington began his episcopal duties in Westminster with a visitation of St Edmund's College, near Ware, and it was here that the controversies which were to plague his career in Westminster began. For a number of years the Oxford convert W. G. Ward had been teaching dogmatic theology to ecclesiastical students at the college. His position at St Edmund's was opposed by a considerable number, including other members of the college staff, since it was unprecedented that a recently converted, married layman should be allowed to teach seminarians. Errington put such restrictions upon his teaching that Ward felt compelled to resign his position. Cardinal Wiseman objected to Errington's decisions and persuaded Ward to withdraw his resignation. Errington was infuriated by Wiseman's actions, since he claimed that before making his visitation he had secured the cardinal's promise that there would be no interference with his decisions. Consequently Errington wrote to the authorities in Rome requesting to be moved, since he felt he could no longer work in harmony with the cardinal. Rome feared that great scandal would be caused by moving him so soon after his appointment; instead of a permanent position elsewhere, therefore, Errington was sent to the vacant see of Clifton in October 1855 as apostolic visitor while a suitable bishop was found. During this appointment he resolved many of the financial problems of the diocese. Errington's ability for managing scarce resources came from a belief in personal austerity and hard work, and he demanded the same from those who worked under him. In some quarters this made him unpopular, and earned him the sobriquet 'the iron archbishop'.

Errington returned to Westminster in February 1857 to conduct a full visitation of that diocese. This led to more disagreements with Wiseman, of the type experienced during the visitation of St Edmund's College. Influential supporters of the cardinal began to voice their suspicions about Errington's loyalty to both the cardinal and the pope, and although by this time Wiseman was convinced that he wanted to be rid of his coadjutor, Errington refused to leave of his own accord. In December 1859 Wiseman arrived in Rome to petition for Errington's removal. After consideration by a special commission it was decided that Errington could no longer remain at Westminster. He was given the opportunity to resign, but declined. On 22 July 1860 Pius IX issued a decree relieving Errington of his coadjutorship and his right of succession to the diocese. Errington submitted and left the diocese, living in retirement for five years.

In 1865, after Wiseman's death, Errington was nominated as his successor by the Westminster chapter, but Pius IX preferred to appoint H. E. Manning. After Errington's removal from Westminster, Pius IX offered him the archbishopric of Trinidad (1863) and the opportunity to restore the Scottish hierarchy (1868). He declined both invitations. In September 1865 he took charge of the parish of Douglas, Isle of Man, and remained there until 1868. In 1869 he was called to the First Vatican Council, where he sided with those who considered it inopportune to define the doctrine of papal infallibility. On his return from Rome, Bishop Clifford engaged him as theology tutor at the newly reopened Prior Park College, near Bath. His reputation for sternness and inflexibility went before him, yet contemporaries often wrote of a gentle and kind side to the archbishop's nature. He taught at Prior Park until a few hours before his death, from bronchitis, on 19 January 1886. He was buried in the college church.

PAUL MOULD

Sources *The Tablet* (23 Jan 1886) · R. Schiefen, *Nicholas Wiseman and the transformation of English Catholicism* (1984) · W. Ward, *The life and times of Cardinal Wiseman*, 2 vols. (1897) · E. Powell, 'Memoir of the Most Reverend George Errington', Westm. DA
Archives Birmingham Archdiocesan Archives, corresp. · Bishop's House, Clifton, Clifton diocesan papers · Bristol RO, corresp. | Sacra Congregazione di Propaganda Fide, Rome, archives · Ushaw College, Durham, letters to Charles Newsham · Ushaw College, Durham, letters to John Walker · Ushaw College, Durham, letters to Nicholas Wiseman · Venerable English College, Rome, Talbot MSS · Westm. DA, letters to Nicholas Wiseman
Wealth at death £580 4s. 4d.: probate, 11 Feb 1886, *CGPLA Eng. & Wales*

Errington, John Edward (1806–1862), civil engineer, was born at Sculcoates, Hull, on 29 December 1806, the eldest son of John Errington and his wife, Harriet. At an early age he was placed with an engineer engaged on public works in Ireland and was trained as a civil engineering surveyor. He then became assistant to Paul Padley on some early railway surveys, which brought him to the attention of John Urpeth Rastrick (1780–1856), whom he assisted in the preparation of plans for the Birmingham–Basford section of the Grand Junction Railway. He first met Joseph Locke, with whom he was to be closely associated for the remainder of his career, on the survey of a proposed Manchester–Stockport railway. In July 1834 he was appointed assistant surveyor on the Grand Junction and when Locke took over sole direction of that railway, he made Errington resident engineer on the line. After its completion in 1837, he took charge of the Glasgow, Paisley, and Greenock Railway and in 1841 began the new harbour works at Greenock.

In 1843, in conjunction with Locke, Errington made the plans for the Lancaster and Carlisle Railway. At this time Locke's practice was very extensive, including continental railways, and Errington took charge of the Lancaster and Carlisle line. When work began on the Caledonian Railway he became partner supervising the construction, as he was on the Clydesdale Junction Railway, the Scottish Central, the Scottish Midland Junction, and the Aberdeen railways. He was involved in some capacity with the entire system of railways from Lancaster to Inverness. After the opening of the larger works in Scotland he joined Locke in London, and devoted his attention to the various additions and branches made to the railways constructed under his own and Locke's superintendence.

Errington became an associate of the Institution of Civil Engineers in 1831 and a member in 1839; he was a member of the council in 1850 and a vice-president in 1861–2, and bequeathed £1000 to the institution. He was involved in various parliamentary deliberations, and the conscientious and clear manner in which he gave his evidence had great weight with the committees concerned.

Errington endeavoured to make railways commercially successful, and at the same time to combine elegance with strength and economy of design. His bridges on the Lancaster and Carlisle and the Caledonian railways, and those across the Thames at Richmond, Kew, and Kingston, showed his success. Latterly he was appointed engineer to the London and South-Western Railway Company after Locke had fallen out with the directors. His plan for the line from Yeovil to Exeter was accepted in 1856. After great difficulties due to tunnelling conditions at Crewkerne and Honiton, the line was opened in 1860. Several branches of this line were also constructed under his direction.

After the completion of this work Errington's health failed; he died at his residence, 6 Pall Mall East, Charing Cross, London, on 4 July 1862, aged fifty-five, and was buried in Kensal Green cemetery, in close proximity to his friend and associate, Locke. Their practice was continued by their assistants W. R. Galbraith, and J. H. Tolmé.

G. C. BOASE, rev. MIKE CHRIMES

Sources *PICE*, 22 (1862–3), 626–9 · *The Times* (7 July 1862), 6 · P. R. Reynolds, 'Paul Padley', *Railway & Canal Historical Society Journal*, 23 (1977) · J. Devey, *The life of Joseph Locke* (1862) · N. W. Webster, *Joseph Locke: railway revolutionary* (1970) · d. cert.
Archives Inst. CE, membership records | Inst. CE, Mackenzie MSS · PRO, Railway records · Sci. Mus., Neumann MSS

Likenesses engraving?, *c.*1853, National Railway Museum; repro. in O. S. Nock, *The Caledonian Railway* (1961) [commemorative brochure]
Wealth at death under £120,000: probate, 17 July 1862, *CGPLA Eng. & Wales*

Errington, William (1716–1768), Roman Catholic priest, was born on 17 July 1716, the son of Mark Errington, gentleman, of Salterton, Durnford, Wiltshire, and his wife, Martha, *née* Baker. His parents had been married in the Church of England at Gosport, Hampshire, on 26 May 1707, and Errington was baptized into the established church on 20 July 1716 at St Thomas's, Portsmouth, Hampshire; but the Errington family's associations were Roman Catholic, and in or about 1737 he was sent to the English College, Douai. He took the college oath in December 1741, and was ordained deacon on 23 September 1747 and priest in December that year. On 26 March 1748 he left for the English mission. In 1758 he published a response to a pamphlet by William Arnold, a convert from protestantism who had then rejected the Catholic church.

By 1760 Errington was living with Richard Challoner, vicar apostolic of the London district (who had mentioned him in a letter to Douai in 1746), and is described in some accounts as his chaplain. The education of English Catholics was of particular concern to Challoner. Although there were Catholic schools for girls and for young children in England, older boys had to travel to the colleges on the continent to complete their education. Challoner authorized Errington to establish a school for boys over the age of twelve whose parents were less prosperous than the gentry families who could send their sons abroad. Errington's first attempts in Buckinghamshire and Wales were unsuccessful, but his third location, at Betley, near Newcastle under Lyme, Staffordshire, with John Hurst as master, was able to attract eighteen pupils. Many of the Catholic gentry had felt that the establishment of a Catholic boys' school would lead to renewed persecution, but it was a Catholic landowner, Thomas Giffard of Chillington, Staffordshire, who helped Errington negotiate the tenancy of a more suitable building, Sedgley Park near Wolverhampton. Its owner, John Ward, first Viscount Dudley and Ward, was criticized for letting his house for a Catholic school, but he defended his actions in parliament and remained a supporter of the project.

The school, initially with twelve pupils, opened on 25 March 1763, and Errington remained in personal authority until the arrival of Hugh Kendal, his appointee, as its first president on 27 May 1763. He then returned to Challoner in London, but continued to be the proprietor of the school and closely supervised its accounts. He also became archdeacon of the chapter of the secular clergy in England and Wales as well as its treasurer. He died in London on 28 September 1768. In his will, made at Red Lion Street, Holborn, on 8 August 1763, he indicated that he wished the chapter to manage the school, but they instead arranged its transfer to John Joseph Hornyold, vicar apostolic of the midland district. A catalogue of his library was published by James Peter Coghlan in 1770.

Sedgley Park School continued until 1873, when it migrated to Cotton Hall, Oakamoor, Staffordshire, and became Cotton College. The college honours Challoner as its founder, but it was Errington who persevered in finding a site and arranging the detail of its establishment, and thus bears much of the responsibility for what might be called the 're-naturalization' of Catholic boys' education in eighteenth-century England.

MATTHEW KILBURN

Sources DNB · E. H. Burton and E. Nolan, *The Douay College diaries: the seventh diary, 1715–1778*, Catholic RS, 28 (1928) · W. Buscot, *The history of Cotton College* (1940) · F. Roberts, *A history of Sedgley Park and Cotton College*, ed. N. Henshaw (1985) · E. H. Burton, *The life and times of Bishop Challoner, 1691–1781*, 2 (1909), 35–7 · G. Anstruther, *The seminary priests*, 4 (1977) · F. C. Husenbeth, *The history of Sedgley Park School, Staffordshire* (1856) · F. Blom and others, *English Catholic books, 1701–1800: a bibliography* (1996) · IGI

Errol, Bert [*real name* Isaac Whitehouse] (1883–1949), singer and female impersonator, was born on 11 August 1883 at 106 Aston Road, Aston, Birmingham, the son of Isaac Whitehouse, brass lock founder, and his wife, Elizabeth Griffiths. He began his career in Birmingham as a concert singer at the age of eighteen. In 1908 he became a full professional, joining Adler's and Sutton's concert party where he sang popular arias in a strong tenor. His subsequent move to one of the then popular 'blackface' troupes, Harry Reynolds's minstrels, began the evolution of the style for which he became famous. His chief function was to play female roles; his operatic strength applied to falsetto enabled him to offer convincing and witty parodies of the divas of the day. He soon abandoned the anonymity of blackface and developed this mixture of comedy and music, making his début at the London Pavilion in 1909 as the Famous Male Soprano and Double-Voiced Vocalist. Much of the act consisted of parodying popular musical comedy actresses; other songs, notably his signature song 'My Sahara Rose', were sung straight to emphasize the real quality of Errol's voice. Both elements were important because they underlined the unique nature of Errol's act. He did not offer a caricature of femininity with exaggerated features; he did not exploit the contrast between his masculine body and a superimposed feminine style; he did not use the physical comedy favoured by many male impersonators who played upon a comic incompetence in dealing with skirts or high heels; rather, he offered a careful and precise impersonation of a particular woman—either a figure from his own imagination or a recognizable actress. The comedy grew out of the accuracy of his observation and the foibles of the character he portrayed, generally a *prima donna* with a roaring ego—but invariably with a talent to match it.

Photographs of Errol show a strong face with a cleft chin, not especially delicate or feminine, upon which a meticulous transformation has been achieved. In one from the 1920s, for instance, the hairdo is smartly contemporary, the shingle favoured by the vast majority of women; it looks natural, as unlike a wig as possible. The make-up is consistent with the contemporary fashion, the lipstick in the Cupid's bow shape familiar from the vamps of the silent movies. The clothes flow smoothly; they

Bert Errol (1883–1949), by unknown photographer, *c.*1930

adhere to the flat-chested ideal of the period rather than offering opportunities for the bosom gags beloved of most caricaturists, and they are luxurious and well-cut.

Before Errol no female impersonator had made a major success in British variety: there were a small number of clubs with drag performers, there were pantomime dames and farces where actors dressed as women, but the delicacy of Errol's parodies was new. He toured widely—in Australia, New Zealand, South Africa, Canada, and the USA. He spent years in American vaudeville, where his glamorous style found an appreciative audience already accustomed to the sophisticated *travesti* of Julian Eltinge and Karyl Norman. He worked for the management of Wyle and Tate for nine seasons in London and the provinces and in 1922 made a rare pantomime appearance in *Cinderella* at the London Hippodrome. The choice is perhaps significant; rather than a dame in isolation, he played one of the ugly sisters (Minnie Mumm) and his counterpart (Maxie Mumm) was not another male but a popular actress, Dolly Harmer, placing the emphasis upon character rather than broad physical jokes and allowing the audience to enjoy an unusually complex form of gender interplay.

Errol's accurate and detailed style of female impersonation had relatively little competition in the popular theatre; the years following both world wars saw a rise in the number of impersonators, many of whom began their careers in all-male revues originally put together to entertain the troops—*Splinters*, for example, began in 1914 and toured the country for two decades after the war; *Soldiers in Skirts*, *Misleading Ladies*, and others achieved brief popularity in the forties and early fifties, the latter launching the career of Danny La Rue. Errol, however, continued to remain what he had always been, a respected solo performer. He died on 29 November 1949 in the Royal Sussex County Hospital, Brighton, of heart failure. He was survived by his wife, Ray, of whom nothing else is known.

FRANCES GRAY

Sources R. Busby, *British music hall: an illustrated who's who from 1850 to the present day* (1976) · R. Baker, *Drag* (1968) · *The Times* (3 Dec 1949) · d. cert. · b. cert. · *CGPLA Eng. & Wales* (1950)
Likenesses photograph, *c.*1930, Hult. Arch. [*see illus.*] · photographs, Mander and Mitcheson theatre collection, London
Wealth at death £2718 6*s.* 3*d.*: probate, 1 March 1950, *CGPLA Eng. & Wales*

Erroll. For this title name *see* individual entries under Erroll; *see also* Hay, William, first earl of Erroll (*d.* 1462) [*see under* Hay family (*per. c.*1295–*c.*1460)]; Hay, Francis, ninth earl of Erroll (*bap.* 1564, *d.* 1631); Hay, Josslyn Victor, twenty-second earl of Erroll (1901–1941).

Erroll, Frederick James, Baron Erroll of Hale and Baron Erroll of Kilmun (1914–2000), politician and businessman, was born in London on 27 May 1914, the only child of George Murison Erroll (1874–1926) and his wife, Kathleen Donovan, *née* Edington (*d.* 1952), daughter of George Brodrick Edington, of Hillhead, Glasgow. His father was an engineer who had changed his name by deed poll in 1914; his previous surname was Bergmans, which was too Germanic-sounding for a man who was about to fight in the First World War. In fact the family came from Rotterdam, where Lord Erroll's grandfather, Theodor John Bergmans, had been a merchant and broker.

Young Freddy Erroll was educated at Oundle School, and spent a year as an engineering apprentice before reading mechanical sciences at Trinity College, Cambridge. He graduated in 1938, and, after travelling in Africa, started work in the engineering department of Metropolitan-Vickers in Manchester. His career was interrupted by war, during which he held a commission in the Territorial Army. By 1945 he had become a full colonel—apparently the youngest TA officer to hold that rank. He had spent the war as a technical adviser on tank construction, a role which took him to Italy, India, and Burma.

Erroll had already shown an interest in public life, having served as chairman of the Engineering Apprentices' Association in the year before he went to Cambridge. Even so, his entry to parliament in 1945 was a surprising break from his previous career. But it seemed an inspired decision. He secured a relatively safe tory seat, Altrincham and Sale, and quickly won a reputation as a lively backbencher, taking part in numerous skirmishes with Labour ministers. He was a conspicuous figure, 6 feet 5 inches tall and athletic (he was a keen swimmer and had rowed at Cambridge); another claim to attention was the fact that he was the youngest MP. Most important, though, was Erroll's unusual technical knowledge. He seemed to epitomize a new breed of tory: good-natured, clever, and hard-working. A party keen to adapt to the post-war world was fortunate to have attracted such a man, and a glittering career seemed to lie ahead.

In one respect, though, Erroll—who on 19 December 1950 married Elizabeth Barrow, daughter of Richard Sowton Barrow, of Exmouth, Devon—was out of step with his contemporaries. He was an enthusiast for the free market at a time when the Conservatives had chosen to accept much of Labour's interventionist approach to economic and social policy. This may explain why he failed to win promotion until 1955, when he became parliamentary secretary at the Ministry of Supply. But this ministry—headed at the time by Reginald Maudling—was not represented in the cabinet. It was therefore a small step up for Erroll when in November 1956 he became parliamentary secretary at the Board of Trade; but even there he was third in the hierarchy, behind Peter Thorneycroft and Toby Low (later Lord Aldington). Nevertheless, Erroll gave ample testimony to his organizational ability, working on schemes to attract new jobs to areas of economic deprivation. It was only a matter of time before he moved further ahead, and in October 1958 he became economic secretary to the Treasury.

Erroll's government posts had exploited his expertise, but he was changing jobs too often to make a lasting impression in any of them. After just one year as economic secretary he migrated again, this time back to the Board of Trade as minister of state, a post which reunited him with Reggie Maudling. Here his dynamic approach to selling British products overseas led him to coin the phrase 'Exporting is fun'. In 1961 he finally reached the cabinet as president of the board, and embarked on an ambitious itinerary, taking in Japan and China among other countries in his attempt to drum up business. In keeping with his free-market beliefs, his strategy was to work towards the general elimination of barriers to trade, regardless of foreign policy considerations. Thus, he felt that economic sanctions against Cuba in the aftermath of the Bay of Pigs fiasco should be kept to a minimum. Harold Macmillan took his advice, despite pressure from President Kennedy and the Foreign Office.

Erroll was still at the Board of Trade when Macmillan stood down as prime minister, but he had not always seen eye to eye with his boss. The most serious disagreement came over resale price maintenance. Many of Erroll's predecessors had contemplated the abolition of this restrictive practice, but Erroll's enthusiasm for the free market led him to drop public hints without permission from a prime minister who recognized that government action could alienate the small shopkeepers—an important body of tory activists. His initiative was stopped in its tracks. Ironically his successor at the Board of Trade, Edward Heath, contrived to force through the legislation. It was the second time that Heath had taken a plum which might have been secured by Erroll, who had been considered in 1960 for the job of chief negotiator with the European Economic Community (EEC).

Heath rejected Erroll's attempt to persuade him not to support Alec Douglas Home for the party leadership, knowing that Erroll supported Maudling, who would have

provided a more formidable obstacle than Home to Heath's future ambitions. Erroll took his opposition to Home to the length of attending a well-publicized meeting with other dissident ministers. Two of these, Enoch Powell and Iain Macleod, subsequently refused to serve under Home. By contrast, both Maudling and Erroll fell into line, although the latter was effectively demoted when he accepted the position of minister of power. However, he felt that the year he spent at the Ministry of Power was his most rewarding government stint; he was particularly proud of having steered the Continental Shelf Bill through parliament, thus ensuring that private companies could begin to explore the fuel reserves under the North Sea.

Erroll won his own seat again in the general election of 1964 with a comfortable majority. But he contracted pneumonia, and felt that he should leave the Commons. Home awarded him a hereditary peerage, with the title Baron Erroll of Hale, in his resignation honours in the same year. With typical humour, Erroll chose 'It will come out all right' as his motto. In keeping with his optimistic motto, he no doubt felt that his illness had been happily timed. Whether or not his party regained office, he no longer had ministerial claims—or ambitions. Instead, he resumed his career in business, chairing Bowater (1973–84) and Consolidated Goldfields (1976–82) among many other companies. This, perhaps, was his proper métier; a large presence, a hearty sense of humour, and a rigorous attention to detail made him an excellent chairman. He also gave his time to the Institute of Directors, whose council he had first joined in 1949. To mark his contribution in the House of Lords (where he served as a member of the select committee on science and technology), he was given a life peerage, with the title Baron Erroll of Kilmun, to ensure continued membership after the expulsion of hereditary peers in 1999. Lively and gregarious to the end, Lord Erroll died in London on 14 September 2000, aged eighty-six. He was survived by his wife Elizabeth. There were no children of their marriage, and his hereditary peerage expired with him.

MARK GARNETT

Sources *The Times* (18 Sept 2000) · *Daily Telegraph* (18 Sept 2000) · *The Guardian* (19 Sept 2000) · *The Independent* (26 Sept 2000) · *WWW* · Burke, *Peerage*
Archives NRA, personal papers | CAC Cam., corresp. with Sir E. L. Spears
Likenesses photograph, 1958, repro. in *Daily Telegraph* · photograph, 1961, repro. in *The Times* · photograph, repro. in *The Guardian* · photograph, repro. in *The Independent*

Erskine family (*per. c.1350–c.1450*), administrators and noblemen, became important in the court politics and government of Scotland in the second half of the fourteenth century. Established in Renfrewshire by the thirteenth century, the Erskines were followers of the Stewarts, and it was after the capture of David II at the battle of Nevilles Cross in 1346, when the king's nephew Robert the Steward (the future Robert II) was governor of Scotland, that **Sir Robert Erskine** (*d.* 1385) assumed a leading role in administration. Already a knight in 1343, by 15 May 1350 he was acting as chamberlain, the crown's chief financial officer, in the name of the absent king. He was involved in the negotiations leading to David's release from captivity in 1357. Although David replaced him as chamberlain with Thomas, earl of Mar, in 1358, Erskine continued to serve as a royal envoy to the English, French, and papal courts, and in 1359 he cited David's unwillingness to release him from his service in justification of a bid to obtain discharge from crusading vows. No later than 12 May 1363, when David II faced a major baronial rebellion sparked partly by his alleged misuse of sums raised to pay for his English ransom, Erskine was reappointed to the chamberlainship, perhaps as a man trusted by both the king and his opponents to control the royal finances. He retained the office until late the following year, and thereafter remained an important royal envoy and administrator, being particularly active in David's negotiations with the English crown during the 1360s. Besides his ambassadorial duties, Erskine also acted as justiciar of Lothian and as custodian at various times of the royal castles of Stirling and Dumbarton. His rewards included Alloa and other lands in the sheriffdom of Clackmannan, granted in regality in 1364, and the barony of Dun, Forfarshire, probably given in 1368 when the grant of Alloa was confirmed.

Towards the end of David's reign Erskine's influence increased because of his association with the king's new mistress, Agnes Dunbar. She was in Erskine's care in 1369, as a result of which more royal patronage was diverted to him and his family. Most notably, in April 1370 he received a lifetime grant of the keepership of Stirling Castle. His place in government was threatened by the unexpected death of David II on 22 February 1371, and he played a significant though rather enigmatic part in the events which occurred between David's death and the accession of Robert II, when William, earl of Douglas, led an armed demonstration at Linlithgow. Douglas's aim has been variously interpreted as either to contest the Steward's claim to the throne or to challenge Erskine's hold on royal offices and his influence in government. Erskine and his allies John and George Dunbar, the brothers of Agnes, were said by Wyntoun to have ended Douglas's demonstration by assembling their own forces and confronting the earl at Linlithgow. Erskine remained as a regular witness to the new king's great seal charters, but in the two years after 1371 he and his son Thomas lost most of their prestigious offices to the earl of Douglas (who became justiciar south of the Forth) and the sons of Robert II (who became custodians of Edinburgh and Stirling castles). Nevertheless Robert received substantial financial compensation for these losses in the form of large one-off payments and annuities from the royal customs, and he continued to witness great seal charters until his death between 21 May and 11 November 1385.

Erskine married twice. His first wife was Beatrice, widow of Sir Archibald Douglas (d. 1333) and daughter of Alexander Lindsay of Crawford. She had died by about 1352, when he married Christian Keith (née Menteith; d.

c.1387), widow of Sir Edward Keith of Sinton, allegedly as a means of settling a quarrel between himself and the Menteiths. A number of grants and confirmations were made jointly to Erskine and his second wife. His heir, however, was **Sir Thomas Erskine** (d. 1403/4), the eldest son of his first marriage. Thomas too had been high in the favour of David II, receiving the lucrative ward of the heiress to the lordship of Brechin and also perhaps the keepership of Edinburgh Castle during 1370. Both the wardship and the constableship were handed over to sons of Robert II after 1371. Despite these setbacks Sir Thomas (he was knighted some time between 1365 and 1370) remained a regular witness to the new king's great seal charters. Like many of the men associated with David II, he found his way into the service of Robert II's eldest son and heir, John Stewart, earl of Carrick (later Robert III); he was paid an 80 merk pension for his service to Carrick and the king throughout the 1380s. Erskine was notably active in the Anglo-Scottish warfare promoted by Carrick in the 1380s and was one of three Scottish knights responsible for the distribution of a French war subsidy in 1385. On 5 August 1388 he was severely wounded at the battle of Otterburn, in which James, second earl of Douglas and eleventh earl of Mar, was killed. Douglas died childless, and his earldom of Mar passed to his sister Isabella and her husband, Malcolm Drummond, who, however, also had no children. Erskine had an interest in Mar through his second wife, Janet Barclay (née Keith; d. c.1413), apparently a great-granddaughter of Gartnait, earl of Mar (d. before 1305), and a claim to be considered as one of the heirs to the earldom should Malcolm and Isabella Drummond remain childless. In 1391 and 1393 he sought and received assurances from the crown that there would be no royal confirmation of any deals made by Countess Isabella that would adversely affect the rights of his own wife in Mar.

Erskine remained active in public life, and on 14 September 1402 he and his son Sir Robert (a knight by 1400) were among the many Scottish lords captured by the English at the battle of Homildon Hill. It is not known whether he had been released before his death between 11 November 1403 and 18 May 1404. His first wife, Mary Douglas, died in childbirth in or before 1370, and his heir, **Robert Erskine**, first Lord Erskine (d. 1451/2), was the son of his marriage to Janet Barclay. Robert's career was dominated by his ultimately unsuccessful efforts to obtain title to the earldom of Mar. His claim was badly affected in August 1404, when the recently widowed Isabella, countess of Mar, married Alexander Stewart, the illegitimate son of Alexander Stewart, earl of Buchan. The couple attempted to arrange for Isabella's earldom to pass to Alexander and his male descendants in heritage. Kinsmen and allies of the Erskines, including Robert Stewart, duke of Albany, then guardian of the kingdom, intervened to ensure that royal approval for this scheme was withheld, and eventually Alexander Stewart had to settle for the right to hold the earldom for his own lifetime. However, in 1426 James I regranted the earldom to Alexander with a descent to Alexander's illegitimate son Thomas and his male heirs. In the event Thomas Stewart predeceased his father and produced no heirs, so that the issue of the succession to Mar was revived again when Earl Alexander eventually died in 1435. Meanwhile Robert Erskine continued his family's tradition of royal service. He was one of the hostages for the release of James I from English captivity in 1424, spending three years in England before attaining his own freedom in 1427, and after his release he served as a royal envoy to England and as custodian of Dumbarton Castle, as well as holding a number of other minor offices. The death of Alexander Stewart, earl of Mar, on 1 August 1435 reopened the debate over the possession of Mar. Erskine attempted to build up local support for his claims to the earldom, but James I took it into his own hands on the grounds that the 1426 grant had stipulated that it should revert to the crown if Earl Alexander's male line failed. But after James's death in 1437 Erskine succeeded in having himself served as the legal heir to Mar in 1438, and from that year onwards he employed the title earl of Mar and Garioch.

Erskine's claims to Mar were not acknowledged by the leaders of James II's minority regime, although about the time he assumed the comital title his standing was acknowledged by his being created a peer of parliament as Lord Erskine. In the 1440s he came to a series of agreements with James II's administration over possession of Kildrummy Castle and the revenues of the earldom. None of these agreements proved binding, and by 1449 it was clear that royal officers had effective control of the earldom. Complaints about the crown's unjust detention of Erskine's rightful inheritance were delivered to meetings of the three estates in April 1449 and January 1450 by his son Thomas, and the dispute was still in progress when Robert died some time between 7 September 1451 and 6 November 1452. The identity of his wife is uncertain, although arrangements were made in 1400 for his marriage to an unnamed daughter of David Lindsay, first earl of Crawford. Robert was succeeded as Lord Erskine by his eldest son, Thomas, whose great-great-grandson John finally became earl of Mar in 1565. S. I. BOARDMAN

Sources J. M. Thomson and others, eds., *Registrum magni sigilli regum Scotorum / The register of the great seal of Scotland*, 11 vols. (1882–1914), vols. 1–2 · G. W. S. Barrow and others, eds., *Regesta regum Scottorum*, 6, ed. B. Webster (1982) · W. Bower, *Scotichronicon*, ed. D. E. R. Watt and others, new edn, 9 vols. (1987–98), vols. 7–8 · The 'Original chronicle' of Andrew of Wyntoun, ed. F. J. Amours, 6 vols., STS, 1st ser., 50, 53–4, 56–7, 63 (1903–14) · G. Burnett and others, eds., The exchequer rolls of Scotland, 2–4 (1878–80) · CDS, vols. 3–4 · J. Robertson, ed., Illustrations of the topography and antiquities of the shires of Aberdeen and Banff, 4, Spalding Club (1862) · W. H. Bliss, ed., Calendar of entries in the papal registers relating to Great Britain and Ireland: petitions to the pope (1896) · Rymer, Foedera · S. I. Boardman, The early Stewart kings: Robert II and Robert III, 1371–1406 (1996) · M. Brown, James I (1994) · C. McGladdery, James II (1990) · Scots peerage, vol. 5

Erskine, Andrew (1740–1793), poet, was born on 10 August 1740 in the parish of Carnbee, Fife, the fifth of six children of Alexander Erskine, fifth earl of Kellie (d. 1756), and his second wife, Janet Pitcairne (1699–1775), daughter of the

physician Archibald *Pitcairne. He spent his early years at Kellie Castle, Carnbee.

The third son in a Jacobite family of declining fortunes, Erskine lived his entire life in straitened financial circumstances. He settled on a military career but had little ambition in that direction. Commissioned lieutenant in the 71st regiment of foot on 13 February 1759, he served until 1763, then later in the 24th regiment of foot (1765–70). He spent as much time as possible on leave, residing either at Kellie Castle with his brother Thomas Alexander *Erskine (1731–1781), the sixth earl, or at New Tarbet in Arrochar parish, Dunbartonshire, the seat of his sister Lady Betty and her husband, Walter Macfarlane.

Writing poetry was more to Erskine's taste than soldiering, especially in the years 1759 to 1764. He contributed fourteen pieces to the first volume of Alexander Donaldson's *A Collection of Original Poems by … Scots Gentlemen* (1760). While some of the poems were serious, Erskine's natural bent was towards burlesque and parody in the manner of Swift and Gay. His work caught the eye of the young James Boswell, who sought out his acquaintance in 1760. Over the next three years they maintained a lively correspondence, visiting each other often. Both contributed heavily to the second volume of Donaldson's *Collection of Original Poems* (1762), and in 1763 published their own correspondence as *Letters between the Honourable Andrew Erskine and James Boswell, Esq.* The letters and Boswell's descriptions in his journals portray Erskine as a tall, dark, rather awkward young man, bashful and indolent, but capable of lively wit and good humour, especially within his family circle. In 1764 there appeared the second edition of his *Two Odes*, on indolence and impudence, and a farce, *She's not Him and He's not Her*.

By 1770 Erskine had resigned his commission, ceased his literary endeavours, and settled into a life of inactivity and obscurity. After the death of Walter Macfarlane in 1767, Lady Betty married Lord Colville of Culross (d. 1770) and took up residence at Drumsheugh House in Edinburgh. Erskine, who never married, lived there for much of the remainder of his life. His occasional letters to Boswell reveal a life of desperate finances, poor health, and recurring melancholy. His principal recreation seems to have been long walks taken alone or with his friend Sir John Whitefoord.

Near the end of his life Andrew Erskine returned briefly to poetry, submitting seven songs for publication in George Thomson's *Select Collection of Original Scottish Airs* (1793); two were accepted. The best-known of these, his most widely reprinted work, 'How sweet the lone vale', appeared in Thomson's third volume of airs (1802), but Erskine did not live to see it printed. In early October 1793, afflicted by illness and depression, he committed suicide by filling his pockets with stones and walking into the sea near his Edinburgh home. J. DAVID HANKINS

Sources Boswell's London journal, 1762–63, ed. F. A. Pottle (1950), vol. 1 of The Yale editions of the private papers of James Boswell, trade edn (1950–89) · The general correspondence of James Boswell, 1757–1763, ed. J. D. Hankins [forthcoming], in The Yale editions of the private papers of James Boswell, research edn (1966–) · C. H. Bennett, 'Letters

between the Honourable Andrew Erskine and James Boswell Esq., 1761–1762', PhD diss., Yale U., 1933 · J. Kay, *A series of original portraits and caricature etchings … with biographical sketches and illustrative anecdotes*, ed. [H. Paton and others], new edn [3rd edn], 2 vols. in 4 (1877) · *Army List* (1759) · *Army List* (1764–5) · *Army List* (1770) · *The Whitefoord papers*, ed. W. A. S. Hewins (1898) · *Scots peerage* · *Register of births and deaths for the parish of Carnbee in the county of Fife* (1742) · C. Pitcairn, *The history of the Fife Pitcairns* (1905) · W. Forbes, letter to James Boswell, 5 Nov 1793, Yale U., Beinecke L., Boswell papers, MS Yale C1303 · *Edinburgh Advertiser* (8 Oct 1793), 231
Archives Yale U., Beinecke L., Boswell papers
Likenesses J. Kay, double portrait, sketch (in later life, with J. Whitefoord), repro. in Kay, *A series of original portraits*, 2, facing p. 56

Erskine, Lady Anne Agnes (1739–1804), friend and trustee of Selina, countess of Huntingdon, was born in Edinburgh, the daughter of Henry David Erskine, tenth earl of Buchan (1710–1767), and Agnes, *née* Steuart (*d.* 1778), daughter of Sir James Steuart, solicitor-general for Scotland. Her brothers were the antiquary David Steuart *Erskine (later eleventh earl), Henry *Erskine, lord advocate of Scotland and politician, and the lord chancellor Thomas *Erskine. The family was very pious and illustrious, with roots in the covenanting tradition. Anne's mother, an accomplished woman, taught her children at home.

In her twenties Lady Anne moved with her father to Walcot near Bath because of the earl's failing health. There she attended the chapel opened by Selina, countess of Huntingdon, in 1765. Links with the countess had previously been made by Lady Anne's grandfather, David, the ninth earl, who had come to know Lady Huntingdon and her minister George Whitefield while himself at Bath. Following the tenth earl's death in December 1767, his funeral service was conducted by Whitefield at Lady Huntingdon's chapel. From now on Lady Anne spent increasing amounts of time with the countess, and for the last few years of Selina's life they lived together in the chapel house at Spa Fields, London, opened by the countess as one of her chapels in 1779. Here Anne wrote many letters for Lady Huntingdon.

Lady Anne was one of four associates to whom the countess bequeathed her chapels and houses in trust shortly before her death in June 1791. The trustees decided that Lady Anne should continue to live in the Spa Fields chapel house and to have responsibility for finding itinerant ministers to serve in the chapels of the connexion. With few financial resources of her own, she was unable to visit the connexion's chapels as the countess had done, and she became reliant on money from various grants, chiefly from the Spa Fields Chapel committee. Much of her time was now taken up with recruiting ministers for the larger chapels and, although some congregations left, the connexion continued to thrive under her supervision.

In her later years Lady Anne's task was made no easier by a long and painful illness. She died, unmarried, in London on 5 October 1804 and was buried at Bunhill Fields, the nonconformist ground at City Road, London. Her place as one of Lady Huntingdon's trustees was now taken by the Revd John Ford; after his death three years later a legal trust was created for the connexion.

E. DOROTHY GRAHAM

Sources E. Welch, 'Erskine, Lady Anne Agnes', *The Blackwell dictionary of evangelical biography, 1730–1860*, ed. D. M. Lewis (1995) · J. B. Cutmore, 'Erskine, Henry', *The Blackwell dictionary of evangelical biography, 1730–1860*, ed. D. M. Lewis (1995) · J. K. La Shell, 'Erskine, Henry David', *The Blackwell dictionary of evangelical biography, 1730–1860*, ed. D. M. Lewis (1995) · A. S Wood, 'Haweis, Thomas', *The Blackwell dictionary of evangelical biography, 1730–1860*, ed. D. M. Lewis (1995) · P. J. Lineham, 'Huntingdon, Selina, countess of', *The Blackwell dictionary of evangelical biography, 1730–1860*, ed. D. M. Lewis (1995) · E. Welch, *Spiritual pilgrim: a reassessment of the life of the countess of Huntingdon* (1995) · B. S. Schlenther, *Queen of the Methodists: the countess of Huntingdon and the eighteenth-century crisis of faith and society* (1997) · P. W. Gentry, *The countess of Huntingdon* (1994) · 'The correspondence of the Revd Brian Bury Collins, MA', ed. A. M. Bradley, *Proceedings of the Wesley Historical Society*, 9 (1914), 83
Archives NL Wales, MSS | Westminster College, Cambridge, Cheshunt Foundation archives
Wealth at death 'few financial resources of her own'

Erskine, Charles, Lord Tinwald (*bap.* 1680, *d.* 1763), judge, was baptized on 25 November 1680 at Alva in Stirlingshire, the third son of Sir Charles Erskine of Alva, baronet (1643–1690), and his wife, Christian Dundas (*d.* 1724/5). His grandfather was Sir Charles Erskine of Alva, seventh son of John Erskine, eighteenth or second earl of Mar, and his second wife, Lady Mary Stuart, daughter of Esmé, first duke of Lennox, and Mary Hope, daughter of Sir Thomas Hope, lord advocate to Charles I. Educated at St Salvator's College in the University of St Andrews (BA, 1696; MA, 1699), Erskine became one of the regents in the University of Edinburgh in 1701, having competed unsuccessfully for a regent's post in St Leonard's College in St Andrews in 1699. With a special interest and aptitude in mathematics he taught Newtonian science in Edinburgh, and his graduating class in 1704 disputed theses considering Newtonian gravity and the works of Leibniz and Descartes. His wide and scholarly interests in natural sciences and natural law are demonstrated by the huge library he collected enthusiastically throughout his life.

In 1707, through the influence of his cousin Mar, he was appointed to a newly established regius chair of public law and the law of nature and nations in Edinburgh. On admission he was given leave to depart for legal study abroad, and he matriculated in the University of Leiden as a law student on 2 February 1708. He stayed there for at least two years, and returned to Edinburgh to be admitted as an advocate on 17 July 1711; he advertised his classes 'on the Laws of Nature and Nations' as starting on 16 November 1711 (*Scots Courant*, 12–16 Nov 1711). He does not seem to have succeeded in attracting a class and abandoned teaching to pursue a career at the bar, though he maintained links with the university's corporate life until he resigned the chair in 1734.

Considered a 'very powerful and successful pleader' Erskine's progress was swift and he 'came almost immediately into great practice' (Allardyce, 1.101). On 21 December 1712 he married Grisel (*d.* in or before 1753), heir of John Grierson of Barjarg, Dumfriesshire. The couple had at least three sons, John (*b.* 1714) and Robert (*b.* 1718), who both died young; James [*see below*]; and four daughters— Christian (*b.* 1715, who married Sir Robert Laurie of Maxwelton), Kathrine (*b.* 1719), Helen (*b.* 1720), and Jean (who married William Kirkpatrick of Lochmaben).

In 1714 Erskine was appointed advocate-depute for the western circuit. He survived his cousin's disgrace and forfeiture after the 1715 Jacobite rising and he was returned as member for Dumfriesshire in April 1722. Having later purchased the estate of Tinwald, just outside Dumfries, he employed William Adam to build an elegant small country house, between 1738 and 1740, in warm, pink, Dumfriesshire stone. He represented the county in parliament until 1741, when Charles Douglas, third duke of Queensberry, who had the greatest interest in the county and had gone into opposition in 1734, successfully put in another candidate. In 1721 he was a leader of the opposition to the admission of Patrick Haldane as a lord of session.

In 1725, having overcome his family's association with Jacobitism to link himself with Archibald Campbell, earl of Ilay, who was now in the ascendant in Scotland, he became solicitor-general, with the novel privilege of pleading within the bar. He served in this office until 1737, when he succeeded Duncan Forbes of Culloden as lord advocate. In 1737 he spoke in the Commons against the punitive measures placed on Edinburgh after the Porteous riots. In 1741 he was elected as member for the Tain burghs; but in 1742, after the fall of Walpole, he was unseated and replaced with Robert Craigie, who also succeeded as lord advocate. Erskine returned to his practice at the bar, and remained until he was appointed to the bench as Lord Tinwald in 1744. When Duncan Forbes died in 1747, Ilay, now third duke of Argyll, wanted the presidency for Erskine, but could not manage it; Erskine gained the compensation of the office of lord justice-clerk in place of Milton in 1748. He was again turned down for the presidency in 1754, when it went to Craigie. In these years he served in the Ilay interest as a commissioner for annexed estates and a trustee for manufactures, playing a role in the reorganization and reconstruction of Scotland.

Erskine's very real intellectual talents led David Hume in 1748 to entrust him with the final decisions on the inclusion of an essay in the philosopher's *Essays, Moral and Political*. In 1753 Erskine, by then a widower, married Elizabeth (1716–1806), daughter of William Harestanes of Craigs, Kirkcudbright, and widow of Dr William Maxwell. He also bought the family estate of Alva when his brother's financial problems led to its sale, necessitating in turn the sale of Tinwald. Remembered as a handsome, educated, elegant, and accomplished man of wit and charm, Erskine died in office on 5 April 1763.

His only surviving son, **James Erskine**, Lord Alva (1722–1796), was admitted advocate on 6 December 1743 and became sheriff-depute of Perthshire in 1748. He was appointed a baron of the exchequer in Scotland in 1754 (probably as compensation for the denial of the presidency of the bench to his father). Complex negotiations

between Argyll, Bute, and Newcastle resulted in his appointment as lord of session in 1761, when he took the title Lord Barjarg; he later exchanged this for Lord Alva. He married first Margaret Macguire (1729–1766), coheir of Hugh Macguire of Drumdour, Ayrshire, on 11 June 1749, and second, on 26 January 1772, Jean (*c.*1725–1797), only daughter of John Stirling of Herbertshire and widow of Sir James Stirling, baronet. Like his father a collector of books, Erskine died on 13 May 1796.   JOHN W. CAIRNS

Sources NL Scot., Erskine-Murray MSS • bap. reg. Scot., NA Scot., OPR index, ext. 873693, 1847632, 2063038 • G. W. T. Omond, *The lord advocates of Scotland from the close of the fifteenth century to the passing of the Reform Bill*, 2 vols. (1883) • *Scotland and Scotsmen in the eighteenth century: from the MSS of John Ramsay, esq., of Ochtertyre*, ed. A. Allardyce, 2 vols. (1888) • A. Murdoch, 'The people above': politics and administration in mid-eighteenth-century Scotland* (1980) • J. S. Shaw, *The management of Scottish society, 1707–1764: power, nobles, lawyers, Edinburgh agents and English influences* (1983) • matriculation register, U. St Andr. • U. Edin. L., special collections division, university archives • *Scots Courant* (12–16 Nov 1711) • *The letters of David Hume*, ed. J. Y. T. Greig, 2 vols. (1932) • *IGI* • *Caledonian Mercury* (6 April 1763) • *Caledonian Mercury* (29 May 1729) • A. Smart, *Allan Ramsay: a complete catalogue of his paintings*, ed. J. Ingamells (1999) • *Scots Magazine*, 58 (1796), 362 • J. Gilhooley, ed., *A directory of Edinburgh in 1752* (1988)

Archives NA Scot., papers • NL Scot., papers, MSS 5070–5138 • NL Scot., corresp. and papers • NL Scot., corresp., MSS and account book [James Erskine] | BL, corresp. with Lord Holdernesse, Egerton MSS 3433–3434 • BL, corresp. with duke of Newcastle, etc., Add. MSS 32715–32903, *passim* • BL, corresp. with Lord Hardwicke, Add. MSS 35446–35449, *passim* • U. Nott. L., corresp. with Henry Pelham

Likenesses A. Ramsay, oils, 1750, Scot. NPG • A. Ramsay, oils, 1750 (James Erskine), Scot. NPG • D. Allan, oils, 1765, Royal Scot. Acad.

Erskine, Claudius James (1821–1893). *See under* Erskine, William (1773–1852).

Erskine, David, second Lord Cardross (*bap.* 1627, *d.* 1671), nobleman, was baptized in Edinburgh on 6 February 1627, the only son of Henry Erskine (*c.*1594–1628), second son of the second marriage of John *Erskine, eighteenth or second earl of Mar (*c.*1562–1634), lord high treasurer, and Margaret, only daughter of the judge Sir James Bellenden of Broughton. Henry was heir to the barony of Cardross at Menteith, Perthshire. The young David was served heir to the barony in March 1637. Although of presbyterian stock, the mature Cardross was one of the few peers to oppose the giving up of Charles I to the Commonwealth army at Newcastle in 1646. His moderation led him to promote the engagement in 1648, but its failure left him out of favour, heavily fined, and debarred from sitting in parliament. The Restoration saw Cardross restored to his seat in parliament. He was appointed to the commission for the plantation of kirks in 1661 and became a commissioner for supply for both Perthshire and Stirlingshire in 1663.

Cardross married first, in 1645, Anne Hope (*bap.* 1625), a daughter of the lord advocate Sir Thomas *Hope of Craighall, to whom his son and heir Henry *Erskine was born, and second, in 1655, Mary, daughter of Sir George Bruce of Carnock, Fife, with whom he had four sons and four

David Erskine, second Lord Cardross (*bap.* 1627, *d.* 1671), by unknown artist

daughters. He died in July 1671, and was buried on 25 July at Holyrood Church in Edinburgh. His second wife survived him. GORDON GOODWIN, *rev.* A. J. MANN

Sources *APS*, 1648–69 · Register House, old parish registers, Canongate, NA Scot., OPR. 685.3/12 [baptism, burial] · register of Great Seal, NA Scot., RMS 62.47 · NA Scot., Bell-Brander MSS, GD 63–105 · NA Scot., Biel MSS, GD 6–855 · NA Scot., Cunninghame Graham MSS, GD 22-1.432 · NA Scot., Earls of Mar and Kellie MSS, 6D 124 · *Scots peerage*, 2.365; 9.52 · *The memoirs of Sir David Erskine of Cardross*, ed. Mrs S. Erskine (1926), 29–30 · Register House, old parish registers, Culross, NA Scot. [second marriage] · *Journal of the Hon. John Erskine of Carnock*, ed. W. Macleod, Scottish History Society, 14 (1893) · GEC, *Peerage*

Likenesses Trotter, line engraving, pubd 1798, NPG · eleventh earl of Buchan, pencil and chalk drawing, Scot. NPG · oils, repro. in Erskine, ed., *Memoirs*, 30 · oils, The Binns, West Lothian [*see illus.*]

Erskine, David, Lord Dun (*bap.* 1673, *d.* 1758), judge and Jacobite sympathizer, was baptized in Dun in spring 1673, the third son and fourth child of David Erskine (*d.* 1710), laird of Dun, and Jean (*d.* 1702), daughter of Sir James Lumsden and widow of Thomas Ramsay. The family had occupied its estate on the edge of Montrose basin since 1375. He studied at the universities of St Andrews and Paris, being called to the Scottish bar on 19 November 1698. Unlike most of his family, he was an episcopalian. In the parliament of 1703 he opposed the union. His elder brothers John and James having died in childhood, in 1710 he both succeeded to the estate and took his seat as an ordinary lord of session by the title of Lord Dun; on 13 April 1714 he was also appointed a lord of justiciary. In 1707 he married Magdalen (*d.* 1736), daughter of John Riddell of the Haining, with whom he had three children:

Anne (*b.* 1709), who married first, in 1730, James Ogilvy (*d.* 1730), styled fourth earl of Airlie, a Jacobite, and second, in 1733, Sir Alexander MacDonald of Sleat; John (1712–1787), the fourteenth laird; and a daughter who died in infancy.

In the Jacobite rising of 1715, Dun supported his kinsman John Erskine, earl of Mar, behind the scenes, although the nature of his activities remains unclear. In 1724 he bought some of Mar's lands and the superiority of the earldom, clearing them of debt and entailing them in 1739 on Mar's son, Thomas, Lord Erskine. Dun's careful economic planning also enabled him to redeem the mortgage on his own estate. Subsequently he was able to authorize the building of a new House of Dun, designed for him by William Adam in the 1730s, on the advice of the earl of Mar. Here Dun's Jacobitism received a lasting memorial in the outstanding plasterwork completed by Joseph Enzer in 1742–3, which provides a remarkable historical reminder of the strength of Jacobite hopes on the brink of the rising of 1745:

> the allegory depicts the Auld Alliance … the return of the exile from oversea, hounds bringing a stag to bay … an enslaved Scot with an English musket pointing at his heart … oak leaves, white roses, and the effulgent renovation of flowers and fertility suggest the positive outcome. (Pittock, 138)

Erskine took no overt role in the 1745 rising, but his brother, James, raised a company in the 2nd battalion, the Forfarshire regiment, and contributed to the capture of the *Hazard* at Montrose, the only Jacobite naval capture of the war.

As Dun was never discovered in explicitly Jacobite activity, he was able to pursue a successful career as a lord of justiciary. In this he was no doubt helped by the Jacobitism of many in the Faculty of Advocates, whose politics were satirized by Defoe. Dun, who had resigned his justiciary gown in 1744, also resigned his office as an ordinary lord in 1753, being succeeded by Boswell's father, Lord Auchinleck. Dun, a broad Scots speaker who fancied himself an English scholar, was widely respected and even loved despite his pedantic talk and starchy manners. He published one book, *Lord Dun's friendly and familiar advices adapted to the various stations and conditions of life* (1754). He died at Dun on 26 May 1758, and was probably buried there. There is a depiction of Lord Dun in his descendant Violet Jacob's historical novel *Flemington* (1911).

MURRAY G. H. PITTOCK

Sources V. Jacob, *The lairds of Dun* (1931) · C. Hartley and W. Kay, *The House of Dun* (1992) · M. Pittock, 'The culture of Jacobitism', *Culture and society in Britain, 1660–1800*, ed. J. Black (1997) · J. Gibson, *Ships of the '45* (1967) · A. Livingstone, C. W. H. Aikman, and B. S. Hart, eds., *Muster roll of Prince Charles Edward Stuart's army, 1745–46* (1984) · Chambers, *Scots.* (1835) · V. Jacob, *Flemington*, ed. C. Anderson (1994) · *DNB* · Anderson, *Scot. nat.*

Archives NA Scot., MSS

Likenesses W. Airman, portrait, repro. in Jacob, *Lairds of Dun*

Erskine, Sir David (1772–1837), writer and antiquary, was the illegitimate son of David Steuart *Erskine, eleventh earl of Buchan (1742–1829). He was appointed an ensign in the 31st regiment on 14 October 1789, and lieutenant of an independent company on 24 January 1791. He returned to the 31st regiment on 6 April 1791, and was promoted to captain on 29 September 1794. On 17 November 1798, he married his cousin, Elizabeth, second daughter of Thomas *Erskine, first Baron Erskine. She died on 2 August 1800, and Ann Ellis became his second wife soon after. Erskine had exchanged to half pay, 132nd regiment, on 10 July 1799, and on 8 May 1806 he was appointed captain of a company of gentlemen cadets at the Royal Military College, Sandhurst. After exchanging to half pay in the Royal York rangers on 10 August 1820, he was appointed a professor at the Royal Military College. The earl of Munster was there placed under his tuition, as were others of William IV's children, and at their request Erskine received the honour of knighthood on 11 September 1830. During his time as a teacher, he produced several literary works, including: *Airyformia, or, Ghosts of Great Note* (1825); *King James the First of Scotland* (1827), a tragedy in five acts; *Love amongst the Roses, or, Guilford in Surrey* (1827), a military opera in three acts; and *Mary, Queen of Scots, or, Melrose in Ancient Times* (1829), a historical melodrama.

Erskine's father died in 1829 and bequeathed to Erskine for life the whole of his disentailed estates, including Dryburgh Abbey, Berwickshire, which thenceforth became Erskine's permanent residence. He was able at this time to indulge his antiquarian interests and he produced *Annals and Antiquities of Dryburgh, and other Places on the Tweed*, the second and revised edition of which appeared in 1836. Erskine, who was FSA Scotland, director of the Royal Academy of Edinburgh, and one of the founders of the Scottish Naval and Military Academy in that city, died on 22 October 1837, aged sixty-five.

GORDON GOODWIN, *rev.* M. CLARE LOUGHLIN-CHOW

Sources *GM*, 1st ser., 70 (1800), 804 · *GM*, 1st ser., 101/1 (1831), 79 · *GM*, 2nd ser., 8 (1837), 652 · R. Inglis, *The dramatic writers of Scotland* (1868) · will, PRO, PROB 11/1887, sig. 831 · War Office, succession book, PRO, 25/213 · *Army List* (1796) · *Army List* (1823), 619 · War Office, half-pay list, PRO, 25/2992, 331 · *LondG* (6–10 May 1806), 569
Archives NRA, priv. coll., sketchbook, mainly of Dryburgh

Erskine, David Montagu, second Baron Erskine (1776–1855), diplomatist, eldest son of Thomas *Erskine, first Baron Erskine, and his wife, Frances, daughter of Daniel Moore MP, was born on 12 August 1776. He was educated at Charterhouse, Winchester, and Trinity College, Cambridge, where he matriculated in 1796. He was called to the bar at Lincoln's Inn in 1802. He did not, however, try to practise law but was elected MP for Portsmouth on 19 February 1806 in place of his father, who had been made lord chancellor. On his father's request to Fox, Erskine was appointed minister-plenipotentiary to the United States of America in July 1806. He had earlier lived there for four years and in 1799 he had married Frances, daughter of General John Cadwallader of Philadelphia and his wife, Williamina. General Cadwallader was a companion of George Washington and one of the leaders of the American War of Independence. They had seven daughters and five sons, one of whom, Edward Morris *Erskine, was also a diplomatist.

Erskine was recalled by Canning in 1809 for exceeding his instructions by offering the withdrawal of the orders in council against the Americans. He remained out of favour and employment until 1824, when, having succeeded his father as second Baron Erskine in November 1823, he was appointed minister-plenipotentiary at Stuttgart, from which place he was promoted to the legation in Munich in January 1828. He remained in Munich for more than fifteen years, during which he had no opportunity of distinguishing himself, and retired on a pension in November 1843. His first wife died on 25 March 1843 and on 29 July 1843 he married Anne Bond, daughter of John Travis of Lancashire. After her death, on 18 April 1851, he married, on 21 December 1852, Anna, daughter of W. C. Cunninghame Graham of Garthmore, Perthshire, and widow of Thomas Calderwood Durham of Largs, Fife. On retiring from Bavaria, Erskine settled at Butler's Green, Sussex, where he died on 19 March 1855; he was buried at Cuckfield. His widow married the Ven. John Sandford and died on 26 March 1886.

H. M. STEPHENS, *rev.* H. C. G. MATTHEW

Sources *GM*, 2nd ser., 43 (1855) · GEC, *Peerage* · HoP, *Commons*
Archives BL, corresp. with Lord Aberdeen, Add. MSS 43141, 43244 · U. Southampton L., corresp. with Lord Palmerston

Erskine, David Steuart, eleventh earl of Buchan (1742–1829), antiquary and political reformer, was born on 1 June 1742 in Edinburgh, the second son of Henry David Erskine, tenth earl (1710–1767), and his wife, Agnes (1717–1778), daughter of Sir James Steuart, bt, and the elder brother of Henry *Erskine and Thomas *Erskine (later first Baron Erskine). He inherited the title Lord Cardross and Auchterhouse on the death of his elder brother, also David, in 1747. He received his early education at home, from his parents (both of whom had studied mathematics under Colin Maclaurin) and from James Buchanan, later professor of oriental languages at Glasgow University. He attended classes at St Andrews University from 1755 to 1759, at Edinburgh University from 1760 to 1762, and at Glasgow University between 1762 and 1763. While at Glasgow he was also taught drawing, etching, and engraving by Robert and Andrew Foulis, and he later published his own etching of the abbey of Icolmkill, with his account of the abbey, in *Transactions of the Antiquaries of Scotland* (vol. 1, 1792). In 1761 he toured the northern highlands and Aberdeen, taking a particular interest in the landscape, culture, and antiquities of the region. His father had hoped to obtain a commission in the guards for him, but in 1762 Cardross had to accept instead a commission in the 32nd regiment of foot, where he rose to a lieutenancy. Through Lord Chatham, a friend of his father's from student days in Leiden, he was appointed secretary to the British embassy in Madrid in 1766. He eventually declined the post, possibly because Sir James Gray, the ambassador, was of inferior rank to himself, but his father's serious illness was probably a more pressing consideration. The tenth earl died on 1 December 1767, and Cardross became the eleventh earl of Buchan.

Soon after his succession to the earldom, Buchan returned to the family estate at Kirkhill and Uphall in Linlithgowshire, and set about remedying its poor financial

David Steuart Erskine, eleventh earl of Buchan (1742–1829), by John Finlayson, pubd 1765 (after Sir Joshua Reynolds, 1764) [in Van Dyck-style costume]

state by applying various improving agricultural practices, such as giving his tenants longer leases of nineteen and thirty-eight years. He has been credited with helping to establish his younger brothers in their careers after their father's death: in 1768 Henry Erskine called at the Scottish bar and Thomas Erskine acquired an ensign's commission in the 1st, or Royal, regiment of foot. Buchan remained on close terms with both his brothers. He married his cousin Margaret (d. 1819), daughter of William Fraser of Fraserfield, in Aberdeen on 15 October 1771. They had no children, but a natural son born to Buchan in 1772, David *Erskine, was brought up in their household, later married Elizabeth, second daughter of Thomas Erskine, and achieved prominence as a writer and antiquary.

After the security of his estates and finances, Buchan's main preoccupations were his curiosity concerning, and desire to celebrate, the ancient kingdom of Scotland, and, apparently contrarily, his political reformism. These were reconciled in his own mind by a 'whiggish intellectual patriotism' (Kidd, 214), which, though lamenting recent and present constitutional degeneracy, honoured what he claimed was a constitutional and even libertarian Scottish past (Steuart, 56–8). Affronted by the post-Union system of electing sixteen Scottish representative peers to sit in the House of Lords, he began his campaign for its reform during the 1768 election. He protested that the system in practice meant little more than the Scottish peers acquiescing in the selection of the administration of the day. Buchan stood against the list of favoured peers and achieved only one vote: his own. He repeated his resistance in 1770

(joined by seventeen other reforming peers, including the earl of Selkirk), in 1774, and in 1780, when he published his *Speech intended to be spoken at the meeting of the peers of Scotland for the general election of their representatives*. However, though Buchan received some celebrity for his unwavering stance on the issue, it does not seem that any real reform was achieved by his actions.

Although Buchan formally retired from active politics after 1780, he retained a keen interest in public affairs, identifying with the whig opposition interest in which his brothers were both active. He had been an ardent supporter of John Wilkes in the 1760s, and he corresponded with Christopher Wyvill and other reformers in the early 1780s. He supported the American colonists during the American War of Independence, partly because of his friendship with Benjamin Franklin, though he served as lieutenant-colonel of the Caledonian band, a volunteer corps established in Edinburgh in 1782 to guard against a possible French invasion. He also corresponded with George Washington, to whom he sent a snuff-box in 1791, supposedly carved from the wood of a tree in which William Wallace had hidden after the battle of Falkirk, and for whom he gave an *Address to the Americans at Edinburgh, on Washington's Birthday* (1811). His regard for America was more than eccentricity, however, and, as well as recommending Scottish scholars for academic positions in American colleges, he also seriously considered settling there himself after the war. During the turbulent 1790s Buchan joined the London Society of the Friends of the People, and communicated with the Society for Constitutional Information in London and also with some of the Scottish branches of the Friends of the People. He wrote *Essays on the Lives and Writings of Fletcher of Saltoun and the Poet Thomson* (1792), in which he praised the ancient Scottish constitution and criticized the corruptions he detected in the present British constitution, and *Letters on the impolicy of a standing army, in time of peace, and, on the unconstitutional and illegal measure of barracks* (1793).

During his long retirement, however, Buchan's primary interest was in Scottish antiquarianism. He had been elected a fellow of both the Society of Antiquaries and the Royal Society in London in 1764, and in 1780 he founded the Society of Antiquaries of Scotland, the achievement for which he is now best remembered. The third earl of Bute was persuaded to serve as president, but it was Buchan, as senior vice-president, who took most responsibility for the organization, to the extent of providing most of the funds for the society's purchase for £1000 of a building in the Cowgate in Edinburgh to house its collections. William Smellie, the printer chiefly responsible for the first edition of the *Encyclopaedia Britannica* (1771), was appointed the keeper of the society's planned natural history collections in 1781, and gave a course of lectures on this subject in the Cowgate building. When the society petitioned for a royal charter, which was granted on 6 May 1783, it was opposed by both the University of Edinburgh (on the grounds that Smellie's lectures competed with its own) and the Faculty of Advocates (since its library was now compelled to contend with the society's collections for documents relating to Scottish history and antiquities).

Besides amalgamating the collections of historical documents and other antiquities belonging to its members, storing them properly, and holding meetings in which members read papers concerning these artefacts, Buchan hoped that the society would encourage the writing of biographies and the collection of portraits of notable Scots, and conduct a topographical survey of the parishes of Scotland. He and his wife contributed numerous donations of money and items for the collections, including books, coins, maps, genealogies, 'a female hummingbird', 'a pair of Chinese lady's shoes', and the standard of the cavalry regiment of his great-grandfather the third Lord Cardross during the revolution of 1688 (Smellie, 46, 92). Buchan also wrote an account of the parish of Uphall for the proposed survey, which was published with several others in the society's first *Transactions Archaeologia Scotica* (1792), but this project was quickly overtaken by the more ambitious *Statistical Account* energetically organized by Buchan's friend Sir John Sinclair of Ulbster. Unfortunately, Buchan never received the level of support in the work of the society from others that he had envisaged, and he gradually withdrew from its meetings from 1787, when the Cowgate building was sold at a considerable loss. He resigned from the society in 1790, and no attempt was made to dissuade him, perhaps because other members found his leadership too domineering. Nevertheless, he continued to assist in various schemes associated with the society, such as John Pinkerton's collection of portraits, and the biographical series, to which he contributed essays on John Napier and George Heriot, as well as those on Fletcher and Thomson. He also served as honorary president of the Literary and Antiquarian Society of Perth (established 1784), and was elected to honorary membership of the Royal Danish Society in 1785 and of the equivalent Icelandic body in 1791, through his friendship with the Icelandic scholar Grímur Jonsson Thorkelin. Besides the works already mentioned, Buchan also published a pamphlet on the trial of Warren Hastings (1786), and several essays (often under the pseudonym Albanicus) in periodicals such as the *Gentleman's Magazine*, the *Scots Magazine*, and *The Bee*, some of which were collected in a volume of essays in 1812.

Buchan was a keen sponsor of the arts and scholarship, taking a particular interest in such men as Robert Burns, James Thomson, John Pinkerton, Gilbert Stuart, and Archibald Constable. He also showed kindness to the young Henry Brougham (though he famously kicked into the street Brougham's 1808 'Don Cevallos' article in the *Edinburgh Review* to make clear his disapproval of it) and founded prizes at the high school in Edinburgh and at Aberdeen University. In 1786 he purchased the Berwickshire estate of Dryburgh Abbey, which the third Lord Cardross had sold when he emigrated to South Carolina. He enlarged and embellished the mansion near the ruined abbey, and this became his principal residence for the rest of his life. He erected a column in the grounds in 1791 to commemorate his own ancestors and, in the same year, a classical temple in honour of James Thomson (together with an obelisk on Ednam Hill, above the poet's birthplace). He established an annual literary festival in Thomson's name in 1791, and added Burns to the roll of honour after Burns's death in 1796. A huge statue of William Wallace was erected on the estate in 1814, and, more practically, a wire suspension bridge was built across the Tweed in 1817.

Many of Buchan's contemporaries thought him at best eccentric and at worst vain and absurd, and in this they have been followed by most later commentators. The story of how in 1819 he tried to storm Sir Walter Scott's sick-room to reassure him that he would personally supervise all the arrangements for Scott's funeral at Dryburgh has been retold many times as evidence of his propensity for the ridiculous. But, as R. G. Cant points out, Buchan was by then an old man in failing health; he had also been very recently widowed, and it is perhaps more accurate to see this incident as another, extreme, example of Buchan's enthusiasm for projects he had set his heart on, a vehement enthusiasm which often led him to try to control events so that they would fall out exactly as he wished. His overbearing administration of the Society of Antiquaries of Scotland can be read in the same light. A maternal line of Scott's ancestors, the Haliburtons, had an ancestral vault at Dryburgh Abbey, which Buchan returned to Scott's family. Both benefited, in the end: Scott died three years after Buchan, and so escaped the earl's meddling in his funeral arrangements, but he was then buried at Dryburgh Abbey, as the earl had hoped. Bruce Lenman suggests that Buchan's unfashionable political views were the real cause of much of the ridicule he suffered in contemporaries' memoirs. Buchan died on 19 April 1829 at Dryburgh Abbey, where he too was buried, on 25 April.

EMMA VINCENT MACLEOD

Sources DNB · R. G. Cant, 'David Steuart Erskine, 11th earl of Buchan: founder of the Society of Antiquaries of Scotland', *The Scottish antiquarian tradition*, ed. A. S. Bell (1981), 1–30 · *Scots peerage*, 2.276–8 · *GM*, 1st ser., 99/1 (1829), 75–8 · A. Fergusson, ed., *The Honourable Henry Erskine* (1882) · B. P. Lenman, 'Aristocratic "country" whiggery in Scotland and the American revolution', *Scotland and America in the age of the Enlightenment*, ed. R. B. Sher and J. R. Smitten (1990), 180–92 · 'Account of the progress of the Society of Antiquaries of Scotland, from 1784 to 1830', *Archaeologia Scotica*, 3 (1831), appx · [A. C. H. Seymour], *The life and times of Selina, countess of Huntingdon*, 2 vols. (1840) · C. Kidd, *Subverting Scotland's past: Scottish whig historians and the creation of an Anglo-British identity, 1689–c.1830* (1993) · earl of Buchan [D. Steuart], *Essays on the lives and writings of Fletcher of Saltoun and the poet Thompson: biographical, critical, and political, with some pieces of Thomson's never before published* (1792) · earl of Buchan, correspondence on parliamentary reform, U. Edin. L., special collections division, Gen. 1736 · *The life and works of Robert Burns*, ed. R. Chambers, rev. W. Wallace, [new edn], 4 vols. (1896) · J. G. Lockhart, *The life of Sir Walter Scott*, [new edn], 10 vols. (1902) · W. Smellie, *Account of the institution and progress of the Society of the Antiquaries of Scotland* (1782) · H. P. Brougham, *The life and times of Henry, Lord Brougham*, ed. W. Brougham, 1 (1871) · J. Kay, *A series of original portraits and caricature etchings … with biographical sketches and illustrative anecdotes*, ed. [H. Paton and others], new edn [3rd edn], 1 (1877), 206–10, 284–9 · Chambers, *Scots.*, rev. T. Thomson

(1875) · *Williamson's Directory for the city and county of Edinburgh* (1786)

Archives BL, corresp. · Mitchell L., Glas., corresp. · NL Scot., corresp. and MSS · U. Edin. L., corresp. and MSS · U. Edin. L., corresp. relating to parliamentary reform | CKS, letters to W. Pitt · N. Yorks. CRO, corresp. with C. Wyvill · NL Scot., letters to T. Coutts; letters to J. Griffiths; corresp. with G. Paton · PRO, letters to Lord Chatham, PRO 30/8 · U. Glas., Murray MSS · V&A NAL, corresp. relating to the memorial for James Thomson

Likenesses J. Reynolds, oils, 1764, National Gallery of South Africa, Cape Town · J. Finlayson, mezzotint, pubd 1765 (after J. Reynolds, 1764), BM, NPG [*see illus.*] · J. Brown, pencil drawing, 1780–81, National Museums of Scotland, Edinburgh; on loan to Scot. NPG · medallion, 1783 (after J. Tassie); plaster replica, Scot. NPG · J. Kay, caricature, etching, 1784, BM; repro. in Kay, *Series of original portraits*, vol. 2, p. 284 · A. Runciman, oils, 1785, Perth Museum and Art Gallery · C. Turner, mezzotint, pubd 1807 (after G. Watson), BM · W. H. Lizars, oils?, 1808 · H. Raeburn, oils, NG Ire. · engraving (as an old man; after oil painting by G. Watson), repro. in Fergusson, *Honourable Henry Erskine* · oils (after J. Reynolds, *c.*1764), U. Edin.

Wealth at death incl. entailed estates at Kirkhill and Uphall in West Lothian; also Dryburgh Abbey estate in Roxburghshire

Ebenezer Erskine (1680–1754), by unknown artist

Erskine, Ebenezer

Erskine, Ebenezer (1680–1754), a founder of the Secession church, was born on 22 June 1680 in Dryburgh, Mertoun, Berwickshire, the fourth son of Henry *Erskine (1624–1696), presbyterian minister in Cornhill, Northumberland, who had been ejected in 1662 by the Act of Uniformity and had returned to live in his place of birth, and his second wife, Margaret Halcro (*d.* 1725) of the Isle of Weir, Orkney. Erskine was educated at Edinburgh University, which awarded him an MA degree in 1697. He subsequently served as tutor and chaplain in the family of his distant relation, the earl of Rothes, a prominent figure in both church and state, who remained his lifelong friend. Erskine was licensed by the presbytery of Kirkcaldy on 11 February 1703 and was ordained to the small rural parish of Portmoak, near Kinross, on 22 September 1703. On 2 February 1704 he married Alison Turpie (1680/81–1720), with whom he had ten children, including one daughter, Jean, who married James Fisher, a co-founder of the Secession church. Another daughter, Alison, married James Scott, a Secession church minister who went with the Anti-Burghers in the split of 1747, though Alison did not, informing him that while he remained her husband he was no longer her minister. After the death of his first wife on 31 August 1720 Erskine married, on 23 January 1724, Mary Webster (*d.* 1751), daughter of James Webster, minister of the Tolbooth parish church, Edinburgh, with whom he had five more children.

Early ministry Though Erskine was diligent and faithful in all his endeavours, in his early years at Portmoak he engaged in a spiritual struggle with the temptation of unbelief. Only after more than four years as a minister was he brought to what he termed in his shorthand diary 'an acquaintance with Christ and religion' (Fraser, 293, 82–3), which transformed first his life and then his ministry. This change began when he accidentally overheard a spiritual conversation between his first wife and his younger brother, Ralph *Erskine. His diligence in preparation and zeal in delivery of sermons were greatly increased, and instead of fixing his attention on a certain stone in the rear wall of the church, he fixed his hearers in their eyes. It was not long before he became a preacher whom multitudes came from considerable distances to hear, particularly during the annual communion seasons, when the Lord's supper was celebrated as the focal point of a series of meetings. In 1728, in his parish of under 1000 inhabitants, wine was ordered for more than 2000 communicants. With his encouragement many of the people of Portmoak began regularly to take notes on his sermons and discourses; so common did the practice become that Erskine occasionally addressed them as the 'scribes'.

Erskine's refusal to take the oath of abjuration was popular with the people at large but gained him the enmity of Alexander Anderson of Falkland and St Andrews, among others. He took an active part in the Marrow controversy, joining with eleven other brethren in the ministry, particularly in drawing up the *Representation and Petition* (1721) and in preparing *Queries, … with the Answers* (1722), the first draft of their answers to the general assembly's commission. As a consequence Erskine suffered substantial personal abuse and the severing of friendships. In 1724 he was considered for a call to the first charge in Kirkcaldy, but after strong opposition, essentially on the grounds of his participation in the Marrow controversy, the 1725 assembly's commission confirmed the synod of Fife's refusal to allow his name to be put before the congregation. Despite three other calls—to Burntisland in 1712, Tulliallen in 1713, and Kinross in 1728—he remained at Portmoak until 1731, when he was called to a newly created third charge in Stirling.

Erskine had consistently expressed his opposition to the 1712 act restoring patronage in Scotland: allowing the patron, whether a local landowner or another, to settle a minister on a parish without, or even against, a call from the people of the parish. The action of the general assembly in 1731, transmitting an overture 'concerning the Method of Planting Vacant Churches', set in motion the events leading to the founding of the Secession church. This act invited presbyteries to send up their opinions in regard to a proposal that whenever a call fell into the hands of a presbytery, *jure devoluto*, the presbytery should meet with the heritors and elders and proceed to elect and call someone to propose to the congregation for approval or disapproval, with the disapprovers to give reasons to the presbytery, which would then be empowered to resolve the matter at its sole discretion. The general assembly recommended that all should take care not to violate this rule. Although the majority of the responding presbyteries expressed opinions hostile to this proposal, the assembly of 1732 passed an act mandating this procedure, thus violating the Barrier Act (1697), which required both the opinion and consent of the presbyteries before 'any General Assembly of this Church shall pass any Acts which are to be binding Rules and Constitution to the Church' (*Acts of the General Assembly of the Church of Scotland*, 260–61, 614). The assembly also refused to receive a representation and petition (published later that year as *A publick testimony; being the representation and petition of a considerable number of Christian people … anent grievances*), which was signed by approximately 2000 people, as well as a similar document signed by forty-two ministers including Erskine. Both documents complained of the evils of patronage. Erskine was among fifteen ministers who protested the assembly's refusal even to hear the petitions. He also spoke against its refusal to receive his dissent from its act.

On his return to Stirling, Erskine preached against this act, but doing so did not satisfy his conscience. After being elected moderator of the synod of Perth and Stirling in October 1732 he preached before the synod a sermon that was later published, *The Stone Rejected by the Builders, Exalted as the Head-Stone of the Corner*, in which he declaimed against the act and against the increasing defections in the Church of Scotland in matters of doctrine and government. Some of his hearers took great offence and after a heated debate the synod voted by a small majority to rebuke him for certain expressions used in his sermon. Erskine and several others appealed against this decision to the general assembly of 1733, but the assembly confirmed the synod's decision and admonished Erskine. Rather than accept this rebuke and admonition Erskine gave in a protest, adhered to by William Wilson, Alexander Moncrieff, and James Fisher. It was read before the general assembly, which ordered all four to 'show their sorrow for their conduct and misbehaviour, in offering to protest', and to retract the same before the meeting of the assembly's commission in August. It further authorized its commission, when it met in November, to proceed to a higher censure if they refused compliance. In due course the commission did just that, by the casting vote of the moderator, thus loosing the four ministers from their charges, declaring their churches vacant, and prohibiting Church of Scotland ministers from communion with them. All four protested this decision as well, and Gabriel Wilson and six others gave in an additional protest, expressing their intention to continue to hold ministerial communion with these four 'dear brethren' as if no sentence had been passed.

Secession church The unintended consequences of this decision were momentous. In December 1733 Erskine

joined Wilson, Moncrieff, and Fisher (with Ebenezer's brother Ralph and Thomas Mair as observers) at Gairney Bridge, south of Kinross, to form the Associate Presbytery. They asserted that they were parting from the prevailing party in the Church of Scotland pending its repentance. But they held it lawful to continue in full communion with those of like mind with them who yet remained in the church. Erskine participated fully in the affairs of the Associate Presbytery throughout the 1730s. At first they agreed that their meetings would be confined to prayer and religious conference, without assuming judicial powers, until it became clear whether or not the established church would be reformed. Early in 1734 the Associate Presbytery published *A testimony to the doctrine, worship, government and discipline of the Church of Scotland, or, Reasons … for their protestation*, complaining of the general assembly's usurpation of the powers of presbytery in regard to ordination and of the assembly's toleration of doctrinal error and refusal to receive protests. After the 1734 assembly instructed the synod of Perth and Stirling to restore all four ministers the synod not only did so but elected Erskine its moderator. But the brethren declined to return on the grounds of the assembly's failure to condemn the previous assembly's action in ejecting them. As Erskine put it, there is a 'great difference between a positive reformation and a stop … given to a deformation' (Fraser, 400).

Just prior to the assembly of 1735 the Associate Presbytery issued *Reasons … why they have not Acceded to the Judicatories of the Established Church*, acknowledging the good done in 1734, but pointing out that most of the evils of which they had complained persisted, and that even the synod's rebuke of Erskine had not been repealed. Although the assembly's acts were generally favourable the presbytery did not accept that a reformation had taken place. As a consequence in August 1735 it voted unanimously to proceed to acts of jurisdiction, and began to comply with requests for ministerial supply. The assembly of 1736 enacted measures that the Associate Presbytery thought praiseworthy, but it also imposed two violent settlements of ministers in parishes in which the vast majority of the people were opposed, and gave Archibald Campbell only a mild warning. In November, Wilson was appointed to train youths for the ministry, and the following spring he began an annual three-month theology course, taught in Latin. In December the presbytery published its judicial testimony, condemning corruptions in the Church of Scotland. Some former friends, particularly John Currie, wrote strongly against them. The ensuing enmity was, with few exceptions, never repaired. At the time of the Porteous riots in September 1736, some even laid the blame for the public unrest on the Associate Presbytery, though ultimately their loyalty to the government was established beyond doubt.

The Associate Presbytery gradually developed into a full-fledged church. In January 1737 the sessions of the Perthshire churches of Abernethy and Kinclaven formally joined (in distinction from their ministers), and the first ruling elders sat in presbytery meetings. In February

Ralph Erskine and Thomas Mair joined formally, as did Thomas Nairn in October and James Thomason the following June. Even eight ministers could not begin to supply the numerous requests they were receiving, however, and the presbytery began licensing young men to preach. The 1738 assembly urged that all possible means be used to reclaim 'these poor deluded people'. But in the following year the Associate Presbytery, constituted as a church court, attended the Church of Scotland's general assembly and gave the assembly a formal declinature of its authority (*Acts and Proceedings of the Associate Presbytery, … Containing their Declinature*, 1739). After a further year's delay, the 1740 general assembly formally deposed all eight members.

Ebenezer Erskine's suspension and ultimate deposition had the effect predicted by the presbytery of Stirling when arguing in the synod: rather than alienate the affections of the people from Erskine, it alienated them from the established church. From the time of his initial suspension to his deposition Erskine continued in the performance of his ministerial duties in the third charge of Stirling as if the general assembly had passed no sentence against him, though in 1735 he declined to serve as moderator of the presbytery on the grounds that no real reformation had occurred in the church. He illustrated this claim by reference to the recent intrusion of James Mackie to the parish of St Ninians in his own presbytery. In his refusal to return to the Church of Scotland, even when invited to do so, he differentiated between the church established by law and the church of Christ in Scotland, maintaining that 'the last is in a great Measure driven into the Wilderness by the first'. In *The testimony and contendings of … Alexander Hamilton … [with] a letter … from Ebenezer Erskine* (1736), he urged on those ministerial brethren who pleaded with him to return to the Church of Scotland to help them preserve the work and testimony of the Lord in it, that it would be the path of safety for them to come out as well.

Erskine remained an active minister in the third charge in Stirling until he was deposed by the general assembly of 1740. On receiving notice of this action the town magistrates immediately evicted him from the church. Being of a 'peaceable disposition', as the town magistrates themselves had testified of him seven years earlier, he kept his supporters from forcing entry by breaking down the doors and instead retired to preach in the open air. A large congregation was quickly gathered, from both Stirling itself and the surrounding area. Erskine continued his ministry among them and, as interest in the Secession church grew, he began preaching in a number of other parishes as well, both near and at a distance.

The Associate Presbytery's concern for evangelism led to a correspondence with George Whitefield, with Ebenezer and his brother Ralph taking the primary part. Whitefield came to Scotland at their invitation, but their first meeting in August 1741 resulted in irreconcilable differences. The Associate Presbytery wished to restrict Whitefield to preaching under their auspices; he believed it his duty to preach the gospel wherever and whenever he

was able. Whitefield went on to take part in the celebrated Cambuslang revival, while the Associate Presbytery denounced the revival and Whitefield's part in it as the work of the devil.

In October 1742 the Associate Presbytery passed an act maintaining the free grace of God, giving particular attention to the doctrines at issue in the Marrow controversy. In 1743 an act for renewing the covenants 'in a way and manner agreeable to our present situation and circumstances' was passed and then implemented. By 1742 there were twenty seceder congregations with regular ministers, with several additional vacant congregations and a considerable number of requests for a minister or probationer. These requests came not only from throughout Scotland, but also from Ireland and America.

Division and later ministry   In the Jacobite rising of 1745 Erskine was an ardent supporter of the government and was even appointed captain of a band of volunteers. For this service he received a letter of thanks at the duke of Cumberland's command, commending him for his zeal and loyalty to the king. It was also in 1745 that the Associate Presbytery constituted itself the Associate Synod. When the synod split over the burgess oath in 1747 Erskine took the more moderate position. The religious requirement of this 1744 oath was designed in respect of the threatened Stuart rising to exclude Roman Catholics from freely engaging in commerce in the cities of Edinburgh, Glasgow, and Perth, requiring them to 'profess … the true religion presently professed within this realm, and authorized by the laws thereof'. Since this clause was interpreted by some as requiring an endorsement of the Church of Scotland, none in the Associate Synod approved of it. Some wished to exclude from the synod any who subscribed it, whereas Erskine maintained in *The True State of the Question* (1747) that even though subscription to the oath was wrong, it should not be grounds for excommunication.

Subsequent to this split Alexander Moncrieff, the Associate Synod's professor of divinity, joined the General Associate (Anti-Burgher) Synod, and Erskine was appointed to serve in this capacity for the Associate (Burgher) Synod. This was only a temporary appointment, however: his son-in-law James Fisher was required to prepare himself for the position, and in 1749 Erskine was relieved of this responsibility. In the winter of 1749–50 he had 'several severe fits of the colic' and gradually became incapable of preaching regularly. Following the death of his second wife, Mary, on 15 March 1751, his nephew James Erskine, his brother Ralph's third son, was ordained as his colleague and successor on 22 January 1752. Erskine contributed to the first part of *The Assembly's Shorter Catechism Explained* (1753), a work which, as completed and revised by James Fisher, was widely influential for over a hundred years. Though he continued to exercise his ministerial duties as he was able, his mental abilities undiminished, his physical state continued to deteriorate until his death in Stirling on 2 June 1754. He was buried 'at the centre of his meeting-house, in a spot opposite the pulpit, where a large stone covered his grave' (Fraser, 454–62).

Erskine was widely admired for his preaching. His demeanour, both in and out of the pulpit, was characterized as noble and dignified. Even the staunch Anti-Burgher Adam Gib told a minister who had never heard Erskine preach, 'Sir, you have never heard the Gospel in its majesty'. The distinctive emphasis of his preaching was God's gracious dealing with men: *God in Christ, a God of Love*, as it was put in the title of one of his sermons of 1752. His first sermons were published during the controversial circumstances of the early 1730s, so as to allow the general public an opportunity to judge of the justice of the charges made against him by the church courts, and were often accompanied by an explanatory note or preface. Later editions and collections of his sermons met an increasing demand as their intrinsic value was more widely recognized. Thus, *A Collection of Sermons* by Ebenezer and his brother Ralph was edited by Thomas Bradbury and published in London in three volumes between 1738 and 1750, and several times reprinted. A full collection of his sermons that was first collected by James Fisher and published in 1761 as *The Whole Works of Ebenezer Erskine* continued to appear for more than a century. A selection, *Beauties*, appeared in 1830. His sermons were also printed in America and the Netherlands, where they have had a lasting influence in certain circles.

DAVID C. LACHMAN

Sources *DNB* · *Fasti Scot.*, new edn, 4.328–9 · D. Fraser, *The life and diary of ... Ebenezer Erskine* (1831) · A. R. MacEwen, *The Erskines* (1900) · J. Harper, 'Memoir', *Lives of Ebenezer Erskine* (1849) · R. Small, *History of the congregations of the United Presbyterian church from 1733 to 1900*, 2 (1904), 663–4 · J. M'Kerrow, *History of the Secession church* (1849) · D. C. Lachman, *The Marrow controversy, 1718–1723: an historical and theological analysis* (1988)
Archives NL Scot., sermons · U. Edin., New Coll. L., notebooks
Likenesses oils, Scot. NPG [*see illus.*]

Erskine, Edward Morris (1817–1883), diplomatist, fourth son of David Montagu *Erskine, second Baron Erskine, and his wife, Frances, daughter of General John Cadwallader of Philadelphia, was born on 17 March 1817. He entered the diplomatic service as attaché to his father at Munich, and after filling subordinate posts was appointed secretary of legation at Turin in 1852. He was transferred to Washington early in 1858, to Stockholm at the end of that year, and in 1860 to St Petersburg as secretary of embassy; he afterwards filled the same role in Constantinople. In 1864 he was appointed minister-plenipotentiary to Greece. During his stay there nothing of importance happened until the 'Dilessi murders' in 1870 (the seizure of Lord and Lady Muncaster and their party by brigands, who killed several of the hostages). Erskine's handling of the affair was much criticized, but in his temperate reaction he reflected the view of the British cabinet, which wished to avoid being pushed into Palmerstonian 'gunboat' diplomacy. In 1872 he was promoted to the legation at Stockholm, and in 1873 made a CB. He remained at Stockholm until 1881, when he retired on a pension.

On 24 July 1847 Erskine married Caroline, daughter of

Edward Morris Erskine (1817–1883), by Carlo Ernesto Liverati, 1842

Robert Hamilton Vaughan and widow of Andrew Loughnan. They had three daughters and a son. She died on 23 October 1877. Erskine died at his home, Neville House, Twickenham, on 19 April 1883.

H. M. STEPHENS, *rev.* H. C. G. MATTHEW

Sources *FO List* (1881) · Burke, *Peerage* · Gladstone, *Diaries* · R. J. H. Jenkins, *The Dilessi murders* (1961)
Archives Bodl. Oxf., letters to fourth earl of Clarendon · Lpool RO, corresp. with fifteenth earl of Derby · PRO, corresp. with Lord John Russell, PRO 30/22
Likenesses C. E. Liverati, drawing, 1842, priv. coll. [*see illus.*]
Wealth at death £3842 14s. 11d.: probate, 6 June 1883, *CGPLA Eng. & Wales*

Erskine, Henry (1624–1696), presbyterian minister, was born on 23 August 1624 in the parish of Mertoun, Dryburgh, in Berwickshire, a younger son of Ralph Erskine of Shielfield and Janet Wilson. Nothing is known of his upbringing or early education save that he was probably influenced in the choice of his future vocation by the earnest piety, preaching, and uncompromising ministry of Alexander Simson, who was pastor at Mertoun from 1597 until the early 1630s. Erskine graduated MA from the University of Edinburgh on 15 April 1645 and after his trials was licensed to the preaching and pastoral ministry by the presbytery of Earlston. In 1652 he married Jean (d. 1670), daughter of John Brown of Park, with whom he had five daughters and three sons. There is some confusion as to the date of his first call and ordination to the charge of Cornhill, a small village in Northumberland some 10 miles south of Dryburgh. Although tradition has ordinarily favoured 1649, a brief biography of his life held in the Wodrow collection in the National Library of Scotland explicitly states that he was ejected from Cornhill a mere three years into his ministry by the Act of Uniformity on 25 August 1662, which would strongly indicate that he was first ordained in 1659.

Erskine's conscientious commitment to a presbyterian ecclesiology with its strong emphasis on the headship of Jesus Christ in and over his church made him unwilling to accept the reimposition of Erastian episcopacy at the restoration of the monarchy in 1660. Immediately after his expulsion from Cornhill he travelled to the royal court in London to petition Charles II for payment of the stipend owing him for his ministerial labours in Northumberland. However, his trip proved fruitless after the king made reimbursement conditional on his conformity to the Act of Uniformity. On the return journey from London to Scotland his ship was forced to take shelter in Harwich harbour and Erskine preached and served to what was presumably a dissenting congregation in that town for the space of six weeks, at the end of which he was called to be their pastor. His wife's reluctance to move away from family and friends, however, compelled him to turn down the offer. He settled in Dryburgh in the home of his brother, from where he unassumingly but surreptitiously continued to minister to kindred spirits within his locality. After the death of his first wife, on 1 September 1674 Erskine married Margaret (d. 1725), daughter of Hugh Halcro of the Isle of Weir, Orkney. Their union produced a further three children, two sons and a daughter.

On 23 April 1682 the laird of Meldrum with a company of soldiers apprehended Erskine while he was conducting divine worship. He was incarcerated firstly at Melrose and then at Jedburgh before being taken to Edinburgh to be arraigned before the privy council. He appeared before the council on 12 May when Sir George Mackenzie, the king's advocate, asked him if he would give his bond to desist from preaching and ministering at conventicles. He courageously and defiantly replied, however, 'I have my commission from Christ, and tho' I were within an hour of my death I durst not lay it down at any mortal man's feet' (NL Scot., Wodrow Qu. LXXV, fol. 191v). On 6 June he was brought back before the court to hear his fate. He was fined 5000 merks and sentenced to confinement on the Bass Rock until the fine was paid in full and he had given an assurance that he would refrain from preaching and pastoral ministry. On the grounds of poor health he successfully appealed against the severity of the sentence, which was commuted to banishment from the kingdom. His nephew John Brown of Park made bond of 5000 merks that Erskine would depart from Scotland within fourteen days.

Erskine spent the first two and a half years of exile living at Parkridge near Carlisle. At the invitation of Philip Gray of Preston, he then took up residence in Monilaws close to his former charge at Cornhill. On 2 July 1685 he was once again apprehended by the militia and confined for a short spell in Newcastle and Wooler prisons but was released on the 22nd of that month by the passing of the Act of Indemnity. In September 1687 he accepted a call to minister to the parish of Whitsome near Berwick and settled in Rivelaw. It was here that Thomas Boston was converted under his preaching at the age of twelve. Boston later recorded in his *Memoirs* that Erskine was 'my father in Christ, and a person eminent for piety, Christian experience, and communion with God' (*Memoirs*, 345). After the revolution of 1688 and the re-establishment of presbyterianism Erskine was called and admitted to the charge of Chirnside near Berwick on 18 September 1690. He died there on 10 August 1696 and was buried that year in the local churchyard. His wife survived him and at least three of his sons followed their father's vocation. Philip Erskine (b. 1657) became rector of Knarresdale, Northumberland; Ebenezer *Erskine ministered at Portmoak and founded the Secession church; and Ralph *Erskine served as minister of Dunfermline. A. S. WAYNE PEARCE

Sources *DNB* · *Fasti Scot.*, new edn, 2.34 · 'Ane Breviar of the life of the Reverend Mr Henry Erskine, minister of the gospel', NL Scot., Wodrow MS Qu. LXXV · *DSCHT* · *Memoirs of the life, time and writings of … Thomas Boston*, ed. G. H. Morrison, new edn (1899); repr. (1988)
Likenesses attrib. J. Medina, oils, Scot. NPG

Erskine, Henry, third Lord Cardross (1650–1693), nobleman, was born in 1650, the eldest of two children of David *Erskine, second Lord Cardross (bap. 1627, d. 1671), and his first wife, Anne (bap. 1625), daughter of Sir Thomas *Hope of Craighall, king's advocate. On 3 March 1671 he married Catherine (d. 1725), daughter of Sir James Stewart of Kirkhill; they would have seven children: David (1672–1745), Charles (d. 1763), Henry, Thomas (1691–1731), Catherine (fl. 1714), Mary (1690–1733), and Anne (1692–c.1716). In June 1671, as master of Cardross, he was infefted in the lordship of Cardross and on 10 July was appointed his father's sole executor. He succeeded his father in the same year.

Cardross was a loyal promoter of presbyterian principles. In June 1674 John King, a covenanter and Cardross's chaplain, was apprehended by order of privy council for keeping conventicles in and around the house of Cardross and was imprisoned in Edinburgh Tolbooth, against which act Lord Cardross unsuccessfully petitioned, although King was liberated on giving a bond of 500 merks. Cited before the council in August 1674 for similar offences, but not appearing, King was then declared a rebel. In May 1675, while Lord Cardross was absent from home, King was seized at Cardross. He was rescued by armed individuals, many of them members of Cardross's household and tenants, for which Cardross was held responsible.

In August 1675 Lord and Lady Cardross, and members of their household, were cited before the privy council as having frequented house and field conventicles. Lord Cardross was found guilty of attending conventicles and of refusing the bond against keeping conventicles as well as inciting ministers to leave their charges and preach illegally. He was fined £1000 sterling and ordered to enter himself a prisoner in Edinburgh Castle. Additionally, he was fined £1350 Scots for refusing to enforce his tenants to give bond against keeping conventicles. He remained a prisoner for four years, during which he was permitted

Henry Erskine, third Lord Cardross (1650–1693), attrib. L. Schuneman

three months liberty (from November 1676 to February 1677), under the pain of 18,000 merks, to attend his wife. While a prisoner he was issued with another fine, in August 1677, to the value of half a year's rent, for having at least two children baptized by unlicensed individuals. In March 1678 he appears among the heritors and life-renters of Linlithgow who had not subscribed the bond against conventicles. He was released from prison in July 1679 on giving bond for his fine, and shortly afterwards presented an account of his sufferings and grievances which the privy council declared was a misrepresentation (February 1680). Being unable to obtain redress, Cardross emigrated to South Carolina where he and his Scottish followers established a colony at Port Royal in 1684. This was soon destroyed by disease and a Spanish attack and he returned to Europe, entered the service of William of Orange, and accompanied him to England in 1688.

Cardross enjoyed the confidence of King William and was a loyal supporter during the revolution. In the summer of 1689 he raised a regiment of dragoons, serving under General Mackay, to which King William appointed him colonel. In the same year he was appointed to assess and oversee repairs required to the castles of Edinburgh and Doune. On 29 July 1689, 'haveing speciall confidence in the loyaltie, couradge and conduct of Henry, Lord Cardross' (*Reg. PCS*, 13.567), the privy council commissioned him to ensure the safeguarding of the inlets of the Forth around Stirling.

Cardross had been elected a member of parliament in June 1672 and in November 1673, and was elected again in March 1689 and April 1690. In May 1689 he was appointed

to the privy council of Scotland, of which he was to prove a diligent member. Interested in both church and state, he was appointed to discuss a union between Scotland and England (23 April 1689) and was a member of the committee for settling church government (9 May 1690). He commanded foot militia in Linlithgow and Peebles (March 1689), as well as being a commissioner for militia in Stirling, Clackmannan, and Perth (1689). Additionally, he was appointed a commissioner of supply for Stirling and Linlithgow (April 1689, June 1690) and for Perth (1690). He was made a justice of the peace for Perth (18 November 1690), was appointed to the commission for visiting universities, colleges, and schools (July 1690), and was a member of the plantation of kirks in July 1690. On 7 November 1689 he was appointed general of the mint, a post which carried with it an annual salary of £300 sterling as well as the benefit of lodgings for himself and his family. In August 1690 Cardross's dragoons were instructed to go north and assess the situation in the highlands. Cardross was entrusted with various other activities, including the examination of prisoners before their release or their imprisonment. In 1690 his fines were remitted and £5000 sterling was awarded to him for his losses. In 1691 his troops were disbanded, despite his offer to keep them together for a further two months at his own expense. He died at Edinburgh on 21 May 1693 from natural causes and was succeeded by his eldest son, David Erskine, later ninth earl of Buchan. ALISON G. MUIR

Sources *Reg. PCS*, 3rd ser. • *APS*, 1648–60; 1670–95 • *CSP dom.*, 1673–6; 1679–80; 1682–4; 1689–91 • *Scots peerage*, vol. 2 • W. H. L. Melville, ed., *Leven and Melville papers: letters and state papers chiefly addressed to George, earl of Melville … 1689–1691*, Bannatyne Club, 77 (1843) • *Journal of the Hon. John Erskine of Carnock*, ed. W. Macleod, Scottish History Society, 14 (1893), introduction, 220–29 • *Historical notices of Scottish affairs, selected from the manuscripts of Sir John Lauder of Fountainhall*, ed. D. Laing, 2 vols., Bannatyne Club, 87 (1848) • H. Mackay, *Memoirs of the war carried on in Scotland and Ireland*, ed. J. M. Hog and others, Bannatyne Club, 45 (1833) • *The memoirs of Sir David Erskine of Cardross*, ed. Mrs S. Erskine (1926) • inventory of Leven and Melville muniments, NA Scot., GD 26 • Cardross writs, NA Scot., GD 15 • Com: Edinburgh testaments, NA Scot., CC8/8/80, fols. 27–30 • GEC, *Peerage*

Archives NA Scot., Edinburgh testaments, CC8/8/80, fols. 27–30 • NA Scot., writs, GD 15 • NRA Scotland, priv. coll., papers and legal proceedings | NA Scot., inventory of Airlie muniments, GD 16 • NA Scot., corresp. with lords Leven and Melville • NA Scot., inventory of Leven and Melville muniments, GD 26 • NA Scot., inventory of Shairp of Houstoun muniments, GD 30

Likenesses attrib. L. Schuneman, oils, Scot. NPG [*see illus.*]

Erskine, Sir Henry [Harry], **of Alva and Cambuskenneth, fifth baronet** (*bap.* 1710, *d.* 1765), army officer and politician, was baptized on 23 December 1710 at Alva, Stirlingshire, the second son of Sir John Erskine, third baronet, who was accidentally killed on 12 March 1739, and his wife, Catherine, second daughter of Henry St Clair or Sinclair, tenth Lord Sinclair. Sir John was a Jacobite leader in the rising of 1715, but was pardoned in return for surrendering to the Treasury his silver mine at Alva. He dissipated his fortune in extravagant mining projects, had to sell his estate, and was employed as manager of the Scottish Mining Company.

Erskine was educated possibly at Eton College and later entered Lincoln's Inn, London. In June 1735 he was commissioned ensign in the 22nd foot commanded by his uncle Colonel James Sinclair (1688–1762), on whom he largely depended in his early career, and in August 1736 he was promoted lieutenant. In 1742 in Minorca the lieutenant-governor, General Philip Anstruther (c.1680–1760), who had been criticized by the opposition in parliament for neglect of duty, suspected Erskine of conspiring against him and had him court-martialled. Erskine was acquitted, but continued bitterly hostile to Anstruther. In March 1743 Erskine was appointed captain in the 1st Royal Scots, then commanded by Sinclair. He served as deputy quartermaster-general, with the rank of lieutenant-colonel, in the blundering expedition against the French Atlantic naval base, L'Orient, in September 1746, commanded by Sinclair, then lieutenant-general, and was wounded. He afterwards served with the 1st Royal Scots in Flanders, where his elder brother, Sir Charles, fourth baronet, a major in the same regiment, was killed at the battle of Val (otherwise Lauffeld or Kisselt) on 2 July 1747. Erskine then succeeded to the baronetcy. In 1748 he accompanied Sinclair as aide-de-camp on his mission to Vienna and Turin.

Elected on the Argyll–Bute interest, Erskine was MP for Ayr burghs from December 1749 to 1754. Attaching himself to Leicester House (the London residence of Frederick, prince of Wales, and centre of his political associates—according to Horace Walpole 'laying a foundation for the next reign'; *Letters*, 3.36), he soon acquired a reputation as an opposition speaker. In February 1751 he attacked the Mutiny Bill and Anstruther's treatment of him in Minorca, which led to a protracted dispute and exacerbated his relations with Anstruther. After the prince of Wales's death (20 March 1751) he supported the administration. In the 1754 general election he contested Anstruther Easter burghs, Fife, and, supported by his kinsmen and Archibald Campbell, third duke of Argyll, defeated the unpopular sitting member, his enemy Anstruther of Airdrie. Reportedly in the constituency Erskine's lively personality and courtly manners won him much popularity. He held the seat until his death. He fostered the alliance between John Stuart, third earl of Bute, and William Pitt the elder, and in 1755 opposed the government. In January 1756, for opposing the subsidy treaties, he was dismissed from the army by order of George II, who continued hostile. He was a friend and confidant of Bute and was dependent on him, and in 1757 took part, as Bute's representative, in the negotiations for a new administration. Shortly after the formation of the 1757 Pitt–Newcastle coalition Bute procured for him the office of surveyor of the king's private roads (which he held 1757–60). In 1760 he was a leading supporter of the Scottish Militia Bill. Following George III's accession in October 1760, in November Erskine was reinstated in the army as major-general (with effect from June 1759). As 'favourite of the Favourite' (Haden-Guest, HoP, *Commons, 1754–90*, 2.403) or in Horace Walpole's words 'a creature of the Favourite' (ibid., 2.404) he assisted Bute politically, on

patronage and elections, and was influential and sought after. He strongly supported Bute's administration. He supported the Grenville administration, requesting from Grenville any vacant military governorship, including in January 1765 the governorship of the ports of the north of Scotland. He was colonel in succession of the 67th foot (October 1760), the 25th foot (May 1761), then the Edinburgh regiment, and—as the king had previously promised—the 1st Royal Scots (December 1762), succeeding his uncle Major-General James Sinclair, who had died in November 1762. In 1765, despite Grenville's protest, the king appointed Erskine secretary of the Order of the Thistle. In the same year he was promoted lieutenant-general. He married on 16 May 1761 Janet, daughter of Peter Wedderburn, Lord Chesterhall, of Chesterhall, and sister of Alexander Wedderburn, afterwards lord chancellor of England and first earl of Rosslyn, and they had two sons and one daughter, the eldest of whom succeeded his maternal uncle as second earl of Rosslyn [see Erskine, James St Clair, second earl of Rosslyn]. Ill in 1764 and 1765, Erskine died at York when returning from Scotland to his residence at Kew, Surrey, on 9 August 1765.

Erskine was an accomplished man, and for some time a 'very fashionable figure in the world of politics' (*Letters*, 3.36). Horace Walpole sneered at him as a military poet and a creature of Lord Bute's. Philip Thicknesse left an account of a transaction in which Erskine, on behalf of Lord Bute, endeavoured to prevent the publication of Lady Mary Wortley Montagu's letters, entitled *An Account of what Passed between Sir Harry Erskine and Philip Thicknesse, Esq.* (1766). Erskine was credited with the authorship of the Scottish march 'Garb of Old Gaul', but Major-General D. Stewart of Garth, a regimental authority, stated that the words were originally composed in Gaelic by a soldier of the 42nd highlanders, and were set to music by Major (later General) John Reid of that regiment, and that several officers claimed to be the English adapters.

H. M. CHICHESTER, rev. ROGER T. STEARN

Sources *Army List* · D. Stewart, *Sketches of the character, manners, and present state of the highlanders of Scotland: with details of the military service of the highland regiments*, 1 (1822) · *Scots Magazine*, 27 (1765), 391 · E. Haden-Guest, 'Erskine, Sir Henry', HoP, *Commons, 1715–54* · E. Haden-Guest, 'Erskine, Sir Henry', HoP, *Commons, 1754–90* · Burke, *Peerage* (1967) · *The letters of Horace Walpole, fourth earl of Orford*, ed. P. Toynbee, 3–4 (1903); 9 (1904) · J. L. McKelvey, *George III and Lord Bute: the Leicester House years* (1973) · *Letters from George III to Lord Bute, 1756–1766*, ed. R. Sedgwick (1939) · R. Cannon, ed., *Historical record of the first, or royal regiment of foot* (1847) · A. M. Brander, *The royal Scots (the royal regiment)* (1976) · J. Black, *Britain as a military power, 1688–1815* (1999) · J. Black, *European warfare, 1660–1815* (1994)

Erskine, Henry (1746–1817), lawyer and politician, was born at Gray's Close, Edinburgh, on 1 November 1746, the third son of Henry David Erskine, tenth earl of Buchan (1710–1767), and of his wife, Agnes (1717–1778); she was the second daughter of Sir James Steuart, first baronet (1681–1727), of Goodtrees, and of his wife, Anne (1687–1736), daughter of Sir Hew Dalrymple (1652–1737), of North Berwick, lord president of the court of session. Henry's elder brother was David Steuart *Erskine, eleventh earl of Buchan (1742–1829), founder of the Society of Antiquaries

Henry Erskine (1746–1817), by James Ward (after Sir Henry Raeburn, c.1805)

of Scotland; his younger brother was Thomas *Erskine, Lord Erskine (1750–1823), lord chancellor from 1806 to 1807. His maternal uncle, Sir James Steuart, second baronet (1713–1780), was the Jacobite political economist.

Formative years Erskine spent his childhood at Uphall, Linlithgowshire, seat of the earls of Buchan. He was educated at St Andrews, in Richard Dick's school and then, from 1760, at the university. He proceeded in 1764 to the University of Glasgow, and in 1766 to the University of Edinburgh. There he attended the classes of Robert Wallace in mathematics, of Hugh Blair in rhetoric, and of Adam Ferguson in moral philosophy, while studying primarily for the bar, to which he was admitted on 20 February 1768. He acquired skill in public speaking at a debating society, the Forum. He began to write poetry and, at that time or later, had several pieces published, notably *The Nettle and the Sensitive Plant* and *The Emigrant: an eclogue occasioned by the late numerous emigrations from the Highlands of Scotland* (1773). The Advocates' Library in Edinburgh owns a manuscript volume of his poems, transcribed about 1780, consisting of a version of *The Emigrant* corrected by his own hand, *Love Elegies Dedicated to Amanda* (1770), pastoral eclogues, and fables, together with epigrams and miscellaneous pieces, including translations and imitations of ancient writers, partly dated between 1769 and 1776. Several of his works were selected for Maria Riddell's *Metrical Miscellany* (1802), but no complete collection of his poems, or of his speeches, ever appeared, greatly admired though these were in his time.

On 30 March 1772 Erskine married Christian (1753–1804), only child of George Fullerton of Broughton Hall, near Edinburgh, comptroller of the customs at Leith, and of his wife, Anne Mary Pringle. They had two sons and two daughters; the elder son, Henry David, succeeded as twelfth earl of Buchan on the death of his uncle in 1829. Erskine's career prospered. Like other fluent advocates in a period when pleadings at the Scots bar were normally written he turned to the general assembly of the Church of Scotland to practise his oratory. From an early age he was regularly elected to it as an elder and he became a partisan of the evangelical party; as such he often clashed with Henry Dundas, his lifelong rival and enemy. In 1778 Erskine was proposed for procurator of the kirk but was beaten by William (afterwards Lord) Robertson, who had the support of Dundas and of his own father, Principal William Robertson of Edinburgh, manager of the moderate party in the assembly.

Office won and lost In politics Erskine first adhered to the Rockingham whigs, whose leadership Charles James Fox took over after the marquess of Rockingham's death. When Fox formed his coalition with Lord North in the spring of 1783 Erskine became advocate and state councillor in Scotland to the prince of Wales, patron of the whigs. Not until August did Erskine displace as lord advocate Dundas, who had been holder of the office since 1775. It is related that just after his appointment Erskine met his predecessor, who had already resumed his stuff gown. After chatting briefly with him Erskine observed, 'I must leave off talking to go and order my silk gown' (the official costume of the lord advocate). 'It is hardly worthwhile for the time you will want it', replied Dundas drily, 'you had better borrow mine'. Erskine was seldom to be capped, and retorted:

> From the readiness with which you make the offer, Mr Dundas, I have no doubt that the gown is a gown made to fit any party. But, however short my time in office may be, it shall never be said of Henry Erskine that he put on the abandoned habits of his predecessor. (Anderson, *Scot. nat.*, 1877, 2.166–71)

His fears for the security of his job proved correct, as he spent only four months in it. Before he could find a parliamentary seat the House of Lords threw out the coalition's East India Bill. The king at once dismissed Fox and North, while Erskine lost his post to Sir Ilay Campbell. On 14 January 1784 Philip Yorke, MP for Cambridgeshire, charged the Fox–North coalition with having lodged £500 in the Bank of Scotland:

> for the purpose of quickening the pace of the Scotch members, and enabling them to use dispatch in coming to town on the first meeting of parliament, by furnishing them with sufficient to defray their travelling expenses, for which they were to apply to the then lord advocate of Scotland. (Cobbett, *Parl. hist.*, 24, 1784, 340)

Dundas, however, exonerated his political opponent as 'incapable of being prostituted into the character of a distributor of the wages of corruption'; any rumours to the contrary 'originated in misinformation' (ibid., 341).

Erskine was still said to be in 'universal requisition', for his abilities and also because 'he reasoned in wit', while his very name 'suggested ideas of wit' (Thorne, 3.708). He remained nevertheless without preferment so long as Henry Dundas and William Pitt the younger held the power that they won at the general election of 1784. He had to content himself as leader and luminary of the inconsiderable faction of Scots whigs, or 'independent friends', as they demurely dubbed themselves. The rest of his career was determined by stubborn partisanship in this forlorn cause, unmatched by political skills that might have made it in any way rewarding. On all but a single occasion in 1785 he was easily and gleefully thwarted by Dundas. The exception occurred when the latter had to resign the post of dean of the faculty of advocates, owing to pressure of work in London. The government opposed Erskine's succession but, thanks to his professional peers, he won the subsequent election. One reason for their esteem is mentioned in Robert Burns's *Extempore in the Court of Session* (1787), where he makes an unfavourable comparison of Campbell's laboured style with the eloquence of his friend Erskine:

> Like wind-driven hail it did assail,
> Or torrents owre a linn, man.

Erskine would have been restored as lord advocate if the whigs had regained office under a regency of the prince of Wales in 1788 or 1789. With transiently brighter prospects he thought to reverse the consolidation of Dundas's electoral dominance in Scotland by alliance with his distant kinsman, but enemy, Sir Thomas Dundas. The pair of them supported agitation for reform of electoral abuses in counties and burghs, while Erskine embraced other liberal causes, notably campaigns against slavery. They commissioned a political survey of Scotland, still of value to historians; it induced in them an excessive optimism that was to be promptly deflated once the prospect of a regency receded again in time for the general election of 1790. Their schemes to seize control in sundry counties came everywhere to nothing. Erskine himself had to withdraw from an intended contest in Fife for lack of support.

Erskine's liberalism also had its limits and did not extend to the sympathy with revolution in France espoused by some whigs. In 1792 he refused to join the Society of Friends of the People, telling the duke of Portland and Sir Gilbert Elliot that, while reform remained desirable in the long run, this was not the time for it. When Edinburgh became the venue for a series of reformers' conventions in 1792–3 Erskine lent his support to moderate resolutions but would have no truck with radicals. In response to their approaches he even declared himself 'a strong aristocrat' (Thorne, 3.708). Yet, as other whigs passed over into support for the government after France declared war on Britain in 1793, Erskine refused to follow. He confirmed his loyalty to a dwindling political opposition by agitating in 1795 against the sedition and treason bills. At a public meeting in Edinburgh he condemned them as unconstitutional, provoking another blast of wrath from Dundas. When he came up for re-election as dean of the faculty on 12 January 1796 he found himself opposed by the minister's nephew, Robert Dundas of Arniston, lord advocate, who received 123 votes to Erskine's 38. This made him a whig martyr, publicly

praised and toasted by Fox and others. It also meant that he would stay out of parliament still longer and be spurned for legal offices to which his seniority at the bar might have recommended him. Even after Dundas had resigned with Pitt in 1801 he took steps to make sure that Erskine would be passed over by the succeeding government too. There was some official correspondence about Erskine's being appointed lord justice clerk in 1802; in 1804 he actually received an offer but he turned it down because he would not come in without his party. So nothing could be done for him. On 7 January 1805 he married again; his second wife was Erskine (*d.* 1845), widow of James Turnbull, advocate, and daughter of Alexander Munro of Glasgow. They had no children.

A reforming lord advocate Erskine's public life at last reached a modest climax when he was reappointed lord advocate early in 1806 under the 'ministry of all the talents', in which his brother Thomas was appointed lord chancellor. When he kissed hands an exchange with the king is said to have taken place in which George III asked, 'Not so rich as Tom?—not so rich as Tom?', to which Erskine replied, 'Your Majesty will please remember that my brother is playing at the guinea table, and I at the shilling one' (Thorne, 3.708). Erskine still found it by no means easy to get into parliament. He had hopes of standing in Linlithgowshire, where he resided at Almondell, but his prospects there were in fact hopeless. Not even the prince of Wales could persuade the whigs' Scottish electoral manager, Francis Rawdon Hastings, second earl of Moira, to back him, in case such an open challenge to the Dundases in a county long controlled by them should provoke a vendetta. At length James Maitland, eighth earl of Lauderdale, created a vacancy in the Haddington burghs, whence the sitting member had gone to the West Indies. Erskine was returned at a by-election and took his seat in parliament for the first time on 22 April; he well knew, however, that he could lose it again at a general election. Since one might be called at any time his search for a safer billet continued. He was reported to have set his sights on the city of Edinburgh, where Henry Dundas was improbably prepared to tolerate him on condition that 'he would come to a clear understanding upon it and not interfere in the interior of town administration or politick' (Fry, 284). The idea was too far-fetched to get anywhere. Erskine contested Linlithgowshire, after all, in the general election of November 1806, polling a mere twelve votes. Already defeated once, he needed the desperate efforts of friends to find refuge in the Dumfries burghs. When the ministry was defeated and the incoming one went to the country six months later Erskine tried again for Linlithgowshire; he raised his vote to fifteen. For this humiliation he blamed, rightly, the Dundases.

Meanwhile as lord advocate—in other words as chief officer of government in Scotland—Erskine had and missed his one chance to dismantle their machine. He set about proving his own credentials not just as a jobber but as a zealous reformer. He made plans to raise ministers' stipends, to revise the poor law, to liberalize the tenure of landed property, to repeal the test act, to improve the defences of Scotland, and to end financial abuse in public offices. He was encouraged by Fox, who agreed that there should be a direct assault on the Dundases, a purge of their creatures, and a systematic electoral offensive against them. But the ministry contained another school of thought on how to deal with Scotland in Grenville and his followers, essentially old whig oligarchs more inclined to take as they found it a country which was, whatever else, politically docile. From the start they were embarrassed by Erskine's sharp and loose tongue, his 'facility and political indiscretion' (Thorne, 3.709), and would have preferred William Adam as a manager of Scottish business far less likely to cause trouble.

Erskine, by contrast, brought with him from his years of frustration rather too many ideas for improving the government of Scotland. At the top of his agenda stood a general change of personnel after decades of the Dundases' cronyism. Erskine appointed a committee of vengeful whigs to weed out the worst cases. Belying a reputation for heroic amiability he urged Fox not to flinch at the resentments that this might cause. Whigs could not put up with any vestige of the old regime and expected 'a just retribution to individuals'; there need not be a 'rigid system of expulsion' but it had to be demonstrated that things had changed for good (Fry, 279). Yet by very reason of their former exclusion the whigs formed only a small and shunned minority in Scotland, carrying about them a whiff of disloyalty and lacking even the minimum of acceptable personnel for repopulation of the political apparatus with their own. Nor, in the event, did they last long enough to make a difference. The Dundases smoothly took over again once they were gone.

Erskine also proposed institutional reforms. One was to be political, entailing the transfer of direct control over Scottish business to the home secretary, who would normally have been an Englishman. Scotland was thus to be governed not by a Scot, as had been the rule since 1707, but by an outsider free of her venality, nepotism, and other reactionary defects. This idea remained a constant of whig politics for most of the nineteenth century and was implemented after 1832, only to produce at length a complete reaction in the popular demand for home rule, and the establishment of the Scottish Office in 1886.

A second reform was to concern the legal system: a total reorganization of the court of session, the highest civil instance, which Erskine thought inefficient and authoritarian. He drafted a bill under the aegis of Grenville, who introduced it in the Lords; it never reached the Commons. This, too, was an Anglicizing measure, if to outward appearance mainly structural in its provisions. It did not fool the Scots bench, which promptly sounded the alarm with expressions of horror at a measure 'subversive of the constitution of the court, and of the fundamental laws of the country, contrary to the Act of Union and in violation of the Claim of Right' (Fry, 283). The principal modern authority has concurred that the bill was one of the most remarkable documents in Scottish legal history: 'It was proposed to remodel the Court of Session on the lines of the courts of common law in England' (Phillipson, 192).

Arousing all but universal opposition, even from whigs, it had no chance of passing before the government fell. Erskine wrote in its defence an anonymous pamphlet, entitled *Expediency of Reform in the Court of Session in Scotland*, but it consisted only of a reprint of two earlier tracts with an introduction. Having lost office he continued to debate the points at issue with his successor, Archibald Campbell Colquhoun. He opposed the less drastic and therefore successful bill introduced by John Scott, Baron Eldon, the lord chancellor, in the next parliament. Outstanding details were referred in 1808 to a commission of inquiry, on which Erskine served, though its recommendations came to little.

Redundancy, death, and assessment Erskine was now out of office and out of parliament. He received assurances of getting back into both if the whigs came into power again but his political career had actually reached its end. There remained a glimmer of hope that he might win judicial preferment. This in its turn was dashed when, on the death of Robert Blair in May 1811, he found himself passed over for succession to the lord presidency of the court of session. Adam got the prince regent's authority to propose him to Eldon, who replied dismissively that 'fitness not politics should be the rule' (Thorne, 3.709). Charles Hope, lord justice clerk, received the appointment instead, though fifteen years junior at the bar to Erskine. Erskine thereupon retired from his professional practice too, and not unexpectedly declined a final electoral contest for Linlithgowshire in 1812. Though his mind was still clear and active his health had already begun to fail; he secluded himself at Almondell, with his garden and his violin. In the spring of 1817 friends again approached the government on his behalf, when he was ill and crippled with debt, to propose him for lord clerk register in place of Colquhoun who, however, recovered from the illness that had been expected to kill him. Erskine died on 8 October 1817; 'his amenity left no sting behind' (*GM*). He was buried in his family's lair at the kirk of Uphall, Linlithgowshire, where a monument to him and to his brother Thomas stands.

Erskine had a contemporary reputation as a man of brilliant gifts: good looks, attractive manner, sparkling wit. Fellow whigs depicted him as the most eloquent speaker at the Scots bar of his time. Henry Brougham praised his 'skilful conduct of the argument, the felicity of the copious illustration, the cogency of the reasoning ... the dexterous appeal to the prejudices of the court' as superior even to the abilities of his brother, the lord chancellor (Brougham, 1.231). Francis Jeffrey recorded that he 'could not only make the most repulsive subjects agreeable, but the most abstruse easy and intelligible. In his profession, indeed, all his wit was argument, and each of his delightful illustrations a material step in his reasoning' (*Scots Magazine*, 79/1, 1817, 292). Though he held strong opinions and never swerved from his allegiance to the whigs, he was a popular man in all companies for, according to Henry Cockburn, 'nothing was so sour as not to be sweetened by the glance, the gaiety, the beauty of Henry Erskine' (Cockburn, 1.93). Yet since he would insist on looking beyond the confines of his natural sphere at the bar and in the social life of Edinburgh the sum of his qualities did not compensate for a fatal lack of political sense—not least when he was faced in Scotland by Dundas, who possessed that sense in the fullest measure. So Erskine never achieved anything much.

MICHAEL FRY

Sources A. Fergusson, ed., *The Honourable Henry Erskine* (1882) · R. G. Thorne, 'Erskine, Hon. Henry', HoP, *Commons, 1790–1820*, 3.708–9 · M. Fry, *The Dundas despotism* (1992) · N. T. Phillipson, 'The Scottish whigs and the reform of the court of session', PhD diss., U. Cam., 1967 · H. P. Brougham, *The life and times of Henry, Lord Brougham*, ed. W. Brougham, 3 vols. (1871) · H. Cockburn, *Life of Lord Jeffrey, with a selection from his correspondence*, 2 vols. (1852) · M. Riddell, *Metrical miscellany* (1802) · DNB · GM, 1st ser., 87/2 (1817), 372 · Chambers, *Scots.*, rev. T. Thomson (1875), 1.547–8 · Burke, *Peerage* (1999)
Archives BL, letters to Lord Grenville, Add. MS 58953 · Mount Stuart Trust Archive, Isle of Bute, corresp. with Bute · N. Yorks. CRO, letters to Sir T. Dundas · NRA, priv. coll., letters to William Adam
Likenesses J. Tassie, paste medallion, 1791, Scot. NPG · P. Turnerelli, marble bust, 1814, Faculty of Advocates, Parliament Hall, Edinburgh · J. Bogle, pencil and watercolour drawing, Scot. NPG · M. Grant, marble relief monument, Scot. NPG · J. Kay, caricatures, etchings, BM, NPG · J. Ward, engraving (after H. Raeburn, *c*.1805), AM Oxf., Hope collection [*see illus.*] · attrib. W. Yellowlees, oils (after H. Raeburn), Scot. NPG

Erskine, Henry Napier Bruce (1831–1893). *See under* Erskine, William (1773–1852).

Erskine, James, sixth earl of Buchan (*d.* 1640), courtier, was the eldest son of John *Erskine, eighteenth or second earl of Mar (*c*.1562–1634), and his second wife, Lady Mary Stuart (*d.* 1644), daughter of Esmé *Stuart, first duke of Lennox (*c*.1542–1583), who married in 1592; William *Erskine (*d.* 1685) was his youngest brother. Nothing is known of his early life. Before 1617 he married Mary Douglas, countess of Buchan, daughter and heir of James Douglas, fifth earl of Buchan, and assumed the title of earl of Buchan. This title was confirmed to him by royal charter, dated 22 March 1617, the countess resigning her rights in his favour, and he was allowed the possession and exercise of all the considerable and ancient honours, dignities, and precedence of former earls of Buchan. A decree of the court of session of 8 July 1628 overturned the ruling of the 1606 decreet of ranking, published when the countess was a minor and unrepresented, which had placed the Buchan earldom below those of Eglinton, Montrose, Cassillis, Caithness, and Glencairn.

After the accession of Charles I, Buchan became one of the lords of the bedchamber, and in that capacity proved a useful link between the Scottish courtiers who dominated the bedchamber under both James VI and I and Charles, and his father, the earl of Mar, who was lord high treasurer of Scotland. Countess Mary died at Holyrood on 20 August 1628, and Buchan subsequently married Dorothy (*d.* 1639?), daughter of Sir Philip Knyvett of Buckenham, Norfolk. He lived chiefly in London, where he died in January 1640, but he was buried at Auchterhouse, Forfarshire. He was survived by four daughters and two sons from his first marriage, including James (*d.* 1664), who succeeded to the earldom, and at least one son, Henry, from his second marriage.

ALSAGER VIAN, *rev.* CHRISTIAN HESKETH

Sources GEC, *Peerage* · R. Douglas, *The peerage of Scotland*, 2 vols. (1892) · *Scots peerage*

Erskine, James, Lord Grange (*bap.* 1679, *d.* 1754), judge and politician, the second son of Charles Erskine, twenty-first or fifth earl of Mar (1650–1689), and his wife, Lady Mary Maule, eldest daughter of George, second earl of Panmure, was baptized on 11 October 1679 at the parish church, Alloa, Clackmannanshire. Educated at the University of Utrecht, he became a member of the Faculty of Advocates on 28 July 1705. Thereafter, through the influence of his elder brother, John *Erskine, twenty-second or sixth earl of Mar, he advanced rapidly. In October 1705 he was appointed principal keeper of the signet. The following October he was raised to the bench, taking the title of Lord Grange. In June 1707 he became a lord of justiciary and in November of that year he was sworn of the Scottish privy council. In July 1710, with Mar now Harley's principal agent in Scotland, Grange was made lord justice clerk. He was dismissed from that post on the accession of George I but remained on the bench.

Grange was a complex figure, politically and personally. He himself took no part in the Jacobite rising of 1715, but, given the prominent role played by Mar, he was never able to dispel strong suspicions—not least in the eyes of Sir Robert Walpole—that he maintained Jacobite connections and this, combined with personal weaknesses, dogged his political career. After Mar's attainder, he devoted himself to recovering his family's forfeited estates and honours. This, and his own financial difficulties, led him to align himself with whichever party he felt could best serve his interests.

Outwardly at least, Grange professed strict presbyterian principles and had a reputation for piety which belied his turbulent private life. He took an active part in the affairs of the general assembly of the Church of Scotland and was a staunch opponent of lay patronage in the appointment of church ministers. As a result he was well regarded by the extreme 'high-flyers'. Generally, however, his reputation among contemporaries was not high. Probably in 1707 he had allegedly debauched and been forced to marry Rachel Chiesley (*bap.* 1679, *d.* 1745) of Dalry [*see* Erskine, Rachel], whose father John had been executed in 1689 for murdering Sir George Lockhart of Carnwath, lord president. Together they had four sons and four daughters, the eldest being born in 1709. A sound lawyer and a man of no little energy, he was nevertheless seen as a libertine, a religious hypocrite, and a profligate. He was a strong believer in witchcraft. He intrigued ceaselessly and was regarded as useful but unreliable by political colleagues.

After the 'Fifteen, Grange attached himself to Archibald Campbell, earl of Ilay, leader of the Argathelian party in Scotland, placing at his disposal the Erskine interests in Stirlingshire, Aberdeenshire, and Clackmannanshire. During the early 1720s he helped Lord Milton, Ilay's sous-ministre, control the general assembly. In 1724, at Ilay's prompting, he submitted a lengthy paper to ministers setting out radical proposals for reforming the highlands. By 1725 he was among the small group of advisers around Milton and helped co-ordinate Argathelian interests at the 1727 election. Despite this, it is clear that Ilay and Milton had serious reservations as to how far Grange could be trusted. Nevertheless, Grange's efforts began to bear fruit. In 1728 he was appointed to the court of delegates, set up to decide claims against the forfeited estates. Then Ilay secured permission for him to purchase Mar's forfeited estates at Alloa for the benefit of his nephew Thomas, Lord Erskine, holding out further hopes of a pardon for Mar and the restoration of the family honours.

In the early 1730s Grange's personal difficulties increased. Thomas Erskine had asked him to prevent Lady Mary Wortley Montagu from acquiring custody of her lunatic sister, Frances, countess of Mar, thus depriving the impoverished Mar of her £1000 p.a. jointure. In April 1731 Grange tried to kidnap Lady Mar and take her to Scotland but was interrupted on the way by Lady Mary with a warrant from the lord chief justice ordering her return. Worse, his wife, Rachel, was an alcoholic and mentally unstable. Not without cause, she suspected Grange of being unfaithful (principally but not only with Fanny Lindsay, a London coffee-house keeper of Scottish origin), publicly accused him of Jacobite intrigue, made an attempt on his life, and forced him to make maintenance payments. 'His health', wrote Robert Wodrow, 'is much broken this winter and spring' (Wodrow, 4.228). Early in 1732 these difficulties were apparently resolved when Grange publicly celebrated his wife's funeral. In reality he had arranged for her to be kidnapped from Edinburgh 'by some highlanders in Lovat tartan' (DNB), Simon Fraser, eleventh Lord Lovat, being a close friend. She was taken up north, eventually to St Kilda where she remained for at least seven years, finally dying in Skye in May 1745.

By early 1732 the opposition in Scotland finally began to stir, encouraged by the growing opposition to Walpole at Westminster and resentment at Ilay's increasing monopoly of patronage. For his part Grange had become dissatisfied with what he saw as Ilay's failure to obtain a pardon for Mar, who had died in May 1732, and the restoration of the family honours. Grange was also in serious financial difficulties. He had approached Ilay seeking to sell his seat on the bench in order to clear his debts but this was refused. Finally, Grange was angered by Argathelian encroachment on what he considered were his electoral interests in Clackmannanshire, Stirlingshire, and Stirling burghs. In September 1733 he therefore defected to the opposition. He was a useful acquisition. He co-ordinated correspondence between the various opposition peers, organized the distribution of propaganda, set up a press in Edinburgh, and published a newspaper called The Thistle. Together with Robert Dundas he prepared a bill to prevent trickery and corruption at elections, but not only did the ministry severely water it down, it added a clause, specifically directed at Grange, to exclude Scottish judges

from sitting in the Commons (Geo II c. 16). He resigned from the bench in May 1734.

At the general election of 1734 Grange stood for Stirling burghs, one of the most venal constituencies in Scotland. Ilay and his supporters made strong efforts to oppose him. With the support of Ebenezer Erskine and other 'high-flying' ministers who were influential in Stirling and Dunfermline and bitterly opposed to Ilay's policy of lay patronage, Grange actually received the votes of three of the five burghs but was outmanoeuvred by the Argathelian presiding officer who returned his opponent. Grange repeatedly petitioned the Commons, without success. He was, however, returned for Clackmannanshire. Despite opposition efforts, the king's list was returned by a large majority at the election of representative peers. The defeated peers resolved to petition the House of Lords, complaining about 'corrupt influence'. Again Grange was at the forefront, co-ordinating the effort and, with Dundas, drew up the required petition. When it was finally presented in February 1735, however, it was summarily dismissed. All Grange's activity had come to nought. The opposition momentum collapsed and Grange returned to the bar in despair. Needing to earn money, he attended parliament infrequently. In March 1735 he supported a bill to reduce the number of playhouses; later he attracted ridicule by making a long speech against the repeal of an act against witchcraft.

By 1737 the opposition to Walpole began to recover. Grange's return to the bar had not been financially successful.

> I mention'd my employment. I once thought it would have been pretty good … but I have neither youth nor ability enough to bear up at the Bar … it is full time to look for some help [i.e. a post], that is not so laborious and fatiguing … there are several employments in the city of London, not great, but such as would do me good. … The other thing I thought of is some employment about the Prince or Princess [of Wales] … I would be less importunate if I did not really need it. (Grange to Marchmont, 18 November 1737, Polwarth MSS, 5.144–5)

Frederick, prince of Wales, made him his secretary for Scotland in April 1738 and during the next few years Grange was part of the opposition to Walpole gathered round Frederick. From at least 1739 onwards, however, Grange was also closely involved in negotiations with Charles Edward Stuart, the Young Pretender, and the French government. In March 1740 Charles Edward's father, James Stuart, the Pretender, wrote thanking him for his 'zealous and loyal disposition' (Cruickshanks). Shortly before Walpole's fall, Grange even approached Pulteney on behalf of James Stuart but was rebuffed.

Grange was returned to parliament for Stirling burghs at the 1741 election, this time without difficulty, but the change of government following Walpole's resignation in February 1742 was of little benefit to him. He had no particular connections with the new secretary of state for Scotland, John Hay, fourth marquess of Tweeddale, and he appears to have fallen out with one of Tweeddale's closest advisers, Lord President Robert Dundas, Lord Arniston, during the aftermath of the 1734 peers' election. Throughout the early 1740s he became increasingly involved in Jacobite intrigues and was in regular touch with the Pretender. He was finally dismissed by the prince of Wales in May 1745. In June he told the Pretender that, with the administration divided and most troops out of the country, 'there never was and never can be such a favourable opportunity to attempt your Majesty's restoration' (Cruickshanks). But when he heard that the Young Pretender might come without troops or arms he condemned the project as 'very weak and very rash', predicting that 'some great misfortune will ensue' (Cruickshanks). True to form, he remained in London throughout the rising. After it collapsed he went back over to the government and in April 1746 was classed as a 'new ally' of the Pelhams. Now almost seventy, he did not stand at the 1747 election but wrote a series of letters to Pelham condemning the electioneering tactics practised by Ilay, now third duke of Argyll.

Grange lived his last years in London. Despite rumours that he received a secret service pension, he remained poor. He died in London on 20 January 1754, the family honours unrestored.   RICHARD SCOTT

Sources *Report on the manuscripts of Lord Polwarth*, 5, HMC, 67 (1961) · E. Cruickshanks, 'Erskine, Hon. James', HoP, *Commons, 1715–54* · R. Scott, 'The politics and administration of Scotland, 1725–48', PhD diss., U. Edin., 1982 · J. Hay, fourth marquess of Tweeddale, correspondence, NL Scot., Yester MSS YP 7044–7119; SYP Acc. 7174 · R. M. Sunter, *Patronage and politics in Scotland, 1707–1832* (1986), 212–29 · J. Erskine, 'Letters of Lord Grange', *The miscellany of the Spalding Club*, ed. J. Stuart, 3, Spalding Club, 16 (1846), 1–67 · G. Brunton and D. Haig, *An historical account of the senators of the college of justice, from its institution in MDXXXII* (1832) · *DNB* · NA Scot., Mar and Kellie muniments · R. Wodrow, *Analecta, or, Materials for a history of remarkable providences, mostly relating to Scotch ministers and Christians*, ed. [M. Leishman], 4 vols., Maitland Club, 60 (1842–3) · *IGI* · Burke, *Peerage* (1999)
Archives NA Scot., corresp. and MSS · NL Scot., memoirs | Hunt. L., letters to earl of London · NL Scot., letters to fourth marquess of Tweeddale
Likenesses attrib. W. Aikman, oils, *c.*1720, Scot. NPG

Erskine, James, Lord Alva (1722–1796). *See under* Erskine, Charles, Lord Tinwald (*bap.* 1680, *d.* 1763).

Erskine, James St Clair, second earl of Rosslyn (1762–1837), army officer and politician, born on 6 February 1762 and baptized at St Marylebone, Middlesex, was the elder son of Lieutenant-General Sir Henry *Erskine of Alva, fifth baronet (*bap.* 1710, *d.* 1765), who had acted as deputy quartermaster-general in the attack on L'Orient in 1746, and his wife, Janet, only daughter of Peter Wedderburn, a Scottish judge of the court of session under the title of Lord Chesterhall, and only sister of Alexander Wedderburn, lord chancellor of England from 1793 to 1801, who was created successively Lord Loughborough and earl of Rosslyn, with remainder in default of issue to James, his nephew. Sir Henry Erskine died on 9 August 1765 and was succeeded by his son James, then only three years old, whose education and career were carefully watched and forwarded by his maternal uncle, Alexander Wedderburn.

Erskine was educated at Edinburgh high school and at Eton College (1772–7) and entered the army reputedly as a cornet in the 1st Horse Guards. In 1778 he became lieutenant first in the 35th foot, then in the 2nd dragoons, and afterwards in the 21st light dragoons. However, the first clear entry in the *Army List* shows him as lieutenant in the 21st light dragoons, on 25 December 1778, with an indication that he did reach that rank in the army on 25 September of that year. He advanced to captain in the 19th light dragoons on 14 July 1780 and transferred to the 14th light dragoons on 4 August 1781. In the following year Loughborough's friend Lord Carlisle, as lord lieutenant of Ireland, appointed Erskine one of his aides-de-camp-extraordinary. He was also appointed assistant adjutant-general in Ireland, and on 28 August 1783 he was promoted major into the 8th light dragoons. In 1782—though under age—he had been elected whig MP for Castle Rising, in Norfolk, a pocket borough, through the influence both of his uncle (who had become lord chief justice of the court of common pleas) and of the Suffolk family. In 1784 Loughborough accepted Carlisle's offer to return Erskine for Morpeth in Northumberland, and Erskine exchanged the seat of Castle Rising for Morpeth, then supposedly a close borough. He soon made his reputation in the House of Commons as a forceful opposition speaker. In February 1785 he was appointed, for life, to the lucrative sinecure (£1852 p.a.) of director of the chancery in Scotland. A member of the group of young whigs around Edmund Burke, he took an effective part in the East India debates of 1786. Through Burke, he was chosen one of the managers of the impeachment of Warren Hastings, and later was nominated a manager in the impeachment of Sir Elijah Impey. While his uncle, Lord Loughborough, was manoeuvring for the chancellorship, he voted against the measures of Pitt. On 9 June 1789 he took the name of St Clair in addition to his own, on succeeding, on the death of Colonel Paterson St Clair, to the estates of his grandmother, the Hon. Catherine St Clair, who had married Sir John Erskine, third baronet; and in 1796 he was elected MP for the Dysart burghs in Fife, a seat which he held until his succession to the peerage. On 4 November 1789 he married Henrietta (or Harriott) Elizabeth Bouverie (*b.* 1771, *d.* 8 August 1810), eldest daughter of the Hon. Edward Bouverie. They had three children: James Alexander Erskine (1802–1866), who succeeded to his father's titles; Henry Francis Erskine (1804–1829), and Anne Erskine (*d.* 1880).

On 14 March 1792 Erskine was promoted lieutenant-colonel into the 12th light dragoons, and in the following year, in which his uncle became lord chancellor, he abandoned active politics and devoted himself to soldiering. He was first sent to the Mediterranean in that year to act as adjutant-general in the army under Major-General David Dundas before Toulon, serving in that capacity there, and in the subsequent operations in Corsica, including the capture of Calvi and San Fiorenzo. He was appointed aide-de-camp to George III and promoted colonel on 20 May 1795, and was in the following year sent to Portugal with the local rank of brigadier-general, from 30 November

1796, to act as adjutant-general to Lieutenant-General the Hon. Sir Charles Stuart, commanding the army there. He was promoted major-general on 1 January 1798 and continued to serve under Stuart, to whom he was second in command at the capture of Minorca in that year, and whom he succeeded as commander-in-chief in the Mediterranean. He returned to England on the arrival of Sir Ralph Abercromby at the end of 1799 and was appointed colonel of the Sussex fencible cavalry, which regiment was, however, reduced in 1800. He commanded a division in Scotland from November 1800 until December 1801, was made colonel of the 9th light dragoons on 1 August 1801 (retaining that appointment until his death), and again commanded a division from June 1803 to 1 January 1805, when he was promoted lieutenant-general.

On 3 January 1805 Erskine succeeded his uncle, the former lord chancellor, as second Lord Loughborough and second earl of Rosslyn, under special clauses in the patents conferring those honours upon him. On his promotion to lieutenant-general he was transferred to the Irish staff, where he commanded the south-western district until 1806. He was then sent on a special mission to Lisbon with Lieutenant-General J. G. Simcoe to report whether the British government should actively assist the Portuguese against Napoleon. The favourable report resulted in the dispatch of Lieutenant-General Sir Arthur Wellesley (later the duke of Wellington) to the Peninsula. Rosslyn was unable to accept a command there because of his seniority to Wellesley, though after the death of Lieutenant-General Sir John Moore his name was mentioned as Moore's possible successor, because of his previous knowledge of the country in 1796. He led a division under Lieutenant-General Lord Cathcart in Denmark in 1807, and under Lieutenant-General Lord Chatham during the Walcheren expedition in 1809, and he commanded the south-eastern district, with his headquarters at Canterbury, from 1812 to 1814. On 4 June 1814 he was promoted general. He was grand master of the freemasons in Scotland from 1810 to 1812. From about 1814 he again turned his attention to politics. A strong tory of the old school, and close friend of the duke of Wellington, he acted as whip to the tory party in the House of Lords for many years, though his favouring Catholic emancipation had been known since 1807. He was appointed GCB in 1820, on the accession of George IV, and lord lieutenant of Fife. After Wellington became prime minister, Rosslyn entered the cabinet as lord privy seal, and was sworn of the privy council. He was also lord president of the council in Wellington's short-lived cabinet of December 1834. Rosslyn died on 18 January 1837 at Dysart House, Fife, aged seventy-four, and was buried in Roslin Chapel, Midlothian.   H. M. STEPHENS, rev. JOHN SWEETMAN

Sources Army List · P. F. Stewart, *The history of the XII royal lancers* (1950) · Burke, *Peerage* (1887) · HoP, *Commons* · GEC, *Peerage*, new edn · J. Wade, ed., *The extraordinary black book*, new edn (1832) · *GM*, 2nd ser., 7 (1837)
Archives NA Scot., corresp. and papers · NRA, priv. coll., corresp. and papers | BL, corresp. with Lord Grenville, Add. MS 59027 · BL, corresp. with Lord Nelson, Add. MSS 34911–34928 · BL, corresp. with Sir Robert Peel, Add. MSS 40312–40415 · NL Scot., letters to

Lord Lynedoch · U. Durham L., letters to second Earl Grey · U. Edin. L., letters to Thomas Chalmers · U. Southampton L., letters to first duke of Wellington
Likenesses G. Hayter, group portrait, oils (*The trial of Queen Caroline, 1820*), NPG · G. Hayter, group portrait, oils (*The House of Commons, 1833*), NPG

Erskine, John, of Dun (1509–1590), landowner and religious activist, was born in the House of Dun, between Montrose and Brechin, the elder son of John Erskine of Dun (*d.* 1513), and of Margaret Ruthven (*d.* 1548), widow of Alexander Stewart, first earl of Buchan (*d.* 1505), and daughter of William *Ruthven, first Lord Ruthven. By the sixteenth century the Erskines comprised a group of powerful landed families, later acquiring the earldoms of Mar and of Kellie. The wealth of the Erskines of Dun, although only a cadet branch, descended from Sir John Erskine, younger brother of Robert, who became the first Lord Erskine earlier in the fifteenth century, is amply attested by the estates of the sixth laird's grandfather and father, who, with a grand-uncle and uncle, were killed at the battle of Flodden in 1513.

Early life Succeeding to the barony as a minor, John Erskine became the ward (and later the client) of his uncle Thomas Erskine of Haltoun, chief secretary to James V from the 1520s and later lord of Brechin and Navar. Sir Thomas had studied at Pavia, but what early education he provided for John, whether at Montrose grammar school, soon to enjoy high repute, or privately, perhaps under his own supervision, is unknown. It seems that John became a student in St Salvator's College, St Andrews, but did not graduate.

Erskine's movements for much of the later 1520s and the 1530s are also largely uncertain. That he studied abroad or travelled overseas with Sir Thomas in the royal service remain only possibilities. Following a contract dated 20 December 1622, he married, probably early in 1523, Lady Elizabeth Lindsay (*d.* 1538), daughter of David Lindsay, eighth earl of Crawford. They had three sons, all of whom lived long enough to marry: the eldest, John (who predeceased his father, perhaps in 1563), Robert (who succeeded to the barony), and James. In 1530 or early 1531 Erskine was the cause of the death of a priest, Sir William Froster, in the bell tower of Montrose. The circumstances are obscure, but Erskine's acknowledgement of responsibility is clear.

Protestant leanings and connection with George Wishart Also impossible to track is Erskine's early exposure to and assimilation of protestant teachings. Ports like Montrose served as a conduit for Lutheran writings from the mid-1520s. Erskine's guardian, Sir Thomas Erskine, has been judged as sharing James V's anti-clericalism while remaining formally Catholic. Erskine of Dun may accordingly have enjoyed his uncle's protection when, during the 1530s and 1540s, he 'began to move from lairdly anti-clericalism towards a true Protestant theology' (Bardgett, 'Erskines from Dun', 5–6). David Straiton, burned for heresy in Edinburgh in August 1534, had 'frequented much the company of the Lard of Dun', according to John Knox (Knox, 1.59). They studied the Bible together. Next year Sir

Thomas took Erskine with him to Paris in order to finalize the king's French marriage arrangements, with the subsidiary purpose perhaps of distracting his nephew from perilous religious interests.

The year 1534 has traditionally been assigned to Erskine's bringing back from the continent Pierre de Marsilier to teach Greek at Montrose grammar school, 'a rare thing in the countrey, nocht hard of befor', according to James Melvill (*Autobiography and Diary*, 39), but Marsilier's introduction now looks likely to have taken place later, probably in the 1540s. However, given his prolonged involvement in town affairs as provost and constable, Erskine probably did support the Greek and New Testament teaching at the school undertaken by his kinsman by marriage and neighbour George *Wishart before this activity occasioned the latter's flight to the continent in 1538. On 29 July that year Erskine's wife died, and probably as early as 1539 he married, according to the Catholic rite amid court festivities in Linlithgow, Barbara De Beirle (*d.* 1572), daughter of Lord Camnecourt and a native of Picardy. Barbara had accompanied Mary of Guise to Scotland the previous year for her marriage to James V and is most unlikely to have had protestant leanings, at least at this date. Erskine's marriage and his continuing association with Mary of Guise and Cardinal Beaton have thus suggested inconstancy in the cause of reform, or (unlike Wishart) a prudent moderation, but when in April 1542 (not, as sometimes thought, 1537) he first received licence to travel abroad on private business, one undeniable motive seems to have been to drink at the sources of protestantism. His son John and his son's tutor Richard Melville, who both accompanied Erskine, went first to hear John MacAlpine (Macchabaeus) in Copenhagen and then to study under Philip Melanchthon in Wittenberg. Melanchthon's biblical humanism could well have inspired Erskine senior to bring back a Greek tutor to Scotland on his return in 1543.

During 1543–5 Erskine was regularly associated with the intrepid Wishart, now back from exile, so that the question has been asked whether Wishart emboldened Erskine or Erskine instructed Wishart. 'The laird of Dun's first steps as a national leader of the nascent Scottish Protestant movement were taken in association with this apostle of the Swiss evangel' (Bardgett, *Scotland Reformed*, 35). When the earl of Arran, governor of Scotland, and Cardinal David Beaton visited Montrose and region in quest of heresy in January 1544, Erskine was consigned to Blackness Castle on the southern shore of the Forth, but not it seems for long. Erskine promoted Wishart's preaching tours around Angus and the Mearns and welcomed him back to Dun from forays into south-west Scotland, but according to Knox, his last journey, to Edinburgh and the Lothians in 1545, was 'sore against the judgement of the Lard of Dune' (Knox, 1.132). After Wishart's execution in 1546 and the assassination of Beaton which followed it partly as an act of revenge, Erskine saw no cause whatever to take to the sword himself. His role in defending Montrose against English seaborne invasion in the late 1540s won royal congratulations.

Supporting John Knox The early 1550s seem to have been quiet years for the laird of Dun, but when John Knox returned from Geneva in September 1555, he was among the first to attend his private exhortations in Edinburgh. He also housed Knox for a month at Dun during his preaching tours. Knox had persuaded him that believers should not take part in the mass, and at Dun they celebrated the Lord's Supper with other notables. Contrary to universal opinion, however, the Erskine whose signature appears fifth on the first protestant band, inviting Knox to return from Geneva, subscribed on 3 December 1557, was not the sixth laird but Lord John Erskine (*c.*1510–1572), later earl of Mar and regent. A comparison of signatures puts this beyond doubt, but there is every reason to assume that Erskine of Dun was among the 'many others' who signed (Knox, 6.675–6).

Less than a fortnight later, such was his versatility, Erskine was among those commissioned to negotiate and witness the marriage in France of Mary Queen of Scots to the dauphin. After his return in 1558 he was chosen by the protestants to be one of the elders to supervise the 'privy kirks' of zealous lay folk meeting for prayer and Bible study. Erskine's subsequent role combined unflinching support for Knox and his colleagues as one of the leading 'lords of the congregation' with a diplomatic civility that more than once during the fraught years from 1559 fitted him to serve as spokesman for the protestants before the queen regent or Mary herself. Knox described him in this context as 'a man most gentill of nature, and most addict to please … in all thingis not repugnant to God' (Knox, 1.318).

In 1559 and 1560 in particular Erskine appeared the key link person between 'the lords' and 'the congregation'. On 6 May 1559 he drafted a letter to the queen regent from 'the professouris of Christis Ewangell, in the Realme of Scotland' which propounded the theory of two kingdoms, civil and ecclesiastical, and he was invited to the convocation at St Andrews on 4 June to plan for 'reformation'. On 23 October he signed the act suspending Mary of Guise from the regency, and on 10 February 1560 signed the instructions to the commissioners sent to Berwick to compact an agreement with the duke of Norfolk on behalf of Elizabeth of England.

Superintendent and moderator At the general assembly of December 1560 Erskine was approved as qualified to preach, and then in 1561 elected superintendent of Angus and Mearns. He was inducted to office by Knox in January 1562 and served until his death, through changes of title, area, and authority. In the acid test of staffing the parishes of the Reformed kirk Erskine had as much success as any superintendent, by making the most of his high social status, landed wealth, and local connections, and perhaps also by not pitching the spiritual requirements too high; in the process he received significant financial rewards, and, given his existing interest in the temporalities of the bishopric of Brechin, it has been suggested that he may have hoped eventually to acquire the see.

Erskine's moderating temper continued to be serviceable. He was the only other person present at Knox's clamorous interview with Mary in mid-1563. When the queen erupted into tears, Erskine, 'a man of meak and gentill spreit, stood besyd, and entreated what he could to mitigat hir anger, and gave unto hir many pleasing wordis of hir beautie, of hir excellence'. On this occasion his words only served 'to cast oyle in the flaming fyre' (Knox, 2.388), but he remained with the queen when Knox was dismissed, and retained her favour thereafter. At the Perth conference at the end of May 1565 on her marriage to Darnley the queen professed her willingness to hear biblical preaching, and 'above all others, she said, she would gladly hear the Superintendent of Angus, (for he was a mild and sweet natured man,) with true honesty and uprightnesse' (Knox, 2.482).

Recognition of similar gifts, together with his firm commitment to the Reformation since 1555, brought Erskine election as moderator of the general assembly on 25 December 1565, 25 June 1566, and 25 December 1566. In 1568–9 he conducted a witch-hunt in Angus and the Mearns, resulting in at least forty accusations, and in 1571 he again wrote in defence of ecclesiastical independence. On 16 August 1672 he was again elected moderator of the general assembly, which had before it the compromise episcopal polity agreed at the convention of Leith in January 1572. Erskine had been instrumental in securing the attendance of the church's commissioners at the convention. Although Robert Wodrow credits him with vigorous opposition to the titular bishops agreed at Leith, consenting to them only 'for peace' (Wodrow, 1.54), Erskine's subsequent conduct revealed this to be an overstatement. His conciliatory influence helped the assembly in August 1572 to agree to the scheme as an interim measure. It was never to be more than patchily and disreputably implemented, yet Erskine supported it to the extent of offering to give up his superintendency once bishops were appointed for St Andrews and Dunkeld.

The Leith provisions were in reality overtaken by the second Book of Discipline of 1578. Erskine played no little part in its drafting, revising, and finalizing. He also moderated a nine-day conference at Stirling Castle in December 1578, when thirteen commissioners invited by the king scrutinized the book. The ministerial participants insisted that they had no warrant to negotiate.

In November 1579 Erskine was named one of the twenty-seven members of the king's council. To the last he served on commissions of the assembly. Even during the crisis of the Black Acts in 1584–5, threatening to subject the kirk to both crown and episcopacy unfettered, Erskine sought safeguards in preference to meek compliance or exile. He persuaded his ministers to sign 'as far as the Word of God allows', with the power of the keys remaining in the kirk's hands.

Death and significance Erskine's wife, Barbara, with whom he had had four sons and two daughters, died on 15 November 1572. Erskine himself died on 22 March 1590. Among his surviving writings were sermons on Matthew 9: 37–8 and Luke 7: 36–50, which represent 'a good percentage of the exceptionally few sermons to have survived from sixteenth century Scotland' (Bardgett, 'John Erskine of Dun', 72); a short dissertation on the respective provinces of civil and ecclesiastical powers; and 'The forme and maner of buriall usit in the kirk of Montrois'. These works show Erskine not only declaring the Reformation's central message of Christ's grace for believing sinners, but also defending the church's spiritual independence. Oecolampadius, the Reformer of Basel, one of whose works Erskine owned, has been proposed as a possible source of this strong advocacy of independent church discipline, while Wishart had translated the First Helvetic Confession of 1536. The evidence indicates Erskine's alignment with the Swiss or Reformed rather than Lutheran stream of continental protestantism.

At the same time Erskine championed the essential jurisdiction of the state, in his typical pragmatism, geared to political and social realities, reflected throughout his career. Not least remarkable for the sixteenth century was the long duration, over fifty years, of his public role. For the most part he succeeded in being well spoken of on all sides. He married a cultured humanity, instinctively conciliatory, to unqualified allegiance to the Reformation. Among his most admirable achievements was his work as superintendent in settling the Reformation into its long future in Angus and the Mearns. D. F. WRIGHT

Sources T. Crockett, 'The life of John Erskine of Dun', DLitt diss., U. Edin., 1924 · F. D. Bardgett, *Scotland reformed: the Reformation in Angus and the Mearns* (1989) · F. D. Bardgett, 'Faith, families and factions', PhD diss., U. Edin., 1987 · F. Bardgett, 'John Erskine of Dun: a theological reassessment', *Scottish Journal of Theology*, 43 (1990), 59–86 · V. Jacob, *The lairds of Dun* (1931) · J. S. McEwen, 'John Erskine of Dun, 1508–91', *Fathers of the kirk*, ed. R. S. Wright (1960), 17–27 · *Miscellany of the Spalding Club*, 4 (1849) · T. Thomson, ed., *A diurnal of remarkable occurrents that have passed within the country of Scotland*, Bannatyne Club, 43 (1833) · W. Macfarlane, *Genealogical collections concerning families in Scotland*, ed. J. T. Clark, 2, Scottish History Society, 34 (1900) · F. D. Bardgett, 'Erskines from Dun and the chapter of Brechin', *Society of Friends of Brechin Cathedral*, bk 39 (1990), 3–15 · A. Sinclair, *Genealogical tree of the ancient family of Erskine of Dun* [n.d.] · R. Wodrow, *Collections upon the lives of the reformers and most eminent ministers*, 1 (1834) · *The works of John Knox*, ed. D. Laing, 6 vols., Wodrow Society, 12 (1846–64) · *The autobiography and diary of Mr James Melvill*, ed. R. Pitcairn, Wodrow Society (1842) · NL Scot. · J. Kirk, *The Second Book of Discipline* (1980) · J. Kirk, *Patterns of reform: continuity and change in the Reformation kirk* (1989) · G. Donaldson, *The Scottish Reformation* (1960) · J. Wormald, *Court, kirk and community in Scotland, 1470–1625* (1981), 169

Erskine, John, seventeenth or first earl of Mar (*d.* 1572), magnate and regent of Scotland, was the third born but eldest surviving son of John, fifth Lord Erskine (*d.* 1555) and his wife, Margaret Campbell, daughter of the second earl of Argyll. As a younger son he was trained for the church, and probably took minor orders. He also obtained the commendatorships of Dryburgh Abbey and Inchmaholme, which had come under his family's control.

Lord Erskine and the Reformation Following the deaths of his elder brothers, Robert in 1547 and Thomas in 1551, John Erskine had to prepare for a secular career. Heir to great estates in central Scotland, especially in Stirlingshire, Renfrewshire, and Clackmannanshire, he also had the advantage of valuable connections at court and with the nobility. As a young man his father had been one of the lords charged with the custody of James V during the latter's childhood, and he later served that king as an ambassador and councillor; he was subsequently also a guardian of the infant Mary, queen of Scots, whom he accompanied to France in 1548. The younger John Erskine is recorded at her residence of St Germain-en-Laye in the following year. His sister Margaret *Erskine [see under James V, mistresses and children of (act. c.1529–1592)], though married to Sir Robert Douglas of Lochleven, was probably the closest to King James of his many mistresses; he might well have married her had the pope been willing to countenance her divorcing her husband. James *Stewart, later earl of Moray, was born of this liaison. Through his mother Erskine was related not only to the earls of Argyll but also to the Stewart earls of Atholl. By 29 January 1557, moreover, he had married Annabella Murray of Tullibardine (d. 1603), whose brother Sir William *Murray was comptroller of Scotland from 1565 to 1582.

When the duke of Châtelherault resigned as regent of Scotland on 12 April 1554, custody of Edinburgh Castle was transferred from him to the fifth Lord Erskine; following the latter's death the following year it became the responsibility of his son. His custody of the castle enabled the younger John Erskine to play a crucial role in events at the end of the decade, as the protestant lords of the congregation struggled against the queen dowager, Mary of Guise, for control of the town. Although he showed his personal support for the cause of religious reform when he visited John Knox at Calder in 1556, and still more when he signed the first protestant bond on 3 December 1557, Erskine nevertheless refused to take sides in the conflict, trying instead to limit the hostilities. In June 1559 he attempted unsuccessfully to dissuade the congregation from attacking Perth, but when the reformers left Edinburgh on 6 November he took their guns into the castle. His avowedly neutral stance irritated Knox, who recorded how Erskine 'would promise unto us no favours. But said, "He must needs declare himself friend to those that were able to support and defend him"' (Knox's History, 1.264). Erskine himself saw his position in more idealistic terms, declaring in December his intention to 'doo that becometh an honest man for the weale of his countrey. As for the castell, he woll not parte with it, but by the order he received it, which was by parliament' (Clifford, 1.631). He had already fired on French troops pillaging the Edinburgh suburbs, and later in December he warned that if the French tried to capture Stirling Castle his guns would bombard the queen dowager in Holyrood House. Mary tried to win Erskine over, and granted him the commendatorship of Cambuskenneth Abbey, but the only concession she obtained in return was an undertaking to admit her to the castle, 'in case there com a greater pour agenst her then she can be able to withstonde … so as she com in such sorte as he may be still master of his charge' (ibid., 1.654). For the time being she stayed outside.

Erskine remained neutral during the early months of 1560. On 19 March he and the fifth Lord Home wrote to Lord James Stewart, Erskine's nephew and a leading member of the congregation, offering to negotiate between Mary of Guise and her adversaries. On 1 April he finally admitted Mary to Edinburgh Castle, perhaps moved by her evident sickness. On 4 June, shortly before her death, he attempted (in vain) to secure for her the spiritual ministrations of the bishop of Amiens, then in the French camp, but that was the limit of his partisanship. During April he had continued his efforts to negotiate peace, and according to Knox he warned Mary on the 30th that a sudden fire at Leith was a sign of God's determination to expel the French from Scotland. The queen dowager died on 11 June, and on 6 July the Anglo-French Treaty of Edinburgh provided for the withdrawal of foreign armies from Scotland. His failure to commit himself to the now-victorious congregation was not held against Erskine, who attended parliament on 1 August and was elected one of the lords of the articles. According to the English ambassador Thomas Randolph, Erskine was among the nobles who now openly declared themselves protestant, 'concluding that this was the faith wherein they ought to live and die' (CSP Scot., 1547–63, 467).

Although Randolph thought him still a papist in October 1560, Erskine was certainly sincere in his conversion, remaining committed for the rest of his life to protestantism and to political alliance with England. On 18 August 1560 he signed the petition that Queen Elizabeth should marry the third earl of Arran. On 27 January 1561 he was in the small minority of nobles who refused to subscribe the Book of Discipline, but his motives seem to have been entirely secular. Knox surmised, probably correctly, that Erskine was unwilling to lose the revenues of his commendatorships, demanded for the maintenance of the reformed church; he could ill afford to do so, having set aside his income from Cambuskenneth to pay off debts inherited from his father. In 1562 he failed to pay the thirds assessed on his ecclesiastical lands.

Relations with Queen Mary On 19 August 1561 Queen Mary returned to Scotland from France. Erskine found no difficulties about serving her. From 19 September he regularly attended meetings of her privy council, while his wife became one of her ladies-in-waiting and his brother Arthur a royal equerry. On 8 November he was given the custody of Stirling Castle, and on 30 June 1562, shortly after he had entertained her at his family seat at Alloa, Mary confirmed to him her mother's grant of Cambuskenneth, and provided his brother Thomas's illegitimate son Adam to the abbacy. In December 1564 he supported the Leicester match for Mary which Lord James (now earl of Moray) and William Maitland of Lethington were trying unsuccessfully to negotiate with England. In the following February he was reportedly hostile to the earl of Lennox, whose son Henry, Lord Darnley, aspired to the queen's hand; Erskine's kinship to the earl of Argyll was thought significant at this point. But he remained loyal to Mary when Moray, Argyll, and the Hamiltons rebelled against the match and against Darnley's elevation at their expense. His efforts to negotiate through his kinsman John Erskine of Dun failed, and when Moray tried to occupy Edinburgh on 31 August he came under fire from the castle guns, directed by his uncle.

By this time Erskine's loyalty to Mary had brought him a long-sought reward. His ancestor Robert, first Lord Erskine, had claimed the earldom of Mar in 1438, but was only permitted to hold it during his lifetime. His son's claim to the title was thwarted, and there is no clear evidence that subsequent lords Erskine revived it. But the fact that on 11 May 1565 Randolph told Sir William Cecil of impending promotions, including that of 'Lord Ersken, earl of Marre which he claims by succession', indicates that the sixth Lord Erskine had not forgotten it (*CSP Scot.*, *1563–9*, 157). Mary needed his support, as she tried to win approval for her marriage to Darnley, and on 23 June she issued a charter granting Erskine the earldom and the lordship of Garioch; in return he relinquished a liferent from the lordship of Menteith. The grant was largely honorific, as the lands of the medieval earldom had long since been dispersed by the crown. It had taken effect by 1 August, when he attended a council meeting as earl of Mar. The new earl played no part in the murder of David Riccio on 9 March 1566 and during that year was among the friends to whom Mary gave jewels as keepsakes; his wife and his daughter Mary were similarly remembered. About the end of July he was again the queen's host at Alloa and went hunting with her and the earls of Bothwell and Moray. Mar avoided, too, any involvement in the murder of Darnley on 10 February 1567.

That murder, and still more Mary's marriage to the fourth earl of Bothwell, had a decisive effect on Mar's relations with the queen. On 19 March 1567 Mary relieved him of the keeping of Edinburgh Castle, entrusting it to a follower of Bothwell's, but on the same day placed the infant Prince James in his care, 'to be conservit, nurist and upbrocht within our said Castell of Striveling under your tutill and governance', and praised Mar's 'treuth and uprichtnes towards us' (*Mar and Kellie MSS*, 1.16). But she failed to win his backing. Mar did not attend the parliament held in April (though some of its legislation benefited him), nor did he sign the so-called Ainslie bond at the end of it approving Mary's marriage to Bothwell, and he did not attend the wedding itself on 15 May. He may simply have resented losing Edinburgh Castle in order to make it easier for Bothwell to overawe the town below. On 1 May Mar was a signatory to a bond undertaking to free the queen (abducted by Bothwell on 24 April), preserve the prince, and bring Darnley's killers to justice. A week later he was reported to be 'witteling' Stirling Castle against Bothwell's alleged intention to seize Prince James.

King's man Together with his title and estates, his custody of the prince made Mar a figure to be reckoned with and also did much to determine his political stance, placing him firmly in the ranks of what soon became the 'king's party', which was opposed to the 'queen's men' who remained loyal to James's mother. The decisive moment in that development was the prince's coronation at Stirling on 29 July. The countess of Mar bore James from the castle to the parish church, and her husband carried him back again afterwards. Shortly afterwards Mar discussed his position with the English ambassador, Sir Nicholas Throckmorton, who found the earl very proud of his responsibility—'He reputes the guard of the young king … a great honour to him'—and resolved to stand by his associates in upholding James's kingship: '"For", said he, "yff I cannot deale syncerely and honestly with these men, whyche be my neryst kynsfolkes and frends, with whom trow ye I can deale well, or betrayeng them and my young master, who wold credyt me hereafter?"' (*CSP Scot.*, *1563–9*, 376–7). Mar subsequently showed himself 'ane nobleman and ane favorar of godlines' by purging the Chapel Royal at Stirling of 'monuments of ydolatrie' (*APS*, *1567–92*, 62), having been present in the confederate army to which Mary surrendered on 15 June at Carberry Hill. On 13 May 1568 he supported Moray, at the battle of Langside.

Mar stood by Moray throughout the latter's regency, resisting Queen Mary's efforts to win him over. In a letter of 17 December 1568 from Bolton Castle she warned him that 'my son is to be taken from you and brought to this country, and Stirling Castle garrisoned by strangers' (*CSP Scot.*, *1563–9*, 584–5). Reassured by a denial from Queen Elizabeth, however, Mar remained unswayed, and later he ignored Mary's charges of ingratitude addressed to him and his wife. His influence kept the shires of his domination largely secure for the regent, and after Moray was murdered, on 23 January 1570, Mar was one of the pallbearers at the funeral in St Giles's, Edinburgh. He was no less firm in his support for Moray's successor as regent, the fourth earl of Lennox. Though his need to devote himself to the care of the young king had led to his being exempted from military service, Mar may have been campaigning against Dumbarton when Moray was killed. In March 1570 he led an attack on Linlithgow, on the route between Stirling and Edinburgh, which burnt the town, and he was engaged in skirmishes there at the end of April. Early in August he accompanied Lennox on a campaign against the Hamiltons in Clydesdale. A year later the queen's men took their revenge by pillaging Mar's house in Brechin, and on 29 August 1571 he was among the nobles forfeited by the Marian parliament in Edinburgh.

Regent of Scotland Shortly afterwards, on 4 September, the queen's men raided Stirling while their adversaries were holding their own parliament there. Their attack was beaten off, but not before Lennox had been mortally wounded, having been saved from capture by a sortie which Mar led from the castle. On the following day Mar was elected to succeed him. The English agent Thomas Randolph wanted to see the forceful and aggressive earl of Morton made regent, but it seems probable that his fellow nobles preferred Mar as a likely peacemaker, at a time when the civil war was becoming increasingly violent. His appointment was followed by a number of defections to the king's men, but Mar took on his new burden without enthusiasm, accepting it only on condition that he could resign 'gif ayther ye heirefter sall find my inhabilitie for the charge Or that I sall find my self owerburdynnit thairin abone my power' (*APS*, *1567–92*, 65–6). Less than three weeks later he was complaining to his predecessor's widow of the 'cairis, restles bussines and daylie danger' to which he was exposed (CSP Scot., 1571–4, 696). Nevertheless, he began his regency with a show of force, making a determined attempt to capture Edinburgh in October. But he lacked both the manpower and the guns needed to break into the town, and retreated to Leith, which increasingly became his headquarters.

Contemporaries were emphatic that throughout his regency Mar was overshadowed by Morton, whom he quickly made his chief lieutenant. The opinion of the English ambassador Henry Killigrew, that 'Morton is the only man for her majesty to account of in this realm', was only one of many to the same effect (CSP Scot., 1571–4, 413). Nevertheless, Mar was both consistent and clear-sighted in appreciating the need for English support, and he began his regency by apologizing to Queen Elizabeth for having taken office without her consent. Having been rewarded with her approval and the promise of £1000 (probably not paid until the following March), he made numerous appeals for assistance from England as the only way to overcome the material weaknesses hampering his war effort. On 22 October, immediately after the failure of his attack on Edinburgh, he asked for 200 guns and 3000 foot soldiers. He did not receive them, however, and the civil war dragged on, with the king's party bogged down before Edinburgh and under pressure from the Hamiltons in the west and the Gordons in the north.

Mar was more successful in his handling of ecclesiastical affairs. Regent Lennox's provision of John Douglas to the archbishopric of St Andrews on 6 August 1571 was seen as unwarranted and high-handed by representatives of a kirk anxious for independence from lay control, and led to protests from John Knox and others. Mar's response was characteristically eirenic. Having initially set up a commission to investigate the issue (its members were largely the same as those of a similar body named by the kirk), he was then offered the chance of a compromise by the intervention in November of his kinsman the widely respected John Erskine of Dun, superintendent of Angus. Acknowledging in response that 'The defaut of the whole standeth in this, that the policie of the Kirk is not perfyte' (Calderwood, 3.164), Mar arranged for an assembly to be held at Leith in January 1572 to discuss the appointment of ministers, and especially of bishops, and the control of the kirk's endowment. The decisions taken at this 'quiet conference' concerning bishops, that election by ministers should follow royal nomination, were not intended to be permanent and soon prompted misgivings in the kirk, but they were sufficient to defuse tension for the time being.

Meanwhile the civil war continued. On 6 March 1572 Mar wrote at length to Queen Elizabeth, repeating earlier appeals for her assistance. Almost simultaneously the governor of Berwick, Baron Hunsdon, reported to Elizabeth that Mar and many other nobles 'would be glad to grant to any reasonable articles of accord' with the Marians, but that Morton, 'who rules the Regent', and others who had benefited from forfeitures were unlikely to agree (CSP Scot., 1571–4, 156). At the end of May the regent handed over to England the seventh earl of Northumberland, a fugitive in Scotland since January 1570, in return for £2000—he needed both the money and English goodwill. Mar was himself sometimes engaged in fighting. On 10 March 1572 he defeated a Marian force outside Edinburgh, and in the following summer he led a raid into Clydesdale, in June, and then an expedition to Dundee, in July. His adversaries responded by destroying his town house in Edinburgh's Cowgate. Beset on every side, unable to secure the English support he needed—Elizabeth even rebuked him for presenting over-hard terms to the queen's men—on 31 July Mar agreed to a two-month truce with Edinburgh's 'Castilians', subsequently extended to the end of the year. On 9 October he announced his intention of leading an expedition against 'the dissobedient subiectis on the bordouris' (CSP Scot., 1571–4, 710–11), but after enjoying Morton's hospitality at Dalkeith he was suddenly taken ill. He made his way to Stirling Castle, where he died on the night of 28/29 October.

The earl and countess of Mar In his will, drawn up on 9 August 1568, Mar instructed that he was to be buried in Alloa church alongside the remains of his ancestors, which were to be transported thither from Cambuskenneth. He also recommended that his wife, whom he named sole executor, should 'use ye counsale of my broder and frends yat ar cum of my hous' in everything concerning 'ye tretment of friendis and intertainment of yame to the kingis grace service for the honoᵣ of the hous' (N&Q, 4th ser., 8.321). As regent he had shown a similar, and entirely conventional, concern for the well-being of his 'hous' by occasionally advancing the interests of its members, as when he granted his own son and heir, another John *Erskine, the ward of Regent Moray's lands on 15 November 1571. In his will he also provided for his daughter Mary, who later married Archibald Douglas, eighth earl of Angus, and for his servants. Contemporary references show that Mar was widely liked and admired for his gentleness and integrity. According to the Diurnal the people of Edinburgh regretted his resignation of the castle in 1567, 'because the said erle of Mar wes ane guid man, and na oppressour of the saidis inhabitantis', and the same source attributed his death to the effects of the civil war—'The maist caus of his deid wes that he lufit peace, and culd nocht have the same' (Thomson, Diurnal, 107, 316–17). To Sir William Drury, writing to Burghley on 14 September 1571, the new regent was 'one of the most constant men of Scotland and wholly given to quietness' (CSP for., 1569–71, 534).

Mar seems to have been a cultivated man. He knew French (Queen Mary wrote to him in that language), possessed a fine collection of silver plate and other household goods, including 'ane bed of reid and yallow silke chakerit … with three courtingis and a covering of reid and yallow taffatie' (Mar and Kellie MSS, 2.30–32), and made a notable contribution to the townscape of Stirling in the form of Mar's Wark. Situated at the head of the town's Broad Street, the Wark is notable for its facade, lavishly ornamented with heraldic and decorative elements. It was also built to carry guns, a reminder that its builder seldom enjoyed the quietness he longed for. Mar lacked the forcefulness and the political skills which he needed to be effective as regent. Thomas Randolph could only say of him that he was 'wiser than some judge of him' (*CSP Scot.*, 1571–4, 282), and Sir James Melville of Halhill, who admired Mar, admitted that 'he was not a gud discimulaire' (*Memoirs of His Own Life*, 180–81). Perhaps Mar was temperamentally better suited to being the young king's guardian. An anonymous poem of 1572, professing to voice the opinions of 'Lady Scotland', referred to James as being well brought up by 'gude Lord Deddy [Daddy], my trew faithfull freind' (Cranstoun, 2.231).

In his task of protecting the king Mar had the assistance of his wife. In the early 1560s she was denounced by John Knox as 'a very Jezebel' and as 'a sweet morsel for the Devil's mouth' (*Knox's History*, 1.344; 2.77), presumably because she was reputed a papist. Nevertheless, on 25 November 1572 parliament decided that James should remain 'under the nutriture of my said lady the countess of Mar his governant' (*APS*, 1567–92, 81). Sir James Melville noted in 1577 that she was 'wyse and schairp, and held the King in gret aw' (*Memoirs of His Own Life*, 262). King James himself appears to have been grateful for her part in his upbringing, for in February 1594 he entrusted his own eldest son, Prince Henry, to the custody of the dowager countess of Mar and her eldest son, the second earl, and referred appreciatively to the good service of the latter's father and grandfather in the same office. Five years later he again praised the countess's former services, while commenting on her great age, 'haveing hir body waist and extenuat be hir former service' (Burton and Masson, 1599–1604, 18). She died in February 1603, having in her will urged her grandson 'to remaine ane constant servand to God continewing in the trew religione, presentlie professit within this realme' (*Fourth Report*, HMC, 526–7).

HENRY SUMMERSON

Sources GEC, *Peerage*, 5.104–6; 8.418–20 · *Scots peerage*, 5.609–15 · *CSP Scot.*, 1547–74 · *CSP for.*, 1569–74 · *Reg. PCS*, 1st ser., vols. 1–2, 6–8 · J. M. Thomson and others, eds., *Registrum magni sigilli regum Scotorum / The register of the great seal of Scotland*, 11 vols. (1882–1914), vol. 4 · M. Livingstone, D. Hay Fleming, and others, eds., *Registrum secreti sigilli regum Scotorum / The register of the privy seal of Scotland*, 4–6 (1952–63), 1548–74 · *APS*, 1424–1592 · *Fourth report*, HMC, 3 (1874) · *Report on the manuscripts of the earl of Mar and Kellie*, HMC, 60 (1904) · H. Paton, ed., *Supplementary report on the manuscripts of the earl of Mar and Kellie*, HMC, 60 (1930) · *N&Q*, 4th ser., 8 (1871), 321 · *The state papers and letters of Sir Ralph Sadler*, ed. A. Clifford, 1 (1809) · [T. Thomson], ed., *The historie and life of King James the Sext*, Bannatyne Club, 13 (1825) · R. Bannatyne, *Memoriales of transactions in Scotland, 1569–1573*, ed. [R. Pitcairn], Bannatyne Club, 51 (1836) · *Memoirs of his own life by Sir James Melville of Halhill*, ed. T. Thomson, Bannatyne Club, 18 (1827) · T. Thomson, ed., *A diurnal of remarkable occurrents that have passed within the country of Scotland*, Bannatyne Club, 43 (1833) · J. Robertson, ed., *Inventories of Mary queen of Scots, 1556–1569*, Bannatyne Club, 111 (1863) · J. Knox, *The history of the Reformation of the Church of Scotland*, sel. edns (1644–1812) · J. Kirk, *The Second Book of Discipline* (1980) · D. Calderwood, *The history of the Kirk of Scotland*, ed. T. Thomson and D. Laing, 8 vols., Wodrow Society, 7 (1842–9) · J. Cranstoun, ed., *Satirical poems of the time of the Reformation*, 1, STS, 20 (1891) · *Stirlingshire: an inventory of the ancient monuments*, 2 vols., Royal Commission on the Ancient and Historical Monuments of Scotland (1963) · J. Cameron, *James V: the personal rule, 1528–1542*, ed. N. Macdougall (1998) · K. M. Brown, *Noble society in Scotland* (2000) · M. Lynch, *Edinburgh and the Reformation* (1981) · R. K. Marshall, *Mary of Guise* (1977) · G. Donaldson, *All the queen's men* (1983) · M. Lee, *James Stewart, earl of Moray* (1953) · G. R. Hewitt, *Scotland under Morton, 1572–80* (1982)
Archives NA Scot., corresp. and papers
Likenesses J. Scougall, oils (after an unknown artist), Scot. NPG

Erskine, John, eighteenth or second earl of Mar (*c*.1562–1634), courtier and politician, was the eldest son of John *Erskine, seventeenth or first earl of Mar (*d*. 1572), and his wife, Annabella Murray (*d*. 1603). His extensive estates were mainly in Stirlingshire (of which he was hereditary sheriff) and Clackmannanshire, and centred on the burgh of Stirling. He also had his family's ancestral barony of Erskine in Renfrewshire, and he inherited claims to estates in the medieval earldom of Mar.

The minority of James VI John Erskine was aged about ten when his father, then regent of Scotland, died on 28 October 1572, having appointed his wife tutor to their children. Countess Annabella was also the senior woman in charge of the young James VI, who called her familiarly Lady Minny. Mar himself was educated alongside the king by his tutors George Buchanan and Peter Young. James's nickname for Mar, John Slaitis, commemorates their educational medium. Mar was also educated at some point by the eccentric intriguer John Colville. His education left him with poor handwriting and spelling, but he could express himself vigorously, and the king's lasting respect for him began with their youthful association.

The tradition which Mar inherited was that of protestantism and the English 'amity', represented by his father and others who had deposed Queen Mary. He was particularly close to Regent Morton; his sister Mary (*d*. 1575) married Morton's nephew the earl of Angus, nominal head of the Douglases, in 1573. Mar's curators in 1578 were his mother, his uncle and heir apparent Alexander Erskine, master of Mar, David Erskine, commendator of Dryburgh, Sir William Murray of Tullibardine, Morton, William Douglas of Lochleven, and Colin Campbell of Glenorchy (Murray's cousin). By 1582 only the first four of these remained.

Mar's entry into politics at sixteen was prompted by Morton's enforced resignation as regent on 15 March 1578. The coalition that ousted Morton included Alexander, master of Mar. The young earl evidently disapproved of his uncle's action and on 26 April demanded the keys of Stirling Castle from him, claiming that he had the hereditary right to be keeper of the castle. There was a scuffle, Alexander's son was killed, and Mar gained possession not just of the castle but of the king—a recurrent theme in the next few years. His backers on 26 April were David Erskine, commendator of Dryburgh, and Adam Erskine, commendator of Cambuskenneth, and Mar rapidly summoned Angus and Morton to join him. Tense negotiations with the anti-Morton faction followed; by July it was agreed that Morton should return to power as head of the council. To cement this, Mar made a bond of friendship on

John Erskine, eighteenth or second earl of Mar (*c*.1562–1634), attrib. Adam de Colone, 1626

27 November with the earl of Argyll, one of Morton's leading opponents.

Mar was now officially keeper of the king and a privy councillor. Government was centred in Stirling Castle, which he commanded, and he received a monthly allowance of £400 to defray council expenses. Closely allied to Morton for the remainder of the latter's period in power, he was active in Morton's campaign against the Hamilton family in the spring of 1579. The king's departure from Stirling in September 1579 had no effect on Mar's prominence. In October 1580 he married Anna Drummond (*d*. 1587), daughter of Lord Drummond, at Kincardine, the king being present. He had 'taken a liking' to her on meeting her in June, and the marriage assisted a political alliance with her brother-in-law, the earl of Montrose (*CSP Scot.*, 1574–81, 447). The marriage was prematurely ended by her death on 23 December 1587 but produced one son, another John *Erskine (*d*. 1653), who later succeeded as nineteenth or third earl.

Mar's circumstances changed with Morton's downfall at the end of 1580. Angus attempted to organize resistance to his uncle's impending execution, and in mid-March 1581 Mar joined his coalition and allowed it to use Stirling as a base. On 28 March he was ordered to hand over Stirling Castle to John Stewart. The master of Mar, who conveyed the order, reported to the king that Mar 'takis heavy in hart that your majestie suld think the castell securer in ony mannis handis nor his' and that he had been warned against the 'evill and desperat course of the earl of Angus'. Mar 'bursted furth' with a desire to leave the country for three years (*Mar and Kellie MSS*, 1.33–4). Initially reconciled to the king while Angus alone went into exile, Mar did

eventually leave (probably joining Angus in England); he was summoned to return in February 1582, when he was 'reponit to his wonted credit with the king, and had his eare' (Moysie, 36).

However, Mar and his pro-English friends were at odds with the dominant figure in the government, the duke of Lennox, and on 23 August 1582 Mar played a leading role in the Ruthven raid, which captured the king and overthrew Lennox. With 120 horsemen he ambushed and scattered a rescue party led by Sir William Stewart. Thereafter he was present at all the Ruthven regime's public occasions. When the regime began to crumble after the king's escape in June 1583, Mar retired to his house and a number of his followers were dismissed from the royal household. In September he was put to the horn for non-payment of taxes. He retreated to Erskine and was ordered to leave the country, on 29 October receiving a royal licence to go abroad for three years. The remission he received on 29 November for the Ruthven raid was probably intended to smooth his path into exile. He went to Argyll, and eventually, in late December, to Carrickfergus in Ireland, where he joined the master of Glamis. There was talk of their going to La Rochelle in France. Instead, however, they returned to Scotland late in March 1584. On 18 April Mar led the so-called Stirling raid, seizing the castle and town of Stirling in an attempt to repeat the Ruthven raid and overthrow the earl of Arran, who had emerged as the leader of the government late in 1583. Mar was soon joined by Angus and the master of Glamis, but superior royal forces assembled against them, and about 21 April he and the other raiders fled to England. In August he was forfeited.

Mar took up residence in Newcastle, and intrigued against Arran's regime. In November he formed an alliance with the exiled leaders of the Hamilton family. On 18 October 1585 Mar, Angus, and the master of Glamis re-entered Scotland, and were joined in the borders by the Hamiltons, the Homes, and the earl of Bothwell. By 1 November they had assembled an army of 3000 which occupied Stirling (where the king and Arran were) almost without bloodshed; Arran and his associates fled or were captured. Mar was restored at the parliament of December 1585, resuming command of Stirling Castle and his position on the council. The success was a lasting one, for the king now emerged as the practical leader of his kingdom and proved willing to govern through the pro-English coalition of which Mar was a leading member.

Courtier and custodian of Prince Henry For the next few years Mar seemed satisfied with his secure position at the royal court. He may have had financial difficulties, having sold many lands to support his political activities in the early 1580s. In July 1587 he procured an act of parliament signalling his intention to recover the long-dispersed lands of the medieval earldom of Mar. He assiduously attended parliaments and conventions, and served on numerous parliamentary commissions. In November 1587 he accompanied the king in a military expedition to the borders. He began witnessing royal charters in

November 1589, perhaps indicating an increase in his political activity. Throughout the 1590s he was one of the most frequent attenders at the privy council other than the officers of state. In June 1592 he was appointed keeper of Edinburgh Castle. In July he fell dangerously ill of a fever, and his life was despaired of. He was still far from well in September, when Chancellor Maitland's enemies put his name forward for the chancellorship; he was reported to have refused the post, which in the event Maitland retained.

On 7 December 1592 Mar made a second, illustrious marriage, arranged by the king: to Mary Stewart (d. 1644), daughter of Esmé Stewart, first duke of Lennox, whom Mar had ousted ten years earlier. The marriage had been arranged in the summer but was postponed through Mar's illness. Mary had been brought up a Roman Catholic, and her sister Henrietta had recently married the Catholic sixth earl of Huntly. Later, in 1609, the king would advise Mar to ensure that Jean Hay (daughter of the ninth earl of Erroll), who was to marry Mar's son and heir, John, was given sound protestant companions because she was suspected of Catholic sympathies—and he mentioned that Mar had done just this with his own wife. The marriage produced seven sons and five daughters. Mary may later have helped to deputize for her husband in some of his duties when he was at court; she had some of his taxation papers in 1629. Mar's relationship with his brother-in-law Ludovick Stuart, second duke of Lennox, thereafter was cordial but not close. On 24 July 1593, when Lennox secretly admitted the outlawed first earl of Bothwell to Holyrood to confront the king, Mar was one of the few who proposed armed resistance. Mar was also one of the most committed opponents of Huntly and his Catholic allies, and on 31 October was appointed by a convention of estates to a commission for their trial—an unpopular service which other nobles avoided.

The king's long-awaited son and heir, Henry, was born in Stirling Castle on 19 February 1594, and Mar was immediately appointed the prince's keeper. The order made Mar and his mother jointly responsible for the prince; Countess Annabella supervised the practical aspects of childcare, as she had done for James, while Mar exercised political responsibility. The appointment was the highest possible statement of the king's trust in Mar, for James wished to ensure that the prince could never be seized and used by his opponents in the way that he himself had been used against his mother in 1567. Queen Anne, however, was furious at being excluded from her son's care, and intrigued constantly against Mar. This was basically a dispute between the royal couple; it meant that Anne would act as a rallying point for Mar's enemies, but also that James would tend to back him against them.

Mar then began to interest himself in the royal finances, apparently taking advice from John Colville. He alleged incompetence or worse on the part of the treasurer (his former ally the master of Glamis) and other financial officials, and succeeded on 11 September 1594 in securing the appointment of a committee of nobles to look into the business. However, Maitland (perhaps mistakenly) took this as an indirect attack on himself, and by January 1595 he had headed the inquiry off. In July 1595 Mar's enemies made a sustained attempt to wrest the prince from his custody, exploiting the feud between the earl and Lord Livingstone which had arisen a month earlier following the killing of one of Mar's servants. The king backed Mar firmly, but in 1596 he awarded the custody of the next royal baby, Princess Elizabeth, to Lord Livingstone. Anne accepted this because Livingstone was her ally against Mar. However, Mar's standing with the king was unshaken, and the queen obtained custody of Henry only in May 1603, when the court's departure for England had removed the issue from Scottish politics. Mar continued to maintain cordial relations with Henry until the prince's death in 1612. Meanwhile his quarrel with Livingstone was settled through assythment (compensation for the killing rather than punishment for the killers) in 1599. A dispute with Huntly was likewise peacefully resolved in 1602.

Administrator and ambassador After Maitland's death, on 3 October 1595, there was much talk of Mar as his successor. Mar himself was less keen than his own supporters, and proposed that the new chancellor should be Walter Stewart, commendator of Blantyre, a fellow schoolmate. James left the post vacant, reportedly promising that he would make no appointment without the advice of Mar and Stewart. In February 1596 the English ambassador pressed unsuccessfully for one of the two to be appointed. Mar co-operated with the Octavian regime of 1596–8, probably because Stewart was one of their number, though they attacked the size of the prince's household at Stirling. On 30 November 1596 Mar was one of the nobles nominally adjoined to the Octavians in their exchequer commission to add legitimacy to their work.

In the presbyterian uprising of 17–19 December 1596 in Edinburgh, Mar played a leading but ambivalent role. He was one of the few councillors present with the king in the tolbooth when the lords and ministers leading the presbyterian movement, rebuffed in their attempts to negotiate with the king, launched an armed uprising in the town. A crowd besieged the tolbooth, intent on ejecting the Octavians from power. Mar and Lord Ochiltree were sent out to negotiate with the leaders in an attempt to disperse the crowd. 'They had great truble and bussines in thaire outgoing, be ressoun of the thronge of pepill'; Mar exchanged some words with Lord Lindsay, a presbyterian leader, 'quhilkis could not be quenched a long tyme' (Moysie, 131). The king fled from the town next day, and Mar did not join him and the rump of the council in Linlithgow. However, on the king's return in force to Edinburgh on 31 December, Mar commanded the troops that occupied Castlehill and West Port. But the king probably did not know that the presbyterian leaders had written to Mar (18 December), as they did to Lord Hamilton and other nobles, seeking his leadership. Unlike Hamilton, Mar felt no urge to confess this to the king, but he may have been tempted by the offer.

One result of the continuing Livingstone feud was that when, in June 1598, the king presented his cherished Act anent Feuding to a convention of estates, Mar spoke out against it, forcing a vote so that the act's passing would not be unanimous. Perhaps only someone as close to James as Mar could have done this without incurring severe displeasure. At another convention of estates in December 1598, 'hearing the noblemen leave all to the king's pleasure', Mar 'said it was not well that they should not freely give their advice as councillors, which the king well allowed of' (*CSP Scot.*, 1597–9, 356). Mar's opposition may explain why James passed him over in at last appointing a chancellor in January 1599, though the new chancellor was the earl of Montrose, a lesser figure with whom Mar was easily reconciled rather than one of his outright enemies such as Huntly. Mar may sometimes have allowed his name to go forward for the chancellorship less through desire for the post than through a wish to keep Huntly out.

Late in 1599 and early in 1600 the major political issue was the king's demand for a huge new tax to prepare to fight for the English succession. Its most unpopular aspect was a new assessment of lands that would be likely to increase taxation permanently. Mar tried to deflect this, putting forward an alternative fiscal scheme, but this was blocked by his rivals. When the time came for a decision, at a convention of estates in June 1600, Mar threw such weight behind the king's proposal that he was perceived as its leading supporter. But after passionate debate the proposal was rejected, principally through opposition from shire and burgh commissioners.

On 5 August 1600 Mar was in the king's company when he visited Gowrie House, and it was to him that James called from an upper window when allegedly attacked by Alexander, master of Ruthven. Mar and others rushed into the house and tried to reach the king by battering on a locked door. Mar's cousin Thomas Erskine (later Viscount Fenton and earl of Kellie), finding another way in, earned a lasting place in royal favour by helping to kill Ruthven.

Mar's solid Anglophile record made him a natural choice when a major embassy to England was planned late in 1600. James believed that the earl of Essex, rather than Sir Robert Cecil, was the likeliest English politician to back his claim to the succession. In December 1600 Essex himself recommended Mar as an ambassador to Elizabeth. Mar was made joint collector of the tax of February 1601 which was intended to support ambassadors' expenses, though he initially had to pay for his own embassy himself. His fellow ambassador was Edward Bruce, commendator of Kinloss, his ally over taxation in June 1600.

Mar and Bruce departed on 18 February 1601, officially to assure Elizabeth of James's friendship, but really to press the queen and others about the succession. Initially the embassy was intended to support Essex in his rivalry with Cecil, but this was abandoned at the last moment when news of Essex's failed uprising arrived. Mar and Bruce had instead to shape their own policy on the spot, which they did with triumphant success. Elizabeth needed Scottish friendship in her Irish wars and agreed to increase the subsidy she paid to James. This was important, but more was to come. Mar and Bruce established a relationship with Cecil, achieving nothing less than a secret understanding that he would after all support James's succession. This assurance transformed the politics of James's remaining years in Scotland. The ambassadors returned on 31 May, and Cecil corresponded clandestinely with Mar thereafter. With this behind him, and with his involvement in the most intimate diplomatic secrets, Mar's favour was now unshakeable. In 1602 he explored the possibility of having his son brought up at the English court.

Between England and Scotland After James succeeded to the English throne in 1603 Mar accompanied him on his progress south, and for a while it seemed as if Mar might establish himself as one of the king's London Scots. He had to return briefly in May to deal with the aftermath of Queen Anne's unsuccessful attempt to seize Prince Henry. In the same month he was named to the English privy council, and in June he and Lennox were the only Scottish recipients of the Garter. In the next few years he received numerous grants of English lands and revenues. Henri IV of France gave him a 'jewell of diamonds', later singled out for mention in his testament.

Mar was proposed by James as one of the union commissioners of 1604, but the Scottish parliament of July 1604 struck his name, and Lennox's, from the commission as they were deemed too committed to the royal vision of union. In December 1605 Mar was the only Scottish member of a seven-man commission to investigate the Gunpowder Plot. Sent to Scotland, he reported to Cecil, now earl of Salisbury, that all was quiet there. In the course of the decade he seems to have gravitated back to Scotland, remaining in close touch with the court by correspondence with his cousin Fenton, a gentleman of the bedchamber.

Like many traditional nobles Mar was never keen on the king's episcopalian programme. In the convention of estates of January 1609 anti-Catholicism was on the agenda, and it was proposed that no heir should succeed to his lands without a certificate of his religious orthodoxy from the bishop. At this, Mar, 'though he is a stern Puritan', joined the opposition and blocked the proposal (*CSP Venice*, 1607–10, 300). Nevertheless, in June 1609 James asked Mar to be the principal collaborator with the earl of Dunbar in managing the royal programme in the forthcoming parliament.

In June 1612 Mar made perhaps his final bid to establish himself at court, seeking the post of master of the horse, but it went to the king's favourite, Robert Carr, Viscount Rochester. Fenton suggested that Mar should bid for the Scottish treasurership instead, but the office remained vacant until 1613 when Rochester (now earl of Somerset) was appointed. In September Fenton thought Mar might become commissioner to the forthcoming Scottish parliament, but Mar was again unsuccessful and consequently felt no reason to be beholden to the king when the parliament assembled in October 1612. Mar now led an attack on the royal taxation plans. The original request was for £800,000 (£66,666 sterling); Mar claimed that the king had told him that he would be satisfied with £120,000 (£10,000 sterling), and offered to ride to court to discuss the matter with him. Parliament eventually agreed on £240,000, whereupon the king protested that he had mentioned £120,000 only as a minimum figure. Fenton passed on James's comment that 'you have ever lyked too mutche to dispute in publike and at sutche tymes' (*Mar and Kellie MSS*, 2.45). Nevertheless, Mar's personal relationship with the king remained close and is evident in correspondence about hunting, an interest they both shared. James in 1620 complained jocularly to him that nobody in Scotland had remembered to send him any hawks: 'if wee be unfurnished frome thence wee shall forgette to cause pay your pension' (ibid., 1.89).

Treasurer of Scotland Mar had been a member of a revived exchequer commission on 15 November 1610, and had sought the treasurership unsuccessfully in 1612. Somerset was dismissed as treasurer on 24 May 1616, and by July James had agreed that Mar should succeed him. Mar and Fenton had cultivated the new favourite, George Villiers (later duke of Buckingham). James, who was planning to revisit Scotland, also thought that English courtiers would be impressed if the treasurer was a senior Scottish nobleman with whom they were familiar. Mar's formal appointment to the post came on 9 December 1616.

The treasurer was responsible for almost all the royal finances, the main exception being parliamentary taxation. On his appointment Mar was expected to agree a demarcation of his duties with the treasurer-depute, Sir Gideon Murray of Elibank, who had acted as treasurer under Somerset and who continued in office. Murray seems to have accepted Mar's appointment willingly in return for a guarantee of continued employment. Mar seems to have been a cautious and reliable treasurer. Jacobean treasurers could become unpopular through trying to restrain royal generosity, and Mar's close relationship with the king helped him. In February 1617 Kellie told him that James was 'not mutche displeased' at his reluctance to endorse payments, and understood financial stringency (*Mar and Kellie MSS*, 2.74). In fact there were few serious problems in Mar's early years, and James gained the justified impression that there would usually be money available for capital projects: the repair of Linlithgow Palace, then Dumbarton Castle, and after that Inverness Castle.

There was a temporary fiscal crisis in 1620–21, met by a freeze on pension payments in July 1620 which preceded, and was probably connected with, the English axe on pensions of 1621. Mar tightened fiscal control by getting himself made collector of the parliamentary tax of 1621–5, waiving the standard £5000 fee. At court in October 1621 he conferred in detail with the king about the need for economy. He learned with horror, soon after this, that the king intended to make a huge gift to the marquess of Hamilton out of the tax proceeds. He enlisted the help of the earl of Melrose in resisting this, writing not only to James himself but also to Prince Charles and to Buckingham. However, James insisted on the payment being made, adding unhelpfully that it should be 'kept as secreate as possiblie maye be for eschewing the importunitie of a number of suters' (*Mar and Kellie MSS*,

1.84). The remaining tax receipts were spent mostly on buying back pensions to courtiers, requiring high-level negotiations in which Mar probably played a large personal part.

During the crisis Sir Gideon Murray died, on 28 June 1621. The king did not appoint a new treasurer-depute, but instead told Mar that 'wee must frome henceforth exacte and expecte from yow that diligence in our affaires which formerlie wee founde in him'—mentioning his efforts to get Linlithgow Palace repaired and game preserved (*Mar and Kellie MSS*, 1.95). According to Lord Napier's vivid but unreliable memoirs, 'the Earle of Mar, thesaurer principall (who could not well brooke a colleg), by means of the Duk of Buckingham, got the tryall of the place solely for a yeare'. But before the end of the year Mar's friends, 'being disapoynted of the hopes hee gave them', endorsed his enemies' efforts to thrust a treasurer-depute upon him (Napier, 4). It would not be surprising if people had been 'disapoynted' in the treasurer during 1622, when he was trying to persuade courtiers to surrender their pensions. Napier became treasurer-depute in October 1622 through the patronage of Hamilton, evidently seeking revenge for Mar's attempt to block his warrant (though Hamilton had been opposed to Mar before and had tried to have his brother made treasurer-depute in July 1621). Napier at first lacked the standing to make trouble for Mar, but they never worked well together.

Mar had long had a puritan reputation, and religion was mentioned in his conference with the king in October 1621. Mar noted to himself that James 'sayd publyklie, Quhy should ye nott ador the Sacramentt and follow the Churche of Ingland. The rest to my aun memorie, quha vilbe his friend' (*Mar and Kellie MSS*, 1.102). Mar evidently disapproved of James's religious policy, which since 1618 had been dominated by the fraught attempt to impose the ceremonies of the five articles of Perth on unwilling ministers and congregations, and he had been distant from his government colleague, Melrose, earlier a staunch supporter of religious innovations. His co-operation with Melrose began in 1621 over finance, and was cemented with a marriage between their children in 1622; it was probably connected with Melrose's shift towards Mar's religious position.

The accession of Charles I in 1625 proved difficult for his father's old Scottish ministers. According to Napier, Mar was 'charg'd home by his enemies with some abuses in the kings presence' but they were unable to substantiate their claims. So they sent to Napier offering to obtain the treasurership for him if he would disclose Mar's alleged misdeeds. Napier claimed that he refused this as dishonourable, but that he was 'evill requited' because Mar never heard of his disinterested conduct (Napier, 10–11). This story probably inflates Napier's role and importance, since he was unlikely to be offered the treasurership. But he seems to have aspired to the post, and to have set himself up openly in opposition to Mar. In October 1625 a commission of exchequer was created that curbed Mar's financial authority, prompting him to write directly to the king in protest on 18 November.

Shortly after this, in January 1626, Mar and the other leading councillors were summoned to Whitehall to discuss recent royal policy initiatives, notably the king's revocation. Mar wrote detailed and vivid notes of the meetings, indicating that he himself took the lead in questioning the legality of the revocation. He and the earl of Nithsdale clashed bitterly, each accusing the other of dereliction of duty. The exchequer commission was also discussed, with Mar claiming that it was a mark of royal distrust. He and his colleagues insisted on their duty to give the king true counsel however unwelcome, and the conference ended with disagreements more evident than before.

In 1627, when the earl of Morton agreed that his eldest son should marry Buckingham's niece, Buckingham proposed Morton as successor to the treasurership in due course. But Mar remained very much in control, and adroitly outmanoeuvred Napier in 1628 when the treasurer-depute attempted to challenge him directly by proposing to take personal responsibility for financing a royal visit to Scotland. Mar's agents persuaded the king that the treasury could not support a visit, and Napier was permanently discredited (though he clung to office until 1631). In the course of the arguments at court, Mar 'fell downe upon his knees with his crutches, and with teares intreated the King to free him of my trouble, and that he could not serve with me' (Napier, 49–50). In 1628 Mar acquired a copy of Sir Robert Cotton's pamphlet *The Danger wherein the Kingdome now Standeth*, circulated by those critical of royal policies in England. He finally demitted office on 3 April 1630, apparently at his own choice, and was succeeded by Morton. This was not the end of his responsibility, for in September 1630 he was asked to take charge of renovating the palaces for a proposed royal visit.

Personal finances: the earldom of Mar The creation of Mar's father as first earl in 1565 had brought with it no right to the lands of the medieval earldom of Mar. The second earl set out to acquire or recover them, even though by 1565 the earldom had been in the hands of the crown or its grantees for some 130 years, and had been substantially dismembered. Mar started his campaign in 1587 by obtaining a portentous act of parliament recognizing him as heir to Isabella Douglas, countess of Mar and lady of Garioch (d. 1408). Several of those who had received crown grants from the earldom entered protests against the 1587 act, but on 20 March 1589 Mar was none the less formally served heir-general to Countess Isabella and began to pursue the possessors of the lands in the courts.

The central issue was possession of Kildrummy, the chief messuage of the medieval earldom. Mar's great case against its possessor, Lord Elphinstone, was brought in 1622 and decided in his favour on 1 July 1626. It was evidently considered wrong for Mar simply to appropriate the lands, and arbiters were appointed to implement the judgment, who agreed that Mar should pay Elphinstone 48,000 merks (£2666 sterling) for Kildrummy. Then in 1628 the earl launched a similar process against 150 lesser proprietors of the earldom, with variable success. The

benefits he reaped seem to have been mainly symbolic, and he stirred up widespread fear and anxiety.

Mar's finances were complicated, and much remains obscure. Sir John Scot of Scotstarvet thought that his estate was 'nothing bettered' during his treasurership, and that he 'sold many lands in his own time' (Scot, 59). In 1617 Mar snapped up the heiress to the earldom of Buchan as a wife for his eldest son by his second marriage, James, but this seems to have brought more costs than benefits. He also spent much on assembling a barony of Cardross in Stirlingshire for Henry, his next son, in the 1600s. On 10 June 1610 Mar was created Lord Cardross, being empowered to transfer that title to Henry. In January 1624 he sought to buy Henry a place in the privy chamber, but the expected vacancy failed to arise. He tried to prevent Henry's intended marriage in 1623–4, but, as Kellie commented to him, Henry 'is willfull, wherein he showes himselfe to be a wadge of the rycht tree, that is of your selfe' (*Mar and Kellie MSS*, 2.191). In the early 1630s Mar seems to have been in financial trouble, possibly through the costs of acquiring the Mar estates as well as subsidizing his eldest son's extravagance. This was temporary, however, and he died a rich man.

Mar's earldom was unlikely to prove financially lucrative, unlike his coal-producing estate at Alloa, but it did provide some excellent highland estates for hunting—Mar's 'chief delight' (Scot, 59), in which he seems to have spent most summers. John Taylor, the Water Poet of London, was a guest at one of his hunts in Braemar in 1618 and left a detailed account of it (Hume Brown, 120–23). In 1628, two years after recovering Kildrummy, Mar built Braemar Castle, partly as a base for hunting and partly perhaps as a defence against possible highland raids.

Mar died in Stirling on 14 December 1634: 'walking in his own hall, a dog cast him off his feet and lamed his leg, of which he died' (Scot, 59). He was buried at Stirling on 7 April 1635. Mar had been on crutches for some years, and in 1627 had needed a bone-setter. In his testament, made on 1 March 1634, he nominated nine arbitrators for any family disputes. There were four Erskines, including Sir George Erskine of Innerteil (with whom Mar had shared James VI's classroom) and his cousin Kellie, along with the earl of Haddington, a longstanding political associate, and his son, Mar's son-in-law. The others, the earls of Kinghorn, Marischal, and Rothes, were also his sons-in-law: all had strongly protestant traditions and (in Rothes's case at least) a record of active opposition to the regime. After the first turbulent decade of his career, Mar had settled down as a loyal servant of the crown; his loyalty was perhaps all the more welcome because he was clearly never a sycophant. But in his later years, the crown's religious and legal innovations placed that loyalty under severe strain.

JULIAN GOODARE

Sources *Report on the manuscripts of the earl of Mar and Kellie*, HMC, 60 (1904); suppl. (1930) · *Reg. PCS*, 1st ser. · *Reg. PCS*, 2nd ser., vols. 1–5 · *CSP Scot., 1547–1603* · *State papers and miscellaneous correspondence of Thomas, earl of Melros*, ed. J. Maidment, 2 vols., Abbotsford Club, 9 (1837) · *APS, 1567–1641* · J. M. Thomson and others, eds., *Registrum magni sigilli regum Scotorum / The register of the great seal of Scotland*, 11 vols. (1882–1914), vols. 4–9 · *CSP dom., 1547–1635* · *CSP Venice, 1603–*

36 • Archibald, Lord Napier, *Memoirs* (1793) • J. Scot, *The staggering state of Scottish statesmen from 1550 to 1650*, ed. C. Rogers (1872) • M. Lee, *John Maitland of Thirlestane and the foundation of the Stewart despotism in Scotland* (Princeton, NJ, 1959) • M. Lee, *Government by pen: Scotland under James VI and I* (Urbana, Ill., 1980) • M. Lee, *The road to revolution: Scotland under Charles I, 1625–1637* (Urbana, Ill., 1985) • *Scots peerage* • K. M. Brown, *Bloodfeud in Scotland, 1573–1625* (1986) • K. M. Brown, *Noble society in Scotland: wealth, family and culture from Reformation to revolution* (2000) • J. Goodare and M. Lynch, eds., *The reign of James VI* (2000) • J. Goodare, 'Parliamentary taxation in Scotland, 1560–1603', *SHR*, 68 (1989), 23–52 • J. Goodare, *State and society in early modern Scotland* (1999) • W. D. Simpson, *The earldom of Mar* (1949) • A. Lindsay, earl of Crawford, *The earldom of Mar in sunshine and in shade*, 2 vols. (1882) • D. Calderwood, *The history of the Kirk of Scotland*, ed. T. Thomson and D. Laing, 8 vols., Wodrow Society, 7 (1842–9) • D. Moysie, *Memoirs of the affairs of Scotland, 1577–1603*, ed. J. Dennistoun, Bannatyne Club, 39 (1830) • [T. Thomson], ed., *The historie and life of King James the Sext*, Bannatyne Club, 13 (1825) • P. Hume Brown, ed., *Early travellers in Scotland* (1891) • M. Lee, ed., 'An unpublished letter of Thomas Hamilton, earl of Melrose', *SHR*, 58 (1979), 175–8 • R. Lockyer, *Buckingham: the life and political career of George Villiers, first duke of Buckingham, 1592–1628* (1981) • A. Lang, *James VI and the Gowrie mystery* (1902) • Stirling testaments, NA Scot., CC21/5/4, 19 Aug 1635 • GEC, *Peerage*, 8.420-24

Archives NA Scot., corresp. and papers, GD 124 • NL Scot., corresp. and papers | NA Scot., letters to Robert Moray **Likenesses** attrib. A. de Colone, oils, 1626, Scot. NPG [*see illus.*] • earl of Buchan, pencil and chalk drawing, 1790–99 (after unknown artist), Scot. NPG **Wealth at death** £75,971 17s. 6d. Scots: Stirling testaments, NA Scot., CC 21/5/4, 19 Aug 1635

Erskine, John, nineteenth or third earl of Mar (*c*.1585–1653), nobleman, was the only child of John *Erskine, eighteenth or second earl of Mar (*c*.1562–1634), and his first wife, Anna, daughter of David, Lord Drummond. Educated initially at home, Lord Erskine travelled in France as a youth; he was admitted to Gray's Inn on 22 May 1603 and was created MA at Oxford on 30 August 1605. He married Lady Jean (*d*. 1668), daughter of Francis *Hay, ninth earl of Erroll (*d*. 1631), on 6 February 1610; the couple had two sons and two daughters. Created a knight of the Bath on 2 June 1610, Erskine was a member of the privy council in July 1615 and in the same year was appointed governor of Edinburgh Castle. He was named an extraordinary lord of session in 1620. Following his father's death, on 14 December 1634, he succeeded as earl of Mar.

Mar's support for the covenanting regime of 1638 earned the king's displeasure, and he was deprived of his command of Edinburgh Castle. In 1641 he was forbidden to attend the privy council, but was reinstated by parliament in the same year. Nevertheless, he was soon accused, along with his son Lord Erskine, of reverting to the king's party. In 1645 the pair were said to have lavishly entertained the marquess of Montrose and the principal officers of his army at Alloa, Clackmannanshire, for which act the marquess of Argyll threatened to sack the family home. Mar's defence of compulsion attracted some sympathy, since the forces of Montrose had plundered the latter town and parts of his adjoining lands, and the earl feared further excesses on their part.

Under pressure from all sides, Mar's political allegiances appear influenced more by his precarious financial affairs than by high principle. His business ventures,

which included a monopoly over the leather trade in Scotland, were largely unsuccessful. In 1638 he resigned his lands in favour of his son to avoid his creditors, and surrendered his heritable offices—including that of sheriff of Stirlingshire—to the king. Compensation of £8000 was granted in November 1641, but probably never honoured. Equally, Mar suffered financially at the hands of the estates, largely owing to his son's continuing support for Montrose. From the sale of certain of his Scottish lands, the earl purchased an estate in Ireland, which he lost during the Irish rising. The value of his estate much depleted, Mar died between January and October 1653. His son John (*d*. 1668) succeeded as twentieth or fourth earl.

VAUGHAN T. WELLS

Sources *Scots peerage* • GEC, *Peerage*, new edn, vol. 8 • *The letters and journals of Robert Baillie*, ed. D. Laing, 3 vols. (1841–2) • testament, NA Scot., CC21/5/7, fols. 361r–362v [Jean Hay] • Anderson, *Scot. nat.* • Foster, *Alum. Oxon.*

Archives NA Scot., corresp. and papers | NA Scot., Mar and Kellie MSS

Erskine, John, styled twenty-second or sixth earl of Mar and Jacobite duke of Mar (*bap.* 1675, *d.* 1732), Jacobite army officer, politician, and architect, was born on the lowland family estate at Alloa, Clackmannanshire, and baptized at Alloa parish church on 21 January 1675. He was the first of four surviving children of Charles Erskine, twenty-first or fifth earl of Mar (1650–1689), and his wife, Lady Mary Maule (1655–1710?), eldest daughter of George, second earl of Panmure.

Family background and education Throughout his life Mar took immense pride in the fact that his father's family was considered to be among the oldest in Scotland, with special ties to the royal Stuart dynasty due to his ancestors' status as hereditary keepers of Stirling Castle and guardians of the royal princes. In fact his first action in the Scottish parliament, where he took his seat in September 1696, was a protest to be put first on any list of the Scottish aristocracy. However, his pride in his ancestry was disproportionate to the family's financial situation. The Erskines had accumulated crushing debts during the civil war, and further mismanagement had reduced the estate to the principal holdings of Alloa, on the Firth of Forth, and Braemar, as well as Kildrummy in Aberdeenshire. These two highland estates were damaged almost beyond repair by the Jacobite forces in spring 1689, probably because Mar's father had by then joined the new government after some prior hesitation. Ranking among the lowest third of his peers in terms of rental income, Mar thus inherited 'more debt than estate' (Master of Sinclair, *Memoirs of the Insurrection in Scotland in 1715*, 1858, 58) when he succeeded his father in May 1689 as twenty-second or sixth earl (dependent on a disputed creation in 1565).

Little is known about Mar's formal education, which was probably somewhat eclectic. He remarked later to his son 'you have been more luckie in your education than I was' ('Mar's legacies', 178). He certainly received some schooling, possibly at Linlithgow, in the 1680s, and went on to attend a few lectures at the University of Edinburgh in 1691–2. By then he had acquired a working knowledge

John Erskine, styled twenty-second or sixth earl of Mar and Jacobite duke of Mar (*bap.* 1675, *d.* 1732), by Sir Godfrey Kneller, *c.*1715 [right, with his son, Thomas Erskine, Lord Erskine]

of Latin, but he did not learn any other foreign language in his youth. It was only in his late forties that he developed his French beyond mere phrases. He did, however, take to drawing and architectural design. In the 1690s the Episcopalian minister Alexander Edwards introduced him to the technicalities of garden design, architecture, and drawing. Henceforward, Mar was 'infected with the desease of building and gardening' (*Stuart Papers*, 5.21), and remained so until his death.

Later in life Mar acquired a reputation for being rather indifferent in religion, but there are frequent remarks hinting at his conviction that the Episcopal church deserved pride of place in Scotland—being, as he put it, 'a medium betwixt the bare unbecomeing nakedness of the Presbiterian service in Scotland, and the gadie, affected, and ostentive way of the Church of Rome' ('Mar's legacies', 186). Accordingly, a private chapel was set up at Alloa about 1700.

Personally, Mar seems to have been not without charm, and even later political enemies referred to him as being a witty conversationalist. There are conflicting descriptions of his physical appearance, but it is certain that he was of low stature, and most probably had some kind of physical disability in the form of a small hump on his back.

Court politician, 1696–1714 From the moment he took his seat in the Scottish parliament in September 1696 to the end of his political career in Britain nineteen years later, Mar was a court politician proper. On the one hand, he needed the salary. But equally important was the boost to his self-esteem that office provided. Although he frequently complained to his brother that he was 'extreamlie wearie of the post I'm in' (Mar to Erskine, 1707, NA Scot., Mar and Kellie MSS, GD 124/15/496/27), he tried hard to emulate his ancestors and also enjoyed being at the centre of political life. An obvious choice of patron for the eager novice was the first duke of Queensberry, who was just emerging as the leading Scottish magnate at court. Quickly, Mar worked his way into the duke's inner circle, and, as a result of this patronage he became a member of the Scottish privy council as early as April 1697. Yet he was desperate to secure a position that was financially more rewarding, and he certainly expected more than the military command (as colonel of a regiment on foot until 1706) which Queensberry was able to grant him in 1701.

Mar's rise at court began when he joined the first commission for the negotiation of the union between Scotland and England. Although the discussions in London came to nothing during winter 1702–3, he once again distinguished himself as an able spokesman and was increasingly seen as Queensberry's lieutenant. His marriage on 6 April 1703 to Lady Margaret Hay (1686–1707), daughter of Thomas, earl of Kinnoull, considerably advanced the connection to the duke of Queensberry on account of Lady Mar's close friendship with the duchess. When his patron was out of favour in 1704, Mar led the opposition to the government of the marquess of Tweeddale 'with so much art and dissimulation that he gained the favour of all the Tories, and was by many of them esteemed an honest man and well inclined to the royal [Stuart] family' (G. Lockhart, *'Scotland's Ruine!' George Lockhart of Carnwath's Memoirs of the Union*, ed. D. Szechi, 1995, 85). It soon became clear that the move towards Jacobitism was nothing but a tactical decision. In fact, after Queensberry's return to power Mar 'returned'—in the harsh words of the Jacobite sympathizer George Lockhart of Carnwath—'as the dog to the vomit and promoted all the Court of England's measures with the greatest zeal imaginable' (ibid.).

Further progress was swift. Owing to his administrative abilities and success as informal deputy of the duke, Mar was made one of the commissioners for the negotiations of the Anglo-Scottish union, and on 29 September 1705 was additionally appointed secretary of state within Scotland, with a salary of £1000. He was certainly the most active speaker for the union, and his reports to London about the Scottish proceedings during the next sixteen months provide the most intimate insight into the negotiations. Although Mar was at no stage able to match magnates such as Queensberry, Argyll, or Hamilton, either financially or in terms of a clientage, he succeeded in establishing himself firmly as a major power in Scottish politics. He successfully campaigned in late 1706 for his younger brother James *Erskine, Lord Grange, to gain an influential legal office, secured a number of positions for his relatives, and in early 1707 became himself sheriff-principal of the sheriffdom of Aberdeen.

By that time Mar's reputation as a skilful amateur architect and garden designer had so advanced among the Scottish aristocracy and gentry that they frequently turned to him for detailed advice about their estates. He had started with small designs for his estate, including a pigeon house or a garden pavilion in 1704; by 1710, probably with the help of James Gibbs (1682–1754), who owed his career solely to Mar's patronage, he was producing elaborate and detailed architectural plans. Several of these were eventually printed, and the 216 surviving plans 'are among the most vivid and colourful of all Scottish architectural drawings' (Gow and Bailey, 251). About twenty different projects can be identified, and the architectural correspondence which Mar conducted throughout his life hints at several of his contributions to buildings and gardens of the British aristocracy. Most members of the Queensberry interest were beneficiaries of his advice, but he also designed plans for English estates such as Bretton Hall and Rokeby Park in Yorkshire. In addition he took some responsibility for the design of the famous House of Dun built for David, Lord Dun. Mar's own estate, Alloa House, Clackmannanshire, gained a reputation for its garden. The combination of a late geometric outline with large vegetable gardens, orangery, orchards, ornamental parterres, and a park of over 2500 acres was at that time unique in Scotland, and visitors 'spok with delight of everything but the filthy naked statues' (David Dalrymple to Mar, 1708, NA Scot., GD 124/15/897). Daniel Defoe gave an overall enthusiastic account of Mar's gardens at Alloa: 'There is, in a Word, every Thing that Nature and Art can do, brought to Perfection', with the town also 'pleasant, well built and full of trade' (D. Defoe, *A Tour through the Whole Island of Great Britain*, letter 13). It was this second aspect with which Mar was most concerned, and his attempts to improve trade proved to be the catalyst for Alloa's industrial development.

Just before the union debate entered the final stage, Mar's son, Thomas, was born in late autumn 1706. After the birth his wife's health deteriorated, and she died on 26 April 1707, just days after her husband took up residence in London. The union negotiations had brought Mar into close contact with the English court circle, especially Sidney, earl of Godolphin, and Robert Harley. These connections proved vital during his further advance in London. He was immediately sworn of the privy council in May 1707. When the Scottish secretaryship ceased with the abolition of the Scottish privy council, Mar was appointed keeper of the signet in early summer 1708. Since Godolphin wanted to rely on the experienced court politician, this office included virtually all the responsibilities and rights of the previous post. Moreover, Mar had already been chosen as one of the representative peers of Scotland in February 1707, and was re-elected in 1708, 1710, and 1713.

Always sensitive to the change of political atmosphere,

Mar increasingly sought the company of Robert Harley, who became his major English patron. The marriage of Harley's daughter Abigail to Mar's brother-in-law George Hay, Viscount Dupplin (and later eighth earl of Kinnoull), certainly eased the way, and Harley secured him a pension of £3000 as early as 1709. In the subsequent Sacheverell crisis Mar voted in favour of the high-church clergyman, and convinced several other Scottish lords to do the same. Thus after the tory victory in the election of 1710 he emerged as the leader of the Scottish court party, and following the death of the duke of Hamilton in 1712 he also became patron to the Scottish Jacobite MPs. It certainly helped him to gain some credit among the Scottish Jacobites that he was now publicly voicing concern about the development of the union, about which 'we had fine hopes … and I think not without good reason, but these hopes have proved vain' (Mar to James Erskine, 1714, NL Scot., MS 5072, fol. 26).

The last two years of Queen Anne's reign saw Mar at the zenith of his career. In London he moved into a fashionable house at Privy Gardens, Whitehall, after being appointed to the re-established secretaryship for Scotland in autumn 1713. The dedication to Mar of an elaborate map of Scotland, printed by the publisher and cartographer Hermann Moll, confirms his status as a major improver, architect, and politician, while Godfrey Kneller's portrait depicts him in lavish attire proudly presenting his nine-year-old son. Arguably his most interesting move was his marriage on 20 June 1714 to Lady Frances Pierrepont (1690–1761), Lockhart's 'buxom vigorous young woman [with] £8000 of portion' (*Letters of George Lockhart of Carnwath*, ed. D. Szechi, 1989, 103); she was the second daughter of the whig politician Evelyn, then earl (later duke) of Kingston, and younger sister of the scholar Lady Mary Wortley Montagu. Thus, just weeks before Queen Anne's death, Mar was able through marriage both to gain new funds for his estate, which was still thousands of pounds in debt, and to attempt to strengthen his ties to the whigs with a view to securing his continued employment.

The Jacobite rising of 1715 The first contact between Mar and the exiled Stuart court probably dates from 1710, but it was only after Queen Anne's death in August 1714 that Mar became seriously engaged in Jacobite conspiracy. It is not unlikely that he had grown up with some sentimental Jacobite feelings, but those had always remained hidden behind his need for profitable court positions. Yet by late 1714 he was running out of options. Keeping up high spirits immediately after the queen's death, he claimed in a letter to his brother that 'I can make as good terms with the other side [the Hanoverian whigs] for myself as any of them' (*Mar and Kellie MSS*, 2.505). However, his central role in the former tory administration negated any efforts to stay in office, since it very quickly became clear that leading tory ministers, with the exception of the earl of Nottingham, had no political future under the new king, George I. Furthermore, it was increasingly apparent that the arrears of £7000 still due to him would not be forthcoming.

Mar's exact role in the overall planning of the Jacobite rising of 1715 is difficult to ascertain. On the one hand, he continued to show outward obedience to the new monarch and even presented an address of loyalty, which included the signatures of twelve highland chiefs. Moreover, he does not appear to have played a major part in orchestrating the initial phase of the rising. Although he was a member of a group of conspirators in London, he apparently had no direct contact with Henry St John, Viscount Bolingbroke, who led all planning from the continent. On the other hand, he boycotted the Scottish election in March 1715, regularly met with James Butler, the duke of Ormond, the major English Jacobite, and, in his first surviving letter to the exiled Stuart court, dating from early July 1715, drew up a detailed invasion scheme. Here he emphasized that there was 'no hope of succeeding in it without the assistance of a regular force' (*Stuart Papers*, 1.520) and asked for at least 20,000 weapons, should there be no foreign assistance. In the latter case he proposed a landing of the Pretender (James Stuart) near Newcastle at the end of September, and advocated a quick joining of the Jacobite forces from Scotland and northern England. Although such scenarios played a role in the plans of the Stuart court, the Scottish and northern risings were never properly co-ordinated with a proposed central rising in the south. Late in July 1715 it became obvious that the plans for the southern rising were an open secret to the government, and the threat of impeachment, which already endangered the earl of Oxford, reached Mar himself. It was most probably a combination of fear of arrest, self-serving careerism, and sentimental attachment to the Stuart family that, at that stage, turned Mar into the only Jacobite to take the initiative.

On 9 August 1715, one day after the birth of his daughter Frances, Mar left London and embarked from Gravesend with some servants and the professional soldier George Hamilton, who acted as his military adviser throughout the rising. He landed near Elie in south-east Fife, and a short ride took him to the estate of the earl of Kinnoull, his former father-in-law, where the small party of eighteen horse was joined by the family's son John Hay. The Erskines' estate at Braemar saw the first council of war, thinly disguised as a hunting party, or *tindal*, on 27 August. On 6 September the standard of 'James the 8th and 3rd' was raised at Braemar among 600 followers. The lack of a proper commission from the Stuart court did not prevent Mar from excelling at the things he did best: sending out orders, canvassing, and gathering supplies. With the help of the printer Robert Freebairn he also took great care in distributing Jacobite propaganda, which skilfully played on Scottish patriotism and anti-union sentiment.

At the beginning of October the Jacobite forces had risen to almost 20,000 men. Apart from Stirling Castle, Mar controlled all of Scotland north of the Firth of Forth. It was undoubtedly the most serious Jacobite threat the British government had faced. Yet it now became apparent that Mar had no military experience whatsoever. Instead of keeping the initiative by laying siege to Stirling Castle and pushing south, he dallied for over a month, thus allowing the government forces under the duke of Argyll to build up strength and move into more favourable positions. The Jacobites' two remarkable military manoeuvres—a quick capture of Perth and the crossing of the Firth of Forth with 2000 men—were most probably based on the initiative of Mar's subordinates. By contrast Mar's conduct throughout the 'Fifteen was 'marked with a disastrous combination of chronic indecision and strategic incompetence' (MacInnes, 200).

These failings were once again in evidence in the one and only battle for which Mar took charge, having on 22 October received a belated royal commission to act as sole commander of the Jacobite forces; on the same date he was appointed duke of Mar in the Jacobite peerage of Scotland. Although the number of soldiers in Mar's force had dwindled somewhat, the Jacobite army still outnumbered the duke of Argyll's forces by three to one, and a decision was finally made to march towards Stirling. About noon on 13 November the two armies met at Sheriffmuir, near Dunblane. After some serious but indecisive fighting which had put both armies into confusion, and parts of them into retreat, Mar and about 4000 Jacobites began to close in on Argyll's remaining 1000 men, who were waiting for a final attack, poorly protected by some mud walls. But Mar, probably under the illusion of having won the battle already, did not order his forces to advance. The government army had lost three times as many men (about 660) as the Jacobites; this made it possible for Mar to claim victory before retreating to Perth. It was obvious, however, that in more than one respect 13 November was the turning point of the rising, by preventing the Jacobites' further advance into the central lowlands. The city of Inverness surrendered to the government forces on the same day, and in the north of England the rising suffered a decisive blow with the capitulation of the English Jacobites at Preston. Moreover, the arrival of James III in Scotland on 22 December failed to stop the numbers dwindling in the Jacobite army.

What followed was a mere six-week epilogue to the rising. Though some were rejoicing at Aberdeen and Dundee, fewer than 5000 Jacobites were still present at Perth when their proclaimed king made his entrance on 9 January 1716. Moreover, a reinforced government army now equipped with heavy artillery was advancing rapidly. To delay its approach Mar gave the order to burn several villages between Perth and Stirling, thus denying shelter and supplies to Argyll's forces, but also fuelling the contempt with which he was increasingly viewed by some of his fellow Jacobites. On 30 January the Jacobites were forced to leave Perth and retreat north. Mar, who had started the 1715 rising, also finished it when on 4 February he persuaded the Pretender to write a farewell letter to the Scots. Sailing from Montrose the next day, James and Mar left behind a perplexed Jacobite army whose leading figures never forgave Mar for his apparent betrayal. On 17 February he was attainted by the Hanoverian authorities and his earldom forfeited.

Jacobite politician and double agent, 1716–1724 In March 1716 Mar arrived in Paris, and one month later he was back in office, this time as James's adviser and secretary of state. The Pretender seems to have had some admiration for Mar, whom he regarded as an experienced politician and, more importantly, as the one man who had raised arms for the Stuart cause in 1715. Yet from the beginning Mar was deeply involved in the internal power struggle at the Jacobite court. Quarrels about who had been responsible for the failure of the rising broke out, and Mar, who himself blamed Bolingbroke, was made the scapegoat by a number of court commentators. His reputation suffered further following his alleged mismanagement of the growing number of exiled Jacobites who now sought refuge at court, thus seriously stretching Jacobite finances. That Mar's solution was seen to favour his own relatives undoubtedly contributed to the increasing tension between the different Jacobite clientage networks. Important leaders such as the duke of Ormond and George Keith, Earl Marischal, had been deeply suspicious of Mar's dealings from the start. This internal struggle prevented the Jacobite court from developing a coherent policy on occasions when the international diplomatic situation would have allowed an alliance with a European power against Hanoverian Britain.

Renewed hostilities between Hanover and Sweden presented just such an opportunity in 1716. The fact that the Swedish king, Charles XII, was widely perceived as a protestant war hero undoubtedly influenced the Jacobites' decision to strengthen the ties with the Swedish court, as a way of counteracting the deep anti-Catholic sentiment hindering the Jacobite movement in Britain. Mar organized diplomatic connections to Charles XII and ordered the English Jacobites to raise money for an invasion force. He probably only realized himself in February 1717 (after the capture of Swedish diplomats in London) that Charles XII had been interested only in the money, and certainly never seriously considered an invasion of England. Mar's other attempt to establish further contact with Peter the Great of Russia proved equally unsuccessful on a political level, though it led to the recruitment of a vast number of Jacobite exiles by the tsar.

In winter 1717 the two constant companions of Jacobite exiles—boredom and homesickness—struck Mar at Urbino: '[I would] die of the spleen', he remarked, 'were it not for building castles in the air of several kinds' (*Stuart Papers*, 5.367). Yet his renewed enthusiasm for architectural drawings was not the only activity with which he fought the despairing mood at the exiled court. Within his limited means he also acted as a patron to musicians, architects, and painters. In his letters he frequently alluded to the lack of court culture in England, combining his Jacobite hopes with his aesthetic preferences for baroque music and architecture. 'Let us hope still', he wrote to his friend James Gibbs, 'there are more polite days a coming when arts will thrive and good performances be cherished by those who have a right taste' (ibid., 2.92).

Nor had Mar cut all ties to his former whig friends. Seeing his political fortunes at the Stuart court slip away (because of Ormond's and Marischal's preparations for another rising with Spanish assistance in early 1719), he resigned his post, renewed an old acquaintance with John Dalrymple, second earl of Stair, and embarked on an attempt to re-establish contact with Westminster. He probably had a hand in his own arrest at Geneva on behalf of the British government in May 1719. After thirteen months of negotiations he succeeded in obtaining payments from Lady Mar's jointure, as well as further financial promises from London and £1000 from the earl of Stair.

Having taken up residence with his family in Paris in 1720, Mar was now interested in acquiring a full pardon, though he also worked hard to remain the major figure in the local Jacobite community. He even informed James III about all his dealings with the British government, pledging his loyalty while carefully hiding the details of his negotiations. In the end this duplicity led to a complete loss of confidence in him by both the Stuart court and London, but for a few years Mar managed to deceive many—and probably even himself—about his real status as a double agent. His role became widely known only in the aftermath of the Atterbury plot, when in May 1722 the British agent Charles Churchill forced Mar to commit himself by writing an incriminating letter to the Jacobite bishop Francis Atterbury, which eventually led to Atterbury's treason trial and his exile. In a desperate attempt to free himself of ongoing rumours and allegations, Mar made a 'fatal mistake' in 1724 (Gregg, 192) when he freely gave his papers to Atterbury. The bishop, distrustful ever since the Swedish affair of 1717, now found proof of Mar's double game and finally convinced the court in Rome to withdraw all confidence from him, though not before he had been elevated to the earldom (1717) and dukedom (1722) of Mar in the Jacobite peerages of England and Ireland respectively.

As Mar's political future darkened, his architectural plans for Alloa became more and more elaborate, while showing a detailed knowledge of the continental discourse on design and architecture. The political allusions to Scottish patriotism in his designs are so obvious that 'they can be understood as an apology ... for his political career' (Stewart, 5). Together with his writings, these plans illustrate Mar's ideological point of view, which, though it always remained secondary to his personal ambition, must be seen as a strong undercurrent in his life. Not unlike his former friend Andrew Fletcher of Saltoun, Mar emphasized the Scots' virtuous and martial spirit. In his 'Jewels of Scotland' (printed in 1896 by the Scottish History Society as part of 'The earl of Mar's legacies') he included detailed advice about a Scottish constitution, suggested an alliance of Scotland and Ireland in a union based on their common Celtic culture, and proposed specific improvements, including the construction of a Firth and Clyde canal, and a plan for a new part of Edinburgh that resembles very much the New Town that was later built. His last letter to the Stuart court dates from May 1727, but his Jacobite career as an architect was far from over, as he kept working on an almost visionary plan for a structure in London that he described as a 'Palace worthy of the Grandeur of the King', referring to James III (Friedman, 115).

Last years and historical reputation The London newspapers regularly reported on the allegedly extravagant lifestyle of Mar and his family. Despite some government payments, however, their financial situation was precarious. In Paris, Mar was already 'treated with insolence by the servants and tradespeople' (A. Raitt to Erskine, 1724, NA Scot., Mar and Kellie MSS, GD 124/15/1247/9). As the years of genteel poverty went on, Lady Mar developed clear signs of severe clinical depression slowly descending into madness. Early in 1728 she was sent back to England to be taken into custody by her sister, Mary. Although—or perhaps because—Mar was, apparently, genuinely devoted to his wife, he did not hesitate to use her case as grounds for a further request for a full pardon from the crown. Obviously homesick, he began a correspondence with the diplomatist Horatio Walpole (later Baron Walpole of Wolterton) and also tried to use his connections with Cardinal Fleury to advance his cause. Although he finally received a limited pardon, his bid for a return to Scotland was explicitly rejected by the prime minister Sir Robert Walpole.

Without regular financial resources, Mar was forced to leave Paris at the end of 1729 to avoid his creditors. Only his daughter, Frances, accompanied him, first to Antwerp and then to Spa. Distrusted by both the Jacobite community and the British government, with no chance of securing a pardon and with limited funds, Mar spent the last three years of his life in a dismal state. Moreover, his health deteriorated. For over a decade he had been suffering from gout, scurvy, and some sort of chronic gastritis, and now his condition worsened markedly. In the winter of 1731–2 he and Frances moved to another fashionable spa, Aix-la-Chapelle. There Mar's last architectural drawing, showing yet another version of his beloved Alloa, was finished in March 1732, with his daughter's assistance. She was also present two months later when Mar died, at Aix-la-Chapelle. His burial place is unknown, but his daughter probably took his remains to Scotland when she visited Alloa for the first time, in November 1732. Mar had desired to be buried in the parish church of Alloa and had even designed a monument in black and white marble for that purpose. His death was reported by the *Gentleman's Magazine*, but he had vanished from the political scene to such a degree that no one—including the Jacobite community—took notice.

Even before his death a Jacobite friend had remarked that 'no man had ever a more glorious game to play & play'd it worse than he has done from first to last' (Lewis Innes to James III, 1729, Stuart papers, Royal Archives, Windsor Castle, 131/174). George Lockhart's contemporary judgment of Mar as 'a man of good sense but bad morals' (*Scotland's Ruine!*, 85) was probably the kindest comment about him in the next two centuries. By the early nineteenth century his poor reputation was firmly established. James Hogg called him 'another Richard III, deformed in his person, but possessed of ambition and an intriguing genius beyond any man living' (J. Hogg, *The Jacobite Relics of Scotland*, 2 vols., reprinted 1874, 2.223). His famous nickname, Bobbing John, which in his lifetime had probably referred only to his physical disabilities, became a synonym for his frequent political double play. It was in the twentieth century, however, that his reputation reached rock-bottom. For historians of Jacobitism, Mar simply was a 'rat' or at best an 'evil genius' (A. Tayler and H. Tayler, *The Old Chevalier: James Francis Stuart*, 1934, 101); by the 1980s Mar was 'a self-centred, monstrously incompetent poltroon' (Lenman, 154). At the same time he has also been rediscovered as one of the most important early modern Scottish art patrons and amateur architects, thus confirming Walter Scott's gentle judgment of his being 'a man of fine taste' (*Tales of a Grandfather*, 1828–30, chap. 63). Arrogant, self-centred, easily offended, and incompetent in things military he certainly was, but he also emerges from his numerous letters as a skilful estate manager, a connoisseur of music and art, a patron of architects, and a charming conversationalist.

CHRISTOPH V. EHRENSTEIN

Sources E. Gregg, 'The Jacobite career of John, earl of Mar', *Ideology and conspiracy: aspects of Jacobitism, 1689–1759*, ed. E. Cruickshanks (1982), 179–200 [most detailed account of Mar's life] · S. Erskine, ed., 'The earl of Mar's legacies to Scotland … 1722–27', *Wariston's diary and other papers*, Scottish History Society, 26 (1896), 151–247 · NA Scot., Mar and Kellie MSS, GD 124 · Mar's plans, NA Scot., RHP 13526–13528 · *Calendar of the Stuart papers belonging to his majesty the king, preserved at Windsor Castle*, 7 vols., HMC, 56 (1902–23) · *Report on the manuscripts of the earl of Mar and Kellie*, HMC, 60 (1904) · Royal Arch., Stuart papers · M. Stewart, 'Lord Mar's plans, 1700–1732', M.Litt diss., U. Glas., 1988 · B. Lenman, *The Jacobite risings in Britain, 1689–1746*, 2nd edn (1995) · P. W. J. Riley, *The English ministers and Scotland, 1707–1727* (1964) · J. Baynes, *The Jacobite rising of 1715* (1970) · I. Grundy, *Lady Mary Wortley Montagu* (1999) · GEC, *Peerage*, new edn · T. Friedman, 'A "Palace worthy of the Grandeur of the King": Lord Mar's designs for the Old Pretender, 1718–30', *Architectural History*, 29 (1986), 102–33 · T. C. Smout, 'The Erskines of Mar and the development of Alloa, 1689–1825', *Scottish Studies*, 7 (1963), 57–74 · P. W. J. Riley, *The union of England and Scotland: a study of Anglo-Scottish politics of the eighteenth century* (1978) · I. Gow and R. Bailey, 'Survey of all other public collections', *Scottish architects' papers: a source book*, ed. R. Bailey (1996), 234–60 · D. Szechi, '"Cam ye o'er frae France?": exile and the mind of Scottish Jacobitism, 1716–1727', *Journal of British Studies*, 37 (1998), 357–90 · M. Bruce, 'The duke of Mar in exile, 1716–1732', *TRHS*, 4th ser., 20 (1937), 61–82 · J. R. Moore, 'Defoe's hand in "A journal of the earl of Marr's proceedings"', *Huntington Library Quarterly*, 17 (1953–4), 209–28 · A. I. MacInnes, *Clanship, commerce, and the house of Stuart* (1996) · R. Wills, *The Jacobites and Russia, 1715–1750* (2000)

Archives NA Scot., corresp. and papers · Royal Arch., corresp. and related material | BL, letters relating to the 1715 rebellion · Hunt. L., letters to earl of Loudon · NA Scot., corresp. with Thomas Kennedy · NA Scot., letters to second earl of Aberdeen · NA Scot., letters to duke of Montrose · NA Scot., letters to Lord Melville · NL Scot., letters to James Stuart [copies] · NL Scot., letters to Alexander Robertson [copies] · PRO, letter-book of the secretary of state, SP 55/1–2 · Royal Arch., Stuart papers · U. Aberdeen L., letters to Lord Lovat

Likenesses J. Smith, mezzotint, 1703 (after G. Kneller), NPG; repro. in R. Sharp, *The engraved record of the Jacobite movement* (1996), p. 181 ff. [including a variation of 1707] · G. Kneller, double portrait, oils, *c*.1715 (with his son), priv. coll.; on loan to Scot. NPG [*see illus.*] · G. F. Ramelli, miniature, *c*.1719 · engraving, *c*.1719–1720, repro. in Stewart, 'An exiled Jacobite's architectural activities: Lord Mar's "House J", its variants and related projects (1716–1731)', *Journal and Annual Report of the Architectural Heritage Society of Scotland*, 14 (1987), 12 • R. Page, engraving, 19th cent. (after G. Kneller), U. Aberdeen, MacBean collection, B2 189 • J. Cook, engraving, 1845 (after W. Hassell), U. Aberdeen, MacBean collection, B2 192 • Chomel, engraving, U. Aberdeen, MacBean collection, B2 186 • S. Freeman, engravings (after G. Kneller), U. Aberdeen, MacBean collection, B2 187, 188 • P. Vanderbank, engraving (after W. Hassell), repro. in G. V. Bennett, *The Tory crisis on church and state, 1688–1730: the career of Francis Atterbury, bishop of Rochester* (1975), 223

Erskine, John, of Carnock (1695–1768), advocate and jurist, was born on 4 November 1695 at Stirling Castle, the eldest surviving son of the six sons and single daughter of Lieutenant-Colonel John Erskine of Carnock (1662–1743), son of David *Erskine, second Lord Cardross, and his second wife, Anne Dundas (d. 1723). His education is obscure, though he is probably the John Erskine who studied in the University of Edinburgh from about 1708 to 1711 and he may subsequently have attended university in the Netherlands to study law. In 1719 he was admitted as an advocate, dedicating his theses to John Campbell, second duke of Argyll, perhaps in connection with his father's military background but also because he hoped for patronage.

'[N]owise ambitious of the palm of eloquence or of celebrity' (Allardyce, 1.144), patronage took time to come and progress for Erskine was slow. In 1719, however, he married Margaret (b. 1697), daughter of James Melville of Balgarvie. The couple had one son, the prominent minister John *Erskine (1721–1803), and a daughter, Elizabeth (b. 1722). After the death of his first wife Erskine married on 14 December 1729 Anne (1706–1779), daughter of James Stirling of Keir. Their children included four sons, James (b. 1731), David (d. 1791), Robert (b. 1734), and Thomas (b. 1742); and a daughter, Christian (b. 1739). Anne was the elder sister of Erskine's father's third wife, Lilias Stirling (d. 1729).

In 1732 Erskine was an unsuccessful candidate for the chair of civil law in the University of Edinburgh in succession to James Craig, the appointment going to Thomas Dundas, a younger son of the prominent squadrone family of Dundas of Arniston. In 1737, however, Erskine was appointed to the chair of Scots law in succession to Alexander Bayne, and while he continued to have some practice at the bar he now directed his main attention to the duties of his chair. He initially taught using Sir George Mackenzie's *Institutions of the Law of Scotland* as his textbook, but in 1754 he published his own *Principles of the law of Scotland: in the order of Sir George Mackenzie's institutions of that law* (1754). This excellent elementary work (the last edition of which was published in 1911) developed out of Erskine's lectures on Mackenzie's book; it was the introduction of generations of Scots lawyers to their legal system and its conceptual approach, mixing Justinian's *Institutes* with a version of natural law derived from the writings of Samuel von Pufendorf, fixed in their minds a powerful map of the law. Erskine was a successful teacher with reasonably sized classes.

In 1765 Erskine resigned the chair and retired to the estate of Cardross, near Port of Menteith, Perthshire, which he had bought in 1746, and devoted himself to completing his *Institute of the law of Scotland: in the order of Sir George Mackenzie's institutions of that law* (1773). Edited by Erskine's son David, a writer to the signet, this posthumously published work provided a powerful account of the law that was soon accorded an authoritative and classic status, its eighth edition (1871) being reprinted as recently as 1989.

Erskine's affairs clearly prospered and he died at Cardross a relatively wealthy man on 1 March 1768. His estate of Carnock passed to his eldest son, John, and on the latter's death, to his son, David. Cardross was settled on Erskine's second son, James, by a post-nuptial marriage contract with Lady Christian Bruce, and later passed to his son, also David.   JOHN W. CAIRNS

Sources *Journal of the Hon. John Erskine of Carnock*, ed. W. Macleod, Scottish History Society, 14 (1893) • *Scotland and Scotsmen in the eighteenth century: from the MSS of John Ramsay, esq., of Ochtertyre*, ed. A. Allardyce, 2 vols. (1888) • *Scots peerage* • m. reg. Scot., OPR index, ext 1109763 • W. W. McBryde, introduction, in J. Erskine, *Institute of the law of Scotland*, repr. (1989) • W. Fraser, *The Stirlings of Keir* (privately printed, Edinburgh, 1858) • H. M. Wellwood, *Account of the life and writings of John Erskine* (1818) • J. M. Pinkerton, ed., *The minute book of the Faculty of Advocates, 1: 1661–1712*, Stair Society, 29 (1976) • records, U. Edin. • *Caledonian Mercury* (Oct 1739) [see also issues in Oct for 1741–2, 1744, 1748–51] • *Edinburgh Evening Courant* (Oct 1741) [see also issues in Oct for 1748–50] • J. Gilhooley, ed., *A directory of Edinburgh in 1752* (1988) • NA Scot., CC 6/5/28
Likenesses D. Lizars, line engraving (after J. Medina), NPG • attrib H. Smith, oils, Parliament Hall, Edinburgh • oils, Faculty of Advocates, Edinburgh
Wealth at death wealthy: NA Scot., CC 6/5/28

Erskine, John (1721–1803), Church of Scotland minister and author, was born probably in Edinburgh, and probably on 2 June 1721, the eldest son of John *Erskine (1695–1768) of Carnock, professor of Scots law at Edinburgh University, and Margaret Melvill (b. 1697) of Belgarvie, Fife. He was educated at the University of Edinburgh, where he first studied law but later switched to theology. Erskine was licensed in 1743 by Dunblane presbytery and was ordained in Kirkintilloch, Dunbartonshire, the following year. He married Christian Mackay (d. 1810), daughter of George, Lord Reay, on 15 June 1746; they had fourteen children, of whom four reached adulthood. Erskine was translated to Culross in 1753 and to New Greyfriars in Edinburgh in 1758; his final move was to Old Greyfriars, Edinburgh, in 1767, where he spent the remainder of his career.

Upon entering the university in the mid-1730s Erskine found himself among an illustrious group of divinity students that included William Robertson, Hugh Blair, Alexander Carlyle, John Home, and John Witherspoon. At the time the University of Edinburgh was just beginning its rise to prominence, and Erskine studied under several celebrated teachers, including Sir John Pringle and John Stevenson, whom he would later praise. But whereas their studies would lead Robertson, Blair, Carlyle, and Home

John Erskine (1721–1803), attrib. Sir Henry Raeburn

into the moderate party in the church, as advocates for applying the principles of the Enlightenment to both the style and content of their preaching, Erskine, like Witherspoon, remained a defender of religious orthodoxy and a supporter of the rival popular party throughout his career.

Erskine began writing for the public even before he entered the ministry, with a pamphlet entitled *The Law of Nature Sufficiently Promulgated to the Heathen World*, published in 1741. The work was written in answer to *The Necessity of Revelation* (1739) by Archibald Campbell, professor of divinity at St Andrews University, which many advocates of orthodoxy considered unsound. A greater impetus to taking up the pen was the preaching of the English evangelist George Whitefield, whose appearances at Glasgow and its vicinity in 1741 and 1742 helped spark a series of religious awakenings known as the Cambuslang revivals. Erskine followed up those events with a pamphlet on *The Signs of the Times Consider'd* (1742), in which he contended that the revivals in Scotland and a set of similar events in British America might signify the approach of the millennium. That discussion marked the beginning of a long-standing interest in America on Erskine's part, and he began an extended correspondence with several religious leaders in America, including Jonathan Edwards and Thomas Prince.

Erskine's interest in publishing never undermined his commitment to his pastoral duties. One of the primary concerns of Erskine's preaching was the realm of practical Christianity, the preaching of virtue and the Christian life rather than theological speculation or ecclesiastical controversy. A contemporary's description of him as

a 'practical and useful preacher' (Somerville, 62) was demonstrated in such sermons as 'The qualifications necessary for teachers of Christianity'—one of his first published works—'The education of poor children recommended', 'On goodness and fidelity', and 'Public spirit'.

Erskine was not averse to discussing controversial topics. One of the pivotal points in his career occurred in 1752 over the issue of patronage, or the right of patrons—usually prominent landowners or the crown—to present candidates for vacant clerical posts. In that year a group of young clergymen led by William Robertson persuaded the general assembly of the church to dismiss an orthodox minister, Thomas Gillespie, for his refusal to participate in the induction of a minister into the parish of Inverkeithing. Robertson and his allies supported patronage as a method of obtaining polished and learned men for the ministry. Although most of Robertson's group were Erskine's former associates, he stood with the opponents of patronage in what came to be known as the popular party.

Throughout his career Erskine was an active figure in ecclesiastical politics, almost always in support of popular party causes. He actively opposed the rights of patrons to impose ministers upon unwilling congregations. In 1748 he took the lead in opposing a measure in the synod of Glasgow and Ayr intended to prohibit ministers from allowing Whitefield to preach from their pulpits. He stood with such other spokesmen for orthodoxy as William Thom of Govan and John Witherspoon—from 1768 president of the College of New Jersey—in opposing British imperial policies towards the American colonies, about which he published three pamphlets, including one issued anonymously in 1769 with the title *Shall I Go to War with my American Brethren?* He was a vocal opponent of the proposal to repeal the penal laws against Roman Catholics in 1778, a call that resulted in rioting in Edinburgh and Glasgow. It was in part the fear of dividing and weakening British protestantism and providing an opening to Catholic France that led him to oppose rigid restrictions on the Americans. Erskine was among the more moderate opponents of repeal, disavowing the rioting that had occurred and arguing that his desire to keep the penal laws in effect did not mean that they should be rigorously enforced; private worship by British Catholics could continue so long as it remained peaceful and discreet.

Erskine's commitment to the party of orthodoxy did not lessen his respect for the achievements of those who pursued the new learning of the Enlightenment. His own sermons were often filled with the language of benevolence and moral sensibility that was so characteristic of the Scottish Enlightenment. Thus in 'The education of poor children recommended' (1774) he described how

in the ordinary course of things, blessings are not immediately and miraculously poured down from heaven; but are, through the seasonable friendly conveyance of one creature, transmitted to another. The Author of all things hath so framed … [the] universe, that every part of it, willingly or unwillingly, promotes that perfection and happiness of the whole, and in particular of the human species. (Erskine, 2.362)

In another sermon, published as *The Influence of Religion on National Happiness* (1756), he offered a defence of religion which one would not have been likely to find among earlier proponents of orthodoxy.

Erskine also shared with others influenced by the Enlightenment a cosmopolitan perspective that led him to look beyond Scottish Presbyterian traditions and revered Scottish works and to translate into English, or to arrange for publication of, a number of religious works by continental and American authors. He edited and arranged for the publication of Jonathan Edwards's sermons *The History of the Work of Redemption* after that author's death, as well as other works by Edwards, Thomas Prince, Solomon Stoddard, Jonathan Dickinson, and other American ministers. Especially during the last decade of his life Erskine devoted himself to disseminating evangelical works from western Europe and America in two volumes entitled *Select Discourses from the American Preacher* (1796–1801), in *Religious Intelligence, and Seasonable Advice from Abroad* (1801), and in *New Religious Intelligence, Chiefly from the American States* (1802).

Yet Erskine's respect for the new learning did not lead him to pursue the sort of literary activities that were undertaken by Robertson, the historian, or Home, the dramatist. Erskine's own writings were overwhelmingly devoted to religious matters; moreover, he cautioned ministers in particular to beware of pursuing the arts and sciences to an extent that might interfere with their primary mission as preachers and pastors. For a minister of the gospel to 'preach what is the result of mere human reason' or mere 'scholastical niceties, metaphysical distinctions, and a fine subtile thread of reasoning', Erskine preached in an early sermon, was one way for a clergyman to 'give offence'.

Erskine possessed the ability, rare among partisans within the Church of Scotland during the eighteenth century, to remain on good terms with his opponents even as he fought their policies. He shared a pulpit at Old Greyfriars with his adversary William Robertson for twenty-six years. Their battles in the general assembly never lessened their respect for one another, and upon Robertson's death in 1793 Erskine preached his funeral sermon, 'The Agency of God in Human Greatness', which he followed with a generous tribute to his deceased colleague.

Erskine died in Edinburgh on 19 January 1803; his own funeral sermons were preached at Old Greyfriars by his friend the Revd Thomas Randall Davidson and his colleague John Inglis. He was survived by his wife, who died on 20 May 1810, and by his only living son, David, who succeeded his father on the estate of Carnock.

Erskine published more than twenty separate works during his lifetime, including eight sermons originally delivered in the pulpit; another fourteen works appeared in *Discourses Preached on Several Occasions* (1798). A second volume, containing twenty-two additional sermons, most not previously printed, was prepared by Sir Henry Moncreiff Wellwood and was posthumously published in 1804.

Erskine is remembered chiefly for his role as a church leader who ably defended religious orthodoxy while maintaining the respect even of those who favoured more modern religious trends. His success was attributable in large part to his ability to fuse the concerns of the new age with traditional Christian doctrine, as well as his obvious dedication to his pastoral duties. *Guy Mannering* contains an extended description of Erskine as a preacher by Sir Walter Scott, whose parents had attended Erskine's congregation. It illuminates the contrast between Erskine, the austere preacher, and his more celebrated colleague William Robertson, whom Mannering had hoped to hear, encountering instead a plain man of very fair complexion, not prepossessing, with a narrow chest and stooping posture. At first Erskine's elocution strikes Mannering as 'imperfect and embarrassed', but as Erskine continues to preach his learning, energetic style, and sincere commitment to promoting practical morality leave Mannering more than satisfied.   NED C. LANDSMAN

Sources H. M. Wellwood, *Account of the life and writings of John Erskine* (1818); repr. with introduction by N. Landsman (1997) • *Fasti Scot.*, new edn, 1.47–8 • J. Kay, *A series of original portraits and caricature etchings ... with biographical sketches and illustrative anecdotes*, ed. [H. Paton and others], 1 (1837), 171–6 • W. Scott, *Guy Mannering, or, The astrologer* (1908) • Chambers, *Scots.* (1870), 1.550–54 • T. Somerville, *My own life and times, 1741–1814*, ed. W. Lee (1861), 62 • J. Erskine, *Discourses preached on several occasions*, 2 vols. (1798–1804)
Archives Mass. Hist. Soc., letter-book | NA Scot., records of the Church of Scotland
Likenesses W. Tassie, paste medallion, 1801, Scot. NPG • attrib. H. Raeburn, oils, Scot. NPG [*see illus.*] • portrait, repro. in Kay, *A series of original portraits*, vol. 1, facing pp. 171, 175

Erskine, John Francis Ashley, Lord Erskine (1895–1953), politician and administrator in India, was born on 12 April 1895, the elder son of Walter John Francis Erskine, twelfth earl of Mar and fourteenth earl of Kellie (1865–1955), and Lady (Susan) Violet Ashley-Cooper (1868–1938). He bore the courtesy title of Lord Erskine, but, predeceasing his father, he never succeeded to the peerage. Erskine was educated at Eton College and at Christ Church, Oxford. He served through the First World War, initially in the Scots Guards and later, in the Argyll and Sutherland Highlanders, attaining the rank of major. The war over, on 2 December 1919 he married Lady Marjorie Hervey (b. 1898), elder daughter of the fourth marquess of Bristol. They had four sons. In November 1922 he was elected as the Unionist MP for Weston-super-Mare, which he represented for the next eleven years, except for a few months in 1924 when the Labour Party was in office. In 1932 he became an assistant whip in the National Government.

Erskine had a keen interest in the affairs of the empire, following particularly closely the round-table conferences of 1930–33 which eventually led to the Government of India Act of 1935. Before it was passed, however, he accepted the governorship of Madras, arriving in India in 1934. Madras represented one of the few unequivocal successes of the previous scheme of constitutional reform drawn up by Edwin Montagu and Lord Chelmsford in 1918 and enacted in 1920. A local 'Justice Party' had emerged to work the reforms with the British government and to keep the nationalist Congress Party at bay. Erskine confidently expected the same to happen after the first elections under the new act, which took place in 1937. But he was to be sorely disappointed. The Congress Party swept to power with its largest majority anywhere in India.

At first, this promised Erskine serious difficulty. The Madras Congress was led by Chakravarti Rajagopalachari, one of Mahatma Gandhi's principal lieutenants. However, Erskine's political skills proved refined, and the 1937–9 Congress ministry co-operated with the British authorities to a degree not initially anticipated. Madras enjoyed two years of relatively stable government. None the less, dénouement came with the approach of war: in 1939 Erskine was obliged to suspend the legislature under section 93 of the 1935 act and impose direct rule by the British executive, as Congress withdrew from office in protest at India's involvement in the war.

Erskine returned to England in 1940 and, soon after, was elected MP for Brighton at a by-election. He was eager to serve in the wartime government but was to be disappointed. He represented a side of the Conservative Party which had long been at odds with the now ascendant Winston Churchill, who had opposed the 1935 Government of India Act. In March 1941 Erskine resigned his seat and retired to his house, Ickworth, near Bury St Edmunds, Suffolk, where he was active in local affairs, especially during the Second World War. But his health steadily deteriorated and, after a major operation, he died at Ickworth on 3 May 1953, at the age of fifty-eight. His wife survived him. Erskine always regarded himself as a Conservative in the liberal tradition, perhaps closest among his generation to R. A. B. Butler, who had drafted the 1935 act. This meant that his political fortunes went into eclipse under Churchill's leadership, and he died before they had a chance to recover in later years. DAVID WASHBROOK

Sources *The Times* (4 May 1953) · C. J. Baker, *The politics of south India* (1976) · Burke, *Peerage* (1959) · d. cert. · *CCI* (1953)
Archives BL OIOC, corresp. and papers as governor of Madras, MS Eur. D 596 | BL OIOC, corresp. with Lord Brabourne, MS Eur. F 97 · BL OIOC, corresp. with Sir Samuel Hoare, MS Eur. E 240 · BL OIOC, corresp. with Lord Linlithgow, MS Eur. F 125
Wealth at death £16,774 12s. 7d.: confirmation, 2 Sept 1953, *CCI*

Erskine, Margaret (d. 1572). *See under* James V, mistresses and children of (*act. c.*1529–1592).

Erskine [*née* Chiesley, Cheislie], **Rachel**, **Lady Grange** (*bap.* 1679, *d.* 1745), victim of abduction, was the daughter of John Cheislie (*d.* 1689) of Dalry and Margaret Nicholson; she was baptized on 4 February 1679 at Edinburgh. On 31 March 1689 her father shot dead Sir George Lockhart, lord president of the court of session, in revenge for a decision in favour of his wife's alimony claim. After torture by the boots he was executed and hung in chains. Probably in 1707 Rachel, who was accounted a great beauty, married James *Erskine (*bap.* 1679, *d.* 1754), a lord of session from 1706 with the title of Lord Grange; consequently Rachel assumed the title of Lady Grange. The couple lived at the foot of Niddry's Wynd, off the High Street in Edinburgh,

Rachel Erskine, Lady Grange (*bap.* 1679, *d.* 1745), attrib. Sir John Baptiste de Medina

and had four sons and four daughters. Rachel was noted for her violent temper and ungovernable rages. The marriage was deeply unhappy; it is claimed that James had debauched her and that she forced him into marriage by threatening his life. By 1730 the marriage was over, owing to James's long absences in London as a sitting MP, but also to his affairs, in particular a long-standing relationship with Fanny Lindsay, a Scottish coffee-house keeper in the Haymarket. James decided to move his family out of Edinburgh and gave Rachel an allowance of £100, but she took to standing beneath his window in Niddry's Wynd, shouting obscenities. She then moved back into Edinburgh, after being denied contact with her children, and continued to harass her husband. She had become a social embarrassment; then, more seriously, she threatened to disclose her husband's involvement in the Jacobite rising of 1715. James's elder brother, the sixth earl of Mar, had led the abortive uprising and Rachel, who claimed to have evidence implicating James, was known to have Hanoverian sympathies.

Lord Grange had already been involved, in 1728, in the forcible abduction of his sister-in-law Lady Mar (Mary Wortley Montagu's sister), who suffered from mental illness; he now planned to remove the threat posed by his wife in a similar fashion. On this occasion he enlisted the help of fellow Jacobites Lord Lovat and Norman MacLeod of Dunvegan. At 11 p.m. on 22 April 1732, after a violent struggle, Rachel was kidnapped from her lodgings in Edinburgh and taken, bound, blindfold, and gagged, on horseback to Linlithgow. She was then moved to Polmaise, Stirlingshire and held there for four months. After being moved through the highlands in great discomfort she was finally placed on the island of Hesker, off North Uist, where she remained for two years. By May 1734 Sir Alexander MacDonald could no longer afford to keep her and she was sent to the remote island group of St Kilda, 42 miles off Uist. There she was held incommunicado, in very primitive conditions and among Gaelic speakers, on the island of Hirta from 1734 to 1742. Meanwhile James announced her death in Edinburgh and held a mock funeral.

Rachel eventually smuggled out a message to her cousin, the lord advocate, in a ball of wool carried by the daughter of St Kilda's minister. Her cousin sent a gunboat for her but before help could arrive Norman MacLeod had her moved to Assynt in Sutherland, and finally to Skye, where all real pretence of looking after her ended and she was reputedly abandoned to live in a local cavern.

Rachel became a romantic figure for later writers. Samuel Johnson mentioned her tale in his *Journey to the Western Isles of Scotland*, and Walter Scott's coadjutor, William Erskine, wrote a romantic poem, *Epistle from Lady Grange to Edward D—*, in which she is portrayed as being sold into a loveless marriage with an older man; the poem suggests she had a younger lover from whom she was parted when sent to St Kilda. In 1897 Alexander Innes Shand wrote a romance, *The Lady Grange*, in which a young couple, Jessie and Malcolm, help Rachel escape from St Kilda and then confront James in Edinburgh. James repents of his actions but Lovat gets wind of this and has Rachel poisoned. Grange helps Jessie and Malcolm emigrate to Virginia before himself dying in penury. In fact Rachel died, at Idrigal on Skye, in May 1745 and was buried at Trumpan on Skye's Waternish peninsula. NICK HERVEY

Sources C. Maclean, *Island on the edge of the world: utopian St Kilda and its passing* (1972), 82–5 · A. I. Shand, *The Lady Grange: a romance* (1897) · K. Macleay, *Historical memoirs of Rob Roy and the Clan Macgregor, including original notices of Lady Grange* (1818), 308–403 · W. Erskine, *Epistle from Lady Grange to Edward D— written during her confinement in the island of St Kilda* (1798) · J. Keay and J. Keay, eds., *Collins encyclopaedia of Scotland* (1994), 358 · bap. reg. Scot. · 'Lockhart, Sir George', *DNB* · IGI

Likenesses attrib. J. B. de Medina, oils, Scot. NPG [*see illus.*]

Erskine, Ralph (1686–1752), minister of the Secession church and poet, was born on 15 March 1686 at Monilaws, near Cornhill, Northumberland, the sixth son of Henry *Erskine (1624–1696), presbyterian minister there, who had been ejected in 1662 by the Act of Uniformity, and his second wife, Margaret Halcro (d. 1725) of the Isle of Weir, Orkney. Evidence of his early piety can be found in notebooks he kept while a youth. He began his studies at the University of Edinburgh in November 1699, apparently completing them in 1704 with an MA degree, though his name is not found in the list of graduates. After spending the summers of 1703 and 1704 in Portmoak, Kinross-shire, where his elder brother Ebenezer *Erskine had recently been ordained, he was employed from about the beginning of 1705 to 1709 as tutor to John Erskine, the future professor of Scottish law, and as chaplain in the family of

Ralph Erskine (1686–1752), by Richard Waitt, 1712

his father, Lieutenant-Colonel John Erskine, an eminent Presbyterian who represented Dunfermline presbytery for forty years as a ruling elder in the general assembly.

Erskine was licensed by the presbytery of Dunfermline on 18 June 1709. After receiving calls to the Fife parishes of Tulliallan and the second charge in Dunfermline in spring 1711, he was prevailed upon by Thomas Buchanan, the senior minister of Dunfermline, to accept the latter, where he was ordained on 7 August 1711. He exercised his responsibilities to the parish diligently, undertaking with his colleague an annual public examination and family visitation for the whole of the parish, then consisting of over 5000 souls. He encouraged a multiplicity of fellowship meetings for prayer and religious conversation and occasionally attended himself. After Buchanan's death in 1715 he was translated to the first charge at Dunfermline on 1 May 1716. Two years of difficulty ensued before the second charge was filled by James Wardlaw, with whom he sustained a harmonious relationship for nearly twenty years.

On 15 July 1714 Erskine married Margaret (d. 1730), daughter of John Dewar of Lassoddie in the adjacent parish of Beath. They had ten children, five of whom survived their mother, who died after a short illness on 22 November 1730. Three of their sons entered the ministry of the Associate Presbytery: Henry, the eldest, served in Falkirk, John in Leslie in Fife, and James (who married Jean, daughter of James Fisher, one of the founders of the Secession church) in Stirling, initially as assistant to his uncle Ebenezer. A fourth son, Ralph, died while studying for the ministry. Margaret, their only surviving daughter, married John Newlands, the editor of her father's sermons. After a period in which Anne Erskine, his brother Ebenezer's second daughter, helped care for his children, on 24 February 1732 he married Margaret Simson, daughter of Daniel Simson, writer to the signet, with whom he had four sons, only one of whom reached maturity.

Though a zealous supporter of George I against the claims of the Stuart pretender, Erskine refused to take the oath of abjuration because he believed it obligated an endorsement of the Anglican church. He played an active part in the Marrow controversy, being the first in the presbytery of Dunfermline to reply to Thomas Boston's letter suggesting concerted action, fully participating in all of the twelve brethren's efforts, and sharing in their ultimate rebuke by the 1722 general assembly. With his brother he refused to comply with the synod of Fife's requirement that those of the Marrow brethren within its bounds subscribe the confession of faith anew. This was due not to any reluctance to subscribe the confession as such, but to his wish to avoid by such subscription implying agreement with the act of the 1720 general assembly condemning the Marrow. From the time of the controversy his published sermons, particularly those of the 1720s, illustrate the doctrines of grace, guard against legalism, and proclaim Marrow doctrine in general. His sermons are full of the love of God and offers of Christ in the gospel.

Erskine's opposition to the Arian heresy in the case of John Simson is reflected in a number of his sermons. In 1733 he was party to an unsuccessful appeal of a case involving the settlement of Robert Stark in Kinross against the will of the people of that parish. Although the general assembly was able to persuade the majority of those parishioners voting at a special meeting called for the purpose of enrolling Stark, Erskine determined never to recognize him as minister of that parish. Concurrent with this case (in which his brother Ebenezer could not participate owing to his own case before the general assembly), he, with Thomas Mair, took great interest in the general assembly's rejection of his brother's appeal against the assembly's rebuke following Ebenezer's critical sermon preached before the synod of Perth in October 1732. Ralph attended the commission meetings in August and November and signed the protest given in by Gabriel Wilson to the commission during November, holding it lawful for them 'to complain to any subsequent Assembly of the Act, and to bear testimony against the same (and other defections) and to hold communion with them as if no such sentence [loosing them from their charges] had been passed'. Subsequently he was present at the Gairney Bridge meeting in which the Associate Presbytery was formed and though he did not join at the time he continued in full fellowship with them, as did other noted like-minded ministers, including John Willison and John Currie, who later wrote zealously against the seceders. He spoke with fervour against the errors of Professor Archibald Campbell of St Andrews, and after the general assembly of 1736 failed to take any serious disciplinary measures against Campbell he appeared before the August meeting of the assembly's commission in an unsuccessful attempt to adhere to the testimony of the four brethren of the Associate Presbytery. After deliberation as to the right course of action he joined the Associate Presbytery, adhering to their judicial testimony in February 1737 and sharing in the subsequent judicial procedures which led to his deposition in 1740. Most of his elders and congregation seceded from the Church of Scotland at that time, but his colleague James Wardlaw did not, even though a meeting of the Associate Presbytery had been held in his house several years previously. A church building seating some 2000 was erected, but Erskine continued to take his turn in the parish church unmolested by the town magistrates until after Wardlaw's death in 1742. Successors to Erskine and Wardlaw were not installed in the parish charge until May 1743 and April 1744, respectively. As the presbytery attempted to supply the pulpit and a minister was called to replace him, Erskine warned the people against leaving his ministry, which he believed was ordained of God.

Erskine participated fully in the work of the Associate Presbytery, including preaching tours throughout Scotland, often in the open. These efforts frequently resulted in the formation of new congregations and the ordination of elders. He also took part in the renewal of the covenants, preaching on this occasion *Covenanted Grace for Covenanting Work* (1744). In this sermon he makes it clear that the basis of this renewal is God's 'Covenant of Grace and Promise' to his people: the obedience promised is not one in which their works earn any reward, but rather an obedience of 'Gratitude and Duty' (10–11). He concludes: 'this Day we have avouched the Lord to be our God, and this Day he hath avouched us to be his peculiar People, formed for himself, to shew forth his Praise' (47).

As the secession attracted growing attention outside Scotland, Erskine began corresponding with Gilbert Tennant, John Wesley, George Whitefield, and others. Whitefield particularly expressed his gratitude for Erskine's sermons. But when Whitefield came to Scotland, substantially at the invitation of the Associate Presbytery, disagreements, particularly over church government and the Associate Presbytery's desire to have him preach exclusively under its auspices, led to an irreparable breach between them. Rather than for them Whitefield preached for their former friends in the Church of Scotland. In the following year he was involved in the Cambuslang revival, a movement which these erstwhile friends pointed to as proof that the secession was schismatic and not of God. For their part, the seceders denounced the revivals as delusion and the work of the devil. Erskine's most extensive publication was a contribution to this controversy: *Faith No Fancy, or, A Treatise of Mental Images* (1745). Essentially a psychological and philosophical treatise it replies to James Robe's claim that 'we cannot think upon Jesus Christ really as he is … without an imaginary idea of him as man'.

In the breach over the burgess oath in 1747 Erskine was persuaded that it was not unlawful to take the oath and boldly maintained this in synodical debate (the Associate Presbytery having constituted itself the Associate Synod, divided into presbyteries, in 1745). Consequently he was the foremost of the first three to have his name removed from the ministerial rolls by the General Associate (Anti-Burgher) Synod. This was a particularly difficult time for him personally as his son John was among those voting so to censure him. It also had the effect of causing some soul-searching by the Burghers, particularly as to the previous conduct of the seceders toward those of like mind whom they had left behind in the Church of Scotland. Erskine wrote a number of pamphlets in this controversy, including *Fancy No Faith, or, A Seasonable Admonition* (1747).

Erskine remained active in the ministry until shortly before his death, though with a variety of ailments which intimated his approaching demise. In 1751 the Associate Synod determined his older brother Ebenezer was more in need than he of the assistance of his son James. When he died in Dunfermline of a 'high fever' (Fraser, 384) on 6 November 1752 Ebenezer commented: 'And is Ralph gone? He has twice got the start of me he was first in Christ; and now he is first in glory' (Fraser, 386). Erskine was buried on 9 November with the attendance of a large body of mourners.

A contemporary obituary characterized him as 'one of the most popular preachers in the church'. About forty of his sermons were published separately during his lifetime, and many of them were reprinted several times. *A Collection of Sermons* by Ralph and Ebenezer, edited by Thomas Bradbury, was issued in London in three volumes between 1738 and 1750. Ralph's own *Sermons, and other Practical Works* was published in two large folio volumes in 1764–5 and was reprinted several times over the course of the next century. A selection was published as *The Beauties* in 1821. Erskine also had a great reputation as a poet, and his *Gospel Sonnets*, first published in 1720 as *Gospel Canticles, or, Spiritual Songs*, was many times reprinted. *Scripture Songs* (1754) was an attempt to turn appropriate passages of scripture into metre for 'the same public use' as the Psalms of David, in accord with an act of the general assembly of 1647 and as recommended by the Associate Synod in 1747. His 'Smoaking Spiritualized', first appended to *An Elegy on the Much-Lamented Death of … Alexander Hamilton* (1739), has often been quoted, the refrain 'Thus think, and smoke tobacco' far more frequently than the verses, 'And when the pipe grows foul within, Think on thy soul defil'd with sin'. Both single volumes and collections of his works were printed in America, and translated into Dutch. In addition to his poetry Erskine was noted for playing the violin, an unusual avocation for a minister in his day. DAVID C. LACHMAN

Sources DNB · *Fasti Scot.*, new edn, 5.30–32 · D. Fraser, *The life and diary of the Reverend Ralph Erskine* (1834) · A. R. MacEwen, *The Erskines* (1900) · R. Small, *History of the congregations of the United Presbyterian church from 1733 to 1900*, 2 (1904), 663–4 · J. M'Kerrow, *History of the Secession church*, rev. edn (1848) · D. C. Lachman, *The Marrow controversy, 1718–1723: an historical and theological analysis* (1988)

Archives Dunfermline Central Library, notebooks · NL Scot., notebooks · U. Edin., New Coll. L., notebooks

Likenesses R. Waitt, oils, 1712, Scot. NPG [*see illus.*] · Buck, line engraving, NPG · T. Chambers, line engraving, NPG

Erskine, Sir Robert (*d.* 1385). *See under* Erskine family (*per. c.*1350–*c.*1450).

Erskine, Robert, first Lord Erskine (*d.* 1451/2). *See under* Erskine family (*per. c.*1350–*c.*1450).

Erskine, Stuart Richard [*known as* Ruaraidh Erskine of Mar] (1869–1960), political activist and Gaelic entrepreneur, was born at 1 Portland Place, Brighton, on 15 January 1869, second of the three sons of William Macnaghten Erskine, fifth Baron Erskine (1841–1913), army officer, and his wife, Caroline Alice Martha, *née* Grimble (*d.* 1922). He spent his early years in Edinburgh, and lived for prolonged periods in Scotland, England, and France. On 18 July 1891 he married Muriel Lilias Colquhoun, daughter of Major-General G. Irving Graham; she died in 1895, the year after the death of their only child, a daughter. On 6 August 1902 he married Maria Guadelupe Zaara Cecilia Heaven y Ramirez de Arellano (*d.* 1956), only daughter of Joseph Robert Heaven of the Forest of Birse, and his wife, the marquesa de Braceras.

Erskine learned Gaelic from a childhood nurse who came from the island of Harris, and this kindled the enthusiasm which was to be a main hallmark of his career. His imagination was fired early by the Irish nationalist movement and these combined influences, together with his family's historic Scottish roots, led to his development as a prominent Gaelic nationalist, whose compelling dream was of a self-governing Celtic Scotland. As essential steps towards the realization of this dream he was actively involved in the fostering of Gaelic consciousness and in the extension of Gaelic usage, especially in the written form. He hoped that a significant extension of Gaelic literary range would contribute to the raising of literary standards, in a reaction against what he saw as the downgrading influence of music-hall and 'pop' culture on Gaelic verse in the second half of the nineteenth century. He probably also viewed his activity as a response to the dominance of folk culture in the Gaelic literary world.

Erskine's literary programme spanned the first three decades of the twentieth century, the first twenty years being especially prolific. His programme was based on the founding and financial support of a series of Gaelic newspapers and periodicals. The first of these was *Am Bàrd* ('The poet'), a bilingual monthly issued in 1901–2. A short-lived weekly Gaelic newspaper, *Alba* ('Scotland'), was published in 1908–9, and a publication devoted to fiction, *An Sgeulaiche* ('The storyteller'), ran as a monthly from 1909 to 1910 and as a quarterly until 1911. A short series of quite bulky annual volumes, *An Ròsarnach* ('The rose garden'), appeared in 1917, 1918, 1921, and 1930. His most substantial and lasting periodical, however, was *Guth na Bliadhna* ('The year's voice'), a quarterly which ran from 1904 to 1925, in bilingual format until 1919 and all-Gaelic thereafter. *Guth na Bliadhna* marked a clear move towards journalistic and modern writing in Gaelic. One of the most prominent contributors was the journalist Angus Henderson, who often chose topics such as the Land Act, land and taxes, schools and education, and deer and deer-forests. The didactic drive behind these articles is clear, but Henderson usually produced a well-balanced discussion and verdict. Donald Sinclair, from Barra, contributed poetry and drama, and a new generation of writers appeared late in the series, with Hector MacDougall and John N. MacLeod, both of whom were to be prolific Gaelic writers for the next three or four decades. The political drive behind the publication was sustained throughout its life, with a movement towards the left (and a hint of communism) appearing in the late war and post-war years. Interviewed in 1956, Erskine at the age of eighty-seven was still a convinced nationalist and talked optimistically of returning to Scotland after his years in France and London. However, it was in England that he died, at St Augustine's Hospital, Chartham, Bridge, Kent, on 5 January 1960.

Erskine himself published a number of books, including fiction, history, an edition of Bolingbroke's political writings (1897) and of *The Earl of Mar's Legacies to Scotland* (1896), *Bordology: the Science of Determining Character by what a Man Eats and Drinks* (1925), and a translation from the Gaelic *The Old Tribute and other Pieces* (1929). Although Ruaraidh Erskine's Gaelic publishing work was not very successful in a commercial sense, it had a positive influence on Gaelic writers, and helped to lay the foundations for the resurgence in Gaelic writing (in fiction, poetry, and journalism) which was to come when he had retired from active work in this field.   DERICK S. THOMSON

Sources D. S. Thomson, ed., *The companion to Gaelic Scotland* (1983) · D. J. MacLeod, 'Gaelic prose', *Transactions of the Gaelic Society of Inverness*, 49 (1974–6), 198–230 · *Gairm*, 16 (1955), 367 · L. MacBean, ed., *The Celtic who's who* (1921), 38 · Burke, *Peerage* (1939) · Burke, *Peerage* (1959) · b. cert. · d. cert.
Likenesses photograph, repro. in *Gairm*

Erskine, Sir Thomas (d. 1403/4). *See under* Erskine family (*per. c.*1350–*c.*1450).

Erskine, Thomas, first earl of Kellie (1566–1639), courtier, was the son of Sir Alexander Erskine of Gogar (*c.*1521–1588x92) and Margaret, daughter of George Home, fourth Lord Home. Erskine was educated with James VI, and became a gentleman of the bedchamber in 1585. He was confirmed in royal favour when at the time of the Gowrie conspiracy at Perth in August 1600 he helped to protect the king and was wounded in the hand in a scuffle with Alexander Ruthven, the earl of Gowrie's brother. Erskine was rewarded with some of the dead earl's lands, and in 1601 he accompanied the duke of Lennox on a diplomatic mission to France. He was admitted to the Scottish privy council on 2 July 1601, and in 1602 sat in the convention of estates.

After James's accession to the English throne in 1603 Erskine was appointed captain of the yeomen of the guard (replacing Sir Walter Ralegh) and began two decades of steady advancement in the new court. Created Lord Dirleton in 1604, he was given the prestigious office of groom of the stole in 1605. In 1606 he was made Viscount Fentoun, being the first Scot granted this newfangled rank. Membership of the English privy council followed in 1610, installation as a knight of the Order of the Garter in 1615, and creation as earl of Kellie in 1619. Kellie devoted his life to the service of the king, but he also showed a strong secondary loyalty, to his cousin John

Erskine, earl of Mar, who was head of the Erskine kin. At court he cultivated Mar's career, and through a constant stream of letters (237 survive for 1612–25 alone) he kept Mar closely in touch with the intricacies of court politics. Mar became treasurer of Scotland in 1616, but Kellie remained a courtier, never gaining the power and the influence over policy that he wanted. On several occasions frustration at this led him to resolve to give up court life and return to Scotland, and he sadly accepted in 1622 that his own limitations would prevent his achieving his ambitions: 'It is not in my power to do as I would, nather can my disposition doe theis things that greater men do for the accomplishment of their desyres' (*Mar and Kellie MSS*, 2.130). Typically, however, he felt he could not leave without establishing another trusted agent to serve Mar at court, and in the end he stayed on. The court was his home and his life.

To Kellie's discontent at lack of real power was added worry at the fact that, in spite of his offices and a number of grants of lands and revenues, the expenditure necessary to maintain his status at court had led to serious financial problems. Temporary relief was obtained through his second and third marriages. He had first married, on 30 November 1587, Anne, daughter of Sir Gilbert Ogilvy of Powrie; after her death he married, in 1604, Elizabeth Pierrepoint (d. 1621), widow of Sir Edward Norreys and sister of the earl of Kingston. Thus he was one of the first to set the fashion for Scots who had come south with King James to marry rich English widows. Elizabeth died in 1621, and gossip claimed that while married to Kellie she, 'having ever lived in a very plentiful way, did now fall into melancholy and much grief, and she never came out of her chamber, and this came out of a consideration of her own wants' (Goodman, 1.389–90), for his extravagance strained their resources. However, friends at court, with King James's support, arranged 'another rich wife' for him, in spite of the fact he was 'old, no comely gentleman, and but a Scots earl, generally known to be very poor'. This was Dorothy Smith (d. in or before 1639), the thrice-widowed daughter of a London silk merchant, her last husband having been Robert Needham, Viscount Kilmorey. She was 'supposed to be very rich in money, plate and jewels' and soon after the marriage, it was alleged:

> Kelly took occasion to break open trunks, to seize upon money and jewels, and there was great discontent between them. Truely Kelly was a very honest natured man, but his own wants and necessity did enforce him to do what he did and therefore he was the more to be pitied. (Goodman, 1.391–2)

This malicious description of Kellie, with its piously sarcastic ending, reflects the bitterness felt against Kellie and other court favourites (especially Scotsmen), who were regarded as parasitic. Another commentator made the same point, listing Kellie as one of four Scots who 'lay suckling at the brests of the state' under King James (Osborne, 1.240).

As a courtier Kellie feared for his future when his royal

patron died, writing to Mar when James was ill in November 1623: 'It may come that young folks shall have their world. I know not if that will be fit for your Lordship and me' (Lee, *Government*, 219). His forebodings were justified. On James's death in 1625 Kellie lamented the loss of a master 'I have waitted on theis fyftye yeares' (*Mar and Kellie MSS*, 2.227), and he also lost office as groom of the stole. Charles I proved sympathetic when Kellie confided 'the straits I am in' (*Mar and Kellie MSS*, 2.236). In December 1626 he promised his father's old friend £10,000 sterling, and he allowed him to retain the captainship of the guard until 1632. But like other old Scottish servants of King James, Kellie quickly lost authority: such men remained at court as 'ghosts of a past era, without respect or influence' (Lee, *Road to revolution*, 33). Kellie died in London on 12 June 1639. Though he had made his career in England, his body was brought to Pittenweem in Fife, where he was buried on 23 June, as the parish contained the castle and lands of Kellie which he had bought in 1613. Aspirations to be a statesman and to gain the wealth he believed appropriate to an earl had failed, but half a century of success as a courtier was consolation. DAVID STEVENSON

Sources DNB · GEC, *Peerage* · *Scots peerage* · M. D. Young, ed., *The parliaments of Scotland: burgh and shire commissioners*, 2 vols. (1992–3) · *Report on the manuscripts of the earl of Mar and Kellie*, HMC, 60 (1904); suppl. (1930) · M. Lee, *Government by pen: Scotland under James VI and I* (1980) · M. Lee, *The road to revolution: Scotland under Charles I, 1625–1637* (1985) · G. Goodman, *The court of King James the First*, ed. J. S. Brewer, 2 vols. (1839) · *The historical works of Sir James Balfour*, ed. J. Haig, 4 vols. (1824–5) · F. Osborne, 'Osborne's traditional memoires', *Secret history of the court of James the First*, ed. W. Scott, 1 (1811), 1–297
Archives NA Scot., MSS | NA Scot., letters to earl of Mar

Erskine, Thomas, ninth earl of Kellie (1745/6–1828), merchant and diplomat, was probably born at Cambo House, near Kingsbarns, Fife, the third son of David Erskine (c.1697–1769), Rothesay herald and later Lyon clerk, and his second wife, Anne Young (b. c.1707), from Fisherrow, near Edinburgh. His paternal grandfather was the Jacobite sympathizer Sir Alexander Erskine of Cambo, second baronet. Connections to the Jacobite cause led to the sequestration of the family's estates in Thomas's childhood. In 1759 Erskine was apprenticed as an accounts assistant to George Carnegie, merchant, in Göteborg, Sweden. As a youth he fathered an illegitimate daughter, Harriet or Henrietta (1763–1829), his only known child. Her mother's identity remains elusive.

In 1765 Erskine began work as a bookkeeper for John and Benjamin Hall, and within two years he became a partner in their company, in which he retained his share until 1798. In 1769 he helped found the Royal Bachelors' Club of Göteborg, though in 1771 he married Ann (c.1750–1829), daughter of Captain Adam Gordon of Ardoch. From 1775 Erskine served as British consul for Göteborg, Marstrand, and other western Swedish ports. In 1787 his daughter Harriet, whom he had adopted, married Johan Henric Engelhart (1759–1832), later professor of medicine at Lund, Sweden. Early in the following decade Erskine established his own business exporting iron, coal, and

timber. In addition he invested in the East India and China trade and undertook business deals in the United States. If commercially progressive, Erskine's politics were reminiscent of an old-fashioned anti-Catholic toryism which led him to share his family's sympathy to the now rapidly waning Jacobite cause. In 1787, for example, he commissioned a set of wine glasses (now in the National Museum of Scotland) for a dinner held in Edinburgh (and attended by Robert Burns) to mark the birth date of Charles Edward Stuart. Three years later he successfully bought back the family's estates.

In October 1799 Erskine became the ninth earl of Kellie, Viscount Fentoun, Lord Dirleton, and Lord Pittenweem following the death of his nephew Charles Erskine who had himself inherited the earldom four years earlier. Kellie now settled permanently at Cambo House. From 1799 to 1809 he was provost of St Andrews, an office which he held (from 1797) alongside the captaincy of the Society of St Andrews Golfers (later the Royal and Ancient Golf Club). During this period he maintained his interest in commerce (his investments included a one-sixteenth share in an East Indiaman, the *Kellie Castle*) and in Scandinavia, sending Scots craftsmen to Sweden to aid the modernizing agriculturalist Carl Georg Stjernwärd, though with limited success.

In 1804 Kellie was elected a representative peer of Scotland, and he was reappointed at the general election of 1807. In the following year he was made a knight commander of the royal order of Vasa by Gustaf IV Adolf of Sweden, an honour he wore with George III's permission. A close friend and admirer of the army officer Sir John Hope (from 1816 fourth earl of Hopetoun), Kellie initiated the commissioning of a portrait of the general, undertaken by Sir Henry Raeburn about 1817–19, for the county hall in Cupar. On Hopetoun's death in 1823, Kellie headed a committee of subscribers to erect the Hopetoun monument on Mount Hill. Kellie's final political position began in June of the following year, when he was appointed lord lieutenant of Fife, succeeding the sixteenth earl of Morton, whose deputy he had been. For several years Kellie had attempted, unsuccessfully, to persuade the prince regent (later George IV) to recognize his eldest grandson, David Engelhart (1792–1841), as his heir. In 1820 he entailed his estate at Cambo on his grandson, who then took the Erskine name and, a year on, became first baronet of Cambo in the second creation. Kellie died aged eighty-two on 7 February 1828 at Cambo House, and was buried at the mausoleum there on 16 February. His personal estate was then worth £49,060 19s. 10d. He was survived by his wife, who died at Cambo on 20 March 1829, and was succeeded as tenth earl by his brother, Methven Erskine, before his death, also in 1829.

MARIANNE MCLEOD GILCHRIST

Sources B. Hildebrand, ed., *Svenskt biografiskt lexicon* (1953), vol. 14, pp. 476–84 · *Scots peerage*, 5.90–94 · H. A. D. Miles and D. B. Brown, eds., *Sir David Wilkie of Scotland* (1987), 209–12 · M. F. Conolly, *Biographical dictionary of eminent men of Fife* (1866), 170 · U. St Andr. L., special collections department, Erskine of Cambo MSS · NA Scot.,

Leven and Melville papers, GD 26/13/297 · J. G. Duncan, 'Scottish trading links with Sweden', *Scottish Local History* (March 1991), 10–13 · records of the commissioners of supply and heritors of Fife, Fife Council Archives, Markinch, Fife · *Fife Herald* (15 July 1824) · *Fife Herald* (29 July 1824) · *Fife Herald* (7 Oct 1824) · M. M. Gilchrist, 'Cupar portraits: works of art in county buildings, Cupar', MS, 1998, Fife Museums Service (East) · G. Dalgleish, 'Objects as icons: myths and realities of Jacobite relics', *Heritage and museums: shaping national identity*, ed. J. M. Fladmark (2000), 90–102 · H. Miles, 'Raeburn's portraits of the 4th earl of Hopetoun', *Scottish Art Review*, 14/2 (1973), 30–36 · will, PRO, PROB 11/1740, fols. 294v–296

Archives U. St Andr., family papers | Fife Council Archives, Markinch, records of the commissioners of supply and heritors of Fife · NA Scot., Leven and Melville papers, GD26/13/297 and 26/13/310

Likenesses oils, after 1799, repro. in Hildebrand, ed., *Svenskt biografiskt lexicon*; priv. coll. · D. Wilkie, oils, 1824–8, County Buildings (Fife Council), Cupar · D. Wilkie, oils, 1829, Musée des Beaux-Arts, Lille, France · D. Wilkie, oil study, priv. coll.

Wealth at death £49,060 19s. 10d.: Erskine of Cambo papers, U. St Andr.

Erskine, Thomas, first Baron Erskine (1750–1823), lord chancellor, was born in Edinburgh on 10 January 1750, the third son of Henry David Erskine, tenth earl of Buchan (1710–1767), and his wife, Agnes (d. 1778), the second daughter of Sir James Steuart of Goodtrees and Coltness, first baronet (1681–1727), solicitor-general of Scotland. Although the family was not flourishing at the time, accounts of their poverty have probably been exaggerated: Erskine was born in a substantial house on the High Street, they owned a country home at Uphall, and they had access to Goodtrees via Lady Buchan's family. The Erskines' distinguished history made their present circumstances relatively humble, however, since the family (the senior branch of which were earls of Mar) had been hereditary custodians of the heir to the throne of Scotland. Erskine would allude in his legal career to his kinship with George III, since both were descendants of the house of Stewart. Indeed, on his maternal side his great-grandfather, Sir James Stewart of Goodtrees, had been lord advocate, although both families had suffered reverses and exile in the Presbyterian cause.

Early life, 1750–1774 As with most children of the aristocracy, Erskine's general education was a combination of learning for cultivation as well as governance, undertaken in a rather haphazard way. But he did enjoy the advantage of direct exposure to the Scottish Enlightenment. His mother was an accomplished woman, and it is likely that his early tuition (like that of his siblings, including his sister Lady Anne Agnes *Erskine) was supervised by her personally, with the aid of her distinguished salon, which incorporated prominent statesmen, ministers of the kirk, and lawyers from the Faculty of Advocates. About this time the family also became acquainted with Allan Ramsay and David Hume. It is not clear whether Erskine had any more formal education before 1760, when the family moved to St Andrews, although he later claimed another Scot who became a barrister, Sir Archibald Macdonald, as his schoolfellow. At St Andrews he and his elder brother Henry *Erskine (1746–1817) were

Thomas Erskine, first Baron Erskine (1750–1823), by Sir Thomas Lawrence, 1802

taught Latin by Richard Dick, later a professor of history in the university, and he also seems to have attended classes in natural philosophy, mathematics, and English, although there is no evidence that Erskine himself was matriculated at St Andrews University. Despite his evident natural curiosity, it is unlikely that such a lively and gregarious boy was always preoccupied with serious books, however: a letter he wrote to his brother David Steuart *Erskine, later eleventh earl of Buchan (1742–1829), in August 1762 relates how they were having dancing lessons, and reading Livy and French during the vacation from classes (Fergusson, 66).

As a younger son Erskine was expected to make his own way in the world, but he hoped that his parents would educate him for a learned profession, or at least purchase a commission in the army, and it was with some disappointment that he left Scotland in 1764 as a midshipman aboard HMS *Tartar*. His family may have arranged special privileges, for the *Tartar* was commanded by a fellow Scot, Sir John Lindsay. Although he was stationed in the West Indies, he was able to indulge himself in further reading, and studied botany. After four years he was promoted acting lieutenant, but his ship was paid off on returning to England in 1768, and since prospects for a commission were so poor in peacetime he determined to change his situation. Lord Buchan had died in December 1767, and on 1 September 1768 Erskine became an ensign in the 2nd battalion of the Royals, having purchased his commission with his inheritance. After an initial posting to Berwick upon Tweed, in 1769 he was stationed at St Helier, Jersey, and during these years he began to develop an aptitude for occasional composition, including both sacred and profane subjects, and writings in poetry and prose, which was maintained throughout his life. The extant specimens written during this period are *Berwick Beauties* (1768), a panegyric on the polite ladies of Berwick upon Tweed, which must have been written for the entertainment of his messmates, and a sermon (1769) on 1 Kings 20, addressed to the soldiers of the Royals at St Helier. Also while he was at St Helier, Erskine wrote an essay on choosing a wife, and it seems this was not merely a theoretical exercise, for on 29 March 1770, at Gretna Green, Dumfriesshire, he married Frances (*d.* 1805), the daughter of Daniel Moore, formerly member of parliament for Marlow in Buckinghamshire. It was a love match: the groom was still under age, and the bride's father initially refused his consent; however, he was soon reconciled, and Erskine's wife accompanied him to his new station at Minorca. There he remained for two years, apparently spending his spare time reading English literature, and perhaps amusing himself by reading prayers and preaching sermons to his regiment, if his table talk is to be credited.

In 1772 Erskine was granted six months' leave, much of which he spent in London, frequenting literary circles and developing a reputation for charm and versatility in conversation. In company one day with James Boswell and Samuel Johnson, he 'talked with a vivacity, fluency, and precision so uncommon, that he attracted particular attention' (Boswell, 1.426). He was promoted lieutenant in April 1773, but two years later he published *Observations on the prevailing abuses of the British army, arising from the corruption of civil government* (1775), a pamphlet which complained about inadequate pay and the inequities of promotion by purchase and 'that Gorgon of corruption, stiled parliamentary interest' (*Observations*, 34). Clearly the glamour of London had contributed to growing disillusionment with the humdrum life of a junior officer without substantial means, and at this point Erskine's mother seems to have encouraged him to remember her family's tradition in the law. As a member of the Scottish aristocracy he must have met the lord chief justice, William Murray, first earl of Mansfield, when he was in London, and would have been encouraged by Mansfield's success in Westminster Hall, as well as that of another Scot, Alexander Wedderburn, who was currently solicitor-general. Certainly by 1775 he had resolved to try his fortune at the English bar, for he was admitted to Lincoln's Inn on 26 April and he sold his commission in September.

Beginnings at the bar and in parliament 1775–1784 At this time the inns of court allowed university graduates two years' dispensation from the time normally required to be eligible for call to the bar, and no doubt this was the primary reason why Erskine matriculated as a fellow commoner at Trinity College, Cambridge, on 13 January 1776. As the son of a nobleman he was entitled to a degree without examination, so he did not have to be in residence, but he may have taken the opportunity for more broad reading, especially in English literature and history. At Cambridge he wrote some more poetry and also composed a formal declamation on the origins of the House of Commons. The last piece prefigures its author's later courtroom rhetoric, which often depended on dramatic appeals to English history, natural rights, and civic republicanism. For Erskine the House of Commons took its origin from one of the accidents of history, the multiplication of royal tenures under Edward I and his successors, which allowed the 'patriot citizen' (Erskine, 'An oration', 101) to take a role in governance, ultimately leading to 'revolution' under Charles I. But this process represented 'the unconquerable spirit of liberty' (ibid., 103), which had been planted in England with Magna Carta, and liberty was legitimized by natural law, not history: Erskine insisted that the 'rights of mankind' were 'sacred and immutable … they are the gift of Heaven' (ibid., 95). His peroration therefore warned that human institutions did not guarantee the maintenance of liberty, and recommended good citizens to keep their attention focused on 'the spirit of the constitution' (ibid., 104), while giving due respect to the state and the existing laws.

Meanwhile Erskine also undertook the much duller experience of reading for the bar, which in his day included an obligatory spell in the chambers of a special pleader. Although the practice came to be ridiculed by barristers who ultimately identified him as the prototype for a more liberal tradition of education, Erskine himself studied under Francis Buller and George Wood, both later common-law judges. Indeed, he seems to have acquired enough black-letter law to become entirely competent, if not outstanding, in the argument of strictly legal issues, although even admirers such as Henry Brougham admitted he was never a truly great lawyer. In addition he probably took advantage of the contemporary vogue for debating societies to improve his skills in formal argument, reputedly being a regular speaker at the Coachmakers' Hall Society, then meeting at the Crown tavern in Bow Lane. This period of Erskine's life was one of some privation. He and his wife had taken modest lodgings in Kentish Town, near Hampstead, and in later life he regaled friends with imaginative accounts of their genteel poverty, by which his growing family depended on the cheapest food, including 'a string of sausages hanging in the fireplace' (*Memoirs … of Thomas Moore*, 4.74). The testimony of Jeremy Bentham, whom he had known since 1776, confirms that he was shabbily dressed, but he seems to have been sustained by a sense of personal destiny, and his lively personality attracted support from a wide circle of friends.

It was important for junior barristers seeking briefs to be active socially, and Erskine's first opportunity for success at the bar came about partly through his conviviality. Having graduated MA at Cambridge in June 1778, he was called to the bar on 3 July. By his own account, a few days earlier his conversation had so impressed a fellow dinner guest that he was given a brief in the case of Captain Thomas Baillie, a naval officer who had charged the governors of the Royal Naval Hospital, Greenwich (of which he was lieutenant-governor), with corrupt administration, and was obliged to show cause in king's bench as to why he should not be prosecuted for a criminal libel. No doubt Baillie was also persuaded by Erskine's previous service in the navy. The hearing took place before Lord Mansfield on 23 November, when counsel were heard in order of seniority, but Francis Hargrave took so long that when he finished Mansfield adjourned until the next day, with only Erskine remaining to speak. Thus Erskine had the night to prepare his speech, and on the following day he made a powerful and courageous attack on the governors of the hospital, especially John Montagu, fourth earl of Sandwich, first lord of the Admiralty, whom he castigated as 'the dark mover behind the scene of this iniquity' (*State trials*, 21.44), and 'a shameless oppressor, a disgrace to his rank, and a traitor to his trust' (ibid.), despite Mansfield's interjections. Moreover, he cited case law to prove that Baillie had not strictly *published* his case, and made an impassioned appeal to popular opinion, arguing that the Admiralty's corrupt practices discouraged 'the heroic ardour of a British sailor' (ibid.) and threatened the continuance of 'a fleet to carry terror all round the globe' (ibid.). Despite this hyperbole, it is doubtful whether Mansfield himself was favourably impressed, for in discharging the rule he complained about arguments which 'charged persons who are not here to defend themselves' (ibid.), and grounded his judgment on the narrow point that Baillie had already been punished by censure and suspension, rather than on Erskine's harangue. But there is no doubt that attorneys would have recognized Erskine's passion and eloquence as potentially powerful weapons before a jury, and the case had established a solid foundation for his career at the bar.

Despite his junior status, Erskine rapidly became the first choice for 'second business' at the bar (Brougham, 'Memoir', in *Speeches of the Right Hon. Lord Erskine*, 1.xiii), especially in cases with a naval or military connection. In January 1779 he acted as legal adviser for Admiral Augustus Keppel at Keppel's court martial in Portsmouth. Although occasioned by Keppel's failure to win a decisive victory over the French off Ushant in the previous June, the trial was essentially a party affair, and no doubt Erskine was retained because his previous attack on Sandwich had identified him as a patriotic opponent of the North government's administration. The court was heavily biased in Keppel's favour, but while he was not able to speak himself Erskine assisted materially by suggesting questions and composing the speech which the admiral delivered. On acquittal Keppel signalled his appreciation by giving him £1000 in return. His rising standing was demonstrated a few months later by being chosen to argue at the bar of the House of Commons in support of the petition of the bookseller Thomas Carnan against a bill giving the two universities and the Stationers' Company a monopoly in the printing of almanacs. For barristers parliamentary hearings represented the cream of their business, and this particular bill was important and controversial, having been introduced by Lord North on behalf of the universities. Erskine rose to the occasion. When he appeared on 10 May he concentrated on public policy arguments for a free press rather than the potential damage to his client, and warned darkly of the political dangers in legislation which sought to limit useful knowledge. He also took the opportunity virtually to recommend himself as a future member of parliament, admitting that he had 'assumed a language fitter, perhaps, for the House than for its bar' (Cobbett, *Parl. hist.*, 20.619). The bill was thrown out. In July Erskine was one of the counsel who appeared in king's bench to argue in mitigation of the judgment against Charles Bourne, a lieutenant of marines who had been found guilty of libel and assault against Sir James Wallace, his former commanding officer on board the *Warrior*. Bourne justified his attacks by alleging humiliating treatment at sea and Wallace's subsequent refusal to accept his challenge to a duel, and Erskine attempted to exculpate him on the basis of the prevailing honour code among officers, referring emotionally to his own service in the navy and declaring: 'Consider what the honor of an officer is, and if their honor is lost, it is their universal ruin' (*Trial of Lieutenant Charles Bourne*, 72–3). But on the other side Edward Law desired the court 'to forget a little the laws of chivalry … [and] to follow a little the law of England' (ibid., 109–10); and in pronouncing judgment the court likewise ridiculed counsel who 'adopted the chimeric notions of knight errants' (ibid., 149). No mitigation was allowed for the assault, and Bourne was sentenced to two years' imprisonment. At the end of the year Erskine appeared in king's bench as one of the counsel for the Madras faction which in 1776 had deposed Lord Pigot, the governor of Fort St George, and made a powerful speech justifying their action according to the principles of 1688. They were subsequently fined the relatively small sum of £1000 each.

Although Erskine's rhetoric did not invariably win the approbation of judges, he consolidated his reputation in jury trials by his defence of Lord George Gordon in January 1781. Gordon was indicted for high treason, on the basis that his leadership of the anti-Catholic crowd which invested parliament in June 1780 and petitioned for the repeal of the recent Roman Catholic Relief Act was construed as levying war against the king under the statute of Edward III. On this occasion Erskine's leader was Lloyd Kenyon, who damaged the prosecution by his cross-examination of their principal witness, and made out a strong case for the strictly constitutional intentions of his client. But contemporaries believed Erskine's final address was decisive in securing Gordon's acquittal. Despite modestly introducing himself as 'a young man of little experience, unused to the bar of criminal courts, and sinking under the dreadful consciousness of my defects' (*State trials*, 21.587), he made a cogent and learned attack on the 'constructive cavil' (ibid., 589) by which the words of Edward III's act had been extended to Gordon's case. He also did not scruple to appeal to popular anti-Catholicism by identifying his ancestors as sufferers in the protestant cause; he repeatedly attacked the attorney-general for dishonourable and unchristian conduct in not showing the indulgence and humanity customary in a cause of blood; and he shamelessly flattered Lord Mansfield, who presided on the bench. After such a triumph Erskine was overwhelmed with work and felt sufficiently confident of his standing to refuse any more junior briefs. Since he had been at the bar for only a few years, such a step effectively disadvantaged many of his seniors, who could not appear with a leader junior in point of seniority. This problem was solved by the grant to Erskine of a patent of precedence at the bar after the king's counsel, dated 16 May 1783, less than five years after he had become a barrister. He was precocious in the achievement of wealth, as well as professional status. In November 1782 he had made a will—occasioned by fighting a duel with one O'Bryen, a surgeon whom he had insulted at Brighton—which revealed that, besides discharging 'considerable debts' (PRO, PROB 11/1680, fol. 130r), he had already made over £9000 since he was called to the bar, an unprecedented sum for a junior counsel. The will left all his property to his wife, for whom he expressed considerable affection, but it is typical of Erskine that he was willing to hazard everything 'from a sense of honour' (ibid.). He was also already developing that consciousness of his own achievements for which he later became notorious, for the will gave instructions for the publication of his speeches, then being revised by his clerk.

Erskine's success at the bar and open avowal of whig principles had brought him to the attention of the parliamentary opposition, and he became an intimate of Charles James Fox and Richard Brinsley Sheridan, who introduced him to the prince of Wales (afterwards George IV). His growing ascendancy in Westminster Hall and mastery of constitutional issues obviously suggested he would be an asset in parliament, and no doubt his patent of precedence was procured by the Fox–North coalition, which had entered into government in April 1783. During the summer recess they arranged for his election as MP for the Admiralty borough of Portsmouth, with the agreement of Keppel, now first sea lord. He was also made attorney-general to the prince of Wales, perhaps in compensation for the loss of his lucrative parliamentary practice. Unfortunately, as friends pointed out at the time, his courtroom triumphs had created unrealistic expectations, and in parliament he suffered by comparison with William Pitt the younger, to whom he was often opposed in debate. He spoke first on 20 November, supporting the motion for a second reading of Fox's India Bill, and reproaching Pitt, who had spoken immediately before him; but the story which has Pitt destroying his confidence on this occasion by studied inattention is most likely apocryphal. Indeed, Erskine spoke on the bill again in the second reading debate on 27 November, when he argued that the exercise of governance by a commercial corporation was 'impolitic and absurd', and reiterated his attack on Pitt, concluding with a solemn pledge to stand for ever by Fox 'at the hazard of every prospect of ambition' (Cobbett, *Parl. hist.*, 23.1293–7). On 17 December, the day the bill was defeated in the Lords, he nailed his colours to the mast by supporting Fox's complaint about the king's declared opposition to the India Bill and carried a motion which committed the house to remedy the 'abuses' in the government of British India and 'consider as an enemy to this country'

any one who counselled the king to dissolve parliament (ibid., 24.226). The ministry was dismissed the next day, and Erskine followed the Foxites into opposition against the minority Pitt government. On 22 December he successfully moved the committee on the state of the nation for an address to the king which begged him not to listen to 'secret advices' (ibid., 24.277) for a dissolution; and in the first debate of the new year he made another strong attack on Pitt, whom he described as 'hatched at once into a minister by the heat of his own ambition' (ibid., 24.313), and who sought to impose on the house by 'fair words, in opposition to the foulest conduct' (ibid.). He also spoke against Pitt's India Bill on 23 January 1784, condemning it as 'a mere piece of patchwork, which could only disgrace the contriver' (ibid., 24.405), and on 16 February he made a substantial speech defending the previous resolution of the Commons which restricted the payment of East India bills under the new ministry. Two days later, in his last speech before the dissolution, he justified the resolutions of the House against the continuance in office of the ministry. At the general election, having been rejected as a candidate for Portsmouth, he stood for the closed borough of Truro, but was defeated and became one of Fox's 'martyrs'. Although out of parliament for six years, in February 1788 Erskine used the opportunity of an appearance at the bar of the Commons on behalf of the East India Company to cast 'a great deal of animadversion and sarcasm on the East India Bill of 1784, and mixed it with much warm eulogium upon that of Mr. Fox' (ibid., 27.78). But he went too far when he suggested the issue before the Commons—Pitt's declaratory bill imposing on the company the costs of transporting soldiers to India—was too important for a late-night debate, and the speaker reproved him for presuming to give advice to the house.

Leader of the bar, 1784–1792 Erskine used his time in the political wilderness to consolidate his professional reputation. At Westminster he practised chiefly in king's bench, but the reports show that from the later 1780s he was also regularly employed in the House of Lords, especially on writs of error and appeals from the Scottish court of session and court of exchequer. His talents were fully exposed only before a jury, however; and besides following the home circuit he received many special retainers for appearances in important trials around the country. His first was the case of William Shipley, dean of St Asaph, who was tried for seditious libel at the Shrewsbury assizes in August 1784. Shipley was indicted for republishing *The Principles of Government, in a Dialogue between a Gentleman and a Farmer*, by Sir William Jones, which had advocated extending the franchise and asserted the right of resistance to unconstitutional authority. In his speech Erskine deliberately revived the party issue of the jury's powers in issues of libel, as animated in *R. v. Woodfall* (1770), and then interpreted narrowly by Lord Mansfield. Against Mansfield he insisted on their right to judge how far the publication was libellous, rather than merely find the fact of publication and confirm the interpretation of the innuendoes averred in the indictment: that the tract referred to the government and the king. Despite the strict direction of Buller, the judge in this case, they returned a verdict 'guilty of publishing *only*', and Erskine contended strongly with Buller that it should be taken in those terms, implying a decision that they found no libel. Buller eventually prevailed on them to agree to a verdict of 'Guilty of publishing, but whether a libel or not the jury do not find', and in the following term Erskine moved for a new trial in king's bench, alleging misdirection by the judge, grounding his argument in an extended dissertation on the origins and rights of juries, in opposition to the recent judicial precedents. Naturally Mansfield and his puisnes ruled against him, the lord chief justice pointedly insisting that recent judicial practice could not be disturbed by 'arguments of general theory, or popular declamation' (*State trials*, 21.1040), and dismissing the essence of Erskine's argument as 'puerile rant' (ibid.). But afterwards Erskine moved successfully in arrest of judgment, on the grounds that the indictment was defective. He subsequently published his argument about the rights of juries, and it substantially informed Fox's Libel Act of 1792.

Despite his association with Fox, Erskine demonstrated his professional independence in December 1789, when he defended the bookseller John Stockdale, who was prosecuted by the government on the basis of an address to the crown moved by Fox in the House of Commons. The Commons had taken exception to Stockdale's publication of *A review of the principal charges against Warren Hastings esq., late governor-general of Bengal* (1787/8), which alleged that the articles of impeachment exhibited against Hastings were unjust, misrepresented and falsified his behaviour as governor-general, and proceeded from the personal animosity of MPs. On this occasion the role of the jury was not in question, since Kenyon had replaced Mansfield as chief justice, and Erskine was able to argue the substantive issue of the libel, insisting on the freedom of the press to question and comment upon proceedings in parliament: 'The people of England are not to be kept in the dark, touching the proceedings of their own representatives' (*State trials*, 22.274). He presented Hastings as the victim of parliamentary oppression, and justified the pamphlet as a 'debt and duty to humanity and justice' in response to the widespread publication of the articles of impeachment before his trial (ibid., 22.259). Kenyon summed up fairly impartially, and the jury found the defendant not guilty. In December 1792 Erskine returned to the issue of press freedom under less favourable circumstances, when he defended Thomas Paine *in absentia*. The government had taken alarm at the popularity of radical opinions in the context of the drift to extremism in France. Paine was indicted for a libel on the revolution and the settlement of the crown and constitution in his *Rights of Man*, part 2, and Sir Archibald Macdonald, the attorney-general, defended the constitution with patriotic and loyal ardour. In reply Erskine made another impassioned speech for the freedom of the press, asserting that Paine was entitled to criticize the constitution, as long as he advocated change by legal means, and comparing its 'abuses' unfavourably with the American constitution

(ibid., 22.427). He also made many self-righteous references to his personal situation, as counsel for an unpopular cause, and insisted:

> From the moment that any advocate can be permitted to say, that he *will* or will *not* stand between the Crown and the subject arraigned in the court where he daily sits to practise, from that moment the liberties of England are at an end. (ibid., 22.412)

Erskine's speech in this case is still remembered by the bar for his articulation of the 'cab-rank rule'—counsel cannot refuse a case simply because it is unpalatable or unpopular—but at the time the jury seems to have been unsympathetic from the start, and returned a guilty verdict without retiring.

Counsel for the radicals, 1793–1800 Following a visit to Paris in September 1790 Erskine had become an enthusiast for the French Revolution and its principles: Samuel Romilly described him at the time as a 'violent democrat', and said he had a coat in the style favoured by the Jacobins, with buttons inscribed 'Vivre libre ou mourir', which he intended to wear in the Commons (*Memoirs of … Romilly*, 1.408). Even as late as 1799 he asserted in court: 'I think I see something that is rapidly advancing the world to a higher state of civilization and happiness, by the destruction of systems which retarded both' (*State trials*, 27.670). But his continuing zeal naturally led to growing estrangement from the more conservative whigs who were horrified by the excesses in Paris, and he was dismissed as the prince's attorney after defending Paine. Nevertheless, his practice continued to prosper. In 1791 he had told his brother that he hoped to clear £10,000 without office, his business 'being greater than ever, and beyond all instance or example since Rufus built the Hall of Westminster' (Fergusson, 389). However, it was his defence of the reformers and radicals inspired by the events in France which sealed his reputation for posterity. The first prosecutions came before the courts in 1793; given his acknowledged principles and previous success, Erskine was automatically first choice as leading counsel for the defence in the most serious cases. In May he failed to save the radical attorney John Frost from the pillory and imprisonment for speaking words in a coffee house against the monarchy, although he suggested to the jury that the situation in France was being used as 'the common stalking horse for all state purposes' (*State trials*, 22.489), and insisted that Frost should have the benefit of the presumption of innocence. But at the end of the year he secured an acquittal for the proprietors and printer of the *Morning Chronicle*, who were prosecuted *ex officio* in king's bench for publishing an advertisement in the name of a radical society in Derby. Against Sir John Scott, the attorney-general, Erskine insisted that the new statute on the law of libel required the jury to consider whether the defendants intended sedition, and not merely that the publication itself was a seditious libel, and the jury followed him to the extent of first returning a special verdict of 'Guilty of publishing, but with no malicious intent' (ibid., 22.1023), which Kenyon refused to accept. In April 1794 he defended

Thomas Walker, of the Manchester Constitutional Society, who was tried at the Lancaster assizes with several others for a conspiracy to overthrow the government and aid the French in case of an invasion. The crown had a weak case, depending on the evidence of one witness; Erskine destroyed his credibility in cross-examination, suggested the prosecution was 'cruel and oppressive', and produced unimpeachable evidence that the witness had perjured himself, upon which the crown gave up the case (ibid., 23.1118).

In May 1794 the government moved more decisively to suppress the growing popular movement for reform. The leaders of the popular societies were arrested, a secret committee of parliament was established to review evidence against them, and habeas corpus was suspended on the grounds that a 'traitorous and detestable conspiracy' (34 George III, c.54, preamble) existed to subvert the constitution and introduce anarchy after the model in France. A special commission was established under Sir James Eyre, lord chief justice of common pleas, to try them for high treason. In his charge to the grand jury, Eyre associated parliamentary reform with treason and French republicanism. True bills were found against twelve, and Erskine was retained for the defence in every case. The indictments alleged constructive treason, in so far as the defendants' plans to summon a national convention and achieve electoral reform amounted to overt acts aimed to alter the constitution against the will of parliament and therefore implied they compassed the king's death. Thomas Hardy, the shoemaker secretary of the London Corresponding Society (LCS), was tried first, in October and early November. The attorney-general, Scott, took nine hours to introduce his case, associating Hardy, the LCS, and the proposed convention with republicanism, Paine, and the revolution in France, and a mass of written and oral evidence was presented, ultimately alleging an armed republican conspiracy. In his speech for the defence Erskine entirely rejected the doctrine of constructive treason and denied that the LCS had any intention beyond parliamentary reform, to be achieved by uniformly constitutional means. He also cited the early works of Edmund Burke and the reforming efforts of Pitt and Charles Lennox, third duke of Richmond, to show that liberal political views did not imply disaffection from the crown. And he did not scruple to enlist the sympathy of the jury by artfully reminding them that Hardy's pregnant wife had died after the shock of his arrest and the invasion of her home by a loyalist mob. The conclusion of his speech was greeted by acclamation from the public in court, and the cry was taken up by the crowds which had been surrounding it, so that he had to go out and bid them to depart in peace. After hearing the evidence for the defence and the closing speeches of junior counsel, Eyre summed the evidence in a way which was clearly hostile to the defence. But despite Eyre's animadversions against the reform societies, his doubts about Hardy's professions of loyalty, and his censure of Erskine for declaring that the people had a right to alter their government, the jury brought in a verdict of not guilty. The trial had lasted eight days in all, and there was jubilation on the streets of London; but the government did not abandon the prosecutions until John Horne Tooke and John Thelwall were also both acquitted, after trials in late November and December which took a further ten days.

As a consequence of his success and extraordinary exertions in these trials, involving almost constant attendance in court from early in the morning until past midnight, and consultations afterwards, Erskine became a national hero. He was described as 'that incomparable defender of national liberty' (*Annual Register*, 1795, 275); medals with his image and appropriate patriotic mottoes were struck; his pictures and busts were reproduced and sold as badges of liberty; and he was presented with the freedom of several corporations. His pre-eminence at the bar was openly acknowledged: even Scott, the attorney-general, felt obliged to warn jurors against his 'plausible and ingenious arguments' and 'the gratification of a brilliant speech' (*State trials*, 27.630). He continued to be retained for the defence in trials for treason and seditious libel. In January 1796 he appeared in king's bench as second counsel for the Unitarian coal merchant William Stone, who was acquitted on an indictment for treason, alleging that he encouraged and sought to assist an invasion from France, in so far as he had collected information about the state of loyalty to the crown in the country for transmission to Paris. As he generously admitted himself, in this case Erskine had little to do after the speech of Serjeant James Adair, the senior counsel for the defence, which adroitly turned the evidence of the crown upon itself and fully exculpated Stone's conduct. In March 1799 Erskine was unsuccessful in his defence of the printers and proprietors of *The Courier*, who were convicted of a libel against the emperor of Russia and imprisoned. And in April he also failed to secure an acquittal for Sackville Tufton, ninth earl of Thanet, and the barrister Robert Fergusson, who were found guilty of a riot at Maidstone, in attempting to rescue Arthur O'Connor from the sheriff after his acquittal for treason. But in the case of the bookseller John Cuthell, who was convicted of seditious libel in February 1799 for selling a pamphlet by Gilbert Wakefield, his speech put a powerful case for the innocence of his client's intention, in so far as he was unaware of the pamphlet's radical nature, and Cuthell escaped with a fine only. And in June 1800 he gained a verdict of not guilty in the case of James Hadfield, who was tried for high treason after firing a pistol at the king in Drury Lane theatre. Hadfield had fought in France, and Erskine was able to establish that wounds received there had rendered him dangerously insane, with the result that he was subsequently imprisoned for life by act of parliament.

Erskine was not wholly engaged in defending state prosecutions at this time. Besides his regular *nisi prius* practice at Westminster and the Guildhall, which centred on commercial cases and prosecutions for 'criminal conversation' (adultery), in July 1796 he appeared at Shrewsbury assizes on behalf of John Warren, bishop of Bangor, who was prosecuted for a riot in attempting to eject Samuel Grindley, claiming to be deputy registrar, from that office.

Daringly, he presented no evidence on behalf of his client, and, despite a hostile summing-up by the judge, he obtained a verdict by neatly deploying the facts proved by the other side to ridicule the prosecution, and associate it with French-style anti-clericalism. And in 1797 he accepted a general retainer as counsel for the Society for Enforcing the King's Proclamation against Immorality and Idleness, successfully prosecuting Thomas Williams in June for publishing Paine's *Age of Reason*, which was judged to be a blasphemous libel because it brought Christianity into contempt. At the trial Erskine referred to his belief in the gospel as the 'great consolation of a life, which, as a shadow, passes away' (*State trials*, 26.662); he cited John Milton, John Locke, and Isaac Newton as witnesses for its truths, and he also asserted that the progress of liberty and happiness depended on the inspiration of Christianity. But he subsequently broke with the society by speaking in mitigation when Williams appeared for judgment and, after returning their fee, declined to appear for them again.

Foxite and reformer, 1790–1800 At the 1790 election Erskine had been returned to parliament for his old seat of Portsmouth, on the interest of Sir John Carter, who dominated the corporation. He spoke first in the December debates about resuming the impeachment of Hastings, a procedure which he had consistently opposed in private and in court. In a long speech, interrupted by exhaustion and resumed a few days later, he maintained that it was a question for judicial determination by the House of Lords, but averred that all the parliamentary precedents, Magna Carta, and 'the great characteristics of English liberty, established for ages' (Cobbett, *Parl. hist.*, 28.1084) were against the continuation of the impeachment. For this effort he was repaid by the stinging sarcasm of Burke, who belittled his reputation for eloquence and suggested he should pay more attention to the facts. Erskine was clearly nettled, and although he addressed the issue again, on 14 February 1791, it was only to explain that he would abstain on Burke's motion for limiting the impeachment. He was treated with more respect in May, when he seconded Fox's motion for an inquiry into the law of libel, referring to his arguments at the bar as justification for legislation, and he defended the resulting bill vigorously when it was debated in committee on 31 May.

In the 1790s Erskine's great political causes were parliamentary reform, the freedom of the press, and opposition to the growing reaction engendered by fear of revolutionary France. On 26 April 1792 he was one of the signatories to the declaration of the 'Society of the Friends of the People associated for the purpose of obtaining a Parliamentary Reform', and on 30 April in the Commons he supported Charles Grey's notice of a motion in that cause, defending the association's popular campaign by pointing out that an appeal to parliament on the issue 'was literally addressing argument to the deaf adder' (Cobbett, *Parl. hist.*, 29.1330). He persisted in the face of growing hostility from the political establishment. In November he promoted a petition for parliamentary reform from the Friends of the People, and in December he condemned

the royal proclamation against sedition and ministerial alarms about France as inflammatory: 'The question was whether the constitution was to be preserved by coercion, or in its spirit and by its own principles' (ibid., 30.57). On 15 December he supported Fox's motion for sending an ambassador to Paris, warning against the horrors of war, and a week later, after the conviction of Paine, he presided at the first meeting of the Friends to the Liberty of the Press, where he made a speech reviewing his career in cases of libel, concluding: 'I belong to the people—they raised me from poverty to affluence—from obscurity to notice—they have a right to demand my services—they shall have them' (*Speech of the Hon. Thomas Erskine at a Meeting*, 14). After he chaired a second meeting of the society, on 19 January, he was parodied in print as 'Counsellor Ego', who admitted he was 'nervously diffident', and wished 'for every man's approbation' (*Proceedings of the Friends to the Abuse of the Liberty of the Press*, 10). But the outbreak of war with France in February made arguing popular causes in the Commons an arduous task, and Erskine and the Foxites were increasingly isolated against the tide of repressive legislation. In March 1793 he spoke against the Traitorous Correspondence Bill, pointing out that it departed from the essence of Edward III's act by criminalizing specific acts, rather than intentions. On 5 January 1795 he discussed the verdicts in the recent treason trials extensively to argue there were no grounds for a continuation of the Habeas Corpus Suspension Act. And in November he deployed all his eminence in cases of treason and sedition as one of the principal opponents of the 'two acts' introduced by the government after the king was mobbed on his way to open parliament. He characterized the Seditious Meetings Bill as 'destructive of the very essence of the constitution ... a direct and gross violation of the Bill of Rights' (Cobbett, *Parl. hist.*, 32.312), and said the Treasonable Practices Bill invested the king with 'the insignia of a tyrant' (ibid., 32.477). At the same time he strongly supported calls for the prosecution of John Reeves, describing his pamphlet on government as 'a book to support the principles of kingly government, which thank God, Englishmen got rid of!' (ibid., 32.624). But he admitted to attending the house infrequently, and often referred to his pressing business in Westminster Hall. His only other major speeches in these years were those in support of Grey's 1793 and 1797 motions for reform, and in opposition to the address in December 1796, when he denied that the French had been the aggressors in the outbreak of war. On this occasion he was silenced by sudden illness, but he published a full version of his argument against the war and in favour of reform in his *View of the Causes and Consequences of the Present War with France*, which appeared in February 1797 and ran to many editions. Having attributed 'the degraded, disgraceful state of this assembly' (ibid., 33.658) to Pitt's maintenance of corruption in May, he seceded from the Commons with Fox from mid-1797 and did not make a major speech again until February 1800, when he returned to condemn the government's rejection of French overtures for peace. His disillusionment was probably personal as well as political:

despite his eminence at the bar, Erskine's demagoguery outside parliament attracted contempt in the Commons, and his dramatic rhetoric was listened to with impatience. As Charles Abbott said in 1795: 'His power of commanding the passions of a jury, so justly celebrated beyond the reputation of all his predecessors in Westminster Hall, wholly fails of its effect in Parliament' (*Diary and Correspondence of Charles Abbott*, 1.24).

Partial eclipse and the chancellorship, 1800–1807 After Pitt's resignation in February 1801, Erskine had high hopes of gaining office, and on 13 November he signalled his approbation of Henry Addington's foreign policy in the Commons by approving the convention with Russia. But it was difficult to navigate through the shifting political currents. Although he had discussions with ministers at this time, his previous radicalism was hard to live down, and his old opponent Sir John Scott was now Lord Chancellor Eldon, with considerable influence over appointments to the bench. He returned to favour with the prince of Wales, however, who made him chancellor of the duchy of Cornwall early in 1802, and in that capacity he spoke in the parliamentary debates of March 1802 and March 1803 about the prince's right to the duchy's revenues. But he briefly returned to partisanship on 7 May 1802 by opposing a vote of thanks for Pitt's services to the nation: although disclaiming 'personal animosity' (Cobbett, *Parl. hist.*, 36.617), he declined to endorse 'acts deserving of an impeachment' (ibid., 36.619). In September 1802, on a visit to Paris as one of Fox's party, he was said to have been mortified when he was introduced to Bonaparte as the prince's chancellor, provoking 'the killing question "Etes vous legiste?"' (Trotter, 267–8). There was more humiliation with the collapse of the peace of Amiens. On 23 May 1803 Erskine embarrassed the whigs by prevaricating in the debate about the renewal of hostilities with France, allowing Pitt to take advantage; and in December he was reported to Fox as making a 'foolish figure' when speaking intemperately to the report on the army estimates, and defending the volunteers against William Windham (Stanhope, 4.109). Erskine's relations with Fox had been strained. In September he advised Addington that he would not follow Fox into a planned coalition with Pitt. But in March 1804 he was forced to reject the offer of the attorney-general's place on discouraging advice from the prince of Wales. After Pitt returned to office he seems never to have spoken again in the Commons, although he was reconciled with Fox at the end of the year and henceforth voted uniformly with the opposition. His practice, meanwhile, had lost some of its glamour and partisan edge, although he continued to be in leading business before king's bench. In December 1803 he appeared for the crown in the trial of the coopers Michael and John Hedges, who were found guilty of a conspiracy to defraud the royal dockyard at Woolwich, and in February 1804 he was successful in arguing the right of volunteers to resign despite the General Defence Act. He cited the decision in his last speech to the Commons on 19 March, persuading Addington to exclude a clause forbidding resignation from the Volunteers Consolidation Bill. His wife, with

whom he had four sons and four daughters, died on 26 December 1805. In November he assisted in the prosecution of the Irish judge Robert Johnson for a libel on the lord lieutenant, but only examined witnesses. His last major appearance was for Dr John Thomas Troy, Catholic archbishop of Dublin, who prosecuted Henry Delahay Symonds for alleging in the *Anti-Jacobin Review* that he concealed knowledge of the 1803 rising in Dublin. On this occasion Erskine's opponent, William Garrow, accused him of introducing 'phantasmagoria' (*State trials*, 29.530) to impress the jury and of manipulating the case to conceal material evidence, but he obtained a verdict and damages for a libel on his client.

The death of Pitt in January 1806, and the subsequent resignation of Eldon with the formation of the Grenville–Fox 'ministry of all the talents', finally removed some of the political impediments to Erskine's further advancement. But Ellenborough (Edward Law) and Sir James Mansfield both refused to leave the common-law bench for the chancellorship, and on 7 February Erskine therefore accepted the great seal himself, becoming Baron Erskine of Restormel Castle in Cornwall, which belonged to the prince's duchy of Cornwall estate. Like many, George Rose thought the appointment was controversial 'not only because of his total inexperience in the Court of Chancery, but from his political attachment to Mr. Fox not having been steady and uniform' (*Diaries and Correspondence*, 2.253–4). Erskine affected to read real property law under the direction of Romilly, however, and usually accepted direction from the chancery bar. As a result his rulings were cautious, and generally did little to advance the development of equity rules. The only new doctrine he ventured—in *Thelusson* v. *Woodford*—was appealed to the House of Lords, although it was affirmed. Romilly had thought him 'totally unfit' (*Memoirs of … Romilly*, 2.134) on appointment, and condemned him for allowing his conduct on the bench to be governed by 'the fear of losing or endangering that vulgar popularity which he values a great deal too highly' (ibid., 2.178). He made a better impression as lord high steward at the trial of Henry Dundas, Viscount Melville, in April and May 1806 for corrupt administration of public funds as treasurer of the navy, where he applied his strictures on the Hastings impeachment by insisting on continuous sittings and abidance by legal rules of evidence and procedure. In June he was named a member of the commission established to inquire into the alleged adultery of Caroline, princess of Wales, and he subsequently acted as the intermediary between her and the king. But it appears that Erskine was rarely consulted by his fellow ministers on substantive political matters, and the death of Fox in September was a blow. The election of a new parliament in December also undermined the position of the whigs. Erskine's main contribution to the Lords centred on legal matters, although he supported the proposed abolition of the slave trade in June, stating the evidence presented had changed his mind on the subject. He was not informed of Lord Howick's bill for allowing Catholics and nonconformists to hold commissions in the army and navy until it was introduced into parliament at the beginning of 1807. Faced with the king's implacable opposition, he argued in cabinet to persuade his colleagues to desist, and in the royal closet for a withdrawal of the demand for a written ministerial promise never again to propose any measure of Catholic relief. On 26 March in the Lords he said that for the ministry to have remained in power upon such a condition was 'contrary to every principle of ministerial duty, and directly in violation of the constitution' (*Hansard 1*, 26 March 1807, 9.259). But he was reluctant to leave office—he told Mackintosh: 'If I had been left where I was I think I could have done some good' (BL, Add. MS 52452, fol. 16)—and before resigning on 7 April he took the opportunity to make Edward Morris, the husband of his daughter Mary (*d.* 1864), a master in chancery.

Declining years and death, 1808–1823 It was difficult for Erskine to find a new role after he left office. He stood up in the Lords within a week of the change in administration to assert that 'the danger to the church is made the stalking-horse upon this occasion' (*Hansard 1*, 13 April 1807, 9.361), suggesting the king had received secret advice to remove his ministers. But the 'no popery' election of mid-1807 decimated the whigs' numbers, and, after speaking in favour of the unsuccessful amendment to the address deploring the dissolution (26 June), Erskine only occasionally manifested active opposition to government measures. His interventions were distinguished by their power and humanity, however. In February 1808 he condemned the expedition to Copenhagen as 'extraordinary, unprecedented, and unjustifiable' (ibid., 8 Feb 1808, 10.354), and on 8 March he moved eight resolutions against the orders in council, arguing unsuccessfully that they were unconstitutional and contrary to the law of nations. He also spoke against the Jesuits' Bark Bill, asserting that to deny medicines to the enemy 'was contrary to the dictates of religion and the principles of humanity' (ibid., 7 April 1808, 10.1321). His main cause in these years was animal welfare: he had always kept pets of various descriptions, including dogs, a goose, a macaw, and even a pair of leeches who he claimed had saved his life. He also wrote a poem which imagines the feelings of a rook upon seeing his companions shot by a bailiff, and of a worm, who lives for a day. On 15 May 1809 he introduced a bill for the prevention of cruelty to animals, arguing that human dominion over them was a moral trust, and particularly deploring the 'most disgusting cruelties practised upon beasts of carriage and burden' (ibid., 15 May 1809, 14.561). It was defeated in the Commons and a subsequent effort was stillborn, but these beginnings prepared the ground for the statute against cruel treatment of cattle, sheep, and horses, which finally passed in 1822 (3 Geo. 4, c. 71). In 1810, when the permanent recurrence of the king's illness revived the issue of the regency, Erskine maintained the prince's claim to full constitutional powers against the restrictions proposed. His hopes of a return to office with the regent were disappointed, however, and although he made a point of speaking for Romilly's law reform bills,

for several years afterwards he virtually retired into private life. In 1807 he had told Grenville 'Public life is nothing to me. I have attained my utmost object, and I have a thousand resources for happiness as a private man' (BL, Add. MS 58965, fol. 134*v*), and in 1811 his achievements were recognized with an honorary LLD from Cambridge, but his personal and social ventures were almost uniformly unsuccessful. Much of his fortune was wasted in American investments, and financial straits forced him to sell the bulk of his property in London. Having bought an estate near Crawley in Sussex, he dabbled in farming; the land was infertile, and he lost heavily when he tried to convert the produce into raw material for manufacturing brooms. In 1815 he accepted the renewal of the war without demur and flaunted himself in London society wearing the Order of the Thistle, granted by the prince on 23 February that year. He also turned to letters. In 1817 and 1818 he published *Armata*, a political romance in two parts, which attempted to distil his life's wisdom about liberty and corruption, care for animals, and moderate law reform into allegory, following the models of *Utopia* and *Gulliver's Travels*. He married Sarah Buck (*d.* 1825), who had been his mistress for many years, at Gretna Green on 12 October 1818, but the union was unhappy, and they separated on 21 June 1821, over five months before the birth of a son, whom Erskine named Hampden.

Notwithstanding his private travails, Erskine rediscovered popular causes with the revival of mass political agitation and the government's return to repression. In 1817 he strenuously opposed the bills for prohibiting seditious meetings and suspending habeas corpus, insisting that the existing laws provided sufficient remedies against seditious words and writings, and imploring parliament 'not to be precipitate but to place confidence in the people, governing them by their affections, the only security for the obedience of a free people' (*Hansard 1*, 24 Feb 1817, 35.546). In November and December 1819 he spoke consistently against the Six Acts, declaring dramatically: 'He wished all the people of this land to know, that he was still in his place, as he ever had been when the rights of the people were invaded' (ibid., 23 Nov 1819, 41.26). Erskine had argued against the abolition of sinecures in 1817, however, and he was forced to defend his popular credentials in *A Short Defence of the Whigs* (1819), which denied the Westminster radicals' claim that they had compromised with 'influence', and justified incremental parliamentary reform. In 1820 he visited Scotland for the first time since he had gone to sea, and was publicly fêted. Despite his friendship with the king, he resisted the bill of pains and penalties against Queen Caroline, locking horns with Eldon and with John Freeman-Mitford, first Baron Redesdale; a frustrated opponent complained:

> His name, in consequence of his great eminence as a barrister, and of his attachment to party, is still such a tower of strength, that three to one against him would have been more conclusive, with many in the House, than two. (*Diary and Correspondence of Charles Abbott*, 3.162)

When the bill was withdrawn he made a speech rejoicing in the restoration of 'the sacred rule of law' (*Hansard 2*, 10

Nov 1820, 3.1747), but George IV was deeply offended. Defending the queen revived Erskine's image as the people's advocate, and he took a patrician interest in the romantic popular causes of Spain and Greece. In 1822–3 he wrote two pamphlets championing the Greek rebellion against the Turks, proposing a diplomatic initiative and private relief efforts. He also affected to speak for the landed interest in *A Letter to the Proprietors and Occupiers of Land* (1823), which called for a return to the provisions of the Elizabethan poor law and supported increased protection, although he had protested against the Corn Law Act in 1822. His financial position continued to be straitened, but even in old age he maintained a lively disposition; in 1818 the American ambassador said he had 'a youthfulness of imagination that imparted its sprightliness to every thing' (Rush, 215). But there had been signs his health was failing in the 1820 debates about Queen Caroline, and late in 1823 he was taken seriously ill on a voyage to visit his brother Lord Buchan in Scotland. He went ashore and was conveyed to Almondell, near Edinburgh, the country house of his late brother Henry, where he died on 17 November 1823. He was buried at Uphall. His wife died on 25 October 1825, having been provided for very inadequately. Erskine was succeeded as second Baron Erskine by his eldest son, David Montagu *Erskine (1776–1855). His fourth son, Thomas *Erskine (1788–1864), became a judge, and his second daughter, Elizabeth (*d.* 1800), was the first wife of Sir David *Erskine (1772–1837).

Significance Although his wit and vitality delighted many, Erskine frequently appeared to be insufferably vain and ridiculous to those who encountered him personally. After meeting him at a dinner Fanny Burney commented, 'The eminence of Mr. Erskine seems all for public life; in private, his excessive egotisms undo him' (*Diary and Letters*, 5.319). But his egoism was not unproductive. Combined with a religious disposition to belief in providence, his extensive reading in English history and literature made him acutely conscious of his role for posterity; he habitually sent his speeches to the press and took early steps for their publication in collected form. As a result his exploits and declarations about the independence of the English bar survived to inspire later generations of lawyers, and are still remembered by barristers in England and its former colonies. Moreover, he helped to make defending criminal and political cases more respectable. Certainly among the next generation of defence counsel there was considerable admiration for his rhetorical and theatrical abilities, as applied to gaining the sympathies of a jury. Indeed, Erskine's contemporary popular appeal derived from his conscious self-fashioning as a patriot citizen fighting constitutional battles in the whig tradition of English history. And the battles were important. His arguments about the freedom of the press to criticize government were a logical corollary of the revolution settlement and a necessary condition for reform, and his insistence on the rights of juries in cases of libel settled the law in a more liberal track. His triumphs in *R.* v. *Hardy* and *R.* v. *Horne Tooke* tended to inhibit government prosecutions of radicals which depended on constructive extensions of the law of treason; and it is arguable that the verdicts in those trials helped to preserve popular subscription to constitutionalist modes of thinking and political action. But although he was by no means a bad lawyer, as well as a consummate advocate, his methods were unorthodox. He:

> successfully undertook to spurn at precedents; to strike out a new path to eminence; to appal or silence the judges themselves; to intimidate, convince, or seduce the juries; to appeal from the understanding to the feelings; to invoke religion in aid of reason; to cite Scripture whenever it suited his purposes; to oppose the Bible against Blackstone; finally to lead captive his audience, and to carry the cause that he defended or espoused, by extorting a sort of involuntary submission, sometimes yielded almost in defiance of evidence, facts, belief, or conviction. (Wraxall, 1.86)

Erskine himself believed that the administration of law could not be reduced to a science. He admitted: 'No man so well acquainted as I am with the events of trials and who has contributed so often myself to produce results not to be anticipated by the strict rules of Law can venture to say particularly what a Jury would determine' (Lord Erskine to Sir J. W. Gordon, 4 Oct 1808, BL, Add. MS 49500, fol. 185). Indeed, it is notable that Romilly was frequently frustrated by him, for Erskine's inclinations and talents were directed to winning great popular victories, rather than the painstaking work which was the stuff of rational law reform. Moreover, despite his public posturing as a man of the people, he was not a genuine democrat: in personal relations he was acutely conscious of his aristocratic breeding and strenuously maintained its honour code; and in public his attitude was that of a patrician who lent his talents to inferiors. In many ways his life story and its representation belong to the Romantic period rather than to the Enlightenment.   DAVID LEMMINGS

Sources State trials, vols. 21–9 · Cobbett, *Parl. hist.*, vols. 20, 23–4, 27–36 · Hansard 1 · Hansard 2 (1820), vols. 1–3 · A. Fergusson, *The Honourable Henry Erskine lord advocate for Scotland, with notices of certain of his kinfolk and of his time* (1882) · DNB · Foss, *Judges*, 8.268–82 · R. G. Thorne, 'Erskine, Hon. Thomas', HoP, *Commons, 1790–1820* · E. Haden-Guest, 'Erskine, Hon. Thomas', HoP, *Commons, 1754–90* · *The speeches of the Right Hon. Lord Erskine at the bar and in parliament, with a prefatory memoir by the Right Hon. Lord Brougham*, ed. J. Ridgeway, 4 vols. (1847) · Henry, Lord Brougham, *Historical sketches of statesmen who flourished in the time of George III, to which is added remarks on party, and an appendix*, 1st ser. (1839), 236–45 · *Memoirs of the life of Sir Samuel Romilly*, 2nd edn, 3 vols. (1860) · will, PRO, PROB 11/1680, fols. 130v–131v · N. W. Wraxall, *Posthumous memoirs of his own time*, 2nd edn, 1 (1836), 80–96 · *The poetical works of the Right Honourable Thomas, Lord Erskine, K.T., with a biographical memoir of his life* (1823) · D. Lemmings, *Professors of the law* (2000) · Earl Stanhope [P. H. Stanhope], *Life of the Right Honourable William Pitt*, 4 vols. (1861–2) · *The diary and correspondence of Charles Abbot, Lord Colchester*, ed. Charles, Lord Colchester, 3 vols. (1861) · *The Beauties of the Anti-Jacobin, or, Weekly Examiner* (1799) · *Diary and letters of Madame D'Arblay*, ed. [C. Barrett], 7 vols. (1842–6), vol. 5, p. 319; vol. 6, p. 42 · *Sketches of the characters of the Hon. Thomas Erskine and James Mingay ... interspersed with anecdotes and professional strictures* (1794) · *Annual Register* (1795), 273–83 · T. Erskine, 'An oration delivered at Cambridge by the Honourable Thomas Erskine, on his taking the degree of Bachelor of Arts', *The Templar, or, Monthly Register of Legal and Constitutional Knowledge*, 1 (1788), 94–105 · W. C. Townsend, *The lives of twelve eminent judges of the last and of the present century*, 2 vols. (1846) · [T. Erskine], *The trial of Lieutenant Charles Bourne, upon the* prosecution of Sir James Wallace, Knt., for an assault (1783) • H. R. Vassall, Lord Holland, *Memoirs of the whig party during my time*, ed. H. E. Vassall, Lord Holland, 2 vols. (1852–4) • *Memoirs, journal and correspondence of Thomas Moore*, ed. J. Russell, 8 vols. (1853–6), vols. 4, 6–7 • *The works of Samuel Parr, LL.D prebendary of St Paul's, curate of Hatton, &c. with memoirs of his life and writings, and a selection from his correspondence*, ed. J. Johnstone, 8 vols. (1828) • *The speech of the Hon. Thomas Erskine, at a meeting of the Friends to the Liberty of the Press, at Free-Mason's Tavern, Dec. 22, 1792, with the resolutions, &c. of that truly patriotic society* (1792) • *Proceedings of the Friends to the Abuse of the Liberty of the Press; on December, the 22nd, 1792. And January 19th, and March 9th, 1793* (1793) • *Declaration of the Friends of the Liberty of the Press; assembled at the Crown and Anchor Tavern, Saturday, January 19, 1793. Written by the Hon. Thomas Erskine; to which is added the other proceedings of the day*, 2nd edn (1793) • *The celebrated speech of the Hon. T. Erskine, in support of the liberty of the press. Delivered at Guildhall, December 18, 1792* (1793) • Holdsworth, *Eng. law*, vol. 13 • S. Rogers, *Recollections*, ed. W. Sharpe (1859), 163–8 • L. G. Mitchell, *Charles James Fox* (1992) • J. A. Lovat-Fraser, *Erskine* (1932) • ER, 33.273–8, 102.927–30 • P. C. Scarlett, *A memoir of the Right Honourable James, first Lord Abinger* (1877) • *The diaries and correspondence of the Right Hon. George Rose*, ed. L. V. V. Harcourt, 2 vols. (1860) • R. Rush, *Residence at the court of London*, ed. B. Rush, 3rd edn (1872) • G. Pellew, *The life and correspondence of … Henry Addington, first Viscount Sidmouth*, 3 vols. (1847) • T. Somerville, *My own life and times, 1741–1814* (1861) • J. B. Trotter, *Memoirs of the latter years of the Right Honourable Charles James Fox* (1811) • *A sketch of the character of the late Lord Erskine* (1823) • J. Boswell, *The life of Samuel Johnson*, new edn, 2 vols. (1906) • BL, Add. MSS 39873, fols. 57–64; 49174, fols. 27–406, esp. 53; 58965, fols. 85–181v; 52451B, fols. 42, 52; 52452, fols. 15, 36; 49500, fol. 185; 49503, fols. 110–18; 49505, fols. 117, 144

Archives Bodl. Oxf., notes and verses • U. Edin. L., corresp. and papers relating to legitimization of his children | BL, Add. MSS 29196, 29475, 35154, 35648, 35649, 36456, 37310, 37416, 37884, 37885, 38275, 39873, 39898, 44992, 45880, 47568, 49173A, 49174, 49500, 49503, 49505, 52451B, 52452, 53804, 53805, 58772, 72844; Egerton MSS 2137, 3260 • BL, letters to Lord Grenville, Add. MS 58965 • BL, corresp. with Lord Holland and Lady Holland, Add. MS 51533 • NRA, priv. coll., letters to earl of Buchan • U. Durham L., letters to second Earl Grey

Likenesses J. Walker, mezzotint, pubd 1783 (after L. Abbott), BM • J. Reynolds, oils, exh. RA 1786, Royal Collection • T. Lawrence, oils, 1802, Lincoln's Inn, London [*see illus.*] • G. Clint, mezzotint, pubd 1803 (after T. Erskine), BM, NPG • J. Nollekens, marble bust, 1815, Royal Collection • R. Westmacott, marble statue, 1830, Lincoln's Inn, London • G. Hayter, group portrait, oils (*The trial of Queen Caroline, 1820*), NPG • K. A. Hickel, group portrait, oils (*The House of Commons, 1793*), NPG • W. C. Ross, oils, NPG • prints, BM

Wealth at death see will, PRO, PROB 11/1680, fols. 130v–131r

Erskine, Thomas (1788–1864), judge, was born on 12 March 1788 at 10 Serjeants' Inn, Fleet Street, London, the fourth son of Thomas *Erskine, first Baron Erskine (1750–1823), and his first wife, Frances (*d.* 1805), daughter of Daniel Moore. He was brought up in Hampstead, where he attended the local grammar school and Mr Foothead's school. He was then sent to Harrow School, where he was taught by doctors Drury and Butler and his schoolfellows included Peel, Aberdeen, Palmerston, Byron, and Hook. Erskine was still a schoolboy when his father became lord chancellor and made his son his secretary of presentation. He matriculated at Trinity College, Cambridge, and being a peer's son, graduated MA without residence or examination in 1811, on the inauguration of the duke of Gloucester as chancellor. In 1807 he entered Lincoln's Inn, and was one of Joseph Chitty's pupils. He became a special pleader in 1810, and practised with success. He was called to the

bar in 1813, and first joined the home circuit but transferred to the western circuit. In 1814 he married Henrietta Eliza, daughter of Henry Trail of Darsie, Fife; they had a large number of children, but only four survived their father.

In 1818 Erskine stood unsuccessfully for parliament as the whig candidate for Lewes. He became king's counsel in 1827, and took a leading place on the western circuit. He was thought by contemporaries to be more exact in his approach to the law than his father, and less flowery in his judgments. When the Bankruptcy Act of 1831 established a court of review of four judges, Erskine was appointed as the chief judge by Lord Brougham (20 October 1831). He was also sworn of the privy council. He was appointed judge of the common pleas on 9 January 1839 in succession to Alan Park on the latter's death, and held this post in conjunction with that of bankruptcy judge until November 1842. As judge of common pleas he presided over the political trials at the spring assizes at York in 1840. His fairness was widely praised even by the *Northern Star*, Feargus O'Connor's paper. He also served as a commissioner for the duchy of Cornwall, and was president of the Trinitarian Bible Society in 1840.

Erskine fell ill with pulmonary tuberculosis and resigned his judgeship in November 1844, but lived for another twenty years, mostly as an invalid. He lived for a time at Little Green, Sussex, but from 1852 normally resided at Fir Grove, Eversley, Hampshire, where he was a close friend of the rector, Charles Kingsley. He died at Bournemouth on 9 November 1864.

J. A. HAMILTON, *rev.* HUGH MOONEY

Sources E. Foss, *Biographia juridica: a biographical dictionary of the judges of England … 1066–1870* (1870) • J. Arnould, *Memoir of Thomas, first Lord Denman*, 2 vols. (1873) • *The life and works of Charles Kingsley*, 19 vols. (1901–3) • D. Lettsom, *Recollections of Dr Rush* (1815) • *CGPLA Eng. & Wales* (1864)

Archives NL Scot., letters to Thomas Carlyle • NL Scot., letters to David Dundas • NL Scot., corresp., incl. Lord Rutherford • NL Scot., letters to Mrs Schwabe • U. Edin., New Coll. L., letters to Thomas Chalmers

Likenesses D. Wilkie, group portrait, oils (*The first council of Queen Victoria, 1837*), Royal Collection

Wealth at death under £25,000: probate, 12 Dec 1864, *CGPLA Eng. & Wales*

Erskine, Thomas, of Linlathen (1788–1870), theologian and advocate, was born in Edinburgh on 13 October 1788, the fifth of seven children born to David Erskine, laird of Linlathen, writer to the signet, who died in Naples on 5 April 1791, and Ann Graham (*d.* 1836). Descended from John Erskine, earl of Mar (*d.* 1572), regent of Scotland and counsellor to James VI, Erskine's great-grandfather was John Erskine of Carnock (1661?–1743), the so-called 'black colonel', who had been instrumental in bringing William and Mary from The Hague in the revolution of 1688 but who remained a staunch covenanter and an enemy to the union. His grandfather was John Erskine of Carnock (1695–1768), professor of municipal law at Edinburgh and author of *The Institutes of the Law of Scotland*. His uncle was Dr John Erskine (1721?–1803), minister of Greyfriars, Edinburgh, and leader of the evangelicals in the general

Thomas Erskine of Linlathen (1788–1870), attrib. Charles Baillod

assembly of the Church of Scotland. Erskine spent much of his childhood in the care of his maternal grandmother, Mrs Graham, one of the Stirlings of Ardoch and a Jacobite who held an Episcopalian service in Airth Castle each Sunday and steadfastly refused to pray for King George. The marriage of strong but divergent political and religious sympathies in his upbringing may account for Erskine's own inability in adulthood to settle comfortably within any established religious and theological tradition, and it doubtless contributed to his notorious eirenic and eclectic spirit.

Early life: laird of Linlathen Erskine was educated at Edinburgh high school and a school in Durham before training for the Scottish bar at Edinburgh University. He passed as an advocate in 1810 and practised in the national capital for some years until, with the early death without issue of his elder brother James (b. 1787) in 1816, he inherited the family estate at Linlathen in Forfarshire. At the age of twenty-eight Erskine relinquished his legal profession and moved to the country with his mother and sisters Christian (1789–1866) and David (1791–1867). For the remainder of his life (apart from some lengthy spells on the continent—notably Germany, Switzerland, and Rome—and some summers on the west coast of Scotland) it was his general pattern of life to spend the spring and summer months at Linlathen and much of the winter in Edinburgh. He had considerable responsibilities as laird of the estate and took these very seriously even during his regular absences. His concern for both the material and spiritual well-being of servants and other dependants was well known, and he became a benefactor of many worthy causes both personal and public in the neighbourhoods of

Monifieth and Broughty Ferry. He took a particular interest in education, endowing the establishment of new schools at Linlathen and in Monifieth, and subscribing £150 in 1857 to the funds for furnishing extra accommodation at Dundee high school for the school of art and the department of modern languages.

While he assumed the role of local laird with grace and enthusiasm, the scope of Erskine's reading and thought stretched far beyond the immediate horizons of his situation. His education furnished him with a firm grounding in the classics, and he was in the habit of reading widely in literature, philosophy, and theology, keeping abreast of developments on the continent and beyond. He would read a portion of the New Testament in Greek each morning, and while still at the bar had already begun to reflect and write on issues of Christian theology and practice, a habit which his new circumstance granted him ample time to indulge and develop. Several extended visits to the continent, a tireless correspondence, and a regular string of notable visitors to his home served to make this laird of a small Scottish estate a highly respected cosmopolitan figure among the educated and literary classes of Britain and Europe. Among the best-known of those who became his friends and correspondents were Madame de Broglie, Thomas Carlyle, Thomas Chalmers, John McLeod Campbell, Charles Kingsley, F. D. Maurice, Adolphus Monod, Prévost-Paradol, A. J. Scott, J. C. Shairp, Dean Stanley, John Tulloch, and Alexandre Vinet.

Theological developments, writings, and connections Erskine is best-known for a string of books written mostly between his thirtieth and fiftieth years. In addition to the potent mixture of Calvinistic preaching and prayer-book liturgy familiar from his youth, and his own close study of the Christian scriptures, Erskine's theological development was shaped by some of his closest acquaintances. One was Thomas *Chalmers.

Erskine first met Chalmers (then minister of Tron Church in Glasgow) in 1818. They became firm friends and regular correspondents, and it was in dialogue with Chalmers that Erskine cut his theological teeth and began to venture his own ideas in a developed form on paper. The first result was the appearance of *Remarks on the Internal Evidence for the Truth of Revealed Religion* in 1820. In this slim volume Erskine developed themes which were to remain characteristic of his teaching to the last. His particular insistence that the spiritual and ethical core of religion cannot be divorced from the objective focus of the doctrines of incarnation and atonement commended itself to many Christian readers in a generation where the more familiar alternatives were either an arid, orthodox dogmatism or a fervent piety cut loose from any doctrinal moorings. The book eventually ran to nine editions and was translated into both French and German. In North America it influenced some of those who, in the 1830s, provoked a disruption in the Presbyterian church in New England, resulting in the clear emergence of distinct 'old' and 'new' theological schools of thought. *An Essay on Faith* appeared in 1822 and pursued similar themes, responding to an emergent theological 'turn to the subject' by insisting that it is with the object of belief and not the nature or structure of the mental act of believing that theology is properly concerned. This book, too, was published in several editions and translated into French.

These earliest writings were warmly received in Erskine's native Scotland as well as abroad. In truth, though, they contained the seeds of developments which would bring his thought into sharp conflict with the official doctrines endorsed and insisted upon by the Church of Scotland to which he formally belonged. Indeed, had he been an ordained rather than a lay member of that church it is likely that sooner or later he would have been called to account for his views and perhaps even deposed from office, a fate which awaited his contemporaries John McLeod Campbell and Edward Irving. The developments in question were already clearly apparent in Erskine's next book, *On the Unconditional Freeness of the Gospel* (1828), which, as its title suggests, insists that salvation is unconditionally free and rooted in a universal forgiving love and atoning work of God for all people alike. Such claims, though they had already been championed in Scotland in the so-called 'Marrow controversy' of 1720, departed significantly from the general tenor of the Westminster confession of faith (which was and remains at the close of the twentieth century the chief subordinate doctrinal standard of the Church of Scotland) and conflicted directly with the ascendant interpretation of it in the so-called federal theology of popular Calvinistic orthodoxy. Erskine cared little for such 'orthodoxies', being confident that the teaching of the Christian scriptures was on his side. There was, though, a personal if not a professional cost to be paid for his open advocacy of such views. Dr Russell, minister of the Ward Chapel Independent congregation of which Erskine, together with his mother and sister, had become a member, visited Linlathen and indicated that, given his public owning of 'heterodox' ideas, it would be best for Erskine to part with the congregation.

About this same time Erskine met a kindred spirit whose teaching and eventual treatment by the church did much to reinforce and further shape his (Erskine's) views. John McLeod Campbell was the young minister of Row (Rhu) near Helensburgh. The views for which, just a few years later, he would be tried and deposed from the ministry of the Church of Scotland were remarkably similar to Erskine's own as expressed in the 1828 book. The supposition of any direct formative influence of either person upon the basic shape of the other's views is, however, difficult to sustain. Campbell's views were formed largely by his early pastoral experiences in Row from 1825 onwards; there is no evidence that he had read Erskine's book prior to forming them (though the possibility that he was familiar with their germinal version in Erskine's earlier writings cannot be excluded). For his part, as already stated, Erskine met Campbell only after his own thoughts on the relevant issues were already developed and committed to print. Encountering him for the first time in Edinburgh where the younger man happened to be preaching, Erskine is recorded as having remarked: 'I have heard today from that pulpit what I believe to be the true gospel', so consonant with his own were the ideas articulated. For the next several summers Erskine lodged at the Gareloch in order to benefit directly from Campbell's preaching and the two became close friends. When Campbell was dragged through the ecclesiastical courts in 1831 Erskine attended several of the meetings and lent him considerable moral support.

Meanwhile Erskine's own views continued to develop. The publication of *The Brazen Serpent* in 1831 and the somewhat prolix and academic *Doctrine of Election* in 1837 saw a significant bolstering of the biblical warrant for a theology whose basic shape had already emerged but which now trespassed into affirmations more identifiably at odds with the orthodox mainstream. The most obvious example of this is Erskine's unashamed universalism—the claim that God will finally redeem all people—though here too he sought to argue for his views through a close appeal to the biblical text and other key Christian doctrines such as incarnation, trinity, and atonement. He was notoriously willing to spend long hours at Linlathen carefully hearing the objections of others to his ideas and answering them. In the last three decades of his long life Erskine published nothing, dedicating his time instead to a more direct and dialogical mode of engagement with others. He pursued this both through a constant correspondence and by entertaining guests at Linlathen. Although his writings merit far more careful attention than they have received as part of the history of theology in Britain, it is probable that it was through these carefully nurtured personal contacts that Erskine had the most influence during his lifetime, shaping the understanding and imagination of a generation of significant figures in public life. His published letters offer a fascinating overview of his contribution in this regard. In his last years he sought to clarify some of his more mature perspectives in a series of essays. These were published posthumously in 1871 as *The Spiritual Order and other Papers*.

Erskine's theology in brief: his death and reputation While no public record of Erskine's baptism has been discovered, it is probable that it was within the Presbyterian tradition of his father's family. His religious formation also owed much to the Episcopalianism of his grandmother, and in adult life he often availed himself of Episcopalian ministry and was in the habit of using the offices of the prayer book for his own private daily devotions. Erskine's religious allegiances, however, were essentially eclectic and more concerned with the pursuit of truth as and where he perceived it than with subscribing or submitting to any tradition. When he died in Edinburgh on Sunday 20 March 1870 his body was taken to Linlathen where, on 28 March, a funeral service according to the rite of 'the English Church' was conducted in the library. He was duly buried in the family plot in the Church of Scotland churchyard in Monifieth.

All contemporary records testify that those who knew Thomas Erskine were impressed above all not by his erudition and intellectual gifts, though these were considerable, but by the generosity and holiness which, woven together in his character and actions, made him a living embodiment of the gospel to the service of which his life was dedicated. TREVOR A. HART

Sources W. Hanna, ed., *Letters of Thomas Erskine of Linlathen*, 3rd edn (1878) · *Dundee Advertiser* (25 March 1870) · *The Scotsman* (31 March 1870) · H. F. Henderson, *Erskine of Linlathen: selections and biography* (1899) · 'Some letters of Thomas Erskine of Linlathen', *Present-day papers*, ed. A. C. Ewing (1870) · 'Some further letters of Thomas Erskine of Linlathen', *Present-day papers*, ed. A. C. Ewing (1871) · T. A. Hart, *Thomas Erskine* (1993) · A. J. Warden, *Angus or Forfarshire: the land and people*, 5 vols. (1880–85), vol. 4 · W. Anderson, *The Scottish nation*, 2 (1869)
Archives NL Scot., corresp. | NL Scot., letters to Thomas Carlyle, MSS 602, 605, 665, 666 · NL Scot., letters to David Dundas, Acc 10719/30 · NL Scot., letters to Mrs Schwabe, MS 9747 · U. Edin., New Coll. L., letters to Thomas Chalmers, CMA4
Likenesses J. Partridge, oils, *c.*1847, repro. in Henderson, *Erskine of Linlathen*; priv. coll. · attrib. C. Baillod, drawing, Scot. NPG [*see illus.*] · F. Holl, stipple (after G. Richmond), BM, NPG

Erskine, Thomas Alexander, sixth earl of Kellie [Kelly] (1731–1781), composer, was born on 1 September 1731 at Kellie Castle, Fife, the eldest of the six children of Alexander Erskine, fifth earl of Kellie (*d.* 1756), landowner, and his second wife, Janet (*d.* 1775), daughter of the Jacobite doctor and poet Archibald Pitcairn. Thomas, who was styled Lord Pittenweem between 1739 and 1756, had violin lessons as a boy, probably from his father's chaplain, and became known locally as Fiddler Tam. He attended Edinburgh high school for two years but left in 1745 when his father was imprisoned for supporting the Jacobite rising (no indictment was made against the fifth earl, and the family retained its property). He was a performing member of the Edinburgh Musical Society by 1750. About 1753 he went on a continental grand tour and spent much of his time in Mannheim, where he studied the violin with Johann Stamitz, an innovative composer and orchestral director.

On the death of his father in 1756 Kellie (or Kelly, as he was usually called) returned to Scotland. He never married, and had little interest in the duties of landownership: in 1769 he sold all his family estates except for Kellie Castle itself. Instead, he lived a sociable, musical life in Edinburgh and London, with occasional trips to the continent. A prominent member of Edinburgh society, Kellie belonged to a drinking society called the Capillaire Club and to the Catch Club; he was a leading member of the grand lodge of freemasons of Scotland and also at the lodge 'Nine Masons' in England. He became an honorary member of the Highland Society of London in 1780. Many anecdotes tell of his heavy drinking, coarse sense of humour, and puns. His face was round and red, prompting the actor Samuel Foote to suggest that sight of Kellie's face would ripen peaches (or cucumbers, in some versions). Kellie became a director of the Edinburgh Musical Society in 1757 and deputy governor in 1767, placing him at the head of the society during its most influential period.

As a composer Kellie has been described as 'arguably Scotland's greatest classical composer' (*New Grove*). He was widely credited with bringing the Mannheim style to Britain. Between 1761 and 1770 Robert Bremner published at least ten of his symphonies, also called overtures, and

including the overture to *The Maid of the Mill* (1765); these were frequently heard in Edinburgh and London, but were eventually superseded by those of Haydn in the 1780s. He also composed songs, at least twenty-four minuets, and some chamber works; very little of his music survives, although a collection of his chamber music, known as the Kilravock partbooks (in private hands) was discovered in 1971. Sir John Hawkins disapproved of the 'tumid extravaganzas of Lord *Kelly*, *Stamitz* and *Richter*' (Hawkins, iv), whereas Thomas Robertson called him 'the greatest secular Musician in his line' in Britain; 'elegance is mingled with fire', he continued, and 'loudness, rapidity, enthusiasm, announce the Earl of Kelly' (Robertson, 436–7). Charles Burney likewise considered that Kellie was 'possessed of more musical science than any dilettante with whom I was ever acquainted' (Burney, 4.1018).

Kellie died on 9 October 1781 in Brussels, on his way home from taking a cure in Europe; he had a stroke and was 'seized with a putrid fever' (Roscoe, 16). On 21 December 1781 the Edinburgh Musical Society gave a funeral concert in his honour. He was succeeded as seventh earl by his brother Archibald. JANE GIRDHAM

Sources J. Purser, *Scotland's music: a history of the traditional and classical music of Scotland from earliest times to the present day* (1992) · D. Johnson, *Music and society in lowland Scotland in the eighteenth century* (1972) · D. Johnson, *Scottish fiddle music in the 18th century: a music collection and historical study* (1984) · J. Burchell, *Polite or commercial concerts? Concert management and orchestral repertoire in Edinburgh, Bath, Oxford, Manchester, and Newcastle, 1730–1799* (1996) · *New Grove* · T. Robertson, *An inquiry into the fine arts* (1784) · W. Cooke, *Memoirs of Samuel Foote*, 3 vols. (1805), vol. 2 · P. C. Roscoe, 'Thomas Alexander Erskine: a biographical note', *MT*, 92 (1951), 14–17 · *GM*, 1st ser., 51 (1781), 492 · *Scots Magazine*, 43 (1781), 557 · H. G. Farmer, *A history of music in Scotland* (1947) · J. Hawkins, 'Memoirs of Dr William Boyce', in W. Boyce, *Cathedral music*, 2nd edn, 1 (1788), i–xi · *GEC, Peerage* · Burney, *Hist. mus.* · *Freemason's Magazine* (Feb 1796) · private information (2004) [Claire Nelson, private correspondence] · *Scots peerage*, 5.89
Likenesses R. Blyth, line engraving, pubd 1782 (after R. Home), NPG; repro. in Johnson, *Music and society* · R. Home, oils, Lincoln's Inn, London · R. Home, oils, Scot. NPG

Erskine, William (*d.* 1685), headmaster, was the seventh and youngest son of John *Erskine, second or eighteenth earl of Mar (*c.*1562–1634), and his second wife, Lady Mary Stuart (*d.* 1644), second daughter of Esmé, duke of Lennox; his parents had married in 1592. Nothing is known of his early life or education. Erskine became a member of the Philosophical Society on 11 September 1661 and, on 22 April 1663, an original fellow of the Royal Society, although he was apparently active only in its early days. On 29 December 1677 he was elected master of Charterhouse, which office he held until his death. John Evelyn judged him 'wise & learned' and 'fitter to have ben a Privy Councelor & Minister of state than laied aside' (Evelyn, 4.262). In fact Erskine's only official appointment was as cupbearer at court. He died at Charterhouse on 29 May 1685. ALSAGER VIAN, *rev.* C. S. KNIGHTON

Sources R. Douglas, *The peerage of Scotland*, 2nd edn, ed. J. P. Wood, 2 (1813), 216 · *Scots peerage*, 5.622 · [R. Smythe], *Historical account of Charter-House* (1808), 238 · Evelyn, *Diary*, 4.262 · *GEC, Peerage* · M. Hunter, *The Royal Society and its fellows, 1660–1700: the morphology of an early scientific institution*, 2nd edn (1994)

Erskine, William, Lord Kinneder (*bap.* **1768**, *d.* **1822**), judge, was baptized on 29 August 1768 at Muthill, Perthshire; he was the son of William Erskine (*d.* 1783), episcopal clergyman at Muthill, and his wife, Helen, *née* Drummond. He was educated at Glasgow University, boarding with the Episcopalian clergyman and author Andrew Macdonald, who influenced him in his development of a passion for English literature in all its forms, and especially its antique forms. Erskine became an advocate in July 1790, and while practising in court soon became a close friend of Walter *Scott, also a young lawyer, who celebrated their youth in a charming poetic epistle. J. G. Lockhart described Erskine as 'the chief literary confidant and counsellor in Scott's prime of manhood' (Lockhart, 1.85).

In this capacity Erskine was instrumental in finding a publisher for *The Chase and William and Helen* (1796), Scott's translation from Gottfried Bürger's German work, and he also induced Monk Lewis to include some ballads of his in *Tales of Terror*, which appeared under a Kelso imprint in 1799. Erskine is now largely remembered for the help he gave Scott in checking topographical and historical details in the latter's amazingly successful series of long, quarto-sized, poems, starting with *The Lay of the Last Minstrel* (1805) and terminating with *The Bridal of Triermain* (1813).

At that time it was considered below the dignity of any professional man to indulge in writing novels, so Scott conspired with Erskine and James and Alexander Ballantyne to market his first fictional prose work anonymously. *Waverley, or, 'Tis Sixty Years Since* appeared in three volumes (1814) and was the forerunner of at least twenty further titles, the manuscripts being carefully copied by Alexander Ballantyne so that the typesetters would not recognize Scott's handwriting, all having been first vetted for historical accuracy by Erskine before being passed to James Ballantyne's printing house.

On 13 September 1800 Erskine married Euphimia (*d.* 1819), daughter of John *Robison (1739–1805), the natural philosopher, and his wife, Rachel. They had two daughters and a son, William, who died in 1811. Erskine was advocate-depute from 1806 to 1809, and was sheriff-depute of Orkney from 1809 until 1822. He played an important part in the organization of Scott's visit to Orkney in 1814, and later advised on details for *The Pirate*. In January 1822, partly as a result of Scott's influence, he was appointed a judge, with the title Lord Kinneder (the spelling of his title varies: Kinneder is the more usual, but he used Kinedder on his bookplate, and that is also Lockhart's spelling; Kinnedder is also found). But within a few weeks of becoming a judge, Erskine, whose wife had died in 1819, was allegedly involved in a sex scandal with a well-known Edinburgh prostitute, Mrs Burt, a charge described by Scott as absolutely groundless and 'a truthless assertion that would have done honour to the invention of the devil himself' (*Letters*, 8.222). Nevertheless, the charge caused Lord Kinneder such distress that he suffered a nervous breakdown, which finally caused pneumonia, from which he died on 14 August 1822. 'If ever a

pure spirit quitted this vale of tears', wrote Sir Walter to a friend, 'it was William Erskine's'. After his death Scott tried to organize a government pension for his family.

ERIC QUAYLE

Sources DNB · *The letters of Sir Walter Scott*, ed. H. J. C. Grierson and others, centenary edn, 12 vols. (1932–79) · *The journal of Sir Walter Scott*, 2 vols. (1890–91) · E. Quayle, *Ballantyne the brave: a Victorian writer and his family* (1967) · J. G. Lockhart, *The life of Sir Walter Scott*, [new edn], 10 vols. (1902) · *IGI*
Archives NL Scot., corresp. with Lord Melville · NL Scot., corresp. with Sir Walter Scott
Likenesses W. Nicholson, watercolour drawing, Scot. NPG

Erskine, Sir William, second baronet (**1770–1813**), army officer, born on 30 March 1770, was the eldest son of Lieutenant-General Sir William Erskine, of Torrie, Fife, first baronet (*d.* 1795), and his second wife, Frances, daughter of James Moray of Abercairney, Perthshire, and widow of George Drummond of Blair Drummond, Perthshire. The younger William's grandfather was Colonel the Hon. William Erskine, deputy governor of Blackness Castle, Linlithgowshire, and elder son of David Erskine, second Lord Cardross. He entered the army as a second lieutenant in the 23rd foot in September 1785 and was promoted lieutenant of the 5th dragoons on 14 November 1787 and captain of the 15th King's light dragoons on 23 February 1791. He first saw service in the campaigns of the duke of York in Flanders in 1793–5 as aide-de-camp to his father. He was appointed to command the British cavalry destined for the continent, in May 1793, and was promoted lieutenant-colonel on 14 December 1794. On 26 February 1796 he exchanged commissions with his brother James Erskine, of the 133rd (Fraser's) foot, and was placed on half pay.

On 19 March 1795 Erskine succeeded his father as second baronet. After his return to England he was in 1796 elected, unopposed and replacing his brother-in-law, MP for the county of Fife (which in 1790 had 188 voters) and supported Pitt's administration. He was promoted colonel on 1 January 1801, was re-elected MP in 1802, and supported Addington's and Pitt's administrations and spoke on defence issues. On 9 June 1803 he was appointed to the 14th (Erskine's) garrison battalion and in 1805 again placed on half pay on the reduction of his battalion. He did not again stand for parliament in 1806, and applied repeatedly for active employment.

Erskine was promoted major-general on 25 April 1808. He was selected for the Peninsula by Sir David Dundas, who had formed a high opinion of him during his service in Germany, though he was already showing signs of mental disorder. In 1809 he joined the duke of Wellington's army in the Peninsula. Lieutenant-Colonel Henry Torrens, military secretary at the Horse Guards, wrote: 'No doubt he is sometimes a little mad, but in his lucid intervals he is an uncommonly clever fellow; and I trust he may have no fit during the campaign, though he looked a little wild before he embarked' (Fortescue, *Brit. army*, 7.419). Wellington wrote to Torrens that Erskine 'I have generally understood to be a madman' (Maxwell, 1.207). Erskine was poor-sighted—'blind as a beetle' (Longford, 217), according to a fellow officer—a drunkard, and incompetent. Wellington tried to get rid of him but failed: Erskine had influence at the Horse Guards. He took command of a brigade of cavalry, and when Major-General Robert Craufurd went home invalided from the lines of the Torres Vedras, Erskine had temporary command of the light division, most unfortunately. He was brave, but his recklessness during the pursuit after Maréchal Masséna in the spring of 1811 nearly ruined the light division on more than one occasion. In particular, at Sabugal, on 3 April 1811, he launched his battalions at the retreating enemy in a fog, and it was only through the skill of his brigadiers, Andrew Barnard and Thomas Beckwith, that a disaster was averted; for when the fog lifted Maréchal Ney was found with his whole *corps d'armée* in a very strong position. After the battle Erskine, already unpopular with the light division and the cavalry, was much criticized by members of both. Later in April his carelessness enabled a convoy to enter the fortress of Ciudad Rodrigo. When Craufurd returned, on 4 May 1811, Erskine was transferred to the command of the cavalry attached to the southern force under the command of Sir Rowland Hill, in succession to General Long. In May, largely due to Erskine's bungling, General Brennier's force was enabled to escape from Almeida: the army at large, which hated Erskine, blamed him. Wellington was furious at 'the most disgraceful military event that has yet occurred to us' (Longford, 254).

Erskine was selected with Thomas Picton, James Leith, and Lowry Cole for the rank of local lieutenant-general in Spain and Portugal in September 1811. He commanded Hill's cavalry in his advance on Madrid in 1812 after the victory of Salamanca, and he covered his retreat when he had to retire from Andalusia, coincidently with Wellington's retreat from Burgos. He had already shown signs of insanity during this period, and at last it became so obvious that he was ordered to leave the army, and Wellington wanted him sent home. On 13 February 1813, at Brozas, Spain, he was in bed with fever, and then threw himself from a window 'in a fit of delirium' (*GM*, 595) and died. He was unmarried, and his baronetcy of Torrie passed in succession to his brothers James and John, and on the latter's death became extinct. Historians have echoed contemporaries' criticism of Erskine; Lady Longford called him 'preposterous' (Longford, 254) and 'ludicrous' (ibid., 256).

H. M. STEPHENS, rev. ROGER T. STEARN

Sources *GM*, 1st ser., 83/1 (1813) • R. G. Thorne, 'Erskine, Sir William', HoP, *Commons* • J. Burke and J. B. Burke, *A genealogical and heraldic history of the extinct and dormant baronetcies of England, Ireland and Scotland*, 2nd edn (1841); repr. (1844) • *Army List* • W. Cope, *The history of the rifle brigade* (1877) • W. F. P. Napier, *History of the war in the Peninsula and in the south of France*, 6 vols. (1828–40) • *The private journal of F. Seymour Larpent, judge-advocate general*, ed. G. Larpent, 2nd edn, 2 vols. (1853) • H. E. Maxwell, *The life of Wellington: the restoration of the martial power of Great Britain*, 1 (1899) • Fortescue, *Brit. army*, vols. 7–9 • E. Longford [E. H. Pakenham, countess of Longford], *Wellington*, 1: *The years of the sword* (1969) • A. J. Guy, ed., *The road to Waterloo: the British army and the struggle against revolutionary and Napoleonic France, 1793–1815* (1990) • R. Muir, *Britain and the defeat of Napoleon, 1807–1815* (1996) • GEC, *Baronetage* • W. Stephen, *History of Inverkeithing and Rosyth* (1921), 83–4 • C. W. C. Oman, *Wellington's army, 1809–1814* (1912), 151

Archives NL Scot., letters to Sir John Halkett

Likenesses R. Cosway, oils, *c*.1810, Royal Collection

Erskine, William (1773–1852), historian of India, was born in Edinburgh on 8 November 1773, the seventh child of David Erskine (*d*. 1791), son of John *Erskine (1695–1768) and writer to the signet, and his wife Jean Melvin (*d*. 1780). Thomas *Erskine (1788–1870) was his half-brother. William was educated at the Royal High School and at Edinburgh University (*c*.1788–1792), where he forged friendships with many of Edinburgh's other ambitiously hopeful young intellectuals, including the poets John Leyden and Thomas Campbell (1777–1844).

Erskine's plans to study medicine were overruled by the family's trustees who, in 1792, apprenticed him to James Dundas, writer to the signet. He stayed with Dundas until 1799, all the while hankering after a job which would give him the income and leisure to pursue intellectual fame. It was in these years, before the appearance of Thomas Campbell's *Pleasures of Hopes* (1799), that Erskine counselled the rising poet against suicide, although his own spirits rose little above despair at the time. In 1798 he published a long poem of his own, *An Epistle from Lady Grange to Edward D—* (2nd edn, 1799), a meditation on the plight of Rachel Erskine, estranged wife of James Erskine, Lord Grange, who had spent her final years confined on the island of St Kilda.

In 1799 Erskine accepted a position as factor to Mr Hay of Drummetzie at Duns, but again his salary and prospects were poor, and in 1803 he leapt at an offer from Sir James Mackintosh, newly appointed recorder of Bombay, to accompany him to India. He already had an elder brother, David, in private trade in India, and Mackintosh, who regarded him as 'one of the most amiable, ingenious, and accurately informed men in the world' (*Memoirs of … Sir James Mackintosh*, 1.331), had promised him the first appointment in his power. He arrived in Bombay in May 1804 and with Mackintosh helped found the Literary Society of Bombay, forerunner of the Bombay branch of the Royal Asiatic Society. In 1808 he was appointed clerk to the small cause court and thereafter a stipendiary magistrate.

On 27 September 1809 Erskine married Mackintosh's second daughter, Maitland (*d*. 1861). They had fourteen children, at least six of whom were born and—against the odds—thrived in India. He was fond of his wife and was a devoted, if somewhat intellectually taxing, father, but the burden of providing for his numerous offspring wore down his spirits and ate into his intellectual confidence. In 1811 the death of his friend Leyden, who had established a reputation as an oriental philologist in a very short time, spurred Erskine to devote himself to oriental studies. He began anew to teach himself Persian and returned to translations he had earlier made of the memoirs of Babur, the first Mughal emperor. Between 1813 and 1821 he also contributed five articles to the *Transactions* of the Literary Society of Bombay, including, in 1813, 'Account of the cave-temple of Elephanta'. In 1820 he was appointed master in equity in the recorder's court of Bombay and, under the admiring patronage of the governor, Mountstuart

Elphinstone, was one of the committee of three which drew up the Bombay code of regulations. In 1823, however, disaster struck when he was accused of embezzling court funds and was sacked. The extent of his guilt remains unclear, but at the very least he had paid insufficient attention to his duties. Consumed by wretchedness, he returned with his family to Edinburgh.

In 1826 Erskine finally published the *Memoirs of Babar*, a combination of his own translation from a Persian version of the *Babur nama* and Leyden's unfinished translation from the Eastern Turkish original. The book was well reviewed but in 1827, still uncomfortable with his Indian disgrace, Erskine shifted his family to Pau, France, where he absorbed himself in insatiable reading. In 1831 he returned to Scotland, to Blackburn House in Linlithgowshire, and began formulating plans for a history of India's Mughal emperors based on original Persian sources. This mammoth task was to occupy him, on and off, for the rest of his life, in between writing articles for the *Edinburgh Review* and completing Sir John Malcolm's *Life of Clive* (1836). In 1836 he became provost of St Andrews, but he resigned after only a year and in 1840 moved everyone again to a cheaper residence in Edinburgh, and thereafter in 1844 to Bonn, before finally returning to Edinburgh for good in 1848. By the summer of 1847 his eyesight had begun to fail and by 1850 he was no longer able to read or edit his writings. With the extreme self-criticism that had characterized all of his labours, he laid aside his Mughal history in the belief that he had wasted his life. He died at Edinburgh on 28 May 1852 and was buried in the churchyard of St John's Episcopal Church, Princes Street.

Erskine's reputation as a scholar stood much higher than he had imagined and his death occasioned warm obituaries in the principal oriental journals. In 1854 his son Claudius James [*see below*] published in two volumes Erskine's *History of India under the two first sovereigns of the house of Taimur, Baber, and Humayun*, a reprint of which was issued in 1974 with an admiring introduction by Peter Hardy, firmly placing Erskine within the intellectual tradition of the French and Scottish Enlightenments. Erskine left over 400 oriental manuscripts which, along with papers Leyden had bequeathed to him, the family sold to the British Museum in 1865. Further European-language papers were presented to the museum in 1888.

Erskine's second son, **Claudius James** [Claude] **Erskine** (1821–1893), one of four brothers to enter the Indian Civil Service, was born at Bombay on 20 May 1821 and educated at St Andrews University, Edinburgh University, and East India College, Haileybury. He arrived in Bombay in 1840, and in 1843 was appointed private secretary to the governor, Sir George Arthur. In 1847 he married Emily Georgina, daughter of Lestock Reid, acting governor of Bombay, and in 1847, following in his father's linguistic footsteps, became oriental translator and deputy secretary in the Persian department. He was especially interested in vernacular education and in 1855, after a short term as secretary to the Bombay general and judicial departments, became the first director of public instruction in western India. Briefly, in 1859, judge of the

Konkan, in 1860 he was appointed to the legislative council of India. He became a judge of the Bombay high court in 1862 and member of the Bombay council in 1865, before ill health forced him to retire in 1867. He died at 66 Oxford Terrace, Hyde Park, London, on 6 June 1893; his wife survived him.

Another of Erskine's sons, **Henry Napier Bruce Erskine** (1831–1893), was also a distinguished member of the Indian Civil Service. He arrived at Bombay in 1853 and in 1869 was appointed collector and magistrate of Nasik. He was commissioner of the northern division of Bombay in 1877–9 and of Sind in 1879–87, in which latter year, just before his retirement, he was appointed CSI. He died suddenly at Cran Hill, Great Malvern, Worcestershire, on 4 December 1893. KATHERINE PRIOR

Sources William Erskine, diary, 1811–50, BL, Add. MS 39945 · J. Douglas, *Glimpses of old Bombay* (1900) · J. Wilson, 'Brief memorial of the literary researches of the late William Erskine, Esq.', *Journal of the Bombay Branch of the Royal Asiatic Society*, 4 (1852–3), 276–84 · P. Hardy, 'Introduction', in W. Erskine, *A history of India under the first two sovereigns of the house of Taimur, Baber, and Humayun*, 2 vols. (1974), vol. 1, pp. vii–xvii · *Memoirs of the life of the Right Honourable Sir James Mackintosh*, ed. R. J. Mackintosh, 2nd edn, 2 vols. (1836) · ecclesiastical records, BL OIOC [W. Erskine and C. J. Erskine] · *DNB* · W. M. Wood, 'Things of India' made plain, or, A journalist's retrospect (1884), 13 · *The Times* (8 June 1893), 1 · *The Times* (15 June 1893), 6 · *The Times* (7 Dec 1893), 1 · BL OIOC, Haileybury MSS [C. J. Erskine and H. N. B. Erskine] · *India Office List* (1892) [H. N. B. Erskine] · *CGPLA Eng. & Wales* (1893) [Claudius James Erskine]
Archives BL, diary and papers, Add. MSS 26603–26616, 26620–26621, 39945 · BL, papers relating to India, Add. MSS 28515–28516, 32630–32631 · BL OIOC, papers relating to India, MSS Eur. A 3–5, B 4–10, C 9–10, D 26–32, E 49–50 | BL OIOC, Elgin collection [Claudius James Erskine] · BL OIOC, Ferguson collection [Henry Napier Bruce Erskine] · NL Scot., letters to Archibald Constable · NL Scot., corresp. with John Leyden · NL Scot., letters to Robert Lundie · NL Scot., corresp. with Robert Lundie and Archibald Lundie
Likenesses oils, 1823, Royal Asiatic Society, Bombay branch
Wealth at death £1222 16s. 11d. Claudius James Erskine: probate, 5 July 1893, *CGPLA Eng. & Wales* · £48,138 6s. 3d. Henry Napier Bruce Erskine: resworn probate, June 1894, *CGPLA Eng. & Wales*

Ervine, St John Greer [*real name* John Greer Irvine] (1883–1971), playwright and novelist, was born in Ballymacarret, a working-class suburb of Belfast, on 28 December 1883, the son of William Irvine and Sarah Greer, both of whom were deaf without speech. When he was barely three his father died, and as a child he spent much of his time in the home of his maternal grandmother, with whom he formed a deep attachment. She died when he was ten and his mother had to struggle to keep him and his sister in decent frugality. He seems to have hated most of the primary schools to which he was sent in his early youth but settled down happily under a notable headmaster, Matthew McClelland, at Westbourne School in Newtownards Road, Belfast. Poverty prevented him from going on to any form of higher education and he became a clerk in a Belfast insurance office at the age of seventeen, soon finding his way to similar work in London. There he joined the Fabian Society and began to write, first for the newspapers and then for the theatre, assuming the name St John Ervine at this time.

Ervine's dramatic career can be seen as falling into three

broad areas: first, his work for the Abbey Theatre, Dublin, between 1911 and 1915; second, his London West End comedies of the 1920s; and third, his return to Ulster themes in the 1930s and 1940s. A one-act play, *The Magnanimous Lover*, brought him into contact with William Butler Yeats, and his first full-length play, *Mixed Marriage*, an exposé of Ulster sectarianism, was produced at the Abbey Theatre by Lennox Robinson in 1911. On 15 July 1911 he married a fellow Fabian, Leonora Mary Davis (1886/7–1965), the daughter of George William Davis, bookseller. Like her husband she was a member of the Fabian reform committee, in opposition to such Fabian liberals as Beatrice and Sidney Webb. In 1913 *Jane Clegg*, a powerful study of a resolutely independent woman, was performed at the Gaiety Theatre, Manchester, with Sybil Thorndike in the title role. In 1915 Ervine was appointed manager of the Abbey Theatre, though his tenure of this post was both brief and turbulent. He made no secret of his concept of the Abbey's role, choosing to see it as one of many repertory theatres in the British Isles rather than as an expression of a separate, national consciousness. A strict disciplinarian, he particularly alienated the company by his draconian insistence that it rehearse twice a day while on tour and by dismissing those players who refused to obey his orders. The actors concerned then formed a new company, the Irish Players, which was to prove a serious rival to the Abbey on the touring circuit in Britain. Much to the relief of Yeats and Lady Augusta Gregory, Ervine resigned as manager in July 1916, having held the post for less than a year. Both his temperament and his political outlook made him seem, in retrospect, a bizarre choice as manager of a national theatre. A unionist and a strong opponent of home rule, he regarded the Easter rising of 1916 as Ireland's supreme betrayal of Britain and of Western civilization. The best thing he did for the Abbey was to give the theatre his fine tragedy, *John Ferguson*, at the end of 1915.

Ervine left Dublin, joined the British army, and in 1918, serving as a lieutenant in the Royal Dublin Fusiliers, was severely wounded in action in France and had to have a leg amputated. The injury troubled him throughout his life, causing frequent pain which he bore with considerable fortitude. After the war he worked as drama critic for the *Morning Post* and *The Observer* and, in 1929, was guest drama critic for the New York *World*, a role in which he aroused considerable public reaction by his caustic comments on the state of the American theatre. His own dramatic output during the 1920s consisted mainly of drawing-room comedies for London's West End theatres, such as *Mary, Mary, quite Contrary* (1923), *Anthony and Anna* (1925), and *The First Mrs Fraser* (1929). With Dame Marie Tempest and Henry Ainley in the cast, this last play ran for more than a year.

Ervine returned to themes of Ulster in 1936 with what proved to be one of his most popular plays, *Boyd's Shop*. This had its first production at the Liverpool Playhouse on 19 February 1936, and the Abbey Theatre opened its production of the play a mere five days later. As well as plays, Ervine wrote a number of novels and some full-length

biographies, as well as a considerable quantity of reminiscential prose which deals mainly with the Belfast of his youth, his contact with other literary figures, and his developing experience of the theatre of his time. His most considerable literary biography is a substantial study of his idol, George Bernard Shaw, which he published in 1956. Five years earlier he had written a hostile study of Oscar Wilde, and, perhaps inevitably, the Ulster realist and puritan proved an incongruous biographer of the doomed Dublin wit, just as he had proved an improbable choice as manager of the Irish National Theatre years before.

A tantalizing figure, Ervine combined an international reputation with an increasingly provincial outlook and an insistence on his love for Ulster with an almost pathological hatred of the rest of Ireland. He spent nearly all his adult life in England, but he was not without honour in his own country. He was one of the first members of the Irish Academy of Letters (founded by Yeats in 1932) and was awarded an honorary DLitt. by the Queen's University, Belfast, in 1945. He was professor of dramatic literature at the Royal Society of Literature from 1933 to 1936. His last years, however, seem to have been rather lonely. His marriage had been childless, a situation which saddened him greatly. His wife died in 1965 and Honey Ditches, his home in Seaton, Devon, was sold as it was too big for him to live in by himself. Two devoted friends, Mr and Mrs Newman, looked after him, first in their own home in Sussex and later in a nursing home. St John Ervine died on 24 January 1971 at Fitzhall, Iping, near Midhurst, Sussex.

JOHN CRONIN

Sources J. Boyd, 'St John Ervine: a biographical note', *Threshold* (summer 1974), 101–15 • P. Howard, 'St John Ervine: a bibliography of his published works', *Irish Booklore* (Aug 1971), 203–9 • S. H. Bell, *The theatre in Ulster* (1972), 81–3 • J. Cronin, 'Introduction', in *Selected plays of St John Ervine*, ed. J. Cronin (1988) • J. Cronin and F.-J. French, 'A selected checklist', in *Selected plays of St John Ervine*, ed. J. Cronin (1988) • *DNB* • m. cert. • d. cert.

Archives BL, corresp. with League of Dramatists, Add. MSS 63376–63377 • Indiana University, Lilly Library, corresp. and papers • JRL, letters to the *Manchester Guardian* • Ransom HRC, corresp., MSS, and literary papers • Royal Society of Literature, London, letters to the Royal Society of Literature | BL, letters to George Bernard Shaw, Add. MS 50533 • U. Birm. L., special collections department, corresp. with Francis Brett Young • U. Leeds, Brotherton L., letters to Thomas Moult • Welwyn Garden City Library, corresp. with Frederic Osborn

Likenesses T. Spicer-Simson, plasticine medallion, c.1920–1929, NPG • E. J. Burra, group portrait, ink, 1932 (*The critics*), NPG • H. Coster, photographs, c.1939, NPG • W. Conor, portrait, 1946, Ulster Museum, Belfast • D. Low, pencil caricature, NPG

Wealth at death £47,197: probate, 3 Sept 1971, CGPLA Eng. & Wales

Esau, Abraham (1864–1901), blacksmith and hero, was born on 12 September 1864 in the northern Kenhardt district of Cape Colony, the eldest son of several children of Adam Esau, semi-skilled general labourer, and his only wife, Martha April, domestic farm servant. Nothing is known of his parents, other than that they led an itinerant working existence for many years on farms and in villages in the northern and north-western Cape Colony, and

Abraham Esau (1864–1901), by unknown photographer

that they were probably illiterate or, at best, semi-literate.

During a settled period of service in the early 1870s as the living-in farm servants of William Seton, a well-off, paternalistic English farmer in the Carnarvon district, the Dutch-Afrikaans-speaking Esau family developed close patronage ties to their master, through whom they absorbed something of the language and culture of Cape British colonists. As a young rural Cape coloured boy in an overwhelmingly Boer-dominated region, Esau grew up in an 'Englische' social milieu, above the menial status of other labouring households, which were customarily bound into ruling Boer culture. He received some intermittently interrupted education at a Methodist mission school in Prieska (1871–9), after which he worked as a self-taught carpenter around Kenhardt until the end of the 1880s. Having accumulated modest means, Esau moved to the small north-western settlement of Calvinia around 1889 or 1890, where he set himself up as an independent blacksmith and local haulier, having acquired mule carts and access to pasturage.

Muscular and enterprising, Esau prospered in the 1890s through his smithy and small transport business, achieving a strong community identity as one of Calvinia's most respectable coloured townsmen and leading artisans, known to the local magistrate for his moral character and temperance activity. In such ways his life mirrored the late nineteenth-century Cape colonial world of independent coloured artisans and craftsmen, a small class of propertied men passionately attached to the multiracial constitutional rights of citizenship, suffrage, and legal equality to which they had come to feel traditionally entitled under a British-influenced Cape political liberalism. Like others of his class and values, the English-speaking Esau was passionately attached to a British South Africa, even if in a remote spot like Calvinia this was an imperial identity he could apprehend but not necessarily comprehend.

As an ordinary, hard-working countryman fond of black neckties, starched shirts, and brown serge jackets, Esau's life might well have coasted along in obscurity, had it not been for the Second South African War of 1899–1902, and the violence it brought to frontier districts of the northern Cape Colony as invading Boer republican forces and local collaborating rebels swept across British territory in the opening months of hostilities. As the Calvinia district became gripped by a siege atmosphere during 1900, Esau's bustling presence, determined manner, and influential oratory put him at the forefront of anti-republican activity. In May 1900 he headed festivities to celebrate the relief of Mafeking, using the opportunity to denounce the Boer cause, much to the chagrin of local pro-republican farmers. In ensuing months Esau drew about him a body of coloured residents as anxious and resolute as he, and in September and October repeatedly petitioned the resident magistrate, Peter Dreyer, to arm a squad of picked volunteers to guard Calvinia. This approach was spurned by the magistracy, which declined to enlist coloured defenders on the official grounds that the war was supposed to be a white man's business. Conspicuous, he rode the countryside on a large black horse brandishing a sabre, and rallied coloured support to the imperial war effort.

For Esau, nothing was more urgent than defending his community against the Boer menace. Increasingly detested by Boers as an 'English coloured' troublemaker, Esau led villagers in preparing makeshift defences, and then in November 1900 he attempted a tactical collaboration with local British forces to aid the imperial cause. Making common cause with the Namaqualand field force intelligence department, Esau established a network of spies and informers, centred on a cellar beneath his stables, to feed information to army intelligence in return for an honourable understanding that imperial troops would be on hand to ensure that Calvinia would not be overrun by invading commandos. He prided himself on his inventiveness as a loyal British spy, but was cruelly misguided in imagining that Nama Land field force troops would come dashing in to provide cover. In effect, he had been palmed off with the empty wave of a British officer's hand.

Calvinia fell to an Orange Free State commando on 7 January 1901, soon joined by other Boers. The brazenly defiant and conspiratorial Esau was clearly destined not to be spared. Aware that he was a marked man, he tried to escape, but was swiftly hunted down and captured. His Boer captors flogged him publicly, trying to extract information about his spy network and to force him to disown his British allegiance. By all contemporary accounts, Esau remained obstinate. The Boers felt the need to eliminate this symbol of British coloured resistance, so a Boer horseman dragged Esau to about 5 miles east of the Calvinia municipal boundary, where, on 5 February 1901, he was shot dead by Stephanus Strydom. Three close associates then stole out to retrieve his corpse, which was laid out on a mule wagon for shuffling mourners to pay homage. The next day the Boer occupation force melted away as a

British column under Lieutenant-Colonel Herbert de Lisle reached Calvinia. At Esau's funeral on 7 February army command draped his coffin with the union flag and posted a firing squad to invest his interment with military honours, not a regular wartime ritual for a black civilian. Esau's death outraged British opinion in South Africa, Britain, and elsewhere. Captain Thomas Eyre-Lloyd, for example, wrote in his diary, 'This is truly a most outrageous and evil act' (Nasson, *Abraham Esau's War*, 131).

Although Esau's murder was a minor incident in a brutal war, his life and wartime conduct acquired the aura of a political martyrdom: he came to epitomize colonial coloured loyalty to the British cause. Contemporary commemoration came from Sir Alfred Milner, the high commissioner, who stated that Esau was 'far more civilised than the average Boer farmer' (Nasson, *Abraham Esau's War*, 132); from Cape politicians in the 1900s; and from the Anglican mission church in Calvinia, which paid him homage through the building of an Abraham Esau memorial chapel in Hantam Street, Calvinia, in 1908. In the area his memory was revived and cited in successive political controversies when coloureds opposed the increasingly dominant Afrikaners: union in 1910, the 1948 election and resultant apartheid, and the 1960 republic referendum. Always disliked by Afrikaner nationalists, the memorial chapel in 1968 was confiscated under the Group Areas Act, sold, and in 1972 demolished. In the 1980s and 1990s Esau's story became widely known through the publication of a biography and other writings on him. Following the end of the apartheid regime, in 1994 a new memorial chapel was due to be built on the original site. In 1995 Abraham Esau's Calvinia grave was finally listed as an official imperial war grave by the South African National Monuments Council. In popular rural oral tradition and folk memory of his area he continues to be remembered as a black martyr of the Second South African War, sometimes metamorphosed into a historical figure of herculean strength and supernatural powers.

BILL NASSON

Sources B. Nasson, 'Esau, Abraham', *New dictionary of South African biography*, ed. E. J. Verwey (1995), 65–7 · B. Nasson, *Abraham Esau's war: a black South African war in the Cape, 1899–1902* (1991) · B. Nasson, 'Abraham Esau's war', *The myths we live by*, ed. R. Samuel and P. Thompson (1991), 111–26 · B. Nasson, 'The war of Abraham Esau, 1899–1901: martyrdom, myth and folk memory in Calvinia, South Africa', *African Affairs*, 87 (1988), 239–65 · B. Nasson, 'The priest, the chapel and the repentant landowner: Abraham Esau revisited', *African Affairs*, 93 (1994), 3–19 · B. Nasson, 'Die lewe en dood van Esau', *Die Suid Afrikaan* (1 Sept 1986), 37–44 · K. Schoeman, 'Die dood van Abraham Esau: ooggetuieberigte uit die besette Calvinia, 1901', *Quarterly Bulletin of the South African Library*, 40 (1985), 56–66 · A. S. Skillicorn, 'The role of the black voter in the 1908 Cape general election', BA diss., University of Cape Town, 1975 · P. Warwick, *Black people and the South African War, 1899–1902* (1983) · C. J. Scheepers Strydom, *Kaapland en die tweede vryheidsoorlog* (1937) · 'Telegram from Sir Alfred Milner to the secretary of state for war, relating to the reported outrage on Esau at Calvinia', *Parl. papers* (1901), 47.563, Cd 464 · encl. in W. Hely-Hutchinson to J. Chamberlain (conf.), 10/2/1901, 18 Feb 1901, PRO, Colonial Office files, CO 48/551/5078 [memorandum from G. V. Fiddes, imperial secretary, 18/2/1901] · *Lloyds Weekly Newspaper* (20 Feb 1901) · *Diamond Fields Advertiser* (7 Feb 1901) · *Graaff-Reinet Advertiser* (17 Feb 1901) · *South African News* (18 Sept 1901) · *Cape Times Weekly* (March 1901) · archive of the resident magistrate, Clanwilliam State Archives Depot, Cape Town, South Africa · Anglo-Boer War files, State Archives Depot, Cape Town, South Africa, attorney-general's department

Archives NAM, Namaqualand field force papers, Anglo-Boer War · State Archives Depot, Cape Town, South Africa, attorney-general's department, Anglo-Boer War files | Clanwilliam State Archives Depot, Cape Town, South Africa, archive of the resident magistrate · PRO, Colonial Office files, CO 48/551/5078

Likenesses oils, c.1898–1900, repro. in Nasson, 'The priest, the chapel and the repentant landowner'; priv. coll. · photograph, repro. in Nasson, *Abraham Esau's war* [*see illus.*]

Esch, Vincent Jerome (1876–1950), architect, was born on 20 July 1876 in Blackheath, London, the son of C. A. Bernard Esch, a merchant banker. The Esch family were devout Roman Catholics. He was educated at Mount St Mary's College in Chesterfield, before training as an architect in the London office of Alfred Purdie. In 1898, at the age of twenty-two, he sailed to India to take up an appointment on the construction of the Bengal–Nagpur railway, and in the course of the next twenty-five years enjoyed a thriving career as an architect based in Calcutta. On the boat out he met and impressed the new viceroy, Lord Curzon, an encounter which gave him an entrée into Calcutta society. In 1900 he married Elsie Harriet (*b.* 1879), daughter of Frederick Latimer, who was then serving as permanent secretary to the viceroy, who was a sponsor at the wedding. Subsequently, Esch was engaged by Curzon for the design of some minor government works, and in 1910 he was appointed superintending architect for the construction of the Victoria Memorial Hall in Calcutta. One of the most ambitious architectural projects undertaken in British India, the memorial had been conceived by Curzon and designed by William Emerson, who particularly recommended Esch for this sensitive task. Besides overseeing the protracted construction of the building (completed in 1921), Esch made substantial contributions to it, including the redesign of the foundations on innovative principles better suited to the difficult, silty site.

Esch's involvement with the Bengal–Nagpur railway culminated with his design of their new head offices at Garden Reach in 1907. The break in his career as an independent architect came when he won the competition to design the Bengal Club on Chowringhee (1907–8; dem.). With its elegant Ionic façade, constructed entirely in precast, probably reinforced mass concrete, this dominated a conspicuous site in the city and established his reputation. His surviving works in the city include the Allahabad Bank, the offices of Duncan Brothers, and a race stand for the Royal Calcutta Turf Club. All these works are notable for combining the latest technology and materials with a restrained colonial classical style.

In 1914 Esch was engaged by the nizam of Hyderabad, Osman Ali Khan, to assist in the redevelopment of that city following its devastation by floods and plague in 1908 and 1911. His contribution was the design of numerous substantial public buildings including the railway station

(1914), the high court (1916), the city high school (1917–20), and the Osmania General Hospital (1918–21). Departing here from the strictly classical style he employed in Calcutta, he developed instead a new style based on the Islamic architecture of southern India, which he found within the nizam's domains. He worked closely with local craftsmen and architects, who continued to produce further public buildings in the city, developing his manner, after his departure. On this subject, he delivered a lecture to the India Society in London in 1942. He thus became one of the most significant practitioners of and apologists for what has come to be known as the Indo-Saracenic movement: the use of Indian sources for architecture in late British India.

In 1923 Esch married Olive Mary, daughter of Charles Hendry Edward, with whom he had one son and one daughter (in addition to two daughters and one son from his previous marriage). On returning to Britain, he settled in London. Although his work in India was recognized, for example by his creation as CVO in 1922, he was never again so successful in securing major commissions. He died on 9 December 1950 at Charlwood, Surrey, where he was also buried.　　　G. H. R. TILLOTSON

Sources priv. coll., Esch MSS · V. J. Esch, 'Examples of modern Indian architecture mainly in Hyderabad state', *Indian Art and Letters*, 16/2 (1942), 49–59 · 'The work of a British architect in India', *British Builder*, 3 (1921), 220–24 · G. H. R. Tillotson, 'Vincent J. Esch and the architecture of Hyderabad, 1914–36', *South Asian Studies*, 9 (1993), 29–46 · P. Vaughan, ed., *The Victoria Memorial Hall Calcutta* (1997) · private information (2004) · m. cert. [Elsie Latimer]
Archives BL OIOC, MSS [copies] · priv. coll. (NRA), MSS
Likenesses F. O. Salisbury, oils, repro. in Vaughan, ed., *Victoria Memorial Hall*; priv. coll.

Escoffier, Georges Auguste (1846–1935), master chef and cookery writer, was born on 28 October 1846 in Villeneuve-sur-Loup (later Villeneuve-Loubet), Alpes-Maritimes, 15 kilometres from Nice, the son of Jean Baptiste Escoffier (*d.* 1909), farmer and village blacksmith. At thirteen Auguste was apprenticed to his uncle François Escoffier, who had opened in 1856 the Restaurant Français in Nice which provided an international cuisine for rich winter visitors and employed a Russian chef.

Chef de cuisine After completing his apprenticeship Escoffier was offered work in Paris by Monsieur Bardoux, owner of the fashionable summer restaurant Le Petit Moulin Rouge. Near the Champs-Élysées, the restaurant attracted the 'demi-monde' of actresses, opera singers, cocottes, and their rich patrons. During the next five years Escoffier worked his way up through the various departments to become *chef saucier* under the direction of the *chef de cuisine*.

Although Escoffier had done his military service in an infantry regiment in 1867, on the declaration of war in July 1870 he was posted as *chef de cuisine* to the headquarters of the army of the Rhine in Metz. Escoffier described his experiences in *Mémoires d'un soldat de l'armée du Rhin*, published in serial form in *La Revue de l'Art Culinaire* during 1894 and 1895. He arrived in Metz in mid-July, and took

Georges Auguste Escoffier (1846–1935), by unknown photographer

part in three weeks of campaigning, which was followed by the ten-week siege of Metz. Escoffier describes collecting a secret farmyard of animals, and stockpiling essentials. He learnt to cook horsemeat. 'On the day Metz surrendered there remained one chicken, a jar of meat extract, a tin of tunny fish and the goat, which I sold' (Herbodeau and Thalamas, 28). Escoffier was the first serious chef to investigate tinned and preserved foods. Later he told Madame Ritz that his experience in Metz gave him the first idea of the potential of tinned foods and of the dire need the world had for them (Ritz, 33).

Following the fall of Metz, Escoffier spent six months as a prisoner of war in Germany, though after two miserable months he found a job as *chef de cuisine* for Marshal MacMahon, from France, imprisoned in Wiesbaden with his staff. Returning to France in April 1871 Escoffier escaped the siege of Paris by taking the last train from Paris to Versailles, where he worked first in Marshal MacMahon's headquarters and then for the officers of the 17th infantry regiment. During this period he learnt from an amateur sculptor the art of making wax flowers for elaborate table decorations. He later exhibited his creations at culinary exhibitions and wrote a book on the subject. After returning to civilian life, from 1872 to 1878 he worked each winter in the south of France, and returned in spring to Le Petit Moulin Rouge as *chef de cuisine*. Despite the military defeat, Paris life blossomed. With little formal education and although the life of a chef was physically very hard, the hours long, and the working conditions unpleasant, Escoffier interested himself in literature, theatre, and opera. His long friendship with Sarah Bernhardt dates from this period (1874). In 1876 be bought premises to set up a restaurant in Cannes; the Faisan Doré opened in 1879, but was then let. Instead, on his marriage in 1878 to Delphine Daphis (*d.* 1935), the daughter of Paul Daphis, a Paris publisher, Escoffier took a position as manager for La Maison Chevet, a famous catering firm in the Palais Royal, with a large government and international clientele.

Hotel cuisine From 1884 Escoffier began writing for the professional journal *La Revue de l'Art Culinaire*. He also wrote with his wife *Traité sur l'art de travailler les fleurs en cire* (1885). A new career and a historic partnership began when Escoffier was asked by César *Ritz in 1884 to manage the kitchens of his recently opened Grand Hotel in Monte Carlo. Ritz brought new ideas to hotel construction, furnishings, and staff organization and deportment, and Escoffier applied to kitchen management some of the same flair for innovation and quality that Ritz evolved for hotels.

The Grand Hotel had 250 rooms, a shopping arcade, electricity from its own steam engine, a 'café anglais', a separate restaurant in a Moorish style in the gardens, and a smoking room. Ritz realized that only first-class cooking would attract and keep the best clientele, and Escoffier took on the challenge of providing high-quality food throughout the day and night for large numbers, yet also providing elaborate gourmet meals for special customers. One long-lasting legacy was the *prix fixe*, a set menu devised to guide the inexperienced through the French *haute cuisine*.

Escoffier recruited and trained teams of chefs to work in Monaco in winter and at the Grand National Hotel in Lucerne, Europe's premier hotel, in summer; meanwhile Ritz engaged teams of specialists in wine, in waiting, and in other aspects of hotel management. They were so successful that in 1890 Ritz was approached by Richard D'Oyley Carte, the opera producer, who had expanded into property development in London and built a modern hotel, next to his theatre, the Savoy. It had opened in 1889 but lost money. Ritz put together a 'little army of hotel men for the conquest of London' (Ritz, 143); Escoffier reorganized the kitchen to provide a suitable working environment for sixty to eighty chefs and found new French staff, and the reopened Savoy Hotel was an immediate and lasting success. Led by the prince of Wales it became the meeting place for London high society and the *nouveaux riches* of the British empire. Madame Ritz, who was involved, described how the food and the ambience lured people from the clubs to dine in public and give great parties there. It allowed ladies, hitherto fearful of dining in public, to be seen in full regalia in the Savoy dining and supper rooms.

Ritz's contract allowed his team to take on freelance work for six months of the year, and they organized hotels all over Europe. Escoffier did not move his home to London—Madame Escoffier and their three children remained in Monte Carlo. In 1886 Ritz formed the Ritz Hotel Development Company, of which Escoffier and his other managers became directors. However, such activities led to Ritz and Escoffier being dismissed from the

Savoy in 1897. The Ritz team threatened to sue for wrongful dismissal: the Savoy's lawyers and accountants built up a counter case against them of financial mismanagement and fraud. After several years the dispute was settled, with Ritz and Escoffier repaying some money to the Savoy. In 1887, employed by the Ritz Company, Escoffier went to Paris to design the kitchens and recruit the chefs for the first Ritz Hotel, in the place Vendôme. Escoffier then returned to London to organize the new Carlton Hotel. From its opening it attracted much of the Savoy's clientele, including the prince of Wales and the Marlborough House set. It paid out a dividend of 7 per cent in its first year to its influential financial and aristocratic backers, and for many years it was considered the finest hotel in London. At the Carlton in 1902, on the night that King Edward VII's coronation was cancelled, Cesar Ritz suffered a nervous breakdown, from which he did not recover.

Escoffier now took over from Ritz as the figurehead of the Carlton and became an international celebrity in his own right, the leading chef of his time, continuing to design kitchens and to tackle such challenges as catering for the new ocean-liners. He continued as a director of the company and manager of the kitchens of the Carlton throughout the difficult war years, coping with both food and labour shortages. Both his sons were in the French army, and his second son was killed in November 1914. For his work in promoting France through its cuisine during these years President Poincaré personally presented him with the cross of the Légion d'honneur in 1919. Escoffier retired in 1920.

Culinary writings and practice In his menus, his cooking, and his writing, Escoffier was the leading exponent of the idea that *haute cuisine* should also be light and healthy. He advocated simplicity, and the banquet style with displays of ornate foods in heavy, rich sauces and indigestible garnishes gave way to dishes cooked for the individual. He insisted that a sense of occasion and luxury should come from flowers, fine china and glass, and specially designed serving dishes and containers (including sculpted ice). In his kitchens he combined the new and the traditional. Modern electric lighting was arranged over stoves and preparation tables to give clear, bright light. Surfaces were designed for high standards of cleanliness. Yet despite the advent of gas and electric cookers, Escoffier continued to rely on natural heat, and flames produced by burning wood and coke. His preferred utensils continued to be of iron and copper.

Escoffier was a devout Catholic, and left-over food from his London kitchens was given to local French nuns for the poor. Physically very small (he always needed specially raised clogs to cook in), and temperamentally reserved, Escoffier worked to improve the morale and working conditions of his chefs and campaigned against the brutality, bad language, and alcoholism endemic in a stressful trade (he provided lemon barley-water in great quantities to cut down alcohol consumption). He encouraged his chefs to dress well and to improve their education. He was involved in setting up educational courses for more formal professional training, including that at the Westminster Technical College. His hotels provided good quarters for staff. Concerned about the long-term insecurity of catering employees, in 1903 he helped to found the Association Culinaire Française de Secours Mutuel.

Escoffier was not good with finance but his talents for organization played an important role in his success. He personally visited his suppliers, commissioned new goods, and sought out new foods. He once described his role in organizing the growing of English-style green asparagus in the 1890s in Lauris in France: he went to the region and personally persuaded the reluctant growers to change their methods, which resulted in improved supply and lower prices in London. In addition, Escoffier and his elder son pioneered the manufacture of gourmet tinned and bottled foods and sauces.

Significance Chefs trained by Escoffier spread his practices of cosmopolitan cuisine throughout the world. However, it was through his writing that Escoffier promoted his ideas, recipes, and practices, and he left a lasting legacy. He rethought the traditional recipes and techniques of French cuisine and described them with a new precision, allowing for experimentation, especially in refining and lightening the essential sauces. In addition he incorporated recipes from other European traditions. In 1903 *Le guide culinaire* was published and became an immediate success. It has gone through numerous editions. In 1912 Escoffier published *Le livre des menus*, a book on kitchen organization and menu preparation based on his work at the Savoy and Carlton hotels. Between 1911 and 1914 he published in London the monthly magazine *Le Carnet d'Épicure*. After retiring he wrote *Ma cuisine, traité de cuisine familiale* (1934) for cooks in private houses.

After an active retirement, not wealthy but much honoured, Escoffier died on 12 February 1935 at 8 bis avenue de la Costa, Monte Carlo, Monaco; his wife died three weeks earlier, in January of the same year. He was buried at Villeneuve-Loubet, where the Escoffier family house later became the Musée de l'Art Culinaire.　　　F. ASHBURNER

Sources E. Herbodeau and P. Thalamas, *Georges Auguste Escoffier* [1955] · M. L. Ritz, *Cesar Ritz, host to the world* (1938) · P. Levey, *Out to lunch* (1986) · T. Shaw, *The world of Escoffier* (1994) · K. James, *Escoffier: the king of chefs* (2002) · A. Escoffier, *The complete guide to the art of modern cookery*, trans. H. L. Cracknell and R. J. Kaufmann (1979) [incl. biographical note by P. Escoffier; Fr. orig. (1903)] · A. Escoffier, *Ma cuisine*, ed. M. Howells, trans. V. Holland [1965] [Fr. orig. (1934)]
Archives Fondation Auguste Escoffier, Villeneuve-Loubet, France
Likenesses portrait, 1926, Parisian Chefs' Society · statue, 1936, Villeneuve-Loubet, Alpes-Maritimes, France · bronze medallion, 1953, Westminster Technical College, London · photograph, repro. in Herbodeau and Thalamas, *Georges Auguste Escoffier*, frontispiece [*see illus.*]
Wealth at death £334 12s. 11d.—in England: administration with will, 12 May 1936, *CGPLA Eng. & Wales*

Escombe, Harry (1838–1899), politician in Natal, the son of Robert Escombe of Chelsea, London, and his wife, Anne, was born at Notting Hill, Middlesex, on 25 July 1838. He was educated at St Paul's School from 1847 until 1855,

before entering the employ of a stockbroker. In 1859 he emigrated to the Cape, and early in 1860 went on to Natal. There he worked for John Robinson as bookkeeper in the office of the *Natal Mercury* and subsequently for Hermon Salomon, general agent, at Pietermaritzburg. He then started a similar business on his own account in Durban but was unsuccessful and so decided to qualify himself as an attorney-at-law. Escombe rapidly became so successful in the courts that he was recognized as the first pleader in Natal, and was often employed in cases of importance. Later he was appointed solicitor and standing counsel for Durban. In 1865 he married Theresa Susan, daughter of Dr William Garbutt Taylor of Durban. They had four daughters, and a son who died young.

In 1872 Escombe was elected for Durban as a member of the colony's legislative council; he was at the time absent in Zululand, commanding the escort that accompanied Theophilus Shepstone to the coronation of King Cetshwayo ka Mpande. At the next general election, in August 1873, he was re-elected, but resigned when the council met. He served with the Royal Durban rifles through the Anglo-Zulu War of 1879–80, and gained a medal. In 1879 he was again elected for Durban to the legislative council. A year later he was re-elected, and placed on the executive council, when he emerged as an outspoken opponent of full responsible government for the colony. In 1880 he was also instrumental in the establishment of a new Natal Harbour Board, and as its controversial chairman (1881–94) he played a leading role in developing at Durban a port which was vital to the economic future of the region. In 1881 he served with the Royal Durban rifles through the First South African War. In the 1882 elections for the legislative council he again opposed Sir John Robinson in his campaign for responsible government, but in the mid-1880s his views on the issue underwent a change. Consequently in 1883 he ceased to be a member of the executive council and in 1885 he lost his seat in the legislature. In 1886 he was re-elected to the legislative council as member for Newcastle.

In 1887–8 Escombe was in England for some time, but hurried back to Natal successfully to defend Cetshwayo's heir, Dinizulu, against the charge of rebellion. Later in 1888 he was elected again to the legislative council as member for Klip River district, but in 1890–91 served as member for Durban, which he continued to represent in the new legislative assembly from 1893 until 1897.

On the advent of responsible government Escombe became, on 10 October 1893, attorney-general in Sir John Robinson's ministry and was appointed QC. On 15 February 1897, after Sir John's health had deteriorated, Escombe became premier, as well as attorney-general, minister of education, and minister of defence. Two of his early measures involved the passing of legislation designed to limit Asiatic immigration and trading in Natal, issues that had long concerned him, though his views on these subjects were more moderate than many of his colonial contemporaries'. In June 1897 he joined the other premiers of colonies in London to celebrate Queen

Victoria's diamond jubilee. Shortly after his return to Natal he was defeated at the polls and accordingly in September 1897 he resigned office in favour of a new ministry under Sir Henry Binns.

On the outbreak of the Second South African War in October 1899 Escombe went to northern Natal to encourage the inhabitants, and remained there until the Boers invaded that part of the colony. Shortly after his return to Durban he died suddenly, on 27 December 1899, and was buried at Durban in the Church of England cemetery.

Escombe was tall and of commanding mien. In speech he was eloquent and often dramatic, and in argument quick and searching. He was an excellent chess player, and fond of astronomy, on which, as well as other subjects, he occasionally lectured at the Durban Institute and elsewhere. He was a keen volunteer, joined the Royal Durban rifles in 1860, became cornet in 1868, and was one of the founders and the first commander of the Natal naval volunteers. He is chiefly remembered in connection with the development of Durban harbour, which owed much to Escombe's persistence in the face of many obstacles. He was sworn of the privy council in 1897, and made an honorary LLD of Cambridge.

C. A. HARRIS, rev. W. R. GUEST

Sources Natal Mercury (28 Dec 1899) · The Natalian (27 March 1908) · South Africa (30 Dec 1899) · J. T. Henderson, ed., Speeches of the late Right Honourable Harry Escombe (1903) · A. Duminy and B. Guest, eds., Natal and Zululand from earliest times to 1910 (1989) · E. H. Brookes and C. de B. Webb, A history of Natal (1965)
Archives Pietermaritzburg Archive Repository, South Africa, Acc. No. A159
Likenesses statue, 1903, Farewell Square, Durban, South Africa · M. Field, portrait, Natal parliament building, Pietermaritzburg, South Africa

Escott, Bickham Aldred Cowan Sweet- (1907–1981), Special Operations Executive officer and banker, was born in Newport, Monmouthshire, on 6 June 1907, the eldest of four children (two sons and two daughters) of Aldred Bickham Sweet-Escott, marine engineer of Newport and Bristol, and his wife, Mary Amy, daughter of Michael Waistall Cowan, inspector-general in the Royal Navy. Educated at the choir school of Llandaff Cathedral and at Winchester College (1921–4), Bickham left the latter early owing to family financial difficulties. He was employed by J. S. Fry & Sons, of Bristol (1924–7), and he continued his studies privately. Through the hard work that characterized his career he took a degree at London University and in 1927 won an exhibition to Balliol College, Oxford, where he took a first in literae humaniores in 1930.

Sweet-Escott joined the British Overseas Bank, where he mastered the politics, personalities, and financial structures of most European countries (1930–8). After serving for a year as personal assistant to Courtaulds' chairman he joined the Secret Intelligence Service, section D, concerned with organizing sabotage, where he foresaw the importance of establishing section D activities in Europe before Nazi occupation. When section D became part of the Special Operations Executive (SOE) his service with the new organization took him to many regions. In 1941 he was in London concerned with the Balkans and Middle East, and became regional director. In July 1941 he went to Cairo, as personal assistant to the head of SOE (Sir Frank Nelson), before returning to London in December to the M (operations) directorate. From July 1942 he was with the SOE mission in Washington, liaising with the office of strategic services (OSS), SOE's opposite number in America. Back in London in 1943 he was briefly head of SOE's Free French section, before returning to Cairo in December to act as adviser to SOE's force 133, a task he carried out until December 1944. From January to December 1945 he was in south-east Asia command as chief of staff to force 136, becoming acting commander during the commander's absence. He was promoted major in 1941, and colonel in 1945.

In Baker Street Irregular (1965) Sweet-Escott gives a reliable and entertaining account of SOE. His experience, outstanding ability, and knowledge of the secrets of the organization repeatedly frustrated his attempts to serve in the field. He was one of the few competent to deal at the top level with SOE's problems, whether in Whitehall, Cairo, Algiers, or Kandy. Whenever and wherever there was a call for staff reinforcement Bickham was the obvious choice.

In 1933 Sweet-Escott had married Doris Katharine Mary, daughter of the Revd Percy George Bulstrode, of Broomfield, Taunton. The marriage was dissolved in 1950 and in the same year he married Beryl Mary (d. 1984), daughter of Trevor Phelps, businessman, of Botha's Hill, South Africa. There were no children of either marriage.

In 1949 Sweet-Escott had become general manager of the Ionian Bank which, helped by his wartime involvement with SOE operations in the Balkans, he rebuilt into a banking force in Greece and those parts of the eastern Mediterranean where Greek and British influence was still important. When the bank to his great regret was taken over in 1958 he joined British Petroleum as group treasurer. BP was at a critical stage in its development, having lost its oil monopoly in Iran, and having 'long lived in its private world of Scottish accountants and Persian oil camps'. It had to find and develop oil elsewhere, and by investing heavily in marketing to reduce its dependence on oil production alone. Sweet-Escott's task was to ensure that financial communities throughout the world 'were aware of BP, understood BP, and trusted BP'. Although at times looked at askance by the old hands, he laid the foundation of much of BP's financial success by his clear-headed guidance, his exceptionally wide banking experience, and his ability to gain the confidence of new colleagues across the world. BP's development during his period of office speaks for his achievement. He retired in 1972.

Sweet-Escott wrote several economic and financial surveys of the Balkans and Greece, including two books for the Royal Institute of International Affairs, of which he was an active member. He was a frequent broadcaster on international affairs. He was visiting professor, international finance, at the City University, London (1970–73), and he worked hard for charitable causes, especially in the field of mental health.

Sweet-Escott was a shrewd judge of character and situations, never afraid to state his views, and unfailingly kind, especially to young people planning their careers. A keen sportsman, in his later years he took up hunting, first stag, then fox, 'pursuing both beasts as if they had been storm troopers'.

Sweet-Escott died on 12 November 1981 at Ipswich.

CHARLES CRUICKSHANK, *rev.*

Sources *The Times* (14 Nov 1981) · *BP shield*, no. 7 (1982) [British Petroleum] · R. E. Wilson and H. A. Jackson, eds., *Winchester College: a register for the years 1901 to 1946* (1956) · private information (1990) [special operations executive adviser] · *CGPLA Eng. & Wales* (1982) · B. Sweet-Escott, *Baker Street irregular* (1965) [autobiog]
Wealth at death £38,905: probate, 12 Jan 1982, *CGPLA Eng. & Wales*

Escott, Thomas Hay Sweet (1844–1924), journalist and newspaper editor, born at Taunton, Somerset, on 6 June 1844, was the eldest son of the Revd Hay Sweet Escott of Hartrow Manor, and Eliza Ball Collins. He was educated at Somerset College, Bath, and Queen's College, Oxford, receiving a second class in the classical schools in 1865. He was lecturer in logic and deputy professor of classics in King's College, London, from 1866 to 1873. He retained his interest in the classics, acting as honorary secretary to the committee that founded the British School at Athens in 1883. But his real interest early lay in journalism; he himself recollected that he wrote his first article (for the *Saturday Review*) in September 1865. He was a leader writer on the *Standard* from 1866 until 1873, and then attempted an unsuccessful publishing venture, the *Hour*, which failed by 1875. He was one of the original staff on the *World* in 1874, and on *Home News*, which circulated primarily in India, and from which he culled his first work in contemporary history, *Pillars of Empire: Sketches of Living Indian and Colonial Statesmen, Celebrities and Officials* (1879). In the same year he brought out what was perhaps his most celebrated work, *England: its People, Polity and Pursuits*, based on three years of travelling and research, during which he claimed to have inspected personally the management of every great landed property, lived among the colliers of Northumberland, and spent a month with the agricultural labourers in the southern and western counties.

In November 1882 Escott became editor of the *Fortnightly Review*, with which he had been associated since 1879. The choice was something of a surprise, for he was following John Morley, who gave the *Fortnightly* its distinctive voice, but it is probable that Escott's lack of a defined political stance helped him to the editorship; it was recorded that 'Mr Escott attended a Board Meeting and gave his views as to the future conduct of the *Review* on a broader and less partisan basis and that his suggestions were approved.' In November and December, Escott published four anonymous articles by Conservatives, and was identified with Lord Randolph Churchill and his 'Fourth Party'; but he also cultivated the friendship of Joseph Chamberlain (who leaked cabinet secrets to him), commissioning the series of articles that were published in book form in 1885 as *The Radical Programme*. In July of that year A. J. Balfour paid tribute to Escott's impartiality. His choice of articles was wide, covering the theatre, imperial and foreign affairs, the franchise question, Ireland, psychical research, and the universities, but he was regarded by later critics as lacking a settled editorial policy, and the *Review* declined in quality and circulation.

Escott continued to write for the *Standard*, *World*, and *Lloyd's Weekly Newspaper*. His health broke down in October 1885. He went abroad in March 1886, and resigned the *Fortnightly* to James Thomas (Frank) Harris less than six months later; Chamberlain and Churchill took up a subscription for his family. Despite never fully recovering from illness, Escott found sufficient outlet for his energies in his literary and historical interests. His output was prodigious, and included in 1913 the first full-length biography of Anthony Trollope (whom he knew personally), and two idiosyncratic works on the press: *Platform, Press, Politics and Play* (1895) and *Masters of English Journalism* (1911). His books were characterized by a lively style, an eye for the telling phrase, and a powerful sense of England and Englishness. He captured the energy and achievements of the Victorian age, but stressed also the continuity of English history. He admired alike the nobility and the English working man, and was at heart perhaps a tory democrat, declaring in 1891 that 'modern Conservatism is successful precisely in proportion as it is an alliance between the aristocratic and democratic elements' (*England*, 345).

Escott belonged to an era when politics and journalism were inseparable. His close contact with politicians of different parties, which he reconciled with his conviction that he was an independent editor, was typical of his age. He drew attention to the 'revolution in journalism' that produced the *Daily Mail*, noting the concentration of newspapers in fewer hands. Yet, though he himself was a practitioner of an older journalism, he did not regret the new, observing that the *Daily Mail* distilled the essence of the news for a busy generation 'as easily as the Iliad or the Odyssey were once packed into a nutshell' (*Social Transformations of the Victorian Age*, 1897, 386). But for all his admiration of the modern age he had few contacts with trade and industry.

Escott married twice. His first wife, whom he married in 1865, was Kate, second daughter of Colonel Charles Liardet (whose pedigree as the English branch of an old Austrian family ennobled by Maria Theresa he proudly announced in his *Who's Who* entry); she died in 1899. He afterwards married Edith, widow of Charles Rawnslay Hilton. In middle age he resembled H. G. Wells in appearance: a rounded figure, with an expression that was both comfortable and alert; he was an inveterate gossip. Escott died at Hove, Sussex on 13 June 1924, being survived by a son and a daughter from his first marriage.

D. GEORGE BOYCE

Sources T. H. S. Escott, *Platform, press, politics and play* (1895) · J. E. Courtney, *The making of an editor: W. L. Courtney, 1850–1928* (1930), 133–42 · *The Times* (17 June 1924) · *WWW* · S. E. Koss, *The rise and fall of the political press in Britain*, 1 (1981), 182–3, 221, 235–45, 252–3, 271 · L. Brown, *Victorian news and newspapers* (1985), 114, 127–38 · *Wellesley index* · D. Griffiths, ed., *The encyclopedia of the British press, 1422–1992* (1992)

Archives BL, corresp. and papers, Add. MSS 58774–58801 | BL, letters to W. E. Gladstone, Add. MSS 44458–44490, *passim* · BL, letters to Sir E. W. Hamilton, Add. MSS 48623–48627 · Bodl. Oxf., letters to Sir Henry Burdett · Hove Central Library, Sussex, letters to Lord and Lady Wolseley · King's AC Cam., letters to Oscar Browning · NL Scot., letters to Blackwoods · NL Scot., corresp. with Lord Rosebery · U. Birm. L., letters to Joseph Chamberlain
Likenesses Spy [L. Ward], cartoon, 2 May 1885, Hult. Arch. · Ape [C. Pellegrini], lithograph, repro. in *VF* (1885), pl. 331 · photograph, repro. in Escott, *Platform, press, politics and play*, frontispiece · photograph, repro. in T. H. S. Escott, *Great Victorians: memories and personalities* (1916), frontispiece
Wealth at death £190: administration, 8 Nov 1924, *CGPLA Eng. & Wales*

Escures, Ralph d' (*c*.1068–1122), archbishop of Canterbury, was the son of Seffrid d'Escures and his first wife, Rascendis. The alternative name de Turbine sometimes attached to him is not recorded before the fourteenth century, and may have originated in a confusion with his successor at Canterbury, William de Corbeil.

Monk and abbot Seffrid, whose name suggests kinship with the lords of Bellême, held extensive lands in the neighbourhood of Alençon, from which he made substantial grants to the abbey of St Martin of Sées, a daughter house of St Evroult founded by Roger de Montgomery, vicomte of the Hièmois, and his wife, Mabel, heir of Bellême; many years later Seffrid died at St Martin's in the monastic habit. Ralph entered the house about 1078, when according to later tradition he was ten years old, and rose to be sub-prior, and then in 1088 prior. In 1089 he became the house's second abbot. He was to hold office under increasingly difficult circumstances for sixteen years. He clearly owed his promotion to more than family influence, for there is remarkable unanimity among contemporaries on his learning and affability. For some time the house prospered. Roger de Montgomery had already taken monks from St Martin's to found a substantial monastery at Shrewsbury about 1083, and in Ralph's time Montgomery's family made extensive further grants of Sées, notably in the lordship of Pembroke and Lancashire. In 1094 Sées also profited from Robert de Bellême's war with Robert Giroie, since part of the former's booty was the arm of St Céneri, which was taken to St Martin. In the meantime, the links between Sées and its mother house remained strong, and Ralph became a close friend of Roger du Sap, abbot of St Evroult from 1091. Many years later Jean de Rheims dedicated his life of St Evroult (now lost) to Ralph, who is described by Orderic Vitalis as very well versed in letters, eloquent, agreeable, and universally beloved.

The death of William Rufus in 1100 was disastrous for St Martin and its abbot. In 1102 Abbot Ralph was in England when Robert de Bellême and his brothers rose against Henry I—after the fall of Bridgnorth the men of Shrewsbury sent Ralph to the king with the keys to the fortress. Count Robert forfeited his English lands and returned to Normandy, bent on creating a near independent lordship based on Bellême. The demands he made on Sées, already heavy, became intolerable, and by 1104 both Bishop Martin of Sées and Abbot Ralph had fled to the protection of King Henry of England. According to William of Malmesbury, England was then full of such exiles, but Ralph was set apart by his unwillingness to burden any of his hosts with too long or exacting a stay. His first documented appearance was at Durham that September, to attend the translation of St Cuthbert to the new cathedral. When doubt was cast on the survival of the saint's uncorrupted body, Abbot Ralph made peace between the contending parties, and himself carried out a detailed examination of the body before proclaiming it as perfect as on the day of death. In 1106 Ralph was at least for a while back in Normandy, where he visited his old acquaintance, Archbishop Anselm, at Bec; he had probably ceased to exercise authority at Sées by this date, although the sources unanimously refer to him as abbot until 1108, and his successor was not elected until 1110.

Bishop of Rochester When Anselm returned to England in 1107 Ralph seems to have attached himself chiefly to the archbishop's household. Certainly he became familiar with the monks of Christ Church, and he came to visit his friend Bishop Gundulf of Rochester in March 1108 as he lay dying. With prophetic foresight Gundulf gave Ralph his episcopal ring. Since Lanfranc's time, at least, the bishopric of Rochester had been recognized as in the archbishop's gift, and on 29 June, Anselm nominated Ralph to the bishopric and took his homage. The next day he was sent to Rochester with the sub-prior of Canterbury and the archdeacon, who invested him with the bishopric. Ralph was consecrated by the archbishop of Canterbury on 9 August; his happy prognostic was 'They are as the angels which are in heaven' (Mark 12: 25).

The people of Rochester remembered Ralph as a friend to their church and liberties, and a handful of charters provide some support for this view. Otherwise he appears only rarely in the sources; late in 1108 he was sent to Southwell to command Thomas, archbishop-elect of York, to come to Canterbury for consecration and to make a profession of obedience, Ralph's first known involvement in the primacy debate which would cast a dark shadow over his later years. By now Anselm was clearly dying, and the next April, Ralph was at Canterbury for his last hours and burial. To the very end Anselm and the monks of Canterbury were preoccupied by the need to secure a profession from Thomas, following the wholly exceptional act of submission of one archbishop to another secured by Lanfranc from Thomas's uncle and predecessor in 1072. The canons of York were no less determined to cast off this humiliating subjection. As Canterbury's representative during a vacancy Ralph continued to press for Thomas's surrender. He also watched over the rights of Canterbury during the long vacancy that followed Anselm's death. It was probably as deputy for the archbishop that he consecrated the crypt chapel at Bury St Edmunds, and promoted Baldwin to the priorate, perhaps in 1112. There was little to indicate that he would soon be called to a much wider stage.

Elevation to Canterbury After a five-year vacancy King Henry, pressed by the pope and the monks of Canterbury, at last took steps to appoint a new archbishop. In April 1114 he summoned his bishops and magnates to Windsor; Bishop Ralph accompanied the prior of Christ Church and a party of his monks, who had also been called. By then Ralph and the aged bishop of Norwich were the only monks among the bishops, and the remainder combined to oppose the king's own choice, Abbot Faricius of Abingdon, demanding a clerk of their own order as vigorously as the monks of Christ Church refused one. In this impasse Ralph emerged as the compromise candidate, a monk but at least a bishop, and of wonderful affability. Nominated on 26 April, and installed at Canterbury on 16 May, he secured his own replacement at Rochester by Abbot Ernulf of Peterborough, a former monk of Christ Church, whom he invested with the bishopric on 28 September. Emissaries set off for Rome late in the year to seek papal confirmation of Ralph's translation and a pallium. According to the letters of support for his election which they carried, the new archbishop was too infirm to make the journey himself, the first sign of the chronic ill health that was to dog his later years.

The ambassadors received at first an icy reception, since Pope Paschal II was already indignant at the reluctance of the English church to refer serious matters to his judgement and to render 'Peter's pence', and an episcopal translation without the previous consent of Rome was conceived as a particular affront. Only the intercession of Abbot Anselm of St Saba, nephew to the late archbishop, at length secured Pope Paschal's agreement, conveyed in letters of the most grudging assent of 30 March 1115. As legate, Abbot Anselm was charged with raising all these matters with the king, as well as with the pallium for Ralph. On 27 June he was received in procession at Canterbury by the archbishop, eight of his bishops, and the communities of Christ Church and St Augustine. Anselm laid the pallium in its silver casket on the high altar of the cathedral, the archbishop swore his oath of fidelity to the pope, and put on the pallium. After enthronement on the seat of St Augustine he proceeded immediately to consecrate Theulf as bishop of Worcester. Very shortly afterwards he appointed John, his sister's son, as his archdeacon.

The dispute with York: diplomatic endeavours The legate also bore a less welcome gift, a detailed requisitory of the pope's grievances against the English church, which he delivered to the king at his court at Westminster in September 1115. It came at a time when the entire Norman episcopate had been suspended for failing to attend a legatine council, and when Thurstan, the archbishop-elect of York, was refusing to make a profession of obedience to Canterbury, and was threatening to seek consecration from the pope. For his part, Ralph refused to consecrate Thurstan unless he professed, even if confronted by a papal command. It was agreed to send the blind but infinitely experienced Bishop William de Warelwast of Exeter to Rome to seek a resolution to these difficulties. A less urgent problem, over the place of consecration to the see of St David's of the queen's chancellor, Bernard, whom

Ralph categorically refused to bless anywhere but at Canterbury, was more easily settled when King Henry arranged that Bernard should make his profession and receive Ralph's blessing at Westminster, the queen's favourite residence.

Late in the year Alexander, king of Scots, wrote to seek the archbishop's advice on finding a new bishop of St Andrews; Alexander's proposal that a new bishop should be consecrated at Canterbury rather than by the archbishop of York must have been extremely welcome, though nothing seems to have come of the proposal immediately. In March 1116 the archbishop was among those who swore allegiance to William Ætheling at Salisbury, an occasion that also saw the king compel Thurstan of York to renounce his see rather than profess to Canterbury, in spite of letters of powerful support from Pope Paschal. Shortly afterwards Thurstan crossed to Normandy to join the king, where he was allowed to resume his status as elect, and continued to press his case. In August, Abbot Anselm returned to Normandy with a new legatine commission for England, a clear indication of the failure of the mission of the bishop of Exeter. A council of English magnates therefore urged Ralph to travel to Rome to present his case, and in September he set out with a substantial company.

Still in Normandy, Ralph fell ill at La Ferté with an ulcer of the face, and for a month his life was despaired of. Further delayed by bad weather, the archbishop and his companions spent Christmas at Lyons. When they reached Rome in March, it was to find the city under assault from the emperor Heinrich V, while the pope had fled to Benevento. The archbishop nevertheless celebrated mass in St Peter's on 12 March, but could communicate with the pope only through messengers, who secured no more than empty courtesy. On the other hand, Thurstan's representatives received unequivocal papal support. Apparently with Paschal's consent, Ralph spent eight days with the emperor, but it became increasingly clear that the rumours of the pope's imminent return to Rome were baseless. By the end of the year Ralph was back at Rouen after much fruitless suffering.

On hearing of the death of Pope Paschal in January 1118, Thurstan left York and joined the king in Normandy, armed with papal letters commanding Ralph to consecrate him without a profession, and hoping for equally determined support from Paschal's successor. Ralph remained with the king, partly no doubt to strengthen the king's resolve to require a profession, partly because the legate Anselm still awaited the king's leave to cross to England to exercise his legation, partly perhaps in the hope that a new pope would be more sympathetic. In September he attended an important royal council at Rouen, where the legate Cono denounced the imperial antipope, and the king took counsel on the war raging along the Norman frontier. The new pope, Gelasius II, proved as staunch a friend to Thurstan as his predecessor, and wrote to Ralph in uncompromising terms commanding him to consecrate Thurstan without a profession, letters that Ralph would always insist he had never seen. Gelasius died suddenly in January 1119, but his successor, Calixtus II, proved no less insistent on Thurstan's rights. The state of war with France and Anjou, and the uncertainty over the pope's movements, yet again frustrated Ralph's attempts to go to plead his case in person, and though a messenger succeeded in delivering a letter of impassioned complaint, this received short shrift from Calixtus. In July (probably in 1119, rather than 1118), as the archbishop was taking off his vestments after mass, he suffered a severe stroke. He made a partial recovery, but his speech was permanently impaired, and his movement restricted; for some time, at least, he could only travel in a litter.

The dispute with York: defeat and death In May, Pope Calixtus had announced his intention of hearing the dispute between Canterbury and York at a council to be held at Rheims in October, to which Ralph and Thurstan were both summoned. A large delegation of English bishops set out, as did Thurstan, but Ralph was too ill, and Canterbury's case was chiefly represented by his half-brother Seffrid, shortly to become abbot of Glastonbury, and his nephew John, the archdeacon. In spite of their protests the pope consecrated Thurstan on 19 October, leaving the issue of the profession to be disputed elsewhere. The king, enraged by what he chose to represent as a breach of faith, forbade Thurstan to enter England and disseised him of his estates. On 4 January 1120, by contrast, Ralph was received with ceremony at Canterbury after an absence of three and a half years; on 4 April he was well enough to consecrate David as bishop of Bangor at Westminster. At this point King Alexander renewed his application for a new bishop of St Andrews, this time specifying Eadmer of Canterbury as his candidate. This was a choice that the archbishop could scarcely oppose, and Eadmer was sent off with the archbishop's blessing and King Henry's leave. Meanwhile, however, the pope's support for Thurstan was unwavering and, faced by a threat of interdict, Henry submitted; at Christmas 1120 Ralph and the other bishops met the king at London and accepted defeat, at least for the moment. Thurstan returned to England and his church a few weeks later.

On 25 November 1120 the king's only legitimate son had drowned in the *White Ship*, two years after his mother's death. Henry's second marriage, to Adeliza of Louvain, was settled with remarkable haste, the marriage taking place at Windsor on 29 January 1121. Ralph was too unwell to perform the wedding, but insisted on taking part in the coronation the following day. His celebrated ease of manner had disintegrated under the pressure of illness and failure, and he broke off the ceremony on seeing the king wearing the crown that it was the archbishop's cherished right to place upon his head. With unexpected restraint the king agreed to untie the thong below his chin, and Ralph was ultimately persuaded to replace the crown and allow the mass to proceed. In the summer he entertained yet another papal legate, Cardinal Pietro Pierleone, later the antipope Anacletus II, at Canterbury and seized the opportunity to display the largely forged privileges of his see. Ralph was again ill at Michaelmas, and so could not attend the council where the king pressed Thurstan once more to agree to make a profession, and with no more success. His last recorded act was to consecrate Gregory as bishop of Dublin at Lambeth on 2 October. By now he was failing fast; he does not certainly attest any later royal charters, and Eadmer has nothing to report of him from then until his death at Canterbury on 20 October 1122. He was buried in the middle of the cathedral nave three days later.

Assessment Ralph's pontificate was in many ways unsuccessful; he struggled long and fruitlessly against ill health and a world that had little place for the exceptional privileges of Canterbury which Lanfranc had secured in very different times. There is a marked difference between the accounts of Anselm and Ralph given by Eadmer, who served them both, and Ralph seems a colourless figure by comparison with his predecessor. For the most part the supporters of York could find little to say for him, yet even one of those could call him worthy of his high office, as it were a lesser pope, barely second to a king to whom he was right arm, heart, and eye. Eadmer, too, speaks of Ralph's shrewd counsel even after his stroke. Elsewhere testimonies to his learning and piety are widespread. The worst that the young William of Malmesbury could say of him was that he could descend into unbecoming frivolity. He was generous to the monks of Canterbury as well as Rochester and his twenty-five surviving charters show him making valuable gifts to Lewes, St Osyth's, and the nuns of Malling. At Abingdon he intervened to make peace when the monks fell out with their abbot; he supported Christina of Markyate in her tribulations; in Wales, Ireland, and Scotland he sought to maintain the influence of Canterbury as vigorously as any of his predecessors.

Apart from a handful of letters on routine business, and a defence of Canterbury's claims over York addressed to Pope Calixtus, impassioned to the point of incoherence and probably to be conceived as the collective work of Canterbury's partisans, only one work of his certainly survives, a sermon on the feast of the Assumption of the Virgin. Originally delivered to the monks of Sées in French, it was translated into Latin at the request of abbots Guillaume of Fécamp and Arnulf of Troarn; travelling under false colours as the work of Anselm it survives in some fifty manuscripts. There was even an Anglo-Saxon translation from the Latin text found in a single manuscript, probably from Canterbury or Rochester. Modest though it is, this celebration of the Virgin's chastity and humility from his happiest years remains Ralph's most apt memorial.

MARTIN BRETT

Sources Ordericus Vitalis, *Eccl. hist.*, 3–6 · *Willelmi Malmesbiriensis monachi de gestis pontificum Anglorum libri quinque*, ed. N. E. S. A. Hamilton, Rolls Series, 52 (1870) · William of Malmesbury, *Gesta regum Anglorum / The history of the English kings*, ed. and trans. R. A. B. Mynors, R. M. Thomson, and M. Winterbottom, 2 vols., OMT (1998–9) · *Eadmeri Historia novorum in Anglia*, ed. M. Rule, Rolls Series, 81 (1884) · Eadmer, *The life of St Anselm, archbishop of Canterbury*, ed. and trans. R. W. Southern, 2nd edn, OMT (1972) · R. Thomson, ed., *Life of Gundulf, bishop of Rochester* (1977) · D. Whitelock, M. Brett, and C. N. L. Brooke, eds., *Councils and synods with other documents relating* to the English church, 871–1204, 2 (1981) • Hugh the Chanter: the history of the church of York, 1066–1127, ed. and trans. C. Johnson, rev. edn, rev. M. Brett, C. N. L. Brooke, and M. Winterbottom, OMT (1990) • A. Wilmart, 'Les homélies attribuées à S. Anselme', Archives d'Histoire Doctrinale et Littéraire du Moyen Âge, 2 (1927), 5–29 • P. Sawyer, ed., Textus Roffensis: Rochester Cathedral Library manuscript A.3.5, 2 vols. (1957–62) • J. Thorpe, ed., Registrum Roffense, or, A collection of antient records, charters and instruments … illustrating the ecclesiastical history and antiquities of the diocese and cathedral church of Rochester (1769) • Bibliothèque Nationale, Paris, MS fr. 18953 [seventeenth-century history of Sées] • 'Livre blanc', Bibliothèque de l'Évêché de Sées, Alençon • Dean and Chapter Muniments, Canterbury, registers A–E • Gallia Christiana in provincias ecclesiasticas distributa, 11, ed. P. Henri and J. Taschereau (1759) • G. Louise, La seigneurie de Bellême: Xe–XIIe siècles, 2 vols. (Flers, France, 1990) • U. Rees, ed., The cartulary of Shrewsbury Abbey, 2 vols. (1975) • J. H. Round, ed., Calendar of documents preserved in France, illustrative of the history of Great Britain and Ireland (1899) • S. Anselmi Cantuariensis archiepiscopi opera omnia, ed. F. S. Schmitt, 6 vols. (1938–61) • Symeon of Durham, Opera • John of Worcester, Chron. • C. Flight, The bishops and monks of Rochester, 1076–1214 (1997) • Reg. RAN, vol. 2 • A. Gransden, ed., The customary of the Benedictine abbey of Bury St Edmunds in Suffolk, HBS, 99 (1973) • D. L. Bethell, 'English Black monks and episcopal elections in the 1120s', EngHR, 84 (1969), 673–98 • D. Bethell, 'Richard of Belmeis and the foundation of St Osyth's', Transactions of the Essex Archaeological Society, 3rd ser., 2 (1966–7), 299–328 • H. A. Wilson, ed., The pontifical of Magdalen College, HBS, 39 (1910) • P. Jaffé, ed., Regesta pontificum Romanorum, rev. G. Wattenbach, 2nd edn, 2 vols. (Leipzig, 1885–8) • The historical works of Gervase of Canterbury, ed. W. Stubbs, 2 vols., Rolls Series, 73 (1879–80) • D. Crouch, The Beaumont twins: the roots and branches of power in the twelfth century, Cambridge Studies in Medieval Life and Thought, 4th ser., 1 (1986) • R. Somerville, ed., Scotia pontificia: papal letters to Scotland before the pontificate of Innocent III (1982) • J. Hudson, ed. and trans., Historia ecclesiae Abbendonensis / The history of the church of Abingdon, OMT, 2 (2002) • J. Raine, ed., The historians of the church of York and its archbishops, 2, Rolls Series, 71 (1886), 228–51, 259–69 • J. H. Round, ed., Ancient charters, royal and private, prior to AD 1200, PRSoc., 10 (1888) • Fasti Angl., 1066–1300, [Monastic cathedrals] • C. H. Talbot, ed. and trans., The life of Christina of Markyate, OMT (1959) • Patrologia Latina, 158 (1853) • N. R. Ker, ed., Catalogue of manuscripts containing Anglo-Saxon (1957) • C. W. Hollister, Henry I (2001) • M. Brett and J. Gribbin, eds., Canterbury, 1070–1136, English Episcopal Acta [forthcoming]

Archives Bibliothèque de l'Évêché de Sées, Alençon, 'Livre blanc' • Canterbury Cathedral, deanery registers A–E | Bibliothèque Nationale, Paris, MS fr. 18953

Likenesses seal, PRO, Ancient Deeds (E 40), A5005, Duchy of Lancaster Ancient Deeds (DL 27), LS 46

Esdaile, James (1808–1859), East India Company surgeon and mesmerist, was born on 8 February 1808 in Montrose, Forfarshire, Scotland, the eldest son of the Revd James Esdaile and his wife, Margaret Blair. He studied at the University of Edinburgh where he graduated MD, and subsequently gained an appointment as assistant surgeon in the East India Company's service in 1830. He arrived in Bengal in 1831, and, apart from a short period in 1846 when he had to accompany a regiment on active field duty, Esdaile spent his working life in and around Calcutta. He suffered from persistent health problems dating from the development of chronic bronchitis and asthma at the age of fifteen. Although the change to a warmer climate had been expected to be beneficial, Esdaile himself held that it had an adverse effect on his state of well-being. He thoroughly disliked India, considering it 'a country injurious to my health and distasteful to me' (Esdaile, Introduction of Mesmerism, 11). His private life was fraught

with grief and he endured much personal hardship: his seventeen-year-old bride died during the voyage to India; his second wife died some years later. Esdaile's continued weak state of health, together with his difficult personal experiences, is thought to have led to his breakdown just four years after his arrival in Calcutta. He was granted an unusually long furlough of nearly three years, part of which he spent travelling, and wrote about his experiences in Letters from the Red Sea, Egypt, and the Continent (1839).

Shortly after his return to work in India, Esdaile was put in charge of Hooghly Hospital, in an area that was then deemed less desirable than Calcutta. His lengthy stay at Hooghly, from 1839 to 1846, did nothing to alleviate Esdaile's dislike of India. Nevertheless, according to his brother he found during this period 'something to dispel the ennui of Indian life' (Esdaile, Mesmerism in India, ix). Esdaile had begun to experiment with mesmerism. During the 1830s and 1840s mesmerism had gained a particularly high profile among medical professionals and the wider public back home in Britain. Esdaile proclaimed 'that his mission was to become "the Apostle of Mesmerism in India"' (ibid.). Although later popular accounts of social life in India suggest that it had by then 'for some time been known that Dr Esdaile … had been making experiments in the jail, and among individuals, in furtherance of his openly professed belief in the mysterious power of mesmerism' (Tayler, 439–40), Esdaile himself stressed that until April 1845, when he performed a major surgical procedure on a mesmerized Hindu convict, he 'had never seen any one mesmerised, nor read a mesmeric book, and had only conversed with one person who had witnessed the mesmeric phenomena' (Esdaile, Introduction of Mesmerism, 13). This presumed first patient suffered from a double hydrocele of considerable proportions on his scrotum. This kind of condition, similar to elephantiasis, was then common in eastern India. No cure was known and surgical removal of these tumours was rare, and widely dreaded at a time when no effective anaesthetic was available. The tumorous growth of one of Esdaile's patients weighed 103 pounds and measured 7 feet in circumference and 2 feet round its neck. The reportedly painless operation undertaken by Esdaile was therefore a major achievement by the standards of the time. Consequently many Indian patients with major tumorous growths travelled from afar to benefit from his painless procedure. Within a short time Esdaile became famous among the indigenous and European communities. Reports of his use of mesmerism in pain inhibition during surgery were also well received in Britain where they helped it to gain credibility in the eyes of some medical practitioners and a general public that had begun to grow weary of the sensationalism surrounding many mesmeric shows and spectacles.

Following a report by Esdaile to the deputy governor of Bengal on his successful first operation and further surgical as well as medical courses of treatment based on mesmerism, he was in November 1846 put in charge of a small experimental mesmeric hospital linked to the Calcutta

Native Hospital. A year later a committee composed of medical and non-medical officials submitted a broadly positive report on Esdaile's painless surgery. This caused the newly appointed governor-general, Lord Dalhousie, to commend Esdaile for his 'ability and zeal' (Dalhousie, 'Bengal, Mesmeric Hospital', no. 23, 9), and to appoint him in 1848 to the prestigious and potentially lucrative position of presidency surgeon and, subsequently, in 1850, to marine surgeon 'in acknowledgment of the service he had rendered to humanity by mitigating largely its sufferings within his own sphere' (Dalhousie to board of guardians of the poor, 3). The committee's report and the admission by a reputedly down-to-earth official such as Lord Dalhousie that he entertained

> no doubt that by Mesmerism, whatever that may be, an influence is exercised over patients, by means of which complete insensibility to pain is produced during the performance of some of the most severe operations to which the human frame can be subjected (Dalhousie, 'Bengal, Mesmeric Hospital', no. 23, 2)

did much to raise Esdaile's and other mesmerists' credibility. However, this was only a partial success as the newly discovered effect of ether as a powerful and more easily administered anaesthetic pushed mesmeric surgery out of its moment in the limelight of medical and public admiration. While recognizing Esdaile's achievement, Dalhousie declined to support the continuation of the Mesmeric Hospital, arguing rightly that ether would enable company surgeons to carry out operations more efficiently and at lower cost. Esdaile continued to carry out mesmeric surgery and medicine in private practice, drawing on the unabated support of influential members of the Bengali nobility and middle classes as well as of a small circle of Europeans. Nevertheless, a small mesmeric hospital established by means of public subscriptions survived only for a year (1848–9), and Esdaile's short-lived superintendence of out-patients at the Sukia Street Dispensary was far removed from his vision of a mesmeric corps in every hospital in India. He returned to Scotland on furlough in 1851 and retired from the company's service as soon as his twenty years' contract came to an end in 1853.

For a while Esdaile continued to publish on the benefits of mesmerism which he considered a gift of God and the 'Medicine of Nature'. He argued that mesmerism should be used with awe and respect by people willing to 'return for a moment to the feet of their mother Nature' (Esdaile, *Mesmerism in India*, 15), rather than for entertainment or evil purposes. Although Esdaile's work and mission received much attention in the 1990s owing to an upsurge of academic interest in heterodox medical practices, during his own time his books were not easily accessible. The memory of his achievements, although lingering longer in India, faded in Britain from the 1850s onwards. Esdaile's attempts to refute any unjustified or sceptical criticism in the 'very forcible language' for which he had been known (Crawford, 413), may be indicative of his disappointment at the disappearance of mesmerism in surgery following

the discovery of ether, especially as he considered the latter to be inferior to the 'natural' mesmeric agency, being a mere 'artificial' remedy and a 'palliative'. He even wrote a note of protest in response to the decision in 1853 by the American congress to award a prize to the discoverer of what it considered as the first anaesthetic, asserting that 'painless surgery by means of Mesmerism had been reduced by me to a regular every-day system in Bengal, long before ether had been heard of' (*Report of the ... London Mesmeric Infirmary*, 20). He became so committed to the cause of mesmerism that he was, in his own words, 'perhaps, the only member of the public service indifferent to ... the good fortune [connected with the position of presidency surgeon and marine surgeon]' (Esdaile, *Introduction of Mesmerism*, 11). Esdaile regretted that 'the routine practitioner will rarely condescend to divide with nature the merit of the cure', and bemoaned the fact that 'if any one pretends to be able sometimes to cure disease by the unassisted powers of nature, he is called a quack, impostor, or fool' (Esdaile, *Mesmerism in India*, 16).

On his return from India, Esdaile became vice-president of the 'London Mesmeric Infirmary', but only occasionally engaged in the practice of mesmerism. He was instrumental in the introduction of the artificial propagation of fish into Scotland, and initiated a scheme for the education of the daughters of academics and the clergy in Scotland. He eventually left Scotland on account of his broken health in favour of the milder climate of Sydenham, Kent, where he settled with his third wife, Eliza Weatherhead, whom he had married probably in 1851, and gradually withdrew into privacy. He died from chronic bronchitis on 10 January 1859 at his home, Elm Bank, Lawrie Road, Sydenham, Kent, and was buried at Norwood cemetery five days later. He was survived by his wife. His death was noted but briefly in only a few medical journals, and his career remained unhonoured by any reference to his professional achievements in the practice of mesmeric surgery and medicine.

WALTRAUD ERNST

Sources J. Esdaile, *Mesmerism in India, and its practical application in surgery and medicine* (1846); repr. (New York, 1976); repr. as *Hypnosis in medicine and surgery* (New York, [1957]) · J. Esdaile, *The introduction of mesmerism (with the sanction of the government) as an anaesthetic and curative agent into the public hospitals of India*, 2nd edn. 1856 (1852) · J. Esdaile, 'On the operation for the removal of scrotal tumours', *London Medical Gazette*, [3rd] ser., 11 (1850), 449–54 · *A record of cases treated in the Mesmeric Hospital, from Nov 1846 to May 1847, with reports of the official visitors* (1847) · *A record of cases treated in the Mesmeric Hospital, from June to Dec 1847, with reports of the official visitors* (1848) · *Report of the Committee appointed by government to observe and report upon surgical operations by Dr J. Esdaile upon patients under the influence of alleged mesmeric agency* (1846) · reopening of the Mesmeric Hospital in Calcutta, 1848, BL OIOC, MS F/4/2401, no. 129.688 · Lord Dalhousie to board of guardians of the poor, Exeter, 1856, NA Scot., MS GD45/14/613 · Lord Dalhousie, Bengal, Mesmeric Hospital, 1848, NA Scot., MS GD45/6/19/1 · J. Esdaile, 'Correspondence: mesmeric facts', *The Englishman and Military Chronicle* (15 Jan 1846) · J. Esdaile, 'Correspondence', *The Englishman and Military Chronicle* (29 May 1846) · F. Mouat and A. F. Lacroix, 'Letters', *The Englishman and Military Chronicle* (10 June 1846) · A. W. [A. Webb], 'Correspondence: mesmerism in Bengal', *Bengal Hurkaru* (14 June 1846) · *Zoist: a journal of cerebral physiology and mesmerism, and their application to human welfare* (1846–54) · D. G. Crawford, 'James Esdaile', *Bengal*

Past and Present, 5 (1910), 52–65 • J. Esdaile, *Letters from the Red sea, Egypt, and the continent* (1839) • *East-India Register and Directory* (1832–44) • *Report of the tenth annual meeting of the London Mesmeric Infirmary* (1859) • *London and Provincial Medical Directory* (1860), 1002 • *BMJ* (22 Jan 1859) • D. G. Crawford, *A history of the Indian medical service, 1600–1913*, 2 vols. (1914) • W. Tayler, *Thirty-eight years in India* (1881) • G. Toynbee, *A sketch of the administration of the Hooghly District, 1795–1845* (1888) • *CGPLA Eng. & Wales* (1859) • d. cert.

Archives BL OIOC, MSS • NA Scot., MSS • SOAS, MSS • Wellcome L., MSS | CUL, Society for Psychical Research, MSS

Wealth at death under £450: probate, 23 Feb 1859, *CGPLA Eng. & Wales*

Esdaile [*née* McDowall], **Katharine Ada** (1881–1950), art historian, was born in London on 23 April 1881, the daughter of Andrew McDowall, secretary to the Girls' Public Day School Trust, and his wife, Ada Benson, sister of E. W. Benson, archbishop of Canterbury, and first headmistress in turn of Norwich, Oxford, and Bedford high schools. Katharine McDowall was educated at Notting Hill high school and was a scholar of Lady Margaret Hall, Oxford. There she read classics, gaining a third in honour moderations in 1903, but the special interest she then showed in antique sculpture already indicated the direction of her future studies. From 1904 onwards she published articles in periodicals such as the *Journal of Hellenic Studies* and the *Numismatic Chronicle* on Greek and Roman coins and on classical portrait sculpture. In 1907 she married Arundell James Kennedy Esdaile (*d.* 1956), secretary of the British Museum from 1926 to 1940, and with him she had a daughter followed by two sons. During the later part of the First World War she worked for the publishers Batsford, with their list of books on British architecture. But it was not until 1919, after the birth of her third child, that she began to focus on intensive study of post-medieval sculpture in England, the subject she made peculiarly her own. With the exception of Lady Victoria Manners's publication of the account book of Nicholas Stone, scholarly attention on English sculpture had hitherto been focused almost exclusively on the medieval period. Esdaile's energetic efforts as both writer and campaigner shifted this markedly. Visiting churches throughout the country and filling almost fifty notebooks in her sprawling hand, she assembled the material for the numerous articles, notes, and letters that appeared continuously from 1920 until her death. The earliest consisted of a series, Studies of English Sculptors from Pierce to Chantrey, that appeared in *The Architect* in 1921 and 1922. These early attempts to write sculptors back into the narrative of British art were followed by the opportunity to introduce these figures to a European audience through her entries on English sculptors included in Thieme and Becker's *Allgemeines Lexicon der bildenden Künstler* from 1924 onwards.

By this date Esdaile had already started work on Roubiliac, the sculptor whose reputation she was to retrieve. A letter to the *Times Literary Supplement* in 1921 about a lost Roubiliac medallion was followed by a series of notes, by a short book in 1924, *Roubiliac's Work at Trinity College, Cambridge*, and finally in 1928 by her monograph *The Life and Works of Louis François Roubiliac*. Despite some wild attributions and unsupported speculations, this work—Esdaile's

most ambitious publication—for the first time assembled Roubiliac's *œuvre* in a way that left no doubt about his importance as an artist. Its rich documentation, most of it completely new, and its use of contemporary anecdotal references from a wide range of sources make it still an essential work of reference. For this and her earlier work on English monuments she was awarded a medal by the Royal Society of Arts in 1928. A year earlier Esdaile had provided a wider context for Roubiliac's work in her *Monumental Sculpture since the Renaissance*, which was the first substantial account to be written of English post-medieval sculpture.

During the late 1920s and 1930s Esdaile's major project was the edition of George Vertue's *Note Books*, published by the Walpole Society between 1930 and 1934. This made available in a proper scholarly form the single most important source for the history of British art in the seventeenth and early eighteenth centuries, and these volumes remain the foundation for work on this period. At the same time Esdaile was relentless in her pursuit of works by neglected sculptors and published a stream of important articles and notes drawing attention to forgotten figures such as Edward Stanton and William Stanton of Holborn, Epiphanius Evesham (seventeenth-century sculptors were especially to her taste), and Sir Robert Taylor, known as an architect but hitherto dismissed as a sculptor. She was also a tireless writer of letters to *The Times*, sometimes announcing new discoveries but as often protesting about the impending demolition or alteration of a building or monument. In 1946 she published a further survey of post-medieval sculpture, *English Church Monuments, 1510–1840*. Arranged thematically, this drew on her very extensive knowledge, but was criticized for failing to provide a European context for the work of English sculptors. Her intention to publish a biographical dictionary of sculptors was never realized (the typescript for part of this is in the National Art Library) but the task was accomplished by her protégé Rupert Gunnis in his *Dictionary of British Sculptors* (1953). During the 1950s the field that Esdaile had effectively established through her pioneering work was being investigated more systematically by scholars such as M. I. Webb (in her monograph on Rysbrack), Terence Hodgkinson, and Margaret Whinney. Although many of her attributions were to be questioned, Esdaile deserves the credit for making English post-medieval sculpture seem worthy of attention, and her work was the foundation on which others built. She died at the Queen Victoria Hospital, East Grinstead, Sussex, on 31 August 1950. Her notebooks and voluminous correspondence were sold by her son Edmund to the library of the Henry H. Huntington Art Collection, San Marino, California.

MALCOLM BAKER

Sources J. Physick and N. Ramsay, 'Katharine Ada Esdaile, 1881–1950', *Church Monuments*, 1/2 (1986), 116–36 • *The Times* (4 Sept 1950) • *ArchR*, 108 (1950), 1027 • *Burlington Magazine*, 92 (1950), 329 • *Country Life*, 107 (July–Dec 1950), 1027 • *DNB* • *CGPLA Eng. & Wales* (1951)

Wealth at death £2442 2s.: administration with will, 21 July 1951, *CGPLA Eng. & Wales*

Esdaile, William (1758–1837), banker and print collector, was born, presumably in London, on 6 February 1758, the fourth son of Sir James Esdaile (1713x15–1793) of Great Gains, Essex, banker, cartouche maker to the army, and one-time lord mayor of London, and his second wife, Mary Major (1731/2–1792). He received a commercial education and was placed as a clerk with the well-established City of London bankers Ladbrooke & Co. In 1781 he joined the new private bank founded by his father and Sir James's son-in-law, Sir Benjamin Hammet, as Esdaile, Hammet, and Esdaile in Birchin Lane, City of London. The bank moved to 73 Lombard Street in 1782 and in 1792 merged with Smith, Wright & Co. On his father's death in 1793 Esdaile took over the firm, which moved to 21 Lombard Street. From 1798 it was known as Sir James Esdaile, Esdaile, Hammet, Esdaile, and Hammet, with a few changes among the junior partners, until 1823, when the firm became Sir James Esdaile, Hammet, Grenfell, and Scott and from 1833 Sir James Esdaile, Esdaile, Grenfell, Thomas & Co. His son describes Esdaile in a private journal as the conscientious and dedicated supervisor of the firm, who had 'neither talent nor inclination for conversation on general subjects, and … knew little or nothing of what was passing out of banking hours' (private information). With the business prospering under his care, Esdaile began to collect under the guidance of two connoisseurs: the Revd Thomas Noble and John Thane (1748–1818), an engraver, printseller, and expert on coins. Esdaile bought an architecturally unpretentious London residence on Clapham Common, situated in park-like grounds, where he housed his growing art collections. In a picture gallery, library, and drawing rooms and in staircases he displayed paintings by Albrecht Dürer, Ostade, Rubens, Jacob van Ruisdael, Salvator Rosa, Richard Wilson, and Thomas Gainsborough, framed drawings by G. B. Cipriani and Francesco Bartolozzi and Sèvres and Chelsea vases. The pride of Esdaile's collection, a very substantial set of prints and drawings kept in specially constructed drawers, included a complete set of etchings by Rembrandt, as well as drawings by Michelangelo, Raphael, Titian, Rubens, and Claude, bought at Sir Thomas Lawrence's sale in 1830. Esdaile also collected drawings by Ostade, Gainsborough, Hogarth, and Wilson, drawings of flowers on vellum, mainly from Lord Bute's sale in 1794, as well as books, coins and medals, marbles, and minerals. Unlike the gentlemen bankers and collectors of the Hope dynasty or Samuel Rogers, Esdaile was not part of the circle of connoisseurs who gravitated towards the Royal Academy and the British Institution. In 1784 Esdaile married Elizabeth Jeffries (1751/2–1811), the only child of Edward Jeffries, treasurer of St Thomas's Hospital, with whom he had two sons and four daughters. His banking business apparently prevented Esdaile from travelling abroad until he visited Italy in 1825 and 1827. He retired from the banking business on grounds of ill health in 1832. The firm fell victim to a financial crisis in 1837 and was quietly wound up. Esdaile passed the winter of 1835–6 at Rome and Naples, but after his return his health began gradually to deteriorate. Having been confined to his bed for nine months, he died at Clapham on 2 October 1837 and was interred at the nonconformist Bunhill Fields burial-ground. His marbles, bronzes, Greek pottery, porcelain, enamels, coins, medals, minerals, and fossils were sold in 1838. In March 1838 and June 1840 Christies held sales of his collection, one of the largest and most valuable in Britain: 621 drawings and 553 prints were sold over seventeen days. Many choice lots went abroad, but the majority were bought by London dealers, realizing a total of £9,409 15s. ALSAGER VIAN, *rev.* HOLGER HOOCK

Sources 'Mr. Esdaile's collections', *GM*, 2nd ser., 14 (1840), 180 · F. G. Hilton Price, *A handbook of London bankers* (1876) · 'The Esdaile crisis', *Three Banks Review*, 70 (1966), 39–48 · H. Malet, 'William Esdaile', *N&Q*, 10th ser., 4 (1905), 481–2 · will, PRO, PROB 11/1885, sig. 712, fols. 97r–98v · *A catalogue of the valuable assemblage of marbles, bronzes, Greek pottery, oriental, Sèvres, & Dresden porcelain, enamels of Limoges, coins, medals, minerals, and fossils, of William Esdaile … which … will be sold by auction, by Messrs. Christie and Manson* (1838) [sale catalogue, 22 March 1838] · private information (1888) · GL, Noble collection, C78 (Sir James Esdaile) · Bunhill Fields burial-ground, interment order books, 1807–11, 1834–9, GL, MS 1092/6, 15 · F. Lugt, *Répertoire des catalogues de ventes publiques*, 2 (The Hague, 1953) · F. Lugt, *Les marques de collections de dessins et d'estampes* (Amsterdam, 1921); repr. (The Hague, 1956)

Archives priv. coll., papers · York University, Toronto, Scott Library, papers | Royal Bank of Scotland, London, Sir James Esdaile, Esdaile, Grenfell, Thomas & Co., GB 1502 ES

Likenesses G. Sharples, pastel drawing, c.1826, NPG · D. Wilkie, oils, 1836 · R. Graves, engraving (after G. Sharples) · T. Lawrence, oils (unfinished), repro. in K. Garlick, *Sir Thomas Lawrence: a complete catalogue of the oil paintings* (1989)

Wealth at death bequests of £60,000 to children; print and drawing collection bequeathed to son-in-law, sold for over £9400 in 1840; remaining real and personal estate bequeathed to a son (not valued): will, PRO, PROB 11/1885, sig. 712; GM

Esdall, Anne (1717/18–c.1795). *See under* Esdall, James (c.1720–1755).

Esdall, James (c.1720–1755), printer and bookseller, was born in Dublin, the third of six sons of James Esdall (d. 1728), a hatter, and his wife, Margaret. Esdall's family was middle-class Irish of the trade culture; and, at a time when social class, religion, and politics were closely linked, the Esdalls were probably protestant, as the principal influences on Esdall's career—his master and mentor, George Faulkner, that prince of Dublin printers, and Esdall's principal compatriot, Charles Lucas, a zealous Irish whig nationalist and polemical writer—were both attached to mostly protestant circles. In a vigorous career of no more than eleven years, Esdall produced a broad range of material for the rapidly expanding Irish markets. Contributing to Dublin's developing status as an international print centre, he and his small family-operated firm launched as many as four Irish newspapers; issued reprints of London editions of popular English novels, plays, and poetry anthologies; printed and sold works by Irish writers; and incurred serious legal penalties by printing and selling inflammatory political material on Anglo-Irish relations and municipal reform in Dublin.

Early beginnings Recorded data on Esdall's early beginnings are thin (Pollard, *Dictionary*, 182–3), but as a true son of the trade culture he was reared and educated accordingly. His apprenticeship at George Faulkner's printing house on Essex Street, Dublin, probably began shortly after his father's death in 1728. Like Faulkner, who learned his trade from the learned London printer and scholar William Bowyer the younger, Esdall received prestigious formal training and invaluable exposure. At Faulkner's busy book hub, with its lively book chat and daily round of commercial dealings, Esdall witnessed at first hand the mechanics and politics of the eighteenth-century Irish print culture. Moreover, in Faulkner himself, Esdall had an imposing career model of the Irish patriot printer, willing to incur both rancour and litigation for his beliefs; and in a city rife with piratical printers, Faulkner also served as a model of correct business practice, notwithstanding his copyright and distribution imbroglios with the English novelist Samuel Richardson. In 1735 Faulkner engaged his promising apprentice in the issue of a slight, but sensitive, anonymous publication, *Observations upon … Holding Ecclesiastical Benefices … together with Fellowships in the University of Dublin*—the first of many career intersections between master and pupil.

On 14 August 1744 Esdall was sworn and admitted free by service of the printers' guild of St Luke the Evangelist; he was paid quarterage from 1744 until 1755, the year of his death. In 1744 he set up as a printer and bookseller on Fishamble Street, Smock Alley, Dublin, the first of his two family-operated establishments. Dublin printers and bookmen doubtless counted Esdall among Faulkner's most enterprising protégés, for during the first half of his career—the years preceding his hazardous association with Lucas in 1749—he achieved an impressive list of imprints; and many of these books and pamphlets were printed on paper manufactured by the Irish home market ('Buy Irish!' the cry of many Dublin tradesmen).

On Fishamble Street, Esdall printed and sold a range of material attractive to Dublin readers with interests political, literary, and feminist. Though the four newspapers he issued reflected largely political material, Esdall's book stock consisted mostly of inexpensive reprints of London imprints. His record of imprints began on 20 March 1744 with an important political text, the *Proceedings of the Sheriffs and Commons of … Dublin … Relating to Controverted Matters in the City*. A shrewd self-promoter, Esdall printed a full-page advertisement on the last page of the book for a recent issue of his, *A Vindication of … Captain Middleton, F.R.S., in a Late Voyage Aboard H.M.S., the "Furace," for the Discovery of the North-West Passage*. On 31 March the firm launched its first of four newspapers, the *Flying Post*, of short duration, followed in October by his *General News-Letter* (ten numbers), an unremarkable digest of domestic and foreign intelligence. Clearly Esdall had not as yet found his voice.

With the relative success of his first year in business, Esdall moved his premises on 16 November 1745 to the Blind Quay, at the corner of Copper Alley on Cork Hill, his base of operations for the next ten years. To his new premises, he brought the capable woman who became his helpmate and unofficial business partner, **Anne Esdall**

[*née* Middleton] (1717/18–*c.*1795), printer and bookseller, whom he had married on 31 August 1745 (*Dublin Courant*, 3 Sept 1745). Esdall now restyled his *General News-Letter* and reissued it under a more assertive and proprietary title: *Esdall's News-Letter*. The paper, which ran (sometimes irregularly) thrice weekly for nearly ten years, spoke to tradesmen and men of business; and it gave a special focus to timely political, urban, and guild news in Dublin and London, as well as in the new American colonies, in Africa, and on the continent. *Esdall's News-Letter* was the economic mainstay of the firm and of Esdall's career; and its income from advertising sales must have been steady, if not robust ('Advertisements are inserted in this paper at a British Half-Crown for the first, and a British sixpence for each time after': no. 400, Wednesday, 13 June 1750). Esdall regularly ran illustrated advertisements for such local establishments as Hibby's Optical Shop, Rourke's Parrot (a clothes shop), and Newman's, where Dubliners could buy 'leather breeches of a black kind, for customers who fancy them' (no. 397, 6 June 1750).

Concurrently with his work on the *News-Letter*, Esdall regularly reprinted, or sold reprints of, English imprints (both new and old) which capitalized on the heated political climate of the mid-1740s—among these *The question of whether Great Britain and Ireland can be otherwise than miserable under a popish king?*; and *The Free Briton's Answer to the Pretender's Declaration … by the Archbishop of Yorke*, followed two years later by a reprint of a popular anonymous London ballad, *Lovat's Ghost*, occasioned by the recent public beheading of a notorious Jacobite intriguer Simon Fraser, Lord Lovat. Other works from this period include new material by Irish writers such as James Eyre Weekes whose poem *The Amazon*, together with *To the Ladies of Dublin* (both 1745), indicates the firm's awareness of Dublin's growing number of women readers. Its output notwithstanding, this first half of Esdall's career was blandly uneventful as compared with the tumult soon to follow.

Troubles and later career, 1749–1754 Esdall's first professional association with Charles Lucas had led to the publication in March 1744 of Lucas's uncharacteristically temperate work, *Divelina libera: an Apology of the Civil Rights and Liberties of the Citizens of Dublin*. Beginning in 1749, however, Esdall's association with Lucas developed into a dangerous partnership, with fatal results for his career. First, Esdall printed in pamphlet format some twenty political addresses by Lucas on Irish constitutional freedom and the corruption of the House of Commons. Second, he furthered his partnership with Lucas by printing Lucas's political newspaper (the fourth newspaper from the Esdall firm), *The Censor, or, The Citizen's Journal*. And, third, he printed in June 1749 Lucas's chief work, the bold *Magna charta libertatum civitatis Dublini*, which he actively promoted in his newspaper (1 June 1749).

The authorities did not share Esdall's enthusiasm. Lucas had manifestly succeeded in focusing strong attention on himself and his polemical writings—and the authorities were keen to stop him and his brisk printer. Finding Lucas's *Charter* thoroughly subversive, the chief justice examined Esdall on 16 June 1749; Esdall admitted to his (and

Lucas's) role in Lucas's political writings (*Censor*, 17). On 11–16 October 1749 the House of Commons resolved that Lucas's newspaper and pamphlets—all printed by Esdall—promoted sedition and insurrection (*The Tryal of Mr Charles Lucas*, 1749; *Collins' Pamphlets*, 54, no. 16). Facing prosecution, Esdall refused to co-operate when summoned to be taken into custody. His subsequent actions remain unclear, though it appears that he went into hiding, was incarcerated, or fled Ireland for London, the continent, or even the new (hospitable) book centres of New York, Boston, and Philadelphia. On 5 December 1749 Anne Esdall, in lieu of her absent husband, was examined by the Commons about 'scandalous' and 'factious libels' emanating from the Esdall firm (*Journals of the House of Commons of … Ireland*, 5.27–8). In May 1750 the grand jury presented Lucas's writings as 'seditious libels' to be publicly burnt, with severe penalties for the author and publisher (Gilbert Library, Dublin, Robinson MS 31, nos. 6 and 7; *Dublin Journal*, 15).

These troubles seriously disrupted the operations and profits of Esdall's firm, resulting in a significant, and evidently irrecoverable, loss of income. In summer 1750 Esdall returned to public life and attempted to recover his recent shortfall with a flurry of new issues and stock; among these were *The Case and Tryal of John Peter Zenger, Printer, for a Libel Against the Government* (a famous case of its kind, with particular applications to Esdall's troubles); Colley Cibber's classical imitations from Horace and Pindar, *A Rhapsody upon the Marvellous* (London, 1751; Esdall reprint, Dublin, 1751); Henry Fielding's essay on urban reform, *Examples of the Interposition of Providence* (London, 1752; Esdall reprint, Dublin, 1752); and Lord Bolingbroke's *Letters on the Study and Use of History* (London, 1752; Dublin reprint, 1752).

James Esdall died in Dublin, aged about thirty-five years, on 24 March 1755. He was survived by his wife and their four children. Esdall's death was mentioned solemnly by his former master and mentor, George Faulkner, whose poignant homage mentioned his former apprentice's short and sad life: 'He suffered very much in Health and Fortune by some certain People whom he espoused', suggesting, perhaps, Lucas's betrayal of Esdall when Esdall most needed him. Faulkner appealed to the public to assist the widow Esdall and her 'four helpless children' (*Dublin Journal*, 25 [1755]; Pollard, *Dictionary*, 183).

The Esdall firm continued after Esdall's death under the direction of Anne Esdall, with the firm's former journeyman, Henry Saunders, who had been taken on in 1749. She had announced these plans in the *Dublin Journal* (1 April 1755). In 1755 she issued *A Vindication of the Conduct of Mr John McCannon* and an edition of Edmund Gibson's *Experimental Philosophy*, sold by Oliver Nelson, an active Dublin bookseller–printer and former business associate of her late husband's. But operations soon foundered, and Mrs Esdall had to liquidate the firm's stock, its equipment, and even the household furniture (*Dublin Journal*, 7 [1755]). Saunders then took over the firm, promptly restyling *Esdall's News-Letter* as *Saunders' News-Letter* (1755–74;

Munter, 243). One of Saunders's apprentices was his former employer's son, William Esdall (d. 1795), husband of Elizabeth Levinge, who was apprenticed to Saunders in 1763 and admitted free of the guild in 1777. After William's death in 1795, Anne Esdall, aged seventy-seven, petitioned the printers' guild for relief. Three guineas were granted (Pollard, *Dictionary*, 182). Anne herself died about 1795.

James Esdall is an important figure in the history of Irish political journalism and Ireland's print culture during the mid-eighteenth century. The necessary man, beneath the blast and counter blast of reputation, lies in the factual record of his life and work. At great personal and professional jeopardy, he was an ardent promoter of Irish talent, Irish writings, and a free Irish press. An ethical businessman in a kingdom rife with surreptitious and unauthorized imprints—not to mention rogue printers—Esdall worked congenially and ethically with stationers and writers in London and in Dublin. In the lineage of protean Irish patriots of his day—Molesworth, Molyneux, Swift, Lucas, Faulkner—James Esdall merits inclusion.

MAUREEN E. MULVIHILL

Sources M. Pollard, *A dictionary of members of the Dublin book trade 1550–1800* (2000) · M. Pollard, 'Control of the press in Ireland through the king's printer's patent, 1600–1800', *Irish Booklore*, 4 (1980), 79–95 · M. Pollard, *Dublin's trade in books, 1500–1800* (1989) · R. Munter, *A dictionary of the print trade in Ireland, 1500–1775* (1988) · R. C. Cole, *Irish booksellers and English writers, 1740–1800* (1986) · J. W. Phillips, *Printing and bookselling in Dublin from 1670 to 1800* (1998) · IGI · ESTC · *The journals of the House of Commons of the kingdom of Ireland*, 5, 12–13, 28 · H. F. Berry, 'The records of the Feltmaker's Company of Dublin, 1687–1841: the loss and recovery', *Journal of the Royal Society of Antiquaries of Ireland*, 6th ser., 1 (1911), 26–45 · R. S. Crane, F. B. Kaye, and M. E. Prior, *A census of British newspapers and periodicals, 1620–1800* (1927); (1979) · early printed books, TCD, library [web page] · L. M. Hudak, *Early American women printers and publishers, 1639–1820* (1978) · C. Petrie, *The Jacobite movement* (1932) · C. Hoy, 'Fletcher, John', *Jacobean and Caroline dramatists*, ed. F. Bowers, DLitB, 58 (1987), 3–26 · R. Mahony, *Swift: the Irish identity* (1995) · M. E. Mulvihill, 'Joseph Esdall', *The British literary book trade, 1475–1700*, ed. J. K. Bracken and J. Silver, DLitB, 170 (1996), 133–7 · M. E. Mulvihill, 'Dublin's inky brotherhood', *Irish Literary Supplement* (autumn 2002), 13–14

Esher. For this title name *see* Brett, William Baliol, first Viscount Esher (1815–1899); Brett, Reginald Baliol, second Viscount Esher (1852–1930).

Eskgrove. For this title name *see* Rae, Sir David, first baronet, Lord Eskgrove (1729–1804).

Esmond, Henry Vernon [*real name* Harry Esmond Jack] (1869–1922), actor and playwright, was the fourth son in the family of fourteen children of Richard George Jack, physician, and his wife, Mary Rynd. He was born at Bridge House, Hampton Court, Middlesex, on 30 November 1869. Educated privately, he went on the stage in 1885, acting mainly in the provinces for four years. In the spring of 1889 he made a hit in a small part in *The Panel Picture* by W. O. Tristram at the Opéra Comique in London, and was afterwards engaged by E. S. Willard and by Edward Terry, chiefly in the parts of old men. On 19 November 1891 he married the actress Eva *Moore (1868–1955), eighth child of Edward Henry Moore, chemist and public analyst for Sussex. They had two daughters, one of whom died in infancy, and a son.

In 1893 George Alexander engaged Esmond to act Cayley Drummle (an elderly man) in A. W. Pinero's *The Second Mrs Tanqueray* at the St James's Theatre; for the next seven years most of his work was done at that theatre, where he had opportunities to show his versatility as well as his accomplishment. Clement Scott called him 'perfect', and A. B. Walkley 'diabolically clever'. His best work was done in parts that gave scope either for boyishness, such as Little Billee in *Trilby* by George Du Maurier—which he played at the Haymarket Theatre with Herbert Beerbohm Tree in 1895—or for fantasy, such as Touchstone, Mercutio, the young Eddie Remon in *The Masqueraders* by Henry Arthur Jones, or Widgery Blake in W. J. Locke's *The Palace of Puck*. After leaving Alexander in 1900 Esmond acted less than before, being more engaged in writing and producing plays.

Esmond wrote about thirty plays. In 1894 he and his wife took the St James's Theatre for a few weeks in order to produce there his comedy *Bogey*, which, although not successful, brought him into notice as a playwright. In 1895 *The Divided Way*, a more serious play, was also produced at the St James's, and in 1897 his success was assured when Charles Hawtrey produced and acted in his comedy *One Summer's Day* (Comedy Theatre). In 1899 *Grierson's Way* (Haymarket Theatre) showed him in gloomy mood, but in 1901 *When we were Twenty-One* (Comedy Theatre) revealed his best vein, that of light, rather sentimental comedy, gay but touched with pathos—the vein in which he also wrote *Eliza Comes to Stay* (Criterion Theatre, 1913), and *The Law Divine* (Wyndham's Theatre, 1918). Less frivolous were two cleverly conceived and written plays, *Billy's Little Love Affair* (Criterion Theatre, 1903) and *The Dangerous Age* (Vaudeville Theatre, 1914). In 1900 and 1914 Esmond visited the United States, and in 1920 Canada, in order to produce and act in his own plays. On the last two visits he was accompanied by his wife, Eva Moore. In private life Esmond was an amusing, excitable, wilful man of much charm. He died suddenly at a hotel in Paris, France, on 17 April 1922.

H. H. CHILD, rev. K. D. REYNOLDS

Sources *The Times* (18 April 1922) · E. Moore, *Exits and entrances* (1923) · personal knowledge (1937) · *WWW* · m. cert. · *CGPLA Eng. & Wales* (1922) · B. Duncan, *The St James's Theatre: its strange and complete history, 1835–1957* (1964) · b. cert.
Likenesses T. C. Turner, two photogravures, c.1895, NPG · W. Hester, caricature, NPG; repro. in *VF* (14 May 1913)
Wealth at death £28,359 18s. 6d.: probate, 14 June 1922, *CGPLA Eng. & Wales*

Esmonde, Laurence, first Lord Esmonde (c.1570–1645), army officer and landowner, was the second son of Walter (also known as William) Esmonde of Johnstown, co. Wexford, and his wife, Margaret, daughter of Michael Furlong of Horetown, barony of Shelmalier, co. Wexford, one of a family of seven daughters and four sons. The Esmondes were of Norman origin in Wexford. In religion Laurence converted from Old English Catholicism to an ardent protestantism and allegiance to Queen Elizabeth I.

Esmonde served with military distinction in the Low Countries against Spain and in Ireland. In September 1599 he was captain of 150 foot under the earl of Essex, and stationed near Naas, co. Kildare. In March 1600 Esmonde was one of Arthur Chichester's captains at Carrickfergus and by mid-September 1600 he was aiding Sir Samuel Bagenal in mustering recruits from the Low Countries at Dundalk. At the battle of Carlingford Pass (13 November 1600) he commanded his company on one of the wings of the battle. By the end of June 1601 Esmonde was captain of 150 foot at Liscannon, in the Briefne, co. Cavan, Ulster. In Fynes Moryson's account of a skirmish at Monaghan in July 1601 he mentions that when Lord Dunsany, commander of Liscannon, took a prey of 1600 cows and came under attack, Dunsany's Irish troops not only lost the prey of cattle in their retreat but

> fell to a flat running away to the Fort so as poor Captain Esmond (who had the command of the Rear, and very valiantly with a few made good the place) was sore hurt and afterwards taken prisoner and forty or fifty of our side slain. (Moryson, 2.437)

Writing to the earl of Shrewsbury, Esmonde volunteered to procure the assassination or at least the banishment of Hugh O'Neill, second earl of Tyrone, then at the height of his power. Esmonde was knighted by Lord Mountjoy in 1603 for his brave services in the war.

At the end of O'Neill's rebellion Esmonde succeeded Sir Josias Bodley as governor of the strategically important fort at Duncannon, co. Waterford, a post he held until his death. In the projected plantations in Wexford county, Esmonde, Sir Edward Fisher, and Sir Walter Parsons were appointed commissioners and, with surveyors and escheators, to survey the confiscated lands, advise on the transplantation of the Kavanaghs, and in general persuade the Wexford Irish 'that nothing was intended to them but good' in the new Jacobean plantation (*CSP Ire., 1611–15*, 450). For his pains Esmonde 'as a servitor and native of Wexford' (ibid., 452) was granted 1500 acres—around Limerick in north Wexford. However, by 1618 investigations into the Wexford plantation had uncovered fraudulent practices with the result that many native Irish wrongfully dispossessed had to have their lands restored. In 1619 Esmonde purchased a grant of some lands in Wicklow from a Sir Patrick Maule. Subsequently he was involved much to his discredit in what was known as the *Phelim MacFeagh O'Byrne case*, when he stood accused of packing juries and torturing witnesses in his quest to wrench lands from the O'Byrnes. Esmonde accumulated much property in the counties of Wexford, Wicklow, Waterford, Kilkenny, and Tipperary. He represented Wicklow in the Irish parliament of 1613 with Sir William Usher and was on 22 May 1622 created Lord Esmonde, baron of Limerick, in co. Wexford (not to be confused with the city of Limerick in south-west Ireland).

During his Connaught expeditions Esmonde had fallen in love with and married the sister of Morrough O'Flaherty. She was as much noted for her devotion to orthodox Catholicism as for her beauty and, fearing lest their child Thomas be brought up a protestant, she fled back with him to her family in Connaught. Thereupon Esmonde repudiated his O'Flaherty wife, without a formal divorce. He married, before December 1628, Elizabeth, second daughter of Walter Butler, the fourth son of James Butler, ninth earl of Ormond. Twice widowed, she had been successively married to John Sherlock and Sir Edward Gough.

Esmonde's zeal for the reformed religion is apparent in his letters to Lord Conway in 1628 warning him of the growth of popery in Ireland, of the establishment of religious orders, even in Dublin, and of the 'hearts of the mere Irish awakened and cheered by the news of our disasters in France' (CSP Ire., 1625–32, 303). In 1639 Esmonde was once again in litigation when summoned before Star Chamber for conspiracy with Lord Mountnorris and Sir Piers Crosby for libelling Lord Deputy Wentworth, whom they had accused of the murder of one Robert Esmonde. During the trial Esmonde wrote that he felt 'the lord deputy's hand heavy against him' (CSP Ire., 1633–47, 216–17).

At the outbreak of the Irish rising, which in due course sparked off the civil war in England, Esmonde continued to hold the garrison of Duncannon. He maintained an ambivalent neutrality between king and parliament. The suspicions of the Catholic confederates were aroused because many of his men were indeed parliamentarian in their sympathies and had broken the cessation—the truce negotiated with the confederates by the marquess of Ormond in September 1643. They advised Ormond 'to have a care of the fort of Duncannon' (DNB). In September 1644 'ould Laurence Esmonde' became caught up in Lord Inchiquin's defection to the parliamentarians; with his officers and many of his men following Inchiquin's example Esmonde retained but a nominal command. The confederate general Thomas Preston laid siege to Duncannon from 20 January to 18 March 1645, 'the verie best siege that was yett in Ireland' (Gilbert, Contemporary history, 1.104). The fort was as much decayed by age as its governor, though Esmonde held out as long as could be expected against the up-to-date siegecraft of Preston's men and he eventually surrendered the fort on St Patrick's day 1645, when 'he began to know himself to be mortal' (Hore, Wexford, 1.13). In fact by this time Esmonde had gone blind so that his lieutenant, Captain Lorcan, took responsibility for the defence of the fort.

Esmonde survived the surrender of Duncannon a couple of months: he died at Adamstown, near New Ross, co. Wexford, on 26 May and was buried at his own church in Limerick, co. Wexford, on the following day. His second wife survived him, and was described the following month as living 'in grief, age and debility' (GEC, Peerage, 5.112). His peerage died with him, while he bequeathed his immense properties to his and his first wife's son, Sir Thomas Esmonde, confederate general of horse in Ireland during the civil wars.

Esmonde was described as a man of 'sanguine complexion, of an indifferent tall stature, compact, solid, corpulent body, with robustious limbs' (DNB). Arthur Annesley, earl of Anglesey, wrote of him as 'an ancient and wise counsellor and soldier' (Hore, Wexford, 1.309). However, it is difficult to assert that he in fact lived up to the family motto, Malo mori quam foedari ('I prefer death to dishonour'). J. J. N. McGURK

Sources CSP Ire., 1603–15; 1625–47 · J. S. Brewer and W. Bullen, eds., Calendar of the Carew manuscripts, 6 vols., PRO (1867–73) · History of the Irish confederation and the war in Ireland ... by Richard Bellings, ed. J. T. Gilbert, 7 vols. (1882–91), vol. 1, pp. 167 ff.; vol. 4, p. xxxvi · F. Moryson, An itinerary containing his ten yeeres travell through the twelve dominions, 2 (1907) · J. T. Gilbert, ed., A contemporary history of affairs in Ireland from 1641 to 1652, 1 (1879), 104 · Burke, Peerage · T. Carte, An history of the life of James, duke of Ormonde, 3 vols. (1735–6); new edn, pubd as The life of James, duke of Ormond, 6 vols. (1851), vol. 2, pp. 55–64 · J. L. J. Hughes, ed., Patentee officers in Ireland, 1173–1826, including high sheriffs, 1661–1684 and 1761–1816, IMC (1960) · T. Carlyle, ed., Cromwell's letters, 3 vols. in 1 (1888), 59–68 · P. H. Hore, History of the town & county of Wexford, 6 vols. (1900–11) · [J. Lodge], ed., Desiderata curiosa Hibernica, 2 (1772), 276 · J. J. N. McGurk, The Elizabethan conquest of Ireland (1997) · P. H. Hore, History of Duncannon fort (1904) · A. Clarke, The Old English in Ireland, 1625–1642 (1966) · F. French, 'Clonegal: its valley and its battle', Journal of the Royal Society of Antiquaries of Ireland, 5th ser., 14 (1904), 346–59 · S. Lewis, A topographical dictionary of Ireland, 2 vols. (1837), vol. 2 Wexford · P. Lenihan, Confederate Catholics at war, 1641–9 (2001) · B. C. Donovan and D. Edwards, British sources for Irish history, IMC (1997) · GEC, Peerage

Archives Arundel Castle, letters to earl of Arundel · Chatsworth House, Derbyshire, letters to Boyle family · CKS, Cranfield MSS, letters, U269/1Hi

Wealth at death accumulation of properties in counties Wicklow, Waterford, Wexford, Tipperary, and Kilkenny indicate great wealth for the period: administration, PRO, PROB 6/21, fol. 47v · payment of £1760 to Cranfield's attorney in the 1620s may be indicative of sound financial status

Espec, Walter (d. 1147×58), baron and justice, succeeded to the Bedfordshire estates held in 1086 by William Spech, possibly his father or maternal uncle, and by c.1122 had acquired (probably from the crown) additional lands centred on Wark, Northumberland, and Helmsley, Yorkshire. Between c.1119 and 1135 Walter Espec witnessed or was addressed in many royal charters, sometimes with Eustace fitz John, and in 1121 he attended an assembly of northern magnates at Durham. By 1130 Espec and Eustace had heard pleas as royal justices in several northern counties, and Espec had also recently been restocking royal manors in Yorkshire and estates in the vacant bishopric of Durham. In 1134 Espec assisted King David of Scots to capture the rebel Malcolm MacHeth; and between, perhaps, 1131 and 1136 attested one of David's charters.

Soon after Henry I's death David invaded England in support of the Empress Matilda's claim to the English crown and to further his own claims to Cumbria and Northumbria. Walter Espec's castle of Wark, on the River Tweed, was captured by David at about Christmas 1135. By February 1136 Espec had accepted Stephen as king (consequently attesting some of his early charters) and, in the treaty agreed between Stephen and David either later that month or in March, the Scottish king surrendered Wark. However, early in 1138 the castle was again besieged by the Scots. On 22 August 1138 Espec was one of the commanders of the army that defeated King David at the battle of the Standard. Ailred describes him there as good, wise, loyal, sagacious in counsel, energetic, brave, able, prudent, far-sighted, gigantic in stature, with a voice like a trumpet, jet-black hair, a long beard, and large dark eyes; and as making an inspiring speech recounting the achievements of the Normans. In November 1138 Espec instructed his Wark garrison to surrender the town to King David. The appointment of King David's stepson, Waldef, to be prior of Kirkham by 1141, suggests that Walter Espec had by then re-established good relations with the Scots, perhaps in the wake of the second treaty between Stephen and David, made in April 1139. It is possible, however, that Walter, whose border estates were still vulnerable to Scottish attack, and whose loyalties may have shifted or been divided, was acting independently of Stephen. Otherwise little is known of Espec's activities. He attested charters of Odo of Boltby, Benedict fitz Gervase, and Robert (II) de Brus in the 1140s or early 1150s. He borrowed a copy of Geoffrey of Monmouth's *Historia regum* from Robert, earl of Gloucester before 1147, and lent it to Custance, wife of Ralph fitz Gilbert, lord of Scampton, Lincolnshire.

Walter Espec was a great patron of the church, founding the Augustinian priory of Kirkham, Yorkshire, in 1121 or 1122, and the Cistercian abbeys of Rievaulx, Yorkshire, and Wardon, Bedfordshire, on 5 March 1132 and 12 December 1136 respectively. Kirkham may have been established on the advice of Walter's uncle, William, rector of Garton and canon of Nostell, who became its first prior. Espec was probably the *advocatus* with whose assistance it was proposed between 1132 and *c*.1140 to establish a new house at Linton for those Kirkham canons who opposed the reception of Kirkham Priory into the Cistercian order. King David's courtier, Ailred, became a monk at Rievaulx *c*.1134 after visiting Walter Espec at Helmsley Castle.

Walter Espec married a certain Adeline. An unreliable source states that he retired to Rievaulx *c*.1153, became a monk, and was buried there on 15 March 1155. He was possibly dead or in retirement when Robert de Ros (*d*. 1162/3) confirmed his gifts to Rievaulx between 1147 and 14 October 1153. Espec's heirs, who accounted for his land in 1158, were William de Bussei, Geoffrey de Trailli, and Robert de Ros, who were sons of his three sisters, Hawise (wife of William de Bussei), Aubreye (wife of Geoffrey (II) de Trailli), and Adeline (wife of Peter de Ros) respectively. Espec's Northumberland and Yorkshire estates descended in the Ros family, while those in Bedfordshire were mainly divided between the Busseis and the Traillis.

PAUL DALTON

Sources J. C. Atkinson, ed., *Cartularium abbathiae de Rievalle*, SurtS, 83 (1889) • W. Farrer, 'The honour of Old Wardon', ed. J. Tait, *Bedfordshire Historical Record Society*, 11 (1927), 1–46 • *Pipe rolls*, 31 Henry I • *Reg. RAN*, vols. 2–3 • St Aelred [abbot of Rievaulx], 'Relatio de standardo', *Chronicles of the reigns of Stephen, Henry II, and Richard I*, ed. R. Howlett, 3, Rolls Series, 82 (1886) • John of Hexham, 'Historia regum continuata', Symeon of Durham, *Opera*, vol. 2 • J. A. Green, *The government of England under Henry I* (1986) • W. Farrer and others, eds., *Early Yorkshire charters*, 12 vols. (1914–65), vols. 1–3, 9–10 • R. Hexham, 'De gestis regis Stephani et de bello standardi', *Chronicles of the reigns of Stephen, Henry II, and Richard I*, ed. R. Howlett, 3, Rolls Series, 82 (1886) • G. H. Fowler, ed., *Cartulary of the abbey of Old Wardon*, Bedfordshire Historical RS, 13 (1930) • *The life of Ailred of Rievaulx by Walter Daniel*, ed. and trans. M. Powicke (1950) • J. E. Burton, *Kirkham Priory from foundation to dissolution*, Borthwick Paper, 86 (1995)
Archives BL, charters, Cotton MS Julius O T

Espin, Thomas Henry Espinell Compton (1858–1934),

astronomer, was born on 28 May 1858 at 5 Crescent East, Birmingham, the only child of Thomas Espinell Espin DD (1824–1912), and his second wife, Eliza Jessop (*d*. 1933), the daughter of a wealthy merchant. His father was rector of Hadleigh, Essex, and professor of theology at Queen's College, Birmingham. Little is known of Espin's early education, but at the age of fourteen he was sent to school at Haileybury College, Hertford. His interest in astronomy was aroused by the bright appearance of Comet Coggia in 1874, and under the pseudonym T. E. E. he contributed his observations to the *English Mechanic*. Espin's precocious talent brought him to the notice of a prominent amateur astronomer, the Revd Thomas William Webb (1806–1885), who requested his help in the revision of his book *Celestial Objects for Common Telescopes*. After Webb's death Espin totally revised the sixth edition of this popular work (1917).

In 1878 Espin went to Oxford, where he studied theology at Exeter College; he graduated in 1881 with second-class honours. At Oxford he had use of the De La Rue telescope at the university observatory. In return he gave astronomy tuition to the students of the Savilian professor, the Revd Charles Pritchard. Following his graduation he was ordained as a curate at West Kirby on the Wirral, only 6 miles from Wallasey, where his father had been rector for fifteen years. Espin was immediately active in the formation of the Liverpool Astronomical Society, and was elected president in 1885. In the same year his father was given the easier living of Wolsingham, co. Durham, which came under the diocese of Chester. Espin followed shortly after and became the second curate at Wolsingham. He lived at 26 Front Street, where he was able to establish his first observatory, housing a 17¼ inch reflecting telescope by George Calver. The instrument was purchased partly through a legacy from Webb. Espin's residency at Wolsingham was shortlived, as in 1888 the bishop of Chester appointed him to the nearby incumbency of Tow Law.

Once established as vicar of Tow Law, Espin embarked on his long career in astronomy, and undertook a visual and spectroscopic survey for unusual red stars. The results were published in the *Monthly Notices of the Royal Astronomical Society* and *Astronomische Nachrichten*. In 1890 he incorporated these and other discoveries in a revised edition of a catalogue of red stars by J. Birmingham. Espin turned his attention after 1900 to using his reflector to measure double stars of moderate separation. Yet he gained his greatest fame in 1910, when he discovered Nova Lacertae (*Monthly Notices of the Royal Astronomical Society*, 71, 1910–11, 189), for which he was awarded the Jackson-Gwilt medal by the Royal Astronomical Society. From 1912 he employed William Milburn (*d*. 1982), a local graduate of Durham University, as his assistant. Espin's will, dated 1920, protected Milburn as principal beneficiary and reversed his earlier intention to endow astronomy at the University of Oxford.

Espin also had an interest in geology: he collected rocks and fossils, which he cut into thin sections. The discovery of X-rays by Roentgen inspired him to construct his own X-ray machine powered by a 24 plate Wimshurst machine. Although primitive, it was for many years used to examine for broken bones. Espin had a shed, open to the elements, erected in his garden in which local sufferers from tuberculosis were treated. He was fiercely independent, disliked constraints on his authority, and saw no need for a local church council. Although generous, later in life he had a detached indifference to the poor of his parish. He never married and appears to have been a misogynist, as he refused to have women in his church choir. He was greatly involved with the running of the church scouts and the Boys' Brigade. For many years he served as a fair but somewhat severe local magistrate.

Espin remained the vicar of Tow Law until his death, after a short illness, on 2 December 1934 at the age of seventy-six. He was buried beside the church he had served for most of his life.   K. L. JOHNSON

Sources Tow Law Local History Group, *The stargazer of Tow Law* (1992) • T. E. R. P. [T. E. R. Phillips], *Monthly Notices of the Royal Astronomical Society*, 95 (1934–5), 319–22 • *Journal of the British Astronomical Association*, 45 (1934–5), 128 • J. B. Hearnshaw, *The analysis of starlight: one hundred and fifty years of astronomical spectroscopy* (1986), 128–9 • A. Brown, 'The life and work of the Rev. T. H. E. C. Espin', MSc diss., U. Durham, 1974 • d. cert.
Archives Bishop Palace Library, Durham • Durham RO • RAS, letters to Royal Astronomical Society
Likenesses pencil sketches, repro. in *Stargazer of Tow Law*; priv. coll. • photographs, repro. in *Stargazer of Tow Law*
Wealth at death £12,399 9s. 10d.: probate, 24 May 1935, CGPLA Eng. & Wales

Espinasse, Isaac (1758–1834), law reporter and legal writer, was the second of four sons of Isaac Espinasse of Mansfield, co. Dublin, and his wife, Mary Magenis. The family descended from an ancient Huguenot family, driven from France by the revocation of the edict of Nantes. He was educated by a private tutor before entering Trinity College, Dublin, in 1768. Here he befriended William Downes (later chief justice of the Irish king's bench) and graduated BA in 1774. He was admitted at Gray's Inn in December 1780, and was called to the bar in February 1787. Espinasse married and had at least one son.

Although Espinasse became a bencher of his inn in June 1809 (at the same time as Edward Christian and George Holroyd), and was treasurer of the inn in 1811, he never rose to eminence in the profession, preferring to concentrate on the *nisi prius* courts. Between 1793 and 1807, he issued a set of reports of cases at *nisi prius* which were among the first to report such cases. Unlike his contemporary John Campbell he did not edit out the 'bad law', and his reports gained a very poor reputation. Lord Denman commented that they 'were never quoted without doubt and hesitation' (*Small v. Nairne*, 1849), while Chief Baron Pollock quipped that he had heard only one half of what was said, and quoted the other. However, in reporting cases which turned largely on questions of evidence Espinasse's reports helped contribute to a development of the law of evidence in the early nineteenth century.

Espinasse also wrote a number of treatises on various aspects of the law. His works were aimed largely at the practitioner on circuit, and included *A Digest of the Law of Actions at Nisi Prius*, which appeared in 1789, reaching a fourth edition in 1812, and *A Treatise on the Settling of Evidence for Trials at Nisi prius* (1819), which was written after he had retired from active practice. The latter was not the product of legal research and learning, but sought rather to record the fruits of his own experience. A second edition in 1825 sought to be more scholarly, with the author stating: 'The names of cases are all given, a task attended with incalculable trouble'. Other works included *Treatise on Bankruptcy* (1825). After his retirement from practice, Espinasse wrote a series of anonymous articles in *Fraser's Magazine*, 'My contemporaries', which contained many humorous anecdotes about the major legal figures of the day, and which were heavily drawn on by later biographers such as William Townsend and Lord Campbell. In these recollections, Espinasse displayed a great sympathy for those on the bench, such as Ellenborough and Heath, who opposed Romilly's desire to reform the criminal law.

Espinasse came from a family which had a long and sometimes stormy relationship with the law. His father had inherited a long-standing lawsuit over land held in trust for a Catholic family, in breach of the Popery in Ireland Acts, which was only settled in the House of Lords, when Isaac was a child. It was appropriate therefore that Isaac and his brothers should have become lawyers in Dublin or London. His youngest brother, Robert (b. 1774), a special pleader, attracted some attention, both legal and social, in the 1820s as a result of the extravagances of his wife, Emilia Petre, who ran up high bills on luxurious goods. When sued for the debts Robert resisted a number of traders successfully, on the grounds that a wife only had implied authority to contract debts in her husband's name for items necessary to her station in life. Isaac's son James also went to law in 1827, after being admitted to Gray's Inn in 1812 and practising for some time as a special pleader; he was appointed a county court judge in 1847. Isaac Espinasse died on 14 February 1834, having suffered ill health for some time.   MICHAEL LOBBAN

Sources Holdsworth, *Eng. law*, 12.110, 13.515 • J. W. Wallace, *The reporters*, 4th edn (1882), 541 n. • A. W. B. Simpson, ed., *Biographical dictionary of the common law* (1984) • Burtchaell & Sadlier, *Alum. Dubl.* • J. Foster, *The register of admissions to Gray's Inn, 1521–1889, together with the register of marriages in Gray's Inn chapel, 1695–1754* (privately printed, London, 1889), 483 • R. J. Fletcher, ed., *The pension book of Gray's Inn*, 2 (1910), 349 • *Legal Observer*, 9 (1834–5), 358 • *Small v. Nairne*, 13 QB 844 • *Espinasse v. Lowe*, BL, Add. MS 36169, fol. 225 • will, PROB 11/1828/146
Wealth at death see will, PRO, PROB 11/1828/146

Essame, Enid Mary [Emma] (1906–1999), headmistress, was born on 5 December 1906 at 10 Carlton Road, Sheffield, the second daughter of Oliver Essame (1874–1959), railway clerk, and his wife, Kate Chandler (1872–1955).

Two younger brothers, Edgar and Gerald, completed the family. She grew up in a middle-class family with a love of literature and the arts and with the expectation that both the girls as well as the boys should receive a good education. The family moved to Leicester when Essame was a child and she attended St Barnabas primary school before winning a scholarship to Wyggeston girls' grammar school. Her progress to school certificate and matriculation exemption was disrupted in 1921 when her father was transferred to Newark, causing her to repeat a year at her new high school, but her academic ability was never in doubt. Meanwhile her father led the Labour Party in Newark and became president of the chamber of commerce, a justice of the peace, and chairman of governors of the local technical college. Essame's mother had become disabled with rheumatoid arthritis and was now confined to a wheelchair but took part in local affairs where she could, becoming chairman of the National Council of Women in Newark. She was a devout Anglican, and the children were baptized and confirmed into the Church of England. Essame won a place to read history at Newnham College, Cambridge, in 1925 and was given a school scholarship to go there. She joined the Student Christian Movement and the International Society. Both her Christian commitment and her interest in people from other cultures were to be seminal influences for the rest of her life.

Teaching and medicine offered the main professional opportunities for women when Essame graduated from Cambridge in 1928. She obtained a grant to study at the London Day Training College run by King's College, London. After qualifying in 1929 as a teacher, she unsuccessfully applied for over fifty jobs in girls' day-schools and eventually, with advice from Miss Strachey, principal of Newnham, applied to Queenswood, a private boarding-school for 240 girls in Hertfordshire. She was to remain there for her entire teaching career. Her influence was to be felt by more than a generation of staff, girls, and parents.

At Queenswood, Enid Essame quickly became known as Emma, a name derived from her initials, E. M. E. She made her mark as a young woman with energy, enthusiasm, ambition, and ideas. She was soon promoted to head of history and became a housemistress. Miss Ethel Mary Trew had been at Queenswood from its Wesleyan foundation in 1894 at Clapham Park, and had been its headmistress from 1897. She and the directors marked Emma out as her eventual successor and in preparation for headship offered her a year's sabbatical (1934–5) to study American educational methods. Essame was awarded the Mary Ewart travelling scholarship by Newnham and obtained a tuition scholarship to teach education at the American University in Washington, DC. She travelled extensively in the United States, visiting schools, colleges, and universities, and wrote a thesis entitled 'The comparative study of private schools in the USA and public schools in Britain'.

On her return voyage to England on the *Aquitania*, Essame discovered that Sir Josiah Stamp (chairman of governors at Queenswood from 1927 until his untimely death in an air raid in 1941) was a fellow passenger. The two spent long hours planning the future of Queenswood. This meeting sustained Essame through the following years, as Miss Trew was far from willing to retire and Essame remained a frustrated headmistress-designate until 1943. Queenswood was fortunate that she turned down other offers of headship in the meantime.

One of Essame's favourite quotations was 'what you can do or dream you can, begin it—boldness has genius power and magic in it' (Goethe). She used all her gifts and talents to steer the school through the years of difficult post-war shortages and financial stringency. She drew up plans to improve and extend the school's facilities. The first successful appeal was launched in 1954 and was followed in 1960 by the foundation of the Queenswood fellowship for parents and friends of the school. By 1971, when Emma retired, Queenswood had a new science building, a new library, an arts and music centre, new staff accommodation, a new pavilion, and a sports hall. The success of these building achievements testified to her ability to inspire parents and governors with her vision of a school that provided excellent opportunities for the full education of its 420 girls.

That vision, however, embraced far more than buildings. The curriculum was kept up to date, and a wide spectrum of sciences and languages was on offer. Essame encouraged public speaking and debating with other schools. She brought eminent speakers and preachers into the school and encouraged full use of London theatre, concerts, and exhibitions. Regular dances were held with the boys from The Leys, Haileybury, and Mill Hill. Upper sixth-formers were called students and given greater independence. Driving lessons were introduced in the 1960s. Emma moved ahead of the times. She foresaw that women would be combining careers with motherhood, and she knew that well-balanced personalities were as important as academic achievements for happy and fulfilled lives. She herself wrote in the pamphlet produced to mark the twenty-first year of her headship in 1965 that her hope for a Queenswoodian was 'the response of a resourceful woman with intellectual curiosity, aesthetic appreciation and the sympathy that bases itself on religious experience'. Although to her younger charges she could appear formidable, beneath the formality was a kind person with a concern for all who came her way. She knew how to listen and combined this with a prodigious memory which enabled her to remember girls and their families long after they had left school.

Essame still found time to pursue her interests outside the confines of a girls' boarding-school. She was an active member of the Council for Education in World Citizenship and of the International New Education Fellowship. She was invited by the British Council in 1953 to go to India and Pakistan to lecture on girls' education in England. In 1961 she visited Nigeria for the British Council, and in 1963 she went to Russia as part of an educational team. In 1957 she visited the USA again and set up staff and pupil exchanges with the Emma Willard School in Troy,

New York. She played a full part in the national educational scene. She was honorary secretary of the Association of Headmistresses of Boarding Schools and its president from 1962 to 1964. She was chairman of the Association of Independent and Direct Grant Schools and was made an honorary life member of the Girls' Schools Association when it was formed in 1974.

Enid Essame retired in 1971 to a house in Potters Bar owned jointly with her great friend Christine Marriott, who had been domestic bursar at the school since 1955. Their friendship grew during the difficult war years, and Marriott's quiet practical common sense and humour complemented Emma's more intellectual seriousness. Essame enjoyed an active retirement, continuing as a justice of the peace (1952–76) and governor of several schools. She regularly attended the meetings of the National Council of Women Graduates, took local adult education courses in philosophy and religion, and went to the theatre and art exhibitions, and she was holding play readings in her home right up to 1998. She was a regular attender at the nearby Methodist church, and her Christian faith and daily practice of prayer were important to her. She attended Old Queenswoodian Association meetings all over the country, warmly welcomed wherever she went and offering understanding and friendship. She and Marriott held open house for family and friends, many of whom were Old Queenswoodians, before Marriott's death in 1998.

Essame herself epitomized the ideals she held for a Queenswoodian. She died peacefully in Potters Bar Hospital on 19 December 1999, aged ninety-three, and was cremated at Garston crematorium, near Watford, on 30 December. A thanksgiving service was held in the school chapel in May 2000, attended by relatives, colleagues, friends, former pupils, and present students and staff. An oak tree was planted in her memory in the gardens of the school she loved and served so well.

AUDREY M. B. BUTLER

Sources M. Nissel, *Emma: a portrait of Enid Essame* (1995) · N. Watson, *In hortis reginae: a history of Queenswood School, 1894–1994* (1994) · H. M. Stafford, *Queenswood: the first sixty years* (1954) [suppl., *The diamond jubilee, 1954–55*] · *The Times* (21 Dec 1999) · E. M. Essame, *Enid Mary Essame* (1965) [pamphlet, Queenswood School, Hertfordshire] · personal knowledge (2004) · private information (2004) [Oliver Essame, nephew] · b. cert. · *WW*
Likenesses W. Narraway, oils, 1971, Queenswood School, Hatfield
Wealth at death £545,930—gross; £541,542—net: probate, 30 Jan 2000, *CGPLA Eng. & Wales*

Essen, Louis (1908–1997), physicist, was born on 6 September 1908 in Nottingham, the younger son and second of the three children of Fred Essen, bespoke bootmaker, and his wife, Ada, daughter of Fred Edson, builder and joiner. Both parents were Strict Baptists (his grandfather Fred Edson had built the Nottingham Strict Baptist Chapel), but Essen 'rejected this strict form of religion from an early age', and 'gradually rejected all religion, forming the view that irrational beliefs lead to intolerance and bigotry causing many of the world's problems' (Essen). He was

educated first at a local board school; he then won a scholarship to the Stanley Road preparatory school in Nottingham, and a county scholarship to the High Pavement School, which was then co-educational. At school he was a keen sportsman, walker, and athlete, as he remained throughout his life. He was head boy at the age of sixteen. He won a scholarship to University College, Nottingham, and graduated with a first-class London external BSc degree in 1928, aged nineteen. He began research, but left in 1929 for the National Physical Laboratory at Teddington, Middlesex. There he remained until he retired in 1970. He married Joan Margery Greenhalgh, a school chemistry teacher, on 6 November 1937; there were four daughters of the marriage.

When Essen joined the National Physical Laboratory, D. W. Dye FRS, a brilliant metrologist, was developing electrical measurements urgently needed in the infant radio industry. Essen joined him to study quartz crystal oscillators as frequency standards and to compare frequencies of radio transmitters; in one form or another frequency standards and their comparisons were his life's work and his fundamental contributions to modern electronic engineering and metrology. Dye died young in 1932, and Essen continued his work. At the outset of the Second World War, Essen's quartz crystal oscillator, with some modifications by the Post Office, was the most reliable of all sources of standard radio frequencies, and it controlled radio frequencies broadcast by the National Physical Laboratory up to 1939. Essen had also made fundamental measurements in physics. When he rotated a horizontal quartz bar oscillator about a vertical axis and found no change in the resonant frequency, he confirmed the result that Michelson and Morley found with an optical interferometer. During the war he developed ways of measuring frequencies and parameters of devices up to 30,000 MHz, the highest used in radar systems. That experience was invaluable after the war.

Essen exploited his wartime work to determine the speed of light. The accepted value largely depended on an extended series of experiments by Michelson over very long paths in air. Essen had investigated metal resonant cavities used in wartime as wavemeters in the field, and he pointed out that the speed of light *in vacuo* might be derived from the resonant frequency of an evacuated cavity of measured dimensions. With a cylindrical cavity resonant at about 3000 MHz he obtained a value some 16 km/sec. greater than Michelson's. That large discrepancy, the result of a novel method, was strongly doubted by some, but Essen confirmed it with an improved cavity, while K. D. Froome did so with a microwave interferometer. Essen's value was very close to the value later adopted by international convention.

Essen already had a high reputation when, in 1950, he visited the United States and saw work under way to establish standards of frequency based on transitions between states in atoms and molecules. He could not start immediately to build apparatus in the National Physical Laboratory, but when he and Froome determined refractive indices of atmospheric gases they did so at a frequency close to that of the hyperfine transition in caesium at about 10,000 MHz that he had selected for his proposed standard. Thus when he could begin construction, he already had a great deal of experience and equipment to hand. In less than a year he and J. V. (Jack) Parry were operating their apparatus as a regular source of standard frequencies, not just for experiments. So he was able, with W. Markowitz of the naval observatory in the USA, to relate the caesium frequency definitively to the astronomical unit of time, the ephemeris second.

Essen strongly advocated replacing the ephemeris second by the atomic standard of frequency and the corresponding unit of time as fundamental units, and so it was done by international agreement in 1968. The standard of length was then a wavelength in the visible spectrum of krypton; its defined value, like that of the standard of frequency, was arbitrary, and the two entailed a value of the speed of light that was subject to experimental uncertainty. Frequencies of atomic transitions can be compared with far finer discrimination than can wavelengths of atomic transitions. Essen pointed out that the speed of light might be taken to have an arbitrary conventional value, with values of lengths being derived from the times taken by electromagnetic signals to traverse them. His observation formed the basis of the modern system of standards in which fundamental quantities, electrical and mechanical, are related to frequency through quantum phenomena. His measurement of the speed of light and his establishment of the atomic frequency standard are at its heart.

Essen was sceptical of the accepted basis and interpretation of Einstein's special theory of relativity, but many found his criticisms unacceptable. Some of his points were valid, and although much of the discussion later seemed misguided, Essen's own experimental work and the basis he established for quantum metrology clarified the status of special relativity, namely that it expresses the fact that the only information we have of distant events is that obtained through electromagnetic signals.

In 1960 Essen was promoted to deputy chief scientific officer by special merit, one of very few at that time in the whole civil service. He was elected to the Royal Society in the same year. He was appointed OBE in 1959 and, among other distinctions, was the first recipient of the Wolfe award of the Department of Scientific and Industrial Research, and the first foreign recipient of the Popov gold medal of the USSR Academy of Sciences. He died in Great Bookham, Surrey, on 24 August 1997, and was survived by his wife and four daughters.   ALAN COOK

Sources A. H. Cook, *Memoirs FRS*, 44 (1998), 143–58 · *Daily Telegraph* (5 Sept 1997) · *The Independent* (3 Sept 1997) · *The Guardian* (6 Sept 1997) · L. Essen, 'Time for reflection', RS [pamphlet prepared for family] · autobiographical notes, RS · *WWW* · personal knowledge (2004) · private information (2004) · *CGPLA Eng. & Wales* (1997)
Archives RS, personal record
Likenesses photograph, 1955 (with Jack Parry), National Physical Laboratory; repro. in Cook, *Memoirs FRS*, 151 · photographs, 1984, repro. in Cook, *Memoirs FRS*, 142 · R. Cook, photograph, repro. in *The Guardian*

Wealth at death under £180,000: probate, 21 Oct 1997, *CGPLA Eng. & Wales*

Essex. For this title name *see* Mandeville, Geoffrey de, first earl of Essex (*d.* 1144); Mandeville, William de, third earl of Essex (*d.* 1189); Geoffrey fitz Peter, fourth earl of Essex (*d.* 1213); Hawisa, *suo jure* countess of Aumale, and countess of Essex (*d.* 1213/14); Bohun, Humphrey (IV) de, second earl of Hereford and seventh earl of Essex (*d.* 1275); Bohun, Humphrey (VI) de, third earl of Hereford and eighth earl of Essex (*c.*1249–1298); Bohun, Humphrey (VII) de, fourth earl of Hereford and ninth earl of Essex (*c.*1276–1322); Bourchier, Henry, first earl of Essex (*c.*1408–1483); Bourchier, Henry, second earl of Essex (1472–1540); Cromwell, Thomas, earl of Essex (*b.* in or before 1485, *d.* 1540); Devereux, Walter, first earl of Essex (1539–1576); Dudley, Lettice, countess of Essex and countess of Leicester (*b.* after 1540, *d.* 1634); Devereux, Robert, second earl of Essex (1565–1601); Devereux, Robert, third earl of Essex (1591–1646); Capel, Arthur, first earl of Essex (*bap.* 1632, *d.* 1683); Capel, William, third earl of Essex (1697–1743); Stephens, Catherine [Catherine Capel-Coningsby, countess of Essex] (1794–1882).

Essex family (*per. c.*1800–*c.*1860), enamellists and miniature painters, came to prominence with the brothers **William Essex** (1784–1869) and **Alfred Essex** (*d.* 1871). Little is known of their parents or childhood, but it appears from the inscription on a miniature by William Essex that William Catt (1777–1853) and Hannah Catt (1777–1823) acted *in loco parentis* at some point in their childhood. Both William Essex and his brother trained as enamellists in the workshop of Charles Muss (1779–1824), enamel painter to William IV, Alfred executing for Muss a very large enamel holy family after Parmigianino (1819; Royal Collection). The methods they learned from Muss were the traditional ones first developed for painting enamel portrait miniatures in the seventeenth century. However, it was the application of these techniques to very large enamel plaques, measuring up to 16 x 18 inches, following the example of Henry Bone and his workshop in the early nineteenth century which distinguished the Essex brothers from earlier enamellers. After training together, the brothers continued to collaborate on large-scale pieces, their shared ambition being to achieve 'effects at least equal to those which are seen in the great Masters, both ancient and modern, whether in Oil or Watercolours' (Essex, introduction) in the demanding medium of enamel. In June 1837 Alfred Essex published a paper on the art of painting in enamel in the *London and Edinburgh Philosophical Magazine* (3rd ser., 10, 442). He later emigrated to South Africa, where he died in 1871, leaving a daughter, Harriet. William Essex and his first wife, Martha, had several children, the first of whom, Martha, was baptized on 13 January 1814.

William Essex went on to become the chief exponent of enamel painting in miniature in the mid-nineteenth century, and was appointed enamel painter to Princess Augusta, Queen Victoria (1839), and to Prince Albert, the prince consort (1841). An exhibition of his work in the

William Essex (1784–1869), self-portrait, 1857

spring of 1839 in London was accompanied by a privately printed catalogue. He had been exhibiting at the Royal Academy since 1818 and continued to exhibit there and at the British Institution and the Society of British Artists until 1864, chiefly miniatures in enamel but also miniatures on ivory and some flower and history subjects in oil. Most of William Essex's enamels were copied from paintings by various artists but they are distinguished by the naturalistic and subtle range of colours which he employed, and particularly his use of brown and yellow pigments in the faces of his subjects, and by his skill as a draughtsman. Good examples are the set of three enamel miniatures framed together of Byron (after a portrait by Thomas Phillips), Sir Walter Scott, and Thomas Moore (both after portraits by Sir Thomas Lawrence), each signed and dated 1849, 1852, and 1853 respectively, sold at Sothebys on 21 July 1988 (lot 55) and reproduced in the catalogue. Several versions of his enamel of Byron are recorded, one of which is in the Victoria and Albert Museum, London. Many of his works are also signed in full on the reverse, with inscribed details of the sitter and the date of the portrait. He also produced decorative panels for snuff-boxes and very small portraits and animal paintings for jewellery. His skills were passed on to his pupils John William Bailey (1831–1914) and William Bishop Ford (1832–1922) as well as his son **William B. Essex** (1822–1852) who followed him into the enamelling profession. However, the critic G. C. Williamson, reflecting the consensus among more recent writers, conceded that while William Essex's works were 'carefully drawn, harmoniously coloured and smoothly executed', those of his son were not 'of equal importance' (Williamson, 2.68). William B. Essex exhibited at the Royal Academy, British Institution, and Society of British Artists from 1845 to 1851. He predeceased his father, dying in Birmingham on 19 January 1852. **Hannah Essex** [married name Bird] (bap. 1832), miniature painter, one of William Essex's daughters by his first wife, Martha, was baptized on 29 May 1832 at the New Jerusalemite Chapel, Cross Street, Holborn. She also produced enamel miniatures, exhibiting at the Royal Academy and British Institution (1854–6) from her

father's address at 3 Osnaburgh Street, Regent's Park, London. William Essex died at his home, at 13 Western Road, Hove, on 29 December 1869 and was survived by his second wife, Catharine. His self-portrait in enamel (1857) was sold at Sothebys on 17 April 1961 (lot 38) but many examples of his work remain in the Victoria and Albert Museum, London, and in the Royal Collection.

V. REMINGTON

Sources Graves, *RA exhibitors* [Hannah Essex] · *The Times* (1 Jan 1870) [William Essex] · *Art Journal*, 14 (1852), 76 [William B. Essex] · W. Essex, *Catalogue of a private exhibition of paintings in enamel executed by Mr W. Essex* (1839) · E. Speel, *Dictionary of enamelling* (1998), 51, colour pl. 25 · E. Speel, 'Enamel portrait miniatures: mid 19th century to the present', *Glass on Metal*, 7/2 (April 1988), 36–8 · G. C. Williamson, *The history of portrait miniatures*, 2 vols. (1904) · D. Foskett, *Miniatures: dictionary and guide* (1987), 408, 411, 536 · B. S. Long, *British miniaturists* (1929), 144–5 · L. R. Schidlof, *The miniature in Europe in the 16th, 17th, 18th, and 19th centuries*, 1 (1964), 240–41 · B. S. Long, *Hand-list of miniature portraits and silhouettes* (1930) · *DNB* · T. J. Gullick, *Painting popularly explained* (1876), 109–10 · A. Peach, 'The portraiture of Byron', PhD diss., U. Lond., 1995 · *CGPLA Eng. & Wales* (1870) [William Essex] · census returns, 1861 · *IGI*
Likenesses W. Essex, self-portrait, enamel miniature, 1857 (William Essex), priv. coll.; Sothebys, 17 April 1961, lot 38 [see illus.]
Wealth at death under £50—William Essex: administration, 1870, *CGPLA Eng. & Wales*

Essex witches (act. 1566–1589) are known from four surviving pamphlets published between 1566 and 1589 describing the lives, and in some cases deaths, of one man and thirty women who were accused of witchcraft in Essex and prosecuted under the Witchcraft Act of 1563. In this period witchcraft was punishable by hanging if a witch was convicted of killing a person, or if he or she committed a second witchcraft offence of any kind. Witches were not burnt in England, and lesser witchcraft offences were punished by imprisonment and the pillory. Because survivals of early modern Essex trial records are among the most numerous in England, and because of the higher than average number of contemporary pamphlets published on Essex cases, the county's witchcraft prosecutions have received more attention than those of most other areas and statistical analysis as well as individual biography is possible.

Early witchcraft trials, 1566–1579 Over the period covered by the pamphlets some 430 people were prosecuted for witchcraft offences in the home counties, which formed the home circuit for judicial purposes, with a peak between 1580 and 1589. Essex, one of these five counties, accounted for nearly 60 per cent of home circuit prosecutions for witchcraft and between 1570 and 1609 fifty-three Essex witches were hanged as against a total of sixty-four executions across all the home counties. This was a high proportion, even allowing for the fact that only about a quarter of the total indicted were actually found guilty and hanged. Accusations were most common in eastern and central Essex, although local episodes of witch accusation could occur anywhere. Many Essex people clearly believed strongly in witchcraft as a threat to them, as a source of healing or divining magic, or as a power which they themselves had come to possess. Women were particularly likely to be accused, often of inheriting their powers or sharing them with other female family members or friends (nearly 90 per cent of all indicted Essex witches were women), and many confessed the accusations to be true. Some may have been convinced that they could and did curse their neighbours, others said they practised only healing magic, while a third group denied all involvement. Some people seem likely—from the pattern of their narratives—to have invented confessions and denials out of mixed motives including, sometimes, a belief that producing any kind of coherent narrative would lead to clemency. Their accusers were equally likely to create an unnaturally neat fiction about the witches out of a combination of incoherent events and unverifiable beliefs about their lives. It is therefore hard to decide, or to find a reliable methodology for assessing, which elements of their stories represent factual and verifiable life events and which are retrospective rationalizations based on fantasy or fiction confabulated under pressure. Both these types of experience represent, however, a biographical reality for the pamphleteers who immortalized these Essex people.

All the villagers are shown in the pamphlets as ordinary people who have been tempted into the felony of maleficent witchcraft for a variety of reasons. In 1566 **Elizabeth Frauncis** (*c.*1529–1579), from Hatfield Peverel, told pre-trial questioners that, aged twelve (at least twenty-five years earlier, the narrative suggests) she was given a white-spotted cat named Satan by her grandmother, Eve. She renounced God and his word and was told to give her blood to the cat. Later she asked the cat for sheep, and to procure her a rich husband. Unfortunately, when the cat prevailed upon her to have sex with the favoured man, he had not married her, and she told the cat to kill him. Fearing pregnancy, she asked the cat for help with abortifacient herbs, and then at its insistence attempted once again to win a husband by what the pamphlet labels 'fornication'. In this attempt she succeeded, but later marital unhappiness prompted her to kill the resultant child, and to lame her husband, whom trial records name as Christopher Frauncis. Her story was printed in *The Examination and Confession of Certaine Wytches at Chensforde in the Countie of Essex* (1566). It suggests that Elizabeth Frauncis felt guilty about sexual events in her younger life, and that, when interrogated on suspicion of witchcraft, she confessed those matters which were on her conscience, rather than the expected punishable acts of harmful magic against neighbours. Equally, the fact that one of her questioners was a churchman may mean that the focus on sin rather than crime in Frauncis's story was his rather than exclusively hers. Assize records suggest that she was not formally charged with any of the matters she confessed—the trial at Chelmsford concentrated on the bewitchment of a child, to which Frauncis pleaded guilty. She was sentenced in July to a year's imprisonment, with four pillory appearances, as the penalty for a first, non-fatal offence. In August 1572 Frauncis was tried again as a witch, for what is rightly described in the assize records as her second offence. However, the indictment had to be redrafted: when tried in March 1573 for the same offence

and found guilty she escaped death (the penalty for a second offence) and was imprisoned and pilloried again (the penalty for a first offence). In April 1579, however, her luck ran out and she was tried, convicted, and hanged for killing a neighbour, Alice Poole, by witchcraft. She pleaded not guilty, but had confessed to the offence in a pre-trial examination which appears in the second Essex pamphlet *A detection of damnable driftes practized by three* [actually four] *witches arraigned at Chelmisforde in Essex* (1579). Frauncis said that she killed Poole, with the help of a dog spirit, because Poole refused to give her yeast—a far more petty motivation than the grand lusts of her first confession thirteen years before.

Agnes Waterhouse (1501/2–1566), Frauncis's neighbour and probably her sister, confessed far more conventional witchcraft offences in 1566 than she did. Waterhouse received the cat, Satan, from Frauncis in exchange for a cake, she said, and used him against neighbours who had angered her, asking him to kill hogs, a cow, and geese, to harm brewing and dairying, to kill a neighbour, and, nine years previously, her own husband. She turned the cat familiar into a toad because poverty forced her to use the wool on which he slept. In July 1566 Waterhouse pleaded guilty in court to killing William Fynee (no mention was made of the more sensational murder of her husband, or the confessed property offences) and she was hanged at Chelmsford on 29 July. She said at her death that she had been a witch for fifteen years, and added that she had always prayed in Latin. The pamphlet emphasized the illegality and ungodliness of this activity, suggesting again the influence of churchmen on some of the confessions of witches, and the thin lines between residual Catholicism, deliberate recusancy, and the practice of secret magical rites with a perceived Satanic tint.

The third witch to be tried at Chelmsford in July 1566 was **Joan Waterhouse** (*b.* 1547/8), Agnes Waterhouse's daughter. She began her pre-trial examination by denying any knowledge of witchcraft, although she said that her mother had attempted to teach her 'this art'. However, shortly afterwards she began to confess that she had tried out the familiar spirit, Satan, in her mother's absence, and used him to punish a neighbour's child, Agnes Browne, for uncharitable acts towards her. Browne is shown in *The Examination and Confession* as giving sensational evidence against both Joan and Agnes Waterhouse, and it seems likely that her stories played a large part in bringing both women to trial, along with Frauncis. She said that she had been 'haunted' by a black dog with an ape's face which had asked for butter, played in the milkhouse, and finally attempted to kill her with a knife which he said belonged to Agnes Waterhouse. Browne was counselled by a clergyman during her alleged experiences, rather as if she were a possession victim, and she had the backing of the pamphlet which treated her as a star witness. However, Joan Waterhouse was acquitted and Browne's credibility in court must therefore be in doubt. Other felonies and witchcraft cases at the 1566 summer assizes went unreported.

Witchcraft was usually thought to have occurred where

disputes arose between victim and suspect, followed by misfortune. The second Essex pamphlet illustrates this well. It contains accusations against four women, Elizabeth Frauncis and three others. The first was **Elleine Smith** (d. 1579), of Maldon, tried and hanged at Chelmsford in April 1579 for killing a child. She had quarrelled with a number of people, including her stepfather, John Chaundeler, when he asked her for money which her mother had given her. Smith's mother, Alice Chaundeler, had been executed for murder by witchcraft in 1574 and her daughter was probably assumed to have inherited her witchcraft as well as her money, especially since John Chaundeler died strangely after their quarrel. Smith was also believed to have hit the child who died and sent a dog spirit to attack her, and to have attacked with a toad spirit a neighbour who refused charity to her son. Her son, as was often the case, also accused his mother of keeping familiar spirits. Margery Staunton of Wimbish, described in the same pamphlet, was refused charity by nine households and was seen to resent this—after which misfortune overtook the households. She escaped punishment because her indictment was wrongly drafted. Finally, Alice Nokes of Lambourne allegedly injured a man who stole gloves from her daughter, and attacked a horse because the ploughman would not speak to her. She was hanged for murder by witchcraft, an accusation not mentioned in the pamphlet.

Late witchcraft trials, 1579–1589 Individual and inter-household quarrels, but also the dynamics of spiralling accusations and ruthless questioning, played a major part in the biggest English witchcraft case of the period, described in W. W.'s *A true and just recorde of the information, examination and confession of all the witches, taken at S. Oses in the countie of Essex* (1582). In February and March 1582 Brian Darcy, an Essex JP and witch-hunter, questioned thirteen women and a man from the villages of St Osyth, Little Clacton, Thorpe, Little Oakley, and Walton and sent them for trial at Chelmsford. The process began modestly enough when a St Osyth servant of Darcy's relative Thomas Darcy, third Baron Darcy of Chiche, complained that a woman whom she had been consulting as a magical healer, **Ursley Kempe** (d. 1582), had killed one of her children and made herself and another child ill. Kempe confessed several attacks on villagers and accused neighbours Alice Newman, **Elizabeth Bennett** (d. 1582), Annis Glascock, and Alice Hunt of witchcraft. She was in turn accused by other informants, including her brother, who said that Kempe had killed his wife for calling her a whore and a witch. Kempe's illegitimate son told the magistrate that she kept spirits, and Newman was described as working in partnership with her, using the same spirits, although she refused to confess anything. Although convicted of the same three offences of murder, Kempe was hanged at Chelmsford in April 1582 while Newman was imprisoned until released by general pardon in 1588—an unusual punishment. After Brian Darcy falsely promised favour to those who confessed, Bennett pleaded guilty to keeping spirits and using them to kill her abusive neighbour and his wife, and was hanged at Chelmsford in April

1582. Glascock apparently confessed nothing, but died in prison (inquest date 11 November 1582) after being convicted of three murders and reprieved. Hunt was acquitted of murder and of killing cows, despite the evidence of her eight-year-old stepdaughter that she kept spirits. Meanwhile her sister, Margery Sammon or Barnes, confessed to the keeping of spirits and incriminated Hunt's next door neighbour, Joan Pechey, saying that she had killed John Johnson, the collector for the poor, for giving her insufficient charity. Newman was also accused (by other informants) of his murder but nobody was formally charged. Pechey refused to confess but died in prison (inquest date 11 November 1582) despite supposedly being discharged without trial. Barnes apparently evaded trial, only to be indicted for keeping spirits in 1583. She was acquitted.

Accusations were also taking place in adjacent villages. Cicely Selles and her husband, Henry Selles, of Little Clacton, were accused of witchcraft by a wealthy neighbour, Richard Ross, and by their own children. Ross also accused them of damaging property and of arson. Henry Selles was not tried, while his wife was acquitted of arson. She was, however, convicted of murdering the son of a neighbour whose daughter had also suffered mysterious illness, supposedly at her hands. Both Selleses died in gaol (inquest dates 31 January and 8 March 1583) after being tried again, with their son Robert Selles, for arson against Ross. This makes it likely that Ross was the force behind their prosecution, especially as they were also accused of, but not charged with, attacking his maid and farm, and killing a child of one of his workers (despite the reluctance of the child's mother to accuse Cicely Selles). Witchcraft accusation could be a way of expressing a more deep-seated hatred—even a feud—here. Alice Manfielde of Thorpe and 55-year-old Margaret Grevell were accused of various offences: impeding farm work by magic, arson, and murder. Manfielde, despite a fulsome confession and further incrimination of existing suspects, was charged only with arson, and was acquitted, while Grevell was acquitted of killing a man whose wife had refused her charity. Elizabeth Ewstace, aged fifty-three, was accused of murder and of causing illness in animals and humans, but was not brought to trial. In Little Oakley, Annis Herd was accused of murder by the parson of Beaumont, but, being charged only with harming animals, was acquitted. Her illegitimate daughter accused her of keeping spirits, and other neighbours described misfortunes which had struck after they refused her charity. Finally, in Walton various accusations of harming animals and causing wind damage were made against Joan Robinson, a comparatively wealthy woman, but were apparently dismissed. The prosecution petered out as accusations became less and less grave, the assize of March 1583 approached and prosecutions were surprisingly unsuccessful in a number of cases.

The desire to publish accounts of witchcraft cases did not, however, fade. In 1589 material from the pre-trial examinations of three more Essex women was published as *The Apprehension and Confession of Three Notorious Witches*.

Joan Cunny [Cony] (*c*.1508/9–1589), of Stisted, was accused of harming and killing her neighbours and causing a damaging storm. She confessed that she had learned her 'art' from a woman who had told her to make a circle on the ground and pray to Satan, at which invocation spirits would appear. She said she had done this twenty years previously, had given her soul to the spirits, taken them home and fed them, and afterwards used them to do various harmful acts. The pamphleteer said that Cunny had two daughters, Margaret and Avis, and two illegitimate grandsons. It was from one of these boys that some of the accusations against Cunny and her daughters came. Cunny was hanged at Chelmsford on 5 July 1589, while Margaret was imprisoned and Avis was sentenced to death, but was reprieved because she was pregnant. Joan Upney of Dagenham was similarly accused with her daughters. She too confessed to learning her witchcraft from a woman who had, this time, brought familiar spirits to her. This woman, named Whitecote, is probably Cecilia Glasenberye (also known as Arnold or Whitecote), a Barking woman executed for witchcraft in 1574, whose story featured in a lost pamphlet of that year and was reprinted in 1595 in *A World of Wonders, a Masse of Murthers, a Covie of Cosonages*. Upney blamed the spirits which Whitecote had given her for harming her neighbours, but was herself convicted of two murders and hanged. Alice Upney, presumably Upney's daughter, was discharged without trial. The pamphlet's final account is of **Joan Prentice** (*d*. 1589), who lived in the almshouse at Sible Hedingham, and confessed that she had a familiar in the shape of a ferret named Satan. She tried to resist his overtures, but let him suck her blood and then used him to harm her neighbours. She said that the ferret disobeyed her instructions to hurt a child and instead killed it, but this excuse did not save her from execution. Prentice was hanged at Chelmsford on 5 July 1589. She named two other women, Elizabeth Whale and Elizabeth Mott, whom she said used the same spirit, but they were discharged without trial.

Each 'witch's' story is subtly different, although there are linking themes, most of which became standard in witchcraft accusations and confessions. In some stories sexual motives meet malice to produce a potent and incredible village Medea: a woman who uses devil-inspired magic to enchant and kill in furtherance of her desires—or feels guilty because she wishes she had. In others poverty leads to begging, which, when refused, prompts designs of revenge on the uncharitable neighbour. Unneighbourly refusal to trade with the witch or less obvious economic or social injuries might equally be revenged. Some cases say more about the alleged victim than the witch: a strong imagination, mental illness, or unexplained disease, combined with naughtiness, teenage crises, or fear, produce a story of peculiar afflictions visited on the innocent by the malignant. Finally, questioners have a great influence over confessions by witches: leading questions were common, and the temptation to say what was expected in the hope of pleasing the magistrate or churchman must have been great.

There are exemplars of each of these life stories in all the pamphlets. Frauncis's sexual adventures are echoed in the fact that a number of the Essex witches had illegitimate children or were accused of causing harm to those who stood in their way sexually. In 1582 Pechey was accused of incest, while Ciccly Selles's husband was alleged to have described his wife as a 'stinking whore'. The 1589 pamphleteer described Cunny and her daughters as 'living very lewdly … no better than naughty packs'. The most common story is, however, that of revenge for uncharity, or economic unneighbourliness such as theft or refusal to trade. At least two thirds of the Essex witches were involved in disputes with neighbours over such matters, and almost all had been insulted, attacked by or had quarrelled abusively with alleged victims. Most were relatively poor; where occupations are known, Henry Selles was an agricultural labourer, Sammon a servant, Bennett the wife of a husbandman, Hunt a mason's wife, and Glascock married to a sawyer. Many of the women were apparently single or widowed (although the convenient legal definition 'spinster' can be misleading here), and the witches accused in these pamphlets are almost exclusively female, mirroring (if exaggerating) the national male : female percentages, where 90 per cent of suspects might be expected to be women.　　　　　　　　　　　　　　　MARION GIBSON

Sources *The examination and confession of certaine wytches at Chensforde in the countie of Essex* (1566) • *A detection of damnable driftes practized by three witches arraigned at Chelmisforde in Essex* (1579) • W. W., *A true and just recorde of the information, examination and confession of all the witches, taken at S. Oses in the countie of Essex* (1582) • *The apprehension and confession of three notorious witches* (1589) • J. S. Cockburn, *Calendar of assize records: Essex indictments, Elizabeth I* (1978) • J. Sharpe, *Instruments of darkness: witchcraft in England 1550–1750* (1996) • A. Macfarlane, *Witchcraft in Tudor and Stuart England: a regional and comparative study* (1970) • M. Gibson, *Early modern witches: witchcraft cases in contemporary writing* (2000) • B. Rosen, *Witchcraft in England, 1558–1618* (1991) • M. Gibson, *Reading witchcraft: stories of early English witches* (1999) • J. S. Cockburn, *Calendar of assize records: introduction* (1985)
Archives PRO, indictment files from assizes, ASSI/35

Essex, Agnes of [*married name* Agnes de Vere], **countess of Oxford** (*b*. 1151, *d*. in or after 1206), noblewoman, was the daughter of Henry of *Essex, royal constable, and his wife, Cecily. Betrothed by her father to Geoffrey de Vere, brother of Aubrey de *Vere, first earl of Oxford, Agnes was raised from the age of three in the earl's household. When she was six Geoffrey took her into his own care, but Agnes refused to accept him as her future husband. The alliance between their families was rescued by her marriage to Aubrey in early 1163. The middle-aged earl had no heir when he made this, his third marriage, with the twelve-year-old Agnes. Although she was not an heiress, she brought him five knights' fees in the eastern counties.

Shortly after his daughter's marriage, Agnes's father was accused of treason and defeated in trial by battle. As a consequence of the scandal, the de Veres sought to have the earl's marriage annulled. The case came before Gilbert Foliot, bishop of London. Agnes fought the annulment, finally appealing to Rome on 9 May 1166. While her case was being reviewed the countess had to endure the earl's displeasure; Bishop Gilbert rebuked Aubrey for having confined Agnes in one of his castles, denying her her marital rights and preventing her attendance at mass. The earl appears to have heeded the bishop, for the couple's first child was most likely born before 1168.

The de Vere case was among those Pope Alexander III considered as he developed the canon law of marriage. Although the extant papal letter does not discuss the specifically legal issues under consideration—it addresses the earl's treatment of Agnes, and threatens excommunication and interdict if he fails to conform to the church's ruling—the pope assumes throughout the validity of the marriage of Agnes to Aubrey. Among the contended issues, that of consent was foremost. The de Veres contended that Agnes's betrothal to Geoffrey invalidated her marriage to Aubrey. As Agnes herself had pointed out, having been raised by the de Veres as Geoffrey's intended bride from the age of three, she had no formal opportunity to consent to or reject the plans made for her. Yet before her twelfth birthday, Agnes had taken the unusual step of writing to her father to express her absolute opposition to the match with Geoffrey. The church accepted that action as sufficient to break their betrothal, freeing her to marry the earl.

Agnes and Aubrey de Vere had at least four sons and a daughter: Aubrey (IV) de Vere, second earl of Oxford; Roger; Robert de *Vere, the third earl; Henry, possibly a clerk of his uncle, Bishop William of Hereford; and Alice, wife of Geoffrey de Say. She witnessed few of her husband's surviving charters, but they were joint founders of a small nunnery at Castle Hedingham, Essex (c.1190), and were benefactors of the de Vere priory at Earls Colne, Essex, and of the hospitallers, of which order the earl's brother was a member. Her husband died in December 1194, and the countess survived him for at least a dozen years. In 1198 she offered the king 100 marks for the right to marry whom she wished; Agnes paid the debt within a year and remained unmarried until her death, which took place in or after 1206. Agnes was buried beside her husband at Earls Colne Priory, Essex.

RaGena C. DeAragon

Sources *Letters and charters of Gilbert Foliot*, ed. A. Morey and others (1967) · GEC, *Peerage*, new edn, 10.205–7 · *Pipe rolls* · H. Hall, ed., *The Red Book of the Exchequer*, 3 vols., Rolls Series, 99 (1896) · J. L. Fisher, ed., *Cartularium prioratus de Colne*, Essex Archaeological Society, occasional publications, 1 (1946) · *Gir. Camb. opera*, vol. 6 · Dugdale, *Monasticon*, new edn
Archives Essex RO, Chelmsford, Earls Colne cartulary
Wealth at death five knights' fees of the honour of Haughley, Suffolk, as dowry; manor of Cockfield, Suffolk, as dower: Hall, ed., *Red book of the Exchequer*

Essex, Alfred (d. 1871). *See under* Essex family (*per. c.1800– c.1860*).

Essex, Hannah (bap. 1832). *See under* Essex family (*per. c.1800–c.1860*).

Essex, Henry of (d. after 1163), administrator and baron, was the son of Robert Fitzsweyn of Essex (d. c.1140), and Gunnora, daughter of Robert Bigod. He inherited from his father the Domesday honour and castle of Rayleigh in Essex. He married first Cecily, who was the mother of most or all of his children, and second Alice, probably the daughter (or possibly the widow) and heir of Robert de Vere (d. c.1151). Alice brought him Robert de Vere's constableship and the barony of Haughley, which had come to Robert through his wife, Alice de Montfort. Henry's children included Henry of Essex the younger, Hugh, Robert, Agnes of *Essex (who married Aubrey de Vere, first earl of Oxford), and Alice (who may have married Geoffrey de Say).

From about 1151 onwards Henry served King Stephen as a royal constable and local justice in Essex. Although Stephen's rival, Empress Matilda, named him as one of those who 'ought to' guarantee her second charter to Geoffrey de Mandeville, and Henry himself reportedly heard the bishop of Winchester's command in 1141 to support the empress, there is no convincing evidence that he ever deserted the king. But upon Stephen's death he moved immediately into the service of Henry II, witnessing for the new king as royal constable at Christmas 1154 and serving with the chancellor Thomas Becket on the first judicial eyre of the reign, in 1156, through nine southern counties. He was sheriff of Hertfordshire in 1155 and of Buckinghamshire and Bedfordshire in 1156 and 1157, and he travelled frequently with the king.

Essex's promising career was blighted, however, by an incident at the battle of Counsylth, during the Welsh campaign of the summer of 1157. Hearing a rumour that Henry II had been killed, he threw away the royal standard and fled, crying out the news. Although the king managed to rally his troops, Essex was replaced as sheriff at Michaelmas of the same year, and his involvement in royal business decreased noticeably thereafter. Even so he retained the office of constable, and served in that capacity in the expedition against Toulouse in 1159. But in 1163 he was finally called to account for his behaviour at Counsylth. Robert de Montfort, whose family had once held Haughley, accused him of treason and defeated him in judicial combat. He was left for dead on the field, but later recovered under the care of the monks of Reading, who had taken his body up for burial at the request of his influential friends. The king mercifully allowed him to enter the monastery, and, although his interest in religious houses had hitherto been confined to some small-scale benefactions to the Premonstratensian priory of Blackwose in Kent, Henry lived out his days as a monk at Reading. His estates were forfeited to the crown.

EMILIE AMT

Sources *Reg. RAN*, vol. 3 · R. Howlett, ed., *Chronicles of the reigns of Stephen, Henry II, and Richard I*, 1, Rolls Series, 82 (1884) · *The chronicle of Jocelin of Brakelond: concerning the acts of Samson, abbot of the monastery of St Edmund*, ed. H. E. Butler (1949) · R. Howlett, ed., *Chronicles of the reigns of Stephen, Henry II, and Richard I*, 4, Rolls Series, 82 (1889) · *Pipe rolls* · L. Helliwell and D. G. Macleod, *Rayleigh castle* (1981) · M. Chibnall, *The Empress Matilda* (1991) · H. M. Colvin, *The white canons in England* (1951)

Essex, James (bap. 1722, d. 1784), architect and antiquary, was born in Cambridge and baptized there at St Botolph's

Church on 25 August 1722, the only child of James Essex (*d.* 1750), joiner, and his wife, Bridget *née* Prigg (*c.*1700–1784). The Essex family appear to have been graziers in the nearby village of Cottenham but the elder Essex already lived in St Botolph's parish in Cambridge when he married in 1721. The connection with St Botolph's endured until the extinction of the family in 1790. Their vault survives to the south of the chancel.

College buildings Essex was educated at King's College Grammar School. Its then site just to the east of King's College chapel and a few hundred yards south of the newly built Senate House symbolized the twin directions of his career: the Cambridge commissions, which were mostly in a classical style, and the Gothic designs and restorations on which his greater fame depends. The Senate House, though designed by James Gibbs, was erected under the supervision of James Burrough, fellow (later master) of Caius and Cambridge's leading architectural amateur, and its rich joinery was provided by the elder Essex. His son began as an assistant in his father's joinery and general building firm and was also taken up by Burrough, who educated him as his architectural assistant and eventual successor. Drawings from Essex's teenage years, now in the British Library, show his early interest in medieval buildings such as Cambridge Castle and the leper chapel at Barnwell. Essex also drew, for published engravings, schemes by established architects, such as Gibbs's for King's College or Burrough's for Trinity Hall, and in time his own designs, starting in 1748 with one for a new court at Corpus Christi College, the originality of which he successfully demonstrated against accusations of plagiarism by the then bursar.

Essex's independent career began on his father's death when he completed the construction of the 'mathematical bridge' at Queens' College, designed by William Etheridge. Shortly afterwards, on 24 June 1753, he married Elizabeth (*c.*1731–1790), daughter of William Thurlbourn, one of the principal booksellers in Cambridge. A year later his son, another James, was born, but he died in 1757 just short of his third birthday. Essex's daughter Miliscent, born in 1756, lived to be her father's assistant in his antiquarian studies. His marriage brought him into the small but closely knit world of Cambridge's middle class, which regularly intermarried with the college fellows. His wife's sister, Martha, married Richard Hayles, surgeon at Addenbrooke's Hospital, and their daughter, Sophia, married Thomas Kerrich, university librarian and eventually Essex's literary executor.

In 1756–60 Essex designed a seventeen-bay range along the river for Queens' College, of which only the south section was built. It set the pattern for most of Essex's new work for colleges, conventional in its classical detailing but convenient in its domestic arrangements. The president of Queens', Dr Plumptre, described it as a 'useful and ornamental building' (Willis and Clark, 2.18). The same adjectives could be used for Essex's reorientation of Emmanuel College in 1771–5, where he created a new entrance front, with a cloister inside to answer those flanking Christopher Wren's chapel opposite but an attached Ionic portico to make a focus in the streetscape. His unexecuted designs for a new court in Corpus and for the newly proposed Downing College remain within the traditions established by Wren and Burrough.

Similar qualities are found in the other type of college work on which Essex was employed, the stone refacing of earlier ranges, a practice begun by Burrough at Peterhouse and Trinity Hall. Although deplored in more recent times, this process not only gave greater aesthetic uniformity but provided larger windows, wider staircases, and more effective chimneys. In the First Court of St John's, Essex provided these amenities by having the south range gutted and heightened by a top storey in stock brick, the contrast with the Tudor red brick left visible at the rear but masked with ashlar to the front. At Nevile's Court in Trinity, although both north and south ranges required extensive rebuilding, Essex retained the Jacobean style of the original, omitting some of the ornament and replacing the gabled dormers with a more generous top storey, and a balustrade to suit the Wren library to the west.

Essex's most ambitious achievement in a classical style was the new chapel erected for Clare College in 1764–9. It was designed in collaboration with Burrough but he died as work began and William Cole, who knew them both, credited the building to Essex. The design cleverly exploits the cramped site, progressing through a domed octagonal ante-chapel, unique for its date, to the elegant barrel-vaulted chapel, fitted out with plaster and woodwork of great refinement.

Evidence for Essex's university and cathedral commissions survives because recorded in their archives. His secular and domestic work is harder to trace, especially because only those of his papers which related to his 'History of Gothic architecture' were retained for eventual lodging at the British Museum. One commission attributable through these papers is Randall House (now Kenmare) in Trumpington Street, Cambridge, of 1768, where Essex unwisely crowded four Palladian windows into a three-bay facade. He had been involved, with Burrough, in the design and building in 1761–3 of Addenbrooke's Hospital, which he then adapted in 1768, a charitable cause which brought together university, town, and county. Essex shared another contemporary interest, bridge building—his first independent job had been the mathematical bridge at Queens'. He went on to rebuild Garret Hostel Bridge in 1769 on the same principles; he had earlier replaced the Great or Magdalene Street Bridge in stone. Both were later demolished but his bridge for Trinity College survives, the 'cycloidal' bridge, so called from the geometry of its arches. He also joined in the contemporary enthusiasm for improving communications. His 'great services, care and attention to improve the Navigation' (Cambs. RO, Common day book, 253) joining Cambridge and Littleport along the Cam and the Ouse rivers earned him the offer of the freedom of Cambridge.

Cathedrals and chapels The twenty-year-old Essex had been noted by Cole as already possessing a serious interest in medieval architecture. To this he added the experience of working on great medieval buildings, restoring King's chapel in 1750–56 and then the cathedrals at Ely and Lincoln. At Ely, Essex was employed in two major structural works, the reconstruction first of the decayed timber lantern over the octagon and, a decade later, of the high roof over the presbytery, where the thirteenth-century coupled rafters were pushing the east gable out of vertical. In both projects the new carpentry is of a high standard and also respects the original construction. The presbytery roof of 1768 maintains the traditional high-pitched and lead-covered profile, unlike the utilitarian low slate roofs preferred at Lichfield and Hereford some fifteen years later. The external detailing of the octagon and lantern Essex left plain, partly from a lack of funds and partly from a distaste for profuse Gothic decoration. More problematic to present-day opinion was the removal of the choir in 1770–71 from its ancient but inconvenient position straddling the crossing into the eastern bays of the presbytery, a reordering Essex favoured although he did not superintend it. The change both opened up vistas along and across the cathedral and also meant that sound and heat no longer disappeared into the octagon. Essex designed new choir and altar screens to east and west in careful conformity with the fourteenth-century stalls, themselves carefully moved, and he recorded the Romanesque pulpitum before its demolition.

Essex's contributions at Ely have largely been swept away but at Lincoln his work has proved more enduring. Careful surveys of the cathedral in 1761 and 1764 were followed by a sequence of repairs and improvements over twenty years. He altered the chapter house roof and St Hugh's chapel off the north-east transept and embellished the choir by a new altar screen and bishop's throne and a comprehensive repaving. His major achievements in the cathedral, and indeed in the history of restoration, were the pierced cresting added to crown the central tower and the refashioning in Gothic of the classical screen walls added at the west end of the nave by Gibbs in 1730. In both designs Essex clearly stated his desire to come 'as near as I could agreeable to the ideas' (Lincoln Chapter Archives, A 14/13, 11) of the original architect. Where new work could be seen in conjunction with old, Essex therefore used detail which was sympathetic in style and material. Despite these major campaigns at Ely and Lincoln and consultations at the cathedrals of Canterbury, Chichester, Salisbury, and Winchester, the commission which gave Essex his name as a church restorer was his rearrangement of the east end of King's College chapel, where he designed blind arcading and pinnacles of convincing Perpendicular form, sympathetic to but not copied from the exterior architecture of the chapel. Here as elsewhere, Essex's shrewd eye found craftsmen who could recreate medieval detail with skill and authority.

The work at King's helped to open the door to commissions in the Gothic style for the polite world beyond Cambridge. Through the recommendation of their mutual friend, William Cole, Essex was asked by Horace Walpole to make designs for Strawberry Hill: first a garden gate derived from Bishop de Luda's tomb at Ely, but then the Beauchamp tower, slender in itself but crucial in giving the house a more romantic asymmetry. For Walpole's friend, Lord Ossory, Essex erected a cross at Ampthill Park, Bedfordshire, in memory of Katherine of Aragon who had lived a prisoner there, and for Lord Hardwicke at Wimpole near Cambridge he executed a large folly castle after drawings by Sanderson Miller.

Antiquarian interests Among his domestic clients Essex could count the two distinguished antiquaries William Cole and Richard Gough, for whom he designed minor alterations, particularly to house their collections of stained glass. More importantly these men became Essex's special mentors in medieval studies. Cole was a close friend from the 1760s, not only introducing Essex to grand clients such as Walpole, but encouraging him seriously to pursue his interest in Gothic architecture. Gough sponsored Essex in the scholarly world of London, securing his election as fellow of the Society of Antiquaries in 1772 and inducing him to produce papers for the society on topics such as 'The development of Lincoln Cathedral', 'The origin and antiquity of round churches', and 'The ancient timber bridge at Rochester', published in successive volumes of *Archaeologia* in 1776 and 1785.

Essex had close links with two other antiquaries of more than local significance. Michael Tyson of Corpus achieved a reputation as an authority on medieval life before his premature death, but left little beyond a series of engravings; it was he who in 1773 accompanied Essex to the Southern Netherlands, his only trip abroad of which Essex's journal (now lost) was published in 1888. James Bentham of Ely was a very different figure, less lively but the author of a substantial history of Ely Cathedral, which he prefaced by tracing the development of medieval architecture in England. Essex assisted with the book in many ways, surveying impressive measured sections of the cathedral as illustrations, and establishing the architectural history of the building. He also had to work closely with Bentham on the cathedral fabric, since Bentham acted as clerk of works during the repairs and alterations Essex undertook at Ely.

What these men prized in Essex was his understanding, exceptional for the period, of how medieval buildings were designed and constructed. The first paper he submitted to the Antiquaries addressed not an individual monument but the general subject of the origins and types of brick building in England. His notes and drawings show that he accumulated evidence of particular features from a wide variety of buildings, mostly in his home areas of East Anglia and the east midlands, but also from as far as Kent and Devon. Essex recognized that to understand Gothic it was not enough to gather eye-catching details, as Walpole and his circle had done at Strawberry Hill. The buildings themselves had to be analysed. 'Time must be spent in measuring their parts, comparing them with each other and ascertaining the proportions they bear among themselves' (BL, Add. MS 6771, fol. 200v).

Essex had no blind admiration for the achievements and techniques of medieval craftsmen. He condemned the builders of King's chapel for risking the safety of the structure by having such a wide and low-pitched roof and replaced the traditional pyramid roof on the chapter house at Lincoln by a hipped design, ungainly in appearance but functional and economical in timber. He accepted that 'we are not to imagine everything done in the past was good architecture, any more than in the present age' (BL, Add. MS 6762, fol. 16v). He was indeed scornful of contemporary neo-Gothic produced 'by our modern builders who mistaking the principles of pure architecture, think they have produced something in the Gothic style when they have collected together a jumble of discordant parts of old buildings' (ibid.). His contemporaries accepted his pre-eminence. Cole, never an indulgent critic, considered that the reredos in King's chapel showed Essex to 'know more of Gothic architecture than anyone I have heard talk of it' (BL, Add. MS 5842, p. 333). In 1773 his reputation gained him the invitation to compete with James Wyatt and Henry Keene to advise on moving the choir at Westminster Abbey.

The achievement which won Essex the greatest academic respect, both in his lifetime and later, was the projected 'History of Gothic architecture', on which he was working for much of his career. Though never brought to fruition in a published volume, his collections were known to scholars such as Richard Gough and were preserved and ordered after his death by his nephew by marriage, the antiquary Thomas Kerrich, who bequeathed them to the British Museum. As early as 1756 Essex planned a book on King's chapel; thirteen years later he was thinking of 'a regular treatise on Gothic Architecture' (Walpole, 1.84). The idea grew, perhaps at Cole's prompting, of a collaborative work in which Essex would write on the 'origin, progress and theory of Gothic … illustrated by plans, elevations and sections' and on geometry, changes in style, prices, and technical terms, but there would also be 'observations on the sculpture, statuary and paintings' to be contributed by Walpole and Tyson (BL, Add. MS 6771, fol. 197). Only Essex persevered, planning on his own account an ambitious survey of the development of architecture from its biblical origins, with illustrated reconstructions of the Israelites' tabernacle and Solomon's temple to its climax in Rome and then through its decadence during the dark ages to its renewed flowering in the middle ages.

Death and significance Essex was a shrewd businessman, accumulating by the time of his death a fortune of over £20,000, derived not only from his building business and architectural practice but also from discreet loans. By the 1770s he had managed to rise socially from joiner to gentleman, though he never moved from the modest Hartshorn tenement on Trumpington Street, Cambridge, first leased from Corpus in 1744 by his father. It was there he died on 14 September 1784, apparently of a paralytic stroke, after some years of increasing infirmity. He was buried in St Botolph's Church, Cambridge. Eight months later his daughter married the Revd John Hammond, fellow of Queens' College and curate of St Botolph's, but she

died in January 1787, followed by her mother in September 1790. The bulk of the family property and papers passed to the family of John Hammond by his second marriage. They were available for study in the 1880s but have since disappeared.

Essex retained a name as one of the most reputable pioneers of the revived Gothic well into the nineteenth century; even Eastlake in 1872 accepted that Essex was the first professional architect to study Gothic. R. Willis and J. W. Clark's *Architectural History of the University of Cambridge* (1886) revealed the range of Essex's secular work but condemned its largely classical nature. Since the Second World War, Essex's reputation has risen again, not only for his Gothic commissions and researches but also for his precocious concern for conservation of buildings in the style.   T. H. COCKE

Sources R. Willis, *The architectural history of the University of Cambridge, and of the colleges of Cambridge and Eton*, ed. J. W. Clark, 4 vols. (1886) • Walpole, *Corr.* • J. Essex, 'Journal of a tour through part of Flanders and France in August 1773', *Cambridge Antiquarian Society, Octavo Publications*, 24 (1888) • Nichols, *Lit. anecdotes*, vols. 5–9 • Nichols, *Illustrations*, vols. 4, 6 • D. R. Stewart, 'James Essex', *ArchR*, 108 (1950), 317–21 • N. Pevsner, 'Walpole and Essex', *Some architectural writers of the nineteenth century* (1972), 1–8 • T. H. Cocke, 'James Essex, cathedral restorer', *Architectural History*, 18 (1975), 20–30 • T. Cocke, ed., *The ingenious Mr Essex, architect, 1722–1784* (1984) [exhibition catalogue, Fitzwilliam Museum, Cambridge, 17 July – 2 Sep 1984] • T. Cocke, 'James Essex', *The architectural outsiders*, ed. R. Brown (1985), 98–113 • Y. Jerrold, 'A study of James Essex of Cambridge: architect and antiquarian', pt 2 diss., U. Cam., school of architecture, 1977 • common day book, Cambridge corporation, 1770–86, Cambs. AS • Lincs. Arch., Lincoln cathedral archives, chapter papers • BL, Add. MS 6771 • BL, Add. MS 6762 • BL, Add. MS 5842 • CCC Cam. • parish register, St Botolph, Cambridge, Cambs. AS [marriage]

Archives BL, papers, Add. MSS 6760–6776 • Cambs. AS, Cambridge, estate and personal papers • CUL, account book • Lincoln Cathedral, Lincoln chapter archives • Winchester College, corresp. relating to work at Winchester College

Likenesses portrait, *c.*1770 (after miniature by W. S. Lambourn?), Downing College, Cambridge, Bowtell MS V f1013 • F. Torond, group portrait, pen-and-ink silhouette, *c.*1780 (with wife and daughter), Worthing Museum

Wealth at death approx. £22,000—of which two thirds given to daughter: Cambs. AS, Probate R 70/46

Essex, John (d. 1744), dancing-master, is of obscure origins, as the place and date of his birth, and his parentage, are unknown. Nothing is known of his early life or his education but by 1702 he was established as a professional dancer at the Drury Lane Theatre, where his repertoire included serious and comic dances. His stage career ended abruptly in 1703, when he made a complaint against the theatre's manager, Christopher Rich, which apparently resulted in his discharge from the company. He did not try to return to the stage, and by 1707 he had moved to Rood Lane (off Fenchurch Street) in the parish of St Dionis Backchurch in the City of London, where he seems to have taught music as well as dancing. Essex had married by 1703, for he and his wife, Catherine (d. 1721), were the parents of a son baptized that year at St Paul's, Covent Garden. Between 1707 and 1715 the registers of St Dionis Backchurch record that John and Catherine Essex had five more children, three of whom died soon after they were baptized.

By 1706 Essex was closely associated with a group of London dancing-masters working to raise the status and reform the practice of dancing, led by Mr Isaac, Thomas Caverley, and John Weaver. Essex subscribed to *Orchesography* (1706), John Weaver's translation of *Choregraphie* (1700), a treatise on dance notation by Raoul Auger Feuillet, and *A Collection of Ball-Dances* (1706), Weaver's notations of six dances by Mr Isaac. Essex himself produced a translation of the introduction to Feuillet's *Recueil de contredances* (1706), a treatise on the notation of country dances, entitled *For the Further Improvement of Dancing* (1710) and containing several notated country dances. A new edition of the work appeared about 1715, dedicated to the princess of Wales, with the notation for a ball dance by Essex entitled *The Princess's Passpied*. Essex wrote music as well as choreographing dances, for *A Collection of Minuets, Rigadoons & French Dances* (1721) included some of his compositions.

Essex's wife was buried on 9 March 1721 but he himself continued to live in Rood Lane, which was given as his address in 1722, when his second book, *The Young Ladies Conduct, or, Rules for Education* appeared. This treatise on female education was conventional, except for its emphasis on the usefulness of dancing. It discussed qualities desirable in women, such as chastity and industry, as well as those to be avoided or corrected, such as pride and vanity; it also identified music, drawing, embroidery, and housewifery as among the proper employments for young ladies. Essex seems to have drawn many of his precepts from *The Adventures of Telemachus*, a translation of Fénelon's *Télémaque*.

Essex maintained his links with other leading dancing-masters, subscribing to Weaver's *Anatomical and Mechanical Lectures upon Dancing* (1721) and Anthony L'Abbé's *A New Collection of Dances* (c.1725), which consisted of theatre dances recorded in notation. His most important book appeared in 1728—*The Dancing-Master, or, The Art of Dancing Explained*, his translation of Pierre Rameau's *Le maître à danser* (1725), which for the first time described how to perform many of the steps notated in Feuillet's *Choregraphie*. Essex added his own preface to the work, in which he provided thumbnail sketches of the dancing-masters Groscourt (to whom the translation was dedicated), Isaac, L'Abbé, Caverley, and the dancer John Shaw, among others; he reserved special praise for John Weaver and the dancer-actress Hester Booth. A second edition of *The Dancing-Master* was published in 1731 and the work was reissued about 1733 with new illustrations by George Bickham the younger. Another edition appeared in 1744, the year that John Essex died; he was buried, alongside his wife, in St Dionis Backchurch on 6 February. His will included a bequest of £20 for John Weaver and divided the residue of his estate between two surviving children, William and Elizabeth. William Essex, whose date and place of birth are unknown, was also a dancing-master and enjoyed a successful career as a dancer at Drury Lane and other theatres between 1724 and 1746. John Essex has been identified as the dancing-master portrayed in the second painting in Hogarth's series *The Rake's Progress* but there is little evidence to support this. MOIRA GOFF

Sources E. L. Avery, ed., *The London stage, 1660–1800*, pt 2: *1700–1729* (1960) · A. H. Scouten, ed., *The London stage, 1660–1800*, pt 3: *1729–1747* (1961) · A. Nicoll, *Early eighteenth century drama, 1700–1750*, 3rd edn (1952), vol. 2 of *A history of English drama, 1660–1900* (1952–9), 292 · J. Nichols, *Biographical anecdotes of William Hogarth, and a catalogue of his works chronologically arranged with occasional remarks* (1781), 14 · Highfill, Burnim & Langhans, *BDA* · R. A. Feuillet, *Orchesography, or, The art of dancing, by characters and demonstrative figures, trans. by John Weaver* (1706) · Mr Isaac, *A collection of ball-dances perform'd at court* (1706) · J. Weaver, *Anatomical and mechanical lectures upon dancing* (1721) · A. L'Abbé, *A new collection of dances* (c.1725) · parish register, London, St Paul's, Covent Garden · parish register, London, St Dionis Backchurch [burial]

Wealth at death over £2000: will, PRO, PROB 11/731, sig. 35

Essex, Margaret (*bap.* 1775, *d.* in or after 1808), composer, was baptized on 30 July 1775 at St Martin-in-the-Fields, London, the youngest of three children of Timothy and Margaret Essex. A brother William was born in 1773. Her elder brother Timothy *Essex was also a composer. Very little evidence of Margaret's life survives, most of it from her printed music. Her publications date from between 1795 (when she was twenty) and 1807. On 2 January 1808 she married John Cambell at St George's, Hanover Square, London. Thereafter her publications ceased and her life remains untraced.

Margaret Essex's connection with Timothy is confirmed by information given on her musical editions, which were all published in London at her own expense by Robert Birchall. Her earliest song, 'Absence', has words by T. Essex and copyright assigned to him. Her address is given here and elsewhere as 2 Newman Street, Oxford Street, London, which matches Timothy's in Doane's *Musical Directory* for 1794. It is unclear whether this Timothy is her father or her brother. The date of 1765? given for Timothy's birth in the *Dictionary of National Biography* is too late for the former but too early for the latter, whose Oxford degree dates from 1806. The fact that Margaret had a very thorough musical education indicates that her father was probably a musician. The publications of T. Essex, however, are undoubtedly those of her brother.

During her years as an active composer around the turn of the century, Margaret Essex was probably employed as a governess or music teacher. All her published compositions are suitable for domestic music-making (songs and chamber music), and at least one is pedagogical. She addressed all but one of her dedications to single women, no doubt the daughters of wealthy families who were her pupils. Her thirteen published compositions comprise ten songs with accompaniment for piano or harp, a set of three accompanied piano sonatas, and two works for solo piano. Her songs demonstrate a genuine melodic gift, subtle and graceful. In particular, her *Select Songs* (six songs published individually between 1802 and 1805) are carefully crafted for the skills of particular performers, presumably the dedicatees. 'Humid seal of soft affection' (no. 3) is a fine example of her lyrical style.

Margaret Essex's output was small by professional

standards but significant in that she was a woman who broke into the public sphere by publishing and copyrighting her works. In other respects she followed the strictures of contemporary society, writing music only for domestic performance, and retiring after her marriage.

JANE GIRDHAM

Sources J. Girdham, 'Margaret Essex', *Women composers: music through the ages*, ed. S. Glickman and M. Schleifer, 4 (New York, 1998) · IGI · Stationers' Hall copyright ledgers · GM, 1st ser., 78 (1808), 85 · *Boyd's miscellaneous marriage index*, ed. Society of Genealogists, 2nd ser. [microfiche] · J. Doane, ed., *A musical directory for the year 1794* [1794]

Essex, Timothy (c.1765–1847), composer and music teacher, was probably born in Coventry about 1765, the eldest child of Timothy Essex and his wife, Margaret. Little is known about his childhood except that his family moved to London, where his two siblings, William (b. 1773) and Margaret (bap. 1775), were born. Essex (or perhaps his father) is listed in Doane's *Musical Directory* for 1794 as a violinist and harpsichordist who performed in the New Musical Fund concerts. He was also listed as a member of the court of assistants for the New Musical Fund in 1805 and 1815. He began publishing his compositions in the early 1790s at his own expense, generally entering them as copyright in the Stationers' Hall ledgers. He also wrote the words to his sister's first published song, 'Absence', in 1795 and owned its copyright.

In 1794–7 Essex and his sister (and probably his parents) lived at 2 Newman Street, London. By 1799 he was married. He and his wife, Jane, had four children, all born in London: Thomas Parr in 1799, Richard Hamilton in 1802, Jane Louisa Paulina in 1806, and Margaret Anna in 1809. On 17 December 1806 Essex was awarded the degree of bachelor of music from Magdalen Hall, Oxford, which was followed by a doctorate in music from Oxford on 2 December 1812.

Essex made his living in large part from teaching music. He ran a 'Musical Academy' at 38 Hill Street, Berkeley Square, and taught at various other establishments, as is indicated by the dedications of some of his songs. For instance, the canzonet 'When Lovely Woman Stoops to Folly' (1797) is dedicated to 'the young ladies at Belle Vue House, Bromly, Kent'; songs from 1804 are dedicated to the 'young ladies' at three other establishments. His songs are pleasantly lyrical, designed for domestic use. Essex also composed pedagogical material, including his *Eight lessons and four sonatinas on a peculiar plan, intended to establish a proper method of fingering on the piano-forte* (1801). He wrote a number of marches and dances for military bands, which he published in full score. A most unusual publication is his *Declaration for the commissioners for the income & property tax, written & the music composed & arranged for the piano forte*. Few if any of his published compositions date from the last thirty years of his life.

Essex was organist, composer, and choir director at St George's Chapel, Albemarle Street, London. He probably wrote his largest publication for this institution: *Harmonia sacrae*, a collection of melodies for the psalms which he selected, arranged, or composed. In 1839 he wrote to the double bass virtuoso Domenico Dragonetti to inform him about a sale of music that included his transcription of madrigals by Cipriano da Rore in modern notation, 'Barr'd and scored', for which Dragonetti owned some original parts. He died on 27 September 1847 at his home in York Buildings, New Road, London.

JANE GIRDHAM

Sources J. Girdham, 'Margaret Essex', *Women composers: music through the ages*, ed. S. Glickman and M. Schleifer, 4 (New York, 1998) · copyright registers of the Worshipful Company of Stationers and Newspaper Makers, London · T. Essex to [Domenico] Dragonetti, BL, Add. MS 17838, fol. 129 · Foster, *Alum. Oxon.* · GM, 2nd ser., 28 (1847), 551 · L. Baillie and R. Balchin, eds., *The catalogue of printed music in the British Library to 1980*, 62 vols. (1981–7) · *Répertoire international des sources musicales*, ser. A/I, 9 vols. (Munich and Duisburg, 1971–81); addenda and corrigenda, 4 vols. (1986–99) · *DNB* · Highfill, Burnim & Langhans, *BDA* · J. Doane, ed., *A musical directory for the year 1794* [1794] · IGI

Essex, William (1784–1869). *See under* Essex family (*per. c.1800–c.1860*).

Essex, William B. (1822–1852). *See under* Essex family (*per. c.1800–c.1860*).

Essinger, Anna (1879–1960), educationist, was born on 15 September 1879 in Ulm, Germany, the eldest of nine children of Leopold Essinger (1853–1934), a Jewish insurance agent, and his wife, Fanny Oppenheimer (1858–1942). She attended school in Ulm until 1893. In 1899 she went to live with an aunt in Nashville, Tennessee, where she became interested in education. At the University of Wisconsin she read German from 1913 onwards for an MA degree, then taught German there as a Pfister fellow. In 1919 she was sent to southern Germany by the American Society of Friends (by whom this non-practising Jew was greatly influenced) to organize the Quaker post-war relief work for children. Then she was involved in establishing further education programmes for working women, but decided, however, that her true vocation lay in educating children.

With the help of her family Essinger founded the co-educational progressive boarding-school, Landschulheim Herrlingen, near Ulm, in 1926. She was in close contact with leading national and international representatives of the New Education Fellowship. The education was based on some fundamental precepts: equal importance of practical and theoretical work; pupils taught in groups according to their abilities and individual work to be encouraged; no learning by rote; no physical punishment; no competitive tests or assessments. In her school English and French were even spoken at table. Teachers were addressed by their nicknames and the informal 'Du'; the headmistress was Tante Anna.

When Hitler came to power in 1933, Essinger realized that her school would have no future in Nazi Germany. With the permission of the British authorities and the support of Quakers and private donors she secretly moved sixty-five Jewish pupils of her school to Bunce Court, a manor house near Otterden, Kent. Bunce Court School employed an equal number of English and German staff and also attracted British pupils. In view of possible emigration of pupils to Palestine modern Hebrew was offered. Practical work was no longer solely taught for pedagogical reasons, but also to make the school self-supporting. Sadly science was neglected in favour of the humanities. There were workshops in which photography, model building, art, and music were taught; an open-air theatre was built by the pupils where plays and operas were performed. Numerous Bunce Courtians, including Gerard Hoffnung, Frank Auerbach, and Frank Marcus, made careers in art, music, and literature, others in science. When the financial situation became precarious because parents were no longer able to send money abroad, the very short-sighted and stout but formidable headmistress made weekly fund-raising trips to London lecturing on the plight of refugee Jewish children.

In November 1938 Essinger was asked to organize Dovercourt Camp, a reception camp of the 'Kindertransports' when 10,000 Jewish unaccompanied children arrived from Nazi Germany shortly after 'Kristallnacht'. A guarantor had to be found for each child while dozens were admitted to her already overcrowded boarding-school. In June 1940 Bunce Court was requisitioned by the military. Trench Hall near Wem, Shropshire, was converted into a makeshift home for the school. Moreover, all male teachers and pupils over sixteen of German nationality were interned. After the war she returned to a dilapidated Bunce Court. The last intake included hidden children from eastern Europe and concentration camp survivors. In 1948 the school closed down, largely because it had fulfilled its purpose.

Essinger, a complex personality, had rescued many hundreds of Jewish children and given them a haven of security in her school family. In her last years she was blind and lived on the Bunce Court estate with three of her sisters who helped her to maintain an enormous correspondence with former pupils, many of whom visited her until her peaceful death at her home, The Bungalow, Bunce Court, on 30 May 1960. She was cremated at Charing, Kent, on 2 June.

Essinger's singular commitment perhaps left her with more admirers of her work than close friends. Professor Leslie Baruch Brent, a former pupil, concluded his funeral oration: 'Anna Essinger devoted herself singlemindedly to the cause of education and the saving of young lives from the persecution of Nazi Germany, and in this she was sustained by an unshakeable faith in the idea of human progress.'   UTA-ELIZABETH TROTT

Sources A. Essinger, *Bunce Court school, 1933–1943* (privately printed, [London], [1943]), 1–13 · A. Major, 'Bunce Court, Anna Essinger and her New Herrlingen School, Otterden', *Bygone Kent*, 10 (1989), 547–53, 623–31, 653–9 · D. M. Potten, 'Des Kindes Chronik' · Wiener Library, London, Bunce Court School and Landschulheim Herrlingen Archive, 1926–1948 · I. Origo, *Images and shadows* (1970) · A. Schubert and P. Schubert, 'Anna's children', television film and video, Süddeutscher Rundfunk, Germany, Holocaust Museum, Washington, DC, deposited · A. Hoffnung, *Hoffnung* (1988) · R. Hughes, *Frank Auerbach* (1990) · private information (2004) [former teachers and pupils; D. M. Potten, niece]
Archives Wiener Library, London, Bunce Court School and Landschulheim Herrlingen Archive
Likenesses photographs, Wiener Library, London, Bunce Court School and Landschulheim Herrlingen Archive
Wealth at death £9422 18s. 9d.: probate, 26 Aug 1960, CGPLA Eng. & Wales

Estaugh [*née* Haddon], **Elizabeth** (1680–1762), Quaker leader and colonial landowner, was born on 5 July 1680 in Bermondsey, Surrey, the second daughter and third child of John Haddon (1654–1724) and his wife, Elizabeth, *née* Clarke (1651?–1724). John Haddon was a convinced Quaker and twice had been fined for voicing his religious views. Like other Quakers he was persuaded by William Penn to look to America for sanctuary. In 1701 he purchased hundreds of acres of land in West Jersey across from Philadelphia. At the time that he signed a land settlement agreement Haddon was a blacksmith in London and unable to accept business offers, which required the taking of oaths of allegiance. The situation changed with the acceptance of affirmations; moreover, Haddon was appointed officer for the Pennsylvania Land Company as well as for the London Lead Company. The latter position made him reluctant to occupy his new property, and indeed he never left England.

Elizabeth Haddon, only nineteen at the time, 'felt a drawing' to fulfil her father's land settlement and was given full power of attorney to transact business in West Jersey. Before she arrived in 1701 her father had already had a dwelling built for her at Cooper's Creek, Newtown township; this now became her home. Elizabeth arrived, thinking that eventually some of her immediate family would follow. This, however, never happened, and with the care of a widowed friend and two faithful manservants she was left to develop what became the large plantation of Haddonfield, an instance 'unique in Quaker records' (Jones, 389).

Auspiciously, Elizabeth Haddon became reacquainted with a Quaker leader John Estaugh (1676–1742), whom she had met at Bermondsey some years earlier and who had arrived in America in 1700 on a religious visit. John and Elizabeth's courtship was celebrated in 'Elizabeth', the only story of Henry Wadsworth Longfellow's *Tales of a Wayside Inn* (1863) to be set outside his native New England. The couple were married in Quaker fashion at Haddonfield on 1 December 1702. Elizabeth said of their forty-year marriage: 'few if any in a married state ever lived in sweeter harmony than we did' (*Journal and Essays of John Woolman*, 532). In 1713 work began on New Haddonfield, the couple's second residence, around which the town of Haddonfield was founded. Though Elizabeth and John Estaugh had no children of their own they were joined, in 1723, by Ebenezer Hopkins, Elizabeth's nephew.

Over the years the Estaughs entertained many Quakers, including John Haslam, a Yorkshire preacher of fifty years' standing. Elizabeth formed a special friendship with Elizabeth Woolman, the sister of John Woolman, a leading Quaker author and an anti-slavery pioneer. Elizabeth Estaugh stayed with Elizabeth Woolman during the latter's final illness, and in 1747 witnessed her will. Elizabeth had long taken an interest in the sick and to this day, at Haddonfield, can be seen her old brewhouse, where she made many 'simples and remedies' to treat inhabitants of her vast settlement. She remained active in Friends' meetings up to her death; for fifty years she was clerk of the women's monthly meeting and so vast was her correspondence that she had to employ several secretaries.

John Estaugh became an agent in his father-in-law's business in the land company in West Jersey; he also undertook a number of visits in the religious ministry of Friends. During one of these, to the small island of Tortola in the West Indies in 1742, he died. After her husband's death Elizabeth maintained her church work and continued to manage the family's estate. She died on 30 March 1762, on Haddonfield plantation, and was buried in the cemetery of the local Friends' meeting-house. Much of her property subsequently passed to the children of Ebenezer Hopkins.

In the testimony of Haddonfield monthly meeting, after Elizabeth's death, it was written: 'Her heart and house were open to her friends, whom to entertain, seemed one of her greatest pleasures' (*Journal and Essays of John Woolman*, 532). Today Elizabeth Estaugh, who is also known by her maiden name of Elizabeth Haddon, is recognized as the founder of the town of Haddonfield, New Jersey, which has a population of 15,000, and is remembered by the state as one of its most significant pioneers.

DAVID SOX

Sources E. A. Lyons, 'Elizabeth Haddon, *c.*1680–1762', *Past and promise: lives of New Jersey women*, ed. J. N. Burstyn (1990), 21–2 · 'Dictionary of Quaker biography', RS Friends, Lond. [card index] · *The journal and essays of John Woolman*, ed. A. Mott Gummere (1922), 21, 33, 531–2, 564 · H. J. Sturge, *Fragmentary memorials of John and Elizabeth Estaugh* (1881) · R. Nicholson, *Contributions to the biography of Elizabeth Estaugh* (Philadelphia, PA, 1894) · L. M. Child, 'The youthful emigrant', *Fact and fiction: a collection of stories* (1847), 8–13 · J. Clement, *Sketches of the first emigrant settlers in Newton Township, Old Gloucester County, Haddonfield, N.J.* (1887) · R. N. Taylor, 'The business papers of John and Elizabeth Estaugh', *Quaker History*, 20 (1931), 13–19 · R. M. Jones, *The Quakers in the American colonies* (1911)
Archives Haddonfield Public Library, New Jersey, MSS
Wealth at death Haddonfield Plantation, New Jersey

Estcourt, Edgar Edmund (1816–1884), Roman Catholic priest, was born on 7 February 1816, the second son of the Revd Edmund William Estcourt (1782–1856), rector of Long Newnton, Wiltshire, and Shipton Moyne, Gloucestershire, and his wife, Bertha Elizabeth, second daughter of Thomas Wyatt of Wargrave, Berkshire. Destined for the church, Estcourt entered Exeter College, Oxford, on 20 February 1834, and proceeded BA in 1838 and MA in 1840. After taking holy orders he served as curate at Cirencester from 1842 to 1845.

Estcourt had come under the influence of the Oxford Movement, and in December 1845, shortly after Newman's conversion to Roman Catholicism, he was received into the Catholic church at Prior Park, near Bath. In 1848 he was ordained priest by W. B. Ullathorne, vicar apostolic of the western district, and on the restoration of the hierarchy in 1850 he was appointed oeconomus of the Birmingham diocese, becoming a canon of St Chad's, Birmingham, in 1852. Here he proved to be a conscientious secretary and assistant to Ullathorne, managing the diocesan temporalities efficiently and acquiring a considerable knowledge of property law. At his funeral, Ullathorne's address praised his 'assiduity, accuracy, punctuality, skill and sound judgement' (*The Tablet*, 670). He also acted as an intermediary between Ullathorne and Newman. Estcourt was a man of schemes: in 1860 he called upon his fellow convert, Newman, to act on a committee to build a new Catholic church in Oxford (and possibly a Catholic college), the first hint of a controversial plan which was to bedevil Newman later in the decade. He also suggested the formation of a society to publish Catholic works of theology, history, and controversy, which was intended to give employment to converts in financial need. A confirmed bibliophile, he was for many years a member of the committee of the London Library.

In 1873 Estcourt published *The Question of Anglican Ordinations Discussed*, a work which he had been researching for more than ten years and which contained an appendix of original documents and facsimiles. Appearing at a time when the validity of Anglican orders was a hotly debated issue, *The Question* attracted considerable attention, and an anonymous reply was published under the title *Anglican orders, a few remarks in the form of a conversation on the recent work by Canon Estcourt*. Estcourt's work was a valuable and scholarly contribution to the debate, unjustly overlooked by the continental scholars whose own work influenced Leo XIII's bull *Apostolicae curae* of 1896. Most of Estcourt's conclusions were endorsed in E. C. Messenger's magisterial work on the subject, *The Reformation, the Priesthood and the Mass* (1936–7). Newman considered that Estcourt's work was 'too antiquarian to be in my line', but recognized its importance in exploring the historical context of the debate, commenting that it created 'an era in [that] great question' (*Letters and Diaries*, 26.184, 237). Estcourt also published *Dogmatic Teaching of the Book of Common Prayer on the Subject of the Holy Eucharist* (1868), which was originally intended as an article for the *Dublin Review*.

In the last years of his life Estcourt was in poor health, and lived in retirement in Leamington Spa, where he died on 17 April 1884, at The Highlands, Heath Terrace, Milverton. He was buried at Kenilworth. He left unpublished an edition of Henry Clifford's *Life of Jane Dormer, Duchess of Feria*, for which he had been collecting materials for twenty-five years. This early seventeenth-century account of the career of Mary I's companion presented the much maligned queen as pious, pure, and noble-minded. It was completed by the Jesuit archivist and scholar Joseph Stevenson (1806–1895), and appeared in 1887.

ROSEMARY MITCHELL

Sources Gillow, *Lit. biog. hist.* · *The Tablet* (26 April 1884), 661, 670 · *The letters and diaries of John Henry Newman*, ed. C. S. Dessain and

others, [31 vols.] (1961–), vols. 11–19 • Foster, *Alum. Oxon.* • Burke, *Gen. GB* • Boase, *Mod. Eng. biog.* • *CGPLA Eng. & Wales* (1884) • d. cert.
Archives Birmingham Roman Catholic Archdiocesan Archives, official papers • Glos. RO, corresp. | Birmingham Oratory, letters to J. H. Newman • Ushaw College, Durham, corresp. with Mgr Searle • Warks. CRO, county notes and papers relating to the duchess of Feria and the Tichborne family
Wealth at death £249 10s. 0d.: probate, 7 June 1884, *CGPLA Eng. & Wales*

Estcourt, James Bucknall Bucknall

Estcourt, James Bucknall Bucknall (1802–1855), army officer, was born on 12 July 1802, the second son of Thomas Grimston Bucknall Estcourt MP (*d.* 1853) of Estcourt, Gloucestershire, and his wife, Eleanor, daughter of James Sutton of New Park, Wiltshire; he was the younger brother of Thomas Henry Sutton Sotheron Estcourt. Educated at Harrow, he purchased a commission as ensign in the 44th foot on 13 July 1820, exchanging on 7 June 1821 into the 43rd foot (Monmouthshire light infantry) before purchasing promotion to lieutenant (9 December 1824) and captain (5 November 1825). Estcourt served with the regiment, which formed part of Lieutenant-General Sir William Clinton's division sent to garrison towns in Portugal (1826–7) during disruption over the succession to the throne. He appears then to have returned with the 43rd to Gibraltar, before sailing for Plymouth and, in 1832, Ireland. From January 1835 until June 1837, he was second in command to Colonel F. R. *Chesney during his expedition to the Euphrates valley, which sought to prove that the river was navigable from within overland reach of the Mediterranean to its mouth on the Persian Gulf, thus shortening the journey to India. Despite a torrid period, during which one steamer was wrecked and twenty lives lost at Basrah on 31 August 1836, Estcourt produced a detailed report for Chesney, anticipating 'no difficulties' in passage during the 'season of high water', provided that accurate knowledge of the deep channel and a vessel of suitable length were acquired. He was less sure about the 'low season', owing to lack of information, though he was confident that local Arabs would not be hostile, once they became used to the steamers.

Estcourt purchased his majority in the 43rd on 21 October 1836, and gained a brevet lieutenant-colonelcy (29 March 1839), before going on half pay as an unattached lieutenant-colonel (25 August 1843). Meanwhile, in 1837, he had married Caroline, daughter of Reginald Pole-Carew, under-secretary of state for the Home department in 1803–4. From February 1848 until 1852, when he did not seek re-election, he sat as Conservative MP for Devizes.

Promoted colonel (11 November 1851), though still on half pay, Estcourt was in Rome when he learned of the proposed expedition to the eastern Mediterranean under Lord Raglan. He hurried back to England seeking appointment as its quartermaster-general, but became instead adjutant-general with the rank of brigadier-general on 21 February 1854. Although he was industrious, tactful, and administratively sound, he had no war experience. Shortly after reaching Turkey his urbanity was tested when he was called upon to quieten angry exchanges

James Bucknall Bucknall Estcourt (1802–1855), by Roger Fenton, 1855

between Lord Cardigan and his superior officer, Lord Lucan, who resented Cardigan's assumption that he held an independent command with the light brigade in Bulgaria. Opting not to 'consider the question … in a formal shape', Estcourt assured Lucan, in June 1854, that Cardigan's 'misapprehensions … have been rectified by private communication from me' (Sweetman, 193–4). The following month, concerned about supply deficiencies, he concluded that the commissariat was 'very defective' and wanting in organization, though as a military officer he had no direct control over that civilian department run by the Treasury. Despite major problems caused by the evident shortcomings in availability and distribution of supplies and the debilitating effect of mounting sickness, as adjutant-general Estcourt was responsible to Raglan for the discipline and effectiveness of the troops in camp, during the landing on the Crimean peninsula in September 1854, and in the field. In the closing stages of the battle of the Alma, Estcourt carried Raglan's order to Lucan, forbidding his cavalry to pursue the defeated enemy for fear of attack from superior Russian forces. Once the siege of Sevastopol had been mounted, Estcourt occupied an outbuilding at Raglan's headquarters on the southern upland. One of Raglan's aides-de-camp noted his 'remarkably kind and courteous disposition', but believed him 'too kind and forgiving' (Calthorpe, 1.88). Only during the hurricane of 14 November 1854 was 'his mien for once disturbed'. As weather conditions before Sevastopol worsened and supplies of food and forage were further reduced, he condemned civilian control of the commissariat as 'a great evil', complained about the 'absence of an organised military conveyance establishment', and despairingly wrote: 'such roads … such ground … such a depth of mud' (Sweetman, 268, 274). Casualties and deaths, through disease and wounds, heightened the inability of the British forces to press siege operations.

Although he was promoted major-general on 12 December 1854, viewed from England the adjutant-general appeared to be failing in his duty. Unwilling or unable to appreciate conditions at the front, successive secretaries of state for war, the duke of Newcastle and Lord Panmure, urged Raglan to dismiss him, and military bureaucrats at the Horse Guards castigated him for failing to forward regular and detailed returns about the state of the army for their gratification. Raglan steadfastly and repeatedly refused to blame or sack Estcourt, insisting that, as a witness of his 'daily labours', he believed him 'perfectly efficient', meriting 'the tribute of warmest approbation' (Hibbert, 232, 255). Panmure retorted that Raglan shouldered 'very grave responsibility' by retaining his adjutant-general in post. On 21 June 1855 Estcourt became ill with cholera and three days later (24 June) he died. He was buried the following day, though Raglan was himself too ill to attend the funeral. Later Lieutenant-Colonel Hamley confirmed Calthorpe's impression of 'a man of remarkably kind and courteous disposition' (268) and A. W. Kinglake, similarly, referred to 'a man greatly loved by Lord Raglan, by all his friends at headquarters, and indeed by all who knew him' (8.261). The *London Gazette* (10 July 1855) announced that Estcourt would have been created KCB had he survived. A royal warrant in 1856 raised Mrs Estcourt (who had spent the winter of 1854–5 in the Crimea and was present at her husband's death) to the rank of a KCB's widow. She died at The Priory, Tetbury, on 17 November 1886.   JOHN SWEETMAN

Sources *Army List* · J. Sweetman, *Raglan: from the Peninsula to the Crimea* (1993) · F. R. Chesney, *The expedition for the survey of the rivers Euphrates and Tigris*, 2 vols. (1850) · R. G. A. Levinge, *Historical records of the forty-third regiment, Monmouthshire light infantry* (1868) · C. Hibbert, *The destruction of Lord Raglan* [1961] · S. J. G. Calthorpe, *Letters from head-quarters … by a staff officer*, 2 vols. (1856) [with illustrations by G. Cadogan]; abridged edn as *Cadogan's Crimea* (1979), vol. 1 · E. Hamley, *The story of the campaign of Sebastopol* (1855) · A. W. Kinglake, *The invasion of the Crimea*, 8 vols. (1863–87), vols. 2–8
Archives Glos. RO, corresp. and papers | NAM, corresp. with Lord Raglan · NAM, letters to Sir George Wetherell
Likenesses R. Fenton, salted paper photograph, 1855, NPG [*see illus.*]

Estcourt, Richard (1668?–1712), actor, was probably born in Tewkesbury, Gloucestershire, in 1668. The few details of his early life that are known can be found in Chetwood's *A General History of the Stage* (1749), but it is uncertain how much fiction is mixed with fact in the account. According to Chetwood, Estcourt, aged fifteen, ran away from the grammar school at Tewkesbury and joined a strolling company performing Nathaniel Lee's

The Rival Queens at Worcester. His father pursued him, so to escape he 'trudg'd it to Chipping Norton … twenty-five long miles in one day' (Chetwood, 140) in female costume. He was caught when obliged to share the bed of the landlord's daughter at an inn. Having been apprenticed to an apothecary in London, he absconded again, Chetwood says, and after two years strolling in England found success in Ireland. However, considering that he was later described as an apothecary by Sir Richard Steele, he probably completed his apprenticeship and practised as an apothecary for a while. About 1688 he fathered a daughter, Charlotte Mary, who became a dancer and married her colleague George Charles Luppino; it is unknown who was Charlotte Mary's mother, or whether Estcourt was ever married.

In 1693 Estcourt spoke a special epilogue for Lord Sydney's departure from Dublin, and in the following years he acted at Smock Alley. He was in Shadwell's *Squire of Alsatia* in the spring of 1698, and he is also recorded as Wheedle in *Love in a Tub*, Sir Joslin Jolly in *She Would if she Could*, and Old Bellair in *The Man of Mode*, all by George Etherege. When James Butler, second duke of Ormond, went to Dublin as lord lieutenant in 1703, Estcourt delivered the poem of welcome at a grand reception.

Estcourt had a song published in 1700, and his play *The Fair Example*, adapted from Dancourt's *Les bourgeoises à la mode*, was first produced at Drury Lane on 10 April 1703. The play ran for three nights at Drury Lane, and was revived in December 1703 and October 1717 at Drury Lane and in 1718 at Lincoln's Inn Fields. When on 18 October 1704 Estcourt played Dominic in Dryden's *The Spanish Fryar* at Drury Lane it was announced as his first appearance on the London stage. He was famous for his mimicry, and Colley Cibber complained that his performance was an uninspired imitation of Anthony Leigh (who had died in 1692) as Dominic. Estcourt was a success with the public, and continued at Drury Lane for that season and the next. His parts included Falstaff, the Gravedigger in *Hamlet*, Trinculo, Blunt in Aphra Behn's *The Rover*, Bluff in William Congreve's *The Old Bachelor*, Bayes in the duke of Buckingham's *The Rehearsal*, Pounce in Richard Steele's *The Tender Husband*, and Antonio in Thomas Otway's *Venice Preserv'd*, and he was the original and admired Sergeant Kite in George Farquhar's *The Recruiting Officer*. He continued to write: according to Chetwood, *The Wife's Excuse, or, Cuckolds Make Themselves* was performed in 1706 with little success, but no other trace can be found of its existence. Better attested is *Prunella*, a satire on the craze for Italian opera performed with *The Rehearsal* at a benefit for Estcourt at Drury Lane on 12 February 1708. Estcourt also produced several popular songs, including patriotic works such as 'Britain's jubilee: a new congratulatory ballad, on … victories … of Marlborough over the French' (*c*.1707) and those intended to celebrate more convivial situations, for example, 'Lard, how man can claret drink' (*c*.1707). He also wrote prologues and epilogues.

Cibber is grudgingly civil in his assessment of Estcourt: because he was 'much sought after in private Companies, he met with a sort of Indulgence, not to say Partiality, for what he sometimes did upon the stage' (Cibber, 165). Others were downright rude:

From Irish Players without Desert,
Whose Acting is not worth a Fart,
Yet they must have vast Salaries for't.
('The Player's Litany', from the *Libera nos &c. Diverting Post*, 21 April 1705)

Estcourt was probably intended: the *Advertisement Concerning the Poor Actors* (1709) gives his income for the 1708–9 season as £363 18*s.* 6*d.* for only fifty-two performances.

Estcourt travelled in the 1706–7 season, perhaps with the duke of Grafton's company, and he played Kite at Bath on 16 September. Back at Drury Lane he was so established that 'Brett assigned his rights [in the Theatre Patent] to Wilks, Estcourt and Cibber' on 31 March 1708. When Rich lost his patent in 1709 Estcourt moved to the Haymarket, but he returned to Drury Lane late in 1710. In this period he undertook the parts of Puzzle in Steele's *The Funeral*, Sir Sampson Legend in Congreve's *Love for Love*, Sullen in Farquhar's *The Beaux' Stratagem*, Captain Otter in Ben Jonson's *The Silent Woman*, Mammon in *The Alchemist* (also by Jonson), and Pandarus in *Truth Found too Late*, Dryden's version of *Troilus and Cressida*. He may by this time already have been in poor health: in *The Tatler* (7 February 1710) Steele advertised a benefit for Estcourt, 'formerly my apothecary, [now] disabled by the gout and stone'.

In December 1711 *The Spectator* announced that Estcourt had taken over the Bumper tavern in James Street, Covent Garden, and would open for business on 1 January. He intended to retire from the stage. That he had some skill in catering is suggested by his appointment as 'providore' to the Beefsteak Club; his badge of office was a golden gridiron on a green ribbon. He gave his last performance on 12 June 1712, as Palmer in *Love in a Tub*. He died on 25 August at the Bumper tavern, but the immediate cause of his death at the age of only forty-four is not recorded. In spite of gout, the Bumper tavern, and his composition of drinking songs, he is not reported an excessive drinker, as some of his contemporaries, including actors, certainly were.

Steele wrote an affectionate account of his friend in *The Spectator* on 27 August.

[T]his extraordinary man ..., in his way, never had an equal in any age before him, or in that wherein he lived. I speak of him as a companion, and a man qualified for conversation. His fortune exposed him to an obsequiousness towards the worst sort of company, but his excellent qualities rendered him capable of making the best figure in the most refined.

Estcourt was also valued for his conversation by Joseph Addison, John Churchill, duke of Marlborough, and Thomas Parnell. Although he was not among the first rank of performers or playwrights in late seventeenth- and early eighteenth-century London, he exhibited professional and social versatility and was evidently well liked among all sections of his audience. **F. H. MARES**

Sources Highfill, Burnim & Langhans, *BDA* · W. Van Lennep and others, eds., *The London stage, 1660–1800*, pt 1: 1660–1700 (1965) · E. L. Avery, ed., *The London stage, 1660–1800*, pt 2: 1700–1729 (1960) · W. R. Chetwood, *A general history of the stage, from its origin in Greece to the present time* (1749), 140–42 · C. Cibber, *An apology for the life of Colley Cibber*, new edn, ed. B. R. S. Fone (1968) · A. Nicoll, *Early eighteenth century drama, 1700–1750*, 3rd edn (1952), vol. 2 of *A history of English drama, 1660–1900* (1952–9) · W. S. Clark, *The early Irish stage: the beginnings to 1720* (1955) · *The Spectator* (1704–12) · *The Tatler* (1709–11) · P. Fitzgerald, *A new history of the English stage*, 2 vols. (1882) · J. Downes, *Roscius Anglicanus*, ed. J. Milhous and R. D. Hume, new edn (1987) · S. Rosenfeld, *Strolling players and drama in the provinces, 1660–1765* (1939)

Wealth at death tavern: *Spectator*, Dec 1711

Estcourt, Thomas Henry Sutton Sotheron (1801–1876), politician, was the eldest son of Thomas Grimston Estcourt (*d.* 1853) of Estcourt, Gloucestershire, MP for Devizes from 1805 to 1827, and for Oxford University from 1827 to 1847, and his wife, Eleanor, daughter and coheir of James Sutton of New Park, Wiltshire. His father took the name Bucknall in 1823 and was a persistent opponent of the reform of Oxford University. His marriage greatly improved the wealth of his ancient Gloucestershire estate. The younger Thomas Estcourt was born on 4 April 1801, and was educated at Harrow School and at Oriel College, Oxford, which he entered on 11 May 1818; he was a leading undergraduate in the days of Copleston, Keble, and Whately. In Michaelmas term 1822, when he was only twenty-one, he was placed in the first class in classics at the same time as his future friends, Lord Ashley, afterwards seventh earl of Shaftesbury, and the Hon. George Howard, afterwards earl of Carlisle and viceroy of Ireland. He took his BA in 1823 and his MA in 1826, and later received the honorary degree of DCL (24 June 1857). He was destined for a political career and, after making the grand tour, he was elected MP for Marlborough in 1829. On 21 August 1830 he married a very wealthy heiress, Lucy Sarah, only daughter of Admiral Frank Sotheron of Kirklington, Nottinghamshire, and Darrington Hall, Yorkshire, and in 1839 on succeeding to the latter property he took the name of Sotheron in lieu of his own. In November 1835 he again entered parliament as MP for Devizes, after a very close election, and held the seat until 1844 when, at a by-election, he was elected unopposed as MP for North Wiltshire; he retained that seat until 1865.

After first taking his seat he soon became known as one of the most promising tory members of the House of Commons; but he inherited his father's disinclination for office, and believed he did enough for his party by speaking often in the house. He was known for his independence, feeling that 'the Task before our leaders ought to be to shew that Toryism is not necessarily antagonistic to Progress' (Stewart, 311). Two years after his father's death (in 1853) he resumed his paternal name of Estcourt (becoming known by the surname Sotheron Estcourt), and in 1858, at the earnest request of his friend Lord Derby, he consented to take office, and was sworn of the privy council and appointed president of the Poor Law Board. He showed himself a competent official, and in March 1859 he succeeded Spencer Walpole as home secretary. The government did not, however, hold together, and in four months Estcourt was glad to retire from office.

Estcourt withdrew altogether from public life in 1863, after a paralytic seizure. He died on 6 January 1876, when he left Estcourt to a younger brother, the Revd Edmund

Hiley Bucknall Estcourt, and Darrington Hall to his nephew, George Thomas John Sotheron-Estcourt, who was created Baron Estcourt in 1903.

H. M. STEPHENS, *rev.* H. C. G. MATTHEW

Sources *The Times* (8 Jan 1876) · Boase, *Mod. Eng. biog.* · R. Stewart, *The foundation of the conservative party, 1830–1867* (1978)
Archives Glos. RO, corresp. and papers | Bodl. Oxf., corresp. with Sir T. G. Wilkinson [some copies] · Lpool RO, letters to fourteenth earl of Derby · Som. ARS, letters to Sir William Joliffe
Likenesses mezzotint, 1863, NPG · J. Phillip, group portrait, oils (*The House of Commons, 1860*), Palace of Westminster, London · engraving, repro. in *ILN* (22 Jan 1876), 76 · wood-engraving (after a photograph by J. Watkins), NPG; repro. in *ILN* (27 March 1858)
Wealth at death under £30,000: probate, 1 March 1876, *CGPLA Eng. & Wales*

Este, Charles (1696–1745), Church of Ireland bishop of Waterford, was born in Whitehall, London, the son of Michael Este of St Margaret's, Westminster. He was educated, as a queen's scholar, at Westminster School, and then at Christ Church, Oxford, where he matriculated on 23 June 1715, graduating BA (1719) and MA (1722). While still at Oxford he co-edited and contributed to *Carmina quadragesimalia ab aedis Christi Oxon* (1729).

Having taken holy orders Este was appointed chaplain to Archbishop Hugh Boulter, whom he accompanied to Ireland in 1724. On 9 January 1726 he was collated, on the presentation of Boulter, to the rectory of Derrynoose, co. Armagh, and in 1730 he was nominated to the archdeaconry of Armagh and the rectories of Aghallow, Killeshill, and Carnteel. Three years later Este resigned these appointments for the chancellorship of Armagh and the rectory of Kilmore, on which living he spent a large sum of money. Through the influence of Boulter and the duke of Newcastle he was raised to the bishopric of Ossory, and enthroned at Kilkenny on 1 March 1736; there he made great additions to the bishop's palace. He was awarded a doctorate of divinity at Dublin University on 9 May 1736, and in October 1740 he became bishop of Waterford. He died on 29 November 1745, probably at Waterford.

ALSAGER VIAN, *rev.* PHILIP CARTER

Sources H. Cotton, *Fasti ecclesiae Hibernicae*, 1–2 (1845–8) · Foster, *Alum. Oxon.*
Likenesses attrib. J. B. van Loo, oils, Christ Church Oxf.

Esten [*née* Bennett; *other married name* Scott-Waring], **Harriet Pye** (1761?–1865), actress, was born, according to her death certificate, in May 1761, at Tooting, Surrey, the natural daughter of Admiral Sir Thomas *Pye (1708/9–1785), and his housekeeper, Anna (or Agnes) Maria *Bennett (d. 1808). She had a brother, Thomas Pye Bennett, who joined the Royal Navy. In February 1784 Harriet Bennett married Lieutenant James Esten, with whom she had two children. The ill success of her husband in a business venture is said to have prompted her to pursue an independent career as an actress.

Esten received her theatrical instruction from her mother. She made her début at Bristol on 19 June 1786 as Alicia in Nicholas Rowe's *Jane Shore*, and acted regularly throughout the 1786–7 season at Bristol and Bath, where the local press dubbed her 'the Bath Abington'. The following summer she joined the company of Richard Daly at

Harriet Pye Esten (1761?–1865), by Samuel De Wilde [as Lady Flutter in *The Discovery* by Frances Sheridan]

Smock Alley, Dublin, where she acted alongside William Holman. In July 1789, while performing in Dublin, she obtained a deed of separation from her husband: Mrs Bennett had agreed to rescue her son-in-law from bankruptcy on condition that he relinquish his wife and children and live abroad.

In January 1790 Harriet Esten took up an engagement with John Jackson in Edinburgh. She made her début as Juliet and 'was received as one scarcely inferior to Mrs Siddons or Mrs Jordan' (Haslewood, 1.6). She then joined the company of Tate Wilkinson at York, where her performance as Shakespeare's Rosalind was received with 'violent applause'. Wilkinson recalls how an enamoured theatre critic of York 'made the press groan with lavish praises of the Esten' (Wilkinson, 3.109).

The popularity of Mrs Esten in the provinces resulted in an engagement for the 1790–91 season at Covent Garden. On 20 October 1790 she made her London début, once more playing Rosalind. 'She is rather small in stature', reported one critic, 'but well made, with a most eloquent eye and a very expressive countenance. Although she is rather underhung, her face may fairly be pronounced pretty, and her figure engaging. Her voice, in the pathetic tones, resembles that of Mrs Siddons, but is more clear and articulate' (*Woodfall's Register*, 21 Oct 1790). Esten performed throughout her first London season 'without receiving any salary; but with the indulgence of appearing in whatever characters she chose' (Gilliland, 2.757). Her first London benefit performance, as Letitia Hardy in

Hannah Cowley's *The Belle's Stratagem*, raised £353 18s. Other roles included Indiana in Richard Steele's *The Conscious Lovers*, Roxalana in Isaac Bickerstaff's *The Sultan*, and Monimia in Otway's *The Orphan*. Thomas Harris, manager of Covent Garden, under strong pressure from the duke of Clarence and Dorothy Jordan, agreed to re-engage Esten for three further seasons on a salary of £11 a week.

In July 1792 Esten obtained the lease of the Theatre Royal, Edinburgh, from Stephen Kemble. The theatre patentee, Douglas, eighth duke of Hamilton (1756–1799), with whom Esten had begun an affair, withdrew from Kemble the authority to perform, thereby obliging him to part with the lease, occasioning considerable local controversy. A year later Esten returned the lease to Kemble for a consideration of £200 per year. In May 1794 she retired from Covent Garden. Two months later she gave birth to a daughter by the duke of Hamilton.

In 1797 James Esten returned from the Caribbean with a fortune estimated at £200,000, which he had accumulated while working as a rent collector for Adam Williamson, the British governor of Santo Domingo. He obtained a divorce from his wife in July, although an action brought against the duke of Hamilton for adultery failed in the House of Lords. The duke died on 1 August 1799, leaving Harriet Esten an annuity of £3000. In the winter of 1802 she made a brief reappearance on the Edinburgh stage, where she earned £50 a night.

On 15 October 1812 Esten married Major John Scott-*Waring (1747–1819), formerly MP for Stockbridge and agent to Warren Hastings. The marriage produced a son, Lieutenant John T. Scott-Waring, and a daughter. Following the death of Major Scott-Waring at their house in Half Moon Street, Piccadilly, Esten raised her children alone. She died at her home, 36 Queen's Gate Terrace, Kensington, on 29 April 1865. Notice of her death 'at a very advanced age' was carried in *The Times* for 2 May 1865. Her death certificate gave her age as 103 years and 11 months. Anne Douglas Hamilton, her daughter by the duke, married Henry Robert, third Baron Rossmore (1792–1860), and died childless in 1844. CHARLES BRAYNE

Sources [J. Haslewood], *The secret history of the green rooms: containing authentic and entertaining memoirs of the actors and actresses in the three theatres royal*, 2nd edn, 2 vols. (1792) · T. Gilliland, *The dramatic mirror, containing the history of the stage from the earliest period, to the present time*, 2 vols. (1808) · T. Wilkinson, *The wandering patentee, or, A history of the Yorkshire theatres from 1770 to the present time*, 4 vols. (1795) · J. Jackson, *The history of the Scottish stage* (1793) · W. S. Clark, *The Irish stage in the county towns, 1720–1800* (1965) · J. F. Fuller, *A curious genealogical medley* (1913) · *The Diary, or, Woodfall's Register* (21 Oct 1790) · GEC, *Peerage* · d. cert. · *CGPLA Eng. & Wales* (1865)
Likenesses Thornthwaite, engraving, 1791, repro. in J. Bell, *Bell's British theatre*, 15 (1797) · engraving, 1793, repro. in *Thespian Magazine* (Feb 1793) · S. De Wilde, portrait, Garr. Club [*see illus.*] · prints, Harvard TC
Wealth at death under £30,000: probate, 23 May 1865, *CGPLA Eng. & Wales*

Estlin, John Bishop (1785–1855), surgeon, son of John Prior *Estlin (1747–1817), schoolmaster, of Bristol, and his second wife, Susanna Bishop (d. 1842), was born at St Michael's Hill, Bristol, on 26 December 1785. He was educated in his father's school on St Michael's Hill, and began his medical training at the Bristol Infirmary in 1804; he continued his studies at Guy's Hospital, London, and became a member of the Royal College of Surgeons, London, in 1806. After further study at the University of Edinburgh, in 1808 he settled in practice at Bristol. His success led him to specialize in ophthalmic surgery, and in 1812 he established in Frogmore Street, Bristol, a charitable dispensary for the treatment of diseases of the eye. He supported it for more than a year at his own cost, and afterwards he managed its affairs for thirty-six years, during which time he treated 52,000 poor patients. He kept careful notes, and published numerous papers on his cases.

Estlin enjoyed a wide reputation as an ophthalmic surgeon, being among the first specialists of this kind in England. In 1843 he was elected a fellow of the newly chartered Royal College of Surgeons of England. In 1817 he married Margaret Bagehot (d. 1821); she died four years later, leaving an only daughter, Mary *Estlin. In 1832 Estlin visited the island of St Vincent, where the warm climate restored his bad health. He obtained and circulated in 1838 a fresh supply of vaccine lymph from cows near Berkeley, Gloucestershire, the region in which Jenner had originally made his discovery of the efficacy of vaccination in the prevention of smallpox. Besides his medical services, Estlin campaigned on temperance, on the abolition of slavery, on the instruction of the poor, on religious toleration, and against the activities of medical impostors. His *Remarks on Mesmerism* (1845) dealt with scientific investigations of phenomena said to be due to hidden forces of nature.

Estlin was a Unitarian with definite theological opinions and wrote in favour of the Christian miracles; one of his publications was *On Prayer and Divine Aid* (1825). Estlin was known for his generosity, upright character, and professional skill, and he became one of the most trusted men in Bristol. He had an attack of right hemiplegia in May 1853 and died on 10 June 1855 at 47 Park Street, Bristol. He was buried locally, in the Lewin's Mead burial-ground. NORMAN MOORE, *rev.* ANITA MCCONNELL

Sources *Bristol Mirror* (16 June 1855) · personal knowledge (1888) · V. G. Plarr, *Plarr's Lives of the fellows of the Royal College of Surgeons of England*, rev. D'A. Power, 2 vols. (1930) · W. James, *Memoir of John Bishop Estlin* (1855) · d. cert.
Archives Boston PL, papers relating to anti-slavery · DWL, corresp. · UCL, letters to the Society for the Diffusion of Useful Knowledge | Bristol RO, papers relating to Rowland Hill testimonial fund
Likenesses E. H. Baily, bust, 1856, Bristol City Art Gallery

Estlin, John Prior (1747–1817), Unitarian minister, was born on 9 April 1747, at Hinckley, Leicestershire, to Thomas Estlin (1716?–1770), hosier, and his wife, Elizabeth Prior (1724?–1789). Educated first by his mother's brother, John Prior, vicar of Ashby-de-la-Zouch, in 1764 he entered Warrington Academy, where John Aikin (1713–1788) taught divinity and Joseph Priestley languages and *belles-lettres*. Conscientious refusal to subscribe the Thirty-Nine Articles prevented him from fulfilling his ambition to become an Anglican clergyman, and in 1771 he became junior colleague to the Revd Thomas Wright of Lewin's

Mead Chapel, Bristol. When Estlin asked in 1791 to be made co-pastor, Wright gently rebuked him for suggesting a possible split in the congregation but agreed to the change, offering to forgo half the differential between their salaries, a gesture the congregational committee refused; Estlin assumed the new position early in 1792. When Wright died in 1797, John Rowe became junior minister.

From his settlement at Bristol, Estlin conducted a school in St Michael's Hill, which produced many distinguished alumni. At the annual reunion of his former pupils in 1807 he was presented with the degree of doctor of laws, which had been procured for him from the University of Glasgow. Estlin's learning and generous character attracted many friends, among them Mrs Barbauld, Robert Hall, Robert Southey, and Samuel Taylor Coleridge, whose letters continued long after he had abandoned his youthful unitarianism.

Of the three children of Estlin's first marriage, to Mary (1753–1783), daughter of Joseph Coates, a Bristol barber and peruke maker, two died in infancy; the surviving son, Joseph, predeceased his father in 1811. Four sons and two daughters were born of his second marriage, to Susanna Bishop (d. 1842) of Bristol; one of the sons, John Bishop *Estlin (1785–1855), became a pioneering eye surgeon.

Estlin was a decided unitarian by 1770 but, in deference to divisions in the congregation, declined to preach on speculative theology, while otherwise making his theological position clear. He retained sympathy and understanding for Arians, who stopped short of maintaining the full humanity of Christ, and for the Church of England; he believed in the benefits of a liturgy, published one largely based on the Book of Common Prayer in 1814, and the next year urged a liturgical service on the Lewin's Mead congregation, but, in view of divided sentiment, did not make an issue of it. His sermons show him in agreement with most points of Priestley's theology and as early as 1791 they foreshadowed the position adopted, under repeated encouragement from Rochemont Barbauld, in *Discourses on Universal Restitution* (1813), which maintained, against the doctrine of eternal torment and the competing belief in annihilation, that all humankind would ultimately be saved.

Suffering from deteriorating eyesight, Estlin gave up his school and resigned his pulpit in June 1817, with a handsome monetary gift from the congregation. He retired to his usual seaside vacation spot in Southerndown, Glamorgan, where he had built a cottage. He died there, on 10 August 1817, from 'a sudden effusion of blood from his lungs' (Barbauld) and was buried in the family vault in Lewin's Mead Chapel.   R. K. WEBB

Sources [A. L. Barbauld], *Monthly Repository*, 12 (1817), 573–5 · correspondence and minute books, DWL, Lewin's Mead MS OD 21, 25, 35 · review of J. P. Estlin, *Discourses on universal restitution*, *Monthly Repository*, 8 (1813), 54–5 · *Unpublished letters from Samuel Taylor Coleridge to the Rev. John Prior Estlin*, ed. H. A. Bright (c.1884); repr. (Folcroft, PA, 1970) · J. Nichols, *The history and antiquities of the county of Leicester*, 4/2 (1811), 693
Archives DWL, Lewin's Mead records
Wealth at death under £4000: PRO

Estlin, Mary Anne (1820–1902), slavery abolitionist and campaigner for women's rights, was born in Bristol, the only child of Dr John Bishop *Estlin (1785–1855), a pioneer ophthalmologist, and his wife (d. c.1822), daughter of the Bagehots of Langport. Her father was the son of a Unitarian minister and she adhered to Unitarianism throughout her life. Mrs Estlin died when Mary was about three years old, and her father did not remarry. In 1832–3 her father spent six months in St Vincent in the West Indies and Mary Estlin accompanied him, seeing at first hand the colonial slave system to which her father was morally opposed. She herself never married, living with her father until his death when she was in her mid-thirties, and thereafter continuing to live in the family home in Park Street, Bristol.

Mary Estlin became a leading British supporter of the radical wing of the American abolitionist movement, which, under the leadership of William Lloyd Garrison, had taken control of the American Anti-Slavery Society in 1839. Both Mary and her father conducted an extensive correspondence with the American abolitionists from 1844 onwards, as well as fostering support for Garrison in the west of England and acting as hosts for visiting American anti-slavery lecturers and fund-raisers. In addition Mary co-ordinated British contributions to the Boston Anti-Slavery Bazaar. In 1851 she was appointed a member of the committee of the Bristol and Clifton Ladies' Anti-Slavery Society. She was largely responsible for persuading the committee to take the unprecedented step of publicly severing links with the British and Foreign Anti-Slavery Society on policy grounds—in particular, the national society's failure to support the American Anti-Slavery Society. The launch of the Bristol society as an independent organization marked the beginning of a period of intense national propaganda by the group under Mary Estlin's direction. She became very influential in transatlantic anti-slavery circles: her advice was increasingly sought by the male leaders of the movement and she acted as a mediator between the rival anti-slavery factions. She maintained her links with American campaigners following abolition, visiting the Garrison family in Boston in 1867–8.

Mary Estlin was also a leading feminist campaigner. She was a member of the executive committee of the Ladies' National Association (1870–86), which co-ordinated the feminist campaign for the repeal of the Contagious Diseases Acts. Josephine Butler, the leader of this campaign, described Mary Estlin and her three Bristol co-workers (the Priestman sisters and Margaret Tanner) as 'a kind of body-guard, a *corps d'élite* on whose prompt aid, singleness of purpose, prudence and unwearying industry, I could and can rely at all times' (Butler, 188–9). Mary was also one of the founding members of the Bristol Women's Suffrage Society (established in 1867), acting as treasurer in its early years. In addition she aided her fellow Unitarian Mary Carpenter's work in the education of destitute girls in Bristol and assisted in the establishment of a hospital for women.

Mary Estlin was described in her obituary by her feminist colleagues as a 'warmly sympathetic and lovable' woman who was 'a staunch Liberal, with advanced views, strongly advocating the rights of her own sex' (*Englishwoman's Review*, 61–3). She was one of a number of prominent female anti-slavery campaigners who became leading feminist activists during the 1860s and 1870s. Mary Estlin died on 14 November 1902 at her home at 36 Upper Belgrave Road, Clifton, near Bristol. CLARE MIDGLEY

Sources *Englishwoman's Review*, 34 (1903), 61–3 · C. Midgley, *Women against slavery: the British campaigns, 1780–1870* (1992) · C. Taylor, *British and American abolitionists: an episode in transatlantic understanding* (1974) · J. E. Butler, *Personal reminiscences of a great crusade* (1896), 188–9 · W. James, *Memoir of John Bishop Estlin* (1855) · S. S. Holton, *Suffrage days: stories from the women's suffrage movement* (1996), 31, 35, 41, 43 · J. R. Walkowitz, *Prostitution and Victorian society: women, class and the state* (1980), 114, 121, 126, 175 · *Special Report of the Bristol and Clifton Ladies' Anti-Slavery Society*, Bristol and Clifton Ladies' Anti-Slavery Society (1852) · *Statements respecting the American abolitionists: by their opponents and their friends*, Bristol and Clifton Ladies' Anti-Slavery Society (1852) · d. cert.

Archives DWL, corresp. and MSS | Boston PL, anti-slavery collection

Wealth at death £17,501 2s. 7d.: probate, 16 Jan 1903, CGPLA Eng. & Wales

Estorick, Eric Elihu (1913–1993), art collector and dealer, was born Elihu Estorick on 13 February 1913 in Brooklyn, New York, the only child of Morris Estorick (d. c.1979), paint manufacturer, and his wife, Sarah, née Cutler (d. c.1969). His parents were Jewish, and had emigrated from Russia in 1905. He was educated at James Madison High School, New York, and from 1930 at Washington Square College, New York University, graduating in 1937. It was at the Gallery of Living Art in Washington Square College, a collection created by Albert Gallatin, that Estorick first discovered modern European art. From 1935 he worked as a research secretary for Waldo Frank, the prominent left-wing novelist and political commentator, and after completing an MA in sociology at the New York University School for Social Research in 1938, he taught sociology at New York University from 1939 to 1941. He published *Stafford Cripps: Prophetic Rebel* in 1941. During the Second World War he worked in Canada and England for the foreign broadcast intelligence service of the United States government, becoming head of the British empire division, and in 1943 wrote the first of several introductions to a series of books by Commonwealth leaders which appeared during the 1940s.

Estorick settled in London in 1947 after his marriage on 12 October that year to Salome Dessau (1920–1989), textile designer and daughter of Henry Dessau, a Nottingham textile manufacturer who had left Leipzig in 1932. They had one son and one daughter. He published a second biography of Cripps, *Stafford Cripps: Master Statesman* (1949), and *Changing Empire: Churchill to Nehru* (1950), a history of the evolution of the British empire into the Commonwealth, becoming closely involved in Labour Party politics. From 1950 to 1953 he worked as archivist for Marks and Spencer, for which his wife was designing lace underwear; he wrote a history of the firm, which remained unpublished.

Estorick began to collect twentieth-century Italian art after the war, and with his wife travelled frequently to Italy in the late 1940s and 1950s, visiting dealers and artists' studios. His interests focused on Italian futurism, the movement launched by the poet Marinetti in 1909 as an attempt to develop an aesthetic based on modern life and technology, especially speed and the machine. He acquired paintings by all the leading futurists, including Giacomo Balla's *La mano del violinista* (1912), Umberto Boccioni's *Idolo moderno* (1911), Carlo Carrà's *Uscita dal teatro* (1910), Gino Severini's *Le boulevard* (1910), and Luigi Russolo's *La musica* (1911). But he also collected works by other modern Italian artists, including sculpture by Medardo Rosso, drawings and sculpture by Emilio Greco, bronzes by Giacomo Manzù and Marino Marini, paintings and drawings by Mario Sironi and Massimo Campigli, still lifes and landscape etchings and drawings by Giorgio Morandi, and two early works, *Melanconia* (1912), and *The Revolt of the Sage* (1916), by Giorgio de Chirico. He also acquired several drawings by Modigliani, including *Caryatid* (1916), and the oil portrait *Dr François Brabander* (1918). He put his collection on show in a series of public exhibitions beginning in 1954, and in 1956 mounted an exhibition, 'Modern Italian Art from the Estorick Collection', composed entirely of works from his own collection, at the Tate Gallery in London. In 1979 the Italian government awarded him the title *commendatore* for his services in promoting Italian art.

In 1960 Estorick gave up collecting and moved to full-time art dealing. He opened the Grosvenor Gallery in Mayfair that year, selling works by artists such as Chagall and Magritte as well as by previously unknown painters, especially from Czechoslovakia. He also turned his attention to modern Russian art, in particular the art of the Russian avant-garde during the revolutionary period, and he mounted an exhibition in 1965 of the works of Oskar Rabin (b. 1928), the leader of 'unofficial art' in Russia in the 1960s, the first one-man show by a living Russian artist. He also mounted the first London exhibition devoted to El Lissitzky, in 1966. This was followed by 'Aspects of Russian Experimental Art, 1900–1925' in 1967. In 1966 he began to buy work by the Russian-born French artist, illustrator, costume and set designer Erté (Romain de Tertoff), whose art deco work had been popular in the 1930s. After the success of the first London Erté exhibition at the Grosvenor Gallery in 1967, when the Victoria and Albert Museum bought many of his works, the Estoricks signed an exclusive contract with Erté, and initiated a series of one-man exhibitions in Europe and the United States which brought him back into the public eye and made him one of the best-selling artists of the 1980s. Estorick published *Erté, the Last Works: graphics and Sculptures* in 1992.

Estorick moved to St Peter, Barbados, in 1975. In the 1980s he made frequent visits to Israel as a benefactor of the Israel Museum in Jerusalem, where he donated a study area as a memorial to his wife after her death in 1989. He was involved in establishing the centre for Jewish art at the Hebrew University, where he helped to document Jewish art from the Soviet Union, and he financed exhibitions in Jerusalem of William Blake, Leon Bakst, Erté, and the Russian avant-garde.

Estorick—described by one observer as 'a large bearded figure with intelligent owl-like eyes and a serious, almost pained expression' (*The Guardian*)—died on 25 December 1993 at Flat 21, 22 St James's Square, Westminster, London, following a heart attack. Shortly before his death he had set up the Eric and Salome Estorick Foundation, and in 1998 the Estorick collection of modern Italian art opened in Northampton Lodge, Islington, London, a permanent collection of eighty works of art, considered to be one of the best collections of modern Italian art outside Italy, with space for temporary exhibitions from other collections and a library of over 2000 books, mainly on early twentieth-century Italian art.   ANNE PIMLOTT BAKER

Sources A. Noble, 'Eric Estorick: a life in pictures', in A. Noble and L. Velani, *Estorick collection of modern Italian art* (1997), 9–31 · *Modern Italian art from the Estorick collection* (1956) [exhibition catalogue, Tate Gallery, London] · Erté, *Things I remember: an autobiography* (1975) · 'The Estorick collection of modern Italian art', *Visiting Arts*, 35 (autumn 1997) · *The Guardian* (29 Dec 1993) · *The Times* (14 Jan 1994) · private information (2004) [Michael Estorick, son] · m. cert. · d. cert. · memoir, 1985, Estorick collection, library · www.estorickcollection.com [modern Italian art]
Archives Estorick Collection of Modern Italian Art, Northampton Lodge, Canonbury Square, Islington, London
Likenesses G. Severini, pen-and-ink drawing, 1956, repro. in www.estorickcollection.com/permanent_collections · photograph, repro. in *The Times*

Estratlinges, John de (*d. c.*1293). *See under* Stradling family (*per. c.*1290–1480).

Estwick, Sampson (1656/7–1739), musician and Church of England clergyman, was, according to Hawkins, one of the first set of children of the Chapel Royal under Henry Cooke, after the Restoration; however, this claim lacks support. Having matriculated at Christ Church, Oxford, on 4 April 1674, aged seventeen (registered among the commoners), he proceeded BA in 1677, MA in 1680, and BD in 1692. He was appointed chaplain of Christ Church on 17 March 1678, serving alongside Edward Lowe, Richard Goodson, and Henry Aldrich (canon from 1682, then dean of Christ Church from 1689). His intimacy with Aldrich gave rise to the line 'I prithee, Sam, fill', in Aldrich's famous smoking catch. Estwick was probably too sympathetic and constant a frequenter of the rehearsals of music held weekly in the dean's lodgings to fall under the extreme penalty dealt unto delinquents by the genial host, namely the restriction for the one evening to small beer, and exclusion from the next meeting. Aldrich's management of the cathedral choir at Christ Church was reputedly excellent, and the case of Estwick is quoted by William Hayes, author of the anonymously published *Remarks on Mr. Avison's 'Essay on Musical Expression'*, as a 'remarkable Instance of the Effect of such an Education: He was not only an excellent and zealous Performer in the Choral-Duty, until extreme Old-Age rendered him incapable of it, but a remarkable fine Reader also'. He was admitted minor canon at St Paul's Cathedral in December 1691; Watkins Shaw rejected Hawkins's assertion that he

became a cardinal there. He continued to serve as chaplain of Christ Church, remaining on the list of chaplains until 1711, and signing regularly in person for the quarterly payments (of £1) until 1700.

Estwick was appointed vicar of St Helen, Bishopsgate, in 1701, and rector of St Michael Queenhithe in 1712, retaining these posts until 1713 and 1739 respectively, but he continued to perform his choral duty at St Paul's Cathedral until near the time of his decease,

> when little short of ninety years of age … Bending beneath the weight of years … but preserving his faculties, and even his voice, which was a deep bass, till the last, he constantly attended his duty at St. Paul's habited in a surplice, and with his bald head covered with a black sattin coif, with grey hair round the edge of it, exhibited a figure the most awful that can well be conceived. (Hawkins)

Estwick died on 16 February 1739, probably in London. The 'Reverend and truly venerable Mr. *Estwick*' was regretted by Hayes as a 'good Man, and a worthy Clergyman' (Hayes), while the *London Evening-Post* of 20 February bore witness to his 'exemplary piety and orthodox principles'. Estwick was said by Hawkins to have been an unsuccessful candidate for the Gresham professorship of music. He attended all the early meetings (from the first held in January 1726) of the Academy of Vocal Music, and his name heads the list of contributors.

Estwick's sermon 'The usefulness of church-musick', preached at Christ Church on 27 November 1696 upon the occasion of the anniversary meeting of the lovers of music on St Cecilia's day, was published in the same year by request of the stewards. In the dedicatory letter Estwick deplores the tendency of the age to 'a neglect, if not a disuse, of church music'. Another sermon, delivered at St Paul's, was published in 1698. His manuscript music is preserved at the Bodleian Library and at the library of Christ Church, Oxford, as well as in the British Library, and the Royal College of Music in London; it includes several odes to be performed at the Oxford Act (university degree ceremonies and special convocations).

L. M. MIDDLETON, *rev.* SUSAN WOLLENBERG

Sources H. Watkins Shaw, 'Estwick, Sampson', *New Grove* · J. Hawkins, *A general history of the science and practice of music*, 5 vols. (1776); new edn, 3 vols. (1875) · [W. Hayes], *Remarks on Mr. Avison's Essay on musical expression* (1753) · Foster, *Alum. Oxon.* · disbursements books; dean's register; battels books, Christ Church Oxf. · W. R. Matthews and W. M. Atkins, eds., *A history of St Paul's Cathedral and the men associated with it* (1957) · T. A. Trowles, 'The musical ode in Britain, c.1670–1800', DPhil diss., U. Oxf., 1992 [esp. chap. 3, 1.32–74, and catalogue, 2.70–72] · minutes book of the Academy of Vocal Music, BL, Add. MS 11732 · S. Estwick, *The usefulness of church-musick, a sermon*, Augustan Reprint Society Publications, 49 (1955)
Archives Bodl. Oxf., MSS · Christ Church Oxf., MSS · Royal College of Music, London, MSS

Estye, George (1560/61–1601), Church of England clergyman and author, was the son of John Estye of Cambridge. He attended school in the town and on 10 February 1577, at the age of sixteen, was admitted as a pensioner to Gonville and Caius College; he graduated BA early in 1581 and proceeded MA in 1584. On Lady Day that year he was elected a fellow of the college. Ordained deacon and priest in the diocese of Lincoln on 25 October 1587, in 1591 Estye was awarded the degree of BTh. He was appointed Greek lecturer in 1592, was Hebrew lecturer from 1594 to 1597, and in 1598 was appointed a scrutator.

At Cambridge, Estye set his hand to a petition against the Arminian views of Peter Baro and later, on 21 January 1596, was one of four deponents to testify against him. Estye's own orthodoxy, however, was not above suspicion: the editorial preface of his published sermons tells the reader that 'in this impression, something is kept back by authority, as namely the proof of the author's judgement, touching Christ's descension into hell'. Estye's resignation from his fellowship of Gonville and Caius on Lady Day 1600 was probably occasioned by marriage to his wife, Triphosa, who survived him (and who later married Matthew Clarke, the mayor of King's Lynn, and its MP). Estye's *Certaine Godly and Learned Expositions* (1603) was later issued by John Stoneham, a scholar of Lynn, admitted to Gonville and Caius College in 1593 under the supervision of Estye, who described him as 'my most loving and most beloved scholar that ever I had' (PROB 11/98, fol. 171).

Despite these Norfolk connections Estye's career in the church began and ended in Bury St Edmunds, Suffolk. Here he acted as town lecturer in the 1590s, preaching at the Monday market-day exercise, attended chiefly by zealous townsmen; it was here that his printed sermons were probably first heard. In 1598 Estye was instituted to the vicarage of St Mary, Bury, where he remained until his death on 2 August 1601. He left money in the trust of Sir John Higham and Sir Robert Jermyn, two of the most eminent puritan worthies of Suffolk, for the establishment of weekly instruction for the prisoners of the gaol at Bury, and of a stock for its poor, though these bequests depended on the fate of his own very vulnerable family— Triphosa Estye had borne at least one male child, still in infancy, and when her husband drafted his will she was thought to be pregnant again. He made careful provision for both the child that was and the one expected but as yet unborn. Estye was buried in the church of St Mary, where a memorial to him was erected with an inscription composed by the bishop of Norwich, Joseph Hall. His *A most Sweete and Comfortable Exposition upon the Tenne Commaundements* was published the next year.

STEPHEN WRIGHT

Sources Venn, *Alum. Cant.* · will, PRO, PROB 11/98, fols. 171–2 · Cooper, *Ath. Cantab.* · P. Collinson, *Godly people: essays on English protestantism and puritanism* (1983) · J. Venn and S. C. Venn, *Admissions to Gonville and Caius College … March 1558–9 to Jan 1678–9* (1887) · ESTC **Archives** BL, letter book, Add. MS 24191 **Wealth at death** modest: PRO, PROB 11/98, fols. 171–2

Étampes, Theobald d' (*c.*1060–*c.*1125), teacher and theologian, took his name from Étampes in the Île-de-France, where he was born. He spent his youth at Caen, in the abbey of St Étienne, where he would have known Lanfranc (*d.* 1089). His correspondence with Queen Margaret of Scotland (*d.* 1093) shows that there was some exploration of the possibility that he might become one of her chaplains—one which attests his ambition, and maybe also an early consciousness of exceptional ability which he wanted to have recognized.

Perhaps before 1089 Theobald went to England, at a time when other scholars from the region were doing the same thing, but not, apparently, to join Lanfranc, as so many others did, but to settle in Oxford. Oxford had a nascent school of some importance from about the time Robert Bloet became bishop of Lincoln in 1094, which was fostered by Walter of Oxford, archdeacon of Oxford from 1111–12. Walter seems to have invited visiting lecturers to the school attached to his collegiate church of St George in the Castle, and Theobald was apparently one of the first and most notable of these.

Theobald is the author of a number of surviving letters in which he describes himself variously as doctor of Caen, master of Caen, and master at Oxford. Several of these letters show him to be a highly competent theologian, and well versed in the topics of the day. Before he went to Oxford he had written to Philip, a friend, on the sins of the flesh, taking the view that lust was less serious than pride. To the bishop of Lincoln he wrote, now as an Oxford master, on penitence and confession in a context of scriptural interpretation; he wrote to Abbot Faricius (*d.* 1117) of nearby Abingdon to insist that he had never taught that unbaptized infants would be saved. The most important of these theological letters is one to Roscelin de Compiègne, a grammarian who had attacked both Anselm of Canterbury and Peter Abelard; Theobald's letter discusses the current issue of the eligibility for holy orders of the sons of priests (in which there was recognized to be potential for nepotism).

Theobald took part in a debate at the beginning of the twelfth century on the question whether a monk ought also to be a priest (taking the view that he should not). The *Rescriptum cuiusdam pro monachis* (*c.*1132–3), written by an anonymous monk in response to Theobald, makes the point that there is no better life than the monastic, and condemns his teaching on the parochial rights of monks. Theobald is attacked as an insignificant little clerk, who is still merely a grammar master, although he had more than 100 pupils. This condemnation must be read as an attempt to diminish the reputation of a teacher of theology who was in fact of considerable standing, and evidently active in the controversies of a highly controversial period.

G. R. EVANS

Sources *Hist. U. Oxf.* 1: *Early Oxf. schools* · F. Barlow, *The English church, 1066–1154: a history of the Anglo-Norman church* (1979) · M. Grandjean, *Laïcs dans l'église* (1994) · R. Foreville and J. Leclercq, 'Un débat sur le sacerdoce des moines au xii siècle', *Analecta Monastica*, 4 (1957), 8–118 · 'Epistola ad Roscelinum', *Libelli de lite imperatorum et pontificum saeculis XI et XII conscripti*, ed. E. Dümmler and others, MGH, 3 (Hanover, 1897) · Bale, *Index* · R. W. Southern, 'Master Vacarius and the beginning of an English academic tradition', *Medieval learning and literature: essays presented to Richard William Hunt*, ed. J. J. G. Alexander and M. T. Gibson (1976), 257–86 · R. Foreville, 'L'école de Caen au xiᵉsiècle et les origines normandes de l'université d'Oxford', *Études médiévales offerts à Augustin Fliche* (1952), 9–19

Etchells, Frederick [*pseud.* Batty Langley] (**1886–1973**), architect and writer, was born at 63 Park Road, Newcastle upon Tyne, on 14 September 1886, the son of John Charles Etchells, a successful engineer, and his wife, Jessie, *née*

Anderson. He was brought up in Macclesfield. From 1908 to 1911 he studied at the Royal College of Art, London, where he came under the influence of W. R. Lethaby and Arthur Beresford-Pite and acquired a feeling for the connection between design and making that remained with him until the last. Like all students at the college he studied architecture, but his particular interest at this time was in stained glass. He is remembered principally for his high spirits and pranks, such as his delight in ringing the college fire alarm 'to stir them all up'. After leaving the college he divided his time between London and Paris, where he came to know Modigliani 'very well', met Picasso at Gertrude Stein's, and sought out Braque in the south of France. In London he struck up an easy friendship with Roger Fry and, through him, with other members of the Bloomsbury group. With them he worked on the murals for the Borough Polytechnic in 1911 and by 1913 he was working regularly for the Omega Workshops set up by Fry with the help of Vanessa Bell and Duncan Grant 'in an attempt to introduce a post-impressionist sense of design and colour into the field of applied arts' (Spalding, 21). At Omega he was remembered by Wyndham Lewis as one of the few artists who was 'any good with his hands' and who had any practical understanding of how to start making or finishing a piece of furniture.

Around this time Etchells was also moving in circles that included Jacob Epstein, Eric Gill, and Spencer Gore. Etchells was one of the signatories of Lewis's letter that marked the rupture in October 1913 between Fry and Lewis. His decision to ally himself with Lewis led to no personal break with Fry, but immediately after that between Lewis and Fry, Etchells started exhibiting with Lewis and H. R. Levinson as one of the English Rebels. In March 1914 he participated with Lewis in the launch of the Rebel Art Centre and in July with the publication of *Blast*, and he continued to exhibit as a Vorticist until his call-up in 1916 [*see* Vorticists].

Etchells's military career was not a success. He recalled later that 'my blond beard, big as a spade, combined with my spectacles and foreign accent to make the French suspect me as a German spy' and he was imprisoned for a short spell in Montauban prison. Worse was to come: he suffered an acute attack of tuberculosis and was invalided out of the army with a septic leg to be discharged from the army in 1917 as permanently disabled. For the remaining year of the war, however, he secured work on the design of Canadian war memorials.

With the end of the war Etchells continued to divide his time between London and Paris, keeping pre-war contacts but painting less. By 1923 he had decided to embark on a career as an architect and formed a partnership with Hugh MacDonald in 1924. The work undertaken by the practice was varied. He was employed under the general supervision of Detmar Blow to produce designs for the Grosvenor estate in Mayfair and Belgravia. Between 1926 and 1929 he worked in conjunction with George Pringle on the redevelopment of Culross, Mayfair. With the resignation of Edmund Wimperis in 1928, Etchells became the

principal architect to the Grosvenor estate, an arrangement that came to an end when Blow broke his connection with the estate in 1933. Among the modest works he undertook for the estate were six neo-Georgian houses in Headfort Place, Belgravia, four Tudor houses in Mount Row, Mayfair, and a Georgian town house in Lees Place, Mayfair, for Lord Kilmarnock. He married Hester Margaret Sainsbury (*b*. 1889/90) on 13 May 1932 and they moved out of London to France House, a Georgian brick house in East Hagbourne, near Didcot, Oxfordshire, which he restored himself.

Although his designs for the Grosvenor estate were essays in traditional styles, Etchells remained in contact with Lewis and maintained his engagement with Paris and modernism. While in Paris he was approached by John Rodker to see if he would be willing to undertake a translation of Le Corbusier's *Vers une architecture*. After publishing a number of books with an exotic and erotic flavour, Rodker was keen to reassert his commitment to modernism and saw Le Corbusier, along with Ezra Pound and T. S. Eliot, as an author whose name would re-establish his radical reputation. The translation was published in 1927, under the title, probably expanded and distorted at Rodker's request, *Towards a New Architecture*. Though Etchells did not meet Le Corbusier, he was sympathetic to continental modernism and by the end of the 1920s was contributing on an occasional basis to the *Architectural Review*, where with his credentials as the translator of *Towards a New Architecture* he was welcomed by the editors, and befriended by John Betjeman. In architectural practice, when opportunity and client allowed, Etchells was an enthusiastic modernist, most evident in his design of 1929–30 for 232–4 High Holborn for the advertising firm Crawfords, a commission he had obtained through his friend Ashley Havenden, who was married to Crawford's daughter. This was the first fully modernist office building in central London. Its clean façade was matched by a modern interior, complete with built-in furniture and stainless steel.

Etchells continued in practice during the 1930s, but the terms of his output mainly changed to small, unassertive modernist houses. His architectural practice still allowed him time for other interests: Betjeman recalls his ability as a harpsichordist with an interest in Tudor music; with MacDonald he founded the Haslemere Press, which enabled him to exercise his typographical skills; he also contributed, under the pseudonym Batty Langley, a number of letters in the manner of an eighteenth-century architect to Betjeman's *Ghastly Good Taste*.

The mid-1930s saw the development of Etchells's interest in restoring medieval churches, the final phase of his architectural practice. Through Edward James, a friend from his days as an artist, he was invited in 1935 to recast the parish church of West Dean, Sussex, working with waxed oak and local materials and installing new stained glass. This led on to a new church, St Bernard's, Sheffield, and the wartime repair and restoration of Abinger church, Surrey, and Holy Trinity, Donnington, near Chichester. This last commission took him back to Chichester and was to lead on to the publication in 1948 with the dean of Chichester, the Very Revd G.W.O. Addleshaw, of *The Architectural Setting of Anglican Worship* in 1948. This in turn was followed by commissions to restore further churches, notably the bomb-damaged St Andrew's, Plymouth, which kept him busy well into the 1950s. Betjeman, a critical observer of church architecture, regarded Etchells's tactful ability as a church restorer as close to genius in his handling of traditional materials such as oak and stone and his feeling for stained glass.

Etchells died on 16 August 1973 at the home to which he had retired at Heather Lodge, 2 Radnor Park West, Folkestone, Kent. His friends remembered him with vivid affection as a great talker and an enthusiast with an irreverent streak and a fondness for jokes against himself. A slight figure, he was remembered by Clive Bell from his time at Omega as having 'red hair and always surrounded by suffragettes' (J. Betjeman, *Architectural Review*, 7 Oct 1973, 271). Frederick Etchells is best remembered by generations of architectural students for his translation into English of Le Corbusier's *Vers une architecture*. It remains unsurpassed; the English-speaking world still knows the heroic rhythms and cadences of Etchells's translation better than those of the original. But his engagement with modernism during the 1920s and 1930s was matched by an understanding and affection for traditional building and the crafts and he spent the post-war years restoring a number of Anglican churches. Indeed the range of Etchells's achievements serves as a reminder of the links in practice, admitted or not, between the arts and crafts movement, Bloomsbury, and many English apologists for the continental avant-garde.   NICHOLAS BULLOCK

Sources b. cert. · m. cert. · d. cert. · F. Spalding, *20th century painters and sculptors* (1990), vol. 6 of *Dictionary of British art* · CGPLA Eng. & Wales (1973)
Likenesses W. Roberts, group portrait, oils, 1961–2 (*The Vorticists at the Restaurant de la Tour Eiffel, spring 1915*), Tate collection; *see illus. in Vorticists (act. 1914–1919)*
Wealth at death £22,018: probate, 30 Oct 1973, CGPLA Eng. & Wales

Ételan, Simon d' [Simon the Norman] (*d.* 1249), administrator, derived from Ételan near Pont-Audemer (Seine-Maritime), though he may have had connections with a minor landowning family in Berkshire. First recorded in the early 1230s, he became a royal clerk; styled *magister*, he had probably studied canon law on the continent, since he was employed by Henry III to act as royal proctor at the papal curia. He went four times to Rome: in 1233 (twice), in 1236, when he petitioned the pope to send a legate to England, and in 1238, when his task was to block the translation of Ralph de Neville from Chichester to Winchester. On this last occasion he also acted on the king's behalf in proceedings over disputed elections to Norwich and Durham. In England, Simon was a commissioner in 1236 to investigate disturbances between the townsfolk and university of Oxford, acted at least once as a papal judge-delegate, and late in 1239 was said to have been one of the king's advisers responsible for harsh measures against the Jews. Early in 1240 he had the custody of the king's rights

in the vacant see of Hereford. His rewards included lands in several southern counties, a prebend at Lichfield, and in 1237 the archdeaconry of Norfolk.

In June 1239 Simon d'Ételan was among the men and women who received the future Edward I from the font at his christening—he may well have been the unnamed Norman who, according to Matthew Paris, watched as Henry III subjected the baptismal offerings to a meticulous scrutiny, and commented, 'God has given us this child, but the lord king is selling it' (Paris, *Chron.*, 3.540). Unpopular because of his sharp tongue and arrogance, Simon nevertheless became a royal councillor, and in 1240 was given the custody of the great seal. But after only a few days he lost it again, for at about Easter he refused to attach the seal to a grant of the proceeds of a tax on wool to Count Thomas of Flanders, Queen Eleanor's uncle, as something contrary to the interests of the crown. For this uncalled-for show of independence he was instantly dismissed, and was deprived of all his benefices except one. He was stripped of his archdeaconry, and although he litigated for its recovery until 1244, failed to achieve it. His lands and goods were seized, including a coffer deposited in the New Temple in London. Simon d'Ételan died in 1249; the notice of his death given by the annals of Dunstable, mistakenly naming him as Simon de Cantilupe, is responsible for the confusion that once masked his identity.   HENRY SUMMERSON

Sources F. M. Powicke, 'Master Simon the Norman', *King Henry III and the Lord Edward: the community of the realm in the thirteenth century*, 2 (1947), 772–83 · Paris, *Chron.*, 3.495, 540, 629; 4.5, 63–4; 5.91 · *Ann. mon.*, 3.152 · R. C. Stacey, *Politics, policy and finance under Henry III, 1216–1245* (1987) · *Fasti Angl., 1066–1300*, [Monastic cathedrals], 66 · D. A. Carpenter, 'Chancellor Ralph de Neville and plans of political reform, 1215–1258', *The reign of Henry III* (1996), 61–73

Ethé, (Carl) Hermann (1844–1917), orientalist, was born in Germany at Stralsund, Pomerania (Prussia), on 13 February 1844, the son of an official land surveyor. He read classics at the University of Greifswald and then oriental philology at Leipzig with Heinrich L. Fleischer, one of the leading Arabic scholars of that period. In 1868 he presented his final thesis to the University of Munich, and was thereby admitted as a private lecturer. During his Munich years he translated from Arabic, Persian, and Turkish, and contributed essays on oriental subjects and German literature to general magazines, selections from which were published in *Morgenlaendische Studien* (1870) and *Essays und Studien* (1872).

In 1872 Ethé was invited by the Bodleian Library, Oxford, to continue the cataloguing of its oriental manuscripts. At the same time, he was entrusted with the preparation of a catalogue of the Persian manuscripts in the library of the India Office. First volumes of each catalogue appeared respectively in 1889 and 1903, but the printing was in both cases only completed after Ethé's death. In 1875 Ethé was appointed as professor at University College, Aberystwyth. For nearly forty years there he taught not only several oriental languages, but also German and Italian.

Meanwhile, Ethé continued to work on the manuscripts in Oxford and London, and contributed many articles on

Persian literature to learned journals in Germany. Apart from his articles on Persian subjects in the ninth edition of the *Encyclopaediu Britannica* (1885), nearly all his publications were written in German. During the 1880s he applied in vain for academic chairs in Germany and for the Laudian chair of Arabic at Oxford University. Though he had settled down permanently in Britain, he kept his German nationality, which brought him into great difficulty at the outbreak of the First World War. In October 1914 a wave of popular anger forced the college to dismiss him. When, in 1916, it became known that Ethé was still allowed to work on the India Office manuscripts, the government was accused in the House of Commons of being too lenient to a German who might very well be a spy.

Ethé left a vivid impression on the minds of several students and colleagues at Aberystwyth. They remembered him as a short, thickset man, who was witty and good-humoured in spite of disappointments in his academic career. Though he never bothered to adapt himself to his foreign environment, he was generally respected for his great learning. Late in life he married Harriet Dora, *née* Wilson. He died at his home, 29 Royal York Crescent, Clifton, Bristol, on 7 June 1917, and was survived by his wife.

Ethé's catalogues, which cover two of the largest collections of Persian manuscripts in the world, are his greatest scholarly achievement. They are particularly valuable because of the meticulous descriptions which laid a solid foundation for further studies. Yet his ambition went beyond the mere recording of philological data. Many of his publications deal with important questions of literary history, which he was often the first to raise. The long article which he wrote for the *Grundriss der iranischen Philologie* (1894–1904) is an authoritative survey of western knowledge about Persian literature at the end of the nineteenth century.   J. T. P. DE BRUIJN

Sources *WWW*, 1941–50 · E. L. Ellis, *The University College of Wales, Aberystwyth, 1872–1972* (1972) · C. H. Herford, 'Impressions of Aberystwyth, 1887–1901', *The college by the sea*, ed. I. Morgan (1926) · testimonials in favour of Hermann Ethé, PhD (Leipzig), candidate for the Laudian professorship of Arabic in the University of Oxford, 1889, Bodl. Oxf. · *Manchester Guardian* (3 Nov 1916) · *The Times* (3 Nov 1916) · J. T. P. de Bruijn, 'Between Hammer and Browne: Hermann Ethé as a historian of Persian literature', *Acta Orientalia Academiae Scientiarum Hungaricae*, 48 (1995) · E. Yarshater, ed., *Encyclopaedia Iranica*, [10 vols.] (1982–) · *CGPLA Eng. & Wales* (1917) · F. Brümmer, *Lexicon der deutschen Dichter und Prosaisten vom Beginn des 19. Jahrhunderts bis zur Gegenwart* (Stuttgart, 1913); repr. (Nendeln, 1975)
Archives U. Wales, Aberystwyth, MSS
Likenesses Ap. Rhobert [H. Lloyd Roberts], cartoon, repro. in Ap. Rhobert, *The Aberdons: 12 caricatures* (1910) · photograph, U. Wales, Aberystwyth
Wealth at death £1559 14s. 3d.: probate, 30 Nov 1917, *CGPLA Eng. & Wales*

Ethelbald. *See* Æthelbald (d. 757); Æthelbald (d. 860).

Ethelbert. *See* Æthelberht I (d. 616?); Æthelberht (779/80–794); Æthelberht (d. 865).

Ethelburga. *See* Æthelburh (*fl.* 664).

Etheldreda. *See* Æthelthryth (d. 679).

Ethelfleda. *See* Æthelflæd (d. 918).

Ethelfrid. *See* Æthelfrith (d. c.616).

Ethelgar. *See* Æthelgar (d. 990).

Ethelhard. *See* Æthelheard (d. 805).

Ethelmær. *See* Elmer (d. 1137).

Ethelnoth. *See* Æthelnoth (d. 1038).

Ethelred. *See* Æthelred I (d. 871); Æthelred (d. 888); Æthelred II (c.966x8–1016); Ailred of Rievaulx (1110–1167).

Ethelstan. *See* Æthelstan (*fl.* 932–956).

Ethelwerd. *See* Æthelweard (d. 998?).

Ethelwine. *See* Æthelwine (d. 992).

Ethelwold. *See* Æthelwold (904x9–984).

Ethelwulf. *See* Æthelwulf (d. 858).

Etherege, George. *See* Etheridge, George (1519–1588?).

Etherege, Sir George (1636–1691/2), playwright and diplomat, was the second child and eldest son of George Etherege (*bap.* 1607, d. 1650) and his wife, Mary, *née* Powney (*bap.* 1612, d. 1699). Etherege's parents were married on 7 October 1634 at Bray, Maidenhead, and the dramatist was probably born in the same parish. Etherege's grandfather, also named George (1576–1658), was a prosperous London vintner who invested in the reorganized Virginian Company (1609) and the Bermuda, or Somers Islands, Company (1615). His name appears in the former's charter as 'George Etheridge, gentleman' (Huseboe, *Etherege*, 3). In 1625 he inherited a half share in the profits of the lease of the manor of Ives, or Ivy, in Maidenhead. He also bought two farms in Kent worth £40 a year in the name of his sons. Some time after 1628 Etherege's grandfather moved from the parish of St Clement Danes, London, to Bray. His son, known as Captain George Etherege, was sent to manage his father's four shares of land amounting to 98 acres in Paget's Tribe, Bermuda, finally returning shortly before his advantageous marriage to Mary, the twenty-two-year-old daughter of Richard Powney, gentleman, of nearby Old Windsor. Both fathers made generous settlements for the young couple.

In 1636, the same year that his first son was born, Captain George used £300 from his father and £300 from his wife's dowry to purchase a place at court as purveyor to Queen Henrietta Maria. This was 'worth about two hundred pounds per annum before the troubles' (Bracher, 'Introduction', xiv). When the queen fled to France in 1644, he probably followed her since he died there in 1650. What is certain is that his father continued to support Etherege's mother and her seven children at his Maidenhead house until his death.

The tradition that as a boy Etherege attended Lord William's Grammar School at Thame cannot be verified and is probably mistaken (Bracher, 'Introduction', xiv). Similarly, the story of his travel to France either as a boy or as a young man, though entirely possible, is not supported by evidence. He nevertheless had a fairly good education. He quotes from Horace in his letters, was well read in English literature and fluent in French: the collection of books he took with him to Europe late in life are those of an educated literary man (Beal, 'Etherege's reading'). Etherege was fourteen when his father died, old enough to experience the upheavals of the civil war and its direct consequences on his family. His mother's second marriage two years later to Christopher Newstead (1597–1662), a suspected royalist and formerly, if briefly, chaplain-extraordinary to Charles I (1641), together with Captain George's place in the queen's court, point to a family converting itself over two generations from City tradesmen into minor royalist gentry.

His grandfather's decision in 1654 to apprentice the eighteen-year-old Etherege to the attorney George Gosnold of Beaconsfield and London is further proof of this ambition. Etherege's signature as witness to Gosnold's legal documents, and his admission to Clement's Inn on 19 February 1659 to study law, show him making the normal progression in his profession.

However, by the time he began study at the inns of court Etherege was financially independent, if in a modest way. A family lawsuit (1656–7) over his inheritance had been resolved in his favour and when his grandfather died early in 1658, he came at the age of twenty-two into the possession of the two farms in Kent worth £40 a year.

Dramatist and man about town The stages in the transformation of Etherege from young lawyer to dramatist and court wit are not well recorded. Copies of his wittily libertine poem, 'The Imperfect Enjoyment', were circulating between 1660 and 1662 (*Poems*, 78). By 1663 he had made the acquaintance of Lord Buckhurst (later earl of Dorset and an important literary patron). In 1662 the nineteen-year-old Buckhurst narrowly escaped a charge of murder and robbery, and in August of the same year he was apparently planning a translation, with four others, of Corneille's *Pompée*. In 1664 Etherege dedicated his first play, *The Comical Revenge, or, Love in a Tub*, to Buckhurst. There he says that the 'Writing of' the play 'was a means to make me known to your Lordship' (*Works*, 1.2). If so, the four familiar verse epistles which the two men wrote to each other in 1663–4, while Buckhurst was out of London, testify to an already well-established relationship. The poems between the twenty-seven-year-old dramatist and the twenty-year-old aristocrat, of which the two by Etherege are known in five manuscript copies, describe their shared pursuit of prostitutes, wine, and pleasure, and are performances on both sides. Signed simply 'Buckhurst' and 'Etherege', a clear proof of Etherege's acceptance in Buckhurst's circle, the verse letters are representative of a group of self-consciously transgressive rakes, transgressive both in vocabulary and sexual openness, for whom masculine camaraderie overrode fine distinctions of rank. But, as in later escapades, Etherege was the older, and probably more experienced, man.

The mores of this small, outrageous, and socially protected group of young libertines is reflected in the character of Sir Frederick Frollick, the hero of *The Comical Revenge*. The play was acted by the Duke's Company at the Lincoln's Inn Theatre. It was licensed and registered on 8 July 1664 and published, probably shortly thereafter, by Henry Herringman, who specialized in court literature, from his shop in the Lower Walk of the fashionable New Exchange. The exact date of the première is unknown, but Evelyn attended a performance on 27 April 1664, so that it was most likely first acted earlier in April. The cast was a strong one and the production was a *succès d'estime*. John Downes, its prompter, later recalled, 'The clean and well performance of this Comedy, got the Company more Reputation and Profit than any preceding Comedy; the Company taking in a Months time at it 1000*l*' (Downes, ed. Milhous and Hume, 25). If so, the play must have monopolized the theatre for a month. Its unprecedented success for the Duke's Players came from the realism of the characters and setting but, above all, from the language in the comic plot, which was supported by an aristocratic love story (in rhymed heroic verse). It established Etherege at twenty-eight as a court wit, author, and man about town in a circle which now included Rochester and the duke of Buckingham as well as Buckhurst and Sedley.

Little is known about Etherege for the next four years. By March 1665 he had addressed a complimentary poem 'To her Excellence the Marchioness of Newcastle after the Reading of her Incomparable Poems' (*Poems*, 90), probably in the hope of some form of patronage from her husband. Other of his verses were circulating in manuscript: one poem, 'To a Lady, Asking him how Long he would Love her', was set to music for three voices by Matthew Locke, Charles II's composer-in-ordinary since 1661, and published in the latest version of John Playford's songbook, *Catch as Catch can* (1667, 194–5). Otherwise, Etherege was no doubt womanizing, gambling, and drinking.

Etherege's second play, *She wou'd if she cou'd, a Comedy*, was first performed on 6 February 1668, again by the Duke's Company at Lincoln's Inn Fields. Herringman, who registered the play on 24 June, was once more Etherege's publisher. Despite a strong cast and a capacity audience, the first performance was disastrous. The king was in the audience along with much of the court. Pepys reports the scene as the audience remained in the theatre sheltering from the rain:

> and among the rest, here was the duke of Buckingham today openly sat in the pit; and there I found him with my Lord Buckhurst and Sidley and Etherige the poett—the last of whom I did hear mightily find fault with the Actors, that they were out of humour, and had not their parts perfect, and that Harris [who played the comic role of Sir Joslin Jolly] did do nothing, nor could do so much as sing a Ketch in it, and so was mightily concerned: which all the rest did through the whole pit blame the play as a silly, dull thing, though there was something very roguish and witty; but the design of the play, and end, mighty insipid.

This account is supported by Shadwell's 'Preface' to *The Humorists* (1671), in which he adds 'that, had it not been for the favour of the *Court*, in all probability it had never got up again; and it suffers for it in great measure, to this very day' (sig. π4ª). In the end the play 'took well' (Downes, ed.

Milhous and Hume, 29) and held its place in the repertory until the mid-eighteenth century.

Etherege, who styled himself 'Esq.' on the comedy's title-page, further benefited from royal favour. Early in 1668 he was appointed as one of the forty gentlemen of the privy chamber-in-ordinary, who waited on the king, and was made secretary to the newly appointed (and knighted) ambassador to Turkey, the Levant merchant Sir Daniel Harvey. The Turkish embassy was the country's most prestigious in rank and salary, bringing the secretary £200 a year. Etherege remained in Turkey almost three years. Although he was bored away from London, he was a shrewd and intelligent observer, who fulfilled his diplomatic role effectively, accompanying Sir Daniel to his audience with the grand signor on 30 November 1669 (Fujimura, 476–8). In July 1670 he fell ill, and left Constantinople in spring 1671. By May 1671 he was in Paris, where his wit amused the English company, before returning to London.

Etherege was by now thirty-five. His habits had not changed. In September 1671 he had an abortive duel 'within the rayles of Covent Garden' with Edmund Ashton (Brett-Smith, 1.xx; Bracher, 'Introduction', xvii). That autumn he also wrote 'A Prologue Spoken at the Opening of the Duke's New Playhouse'. The new theatre at Dorset Gardens was built for Betterton's company and opened on 9 November 1671 with a performance of Dryden's *Sir Martin Mar-All*, originally played at the Lincoln's Inn Theatre in 1667. In the meantime, three of Etherege's poems had been printed in a verse miscellany, *The New Academy of Complements* (1669), and nine more appeared shortly after in *A Collection of Poems, Written on Several Occasions* (1672). He is unlikely to have had any hand in their publication, regarding himself as a gentleman writer, but that did not preclude a long friendship with Thomas Betterton (1635–1710), actor–manager of the Duke's Company who had taken important roles in Etherege's plays. By 1676 he appears to have been in the service of Mary of Modena, duchess of York and wife of the future James II. In the 'Dedication' to *The Man of Mode* Etherege writes, 'I hope the honour I have of belonging to You, will excuse my presumption', claiming that his new comedy is 'the first thing I have produc'd in Your Service' (*Works*, 2.183). The first recorded performance, which may also have been the première, of Etherege's third and last play, *The Man of Mode, or, Sir Fopling Flutter*, was acted before the king on 11 March 1676 at the Dorset Gardens Theatre. The king's presence at this performance, that of his court at later performances, along with Sir Car Scrope's prologue and song, Dryden's epilogue, and the printed dedication to the duchess of York, all testify to the court-centred ethos of Etherege's comedy. The play was licensed on 3 June and published by Herringman, probably shortly thereafter.

It was an immediate and lasting success. The strong cast included Betterton as the lead character, Dorimant, with his wife playing Bellinda, while the young Mrs Barry probably took the part of Mrs Loveit. Downes remembered that 'this Comedy being well Cloath'd and well *Acted*, got a great deal of *Money*' (Downes, ed. Milhous and Hume, 39).

Etherege's characters were immediately regarded as portraits of living people. Although Dorimant has been most frequently identified with Rochester, at the time he was also seen as representing the duke of Monmouth (and his affair with Moll Kirke) or alternatively as Buckhurst. Sir Fopling was variously believed to be based on Edward Villiers, 'Beau' Hewitt, or Etherege himself (see J. Spence, *Observations*, ed. J. M. Osborn, 1966, 2.638). Looking back in 1722, John Dennis was to claim that Etherege's play was 'well receiv'd, and believ'd by the people of *England* to be the most agreeable Comedy for about Half a Century' (Dennis, 2.243).

In the same summer Etherege was involved in the notorious episode of Rochester's attack on the watch at Epsom. Despite the playwright's efforts as peacemaker, a bystander, Mr Downs, was killed, and Rochester, Captain Bridges, and Etherege had to abscond (*Correspondence of the Family of Hatton … 1601–1704*, ed. E. M. Thompson, Camden Society, new ser., 22, 1878, 133–4). Once again Etherege was the older man, forty to Rochester's late twenties. Not long after, in December 1677, Fleetwood Shepherd was 'run with a sword under the eye endeavouring to part Buckley and Etheridge squabbling in a taverne' (Brett-Smith, 1.xxvii–viii).

At some point between November 1677 and 1679 Etherege acquired a knighthood and was married. It was rumoured that the dramatist bought his knighthood in order to marry a 'rich old widow' (Brett-Smith, 1.xxviii–ix). Mary Arnold, *née* Sheppard (d. 1691/2), was the daughter of a London merchant, from whom she inherited £100 and half his goods and household stuffs. At some point before 1648 she had married Edmund Arnold, a successful London lawyer, on whose death in 1676 she inherited a further £600 together with £240 in annual rents and profits from the manor of Furthoe in Northamptonshire (Bracher, 'Introduction', xvii). As the first of her two sons, who both died as children, was baptized in August 1648, she was probably in her mid- or late forties when she married the somewhat younger Etherege (Nichol, 419–22). The tone of Etherege's one extant letter to her suggests that there was some coldness on her side (13 March 1687, *Letters*, 100), though the couple went to law together in 1687 to recover £300 which she had lent to a London skinner, John Rowley, while she was still a widow.

Etherege's passion for gambling is well attested. Looking back on his London life, he wrote to the earl of Sunderland, 'I can assure your Lordship that I find I can live without play, a thing my best Freinds will hardly believe' (3 Dec 1685, *Letters*, 12), and he had always placed women and gambling above the pleasures of wine ('Mr Dryden's Letter to Sir George Etherege', ll. 53–4). Satires of the early 1680s describe him as suffering both from the pox and from an ageing wife, and if the 'Sr Fopling' depicted in Thomas Wood's *Juvenalis redivivus* (1683) is Sir George, he was not only gambling away '*Grannum's* old Gold' at Locket's while leaving his 'Lowsy Footmen' unpaid, but had to flee the country. His 'Song on Basset' celebrating the new card game introduced to England in 1677, which he had played at the duchess of Mazarine's London house (*Poems*, 11–12, 86), gives credence to these charges.

Diplomatic career Etherege nevertheless remained in the duke of York's favour. He is listed as one of the pensioners in his household in September 1682 at £100 a year, and when James became king in 1685, Sir George was swiftly appointed to the post of resident at Ratisbon (Regensburg, Bavaria). He reached Regensburg on 21 November 1685 after a leisurely journey, which included a stay at The Hague.

His personal, social, and diplomatic life for the next four years is the most fully recorded part of Etherege's life, or that of any other Restoration writer. Not only are many of his personal letters preserved but no fewer than six versions of his letter-books were made (two of which are unlocated). The multiplicity of manuscript texts of his official correspondence reveals the complications of the political world into which Etherege had moved. Etherege's official copy of the letter-books is now at Harvard and has been edited by Bracher (1974). These two volumes were transcribed by Etherege's secretary, Hugo Hughes, with Etherege's autograph corrections. Unknown to his master, Hughes was transcribing parts of Etherege's official letters along with excerpts from his personal correspondence with a view to discrediting his employer's professional integrity with his superiors. Hughes disapproved equally of the resident's rakish lifestyle and his pro-Stuart politics. The resulting manuscript is now in the British Library, and has been transcribed and edited by Rosenfeld (1928). Hughes, along with associates in England and the Dutch representative at the Diet, Pierre Valkenier, was part of the whig and protestant plan to replace the Catholic James II with William of Orange. The three other extant versions of the letter-books were further copies for Hughes's allies or were made by them. Peter Beal found a further cache of Etherege's papers left behind at Regensburg when he gave up his post in 1689. These include some 116 letters to Etherege, substantially filling out the printed correspondence and papers (Beal, *Index*, 446–68). They are unpublished, but are described by Beal and throw important light on Etherege's performance as a diplomat.

Etherege's post as resident at the German imperial Diet at Regensburg was the lowest rank in the diplomatic service. His role was purely that of an observer with no official powers to treat with the other envoys there. His duties were to write dispatches to his immediate superior, Lord Middleton, reporting any developments, and to send on any political news he could pick up, while representing his king with appropriate dignity. All of this depended on establishing good relations with the other diplomats at Regensburg. Although Etherege was efficient at reporting to the secretary of state, generally twice a week, the first year of his mission was, to the delight of Hugo Hughes, unfortunate. Even before reaching Regensburg, Etherege had, Hughes reported, lost £250 gambling at The Hague, and went on to caress 'every dirty Drab that came in his way from Holland to this place' (*Letters*, 292). Once in

Regensburg, Etherege refurbished the lodgings of the previous resident, Edwin Poley, and established his household, but he was once more bored away from London and oppressed by the stiff formality of his fellow diplomats. He wrote, 'London is dull by accident, but Ratisbonne by Nature' (ibid., 153). Hughes reported on the new resident's gambling, his drunken brawls, and the very public affair with a travelling actress from Nuremburg (ibid., 299–303) which scandalized the local community and only ended when Etherege ran out of money. According to Hughes, Etherege had destroyed his credibility as a diplomat.

However, in spring 1687 Etherege found that his reputation in Paris, Vienna, and London was being threatened by letters written by the count of Windischgratz, the emperor's co-commissioner. Thereafter he mended fences and took his duties increasingly seriously. Etherege's diplomatic post, traditionally regarded as an unimportant one, was certainly taken seriously in England. Sir Gabriel Sylvius told him as early as 11 January 1686, 'You are got into a station, where there is more to be done, & more to bee seen than in all Europe besides' (Beal, *Index*, 447). This analysis cannot have applied to the Diet itself, which had been meeting in Regensburg since 1663, and which, as Etherege complained, never did anything. Rather, its importance lay in the opportunity it gave for gathering intelligence. The eagerness with which his dispatches were awaited in London by July 1688 is indicative of his professional success in this respect.

Apart from his diplomatic duties, Etherege employed musicians, a fencing-master and a dancing-master, played tennis, and went hunting. He also had a library of at least sixty-four titles and over ninety volumes, including Dryden's *The Hind and the Panther* (1687), while letters from England kept him up with the news. Etherege was to claim that his creative imagination had deserted him, but the two familiar verse letters he wrote to Lord Middleton at some time between January and April 1686 (*Poems*, 115) as supplements to his official dispatches, show his abilities in this male verse genre to be undiminished. They, as much as Dryden's verse letter in response, demonstrate his intelligent playfulness, but at the same time express the nostalgia for his past in London which appears in his letter to John Cooke, written on 28 November 1687:

> You can do no less than pitty me who have been forc'd from the shoar of delightfull Thames to be confin'd to live on the banks of the unwholesome Danube where we have been this moneth choak'd with fogs, and cannot now set a foot out of doors, without being up to the knee in snow. (*Letterbook*, 293)

The bawdy verse letters to Middleton, his friend and immediate superior, like his similar exchanges with Buckhurst in the early 1660s, say much about the way in which Etherege's literary gifts helped his career at key stages. And this applied as much to the former duke of York. In December 1685 the continuing popularity at court of *The Man of Mode* led James II to hope Etherege would write another comedy, an expectation which had turned into a request by 5 March 1686, communicated to him by Lord Middleton:

Since you made no answer to what the King had commanded me to acquaint you with, I mean your writing a play, I should not have troubled you with it, if his Majesty had not again renewd his commands in that matter, so that I must tell you, he does seriously expect it from you.   (Beal, *Index*, 447)

But Etherege had given up writing plays. As he told Buckhurst, now earl of Dorset, on 27 February 1687, he had 'lost for want of exercise the use of fancy imagination' (*Letterbook*, 239).

But if he would not write a comedy for his king, Etherege remained deeply loyal to the Stuart cause against his better interests. At considerable expense he organized elaborate celebrations for the birth of the prince of Wales on 6 July 1688. Festivities began with a 'Te Deum' at the Scottish Benedictine monastery on Sunday 25 July, followed by a dinner for the ministers at the Diet in Etherege's second residence at the Wildische Haus (now 3/4 Arnulfplatz), and continued for another two days (*Letters*, 214–16, 279–85; Beal, *Index*, 446). But his dispatches to England were desperately urging Middleton and Sunderland to warn the king of the seriousness of the Williamite plans to force him to give up the throne in favour of a protestant succession. By now, however, it was too late, and James II fled England on 23 December 1688. On 18 January 1689 Etherege learned that James had arrived in Paris. Shortly after, he left Regensburg to join the Stuart court in exile just as his father before him had done, and reached Paris by 20 February. It may be that he could not have returned to London because of debts. Although there is no record of his membership of James's court, Abbot Fleming was put in charge of his affairs in Regensburg by James on 20 July 1689. There were rumours in February 1691 that he had died in Paris, but his nephew, George, later testified that he had died there 'on or about' 10 May 1692 without issue (Bracher, 'Introduction', xxiii). He probably died a Catholic: his friend Abbot Placidus Fleming added against Etherege's name in the monastery's syllabus of benefactors 'Obiit Parisiis factus Catholicus' (ibid.), though there is no further evidence of Etherege's surprising conversion.

No portrait of Etherege is known. The adjectives with which Etherege was characterized by his contemporaries, 'easy' and 'gentle', seem to have described not only his literary style but also his social behaviour. Writing some sixty years later, William Oldys cited the account of Etherege given him by the veteran actor John Bowman (*c*.1651–1739), who had been a member of the Duke's Company:

Sir George was, in his person, a fair, slender, genteel man; but spoiled his countenance with drinking and other habits of intemperance; and in his deportment, very affable and courteous, of a sprightly and generous temper; which with his free, lively, and natural vein of writing, acquired him the general character of *Gentle George* and *Easy Etherege*. (*Biographia Britannica*, 3.844)

This fits well enough with the man as he appears in his letters and his early association with Buckhurst and Sedley. However, one story, again one which was reported at second hand after his death, suggests that his gentility depended heavily on a strong sense of his own class and

gender. Birch reported that he had been told by Otway of a dispute at Locket's when

some Company there, who were highly incensed at some ill manage of their Entertainment or attendance, were all in a violent Passion with the waiters, so that Mrs Locket came up; when Sr Geo. told her they were so provoked that he could find it in his Heart to pull the Nosegay out of her Bosom and throw the flowers in her Face, wch turned all their anger to a Jest. (Brett-Smith, 7.xxxi n. 3)

One feature of Etherege's character agreed on by himself, his friends, and his enemies, was his laziness. The eight-year gap between his second and third comedies, despite his having 'more fancy, sense, judgement and wit' than any of his contemporaries, was attributed by the author of 'A Session of the Poets' (1676) to his 'crying sin idleness' (*Poems on Affairs of State*, 1.353). Years later Etherege was provoked by Dryden's verse letter to him in Regensburg to assert his own pre-eminence in laziness. 'If you persist in your claim to Laziness, you will be thought as affected in it as Montaigne is, when he complaines of want of memory', he wrote on 20 March 1687, continuing 'I (whose every action of my life is as a witness of my Idleness) little thought that you … durst have set up to be my Rival' (*Letters*, 102–3). Yet judging by the regularity of his diplomatic correspondence from Regensburg he was less lazy than content to place a premium on pleasure, whether in women, gaming, or male friendship, if these had to be set against the demands of business. Dryden was indeed an immensely hard-working and ambitious poet and author: for Etherege, writing, whether of letters, verse, or plays, was a way to preferment and social recognition. Only in that sense was he a gentleman who wrote with ease. Failure to raise, and to maintain, the interest of his superiors in rank and position through his writing would have foreclosed the success of his diplomatic career.

The importance of Etherege's role at Regensburg has been traditionally underrated. Yet even though his correspondence proves the seriousness with which he undertook the actual work required of him, his letters have real value if read as literature. The virtues of his letters, official and unofficial, are those of clarity, liveliness, and immediacy, based on shrewd (and amused) observation of Regensburg society, all expressed through a style which approximates to a colloquial spoken language. Dryden, himself a master of prose, was not flattering Etherege when he said 'I will never enter the lists in Prose with the undoubted best author of it which our nation has produced' (*Letters*, 276).

It is precisely that ability to catch vernacular speech in a variety of linguistic registers, from tradesmen and servants to young men and women about town (as well as their unfashionable elders), which at once distinguished his 'talking plays' from his immediately contemporary rivals, and pointed the way for subsequent writers of Restoration comedy. Yet for all the early objections that his plays lacked 'plot' his three plays catch the moment of a rebellious younger generation opposed to relationships between the sexes based merely on interest. At the same time, in particular *The Man of Mode*, they give a sceptical analysis of the stresses between libertinage, love, sexuality, and money. His final commitment to the exiled James II, and his probable last-minute conversion to Catholicism, suggest that in the final analysis Etherege may have been as much an idealist as a cynic.   JOHN BARNARD

Sources *The dramatic works of Sir George Etherege*, ed. H. F. B. Brett-Smith, 2 vols. (1927) · *The poems of Sir George Etherege*, ed. J. Thorpe (1963) · *The letterbook of Sir George Etherege*, ed. S. Rosenfeld (1928) · *Letters of Sir George Etherege*, ed. F. Bracher (1974) · P. Beal and others, *Index of English literary manuscripts*, ed. P. J. Croft and others, [4 vols. in 11 pts] (1980–), vol. 2, pt 1, pp. 443–59 · P. Beal, '"The most constant and best entertainment": Sir George Etherege's reading in Ratisbon', *The Library*, 6th ser., 10 (1988), 122–44 · *Biographia Britannica, or, The lives of the most eminent persons who have flourished in Great Britain and Ireland*, 3 (1750), 841–9 [account of Etherege by William Oldys] · F. Bracher, 'Etherege as a diplomat', *Harvard Library Bulletin*, 17 (1969), 45–60 · F. Bracher, 'Etherege at Clement's Inn', *Huntington Library Quarterly*, 43 (1979–80), 127–34 · J. Dennis, 'A defence of Sir Fopling Flutter, a comedy written by Sir George Etheridge', *The critical works of John Dennis*, ed. E. N. Hooker, 2 (1943), 241–50 · J. Downes, *Roscius Anglicanus, or, An historical review of the stage* (1708) · J. Downes, *Roscius Anglicanus*, ed. J. Milhous and R. D. Hume, new edn (1987) · T. Fujimura, 'Etherege at Constantinople', *Publications of the Modern Language Association of America*, 72 (1956), 465–81 · B. Harris, *Charles Sackville, sixth earl of Dorset: patron and poet of the Restoration* (1940) · Highfill, Burnim & Langhans, *BDA* · A. R. Huseboe, 'The mother of Sir George Etherege', *N&Q*, 220 (1975), 262–4 · A. R. Huseboe, *Sir George Etherege* (1987) [Huseboe lists the important ser. of articles and notes by D. Foster based on archival research into Etherege and his family, and pubd between 1922 and 1932 on p. 135.] · W. Van Lennep and others, eds., *The London stage, 1660–1800*, pt 1: *1660–1700* (1965) · J. W. Nichol, 'Dame Mary Etherege', *Modern Language Notes*, 64 (1949), 419–22 · G. de F. Lord and others, eds., *Poems on affairs of state: Augustan satirical verse, 1660–1714*, 7 vols. (1963–75), vol. 1 · F. Bracher, introduction, in *Letters of Sir George Etherege*, ed. F. Bracher (1974), xi–xxv · H. F. B. Brett-Smith, 'Introduction', *The dramatic works of Sir George Etherege*, ed. H. F. B. Brett-Smith, 2 vols. (1927), 1.xi–lxxxiii · S. Rosenfeld, 'Introduction', *The letterbook of Sir George Etherege*, ed. S. Rosenfeld (1928), 1–51

Archives Bischöflicher Zentralbibliothek und Zentralarchiv, Regensburg, MSS · BL, letter-book, Add. MS 11513 · BL, letters to the secretary of state, Add. MSS 41805–41837, 41840–41841 · Bodl. Oxf., MSS · Harvard TC, MSS · Harvard U., Houghton L., letter-books · PRO, MSS, SP 9/19, SP 81/86 · U. Birm., letter-book | Berks. RO, Trumbull corresp. · Yale U., Osborn collection, Poley MSS, MSS

Etheridge [Etherege], **George** (1519–1588?), physician and classical scholar, was born in Thame, Oxfordshire. Presumably educated at Thame Abbey before going to Corpus Christi College, Oxford, he was admitted as a scholar there on 11 November 1534 aged fifteen years and one month. A pupil of John Shepreve, Etheridge graduated BA on 15 February 1539 and was elected a probationary fellow six days later. Made a full fellow on 26 February 1541, he graduated MA on 20 June 1543 and was appointed a college lecturer in Greek the same year. On taking his BM degree in autumn 1545 Etheridge resigned his college positions to take his 'place among the physicians' (Etheridge, *In libros Pauli Aeginetae*, sig. A4v). Two years later, in January 1547, he was appointed regius professor in Greek.

At Christ Church, Etheridge was one of the few lecturers not to take pupils. As a classicist he was widely esteemed for his linguistic precision, his gift of poetry, and his skill as a translator. Pits knew of his translation of the works of Justin Martyr into Latin, as well as of an abridged version of the psalter, in Hebrew, neither of which survive. As a medical doctor he was similarly valued by his colleagues who, according to Etheridge's own testimony, showed respect for his double vocation: 'The great physicians … showed me much kindness' when teaching Greek in the university (Etheridge, *In libros Pauli Aeginetae*, sig. A4v). He was among the few Oxford physicians to publish a text-book of medicine and pharmacology, *In libros Pauli Aeginetae*. Written specifically for the training of medical students, together with the works of Edward Wotton and Matthew Gwynn it formed 'the sum total of known works in Latin of all the Oxford medical graduates of the century' (*Hist. U. Oxf.* 3: *Colleg. univ.*, 242).

While Etheridge showed some initial support for the royal supremacy in 1538 when he was among a group of fellows censoring the continued appeal to papal supremacy in Corpus Christi College, like many Catholics he had to vacate his chair in 1550 following a royal visitation to the university. Reinstated within a month of Mary's accession, he was present at the trial of Latimer and Ridley in 1555 where he demanded that Ridley should be gagged at his degradation from the priesthood. 'A forward person against the Protestants in Queen Mary's reign', in April 1559 Etheridge was deprived of his lectureship almost immediately after his refusal to take the oath of supremacy following the accession of Elizabeth I (Wood, *Ath. Oxon.*, 1.546f.). Following his dismissal from office, Etheridge moved from his quarters in Christ Church to William Hall in Kibald Street, which he had rented from the university. There he practised to great acclaim as a medical doctor, provided 'a refuge for poor scholars, granted hospitality to clergy, and his lavish liberality provided for all necessities of the Catholics' (Pits, 785). Wood reports that he counted William *Gifford, later Catholic archbishop of Rheims, among his students at William Hall 'who received from him the rudiments in grammar, music and partly in logic' (Wood, *Ath. Oxon.*, 1.547).

As a 'confessor of the orthodox faith' (Pits, 784), Etheridge was purportedly interrogated and imprisoned frequently, both in Oxford and London. While his opposition to Elizabethan claims to sovereignty was well established, in 1566 he none the less dedicated a Greek ode to the queen on the occasion of her visit to the university, in which he reminded her of the achievements and the faith of Henry VIII. Etheridge probably died in 1588.

J. ANDREAS LÖWE

Sources G. Etheridge, *Aeneidos liber secundus graecis versibus redditus* (1553) · G. Etheridge, *In libros Pauli Aeginetae* (1588), sig. A4v, A5r · *Acta Henrici Octavi carmine, Graece*, BL, Royal MS 16 C.x., fols.1–38 · CCC Oxf., *Liber Adm. I*, fols.17v, 25v; *Libri Magni II*, fol.115v · fellows' bonds, 26 Feb 1541, CCC Oxf. · Christ Church Oxf., MS x (1) c.1, 3, 5, 6 · Dean and chapter of Christ Church, Christ Church Oxf., MS i. B. 1, fols.1, 3v · long rolls, 1546–7, Queen's College, Oxford · Bodl. Oxf., MS Wood F. 28, fol. 186v; C. 8, fol. 7; MS Top. Oxon. e. 111, fol. 3 · *APC*, 1552–4, 333 · *LP Henry VIII*, 13/2, nos. 218, 561 · *CSP dom.*, 1547–80, p. 171, no.14 · *CSP Rome*, 1558–71, 68 · *The acts and monuments of John Foxe*, new edn, ed. G. Townsend, 7 (1847), 544 · J. Pits, *Relationum historicarum de rebus Anglicis*, ed. [W. Bishop] (Paris, 1619),

748ff. • Wood, *Ath. Oxon.*, new edn, 1.546 • Wood, *Ath. Oxon.: Fasti* (1815), 107, 118, 122 • Foster, *Alum. Oxon.* • T. Fowler, *The history of Corpus Christi College*, OHS, 25 (1893), 86, 104, 370 • J. G. Milne, *The early history of Corpus Christi College, Oxford* (1946), 29, 33 • H. E. Salter, *Survey of Oxford*, 1, ed. W. A. Pantin, OHS, 14 (1960), 256 • F. G. Lee, *The history, description and antiquities of the prebendal church of the Blessed Virgin Mary of Thame* (1883), 527 • *Hist. U. Oxf.* 3: *Colleg. univ.*, 26, 40, 238, 242, 355, 374 • Emden, *Oxf.*, vol. 4

Etheridge, John Wesley (1804–1866), Wesleyan Methodist minister and Semitic scholar, was born at Youngwoods, a farmhouse near Newport, Isle of Wight, on 24 February 1804. His father was a Methodist local preacher and had been urged by Wesley to enter the itinerant ministry, but refused. His mother was Alley Gray, daughter of a naval officer. As a youth Etheridge was thoughtful and studious. He was privately educated and began to preach in 1826. Towards the end of 1827 the president of the conference sent him to Hull to assist Dr Joseph Beaumont, whose health had broken down. At the Bristol conference in August 1831 Etheridge was received into full connexion, being then second minister in the Brighton circuit. During that year he married Eliza Middleton. They had a daughter who, under her father's teaching, became a remarkable Hebrew scholar and linguist. He took delight in the sacred literature and languages of the East, and most of his works related to these subjects. During several years of indifferent health he lived in Devon, Guernsey, and then France, where he availed himself of the libraries for carrying on his favourite studies, and helped in the missions at Paris and Boulogne. He wrote extensively on the history and writings of the Syriac churches, revealing an impressive knowledge of the Jewish, biblical, and rabbinic literature of the early Christian era. The University of Heidelberg in 1847 conferred upon him the degree of PhD in recognition of his exact scholarship and contributions to learning.

Etheridge resumed circuit work on his recovery to health in 1846 and laboured successfully in Bristol, Leeds, and London. From 1853 he served in the Cornwall district at Penzance, Truro, Falmouth, St Austell, and Camborne. During this period he completed official biographies of two key figures in Methodism, Adam Clarke (1858) and Thomas Coke (1860). Etheridge died at Camborne on 24 May 1866, leaving an unpublished biography of John Fletcher in manuscript form.

W. B. LOWTHER, *rev.* TIM MACQUIBAN

Sources W. Hill, *An alphabetical arrangement of all the Wesleyan-Methodist ministers, missionaries, and preachers*, rev. J. P. Haswell, 9th edn (1862) • *Minutes of the Methodist conferences, from the first, held in London by the late Rev. John Wesley …*, 20 vols. (1812–79) [1866 conference] • N. B. Harmon, ed., *The encyclopedia of world Methodism*, 2 vols. (1974) • J. Harris, *A tear and a floweret* (1871)

Likenesses portrait, repro. in T. Smith, *Memoirs of J. W. Etheridge* (1871)

Wealth at death under £6000: resworn administration, June 1877, *CGPLA Eng. & Wales* (1867)

Etheridge, Richard Albert [Dick] (1909–1985), trade unionist, was born on 27 December 1909 in Halesowen, son of Alfred and Berthie, *née* Rudge. Shortly afterwards the family moved to Birmingham, where Alfred ran a café.

Dick attended St Thomas's School and Handsworth Technical School. His first job was with a chemist; in 1928 he moved to a garage, but when this closed during the depression, he moved into the family café business. In 1933 he married Lily May Thomas. They set up home in Halesowen and had three children.

In 1933 Etheridge became a clandestine communist. The typical Black Country combination of radicalism, economic enterprise, and deep alienation that formed his cultural inheritance seems to have been transmitted largely by his grandmother, a second-hand clothes dealer. During the 1930s he was secretary of the Halesowen Trades Council and a Labour Party member. He became an open communist about 1938.

In 1940 Etheridge went to work at Austin's Longbridge works as a lathe operator. He joined the Amalgamated Engineering Union (AEU) and in 1941 was elected a shop steward. During the war years he took correspondence courses with the National Council of Labour Colleges. These taught him committee and secretarial skills. In 1945 he became convener of the shop stewards' works committee. After the war, despite a considerable increase in union membership, the works committee was still not strongly established. There was a continuing conflict between the AEU and the Transport and General Workers Union (TGWU), and the latter withdrew its shop stewards from the works committee. The 1951 'Pegg and Bills' strike over the dismissal of two National Union of Vehicle Builders (NUVB) shop stewards foundered on the rock of inter-union strife. TGWU members returned to work, saying that Etheridge was only interested in his communist 'comrade', Sid Pegg: TGWU leaders disregarded the fact that Bills, the other NUVB shop steward dismissed, was not a communist. Etheridge, as convener, involved the works committee in campaigns that emphasized the common interests of the workforce. One related to canteen facilities and another to transport to work. More fundamental was the reduction of working hours to forty-two per week.

Etheridge was active in the Communist Party's Halesowen branch and on the Birmingham and midland committees. In 1950 he stood unsuccessfully for parliament in Birmingham, Northfield. He played a major part in formulating Communist policy on the motor industry. From 1961 to 1973 he was a member of the national executive committee. In the AEU he served on the Birmingham district committee and as a member of no. 16 divisional committee. In 1958 and on five occasions subsequently he was elected to the union's annual policy-making national committee. From 1963 to 1974 he was a member of the AEU's delegation to the TUC. From 1965 until 1975 he was president of the Birmingham west district.

In 1956 there were major strikes at Norton, Standard Motors, and British Motor Corporation (BMC) concerning automation and redundancies. Etheridge played a major role in the BMC strike. To him the partial victory achieved was less important than the simple fact of united action by members of all unions.

When the controversy over Hungary broke out in 1956,

Etheridge's first priority was to maintain the unity of the Austin works committee. He persuaded them to refuse to discuss the issue on the grounds that it was political. Etheridge's position at Longbridge was not entirely secure in his first ten years as convener. His communist views naturally provoked hostility on the part of supervisors and senior management. None the less, his role in mediating between rival unions (particularly in brokering a labour mobility agreement under the terms of which only tiny parts of the plant were to be the exclusive preserve of any one union) and in articulating grievances before they reached a critical phase was sufficiently appreciated to protect him from dismissal. From the late 1950s his employers provided him with an ever greater degree of recognition within the plant and with steadily enhanced facilities. In the late 1940s he had had to obtain permission every time he wished to leave his machine; by the 1960s he was a full-time convener with an office, telephone, and unrestricted access to all areas of the plant. Contemporaries commented that his was the best-known face at Longbridge.

During the 1960s Etheridge and the works committee faced a recurring crisis of confidence in respect of labourers, storemen, and other 'indirect' workers (those not employed directly on the production lines) at Longbridge. The indirect workers repeatedly ignored the plant's internal procedures and committee. Etheridge was unable to resolve this problem. In 1968 he became co-chairman of the federal British Leyland Motor Corporation (BLMC) shop stewards' committee. Two matters dominated the remainder of his working life. One was the negotiation of a new BLMC wage structure, a variant of measured day work. Only when the principle of mutuality was introduced did the shop stewards accept the new system. The second was industrial relations legislation.

As Longbridge convener, Amalgamated Union of Engineering Workers district president and TUC delegate, and Communist national executive committee member, Etheridge played a significant role in the campaign which eventually made the Industrial Relations Act of 1971 inoperable. He and the Longbridge works committee supported the unofficial Liaison Committee for the Defence of Trade Unions which played an important role in co-ordinating and stimulating the activities of shop stewards and rank-and-file opponents.

Etheridge retired on 21 February 1975. Over the years he devoted much time and effort to writing, broadcasting, public speaking, and lecturing. Much of his public speaking was undertaken at AEU branch dinners and socials. From the early 1960s he was regularly invited to rotary clubs, discussion groups, and, increasingly, colleges (to lecture on industrial relations). During the 1960s and 1970s he was frequently interviewed on television and radio.

A teetotaller, non-smoker, and non-gambler but a great trencherman, Etheridge was fascinated by Black Country lore. His favourite authors were Gorky, Jerome K. Jerome, and Kipling. For many years he took family holidays near Aberystwyth in a caravan that he built himself. He also travelled overseas, visiting Cuba, Romania, the Soviet Union, and Germany. Over 6 feet tall, broad-shouldered, and robust, Etheridge was accustomed to good health. For many years, however, he had to wear spectacles and his eyesight began to fail several years before his death. He died at Halesowen on 17 March 1985, following two severe strokes. ALISTAIR G. TOUGH

Sources G. Turner, *The Leyland papers*, 2nd edn (1973) · J. Salmon, 'Organised labour in a market economy', PhD diss., Warwick University, 1983 · M. Terry and P. K. Edwards, eds., *Shop-floor politics and job controls* (1988) · R. Croucher, *Engineers at war, 1939–1945* (1982) · G. Turner, *The car makers*, rev. edn (1964) · R. Hastings, 'The labour movement in Birmingham, 1927–45', MA diss., U. Birm., 1959 · J. F. B. Goodman and T. G. Whittingham, *Shop stewards in British industry*, 2nd edn (1973) · E. Frow and R. Frow, *Engineering struggles* (1982) · P. Pagnamenta, *All our working lives* (1984) · J. B. Jefferys, *The story of the engineers, 1800–1945* [1946] · Warwick University, Coventry, West Midlands, Etheridge MSS · personal knowledge (2004) · private information (2004)

Archives U. Warwick Mod. RC, corresp. and papers | University of Warwick, British Leyland Trade Union Committee Archive, west midlands, University of Warwick British Motor Industry Heritage Trust Archive

Wealth at death under £40,000: probate, 24 Oct 1985, *CGPLA Eng. & Wales*

Etheridge, Robert (1819–1903), palaeontologist and museum curator, was born at Ross, Herefordshire, on 3 December 1819, the elder of the two sons of Thomas Etheridge, a Gloucester shipper, and his wife, Hannah Pardoe. Details of his education are uncertain; Etheridge is said to have attended a private school in Ross, where in return for assistance towards university entrance he briefly served as a school usher, but he appears to have been largely self-educated. However, it appears that his paternal grandfather, harbour master at Bristol, encouraged him to form a 'museum' of local specimens. In the 1840s Etheridge partnered his brother in a Cheltenham drapery business, then spent some time as a school tutor in Bristol, before returning to a more lucrative position in business, as a silk mercer, probably in Cheltenham. On 21 April 1845 he married Martha Smith, in Atcham, Shropshire; they had one son, Robert Etheridge junior (1846–1920), a palaeontologist, who became curator at the Australian Museum in Sydney.

Etheridge attended lectures at the Bristol Philosophical Institution, where he came under the guidance of William Sanders, and the curator Samuel Stutchbury (1798–1859). In 1850 Etheridge was appointed curator at the institution and for five years he also lectured on vegetable physiology and botany in the Bristol Medical School and geology at the Bristol Mining School. An active member of the Cotteswold Naturalists' Club by 1848, he was introduced to Roderick Murchison, then director-general of the geological survey, during a visit to Tortworth Court in 1856.

Etheridge's extensive knowledge of Jurassic fossils and Cotswold geology led to an appointment, on 1 July 1857, as an assistant naturalist at the geological survey; he was appointed palaeontologist in July 1863. He identified, curated, and exhibited the fossils collected by the survey's field geologists at the Museum of Practical Geology. His various lists and reports were included in the survey *Memoirs* published between 1858 and 1881. Etheridge prepared a museum catalogue (1865) and for fifteen years assisted Professor T. H. Huxley at the Royal School of Mines as a demonstrator in palaeontology. In recognition of his work on the compilation of a catalogue (*Fossils of the British Islands*) recording the geological occurrence and published references of all known British fossils, the Geological Society awarded him the balance of the Wollaston fund (1871) and the Murchison medal (1880). The volume on Palaeozoic fossils (1888) was the only part to be published.

In 1881 Etheridge was appointed assistant keeper in the department of geology at the British Museum. He was immediately involved in the reorganization of the palaeontological collections following the transfer of the natural history departments from Bloomsbury to South Kensington. His son Robert Etheridge, then an assistant at the museum (1878–87), was among those engaged in this task. Etheridge retired in 1891, but was re-employed for two years until the Treasury vetoed any further continuation. He described material collected by others from many parts of the world. A permanent exhibit devoted to British stratigraphy and palaeontology has been considered to be his most significant contribution. Yet it was the reliability of his work, together with his encouraging attitude, that were seen as his greatest achievements (Geikie and others).

Etheridge was elected FRS in 1871, served on the council (1884) and became a vice-president of the Royal Society. He was elected a fellow of the Geological Society of London in 1854, served on its council (1863–8, 1872–8, 1880–83, 1892–4), and was serving as its president (1880–82) when he moved to the British Museum in 1881. The following year he was president of Section C of the British Association meeting held at Southampton. He served as treasurer of the Palaeontographical Society from 1880 to 1903, and in 1890 was created an honorary fellow of King's College, London. Etheridge was an assistant editor of the *Geological Magazine* from 1865 until his death.

In 1866 Etheridge examined the controversial confused sequence of rocks occurring in north Devon that are now known to be alternations of marine Devonian and Old Red Sandstone. His paper (1867) dealing with the physical structure of that region and the value of its Devonian fossils has been regarded as his most important (H. Woodward, *Geological Magazine*, 43). Throughout his life he maintained a keen interest in the geology of the Bristol area and south-west England, particularly the Rhaetic beds, and the Devonian system. In recognition of this, in 1896, Etheridge was awarded the first Bolitho medal of the Royal Geological Society of Cornwall. Later, as a consultant geologist he was involved in aspects of water supply for Bristol, Plymouth, and London, as well as being regarded as an authority on the coalfields of southern Britain.

Etheridge's early lecture course entitled *Geology: its Relation and Bearing upon Mining* was published in 1859, his *Stratigraphical Geology and Palaeontology* in 1887. He was responsible for the third edition of John Phillip's *Illustrations of the Geology of Yorkshire* (part 1, 1875), and for rewriting the second edition of Phillip's *Manual of Geology* (part 2, 1885). Etheridge also assisted Dr J. J. Bigsby in the preparation of *Thesaurus Siluricus* (1868) and *Thesaurus Devonico-Carboniferus* (1878).

Always active and genial, Etheridge was distinguished by his courtesy and readiness to assist. Following the death of his first wife he married Helen (*b*. 1838/9), originally a native of East Leake, Nottinghamshire. She too predeceased him; his third wife, Anna Letitia, survived him. Etheridge died after a severe cold and bronchitis on 18 December 1903 at his home, 14 Carlyle Square, Chelsea, London, and was buried in Brompton cemetery.

R. J. Cleevely

Sources H. Woodward, 'Robert Etheridge', *Geological Magazine*, new ser., 5th decade, 1 (1904), 42–8 [bibliography, see also frontispiece] · H. B. Woodward, 'A memoir of Robert Etheridge, FRS', *Proceedings of the Bristol Naturalist's Society*, new ser., 10/3 (1904), 175–87 [for 1903, portrait] · H. B. W. [H. B. Woodward], *PRS*, 75 (1905), 258–61 · H. B. Woodward, 'Robert Etheridge', *Nature*, 69 (1903–4), 181–2 · A. Geikie, presidential address, *Quarterly Journal of the Geological Society*, 60 (1904), lxviii–lxxi · H. Woodward, *A brief notice of the scientific labours of Robert Etheridge: with a list of the titles of his published works and memoirs* (privately printed, London, 1891) · A. S. Woodward and others, 'The department of geology', *The history of the collections contained in the natural history departments of the British Museum*, ed. E. R. Lanicester, 1 (1904), 197–9, 198 [in 'Department of Geology'] · J. S. Flett, *The first hundred years of the geological survey of Great Britain* (1937), 67, 82, 105, 246 · J. R. Norman, *Squire: memories of Charles Davies Sherborn* (1944), 30 · W. T. Stearn, *The Natural History Museum at South Kensington: a history of the British Museum (Natural History), 1753–1980* (1981), 231, 233–4 · H. S. Torrens and M. A. Taylor, 'Collections, collectors and museums of note: no. 55: geological collectors and museums in Cheltenham', *Geological Curator*, 5 (1988–94), 175–211, esp. 185–6 · 'Familiar faces no. 51: Robert Etheridge, esq.', *Mining Journal* (6 Feb 1892), 140 · census returns, 1871, 1891

Archives BGS · NHM · Yorkshire Museum, York | NHM, corresp. with Richard Owen

Likenesses group portrait, photograph, 1881, NHM; repro. in P. J. P. Whitehead and C. Keates, *The British Museum (Natural History)* (1981), 11 · W. Blackwood and Sons, photograph, repro. in Woodward, 'Memoir of Robert Etheridge, FRS', frontispiece · A. W. Cox and H. Cox, photograph, BGSL · Maull & Co., BGSL · Maull & Fox, photograph, NHM · Power, photograph, NHM; repro. in Woodward, 'Memoir of Robert Etheridge, FRS', pl. 3 · photograph, repro. in *The Mining Journal*

Wealth at death £6695 12*s*. 6*d*.: probate, 9 Feb 1904, *CGPLA Eng. & Wales*

Ettrick. For this title name *see* Napier, Francis, tenth Lord Napier of Merchistoun and first Baron Ettrick (1819–1898).

Etty, William (1787–1849), painter, was born at 20 Feasegate, York, on 10 March 1787, the seventh child of Matthew Etty (1743–1818) and Esther, *née* Calverley (1754–1829). His father was a baker and miller; Esther Etty was of gentle birth and a forceful character. Etty recalls in his 'Autobiography' (published in the *Art Journal*, January 1849), that the 'first panels on which I drew were the boards of my father's shop floor' (Etty, 13), and he graduated from white chalk to watercolour and crudely made oil paints. Alexander Gilchrist, Etty's first biographer,

William Etty (1787–1849), self-portrait, 1825

records that his uncle William showed artistic talent, but an austere Wesleyan Methodist upbringing was not very conducive to Etty's development as an artist (Gilchrist, 1.21–2).

Early years After a rudimentary schooling Etty had to serve a seven-year apprenticeship to a printer at Hull from October 1798 to 1805. He worked for three weeks as a journeyman printer, before his prosperous uncle William (1740–1809), a manufacturer of gold lace, invited him to his house at 3 Lombard Street, London, in November 1805. Etty's elder brother Walter (1774–1850), who supported him financially for many years, became a partner in the gold lace firm of Bodley, Etty, and Bodley in 1809. Etty had to overcome the twin disadvantages of a deficient education and a late start in his profession; he spent a year drawing from prints and from nature, besides copying from antique casts in J. B. Gianelli's cast shop, near Smithfield, in preparation for the Royal Academy Schools, where he was enrolled in January 1807. His generous uncle paid 100 guineas' premium in July 1807 to enable Etty to study for a year with Sir Thomas Lawrence. He learned to imitate something of Lawrence's style and later earned money by making copies for him.

Student years More immediately important to Etty were John Opie's lectures on painting to the Royal Academy students (published in 1809), that fired Etty's ambition to become a history painter. Opie extolled the work of Titian and Rubens, two artists whose techniques greatly differed, but by whom Etty was inspired to paint the female nude in succulent textures and full-blooded colour, an innovation that later established his reputation and, less agreeably, invited censure from contemporary critics. Henry Fuseli, keeper of the Royal Academy Schools, widened Etty's intellectual horizons; and John Flaxman, appointed professor of sculpture in 1810, both by his lectures and by the example of his line engravings of antique subjects provided him with an iconographic vocabulary. Etty's lifelong devotion to the Royal Academy life school provoked comment from his fellow Academicians. On his uncle William's death in May 1809, Etty received a handsome legacy and moved into a succession of lodgings, until, in 1824, he settled at 14 Buckingham Street, Strand, London. He lived there until his retirement in June 1848 when he moved to a house in Coney Street, York, which he had bought for £1100 two years before.

Etty advanced slowly in comparison with successful near-contemporaries such as David Wilkie, and between 1808 and 1811 strove to improve his anatomical knowledge by studying anatomical atlases and prints of antique sculpture. In 1811 he sold, for 25 guineas, a *Sappho*, from the British Institution exhibition, and showed *Telemachus Rescues Antiope from the Fury of the Wild Boar* at the Royal Academy. Thereafter, he became a regular contributor to the academy summer exhibitions. Some family portraits of 1811 apart, none of his early exhibited works has survived, but seven sketchbooks covering the period 1810–35 in York City Art Gallery provide evidence of his powers of draughtsmanship, of his artistic development, and of which old masters interested him on his travels. *Manlius Hurled from the Rock* (1818; Birmingham Art Gallery), exhibited at the British Institution in 1819, is the first of his surviving early heroic works. A somewhat drily painted academy male nude is seen back view, plunging through space to its doom; influenced by antique sculpture and Michelangelo, it shows Etty's ambitious approach to history painting. Far more appealing are two highly competent large half-length portraits, *The Rev. Robert Bolton* and *Mrs Robert Bolton and her Children*, painted in 1818 (New York Historical Society, New York). Although grandly conceived, with classically inspired poses, they have an unforced naturalism that Etty would have learned from Lawrence, while avoiding his master's glittering finish. The portrait *Miss Arabella Mary Jay* (1818; National Gallery, London) is more obviously in the Lawrence style.

First visits to France and Italy Etty travelled to France in early January 1815, arriving at Calais, from where he wrote to his brother Walter; this letter is the only evidence of the visit. Whether he reached Paris or not is unknown; in September 1816 he embarked for Italy, travelling to Paris and Dijon *en route* for Switzerland and Florence. Alone, ill, unrequited in love, and homesick as he was, his first Italian expedition was a failure, and he returned to Paris in late October, staying a month. He entered the neoclassicist painter Jean-Baptiste Regnault's studio briefly, besides studying at the Académie des Beaux-Arts. Etty began collecting prints assiduously; these were later to be an iconographic treasure trove.

Early successes Two paintings sent to the Royal Academy exhibition of 1820 won Etty some critical attention: *The Coral Finder: Venus and her Youthful Satellites Arriving at the Isle of Paphos* and *Drunken Barnaby* (both priv. colls.); the latter was an uncharacteristic essay in the domestic genre popularized by William Mulready and Wilkie. *The Coral Finder* is the first of those serene mythological compositions that Etty made so peculiarly his own, and which surprised both the public and his fellow artists by their freshness and apparent originality. He sold it for £30 to a pianoforte maker, and won a commission from Sir Francis Freeling, secretary to the Post Office. This was for *Cleopatra's Arrival in Cilicia* (exh. RA, 1821; Lady Lever Art Gallery, Port Sunlight), a subject taken from Plutarch's *Life of Antony* and Shakespeare's *Antony and Cleopatra*. The palette is still somewhat gaudy and the scale of the boat to its occupants absurdly idiosyncratic; although both the *Coral Finder* and the *Cleopatra* are indebted to Titian, Etty was principally inspired by the crowded allegorical compositions of Regnault and the eclecticism practised by contemporary academic painters. There are echoes of Rubens's *The Landing of Marie de Médicis* (Louvre, Paris), in the figures of the Triton and sea-nymphs, which Etty had admired in 1816. The *Cleopatra*, praised by reviewers, also provoked the first of those charges of indecency that were to persist until the late 1830s. The *Times* critic wrote:

> we take this opportunity of advising Mr Etty, who got some reputation for painting *Cleopatra's Galley*, not to be seduced into a style which can gratify only the most vicious taste. Naked figures, when painted with the purity of Raphael, may be endured: but nakedness without purity is offensive and indecent, and in Mr Etty's canvass is mere dirty flesh. (*The Times*, 19 Jan 1822)

The 'canvass' referred to was a preliminary study for *Youth on the Prow and Pleasure at the Helm* (1832; Tate collection), exhibited at the British Institution. Clearly, Etty had struck a new note, but the literal directness with which he painted the female nude, a quality admired by Eugène Delacroix, annoyed his critics. He made no attempt to idealize or 'etherealize' the female form, and fell foul of the emerging cult of respectability, led by the sabbatarian evangelicals of the Clapham Sect.

Etty's grand tour Accompanied by a fellow student, Richard Evans, Etty set off in June 1822 on his grand tour, only returning to England in early January 1824. He benefited greatly from his experiences, studying intensively and travelling as far as Naples, where he spent a month, with prolonged stays in Rome and, above all, in Venice, which became a second home and where he remained for almost nine months: 'dear Venice—Venezia, cara Venezia! thy pictured glories haunt my fancy now! Venice, the birthplace and cradle of colour, the hope and glory of my professional life' (Etty, 38). He was welcomed by the British vice-consul and by the artists of the Accademia, who nicknamed him Il Diavolo for the speed with which he painted nude studies, and they elected Lawrence and him honorary academicians. Extensive correspondence with his brother Walter and with Lawrence enables us to follow Etty's peregrinations closely and gauge what most interested him. He copied industriously, making many 'memorials' of paintings by Titian, Tintoretto, and Veronese, as well as a full-size copy of Titian's *Venus of Urbino* (Royal Academy of Scotland, Edinburgh) in the Uffizi, Florence, and of Titian's *Sacred and Profane Love* in the Borghese, Rome. Back in Paris by November 1823, he stayed on into the new year to paint copies in the Louvre after Rubens's 'water nymphs' (from the *Landing of Marie de Médicis*), Veronese's *Marriage of Cana*, and Poussin's *Le déluge: l'hiver*. These were artists whom Delacroix admired at about the same time, and for a brief moment Etty and Delacroix pursued similar interests; Delacroix met Etty in London in 1825, but there is no evidence of any close professional friendship.

Academic honours Etty's foreign tour had greatly increased his self-confidence and skill; he simplified his compositions, and *Pandora Crowned by the Seasons* (City Art Gallery, Leeds), shown at the 1824 Royal Academy exhibition, reflects this greater maturity. The flattened diamond-shaped grouping of the main figures around Pandora became, with variations, a favourite formula throughout the rest of his career. The paint handling is now far more subtle, the palette more harmonious, and the general tonality cooler. Lawrence bought the painting for 300 guineas, a welcome accolade. Still more welcome was his election as an associate of the Royal Academy on 1 November 1824. In 1818 Etty had hired an assistant, George Henry Franklin, who served him for thirty years until they became estranged. Some of the poorer imitations of Etty's life studies may be Franklin's work. Notwithstanding his uncle's legacy, Etty was still heavily dependent on his brother Walter's financial help; his move to larger quarters in Buckingham Street in June 1824 caused him considerable anxiety. A niece, Elizabeth, kept house for him from about 1819 to his death. As late as May 1831, Etty owed Walter £804, Walter having paid out £3937 on Etty's behalf and received £3133 (Gilchrist, 1.358–9); by 1841, however, all outstanding debts had been paid, and Etty had £300 invested in 3 per cent bank stock. By the end of November 1845 he had £8500 so invested, but at his death this had doubled to £17,000 in funds. This dramatic turnaround was largely due to the emerging class of self-made men such as the Birmingham pen-nib manufacturer Joseph Gillott, and Daniel Grant, a Manchester cotton magnate, who patronized Etty, and to the dealers who promoted his work.

The years 1825–40 undoubtedly form Etty's 'heroic' period, to which belong most of the *grandes machines*, beginning with *The Combat: Woman Pleading for the Vanquished—an Ideal Group* (NG Scot.), shown at the Royal Academy in 1825. This illustrates an abstract virtue, Mercy, and is shorn of any underlying historical or mythological story. Although the figures recall combat scenes in the metopes of the Elgin marbles, there is a pervasive tempestuous romanticism. More classically inspired was the large *Judgment of Paris* (Lady Lever Art Gallery, Port Sunlight), commissioned by Lord Darnley for £500, and shown at the Royal Academy in 1826. Etty reinvigorated a hackneyed subject, and *The Times* praised him for his 'brilliant and harmonious colouring, combined with graceful grouping and careful execution, such as no artist of the present day can equal' (29 April 1826). The general composition derives from a Flaxman engraving of the subject, from Rubens, and, ultimately, from a Marcantonio Raimondi engraving after a lost *Judgment* by Raphael. The *Judith and Holofernes*, shown at the Royal Academy in 1827, was the first of a trilogy, based on the Apocrypha story, illustrating the theme of patriotism. The Royal Scottish Academy, having bought the *Judith*, in 1829 commissioned Etty to paint two pendants, which were exhibited in 1830 and 1831; all three pictures are now in the National Gallery of Scotland. Some of the oil sketches for the central panel have a vigour and brilliance quite unlike any other contemporary English artist's work. The fluent brushstrokes, glazing of half-tones, and brilliant colour appear again in his *Self-Portrait* (Manchester City Galleries) of 1825, showing him in classical cameo-like profile, but infused with a brooding introspection that places it with similar works of the French Romantic school.

Etty's portraits, usually of friends and relatives, are among his most attractive creations, being notable for a direct, sympathetic insight into character, especially so for the male sitters; while in his female portraits he captures equally well the charm and freshness of youth or matronly gravitas. He began to paint still lifes as self-sufficient subjects in September 1839; they have the same delightful fluency, and are unusual in English art of the time. Early in his career he had thought of becoming a landscape painter, and the several landscapes he painted in the 1840s have an atmospheric vividness that makes one regret he did not paint more of them.

Etty became a Royal Academician in February 1828, and presented his diploma work, *Sleeping Nymph and Satyrs* (Royal Academy), that October. A large work (51 in. x 70½ in.), it has a simple monumentality and mingles Venetian colour with a Poussinesque composition. The nymph is displayed in a twisting pose and the two satyrs struggle between themselves to reveal her, thus providing a dynamic tension which Roger Fry found disturbing. Etty, in Paris during the 1830 July revolution, made five copies in the Louvre, including one of Giorgione's *Fête champêtre* (priv. coll.), and another of Ruisdael's *Fresh Breeze: Sea Coast*. Perhaps as a respite from his heroic compositions, he began to paint, in 1831, a new type of subject matter, *Window in Venice during a Festa* (Tate collection). This shows a group of three elegantly dressed young women, two of whom lean out over a vine-clad balcony observing the festive crowd hidden from view. It is the secular equivalent of the Venetian *sacra conversazione*, and was bought by an army contractor, Robert Vernon, for £120. Vernon bequeathed 160 paintings, mostly by contemporary English artists, including eleven Ettys, to the National Gallery, London, in 1847.

Prosperity and decline Etty's later religious subjects included, among others, the figures of Moses and Aaron for the church of St Edmund, King and Martyr, London, in

1833, and two versions of the Prodigal Son, in 1836 and 1841; they culminated in an ambitious trilogy devoted to the life and martyrdom of Joan of Arc (exh. RA, 1847), on which he spent much time and effort, even travelling in 1843 to Rouen, Paris, and Orléans to gather impressions of places connected with St Joan. The engraver C. W. Wass and the dealer Richard Colls jointly bought all three for 2500 guineas as a speculation. Wass engraved them, but the paintings were split up, and only the left and central panels seem to have survived: the former, *Joan of Arc, on Finding the Sword*, in a private collection, and the latter, *Joan of Arc Making her Sortie*, in a museum at Orléans. They measure 6 feet 6 inches by 9 feet 9 inches and 15 feet by 9 feet 9 inches respectively, and do not add much lustre to Etty's reputation. By the 1830s Etty had abandoned his Methodist roots, becoming increasingly attached to high Anglicanism, and at times wistfully recalling the glories of the 'old faith'. As late as November 1847, he sought Sir Charles Eastlake's advice on the merits of Roman Catholicism, but unlike A. W. N. Pugin, whom he knew and admired, he did not become a convert. He campaigned vigorously in defence of York Minster and the preservation of the British medieval heritage, against the vandalisms of modern 'restorers'. He served on the council of the South Kensington School of Design and championed the establishment of such a school at York, which opened in 1842.

By the late 1830s, Etty's work began to show signs of unevenness and his brushwork became looser; physically, the artist increasingly suffered from rheumatism and asthma. He had resigned himself to bachelorhood. Short in stature, his face scarred by smallpox, with sandy hair and a 'shrill and feeble tone of voice' (so noted the actor, William Macready, in his diary, in 1822), Etty, although much liked by many friends, was probably too easily rebuffed (and impecunious) to find a wife (F. Pollock, ed., *Macready's Reminiscences, and Selections from his Diaries and Letters*, 1875, 1.xvi, p. 266). Perhaps his devotion to the female nude was a form of sublimation. Yet he could still produce large mythological works, such as *The Sirens and Ulysses* (exh. RA, 1837; Manchester City Galleries), almost 10 by 15 feet, and *Pluto Carrying off Proserpine* (priv. coll.) shown at the Royal Academy in 1839, that again caused some critics to complain of indecency, charges that he repudiated. He was invited by the prince consort in 1843 to submit a design for one of eight lunettes in a new summer pavilion in the gardens of Buckingham Palace, to illustrate Milton's *Masque of Comus*. He could not master the unfamiliar medium of fresco, and eventually painted a version in oils: *Circe* (Art Gallery of Western Australia, Perth), and a new subject, *Hesperus* (Lady Lever Art Gallery, Port Sunlight), shown at the Royal Academy in 1844. In 1840 and 1842, he visited the Low Countries and lower Rhineland to see altarpieces by Rubens.

At a private view on 9 June 1849, Etty had the satisfaction of seeing 133 of his paintings, spanning 1820–48, exhibited in London at the Society of Arts, Adelphi; the exhibition ran for three months, and was warmly praised by fellow artists, but received mixed reviews. Etty had a genuine gift for beautifully fresh brushwork and a spontaneity of expression that was justly admired; but he was wedded to the grand history piece as his chosen vehicle to paint 'some great moral on the heart' (Etty, 40). He was neither the Ingres nor the Delacroix of the British school; his considerable native talent was too often constrained by an outmoded classicism. His reputation was not well served by pressure from dealers to produce small, easily saleable pictures, in his later years. A man of strong feelings and simple piety, he succumbed to an unusually fierce attack of asthma on 3 November; ten days later, speaking serenely of death's mystery—'wonderful, wonderful, this death'—he died at his home in Coney Street, York, in the evening of 13 November 1849. He was buried, with full public honours, in St Olave's churchyard, York, on 23 November. In May 1850, the contents of his studio were sold at Christies over seven days for £5186 16s. 6d. Substantial holdings of Etty's paintings are in the Tate collection and York City Art Gallery.   DENNIS FARR

Sources A. Gilchrist, *Life of William Etty RA*, 2 vols. (1855) · D. Farr, *William Etty* (1958) · W. Etty, 'Autobiography', *Art Journal*, 11 (1849), 13, 37–40 · W. Gaunt and F. G. Roe, *Etty and the nude* (1943) · D. Farr, 'An Etty sketchbook', *The Connoisseur*, 153 (1963), 255–9 · MSS, City Art Gallery, York · BL, Add. MS 38794 · MSS, City Reference Library, York · I. Bignamini and M. Postle, *The artist's model* (1991) [exhibition catalogue, University Art Gallery, Nottingham, 30 April – 31 May 1991, and Iveagh Bequest, Kenwood, 19 June – 31 Aug 1991] · R. W. Liscombe, 'The commencement of real art', *Apollo*, 103 (1976), 34–9 · D. Ojalvo, 'Jeanne d'Arc délivrant Orléans par Etty', *Revue du Louvre et des Musées de France*, 33 (1983), 434–5 · G. Reynolds, 'Life of William Etty', *TLS* (12 Sept 1980), 988 · W. Vaughan, 'The artist's model', *Art History*, 15 (1992), 263–5 [review] · private information (2004)
Archives City Art Gallery, York, MSS · City Reference Library, York, letters and memorabilia · FM Cam., corresp. and album · Kensington Central Library, corresp. · priv. coll., family MSS and pictures · RA, MSS · RSA, scrapbook and letter-books | BL, letters to Walter Etty, Add. MS 38794 · Man. CL, letters to Royal Manchester Institution · priv. coll., letters to Joseph Gillott and account books
Likenesses W. Etty, self-portrait, oils, 1825, Man. City Gall. [*see illus.*] · W. Etty, self-portrait, pen and brown ink drawing, c.1834, AM Oxf. · D. O. Hill and R. Adamson, calotype, c.1844, Ransom HRC, Gernsheim collection; oil copies, NPG · C. H. Lear, three pencil drawings, 1845, NPG · H. Baines, drawing, 1847, King's Lynn Museum and Art Gallery · M. Noble, marble bust, 1850, NPG · G. Adams, medal, 1872, NPG · G. W. Milburn, bronze statue, 1910–11, York City Art Gallery · W. Etty, self-portrait, oils, priv. coll. · W. Etty, self-portrait, oils, second version, Harvard U., Fogg Art Museum · W. Nicholson, drawing, Royal Scot. Acad. · W. Nicholson, pencil and watercolour drawing, Scot. NPG · J. Watkins, photograph, NPG · oils (after photograph by Hill & Adamson, 1844), NPG
Wealth at death £17,000—in 3% bank stock, plus a house in Coney Street, York, bought for £1100 in 1846, and numerous unsold paintings in his studio: Gilchrist, *Life*

Eu. For this title name *see* Alice, *suo jure* countess of Eu (d. 1246); Bourchier, Sir William, count of Eu (c.1374–1420).

Euddogwy [St Euddogwy, Oudoceus] (*supp. fl.* **late 6th cent.**), holy man and supposed bishop, was founder of the church of Llandogo in Monmouthshire, but by the twelfth century he had been appropriated by the expanding see of Llandaff and erroneously turned into its third bishop. Euddogwy (from Old Welsh Oudocui), or in the Latin form Oudoceus, is one of the most problematic of the Welsh saints, and may largely be the product of the ecclesiastical propaganda underlying the Book of Llandaff, compiled under Bishop Urban in the twelfth century and intended to provide the episcopal church with a demonstrable early history. The only extant account of the life and deeds of St Euddogwy is the brief *Vita sancti Oudocei* found in the Book of Llandaff; it is very derivative in content. It states that the saint's parents were Budig, son of Cybrdan of Cornwall, and Anawfedd, daughter of Ensig of Dyfed and sister of St *Teilo (supposedly second bishop of Llandaff). Budig had allegedly promised his sons as disciples to Teilo, and so, following the end of the 'yellow pestilence' (presumably meant to be that which raged in Britain during the 550s), Teilo travelled to Cornwall and brought the young Euddogwy back with him to Llandaff, where he was eventually to succeed Teilo as bishop.

G. H. Doble argued convincingly that the author of this life simply created a series of fictional early bishops of Llandaff by extracting their names, including a 'Eudoce episcopus', from a list of witnesses to charters appended to the life of St Cadog in BL, Cotton MS Vespasian A.xiv. Furthermore, while much of the life of Euddogwy is concerned with confirming the territorial extent and ecclesiastical privileges of the church of Llandaff, towards its conclusion it shifts rather awkwardly to describe the deeds of Euddogwy as a hermit dwelling on the banks of the Wye, where he founds the church of Llandogo (called Lann Einniaun) in what is now Monmouthshire. The author explains this sudden shift by claiming that Euddogwy had resigned the episcopacy of Llandaff before departing for the Wye, even though elsewhere he claims that Euddogwy would die while still performing his episcopal duties. The feast day is given as 2 July. The patron of Llandogo is probably a very minor Monmouthshire saint, with no connection whatsoever to Llandaff, whom the author of the life has attempted to identify with his subject on account of their onomastic similarity. The Euddogwy of Llandogo has left very little trace of a cult, except for the notice in a document from the end of the twelfth century of a *Fons Sancti Eudaci* ('Fountain of St Eudacus') located in the parish of Dixton, near Monmouth. It seems likely, therefore, that St Euddogwy, bishop of Llandaff, was created wholesale during the composition of his life, partly from the name form Eudoce occurring in another twelfth-century life, and partly from Euddogwy, a local Monmouthshire saint of little consequence, in order to furnish the episcopal church of Llandaff with a suitable early bishop. Consequently, any treatment of him as a historical figure is to be suspected.

                                            DAVID E. THORNTON

Sources J. G. Evans and J. Rhys, eds., *The text of the Book of Llan Dâv reproduced from the Gwysaney manuscript* (1893) · A. W. Wade-Evans, ed. and trans., *Vitae sanctorum Britanniae et genealogiae* (1944) · G. H. Doble, *Lives of the Welsh saints*, ed. D. S. Evans (1971) · J. W. James, 'The Book of Llan Dâv and Bishop Oudoceus', *Journal of the Historical Society of the Church in Wales*, 5 (1955), 23–37

Eugenius I (*d. c.*360). *See under* Eugenius I–VIII (*act. c.*350–763).

Eugenius II (*fl.* 419–452). *See under* Eugenius I–VIII (*act. c.*350–763).

Eugenius III (*fl.* 535–558). *See under* Eugenius I–VIII (*act. c.*350–763).

Eugenius IV. *See* Eochaid Buide (*d. c.*629) *under* Dál Riata, kings of (*act. c.*500–*c.*850).

Eugenius V. *See* Eochaid (*d.* 697), *under* Dál Riata, kings of (*act. c.*500–*c.*850).

Eugenius VI (*fl.* 687–697). *See under* Eugenius I–VIII (*act. c.*350–763).

Eugenius VII (*fl.* 698–715). *See under* Eugenius I–VIII (*act. c.*350–763).

Eugenius I–VIII (*act. c.*350–763), Scottish kings, appear in the pages of John Fordun and later historians among the real and fictitious early rulers of a realm made up at first of lands extending between north-east Ireland and Argyll and later of portions of mainland Scotland. Given cohesion by their Latinate names, for the positive scholarship of the late nineteenth century they formed a group providing a yardstick whereby issues of historical identification and authenticity could be judged. A century later, although some problems of identity remain, they had become interesting principally for the light they shed upon the varying concerns of the historians who described, or invented, their deeds.

Eugenius I (*d. c.*360), reported to have been killed in a battle between Scots and Picts in which the latter owed their victory to Roman allies, **Eugenius II** (*fl.* 419–452), who appears as a model ruler in the pages of Buchanan, and **Eugenius III** (*fl.* 535–558), a notable warrior against the Saxons and Picts, do not occur in authentic king-lists and are first recorded only in Fordun's fourteenth-century compilations. There is no reason to suppose that Fordun himself created them, but the stages by which they came to enjoy the standing of historical figures cannot be traced.

With the last five kings, however, all of whom fall within the purview of the kings of *Dál Riata, the sequence begins to coincide with ascertainable fact, even if it all too often demonstrates historical plausibility only through the faithfulness with which it reflects the inadequacies of the surviving sources. The recurrent name of Eugenius can now be seen as disguising identities that were culturally and linguistically Celtic. Thus Eugenius IV (*fl.* 606–622) is identifiable with *Eochaid Buide (*d. c.*629) [*see under* Dál Riata, kings of (*act. c.*500–*c.*850)], and Eugenius V (*fl.* 684–687) appears to have been identical with *Eochaid son of Domangart (*d.* 697) [*see under* Dál Riata, kings of (*act. c.*500–*c.*850)] and thus placed a decade too early, while **Eugenius VI** (*fl.* 687–697) and **Eugenius VII** (*fl.* 698–715) seemingly represent a confused duplication of a king named Ewen or Eogan, the son of *Ferchar Fota

[*see under* Dál Riata, kings of (*act. c.*500–*c.*850)], who reigned for either thirteen or sixteen years after the death of his father. Ferchar, who died in 697, was apparently ruler of Lorne rather than of Dál Riata, and this was probably also true of his descendants, although they certainly aspired to a wider dominion. They appear as kings only in the Latin lists. Among them was another *Ewen or Eogan [*see under* Dál Riata, kings of (*act. c.*500–*c.*850)], the son of *Muredach [*see under* Dál Riata, kings of (*act. c.*500–*c.*850)], who probably lies behind Eugenius VIII (*fl.* 761–763), though it is impossible to be certain when he ruled—his father lost his kingship in 736, and his successor, Aed (or Áed) Find, may have begun to rule in 748. His kingship too was presumably confined to Lorne.

Historiographically the kings named Eugenius served diverse purposes. For Fordun and Walter Bower, in particular, the first three helped to buttress the Scottish origin-myth, giving antiquity and continuity to a succession of early kings stretching back into a satisfyingly distant past. For sixteenth-century writers they all provided grist for ideological mills, providing models of kingship according to each historian's requirements. Hector Boece had clear-cut ideas as to what constituted good and bad kingship, and shaped his regal images accordingly. Thus Eugenius IV, benefiting from the teaching of St Columba in his youth, proved an exemplary ruler who was more concerned to defend his realm than to extend it. Rigorous to malefactors, he was just and generous to the law-abiding. Eugenius VIII, on the other hand, though also a stern upholder of law and order, was increasingly given to brothels, taverns, and the pursuit of avarice, and was consequently murdered by his nobles. For George Buchanan, writing after the Reformation, the kings named Eugenius, like the other early Scottish rulers, provided a means whereby details taken from Boece could be redirected, using rhetorical skills based upon a mastery of Tacitean Latin, to project upon the past Buchanan's ideal of a strictly limited monarchy. Hence his accounts of reigns like that of Eugenius VII, chosen king by the army and later obliged to stand trial for killing his wife.

The place of the eight Eugenii in the succession of Scottish kings was not maintained by words alone, for in the mid-1680s they were also immortalized, after a fashion, in the remarkable collection of royal 'portraits' at Holyrood Palace which the Dutchman Jacob de Wet, under a contract of 26 February 1684, undertook to produce within two years for a total of £240. One hundred and ten pictures were promised, and while not all appear to have survived, every Eugenius is still represented. The problem of differentiating so many rulers, a high proportion of them non-existent, greatly taxed the painter's slender powers of invention, though he did his best with beards, hats, hairstyles, and expressions; thus Eugenius II contemplates posterity with a complacent smirk, Eugenius IV with a shifty leer. A rare touch of imagination gave a family likeness to the entire series by endowing each king with the nose of Charles II.

Then in 1729 Father Thomas Innes published his *Critical Essay on the Ancient Inhabitants of the Northern Parts of Britain or Scotland*, and in it he both demolished the historicity of the pre-sixth-century king-lists provided by Fordun and Bower and showed in detail how in relating the fortunes of early kings, whether they existed or not, Boece and Buchanan had manipulated their sources for ideological purposes, in the process creating narratives riddled with anachronisms and inconsistencies. Eugenius VIII was among the kings Innes chose to demonstrate how 'none of all these [medieval] historians … have so much as one of the many instances or examples, related by Boece … of the Scottish nobility calling their kings to account, or claiming the power to judge them' (Innes, 152). The blow dealt by Innes to the mythical history of early Scotland proved mortal, and thereafter Eugenius I–VIII, their milieu, ancestors, and descendants, were increasingly left to the meticulous investigation of scholars like W. F. Skene in the nineteenth century and M. O. Anderson in the twentieth.   HENRY SUMMERSON

Sources J. Fordun, *Chronica gentis Scotorum*, ed. W. F. Skene, 2 vols. (1871–2) · W. Bower, *Scotichronicon*, ed. D. E. R. Watt and others, new edn, 9 vols. (1987–98), vol. 2 · *John Major's 'History of Great Britain'*, *1521*, ed. A. Constable, Scottish History Society, 10 (1892) · H. Boethius, *Chronicle of Scotland*, trans. J. Bellenden (1540); repr. (1977) · G. Buchanan, *Rerum Scoticarum historia*, ed. R. Freebairn (1727) · T. Innes, *A critical essay on the ancient inhabitants of the northern parts of Britain or Scotland* (1729); repr. (1879) · M. O. Anderson, *Kings and kingship in early Scotland*, rev. edn (1980) · C. Kidd, *Subverting Scotland's past* (1993) · D. Broun, 'The birth of Scottish history', *SHR*, 76 (1997), 4–22 · 'The contract with James Dewitte, painter, for the portraits of the kings of Scotland in the palace of Holyrood', *Bannatyne miscellany III*, ed. D. Laing, Bannatyne Club, 19B (1855), 327–42

Eumorfopoulos, George (1863–1939), art collector, was born at 43 Bedford Street South, Mount Pleasant, Liverpool, on 18 April 1863, the eldest son of Aristides George Eumorfopoulos, and his wife, Mariora Scaramanga. His father was a Greek merchant whose family originally came from the island of Chios. George entered the firm of Ralli Brothers, merchants, of London, of which for a time he was representative in south Russia; he rose eventually to be vice-president and retired in 1934. On 10 June 1890 he married Julia (1864/5–1943), daughter of George Emanuel Scaramanga, merchant, of Tiltwood, Sussex; the couple had no children.

Soon after his marriage, Eumorfopoulos started collecting: beginning with European porcelain, he moved on to Chinese. It was a time when knowledge of Chinese art in the West was about to expand rapidly: archaeology and railway construction in north China cut into tombs richly furnished with pottery figures and vessels of the first to the tenth century. In his preface to the first of the six volumes of R. L. Hobson's monumental catalogue of his Chinese and other Eastern ceramics (1925–8), Eumorfopoulos recorded that it was in 1906 that he saw the first specimens of tomb wares: 'First came the Han, then the Tang (figures of horses and camels first in 1910), and lastly the Wei' (Hobson, *The George Eumorfopoulos Collection*, vii). His collection grew rapidly until it became remarkably representative of the ceramics of the Song and earlier periods.

Eumorfopoulos then launched out into the field of Chinese archaic bronzes and jades, and eventually of sculpture and paintings as well, until his collection became the greatest of his time. Eumorfopoulos had intended to bequeath his collection to the nation, but in 1934 he found it necessary to realize a part. Accordingly, he offered the national museums all that they required of the Chinese section for £100,000, a sum estimated at the time to be well under half the market value. The money was found, and a division between the British and Victoria and Albert museums was made on a basis of three to two.

Eumorfopoulos and his wife lived firstly at Clandon, Surrey, before moving to London, where a two-storey museum was added to the back of their home at 7 Chelsea Embankment. Here they were always ready to show the collection, and their Sunday afternoons became a feature of London life for those in artistic circles. Eumorfopoulos was a short and slight figure, with pale blue eyes and a large nose. His manner was generally reserved and even a little severe, but he talked with enthusiasm about his collection. Fellow connoisseurs found him congenial: W. G. Constable, director of the Courtauld Institute, described him as 'one of the kindest and most generous of men'. Constable recalled Eumorfopoulos's simple lifestyle: apparently he travelled to work on the underground, and his only personal indulgence was 'a vast plate of ice-cream at Sunday lunch' (Constable, 119). After the sale of 1934, Eumorfopoulos still continued to buy Chinese antiquities; his taste was wide, however, ranging from Islamic and medieval art to modern European painting and sculpture. The vitality of his judgement is shown in the remarkable examples of contemporary work which he acquired, largely through his patronage of young artists, in particular sculptors: he owned paintings by Matisse and sculptures by Barbara Hepworth. He also supported archaeological studies and was one of the founders of the Oriental Ceramic Society and its first president from 1921 until his death at 7 Chelsea Embankment on 19 December 1939. His remaining collections were sold at auction by Sothebys from 28 to 31 May and on 5 and 6 June 1940 and, after his widow's death, in 1944. His collection is represented in the major national collections of Chinese art.

BASIL GRAY, *rev.* M. TREGEAR

Sources R. L. Hobson, 'George Eumorfopoulos', *Transactions of the Oriental Ceramic Society*, 17 (1940), 9–10 · *The Times* (20 Dec 1939) · private information (1949) · b. cert. · m. cert. · d. cert. · R. L. Hobson, *The George Eumorfopoulos collection: catalogue of the Chinese, Corean and Persian pottery and porcelain*, 6 vols. [1925–8] · W. P. Yetts, *The George Eumorfopoulos collection: catalogue of the Chinese and Corean bronzes, sculpture, jades, jewellery and miscellaneous objects*, 3 vols. (1929) · L. Binyon, *The George Eumorfopoulos collection: catalogue of the Chinese frescoes* (1927) · L. Binyon, *The George Eumorfopoulos collection: catalogue of the Chinese, Corean and Siamese paintings* [1928] · W. G. Constable, 'Some notes for an obituary [pt I]', *Apollo*, 77 (1963), 116–19
Likenesses G. Frankl, drypoint print, *c.*1938, V&A · D. Gordine, bronze head, V&A · I. Mestrović, bust, BM
Wealth at death £104,657 13s. 1d.: probate, 4 April 1940, *CGPLA Eng. & Wales*

Euphemia [*née* Euphemia Ross] (*b.* in or before **1329**?, *d.* **1388/9**), queen of Scots, consort of Robert II, was the daughter of Hugh *Ross, fourth earl of Ross (d. 1333) [see under Ross family], and his second wife, Margaret Graham, and was possibly one of the children born before her parents obtained a retrospective papal legitimation of their marriage in November 1329. She married John *Randolph, third earl of Moray, who was killed at the battle of Nevilles Cross in 1346. She remained unmarried for almost a decade, until in 1355 a papal dispensation, styling her countess of Moray and widow of John Randolph, was granted for her marriage to Robert the Steward (1316–1390). Euphemia's property rights as the widow of the earl of Moray probably allowed the Steward to claim control of the former Randolph lordship of Badenoch, while the marriage also served to cement Robert's relationship with Euphemia's brother William *Ross, fifth earl of Ross [see under Ross family (per. c.1215–c.1415)].

On 22 February 1371 Euphemia's husband succeeded to the Scottish throne as *Robert II. Although she was recognized and styled as queen from the moment of his succession, her formal coronation took place much later than the new king's. Whereas Robert was crowned on 27 March 1371, Walter Bower's Scotichronicon suggests that Euphemia's coronation occurred between 6 December 1372 and 24 March 1373, in a service conducted at Scone by Alexander Kininmund, bishop of Aberdeen. The delay may have been caused by some uncertainty about the status of David II's recently divorced queen, Margaret Logie, who had set out to the papal court in 1372 in order to protest against her exclusion from her rights as queen of Scots. Scottish clergymen, in particular, may have been unwilling to conduct a ceremony which created a new queen of Scots and pre-empted papal judgement on the issue. Euphemia does not appear in any contemporary accounts as an active or influential figure in the life of the kingdom, and this may partly reflect the transfer of Robert II's affections to his long-term mistress, Mariota Cardeny, a relationship which was openly acknowledged as early as March 1372.

The marriage of Euphemia and Robert produced two sons, David *Stewart and Walter *Stewart, but the king's nearest male heirs were the three sons of his first wife, Elizabeth Mure: John (the future Robert III), Robert, and Alexander. The place of David and Walter in the royal succession was detailed in an entail of 4 April 1373, which stipulated that only after the failure of the male lines descending from the three sons of Robert II and Elizabeth Mure could they or their male heirs succeed to the throne. Perhaps it is significant that Euphemia was not crowned queen until shortly before the entailing of the royal title. Euphemia's sons were, however, the beneficiaries of substantial royal patronage after 1371. David became earl of Strathearn and Caithness and lord of Urquhart before his death (1386?). All three titles may have been acquired by David partly through his mother's rights as a kinswoman of Malise, eighth earl of Strathearn and Caithness, and as the widow of John Randolph. Euphemia's second son, Walter, married the heiress to the lordship of Brechin in 1378 and went on to obtain the earldoms of Atholl and Caithness early in the fifteenth century. In March 1437

Walter was executed for his involvement in the assassination of his nephew, James I.

Euphemia and Robert II also had at least two daughters, Egidia and Elizabeth. Egidia was married about 1388 to William Douglas of Nithsdale, an illegitimate son of Archibald Douglas, third earl of Douglas and lord of Galloway; William was killed in 1391 in a quarrel with English knights at Königsberg, during preparations for an expedition against the pagan Lithuanians. A dispensation for Elizabeth's marriage to David Lindsay, lord of Glen Esk (created earl of Crawford in 1398), was obtained in 1375 and the couple were married before 1384.

In an addition to a fifteenth-century manuscript of Bower's Scotichronicon, Euphemia is said to have died on 20 February 1388 and to have been buried in Dunfermline Abbey. The intended date may be 20 February 1389, as she was apparently alive on 19 June 1388, but dead by 23 February 1389. A conventional and stylized representation of her as queen is to be found on a seal dating from 1375, which depicts her standing between the arms of the Scottish kingdom and those of the earldom of Ross.

S. I. BOARDMAN

Sources W. Bower, Scotichronicon, ed. D. E. R. Watt and others, new edn, 9 vols. (1987–98), vol. 7 · Scots peerage, 6.296–7 · Scots peerage, 7.235–9 · S. I. Boardman, The early Stewart kings: Robert II and Robert III, 1371–1406 (1996) · APS, 1124–1423
Likenesses seal

Euphemia of Wherwell. See Walliers, Euphemia de (d. 1257).

Eurich, Richard Ernst (1903–1992), painter, was born at 7 Lindum Terrace, Manningham, Bradford, on 14 March 1903, the second child in the family of two sons and three daughters of Frederick William Eurich, bacteriologist, and his wife, Margaret Gwendolyn, née Carter-Squire. His father was a celebrated research bacteriologist for the Anthrax Investigation Board and later professor of forensic medicine at the University of Leeds. His ancestors had migrated from Germany to Bradford in the early nineteenth century. Apart from four years boarding at St George's School, Harpenden, Eurich's childhood was spent in the centre of Bradford, a city whose bustling industrial life was to provide a rich visual source for some of his mature art. After two years at Bradford grammar school, his professional artistic training began at Bradford School of Arts and Crafts in 1920; four years later he entered the Slade School of Fine Art (1924–7). His training there under the remarkable professorship of Henry Tonks was almost entirely in drawing, and indeed his earliest successes after he left were with a series of highly finished, often large-scale drawings of figures in interiors. These came to the attention of the collector and founding father of the Contemporary Art Society, Sir Edward Marsh; not only did he buy several of them but he also introduced Eurich to Eric Gill, who, impressed, recommended him to his own gallery, Goupil.

It was at the one-man show that the Goupil Gallery gave him in 1929 that Eurich met the only contemporary artist who ever exerted any major influence on his work: Christopher Wood. At this point Eurich was still uncertain of his future direction and was under doctor's orders to give up drawing because of deteriorating eyesight. Wood's straightforward advice to Eurich at this, their only meeting (Wood died a year later), 'to paint the things you love', changed the course of Eurich's career. For Eurich this came to mean, above all, painting the sea; childhood visits to Whitby and later to cousins at Weymouth, where he struggled to teach himself to paint on the windswept shingle bar of Chesil Beach, had instilled in him a profound fascination with the structure and movement of the sea. The immediate consequence was that he spent winter 1932–3 working in a cottage in Lyme Regis on the Dorset coast, where he evolved a style and subject matter based on coastal scenes and harbours. Lyrical and painterly in character, these brought him considerable success during the 1930s in a series of shows at Rex Nankivell's well-regarded Redfern Gallery. Now earning a steady living as a painter, he married, on 15 September 1934, Mavis Llewellyn Pope (b. 1906/7), art lecturer, and daughter of Frederick John Pope, Methodist minister. After their marriage they went to live at Dibden Purlieu, close to Southampton Water. There they built the house, Appletreewick, in which they lived together until Eurich's death nearly sixty years later.

This pattern of life was sharply interrupted by the Second World War. A Quaker by upbringing, Eurich had strongly pacifist instincts and initially worked as an ambulance driver before an approach from the War Artists' Advisory Committee offered more regular work as a war artist. This came principally through his remarkable painting *Withdrawal from Dunkirk* (1940)—a complex, detailed work of astonishing technical assurance, painted in just six weeks only a month or so after the event itself. Exhibited at the National Gallery's war art exhibition in August 1940, it created a public sensation and led to Eurich being appointed a full-time, salaried war artist to the Admiralty in March 1941. There then followed a period of four years' intense work, during which his vividly imagined reconstructions of incidents at sea, shipwreck survivors, and naval raids, painted in a highly idiosyncratic manner that combined elements of J. M. W. Turner and Christopher Wood with Breugel, Cranach, and Northern Renaissance art, won him enormous critical admiration.

A career as an artist recording public events and occasions beckoned but, in the years after the war, Eurich, exhausted by his efforts, turned his back on the prospect and, for a time, on sea subjects also. In the period of introspection that followed he started writing the massive autobiographical memoir that provided later scholars with an insight into his development as an artist. Its rich evocation of his Bradford childhood also provided a new vein of subject matter for his painting, consisting largely of lyrical evocations of childhood together with more surrealistic imaginings of children's stories and folk songs, as well as more straightforward representations of the Yorkshire landscape of Wharfedale that he had explored as a

boy. They were not so popular with the public, however, and Eurich, forced to take up teaching for the first time in his career, worked at Camberwell School of Arts and Crafts from 1949 to 1968. It was not a role he ever enjoyed particularly, though all the evidence is that he was an extremely conscientious and supportive teacher. Then a highly successful one-man show at Tooth's Gallery in 1968, his first in London for a decade, marked the beginning of a modest but steady revival in his critical fortunes that led to a first retrospective at Bradford Art Gallery in 1980, regular one-man shows at the Fine Art Society, and, in 1991, shortly before his death, an impressive show of his war art at the Imperial War Museum.

Eurich continued to work more or less until his death. His late style developed a delicate pale colouring and feathery brushstroke, ideal for rendering the quirky observations of everyday life along nearby Southampton Water and mysterious poetic recollections of the past that formed the basis of his late work. The dedication to painting was typical too of the tenacious individualism of an artist who painted virtually every day of his working life, for the most part in a shed at the bottom of his garden, and only latterly in a purpose-built studio attached to the house. Though there was something of the reclusive in his temperament, there was, equally, nothing misanthropic about it. He was always a man of the sweetest temperament, a spry, sprightly, neatly built figure who drove a car very well right into his late eighties—his only disability in later years being an increasingly serious deafness. This working life was, remarkably, sustained against a private life that involved several personal tragedies: the death of an infant daughter at the end of the war and the deaths of his only son, the gifted documentary photographer Crispin Eurich, in 1977, and, at the same period, of a much loved son-in-law.

Eurich was elected ARA in 1942 and RA in 1953 and appointed OBE in 1984. His work is held in numerous public collections, principally the Tate collection, the National Maritime Museum, and the Imperial War Museum. He was awarded an honorary doctorate by Bradford University in 1989. He died of cancer of the colon at the Royal South Hampshire Hospital, Southampton, on 6 June 1992. He was survived by his wife, Mavis, and two daughters, Caroline and Philippa.

NICHOLAS USHERWOOD

Sources *The edge of all the land: Richard Eurich, 1903–1992* (1994) [exhibition catalogue, Southampton Art Gallery, 1994; incl. introduction and notes by N. Usherwood] · *Richard Eurich: from Dunkirk to D-Day* (1991) [exhibition catalogue, IWM, 1994; incl. notes by N. Usherwood and A. Weight] · *Richard Eurich RA* (1980) [exhibition catalogue, Bradford Art Gallery] · *Richard Eurich (1903–1992): visionary artist* (2003) [exhibition catalogue, Southampton Art Gallery, 2003; incl. introduction and notes by E. Chaney and C. Clearkin] · R. Eurich, 'As the twig is bent' (c.1955) [unpublished autobiographical memoir] · private information (2004) · personal knowledge (2004) · *The Times* (9 June 1992) · *The Independent* (10 June 1992) · WWW · b. cert. · m. cert. · d. cert.

Archives IWM, London · priv. coll., private family archives and papers · Tate collection, autobiography, corresp., and papers

Likenesses R. E. Eurich, self-portrait, 1932, Fine Art Society, London · R. E. Eurich, self-portrait, 1938, Bradford Art Galleries and Museums
Wealth at death £55,490: probate, 15 Feb 1993, CGPLA Eng. & Wales

Eusden, Laurence (1688–1730), poet, was baptized on 6 September 1688, at Spofforth, Yorkshire, where his father, Laurence Eusden (d. 1699), was rector. He went to St Peter's School, York, and was admitted as pensioner (aged sixteen) at Trinity College, Cambridge, on 24 March 1705. He graduated BA in 1708, MA in 1712. On 2 April 1706 he became a scholar of his college, was admitted as a minor fellow on 2 October 1711, and advanced to a full fellowship on 2 July 1712. He became third sublector on 2 October 1712, and a year later was admitted as second sublector. He drew no stipend after 1720, but continued at least occasionally in residence until 1725.

Eusden, a whig, was not among the Trinity fellows hostile to the master, Richard Bentley; he wrote a congratulatory poem to Bentley on the refurbishment of the college chapel. He also wrote sensuous love poetry, including translations of Claudian and Musaeus, and a faintly risqué satire of women, *Verses at the Last Publick Commencement in Cambridge* (1714). He was one of the largest contributors to a collection of English versions of Ovid's *Metamorphoses* by Dryden, Garth, and others (1717).

Meanwhile Eusden's verse compliments to Addison, Lord Halifax, and the duke of Newcastle brought him the patronage of highly placed whigs. Listed by Steele among *Spectator* and *Guardian* authors, Eusden was credited (by John Nichols) with letters in *Spectator* numbers 54, 78, and 87 (1711), and *Guardian* numbers 95 and 124 (1713). Eusden certainly contributed translations from Claudian in *The Guardian* (127 and 164) which were reprinted with ten other poems by him in Steele's *Miscellanies* (1714). He was one of seven poets granted the honour of having their commendatory verses on Addison's *Cato* prefixed to the seventh edition of the play (1713). His lines 'To a Lady that Wept at Hearing Cato Read' in Steele's *Miscellanies* (1714) were promptly parodied by Pope as 'On a Lady who P—St at the Tragedy of Cato'.

In 1717 Eusden published a flattering epithalamium on the duke of Newcastle's marriage to Lady Henrietta Godolphin. His reward came when Nicholas Rowe died a year later and Newcastle, as lord chamberlain, made Eusden poet laureate. Over the next ten years he produced a steady drip of adulatory new year odes, birthday odes, and other conventional laureate verse addressed to members of the royal family, alongside complimentary verse addressed to actual or potential aristocratic patrons.

Eusden was ridiculed by the duke of Buckingham in 'The election of a poet laureate' (*Works*, 1723); Thomas Cooke wrote of him in *The Battle of the Poets* (1725) as 'a laurel'd Bard … Who has by few been read, by fewer prais'd'; and Swift satirized his laureate verse in 'Directions for a Birth-Day Song' (1729, first printed 1765). Pope joined the attack in *Peri Bathous* (A. Pope and J. Swift, *Miscellanies in Prose and Verse*, 1728), *Dunciad* (1728), and *Dunciad variorum* (1729), and continued it, with further variations,

in the *Epistle to Arbuthnot*, *Imitations of Horace: Ep.II.i*, and *Dunciad* (1743), well after his target's death. Pope accuses Eusden repeatedly and equally of dullness and drunkenness. The second charge is reiterated in Richard Savage's preface to his *An Author to be Lett* (1729), but it is not known whether the accusation is well grounded or is the common taunt that a poet craves the laureateship solely for the perquisite of sack. Thomas Gray's well-known punning remark in a letter to William Mason (19 December 1757) that 'Eusden was a person of great hopes in his youth, though at last he turned out a drunken parson' might be based on Pope's satire, rather than independent testimony.

Eusden never replied to the many attacks upon his character and poetry. Whatever his character, his poetry has little merit. He was ordained deacon (Lincoln diocese) on 20 September 1724, and priest on 25 March 1729. He was chaplain to Richard Verney, Lord Willoughby de Broke, from 1725 to 1730, when he became rector of Coningsby, Lincolnshire, a living he obtained through the favour of a Mr Cotesworth. Eusden died at Coningsby on 27 September 1730, and was buried there three days later. He left behind him in manuscript a translation of the works of Tasso with a life of that poet. The sale catalogue of his library was dated 1763. His portrait, painted in the 1720s by Saunders (1682–c.1735) of Cambridge, had not been traced.

JAMES SAMBROOK

Sources senior bursar's audit books, admissions and admonitions, 1560–1759, Trinity Cam. · Venn, *Alum. Cant.* · J. Nichols, ed., *A select collection of poems*, 4 (1780), 128–63, 226–49 · R. Shiels, *The lives of the poets of Great Britain and Ireland*, ed. T. Cibber, 4 (1753), 193–7 · Nichols, *Illustrations*, 2.616–17 · Nichols, *Lit. anecdotes*, 3.637 · D. F. Foxon, ed., *English verse, 1701–1750: a catalogue of separately printed poems with notes on contemporary collected editions*, 2 vols. (1975) · R. J. White, *Dr Bentley: a study in academic scarlet* (1965) · R. Steele and J. Addison, *The Spectator*, ed. D. Bond, 5 vols. (1965) · R. Steele and others, *The Guardian*, ed. J. C. Stephens (1982) · E. K. Broadus, *The laureateship* (1921), 113–19 · *IGI* · parish register, Coningsby, 1730
Likenesses J. Richardson, black chalk drawing, BM

Eustace (II) [Eustace aux Gernons], **count of Boulogne** (d. c.1087), magnate, was the eldest son of Eustace (I), count of Boulogne and Lens, and of Matilda, daughter of Lambert, count of Louvain. In 1036, and before his succession to the countship of Boulogne, Eustace (II) married Godgifu (or Goda; d. c.1047), daughter of King *Æthelred II and formerly wife of Drogo, count of the Vexin (d. 1035). The marriage fostered an alliance between Eustace and Godgifu's brother, *Edward the Confessor, and the sons of her first marriage, *Ralph, earl of Hereford (d. 1057), and Walter, count of Amiens and the Vexin (d. 1063). Eustace and the counts of Ponthieu and the Vexin used the alliance with Edward to prevent annexation into the Norman or Flemish polities and Edward used the Boulonnais-Picard alliance to counter-balance Flemish aid to his Danish adversaries. Eustace's defence of his alliance with Edward against the newly allied counts of Normandy and Flanders prompted a conflict in 1051–2 with Earl Godwine and his sons, who favoured a pro-Flemish policy. In addition to pursuing ties with the English king to forestall

Eustace (II), count of Boulogne (*d. c.*1087), embroidery (Bayeux Tapestry) [right, holding the banner]

Flemish incorporation, Eustace continued his father's strategy of allying with the nobility of Lower Lorraine. In 1047–9 Eustace joined his maternal kin in the war between Duke Godefroi of Lower Lorraine, and the holy Roman emperor, Heinrich III.

Shortly after the death of his first wife, Eustace about 1049 married Ida of Lorraine (*d.* 1113), in order to strengthen his alliance to her father, the duke. The defeat of Eustace and his allies in Lorraine in 1049 and in England in 1052 encouraged the count's support of his Picard and northern Norman kin and allies in the rebellion of Guillaume d'Arques against his nephew the duke of Normandy. The failure of this rebellion led to a period of quiescence and limited co-operation with Count Baudouin (V) of Flanders. In 1066 Eustace changed his family's traditional hostility towards the Norman dukes and joined William of Normandy in the conquest of England. His contributions to the conquest were praised in the *Carmen de Hastingae proelio* and portrayed on the Bayeux tapestry. It was here that his moustaches (giving rise to the epithet 'aux Gernons') were immortalized. After a brief estrangement, Eustace and William the Conqueror fought to oust Robert of Flanders, who had usurped the countship from his nephew in 1071. The coalition against Robert included Eustace's brother-in-law Duke Godefroi of Lower Lorraine and, initially, the French king, whose support was encouraged by Eustace's brother Godefroi, bishop of Paris. Despite Robert of Flanders's victory, William and Eustace remained allies and William restored to Eustace the extensive estates he had received shortly after the conquest of England. Domesday Book reveals that the count held lands in eleven counties, with the majority of his holdings in Essex. These estates produced an annual

income of approximately £770, placing Eustace among the wealthiest lay magnates.

Eustace's marriage to Ida of Lorraine produced three children: Eustace (III), count of Boulogne; Godefroi de Bouillon, duke of Lower Lorraine and later defender of the Holy Sepulchre; and Baudouin I, king of Jerusalem. Eustace also had a bastard son, Geoffroi, who married Beatrice, daughter of Geoffrey de Mandeville. Ida worked to reform monasticism in Boulogne with the encouragement of Anselm of Bec and Hugh, abbot of Cluny, and was considered a saint by her contemporaries. She used her dower lands in Lorraine and well-placed monastic foundations to aid her husband and sons in the maintenance of the family's power. In the early 1080s a genealogy of the comital family of Boulogne was produced which stressed Eustace's Carolingian descent through his mother, Matilda, and his marriage to Ida of Lorraine, and also reflected the prestige the family had gained through Eustace's military prowess. At Eustace's death, *c.*1087, he was the tenth largest landholder among the Anglo-Norman nobility and a wealthy and independent count in northern France.

HEATHER J. TANNER

Sources H. J. Tanner, 'The expansion of the power and influence of the counts of Boulogne under Eustace II', *Anglo-Norman Studies*, 14 (1991), 251–86 · *ASC*, s.a. 1048, 1052 [texts D, E] · L. C. Bethmann, ed., 'Genealogia comitum Bulonensium', [*Chronica et annales aevi Salici*], ed. G. H. Pertz, MGH Scriptores [folio], 9 (Hanover, 1851); repr. (Stuttgart, 1963), 299–301 · A. Farley, ed., *Domesday Book*, 2 vols. (1783) · J. H. Round, 'The counts of Boulogne as English lords', *Studies in peerage and family history* (1901), 147–80 · *The Carmen de Hastingae proelio of Guy, bishop of Amiens*, ed. C. Morton and H. Muntz, OMT (1972) · A. Le Miré and J. Fopens, *Opera diplomatica et historica*, 4 vols. (1723–48), 1.159–61 · F. Barlow, *Edward the Confessor*, 2nd edn (1979), 97–9, 104–14 · *The Gesta Guillelmi of William of Poitiers*, ed. and trans. R. H. C. Davis and M. Chibnall, OMT (1998), 132–3, 138–9, 182–5 · *The Gesta Normannorum ducum of William of Jumièges, Orderic Vitalis, and Robert of Torigni*, ed. and trans. E. M. C. van Houts, 2 vols., OMT (1992–5) · S. A. Brown, 'The Bayeux tapestry: why Eustace, Odo, and William?', *Anglo-Norman Studies*, 12 (1989), 7–28 · *Reg. RAN*, 1.9, 45 · D. Bates, ed., *Regesta regum Anglo-Normannorum: the Acta of William I, 1066–1087* (1998) · A. Bridgeford, 'Was Count Eustace II of Boulogne the patron of the Bayeux tapestry?', *Journal of Medieval History*, 25 (1999), 155–85 · H. J. Tanner, 'Between Scylla and Charybdis: the political role of the comital family of Boulogne in northern France and England (879–1159)', PhD diss., U. Cal., Santa Barbara, 1993
Archives Canterbury Cathedral, archives, charter F130 · Westminster Abbey archives, charter 968
Likenesses embroidery (Bayeux Tapestry), Bayeux, France [*see illus.*]
Wealth at death English landholdings yielded £770 p.a.; value of county of Boulogne and Lens is unknown: Tanner, 'The expansion', 278–85; C. W. Hollister, 'Magnates and "Curiales" in Early Norman England', *Viator* 8 (1977), 68–9

Eustace, **count of Boulogne** (*c.*1129–1153), claimant to the English throne, was the eldest son of King *Stephen (*c.*1092–1154) and *Matilda of Boulogne (*c.*1103–1152). He was the elder brother of *William (William of Blois), earl of Surrey (*c.*1135–1159), and *Mary (Mary of Blois), countess of Boulogne (*d.* 1182). His date of birth has to be surmised from his knighting and investiture of the honour of Boulogne in late 1146 or early 1147. If he was eighteen at this time he was born in 1129: he may have been a year or two younger, but no more, for he occurs in one of his parents' charters dated not later than 30 August 1131. Eustace was a Boulogne family name, but his father's coup in claiming the English crown in December 1135 moved him onto the wider stage of Anglo-Norman politics.

On this stage, however, Eustace would never enjoy more than a subordinate role. Of the numerous mentions of Eustace in charters and in chronicles, all but a few relate to his position as his father's intended heir. As such, he did homage to the French king for Normandy in 1137. As such, he was betrothed in some state within France to Constance, the sister of Louis VII (r. 1137–80), in February 1140—if the marriage did not take place at the same time, it took place very soon afterwards. As such, in 1141, with his father in captivity after the battle of Lincoln, his still powerful family asked for the release to him of the Boulogne lands and other family estates. This the Empress Matilda and her party refused. Both for the Angevins and the house of Blois it was all or nothing. Henry of Anjou, the son of the empress, claimed to be the lawful heir to England and Normandy: Eustace could claim to be the legitimate heir of an anointed king. In the late 1140s the issue was joined between them. Henry always had the initiative. He came to England in 1149, and was knighted at Carlisle; but Eustace pursued him through the west country, and Henry left England with little achieved. Eustace then followed him to France in 1151, as an ally of his brother-in-law Louis VII; but the French king then accepted Henry's homage as duke of Normandy. In the following year also he was in France, as part of a wider coalition of Henry's enemies; but Henry's control of the duchy remained unshaken.

In diplomatic manoeuvrings ultimately equally fruitless Stephen had attempted to follow Capetian custom, and have Eustace crowned in his own lifetime. His mother assiduously cultivated Archbishop Theobald (d. 1161); but all to no avail. The papacy referred to English custom, and declined to approve Eustace's coronation. By the end Eustace alone believed in the legitimacy of his cause. That stage was reached after the second siege of Wallingford in July 1153, after Duke Henry had invaded England and attracted widespread support. Stephen was persuaded to agree to terms, at which Eustace withdrew from the court, 'greatly vexed and angry because the war, in his opinion, had reached no proper conclusion' (Gesta Stephani, 238–9). Very soon afterwards, on about 17 August 1153, he died in East Anglia. He had wasted the lands of Bury St Edmunds, and that powerful saint was seen by some as implicated in his death; others said more simply that he had died of a broken heart. He died childless, and was buried at Faversham Abbey.

The reputation Eustace left behind was mixed. In the courtly world he was seen as a true son of his father, able to 'meet men on a footing of equality or superiority as occasion required' (Gesta Stephani, 208–9). In the countryside he was a lord no less demanding than his peers, 'a bad man … he robbed the lands and levied heavy taxes' (ASC, 202). His wife, the Countess Constance, was remembered as 'a good woman' (ASC, 202), but she did not linger in her adopted land, and early in 1154 married Raymond (V), count of Toulouse.   EDMUND KING

Sources Reg. RAN, vol. 3 · R. H. C. Davis, King Stephen, 3rd edn (1990) · K. R. Potter and R. H. C. Davis, eds., Gesta Stephani, OMT (1976) · John of Salisbury, Historia pontificalis: John of Salisbury's memoirs of the papal court, ed. and trans. M. Chibnall (1956) · ASC · Henry, archdeacon of Huntingdon, Historia Anglorum, ed. D. E. Greenway, OMT (1996) · The chronicle of John of Worcester, 1118–1140, ed. J. R. H. Weaver (1908) · R. Howlett, ed., Chronicles of the reigns of Stephen, Henry II, and Richard I, 4, Rolls Series, 82 (1889) · muniments, Merton Oxf., 5525 no.1

Eustace (d. 1215), administrator and bishop of Ely, is likely to have been of Norman or French origin. A student at the schools of Paris, alongside Gerald of Wales, who became a lifelong friend, he seems to have been a 'consistent benefactor' to the abbey of St Victor, while Roger of Wendover's description of him as 'a man of learning both divine and secular' (Flores historiarum, 2.114), as well as Gerald's reference to his skill in law, points to a legal as well as a theological training. He is first recorded in 1177 as a clerk of Robert Foliot, bishop of Hereford, and seems to have remained at Hereford, where he became a canon, until at least 1186. By 1190 he was parson of Withcall, Lincolnshire. It is not known when he entered the king's service, but he must have done so well before 20 April 1194, when he acted as deputy for the chancellor in issuing a royal charter at Winchester. Ecclesiastical preferment followed. By 5 May 1194 Eustace was dean of Salisbury, and in 1196 he became successively dean of Richmond, Yorkshire, and treasurer of York. From 1194 onwards he was constantly in attendance on Richard I in Normandy; referred to as the king's seal-bearer, he also continued to act in the place of the chancellor, William de Longchamp. When Longchamp died, on 31 January 1197, Eustace succeeded him as bishop of Ely, the election taking place at Vaudreuil on 10 August 1197; but the king's needs—Eustace was sent to represent Richard at an assembly summoned for 22 February 1198 to elect a new German emperor—prevented his being consecrated until 8 March following, when Archbishop Hubert Walter performed the ceremony in St Katherine's Chapel, Westminster. Later that year, between 18 and 22 May, Eustace was formally appointed chancellor. In October and November 1198 he acted as a justice at Westminster, the only occasion on which he is recorded as having done so. But he then returned to the king's side, and in January 1199 was sent by Richard to the French king to declare an end to the existing truce.

Following the death of Richard I, Eustace was replaced as chancellor by Hubert Walter on 27 May 1199. But this does not mean that he was out of favour with the new king, whose coronation he attended on the same day, and from whom he obtained a charter confirming Ely in its liberties on 23 August. He accompanied John to Normandy in 1200, was present when William, king of Scots, did homage at Lincoln on 21 November, and in both 1202 and 1204 was sent on unsuccessful embassies to the French king. However, although his attestations of royal charters show that he still came to court with some regularity, his energies were increasingly absorbed by the administration of his diocese, and still more by his frequent employment by Pope Innocent III (*r.* 1198–1216) as a judge-delegate and as an executor of papal mandates. In 1199–1200 he was first a judge-delegate and then an arbitrator in the bitter dispute between Archbishop Hubert Walter and the monks of Canterbury over the former's plans for a collegiate church at Lambeth. In 1200 and 1201 he devoted much time to promoting the canonization of Gilbert of Sempringham. An arbitrator between Bishop Savaric of Bath and the monks of Glastonbury, in 1203 he was appointed to investigate the miracles of Wulfstan of Worcester. In the latter year, and again in 1206, he was employed as an arbitrator in the quarrel between the monks of Evesham, their abbot, and the bishop of Worcester. Towards the end of his life he became deeply involved in the disputes over the election of Hugh of Northwold to be abbot of Bury St Edmunds. The recipient of at least thirty-five letters from the pope, he also addressed correspondence to Rome, on 19 December 1204 drawing from Innocent the celebrated letter *Pastoralis officii diligentia*, which contained rulings on some nineteen points of law, every one of which later passed into the law of the church.

Eustace was also closely involved in the difficulties that faced the English church as a result of King John's refusal to accept the election of Stephen Langton as archbishop of Canterbury. Following Innocent III's consecration of Langton on 17 June 1207 the monks of Canterbury who had elected Langton were expelled from their monastery. The pope appointed Eustace, together with William de Ste Mère-Église, bishop of London, and Mauger, bishop of Worcester, all of them former royal servants, to negotiate with King John. Negotiations dragged on until 23 March 1208, when the bishops issued an interdict on England. The king's reprisals were thorough, and a complete seizure of all clerical property began, followed by piecemeal negotiations for its recovery. But those clergy who fled abroad, who inevitably included the three executors of the interdict, did not recover their possessions until 1213. Eustace continued to be involved in Innocent's efforts to put pressure on John, and made several visits to England in aid of these. But negotiations always broke down, and Eustace was present at Arras when John was excommunicated in November 1209. Late in 1212 Eustace went to Rome with Langton and the bishop of London in order to complain of John's oppression of the English church, a visit claimed by some chroniclers—implausibly—to have led the pope to declare John deposed.

When the crisis was resolved on 15 May 1213, by John's becoming a papal vassal, Eustace returned to England, and was present at Winchester when the king received absolution on 20 July, and at St Paul's, London, when John took an oath of fealty to the pope on 3 October. As part of the settlement John was ordered to pay 100,000 marks to the papal legate, Nicolò of Tusculum, Archbishop Langton, and Eustace of Ely as an earnest of restitution to the ecclesiastics who had suffered serious losses in the previous seven years. Eustace's own damages were variously estimated at £750 and £1050. Finally, at a great council held in St Paul's, London, presided over by the legate, the interdict was formally lifted by Bishop Eustace on 2 July 1214. As John passed from conflict with the pope to confrontation with the barons, Eustace was one of the bishops wooed by the king, who on 15 January 1215 transferred to him the crown's rights of patronage over Thorney Abbey. He is said to have played a leading part in negotiations between John and the rebels, before he died at Reading on 3 February 1215. He was buried in Ely Cathedral, before St Mary's altar, on the south side of the choir.

When circumstances permitted, Eustace was an active bishop. His statute on the tithing of lambs is one of the earliest acts of English diocesan legislation to survive. He appears to have rebuilt and endowed the church of St Mary in Ely; he gave land in Witcham, Somersham, and March to the convent of Ely; and he assigned the church of Impington to the monastic precentor, in order to provide for books. He is also credited with the construction of the Galilee porch at the west end of his cathedral church (though little of his work now survives), with the endowment of a light at the lady altar, and with a grant of land on the west side of the convent enclosure to make a cellar for the monks. Finally, the Ely chronicle records that he gave a number of vestments, a gold chalice and pyx, silver basins and spoons, a pastoral staff, and a little gold cross containing a fragment of the True Cross. Variously praised for his learning, discretion, and authority, Eustace was clearly widely admired by his contemporaries.

DOROTHY M. OWEN

Sources *Fasti Angl., 1066–1300*, [Monastic cathedrals] · *Fasti Angl., 1066–1300*, [Salisbury] · *Selected letters of Pope Innocent III concerning England, 1198–1216*, ed. C. R. Cheney and W. H. Semple (1953) · C. R. Cheney, 'King John and the papal interdict', *The papacy and England* (1982) · C. R. Cheney, *Pope Innocent III and England* (1976) · C. R. Cheney, *Hubert Walter* (1967) · J. Barrow, ed., *Hereford, 1079–1234*, English Episcopal Acta, 7 (1993), 145, 147, 149, 152, 163 · F. M. Powicke and C. R. Cheney, eds., *Councils and synods with other documents relating to the English church, 1205–1313*, 1 (1964), 41 · [H. Wharton], ed., *Anglia sacra*, 1 (1691), 363–4 · J. Bentham, *The history and antiquities of the conventual and cathedral church of Ely*, ed. J. Bentham, 2nd edn (1812), 148–9 · Emden, *Oxf.*, vol. 3 · *Chancery records* (RC) · *Pipe rolls, 2 Richard 1* · *Pipe rolls, 2, 3, 5, 11 John* · L. Landon, ed., *The cartae antiquae: rolls 1–10, printed from the original in the custody of the master of the rolls*, PRSoc., 55, new ser., 17 (1939) · L. Landon, *The itinerary of King Richard I*, PRSoc., new ser., 13 (1935) · D. M. Stenton, ed., *Pleas before the king or his justices, 1198–1212*, 3, SeldS, 83 (1967), 134 · *Ann. mon.*, vols. 1–4 · *Gir. Camb. opera*, 3.75, 232, 297 · *The historical works of Gervase of Canterbury*, ed. W. Stubbs, 1: *The chronicle of the reigns of Stephen, Henry II, and Richard I*, Rolls Series, 73 (1879), 544, 551; 2.95, 100, 106–7 · *Chronica magistri Rogeri de Hovedene*, ed. W. Stubbs, 4, Rolls Series, 51 (1871) · *Rogeri de Wendover liber qui dicitur flores historiarum*, ed. H. G. Hewlett, 3 vols., Rolls Series, [84] (1886–9), vol. 2 · *Memoriale fratris Walteri de Coventria / The historical collections of Walter of Coventry*, ed. W. Stubbs, 2, Rolls Series, 58 (1873), 217, 219 · W. D. Macray, ed., *Chronicon abbatiae de Evesham, ad annum 1418*, Rolls Series, 29 (1863) · *Radulfi de Diceto … opera historica*, ed. W. Stubbs, 2: *1180–1202*, Rolls Series, 68 (1876), 159 · *VCH Cambridgeshire and the Isle of Ely*, 4.83

Eustace fitz John (*d.* 1157), justice and baron, was the son of John fitz Richard (*b.* before 1056), a minor tenant-in-chief in Essex and Norfolk, and an unknown mother. He

Eustace fitz John (*d*. 1157), coin

succeeded Serlo de Burg, who is said (perhaps wrongly) to have been his uncle and to have founded the castle of Knaresborough, as the farmer of the royal manors of Knaresborough and Aldborough. He had two brothers, *Pain fitz John and William, and two sisters, Agnes and Alice. Like his brother Pain, Eustace became attached to the court of Henry I, and between 1114 and 1133 was a regular witness of Henry's charters. In the only extant pipe roll of Henry's reign he appears as a justice itinerant in the north, acting in conjunction with Walter Espec. He won Henry's special favour, receiving grants that made him very powerful in Yorkshire and Northumberland, including the manor of Malton in the North Riding of Yorkshire, and was reputed to be a man of great wisdom and counsel. His main places of residence were Alnwick and Malton and he was also custodian of Bamburgh Castle and of the castle and honour of Tickhill (sometimes known as Blyth). After the death of Henry I, Eustace submitted to King Stephen (by Easter 1136), and appears to have been employed by Stephen as a justice in the north. His castle of Alnwick was captured by the Scots before 5 February 1136, but was returned by 22 March 1136. He supported Stephen's invasion of Scotland early in 1138, but afterwards was arrested by Stephen and deprived of the castles Henry I had given him, including Bamburgh. As a result he joined David, king of Scots, when he invaded the north of England again after Easter 1138, and intended to give his own castle of Malton to the Scots. He was present at the battle of the Standard, where he and his followers fought alongside the men of Cumbria and Teviotdale in the second line of King David's host. Wounded in the battle, he escaped to one of his castles, after which his town and fortress of Malton were besieged by English forces. By 1142 Henry of Scotland, earl of Northumberland, had restored him to his Northumberland possessions and granted him extensive lands in the honour of Huntingdon. Eustace

supported the attempt by the Scottish chancellor, William Cumin, to establish himself as bishop of Durham in 1141, helped to arrange a truce between Cumin and Bishop William de Ste Barbe in 1143, and thereafter allied himself with the earls of Chester and York in what appears to have been an attempt to restore his power, and probably also to promote Scottish authority, south of the Tees. Coins bearing his name were minted at York in Stephen's reign, and, probably between 1149 and *c*.1151, he destroyed Gilbert de Gant's castle of Hunmanby in Yorkshire in a war fought for control of the earldom of Lincoln, to which Gant was a claimant. Towards the end of Stephen's reign Eustace made a grant to his son, William de Vescy, perhaps as a means of securing William's succession to his lands; this grant was confirmed by Duke Henry of Normandy in 1153–4.

Eustace was a lavish patron of the church and the special friend of new orders of regulars. His name appears in the witness list of the document purporting to be the charter by which his colleague Walter Espec founded Rievaulx, the first Cistercian house established in Yorkshire. When the first monks of Fountains were in the direst distress and had given away their last loaves in charity, Eustace's timely present of a load of bread from Knaresborough was looked on as little less than a miracle. He also made important gifts of lands to Fountains. In 1147 he founded the abbey of Alnwick for Premonstratensian canons as a daughter house of Newhouse Abbey, which had been the first Premonstratensian community established in England. He was a friend of St Gilbert of Sempringham, and established two of the earliest Gilbertine houses in England. One, probably founded in 1150–51, was a foundation for canons at Old Malton in Yorkshire. The other, founded by Eustace in conjunction with his second wife, Agnes, probably in 1151, was a community for canons and nuns at Watton in the same county. He also made grants to the monks of St Peter's, Gloucester, and to the Augustinian canons of Bridlington.

Eustace made two rich marriages. His first wife, whom he probably married before 1130, was Beatrice, daughter and heir of Ivo de Vescy. She brought Alnwick to Eustace. She died at the birth of their son, William, who adopted the name of Vescy, and was active in the king's service during the reign of Henry II, being sheriff of Northumberland between 1157 and 1170. He was the ancestor of the barons de Vescy. William's son Eustace was prominent among the northern barons whose revolt from John led to the issue of Magna Carta. Eustace fitz John's second wife was Agnes, daughter of William Fitznigel, baron of Halton and constable of Chester, one of the leading lords of the earldom of Chester. They were probably married by 1135 and had a son, Richard Fitzeustace, the ancestor of the second line of Lacys. After the childless death of Fitznigel's son and heir, William, in 1143 or 1144, Eustace obtained from Earl Ranulf (II) of Chester a grant of Fitznigel's estates and titles, in which he was recognized as leading counsellor to the earl, above all the nobles of Ranulf's lands (Barraclough, 28). In his new capacity he took part in Henry II's first expedition into Wales, and was slain in July 1157 when the king's army fell into an ambush near Basingwerk. He was then an old man. Roger of Howden described Eustace as a one-eyed worthless traitor (*Chronica … Hovedene*, 1.193), but the Alnwick chronicle, while also referring to this physical disability, states that Eustace was an energetic and lawful man.

T. F. TOUT, *rev.* PAUL DALTON

Sources GEC, *Peerage* · J. A. Green, *The government of England under Henry I* (1986) · G. Barraclough, 'Some charters of the earls of Chester', *A medieval miscellany for Doris Mary Stenton*, ed. P. M. Barnes and C. F. Slade, PRSoc., new ser., 36 (1962), 25–34 · P. Dalton, 'Eustace fitz John and the politics of Anglo-Norman England: the rise and survival of a twelfth-century royal servant', *Speculum*, 71 (1996), 358–83 · Dugdale, *Monasticon*, new edn · *Pipe rolls*, 31 Henry I · Symeon of Durham, *Opera*, vol. 2 · R. Hexham, 'De gestis regis Stephani et de bello standardi', *Chronicles of the reigns of Stephen, Henry II, and Richard I*, ed. R. Howlett, 3, Rolls Series, 82 (1886) · *Reg. RAN*, vols. 2–3 · W. Farrer and others, eds., *Early Yorkshire charters*, 12 vols. (1914–65), vols. 2, 12 · St Aelred [abbot of Rievaulx], 'Relatio de standardo', *Chronicles of the reigns of Stephen, Henry II, and Richard I*, ed. R. Howlett, 3, Rolls Series, 82 (1886) · R. Howlett, ed., *Chronicles of the reigns of Stephen, Henry II, and Richard I*, 1, Rolls Series, 82 (1884) · W. Dugdale, *The baronage of England*, 2 vols. (1675–6), 91 · *Chronica magistri Rogeri de Hovedene*, ed. W. Stubbs, 1, Rolls Series, 51 (1868), 193

Archives BL, cartulary of Malton Priory, Cotton MS Claudius D.xi. · Bodl. Oxf., Dodsworth MSS, charters [copies] · PRO, charters [copies]

Likenesses coin, BM [*see illus.*]

Eustace the Monk (*c.*1170–1217), Benedictine monk, sea captain, and pirate, was the son of Baudoin Busket, a lord of the county of Boulogne. According to his biography, Eustace studied black magic in Toledo, returned home to become a monk at the abbey of St Samer near Calais, and then left the monastery to avenge the murder of his father. Other evidence suggests that his father died soon after 1190 and proves that by the early 1200s Eustace was the seneschal of the count of Boulogne, Renaud de Dammartin. About 1204, however, the two quarrelled and Eustace became a fugitive: it is with his adventures in the next year or so that the thirteenth-century romance biography, composed between 1223 and 1284 by an unknown poet from Picardy, is principally concerned. Hiding out in the forest, Eustace duped and humiliated Renaud in a series of daring escapades, appearing before him in numerous disguises, ambushing him and his men, and time and again making off with his horses. These adventures have obvious links both with the romance *Fouke le Fitz Waryn* and the tales of Robin Hood.

From 1205 onwards the main outlines of Eustace's career can be followed in the records of the English government as well as in the biography. He established himself in the Channel Islands and from there preyed upon shipping in the channel. Much of this was piracy on his own account, but from 1205 until 1212 Eustace was also employed intermittently by King John, whose conflict with Philip Augustus, king of France, was reaching its climax. Indeed, the biography asserts that when Eustace first offered his services to John (probably in 1205), he was given command of thirty ships.

A decisive change of allegiance, however, took place in 1212, when Renaud Dammartin became John's ally and turned the king against Eustace, who consequently entered the service of King Philip. In 1216 it was Eustace who commanded the fleet that ferried Philip's son, Louis, across to England when the latter mounted his bid for the English throne. In August of the following year he commanded another fleet bringing Louis much needed reinforcements. This was met off Sandwich on 24 August 1217 by an English force under Hubert de Burgh. Eustace's flagship was surrounded and captured. Eustace himself, discovered hiding in the ship's bilges, offered huge sums for his life but, hated as he was by the men of the Cinque Ports, he was given only one choice: whether to have his head cut off on the ship's rail or on the side of the trebuchet that was being brought as deck cargo to England. Matthew Paris included the beheading in his dramatic account of the battle without revealing the preferred block.

Under the peace of Kingston–Lambeth, in the following month, Louis promised to ensure that Eustace's brothers vacated the Channel Islands. Eustace had played a significant part in the struggle between Angevin and Capetian royal houses, but, as with the case of his contemporary, Fulk Fitzwarine, it was his exploits as a fugitive on the run from authority that really appealed to his biographer.

D. A. CARPENTER, *rev.*

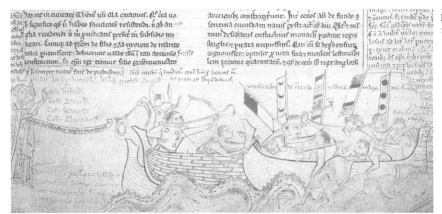

Eustace the Monk (*c.*1170–1217), drawing [far right]

Sources D. J. Conlon, ed., *Li romans de Witasse le Moine*, University of North Carolina, Studies in Romance Languages and Literature, 126 (1972) · J. C. Holt, *Robin Hood* (1982) · Paris, *Chron.*
Likenesses drawing, CCC Cam., MS 16, fol. 52 [*see illus.*]

Eustace, James, third Viscount Baltinglass (1530–1585), nobleman and rebel, was the eldest son and heir of Sir Roland Eustace, later second Viscount Baltinglass (1504–1579), and Joan, daughter of James Butler, Lord Dunboyne. The family had a long and distinguished record of royal service in Ireland, in both central and local government. This loyalty was rewarded when Thomas, James's grandfather, was granted the viscountcy and lands of Baltinglass, a dissolved abbey in Wicklow, by Henry VIII in 1541. Although Sir Roland continued the tradition of government service after his succession as viscount in 1549, he was a vehement opponent of the cess, the state's policy of arbitrary taxation for victualling the army in Ireland. After his release from some months' imprisonment in 1577–8, he engaged in a bitter dispute with Marshal Nicholas Bagenal over oppressive billeting of the army on his estate at Kilcullen, co. Kildare.

On his father's death in 1579, James succeeded to the title and estates. His early education had been under the tutelage of Norman Eustace, a cousin and Roman Catholic priest. In 1567 James was admitted to Gray's Inn, London. By then he was married to Mary (*b. c.*1548), daughter of Sir John Travers, master of the ordnance in Ireland; the marriage was childless. While a student in London, Eustace may have been confirmed in his zeal for Catholicism. On his return to Ireland, he came under the influence of the Jesuit Robert Rochford and of Edmund Tanner, Roman Catholic bishop of Cork, and he travelled to Rome in the mid-1570s.

Eustace's recusancy was manifested when he was fined and imprisoned by the court of high commission for flouting the Act of Uniformity in 1578. His religious disaffection led him to question the right of Queen Elizabeth to be monarch of Ireland. Influenced by radical priests such as Rochford and Tanner, Eustace was prepared to take militant action which, for him, was the logical imperative of the papal bull of excommunication of the queen. Although viewed as 'a very simple man without wisdom, manhood or any other quality meet to embrace such an enterprise' (PRO, SP 63/79/26, i), Baltinglass organized a conspiracy comprising some of the leading lords in Leinster and elsewhere. Both the earl of Kildare and the baron of Delvin were implicated in plans for an uprising but withdrew on its eve. Concurrently with renewed insurrection in Munster, Baltinglass prepared for a military campaign, drawing in his fellow gentry of the pale and the Gaelic clans of southern Leinster, led by Feagh McHugh O'Byrne. The paramount chieftain of central Ulster, Turlough Luineach O'Neill, also evinced interest. With the help of prominent Dublin merchants (who supplied him with munitions) and the blessing of the priests, Baltinglass declared himself to be in rebellion against Queen Elizabeth in mid-July 1580, rejecting her claim to be supreme governor of the church as a woman 'uncapax of all holy order', and condemning 'the oppression of poor subjects under pretence of justice' (PRO, SP 63/74/62).

The administration of Arthur, Lord Grey of Wilton, feared that a countrywide campaign with continental aid was imminent. The alarm became more acute when Baltinglass, Feagh McHugh O'Byrne, and their allies inflicted a severe defeat on the English forces in Glenmalure in Wicklow on 25 August 1580. This ambush deterred the state army from campaigning in the mountainous countryside, and thereafter the uprising took the form of raid and counter-raid in the southern pale. The state's effort was not helped by the ambiguous stance of the earl of Kildare who, with the baron of Delvin, was arrested and imprisoned in Dublin Castle at Christmas 1580. A confederacy of Delvin's connections in Meath and Kildare failed to aid Baltinglass militarily, however, and by the spring of 1581 Grey's attritional war had begun to succeed. The massacre of a continental force at Smerwick in November 1580 and the wearing down of the Munster rebels dashed hopes of extra-provincial assistance, and a series of arrests and surrenders of Baltinglass's relatives and allies left him with a dwindling force. Eventually he opted to flee the country with the aid of some Wexford sailors, and sailed for the Iberian peninsula to seek more support from the Spanish king.

The trials of the captured rebels took place in November 1581, and at least twenty were convicted of treason and executed. Among these were Baltinglass's brother, Walter, and several cousins and followers, many of whom went to the scaffold professing their Catholicism. The estates of the rebels, including those of the viscount, were confiscated in the aftermath of the uprising, the act of attainder finally passing through the Irish parliament in 1585. Having spent time in Lisbon and Rome, Baltinglass had moved to Madrid by 1584. His embassy at the court of Philip II of Spain did not bear fruit, though his presence there was a source of alarm to the authorities in Dublin Castle. He died at Madrid on 24 November 1585.

Viscount Baltinglass's rebellion emanated from his own zeal for the restoration of Catholicism as the official state religion, and he struck a chord with opponents of state political and religious policies in many parts of Ireland. A small group of priests orchestrated the enterprise, but the failure of the earl of Kildare to commit himself was a major blow to the viscount's hopes. Most of the disaffected palesmen eschewed military confrontation, preferring to use constitutional means in pursuit of their political ends. Undoubtedly, however, the bravery of Baltinglass and his followers served to galvanize many of the Old English population into recusancy.

COLM LENNON

Sources Jan 1577–Jan 1584, PRO, SP 63/57–8; 63/61; 63/74–90; 63/92–8; 63/101–14 · *CSP Ire., 1574–85* · E. A. O'Connor, 'The rebellion of James Eustace, Viscount Baltinglass, 1580–1', MA diss., National University of Ireland, Maynooth, 1989 · P. F. Moran, ed., *Spicilegium Ossoriense*, 3 vols. (1874–84) · E. F. Tickell, 'The Eustace family and their lands in county Kildare', *Journal of the Kildare Archaeological Society*, 13 (1955–60), 270–87, 307–41, 364–413 · H. C. Walshe, 'The rebellion of William Nugent, 1581', *Religion, conflict, and coexistence in Ireland: essays presented to Monsignor Patrick J. Corish,* ed. R. V. Comerford and others (1990), 26–52 · J. S. Brewer and W. Bullen, eds., *Calendar of the Carew manuscripts, 2: 1575–1588*, PRO (1868) · *CSP Spain, 1580–86* · M. V. Ronan, *The Reformation in Ireland under Elizabeth, 1558–1580* (1930) · J. Kingston, 'The Catholic families of the pale: Eustace', *Reportorium Novum*, 2 (1958), 245–56 · J. S. Brewer and W. Bullen, eds., *Calendar of the Carew manuscripts, 1: 1515–1574*, PRO (1867) · *DNB*

Eustace, John Chetwode (1761–1815), antiquary and Roman Catholic priest, was born in Ireland. His father's family, of Anglo-Norman descent, had long been settled in co. Kildare, while his mother was a Chetwode (otherwise Chetwood), an old Cheshire family. After education at the Roman Catholic Sedgeley Park School, Staffordshire, *c.*1775, he is said to have tried his vocation briefly with the English Benedictines at St Gregory's, Douai. On returning to Ireland, he was ordained for the diocese of Kildare and Leighlin, and in 1795 was appointed professor of rhetoric at the newly established college of Maynooth. In October 1796 he presented Edmund Burke with a copy of the verses he had composed for the inauguration of the college by the lord lieutenant, Lord Camden, whom he declined to eulogize. Burke found the piece full of spirit, evidence that 'bad as things are in Ireland, principle is not quite dead' (*Correspondence*, 102).

From 1798 Eustace served for two years as chaplain to Sir William Jerningham at Costessey, Norfolk, and henceforth made his career in England. In 1801–2 he travelled in Italy as tutor and companion to three young gentlemen who included John Cust (later Lord Brownlow). In 1805 he moved to Cambridge to act as tutor–companion to George Petre, nephew of the tenth Lord Petre, the first Roman Catholic to attend the university (as a member of Jesus College) since the Reformation—though barred from taking a degree, and liable to fines for non-attendance at chapel. Eustace moved in Cambridge literary circles, and was encouraged by the antiquary and traveller Edward Daniel Clarke, a fellow of Jesus, to prepare the journal of his Italian tour for publication. He later accompanied Petre on a further tour of Dalmatia, western Greece, Sicily, and Malta. His moderate whig principles are evident in the *Political Catechism* which he published anonymously in 1810. By now he had settled at Great Chesterford, Essex.

When Eustace's two-volume *Tour through Italy* was eventually published in 1813, it won him instant celebrity, and the work (from 1815, entitled *A Classical Tour through Italy and Sicily*) went through eight editions between 1813 and 1841, becoming the standard vade-mecum of classical tourists. While the guide was antiquarian in tone, with an aesthetic preference for pure classicism over the Gothic and baroque styles, it was eloquent in its denunciation of contemporary absolutism and its championship of Italian liberty. Rejecting papal infallibility as 'absurd', and sceptical in his attitude towards miracles and relics, Eustace was ahead of his time in advocating a vernacular liturgy and urging the adoption within the Papal States of the principles of constitutional government. John Cam Hobhouse, in his annotations to *Childe Harold*, dismissed the *Tour* as inaccurate and derivative (*Byron: Complete Poetical Works*, 2.262–3)—a judgement which is ungenerous and unjust.

In June 1814 Eustace accompanied lords Carrington and Essex on a visit to Paris. His *Letter from Paris to George Petre, Esquire* (1814), which was reprinted eight times in its year of publication, depicted the effect on Parisian society of war and 'revolutionary madness' (*Letter from Paris*, 1).

Eustace wore his learning lightly, and his polish and conversational charm made him popular in English aristocratic and literary society. Though he maintained friendly relations with Anglican clergymen, he was an eloquent champion of Roman Catholic liberties, which he defended in a celebrated exchange with the bishop of Lincoln in 1812. However, his ecumenism earned him the hostility of his ecclesiastical superior Joseph Milner, who delated him to Rome as a latitudinarian. Milner was later to write that 'instead of gadding with Protestants through classical scenes, he [Eustace] ought to have been teaching Irish Catholics their catechism' (*Orthodox Journal*, August 1819, 303).

Eustace returned to Italy in 1815, and was collecting material for a supplement to the *Classical Tour* when he contracted malaria at Naples, where he died on 1 August 1815. He was interred in Naples in the church of the 'Crocelle', where a Latin inscription by the *abate* Campbell marked his monument (Clayton). His projected supplement was completed by Sir Richard Colt Hoare and published in 1819. At the time of his death Eustace's literary reputation was such that he was said to have been offered an advance of £2000 by his publisher, John Murray, for a didactic poem on 'the culture of the youthful mind' (*Byron's Letters and Journals*, 5.263).

G. MARTIN MURPHY

Sources Gillow, *Lit. biog. hist.* · J. Clayton, *Sketches of biography* (1825), 375–402 · *Catholic Magazine*, 1 (1831), 60, 306–7 · *Catholic Magazine*, 2 (1832), 96–8, 200–02 · *Catholic Magazine*, 3 (1833), 32 · B. N. Ward, *The eve of Catholic emancipation*, 3 vols. (1911–12), vol. 1 · F. C. Husenbeth, *The life of … John Milner* (1862), 398–9, 401–5 · *The correspondence of Edmund Burke*, 9, ed. R. B. McDowell and J. A. Woods (1970), 102 · *Lord Byron: the complete poetical works*, ed. J. J. McGann, 2 (1980), 262–3 · G. Oliver, *Collections illustrating the history of the Catholic religion in the counties of Cornwall, Devon, Dorset, Somerset, Wilts, and Gloucester* (1857), 513–14 · P. J. Corish, *Maynooth College, 1795–1995* (1995), 17, 32, 453 · J. H. Whitfield, 'Mr Eustace and Lady Morgan', *Italian studies presented to E. R. Vincent* (1962), 166–89 · *GM*, 1st ser., 85/2 (1815), 372 · *Byron's letters and journals*, ed. L. A. Marchand, 5 (1976) · J. P. Smith, 'The Catholic registers of Costessey or Cossey Hall, Norfolk', *Miscellanea, XII*, Catholic RS, 22 (1921), 276–303, esp. 280

Archives BL, corresp., Add. MSS 22976, fol. 273; 39312 | Sheff. Arch., Fitzwilliam MSS

Eustace, Sir Maurice (1590×95–1665), lord chancellor of Ireland and speaker of the Irish House of Commons, was the eldest son of the three sons and five daughters of John FitzWilliam Eustace (d. 1623) of Harristown, co. Kildare, and his wife, Catherine. His father was a protestant member of a largely Catholic old English family based in counties Kildare and Carlow, and was reported to have raised his children 'in the true religion and good literature' (*CSP Ire., 1647–60*, 103). Maurice entered Trinity College, Dublin, in 1610, graduating BA in 1615, proceeding MA in 1618, becoming a fellow of the college in 1617, and lecturing in Hebrew. He seemed destined for an ecclesiastical career, but turned to the study of law and entered Lincoln's Inn on 24 May 1619, where he secured an allowance from the king on the recommendation of the privy council. He was called to the English bar on 20 June 1625 and admitted to King's Inns, Dublin, on 25 January 1627 or 1628. 'According to his own account, he always took time by the forelock, studying most at seasons when others played and arousing apprehension lest he should over-exert himself' (Ball, *Judges*, 1.263). Reckoned a leading counsel he was rumoured to earn 'forty gold pieces in a morning' (Ball, *Judges*, 1.264). He was confirmed in possession of his father's property in co. Kildare in 1627 and received grants of lands and property there and in counties Carlow, Wexford, and Dublin, augmenting them with leases. In 1629 he received a king's letter which appointed him king's serjeant for Ireland, but the post had already been filled; he secured the post when next vacant in 1634. In 1633 he married Charity, or Cicely (1605/6–1672), daughter of Sir Robert Dixon, lord mayor of Dublin and a Kildare landowner, and his wife, Maud Bee.

From 1637 Lord Deputy Wentworth permitted Eustace to act as an assize judge on the basis of his post as serjeant. He was elected to the Irish parliament for Athy in 1634, and in 1640 was returned for co. Kildare and elected as speaker. His speech on the opening of parliament celebrated a land at peace, in contrast to much of Europe and to the recent Irish past: now 'every one of us doth sit in Safety at Home under his own Roof; our Swords are turned into Plow-shares, and we have wholly forgotten the Use of War'. He alluded to the 'great and high Honour' bestowed on Ireland in having a parliament which could not be bound by that of England, a matter of some controversy within a few years (*Journal of the House of Commons … Ireland*, 1.135–6).

Eustace was knighted in 1640. As compensation for loss of practice while acting as speaker he was awarded £1000 in 1641 and reversions to leases of former monastic lands in counties Galway and Kildare in 1645. Ormond, the royalist lord lieutenant, named him one of his executors in 1642, and he was appointed to treat with the confederate Catholics for a cessation in 1643. His wartime losses were recognized through successive grants of confiscated land and of office: escheator of Leinster on 9 February 1644, reversion to the post of master of the rolls on 22 January 1645, deputy attorney-general in 1646. He acted as an adviser to Ormond in negotiations for a peace settlement with the confederates from 1644, though by June 1645 he expressed his frustration with 'this ungrateful people [who] goe about to worke upon his Majestie's necessities … to their own inevitable ruin' (Gilbert, 4.339). Yet after Ormond had departed, handing Dublin over to the English parliamentarians in 1647, Eustace spoke up for accommodation, urging Ormond to overcome the fact that the Catholics 'deserved verie ill' and to undertake the 'glorious work to preserve a nation from extirpation' and perhaps 'introduce a perpetuall settlement' of the country (ibid., 6.206–7).

Eustace was arrested by the parliamentarian authorities and detained at Chester, perhaps for as long as seven years. In 1655 he resumed his legal practice in Dublin, still not above suspicion, but was favoured by Henry Cromwell. He was even named to a committee to consider a second college for the University of Dublin. As the restoration of Charles II loomed he was named one of the Irish convention's commissioners to the new monarch.

With the Restoration Eustace received his reward. He claimed he was 'now grown too old to perform any public service. I desire no such post' (Ball, *Judges*, 1.272). Even so he was appointed lord chancellor of Ireland on 9 October 1660 with fee of £1000 and supplementary pension of £1500, and was sworn in as one of three lords justices on 1 January 1661. He received confirmation of his inheritance, with substantial additional awards in counties Kildare and Dublin. The house he had built at Harristown had been destroyed in 1648 but he now built there again. Yet he was already expressing concern that the projected land settlement would be too favourable to the adventurers and soldiers of the 1650s. He found himself at odds with his fellow lords justices, Mountrath and Orrery, both of whom had served the Commonwealth regimes, and whom he accused of failing to discriminate between 'the noisome goats and the harmless sheep' among recent settlers in the kingdom (ibid., 1.273). Most of the lands secured to him in 1662 were in fact regranted to 'innocents' from the earlier confiscations. He appears to have acted in the interests of the Catholic branches of the Eustaces who had suffered confiscation of their property; much of it was awarded to him and subsequently handed back or bequeathed to his kin. Instead he appears to have made purchases, notably of the Portlester estate in co. Meath, once associated with the family. 'In office, he was to prove cavalier to the point of embarrassing his patron', Ormond (Clarke, 300). In 1661 Ormond had criticized his allowing Catholic lawyers (including ex-confederates) to practise and his approving Catholic appointments to the commission of the peace. He also acted to quash attempts to exclude Catholic peers from the Irish Lords.

Eustace's term as lord justice ended when Ormond was sworn in as lord lieutenant on 27 July 1662, but he remained as chancellor. By 1662 he was reported to have succumbed to successive bouts of 'melancholy' and by 1663 Clarendon was searching for a possible successor, hoping Eustace would be willing to retire. Though excused from attending the privy council through ill health any threat to his office seems to have 'acted as a tonic' (Ball, *Judges*, 1.275). In March 1664 Ormond admitted to Clarendon that he found Eustace, as chancellor, 'not so fit as he hoped' and he would 'not be disobliged if a fitter man were put in his place' (Ogle and others, 5.381).

Eustace owned a 'magnificent house' in Dame Street, Dublin (McGrath, 152), later building a house at nearby Chapelizod. He sold his lands in this area to the crown to be incorporated in the Phoenix Park, then being developed by Ormond, though only half the purchase price of £10,000 had been paid over at his death. At Baltinglass, co. Wicklow, he undertook to build and endow church, school, bridge, and market, which led to the town being elevated to a parliamentary borough, with civic rights vested in him. Charles II offered him a peerage but, lacking legitimate children, he suffered 'even greater melancholy' over the succession to his lands and potential title, and the latter had not been passed at the time of his death, following a 'paralytic attack' (Ball, *Judges*, 1.274–5) in 1665, probably on 22 June. He was accorded a state funeral at St Patrick's Cathedral, Dublin, on 7 July; but it may be that his body had already been buried or was afterwards reinterred on ancestral lands at Castlemartin, co. Kildare, where he had wished to be buried. His estate passed partly to his natural son, Maurice, but mostly to his nephews, John and Maurice, while his will allowed for funds for a lectureship in Hebrew in Trinity College, Dublin.

Eustace's career exemplified a variation on the difficulties faced by the old English gentry from whom he sprung. Though his protestantism spared him the dilemma of squaring loyalty to faith and crown, his abiding concern was to secure the position and loyalty of his kin and with them of the old colony in Ireland. His efforts were not in vain, but he was swimming against the tide of the rise of the 'New English' in Ireland, and even in the pale, where the Eustaces had been a force for centuries.

R. M. ARMSTRONG

Sources B. McGrath, 'A biographical dictionary of the membership of the Irish House of Commons, 1640–1641', PhD diss., University of Dublin, 1997 · E. F. Tickell, 'The Eustace family and their lands in co. Kildare', *Journal of the Kildare Archaeological Society*, 13/pts 2–3 (1946–63), 307–41, 364–413 · F. E. Ball, *The judges in Ireland, 1221–1921*, 2 vols. (1926) · *History of the Irish confederation and the war in Ireland … by Richard Bellings*, ed. J. T. Gilbert, 7 vols. (1882–91) · L. J. Arnold, *The Restoration land settlement in county Dublin, 1660–1688* (1993) · R. Lascelles, ed., *Liber munerum publicorum Hiberniae … or, The establishments of Ireland*, later edn, 2 vols. in 7 pts (1852) · J. R. O'Flanagan, *The lives of the lord chancellors and keepers of the great seal of Ireland*, 2 vols. (1870) · *CSP Ire., 1625–70 · Journal of the House of Commons … Ireland*, 28 vols. (1753–91) · *Calendar of the Clarendon state papers preserved in the Bodleian Library*, ed. O. Ogle and others, 5 vols. (1869–1970) · F. E. Ball, 'Some notes on the Irish judiciary in the reign of Charles II [pt 1]', *Journal of the Cork Historical and Archaeological Society*, 2nd ser., 7 (1901), 26–42, vii–ix · A. Clarke, *Prelude to Restoration in Ireland* (1999) · W. P. Baildon, ed., *The records of the Honorable Society of Lincoln's Inn* [incl. *Admissions*, 2 vols. (1896), and *Black books*, 6 vols. (1897–2001)]

Eustace, Roland Fitz. *See* FitzEustace, Roland, first baron of Portlester (*d.* 1496).

Euston Road School (*act.* 1937–1939), artists, was the staff and former students of the School of Drawing and Painting, which opened on 4 October 1937 at 12 Fitzroy Street, London, under the direction of Claude *Rogers (1907–1979), Victor *Pasmore (1908–1998), and William *Coldstream (1908–1987), and which moved its premises to 314/316 Euston Road in February 1938. The terms 'Euston Road group' and 'Euston school' first appeared in print in a review, 'Present and future', by Clive Bell (1881–1964), in the *New Statesman and Nation* (5 November 1938), with reference to the aforementioned painters together with (Frank) Graham *Bell (1910–1943) and Lawrence *Gowing (1918–1991). Although Bell did not officially teach at the school he was closely involved in its theoretical basis.

Gowing, who greatly admired Bell's intellect, was an outstanding student who in his later career described himself as 'pupil of William Coldstream'. What all these painters had in common was a certain probity of approach towards representational painting; technically it involved measuring proportional relationships of distances (to a greater or lesser degree), an acute eye for subtle tonal and colour relationships, and a restrained but highly sensitive touch with the brush. They shared a desire to make their realist art accessible to 'the man in the street'; this last characteristic had strong socialist overtones, promoted most by Bell and to a lesser degree by the others.

In April 1938 Bell and Coldstream spent three weeks in Bolton, Lancashire, staying in a working-class boarding-house and painting cityscapes with smoky factory chimneys as part of a scheme devised by Tom Harrisson (1911–1976), for his Mass-Observation experiment, to see how Boltonians would respond to paintings of their city in several different styles. Ironically Bell's and Coldstream's two realistic views of Bolton (Coldstream's now in the National Gallery of Canada, Ottawa) were not particularly popular with the people surveyed. In November 1938 an exhibition, 'Fifteen paintings of London', was held at the Storran Gallery, which included the Euston-Roaders. Wishing to draw in a random cross-section of the ordinary public, the organizers sent out private view cards to everyone named Brown (some allege that it was Green) in the Post Office directory. In retrospect four of the most memorable paintings there were Coldstream's *St Pancras Station* (priv. coll.), Pasmore's *The Flower Barrow* (Art Gallery of South Australia, Adelaide), Rogers's *Regent's Park* (Laing Art Gallery, Newcastle), and Gowing's *Mare Street, Hackney* (Shrewsbury Technical College, Shropshire). Comparable to these is Bell's *The café* (Manchester City Galleries), showing members of the group at a breakfast counter, which was first exhibited with the down-to-earth title *Forty-Four Goodge Street*.

The Euston Road School became known for its teaching of objective observation. But this was not done in a narrow or doctrinaire manner, as their prospectus makes clear:

> The direct contact and exchange of ideas between artists and students is important and is an advantage which hitherto students have been able to enjoy only through private acquaintanceship. In teaching, particular emphasis will be laid on training the observation, since this is the faculty most open to training. No attempt, however, will be made to impose a style and students will be left with the maximum freedom of expression.

Visiting teachers included Vanessa Bell (1879–1961) and Duncan Grant (1885–1978), two older Bloomsbury painters whose English version of post-impressionism, congenial as it no doubt seemed to some students, had little in common with the dynamics of the younger principals. The atmosphere was casual but not undisciplined. The difference in personalities of the teachers was remarkable: Rogers large and ebullient, very practical in his advice and adept at demonstration; Pasmore very friendly but engrossed in his own work, breaking off every now and then to boom out gnomic pronouncements; and Coldstream, the least visible, dashing in and out between commissioned portrait sittings and other urgent affairs but, as the most rigorous of them all in his methodology, exercising an enormous influence over his admirers. One of these was B. A. R. (Sam) Carter (b. 1909), who later taught with Coldstream at the Slade School of Fine Art for many years, and who was to write an authoritative article on the history of perspective for *The Oxford Companion to Art* (1970). What gave the school a special social kudos, however, was probably its Bloomsbury ambience and literary connections. Both Adrian Stokes (1902–1972), the writer and critic whose book *Colour and Form* was published in 1937, and the poet Stephen Spender (1909–1995) regularly attended the life classes. An apocryphal story is that one day Spender came in and announced to Bell (who was then barely surviving on a meagre income as a journalist), 'this morning I decided to give up poetry and become a painter'. 'Well now isn't that interesting', snapped Bell, 'because this morning I decided to give up painting and become a poet!'

With the outbreak of the Second World War, in September 1939, the Euston Road School closed its doors and the principals dispersed. During the months known as the phoney war Bell and Rogers retreated to paint and grow vegetables at Rodwell House in Suffolk, which was owned by Helen Anrep (1885–1965), who had befriended and encouraged the young painters ever since she lived at Gordon Square with Roger Fry (1866–1934). Coldstream and Pasmore remained in London, in adjacent studios in Fitzroy Street, and early in 1940 ran a one-day-a-week rump life class with half a dozen students. A small wartime exhibition, 'Members of the Euston Road group'—organized by the Contemporary Art Society at the behest of Sir Kenneth Clark (1903–1983)—was held at the Ashmolean Museum, Oxford, in 1942, when most of the members were in the armed forces (Bell was killed in training in 1943). Coldstream became a war artist, painting portraits of Indian army regular soldiers at a transit camp in Egypt in 1943–4; *Havildar Ajmer Singh* (*Man in a Yellow Turban*), in the Tate collection, London, is an outstanding example. He also painted some pure, Corot-like landscapes of war zones during the Italian campaign of 1944–5. Pasmore meanwhile developed a new discipline in his painting after his release from imprisonment as a conscientious objector. He produced a series of paintings of the River Thames at Hammersmith in which the drawing and design became, in stages, increasingly formalized; he regarded this as a logical development from the objective approach of the Euston Road painters. His 'last and final Euston School painting' (his words) was *The Studio of Ingres* (1945–7; ex. Sothebys, 18 June 1997), in which the pose of his nude female model is a tribute to Ingres, although she is freshly observed from life (MS Pasmore, priv. coll.). Thereafter he changed direction completely—while holding it to be a logical move—to abstract art, and pursued this for the rest of a distinguished career.

In 1945 Pasmore, teaching painting at Camberwell School of Arts and Crafts, persuaded the principal to employ Coldstream, Rogers, and Gowing as well; a new post-Euston Road dialogue continued there for three or four years. Two more group exhibitions were held: 'The Euston Road School and others' (May 1948; Wakefield Art Gallery, Yorkshire), organized by the painter William Townsend (1909–1973), which included several much younger artists; and a more historical one that was toured by the Arts Council during 1948 and 1949. That was the last time that the term Euston Road School was used officially. By then the principals had all gone their separate ways, Coldstream taking some of the best students with him to the Slade School, but leaving behind at Camberwell a strong tradition of training in representational painting that continued there for many years.

BRUCE LAUGHTON

Sources B. Laughton, *The Euston Road School* (1986) · A. Bowness and L. Lambertini, *Victor Pasmore*, 1 (1980) [includes text by the artist] · *The paintings of William Coldstream, 1908–1987* (1990) [exhibition catalogue, Tate Gallery, London, 1990] · b. cert. [Edwin John Victor Pasmore] · m. cert. [Wendy Blood] · *WW* · personal knowledge (2004) · *The Times* (26 Jan 1998)
Archives Tate collection · Tate collection, corresp., journals, and MSS [Sir William Menzies Coldstream] | Tate collection, album of Christmas cards [Pasmore, Victor] · Tate collection, corresp. [Gowing, Lawrence] · Tate collection, corresp. and MSS [Bell, Graham] [photocopies] · Tate collection, corresp. with Lord Clark [Bell, Graham] · Tate collection, corresp. with Lord Clark [Coldstream, William] · Tate collection, corresp. with Lord Clark [Gowing, Lawrence] · Tate collection, corresp. with Lord Clark [Pasmore, Victor] · Tate collection, letters to Sir William Coldstream [Pasmore, Victor] · Tate collection, letters to C. G. H. Dicker [Coldstream, William] · U. Birm. L., corresp. with Lord Avon [Coldstream, William] · UCL, corresp. relating to Arts Council [Coldstream, William] · UCL, The Townsend Journals | SOUND BBC Sound Archives
Likenesses photograph, c.1938, Tate collection, Tate Gallery archive, Claude Rogers papers; repro. in Laughton, *Euston Road School*, 171 · photograph, c.1939, repro. in *Paintings of William Coldstream*, 110

Eva fitz Harding (d. c.1173), monastic patron, was the wife of *Robert fitz Harding, a wealthy citizen of Bristol and lord of Berkeley, whom she had probably married by c.1140. According to later tradition she was associated with Robert in the foundation of the abbey of St Augustine, Bristol. Early charters of Robert recording grants to this house do little to suggest that she played an important role. But the fifteenth-century Abbot Newland's roll states that both Robert and Eva were prayed for daily as founders of the abbey, and that the anniversary of Eva's death, as founder, was marked by the feeding of fifty poor men. As 'Domina Eva' she witnessed charters of her husband, which can be dated c.1150–70. Eva and Robert had five sons and three daughters. One son, Henry, was archdeacon of Exeter from 1162 to 1188. Eva died on 12 March c.1173.

According to the fifteenth-century evidence of both Abbot Newland and Robert Ricart, town clerk of Bristol, Eva was buried by the side of her husband in the quire next to the abbot's stall. This is unlikely to have been the case, however: late twelfth-century monastic founders were generally buried in the chapter house or cloister. Ricart also states that Eva was the founder of a community of nuns, the Magdalenes, and that she became its prioress.

This must refer to the nunnery of St Mary Magdalene situated on St Michael's Hill. If this was a separate foundation it is probable that she would have been buried there, and Robert and Eva may have been founders of a double community or at least linked establishments. Early charters refer to the community of St Mary Magdalene as a hospital and reveal the presence of both brothers and sisters. Perhaps the women were originally linked to St Augustine's for the provision of alms and developed as a more separate community later. Before his death on 5 February 1171 Robert entered the abbey as a canon. Eva may have taken the veil at St Mary Magdalene's at the same time.

Eva's parentage is not established. Later tradition claimed that she was of royal blood—the daughter of Estmond and a sister of William the Conqueror called Godiva. Claims of royal descent from the king of Denmark were made for Robert, and it is probable that these reflect a desire to accentuate the founders' importance to their communities rather than any historical accuracy.

S. P. Thompson

Sources I. H. Jeayes, 'Abbot Newland's roll', *Transactions of the Bristol and Gloucestershire Archaeological Society*, 14 (1889–90), 117–30, esp. 125–6 · *The maire of Bristowe is kalendar, by Robert Ricart*, ed. L. Toulmin Smith, CS, new ser., 5 (1872), 22 · I. H. Jeayes, *Descriptive catalogue of the charters and muniments in the possession of the Rt. Hon. Lord Fitzhardinge at Berkeley Castle* (1892), xi, 5, 8, 15 · J. Smyth, *Lives of the Berkeleys* (1883), vol. 1 of *The Berkeley manuscripts*, ed. J. Maclean (1883–5), 44, 59 · *DNB* · J. C. Dickinson, 'The origins of St Augustine's Bristol', *Essays in Bristol and Gloucestershire history: the centenary volume of the Bristol and Gloucestershire Archaeological Society*, ed. P. McGrath and J. Cannon (1976), 109–26 · C. D. Ross, ed., *Cartulary of St Mark's Hospital, Bristol*, Bristol RS, 21 (1959), 205–7 · F. Barlow, ed., *Exeter, 1186–1257*, English Episcopal Acta, 12 (1996), 307 · R. B. Patterson, 'Robert fitz Harding of Bristol: profile of an early Angevin burgess–baron patrician and his family's urban involvement', *Haskins Society Journal*, 1 (1989), 109–22 · O. Barton, 'Our oldest families: the Berkeleys', *The Ancestor*, 8 (1904), 73–6 · R. Atkyns, *The ancient and present state of Glostershire*, 2nd edn, 2 pts in 1 (1768), pt 1, p. 136 · GEC, *Peerage* · S. Thompson, *Women religious: the founding of English nunneries after the Norman conquest* (1991), 45–6 · G. R. C. Davis, ed., 'Cartulary of St Augustine's Abbey, Bristol', *Medieval cartularies of Great Britain: a short catalogue* (1958), no. 77 [microfilm, Bod. MS Film Dep. 912, and Gloucester RO, T66/M.F.1071] · BL, Additional charter 6518

Evan [**Evans**], **Edward** (1716–1798), nonconformist minister and poet, was born in March 1716 in Tir Evan Rhys, a farmhouse at Llwydcoed, Aberdâr, Glamorgan, the son of Ifan ap Siôn ap Rhys, a weaver and smallholder noted for his geniality and fondness for poetry. Reputedly a skilled harpist when he was only eleven years old, Evan's services in that capacity were later frequently in demand. The *englynion* he sang in the eisteddfod held in Cymer, Glamorgan, on 1 March 1735 show that, although he was then only eighteen years old, he was already taking an intelligent interest in Welsh prosody. He received very little education in his early, formative years, but he was later taught by James John, a hooper and farmer from Aberdâr, who was well read in both Welsh and English and a fairly good poet.

After working for a few years as a weaver, Evan was apprenticed, at the age of twenty-three, to carpentry and glazing under Lewis Hopkin (1707/8–1771) at Hendre Ifan Goch, in the parish of Llandyfodwg, Glamorgan, and it was his close association with Hopkin which explains the main features of his career as a Welsh bard and nonconformist. Under his guidance Evan applied himself to mastering the Welsh strict metres and the contents of the bardic grammar, and he soon set about composing an 'exemplifying ode', that is, a composition incorporating one of each of the canonical twenty-four strict metres. It was probably Hopkin who also aroused his interest in English literature, and Evan's work contains Welsh translations of some of the poems of Pope, Samuel Butler, Bishop Horne, and Isaac Watts. It may also have been under the influence of Hopkin and the religious congregation at Cymer, Porth, that Evan became a nonconformist.

Edward Evan worked for many years as a carpenter and glazier—in seventeen parishes in all. After his first marriage in 1744 to Margaret Thomas of Penderyn (*d.* 1774), he settled for a while at Cefnpennar Isaf, Glamorgan, but in 1749 he moved to the farm of Ton-coch, above Dyffryn House, Mountain Ash, where he remained until his death in 1798. About 1748 (or possibly a little earlier), he joined the nonconformist congregation at Cwm-y-glo, and when a separate church—'the Old Meeting-House'—was later established near Aberdâr, he became one of its most prominent members and a preacher. An orthodox Calvinist in his earlier days, according to Edward Williams (Iolo Morganwg; 1747–1826), he later turned towards Arminianism and, later still, to Arianism. However, he did not take a prominent part in contemporary theological disputations. Some of his political views were of a distinctly radical nature. From 1 July 1772 until 1796 he was pastor of the Old Meeting-House. About 1776 he married Mary Llywelyn of Rhigos (1733–1824). The second marriage produced two sons, Edward (1776?–1862), and Rhys (1779–1867), who was of some literary repute and an ardent supporter of eisteddfodau.

During his lifetime Evan published two prose works: *Gwersi i blant a dynjon jeuaingc, mewn dau gatecism* (1757), a Welsh translation of one of Samuel Bourn's catechisms; and *Golwg ar gynheddfau gwasanaeth, ac anrhydedd gwasanaethwyr Crist* (1775), a sermon delivered at one of the Presbyterian gatherings. He also published in 1767, jointly with Lewis Hopkin, a Welsh translation in the *cywydd* metre of the book of Ecclesiastes, a translation first begun by David Thomas (*d.* 1735), who proceeded no further than the first chapter.

Evan died at Ton-coch on 21 June 1798, aged eighty-two, and was buried in St John's churchyard, Aberdâr. After his death some of his poetry was published at Merthyr Tudful under the title *Caniadau moesol a duwiol* (1804). Three enlarged editions were later published under the title *Afalau'r awen*—at Merthyr in 1816 and 1837, and at Aberdâr in 1874. His verse, which shows that he remained a jovial character to the end of his days, was very popular among the Welsh inhabitants of upper Glamorgan. He became a somewhat romantic figure after it was claimed in the *Gentleman's Magazine* in November 1789 that he and Iolo Morganwg were by then the only surviving legitimate descendants of the 'Ancient British Bards'.

C. W. Lewis

Sources R. T. Jenkins, 'Bardd a'i Gefndir (Edward Ifan o'r Ton Coch)', *Transactions of the Honourable Society of Cymmrodorion* (1946–7), 97–149 · G. J. Williams, *Traddodiad llenyddol Morgannwg* (1948), 245–50 [and other references in index] · C. W. Lewis, 'The literary history of Glamorgan from 1550 to 1770', *Glamorgan county history*, ed. G. Williams, 4: *Early modern Glamorgan* (1974), 535–639, esp. 618–19 · E. Evan, *Afalau'r awen*, 4th edn (1874) · G. J. Williams, *Iolo Morganwg a chywyddau'r ychwanegiad* (1926), 3, 200 · *GM*, 1st ser., 59 (1789), 976 · I. Morganwg [E. Williams], NL Wales, MS 13159A (Llanover MS C. 72), 142–5 · L. Hopkins, *Y fel gafod* (1813), 98–9, 101 · *Yr Ymofynnydd* (1847), 149–53 · *Yr Ymofynnydd* (1854), 58 · *Yr Ymofynnydd* (1892), 206 · Iolo Fardd Glas, *Cyfaill y Cymru* (1797), 12–13 · J. J. Evans, *Dylanwad y chwyldro Ffrengig ar lenyddiaeth Cymru* (1928)
Wealth at death almost certainly modest

Evance, Sir Stephen

Evance, Sir Stephen (1654/5–1712), goldsmith and entrepreneur, was born at New Haven, New England, the son of John Evance, a London merchant who had emigrated to Virginia in 1635 and traded with the Caribbean islands. Evance presumably spent his youth in New England but in 1669, when he was fourteen and perhaps as a result of his father's recent death, he was sent to London as an apprentice to the Goldsmiths' Company. He prospered there, being admitted a freeman of the company in 1676 and elected prime warden in 1691. During these years he became acquainted with leading figures in many of the larger trading companies, notably the Hudson's Bay Company, for which by 1681 he had become the principal cashier, responsible for most of its financial transactions. His work for the company concentrated on the sale of North American furs, and on establishing trade with Russia in furs and hemp. Within twenty years he owned more than £4300 in stock, but his own considerable loans to the company, on which it often depended to remain solvent, were frequently jeopardized by late or incomplete reimbursements. The profits from his investments, when paid, were dispersed among diverse business interests, which included leasing a trading ship, purchasing stock in the White Paper Makers', Royal African, and East India companies, financing various schemes for manufacturing steel, guns, and hollow sword blades, exploiting royal copper mines in New England, and developing a newly invented air pump to allow divers to salvage wrecks.

From 1689 Evance became one of the crown's main domestic lenders. In that year alone he raised loans to the crown amounting to £175,000, and in addition supported the government's commitments to supplying armies in Ireland and Flanders, and provided subsidies for the allies in Europe. He was able to finance these enterprises by drawing bills of exchange on the Amsterdam market while accepting payment in the form of government debt. Evance was rewarded for these endeavours by a knighthood and several gifts of money, as well as being appointed the king's jeweller and a commissioner of excise and wine licences.

His support for the government would explain Evance's return to parliament in 1690 for Bridport, a borough recently granted a new charter and comprising a reduced corporation purged of all court opponents. Outside the house, Evance's natural opposition to the formation of the Bank of England, which threatened his financial activities, was criticized by the lords justices, but this posed no immediate threat to his importance as a financier and man of business. However, early the following year he was censured for accusing two of his fellow excise commissioners of Jacobitism, and when he was threatened with a prosecution for defamation his backers considered that his financial usefulness to the government was outweighed by both his political liability and emerging evidence of irregularities in his government contracts; by the summer he had been removed from the excise commission.

Evance's political career was swiftly terminated by this crisis but his involvement in public life, and in a variety of entrepreneurial schemes supported by his business contacts, continued to occupy him. In 1700 he was appointed, for the second time, governor of the Hudson's Bay Company, and the following year he led a consortium to raise a voluntary subscription of £1 million to create a company manufacturing woollen goods. He also attempted to secure a private bill for the company's incorporation. By 1702 Evance's private trading had brought him into contact with Thomas Pitt, governor of Madras, and the latter's son Robert, and when Robert returned from Madras with his father's celebrated diamond Evance was chosen as its custodian. Soon afterwards Evance embarked on an unsuccessful speculative enterprise insuring merchants, but as his losses overwhelmed him so did his business partners desert him. He was declared bankrupt early in January 1712, reputedly owing more than £100,000. On 5 March, at Woodford, in the house of Sir Caesar Child, a relative, he hanged himself from an attic window. He was unmarried, and his remaining stock, held in trust for him and amounting to £4000, was settled on his niece.

HENRY LANCASTER

Sources apprentice books, Goldsmiths' Hall, London, esp. apprentice bk II, fol. 182 · E. E. Rich, ed., *Hudson's Bay copy booke of letters* (1957) · N. Luttrell, *A brief historical relation of state affairs from September 1678 to April 1714*, 6 vols. (1857); repr. (1969) · E. Rich, *The history of the Hudson's Bay Company, 1670–1870*, 1: *1670–1763* (1958) · F. G. Hilton Price, *A handbook of London bankers*, enl. edn (1890–91) · *CSP dom.*, 1689–1700 · W. A. Shaw, ed., *Calendar of treasury books*, 9–15, PRO (1931–5) · *British Mercury* (5–7 March 1712) · BL, Add. MS 22851, fols. 123–8 · S. Quinn, 'Gold, silver, and the Glorious Revolution: arbitrage between bills of exchange and bullion', *Economic History Review*, 2nd ser., 49 (1996), 486 · *Le Neve's Pedigrees of the knights*, ed. G. W. Marshall, Harleian Society, 8 (1873), 435 · J. C. Hotten, *The original lists of persons of quality* (1874), 84
Wealth at death approx. £4000: BL, Add. MS 22851, fols. 123–8

Evans, Abel

Evans, Abel (1675–1737), Church of England clergyman and poet, son of Abel Evans and his wife, Sarah, *née* Spalding (*bap.* 1638?), was baptized at St Mary, Whitechapel, Stepney, on 26 February 1675. He entered Merchant Taylors' School, London, on 11 March 1685, matriculated from St John's College, Oxford, on 2 July 1692, and proceeded to the degrees of BA in 1696, MA on 23 March 1700, BD on 26 April 1705, and DD on 16 May 1711. He was ordained in 1700 and presented to the college living of St Mary's, Kirtlington, near Oxford, but retained his college fellowship until 1724. He resigned Kirtlington on 4 June 1707.

Evans's low-church sermon at the university church on 23 August 1705 vexed the Oxford tories, but its praise of the duke of Marlborough earned him the favour of the duchess, who sent him a gift of venison. In December 1706 he further antagonized colleagues by publicly reflecting upon the president and most of the fellows of his college, for which he was deprived on 20 February 1707 of the chaplaincy which he had held for only eight months.

About 1709 Evans fell into line with the preponderant toryism and high-churchmanship of Oxford, was reinstated in his college chaplaincy (which he held until February 1713), and served at various later times as senior bursar, dean of divinity, and vice-president. As a tory he also wrote *The Apparition*, 'a dialogue betwixt the Devil and a Doctor concerning the rights of the Christian Church', published in January 1710. This long satire in heroic couplets against Matthew Tindal, the deist, was popular enough to run into four authorized editions and five piracies.

Evans's *Vertumnus* (June 1713), an epistle in octosyllabic couplets to Jacob Bobart (1641–1719), the botanist, is shorter and more agreeable. The modern attribution of a Miltonic imitation, *Pre-Existence* (1714), to Evans is highly unlikely (Chapin, 178–80).

On 31 July 1713 Evans was presented to the college living of St Giles', Oxford. Thomas Hearne noted the politics of his sermons, from ultra-toryism on 25 September 1715, when Evans hinted that George I was a usurper, to 'a most vile, Whiggish Sermon' on 30 January 1719 (*Remarks*, 5.121, 6.294). Hearne concluded that Evans was seeking preferment from the whigs, but in the event Evans's college remained his only ecclesiastical patron. It provided him with the vicarage of St Andrew, Great Staughton, Huntingdonshire, where he was incumbent from 3 January to 6 December 1723, and the rectory of St Dunstan, Cheam, Surrey, to which he was presented on 31 May 1724 and where in less than three years he was 'at odds wth all his Parish, & talks of Law, but is yet got no farther than Epigrams' (*Correspondence of Edward Young*, 54).

Evans is remembered as an epigrammatist, though the originality of his well-known epitaph on Vanbrugh beginning 'Lie heavy on him, Earth' has been questioned; also as the admirer and friend of Alexander Pope, who praised him in *The Dunciad* (1728, 2.108). Although the Cheam benefice had been held by no fewer than five bishops, Evans was still rector when he died there on 18 October 1737; he was buried there four days later. He never married. He was survived by two widowed sisters and a niece, who administered his estate. Six naturalized, 'realistic' pastorals by Evans, variously dated from 1707 to 1726, were first printed in volume 5 of Nichols's *Select Collection of Poems* (1782); they were from a manuscript, now lost, which, it seems, contained at least thirteen pastorals.

JAMES SAMBROOK

Sources *Remarks and collections of Thomas Hearne*, ed. C. E. Doble and others, 11 vols., OHS, 2, 7, 13, 34, 42–3, 48, 50, 65, 67, 72 (1885–1921), vols. 1–8 • Foster, *Alum. Oxon.* • *The correspondence of Alexander Pope*, ed. G. Sherburn, 1–2 (1956) • *IGI* • *The correspondence of Edward Young, 1683–1765*, ed. H. Pettit (1971), 54 • J. Nichols, ed., *A select collection of poems*, 8 vols. (1780–82), vols. 1, 3 • C. Chapin, 'The poems of Abel Evans, 1679–1737', *N&Q*, 236 (1991), 178–81 • C. J. Robinson, ed., *A register of the scholars admitted into Merchant Taylors' School, from AD 1562 to 1874*, 1 (1882), 314 • private information (2004) [keeper of the archives, St John's College, Oxford] • C. J. Marshall, *History of Cheam and Sutton* (1936), 33 • J. Carswell, *The old cause: three biographical studies in whiggism* (1954), 134–5
Archives BL, letter to Jacob Tonson, Add. MS 28275, fol. 82

Evans, Anne (1820–1870). *See under* Evans, Arthur Benoni (1781–1854).

Evans, Arise [Rhys, Rice] (*b. c.*1607, *d.* in or after **1660**), prophet, usually known by his adopted name of Arise Evans, was born a mile from Barmouth, in the parish of 'Llangluin', presumably Llangelynnin. Rhys or Rice Evans was the son of Evan Evans (*d. c.*1614), who was a prosperous member of the gentry class, rich enough to subvent a local curacy by the gift or loan of a 'little Tenement of Land' (Evans, 2). Arise Evans claimed that he could trace his lineage back six generations, and beyond that to legendary times. He had at least two older siblings and one younger brother, perhaps a half-brother (ibid., 1–3, 35).

Evans's native tongue was Welsh. He was educated by a local clergyman, and learned to read English at a young age and with such facility that 'all concluded that God had designed me for some great work' (Evans, 2). However, his father died when he was seven, leaving a will which apportioned property to his named family but from which Arise's name was excluded, presumably because it had not been revised since his birth. His mother shortly remarried, and he moved with her to 'a place four miles off, called *Maisellan Kaderise*', probably the Maes-y-llan farmstead near Llanfihangel-y-Pennant, on the south-west flank of Cadair Idris (ibid., 6). He worked in several other households until he was contracted to work for a tailor from Chester. At eleven he returned to his mother, now widowed a second time, in Maes-y-llan.

About the age of fourteen Evans began to experience visions. A third marriage took his mother to Wrexham, together with Arise. His contract with his first employer was fulfilled, and he was bound apprentice to another tailor, Hugh Jones, also of Chester, an autodidact, who recognized both intelligence and spirituality in Evans, and encouraged both. Jones was responsible for the nickname Arise: he told Evans to call himself by that name and reproved those who called him Rhys or Rice, maintaining, as Evans relates, 'they knew not the English of my name, giving me a charge not to answer any but such as did call me Arise. … This is the main cause why I write myself Arise, for there was a great providence of God in bringing me to understand my name' (Evans, 11–12). On completing his apprenticeship, Arise worked as journeyman tailor in Coventry and then, from 1629, in London, where he lodged in Creed Lane by Blackfriars Gate, moving by 1633 to Salisbury Court. His lapsed spirituality was reanimated by a sermon he heard at Blackfriars Church, and an intense period of Bible study, confirmed by recollection of earlier visions, led him to understand that 'the King and the Kingdom was to be destroyed suddainly' (ibid., 17). His distracted and inspired condition lost him his journeyman employment, forcing him to seek out new masters, where, sitting at the shop-board, he 'beheld the Angel of the Lord all in white, stood upon the shop-board with a flaming sword in his hand ready to destroy me' (ibid., 20).

Confirming his fears by randomly consulting the Bible, Evans felt thus prompted to communicate his prophecy of doom to Charles I, whom he followed to Greenwich, and he gave him the news in a letter presented as a petition. His landlord subsequently declined to give him further lodging out of fear of reprisal. Realizing that his first communication had been ignored, and prompted by further visions, he returned to Greenwich, declaring his revelation publicly to bishops and other worthies around the court.

Evans was then prompted to seek out Robert Devereux, third earl of Essex, in his London house, and to prophesy to him that he would be general of an army that would 'execute judgement upon the Court' (Evans, 28). Essex rewarded him but 'turned it all into a jest' (ibid., 29). While to prophesy that Charles I would face difficulties may have been unremarkable, his identification in 1633 of the future role of Essex, documented with plausible circumstantial detail in his own account, must have seemed singularly uncanny by 1642, and he frequently cites this success in substantiation of his later prophecies.

Most of Evans's prophetic utterances related to English politics, and though he anticipated the civil war he was not himself a puritan. Indeed, when at Essex's presumably amused suggestion he repeated his prophecy to Robert Greville, Baron Brooke, he defended the Church of England to Brooke's puritan chaplain (Evans, 30). Arise returned to Wales to advise his relatives of the impending crisis, though his sanity was questioned and with his family's consent he was kept in custody until his mental health improved. He married, probably in 1635, though promptly left his wife to return to London, lodging in Blackfriars, and frequenting the court and Somerset House to repeat his prophecies. He was arrested and brought before Sir Francis Windebank, to whom he retorted, 'you are the Kings Secretary, and I am Gods Secretary' (ibid., 46). He was sent close prisoner to the Gatehouse in Westminster, where he remained until 1637, when his wife successfully petitioned for his release. He returned with her to Wrexham and had children before returning to London, once more settling in Blackfriars and working as a journeyman tailor.

Prompted by a voice heard in a trance, Evans attacked Anabaptists and other sectaries, pursuing with reproofs the General Baptist Thomas Lambe the soap-boiler and defending the Church of England. Moving frequently in such radical circles in the mid-1640s and maintaining his own prophetic status, he was rumoured to have represented himself as Jesus Christ. Thomas Edwards, the great heresiographer, basing his account on this incorrect intelligence, included him in the second part of *Gangraena* as 'one Sectarie who maintained and affirmed he was Jesus Christ' (Edwards, 2.173). The Independents in Lambe's circle regarded him as 'a Decoy sent to catch them', and drove him from their company (Evans, 59). He was arrested for the alleged blasphemy and brought before the recorder, Sir John Glynne, at the Old Bailey, and later before his deputy, who remanded him to Bridewell. He signed a confession:

> I know the Bench and people thought I recanted, but alas they were deceived, for I never beleeved nor understood my self any otherwise then thus. ... [Christ] is my Saviour, and I am but his bought servant to do his will.   (ibid., 65)

At the following sessions, he was released.

Evans detected a concerted presbyterian conspiracy to imprison him or have him secured in Bedlam, and in the late 1640s, while retaining his loyalty to the captive king, in reaction he sought out Cromwell and his circle, visiting him and Henry Ireton at Cromwell's house in Drury Lane, and urging him to release Charles I and restore him to power.

Evans published about twenty-five pamphlets. The overwhelming majority date from the period 1652–5. Several are addressed to Cromwell, and the recurrent theme is that Charles II should be restored and that Cromwell is the destined agent to accomplish that task. The idiom is generally prophetic, and sometimes he bases his prophecies on interpretations of the visionary experiences of others, as in *The Bloudy Vision of John Farly* (1653) or *A Message from God by a Dumb Woman* [*Elinor Channel*] *to the Lord Protector* (1653). These tracts are either printed for the author to be sold at his house in Long Alley in Blackfriars, or bear the spoof imprint of 'Giles Convert', in allusion to the most active publisher of radical tracts, Giles Calvert. His autobiography and apologia, *An eccho to the voice from heaven, or, A narration of the life, and manner of the special calling, and visions of Arise Evans* (1652), is both a vivid evocation of the radical margins of London political and religious life in the 1640s and fascinating documentation, from an age of faith, of a mind obsessed with intrusive and delusional thoughts. As early as 1652, Evans referred to himself as 'being old, not able to labour' (Evans, 84), and it is unlikely that an unemployed journey-tailor could have financed such a publishing campaign without the assistance of presumably royalist funding.

Evans's last publication, *To the most High and Mighty Prince, Charles II*, dates from 1660. Early in the Restoration John Aubrey, citing Elias Ashmole as his source, relates that he was touched for the King's Evil:

> Arise Evans had a fungous nose, and said it was revealed to him that the king's hand would cure him, and at the first coming of King Charles II into St James's Park he kissed the king's hand, and rubbed his nose with it, which disturbed the king, but cured him.   (Aubrey, 128)

No later life record is known. Since so much of his prophetic output had related to anticipating the Restoration, the absence of further publication claiming credit and personal justification may suggest he died shortly after his meeting with the restored king.

THOMAS N. CORNS

Sources A. Evans, *An eccho to the voice from heaven* (1652) · T. Edwards, *Gangraena, or, A catalogue and discovery of many of the errours, heresies, blasphemies and pernicious practices of the sectaries of* this time, 2 (1646), 173 • M. Tolmie, *The triumph of the saints: the separate churches of London, 1616–1649* (1977) • *Ordnance survey of England and Wales: OS map 59*, Ordnance Survey (1878) • *DNB* • J. Stow, *A survey of London*, rev. edn (1603); repr. with introduction by C. L. Kingsford as *A survey of London*, 2 vols. (1908); repr. with addns (1971) • J. Aubrey, *Miscellanies upon various subjects* (1857), 128 • J. M. Dodgson, *The place-names of Cheshire, 5/1: The place-names of the city of Chester*, English Place-name Society, 48 (1981), 5–7

Evans, Arthur Benoni (1781–1854), writer, was born at Compton-Beauchamp, Berkshire, on 25 March 1781, son of the Revd Lewis Evans (1755–1827) of Basaleg, Monmouthshire, vicar of Froxfield, Wiltshire, and his wife, Ann, eldest daughter of Thomas Norman. Lewis Evans was a well-known astronomer, and held for many years the professorship of mathematics at the Royal Military Academy, Woolwich. Arthur Evans was educated at the college school, Gloucester, of which his uncle and namesake was headmaster; his courageous character earned him the nickname the Bold Arthur. He went up to St John's College, Oxford, in October 1800, and graduated BA on 21 February 1804, MA in 1820, and BD and DD in 1828. In addition to Greek and Latin, he learned Hebrew, French, Italian, Spanish, German, and Icelandic. His other interests included music—he played several instruments—and art; he sketched in pencil, crayon, and sepia. He also studied geology and botany, and his knowledge of Greek, Roman, and English coins, of which he had a large collection, was considerable.

Evans was ordained to the curacy of Hartpury, Gloucester, in August 1804, and after receiving priest's orders in September 1805 was in the following month appointed professor of classics and history in the Royal Military College, then just established at Great Marlow, Buckinghamshire. He moved with the college to Sandhurst in October 1812. In June 1819 he married Anne (1791–1883), third daughter of Captain Thomas Dickinson RN of Bramblebury, near Woolwich, with whom he had four sons and two daughters.

Evans resigned his chair at the Royal Military College in 1822, and went to Britwell, near Burnham, where he prepared pupils for the universities and served the curacy of Burnham until 1829. In that year he accepted the headmastership of the free grammar school at Market Bosworth, Leicestershire. He also held successively the curacies of Bosworth, Carlton, and Cadeby between 1829 and 1841. Clerical appointments never brought Evans more than £100 a year, but as a schoolmaster he was very successful and prosperous. His publications included sermons, poems, and pastoral and polemical works, as well as *Leicestershire Words, Phrases, and Proverbs* (1848), which was reprinted by the English Dialect Society in 1881. He died at the free grammar school, Market Bosworth, on 8 November 1854.

One of Evans's sons, John *Evans (1823–1908), became a leading archaeologist and numismatist, serving as treasurer of the Royal Society (1878–98) and president of the Society of Antiquaries (1885–92). Another, Sebastian *Evans, was a designer for glass work and a poet; he also edited the *Birmingham Daily Gazette* from 1867 to 1870, and was for some time the editor of *The People*, a Conservative

Sunday journal. Evans's daughter, **Anne Evans** (1820–1870), author, was born on 4 June 1820, probably at Britwell Court, near Burnham. She never married, and after the death of her father she moved to Kensington. Her health broke down in 1867, and she was an invalid until her death on 19 February 1870. Anne Evans wrote poetry and music, which were edited and published with a memoir after her death by Anne Thackeray Ritchie (1880). Lady Ritchie described her as a 'diffident woman, who … unconsciously touched and influenced us all by her intense sincerity of heart and purpose' (Ritchie, viii).

G. C. BOASE, *rev.* MARI G. ELLIS

Sources *GM*, 2nd ser., 43 (1855), 100–02 • Foster, *Alum. Oxon.* • *Men of the time* (1887) • A. T. Ritchie, 'Memoir', in A. Evans, *Anne Evans: poems and music*, ed. A. T. Ritchie (1880)

Evans, Sir Arthur John (1851–1941), archaeologist, was born at Nash Mills, Hemel Hempstead, on 8 July 1851, the eldest of the three sons of the distinguished archaeologist and numismatist Sir John *Evans, and his first wife, Harriet Ann, younger daughter of his maternal uncle John Dickinson, paper maker. Joan *Evans was his much younger half-sister. Arthur resembled his father in features and tastes, and as early as 1866 accompanied him on his first visit to the Somme gravels, and himself found a 'palaeolith' *in situ*. He became a collector, a draughtsman, and a linguist; unusual short sight did not debar him from enjoyment of country life, and enabled him to detect minute details such as artists' signatures on Greek coins and gems.

From the preparatory school of C. A. Johns, a naturalist, at Chipperfield, Hertfordshire, Evans entered Harrow School, reaching the sixth form in 1867. He was placed fourth in the examination for leaving scholarships in April 1870, distinguishing himself in English literature, Greek and Latin verse, modern languages, and natural science, and by editing *The Harrovian* and a satirical *Pen-Viper* which was suppressed. He was already an ardent liberal, and a keen Slav partisan in Balkan politics. In October 1870 he entered Brasenose College, Oxford, and was placed in the first class in modern history in 1874.

A year's study at Göttingen was preceded and followed by adventures in Bosnia (1871), Herzegovina, Finland, and northern Scandinavia (1873–4), and in 1875 Evans sent to the *Manchester Guardian* letters republished in 1876 as *Through Bosnia and the Herzegovina on Foot, during the Insurrection, August and September 1875*; this was followed by *Illyrian Letters* (1878). In 1878 he married Margaret, eldest daughter of the historian Edward Augustus *Freeman, an accomplished and devoted comrade until her death in 1893. At Ragusa he found in the Casa San Lazzaro a convenient centre for the study of language, antiquities, and customs, and spent six years there in all. During the Crivoscian insurrection of 1882 he was arrested and condemned to death by the Austrians, but was reprieved and expelled. His political ideal was a 'South Slavonic monarchy built out of Austria and the Balkans'; to this he recurred vigorously in 1914–16 and later he saw it temporarily realized.

Sir Arthur John Evans (1851–1941), by Sir William Blake Richmond, exh. RA 1907

His archaeological studies in these years were published in *Archaeologia*, volumes 48 and 49 (1884, 1885), and summarized in his unpublished Ilchester lectures delivered at Oxford in 1884, and in his Rhind lectures given at Edinburgh in 1895. In Italy and Sicily he collected vases and coins, and wrote articles entitled 'The "Horsemen" of Tarentum' (*Numismatic Chronicle*, 9, 1889) and 'Syracusan "medallions" and their engravers' (ibid., 11, 1891).

With this wide experience and equipment Evans was in 1884 appointed keeper of the Ashmolean Museum at Oxford which had fallen into neglect and whose collection was overlapped by the classical sculpture and vases of the Randolph Gallery in Beaumont Street, where Sir W. M. Ramsay, the first occupant of the Lincoln and Merton chair of classical archaeology and art, was provided with a small space for a library and a cast collection. With the munificent help of C. D. E. Fortnum and Greville Chester the collections were removed in 1894 to a new building behind the Randolph, repeatedly enlarged and always overflowing, and in 1908, after many years of controversy and negotiation, the combined institutions were supplied with a single board of visitors.

The conditions of Ashmole's keepership prescribed travel and lectures, and Evans took full advantage of both. In 1890 he gave a summer course on British prehistoric antiquities, but he was not a popular lecturer, and most of his later discoveries were announced at meetings of the British Association. Meanwhile he excavated a Roman villa at Frilford, near Oxford, and in 1891 the late Celtic

urnfield at Aylesford in Kent. In 1893 he acquired an estate called Youlbury, near Oxford, and created there an earthly paradise and a second home to three generations of friends.

In his Rhind lectures, Evans studied the highly controversial question of the influence of ancient oriental cultures on those of early Europe. As a young man he had been influenced by the work of Heinrich Schliemann at Troy, Mycenae, and Tiryns, by Wolfgang Helbig's *Das homerische Epos* (1884) with its Italian archaeology, and by Arthur Milchhoefer's *Die Anfänge der Kunst in Griechenland* (1883) inferring from the geographical distribution of certain engraved seal-stones that Crete had been a principal centre of 'Mycenaean' culture. In 1889 the Ashmolean acquired such a seal-stone from Greville Chester; Evans found others in Athens (1893) and in the Berlin Antiquarium. Such surface finds could be explored even in a malcontent province of Turkey. In 1893 came news of painted pottery in the Candia Museum from the Kamárais cave on Mount Ida, identical with 'Aegean imports' announced by Sir Flinders Petrie from Kahun, a twelfth dynasty site in the Fayyum. The same year Evans announced his clue to the existence of picture-writing in Greek lands, and in March 1894 he travelled in Crete, collecting from the peasant women many prehistoric seal-stones inscribed with pictorial signs. He copied a clay tablet (afterwards destroyed) with a linear inscription, and noted masons' marks on pre-Hellenic walls. These finds were announced to the British Association in August (*Journal of Hellenic Studies*, 14, 1894) and extended in subsequent years (ibid., 17, 1897). The general bearing of these discoveries was communicated to the British Association in 1896 (*The Eastern Question in Anthropology*) and their significance for Greek religion in 'Mycenaean tree and pillar cult' (*Proceedings of the British Association*, 1896; *Journal of Hellenic Studies*, 21, 1901). In 1897, when war was imminent between Greece and Turkey, he explored the 'megalithic' structures of Tripolitania, finding them to be Roman oil-presses.

In 1894 Evans had acquired a share, under Ottoman law, of the estate at Kephála, near Candia, classical Knossos, where 'Mycenaean' remains had been found in 1878; so when the Turks evacuated Crete in 1899 he was able at once to gain full possession, and excavate in association with the British School of Archaeology at Athens and its director, D. G. Hogarth. There was no overload of later remains, and some of the best finds were close to the surface. The first season (1899–1900) revealed an elaborate palace, of the late Bronze Age (*c*.1700–1200 BC), with many clay tablets inscribed in the 'linear' script already detected, superimposed upon earlier buildings with 'Kamárais' pottery (*c*.2000 BC), brilliant frescoes, and imported Egyptian and Babylonian objects. Work continued for eight seasons, followed by intermittent enterprises in the 'palace', its suburbs, and cemeteries. The principal works of art were exhibited in London in 1903, and more fully in 1936. The first volume of *Scripta Minoa* was published in 1909, the second in 1952, and *The Palace of Minos at Knossos* in four volumes between 1921 and 1935 (index, 1936). Concurrent excavations by Italians at Phaestos and Hagia Triada, by the French at Mállia, by Americans at Gourniá, Mochlos, and other sites, and by the British School at Praesos, Palaikastro, and Zakro, supplemented the record of Knossos, and made it necessary to present the new prehistoric culture as a whole. Evans christened it 'Minoan', after the legendary Cretan ruler Minos, and proposed in advance a ninefold classification into 'early', 'middle', and 'late', each subdivided into periods I, II, and III, to correspond with major phases of civilization both in Crete and in Egypt, and with extensive demolitions and reconstructions at Knossos. Below the early Minoan lay a deep Neolithic deposit, and above the latest Minoan a rapid replacement of Bronze Age by early Iron Age occupancy. Less symmetrical crises were the great earthquakes which ended Middle Minoan II (*c.*1700 BC) and Late Minoan II (the specifically 'palace' style, *c.*1400 BC). In Late Minoan III a growing divergence between the culture of Crete and that of the 'Mycenaean' or 'Helladic' mainland marked the growing predominance of the latter over a wide colonial region, from Cyprus to Sicily. This preliminary scheme for classification was published in Athens in 1905, London in 1906, and Rome in 1912. The distinction of a separate mainland culture was never accepted by Evans.

The deep substructures of the palace of Knossos having become choked with hillwash before they collapsed, staircases and even floors could be reconstructed to an unusual extent, to the third storey and even above it. Wall frescoes, shattered or insecure, were removed to the museum and replaced by copies; courtyards were paved, and much skilful restoration—preferred to mere consolidation—made the complex structure vividly intelligible as the abode of a vigorous and original mode of life. Evans's villa overlooking the site served as an abode for a curator and for visiting archaeologists, and a considerable estate contributed to the endowment. In 1926, being no longer able to supervise it personally, Evans agreed with the Greek government to convey the whole property in trust to the British School of Archaeology at Athens, but he returned to excavate the 'royal tomb' hard by in 1931. *A Handbook to the Palace of Minos at Knossos*, by John Devitt Stringfellow Pendlebury, the then curator, was published in 1933. Both palace and museum were undamaged in the German invasion of 1941.

Resigning the keepership of the Ashmolean in 1908, and completing *Scripta Minoa I*, Evans gained time for other interests. Always a strong liberal, in 1909 he was induced to offer himself as tariff reform candidate for the University of Oxford; but there were cross-currents, and he was persuaded by Lord Lansdowne to withdraw. Balkan affairs were becoming urgent, and Lord Curzon was pressing university reforms upon Oxford. Evans was of an age and eminence to preside over many learned societies. He was a founder of the British School at Athens (1886) and of the British Academy (1901). In 1909 he received the royal gold medal of the Royal Institute of British Architects, an honour rarely conferred upon a layman; in 1911 he was knighted. He was the fourth generation of his family to be

elected (1901) a fellow of the Royal Society and in 1936 he received its Copley medal, to add to the gold medals of the Swedish Academy and the Society of Antiquaries, and many other academic and scientific distinctions. Honorary degrees were conferred on him by the universities of Edinburgh, Dublin, and Berlin, and he was an honorary fellow of his own college, Brasenose.

During the war years Evans was president of the Society of Antiquaries (1914-19) and of the British Association (1916-19), and as a trustee of the British Museum helped, in 1918, to rescue that institution from the Air Board, and hasten its rehabilitation. He took an active part in South Slav politics, Italy now replacing Austria as the oppressor of nationalities.

Although his health was normally excellent, and his physical energy inexhaustible—'he never worked when he was tired, and was seldom too tired to work'—a severe operation in 1938 restricted Evans's movements to local explorations near his home, but in 1939 he went by air to Geneva, returning along the Rhine. Until the summer of 1941 he went frequently to the Ashmolean Museum, and another operation did not prevent him from receiving on his ninetieth birthday the congratulations of the Hellenic Society and the British School at Athens, and showing with pride his account of a newly traced Roman road from Oxford to the south coast. Three days later, on 11 July 1941, he died at Youlbury.

In a very long career Evans made generous use of great gifts, wide experience, and ample means, for he inherited two fortunes in middle life, when Cretan work was most costly. His knowledge was wide and profound, his judgement and flair unerring, and his encouragement of others unfailing. He had a genius for friendship, and was most at home among simple people. He loved children and guests, outdoor life, and his woods and gardens at Youlbury, which he intended as a 'private open space' in concert with the Oxford Preservation Trust, together with the 'Jarn' mound raised on the crest of Boars Hill, and its wild garden. He was a generous patron of the Boy Scouts, giving them a training station at Youlbury and an interest in his long study of beacons, and of craftsmanship of all kinds. In his greater enterprises he enlisted the loyal help of many different allies, learned and simple, and in Crete he was a popular hero after the liberation. In archaeology, although his historical knowledge was wide, and his political views emphatic, his strength, like his father's, was as a critic of craftsmanship and style. Here his judgements were seldom challenged, and always supported by strictly archaeological evidence, often of his own discovery: as he put it '*omne ignotum pro falso* is a dangerous motto in the Minoan field' and more widely.

In person Evans was of small build, thickset, of great strength and endurance, with a dark complexion and aquiline features. A fine portrait of him in his prime, by Sir William Richmond (1907), is in the Ashmolean Museum.

Evans was a man of such formidable authority that his interpretations, though challenged in his lifetime, aroused much greater controversy after his death. The discovery in 1952 by Michael *Ventris that the majority of the tablets in 'linear' script excavated by Evans at Knossos were written in an early form of Greek necessitated a radical reappraisal of Evans's views: for Greek had not been the inherited language of Minoan Crete. Either, therefore, palatial Knossos in its heyday had been under the domination of Greek-speaking Mycenaeans, or the inscribed tablets, over 4000 in number, must all date to the period after the fall of the palace, which Evans had dismissed as one of an occupation by 'squatters'. This latter alternative was supported by the late dating of other tablets in this 'Linear B' script from mainland Greek sites. A new line of attack then developed: that the fall of palatial Knossos must itself be brought down to c.1200 BC. This proposal, originally advanced by L. R. Palmer in 1960 in a tendentious form which involved falsification of the stratigraphy on Evans's part, was soon moderated; but, even a hundred years after Evans's first discovery of the script, it has still not led to a consensus. The one point on which scholars are now united is that Evans seriously overrated the dominance of Crete in the civilization of the prehistoric Aegean, and correspondingly undervalued the strength and independence of the culture of the Greek mainland and, to a lesser extent, of the Cyclades.

J. L. MYRES, *rev.* A. M. SNODGRASS

Sources J. Evans, *Time and chance: the story of Arthur Evans and his forebears* (1943) · J. L. Myres, 'Sir Arthur Evans, 1851–1941', *PBA*, 27 (1941), 323–57 · J. L. Myres, *Obits. FRS*, 3 (1939–41), 941–68 · *Slavonic Review* (1946) · personal knowledge (1959) · W. D. Niemeyer, 'Mycenaean Knossos and the age of Linear B', *Studi Micenei ed Egeo-Anatolici*, 23 (1982)
Archives AM Oxf., Knossos notebooks and papers; photographs, plans, and maps of Knossos excavations, press cuttings, offprints, etc. · JRL, letters to the *Manchester Guardian* · S. Antiquaries, Lond., corresp. about his planned publications on Knossos · UCL, school of Slavonic and east European studies, papers relating to the Balkans | BL, corresp. with Macmillans, Add. MS 55219 · Bodl. Oxf., corresp. with J. L. Myres
Likenesses W. B. Richmond, oils, exh. RA 1907, AM Oxf. [*see illus.*] · F. Dodd, pencil drawing, 1935, NPG · D. Evans, marble bust, 1936, AM Oxf. · R. Guthrie, crayon drawing, 1937, AM Oxf. · bronze bust, Knossos, Crete, Greece
Wealth at death £182,460 14s. 0d.: probate, 12 Dec 1941, *CGPLA Eng. & Wales*

Evans, Benjamin (1740–1821), Independent minister, was born on 23 February 1740 at Ffynnon Adda, Meline, Pembrokeshire, the son of Daniel Evans, farmer and drover, and his wife, Ann. After attending schools in Glandŵr and Monkton, in Pembrokeshire, he completed his formal education at the Haverfordwest grammar school, aged fifteen, without attending a dissenting academy.

Though his father was a Baptist, Evans and his mother joined the Independents at Moylgrove, where he was baptized on 24 March 1764. He began to preach, and undertook a preaching tour through south Wales. Influenced by Lewis Rees, he went to the north in 1768 for a trial period at Llanuwchllyn, Merioneth; being approved, he was ordained minister there in 1769. There were sixty members and 600 'hearers'. He married about 1770 Ann Lloyd,

daughter of the Revd Daniel Lloyd of Brynberian; apparently, there were no children. The Independents encountered considerable persecution in north Wales, and he obtained in 1772 a high court judgment compelling the magistrates to register a house for the purpose of worship at Cutiau, near Barmouth. He moved in 1777 to Albany Church, Haverfordwest, and thence to Tre-wen, Cardiganshire, in June 1779, where he remained for over forty years until his death.

Evans was a high Calvinist by persuasion, and steadfastly opposed the advance of Arianism and Arminianism in the area. His predecessor at Tre-wen had Arminian sympathies, but Evans, showing great tact, gradually and successfully led back the congregation to Calvinism. His members founded several new churches, of which he took charge. He was also a pioneer of the Sunday school movement. The distribution of tracts among his members by the Baptists obliged him to defend his position on infant baptism, which he did most ably, bringing him into dispute with William Richards of Lynn, who argued the opposite viewpoint. Evans published (in Welsh) *Letters on Baptism* in two editions (1788 and 1789), a translation of Mathias Maurice's *Social Religion* (1797), and two works on the sufferings of the black slaves in the West Indies, as well as sermons, catechisms, hymns, and poetry.

Evans was a rather short man of strong and shapely build, with an intense look. An acknowledged leader of his denomination, Evans's services to his countrymen, through the pulpit and the press, were very great. He was taken ill in 1816, and died in Tre-wen on 2 March 1821, survived by his wife. He was buried in Hawen Chapel.

D. R. L. JONES

Sources J. T. Jones, *Geiriadur bywgraffyddol o enwogion Cymru*, 1 (1867) · J. Bulmer, *Memoirs ... of the Rev. Benjamin Evans* (1826) · T. Rees and J. Thomas, *Hanes eglwysi annibynol Cymru*, 4 (1875) · R. T. Jenkins, *Hanes cynulleidfa hen gapel Llanwchllyn* (1937) · *DWB* · will proved, 1821, NL Wales [Benjamin Evans, Tre-wen, parish of Brongwyn, St Davids PR] · W. Rowlands, *Cambrian bibliography / Llyfryddiaeth y Cymry*, ed. D. S. Evans (1869)
Wealth at death under £100; left entire estate, incl. house and fields, to wife: will, 1821, NL Wales

Evans, Beriah Gwynfe (1848–1927), journalist and author, was born at Bailey Street, Bryn-mawr, Brecknockshire, on 12 February 1848, the son of a notable Congregationalist minister and writer, Evan *Evans (1804–1886), and his wife, Mary Valentine. Evans was educated at the Beaufort British school and through 'private study'; he began his career as a schoolteacher at Gwynfe (which he adopted as a second forename) and Llangadog, Carmarthenshire. On 28 July 1871 he married Anne, the daughter of Michael Thomas, a farmer, of Y Neuadd, Gwynfe. Their second son, William John Evans, became a prominent figure in Welsh educational and cultural life.

Beriah Evans soon developed other aspirations beyond schoolteaching, notably as a writer. At a youthful age he became a pioneer of Welsh-language drama and won a prize at the Llanberis national eisteddfod in 1877 for his play on the fifteenth-century nationalist leader, Owain Glyndŵr. He established in 1880 a new literary monthly,

Cyfaill yr Aelwyd ('Friend of the Hearth'), which continued to be published until 1894, and became increasingly active as an author. He was also the active secretary of the Society for the Utilization of the Welsh Language, a body of educationists and scholars formed in 1885 to press for Welsh to be recognized as a grant-earning subject under the elementary education code on an equal footing with other languages: its objective was achieved a few years later.

Evans, however, was now more involved with political journalism, and at this time also began a long and momentous association with David Lloyd George. In 1887 he left schoolteaching for journalism, becoming editor of the Welsh section of the *Cardiff Times* and the *South Wales Daily News*. In 1892 he moved to Caernarfon, in Lloyd George's own constituency, to become until 1895 managing editor of the Welsh National Press Company, a company with which Lloyd George was involved and which published the influential weekly *Y Genedl Gymreig* along with the *North Wales Observer* and other newspapers. He was also the long-term Welsh correspondent of the *Liverpool Mercury* and *Liverpool Daily Post*. In 1895 he joined Lloyd George as secretary of the Cymru Fydd league, seeking to unite Welsh Liberalism behind the cause of Welsh self-government. But for all his efforts the movement collapsed early in 1896 through acrimony between north and south Wales Liberals.

Evans then turned back to dramatic and literary activities. He was prominent on the gorsedd of the national eisteddfod; he wrote the satirical political tract *Dafydd Dafis* (1898), and a work on Welsh revivalists, *Diwygwyr Cymru* (1900). His play on Owain Glyndŵr was performed during the investiture of Edward as prince of Wales at Caernarfon in 1911. Later, in 1917, he became editor of the important Independent weekly newspaper, *Y Tyst*.

During the Second South African War Evans was among the majority of Welsh Liberals who supported the imperial cause, contrary to Lloyd George's passionate pro-Boer sympathies. However, Evans continued to be close to Lloyd George's brand of radical Liberalism. His newspapers campaigned hard for the 1909 budget and the remainder of Lloyd George's social policies. After the First World War began he wrote his best-known work: a highly eulogistic biography, *The Life Romance of David Lloyd George* (n.d., 1915), published in a Welsh-language version in Utica, New York, in 1916. It drew on his previous relationship with its subject, while his conclusion speculated prophetically on Lloyd George becoming head of a post-war coalition government to promote imperial reconstruction.

Yet it was during the war that Evans, like other older radicals, began to drift away from his old hero. He now worked closely with the Welsh home-rule enthusiast Edward Thomas John, and he campaigned strongly to promote federal home rule in the wartime and post-war years. He also became far more sympathetic to the Labour Party. But, as throughout his career, it was his nationalism that dominated Evans's political stance, and in 1920 he defined his outlook as 'Welsh Nationalist'. He continued

to back John's abortive efforts on behalf of Welsh self-government, and in his last years joined the nascent nationalist party, Plaid Cymru, as did his son William John. He died in his home, Pen-y-bryn, East Twthill, Caernarfon, on 4 November 1927.

Evans is a notable representative of the nonconformist Liberalism that dominated Welsh politics following the general election of 1868. He was bound up with its achievements—church disestablishment, educational reform, recognition of the Welsh language and culture—along with the social and international aspirations of Liberalism. But in his later years he became a disillusioned critic of the failures of the national movement of his time, and of its inability to persuade the Welsh people to take self-government seriously or to promote the language with sufficient zeal. Short of stature with a neatly trimmed beard, he was a talented man whose outlook became increasingly out of date. After 1918 he was largely forgotten, while his historical plays fell out of fashion. Yet as a crusading journalist he played a major part in the civic Liberalism of Wales during Lloyd George's heyday between 1890 and 1918. Ideologically, Evans straddles the divide between the Liberal nationalism of the late-Victorian period, committed to national equality for Wales within the United Kingdom, and the cultural aspirations and political separatism of twentieth-century nationalists.   KENNETH O. MORGAN

Sources NL Wales, Timothy Lewis papers · papers of T. E. Ellis, Stuart Rendel, D. Lloyd George, E. Morgan Humphreys, NL Wales · E. Evans, 'Beriah Gwynfe Evans: ei fywyd a'i waith', PhD diss., U. Wales, Aberystwyth, 1989 · E. M. Humphreys, *Gwŷr enwog gynt: yr ail gyfres* (1953) · K. O. Morgan, *Wales in British politics, 1868–1922*, 3rd edn (1992) · K. O. Morgan, *Rebirth of a nation: Wales, 1880–1980* (1981) · K. O. Morgan, ed., *Lloyd George: family letters, c.1885–1936* (1973) · A. Mee, ed., *Who's who in Wales* (1921) · *DWB* · B. G. Evans, *Dafydd Dafis* (1898) · B. G. Evans, *The life romance of David Lloyd George* [1915] · b. cert. · m. cert. · d. cert.
Archives NL Wales, corresp. and papers | NL Wales, David Lloyd George papers · NL Wales, E. Morgan Humphreys papers
Likenesses photograph, repro. in Morgan Humphreys, *Gwŷr enwog gynt*, facing p. 120
Wealth at death £1289 17s. 4d.: probate, 13 Feb 1928, *CGPLA Eng. & Wales*

Evans, Brooke (1797–1862), nickel refiner, was born in Bull Street, Birmingham, the son of a woollen draper and tailor. He went to school in Singer's Hill, Birmingham, and Aldridge, Staffordshire. On leaving school at the age of fifteen he was apprenticed to a gun maker, and made his first acquaintance with metallurgy.

Having served his apprenticeship, Evans travelled to the United States, and entered into partnership with a gun maker in New York. He was only partially successful in this trade, and he returned to England in 1826. He then went off prospecting in Central America, where he became an indigo planter and merchant in Guatemala. In the course of a voyage home, the captain of his ship and several of the crew were seized with yellow fever in the Gulf of Mexico. Evans apparently took command of the ship, and navigated her successfully to the British Isles. He afterwards purchased a small business in the glass and lead trade at Stratford upon Avon, where he lived six years with his sister. This business prospered, and enabled him to save up to £6000.

Charles Askin, a veterinary surgeon who was greatly interested in chemistry and metals, was a friend of Evans. While staying in Warsaw, Askin had discovered that a white metal called argentan contained nickel and he and Evans experimented with methods of refining nickel from speiss (an impure mixture of cobalt, nickel, and other metals), left after the preparation of cobalt blue for painting pottery. They were successful, and Askin went into partnership with Messrs H. and T. Merry to manufacture German silver, an alloy of nickel, copper, and zinc. Askin gained £1500 from the venture, and subsequently went into partnership with Evans. In 1835 they built works in Birmingham, where they successfully produced refined nickel from nickel-speiss. The demand for Evans and Askin's refined nickel and German silver increased rapidly, because it was durable, attractive, and able to be stamped, spun, cast, and wrought.

The speiss produced by the cobalt blue manufacturers was quite insufficient for their requirements, however, and Evans explored Europe for new sources of ores containing nickel. He heard of its existence at the mines of Dobschan in Hungary, visited the place, and bought all the ore for which he could afford to pay, although this new ore contained half as much cobalt as nickel. As cobalt was detrimental to the German silver, and as Askin could not by his mode of refining separate these metals, new techniques had to be developed. The demand for nickel was meanwhile steadily increasing, especially from the Birmingham electroplating business of Elkingtons; and by steady perseverance Evans and Askin discovered a process by which they obtained refined nickel in large quantities. To meet the demand Askin visited some nickel mines near Geisdal in Norway in 1847, where he died suddenly on 25 August. He was taken home and buried at Edgbaston. The nickel business was continued by Evans, who died at Edgbaston on 15 September 1862 and was buried near his partner. The firm of Evans and Askin was taken over by Henry Wiggin, who had joined the business in 1842 and had become a partner six years later.

ROBERT HUNT, rev. CARL CHINN

Sources J. A. Langford, ed., *Modern Birmingham and its institutions: a chronicle of local events, from 1841 to 1871*, 2 (1877) · 'The electro-plate trade and Charles Askin', *Birmingham Daily Mail* (11 Dec 1878) · S. Barker, 'Nickel German silver manufacture', *Birmingham and the midland hardware district*, ed. S. Timmins (1866) · D. E. C. Eversley, 'Industry and trade, 1500–1880', *VCH Warwickshire* · R. Wrightson, *Wrightson's new triennial directory etc.* (1818) · A. W. Wills, 'The chemical trades', *Birmingham and the midland hardware district*, ed. S. Timmins (1866)

Wealth at death under £35,000: resworn probate, Nov 1863, *CGPLA Eng. & Wales*

Evans, Caleb (1737–1791), Particular Baptist minister and college head, was born on 12 November 1737 in Bristol, the first child of Hugh Evans (1712–1781), Particular Baptist

minister and principal of the Bristol Baptist Academy, and his first wife, Sarah Browne (d. 1751), daughter of Joseph Browne of Bristol. Educated at Mile End Academy, Middlesex, Caleb received baptism as a believer at Little Wild Street Baptist Church, London, on 29 November 1753. He assisted Josiah Thompson at Unicorn Yard, London, from 15 September 1758, moving to Broadmead, Bristol, to assist his father on 12 August 1759. He was ordained co-pastor on 18 August 1767 and appointed tutor at Bristol Academy, succeeding his father as principal in 1781. Caleb married Sarah Jeffries (d. 1771), only daughter of the Revd Joseph Jeffries and his second wife, Miss Rickard, at St Andrew's, Pershore, on 19 April 1762; they had five children. Following her death on 7 November 1771, he married Sarah Hazle (d. 1817), only daughter of William and Judith Hazle of Bristol, at St James's, Bristol, on 7 December 1774.

Primarily Evans was concerned to provide able and evangelical ministers for English and Welsh Baptist churches. In 1770 he separated the academy from Broadmead church and put the academy on a sound financial basis as the Bristol Education Society, which provided voluntary support from individuals and churches for the education of 'pious candidates for the ministry ... [and] the encouragement of missionaries to preach the Gospel' (C. Evans, *The Kingdom*, 1775, 24). This significant breakthrough in Baptist ministerial training led to the formation of other Baptist colleges in England and Wales. In America a Bristol student, William Staughton (1770–1829), used Evans's model as the basis for Columbian College, the first American national Baptist university, now George Washington University. Evans received two honorary doctorates, one from Rhode Island College (1789), the other from King's College, Aberdeen (1790).

Evans's ordination statement in 1767 indicated his early commitment to the evangelical Calvinism propounded by Jonathan Edwards in America, and he commended Edwards to all his students. One student, John Sutcliff (1752–1814), minister at Olney, Northamptonshire, was profoundly influenced by Evans's commendation of Edwards and initiated prayer for revival on the Edwards pattern among local Baptist churches in 1784. He introduced Andrew Fuller, founder of the Baptist Missionary Society in 1792, to Evans's *An Address to the Serious and Candid Professors of Christianity* (1772), in which Evans uses the insights of Edwards to explain the distinction between natural and moral ability in man. Fuller's *The Gospel Worthy of All Acceptation* (1785), which quoted pages 11–13 of Evans's book verbatim, provided the theological key to liberating English Baptists from a sterile high-Calvinism into a vibrant, worldwide, missionary community. Evans himself undertook itinerant evangelistic preaching tours with students, the first to Cornwall in 1773. In 1769 Evans and John Ash of Pershore edited *A Collection of Hymns Adapted to Public Worship*, the first congregational Baptist hymnbook, which had 412 hymns, 275 of which were by Baptists, including some by Evans's personal friend Anne Steele.

Evans was a Hanoverian loyalist who celebrated annually Guy Fawkes night and King William's landing at Torbay on 5 November. In his *Political Sophistry Detected* (1776), he claimed the 'great *American question*' was intricately interwoven with 'the British constitution and British liberty', and that American resistance was 'one of the best causes in the world' (14, 35). In his *British Constitutional Liberty* (1775), he advocated radical political reform but refuted republican ideals. When John Wesley contended the king had power to tax his subjects without their consent, Evans disagreed. In *A Letter to Mr. Wesley* (1775) Evans charged Wesley with inconsistency, for in Bristol Wesley had supported an American-born radical parliamentary candidate, Henry Cruger. In addition Wesley, in his *Calm Address*, was not only guilty of serious plagiarism of Samuel Johnson's *Taxation No Tyranny* but also defended the legitimacy of the taxation of the American colonists, who had no parliamentary representation. In *A Letter to Mr. Wesley* Evans exposed these issues and eventually received a public apology from Wesley in *The Gazetteer* on 13 December 1775. The infamy of the slave trade was opposed vigorously in works by both authors. Among Evans's thirty pamphlets and sermons, those already listed, together with *The Remembrance of Former Days* (1779) and *British Freedom Realized* (1788), provide a comprehensive survey of his political thought.

In May 1791 Evans had a paralytic stroke; a second at Bristol on 9 August 1791 was fatal. His funeral at Broadmead, Bristol, was conducted by the Revd Samuel Stennett, and the Revd John Tommas spoke at the interment in Redcross Street burial-ground, Bristol, on 16 August 1791.

ROGER HAYDEN

Sources Bristol Baptist College, Clifton Down, Bristol, Caleb Evans MSS · church minute books, Broadmead Baptist Church, Bristol · notebook of Caleb Evans, Broadmead Baptist Church, Bristol · *Family chronicle of the descendants of Thomas Evans of Brecon, 1678–1857* (privately printed, [n.d., c.1870–c.1890]) · N. S. Moon, 'Caleb Evans: founder of the Bristol Education Society', *Baptist Quarterly*, 24 (1971–2), 175–90 · D. M. Lewis, ed., *The Blackwell dictionary of evangelical biography, 1730–1860*, 2 vols. (1995) · R. Hayden, 'Evangelical Calvinism among eighteenth-century Baptists with particular reference to Bernard Foskett, Hugh and Caleb Evans and the Bristol Baptist Academy, 1690–1791', PhD diss., Keele University, 1991, 209–40 · church books, Regent's Park College, Oxford, Angus Library · H. Abelove, 'John Wesley's plagiarism of Samuel Johnson and its contemporary reception', *Huntington Library Quarterly*, 59 (1997–8), 73–9
Archives BGS, geological sections · Bristol Baptist College, Bristol, MSS · Broadmead Baptist Church, Whippington Court, Bristol, notebook · NHM, notes and drawings
Likenesses oils, c.1780–1789, Bristol Baptist College

Evans, Caleb (1831–1886), geologist, was born on 25 July 1831 at 7 Pullins Row, Islington, the third of five children of John Evans (*d.* 1846), barrister, and his wife, Frances (*d.* 1848), daughter of George Knight of Headcorn, Kent. He was educated at University College School, London, until 1846, when the death of his father forced him to begin work, initially in a solicitor's office. From 1852 he was (like his elder brother) a clerk in the chancery pay office, until ill health forced his early retirement in 1882.

Evans's involvement with geology began after he attended lectures given in 1855 by, among others, the eminent anatomist Richard Owen. Evans excelled as a collector, and from 1858 specialized in the fossils of the Tertiary formations of the south of England, taking advantage in particular of exposures made in south London by the Metropolitan Board of Works in the course of its major sewerage schemes of the 1860s. He also collected extensively from the Chalk, and, during his annual vacations, investigated the strata of the Isle of Wight, Lyme Regis, Weymouth, Swanage, and Portsmouth. His geological work found formal expression in numerous scientific papers and field-meeting reports, published mainly in the *Proceedings of the Geologists' Association*; the most notable of these were 'On some sections of Chalk, between Croydon and Oxtead' (1870), and 'Geology of the neighbourhood of Portsmouth and Ryde' (1871). The former paper marks the first English attempt to subdivide the Chalk, an important geological formation in southern England, into zones correlatable with those previously established in continental Europe. Certain fossil crabs that Evans collected from the Lower Tertiary sediments of Portsmouth were subsequently described (by Henry Woodward) as new species. Evans also constructed geological models or relief maps, of England and Wales, and of specific areas therein, by pasting layer upon layer of cartridge paper to achieve the required topography, and then colouring the rock outcrops appropriately.

Because he was an amateur, most of Evans's geological work reached fruition under the auspices of the Geologists' Association. This he joined in February 1859 as one of its earliest and most active members, serving on its general committee for many years, acting as an auditor of its accounts, and leading its members on field meetings. On the strength of his geological work, in 1867 he was admitted as a fellow of the Geological Society of London. Evans never married, but domestically remained part of a tightly knit family, living for many years with his unmarried sisters and brother in Hampstead, where he died at 3 Downshire Hill on 16 September 1886.

ERIC F. FREEMAN

Sources *Proceedings of the Geologists' Association*, 10 (1887), 29–30 · private information (1888) · will, proved, 25 Oct 1886, Principal Registry, fol. 858 · 'Dr Williams's Library', PRO, RG 5 129 entry 2223 · will of Frances Evans, PRO, Prob 11/2081, fols. 380–81 · census returns, 1871, PRO, RG 10/189, fol. 76; 1881, RG 11/168, fol. 43 · will of John Evans, PRO, Prob 11/2046, fol. 279*v* · J. W. Judd, *Quarterly Journal of the Geological Society*, 43 (1887), 47–8 · *Geological Magazine*, new ser., 3rd decade, 4 (1887), 141–2 · *DNB* · membership lists, Geologists' Association
Archives BGS, geological sections · NHM, notes and drawings
Wealth at death £4188 3s. 11d.: probate, 25 Oct 1886, *CGPLA Eng. & Wales*

Evans, (David) Caradoc (1878–1945), novelist and short-story writer, was born on 31 December 1878 at Pant-y-croi, Llanfihangel-ar-arth, Carmarthenshire, the fourth of the five children of William Evans (1849–1882), auctioneer, and his wife, Mary (1848–1934), daughter of William Powell and his wife, Mary. His childhood was spent at Rhydlewis, Cardiganshire, where his widowed mother worked a 9 acre smallholding. Forced to leave the Rhydlewis board school at fourteen, Evans became an apprentice draper, suffering the tyranny of 'living in' at various south Wales and London stores. He read Robert Blatchford's socialist *Clarion* and the French and Russian short-story writers, and, following evening classes at the Working Men's College, took his chance in Fleet Street.

By 1915 Evans had become editor of *Ideas* (a Hulton's popular weekly) and had begun to publish the stories that would make his literary reputation. *My People* (1915) debunked the myth of rural Wales: Evans's Manteg (a fictionalized Rhydlewis) is a place of greed and violence, of patriarchal repression and chapel terrorism, all beneath the veneer of religion. Visceral Welsh antagonism countered London critical praise. Sermons were preached against him, his East Sheen windows stoned, and efforts made to suppress his book. *Capel Sion* (1916) and *My Neighbours* (1920) followed, the latter exploiting comic fantasy in its satire on the London Welsh—who in turn responded by wrecking a 1925 performance of *Taffy*, Evans's only play.

Evans published little in the 1920s outside assaults on Liberal nonconformity, judged a politically repressive force, stifling the intellect and imagination. As a journalist he prospered, first with the *Daily Mirror* (1917–23), then as acting editor of *T.P.'s Weekly* (1923–9), a middlebrow literary journal. An acquaintance described him at this time, his:

> hollow strong face, the mouth large, the eyes small and piercing, beneath a black felt hat, of which the turned-down brim keeps even the high cheek-bones of the creature in shadow. The speech is swift, hissing; the views it conveys invariably violent and violently phrased. (Blake, 61)

It was the violence of protest; his kindness and courtesy were manifest.

Nothing to Pay (1930), Evans's fine first novel, is a Swiftian fable of money worship in the underworld of drapery. His pleasure at its reception—H. G. Wells thought it 'true in all substantial particulars' (Wells, 147)—hid an inner turmoil. He had lost his job when *T.P.'s Weekly* folded and was involved with Marguerite Barczinsky [*see* Evans, Marguerite Florence Laura (1886/7–1964)], a best-selling novelist under the pseudonyms Countess Barcynska and Oliver Sandys, who urged that he abandon Fleet Street to become a full-time writer. With her he left London and his wife, Rose Jessie, *née* Sewell (*b.* 1876), the Lambeth jobmaster's daughter he had married on 25 December 1907.

At first the move seemed justified. Remarried on 22 March 1933 and settled at Aberystwyth, Evans published two more novels: the moderately successful *Wasps* (1933) and *This Way to Heaven* (1934), a critical disaster. Again his writing dried up, though controversy still clung around 'the best-hated man in Wales' (Stokes, 135): his portrait, by Evan Walters, was refused a Welsh showing (and knife-slashed across the throat while on display in London), and his draft for a broadcast talk rejected by the BBC in Wales. Yet the excellence of Evans's writing and his courage as dissident won the admiration of Dylan Thomas and other English-language writers in Wales, for whom he became the founding father of a new 'Anglo-Welsh' literature.

'I like stories that are gloomy, morose and bitter', said Evans, explaining his lifelong obsessions; 'an angry man is nearer himself than a happy man' (Evans, *Fury Never Leaves Us*, 131). None the less his later stories show a broadening of vision: *Pilgrims in a Foreign Land* (1942) and *The Earth Gives All and Takes All* (1946) move into fantasy and folk tale through a more consciously poetic idiom. Caradoc Evans died of heart failure at Aberystwyth and Cardiganshire General Hospital on 11 January 1945, and was buried on 16 January at Horeb Chapel, next to Brynawelon ('hill of breezes'), the Evans' home at New Cross. During the second half of the twentieth century his critical reputation in Wales improved, and few serious critics would now react to his depiction of Welsh life with the ferocity of his original commentators.

JOHN HARRIS

Sources O. Sandys, *Caradoc Evans* (1946) · J. Harris, 'Caradoc Evans, 1878–1945: a biographical introduction', in C. Evans, *Fury never leaves us: a miscellany of Caradoc Evans*, ed. J. Harris (1985), 9–45 · T. Williams, *Caradoc Evans* (1970) · G. Jones, 'A mighty man in Sion: Caradoc Evans, 1878–1945', *Background to Dylan Thomas and other explorations* (1992), 72–88 · D. Jenkins, 'Community and kin: Caradoc Evans "at home"', *Anglo-Welsh Review*, 53 (1974), 43–57 · G. Green, 'Caradoc', in C. Evans, *The earth gives all and takes all* (1946), vii–xxxiv · S. Stokes, 'Crust and crumb', *Personal glimpses* (1924), 135–9 · G. Blake, 'Strangers within the gate', *The book of Fleet Street*, ed. T. M. Pope (1930), 61–2 · H. G. Wells, *Experiment in autobiography: discoveries and conclusions of a very ordinary brain (since 1866)*, 1 (1934), 147–8; facs. edn (1984) · m. certs. and divorce papers · d. cert.

Archives NL Wales, corresp. and literary MSS · NL Wales, drafts of unpublished MSS and corresp.

Likenesses photograph, 1920–29, NL Wales · E. Walters, oils, 1930, NMG Wales · Matt [M. Sandford], caricature, repro. in Stokes, 'Crust and crumb', facing p. 136

Wealth at death £81 6s. 5d.: administration, 5 April 1945, CGPLA Eng. & Wales

Evans, Sir (Robert) Charles (1918–1995), surgeon and mountaineer, was born in Liverpool on 19 October 1918, the son of Robert Charles Evans (1882–1918), solicitor, and his wife, Edith Lloyd, *née* Williams (1883–1966). His father, a second lieutenant in the 15th Welsh regiment, was shot dead by a German prisoner on 24 August 1918, and Evans was brought up in Dyffryn Clwyd, Denbighshire, principally by his mother. In childhood he spoke Welsh as his first language. He won a scholarship to Shrewsbury School, which he attended from 1931 to 1937, and another to University College, Oxford, at a time when his love of mountains was already well established. He had been introduced to the Welsh hills by Patrick Childs, a master at Shrewsbury, and by 1939 he had already climbed in Wales, Scotland, Ireland, and the Alps. He qualified in medicine in December 1942, and the following year joined the Royal Army Medical Corps before serving in India, Burma, Vietnam, and Borneo. He was mentioned in dispatches in 1945 for his courage as a regimental medical officer crossing the Irrawaddy. He made two brief treks in the Himalayas during this period—to Kumaon and along the Singalila Ridge, in sight of Kanchenjunga, third highest mountain in the world. Within a decade he was chosen to lead the expedition that first climbed it.

Evans practised as a surgical and neurosurgical registrar

Sir (Robert) Charles Evans (1918–1995), by unknown photographer, 1953

in Liverpool between 1947 and 1957; during this period his mountaineering prowess blossomed. He was to remark that because of this focus of his life he was the oldest middle-grade surgical registrar in the National Health Service. In the Alps in 1949 his season was marred by the tragic fatality of his companion Richard Hull on the Brouillard Ridge of Mont Blanc. Though injured, having broken Hull's fall, Evans descended alone to Courmayeur to summon help. His first Himalayan expedition was to Annapurna II with Bill Tilman in 1950. He visited Kulu (India), attempting Deo Tibba in 1951, and in 1952 he was deputy leader on the expedition to the 8000 metre peak Cho Oyu, under Eric Shipton. Competence, imperturbability, kindness, exceptional organizational ability, and a quiet wit were the qualities for which his colleagues remembered him. Following Cho Oyu he stayed on in Nepal to explore the upper Barun valley.

In 1953 Evans was appointed deputy leader of the British Everest expedition under John Hunt, who had replaced Eric Shipton. Evans and Tom Bourdillon made the first ascent of the south summit of Mount Everest on 26 May 1953. Faulty oxygen apparatus and lack of time prevented them from reaching the main summit, which was climbed by Edmund Hillary and Tenzing Norgay several days later. How different Evans's life would have been if he had been one of the summit pair. Nevertheless he was soon chosen to lead the 1955 British expedition to Kanchenjunga, a peak harder and demanding more commitment than Everest itself, and scarcely less high. The ascent by two parties, George Band with Joe Brown, and later Norman Hardie with Tony Streather, on 25 and 26 May made this expedition a model of its kind. 1957 was Evans's last expedition, to Annapurna IV. On 14 August the same year he married (Denise) Nea Morin (b. 1931), a teacher, and also in her own right a distinguished climber from a mountaineering family. There were three sons of the marriage.

In the late 1950s symptoms of Evans's neurological illness began. Multiple sclerosis soon disabled him, marking the end of active climbing. He moved laterally from neurosurgery into university administration, and became principal of the University College of North Wales, Bangor, in 1957. This post, which he held until 1984, brought him into conflict with Plaid Cymru, in particular over the appointment of non-Welsh academic staff. Despite these difficulties (which saddened him greatly), and those of his progressive illness, he presided over a flourishing university that tripled in size and established departments of international repute in oceanography, marine biology, electronics, and forestry.

Evans's four books portrayed his modesty, accuracy, and humour. *Eye on Everest* (1955) was a gentle book of the sketches he made in 1953, sometimes mocking the neo-imperial aspects of the Everest expedition. *On Climbing* (1956) was in part an autobiography, understated and dwelling more on climbs he had enjoyed than those for which he was well known. *Kanchenjunga: the Untrodden Peak* (1956) was the story of this great expedition which he led. His final book, *A Doctor in the XIVth Army*, was published posthumously in 1998; this recorded the campaign by the 'forgotten army' against the Japanese forces. Evans's diaries, on which the book was based, were meticulous, frank, and full of understanding. He described the poor physical condition and privation that Japanese prisoners suffered in British hands, as well as *vice versa*, and recalled how at the trial of a Japanese Lieutenant-Colonel Sumida for war crimes, a British civilian witness named Robert Scott had been summoned to identify his torturers: 'At this the Japanese all rose and gave Scott a formal bow of recognition; a faint smile passed between the two' (Evans, *A Doctor*, 191).

Evans received a string of academic honours throughout his life and was knighted in 1969. He was a member of the council of the Royal Geographical Society in 1960–61 and president of the Alpine Club from 1967 to 1970. He died of pneumonia at a nursing home in Deganwy, north Wales, on 5 December 1995, and was cremated at Colwyn Bay on 11 December. He was survived by his wife and three sons.

CHARLES CLARKE

Sources *Alpine Journal*, 99 (1994), 334–41 · *The Times* (9 Dec 1995) · *The Independent* (12 Dec 1995) · *The Guardian* (19 Dec 1995) · C. Evans, *Eye on Everest* (1955) · C. Evans, *Kanchenjunga: the untrodden peak* (1956) · C. Evans, *On climbing* (1956) · C. Evans, *A doctor in the XIVth army: Burma, 1944–1945* (1998) · *WWW* · private information (2004)

Archives Alpine Club, 55 Charlotte Road, London, records · priv. coll., MSS | FILM BBC, Kanchenjunga film · priv. coll., Annapurna IV film
Likenesses photograph, 1953, RGS [*see illus.*] · J. Merton, oils, 1972, U. Wales, Bangor · group photograph, Alpine Club, London · photograph, repro. in *The Times* · photograph, repro. in *The Independent* · photograph, repro. in *The Guardian*
Wealth at death £94,135: probate, 31 Jan 1996, *CGPLA Eng. & Wales*

Evans, Sir Charles Arthur Lovatt (1884–1968), physiologist, was born on 8 July 1884 in Birmingham, the son of Charles Evans, music teacher, and his wife, Alice Harriett Hipkins. His interest in science appeared to be uninfluenced by his family background. He was educated at Birmingham Upper High Street elementary school and the council secondary school, Waverley Road, which he entered on the science side at the age of thirteen. Chemistry was taught by a master who went round a number of schools, and the young Lovatt Evans left school at the age of fourteen in order to become an assistant to this itinerant teacher. He furthered his education by correspondence courses and by studying at the Birmingham Municipal Technical School. At the age of sixteen he started work in the department of physiology in Mason Science College, Edmund Street, Birmingham. He then matriculated as an external candidate of the University of London in 1907, and graduated as BSc in 1910. During that period he earned his living as steward in the physiology department and by a series of teaching posts: lecturer in physiology at Handsworth Technical School (1902–8), demonstrator in physiology at the Birmingham Midland Institute (1904–7), and interim lecturer in physiology, University of Birmingham. He retained much affection for that university and great interest in it.

In 1911 Lovatt Evans married Laura Stevenson (*d.* 1964) from Hanley, Stoke-on-Trent, the daughter of an opera singer. They had two daughters, one of whom lived in Copenhagen at the beginning of the Second World War and worked for a time as assistant to Professor S. A. S. Krogh.

When Lovatt Evans graduated in 1910, he intended to make a career in chemistry. But at the conclusion of the examination he was offered the Sharpey scholarship by E. H. Starling in the department of physiology at University College, London. This was the beginning of an association and friendship which lasted until Starling's death in 1927. He worked with Starling for five years, mainly on the metabolism of the heart, and during this period he also studied medicine at University College Hospital, qualified MRCS, LRCP, in 1916, and in addition obtained the degree of DSc.

Lovatt Evans then joined the Royal Army Medical Corps and continued his association with Starling at the Royal Army Medical College at Millbank, London, where Starling was in charge of the anti-gas department. For two years he was occupied with a number of problems related to gas warfare: the effects of arsine, phosgene, hydrocyanic acid, and mustard gas; general anti-gas training at

Sir Charles Arthur Lovatt Evans (1884–1968), by Lafayette, 1928

Aldershot; the efficiency of respirators; and field trials, held on Porton Down.

After demobilization in 1918 Lovatt Evans was appointed to the chair of experimental physiology in Leeds. He made a considerable impact on physiology in a short time, for this appointment came only eight years after his first degree and part of that time had been spent in qualifying in medicine and in performing war work. However, he remained in Leeds for only one year, leaving to accept an invitation by H. H. Dale to join the staff of the National Institute for Medical Research in Hampstead, from which he went in 1922 to the chair of physiology at St Bartholomew's Hospital, London. In 1926 he went to the Jodrell chair of physiology in University College, London. His two predecessors in that chair were still working in the department as Foulerton professors of the Royal Society. Starling died in 1927, but A. V. Hill and Lovatt Evans worked together for twenty-three years. They had a common interest in the application of the methods of the exact sciences to biological problems. Lovatt Evans worked on the chemical side and Hill on the physical.

During the Second World War Lovatt Evans left London to work at the Chemical Defence Experimental Establishment at Porton Down. He later resumed his chair at University College until his retirement in 1949, when he returned once more to Porton and continued to work there until shortly before his death.

Lovatt Evans had only a relatively short time in which to undertake research. His early struggles meant that he was twenty-six when he graduated, and his first period at University College was partly occupied in obtaining a medical qualification. Only after the war was he free to pursue academic research. His first interest with Starling was the metabolism of the heart and lungs studied by Starling's heart–lung preparation, and it was here that he became interested in the role of lactic acid in muscle metabolism. He published a number of papers on cardiac, voluntary, and smooth muscle in relation to lactic acid and heat production. During this work he developed the heart oxygenator preparation which enabled the metabolism of the heart to be studied without the complication of the lungs. This early work of Starling and Lovatt Evans laid the foundations for open-chest surgery. He later published a series of papers with F. G. Young and others on the conditions affecting the storage of glycogen.

Lovatt Evans's early interest in problems related to chemical warfare was renewed in 1939, and again in 1949, when he retired from the Jodrell chair. He became interested in anticholinesterones and analysed the ways in which they affected respiration by bronchoconstriction, by neuromuscular block, and by central respiratory failure. He investigated sweating in the horse, finding it to be controlled by adrenaline in the blood rather than by nervous control. His last published work was on the toxicity of hydrogen sulphide, and at the age of eighty-three he cannulated the six different blood vessels required and carried out the titrations to estimate the sulphide concentrations.

Lovatt Evans made a great contribution to teaching by his fourteen editions of Starling's *Principles of Human Physiology* (1930–58). He also wrote *Recent Advances in Physiology*, which ran to four editions and included Spanish translations. His administrative skills were exercised at University College, and the Royal Veterinary College, London, where he acted as chairman of the council (1949–63). He was the first honorary fellow of the college. He also served on the Medical Research Council in 1947–50, and was chairman of the military personnel research committee from 1948 to 1953.

Lovatt Evans was among the first physiologists to recognize the importance of the new subject of biochemistry. He was a founder member of the Biochemical Society, but always hoped that the two disciplines would keep close together, and for a considerable time the annual general meetings of the Biochemical and Physiological societies took place on successive days at University College.

Lovatt Evans was elected FRS in 1925. He was Sharpey-Schafer lecturer (University of Edinburgh, 1939), Louis Abrahams lecturer (Royal College of Physicians, 1946), Stephen Paget lecturer (Research Defence Society, 1949), first Bayliss-Starling lecturer (Physiological Society, 1963), and William Dick memorial lecturer (Edinburgh, 1965). He was an honorary member of the Physiological Society, the Biochemical Society, the Italian Society of Experimental Biology, and the Ergonomics Society (of which he was a founder member); and a foreign member of the Royal Physiographical Society, Lund. He was a fellow of University College, London, and of the Royal Veterinary College.

In 1934 he received the LLD from the University of Birmingham, and in 1957 the LLD from the University of London. He was knighted in 1951.

Straightforward and friendly, Lovatt Evans could establish an immediate rapport with a wide range of people. His early struggles made him appreciate independence in others, and he believed in letting people show what they could do on their own without too much assistance (a belief which he inherited from his father). He was widely read and also had some skill in painting in watercolours. His knowledge of the early physiologists was profound and he was an excellent raconteur.

Lovatt Evans's greatest characteristic was perhaps a capacity to inspire confidence in both his friendship and his judgement. In later years he went to live at Hedgemoor Cottage, Winterslow, near Salisbury, where he looked after his wife during a trying illness, and after her death lived alone in his cottage. He died within a year of giving up active work, on 29 August 1968, at Hedgemoor Cottage. D. H. SMYTH, *rev.*

Sources I. de B. Daly and R. A. Gregory, *Memoirs FRS*, 16 (1970), 233–52 · personal knowledge (1981) · *CGPLA Eng. & Wales* (1968)
Archives LUL, laboratory notebooks · Wellcome L., scientific corresp. and papers | CAC Cam., corresp. with A. V. Hill
Likenesses Lafayette, photograph, 1928, NPG [*see illus.*] · W. Stoneman, photograph, RS · photograph, repro. in *Memoirs FRS*
Wealth at death £84,569: probate, 18 Oct 1968, *CGPLA Eng. & Wales*

Evans, Charles Smart (1778–1849), singer and composer, was born in London. He was a chorister at the Chapel Royal under Edmund Ayrton, and on 14 June 1808 became a gentleman of the Chapel Royal. His name appears among the alto singers in the chorus of the Ancient Concerts of 1798, and he took part with John Braham and others in the music performed at Weber's funeral in 1826. Four of Evans's partsongs gained prizes from the glee and catch clubs namely, 'Beauties, have you seen a toy?' (1811), 'Fill all the glasses' (1812), a setting of William Linley's 'Ode to the Memory of Samuel Webbe' (1817), and 'Great Bacchus' (1821). He was also the composer of many songs and some anthems, and for several years served as organist at St Paul's, Covent Garden. He later became a Roman Catholic and a member of the choir which sang at the chapel of the Portuguese embassy in South Street, Grosvenor Square, for which he wrote a Magnificat and several motets. These were included in Novello's *Collection of Motets*. Evans died in London on 4 January 1849.

L. M. MIDDLETON, *rev.* DAVID J. GOLBY

Sources W. H. Husk, 'Evans, Charles (Smart)', Grove, *Dict. mus.* (1954) · *Quarterly Musical Magazine and Review*, 8 (1826), 127 · Gillow, *Lit. biog. hist.*

Evans, Christmas (1766–1838), Baptist minister, was born on 25 December 1766, at Esgair Wen, a thatched cottage in the parish of Llandysul, Cardiganshire, the son of Samuel Evans, shoemaker, and his wife, Joanna Lewis. They had three children, a daughter and two sons; Christmas was their second child. His father died in 1775, when Evans was only nine years old, and left the family in a state of complete destitution. The next four years Evans spent with James Lewis, his mother's brother, at Bwlchog in the parish of Llanfihangel-ar-arth in Carmarthenshire. He left him to become a farm servant, working at various places, including Castellhywel, the home of David Davis (1745–1827), the learned Arian minister of the Arminian congregation at Llwynrhydowen. In 1783 Evans underwent conversion during a revival there and became a member of the church. He was given a basic education by Davis in his school, learning to read Welsh, and acquiring some knowledge of English.

Evans began to preach at cottage meetings, but as the strict rules of the Presbyterians required an academic education for their ministers, he gravitated towards the Baptists, who had no such limitations, in order to enter the ministry. In 1788 he was baptized in the River Duar at Llanybydder in Carmarthenshire by Timothy Thomas (1754–1840), and joined his Baptist congregation at Aberdyar. Earlier, he had lost one eye in an accident but according to the Baptist minister Robert Hall (1764–1831) his surviving eye was one 'that could light an army through a wilderness on a dark night' (W. Morgan, 25).

In 1776 the Baptists had launched their mission to north Wales. At the assembly held at Maes-y-Berllan, Brecknockshire, on 8–11 June 1789, representatives from the new churches in north Wales pleaded for ministerial help. Christmas Evans volunteered his services and had a successful preaching tour in Anglesey and Caernarvonshire. In August 1789 he was ordained at Salem, Ty'ndonnen, in the parish of Botwnnog to serve the Baptists of Llŷn. On 23 October 1789, at Bryncroes parish church, he married Catherine Jones, a member of his congregation. They had no children.

During the autumn of 1789 Evans experienced a transformation of spirit due to a profound realization of the wonder of God's grace, and the discovery of the significance of the Welsh revivalist tradition. At once his preaching became more vivacious and dramatic, marking the incursion of the Methodist spirit into the Baptist pulpit. On Christmas day 1791 he moved to Anglesey to act as minister to all the Baptist churches in the island. He lived at Llangefni, where the leading chapel, Cil-dwrm, was situated. Between 1795 and 1798 the minister of Ramoth, Merioneth, John Richard Jones (1765–1822), sought to persuade his fellow Baptists of the validity of the anti-evangelical teachings of Robert Sandeman (1718–1771) and Archibald McClean (1733–1812), and in 1798 initiated a split among the churches. For a time Christmas Evans was attracted to these views, but as he later confessed, Sandemanian opinions drove away his 'spirit of prayer for the salvation of sinners'. He resumed his orthodoxy, and became the central figure in a great Baptist movement in Anglesey. Although for many years his salary was only £17 a year, he ruled over the Anglesey Baptists with a rod of iron; he built new chapels, and made at least two long and laborious preaching journeys every year all over Wales to collect money to pay off the chapel debts, which often weighed heavily upon him. These tours boosted his reputation, as crowds flocked to hear his sermons. Evans alternated humour and pathos effectively, and his startling power of declamation exercised extraordinary influence over his auditors.

On 22 October 1823 Catherine Evans died; in the same year Evans suffered much ill health. His wounded eye often troubled him, and he was periodically threatened with blindness. At last the Baptist churches of Anglesey threw off the yoke of Evans's ministry, aiming to become independent churches: his position as a sort of Baptist bishop was no longer tenable. He bitterly resented their choosing ministers without reference to him, and a lawsuit about a chapel debt added to his difficulties. In 1826 he gladly accepted the ministry of Tonyfelin Chapel in Caerphilly in Glamorgan.

Evans ministered very effectively at Caerphilly for two years. On 23 April 1828 at Eglwysilan parish church, he married as his second wife Mary Jones, who had been his maid at Llangefni. They had no children. But difficulties with his flock again arose, causing him to move to Cardiff in September 1828; but the constitution of that church was so democratic that his autocratic ways again created problems, and in 1832 he made his final change to Caernarfon. Despite the dissensions of the thirty church members, the drunkenness of some, and the pressure of a debt of £800, he was not unhappy.

While on a journey to collect money towards the chapel debt in south Wales, Evans was suddenly taken ill, and died on 19 July 1838 in the house of the Revd Daniel Davies in Oxford Street, Swansea, attended by his wife. On 23 July he was buried with great honour in the burial-ground of the Bethesda Welsh Baptist Chapel at Swansea.

Christmas Evans was a complex character. He was generous to a fault, an untiring worker, perfectly sincere, and a man of deep spirituality. And yet he was impulsive and wayward. He could be dictatorial in his pastoral work and could not suffer criticism with equanimity. Apart from his sermons, published in Welsh, his only other publications were some Welsh hymns and tracts. But there is no doubting his extraordinary influence as a preacher: huge crowds gathered to hear him and his converts were legion. His vivid imagination transformed biblical stories and parables into gripping dramas. Although he sought by hard reading to overcome the limitations of his lack of education, he never acquired the equipment to make a sophisticated contribution to theology. Nevertheless he had a significant place in the growing influence of evangelicalism in nineteenth-century Wales.

T. F. TOUT, rev. R. TUDUR JONES

Sources J. T. Jones, *Christmas Evans* (1938) · D. D. Morgan, *Christmas Evans* (1991) · W. Morgan, *Cofiant, neu hanes bywyd … Christmas Evans* (1839) · D. R. Stephen, *Memoirs of the late Christmas Evans* (1847) · D. M. Evans, *Christmas Evans: a memoir* (1863) · David Owen, *Christmasia* (1861) · Owen Jones, *Great preachers of Wales* (1885), 159–224 · E. P. Hood, *Christmas Evans* (1881) · O. Thomas, *Cofiant y Parch. John Jones, Talsarn* (1874), 942–54 [biography of John Jones, Talsarn] · J. Rowlands, *Cofiant … Daniel Davies, DD* (1879), 178–9

Archives NL Wales, account book with sermon notes · NL Wales, notebook · NL Wales, notebooks, sermons · NL Wales, sermon notes • NL Wales, sermon notes and MSS • U. Wales, Bangor, sermon notes

Likenesses Freeman, stipple, pubd 1822 (after Branwhite), NPG • N. Branwhite, portrait, probably NL Wales • W. Roos, oils, NMG Wales • W. Williams (Ap Calidfryn), oils (after H. Hughes), Cardiff Baptist College • portrait, probably NL Wales • Staffordshire porcelain statuettes

Evans, Cornelius (*fl.* **1648**), impostor, is said to have been born at Marseilles, of a Welsh father and a Provençale mother. Nothing is known of his early life, but it was reported in 1648 that he spoke English 'not perfectly and in another dialect than it is usually pronounced by Englishmen' (*Kingdomes Weekly Intelligencer*, 955). Despite his slight resemblance to Charles Stuart, prince of Wales—the future Charles II—he was 'shorter than the Prince by the head, a little bowed in his shoulders, with hands like to a butcher's boy's hands' (*A Declaration*, 1). Evans himself claimed that he was a poor gentleman who had been in the service of the king, but a parliamentarian newsletter sneered that he was 'well known in London especially at some of the common gaols' (*Perfect Weekly Account*, 29 May 1648). In early May 1648 Evans was lodging in the house of Nicholas Evans, a seaman, in the parish of St Katharine by the Tower, London. Seeking shipboard work, but failing to find it, he set out on foot shortly afterwards for the channel ports.

Whether Evans had yet hatched the idea of impersonating Prince Charles is unclear. Having walked from London to Dover, he set off for Deal, and there fell into the company of dissident sailors from the ship *Providence*. At this meeting the idea of an imposture (whoever suggested it) was agreed. Evans later tried to implicate Vice-Admiral Thomas Rainborowe in the business, but he and his new friends quietly left Deal, where Rainborowe was governor, and made instead for Sandwich, the sailors by means of a longboat, and the 'prince' on foot. It was here that his imposture was launched. Arriving probably on 17 May, Evans refreshed himself at the Bell tavern, with a butcher, Casimir Mathew, and a victualler, Charles Baron, while the sailors (including some officers) spread the news of the princely presence. A Captain Henry Foster was persuaded of Evans's royal status and presented him to William Mandey, the mayor. To Mandey the visitor explained that his mother, Queen Henrietta Maria, had sought to poison him, forcing him to flee in haste from France. When it was proposed to carry him to London so that parliament could verify his credentials, Evans found a reason for refusal which conflicted with his first explanation: Kent and other counties:

> had declared their affections to settle him and his father in their rights, and that therefore he was come over to join with them, and that his intent is to assist them to the bringing of the king his father to London. (*A Letter from Kent*, 5)

It seems that Evans had concocted the poisoning story in advance, but that a sceptical response decided him to risk taking advantage of the loud rumblings of rebellion newly heard in Kent.

Despite this inconsistency, Evans's claims were treated as true until proved otherwise. Lodged at Captain Foster's house, he held court: 'many gentlemen and women came daily to kiss his hand, and many presents he had made him' (*A Letter from Kent*, 6). A gentlewoman, revealed Evans later, brought him 'one hundred pieces of gold and three bunches of asparagus' (*JHL*, 1647–8, 300). He had arrived in Sandwich 'in an old black ragged suit, with no companions but lice', but the authorities accepted that this misfortune stemmed from the hardships of his escape (Carter, 43). They put to work the tailors of the town, and on Sunday 21 May the eminent visitor was able to attend church:

> in a rich suit lined with crimson satin, and laced with gold and silver lace. One Thomas Richards, a man of an extraordinary stature, was chosen to carry the sword … [he] walking before him in a slow and stately posture, commands the people to bear back: and cries out, 'Room for the Prince'. (*Kingdomes Weekly Intelligencer*, 953)

At Foster's house dinner was taken in the grand manner, 'trumpets sounding his meat to the table most commonly' (Carter, 44). Evans promised a knighthood to his host and posts to various others.

Evans's imposture was reported to have received crucial support: 'certain ancient servants of the king then in the town being desired to give their attestation who by a great mistake did all affirm that it was the prince' (*Kingdomes Weekly Intelligencer*, 953–4). The presence of navy officers and sailors may also have exerted influence, especially if, as seems likely, they were armed. The mayor and jurats were suspicious, and sent to parliament a detailed description of their guest, set down by the town clerk, James Thurburne. On 20 May the committee of both houses wrote back, explaining that whereas Thurburne had depicted a blond-haired man with light skin:

> the Prince himself is of a black complexion and very black hair—we are fully satisfied he is only an imposter, and doth now appear of purpose to raise tumults and insurrections in the county. We therefore desire you to take special care for securing the person of the above said man. (*CSP dom.*, 1648–9, 73)

But in Sandwich there were the sailors, and many others, who believed Evans's claims. Even doubters understood his value as a figurehead:

> it is believed by most of judgement that it is not the prince; but that he was one that was appointed to have been reputed so, to have animated the cavaliers to join in a speedy body, out of this and some other counties. (*A Letter from Kent*, 6)

Meanwhile there had arrived at Dover a servant to the queen, Sir Thomas Dishington, who was startled to hear of his young master's presence at Sandwich, since he had only just received from the real prince a letter sent from the court of St Germain, in Paris. He persuaded the mayor of Dover to send an express to Sandwich, explaining that Charles was still in France. But Mandey was unmoved, so on Saturday 20 May Dishington hastened there himself. What he found on arrival was Evans, 'delighting himself in the town haven with the pleasures of hunting the duck … in a boat attended by many of the chiefest inhabitants' (*Kingdomes Weekly Intelligencer*, 955). As Carter remarked, this was 'indeed a Welsh prince but not the prince of Wales'; Sir Thomas, 'being much incensed, called him villain, and counterfeit rogue' (Carter, 43). But Evans had already grown accustomed to his part, and was equal to the challenge. Feigning high indignation, he 'commands the Mayor to clap Sir Thomas up in prison for his treason; the mayor presently obeys his command' (ibid.). The mayor may have had less choice than this implies, for as Dishington explains, it was the mayor 'with 20 or 30 mariners' who effected his arrest, and 'presently committed me to the common gaol'. There he remained until, on Sunday, several friends arrived from Dover to vouch for him (*A Declaration*, 1). In the evening Dishington was released. Confronting Evans for a second time, he demanded to know the names of the prince's servants, and posed other questions designed to expose before the governors of Sandwich the falsity of the man he knew to be a fraud.

Evans's failure to answer was not immediately fatal to his scheme. The authorities did not rearrest Dishington, and gave him permission to leave the town. Many of the inhabitants, however, had other ideas:

> the women, and mariners would have stoned me in the streets, for not confessing that rogue to be the Prince: when we got to our horses, they refused to let us out at Dover gate, and beat us back with halberts, we were forced to take us to Canterbury gate, where with much ado we got out. (*A Declaration*, 2)

It is also likely that the defectors from the *Providence* remained in Sandwich and continued to champion Evans's cause. Caught between conflicting forces, it seems that the town authorities, though aware that his imposture could no longer be doubted, still hesitated to arrest and expose the counterfeit prince.

On Tuesday 23 September parliament sent a second order demanding that Evans be secured, and instructed Rainborowe to take him by force if the Sandwich authorities should prove obstructive. That day, however, rebel Kentish troops under the command of Sir Richard Hardress and captains Hamond and Carter gained entry to the town and quickly imposed their authority. Would they recognize the pretended prince? At first the rebel commanders were uncertain. Captain Carter paid Evans a visit 'to satisfy not only himself, but some deputy lieutenants in the county whether it were he or not' (Carter, 43). By Friday, it seems, they too had become convinced of Evans's imposture and sought to persuade him to leave quietly with them, for 'the hearts of the people were much inclined to him' (ibid., 44). But Captain Foster, Evans's host, was one of the believers. When the 'prince' declined the rebel leaders' offer of a coach, Foster refused to admit them, even when confronted by sixty musketeers; and 'now the whole town grew into a mutiny, and distraction' (ibid., 45). The officers:

> commanded all houses and shops to be shut up. Meanwhile this young imposter, ranting in his new invested authority, waves his hat and plume out at the window, calling out, 'raise the town, raise the town; seamen, stand to me seamen', throwing out handfuls of money into the streets among the people, which began to swarm up and down in throngs and tumults;

these street scenes 'would have ended in much mischief, had not the gentlemen bestirred themselves resolutely, and undauntedly in the quelling of them' (ibid.).

At length Evans was taken by his followers from the house, 'through the backside; and some seamen waiting purposely at the waterside, transported him immediately over into the Isle of Thanet' (Carter, 45). Here, it seems, Evans may have been handed over to the parliamentarian authorities by means of Sir Nicholas Crisp, the customs farmer and sequestered royalist of Birchington, Thanet, for the committee of both houses summoned him to appear before them on Saturday 27 May and that day or the next Evans was found in Thanet, 'at Mr Crispe's house at supper' (Carter, 46). Taken to Rochester and examined by the mayor, Philip Ward, and a JP, George Newman, Evans made a full written confession which revealed his true identity. He was taken to London and appeared before the House of Lords, who consigned him to Newgate. Mysteriously, Evans was able, or was enabled, to escape from his confinement. On 5 June he signed a letter addressed to his role model, the prince of Wales, in which he recommended his services. It may be assumed that Charles did not reply. The following month the real prince left for England to reclaim it for the Stuarts, but the attempt met with no more success than that of his imitator. Evans had already vanished into the mist, as quickly as he had appeared.   STEPHEN WRIGHT

Sources *JHL*, 10 (1647–8) • M. C. [M. Carter], *A … true … relation of that as honourable as unfortunate expedition of Kent, Essex, and Colchester* (1650) • *A letter from Kent of the rising at Rochester* (1648) [Thomason tract E 443(26)] • *Kingdomes Weekly Intelligencer*, 262 (23–30 May 1648) [Thomason tract] • *CSP dom.*, 1648–9 • B. Capp, *Cromwell's navy: the fleet and the English revolution, 1648–1660* (1989) • *A declaration from the City of London … also a message concerning Prince Charles, read in the House of Lords, from Sir Thomas Dishington* (27 May 1648) [Thomason tract E 445(2)] • *Perfect Weekly Account*, 12 (24–31 May 1648) [Thomason tract] • R. Scrope and T. Monkhouse, eds., *State papers collected by Edward, earl of Clarendon*, 3 vols. (1767–86), vol. 2, pp. 405–6 • *Report on the Pepys manuscripts*, HMC, 70 (1911) • *Perfect Weekly Account*, 11 (17–24 May 1648) [Thomason tract] • *Collections relating to the family of Crispe* (1882–3), vol. 1

Evans, Daniel (1774–1835), Independent minister, was born at Maindala, Eglwyswrw, Pembrokeshire, on 16 January 1774. As a youth he received little education and was apprenticed as a tailor. He frequently attended prayer meetings in private houses and, at the age of fifteen, became a member of the Independent church. Soon afterwards, in 1792, he began preaching with great enthusiasm from house to house. He thus trained himself for his future work, and became very successful as a missionary. His first settlement was at Llanwrtyd, Brecknockshire, as co-pastor with the Revd Isaac Price, from 1796 to 1799. In 1799 he accepted a call to Bangor, where his congregation had but twenty-five members, who were unable to pay him a sufficient wage. Supported partially by his own private means, he worked extremely hard and succeeded in enlarging his own congregation, as well as establishing seven new ones in the immediate neighbourhood, and extending his ministry as far as the Conwy valley. In 1808 he moved to Mynydd-bach, near Swansea, where he was again exceptionally successful. During a period of only six months, in 1828–9, he added no fewer than 650 to the membership of his churches and Mynydd-bach became the mother church of a cluster of Independent chapels in a district extending over much of the Swansea valley and Swansea itself.

Evans's published works, which were all in Welsh, included several biographies and religious commentaries, and a volume of sermons published posthumously. He died at Mynydd-bach on 3 March 1835.

R. M. J. JONES, *rev.* MARI A. WILLIAMS

Sources NL Wales, Henry Blackwell papers, MS 9257 · T. Rees and J. Thomas, *Hanes eglwysi annibynol Cymru*, 2 (1872), 23–6 · *DWB* · J. T. Jones, *Geiriadur bywgraffyddol o enwogion Cymru*, 1 (1867)
Archives NL Wales

Evans, Daniel [*pseud.* Daniel Ddu o Geredigion] (1792–1846), poet, was born at Maesymynach in the parish of Llanfihangel Ystrad, Cardiganshire. His father, David Evans, was a prosperous farmer, and he was the second of three sons. He was educated at Lampeter grammar school under Eliezer Williams, and subsequently went to Jesus College, Oxford. His BA (1814) was followed by his MA (1817) and BD (1824). He took holy orders and, although elected to a fellowship, chose to reside mainly in Wales.

Daniel Ddu became involved with the 1819 eisteddfod organized by the Dyfed Cambrian Society, whose members sought to revive the old institution. In the same year he was elected poet to the London Gwyneddigion Society. It was in 1823, however, that he gained prominence as a poet, winning two major prizes at the Carmarthen eisteddfod for his strict-metre poetry, but his popularity in his home county was based on his simplistic love and nature verses. Several of his pieces were published in pamphlet form. His collected works appeared in 1830, entitled *Gwinllan y bardd*, followed in 1872 by an enlarged second edition, collected mainly from unpublished sources, and a third edition in 1906. The few English poems in the collection are of very inferior merit.

A sensitive man—as is evident in his love poems and his verses to nature's mute sufferers—prone to depression, Daniel Evans died by his own hand in Maesnewydd, Llanwnnen, Cardiganshire, on 28 March 1846, and was buried on 1 April in the churchyard of Pencarreg in Carmarthenshire. E. H. Rowland summarizes his century's verdict on his works: 'one of the most deservedly admired of modern Welsh poets' (Rowland, 53), but his reputation has diminished, and he merited only a passing reference in the 1986 *Oxford Companion to the Literature of Wales*.

A. CYNFAEL LAKE

Sources G. J. Williams, 'Daniel Ddu o Geredigion a'i gyfnod', *Y Llenor*, 5 (1926), 48–59 · B. Williams [Gwynionydd], *Enwogion Ceredigion* (1869), 64–6 · M. Howell, 'Daniel Ddu o Geredigion', *Cymru*, 17 (1899), 205–6 · I. Foulkes, *Geirlyfr bywgraffiadol o enwogion Cymru* (1870), 177–8 · Foster, *Alum. Oxon.* · E. H. Rowland, *A biographical dictionary of eminent Welshmen who flourished from 1700 to 1900* (privately printed, Wrexham, 1907), 53–4 · J. T. Jones, *Geiriadur bywgraffyddol o enwogion Cymru*, 1 (1867), 102 · A. E. Jones, 'Daniel Ddu o Geredigion', *Cymru*, 16 (1899), 183–7 · R. Williams, *Enwogion Cymru: a biographical dictionary of eminent Welshmen* (1852) · G. Jones, *Enwogion Sir Aberteifi* (1868) · bishops' transcripts, St David's, Pencarreg, Carms., 1846
Likenesses oils?, U. Wales, Lampeter · portrait, repro. in Howell, 'Daniel Ddu', 205

Evans, Daniel Silvan (1818–1903), Welsh scholar and lexicographer, born at Fron Wilym Uchaf, Llannarth, Cardiganshire, on 11 January 1818, was the son of Silvanus Evans, a farmer, and his wife, Sarah. He attended a nearby school for two months at a house called Pen-cae, kept by Thomas Thomas, and subsequently several other short-lived local schools, mostly during the winter months. Having started to preach to the Independent congregation of which he was a member, he decided to train for the ministry, and he attended Thomas Phillips's school at Neuaddlwyd (1838–40) and the Brecon Independent college (from 1840). He soon left the college, however, and kept school for five years before entering St David's College, Lampeter, in 1846, with the intention of taking holy orders in the established church. He was ordained deacon in 1848 and priest in 1849. His first curacy was at Llandegwning and Penllech, Caernarvonshire (1848–52), his second at Llangïan in the same district (1852–62). In 1862 he became rector of Llanymawddwy near Machynlleth, and in 1876 exchanged to the neighbouring rectory of Llanwrin; the greater part of his life's work was done in these two retired parsonages.

Although Evans's first publications were two collections of his own poems and hymns (1843 and 1846), the study of the Welsh language soon absorbed all his attention. In 1847 he started publishing his first significant work, an English-Welsh dictionary, which was finished in 1858. He was a keen editor and translator. Among many other literary projects he contributed articles to *Y Gwyddoniadur* and edited *Y Brython* from 1858 to 1860. He produced two editions of Ellis Wynne's *Bardd Cwsc* (1853, 1865), contributed translations to Skene's *The Four Ancient Books of Wales* (1868), and edited William Rowlands's *Cambrian Bibliography* in 1869. He edited Thomas Stephens's *Literature of the Kymry* (1876) and Lewis Morris's *Literary Remains* (1878).

Evans's main interest, and most significant work, was in the field of lexicography. In 1887 the first part of his *Dictionary of the Welsh Language* was published, followed by further volumes. All important words were illustrated by examples of their use from Welsh literature. Evans had produced over 1900 pages at the time of his death, but had only reached the letter E.

In later life Evans's eminence as a Welsh scholar received full recognition. In 1868 he received the honorary degree of BD from Lampeter; from 1875 to 1883 he was lecturer in Welsh in the University College of Wales, Aberystwyth; in 1897 he was elected to a research fellowship in Jesus College, Oxford, and in 1901 the newly established University of Wales gave him the honorary degree of DLitt. He was made honorary canon of Bangor in 1888, prebendary of Llanfair in 1891, and chancellor of the cathedral in 1895. From January 1872 to August 1875 he was editor of *Archaeologia Cambrensis*.

Evans married Margaret (d. 1889), daughter of Walter Walters, a farmer, on 16 February 1846. He died on 12 April 1903 at the rectory, Llanwrin, and was buried at Cemais, Montgomeryshire. A headstone and tablet were placed on his previously unmarked grave in 1956 and unveiled by a former professor of Welsh at the University College of

Wales, Aberystwyth, T. H. Parry-Williams. Three sons and three daughters predeceased Evans; his surviving son, John Henry Silvan Evans, assisted his father in his lexicographical work. This, together with many of Evans's editorial publications, is still consulted by scholars today.

J. E. LLOYD, rev. BETI JONES

Sources DWB · T. Parry, Transactions of the Honourable Society of Cymmrodorion (1981), 109–25 · M. D. Jones, 'Geiriadur Daniel Silvan Evans', Journal of the Welsh Bibliographical Society, 8 (1954–7), 24–38, 64–80 · D. Samuel, 'Sylvaniana', Y Geninen, 23 (1905), 15–22 · T. R. Roberts, Eminent Welshmen: a short biographical dictionary (1908), 95–6 · Bye-Gones Relating to Wales and the Border Counties, new ser., 8 (1903–4) [22 April 1903] · m. cert. · d. cert.
Archives NL Wales, corresp., notebooks, and papers · U. Wales, Bangor, MSS | Hergest Trust Archives, Kingston, letters to R. W. Banks · NL Wales, letters to T. C. Edwards · NL Wales, letters to Benjamin Williams (Gwynionydd), notebook
Likenesses photograph, c.1900, NL Wales

Evans, Sir David Gwynne (1909–1984), microbiologist, was born in Atherton, Lancashire, on 6 September 1909, third of the four children of Frederick George Evans from Pembroke, an Atherton headmaster, and his wife, Margaretta Eleonora Williams, a schoolteacher from Bangor. His elder brother, Meredith *Evans, was professor of physical chemistry at Leeds and Manchester and a fellow of the Royal Society.

Evans left Leigh grammar school in 1928 and after two years with the British Cotton Growers' Association went to Manchester University, where he graduated in physics and chemistry in 1933 and gained an MSc degree a year later. Evans then joined the Manchester University department of bacteriology under Professor H. B. Maitland and so started his career in microbiology. Their research on H. pertussis led to his lifelong interest in whooping cough. He took his PhD in 1938. In 1937 Evans married Mary, a fabric designer and artist, the daughter of Ben Darby, district electrical engineer, of Atherton. They had two children.

In 1940 Evans went to the department of biological standards at the National Institute for Medical Research, Hampstead, London, under Percival Hartley. He worked on clostridial antitoxin standardization and tetanus vaccination schedules. In 1947 he returned to Manchester University as reader in the bacteriology department. In spite of heavy teaching commitments he and his associates continued their research into whooping cough and clostridial toxins. He became secretary of the Medical Research Council (MRC) whooping cough vaccination committee which organized the trials of H. pertussis vaccines that led to the establishment of a British standard vaccine.

In 1955 Evans went back to Hampstead as director of the new biological standards control laboratory which was formed initially to monitor polio vaccines and formulate tests for their safety and potency. In 1958 he also became director of the parent department of biological standards. In 1957 he was appointed chairman of the MRC committee on the standardization of freeze-dried BCG vaccine, which was successfully introduced as a replacement for the current liquid one: in consequence he was invited to be president of the international symposium on BCG vaccine at Frankfurt-am-Main in 1970.

From 1961 to 1971 Evans was professor of bacteriology and immunology at the London School of Hygiene and Tropical Medicine. He became secretary and then chairman of the MRC's measles vaccine committee and organized trials of this product in children. He served on the World Health Organization's expert panel on biological standardization, the Central Health Services Council, the British Council medical advisory committee, and the MRC.

From 1964 Evans became involved with veterinary problems, being on the governing body of the Animal Virus Research Institute, at Pirbright, and on the Northumberland committee investigating the foot-and-mouth disease outbreaks of 1967. In 1971 the Joint Racing Board asked him to undertake a study of influenza in racehorses and in 1972 he became a member and then chairman (1973–9) of the board's veterinary advisory committee. He organized an investigation into contagious equine metritis which identified the agent responsible and recommended methods of prevention. In 1971–2 Evans was director of the Lister Institute and struggled in vain to save its Chelsea laboratory from financial failure. In 1972 he was appointed director of the new National Institute for Biological Standards and Control in order to prepare for its transfer in 1976 from the MRC to the National Biological Standards Board and its move to South Mimms. From 1973 he was on the committees of safety of medicines and the British and European pharmacopoeia commissions. In 1976 Evans went to Oxford and taught medical students at the Sir William Dunn school of pathology until 1979, when he retired to north Wales.

Enthusiasm and commitment were Evans's main attributes both in his scientific and social life, and he was an outstanding teacher, who had the ability to present subjects lucidly and simply. He always had time to listen to others and to bring out the best in them. He was always welcome at social as well as at scientific functions, and he liked to take colleagues on trips to the Lake District and Snowdonia, places he loved very much. Opera was his special interest and later in life he enjoyed gardening.

Evans gained his DSc in 1948, and was elected FRS in 1960 and FRCPath in 1965. In 1968 he was awarded the Stewart prize by the British Medical Association for his studies on epidemiology, and in 1977 he received the Buchanan medal of the Royal Society because his work had 'revolutionized the picture of childhood disease'. In 1969 he was appointed CBE and in 1977 he received a knighthood. He was president of the Society of General Microbiology (1972–5) and received an honorary doctorate from Surrey University in 1982. Evans died at Rhos-on-Sea, Colwyn Bay, on 13 June 1984.

J. O'H. TOBIN, rev.

Sources A. Downie, E. Smith, and J. O'H. Tobin, Memoirs FRS, 31 (1985), 171–96 · personal knowledge (1990)
Likenesses W. Bird, photograph, 1960, RS
Wealth at death £9868: probate, 20 Aug 1984, CGPLA Eng. & Wales

Evans, David Morier (1819–1874), financial journalist, was the son of Joshua Lloyd Evans of Llanidloes, Montgomeryshire. He formed an early connection with journalism, and became assistant city correspondent on *The Times*, a post that he occupied for several years, and left to assume the direction of financial articles in the *Morning Herald* and *Standard*. He left *The Standard* at the end of 1872, and in the following March, with Tom Hamber, started a paper called *The Hour* as an ultra-protestant tory paper. Evans spent his entire fortune on it, being adjudged bankrupt on 19 December 1873 (though he left about £4000 when he died a month later). The paper limped on until 1876 when Disraeli heard of its death with 'a pang' (Escott, 204). Evans's health broke down under the strain of his financial difficulties, and he died, from cirrhosis and general dropsy, at Albion House, King Edward's Road, South Hackney, London, on the morning of 1 January 1874, aged fifty-four. His wife, Jemima, survived him, with several children. He was buried in Abney Park cemetery, Stamford Hill, the funeral being attended by a large number of fellow journalists among whom he was popular.

In addition to his regular work, Evans was connected with several other commercial and financial periodicals, among them the *Bankers' Magazine*, to which he was one of the principal contributors, *The Bullionist*, and the *Stock Exchange Gazette*. He also conducted the literary and statistical departments of the *Bankers' Almanac and Diary*. He recognized the significant role of 'panics' in nineteenth-century financial history and two of his books are valuable records, anticipating much subsequent historical work: *The Commercial Crisis, 1847–8* (1849) and *History of the Commercial Crisis, 1857–8* (1859). He also published (anonymously) *The City, or, The Physiology of London Business* (1845); *City Men and City Matters* (1852); *Facts, Failures, and Frauds* (1859); and *Speculative Notes* (1864).

ALSAGER VIAN, *rev.* H. C. G. MATTHEW

Sources *The Times* (2 Jan 1874) · *Men of the time* (1872) · *The Standard* (6 Jan 1874) · T. H. S. Escott, *Masters of English journalism* (1911) · *CGPLA Eng. & Wales* (1874)
Wealth at death under £4000: probate, 10 June 1874, *CGPLA Eng. & Wales*

Evans, Dorothy (1888–1944), activist and organizer, was born on 6 May 1888 at 14 St Paul's Road, Kentish Town, London, daughter of Edward Evans, commercial clerk, and his wife, Marian, *née* Smith. Little is known of her parents beyond the occupation of her father. Dorothy Evans was educated at North London Collegiate School, trained as a teacher at Dartford College of Physical Education, and worked briefly as a teacher of gymnastics before resigning to commit herself full-time to the cause of women's suffrage in 1909. From this point she began a lifelong career of political activism and organization, primarily in relation to issues of women's inequality.

As an active member of the Women's Social and Political Union (WSPU), Dorothy Evans was deeply committed to militant tactics of civil disobedience in pursuit of women's suffrage. She was arrested and imprisoned on numerous occasions, undertaking hunger and thirst strikes and suffering forced feeding. In 1910 she was first arrested for failing to pay a dog licence on the grounds that women should not be taxed unless they had political representation. Involvement in a window-smashing campaign in the West End in 1912 resulted in her first imprisonment. The next year her loyalty to the WSPU and its leadership led to the trusted role of liaison officer between the WSPU headquarters in London and its exiled leader Christabel Pankhurst in Paris. To move freely between the two capitals Dorothy Evans was forced to travel in disguise.

As a key activist and organizer, Dorothy Evans was sent by the WSPU to the north of Ireland to increase agitation for women's suffrage. In 1913 she was arrested for being in possession of explosives during an abortive attempt to blow up Lisburn Castle. For this and other activities in Ireland she was charged with conspiracy. However, as on other occasions, her court appearances and prison terms were disrupted by repeated hunger and thirst striking. In 1914 she was released from prison under the government's wartime amnesty for suffragette prisoners.

Shocked by the scale of suffering caused by the First World War, Dorothy Evans became a 'whole-hearted pacifist', speaking in favour of international arbitration at public meetings (Whately, 46). After the war she continued to devote her time and energy to feminist causes, working with other suffragettes in the newly formed Six Point Group which was committed to securing legal equality between the sexes. During the 1920s her commitment to issues concerned with legal equal rights for women, such as equal pay and women's right to custody of their children and to retain their nationality on marriage, linked her with the 'old' feminism rather than the 'new', or special needs, feminism espoused by Eleanor Rathbone and her National Union of Societies for Equal Citizenship. Although a committed socialist and pacifist during this period, she was always prepared to put aside issues of personal political affinity to work for equality with women across the political spectrum.

In the mid-1930s, together with socialist feminists such as the Labour MP Edith Summerskill, Dorothy Evans became convinced, through her concern for the welfare of married women and housewives, that feminist groups should shift their focus of concern to married women's position in the home. At the same time, she believed it was necessary for feminism to reach out to working-class women by building alliances with the labour movement. She was instrumental in founding the Married Women's Association, a key feminist organization of the 1940s and 1950s committed to securing the legal and economic rights of housewives.

Dorothy Evans's interest in the position of married women and housewives was particularly notable given that her personal opposition to the institution of marriage was well known. Although involved in a long-term relationship with A. Emil Davies, treasurer of the Fabian Society, with whom she had a daughter, she never married. According to her biographer, Monica Whately, she believed in a 'partnership held together by love, comradeship and mutual respect and not by legal ties' (Whately, 47). In the mid-1930s she also began a long-term lesbian relationship with the feminist and pacifist activist Sybil Morrison.

During the Second World War Dorothy Evans continued to work full-time for equality. She was appointed secretary of Women for Westminster, a national organization committed to increasing women's representation in parliament. During the same period she was also largely responsible for researching and framing the Equal Citizenship (Blanket) Bill. Although unsuccessful, this attempted piece of legislation stands as a fitting testimony to Dorothy Evans's political aspirations, since it was intended to rectify in one stroke all instances of discrimination against women on the statute book.

By the time of her death in 1944, Dorothy Evans had become a leading figure in women's politics. Despite what was for the period an unconventional lifestyle, she appears to have gained the respect, admiration, and support of a wide range of women, including those who disagreed with her on moral or religious grounds. She was also one of the few feminists able to bridge the generation gap between older women, like herself, who had been involved in the suffrage struggle, and younger women who had come into politics during the 1930s and 1940s. According to Bee Serota, a young member of the Six Point Group in the early 1940s, Dorothy Evans had 'this tremendous quality of being able to encourage young people and not necessarily to think as she thought, but to do things themselves' (Blackford, 89). On 28 August 1944 at the age of fifty-five Dorothy Evans died of cancer in Canniesburn Auxiliary Hospital, Bearsden, Glasgow. Active in women's politics even in the late stages of her illness, she was in Glasgow to address a public meeting. She left her body for medical research.   CATHERINE BLACKFORD

Sources C. Blackford, 'Ideas, structures and practices of feminism, 1939–64', PhD diss., University of East London, 1996 · M. Pugh, *Women and the women's movement in Britain, 1914–1959* (1992) · M. Whately, *Dorothy Evans and the Six Point Group* (1945) · b. cert. · d. cert. · private information (2004) [Lyndal Evans]

Archives Women's Library, London, corresp. and drafts relating to women and the civil service

Wealth at death £3407 8s. 4d.: probate, 29 June 1945, *CGPLA Eng. & Wales*

Evans, Edgar (1876–1912), polar explorer, was born at Middleton Cottage, Rhosili, Gower, Glamorgan, on 7 March 1876, the sixth of the eight surviving children of Charles Evans, mariner, and his wife, Sarah, *née* Beynon. His parents moved to Swansea, where he was educated at St Helen's School. On leaving school he worked at the Castle Hotel, Swansea, but he was determined to follow his father to sea and joined the Royal Navy at the minimum age of fifteen. He began his training in 1891 on HMS *Ganges* at Falmouth and became an ordinary seaman in 1894. Strongly built, he served as a physical training instructor at HMS *Excellent*, the gunnery school at Portsmouth, and in 1899 he joined the *Majestic*, where he came to the notice of Lieutenant Robert Falcon Scott. When

Scott began recruiting for the National Antarctic Expedition of 1901–4, he applied to the Admiralty for Evans's services, and Evans signed on to the expedition ship *Discovery* as a petty officer second class in London on 27 July 1901.

Around 5 feet 10 inches tall and over 13 stone, with rugged features and an extrovert character, Evans readily adapted to the harshness of Antarctic life. In October 1903 he and Leading Stoker William Lashly were selected by Scott for an arduous sledging expedition to the high plateau of Victoria Land, during which they covered 1098 miles at an average of 15.4 miles a day. Scott later wrote: 'With these two men behind me our sledge seemed to become a living thing, and the days of slow progress were numbered' (Scott, *Discovery*, ii.259). On 14 December, during the return journey, Scott and Evans fell to the length of their harness into a deep crevasse and were saved by Lashly, who managed to anchor the sledge and enable them to climb to safety. Strong bonds of mutual respect were forged between the three men, and Scott emerged from the 'western journey' with a better understanding of life on the lower decks, and the strong conviction 'that one would have to search far for a better sledge-companion than the British bluejacket' (ibid., i.486).

When the *Discovery* returned to England in September 1904 Evans was promoted to petty officer first class (backdated to April 1904). He returned to HMS *Excellent* to qualify as a gunnery instructor and on 13 December 1904 married his first cousin Lois Beynon (*c*.1879–1952), daughter of William Beynon (Evans's maternal uncle), licensee of the Ship Inn, Middleton. They had two sons and a daughter and lived at Portsmouth, where Evans completed his gunnery training at HMS *Vernon*.

In spring 1910 Petty Officer Evans joined Scott's second Antarctic expedition, which aimed to be first to the pole. He had no romantic illusions about polar life and went because Scott asked him to, and because of the prospect of promotion if the pole were reached. With his *Discovery* mess mates Petty Officer Tom Crean and Chief Stoker William Lashly, Evans helped fit out the expedition ship *Terra Nova*, which left Cardiff for the southern oceans in June. Evans was the dominant personality in the mess deck, but when he fell drunk into the dock at Lyttelton, New Zealand, Scott dismissed him from the expedition. Evans pleaded to be taken back and Scott soon relented: he regarded Evans (as he later wrote) as 'a giant worker with a really remarkable headpiece', and at the Cape Evans expedition base he became 'sledgemaster', in charge of all rigging and repairs (Scott, *Scott's Last Expedition*, 389). He also guided the geological expedition to the western mountains in January to March 1911. Few at Cape Evans that winter doubted that 'Taff' would be involved in the pole attempt the following summer, a proud representative of Wales and the lower deck.

The main polar party left base on 1 November 1911, and on 4 January 1912 the last supporting party turned back on the polar plateau at 87°32′ south. Evans was a member of the five-man team that reached the pole on 18 January already aware that the Norwegians had beaten them there. They began the return journey of more than 800 miles with lowered spirits and with the daily minimum temperature nearing -20 °F. Their fatigue was intensified by dehydration and malnutrition. This affected Evans, the biggest man, most acutely. He was constantly hungry, and it is possible that he had incipient scurvy. A deep cut on his hand refused to heal and became infected, and he suffered painful frostbite to his face and fingers. On 4 February he fell waist-deep into a crevasse, and there were further falls on the Beardmore glacier. The scant evidence available suggests either that one of these falls induced a slow brain haemorrhage leading to his death, or that he was afflicted by high-altitude cerebral oedema. He became withdrawn and depressed, a shadow of his former self, and on 16 February collapsed near the foot of the glacier, 'sick and giddy and unable to walk' (*Edward Wilson: Diary*, 243). Next morning he 'declared as he always did that he was quite well', but soon dropped behind in the march (Scott, *Diaries*, 2, 17 Feb 1912). His companions returned to find him 'on his knees with clothing disarranged, hands uncovered & frostbitten and a wild look in his eyes' (ibid.). He died in the camp abreast of Monument rock, at the foot of the Beardmore glacier, that night, on 17 February 1912.

In the words of Apsley Cherry-Garrard, 'Seaman Evans was the first to crack', and his reputation has suffered accordingly (Cherry-Garrard, 378). On the outward march the two doctors in the party, Edward Wilson and Edward Atkinson, agreed that if a rating was to be included in the pole party it should be William Lashly, and not Evans. Events seemed to confirm this judgement. Lashly's remarkable resilience during his return journey from 4 January to 22 February, which was indeed matched by Tom Crean, contrasts markedly with Evans's rapid decline. That Scott placed such faith in the latter has furnished his critics with an example of his failings as expedition leader. Modern research, though, emphasizes how far Edgar Evans's well-proven strength and polar experience were fatally undermined by a combination of dietary deficiencies, illness, and injury. That he started in his place on the traces on 17 February and began to pull is fitting enough testimony to what Scott once called his 'undefeatable' spirit.

Edgar Evans was commemorated with his four companions at the cairn erected at 79°50′ south by the relief expedition in November 1912 and on the jarrah wood cross later erected at Observation Hill on Hut Point, Ross Island. News of his death first reached Swansea on 10 February 1913, and on 27 January 1914 a memorial plaque was unveiled inside Rhosili church. He was posthumously awarded the polar medal, which was received by his widow in July 1913. The Evans Glacier (83°47′ S, 170°00′ E), Evans Névé (72°45′ S, 164°30′ E), and Evans Piedmont Glacier (76°44′ S, 162°40′ E) in the Antarctic were named after him. MARK POTTLE

Sources G. C. Gregor, *Swansea's Antarctic explorer: Edgar Evans, 1876–1912* (1995) · R. F. Scott, *The diaries of Captain Robert Scott: a record of the second Antarctic expedition, 1910–1912*, 6 vols. (1968), vol. 2 · R. F. Scott, *Scott's last expedition: the journals* (1951–64) · R. F. Scott, *The voyage of the 'Discovery'*, 2 vols. (1905) · *Edward Wilson: diary of the 'Terra Nova' expedition to the Antarctic, 1910–1912*, ed. H. G. R. King (1972) · A. Cherry-Garrard, *The worst journey in the world: Antarctic, 1910–1913* (1951) · *Under Scott's command: Lashly's Antarctic diaries*, ed. A. R. Ellis (1969) · *The quiet land: the diaries of Frank Debenham*, ed. J. Debenham Back (1992) · *The Norwegian with Scott: Tryggve Gran's Antarctic diary, 1910–1913*, ed. G. Hattersley-Smith (1984) · E. R. G. R. Evans, *South with Scott* (1921); repr. (1962) · H. G. Ponting, *The great white south* (1921) · S. Solomon, *The coldest March: Scott's fatal Antarctic expedition* (2001) · S. Wheeler, *Cherry: a life of Apsley Cherry-Garrard* (2001) · A. F. Rogers, 'The death of chief petty officer Evans', *The Practitioner*, 212 (1974), 570–80 · R. Mear and R. Swan, *In the footsteps of Scott* (1987) · E. Huxley, *Scott of the Antarctic* (1977) · R. Huntford, *Scott and Amundsen* (1993) · G. Seaver, *'Birdie' Bowers of the Antarctic* (1938) · b. cert.

Likenesses Ponting, group portrait, photograph, 1912, repro. in Solomon, *Coldest march* · J. J. Jones, two oil paintings, *c*.1966, Swansea Museum · P. Chatfield, marble bust, Swansea Museum · Ponting, photograph, repro. in Solomon, *Coldest march*, 229

Evans, Dame Edith Mary (1888–1976), actress, was born on 8 February 1888 at 12 Ebury Square, London, the daughter of Edward Evans, a minor civil servant, and his wife, Caroline Ellen Foster; a brother born in 1886 died at the age of four. Evans was educated at St Michael's Church of England School, Pimlico, before being indentured in 1903 at the age of fifteen as a milliner to a Mr Blackaller in the Buckingham Palace Road. On 9 September 1925 she married a petroleum engineer, George (Guy) Booth (1882/3–1935), whom she had known since she was sixteen; the marriage was childless.

Evans's first appearance on the stage, as an amateur, was with Miss Massey's Streatham Shakespeare Players in the role of Viola in *Twelfth Night* in October 1910. In 1912 she was discovered by the noted producer William Poel and made her first professional appearance for Poel at the Cambridge University Examination Hall in August of that year, playing the role of Gautami in an obscure sixth-century Hindu classic, *Sakuntala*. Her talents were then noted by novelist George Moore who became her passionate mentor and was responsible for her being engaged at the Royalty Theatre, Dean Street, in February 1914 on a year's contract at a salary of £2 10s. a week. She had earlier aroused considerable attention with her performance as Cressida in *Troilus and Cressida* directed by Poel for the Elizabethan Stage Society in the King's Hall, Covent Garden, and subsequently at Stratford upon Avon. Her extraordinary career was to span sixty-six years: she performed without a break until a few months before her death, her final public appearance being a BBC radio programme before an invited audience in August 1976.

From the outset Evans was a leading player ('God was very good to me', she once remarked, 'he never let me go on tour') and was dedicated to the truth, saying that 'I don't think there is anything extraordinary about me except this passion for the truth', and indeed it is difficult to call to mind any other leading actress of the twentieth century who had such single-minded application towards her profession. She played over 150 different roles in the course of her long career and created six of the characters of George Bernard Shaw: the Serpent, the Oracle, the She-Ancient, and the Ghost of the Serpent in *Back to Methuselah* (1923); Orinthia in *The Apple Cart* (1929); and Epifania in *The Millionairess* (1940). She gave what many consider to be

Dame Edith Mary Evans (1888–1976), by Sasha, 1929

definitive performances as Millamant in *The Way of the World* (1924), Rosalind in *As You Like It* (1926 and 1936), the Nurse in *Romeo and Juliet* (1932, 1934, and 1961), and, most notably, as Lady Bracknell in *The Importance of being Earnest* (1939). Indeed she became so identified with Lady Bracknell in the public eye that she grew to hate the role.

Evans began her film career in a silent film called *A Welsh Singer*, made for Henry Edwards at Walton-on-Thames studios in 1915, but then concentrated on stage roles until Emlyn Williams directed her in his own film *The Last Days on Dolwyn* in 1948, the same year as she appeared in Thorold Dickinson's widely admired *The Queen of Spades*. Although she re-created two of her most famous stage roles for the cinema—Lady Bracknell and Mrs St Maugham from Enid Bagnold's *The Chalk Garden*—they are but pale versions of the originals and she herself was not proud of them. Perhaps her most rounded screen performance was as Mrs Ross in *The Whisperers* (1966), for which she received the Golden Bear for best actress at the Berlin Film Festival, the British Academy award, the New York Film Critics' award, and was nominated for an American Oscar and other international prizes. Her last screen performance (in which she sang and danced) was in *The Slipper and the Rose* (1975) when she was eighty-seven.

Evans's most widely admired asset was her voice, a highly individual instrument, often imitated but never surpassed. She often professed herself unaware of the extraordinary effect it had on her audiences, but she set great store by clear diction, and in her later years openly criticized the slovenly standards of speech prevalent in the theatre. Belonging as she did to the old school, she imposed severe disciplines on herself and, although she liked to be in complete control of her audiences, always kept them at a distance, becoming over the course of the years a remote and finally very lonely figure. She had a love for and natural feeling for poetry; her taste was catholic and when she felt unable to undertake the task of learning any new roles she embarked on a highly successful one-woman show of poetry readings (1973), and indeed her last appearance on any West End stage, on 5 October 1974, took place during a revival of this entertainment.

Evans was the complete actress, dedicated, always professional, sublimating all other aspects of her life in the service of the theatre. A prime mover and lifelong supporter of British Actors' Equity, though not actively political, she was honoured by being appointed DBE in the new year's list of 1946. She also received four degrees *honoris causa* from the universities of London (1950), Cambridge (1951), Oxford (1954), and Hull (1968). Walter Sickert painted her, Shaw flirted with her, playwrights queued to write for her, but she remained curiously untouched by fame and whenever she was not active in the theatre or the film studios, retired to her Elizabethan manor house in Kent, there to tend her garden, read, 'recharge my batteries', and watch football on television.

Evans was a Christian Scientist, a devout woman who frequently did good by stealth, and when she died she left the bulk of her considerable estate for the benefit of the Actors' Charitable Trust. James Agate wrote of her 'there has never been a more versatile actress', and indeed her unique way of acting must place her among the immortals. She said of herself 'I can't imagine going on when there are no more expectations' but she fulfilled those expectations to the very end of her days and died in harness. 'Marking ages', she said, 'is a sign of deterioration. Age has nothing to do with me.' Edith Evans died at her home, The Gatehouse, Kilndown, Kent, on 14 October 1976.   BRYAN FORBES, *rev.*

Sources B. Forbes, *Ned's girl* (1977) · J. C. Trewin, *Edith Evans* (1954) · J. Batters, *Edith Evans* (1977) · personal knowledge (1986) · *The Times* (15 Oct 1976) · *CGPLA Eng. & Wales* (1976) · b. cert. · m. cert.

Archives King's Cam., letters and postcards to G. H. W. Rylands · Theatre Museum, London, corresp. with Christopher Fry | FILM BFI NFTVA, *Parkinson: the interviews*, BBC 1, 3 Aug 1996 · BFI NFTVA, documentary footage · BFI NFTVA, performance footage | SOUND BL NSA, Bow dialogues, 28 Jan 1969, C 812/20 C25

Likenesses Sasha, photograph, 1929, Hult. Arch. [*see illus.*] · W. Lewis, pencil and wash drawing, 1932, AM Oxf. · E. Gabain, oils, *c.*1935, City of Stoke-on-Trent Art Gallery · W. R. Sickert, oils, *c.*1935, Leeds City Art Gallery · W. R. Sickert, oils, 1937, Bradford City Art Gallery · Madame Yevonde, photograph, 1937, NPG · R. Buhler, oils, 1959, Royal Shakespeare Theatre, Stratford upon Avon · A. McBean, bromide print, 1959, NPG · G. Argent, photograph, 1970, NPG · C. Beaton, photograph, NPG · H. Coster, two photographs, NPG

Wealth at death £130,545: probate, 3 Dec 1976, *CGPLA Eng. & Wales* · £1000: probate, 14 April 1977, *CGPLA Eng. & Wales* (1976)

Evans, Edmund (1826–1905), wood-engraver and printer, was born in Southwark, London, on 23 February 1826, the son of Henry Evans and his wife, Mary, and baptized on 9 April 1826 at St Mary Magdalen, Bermondsey. Following a brief education at a school in Jamaica Row kept by Bert Robson, an old sailor, in 1839, at the age of thirteen, he became 'reading boy' in Samuel Bentley's printing firm in Shoe Lane. When an overseer found that the boy had a talent for drawing, his parents apprenticed him in 1840 to Ebenezer Landells, a wood-engraver who had been a pupil of Thomas Bewick. As Evans wrote later in his *Reminiscences*: 'I experienced great enjoyment in my beginning engraving; the work was quite to my liking, and the relief of getting to work at 9 o'clock, instead of 7, made me feel quite a young gentleman' (*Reminiscences*, 8). The artist Myles Birket Foster, one year older than Evans, was also apprenticed to Landells, and a friendship grew up between the two young men which developed into a long collaboration; Foster later provided many of the designs which Evans engraved and printed.

When Evans's apprenticeship was completed in May 1847 he started business as a wood-engraver on his own account; he first took small premises in Wine Office Court, Fleet Street, but in 1851 moved to 4 Racquet Court (later expanded to include 116 and 119 Fleet Street). He was soon getting orders from publishers and employing assistants, including his younger brothers Wilfred and Herbert. Although he was a talented engraver in black and white, particularly of landscapes and flora and fauna, Evans made his name by exploiting a growing market for books with illustrations printed in colour. His first printing in colour was for Ida Pfeiffer's *Visit to the Holy Land* (1852), published by Ingram, Cooke & Co.: he engraved the blocks for three printings, in delicate shades of brown, pale blue, and pale yellow. There was, of course, nothing new about colour printing of this kind at that date: George Baxter's plates had been familiar for nearly twenty years, and colour printing from woodblocks in cheap children's books had been done by the firm of Gregory, Collins, and Reynolds between 1843 and 1849. Evans's undoubted achievement as a colour printer was as a popularizer rather than a pioneer. Although he was generally responsive to minor innovations and improvements—some of which he introduced himself—he was not responsible for the discovery or adoption of any major technological advances and his printing methods always remained based on the wood-engraving technique which dominated mid-century illustration. The new photomechanical methods of the 1890s were to pass the aged printer by.

The profitable basis of Evans's colour-printing business was established when Ingram Cooke asked him to start printing book covers in three colours for the new railway bookstall market. Speed, cheapness, and bright colours were the prime requisites, and Evans was particularly successful in mixing bright inks. He also introduced the use of yellow glazed paper, more serviceable than the previously used white. The yellow-backs, as they were known, were enormously popular. (Evans's own collection of more than 350 proofs of his yellow-back and other book covers passed, via Sir Michael Sadleir, into the Constance Meade collection, now in the Bodleian Library in Oxford.) Evans then turned almost entirely to colour engraving and printing: a popular employer (although an

overtrusting businessman), he may have employed as many as thirty engravers during the 1860s and 1870s. His cheap three- or two-colour printing for publishers was sometimes astonishingly poor, but it is his higher quality work that won him his reputation. *Sabbath Bells Chimed by the Poets* (1856) was his first book with illustrations engraved and printed by him in full colours, after drawings by Birket Foster: with hand-coloured initials, it is a very pretty book indeed. Devised by Joseph Cundall, it was printed by the Chiswick Press, and the illustrations were presumably overprinted on the Chiswick Press sheets, in four or five colours, by Evans. Later editions of the book, in 1861, 1862, and after, were reset and entirely printed by Evans.

In the 1860s Evans established himself as the leading and the best woodblock colour printer in London. In 1860 Routledge published M. E. Chevreul's *The Laws of Contrast in Colour*, an important text illustrated with seventeen plates printed by Evans in up to about ten colours, brilliant in colouring and exciting as compositions. In 1864 came the substantial *A Chronicle of England*, written and illustrated by James Doyle, the elder brother of Richard Doyle: the many small illustrations, set in the text, are as bright as if they had just been painted. Exhibiting Evans's colour printing at its very best, they rival anything that Baxter ever did. Even more splendid was the Longman edition of Richard Doyle's masterpiece *In Fairyland* (1870), which contained sixteen plates printed by Evans in from eight to twelve colours: it is one of the most entrancing children's books ever made.

The next big development in commercial colour printing in Britain came with the publication of the Toy Books, introduced by Routledge and Warne in the mid-1860s. These children's books consisted of six pages of text and six pages of colour, printed on one side only, bound in paper covers, measuring about 10½ by 9 inches. The first titles were printed by Evans, but soon they became so popular that most of the other colour printers in London were called in. Those printed by Evans and the Dalziel brothers were printed from woodblocks; Kronheim and G. C. Leighton printed mostly from wood or metal, sometimes combined with lithography. The demand for Toy Books became so great that—like other printers—Evans turned publisher, and commissioned the artists himself. He commissioned Walter Crane to illustrate the first of these de luxe books, *The Baby's Opera* (1877); Crane designed between forty and fifty Toy Books, all printed and many commissioned by Evans, between 1865 and 1886. In 1878 Evans followed up this shrewd and successful move by engaging Randolph Caldecott to provide two Christmas Toy Books, *John Gilpin* and *The House that Jack Built*: the illustrator went on to produce two such books every year, sixteen in all, of which many more than a million copies have been printed. They remain in print and are still popular.

Evans's next protégé was Kate Greenaway: her first commission appears to have been for an Aunt Louisa's Toy Book from Kronheim & Co., *Diamonds and Toads* (1870), which is far more interesting than her later insipid work. In 1877 she took a book of her own verses and drawings to

Evans, who immediately accepted them and obtained Routledge's agreement to publish them in a 6-shilling book to be called *Under the Window*. He printed 20,000 copies, which soon sold out, and he had great difficulty in keeping up with demand: *Under the Window* was still in print in 1972. Greenaway never allowed anyone other than Evans to engrave and print her illustrations, clearly recognizing how much Evans's interpretative skills and ability to match medium to style contributed to the final appearance of her work.

In 1864 Evans married Mary Spence Brown, a niece of Birket Foster, and they went to live in the village of Witley in Surrey; their neighbours included George Eliot and the Allinghams and their visitors Kate Greenaway and other artistic protégés. Evans retired from business in 1892—the success of his firm meant that he had left off engraving some years before—and settled in Ventnor in the Isle of Wight. He died there at his home, Belgrave View, Zig Zag Road, on 21 August 1905 and was buried in Ventnor cemetery. His business was carried on by his sons Wilfred and Herbert (he also had three daughters) and was amalgamated with another firm, W. P. Griffith Ltd, in 1953: in 1966 Evans's grandson Rex Evans was managing director.

In his old age Evans wrote his *Reminiscences*, which were published, with illustrations and a selective list of his colour printing, by the Clarendon Press, Oxford, in 1967. The original manuscript is not now known to exist. The copy used for publication in 1967 was a typescript of 102 numbered pages—uncorrected, with gaps, and clearly never read by Evans. Some of its deficiencies clearly derive from its original: it contains typing errors and numerous inconsistencies and mistakes, such as might be expected in the unchecked reminiscences of a seventy-year-old man. Nevertheless, it offers a unique insight into the nineteenth-century wood-engraving and colour-printing world. It was presented by Rex Evans to the Constance Meade collection, which includes many of Evans's books and proofs. RUARI MCLEAN

Sources *The reminiscences of Edmund Evans*, ed. R. McLean (1967) · *British and Colonial Printer and Stationer* (7 Sept 1905), 3 · R. K. Engen, *Dictionary of Victorian wood engravers* (1985) · R. McLean, *Victorian book design and colour printing*, rev. edn (1972) · Bodl. Oxf., Constance Meade collection · 'Some notes on the history of printing in colour', *British and Colonial Printer and Stationer* (31 March 1904), 229–31 · M. Hardie, *English coloured books* (1906) · *DNB* · d. cert. · IGI
Archives U. Cal., Los Angeles, MSS, drawings, sketches
Likenesses pencil, repro. in McLean, ed., *Reminiscences* · photograph, repro. in McLean, ed., *Reminiscences*
Wealth at death £11,098 18s. 1d.: resworn probate, 13 Oct 1905, CGPLA Eng. & Wales

Evans, Edward (*b.* 1573/4), Church of England clergyman, was the son of a clergyman from West Meon, Hampshire. He was educated at Winchester College, matriculated at New College, Oxford, on 10 October 1594, aged twenty, and was admitted a fellow there in 1595, graduating BA in 1598 and proceeding MA in 1602. On the presentation of the college he was vicar of Heckfield, Hampshire, briefly in 1601–2, and of Chesterton, Oxfordshire, between 1604 and 1610.

Since he was apparently 'a noted preacher of his time in the university' (Wood, *Ath. Oxon.* 2.168), it was almost certainly he who published in 1615 *Verba Dierum, or, The Dayes Report of Gods Glory*, based on sermons or lectures given in Oxford, rather than the Edward Evans (*b. c.*1582) of Denbighshire and Christ Church to whom Wood gave credit for the work (Wood, *Ath. Oxon.: Fasti*, 1.299). Dedicated only to 'the honour and glory of the holiest of all, the Almightie and most high King of Kings and Lord of Lords, Father of Lights, Maker of all Things, fountain of all glory', and stiff with explanations of Greek, Hebrew, and Arabic meanings, the work celebrates the knowledge of God written in the world as well as the Bible, approves 'rites and ceremonies … royaltie and magnificence' as 'very singular means of the advancement of the glory of the most glorious', affirms holy days, and stresses the importance of the laity's acting as a spiritual priesthood, speaking and preaching by their good lives and conversation, for 'beautifying ourselves sets forth the glory of God'.

Describing himself on the title-page as 'Preacher and Minister of Godsword', Evans does not at that date appear to have been beneficed, but is probably the same man who was vicar of Leckford, Hampshire, in 1627. There is no other indication of his later career or date of death.

GORDON GOODWIN, *rev.* VIVIENNE LARMINIE

Sources Foster, *Alum. Oxon.* · Wood, *Ath. Oxon.*, new edn, 2.168 · Wood, *Ath. Oxon.: Fasti* (1815), 299, 317 · E. Evans, *Verba dierum, or, The dayes report of Gods glory* (1615) · W. J. Oldfield, 'Index to the clergy whose ordination, institution, resignation, licence or death is recorded in the diocesan registers of the diocese of Oxford … 1542–1908', 1915, Bodl. Oxf., MS Top. Oxon. c. 250, 1, fol. 121v; 2, fol. 420v

Evans, Edward. *See* Evan, Edward (1716–1798).

Evans, Edward (1789–1835), printseller, was probably born in London. He was the founder of a noted London print dealership which was eventually inherited by his two sons. Almost nothing is known of Evans's early life except that he trained as a compositor at the printers Nichols & Son in Red Lion Passage, Fleet Street. His *Gentleman's Magazine* obituary records that the firm of Nichols & Son quickly elevated him to the more senior position of reader on account of his efficiency and speed. Despite this advancement, Evans was obviously a man of determination. Having saved a small capital sum he decided to set himself up in business as a printseller with a specialist interest in engraved historic portrait heads. Although published without a date, Evans's *Catalogue of a Collection of Engraved Portraits* indicates the extensive stock of upwards of 20,000 English and foreign portrait prints that was available at his Great Queen Street shop. Evans was particularly well suited to this trade. First he was remembered for his 'cleverness and industry' (*GM*, 1860, 434) in arranging his complicated stock into a taxonomy which met the needs of his customers and, second, as an 'amiable, good-tempered man' (*GM*, 1835, 105), he was able to develop close relationships with a number of collectors and literary men. For example, the antiquarian Mark Noble frequently consulted him on matters of biographical research and, in return, Evans supplied him with detailed accounts of the information inscribed on various prints.

The enterprise prospered, and following Edward Evans's death, at Great Queen Street, Lincoln's Inn Fields, on 24 November 1835, his wife, Anne, continued the business with their eldest son, **Edward David Evans** (1818–1860). He too attained a reputation for his knowledge of rare portrait prints. Edward David Evans died on 15 August 1860, at the age of only forty-two, at his home, 3 Circus Road, St John's Wood. He was survived by his wife and four children, and the business continued trading, as A. E. Evans & Son, under the guidance of his brother Albert Evans, from new premises at 403 Strand.   LUCY PELTZ

Sources Boase, *Mod. Eng. biog.* · E. Evans, *Catalogue of a collection of engraved portraits*, 2 vols. [1836–53] · D. Bank and A. Esposito, eds., *British biographical index*, 4 vols. (1990) · *GM*, 2nd ser., 4 (1835) · *GM*, 3rd ser., 9 (1860), 434 [Edward David Evans]

Evans, Edward David (1818–1860). *See under* Evans, Edward (1789–1835).

Evans, Edward Ratcliffe Garth Russell, first Baron Mountevans (1880–1957), naval officer, was born in London on 28 October 1880, the second of the three sons and the third child of Frank Evans, barrister, and his wife, Eliza Frances Garth. From the first he was of an adventurous disposition and more than once ran away from home; although not the eldest son, he was always the ringleader. He and his elder brother went in due course to Merchant Taylors' School, London, whence they were soon expelled for repeatedly playing truant. Evans was then sent to a school for 'troublesome boys' at Kenley, where he was very happy. He went on to Warwick House School, Maida Vale, from where he passed into the *Worcester*, mercantile marine training ship. Two years later he obtained a naval cadetship.

Evans's first ship in the Royal Navy was the *Hawke*, in the Mediterranean Fleet, a good ship for one who loved 'clean, well-run ships and well-dressed, smart men-at-arms', for she was famous for those qualities. He was later appointed to the training sloop *Dolphin*, where the experience of handling a ship under sail alone was of inestimable value to him. In 1900 he was promoted sub-lieutenant and in 1902 he was selected, chiefly on account of his superb physical fitness, to be second officer of the *Morning*, the relief ship sent out by the Royal Geographical Society to the first Antarctic expedition of R. F. Scott. The *Morning* located the *Discovery* fast in the ice; but after revictualling her was obliged to leave her there for a second winter. In January 1904 the *Morning* returned, accompanied by the *Terra Nova*; the *Discovery* broke out of the ice in February, and the three ships returned home.

Evans, who had been promoted lieutenant in 1902, returned to naval duty and qualified as a navigating officer. In 1909 he was selected by Scott himself as second in command of his second expedition and captain of the *Terra Nova*, which left England in June 1910. He accompanied Scott in January 1912 to within 150 miles of the pole, where he turned back. Struck down by scurvy he was saved only by the devotion of his two companions, Chief

Edward Ratcliffe Garth Russell Evans, first Baron Mountevans (1880–1957), by Philip A. de Laszlo, 1920

Stoker Lashly and Petty Officer Crean. After a brief period of convalescence in England, which he devoted to raising money for the expedition, he returned to take command of the *Terra Nova* in New Zealand and sailed south, only to find on arrival at Cape Evans in January 1913 that Scott had died in an unparalleled period of bad weather when returning from the pole in March of the previous year. After bringing home the expedition and clearing up its affairs Evans went on half pay and spent some time lecturing in Canada and the United States. He had been promoted commander in 1912.

In the summer of 1914 Evans resumed naval service in command of the *Mohawk*, destroyer, in the Dover patrol. He went on to command various ships in the patrol, the one for which he was best-known being the *Broke*. In April 1917 the *Swift*, under Commander Ambrose Peck, and the *Broke* were sent out to counter-attack six German destroyers which had just bombarded Dover harbour. They met the enemy on opposite courses and at once fired torpedoes and turned to ram. The *Swift* was unsuccessful, passing through the enemy line, but the *Broke* rammed the G.42 and sustained forty casualties while the ships were locked together. There were no more German raids on Dover. This action struck the public imagination as the first in which ships came to close quarters in the old style, and he was always thereafter known as 'Evans of the *Broke*'. Peck and he were both appointed to the DSO and promoted captain. He became chief of staff to the admiral of the Dover patrol, Sir Reginald Bacon. When Roger Keyes took over the command Evans was eventually relieved, and until the end of the war, in the scout *Active*, was employed on escorting convoys to and from Gibraltar.

Evans paid off the *Active*, without orders, after the armistice, and following a period on half pay which he spent in Norway, he was for some months senior naval officer at Ostend, leaving only when all the mines had been swept up and the scars of war removed. He went next (1920–22) to the small cruiser *Carlisle* on the China station where he distinguished himself by swimming with a line to rescue the survivors on the steamer *Hong Moh*, ashore near Swatow (Shantou), an exploit which again brought him before the public. After another leave in Norway he became in 1923 captain of the auxiliary patrol, later renamed the fishery and mine-sweeping flotilla, in the sloop *Harebell*. It was an appointment after his own heart, for he was his own master and was able to visit many out-of-the-way places, a rare privilege at that period. In 1926 he received one of the plums for a captain, the command of the battle cruiser *Repulse*, which he held until shortly before his promotion to rear-admiral in February 1928.

Evans's first flag command was the Australian squadron (1929), with his flag in the cruiser *Australia*. He was immensely popular in the commonwealth, where his unconventional ways were fully appreciated. When he left in 1931, instead of inspecting each ship 'in all the dingle-dangle of braid', he entertained some 2000 ratings and their wives at a cinema. He was promoted vice-admiral in 1932 and in the following year became commander-in-chief on the Africa station, where again he was immensely popular. But he was much criticized when acting in 1933 as high commissioner in the absence of Sir Herbert Stanley for his handling of the case of Tshekedi *Khama, the regent of the Ngwato tribe in Bechuanaland, who had ordered the flogging of a European accused of assault and known to be seducing African women in tribal territory. Evans travelled to Bechuanaland in state, accompanied by a strong force of armed sailors, suspended Tshekedi, and expelled the European. Tshekedi was recognized as, on the whole, an enlightened and capable chieftain and after a few weeks Evans reinstated him. It was thought that the case would have been better handled with less ostentation, but that was not Evans's way. While on the Africa station he attempted to renew his acquaintance with the Antarctic, shifting his flag in 1934 to the sloop *Milford* and visiting Bouvet Island to check its position on the charts; but he was unable to continue to the south as the *Milford*'s coal supply had been depleted by heavy weather.

Evans next served as commander-in-chief at the Nore (1935–9), an appointment which provided little scope for his special talents; but during his tenure he was promoted admiral (1936) and received the freedom of Dover (1938) and Chatham (1939), and many other distinctions. In the spring of 1939 he was made a regional commissioner for London under the civil defence scheme. After the German invasion of Norway in 1940 he was sent there to establish liaison with the king. On his return he was at first employed in organizing the defence of aircraft factories and only when that was completed did he resume his duties as regional commissioner. His energy and fearlessness through the blitz on London were an inspiration to all who served under him. He retired from the navy in 1941 but continued to hold his post in civil defence until the end of the war. In 1945 he was one of the seven selected for peerages, ostensibly to strengthen the Labour Party in the House of Lords, taking the title of Baron Mountevans. He had been appointed CB (civil, 1913, military, 1932) and KCB (1935).

Evans was not a typical naval officer, except in his skill as a seaman. He revelled in publicity and was never happier than when in the public eye. That trait, which in a lesser man would have provoked severe criticism, was recognized as being part of his make-up and excused; for he was as universally popular with those brother officers who knew him personally as he was with the lower deck.

Evans was twice married: first, in 1904, to Hilda Beatrice (d. 1913), daughter of Thomas Gregory Russell, barrister, of Christchurch, New Zealand. There were no children. Second, in 1916, he married Elsa (d. 1963), daughter of Richard Andvord, *statshauptman* of Oslo. They had two sons.

Evans was elected rector of the University of Aberdeen in 1936, a very unusual distinction for a serving officer, and he was re-elected in 1939. He wrote a number of books, one of the first being *South with Scott* (1921) which he wrote to beguile the tedium of his voyage to China to take command of the *Carlisle*. Exploration was the theme of most of his books, but he also had a flair for writing for boys. Mountevans died at Golaa, near Oslo, in his beloved Norway on 20 August 1957, and was succeeded by his elder son, Richard Andvord Evans (b. 1918).

H. G. Thursfield, *rev.*

Sources Lord Mountevans [E. R. G. R. Evans], *Adventurous life* (1946) · E. Evans, first baron Mountevans, *Happy adventurer: an autobiography* (1951) · R. Pound, *Evans of the Broke* (1963) · private information (1971) · personal knowledge (1971) · *WWW* · *The Times* (22 Aug 1957) · *CGPLA Eng. & Wales* (1957)

Archives Scott Polar RI, corresp., notebooks, and papers | FILM BFI NFTVA, 'British Antarctic expedition, 1910–1913', 1924 · BFI NFTVA, news footage · IWM FVA, actuality footage · IWM FVA, news footage

Likenesses P. A. de Laszlo, oils, 1920, priv. coll. [*see illus.*] · photograph, 1928, Hult. Arch. · S. M. Brown, portrait, 1937, NMG Wales · W. Stoneman, photograph, 1947, NPG · W. A. Bowring, portrait, priv. coll. · M. Grixoni, portrait, priv. coll. · photographs, Scott Polar RI

Wealth at death £16,191 8s. 3d.: administration with will, 18 Nov 1957, *CGPLA Eng. & Wales*

Evans, Ellis Humphrey [*pseud.* Hedd Wyn] (1887–1917), poet, was born on 13 January 1887 at Pen-lan in the village of Trawsfynydd, Merioneth, and brought up at Yr Ysgwrn, a farm about a mile distant and facing Cwm Prysor. He was the eldest child of Evan Evans (1852–1942) and his wife, Mary, *née* Morris (1862–1950), a maidservant, the daughter of David Morris, blacksmith, of the same village. He received his elementary education at the village school and then helped his father on the family farm, although his heart was not in farming. The district had a rich Welsh-speaking culture in which poets enjoyed great prestige; the writing of verse in both the free and strict metres was the boy's only interest, and from the age of nineteen he began winning prizes at local eisteddfods. Brought up in a religious home, he attended Sunday school regularly at Ebenezer, a Congregationalist chapel in the village, and was steeped in the Bible, but, a handsome and naturally charming man, he was not averse to the company of young women; he had several sweethearts but did not marry. Under the influence of the poet R. Silyn Roberts, with whom he used to go fishing, he was attracted to socialism.

Although he wrote several lyrics of lasting merit, such as the one to the River Prysor, Hedd Wyn (the bardic name by which he was generally known can be rendered in English as 'blessed peace') is remembered mainly not on account of his poetry but because of his death in action during the First World War. Early in 1917 he enlisted with the 15th battalion of the Royal Welch Fusiliers, which left for Flanders in June, and was killed in the battle for Pilkem Ridge on 31 July.

At the national eisteddfod held at Birkenhead in the following September, and in the presence of David Lloyd George, who made a speech calling for victory against Germany no matter what the cost, a poem entitled 'Yr arwr' ('The hero'), which had been posted from the trenches by a poet using the pseudonym Fleur-de-lis, was awarded the oaken chair, the prize traditionally reserved for the author of the winning poem in strict metre. When it was announced from the stage that its author was Hedd Wyn, and that he had been killed on the western front, the chair was draped in black, causing great emotion in the audience, and the usual pageantry did not take place. A number of his fellow poets then paid tribute in verse to Hedd Wyn, whose only ambition had been to win the major competition at the festival. To many in Wales, which lost a disproportionate number of its young men on the field of battle, Hedd Wyn's death seemed to represent the sacrifice of a whole generation.

The Irish poet Francis Ledwidge was killed at Ypres on the same day as Hedd Wyn; both poets were buried in the military cemetery at Artillery Wood near Boesinghe, where the Welshman's gravestone bears the words 'Y prifardd Hedd Wyn' ('The chief poet Hedd Wyn'), a bardic title bestowed on those who distinguish themselves by winning the principal literary prizes at the national eisteddfod.

A collection of Hedd Wyn's poems, edited by J. J. Williams, was published under the title *Cerddi'r bugail* ('Poems of the Shepherd') in 1918; it included 'Yr arwr', which relates the myth of Prometheus to Christian symbolism and was written under the influence of Shelley's poem 'The Revolt of Islam'.

The sequence of *englynion* by R. Williams Parry beginning 'Y bardd trwm dan bridd tramor' ('The poet who lies heavily under foreign soil'), often sung to harp accompaniment and the tune 'Troytes Chant', was composed in memory of Hedd Wyn; the bronze statue portraying the poet as a shepherd which stands in the centre of Trawsfynydd was unveiled by his mother in 1923. The film *Hedd Wyn*, made in 1992, was nominated for an Oscar; its author, Alan Llwyd, also wrote a biography of the poet,

Gwae fi fy myw (1991). The poet's home, Yr Ysgwrn, which has not changed much since the poet's day, is now a small museum dedicated to his memory; among the artefacts on display is the 'black chair of Birkenhead'.

MEIC STEPHENS

Sources A. Llwyd, *Gwae fi fy myw: cofiant Hedd Wyn* (1991) • W. Morris, *Hedd Wyn* (1969) • D. Jones, 'Rhai sylwadau ar farddoniaeth Hedd Wyn', *Ysgrifau Beirniadol*, 6 (1971) • B. Phillips, 'A fine day's work', *Planet*, 72 (Dec 1988/Jan 1989)
Archives NL Wales, MSS • Yr Ysgwrn, Trawsfynydd, MSS
Likenesses bronze statue, Trawsfynydd • photographs, repro. in Llwyd, *Gwae fi fy myw* • portrait, Yr Ysgwrn, Trawsfynydd

Evans, (Emyr) Estyn (1905–1989), geographer, was born on 29 May 1905 at 12 Havelock Terrace, Shrewsbury, Shropshire, the fourth of the five children of the Revd George Owen Evans (1865–1920), and his wife, Elizabeth (1864–1944), *née* Jones. His parents were both Welsh-speaking and the Revd Evans—a Methodist—later moved from Shrewsbury to a poorer parish across the Welsh border. Estyn Evans was educated at Welshpool county school (1915–22) before going to the University College of Wales, Aberystwyth, in 1922 to study geography and anthropology under the tutelage of H. J. Fleure. After graduating with a BA in 1925, Evans was prevented by tuberculosis from undertaking postgraduate study at Oxford and it was not until 1928—albeit then aged only twenty-three—that he was appointed to the first post in geography at Queen's University, Belfast. Two days after his successful interview, he met his future wife, Gwyneth Lyon Jones (1908–2003); they married on 27 August 1931 and had four sons, David (b. 1934), Colin (b. 1939), Edwin (b. 1943), and Alun (b. 1944).

Evans struggled long and hard during the 1930s, and the straitened years of the Second World War, to establish his discipline and department in Queen's, encountering an often hostile academic environment in which geography was for long regarded as an adjunct to geology. Consequently, it was only in 1947 that geography was granted the status of a single-honours course, and not until 1955 that Evans was able to offer a first-year course in his own subject. He was appointed professor of geography in 1945, in which post he remained until resigning in 1968 to accept the university's invitation to become the first director of the newly established Institute of Irish Studies. What was by then a flourishing department of geography was by no means his only achievement. He was awarded the degrees of MA (1931) and DSc (1939) from Aberystwyth, together with five honorary degrees. Evans was also instrumental in originating departments of archaeology (1948) and social anthropology (1960) at Queen's, and played a leading role in the creation of the Ulster Folk Museum at Cultra, co. Down (established in 1958), which was designed to record a way of life then fast disappearing. In 1970, the same year in which Queen's appointed him emeritus professor in geography and Irish studies, he was appointed CBE.

Because Evans published largely in Ireland, his work was never as well known in Britain as it deserved. In contrast, however, he was widely recognized in the United

States and is often compared to the influential Berkeley geographer Carl Sauer. Evans's geographical context was dominated by Ireland and its setting on the Atlantic margins of Europe. Fascinated by borders and frontiers, and the infinite variety of folk adaptations to a bewildering array of environments, he created an Ireland of regional diversity in which differences were as important as similarities. It was a moral world, too, for while Evans had long lost his father's faith, his geography is defined by a humanistic vision of the total inheritance of Irish heritage, irrespective of formal creeds. For Evans, Irishness was a complex fusion of processes operating at a variety of scales from the intimacy of locality to the wider embrace of the Atlantic world. This vision of a pluralistic place was—and remains—a powerful riposte to the simplifying certainties of traditional Irish nationalism.

Evans published numerous academic papers, archaeological surveys, excavation reports (especially that on Lyle's Hill, co. Antrim), and contributions to reviews, magazines, and newspapers, many posthumously collected in *Ireland and the Atlantic Heritage* (1996). His output is dominated, however, by seven books, of which the most enduring in popular terms is *Irish Folk Ways* (1957). In the contemporary context, however, the most important may be *Mourne Country* (1951), now widely recognized as a classic study of the interrelationships between place and identity, and *The Personality of Ireland* (1973). The latter is not an easy book, but it distils Evans's vision of Ireland as a complex and diverse place, a conceptualization which provides his work with an enduring relevance as subsequent generations seek to break down the malevolent legacy of ethnic conflict. Following his death in Belfast on 12 August 1989 after a long illness and his cremation on 15 August at the Roselawn crematorium, Belfast, it was entirely appropriate that Evans's life's work was marked by a memorial service held on 9 December 1989 at the Ulster Folk Museum, the institution which embodied his belief that regional diversity should be seen as a source of richness and integration rather than division.

BRIAN GRAHAM

Sources G. Evans, 'Estyn: a biographical memoir', in E. E. Evans, *Ireland and the Atlantic heritage: selected writings* (1996), 1–19 · R. E. Glasscock, 'Obituary: E. Estyn Evans, 1905–1989', *Journal of Historical Geography*, 17 (1991), 87–91 · B. J. Graham, 'The search for common ground: Estyn Evans's Ireland', *Transactions of the Institute of British Geographers*, new ser., 19 (1994), 183–201 · WW · R. H. Buchanan, 'Obituary: Emyr Estyn Evans, 1905–1989', *Ulster Folklife*, 36 (1990), 1–3 · J. Campbell, 'Ecology and culture in Ireland', in E. E. Evans, *Ireland and the Atlantic heritage: selected writings* (1996), 225–44 · E. E. Evans, 'Beginnings', in J. A. Campbell, E. E. Evans, and W. Kirk, *Geography at Queen's: an historical survey* (1978), 5–15 · private information (2004)

Archives Ulster Folk and Transport Museum, Cultra, co. Down

Likenesses R. Piper, drawing, *c*.1967, Queen's University, Belfast · R. Wilson, drawing, *c*.1970, Queen's University, Belfast

Wealth at death £57,745: probate, 10 Nov 1989, *CGPLA NIre*.

Evans, Evan [*pseud.* Ieuan Fardd; *called* Ieuan Brydydd Hir] (1731–1788), scholar and poet, was born on 20 May 1731 at Cynhawdref farm in the parish of Lledrod, Cardiganshire. The son of Jenkin Evans (*d. c*.1758), a farmer, and his wife, Catherine (*d*. 1788), he sat at the feet of Edward Richard at his celebrated school in Ystradmeurig before entering Merton College, Oxford, in December 1750. He left without graduating, but by 1754 he was an ordained priest and he spent the following two decades wandering disconsolately from curacy to curacy. He served in at least eighteen different cures in England and Wales, and became an instantly recognized figure among his countrymen. He adopted the bardic name Ieuan Fardd (Ieuan the Poet), but since he was an extraordinarily tall and lean man his contemporaries normally referred to him as Ieuan Brydydd Hir (Ieuan the Tall Poet) or Longobardus.

For much of his life Evans was preoccupied by two issues of critical importance in eighteenth-century Wales. The first was the Anglicization of the established church in Wales, the direct result of the appointment of non-Welsh prelates. Evans despised the absentee 'Esgyb-Eingl' ('Anglo-bishops') who passed over deserving Welsh clergymen in favour of pliant, non-Welsh-speaking timeservers, and became convinced that ardent and outspoken Welsh patriots within the church would always be denied affluent and permanent preferments. As avenues of advancement were closed to him, he began to thunder and rage against his *bêtes noires*, the Anglo-bishops and the place-hunters and sycophants who preached 'horrid unintelligible jargon' in Welsh pulpits. In 1764–5 he completed an unpublished polemic entitled 'The grievances of the principality of Wales in the church considered', the most sweeping indictment of the established church since the publication of Erasmus Saunders's tract on the diocese of St David's in 1721. Since the manuscript was riddled with barbed references to 'ravenous wolves', 'ignorant bunglers', and 'useless rogues' who had turned the church into a 'house of Merchandise and a den of thieves' (NL Wales, MS 2009B), it is not surprising that the Society of Cymmrodorion was reluctant to publish it. Convinced that bishops looked upon him with 'an evil eye' (Owen, 2.620), however, Evans continued until his dying day to vent his spleen on arrogant English churchmen, tithe-grabbing landowners, and the new Methodist enthusiasts.

Evans's second preoccupation was the sorry plight of Welsh culture. At a time when Wales lacked major cultural institutions and libraries, he resolved to concentrate on fostering the cause of Welsh scholarship. Influenced by Edward Richard and Lewis Morris, he joined the Morris circle and spent his leisure hours seeking out and copying manuscripts of literary and historical interest. He tramped the length and breadth of Wales in search of unpublished manuscripts in private libraries, many of which had been subjected to the ravages of mildew, mice, rats, and rain. His manuscripts and books were so numerous that two men and horses were required to move his library in 1767. He established fruitful links with the poet Thomas Gray and the antiquary Thomas Percy, and his joy was boundless when he discovered valuable texts such as 'Y Gododdin' and the work of Taliesin. His knowledge of the contents of Welsh manuscripts was second to none, and his major work, *Some Specimens of the Poetry of the Antient Welsh Bards* (1764), has been widely acclaimed as a seminal landmark in the history of Welsh scholarship. This was the first attempt to interpret the works of the Poets of the Princes and to chart the development of Welsh poetry from the sixth century to the Tudor period. It established Evans's reputation as the greatest Welsh scholar since Edward Lhuyd. Evans also composed *awdlau*, *cywyddau*, and *englynion*, mainly for the benefit of his patrons and companions, and his most celebrated poem is 'Llys Ifor Hael' ('The court of Ifor the Generous'), a series of *englynion* lamenting the demise of the heroic poetic tradition which he composed in 1779 during a visit to the ruins of the court of Ifor Hael (Ifor ap Llywelyn) at Gwernyclepa, near Basaleg, Monmouthshire.

Increasingly, however, Evans became a misanthropic, disorganized, and dishevelled figure, given to fits of melancholic depression which he sought (unsuccessfully) to relieve by imbibing prodigious quantities of alcohol. During the 1770s the second Sir Watkin Williams Wynn (1749–1789) took pity on him and gave him a modest pension and access to the literary treasures at the Wynnstay library. But Evans remained at odds with himself and the world around him. His writings became passionately patriotic and Anglophobe, and in the preface to a collection of translated sermons in 1776 he berated the likes of Williams Wynn for 'wearing the badge of their vassalage, by adopting the language of their conquerors, which is a mark of the most despicable meanness of spirit' (E. Evans, *Casgliad o bregethau*, 1, 1776, sig. B3). Similarly, in his best-known English poem—*The Love of our Country*, published in 1772—he depicted Owain Glyndŵr as a popular hero rather than as a bandit rebel in order to instil into his fellow countrymen greater pride in their national heritage.

During the latter years of Evans's life Paul Panton and Thomas Pennant sought to relieve his penury by inviting subscriptions from well-wishers on his behalf, and in 1787 Panton also purchased his remarkable collection of manuscripts, much of which entered the public domain when *The Myvyrian Archaiology* was published in three volumes between 1801 and 1807. Although Evans's burning patriotism and hard-hitting criticisms did not endear him to the establishment in Wales, he was highly regarded as a scholar. Unmarried and virtually penniless, he died on 4 August 1788 in the remote farmhouse where he had been born, and was buried in Lledrod churchyard. Such a gifted man deserved a better fate than a life of penury and neglect. GERAINT H. JENKINS

Sources D. S. Evans, ed., *Gwaith … Evan Evans (Ieuan Brydydd Hir)* (1876) · A. Lewis, 'Evan Evans ('Ieuan Fardd'), 1731–1788: hanes ei fywyd a'i gysylltiadau llenyddol', MA diss., U. Wales, 1950 · *The correspondence of Thomas Percy and Evan Evans*, ed. A. Lewis (1957), vol. 5 of *The Percy letters*, ed. C. Brooks, D. N. Smith, and A. F. Falconer (1944–88) · A. Lewis, 'Ieuan Fardd a'r Llenorion Saesneg', *Llên Cymru*, 7 (1962–3), 172–92 · G. Morgan, *Ieuan Fardd* (1988) · G. H. Jenkins, *The foundations of modern Wales, 1642–1780* (1987) · *DWB* · NL Wales, MS 2009B · *Additional letters of the Morrises of Anglesey, 1735–1786*, ed. H. Owen, 2 vols. (1947–9) · NL Wales, Panton MS 18, 23
Archives BL, corresp. and papers, Add. MSS 14884–15085, *passim* · NL Wales, corresp. and papers; 'Miscellanies' mainly in his hand; commonplace book | BL, corresp. with Bishop Percy, Add. MS 32330

Evans, Evan [*called* Evans Bach Nantyglo] (**1804–1886**), Congregational minister, was born at Gellillyndu, Llandewibrefi, Cardiganshire, on 8 March 1804, the son of David Evans, a member of Daniel Rowland's Calvinistic Methodist congregation. In 1824 he moved to industrial Monmouthshire, becoming a schoolmaster at Pontypool and later at Goetre and Nant-y-glo. He began preaching with the Methodists in 1825 and was an ardent supporter of the Sunday school movement and the education of children, editing the monthly publication, *Cyfaill Plentyn* ('Companions of children'), from 1835. After 1830 he became a complete abstainer, and was a powerful advocate for the temperance cause, suffering persecution because of his views. Changing convictions led him to join the Congregationalists at the nearby community of Beaufort, Brecknockshire, in 1847. Becoming a popular minister for his new denomination at Llan-giwg, Glamorgan, in 1852, he subsequently moved to chapels in southern Monmouthshire, at Risca and Machen and then Risca alone, from 1857 to 1860. In 1869 he emigrated to America, following his father and other family members who had left Wales in 1833. Initially settling at Oakhill, Ohio, he travelled and preached in various places before establishing the first Welsh church in Arkansas at Curtis in 1881. His wife, Mary Valentine of Beaufort, whom he had married about 1830, died in January 1886; Evans himself died in Curtis, Arkansas, on 29 October 1886. They were survived by three children, one of whom, Beriah Gwynfe *Evans (1848–1927), became a prominent Welsh nationalist, journalist, and pioneer dramatist.

In addition to his periodical work and contributions to many journals, such as *Cyfaill yr Aelwyd* ('Companions of the hearth', volumes 6 and 7), on contemporary issues, Evans was the author of five books: *Rhodd mam i'w plentyn* ('Mother's gift to children', 1833), *Y cyfammod gweithredoedd* ('Covenant of deeds',), *Ffordd Duw yr y cyssegr a'r mor* ('God's way in the sacred sea', 1842), and two volumes of sermons, *Arthrawiaeth a dyledswydd* ('Doctrine and duty', 1865–6). He also translated six works on theology and religion into Welsh. At the time of his death he was working on his reminiscences of eighty years of changes in Wales, a work which was never completed.

R. M. J. JONES, *rev.* WAYNE K. D. DAVIES

Sources *DWB*, 232 · *Cyfaill yr Aelwyd* (1887), 147–51 · *Bye-Gones Relating to Wales and the Border Counties*, 8 (1886–7), 189 · T. Mardy Rees, ed., *Notable Welshmen, 1700–1900* (1908), 391 · D. Morgan, ed., *Gwyr llên y bedwaredd ganrif ar bymtheg a'u cefndir* (1968)

Evans, Evan Herber (**1836–1896**), Congregational minister and college head, the eldest son of Josiah Evans (1814–1876), a blacksmith, and his wife, Sarah, *née* James (1817–1894), was born at Pant-yr-onnen, near Newcastle Emlyn, Carmarthenshire, on 5 July 1836. He spent some early years with his grandfather Jonah Evans at Pen-yr-herber, whence, in 1873, he adopted his second name. He received his early education at the private grammar school of John Davies in Adpar, Newcastle Emlyn, and at the British School in Llechryd. He was apprenticed to a local draper at

Rhydlewis from 1850 to 1853 and after a year's further service in Pontypridd and Merthyr Tudful he moved to Liverpool. Here, in 1857, he started to preach in the Welsh Congregational church (the Tabernacle), Great Crosshall Street, then under the pastorate of John Thomas (1821–1892). After twelve months' preparatory training at the Normal College, Swansea, he entered the Memorial College, Brecon, in 1858, where he remained for four years. He was ordained as pastor of Libanus church, Morriston, on 26 June 1862, and almost immediately he became one of the leading Welsh preachers. After three years at Morriston (during which time a debt of £2000 was paid off the chapel) he moved in October 1865 to Caernarfon to undertake the charge of a small church, Salem, established only two or three years previously, and still heavily in debt. Before he left it, in April 1894, it had the largest congregation of any Congregational church in north Wales, the chapel having been enlarged in 1890.

Evans was elected chairman of the Union of Welsh Independents in 1886, and delivered his address, entitled 'The answers of Christ to the questions of the age', at Aberdâr.

On 20 September 1865 Evans married Jenny (b. 1841/2), only daughter of John Hughes, jeweller, of Caernarfon; she died on 10 May 1875, leaving an only daughter, Lizzie, who married the Revd O. L. Roberts of Liverpool. On 28 September 1877 Evans married, secondly, Annie Ellen (1842/3–1927), the only daughter of Owen Jones, of Waterloo House, Caernarfon, who survived him. Their only child, Owen Herber, died in infancy on 27 May 1883.

In 1891 Evans was elected chairman of the Congregational Union of England and Wales, and his first presidential address, entitled 'The free churches and their opportunities', delivered at the City Temple, London, was described by Dr A. M. Fairbairn of Mansfield College, Oxford, as 'magnificent'. His second address, delivered at Bradford in October 1892, 'A living church', was (by special vote of the assembly) ordered to be printed in a cheap form for general circulation. In 1891 he became lecturer on homiletics at Bala–Bangor Congregational college. In 1894 he became its principal.

Throughout his life Evans took an active part in local politics; he was elected on the first school board at Caernarfon in 1874, and on the first county council in 1888. He declined, however, to stand as Liberal candidate for Caernarfon boroughs in May 1885 and April 1890. In 1895 he was appointed to the commission of the peace for Caernarvonshire, apparently an honour never previously conferred on a Welsh dissenting minister. He was awarded an honorary doctorate in divinity by the University of Miami, Ohio, in 1887.

Evans acted as editor of Y Dysgedydd ('The instructor'), one of the monthly magazines of the Welsh Congregationalists. From December 1873 to May 1880 he shared its editorship with Robert Thomas 'Ap Vychan', but had sole charge of it from 1880 until his death. A selection of his editorial notes was issued shortly after his death by his son-in-law, O. L. Roberts, under the title of Nodiadau Herber (1897). His brother, the Revd W. Justin Evans, also edited a volume of his sermons entitled True and False Aims and other

Sermons (1897) including reprints of his two addresses from the chair of the Congregational Union. A volume of his Welsh sermons, entitled Goleuni yn yr hwyr (1904), was edited by his son-in-law. Evans had just completed, before his final illness, a chapter which he was contributing to a biography of Dr John Thomas of Liverpool, and a short life of David Rees of Llanelli, which appeared posthumously.

But it was as a preacher that Evans was chiefly remembered: unoriginal in content, his sermons were practical rather than dogmatic, but his physique, his voice, the cast of his sermon, his entire personality, all combined to win him a position unequalled by any living preacher. Probably no other Welsh preacher so often appeared in English pulpits; between 1873 and 1877 he turned down several calls to minister to Congregational churches at Bishopsgate, Bath, and Brighton, and Westminster chapel and Harecourt chapel, London. Evans died on 30 December 1896 at his home, The Roft, Upper Bangor, and was buried there on 4 January 1897 in the Glanadda cemetery.

D. L. THOMAS, rev. HUW WALTERS

Sources H. E. Lewis, The life of E. Herber Evans DD (1900) • Y Dysgedydd, 76 (Feb 1897) [special memorial issue] • Western Mail [Cardiff] (31 Dec 1896) • Y Tyst (6 Jan 1897) • Y Geninen, 15 (1897) • DWB • Congregational Year Book (1898), 177 • R. Tudur Jones, Yr undeb (1975), 58–9, 387–8 • T. Rees and J. Thomas, Hanes eglwysi annibynol Cymru, 3 (1873), 245–6 • T. Rees and J. Thomas, Hanes eglwysi annibynol Cymru, 5 (1891), 295 • d. cert. • m. certs.

Archives NL Wales, MSS

Likenesses Lafayette of Dublin, photograph, NL Wales • Walker & Boutall, process reproduction (after photograph by Lafayette), NL Wales

Wealth at death £684 18s. 10d.: probate, 30 March 1897, CGPLA Eng. & Wales

Evans, Florence Annie [Nancy] (**1915–2000**), singer and teacher of singing, was born on 19 March 1915 at 36 Granville Road, Wavertree, Liverpool, the first daughter and second of the three children of Thomas Herbert Evans (1887–1972), monumental mason, and his wife, Florence Jones (1885–1967). Educated at Calder high school, Liverpool, Evans was a protégée of one of Lancashire's leading conductors and teachers, John Tobin. A mezzo-soprano, at the age of seventeen she made her operatic début in her home town as the Sorceress in Purcell's Dido and Aeneas, in performances conducted by Tobin. At the age of eighteen she gave her first solo recital, with Tobin in Liverpool, and made her London recital début with Gerald Moore at the Aeolian Hall. 1934 also saw her first broadcast for the BBC (in Pergolesi's Stabat mater), and while still in her teens she made her London stage début, in Sullivan's The Rose of Persia at the Prince's Theatre. Her father (who was proudly supportive of her career) commissioned Decca to make a private recording of her singing Strauss's 'Morgen', and the company immediately signed her (still aged just nineteen) to sing the title role in the first ever complete recording of Purcell's Dido and Aeneas. Glyndebourne Opera's John Christie paid for her to have further singing lessons with Jani Strasser, and in 1938 she joined the Glyndebourne chorus, in which she sang alongside Peter Pears in Don Giovanni, Le nozze di Figaro, Macbeth, and Don Pasquale. In the following year she was engaged for a season at Covent

Florence Annie [Nancy] **Evans** (1915–2000), by Bert Hardy, 1948 [as Polly Peachum in *The Beggar's Opera* by Benjamin Britten]

Garden, singing the Flower Maiden and the Voice on High in *Parsifal* under Weingartner, the Shepherd Boy in *Tosca* under Gui, and Rossweisse in *Die Walküre* under Beecham. There she met her first husband, (Harry) Walter *Legge (1906–1979), Beecham's assistant artistic director, whom she married on 14 July 1941. Their daughter Helga was born the following year.

During the war years Evans continued her vocal studies with Maggie Teyte, and because of the circumstances of war her career became very diverse and often hectic. In 1940 she joined Tommy Trinder and the Crazy Gang in *Top of the World* at the London Palladium, and during the 1941–2 season she sang Valencienne in *The Merry Widow* at His Majesty's, giving nine performances a week for ten consecutive months. She also toured extensively with the Entertainments National Service Association, giving concerts throughout England, the Netherlands, Belgium, France, and the Middle East, and towards the end of the war she made her début at the BBC's Promenade Concerts under Adrian Boult.

Evans's post-war career was launched back at Glyndebourne when in 1946 she alternated with Kathleen Ferrier, singing Lucretia in the première of Britten's first chamber opera *The Rape of Lucretia*. This set the seal on the rest of her personal and professional life. By now estranged from her first husband, Nancy fell in love with the opera's producer, Eric John *Crozier (1914–1994). She eventually divorced Legge in 1948, and she and Crozier married on Boxing day (26 December) 1949. At Glyndebourne she also fell under the spell of Benjamin Britten and his music, and Crozier and Britten were undoubtedly the most formative influences of her post-war career. She was a founder member of the English Opera Group and a founder artist of the Aldeburgh Festival, creating the parts of Nancy in *Albert Herring* (a role lovingly written for her by Britten and Crozier, by now Britten's librettist), Polly in Britten's version of *The Beggar's Opera*, Dido in Britten's edition of Purcell's *Dido and Aeneas*, and Lucinda in Arthur Oldham's *Love in a Village*. Britten also wrote *A Charm of Lullabies* for Evans, for a Holland Festival recital she gave with

Felix de Nobel at The Hague in 1948. During this time she continued her vocal studies with Eva de Reusz.

Aside from her Aldeburgh connections, Nancy sang at the first and many subsequent Edinburgh festivals, and regularly appeared at the Three Choirs, Holland, and Leith Hill festivals. She enjoyed a highly productive relationship with the BBC and made over 300 broadcasts during her career, including regular recitals, concerts, and studio operas—notably in the title roles of *Venus and Adonis*, *Julius Caesar*, and *Carmen*. She was the mezzo-soprano soloist in the first televised *Messiah*, with the Huddersfield Choral Society under Sir Malcolm Sargent, and she performed at the BBC Promenade Concerts for no fewer than thirteen successive seasons. It was her return to Glyndebourne that interrupted this extraordinary (and during her lifetime probably unbeaten) record, with appearances in *Die Zauberflöte* under Sacher, and alongside Crespin and Söderström in the legendary *Der Rosenkavalier* of 1960.

During a long career, embracing a very catholic range of repertory, Nancy Evans's recital accompanists included, besides Moore and de Nobel, Newton, Beecham, Britten, and Poulenc. She sang extensively with some of the greatest conductors of the twentieth century, including Ansermet, Barbirolli, Beecham, Boult, Britten, Goodall, Gui, Krips, Lambert, Münch, da Sabata, Sacher, Susskind, Sargent, Scherchen, Schwarz, Weingartner, and Henry Wood. She premièred works by Britten, Berkeley, Vaughan Williams, and Malcolm Williamson and gave important UK premières of works by Copland, Duruflé, Hindemith, Honegger, and Stravinsky.

From 1961 to 1965 Nancy Evans was president of the Society of Women Musicians, a role she relinquished when she and Eric Crozier moved from Kent to settle in Church Field Cottage in Great Glemham, Suffolk, the home they had acquired in the early days of the Aldeburgh Festival. Here she began to develop her second career as teacher (first at the Colchester Institute from 1966 to 1978) and adjudicator, notably for the Kathleen Ferrier, Maggie Teyte, and Miriam Licette memorial prizes and the Benson and Hedges award. She continued to perform, premièring Malcolm Williamson's *The Growing Castle* in 1968, and her singing career continued into the early 1970s, almost forty years after it had begun. From 1973 she taught every year at the Britten–Pears School, and in 1979 Pears invited her to become his co-director of singing studies, a role she continued to fulfil with great commitment, enthusiasm, and generosity beyond Pears's death in 1986 and until her own retirement in 1990.

The long and distinguished careers shared by Nancy Evans and Eric Crozier were acknowledged in 1990 when both were appointed OBE in the same honours list. Crozier died four years later, while on holiday with Nancy in Granville, France. The great solace of Nancy's last years was her daughter Helga and three grandchildren (Ruth, Timothy, and Benjamin), resident close by in Great Glemham since the mid-eighties. When she died (in Alderton House, a nursing home at Leiston, near Aldeburgh) on 20 August 2000, the substantial and warm obituaries in all the UK broadsheets recalled, as one of them described her, 'one of the best-loved personalities in the musical world' whose 'good looks and appealing personality complemented her attractively warm singing … a vibrant, evenly produced mezzo, which she deployed expressively and with an innate musicality … remarkable for its clear diction, while her sparkling personality brought charm and vitality to her roles … exceptionally attractive and an excellent actress'. She was also credited with being a 'strict teacher' but 'a sympathetic one' and a 'discerning adjudicator', and readers were reminded of 'her gentle wit' and 'her marvellous sense of fun'. Her funeral was held on 25 August 2000 at Great Glemham church, where she was buried on the same day, and a memorial concert was held on 1 April 2001 in Aldeburgh parish church. The 2001 Aldeburgh Festival opened with a new production of Britten's *The Rape of Lucretia* dedicated to her memory.

JOHN EVANS

Sources private information (2004) [family] · transcript of J. Evans and N. Evans, filmed autobiographical interview, priv. coll. · J. Calder, *The Independent* (22 Aug 2000) · *The Times* (23 Aug 2000) · *Daily Telegraph* (23 Aug 2000) · T. McDonald, *The Guardian* (24 Aug 2000) · E. Crozier and N. Evans, 'After long pursuit', Britten–Pears Library, Aldeburgh, Suffolk [memoirs] · b. cert. · m. cert. · *New Grove*

Archives Britten–Pears Library, The Red House, Aldeburgh, Suffolk, papers and recordings | FILM BFI NFTVA | SOUND BBC Sound Archives · BL NSA · Decca Records and EMI (HMV) Archives

Likenesses B. Hardy, double portrait, photograph, 1948 (with Peter Pears), Hult. Arch. · B. Hardy, photograph, 1948, Hult. Arch. [*see illus.*] · E. Auerbach, photograph, Britten–Pears Library collection · M. Cosman, line drawing (as Polly Peacham), Britten–Pears Library collection · A. McBean, photograph, Britten–Pears Library collection · photographs, Britten–Pears Library collection

Evans, Frederick Henry (1853–1943), bookseller and photographer, was born in Whitechapel, London, on 26 June 1853, the son of John Cleland Evans, a music teacher. He spent his early years as a clerk in the accounts department of a London business. After purchasing a Ross microscope, he bought a camera in 1883 for both photomicroscopic and landscape photography from George Smith, owner of the Sciopticon Company, which made lantern slides from Evans's negatives by the woodburytype process. In 1887 he received the Photographic Society of London's medal of honour for his photomicrographs. His insistence upon fine detail and tonal gradation in photography may have its origin with the lantern slide, a medium which he praised in his later writings. His lifelong engagement with the photography of cathedral architecture was begun on a visit to Salisbury Cathedral. Some of his first photographs of cathedrals were shown at the Photographic Society of London's annual exhibition of 1890, and in the following year he was elected a member of the London and Provincial Photographic Association.

Evans's love of literature and fine printing made him a constant visitor to a bookshop owned by Edward Jones in Queen Street, Cheapside, London; when he was offered a partnership in the business about 1890, he secured it with a loan from his father. When Jones died suddenly the bookshop was left with Evans. He became interested in portraiture about 1891, and he photographed George Bernard Shaw, Arthur Symons, and (most famously) Aubrey Beardsley, whom he captured in the pose of the Notre Dame gargoyle known as Le Stryge. In 1896 Evans made a series of photographs of Kelmscott Manor, the home of William Morris, for whose lectures on architecture he had provided lantern slides; he assembled a group of these photographs in a memorial portfolio after Morris's death. In 1908–9 he produced a series of landscapes for a memorial edition of the poems of George Meredith.

Evans's first major exhibition, of 120 cathedral photographs, was held in March 1897 at the Architectural Club in Boston, Massachusetts. He retired from his bookshop in 1898, and on 26 November 1900 married Ada Emily Longhurst, daughter of James Longhurst, a builder; the couple had three children: Barbara, Evan, and Geoffrey. Evans now gave his full attention to the making of fine photographs and writing critical and technical articles on his chosen medium, the platinum print. In 1900 he was elected to the Linked Ring Brotherhood and a one-man show of his photographs was held at the Royal Photographic Society in April. In 1903 his work was featured in Alfred Stieglitz's magazine *Camera Work* with a portfolio of cathedral photographs. In his best-known photograph, *A Sea of Steps* (1903), of Wells Cathedral, he subjects the form of spiralling stairs to the flattening effect of the telephoto lens in order to express the difficulty of spiritual ascent.

In 1905 Evans collaborated with the writer Theodore Andrea Cook on a *Country Life* magazine commission to photograph the French châteaux for *Twenty-Five Great Houses of France* (1916). Evans's interest in the expression of symmetry in nature was reinforced by Cook's researches into the vitalism of the spiral form in mathematics, astronomy, botany, and the structure of the spiral staircase as illustrated by Evans in Cook's *The Curves of Life* (1914). About 1911 he compiled albums of his 'harmonograph' drawings, spiral patterns made by the oscillations of a pair of pendulums set in harmonious ratios. His knowledge of the writings of Emanuel Swedenborg and Jakob Boehme underpinned his sense of physical and spiritual correspondences. In 1911 he produced a series of photographs of the interior of Westminster Abbey in London, many of which were published in *Country Life* (1911–19).

In 1919 Evans sold 400 items from his large collection of rare and fine-printed books at Mitchell Kennerley's Anderson Galleries in New York. Between 1912 and 1925 he printed portfolios of platinum reproductions of woodengravings by William Blake, Hans Holbein, and Edward Calvert, and ink drawings by Beardsley. He was elected an honorary fellow of the Royal Photographic Society in 1928. Frederick Henry Evans died on 24 June 1943 at his home at 32 Rosemont Road, Acton, Middlesex; he was survived by his wife.

ANNE HAMMOND

Sources A. Strasser, 'Evans: photographer', *The Saturday Book* [ed. L. Russell], 3 (1943), 149–64 · B. Newhall, *Frederick H. Evans* (1973) · *Frederick H. Evans: selected texts and bibliography*, ed. A. Hammond (1992) · m. cert. · d. cert. · *CGPLA Eng. & Wales* (1943)

Likenesses self-portrait, photograph, c.1895–1900, repro. in Hammond, ed., *Frederick H. Evans*, frontispiece · G. B. Shaw, photograph, c.1901, National Museum of Photography, Film and Television, Bradford, Royal Photographic Society collection · E. O. Hoppé, photograph, International Museum of Photography, George Eastman House, Rochester, New York

Wealth at death £12,478 5s. 1d.: probate, 12 Nov 1943, CGPLA Eng. & Wales

Evans, Sir Frederick John Owen (1815–1885), naval officer and hydrographer, son of John Evans, master RN, was born on 9 March 1815. He entered the navy as a second-class volunteer in 1828. After serving in the *Rose* and the *Winchester* he was transferred in 1833 to the *Thunder*, Captain Richard Owen, and spent three years in surveying the coasts of Central America, the Demerara River, and the Bahama banks. Evans subsequently served in the Mediterranean on the *Caledonia* (flagship), *Asia*, *Rapid*, *Rolla*, *Dido*, and *Wolverene*, passing through the different ranks of the 'master's' line, the officers then charged with the duties of navigation. In 1841 Evans was appointed master of the *Fly*, and for the next five years surveyed the Coral Sea, the great barrier reef of Australia, and Torres Strait. Beete Jukes, the geologist, was on the *Fly*, and wrote an account of the expedition. Shortly after his return to Britain Evans married, on 12 November 1846, Elizabeth Mary, eldest daughter of Captain Charles Hall RN, of Stoke, Plymouth.

After a short spell of duty in the Isle of Man, Evans returned in 1847, in the *Acheron*, to New Zealand, where he spent four years in surveying. During the Russian war he served on the *Lighting*, Captain Bartholomew Sulivan, in the Baltic, where he received the special thanks of Sir Charles Napier for his share in piloting the fleet through the Aland isles.

By this time Evans had become known by his scientific qualifications, and in 1855 he was appointed superintendent of the compass department of the navy. He had at once to consider a difficult problem, the use of the compass in iron ships and armourclads. In co-operation with Archibald Smith, he accomplished the task satisfactorily, and he contributed seven papers, on the magnetism of ships, to the *Philosophical Transactions* of the Royal Society, of which he was elected fellow in June 1862. This work was critical to the safe navigation of iron warships.

In 1858 Evans prepared a *Chart of Curves of Equal Magnetic Declination*, published by the Admiralty. In 1860 he wrote a valuable *Report on Compass Deviations in the Royal Navy*, on the magnetic character of the various iron ships in the navy, and also of the *Great Eastern*. His most important work was the *Admiralty Manual for Deviations of the Compass* (1862), of which Smith and himself were joint editors. A simple account of the same subject was issued by Evans in 1870 as an *Elementary Manual for Deviations of the Compass*. These became standard textbooks, and were translated and adopted by the major maritime nations.

Evans later devoted much attention to terrestrial magnetism. He compiled the magnetical instructions for the observers on the *Challenger* in 1872, and delivered a lecture on the 'Magnetism of the earth' to the Royal Geographical

Sir Frederick John Owen Evans (1815–1885), by unknown photographer, c.1884

Society in 1878. He was made a staff commander in 1863, staff captain in 1867, and full captain in 1872. In 1865 he was appointed chief naval assistant to the hydrographer to the Admiralty, Captain G. H. Richards, whom he succeeded in 1874. He was made CB in May 1873, and KCB in May 1881. He was vice-president of the Royal Geographical Society from 1879 to 1881, and president of the geographical section of the British Association in 1876. In 1881 he contributed a paper to the latter on 'Oceanic or maritime discovery from 1831 to 1881'.

After resigning the post of hydrographer in August 1884, Evans was appointed one of the British delegates to the international conference held at Washington in 1885, to fix a prime meridian and universal day. He died at his residence, 21 Dawson Place, Pembridge Square, Bayswater, London, on 20 December 1885. He was the only officer to join the hydrographic service as a master who rose to be hydrographer of the navy.

W. J. HARRISON, *rev.* ANDREW LAMBERT

Sources G. S. Ritchie, *The Admiralty chart: British naval hydrography in the nineteenth century* (1967) · H. N. Sulivan, *Admiral Sir B. J. Sulivan, 1810–1890* (1896) · A. E. Fanning, *Steady as she goes: a history of the compass department of the admiralty* (1986) · *Nature*, 33 (1885–6), 246–8 · *Proceedings* [Royal Geographical Society], new ser., 8 (1886), 112–13 · *The Times* (22 Dec 1885) · Boase, *Mod. Eng. biog.* · Kelly, *Handbk* (1879)

Archives CUL, letters to Lord Kelvin

Likenesses photograph, c.1880, repro. in Fanning, *Steady as she goes*, 390 · photograph, c.1884, NMM [*see illus.*]

Wealth at death £11,316 15s. 3d.: probate, 14 Jan 1886, CGPLA Eng. & Wales

Evans, Frederick Moule (1832/3–1902), printer, was born at Southwark, Surrey, the son of Frederick Mullett *Evans (1803–1870), printer and publisher. Fred, as he was universally known, was one of eight children who survived to adulthood, including three brothers whose names are known (Tom, Lewis, Godfrey) and three sisters, one of whom was Elizabeth Matilda Moule Evans (Bessie). Almost nothing has survived about Fred's childhood; his mother died when he was in his teens. The principal publications of his father's firm were the works of Charles Dickens (his novels, his periodical *Household Words*, and the newspaper the *Daily News* which Dickens edited for a few weeks in 1847), the hugely successful humour magazine *Punch* and books by its staff, many of Thackeray's novels, and assorted other periodicals that could be profitably printed on their large presses. Fred and the sons of his father's partner, William Bradbury, were apparently often in company together, and they grew up with the expectation that they would go into the family business. The story goes that Fred, along with Henry Bradbury and William Hardwick Bradbury, printed the sheets of Charles Dickens's serial novel *David Copperfield* (1849–50) behind locked doors so that there would be no possibility that the shop workmen would leak news about the next instalments ahead of publication. Analogous precautions had been taken in the preceding decade during the printing of *Nicholas Nickleby*. This same concern for security led Fred to be chosen to act as the sole in-house proofreader of the early chapters of *Little Dorrit* in 1856.

Evans's father, known within the firm as Pater, was kind, genial, loyal, and much beloved by his staff and associates, and this affection appears to have extended to the son, who enjoyed a warm relationship with the members of the *Punch* staff. In the early 1860s he and W. H. Bradbury began to make occasional appearances at the staff's famous Wednesday evening dinners, long a central ritual of the firm, and in time Evans became a frequent member of that convivial assembly. Just as his father had been more closely involved with the professional and social lives of the *Punch* writers and artists than had the firm's senior partner, so Fred Evans appears to have enjoyed a greater familiarity with the magazine's staff at this period than did Bradbury's sons. Fred and his wife, Amy, turn up frequently in accounts of dinners, parties, and outings. He was particularly close to Shirley Brooks, versatile writer, assistant editor of *Punch* under Mark Lemon, and Lemon's successor as editor in 1870, with whom he shared an interest in freemasonry. With Charles Knight, Evans stood godfather to Brooks's eldest son, Reginald, in 1865, and appears to have kept Brooks informed of the firm's dealings. Throughout the early 1860s he assisted his father, whose health became ever more precarious, in managing the day-to-day business of the firm.

Those years tried the strength of all who worked for Bradbury and Evans. Dickens's sudden and violent break with the firm in 1858 over its failure to insert in *Punch* his self-justifying notice about his separation from his wife fell particularly hard on the Evans family. 'Pater' Evans had at Dickens's request agreed to act as co-trustee (with Mark Lemon) for his wife, Catherine Dickens, when the separation was being negotiated, and this closeness to the situation, as well as the long and trusting relationship between the two men, seems to have focused Dickens's enraged sense of betrayal squarely on the elder Evans. He forbade his children to enter Evans's house, and after writing a brief and angry note never wrote or spoke to him again. To make matters even more painful for the two families, Charles Dickens jun. and Fred's sister Bessie had been intended for one another since childhood, and had fallen in love, but Dickens now sternly opposed the match. Litigation between Bradbury and Evans and Dickens over the latter's insistence on closing *Household Words*, which had been a valuable common property, added to the bitter feelings, as did the rivalry between their respective new periodicals, Dickens's *All the Year Round* and Bradbury and Evans's *Once a Week*. Finally, in a tangled dispute at this same time between Dickens and Thackeray involving the writer Edmund Yates and the Garrick Club, Charley Dickens took the part of Thackeray against his father, publishing an article in *Punch* critical of Yates, whom the elder Dickens had defended and advised. As a result, Dickens withdrew his son's name from candidacy at the Garrick, and when Charley and Bessie were married in November 1861 Dickens refused to attend the wedding and tried to dissuade his friends from going.

Quite apart from their personal estrangement from an important friend, the firm of Bradbury and Evans never entirely recovered as publishers from the break with Dickens, gradually retreating from book publishing over the following decade, though retaining their work as jobbing printers and continuing to take great pride in their proprietorship of *Punch*. W. H. Bradbury and his sister, Edith, had each married into the wealthy Agnew family, art dealers in Manchester, and during the 1860s the Agnews became closely involved in the business affairs of the Bradbury and Evans firm. In failing health and depressed by the deaths of Thackeray and John Leech and the continued estrangement from Dickens, the founding partners retired in 1865 to leave their sons in charge and formally to take the Agnews into partnership in the firm, which was reconstituted and renamed 'Bradbury, Evans and Company'. The elder Evans invested disastrously with Fred and with Charley Dickens in a papermaking company, which Dickens predicted in June 1868 'is coming to irretrievable bankruptcy, smash, and ruin' (*Letters of Charles Dickens*, 12.139). Pater Evans lost all his savings and had to appear before the bankruptcy court later that year. In 1869 the elder Bradbury died, followed in June 1870 by his partner Evans, leaving the sons without their fathers' counsel. Within a year, Shirley Brooks recorded in his diary that the prospects for Fred Evans's position in the business looked unpromising, and in the summer of 1872 he noted that William Hardwick Bradbury and his in-laws the Agnews planned to force Evans to retire quietly. The Agnews had threatened to withdraw their capital unless Evans and the younger Bradbury came up with capital funds of their own. In July they made a proposal whereby Evans could remain at the firm at a reduced salary for three years, a proposal that Charles Dickens jun. and his solicitor advised Evans not to accept. After a furious argument with Bradbury that convinced Evans he could not work with him again, he began negotiations for an immediate departure. Shortly thereafter he left the firm for a payment of £5000, of which £3000 cleared his outstanding debts to the business. In justifying the move, Bradbury and Thomas Agnew suggested privately that Fred had done no work and been useless in the firm; they announced at the *Punch* dinner that Evans had chosen to leave of his own accord and that the firm thereafter would be renamed Bradbury, Agnew, & Co.

Shortly after leaving the firm that his father had co-founded, Fred Evans went into business as printer with Charley Dickens. In February 1873, to their great joy, he and Dickens succeeded in securing the printing contract for the Crystal Palace at Sydenham, which had become a vastly popular venue for musical entertainment. Thereafter the firm's imprint became 'Charles Dickens and Evans, Crystal Palace Press' and the printing works occupied the south end of the basement, where Crystal Palace visitors could observe the machines in operation. In addition to guidebooks and notices for the Crystal Palace, the firm also printed plays written to be performed there, such as E. L. Blanchard's *The Grand Pantomime Cinderella, or, Harlequin and the Glass Slipper, the Magic Pumpkin, and the Butterflies' Ball and Grasshoppers' Feast* (1874). The printing of the magazine *All the Year Round*, of which Charley, following his father's death in 1870, had become editor, was another source of work. This connection also provided work in the form of volumes of material reprinted from the magazine, such as Walter Austin's *One Dinner a Week and Travels in the East* (1884). In 1879 the firm printed the younger Dickens's two-volume edition of the autobiography of Charles James Mathews, the comedian, whom his father had greatly admired.

For Chapman and Hall the firm printed a number of books, including Charles Dickens's and Wilkie Collins's, *The Lazy Tour of Two Idle Apprentices* (1890), a collection of pieces from *Household Words*, and William H. Ablett's *Farming for Pleasure and Profit* (1879). Charley Dickens's own popular *Dictionary of London*, which first appeared in 1887 and went through several editions, provided what must have been another lucrative printing job, as did his *Dictionary of the Thames* and other guides. Kelly's directory of 1885 lists the business's premises as '24 Great New Street, Fetter Lane, E. C. and Crystal Palace S. E.' By 1896, however, the firm of Dickens and Evans was 'extinct' (Berkeley, 283). Fred, like his father, was a member of the Garrick Club, to which he was elected in 1852. He resigned at the end of December 1901, perhaps because of failing health. He died at 3 Chartham Terrace, Ramsgate, Kent on 3 March 1902, aged sixty-nine. He was survived by his wife.

Robert L. Patten and Patrick Leary

Sources *The letters of Charles Dickens*, ed. M. House, G. Storey, and others, 12 vols. (1965–2002) • 'Some London printing offices: No. 5, Bradbury, Agnew, & Co.', *London, Provincial, and Colonial Press News* (Nov 1884), 27–9 • 'Mr. Punch at dinner: centenary of a famous printery', *British and Colonial Printer and Stationer* (28 Jan 1926), 63–

4 • G. S. Layard, *A great 'Punch' editor* (1907) • 'Incidents of my life', *London, Provincial, and Colonial Press News* (Sept 1886), 17–20; (Dec 1886), 17–21 • *Kelly's directory of stationers, printers, booksellers, publishers and papermakers of England, Scotland, and Wales* (1885) • *The Times* • E. Berkeley jun., *Autographs and manuscripts: a collector's manual* (1978) • d. cert.
Archives *Punch* Library, London, letters and account books
Likenesses A. Bassano Ltd, photograph, repro. in M. H. Spielmann, *The history of 'Punch'* (1895), 37

Evans, Frederick Mullett (1803–1870), printer and publisher, grew up in London. He later recalled as a schoolboy meeting Benjamin Disraeli, who, like Frederick's elder brother Thomas Mullett Evans, was a solicitor's clerk with the City firm of Swaine and Stevens, Frederick's Place, Old Jewry. Thomas Evans invested with Disraeli in Latin American mining shares, losing all his money in the market collapse of 1825 and going heavily into debt; despite the burden of those debts he moved to Bristol and later became a partner in the solicitor's office of Ball and Evans. After his schooldays ended Frederick was employed in a printing business in Southampton before joining with William *Bradbury (1800–1869) in London in 1830 to found the printing firm of Bradbury and Evans, located in Bouverie Street and Lombard Street, Whitefriars. After opening a printing works dominated by a large steam-driven rotary press of the latest design, and advertising the firm as one capable of handling the demanding task of printing newspapers and other periodicals, Bradbury and Evans soon had such major clients as the Chambers brothers in Edinburgh, for whom they printed *Chambers's Edinburgh Journal* and *Chambers's Cyclopedia*, as well as Richard Bentley, Alexander Maxwell, Edward Moxon, and Edward Chapman and William Hall. In the 1850s they became the main printers for Smith, Elder, and obtained additional work from Macmillan. The firm also printed several weekly newspapers, while assisting other printers in meeting deadlines for such periodicals as the *London Journal* and the *Illustrated London News*. Early and long-continued specialities were the printing of legal and parliamentary reports as well as of works on gardening and botany, including Joseph Paxton's *Horticultural Register*. Bradbury and Evans were said to have been the first printers in Britain to adopt the French process of stereotyping, an innovation consistent with their growing reputation for uncommon skill and efficiency.

Publishing *Punch* In December 1842 Bradbury and Evans were persuaded to become not merely the printers but the proprietors of the struggling new comic magazine *Punch*. With Mark Lemon as editor and a stable of brilliant comic writers and artists, the magazine within a few years became a national institution, selling over 40,000 copies a week and bringing in some £10,000 a year to the firm. *Punch*'s success created a ready market for other books by its writers and artists, and Bradbury and Evans subsequently published volumes written or illustrated by such associates as Douglas Jerrold, Gilbert Abbott à Beckett, William Makepeace Thackeray, Albert Smith, Percival Leigh, Shirley Brooks, John Leech, Richard Doyle, Horace Mayhew, Francis Burnand, Charles Keene, and Mark

Lemon, many of them made up of material reprinted from the magazine. Lemon's early decision to retain a core group of contributors on salary in lieu of paying for all contributions by the piece, a policy made possible by Bradbury and Evans's ability and willingness to provide the necessary capital, gave the magazine an unusual cohesiveness and stability. From the beginning of their ownership, the proprietors hosted a weekly dinner for the *Punch* staff—originally on Saturdays, then on Wednesdays—that became a central ritual of the magazine and the firm, and at which Evans was a constant fixture and jovial presence. A man of kindly and expansive temperament and Pickwickian appearance, he maintained warm personal friendships with the staff, to whom he was known simply as Pater and for whom he served as the main point of contact with the firm in negotiations over books, pay, loans, and other matters. When Doyle threatened to quit over the magazine's anti-Catholic tone, for example, it was Evans who tried, unsuccessfully, to persuade him to stay. Similarly, Evans undertook the delicate task of explaining to Jerrold why a secret agreement with Dickens had pre-empted Jerrold's idea of editing a weekly magazine to be published by the firm. Most crucially, the willingness of Evans and his partner to act as bankers for the magazine's writers and artists meant that almost all the members of the staff routinely borrowed money from the proprietors, usually with no other collateral than their salaries and the payments expected for future work for *Punch*. Evans proclaimed in later life that the friendly feeling between the firm and the staff was the key to the magazine's success, and that the friendships that had come to him through *Punch* had given him some of the happiest moments of his life. It is clear that the firm's resolute financial backing of the magazine, as well as of its writers and artists individually, enabled it to thrive in a highly competitive periodical market in which many less stoutly supported and carefully managed magazines faltered. In return, *Punch* proved itself the mainstay of the firm's finances and reputation and a continuing source of pride to both proprietors.

Thackeray and Dickens Thackeray had served on the *Punch* staff for several years when he brought to Bradbury and Evans his first full-length novel, after trying to place it elsewhere; published in monthly numbers as *Vanity Fair* in 1847–8, coincident with *Dombey and Son*, it immediately established Thackeray's reputation as a major new novelist. Although Thackeray soon left *Punch* out of dissatisfaction with both its politics and its rate of pay, he maintained warmly cordial relations with the firm, which published *Pendennis* (1848–50), *The Newcomes* (1853–5), and *The Virginians* (1857–9) as well as several minor works, and continued to welcome his attendance at the Wednesday evening dinners. During his time as a *Punch* contributor Thackeray had dealt primarily with Evans rather than with Lemon, and in negotiating his book contracts he turned to Evans again. Typically, Evans and Thackeray relied on gentleman's agreements that were somewhat easy-going, not binding the novelist beyond the current book. When, in 1852, Thackeray took *Henry Esmond* to George Smith, Bradbury and Evans made no difficulties, printing it just

as they had other Smith, Elder works. In 1859, after Bradbury and Evans's edition of *The Virginians* sold poorly, Smith offered Thackeray sums to edit and write for the new *Cornhill Magazine* that Bradbury and Evans could not hope to match. Despite these interruptions in the business relationship, Thackeray always loyally considered the Whitefriars firm his principal publishers, and over the years the connection would prove an almost uniformly friendly and profitable one for both parties. Evans and his partner resented Smith's attempts, soon after Thackeray's death in 1863, to buy their shares in the novelist's copyrights, but ultimately they were persuaded to sell these valuable properties along with back stock for £3750, a move perhaps occasioned by a decline in the firm's finances.

In Thackeray and Charles Dickens, Bradbury and Evans found themselves the publishers, for a time, of the two most acclaimed novelists in the English-speaking world. As printers for Chapman and Hall they had become acquainted with Dickens in the late 1830s. In 1844, dissatisfied with Chapman and Hall, Dickens proposed to his printers that they become his publishers as well. Despite the firm's initial reluctance, on 1 June Dickens entered into agreements that constituted Bradbury and Evans for the ensuing eight years his publishers as well as printers, with a quarter share in all future copyrights, in exchange for a large cash advance. In December 1845 they, along with Joseph Paxton and others, agreed to launch a Liberal morning paper, the *Daily News*, as a political and commercial rival to *The Times*, with Dickens as editor. The venture proved catastrophically expensive: Dickens left after a few weeks, a lowering of the price to 2s. 6d. proved a disastrous experiment, and the investors, Bradbury and Evans prominent among them, lost tens of thousands of pounds. This failure haunted Evans for years afterwards, and on his retirement in 1865 he warned his son and Bradbury's to 'avoid Daily Newses' (diary of Henry Silver, Punch Library, London, 1 Nov 1865). By contrast, the publishing of Dickens's books, on terms highly favourable to the author, was substantially and steadily profitable for all concerned. Evans bore principal responsibility for drafting terms renewing the firm's publishing agreement with Dickens in 1852. As they had done with Thackeray, they voluntarily renounced their 10 per cent commission as a charge against expenses before the profits were divided, and the novelist happily accepted. Over a period of fourteen years Bradbury and Evans published for Dickens some of the most memorable novels in the language: four of the Christmas books, *Dombey and Son*, *David Copperfield*, *Bleak House*, and *Little Dorrit*. In 1850 the firm became part owners with Dickens of the twopenny weekly *Household Words*, which Dickens edited with W. H. Wills. For nine years the magazine featured a range of innovative fiction and lively reporting that proved highly popular, its circulation rivalling that of *Punch* itself.

Throughout this period of expansion the Bradburys and Evanses socialized a great deal with the Dickenses; they were frequently guests at celebratory dinners and during the 1850s they visited Dickens during his summer holidays at Boulogne. Dickens was especially close to Evans and his family, and because it was through Evans that much of Dickens's business with the firm was conducted, the Evanses were often brought within the highly charged ambit of Boz. In the first performance of Dickens's amateur production of Ben Jonson's *Every Man in his Humour* (20 September 1845), Evans played Roger Formal; he frequently dispatched proofs, presentation copies, and other materials at Dickens's behest; and in the 1857 production of *The Frozen Deep* several of his sons had non-speaking roles. Evans sometimes made mistakes which irritated Dickens, and several times his staff, especially his manager Captain Felix Joyce, occasioned ruptures which Evans, kindly and generally placatory, smoothed over. But on the whole the friendship deepened through the years, and was as much treasured by Catherine Dickens as by her husband.

Break with Dickens All this conviviality was eclipsed within months during autumn 1857, when Dickens decided to separate from Catherine. The dissolution of the marriage was fraught with family tensions on all sides. Dickens asked Mark Lemon and Evans to represent Catherine, and they were named her trustees under the deed of separation that was at last negotiated. Evans had been reluctant to undertake this responsibility, but consented after Dickens insisted that he should like no one better. In the face of rumours that he had taken up either with her sister Georgina Hogarth, who lived with them, or with an unnamed actress (Ellen Ternan), Dickens decided in the early summer of 1858 to publish an explanation and defence of his actions in *Household Words*, sending copies also to *The Times*, which printed it, and to *Punch*, which did not. Dickens had never explicitly requested that the statement be printed in the latter, and it seems never to have occurred to either Lemon or Evans that *Punch* would be an appropriate place to do so, yet after the fact Dickens chose to consider the notice's non-appearance as a deliberate personal betrayal by his old friends and associates. With a dispatch that startled and angered Evans and his partner, Dickens moved at once to end their long business relationship. He ceased production of *Household Words*, returned to Chapman and Hall, and started a new journal, *All the Year Round*, into which the old journal, whose copyright and stock he outbid his former publishers to acquire, was incorporated. Bradbury and Evans soon began publication of a rival periodical, *Once a Week*, that drew upon the firm's long experience with woodblock printing, and its relationships with prominent artists, to present lavishly illustrated serialized novels. Evans had initially extracted a half-promise from Thackeray to contribute, which would have given the magazine a big name to offset its Dickensian rival, but the terms of Thackeray's subsequent agreement with George Smith to write two novels for the *Cornhill Magazine* forbade him to write for any other journal. Despite this early misstep the magazine soon set the highest standard of illustration of any periodical of its time, and attracted contributions from a wide variety of writers and artists. His work on behalf of *Once a Week* brought

Evans the friendship of such authors as Harriet Martineau, who had long heard of him as 'one of the best men in the world;—and a capital man of business too, and full of knowledge' (*Harriet Martineau's Letters*, 196). The magazine's circulation, however, never matched its critical esteem, and three successive editors failed to slow its decline. Expensive to produce and lacking a consistently attractive series of novels, *Once a Week* became a financial burden on the firm over the following decade, and was at last sold to James Rice in 1869.

The break with Dickens was a great blow to the Bradbury and Evans firm, entailing as it did the loss of not only the publishing profits from the books of this most popular of novelists and the journal *Household Words* but also the printing contracts for those works. The break also cost the firm the opportunity to publish such members of Dickens's circle as Wilkie Collins, who shortly before had expressed to Evans his hopes for a long relationship with the house. Bradbury and Evans never recovered as book publishers, ultimately failing to establish such continuing personal and contractual relationships with other marketable authors as might have made up the loss of Dickens. Although it published new books by Thackeray, Surtees, and some others in the years to come, the firm gradually returned to its more modest earlier roles as jobbing printers and as proprietors of *Punch*, eventually publishing only reprints and other books associated with the magazine and its staff.

The personal consequences of the break were particularly painful for Frederick Evans and his family, as it was Evans, for reasons that remain obscure, who bore the brunt of Dickens's cold ferocity. Accusing Evans of having been 'false' to his name 'under the only great wrong it has ever known' (22 July 1858; *Letters of Charles Dickens*, 9.608), Dickens vowed never to speak to him again, and attempted to sever all contact between the two families. 'I absolutely prohibit', he told his wife and son, any of his children 'ever being taken to Mr. Evans's house' (July 1858; ibid., 8.602–3). This prohibition was particularly difficult for Charley Dickens, who had been 'engaged' since infancy to Bessie Evans, whose name, Dickens complained after their marriage, 'is odious to me' (23 Dec 1861, ibid., 9.548). Despite this opposition the two were married on 19 November 1861 at St Mark's, Regent's Park; Dickens did not attend and told friends that he expected them not to enter Evans's house either. Dickens eventually healed the breach with his son's family, but the estrangement from Evans was never repaired. In 1864 Evans hoped to secure the printing of *Our Mutual Friend*, and with it a possible avenue towards reconciliation with Dickens, but though Dickens was at first open to the idea this last approach was rebuffed, possibly through the intervention of John Forster and Frederic Chapman, and the printing contract went instead to the Clowes firm. As late as 1867 Evans, who claimed that he never could discover how he had so deeply offended Dickens, still held out hope for making things up with him, but this was not to be.

Judging by a remark that he made one evening at the

Punch table, that no man knows complete happiness until he is married, Evans's own marriage may be presumed to have been a happy one. His wife appears to have been of the same family as the Revd Henry Moule of Dorset, inventor of the earth closet, and at least two of the children bore her family name. Eight of the Evanses' twelve children survived to adulthood, including Frederick Moule (Fred) *Evans (1832/3–1902); Thomas Evans (married 4 March 1872); Lewis Evans, who became rector of Leathley; Godfrey Evans; the second eldest daughter, Elizabeth Matilda Moule (Bessie) Evans (1839–1907); and two other daughters, the elder of whom was married in August 1860. One child, a daughter, died at the age of five at Worthing in Sussex. Their mother died about 1850, leaving Evans with the responsibility for raising the children, which he seems conscientiously to have done. Eager for grandchildren, he was intensely delighted when Bessie gave birth to Mary Angela Dickens in autumn 1862.

Evans was remembered by one author as 'a round, ruddy, genial, cheery, busy little man' much beloved by the *Punch* men (Hatton, 160). Yet he became increasingly prone to fits of despondency as personal sorrows multiplied in the last ten years of his life. His partner's eldest son, the talented printer Henry Bradbury, committed suicide in September 1860, allegedly because one of Evans's daughters would not marry him. In the aftermath of the deaths of Thackeray and of John Leech, increasingly fragile health and spirits impelled both founding partners to relinquish control of the firm in 1865 to their sons and to William and Thomas Agnew, prominent Manchester art dealers who at the same time were taken into partnership to supply the firm with much needed capital. Evans's disastrous investment, with his son and Charles Dickens junior, in a papermaking company led to the loss of his savings and an appearance before the bankruptcy court in December 1868, which entailed the further embarrassment of his temporary ouster from the Garrick Club. Increasingly nervous and despondent, Evans fell seriously ill in the autumn of 1869. On 25 June 1870 he died at the house of his son Fred, 18 Albert Road, St Pancras, London; he was memorialized in *Punch* as a 'warm-hearted, faithful friend' (2 July 1870, 7).

ROBERT L. PATTEN and PATRICK LEARY

Sources *The letters of Charles Dickens*, ed. M. House, G. Storey, and others, 12 vols. (1965–2002) • J. Forster, *The life of Charles Dickens*, ed. J. W. T. Ley (1928) • *The letters and private papers of William Makepeace Thackeray*, ed. G. N. Ray, 4 vols. (1945–6) [with 2 vol. suppl., ed. E. F. Harden (1994)] • M. H. Spielmann, *The history of 'Punch'* (1895) • R. L. Patten, *Charles Dickens and his publishers* (1978) • D. Dixon, 'Bradbury and Evans', *British literary publishing houses, 1820–1880*, ed. P. J. Anderson and J. Rose, DLitB, 106 (1991) • *Benjamin Disraeli letters*, ed. J. A. W. Gunn and others (1982–) • *The George Eliot letters*, ed. G. S. Haight, 9 vols. (1954–78) • C. Fox, *Graphic journalism in England during the 1830s and 1840s* (1988) • 'Mr. Punch at dinner: centenary of a famous printery', *British and Colonial Printer and Stationer* (28 Jan 1926), 63–4 • R. D. Altick, *'Punch': the lively youth of a British institution, 1841–1851* (1997) • P. Shillingsburg, *Pegasus in harness: Victorian publishing and W. M. Thackeray* (1992) • J. Hatton, 'The true story of Punch', *London Society* (Aug 1875), 152–61 • *Harriet Martineau's letters to Fanny Wedgwood*, ed. E. Sanders Arbuckle (1983) • 'Some London printing offices: No. 5, Bradbury, Agnew, & Co.', *London, Provincial and Colonial Press News* (Nov 1884), 27–9 • *The Times* • *Punch* (2 July 1870), 7

Archives *Punch* Library, London, account books and letters • Bodl. Oxf., corresp. | Bodl. Oxf., Bradbury and Evans papers • Yale U., Beinecke L., Bradbury collection

Likenesses A. Bassano Ltd, photograph, repro. in Spielmann, *The history of 'Punch'*, 37

Evans, (Michael) Gareth Justin (1946–1980), philosopher, was born on 12 May 1946 in Queen Charlotte's Hospital, Hammersmith, London, the third of the four children of (Howell) Justin Evans, of Larkhall estate, Wandsworth, social welfare secretary and later a sports administrator, and his wife, Gwladus Tudor Davies. He was educated at Granton primary school, London (1952–7), Dulwich College (1957–63), and University College, Oxford (scholar, 1964–7: first-class honours in philosophy, politics, and economics, 1967; Webb Medley prize for economics, Henry Wilde prize for philosophy). He was a senior scholar of Christ Church, Oxford (1967–8), and a Kennedy scholar at Harvard University and the University of California, Berkeley (1968–9). He was a fellow of University College, Oxford, from 1969 to his death, at first as praelector (tutor) in philosophy, and in 1979–80 as a professorial fellow in conjunction with his university appointment as Wilde reader in mental philosophy. He also held visiting positions at the University of Minnesota (1971) and the Massachusetts Institute of Technology (1977–8).

Evans wrote a number of articles on topics in linguistics and the philosophy of language, the philosophy of mind, and metaphysics. His shorter works were assembled in his *Collected Papers* (1985). These papers display a striking range. To cite some examples, 'The causal theory of names' synthesizes insights from the causal and description theories of names in a conception that stresses the role of information in determining what names denote; 'Things without the mind' is a sustained reflection on the connection between objectivity and spatiality; and 'Molyneux's question' (posthumously published) considers the spatiality of vision and of perception in general. 'Identity and predication' discusses the relation between a language's predicative resources and its capacity to single out objects, with an eye to W. V. Quine's thesis of the inscrutability of reference. 'Semantic structure and logical form' takes issue with Donald Davidson's conception of structurally valid inferences. 'Pronouns, quantifiers, and relative clauses' attacks the thesis that all uses of pronouns can be understood either as vernacular equivalents of bound variables or as mere shorthand for anaphoric antecedents.

But Evans's most important work is *The Varieties of Reference* (1982), which was published after his death from manuscripts he had been reworking for years, on a set of topics that had engaged him all his professional life; some parts reflect new thinking he had done in preparation for a graduate seminar that was interrupted by his final illness. *The Varieties of Reference* is noteworthy both at a general level and in detail.

At the general level Evans trenchantly challenges a common assimilation between Frege's conception of sense, as applied to singular terms, and the leading idea of Russell's theory of descriptions. The point of the notion of sense is to ensure that thoughts can be individuated in a way that allows their attribution to be controlled by the purpose of finding thinkers rational. For instance, on the ground that a person's rationality is not put in question by, say, believing that the morning star is now visible but not believing that the evening star is now visible, we are to find two different thoughts expressed by those two 'that' clauses; 'the morning star' and 'the evening star' present the same object in two different ways. The point of the theory of descriptions, by contrast, is to ensure that thoughts are available to be expressed even if objects putatively referred to in the putative expression of them do not exist; thus (Russell's example) 'The present King of France is bald' expresses a thought even though there is no present king of France. Assimilating Frege's thinking to this part of Russell's thinking implies that a Fregean conception of singular thoughts, according to which it matters how objects are presented in them, cannot make room for thoughts whose very thinkability depends on the existence of the objects they are about. But Evans separates the Fregean idea of modes of presentation of objects from the Russellian idea of specifications that partly determine the content of thoughts even if nothing fits them. The idea that results—a conception of object-dependent thoughts that allows entertaining such a thought to be a configuration in a rational mind—has important and still widely unappreciated consequences for the philosophy of mind and language. It points to a picture in which meaning and mindedness are in a radical way determined by how a person is situated in the world.

At the level of detail the book contains brilliantly perceptive discussions of many topics: perhaps most notably demonstrative thought and speech about objects that are perceptually present to the thinker, and—connected to but distinguished from that—thought and speech in which the thinker himself figures in the first person.

Evans was an imposing figure, often bearded and with a shock of dark curly hair; his eyes twinkled behind metal-framed spectacles. He had a famously boisterous laugh, and he gave an impression of constant motion; his physical vigour seemed to match his intellectual energy. He was a keen motorcyclist, an avid squash player, and an enthusiastic handyman at a house of which he was part owner, in the south of France. His teaching was lively and charismatic; his graduate classes in particular attracted a devoted following and were influential in setting a philosophical tone for many Oxford graduate students, and thereby to some extent in Oxford philosophy in general, in the 1970s.

Evans's untimely death cut short a career of immense promise. In his later work his brilliance was increasingly in the service of deep reflection. He himself, facing death with a characteristic thoughtfulness, modestly rejected the tempting comparison with F. P. Ramsey; but many think Evans's death merits a similar regret for achievements there might have been.

In 1978, in Mexico, Evans suffered a serious gunshot wound, in what was presumed to be a botched attempt at kidnapping whose target, the Mexican philosopher Hugo Margain, was killed. He married on 11 June 1980 Antonia Phillips (b. 1950/51) his companion of several years, a university lecturer, daughter of John Charles Phillips, artist. He died of cancer in London on 10 August 1980, and was buried in Wolvercote cemetery, Oxford, on 14 August. His wife survived him. JOHN McDOWELL

Sources personal knowledge (2004) · private information (2004) · *The Times* (12 Aug 1980) · b. cert. · m. cert. · *CGPLA Eng. & Wales* (1980)
Likenesses photograph, Oxford University Press (?)
Wealth at death £31,278: probate, 1 Dec 1980, *CGPLA Eng. & Wales*

Evans, George (*bap.* 1631, *d.* 1702), antiquary, was baptized in the abbey church, St Albans, on 19 February 1631, the son of George and Mary Evans. He was probably educated at the free school and thereafter was admitted to Jesus College, Cambridge, graduating BA in 1650 and proceeding MA in 1653. He was a fellow from 1650 to 1658, and was awarded a doctorate in divinity in 1665. By this time he had been admitted a canon of Windsor (26 July 1660) and on 6 May 1663 he was given a lease of the rectory and parsonage of St Benet Fink, London, by the college of canons. He was also, on 26 March 1667, instituted rector of the parish of Hitcham, Buckinghamshire, where he seems to have spent some time.

Evans and his wife, Rebecca, had five sons and four daughters; a son and a daughter were buried in the churchyard at Hitcham in 1685 and 1690 and his daughter Mary married there in 1697. He seems to have been an affectionate father, asking to be buried 'as near my dear children ... as conveniently can be' and 'with as much privacy and little expense as well may be' (PRO, PROB 11/454, sig. 45). He also had a lively interest in the past and present of St George's Chapel, Windsor; two volumes of his notes of deeds and memoranda of events concerning the college survive in the chapter library. Some of his work was published in *The Antiquities of Berkshire* (1719) by his friend Elias Ashmole, with whom he corresponded over a number of years. Evans died at Hitcham on 2 March 1702 and was buried in the churchyard there four days later; his wife survived him. In addition to the advowson of Hitcham, he owned land and property in Buckinghamshire, Huntingdon, and Cambridgeshire, and had lent about £170 to the crown to be repaid as annuities from the excise. Among his bequests were gifts to the free school of St Albans, the college of Windsor, and the poor of St Albans and New Windsor. JOAN A. DILS

Sources Venn, *Alum. Cant.* · will, PRO, PROB 11/454, sig. 45 · E. Ashmole, *The antiquities of Berkshire*, 3 (1719), 275 · parish register, St Albans Abbey, 19 Feb 1631, Herts. ALS, D/P90/1/1 · parish register, Hitcham, Buckinghamshire, Bucks. RLSS, 6 March 1702 [burial] · S. L. Ollard, *Fasti Wyndesorienses: the deans and canons of Windsor* (privately printed, Windsor, 1950) · R. R. Tighe and J. E. Davis, *Annals of Windsor*, 2 vols. (1858), vol. 1, p. 61 · mandamus appointing George Evans, canon, 26 July 1660, St George's Chapel, Windsor · lease to

George Evans of the rectory and parsonage of St Benet Fink, London, 6 May 1663, SGC XVI.2.74

Archives Royal Arch., SGC IV.B.16–17 · St. George's Chapel, Windsor, antiquarian notes · St. George's Chapel, Windsor, two volumes of deeds and memoranda relating to the College of Canons, Windsor

Wealth at death approx. £400: will, PRO, PROB 11/454, sig. 45

Evans, Sir George de Lacy (1787–1870), army officer, was born on 7 October 1787 in Moig, co. Limerick, the third son of John Evans, a small landed proprietor, and his wife, Mary Ann, a descendant of the Anglo-Norman family of de Lacy, which had a distinguished military tradition. Evans attended the Royal Military Academy, Woolwich, before joining the army in India as a volunteer in 1806. Appointed ensign in the 22nd foot on 1 February 1807, he displayed an instinctive boldness and daring in the campaign against Amir Khan, and was promoted for gallantry to the rank of lieutenant on 1 December 1808. He served under Major-General the Hon. John Abercromby in the capture of Mauritius (1810) but declined an appointment on Sir John Malcolm's mission to Persia, preferring active service in the Deccan. In March 1812 he exchanged into the 3rd dragoons, then serving with Wellington in the Peninsula. He participated in the rear-guard action during the retreat from Burgos (1812) and, despite being wounded in the action at the Hermoza River, remained in the saddle as an example to his men. He led several cavalry charges at Vitoria (21 June 1813), earned plaudits for his daring in the battle of Sorauren, had a horse shot from under him at Bayonne, and served in the actions of Nivelle, Orthez, and Tarbes. In the battle of Toulouse (10 April 1814) he was twice wounded and had two horses shot from under him. Ever eager for combat, he served as an engineer in the trenches before San Sebastian and in the siege of Pamplona. Apart from a brief attachment to the quartermaster-general's department (13 March – 25 May 1814), and the award of the military general service medal with bars for Vitoria, the Pyrenees, and Toulouse, his Peninsular services were unrecognized, leaving him deeply embittered about the purchase system of promotion in the army.

Evans found further action in the Anglo-American War, during which he served on the staff of Major-General Robert Ross. He had another two horses shot from under him in the battle of Bladensburg (24 August 1814), took part in the retaliatory burning of public buildings in Washington, and served in the abortive assault on Baltimore. As the only soldier in the naval operations which preceded the battle of New Orleans, he earned the naval general service medal, and subsequently participated in the disastrous attacks on New Orleans (December 1814 and January 1815), where he was twice wounded but praised for his 'indefatigable zeal and intelligence'. Mentioned five times in dispatches from the United States, Evans was promoted captain in the 5th West India regiment (12 January 1815), and gained a brevet majority (11 May 1815) on his appointment as deputy quartermaster-general with the duke of Wellington's army in the Southern Netherlands. He served at Quatre Bras and then at Waterloo (18 June 1815),

Sir George de Lacy Evans (1787–1870), by Roger Fenton, 1855

where he had two horses shot or sabred from under him but gave the order for the advance of the Union brigade of cavalry and assisted in reorganizing the brigade after its charge. Made a brevet lieutenant-colonel on 18 June 1815, he remained on the staff of the army of occupation until its withdrawal from France.

Placed on half pay (25 April 1817) and frustrated in his hopes for further military employment, Evans immersed himself in radical politics. A Russophobe, he wrote two alarmist books which sounded the tocsin over a possible Russian threat to the empire. They prompted an official inquiry by the India board (1830) into the state of Britain's imperial defences and advanced his political credentials. Adopted as the radical candidate for Rye, he narrowly won and lost elections in 1830 before regaining his seat in the pre-reformed parliament in 1831. An assiduous MP, he regularly attended meetings in Rye and spoke in parliamentary debates, but was never a good orator. He based his speeches upon masses of factual data and lengthy quotations, and was often criticized as inaudible and sometimes incoherent. Nevertheless he promoted many radical causes, such as electoral reform, the ballot, triennial parliaments, Polish independence, Irish reform, and the separation of church and state. He advocated the abolition of slavery, military flogging, the purchase system, and the corn laws, and deplored the use of the yeomanry to maintain public order. His extreme radicalism, together with boundary changes, lost him elections in Rye and Westminster in 1832, but in 1833 he defeated Sir John Cam Hobhouse in a Westminster by-election, profiting from a tory candidacy which split the anti-radical vote. In the Commons he championed the causes which concerned many of his metropolitan constituents, including the burdens of assessed taxation on houses and windows, the powers of the Metropolitan Police, and the Poor Law Amendment Act. He was re-elected in January 1835. On 21 June 1834 he married Josette Hughes (*née* Arbuthnot), a wealthy widow. They had no children.

In May 1835 General Alava, the Spanish ambassador in London, obtained the permission of the king and of Lord Melbourne's ministry to raise a force of 10,000 volunteers, which would be known as the British Legion, to support the Spanish constitutional cause against the Carlist insurrection. While tories disparaged the volunteers as mercenaries Evans, a prominent advocate of the constitutional cause in Spain and Portugal, accepted the offer of command. Now politically and financially secure, and with the local rank of lieutenant-general and a salary of £5000 a year from Madrid, he yearned for field command. When Evans assumed command of the legion in San Sebastian in August 1835 he found his corps undermanned (with only some 7000 effective soldiers), untrained (as training had been banned in Britain), and bereft of experienced officers (as the duke of Wellington and Lord Hill, the commander-in-chief, had explicitly condemned military service in Spain). Still willing to proffer support to the Spanish cause, Evans marched his forces over 150 miles to Vitoria in December, assisted in the skirmish at Arlaban (16 January 1836), and, accompanied by a battalion of Royal Marines under Lord John Hay, raised the siege of San Sebastian (5 May 1836) after a fierce battle. The Madrid authorities, none the less, utterly neglected the legion, leaving officers and men with mounting arrears of pay, inadequate supplies and reinforcements, and scant medical support, especially at Vitoria when fever and dysentery swept through the ranks. Throughout the summer of 1836 Evans had to cope with falling morale, contractual disputes, and dissension over the lack of pay and medals (he even dismissed several hundred mutineers from the legion's service). The legion repulsed formidable Carlist attacks on its lines on 31 May, and 6 and 9 June, and mounted an abortive assault on Fuenterrabía (11 July 1836) before withstanding a massive Carlist offensive on 1 October 1836. In this battle Evans was slightly injured, but took even greater risks by conspicuously riding from one part of the line to another in complete disregard for his personal safety. Thereafter the legion endured several months of grinding inactivity until it received the long-awaited reinforcements of 210 officers and 5135 men. Now able to take the field with some 9000 troops (supported by Royal Marines and Spanish forces), Evans launched a disastrous attack upon the Carlist lines at Hernani (15 March 1837), losing 900 men killed and wounded. Only the arrival of General Espartero's army of 14,000 men enabled Evans to resume his offensive, and, on 14 May 1837, the combined forces stormed the heights overlooking Hernani. They then seized the towns of Oyarzun, Irun, and Fuenterrabía (18 May 1837), with the last garrison surrendering after Evans had spared the prisoners of Irun. Although the Spanish authorities belatedly recognized the achievements of the legion, Evans and the majority of legionnaires declined requests to re-engage and left Spain. Evans received the grand crosses of San Fernando and of Charles III.

Evans encountered a mixed reception on his return to London. Despite promotion to the rank of colonel on 10 January 1837, re-election for Westminster in July, and the appointment as KCB in August 1837, Evans found his military achievements derided by Conservatives in the press and parliament. Having failed after an ineffectual speech to assuage criticisms in the house, Evans continued to press Madrid over the legion's arrears of pay and sought to defend his actions in a book entitled *Memoranda of the Contest in Spain* (1840). This preoccupation with the legion, coupled with divisions among Westminster Liberals, left his constituency vulnerable to a revival of Conservative fortunes in the general election of 1841. Narrowly defeated at the polls, Evans remained a prominent figure in radical politics by participating in the campaign for the repeal of the corn laws. Re-elected for Westminster at a by-election in 1846 (and at the subsequent general elections of 1847 and 1852), he continued to promote local Westminster grievances and army reform in the Commons, but aroused increasing criticism from ultra-radicals within his constituency by tempering his support for the more extreme Chartist proposals.

Evans's military career revived, however. Promoted to the rank of major-general (9 November 1846), he was given a brigade command at the Chobham camp exercise in the summer of 1853. Having impressed Lord Hardinge, the commander-in-chief, he was appointed colonel of the 21st Royal North British Fusiliers (29 August 1853) and given command of the 2nd division in the Crimea, with a subsequent promotion to lieutenant-general on 20 June 1854. He was always concerned about the health and morale of his men, choosing camp sites with care in Bulgaria to minimize losses from cholera and authorizing recreational sports to relieve boredom and sustain morale. At the battle of the Alma (26 September 1854), he not only led his forces with distinction, taking them across the river to the relief of the light division, but also maintained the offensive by prompting the duke of Cambridge to provide support with the 1st division. Though severely wounded at the Alma and weakened by illness, he commanded his men in their successful repulse of a Russian sortie from Sevastopol (the battle of little Inkerman, 26 October 1854). After a fall from his horse Evans was hospitalized, but returned to his division during the main battle of Inkerman (5 November 1854), inspiring officers and men without undermining the command of Major-General Pennefather. Debilitated by his exertions, Evans retired from the war and returned as a national hero. He received a vote of thanks from the House of Commons and a GCB in July

1855. He was appointed grand officer of the Légion d'honneur in 1856, and received both an honorary DCL from Oxford University and the Turkish order of the Mejidiye.

Although Evans deprecated parliamentary criticism of the Crimean army and deplored the cessation of hostilities in January 1856, he remained passionately committed to army reform. This became his main concern during his last ten years in parliament (retaining his Westminster seat without opposition in the elections of 1857 and 1859). He served on several royal commissions and select committees, spoke in army debates, championed the volunteer movement of 1859, and repeatedly pressed for the abolition—in whole or in part—of the purchase system. His dismal oratory, laced all too often with personal invective, failed to sway the house, and he found that the press was much less interested in the issue after the army's suppression of the Indian mutiny. Evans lost further credibility as a reformer and dissipated his energies by promoting the cause of the local European forces of the East India Company. He bitterly opposed the European Forces (India) Bill (1860) and so found himself isolated from both front benches and ignored by the metropolitan press. Despite promotion to the rank of general on 10 March 1861 he achieved little as an army reformer, and attended parliament less and less frequently on account of recurrent illnesses. He retired from political life at the dissolution of 1865 and died at his home, 6 Great Cumberland Place, London, on 9 January 1870, aged eighty-two.

EDWARD M. SPIERS

Sources E. M. Spiers, *Radical general: Sir George de Lacy Evans, 1787–1870* (1983) · M. K. Wells, 'Westminster's general: the military and political career of Sir George de Lacy Evans', MA diss., Texas Tech University, 1983 · J. H. Gleason, *The genesis of Russophobia in Great Britain: a study of the interaction of policy and opinion* (1950) · E. Holt, *The Carlist wars in Spain* (1967) · G. H. Jenkins, *The army in Victorian society* (1977) · E. M. Spiers, *The army and society, 1815–1914* (1980) · A. Somerville, *History of the British legion, and war in Spain, with an appendix, containing every officer's name, rank, and service, that was in the expedition* (1839) · A. W. Kinglake, *The invasion of the Crimea*, [new edn], 9 vols. (1877–88) · A. Bruce, *The purchase system in the British army, 1660–1871*, Royal Historical Society Studies in History, 20 (1980) · *The Times* (13 Jan 1870), 1 · G. de Lacy Evans, *Memoranda of the contest in Spain* (1840) · Deed no. 227572, Registry of Deeds, Dublin, Book 340 · 'Pedigree of De Lacy Evans', Genealogical Office, Dublin Castle, MSS 176, 177

Archives NL Ire., MSS · priv. coll., MSS | BL, Aberdeen MSS · BL, letters to Lord Carnarvon, Add. MS 60785 · Bodl. Oxf., letters to Lord Clarendon · NAM, Raglan MSS · U. Nott., Newcastle MSS · U. Southampton L., Broadlands MSS · U. Southampton L., corresp. with Lord Palmerston

Likenesses M. O'Connor, lithograph, pubd 1833, BM, NPG · M. Gauci, lithograph, pubd 1834 (after A. E. Chalon), BM, NPG · miniature, *c.*1840, NPG · R. Fenton, photograph, 1855, NPG [*see illus.*] · R. Fenton, photographs, 1855–60, NAM · D. J. Pound, engraving, *c.*1856, NAM · G. Zobel, mezzotint, pubd 1856 (after R. Buckner), NPG · photograph, *c.*1856, NAM · E. Edwards, photograph, NPG; repro. in *Portraits of men of eminence*, 3 (1865) · J. H. Lynch, lithograph (after photograph by R. Fenton, *c.*1855), BM, NPG · marble bust, Brighton Pavilion · photographs, NPG

Wealth at death under £80,000: probate, 2 July 1870, *CGPLA Eng. & Wales*

Evans, George Essex (1863–1909), poet and journalist, was born at Cumberland Terrace, Regent's Park, London, on 18 June 1863, the son of John Evans (1795/6–1864), and his wife, Mary Ann Owen. His father was a QC and for five years a member of parliament, and died when George Evans was only a few months old. Evans attended Haverfordwest grammar school, Pembrokeshire, and after studying at St James's Collegiate School in Jersey in the Channel Islands, he left with his brother and two sisters for Queensland in 1881. They began farming at Allora, in the Darling Downs, but were unsuccessful, and George tried teaching in a private school and afterwards entered journalism. In 1888 he obtained an appointment in the public service, eventually becoming district registrar at Gympie and later at Toowoomba, in northern Queensland, the town with which his name is closely associated.

Evans's literary career dates from about 1885, when he began to contribute to *The Queenslander*; throughout his life he wrote for the press in both prose and verse. His first volume of poetry, *The Repentance of Magdale Despar*, was published in 1891 and received some attention. The title poem, one of several of Evans's long narrative and philosophical poems, tells of the tragedy of a young woman's faithlessness to an elderly husband. Evans also worked for a time with the poet A. B. (Banjo) Paterson on the literary annual, *The Antipodean*, which, however, eventually failed. He was also for a considerable time the literary director of the government tourist bureau. His first volume was followed by *Loraine* (1898) and *The Secret Key* (1906). On 6 November 1899 Evans married Blanche Hopkins, the young widow of E. B. Hopkins, of Goodar station, near Goondiwindi, and the daughter of the Revd William Eglinton. They had one son.

In 1901 Evans was awarded a prize of £50 for his 'Ode for Commonwealth Day'. As founder of the Austral Association, he was a prime mover in establishing national festivals of music, art, and literature. During the last two years of his life he wrote on the resources of his adopted state for the Queensland government.

Evans died suddenly at the Toowoomba Hospital during the musical festival of the Austral Society on 10 November 1909, exactly seven months after Swinburne, who was, with Kipling, one of the poets he most admired. His wife survived him. His death was announced from the stage of the auditorium, holding 8000 people, which he had been instrumental in converting from a former gaol. At the time of his death he was widely respected as the unofficial poet laureate of Queensland and of Toowoomba. On his death the prime minister, Alfred Deakin, spoke of him as a great national patriotic poet. There is a monument to him in Toowoomba and an annual George Essex Evans pilgrimage and memorial lecture. A collected edition of his works, published in 1928 under the editorship of Firmin McKinnon, contained over a hundred poems, some never before published in book form.

During his lifetime Evans was probably best-known for the frequently anthologized 'The Women of the West' and the patriotic 'An Australian Symphony'. The former celebrated those pioneer women who left the city and accompanied their husbands into the plains, but celebrated them in markedly ambivalent terms:

The red sun robs their beauty, and, in weariness and pain,
The slow years steal the nameless grace that never comes
  again.

Admirers of 'An Australian Symphony' may similarly have missed the underlying melancholy of the poem. After celebrating Australia's uniqueness in its opening lines:

Not as the songs of other lands
Her song shall be

the poem introduces elements of sadness and weirdness into its descriptions of the Australian landscape and psyche, ending with speculation as to whether the country's silence will ever be converted into song. Under the influence of his near contemporary James Brunton Stephens, Evans wrote a number of philosophical poems. These are sad, usually tragic monologues in which the poet suggests the futility of man's attempts to interfere with the course of destiny: they postulate a God who is seen in terms of a passionless power. Evans was a competent but derivative craftsman, whose reputation, especially outside Queensland, has declined markedly since his death.

G. S. WOODS, rev. LAURIE CLANCY

Sources M. D. O'Hagan, 'Evans, George Essex', *AusDB*, vol. 8 • *The collected verse of George Essex Evans*, ed. F. McKinnon (1928) • E. M. Miller and F. T. B. Macartney, *Australian literature: a bibliography to 1938, extended to 1950* (1956) • W. H. Wilde, J. Hooton, and B. Andrews, *The Oxford companion to Australian literature*, 2nd edn (1994) • K. L. Goodwin, *A history of Australian literature* (1986) • R. Fitzgerald, 'George Essex Evans: poet of Toowoomba', *Image*, 1 (1989), 53–6 • H. A. Kellow, *Queensland poets* (1930) • H. A. Tardent, *The life and poetry of George Essex Evans* (1913) • *WWBMP*, vol. 1 • Boase, *Mod. Eng. biog.*

Evans, George Ewart (1909–1988), historian and writer, was born on 1 April 1909 in Abercynon, Glamorgan, one of the eleven children, seven boys and four girls, of William Evans, shopkeeper, of Abercynon. He was one of the eight children of his father's second marriage, to Janet Hitchings of Maesteg. He was educated at Mountain Ash grammar school, and then University College, Cardiff, where he went as a trainee teacher on a Glamorgan county council scholarship, winning a college bursary *en route*. He read classics and graduated in the summer of 1930 with a lower second-class degree. There followed a year of professional training, at the end of which he obtained his diploma in education and became unemployed. As he himself bitterly remarked in his autobiography: 'You swore to teach but the Board of Education … could not provide you with the opportunity.'

When Evans finally found work in 1934 it was quite another aspect of his career which gave him the necessary qualifications. From his late boyhood Evans had been a fine rugby player and an excellent runner. He had played rugby both for the renowned Mountain Ash 'Old Firm' before university, and for University College as an undergraduate. His running was in the rougher school of the old Welsh working-class semi-professional track, where, by side bets, he gained the money to finance part of his university career. It was this athleticism which got him his first job in 1934, as a games master at the newly opened Sawston Village College, Cambridgeshire, where he met Florence Knappett, who was later to become his wife.

Evans's move to East Anglia, although it happened by chance, was to prove momentous in what was to be his final career—that of writer and historian of rural life. By 1934 he had already decided, as he later wrote, that 'I did not care ultimately what kind of job I took. I determined that my real work henceforth would be to write.' In the following years he published a number of short stories, poems, and articles and became closely associated with the group around Keidrych Rhys's magazine *Wales*, and the London-based *Left Review*. These pieces are, in some ways, very much of their time, and yet they also show a close sense of the realities of life in south Wales which distinguish them from the run-of-the-mill socialist-realist fiction of the period.

In October 1941 Evans was called up into the Royal Air Force. Restricted because of his increasing deafness to home-based and ground-based duties, he served as a radio technician in 206 squadron, Coastal Command. After his wartime service Evans published a full-length novel, *The Voices of the Children* (1947), but it was badly received outside Wales. In the 1940s he suffered recurrent moods of black depression, in which he constantly questioned his own abilities, and felt a despair which was exacerbated by his deafness, which made it virtually impossible to find work as a teacher.

In 1948 Evans moved to Blaxhall in Suffolk, where his wife had been appointed village schoolteacher, and it was out of Blaxhall that his first book about English rural life, *Ask the Fellows who Cut the Hay*, came in 1956. The book was based on interviews with the older inhabitants of the village about their lives, their work, and their communities. This was a technique used in folk-life studies, and one which was beginning to find favour in the world of radio, but it was still well outside the bounds of conventional academic history. The book, however, was a success and in the next ten years three more followed. Part of their popularity certainly rested on the English nostalgia for a lost rural past, but, like Evans's earlier fiction, they contained a great deal more than that. Evans also lectured widely, particularly for the Workers' Educational Association. In the late 1960s, with the emergence of the technique of oral history in British academic life, there followed a period of stimulating, if not always easy, contact with academic life, especially the University of Essex, where Evans was Major Burrows lecturer in 1972 and a visiting fellow from 1973 to 1978. His books from this period, particularly *Where Beards Wag All* (1970), *The Days that we have Seen* (1975), and *From Mouths of Men* (1976), represent his best work. Careful and beautifully crafted, they remind the reader that Evans remained a writer as much as a historian. In the 1980s his relationship with academe, never easy, became more tense. His book on the myth of the hare, *The Leaping Hare*, written in 1972 with David Thomson, had been dismissed by academic anthropology, and he felt that oral history was moving away from its roots into ever wilder areas of theory, while neglecting the ordinary people. Some of these feelings are present in his fine volume of autobiography, *The Strength of the Hills* (1983), and in his last book, the much less satisfactory *Spoken History* (1987).

Through all this Evans retained much of his Welshness. Although not tall, he was an upright figure who kept his rugby-playing physique until late in life. He was a native Welsh speaker, and retained a clear Welsh accent all his life, which was often a shock to those who knew him only through his books and assumed he was East Anglian. His past also shaped him in other, more fundamental, ways. Politically he was born into a radical family; he was named Ewart after William Ewart Gladstone, and that radicalism never left him. He was a member of the Communist Party in the 1930s and remained very close to communism throughout his life. His politics and his Welshness drew him back in the 1970s to the subject matter of Wales, and in his last books he became a chronicler of the end of the south Wales coal industry, as he had earlier been the recorder of the end of horse-based agriculture in England.

Evans remained very much an outsider to the academic world. His honesty, which was often blunt, and always based on a deep distrust of the English ruling élite, ill fitted him for English universities, and it is perhaps not surprising that it was at the politically radical University of Essex of the 1970s that he seemed happiest. He was awarded an honorary DU by Essex in 1982, and an honorary DLitt by the University of Keele in 1983. In 1971 he was president of the anthropology section of the British Association for the Advancement of Science meeting at Swansea.

In 1938 Evans married Florence Ellen, daughter of Albert George Knappett, clerk in the stock exchange. They had a son, who became a director of Faber and Faber, Evans's publishers, and three daughters, one of whom married David Gentleman, who illustrated many of Evans's books. Florence was a key figure in Evans's life, supporting him with her teaching in the 1940s and early 1950s, when otherwise he would not have been able to write, as well as being a gentle but firm commentator on his work, of which she said once, '[it was] a bit creepy … listening to all those dead voices'. Evans died on 11 January 1988 at Brooke, Norfolk, where he had lived since the 1970s. ALUN HOWKINS, *rev.*

Sources G. E. Evans, *The strength of the hills* (1983) · G. Williams, *George Ewart Evans* (1991) · personal knowledge (1996) · private information (1996) · CGPLA *Eng. & Wales* (1988)

Archives NL Wales, corresp., papers, literary MSS, local history notes, diaries

Wealth at death under £70,000: probate, 26 April 1988, CGPLA *Eng. & Wales*

Evans, Sir Geraint Llewellyn (1922–1992), singer, was born on 16 February 1922 at 55 William Street, Cilfynydd, Glamorgan, the only son of William John Evans (1899–1978), miner, and his wife, Charlotte May, *née* Thomas (1901–1923). His mother died in childbirth when her son was seventeen months old, and the daughter she then bore did not long survive her. His father thereupon returned to live with his own parents, and Evans was brought up by his maternal grandparents in Cilfynydd. The family was Welsh speaking, and Welsh was Evans's first language before he learned English. He was aged ten

Sir Geraint Llewellyn Evans (1922–1992), by Arnold Newman, 1978

when his father remarried, and the boy moved with his father and stepmother to Hopkinstown, in the Rhondda valley. He attended local schools and Lan Wood School, Pontypridd, until the age of fourteen, when he returned to live with his grandparents and took his first job as a shop assistant and window-dresser in nearby Pontypridd.

On his afternoons off Evans began taking singing lessons in Cardiff, sang with the Bethel Methodist Chapel choir in Cilfynydd (he remained a Methodist all his life), appeared in *Lilac Time* with a local dramatic society, made his first solo broadcast for BBC Wales, aged seventeen, and took the title role in a Bethel Chapel costumed performance of Mendelssohn's oratorio *Elijah*. He followed the local trend as a keen enthusiast for rugby football, but was prevented from active participation by the asthma from which he suffered when young. On the outbreak of the Second World War he volunteered for the Royal Air Force and was trained as a radio mechanic, serving in France, Belgium, and Germany, and taking part in forces entertainments at home and abroad. At the war's end he was posted to British Forces Network, broadcasting from Hamburg, where he sang regularly with the radio chorus and began professional vocal training with the lieder singer Theo Herrmann, a Viennese baritone of distinction then resident in Hamburg.

On demobilization Evans took a gamble in deciding to pursue a singing career, and a reluctant local authority was persuaded to give him a serviceman's vocational grant to attend London's Guildhall School of Music and Drama. There he made his operatic début in 1948 as Don

Alfonso in a student production of Mozart's *Così fan tutte*. After a successful audition at Covent Garden he was engaged as principal baritone at £12 per week. On the prospects of a regular income he proposed to Brenda Evans Davies (*b.* 1920), a neighbour and schoolteacher from Cilfynydd, and they were married on 27 March 1948 at Moriah Chapel, Cilfynydd. Their marriage remained steadfast until his death, and they had two sons, Alun and Huw. His wife was a constant source of strength and support throughout his career, giving perceptive criticism when she thought it was needed.

Evans made his début with the Covent Garden Opera on 21 January 1948 in the brief but exposed role of the Nightwatchman in *Die Meistersinger von Nürnberg*, the first Wagner production there since the war. A decade later he had progressed to Beckmesser, the crotchety town clerk in the same opera, which became one of the half-dozen roles most closely associated with him, of the seventy-three roles in fifty-three operas which he performed in his career. Before this he had already launched a Figaro at Covent Garden that proved ideally suited to his voice and personality, and which he would sing more than 500 times around the world. Together with his seedy Leporello in *Don Giovanni* and his happy-go-lucky Papageno in *The Magic Flute*, this formed part of a trilogy of Mozart roles that always showed to advantage his sense of musical style and his talent for stage character.

Evans acknowledged that he preferred the opera stage to the concert platform, the physical process of costume and make-up enabling him to take on another identity altogether. In search of a convincing portrait he would sometimes invent for himself backgrounds to the characters he sang, and these were always built 'from the feet up'. His Mozart characters were polished at the Glyndebourne Festival in Sussex, where he sang at ten annual festivals, from 1950 to 1959, and where, in 1957, he first assumed the title role in Verdi's *Falstaff*, a role that was to bring him lasting fame and launch him on more than two decades of international travel.

Evans's engagements abroad included an unprecedented twenty-four consecutive annual seasons at San Francisco, for which he received the San Francisco Opera medal acknowledging his 'exceptional contributions'; the Vienna Staatsoper, where he was invited to join the resident company by the conductor Herbert von Karajan, but chose instead to remain at Covent Garden; the Chicago Lyric Opera, for several seasons from 1961; and La Scala, Milan, where the stage crew in 1960, puzzled by his fluent if Welsh-inflected Italian as Figaro and his strange name, decided he must be Sicilian (Evans, 149). The Salzburg Festival also engaged him for nine consecutive years. His début role was, inevitably, Figaro, which had never previously been sung at Salzburg by anybody from Britain, so he felt not a little insulted that a BBC television crew, sent there to make a documentary feature, interviewed his co-stars and ignored him completely (ibid., 164). Ignoring the achievements of British singers abroad was, he found, endemic in the attitude of British officialdom. He would frequently be invited to receptions given for their singers by the German, Austrian, French, Polish, and other embassies, but he was able to reciprocate only 'a couple of times' at the British embassy. Yet he made sure that, whenever possible, he put in a good word abroad for fellow singers he knew in Britain (especially if they were Welsh), to a point where Britain's international operatic prestige had never been higher.

At home Evans felt privileged to work with Benjamin Britten, creating roles in the premières of *Billy Budd* and the coronation opera, *Gloriana*, as well as singing in other operas including *Peter Grimes* and a ripely seasoned Bottom in *A Midsummer Night's Dream*. *Peter Grimes* and *Billy Budd* were two of his first choices when he was invited to direct his own productions in the USA, where he also directed *Falstaff*, *The Marriage of Figaro*, and *Don Pasquale*, and he harboured some regret that more was not made of his experience in this way among British companies. Much of his professional success was due to his sense of ensemble, of being part of a team working together in a combined artistic endeavour rather than in individual rivalry. Late in his career he appeared with both the Welsh National Opera and the Scottish Opera to sing several of his best loved roles, and added new roles in operas composed for him by Norman Kay and the Welsh composer Alun Hoddinott. He felt some disappointment that more use of his great talent was not made for recording purposes, although he recorded his 'signature role' of Figaro under both Otto Klemperer and Daniel Barenboim, Falstaff under Georg Solti, *Die Meistersinger* with Herbert von Karajan, and *Peter Grimes* with Britten.

Evans made his farewell appearance at Covent Garden on 4 June 1984 as the quack Doctor Dulcamara in Donizetti's *L'elisir d'amore*, chosen so he could offer the doctor's supposed 'love-potion' all around as a token of thanks to fellow artists and audiences alike. In retirement at Trelawney, the harbourside house at Aberaeron, Cardiganshire, bought as a holiday home in 1966, he was occupied with programmes for Harlech Television, including master classes and occasional coaching. He was appointed CBE in 1959, was knighted in 1969, and, besides various academic fellowships, became a freeman of the City of London in 1984. He died of a heart attack at Aberystwyth on 19 September 1992 and, after cremation, his ashes were interred at the church of Llanddewi Aber-arth, near Aberaeron, on 11 November. He was commemorated by a service of thanksgiving at Westminster Abbey, London, on 27 November that year, for the life of a great artist and a lovable man.

NOËL GOODWIN

Sources G. Evans, *A knight at the opera* (1984) · *The Times* (21 Sept 1992) · *The Independent* (21 Sept 1992) · private information (2004) [B. E. Evans] · personal knowledge (2004)

Archives priv. coll. | FILM priv. coll., performance footage | SOUND BL NSA, documentary recordings · BL NSA, performance recordings

Likenesses photographs, 1948–73, Hult. Arch. · O. Lancaster, portrait, 1958 (as Falstaff), priv. coll. · A. Blatas, watercolour sketch, 1970, priv. coll. · A. Newman, photograph, 1978, NPG [*see illus.*] · D. Griffiths, portrait, 1982, priv. coll. · I. R. Jones, bust, 1984, NMG Wales · I. Roberts-Jones, bronze bust, *c.*1984, NPG · A. Blatas, portrait (as Falstaff), NMG Wales · J. Bratby, portrait, priv. coll. ·

R. Harries, bust (as Falstaff), Royal Opera House • J. Piper, portrait, priv. coll.

Wealth at death £84,228: probate, 21 Jan 1993, *CGPLA Eng. & Wales*

Evans, (Thomas) Godfrey (1920–1999), cricketer, was born on 18 August 1920 at 20 Woodgrange Avenue, Finchley, Middlesex, the second son of Arthur Gordon Lockwood Evans, master builder, and his wife, Rose Elizabeth, *née* Allen. His father was abroad for much of the time and within a few months of his birth the family moved to Sheldwich, near Faversham, Kent. In 1928 Evans joined his elder brother, John Gordon (Jack), at Kent College, Canterbury, where his sporting prowess led to captaincies at soccer, hockey, and cricket, his swashbuckling batting being especially impressive. He also whipped-in for a hunt and boxed lightweight. On leaving school he briefly turned professional, but his third fight was very bruising and as he had joined the ground staff at Kent County Cricket Club at sixteen, he was instructed to abandon boxing to avoid the risk of damage to his eyesight.

Inspired by Kent's wicket-keeping traditions, Evans proved a natural keeper. In 1939 he played his first county game as a batsman and in four further matches before war intervened he was able to show his flair behind the stumps. After Dunkirk the recruiting age was lowered to nineteen; in June 1940 Evans joined the army, and was posted to the Royal Army Service Corps where he rose to the rank of sergeant. On 25 January 1941 he married Jean Beatrice (1921/2–1966?), a clerk and daughter of Charles Henry Tritton, electrical engineer. Their son was named Howard Leslie after two of his admired Kent players. The marriage did not last, however, and was dissolved.

While stationed at Aldershot, Evans played in several wartime matches. In 1946 he took over from Kent batsman and wicket-keeper Leslie Ames in a test match against India, and took part in the winter tour to Australia. There England was outplayed, but Evans shone, setting two unusual records: Australia scored 1054 runs before he let a bye; and at Adelaide, contrary to his usual custom, he batted for 95 minutes before scoring, and helped Denis Compton force a draw. A subsequent batting record was truer to his attacking style: 98 runs of his century before lunch at Lord's against India in 1952.

'Godders', as he was known, hit seven first-class hundreds, including another in tests: upon going in at 88 for 5 against the West Indies at Old Trafford in 1950 he scored 104 of 161 in a 'hare and tortoise' partnership with Trevor Bailey. His test average at 20.49 was not in Ames's class, or even Knott's, his successor, but coupled with brilliant keeping it ensured that he played 91 tests for England, a wicket-keeping record until Knott overtook it. He was only once excluded, as the scapegoat for humiliating defeat in 1948. Australia piled up an unmatched fourth innings winning total of 404 for 3 with Evans failing to stump Arthur Morris and Don Bradman early in their decisive 301 partnership. Unabashed he bounced right back and was soon rated the world's best. Evans's final test was against India in 1959. One stumping took his total in

tests to 46 plus 173 catches, another record until Knott surpassed it. Yet he missed other chances, and was dropped. Second best was no good for him and he promptly retired from county cricket too. In 1960 he was appointed CBE and published his first book, *The Gloves are Off*. Three more followed.

In 258 matches for Kent, Evans scored 9325 runs, averaging 21.38. In an emergency he played a final game against Yorkshire in 1967. His three catches brought his total to 451 plus 103 stumpings, many off Doug Wright. Doug bowled faster than most spinners, gaining unusual lift and turn, which foxed lesser wicket-keepers. With his 17-yard run, Wright bowled an occasional faster ball that was so quick that he had to signal Evans to retreat. Yet to underline his range of skills Evans always stood up to Bedser swinging the ball late and fast. Bedser appreciated the way this discomforted batsmen, and gave him a clearer target. Another of Evans's great assets was his ability to shrug off error, which Knott regarded as the most important lesson he learned from him. Typically Evans once responded to dropping a catch off Bedser by calling 'Bowl at the wicket, Alec!' Yet another attribute caused Colin Cowdrey to rate Evans the best of Kent's great trio. 'He lifted teams with his tireless energy, and extrovert enthusiasm. A tonic for weary fielders was the way he made bad returns look good by scooping the ball up and flourishing it over the bails.' His stamina was exceptional, both on the field and when partying the night away.

'Godders' continued to enjoy charity games for Lord's Taverners and International Cavaliers. Instantly recognizable with his bushy white whiskers and jaunty walk, he remained outstandingly popular with the public. The ebullient Evans never settled to work, his jobs ranging from cheap-jewellery salesman to chicken farmer and publican. On 15 October 1973 he married Angela Joy Peart (b. 1939/40), his employee at the Jolly Drover, Rogate, Sussex. They had a daughter, Abigail. Evans was partial to a bet and his most appropriate job was as adviser to Ladbroke's in setting test odds. This second marriage cooled and in later years Evans was living at Rushden, Northamptonshire, with a partner, Mary Katherine Wills-Evans.

Throughout his life Evans took triumph or disaster in his stride and met misfortune with a grin. One of his matches for the Old England XI was at the Oval against Rachel Heyhoe's world cup winning team. The ladies enjoyed his sprightly antics and irreverent comment. In a special match to celebrate his seventieth birthday Evans still kept wicket with a flourish. An exceptional cricketer and a great entertainer, he was a true 'people's champion'. He suffered a heart attack at the Cricketers' Club, London, and was taken to Northampton General Hospital where he died on 3 May 1999.   A. Pawson

Sources *Wisden* • J. Evans, *Images of Kent cricket* (2000) • *The Guardian* (4 May 1999), 18a–f • N. Harris, *The Independent* (4 May 1999) • *Daily Telegraph* (4 May 1999) • T. Corbett, *The Scotsman* (4 May 1999) • personal knowledge (2004) • private information (2004) [family and friends] • *Kent Messenger* (7 May 1999), 65 • b. cert. • d. cert.
Likenesses photographs, 1940–60, Hult. Arch. • photograph, repro. in Corbett, *The Scotsman* • photograph, repro. in Harris, *The Independent* • photograph, repro. in *The Times* • photograph, repro.

in *Daily Telegraph* · photograph, repro. in *Kent Messenger* · photograph, repro. in *The Guardian*
Wealth at death under £200,000: probate, 1999

Evans, Sir Guildhaume Myrddin- (1894–1964), civil servant, was born at Clynmawr House, Blaenau Gwent, Monmouthshire, on 17 December 1894, the second son of Thomas Towy Evans, a Baptist minister, and his wife, Mary James. He was educated at Llandovery and Christ Church, Oxford, where he obtained first-class honours in mathematical moderations in 1914, and took his BA degree in 1919. On the outbreak of the First World War he was commissioned in the South Wales Borderers, and served in France and Flanders. In 1917 he was invalided out of the army, and he then joined the prime minister's secretariat. Two years later he became assistant secretary to the cabinet, and for the next ten years he was an assistant principal in the Treasury. On 16 April 1919 he married Elizabeth (1889/90–1981), daughter of Owen Watkin, farmer, of Sarn, Caernarvonshire; there were two sons of the marriage.

In 1929 Myrddin-Evans moved to the Ministry of Labour, and in 1935 became deputy chief insurance officer under the new Unemployment Acts. Then, in 1938, he was appointed head of the international labour division of the Ministry of Labour. From this time until his retirement in 1959 he led nearly all the British delegations to international labour conferences, and it was at once the most congenial as well as the most successful period of his career. During the Second World War he served as head of the production executive secretariat, and he also acted as adviser on manpower problems to both the American and Canadian governments. He was a member of the British delegation to the San Francisco conference in 1945 which established the United Nations, and he served in the British delegation to the general assembly of the UN between 1946 and 1953. But his outstanding achievement was his work for the International Labour Organization (ILO). He had become the representative of the British government on the governing body of the ILO in 1945, and he was soon elected chairman. In the early months of 1946 negotiations began between the ILO and the UN; and the conclusions of these often difficult discussions, formally embodied in a detailed agreement, owed much to the tact, skill, and competence of the two respective chairmen: Myrddin-Evans for the ILO and Sir A. Ramaswami Mudaliar, of India, for the UN. Myrddin-Evans was chairman of the ILO for three periods of office—a rare occurrence—and he was the first civil servant ever to be elected president of the International Labour Conference. This was in 1949.

Myrddin-Evans enjoyed great esteem within the ILO and was known all over the world for his remarkable knowledge of international labour conditions and problems. His contribution to the growth and development of the ILO was widely appreciated, and the warmth of his reception on his many visits to different parts of the world was a matter of deep personal satisfaction. On the eve of his retirement from the Ministry of Labour he was appointed chairman of the Local Government Commission for Wales. He greatly appreciated the compliment; and he showed himself once more as an admirable chairman: thorough, positive, always helpful, and able to win the respect and the affection of his committee. The commission's report was published in 1963, a year before his death.

Myrddin-Evans was an active churchman all his life. For many years he was a member of the council of the Baptist Union, and for a time he served as secretary of the Bloomsbury Central Baptist Church in London. In 1934 he published, with Thomas Chegwidden, *The Employment Exchange Service of Great Britain*. He was appointed CB in 1945 and KCMG in 1947. Myrddin-Evans died at his London home, 6 Chester Place, Regent's Park, on 15 February 1964.   JOHN SAVILLE, *rev.*

Sources *The Times* (17 Feb 1964) · *Western Mail* (17 Feb 1964) · private information (1981) · b. cert. · m. cert. · *CGPLA Eng. & Wales* (1964)
Likenesses W. Stoneman, photograph, 1949, NPG
Wealth at death £16,146: probate, 1 May 1964, *CGPLA Eng. & Wales*

Evans, Horace, Baron Evans (1903–1963), physician, was born on 1 January 1903 at Dowlais, near Merthyr Tudful, Wales, the elder son of Harry Evans, musician, and his wife, Edith Gwendolen Rees. His grandfather was a pharmacist in Dowlais and his father, who conducted the famous Dowlais Choir, subsequently became a prominent musician in Liverpool and conductor of the Liverpool Philharmonic Orchestra. Horace Evans was educated at Liverpool College, at the Guildhall School of Music, and at the City of London School.

In 1921 Evans entered the London Hospital medical college on a science scholarship. His student career was undistinguished, and though he qualified in 1925, and took his MB BS in 1920, he failed his MRCP examination. None the less he was selected by Arthur Ellis as house physician to the medical unit of the London Hospital, following which he held a series of appointments—surgical, obstetric, and in anaesthetics and pathology—which provided a broad basis for his future career as a general physician. In 1929 he married Helen Aldwyth Davies, daughter of a former high-sheriff of Glamorgan; they had two daughters. Evans passed the MRCP examination in 1930, took his MD in the same year, and was made FRCP in 1938.

In 1933 Evans became assistant director of the medical unit at the London Hospital, where he carried out research into nephritis and hypertension, collecting the accurate clinical information on which Ellis subsequently based his classification of nephritis. Ellis gave an account of this work in his Croonian lectures on the natural history of Bright's disease, delivered at the Royal College of Physicians in 1941. At the end of these lectures, which were published in *The Lancet* in January 1942, Ellis mentioned that he, Evans, and Clifford Wilson (Evans's successor as assistant director of the medical unit at the London) were to produce a book detailing their research. The brown book, as it was known at the hospital, was never published.

By the time Evans had relinquished his post he had built up a highly successful consulting practice. He was appointed assistant physician to the London Hospital in 1936 and full physician in 1947. He subsequently became consulting physician to the Royal Navy and to the Royal Masonic Hospital, the Royal Buckinghamshire Hospital, the Poplar Hospital, the King Edward VII Hospital for Officers, and the King Edward VII Sanatorium at Midhurst. In 1946, on the recommendation of Lord Webb-Johnson, Evans succeeded Lord Dawson of Penn as physician to Queen Mary; he became physician to George VI in 1949, and from 1952 until his death was physician to Elizabeth II. This distinguished service brought him many honours. He was appointed KCVO in 1949 and GCVO in 1955, and in 1957 was created Baron Evans, of Merthyr Tudful.

Evans was a general physician of a high order and he grew in stature as his work expanded in breadth and importance. Yet it is doubtful if he would have achieved such high distinction had Ellis not singled him out. Ellis could recognize special promise in his students and selected Evans at a time when he showed no particular academic ability or evidence of the great personal qualities which emerged later. It was from Ellis that Evans learned the fundamental clinical discipline of careful, unhurried, and informed history-taking and physical examination, as well as a profound suspicion of dogma and theory, and a proper humility when faced with a difficult clinical problem.

Evans realized, and impressed on all those he taught, that the explosive growth of the biological sciences, and the increasing dependence of the traditional physician on the laboratory worker for technical information about his patients, increased rather than diminished the need for the personal physician with a critical judgement based on broad general experience. In Evans this basic discipline was grounded in a personality of resilience, compassion, and understanding, combined with a remarkable physical presence, in the sickroom and the hospital ward, of which all who came in contact with him became instantly aware. At the London Hospital, Evans gave freely of his time to the nursing staff. His clinical teaching was simple, practical, and reflected the immense experience of 'problem' disorders which came his way from all parts of the world.

Outside the hospital Evans's interests included the activities of the Medical Society of London, of which he became president, the British Heart Foundation, of which he was a founder member, and the Royal College of Physicians, which he served as examiner, senior censor, and vice-president. His greatest service to the college was, however, the part he played in its transfer from Trafalgar Square to Regent's Park and its receipt of magnanimous financial support from the Wolfson Foundation, of which he was a trustee. His many professional distinctions included the Hunterian professorship of the Royal College of Surgeons, and the Croonian lectureship of the Royal College of Physicians (1955).

While his voice, his appearance, his gait, and his attitude at the bedside always appeared to indicate an unhurried personality, Evans appeared to have few relaxations.

His main diversion was the racecourse—he never missed Ascot—and he was an excellent judge of horses. He was also a regular visitor to Monte Carlo. Much of Evans's sympathy and understanding stemmed unfortunately from his personal family misfortunes. His younger daughter died in tragic circumstances and his wife suffered prolonged ill health; but even during his own final illness, from which he died in Beaumont House, Beaumont Street, London, on 26 October 1963, he showed immense fortitude, imperturbable humour, and continuing interest in students, patients, and the colleagues who sought his help and advice. He was survived by his wife.

CLIFFORD WILSON, rev. MARK W. WEATHERALL

Sources BMJ (2 Nov 1963), 1133–5 · The Lancet (2 Nov 1963), 949–50 · The Times (28 Oct 1963) · The Times (31 Oct 1963) · The Guardian (28 Oct 1963) · Munk, Roll · 'In memoriam Lord Evans', Annals of the Royal College of Surgeons of England, 33 (1963), 387–9 · CGPLA Eng. & Wales (1964)

Likenesses J. Aris, oils, 1966 (after unknown artist; after J. Gunn), RCP Lond. · J. Gunn, oils, London Hospital

Wealth at death £90,287: probate, 27 Jan 1964, CGPLA Eng. & Wales

Evans, (Benjamin) Ifor, Baron Evans of Hungershall (1899–1982), literary scholar and college administrator, was born in Soho, London, on 19 August 1899, the younger son of Benjamin Evans, journeyman carpenter, and his wife, Ann Powell, both of whom came from Wales. He was educated at the Stationers' Company School and at University College, London, obtaining a first-class honours degree in English (1920), a teaching diploma with honours (1921), and an MA with distinction (1922). He won several college prizes and medals and the Early English Text Society's prize (1920), and became president of the union. His first post was as lecturer in English at Manchester University (1921–4). In 1923 he married Marjorie Ruth, daughter of John Measures, of Ifield, Sussex. She was a fellow student at University College. They had one daughter, Mary (or Hilary) Ann (b. 1931).

Evans was professor of English at University College, Southampton (1925–6), Sheffield University (1926–33), and Queen Mary College, London (1933–44); he also worked for the Ministry of Information (1939–41), and spent the years 1940–44 as educational director of the British Council. He was principal of Queen Mary College from 1944 to 1951 and provost of University College, London, from 1951 to 1966. Part-time commitments included service as vice-chair of the Arts Council (1946–51); chair of Thames TV's educational advisory council, of the Linguaphone Institute, of the Observer Trust (1957–66), and of the Royal Society of Literature (1975–7) (and its vice-president in 1974); he was an executive member of the British Council (1950–54), governor of the Old Vic and Sadler's Wells theatres; and trustee of the British Museum.

The springboard for this diverse career was a deep love of English literature. Evans's A Short History of English Literature (1940) and A Short History of English Drama (1948), commissioned for Penguin Books' Pelican series, are classic and accessible concise introductions for the student of literature and the general reader. Other titles in Evans's long

(Benjamin) Ifor Evans, Baron Evans of Hungershall (1899–1982), by Sir William Coldstream, 1958–60

and varied list of publications include *English Literature between the Wars* (1948), *The Language of Shakespeare's Plays* (1952), *Literature and Science* (1954), and *English Poetry in the Later Nineteenth Century* (1933; rev. edn, 1966). A very precise kind of textual scholarship is firmly evinced in his edition (with W. W. Greg) of *The most Virtuous and Godly Susanna* and *Jack Juggler* (both 1937, for the Malone Society). Evans's main gift, however, lay in exposition. A witty and pithy lecturer, lucid and sensible, he also wrote works which generations of students have found valuable.

Evans's work in the University of London, hard hit by the Second World War, deserves special mention. In 1945 he restored the fortunes of Queen Mary College, when it returned after evacuation to a set of bomb-scarred buildings in a devastated area: seeing the area's potential, he set about acquiring land which doubled the college's site and made possible the expansion necessary for its survival as bearer of light in a dark corner of London. His subsequent appointment as provost of University College crowned his career: it brought his varied abilities and his intense loyalty back, when they were most needed, to an institution he loved. Reconstruction after catastrophic bombing had barely begun and the college was just settling down after wartime dispersal. Evans's energy and leadership brought all the threads together and released a creative spirit of unity and co-operation. The college's needs, particularly for building purposes, far outstripped support available from the University Grants Committee, despite generous help from the university court, and

Evans realized that he must fund-raise if University College was to prosper in teaching and research and to provide adequate student living accommodation. He was remarkably successful in attracting benefactions, and enjoyed the careful preparation, the discreet matching of potential donor with appropriate cause, and the interplay of foresight, patience, timing, and presentation involved. He managed these operations with a rare combination of drive and charm. He raised about £200,000 each year he was provost from sources such as Marks and Spencer, Lord Mark's Charitable Trust, the Wolfson Foundation, the Wellcome Trust, and the Max Rayne Foundation.

Evans maintained that the provost of University College had no powers and few duties, the latter consisting mainly in chairing professorial board meetings, attracting good heads of departments, and then backing them. As to powers, he needed no formal statement; his persuasiveness and evident disinterestedness and dedication combined to melt opposition. Regarding his style as a chairman his obituarist in *The Times* wrote, with some justice, of the 'affectionate disdain' with which he treated his colleagues; though 'affectionate leg-pulling' might have been more accurate. During a discussion on tree planting in the college quadrangle, one professor opined that 'trees should be chosen that will flower at times when we can enjoy them'; to which Evans replied: 'Then, my dear professor, we must have trees that will flower between 11 a.m. on Tuesdays and 4 p.m. on Thursdays.' His irony could also be self-directed; he once said: 'Bill Coldstream painted my portrait, and I've been trying to look like it ever since.'

Evans had a love–hate relationship with the federal University of London. He endorsed the dictum of Lord Beveridge that it could achieve more than could its component colleges separately; but it irked him when the desire of University College to introduce new material into syllabuses was baulked by boards of studies because not every college could teach it. He welcomed the Saunders reforms of 1966, which gave more freedom to colleges within the federal framework. He had earlier helped to found the university students' union and later worked for the erection of its building. He discharged the duties of public orator with elegance. After retirement he became director of the Wates Foundation—an interesting example of enterprising poacher turned generous gamekeeper.

Evans was knighted in 1955 and in 1967 became a life peer. He received honorary degrees from Paris and Manchester, and became an officer of the Légion d'honneur and commander of the orders of Orange Nassau and Dannebrog. Evans died at his home, Hungershall Lodge, Tunbridge Wells, on 28 August 1982.

ARTHUR TATTERSALL, *rev.*

Sources WWW · A. Kimmens, 'Lord Evans of Hungershall, Benjamin Ifor Evans, university administrator', *Annual Obituary* (1982), 407–8 · *The Times* (1 Sept 1982) · *Debrett's Peerage* (1995) · personal knowledge (1990) · private information (1990)
Archives BL, corresp. with Marie Stopes, Add. MS 58499 · CAC Cam., corresp. with A. V. Hill · NL Wales, corresp. with Thomas Jones · Tate Collection, corresp. with Lord Clark · UCL, corresp. with J. Z. Young

Likenesses W. Stoneman, photograph, 1946, NPG · W. Cold-stream, oils, 1958–60, UCL [*see illus.*] · H. Coster, photographs, NPG
Wealth at death £145,460: probate, 3 Nov 1982, CGPLA Eng. & Wales

Evans, James Harington (1785–1849), religious controversialist, was born at Salisbury, Wiltshire, on 15 April 1785, the only child of Dr James E. Evans (*d.* 1825), priest-vicar of Salisbury Cathedral and master of the cathedral grammar school, and his wife, Sarah Evans (*d.* 1803). From birth Evans was destined for the church. He was educated at the cathedral school and privately by his uncle, the Revd Isaac Hodgson. At the age of fourteen he was elected scholar of Wadham College, Oxford, where he took his BA in 1803, became a fellow in 1805, and took his MA in 1808. He was ordained deacon by Charles Moss, bishop of Oxford, on 12 June 1808, and priest by Brownlow North, bishop of Winchester, on 9 December 1810. He spent some time during 1809 at Worplesdon, Surrey, before becoming, for a short while, curate of Enville, Staffordshire. On 24 April 1810 Evans married Caroline Joyce (1787–1831), younger daughter of Thomas Joyce, of Freshford House, Somerset, with whom he had three children. In the autumn of that year he was appointed curate of Milford and Hordle, Hampshire. Here, in the aftermath of the tragic death of his infant son in February 1812, Evans came to embrace the teachings of 'serious religion'.

In 1815 Evans became a leading figure in the Western Schism, an antinomian clerical and lay secession from the Church of England. During the first phase of the Schism, Evans helped to establish a chapel which the seceders had erected at Milford. In January 1816, as the Schism entered into a new and more geographically diverse phase, he moved to Walford House, Durston, Somerset, the home of the leader of the Schism, George Baring. Four months later Evans and his wife were baptized by immersion at the Octagon Chapel, Taunton; he then became a frequent preacher at the chapel and in many of the surrounding towns and villages. In November 1816, as the adherents of the Schism began to disperse nationally, he moved to London, where he preached initially at the Swiss church in Endell Street, and later at the chapel at Cross Street, Hatton Garden, where he formed a church. Evans benefited from the patronage of two of the Schism's leading lights, Harriet Wall and Henry Drummond; in 1818 Drummond presented Evans with a life interest in a chapel in John Street, Holborn.

Although Evans developed no formal theological system, he advanced a number of highly unorthodox doctrines (derived largely from his having read Isaac Watts on the Trinity), which were for a time held in common by most of his fellow seceders. In his *Dialogues on Important Subjects* (1819) Evans sought to undermine the divine triunity of the godhead. Consequently he was accused publicly of advancing Sabellianism, a charge he vigorously denied. By 1823, however, having cut his ties with the excesses of the Baring party, Evans adopted standard Trinitarian and Christological positions, his *Letters to a Friend* (1826) being

published in order to re-establish his evangelical credentials. He remained, nevertheless, uncertain over the correct mode of baptism. This led, briefly, to his severing his connections with John Street Chapel. By 1824, however, after once again changing his views on baptism, he reorganized the John Street congregation, the members continuing to hold various views on the subject.

Evans remained within the ranks of Christian orthodoxy for the remainder of his life, eventually achieving a certain prominence within nonconformist circles. In the late 1820s, when Drummond became closely tied to Edward Irving and the English prophetic movement, the two parted company, Evans denouncing Irvingism as a dangerous heresy. His first wife having died in 1831, on 25 January 1833 Evans married Elizabeth, daughter of Robert Merttins Bird of Taplow, Buckinghamshire, an administrator in India.

Although Evans never came to regret his secession, he responded charitably when, in 1842, his son, James Joyce Evans, was ordained into the Church of England. Five years later, in 1847, he retired from John Street Chapel. He died in an accident on 1 December 1849 at Stonehaven during a tour of Scotland, and was buried in Highgate cemetery, Middlesex, five days later. The *Christian Observer* noted drily (in a phrase coined earlier by Dr Johnson to describe Isaac Watts) that, as a man of education and talent, Evans was to be admired 'in almost everything "except his Nonconformity"'.   GRAYSON CARTER

Sources J. J. Evans, *Memoir and remains of the Revd James Harington Evans* (1852) · 'A brief account of the Rev. James Harington Evans, M.A.', J. H. Evans, *Three funeral sermons* (1850) · G. Carter, 'Evangelical seceders from the Church of England, c.1800–1850', DPhil diss., U. Oxf., 1990 · *Baptist Magazine*, 42 (1850), 36–8 · *Christian Observer* (1852), 789–90 · Foster, *Alum. Oxon.* · A. J. Willis, *Winchester ordinations, 1660–1829, from records in the Diocesan registry, Winchester*, 1 (1964), 126 · IGI · *Hampshire Chronicle* (22 Jan 1816) · *Hampshire Chronicle* (5 May 1817) · *Salisbury and Winchester Journal* (22 July 1816)
Likenesses copper engraving, priv. coll. · steel engraving (after sculpture by C. W. Wass), repro. in Evans, ed., *Memoir and remains*, frontispiece

Evans [*née* Galloway], **Janet** (*d.* 1822x30?), revolutionary, was born into a comfortable London family. Her brother Alexander Galloway was a mathematical machine maker and an officer of the London Corresponding Society. Janet married his close political colleague Thomas *Evans (*b.* 1763, *d.* in or before 1831), self-styled 'Citizen and Baker, but by profession an Artist' (Bodl. Oxf., MS Eng. hist. c. 296), at some time before May 1794. The couple lived and worked as print colourers in Soho, but by 1796 had moved to 14 Plough Court, Fetter Lane. Here they hosted committee meetings of the Corresponding Society (of which Thomas was now secretary) and of an overlapping revolutionary circle. It was on Plough Court that revolutionary conspiracy in the capital hinged, until 18 April 1798 when Evans, Galloway, and others were arrested. Janet, pregnant and nursing her infant son, Thomas John, was herself detained without trial for a while. She bore stillborn twins soon after.

Janet Evans campaigned vigorously not only for her husband's release but, with Sir Francis Burdett, against conditions and corruption in the prison's regime generally. She was at one point banned from visiting her husband for signalling messages to others imprisoned with him and for inciting a riot outside the gates. Initially she relied on subscriptions organized by Francis Place, but in October 1799 she received a sizeable legacy on the death of her father. This she used to establish Thomas as a patent brace and steel spring manufacturer, following his release in March 1801.

Janet's family remained committed to ultra-radical politics. From 1801 the London revolutionary circle was closely associated with Thomas Spence, and Evans assumed its leadership when Spence died in 1814. Janet and her son, T. J. Evans, quickly became prominent figures within the group. In all likelihood she helped to shape her husband's opinions, for when the Spenceans split in 1819 the role of women among them was one of the issues contested. Janet was attacked as Thomas Evans's 'brandy fac'd Dulcina … "As long as I the breeches wear, I will have all the pelf"' (Wedderburn). There is no corroborative evidence of her drinking heavily, which the contemporary term 'brandy-faced' implies, but she was clearly a strong personality: 'Mrs Evans is more furious than ever and bids open defiance', reported one informer after the Spenceans' failure to turn the Spa Fields meeting of December 1816 into a radical *coup d'état* (PRO, HO 42/158, 27 Jan 1817). These machinations led to the arrest of her husband and son. Janet wrote extensively to the press and government, demanding their release, while issuing Spencean propaganda from a shop she had begun to support herself. She also smuggled political material in and out of prison and was described by a spy as 'endeavouring to *revive Spenceanism*, and disseminate sedition and disafection [*sic*]' (PRO, HO 42/172, 2 Dec 1817).

However, the family's economic and political fortunes changed sharply in the wake of Thomas Evans's second detention; while Galloway was now a major London engineering employer, Evans's imprisonment caused his business to collapse. On his release the Evanses were politically marginalized. They ran a coffee shop and radical newsroom until, early in 1820, Galloway funded Evans junior's purchase of the *Manchester Observer*, and the family moved north. Evans senior began a printing business and they seemed settled, until T. J. Evans was prosecuted for libelling the army; he was gaoled and the newspaper had to be sold. In the summer of 1822 the family returned to London. Henceforward nothing is known of Janet, while Thomas disappeared from view after 1824 and had died by 1831. They may both have died by 1829–30, by which time letters between Place, Galloway, and T. J. Evans mention neither. The couple's own correspondence reveals a warm marriage of equals and confirms that Janet was more than merely supportive of revolutionary principles. For two decades she kept open house for political fellow travellers and their families. From 1798 to 1801, and again in 1817, Janet Evans helped to keep London ultra-

radicalism afloat, but the full scope of her contribution to the revolutionary tradition in the capital can only be guessed.

MALCOLM CHASE

Sources I. McCalman, *Radical underworld: prophets, revolutionaries, and pornographers in London, 1795–1840* (1988) • M. Chase, 'Evans, Thomas', *DLB*, vol. 8 • R. Wells, *Insurrection: the British experience, 1795–1803* (1983) • 'Particulars of the arrest of Thomas Evans', Burdett MSS, 1798, Bodl. Oxf., MS Eng. hist. c. 296/63–6 • R. W. [R. Wedderburn], *A few lines for a double-faced politician* [1819] • home office papers, PRO, HO 42/158, 42/166, 42/168, 42/172, 44/5 • privy council papers, PRO, PC 1/42/A144, A158; PC 1/44/A161 • BL, Place MSS, Add. MSS 27808, fols. 91, 98ff.; 27809, fols. 95–9; 27816, fols. 540ff.; 27851, fols. 6–7; 35152, fols. 60–63; 37930, fol. 30 • *Reformists' Register* (25 Oct 1817) • *The Forlorn Hope*, 1 [1817], cols. 6–10 • *Independent Whig* (18 Jan 1818) • T. Evans, *A brief sketch of the life of Mr Thomas Spence* (1821)

Archives PRO, Home Office papers • PRO, Privy Council papers

Evans, Dame Joan (1893–1977), scholar and author, was born at Nash House, Abbots Langley, Hertfordshire, on 22 June 1893, the only child of Sir John *Evans (1823–1908), archaeologist and numismatist, and his third wife, Maria Millington Lathbury (1856–1944), daughter of Charles Crawford Lathbury of Wimbledon. There were three sons and two daughters by Sir John's first marriage. Joan's half-brother Sir Arthur *Evans, of Knossos fame, was forty-two years her senior. As the child of an elderly, distinguished father and a mature, academic mother, she had a somewhat solitary childhood, depending for close affection on her nanny, Caroline Hancock, to whose memory she dedicated her memoir *Prelude and Fugue* (1964), and who stayed with her for nearly sixty-seven years. The only man she might have married was killed in the First World War. Her father died when she was fifteen but the bond between them was already forged, and she knew by instinct that some form of scholarship would be the guiding motif of her life.

Joan Evans was educated at Coram School, Watford, Berkhamsted Girls' Grammar School, and then from 1914 at St Hugh's College, Oxford, where she took a diploma in archaeology (with distinction) in 1916, a certificate of letters in 1919, and a BLitt in 1920. From 1917 to 1922 she was the college's librarian (initially temporarily). In 1931 she became honorary librarian of the Courtauld Institute, London. Her interests were always far-ranging, but in view of her later concentration on medieval France, it may seem surprising that her first book was *English Jewellery from the 5th Century BC to 1800* (1921). Much later she published *A History of Jewellery, 1100–1870* (1953). She had a true collector's flair and, just as her father avidly collected British flints, she early began to collect gems and jewels. The Ashmolean Museum, Oxford, the Birmingham City Art Gallery, and, above all, the Victoria and Albert Museum, were to be the beneficiaries. From this time she published numerous articles on jewellery and medieval artefacts and occasionally edited French medieval texts.

In 1931 came Evans's ground-breaking book, *Pattern: a Study of Ornament in Western Europe from 1180 to 1900*, and in 1939 *Taste and Temperament*; but these were subsidiary interests. She truly discovered her abiding interest with *Life in Mediaeval France* (1925), which was followed by

Monastic Life at Cluny, 930–1157 (1936), *Art in Mediaeval France* (1948), *English Art, 1307–1461* (1949), *Cluniac Art of the Roman-esque Period* (1950), *Dress in Mediaeval France* (1952), and her edition of *The Flowering of the Middle Ages* (1966). These works remain vital general works of reference, despite the further researches of others. France was the passion of her life. In the preface of *Art in Mediaeval France*, a work which was dedicated to archaeologists and antiquaries who had fought for France during the Second World War, Evans vividly recalled her childhood visits to France, when a 'mediaeval cycle of times and seasons, traditions and beliefs' still governed much of everyday life, now much altered. Despite the ravages of the revolution and the recent war, she firmly believed that 'by force of memory and imagination and love we may mend the shining chain; not France, nor her history, nor the memorials of that history can die' (*Art in Mediaeval France*, x–xi). To this end, she devoted some of her considerable private means, in the same year that she published this seminal work, purchasing and presenting to the municipality of Mâcon the Cluniac Chappelle des Moines de Berzé. A plaque commemorates the gift. In the 1930s and 1940s she had also worked on a later period of French history and had written biographical studies of Chateaubriand (1939), Madame de Sérilly (1946), and Joseph Joubert (1947). In *Prelude and Fugue* she chillingly describes the bombers going overhead at dawn on D-day: 'That dawn indeed it seemed as if all the world was changing. My mother who had dominated my life for so long, lay dead; the France that I loved was being attacked by her allies; and everything seemed in flux.'

Joan Evans was a woman of strong family loyalties. In 1943 she published *Time and Chance: the Story of Arthur Evans and his Forebears* and in 1956 *A History of the Society of Antiquaries*. Sir John and Sir Arthur had both been presidents of the antiquaries. She became the first woman president (1959–64), and in 1973 received the gold medal of the society. She was proud of the fact that she had been elected president in her own right with no suspicion of nepotism. From 1948 to 1951 she had been president of the Royal Archaeological Institute. She was a chevalier of the Légion d'honneur. Many other honours fell to her: she was DLitt, London (1930), DLitt, Oxford (1932), honorary LLD, Edinburgh (1952), honorary LittD, Cambridge (1956), honorary FRIBA, and a fellow of the Royal Historical Society and the Royal Society of Literature. In 1976 she was appointed DBE. She was at various times a trustee of the London Museum and of the British Museum and a member of the advisory council of the Victoria and Albert Museum. She was also a sympathetic and generous person. Her gifts to individual friends and scholars were anonymous and numerous. She was a major benefactor of St Hugh's College, and bought for it part of its present site; she was elected to an honorary fellowship in 1936, and returned to the college as a supernumerary fellow in 1951. She helped to secure for the National Trust the ridge above Wotton under Edge, where she lived for the second half of her life.

One unusual episode should be mentioned. In 1911 Miss Moberley and Miss Jourdain, successive principals of St Hugh's, published *An Adventure*, an account of a psychic experience which they believed had occurred to them on a visit to Versailles. They left the copyright to Joan Evans and she edited its fifth edition (1955). Despite her admiration for these ladies she was eventually convinced that the experience was hallucinatory and in 1971 she forbade further reprinting. In October 1976 she published her own view of the affair in 'An end to *An adventure*', in *Encounter* (vol. 47).

Joan Evans considered herself a Victorian, and her air of authority and her bearing were splendidly of that period. In appearance she was very like her father, a fact noted by her mother's French friends who remarked that this was 'tactful' as her father was seventy when she was born. Her rapport with the nineteenth century was shown in 1956, when she co-edited Ruskin's diaries with J. H. Whitehead, and in 1966 when she edited *The Victorians*, a selection of extracts and illustrations that tell us almost as much about herself as about them. It was in character that she retained some of the heavy Evans family furniture in her home, Thousand Acres, Wotton under Edge, where she died on 14 July 1977. Her body was cremated. Of her writings it has been rightly said that she published too much too quickly; she can be faulted on detail. This, however, does not diminish her achievement overall, which was of an inspirational nature. She was a scholar with an overriding sense of beauty and visual awareness, inspired by the vision implied in Ruskin's phrase 'the lamp of beauty'.

KENNETH GARLICK

Sources J. Evans, *Time and chance: the story of Arthur Evans and his forebears* (1943) · J. Evans, *Prelude and fugue* (1964) · C. N. L. Brooke, 'Memorial address', *Antiquaries Journal*, 58 (1978), 9–12 · *The Times* (15 July 1977) · personal knowledge (2004) · *WWW* · b. cert. · d. cert.

Likenesses P. Greenham, oils, 1977, St Hugh's College, Oxford

Wealth at death £270,919: probate, 12 Oct 1977, *CGPLA Eng. & Wales*

Evans, John (*b.* 1594/5?, *d.* in or after 1659), astrologer and medical practitioner, was of Welsh origin. He was well educated and had obtained an MA degree by 1621. He was probably the John Evans of Flint who matriculated at Corpus Christi College, Oxford, in 1615, aged twenty, and proceeded BA the following year; though several namesakes attended Oxford in this period, this is the most likely identification. Evans became a minister, serving probably in the diocese of Worcester and later as curate of Enfield, Staffordshire, where his name occurs between 1620 and 1625.

In 1625, when he was living at Four Ashes, Enfield, Evans offered tuition in English, Latin, Greek, Hebrew, writing, and mathematics. He published an almanac for 1613, calculated for Worcester and dedicated to the bishop of Worcester (Henry Parry), and others for 1625 and 1629–31, calculated for Shrewsbury. They contain pious exhortations in verse, extracts from Du Bartas's *Divine Weeks*, and astrological advice. His *The Palace of Profitable Pleasure* (1621), dedicated to James I, was a simple dictionary and grammar with arithmetical tables, while his *The Sacrifice of a*

Contrite Heart (1630), a book of prayers and meditations, utilized some of his almanac material and included prayers for the conversion of the Jews and the overthrow of the Roman Antichrist.

In 1633 Evans published an *Ephemerides* for five years, based on the tables of David Origanus. About 1630 he was forced to flee Enfield 'for some Offences very scandalous' and settled in London, first in the Minories, in Aldgate, then in Gunpowder Alley near Fetter Lane, where he scraped a living by practising astrology and chemical medicine. In 1632 a friend took the young William Lilly to meet him as 'an excellent wise man' in astrology. Lilly describes finding him living in squalor and in bed with a hangover, 'if it be lawful to call that a Bed whereon he lay'. None the less he agreed to teach Lilly astrology, and did so very effectively for seven or eight weeks despite a library comprising only two books. Lilly later penned a vivid portrait of his tutor: 'of a middle Stature, broad Forehead, Beetle-brow'd, thick Shoulders, flat Nosed, full Lips, downlook'd, black curling stiff Hair, splay-footed', dishonest, and 'much addicted to Debauchery, and then very abusive and quarrelsom, seldom without a black Eye, or one Mischief or another' (Lilly, 21). They parted company when Evans gave a blatantly false resolution to a client, observing cynically that 'he had a Wife and Family to provide for' (Lilly, 23).

Though a rogue, Evans was no impostor. Lilly admired his 'piercing Judgment' (Lilly, 21) and Richard Napier thought Evans his superior in some branches of the art. Evans also practised the invocation of spirits, both in Staffordshire and London. On one occasion, he told Lilly, he raised a spirit at the request of Sir Kenelm Digby and was transported bodily from the Minories to a field near Battersea. Evans's daughter Ellen also practised the invocation of spirits. A considerable part of Evans's income came from his antimonial cups, which he promoted in *The Universal Medicine, or, The Vertues of the Antimoniall Cup* (1634). He claimed to have used his cup safely for three years, citing Sir Thomas Myddelton, a former lord mayor, as proof of its virtues. However, some abusive remarks about the eminent physician Sir Théodore de Mayerne brought Evans to the attention of the College of Physicians of London, and on hearing that two of Evans's patients (Sir Nathaniel Kitch and Lady Amy Blunt) had died of severe vomiting, it ruled that he was a dangerous charlatan. The college pressed Archbishop Laud to take action, and on Laud's orders all remaining copies of Evans's book were seized and destroyed. Laud also summoned him before the court of high commission in June 1635, where he proved unable to produce his holy orders and was detained for behaving 'contemptuously'. The case dragged on until November, when Evans was discharged on promising not to practise medicine in or near London.

Little is known of Evans's later years. He is said by Anthony Wood, very plausibly, to have 'lived in several places, and in obscure conditions' (Wood). He may be the John Evans intruded as rector of Yeovilton, Somerset, in 1647. In 1659 he surfaced as rector of Littleton upon Severn, Gloucestershire, announcing in a London newspaper

that his cup was still much in demand and could be obtained through a relative in the capital. Nothing more is heard of him after this date.   BERNARD CAPP

Sources B. S. Capp, *Astrology and the popular press: English almanacs, 1500–1800* (1979) · W. Lilly, *Mr William Lilly's history of his life and times: from the year 1602, to 1681*, 2nd edn (1715); repr. with introduction by K. M. Briggs (1974) · C. Goodall, *The Royal College of Physicians of London founded and established by law* (1684), 442–3 · *CSP dom.*, 1635–6 · Foster, *Alum. Oxon.* · Wood, *Ath. Oxon.*

Evans, John (*c.*1652–1724), East India Company chaplain and Church of Ireland bishop of Meath, was born into a Welsh-speaking family at Plas-du, Llanarmon, Caernarvonshire. Although the precise details of his parentage and early life remain obscure, it seems most likely that he was the son of Ynyr Evans of Plas-du, and that he was the John, son of Bonner (an Anglicization of ab Ynyr or Bynyr), who matriculated at Gloucester Hall, Oxford, in 1668 (when his age was given as sixteen), but left the university without taking a degree.

After ordination Evans served as a curate at St Magnus the Martyr, Thames Street, London, and then at Isleworth in Middlesex, where he came to the attention of Sir Joseph Ashe, first baronet, governor of the East India Company. Through Ashe's recommendation Evans was appointed in 1678 as the company's first chaplain in India, at £100 a year. On 13 February 1679 he married Elizabeth Trenchfield, sister of the interloping merchant Richard Trenchfield, and himself became drawn into the interloping trade. He thus attracted the unwelcome attentions of William Hedges, the agent sent out by the company in 1682, who reported that Evans 'busies himself too much in trade and merchandise for a man of his coat, being certainly one of the greatest traders in Hugli' (*Diary of William Hedges*, 1.140). Furthermore, Evans was regarded by those who had business dealings with him as a 'great knave' (ibid.). In consequence, Evans lost the trust of the company directors, who disparaged him as 'the quondam minister but late great merchant', and as the 'politic padre' (ibid.), and he was eventually dismissed from the chaplaincy in 1692. He made his own way back to England, took his bachelor's and doctor's degrees in divinity at Oxford in 1695, and secured a parish in his native county, though whether his advancement was the product of political influence or a tribute to the power of his money is unclear. He was certainly wealthy enough from his trading days to maintain a residence in Bloomsbury, Middlesex (which suggests that he may well have been an absentee rector), and he kept up his contacts with East India merchants.

In 1699 Evans was said to be actively soliciting the likely vacancy in the bishopric of St David's, and in 1701 he succeeded in obtaining Bangor. A staunch whig, Evans soon showed his party colours in convocation, where in 1702 he caused a minor furore by accusing the leading high churchman Francis Atterbury of lying, in return for which Atterbury's high-church friends maliciously questioned the legitimacy of Evans's own summons. In the Lords he was a reliable junto whig and he regularly subscribed to partisan protests. He was also a founder member of the

Most Honourable and Loyal Society of Ancient Britons, the first Welsh club to be established in London, which had a strong party-political bias. His active involvement in the Society for Promoting Christian Knowledge and in the Society for the Propagation of the Gospel is evidence that he was more than a political prelate, but it was undoubtedly his whiggism that earned him translation to the lucrative Irish see of Meath in 1716, at a time when he supposedly had his pick of several vacancies. In Ireland as in England Evans did not flinch from political controversy; he became a prominent spokesman for the English interest in the Irish House of Lords, in particular over the issue of the appellate jurisdiction of the house.

Evans's correspondence with William Wake, archbishop of Canterbury, reveals him to be not only a man of firm principles and unquenchable loyalty to administration, but one of passionate temper. Evans felt keenly his political isolation in Ireland, where he and a coterie of like-minded bishops, including his old friend William Nicolson of Derry, took prime responsibility for the defence of the ministry's position in parliament, and his often querulous commentary on the intrigues of his 'patriot' opponents, imputing to them the most extreme views (extending as far as the contemplation of armed rebellion in support of Irish legislative independence), sometimes suggests an imbalance in his own psychology. He carried his political vendettas over into ecclesiastical affairs, especially in his quarrel with Jonathan Swift, who held a living in Evans's diocese. At an episcopal visitation in 1718 words passed between the two men which resulted in Swift reminding his bishop that he was speaking to a clergyman and not a footman. When Swift did not attend subsequent visitations Evans petulantly refused to accept his proxy. Swift's letters of self-justification included the memorable reproof: 'I am only sorry that you, who are of a country famed for good nature, have found a way to unite the hasty passion of your own countrymen, with the long, sedate resentment of the Spaniard' (*Correspondence*, 2.388–90). At the same time, however, Evans showed himself to be a determined opponent of clerical absenteeism (which again involved him in conflicts with Swift), and a surprisingly disinterested steward of the material interests of the church. His energetic pursuit of a legal case against an influential tenant, Henry St George, for the renegotiation of an over-indulgent lease eventually provoked Irish MPs to introduce a bill to preserve the rights of tenants at the expense of the church, which the bishop duly opposed in the Lords.

Evans died suddenly in Dublin on 2 March 1724, after having been 'afflicted with a violent fit of the gout about ten days' (BL, Add. MS 6116, fol. 132), and was buried in the churchyard of 'Little St George's' Chapel in Temple Street in Dublin. His wife evidently outlived him, but there is no mention in contemporary correspondence of any surviving children, although at least one son (John) had been born in India. In his will, described by Swift as the 'wise' act of a 'fool' (*Correspondence*, 3.11), he bequeathed £1000 for the building of an episcopal palace at Ardbraccan in co.

Meath (which was completed only in 1776), a much smaller sum of money to endow his first rectory in Caernarvonshire, and the residue of his personal estate for the benefit of poorer clergy in England and the churches of his Irish diocese. D. W. HAYTON

Sources M. Martyn, 'John Evans, East India chaplain', *History Today*, 26 (1976), 670–77 · DNB · DWB · Christ Church Oxf., Wake MSS Arch. W. Epist. 12–13 · *The diary of William Hedges … during his agency in Bengal; as well as on his voyage out and return overland (1681–1687)*, ed. R. Barlow and H. Yule, 1, Hakluyt Society, 74 (1887), 118, 140, 163, 165, 195–6 · *The correspondence of Jonathan Swift*, ed. H. Williams, 5 vols. (1963–5) · I. Ehrenpreis, *Swift: the man, his works and the age*, 3 vols. (1962–83), vol. 3, pp. 50–58, 158–63, 170–80 · P. McNally, '"Irish and English interests": national conflict within the Church of Ireland episcopate in the reign of George I', *Irish Historical Studies*, 29 (1994–5), 295–314 · J. E. T. Rogers, ed., *A complete collection of the protests of the Lords*, 1 (1875), 164, 200–21 · L. A. Landa, 'The insolent rudeness of Dr Swift', *Modern Language Notes*, 68 (1953), 223–6 · M. Clement, *The SPCK and Wales, 1699–1740* (1954), 27–8, 66 · E. D. Evans, 'The Rev. George Lewis, rector of Dolgellau, 1715–23', *Journal of the Merioneth Historical and Record Society*, 11 (1990–93), 19–35 · BL, Add. MS 28882, fol. 231 · BL, Add. MS 6116, fol. 152 · CSP dom. · E. B. Fryde and others, eds., *Handbook of British chronology*, 3rd edn, Royal Historical Society Guides and Handbooks, 2 (1986) · Foster, *Alum. Oxon.*

Archives BL, Add. MSS 28882, 28927, 6116 | BL, Stowe MS 220 · Christ Church Oxf., Wake MSS, vols. 12–13, Arch. W. Epist. · TCD, corresp. with William King

Likenesses attrib. M. Dahl, oils, LPL; repro. in Martyn, 'John Evans', 670

Wealth at death £1140 specifically appropriated in will, PRO, PROB 11/597, sig. 93: DNB

Evans, John (*c*.1677–1718), actor and theatre manager, was probably born in Ireland, but no details are known. He joined the Smock Alley troupe in Dublin in 1699 and was later associated with Thomas Elrington, Thomas Griffith, and Joseph Ashbury in the management of the theatre. In 1707–8 he played Friar Andrews in Mary Pix's *The Spanish Wives*, and on 2 December 1709 he received a benefit in Dublin. He then travelled to England, and is listed in Thomas Betterton's company at the Queen's Theatre in the Haymarket for the 1709–10 season. Billed as 'lately arrived from the theatre in Dublin', he took over the role of Kite in George Farquhar's *The Recruiting Officer* from Richard Escourt on 16 March 1710. On 14 April he performed the title role in *The Spanish Fryar*, and on 4 May he played Falstaff in *King Henry the Fourth* for his benefit before returning to Ireland. In 1714 his Dublin company played a summer season at Cork. According to William Chetwood, Evans was invited to a tavern, where he illadvisedly proposed the health of Queen Anne. A duel ensued with a Jacobite officer whom Evans disarmed. Although the incident ended with reconciliation, a story spread that Evans had insulted the army. When the company returned to Dublin, Evans's performance as Alexander in Nathaniel Lee's *The Rival Queens* was stopped until he publicly apologized. A voice from the pit cried, 'Kneel, you rascal.' 'I'll kneel to none but God, and my queen!', said Evans. Although it has been reported that this reply and subsequent kneeling satisfied both Evans and his opponents, according to Chetwood the situation was only calmed by army officers who knew the history of the original quarrel.

In 1715 Evans returned to London for an engagement at Drury Lane. On 22 January he played Claudius in *Hamlet* and during the rest of the season revised his earlier roles of Kite, the Spanish Fryar, and Falstaff. On 21 March he played Aquilius in Lee's *Mithridates, King of Pontus* for Thomas Elrington's benefit. At his own benefit, 'at the desire of several Ladies of Quality' on 28 March, he took the part of King Harry the Eighth in *Virtue Betray'd* by John Banks, alongside Anne Oldfield. Back in Dublin in 1715 Evans played Alcibiades in *Timon of Athens*, Thomas Shadwell's version of Shakespeare's play, and Lieutenant Story in *The Committee, or, The Faithful Irishman*, by Sir Robert Howard. He was seen in Charles Shadwell's *Irish Hospitality* at Smock Alley Theatre in 1717 and was again in London in 1718 playing at Lincoln's Inn Fields. On 26 September he appeared as Dorax in John Dryden's *Don Sebastian, King of Portugal*, which was followed by performances as Kite, Falstaff, the Spanish Fryar, Alexander, Tamerlane, and Cato. On 3 October he played Flip in Charles Shadwell's *The Fair Quaker of Deal*, a performance which ended in an uproar of drawn swords and pelted apples as a result of a gentleman's being denied admittance backstage. He appeared last as Tamerlane on 4 November 1718. On the journey back to Ireland, Evans became ill with fever at Whitchurch, Shropshire, and was taken to Chester for medical care. He died there, probably in December 1718, and was privately buried in the cathedral without monument or inscription.

According to Chetwood, Evans was an actor of good reputation in Ireland who had a harmonious voice and just delivery. Unfortunately he was also considered gross, indolent, and lacking in delicacy. He has sometimes been ascribed later dates, as a John Evans performed in the 1723 London season; however, this Evans did not play any of the parts in Evans's usual repertory, and Chetwood is almost certainly correct in stating that Evans the actor–manager died in 1718.   ROBERTA MOCK

Sources W. R. Chetwood, *A general history of the stage, from its origin in Greece to the present time* (1749) · B. R. Schneider, *Index to 'The London stage, 1660–1800'* (1979) · W. C. Russell, *Representative actors* [1888] · Genest, *Eng. stage* · R. Hitchcock, *An historical view of the Irish stage from the earliest period down to the close of the season 1788*, 2 vols. (1788–94) · Highfill, Burnim & Langhans, *BDA* · G. B. Bryan, *Stage lives: a bibliography and index to theatrical biographies in English* (1985) · E. L. Avery, ed., *The London stage, 1660–1800*, pt 2: 1700–1729 (1960)

Evans, John (*c*.1678–*c*.1743), army officer and politician in America, was the son of Thomas, a Welsh sailor and old friend of William Penn, proprietor of Pennsylvania. Penn described Evans as having 'more of the rake in his character than of anything else' (*New Jersey Historical Society Proceedings*, 8.131). His behaviour while in Philadelphia with Penn's son, William junior, when they got into a tavern brawl, only served to enhance this reputation. Nevertheless, Penn believed Evans to be incorruptible as deputy lieutenant and not to be swayed by the factions in the colony.

Penn appointed Evans deputy lieutenant of Pennsylvania in 1704, to 'take care in all things to keep within the compas of & to keep up the powers of my Graunts ... and in no wise suffer them to be broken in upon by any refractory or factious persons what ever', but this proved an impossibility. Penn did not make clear to the new appointee the problems in the colony arising from divisions between the anti-proprietary and proprietary groups, and the split between the three lower counties of Delaware, dominated by the Church of England, and the Quaker-dominated three upper ones of Pennsylvania. This became obvious when Evans called a meeting of all the counties on 10 April 1704. When the Delaware representatives withdrew from the Philadelphia assembly after disagreements, Evans allowed them to form their own assembly in Delaware. Evans's military approach and his Church of England sympathies only exacerbated the anti-proprietary feeling in the colony and united its factions. However, he did have some success in keeping the Quaker-dominated assembly in Philadelphia from encroaching upon the proprietor's prerogatives. He was able to defeat the move to have judges appointed on good behaviour instead of by the proprietor. He also stymied the impeachment attempt against Penn's secretary, James Logan, by arguing that without an upper house the process could not be carried out.

On 14 May 1706 Evans continued to overstep himself in an effort to get the pacifist-dominated Pennsylvania assembly to support the cost of the defence of the colony against a possible French invasion. The exasperated Evans raised a false alarm by concocting an emergency, claiming that the French were heading up the Delaware River on the next tide. Panic ensued when Evans ran into the street brandishing a sword and calling men to arms. People grabbed their valuables and sailed their boats upriver, creating congestion on the creeks north of Philadelphia. When no such invasion occurred, Evans tried to justify the farce to the Board of Trade a year later by claiming that he did it so 'that I might know in case of real necessity what to expect from the people' (*CSP col.*, 554).

Ultimately, Evans succeeded in uniting all of the factions against him when he gave the assent to a duties bill passed by the Delaware legislature which claimed the right to collect imposts from any vessel sailing in and out of the Delaware River. Evans enforced the measure by building a fort complete with cannons along the river to fire upon any ships that refused to pay. This was the last straw, and Penn had little option but to sack Evans in 1709 and annul the act. However, although he accepted that Evans's behaviour necessitated his dismissal, Penn clearly felt that his hand had been forced, for he recommended that his disgraced deputy should be appointed as first royal governor of Pennsylvania in the event that the colony should succeed in surrendering. Evans continued to reside in the colony after his removal from office, possibly in hope of a reappointment.

In 1709 Evans married Rebecca Moore, daughter of the advocate of the Admiralty court, J. Moore. After leaving

Pennsylvania that year he lived at Pentre Manor, Denbighshire, Wales. He had one daughter. Evans died about 1743. MARY K. GEITER

Sources E. D. Neill, 'Memoirs of John Evans', *New England Historical and Genealogical Register*, 26 (1872) · J. M. Seaver, *Evans family records* (Philadelphia, 1929) · *The papers of William Penn*, ed. M. M. Dunn, R. S. Dunn, and others, 4 (1987) · *New Jersey Historical Society Proceedings*, 8 · *CSP col.*, vol. 23 · *Correspondence between William Penn and James Logan … and others, 1700–1750*, ed. D. Logan and E. Armstrong, 2 vols. (1870–72) · P. Thompson, *Rum punch & revolution: taverngoing & public life in eighteenth-century Philadelphia* (1999)

Evans, John (1679/80–1730), Presbyterian minister and historian, was born at Wrexham, Denbighshire, the son of John Evans (1628/9–1700), dissenting minister and schoolmaster, and his wife, Katherine (*bap.* 1638), widow of Vavasor Powell (1617–1670), Independent minister, and the fifth daughter of Gilbert Gerard of Crewood, parliamentarian colonel. His great-grandfather and grandfather were successively rectors of Penegoes, Montgomeryshire. After a brief spell at Magdalen College, Oxford, from where he was expelled in 1648, John Evans senior was ordained priest on 28 November 1648, yet soon had doubts about the established church. Briefly master of Bala School, Merioneth, he was appointed master of Oswestry grammar school in July 1657, on Cromwell's recommendation. Ejected in 1662, when he refused to subscribe to the Act of Uniformity, he went to live in Wrexham, where in February 1668 he was chosen pastor of the Independent chapel. Licensed as a Congregational minister on 22 May 1672, he came to share his wife's Baptist views; by 1689 his congregation included Baptists as well as Independents and Presbyterians, although the Presbyterians withdrew in 1691.

The younger John Evans was educated first in London, under Thomas Rowe, and from 26 May 1697 at Richard Frankland's academy at Rathmell, Yorkshire, which was continued by Timothy Jollie. Following his father's death, on 16 July 1700, Evans was taken into the household in Boreatton, Shropshire, of Mrs Hunt, widow of Rowland Hunt and sister of Lord Paget, ambassador to the Porte. While living there he studied under James Owen and, according to Harris, read the whole of Matthew Poole's five-volume biblical commentary in Latin and the works of all the Christian writers of the first three centuries after Christ. On 18 August 1702 he was ordained minister at Wrexham, after which he took charge of the new Independent congregation there. In 1704 he was invited to join the ministry at Dublin but was dissuaded from accepting it by Daniel Williams, who offered to take him as his assistant in London. Evans served as assistant at the meeting-house in Hand Alley, Westminster, until Williams's death, in 1716, when he was chosen as his successor. Under Williams's influence he was persuaded to join the Presbyterians in London, rather than the Independents, as was his original intention.

Evans was an eloquent and popular preacher. A man of tolerant views, he played a prominent role on the side of the non-subscribers in the Salters' Hall controversy in 1719. His appreciative congregation built him a new chapel in New Broad Street, Petty France, that opened on 14 December 1729. He also acted as Sunday evening preacher for several years until 1716, and in October 1723 he was elected preacher of the Merchants' Lecture at the same place. Over twenty of his sermons were published separately, yet his most successful publication was a collection, *Practical Discourses Concerning the Christian Temper: Thirty-Eight Sermons* (2 vols., 1723); a fourth edition appeared in 1737 and it was still being reprinted as late as 1812. In the preface to the sermons Isaac Watts declared that 'they contain, perhaps the most complete summary of those duties which make up the Christian life, that hath been published in our age' (Wilson, 2.216). The collection was also highly praised by Philip Doddridge, who regarded it as among the best practical treatises in English. Evans's *Sermons on various subjects, preach'd to young people; designed for the promoting of early piety* (1725) was reissued in 1802, together with Dr John Erskine's memoir of the author. Evans also published his side of a correspondence with Dr John Cumming, minister of the Scottish church at London Wall, 'concerning the regard which ought to be had to Scripture consequences', and commented on the epistle to the Romans for the New Testament commentary left unfinished by Matthew Henry. In November 1728 he was awarded the degree of DD from Edinburgh University.

Early in his career Evans had shown an interest in the history of dissent when he edited Charles Owen's account of his brother James Owen, who kept a dissenting academy first at Oswestry and then at Shrewsbury; this was published in 1709. He formed a plan to write a comprehensive history of nonconformity from the Reformation to the civil war and collected a large quantity of materials, some of which were donated, such as Thomas Dixon's information about Cumberland and Westmorland congregations, but most of which he acquired at great expense. He read exhaustively and accumulated a fine library that amounted to 10,000 volumes at his death. Ill health prevented him from writing more than a sixth of the intended three-volume history, but he compiled an invaluable list of the members of Baptist, Independent, and Presbyterian congregations in England and Wales from 1715 to 1729, which is preserved at Dr Williams's Library, London.

On 7 December 1708 at St Katharine by the Tower, London, Evans married Elizabeth, the wealthy daughter of John *Quick (*bap.* 1636, *d.* 1706), ejected minister, and his wife, Elizabeth Cook (*d.* 1708). With his wife's fortune and his own savings Evans unwisely speculated in the South Sea Company, and lost all his investment. His last years were troubled by financial difficulties, which he kept secret, and his health rapidly worsened. Described as being of 'uncommonly tall stature, yet not a lusty man' (Wilson, 2.219), Evans died, aged fifty, on 16 May 1730, of dropsy and other complications, and was buried in Dr Williams's vault in Bunhill Fields, London; William Harris preached the funeral sermon at New Broad Street, Petty

France. Evans was survived by his wife and by one of his daughters, Elizabeth; his library was sold at auction to provide a much needed income for them.

ALSAGER VIAN, *rev.* S. J. SKEDD

Sources W. Harris, *Finishing the Christian course considered and argued: a funeral sermon preached on the death of John Evans* (1730) • J. Erskine, *Brief account of John Evans, D.D.* (1802) • *Calamy rev.*, 184–5 • W. Wilson, *The history and antiquities of the dissenting churches and meeting houses in London, Westminster and Southwark*, 4 vols. (1808–14), vol. 2, pp. 212–21 • *DWB* • *IGI*
Archives DWL, MSS and historical collections
Likenesses Hopwood, engraving (after Baxter, 1809), repro. in Wilson, *History and antiquities*, facing p. 212 • oils, DWL

Evans, John (*d.* 1779), Church of England clergyman and biblical commentator, was born at Meini Gwynion, Llanbadarn Odwyn (Llangeitho), Cardiganshire, and is said to have been educated at the University of Oxford. His first curacy was that of Llannarth, from where he moved to Portsmouth, also as curate. He is credited with being the John Evans who translated a work on the sacraments by Jabez Earle in 1735. In 1765 Evans published his *Cyssondeb y pedair efengyl* ('Harmony of the four gospels'). This was the first commentary in Welsh on any portion of the Bible, being five years earlier than the commentary of Peter Williams; a second edition was published in 1804. Evans is supposed to have seen through the press the Welsh Bible of 1769, which ran to 20,000 copies, and he also translated into Welsh Bishop Francis Gastrell's *The Christian Institutes* in 1773. He died at Portsmouth in 1779.

R. M. J. JONES, *rev.* DYLAN FOSTER EVANS

Sources B. Williams [Gwynionydd], *Enwogion Ceredigion* (1869), 73–5 • *DWB* • E. Rees, ed., *Libri Walliae: a catalogue of Welsh books and books printed in Wales, 1546–1820*, 1 (1987), 241 • J. Ballinger, *The Bible in Wales: a study in the history of the Welsh people* (1906), 44, 48, 53

Evans, John (1767–1827), General Baptist minister, was born at Usk, Monmouthshire, on 2 October 1767. He traced his descent through an almost unbroken line of Baptist preachers from the time of the Commonwealth. After some schooling at Bristol, in November 1783 he became a student at the Bristol Baptist college, over which his relative, Dr Caleb Evans, presided as theological tutor. In 1787 he matriculated at King's College, Aberdeen, where he remained for three years. He then spent a year at the University of Edinburgh, where he graduated MA. He returned to England in 1791.

Having some doubts about Calvinist doctrine, Evans accepted an invitation from the morning congregation of General Baptists in Worship Street, London, where, after officiating for a few months, he was chosen pastor and ordained on 31 May 1792. He remained at Worship Street for the rest of his life. Immediately on assuming this office, Evans published *An address humbly designed to promote the revival of religion, more especially among the General Baptists* (1793). Two years later he opened a seminary, located first at Hoxton Square and subsequently at 7 Pullin's Row, Islington, where he taught for about thirty years.

In August 1795 Evans married Mary, daughter of John *Wiche, General Baptist minister at Maidstone. They had

four sons. In 1815 Evans was attacked by a degenerative disease which within two years deprived him of the use of his legs. In 1825 he withdrew from the Society of Antiquaries, to which he had been elected a fellow in 1803, and resigned his school, having in December 1821 lost his third son, the Revd Caleb Evans, who had been his intended successor. Although obliged to be carried from his couch to the pulpit, he continued to preach until a few weeks before his death at his home in Pullin's Row, Islington, on 25 January 1827. He was a liberal-minded man, knowledgeable on a wide range of subjects.

Evans's writings, some forty in number, comprise sermons, tracts, prefaces, biographical and topographical notices, and school books. He is best-known for his *Sketch of the Denominations of the Christian World*, which first appeared in early 1795 in the form of a shilling pamphlet. Its rapid sale called for a second edition in July of the same year, and during the next thirty years fourteen successive editions were circulated; a fifteenth edition had been completed by the author immediately before his last illness. The book was translated into Welsh and various other languages, and several editions were issued in America, initially at Boston (1807). A sequel to the *Sketch*, entitled *A Preservative Against the Infidelity and Uncharitableness of the Eighteenth Century* (1796), was later issued as *The Golden Centenary* (1806). Other significant works included *General Redemption the Only Proper Basis of General Benevolence: a Letter to Robert Hawker* (1809). *Complete Religious Liberty Vindicated* (1813) considered the petition for the abolition of all penal statutes by the dissenting ministers of London and Westminster.

GORDON GOODWIN, *rev.* L. E. LAUER

Sources E. C. Starr, ed., *A Baptist bibliography*, 7 (1961), 116–26 • *GM*, 1st ser., 97/1 (1827), 368–71 • *Annual Biography and Obituary*, 12 (1828), 82–93 • R. Williams, *Enwogion Cymru: a biographical dictionary of eminent Welshmen* (1852) • S. Lewis, *The history and topography of the parish of St Mary, Islington* (1842), 166, 349
Likenesses H. Meyer, mezzotint, pubd 1812 (after J. Hazlitt), BM • R. Woodman, stipple (after J. Wiche), NPG • Woodman, portrait, repro. in M. Evans, *Tracts, sermons and funeral orations* (1826)

Evans, John (*b.* 1767/8, *d.* in or after 1812). *See under* Evans, John (1784–1831).

Evans, John (*bap.* 1774, *d.* 1828), printer, was born at Bristol, the son of David and Mary Evans, and baptized on 16 January 1774 at St Philip and St Jacob's Church. Nothing is known of Evans's early life.

Evans was variously proprietor, printer, and editor of a number of local newspapers, none of which was a great success. In June 1808 Evans became the proprietor of the *Bristol Mercury* and from about 1812 he took into partnership John Grabham. Evans retired on 7 March 1814 to set up as a printer. He produced the Bristol directories for the years 1815–17 from his premises at 7 St John Street as well as three books by his namesake, the Revd John Evans: *The Substance of an Oration … on the Death of William Peter Lunell* (1811), *Remains of William Reed* (1815), and *Historical Account of the Church of St Mary Redcliffe* (1815). On 7 August 1817 Evans published the first number of the *Bristol Observer*, a weekly journal, printed by John Sharp until 1823 when the Bristol directory gives Evans as the printer. He was living at 13 Kingsdown Parade and contributed many articles to the *Observer*, but the paper ended on 1 October 1823 after 322 numbers had been published. That year Evans also published *Practical Observations on the due Performance of Psalmody*. In 1824, while living at 9 Somerset Street, Kingsdown, he put together a *Chronological outline of the history of Bristol, and the stranger's guide through its streets and neighbourhood*, a storehouse of entertaining facts, but the book was not a success. He applied for financial assistance from the corporation of Bristol, which awarded him £20 on the delivery of four copies of his book. He then left the printing profession and went to work as a clerk in the Phoenix Glasshouse.

Evans's wife died at the end of 1827 and early in 1828 he left Bristol for London to go into business with a printer named Maurice of Fenchurch Street. Maurice was also the proprietor of the newly decorated Brunswick Theatre in Well Street, Wellclose Square. Evans and Maurice were among the ten people killed when the theatre suddenly collapsed on the morning of 28 February 1828. Twenty others were injured. The company was rehearsing the evening's performance of *Guy Mannering*

> when suddenly a crackling noise was heard from the wrought-iron roof of the building, and almost instantaneously it fell in with a tremendous crash, throwing the front wall of the theatre into the street. The shouts and wailings of the persons inclosed within the theatre were of the most pitiable description. (*GM*, 264)

Evans left two young daughters and a son. A subscription was taken for their benefit in Bristol and £200 was raised. His son, William *Evans (1809–1858), became a landscape painter, styled Evans of Bristol.

JANE POTTER

Sources *DNB* · *GM*, 1st ser., 98/1 (1828), 264, 375–6 · *Chronological outline of the history of Bristol* (1824) · C. R. Hudleston, 'John Evans of Bristol', *Bristol and Gloucestershire Archaeological Society Transactions*, 61 (1939), 196–8

Evans, John (1779–1847), Calvinistic Methodist preacher, was born at Cwm Gwen, Pencader, Carmarthenshire, in October 1779, the son of John Evans and his wife, Rachel. His parents gave him a religious education, and he could read his Bible when he was four. He was sent to the best schools within reach, and under Mr Jones of Maesnoni he is supposed to have learned Latin, Greek, and Hebrew. As a boy he often preached without hearers. His parents were members, and his father a deacon, of the Independent church at Pencader. At the age of fourteen he was taken to hear David Jones of Llan-gan, one of the great Methodist preachers of the day. At sixteen, when his father had failed to persuade him to join the Independent church, he joined the Calvinistic Methodists and in 1796 began to preach at Llanpumsaint, where he had opened his own school. At nineteen he went to the Presbyterian college, Carmarthen, but soon left, though his tutor, the Revd D. Peter, thought highly of him. He married Mrs Jones, a widow of Llwyn Ffortun, Llanegwad, about 1808, and the year after his marriage he received deacon's orders, after examination, from Richard Watson, bishop of Llandaff.

He held several curacies in succession—at Mynyddislwyn, Monmouthshire, and Bridgend and Laleston in Glamorgan—for short periods, and wherever he went he filled the churches. Great opposition was raised by some against his 'Methodistic ways' and he was returned to Llwyn Ffortun. His last curacy was at Llanddowror. He could not confine himself to his own church, and often preached off tombstones to crowded assemblies. He soon found, however, that the episcopal church was no proper place for him, and he returned to his old friends the Calvinistic Methodists, though he preached also among the Baptists or Congregationalists, and was everywhere welcome, and followed by an admiring multitude.

After the death of his first wife he married Rachel Davies of Pen-twyn, Llan-non, Carmarthenshire, and he spent the remainder of his life at her home. As he advanced in years he became much troubled with melancholia, and sometimes he had to be fetched from his bed to his pulpit duties. He died on 6 October 1847, and was buried at Pentwyn Chapel, Llan-non.

R. M. J. JONES, *rev.* MARI A. WILLIAMS

Sources O. Thomas, *Cofiant y Parch. John Jones, Talsarn* (1874), 872–8 · *Y Drysorfa*, 17 (1847), 353–4 · T. J. Williams, *Bywyd y Parch John Evans, Llwynfforttun* (1848) [biography] · L. Edwards, *Traethodau Llenyddol* (1867), 310–26 · *DWB* · J. T. Jones, *Geiriadur bywgraffyddol o enwogion Cymru*, 1 (1867)

Archives NL Wales, Calvinistic Methodists archive

Likenesses H. Hughes, oils, 1839, U. Wales, Aberystwyth, Welsh Independents' College, faculty of theology · R. Woodman, engraving, 1841 (after H. Hughes), NL Wales

Wealth at death under £2000: will, CM archives, 8876, NL Wales

Evans, John (1784–1831), schoolmaster and writer, was born in Bristol and educated there by John Prior Estlin, a Unitarian minister and schoolmaster. He married Lucy, daughter of Bernard Hickason, a Bristol custom house officer, in or after 1807. He kept a school in Bristol from about 1809 to about 1825 at various addresses in Clifton, except for a short period around 1816 when his school was at 1 Somerset Street, Kingsdown. From 1816 to 1820 he was also minister of the Presbyterian congregation at the Old Meeting-House, Marshfield, and for a shorter time at the Grove Meeting, Bradford-on-Avon, where Presbyterians had adopted Unitarian views. He moved to Bath and then to London, where he had a school in Drummond Street, Euston Square. He died in London in December 1831 and was survived by his wife. Besides some schoolbooks Evans wrote *An Oration on the Doctrine of Philosophical Necessity* (1809) and *The Ponderer* (1812), a series of essays originally published in the *Bristol Mercury*. More important are his topographical works, including *The Picture of Bristol ... Including Biographical Notices of Eminent Natives* (1814), which appeared in various forms and editions, and the second volume of *The History of Bristol* (1816), the first volume having been written by John Corry. This last work was soon eclipsed by Samuel Seyer's history of the city (1821–3) and was criticized for being very largely drawn from the works of William Barrett (1733–1789). Evans also edited, with a memoir, the *Remains* (1815) of William Reed of Thornbury.

Evans is to be distinguished from **John Evans** (*b*. 1767/8, *d*. in or after 1812), who was also a schoolmaster, topographer, and sometime resident of Bristol. He was the son of Benjamin Evans of Lydney, Gloucestershire. He matriculated on 4 April 1789, aged twenty-one, at Jesus College, Oxford, and graduated BA in 1792. He kept a boarding-school at Colston's Parade, Bristol, and in 1807 at Winterbourne Court, near Bristol. He was the author of *A Tour through Part of North Wales* (1800) and *Letters Written during a Tour through South Wales* (1804). He also wrote volume 12, on *North Wales*, and contributed to volume 11 of *The Beauties of England and Wales*, compiled by E. W. Brayley and J. Britton. At the time of his last publication, in April 1812, Evans was residing at Delancy Place, Camden Town, London. He had intended to write the account of south Wales for the *Beauties*, but died shortly after the completion of the first part of the undertaking.

These two John Evanses must further be distinguished from their namesake the Bristol writer John *Evans (*bap.* 1774, *d*. 1828).   ELIZABETH BAIGENT

Sources C. R. Huddleston, 'John Evans of Bristol', *Transactions of the Bristol and Gloucestershire Archaeological Society*, 61 (1939), 196–201 · I. Gray, *Antiquaries of Gloucestershire and Bristol*, Bristol and Gloucestershire Archaeological Society Records Section, 12 (1981) · *GM*, 1st ser., 102/1 (1832), 372–3, 651 · Foster, *Alum. Oxon.* · C. R. J. Currie and C. P. Lewis, eds., *English county histories: a guide* (1994) · *Christian Reformer, or, New Evangelical Miscellany*, 18 (1832), 42 · J. Murch, *A history of the Presbyterian and General Baptist churches in the west of England* (1835) · *Corrections and additions to the Dictionary of National Biography*, Institute of Historical Research (1966)
Wealth at death see administration, Huddleston, 'John Evans', 200

Evans, John [*pseuds.* I. D. Ffraid, Adda Jones] (1814–1875), Welsh scholar and businessman, was born at Tŷ Mawr, Llansanffraid Glan Conwy, on 23 July 1814, the son of David and Grace Evans. His education consisted of two periods, at Abergele in 1824 and at Wrexham in 1830. He started work in his uncle's shop when he was eleven, and by the age of sixteen he had written *Hanes yr Iddewon* (1831). He then edited *Difyrwch bechgyn Glanau Conway* (1835), a volume of poetry which included some of his own work. On 9 November 1836 he married Ann (1817–1850), daughter of Thomas Williams, a grocer of Llansanffraid. They went on to have six children.

Evans continued his study, and his effort as a lexicographer is found in *Geiriadur Saesneg–Cymraeg* (1847), which included a glossary of herbs. His first wife died in 1850, and in 1853 he married Hannah, who survived him. From January 1869 to December 1874 Evans contributed a series of 483 satirical letters, published as 'Llythyrau Adda Jones' in *Baner ac Amserau Cymru*. His lasting contribution, however, is his translation of *Paradise Lost* (*Coll Gwynfa*, 1865), although he also translated *The Life of Dick Turpin* (*Bywyd Turpin Leidr*, 1835) and Young's 'Night Thoughts' (NL Wales, MS 4757), which remain unpublished.

Evans combined his literary work with a thriving business career, eventually taking over his uncle's shop and running four other businesses—a nail factory, a sawmill, a watermill, and another shop. Ordained in the Calvinistic Methodist church in 1853, he never accepted a call, but

preached regularly, and also campaigned for the Liberation Society and for temperance, and was an enthusiastic attender of eisteddfods. His bardic name was given credence when he was accepted into the order of bards at the national eisteddfod held at Denbigh, on 7–10 August 1860. He was presented with a national testimonial in 1869. John Evans died of pneumonia at Llansanffraid Glan Conwy on 4 March 1875, and his remains were interred in the burial-ground of his native parish on 10 March.

       D. BEN REES

Sources DWB · L. Edwards, 'Coll Gwynfa', *Traethodau llenyddol* (1867), 71–9 · M. Stephens, ed., *Cydymaith i lenyddiaeth Cymru* (1986), 202 · G. Bowen and Z. Bowen, *Hanes gorsedd y beirdd* (1991), 197 · *Y Drysorfa*, 20 (1850), 287–8 · W. L. Roberts, 'Bywyd a gwaith John Evans (I. D. Ffraid)', MA diss., U. Wales, Bangor, 1950 · *Y Faner* (24 March 1875) · d. cert.
Archives NL Wales
Wealth at death under £200: probate, 21 Feb 1876, *CGPLA Eng. & Wales*

Evans, Sir John (1823–1908), archaeologist, numismatist, and paper manufacturer, was born on 17 November 1823 at Britwell Court, Burnham, Buckinghamshire, the second son of the Revd Arthur Benoni *Evans (1781–1854), schoolmaster, cleric, and author, and his wife, Anne (1791–1883), daughter of Captain Thomas Dickinson RN (1754–1828) of Bramblebury, near Woolwich, who was superintendent of shipping in the ordnance service. His grandfather was Lewis *Evans (1755–1827), an astronomer and first mathematical master at the Royal Military Academy, Woolwich. Evans's five siblings included the poet and musical composer Anne *Evans (1820–1870) [*see under* Evans, Arthur Benoni] and the journalist Sebastian *Evans (1830–1909).

Early in 1829 Evans and his older brother Arthur (1822–1850) were sent to Mrs Brown's school at Datchet, Buckinghamshire. However, from August of that year they attended the free grammar school at Market Bosworth, Leicestershire, where their father had become headmaster. Here John and Arthur Evans were encouraged by their father to join him in the pursuit of his interests in numismatics and fossils. In March 1839 they were sent to Germany to learn the language, under the charge of Wyndham Knight (a former pupil of their father). The boys travelled to Cotta, near Dresden, where they remained for about six months, long enough for John Evans (a gifted linguist) to acquire a thorough knowledge of German. On the return journey to Market Bosworth, John was taken by his father to be entered at Brasenose College, Oxford, but an offer of employment from his uncle, the paper manufacturer John Dickinson (1782–1869) of Nash Mills, Hemel Hempstead, secured him a career in business.

A career in business Evans arrived at his uncle's house, Abbot's Hill, in April 1840. As a novice in the firm of John Dickinson & Co., which comprised not only mills in Hertfordshire but also regional branches, Evans was placed under a Mr Tyers, who was in charge of the paper mill accounts. Dickinson arranged for his nephew to reside in two rooms built on to Mr Tyers's cottage, which was

Sir John Evans (1823–1908), by John H. Pinches, 1887

located opposite the lodge at Nash Mills; here Evans filled his spare time with numismatic and antiquarian studies.

Against John Dickinson's wishes, Evans married his uncle's daughter, Harriet Ann (1823–1858), on 12 September 1850 in the parish of Abbots Langley, Hertfordshire. The couple had five children; their eldest son was the explorer and archaeologist Sir Arthur John *Evans (1851–1941). The Evanses spent their early married life in the village, in the Red House, designed for them by Dickinson. In June 1856 they took possession of Nash House, the residence at Nash Mills, from Charles Longman, a partner in Dickinson's firm. At home Evans was never too busy to receive visitors, give advice, or show his collections to those interested; he enjoyed conversation and appreciated a jest.

John Dickinson made Evans a junior partner in the firm in the same year in which Evans married. Evans took an active interest in the paper manufacturing industry and proved himself to have a great capacity for business, both public and private. His influence on the paper trade was significant. He was involved in founding the Paper Makers' Association (1856) and the Paper Makers' Club; he was the first president of both bodies. He also helped build up the fortunes of the firm, and from 1856 managed the mills.

Business concerns also led Evans to an interest in geology. In 1852 the company secured an injunction against the Grand Junction Canal Company concerning rights to the local water supply (vital to the paper-making process). As a result Evans made a thorough investigation of the local geology and hydrological and meteorological processes in order to understand the controlling factors of the mill's water supply, which made him a recognized authority in this field.

Despite an active career Evans, with his wife, found time to be involved in improving local education. Harriet Evans established a library for the mill and a school for the village girls, and Evans founded a school for boys at Frogmore End (1854–5). However, in 1857 Harriet became ill after the birth of their fifth child; she died on 1 January 1858. On 23 July 1859 Evans married another cousin, Frances (1824/5–1890), daughter of the merchant Joseph Phelps (1791–1876) of Funchal, Madeira; the couple had no children.

Despite almost daily engagements in London, Evans resided at Nash House for fifty years, and was a prominent and active figure in local politics. In 1871 he was sworn in as a magistrate for the county of Hertfordshire, by 1876 he was deputy lieutenant, and in 1881 he was appointed high sheriff. Similarly, he was chairman of quarter sessions and of the county council for a number of years. He was founder and president of the Watford (Hertfordshire) Natural History Society, vice-president of the East Hertfordshire Archaeological Society, and an active member from its foundation in 1845 of the St Albans and Hertfordshire Architectural and Archaeological Society. In 1885, shortly before retiring from business, Evans made the decision to convert the firm of John Dickinson & Co. into a private limited company.

Archaeology, geology, and numismatics Throughout a successful business career Evans retained a thirst for knowledge and an insatiable desire to uncover the secrets of the past. Litigation over water rights brought him into contact with the geologist and wine merchant Sir Joseph Prestwich (1812–1896). Despite representing opposite sides in the case they became close friends and often 'geologized' together. In 1859 they travelled to France to assess the authenticity of a collection of chipped flints discovered by Boucher de Perthes. In 1847 Perthes put forward his (widely contested) theory that the flints represented evidence of the existence of prehistoric man in the Somme valley. The investigation made by Prestwich and Evans corroborated his theory, and in turn formed a stepping stone to the general acceptance of the antiquity of man in western Europe. Evans presented his findings on the subject to the Society of Antiquaries (of which he became a fellow in 1852) and in a paper in 1860 (*Archaeologia*, 38, 1860, 280). His meticulous attention to detail and his powers of observation were undoubtedly reflected in his success as a collector and scientist.

The geological expedition to the valley of the Somme with Prestwich, one of many such journeys, was a turning point in Evans's scientific career. His studies became focused on discovering the traces of prehistoric man both on the continent and in the British Isles, with especial attention to river gravel and cave deposits. He collected stone and bronze implements from all over the world and wrote two standard works on the classification, origin, and manufacture of these prehistoric artefacts. The first work, *The Ancient Stone Implements, Weapons and Ornaments of Great Britain*, appeared in 1872 (2nd edn, 1897) and was translated into French in 1875; the second work, *The Ancient Bronze Implements, Weapons and Ornaments of Great Britain and Ireland*, was published in 1881 and translated into French in the following year.

Evans's predilection for geology and fossils remained unchanged throughout his life and, though chiefly occupied with archaeological researches, he published an important paper, 'On portions of a cranium and of a jaw, in the slab containing the fossil remains of the *archaeopteryx*' in the *Natural History Review* (new ser. 5, 415–21) in 1865. When Evans examined the fossilized remains of an *archaeopteryx* contained within the Solenhofen slab at the British Museum he found evidence of the brain and a jaw with teeth, features previously unnoticed by Sir Richard Owen, superintendent of the museum's natural history departments. Furthermore, Evans established analogous characteristics in the *archaeopteryx* and the brain cavities and beaks of modern birds, such as the jay and woodcock, providing support for Darwin's recent theory of the origin of species.

In 1848 Evans presented a paper to an archaeological society at St Albans on gold coinage in Britain before the Roman invasion. He communicated a similar paper in 1849 to the Numismatic Society of London, which he had recently joined. Evans was awarded the Prix Allier de Hauteroche of the Académie des Inscriptions et Belles-Lettres for his first book, *The Coins of the Ancient Britons* (1864). Here he used a systematic, scientific approach, drawing together a wealth of information, to chart the evolution of ancient British coin design from an original prototype, believed to be the gold stater of Philip II of Macedon. A supplement followed in 1890. He was also the author of an important paper in the *Numismatic Chronicle* (1865) on the distinction between the 'short-cross' pennies of Henry I, Richard I, John, and Henry III.

Evans based his major works on, and illustrated them with, examples from his own extensive collections. These comprised not only ancient British coins, and Bronze Age, neolithic, and palaeolithic implements and weapons, but also Greek, Roman, Saxon, and English gold coins, medals, rings, seals, and remains of extinct animals and fossils. He presented some of his collection to the British Museum, and other parts were put on display in the John Evans Room at the Ashmolean Museum, Oxford.

Honours and recognition For a businessman, Evans's scientific and literary achievements are remarkable. He was one of the first men of trade to be elected a fellow of the Royal Society (1864). He twice served on the society's council, was nominated vice-president in 1876, and from 1878 to 1898 was treasurer; in 1884 he prepared and delivered the anniversary address when the president, Thomas Huxley, was absent. A fellow of the Geological Society from 1857, Evans was one of its honorary secretaries from 1866 to 1874, was president for two years (1874–6), and acted as foreign secretary from 1895. In 1880 he received the Lyell medal for his distinguished services to geological science, especially post-Tertiary geology. In 1876 Evans was appointed vice-president of the Society of Antiquaries, and was later elected president (1885–92); in turn he became an ex-officio trustee of the British Museum, and was later elected a permanent trustee, playing a very active role in the museum's management. At the time of

his death Evans was one of the oldest members of the society, having been a fellow for fifty-six years.

By 1887 nearly seventy papers had been contributed by Evans to the *Numismatic Chronicle*, the journal of the Numismatic Society. From 1861 he was joint editor of the journal, and after twenty years as honorary secretary of the society (1854–74) he was elected president and served in that role from 1874 until his death. In 1887 the society awarded him its jubilee medal (engraved by Pinches), struck in gold, in recognition of his distinguished services to numismatics. Furthermore, in 1899, his fiftieth year of membership of the society and the twenty-fifth year of his presidency, he was presented with a bronze medallion, executed by Frank Bowcher. His portrait appears on both medals.

Evans served as president of the Anthropological Institute from 1877 to 1879, the Institute of Chemical Industry from 1892 to 1893, the Egypt Exploration Fund from 1898 to 1905, and the Midland Institute in 1899. He was also chairman of the Society of Arts from 1900 to 1901, chairman of the Lawes Agricultural Trust committee, and an associate of the Institution of Civil Engineers, which he joined in 1859. In 1861 Evans joined the British Association for the Advancement of Science and regularly attended its meetings; between 1870 and 1890 he presided over either the anthropological or geological section at a number of meetings. As president of the association (1897–8) he delivered the address at the Toronto meeting on the antiquity of man.

Evans was among the foremost figures of British archaeology of his time, and his scientific approach to the subject enabled great advances to be made. His intellect and attainments were honoured by a great many learned societies and institutions, at home and abroad. He was elected a corresponding member of the Institut de France in 1887, and he held honorary degrees from various universities, including DCL Oxford (1877), LLD Dublin (1878), ScD Cambridge (1890), DCL Toronto (1897), and LLD Trinity College, Toronto (1897). Evans was perhaps proudest of an honorary fellowship (1903) of Brasenose College, Oxford, the college to which he had been entered for matriculation some sixty-four years before. In 1881 the king of Portugal made Evans a commander of the order of St Iago da Espada; in 1892 Queen Victoria made him a knight commander of the Bath; and in 1906 the prince of Monaco created him an officer of the order of St Charles.

Final years When Evans resolved in 1904 to leave Nash House he selected a plot of land on the edge of Berkhamsted Common as the site of his new home, to be named Britwell after his birthplace. In 1906 he settled there with his third wife, Maria Millington Lathbury (1856–1944), also an archaeologist, and daughter of Charles Crawford Lathbury of Wimbledon; they had married on 29 July 1892 (Evans's second wife, Frances, having died on 22 September 1890). Their only child was the historian Dame Joan *Evans (1893–1977). Evans was not long to enjoy his new residence: his health began to fail and he died there on 31

May 1908, after an operation for cancer. His body was laid to rest in Abbots Langley churchyard on 4 June. He was survived by his wife, two sons, and two daughters.

YOLANDA FOOTE

Sources J. Evans, *Time and chance: the story of Arthur Evans and his forebears* (1943) · J. Evans, *Prelude and fugue* (1964) · A. G., *PRS*, 80B (1908), l-lvi · *The Paper-maker and British Paper Trade Journal* (June 1908), 762–4 · *Report of Egypt Exploration Fund* (Nov 1908), 1–4 · *The World's Paper Trade Review* (June 1908), 16 · Paper and Pulp, supplement to, *Paper Making* (July 1908), 284 · *Proceedings of the Society of Antiquaries of London*, 2nd ser., 22 (1907–9), 469–71 · *WWW*, 1897–1915 · *The Paper Makers' Monthly Journal* (June 1908), 197 · *The Herts and Watford Observer* (6 June 1908) · L. Forrer, 'Correspondance anglaise', *Gazette Numismatique Française*, 3 (1899), 307–8 · *DNB* · *Men and women of the time* (1899) · *Numismatic Chronicle*, 3rd ser., 7 (1887) · *Numismatic Chronicle*, 3rd ser., 19 (1899) · d. cert.

Archives AM Oxf., notebooks, corresp., etc. | CUL, letters to Sir George Stokes · Salisbury and South Wiltshire Museum, letters to A. H. L. F. Pitt-Rivers · U. Edin. L., special collections division, letters to Sir Charles Lyell

Likenesses photograph, *c*.1855, repro. in Evans, *Time and chance* · J. H. Pinches, copper medal, 1887, NPG [see illus.] · J. H. Pinches, gold medal, 1887, Numismatic Society, London · H. Herkomer, photograph, 1890, repro. in Evans, *Time and chance* · F. Bowcher, bronze medallion, 1899, Numismatic Society, London · A. S. Cope, oils, exh. 1900, RS · J. Collier, oils, 1905 (loaned by A. L. Evans), AM Oxf. · J. Collier, oils, 1905, Shire Hall, Hertford · A. S. Cope, oils, RS · H. von Herkomer, monotype, Somerville College, Oxford · W. Richmond, marble relief, St Lawrence the Martyr Church, Abbots Langley, Hertfordshire

Wealth at death £147,347 7s. 9d.: probate, 28 July 1908, *CGPLA Eng. & Wales*

Evans, John [*known as* John Evans Eglwysbach] (1840–1897), Wesleyan Methodist minister, was the eldest son of David and Margaret Evans of Tŷ Du, a small farm in the parish of Eglwys-bach, Denbighshire, where he was born on 28 September 1840. The name of his native parish became associated with him, and was the name by which he was popularly known in Wales. He was educated at the national school of the parish and, after leaving, he acted as his father's shepherd, using his spare time for private study. At the age of seventeen, he began preaching, and soon became a well-known and popular preacher with his congregations. He was accepted for the ministry in 1860, but owing to ill health was unable to proceed to a theological college. His first appointment was as a local preacher in Anglesey in 1861, before he moved to Mold in 1863, and was fully ordained in 1865. He moved on to minister at the following circuits: Liverpool (1866); Bethesda (1869); Liverpool (1872–8); London (1878–86); Bangor (1886–9); Oswestry (1889–90); and Islington, London (1890–93). He also visited the USA on extensive preaching tours in 1873 and 1887. During his earlier ministries in Liverpool and London he strove to compensate for his lack of collegiate training by attending evening classes, becoming an associate of King's College, London. In 1884 he was elected a member of the legal hundred of the Wesleyan conference, and in 1895 became chairman of the South Wales district. During the last four years of his life he organized and vigorously conducted a 'forward movement' mission in Glamorgan, its headquarters being at

Pontypridd. So successful did his work prove that arrangements had been made to enable him to exchange it in another year for that of peripatetic evangelist for the whole of Wales, but the strain of the Glamorgan mission proved too great. Early in 1897 he had to abandon all his literary work, but he did not reduce his ministerial role, and on 23 October 1897 he died suddenly of heart failure at St Domingo Vale in Liverpool (where he had gone to preach); he was buried there on 27 October at Anfield cemetery.

Evans was married twice: first, in 1873, to Charlotte (*d.* 1884), daughter of John Pritchard of Liverpool; and second, in 1886, to Clara Kate, daughter of James Richardson of Duke Street, Manchester Square, London. His second wife, by lecturing and conducting mission services, shared the burden of her husband's evangelistic work. Both she and a family of six children survived him. He was commemorated at Pontypridd by a memorial chapel, erected by public subscriptions drawn from all parts of Wales.

Eglwysbach takes rank among the greatest of Welsh pulpit orators, and was probably the most eloquent that Wesleyan Methodism produced in nineteenth-century Wales. While in Liverpool he was often described as 'the Welsh Spurgeon', but in his style of preaching he resembled William Morley Punshon more closely. A contemporary commented that 'his power as a preacher of the gospel is well known in England and America, but especially in the Principality … the church at Eglwysbach will ever have reason to be proud that it brought up one of the ablest preachers in the Welsh language' (D. Young, *The Origin and History of Methodism in Wales*, 1893, 451). His missionary zeal and great charm made him an influential figure, and it was said that he converted thousands during the course of his life.

Evans had strong literary tastes, and his output as a Welsh-language writer was considerable, given his activity as preacher and lecturer. His most important work was a Welsh biography of John Wesley (1880), a revised translation of whose sermons he also brought out in 1887. He published three volumes of sermons and contributed largely to the magazines of his own connexion, and edited *Y Winllan* (1878–9) and *Y Fwyell* (1894–7), a monthly journal connected to the Pontypridd mission. In the latter appeared in 1896–7 a long series of autobiographical chapters which he did not live to complete.

D. L. THOMAS, *rev.* MARI A. WILLIAMS

Sources J. Humphreys, *John Evans, Eglwysbach* (1913) · T. Hughes and J. P. Roberts, *Cofiant* (1903) · *DWB* · *Y Geninen*, 16 (1898), 13–19 · *Ceninen Gŵyl Dewi*, 18 (March 1900), 27–9 · *Yr Eurgrawn*, 89 (Dec 1897) [memorial issue] · *Methodist Recorder* (29 Oct 1897) · *Methodist Times* (29 Oct 1897) · *Caernarvon Herald* (2 Nov 1897) · *Y Fwyell*, 2–3 (1896–7)

Archives NL Wales · NL Wales, J. D. Owen MSS

Likenesses A. Hughes, photograph, *c*.1860, repro. in Hughes and Roberts, *Cofiant*, 233 · photograph, *c*.1880, repro. in Hughes and Roberts, *Cofiant*, 377 · A. Hughes, photograph, *c*.1890, repro. in Hughes and Roberts, *Cofiant*, 537 · Meisenbach, photograph, *c*.1896, repro. in Hughes and Roberts, *Cofiant*, 140 · oils, NMG Wales

Wealth at death £442 10s. 0d.: probate, 27 April 1898, *CGPLA Eng. & Wales*

Evans, John Gwenogvryn (1852–1930), palaeographer, was born at Ffynnon-felfed, Llanybydder, Carmarthenshire, on 20 March 1852, the only son of Thomas Evans, farmer, and his wife, Margaret, *née* Rees. When he was a year old his parents moved to Llanwenog, Cardiganshire, the parish from which he later coined his middle name. He attended local schools until the age of fourteen, and then spent four years apprenticed to his uncle, David Rees, a grocer in Lampeter. At eighteen, after an accident, he returned to school, first at Carmarthen School under Alcwyn C. Evans, then at Pont-siân grammar school under Gwilym Marles. In 1872 he was admitted, as a candidate for the ministry, to the Presbyterian college, Carmarthen, where he stayed until 1875. After a short period in 1874–5 as assistant master at Milton College, near Rugby, he was ordained as a Unitarian minister in August 1876 and returned to Carmarthen as pastor of the Unitarian church, Parc-y-felfed. Evans married Edith (*d.* 1923), youngest daughter of the Revd Stephenson Hunter, principal of the Presbyterian college, Carmarthen, on 16 October 1877. They had two sons (Emrys and Tringad) and one daughter (Myfanwy). From 1877 to 1880 Evans served in Preston, Lancashire, but ill health brought about by a childhood case of typhoid fever and loss of voice forced him to give up the ministry.

Evans entered Owens College, Manchester, in early 1880 to study natural sciences, but left for Oxford before the end of the year. Pulmonary tuberculosis prevented him from working for a degree, and, having taken medical advice, he embarked in August 1881 on a sea voyage to Australia, followed by a period of time at the Swiss resort of Davos-Platz. Evans returned to Oxford in 1882 and settled at 7 Clarendon Villas, and later that year published (privately) the journal kept by himself and his fellow passengers, *The 'Homeward Bound': an occasional paper published at sea during the voyage of the ship 'Sobraon' from Melbourne to London, 1882.* It was his first publication. Evans attended the lectures of Professor Sir John Rhŷs on the *Mabinogion*, and the intense interest in Welsh palaeography that was born at this time enabled him to some extent to conquer his illness, although his health remained poor for the rest of his life. The first fruit of his interest in transcribing the Red Book of Hergest (Jesus College, Oxford, MS 111) was 'A collection of Welsh proverbs', which was awarded the prize at the 1884 Liverpool national eisteddfod, and was published in its 1885 *Transactions*.

Recognizing the weaknesses in the edition of the *Mabinogion* by Lady Charlotte Guest led Evans to make a transcript of the tales from the red book, and later from the White Book of Rhydderch (NL Wales, Peniarth MS 4–5). His copying was extraordinarily faithful to the original, reproducing all the manuscript's features, including such elements as lineation, corrections, and marginalia. Rhŷs agreed to act as co-editor, and in 1887 Oxford University Press issued the first of the series of Old Welsh Texts, *The Text of the Mabinogion and other Welsh Tales from the Red Book of Hergest.* The transcription and publication of early Welsh

texts occupied Evans for the next forty years. In most cases he set his own type, and while he remained in Oxford this work was done directly from the manuscripts in the interest of accuracy. Evans's concern with palaeography next led him to produce a *Facsimile of the Black Book of Carmarthen* (1888; repr. 1908), followed by *The Text of the Bruts from the Red Book of Hergest* (1890) and *The Text of the Book of Llan Dav* (1893), both co-edited by Rhŷs.

The University of Oxford conferred an honorary degree of MA on Evans in 1887, and he was made DLitt *honoris causa* by Oxford in 1901 and by the University of Wales in 1905. He was granted a civil-list pension of £200 in 1893 (backdated to 1892), and in 1894 was appointed inspector of Welsh manuscripts for the Historical Manuscripts Commission. His *Report on Manuscripts in the Welsh Language* appeared in seven parts between 1898 and 1910. It is a monumental work, dealing succinctly with the contents of some 900 manuscripts, ranging in date from about 1100 to 1800. His inspectorate allowed him to take an active part in the negotiations in 1905 concerning the purchase of the Peniarth manuscript collection, and he was closely involved in the decisions regarding the founding and choice of location of the new National Library of Wales. After its foundation, he became the privy council's nominee to the library's council. He served as justice of the peace for Cardiganshire and as a member of the council of the University College of Wales, Aberystwyth.

Evans retired in 1905 to Tremfan, Llanbedrog, Caernarvonshire, where he continued to produce diplomatic editions of early Welsh texts on a small hand press. The products of this period of Evans's work are nothing short of astonishing, marked by an extremely high level of accuracy produced by hand-typesetting with the utmost care. During his first two decades at Tremfan, Evans produced *The Black Book of Carmarthen* (1906; students' edition, 1907); *The White Book Mabinogion: Welsh Tales and Romances* (1907 [1909]); *The Text of the Book of Aneirin* (1908 [1910]); *Kymdeithas Amlyn ac Amic* (1909); and the *Facsimile of the Chirk Codex of the Welsh Laws* (1909 [1920]). There are frequent discrepancies between the actual date of publication and the title-page date for Evans's work during this period. From 1909 onwards, however, Evans became interested in the interpretation of texts, especially the *hengerdd* poetry of Aneirin and Taliesin. His theories were presented in his commentaries to *The Text of the Book of Taliesin* (1910); *Facsimile and Text of the Book of Taliesin* (1910 [1916]); *The Poetry in the Red Book of Hergest* (1911); *Poems from the Book of Taliesin, Amended and Translated* (1915 [1916]); and *The Book of Aneirin Revised and Translated*, volume 2 (1922 [1924]; students' edition, 1934). The translations and (often radical) revisions that Evans proposed found virtually no acceptance by scholars, and reviews of his work were unfavourable. Most serious was the lengthy critical article by Sir John Morris-Jones in 'Taliesin' (*Y Cymmrodor*, 28, 1918), to which Evans replied in 'Taliesin, or, The Critic Criticised' (*Y Cymmrodor*, 34, 1924). In the last decade of his life Evans published *Poetry by Medieval Welsh Bards*, vol. 2 (Llanbedrog, 1926), as well as two volumes in a planned series Welsh Classics for the People: a reprint of the 1588 translation of the book of Job by Bishop William Morgan, *Llyvyr Iob* (1888), and *Pedeir Kainc y Mabinogi* (1905). A facsimile of the 1546 edition of *Oll Synnwyr Pen Kembero* of William Salesbury was intended for the series, but was published by the Guild of Graduates of the University of Wales in 1902.

Evans's wife died in 1923 and was buried in the grounds of Tremfan. He survived her by seven years, dying at Tremfan on 25 March 1930, and was buried in the same grave.

DAVID N. KLAUSNER

Sources 'John Gwenogfryn Evans', *Cymru*, 4 (1893), 77–9 · J. Vendryes, 'John Gwenogfryn Evans', *Revue Celtique*, 47 (1930), 280–82 · *The Unitarian students at the Presbyterian College, Carmarthen* (1907) · NL Wales, J. G. Evans papers · *DWB*
Archives NL Wales, corresp. and papers · NL Wales, corresp. and papers incl. MSS collection · NL Wales, family MSS · NL Wales, papers and collections | NL Wales, letters to D. R. Daniels · NL Wales, letters to D. S. Evans · NL Wales, letters to Sir Evan Vincent Evans and L. M. Williams · NL Wales, letters to T. G. Jones · NL Wales, letters to Sir J. H. Lewis and Lady Lewis · NL Wales, letters to Edward Owen
Likenesses photograph, repro. in 'John Gwenogfryn Evans', 77
Wealth at death £11,179 1s. 10d.: probate, 26 June 1930, CGPLA Eng. & Wales

Evans, John Thomas (*bap.* 1770, *d.* 1798), explorer, was born in the farmhouse of Gwredog Uchaf in Caernarvonshire, the son of Thomas Evans (*d.* 1788) and his wife, Anne. Baptized on 14 April 1770, he was the product of a pious home. His father, a farmer, gained some distinction as an itinerant preacher and was one of the first Methodists in Caernarvonshire. After attending the village school Evans had established himself in London by the spring of 1792. He believed, with others, in the story of the pre-Columbian discovery of America by a twelfth-century Welsh prince, Madoc, and his mythical descendants, the white-skinned, Welsh-speaking Padoucas. This persistent legend was revitalized by the Nootka Sound crisis of 1790, which gave old legends of a British prior claim to America contemporary political relevance. The Padoucas were identified with a real people, the Mandans, on the upper reaches of the Missouri. Iolo Morganwg resolved to find them. In May 1792 it was mentioned for the first time that Iolo would be accompanied by Evans. Although Iolo fell desperately ill, Evans was undeterred: he borrowed money for his steerage passage and reached Baltimore in October.

Evans walked to the home of the influential Welsh-American Baptist the Revd Samuel Jones in Philadelphia to seek advice. Back in Baltimore, he became a merchant's clerk and spent the winter of 1792 there, whence he wrote: 'Either Death or Liberty … so it is with me, either the Madogion or death' (J. Evans to E. Williams, 22 Nov 1792, NL Wales, 13222). In February 1793 he consulted Samuel Jones for a second time, who tried to dissuade him, but without success. He left Philadelphia in March and in May reached New Madrid in Spanish Louisiana. He set out for the Illinois, and for eighteen months after his arrival dropped out of sight. It seems likely that a frontier merchant found employment for him as a surveyor or general agent. He became embroiled in the imperialist and trading tensions of the frontier, and was imprisoned by the

Spanish as a British spy for two days in St Louis. The US supreme justice in the Northwest Territory interceded and effected an introduction for him to the Spanish governor. The Spanish realized that even if he failed to find the Welsh Indians, he might find a great deal more.

Evans had already met the experienced explorer James Mackay, who was to be the leader of a full-scale Spanish scientific expedition. Mackay and Evans set out in mid-August 1795 aiming to reach the Pacific for Spain. By November they were in Omaha territory, where they wintered. Early in 1796 Evans and a detachment set out to find the Mandans. Mackay supplied him with detailed charts and instructions. For over six months Evans lived among the Mandans and held them to their Spanish allegiance. The Missouri Company unravelled behind him and in May 1797, facing pressure from the British Northwest Company, he had to leave. On 15 July he reported to Samuel Jones from St Louis that 'there is no such people as the Welsh Indians' (Williams, 'Mission to the Madogwys', 600–01), although the letter was not in his usual style, and may have been censored by the Spanish. The report was published in the American and then the Welsh press. Through the winter of 1797–8 Evans was a surveyor in upper Louisiana, in the employ of Americans. His months on the Missouri had undermined his health; without pay, he returned to St Louis. Suffering from nervous depression, Evans began to drink heavily. He moved into the household of the enigmatic Spanish empire builder Jacques Clamorgan, and went down to New Orleans on his behalf to secure assistance for another expedition. The governor of New Orleans observed that the strength of liquor had deranged his senses. Evans died in poverty in New Orleans in June or July 1798.

According to an oral tradition, Evans claimed while drinking that he knew more about the Welsh Indians than anyone would ever know, but that he had been paid to keep his mouth shut. A more concrete legacy was the striking resemblance between the instructions drawn up for a later explorer, Meriwether Lewis, and those which James Mackay drew for John Evans's visit to the Mandans in 1796.

HYWEL MEILYR DAVIES

Sources D. Williams, 'John Evans's strange journey', *Transactions of the Honourable Society of Cymmrodorion* (1948) · G. A. Williams, 'John Evans's mission to the Madogwys, 1792–1799', *BBCS*, 27 (1976–8), 569–601 · A. P. Nasatir, 'John Evans: explorer and surveyor', *Missouri Historical Review*, 25 (1931) · B. de Voto, *The course of empire* (1962) · R. Deacon, *Madoc* (1966) · G. A. Williams, *Madoc: the making of a myth* (1979) · G. A. Williams, 'Welsh Indians: the Madoc legend and the first Welsh radicalism', *History Workshop Journal*, 1 (1976), 137–54 · A. P. Nasatir, *Before Lewis and Clark*, 2 vols. (1952) · H. M. Davies, *Transatlantic brethren: Rev. Samuel Jones (1735–1814) and his friends* (1995) · J. Evans to E. Williams, 22 Nov 1792, NL Wales, MS 13222, fols. 315–16
Archives Hist. Soc. Penn., Mrs Irving H. McKesson Collection · NL Wales, Mysevin MSS

Evans [*née* Canual or Canval], **Katharine** (*c.*1618–1692), Quaker missionary, declared to the Maltese inquisition in 1658 that she was the daughter of Anne and Roger 'Canual' and that she was then aged about forty; this was an Italian rendering of her maiden name, which may have been Canval. At an unknown date she married John Evans (*d.* in or after 1690), a yeoman. Before her conversion to Quakerism, she was a member of the Church of England, then a Baptist, and eventually an Independent. Presumably the Evans family converted to Quakerism in the summer of 1654 together with Thomas Murford, who was arrested in 1655 because he disturbed a minister in Bath Abbey and whose wife, Jane, was probably John Evans's sister.

Possibly between the end of 1655 and the beginning of 1656 Katharine Evans went to the Isle of Man. She was banished from the island, and probably shortly thereafter went to Ireland. There she was interviewed by Henry Cromwell and was placed under arrest for four days. At the end of May 1657 she was arrested and publicly whipped in the market square of Salisbury. Shortly after this, together with Murford, she returned to the Isle of Wight. Afterwards she preached in Portsmouth, Salisbury, and Warminster and in all these places was received with fiery abuse. In the winter of 1657 Evans felt inspired to go to Alexandria and during 1658 went twice to London to organize her journey. In London she met Sarah *Cheevers who, independently, had felt the same inspiration. They set out for the Mediterranean in the autumn of 1658. After a short stay in Leghorn the two women got passage in a Dutch ship that reached Malta on 21 December 1658. A few days after their arrival they were interrogated by the Inquisition and arrested. After three months of detention in the house of the English consul in La Valletta, they were taken to the Inquisition prison in Birgu at the beginning of April 1659. The imprisonment of the two women lasted until the summer of 1662. During their stay in the Inquisition prison, the Quaker Daniel Baker went to Malta. He met the inquisitor and the new consul to intercede for them. Their freedom was requested by English shipmasters who visited the island, and by the consul. However, it was probably only through the intercession of Ludovic Stuart, seigneur d'Aubigny, lord almoner to Queen Henrietta Maria and Jansenist abbot of Haute Fontaine and canon of Notre Dame, who had been contracted by the Quakers Gilbert Latey and George Fox, that the two women were released in the summer of 1662. After staying almost three months in the consul's house, they got passage on the *Sapphire* and returned to England. Their letters and the accounts of their travels to Malta, arrest, and imprisonment, recounting their sufferings, fasting, and visions, were taken to England by Daniel Baker and published in 1662 (shortly before the announcement of their release). This miscellany of documents was republished in 1663 with the account of the last period of detention and of their release.

On 6 September 1663 Katharine Evans was arrested at Rochester, Kent, but released a few days later. According to the Quaker annalist John Whiting, she went to Scotland in 1663 together with Sarah Cheevers, and then they went to Ireland. They returned to England in May 1664 (Whiting, 221). On their way back they were arrested at Wiveliscombe, Somerset, and remained in prison for a few months. Shortly after their release Sarah Cheevers died.

After the death of her friend, Katharine Evans continued her missionary work. In 1666 she was imprisoned at Welshpool, Montgomeryshire. In 1671 she was back in Ireland where she was arrested at Wicklow. On 29 January 1681 she was arrested at Bristol. She died in June 1692.

STEFANO VILLANI

Sources D. Baker, ed., *This is a short relation of some of the cruel sufferings (for the truths sake) of Katharine Evans and Sarah Cheevers in the inquisition of the isle of Malta* (1662) · *A true account of the great tryals and cruel sufferings undergone by those two faithful servants of God Katharine Evans and Sarah Cheevers* (1663) · 'Examen Sarah Cheevers, Catherina Evans', Archivum Inquisitionis Maltae, Mdina, sezione processi criminali, vol. 70A, caso 3, fols. 23–5 · 'Denunc. Mulieres Anglas', Maltese Inquisition Archives, sezioni processi criminali, vol. 71B, caso 307, fols. 675–81 · 'Denunc. Joannem Remigio', Maltese Inquisition Archives, sezione processi criminali, vol. 71A, fols. 270r–275v (caso 163) · T. Morford, *The cry of oppression* (1659), 18–19 · S. Villani, *Tremolanti e Papisti: missioni quacchere nell'Italia del seicento* (Rome, 1996) · J. Whiting, *Persecution expos'd, in some memoirs relating to the sufferings of John Whiting, and many others of the people called Quakers for conscience sake, in the west of England …* (1715), 219–23 · J. Besse, *A collection of the sufferings of the people called Quakers*, 2 vols. (1753), vol. 1, pp. 41, 55, 149, 151, 229, 269, 293, 479, 576, 584–5, 597, 648; vol. 2, p. 495 · [G. Fox and E. Pyot], *The west answering the north* (1657), 84–5 · H. J. Cadbury, 'Friends and the inquisition at Malta', *Journal of the Friends' Historical Society*, 53 (1972–5), 219–25 · P. Mack, *Visionary women: ecstatic prophecy in seventeenth-century England* (1992)

Evans, Sir (Worthington) Laming Worthington-, first baronet (1868–1931), politician, was born at Broadstairs, Kent, on 23 August 1868, the elder son of Worthington Evans (1827–1901) of Isleworth and his second wife, Susanna Jane (*d.* 1891), daughter of James Laming, of Birchington Hall, Kent. He was educated at Eastbourne College, and was articled to his father, a solicitor in the City of London, at the age of seventeen, being admitted a solicitor in 1890 and eventually becoming head of the firm of Worthington Evans, Dauney & Co. On 5 November 1898 he married Gertrude Annie (*d.* 1947), younger daughter of William Hale, of London; they had a son and a daughter. During this period he published *Notes on the Companies Acts* and his expertise in this field prompted his appointment as member of the Board of Trade committee for the reform of company law in 1905. In 1906 he unsuccessfully contested the borough of Colchester as a Conservative, but at the general election of January 1910 Evans gained the seat (which in 1918 became the Colchester division), and he held it until in 1929 he was returned for the St George's division of Westminster by a very large majority.

In the Commons, Worthy, as he was widely known, immediately established his reputation as a skilful parliamentary tactician and effective debater during the passage of Lloyd George's National Insurance Bill. Using the actuarial knowledge and experience of friendly societies acquired as a City solicitor, Evans assembled a small committee to decide what to commend and what to condemn in a measure his party wished to welcome in principle but attack in detail. During 1911 he also joined Lord Hugh Cecil, F. E. Smith, and others in a group seated below the gangway committed to harrying the Liberal government in a manner reminiscent of the Fourth Party in the 1880s.

On the outbreak of war in 1914 Evans served at York as inspector of administrative services to northern command with the temporary rank of major. In May 1915 he was appointed parliamentary private secretary to the financial secretary to the War Office, and from January to December 1916 he was controller of the foreign trade department of the Foreign Office. During the Lloyd George wartime coalition he served as parliamentary secretary (later also financial secretary) to the Ministry of Munitions until July 1918, when he became minister of blockade and under-secretary at the Foreign Office, serving until the general election in December. He was created a baronet on 15 November 1916, when he assumed by royal licence the additional surname Worthington and was sworn of the privy council in September 1918.

During the post-war coalition Worthington-Evans became increasingly closely involved with Lloyd George as a loyal member of his inner circle. Having proved a competent minister of pensions since January 1919, he became minister without portfolio in April 1920 with a seat in the cabinet, and from February 1921 until October 1922 he served as secretary of state for war. From spring 1920 Worthington-Evans attended many of the post-war conferences with the prime minister and played a particularly significant role in negotiations over German reparations. He was also one of seven British negotiators who agreed the Irish treaty in December 1921. He was appointed GBE in June 1922. In domestic affairs his pre-war support for the Unionist Social Reform Committee made him sympathetic to the coalition's social reform aspirations: he worked sympathetically with Addison and demonstrated an enlightened attitude as pensions minister by increasing old age payments. Politically, Worthington-Evans supported 'fusion' between the coalition parties in 1920 and was a vocal advocate of an early general election in December 1921 to achieve the same objective by the back door. As a result, at the decisive Carlton Club meeting in October 1922 he was one of the 'first-class brains' who remained loyal to Lloyd George and went into the political wilderness rather than join the bulk of his party in office.

During the next year Worthington-Evans was torn between supporting his party and coalition, and between loyalty to the rejected Conservative former ministers under Austen Chamberlain and the pursuit of his own personal ambitions under Bonar Law. Although he remained formally committed to the Chamberlainite group and its strategy of abstaining from office until the collapse of the Law government opened the way for a renewed coalition, from the outset he was rightly suspected of being anxious to desert and return to office at any cost. After being considered for the Ministry of Health early in 1923, he accepted from Baldwin the office of postmaster-general in May 1923, explaining to Chamberlain, 'I don't want to see the Baldwin Government fail, if it fails the Tory party fails' (Dutton, 204).

The transition did little for Worthington-Evans's reputation either with his former Chamberlainite allies who despised his careerist disloyalty or with his new cabinet colleagues—particularly as he relentlessly and publicly manoeuvred for promotion during 1923. Probably because of his suspect loyalties, he was the only ministerial protectionist not to be consulted about the revival of tariff reform before its announcement to cabinet in October 1923, but he soon became part of the inner group directing election strategy. His compromising involvement in the 'Birkenhead plot' to displace Baldwin and create an anti-socialist coalition between the Unionist losses in the general election of December 1923 and the fall of Baldwin's government in January 1924 forfeited much of this new acceptance. His return to the War Office in Baldwin's second ministry of 1924–9 was notable largely for his continued reduction in army estimates over five successive years.

As a politician Worthington-Evans possessed several substantial strengths. By common consent he was clever, a shrewd judge of political and electoral strategy, and possessed of a broad vision on complex questions well beyond his own department. He was also an effective debater capable of speaking at short notice on a wide variety of topics and an excellent chairman of committees. Above all, his real interest and expertise in finance made him an authoritative and valued adviser on these matters throughout his career. Yet despite this ability and a genial personality, his progress was inhibited by three significant defects. First, his booming voice and rather loud manner, attributed to his lack of public-school and university education, suggested an air of unpolished vulgarity which created disdain in some quarters within the party. Second, his earlier attachment to Lloyd George, his alignment with the Chamberlainites after 1922, and his support for an anti-socialist arrangement with the Liberals after electoral defeats in 1923 and 1929 reinforced the damaging taint of coalitionist sympathies in a party hostile to such sentiments after the Carlton Club revolt. Finally, there was the omnipresent suspicion of unbridled ambition and cynical opportunism. Always conspicuously supporting the person most able to further his own career, after Worthington-Evans's shift in allegiances in May 1923 Curzon's phrase 'worthy reasons' became a euphemism for such brazen opportunism (Gilbert, 5.133). Two months later, his efforts to use the Post Office public relations department to accelerate his ministerial promotion in Baldwin's first government were such a 'dreadful fiasco' that Attlee still recalled them with disdain over a quarter of a century later (H. Nicolson, *Diaries and Letters, 1945–1962*, 1968, 136). Thereafter, Austen Chamberlain spoke for many in the valedictory comment that Worthington-Evans 'was a very useful member of our counsels & personally a very good fellow tho' a bit of a bounder in manner' (*Austen Chamberlain Diary*, 363). Although perhaps he possessed many of the qualities necessary to fulfil his principal ambition of becoming chancellor of the exchequer, this background and reputation always precluded him from serious consideration. A heart condition meant that he suffered from periodic poor health throughout the late 1920s, and he died suddenly in his sleep at his residence at 6 Eaton Place, London, on 14 February 1931.   ROBERT C. SELF

Sources Worthington-Evans papers, Bodl. Oxf., MS Eng. hist. c. 890–940, d. 424–7, e. 319–20, f. 26 · W. Churchill, *The Times* (16 Feb 1931) · *The modernisation of conservative politics: the diaries and letters of William Bridgeman, 1904–1935*, ed. P. Williamson (1988) · K. O. Morgan, *Consensus and disunity: the Lloyd George coalition government, 1918–1922* (1979) · L. S. Amery, *My political life, 1: England before the storm* (1953) · *The Austen Chamberlain diary letters: the correspondence of Sir Austen Chamberlain with his sisters Hilda and Ida, 1916–1937*, ed. R. C. Self, CS, 5th ser., 5 (1995) · M. Gilbert, *Winston S. Churchill, 4: 1916–1922* (1975); 5: *1922–1939* (1976) · D. J. Dutton, *Austen Chamberlain: gentleman in politics* (1985) · J. Ramsden, *The age of Balfour and Baldwin, 1902–1940* (1978) · Burke, *Peerage* (1967) · *Dod's Parliamentary Companion* · *CGPLA Eng. & Wales* (1931) · *DNB*
Archives Bodl. Oxf., corresp. and papers, MSS Eng. hist. c. 890–940, d. 424–427, e. 319–320, f. 26 · PRO, MUN 4/396–451 | HLRO, corresp. with Andrew Bonar Law · IWM, corresp. with Sir Henry Wilson · U. Birm., Austen Chamberlain MSS |SOUND BL NSA, recorded talk
Likenesses W. Stoneman, photograph, 1925, NPG · M. Webb, plaque, St Margaret's Church, Westminster
Wealth at death £118,562 15s. 7d.: probate, 16 April 1931, *CGPLA Eng. & Wales*

Evans, Lewis (*b.* **1532/3**, *d.* in or after **1576**). *See under* Evans, Lewis (*fl.* 1565–1571).

Evans, Lewis (*fl.* 1565–1571), religious controversialist, was of unknown parentage and bore a name common in the Elizabethan church, especially at the University of Oxford. Anthony Wood listed him as an Oxonian, but gloomily mentioned half a dozen namesakes and confessed, 'I cannot tell' which of them was the writer (Wood, *Ath. Oxon.*, 1.411). Others have favoured **Lewis Evans** (*b.* 1532/3, *d.* in or after 1576), Church of England clergyman, the Flintshire man elected student of Christ Church, Oxford, in 1552 at the age of nineteen, though Wood argued that the author, who mentioned no degrees on his title-pages, was from either Oxfordshire or Monmouthshire but not a graduate. Compared with others, Evans 'can hardly be regarded as a serious controversialist', and there is no certainty that he had the education implied in the Christ Church identification (Southern, 116).

About the time of the Council of Trent's definite prohibition in 1564 of 'church papistry' (Roman Catholic attendance at Church of England services), Evans seems to have abandoned his initial conformity to the Elizabethan settlement. He must have gone to the diocese of London, for in 1565 he recalled being before the bishop, Edmund Grindal, at Fulham Palace 'sundrie times for religion'—'I founde at youre handes a certayne kinde of favour' (Evans, *Certaine Tables*, sig. A2r). By 1565 he had withdrawn to the Catholic printing centre of Antwerp, where he published Willem van der Lindt's *Certaine tables … translated into Englishe by Lewys Evans and by hym intituled the betraying of the beastlines of heretykes* and also *A Brieve Admonition unto the Nowe Made Ministers of England* (signed by him at Louvain). Evans insisted that Catholics' political loyalty exceeded that of their protestant critics, and exhibited a particular interest in the sexual misconduct of protestant clergy. In

this latter preoccupation he exceeded co-religionists such as Thomas Harding and John Rastell. He did not engage directly with Church of England opponents such as John Jewel, bishop of Salisbury, nor they with him, though James Calfhill noted that he could have said worse things about Catholics' morality 'if I had Lewis Evans his vein' (Calfhill, 331).

By 1568 Evans was back in England, was imprisoned briefly, and published a protestant tract, *The Castle of Christianitie, Detecting the Long Erring Estate … of the Romaine Church*. The title-page quoted Ecclesiastes: 'Be not ashamed to confesse thine errour, for he that is wise will remember himselfe.' The dedication to Elizabeth I thanked her for overlooking his drinking 'of the puddell of ignorancy, of the mudde of idolatrie, of the ponde of superstition' (Evans, *Castle*, sig. Dv). He espoused patriotism, continuing in *A Short Treatise of the Mistery of the Eucharist* (1569) that Catholics should 'understande where they were brought up … They knowe what I meane, and they be not ignorant what I doe know' (sig. A3r). The northern rising provided the occasion for *The Hatefull Hypocrisie and Rebellion of the Romish Prelacie* (1570), which he began by refuting rumours that he had heard in 'the university of Oxforde' and London 'that I had revolted from the gospell, and … agayne gonne beyonde the seas … that I was deade' (Evans, *Hatefull Hypocrisie*, 'To the reader', sig. A4r). It, and *The Castle of Christianitie*, continued his favoured accusations of disloyalty and incontinence, merely reversing the direction of his arguments from those he had made in 1565. In summer 1571 he was at Denbigh—he told Robert Dudley, earl of Leicester, that he was seizing for the bishop of Bangor, Nicholas Robinson, 'sediciouse and trayterouse' prophecies. Moreover, 'there came hyther of late a Welshe booke wrytten by some of Rome … At the busshop's request I translated yt into English, and soe doe aunswere yt' (*Bath MSS*, 5.182). This was Morys Clynnog's catechism, to which Evans published his *Brief Answer* that year.

The career of the Lewis Evans who was at Christ Church is clearer, but accords in some respects with the details of the life of the controversialist as they are known. He had Thomas Francis, later regius professor of physic, as tutor. Having entered under Edward VI's religious dispensation, he weathered later changes to graduate BA on 1 February 1554, proceeding MA in July 1557 and BD in February 1562. He was ordained subdeacon at Oxford in December 1557. Probably he was the MA presented in November 1561 to the rectory of Waterstock, Oxfordshire, by Elizabeth, widow of Sir Thomas Cave. He left Christ Church some time between Michaelmas 1562 and Michaelmas 1563, conceivably for Waterstock—but this would also be a plausible time for a reversion to Catholicism. An argument against the controversialist's being Evans of Christ Church is that the latter seems to have retained Waterstock—although it might have been sequestrated—and was given dispensations to hold pluralities with it by Matthew Parker, archbishop of Canterbury, in May 1566 and by the faculty office in May 1567. This allowed him to become rector of Westwell in Oxfordshire, a Christ

Church living, worth under £8 per annum. As Waterstock was worth £10 16s. per annum, his circumstances were still not lavish, but he also held a third Oxfordshire rectory, Ducklington, worth £24 10 s. per annum. He resigned Westwell by October 1574 and was replaced at Waterstock in May 1576, apparently being deprived and certainly departing rather than dying. Later references are probably to namesakes, especially the graduate of Oriel College, Oxford, who died in 1585, and has been identified as canon of Wells in 1566, MA in 1570, and chaplain to Ferdinando Stanley, Baron Strange, in 1576.

Wood believed the controversialist Evans became a schoolmaster, which tends to identify him with the editor of John Withal's *Shorte Dictionarie* (1574)—published with a dedication to Leicester—and possibly also with the author of *Abridgement of Logique* (1568). The dedication of the latter to Grindal, who is thanked for 'clemencie' towards the author, might recall that of *Certaine Tables*, but the book's classical interests have little in common with those of the religious polemics and more with that of a fragmentary translation of Horace by 'Lewis Evans scholemayster', whose date of 1565 makes it unlikely that he was the controversialist (sig. A7v). Ultimately the controversialist's career is obscure except for the information he gives about himself—the Christ Church identification is tempting but unproven. Evans the controversialist was remembered for self-contradiction; although he was listed in or before 1588 as both 'papist' and protestant divine, it is confirmed that he was then dead (*Salisbury MSS*, 13.394).

JULIAN LOCK

Sources L. Evans, *The castle of Christianitie, detecting the long erring estate as well of the Romaine church as of the byshop of Rome together with the defence of the Catholique church* (1568) · L. Evans, *The hatefull hypocrisie and rebellion of the Romish prelacie* (1570) · [W. van der Lindt], *Certaine tables ... intituled the betraying of the beastlines of heretykes*, ed. L. Evans (1565) · Wood, *Ath. Oxon.*, new edn, 1.411–12 · A. C. Southern, *Elizabethan recusant prose, 1559–1582* (1950) · private information (2004) [J. Curthoys, archivist, Christ Church, Oxf.] · transcripts from Christ Church archives, Bodl. Oxf., MS Wood C. 8 · *Calendar of the manuscripts of the marquis of Bath preserved at Longleat, Wiltshire*, 5 vols., HMC, 58 (1904–80), vol. 5, p. 182 · *Calendar of the manuscripts of the most hon. the marquis of Salisbury*, 24 vols., HMC, 9 (1883–1976), vol. 13, p. 394 · J. Calfhill, *Answer to John Martiall's 'Treatise of the cross'*, ed. R. Gibbings, Parker Society (1846) · PRO, SP 12/76; 100

Evans, Lewis (*c.*1700–1756), cartographer and geologist, was born in Llangwnnadl, near Pwllheli, Caernarvonshire. Of his early life and parentage nothing is known. By 1736 he was a surveyor and map maker in Philadelphia. His first known work is 'A map of that part of Bucks County released by the Indians to the proprietaries of Pensilvania in September 1737' (1738, Logan MSS, Historical Society of Pennsylvania, Philadelphia), which showed the important land purchase by James Logan who had commissioned Evans to make the map. Evans wanted to make further maps of Indian lands which the colonial proprietors wanted to secure to enable the colony's peaceful westward expansion. In 1743 he and John Bartram the botanist were granted permission to accompany Conrad Weiser, provincial Indian agent, into Indian lands west of the settled parts of Pennsylvania and New York. Posing as a disinterested scientific observer, Evans was able, under Weiser's protection, to penetrate further westward than any other geographer to date. In 1746 he reduced a map for the board of proprietors of New Jersey and the knowledge he gained thereby and from seeing the maps which passed through the Pennsylvania land office and from further travel enabled him in 1749 to produce 'A map of Pensilvania, New-Jersey, New York and the three Delaware counties' which was the first delineation of so large a part of the territory in such detail. He was, however, aware that further advances depended on his being able to survey in the field, not just bring together pre-existing knowledge, but such surveys were impossible in Indian territory.

In 1749 and 1750 Evans drew for Thomas Penn maps of the areas west of the settled part of Pennsylvania to help Penn decide which tract he should next purchase from the Indians, but Penn's 1750 plan that Evans and Bartram make a westward reconnaissance trip under a scientific cloak came to nothing. At the same time Evans gave Pehr Kalm, the Swedish naturalist, a map and geological information to guide him on his travels on the continent. On his return to Philadelphia, Kalm gave Evans geographical information about the areas he had visited. The manuscript of the map drawn by Evans for Kalm has not survived and just one engraved copy is known (facsimile in Jörgensen, 27). The map covers New Hampshire, Massachusetts, Rhode Island, Connecticut, part of Lake Ontario, and the St Lawrence River as far as Quebec, as well as the middle Atlantic colonies shown on his 1749 map, although Kalm complained in retrospect, in a letter of 30 October 1777 to Pehr Wargentin, 'Alla orter, dem jag i America besökte, finns wäl ej här antecknade' ('none of the places which I visited in America is shown'; Jörgensen, 28). Kalm's published accounts of his journey included maps based on Evans's 1749 map.

In 1751–2 Evans lectured in various colonies on natural philosophy including electricity in which he had been instructed by Benjamin Franklin. In 1752 he reissued his 1749 map and published *A Brief Account of Pennsylvania* (1753). Piqued to find that he had been induced by Penn to include topographical information which was erroneous but which bolstered Penn's position in the Pennsylvania–Maryland border dispute, he undertook work for Penn's rival Lord Baltimore in 1753–4, trying in vain to unearth archival material which would bolster Baltimore's position. This in turn put him in bad odour with Penn who then did not commission him to map the western part of the colony as part of his strategy to ward off French claims. Instead Evans prepared a map on his own initiative. His 'General map of the middle British colonies' was accompanied by a booklet entitled *An Analysis of a General Map* (both published in 1755). The latter described as treasonable the British authorities' failure to consolidate claims to the rich Ohio country. While his condemnation grew intemperate he also attracted criticism in the press for the effect his maps had allegedly had on the prosecution of the war against the French, he having provided

General Braddock with two maps for military purposes. Finally he was indicted for libel against Robert Morris Hunter, governor of Pennsylvania, for allegations in the 1755 pamphlet. He was imprisoned in New York city in the spring of 1756. Suffering from 'a lingering indisposition' he was released on 8 June 1756, but he died there on 11 June. He left an eleven-year-old daughter, but no details of a marriage are known.

Since his death Evans has been hailed as a prescient scientific observer—ironically just the pose he adopted to cover his original political purpose. His map of the Atlantic colonies in its 1749 and 1752 states, his essay, and his journal of his 1743 journey, of which the original is lost but which was published in Thomas Pownall's *Topographical Description of such Parts of North America as are Contained in the (Annexed) Map* (1776), show him to have been a keen and knowledgeable observer of the natural world, including its geology, geomorphology, and meteorology. He has been hailed as the first to recognize in America signs of isostatic adjustment. This process is held to occur when erosion strips material from an area and it becomes lighter and rises. The area where the eroded material is deposited becomes correspondingly heavier and sinks. The term 'isostasy' was coined in 1889, but nearly 150 years earlier Evans had described the process. He described the transport of eroded material from the Appalachians to the plains below, and the isostatic adjustment which would take place if the Great Lakes were drained of all or some of their water (he had inferred the existence of earlier larger lakes from raised beaches around Lake Ontario). His map has also been hailed as 'the first known document to show oil at the industry's birthplace' (facsimile edition by the Ethyl Corporation, 1953). He was certainly an astute and knowledgeable observer, and an ambitious cartographer, though these skills were in his lifetime bent largely to political ends.

ELIZABETH BAIGENT

Sources W. Klinefelter, *Lewis Evans and his maps* (1971) [incl. facs.] · G. W. White, 'Lewis Evans' early American notice of isostasy', *Science*, 114 (1951), 302–3 · G. W. White, 'Lewis Evans (1700–56): a scientist in colonial America', *Nature*, 177 (1956), 1055–6 · A. Jörgensen, 'Lewis Evans' karta över Pehr Kalms resor', *Nordisk Tidskrift över Bokoch Biblioteksväsen*, 33 (1936), 23–8 [facs. of Evans's map at p. 27]
Wealth at death very small estate: will, 1756, office of the register of wills, Philadelphia, will no. 273; Klinefelter, 'Lewis Evans', 9, fn 19, 54

Evans, Lewis (1755–1827), mathematician, was the son of the Revd Thomas Evans of Basaleg, Monmouthshire. He matriculated at Merton College, Oxford, on 16 December 1774, but left the university without a degree. In 1777 he was ordained by the bishop of Lichfield and Coventry, and was for a year curate at Ashbury, Berkshire. He then served for ten years as residential curate of Compton, Berkshire, during which time he married Ann, the daughter of Thomas Norman. They had at least two sons, Thomas Simpson *Evans and Arthur Benoni *Evans, and two daughters. In 1788 Evans moved to the vicarage at Froxfield, Wiltshire, and he retained the living until his

death. In 1799 he was appointed first mathematical master at the Royal Military Academy, Woolwich, a post he held until 1820.

In later life Evans devoted much of his time to astronomy. He possessed several valuable instruments, notably the fine transit by Edward Troughton, later known as the 'Lee circle' and preserved by the Royal Astronomical Society. For many years he employed himself as a skilful and successful observer, and he had his own private observatories at Froxfield (1788–99) and at Woolwich (1799–1820). He contributed several papers to the *Philosophical Magazine*. Evans was elected FRS on 29 May 1823, and was an early fellow of the Astronomical Society. He died at the vicarage, Froxfield, on 19 November 1827.

GORDON GOODWIN, rev. ANITA MCCONNELL

Sources *Monthly Notices of the Astronomical Society of London*, 1 (1827–30), 53 · *Journal for the History of Astronomy*, 17/4 (1986) [*The Greenwich list of observatories*, ed. D. Howse], esp. 71, 83 · *GM*, 1st ser., 97/2 (1827), 570 · private information (1888)
Archives MHS Oxf., corresp., notebooks, and MSS
Likenesses oils, RAS
Wealth at death under £2000: PRO, death duty registers

Evans [née Jervis], **Marguerite Florence Laura** [*pseuds.* Countess Barcynska, Oliver Sandys] (**1886/7–1964**), novelist, was born at Henzada, Burma, the eldest of the three children of Henry Pruce Jervis (1855/6–1927), army officer, and his wife, Florence Mary Dorinda (1865/6–1941). She spent her childhood partly in India, where her father was lieutenant-colonel in the Bombay infantry, and partly with an aunt in London, where she was educated privately. A spell at the Academy of Dramatic Art launched her into acting, if with no real success; simultaneously she kept up writing, having at the age of thirteen placed a story in *Household Words*.

On 17 July 1911 Marguerite married Armiger Barczinsky (1861?–1930), a Polish-born journalist (Armiger Barclay) some twenty-five years her senior and, like her father, an aloof disciplinarian; he promised that under his tutelage she would fulfil her literary ambitions (an invention amusingly caught in her volume of autobiography). Stories and serials followed, and books under the name Marguerite Barclay; then came *The Honeypot* (1916) by 'Countess Barcynska', a novel of the stage whose remarkable success made its pen-name a valuable property and a bone of contention when, soon afterwards, the couple agreed to part.

Living now with her son Nicholas (*b.* 1916), Marguerite resolved that whatever her relations with men, henceforth through her writing she would preserve her financial independence. Quickly she hit her stride, averaging four novels a year, either as Countess Barcynska or as Oliver Sandys—the additional pseudonym deriving from her mother's family. Whatever the authorial disguise, she produced a dependable product, stronger on characterization than on plot, with some freshness of detail and a sunny vision of life—'personally, I'm all for the happy ending' (Sandys, *Full and Frank*, 616). Her serials for women's magazines—channelled through Winifred Johnson, an Amalgamated Press editor with a finger on

Marguerite Florence Laura Evans (1886/7–1964), by unknown photographer

the popular pulse—were recycled as romantic novels for the publishers Hurst and Blackett. Film rights swelled her income (*The Pleasure Garden* brought Alfred Hitchcock his first success), and on £1000 a year she enjoyed the rewards of best-sellerdom, including a chauffeur and limousine.

Widowed in 1930, Marguerite moved out of London with the writer (David) Caradoc *Evans (1878–1945), whom she married on 22 March 1933. It seemed an improbable coupling—'like a redbrick Nonconformist chapel in the shadow of an English parish church', thought Frank O'Connor—and indeed little in their background united them: Marguerite was upper-class tory while Evans, the Welsh iconoclast, had risen in Fleet Street. Yet their devotion to writing was absolute (she worked a six-hour day) and she never doubted Evans's genius. They settled at Aberystwyth, where in 1935 Marguerite founded Countess Barcynska's Rogues and Vagabonds, a repertory theatre company bringing sleek productions of West End successes to the town and outlying villages. In 1937 the family left Wales for Ruislip, a move which Marguerite hoped might further her son's prospects as an actor, but the outbreak of war drove them back to Aberystwyth. All the while she continued to write, her novels packed with people and events around her, including an Evans figure as the type of temperamental genius.

With his death in 1945 Marguerite turned increasingly to a spiritualism that accorded with her Christian faith. Her last years, at Little Stretton, Shropshire, were exceedingly difficult: the market for her fiction had collapsed

and she survived on a literary services pension. Besides some 130 novels, she published (as Oliver Sandys) an autobiography (*Full and Frank*, 1941) and a biography of her husband (*Caradoc Evans*, 1946); both are intimate and revealing, and moderately sound on fact. Marguerite died of heart failure at Shrewsbury Hospital on 10 March 1964 and was buried on 13 March in her husband's grave at Horeb Chapel, next to Brynawelon, their home at New Cross, near Aberystwyth.   JOHN HARRIS

Sources O. Sandys, *Full and frank: the private life of a woman novelist* (1941) · O. Sandys, 'In the days of my youth', *T. P.'s Weekly* (17 Nov 1928) · F. O'Connor, 'Author's stormy married life', *Evening News* [London] (Sept 1946) [review of O. Sandys, *Caradoc Evans* (1946)] · d. cert.

Archives NL Wales, letters

Likenesses E. Walters, oils, *c*.1931, NMG Wales · pencil sketch, repro. in *Modern Society* (16 Aug 1913) · photograph, repro. in Sandys, *Full and frank*, frontispiece [*see illus.*]

Evans, Marian [*pseud.* George Eliot] **(1819–1880)**, novelist, was known under several names during her life: Mary Anne Evans (at birth), Mary Ann Evans (from 1837), Marian Evans (from 1851), Marian Evans Lewes (from 1854), and Mary Ann Cross (1880).

Early life She was born Mary Anne Evans on 22 November 1819 at South Farm on the Arbury estate in the parish of Chilvers Coton, Warwickshire, the third child of the second marriage of Robert Evans (1773–1849), manager of the large estates of the Newdigate family of Arbury Hall. Robert Evans's work on the estate was wide-ranging. He not only surveyed land and buildings, managed relations with the tenant farmers on the estate, collected rents, oversaw repairs, and arranged the buying and selling of land, but was also involved in negotiations with road builders and coalmining businesses in the area. His journals and correspondence with Francis Newdigate show Evans to have been an inventive and inconsistent speller, but a man of integrity and determination, and one in whom his employer invested a great deal of trust and authority. The eponymous hero of George Eliot's first full-length novel, *Adam Bede* (1859), is based in some respects—particularly in regard to his pride in his work and his determination of character—on Robert Evans.

Robert Evans's first wife, Harriet Poynton, with whom he had a son, Robert (1802–1864), and a daughter, Fanny (1805–1882), died in 1809. In 1813 he married Christiana Pearson (1788?–1836), the daughter of a local farmer. The children of this marriage were Christiana, known as Chrissey (1814–1859), Isaac (1816–1890), and Mary Anne, the youngest, born in 1819. Twin sons were born in March 1821, but survived only a few days.

In the spring of 1820, when Mary Anne was only a few months old, the family moved from South Farm to a house known as Griff, situated just off the main road between Nuneaton and Coventry. This was her home until she was twenty-one. It was a large house with stables and outbuildings, a dairy and farmyard, and an orchard. In her semi-autobiographical sketch, 'Looking backward', found in her last published work, *Impressions of Theophrastus Such* (1879), George Eliot describes her native country as 'fat

Marian Evans [George Eliot] (**1819–1880**), by Sir Frederic William Burton, 1865

central England' with its elms, buttercups, and tree-studded hedgerows, but she remembers also the coalmining, the building of roads and railways, the cutting of canals to carry the coal from the mines. It was not all lush, rural, idyllic; many of the local villagers worked in the pits and lived in poor cottages on the Newdigate estate, and some of the tenant farmers lived in conditions of poverty rather than plenty. It was this varied nature of the rural life of her childhood that she later drew on for her novels, having as a child noticed the contrast between the lives of the tenants and that of the landed family at the magnificent Arbury Hall, where she was allowed, as a clever and serious schoolgirl, to browse in the family library.

At five Mary Anne boarded with Chrissey at Miss Lathom's school in nearby Attleborough; in 1828, when she was nine, she became a boarder at Mrs Wallington's school in Nuneaton. Here she came under the strong religious influence of an evangelical teacher, Maria Lewis, to whom most of her earliest extant letters—earnest, pious, and rather self-righteous—are addressed. From thirteen to sixteen she attended a school in Coventry run by Mary and Rebecca Franklin, the daughters of a Baptist minister. Religious dissent was strong in the midlands at this time; there were chapels of all denominations: Baptist, Wesleyan, Unitarian, Quaker, Congregationalist. Though her own family belonged to the middle-of-the-road Anglican community, Mary Anne herself was strongly evangelical. As a teenager she alarmed her brother Isaac by taking her

piety to extremes, frowning on theatregoing and neglecting her appearance—going about 'like an owl', as she said, 'to the great disgust of my brother' (Cross, 1.157).

At the Franklins' school Mary Anne won prizes in French and in English composition, and was known for her fine piano playing. Her schoolfellows later remembered her as a serious, clever girl, but a shy and sensitive one, who hated performing in public, and who often ran out of the room in tears. At Christmas 1835, when she was just sixteen, Mary Anne came home to a domestic crisis. Her mother, who had been in poor health since the death of the twins, was dying painfully of breast cancer.

After her mother's death in February 1836, Mary Anne stayed at home to help her sister Chrissey keep house. Her brother Isaac was now helping his father with the estate business, and would eventually take over from him, working for the next generation of the Newdigate family. In May 1837 Chrissey married Edward Clarke, a doctor in nearby Meriden. Mary Anne was bridesmaid, and when signing the register after the wedding, she dropped the 'e' from her forename. She now became housekeeper for her father and her brother Isaac. Although her schooling had ended with her mother's death and the assumption of domestic duties, she had continued to read widely and had lessons at home in Italian and German from a visiting tutor, Joseph Brezzi. She also read, under Maria Lewis's guidance, improving works such as the life of Wilberforce.

Isaac married in 1841, and it was decided that he and his wife, Sarah, should live at Griff. Robert Evans retired as agent to the Newdigates, and he and Mary Ann found another house. In March 1841 they moved to a comfortable house in Foleshill, on the outskirts of Coventry. Perhaps Robert Evans hoped that his youngest daughter would find a suitable husband in Coventry despite her plain looks and serious demeanour. Instead, she made a new set of friends who were to have an important influence on her future life.

Mary Ann Evans's piety at the age of twenty was remarkable even in an age of pious evangelicalism among the provincial middle and lower classes. The correspondence between her and Maria Lewis was serious, preoccupied with religious matters, and somewhat sentimental. Mary Ann christened Miss Lewis Veronica, signifying 'fidelity in friendship', and was in turn given the name Clematis, which meant, appropriately enough, 'mental beauty'. In their correspondence they discussed their reading, mostly of religious and morally edifying works. One such letter, written by Mary Ann in March 1841, ends with a paragraph full of earnest spiritual aspirations:

> May we both in our diverse but I trust converging paths be upheld and guided by the staff of Divine consolation and the light of Divine Wisdom. How beautiful is the 63d Psalm. 'Because Thy loving kindness is better than life my lips shall praise thee. Thus will I bless thee while I live, I will lift up my hands in thy name, my soul shall be satisfied as with marrow and fatness, and my mouth shall praise thee with joyful lips' etc. I feel strongly reproved by this picture of entire satisfaction in God as a portion. (*Letters*, 1.82)

Like her semi-autobiographical fictional character Maggie Tulliver in *The Mill on the Floss*, Mary Ann eventually reacted against such extreme piety and saintliness. Her intellectual curiosity led her to read widely in non-religious literature: Shakespeare, Scott, Cervantes, Schiller, Thomas Carlyle. After the move in 1841 to Foleshill she also came under the influence of the attractive Bray family of Coventry.

Life in Coventry Charles Bray (1811–1884) was a wealthy ribbon manufacturer, a progressive in politics, and a philanthropist who used his wealth to set up schools and to support hospitals, all with a view to improving the social conditions of the poor. He was a freethinker in religion, a robust and original man, who did not care what his neighbours thought of him. In his autobiography, *Phases of Opinion and Experience during a Long Life* (1884), Bray remembered with pride how his large house, Rosehill, was a Mecca for radicals and intellectuals who enjoyed the 'free-and-easy mental atmosphere' and 'the absence of all pretension and conventionality' which prevailed there. According to him, 'Every one who came to Coventry with a queer mission, or a crotchet, or was supposed to be "a little cracked", was sent up to Rosehill' (Bray, 69–70).

Along with his quiet wife, Cara, herself inclined to piety but not an orthodox Christian, and Cara's sister and brother, Sara and Charles Hennell, Bray offered Mary Ann an intellectually challenging milieu. Already bookish and well read in several languages, she became interested in historical accounts of the Bible—one by Charles Hennell and several by German Biblical historians—which cast doubt on the accounts of miracles and on the supernatural elements in the gospels.

By the end of 1841, at the age of twenty-two, after reading, among other works of historical scholarship, Charles Hennell's *Inquiry Concerning the Origin of Christianity* (1838), Mary Ann had come to the view that Christianity was based on 'mingled truth and fiction' (*Letters*, 1.28). On 2 January 1842 she refused to go to church. Her action resulted in anger and silence on the part of her father, which lasted for some months. Her brother Isaac told her she was jeopardizing the family's good name by associating with Coventry radicals and infidels. He despaired of her ever finding a husband, now that she was adding unorthodox opinions to her plain appearance. Robert Evans almost turned his daughter out of the house, but eventually he relented, and from then on an uneasy truce existed between them. She continued to keep house for him until he died in 1849, trying to be a dutiful daughter, but reserving the right to hold her own opinions on the subject of religion and to continue her friendship with the Brays.

At Rosehill, Mary Ann met many liberal thinkers, including the social philosophers Herbert Spencer and Harriet Martineau, the social experimentalist Robert Owen, the radical publisher John Chapman, and Ralph Waldo Emerson on his visits from America. At the end of 1843, when Charles Hennell married Rufa Brabant, it was arranged that Mary Ann should take over from Rufa the

translation of David Friedrich Strauss's scholarly investigation of the gospels published in 1835–6, *Das Leben Jesu, kritisch bearbeitet* (*The Life of Jesus, Critically Examined*). Mary Ann was the obvious person to take on the task. She was the most learned member of the Bray–Hennell circle, having made a close study of the Bible, first as ardent evangelical, then as historical critic. And she knew German. In 1846 John Chapman published, in three volumes, her translation of this work, which painstakingly investigated the events of Christ's life as told in all four gospels and found them to be not historical, but mythological—the wished-for fulfilment of Old Testament prophecies. Mary Ann received £20 for her labours.

Chapman was also to publish *The Essence of Christianity* (1854), her second translation of a German work demystifying scripture, Ludwig Feuerbach's *Das Wesen des Christenthums* (1841). The translation was the only work to be published under her name, Marian Evans. Both Strauss, and, more particularly, Feuerbach had an influence on her own position, illustrated widely in her novels, as a humanist for whom relations between people have all the sanctity reserved in orthodox religion for the relationship between the individual and God.

Though still a serious young woman, inclined to depression and self-doubt and painfully conscious of her plain appearance, Mary Ann began to show that she was not just formidably intelligent and knowledgeable, but also sharp-witted and imaginatively gifted. In October 1846 Charles Bray received a letter in which she gave evidence that she possessed all the qualities required of a novelist: wit, wisdom, imagination, and an ability to turn her own experience to good account fictionally. She exploits with playful ease the hard intellectual labour, not without its *longueurs*, of translating Strauss's work in her description to Bray of a (fictitious) visit from a Professor Bücherwurm of Moderig University (Professor Bookworm of Musty University):

> Down I came, not a little elated at the idea that a live professor was in the house, and, as you know I have quite the average quantity of that valuable endowment which spiteful people call assurance, but which I dignify with the name of self possession, you will believe that I neither blushed nor made a nervous giggle in attempting to smile, as is the lot of some unfortunate young ladies who are immersed in youthful bashfulness. (*Letters*, 8.13)

Professor Bücherwurm is, by his own account, 'a voluminous author—indeed my works already amount to some 20 vols.—my last publication in 5 vols. was a commentary on the book of Tobit'. He has come to England in search of a wife who will double as the translator of his scholarly works, and he is idiosyncratic enough to desire, 'besides ability to translate, a very decided ugliness of person and a sufficient fortune to supply a poor professor with coffee and tobacco, and an occasional draft of schwarzbier, as well as to contribute to the expenses of publication'. He expresses himself satisfied that Mary Ann fulfils these criteria, though he regrets that she has no beard, 'an attribute which I have ever regarded as the most unfailing indication of a strong-minded woman'.

Mary Ann tells Bray how delighted she was by this proposal, since she is desperate to be saved from the 'horrific disgrace of spinster-hood' and to be taken away from England. The letter turns her learning to light-hearted and witty account, and makes a brave joke about her plain looks and her anxiety that, at the age of nearly twenty-seven, she may not find a husband, as well as providing a shrewd preparatory sketch for Mr Casaubon in *Middlemarch*. Furthermore, her ability here to illustrate her story by means of allusions, analogies, and metaphors drawn from literature, science, religion, and history gives a foretaste of the distinctiveness of her gifts as a novelist with a truly remarkable range of reference.

The next few years were for Mary Ann a lonely and painful time. She had to nurse her father through a long illness, during which he was demanding and often ungrateful. She was exhausted, physically and emotionally, when he died on 31 May 1849. Robert Evans was buried in Chilvers Coton churchyard, next to his wife. His property was divided between his sons Robert and Isaac; Fanny and Chrissey, who had been given £1000 each when they married, received another £1000 in his will, as well as household items. Mary Ann was left £2000 in trust, a sum which, when invested, would yield about £90 a year in interest, not quite enough to live on without supplementary earnings, but enough to encourage her to consider living independently. She might have gone to live with her married brother Isaac, resigning herself to a life of plain sewing, playing the piano, and reading to her nephews and nieces in a household of conventional religious and social observance which was to her stiflingly narrow. But she knew that she and Isaac disagreed about everything: politics, religion, and the duties of younger sisters to obey their older brothers. Although she got on better with her sister Chrissey, married to Edward Clarke, a struggling doctor (who died in 1852), she had no wish to settle with Chrissey's family either.

While Mary Ann wondered what to do next, the Brays generously offered to take her with them on a trip to Switzerland and Italy. After six weeks of travelling, the Brays returned to England, leaving her in Geneva, where she bravely took lodgings and spent a winter trying out her new found independence, and taking stock. A sympathetic family, the D'Albert Durades, took her in as a paying guest. François D'Albert Durade, who later translated several of her novels into French, was an artist. He painted her portrait in February 1850, representing her as modest, pensive, long-faced, but pleasant looking. Mary Ann spent her time in Geneva reading, walking, learning mathematics, and continuing with a translation (never to be finished) of Spinoza's *Tractatus theologico-politicus* which she had begun during her father's illness.

When she returned to England in March 1850, Mary Ann had more or less made up her mind to move to London and pursue a career in journalism. A short stay with Isaac and his family at Griff, followed by a rather less painful visit to Chrissey at Meriden, convinced her that she could not make her home among them. The decision to move to London was a momentous one, and was accompanied by a change of name. She now called herself Marian Evans, and in January 1851 she took up lodgings in the Strand.

Journalistic career in London Thanks to the Brays, Marian Evans had an immediate entrée into the world of radical politics and journalism, of free thinking, and in some cases of free living too. The Chapman household at 142 Strand was itself a most unconventional one. The three-storey building, looking over Somerset House and the Thames at the back, was both the workplace and the home of the publisher John Chapman, who specialized in publishing works of a left-wing or sceptical tendency. He had been impressed by Marian's intellect and by her stamina in completing the translation of Strauss. He came to value these qualities even more when in 1851 he bought the great radical periodical, the *Westminster Review*, first set up in the 1820s to further the cause of political and social reform in the long run-up to the Reform Act of 1832. Marian Evans became, in effect, the editor of the *Review*, as well as one of its best and most widely admired reviewers.

On the upper floors of 142 Strand lived Chapman's family and a number of lodgers—mainly literary people whose books he published or who wrote for the *Westminster Review*. Chapman held Friday night parties, when writers gathered to talk about literature and politics of a mainly radical kind. It was through Chapman that Marian Evans met Herbert *Spencer (1820–1903) and his friend, the critic George Henry *Lewes (1817–1878), with both of whom she was to fall in love. But first she succumbed to the charms of Chapman himself. He was handsome, worldly, successful, and his admiration for her abilities flattered Marian. Chapman lived with his wife, Susanna, a woman fourteen years older than he was—Chapman was thirty in 1851—their two children, and the children's governess, Elisabeth Tilley, who was also Chapman's mistress.

Into this unusual household came Marian Evans, a provincial young woman of plain and earnest appearance but of strong will and strong passion. Over the next few months a comedy was played out, with Chapman arousing the jealousy of both his wife (who seems to have accepted the governess's role in their lives) and his mistress by the attention he gave to the new guest. He visited Marian Evans's room, where she played the piano for him and taught him German. They were caught holding hands. Mrs Chapman and Elisabeth joined forces to expel the interloper, sending her, literally, to Coventry, where she fled in tears to the Brays, upset by Chapman's assurances that he admired her mental beauty (Clematis again), but found her lacking in physical charm.

Sensibly, Marian abandoned all hopes of Chapman as a lover and—establishing a pattern which she was also to follow with Herbert Spencer—settled down to a friendly, professional relationship with him. The women at 142 Strand relented, and in the autumn of 1851 Chapman brought Marian back to London, where she began to guide him in the editorial department of the *Westminster Review*. He was the nominal editor, while she, from a mixture of diffidence, modesty, and fear of playing a public role, was happy to remain behind the scenes, doing the work and letting Chapman put his name to it.

Marian's social life blossomed in London. Sometimes accompanied by Chapman, she attended lectures in geometry at the new Ladies' College in Regent's Park, later renamed Bedford College. She also frequently walked across the Strand to see plays put on at the Lyceum Theatre in Catherine Street (now Aldwych). Among these was *The Game of Speculation*, G. H. Lewes's successful adaptation of Balzac's *Mercadet*, which opened at the Lyceum in October 1851 and ran for ninety-four performances. It was in October 1851, too, that Marian Evans first met Lewes. Chapman introduced them on 6 October at William Jeffs's bookshop in the Burlington Arcade. Marian reported to the Brays that Lewes was 'a sort of miniature Mirabeau in appearance', a reference to his slight physique and plain looks (*Letters*, 1.367).

Marian worked closely with Chapman on the *Westminster Review* until 1854. She was invaluable to him with her sharp brain, wide knowledge, willing labour, and ability to deal tactfully yet firmly with touchy contributors. Chapman himself lacked all these qualities, as one of the chief contributors and supporters of the *Review*, George Combe, pointed out to him. Combe was a well-known phrenologist, a practitioner of that 'science' by which character was to be read by feeling the contours of the head. In 1851 he felt Marian Evans's bumps at Bray's house, and concluded, 'she appeared to me the ablest woman I have seen', having 'a very large brain', and large bumps of 'concentrativeness', and 'love of approbation' (*Letters*, 8.27–8). He advised Chapman in December 1851 to 'use Miss Evans's tact and judgment as an aid to your own', continuing, 'She has certain organs large in her brain which are not so fully developed in yours, and she will judge more correctly of the influence upon other persons of what you write and do, than you will do yourself' (ibid., 8.33). On hearing three years later that Marian Evans had gone to Germany with the married G. H. Lewes, Combe was horrified. He wrote to Bray in November 1854: 'I should like to know whether there is insanity in Miss Evans's family; for her conduct, with *her* brain, seems to me like morbid mental aberration' (ibid., 8.129).

Marian gained from the partnership with Chapman a widened social circle, the experience of running a review under cover of anonymity, the freedom to take decisions, and the chance to review works for the *Westminster* on topics ranging from English, French, and German literature to science to philosophy to evangelical sermons. Although at first she worked in return for board and lodgings at Chapman's house, from 1855 she was paid between £12 and £20 per article, earning between £60 and £120 per annum for her journalism (*Letters*, 7.358–9). She found her voice as a writer in her work for the *Westminster Review* from 1851 to 1856. In the essayist, increasingly confident, wide-ranging, witty, and rhetorically complex, we can see many of the characteristics of the future novelist George Eliot.

Marian Evans's social position as a single working woman in London in the early 1850s was extremely unusual. Generally, women of small means either married (whereupon their income promptly became their husbands' property under the law) or took jobs as governesses or live-in companions to rich relations or acquaintances. Marian herself had thought of becoming a teacher in Leamington Spa when her father threatened to make her leave the house in 1842, but had not relished the idea of becoming a domestic slave in a strange household or boarding establishment. On the other hand, there was a risk attached to cutting loose. Her brother disapproved of the move to London, making her feel that she would no longer be welcome in his home, even for visits. She was now in a society composed entirely of men, and though it was intellectually stimulating to associate with them freely, she was risking her reputation in doing so. She must often, too, have missed the companionship of a female friend in London, although she still corresponded with Cara Bray and Sara Hennell in Coventry.

In one letter to them in May 1852 Marian reported a great occasion at 142 Strand. On 4 May Chapman held a meeting of publishers, writers, and booksellers to protest against the Booksellers' Association, a cartel of larger publishers which fixed the price of books, prohibiting small publishers like Chapman from offering discounts. Dickens took the chair, 'preserving', according to Marian, 'a courteous neutrality of eyebrow, and speaking with clearness and decision' (*Letters*, 2.23). Many famous liberals and radicals were there: Herbert Spencer, Lewes, the scientist Richard Owen, Wilkie Collins, and many more distinguished men. Marian Evans was also there—the only woman.

Marian's position was a remarkable one, as several of her acquaintances noted. In 1885 William Hale White read the biography of George Eliot written by John Walter Cross (1840–1924), whom she had married in 1880, and was moved to write his recollection of Marian Evans, who had been his fellow lodger in the Strand in the early 1850s:

> She was really one of the most sceptical, unusual creatures I ever knew, and it was this side of her character which was to me the most attractive ... I can see her now, with her hair over her shoulders, the easy chair half sideways to the fire, her feet over the arms, and a proof in her hands, in that dark room at the back of No. 142, and I confess I hardly recognize her in the pages of Mr Cross's—on many accounts—most interesting volumes. I do hope that in some future edition, or in some future work, the salt and spice will be restored to the records of George Eliot's entirely unconventional life. (*The Athenaeum*, 28 Nov 1885)

Hale White was right. Cross took great liberties with his wife's letters, removing any phrases he thought controversial or compromising (*Letters*, 1.xiii). One wonders what Cross would have made of a letter to Chapman in February 1856, in which Marian vigorously urges him not to print in the *Westminster* an article by a Miss H on the French woman writer George Sand. She describes Miss H (Matilda Hays) as 'one of the numerous class of female scribblers who undertake to edify the public before they know the proper use of their own language'. The article is made up of 'feminine rant of the worst kind, which it will be simply fatal to the Review to admit' (Ashton, 'New George Eliot letters', 121–2). Further, 'I would not trust the most ordinary subject, still less the most delicate, to a woman who writes such trash'; and 'Everything she says about George Sand is undiscriminating Bosh'.

All of Marian's letters to Chapman about the conduct of the *Review* are like this, confident, wide-ranging, managerial, even magisterial towards her employer, the attractive, desirable, but intellectually inferior man of the world.

This unconventional young woman, who had attended lectures, theatre, and opera during 1851 with Chapman, was soon going to the theatre and opera with Herbert Spencer. By June 1852 Marian was reporting to the Brays that she and Spencer were seen so often in one another's company that 'all the world is setting us down as engaged' (*Letters*, 2.35). Marian would have liked nothing better, but Spencer was less keen. In July Marian went off alone to Broadstairs on holiday; from there she sent several managing letters to Chapman about the *Westminster Review*, careful letters to Combe, whom Chapman was pressing for money to help the *Review* out of a financial crisis, and, at the same time, love letters to Spencer. She wrote begging him to visit her at Broadstairs. All her passion and pride and humour are on display, as well as her loneliness and uncertainty:

> Dear Friend
> No credit to me for my virtues as a refrigerent. I owe them all to a few lumps of ice which I carried away with me from that tremendous glacier of yours. I am glad that Nemesis, lame as she is, has already made you feel a little uneasy in my absence, whether from the state of the thermometer [a reference to the very high temperatures that July] or aught else. We will not inquire too curiously whether you long most for my society or for the sea-breezes. If you decided that I was not worth coming to see, it would only be of a piece with that generally exasperating perspicacity of yours which will not allow one to humbug you. (An agreeable quality, let me tell you, that capacity of being humbugged. Don't pique yourself on not possessing it.)   (ibid., 8.50–51)

Spencer did visit Marian briefly in Broadstairs and obviously discouraged her, for a week later she wrote again, almost proposing marriage to him:

> Those who have known me best have always said, that if ever I loved any one thoroughly my whole life must turn upon that feeling, and I find they say truly. You curse the destiny which has made the feeling concentrate itself on you—but if you will only have patience with me you shall not curse it long. You will find that I can be satisfied with very little, if I am delivered from the dread of losing it.   (*Letters*, 8.56–7)

Finally, she asserts her sense of self-worth, admitting that probably 'no woman ever before wrote such a letter as this', but insisting she is not ashamed, 'for I am conscious that in the light of reason and true refinement I am worthy of your respect and tenderness, whatever gross men or vulgar-minded women might think of me' (ibid., 8.57).

These letters to Spencer give some insight into how, when she came to write fiction, George Eliot could be so penetrating in her analyses of the complex relations between men and women, both those who marry and those—like Maggie Tulliver with Stephen Guest and Philip Wakem, or like Gwendolen Grandcourt with Daniel Deronda—who have intimate relationships which do not end in marriage.

Life with G. H. Lewes   By 1853 G. H. Lewes had replaced Spencer in Marian Evans's affections, and fortunately he returned them. He, too, was a regular contributor to the *Westminster Review*, as well as theatre critic for *The Leader*, the weekly paper which he co-edited with his friend Thornton Hunt. Lewes, two years older than Marian, had had a busy and varied career. From an insecure background, brought up by his mother and a hated stepfather, with a miscellaneous schooling, he had worked his way to prominence in literary London by means of prodigious talent, versatility, and hard work.

When Marian Evans met Lewes in Jeffs's bookshop in October 1851 he was already the author of a popular history of philosophy; two novels; several plays and adaptations of French farces, some of which Marian saw at the Lyceum with Chapman or Spencer; a biography of Robespierre; and hundreds of articles and reviews. He was planning a life of Goethe. He had acted successfully with Dickens's amateur theatre company, and had even toyed with the idea of going on the stage professionally. Like Marian he was fluent in French and German, and widely read in literature, philosophy, and science. He had no religious faith. He was married and unable to sue for a divorce.

In February 1841 Lewes had married Agnes Jervis (1822–1902), the beautiful eighteen-year-old daughter of a radical MP, Swynfen Jervis. They had agreed to have an open marriage, the result of which was that in addition to having three surviving sons by Lewes, Agnes had by 1851 borne two children whose father was not Lewes, but his friend Thornton Hunt. She was to have two more children by Hunt in 1853 and 1857. Lewes, having entered on this open marriage, registered the first two of these children as his own. When he subsequently met and fell in love with Marian Evans, he could not sue for divorce, as under the terms of the law he had condoned his wife's adultery by registering the births of her children by Hunt in his own name. Though he was by 1853 disillusioned with his domestic arrangements—and notably did not register the birth of Agnes's daughter Ethel, born in October 1853—he had disqualified himself from ever seeking a divorce.

He had, however, left Agnes, probably in 1852, although he visited her and his children frequently at their home in Kensington, supported them financially, and was generous to Agnes for the rest of his life, as was Marian after his death. Agnes, who outlived them both by many years, living on until 1902, received amounts of between £100 and £250 per annum (Haight, *Biography*, 370, 460–61, 491). According to Marian's close friend Barbara Leigh Smith (later Mme Bodichon), Lewes and Marian chose not to have children of their own (ibid., 205). Marian, who instinctively shrank from publicity and from scandal—though ironically the great decisions of her life involved her in both—did not want to bear children who would suffer from having parents who were not married.

In October 1853 Marian moved to new lodgings at 21 Cambridge Street, Hyde Park Square, where she could receive Lewes less publicly than at 142 Strand. It has long been thought that their liaison dated from this move of hers, but it can be shown that they were probably intimate by the end of 1852 or beginning of 1853. In fact, it seems that Marian was already attracted to Lewes while she was still 'in love' with Spencer (Ashton, *Lewes*, 132–43). She knew from her own experience that it is possible to be confused in one's emotional life, and the heroines of George Eliot's novels are often in a state of doubt about their feelings. Maggie Tulliver, the most obviously autobiographical of them, certainly loves two men at once—or three, when one considers that her deepest feelings are those for her brother Tom. We can see something of a similar dilemma in Marian's life in the letters she wrote to the Brays during 1852–3.

Surprisingly perhaps, the Brays did not much like Lewes. Unorthodox though they were, they thought him bohemian, flippant, metropolitan, not quite respectable (though this showed some hypocrisy on Bray's part, since he kept a mistress by whom he had a daughter, Elinor, whom he and Cara, who was childless, had adopted).

Throughout 1852 and early 1853 Marian was meeting Lewes regularly in the company of Spencer, with whom Lewes was friendly, and her letters to the Brays during the 'romance' with Spencer often mention Lewes too. In June 1852 the Brays were obviously trying to bring Spencer to the brink of a proposal to Marian. They invited Spencer to visit them in Coventry later that summer, when Marian would also be there. Marian connived at the matchmaking. Lewes was also invited to visit, though not at the same time as Spencer. Marian's response was a rather excited and contradictory one:

> *Entre nous*, if Mr Lewes should not accept your invitation now, pray don't ask him when I am with you—not that I don't like him—*au contraire*—but I want nothing so Londonish when I go to enjoy the fields and hedgerows and yet more, friends of ten years' growth. (*Letters*, 2.37)

In the end, Marian visited the Brays alone at the end of October, having clarified her position with Spencer in Broadstairs in July. Meanwhile, she had been reading on this holiday Lewes's not very good novel *Rose, Blanche and Violet* (1848), and her letters from this point on have frequent references to his articles for the *Westminster* and his activities as theatre critic of his own weekly newspaper, *The Leader*. Soon she was going to the theatre with Lewes, not Spencer. On her thirty-third birthday, 22 November 1852, she wrote to the Brays describing her day. After lunch she had just got down to work when, 'with two clear hours before dinner, rap at the door—Mr Lewes—who of course sits talking till the second bell rings' (*Letters*, 2.68).

Marian found herself often defending Lewes against criticism. She told Cara Bray in April 1853 that Lewes was 'a man of heart and conscience wearing a mask of flippancy' (*Letters*, 2.98). In December 1853 she wrote a strong letter to Chapman, trying to get him to refuse an article by the new star on the scientific horizon, T. H. Huxley, in which Huxley attacked Lewes's book, *Comte's Philosophy of the Sciences*, praising Harriet Martineau's rival book, an abridged translation of Comte's work. Lewes's book had

been published by Bohn, Martineau's by Chapman himself. Marian frankly advises Chapman to 'expunge' Huxley's review from the *Westminster*:

> My opinion is, that the editors of the Review will disgrace themselves by inserting an utterly worthless & unworthy notice of a work by one of their own writers—a man of much longer & higher standing than Mr. Huxley, & whom Mr. H's seniors in science & superiors both in intellect & fame treat with respect. (Ashton, 'New George Eliot letters', 120)

In another letter written probably on the same day, she added, 'Do you really think that if you had been the publisher of Mr. Lewes's book and Bohn the publisher of Miss Martineau's, Mr. Huxley would have written just so? "Tell that to the Marines"' (*Letters*, 2.133).

It was probably in late 1852 or early 1853 that Marian and Lewes became lovers. Some time in 1853 they reached a momentous decision—more significant for her than for him—the decision to live together openly as man and wife. Once more Marian Evans changed her name, though not legally. From now on she called herself Mrs Lewes or Marian Evans Lewes. Although it was not uncommon for Victorian men to have mistresses—as Bray, Chapman, and Wilkie Collins did—such arrangements were usually kept quiet. This was different. Marian and Lewes made no secret of their liaison, which they considered a true marriage. Marian's reputation suffered most. As she wrote in September 1855 to her old friend Cara Bray, who at first could not bring herself to see Marian:

> Light and easily broken ties are what I neither desire theoretically nor could live for practically. Women who are satisfied with such ties do not act as I have done—they obtain what they desire and are still invited to dinner. (*Letters*, 2.214)

George Eliot often puts her heroines in difficult—even dangerous—emotional situations in which they attract criticism from society for breaking, or appearing to break, its social rules. Dorothea begins to love Will Ladislaw even while she is dutifully married to Mr Casaubon; it is a tribute to George Eliot's power as a writer, and her knowledge of human nature, that she persuades us that Dorothea herself is unaware of her feelings for Ladislaw. She shows, of course, that Mr Casaubon himself is all too aware of the attraction between his young wife and his young cousin.

The Mill on the Floss, her most autobiographical novel in the portrayal of the childhood relationship between Tom and Maggie Tulliver, is also the novel in which George Eliot comes closest to describing prohibited relationships. Maggie falls in love with Stephen Guest against all her wishes and her sense of prior duties. They elope together, and then Maggie returns without consummating the affair, but to all appearances the fallen woman. George Eliot launches a strong attack on society's way of thinking the worst in relations between the sexes, pointing out how much harder public opinion is on the woman in such situations than on the man:

> It was soon known throughout St. Ogg's that Miss Tulliver was come back: she had not, then, eloped in order to be married to Mr Stephen Guest—at all events, Mr Stephen Guest had not married her—which came to the same thing,

so far as her culpability was concerned. We judge others according to results; how else?—not knowing the process by which results are arrived at. If Miss Tulliver, after a few months of well-chosen travel, had returned as Mrs Stephen Guest—with a post-marital trousseau and all the advantages possessed even by the most unwelcome wife of an only son, public opinion, which at St. Ogg's, as elsewhere, always knew what to think, would have judged in strict consistency with those results.

   …

   But the results, we know, were not of a kind to warrant this extenuation of the past. Maggie had returned without a trousseau, without a husband—in that degraded and outcast condition to which error is well known to lead; and the world's wife, with that fine instinct which is given her for the preservation of society, saw at once that Miss Tulliver's conduct had been of the most aggravated kind. (*The Mill on the Floss*, bk 7, chap. 2)

In 1854 Lewes and Marian, after telling only a few friends of their plans, embarked publicly on their unorthodox relationship. They did so out of England. As Lewes needed to visit Weimar and Berlin to research his life of Goethe, it was to Weimar that they went together in July 1854, Marian sending her famous telegram on 19 July to Charles and Cara Bray and Sara Hennell:

Dear Friends—all three
   I have only time to say good bye and God bless you. Poste Restante, Weimar for the next six weeks, and afterwards Berlin. (*Letters*, 2.166)

While acquaintances in London and Coventry discussed the liaison (with Chapman and Bray joining in the head-shaking and moralizing), Marian and Lewes settled down to hard work and social pleasure at Weimar. Lewes worked on his biography of Goethe, helped in the translation of extracts by Marian. She also spent time translating Spinoza's *Ethics*, a work which, with its stress on man's self-love being naturally balanced by the love of society and a natural sympathy with others of his species, was at least as influential on George Eliot's own humanism as were Feuerbach's and Comte's versions of the religion of humanity. Unfortunately, Lewes quarrelled with the publisher Bohn on their return to England about the financial terms for Marian's translation, which remained unpublished until 1981.

In Weimar the Leweses met the composer Franz Liszt, who was living with a married woman without raising eyebrows. Marian and Lewes, too, were able to go about together without shocking anyone. But on their return to England in March 1855, Marian found that she was no longer accepted in mixed society. She and Lewes found lodgings first at Clarence Row, East Sheen, then at 8 Park Shot, Richmond, where they remained until February 1859, by which time George Eliot had sprung on the world with the publication of *Scenes of Clerical Life* in 1858 and the extremely successful *Adam Bede* in February 1859. Their male friends from the *Westminster Review* circle visited, of course, as before, but did not bring their wives. Marian had to tell her enthusiastic feminist friend Bessie Parkes to address letters to Mrs Lewes, not Miss Evans, so as not to arouse the suspicion of the landlady. Lewes was invited out to dinner, but not Marian.

In 1856 Marian, encouraged by Lewes, first tried her hand at fiction. Despite the anonymity of her journalism, she was already well known in London's literary circles as the author of several trenchant articles and reviews in the *Westminster Review* on a variety of subjects, including the writing of fiction. In her article 'The natural history of German life' (July 1856) she advocated a particular (Spinozan) kind of realism in art: 'The greatest benefit we owe to the artist, whether painter, poet, or novelist, is the extension of our sympathies'; and 'Art is the nearest thing to life; it is a mode of amplifying our experience and extending our contact with our fellow-men beyond the bounds of our personal lot' (*Essays*, 270–71). These remarks read like a manifesto for the kind of fiction she was very soon to write herself.

One of the last articles Marian wrote for Chapman before beginning 'The Sad Fortunes of the Reverend Amos Barton', the first of the three stories which made up *Scenes of Clerical Life*, was a sparklingly witty attack on the 'left-handed imbecility' of certain minor female novelists. Called 'Silly novels by lady novelists', and published in the *Westminster Review* in October 1856, it divides the novels according to certain classes: 'the *mind-and-millinery* species', 'the *oracular* species', and 'the *white neck-cloth* species'. This last type represents evangelicalism, a subject Marian knew much about from her early life as well as from her wide reading. She criticizes those contemporary novelists who mix evangelical religion with high society. 'The real drama of Evangelicalism', she writes, 'for any one who has genius enough to discern and reproduce it—lies among the middle and lower classes' (*Essays*, 318). Whereupon she set about showing how it could, and should, be done.

The emergence of George Eliot Partly because of her anomalous social position, and partly because she had always liked to work anonymously, Marian Evans chose to write under a pseudonym. In November 1856 Lewes sent the manuscript of 'Amos Barton' to the Edinburgh publisher John Blackwood, saying it was by a 'shy, ambitious' friend of his (*Letters*, 2.269, 276). No name was given for this unknown author, and Blackwood actually began corresponding, via Lewes, with 'My Dear Amos'. He knew he was dealing with a potentially great writer, telling his mysterious correspondent in January 1857 that he had recently confided to Thackeray that he had 'lighted upon a new Author who is uncommonly like a first class passenger' (ibid., 2.291). Marian replied to this praise on 4 February 1857, signing herself for the first time George Eliot. The name was chosen, as she later told Cross, because George was Lewes's forename and Eliot was 'a good mouth-filling, easily pronounced word' (Cross, 1.431).

Other Victorian women published under male pseudonyms: most famously, the Brontë sisters had published their works in the 1840s under the names Currer, Ellis, and Acton Bell. But it would be wrong to think that women found it necessary to hide behind a masculine name in order to be published and appreciated. Novel writing had long been recognized as a genre suitable for women to write—particularly the novel of social manners, a subject which they could be expected to know about. Fanny Burney and Maria Edgeworth had written under their own names at the beginning of the century, and Elizabeth Gaskell was happy to write her novels without recourse to a pseudonym.

But Marian Evans was known as the freethinking radical of the *Westminster Review*, the 'strong-minded woman', as Carlyle called her (*Letters*, 2.176n.), and the woman who was living with a married man. She needed the protection of a pseudonym. It also suited her constitutional diffidence and fear of failure to conceal her identity, as it had suited her to be the unnamed though independent and managing editor of Chapman's *Westminster Review*. Moreover, once it was known that George Eliot was Marian Evans, or Mrs Lewes, the pseudonym endured, in contrast to the Bell pseudonyms of the Brontës. One probable reason for this was the difficulty her contemporaries experienced in addressing or naming the author—was she to be called Miss Evans, or Mrs Lewes? The pseudonym solved the problem. Another reason may be the strong narrative voice of George Eliot, with its echoes of the genial, man of the world tone of a Fielding or a Scott, together with the range of reference employed by a narrator who seems equally *au fait* with the domestic (and hence usually female) and the public and professional (usually male) spheres.

The three stories which together make up *Scenes of Clerical Life*—'The Sad Fortunes of the Rev. Amos Barton', 'Mr Gilfil's Love Story', and 'Janet's Repentance'—have some awkwardness of structure. Their slow expositions, intended to embody George Eliot's Wordsworthian view that there is abundant passion and interest in ordinary working lives, are followed by hasty, even melodramatic conclusions. But with their deft contextualizing and strong dialogue, they indicated the arrival of a fresh new talent among Victorian writers of fiction. The *Scenes of Clerical Life* were published serially in *Blackwood's Magazine* from January to November 1857, often appearing on facing pages with Lewes's lively work of popularizing marine biology, *Sea-Side Studies*, which was being serialized at the same time. Marian was paid £260 for the serialization in *Blackwood's*, and £180 for the separate publication in book form which followed in 1858 (*Letters*, 7.359–60). Meanwhile, she had taken the decision to tell her family in Warwickshire of her new life with Lewes. She wrote to Isaac, who, when he ascertained that her marriage was not a legal one, instructed his solicitor to inform his sister that he wished to have no more contact with her. He prevailed on their sister Chrissey and half-sister Fanny to stop corresponding too. It was a blow to Marian's feelings, although she was not surprised at Isaac's disapproval, having encountered it at the time of losing her faith and again when she made the move to London.

Encouraged by the success of her three clerical stories, Marian soon set about writing her first full-length novel, *Adam Bede*, which brought her instant fame on its publication in February 1859. Dickens admired it (and guessed the author was a woman); Elizabeth Gaskell was flattered to be asked if she had written it. The novel evokes pastoral romance and the picturesque qualities of country life around 1800, while at the same time embodying George Eliot's ideas of realism as expounded in her essays and in *Scenes of Clerical Life*. She catches the ugliness as well as the beauty, the unkindness as well as the neighbourliness, of country life. A conventional story of the seduction of a young country woman, Hetty Sorrel, by the squire in waiting, Arthur Donnithorne, is handled in a distinctly unconventional way, with several chapters devoted to the pregnant Hetty's lonely and desperate journey in search of her lover. Also, unusually, George Eliot wins the reader's interest for her saintly heroine, Dinah Morris, the Methodist preacher modelled in some respects on Marian's aunt Elizabeth Evans, wife of her father's brother Samuel, who had converted to Methodism as a young man.

Inevitably, gossip got to work, both in London's literary circles, where Herbert Spencer let out the secret of the authorship, and in Warwickshire, where readers, including members of Marian Evans's estranged family, recognized characters and settings in both *Scenes of Clerical Life* and *Adam Bede*. Authorship was claimed for a midlands man called Joseph Liggins, who, although he himself never went into print on the subject, allowed others to do so without refuting the claim. The 'Liggins business' lasted for two years, with letters being written in *The Times* and the pro-Liggins faction, which included Mrs Gaskell, refusing to accept Blackwood's public statements denying that Liggins was the author. The business of keeping her identity secret, although important to the sensitive Marian, caused her anguish, and the persistence of the Liggins myth, combined with the rumours of literary London, led her at last to admit defeat and allow it to be known, in June 1859, that George Eliot was Marian Evans, alias Mrs Lewes.

Marian's friends were, on the whole, pleased, although Sara Hennell felt jealous and suddenly left behind by a friend now departed into 'glory', and Herbert Spencer also showed resentment at his friend's tremendous success (*Letters*, 3.49n., 95–6). Cara Bray, who had taken a long time to accept the liaison with Lewes, wrote warmly congratulating her friend, and robust feminist friends like Bessie Parkes and Barbara Bodichon were jubilant both at her success and at the discomfort of those who disapproved of her life.

On discovering the identity of George Eliot, many readers and critics were shocked to find that the novelist they had welcomed for her humanity, her humour, her tolerance, and the moral—though neither moralistic nor religious—ethos of her work was none other than the freethinking, free-loving (as the caricature of her relationship with Lewes went) Marian Evans. In due course society adjusted to the shock of finding that one of its greatest writers was an unbeliever and a woman in a compromising social position. By the time George Eliot's sixth and greatest novel, *Middlemarch*, had appeared in 1871–2, her status as England's finest living novelist was assured.

But at the time of *Adam Bede* itself, Marian found that her enjoyment of its success—with accolades in all the journals and sales of more than 10,000 copies in the first year, well beyond her, or Blackwood's, wildest dreams—was soured by the Liggins problem and the uproar in some

quarters which followed on the lifting of the veil of anonymity. Only Lewes's encouragement and cheerfulness
and Blackwood's firm and friendly support—he sent her
an extra £400 for *Adam Bede* on top of the £800 he had originally paid for it, in order to give her a fair share in its
unexpected success—kept her from giving up fiction and
even, according to Lewes in September 1859, leaving England altogether to get away from the 'fools' who 'obtrude
themselves upon her' (*Letters*, 8.245). Marian's debt to
Lewes is eloquently expressed on the manuscript of the
novel (now in the British Library), which she dedicated to
him: 'To my dear husband, George Henry Lewes, I give this
M.S. of a work which would never have been written but
for the happiness which his love has conferred on my
life.'

The painfulness of having her domestic situation discussed and judged by all and sundry finds indirect expression in 'The Lifted Veil', an uncharacteristically gloomy,
even morbid, tale of second sight and hatred which Marian wrote early in 1859, as *Adam Bede* was being published
to acclaim and work on her next novel, *The Mill on the Floss*,
had begun. Both the short story and the new novel bear
witness to the distress and depression against which Marian was struggling, despite her domestic happiness with
Lewes and her success as a novelist. The miracle is that *The
Mill on the Floss*, with its tragic plot based on the loving yet
mutually thwarting relationship between Tom and Maggie Tulliver, and its bold approach to the difficulties of sexual attraction, should also be such a humorous work. It is
evidence of Marian's ability—seen in miniature in the
comic letter to Bray in 1846—to turn painful personal
experience to comic, as well as tragic, account.

During the writing of this novel Marian learned that her
sister Chrissey was dying of consumption. In February
1859 Chrissey wrote, regretting the break in their relations. She died on 15 March. It is hardly surprising that
Marian's bitter feelings towards Isaac find expression in
some harsh authorial remarks about Tom Tulliver in *The
Mill on the Floss*. Family life had been a battle for her; she
had been at odds with her father and brother, and
estranged from Chrissey, though they had been close and
Marian had helped her sister financially on the death of
her husband in 1852, when Chrissey had been left with six
young children and little money. *The Mill on the Floss* illustrates in several of its relationships the remark made by
the narrator of *Adam Bede*: 'Nature, that great tragic
dramatist, knits us together by bone and muscle, and divides us by the subtler web of our brains; blends yearning
and repulsion; and ties us by our heartstrings to the beings
that jar us at every movement' (chap. 4). Yet *The Mill on the
Floss* is also full of the rich comedy of family life as represented mainly by the three Dodson aunts of Tom and Maggie. The novel's form displays on a fictional level the serious intellectual engagement that she had with the
nineteenth-century debate on evolution—Darwin's *Origin
of Species* was published late in 1859, only a few months
before *The Mill on the Floss* appeared.

With *Adam Bede*, George Eliot had become a best-selling
author. Accordingly, Blackwood offered her £2000 for her
second novel, with a royalty of more than 30 per cent
(Haight, *Biography*, 318). *The Mill on the Floss* was published
in April 1860, and within four days had sold 4600 copies.
By the end of 1860 it had earned Marian the impressive
amount of £3865 (*Letters*, 7.360). Marian and Lewes had
gone abroad on an extended trip to Italy late in March to
avoid the inevitable comments on the recently revealed
identity of the author. They visited all the major Italian
cities; in Florence, Lewes drew Marian's attention to the
history of the city in the late fifteenth century, particularly the role in public life played by the Dominican monk
Savonarola, who led a religious revival after the fall of the
Medici family but was tried and executed as a heretic in
1498. In due course George Eliot was to base her historical
novel *Romola* (1863) on his story.

In June 1860 Marian and Lewes travelled to Hofwyl in
Switzerland, where Lewes's three sons, Charles, aged
nearly eighteen, Thornie, aged sixteen, and Herbert, aged
fourteen, were at school. They brought Charles back to
London with them; he studied for the civil service exams
and took up a job as clerk in the Post Office. Because of the
inconvenience for Charles of travelling to work daily from
the Leweses' home in Wandsworth, they moved into London, first in September 1860 to 10 Harewood Square, near
Regent's Park, then round the corner to 16 Blandford
Square in December. Gradually, Marian began to go out to
concerts, theatre, and dinner-parties, finding that she was
becoming more welcome in general society than she had
been on her return from Germany with Lewes in 1855.
Samuel Laurence painted her portrait, completing it in
September 1860. Lewes did not like it, but Blackwood, recognizing the 'sad pensive look' which had struck him
when he first met her, bought it to hang in his office in
Edinburgh (*Letters*, 3.343).

George Eliot's next work was the short novel *Silas
Marner*, begun in November 1860, and finished in March
1861. She experienced much less depression and fewer
delays than was usual for her in its composition. With its
happy ending, its legendary plot of the miser who turns
into a philanthropist and finds happiness in adopting a
child, it is different from her other novels, while sharing
their humour and breadth of understanding. Though contemporary readers were, on the whole, fondest of *Adam
Bede* among her novels, the response to *Silas Marner* was
gratifyingly warm. Eight thousand copies were sold by the
end of 1861, bringing her £1760 (Haight, *Biography*, 341).

By contrast, *Romola* proved the most difficult novel to
write and in the long run the least popular of George Eliot's works. It was certainly the one on which she laboured
for longest and not, it must be admitted, to altogether
happy effect. *Romola* was thoroughly researched for (too
much so, according to Lewes and to many readers and critics), both in Italy and in the reading room of the British
Museum, but the writing went slowly and by fits and
starts. The resulting novel, though full of fine things, is
too cramped, crowded, and laborious to come to life
imaginatively. It falls short, in places, of George Eliot's
own requirement, articulated in a letter of 1866, that 'aesthetic teaching', 'the highest of all teaching because it

deals with life in its highest complexity', should never lapse 'from the picture to the diagram' (*Letters*, 4.300).

While Marian was writing *The Mill on the Floss*, relations with her supportive publisher John Blackwood had become strained. She felt he had not done enough to dispel the Liggins myth and feared, not without justification, that he was nervous about the public response to that novel now that the identity of George Eliot was widely known. When George Smith, a London publisher with money to spare and a new journal, the *Cornhill Magazine*, to launch, offered Lewes the editorship of the journal and George Eliot an unprecedented £10,000 to publish *Romola* in twelve monthly parts in the *Cornhill*, beginning in July 1862, she accepted, though with a bad conscience. Trying to keep up with the relentless pace of part publication proved a nightmare for her. The novel also fell rather flat with critics and the public. Though Marian voluntarily took £7000 rather than the offered £10,000, Smith still lost money on it. She felt guilty towards him for his loss and also towards Blackwood for having deserted him.

Later works The Leweses, now comfortably off thanks to Marian's earnings, searched for a larger house. They found The Priory near Regent's Park. Lewes's friend, the designer Owen Jones (chief designer of the Crystal Palace), was commissioned to decorate the living rooms at considerable expense, and in November 1863 the Leweses moved in and entered on a splendid style of living. Here at The Priory they soon began to hold regular Sunday afternoon parties for friends and visitors, including Darwin, Huxley, Spencer, Henry James, and the artist Frederic Leighton, who illustrated *Romola*.

At last the Leweses were being invited out together by literary friends and admirers. Although it was not until 1877 that Marian was introduced to royalty in the person of Queen Victoria's daughter Princess Louise, the queen herself had read all of George Eliot's novels, admiring *Adam Bede* so much that in 1861 she had commissioned Edward Henry Corbould to paint two scenes from the novel—one of Dinah Morris preaching, the other of Hetty Sorrel making butter in the dairy.

In 1865 Frederic Burton drew Marian's portrait, which he gave to the National Portrait Gallery in 1883. Friends reckoned that this was the best likeness of the few she allowed to be taken. Like Laurence's, it shows a melancholy long-faced woman with abundant brown hair and intelligent but sad eyes. Contemporaries who saw her agreed with her own estimate of her appearance as plain (and many enjoyed noticing that Lewes, too, was ugly); Henry James summed it up best, perhaps, when he wrote to his brother William in 1878: 'The great G.E. herself is both sweet and superior, and has a delightful expression in her large, long, pale equine face' (Ashton, *George Eliot*, 275).

As agitation grew during 1866, leading finally to the passing of the second Reform Act of 1867, George Eliot returned for her next novel to England and to the familiar midlands countryside of her early novels. *Felix Holt, the Radical* (1866) takes for its subject and milieu the upheavals of society at the time of the first Reform Act of 1832. She once more approached her old publisher John Blackwood, who responded with warmth to her return, offering her £5000 for the copyright for five years (Haight, *Biography*, 384). Blackwood appreciated, as did her readers, the richly observed social scene, although the election riot on which the plot turns, based in part on a polling-day riot which occurred in her native Nuneaton in 1832, is a rather tame affair, and Felix Holt himself is unconvincing both as a radical and as a hero. There is also an over-elaborate mystery about exchanged identities and legal arrangements of estates, not unlike that in Dickens's most recent novel, *Our Mutual Friend* (1865) and in Wilkie Collins's works. *Felix Holt* was less successful than *Adam Bede*, *The Mill on the Floss*, or *Silas Marner*, although nearly 5000 copies were sold in the first year (ibid., 387).

In December 1866 Marian and Lewes visited Spain. Lewes's health was poor, and the journey was gruelling, but both had long wished to see Granada and the Alhambra. While on this visit, Marian had the idea of writing about the expulsion from Spain of the Moors and the Gypsies in the 1490s, and the result was *The Spanish Gypsy* (1868). The Gypsy of the title, Fedalma, has to choose between duty to her race and love of a Catholic duke. As with *Romola*, the conception and execution are less than successful, the more so as, after some deliberation, she cast this story in the form of a dramatic poem in blank verse. One of her most sympathetic and astute critics, Richard Holt Hutton, noticed that 'verse to her is a fetter, and not a stimulus'; Henry James asked readers to imagine what it would be like if Tennyson wrote a novel or George Sand a tragedy in French alexandrines (Ashton, *George Eliot*, 294).

Though the response to *Romola*, *Felix Holt*, and *The Spanish Gypsy* was polite, Marian was aware of a drop in her popularity. She could not know that her next work, an amalgam of two stories begun and abandoned, would be acclaimed her masterpiece. It was the result of a brilliant idea to knit together her story about the arrival of a young doctor in a midlands town shortly before the Reform Act of 1832 and a second story, 'Miss Brooke', about the marriage choice of an idealistic young woman of the landed gentry.

Middlemarch was not, however, written under the most auspicious circumstances. During its slow production Marian battled against self-doubt and illness. Not only did she suffer from the usual agonies of composition; she and Lewes spent the summer of 1869 nursing Lewes's second son, Thornie, through the excruciatingly painful illness of tuberculosis of the spine, of which he finally died, aged twenty-five, in October 1869. The irrepressible Thornie had failed his civil service examinations in 1863 and had gone out to Africa to farm. The venture, undertaken with his younger brother Herbert, was not wholly successful financially, and Thornie had contracted his fatal illness in Natal. Lewes sent him money to take the passage home, in the hope that he might be cured in England. Instead, he came home to die.

By May 1871 it was clear to Marian and Lewes that *Middlemarch* was becoming too long to fit the usual three-volume format. Lewes suggested to Blackwood that, on the model of Victor Hugo's *Les misérables*, it should be brought out in eight parts at two-monthly intervals, and subsequently published in four volumes. This mode of publishing was duly adopted, and the novel appeared to public delight from December 1871 to December 1872. About 5000 copies of these 5*s*. parts were sold. By 1879 nearly 30,000 copies had been sold in one edition or another, earning Marian about £9000. This astonishingly fully realized 'study of provincial life'—the subtitle of the novel—brought the author admiring reviews and letters from friends and strangers enthusing about her understanding of human life, male and female, rich and poor, professional and domestic, married and unmarried, happy and unhappy.

In *Middlemarch*, the social changes of the early 1830s are thoroughly absorbed into the multiple plot connections between individuals—what the narrator calls 'the stealthy convergence of human lots' (chap. 2). And George Eliot shows more than ever before her ability to enter imaginatively into the consciousness of every kind of human being, from the naive, aspiring Dorothea Brooke to the petrified pedant Casaubon, from the ambitious Dr Lydgate to his ill-matched unresponsive wife, Rosamond, from the loud merchant and mayor Vincy to his brother-in-law, the evangelical banker Bulstrode. The portrayal of the two unhappy marriages, the Lydgates' and the Casaubons', drew praise from Freud; Henry James wrote of the 'painful fireside scenes between Lydgate and his miserable little wife' that there was 'nothing more powerfully real' and 'nothing certainly more *intelligent*' in all English fiction (Ashton, *George Eliot*, 325).

On a visit to Germany in the summer of 1873 the Leweses visited the spa town of Bad Homburg. There they witnessed a scene of international gambling at the casino which was to provide material for the striking opening of George Eliot's next and last novel, *Daniel Deronda*. Like *Middlemarch*, it appeared in eight parts, this time monthly during 1876. While creating once more a panorama of social classes and opinion and showing how individuals interact at times of social change, this novel spreads its net even wider than its predecessor, taking in the English aristocracy at one end of the scale and poor London Jews at the other end. George Eliot's ambitious plot brings the two extremes into close contact through the figure of Deronda himself; her comic treatment of the ludicrous hunting and shooting county set is daringly offset by her respectful description of the Jewish religion and culture embodied in the ailing scholar Mordecai.

Marian was aware, as she admitted in April 1876, that 'the Jewish element' would be 'likely to satisfy nobody' (*Letters*, 6.238). Certainly, though the novel sold well, and earned its author over £9000, and though Blackwood, while not keen on the parts exclusively concerned with Mordecai's philosophy and vision of a Jewish homeland, saw that the work was full of brilliance, critics were puzzled, praising the 'English' parts for the familiar humour and insight, while they felt awkward about the 'Jewish element'.

There are a number of possible reasons why George Eliot turned to the vision of a Jewish homeland. By *Middlemarch* she had gone as far as it was possible to go in the imaginative study of English provincial life. Marian's wide intellectual curiosity, in evidence from her earliest years through her learning of foreign languages, translations of Spinoza, Strauss, and Feuerbach, and critical appreciations of Goethe, George Sand, and other European authors, and reinforced in recent years by frequent visits abroad, led her to set the scene of *Daniel Deronda* partly outside England. She had become interested in Judaism, through her friendship with Emanuel Deutsch, an orientalist employed by the British Museum, who taught her Hebrew. Deutsch had a vision of a Jewish homeland in the East; he travelled to Palestine, and died in Alexandria in 1873. Marian sympathized with his idealism, and was also irritated by the routine antisemitism she encountered among her acquaintances. She told Blackwood that she had wanted in *Daniel Deronda* to 'widen the English vision a little' (Ashton, *George Eliot*, 348).

Last years Marian was exhausted at the end of writing another long novel. In November 1876 she and Lewes found a country house, The Heights, in Witley, near Haslemere in Surrey, which they bought with a view to spending the summers there. But they were to enjoy only two idyllic summers, and even those were overshadowed by anxiety about Lewes's failing health. He died of enteritis and cancer on 30 November 1878, aged sixty-one, and was buried in the dissenters' part of Highgate cemetery on 4 December. Marian was too distraught to attend. She was plunged into loneliness, filling her journal with verses from Tennyson's great poem of mourning, *In Memoriam* (1850), as Queen Victoria had also done after the death of Prince Albert.

Without Lewes to help, Marian was unable to decide whether to publish her rather heavy and subdued set of ironic character sketches, *Impressions of Theophrastus Such*, which Blackwood eventually brought out in 1879. She spent her time preparing the last two volumes of Lewes's five-volume work of physiology and psychology, *Problems of Life and Mind* (1874–9), for the press, and arranging for the founding of a George Henry Lewes studentship in physiology at the University of Cambridge. For months she would not see her friends, even the adoring younger women Edith Simcox and Elma Stuart, who had attached themselves to her in recent years. She could bear to be visited only by Lewes's one remaining son Charles and by the friend who had found the house at Witley for them, the banker John Walter Cross.

Cross's mother had died within a few days of Lewes. He, a bachelor of forty who had lived with his mother and sisters, needed consolation too. Several months later he asked Marian, more than twenty years his senior, to marry him. She hesitated, still devastated by the loss of Lewes and acutely aware of the great age difference, but in the spring of 1880 she agreed to marry Cross. Despite her lack of religious affiliation, and presumably in deference to the Cross family, they were married in St George's, Hanover Square, on 6 May 1880. Charles Lewes gave her away.

She and Cross went on their honeymoon to Italy, leaving behind a startled public and some disapproving friends. She now reverted to her childhood forename, calling herself Mary Ann Cross, and seemed destined to shock once more with the last great decision of her life. If the orthodox had shaken their heads at the 'elopement' with Lewes, both they and the non-orthodox found it hard to adjust to her sudden marriage to a man much younger than herself. One positive—if meagre—result was a brief letter of congratulations from her estranged brother Isaac, content that his wayward sister, whom he had always known as Mary Ann, was now legally married.

Mary Ann's happiness was short-lived. Cross became depressed on the honeymoon and fell, or threw himself, from the balcony of their Venice hotel into the Grand Canal. Though little is known about the details of his illness, it fuelled gossip at home, with many a club-going acquaintance of Cross's commenting on both the age gap and the intelligence gap between husband and wife. According to Edith Simcox, whose autobiography is one of the few sources of information about Cross, he had suffered from bouts of depression before his marriage (Ashton, *George Eliot*, 377).

Back home by the end of July, the Crosses went to Witley to recuperate. Mary Ann suffered from recurring kidney trouble. On 3 December 1880 they moved into their splendid new house, 4 Cheyne Walk, by the Thames at Chelsea. Less than three weeks later, on 22 December, she died of the kidney disease she had suffered from for several years, exacerbated by a throat infection.

Cross inquired about the possibility of burial in Westminster Abbey, where Dickens and other great writers had been buried. Herbert Spencer was among those who thought that George Eliot, too, should have her place in Poets' Corner. But many felt that her denial of Christian faith, as well as her 'irregular' (though monogamous) life with Lewes, ruled this out. Cross dropped the idea, and on 29 December she was buried instead alongside Lewes in the dissenters' part of Highgate cemetery. It was fitting that she should be laid to rest beside the man who had cherished her and encouraged her genius, overriding her tendency to paralysing self-doubt and despondency. But it was also fitting that in 1980, 100 years after her death, a memorial stone was finally established in Poets' Corner, so that this great writer should be seen to be honoured in the same way as others who have enriched, as she undoubtedly did, the national literature.

Reputation George Eliot was one of the greatest Victorian writers. Recognized as such in her lifetime, when, like Dickens, she was both an admired and a commercially successful novelist, she suffered a temporary decline in reputation in the decades following her death. This was largely due to her husband's well-meaning but misguided efforts, in the biography he published in three volumes in 1885, to portray her as respectable despite her unorthodox relationship with Lewes. Cross, who had only got to know her in 1869, when she was fifty, who was in awe of his famous older wife, and who was, in addition, not a natural writer, gave a picture of her as a stuffy, sibylline figure.

Not only did he silently change passages in her letters, removing her trenchancy, her 'salt and spice', as Hale White noticed, but he omitted much, including the whole history of her relationship with Chapman. Cross may also have destroyed the pages of George Eliot's journal relating to her life in London up to the journey to Germany with Lewes. The extant journals, which remained unpublished until 1998, begin in July 1854, with evidence that the first forty-six pages have been removed (Haight, *Biography*, xv).

Everything that was unusual, strong-minded, and racy about her was left out of the picture, and by the 1890s George Eliot was being described as a heavy, humourless writer. For example, in 1890 the critic W. E. Henley characterized her—surely without having read the novels—as 'George Sand *plus* Science and *minus* Sex' (Carroll, 42). Leslie Stephen was an honourable exception to the general depreciation of her; he wrote an admiring volume on her in the (in this case ironically named) English Men of Letters series in 1902, and he was the author of the sympathetic entry on George Eliot in the *Dictionary of National Biography*.

It was Stephen's daughter Virginia Woolf who began the true rehabilitation of George Eliot's reputation with an essay in the *Times Literary Supplement* in 1919, the centenary of George Eliot's birth, in which she famously remarked that *Middlemarch* was 'one of the few English novels written for grown-up people' (Carroll, 43). Thereafter George Eliot was influentially praised by F. R. Leavis in *The Great Tradition* (1948); and with the great biographical and editorial work done by Gordon Haight in his nine-volume edition of her letters (1954–5, 1978) and his thorough documentary biography (1968), appreciation of George Eliot's greatness, and interest in all aspects of her life and work, were restored.

The last decades of the twentieth century saw all George Eliot's works republished, and her journals and working notebooks published for the first time. All the novels are available in paperback, and *Middlemarch* in particular is taught on many school and university English literature courses. Although not so frequently adapted for radio, television, and film as Dickens's, George Eliot's novels have had some notable BBC television adaptations: *Daniel Deronda* in 1970 and 2002, *Silas Marner* in 1985, and *Middlemarch* in 1994. The *Middlemarch* production resulted in paperback editions of the novel entering the best-seller lists for the first time since the novel's original publication, making George Eliot once more that rare phenomenon, a novelist whose success can be measured in both sales figures and critical esteem.

Marian's was a difficult life, but a brave and extremely interesting one. Curious, sceptical, critical, and even rebellious by nature, she was also timid, self-doubting, longing to conform where she felt compelled to rebel. This complex and conflicting combination of traits can be seen in all the important relationships of her life: with her father Robert Evans, her brother Isaac, the partner of her life, G. H. Lewes, and John Walter Cross, her husband of a few months. The combination can also be seen, duly transformed by her extraordinary imaginative and narrative gift, in the ambitious handling of human problems in her novels, where she skilfully, sympathetically, and wittily puts difficult choices before her characters, showing their frailty in both comic and tragic mode and analysing their often mixed and confused motives.

As a novelist George Eliot managed to be both a moralist and a realist. She appreciated in Goethe's novel *Wilhelm Meister's Apprenticeship* his honesty in depicting 'irregular relations in all the charms they really have for human nature', while also representing 'every aspect of human life where there is some trait of love, or endurance, or helplessness to call forth our best sympathies' (*Essays*, 145, 146). Art should extend our sympathies by opening our imaginations to understand unheroic, even dislikeable, characters like Mr Casaubon and Mr Bulstrode, even while we judge their faults. It was George Eliot's special gift to apply her wide knowledge, penetrating analytical intelligence, and humorous sympathy to the depiction of characters, their motivation, and their interaction in a densely realized social milieu. All her novels illustrate the famous remark made by the narrator in *Felix Holt*: 'There is no private life which has not been determined by a wider public life' (chap. 3). She experienced as much in her own unusual life, which became so cosmopolitan from unpromising provincial beginnings, and so adventurous intellectually and socially—particularly for a woman in the nineteenth century—after a timid, conventional early life. Yet she delved deep into that provincial and conventional past for much of the material—the felt life—which animated her fiction. As Lewes remarked in 1873 to a Coventry friend of Marian's early years, 'she forgets nothing that has ever come within the curl of her eyelash' (Ashton, *George Eliot*, 205). All the phases of her experience, from piety to scepticism, from family life to social exile, from provincial obscurity to professional fame, with the pleasures and pains associated with families and small communities and associated also with expulsion, exile, or escape from them, are absorbed by the philosophical intelligence, literary allusiveness, and strong sense of dialogue and structure in those fine novels of George Eliot.

ROSEMARY ASHTON

Sources *The George Eliot letters*, ed. G. S. Haight, 9 vols. (1954–78) · G. S. Haight, *George Eliot: a biography* (1968) · R. Ashton, *George Eliot: a life* (1996) · J. W. Cross, ed., *George Eliot's life as related in her letters and journals*, 3 vols. (1885) · R. Ashton, *G. H. Lewes: a life* (1991) · R. Ashton, 'New George Eliot letters at the Huntington', *Huntington Library Quarterly*, 54 (1991), 111–26 · *Essays of George Eliot*, ed. T. Pinney (1963) · *Selected critical writings*, ed. R. Ashton (1992) · D. Carroll, ed., *George Eliot: the critical heritage* (1977) · G. S. Haight, *George Eliot and John Chapman: with Chapman's diaries* (1940); 2nd edn (1969) · W. H. White, 'George Eliot', *The Athenaeum* (28 Nov 1885) · C. Bray, *Phases of opinion and experience during a long life* (1884) · L. Stephen, *George Eliot* (1902) · F. R. Leavis, *The great tradition* (1948) **Archives** BL, letters, Add. MS 61891 · BL, papers, Add. MS 54338 · Bodl. Oxf., notebook · Coventry Central Library, collection relating to Evans · Hunt. L., letters · NYPL, diary · Yale U., Beinecke L., corresp., journals, and literary MSS | BL, letters to Lady Dilke, Add. MS 43907 · BL, notebook for *Romola*, Add. MS 40768 · BL, letters mainly to Jane Senior, Add. MS 75298 · BL, letters to Herbert Spencer, Add. MS 65530 · BL, letters to Elma Stuart, Add. MS 37952 · Girton Cam., letters mainly to Bessie Rayner Parkes · NL Scot., corresp. with Blackwoods · NL Scot., corresp. with George Combe · Nuneaton Library, notebook, music exercise book, and letters to Mrs Cash · NYPL, Henry W. and Albert A. Berg Collection of English and American Literature · Trinity Cam., letters to Henry Sidgwick · UCL, letters to James Sully **Likenesses** C. Bray, watercolour drawing, 1842, NPG · F. D'A. Durade, oils, 1850, NPG · S. Laurence, chalk drawing, 1860, BM · S. Laurence, crayon drawing, 1860, Girton Cam. · F. Burton, chalk drawing, 1865, NPG [*see illus.*] · L. C. Dickinson, ink drawing, 1872, NPG · L. T. Alma-Tadema, pencil drawing, 1877, NPG · Princess Louise, pencil drawing?, 1877, Yale U., Beinecke L. · P. Rajon, etching, 1884 (after photograph, 1858), NYPL · F. W. Burton, chalk drawing, Birmingham Museums and Art Gallery · silhouette, NPG **Wealth at death** under £45,000: probate, Feb/July 1881, resworn

Evans [*née* Webb], **Matilda Maria** (1843/4–1909), local politician and social reformer, daughter of Richard Webb, herald chaser, emerged from an obscure background. Nothing is known of her early life, but on 17 March 1870 she married Henry Evans, a photographer's publisher. She was widowed by 1881 and returned to live with her mother, Rachel Webb, at 53 Sidmouth Street, St Pancras, London. She had children from the marriage and earned her family's living as a photographic publisher and print seller from commercial premises at 4a Duncannon Street, in the Strand, London. The earliest reference to any political activity on the part of Matilda Evans relates to the 1886 election for the Strand poor-law union, in which she polled 813 votes, finishing eleventh in the contest for the ten positions as guardian for the parish of St Martin-in-the-Fields. She contested the election again in 1887, this time with success: she became the first woman guardian on the Strand board. Attending her first meeting on 19 April, she was elected to serve on the finance committee and general purposes committee and soon became a high-profile figure in London government, one who was especially interested in the need to ensure sound financial management of the ratepayers' money and the welfare and training of girls. Indeed, by 1893 Louisa Tempe Mallet (member of the inner circle of the Women's Local Government Society) was quoting her example in an article promoting women's work in local government written for the *Women's Herald*. According to Mrs Mallet, 'everybody knows the story of the Strand workhouse school, where the first woman guardian discovered that one bath, with water unchanged, was considered adequate for the ablutions of sixty girls, and one brush and comb for their toilet' (Mallet, 10). In 1889 Mrs Evans was joined by Emma Stevens, a fancy goods importer, and Margaret Painton.

Apart from her poor-law work, in 1888 Mrs Evans also stood as an independent candidate for Westminster in the triennial election for the London school board, but finished at the bottom of the poll. Unlike most of those serving on the board she was not relying on the support of any association, political or otherwise, neither did she enter the fray as a supporter of free education or free school meals. In fact, her main concern was to avoid excessive expenditure. Consequently, in the autumn of 1888 the feminist *Women's Penny Paper* paid tribute to her sound business ability as a guardian and her 'eagle eye' for abuses: 'To the pauper children she is an invaluable friend, and, if returned to the larger Board, the interests of the rising generation will be safe in her hands' (*Women's Penny Paper*, 1). Despite her lack of success, it was in the same year that she was approached by Annie Leigh Browne of the newly established Society for Promoting the Return of Women as County Councillors (which became in 1893 the Women's Local Government Society) to allow herself to be nominated as a candidate for the London county council, an invitation which she refused. In 1891 she was again unsuccessful in the elections for the school board, but three years later was invited to join the vestry for St Martin-in-the-Fields.

Oddly enough Mrs Evans had attended vestry meetings regularly for ten years owing to her misgivings about the over-assessment of her rates. Indeed she told the 1896 conference of the Women's Emancipation Union that the driving force behind her interest in municipal affairs was a sense of injustice, reinforced by anger at her subsequent treatment by the male judiciary and local vestry (Ignota, 387–9). Initially excluded from all committees except the housing of the working classes committee, hard work and consistent attendances at vestry meetings were rewarded when on 28 May 1896 Mrs Evans was elected to serve on the works and general purposes committee, the finance committee, the improvements committee (dealing with issues arising from the Strand Improvement Bill), and the lighting committee. By 1899 she was serving on all vestry committees except one; the most important of those on which she acted was the works and general purposes committee, which determined the planning implications of road works, gas and water pipes, new sewers, and electric and telephone wires.

Down to the turn of the century Matilda Evans devoted herself to her work as a vestrywoman and poor-law guardian until she was unseated as a result of a petition lodged against her in July 1899 by an unsuccessful candidate, John Theodore Audy, for a technical infringement of the Corrupt Practices Act. In the event she was found guilty of illegal practices under the Municipal Corporations Act of 1882 (because she paid a certain F. Barrow 10s. for the conveyance of electors to and from the poll at the election on 15 May) and her election was declared void. It seems that the decision not only caused much local indignation but precipitated much comment in the press concerning the severity of the penalty imposed by comparison with other election petitions. By the judgment of the commissioners Mrs Evans was compelled to resign her seat on the Strand board of guardians, and in the opinion of the Women's Local Government Society, the 'withdrawal of her able and disinterested work as Guardian, as member of the Vestry, and as Overseer, is a very serious loss in the local administration of the Strand' (WLGS report, 1899–1900, 17). In 1909 she was an unsuccessful candidate for the London county council. She committed suicide at 17 Panton Street, Haymarket, London, on 14 June 1909. Her work illustrated both the difficulties and the achievements of women entering local government in the late nineteenth century.   JANE MARTIN

Sources Ignota [L. E. Wolstenholme Elmy], 'Women in local administration', *Westminster Review*, 150 (1898), 387–9 • L. T. Mallet, 'The work of women in workhouses and on county councils', *Women's Herald* (28 Jan 1893), 10 • St Martin-in-the-Fields vestry minutes, 1894–1900, City Westm. AC • Strand board of guardians minutes, 1887–1900, City Westm. AC • *Women's Penny Paper* (24 Nov 1888) • *Englishwoman's Review* (15 Feb 1881) • *Englishwoman's Review* (15 Aug 1887) • Women's Local Government Society minutes, LMA: 9 Nov 1888, 17 Nov 1888, 6 Dec 1888, 10 Dec 1888, 13 Dec 1888, 20 Dec 1888 • Women's Local Government Society reports, LMA: 1893, 1899–1900 • d. cert. • census returns, 1881 • 1870 marriage registers index, freebmd.rootsweb.com [March 1870, St Giles, 1b.553] • m. cert.
Archives LMA, Women's Local Government Society MSS
Wealth at death £2015 7s. 9d.: probate, 2 July 1909, *CGPLA Eng. & Wales*

Evans, Meredith Gwynne (1904–1952), physical chemist, was born at 15 Kay Street, Atherton, Lancashire, on 2 December 1904, the son of Frederick George Evans, an elementary schoolmaster, and his wife, Margaretta Eleanora Williams. From his father's school Evans won a county scholarship to Leigh grammar school. From there he went in due course to Manchester University to study chemistry and graduated with first-class honours in 1926. Both his younger brothers also became scientists: A. G. Evans was later professor of chemistry at University College, Cardiff, and D. G. *Evans was later professor of bacteriology and immunology in the London School of Hygiene and Tropical Medicine. Between 1926 and 1934 Evans was successively research scholar, assistant lecturer, and Sir Clement Royds scholar at Manchester. On 4 August 1931 he married Milly, née Trafford, an elementary schoolteacher. They had one son and one daughter.

A turning point in Evans's career came when he was awarded a Rockefeller fellowship to work with Professor Hugh S. Taylor at the Frick Chemical Laboratory at Princeton University in 1934–5. A year later he returned to a full lectureship at Manchester, where Michael Polanyi had recently arrived as professor of physical chemistry. Similarity of chemical interests brought the two men closely together and led to a fruitful period of collaboration which had a great influence on the development of the Manchester school of physical chemistry.

Evans's reputation grew quickly and in 1939 he was appointed professor of inorganic and physical chemistry at the University of Leeds, but his first six years there were disrupted by wartime activities. He joined Professor R. Whytlaw-Gray in researches connected with chemical warfare problems, particularly in the behaviour of smokes. This was a difficult period for Evans and his health suffered severely as a result of overwork. Fortunately he recovered and after the war was able to set about the development of the Leeds school to good effect. In January 1949 he returned to Manchester to succeed Polanyi in the chair of physical chemistry.

Evans was elected FRS in 1947 and served for a period on the council. He was also a vice-president of the Faraday Society. He served on the Ministry of Supply's Advisory

Council on Scientific Research and Technical Development and the government's Advisory Council on Scientific Policy. He paid numerous visits overseas as guest lecturer to many universities. His considerable scientific reputation, acquired during a relatively short career, was in the physical chemistry of reaction mechanisms, an interest much stimulated by his association with Polanyi. He worked on the kinetics and thermodynamics of reactions, transition state theory, applications of quantum mechanics, and the study of polymerization. His close collaboration with Polanyi enabled him to begin to apply the principles of quantum mechanics to systems which could not be tackled rigorously, thereby achieving a more detailed explanation of the rates of the simpler gas and liquid phase reactions.

Outside science Evans had wide tastes in reading, and an appreciation of good music; living in Manchester, he had a particular interest in the Hallé Orchestra. After a serious illness, and still a relatively young man, he died at his home, Mayfield, Beaufort Road, Sale, near Manchester, on Christmas day, 1952.

H. W. MELVILLE, rev. JOHN SHORTER

Sources H. W. Melville, *Obits. FRS*, 8 (1952–3), 395–409 · private information (1971) · personal knowledge (1971) · b. cert. · m. cert. · d. cert.

Likenesses N. Uri, photograph, 1948?, RS · W. Stoneman, photograph, RS

Wealth at death £1154 10s. 0d.: probate, 29 April 1953, *CGPLA Eng. & Wales*

Evans, Merlyn Oliver (1910–1973), painter and printmaker, was born in Llandaff, Cardiff, on 13 March 1910, the only child of Pryce Oliver Evans, an analytic chemist, and his wife, Minnie Veronica Edwards, a former nurse. Although the family moved to Rutherglen, Glasgow, in 1913, Evans always referred to himself as Welsh. He was educated at Rutherglen Academy, Glasgow, from 1917, and from 1925 to 1927 at Allan Glen's School, Glasgow, noted for its bias towards technical and scientific subjects. As a child, he proved adept at technical drawing, yacht modelling, and kite design. From the age of ten he received free private tuition in drawing and painting from John Houston RSA and his brother Charles. From 1927 to 1931 he attended Glasgow School of Art, exhibiting at the Royal Scottish Academy in 1930, and in 1931, when he won the £50 Haldane travelling scholarship and a scholarship to the Royal College of Art.

Evans was deeply affected by the poverty and violence he witnessed in Glasgow during the depressed years of the late twenties, and by 1930 he had begun to develop a highly personal abstract style, feeling that the lyrical naturalism in which he was already highly competent was inadequate to the reality around him. His experimental drawings and paintings at this time, combining plant, crustacean, and mechanical forms, announce a lifelong commitment to morphological abstraction, and to the idea that art should be an engagement with life, reflecting psychological, ethical, and political concerns. This conviction was intensified by firsthand experience, in Berlin, Copenhagen, and Paris in 1931 and 1932, of the work of Juan Gris, Lyonel Feininger, Klee, Kandinsky, Mondrian, Ernst, and Stanley Hayter among others.

Evans was not happy at the Royal College, where abstraction was discouraged. Not permitted to study sculpture, he took private lessons from a stonemason. Although he made few stone carvings, there remained a strong sculptural quality to his imagery, and he always favoured the intaglio graphic techniques, engraving and etching, that make possible the high definition and contrast of forms in pictorial space. He left the college in 1933 after only one year. Surrealism early became an influence, and in 1936 he exhibited several works in the International Surrealist Exhibition in London. He associated with the surrealist group around Roland Penrose, Humphrey Jennings, and Herbert Read, but remained, characteristically, independent of it. His work through the thirties assimilated a wide range of influences, from analytic cubism to vorticism to surrealism, and from ancient and ethnographic art. His subject matter became increasingly social and political, reflecting his growing concern over economic distress at home and political disaster in Europe.

In 1934 Evans married Phyllis Sullivan, a former fellow student at the Royal College of Art, and moved to Streatham in south London. He taught art at Wilson's Grammar School, Camberwell, from 1934 to 1936, and at Riemann's design school in Belgravia from 1936 to 1938. In 1937 he exhibited with the Artists' International Association, the London Group, and in 'Surrealist Poems and Objects' at the London Gallery. In 1938 he moved with his wife and their infant son and daughter to Durban, South Africa, to teach at Natal Technical College. The European crisis continued to preoccupy him, however, and in paintings that made explicit reference to economic depression, atrocity, and war Evans declared himself a political artist. His style, with its interlock of the organic and the mechanical, and its grotesque morphologies, proved highly effective as a response to the anguish of the time.

In August 1942 Evans joined the South African army 14th armoured brigade, and saw action in north Africa, and with the Eighth Army in Italy, where he was awarded the Italian star. Demobilized in 1945, and his marriage recently dissolved, he returned to London. After a refresher course in etching and aquatint at the Central School in 1946, he embarked on a distinguished printmaking career, in theme and image parallel to his painting. Through the late 1940s he continued to treat of political and philosophical themes in pictorial allegories that drew upon eclectic sources, with recognizably human forms in theatrical space.

In 1950 Evans was married again, this time to Marjorie Few, a concert pianist. After living and working in Mecklenburgh Square for some years he finally settled at 40A Downshire Hill, Hampstead, setting up a studio in a nearby disused nineteenth-century church. In the mid-fifties Evans's work became more abstract, its imagery deriving from wharfside and industrial landscape. By the early sixties architectural and mechanomorphic forms in the paintings and prints had given way to starkly silhouetted quasi-geometric shapes against flat grounds. The expressive vehemence of *Vertical Suite in Black* (1958), and further series of aquatints and mezzotints, established Evans as one of the great printmakers of the post-war era. As his work became increasingly geometric he maintained that its implications were always indirectly figurative. His first retrospective was held at the Whitechapel Gallery in 1956; later important exhibitions included those at McRoberts and Tunnard, London (1963), the Art Institute of Chicago (retrospective, 1967), Marlborough Fine Art, London (1968), and the Victoria and Albert Museum (graphic work, 1973).

Evans was a handsome man, witty and sardonic, whose temperament combined passion and intellectuality. His love of speculation and argument was informed by his studies in psychology, philosophy, politics, mechanics, optics, and the history and techniques of art. He was deeply read in modernist literature and contemporary poetry. He played the piano and trumpet well enough to amuse his friends with stylish pastiches and improvisations. He was practical and ingenious, and a good craftsman. All these aspects of the man found expression in his work as an artist. He was also a gifted writer and teacher. Evans died at 40A Downshire Hill, Hampstead, London, on 31 October 1973; his second wife survived him.

MEL GOODING

Sources M. Gooding and others, *Merlyn Evans, 1910–1973: a retrospective exhibition* (1988) [exhibition catalogue, Mayor Gallery and Redfern Gallery, London] · *The political paintings of Merlyn Evans, 1930–1950* (1985) [exhibition catalogue, Tate Gallery, London] · *The graphic work of Merlyn Evans* (1972) [exhibition catalogue, V&A] · *Merlyn Evans* (1956) [exhibition catalogue, Whitechapel Art Gallery, London] · M. Chamot, D. Farr, and M. Butlin, *The modern British paintings, drawings and sculpture*, 2 vols. (1964–5) [catalogue, Tate Gallery, London] · P. Huxley, ed., *Exhibition Road: painters at the Royal College of Art* (1988) · A. Robertson and others, *Surrealism in Britain in the thirties: angels of anarchy and machines for making clouds* (1986) [exhibition catalogue, Leeds City Art Galleries, 10 Oct – 7 Dec 1986] · *CGPLA Eng. & Wales* (1974)
Archives Tate collection, corresp., sketchbooks, and papers
Likenesses M. Evans, self-portrait, pencil, repro. in *Political paintings* · D. Grass, photograph, repro. in *Graphic work* · photograph, repro. in Gooding, *Merlyn Evans*
Wealth at death £18,505: administration, 2 April 1974, *CGPLA Eng. & Wales*

Evans, Philip [St Philip Evans] (1645–1679), Jesuit, was born in Monmouthshire to William Evans and his wife, Winifred, *née* Morgan. His sister was professed as a Blue Nun in Paris and became known as Sister Barbara Catherine. Philip Evans was educated at the English College, St Omer, and on 8 September 1665 he entered the Society of Jesus. After the completion of his noviciate at Watten and further studies he was ordained priest at the English College, Liège. In 1675 he was sent to conduct missionary work in south Wales and lived at the Jesuit college at Cwm in Llanrothal parish on the Monmouthshire–Herefordshire border. It has also been suggested that he was an occasional visitor to the Catholic household of the marquess of Powis at Powis Castle, but in 1678 he was a guest of Thomas Gunter, a recusant who lived at Abergavenny,

Philip Evans [St Philip Evans] (1645–1679), by Alexander Voet, pubd 1683

and he lived at the home of Charles Proger of Wern-ddu in Llandeilo Bertholau in Monmouthshire.

On 4 December 1678, at the height of intense persecution of Roman Catholics during the Popish Plot, Evans was captured at the house of his loyal friend and patron, Sir Christopher Turberville of Sker House, near Porth-cawl in Glamorgan. He was quickly brought before Judge Richard Lougher and was later offered bail by Sir Edward Stradling if he agreed to swear to the oaths of allegiance and supremacy. He refused to comply with this request and was consequently committed to gaol for three weeks, possibly in the Black Tower of Cardiff Castle. During this period of confinement he was kept in an underground cellar and allowed no visitors.

Evans's persecutors had difficulty finding witnesses willing to testify against him or to produce any evidence of his being a priest. Eventually they forced an old poor woman and her daughter to testify upon oath that they had witnessed him say mass as well as preach in Latin, English, and Welsh. On 8 and 9 May 1679, after being confined for five months, he was brought before the spring assizes in the Shire Hall in Cardiff and charged with being a Roman Catholic priest. Mayne Trott, an apostate, and two female witnesses were subpoenaed by John Arnold of Llanfihangel Crucornau in Monmouthshire to give evidence against him. Earlier in November 1678 Arnold, the main persecutor of Roman Catholic priests in south Wales, had offered £200 in addition to the £50 reward the government had tendered for the apprehension and conviction of any Jesuit. Trott's unsubstantiated evidence implicated Evans in the alleged plot, and upon the further evidence of the two women he was condemned to death. He was sentenced to be hanged, drawn, and quartered by Judge Owen Wynne under the statute of 27 Elizabeth for being a priest.

The execution was delayed until 22 July 1679, when Evans was taken from Cardiff gaol with Father John Lloyd. Both priests were put in a cart and with their arms tied behind them they were taken to Gallows Field. Evans was the first to be executed. Before mounting the gallows he knelt and kissed them, cried out 'welcome good cross' (Ellis, 120), and then began praying. The ladder to the gallows was too short and consequently it moved when his neck was placed in the noose. One of the sheriff's bailiffs therefore took hold of his legs and twisted them after his body. He was later disembowelled while still conscious, decapitated, and quartered.

It has been recorded that Evans was

> remarkable for his unaffected candour and modesty; he had a cheerful and open countenance, marked by religious gravity. He was diligent in prayer, most observant of discipline, and obedient to the very nod of his Superior; and in his earnest desire to comply with the wishes of all, he made himself universally beloved. (Gillow, *Lit. biog. hist.*, 187)

Shortly after the execution of the two Jesuits 'Short memorandums' about them were published at London; on 25 October 1970 Paul VI canonized Evans as one of the forty martyrs of England and Wales.

RICHARD C. ALLEN

Sources M. Tanner, *Brevis relatio felicis agonis* (1683) · [J. Keynes and T. Stapleton], *Florus Anglo-Bavaricus* (Liège, 1685) · *DNB* · J. H. Canning, 'The Titus Oates plot in South Wales and the marches, 2: The Cardiff martyrs: the Venerables Philip Evans, S.J. and John Lloyd', *St. Peter's Magazine*, 3 (1923), 38–47 [portrait] · H. Foley, ed., *Records of the English province of the Society of Jesus*, 5 (1879), 882–91; 7 (1882–3), 232 [portrait] · Gillow, *Lit. biog. hist.*, 2.186–7 · M. M. C. O'Keefe, 'The Popish Plot in south Wales and the marches of Gloucester and Hereford', MA diss., National University of Ireland (University College, Galway), 1970 · T. P. Ellis, *The Catholic martyrs of Wales, 1535–1680* (1933), 75–9 · R. P. Matthews, 'Roman Catholic recusancy in Monmouthshire, 1608–89. A demographic and morphological analysis', PhD diss., U. Wales, Cardiff, 1996 · B. L. Norton, 'Recusancy in south Wales, 1600–1840', MA diss., U. Wales, Cardiff, 1996 · D. A. Bellenger, ed., *English and Welsh priests, 1558–1800* (1984) · *The Catholic martyrs of England and Wales*, Catholic Truth Society, 2nd edn (1979) · R. Challoner, *Memoirs of missionary priests*, another edn, 2 vols. (1803), vol. 2, pp. 214–29 · J. H. Matthews, 'Mass in penal times', *St. Peter's Magazine*, 9 (1929), 322–6 · J. C. H. Aveling, *The handle and the axe: the Catholic recusants in England from Reformation to emancipation* (1976), chaps. 8–9 · P. P. Murphy, 'Catholics in Monmouthshire, 1533–1689', *Presenting Monmouthshire*, 21 (1966), 33–8 · P. P. Murphy, 'The Jesuit College of the Cwm, Llanrothall', *Severn and Wye Review*, 1/6 (1970–72), 135–9 · J. Bossy, *The English Catholic community, 1570–1850* (1975) · E. T. Davies, 'Popish Plot in Monmouthshire', *Journal of the Historical Society of the Church in Wales*, 25 (1976), 32–45 · P. Jenkins, 'Anti-popery on the Welsh marches in the seventeenth century', *HJ*, 23 (1980), 275–93 · G. Holt, *The English Jesuits, 1650–1829: a biographical dictionary*, Catholic RS, 70 (1984)

Archives Cardiff Central Library, Phillips MSS, 'Short memorandums upon the deaths of Mr. Philip Evans … 22nd day of July, 1679', MS 21183
Likenesses A. Voet, line engraving, NPG; repro. in Tanner, *Brevis relatio felicis* [see illus.] · group portrait, line engraving (*Titus Oates and Jesuits*), BM · portraits, repro. in Canning, 'The Titus Oates plot' · portraits, repro. in Foley, *Records of the English province*, 5

Evans, Richard (1783?–1871), portrait painter and copyist, was born in Shrewsbury, Shropshire. He was possibly the Richard Evans who was baptized on 1 August 1783 at St Mary's, Shrewsbury, the son of Robert Evans and his wife, Elizabeth. About 1804 he followed his friend David Cox from Birmingham to London, taking lodgings near him. Evans was poor in those days and Cox, who was more proficient in landscape painting, lent him many of his indian ink sketches to copy and sell in order to support himself. Eventually he turned to portrait painting and worked as an assistant to Sir Thomas Lawrence making duplicate copies of his master's portraits of members of the royal family. In 1814 Evans visited the Louvre in Paris and was one of the first Englishmen to copy the pictures there collected. He exhibited at the Royal Academy for the first time in 1816 from 26 Southampton Street, London, sending a portrait entitled *Mr Sadler the Aeronaught*. In all he exhibited forty-two pictures at the academy and six at the British Institution. From 86 Newman Street, London, he exhibited at the Royal Academy in 1818 a portrait *His Majesty Henry Christophe, King of Haiti* (who in 1820 was deposed and committed suicide) and another of his son Prince Victor Henry, prince royal of Haiti (who with others was bayoneted to death).

In 1821 Joseph Farington recorded in his diary that the architect John Nash had 'employed an English painter [Evans] to copy the works of Raphael in the Logio at Rome. Evans is now in the city proceeding on the work … the copies … are meant to embellish Mr. Nash's Gallery' in Regent Street (Farington, *Diary*, 16.5745). He also copied pictures by old masters and painted portraits. On giving up his studio he gave one of his fresco studies to the attendant who swept his studio. Years afterwards, he was astonished to find this identical work hanging in the South Kensington Museum. It was described as a genuine piece of antique fresco painting depicting *Ganymede Feeding the Eagle*, from a tomb in the neighbourhood of Rome. He examined his original sketch of the subject, made a special journey to London, and convinced Mr Redgrave, the director-general for art, that the work was really his and not antique.

From about 1826 Evans was living at 15 Newman Street (remaining there until after 1845), sending to the Royal Academy a portrait, *Admiral Sir Edward Owen KCB*, which had been commissioned by the corporation of Shrewsbury (Evans's birthplace). Other portraits of important sitters he exhibited at the Royal Academy include in 1828 the Russian ambassador Count Vorontsov; Alderman Carden in his ninetieth year, painted for the corporation of Worcester in 1834, and Nelson's captain, Rear Admiral Sir Thomas Masterman Hardy. His portrait of Harriet Martineau (National Portrait Gallery, London) exhibited in the same year received such 'brutal comment' by a notorious critic of the *Morning Chronicle* that the critic was dismissed. The National Portrait Gallery also hold his portraits of the radical politician Sir Francis Burdett, the poet Thomas Campbell, his master, Sir Thomas Lawrence, John Nash, and the architect Sir Jeffry Wyatville.

After 1845 Evans seems to have ceased portrait painting. His wife, Margaret Bridger (*c*.1782–1857), a British subject, was born in America. By 1851 they had moved to Southampton, and were living at Bugle Street. From there he sent two pictures to the British Institution in 1856, *Gipsies by Moonlight*, 30 guineas, and *A Monk of Val Ombrosa*, 40 guineas. When more than eighty-five years old he executed a large picture, *The Death of Aesculapius*, whom he had depicted in two other paintings: one at the Royal Academy in 1830 and another in 1832 at the British Institution.

After being stricken with paralysis for eighteen days Evans died on 9 November 1871 at his home, 5 Bugle Street, Southampton, Hampshire, aged eighty-seven. Other examples of his work are in the British Museum, and the Victoria and Albert Museum, London, and Southampton City Art Gallery.

L. H. CUST, rev. MERVYN CUTTEN

Sources A. Davies and E. Kilmurray, *Dictionary of British portraiture*, 4 vols. (1979–81) · Redgrave, *Artists* · B. Stewart and M. Cutten, *The dictionary of portrait painters in Britain up to 1920* (1997) · Graves, *Brit. Inst.* · N. N. Solly, *Memoir of the life of David Cox* (1873), 13 · *Art Journal*, 34 (1872), 75 · *Hampshire Telegraph* (1871) · R. Parkinson, ed., *Catalogue of British oil paintings, 1820–1860* (1990) [catalogue of V&A] · *CGPLA Eng. & Wales* (1872) · IGI
Likenesses R. Evans, self-portrait, 1834, NPG · C. C. Vogel, drawing, 1837, Staatliche Kunstsammlungen, Dresden, Germany
Wealth at death under £800: resworn administration, Aug 1876, *CGPLA Eng. & Wales* (1872)

Evans, Robert Harding (1777–1857), bookseller and auctioneer, was born on 6 December 1777 in Westminster, the son of Thomas *Evans (1742–1784), a bookseller in the Strand, and his wife, Ann. He entered Westminster School in 1788, and was afterwards apprenticed to Thomas Payne, bookseller, of Charing Cross. He succeeded to the business of James Edwards of Pall Mall, but in 1812 took up auctioneering, his first sale being the library of the duke of Roxburghe. Between 1812 and 1847 many of the great libraries sold in England passed through his Pall Mall saleroom; his own marked set of catalogues is in the British Library.

On 22 October 1833 Evans married Susannah (*d.* 1861), eldest daughter of Thomas Baker of Limehouse. They had at least five children, including Thomas (*b.* 1804), who was also educated at Westminster, and Charles, both of whom followed their father's trade. Possessing an excellent memory and a rich store of information, Robert Evans was in the habit of discoursing upon the books passing under his hammer. His expertness as an auctioneer was not, however, matched by business acumen and he and Charles were declared bankrupt in 1846. He survived this calamity and recommenced trading, probably about 1849, in partnership with both sons.

Evans took a keen interest in politics and in the history of the whig party, reflected in the books which he published between 1809 and 1851. Among the eight works

bearing his imprint were a four-volume set of old ballads compiled by his father, which he enlarged and revised from the edition of 1784; a nine-volume set of Euripides' works in Latin and Greek (1821), in which he assisted the editors; and the *Historical and Descriptive Account of the Caricatures of James Gillray* (1851), which he wrote with Thomas Wright. Two books attributed to him in the *Dictionary of National Biography*, *Six Letters of Publicola* (1810) and *A Letter … on Reform* (1817), are now considered to be by Robert Harding Evans (1784–1821), editor of parliamentary reports.

Evans died at his house in Edward Street, Hampstead Road, London, on 25 April 1857. ANITA MCCONNELL

Sources M. Vaulbert de Chantilly, *Robert Harding Evans of Pall Mall: auction catalogues 1812–1846: a provisional list* (2002), iii–xii · *GM*, 3rd ser., 2 (1857), 734–5 · I. Maxted, *The London book trades, 1775–1800: a preliminary checklist of members* (1977), 76 · *LondG* (7 July 1846); (9 Oct 1846); (10 Nov 1846) · *LondG* (1 June 1849), 1816 · *Old Westminsters*, 1.315 · Nichols, *Lit. anecdotes*, 6.436 · DNB
Archives BL, letters to Lord Sheffield, Add. MS 61985
Likenesses Freeman, engraving, repro. in T. F. Dibdin, *The bibliographical decameron*, 3 (1817), 51 · stipple (after W. Behnes), BM

Evans, Robert Wilson (1789–1866), Church of England clergyman and author, second son of John Evans (1756–1846), a surgeon of Llwyn-y-groes, near Oswestry, and his wife, Jane Wilson, was born at the Council House, Shrewsbury, on 30 August 1789. He was educated under Samuel Butler at Shrewsbury School, and entered Trinity College, Cambridge, in 1807. There he became seventh wrangler and second chancellor's medallist, proceeding BA in 1811, MA in 1814, and BD in 1842. He was elected a fellow in 1813 and classical tutor of his college in 1814, becoming a colleague of George Peacock, afterwards dean of Ely. Ordained in 1815 he was presented to the Trinity College living of Aysgarth, Yorkshire, in 1825, where he resided in the long vacations, acquiring experience of parochial ministry. This inspired the religious tale *The Rectory of Valehead* (1830; 15th edn, 1852), his most popular work.

Although a scholarly man, contributing five volumes to the Theological Library series, Evans preferred parish work to university teaching, and resigned his tutorship in 1836 when his former headmaster, Samuel Butler, bishop of Lichfield, made him his examining chaplain and collated him to the vicarage of Tarvin, Cheshire. His ministry there and his addresses to ordinands provided the material for his *The Bishopric of Souls* (1842; 5th edn, 1877), a handbook describing the various aspects of a clergyman's work. Highly regarded by J. B. Lightfoot, Evans's book now stands as a vivid account of the methods and aims of the early Victorian clergy in rural parishes (see O. Chadwick, *The Victorian Church*, part 2, 1972, 171–4). In 1842 he accepted the Trinity College living of Heversham, Westmorland, in the Lake District, which was congenial to one who had a deep attachment to the countryside. One of his first acts was to build a new vicarage house on the shoulders of Heversham Head, a spot from which he could command an extensive view of the Westmorland scenery. From 1856 to 1865 he was archdeacon of Westmorland. He maintained his literary output, contributing to the *Christian Remembrancer* as well as publishing parochial sermons, charges to the clergy, and hymns. Evans died, unmarried, at Heversham vicarage on 10 March 1866. In 1869 his friends endowed in his memory the Evans prize at Cambridge, awarded to those students who distinguished themselves in the theological examination.

M. C. CURTHOYS

Sources E. Bickersteth, 'Memoir', in R. W. Evans, *The bishopric of souls*, 5th edn (1877) • Venn, *Alum. Cant.* • Boase, *Mod. Eng. biog.* • R. Williams, *Enwogion Cymru: a biographical dictionary of eminent Welshmen* (1852) • J. R. Tanner, ed., *Historical register of the University of Cambridge … to the year 1910* (1917)

Archives Trinity Cam., letters to William Whewell

Likenesses J. Brown, engraving, repro. in Evans, *Bishopric of souls*, frontispiece • photograph, repro. in *The Church of England photographic portrait gallery*, Church of England (1859), 33

Wealth at death under £10,000: probate, 13 April 1866, *CGPLA Eng. & Wales*

Evans, Rudolph Bayfield [Rudy; *performing name* André de Dakar] (1897–1987), singer, actor, and entrepreneur, was born at Monkey Hill, Panama, on 23 February 1897, the eighth son and ninth of the ten children of Edward John Rhodes Evans (*b.* 1853), a land and property owner, and his wife, Emma Evangeline (*b.* 1863). Both parents were Jamaican. He was baptized into the Church of England as Rodolph Bayfield Evans at St John's Church, Monkey Hill, on 11 April 1897 and grew up in Kingston, Jamaica, where he attended Wolmer's School.

In 1915 Evans was among the many Caribbean men who volunteered for war service and joined the British West Indies regiment. In France he reached the rank of sergeant and won the Military Medal. On returning home, he attended farm school with the intention of becoming a veterinary surgeon. He also worked as a photographer, but his fondness for singing predominated, and he made concert appearances in Kingston before returning to Europe. He left behind a daughter, Evadne (*b. c.*1915).

By early 1926 Evans was living in Belgium. He possessed a fine tenor voice and, as Rodolphe Bayfield Evans, soon found work as a singer and actor. He then travelled to London, where as Bayfield Evans he worked with leading British dance-band musicians at the Savoy Hotel and recorded. In Brussels in 1929 he married Germaine Marie Gertrude Louis (1907–2000), a pianist. They moved to Paris, where Evans changed his first name to Rudolph and sang with several notable jazz groups and also taught singing and dancing. He formed a song-and-dance act for solo cabaret appearances in France and Egypt, and travelled to Italy before settling in London in 1936. There he became a familiar figure in Soho and Mayfair nightlife and was later joined by his wife. He sang with fashionable all-black dance bands and played drums before forming a vocal harmony duo with the Guyanese pianist Stanley Carter.

Evans's ambition was to become a nightclub entrepreneur. The Second World War was his saviour. Because of the segregation that divided the American forces, a need existed for places where black war workers could socialize freely. When Evans opened his Caribbean Club in 1944 he had unofficial Colonial Office backing. Situated in Denman Street, near Piccadilly Circus, this was originally intended as a place where Caribbean and African American officers could relax. The club, which provided work for local black people, especially women, was renowned for the quality of its music, its food, and its colourful atmosphere, and its clientele ranged from civil servants to bookmakers, and from prostitutes to the aristocracy, the more famous including Django Reinhardt, Pearl Bailey, Jacob Epstein, James Mason, and Pablo Picasso. Other musicians took inspiration from the resident Caribbean Trio, which featured Lauderic Caton's inventive guitar, while the genial Evans presided nightly, closing the proceedings by singing love songs in French. He also opened the Antilles, a bottle party, where local modern jazz musicians played with the new wave of Caribbean arrivals. In 1945, having divorced his first wife, he married Viola Mari Mathilde Lyberg-Bondesen (Marie; *b. c.*1901), a nurse, the daughter of Hans Christian Olsen, a Danish armaments manufacturer, and the former wife of Carl Lyberg-Bondesen. They had known each other since 1936. Their son, André Rudolph Evans, later known as André de Dakar, was born in 1941.

The Caribbean Club remained open until 1953. With its success, Evans had realized one of two ambitions; his second was to star in *Othello*. Before the war he had acted in Brussels and Paris and in the Paul Robeson film *Jericho* (1937); now he found work on the stage and on both the large and the small screen. Under the name André Dakar or André de Dakar his film roles included *Men of Two Worlds* (1946) and *Beyond Mombasa* (1957) and, on television, John Hopkins's controversial play *Fable* (1965). Playing father figures, he became a ubiquitous and dependable performer, although his readings of *Othello* were confined to cultural and commemorative events organized by other black British artists. In the 1950s he formed a relationship with Joan Elizabeth Mary (1921–1994), an office services supervisor in local government, and the daughter of William James Clive Pelling, a sales manager. They married on 4 March 1970 following his second divorce; their children were Rhoda Elizabeth Evans de Dakar, the singer known as Rhoda Dakar (*b.* 1959), and Clive Edward Evans de Dakar (*b.* 1963).

Ramrod-straight and refined, Evans always wore a hat and three-piece suit, sported a carnation buttonhole, and carried a silver-topped cane. He was admired for his dress sense and deportment, for his acting ability, and for a voice that became richer and more resonant with maturity. On leaving the nightclub life, he found a new profession. A lifelong adherent of homoeopathy, he had studied physiotherapy in France and now began to practise chiropody. Living in Brixton, where he was regarded as a knowledgeable community elder, he was in constant demand for his services.

Rudy Evans displayed entrepreneurial endeavour at a time when this required stamina, inventiveness, and a pioneering spirit. Through organizing the Caribbean Club at a time of national crisis and continuing to run it in the immediate post-war period, he established a specifically Jamaican presence in London before the major wave of

Caribbean settlement began. As an artist, he had no desire to embrace any vernacular tradition; indeed, it can be said that, given some of the stereotypes of the day, he admirably side-stepped the typecasting of African peoples that then prevailed. He sang easily and rhythmically within contemporary dance-band conventions at a time when great individuality was not required, although the absence of suitable film parts for older black men limited him to supporting roles as an actor. However, he was a respected figure among fellow professionals, celebrated for his longevity as a Caribbean artist and his visibility at the centre of a changing black community. He died on 30 December 1987 at the Dulwich Hospital, East Dulwich, London, following a stroke, survived by his wife, Joan, and his four children. VAL WILMER

Sources 'Jamaican home on visit after 42 years', *Daily Gleaner* [Kingston, Jamaica] (16 March 1967), 26 · S. Jackson, *An indiscreet guide to Soho* (1947), 10–11 · B. Rust, *Jazz records: A–Z, 1897–1942*, 4th edn (1978) · B. Rust and S. Forbes, *British dance bands on record, 1911–1945*, 2nd edn (1986) · S. Bourne, *Black in the British frame: black people in British film and television, 1896–1996* (1998) · R. Ottley, *No green pastures* (1952), 24 · personal knowledge (2004) · private information (2004) · parish register, St John, Panama [baptism] · m. certs. · d. cert.

Likenesses Yvonne, photographs, c.1942, priv. coll. · B. Hardy, photographs, 1949, Hult. Arch. · photographic stills, BFI · photographs, priv. coll.

Evans, Samuel (1762–1835). *See under* Evans, William (1798–1877).

Evans, Sir Samuel Thomas (1859–1918), politician and judge, was born on 4 May 1859 at Skewen, near Neath, Glamorgan, the only son of John Evans, grocer, and his wife, Margaret, *née* Thomas. After school in Swansea, he took his LLB at London University and was admitted as a solicitor in 1883, starting practice in Neath. On 10 February 1887 Evans married his first wife, Rachel Rees (*d.* 1889), daughter of William Thomas of Skewen; they had one son.

In 1890 Evans was elected member of parliament for Mid-Glamorgan, which he represented without a break until promoted to the bench twenty years later. In 1891 he was called to the bar by Middle Temple and soon became one of the busiest juniors on the south Wales circuit. In 1901, after less than ten years at the bar, he became queen's counsel in the hope of reducing the strain of combining legal work in Wales with parliamentary work in London. The change brought him little relief, however. He never established any great connection with London solicitors and his practice continued to be dependent on his Welsh connections, with the result that his parliamentary work suffered from his frequent absences in Wales. Nevertheless, he soon made his mark as a promising member of the radical wing of the Liberal Party.

Evans was impetuous and combative, and not always conciliatory to those with whom he disagreed. He was an eager and humorous debater, with a rapid delivery, and a keen fighter for the Liberal Party, whether in power or in opposition. He was a particularly active critic in debates surrounding Balfour's Education Bill of 1902, which he opposed, and in supporting the Licensing Bill of 1908 and arguing against women's suffrage. His criticisms of the Church of England, informed by his nonconformist beliefs, could be bitter and prejudiced. He seemed destined for political rather than legal success.

On 21 February 1905 Evans married his second wife, Blanche De Pinto, a widow, daughter of Charles Rule of Cincinnati, Ohio; they had one daughter.

From 1906 to 1908 Evans was recorder of Swansea. In 1908 he became a bencher of the Middle Temple and in the same year was appointed solicitor-general by Sir Henry Campbell-Bannerman, staying on in Asquith's government.

In 1910 Evans reluctantly, but knowingly, abandoned his political career by accepting appointment as president of the Probate, Divorce, and Admiralty Division of the High Court in succession to Sir John Bigham. He had few qualifications and his experience had been in workmen's compensation and trade union cases. His appointment was not popular at the bar, and he did little at first to remove the prejudice. He allowed his indifference to the traditions of the court to be too apparent, and his brusqueness gave unnecessary offence. But he threw himself into the work of the court, even spending vacations at sea so that he could study the technique of Admiralty work. His decision in 1911 in the dispute which arose out of the collision in Cowes Road between the liner *Olympic* and HMS *Hawke* illustrated his capacity for mastering technical details and of patiently reconstructing the story out of a tangled mass of conflicting evidence. He had already proved himself a competent, if not distinguished, judge, when the outbreak of the First World War in 1914 brought him a great and unexpected opportunity.

Evans's reputation among his contemporaries as a judge of the first rank rested on the series of judgments in prize which he delivered during the war. For the first time in England since the Crimean War a prize court began to sit, under his presidency, on 4 September 1914. Prize law consisted, except for a few Crimean War decisions, almost entirely of the principles laid down by Lord Stowell to meet the relatively simple conditions of international commerce and naval warfare during the Napoleonic wars. Clearly those principles could not fairly be applied as they stood to modern naval warfare, but needed to be adapted to meet the new conditions. Any modification would affect neutral traders, and might lead to diplomatic controversies. The judge presiding over the prize court had therefore to be bold enough to develop the law to meet the new conditions, while striking a balance between British interests and those of neutrals. The reasons for his decisions had to demonstrate to the world the determination of the English courts to dispense justice impartially.

Evans rose to the task better than even his promoters had anticipated. Not content to shelter under Stowell, Evans relied on the principle of international law, cited in the *Odessa* case, that old doctrines might be extended or new principles developed in accordance with the general feeling of the times, precedents being seen as guidelines to be treated seriously and with respect but not as absolute dictates to modern legal judgments.

Evans had no specialist knowledge of the laws of naval warfare, but was nevertheless able to deliver judgments which were lucid, cogent, and informed by the expertise of others. In the case of the *Kim*, for example, Evans applied, for the first time in an English court the doctrine of 'continuous voyage' to the carriage of contraband goods. Adopting American Civil War precedents, he held that although the immediate and ostensible destination of such goods might be neutral, they would nevertheless be subject to criminal law if their ultimate destination was to the enemy. In that of the *Leonora*, he held that the so-called 'reprisals' order in council of 16 February 1917 was consistent with established principles of international law. These two cases raised fundamental questions affecting the legality of the naval policy of the allies, and had serious political consequences.

In the case of the *Möwe*, Evans greatly relaxed the traditional rule denying to an enemy subject the right to appear and to argue his case before the court concerned. In the case of the *Hamborn*, he held that the national character of a ship for prize purposes is not necessarily that of the flag she is entitled to fly, nor the country where the owning company is incorporated, but the country which has effective control over the ship's movements.

Evans's judgments in prize were reported in the ordinary series of *Law Reports*, and were also collected together in *British and Colonial Prize Cases* and in *Lloyds's Prize Cases*. His skill as a judge rested less on his intimate knowledge of the detail of his cases than on his ability to develop the principles inherent in the law to make them applicable to new legal problems. Yet his judgments in the *Kim* case show that he was able to make sense of a bewildering mass of detail, and his handling of complicated commercial transactions revealed his acuity in exposing attempts to deceive the courts. He was often accused of being too ready to condemn, and it is certainly true that he was quick to detect fraud and deal with it sternly.

Evans was created GCB in 1917, and he was offered, but declined, a peerage. He died of post-operative bleeding at 19 Lansdowne Place, Hove, Sussex, on 13 September 1918. He was survived by his second wife.

J. L. BRIERLY, rev. HUGH MOONEY

Sources *The Times* (14 Sept 1918) · letter, *The Times* (19 Oct 1918) · b. cert. · m. certs · d. cert.
Archives NL Wales, corresp. and papers | NL Wales, letters to James Clement
Likenesses G. Frampton, marble bust, 1921, Law Courts, London · C. Williams, portrait, 1927, Middle Temple, London · C. P. Hawkes, ink and wash drawing, NPG · Spy [L. Ward], caricature, mechanical reproduction, NPG; repro. in *VF* (12 Feb 1908)
Wealth at death £49,736 12s. 11d.: probate, 6 Oct 1918, *CGPLA Eng. & Wales*

Evans, Samuel Thomas George (1829–1904). *See under* Evans, William (1798–1877).

Evans, Sebastian (1830–1909), artist and author, was born on 2 March 1830 at Market Bosworth, Leicestershire, the youngest son of the Revd Arthur Benoni *Evans (1781–

1854) and his wife, Anne Dickinson (1791/2–1883), daughter of Captain Thomas Dickinson RN. Sir John *Evans (1823–1908) was his elder brother. After an early education under his father at the free grammar school of Market Bosworth, he won a scholarship to Emmanuel College, Cambridge, in 1849. He graduated BA in 1853 and proceeded MA in 1856. He showed early promise as an artist and developed an aptitude for Latin and English verse. While an undergraduate he published a volume of sonnets on the death of the duke of Wellington (1852). On leaving university Evans became a student at Lincoln's Inn, London, on 29 January 1855 but was soon after appointed secretary of the Indian Reform Association; in that capacity he was the first person in England to receive news of the Indian mutiny. In 1857 he resigned the secretaryship and became manager of the art department of the glassworks of Messrs Chance Bros. & Co. at Oldbury, near Birmingham. He held this post for ten years, and designed many windows, including one illustrating the legend of Robin Hood for the International Exhibition in London in 1862. On 6 April 1858 he married Elizabeth (*b.* 1832/3), youngest daughter of Francis Bennett Goldney, a founder of the London Joint-Stock Bank; they had two sons.

Evans took a growing interest in politics as an enthusiastic Conservative supporter; his work for the Indian Reform Association had brought him into contact with John Bright, the outspoken political reformer, and at Birmingham he met Joseph Chamberlain, with whom, in spite of their political differences, he made a lasting friendship. In 1867 Evans left the glassworks to become editor of the *Birmingham Daily Gazette*, a Conservative newspaper. In 1868 he unsuccessfully contested Birmingham for the Conservative Party and also helped to form the National Union of Conservative and Constitutional Associations. In the same year he took the degree of LLD at Cambridge. In 1870 he left the *Gazette* to pursue a legal career, and on 17 November 1873 he was called to the bar at Lincoln's Inn, then joined the Oxford circuit. However, he still found time for both political and journalistic activity, writing leading articles for *The Observer* and contributing esoteric articles and stories to *Macmillan's* and *Longman's* magazines. In 1878 he co-founded *The People*, a weekly Conservative newspaper, which he edited for the first three years of its publication. When, on the eve of the general election of 1886, the editor of the *Birmingham Daily Gazette* died suddenly, Evans resumed the editorship through this critical period.

Evans continued to pursue his artistic and poetic interests and exhibited pictures in a variety of media at the Royal Academy and elsewhere. He also enjoyed woodcarving, engraving, and bookbinding. As a poet he combined a taste for medievalism with a humour which lacked the self-consciousness of the Pre-Raphaelites. He published three further collections of poems, most notably *Brother Fabian's Manuscript and other Poems* (1865). He was an excellent translator in verse and prose from medieval and contemporary French, Latin, Greek, and Italian.

In 1898 he published *The High History of the Holy Graal*, a version of the old French romance of 'Perceval le Gallois', as well as an original study of the legend entitled *In Quest of the Holy Graal* (1898). A curious and eerie watercolour entitled *The Ancients of the World*, of about 1870 (priv. coll.), is representative of the esoteric philosophy evident in both his writing and paintings; it is reinforced by an accompanying text describing the Greek mystic symbolism of the image.

Evans's versatility and social charm brought him a varied circle of acquaintances. He knew William Makepeace Thackeray, Charles Darwin, Thomas Huxley, J. H. Newman, Matthew Arnold, and John Ruskin. In 1885 he met Edward Burne-Jones, who became an intimate friend and close companion during his last days until Burne-Jones's death in 1898; he shared Evans's interests in medieval legend and illustrated his history of the grail. Towards the end of his life Evans retired to Abbot's Barton, Canterbury, Kent, where he died on 18 December 1909; his wife survived him. After a funeral service in Canterbury Cathedral, he was buried in St Martin's Church, Canterbury, on 22 December. F. L. BICKLEY, rev. ROWENA WILLIAMS

Sources *Men and women of the time* (1891) · *The Times* (20 Dec 1909) · m. cert. · d. cert. · J. Foster, *Men-at-the-bar: a biographical hand-list of the members of the various inns of court*, 2nd edn (1885) · A. H. Miles, ed., *The poets and the poetry of the century*, 5 (1892) · G. Burne-Jones, *Memorials of Edward Burne-Jones*, 2 vols. (1904) · Venn, *Alum. Cant.* · *Burne-Jones talking: his conversations, 1895–1898, preserved by his studio assistant Thomas Rooke*, ed. M. Lago (1982)

Archives AM Oxf., papers

Likenesses P. H. Delamotte, silverpoint drawing, *c.*1856 · W. T. Roden, portrait, 1868, repro. in J. Johnson, *Works exhibited at the Royal Society of British Artists … and the New English Art Club* (1975)

Wealth at death £1679 12s. 6d.: probate, 11 April 1910, *CGPLA Eng. & Wales*

Evans, Stanley George (1912–1965), Church of England clergyman and Christian socialist, was educated at Westminster City School, King's College, London, and the College of the Resurrection, Mirfield. In spite of his pastoral and intellectual gifts, after ordination in 1935, and curacies in Shepherd's Bush, Islington, and Plaistow, he spent many years in the ecclesiastical wilderness before becoming a parish priest in Dalston, east London, in 1955. There is little doubt that this was entirely due to his political views which were closely allied to those of the Communist Party. Evans married Anastasia Cecilia Nicholson and they had two daughters.

In the 1930s Evans was heavily involved in opposition to fascism and supported the republican cause in the Spanish Civil War. He was one of the founders of the Russia Today group which grew into the British Soviet Friendship Society. He led many visits to the USSR and countries of eastern Europe throughout the cold-war years, and was the *Daily Worker* correspondent at the trial of Cardinal Mindszenty in 1949. He followed the Communist Party line fairly closely and preached a glowing, uncritical, sermon on the death of Stalin in 1953. However, after the Twentieth Congress of the Communist Party of the Soviet Union, and the invasion of Hungary, in 1956, he became a more open socialist, holding views akin to the socialist humanism of the New Reasoner group. He remained a Marxist in his political thinking until his death.

Evans played an important role from the 1940s to the 1960s, both in his intellectual nourishment of the socialist Christian constituency, and in providing links for Christians with the USSR and the countries of the eastern bloc. He was a regular visitor to all the Warsaw pact countries, wrote a history of Bulgaria, and was the editor of the *New Central European Observer* during the 1940s. He was responsible for a whole series of small journals—*Religion and the People*, which he edited from 1946 to 1957, *Magnificat*, and *The Junction* (named after Dalston Junction railway station) from 1958 until his death. The latter was subtitled 'a journal of Anglican realism', and it was as an Anglican realist that he wished to be known. He was the key figure in the Council of Clergy and Ministers for Common Ownership, founded in 1942, which became the Society of Socialist Clergy and Ministers, and was one of the leaders of the Christian Socialist Movement, founded in 1960.

In many areas Evans was ahead of his time. He was writing on race and South Africa in 1944. In 1957 he argued that the old confessional divisions within world Christianity had become less important than the division about the nature of the kingdom of God, and its relation to the structures of this world (Leech, 'Back street pastor', 188). Much of his thinking anticipated liberation theology, though the term was not used until three years after his death.

In his theology Evans was traditional and orthodox, and very critical of what he saw as relativizing trends in theology and ethics. At Holy Trinity, Dalston, where he was vicar from 1955 to 1960, the life of the parish was focused on the parish eucharist and the parish meeting. Celebration and debate were seen as inseparable, heart and head were fully engaged. Evans had a strong sense of the place of liturgy in shaping the corporate identity of the Christian community. In an interview on BBC radio about 1962, he spoke prophetically and with great perception about the future possibilities for a people's liturgy. Liturgy, he pointed out, had for many centuries been separated from the people, becoming something performed above the people's heads, by clergy or choir. A central problem for the late twentieth century was the lack of a common language and a common cultural form. Most thinking about liturgy had tended to focus on the rite rather than on the production of the whole liturgical act. Evans stressed that the Christian community at worship is 'not ever an audience. They are an expressive community, if you like, an orchestra. The distinction between the audience and the players … does not exist in Christian liturgy. We have built up an area in which it does exist and we have destroyed Christian liturgy in doing so' (private information).

In 1960 Evans became chancellor of Southwark Cathedral and the first principal of the Southwark ordination course. In a sermon delivered at Southwark Cathedral in September 1963 he argued against the seminary model of theological education, and strongly opposed the class bias in clergy selection: 'the idea of clergy drawn from only one class of a class-divided society is one of the most dangerous of very modern Anglican innovations' (archives of

S. G. Evans, Hull University). His smallest book, *The Church in the Back Streets* (1962), is in some ways his most important. Here he confronted the crisis of the church in the inner city, which had been the context for all his ministry. Evans died in a car accident on 11 September 1965 returning from an anti-nuclear demonstration. He was declared dead at Grantham and Kesteven General Hospital, Grantham, Lincolnshire.　　　　KENNETH LEECH

Sources S. G. Evans, archives, U. Hull, Brynmor Jones L. · C. Bryant, *Possible dreams: a personal history of the British Christian socialists* (1996) · K. Leech, 'A prophet of revolutionary orthodoxy', *The Times* (13 Sept 1975) · K. Leech, 'Stanley Evans: the kingdom of God in the back streets', *Spirituality and pastoral care* (1989), 95–104 · K. Leech, 'Back street pastor: the eucharistic politics of Stanley Evans', *The eye of the storm: spiritual resources for the pursuit of justice* (1992), 183–9 · K. Leech, 'Stanley Evans: back street pastor', *Paragon Review* [Hull University Archives] (1995), 5–7 · A. Wilkinson, *Christian socialism: Scott Holland to Tony Blair* (1998) · WWW · d. cert. · private information (2004) [tape of BBC radio discussion of liturgy] · *CGPLA Eng. & Wales* (1965)

Archives U. Hull, corresp., MSS, and sermons | SOUND BL NSA, current affairs recording

Wealth at death £7046: administration, 1 Dec 1965, *CGPLA Eng. & Wales*

Evans, Theophilus (1693–1767), Church of England clergyman and author, was born on 19 or 20 February 1693 at Penywennallt, in the parish of Llandygwydd, in south Cardiganshire, the son of Charles Evans (*d.* 1730) and his wife, Elinor Beynon. Little is known of his early education, but it is likely that he attended Carmarthen grammar school, and some circumstantial evidence suggests that he went on to Jesus College, Oxford, but that he left without graduating. He married Alice Bevan of Gelligaled, Glamorgan, some time in 1719–20 and raised three sons (Charles, Theophilus, and Michael) and two daughters (Elinor and Sarah). His favourite grandchild, Theophilus *Jones, author of the celebrated *A History of the County of Brecknock* (2 vols., 1805–9), described him, with pardonable exaggeration, as one who 'had perhaps as much of the milk of human kindness as any man who ever lived: of the value of money he knew little, books were his only treasures' (Jones, 2.276).

Three factors moulded Evans's career—his gentry blood, his warm attachment to the Anglican church, and his love of literature. His great-grandfather Griffith ab Evan Jenkin (who lived to be 100) and his grandfather Evan Griffith (popularly known as Captain Tory) were uncompromising royalists and churchmen. From an early age, therefore, Evans was taught to believe that dissent was not only a grave threat to the Anglican cause but also inimical to peace and good order. During his highly productive and sometimes controversial fifty years' service as an Anglican clergyman in Cardiganshire and Brecknockshire, he published an appreciable number of sermons and devotional works (mostly translations of English bestsellers) in which he regularly vilified 'heretical' sects, 'levelling' Roundheads, and, most of all, 'arrogant' enthusiasts. Methodism was anathema to him. He parted company with his patron, Marmaduke Gwynne of Garth, Brecknockshire, when the latter fell under the spell of the prominent Methodist Howel Harris in 1737, and he publicly chastised William Williams (Pantycelyn), who served as his curate in 1740–43, and Daniel Rowland. In *The History of Modern Enthusiasm* (1752) he denounced all the allegedly 'heretical' sects which had sprouted since the Reformation and, as vicar of Llangamarch, Brecknockshire, he proudly declared in 1762 that his parish was an unblemished Anglican fiefdom: 'No Papists, nor any popish School. No Presbyterians, Independents, Anabaptists, or Quakers' (Church in Wales records, archdeaconry of Brecon, 1762).

Theophilus Evans was born and bred in the Vale of Teifi, an area highly regarded at the turn of the seventeenth century for the vigour of its spiritual life and the richness of its literary inheritance. Like many other gifted authors, antiquarians, and poets in the locality he learned to transcribe, translate, and compose at an early age, and his most celebrated work, *Drych y prif oesoedd* ('Mirror of the primitive ages'; (1716)), was published when he was twenty-three. In this vivid and uncritical epic, Evans not only celebrated what he considered 'Anglican' values in the early British church but also the 'British history' which had been so mercilessly pilloried since the days of Polydore Vergil. He considered the cynical attitude of English historians towards Brutus and Arthur both humiliating and unjust, and he unashamedly extolled the glorious origins of the Welsh by offering a Welsh-language version of the thesis of the Breton monk Paul-Yves Pezron that the Welsh were directly descended from Gomer, son of Japhet, son of Noah. Writing in robustly patriotic vein, Evans portrayed the history of Wales as a pageant of alien usurpations, bitter defeats, and epic victories. For the first time in their history, the Welsh were provided with a printed account of their own history in their native tongue. *Drych y prif oesoedd* caught the imagination of the Welsh reading public and ran to five editions in the eighteenth century. Sixteen editions were published in the nineteenth century and even by the twilight years of the Victorian age it was still far and away the most popular history book in Welsh.

In 1763 Evans made over the living of Llangamarch, Brecknockshire, which he had held since 1738, to his son-in-law Hugh Jones, though he retained the living of Llanfaes, Brecon, until his death on 11 September 1767 at his home, Llwyneinon, Llangamarch, Brecknockshire. He was buried in Llangamarch churchyard. Local inhabitants probably remembered him as the discoverer of the celebrated spring at Llanwrtyd Wells or as the hammer of Welsh dissenters and Methodists, but his posthumous fame rests on the triumphant success of *Drych y prif oesoedd*, undeniably one of the classics of Welsh prose.

GERAINT H. JENKINS

Sources G. H. Jenkins, *Theophilus Evans (1693–1767): y dyn, ei deulu, a'i oes* (1993) · T. Evans, *Drych y prif oesoedd*, ed. D. Thomas (1955) · T. Evans, *Drych y prif oesoedd: yn ôl yr argraffiad cyntaf: 1716*, ed. G. H. Hughes (1961) · DWB · M. Stephens, ed., *The Oxford companion to the literature of Wales* (1986) · T. Jones, *A history of the county of Brecknock*, 2 vols. (1805–9) · Church in Wales records, archdeaconry of Brecon, 1762, NL Wales

Wealth at death see will, NL Wales, BR/1768/52

Evans, Thomas (*d.* 1633), Church of England clergyman and poet, matriculated at St John's College, Cambridge, at Michaelmas 1608; nothing is known of him before this date. He graduated BA from Corpus Christi College, Cambridge, in 1612–13, MA in 1616, and BD in 1622. Between 1618 and 1619 he was rector of St Helen, Bishopsgate, London, and he was rector of Little Holland, Essex, from 1618 until his death in 1633.

Evans was the author of one publication: *Oedipus: three cantoes wherein is contained 1 his unfortunate infancy, 2 his execrable actions, 3 his lamentable end, by T.E. Bach: Art. Cantab.* (1615). This long poem in iambic pentameter quatrains narrates the story of Oedipus in straightforward chronological order. There is an elaborate prose dedication (signed Thomas Evans) to John Clapham, one of the six clerks of chancery, which describes the poem as 'the first child, but not the heyre of all the father's wit': no further publication by Evans is known, although his name is associated with verses in at least one manuscript miscellany with a Cambridge University connection (BL, Add. MS 15227). THOMPSON COOPER, *rev.* MATTHEW STEGGLE

Sources Venn, *Alum. Cant.*, 1/2.109

Evans, Thomas (1738/9–1803), bookseller, was born in Wales and although the identity of his parents is unknown, his background, by all accounts, was humble, with the *Gentleman's Magazine* discerning 'very little to boast of in point of [his] origin' (*GM*, 696). Evans eventually moved to London, where at first he lived with and served as porter to William Johnston, a bookseller in Ludgate Street, and on 23 April 1776 was made free of the Musicians' Company. It was by 'industry and perseverance' that he became an 'eminent bookseller' (ibid.), working in the centre of London's book trade precinct from several addresses in Paternoster Row between 1770 and 1797. For a number of years during the early 1770s Evans was publisher of the *Morning Chronicle* and *London Packet*, by means of which he became acquainted with many literary characters of the day. Although friendly with many members of London's literati, his association with the Irish writer Oliver Goldsmith was less amicable as a result of one article, reflecting upon Goldsmith and Miss Horneck, a female acquaintance, published by Evans in the *Morning Chronicle*. Goldsmith was so incensed by the article that he resorted to a physical confrontation, but Evans reputedly defended himself 'in a true pugilistic style', and in a few moments the author of *The Vicar of Wakefield* 'was disarmed, and extended on the floor, to the no small diversion of the by-standers' (ibid.). Goldsmith was subsequently indicted for an assault and compromised by paying £50 to a Welsh charity.

By 1779 Evans had taken control of the extensive bookselling business of Hawes, Clarke, and Collins at 32 Paternoster Row, and was by this time a competent master of his trade, training apprentices who, according to the *Gentleman's Magazine*, became 'ornaments of their profession' (*GM*, 696). Evans had married a woman named Ann about this time and was the father of his only son, James Evans. In 1789, father and son were working together, but

the following year James was trading alone and married a daughter of Archibald Hamilton II. In 1792 James was made free of the Stationers' Company, but on 18 July 1795 he was declared bankrupt and went to America before returning to England, where he died in poverty eighteen months before his father. Thomas Evans, by contrast, had amassed a significant personal fortune and was able to retire in 1797, before separating from his wife the following year, apparently on account of her partiality for one of her sons.

Evans died, aged sixty-four, on 2 July 1803 at his lodgings in Chapter House Court, London, after suffering from a short and unknown illness. Considered by some contemporaries as a man of rough and eccentric habits, Evans requested in his will that he was to be buried without a coffin, that his grave should not have a tombstone, and that the funeral would cost no more than 40 shillings. His son was to be a beneficiary of his will to the amount of £200, while to his wife he bequeathed £40 a year and a further £20 per annum to a niece, Sarah Morgan, as well as a share of his property to his sister, Eleanor Vaughan. The remainder of his estate was left to his friend of forty years and fellow bookseller, Christopher Brown.

MICHAEL T. DAVIS

Sources *GM*, 1st ser., 73 (1803), 696 • C. H. Timperley, *Encyclopaedia of literary and typographical anecdote*, 2nd edn (1842); repr. (1977) • H. R. Plomer and others, *A dictionary of the printers and booksellers who were at work in England, Scotland, and Ireland from 1726 to 1775* (1932) • I. Maxted, *The London book trades, 1775–1800: a preliminary checklist of members* (1977) • C. Humphries and W. C. Smith, *Music publishing in the British Isles, from the earliest times to the middle of the nineteenth century: a dictionary of engravers, printers, publishers, and music sellers* (1954) • will, 1803, PRO, PROB 11/1397, sig. 697 • *DNB*
Wealth at death reportedly significant: will, PRO, PROB 11/1397, sig. 697

Evans, Thomas (1742–1784), bookseller, left no record of his parents or origin. He was apprenticed in London in 1757 for £40 to Charles Marsh, whose shop was registered as in St Martin-in-the-Fields (but later in Round Court in the Strand and in Charing Cross). A handwritten note on a copy of Marsh's poem *The Library* (1766; Nichols, 3.647) suggests that Evans carried on at Marsh's shop beyond his apprenticeship, perhaps even under Marsh's successor Samuel Leacroft (1767), until he set up his own shop at 50 Strand, near the York Buildings, in 1774.

Evans was a 'literary' bookseller who, as Nichols says, 'favoured the world with elegant editions of complete collections of the works of some very eminent poets' (Nichols, 6.435). Among these multi-volume editions (some of which Evans personally edited) were the works of Beaumont and Fletcher, George Villiers, Matthew Prior, Richard Savage, Oliver Goldsmith (the first collected edition), and François Rabelais. Other notable publications included Shakespeare's *Poems*, Evans's own four volumes of *Old Ballads, Historical and Narrative*, Nicholson's *The English, Scotch, and Irish Historical Libraries*, Caradoc of Lhancarvan's *History of Wales*, and a revised edition of Francis Peck's *Desiderata curiosa*. The dedicatees of some of these works reflect Evans's circle of friends and acquaintances: Sir Joshua Reynolds, Richard B. Sheridan, Samuel

Foote, and David Garrick. Pieces of his correspondence with Garrick are extant. Evans's engaging conversation and lively humour delighted fellow booksellers who met weekly at the Grecian Coffee House, a club that included Thomas Davies, Lockyer Davis, James Dodsley, Thomas Longman, Thomas Payne, Thomas Cadell, Robert Baldwin, and John Nichols, with most of whom Evans issued joint publications.

Evans died at 50 Strand, London, on 30 April 1784, and his closest friend, Cadell, served as the executor of his will (witnessed by Isaac Reed and William Fell) and was appointed guardian to Robert Harding *Evans, the only son of Evans and his wife, Ann, who survived him. Robert was only six years old at the time of his father's death, and in 1792 Cadell apprenticed the young Evans to Thomas Payne at Mew's Gate for £120. About 1804 Robert Evans took over the bookselling business of James Edwards in Pall Mall but then abandoned it about 1812 to become a celebrated auctioneer of private libraries. In a laudatory two-column obituary, Nichols says nothing of the cause of Evans's early death (*GM*, 1st ser., 54/1, 396). Thomas Evans should not be confused with a contemporary bookseller of the same name, the one Goldsmith caned and whose bookshop was variously located at 20 and 54 Paternoster Row and 429 Strand.   JAMES E. TIERNEY

Sources Nichols, *Lit. anecdotes* · H. R. Plomer and others, *A dictionary of the printers and booksellers who were at work in England, Scotland, and Ireland from 1726 to 1775* (1932); repr. (1968), 85 · *GM*, 1st ser., 54 (1784), 396 · *DNB* · I. Maxted, ed., *The British book trades, 1710–1777: an index of the masters and their apprentices* (1983), no. 1037a · H. Hammelmann, *Book illustrators in eighteenth-century England*, ed. T. S. R. Boase (1975), 46, 60, 66, 76, 77 · *The letters of David Garrick*, ed. D. M. Little and G. M. Kahrl, 3 (1963), 957–8, 965, 1283–4 · *The private correspondence of David Garrick*, ed. J. Boaden, 2 (1832), 268 · D. F. McKenzie, ed., *Stationers' Company apprentices*, [3]: *1701–1800* (1978) · *Poems written by Mr William Shakespeare* [1775] · will, PRO, PROB 11/1116, sig. 256

Evans, Thomas (*b.* 1763, *d.* in or before 1831), insurrectionist, emerged from obscurity in 1793 as a member of the *London Corresponding Society. In 1797 he became the society's secretary at a time when government repression was punitive. Intelligence sources linked Evans closely with revolutionary tendencies. He was one of twelve United Englishmen arrested on 18 April 1798; an alleged correspondence between the United English and Irish movements, in his hand, was also seized, and he was detained without trial for three years. His wife, Janet, *née* Galloway (*d.* 1822x30?) [*see* Evans, Janet], gave birth to their only surviving child, Thomas John, shortly before his arrest.

In the picaresque career that followed his release in March 1801 Evans worked as a bracemaker, bawdy print-colourer, coffee-house keeper, and printer. His links with revolutionary elements were maintained, and he attempted to blackmail his erstwhile associate Francis Place over his role in 1810 as jury foreman at the coroner's inquest into the death of Joseph Sellis, rumoured to have been murdered by the duke of Cumberland. Evans was also involved in more reputable activities, for example on the 1812 election committee for Francis Burdett and

Thomas Cochrane. Most of his energy was devoted to promoting the agrarian ideas of Thomas Spence, on whose death in 1814 Evans became leader of the Society of Spencean Philanthropists. His *Christian Policy: the Salvation of the Empire* (1816) combined Jacobin, Spencean, and millenarian ideas. It aroused considerable notice, and was attacked by Southey in the *Quarterly Review* and by Malthus in the fifth edition (1817) of his *Essay on Population*.

The putative revolutionary now chose to distance himself from those Spenceans, led by Thistlewood and Watson, who were prepared to compromise agrarian ideals for short-term gains in popularity. As a result, Evans took no part in the Spa Fields conspiracy of 1816. Yet he was considered sufficiently dangerous to be arrested in February 1817 on charges of high treason. Imprisonment and his doctrinaire views marginalized him among London ultra-radicals, though he courageously organized a public fund to support the families of those arrested at Cato Street in 1820. Shortly afterwards he moved to Manchester, where his son was enjoying a brief tenure as proprietor and editor of the radical *Manchester Observer*. His son's interest in the paper had to be sold following prosecution in April 1821 for 'libelling the army'. The elder Evans supported the family from the proceeds of a printing business (which published his biography of Spence, the first, in 1821), but on the son's release in April 1822 they headed back to the capital. Evans now campaigned for Carlile's defence, and for the London Mechanics' Institute. Then, in February 1824, he spoke at a celebration of Paine's birthday before passing into an obscurity as total as that from which he had emerged thirty years before. Correspondence between his son and Francis Place in 1831 indicates that Thomas Evans had died before that date.

MALCOLM CHASE

Sources M. Chase, 'Evans, Thomas', *DLB*, vol. 8 · I. McCalman, *Radical underworld: prophets, revolutionaries, and pornographers in London, 1795–1840* (1988) · M. Chase, *The people's farm: English radical agrarianism, 1775–1840* (1988) · G. Claeys, 'Thomas Evans and the development of Spenceanism, 1815–16', *Bulletin of the Society for the Study of Labour History*, 48 (1984), 24–30 · Bodl. Oxf., MSS Burdett · BL, Add. MS 27808, fol. 229
Archives BL, Place MSS · PRO, Home Office and Treasury Solicitor's MSS

Evans, Thomas [*pseud.* Tomos Glyn Cothi] (1764–1833), Unitarian minister and poet, son of Ifan and Hannah Evans, was born at Capel Sain Silin, near Brechfa, Carmarthenshire, on 20 June 1764. His father was an independent-minded weaver who bought books and essays for his children, including the religious works of Joseph Priestley, the English Unitarian. The prevailing theology in the neighbourhood was Calvinism; Evans, from an early age, was nicknamed Priestley Bach (Little Priestley) on account of the influence of Priestley on his theological development. In order to worship with like-minded friends he used to walk to Alltyblaca, 12 miles away, to hear David Davis of Castellhywel preach sermons of an Arian type. As an adult he began to preach in his father's house, a part of which he got licensed for this purpose; eventually a chapel was built for him.

A democrat as well as a dissenter, Evans preached the rights of man, lamented the use of fast days to pray for military success, and advocated peace during the war with revolutionary France. As well as translations from Priestley and Theophilus Lindsey, he published three editions (1795–6) of the *Miscellaneous Repository* or *Drysorfa Gymmysgedig* to bring the benefits of enlightenment and dissent to his Welsh audience. The journal gave political news of the state trials against the English 'Jacobins'. It was once thought that he had translated 'La Marseillaise' into Welsh.

In 1801, on the information of a spy belonging to his own congregation, Evans was apprehended, tried, and sentenced by Judge Harding to be imprisoned for two years in Carmarthen gaol, and to stand in the pillory. He was charged with singing, in English, a seditious song, an accusation which he consistently denied. Evans was the political victim of anti-Unitarian prejudice and malicious gossip; during his imprisonment he met with great sympathy and compiled an English–Welsh dictionary.

Evans became minister of the Old Meeting-House, Aberdâr, in 1811, the same year in which he published a collection of hymns for Unitarian worship (*Cyhoeddiad o hymnau*). He was married to Ann Davies, with whom he had eleven children. Of the Welsh dissenters and democrats of the period of the French Revolutionary and Napoleonic wars, Evans was the most sustained and persistent in his radicalism. One of a 'little knot of men, sturdy old republicans' (Evans, *Dylanwad y Chwyldro Ffrengig ar lenyddiaeth Cymru*, 96) in the industrial area of Merthyr Tudful, he died, after a short illness, on 29 January 1833 at Mill Street, Aberdâr, Glamorgan.

HYWEL MEILYR DAVIES

Sources G. D. Owen, *Thomas Evans (Tomos Glyn Cothi)* (1960) · J. J. Evans, *Morgan John Rhys a'i Amserau* (1935) · J. J. Evans, *Dylanwad y chwyldro Ffrengig ar lenyddiaeth Cymru* (1928) · *Yr Ymofynnydd* (July 1933) [memorial issue] · T. Oswald Williams, *Undodiaeth a rhyddid meddwl* (1962) · David Davies, *The influence of the French Revolution on Welsh life and literature* (1926) · Jacob Davies, ed., *Crefydd a gweriniaeth yn hanes yr hen dŷ cwrdd Aberdâr* (1951) · *Seren Gomer* (March 1833), 94
Archives NL Wales, notes and MSS

Evans, Thomas [*pseud.* Telynog] (1840–1865), Welsh-language poet, was born at Cardigan on 8 September 1840, the son of Thomas Evans, ship carpenter. His early education was very rudimentary. At the age of eleven he was apprenticed on a coasting vessel, but his treatment was so bad that he ran away to Aberdâr and worked in a coalmine in Cwm-bach. From here he sent a letter to his mother, written in verse (his first attempt), apprising her of his whereabouts.

When Evans was about fifteen he devoted his leisure hours to music and attracted public attention as a singer. Shortly after this he competed successfully at a small eisteddfod, held at his chapel, for the best poem on humility. This brought him to public notice, and from this time his name was constantly in the local papers and mentioned in connection with eisteddfods, where, under the bardic name Telynog, he won no fewer than twenty

prizes. His achievement is all the more marked when one considers that during all this time he was working as a collier. His last six years were spent in constant battle first with dyspepsia, and then with consumption. He died on 29 April 1865 and was buried in the Aberdâr cemetery. At the time of his death 'he was regarded as one of the most promising poets of Wales' (*DWB*).

Evans's poetical works, including the lyrics 'Blodeuyn bach wyf fi mewn gardd' and 'Yr haf', were collected and arranged by Dafydd Morganwg, and published by subscription in a limited edition. The volume was prefaced by a brief memoir by Howel Williams.

R. M. J. JONES, *rev.* M. CLARE LOUGHLIN-CHOW

Sources H. Williams, 'Byr gofiant o'r awdwr', in *Barddoniaeth Telynog*, ed. D. Morganwg, new edn (1870) · *DWB*

Evans, Thomas Simpson (1776/7–1818), mathematician, born in Ashbury, Berkshire, was the eldest son of Lewis *Evans (1755–1827), the curate of Ashbury, and his wife, Ann Norman, and was baptized at Ashbury in August 1777. He was named after Thomas Simpson, the mathematician. On 12 February 1796 he was appointed assistant to Nevil Maskelyne at the Royal Observatory, Greenwich. However, shortly after marrying Deborah Mascall, governess to Maskelyne's daughter Margaret and daughter of John Mascall of Ashford, Kent, on 7 June 1798, he left the Royal Observatory. He took charge of a private observatory at Blackheath belonging to William Larkins, formerly accountant-general to the East India Company at Bengal. Some time after the death of Larkins on 24 April 1800, he was appointed mathematical master under his father at the Royal Military Academy, Woolwich. There he continued until 1810, when he accepted the mastership of the mathematical school at New Charlton, near Woolwich. He left this position in 1813 to become master of mathematics at Christ's Hospital, London. He appears to have held the degree of LLD and to have been a fellow of the Linnean Society. He and his wife had five children: Thomas Simpson Evans (1798–1880), vicar of St Leonard, Shoreditch; Aspasia Evans (1799–1876); Herbert Norman Evans MD (1802–1877), a great book collector; Arthur Benoni Evans (*d.* 1838); and Lewis Evans (1815–1869), headmaster of Sandbach Free Grammar School, Cheshire.

Evans died in London on 28 October 1818, aged forty-one. He left a completed translation of Antonio Cagnoli's *Trigonometria piana e sferica* besides other translations from foreign scientific works and a vast collection of unfinished papers in several branches of science. He also contributed various articles to the *Philosophical Magazine*. Apart from these he wrote a comprehensive account of the Royal Observatory, its instruments, and the role of the assistant, and brief biographies of the astronomers royal, all of which appeared in John Evans's *Juvenile Tourist* (3rd edn, 1810). His library was considered one of the most valuable collections of mathematical and philosophical works in the kingdom.

GORDON GOODWIN, *rev.* H. K. HIGTON

Sources D. Howse, *Nevil Maskelyne: the seaman's astronomer* (1989) · E. G. R. Taylor, *The mathematical practitioners of Hanoverian England, 1714–1840* (1966) · J. Evans, *The juvenile tourist*, 3rd edn (1810)

Likenesses stipple, silhouette, BM

Evans, (Sydney Edmund) Tolchard (1901–1978), popular song composer, was born on 20 September 1901 at 238 Portnall Road, West Kilburn, London, the son of (Edmund) George Evans, a commercial clerk and later an engineer, and his wife, Maud Mary, *née* Tolchard. While he was still a boy the family moved to nearby Willesden, and he lived in the area for the rest of his life. He grew up in a musical family, his father playing several instruments and his sister becoming an orchestral violinist. He took his first piano lessons at six and quickly displayed a musical ear and a talent for extemporization. He studied orchestration and conducting and had an early ambition to be a serious composer, but in 1919 he joined the Lawrence Wright popular music publishing company as office boy, gaining valuable contacts in the popular music industry and seeing his first songs in print.

In 1924 Evans left to work as pianist for silent films and dance bands, and by 1925 he had his own band at the Queen's Hotel, Westcliff-on-Sea. He later moved to the Palace Hotel, Southend, where he remained for most of the 1930s. Also in 1925 he enjoyed modest success as a songwriter when 'Every Step towards Killarney' was performed by the Savoy Havana Band. His first international hit came in 1926 with 'Barcelona', which built on the popularity of the continental hit song 'Valencia'. About this time he and his regular lyricists Stanley J. Damerell and Robert Hargreaves formed the Cecil Lennox Music Company to publish their songs. These included 'Dreamy Devon' in 1930, and 'Lights of Paris' and 'Life's Desire' in 1931, in which year they also achieved their greatest success with another Spanish-flavoured number, 'Lady of Spain'. Because of its unfamiliar *paso doble* rhythm, it was turned down by several bands before being launched by Jack Payne. It went on to achieve international success and ultimate classic status in Spain itself.

On Christmas day 1931 Evans married Phyllis Elizabeth Mayhead (*b.* 1906/7); they had two sons. In the following year he enjoyed another major British song success with an old-time comedy chorus number, 'Let's All Sing like the Birdies Sing', that rapidly caught on when broadcast by Henry Hall. In 1934 came a series of songs with one-word titles—'Faith', 'If', and 'Unless'—and in 1935 he produced 'The Song of the Trees' and 'There's a Lovely Lake in London'. At one time four of Evans's songs were being used by major London dance bands as signature tunes, while another was similarly used by the commercial radio station Radio Normandy. He continued to turn out popular dance numbers during the 1940s, among them 'I Hear Your Voice' (1942) and 'Sailor, who are You Dreaming of Tonight?' (1944). As bandleader he was featured on BBC radio, notably with his *Tuneful Twenties* series in 1949 and *John Bull's Band* in 1951.

Also in 1951 Evans's songwriting career enjoyed a boost when a recording of 'If' by Perry Como sold over a million copies. On the back of it, Evans spent three months in the USA in 1952, a year which saw another million-seller in Eddie Fisher's recording of 'Lady of Spain'. Back in Britain

the song 'Ev'rywhere' won an Ivor Novello award in 1955, as did 'My September Love' and 'I'll Find You' in 1957. Both the latter went into the hit charts in recordings by David Whitfield, the former reaching number three and the latter being featured in the film *The Sea Wife* starring Richard Burton. After recovering from a nervous breakdown, Evans enjoyed his final song success with his own recording of 'The Singing Piano' in 1959.

Besides writing background music for other films and television, Evans also appeared on such television shows as *The Black and White Minstrel Show* and *The Billy Cotton Band Show*. A popular, sometimes outspoken person, known as Tolch, he was ever willing to turn out a song in response to a telephone call, and his total output supposedly exceeded 1000 songs. Increasingly unfashionable, however, these began to accumulate unpublished in a trunk in the garage of his home at 53 Hardinge Road, Kensal Rise. In 1973–4 he won an Ivor Novello award for outstanding services to British music and in 1976 was featured on the radio programme *Desert Island Discs*. As luxury item he chose a pile of manuscript paper to write non-commercial music, and his selected book was the works of Voltaire, whose sense of humour he claimed to share. He died at the Central Middlesex Hospital, Park Royal, London, on 12 March 1978, and was survived by his wife.   Andrew Lamb

Sources E. Rogers and M. Henessy, *Tin Pan Alley* (1964) • M. White, *You must remember this …* (1983) • *Desert island discs*, 28/30 April 1976 [BBC Radio 4] • P. Gammond, *The Oxford companion to popular music* (1991) • b. cert. • m. cert. • d. cert. • *CGPLA Eng. & Wales* (1978)
Archives SOUND BL NSA, performance recordings
Likenesses photograph, repro. in P. Cliffe, *Fascinating rhythm* (1990), 68
Wealth at death £44,969: probate, 7 July 1978, *CGPLA Eng. & Wales*

Evans, Sir Trevor Maldwyn (1902–1981), journalist, was born in Abertridwr, Glamorgan, on 21 February 1902, the only son and elder child of Samuel Evans, a police sergeant, and his wife, Margaret Jones. He was educated at Pontypridd grammar school. When he was fifteen his father was killed in a railway-crossing accident and in order to bolster the family finances Evans put aside his ambition to go to the University College of Wales, Aberystwyth, to train as a teacher. Instead he went down the local pit and, for four years, worked as a trainee electrician until the miners' strike of 1921 threw him out of work. Evans went to night school, obtained a London matriculation certificate, became a pupil teacher, and added to his earnings by doing freelance reporting for the *Glamorgan Free Press*, for a payment of 5*s.* a column. One week the paper left out his column, so Evans tramped over the hills to Pontypridd and confronted the editor, who at once appointed him as his assistant. His life's work in newspapers had begun.

In 1926 he moved to the *Daily Dispatch* in Manchester; in 1928 to the *Daily Mail*, and in 1930 to the *Daily Express* as news editor in the Manchester offices. That year he also married Margaret (Madge) Speers, daughter of John Best Gribbin, journalist, of Heaton Moor, Cheshire. They had a son and a daughter: Richard Trevor, who became a senior journalist on the *Financial Times*, and Marilyn Speers, King Edward VII professor of English literature at Cambridge University.

In 1933 Evans moved to the *Daily Express* London office and became one of a renowned editorial team—to be known as the 1933 Club—that Arthur Christiansen, editor at the age of twenty-nine, was building up around him. Increasingly, during these years, Evans had become a writer deeply involved in labour and industrial affairs. These had been years of depression and unemployment; the trade unions were emerging as a powerful influence in Britain and Evans, with his mining background and a steadfast devotion to the miners' cause, saw a supreme opportunity to pioneer a new era in industrial reporting.

Evans was not alone in this ambition. Two other distinguished Fleet Street industrial correspondents, Ian Mackay (of whom he later wrote a biography, 1953) of the *News Chronicle* and Hugh Chevins of the *Daily Telegraph*, joined him in establishing a standard of reporting that did justice to the growing importance of industry and labour in national life. They cultivated close and friendly relations with employers, unions, and civil servants. Evans in particular practised a rare political detachment; within the National Union of Mineworkers, for example, he was on intimate terms with right-wing leaders such as Will Lawther and Sam Watson, as well as with communists such as Arthur Horner. The respect he gained on all sides of politics and industry was shown by the fact that in the course of his career Evans was offered a high appointment with the Federation of British Industries and invited to stand for parliament by the Labour Party. He turned down both offers, preferring to stay with journalism. Yet these relationships never robbed him of a fearless invective when he considered that either employers or unions were guilty of conduct that fell short of the highest standards.

Evans was a widely known and respected writer at all important industrial conferences, especially the Trades Union Congress. He acquired an easy sociability that often masked a steely determination to get every detail of a story right and in the correct perspective. He was a superb after-dinner speaker and raconteur, fluent, engaging, with a touch of Welsh exuberance. He put his diplomatic skills to good use, especially during the war years, and he told the story of one famed occasion when he tried to bring together those two irreconcilables, Ernest Bevin, then minister of labour, and Lord Beaverbrook, then minister of production. He arranged a dinner party at Beaverbrook's home. 'A nice place you have here,' said Bevin on arrival. 'Yes,' replied Beaverbrook, 'and I expect you fellows will take it away from me some day.' Bevin departed at once without his dinner. Temperamental incompatibility had, for once, defeated Evans's diplomacy. He later wrote a biography of Bevin (1946).

Evans became a director of Express Newspapers, but the executive role never greatly appealed to him; he remained always the good reporter. He also became chairman of the London Press Club, later vice-president, and finally honorary life member emeritus. He was appointed to the Press Council in 1964 and served as a member until 1975.

Throughout all this full life, he found time to teach and inspire a new generation of industrial reporters. Many of his pupils achieved fame both in newspapers and in public life. He was appointed CBE in 1963 and was knighted in 1967.

Evans died suddenly on 10 June 1981, while travelling from his home in Kingston upon Thames, Surrey, to a meeting at the London Press Club. His wife survived him. He was cremated at Putney Vale on 15 June.

EDWARD PICKERING, *rev.*

Sources *The Times* (11 June 1981) · *The Times* (12 June 1981) · A. C. H. Smith, *Paper voices: the popular press and social change, 1935–1965* (1975) · D. Griffiths, ed., *The encyclopedia of the British press, 1422–1992* (1992) · A. J. P. Taylor, *Beaverbrook* (1972) · private information (1990) · *CGPLA Eng. & Wales* (1981) · WWW

Archives FILM BFI NFTVA, news footage | SOUND BL NSA, performance recording

Wealth at death £110,500: probate, 24 Sept 1981, *CGPLA Eng. & Wales*

Evans, Sir (Evan) Vincent (1851–1934), journalist and promoter of the Welsh national revival, was born at Nantcol in the parish of Llangelynnin, Merioneth, Wales, probably on 18 November 1851. He was the elder son of Lewis Evans, a farmer, and his first wife, Ann, *née* Lewis. The registration of the birth cannot be traced. Following his mother's death, after the birth of a second son, the family moved in 1856 to Tynllyn, Trawsfynydd, in the same county, where Evans was brought up by his grandmother. He was for some years a pupil teacher in the national school at Trawsfynydd and later an assistant in the village store. In 1872 he moved to London, where he adopted the name Vincent, after his grandfather Evans Vincent, and where he remained until his death. He was first employed in a solicitors' office and then by Harding, Whinney & Co., accountants, through whom he was put in touch with the Chancery Lane Safe Deposit and Offices Company Ltd, the service of which he then entered, becoming first secretary and afterwards managing director.

In his youth Evans had been the local correspondent of *Baner ac Amserau Cymru*. He was again attracted to journalism in London, becoming a member of the parliamentary press gallery. Throughout his life he continued his connection with the Welsh-language press, and particularly from 1883 with the *South Wales Daily News* (for the London letter of which he was for many years largely responsible, as he was for that of *Baner ac Amserau Cymru* from 1878). He became a familiar figure in the dining-room and smoking-room of the House of Commons, was close to the younger members of parliament from Wales, and welcomed the advent of his neighbour David Lloyd George to London on his election as member for Caernarfon boroughs in 1890.

In 1881 Evans married Annie Elizabeth (*d.* 1898), daughter of Thomas Beale of Oxford. They had one daughter and a son, Lewis Noel Vincent Evans, later CB and deputy director of public prosecutions. Also in 1881 Evans became the first secretary and editor of the publications of the newly established National Eisteddfod Association. In 1884 he was made a member of the Honourable Society of Cymmrodorion, the council of which he joined in 1886.

He became secretary in 1887, and later undertook the editorship of the society's publications, which became important academic and research publications. He revived the fortunes of the society, broadening the sphere of its interests and re-establishing its relevance for the needs of Wales. Under his guidance it became once more an influential literary and social force. Evans's work was recognized with the award of the society's medal in 1923. The link between the society and the eisteddfod was strengthened when the Cymmrodorion national eisteddfod section was formed in 1893 with Evans as secretary. He retained his offices in all these institutions until his death.

The strong national feeling which manifested itself in Wales during the last two decades of the nineteenth century looked to the 'London Welsh' for guidance, and Evans's interests and associations connected him with many bodies, in particular the university colleges at Aberystwyth and Bangor of the University of Wales, of which he was a governor, and which in 1922 conferred upon him the honorary degree of LLD. He was elected a fellow of the Society of Antiquaries and of the Royal Historical Society. Among other offices he was chairman of the Royal Commission on the Ancient and Historical Monuments of Wales and Monmouthshire, a governor of the Welsh National Museum and the National Library of Wales, president in 1918 of the Cambrian Archaeological Society, vice-chairman of the executive committee of the Welsh Bibliographical Society, and treasurer of the Welsh Folk-Song Society. He also took a large part in organizing and recruiting the London Welsh battalions during the First World War. Although he could make no claim to scholarship—a friend remarked that his appointment as chairman of the royal commission 'owed more to his business aptitude and experience of public affairs than to his knowledge of archaeology' (*Archaeologia Cambrensis*, 90, 1935, 167)—many articles of useful comment and careful compilation by Evans appeared in the *Cymmrodor*, the *Transactions* of the Cymmrodorion Society, *Welsh Outlook*, *Bye-gones*, *y Traethodydd*, *y Geninen*, and other journals. His presidential address appears in *Archaeologia Cambrensis*, 19 (1919).

Evans, who was knighted in 1909 for his services to Wales and appointed CH in 1922, was of sturdy build, somewhat above the middle height, with a large and striking head. He was of 'a strong and obstinate will' (*Welsh Outlook*, 1920, 12), but his effective administrative abilities and experience of public life made his views respected for their impartiality and soundness. He died at his home, 64 Chancery Lane, Holborn, London, on 13 November 1934 and was cremated at Golders Green on 16 November.

H. E. JAMES, rev. BRYNLEY F. ROBERTS

Sources J. C. Cecil-Williams, *Transactions of the Honourable Society of Cymmrodorion* (1933–5), 183–90 • R. T. Jenkins and H. M. Ramage, *A history of the Honourable Society of Cymmrodorion* (1951), 193–5 • W. E. Davies, *Welsh Outlook*, 7 (1920), 9–12 • *Transactions of the Honourable Society of Cymmrodorion* (1922–3), 208–9 • T. E. M., *Archaeologia Cambrensis*, 90 (1935), 167 • *DWB*
Archives NL Wales, corresp. and papers • NL Wales, Cymmrodorion Archives | NL Wales, letters to John Glyn Davies • NL Wales, letters to Thomas Iorworth Ellis, Annie Hughes-Griffiths, and Peter Hughes-Griffiths • NL Wales, corresp. with E. T. John • NL Wales, letters to Sir Henry Haydn Jones • NL Wales, corresp. with Sir John Herbert Lewis • NL Wales, letters to Edward Owen • NL Wales, letters to Mary Williams
Likenesses W. Oliver, oils, 1892, NMG Wales • W. G. John, bust, c.1910, NL Wales • Swaine, photograph, 1916, NL Wales • W. Stoneman, photograph, 1923, NPG • Elliott & Fry, photograph, NL Wales • C. Morris, oils, NL Wales
Wealth at death £9919 19s. 5d.: probate, 17 Dec 1934, CGPLA Eng. & Wales

Evans, William (*d.* 1718), Independent minister and tutor, is of unknown parentage, and the year and place of his birth are likewise unknown. He was educated at Rhys Prydderch's school at Ystradwallter, and was later taught by Stephen Hughes. He was ordained at Pencader, Carmarthenshire, in 1688, where he then ministered and taught a school. With very slender means of subsistence, he had to rely largely on his wife's small private income. In 1703 he moved to Carmarthen to take charge of the Independent causes in the area, and to keep a school (assisted by the SPCK) for poor children. From 1704 he received in his house students for the dissenting ministry, thus establishing an academy which succeeded those at Brynllywarch and Abergavenny. He was patronized by the Presbyterian and Congregational funds in London and by wealthy dissenters.

Evans educated a number of prominent ministers at his academy, including some who became noted authors, such as Matthias Maurice and Christmas Samuel. A man of immense energy, he maintained a close connection with his former charge at Pencader, and he achieved a coup by securing for dissenting worship the erstwhile Anglican chapel at Llan-y-bri, near Carmarthen. In 1707 he published in Welsh *The Principles of the Christian Religion*, a translation of the shorter catechism of the Westminster assembly, and in 1714 published *Gemau doethineb* ('Gems of Wisdom'), by his old mentor Rhys Prydderch. Evans's wife was named Katherine, but no other details of the marriage are known; two sons and a daughter are mentioned in his will of 1716. Following Stephen Hughes's death, Evans came to be regarded as the new leader of dissent in Carmarthenshire. A man of superior attainments as scholar, preacher, and educator, he devoted himself with great diligence to his work. Jeremy Owen called him 'God's gift to his people … a public blessing' (Jenkins, 207). He died in January 1718 in Carmarthen Town, survived by his wife.

D. R. L. JONES

Sources J. E. Lloyd, *A history of Carmarthenshire*, 2 (1939) • A. Gordon, ed., *Freedom after ejection: a review (1690–1692) of presbyterian and congregational nonconformity in England and Wales* (1917) • G. H. Jenkins, *Literature, religion and society in Wales, 1660–1730* (1978) • *DWB* • will, proved, 1718, NL Wales [William Evans, Carmarthen, parish of St Peter, St Davids PR] • R. T. Jones, *Hanes Annibynwyr Cymru* (1966) • H. McLachlan, *English education under the Test Acts: being the history of the nonconformist academies, 1662–1820* (1931), 52–3
Wealth at death £340 bequests; plus a house with garden and barns; effects and residue: will, St Davids PR

Evans, William (*d.* 1776?), Presbyterian minister and lexicographer, was probably born in Carmarthenshire, perhaps in Cefngwili, Llanedi. He is believed to have been educated at Carmarthen Academy under Dr Jenkins between 1768 and 1772. His chief claim to notice is based on his work *A New English–Welsh Dictionary*, compiled while he was a student and published in 1771. This was used by William Richards as a source for his own dictionary of 1798, but was not fully superseded as a second edition appeared in 1812. The dictionary was described by the bibliographer the Revd D. Silvan Evans as a not irresponsible work. William Evans was for some years pastor of the Presbyterian congregation at Sherborne, Dorset, but, in 1776, owing to poor health, he took charge of a congregation at Moretonhampstead, Devon. However, he was able to remain in this post only for a few weeks, and probably died shortly after taking it up.

R. M. J. JONES, *rev.* DYLAN FOSTER EVANS

Sources S. N. S., 'Enwogion Annghofiedig', *Yr Ymofynydd*, 12 (1887), 268–70 • W. D. Jeremy, 'Nodynau Gwasgarog', *Yr Ymofynydd*, 13 (1888), 19–20 • S. N. S., 'Nodynau Gwasgarog', *Yr Ymofynydd*, 13 (1888), 43–4 • T. Davies, letter, *Cymru*, 28 (1905), 223 [O. M. Edwards] • W. Richards, *Geiriadur Saesneg a Chymraeg: An English and Welsh dictionary* (1798) • E. Rees, ed., *Libri Walliae: a catalogue of Welsh books and books printed in Wales, 1546–1820*, 1 (1987), 248 • *DWB* • W. Rowlands, *Llyfryddiaeth y Cymry*, ed. D. S. Evans (1869), 526

Evans, William [*known as* William Evans of Eton] (1798–1877), watercolour painter, was born probably at Eton College on 4 December 1798, the elder son of **Samuel Evans** (1762–1835), a topographical draughtsman from Flintshire, who taught drawing to the youngest daughters of George III before 1795. Samuel succeeded Richard Cooper as drawing-master at Eton College in 1808, and retired in 1822 to Droxford, Hampshire, near the birthplace of his wife, Ann Knight (1775–1852). His views of Wales were engraved, and he produced coloured chalk and watercolour pictures for his pupils to copy.

After attending Eton College, William Evans abandoned a medical training to assist his father in 1819, and was appointed drawing-master of Eton by the headmaster, John Keate, whose children he was teaching, in 1823. William Collins and Peter DeWint gave him lessons, and he was elected an associate of the Society of Painters in Water Colours on 11 February 1828, becoming a full member on 7 June 1830. His early work *The Brunswick and Winchester Towers from the Locks, Windsor* (1829) was acquired by Margaret Carpenter. The influence of his bohemian friends George Cattermole, Edwin Landseer, and above all John Frederick Lewis becomes increasingly evident on his technique during the 1830s. In 1836 he toured Connemara, returning to this remote area with his former pupil Thomas Gambier Parry in 1838.

Evans married Jane Grace Jackson (*b.* 1801) from Droxford in 1822; she died in 1837, leaving him with eight children. Encouraged by his colleagues George Selwyn and Edward Coleridge, he acquired Mrs Vallency's boys' house in 1839, and became an Eton 'dame'. Enlightened discipline prevailed at Evans's and it attracted a talented mixture of pupils. In the mid-1830s he depicted cricket and the wall game on the playing fields, and the pageantry of the fourth of June regatta. His two Eton *Montem* pictures were exhibited in 1844, lithographed in 1852, and

William Evans [of Eton] (1798–1877), by Margaret Sarah Carpenter, *c.*1825–30

acquired by Lord Braybrooke in 1863; these remain his best-known works. In 1844 he recorded the visit of Tsar Nicholas I for Queen Victoria, and in 1846 began a lifelong friendship with the sixth duke and duchess of Atholl, which involved tutoring their son, Lord Tullibardine. Blair Atholl inspired several highland pictures, including *Sheep Shearing* (1848). To compete with the brilliance of oil paint, his large exhibition watercolours consist of increasing layers of pigment and highlight.

A broken jaw in 1844 left Evans with chronic pain which affected his painting arm, and opium was prescribed. His daughters began to help in the running of his house, Jane (1826–1906) becoming a school legend. Evans reacted with hostility to Henry Cole's plans to reform the teaching of art in schools and resigned as drawing-master in 1853 to concentrate on his exhibition work, sending three pictures to the 1855 Paris Universal Exhibition. After 1845 he generally added 'of Eton' to his signature in distinction from William Evans of Bristol (1809–1858), who shared his Welsh repertoire. He canvassed for the election of John Frederick Lewis as president of the Society of Painters in Water Colours, acted as his right-hand man, and never forgave him for his sudden resignation in 1858. He proposed the introduction of winter exhibitions at the society, after it failed to leave the Pall Mall premises in 1859. Cannes reinvigorated him in 1868–9, and he sent his last subject from Burnham Beeches to the 1874 exhibition. He died on 31 December 1877 at Evans's and was buried in Keate Lane cemetery, Eton.

Samuel Thomas George Evans (1829–1904), son of William Evans, was born in Wales on 26 May 1829. He attended Eton (1842–8) and a Paris art school before assisting his father at Eton from 1849 to 1853; he succeeded him as drawing-master in 1854. When in 1888 art became part of the school curriculum, he ran the first drawing schools. In 1899 he published a manual on elementary drawing. He had sketched alongside his father, and even completed exhibition work for him. Similar compositions were chosen by both artists, especially popular Eton and Windsor views. Having trained at the Royal Academy Schools in 1849 he showed his first works there. On 8 February 1858 he was elected an associate of the Society of Painters in Water Colours, but although a regular exhibitor, he had to wait until 1894 for full membership. Anne, duchess of Atholl, befriended him bringing him royal patronage: he taught Princess Beatrice and Prince Leopold in 1867–8, and Queen Victoria commissioned *In the Woods Near Balmoral* from him in 1874. On 1 August 1863 he married Susan Bros and they had four children. After his honeymoon Evans built a chalet and boathouse by Lake Hallstadt, and the Austrian Tyrol inspired many of his watercolours. In his last decade he painted seascapes from the south coast. He died on 1 November 1904 at the Old Watercolour Society's galleries in Pall Mall, London, and was buried at Eton. His son, William Sidney Vernon Evans (1869–1943), assisted him after 1893, and became the last Evans to be drawing-master at Eton (1904–22).

LOUISA M. CONNOR BULMAN

Sources *Art Journal*, new ser., 25 (1905), 34 · L. M. Connor, *William Evans of Eton, 1798–1877* (1998) · E. G. Parry, *Annals of an Eton house* (1907) · J. L. Roget, *A history of the 'Old Water-Colour' Society*, 2 vols. (1891) · *The Royal Watercolour Society: the first fifty years, 1805–1855* (1992) · S. Fenwick and G. Smith, eds., *The business of watercolour: a guide to the archives of the Royal Watercolour Society* (1997) · D. Millar, *The Victorian watercolours and drawings in the collection of her majesty the queen*, 1 (1995) · Redgrave, *Artists* · Wood, *Vic. painters*, 3rd edn · M. Hardie, *Water-colour painting in Britain*, ed. D. Snelgrove, J. Mayne, and B. Taylor, 3 vols. (1966–8) · J. Barbour, 'William Evans and his Droxford connection', *Hatcher Review*, 36 (1993), 33–46 · Evans family Bible, Eton · Eton College school lists · W. Evans, diary, Eton
Archives Blair Atholl, Perthshire, corresp. · Eton, diary | Bankside Gallery, London, Old Watercolour Society archives
Likenesses M. S. Carpenter, red chalk drawing, *c.*1825–1830, priv. coll. [*see illus.*] · J. F. Lewis, watercolour, 1828, priv. coll. · G. Richmond, red chalk drawing, 1840, Eton · F. G. Cotman, oils, priv. coll. · A. Evans, photograph (Evans, SamuelThomas George), Annie Evans album · J. F. Lewis, watercolour, Yale U. CBA · photograph, Blair Atholl, Perthshire, photo album 185 · photograph, Eton, Annie Evans album · photograph (Evans, Samuel Thomas George), Blair Atholl, Perthshire, Album 1
Wealth at death £9000: resworn probate, Dec 1879, *CGPLA Eng. & Wales* (1878)

Evans, William (1809–1858), watercolour painter, known both as Evans of Bristol and as Welsh Evans to distinguish him from William Evans of Eton, was probably born in Bristol, where his father, John *Evans (*bap.* 1774, *d.* 1828), was a printer. Nothing is known of William's early life. He was taught drawing in Bristol by Francis Danby (*c.*1824–*c.*1826) and between 1827 and 1832 was himself giving drawing lessons in Clifton. In 1832–3 he was a member of a sketching club in Bristol whose members also included W. J. Müller and J. S. Prout. A drawing, *Chepstow Old Toll Gate*, dated 1834 (NL Wales, Aberystwyth), provides evidence of an early visit to Wales, perhaps in the company of friends from the sketching club, and he certainly toured with Müller, who seems to have been his closest companion, in 1842. The *View of Snowdon* (City of Bristol Museum and Art Gallery) is dated 1843, suggesting that by this time north Wales provided the main focus for his work.

From about 1844 Evans lodged at Tŷ'n-y-cae, a cottage near the Fairy Glen at Betws-y-coed in the Conwy valley, and thereby became one of the first resident painters of the artists' colony popularized by David Cox, whose annual summer visits to the village commenced in that year. Evans's relationship with the increasing number of painters, both summer visitors and residents, who frequented Betws-y-coed at this time is unclear, but the paucity of references to him in letters and diaries suggests that he may have been less sociable than many of his contemporaries. He certainly lived in poverty and dire conditions at Tŷ'n-y-cae but produced some of the most lyrical landscape watercolours of the period there, as open and fluid as the later works of Cox, along with studies of domestic interiors and of the local people which reflect his earlier contact with Müller. Among the small number of his works which survive in public collections, the *Autumn Landscape, North Wales* (BM), painted about 1844, is characteristic of his style in the Betws-y-coed period.

Subjects from other parts of Wales and from England demonstrate that Evans continued to travel in the 1840s. However, his health began to decline and he went to Italy in 1852, spending the winter successively at Genoa, Rome, and Naples. Evans settled in London probably in late 1854. His work was held in high esteem by his contemporaries in the Old Watercolour Society, where his work was exhibited between 1845 and 1859. He died at 143 Marylebone Road, London, on 8 December 1858, the cause of death given as asthma.

PETER LORD

Sources P. Lord, *Clarence Whaite and the Welsh art world: the Betws-y-Coed artists' colony, 1844–1914* (1998) · F. Greenacre, *William Evans of Bristol* (1987) [exhibition catalogue, Martyn Gregory Gallery, London, 10–28 Nov 1987] · Bankside Gallery, London, Royal Watercolour Society MSS · *Art Journal*, 21 (1859), 29, 135–6 · d. cert.
Archives Bankside Gallery, London, Royal Watercolour Society · NL Wales

Evans, William (1864–1934), grocer and soft drinks manufacturer, was born at Trellwyn Uchaf Farm, near Fishguard, Pembrokeshire, Wales, on 24 August 1864, the oldest of the fourteen children of Thomas Evans (*b.* 1842/3), farmer, and his wife, Maria Francis (*b.* 1844/5). He was educated at Jabez Chapel school and Pontvane School, Pembrokeshire. At the age of twelve he became an apprentice to James Rees, a Haverfordwest grocer, and at sixteen he went to work in alderman William Thomas's grocery store at Aber-big, Monmouthshire. At nineteen he became manager of the Porth branch of Peglers' Stores in the Rhondda valley, Glamorgan.

In 1885, in partnership with his former employer, William Thomas, Evans opened a grocery and provision shop in Hannah Street, Porth, a central location for serving the rapidly growing population of the Rhondda valleys. On 27 July 1886 he married Annie Jane Evans (d. 1949), a native of Aberystwyth, whose father had established a butcher's shop in Hannah Street, Porth. There is no record of any children.

In 1888 Thomas left the partnership, although the business continued as Thomas and Evans, with William Evans in sole control. From a single grocery store, the business gradually expanded. A bakery was added in 1890, followed by branch shops at three other locations by 1895. In 1897 Evans, an adherent of the temperance movement, became interested in the manufacture of soft drinks following a chance meeting with an Indian 'quack doctor'. Production of soft drinks at Porth, comprising hop bitters, ginger beer, and lemonade, under the label Welsh Hills Mineral Waters, commenced at the beginning of the twentieth century. From these small beginnings the Corona business emerged.

Before the First World War, the expansion of production and distribution of the soft drinks was confined to the south Wales region, but following the change of name from Welsh Hills to Corona in the early 1920s, the business mushroomed. By the time of Evans's death, in 1934, there were about twenty-seven factories and fifty depots throughout England and Wales. A key factor in the success of Thomas and Evans was Evans's ability to assess the customer's needs and develop methods of satisfying them. In the case of Corona this involved doorstep deliveries, a concept he had pioneered at Porth with his grocery business. From this retail base, a notable development was the formation of a chain of small, fully stocked, local grocers' shops (the Terry shops), a forerunner of the later Spar and Mace grocery chains.

Evans did not regard business as simply a means of self-aggrandizement through profit maximization: 'In his expressed view, commerce, properly conducted, conveyed advantage not only to the provider of capital and enterprise, but also to customer and employee, and beyond these to the community at large, and the nation as a whole' (Jones, 35). In 1920 Evans made a gift of 200 acres of ground for the creation of a public park for the benefit of the inhabitants of Porth. A deeply committed Baptist, he was connected with Salem Chapel, Porth, for nearly forty years, being both a deacon and treasurer, and in 1930–31 he was president of the Welsh Baptist Union. A Liberal, in 1910 he became a Glamorgan county councillor, serving for a time as chairman of the finance committee, and in 1917 he was appointed a JP for Glamorgan.

William Evans died of a stroke at Bronwydd, Porth, his home for much of his later life, on 27 September 1934. He left £287,658 gross, and was succeeded in the control of Thomas and Evans, a private limited company since 1920, by his brother Daniel Francis (Frank) Evans (1875–1940), a business partner since the early 1890s. In the 1950s Thomas and Evans was acquired by Beechams Ltd.

Trevor Boyns

Sources O. V. Jones, *William Evans, 1864–1934* (1982) · A. Mee, ed., *Who's who in Wales* (1921) · *Who's who in Wales*, 2nd edn (1933) · *Western Mail* [Cardiff] (28 Sept 1934) · d. cert. · *CGPLA Eng. & Wales* (1934)
Likenesses photographs, repro. in Jones, *William Evans*
Wealth at death £287,658—gross: probate index, Llandaff, 1934

Evans, William [*pseud.* Wil Ifan] (1883–1968), writer, was born on 22 April 1883 at Vale View, Cwm-bach, Llanwinio, Carmarthenshire, the sixth son of the nine children of the Revd Dr Daniel Evans (1850–1928) and Mary Davies (1853–1932). His father was heavily involved in local politics and culture; he was also editor of the journal *Y Celt*. In 1890 he accepted a call to Cwmafan, near Port Talbot, and his son was educated at the local school, then Port Talbot county school (1893–1900) and the University College of Wales, Bangor, where he graduated BA in 1905; he then spent a year at Mansfield College, Oxford.

Evans was ordained in 1906 at the English-speaking Congregational church at Dolgellau, and met there his future wife, Nesta Wyn Edwards (1883–1968), an organist and a first-class honours graduate of the University College of Wales, Aberystwyth. They were married on 28 December 1910 and settled at Bridgend, Glamorgan, where he had moved in 1909 as minister of the English Congregational church. In 1916 he accepted a call to Richmond Road English Congregational Church, Cardiff, but in 1925 he returned to Bridgend to serve as minister. He was well loved; the *Glamorgan Gazette* in 1925 referred to his 'winning gifts of rich humour, geniality and kindness'.

By this time Evans had become a well-known bardic figure, having won the crown at the national eisteddfod of Wales on three occasions: in Abergavenny (1913), Birkenhead (1917), and Pwllheli (1925). He was extremely skilled at writing lyrics in both Welsh and English. The volumes *Songs of the Heather Heights* (1914), *A Quire of Rhymes: Short Poems* (1943), *Where I Belong* (1946), and *Further Poems* (1955) praised the beauty of the countryside of west Wales and the Vale of Glamorgan. A convinced pacifist, he voiced his anti-war philosophy in *Dail iorwg* ('Ivy Leaves'; 1919) and *Unwaith eto* ('Once more'; 1946), while 'Atgof' ('Memory') is perhaps his finest lyric on the subject. He wrote a great many poems for the eisteddfod movement, poems that were recited in chapel and cultural gatherings. These were compiled in *Darnau adrodd* (1932) and a follow-up, *Darnau newydd* (1944).

Evans also edited the poems of Thomas Jones (1820–1876) as *Gweithiau Taliesin o Eifion* (1922) and published three volumes of prose in Welsh, *Gweithio englyn* (1948), an introduction to traditional versecraft, *Y filltir deg* (1954), and *Colofnau Wil Ifan* (1962), which included a selection of his weekly columns for the daily newspaper *Western Mail*. He collaborated with musicians such as David Evans, Haydn Morris, and T. Hopkin Evans in writing or translating a variety of songs. His admiration for D. Afan Thomas (1881–1928) led him to write a biography, *Afan: a Welsh Music Maker* (1944).

Evans was also a playwright. *Dreams Come True* (1916), a biblical drama in three acts, was followed by the Welsh-language plays *Y dowlad* (1922), *Yr het goch* (1933), *Helbulon llenor* (1938), and *Flynyddoedd o flaen Adda* (1938).

In addition to contributing cartoons for the *Western Mail*, Evans was a regular columnist and broadcaster. He retired as pastor of Bridgend in 1947, and that same year was made an honorary MA by the University of Wales. Between 1947 and 1950 he was archdruid of the national eisteddfod and, at a service to celebrate the coronation of Queen Elizabeth II in 1953, he became the first nonconformist ever to preach from the pulpit of the Anglican cathedral in St David's, Pembrokeshire.

Evans died on 16 July 1968 at his home at 14 Park Street, Bridgend, six months after the death of his wife; he was buried at Rhyd-y-main, Merioneth. A collection of his poems, *Bro fy mebyd a cherddi eraill*, published in 1998, includes the most impressive of his lyrics from his volumes *Dros y nyth* (1915), *Dail iorwg* (1919), *Plant y babell* (1922), *O ddydd i ddydd* (1927), *Y winllan las* (1936), *Unwaith eto* (1946), and *Haul a glaw* (n.d.). A Bridgend road is named in his memory.   D. BEN REES

Sources E. D. Jones and B. F. Roberts, eds., *Y bywgraffiadur Cymreig, 1951–1970* (1997), 57 · M. George, 'Wil Ifan: bardd "bro Fy mebyd"', *Llynfi ac Afan, Garw ac Ogwr*, ed. H. Edwards (1998), 274–300 · D. Jones, ed., *Bro fy mebyd a cherddi eraill* (1998) · E. Evans, 'Atgofion am Wil Ifan', *Barn* (1983), 19–22 · D. B. Rees, 'William Evans (Wil Ifan)', *Pymtheg o Wŷr llên yr ugeinfed ganrif* (1972), 17–19 · H. J. Williams, *Bibliography of Welsh and English works of Wil Ifan* (1959) · D. B. Rees, *Cymry adnabyddus, 1952–1972* (1978) · private information (2004) [family] · d. cert. · m. cert. · *CGPLA Eng. & Wales* (1968)
Archives Anglesey County RO, papers · NL Wales, corresp. | NL Wales, letters to W. Rhys Nicholas | SOUND BBC Radio Wales, Llandaff, Cardiff, Wales · Radio Cymru
Likenesses photograph, repro. in Rees, 'William Evans' · photographs, repro. in George, 'Wil Ifan', 275, 287
Wealth at death £2197: probate, 6 Sept 1968, *CGPLA Eng. & Wales*

Evans, Sir William David (1767–1821), lawyer, was born in London on 25 May 1767, the son of John Evans and his wife, Janet, *née* Butterfield. Educated at Harrow School (1779–80), on attaining his sixteenth year he was articled to a Warrington solicitor, in whose office he relieved the tedium of business hours by courting the muses. He was admitted an attorney in February 1789, and practised at Leigh, Lancashire. In 1790 he married Hannah (*d.* 1832), daughter of Peter Seaman of Warrington. After being admitted as a student of Gray's Inn, on 29 January 1789, he was called to the bar in February 1794. He joined the northern circuit, residing in Liverpool, and practised there several years as a special pleader and conveyancer. He published an enlarged edition of *Salkeld's Reports* (3 vols., 1795), *Essays on the Action for Money Lent and Received* (1802), *A General View of the Decisions of Lord Mansfield in Civil Causes* (2 vols., 1803), and *A Treatise on the Law of Obligations and Contracts, from the French of Pothier* (2 vols., 1806). He moved to Manchester in 1807, and established a lucrative practice. His *Letter to Sir S. Romilly on the Revision of the Bankrupt Laws* (1810) influenced subsequent legislation. He strongly favoured Roman Catholic emancipation, and in 1813 published *Letters on the Disabilities of the Roman Catholics and Dissenters*. In 1813 he was appointed the first Manchester stipendiary magistrate. In 1815 he was appointed vice-

Sir William David Evans (1767–1821), by Edward Scriven

chancellor of the county palatine court of Lancaster, holding these offices concurrently until 1818. Meanwhile he published more legal works including *The Practice of the Court of Common Pleas of Lancaster* (1814), *A Charge to the Grand Jury at Preston* (1817), *A Collection of Statutes Relating to the Clergy, with Notes* (1817), and *A Collection of the Statutes Connected with the General Administration of the Law … with Notes* (8 vols., 1817 and later editions). He collected material for other works, but did not live to finish them. Sir Charles Harcourt Chambers's *Treatise on the Law of Landlord and Tenant* (1823) was compiled from his notes, and he left a manuscript 'Life of the chancellor d'Aguesseau' which Charles Butler used in his work on d'Aguesseau.

In 1817 Evans unsuccessfully applied for a vacant judgeship, but in 1819 he was appointed recorder of Bombay (at £7000 a year) and was knighted. On the voyage out he wrote *A Treatise upon the Civil Law* and initiated a weekly literary publication to entertain his fellow passengers. He began his duties in India with great promise of success, but fell victim to a pre-existing condition, presumably aggravated by the climate, and died at Bombay on 5 December 1821.   C. W. SUTTON, *rev.* ROGER T. STEARN

Sources Nicholson, *Memoirs of Sir W. D. Evans* (1845) · *GM*, 1st ser., 92/1 (1822), 563 · W. T. J. Gun, ed., *The Harrow School register, 1571–1800* (1934)
Likenesses E. Scriven, stipple, BM, NPG [*see illus.*]

Evans, William Edward (1801–1869), Church of England clergyman and naturalist, was born on 8 June 1801 at Shrewsbury, son of John Evans MD, and his wife, Jane Wilson Evans (1756–1846). He inherited a taste for poetry and natural history from his father, who wrote a poem in four books on bees (1806–13). A brother, Robert Wilson *Evans (1789–1866), became archdeacon of Westmorland. From

Shrewsbury School, where Samuel Butler was then head-master, Evans gained a scholarship at Clare College, Cambridge, where he graduated BA in 1823 and MA in 1826. He was ordained deacon in 1824 and priest in 1825. From 1825 to 1829 he served as curate of Llanymynech, his father's native parish. When he married his cousin, Elizabeth Evans, he was presented to the perpetual curacy of Crig-gion, Montgomeryshire. This, however, he resigned in order to live at Burton Court, Leominster, which his wife had inherited, and to hold the sole charge of the parish of Monkland (1832–50). In 1841 he was appointed prebendary of Hereford and prelector of the cathedral.

Evans was an eloquent and effective preacher, a keen naturalist, and an excellent angler. His chief work is *The Song of the Birds, or, Analogies of Animal and Spiritual Life* (1845), in which the habits of birds were shown to offer spiritual lessons. The twenty-two chapters on British song birds revealed the carefulness and accuracy of Evans's observations. His other works included *The First Revelation of God to Man* (1849), a series of sermons on Genesis, *An Order for Family Prayer* (1844), and a *Letter to the Bishop [of Hereford] on Diocesan Education* (1850).

After holding Monkland for eighteen years, in 1850 Evans accepted the living of Madley with Tibberton, Here-fordshire. In 1861 he became canon of Hereford Cathedral. His health failed in the last two or three years of his life, and he died in the close, Hereford, on 22 November 1869. Memorial windows were erected in Llanymynech church to commemorate Evans, and his father and brother. Evans left one daughter and three sons.

M. G. Watkins, rev. Mari G. Ellis

Sources Venn, *Alum. Cant.* · Crockford (1865) · D. R. Thomas, *Esgobaeth Llanelwy: the history of the diocese of St Asaph*, rev. edn, 3 vols. (1908–13), vol. 3, p. 35 · review of *The songs of the birds* by W. E. Evans, *The Athenaeum* (19 July 1845), 715 · Boase, *Mod. Eng. biog.*
Wealth at death under £7000: administration, 16 Feb 1870, *CGPLA Eng. & Wales*

Evanson, Edward (1731–1805), Church of England clergy-man, was born at Warrington on 21 April 1731, the son of Thomas Evanson, mercer, and his wife, Margaret. His uncle, John Evanson, rector of Mitcham, Surrey, educated him, and sent him to Emmanuel College, Cambridge, in 1745. He took the degree of BA (1750), and MA (1753). He was ordained deacon and became curate to his uncle, who also kept a school where Evanson assisted. He was ordained priest on 21 September 1755. In 1766 he became vicar of South Mimms, near Barnet. In 1769 the lord chancellor, Lord Camden, gave him the vicarage of Tewkesbury, at the request of John Dodd, MP for Reading. The bishop of Worcester, Richard Hurd, introduced Evanson, as a member of his own college, to William Warburton, bishop of Gloucester, who, on the strength of Hurd's introduction, gave him also the perpetual curacy of Tredington, Worcestershire. In August 1770 he exchanged South Mimms for Longdon in Worcestershire.

Evanson soon began to show doubts about the trinitarian orthodoxy. He wrote to the archbishop of Canterbury, Frederick Cornwallis, who was then discussing with the bench possible changes to the liturgy, and asked for his objections to the Nicene and Athanasian creeds to be considered. Cornwallis never replied and Evanson adapted the liturgy to his own opinions. His sermon on the resurrection on Easter day (31 March 1771) was an additional provocation and a prosecution was instituted by Neast Havard, town clerk of Tewkesbury, and others, in the consistory court. In 1772 Evanson published anonymously a pamphlet upon *The Doctrines of a Trinity and the Incarnation of God*. His heterodox views were symptomatic of a growing sense of dissatisfaction among some Anglican clergy-men with traditional trinitarian formulations. The Feathers Tavern Association was a London lobbying group formed in July 1771 to press for the abolition of clerical subscription to the Thirty-Nine Articles and lay subscription to them in the universities. A petition presented to parliament in 1772 was rejected, which contributed to Theophilus Lindsey resigning his orders and establishing a Unitarian chapel.

Evanson's case was heard before the bishop of Gloucester on 16 January 1775. Some technical objections led to the failure of the prosecution; but appeals were made to the court of arches, and afterwards to the court of delegates. He was popular in the parish, and his court expenses were paid by a subscription of his Tewkesbury parishioners; his Longdon parishioners expressed their willingness to accept his alterations of the services. Alexander Wedderburne, the solicitor-general, defended him gratuitously, and on 31 May 1775 appointed him his chaplain. In 1777 Evanson published *A Letter to the ... Bishop of Litchfield and Coventry* in which he argued that 'either the christian revelation is not true, or the religion of every orthodox church in Europe is fabulous and false' (E. Evanson, *A Letter*, 1777, 127). He argued that the prophecies foretold the great apostasy of trinitarianism. This overtly heterodox statement naturally led to his resignation from his living, in a letter to his bishop dated 22 March 1778. Evanson's case illustrated the difficulty of maintaining doctrinal orthodoxy in the Church of England by the system of ecclesiastical courts. Rather, the problem was resolved when Evanson resigned as a matter of conscience.

Evanson returned to Mitcham, and set up a school. The father of one of his pupils, Colonel Evelyn James Stuart, son of the earl of Bute, settled an annuity upon him, which was paid until his death. He held family services, using Samuel Clarke's version of the liturgy, with additional changes of his own. He administered the Lord's supper to visitors, maintaining that it was the only sacrament and intended for all social gatherings. He also wished to set up a society of 'Christo philanthropists' to hear expositions of the authentic scriptures. He debated the sanctity of the sabbath with Joseph Priestley. Their exchanges were collected and published by Evanson with a letter to Priestley as *Arguments Against the Sabbatical Observance of the Sunday* (1792). In 1792 he also published *The Dissonance of the Four Generally Received Evangelists, and the Evidence of their Authenticity Examined*. In this early work of biblical criticism he rejected the gospels according to Matthew, Mark, and John, the epistles to the Romans, Ephesians, Colossians, and Hebrews, and those of James, Peter, John, and Jude, besides part of the other books of the New Testament. He was again answered by Priestley (in reply to whom he published in 1794 *Letter to Dr. Priestley's Young Man*), expelled from a book club, and 'pestered by anonymous letters'. Thomas Falconer also replied to him in a course of Bampton lectures published in 1811. Evanson also published *Reflections upon the State of Religion in Christendom* (1802) and *Second Thoughts on the Trinity* (1805).

On 27 July 1786, in London, Evanson married Dorothy (*b.* 1751), daughter of Robert Alchorne, a respectable merchant of Old Jewry, London, and his wife, Margaret. His bride probably brought him a fortune, as he afterwards bought an estate at Great Blakenham, Suffolk. He retired to Great Bealings, near Woodbridge, thence to Lympston, Devon, where he preached to a Unitarian congregation, and finally to Coleford in Devon where he died on 25 September 1805. He was survived by his wife. Two volumes of his collected sermons were published in 1807.

[ANON.], rev. S. L. COPSON

Sources G. Rogers, 'Some account of the life, religious opinions, and writings, of Edward Evanson', in E. Evanson, *Sermons*, 2 vols. (1807) · *GM*, 1st ser., 75 (1805), 1233–6 · M. Neast, *A narrative of the origin and progress of the prosecution against the Rev. Edward Evanson* (1778) · Nichols, *Lit. anecdotes*, 6.483 · G. M. Ditchfield, 'Antitrinitarianism and toleration in late eighteenth century British politics: the Unitarian petition of 1792', *Journal of Ecclesiastical History*, 42 (1991), 39–67 · J. Dybikowski and M. Fitzpatrick, 'David Williams, John Jebb and liturgical reform', *Enlightenment and Dissent*, 9 (1990), 106–13 · J. Stephens, 'The London ministers and subscription, 1772–1779', *Enlightenment and Dissent*, 1 (1982), 43–7 · *Monthly Magazine*, 20 (1805), 477–83 · IGI

Evatt, Herbert Vere (1894–1965), politician and judge, was born on 30 April 1894 at East Maitland, New South Wales, Australia, the third of six surviving sons of John Ashmore Hamilton Evatt (*d. c.*1901), a publican born in India, and his Sydney-born wife, Jane Sophia Gray. His father came from an Anglo-Irish family and emigrated to Australia at the age of sixteen after being educated in Dublin and Charterhouse School in England. His mother was the daughter of an Australian engineer and his Irish-born wife. Evatt's father died when he was seven years old and his mother moved the family to Sydney. Evatt was an outstanding student, winning scholarships to Fort Street high school and the University of Sydney whence he graduated BA (1915), MA (1917), LLB (1918), and LLD (1924). Although a robust sportsman, he suffered from poor eyesight and was rejected for military service in the First World War, in which two of his brothers were killed. On 27 November 1920 Evatt married Mary Alice Sheffer (1898–1973), a fellow arts student at the University of Sydney and tutor at St Andrew's College who, although born in the United States, had lived in Sydney since early childhood. The Evatts settled in Sydney and adopted a son and a daughter, moving to Canberra after Evatt entered federal politics.

Evatt's legal career, in which he was spectacularly successful, was the main focus of his life until 1940. While

Herbert Vere Evatt (1894–1965), by Walter Stoneman, 1942

studying law Evatt landed the plum job of associate to the chief justice of New South Wales, Sir William Cullen, who was also chancellor of the University of Sydney. After graduation he was admitted to the New South Wales bar. He appeared as a junior in the high court in 1919 and took silk in 1929, having built up a leading practice within a decade. In 1930 he was appointed to the high court at the exceptionally young age of thirty-six and served for a decade as one of its leading judges.

Evatt's judicial appointment was political. Deeply committed to radical liberalism and social democracy as a young man, Evatt had joined the Labor Party and entered the New South Wales parliament in 1925 as a member for Balmain, an inner suburb of Sydney and strong Labor precinct. Labor won the election and Evatt stood for a ministerial post in the new Labor government but was unsuccessful. Evatt's political prospects waned because of his opposition to the strong-arm premier, Jack Lang, who would be dismissed by the governor, Sir Philip Game, in 1932. Evatt lost party endorsement in 1927, stood successfully as an independent but was expelled from the Labor Party. Nevertheless, he and Edward McTiernan, a Labor colleague who had become New South Wales attorney-general in 1925, were appointed to the high court by an assertive federal Labor caucus and cabinet, against the wishes of Prime Minister Scullin and Attorney-General Brennan who were overseas at the time.

Evatt was a judge in the Australian high court for ten years where his constitutional jurisprudence favoured government powers and took account of the policy consequences of judicial decisions. He supported expansive interpretation of the commonwealth government's jurisdiction over telecommunications and its external affairs power, and narrow interpretation of the restrictive guarantee of interstate free trade mandated by section 92. In his purposive approach Evatt was at odds with the great legalist Sir Owen Dixon who had been appointed in 1929 and increasingly dominated the court, serving as chief justice from 1952 to 1964. Some have interpreted Evatt's decision to quit the court in 1940 as recognition that he could only ever be second to Dixon.

During his decade in the high court Evatt was also a prodigious researcher and writer. He published *The King and his Dominion Governors* (1936), an authoritative work on the conventions of responsible government and the reserve powers of the monarch and their viceregal representatives. This book was stimulated by Governor Game's sacking in 1932 of his old adversary Premier Jack Lang, and was cited extensively in the debate over Sir John Kerr's sacking of Prime Minister Gough Whitlam in 1975. Evatt also published historical studies of the Tolpuddle martyrs, *Injustice within the Law* (1937), the colonial revolt against Governor William Bligh, *Rum Rebellion* (1938), and *Australian Labor Leader* (1940), a political biography of W. A. Holman, an earlier New South Wales Labor premier whom he admired.

With impeccable timing, Evatt resigned from the high court to enter the commonwealth parliament as the Labor member for Barton in the election of September 1940 that produced a hung parliament. The Menzies–Fadden coalition government carried on but was unable to provide the strong government required for wartime. When the two independent members who held the balance of power switched their support to Labor, the Curtin government was sworn in on 7 October 1941. Evatt became attorney-general and minister for external affairs and held both senior cabinet posts throughout Labor's 'golden era' of federal government from 1941 to 1949. He was a senior minister during the decade of war and post-war reconstruction, serving under prime ministers Curtin who died in July 1945 and Ben Chifley who lost the December 1949 election and died in July 1951. Evatt would succeed Chifley as leader of the federal Labor Party in opposition.

As attorney-general Evatt was influential in shaping Labor's constitutional and legal agenda but only modestly successful in implementing it. Evatt masterminded Australia's assertion of sovereignty in external affairs through making its own declaration of war on Japan on 8 December 1941—previously such decisions were entrusted to Britain—and adopting the statute of Westminster in 1942. An ambitious attempt to expand commonwealth government powers for post-war reconstruction and guarantee freedom of religion and speech in the constitution was defeated at referendum in 1944. However, a broad power over social services that provided the constitutional basis for the post-war welfare state was successfully carried in 1946. Evatt protected the integrity of the high court although its ageing judges persistently

overturned Labor's more ambitious socialist and centralist legislation. He reversed a cabinet decision of 1945 proposing to pack the court by appointing three new judges, and subsequently made only one appointment of a conservative judge to restore its bench to seven. Evatt insisted on arguing the *Bank Nationalisation* case himself before the high court in 1948 and the privy council in 1949 but neither court would accept his restrictive view of the constitutional guarantee of free trade over the now dominant libertarian view of Dixon. Evatt's civil libertarian record was less than perfect: numbers of loyal Australian citizens of Italian and German background were interned for years during the war. Evatt's 'finest hour' as champion of human rights was in 1951. In that year he spearheaded the campaign that narrowly defeated the Menzies government's proposal to pass a constitutional amendment banning the Communist Party, after legislation to that effect had been ruled unconstitutional by the high court.

As minister for external affairs Evatt worked tirelessly to affirm Australia's independent status and articulate an independent foreign policy. This entailed reorienting Australia's outlook towards the Asia Pacific and building up the department of external affairs. He sought to balance Australia's increasing reliance on the United States by reaffirming British links and a larger role for small and medium powers in world affairs. Evatt championed the cause of the United Nations and contributed significantly to the founding conference at San Francisco in 1945. He was elected president of the United Nations general assembly for its third session in 1948–9. Although often controversial, Evatt's contribution to Australian foreign policy and international affairs was probably his greatest achievement.

In contrast, Evatt's political career as leader of the opposition and the Labor Party from 1951 to 1960 was disappointing. Evatt was no match for Prime Minister Menzies, who led a rejuvenated Liberal–Country Party coalition government to power in December 1949 and dominated Australian politics until he retired in 1967. Just before Evatt became leader, Labor had lost the snap election of 1951 that gave Menzies control of the senate. Under Evatt, Labor lost narrowly in the 1954 election, and by large margins in both 1955 and 1958. The turning point in Labor's fortunes, that kept the federal Labor Party in opposition until 1972, was the party split that Evatt precipitated in 1955. Evatt had become mired in controversy surrounding the 1954 Petrov royal commission investigating Soviet espionage in Australia. In defending his shaky leadership position, Evatt attacked the 'movement' of B. A. Santamaria that was warring against communists for control of Victorian trade unions. The dispute between 'left' and 'right' engulfed the Labor Party; leading right-wing, and mainly Catholic, members of the Victorian party were excluded from the 1955 federal conference in Hobart. This group formed the Anti-Communist Labor Party that, after a similar sectarian split in Queensland in 1957, became the Democratic Labor Party and kept Evatt and Labor out of office by giving its preferences to the Menzies coalition.

With Labor's electoral chances ruined Evatt's leadership became increasingly inept and erratic.

In failing health, Evatt finally retired from politics on being appointed chief justice of New South Wales by an accommodating state Labor government in February 1960. He suffered a stroke in March 1962 and resigned later in the year. Evatt spent the last years of his life being cared for in Canberra, where he died in the suburb of Forrest, on 2 November 1965. He was given a state funeral and was buried with Anglican rites in Canberra.

BRIAN GALLIGAN

Sources G. C. Bolton, 'Evatt, Herbert Vere', *AusDB*, 14.108–14 · K. Buckley, B. Dale, and W. Reynolds, *Doc Evatt* (1994) · P. Crockett, *Evatt: a life* (1993) · A. Dalziel, *Evatt the enigma* (1967) · K. Tennant, *Evatt: politics and justice* (1970) · A. Renouf, *Let justice be done: the foreign policy of Dr. H. V. Evatt* (1983) · W. J. Hudson, *Australia and the new world order: Evatt at San Francisco, 1965* (1993) · P. G. Edwards, 'Evatt and the Americans', *Historical Studies*, 18 (1978–9), 546–60 · D. Day, 'H. V. Evatt and the "Beat Hitler First" strategy', *Historical Studies*, 22 (1986–7), 587–603
Archives Flinders University, Adelaide, papers | SOUND BL NSA, documentary recording
Likenesses W. Stoneman, photograph, 1942, NPG [*see illus.*] · photographs, 1945–8, Hult. Arch.

Eve, Sir Harry Trelawney (1856–1940), judge, was born in London on 13 October 1856, the only son of Thomas Eve, a Jamaica merchant, and his wife, of whom little is known. He was educated privately and at Exeter College, Oxford, where he matriculated on 14 October 1876, graduating BA and MA in 1883, going on to choose the bar as his career. He read in the chambers of Charles Swinfen Eady, afterwards master of the rolls, and was called to the bar by Lincoln's Inn in 1881, taking silk in 1895.

On 24 June 1879 Eve married Beatrice Wright, daughter of Henry Strangways Hounsell; they had one son (who was killed in action in 1917) and two daughters (the younger of whom predeceased her father). He became a bencher of Lincoln's Inn in 1899. Eve entered parliament in 1904 as Liberal member for the Ashburton division of Devon. He retained his seat by a large majority at the general election of 1906 but retired from politics in 1907 on his acceptance of a judgeship in the Chancery Division. He was elected an honorary fellow of Exeter College, Oxford, and knighted in the same year. He retired from the bench in 1937 and was sworn of the privy council.

Eve was regarded as being a thoroughly sound judge. His grasp of equity was comprehensive and so it is unclear why he never advanced to the Court of Appeal, despite having sat there on many occasions.

Eve was involved in many interesting cases and one of his earliest decisions was in *Cope v. Crossingham* in 1908. This concerned section 4 of the Trade Union Act (1871), which provided that nothing in the act should enable any court to entertain any legal proceeding for the object of 'directly enforcing' certain trade union agreements. In *Cope v. Crossingham* the members of a branch of a trade union passed a resolution that they would secede from the parent society and distribute the funds of the branch among themselves. This resolution was contrary to the rules of the trade union, and its trustees sought a declaration that the resolution was *ultra vires*, and an order that the funds should be paid over to them according to the rules. Eve held that they had sufficient interest in the property of the branch to maintain the action and were not prevented by section 4 from doing so; further, he declared the proposed distribution of the funds to be *ultra vires*, but on the other hand he refused to administer the funds of the union by making any order for the payment over of the funds to the head trustees. He pointed out that the declaration would prevent misapplication of the funds but did not feel it his duty to lay down the exact method of appropriation.

Other well-known decisions during the course of Eve's career included *Powell v. Hemsley* (1909), a frequently cited authority on covenants restrictive of the user of land; *Re Pryce* (1917), on a covenant in a marriage settlement to settle the after-acquired property of the wife; *Hill v. Peters* (1918), on mortgage priorities; *Wise v. Whitburn* (1924), on the determination of the moment at which persons cease to hold property as executors and begin to hold it as trustees; *Re Bathe* (1925), on the validity of conditions in wills in partial restraint of marriage; and *Cummins v. Bond* (1926). This last case attracted a great deal of attention as it concerned a spiritualist medium who claimed to have produced a script entitled *The Chronicle of Cleophas* by automatic writing. Eve held that the medium was the owner of the copyright in it and entitled to restrain a person who was present at the séances at which it had been written from publishing it, annotated by himself, in book form.

Eve also passed many judgments on the subject of charitable trusts. He was quick to absorb and apply the property legislation which came into effect in 1925, and his application of it was well balanced and never unduly conservative. Eve maintained until his death an interest in politics, publishing a paper entitled *The present parliament: a complete analysis of each member's vote on all the principal divisions* (1880), and in farming. He died at Eldon House, Lower Bourne, Farnham, Surrey, on 10 December 1940.

H. G. HANBURY, rev. SINÉAD AGNEW

Sources J. Foster, *Men-at-the-bar: a biographical hand-list of the members of the various inns of court*, 2nd edn (1885), 145 · *WWW* · Allibone, *Dict.* · W. P. Baildon, ed., *The records of the Honorable Society of Lincoln's Inn: admissions*, 2 vols. (1896), vol. 2, p. 386 [Chapel registers] · *The Times* (11 Dec 1940) · E. Kilmurray, *Dictionary of British portraiture*, 3 (1981), 65
Likenesses W. Stoneman, photograph, 1930, NPG · E. Clegg Williams, oils, Exeter College, Oxford · portrait, repro. in *ILN*, 124 (1904), 72
Wealth at death £59,268 15s. 11d.: probate, 6 May 1941, *CGPLA Eng. & Wales*

Eveleigh, John (1748–1814), college head and university reformer, was born on 22 February 1748, and baptized on 17 March 1748 at Winkleigh, Devon, the eldest of the three sons of John Eveleigh (1716?–1770), rector of Winkleigh, and his wife, Martha, daughter of John Scobell of Nutcombe, Devon. Having matriculated from Wadham College, Oxford, on 15 May 1766 he was elected Goodrich and Pigott exhibitioner of his college in the same year and admitted scholar on 25 September 1767; he was again elected Goodrich exhibitioner, in 1767 and 1769, and was Hody exhibitioner from 1767 to 1770. He graduated BA on 19 January 1770 and was elected fellow of Oriel College on 30 March; he proceeded MA on 25 November 1772, BD on 17 November 1782, and DD on 7 May 1783.

Eveleigh served as vicar of St Mary the Virgin, Oxford, from 1778 until 1781, when he was elected provost of Oriel College on 5 December, in succession to John Clarke. As head of house he also became prebendary of Rochester Cathedral. On his election as college head Eveleigh was released from the statute that prevented college fellows from taking a wife, and married Dorothy, daughter of William Sanford (c.1711–1783), sometime fellow of All Souls. They had a daughter, Jane Dorothy, who was baptized on 14 June 1788 at Lechlade; she married John Heathcote Wyndham, rector of Corton, on 26 April 1813.

Eveleigh proved to be a highly successful provost, and under him the college entered its most illustrious period. Keen to raise its intellectual standing, and frustrated by the restrictions on some fellowships, Eveleigh invited the brilliant young scholar Edward Copleston to accept a vacant fellowship in 1795, even though Copleston did not conform to the stipulation that the candidate should be a native of Wiltshire. Copleston's election and the subsequent method of examining candidates set the pattern for open competition and election on intellectual merit that was soon adopted by other colleges. Furthermore this reform enabled Oriel to attract many other high-calibre fellows, such as John Keble, Richard Whately, and Edward Hawkins, who guaranteed the college's intellectual preeminence in Oxford into the mid-nineteenth century.

Eveleigh's innovation at Oriel of selecting fellows by setting them four days of examinations prompted him to suggest that the university should adopt a similarly rigorous system to examine undergraduates. Together with Cyril Jackson, dean of Christ Church, and John Parsons, master of Balliol, Eveleigh secured the examination statute of 1800. This stipulated that candidates for the degree of BA should undergo public examination in grammar, rhetoric, logic, moral philosophy, mathematics, physics, and the Christian religion, notably the doctrinal articles of the Church of England. An additional examination was established for those undergraduates who wished to compete for an honours degree, and the best twelve candidates were ranked according to merit. The new examinations succeeded and a further university statute, of 1807, abolished the list of the twelve best candidates and instead listed candidates alphabetically in two classes, the origins of first- and second-class degrees.

Vicar of Aylesford from 1782 to 1792, Eveleigh delivered the Bampton lectures in Oxford in 1792, which were published as *Eight Sermons* in the same year; a second edition, with four additional sermons, appeared in 1794, a third edition, in two volumes, in 1814. He also brought out *The Doctrine of the Holy Trinity* (1791) and a few separate sermons. In failing health, Eveleigh spent the summer of 1814 in Brighton, and died at Oxford on 10 December 1814; he was buried in St Mary the Virgin six days later. In his

funeral sermon Copleston, who succeeded him as provost, praised Eveleigh's achievements as a university reformer and hailed him as 'one of the most strenous originators of the present system of classes and honours' (Copleston, 28).   S. J. SKEDD

Sources *Hist. U. Oxf.*, vols. 5–6 · D. W. Rannie, *Oriel College* (1900) · M. Pattison, *Memoirs of an Oxford don*, ed. V. H. H. Green (1988) · W. J. Copleston, *Memoir of Edward Copleston* (1851) · *GM*, 1st ser., 84/2 (1814), 676 · J. W. Burgon, *Lives of twelve good men*, 2 vols. (1885) · Foster, *Alum. Oxon.* · *DNB*

Likenesses R. Dighton, caricature, coloured etching, pubd 1808 (*A view from Oriel College, Oxford*), NPG · J. Hoppner, oils, Oriel College, Oxford

Evelinge, Elizabeth [*name in religion* Catharine Magdalen] (1596/7–1668), abbess of Aire and translator, took vows at the English convent of the Poor Clares at Gravelines on 22 July 1620, aged twenty-three, adopting the name Sister Catharine Magdalen. Nothing is known of her family, though the Rose Evelinge who joined the convent on the same day and the Mary Evelinge who joined it the following year were probably younger sisters. At some point she transferred to the offshoot house at Aire, where she served as portress and mistress of novices before becoming abbess, in which role she is said to have served for twenty-five years before her death there on 23 September 1668.

Evelinge's obituary, written by a colleague, credits her with 'a more polished way of writing above her sex' (Hunnybun, 52). This seems to corroborate Luke Wadding's rather vague statement that she wrote a number of translations, including one derived from his own writings entitled *The History of the Angelicall Virgin Glorious St. Clare* and printed at Douai in 1635 by Martin Bocart. However, this text names its translator on its title-page, and identifies her as Magdalen Augustine (Catharine Bentley), another and more senior nun at Aire. The problem seems insoluble, though A. F. Allison suggests that it may be evidence of collaborative translation practices (Allison, 37).   MATTHEW STEGGLE

Sources W. M. Hunnybun, 'Registers of the English Poor Clare Nuns at Gravelines … 1608–1837', *Miscellanea, IX*, Catholic RS, 14 (1914), 25–173 · A. F. Allison, 'Franciscan books in English, 1559–1640', *Biographical Supplement*, 3/1 (1955), 16–65 · O. Valbuena, introduction to Sister Magdalen Augustine, *The history of the angelical virgin glorious S. Clare*, www.wwp.brown.edu/texts/rwoentry.html [Renaissance women online]

Evelyn, Sir George Augustus William Shuckburgh, **sixth baronet** (1751–1804), mathematician, was born George Augustus William Shuckburgh on 23 August 1751, the eldest son of Richard Shuckburgh (1728–1772) of Limerick and his wife, Sarah, daughter of Captain John Hayward RN, of Plumstead, Kent, and widow of Edward Bate. Sir Richard Shuckburgh (1596–1656) was his direct ancestor. Shuckburgh was educated at Rugby School from June 1760 until he entered Balliol College, Oxford, in April 1768, graduating BA in 1772. On the death of his uncle, Sir Charles Shuckburgh, fifth baronet, on 10 August 1773, he succeeded to the baronetcy and the family estates at Shuckburgh, Warwickshire. He was elected to the Royal

Society in December 1774, by which time he had already departed on a tour of Europe.

The weather diary which Shuckburgh maintained during this period shows that he spent the winter of 1774–5 in Amiens, the following summer in Paris, then travelled via Lyons, where he was admitted to the Académie des Sciences, Belles-Lettres et Arts, and reached Geneva in July 1775. Shuckburgh was particularly interested in the heights of the Alps, and in the structure and quality of the atmosphere. He took with him on his travels two fine travelling barometers by Ramsden, from which he could ascertain his altitude, also small hygrometers and an anemometer. From Geneva he went to Chamonix to explore its glacier, and continued over the Alps via Turin and Bologna to Florence, where he stayed for the rest of the winter. In the summer of 1776 he toured the Italian cities as far south as Rome, before returning to Paris, thence to London, which he reached in September 1776.

After his grand tour Shuckburgh frequently travelled within Britain, and occupied himself with various scientific experiments. He was elected to the Society of Antiquaries in 1777, and was among the medical and political membership of the Eumelean Club, which met in a tavern in Bond Street, Westminster. On 27 September 1780 he was returned to parliament for the county of Warwick, and retained the seat until his death. He mostly supported Pitt and Fox; one of the few subjects on which he spoke in the house was applied mathematics, on which he presented several papers to the Royal Society. In 1790 he was one of the committee that declined the petition of Thomas Mudge who was seeking a reward for his chronometer, and he spoke on the debate in 1793. In February 1796 he actively supported the public purchase of John Hunter's museum, which was given into the care of the Royal College of Surgeons.

Shuckburgh's first marriage, on 3 July 1782 to Sarah Johanna (1755–1783), daughter of John Darker, merchant and MP for Leicester, was brief; on 10 April 1783 she died at Bristol where she had gone to take the medicinal waters. His second marriage, on 6 October 1785 at St Margaret's, Westminster, was to Julia Annabella (1757–1797), daughter of James Evelyn of Felbridge, Surrey. Their only child, Julia Evelyn Medley Shuckburgh, was born in her father's town house, in Park Street, Westminster.

The painstaking barometric measurements made by Shuckburgh and General William Roy in Savoy, concerning the heights of mountains, were published in 1777. Shuckburgh also toured Wales in 1779, taking barometric readings at the foot and summit of Snowdon. Astronomy was another of his interests; his observatory at Shuckburgh was equipped with an equatorial telescope and other instruments by Jesse Ramsden. From 1780 Shuckburgh began to consider how best to set up a universal measure of length, such that if the physical standard should be destroyed, the measure could be reconstructed from first principles. He devoted much time to determination of standards of length, capacity, and weight. In contrast to similar work being undertaken in France, where

the metre was taken as one part in ten million of the distance between pole and equator along a great circle, Shuckburgh chose to derive the yard by reference to the length of a pendulum beating seconds. He procured the apparatus which John Whitehurst had constructed before his death, and obtained a chronometer from Arnold, and from the instrument maker Edward Troughton a 5 foot standard, fitted with reading microscopes, and a precision beam balance. The microscopes allowed a far more accurate measurement than the beam-compasses used hitherto, and did not need to be in contact with the standard. In the event, Whitehurst's apparatus was unequal to the task, but with the aid of Whitehurst's data, and comparisons with existing standards dating from the reign of Henry VII, Shuckburgh achieved his aim. For this work, the Royal Society awarded him its Copley medal.

The condition of inheritance following the death of his father-in-law in 1793 required Shuckburgh to adopt the name of Evelyn, which he took by private act of 1794, being henceforth known as Shuckburgh Evelyn. Another private bill dealt with enclosure of his lands, possibly in connection with the construction of a canal through this area. He died at Shuckburgh Park on 11 August 1804 and was buried on 20 August at Shuckburgh church, alongside his wives. His daughter married in 1810 Charles Cecil Cope, third and last earl of Liverpool.

ANITA MCCONNELL

Sources HoP, *Commons* · 'The family of Shuckburgh', *Miscellanea Genealogica et Heraldica*, 2nd ser., 3 (1888–9), 279, 280, 357 · F. L. Colvile, *The worthies of Warwickshire who lived between 1500 and 1800* [1870], 691–2 · *GM*, 1st ser., 74 (1804), 793 · J. Britton, E. W. Brayley, and others, *The beauties of England and Wales, or, Delineations topographical, historical, and descriptive, of each county*, [18 vols.] (1801–16), vol. 15, pt 2, p. 96 · Nichols, *Lit. anecdotes*, 2.638; 3.623; 8.16 · T. Thomson, *History of the Royal Society from its institution to the end of the eighteenth century* (1812), 524–5 · C. Hutton, *A philosophical and mathematical dictionary*, new edn, 2 (1815), 389 · G. Shuckburgh Evelyn, 'An account of some endeavours to ascertain a standard of weight and measure', *PTRS*, 88 (1798), 133–82 · R. E. Zupko, *Revolution in measurement* (1990)

Archives CUL, astronomical observations · Meteorological Office, Bracknell, Berkshire, National Meteorological Library, meteorological journals · Warks. CRO, MSS | Birm. CA, letters to Boulton family · NL Scot., letters to John Lloyd · RS, corresp. with Sir Joseph Banks

Evelyn, Sir John (bap. 1591, d. 1663/4), politician, was baptized on 20 October 1591 in Kingston, Surrey, the second son of John Evelyn (d. 1627), manufacturer, of Godstone in the same county, and his wife, Elizabeth, daughter and heir of William Stephens of Kingston. The family fortune had been established by Evelyn's grandfather, who had acquired the monopoly of making gunpowder under the Tudors.

Evelyn matriculated as a pensioner at Emmanuel College, Cambridge, in 1606 and entered the Middle Temple in 1610. On 24 November 1618 he married Thomazine, daughter of William Heynes of Chessington, Surrey, and soon after built a large family house at Godstone at the alleged cost of £9000. He succeeded to his father's business in 1627, by which time the gunpowder monopoly was under attack and the business itself in financial difficulty.

In an attempt to defend his position Evelyn secured election to parliament for Bletchingley, Surrey, the following year and immediately introduced a bill, which was lost in committee, for the easier supply of saltpetre. After finally losing the contract to supply gunpowder in 1636, he petitioned for compensation for losses but it was several years before he was cleared of all responsibility for the failure to maintain supplies.

In 1640 Evelyn was re-elected to the Long Parliament in which his nephew, Sir John *Evelyn (1601–1685) of Wiltshire, sat for Ludgershall; he was 'galled' at the attacks on the family's monopoly. He was knighted in June 1641, and as late as December he urged consultation with the king over suppression of the Irish rising. A reluctant supporter of parliament after the outbreak of civil war, Evelyn was only persuaded to subscribe the oath of loyalty to Robert Devereux, third earl of Essex, on threat of imprisonment. With the failure of peace moves Evelyn's allegiance to parliament faltered in August 1643: he retired to Godstone but came under suspicion following the interception of a letter which seemed to suggest that he and his nephew were preparing to make their peace with the king. When interrogated by a Commons committee he failed to answer questions 'clearly and ingenuously' (HoP, *Commons, 1640–60*) and was suspended from the house for over a year.

Evelyn's subsequent political actions, unlike his nephew's, were commended by the diarist, Sir Simonds D'Ewes, as those of a 'gallant and honest man' (BL, Harley MS 165, fol. 157). He favoured accommodation with the king and in February 1648 acted as teller against upholding the vote of no addresses. He did not sit in parliament after Pride's Purge in December 1648 but took his seat after the readmission of the secluded members in February 1660, and was re-elected to the Convention Parliament (April 1660).

Reconciled to death 'with patience and comfort' by 'seeing what befell my soverign lord and master King Charles I the best of men' Evelyn was buried in Godstone on 18 January 1664 (HoP, *Commons, 1640–60*). Four of his seven children survived him. His elder son was created a baronet at the Restoration in 1660, and the younger entered parliament for Bletchingley as an exclusionist.

E. A. REID, *rev.*

Sources 'Evelyn, Sir John (1591–1664)', HoP, *Commons, 1640–60* [draft] · M. W. Helms and J. S. Crossette, 'Evelyn, Sir John I', HoP, *Commons, 1660–90*, 2.280–81 · Keeler, *Long Parliament* · BL, Harley MS 165, fols. 156–9 · *IGI* · Venn, *Alum. Cant.*

Evelyn, Sir John (1601–1685), politician, was born on 11 August 1601 in Kingston, Surrey, the first son of George Evelyn (d. 1636) of West Dean, Wiltshire, clerk in chancery, and his wife, Elizabeth, daughter of Sir John Rivers of Chafford, Kent. The nephew of Sir John *Evelyn (*bap.* 1591, d. 1663/4) of Surrey, MP, and cousin of the diarist John Evelyn (1620–1706), he was educated at Merchant Taylors' School, Emmanuel College, Cambridge (BA 1619), and the Middle Temple. On his marriage on 2 April 1622 to Elizabeth, daughter of Robert Coxe, grocer, of London, he had land in Hampshire, Surrey, and Wiltshire settled on him.

Evelyn was knighted in 1623. He first entered parliament for Wilton, Wiltshire, in 1626. Ten years later he succeeded to an estate allegedly worth £2000 per annum but heavily encumbered with debt. He was among the Wiltshire justices reproved for obstructing royal purveyors of timber for the navy in 1637 and he refused a contribution to the expenses of the bishops' war two years later. Elected in 1640 to both the Short and Long parliaments for Ludgershall, Evelyn supported 'root and branch' reform of the church, and in the summer of 1642 urged preparation for war. Although he was proclaimed a traitor for his activities against the Wiltshire royalists and refused access to the royal presence in November 1642, Evelyn, with his uncle, contemplated making terms with the king in August 1643. Suspended from the Commons for a year following the interception of an incriminating letter, he secured his readmittance, according to the diarist Sir Simonds D'Ewes, only by promising to work with the Independents.

Thereafter D'Ewes accused Evelyn of doing his utmost to 'kindle a fire' between England and Scotland and to hinder a church settlement on presbyterian lines (BL, Harley MS 165, fols. 156–7). For the next four years Evelyn was politically prominent: he became a leading member of the group around Oliver St John, termed the 'Royal Independents', and in Commons divisions frequently acted as teller with Sir Arthur Hesilrige against Denzil Holles and Sir Philip Stapleton. Siding with the army revolt in 1647 against the presbyterian leadership in parliament, in January 1648 Evelyn became a member of the committee of both kingdoms. He was a teller for the motion to make no further addresses to the king and was later involved in plans to make a new peace approach to disengage Charles I from the Scots; during the Newport negotiations he urged that extremist measures should be tempered while negotiations continued.

Evelyn abstained from the Commons after Pride's Purge in 1648, and went into retirement until the return of the secluded MPs to the Long Parliament in February 1660, when he became a councillor of state. He was elected to the Convention Parliament (April 1660) for Ludgershall (on a double return) and Stockbridge. 'A long lived, happy man' (HoP, *Commons, 1660–90*, 2.281), Evelyn died on 26 June 1685; his wife may well have predeceased him. He was survived by two daughters, one of whom he cut out of his will with 5s. because of her marriage to a tory.

E. A. REID, *rev.*

Sources 'Evelyn, Sir John (1591–1664)', HoP, *Commons, 1640–60* [draft] · M. W. Helms and P. Watson, 'Evelyn, Sir John II', HoP, *Commons, 1660–90*, 2.281 · V. Pearl, 'The Royal Independents in the English civil wars', *TRHS*, 5th ser., 18 (1968), 69–96 · *JHC*, 2 (1640–42) · *JHC*, 6 (1648–51) · BL, Harley MS 165, fols. 156–7

Evelyn, John (1620–1706), diarist and writer, was born on 31 October 1620 at Wotton in Surrey, the second son and fourth child of Richard Evelyn (1590–1640) and his wife, Eleanor (1599–1635), daughter of John Stansfield (d. 1627) and his wife, Elianor, *née* Comber (d. 1613). Evelyn believed that his family came from Shropshire and ultimately from

In July 1641, in the company of Mary, princess royal, Evelyn made his first journey to the continent, remaining in Holland and Belgium until the following October. A year later he was present at the battle of Brentford, but realizing that he could do the king's side no service, he procured another licence to travel and by November 1643 he was in Calais. This was the beginning of a visit that lasted nearly four years, to France and Italy, a journey on which Thomas Howard advised him, and which has become one of the great seventeenth-century examples of the grand tour. At the end of that tour, in June 1647, Evelyn married Mary Browne [see Evelyn, Mary (c.1635–1709)], the daughter of the English resident in Paris, Sir Richard Browne, though they did not cohabit until three years later.

At the age of eleven Evelyn began to keep the notes from which his best-known work, the *Diary*, was subsequently composed. Probably it began in the same sort of almanac that he used for the year 1637 and that is in the library of Balliol College. He did not put these notes into the form of what is now the *Diary* until the 1680s, and many of the entries about the continent, Beer points out (Evelyn, *Diary*, 1.87–101), make use of later guidebooks that refer to things Evelyn could not have seen himself. Certainly the diary contains both his personal reflections and what is more like news reporting. It exists in essentially two forms: a work called *De vita propria* which covers the period from 1620 to 1644 (which Beer prints separately), and another called the *Kalendarium* which covers his life from 1620 to 1697 (BL Add. MSS 78323–78325) and covers much of the material in *De vita propria* though with significant variations. In addition there are some loose sheets covering the period between 1697 and 1706, and a later transcript of *De vita propria* made by his grandson Sir John Evelyn (BL, Add. MS 78326) in 1737. Beer's edition of the *Diary* supersedes all others and, with Evelyn's correspondence, provides the primary basis of his life record. Like most of Evelyn's manuscripts, these are all now in the British Library.

The interregnum and *Elysium Britannicum* Evelyn's return to England in 1647 signalled his first engagement with property: both that which he had inherited in 1640 from his father and the lease of Sayes Court, Deptford, a 200 acre estate (Evelyn, letter copybook, 2, fol. 22v, letter 469 (467)) which his father-in-law had held from the crown. The execution of Charles I in 1649 was for him a dark day that he never forgot or forgave, and it confirmed him in a suspicion of public life that remained with him in spite of his later contribution to it. In 1652 his wife moved to London and gave birth to their first child, Richard (1652–1658). He was the first of eight children, only four of whom reached adulthood. John Stansfield (1653–1654), George (1657–1658), and a second Richard (b. and d. 1664) died in infancy. John *Evelyn (1655–1699), the only son to survive childhood, was never well, and two of his sisters, Mary *Evelyn (1665–1685) [see under Evelyn, Mary (c.1635–1709)] and Elizabeth (1667–1685), died young of smallpox. Only Susanna (1669–1754) outlived her father.

The deaths of three young children in the 1650s, as well as the increasingly hostile climate of the interregnum,

John Evelyn (1620–1706), by Robert Walker, 1648

Normandy. From his great-grandfather John, who first brought the invention of gunpowder into England, his grandfather George (1526–1603) inherited the patent for its manufacture that descended in the family until the outbreak of the civil war.

Education and the grand tour Evelyn's father, Richard, who was the only son of George's second marriage (to Joan Stint), inherited Wotton with about 700 acres of land. He was worth £4000 a year, and became sheriff of Sussex and Surrey in 1633. Having been sent to stay with his maternal grandfather in Lewes at the age of five, Evelyn began to draw and sketch even before he went to school in 1630 and kept a diary in the following year. In 1632 his father wanted to send him to Eton College but was persuaded by his son to allow him to stay at the free school in Southover, a school where (Evelyn later believed) he had an inadequate education at the hands of Edward Snatt. His mother died in 1635 of an excessive remorse, Evelyn claimed, for the death of his sister Elizabeth (1614–1634) and other children dead in infancy. On 13 February 1637 Evelyn and his two brothers were admitted to the Middle Temple where his tutor was his later fellow traveller on the continent Thomas Henshaw. In April 1637 Evelyn was admitted fellow-commoner of Balliol College, Oxford, and matriculated on 29 May. His tutor was meant to be Ralph Bathurst (later a friend, and supervisor of his son's education) but instead he was assigned to George Bradshaw, whom Evelyn later believed negligent in his duty. Like many of his rank, he left without a degree.

darkened Evelyn's youthful exuberance but established his lifelong interest in pedagogy and education. This was first reflected in his translation of St John Chrysostom's *Golden Book* (1659), which Evelyn dedicated to the memory of his first son, the infant prodigy Richard, the subject of a moving tribute in his *Diary*. In a letter to Samuel Hartlib in 1660 Evelyn also praised the usefulness of John Comenius's *Orbis sensualium pictus* (1659) to children's education (Evelyn, letter copybook 2, fol. 22v, letter 467 (165)). Later he both employed Milton's nephew Edward Phillips as tutor to his son John and encouraged him to contribute to Edmund Gibson's 1695 edition of William Camden's *Britannia* to which he himself contributed. A series of unpublished treatises on educational subjects (BL, Add. MS 15950) and later letters to Samuel Pepys, Charles Spencer, Robert Berkeley, and Francis Godolphin also represent this tutorial side of his character. He first met William Wotton, the instigator of the ancients and moderns controversy, as a child prodigy, and although Evelyn himself was never simply an ancient or a modern, he encouraged Wotton in his part in the controversy and urged him to write the life of Robert Boyle.

In 1652 Evelyn began to create the garden at Sayes Court, a project that signalled the beginning of his serious interest in botany and garden history. This led to his writing the *Elysium Britannicum* (BL, Add. MSS 78342–78344), an encyclopaedic history of gardens and gardening practices that occupied him for most of his life. It was first proposed to Sir Thomas Browne in 1655 and publicly announced in Evelyn's *The French Gardiner* (a translation of Nicolas de Bonnefons's *Le jardinier françois*) in 1659. The *Elysium* project led also to the extensive 'information exchange' on horticulture that grew out of garden making, an exchange that is reflected in Evelyn's two letter copybooks (BL, Add. MSS 78298–78299) and elsewhere. Learned as the intention of the project was, it also attracted the correspondence of many ordinary gardeners or 'planters of coleworts', as Evelyn frequently described himself. Among these were George London and Henry Wise, the founders of the Brompton nursery, and Moses Cook, the gardener at Cassiobury who, like John Rose, another of Evelyn's correspondents, became a partner in that enterprise.

Through Samuel Hartlib's 'Office of address', Evelyn also came to know John Beale, a pioneer of pomiculture in Herefordshire, who introduced Evelyn to Le Gendre's *Manière de cultiver les arbres fruitiers* which Evelyn translated and published in 1660 as *The Manner of Ordering Fruit-Trees*. Beale also contributed to Evelyn's *Pomona* (1664), and offered extensive material for *Elysium Britannicum* (BL, Add. MSS 78312, 78313). In a robust and extensive correspondence in the early 1660s Beale also challenged Evelyn to redefine his thoughts about the nature of gardens. Beale encouraged him to move away from the French model of Pierre Morin which was the source of the first flower garden at Sayes Court, and to pursue the idea of extensive or rural gardening with trees that Evelyn also discussed in letters with Sir Richard Browne (BL, Add. MS 78306).

Having experimented with garden design at Wotton in 1643 and again in 1652 Evelyn went on to create a garden for his old neighbours and friends the Howards at Albury. He also consulted with Arthur Capel, earl of Essex, about the design of Cassiobury, the first garden to be made entirely with trees. And at Euston, Lord Arlington's estate in Suffolk, he recommended laying out the grounds in a way that anticipated the landscape gardens of the mid-eighteenth century.

Evelyn's interest in science led to other research and publication. The first book of his translation of Lucretius's *De rerum natura* was published in 1656 (*An Essay on the First Book of T. Lucretius Carus De rerum natura*), though the remaining books were not published until 2000 (ed. M. Repetski). The abortion of this project was due partly to Evelyn's disgust with the slovenly proof-reading of the text in his absence, a problem that was to continue to plague his books. There are also documents on scientific subjects among his manuscripts. His 'Coelum sanitatis' (BL, Add. MS 78346), a translation of an anonymous alchemical work, represents his belief that translation was part of the work of extending Bacon's *Great Instauration*. More significant are his 'Medicus itinerarius' and related papers (BL, Add. MSS 78336–78338) as well as the famous anatomical tables done for him in Padua in 1646 and published in the *Philosophical Transactions* in 1702 (12, no. 158). There are also manuscripts on mathematics, physics, mechanics (BL, Add. MS 78333), natural history, and chemistry (BL, Add. MSS 78335, 78346), in the last of which he was instructed by Nicholas Le Fèvre in Paris. The most complete of Evelyn's library catalogues (1687, BL, Add. MS 78632) also indicates his interest in books on all these subjects, as well as grammar, law, philology, philosophy, poetry, mechanics, and theology.

Many of Evelyn's books and manuscripts were alienated from the collection both before and after his death, not least by William Upcott, the editor of his *Miscellaneous Writings* (1825). The chief dispersal of his library, however, was in the Christies sale of 1977 when his collection of prints, largely purchased in Italy, and his furniture (including two cabinets for his collection of curiosities) were also sold. Most of the books from Evelyn's library containing significant marginalia are now in the British Library and have their own pressmark (EVE). (An alphabetical list of them was published by Michael Hunter in *John Evelyn in the British Library*, 1995). The marginalia in these books reflect Evelyn's sense of a text as cumulative and exemplify his refusal to see any document as complete.

In 1664 Evelyn's friend Abraham Cowley wrote and dedicated an essay and pindaric ode on gardens to Evelyn; Evelyn's pindaric ode in reply is less well known. He later revised the ode for another gardening friend, the second countess of Clarendon, about her garden at Swallowfield. Apart from the Lucretius translation, all of which is in verse, there is a considerable body of occasional poetry among his manuscripts, including the letters. He also wrote a play, *Thersander*, and advised his cousin Sir Samuel Tuke on his translation of the Spanish play *The Adventures of Five Hours* (1663).

Evelyn's pioneering work on tree cultivation (*Sylva*,

1664) and on soils (*A Philosophical Discourse of Earth*, 1676; in later editions entitled *Terra: a philosophical discourse*) were both outgrowths of the *Elysium Britannicum*. Although primarily intended to encourage tree planting after the devastation of the civil war, *Sylva* was a learned work addressed more to gentlemen than to foresters. In it he introduced the word 'avenues' into the English language of landscaping. By its fourth edition it contained 'an Historical Account of the Sacredness and Use of Standing Groves' that demonstrates its relation to the *Elysium* project. *Sylva*'s handsome reissue with additional plates by Alexander Hunter in 1776 gave it a renewed popularity. The subjects of both *Sylva* and *Terra* are also extensively represented in his manuscript collections, including his incomplete treatise on staves (BL, JE MS D13.2) and his notes on husbandry (BL, Add. MS 78340). Never more than an amateur scientist, Evelyn was none the less one of the virtuosi who formed the Georgical committee of what became the Royal Society in 1661. In 1659 (Evelyn, letter copybook, 2, fol. 19, letter 159 (155), 1 Oct 1659), he both proposed a model for the society to his friend Robert Boyle and contributed to Boyle's *A History of Cold* (1665, pp. 407–9).

In his lifetime Evelyn also published works that were part of the unpublished *Elysium Britannicum: Kalendarium hortense* (1664) and *Acetaria* (1699), as well as a paper in the *Philosophical Transactions* in 1670 on Lord Sandwich's discovery in Spain of an early seed drill, the 'sembrador' (5.60). In the twentieth century a further *Elysium*-related document was published: his *Directions for the Gardiner at Sayes Court* (1932). Also related to the *Elysium* were Evelyn's translation of Nicolas de Bonnefons's *Le jardinier françois* (1659), a book Evelyn believed the best introduction to vegetable gardening, and *The Compleat Gard'ner* (1693), a translation of the work by la Quintinie in which Evelyn was probably assisted both by Thomas Creech and George London who, with Thomas Wise, brought out a condensed version in 1699. His wife's work in the still room also contributed to the *Elysium* proposal, as did his own notes on culinary and other subjects (BL, JE MS D4). Throughout Evelyn's correspondence from 1660 onwards there are also many letters related to what Evelyn frequently called 'my hortulan affair'.

The Restoration Evelyn's earliest publications were essentially royalist tracts: *A Character of England* (1659), *An Apology for the Royal Party* (1659), and *The Late Newes from Brussels Unmasked* (1660). All of them were published before the Restoration. Although, like his father, Evelyn was loath to be drawn into public life, much of his life after 1660 was involved with public affairs of one sort or another. *Fumifugium* (1661), the first English book on pollution, announces his commitment to the improvement of public life, evident in his agreement to serve as a commissioner of the sewers the previous year. Thereafter he found himself on other committees of this kind: for licensing hackney coaches (1663), reforming the streets (1662–4), regulating the Royal Mint and Gresham College (1663), repairing St Paul's Cathedral (1666), or even for replanning London after the great fire (1667, *London*

Revived, ed. E. S. de Beer, 1938), a disaster of which he wrote a powerful account in his *Diary*.

These were far less important and time-consuming than Evelyn's appointment to the commission for the sick and wounded in the Second and Third Anglo-Dutch Wars (1664–7; 1672–4) that consumed a large part of his energy and resources for the better part of a decade. He was also a member of the council for foreign plantations (later trade and plantations, 1670–74). Already an investor in the East India Company, Evelyn was thereby enabled to pursue his interests in botany, exploration, and trade, interests that led to his friendship with William Dampier. He was also a commissioner of the privy seal in the difficult period preceding James II's abdication (1685–7), and treasurer of the commissioners for erecting Greenwich Hospital (1695–1703).

The corruption of public and private life, especially at court, is a theme that runs through Evelyn's correspondence. It appears as early as his description of dissolute public gatherings in *A Character of England* (1659) and reappears in his argument for legal restraint on luxury in *Tyrannus, or, The Mode* (1661). Not surprisingly it also appears in the writing of his pious and studious daughter Mary.

In spite of his desire to avoid the court, Evelyn found it necessary to pursue great men of office in an attempt to settle legal cases. One was over the ownership of Sayes Court that had been thrown into question by the civil war. The other was over the money owed to Evelyn's father-in-law for his work as English agent of the crown in Paris during the interregnum. Although Charles II had promised to reimburse Sir Richard, this claim was not settled until 1687. In the meantime Sir Richard's brother-in-law was suing for reimbursement of the money that he had lent Sir Richard for his expenses at that time.

While his son John went abroad in 1675 in the household of the first Lord Berkeley, Evelyn stayed behind to manage the Berkeley estate and later advised Lady Berkeley on the development of what is now Berkeley Square. He was also a lifelong friend of Anne Digby, wife of the second Lord Sunderland, the wily prime minister in all but name. Arlington, Clarendon, Clifford, Fox, Godolphin, Mordaunt, and Osborne were all his close acquaintants, but he was never at the centre of politics, nor wished to be, and his literary controversy with Sir George Mackenzie in 1665 about whether the public or the private life was to be preferred was as much an old-fashioned exercise in academic disputation as an endorsement of public employment. Commanded by Charles II to write about the history of the conflict between the Dutch and the English over the sovereignty of the seas (BL, Add. MS JE Gq), Evelyn found his labours rejected as malapropos in a time of peace. The introduction was published as *Navigation and Commerce* in 1674, but the rest of his history, given to Pepys for his proposed history of the navy, was lost.

Later works Although Evelyn continued to be interested in the work of the Royal Society, he was increasingly out of sympathy and touch with the direction that it took—towards an exclusivist science and away from the arts and the wide range of humanist interests that had been part of its early mandate. His attitude to knowledge was essentially encyclopaedic rather than taxonomic, connotative rather than denotative. He celebrated Boyle's invention of the air-pump and recognized how it might be used to vacuum-pack food, but he was disgusted by the cruelty of a dog's vivisection in 1667. The great works of his later life are on the arts: *Sculptura* (1661); his translations of Gabriel Naudé's *Advis pour dresser une bibliothèque* (*Instructions Concerning Erecting of a Library*, 1661) and of Roland Fréart's *Parallèle de l'architecture antique et de la moderne* (*Parallel of Architecture*, 1664) and *Idée de la perfection de la peinture* (*Idea of the Perfection of Painting*, 1668); and *Numismata* (1697).

Sculptura, or, The History, and Art of Chalcography and Engraving in Copper represents Evelyn's project (evident as early as his manuscript notes from the 1650s) to fulfil one of Bacon's recommendations to compile a history of trades. But *Sculptura* also recognizes the earlier work of Giacomo Favi, who is celebrated in its preface by Samuel de Sorbière. Evelyn's manuscript 'Trades. Secrets and receipts mechanical' (BL, Add. MS 78341) and its variant, 'Circle of mechanical trades' at the Royal Society, were motivated by his desire to protect the arts from vulgarization by defining their function. As with *Elysium Britannicum*, *Sculptura* was concerned more with the skills of the artist and virtuoso than the mere mechanic. The book announces the invention of the mezzotint, as represented by one done by Prince Rupert, but it is concerned to guard that invention from being 'prostituted'.

Whether Evelyn discovered the woodcarver Grinling Gibbons (as he claimed, Evelyn, *Diary*, 3.567) has been disputed, but certainly Evelyn was interested in the encouragement of artists of all kinds. His translation of Fréart's *Parallèle de l'architecture antique et de la moderne*, augmented by an account of modern architects in the third edition published just after his death, celebrates his friend Wren and refutes the claim that Lord Burlington rescued Palladio from obscurity. His translation of Fréart's *Idée de la perfection de la peinture* reflects his own keen interest in painting as a young man as well as his own landscape and portrait drawings and those of his wife and daughter. His portrait was painted by Chanterell when he was six and again by van der Borcht when he was twenty. His best-known portraits are by Walker in 1648 (now in the National Portrait Gallery) and Kneller in 1679 and 1685, but perhaps the most engaging is the drawing made in 1650 by Nanteuil that was subsequently engraved. Evelyn also continued to number among his friends such painters as Lely, Kneller, and Verrio. His friendship with Wren grew out of several architectural projects in which they were both interested—the Sheldonian Theatre at Oxford, the rebuilding of Whitehall, Chelsea Hospital, and the rebuilding of St Paul's. And Evelyn spent a good deal of time in 1667 ensuring that the great collection of classical inscriptions assembled by his friend Thomas Howard, earl of Arundel, be given a home at Oxford. For this he was awarded a DCL by the University of Oxford in 1669.

Evelyn's *Numismata* is as much about the depiction of physiognomy as it is about its ostensible subject, medals.

Ranging as it does over a wide range of subjects, it reflects at the end of Evelyn's life his continuing commitment to the plurality of knowledge. In it is also contained the story of the motto by which Evelyn is still best known to the general public, *Decus et tutamen* ('an ornament and a defence'), suggested by him to Sir Henry Slingsby for the new milled coinage and still on the English £1 coin. This motto is the title of John Brydall's book on the laws of England, a work that Evelyn listed in the 1687 catalogue of his library. One of the four catalogues of his books, it represents his lifelong concern for book collecting and cataloguing that led him to translate the *Advis pour dresser une bibliothèque* (1661) by Cardinal Mazarin's librarian Naudé. He also offered advice to Arlington and Pepys about their libraries, arranged the gift of the library of Henry Howard, sixth duke of Norfolk, to the Royal Society, and encouraged the establishment of a public library at St James's Palace under the care of his friend Richard Bentley.

Collections of the writings of others also constitute a major part of what is one of the more extensive sorts of writing by Evelyn, the religious. Among his posthumously published works (1850) is his 830-page *History of Religion* (BL, Add. MS 78367). Begun by him in 1657, it was added to as late as 1704 and arose from Evelyn's doubts about his own religion during the persecution of the Church of England in the interregnum. In part it is a response to the conversion to Roman Catholicism in this period both of John Cosin, the son of his friend Bishop Cosin, and of Evelyn's distant cousin Thomas Keightley. But it also represents Evelyn's long-standing interest in religious subjects, an interest reflected in the large number of clergy who were among his friends, including many bishops and most of the archbishops of Canterbury from the Restoration until his death. Evelyn's falling-out with his brother-in-law William Glanville near the end of his life was because of the latter's Socinianism (disbelief in the Trinity), a subject on which he had a firm and outspoken position.

Among Evelyn's manuscripts are his annotated Bible (BL, Add. MSS 78360–78361), his collection of lectures from the New Testament (BL, Add. MS 78363), and his 'briefe Account of divers Sermons' (BL, Add. MS 78365), on some of which he drew for the *Diary*. He also published three other works on religion: *Another Part of the Mystery of Jesuitism* (1664), a translation of a work by Antoine Arnauld; *The Pernicious Consequences of the New Heresie of the Jesuites* (1666), a translation of a work by Pierre Nicole; and *The History of the Three Late Famous Impostors* (1669), accounts of three religious cheats, two of them gleaned from Pietro Cesii and the third from Sir Paul Rycaut.

Even Evelyn's letter to Boyle about the buildings for a Royal Society (Evelyn, letter copybook, 159) reflects his religious interests. It sounds as much like a proposal for a monastery as an academy. Among his religious papers there are also devotional collections and offices from the interregnum, most of them composed for Margaret *Godolphin between 1672 and 1675 (BL, Add. MSS 78375–78385). Much has been made of the apparently pathological element in Evelyn's attachment to her, but this approach fails to consider the intense strain of high-church devotion that existed, largely apart from the court, in the late seventeenth century. Evelyn first met Margaret in 1672, and the anniversary of her death in childbirth in 1678 is one that he never forgot. A maid of honour to Catherine of Braganza, she represented to him everything that the court was not: intelligence, piety, and modesty.

After the death in 1691 of his nephew John, the last surviving son of Evelyn's elder brother George, Evelyn arranged to inherit the family estate, Wotton, and he moved there with his wife in 1694, leaving Sayes Court in the hands of his son-in-law William Draper. Evelyn's inheriting Wotton was not without challenge by his brother's granddaughters: he had to contest a case in the House of Commons in 1698, the year before his brother's death. In 1696 Sayes Court was let to Admiral Benbow, who in turn sublet it (through William III) to the youthful Peter the Great, thereby precipitating its ruin. Although Evelyn continued to travel to London about Greenwich Hospital business his life was based at Wotton; it was at his son's house in Dover Street, London, that he died at the age of eighty-five on 27 February 1706. He was buried in the chancel of Wotton church.

Long dismissed as a virtuoso dabbler in the arts and sciences, Evelyn has now come to be recognized as a scholar and participant in the reception of the new science of the seventeenth century. Over a period of more than half a century his voluminous correspondence reflected and extended the social and scientific interchange of his time. His enthusiasm for horticulture in particular, both in his own garden at Sayes Court and in his correspondence and publications, translated continental ideas into England and laid the groundwork for the English landscape garden of the eighteenth century.

DOUGLAS D. C. CHAMBERS

Sources P. Beal and others, *Index of English literary manuscripts*, ed. P. J. Croft and others, [4 vols. in 11 pts] (1980–), vol. 2, pt 1, pp. 461–87 · Evelyn, *Diary* · J. Evelyn, letter copybooks, RS · G. Keynes, *John Evelyn: a study in bibliophily with a bibliography of his writings* (1968) · *Evelyn's furniture* (1977) [sale catalogue, Christie, Manson & Woods, London, 31 March 1977] · *English, old master and modern prints* (1977) [sale catalogue, Christie, Manson & Woods, London, 26 July 1977] · *The Evelyn library*, 4 vols. (22 June 1977–13 July 1978) [sale catalogues, Christie, Manson & Woods, London, 22–3 June 1977; 30 Nov – 1 Dec 1977; 15–16 March 1978; 12–13 July 1978] · *Valuable printed books and a few manuscripts* (1978) [sale catalogue, Christie, Manson & Woods, London, 8 Nov 1978] · *The Evelyn family library* (1977) [sale catalogue, Christie, Manson & Woods, London, 12 Oct 1977] · F. Harris, 'Living in the neighbourhood of science: Mary Evelyn, Margaret Cavendish and the Greshamites', *Women, science, and medicine, 1500–1700*, ed. L. Hunter and S. Hutton (1997), 198–217 · M. Hunter, 'John Evelyn in the 1650s: a virtuoso in quest of a role', *Science and the shape of orthodoxy: intellectual change in late seventeenth-century Britain* (1995), 67–98 · M. Hunter, *Establishing the new science: the experience of the early Royal Society* (1989) · T. O'Malley and J. Wolschke-Buhlmann, *John Evelyn's Elysium Britannicum and European gardening* (Dumbarton Oaks Research Library, Washington, 1997) · 'John Evelyn in the British Library', *Book Collector*, 44/2 and BL (1995) · G. de la Bédoyère, ed., *Particular friends: the correspondence of Samuel Pepys and John Evelyn* (1997) · G. de la Bédoyère, 'John Evelyn's library catalogue', *Book Collector*, 43/4 (1994) · J. Evelyn, *Elysium Britannicum, or, The royal gardens*, ed. J. Ingram (2001) · Pepys, *Diary* · M. Hunter, *The Royal Society and its fellows, 1660–1700: the morphology of an early scientific institution* (1982) · *DNB* · GEC, *Baronetage* · HoP, *Commons, 1660–90* · Munk, *Roll* · GEC, *Peerage*

Archives Balliol Oxf., almanacs · BL, Add. MSS, Evelyn MSS · BL, collection of annotated pamphlets and engravings · BL, corresp., notes, and papers, Add. MSS 15948, 15950 · BL, diaries and papers · Bodl. Oxf., notes on John Aubrey's *Monumenta Britannica* · Harvard U., Houghton L., letters and literary MSS · Magd. Cam., essays on the fishery and notes · PRO, 'Narrative of the encounter between the French and Spanish ambassadors', SP 29/43/12 · RS, essays, lectures, and papers · RS, letter-books · U. Cal., Los Angeles, William Andrews Clark Memorial Library, letters and papers · Yale U., Beinecke L., annotated 'publick employment preferr'd' · Yale U., Beinecke L., letters | Arundel Castle, West Sussex, copy of earl of Arundel's 'Remembrances' · BL, letters to Sir Hans Sloane, Sloane MSS 4037, 4039, 4075 · Bodl. Oxf., autograph, Ashmole, Rawlinson, Tanner MSS · Helmingham Hall, Stowmarket, letters to Lord Huntingtower · Ransom HRC, letters to Samuel Pepys and papers · Trinity Cam., corresp. with Richard Bentley

Likenesses H. van der Borcht, oils, 1641, NPG · R. Walker, oils, 1648, NPG [*see illus.*] · R. Nanteuil, line engraving, 1650, BM, NPG · R. Gaywood, etching, 1654, BM · G. Kneller, oils, 1689 · T. Bragg, line engraving (after G. Kneller), BM, NPG; repro. in W. Bray, ed., *Memoirs of John Evelyn*, 2 vols. (1818)

Wealth at death in 1703 total annual revenue recorded as £2328: Harvard U., Houghton L., Houghton MS 992.2, p. 23 · bequeathed annuity of £144 p.a. to granddaughter; left grandson (only male heir) £2300 and £300, plus remaining estate and books: will, 20 Feb 1706, BL, Evelyn MSS, BL JEI 11, copy in PRO B1/55

Evelyn, John (1655–1699), translator and government official, was born on 14 January 1655, at Sayes Court, Deptford, Kent, the third but eldest surviving son of the diarist, John *Evelyn (1620–1706) and his wife, Mary *Evelyn (c.1635–1709), daughter of Sir Richard Browne, of Sayes Court. In his early years Evelyn was brought up at Arundel House among the children of Henry Howard, later sixth duke of Norfolk. However in 1662 Evelyn's father put an end to the association with the Howard children, 'for fear of their perverting him in the popish religion' (Evelyn, 3.326). From 1663 to 1665 Evelyn was tutored by Edward Phillips, a nephew of the poet John Milton, and from 1665 to 1667 by Ralph Bohun. He entered Trinity College, Oxford, in 1667 under the care of the president of the college, Dr Ralph Bathurst. He matriculated on 2 May 1668, and left Oxford the following year. In 1672 Evelyn was admitted to the Middle Temple by the solicitor-general, Sir Francis North, and was called to the bar in 1683. During the time of his education he had been presented on separate occasions to the queen mother, Henrietta Maria, and to Charles II, and had been with the court party in Dover and Calais during the negotiations of the secret treaty of Dover. At the age of eighteen Evelyn received instruction and advice from the Anglican bishop of Chichester 'before he received the Holy Sacrament'. In 1675 Evelyn travelled to France in the entourage of the English ambassador, Lord Berkeley. On 24 February 1680 Evelyn married Martha (c.1660–1726), daughter of Lady Martha Stonhouse by her first husband, Richard Spencer, a London merchant. Although the marriage produced two sons and three daughters, only a son and a daughter survived infancy. The marriage settlement included a dowry of £5000 plus a jointure of £500 a year after the death of Evelyn's parents.

Evelyn's work as a translator included *Of Gardens: Four

Books, First Written in Latine Verse by Renatus Rapinus, and now Made English (1673), a version of François de Chassepol's French work, translated as The History of the Grand Visiers (1677), and Plutarch's 'Life of Alexander the Great' for Plutarch's Lives by Several Hands (1683–6). He contributed some prefatory Greek hexameters, which he had written at the age of fifteen, to his father's work, Sylva (8th edn, 1678), as well as a reprint of the second book of his translation of Rapin's Hortorum liber. He also had several poems published in the third edition of Dryden's Miscellanies (1702) and in John Nichols's Collection of Poems.

Evelyn's career in government commenced in 1687, when he was employed in Devon on a commission from the Treasury lords about concealed lands. In December of the following year he joined William of Orange at Abingdon, and, as a volunteer in Lord Lovelace's troop, helped to secure Oxford. In 1690 he purchased the chief clerkship of the Treasury, a post from which he was removed within a year. In early 1692 he was appointed as one of the seven commissioners of the revenue in Ireland. Although Evelyn was pleased with the appointment, his father considered it to be 'far from my wishes' and could only hope that 'I may yet see him in prosperity again' (Evelyn, 5.92, 113). His father's wishes were not to be fulfilled, and after four years in Ireland, Evelyn returned to England in ill health. Thereafter he spent his remaining years in England. Evelyn died on 24 March 1699, at Berkeley Street, London, from the illness which he had contracted in Ireland. He was buried in the family vault in Wotton, Surrey.

C. I. McGRATH

Sources Evelyn, Diary · Evelyn MSS, BL · Foster, Alum. Oxon. · Wood, Ath. Oxon., new edn · R. Lascelles, ed., Liber munerum publicorum Hiberniae … or, The establishments of Ireland, later edn, 2 vols. in 7 pts (1852), vol. 1, pt 2 · C. I. McGrath, 'The Irish revenue system: government and administration, 1689–1702', PhD diss., U. Lond., 1997
Archives BL, MSS; family MSS | PRO, minutes of the Irish revenue commissioners, cust 1/3 · PRO NIre., De Ros MS D638/30/12

Evelyn [née Browne], **Mary** (c.1635–1709), correspondent, was the only child of Sir Richard *Browne (1605–1683) and his wife, Elizabeth, née Pretyman (1610–1652). Mary spent most of her childhood and adolescence in France, where her father represented Charles I. She married John *Evelyn (1620–1706) on 27 June 1647 in Paris; she was twelve or thirteen, he was twenty-six. She returned to England in June 1652, residing with her husband first at Sayes Court, in Deptford, and later at Wotton, in Surrey. She gave birth to five sons (Richard, John Stansfield, John *Evelyn, George, and Richard), and three daughters (Mary [see below], Elizabeth, and Susanna). The recipient of a careful humanist education, she played an important role in educating her children, only the youngest of whom survived her. She was fluent in French, knew Italian, and studied mathematics and drawing. Though her marriage and family duties in many ways limited her intellectual pursuits her marriage was both a friendship and a partnership. Her husband's plan for an otherwise all-male mathematical college included her, and she designed the frontispiece for his 1656 translation of Lucretius. After his death she said

of him that 'His care of my Education was such as might become a Father a Lover a Friend and Husband' (Evelyn, Diary, 1.37). She died on 9 February 1709 at her home in Dover Street, London, and was buried on the 14th at Wotton.

After the publication of the diary of her husband, John Evelyn, in 1818 Mary Evelyn became with him a model of Anglican piety and domestic virtue. Though her husband credits her with authorship of The picture of the Princess Henrietta, published as a broadsheet in 1660, the attribution has been questioned (see Hiscock, 45), and it is in her correspondence that her wit, perceptiveness, and strength of character are most evident. Her letters to her son's tutor at Oxford, Ralph Bohun, were circulated by him among his university acquaintance for several years, providing Mary with an opportunity to engage Oxford dons on topics that included theatre and literature (see Harris, 'Living in the neighbourhood of science', 208; Harris, 'Letterbooks', 210–14).

Mary Evelyn (1665–1685), the sixth of eight children born to John and Mary Evelyn, is credited with authorship of Mundus muliebris, a brief satire in tetrameter couplets on fashionable women's clothing, accoutrements, and behaviour, first published in 1690. Sole attribution of the piece to her is questionable: de Beer points out that the one reference to the work in her father's diary may suggest that she contributed to rather than wrote it (see Evelyn, Diary, 4.423; Nevinson, 5–12; Greer and others, 324). Other writings in Mary Evelyn's hand survive; these are primarily religious meditations and rules for her own conduct. She was dutiful and devout, playful and pious, and her death at the age of nineteen grieved her family deeply. She spent most of her short life at the family home at Sayes Court, Deptford. She studied French and Italian, history and literature, music and dancing. After her death her father eulogized her in his diary: 'The justnesse of her stature, person, comelinesse of her Countenance and gracefullnesse of motion, naturall, & unaffected (though more than ordinaryly beautifull), was … of the least, compar'd with the Ornaments of her mind' (Evelyn, Diary, 4.421). Her mother described her to a correspondent: 'The papers which are found in her cabinet discover she profited by her readying—such reflections, collections out of Scripture, confessions, meditations, and pious notions, evidence her time was not spent in the trifling way of most young women' (H. Evelyn, 107). Another important role model was Margaret *Godolphin (1652–1678), a family friend with whom Mary's father signed a pact of friendship using a symbol that Mary was to adapt in her own journal (Evelyn papers, MS ME 13). During an extended visit to Rebecca, Viscountess Falkland, in late 1684 and early 1685 Mary was exposed to smallpox. She returned to Sayes Court, where she fell ill, and died on 14 March 1685. She was buried on 17 March in St Nicholas's Church, Deptford.

JOAN K. PERKINS

Sources Evelyn, Diary · BL, Evelyn papers · W. G. Hiscock, John Evelyn and his family circle (1955) · F. Harris, 'The letterbooks of Mary Evelyn', English Manuscript Studies, 1100–1700, 7 (1998), 202–15 · F. Harris, 'Living in the neighbourhood of science: Mary Evelyn,

Margaret Cavendish and the Greshamites', *Women, science, and medicine, 1500–1700*, ed. L. Hunter and S. Hutton (1997), 198–217 · 'Mary Evelyn', *Kissing the rod: an anthology of seventeenth-century women's verse*, ed. G. Greer and others (1988), 324–32 · J. L. Nevinson, *Mundus muliebris* (1977) · H. Evelyn, 'John Evelyn, author of *Sylva*', *The history of the Evelyn family* (1915), 63–131 · J. Perkins, 'Introductory note to Mary Evelyn's *Mundus muliebris*', *The early modern Englishwoman: a facsimile library of essential works, 1500–1750*, series 2, part 3: *Printed writings, 1641–1700*, ed. B. Travitsky and P. Cullen [forthcoming] · T. Hofmann and others, 'John Evelyn's archive at the British Library', *Book Collector*, 43/4 (1995), 147–209 · G. Keynes, *John Evelyn* (1968) · A. Ponsonby, *John Evelyn* (1933) · G. de la Bédoyère, *Particular friends* (1997) · R. Kroll, '"Living and breathing statues": domesticating Epicurus', *The material world* (1991), 140–79 · J. Evelyn, *Life of Mrs. Godolphin*, ed. H. Sampson (1939) · J. Fitzmaurice, 'The Cavendishes, the Evelyns, and teasing in verse and prose', *Journal of the Rocky Mountain Medieval and Renaissance Association*, 16–17 (1995–6), 161–86 · J. K. Welcher, *John Evelyn* (1972) · J. Bowle, *John Evelyn and his world* (1981) · B. Saunders, *John Evelyn and his times* (1970)

Archives BL, Add. MSS., 15949, 15950, 34702

Likenesses Nanteuil, drawing, 1650, Wotton House; repro. in Evelyn, *Diary*, 2 · portrait (Mary Browne Evelyn?; as a very young girl), Wotton House; repro. in Evelyn, 'John Evelyn', following p. 88

Wealth at death a small sum of money and some trinkets; Mary Evelyn (1665–1685): BL, Evelyn papers, MS ME12; will, Evelyn, *History of the Evelyn family*

Evelyn, Mary (1665–1685). *See under* Evelyn, Mary (*c*.1635–1709).

Evens, George Bramwell (1884–1943), broadcaster, was born on 15 February 1884 at 3 Argyle Street, Anlaby Road, Kingston upon Hull, the only child of George Matthew Evens (1860–1920), a Salvation Army officer, and his wife, Matilda (1862?–1945), daughter of Cornelius Smith and his wife, Polly. His father was of Huguenot descent and his mother of Gypsy stock, hence his later assumption of the pseudonym Romany when he commenced the natural history radio broadcasts for children in 1931 which established his reputation as one of the most popular children's broadcasters of the era. He was also the nephew of the celebrated evangelist and preacher Gypsy Rodney *Smith (1860–1947).

Evens's early years to the age of seven were very unsettled after his father left the Salvation Army to become an itinerant evangelist in 1885. Although he sang on public platforms at prayer meetings from the age of four, his early education was disrupted. Indeed, he only attended elementary school regularly from 1891 when his father became a Wesleyan home missioner in Liverpool, subsequently transferring to higher grade school in Aspeen Grove, Lodge Lane, Liverpool. His interest in wildlife was nurtured even in the predominantly urban environment of Liverpool. Visiting the docks with his father, he became fascinated by the rats leaving the holds of ships along the mooring ropes, and he took regular country walks with his dog Floss around Aigburth. He reared mice, rabbits, and pigeons, and when he was sent to Epworth College at Rhyl at the age of thirteen, he always took a pigeon with him to release on arrival to let his parents know he had reached his destination safely. He spent four years at Epworth College, emerging as a good athlete, captaining

George Bramwell Evens (1884–1943), by Ronald Howgate

both the school soccer and cricket teams, and an accomplished pianist. Recognizing an increasingly compelling vocation for the ministry, he proceeded to Queen's College, Taunton, as a divinity student in 1902, where he also contributed his first articles on ornithology to the school magazine. He was accepted as a candidate for the Wesleyan ministry and entered the Wesleyan Theological College at Handsworth, near Birmingham, in 1905.

After leaving college Evens was stationed at Dalston in the East End of London, where he married on 1 August 1911 Eunice (1887–1976), the daughter of Owen Thomas, a Congregational minister. They had a son and a daughter. They soon moved north, where Evens was to spend the remaining years of his ministry in the urban centres of Goole, Carlisle, Huddersfield, and Halifax. His longest pastorates were for twelve years at Carlisle (1914–26), where he began lecturing on natural history and writing articles for the *Cumberland News* and the *Methodist Recorder* under the pseudonym The Tramp and for ten years at Halifax (1929–39), where he reached the height of his fame as an author and broadcaster. He seized every opportunity to explore the surrounding countryside in these urban appointments, taking his fishing rod with him to Methodist synods in rural locations and purchasing an authentic horse-drawn vardo from Gypsies at a Cumbrian fair in 1921 to provide him with a well-equipped rural retreat.

Evens's longing for the outdoors and his artistic temperament produced a distinct lack of enthusiasm for chapel and circuit administration, much of which devolved upon his wife. Her organizational skills enabled him to combine a growing programme of speaking and broadcasting engagements with his demanding pastoral ministry. However, he possessed both a great affinity for people, especially young people, and an ability to move congregations in his preaching and conduct of worship. His sermons were eloquent in their simplicity and imbued with optimism and thankfulness. He was no scholar, and did not attempt to explain many of the great mysteries of the Christian faith. Modest and good-humoured, he was of striking appearance. Over 6 feet tall, with unusually broad shoulders, he had long raven-black hair, swept back to reveal a broad forehead, heavy eyebrows, piercing dark hazel eyes, swarthy cheeks, and a strong nose and chin. In his younger days he sported a dark moustache, invariably smoked a pipe, and never wore a hat.

For technological reasons Evens's pioneering *Out with Romany* radio broadcasts between 1931 and 1943 were confined to the studio, with all the sound effects of the natural world created synthetically. They took the form of imaginary descriptive rambles accompanied by his cocker spaniel Raq and his young friends Muriel Levy and Doris Gambell; it later emerged that Levy was an experienced children's writer, married with a child of her own, and that Gambell was an accomplished concert singer. The broadcasts appeared so realistic that few doubted their authenticity, and there was widespread amazement and disappointment, not least from the performers themselves, when the *Radio Times* unexpectedly revealed in 1942 that they were studio reconstructions. Their spontaneity derived from Evens's confident improvisation from a skeletal script, his ability to communicate with listeners personally, and his technique of seeming unaware that the microphone was present. 'Just as he had no special voice reserved for pulpit utterances', his wife later observed, 'so before the microphone he talked and laughed as naturally as he did at home' (Evens, 141).

Evens's detailed and unusual knowledge of the countryside, acquired more by observation than by scientific study, was impressive. There was, however, some initial reluctance within the BBC to transmit the broadcasts of an enthusiastic amateur nationwide until calculations of audience figures underlined their immense popularity. The programme consistently headed listener request polls, and it was estimated that at their peak some 13 million listeners tuned into his broadcasts, of whom 9 million were adults. The programme became compulsive listening during the wartime blackout and was even parodied by the comedy programme *ITMA*. The drama critic Herbert Farjeon in June 1942 pronounced it 'the BBC's best creation' (Evens, 113), while the broadcaster Terry Waite later recalled that 'Romany introduced thousands of children of my generation to the wonders of the countryside' (Loveridge, *Romany Returns*, foreword). The programme also stimulated such a demand for Evens to give

public lectures that he acquired an agent in 1932, and travelled extensively throughout the north of England and the midlands. He also wrote no fewer than ten books, published between 1929 and 1944, many of them illustrated with his own photographs of wildlife. He received daily a heavy mailbag, with correspondents often enclosing specimens for him to identify, including dead birds and beetles, some in an advanced state of decay. The impact of his unrivalled influence as a naturalist was to raise awareness of the dangers that the countryside faced, and of the growing need to maintain a balance between agriculture and the world of nature.

Evens was never robust in health. A congenital heart murmur had rendered him unfit for military service in both world wars, and almost prevented him from entering the Wesleyan ministry. In later life he was plagued with duodenal ulcers, and following surgery he retired prematurely from the Methodist ministry in 1939. After suffering a coronary thrombosis while gardening, he died suddenly at his home, 35 Parkway, Wilmslow, Cheshire, on 20 November 1943. His death was announced in national news bulletins and was followed by fulsome tributes on *Children's Hour* and in the *Radio Times*, which mourned him as 'one of the great personalities of radio, a man who made millions of friends by his genius for being just himself' (Evens, 248). He was cremated at Manchester crematorium on 24 November and his ashes were scattered near Penrith, on the Cumberland fells, where a memorial birdbath was later erected.

JOHN A. HARGREAVES

Sources E. Evens, *Through the years with Romany* (1946) · G. Loveridge, *Romany returns* (1995) · H. L. Gree, *The spirit of Romany* (1945) · *Halifax Courier* (22 Nov 1943) · *Stockport Advertiser* (26 Nov 1943) · *Sunday Dispatch* (21 Nov 1943) · *Sunday Express* (21 Nov 1943) · *Manchester Guardian* (23 Nov 1943) · *Daily Mail* (22 Nov 1943) · *Altrincham and Wilmslow Advertiser* (26 Nov 1943) · *Carlisle Journal* (23 Nov 1943) · *News Chronicle* (22 Nov 1943) · *Methodist Recorder* (25 Nov 1943) · J. A. Hargreaves, *Halifax* (1999) · CGPLA Eng. & Wales (1944) · b. cert. · m. cert. · d. cert. · private information (2004) [R. Watt]
Archives SOUND BBC WAC, performance recording
Likenesses photographs, 1891 (aged seven), repro. in Evens, *Through the years with Romany* · photographs, 1911–14, repro. in Loveridge, *Romany returns* · W. Scott, photograph, 1930 (with Mrs G. B. Evens), repro. in Evens, *Through the years with Romany* · R. Howgate, photograph, repro. in Evens, *Through the years with Romany*, frontispiece [see illus.] · Longbotham, photographs, repro. in Evens, *Through the years with Romany* · R. Nicholson, photographs, repro. in Evens, *Through the years with Romany* · photograph, repro. in Evens, *Through the years with Romany*
Wealth at death £3588 5s. 8d.: probate, 24 March 1944, CGPLA Eng. & Wales

Everard [Eborard] (d. 1147), bishop of Norwich, was once considered to have been a member of the Montgomery family, identifiable with the Everard, son of Roger, earl of Shrewsbury, who attested several charters of Henry I. It now seems almost certain that he was the son or nephew of Nigel the Doctor, a substantial Domesday tenant who held the royal manor and the church of Calne, Wiltshire, and who held the prebend of Mora in St Paul's Cathedral before Everard himself, whose own successor therein was his nephew, William of Calne. The later Norwich chronicler Bartholomew Cotton states that Everard was archdeacon of Salisbury, and William of Malmesbury relates in his account of St Osmund, bishop of Salisbury, how, when he was one of Osmund's archdeacons, Everard was miraculously cured by the intervention of St Aldhelm. These lucrative benefices were almost certainly the reward for service to the crown, for in his old age, in a letter to the pope, Everard stated that he had been present when William Rufus and Archbishop Lanfranc had communed with the bishops and barons of England, that is, between 1087 and 1089, and had attended most royal and ecclesiastical councils thereafter, first as a royal chaplain and then as bishop. All this suggests that he must have been born in or before the late 1060s.

It is almost certain that Everard's appointment as the second bishop of Norwich, two years after the death of Herbert de Losinga in 1119, was at the royal command, but a form of election at least was held and the result announced to the archbishop by the 'clergy and people of the church of Norwich' (Landon, 197–8). He was elected shortly after 13 March 1121, royal assent was given immediately, and he was consecrated at Canterbury on 12 June 1121. He was thereafter present at most of the great ecclesiastical occasions which occurred during his pontificate, such as legatine councils and the consecration of the Conrad choir at Canterbury Cathedral in 1130, but despite his previous background, he was seldom at the royal court after 1121, except for major assemblies. As bishop, Everard attested only eight charters for Henry I and a further thirteen for King Stephen. In his personal life he was an old-fashioned, pre-Gregorian figure. He certainly had children, for whom William d'Aubigny, first earl of Arundel, instructed his monks of Wymondham to pray, and, as bishop, Everard was surrounded at Norwich by a multitude of nephews, of whom at least ten occur as witnesses to his charters, as does his own brother Arthur. These family preoccupations did not, however, divorce him from the monks of his cathedral priory, and despite the hostility of some contemporary secular bishops to the Benedictines, he was remembered by the monks of Norwich as one who had cherished them with great affection.

Everard completed the construction of Norwich Cathedral church, inaugurated by his predecessor, with little financial help from the magnates of the region. He assisted the monks in the establishment of St Paul's Hospital at Norwich and ratified the establishment of a cell at Hoxne, Suffolk; he accepted their complaints against the exactions perpetrated by his officials, and he confirmed to them the levy from the parishes of the diocese granted to them by Bishop Herbert. He was criticized, however, for the alienation to the sheriff and another knight during the early years of Stephen's reign of two estates, Blickling and Cressingham; this he did without consultation with monks or archdeacons, probably to avert worse depredations by the sheriff. Everard also appears to have been extremely doubtful of the validity and veracity of the martyrdom and burgeoning cult of the boy saint William, allegedly ritually murdered by the Norwich Jews (the charge was first made at a synod, held before the bishop at Norwich, of all the priests in his diocese). He was cautious in the face of the enthusiasm of a strong faction within the priory, but he did authorize the first removal of the body from Thorpe Wood to the monks' cemetery.

Within the diocese at large Everard issued confirmations for several of the lavishly endowed monasteries whose foundation transformed the landscape and landholding pattern of East Anglia in the early twelfth century. The most important administrative development was the clearer definition of the responsibilities of the archdeacons, now increased to four in number, for whom territorial titles were used for the first time, albeit sporadically. In his episcopate, too, there appear as witnesses to charters a multitude of rural deans, who carried episcopal authority down to the most local level.

Everard's last recorded public appearance in England was in the early months of 1145, in the company of the papal legate Imar of Tusculum. During this year he resigned his bishopric. Henry of Huntingdon, in his letter 'De contemptu mundi', states that he was deposed because of his cruelty, but this is a strangely improbable allegation which is nowhere corroborated. He retired to the Cistercian monastery of Fontenay (Côte-d'Or), and his description of himself to the pope, in a letter supporting the metropolitical jurisdiction of Canterbury over Wales, as 'joined by love and desire to the poor of Christ', suggests that he became a monk (*First Register of Norwich Cathedral Priory*, 70). It is likely that he played a major role in the construction of the abbey church. It was certainly at the abbey that he died; he was buried first (before 21 September 1147) in the chapel of St Paul, and subsequently before the high altar, where his tombstone bears a fine effigy of a bishop in pontificals. CHRISTOPHER HARPER-BILL

Sources C. Harper-Bill, ed., *Norwich, 1070–1214*, English Episcopal Acta, 6 (1990) • L. Landon, 'Everard bishop of Norwich', *Proc. Suffolk Institute of Archaeology*, 20 (1930), 186–98 • *Bartholomaei de Cotton … Historia Anglicana*, ed. H. R. Luard, Rolls Series, 16 (1859) • H. W. Saunders, ed., *The first register of Norwich Cathedral priory*, Norfolk RS, 11 (1939) • D. Whitelock, M. Brett, and C. N. L. Brooke, eds., *Councils and synods with other documents relating to the English church, 871–1204*, 2 (1981) • Henry, archdeacon of Huntingdon, *Historia Anglorum*, ed. D. E. Greenway, OMT (1996) • J. B. Corbolin, *L'abbaye de Fontenay* (1882)
Likenesses effigy (in pontificals on tomb), Fontenay Abbey • seal on documents

Everard, Edmund (*fl.* 1673–1691), informer, is of obscure origins, but may have been of Irish descent. He was apparently employed as an agent to the French court, and was also employed for a time as an assistant secretary to the duke of Monmouth. A Catholic during his time in France, it was claimed that by 1678 he had become a protestant. He appears to have associated with a number of Irish exiles while in Paris, and in his printed version of events there he claimed that in 1673 he met the future Catholic plotter Edward Fitzharris. Everard was also to claim that he had uncovered a popish plot to remove Charles II from the throne in a manner that was very similar to the alleged plot of autumn 1678. When it was discovered that Everard had knowledge of this plot he maintained that he had been threatened with punishment unless he kept quiet. However, another version of the Paris sojourn was that Everard had himself actually threatened some persons there, especially Monmouth, for the non-payment of his arrears. In the event, on visiting London in December 1673 Everard was arrested for treasonable designs. He was incarcerated in the Tower and interrogated for a design to poison 'some great person', whom some thought to be the duke of Monmouth (*Fourth Report*, HMC, 234). Everard was later to state that he had been threatened with the rack while in the Tower.

Everard was finally discharged from the Tower in January 1678. With the outbreak of the Popish Plot scare he naturally became a minor informer on the scene, claiming to be a precursor of Titus Oates and attacking Slingsby Bethell and later Sir Robert Walsh in print. Being an opportunist, Everard was frequently to change his stories, as well as sides, in the years that followed. He gave evidence before the Lords committee and was involved with Edmund Warcup JP, the notorious hunter of papists, as well as the many Irish witnesses who flooded into London. At length in February 1681 Everard once more became involved with Edward Fitzharris. The latter wrote a libellous pamphlet, *The True Englishman Speaking Plain English in a Letter from a Friend to a Friend*, advocating the deposition of Charles II and the exclusion of the duke of York. It seems that Fitzharris hoped to plant this pamphlet in the home of a prominent whig and then make a 'discovery'. Fitzharris contacted Everard to forward this scheme and this was to lead to Fitzharris's death. Everard, whose loyalties were, at least temporarily, whiggish, drew Fitzharris into a trap, duping him into betraying the entire scheme before Sir William Waller, who promptly arrested him and sent him to Newgate on a charge of high treason. Everard gave evidence against Fitzharris at his trial and made an assortment of other unsubstantiated claims that netted him various sums from the secret service fund.

By 1682 Everard had joined the court faction, but still gave evidence against Warcup, who faced counter-accusations of conspiracy to suborn witnesses. He was also to claim that various nonconformist ministers had offered him a pension if he would retire to the Netherlands. In due course he did so, but for reasons of his own. In the Netherlands in the 1680s he worked as a merchant and spy for Sir Bevil Skelton and was used to spy on his former whig friends. Once they discovered this Everard's life was threatened, his goods were seized, and his debts called in. With the collapse of James II's government Everard seems to have changed sides once more, as by 1691 he was giving evidence against Jacobites and made various accusations in that year. Visiting their haunts in the Netherlands and Flanders he also took to uncovering military intelligence against the French army. He was placed in the Tower in 1691, but disappeared from view shortly afterwards. The date of his death is unknown.

ALAN MARSHALL

Sources E. Everard, *The depositions and examinations of Mr E. Everard concerning the horrid Popish Plot* (1679) • E. Everard, *Discourses on the present state of the protestant princes of Europe* (1679) • *Fourth report,* HMC, 3 (1874) • R. Walsh, *A true narrative and manifest … by Sir R. W. which he is ready to justify as relating to the plot* (1679) • *Report on the manuscripts of Allan George Finch*, 5 vols., HMC, 71 (1913–2003), vol. 3 • 'The journals of Edmund Warcup, 1676–84', ed. K. G. Feiling and F. R. D. Needham, *EngHR*, 40 (1925), 235–60 • *CSP dom.*, 1673–85 **Archives** BL, letters to Lord Middleton, B. Skelton, etc., Add. MSS 41804–41819

Everard, Edward Cape (b. 1755, d. in or after 1818), dancer and actor, was born on 3 February 1755 at the White Hart at Tottenham High Cross, Middlesex, the elder son of Edward Everard (1728–1755), the innkeeper of the White Hart, and his wife, Ann, née Sowerby. Following the death of his father ten months later, his mother—already pregnant with a second son—entrusted him to his godfather, a dresser at Drury Lane who also kept theatrical lodgings, and returned to her home town of Carlisle. Everard detested his guardian, Cape, whom for eighteen years he took to be his father, and suppresses his Christian name in his autobiography. By the age of four Everard had learned to dance. Cape introduced him to David Garrick at a moment when the theatre needed fairies and Lilliputians, and his career, as Master Cape, began. His dancing improved after lessons from Jean-Georges Noverre, and for ten years from the age of seven he himself taught the art to 'some of the first families in London' (Everard, 11). When he was twelve he appeared before the young prince of Wales (afterwards George IV) and his brother Prince Frederick and was noticed by George III. He danced at Drury Lane and acted boys' parts, such as Arthur in *King John*, until he was eighteen. Garrick became his patron; long afterwards Everard was briefly his amanuensis. 'Doctor Johnson and Doctor Goldsmith knew me from infancy' he wrote (ibid., 71). Such connections were later to be helpful.

At the age of eighteen Everard abandoned his godfather and henceforward appeared under his own name. By then he had spent two summers in theatres at Plymouth and Portsmouth, dancing and acting in parts which he would never have been given at Drury Lane. Indeed, in the autumn of 1773 George Garrick told him that he was too big for boys' parts and not ready for adult roles, but that he could stay on, on a low wage (£1 5s.), combining acting with helping rehearse the dancers. He accepted under protest and remained for a few years longer, working in the summers for Samuel Foote at the Haymarket and at Brighton, Exeter, and Bristol. He married an actress, Ann Gibson (b. 1756), probably in 1776. They had two children, one of whom certainly died in infancy; there is no record of the other. At the end of that season Everard resolved to leave Drury Lane, but the management discharged him first.

Everard then became a strolling actor, with occasional brief periods attached to a theatre. He records everything in his autobiography, which is important evidence of the contemporary state of provincial theatre. It is full of complaint, but also contains lively anecdotes and shrewd comments on other players, for he had acted with the best. Although qualified, he did not benefit from the pension fund Garrick had set up for decayed actors. He blames Robert Baddeley for this, whom he alleged maliciously refused to accept a late contribution.

Everard was briefly a member of almost every theatrical company outside London, playing (when he could) such high-comedy parts as Sir Peter Teazle in Richard Brinsley Sheridan's *The School for Scandal* and Lord Ogleby in Garrick and George Colman the elder's *The Clandestine Marriage*. He never stayed long even in the poorest of them, for he was demanding, jealous over parts, and bitter over claims for benefit nights. In bad times he would book local assembly rooms and give recitations, usually with support from the gentry. Once he became a private tutor in London. In 1805 he contrived to get back to Drury Lane: pressure from the lord chancellor, John Scott, first Baron Eldon, a connection of his wife's family, brought him the humble role of one of the forty thieves in *Ali Baba*, on a pittance. Everard remained at that level for the next two seasons, although in 1806 he organized a benefit for himself at the Haymarket, exploiting the goodwill of more successful former colleagues. In May 1808 Drury Lane discharged him again. He went back to the old road, but in November, at Leek, Staffordshire, he had had enough and resolved to retire. He walked to Scotland, surviving on his recitations, and settled in Edinburgh, where his wife had connections. The management of the theatre there gave him a few small parts which he took in spite of his vow, and granted him benefits in 1817 and 1818. But that was the end. He wrote his autobiography when old, sick, and impoverished, and he probably died within a few years.

JOHN LEVITT

Sources E. C. Everard, *Memoirs of an unfortunate son of Thespis* (1818) · Highfill, Burnim & Langhans, *BDA* · S. V. Troubridge, *The benefit system in the British theatre* (1967) · G. W. Stone, ed., *The London stage, 1660–1800*, pt 4: 1747–1776 (1962) · C. B. Hogan, ed., *The London stage, 1660–1800*, pt 5: 1776–1800 (1968) · A. Hare, *George Frederick Cooke: the actor and the man* (1980)
Likenesses J. Zoffany, group portrait, oils, 1762 (in *The farmer's return*), Theatre Museum, London; repro. in Highfill, Burnim & Langhans, *BDA*, 2.287
Wealth at death negligible: Everard, *Memoirs*

Everard, Frederick Thomas [*formerly* Friedrich Thomas Eberhardt] (**1858/9–1929**), shipowner, was of German origins, beginning life with the surname Eberhardt, which he prudently changed in the First World War. He became foreman shipwright for A. H. Keep, a barge builder at Greenhithe, in Swanscombe, Kent, after a period in its Battersea yard. He was so successful that by 1880 he was yard manager, and bought the site to operate it himself. About a decade later he moved into barge owning, though not with one of his own construction, but perhaps as payment for a debt from the cement makers Knight and Bevan.

The fleet was built up until, by his death in 1929, it numbered about fifty vessels. Although Everard started with sailing barges, and throughout his life retained a strong belief in their utility and profitability, he was not immune from changes around him and encouraged the shift to powered craft, which Everards began just before the First World War. The firm went into both steam and motor coasters. Interestingly, given the criticisms usually levelled at British shipowners for being slow to adopt diesel technology, Everards owned a motorship before it did a steam-engined vessel, and operated more motorships than steamers throughout the inter-war period. By 1939 its fleet comprised nearly forty motor coasters as against about ten steamships and twenty-five sailing ships. Thus the firm was able to compete against the Dutch motor coasters which began to appear in the British coastal trade.

Everard married Susan Ann Spooner (1862–1944), daughter of William Martin Spooner, mariner, on 8 March 1885. They had three sons and one daughter, all of whom were encouraged to take an interest in the firm. Everard ensured his two eldest sons received a thorough technical training at the Greenhithe yard and in the shipyard of Fellows at Great Yarmouth. His youngest son was trained as an engineer at the firm of Plenty & Son at Newbury, which made marine diesel engines, and which was acquired by Everards in 1932. His daughter, Alice Ethel, the eldest of the four children, also helped with the business, especially on the bookkeeping and office management side, remaining undistracted by marriage. By the First World War all four children were playing an active part in the firm with William taking the lead in strategy and the operational side, Frederick in the construction and repair of barges. When the private firm was converted to a limited liability company in 1922 Everard was governing director, and the other four directors were his children; the shares were split equally among these five.

One of Everards' strengths in the 1920s was its enterprise. Apart from being among the first British firms to operate diesel ships, it also sought and found new trades, such as coastal tankers with steam heating coils, which allowed it to carry edible fish and vegetable oils at the correct temperature for easy pumping. It also spread its risks by operating in a wide range of trades such as coal, clay for cement making, china clay, and grains. The firm was also good at fostering a spirit of friendly rivalry among its skippers, encouraging them to make fast passages and paying them a form of piece rate—on shares—to ensure the minimum time spent in harbour. The founder was also careful with the finances, ensuring profits were ploughed back into more vessels, and employing external sources of finance, such as the Midland Bank, using the fleet as collateral. During the First World War the firm received 'financial help' (Wilson, 173) from Van den Berghs in return for carrying oils to the Netherlands and margarine back to the UK. The association lasted into the Unilever era and beyond the Second World War.

Everards has been described as 'a paternalistic company demanding acquiescence, in return for which they looked after their own' (Durham, 111). At times this meant the skippers were driven to improve productivity or were subject to sarcastic comment if they were slow on a passage. The good side was small unexplained gifts and thoughtfulness to the crews, and the provision of over fifty houses in Greenhithe for the crews' occupation, appropriately in Port and Starboard Avenues. Everards also used barge racing as a method of motivating its crews and advertising its services. The founder of the firm was a keen supporter of the Thames and Medway races, and his sons kept up this tradition until well into the 1960s. Although never as large scale as the largest barge owners, such as E. and J. Goldsmith of Grays or the London and Rochester Trading Company of Kent, Everards was built on stronger foundations and endured.

Everard has been described as calm and restrained, a gentleman of the old school, genuinely concerned for his crews. He was active in the local community, presenting a flagstaff to celebrate the relief of Mafeking in 1900 to St Mary's Greenhithe, the local parish church, of which he was a churchwarden from 1909 to 1920. In 1925 he donated land on which to build a rectory. He was widely liked and respected. He died on 8 June 1929, aged seventy, at his house, The Warren, High Street, Greenhithe, and was probably buried in St Mary's.   JOHN ARMSTRONG

Sources K. S. Garrett, *Everard of Greenhithe* (1991) · G. Romilly, 'F. T. Everard & Sons Ltd', *Progress*, 223 (1949), 26–32 · Companies House, London, file 180834 · D. Durham, *The last sailorman* (1989) · *A short history of the parish church of Greenhithe* (1956) · J. Uglow, *Sailorman: a barge-master's story* (1975) · B. Roberts, *Last of the sailormen* (1960) · C. V. Waine, *Steam coasters and short sea traders* (1976) · C. Wilson, *The history of Unilever: a study in economic growth and social change*, 2 (1954), 173 · F. G. G. Carr, *Sailing barges* (1989) · H. Benham, *Down tops'l* (1951) · H. Benham, *Last stronghold of sail* (1948) · B. Roberts, *Breeze for a bargeman* (1981) · F. G. Willmott, *Cement, mud, and 'muddies': a history of the APCM barges* (1977) · *CGPLA Eng. & Wales* (1930) · d. cert. · m. cert.
Archives Companies House, London, file 180834
Likenesses portrait, repro. in Garrett, *Everard of Greenhithe*, 6
Wealth at death £27,602 17s. 3d.: resworn probate, 30 April 1930, *CGPLA Eng. & Wales*

Everard, Harry Stirling Crawfurd (1848–1909), writer on golf, was born at Claybrook House, Leicestershire, on 30 January 1848, the only son of Henry Everard of Gosberton, Lincolnshire, and his wife, Helen Maitland. After attending Eton College (1862–6) he entered Christ Church, Oxford, matriculating on 23 May 1866 and graduating BA in 1871. In 1867 he became a student of the Inner Temple but was not called to the bar. He settled in St Andrews, his wife's home, and took up golf with great enthusiasm, having been a keen player of tennis and cricket as well as a swimmer and a competitive pedestrian. His golfing style was eccentric but effective and he became a formidable player, winning the Royal and Ancient Golf Club's silver medal in 1889, the Calcutta cup in 1890, and the silver cross in 1891, as well as collecting medals and championships at Montrose and Carnoustie.

Everard's playing enthusiasm was matched by extensive writing in support of the game at the time of its greatest boom in Britain. He contributed articles to the *Scots Observer*, the *National Observer*, *The Spectator*, the *Saturday Review*, and many of the growing number of specialist periodicals. In addition he published *Golf in Theory and Practice* (1897; 3rd edn, 1898), *The History of the Royal and Ancient Golf Club of St Andrews* (1907), and provided chapter 8, 'Some celebrated golfers', for the golf volume of the Badminton Library (1890). His writing was like his play,

cumbersome, laboured yet accurate, with 'much valuable, if rather elaborate instruction' enriched by many anecdotes.

Everard married Annie, eldest surviving daughter of Colonel Robert Tod Boothby of St Andrews, in 1880; they had two sons and two daughters. Everard died, after a short illness, on 15 May 1909 at his home at Rathmore, St Andrews; his wife survived him. His funeral at St Andrews, on 19 May, was attended by many keen golfers, the Royal and Ancient's silver clubs and balls, draped in crêpe, being carried in procession by club officials.

J. R. LOWERSON

Sources DNB · *The Times* (17 May 1909) · *The Times* (20 May 1909) · *The Times* (7 Oct 1909)
Wealth at death £70,383 16s. 4d.: confirmation, 21 Sept 1909, *CCI* · £74,066 8s. 5d. plus real estate: *The Times* (7 Oct 1909)

Everard, John (1584?–1640/41), preacher and religious controversialist, has been identified as the John Everard born on 19 April 1584 and baptized the same day at St Peter's, Deene, Northamptonshire, the second child and eldest son of Christopher Everard (d. 1608), rector there, and his wife, Elizabeth Diggles, *née* Palladay. Some circumstantial evidence supports this, but the preacher himself did not name his parents and there were at least two John Everards whose early lives have been confused [see Everard, John (b. 1586/7?)]; it is just possible, given his later connection with the Rich family, that he was a member of the puritan Everard family of Essex rather than of the Leicestershire and Northamptonshire family, several of whom were recusants. Although he claimed that he had wasted his youth in ignorance and error, he was certainly well educated, since in later life he translated from Greek, Latin, and possibly Arabic, and it is plausible that he was one of the John Everards admitted to Clare College, Cambridge, either in 1597, as a Leeds scholar, or in 1603. The former graduated BA in 1601, and one proceeded MA in 1607. Given that he later held benefices, it is likely that it was he who was made a deacon in 1606 and who was ordained priest in 1609 in the diocese of Peterborough. He may have been the John Everard who in 1610 presented himself at the English College in Rome as a convert to Catholicism, only to repudiate his new faith in print the following year, but the internal contradictions in this man's testimony further weaken an already unproven link.

By 1618 John Everard the preacher was a lecturer at St Martin-in-the-Fields, Westminster. He may have been the John Everard or Everett who with his wife Frances had three children baptized in the parish, John (bap. 1617, d. 1621), James (bap. 1627), and Frances (bap. 1630, d. 1632); equally, the children's father may have been a John Everett (d. 1631). Everard the lecturer was probably the man who proceeded BD from Cambridge in 1619; by the 1620s he was known as Dr Everard, although there is no record of this degree. He quickly attracted unfavourable attention for outspokenness. By about the beginning of 1618 he had attacked the administration of the court of orphans, for which the lord mayor and aldermen of London were responsible, and he had been censured by the

This is the Shadow of that Houſe of Clay
Where dwelt a Soule who richly did Diſplay
Such Light of Trueth abroad, as did Unſeal
The Book of God and Hidden Things Reveal;
But hauing left That Houſe now dwells Aboue;
In thoſe Bleſs'd Manſions of pure Light & Loue.
T. Croſs ſculpſit   M:B:

John Everard (1584?–1640/41), by Thomas Cross, pubd 1659

bishop and admonished that if he spoke the truth it should not be before a large number of people. Plainly trouble was feared. In the same year Everard published a sermon preached at St Andrew's Holborn, as lecturer at St Martin-in-the-Fields: in *The Arriereban* he expounded godly attitudes to war, believing that malicious people desired to disgrace him, perhaps for stating that God's power, much more than the king's, was not to be questioned, and for the general implication that war against Spain would be in a good cause, as parliament urged. Over Christmas 1620 he prayed that the English might be delivered from a Catholic king, as they already were from Catholic bishops—a direct challenge to the proposed terms of the Spanish marriage. In February 1621 he attacked the Spanish match directly in a sermon in St Martin's, and was imprisoned in the Gatehouse for about six months, after which he asked pardon and promised amendment.

Soon after this Everard was presented to the living of Hinton Martell in Dorset, and in 1622, ironically by James I, to Wilby in Northamptonshire, which he held until 1627. However in August 1622 he attacked the liberation of all Roman Catholic priests and refusers of the oath of supremacy in connection with the Spanish marriage, and

consequently was committed to the Marshalsea prison. After his release, in December he visited Tregony in Cornwall and, as the result of seeing a triple sun in the sky, published an anonymous tract, *Somewhat Written by Occasion of Three Sunnes Seen at Tregnie* (1622), warning that God 'is whetting his sword, and making ready his quiver for impenitent sinners', because most of the church was deceived, implicitly by Roman Catholicism. In March 1623 he was once again imprisoned for expressing unease about the Spanish match. Powerful friends such as Francis Bacon, Lord Verulam, had repeatedly pleaded for his release, but finally James I's patience wore out. He is reported to have said, 'Who is this Dr Ever-out you come so oft about? his name shall be Dr Never-out'. In all, Everard stated that he was imprisoned six or seven times.

By 1626 the emphasis of Everard's preaching began to change. He was investigated by Bishop George Montaigne of London for arguing that it was unlawful to pray for temporal blessings. This marks a step towards the more contemplative content of his later sermons, like *The Rending of the Vail*. Influenced by the Dominican mystic Johannes Tauler (1300–1361), Everard increasingly expounded on humility, simplicity, and letting God have his way in individual lives as important themes. He then became chaplain to Henry Rich, Lord Holland, and moved to Holland House in Kensington. He was also lecturer at the parish church by September 1628, by which time he was renowned as a preacher, drawing a very wide auditory from all sections of society. Sermons preached in city churches like St Giles Cripplegate may date from this time.

According to Rapha Harford, who knew Everard well—and who wrote a foreword to the 1659 edition of Everard's *The Gospel Treasury Opened*—bishops attacked him and deprived him of benefices worth £400. Perhaps these were actually lectureships. Certainly he was not rector of Fairstead, Essex, as has been assumed; John Etheridge was incumbent by 1628, and resigned in 1643. The John Evered of Fairstead summoned and dismissed by the court of high commission in 1636 was more likely to have been a member of the Everard family of Essex. It seems certain, however, that he was deprived of substantial sources of income. According to Harford his reaction was to kneel in court, praising God, and saying, 'The earth is the Lord's and the fulness thereof: therefore I will not fear', and, with St Stephen, 'Lay not this sin to their charge' (Everard, c4). He refused to submit, though William Laud reputedly threatened to bring him to a morsel of bread.

In the late 1630s Everard was the dominant figure influencing London separatism outside the Baptists, though probably not formally separated. Many of his sermons were preached at 'public meeting places' in Kensington, and fashionable Middlesex villages like Islington, and he also preached privately, especially in Kensington. He is mentioned as a separatist in 1638, and may have had links with the Familists, one of whom he helped. By this time he was influenced by Henry Niclaes, and the medieval *Theologia Germanica* favoured by Martin Luther. He translated the latter at this time, and made copies for the earls of Holland and Mulgrave. His other translations included 'The letter and the life, or, The flesh and the spirit' and, from works by Sebastien Franck, 'The tree of life' and 'The vision of God'. Their thought later had an influence on the early Quakers, probably partly through his preaching. Some or all of these books were copied by Woulston, a Chancery Lane scrivener, and bound by Rapha Harford.

In November 1637 the privy council issued a warrant to search Everard's house in Fulham, seize all his papers, and remove those concerning the state. Perhaps these provided material for his trial by the high commission, where he was, according to Harford, falsely accused. He was charged with keeping conventicles and on 11 July 1639 fined £1000 for teaching and publishing heretical doctrine. Such a crippling fine must have been intended to be unpayable, and he was imprisoned. Though negotiations about his submission began in November, only after conferring with the bishops of Ely and Rochester, and reference to Archbishop Laud, did he finally read his submission kneeling in June 1640. He was released from clerical suspension, and in July his fine was remitted. He predicted the downfall of bishops should there be a parliament which the king could not dissolve.

William Penn described Everard as a renowned Independent, and as the great spiritual separatist. He was princely in presence and behaviour, yet able to mix with the humblest if they wished to learn. His greatest desire was to share his faith clearly with others, and he counted all his intellectual gifts as dung beside knowing Christ crucified. His words are notable for their love: 'Beloved' is his usual way of addressing his hearers, and his sermons burn with an eagerness for his hearers to share in a deep encounter with God which he plainly experienced. He describes how, to a repenting and bleeding soul, God appears 'in Mercy and Love, and Marrieth himself to them, and as he communicates to them his sweet Loves, so their *Wills* and their *Loves* are swallowed up in his' (Everard, 7). His portrait, engraved by T. Cross, shows a plump man, ruffed and gowned, with a little goatee beard, and dark, curly, shoulder-length hair. The verse beneath catches the spirit of his admirers' views:

This is the Shadow of that House of Clay
Where dwelt a Soule who richly did Display
Such Light of Trueth abroad, as did Unseal
The Book of God and Hidden Things Reveal.
(ibid., frontispiece)

Everard died in Fulham, Middlesex, leaving a modest sum, at the end of 1640 or in early January, 1641, when administration of his goods was granted. In 1658 Elias Ashmole published *The Way to Blisse*, an anonymous work of natural philosophy dated by Ashmole to the late sixteenth or early seventeenth century, to which 'the industrious Dr Everard' ('To the Reader') had added explicatory marginal notes. ELIZABETH ALLEN

Sources CSP dom., 1611–26; 1636–41; 1648–9 • A. Kenny, ed., *The responsa scholarum of the English College, Rome*, 1, Catholic RS, 54 (1962), 227–9 • J. Everard, *The gospel treasury opened* (1659) [including foreword by Rapha Harford] • H. I. Longden, *Northamptonshire and Rutland clergy from 1500*, ed. P. I. King and others, 16 vols. in 6, Northamptonshire RS (1938–52), vol. 4, p. 255 • *The letters of John Chamberlain*, ed. N. E. McClure, 2 (1939), 350, 439, 486 • M. Tolmie, *The triumph of the saints: the separate churches of London, 1616–1649* (1977), 34–5 • O. C. Watkins, *The puritan experience* (1972), 218–19 • Venn, *Alum. Cant.* • J. V. Kitto, ed., *The register of St Martin-in-the-Fields, London, 1619–1636*, Harleian Society, register section, 66 (1936), 46, 70, 153, 167, 264, 271 • BL, 4454 df17 [note at the back by A. Benezet] • *DNB* • T. Mason, ed., *A register of baptisms, marriages, and burials in the parish of St Martin in the Fields … from 1550 to 1619*, Harleian Society, register section, 25 (1898), 51 • Peterborough diocesan institution book, Northants. RO, 4, fol. 63v; Arch 42, fol. 413 • GL, MSS 9168/19, fol. 48v; 9537/13, fols. 17, 56; 9531/15, fol. 113v • J. Nichols, *The history and antiquities of the county of Leicester*, 4/2 (1811), 522 • W. C. Metcalfe, ed., *The visitations of Essex*, 1, Harleian Society, 13 (1878), 193, 395

Likenesses T. Cross, line engraving, BM, NPG; repro. in Everard, *The gospel treasury opened* [see illus.]

Everard, John (b. **1586/7?**), Roman Catholic convert and author, presented himself in 1610 at the English College, Rome, giving a somewhat confusing account of his life thus far. He was two months short of either his twenty-third or his twenty-fourth birthday, and had been born a younger son at Deene, Northamptonshire. His father, who had died two years previously, a gentleman worth £100 a year, was an 'Anglicanus' (Kenny, 223), but his father's twin sister, Mary Brudenell, was a Catholic, as was their nephew, Richard Everard of Leicester. This suggests that John was the son of Humphrey Everard of Whittington, Staffordshire, an identification strengthened by his reference to an elder brother was a 'captain with the heretics in Belgium'; this could be Michael Everard, son of Humphrey, later killed while fighting in the service of the United Provinces, or Edward Everard (b. c.1575). However, John also refers to his mother, née Diggles, who had remarried Richard Smith (d. 1615), rector of Bulwick and canon of Peterborough. This woman appears in other sources as the Elizabeth Diggles, née Palladay, who on 8 May 1581 married the rector of Deene, Christopher Everard (d. 1608), a first cousin of Humphrey Everard. Elizabeth and Christopher Everard's second child and eldest son, another John Everard, was born and baptized on 19 April 1584; two sisters and two brother also survived their father, just as John of Rome claimed in his own case.

This is not the limit of confusion over which of the second cousins called John Everard presented himself at Rome. The convert says that, after private education of about eight and a half years, at the age of eleven or twelve, he went to Clare College, Cambridge, where he studied under the principal, Thomas Byng (d. 1599), and after four years graduated and became a fellow. College records reveal one John Everard admitted as a Leeds scholar in 1597, who graduated BA in 1601, and another admitted in 1603; neither seems to have been a fellow, but one proceeded MA in 1607. John of Rome, however, recalled that he had caught the plague in Belgium when he was seventeen, which does not indicate uninterrupted residence in Cambridge. His stay at university was long enough for his reading in the works of Cardinal Bellarmine and Thomas Stapleton to lead him into the Catholic faith. He claimed that, having gone to the English Jesuits' College at St

Omer, he was reconciled to the Roman Catholic church by John Floyd, although Everard does not appear in the register there. Under the name Edward Smith, in 1610 he was admitted to the English College at Rome as a probationer, but he left after two or three months because he was afflicted with dizziness in the head during his studies, and because he was unable to agree with his fellow students.

It must have been this John Everard who, following his return to England, published under that name in 1611 *Britanno-Romanus, sive, Angligenarum in Collegio Romano vitae Ratio*. A detailed account in Latin of how the college worked, it exhibited hostility to the Jesuits who ran it, and evidently marked Everard's reconversion to protestantism. The later life of the author, and in particular his relationship to the protestant preacher John *Everard (1584?–1640/41), is uncertain.   VIVIENNE LARMINIE

Sources A. Kenny, ed., *The responsa scholarum of the English College, Rome*, 1, Catholic RS, 54 (1962), 223–9 · Venn, *Alum. Cant.*, 1/2.110 · private information (2004) [archivist, Clare College, Cambridge] · H. Foley, ed., *Records of the English province of the Society of Jesus*, 4 (1878), 611; 6 (1880), 257 · J. Nichols, *The history and antiquities of the county of Leicester*, 4/2 (1811), 522 · J. Wake, *The Brudenells of Deene* [1953], 91, 94, 98–100 · H. I. Longden, *Northamptonshire and Rutland clergy from 1500*, ed. P. I. King and others, 16 vols. in 6, Northamptonshire RS (1938–52), vol. 4, p. 255; vol. 12, pp. 227–9

Everard, Sir Mathias (d. 1857), army officer, was the third son of Thomas Everard of Randilestown, co. Meath, and his wife and cousin, Barbara, daughter of O'Reilly of Ballinlough Castle and sister of Sir Henry Nugent. He was appointed ensign in the 2nd (or Queen's) regiment at Gibraltar on 28 September 1804, and became lieutenant on 21 March 1805. In December 1805 the company to which he belonged, with two others of his regiment and two of the 54th foot, were captured on their voyage home from Gibraltar by a French squadron under Admiral Guillaumet, bound for Mauritius. The troops were put on the frigate *La Volontaire* and carried about for three months, until *La Volontaire* went into Table Bay for water, ignorant of the recapture of the Cape by the British, and surrendered to the shore batteries. The troops were landed, and the companies of the Queen's did duty for some months at the Cape; those of the 54th, to which Everard appears to have been temporarily attached, were sent with reinforcements to the River Plate, and acted as mounted infantry with the force under Sir Samuel Auchmuty. Everard led the forlorn hope at the storming of Montevideo on 3 February 1807, when twenty-two out of thirty-two men with him were killed or wounded. For this he received a sword of honour from the Patriotic Fund at Lloyd's and the freedom of the city of Dublin.

Everard was promoted, on 23 April 1807, to a company in the 2nd battalion, 14th foot, with which he served at Corunna and in the Walcheren expedition. During the latter he was thanked in general orders for his conduct at the siege of Flushing (12 August 1809), when the flank companies of the 14th, one of which he commanded, supported by the rest of the battalion, in conjunction with some of the German legion, stormed one of the enemy's batteries and effected a lodgement within musket-shot of the walls.

Everard was subsequently transferred to the 1st battalion of his regiment in India, and commanded it at the siege of Hathras in 1817. He commanded a flank battalion in the operations against the Pindaris in 1818–19, was made regimental major on 10 July 1821, and commanded it at the storming of Bharatpur on 29 December 1825. The 14th headed one of the columns of assault at Bharatpur, and unsupported cleared the breach after the premature explosion of a mine and effected a junction with the other column led by the 59th foot—the steadiness and discipline of these two regiments, according to Lord Combermere, 'deciding the fate of the day'. Everard was made CB in 1826 and a brevet lieutenant-colonel.

Everard became regimental lieutenant-colonel in 1831, and commanded the regiment for a period of sixteen years in the UK, the West Indies, and North America. He was made KH in 1831 and major-general on 11 November 1851, and received a distinguished service pension. Everard, who had succeeded his elder brother in the family estate, died at Southsea, unmarried, on 20 April 1857.

H. M. CHICHESTER, *rev.* JAMES LUNT

Sources Burke, *Gen. GB* · R. Cannon, *Historical record of the second or queen's regiment* (1852) · R. Cannon, ed., *Historical record of the fourteenth, or the Buckinghamshire regiment of foot* (1845) · *GM*, 3rd ser., 2 (1857), 618 · *The path of glory: being the memoirs of the extraordinary military career of John Shipp*, ed. C. J. Stranks (1969), 139–52 · *Army List* · H. O'Donnell, *Historical records of the 14th regiment* (1893) · A. J. Barker, *The West Yorkshire regiment* (1974), 28 · Boase, *Mod. Eng. biog.*

Everard, Sir Richard, baronet (1683–1733), colonial governor, was born on 24 June 1683 at Langleys, Much Waltham, Essex, the son of Sir Hugh Everard (d. 1706) and his wife, Mary, daughter of John Browne (1642–1702/3) of Salisbury, Wiltshire, surgeon to Charles II and William III. Everard became a captain in Queen Anne's army and may have been with the force of Admiral Sir George Rooke that attacked Gibraltar in 1704, where Everard remained in garrison for eighteen months. On returning to England he resigned his commission. This was about the time (January 1706) that he succeeded to the baronetcy and sold the family property to pay debts; he then purchased property at Broomfield Green. In St Alfege Church, London, on 13 June 1706, he married Susannah, daughter of Richard Kidder (1633–1703), bishop of Bath and Wells.

Everard became involved in colonial affairs in America when complaints from the council of North Carolina against Governor George Burrington, delivered to the lords proprietors by Chief Justice Christopher Gale, led to Burrington's removal from office in January 1725. At the meeting of the proprietors at which this action was taken a letter was read from Everard, seeking the governorship. It was promptly consented to and a formal appointment made on 7 April. This was approved by the crown, and Everard was required to post a bond to enforce the acts of trade. He was soon granted 2000 acres of land in the colony, and in May 1726, after she had joined her husband in

North Carolina, Lady Everard was granted 3000 acres. Burrington received notice of his dismissal on 17 July, when Everard appeared in Edenton before the council and took the oath of office.

Everard was the last proprietary governor of the colony. After the purchase of Carolina by the crown in 1729 he remained in office until 25 February 1731, when Burrington returned to succeed him as the first royal governor of the province. Between the time of his dismissal and July 1726 Burrington remained in North Carolina, where he was the cause of considerable political unrest as well as responsible for several physical attacks on Everard and other leaders with whom he disagreed. It was a time of distress for many people and factions developed that contributed to unstable conditions throughout most of Everard's administration.

In spite of the opposition Everard attempted to maintain peace and to abide by his instructions. He worked with local leaders as far as possible and was concerned for the welfare of the colony. For example, because of poor port facilities most of North Carolina's exports were shipped through Virginia but officials there began to charge excessive fees for this service or to prohibit it entirely. Everard attempted to persuade the Board of Trade to declare a port on the Nansemond River in Virginia free to Carolinians for shipping tobacco. He further demonstrated genuine concern in maintaining peace between American Indian communities in North Carolina and those in Virginia. Two new counties, New Hanover and Tyrrell, were created during his term of office.

It was apparent from the time of Everard's appointment that the crown was intent on purchasing the proprietary rights in Carolina, and it fell to Everard to co-operate with Virginia in running the boundary between the two colonies. For that purpose he commissioned in 1727 Christopher Gale, John Lovick, and William Little, each of whom had friends in England in common with Everard and who up to that point had been strong supporters of the governor. He also named Edward Moseley to the commission. The line was fairly run and North Carolina retained land long in dispute with Virginia.

Knowing from the beginning that North Carolina was likely to become a royal colony Everard seems to have worked diligently to improve conditions in North Carolina while at the same time attempting to please officials at home. Perhaps he hoped for future royal favour. He strictly obeyed his instructions that the granting of land cease; this was a reversal of the practice recently followed by Burrington in violation of directions from home. He had continued to permit land to be taken up, however, particularly in the Cape Fear region, an area rapidly developing and with the prospect of a good seaport. It may have been Everard's action in this respect that displeased popular leaders in the colony and turned some of Everard's oldest supporters against him. By mid-1728 it had become clear that Burrington, then in England, was again in the crown's favour and that upon sale of the colony he was likely to return to office. After all, one of the charges against Burrington had been that he was suspected of working with South Carolina, a royal colony that favoured a shift from proprietary to royal control for North Carolina. With this about to become a reality Everard realized that his days in office were limited and he changed his policies. Land sales were resumed and much land was taken up through the use of blank patents, documents signed by the proper officials but with the quantity and location of the land filled in by the new owner and inadequately recorded as a means of avoiding the payment of quitrents. Everard also approved the issuance of £40,000 in paper currency, something for which the assembly rewarded him with the gift of £500. Although Burrington was named the new governor of North Carolina when it became a royal colony in January 1730 he did not arrive until February 1731. Shortly afterwards the Everards left for England by way of Virginia.

Sir Richard and Lady Everard were the parents of four children: Richard (c.1709–1742), who succeeded to the baronetcy but died a widower without children; Hugh (d. 1745), who succeeded his brother but also died childless, upon which the baronetcy became extinct; Susannah, who married David Meade in Virginia in 1731 and from whom descended many prominent families in Virginia and North Carolina; and Anne, who married George Lathbury in England. Susannah Meade bought a house in Halifax, North Carolina, where she lived after the death of her husband. Sir Richard died at his home in Red Lion Street, London, on 17 February 1733 and was buried in Much Waltham. He had been a member of the lodge of freemasons at Ross Tavern without Temple Bar in London.

WILLIAM S. POWELL

Sources M. D. Haywood, *Sir Richard Everard, baronet, governer of the colony of North Carolina and his descendants in Virginia* (1897) · E. L. Lee, *The lower Cape Fear in colonial days* (1965) · H. J. Peet, ed., *Chaumiere papers, containing matters of interest to the descendants of David Meade* (1883) · W. L. Saunders and W. Clark, eds., *The colonial records of North Carolina*, 30 vols. (1886–1907), vols. 2–5 · R. J. Cain, ed., *North Carolina higher courts minutes, 1724–1730* (1981) · CSP col., vols. 34–9 · P. Marambaud, *William Byrd of Westover, 1674–1744* (1966) · W. S. Powell, ed., *Dictionary of North Carolina biography*, 6 vols. (1979–96) · GEC, *Baronetage*, vol. 2

Archives PRO, State Papers, Colonial Series, America and West Indies, vols. 34–9 · State Archives, Raleigh, North Carolina, governor's papers

Everard, Robert (*fl.* 1647–1664), religious controversialist, whose parentage and date of birth are unknown, probably had humble origins as he later described himself as a 'poor man' (Clarke, *Puritanism and Liberty*, 42). He served in parliament's New Model Army, in Cromwell's regiment; he was a trooper in Cromwell's cavalry regiment by autumn 1647. At the end of April 1647 the soldiery of the New Model Army began to elect two agitators from each regiment to express their grievances with parliament. About late September it seems that disillusionment with the army grandees led to new agents being selected by five regiments, although these did not replace the old agitators. Everard was one of these new agents. In this capacity he was a signatory to (but may not have been involved in the composition of), among other documents, *The Case of the Armie Truly Stated, to-Gether with the Mischiefes* (18 October), and *An Agreement of the People for a Firm and Present Peace* (3 November). On 27 October he presented *An Agreement of the People* at the army headquarters in Putney. This led to the celebrated Putney debates of 28 October to 1 November 1647 at which officers, soldiers, and civilians debated how best to negotiate a settlement for the nation. On the first day of these debates the army secretary, William Clarke (then unaware of Everard's name) recorded his speeches under the name 'Buff-Coat'. Everard spoke with commitment at Putney, on the side of the Levellers and those influenced by them. He clearly wished to guide the debates towards agreement, but his main concern was that such an agreement should be speedily reached. He showed that he had little time for the prevarications of senior officers, on the second day he warned them: 'yett this message God hath sent mee to you, that there is great expectation of suddaine destruction; and I would bee loath to fill uppe that with words' (*Clarke Papers*, 1.286).

In 1649 there were a series of Leveller mutinies caused by opposition to the Irish campaign, and the perceived failure of the army grandees to fulfil the obligations set down in their early engagements. Everard was involved in these mutinies. In May 1649 one pamphlet records a Captain Everard with a 'considerable party' fighting with some of the lord-general's forces (*The Declaration*, 3). Twenty prisoners were taken by Everard's troop, and almost the same number were killed. He is said to have been riding westward to meet other mutineers, and the pamphlet later locates him (this time identified as Mr Everard) and his party near Oxford. His army career may have ended after the mutinies, although one source suggests that it ended after the battle of Worcester in September 1651 (Everard, *Antidote*, 1–2).

Everard tried a number of the different varieties of Christianity which abounded during his early life before settling upon the General Baptist faith. He fully enunciated his General Baptist beliefs in his first pamphlet, *The Creation and Fall of Adam* (1649; 2nd edn, 1652). In this pamphlet he used both argument from observation and scripture to demolish the idea of original sin. It seems that on first publication this pamphlet had some impact on the wider General Baptist movement. *The Faith and Practice of Thirty Congregations* (1651), which was largely signed by Leicestershire and Lincolnshire Baptists, was printed as an appendix to the second edition of this work, although the exact relationship of Everard to these congregations remains unclear. Whatever his influence over these congregations was, it seems to have declined significantly before the end of the interregnum. He was to return to the question of the status of nature, which he had first written about in *The Creation and Fall of Adam*, in *Nature's Vindication* (1652). Here he attempted to disprove the view that nature itself was fundamentally evil, by scriptural means. *The Creation and Fall of Adam* elicited a hostile response from the presbyterian minister Nathaniel Stephens in *Vindiciae fundamenti, or, A Threefold Defence* (1658).

In 1650 Everard continued to expound General Baptist beliefs in *Baby-Baptisme Routed*. This pamphlet is no longer extant, but it attracted a similarly unfavourable response from Nathaniel Stephens, *A Precept for the Baptisme of Infants* (1651), which prints extracts from the lost Everard pamphlet. Stephens also makes it clear that this pamphlet debate grew from a series of disputes concerning paedobaptism in Earl Shilton, Leicester.

By March 1652 Everard had been in Newcastle, seemingly on a proselytizing mission. According to his own account he resided there for about four months, preaching three or four times a week. He may have been encouraged from within the army garrison, particularly by Lieutenant-Colonel John Mason. His behaviour in Newcastle, however, brought the opprobrium of the resident ministers. In a letter to Cromwell, and 'Articles exhibited against Captain Robert Everard', they outlined some of their criticisms of him. These range from claims that he untruly said that he could discourse in Hebrew and Greek, to allegations that he drunkenly interrupted one of the presbyterian Cuthbert Sydenham's services. They then wrote of the unorthodox theological positions which they believed that he held—highlighting his stances on election and original sin. He responded to these criticisms in *An Antidote for the Newcastle Priests* (1652), refuting many of the criticisms and clarifying his views. He also used the pamphlet to attack the ministers themselves. Their views on paedobaptism and their collection of tithes attracted most censure, Everard even claimed: 'I believe, so long as a hireling Minister remains in this Nation, it will not be absolutely free from tyranny and slavery' (Everard, *Antidote*, 12).

Everard's final Baptist pamphlet, *Robert Everard's Three Questions* (1655), concerns whether or not there was any scriptural warrant for the practice of laying on of hands. It records a debate which he entered into with Benjamin Morley. Everard's pamphlet is printed with another pamphlet that enters into this debate, Thomas Morris's *A Messenger Sent* (1655), itself a response to Morley's *A Vindication of … the Laying on of Hands* (1653).

Very little is known of Everard's life in the following nine years. He re-emerges in print in 1664 to detail his recent conversion to Roman Catholicism. At one point after the Restoration he met a lay Catholic gentleman who questioned the basis of his faith and convinced him, with the help of some Roman Catholic tracts, to convert. This conversion appears to have been emphatic and complete. He renounced not only his religious beliefs, but also asked Charles II for forgiveness for the part he played in the New Model Army. The pamphlet which he published, *An Epistle to the Several Congregations* (1664; rev. 2nd edn, 1664), elicited responses from a number of different perspectives. The General Baptist Jeremiah Ives responded in *Rome is No Rule* (1664); the Quaker Francis Howgill in *The True Rule, Judge and Guide* (1665); the presbyterian biblical commentator Matthew Poole replied in the appendix of *The Nullity of the Romish Faith* (1666); Joseph Harrison in *The Popish Proselyte* (1684). All of these responses are hostile, and they are perhaps testament to the fear within nonconformist groups after the Restoration that they might become associated with Roman Catholicism.

GEORGE SOUTHCOMBE

Sources R. Everard, *An antidote for the Newcastle priests* (1652) • R. Everard, *An epistle to the several congregations*, rev. 2nd edn (1664) • W. Poole, 'Frail originals: theories of the fall in the age of Milton', DPhil diss., U. Oxf., 2000 • *The Clarke papers*, ed. C. H. Firth, 1, CS, new ser., 49 (1891) • N. Stephens, *A precept for the baptisme of infants* (1651) • *The declaration of the Levellers concerning Prince Charles* (1649) • A. Woolrych, *Soldiers and statesmen: the general council of the army and its debates, 1647–1648* (1987) • I. Gentles, *The New Model Army in England, Ireland, and Scotland, 1645–1653* (1992) • R. Howell, *Newcastle upon Tyne and the puritan revolution: a study of the civil war in north England* (1967) • T. K. Gulley, 'The General Baptists in early Stuart and revolutionary England', PhD diss., University of Wisconsin, Madison, 1994 • N. Smith, *Perfection proclaimed: language and literature in English radical religion, 1640–1660* (1989) • W. Clarke, *Puritanism and liberty*, ed. A. S. P. Woodhouse, 3rd edn (1986) • private information, 2004 [P. Baker] • *The Levellers (falsly so called) vindicated* (1649)
Archives Hunt. L., letters

Everard, Thomas (1560–1633), Jesuit and translator, was born on 8 February 1560, and baptized on 10 February at Linstead Parva, Suffolk, the son of Henry Everard (*d.* 1596), of Pond Hall, Linstead Magna, and Catherine Gawdy. His father was imprisoned in 1578–9 in the common gaol at Bury St Edmunds for refusing to conform to the established church. He was repeatedly fined for recusancy from 1581 until his death in 1596, leaving the estate heavily in debt with accumulated unpaid fines. In 1572 Thomas Everard entered Jesus College, Cambridge, where he remained for two years, and then possibly enrolled at one of the inns of court as did his brothers. At the age of thirty, in 1590, he met the Jesuit John Gerard either in London or, more probably, at Lawshall, Suffolk, where Gerard was living with Henry and Elizabeth Drury. A number of Catholics from the eastern counties visited Gerard there for instruction and to make the spiritual exercises under his direction. Among them were Everard and his cousin Anthony Rous of Dennington. As a result of Gerard's influence both men left England in 1591 to enter the English College at Rheims, receiving the diaconate in 1592 and priest's orders later in the same year. In 1593 Everard entered the Society of Jesus at Tournai and followed the course of Jesuit formation at houses in the Spanish Netherlands until his final profession in 1604.

Everard was sent to join John Gerard in London in 1605. Gerard referred to him in his autobiography as Everett, not a pseudonym but a common variant of Everard. In the aftermath of the Gunpowder Plot, Robert Cecil had ordered a particular search to be made for Gerard. Everard, who was considered to resemble him, had two narrow escapes from arrest, once when tracked to Gerard's house and the second even more dramatically as he was preparing to say mass on Maundy Thursday. As it was thought to be too risky for him to remain in London he moved to East Anglia, where for five years he tramped the counties of Norfolk and Suffolk saying mass and strengthening the scattered Roman Catholic communities. In Suffolk he met his cousin Anthony Rous who had weakened under the rigours of the missionary life. In 1608 he had betrayed a fellow priest, Thomas Garnet SJ, and abandoning his Roman Catholic priesthood retired to be incumbent of the Church of England parish of Sweeting, Norfolk. Everard appears to have reconciled him to the Roman Catholic church as in 1613 both returned to Flanders, Everard to St Omer and Rous to Louvain.

An able linguist, Everard continued to work on the translations into English of spiritual classics from Latin, Spanish, and Italian originals which he had begun during the final years of his Jesuit training. Those published, mostly in St Omer, include two works of Luca Pinelli, published as *The Mirrour of Religious Perfection* (1618) and *Meditations upon the … Sacrament* (1622); *The Paradise of the Soule* by Albertus Magnus (1617) and translation of works by Francisco Arias and St Francis Borgia were included in the compilation *A Treatise of Mental Prayer* (1617). Less certainly he may have been involved in two translations of the works by Fulvio Androzzi published as *Certaine Devout Considerations of Frequenting the Blessed Sacrament* (1606) and *Meditations uppon the Passion* (1606). Later works included an adaptation of works by Luis de la Puente, published as *Meditations upon the Mysteries of our Faith* (1624), of St Francis Borgia published in *The Practice of Christian Workes* (1620), and, perhaps in collaboration with John Heigham, *An Instruction how to Pray and Meditate Well* (1618) from the work of Ignacio Balsamo. Finally, he may have been responsible for three posthumous translations from Bellarmine published from 1638 to 1641.

In 1618 Everard was back again in Suffolk where he was arrested and imprisoned, and was finally exiled from England in 1620. In 1623 he attempted to return to England disguised as a soldier and using the pseudonym of Harrison, but was arrested on arrival at Dover and imprisoned in the castle for three months. He was then bound over in the sum of £100 to appear before the magistrates in London. For the last ten years of his life he divided his time between Suffolk and London, continuing with his translations. Contemporary accounts describe his increasing lameness and the loss of power in his arms and finally his blindness, so that in London he could not go about nor read. When he could no longer work he filled his time with vocal and mental prayer. It was remarked that he returned to the familiar patterns of prayer taught him as a child, the rosary and in particular, the much loved Jesus psalter of pre-Reformation English Catholic piety. He died in London on 16 May 1633.

JOY ROWE

Sources A. F. Allison, 'An early 17th century translator: Thomas Everard', *Biographical Studies*, 2 (1953–4), 188–215 • M. Tanner, *Societas Jesu apostolorum imitatrix* (Prague, 1694) • P. de Ribadeneira, *Bibliotheca scriptorum Societatis Jesu opus inchoatum* (Rome, 1676) • H. Foley, ed., *Records of the English province of the Society of Jesus*, 1–2 (1875–7); 4 (1878); 6 (1880) • T. M. McCoog, *English and Welsh Jesuits, 1555–1650*, 2 vols., Catholic RS, 74–5 (1994–5) • G. Anstruther, *The seminary priests*, 1 (1969), 19 • *John Gerard: the autobiography of an Elizabethan*, trans. P. Caraman, 2nd edn (1956) • BL, Egerton MS 2713 • H. Bowler, ed., *Recusant roll no. 2 (1593–1594)*, Catholic RS, 57 (1965) • W. A. Copinger, *The manors of Suffolk*, 7 vols. (1905–11), vol. 2 • W. Hervey, *The visitation of Suffolk, 1561*, ed. J. Corder, 2 vols., Harleian Society, new ser., 2–3 (1981–4) • Norfolk RO, MS DN/D15 9/1a • Venn, *Alum. Cant.* • *Report on the manuscripts of the family of Gawdy, formerly of Norfolk*, HMC, 11 (1885) • H. Bowler, *Recusants in the* *exchequer pipe rolls, 1581–1592*, ed. T. J. McCann, Catholic RS, 71 (1986)

Archives Archives of the British Province of the Society of Jesus, London · BL, Gawdy corresp., Egerton MS 2713 · Norfolk RO, recusancy indictments, DN/D15 9/1a

Everard, William (*bap.* 1602?, *d.* in or after 1651), Digger, supposedly came from Reading. A William Everard was baptized on 9 May 1602 in the parish of St Giles, Reading, as William Evered. It appears that aged fourteen this William Everard was apprenticed on 14 August 1616 to Robert Miller of the Merchant Taylors' Company, London, for the term of eight years; his name appears in the apprentice binding book as William Everad, son of William Everad, yeoman of Reading, Berkshire. It does not appear that this William Everard completed his term of apprenticeship, though it is noteworthy that Everard's future associate Gerrard Winstanley was a freeman of the Merchant Taylors'. It may be assumed that William Everard's family was poor for no one with the name Everard was assessed in the borough of Reading for a parliamentary subsidy between 1625 and 1641. On 20 February 1642 'William Everet' took the protestation oath in St Lawrence, Reading—a parish where John Pordage (1607–1681) was to become successively curate and vicar. In the early months of 1643 William Everard seems to have been acting as a parliamentarian spy for Sir Samuel Luke, scouting mainly in the Berkshire and Oxfordshire area. Perhaps he was captured on one of these sorties, for William Everard is not heard of again until May 1647, when his name appears as an ensign on a petition voicing the grievances of the army under the command of Sir Thomas Fairfax. Implicated in a plot to kill Charles I and subsequently detained at Windsor in the marshall-general's custody, William Everard was one of several men who in December 1647, while awaiting court martial, petitioned Fairfax against the injustice of their imprisonment. Some time afterwards Everard was cashiered from the army.

In 1648, after spending the night in Kingston, Surrey, William Everard was imprisoned by the bailiffs of the town, allegedly at the instigation of 'Ministers, and some common people'. Everard's companion, Gerrard Winstanley, defended him in a work entitled *Truth Lifting up its Head above Scandals* (the preface to the reader is dated 16 October 1648). According to Winstanley 'the Redding man, called after the flesh, William Everard' had reportedly held blasphemous opinions 'as to deny God, and Christ, and Scriptures, and prayer'. Winstanley declared Everard and himself innocent of these slanders (*Works of Gerrard Winstanley*, 103). Everard was soon the cause of scandal again. On 6 March 1649 he was bound by recognizance to appear at the Middlesex sessions of the peace to 'answer his goeing in a threateninge manner into Staines Church w[i]th a longe hedginge bill in his hand, and shakinge it at the Minister' saying to him 'come down thou sonne of perdition come downe' (LMA, MJ/SR 1025/60).

In April 1649 Everard attained even greater notoriety. On Sunday 8 April, together with four others, all described as living at Cobham, he went to St George's Hill in Surrey and began digging the earth. The men 'sowed the ground with parsenipps, and carretts, and beanes'. The following day they returned with others and burned part of the heath. By the end of the week between twenty and thirty people 'wrought all day at digging' (Firth, 2.210, 210–11). Everard and Winstanley were the acknowledged leaders of the group, who called themselves 'True Levellers'. It was said of Everard that he 'is no other then a madd man' and that he 'termeth himself a prophett' (Firth, 2.212, 210). Indeed, he had used a vision—one of the lowest forms of prophetic dispensation—to justify the new communal enterprise. Describing them as a 'new fangled', 'disorderly and tumultuous sort of people', complaints were soon made to the council of state against the Diggers (Raymond, 393; Firth, 2.209–10). In response two troops of horse were dispatched to Surrey, Everard and Winstanley were questioned, and the rest of the group dispersed. On Friday 20 April, Everard and Winstanley were taken to Whitehall before Lord General Thomas Fairfax. According to one report, frequently reprinted in the newsbooks, Everard and Winstanley refused to remove their hats in deference to Fairfax. Moreover it was said that Everard had asserted that:

> he was of the Race of the Jewes, & that all the liberties of the people were lost by the coming in of William the Conquerour; and that ever since, the people of God have lived under tyranny and oppression.

The 'time of deliverance was at hand, and God would bring his people' out of their Egyptian 'slavery'. It was the declared intent of the True Levellers to 'restore the Creation to its former Condition' and to fulfil the prophecy of Ezekiel 36:35 that they shall say 'This Land which was barren and wast is now become fruitfull and pleasant like the Garden of Eden' (Raymond, 394). In accordance with the prescriptions of Matthew's gospel they intended to feed the hungry and clothe the naked. As such, the True Leveller programme could be described as the millennial yearning of a group identifying themselves as God's elect people, who sought a return to a time before the bondage of the 'Norman yoke', a return to the simple precepts of apostolic Christianity, a return to the prelapsarian purity of paradisical Eden in anticipation of Christ's return on earth. Days after the incident the Diggers issued their first manifesto, *The True Levellers Standard Advanced*, the London book collector George Thomason dating his copy 26 April 1649. The names of William Everard and Gerrard Winstanley headed the list of fifteen subscribers (*Works of Gerrard Winstanley*, 259, 266). Everard's name does not appear in connection with the Diggers again, though in May mistaken reports in the press placed him with the Leveller mutiny in Oxfordshire, the newsbook writers confusing him with the army agitator Captain Robert Everard.

In August 1649 Everard appeared at Bradfield, Berkshire, where John Pordage was rector, although Pordage was to claim that Everard's appearance was in the form of 'a spirit', with 'his wearing apparel, Band, Cuffs, Hat, &c.' (Pordage, 72). The following summer Everard reappeared at Bradfield, this time in the guise of a harvest worker, much in the manner of his former comrade Winstanley, who had found employ as a wheat thresher on Lady Eleanor Douglas's estate at Pirton, Hertfordshire. Then, on Sunday 8 September 1650, there was bedlam in Bradfield. It was reported that Pordage had fled the local church in a 'Trance, running out … and bellowing like a Bull', before retiring to his rectory. The previous Sunday, 1 September, a thirteen-year-old boy called William Snelling had recited mysterious verses proclaiming 'the great Jehova'. The likelihood is that Pordage, Everard, and 'one Tawny, who stiled himself King of the Jews' had been together at the rectory in Bradfield on or about that day. This 'Tawny' was Theaurau John Tany, the self-proclaimed prophet and lord's high priest of the Jews. Local suspicions, however, pointed to 'one Everet', 'reputed to be a Conjurer' and a 'man suspected to be a Sorcerer or Witch', as the malefic presence in the parish (*A most Faithful Relation*, 2, 4; Pordage, 9, 11–12; Fowler, 54, 59–60; Bodl. Oxf., MS Rawl. D 864, fol. 233v; a riddle, 1 Sept 1650?). This 'Everet' was William Everard, and shortly after, in September 1650, Everard was seen in a 'frantick posture' in London (*A most Faithful Relation*, 4). In October he was apprehended. His ravings proved to be feigned and he was committed to Bridewell on the instructions of the council of state. His wife failed to find the money necessary to have him removed to Bethlem Hospital. All the while Everard's 'distracted' state persisted. In November he was 'manacled' for violent and desperate behaviour, and in December it was reported that 'many of Ranting Everard's party are lunatick, and exceedingly distracted; they talk very high against the Parliament, and this present Government; for which some of them have received the lash' (court minute book of Bridewell and Bethlem Hospital, MS 33011/9, pp. 464, 471; *The Ranters Recantation and their Sermon*, 1650, 6). By February 1651, Everard had become so 'distracted' and 'outragious' that he could no longer be kept in Bridewell 'without danger'. It was ordered that he be removed to Bethlem Hospital, 'there to be kept with diett phisick' (court minute book of Bridewell and Bethlem Hospital, MS 33011/9, p. 484). On 19 March 1651 William Everard was sent to Bethlem Hospital; he was never heard of again.

ARIEL HESSAYON

Sources parish register, St Giles, Reading, Berks. RO, D/P 96/1/2 · Merchant Taylors' Company, apprentice binding book, 1613–16, GL, microfilm 315, 7.287 · court minute book of Bridewell and Bethlem Hospital, GL, MS 33011/9, 464, 469, 471, 473, 476, 478, 484, 486 · recognizance of William Everard of Reading, 6 March 1649, LMA, MJ/SR 1025/60 · protestation returns, St Lawrence, Reading, Berkshire, HLRO, main papers collection · *His majesties declaration to all his subjects* (1647), 37–8 · *The declaration and standard of the Levellers of England* (1649) · *A most faithful relation of two wonderful passages* (1650), 2, 4 · [C. Fowler], *Daemonium meridianum: Satan at noon* (1655), 53–6, 59, 60 · J. Pordage, *Innocence appearing through the dark mists of pretended guilt* (1655), 9, 11–12, 68, 72–3 · G. Winstanley, 'To the gentle reader', *Truth lifting up its head above scandals* (1649) · A. Hessayon, 'Gold tried in the fire': the prophet Theaurau John Tany and the puritan revolution [forthcoming] · *The Clarke papers*, ed. C. H. Firth, 4 vols., CS, new ser., 49, 54, 61–2 (1891–1901), vol. 1, p. 419; vol. 2, pp. 209, 212 · *The works of Gerrard Winstanley*, ed. G. Sabine (1941) · J. Raymond, ed., *Making the news: an anthology of the newsbooks of revolutionary England* (1993)

Everden, John (*fl.* 1294–1315), Benedictine monk and chronicler, derived his surname from either Great Eversden or Little Eversden, villages near Caxton in Cambridgeshire. At an unknown date he became a monk of Bury St Edmunds, and by 1294 was kitchener and by 1296 cellarer, holding the latter office for about twenty years. The thirteenth-century chronicle of Bury St Edmunds Abbey records that in 1299 John Everden, cellarer, stayed at the cellarer's manor of Warkton (near Kettering in Northamptonshire), endeavouring to obtain the manor's disafforestment. The chronicle records that he was successful and that he visited Warkton again the next year, this time defending the abbey's right to a certain pasture. In 1302 Everden was one of the six delegates chosen by the monks to elect their new abbot, and he was the delegate chosen to announce the election of Thomas Tottington to the rest of the convent. In 1306–7 he was one of Abbot Thomas's two proctors at the parliament in Carlisle, and again in 1309 at the parliament at Westminster. The abbey's registers have a number of entries for the period between November 1296 and November 1315 recording some of Everden's other activities, mainly on business relating to the cellarer's office.

Everden was evidently a monk of some, but not outstanding, importance. He owes his subsequent reputation to the attribution to his authorship of part of the Bury chronicle. This originated as a chronicle from the creation of the world to 1265 by the Bury monk, John of Taxster (d. 1265). Some time before the end of the 1270s Taxster's chronicle was revised at Bury. This new recension survives complete in only two copies, London, College of Arms, Arundel MS 30, and West Suffolk Record Office, MS A 8/1, both of the late thirteenth or early fourteenth century. The text has significant variants from Taxster's work. For instance, it omits the notice under 1244 that Taxster took the habit in that year, and a notice under 1264 about the siege of Gloucester by the Lord Edward, but adds to Taxster's narrative a note (an addition, not by the original scribe in Arundel MS 30 but incorporated in MS A 8/1) under 1255 *hic attonsus fui*, and a paragraph under 1264 about the fine of 800 marks imposed on Bury St Edmunds Abbey by the parliament at Winchester. This revised version of Taxster's chronicle was the basis of two continuations, to 1296 and 1301 respectively, both valuable sources for Edward I's reign. The 1265–96 continuation was borrowed from by chroniclers in a number of monasteries, most of them in East Anglia: Bartholomew Cotton (d. 1321/2) at Norwich, the chronicler known as John of Oxnead at St Benet of Hulme, and the Peterborough chronicler were especially indebted to it. This continuation, together with the revised version of Taxster's chronicle, is the section of the Bury chronicle usually attributed to John Everden, who, it has been supposed, was the monk whose tonsuring the chronicle records under 1255.

The reason for the chronicle's attribution to Everden is to be found in Arundel MS 30. This manuscript is of Bury provenance and contains, besides the chronicle, a miscellaneous collection of treatises and notes, in various thirteenth- and fourteenth-century hands. It has the best, and only complete, copy of the 1265–96 continuation, and the unique copy of the 1296–1301 continuation. In the margin by the passage recording Everden's expeditions to Warkton in 1299 and 1300 is a sketch of the head of a man—apparently a rustic—hooded. Arundel MS 30 was once owned by the antiquary and bibliographer John Bale (d. 1563). Quite possibly it was because of the above reference to Everden in the text that Bale attributed the whole Bury chronicle to him. Bale may also have supposed that the marginal sketch represented Everden. Until the twentieth century scholars concurred with the attribution in so far as it referred to the 1265–96 continuation, although Liebermann in 1888 pointed out that the known evidence for Everden's authorship is extremely weak. Then in 1943 V. H. Galbraith reiterated Liebermann's doubts, and further research has yielded nothing to substantiate the attribution. Bale attributed four other works, besides the chronicle, to Everden, copies of all of which are in Arundel 30. Nothing is known to corroborate these attributions. It would seem that Bale, having attributed the chronicle in Arundel MS 30 to Everden, concluded that these other works in the manuscript must likewise have been by him.

ANTONIA GRANSDEN

Sources Bale, *Cat.*, 410, no. XL · A. Gransden, ed. and trans., *The chronicle of Bury St Edmunds, 1212–1301* [1964], xvi–xxix, xli, 158–9 and nn. 2–3 · R. Pauli and F. Liebermann, eds., [*Ex rerum Anglicarum scriptoribus*], MGH Scriptores [folio], 28 (Stuttgart, 1888), 584 and n. 9 · V. H. Galbraith, 'The St. Edmundsbury Chronicle, 1296–1301', *EngHR*, 58 (1943), 51–78, esp. 51–6 · T. Arnold, ed., *Memorials of St Edmund's Abbey*, 2, Rolls Series, 96 (1892), 305, 310, 317 · *RotP*, 1.191 · G. Digard, M. Faucon, A. Thomas, and R. Fawtier, eds., *Registres de Boniface VIII*, 3 (1921), cols. 482–3, no. 4671 · [W. H. Black], *Catalogue of the Arundel manuscripts in the library of the College of Arms* (1829), 44–57 · *Bartholomaei de Cotton … Historia Anglicana*, ed. H. R. Luard, Rolls Series, 16 (1859), lvi–lvii · E. Clarke, *Bury chroniclers in the thirteenth century* (1905), 4, 8–10 · BL, Harley MS 230, fols. 60, 69, 69v, 70v, 80 · BL, Harley MS 638, fols. 178–178v, 179v, 182v · BL, Harley MS 645, fols. 63v, 69v, 70, 145 · A. Gransden, 'A critical edition of the Bury St. Edmund Chronicle in Arundel MS 30 (College of Arms)', PhD diss., U. Lond., 1956
Archives Coll. Arms, Arundel MS 30 · West Suffolk RO, MS 8/1

Everdon, Silvester of (d. 1254), administrator and bishop of Carlisle, came from Everdon in Northamptonshire; his parentage is unknown, but he was related to the locally important family of Thrupp or Thorp. Instituted vicar of Everdon in 1219, by 1229 he was in the service of the chancellor, Ralph de Neville (d. 1244), and made his career in the chancery thereafter, his advance being marked by his presentation to a number of valuable livings, culminating in the archdeaconry of Chester in 1245. In 1242 he was entrusted with the custody of the exchequer seal, this being a temporary substitute for the great seal, which went to Gascony with Henry III, and in 1244 he became temporarily keeper of the great seal itself, though he was never formally appointed chancellor. In 1246 the seal was committed to him again. He was by this time increasingly active in court circles, in 1243 receiving a gift of robes from the king, and according to Matthew Paris coming to be regarded as 'the king's faithful clerk, dear and close, obtaining the first place in the chancery, where he served

him wisely' (*Flores historiarum*, 2.322). Royal favour and personal piety—in 1235 he appears to have gone on pilgrimage to Santiago de Compostela—made him a natural candidate for a bishopric, and in 1246 he was elected bishop of Carlisle, but at first refused promotion, apparently because he had qualms about accepting high spiritual office in return for secular administrative work. He was persuaded to change his mind, probably by the king, who provided him with pontifical vestments; the temporalities were restored on 8 December 1246, and he was consecrated bishop on 13 October 1247.

Everdon proved an effective and conscientious diocesan, settling disputes, ensuring that vicars received proper stipends, and safeguarding the rights and property of the see of Carlisle, most notably by bringing to a satisfactory conclusion in 1249 the long-running dispute over their respective endowments between the bishops and the canons of Carlisle Cathedral priory. In 1251–2 he returned to the king's service, acting as a justice itinerant at eyres for Yorkshire, Nottinghamshire, Derbyshire, Warwickshire, and Leicestershire, though his role appears to have been primarily that of a figurehead, since he did not attend all the sessions, and was restricted in the exercise of his judicial functions by being forbidden to act in the absence of more experienced colleagues. In May 1253 he attended parliament at Westminster, and formed one of a delegation of bishops which asked Henry III to respect the liberties of the church, particularly over episcopal elections; Henry's response was to ridicule the petitioners by reminding them that they owed their own promotion to his influence, Everdon being derided as having been formerly *clericorum meorum clericulus* ('the littlest of my clerks'; Paris, 5.374). But he remained in the king's favour and service, and was on his way to court in March 1254 when he was thrown from his horse near Northampton, suffering injuries from which he died a few days later.

HENRY SUMMERSON

Sources H. Summerson, 'The king's *clericulus*: the life and career of Silvester de Everdon, bishop of Carlisle, 1247–1254', *Northern History*, 28 (1992), 70–91 · C. M. L. Bouch, *Prelates and people of the lake counties: a history of the diocese of Carlisle, 1133–1933* (1948) · Chancery records · Paris, *Chron.*, vols. 4, 5 · H. R. Luard, ed., *Flores historiarum*, 3 vols., Rolls Series, 95 (1890), vol. 2
Archives PRO

Everest, Sir George (1790–1866), geodesist and military engineer, was born in Greenwich on 4 July 1790, the third of six children and the eldest son of (William) Tristram Everest (1747–1825), a lawyer at Greenwich, and his wife, Lucetta Mary Smith (d. 1809). He was educated at the Royal Military College, Marlow, and the Royal Military Academy, Woolwich (1805), before joining the East India Company as a cadet in 1806. That year he sailed for India as second lieutenant in the Bengal artillery. After seven years' service, about which little is known, he was sent to Java, where from 1814 to 1816 he surveyed the island at the request of the lieutenant-governor, Stamford Raffles. He was chosen for this task because of his proficiency in mathematics and astronomy. He then returned to Bengal and spent the next two years improving the navigation of

Sir George Everest (1790–1866), by Maull & Fox

the rivers connecting the Ganges and the Hooghly. The success of these engineering works brought him to the notice of William Lambton, superintendent of the great trigonometrical survey of India, and as a result Everest was appointed chief assistant on the survey in 1817. He delayed joining it in order to survey a line for a visual telegraph (for the transmission of messages by semaphore) from Calcutta to Benares, a distance of 400 miles. In 1818 he joined Lambton at Hyderabad and began surveying.

There were three main surveying projects current in India at the time: the revenue survey, the topographical survey, and the trigonometrical survey. Lambton and Everest were associated with the last of these projects, which was of international geodetic importance because of its part in determining the figure of the earth. Lambton had begun the work of measuring a meridian arc north from Cape Cormorin, and Everest's task was to complete the arc. From the start he was hampered by inadequate staff and instruments, but was insistent that work be carried out to the greatest degree of precision possible. This meant he had to do much of the fieldwork himself, particularly in its early stages, and this in turn worsened his already poor health. In 1820, while he was surveying in a swampy and malarial part of the nizam of Hyderabad's territory, he contracted malaria for the second time and he was ordered to the Cape of Good Hope to recuperate.

He used his time to investigate a meridian arc measured in southern Africa in the mid-eighteenth century. In 1821 he returned to India and continued work. On the death of Lambton in 1823 Everest was appointed superintendent of the survey and began to extend his predecessor's work northwards from the valley of Berar, insisting on working in the field even though half paralysed from the effects of fever and rheumatism. In November 1824 he measured a base-line in the Sironj valley, and in 1825 had carried the observations on to Bhaorasa when his health gave way and he returned to England, bringing work on the arc to a halt.

Although initially too ill to work, Everest used his time in England to good effect. He had three main aims: the first was to win the unequivocal support of the East India Company for the completion of the measurement of the arc, the second was to investigate the methods and instruments in use by the Ordnance Survey, and the third was to secure lasting improvements in the instruments available in India. He achieved the first at least in part by winning interest in scientific circles for the continuation of the arc, in which connection he was elected fellow of the Royal Society on 8 March 1827. By 1830 the company had abandoned earlier plans to use astronomical methods to survey the northern plains, and Everest was charged with extending the work by trigonometrical means whatever the cost. Everest achieved his second aim particularly through contact with Thomas Colby of the Ordnance Survey in Ireland; he returned to India with compensation bars modelled on Colby's. He achieved his third aim by persuading the East India Company to engage Henry Barrow to travel to India to make and maintain mathematical instruments for the survey. While in England he published *An Account of the Measurement of the Arc of the Meridian* (1830).

Everest went back to India in June 1830 to become, in addition to superintendent of the trigonometric survey, surveyor-general of India. His administrative duties were thus considerably increased, and this delayed his return to scientific work on the great arc until 1832. However, despite further bouts of sickness, he was able to see the work through to completion in 1841 under Andrew Scott Waugh, by which time an arc of meridian more than 21° in length had been measured from Cape Comorin to the northern border of British India. He worked tirelessly, in the field and at survey headquarters, to ensure the steady progress and high scientific standard of the survey work. These years were marred by a quarrel between Everest and Thomas Jervis whom, without consulting Everest, the East India Company had provisionally appointed as his successor. In that capacity, Jervis had lectured to the Royal Society in London on the inadequacies of the present Indian survey and had gathered support among fellows for improvements. Everest, always rather hot-tempered and devoted to the survey, reacted furiously to this criticism in effect of himself and Lambton, publishing *A Series of Letters Addressed to the Duke of Sussex as President of the Royal Society* (1839). The letters are stinging attacks on the fellows of the Royal Society for meddling in matters of which they know little. In the end the affair came to nothing: the Royal Society retreated into inaction and Jervis resigned in 1841 and thus never succeeded Everest. In November 1842, the arc complete, Everest resigned, successfully recommending Waugh as his successor. He left the administration in good order, having in Thomas Renny-Tailour and Waugh officers in whom he had great trust and having promoted to positions of considerable importance local staff such as the computer Radhanath Sickdhar and the instrument maker Saiyid Mir Mohsin Hussain.

The price of Everest's trigonometrical success, however, was the relative neglect of topographical survey. This latter was pursued *ad hoc* and for its neglect Everest was criticized at the time by Henry Prinsep, member of the Council of India, and later by some historians. Edney (289) defends Everest, pointing out that the great trigonometrical survey was seen as the fundamental geographical project and the other surveys as secondary in the sense that their results could be contained within the 'archive structure' of the great trigonometrical survey.

On 16 December 1843 Everest retired and returned to England. There he married, on 17 November 1846, Emma (*b.* 1822/3), the eldest daughter of Thomas Wing, a lawyer of Gray's Inn and Hampstead; they had four daughters and two sons. Everest wrote *An Account of the Measurement of Two Sections of the Meridional Arc of India* (2 vols., 1847), for which he received the medal of the Royal Astronomical Society. He was elected an honorary member of the Asiatic Society of Bengal and fellow of the Royal Asiatic and Royal Geographical societies. He was as active as his health allowed in his masonic lodge and at the Athenaeum. He reached the rank of colonel with effect from 1854, was named CB on 26 February 1861 (having solicited this honour in memoranda to the directors of the East India Company as early as 1838), and knighted on 13 March 1861. He served on the council of the Royal Society from 1863 to 1865, was a member of the council and a vice-president of the Royal Geographical Society, and was a manager of the Royal Institution from 1859 to his death. He died at his home, 10 Westbourne Street, Hyde Park Gardens, London, on 1 December 1866, survived by his wife and children, and was buried on 8 December in St Andrew's churchyard, Hove.

Everest is chiefly remembered not for his geodetic work, but because his name was given in 1856 by his successor in India, Andrew Waugh, to Peak XV in the Himalayas. Mount Everest (originally Mont Everest), at 29,028 feet, is the highest summit in the world. It was exceptional to name a feature after a European, since the surveyors were normally scrupulous in using local names. In this instance, however, no local name could be agreed on. Everest's scientific achievements have inevitably lasted less well. His great vision was to calculate the figure of the earth, comparing his great arc with arcs in higher latitude, particularly that from Spain to Scotland, and F. G. W. Struve's western Russian arc, as well as the short arc in Peru. Astronomical measurements along the Indian great arc were subsequently found to be too disturbed by the attraction of the Himalayas, and to be too inaccurate in its southernmost part (that is, the part for which Lambton was responsible) to make it reliable. Everest's figure was soon superseded and, although he had made considerable procedural and technical improvements in surveying, he left no major scientific discovery or invention as his legacy. By the later twentieth century satellite technology had completely changed the method of calculating the figure of the earth. Everest's importance was as a man of vision who with immense determination carried out his plan to the limits of precision then possible, without regard to his own comfort or that of those around him, and whose achievement was of great importance to contemporary geodesy and to the accurate surveying of India.

ELIZABETH BAIGENT

Sources R. H. Phillimore, ed., *Historical records of the survey of India*, 4 (1958) · 'Colonel Sir George Everest', *Proceedings of the Bicentenary Conference of the Royal Geographical Society, 8th November 1990* [London 1990] (1990), 34–50 · J. Insley, 'Making mountains out of molehills? George Everest and Henry Barrow, 1830–9', *Indian Journal of History of Science*, 30 (1995), 47–55 · M. H. Edney, *Mapping an empire: the geographical construction of British India, 1765–1843* (1997) · J. R. Smith, *Everest: the man and the mountain* (1999) · C. R. Markham, *A memoir on the Indian surveys* (1871)

Archives BL OIOC, MSS · National Archives of India, New Delhi, corresp. and papers relating to survey of India · Royal Artillery Institution, Woolwich, London, papers · RS, papers relating to survey of India | BL, letters to Charles Babbage, Add. MSS 37183–37200, *passim* · PRO, corresp. with Lord Ellenborough, 30/12 · RGS, letters to Royal Geographical Society

Likenesses attrib. W. Tayler, pencil drawing, 1843, NPG · Burrard, oils (after a photograph), Royal Artillery Museum, Woolwich, London · Elliott & Fry, photograph, NPG · Maull & Fox, photograph, NPG [*see illus.*] · Russell & Sons, photograph, NPG

Wealth at death under £70,000: probate, 14 Jan 1867, *CGPLA Eng. & Wales*

Everett, James (1784–1872), Methodist minister and religious writer, was born on 16 May 1784 at Alnwick, Northumberland. He was the second son of John Everett and his wife, Margaret Bowmaker. Everett's father died while he was young, and the boy soon learned to help his mother. After a short time at a private school in Alnwick he was apprenticed to a grocer and general dealer, where he was given to practical jokes. In 1803 he was converted and joined the Wesleyan Methodist Society. He began to preach in Sunderland in 1804 but refused an offer made in the same year to send him to Hoxton Academy to prepare for the Independent ministry. He showed such preaching power that in 1807 he was accepted for the itinerant ministry among the Wesleyans. His first circuits were Sunderland, Shields, and Belper in Derbyshire. In August 1810 he married Elizabeth Hutchinson of Sunderland. From an early period he took careful notes of the celebrated characters whom he met, and thus preserved recollections of Robert Southey, the poet laureate, James Montgomery, the hymn writer, William Dawson, the preacher, and many others. From 1810 to 1821 he served in a variety of Yorkshire towns, and also spent two years in Manchester (1815–17) under Adam Clarke, who became a close friend. He was enrolled as a member of the Literary and Philosophic Society there.

On account of a serious throat complaint in 1821, Everett gave up the regular ministry and became a bookseller and writer, first in Sheffield and afterwards in Manchester. He had been collecting materials for the history of Methodism in those towns, part of which he published in 1823 and 1827. Everett preached occasional and special sermons while in business, and extended his popularity. In 1834 he resumed full ministerial work at Newcastle upon Tyne, and from there moved to York in 1839. Through failure of health he was again made a supernumerary minister in 1842, but remained in York, writing more actively than ever. His main contributions were in the areas of biography and church history, and he displayed a talent for poetry through his friendship with James Montgomery, editor of the *Sheffield Iris*. His accounts of the lives of Adam Clarke (1843, 1849), William Dawson (1844), Samuel Hick, the village blacksmith (1848), and William Crister, the Wallsend miner (1851), were very popular and went into many editions. His verses on the death of Joseph Benson (1823) and the *Sacred Grave* (1831) were widely read.

The most important event in Everett's life was his expulsion from the Wesleyan conference in August 1849. For many years he had been opposed to the policy and working of conference, and had published critical comments in works such as *The Disputants* (1835), in which he argued against the scheme for starting a theological college for the training of ministers. He defended Adam Clarke and Richard Watson in the dispute concerning the doctrine of the eternal sonship of Christ against Bunting and his party, to whose perceived autocracy he became deeply opposed. He was an encourager of the religious revival that the American James Caughey brought to York and other places, in opposition to the more orthodox and static preaching style of Robert Newton and Wesleyan conservatives. He was the author of the chief part of *Centenary Sketches of Ministerial Character* (1841), a work in two volumes containing disparaging sketches of the preachers with a humorous but satirical tone. In 1845 and following years certain clandestine pamphlets, called *Fly Sheets*, were circulated widely, bearing neither printer's nor publisher's names. They contained serious charges against the leading men of the conference, reflecting both on their public actions and on their personal character. A general suspicion attributed the authorship of these pamphlets to Everett. He was brought before the conference and questioned respecting them, but declined to give any answer. After further inquiry and discussion he was formally expelled. Everett then took the lead in an agitation against the conference which shook the entire Wesleyan connexion, and resulted in the loss of more than 100,000 members and adherents. Some of the seceders joined others who had previously left the 'old body', and formed a new denomination which they styled the United Methodist Free Churches. Everett was elected the first president of their assembly, which met at Rochdale in July 1857. To the end of his life Everett remained a minister of this denomination, filling its pulpits as health and opportunity permitted.

Everett lived for some years in Newcastle, and finally in Sunderland. He wrote many articles for magazines and printed a few poems. In July 1865 his wife died, leaving no children. Everett, as a connoisseur of books and manuscripts, had formed a large collection of Methodist literature and artefacts, revealing a fascination for curious and unusual items. Much of the collection he disposed of to Luke Tyerman, the biographer of Wesley. Everett died at Tavistock Place, Sunderland, on Friday 10 May 1872, and his library was bought for Ranmoor College, the theological institution of the United Methodist Free Churches. W. B. LOWTHER, *rev.* TIM MACQUIBAN

Sources R. Chew, *James Everett: a biography* (1875) · W. Hill, *An alphabetical arrangement of all the Wesleyan-Methodist ministers, missionaries, and preachers*, rev. J. P. Haswell, 9th edn (1862) · *Minutes of the Methodist conference* · N. B. Harmon, ed., *The encyclopedia of world Methodism*, 2 vols. (1974)
Archives JRL, diaries, corresp., and papers | Sheff. Arch., corresp. with James Montgomery
Likenesses H. Adlard, stipple (after Parry), BM, NPG; repro. in J. Holland and J. Everett, *Memoirs of the life and writings of James Montgomery*, 7 vols. (1854–6) · W. H. Egleton, stipple (after H. Anelay), NPG

Everett, Joseph David (1831–1904), physicist and mathematician, was born at Rushmere, near Ipswich, Suffolk, on 11 September 1831, the eldest son of nine children of Joseph David Everett, a landowner and farmer of Rushmere, and his wife, Elizabeth, eldest daughter of John Garwood, corn merchant of London. A younger brother, Robert Lacey Everett (*b.* 1833), was MP successively for the Woodbridge division (1885–6, 1892–5) and for south-east Suffolk (1906–10).

Everett was educated at Mr Buck's private school at Ipswich. On leaving he attended higher classes in mathematics at the Ipswich Mechanics' Institution under Stephen Jackson, proprietor of the *Ipswich Journal*, who advised him to follow an academic life. Everett's father, however, was unable to finance his plans to study at university owing to losses in an agricultural depression. After a short experience of teaching at a private school at Newmarket, at which Charles Haddon Spurgeon was a colleague, he became, in 1850, mathematical master at Mr Thorowgood's school at Totteridge, near Barnet. At this school Everett taught the young George Carey Foster and published a guide to the 'Protean' geometrical puzzle, which he had invented as a schoolboy, in 1853. In 1854 he gained one of Dr Williams's bursaries which enabled him to become a student at Glasgow College (later University). After a most successful course he graduated MA in 1857 with first-class honours in mathematics and natural philosophy and second-class honours in classics and mental philosophy.

Everett had thought of entering the ministry but gave up the idea and, after acting for a short time as secretary of the Meteorological Society of Edinburgh, Everett was appointed professor of mathematics in King's College, Windsor, Nova Scotia, in 1859. In Canada, Everett undertook observations on meteorology and underground thermometry; these were published in the *Transactions of the Royal Society of Edinburgh*, of which he was elected a fellow in 1863. He married, on 3 September 1862, Jessie (*b.* 1840/41), daughter of the Revd Alexander Fraser, of the Frasers of Kirkhill, Inverness, Congregational minister of Ewing Place Chapel, Glasgow, who officiated. Finding the isolation of this colonial outpost too great he returned to Glasgow in 1864 as assistant to Dr Hugh Blackburn, professor of mathematics in the university (1849–79). He then worked for a time in Sir William Thomson's laboratory on the rigidities of glass, iron, and copper, drawing great inspiration from this experience. From 1867 until his retirement in 1897 Everett was professor of natural philosophy in Queen's College, Belfast, serving on the college council from 1875 to 1881; he was also a fellow of the Royal University of Ireland.

At Belfast, Everett taught many who distinguished themselves in science, notably John Perry and Joseph Carmor. Bereft of a laboratory, however, Everett's researches focused on his roles as secretary and subsequently chairman of the committee of the British Association for investigating the rate of increase of underground temperature downwards (1867–1904). He also devoted much energy to textbooks, translating and editing Deschanel's *Physics* in 1870. Later editions of this extremely popular text became effectively Everett's own work. As secretary of the committee for the selection and nomenclature of dynamical units (1871–3) Everett was highly instrumental in introducing the centimetre-gramme-second (CGS) system of metric units. The introductory guide to this subject that the Physical Society of London commissioned from him was widely translated after its publication in 1875, and was crucial to the successful campaign for the CGS system to be adopted internationally in 1881 at the International Congress of Electricians held in Paris.

Although Everett undertook a number of mathematical projects concerned with optics and methods of calculation he regarded it as his special mission to expound clearly the results of others. In his books and his lectures he spared no pains to make his statements precise and compact and to bring them up to date. The pedagogically inspired clarity of his work can be seen most palpably in his *Elementary Text Book of Physics* (1877), and his *Outlines of Natural Philosophy* (1887). The calibre of Everett's work was acknowledged by his election as a fellow of the Royal Society in 1879.

Everett had many interests outside his professional work. He invented a system of shorthand which he published (1877 and 1883), and from 1868 he was one of the pioneers of cycling, inventing a spring hub attachment for the spokes of bicycle wheels. From 1896 Everett became an enthusiastic golfer.

After he retired in 1897, Everett and his family moved from Belfast to London and eventually settled at 11 Leopold Road, Ealing. He devoted himself to the tasks of refereeing scientific papers for publication, joining his daughter Alice in working at entries for the Royal Society *Catalogue of Scientific Papers* and translating Hovestadt's treatise on Jena glass (1902). Everett also involved himself most actively in the scientific societies in London, especially the Physical Society, of which he was vice-president 1900–04. Everett latterly gave important evidence on temperatures below ground to the royal commission on coal supplies, and had just finished correcting proofs of this when he died unexpectedly from heart failure at Ealing on 9 August 1904; he was buried at Ipswich. Everett left his wife, three daughters, one of whom, Alice, did valuable astronomical work at Greenwich observatory, and three sons, of whom the second, Wilfred, became professor of engineering in the Government Engineering College, Sibpur, Calcutta. After his death the genial and devout Everett was cherished for his work in connecting together and clarifying the researches of his contemporaries, and for his compelling advocacy of the metric system in scientific publications.

C. H. Lees, rev. Graeme J. N. Gooday

Sources J. P. [J. Perry], *PRS*, 75 (1905), 377–80 · *Proceedings of the Physical Society*, 19 (1903–5), 11–13 · *The Times* (12 Aug 1904) · private information (1912) · m. cert. · d. cert. · *CGPLA Eng. & Wales* (1904) **Archives** CUL, Society for Psychical Research archives, diaries · Queen's University, Belfast, letters | Air Force Research Laboratories, Cambridge, Massachusetts, letters to Lord Rayleigh **Likenesses** W. R. Symonds, oils, *c.*1898, Queen's University, Belfast **Wealth at death** £9117 3*s.* 9*d.*: resworn probate, 31 Aug 1904, *CGPLA Eng. & Wales*

Everett, Kenny [*real name* Maurice James Christopher Cole] (1944–1995), broadcaster and comedian, was born on 25 December 1944 at 14 Hereford Road, Seaforth, Liverpool, the son of Thomas Cole, Mersey tugboat mate and later tugboat captain, and his wife, Elizabeth Margaret, *née* Haugh. He was educated at St Bede's secondary modern school, Liverpool. While growing up he was inspired by radio comedy, especially wacky programmes such as *The Goon Show*, and developed a talent for mimicry. On leaving school he worked in a bakery, where he cleaned sausage-roll trays for three months, before joining an advertising agency and, two years later, moving on to the advertisement department of a shipping publication, the *Journal of Commerce*. Longing to break into radio, he bought two tape recorders and started to make his own programmes of music and comic monologues, drawing on the style of BBC Light Programme host John Jackson, who skilfully edited clips from comedy albums. After he sent a tape to the BBC 'The Maurice Cole Quarter of an Hour Show' was broadcast on the Home Service programme *Midweek*, with the young hopeful being interviewed by its presenter, Ronald Fletcher. However, Cole failed to impress producer Derek Chinnery at a subsequent audition, and he returned to Liverpool. Hoping that the independent pirate stations might be more sympathetic to his irreverent style, he sent the same tape to the original Radio London and was immediately taken on as a disc jockey, at £15 a week. Radio Luxemburg and offshore pirates such as Radio Caroline and Radio London were giving young people who had grown up since the Second World War the pop music they wanted, in sharp contrast to the BBC's stuffier approach.

Like other pirate radio disc jockeys at Radio London

Kenny Everett (1944–1995), by Lewis Morley, 1960s [with his wife, Lee Middleton]

such as Ed Stewart, Dave Cash, and Pete Brady, who all later joined BBC Radio 1, Cole had to change his name for legal reasons. As a result he became Kenny Everett, after an American film comedy star named Edward Everett Horton, and began a controversial broadcasting career that combined inventive brilliance with unremitting disrespect, which frequently landed him in trouble. His time at Radio London was short as a result of his sacking for criticizing the sponsor of the station's evangelist programme, *The World Tomorrow*. However, after a short time at Radio Luxemburg, he once again sought to work for the BBC, at a time when it was planning the launch of Radio 1, Britain's first land-based pop station, and the government was outlawing the pirates through the Marine Offences Act. In May 1967 he was heard reviewing the Beatles' classic album *Sergeant Pepper's Lonely Hearts Club Band* for the BBC's Light Programme, which four months later was turned into the new Radio 1 and Radio 2. Everett, who along with other former pirate disc jockeys joined Radio 1, presented the Wednesday edition of *Midday Spin* before hosting his own Sunday-morning show, and in 1968 landed a 45 minute weekday evening programme, *Foreverett*. When that finished after five months, he presented a Saturday-morning programme. However, he upset his bosses again when in 1970 he made a quip about the transport minister John Peyton's wife, Mary, who had just passed her driving test—'probably slipping the examiner a fiver', he jested. He was sacked but two years later was asked to return to the BBC to present a Saturday-morning show for Radio 1, which was safely recorded at his studio in Wales the previous day, ensuring that nothing offensive would slip into the programme. In 1969 he married Lee Middleton, with whom he co-authored *The Lee and Kenny Everett Cookery Book* (1976). There were no children of the marriage.

Everett was let out of the BBC's straitjacket when he joined Capital Radio in London, which started broadcasting as the first independent pop music station in Britain, in October 1973. He landed the plum job of presenting the breakfast show and revived his Radio London partnership of the 1960s with Dave Cash by teaming up with him again in *The Kenny and Cash Show*, an early treat for listeners to the new commercial station. Eighteen months after joining Capital he took an overdose of Mandrax, which he used as a sleeping pill, although he admitted in his autobiography, *The Custard Stops at Hatfield* (1982), that he had been taking drugs and drinking since the 1960s. He moved to weekend shows on Capital until his departure from the station in 1980. During his time there he created the serial *Captain Kremmen*, whose hero waged intergalactic battles with the man-eating Krells. This space cowboy was inspired by Everett's childhood memories of comic-book superheroes such as Dan Dare and Flash Gordon.

Everett's next step was into television. He had previously co-presented the 1968 series *Nice Time* with Jonathan Routh and Germaine Greer and hosted his own programme, *The Kenny Everett Explosion*, in 1970, as well as being the voice behind the prizes in Bob Monkhouse's noughts-and-crosses game show, *Celebrity Squares*. But he made his biggest impression to date in *The Kenny Everett Video Show* (1978–80) on ITV, featuring electronic trickery and madcap sketches in which he unleashed such characters as leather-clad biker Sid Snot and fastidious hair stylist Marcel Wave, as well as a cartoon-strip serial of Captain Kremmen. They were accompanied by Arlene Phillips's scantily clad, raunchy dance troupe Hot Gossip, and the buxom Miss Whiplash, played by Cleo Rocos. The programme won international awards and Everett's voice helped another television game show to success, with the launch in 1979 of *Blankety Blank*, hosted by Terry Wogan. After another ITV show, *The Kenny Everett Video Cassette* (1981), the zany star switched channels to the BBC for *The Kenny Everett Television Show*, subsequently retitled *The Kenny Everett Show* (1982–8). Although the programme lost the bite of the original ITV series—the equivalent of switching from Radio 1 to Radio 2—Everett still attracted audiences of up to 15 million with a repertoire of characters that now included the skinhead yob Gizzard Puke, Beau D'Iddley of the foreign legion, and drag starlet Cupid Stunt, complete with latex boobs. Everett insisted throughout that it was 'all done in the best possible taste', a line from the mouth of Cupid, who would cross her legs with a total lack of discretion. Another new creation in the BBC series was the 'Bee Gees', with Everett playing all three pop star brothers as well as the interviewer asking them questions, which were answered with lines from their songs: 'How do you sell so many records?'—'Because we're living in a world of fools'.

Lending his support to the Conservative Party during the 1983 British general election campaign, Everett caused uproar with his call of 'Let's bomb Russia!' as he took to the stage at a Young Conservatives' rally. This error of judgement, followed by a threat to kick away Labour Party leader Michael Foot's walking stick, led to widespread criticism and his own vow to keep out of politics in future. One new experience for him was acting in a feature film, playing a tin-legged, schizoid scientist investigating a sinister manor house in the spoof horror picture *Blood Bath at the House of Death* (1983). When Everett's television series finally finished, his screen profile diminished, although he hosted the science-based quiz *Brainstorm* (1988) and the daytime quiz show *Gibberish*. By then he had once more returned to and left BBC radio. Presenting a Radio 2 show, he was again sacked in 1984, this time for telling an offensive joke about the prime minister, Margaret Thatcher. Four years later he experienced another revival when he joined the newly launched Capital Gold, playing classic pop hits on the London station that also hired former Radio 1 disc jockeys Tony Blackburn and David Hamilton. Everett savoured his six years with the station and enjoyed his longest run in a daily radio show. In 1991 he also took to the West End stage as the Billiard Marker in composer Mike Batt's short-lived musical *The Hunting of the Snark*, based on Lewis Carroll's nonsense poem and performed at the Prince Edward Theatre. In 1994 Everett's contribution to broadcasting was recognized with a gold award from the Sony Radio Awards judges, who noted that his comic talent and wacky style had 'consistently bewitched audiences'.

Everett left Capital in 1994 after being diagnosed with AIDS, having known that he was HIV-positive since 1989. His marriage to Lee Middleton was dissolved in 1984 and he subsequently lived with a former Soviet Red Army soldier, Nikolay Grishanovich, who died of AIDS in 1991. Everett died of AIDS-related bronchopneumonia on 4 April 1995 at his home, 91 Lexham Gardens, Kensington, London, and was cremated following a funeral service at the church of the Immaculate Conception, Mayfair, on 10 April.   ANTHONY HAYWARD

Sources K. Everett, *The custard stops at Hatfield* (1982) • D. Lister, *In the best possible taste: the crazy life of Kenny Everett* (1996) • *The Independent* (5 April 1995) • *The Independent* (11 April 1995) • *The Times* (5 April 1995) • T. Vahimagi, ed., *British television: an illustrated guide* (1994) • J. E. Lewis and P. Stempel, *The ultimate TV guide* (1999) • b. cert. • d. cert.
Archives FILM BFI NFTVA, *Heroes of comedy*, Channel 4, 9 Feb 1998 • BFI NFTVA, 'The unforgettable Kenny Everett', ITV, 31 March 2000 • BFI NFTVA, documentary footage • BL NSA, performance footage |SOUND BL NSA, 'Radio radio', BBC Radio 1, 18 Jan 1986, B636/1 • BL NSA, 'In the best possible taste', 26 May 1995, V3475/1 • BL NSA, *Radio lives*, BBC Radio 4, 13 July 1995, H71763 • BL NSA, documentary recordings • BL NSA, performance recordings • *Foreverett* (4 parts), BBC Radio 2, April 1997
Likenesses L. Morley, photograph, 1960–69, NPG [*see illus.*] • photographs, 1964–80, Hult. Arch. • photograph, repro. in *The Independent* (5 April 1995) • photograph, repro. in *The Times* • photographs, repro. in Lister, *In the best possible taste*
Wealth at death £357,438: probate, 9 Aug 1995, *CGPLA Eng. & Wales*

Everett, Sir William (1844–1908), army officer, born on 20 April 1844, was the son of Thomas Ellis Everett, rector of Theddingworth, Leicestershire, and Gertrude Louisa, daughter of Joshua Walker, formerly MP for Aldborough. After a term in 1856 at Marlborough College, he entered Sandhurst, and was commissioned as ensign in the 26th Cameronians regiment on 28 June 1864. In August he was transferred to the 33rd regiment; he was promoted lieutenant in January 1867, and made adjutant in November 1868. An excellent draughtsman, from 1870 to 1878 he was instructor in military drawing at the Royal Military Academy, Woolwich. In 1870 he married Marie Georgina,

daughter of Pietro Quartano di Calogeras of Corfu. They had no children. He passed Staff College in 1878.

In 1879 he was employed on the Turco-Bulgarian boundary commission under Sir Edward Bruce Hamley, and in July was appointed vice-consul at Erzurum. In July 1880 he served on a Turco-Persian frontier commission. During the 1881 famine he was active at Erzurum in administering Lady Strangford's relief fund. From September 1882 until the end of 1887 he was consul in Kurdistan. A Roman Catholic Armenian attempted to assassinate him in April 1884, and severely injured him. He was made CMG on 6 August 1886.

From January 1888 until September 1892 Everett was professor of military topography at the Staff College. He left his regiment, in which he had become major, in July 1881, for an unattached lieutenant-colonelcy. He was employed in the intelligence division of the War Office as assistant adjutant-general, with the rank of colonel, from June 1893 to March 1901. From 1895 to 1900 he worked on commissions on west African frontiers, and was made KCMG in June 1898. He was in charge of the intelligence division during 1899 (a time of exceptional stress). Sir William retired on 20 April 1901 and died at Interlaken of heart failure on 9 August 1908. He was buried at Dunsfold, near Godalming, survived by his wife.

                           E. M. LLOYD, *rev.* JAMES FALKNER

Sources *The Times* (12 Aug 1908) • *Army List* • *Hart's Army List* • Susan, countess of Malmesbury [S. Ardagh], *The life of Major-General Sir John Ardagh* (1909) • private information (1912)
Archives St Ant. Oxf., Middle East Centre, corresp. and papers
Wealth at death £3739 10s. 9d.: probate, 11 Sept 1908, *CGPLA Eng. & Wales*

Everitt, Allen Edward (1824–1882), artist, was born on 10 April 1824 at 59 Newhall Street, Birmingham, the son of Edward Everitt (1793–1880) and his wife, Harriet Parkes (1797–1877), and grandson of Allen Everitt (1759–1851), successive proprietors of the principal artists' repository in the city. His maternal grandfather was David *Parkes, the Shropshire antiquary.

Taking drawing lessons in early life from David Cox, Everitt soon showed a special talent for the illustration of old buildings and interiors. With J. G. Jackson he contributed the illustrations to *The Churches of Warwickshire*, a survey initiated in 1844 by William Staunton and Matthew Bloxham, and made a series of watercolours of Aston Hall for a book by his friend Alfred Davidson, *A History of the Holtes of Aston* (1854). Between 1848 and 1860 he undertook several continental tours to the old towns of Belgium, France, and Germany, and showed watercolours at the Royal Academy in 1857 and 1858, and at other London exhibitions.

In 1857 Everitt joined the Royal Society of Artists in Birmingham, of which he became honorary secretary in 1858, a post that he held until his death. A respected drawing master in the midlands, for many years he taught drawing at the Birmingham Deaf and Dumb Institution, of which he was also virtually the secretary. In 1870 an archaeological section of the Midland Institute was formed, and Everitt was appointed one of the honorary secretaries of what was to become the Birmingham and Warwickshire Archaeological Society, contributing many papers to its *Transactions*. He also illustrated J. T. Bunce's *History of Old St. Martin's* (1875), the parish church of Birmingham. Everitt was also for some time a member of the general council of the Midland Institute. In June 1880 he accepted the post of honorary curator of the Free Art Gallery, a municipal institution which was the forerunner of the Birmingham Museum and Art Gallery.

On 1 May 1880 Everitt married Frances Hudson (*b.* 1835/6) of Moseley, and they received as a gift from the Society of Artists a magnificent carved and painted cabinet designed by J. H. Chamberlain (known as the Everitt cabinet; Birmingham Museum and Art Gallery). Everitt lived in Edgbaston, first in George Road and from 1855 at The Grove, 28 Frederick Road, where he died, of congestion of the lungs, on 11 June 1882; he was buried in the churchyard of St Bartholomew (Edgbaston Old Church). His very large collection of topographical drawings, invaluable as a record of the appearance of the west midlands in the mid-nineteenth century, is now at the Birmingham Museum and Art Gallery.

W. J. HARRISON, *rev.* STEPHEN WILDMAN

Sources *Birmingham Daily Post* (12 June 1882) · S. Price, *Town and country in the Victorian west midlands: the watercolours and drawings of A. E. Everitt of Birmingham, 1828–1882* (1986) · private information (1888) · *Birmingham Gazette* (12 June 1882) · m. cert. · d. cert.
Likenesses portrait, *c.*1834, Birmingham Museums and Art Gallery · J. Pratt, oils, 1881, Birmingham Museums and Art Gallery
Wealth at death £8511 18s. 1d.: probate, 8 Sept 1882, CGPLA Eng. & Wales

Eversden, John of. *See* Everden, John (*fl.* 1294–1315).

Evershed, John (1864–1956), astronomer, was born on 26 February 1864 at Gomshall, Surrey, the seventh of eight children (four boys and four girls) of John Evershed, a tanner, and his wife, Sophia, the daughter of David Brent Price of Portsmouth. Up to his father, who owned Gomshall tannery, his family had been yeoman farmers in Surrey for over 600 years. Evershed was educated at Unitarian schools in Brighton and Kenley, near Croydon (where Neville Chamberlain was a fellow student). He was interested in astronomy from early on, and his skills in building instrumentation were encouraged by his elder brother Sydney (*d.* 1939), who designed electrical apparatus for the Royal Navy.

Evershed's first employment was with a firm of chemical manufacturers in London whose products he analysed and tested. He continued his astronomical activities, and in 1890 became one of the founder members of the British Astronomical Association. He later acquired an 18 inch telescope and spectrograph from another amateur, A. C. Ranyard, and was soon making systematic monochromatic observations of the sun. He also (in 1895) provided an important laboratory confirmation that the emission of the characteristic spectra of gases and vapours was caused by heat alone.

Evershed's employers granted him leave of absence to take part in solar eclipse expeditions, and these became a continuing feature of his life. The first (to Norway in 1896) was unfruitful on account of clouds; but it was there that he met Mary Acworth [*see* Evershed, Mary Acworth (1867–1949)], the daughter of Major Andrew Orr, whom he married in 1906. They worked together on solar observations for many years and participated in other eclipse expeditions, to Talni (India) in 1898, Maelma (Algeria) in 1900, Pineda de la Sierra (Spain) in 1905, Yorkshire in 1927, and a few miles south of Athens in 1936, from the deck of the P. & O. liner *Strathaird*. The 1898 eclipse was particularly important for Evershed. He travelled to India via the USA, where he held long discussions with the leading solar physicist, G. E. Hale. At the eclipse he obtained the first observational verification of the Balmer continuum in the far ultraviolet.

In 1906, at the instigation of Sir William Huggins, then president of the Royal Society, Evershed was appointed assistant director of Kodaikanal observatory in India, and in 1911 he became director. He overhauled and greatly improved the instruments and constructed a large spectrograph with a diffraction grating made by A. A. Michelson. The high altitude of Kodaikanal allowed him to make an outstanding sequence of solar spectroscopic observations. These led to the discovery of the Evershed effect—a radial circulation of gases in sunspots, which flow outwards at a low level and inwards at a higher level. In recognition of this and other solar discoveries he was elected FRS in 1915 and was awarded the gold medal of the Royal Astronomical Society in 1918.

When Evershed retired from Kodaikanal in 1923 he was appointed CIE. He returned to England and constructed a solar observatory at Ewhurst, Surrey, furnished with a coelostat and spectrographic equipment in an underground chamber. He used hollow prisms filled with liquid having a very high dispersive power, together with an ingenious arrangement of plane mirrors which enabled him to pass the solar beam back and forth through the prisms as many as eight times. In this way, very high dispersions were obtained. His measurements of small line shifts, both in India and England, proved very relevant to the debate on proofs of Einstein's general theory of relativity, which began as the First World War ended.

For detecting and measuring Doppler shifts Evershed devised an ingenious method consisting of superimposing a positive made from one negative spectrogram upon another negative taken in different conditions. For example, an east-limb positive would be superimposed on a west-limb negative with the comparison-spectrum (iron-arc) lines in register. The relative displacement of the solar lines would be immediately apparent and could be measured directly. Evershed also measured solar spectrograms made at Mount Wilson, California, by G. E. Hale, which were thought to show a general magnetic field. He satisfied himself (and Hale) that they gave no evidence of such a field.

Although Evershed's main concern was solar observation, he was interested in spectra of all sorts. Thus he was the first to supply the explanation of the 'stationary' calcium lines in stellar spectra in which other lines showed large Doppler shifts. He pointed out that this could only be due to calcium atoms in space.

Evershed's first wife died in 1949; in 1950 he married Margaret Grace Randall (there were no children from either marriage). He closed his observatory in 1953 and presented many of his instruments to the Royal Greenwich Observatory. However, he continued his lifelong interest in lepidoptery. He died at Highbroom, Ewhurst, Surrey, on 17 November 1956.

F. J. HARGREAVES, rev. A. J. MEADOWS

Sources F. J. M. Stratton, *Memoirs FRS*, 3 (1957), 41–51 · J. Evershed, 'Recollections of seventy years of scientific work', *Vistas in Astronomy*, 1 (1955), 33–40 · personal knowledge (1971)
Archives CUL, papers · RAS, corresp. and papers | California Institute of Technology, Pasadena, California, corresp. with G. E. Hale
Likenesses V. Coverley-Price, portrait; formerly priv. coll. · photograph, repro. in Stratton, *Memoirs FRS* · photographs, RAS
Wealth at death £21,787 0s. 11d.: probate, 11 Feb 1957, *CGPLA Eng. & Wales*

Evershed [*née* Orr], **Mary Acworth** (1867–1949), astronomer and literary scholar, was born on 1 January 1867 at Plymouth Hoe, the fifth child and third daughter of Andrew Orr (*d.* 1870), an officer in the Royal Artillery, and his wife, Lucy Acworth. Her father died when she was only three years old and the family went to live with their maternal grandfather, a priest in the Church of England, first at Wimborne and then at South Stoke near Bath. Mary and her youngest sister, Lucy, the close companion of her childhood, were educated entirely at home. When Mary was twenty the two sisters travelled abroad to study languages and the arts. They spent the years 1888–90 in Florence where they began studying the work of Dante and where Mary, who from an early age had an interest in astronomy, became fascinated by the astronomical references in Dante's poetry. Following this, their mother and all four daughters lived for five years in Australia, near Sydney in New South Wales, where Mary got to know the astronomer John Tebbutt at his observatory at Windsor. Finding that there existed no simple star charts of the southern sky she produced *An Easy Guide to the Southern Stars* (1897) with a foreword by Tebbutt.

The Orr family returned to England in 1895. Mary, already since 1891 a member of the Astronomical Society of the Pacific, joined the British Astronomical Association in London and strove to become a serious amateur observer. From 1900 onwards at her home in Frimley, Surrey, she used a 3 in. refractor to make observations of variable stars; she appeared in Stroobant's list of the world's astronomers compiled for the year 1902.

In 1906 plans were afoot for Miss Orr to work with E. T. Whitaker, whose wife was a cousin of hers, at Dunsink observatory, Dublin, presumably on a voluntary basis. These came to nothing with her marriage to John *Evershed (1864–1956), whom she had first met in 1896 on the British Astronomical Association's clouded-out eclipse expedition to Norway. She moved with him to India on his appointment as assistant director of the Kodaikanal observatory.

The Eversheds spent the years 1906–23 in Kodaikanal, Evershed being promoted to director of the observatory in 1911. The observatory was entirely devoted to solar work in which Mrs Evershed, though not a formal member of staff, took a keen interest. She published in 1913 an important paper on active solar prominences, illustrated with a number of fine spectroheliograms. She also acted as her husband's assistant on an expedition to observe the total solar eclipse of 1922 in Australia, and on his expeditions to Kashmir and to New Zealand to test astronomical observing sites.

Mrs Evershed's early years in India were largely taken up with her study of the astronomy of Dante, published in her book *Dante and the Early Astronomers* (1913). Much of the research had been done before her marriage, and as author she adopted the style 'M. A. Orr (Mrs John Evershed)'. The book, comprising the history of astronomy until the age of Dante and an elucidation of the numerous astronomical allusions in Dante's writings, has been described by Dorothy Sayers, a translator of the first two books of the *Divina commedia*, as 'quite the best guide available to Ptolemaic astronomy and to Dante's handling of celestial phenomena' (Sayers, bibliography). *Dante and the Early Astronomers*, published by a firm of scientific publishers, did not reach a wide public. A second edition, prepared by Barbara Reynolds, who came across a copy of the book by chance some thirty years after its first appearance, was published in 1956 after Mrs Evershed's death; this remains a standard work of reference in Dante bibliographies.

On their return from India the Eversheds settled in Ewhurst, Sussex, where Evershed remounted his solar apparatus. His wife took part with him in two further eclipse expeditions, but her own interests were now principally in the history of astronomy about which she published a number of articles in the *Journal of the British Astronomical Association*. In 1930 she founded the association's highly successful historical section. She organized an international team to assemble and publish *Who's Who on the Moon* (1938), an index of all named lunar formations including more than 600 personal names complete with miniature biographies.

The Eversheds had no children, but their nephew, Andrew David Thackeray (son of Mrs Evershed's sister Lucy) became a distinguished astronomer and director of the Radcliffe Observatory, Pretoria, South Africa. Mary Evershed died at her home, Highbroom, Ewhurst, Surrey, after some years of failing health, on 25 October 1949.

M. T. BRÜCK

Sources B. Reynolds, *Italian Studies*, 5 (1950), 72–5 · B. Reynolds, 'Introduction', in M. A. Orr, *Dante and the early astronomers*, 2nd edn (1956), 17–20 · A. D. Thackeray, *Monthly Notices of the Royal Astronomical Society*, 110 (1950), 128–9 · *The Observatory*, 70 (1950), 31–2 · A. C. Crombie, *Italian Studies*, 11 (1956), 98–100 · J. Evershed, 'Recollections of seventy years of scientific work', *Vistas in Astronomy*, 1 (1955), 33–40 · *The comedy of Dante Alighieri*, trans. D. L. Sayers, 2: *Purgatory* (1955) · private information (2004) · M. T. Brück, 'Mary Acworth Evershed (née Orr) (1867–1949), solar physicist and Dante scholar', *Journal of Astronomical History and Heritage*, 1 (1998), 45–59 · *The Times* (28 Oct 1949)
Archives RAS, J. Evershed MSS

Wealth at death £9254 12s.: probate, 10 Jan 1950, *CGPLA Eng. & Wales*

Evershed, (Francis) Raymond, Baron Evershed (1899–1966), judge, was born on 8 August 1899 at his father's house at 8 Clay Street, Stapenhill, Burton upon Trent, the only child of Frank Evershed, a solicitor, fourth son of Sydney Evershed MP JP of Albury House, Burton upon Trent, and of (Frances) Helen, daughter of Thomas Barnabas Lowe, also of Burton upon Trent. He was educated at Clifton College and Balliol College, Oxford (1919–21), where he obtained a second-class degree in *literae humaniores*. During the First World War he served in France as a second lieutenant in the Royal Engineers in 1918–19.

As often happens, Evershed followed his father into the law but chose the other branch of the legal profession. He obtained a certificate of honour in the bar final examinations and was called to the bar by Lincoln's Inn in January 1923. He then embarked on a highly successful career as a barrister in Chancery chambers, long since demolished, at 11 New Court, Carey Street, London. From his earliest days he was marked out as one of the high-flyers of his generation. His ability and easy manner inspired confidence, and he quickly acquired an extensive Chancery practice. After barely ten years, and at the amazingly young age of thirty-three, he became a KC in 1933. As a silk he regularly appeared in the most important cases, in the House of Lords and the privy council. In 1938, while still in his thirties, he was elected a bencher of his inn.

During the Second World War, Evershed undertook public duties. From 1939 to 1942 he was chairman of the Central Price Regulation Committee, concerned with the fixing of prices over a wide range of consumer goods. From 1942 to 1944 he was regional controller of the Nottinghamshire, Derbyshire, and Leicestershire coal-producing region, where the maintenance of essential coal production called for the delicate handling of relations between owners and miners. It was on his recommendation that the first nationalization of a coalmine took place, when the state took over Clifton colliery at Nottingham in November 1942.

Evershed's judicial career started in April 1944 on appointment as a justice of the Chancery Division of the High Court. Aged forty-four, he was one of the youngest persons ever appointed to the High Court bench. He was accorded the customary knighthood. Further elevation followed rapidly. After a mere three years, in April 1947 he was appointed to be a lord justice of the Court of Appeal and sworn a member of the privy council. In 1949 Lord Greene, the master of the rolls, was appointed a lord of appeal in ordinary and Sir Raymond Evershed succeeded him. He continued as master of the rolls for thirteen years, longer than any of his predecessors since Lord Esher in the nineteenth century, though on his retirement from that office in 1962 he was slightly younger than the judge appointed to succeed him, Lord Denning. He was raised to the peerage on 20 January 1956.

Evershed married, on 19 December 1928, (Cicely) Elizabeth Joan, only daughter of Sir Charles Alan Bennett, later a justice of the Chancery Division. There were no children

of the marriage. Evershed was a sturdy figure of medium height, dark, and good looking. He was a kindly man and delightful company, with a ready smile, popular as well as respected. He was much in demand as a speaker and his elegant wit and endearing phrases and manner always charmed his audience. He had a notable capacity to make and retain friends, always a sure guide to innate warmth and humanity.

Lord Evershed was a sound lawyer and distinguished judge. This is no mean praise, because judging calls for more skill than is generally appreciated. As elsewhere, the more accomplished the performance, the easier it looks. In addition to intellectual ability and an adequate knowledge of law and legal procedure, a good judge needs fair-mindedness, discerning judgement, and much common sense, tact, endless patience and courtesy, an authoritative presence in court, diligence, and decisiveness. Evershed was endowed generously with these diverse qualities.

Despite this, and despite Evershed's meteoric rise, the ultimate accolade of greatness as a lawyer and judge eluded him. Incisiveness and flair in the marshalling and articulation of legal principles are the hallmarks of a great appeal judge. The master of the rolls, as presiding judge in the civil division of the Court of Appeal, is uniquely well placed to display these qualities and guide the development of the law. Both Lord Evershed's predecessor as master of the rolls, Lord Greene, and his successor, Lord Denning, left an enduring mark on English law in a way Lord Evershed did not. His judgments were often prolix and lacked clarity. They are not a source of crisp reasoning and cogent statements of the law. His contribution to shaping the future of equity, his own field of law, was disappointingly limited, given the many years he held his high office at a time of post-war questioning and change.

Evershed's services were much sought for extra-judicial duties, legal and non-legal alike. While still a High Court judge he was chairman, from 1945 to 1946, of the commission on wages and conditions of labour in the cotton-spinning industry. He was chairman of committees of inquiry into dock wages in 1945, and into prices and production of textile machinery in 1946.

Every generation, prompted by uneasy consciousness of the delays and cost of court proceedings, makes its own contribution to the endless quest for speedier and cheaper justice. In 1947 Evershed was appointed chairman of a committee to inquire into the practice and procedure of the Supreme Court. The committee spent six years examining the rules which had mainly been introduced in 1875 to govern the newly created, single Supreme Court. By the middle of the twentieth century this code had distinctly aged and become an ill-assorted patchwork. Following three interim reports the committee reported finally in 1953 with more than 200 recommendations. These recommendations fashioned improvements, none startlingly radical, in the civil courts procedure. These endured for half a century until the next overall review was undertaken by Lord Woolf, who himself later became a master of the rolls, in the mid-1990s.

In 1949 Evershed was made chairman of the Historical Manuscripts Commission. From 1950 he was United Kingdom member of the Permanent Court of Arbitration at The Hague. In 1956 he became chairman of the law advisory committee of the British Council. He did not lack for honours in recognition of his contribution to national life. He was elected an honorary fellow of Balliol College in 1947. In 1950 he was made an honorary freeman of his home borough of Burton upon Trent. In 1951 he became president of Clifton College, and in 1960 chairman of the Pilgrim Trust. He received an honorary doctorate from Oxford University in 1955 and from many other universities in Britain and abroad. In 1958 Lincoln's Inn elected him as treasurer, its highest office.

In 1962 Lord Evershed resigned as master of the rolls on appointment as a lord of appeal in ordinary. By then his best years as a judge were past. He retired in 1965. He died at St Andrews Hospital, Northampton, on 3 October 1966, after suffering a sudden heart attack. The title became extinct on his death.   NICHOLLS OF BIRKENHEAD

Sources *WWW* · *The Times* (4 Oct 1966) · *DNB* · Burke, *Peerage* (1967) · private information (2004) · personal knowledge (2004) · *Law reports* · d. cert.
Archives PRO, official papers, HMC 3 · Staffs. RO, corresp., photographs, and publications | Bodl. Oxf., corresp. with A. L. Goodhart, MS Eng. c. 2884 · Bodl. Oxf., corresp. with Lord Monckton · Bodl. Oxf., corresp. with Lord Woolton · PRO, letters to Sir Hilary Jenkinson, PRO 30/75/2, 53, 54 | SOUND BL NSA, recorded talk
Likenesses H. Coster, photographs, *c.*1940, NPG · W. Stoneman, photograph, 1944, NPG · N. Hepple, group portrait, oils, 1958 (*A short adjournment*), Lincoln's Inn, London · N. Hepple, oils, 1958, NPG · W. Bird, photograph, 1962, NPG
Wealth at death £20,858: probate, 23 Nov 1966, *CGPLA Eng. & Wales*

Eversley. For this title name *see* Lefevre, Charles Shaw-, Viscount Eversley (1794–1888); Lefevre, George John Shaw-, Baron Eversley (1831–1928).

Eves, Reginald Grenville (1876–1941), painter, was born on 24 May 1876 in London, the son of William Henry Eves JP and his second wife, Anne Grenville. As a child he showed a talent for painting and drawing, and while at University College School, London, he won the Trevelyan Goodall scholarship in art, which took him to the Slade School of Fine Art. He worked there under Alphonse Legros, Frederick Brown, and Henry Tonks and won a Slade studentship.

Eves left the Slade School in 1895 and spent the next five years living on a farm near Holwick, Yorkshire, where he devoted his time to painting landscapes, animals, and portraits. In 1901 he returned to London and took a studio in Fitzroy Street; in the same year he exhibited for the first time at the Royal Academy. In 1903 he married Bertha Sybil, an artist and the younger daughter of Philip Oxenden Papillon JP and deputy lieutenant, of Crowhurst Park, Battle, Sussex, and Lexden Manor, Colchester; they had one son, Grenville Eves.

Success did not come quickly to Eves, and it was not until 1912, when his portrait of Sir Herbert Cozens-Hardy drew considerable praise, that he became a regular exhibitor at the academy. From then until his death in 1941 he exhibited every year (with the exception of 1931) never fewer than two paintings. He also exhibited at the Royal Institute of Oil Painters, the Paris Salon (where he won a gold medal in 1926), and elsewhere. His sitters were for the most part men, but his portraits of the queen of Spain (1921) and Miss Kyra Nijinsky (1935) showed that he could be equally successful in painting women. During his career he painted many of the most prominent figures in British public and artistic life. His portraits of George VI (1924), Sir Ernest Shackleton (1921), Thomas Hardy (1923), Sir Frank Benson (1924), Stanley Baldwin (1933), Lord Jellicoe (1935), Geoffrey Fisher, archbishop of Canterbury, Leslie Howard, Sir Frederick Pollock (*c.*1926), Sir William Watson (1929?), and Sir Charles Scott Sherrington (1927) are in the National Portrait Gallery; another portrait of Hardy (1924) and one of Max Beerbohm (1936) are in the Tate collection, the latter having been purchased by the Chantrey bequest in 1937. Although the majority of these are now perceived as unimaginative, the status of his sitters indicates that Eves achieved a highly successful portrait practice.

In 1931 there was a controversy concerning some architectural paintings which Eves had sent to the Royal Academy and which were rejected on the ground that a photographic process had been used at one stage in their production. Eves claimed ignorance of the regulation forbidding such a practice. This slight conflict did not, however, hold up his advancement, for in 1933 he became an ARA and in 1939 an RA. In 1940 he was appointed an official war artist, and in 1941, at the time of his death, eight portraits by him of war leaders were on exhibition at the National Gallery.

Eves had a remarkable gift for catching and fixing a characteristic expression. He developed a trademark style in which loosely worked backgrounds and unfinished edges give the impression of a spontaneous sketch. Although he worked mainly in portraiture, he also painted landscapes in oil and watercolour in a style which owed something to Whistler and Philip Wilson Steer. Eves died at 25 Bridge Street, Middleton in Teesdale, co. Durham, on 14 June 1941. A retrospective exhibition of his work was held at the gallery of the Royal Society of British Artists in 1947.   JAMES LAVER, rev. BEN WHITWORTH

Sources A. Windsor, ed., *Handbook of modern British painting, 1900–1980* (1992) · *WWW, 1941–50* · *WW* (1938) · F. Spalding, *20th century painters and sculptors* (1990), vol. 6 of *Dictionary of British art* · A. Jarman and others, eds., *Royal Academy exhibitors, 1905–1970: a dictionary of artists and their work in the summer exhibitions of the Royal Academy of Arts*, 3 (1978) · Graves, *RA exhibitors* · B. Stewart and M. Cutten, *The dictionary of portrait painters in Britain up to 1920* (1997) · *CGPLA Eng. & Wales* (1941) · *The Times* (16 June 1941)
Likenesses R. G. Eves, self-portrait, oils, 1908, NPG · J. S. Sargent, pencil, 1913, repro. in sale catalogue (1973) [Phillips, Son, and Neale, London, 30 Oct 1973]
Wealth at death £5966 3s. 5d.: probate, 22 Aug 1941, *CGPLA Eng. & Wales*

Evesham, Dominic of (*d.* in or before 1150), Benedictine monk and hagiographer, was perhaps born of English parents, as some slight linguistic evidence suggests. He seems to have become a monk at the Benedictine abbey of Evesham during the abbacy of Walter (1078–1104), probably during its latter years—he was not a monk in 1077, and knew only at second hand about some remarkable events at Evesham in Walter's earlier years. Dominic was an Evesham monk before Walter died, however, but was not highly placed in a list of the convent that was drawn up soon afterwards. In due course he became prior, and in that capacity represented his abbot in 1125 at the consecration of the abbot of Tewkesbury and witnessed his abbot's charters in 1130 and probably 1133. But by 1150 there was a different prior, and the inference is that Dominic was dead. Evesham Abbey observed his obit every year on 11 October.

Although Evesham Abbey was not very notable for its writings in Abbot Walter's day, Walter himself was believed to be 'greatly learned in both liberal and grammatical literature' and he encouraged the monks to study; 'he made many books' (*Chronicon abbatiae de Evesham*, 96–7). Dominic's chief literary interest was in miracle stories connected with the house. It was probably before 1100 that he rewrote Byrhtferth of Ramsey's life of Evesham's founder, St Ecgwine (*d.* 717), which he rendered in a more conventional and polished style to agree with Anglo-Norman taste, and in or after 1104 he added his own collection of stories about Ecgwine's posthumous miracles, from the late tenth-century revival of Evesham to the abbacy of Walter. Together Dominic's life and miracles of St Ecgwine have been praised for their clarity and elegance. The life was published by M. Lapidge in *Analecta Bollandiana*, 96 (1978), 65–104. The miracles are in Hereford Cathedral Library, MS P.vii.6, and a thirteenth-century Evesham version of them, with no significant changes, was published in *Chronicon abbatiae de Evesham* (pp. 36–67). Dominic also collected miracles of St Odulf (*d.* 855), a Brabantine missionary whose relics were given to Evesham in the early eleventh century. The stories evidently dated from that time to the abbacy of Maurice (1104–*c.*1121) and seem to have been appended to a life lightly adapted, perhaps by Dominic, from that usually ascribed to Cappidus of Stavoren. The life and Dominic's miracles of St Odulf, or versions of them, are probably those in Bodl. Oxf., MS Rawl. A.287, folios 116v–119v, from which the miracles were published in *Chronicon abbatiae de Evesham* (pp. 313–20).

Dominic's most widely read collection, and one that became more influential than he could have foreseen, was of fourteen miracles of the Virgin Mary, Evesham's patron. He appears to have compiled it after *c.*1121—one of the stories probably came from Abbot Robert, appointed about then—and under the influence of a contemporary compilation of miracles of the Virgin now ascribed to Anselm, abbot of Bury (*d.* 1148). William of Malmesbury's collection of miracles of the Virgin borrowed seven or eight stories from Dominic's, and all three English collections were amalgamated by the mid-twelfth century. In that form they laid the foundations of a new genre, devoted to the Virgin herself rather than to places or saints that she had honoured, which was to permeate the culture of western Europe. Dominic later made a collection of eleventh-century miracle stories associated with Evesham called *Acta proborum virorum* ('Deeds of good men'), in which he listed his own earlier miracle collections. It was published in *Chronicon abbatiae de Evesham* (pp. 320–25). There is no evidence to confirm the suggestion that Dominic revised (to 1078) and continued the Evesham *Gesta abbatum* ('Deeds of the abbots'); those parts of the *Gesta* (printed in *Chronicon abbatiae de Evesham*, 69–98) are unlike Dominic's known writings in genre and style. Nor has it been demonstrated that a lost life of St Wigstan (*d.* 849), whose relics lay at Evesham, was Dominic's work, though a version of it was written at Evesham in the thirteenth century (published in *Chronicon abbatiae de Evesham*, 325–37).

D. C. COX

Sources W. D. Macray, ed., *Chronicon abbatiae de Evesham, ad annum 1418*, Rolls Series, 29 (1863) · J. C. Jennings, 'The writings of Prior Dominic of Evesham', *EngHR*, 77 (1962), 298–304 · 'Dominic of Evesham, *Vita S. Ecgwini episcopi et confessoris*', ed. M. Lapidge, *Analecta Bollandiana*, 96 (1978), 65–104 · R. W. Southern, 'The English origins of the "miracles of the Virgin"', *Mediaeval and Renaissance Studies*, 4 (1958), 176–216 · J. C. Jennings, 'The origins of the "Elements series" of the miracles of the Virgin', *Mediaeval and Renaissance Studies*, 6 (1968), 84–93 · P. Carter, 'The historical content of William of Malmesbury's "Miracles of the Virgin Mary"', *The writing of history in the Middle Ages*, ed. R. H. C. Davis and J. M. Wallace-Hadrill (1981), 133–7 · BL, Cotton MS Vespasian B.xxiv, fol. 56 [dated by J. Stow, *A survey of London*, ed. C. L. Kingsford, 2 vols. (1908), 1.195] · Dugdale, *Monasticon*, new edn, 2.4n · BL, Lansdowne MS 427, fols. 16v, 34 · A. Gransden, *Historical writing in England*, 1 (1974), 113–14 · *Letters and charters of Gilbert Foliot*, ed. A. Morey and others (1967) · C. Neuhaus, ed., *Die lateinischen Vorlagen zu den alt-französischen Adgar'schen Marien-Legenden*, 1 (1886), 9–28 · H. Kjellman, ed., *La deuxième collection anglo-normande des miracles de la Sainte Vierge* (1922)
Archives Bodl. Oxf., MS Rawl. A.287, fols. 116v–119v · Hereford Cathedral Library, MS P.vii.6

Evesham, Epiphanius (*fl.* 1570–*c.*1623), sculptor, painter, and metal-engraver, was born in or before 1570, perhaps on the feast day of the Epiphany (6 January), the fourteenth and youngest son of William Evesham (1518/19–1584) and his wife, Jane (*d.* 1570), daughter of Alexander Howarth (or Howorth) of Burghill. His childhood is obscure and there is no reliable evidence as to his training. His first recorded work is a sundial (Hereford City Museum and Art Gallery) which he made in 1589 for John Evesham, probably one of his brothers of that name. The family was in London when William died, on 12 June 1584, and during the 1590s Epiphanius appears to have had his workshop in the capital. Two signed memorial tablets at Mersham and Hythe in Kent bear dates of death in this decade.

By 1600 Evesham had moved to Paris where he lived until at least 1615. He worked for a while with the sculptor Mathieu Jacquet before attempting to strike out on his own, but was called to account by the city's guild of painters and sculptors for claiming to practise their art while being in reality no more than a 'sawer and polisher of marble'. He finally became a master in the guild in 1604. His stay abroad is well documented—far better than his life in England—but his major works of that period all appear to be lost. They included a group of Neptune on three sea horses, perhaps intended for a fountain, which Evesham caused to be cast in metal under a subcontract of 1601, a tomb slab commemorating the archbishop of Sens in the cathedral of Notre Dame (1606–7), and a more elaborate memorial with a kneeling effigy, erected to Jacques de Poyanne in the church of the convent of the Grands Augustins (1611). In documents dating from between 1608 and 1614 Evesham is referred to both as a sculptor and as a painter, and he may well have begun three pictures that included votive portraits of himself and members of his family and which, in 1611, he commissioned another artist to complete.

Evesham returned to England about 1617 and, so far as is known, confined himself to tomb sculpture thereafter. The signed monument to Sir Thomas Hawkins and his wife at Boughton under Blean, Kent, must date from about 1618: it shows a skill in pictorial relief carving which is rare in early seventeenth-century English sculpture. His mature manner is also exemplified by the tomb chest of Edmund West (d. 1618) at Marsworth, Buckinghamshire, with its signed effigial brass and series of carved panels, some incised, others in relief. The subject matter of the panels is not entirely clear, but part of it is on the theme of death and resurrection, and he defied protestant convention by including a figure of Christ who is shown as the redeemer, risen from the grave. Another brass was destroyed in the great fire of London: it was the memorial in Old St Paul's to the poet John Owen (d. 1622) and gave rise to John Penkethman's encomium on Evesham as 'that most exquisite artist' (Epigrams of P. Virgilius Maro, sig. D3v).

By the mid-1620s Evesham may have been in financial straits. His kinsman Richard, earl of Cork, noted in October 1628 that the sculptor had begun a monument to Cork's eldest son, the Hon. Roger Boyle, but had pawned the work. It had to be finished by another artist, James White of Long Acre, and was eventually erected in St Nicholas's, Deptford, London. The final phase of his career is best represented by the monument to Christopher Roper, Lord Teynham (d. 1622), at Lynsted, Kent. The deceased is shown recumbent, mourned by his wife who kneels over him, and by his sons and daughters who are shown in relief on a pair of panels fixed to the tomb chest. The highly expressive panel of the grief-stricken daughters is a minor masterpiece and sufficient in itself to explain Penkethman's enthusiasm for the work of its creator.

This small group of authenticated church monuments has formed the basis of some fifty attributions. Few of them, however, stand up to close scrutiny and they have had the effect of artificially extending Evesham's career into the 1630s. Figured panels of alabaster which closely resemble those on the Hawkins and Teynham monuments have been cited in support of two attributions which remain convincing. The memorial to Sir Adrian Scrope (d. 1623) at South Cockerington, Lincolnshire,

shows the subject's offspring kneeling against the tomb chest like the Teynham and Hawkins children, while the monument to Richard, Lord Rich (c.1620–21), at Felsted, Essex, is grandly embellished with scenes from the life of the deceased. There are also substantial reasons for attributing to Evesham the monuments to Cicile and Ellenor, the wives of Sir John Denham (c.1619), at Egham, Surrey, and to Sir Justinian Lewin (d. 1620) at Otterden, Kent.

It has been suggested that Evesham was a Catholic recusant. His connection with Paris, at that time a Catholic stronghold, combined with the fact that he had recusant patrons in England, and the exceptional range of religious images which occur in his work all seem to support this theory but his name has yet to be traced in the contemporary annals of the Catholic faith. He is known to have married; however, no further details of his family, nor the date and place of his death are known. ADAM WHITE

Sources A. White, 'A biographical dictionary of London tomb sculptors, c.1560–c.1660', Walpole Society, 61 (1999), 1–162, esp. 49–55 · M. Jurgens, 'Quelques actes inédits concernant Epiphanius Evesham', Bulletin de la Société de l'Histoire de l'Art Français (1960), 175–82 · M. F. de Guilhermy, Inscriptions de la France du Ve siècle au XVIIIe, 2 (1875), pp. 343–4 · M. F. de Guilhermy, Inscriptions de la France du Ve siècle au XVIIIe, 4 (1879), pp. 356–8, 362–4 · G. M. Leproux, 'La Corporation des Peintres et Sculpteurs à Paris dans les premières années du XVIIe siècle', XVIIe Siècle, no. 201 · M. Whinney, Sculpture in Britain, 1530 to 1830, rev. J. Physick, 2nd edn (1988), 56–60 · The epigrams of P. Virgilius Maro, and others … Englished by J. P., love of learning, ed. and trans. J. Penkethman (1624)

Evesham, Hugh of (d. 1287), physician and cardinal, was born, and possibly educated, at Evesham, before first making his name at Oxford University, where he distinguished himself as a peacemaker in various university disputes between 1267 and 1274. However, he sided with the Dominicans against the Franciscans in their battle over evangelical poverty in 1269. In 1275 he was granted licence, as archdeacon of Worcester, to study abroad for a year. Archbishop John Pecham (d. 1292) referred in correspondence to acquaintance with Hugh 'vel in curia vel in scholis' ('both at the curia and in school'; Martin, 1.219). The men were near contemporaries and it is likely that they knew each other at Oxford and at Paris and, later on, at the papal court, probably before 1279.

By the early 1270s Hugh was styled king's clerk, serving Edward I and his mother, Eleanor of Provence, probably as a medical adviser. By 1279 he was being referred to in English documents as a famous physician. Hugh enjoyed numerous royal and ecclesiastical incomes and honours, especially in the diocese of York, where he was presented to the rectories of Hemingbrough and Spofforth, and became prebendary of Bugthorpe in 1279. In the same year, his friend William de Wickwane (d. 1285) was chosen ahead of Hugh as archbishop of York and in 1282 asked him to mediate at Rome in William's disputes with the archbishop of Canterbury and the bishop of Durham.

Hugh, like many church officials, found the vogue for alchemical medicine at the papal court during the latter part of the thirteenth century an excellent road to papal patronage. Either Nicholas III (r. 1277–80) or Martin IV (r. 1281–5) commissioned him to find a cure for a fever raging around Rome, and it is possible that he became a medical adviser to Martin in 1280. The pope created him cardinal-priest of San Lorenzo in Lucina on 23 March 1281, a position he held until his death at Rome on 27 July 1287. He was buried in his own church of San Lorenzo. Rumour persisted that Hugh died by poisoning, but such stories were common explanations for sudden death from any unknown cause. He had remained archdeacon of Worcester until his death, and in his will he made a bequest to at least one of his Worcestershire kinsmen.

Early bibliographers record several works by Hugh, including *Super opere febrium Isaac*, a commentary on the book on fevers of Isaac Israeli, beginning 'Quoniam de filii bonitate sicut' (Thorndike and Kibre, col. 1270), but this has been lost. A sermon for Septuagesima Sunday by him survives in a Bodleian Library manuscript (Bodl. Oxf., MS Bodley 50, fols. 299v ff.). Most interesting are his surviving medical writings, all but one of which appear in company with those of the English Cistercian, Cardinal John of Toledo. John, who died in 1275 and was also a papal physician, was sometimes called the white cardinal, and his association with Hugh, once an advocate of the Dominicans, perhaps explains the name *atratus* ('black'), sometimes attached to Hugh's name. Gloucester Cathedral, MS 18, folio 273v, contains a recipe 'secundum magistrum H. de Eveham contra phisum' ('a recipe against consumption'). Manuscript 1246 in the Biblioteca Riccardiana at Florence has a panacea attributed to *dominus Ugo cardinalis* contained in *Liber de sanitate conservanda a Johanne de Toleto compositus* (fol. 32v). The two men are mentioned again in a collection of medical/alchemical recipes found in Munich, Bayerische Staatsbibliothek, MS 405 (fol. 102). A treatise on medical alchemy found in Paris, Bibliothèque Nationale, MS Lat. 7817, fol. 54, contains a recipe for *aurum potabile* (a medical/alchemical concoction). In it, both Hugh and John affirm the usefulness of the preparation, which is said to have been a secret ingredient used in the food of all the cardinals, to liven them up and improve their memories.   FAYE GETZ

Sources A. P. Bagliani, *Medicina e scienze della natura alle corte dei papi nel duecento* (1991) · Emden, *Oxf.* · C. H. Talbot and E. A. Hammond, *The medical practitioners in medieval England: a biographical register* (1965) · F. M. Getz, 'The faculty of medicine before 1500', *Hist. U. Oxf. 2: Late med. Oxf.*, 373–405 · F. Getz, 'Medical practitioners in medieval England', *Social History of Medicine*, 3 (1990), 245–83 · L. Thorndike and P. Kibre, *A catalogue of incipits of mediaeval scientific writings in Latin*, rev. edn (1963) · *Registrum epistolarum fratris Johannis Peckham, archiepiscopi Cantuariensis*, ed. C. T. Martin, 3 vols., Rolls Series, 77 (1882–5) · J. W. W. Bund, ed., *Register of Bishop Godfrey Giffard, September 23rd, 1268, to August 15th, 1301*, 2 vols., Worcestershire Historical Society, 15 (1898–1902) · Gloucester Cathedral, MS 18, fol. 273v · 'Liber de sanitate a Johanne de Toleto compositus', Biblioteca Riccardiana, Florence, MS 1246, fol. 32v
Archives Bodl. Oxf., sermon, MS Bodley 50, fols. 299v ff. · Gloucester Cathedral, MS 18, fol. 273v | Bayerische Staatsbibliothek, Munich, MS 405, fol. 102 · Biblioteca Riccardiana, Florence, MS 1246, fol. 32v · Bibliothèque Nationale, Paris, MS Lat. 7817, fol. 54

Evesham, Randal [Ranulf] **of** (*d.* 1229), abbot of Evesham, was born at Evesham but became a monk of Worcester, as did his brother Ralph (or Radulf). In 1203 he was joint leader of some Worcester monks sent to Rome with evidence to support Wulfstan's canonization, and became prior of Worcester on 24 December. Randal was elected bishop of Worcester on 2 December 1213 but renounced the see in favour of the king's chancellor, and on 20 January 1214 a divided Evesham chapter accepted the advice of the papal legate, Nicolò of Tusculum, to elect Randal abbot. Thomas of Marlborough (*d.* 1236), his closest aide, was perhaps untruthful in stating that Randal, when prior of Worcester, already had a seat in the Evesham chapter, for Thomas was trying to prove that only monks of Evesham ought to be elected abbots.

Randal arrived at Evesham on 22 January 1214, and on 9 March was blessed by the legate in St Mary's Abbey, York. Though mild, he restored discipline and prudence to Evesham's internal affairs after the misrule of his predecessor, Roger Norreys (*d.* 1223). In 1215 he and Thomas were in Rome for the Lateran Council, and obtained papal confirmation of Evesham's administrative customs and of the revenues due to each obedientiary. Under Randal the abbey paid off its debts, improved its buildings and estates, and endowed its church with ornaments. He attended the translation of St Wulfstan's relics at Worcester in 1218, but the next year was prevented at a Worcester synod from either wearing his mitre or enjoying the precedence he claimed on the strength of it. Randal was a president of the Benedictine general chapter for the southern province in 1219 and 1225, a justice on eyre in 1221, an arbitrator between the bishop and convent of Worcester in 1224, and a witness to the reissue of Magna Carta in 1225. He died on 17 December 1229, probably at Evesham Abbey.   D. C. COX

Sources W. D. Macray, ed., *Chronicon abbatiae de Evesham, ad annum 1418*, Rolls Series, 29 (1863), 205–22, 254–72 · *Ann. mon.*, 4.391–2, 4.398, 4.402, 4.409–11, 4.416–17 · W. A. Pantin, ed., *Documents illustrating the activities of ... the English black monks, 1215–1540*, 3 vols., CS, 3rd ser., 45, 47, 54 (1931–7), vol. 1, pp. 15–17 · D. Crook, *Records of the general eyre*, Public Record Office Handbooks, 20 (1982), 76 · W. Stubbs, ed., *Select charters and other illustrations of English constitutional history*, 9th edn (1913), 350
Likenesses seal and counterseal (attached to PRO E 329/83), PRO

Evesham, Walter. *See* Odington, Walter (*fl. c.*1280–1301).

Eveske, Elias l' (*d.* in or after **1259**), financier and leader of the Jewish community in England, was the eldest of the several sons of Benedict l'Eveske of London. Born before 1200, he became a prominent figure during the 1220s, and by the 1230s was firmly established as one of the leading members of the London Jewish community. In 1237 and 1241 he served the crown as a tax assessor and collector, and in 1238 was a commissioner against coin-clipping. It was also during these years that he began lending money and selling bonds to members of Henry III's court. In 1243 the king appointed him archpresbyter, thus establishing him as the administrative head of the English Jewish community and the chief Jewish official at the Jewish exchequer.

The period of l'Eveske's archpresbyterate was disastrous for English Jewry. Savage royal taxation, crushing inheritance fines, and accusations of ritual murder devastated Jewish communities throughout the realm. As archpresbyter, l'Eveske was directly involved in implementing the king's destructive policies. He cannot have done so happily, and in 1254 he petitioned, unsuccessfully, for permission for the Jews of England to depart the realm. At the same time, however, he used his influence at the exchequer to secure tax reductions and exemptions for himself and his brothers, thus placing an even heavier burden of taxation upon others.

The resulting divisions within the London Jewish community finally brought about l'Eveske's downfall. His favourable tax assessments were revoked. In 1249 and again in 1252 he was accused of malfeasance in office, but both times he was restored to office. In June 1257, however, he was accused of having fraudulently transferred several debts to Richard, earl of Cornwall (d. 1272), on which l'Eveske then continued to collect payment. He was convicted and deposed from office. Hagin and Cresse, sons of Master Moses of London, thereupon paid the king 3 gold marks on behalf of the English Jewish community for his promise never to restore l'Eveske to the archpresbyterate, and to allow the community in future to elect their archpresbyter. In February 1258 Hagin succeeded l'Eveske as archpresbyter.

In December 1258, however, Elias l'Eveske was accused by Cresse, the brother of Hagin, of having ordered his servant, John Forncett, to make a murderous attack upon Hagin in a London street. Hagin was too gravely wounded to appear in court, but l'Eveske, with his two sons, did appear, and in January 1259 all three converted to Christianity, thus ending the case against them. As they were converts, their property escheated to the king, who sold it, for 400 marks, to Master Elijah Menahem (d. 1284), brother to Cresse and Hagin. L'Eveske's sons took the baptismal names Adam and Nicholas, but his own new name is unknown, as is his fate after this date. His wife has not been identified. They had at least three children. Their daughter Hannah married Josce, archpresbyter from 1207 until 1236. One son, Isaac, was active in his father's business of lending money. The other son is unknown. No other sons are recorded; it may be presumed, therefore, that these were the two sons who converted with their father to Christianity.　　　ROBERT C. STACEY

Sources Chancery records · Paris, Chron. · exchequer, treasury of receipt, receipt rolls, PRO, E 401 · justices itinerant, assize rolls, PRO, JUST 1/1187 m. 10 · I. Abrahams, H. P. Stokes, and H. Loewe, eds., Starrs and Jewish charters preserved in the British Museum, 3 vols. (1930–32) · J. Hillaby, 'London: the 13th-century Jewry revisited', Jewish Historical Studies, 32 (1990–92), 89–158 · H. P. Stokes, Studies in Anglo-Jewish history (1913) · J. M. Rigg and others, eds., Pleas rolls of the exchequer of the Jews, 5 vols. (1905–92) · R. C. Stacey, 'The conversion of Jews to Christianity in thirteenth-century England', Speculum, 67 (1992), 263–83

Evill, Sir Douglas Claude Strathern (1892–1971), air force officer, was born on 8 October 1892 at Broken Hill, New South Wales, Australia, the only child of Frederick Claude Evill, a general practitioner, of Barnet, Hertfordshire, and his wife, Sybella Strathern Murray, of Kingsclere, Hampshire. A first cousin of Air Chief Marshal Sir Arthur Longmore, Evill always thought of him more as a brother.

Educated privately in Hertfordshire and from 1905 as a cadet at the Royal Naval College at Osborne and Dartmouth, Evill excelled as a student. Despite his slight build, he was also good at all games, and from the beginning he was recognized as a natural leader. He was commissioned in May 1913, and while on leave in the summer of that year he stayed at Upavon with Longmore, who was there as one of the naval instructors at the Central Flying School. Already more a thinker than a man of action, Evill took Longmore's advice and learned to fly at a civil school at Hendon. On 13 June 1913 he received the recognized aviator's certificate, but he failed in his repeated requests over the course of the next year for transfer to the Royal Naval Air Service, and at the time of the outbreak of the First World War he was serving in destroyers. In December 1914, however, he was finally transferred to the Royal Naval Air Service.

Evill spent most of the war on operational flying in France, and in 1916 he was awarded the DSC. In 1919 he was granted a permanent commission in the Royal Air Force and was awarded the AFC. Over the next four years he commanded early flying boat bases, and attended the course at the Staff College, Camberley. He married on 8 October 1920 Henrietta Hortense (d. 1980), daughter of Sir Alexander Drake Kleinwort, bt. They had three sons and two daughters.

In 1923 Evill went to Iraq to command 70 squadron. After returning to England in 1925 he became, with promotion to wing commander, an instructor at the RAF Staff College. Four years later he was appointed assistant commandant of the RAF College, Cranwell, of which the commandant during part of his time there was Arthur Longmore. In 1932, with promotion to group captain, he was appointed assistant commandant of the RAF Staff College, and a year later he attended the course at the Imperial Defence College.

In 1934 Evill became deputy director of war organization at the Air Ministry. This led, after his promotion to air commodore earlier in the year, to his being appointed in September 1936 senior air staff officer of Bomber Command. Two years later he became, with promotion to air vice-marshal, the air officer in charge of administration of the command. In January 1937 he was a member of the important mission to Germany, led by Air Vice-Marshal Christopher Courtney, on a tour of inspection of the new Luftwaffe. Just before the outbreak of the Second World War, Evill was briefly the British air deputy on the staff of the supreme war council at the time when the views held by the French conflicted seriously with those of the RAF. In February 1940 he was appointed senior air staff officer of the ill-fated British air forces in France.

Immediately after the evacuation from France, and with appointment as CB (1940), Evill was appointed senior air staff officer to Air Chief Marshal Sir Hugh Dowding, the air officer commanding-in-chief, Fighter Command. He served in this vitally important post during the whole of the battle of Britain, the blitz, and the offensive fighter operations of 1941. Commenting on Evill's work—which was unique in operational command appointments—Dowding later stated: 'I could not have had a sounder or more reliable man supporting me. He was always there, always on the job, and always so pleasant in that quiet way of his.' As Dowding's right-hand man, Evill was all too well aware of the arguments that developed over fighter tactics towards the end of the battle of Britain, and in particular the idea of big-wing formations promoted by Air Vice-Marshal Leigh-Mallory. He thought it his duty to shield Dowding from the details of what he viewed as unnecessary wrangling within the command; and he was strongly critical of the intervention by the Air Ministry in what he described as a 'stupid controversy', which led to Dowding's removal. He always thought that the treatment Dowding received was 'deplorable'. Towards the end of his time at Fighter Command, Evill suffered a grievous blow when one of his sons, William, who was only eighteen, was killed while serving as a pilot in Bomber Command. Sholto Douglas was to comment later on Evill's composure at the time of his son's death, and added: 'I admired Evill for the firm but gentle control of his manner, which was a feature that won for him the affection of everybody with whom he came in contact' (S. Douglas, *Years of Command*, 1966, 97).

Early in 1942 Evill became, with promotion to air marshal, head of the RAF delegation in Washington, where he served until March 1943. He returned, after being created KCB, to the United Kingdom on appointment as vice-chief of the air staff and additional member of the Air Council. He continued in this post for the remaining years of the war, becoming an air chief marshal, with elevation to GBE, in January 1946. A year later he retired from the RAF. He had by then received from the Americans the Legion of Merit (commander), from the French promotion to commandeur of the Légion d'honneur which he had first received in 1917, from the Poles the order of Polonia restituta, and from the Czechs the order of the white lion.

During the early years of his retirement Evill was active as honorary air commodore of no. 3617 (County of Hampshire) fighter control unit, and as a member of the council of the King Edward VII Hospital for officers. For two years between 1947 and 1949 he was director-general of the English Speaking Union. In later years he became afflicted with severe arthritis. He died at his home, South Lawn, Cheriton Close, Winchester, on 22 March 1971. At the memorial service for Evill, Air Chief Marshal Sir Donald Hardman concluded his address with the apt and touching comment: 'He was a very perfect gentle knight.' He was also a markedly devout man with, throughout his life, a pronounced sense of duty that led him to place service interests first, even before those of his family, in the ordering of that life.

ROBERT WRIGHT, *rev.* CHRISTINA J. M. GOULTER

Sources RAF, air historical branch · *The Times* (24 March 1971) · personal knowledge (2004) · private information (2004) · J. P. Ray, *The Battle of Britain: new perspectives* (1994) · V. Orange, *Sir Keith Park* (1984) · Burke, *Peerage* (1967)

Archives Royal Air Force Museum, Hendon, department of research and information services, corresp., diaries, and logbooks | FILM BFI NFTVA, news footage
Likenesses T. Dugdale, portrait, IWM
Wealth at death £72,258: probate, 11 June 1971, *CGPLA Eng. & Wales*

Ewald, Alexander Charles (1842–1891). *See under* Ewald, Ferdinand Christian (1802–1874).

Ewald, Ferdinand Christian (1802–1874), Christian missionary to the Jews, was born of Jewish parentage near Bamberg, and joined the Christian faith in 1822. As a Lutheran minister he came under the aegis of the London Society for Promoting Christianity among the Jews and studied at its seminary at Palestine House, Bethnal Green, before entering the society's service in 1832. He worked for a decade among the oppressed and lowly communities of north Africa, selling bibles and distributing tracts, preaching and persuading. In 1836 he was ordained by the bishop of London, and returned to the Mediterranean coast until repeated attacks of ophthalmia forced him to return to London in 1841. He was then appointed chaplain to Michael Solomon Alexander, first Anglican bishop of Jerusalem and, like Ewald, a convert, and wrote of their work in *The Journal of Missionary Labours in Jerusalem, 1842–1844* (1846). Continued ill health obliged him to return home again in 1851, when he became head of the society's London mission. He was employed there until 1870. During that time hundreds of Jews were baptized out of the thousands he had instructed, and he helped the society to set up a 'Wanderers' Home' for the assimilation of convert Jews into their new community.

Ewald published in 1856 a German translation of the Talmudic treatise *Abodah Sarah* ('Idolatrous worship'), for which he was awarded a doctorate of philosophy by the University of Erlangen. In 1872 he was awarded by Archbishop Tait the Lambeth degree of bachelor of divinity, in recognition of his proficiency in Hebrew and oriental learning, as well as for his prominent services to the society. He died at his home, 14 Woodside Villas, Gipsy Hill, Upper Norwood, London, on 9 August 1874.

His son **Alexander Charles Ewald** (1842–1891), writer, was born in Jerusalem in 1842. He was educated abroad and appointed by open competition to a clerkship in the Public Record Office in August 1860; he was promoted senior clerk in 1872. His main responsibility was the completion of Sir Thomas Duffus Hardy's work of calendaring the Norman rolls of Henry V; Ewald's calendars were printed in the deputy keeper's reports (vols. 61–2, 1880 and 1881); Ewald also prepared for this précis the glossary of French words. Within the Public Record Office he was left behind in an increasingly competitive and professionalized service, but found his métier by writing for a wider public a great many popular works of biographical and historical character. Compilations of general English history and constitutional development were followed by *Our Public Records: a Brief Handbook to the National Archives* (1873), a serviceable but inadequate introduction. A life of Charles Edward Stuart, the Young Pretender, first published in 1875 (and apparently written partly in official time), enjoyed minor reputation, and among other works Ewald prepared a two-volume biographical compilation on Disraeli (1883) and a life of Sir Joseph Napier, the Irish lord chancellor (1887; rev. edn, 1892). Scarcely anything from his extensive literary output is worthy of remembrance, however, not even *How to Pass: a Civil Service Textbook* (1867). A pseudonymous novel, *Harry Disney: an Autobiography* by Atholl de Walden (3 vols., 1871), is attributed to him.

Ewald is reported to have been in line for promotion in his department at the time of his premature death at his home, 31 Victoria Road, Upper Norwood, on 20 June 1891. He was survived by his wife, Amelia Isabella.

ALAN BELL

Sources W. T. Gidney, *History of the London Society for Promoting Christianity among the Jews, 1809–1908* (1908) · J. F. A. de la Roi, *Ferdinand Christian Ewald: ein Lebensbild aus der neueren Judenmission* (Gütersloh, 1896) · *The Times* (22 June 1891) · *The Times* (25 June 1891) · *The Athenaeum* (27 June 1891), 831 · J. D. Cantwell, *The Public Record Office, 1838–1958* (1991) · *CGPLA Eng. & Wales* (1874) · *CGPLA Eng. & Wales* (1891) · *DNB* · Venn, *Alum. Cant.*

Wealth at death under £3000: probate, 22 Aug 1874, *CGPLA Eng. & Wales*

Ewart, Alfred James (1872–1937), botanist, was born at 12 Noel Street, Toxteth Park, Liverpool, on 12 February 1872, the second of the four sons of Edmund Brown Ewart and his wife, Martha Williams. His father, who was of Scottish descent, was a lecturer in chemistry and director of the chemical laboratory of the Liverpool Institute; he was a nephew of the politician William Ewart. Ewart was educated at the Liverpool Institute and at the University College (later Liverpool University), where he read for a London degree, graduating BSc with first class honours in botany in 1893. He was appointed a demonstrator in botany at the University College, but the following year (1894) he was awarded an 1851 Exhibition scholarship. He went to Leipzig where he studied plant physiology under Wilhelm Friedrich Philipp Pfeffer and obtained the degree of PhD in 1896. An extension to his studentship allowed him to travel to Java, to work under Melchior Treub in the laboratory of the botanical garden at Buitenzorg (Bogor).

After Ewart's return to England in 1897, he was awarded a DSc (London), and began an association with Mason College, Birmingham (from 1900, Birmingham University), which lasted until 1905. Following his matriculation as a non-collegiate student in 1898 he also worked as an extension lecturer at the botanic garden at Oxford. He later graduated BSc (1906) and was awarded a DSc in 1910. It was in Oxford, on 17 December 1898 that Ewart married Florence Maude Donaldson (1864–1949) [*see below*], daughter of Frederick William Donaldson, who was an accomplished violinist. The couple had met several years earlier in Leipzig.

In 1900 Ewart returned to Birmingham. Following several years of teaching at King Edwards School, the Municipal Technical School, and the university he was, in 1906, appointed to the foundation chair of botany and plant physiology at the University of Melbourne. For the first sixteen years of his tenure of the Melbourne chair he held the dual office of professor of botany and plant physiology and government botanist. Half of each day he spent in the national herbarium at South Yarra, and the remainder in the university at Carlton on the opposite side of the city. In 1921 the chair of botany was made a full-time position, and in 1929 Ewart moved his department to a new building dedicated to botany: previously he had shared the laboratory with the zoology school. Following the dissolution of his marriage on 24 December 1929, Ewart married Elizabeth Bilton, a teacher some twenty-five years his junior, on 9 February 1931. She was the daughter of David Richard Bilton, a grazier, of Craigie, Victoria.

Ewart's contributions to botany cover a wide field. Trained as a physiologist, he is remembered as the translator of Pfeffer's *Physiology of Plants* (3 vols., 1900–06) and as the author of important contributions on *The Physics and Physiology of Protoplasmic Streaming in Plants* (1903) and 'The ascent of water in trees' (*PTRS*, 198B, 1906; 199B, 1908). After his emigration to Australia, work of a taxonomic nature and problems of applied botany had to occupy most of his time. He did much for the education of foresters and in 1925 published *A Handbook of Forest Trees for Victorian Foresters*. Inevitably problems of weed identification and control took a large part in his career as a government botanist. In 1930 he published his most important floristic work, *Flora of Victoria*. Towards the end of his life he made a useful contribution towards identifying the causes of the poisoning of stock and horses in central and Western Australia.

Ewart was a man of robust physique and somewhat choleric disposition. He became involved in a number of bitter controversies which prevented his taking as large a part in the development of botanical work in Australia as might have been expected from one of his ability and standing. He was elected a fellow of the Linnean Society in 1898 and FRS in 1922, and was an active member of the Royal Society of Victoria. A man of simple tastes, he delighted in country life and in good music. Ewart died in East Malvern, Melbourne, on 12 September 1937, survived by his second wife and the two sons of his first marriage.

Florence Maude Ewart [*née* Donaldson] (1864–1949), violinist and composer, was born at 127 Leighton Road, Kentish Town, London, on 16 November 1864, the daughter of Frederick William Donaldson, clerk to a glass manufacturer, and his wife, Elizabeth Lewis. Her elder brother was Frederic Lewis *Donaldson (1860–1953), leader of the Christian Social movement. Early an accomplished violinist, she won a scholarship to the National Training School for Music, Kensington, gaining a diploma in 1882. Following periods of further study at the Hochschule für Musik, in Leipzig, and under Joseph Joachim, in Berlin, she returned to Birmingham where she gave violin recitals and, until 1894, conducted an orchestra. It was about this time that Donaldson began composing pieces, including her first opera *Ekkehard*. After her marriage in 1898 she had two sons, born in 1900 and 1902. Following her emigration to Australia, Ewart complained of a rheumatic condition and turned increasingly from performance to composition. She returned to Europe in 1910, 1916, and 1920–21, possibly in an attempt to have her large-scale works performed, but also possibly because of an unhappy domestic life. From late 1924 to mid-1928 she was in Europe again, studying with Ottorino Respighi and Giacomo Settacciole. It was during this period that Alfred Ewart petitioned for divorce; a decree absolute was granted on 24 December 1929.

Ewart's works include six operas (one written under the pseudonym Sonia Aldon), five works for voice and orchestra, forty-six songs, and a number of instrumental works (including at least one string quartet). Her last opera, *Pepita's Miracle*, is dated 1945. She died in early November (probably on the 8th) 1949 at her home in South Yarra, Melbourne. T. G. B. OSBORN, rev. PETER OSBORNE

Sources W. Stiles, *Obits. FRS*, 2 (1936–8), 465–9 · T. G. B. Osborn, *Proceedings of the Linnean Society of London*, 150th session (1937–8), 314–17 · *Nature*, 141 (1938), 17 · private information (1949) · T. C. Chambers, 'Ewart, Alfred James', *AusDB*, 8.448–50 · M. T. Radic, 'Ewart, Florence Maud', *AusDB*, 450–51, vol. 8 · *WWW* · F. E. Patton, 'Ewart [née Donaldson], Florence Maud', *The new Grove dictionary of women composers*, ed. J. A. Sadie and R. Samuel (1994) · *CGPLA Eng. & Wales* (1938) · b. cert. [Alfred James Ewart] · b. cert. [Florence Maude Donaldson]
Likenesses photograph, repro. in Stiles, *Obits. FRS*
Wealth at death £877 10s. od.—in England: Australian probate, sealed in England, 3 Sept 1938, *CGPLA Eng. & Wales*

Ewart, Charles Brisbane (1827–1903), army officer, born at Coventry on 15 February 1827, was the fourth son of Lieutenant-General John Frederick Ewart (d. 1854) and his wife, Lavinia Isabella Brisbane. Sir John Alexander *Ewart was his elder brother. After passing with credit through the Royal Military Academy at Woolwich Ewart was commissioned second lieutenant in the Royal Engineers on 18 June 1845. Promoted lieutenant on 1 April 1846, he served in England, Ireland, and Gibraltar. In January 1854 he accompanied General Sir John Fox Burgoyne on a mission to examine the defences of the Dardanelles. After surveying the ground at Gallipoli, Ewart went to Varna, and acted as brigade major while assisting in the preparations for the arrival of the allied army. He served in the Crimea, including at the battles of the Alma, Balaklava, and Inkerman, was promoted captain on 13 December 1854, and was acting adjutant throughout the siege of Sevastopol. Mentioned in dispatches, he was promoted brevet major on 2 November 1855, and acted as major of brigade to the Royal Engineers until the troops left the Crimea in June 1856.

From 1856 to 1884 Ewart held various posts in England and overseas, including deputy director of works for barracks, 1872–7. He was steadily promoted, being made CB and, in April 1884, a member of the ordnance committee. He married in 1860 his second cousin, Emily Jane, daughter of Peter Ewart, rector of Kirklington, Yorkshire, and sister of Major-General Sir Henry Peter Ewart, crown equerry; they had three sons and two daughters.

Promoted major-general on 27 January 1885, Ewart was sent with the Sudan expedition under Sir Gerald Graham as a brigadier-general in command of the base and line of communications, including the general supervision of the railway construction from Suakin to Berber, and was mentioned in dispatches. He was lieutenant-governor of Jersey from November 1887 until November 1892. He was promoted lieutenant-general on 20 July 1888, retired on 15 February 1894, and was made a colonel-commandant of his corps on 30 March 1902. He died at the Norfolk Hotel, Folkestone, on 8 August 1903, and was buried at Folkestone. R. H. VETCH, rev. JAMES FALKNER

Sources *The Times* (10 Aug 1903) · *Army List* · *Hart's Army List* · W. Porter, *History of the corps of royal engineers*, 2 vols. (1889) · *Royal Engineers Journal*, 33/394 (1 Sept 1903), 204–5 · *CGPLA Eng. & Wales* (1903)
Wealth at death £3524 7s. 8d.: probate, 19 Aug 1903, *CGPLA Eng. & Wales*

Ewart, Florence Maude (1864–1949). *See under* Ewart, Alfred James (1872–1937).

Ewart, Gavin Buchanan (1916–1995), poet, was born on 4 February 1916 at 25 Norfolk Crescent, London, the first of three children of George Arthur Ewart (1886–1942), gynaecologist, and his wife, Dorothy Hannah, née Turner (1889–1979). George Ewart was the son of James Coffar Ewart FRS (1851–1933), Darwinist and regius professor of natural history at Edinburgh University. Gavin Ewart went to Wellesley House, a preparatory school in Broadstairs, Kent, from 1924 to 1929, and from there to Wellington College, Crowthorne, Berkshire, where he stayed until 1933.

Already Ewart had begun to write poetry; by the age of fourteen he had written several short plays and he contributed poetry to the Wellington *Year Book*, and also *Out of Bounds*, the magazine edited by his Wellington contemporaries Esmond and Giles Romilly; the magazine attacked the public schools as a breeding-ground of (in the Romillys' words) 'Reaction, Militarism and Fascism' (Philip Toynbee, *Friends Apart*, 1954, 15). *Out of Bounds* published Ewart's fourteen-verse poem 'The Fourth of May', written in the summer of 1934, with the opening lines:

> My dear old school goes back today,
> Fumbling for tips and 'Goodbye, old boy,'
> Shall we give it a cheer?
> Let us pray for its members, past and present,
> Let us remember how unpleasant
> Most of them were.

His pungent and sarcastic farewell to Wellington included a daring reference to masturbation:

> So we were onanists; beds at night
> Used to respond with continual slight
> Creaks of their springs

at the time an unmentionable subject; Ewart's poem so scandalized his housemaster that he wrote to say it would not be a good thing for Ewart to visit the school for at least three years.

The youthful Ewart had thus staked out some of the territory he would exploit in later years. But this he had already done with the poem that represented his first adult success, 'Phallus in Wonderland', written shortly after his seventeenth birthday, which Geoffrey Grigson published in *New Verse*. The poem was much influenced by T. S. Eliot and Ezra Pound; considering it immature, Ewart omitted it from his first published collection, *Poems and*

Songs (1939), but he included it in his *Collected Poems, 1933–1980* (1980).

In 1934 Ewart went up to Christ's College, Cambridge, as an exhibitioner to read classics, but changed to English at the end of his first year, becoming a pupil of F. R. Leavis. He was literary editor of *Granta* for the year 1936–7 and he went down in 1938 with a second in finals, hoping to follow the profession of poet; to earn a living, he did secretarial work for various authors and worked as a salesman for a firm of fine art publishers. His larger ambition seemed closer to fulfilment when the Fortune Press, under the notorious R. A. Caton, published *Poems and Songs* in 1939. The most noticeable influence this time was that of W. H. Auden, whom he always considered the greatest English-language poet of the twentieth century; however, the best-known poem in the book is probably the squib 'Miss Twye', a ribald quatrain anticipating Ewart's later light verse.

War service stalled Ewart's progress as a poet. He was called up in June 1940 to the East Surrey regiment, and in May 1941 he was commissioned in the Royal Artillery. He served in anti-aircraft batteries in north Africa and Italy, and although he later denied any talent for 'war poetry', his *Collected Poems, 1933–1980* includes nine 'war poems' written between 1940 and 1946: one of them, 'When a Beau goes in', became a well-known anthology piece ('Beau' was wartime slang for Beaufighter, the twin-engined fighter aircraft introduced in 1940).

Ewart was demobilized in May 1946 with the rank of captain, and soon afterwards M. J. Tambimuttu, proprietor of Editions Poetry London, took him on as production manager. Ewart was also working for the British Council, helping to select books for overseas distribution, but in 1949 the council was drastically pruned as a result of government cuts and at roughly the same time Tambimuttu went to live in the United States: Editions Poetry London collapsed. Out of a job, Ewart now began the occupation he remained in until 1971: he became an advertising copywriter. He worked for a succession of agencies—Royds, the London Press Exchange, Notleys (later Saatchi and Saatchi), and finally J. Walter Thompson.

Ewart found the work uninteresting and the clients tiresome, and his talents as a poet were neglected, although he would sometimes write during quiet periods in the office and had occasional poems accepted by, among others, the *New Yorker* and the *New Statesman*. Nor was he the only aspiring writer to look for a livelihood in advertising: another—at Royds—was the Australian émigré poet Peter Porter. Ewart's friendship with Porter (they remained friends for the rest of Ewart's life) prompted him to start writing seriously again. Alan Ross, editor of the *London Magazine* and director of London Magazine Editions, persuaded him to put together the collection which appeared in 1964 with the title *Londoners*, with illustrations by Colin Spencer. This volume, consisting of verse portraits of eighteen London landmarks, was competent rather than inspired, and sold few copies.

Londoners was succeeded in 1966 by *Pleasures of the Flesh*, and now Ewart's distinctive voice began to be heard in verse that was witty, nimble, comprehensible, and metrically resourceful, able to handle the erotic and the satirical with equal verve and confidence; one note clearly heard, however, is of restlessness and vexation with the dullness of his work. Matters came to a head in 1971 when J. Walter Thompson made Ewart redundant. On 24 March 1956 he had married Margaret (Margo) Adelaide Bennett (*b.* 1922), and by now they had two children, Jane Susan (*b.* 1956) and Julian Robert (*b.* 1958). Ewart took a job as a schoolmaster, and for two terms taught O and A level English at several local schools, principally a south London comprehensive. This excursion into a new profession was not a success—he found his pupils ill-motivated and mischievous—but Ewart's confidence as a writer was strengthened by the Cholmondeley award for poetry in 1971, and he resolved once more to make a living as a poet. Indeed his poetic output began to increase rapidly and he was becoming a well-liked member of the literary community. Aware of his debt to Peter Porter, he dedicated to him his next book, *The Deceptive Grin of the Gravel Porters* (1968). His next volume, *The Gavin Ewart Show* (1971), is a collection of mature, confident poetry, displaying his talent for metrical dexterity and encompassing a range of feeling and personal experience. As in the next volume, *An Imaginary Love Affair* (1974), many of the poems reflect a conflict between the anguish of romantic love and the deeper satisfaction of a secure marriage; and in later volumes too, he appears to settle, or at least suppress, this conflict with the help of the bawdy wit and irreverence for sexual convention for which he was now known.

Ewart was elected chairman of the Poetry Society for the year 1978–9 and when the Oxford professorship of poetry became vacant in 1984 he stood as 'the Cambridge candidate'. He won few votes; John Wain was elected. Meanwhile he edited books of light verse, children's verse, and school songs, and the appearance in 1980 of his first collected volume (*The Collected Ewart*, dedicated to his wife) demonstrates his productiveness no less than his gifts. He was by now very much the professional poet: writing reviews and taking part in radio programmes; his work appearing in literary periodicals (the *Times Literary Supplement*, the *London Magazine*, *Ambit*); and becoming a familiar figure at poetry readings. An awkward public performer at first, he rapidly improved; in his last decade he was acknowledged as a virtuoso reader—witty yet modest, his voice melodious and his manner confident, making the most of his poetry's numerous technical stunts and devices.

Ewart published a second *Collected Poems* covering the years 1980–90, it and the 1980 volume totalling almost 900 pages. Then came in 1993 his *85 Poems*, and he continued unstoppably, writing for periodicals and in letters to his friends. Verse came to him spontaneously: 'found' poetry, in newspapers and speech, pleased him, and so did experiments with metre and rhyme. His fluency and wit and his gleeful use of sexual imagery (he was the second most prolific contributor to *The Faber Book of Blue Verse*, 1990) usually gave him the status of 'light' poet and he said he was 'most proud' of the Michael Braude award for light verse which the American Academy gave him in 1991. Yet at heart his was serious poetry, admired by such contemporaries as Philip Larkin, Stephen Spender, Anthony Thwaite, Alan Brownjohn, and Peter Porter, who said of him 'There is simply more of the observable surface of our world in his poetry than in most of his contemporaries', and more of its humour and moral seriousness' (personal knowledge).

Ewart had been handsome as a young man and in his latter years he was still noticeably so: humorous, engaging, sociable, widely read, with many friends, and fond of music, especially 1930s jazz, Mozart, and Richard Strauss. He died of prostate cancer in Trinity Hospice, in Clapham, south London, on 23 October 1995. He was a declared atheist and a member of the Humanist Society and he was cremated on 30 October at Putney Vale crematorium, south London. At his request, the congregation, of fellow poets and writers as well as family and friends, were played the last of Strauss's *Four Last Songs*, his setting of Joseph von Eichendorff's 'Im Abendrot' ('At dusk').

PAUL VAUGHAN

Sources personal knowledge (2004) · private information (2004) [Peter Porter; Margo Ewart, widow] · m. cert. **Archives** Emory University, Atlanta, Georgia, papers · NL Scot., corresp. and literary papers · NL Scot., corresp. and papers · priv. coll., letters, diaries, papers, etc. · U. Hull, MSS · U. Texas, papers **Likenesses** photograph, NPG · photographs, priv. coll. **Wealth at death** £67,696: probate, 6 Feb 1996, *CGPLA Eng. & Wales*

Ewart, Sir John Alexander (1821–1904), army officer, was born at Sholapur, Bombay, on 11 June 1821, the third son in a family of four sons and a daughter of the Peninsular veteran Lieutenant-General John Frederick Ewart (d. 1854) and his wife, Lavinia Isabella, eldest daughter of Rear-Admiral Sir Charles *Brisbane. Joseph *Ewart was his grandfather and Charles Brisbane *Ewart was his younger brother.

Educated at the Royal Military College, Sandhurst (1835–8), where he obtained special distinction, Ewart on 27 July 1838 was commissioned ensign in the 35th (Royal Sussex) regiment. He was promoted lieutenant on 15 April 1842. He was a good cricketer and captain of the regimental eleven, and was elected to the MCC in 1848. After garrison duty at Cape Town and Mauritius, Ewart exchanged into the 93rd Sutherland Highlanders in 1846, and became captain on 12 May 1848, brevet major on 12 December 1854, major on 29 December 1854, and brevet lieutenant-colonel on 2 November 1855.

Ewart served with the 93rd throughout the Crimean War. He was at the battle of the Alma (20 September) and at the occupation of Balaklava (25 September), being appointed a deputy assistant quartermaster-general the next day. At the battle of Balaklava (25 October) he commanded the 6th company of the 'thin red line'. On 5 November at Inkerman he was the first to inform Raglan of the Russian advance. He took part in the early siege operations before Sevastopol, and in May accompanied the expedition to the Sea of Azov and was present at the capture of Kerch and Yenikale. He returned to the besieging force before Sevastopol and was engaged in the

assaults on 18 June and 5 September. He received Piedmontese, French, and Turkish decorations.

Ewart served with the 93rd in India during the mutiny. He took part in an engagement near Bunni, holding for a short time a command consisting of three squadrons of cavalry, five guns, and 500 infantry. On 16 November 1857 he commanded the leading party at the assault of the *sikandarabagh*, during which he personally captured a colour and received two sabre wounds. He was recommended for the Victoria Cross without result. On 1 December 1857 he was again very severely wounded by a cannon shot at Cawnpore, his left arm being carried away. He was made CB on 24 March 1858 and promoted lieutenant-colonel on 16 April 1858.

On 16 November 1858 Ewart married Frances (d. 1873), eldest daughter of Spencer Stone of Callingwood Hall, Stafford. They had one daughter and four sons, including Sir John Spencer *Ewart.

Promoted colonel on 26 April 1859 and aide-de-camp to Queen Victoria the same year, from 1859 to 1864 Ewart commanded the 78th Ross-shire Buffs. Major-general on 6 March 1869 and lieutenant-general on 1 October 1877, he commanded from 1877 to 1879 the Allahabad division of the Indian army. In 1881 he published his two-volume autobiography, *The Story of a Soldier's Life*. He was made general on 13 January 1884. In 1883–4 he was honorary colonel of the 1st battalion Duke of Edinburgh's regiment, from 1884 to 1895 of the 92nd Gordon Highlanders, and from 1895 to 1904 of the Argyll and Sutherland Highlanders. In 1887 he was created KCB. He was promoted GCB two days before his death, which took place on 18 June 1904 at his residence, Craigcleuch, Langholm, Dumfriesshire. He was buried in the cemetery of Stirling Castle.

H. M. VIBART, rev. ALEX MAY

Sources *Army List* · J. A. Ewart, *The story of a soldier's life*, 2 vols. (1881) · R. H. Burgoyne, *Historical records of the 93rd Sutherland highlanders* (1883) · P. Groves, *History of the 93rd Sutherland highlanders* (1895) · A. W. Kinglake, *The invasion of the Crimea*, 8 vols. (1863–87) · G. B. Malleson, *History of the Indian mutiny, 1857–1858: commencing from the close of the second volume of Sir John Kaye's History of the Sepoy War*, 3 vols. (1878–80) · C. Hibbert, *The great mutiny, India, 1857* (1978) · Burke, *Peerage* · WWW **Archives** NRA Scotland, priv. coll., papers **Likenesses** photograph (after portrait, 1839), repro. in *Journal of the Queen's Regiment* (July 1967), 45 · portrait, repro. in *The Thin Red Line* (June–July 1904) **Wealth at death** £18,890 7s. 5d.: confirmation, 7 Sept 1904, CCI

Ewart, Sir John Spencer (1861–1930), army officer, was born at Callingwood Hall, near Burton upon Trent, Staffordshire, on 22 March 1861, the eldest son of General Sir John Alexander *Ewart (1821–1904), a veteran of the Crimean War and the Indian Mutiny, and his wife, Frances (d. 1873), daughter of Spencer Stone. He was educated at Marlborough College (1876–9), before attending the Royal Military College, Sandhurst (1880–81), which he left with the sword of honour. He joined the Queen's Own Cameron Highlanders at Gibraltar in 1881, and, in the following year, saw active service at the battle of Tell al-Kebir (13

September 1882). Spencer Ewart also served with his regiment throughout the Nile expedition of 1884–5, attributing its failure to Viscount Wolseley's use of whaleboats to navigate the Nile (Ewart's diaries, 6 Feb 1885, Monro MSS, NA Scot.), and with the Sudan frontier force in 1885–6. In the latter expedition he was adjutant of the battalion and garrison adjutant, serving as a staff officer at Koshe during its investment (12–29 December 1885) and in the battle of Giniss (30 December 1885). He was mentioned in dispatches and awarded the order of the Mejidiye (5th class). On 26 December 1891 Spencer Ewart married Robin, daughter of Major George William Platt, of Bridge of Allan, Stirlingshire; they had one daughter. He passed out of the Staff College, Camberley, in the same year, and two years later was appointed aide-de-camp to the general officer commanding-in-chief, Scottish command. For five years from 1893 he was military secretary to the governor of Malta, before rejoining his battalion in 1898 during the final stages of the Sudan campaign. He extolled the achievements of the Cameron Highlanders, praised the quality of the Sudanese soldiers, and defended the much-criticized leadership of Major-General William F. Gatacre, on whose divisional staff he served. Spencer Ewart was present at the battle of Omdurman (2 September) and, besides being mentioned again in dispatches, was awarded the brevet of lieutenant-colonel.

After a brief service as deputy assistant adjutant-general, western district, Spencer Ewart saw further active service in the Second South African War. Initially base-commandant at East London and of the lines of communication to Stormberg, he later participated in the advance to the relief of Kimberley as brigade-major of the 3rd (Highland) brigade. At the battle of Magersfontein (11 December 1899) he distinguished himself in the rallying of the brigade when it was unexpectedly attacked in the act of deploying into fighting formation at the foot of Magersfontein Hill. After the battle he fiercely defended the tactics of Major-General Andrew Wauchope, but castigated the frontal attacks launched by Lord Methuen, doubting that 'there was ever such a display of military incapacity' (Ewart's diaries, 11 Dec 1899). Spencer Ewart saw more action at Koodoosberg (2–4 February 1900), and was shortly afterwards appointed assistant adjutant-general of the 9th division, with which he was present at the actions of Paardeberg (27 February 1900), Poplar Grove (7 March), and Driefontein (10 March). He also took part in the occupation of Bloemfontein (13 March) and the engagements at Waterval Drift (30–31 March), Vet River (5 May), Blaauwberg (26 May), and Roodepoort (30 May). Passing on to the 10th division, Spencer Ewart served in the same capacity in the operations at Wittebergen (20–21 July), Retief's Nek (23 July), and Slaapkranz (28 July), ending up as quartermaster-general at Pretoria where he remained until May 1902. For his services in the campaign he was twice mentioned in dispatches, created CB (1902), and promoted brevet colonel. The war had left its mark on Spencer Ewart's politics. Although 'a Liberal in sentiment', he detested the activities of the pro-Boers and would not vote thereafter for 'a party led by that unpatriotic person—Campbell-Bannerman' (ibid., 16 January 1906).

Spencer Ewart now entered upon a long career at the War Office. He was appointed assistant military secretary in October 1902, and became deputy military secretary in the following year and military secretary in March 1904. As director of military operations (1906–10), he provided crucial support for the army reforms of Richard Burdon Haldane, the Liberal secretary of state for war (1906–10). It was his suggestion that the militia depots should serve as 74 reserve battalion cadres which could become draft-producing battalions on mobilization. As Haldane remarked, this 'worked like magic with the generals' (Haldane to Campbell-Bannerman, 9 Jan 1907, Campbell-Bannerman MSS, BL). Spencer Ewart remained concerned about the shortage of officers for mobilization, favouring the promotion of non-commissioned officers and the creation of the Officers' Training Corps. He also supported the Territorial Force, describing the National Service League's alternative of home defence as a 'strategic fallacy' (Ewart diaries, 12 July 1909). In 1910 he was appointed director-general of the Territorial Force and a few months later, adjutant-general to the forces and second military member of the Army Council. In the same year he became aide-de-camp to George V, a position he held until 1914. In 1911 he was promoted lieutenant-general and created KCB.

During the Curragh incident in March 1914 Spencer Ewart drafted a written assurance for Brigadier-General Hubert Gough that the army would not be used to coerce Ulster. When this document, as amended in cabinet and amplified by two paragraphs written by the secretary of state for war, was repudiated by Prime Minister Asquith, Spencer Ewart, Colonel J. E. B. Seely, the secretary of state for war, and Sir John French, the chief of the Imperial General Staff, resigned. Within a few weeks Spencer Ewart was appointed general officer commanding in chief, Scottish command, a post that involved raising large numbers of recruits and making provision for home defence, which he discharged until his retirement in 1918. In that year he became honorary colonel of the 4th battalion of his own regiment, and was colonel of the regiment from 1914 to 1929. He worked prodigiously on behalf of the Cameron Highlanders, writing articles in the *79th News*, supporting the regimental association, and co-authoring several volumes of the regimental history. He also supported the creation of the Scottish war memorial. Although he was renowned for his wit and intellect, Spencer Ewart was deeply disappointed by the fact that the Curragh incident had ruined his career, ensuring that he never held field command, was passed over for promotion to general, and was never invited to visit the armies on the western front.

Spencer Ewart died on 19 September 1930 at Craigcleuch, Langholm, Dumfriesshire, where he had lived since shortly before his marriage. He was buried at Westerkirk, Dumfriesshire, on 23 September.

EDWARD M. SPIERS

Sources I. F. W. Beckett, ed., *The army and the Curragh incident, 1914* (1986) · E. M. Spiers, *Haldane: an army reformer* (1980) · I. Beckett and J. Gooch, eds., *Politicians and defence: studies in the formulation of British defence policy, 1845–1970* (1981) · J. Gooch, *The plans of war: the general staff and British military strategy, c.1900–1916* (1974) · E. M. Spiers, ed., *Sudan: the reconquest reappraised* (1998) · A. J. McNeill, 'Further reminiscences of a subaltern', *Cabar Feidh: The Quarterly Magazine of the Seaforth Highlanders*, 7 (1934), 12–15 · 'Obituary: Lieutenant-General Sir John Spencer Ewart', *The 79th News*, 192 (Oct 1930), 611–14 · *The Times* (20 Sept 1930), 12 · NA Scot., Monro of Williamwood MSS, Ewart's diaries · BL, Campbell-Bannerman MSS · *CCI* (1931) · *DNB*
Archives NRA Scotland, priv. coll., diary and papers · PRO, Committee of Imperial Defence minutes | BL, Campbell-Bannerman MSS · CAC Cam., Esher MSS · NA Scot., Monro of Williamwood MSS · NL Scot., Haig diary · NL Scot., Haldane MSS · U. Lond., Institute of Commonwealth Studies, corresp. with Richard Jebb | FILM IWM FVA, documentary footage · IWM FVA, news footage
Likenesses photograph, repro. in *79th News*
Wealth at death £25,244 15s. 11d.: confirmation, 2 March 1931, *CCI*

Ewart, Joseph (1759–1792), diplomat, was born on 30 April 1759, the eldest son of the minister of Troqueer in Kirkcudbrightshire. He attended a local school before entering Edinburgh University, where he took the degree of MA. He then acted as travelling tutor to John Macdonald of Clanranald, and while abroad he met Sir John Stepney, the British envoy at Dresden. On Stepney's transfer to Berlin in October 1782 Ewart became his private secretary. Ewart remained at the embassy after Lord Dalrymple succeeded Stepney and served as secretary of legation from October 1785 and as chargé d'affaires from May 1787 to July 1788, when he was appointed envoy-extraordinary and minister-plenipotentiary. In 1785 he married a daughter of Count Wontensleben, with whom he had a son and two daughters.

In Berlin, Ewart worked hard to re-establish a close relationship between Britain and Prussia and played a significant role in concluding the general defensive alliance between the two countries that was signed in Berlin on 13 August 1788; this completed the triple alliance between Britain, Prussia, and the Netherlands. Ewart then pressed for a consolidation of the alliance to put pressure on Russia, then engaged in war against Turkey, to make peace and return conquered territory to Turkey—in particular the Black Sea port of Ochakov. On leave from Berlin in autumn 1790 Ewart presented his case to William Pitt, arguing that it was in Britain's interest to join Prussia in thwarting Russia's expansionist plans in the east. By early 1791 Pitt appeared committed to enforcing a peace treaty on Russia and began preparing for war against Russia; by mid-March 1791 a Baltic squadron in Spithead was ready to go into action. However, in the face of growing hostility to a war in both parliament and the press, Pitt backed down. In April he ordered Ewart to return to Berlin to persuade Prussia to adopt a more conciliatory policy towards Russia. Ewart was a broken man and was held responsible for the deterioration in relations with Prussia. To add to his difficulties, he bungled the legal issues involved in arranging the marriage of Frederick, duke of York, to Princess Frederica Charlotte, the king of Prussia's eldest daughter. He was granted permission to return home on grounds of ill health and left Berlin on 22 October 1791, with a pension of £1000 per annum and the promise of the Order of the Bath.

Ewart died shortly afterwards, on 27 January 1792, at his brother's home in Bladud's Buildings in Bath, where he had gone to recover his health; he was buried in Bath Abbey. The fact that he died in delirium gave rise to rumours that he had either been poisoned by a Russian agent or gone mad as a result of political disappointments, but the delirium appears to have resulted from acute appendicitis.

H. M. STEPHENS, *rev.* M. J. MERCER

Sources D. B. Horn, *Great Britain and Europe in the 18th century* (1967), 165, 173–4, 223 · J. Ehrman, *The younger Pitt*, 3 vols. (1969–96), esp. vol. 2, pp. 7–31 · A. W. Ward, *The Cambridge history of British foreign policy, 1783–1919*, ed. A. W. Ward and G. P. Gooch, 3 vols. (1922–3), vol. 1, pp. 177–81, 190–208 · D. G. Barnes, *George III and William Pitt, 1783–1806: a new interpretation based upon a study of their unpublished correspondence* (1939); repr. (1965), 229–31 · *GM*, 1st ser., 62 (1792), 94 · S. T. Bindoff and others, eds., *British diplomatic representatives, 1789–1852*, CS, 3rd ser., 50 (1934) · J. H. Rote, *William Pitt and national revival* (1911), 311–13, 629–30
Archives NRA Scotland, priv. coll., corresp. and papers · PRO, letter-books and corresp., FO 353 | BL, letters to Lord Grenville, Add. MS 59017 · BL, corresp. with Sir R. M. Keith, Add. MSS 35526–35544, *passim* · BL, letters to duke of Leeds, Add. MSS 28060–28066 · BL, corresp. with duke of Leeds, Lord Auckland, and Lord Grenville, Add. MSS 34425–34460, *passim* · Bodl. Oxf., corresp. with Sir James Bland Burges · Derbys. RO, corresp. with Lord St Helens and diplomatic papers · NL Scot., corresp. with Hugh Elliot · NL Scot., corresp. with Sir Robert Liston · PRO, letters to William Pitt, PRO 30/8

Ewart, Mary Anne (1830–1911). *See under* Ewart, William (1798–1869).

Ewart, Peter (1767–1842), engineer, was born on 14 May 1767 at Troqueer Manse, near Dumfries, the son of the Revd John Ewart, minister in Troqueer parish and his wife, Mary (*née* Corrie). He was the ninth of eleven brothers and sisters, some of whom also had distinguished careers. His eldest brother was Joseph *Ewart, who became a diplomat; and his brother William was a merchant and partner of John Gladstone (father of W. E. Gladstone) in Liverpool.

After early education at a local school, Ewart at the age of fifteen attended lectures at Edinburgh University, where his cousin John Robison (1739–1805) was professor of natural philosophy. (It was this connection that later commended him to James Watt.) At about the same time he was apprenticed to John Rennie (1761–1821), then a millwright in Haddingtonshire. In 1784 Rennie, when commissioned by Watt to help with the erection of the Albion Mills, Blackfriars, took Ewart with him to London. Four years later Ewart was at work on a water-wheel for Matthew Boulton's rolling mill in Birmingham. At this time markets for Watt's rotative steam engine were opening up in the growing cotton and woollen textile industries; and in 1789 Boulton and Watt sent Ewart to Manchester to erect a Watt engine for Peter Drinkwater. In 1790 Ewart became Boulton and Watt's northern area representative. This brought him into contact with other leaders of the industrial revolution, such as George Lee (who married his youngest sister, Mary Ewart), Benjamin Gott, Samuel Oldknow, and William Strutt.

The problems of dealing with unreliable component suppliers were so frustrating that, in 1792, Ewart resigned as area representative and went into partnership with Oldknow as a cotton spinner. When Oldknow's enterprise failed, Ewart found, in 1793, a new partner in Samuel Greg, of Quarry Bank Mill, Styal, near Manchester. Here he improved the water power resource by building a masonry dam on the River Bollin and this work, together with the mill, is now maintained by the National Trust. At Styal, Ewart may well have made a significant contribution to the development of water power and the design of water-wheels, and in addition he installed a Boulton and Watt engine, as a standby power source.

The Greg partnership ended in 1811, when Ewart concentrated his efforts on his own mill in Manchester. The extent to which this move was due to a new and quite different interest can only be conjectured. He had joined the Manchester Literary and Philosophical Society in 1798; in 1812 he became, with John Dalton, a vice-president of the society. His wide experience of steam and water power on the one hand and his knowledge of mathematics and natural philosophy on the other made him unusually well qualified to pronounce on the vexed questions of power, force, and work, still veiled in confusion. An attack, probably by John Playfair, in the *Edinburgh Review* (12, 1808, 120–130) on W. H. Wollaston's Bakerian lecture, and on John Smeaton's experiments between 1759 and 1782, was the occasion for the longest (153 pages) and most important of the four papers Ewart published, 'On the measure of moving force' (1813). This was a sustained plea that British mathematicians and natural philosophers should take account of the concept of 'living force' or *vis viva* and the related measure of work (force times distance), advocated strongly by Smeaton, supported by Wollaston, and used by most engineers.

The received doctrine that momentum (mv) is the true measure of the force was supported by the fact that momentum is conserved when inelastic bodies collide, while *vis viva* (mv²) is apparently not conserved. Ewart, following Smeaton, argued that the apparent loss of *vis viva* was accounted for by the 'change of figure' of the colliding bodies. And, having countered the theoretical objections to *vis viva*, he pointed out that a wide range of manufacturing processes depend on 'change of figure' and that the losses entailed can be accurately calculated. The received doctrine cannot account for 'change of figure'. An insight, in the paper, was his assertion, contrary to the Edinburgh critic, that to a given quantity of heat, used in a steam engine, there must correspond a fixed amount of work. Ewart knew, of course, that in all practical engines the full amount of work could never be realized. He did not, however, recognize that heat could be converted into work.

This was the longest paper yet published, and for a long time to come, in the Manchester *Memoirs*. Ewart acknowledged John Dalton's support and 'candid encouragement' in writing it and it may be assumed that Dalton had advocated publication in its entirety. Moreover, Dalton dedicated the first part of volume 2 of his *New System of Chemical Philosophy* (1827) jointly to Ewart as a friend and 'for the able exposition and excellent illustrations of the Fundamental Principles of Mechanics in his essay on the measure of moving force'. James Watt, and his son James Watt Junior, seem to have approved of the work too. Apart from its originality, in the British context, and the knowledge of continental ideas that it revealed, the paper is of some significance as a distinctive contribution to the new, Manchester, school of science; and James Prescott Joule, a loyal pupil of Dalton, established his comprehensive ideas on energy and the mechanical theory of heat on the basis of the doctrines of *vis viva* and the related 'measure of moving force'.

Ewart left Manchester in 1835, when he was appointed the first chief engineer and inspector of machinery for the navy's steam ships. He died on 15 September 1842, as a result of an accident in Woolwich Dockyard, when a chain carrying a very heavy load suddenly snapped. It is not known whether his wife, formerly Miss Kerr, whom he had married in 1802, survived him.

DONALD CARDWELL

Sources P. Ewart, 'On the measure of moving force', *Memoirs of the Literary and Philosophical Society of Manchester*, 2nd ser., 2 (1813), 105–258 · W. C. Henry, 'A biographical note of the late Peter Ewart', *Memoirs of the Literary and Philosophical Society of Manchester*, 2nd ser., 7 (1846), 113–36 · E. Hodgkinson, 'Some account of the late Mr Ewart's paper "On the measure of moving force"', *Memoirs of the Literary and Philosophical Society of Manchester*, 2nd ser., 7 (1846), 137–56 · J. Walker, presidential address, *PICE*, 2 (1843), 22–31, esp. 25–9 · J. P. Joule, *The scientific papers of James Prescott Joule*, 2 vols. (1884–7); repr. (1963) · A. E. Musson and E. Robinson, *Science and technology in the industrial revolution* (1969) · R. S. Fitton and A. P. Wadsworth, *The Strutts and the Arkwrights, 1758–1830: a study of the early factory system* (1958) · *Partners in science: letters of James Watt and Joseph Black*, ed. E. Robinson and D. McKie (1970) · R. L. Hills, *Power in the industrial revolution* (1970) · R. L. Hills, *Power from steam: a history of the stationary steam engine* (1989) · M. B. Rose, *The Gregs of Quarry Bank Mill: the rise and decline of the family firm, 1750–1914* (1986) · Birm. CL, James Watt MSS, C2/12.27 · R. L. Hills, 'Peter Ewart, 1767–1842', *Manchester Memoirs*, 127 (1987–8), 29–43 · D. S. L. Cardwell, *From Watt to Clausius: the rise of thermodynamics in the early industrial age* (1971); repr. (1989), 82–3

Archives Birm. CA, letters to Boulton and Watt · JRL, Oldknow MSS · Man. CL, Greg MSS · Man. CL, Oldknow MSS

Likenesses portrait, Man. CL

Ewart, William (1798–1869), politician, was born on 1 May 1798 at 7 Queen Square in Liverpool, the second of the four sons of William Ewart (1763–1823), merchant, and his wife, Margaret (1773–1844), daughter of Christopher Jaques of Bedale, Yorkshire. Descended from a Kirkcudbrightshire family, William Ewart senior, who was the brother of the diplomatist Joseph Ewart and godfather of the future statesman William Ewart Gladstone, had made his fortune as a general commission merchant, and was senior partner in the firm of Ewart, Rutson & Co. of Liverpool. His son and namesake was educated at Eton College from 1811, and proceeded in 1817 to Christ Church, Oxford, where he won the college prize for Latin verse in 1819 and the Newdigate prize the following year. He graduated in 1821, undertook a two-year tour of the continent, and, having been admitted to the Middle Temple in March 1820, was called to the bar on 26 January 1827. On 15 December 1829 at Prestwich he married his first cousin Mary Anne (1805–1837), the daughter of his father's youngest sister, Mary, and the Manchester cotton merchant George Augustus Lee of Singleton.

Ewart, who was elected for Bletchingley at a by-election in July 1828, took his seat in the Commons on 5 February and made his maiden speech in favour of Catholic emancipation on 27 March 1829. He was left without a constituency in 1830, but, following the death of William Huskisson later that year, he was narrowly elected for Liverpool after a fierce contest. Although unseated on petition by the house on 28 March 1831, he regained his seat at the general election in May, and held it until 1837. A Liberal with radical leanings, who advocated the ballot, reform of the established church, abolition of colonial slavery, and repeal of the corn laws, he was active in parliament, speaking on general topics 'with considerable ease, and with much rapidity … without being eloquent' (Grant, 289–90). In 1832 he secured the passage of an act to end the use of capital punishment in cases of theft of money or animals from a dwelling house (2–3 Will. IV c. 62), and in subsequent years succeeded in obtaining other legislative steps towards the total abolition of the death penalty. On 1 August 1833 he made the first of a series of annual motions for equalization of the duties on East and West Indian sugars, as an indirect attack on the use of slave labour in the West Indies. Other humanitarian achievements of his included the acts of 1834, to end the hanging of the bodies of prisoners in chains (4 & 5 Will. IV c. 26), and of 1836, to allow felons to be defended by counsel (6 & 7 Will. IV c. 114).

Having been defeated at Liverpool and Kilkenny borough in 1837, Ewart lost a by-election at Marylebone in March 1838, but returned to the Commons as member for Wigan in March 1839. In *The Reform of the Reform Bill* (1837) he urged the case for widening the scope of political changes, and in a major intervention in the Commons on 28 January 1840, called for these to be extended to the realms of free trade and national education. At the general election of 1841 he returned to his family's Scottish roots, becoming member for Dumfries burghs, which he represented for the next twenty-seven years. In the 1840s he continued to press for free trade, being involved in the activities of the Anti-Corn Law League. Strongly internationalist in his outlook, he also attended several peace congresses in Europe. He maintained consistent opinions on public finance, arguing for a system of more direct taxation in a published speech (28 May 1847). Other speeches which were separately printed were those on capital punishment (10 June 1856) and European settlement in India (16 March 1858), in which he expressed the hope that 'our mission there would be for the benefit of the Natives themselves' (Munford, 145). He chaired a select committee on this question, which provoked John Warden to write his *Letter to William Ewart*. The select committee on the adoption of the metric system, which he

also chaired, led to the permissive act of 1864 (27 & 28 Vict. c. 117). On 3 May 1864 he secured the appointment of a royal commission on capital punishment, on which he served from July 1864 to January 1866.

Ewart's concern to promote education and public libraries, which was largely motivated by a wish to improve the economic and social status of the lower classes, began in 1836, when his select committee's report on arts and manufactures led to the creation of the School of Design at Somerset House, London. He spoke often on education—for instance, on the need to free it from church domination (20 June 1839)—and in 1841 requested that an annual ministerial statement be made to parliament. In the autumn of 1846 he explained to Lord John Russell that while he was against large-scale public provision of education, he was 'rather desirous of combining the voluntary system with government inspection and public encouragement of it' (Baines, 135). He endeavoured to introduce competitive examinations for entry to the civil and diplomatic services (1845 and 1852), and the army (1847). He supported the Museums Act of 1845, which enabled town councils to levy rates to pay for local museums, and was instrumental in securing the extension of this scheme to libraries, chairing the select committees which were appointed in 1849 and 1850. The resulting Libraries Act of 1850 (13 & 14 Vict. c. 65) established what ultimately became a nationwide system of public library provision. He sponsored an amendment bill in 1855, and on the introduction of another on 27 February 1866, Gladstone told the Commons that Ewart's name was 'associated with many achievements of public utility, but with this act of legislation [of 1850], I think, he may feel assured that his name will be associated not only during his life, but after he is gone' (Munford, 151).

Ewart, who retired from parliament in 1868, died of pneumonia on 23 January 1869, at Broadleas, near Devizes, Wiltshire, which had been his country residence since 1854. He was buried on 28 January at Bishops Cannings, Wiltshire, where his next younger brother, Joseph Christopher Ewart (1799–1868), who was Liberal member for Liverpool from 1855 to 1865, had recently been interred. He left the bulk of his estate, which included personalty sworn under £70,000, to his only son, William Lee Ewart (1836–1892), and provided for the two of his four daughters who survived him. His eldest daughter, **Mary Anne Ewart** (1830–1911), was an early patron of higher education for women. She was a benefactor and governor of Newnham College, Cambridge, Somerville College, Oxford, and Bedford College, London. She also started and administered a teachers' education loan fund for aspiring women teachers of limited means. Ewart, who was described by Benjamin Robert Haydon as 'a keen little man' (*Diary*, ed. Pope, 3.356), was a slightly built figure of respectable character, who applied himself diligently to the introduction of many social improvements over a long career. He was an advanced Liberal, whose political philosophy was based on a desire for better public administration, and this was expressed in all his concerns, which ranged from the organization of business in the

Commons to the establishment of free public libraries. The Ewart Library in Dumfries is named in his honour, and a bust of him is displayed in the Ewart room at the Library Association headquarters in London.

S. M. FARRELL

Sources W. A. Munford, *William Ewart, M.P., 1798–1869: portrait of a radical* (1960) · E. Baines jun., *Letters to the Right Hon. Lord John Russell* (1846), 135–41 · J. Minto, *A history of the public library movement in Great Britain and Ireland* (1932) · T. Kelly, *A history of public libraries in Great Britain, 1845–1965* (1973) · *Dumfries and Galloway Standard and Advertiser* (27 Jan 1869) · *Devizes and Wiltshire Gazette* (28 Jan 1869) · *The Times* (28 Jan 1869) · *ILN* (6 March 1869) · J. Warden, *Letter to William Ewart* (1859) · H. E. M. James and W. A. James, *Pedigrees of the family of James of Culgarth, West Auckland, and Barrock, and their kinfolk* (1913), no. 28 · [J. Grant], *Random recollections of the House of Commons*, 5th edn (1837) · *The diary of Benjamin Robert Haydon*, ed. W. B. Pope, 5 vols. (1960–63) · M. Taylor, *The decline of British radicalism, 1847–1860* (1995) · B. A. Clough, 'In memoriam Miss Mary Ewart', *Newnham College Letter* (1911), 41–5 · *IGI* · *CGPLA Eng. & Wales* (1911)
Archives NRA, priv. coll. | BL, corresp. with W. E. Gladstone, Add. MSS 44374–44375 · BL, corresp. with Sir Robert Peel, Add. MSS 40416–40593, *passim* · Man. CL, Manchester Archives and Local Studies, letters to Edward Edwards · W. Sussex RO, corresp. with Richard Cobden
Likenesses G. Hayter, group portrait, oils (*The House of Commons*, 1833), NPG · bust, Library Association, London; repro. in Munford, *William Ewart*, 145 · oils, Eton · portrait, priv. coll.; repro. in Munford, *William Ewart*, xiv · portrait, priv. coll.; repro. in Munford, *William Ewart*, frontispiece · wood-engraving, NPG; repro. in *ILN* (6 March 1869), 237
Wealth at death under £70,000: probate, 9 March 1869, *CGPLA Eng. & Wales* · £58,750 1s. 5d.—Mary Anne Ewart: probate, 25 March 1911, *CGPLA Eng. & Wales*

Ewart, Sir William, first baronet (1817–1889), linen manufacturer, politician, and philanthropist, was born on 11 November 1817 in Sydenham, on the outskirts of Belfast, the eldest son of William Ewart (1789–1873) and Mary Anne, *née* Rosen. He was educated at the Belfast Royal Academy, and was then employed in his grandfather's firm of William Ewart & Son, becoming a partner in 1843. In 1840 he married Isabella Kelso, daughter of Lavens Mathewson of Newtownstewart, co. Tyrone. They had nine sons and five daughters, of whom nine children survived him. As a partner he was the dominant influence in the business and a powerful figure in the linen industry generally, so much so that when he died, the *Northern Whig* described him, with a touch of hyperbole, as the 'father of our staple trade in Belfast' (*Northern Whig*, 5 Aug 1889).

Ewart's grandfather, also William Ewart (1759–1851), had moved to Ballymacarret, close to Belfast, from Hillsborough, co. Down, about 1790, and became involved in the newly developing cotton industry. In 1814 he formed a partnership with his eldest son, Ewart's father. About 1840 the firm diversified into flax spinning, thus following a trend initiated by Andrew Mulholland a decade earlier and taken up by an increasing number of Belfast cotton producers, who exploited the comparative advantages that wet flax-spinning techniques offered. The Ewarts were unusual only in that they had been manufacturers of cloth rather than spinners.

The Ewarts' first mill, powered by water, was on the Crumlin Road. Power-loom weaving was added about 1850, and in 1852 they purchased the Glenbank bleaching works. In 1859 the firm moved to extensive warehouses at 11 Donegal Place, though it kept its mills on the Crumlin Road. On the eve of the American civil war and the subsequent cotton famine, the Ewarts were already in possession of a vertically integrated business and well placed to meet the increasing demand for linen. By now Ewart was in full control.

By good management, Ewarts survived the post-war depression and, indeed, prospered by buying up the assets of less enterprising competitors. For example, in 1876 it bought the premises of the Bedford Street Weaving Company and in the same year purchased the Mountain mill, Ligoniel, from Waring and Duncan. During the trade depression of 1883, in order to protect the family wealth, Ewart turned the business into a limited liability company, with a capital of £500,000. There were six partners: Ewart himself, and five sons.

Part of the success of Ewarts can be attributed to tight family control both before and after the adoption of limited liability. Five of Ewart's six surviving sons entered the business. Two of them were resident in New York and attended to American sales. The reputation of the firm as an employer was mixed. According to a contemporary source, Ewart, on winning a legal case with a rival firm over water rights, was cheered by an 'enthusiastic crowd' all the way from the court house to his office. After he acquired the Mountain mill he built 500 dwelling houses at Ligoniel for his employees. On the other hand, in 1870 the firm was fined £13 10s. for employing labour between 8 p.m. and 11 p.m. in breach of the Factory Acts, and had repeatedly been reported for serious infringements in its spinning mills. When Ewart died, the firm had between 5000 and 6000 employees and an annual wage bill of £150,000. It operated 33,500 spindles and 2000 power looms.

In common with many other Belfast manufacturers during the nineteenth century, Ewart played an active part in the political, philanthropic, and religious life of the city. He was a member of the Belfast corporation for twenty-five years and mayor in 1859 and 1860. He was elected for Belfast City as a Conservative at a by-election in 1878; he held the seat in 1880. In 1885 he moved to North Belfast as a result of boundary changes. He was created a baronet in 1887. He was a justice of the peace for Belfast, Antrim, and Down, served on the boards of several charitable institutions, as well as trade bodies such as the Flax Supply Association, the Linen Merchants' Association, and the Belfast chamber of commerce.

Ewart was a staunch member of the Church of Ireland and was a member of the representative board set up in 1869 after disestablishment. In this role he was active in putting the financial affairs of the church on a sound footing. According to his obituary, 'there was hardly a church throughout Belfast which had not received of his liberality' (*Northern Whig*, 5 Aug 1889). He died in London at 14 Albemarle Street, Piccadilly, on 1 August 1889 and was buried in Belfast five days later. News of his death arrived in Belfast on a Saturday, in time for five churches to hold memorial services on Sunday and for the encomiums to be reported at length in the press the following morning. He opposed, however, the building of a cathedral in Belfast, arguing that it would detract from the erection of parish churches required by a growing population. He was succeeded by his eldest son, William Quartus Ewart (1844–1919).   L. A. CLARKSON

Sources *Northern Whig* (2 Aug 1889) [notice of death] · *Northern Whig* (5 Aug 1889) · *Belfast News-Letter* (5 Aug 1889) · H. C. Lawlor, 'The Ewarts of Belfast (formerly of Hillsborough)', *Fibres & Fabrics Journal*, 10/7 (April 1943), 178–80 · E. Boyle, 'Ewart, Sir William', *DBB* · E. Boyle, 'Linenopolis: the rise of the textile industry', *Belfast: the making of the city, 1800–1914*, ed. J. C. Beckett and others (1983) · I. Budge and C. O'Leary, *Belfast: approach to crisis. A study of Belfast politics, 1613–1970* (1973) · d. cert.
Archives PRO NIre., papers
Wealth at death £313,127: *Northern Whig* (5 Aug 1889)

Ewart-Biggs. For this title name *see* Biggs, (Felicity) Jane Ewart-, Baroness Ewart-Biggs (1929–1992).

Ewbank, John Wilson (*c*.1779–1847), painter, was born at Gateshead, co. Durham, and was adopted when a child by a wealthy uncle who lived at Wycliffe, on the banks of the Tees, Yorkshire. It was intended that Ewbank should become a Roman Catholic priest and he was therefore sent to Ushaw College, near Durham. He absconded, however, and became an apprentice to T. Coulson, an ornamental painter in Newcastle. On visiting Edinburgh with his master, Ewbank was encouraged to study under Alexander Nasmyth, and he soon set up in practice as an independent artist and drawing-master. The vigour and accuracy of his sketches from nature were especially admired; a series of fifty-one drawings of Edinburgh, by him, were engraved by W. H. Lizars for Dr James Browne's *Picturesque Views of Edinburgh* (1825). Another view of the city, *View of Edinburgh from Inchkeith*, was one of his finest landscapes. His reputation, however, was chiefly established by his small-scale marine paintings, which reflected the influence of Dutch seventeenth-century artists, such as Willem Van de Velde, and he was considered one of the foremost marine artists of this period. During the late 1820s he turned to subject matter of a more ambitious character, painting *The Visit of George IV to Edinburgh*, *The Entry of Alexander the Great into Babylon* (exh. RA, 1826), and *Hannibal Crossing the Alps* at the apogee of his career. His annual income at this point was said to be no less than £2500, and in 1826 he was nominated a founder member of the Royal Scottish Academy. He exhibited numerous paintings at the academy between 1827 and 1833 as well as twenty-seven works (mostly shipping and coastal views) at the Carlisle Academy between 1825 and 1833.

At a late stage in his career, however, Ewbank became an alcoholic and he descended into extreme poverty. His pictures were frequently painted in the bar of a public house or in his own squalid home. According to one obituarist:

a solitary chair and a pile or two of bricks formed the only articles in the shape of furniture to be seen—the window-sill serving for his easel … [the pictures] were generally painted on tin, within an hour or two, and sold on the instant, wet and unvarnished, for sixpence or a shilling, which was

immediately spent in ministering to his sensual gratifications.   (*GM*, new ser., 29, 1848, 668)

Ewbank died, apparently unmarried, of typhus fever, in the infirmary at Edinburgh on 28 November 1847. Examples of his work are in the National Gallery of Scotland, Edinburgh; the Shipley Art Gallery, Gateshead; the British Museum, London; the Laing Art Gallery, Newcastle; the Sutherland Art Gallery; and Tyneside Public Libraries.   GORDON GOODWIN, *rev.* V. REMINGTON

Sources *GM*, 2nd ser., 29 (1848), 668 · *Art Union*, 10 (1848), 51 · E. H. H. Archibald, *Dictionary of sea painters*, 2nd edn (1989) · P. J. M. McEwan, *Dictionary of Scottish art and architecture* (1994), 194 · Thieme & Becker, *Allgemeines Lexikon* · C. B. de Laperriere, ed., *The Royal Scottish Academy exhibitors, 1826–1990*, 4 vols. (1991)

Ewbank, Thomas (1792–1870), writer on hydraulics and physics, was born at Barnard Castle, co. Durham, on 11 March 1792. When thirteen years of age he began work as a plumber and brass-founder. In 1812 he went to London, where he was employed in making cases for preserved meats. His spare hours were given to reading. In 1819 he emigrated to America, and the following year commenced business in New York as a manufacturer of lead, tin, and copper tubing.

In 1836 Ewbank was able to retire from business and devote himself to studying and writing on mechanical matters. In 1845–6 he travelled in Brazil, and on his return to New York published an account of his travels, *Life in Brazil* (1856). He was appointed commissioner of patents by President Taylor in 1849, but was criticized for the manner in which he fulfilled the duties of his office, which he held until 1852.

Ewbank was one of the founders and a president of the American Ethnological Society. He wrote on a variety of subjects, including hydraulic machinery for raising water; the physical relationship of man to the earth; matter and force; and inorganic forces ordained to supersede human slavery. He also wrote a number of other papers on scientific subjects, ranging from the ingenuity of spiders to the design of steam engines, many of which appeared in the *Transactions of the Franklin Institute*. One of his papers on marine propulsion attracted some attention in Europe. He died at New York on 16 September 1870.

FRANCIS WATT, *rev.* R. C. COX

Sources *Men of the time* (1868) · *Catalogue of scientific papers*, Royal Society, 19 vols. (1867–1925)

Ewen (*d*. 763). *See under* Dál Riata, kings of (*act. c.*500–*c*.850).

Ewen, John (1741–1821), songwriter, was born in Montrose, of poor parents, and received only a very slender education. Having saved a few pounds working as a travelling merchant he went in 1762 to Aberdeen, where he opened a small hardware shop. This appears to have prospered, but the chief rise in his fortunes was owing to his marriage, on 3 March 1766, to Janet, one of two daughters of John Middleton, a yarn and stocking maker in Aberdeen. Through Janet, who died shortly after giving birth to a daughter, Ewen came into possession of half his father-in-law's property.

Gradually Ewen came to be recognized as one of the

most respectable public characters of Aberdeen. Trevor Royle suggests that he probably based 'O weel may the boatie row', published anonymously in Johnson's *The Scots Musical Museum*, 'on an older fragment' (Royle, 102). Burns described it as 'a charming display of womanly affection mingling with the concerns and occupations of life. It is nearly equal to "There's nae luck about the house"'.

Ewen died on 21 October 1821, leaving, after the payment of various sums to the public charities of Aberdeen, about £14,000 to found a hospital in Montrose to maintain and educate boys. The will was challenged by his estranged daughter and, after conflicting decisions in the Scottish court of session, was appealed to the House of Lords. There, on 17 November 1830, the settlement was set aside because the deed was imprecise on the sum to be accumulated by the trustees before building, and on the number of boys to be educated.

T. F. HENDERSON, *rev.* JAMES HOW

Sources W. Bannerman, *The Aberdeen worthies: or, Sketches of characters resident in Aberdeen* (1840) · W. Stenhouse, *Illustrations of the lyric poetry and music of Scotland* (1853) · Irving, *Scots.* · T. Royle, *The Macmillan companion to Scottish literature* (1983) · m. reg. Scot.
Archives University of Guelph Library, Ontario, papers
Likenesses oils, Scot. NPG
Wealth at death over £14,000: *DNB*

Ewen, William (*c.*1720–1777), merchant and revolutionary politician in America, was born in England; details of his parents and upbringing are unknown. Ewen moved to the American colonies as an apprentice to the trustees of the Georgia corporation in 1734. After working in the public stores in Savannah for two years, he took up a land grant on Skidaway Island, a settlement designed by James Oglethorpe for defence against the Spanish in Florida. There, for four years, as a 'young single man', he diligently worked his 16 acres hoping for success as a farmer. John and Charles Wesley, who visited the island, described it as about 6000 acres, having a small village on the east coast, with up to nine families, a small fort, a substantial house, and several huts, with about 20 acres of cleared land. Ewen worked his land until 1740, when only he and one other family remained. In 1739 he produced 9 bushels of corn and half a bushel of peas, but none of the rice, potatoes, olives, silk, or exotic goods desired by the trustees. In 1740 his yields further declined. Plagued by and incensed at the trustees' determined attitude against slavery and land ownership in fee simple, and their insistence upon controlling the economy through 'sola bills', Ewen became one of their most outspoken critics. The uninformed opinions of the rich and absentee trustees, who wanted the settlers to cultivate a 'Garden of Eden' of mulberry and orange trees, olives, and grapevines, especially infuriated Ewen. He sarcastically wrote:

> I need not amuse your Honrs., with the many Curiossities that may be raised here (with care and pains) … but those are things that will not Satisfye a man when he is hungry; nor cloathe him when he is Naked; for many times; I have had; no other provisions to eat but Homony and Salt; tho I have used my utmost endeavors.

Convinced that the problem lay in the absence of authority in Georgia, Ewen entered politics and became a lifelong supporter of local government.

Ewen sided with the settlers against the trustees and the British government at almost every opportunity. In 1744 a committee of five, headed by Ewen, suggested revisions to the colonial Georgia charter to allow slavery and to remove the tail-male restriction on landholding. When the first provincial assembly convened in Savannah in January 1751, Ewen represented the Abercorn and Goshen districts on the outskirts of Savannah. After the colony reverted to royal control in 1752, Ewen, who had already sold lumber and pottery even before he left Skidaway, became a merchant and, within a decade, one of the richest men in the southern American colonies. He remained active in politics, serving on a panel of judges in civil cases and opposing the Stamp Act and the Townshend duties of 1767. By 1766 Ewen, unlike his contemporaries James Habersham and Noble Jones, had joined the 'Liberty Boys', and he later became a supporter of the Continental Association, which urged non-importation of British products. In 1775 the new fourteen-member council of safety elected Ewen its first president, thus completing the shift of control from Georgia's last royal governor, Sir James Wright, to the new provincial congress of the rebels.

William Ewen represented a poorer class of Britons who went to the American colonies, yet through outstanding skill, courage, hard work, and a long life he obtained remarkable wealth and status. Unlike many of his contemporaries Ewen chose to rebel rather than remain loyal to Britain during the revolution, thus exemplifying the nature of that event as a civil war as well as a rebellion for independence. Ewen died in Savannah, Georgia, in 1777.

MILTON READY

Sources W. J. Northen, *Men of mark in Georgia*, 1 (1974) · R. S. Davis, *Georgians in the revolution* (1986) · H. E. Davis, *The fledgling province: social and cultural life in colonial Georgia, 1733–1776* (1988) · J. M. Johnson, *Militiamen, rangers and redcoats: the military in Georgia, 1754–1776* (Macon, Ga, 1992) · C. Howell, *History of Georgia*, 1 (1926) · A. Johnson, *Georgia as colony and state* (1970) · K. Coleman, *Colonial Georgia: a history* (1976) · S. B. G. Temple and K. Coleman, *Georgia journeys* (1961) · *Memoirs of Georgia* (1899)

Ewens [*alias* Newport], **Maurice** (*c.*1611–1687), Jesuit, was born in Dorset, the son of John Ewens and his wife, Elizabeth Keynes, who was niece of James Keynes of Compton Pauncefoot, Somerset. His brother may have been the Jesuit Matthew Newport. He may also have been related to the Ewens family of Wincanton, Somerset, which was granted arms in 1578; a James Ewens was noted as a recusant in 1610.

Ewens went to the Jesuit college in St Omer in or before 1623. He remained there until 1628, when he went to the English College, Rome, where he was ordained a priest on 30 November 1634. He left Rome the following year to join the Jesuits at Watten, assuming the name of Newport; he also occasionally used Keynes as an alias. He remained at Watten for at least a year, after which there followed a period of teaching at St Omer: he was professor of syntax in 1638 and professor of rhetoric in 1641. In the latter year he also composed a tragedy for a private performance by the students at St Omer on 13 August. In 1644 he was sent to England, where he was based at the residence of St Thomas of Canterbury in Hampshire. Between 1645 and 1649 he was in Devon, at the residence of Blessed Stanislaus, and was professed of the four vows at Arlington on 23 November 1648. During 1651–2 he was in Oxfordshire, and in 1653 he was sent to the London district, where he served as rector in 1666.

In 1665 Newport published in London a Latin poem of congratulation to Charles II, *Sereniss. principi Carolo Secundo mag. Brit. Fran. et Hib. regi votum candidum vivat rex*. It evidently proved popular, going through at least four editions during Newport's lifetime. His Latin poem upon the birth in 1677 of the duke of Cambridge (who lived only twenty-five days—17 November to 12 December 1677) is bound with the 1676 edition of *Sereniss.* in the Huntington Library copy. An English translation of part of the *Vivat rex* poem appeared in 1695, the translator praising the original for '[t]he Purity of the Latin, and the Excellency of the Thoughts' (*The Double Eternity, or, The Inevitable Choice*, sig. B1r).

At the outbreak of the Popish Plot in 1678 Newport was hotly pursued but escaped to the continent. During 1679–80 he was in the college of Ghent and from 1685 at Liège. He finally returned to London, where he died on 4 December 1687. According to the *Dictionary of National Biography* Newport also wrote the manuscript treatise 'De scientia Dei', which survives in Salamanca.

THOMAS H. CLANCY

Sources T. M. McCoog, *English and Welsh Jesuits, 1555–1650*, 2, Catholic RS, 75 (1995), 252 · T. M. McCoog, ed., *Monumenta Angliae*, 2: *English and Welsh Jesuits, catalogues, 1630–1640* (1992), 419 · H. Foley, ed., *Records of the English province of the Society of Jesus*, 7/1 (1882), 236–7 · Gillow, *Lit. biog. hist.*, 2.192–3 · G. Holt, *St Omers and Bruges colleges, 1593–1773: a biographical dictionary*, Catholic RS, 69 (1979) · W. H. McCabe, *An introduction to Jesuit theater*, ed. L. J. Oldani (1983) · G. Anstruther, *The seminary priests*, 2 (1975) · A. Kenny, ed., *The responsa scholarum of the English College, Rome*, 2, Catholic RS, 55 (1963)

Ewer, Isaac (*d.* 1650/51), army officer and regicide, was a close relation and possibly son of Richard Ewer of Hatfield Broad Oak, Essex, and may have been related to the Ewers of Pinner, Middlesex, and Cheshunt, Hertfordshire. He was living at Hatfield by 1633, having by that year married Joan (*d.* in or before 1649), daughter of Thomas Thurloe, rector of Abbot's Roding, Essex, and sister of John *Thurloe (*bap.* 1616, *d.* 1668), later Cromwell's secretary of state. Ewer's assessment for 9s. of ship money and post as a surveyor of highways for Hatfield in 1636 suggests he was of middling sort status. After joining parliament's army some time after the outbreak of civil war, he captained a troop of horse by 1643. In March 1645 he was major of the dragoons in the eastern association. Later that year he was appointed lieutenant-colonel to Robert Hammond's foot regiment in the New Model Army, succeeding Hammond as colonel in October 1647.

At The Garter inn in Windsor on 20 April 1648 Ewer was overheard plotting with other officers to threaten to disarm the city of London and extract £1 million in order to

wage war on their enemies. During the second civil war, his regiment was at first employed in south Wales and was then left by Cromwell to besiege Chepstow Castle. Ewer took Chepstow on 25 May 1648, killing the governor, Sir Nicholas Kemish, and his subsequent report earned him parliament's thanks. The regiment was then ordered to Essex, where Ewer was one of the commissioners who signed the articles for the surrender of Colchester and was presumably a member of the council of war that condemned Lucas and Lisle. Soon after he was appointed governor of Portsmouth and on 20 November 1648 headed the deputation which presented the army's remonstrance against the treaty with the king to the House of Commons.

With the army resolved to bring the king to trial, Ewer was ordered to convey Charles's then custodian, the doubting Hammond, from the Isle of Wight, where he arrived on 26 November 1648; he was eventually forced to arrest his former colonel, leaving his subordinates to remove the king to Hurst Castle. Appointed one of the king's judges, Ewer attended the high court every day and signed the death warrant [*see also* Regicides]. He later recounted a story that Cromwell and Henry Marten playfully splashed each other's faces with ink after the warrant was signed.

Ewer's foot regiment was selected by lot for Ireland on 20 April 1649, prompting him to draw up his will on 1 August, 'not knoweinge whether God maie ever bring mee backe againe' (PROB 11/215, fol. 149v). His regiment distinguished itself at Drogheda, and on 26 March 1650 Ewer was instrumental in Cromwell's capture of Kilkenny. He was at Clonmel on 9 May, and served under Ireton at Waterford, which fell on 6 August. He is last heard of marching towards Kilkenny on 31 October 1650; he died of plague in Ireland in either the final months of 1650 or in the first two months of the new year, and was buried at Waterford. His will was proved on 25 February 1651 by John Thurloe, who became guardian to his children.

ANDREW J. HOPPER

Sources R. K. G. Temple, 'Ewer (or Ewers), Isaac', Greaves & Zaller, BDBR · I. Gentles, *The New Model Army in England, Ireland, and Scotland, 1645–1653* (1992) · T. Herbert, *Memorials of the last two years of the reign of Charles I* (1813) · Thurloe, *State papers*, vol. 5 · *Oliver Cromwell's letters and speeches with elucidations*, ed. T. Carlyle, 3rd edn, 3 vols. (1849), vols. 1–2 · T. Reilly, *Cromwell, an honourable enemy: the untold story of the Cromwellian invasion of Ireland* (1999) · DNB · CSP dom., 1644–50 · M. Noble, *The lives of the English regicides*, 1 (1798) · B. Whitelocke, *Memorials of English affairs*, new edn, 4 vols. (1853), vols. 2–3 · *JHC*, 8 (1660–67) · Wood, *Ath. Oxon.*, 2nd edn · will, PRO, PROB 11/215, fols. 149r–150r
Archives BL, Egerton MS 2647 · Bodl. Oxf., MSS Tanner 57/1, 2 · Essex RO, D/DBa Al; Q/SR 285/16 and 293/44; T/A 42
Wealth at death wealthy: will, PRO, PROB 11/215, fols. 149r–150r

Ewer, John (1703–1774), bishop of Bangor, was born at Belchamp St Paul, Essex, in March 1703 and baptized there on 16 March. He was the son of Edward Ewer, who came from a whig Hertfordshire family distantly connected with Lord Shaftesbury and the duke of Rutland, and his wife,

Susannah. Ewer was educated at Eton College, where he was elected as a king's scholar in 1716, and proceeded to King's College, Cambridge, in 1723. He graduated BA in 1728, MA in 1732, and DD in 1756; he was elected to a fellowship in 1727 but in 1756 failed in a bid for the provostship as the duke of Newcastle's candidate. In June 1728 he returned briefly, as an assistant master, to Eton where he was tutor to the marquess of Granby. His reward for this service came in 1735 with his presentation to the living of Bottesford, the church being the closest to the Manners's seat at Belvoir Castle. He was ordained priest on 1 June 1735. In 1738 the duke of Rutland obtained a canonry of Winchester for Ewer, though Ewer's attempt to gain the income from the preceding vacancy in the canonry failed. In 1741 Ewer accompanied Lord Granby on the grand tour, which included Europe and Asia Minor. In September 1743 Ewer married Elizabeth, daughter of Thomas Barnardiston of Suffolk; they had two daughters.

In 1749 Ewer was presented to the living of Dengie, Essex, and in 1751 to that of West Ilsley, Berkshire; later that year he was collated to the prebend of Moreton-cum-Whaddon in Hereford Cathedral. In January 1761 the duke of Rutland unsuccessfully sought the vacant bishopric of St David's for Ewer. However later that year Ewer was nominated to the see of Llandaff, though he may have delayed his consecration in the hope of a better appointment. He was consecrated at Lambeth on 13 September 1761 by Archbishop Thomas Secker and other bishops. He was permitted to retain his living of West Ilsley and his canonry of Windsor *in commendam*. In the absence of an episcopal residence at Llandaff he lived principally in Berkshire. Ewer's primary visitation at Llandaff was held in 1763 and a further visitation in 1768. It was during Ewer's episcopate that the cathedral choir was repaired. On 20 December 1769 he was translated to Bangor, where he held a visitation in 1771, taking care to send out visitation questions in English and in Welsh. He died on 28 October 1774 at his home near Worcester. He was survived by his wife and one of his daughters, Margaret Frances. Two years later his large library was sold in London.

Ewer's published sermons include those delivered on 12 March 1762, before the House of Lords, and on 10 April 1766, before the president and governors of the London Hospital at Whitechapel. His third published sermon, before the Society for the Propagation of the Gospel in Foreign Parts at St Mary-le-Bow on 20 February 1767, sparked a major controversy; one historian has claimed that 'no Anglican prelate of the eighteenth century committed as great an indiscretion' (Bridenbaugh, 293). Ewer attacked the 'scandalous neglect' of the American colonies by the government in denying them a resident episcopate. He also argued that the British had placed the American colonies under the great burden of having to travel to England for ordinations. Ewer was as firm in condemning the colonists for failing to use episcopally ordained ministers and claimed that this was contrary to the royal charter of those colonies. Bishop Warburton was to repeat Ewer's claims some months later. Ewer's sermon

was attacked in the *St James's Chronicle* and the *London Chronicle*. The pamphlet war that followed, in both England and America, focused on whether Anglican episcopacy would be a benefit or a hindrance for American colonists. Those colonists who rejected Ewer's arguments included John Devotion, who termed them 'Llandaff's Whines', and William Livingstone, who viewed Ewer as a 'haughty prelate'. The significance of Ewer's sermon was that it formed part of the growing unease at British policy towards the American colonies among the Anglican episcopate. WILLIAM GIBSON

Sources Venn, *Alum. Cant.* · J. N. Dalton, ed., *The manuscripts of St George's Chapel, Windsor Castle* (1957) · *The manuscripts of his grace the duke of Rutland*, 4 vols., HMC, 24 (1888–1905), vol. 2 · W. Stubbs, *Registrum sacrum Anglicanum* (1858) · Nichols, *Lit. anecdotes* · J. R. Guy, *The diocese of Llandaff in 1763* (1991) · N. Sykes, *Church and state in England in the XVIII century* (1934) · J. Ewer, *A sermon preached before the Incorporated Society for the Propagation of the Gospel in Foreign Parts at the Anniversary Meeting … St Mary le Bow … 20 February 1767* (1767) · C. Bridenbaugh, *Mitre and sceptre: transatlantic faiths, ideas, personalities, and politics, 1689–1775* (1962) · D. A. Winstanley, *The University of Cambridge in the eighteenth century* (1922) · GM, 1st ser., 44 (1774) · M. L. Clarke, *Bangor Cathedral* (1969) · will, PRO, PROB 11/1003, fols. 14r–15r

Wealth at death over £500; £100 p.a. to his widow; also library sold by beneficiaries: will, PRO, PROB 11/1003, fols. 14r–15r

Ewer, William Norman (1885–1977), journalist, was born at Hornsey, London, on 22 October 1885, the only son of William Thomas Ewer, silk merchant, and his wife, Julia Stone. Scholarships took Ewer to Merchant Taylors' School, London, and Trinity College, Cambridge, where in 1907 he took a middle first in the mathematical tripos—he was classed as fifteenth wrangler out of thirty-one. He won the members' English prize in 1908 and in the same year took a first in part two of the history tripos.

Ewer's eye was on the civil service but he became secretary to the future Liberal MP for West Ham, Baron M. A. de Forest, who used his Austrian title in Britain by royal licence, yet was a radical. Thus Ewer met George Lansbury, MP for the adjoining constituency. In 1912 Lansbury became one of the founders of the *Daily Herald* and recruited Ewer as one of 'Lansbury's lambs', a brilliant flock that included G. D. H. Cole, Francis Meynell, Harold Laski, Gerald Gould, and William Mellor. The paper had no central policy; yet it was usually opposed to the official policy of the labour movement, preached syndicalism, backed every strike, encouraged the suffragettes in their law breaking militancy, and rejoiced over the two Russian revolutions.

In 1914 the *Herald* was reduced to a weekly for the duration of the war and in 1916 Ewer, a political conscientious objector (like several of his colleagues) was drafted to Cliveden to tend the pigs of W. W. Astor. In 1919, when the *Herald* resumed daily publication, Ewer became foreign editor and went to the Paris peace conference. For the next thirty years he was to attend every great international conference. He was a bitter critic of the Versailles treaty; he exposed more than once the inadequacies of the blue book which described events in the days leading up to the war; and he told the Foreign Office on the day of its publication that the Zinoviev letter was a forgery.

When the *Herald* was taken over by the Trades Union Congress and the Labour Party in 1922 it lost much of its gaiety, *élan*, and incompetence. Most of the lambs wandered away but Ewer stayed on, although he was a member of the Communist Party and was to remain so until 1929. In that year he wrote an article for the communist *Labour Monthly*, an intellectual review of which he was joint founder. Ewer suggested that Anglo-Russian problems were not wholly ideological but derived also from the two countries' old rivalries as Asiatic powers. Next month the editor, R. Palme Dutt, who had been away, denounced Ewer's piece as being 'in glaring contradiction to the line of the *Labour Monthly* and of the revolutionary working class'. The political bureau also repudiated the article, and Ewer was expelled from the party. He was eventually to become the holder of orthodox Labour views and a resolute anti-communist.

To generations of journalists Ewer was known as Trilby, a nickname given to him in youth because, like the heroine of George Du Maurier, he liked to go barefoot. Ewer is remembered for a laconic quatrain, famous throughout the English-speaking world. In the 1920s a guest at the Savage Club asked Benno Moisewitsch if there was any anti-semitism in the club. 'Only among the Jews', the Jewish pianist answered, and Ewer spontaneously murmured:

How odd
Of God
To choose
The Jews.

The *Oxford Dictionary of Quotations* also gives the lines ending each stanza of his 'Five Souls' (1917), often recited at pacifist meetings:

I gave my life for freedom—this I know:
For those who bade me fight had told me so.

In his late seventies, as the doyen of diplomatic correspondents, Ewer remained an upright, sturdy figure, distinguished by his white head, sceptical, penetrating eye, and a well-modulated bass voice. His pieces for the *Herald* were models of clarity and concision, and the BBC Overseas Service gave him frequent opportunities to express himself at adequate length. It was to the amiable Trilby that young journalists would turn to interpret for them the contrived circumlocutions of Foreign Office spokesmen, and they found it hard to believe that this urbane and companionable man had once belonged to the far and fiery left. When he was appointed CBE in 1959 stories were retold of the way he had rebuked Mussolini for an anti-British remark, and silenced even Vishinsky at a Moscow press conference.

Ewer retired, aged seventy-nine, in 1964, as the *Herald* was transformed into *The Sun*. That year his wife, Monica, whom he had married in 1912, died. She was daughter of William Marcus *Thompson, who had edited the radical *Reynolds's Newspaper*. She wrote fifty romantic novels and countless articles. They had one son, Denis William Ewer, who became professor of zoology at the University of

Ghana and a fellow of the Royal Society of South Africa. Ewer died on 25 January 1977 at Great Missenden, Buckinghamshire. JOHN BEAVAN, *rev.*

Sources personal knowledge (1986) · private information (1986) [D. W. Ewer, W. Forrest, A. Wykes] · *The Times* (31 Jan 1977) · *The Times* (7 Feb 1977) · *Daily Herald* · *Daily Worker* · People's History Museum, Manchester, Communist Party archive · G. Lansbury, *The miracle of Fleet Street* (1925) · R. Postgate, *The life of George Lansbury* (1951) · F. Williams, *Dangerous estate: the anatomy of newspapers* (1957) · *CGPLA Eng. & Wales* (1977)
Wealth at death £34,164: administration, 21 April 1977, *CGPLA Eng. & Wales*

Ewin, William Howell (*bap.* 1731, *d.* 1804), usurer, was born in Cambridge, where he was baptized on 3 February 1731 at St Sepulchre's. He was the son of Thomas Ewin, formerly a grocer, and later a brewer in partnership with a Mr Sparks, and Susanna, *née* Howell, the daughter of a Cambridge coal merchant. He had a sister named Sarah. He was educated at St John's College, Cambridge, which he entered on 15 March 1749, and graduated BA in 1753, MA in 1756, and LLD on 11 June 1766. He is said to have received a diploma of LLD from Edinburgh in or about 1778, but his name does not occur in the 1858 catalogue of graduates. At the death of his father Ewin inherited his share of the brewing business and a substantial fortune, which he largely increased by private usury. He joined the commission of the peace for the town and county of Cambridge, and in 1769, along with his former college tutor, William Samuel Powell, delayed the implementation of an act for better paving, lighting, and public order in the town. The antiquarian William Cole wrote:

My friend, Dr. Ewin, by being much of his father's turn, busy and meddling in other people's concerns, got the ill will of most persons in the town and university. ... The gownsmen bore him a particular grudge for interfering much in their affairs. ... They often broke the doctor's windows, as they said he had been caught listening on their staircases and doors. ... Dr. Ewin, as did his father, squinted very much

which resulted in him receiving the nickname of Dr Squintum (BL, Add. MS 5804, fol. 68*b*).

In January 1777 it was reported that Ewin had loaned money to William Bird, a scholar at Trinity College, at a high rate of interest. Between 1775 and 1776 Bird, then a minor without a father, had been lent £750 and was required to repay Ewin a total of £1090; failure to do so had led to Bird's imprisonment in a sponging-house for debtors. This 'usurious affair', as Cole terms it, came to light at a very unlucky time, for Ewin had been promised the chancellorship of the diocese of Ely, which was to fall vacant in the following May. However, eighteen months elapsed before the university took action. The trial took place at the vice-chancellor's court on 14 October 1778, and on 21 October Ewin was sentenced to be suspended from all degrees taken, or to be taken, and expelled from the university. The delegates on his appeal confirmed the suspension, but revoked the expulsion. He thereupon applied to the court of king's bench for a mandamus to restore him to his degrees. After lengthy discussions the court awarded the writ in June 1779, on the ground that, as no university statute expressly forbade usury or the lending of money to minors, the vice-chancellor's court had no jurisdiction in the case. Lord Mansfield, however, censured Ewin's conduct in the strongest terms, and stigmatized him as 'a corrupter of youth and an usurer'. He suggested that Ewin be removed from the commission of the peace and that a statute should be passed to meet such cases in the future (Cooper, 4.388–9, 392). On 20 October 1779 Ewin was restored to his degree of LLD, but two years later was dismissed from the county commission.

Eventually Ewin settled at Brentford where, according to his obituary, 'his strict attention to the administration of parochial concerns' and his readiness to 'condemn every species of idleness and imposition, created him many enemies, particularly among the lower orders of people' (*GM*). He died at Brentford Butts on 20 or 29 December 1804, aged seventy-three, and was buried in the chapel of New Brentford, with a monument by John Flaxman. He is thought to have left property amounting to over £100,000 to his sister Sarah, who died in 1808.

GORDON GOODWIN, rev. HEATHER SHORE

Sources R. F. Scott, ed., *Admissions to the College of St John the Evangelist in the University of Cambridge*, 3: *July 1715 – November 1767* (1903) · Nichols, *Lit. anecdotes* · C. H. Cooper and J. W. Cooper, *Annals of Cambridge*, 5 vols. (1842–1908) · D. Lysons, *The environs of London*, 4 vols. (1792–6) · *GM*, 1st ser., 74 (1804), 1174 · BL, Add. MS 5804, fol. 68b
Likenesses print, 1773
Wealth at death over £100,000: *GM*

Ewing, Alexander (1814–1873), Scottish Episcopal bishop of Argyll and the Isles, was born in Aberdeen on 25 March 1814, the eldest of the two sons and one daughter of John Ewing, advocate in Aberdeen, from Loch Lomond, and his wife, Elspet Aitken. After their parents' early deaths, the children were cared for by an uncle. Alexander developed an early love of poetry and languages. He was educated at the Marischal College of Aberdeen and a private school in Chelsea, where he was deeply influenced by an evangelical schoolmaster. From 1831 until 1835 he attended classes at the University of Edinburgh. He was married in 1835 to Katherine Stewart (1816–1856), daughter of Major Ludovic Stewart of Pittyvaich, Banffshire: they had three sons and two daughters. Much of their early married life was spent in Italy because of Ewing's poor health. In 1838 he was ordained, returned to Italy, and then undertook charge of the Episcopal chapel in Forres for three years.

After his consecration as bishop of Argyll and the Isles in 1847 Ewing lived in Lochgilphead and struggled with the problems of his diocese, Calvinism in Scotland, and factional struggles in the Episcopal church. Most of his flock had been lost to emigration, but there were still 1500 in Appin, usually with no priest, and remnants elsewhere. Ewing founded the Highland and Islands Episcopal Fund to provide houses and books for his clergy and schoolteachers. But he failed to learn Gaelic, and he never managed to train enough priests who did. Taken together with his absences for reasons of health, Ewing's work as a bishop was not successful.

With regard to Italy, Ewing had hopes of providing espiscopacy to the Waldensians, but they did not want it, and his dream of a non-papal Catholicism in northern Italy came to nothing. With regard to Calvinism, Ewing had joined Thomas Erskine of Linlathen as early as 1836 in opposing predestination, and he later came close to a doctrine of universal salvation. It was thought that if Calvinism were undermined the presbyterian churches would give up their people to the Episcopal church; in fact the slow waning of Calvinism in the presbyterian fold took away the one advantage the Episcopalians possessed, and doomed them to irrelevance.

Factionalism in the Episcopal church centred on doctrines of the eucharist. Ewing's own views tended almost to the receptionist interpretation; he had been abroad during the key years of the Catholic revival, was unmoved by their sacramental doctrine, and resented an incursion of Oxford Movement clergy from England. The latter did in Scotland what they could not do in England, causing protestant zealots, whom Ewing also disliked, to oppose them with constant litigation. In 1858 Ewing wrote an open letter complaining of these controversies without which, 'at the time of the great Presbyterian disruption … we should have absorbed within our pale the bulk of the sober-minded and educated of Scotland'. Describing himself as the only bishop born, ordained, and consecrated in Scotland, Ewing none the less found a solution to the troubles of the Episcopal church in its future alignment with, or incorporation into, the Church of England. There its tumult would be more easily contained, and the trouble-making English clergy would go home. Ewing furthered his scheme by his opposition to the use of the Scottish liturgy and his assistance, with the archbishop of Canterbury and the bishops of London and Oxford, in the celebration of a Eucharist service at Westminster Abbey. But, since incorporation would have required parliamentary approval, and alignment not much less, the scheme was impractical, but it was typical of the man—a confirmed protestant whose love of the ancient Celtic church bred no interest in returning to its traditions.

Ewing's first wife died in 1856; he married his second wife, Alice Louisa, daughter of George Sholto Douglas, seventeenth earl of Morton, in 1862. They had one son. In his last years Ewing wintered in the warmth of Pollok House in Glasgow, still working with Erskine on theological projects. He died at Westmill rectory in Hertfordshire on 22 May 1873. His widow survived him until 1913. Perhaps the most interesting Scottish bishop of his day, he was remembered for his scholarship and his good nature, rather than for any accomplishment.

GAVIN WHITE, rev.

Sources A. J. Ross, *Memoir of Alexander Ewing, DCL, bishop of Argyll and the Isles* (1877) · Bishop of Argyll [A. Ewing], *A letter to the right reverend the primus of the Scottish Episcopal church from the bishop of Argyll* (1858)
Archives Argyll and Bute archives, private ledger, letters and papers, ref. EC1 · LPL, journal and papers, MS 1597 | BL, corresp. with W. E. Gladstone, Add. MS 44152 · LPL, corresp. with A. C. Tait

Wealth at death £6980 15s. 5d.: confirmation, 13 Oct 1873, NA Scot., SC 51/32/19/192–198

Ewing, Sir (James) Alfred (1855–1935), engineer and cryptographer, was born on 27 March 1855 at 109 Nethergate, Dundee, the youngest of the three sons of James Ewing (1810–1886), minister of St Andrew's Free Church, Dundee, and his wife, Marjory, eldest daughter of John Ferguson, a Glasgow solicitor. He was educated at the West End Academy and at Dundee high school. In 1871 he was awarded a school-leaver's scholarship that enabled him to read engineering at Edinburgh University, where he studied under H. C. Fleeming Jenkin and P. G. Tait, who both recognized his unusual ability. Jenkin was then engaged with Sir William Thomson in making and laying submarine telegraph cables for the Great Western Telegraph Company, and Jenkin arranged that Ewing should assist in this work during summer vacations. Ewing accepted this offer and carried out three successive cable-laying expeditions to Brazil and the River Plate, returning periodically to Edinburgh for the university teaching sessions. Consequently, he did not graduate until 1878.

In the same year, after briefly teaching engineering at the Watt Institute in Edinburgh, on Jenkin's recommendation Ewing was appointed professor of mechanical engineering and physics at the Imperial University of Tokyo for three, subsequently extended to five, years. In 1879, at the British legation in Tokyo, he married Annie Maria Thomasina Blackburn (1854–1909), daughter of Thomas Blackburn Washington, of Claymont, West Virginia, and a descendant of George Washington, who was visiting Japan with her stepfather, an American missionary. A son and daughter were born in Tokyo. In Japan Ewing investigated earthquakes, claiming later to have experienced 300 of them in just five years. In a specially built observatory he developed a new form of seismograph which allowed him to make a continuous record of the earth's movements. The results of his research, which was continued by his geological colleague John Milne, were first published in the *Memoirs* of the science department of the University of Tokyo in 1883, the year in which he was appointed professor of engineering in the newly endowed University College of Dundee. Here he completed experimental work on magnetism that he had also begun in Japan while teaching physics. In experiments on the effect of stress on metals, Ewing found that the thermoelectric effect lagged behind the applied stress. Further investigation showed that the phenomenon, which he termed hysteresis (from Greek, to be late), was general in mechanical and electrical systems where the behaviour of a body during the reversal of stress is different from its behaviour in the corresponding part during the increase of stress. In a careful study of magnetism in 1883, he showed that the work done in a cycle of magnetization and demagnetization of iron was proportional to the hysteresis loop. Ewing's work on hysteresis proved fundamental in understanding and preventing energy losses in transformers and electric motors.

In 1890 the professorship of mechanism and applied mechanics at Cambridge fell vacant, and on the advice of

Sir (James) Alfred Ewing (1855–1935), by Bassano, 1915

the electrical engineer John Hopkinson, Ewing successfully applied for the chair. In his inaugural lecture the following year Ewing stressed the need for laboratory training to stimulate students' interest and habits of observation and of independent thought, as well as to make the dry bones of science start into life. During his tenure the Cambridge engineering school grew at an almost embarrassing rate: the mechanical sciences tripos was instituted (1892); a laboratory was founded (1894); and in 1899 a wing was opened in memory of Hopkinson. Ewing did little research at Cambridge, though he found time to write textbooks—*The Steam Engine* (1894; 4th edn, 1926) and *The Strength of Materials* (1899)—and to give the Royal Society of Arts an original course of lectures on refrigeration in 1897; the latter was published as *The Mechanical Production of Cold* (1908). In 1898 Ewing became a fellow of King's College, Cambridge. He was offered, but refused, the post of director of the National Physical Laboratory in 1899.

In 1903 Ewing was called to a wider sphere of action. The Admiralty was about to introduce for naval officers a new scheme of education and training promoted by W. W. Palmer and Sir John Fisher, into which a large element of engineering knowledge was to be infused. Ewing accepted the post of director of naval education and threw himself into his new duties with characteristic enthusiasm. He organized a system of scientific and engineering training that was eminently practical and included much experimental work, preliminary to the exposition of theory. He directed the preparation of several textbooks for young officers, and continued to supervise the work of naval education until 1916. He was also a member of the Ordnance board from 1906 to 1908, when Sir Philip Watts was building dreadnoughts; and from 1903 to 1906 a member of the explosives committee which improved the quality and manufacture of cordite. Following the death of his first wife, in 1911 he married Ellen Lina, daughter of John *Hopkinson and sister of the engineer Bertram Hopkinson. They had one son and she outlived her husband.

On the outbreak of war in 1914 Ewing was asked by Rear-Admiral H. F. Oliver, then director of the intelligence division of the naval staff, to decipher some wireless 'intercepts' from German stations, there being no department to which to refer them. This was the beginning of 'Room 40' in the old buildings of the Admiralty, where the task of deciphering the German messages under Ewing's supervision was facilitated by the opportune discovery in 1914 of the highly confidential signal book of the German navy on the body of a drowned signalman from the *Magdeburg*. Ewing's cryptographic work led up to the great naval battles of Dogger Bank (1915) and Jutland (1916), the arrest of Roger Casement, the loss of his armament off Tralee, and the revelation of the Zimmermann telegrams that brought the United States of America into the war. In May 1916 Ewing was offered the principalship and vice-chancellorship of Edinburgh University. It was intended that he should continue to superintend Room 40, but he found after a year that the claims of Edinburgh were too demanding to make the double duty practicable or desirable. Nevertheless, he found time to compose a useful textbook, *Thermodynamics for Engineers* (1920). Under his headship, from 1916 to 1929, Edinburgh University passed through a period of development and expansion. When Ewing received the freedom of the city in 1929, the lord provost, Sir Alexander Stevenson, noted that since 1916 no fewer than thirteen new chairs had been established besides a number of lectureships; a new degree in commerce had come into being; and the degree of PhD instituted for postgraduate research. The increase in the number of teaching staff involved an extension scheme of new buildings, known as the King's Buildings, on a large area about a mile and a half from the Old College, where independent blocks were erected for chemistry and zoology while provision was made, and plans prepared, for geology and engineering. These were carried out after Ewing's resignation in 1929, when he retired to Cambridge, where he had been elected an honorary fellow of King's College in 1903.

Ewing was elected FRS in 1887 and was awarded a royal medal by the Royal Society for his magnetic research in 1895. He was elected FRS (Edinburgh) in 1878 and was president from 1924 to 1929. He was appointed CB in 1907 and KCB in 1911. He received the Japanese order of the Precious Treasure and honorary doctorates in science from the universities of Oxford, Cambridge, Durham, and Sheffield, and in law from Edinburgh, St Andrews, and Glasgow. He was awarded the Albert medal of the Royal Society of Arts in 1929. He was president of the British Association in 1932, and received the freedom of Dundee in 1933. He gave the James Forest lecture to the Institution of Civil

Engineers in 1899 and in 1928; the Rede lecture at Cambridge in 1904; the second Kelvin lecture to the Institution of Electrical Engineers in 1910; and the Hibbert lecture at Cambridge in 1933. He participated in innumerable committees dealing with engineering problems and the applications of science, including many connected with the Department of Scientific and Industrial Research, and the bridge stress committee, which he chaired from 1923 to 1928.

A keen walker and amateur astronomer, Ewing spent most of his holidays in Switzerland. Although his researches on hysteresis, seismography, thermodynamics, and refrigeration were important, and his cryptographic services were of vital significance during the First World War, his greatest influence was felt in establishing engineering education. Here his abilities as an admirable and efficient chairman and administrator with a persuasive tongue proved invaluable, while his textbooks moulded the thought of several generations of engineers. His involvement of Japanese students in research was also of considerable influence on the first generation of Japanese physicists.

In retirement Ewing became much concerned that human ethical development had failed to keep pace with advances in science and technology, and these concerns were reflected in his discursive *An Engineer's Outlook* (1933). He died of heart disease at his home, 5 Herschel Road, Cambridge, on 7 January 1935. A devout Christian all of his life, he left a sum of money for the maintenance of King's College chapel. The James Alfred Ewing medal for distinction in research was established by the Institution of Civil Engineers in his memory in 1938.

E. I. Carlyle, *rev.* W. H. Brock

Sources R. T. Glazebrook, *Obits. FRS*, 1 (1932–5), 475–92 · T. H. Beare and others, *Nature*, 135 (1935), 137–40 · E. Griffiths, 'Sir Alfred Ewing', *Proceedings of the Physical Society*, 47 (1935), 1135–6 · A. W. Ewing, *The man of Room 40: the life of Sir Alfred Ewing* (1939) · J. A. Ewing, *An engineer's outlook* (1933) · J. A. Ewing, *The university training of engineers* (1891) · S. Dostrovsky, 'Ewing, James Alfred', *DSB* · O. Checkland, *Britain's encounter with Meiji Japan, 1868–1912* (1989) · T. J. N. Hilken, *Engineering at Cambridge University, 1783–1965* (1967) · R. V. Jones, 'Alfred Ewing and "Room 40"', *Notes and Records of the Royal Society*, 34 (1979–80), 65–90

Archives Laing Art Gallery, Newcastle upon Tyne, report on the *Turbinia* · priv. coll., letters to Dundee Society of Engineers | NA Scot., corresp. with Arthur Balfour · NMM, letters to Sir Julian Corbett

Likenesses Bassano, photograph, 1915, NPG [*see illus.*] · D. G. Shields, oils, 1919, U. Cam., department of engineering · H. Lintott, oils, 1929, U. Edin. · W. Stoneman, photograph, 1931, NPG · C. Muirhead, bronze bust, probably priv. coll. · photographs, repro. in Ewing, *Man of Room 40*

Wealth at death £38,058 6s. 4d.: resworn probate, 15 Feb 1935, *CGPLA Eng. & Wales*

Ewing, Greville (1767–1841), Congregational minister, the youngest son of Alexander Ewing, a teacher of mathematics, and his wife, Jacobina, was born on 27 April 1767 in the parish of Old Greyfriars, Edinburgh. He studied with considerable distinction at the high school and university there, and then decided, much against his father's wishes, to prepare for the ministry of the Church of Scotland. He was ordained in 1793 as associate minister of Lady Glenorchy's Chapel, Edinburgh, where he soon acquired wide popularity as a preacher. Missions attracted much of Ewing's attention, and in 1796 he took an active part in the formation of the Edinburgh Missionary Society, becoming its first secretary. He was also co-founder of the *Missionary Magazine*, which he edited for three years from its foundation in 1796. When Robert Haldane of Airthrey planned a mission to India, Ewing was appointed to go out, but the directors of the East India Company refused to sanction the undertaking, and it was abandoned. His association with the Haldanes involved him in an itinerant mission during the winter of 1798 on behalf of the newly formed Society for Propagating the Gospel at Home, and subsequently in the establishment of preaching centres in many parts of Scotland.

Finding the Church of Scotland inflexible, Ewing resigned his ministry at Lady Glenorchy's Chapel in 1798 and left the church. In July 1799 he became minister of the Glasgow Tabernacle, which connection he retained until 1836. Ewing embraced Congregational principles wholeheartedly and engaged in disputes with the Haldanes over church order and baptism. He defended his position in print in 1807 and 1809, and published *An Essay on Baptism* in 1823.

Ewing assisted in the foundation of the Glasgow Theological Academy in 1809 and of the Congregational Union of Scotland in 1812. He remained a tutor at the academy until 1836, training the first generation of Scottish Congregational ministers in moderate Calvinism. He did much to promote the study of the Bible in the original languages, publishing in 1801 a Greek grammar and lexicon for students of the New Testament which ran to several editions. In 1821 he was awarded a DD by Princeton College, New Jersey.

Ewing married three times. His first wife, Anne Innes of Gifford, whom he married on 13 November 1794, died nine months later. In 1799 he married Janet Jamieson, who died on 18 January 1801, having borne a daughter, Ewing's only child. He married third, on 15 November 1802, Barbara, daughter of Sir James Maxwell, sixth baronet, of Pollok, and Frances Colquhoun; she died on 14 September 1828 as the result of an accident at the Falls of Clyde. Ewing published a memoir of her, which reached a second edition in 1829.

During the last few years of his life Ewing was in poor health, and had to discontinue his regular work. He died suddenly on 2 August 1841 in Glasgow, and was buried on 6 August at Eastwood.

W. G. BLAIKIE, rev. DAVID HUDDLESTON

Sources J. J. Matheson, *A memoir of Greville Ewing* (1843) • H. Escott, *A history of Scottish Congregationalism* (1960) • W. D. McNaughton, *The Scottish Congregational ministry, 1794–1993* (1993) • DSCHT
Likenesses J. Kay, etching, 1797, BM, NPG • H. Dawe, mezzotint, pubd 1826 (after J. Campbell), BM • J. Horsburgh, stipple and line engraving (after J. Graham, 1838), NPG; repro. in Matheson, *Memoir of Greville Ewing* • W. Ridley, stipple, BM, NPG; repro. in *Evangelical Magazine* (1804)

Ewing [*née* Gatty], **Juliana Horatia** (1841–1885), children's writer, was born in the vicarage at Ecclesfield, near Sheffield, on 3 August 1841, the second of eight children of Alfred *Gatty (1813–1903), Church of England clergyman, and his wife, Margaret *Gatty, *née* Scott (1809–1873). Educated primarily by her mother, Juliana (Julie) was the leader in the children's botanical, theatrical, and literary activities, and their chief story-teller. She was known as Aunt Judy not only to her family but to the readers of her mother's works: *Aunt Judy's Tales* (1859), *Aunt Judy's Letters* (1862), and *Aunt Judy's Magazine* (1866–82). In the parish as well as the vicarage, she and her three sisters were as good as curates—better, because unpaid—but she was enthusiastic in this work, and was responsible for establishing the Ecclesfield village library. Her first stories appeared in Charlotte Yonge's *Monthly Packet*, and in book form in 1862 (*Melchior's Dream and other Tales*). Apart from one youthful Gothic tale, she concentrated her professionalism and perfectionism on children's stories and verse, eventually making an eighteen-volume SPCK series. Most of her work appeared first in *Aunt Judy's Magazine*. After their mother's death, she and her sister Horatia assumed the editorship, but after two years her sister continued as sole editor.

In 1866, Juliana Gatty renewed acquaintance with Major Alexander (Rex) Ewing (1830–1895) of the army pay department. His church connections, talents, and tastes suited a family where books, music, and animals were abundant, but his financial prospects were poor, and she was deemed too delicate for army life. Despite initial discouragement, they married with the Gattys' blessing on 1 June 1867, and embarked within days for Canada. They spent two years in Fredericton, New Brunswick, as the colony adjusted to its new status as part of the Canadian confederation. Juliana Ewing's reassuring letters home are full of lively details and sketches; she and her husband were a happy couple, sharing many interests. They studied with John Medley, the bishop, and were stalwarts of the cathedral, where her husband played the organ and composed hymns. Juliana Ewing continued to contribute to *Aunt Judy's Magazine*, concluding *Mrs. Overtheway's Remembrances* (1866–8; 1869) from Canada, and sending the first of a series of *Old-Fashioned Fairy-Tales* (1869–76; 1882), in emulation of the oral folk-tale. Only when they were ordered home did her homesickness become evident, and their return to Ecclesfield, accompanied by a rescued dog and innumerable botanical specimens, was a triumphal occasion.

Alexander Ewing was posted next to Aldershot, where they lived very happily until 1877, although Ethel Smyth's impressions of Juliana at this time are not entirely sympathetic. Her admiration for military life grew, although it was never wholly uncritical; 'Jackanapes' (1869; 1883) celebrated military honour in the face of a civilian standard of judgement she thought increasingly material and commercial. 'The Story of a Short Life' (1882; 1885) similarly presented a military ethos as a source of great strength and goodness. In addition to short stories, the Aldershot years saw three longer works: *A Flat-Iron for a Farthing* (1870–71; 1872), *Six to Sixteen* (1872; 1875), and *Jan of the*

Juliana Horatia Ewing (1841–1885), by Frederick Hollyer

she republished poems in illustrated shilling books. Herself a talented visual artist, she habitually took great pains in discussions with her illustrators, among them George Cruikshank and Randolph Caldecott.

Alexander Ewing returned in 1883, and they settled outside Taunton in Somerset, where Juliana Ewing established a garden and wrote *Mary's Meadow* (1883–4; 1886) and letters on gardening for *Aunt Judy*. Her 'neuralgia' (probably cancer) grew worse; she went to Bath, underwent two operations, and died there on 13 May 1885. Her grave in the Trull churchyard, near Taunton, where she was buried on 16 May, was so heaped with flowers from admirers that no soil was visible. Realistic and rarely oversentimental, her books were greatly admired by E. Nesbit, and they retain their attraction for the reader who appreciates humour, country life, happy but interesting families, and a sensibility distinctly but not dismally Victorian.   SUSAN DRAIN

Sources H. K. F. Eden, *Juliana Horatia Ewing and her books* (1885) · C. Maxwell, *Mrs Gatty and Mrs Ewing* (1949) · *Canada home: Juliana Horatia Ewing's Fredericton letters, 1867–1869*, ed. M. H. Blom and T. E. Blom (1983) · G. Avery, *Mrs Ewing* (1961) · M. Laski, *Mrs Ewing, Mrs Molesworth, and Mrs Hodgson Burnett* (1950) · C. Mills, 'Choosing a way of life: *Eight cousins* and *Six to sixteen*', *Children's Literature Association Quarterly*, 14/2 (1989), 71–5 · D. E. Hall, 'We and the world: Juliana Horatia Ewing and Victorian colonialism for children', *Children's Literature Association Quarterly*, 16/2 (1991), 51–5 · J. Plotz, 'A Victorian comfort book: Juliana Ewing's *The story of a short life*', ed. J. H. McGarran, *Romanticism and children's literature in nineteenth-century England* (1991), 168–89 · *CGPLA Eng. & Wales* (1885)

Archives Sheff. Arch., corresp., diaries, commonplace book, and MSS | U. Reading L., letters to George Bell & Sons Ltd, publishers

Likenesses F. Hollyer, photograph, National Museum of Photograph, Film and Television, Bradford, Royal Photographic Society collection [*see illus.*] · F. Largs, photograph, repro. in Eden, *Juliana Horatia Ewing* · photograph, repro. in Maxwell, *Mrs Gatty and Mrs Ewing*

Wealth at death £3015 0s. 10d.: probate, 21 Sept 1885, *CGPLA Eng. & Wales*

Windmill (1872–3; 1876). The second of these, a novel about an orphan girl growing up, Rudyard Kipling claimed to have known almost by heart. It drew upon her husband's knowledge of India, and her own early memories of her Ecclesfield home.

Juliana Ewing's Anglican faith and practice were a source of great strength to her; unlike her mother, she felt no need to preach it explicitly, though the values of service, self-denial, and generosity are frequent themes in such stories as 'The Brownies' (1865), 'Lob-Lie-by-the-Fire' (1874), and 'Madam Liberality' (1873). The Baden-Powells borrowed the idea of the brownies for the younger branch of the Girl Guides; in the person of Madam Liberality her family recognized Julie herself.

After Aldershot, the Ewings entered an unsettled period, living briefly near Manchester and York, before Alexander Ewing was posted to Malta in 1879. Despite ill health, Juliana planned to follow in the autumn, but got no further than Paris before breaking down. She returned to England, where she stayed with relatives and friends, hoping for better health. William Jenner diagnosed neuralgia of the spine; she continued to be unable to travel, and frequently exhausted herself with work. Her husband was posted to Ceylon in 1881, and his remittances to his wife were often insufficient. Disappointed that she made so little from her books, she almost took Ruskin's advice to declare herself independent of a commercial publisher, but she gave *Daddy Darwin's Dovecote* (1881; 1884) to Bell as usual. In an attempt to reach a broader audience,

Ewins, Arthur James (1882–1957), chemist, was born on 3 February 1882, in Norwood, London, the elder son of Joseph Ewins, a railway platelayer on the South Eastern Railway, and his wife, Sophia Wickham. He won a scholarship to the Alleyn's School where he received a better grounding in the basic natural sciences than was then available to most schoolboys. In 1899, with others from the same school, he entered the Wellcome Physiological Research Laboratories as a research assistant. These laboratories had recently been established by Henry Wellcome to produce remedies such as the recently discovered serum antitoxins, in conditions that also provided facilities for their proper control and development. The Wellcome laboratories also provided opportunities for research in a wide range of therapeutic sciences including biochemistry and pharmacology.

Ewins worked there initially as an assistant to John Mellanby, then, for a further and longer period, as assistant to George Barger. He had the opportunity of co-operating intimately in a wide variety of research problems in biological, organic, and pharmaceutical chemistry. Many publications between 1905 and 1911 bore the names of

Ewins and Barger, and their close association extended to other work published by Barger alone, or by Barger and H. H. Dale, who had joined the Wellcome laboratories in 1904 and was later to become their director. When Barger left the laboratories for an academic appointment in 1909, Ewins, who had graduated BSc in 1906 by taking evening classes at the University of London, was appointed to succeed him as head of the chemical division; thereafter his researches were largely associated with those of Dale and P. P. Laidlaw. Work with Barger had been largely concerned with the activities and chemistry of ergot of rye—its specific alkaloids, and the series of putrefactive amines found in extracts prepared from it. In co-operation with Laidlaw, Ewins found and synthesized, from tryptophan, another member of this series of amines, 3-β-aminoethylindole, a close relative of the now widely investigated serotonin (5-hydroxy-tryptamine). Then in 1914, from an extract of ergot in which a peculiarly unusual and intense activity had been observed, Ewins isolated the responsible constituent and found it to be acetylcholine. Subsequently acetylcholine was found to be of considerable physiological interest, as its transmitter functions, at ganglionic and some end-organ sites in the autonomic nervous system, and neuro-effector junctions in the peripheral nervous system, were increasingly recognized. Further study of the actions of acetylcholine enabled Ewins to remove a long-standing puzzle from pharmacology, by showing that the so-called 'artificial muscarine' was a nitrous acid ester of choline.

In 1914 Ewins moved with Dale from the Wellcome laboratories as a member of the staff of the newly created National Institute for Medical Research of the Medical Research Council. Almost immediately the outbreak of war diverted them from their research plans; Ewins became Dale's principal colleague in the creation and application of new standards for the safety and efficacy of supplies of essential remedies such as Salvarsan, prepared on an emergency basis by manufacturers in Britain and allied countries to replace those from Germany. This responsible work brought Ewins into contact with the directorate of Messrs May and Baker who, in 1917, offered him the position as director of their research department.

The rest of Ewins's working life was spent in their service. Until his retirement in 1952 there were few scientific publications bearing his name among those issued from the laboratories he directed. His own essential part, however, in the initiative and enterprise which they represented, was explicitly recognized by the members of his scientific staff, and was well known to the many others with whom he shared interests and retained friendly contacts. He never had the urge of the academic scientist to penetrate to the theoretical roots of a problem, or into essentially new territory. On the other hand, he showed, in this major part of his career, a remarkable ability to recognize and exploit the practical possibilities of therapeutic developments. He and his team were the first, for example, to develop the chemotherapeutic possibilities of the anti-protozoal agents, the diamidines, which Harold King and Warrington Yorke had discovered. This work rapidly led to Pentamide, a drug which gave protection against sleeping sickness. When, from 1935 onwards, the anti-streptococcal action of Prontosil had been discovered by G. Domagk, and that of its sulphanilamide moiety by Tréfouël, D. Bovet, and F. Nitti, it was Ewins and his collaborators, again, who recognized the chemotherapeutic possibilities for bacterial infections and produced the first derivative with a more potent and specific action, Sulphapyridine. This was first issued as 'M & B 693', and radically improved the prospect of sufferers from pneumococcal pneumonia, among them Winston Churchill during the Second World War. A wartime acknowledgement by Churchill to 'M & B' was wittily associated with his doctors, Moran and Bedford, but also served to bring the pharmaceutical company to popular attention. Ewins's most important service to the progress of medicinal chemistry, in this country and in the world at large, was in the practical development of researches on the chemotherapy of infections. His work was recognized by the award of a DSc from the University of London in 1914 and he was elected FRS in 1943.

Ewins married in 1905 Ada Amelia, daughter of James Webb, an inspector of weights and measures; they had one son and one daughter. He died at Springfield House, Kempston, Bedfordshire, on 24 December 1957.

H. H. DALE, rev. E. M. TANSEY

Sources H. H. Dale, *Memoirs FRS*, 4 (1958), 81–91 · *Chemistry and Industry* (22 Feb 1958), 224–5 · J. Slinn, *A history of May & Baker, 1834–1984* (1984) · E. M. Tansey, 'Sir Henry Dale and autopharmacology: the role of acetylcholine in neurotransmission', *Essays in the history of the physiological sciences*, ed. C. Debru (1995), 180–93 · E. M. Tansey, 'Chemical neurotransmission in the autonomic nervous system: Sir Henry Dale and the discovery of acetylcholine', *Clinical Autonomic Research*, 1 (1991), 63–72 · *The Times* (30 Dec 1957) · *CGPLA Eng. & Wales* (1958)

Archives GlaxoSmithKline, Greenford, Middlesex, letters · May and Baker archives, papers · National Institute for Medical Research, London, corresp. · PRO, Medical Research Council archives, corresp. | RS, Dale MSS, corresp.

Likenesses W. Stoneman, photograph, 1954, NPG · group portrait, photograph, Wellcome L. · photograph, repro. in Dale, *Memoirs FRS* · photographs, repro. in Slinn, *History of May and Baker*

Wealth at death £16,422 1s. 6d.: probate, 2 April 1958, *CGPLA Eng. & Wales*

Eworth, Hans (d. 1574), painter, of Netherlandish origin, is first recorded as a freeman of the Antwerp guild of St Luke in 1540. He is listed there as Jan Eeuworts, and his name appears variously in other sources as Ewottes, Eywooddes, and even possibly Suete, among other forms. Probably attracted to England in the aftermath of the death of Hans Holbein, in 1543, he is first recorded in London in 1549. On 19 October 1550 he was granted letters of denization, and he is listed thereafter in various City parishes, the last being St Bride's, in the ward of Faringdon Without, where he was described in 1571 as 'Haunce Evance, pictorer, a denizen, borne in Anwarpe, came into the realm about xxviii yeres past, Douch' (Cust, 5). In 1572 he was brought in by the musician Alfonso Ferrabosco to design the tournament staged to greet the French embassy in June of that year. Payments indicate that he continued to be employed by the revels office for the next two years.

It is known that Eworth can be associated with a long series of signed pictures bearing the monogram 'HE'. In the eighteenth century this was wrongly equated with Lucas de Heere and it was only in 1913 that Lionel Cust made the connection with Eworth, thanks to his listing as a painter in the inventory made in 1590 of the pictures belonging to John, first Baron Lumley. Some twenty-five paintings have so far emerged either signed or as pendants to signed ones. About a dozen more are firmly attributable. The earliest, *A Turk on Horseback* (priv. coll.), is dated 1549 and the latest, *Allegory of the Wise and Foolish Virgins* (Statens Museum for Kunst, Copenhagen), 1570. Among them are subject pictures but in the main they are portraits, including a major group of Mary I, to whom Eworth acted as court painter, albeit without any official status. The most important of these is dated 1554 (Society of Antiquaries, London). Many but by no means all of his sitters were adherents of the old faith, including Mary Neville, Baroness Dacre (painted twice, 1559 and undated; NPG and National Gallery of Canada, Ottawa), Nicholas Heath, archbishop of York (1566; NPG), Anthony Browne, first Viscount Montague (1569; NPG), Henry Stewart, Lord Darnley, and his brother Charles, earl of Lennox (1562 and 1563; both Royal Collection), and Thomas Howard, fourth duke of Norfolk, with his second wife (1562 and 1563; both priv. coll.). It is noticeable that the young Elizabeth I did not sit for him; there was a sharp decline in royal portraiture during the 1560s.

Eworth was the most distinguished foreign painter to work in England in the Tudor period after Holbein. His portraiture, like Holbein's, is remarkable for its wide variation in scale and included miniatures; small-, two-thirds-, and life-scale; and embraced everything from head and shoulders to full-length. His style stemmed from that of Jan van Scorel, using a strong, three-dimensional rendering of the features, and modified by late Holbein with its concern for a dazzling and exact record of magnificent dress and jewels. His work has a high degree of finish and gloss. Although some of his portraits include backgrounds, particularly his early work, he gradually evolved a formula of placing the sitter against a plain ground upon which the shadow of the figure was cast and the age and date inserted in an idiosyncratic script. Fine examples of his work are in the National Portrait Gallery and the Tate Collection, London. Eworth died in 1574.

ROY STRONG, *rev.*

Sources R. Strong, 'Hans Eworth: a Tudor artist and his circle', *The Tudor and Stuart monarchy: pageantry, painting, iconography*, 1 (1995), 93–133 · R. Strong, 'Hans Eworth reconsidered', *The Tudor and Stuart monarchy: pageantry, painting, iconography*, 1 (1995), 135–45 · R. Strong, *The English icon: Elizabethan and Jacobean portraiture* (1969), 83–106 · S. Foister, 'Nobility restored', *Antique Collector*, 4 (1986), 58–60 · L. Cust, 'The painter HE', *Walpole Society*, 2 (1913), 5

Exeter. For this title name *see* Holland, John, first earl of Huntingdon and duke of Exeter (c.1352–1400); Beaufort, Thomas, duke of Exeter (1377?–1426); Holland, John, first duke of Exeter (1395–1447); Holland, Henry, second duke of Exeter (1430–1475); Courtenay, Henry, marquess of Exeter (1498/9–1538); Courtenay, Gertrude, marchioness of Exeter (d. 1558); Cecil, Thomas, first earl of Exeter (1542–1623); Cecil, Frances, countess of Exeter (1580–1663); Cecil, David George Brownlow, sixth marquess of Exeter (1905–1981).

Exeter [Canterbury], **Joseph of** (*fl. c.*1180–1194), poet, appears to have been one of those rare figures of lowly origins whose education and family connections brought him to some degree of temporary prominence in the second half of the twelfth century, when his uncle, Baldwin of Forde, became archbishop of Canterbury in 1185. Joseph is widely acclaimed as one of the best medieval Latin poets of the traditional school. John Leland claims to have seen a fragment of Joseph's lost epic *Antiocheis* at Abingdon, from which he learned that Joseph was born at Exeter; when specific, contemporary or near contemporary evidence gives Magister Joseph Anglicus or Joseph Cantuariensis. The latter name presumably originated in the period when Joseph was acting in some secretarial capacity to his uncle. He appears to have earned the title of *magister* just before 1188.

Although there is no evidence, it is reasonable to assume that Exeter was the place of Joseph's early education, probably due to the influence of Baldwin, who was archdeacon of Exeter before becoming abbot of the Cistercian abbey of Forde in Devon. The Exeter clergy were well known for their learning and literary activities. Joseph's letters to his friend and spiritual adviser, Guibert, abbot of Florennes from 1188 to 1194, and then of Gembloux, reveal that he then followed the pattern of most of his compatriots and continued his education in France, though he did not go to the more favoured schools of Orléans or Paris, but to Rheims, where the Exeter clergy had been offered refuge during the Becket controversy. While there he obviously took advantage of the good library and plentiful leisure time to write his epic on the Trojan War before presumably being called to Canterbury by his uncle. He had returned to Rheims to continue his studies in theology and canon law by 1189, when he complains of being short of money and books, but in the following year had to accompany Baldwin on the third crusade as official verse chronicler. In a letter to Guibert he reveals his lack of crusading fervour by expressing concern over his likely seasickness, the poor quality of the food he will have to endure, and the almost certain illnesses that will result. Baldwin's death in 1190 probably released Joseph from his crusading obligations, but perhaps lack of money or opportunity prevented him from returning immediately, because he did write his verse account of the crusade. The last extant reference to him is a letter of Guibert written in 1194 indicating that he was a teacher in Jodoigne (not Gueldres as often stated) in Belgium, but that he was still trying to continue his religious studies. Their correspondence indicates that Joseph had great difficulties for much of his life in devoting himself to the Christian life and even his teaching post in Jodoigne appears to have been in a school set up by the municipal authorities.

Joseph wrote in classical metre, in the style of Lucan. In fact his six-book poem on the Trojan War, which was known in his time as *Ylias* or *Ylias Daretis Phrygii*, was still thought to be a classical Latin poem as late as the seventeenth century. The title *De bello Trojano* or *Bellum Trojanum* is a sixteenth-century invention. The work is based on the pseudo-historical account of the war by Dares the Phrygian, and as such appears to be in the Rheims tradition of historical epics (comparable with, for instance, Gautier of Châtillon's *Alexandreis*). Joseph wrote it *c*.1180, and added short passages when he presumably thought them politically expedient; praise of Henry, the Young King, on his death in 1183, a dedication to Baldwin (soon after 1185), and reference to his role as chronicler of the forthcoming crusade (probably in 1189 or 1190). At least five manuscripts of the text, all from the thirteenth century, are extant: London, Westminster Abbey, MS 18; Cambridge, Corpus Christi College, MS 406; Bodl. Oxf., MS Digby 57; Admont Stiftsbibliothek, MS 128; Paris, Bibliothèque Nationale, MS Lat. 15015. A sixth manuscript, from the fourteenth century, is said to be in Italy. In the Paris and Admont manuscripts there are glosses whose material is partly the work of Joseph himself. These often cite variant readings not contained in extant manuscripts, and thus point to a somewhat larger diffusion of the text. Only fragments of his epic on the third crusade, *Antiocheis*, are extant, published by William Camden in his *Remaines* (1657). They concern Brutus and King Arthur. Other secular works attributed to Joseph appear to be due to John Bale's imagination. However, in his spiritual struggles Joseph turned to religious poetry, and there are five metrical poems on the theme of virginity and a rhythmical sequence with two-syllable rhyme on the life of St Martin of Tours, to be found in some manuscripts of Guibert's collected correspondence.   KEITH BATE

Sources *Joseph Iscanus: Werke und Briefe*, ed. L. Gompf (1970) · Joseph of Exeter, *Trojan War, I–III*, ed. and trans. A. K. Bate (1986) · G. Riddehough, 'Joseph of Exeter: a forgotten poet', *Journal of English and Germanic Philology*, 46 (1947), 254–9 · A. K. Bate, 'Joseph of Exeter, religious poet', *Medium Aevum*, 40 (1971), 222–9 · *The historical works of Gervase of Canterbury*, ed. W. Stubbs, 2 vols., Rolls Series, 73 (1879–80)
Archives Admont Stiftsbibliothek, MS 128 · Bibliothèque Nationale, Paris, MS lat. 15015 · Bodl. Oxf., Digby MS 57 · CCC Cam., MS 406 · Westminster Abbey, MS 18

Exeter, Stephen of (*b*. 1246, *d*. in or after **1275**?), annalist, is the presumed author of the work known as *Annales domus Montis Fernandi ab anno XLV usque ad annum MCCLXXIV*, the annals of Multyfarnham. The original manuscript is in Trinity College, Dublin. According to the annals, Stephen was born in 1246, and entered the religious life in 1263; the mendicant entries of that period indicate that he joined the Franciscan order. He was probably a member of the family of Richard of Exeter, justiciar of Ireland, who is mentioned eight times in the annals (these include his three marriages, the birth of his son John, and his assumption of the position of justiciar of Ireland). The only association with Multyfarnham (Westmeath) is that, according to James Ware, the manuscript may have been in the library of Sir Francis Shane, who sacked the friary there in

1601. The annals expand after 1261 and internal evidence suggests a date of composition of 1272–4 and a Connacht origin. An explanation for the cessation of the annals in 1274 may be that the author was absent from the country; in 1274–5 a Franciscan friar, Stephen of Exeter, was sent by the justiciar of Ireland, Geoffrey de Geneville, to the king to report on the state of Ireland. He returned to Ireland in 1275; it is not known when he died.

      BERNADETTE A. WILLIAMS

Sources TCD, MS 347 · Bodl. Oxf., MS Rawl. B. 496, fols. 32*r*, 41*v* · Bodl. Oxf., MS Misc. 614, fol. 113 · BL, MS Add. 4789, fol. 136*r* · A. Smith, ed., 'Annales de Monte Fernandi / Annals of Multifernan', *Tracts relating to Ireland*, Irish Archaeological Society, 2/2 (1842), 15 · G. O. Sayles, ed., *Documents on the affairs of Ireland before the king's council*, IMC (1979), 8 · H. S. Sweetman and G. F. Handcock, eds., *Calendar of documents relating to Ireland*, 5 vols., PRO (1875–86), vol. 3, pp. 81, 105 · H. Walton, 'The English in Connacht, 1171–1333', PhD diss., University of Dublin, 1980 · K. Simms, 'The O'Hanlons, the O'Neills and the Anglo-Normans in thirteenth century Armagh', *Seanchus Ard Mhacha*, 9 (1978–9), 70–94 · D. Mooney [D. Moneyus], 'Brussels MS 3947. De provincia Hiberniae s. Francisci', ed. B. Jennings, *Analecta Hibernica*, 6 (1934), 12–138, esp. 92–100
Archives TCD, MS 347

Exeter, Walter of (*supp. fl.* 1301), supposed writer, is said by the sixteenth-century bibliographer John Bale to have written a 'Life of Guy, earl of Warwick', in 1301 at the instance of one Baldwin, a citizen of Exeter. Bale saw this work, which does not survive, in the bookshop of Gerbrand Harkes in Oxford. It is likely to have been a version of the medieval romance of *Guy of Warwick. Bale conjectures that Walter was a mendicant friar, though he gives the place at which Walter wrote his work as St Caroc, Cornwall, which was in fact a cell of the Cluniac house of Montacute, Somerset. Another Walter of Exeter listed by Bale is a ghost, created by Henry Kirkestede by misreading a reference to Walter Map, archdeacon of Oxford, in a copy of Higden's *Polychronicon*.   MARIOS COSTAMBEYS

Sources R. Sharpe, *A handlist of the Latin writers of Great Britain and Ireland before 1540* (1997)

Exeter, William of (*fl. c.*1200). *See under* Exeter, William (*d.* 1359).

Exeter [Newetone], **William** (*d.* 1359), physician and theologian, probably came from Newton Abbot, Devon, but nothing is known of him before 28 July 1318, when he was provided to the rectory of Stoke in Teignhead, Devon, at the request of Walter Stapeldon, bishop of Exeter (*d.* 1326), except that he had already studied arts at Oxford. He was MA by 1319 and proceeded to study medicine, becoming doctor of medicine by 1327, and of theology by 1336. He was a fellow student of John Grandison (*d.* 1369), later bishop of Exeter and his patron, while in 1327 he was one of the delegates of the university at the confirmation of the election of a new chancellor by the bishop of Lincoln. His determination against the views of William Ockham and other friars on church property was probably an Oxford theological lecture given in or shortly before 1336. However his real practice seems to have been medicine; he was a king's clerk, perhaps in that capacity, in 1330, and physician to Queen Philippa, the foremost patron of the profession, in 1336, still in 1344, and probably as late as 1354. Through her patronage and that of Edward III he was amply rewarded: canon of Exeter in 1331, canon and then subdean of York (1336–43); precentor, then chancellor of Lincoln (1337–44) and prebendary of North Kelsey (1337–59); and finally rector of Great Brington in Northamptonshire (1344–c.1359). Perhaps Exeter's vacation of his most lucrative benefices in the mid-1340s, closely followed by his acceptance of a rectory with cure of souls, marked a decision to retire from medical practice into the country; if so, he was disappointed, since Queen Philippa insisted on his presence for at least another five years, and probably for longer. He was also one of Edward III's representatives in a mission to Philippe VI of France in January 1340, and had protection for going overseas on his service on 16 January 1354. Presumably his connection with Queen Philippa explains his bequest of books to her college at Oxford in 1359, the year of his death.

The only literary evidence of Exeter's medical practice occurs in a remedy for deafness attributed to him in the fifteenth-century *Liber de diversis medicinis*, which used Oxford sources. Bale saw his *Determinatio contra Ockham et alios fratres pro ecclesiae proprietate* and another of his works, *De generatione Christi* at Queen's College, presumably his own copies; the *Determinatio* is extant in a Paris manuscript.

William Exeter the physician is not to be confused with the **William of Exeter** (*fl.* before 1220) who was author of a treatise on the eight beatitudes in a Laudian manuscript at Oxford (Bodl. Oxf., MS Laud misc. 368). This author, of whom nothing further is known, must have lived before *c.*1220, the date of the manuscript, and was possibly a monastic writer. JEREMY CATTO

Sources W. Exeter, 'Determinatio contra Ockham', Bibliothèque Nationale, Paris, MS Lat. 3183 · William of Exeter, 'Tractatus de octo beatitudinibus', Bodl. Oxf., MS Laud misc. 368 · *Liber de diversis medicinis*, ed. M. S. Ogden, EETS, old ser., 207 (1938) · F. C. Hingeston-Randolph, ed., *The register of Walter de Stapeldon, bishop of Exeter* (1892) · F. C. Hingeston-Randolph, ed., *The register of John de Grandisson, bishop of Exeter*, 3 vols. (1894–9) · W. H. Bliss, ed., *Calendar of entries in the papal registers relating to Great Britain and Ireland: petitions to the pope* (1896) · Bale, *Index*, 124 · F. Pelster, 'Ein Kontroverse zwischen englischen Dominikanern und Minoriten', *Archivum Fratrum Praedicatorum*, 3 (1933), 57–80 · Emden, *Oxf.*, 1.659–60 · C. H. Talbot and E. A. Hammond, *The medical practitioners in medieval England: a biographical register* (1965) · *Fasti Angl., 1300–1541*, [York] · *Fasti Angl., 1300–1541*, [Lincoln] · *Fasti Angl., 1300–1541*, [Exeter]

Archives Bodl. Oxf., MS Laud misc. 368 [William of Exeter]

Exley, Thomas (1775–1855), natural philosopher and scriptural commentator, was born in Gowdall, Yorkshire. Little is known of his first thirty years. He is sometimes described as an MA, but it is not known if he attended a university. However, it is certain that he maintained an interest in a wide spectrum of academic and literary disciplines, for in 1812 he co-authored, with the Revd William Moore Johnson, the four volume *Imperial encyclopaedia, or, Dictionary of the sciences and arts; comprehending also the whole circle of miscellaneous literature*. About the time of this publication Exley was employed as a mathematics instructor in a Bristol school, a situation he retained until his retirement in 1847. During the first half of his life he was also involved in a variety of theological disputes, especially concerning the eternal Sonship of Jesus. In 1817–18 he joined forces with his brother-in-law, Adam Clarke, to answer a number of pamphlets which maintained that even after his ascension into heaven, Jesus was not the equal of the Father.

Exley is best remembered for his controversial scientific speculations. As a natural philosopher he explicitly rejected the complex series of attractive and repulsive spheres which he insisted corrupted the matter theories of Newton and Boscovich, and instead proposed a system of subtle and gross particles for which there were no eighteenth-century precedents. This system was developed in many works, including his *Principles of Natural Philosophy* (1829) and his *New Theory of Physics* (1841). In particular he posited the existence of four types of matter: common or tenacious, electric, ethereal, and microgenic. He first proposed the existence of microgen, 'exceedingly small atoms', at the 1838 meeting of the British Association for the Advancement of Science. Although his account fared poorly in the philosophical market place, he contended that their presence could account for 'miasmata of marshes, infections, odiferous effluvia, and other phenomena' (Exley, 34), as well as animalcules and their ova.

Exley employed his conception of matter and forces to tackle a multitude of other problems in chemistry and optics. In chemistry he produced novel formulations of atomic combinations, gaseous vapours, and specific gravities. In addition, he exploited his conception of common matter, ether, and short-range attractive and repulsive forces in order to develop a sophisticated account of optical phenomena such as flexion, refraction, and polarization. In his *Physical Optics, or, The Phenomena of Optics Explained According to Mechanical Sciences* (1834) he supposed that light was caused by high-speed ether particles and, as one of the last supporters of the projectile theory of light, sided with David Brewster, Henry Brougham, Richard Potter, and John Barton against G. B. Airy, William Whewell, and John Herschel. However, Exley's explanations of optical phenomena met with vehement opposition. At the 1836 meeting of the British Association in Bristol he suffered an energetic assault by John Dalton, who ridiculed his explanation of the aurora borealis.

Exley was married, but the name of his wife is not known. A son, John Thomas, was admitted to St John's College, Cambridge, in 1834. Towards the end of his life Exley toiled hard to reconcile the latest scientific work with scripture. In 1844, the same year that Robert Chambers's *Vestiges of the Natural History of Creation* was published, Exley brought out his *Commentary on Genesis*, which attempted to elucidate the Mosaic account of creation and the tale of the deluge in terms of modern concepts such as the electric fluid and caloric. Returning to Hebrew texts, and utilizing his own conception of the ether, microgen, and recent geological facts, Exley developed astonishing explanations for the chaos, the creation of the animal kingdom, the flood, the Holy Ghost and God's superintending providence. Despite the remarkable nature of the narrative, little attention was paid to the text. Exley died at his home in Cotham Park Road, Bristol, on 17 February 1855 in relative obscurity. KEVIN C. KNOX

Sources G. Cantor, *Optics after Newton* (1983) · J. Morrell and A. Thackray, *Gentlemen of science: early years of the British Association for the Advancement of Science* (1981) · *Report of the British Association for the Advancement of Science* (1836–48) · Venn, *Alum. Cant.* · T. Exley, *A commentary on Genesis* (1844)
Likenesses I. Thompson, stipple, pubd 1819 (after Braithwaite), NPG

Exmew, William (*c*.1507–1535), Carthusian monk, was apparently born in London about 1507, probably the son of Sir Thomas Exmew, goldsmith, alderman of London from 1506 onwards and lord mayor in 1517, the year in which he was also knighted. After Sir Thomas's death, on 6 February 1529, his stepson, John West, a friar observant at Greenwich, wrote to Cardinal Wolsey concerning the estate of his mother, Lady Elizabeth Exmew, who had died on 14 February in the previous year. Exmew apparently studied at Christ's College, Cambridge, though no degree is recorded. Maurice Chauncy, a fellow monk of the London Charterhouse, who greatly admired Exmew, attests his competence in both Latin and Greek. An Elizabeth Exmew, who may have been William Exmew's sister, a Dominican nun at Dartford, remained faithful to her vocation even after the suppression, dying in a Dominican convent near Bruges as late as 6 February 1585. In 1522 Sir John Thurston, goldsmith and alderman of London, left W. Exmew the substantial legacy of £100.

The date of Exmew's entry into the London Charterhouse is unknown, but Bishop Cuthbert Tunstall's register records his ordination in 1529. Exmew was soon made vicar despite his youth, and acted also as confessor to his prior, John Houghton. Some time after 29 May 1534 he was appointed procurator in place of Humphrey Middlemore, who then became vicar. During Prior Houghton's imprisonment in the Tower for initially refusing the oath to the succession in 1534, and after the prior's martyrdom in 1535, the onus of running the house fell on the vicar and the procurator. The efforts of Cromwell's agent Thomas Bedyll to persuade Exmew, Middlemore, and Sebastian Newdigate to acknowledge Henry VIII as supreme head of the church in England, made on 4 May 1535, the very day of the martyrdom of Prior Houghton, were unsuccessful. On 25 May the three were summoned to Cromwell's house in Stepney and, after examination, were imprisoned, first, according to Chauncy, in the Marshalsea, then in the Tower, where they were chained upright, being offered only meat, which their rule forbade them to eat. After being tried at Westminster, they were hanged in their habits at Tyburn on 19 June 1535. All three were beatified in 1886. By a misunderstanding of the colophon (fol. 95*v*) to the copy which he made of *The Cloud of Unknowing*, which is today preserved at St Hugh's Charterhouse, Parkminster, William Exmew has sometimes been credited with the authorship of that anonymous fourteenth-century mystical treatise. JAMES HOGG

Sources register of Bishop Tunstall, 1522–30, GL, MS 9531/10 · *LP Henry VIII*, vols. 4/3, 7–8 · M. Chauncy, *Historia aliquot martyrum Anglorum maxime octodecim Cartusianorum sub Henrico octavo ob fidei confessionem et summi pontificis jura vindicanda interemptorum* (1888) · L. Hendriks, *The London Charterhouse: its monks and its martyrs* (1889) · V. M. Doreau, *Henri VIII et les martyrs de la Chartreuse de Londres* (1890) · D. Mathew and G. Mathew, *The Reformation and the contemplative life: a study of the conflict between the Carthusians and the state* (1934) · L. E. Whatmore, 'Some new facts about Bl. William Exmew', *Pax*, 36 (1946), 180–83 · L. E. Whatmore, 'Some new facts about Bl. William Exmew', *Pax*, 37 (1947), 9–13 · L. E. Whatmore, 'The Carthusians under King Henry the Eighth', *Analecta Cartusiana*, 109 (1983) · M. G. Sargent, 'William Exmewe, Maurice Chauncy and *The cloud of unknowing*', *Analecta Cartusiana*, 35/4 (1984), 17–20 · W. Beutler, 'Vicente Carducho in El Paular', *Analecta Cartusiana*, 130/12 (1997), 248–9 · D. Knowles [M. C. Knowles], *The religious orders in England*, 3 (1959) · E. M. Thompson, *The Carthusian order in England* (1930) · Venn, *Alum. Cant.*
Archives St Hugh's Charterhouse, Parkminster, Sussex, Exmew's copy, written out by himself, of *The cloud of unknowing*
Likenesses V. Carducho, oils (his martyrdom), Prado Museum, Madrid, Spain · oils, Charterhouse of Trisulti · oils, St Hugh's Charterhouse, Parkminster, Sussex · oils, English College, Rome, Italy

Exmouth. For this title name *see* Pellew, Edward, first Viscount Exmouth (1757–1833).

Exotic visitors (*act. c*.1500–*c*.1855), both free and pressed, give a unique insight into the way English people regarded distant lands and their peoples.

Forerunners The earliest visitor whose name has come down to us is the Greek mariner Pytheas, who in the fourth century BC sailed from Marseilles to trade for British supplies of tin. Only his *periplus*—the route—of this voyage has survived, and he reached these shores before the inhabitants were sufficiently literate to mark his arrival. Over the following centuries soldiers drawn from all parts of the Roman empire, merchants and envoys from Europe, came in such numbers that their appearance was unremarkable. Occasionally official visitors arrived from more remote civilizations. One such was Emperor Manuel II of Byzantium, who in 1400–01 travelled to Paris and London to appeal for men and money to help him resist the Turkish invasion. Henry IV gave him a royal reception, but nothing more; nevertheless his visit was of cultural significance and facilitated closer relationships between Byzantium and the Western world during the early Renaissance.

With the discovery of the New World and the commencement of ocean voyages, men, women, and children were brought back from the Americas and often aroused such interest by their exotic appearance and behaviour that they were taken as curiosities to be paraded before the monarch and nobility [*see* American Indians in England (*act. c*.1500–1609)].

Africans Dark-skinned people from Africa, generally described as 'Moors', had long been known in England since the Muslim occupation of Spain led to their settlement in Western Europe. Portuguese ships had already established trading posts on the Atlantic coast from Morocco to Guinea and the kingdom of Benin, on the equator, before English privateers began to realize the wealth of gold, ivory, and slaves, which could be obtained there. Two Moroccans at least must have found their way to England by the early 1550s, for James Alday, former pirate, in a letter to Michael Lok, master, states 'in the first voyage to Barbary there were two Moores, being noblemen, whereof one was of the king's blood, conveyed by the … master, Thomas Windham, into their countrey out of England' (Hakluyt, 6.137). This first voyage, of 1553, proceeded to Guinea and Benin. Three ships sailed under Thomas Windham and a Portuguese master, Pinteado, both of whom died on the voyage. From a later voyage Hakluyt reports: 'They brought with them certain blacke slaves, whereof some were tall and strong men, and could wel agree with our meates and drinkes, The colde and moyste aire doth somewhat offend them' (ibid., 6.176).

A Russian ambassador Until the twelfth century Kievan Russia had maintained contacts with the West, through commerce and royal marriages, and from this period dates the arrival of Rabbi Iza, or Isaac of Tchernigoff, who in 1181 encountered in London his fellow rabbi Moses ben Isaac, a man known only from his early Hebrew tombstone, mentioned by John Stow. But the Tartar invasions had severed that link, and to England at least, Russia was a vast and shadowy realm, beset by a harsh climate and populated by uncouth people and fantastic beasts. On 28 February 1557 Osip Nepea, representative of Ivan IV, passed through the streets of London accompanied by the lord mayor and aldermen from Smithfield to his lodging at Fenchurch Street. Nepea's arrival came in the wake of Richard Chancellor's journey in 1553 to the White Sea and thence to Moscow, which reopened the prospect of profitable trade and leading, in London, to the foundation of the Muscovy Company in 1555. Nepea and his suite brought with them large quantities of wax, oil, and furs as a private speculation.

Visitors from oriental lands The Chinese seem to have had little interest in the lands from which the European strangers had come, and there is no record of anyone from China coming to England. However, Thomas Cavendish, on his circumnavigation of 1587–8, captured near the point of Lower California the Manila galleon *Great St Anna*, and besides the rich prize of gold and merchandise took off her five boys, two from Japan and three from Luzon, in the Philippines; the youngest of those from Luzon, being about nine years old, later found a home with the countess of Essex. William Barlow, who was interested in the origins of the ship's compass, spoke with at least one from each region, learning that in those parts the sailors found north by floating a magnetic needle in a china bowl of water (W. Barlow, *Magnetical Advertisements*, 1616, A3r–A4v).

It is not known who the first people were to reach England from the Indian sub-continent, but Patrick Copeland, a man with missionary interests, returned from India in 1614 bringing with him an intelligent young Indian who became the first of his race to be baptized into the Church of England. After religious instruction from Copeland, the Indian was baptized on 22 December 1616 with the name

of Peter, which King James had selected for him. The ceremony took place at St Dionis Backchurch before an assembly which included members of the privy council, the lord mayor and aldermen, and representatives from the East India and Virginia companies. Peter's parentage is unknown, his place of birth being given only as 'Bay of Bengal'. The East India Company provided money for his education, which included Latin. Copeland and Peter sailed back to India on the *Royal James*.

In 1690 a broadsheet advertisement invited Londoners to view 'The Painted Prince', a tattooed man from the East Indies who was 'exposed every day from 16 June at his lodgings at the Blew Boars Head in Fleet Street, where he will continue for some time if his health will permit'. The price was 6*d.*, or 1*s.* for 'the best places' (BL, 551.d.18 (2)). For upper-class persons, the prince would visit private homes by arrangement. This decorated individual, known as **Prince Giolo** (*fl.* 1690), had been brought to London by the seaman William Dampier. He was born in Miangis, or Gilolo, a small island near Mindanao, in the Philippines, where he and his mother had been captured by pirates from Celebes and sold into captivity, eventually arriving at Fort St George in India, where Dampier bought them, the mother dying shortly afterwards. By means of Malay, which Dampier and Giolo both spoke imperfectly, Dampier gathered that he was the son of the king of Miangis, and had a wife and five children. On arrival in England, Dampier sold a share in Giolo, and was soon obliged to sell his remaining rights. In London, Giolo was seen by a Dutch merchant who spoke the language of the Celebes, which Giolo had picked up during his captivity. The Dutchman was prevailed on to extract from Giolo some account of his life, and this was subsequently published by Thomas Hyde, orientalist and librarian of the Bodleian Library, as *An account of the famous Prince Giolo, son of the King of Gilolo, now in England, with an account of his life, parentage, and his strange and wonderful adventures; the manner of his being brought to England* (1692). The frontispiece showed Giolo to be tattooed on his body and limbs; it was explained in the broadsheet that 'the more admirable back parts afford us a lively Representation of one quarter part of the World upon and betwixt his shoulders, where the Arctic and Tropick Circles meet in the North Pole upon his Neck. All the other Lines, Circles and Characters are in such exact Symmetry' (BL, 551.d.18 (2)). Before he died of smallpox in Oxford, Giolo had to compete with numerous other proclaimed giants, dwarves, fairies, and monsters currently exhibited; one such, on view in Bartholomew fair, was 'a prodigious monster lately brought over by Sir Thomas Grantham from the Great Mogul's Countrey, being a man with one Head and two distinct Bodies, both Masculine' (BL, 551.d.18 (11)), also priced at 6*d.* and 1*s.*

The Pacific and Australia The main thrust of British exploration of the Pacific and its island societies came only in the second half of the eighteenth century. In the throes of the debate about 'the noble savage', James Cook's second voyage in 1772–5 brought to England a young man named *Omai (c.1753–c.1780), a native of the island of Raiatia, whose affable behaviour endeared him to London society.

A rather different culture was discovered in Australia, where in 1789 an Aborigine named *Bennelong (c.1765–1813) was captured and brought to Sydney Cove, the intention being to learn more about the language and customs of his people. He accompanied Governor Arthur Phillip on his return to England in December 1792, where he was presented to George III. Bennelong's return was delayed until early in 1795, by which time the cold weather and homesickness had made him disconsolate. Having reached Sydney in September, he found it hard to readjust to life in his own community, whereupon he took to heavy drinking.

John Savage, ship's surgeon, spent some time around 1805 in the Bay of Islands, New Zealand, before publishing an account of his experiences in 1807. He took an interest in the Maori and their way of life. From the several who offered to accompany him to Europe he selected **Te Mahanga** (*fl.* 1805), whom he described as a healthy, stout young man from an upper-class family. Te Mahanga was, like Omai, amiable and generally cheerful in character. He took a great interest in everything he saw during the long voyage, during which they touched at St Helena and Cork, and it became obvious that he had exceptionally good sight and hearing. On reaching London, Te Mahanga was amazed by its size and population; he became gloomy on realizing that he would not be a figure of importance there as he had been among his own people, but is said soon to have reverted to his naturally happy state. In Savage's house he lived with the servant boy who had been his companion on the voyage. He was introduced to Earl Fitzwilliam, Savage's patron, and entered the mansion with becoming respect, greeting Lady Fitzwilliam and her family, and delightedly examining the furniture and paintings. On later occasions he was taken to St Paul's Cathedral, where he was impressed by its great size and its numerous monuments. The ironmongery and clothes shops always caught his fancy, as did the carriages, and he enjoyed looking at people's faces and their expressions. However, he found London ill-served with fish and potatoes, two commodities by which he judged the quality of life. Te Mahanga's stay was brief; a few weeks later he was returned to New Zealand with Captain Skelton of the *Ferret*, a whaler, taking with him various coopers' and carpenters' tools.

Three representatives from the far south of South America were brought to London by Robert Fitzroy (1805–1865), captain of the surveying ship HMS *Beagle*, which in February 1830 was working round Tierra del Fuego. Fitzroy's capture of some Yahgans had been made with the intention of using them as a bargaining counter to recover a stolen whaleboat and other items of clothing and equipment. Eventually he conceived the idea of taking some young persons to England, and educating them so that on return they could 'civilize' their own people. All were named according to whim: from one group, **York Minster** (*b. c.*1804, *d.* in or after 1851), a somewhat sullen man of about twenty-six; **Boat Memory** (1809/10–1830), a woman, aged twenty; **Fuegia Basket** (*b.* 1820/21, *d.* in or after 1851), a girl aged nine; and from another group,

speaking a different dialect, **Jemmy Button** [*formerly* Orundellico] (*b.* 1815/16, *d.* in or after 1855), a boy aged fourteen. On arrival at Plymouth in September 1830 Fitzroy offered them to the British government, which declined responsibility, although agreeing to assist in their support and to offer free passage back to their homeland. With many British vessels passing through the dangerous waters around Tierra del Fuego, the Admiralty, like Fitzroy, may have seen the advantage of having friendly natives on hand.

The Fuegians were lodged near Plymouth, but although they were immediately vaccinated, Boat Memory contracted smallpox and died. The remaining three were then sent to a school at Walthamstow, where Fitzroy kept an eye on them while accumulating a store of articles donated by well-wishers against their return. In the summer of 1831 he was commanded to bring them to court. William IV, the 'sailor king', questioned Fitzroy about their lives, while Queen Adelaide gave Fuegia Basket a bonnet, a ring, and a purse of money for clothes. The Fuegians embarked on *Beagle* with Fitzroy in late 1831. From the diary of Charles Darwin, naturalist on this voyage, we learn that York Minster was a short, thick, powerful man, reserved, taciturn, and jealous of any attention paid to Fuegia Basket, whom he intended to marry; that she was quick in learning, especially languages, as she acquired some Portuguese and Spanish during the year-long voyage; and that Jemmy Button was passionate, but pleasant and rather a dandy. Because of bad weather all three agreed to be left on Navarino Island off Tierra del Fuego with Jemmy Button's people, where they were put ashore with a young missionary, Richard Matthew, and an utterly impractical load of agricultural and domestic stores. The outcome was inevitably disastrous. Matthew had to be rescued and taken off within days, while the returnees adopted their previous way of life. York Minster built a boat and departed one night with Fuegia Basket and everything that had been left for them. Other missionaries followed: Allen Francis Gardiner (1794–1851) tried three times to found a settlement before he and his associates died of starvation in 1851. Captain William Parker Snow (1817–1895) reported that York Minster and Fuegia Basket had been seen in 1851, and he himself met and spoke with Jemmy Button in 1855.

The sad episode of Fitzroy and the Fuegians showed the mutual lack of understanding between Englishmen and the people of tribal societies whom they saw as thieving and degenerate, existing on a distressingly primitive level. The Fuegians were not a new discovery, for ships had been passing through their region for centuries. Possessed of considerable intelligence and the skills necessary to survive, like many tribal people, they held everything in common and could not understand the European possessiveness. The Indian who had been baptized as Peter in 1616 returned to his country as a missionary for Christianity; it was now Fitzroy's ambition to convert some Fuegians to a European, and Christian, style of life in order to provide a waystation for ships in distress. His actions led to the worst possible results, which tailed on for many years. When emigrants of European stock settled in the region in the late nineteenth and early twentieth centuries it resulted in the virtual extermination of the Fuegian tribes.

Conclusion Over the four and a half centuries covered here, the treatment accorded to exotic visitors varied according to their perceived level of civilization, a perception which in turn was influenced by the cultural fashions in London. Whereas the Spanish conquistadors had come upon the urban civilizations of central and Andean America, the English explorers encountered on the eastern margins of the New World what were seen as utterly unfamiliar and primitive beings. There was no need to fight them for the riches they possessed, and the few that were captured, rather as strange animals, were brought back to be exhibited partly to support the explorers' accounts and partly to enhance their prestige with the crown or their patrons. No sustained effort was made to learn the native languages or to understand their social structure.

The eighteenth century was perhaps the heyday of sophisticated scrutiny of exotics. Influenced by Jean-Jacques Rousseau and the concept of the 'noble savage', serious attempts were made to accord respect to native peoples, and to understand their societies. The English ships trading with West Africa, India, and south-east Asia were following in the wake of earlier European voyagers, and found themselves confronting inhabitants of alien, but recognizable, civilizations. Often there was some language in common, and a mutual curiosity, which led natives of these parts to embark willingly, in order to see the lands from which these Europeans had come. Once in England, those from the upper strata of their own society adopted English dress and diet, behaved with the accepted social graces, and came to like European music and fine arts. The counter-example of the Fuegians showed what could happen when Englishmen tried to change apparently primitive societies, not simply to treat exotic foreigners as objects of curiosity and wonder.

ANITA MCCONNELL

Sources R. Hakluyt, *The principal navigations, voyages, traffiques and discoveries of the English nation*, 2nd edn, 3 vols. (1598–1600); repr. 12 vols., Hakluyt Society, extra ser., 1–12 (1903–5) • M. S. Anderson, *Britain's discovery of Russia, 1553–1815* (1958) • J. Stow, *Chronicle* (1580), 872, 875 • G. Best, *The three voyages of Martin Frobisher, in search of a passage to Cathaia and India, by the north-west, AD 1576–8*, 2 vols. (1578); repr. (1938) • D. F. Lach and E. J. van Kley, *Asia in the making of Europe*, 3, bk 1 (1993), 285 • H. Das, 'The early Indian visitors', *Calcutta Review*, 3rd ser., 13 (1824), 83–114 • J. Jacobs, 'The first Russian in England', *The Academy*, 34/868 (1888), 404–5 • E. Dark, 'Bennelong', *ANB*, 1.85–6 • J. Savage, *Some account of New Zealand, particularly the Bay of Islands and surrounding country* (1803) • T. Hyde, *An account of the famous Prince Giolo* (1692) • W. P. Snow, *A two years cruise off Tierra del Fuego, the Falkland Islands*, 2 vols. (1857) • N. Hazelwood, *Savage: the life and times of Jemmy Button* (2000)

Exshaw, Charles (*d.* 1771), painter and art dealer, was born in Dublin, the son of John Exshaw (*d.* 1746). He trained there under Francis Bindon, who may have encouraged him to travel abroad. Exshaw left Dublin in 1747 to study in Paris and Rome; he presumably went straight to Paris as

he was awarded a medal at the Académie Royale de Peinture et de Sculpture in 1749. This had distinct resonance back home where the international success of a local youth was greeted as a great triumph.

After his stay in France, Exshaw went on to Flanders and then Italy, where one 'Carlos Exshaw' is recorded as passing through Capua in the company of the artist Richard Hayward on 27 September 1753. During his travels Exshaw assembled a large collection of paintings and on his return to Dublin in 1755 hired Geminiani's rooms to auction this 'curious and valuable collection of paintings, statuary and drawings' (Strickland), the first of a number of sales Exshaw was to hold. The catalogue announced that the artist would soon return to Italy to continue collecting for the Dublin market. True to his promise, Exshaw departed for the continent soon after, but went first to France to continue his studies under Charles Van Loo before returning to Italy. In the first years of the 1760s Exshaw divided his time between making and buying art. In Amsterdam, for example, he etched several sensitive plates after Rembrandt, notably *St Peter's Bark in a Storm*; he also purchased the art collection of Count Colloredo. After his return to Ireland, this block purchase formed the basis of his next two sales at Geminiani's auction rooms.

Evidently Exshaw had some skill as an entrepreneur but apart from his sales of foreign art he had few notable successes. In 1762 he attempted to establish a drawing academy at his London lodgings in Maiden Lane. The comment by Edward Edwards on the 'pompous advertisement announcing … drawing in the manner of the Caracci' is, no doubt, indicative. Only two pupils subscribed to Exshaw's academy and so the venture failed. With his painting *Edward the Black Prince at the Battle of Cressy*, Exshaw was also unsuccessful in his attempt to win the Society of Arts' premium for history painting in 1764.

The rest of Exshaw's career appears uneventful. Living in London at Mr Rummer's in Denmark Street, Soho, he exhibited two paintings at the Society of Arts in 1764 including *A View of Salisbury from Harnham Hill*. Charles Exshaw died early in 1771, probably in London, and his drawings and pictures were sold in April 1771 at Exeter Change.

LUCY PELTZ

Sources Graves, *Soc. Artists* • Redgrave, *Artists* • W. G. Strickland, *A dictionary of Irish artists*, 2 vols. (1913) • J. Ingamells, ed., *A dictionary of British and Irish travellers in Italy, 1701–1800* (1997) • J. C. Smith, *British mezzotinto portraits*, 4 (1882–4) • E. Edwards, *Anecdotes of painters* (1808); facs. edn (1970) • J. Strutt, *A biographical dictionary, containing an historical account of all the engravers, from the earliest period of the art of engraving to the present time*, 2 vols. (1785–6)

Exton, John (*c.*1600–1668), civil lawyer and judge, is of obscure origins. He was admitted a pensioner at Christ's College, Cambridge, in July 1617, and migrated to Trinity Hall, Cambridge, in March 1619. He graduated BA in 1620 and MA in 1623. Exton married on 18 June 1623 Thomasina, daughter and coheir of Ralph Brooke, York herald, of London. He received the degree of LLD in 1634, and was admitted to the court of arches on 31 June 1635. On 13 February 1636 he entered Doctors' Commons, being active as an advocate in London courts 1638–40. In 1647 he served as treasurer of Doctors' Commons.

Exton may have been an admiralty judge as early as 1647, serving with William Clark, and continued by patent from parliament in 1649. He was certainly an admiralty judge in 1651, when together with Clark he was appointed by act of parliament until 1 December 1651, but he was not one of those appointed by the act of 1653. At the Restoration the post was under the nomination of the lord high admiral and went to the pre-war incumbent Robert Zouche, who died almost upon taking office. His successor Thomas Hyde soon followed him to the grave, so on 26 October 1661 Exton was appointed.

Samuel Pepys heard Exton give a charge on 17 March 1663, which he found 'somewhat dull, though he [Exton] would seem to intend it to be very rhetorical' (Pepys, 4.76). Admiralty jurisdiction had been much curtailed by the encroachment of the common law. In 1664 Exton published *The Maritime Dicaeologie, or, Sea-Jurisdiction of England*, which made the case for a wider jurisdiction. Although it had little practical effect, it was later reprinted three times in the mid-eighteenth century because it offered a good history of the court.

Exton was buried on 22 October 1668 in St Benet Paul's Wharf, London. His will, with a codicil dated 12 October 1668, gives his residence as St Margaret's, Westminster. He left two-thirds of his estate to his elder son, Sir Thomas *Exton, also an admiralty judge, and one-third to his younger son, Everard.   STUART HANDLEY

Sources G. D. Squibb, *Doctors' Commons: a history of the College of Advocates and Doctors of Law* (1977), 175 · B. P. Levack, *The civil lawyers in England, 1603–1641* (1973), 229 · will, PRO, PROB 11/328, fol. 323v–r · J. C. Sainty, ed., *Admiralty officials, 1660–1870* (1975), 123 · J. Haydn, *The book of dignities: containing rolls of the official personages of the British empire* (1851) · Venn, *Alum. Cant.* · W. A. Littledale, ed., *The registers of St Bene't and St Peter, Paul's Wharf, London*, 4, Harleian Society, register section, 41 (1912), 24, 62 · Pepys, *Diary*, 4.76 · C. H. Firth and R. S. Rait, eds., *Acts and ordinances of the interregnum, 1642–1660*, 3 vols. (1911), vol. 2, pp. 510, 712–13 · Holdsworth, *Eng. law*, 12.626–7, 646 · IGI

Exton, Nicholas (d. 1402), mayor of London, was a member of the fishmongers' guild, for whom, and for the other city victualling guilds, he was to be an active spokesman in the early 1380s. He had served, rather precociously, as MP for Middlesex in 1369. In 1382 he began the first of his eight terms as alderman for Billingsgate—then, as later, the London ward most closely associated with the fish trade. John Northampton (d. 1398) was then in the middle of his tumultuous two-year mayoralty. Northampton's mildly populist programme—demanding increased electoral influence for crafts rather than wards, and a reduction of food prices to encourage price competition—was regarded as extreme and unsettling by the powerful grocers and fishmongers, and by other established interests. Exton, who gravitated naturally to the following of Northampton's leading opponent, the grocer Nicholas Brembre (d. 1388), quickly established himself as an ardent advocate of the fishmongers and related groups.

On 10 August 1382 pro-Northampton aldermen and others called for his resignation as alderman 'for opprobrious words used to the aforesaid mayor' (Sharpe, *Calendar of Letter-Books*, H, 196), and Exton, claiming a personal wish to be discharged of office, was in fact removed five days later. Yet in September 1382 he addressed parliament on behalf of the fishmongers, evidently arguing with some satiric force that if current measures on the sale of fish were approved, then any non-citizen should be able to sell any merchandise he chose in the city. During this period of heightened debate one group of fishmongers was hauled into court, one of their number reputedly having said that 'he and all the other fishmongers of London were bound to put their hands under the feet of Nicholas Extone for his good deeds and words on behalf of the mistery' (Sharpe, *Calendar of Letter-Books*, H, 203).

Exton's political fortunes improved with the election of Nicholas Brembre as mayor, an office he held from 1383 to 1386. He was among Brembre's supporters present at Northampton's conviction on 15 August 1384, and shortly thereafter was elected sheriff by the commonalty in 1384, and returned to his aldermanry in 1385. Elected mayor in his own right from 1386 to 1388, he continued to co-operate closely with his predecessor Brembre. In pursuance of Brembre's programme he arranged a meeting of the common council on 12 March 1387, with a selectively augmented membership, at which agreement was reached to burn the jubilee book of city ordinances, first compiled in 1377 (the jubilee of Edward III), and containing regulations for the victualling trades and other reformist material sponsored by John Northampton and others.

Certain equivocations may be seen in Exton's conduct as mayor during the difficult period in 1386–8, when the lords appellant sought to limit Richard II's power. The king sought by varied means to secure London's support, and on 5 October 1387 Exton tried to induce the craft guilds to subscribe to a pro-Ricardian oath of loyalty. Knighton claims that he sought, unsuccessfully, to raise troops in London in defence of the king's prerogative. But Knighton also represents Exton as blocking an anti-parliamentary scheme by Richard in 1386, and as saving London from forcible entry in December 1387 by opening the city's gates to the lords appellant once their victory had become certain. During the Merciless Parliament of 1388 Brembre was condemned to death along with other Ricardian loyalists, with Exton evidently assenting to the view that his sometime ally had been guilty of the treasons with which he was charged. On 13 October 1388 the more moderate Nicholas Twyford (d. 1390/91) was elected mayor.

A strongly partisan figure, Exton nevertheless belonged to a ruling oligarchy whose shared interests often made it a force for stability in London's affairs, and especially in the city's dealings with the crown. Moreover, some of his offices, such as that of mayor of the staple of Westminster, helped to align him with interests outside the oligarchy, a consideration that may have helped him to weather a difficult period unscathed. He received royal preferment throughout the unsettled years from 1387 to 1389. At the

Cambridge parliament of October 1388 he received a pardon for all treasons and felonies, and on the same occasion notification was made prohibiting citizens from spreading rumours that he had sought the derogation of city liberties. He sued successfully for moneys owed him by Nicholas Brembre, lost in forfeit, receiving from the king a Spanish sword and other items in pawn, and he later purchased many of Brembre's forfeited possessions. In 1392 he stood with a broad political cross-section of elected officials in bearing Richard II's wrath during the latter's celebrated 'quarrel with the city'.

Exton appears to have lived in retirement during the last decade of his life. No children are recorded of either of his two marriages, to Katherine and (c.1382) to Johanna. In his will, made in 1393 but not proved until 20 February 1402, he left properties in the London parish of All Hallows Gracechurch to his brother John Curteys, and other rents to the rector, Henry Cokeham, for anniversaries and prayers.   Paul Strohm

Sources R. R. Sharpe, ed., *Calendar of letter-books preserved in the archives of the corporation of the City of London*, [12 vols.] (1899–1912), vols. G–H • A. H. Thomas and P. E. Jones, eds., *Calendar of plea and memoranda rolls preserved among the archives of the corporation of the City of London at the Guildhall*, 2–3 (1929–32) • R. R. Sharpe, ed., *Calendar of wills proved and enrolled in the court of husting, London, AD 1258 – AD 1688*, 2 (1890) • S. L. Thrupp, *The merchant class of medieval London, 1300–1500* (1948) • R. Bird, *The turbulent London of Richard II* (1949) • L. C. Hector and B. F. Harvey, eds. and trans., *The Westminster chronicle, 1381–1394*, OMT (1982) • *Chronicon Henrici Knighton, vel Cnitthon, monachi Leycestrensis*, ed. J. R. Lumby, 2 vols., Rolls Series, 92 (1889–95) • *RotP*, vol. 3 • deeds and wills, CLRO, 130 (69) • *LBH*
Archives CLRO, hustings rolls, wills, and deeds, 130 (69)
Wealth at death approx. £1000?—tenement and other rents

Exton, Sir Thomas (*bap.* 1631, *d.* 1688), lawyer and politician, was baptized at St Andrew's, Holborn, on 2 June 1631, the first surviving son of John *Exton (*c.*1600–1668), admiralty judge, and his wife, Thomasina (*d.* in or before 1667), daughter of Ralph Brooke, York herald. He was educated at Merchant Taylors' School, London, from 1637 to 1643 before matriculating from Trinity Hall, Cambridge, in 1647. He entered Gray's Inn on 28 December 1649. He became a fellow of Trinity in 1651, graduating LLB in 1652. In 1659 he was called to the bar at Gray's Inn and in 1662 received his LLD. In 1663 Exton resigned his fellowship and was named chancellor of the diocese of London. He married on 19 January 1664 Isabella (1625/6–1673), daughter of Robert Hore, apothecary, of London, the widow of Thomas Prujean of Hornchurch, Essex. They had a son and a daughter. On 22 June 1664 he became an advocate at Doctors' Commons. He succeeded his father in 1668 and received two-thirds of his estate, the remaining third going to his brother Everard, a proctor.

Exton was knighted on 23 November 1675, and on the following day took office as advocate-general. On 10 November 1676 he was admitted master of Trinity Hall. He was elected to all three Exclusion Parliaments for the University of Cambridge, being noted as 'vile' by the first earl of Shaftesbury. In his first parliament he made several recorded speeches and voted against the Exclusion Bill. In 1680, together with Sir Richard Lloyd, he printed *The Case*

of the Merchants Concerned in the Loss of the Ship Virgin. Exton was reappointed advocate-general on the accession of James II and re-elected to parliament for Cambridge University. On 6 July 1686 he was promoted to judge of the Admiralty, and he also succeeded Sir Richard Lloyd as dean of arches. No sooner had he become a judge than he became embroiled in the controversy over the suspension of Dr Sharp for preaching sermons against Catholicism. He reputedly advised King James in favour of suspending the divine, and then advised Bishop Compton that he could safely refuse to comply with the order from the ecclesiastical commission. As a result Exton himself was hauled before the ecclesiastical commissioners in November to justify his conduct, and he lost his Admiralty judgeship in December. In 1688 he gave evidence that the handwriting on the petition of the seven bishops was that of Archbishop Sancroft.

Exton died on 5 November 1688: 'his heart was broke through cowardice, for he never looked up after he was put forth of the Admiralty and reprimanded by the commissioners' (*Downshire MSS*, 1.305). He was buried on 8 November in St Benet Paul's Wharf, London. His will, made on 20 March 1688, reflected on his 'several losses in my estate', and thus his inability to add to the portion of his daughter Bridget following her recent marriage to Sir John Sudbury. Most of his estate went to his son, John, who followed the same profession as his father.
          Stuart Handley

Sources HoP, *Commons, 1660–90* • Sainty, *King's counsel* • Venn, *Alum. Cant.* • G. D. Squibb, *Doctors' Commons: a history of the College of Advocates and Doctors of Law* (1977), 35, 117, 179 • *The autobiography of Sir John Bramston*, ed. [Lord Braybrooke], CS, 32 (1845), 247–51 • *Report on the manuscripts of the marquis of Downshire*, 6 vols. in 7, HMC, 75 (1924–95), vol. 1, pp. 25, 185–6, 305 • A. Grey, ed., *Debates of the House of Commons, from the year 1667 to the year 1694*, 10 vols. (1763), vol. 6. p. 436; vol. 7, pp. 103–4 • will, PRO, PROB 11/393, sig. 148 • G. W. Keeton, *Lord Chancellor Jeffreys and the Stuart cause* (1965), 412 • H. E. Maldon, *University of Cambridge college histories: Trinity Hall* (1902), 161–2 • B. P. Levack, *The civil lawyers in England, 1603–1641* (1973), 229 • N. Luttrell, *A brief historical relation of state affairs from September 1678 to April 1714*, 1 (1857) • *State trials*, 12.287 • W. A. Littledale, ed., *The registers of St Bene't and St Peter, Paul's Wharf, London*, 2, Harleian Society, register section, 39 (1910), 47 • W. A. Littledale, ed., *The registers of St Bene't and St Peter, Paul's Wharf, London*, 4, Harleian Society, register section, 41 (1912), 81

Eyden, Jeremiah van der (*d.* 1695), portrait painter, a native of Brussels, was a pupil of Adrien Hanneman at The Hague in 1658. He travelled to England and was employed by Sir Peter Lely to paint the draperies in some of his portraits. On his marriage he settled in Northamptonshire, where he worked as a portrait painter for the duke of Rutland, producing made-up portraits of the first eight earls of Rutland for Belvoir Castle. Similar imaginary portraits of the fourteenth- and fifteenth-century Montagues by van der Eyden hang in Boughton House, Northamptonshire, perhaps commissioned by Ralph, first duke of Montagu. These are recorded in the 1718 inventory of Boughton House as 'six hole length pictures in gold and black frames'. Van der Eyden was also patronized by Lord Sherard of Stapleford, Leicestershire, at whose house he died in September 1695. The parish register for that year contains the entry 'Mr Jeremiah Vanroyden was buried Sept. ye 17'. CAMPBELL DODGSON, *rev.* SARAH HERRING

Sources E. K. Waterhouse, *The dictionary of British 16th and 17th century painters* (1988) · C. H. C. Baker, *Lely and the Stuart portrait painters: a study of English portraiture before and after van Dyck*, 2 (1912), 195 · A. von Wurzbach, *Niederländisches Künstler-Lexikon*, 1 (Vienna and Leipzig, 1906), 522 · D. O. Obreen, *Archief voor Nederlandsche kunstgeschiedenis*, 5 (Rotterdam, 1882–3), 145 · C. Kramm, *Geschiedenis van de beeldende kunsten in der Nederlanden*, 1–2 (Amsterdam, 1864), 469–70 · T. Murdoch, ed., *Boughton House: the English Versailles* (1992), 22, 91 · I. Eller, *History of Belvoir Castle* (1841), 288 · H. Walpole, *Anecdotes of painting in England: with some account of the principal artists*, ed. R. N. Wornum, new edn, 3 vols. (1888), vol. 2, p. 105 · parish register, Stapleford, Leics. RO [burial]

Archives NRA, Rutland papers

Eyles, Sir Francis, first baronet (*c.*1650–1716), merchant and financier, was the son of John Eyles (*d.* 1662), woolstapler and mercer of Devizes, and his wife, Mary (*d. c.*1666). He was the younger brother of Sir John *Eyles. On 26 May 1669 he was apprenticed to Thomas Cooper, haberdasher of London, and he took his freedom in that company on 28 February 1677. The date of his marriage to Elizabeth, daughter of Richard Ayley of London, merchant, is unknown, but his son and heir, John, was born in 1683.

Eyles was a commission agent in the Atlantic sugar trade in partnership with his brother John, dealing principally with Barbados, where dissenters had built up an effective business network. Although John probably founded the firm of Eyles & Co. and was the senior partner, both brothers are named in documents pertaining to the firm among the records of the Royal Africa Company. On 13 September 1689 they jointly lent £4000 to the new government. The privy council registers mention in passing a Francis Eyles trading to Barbados on 15 November 1690, and the Treasury papers of 1690 describe him as one of the most considerable traders to Barbados in the same year.

Eyles, however, had multiple economic interests. In July 1691 he petitioned the Treasury to pay him out of the funds allocated to reduce Ireland for providing shipping for army stores needed in Ireland. The commissioners of transportation had issued certificates for half the money due, but he had received nothing in eight months. In September 1692 he was engaged in the trade to Madeira and from 1697 onwards he was a director of the Bank of England. From 1695 to 1698 he also served as a director of the East India Company. On 1 July 1697, as deputy governor, he was called in to explain what arrangements the company had made for the provisioning of naval escorts supplied by the Admiralty, and he appealed unsuccessfully for the need for secrecy.

From 1697 Eyles also acted as agent for Barbados, presenting accounts and petitions and supplying information. On 2 November 1697 he petitioned the Board of Trade to maintain the ratio of white to black people in Barbados. On 9 May 1698 he tried to secure payment to Francis Bond, president of the council of Barbados, of an allowance of £600 out of the 4½ per cent duty. On 5 November

1700 he was reappointed agent for two years by the assembly in Barbados.

Eyles's major fortune was probably made as a financier during the French wars, supplying bills of exchange to maintain the army in Flanders. In 1696 he proposed to provide £100,000 in bills of exchange payable in Amsterdam at a rate of 10 guilders 8 stivers. He also volunteered to speak to possible subscribers at Mercers' Hall to see what rate on bills would attract lenders. On 24 April 1697 he was made a trustee for managing subscriptions for circulating exchequer bills of credit, which had been authorized by parliament to remedy a shortfall in several funds.

On 11 May 1697 Eyles supplied 330,000 guilders in return for £30,000 in tallies and orders charged on the 3s. aid plus £4500 in satisfaction for loss or discount. On 1 April 1698 he was one of those questioned when the Lords investigated false endorsements of exchequer bills by Marriott and Knight. But he was still listed, on 4 April, among those providing bills of exchange (repaid in exchequer bills) for the earl of Ranelagh to send to Flanders. Eyles claimed on 8 April 1698 that he had supplied £21,000 to Mr Schuylenberg.

On 18 May 1698 Eyles and his brother were among several merchants who received payment for jointly providing 480,000 florins. On 22 February 1699 he was a member of a syndicate which advanced £300,000 at 8 per cent. On 11 June 1701, together with his brother, he proposed to give letters of credit for the continental army payable in Amsterdam or Rotterdam at sight at a rate of 11 guilders current money for every pound. The Treasury accepted the offer, but for a minimum period of twelve months. On 18 March 1704 he was named one of the three commissioners of account and on 21 March 1706 he was named one of the seven managers appointed to remit £250,000 to Prince Eugene in Italy.

Eyles was elected an assistant of the Levant Company (1703–4) and was a director of both the Old East India Company (1709–10) and of the New East India Company (1702–5, 1706–9). He continued to serve as a director of the Bank of England until 1715 and was deputy governor (1705–7) and governor (5 April 1707 to 1709). He took no position on the question of whether a rapprochement between the bank and the new tory ministry in 1710–13 required a change of leadership at the bank.

Eyles was elected alderman for the London ward of Bridge Without on 23 January 1711 and he stayed on the court until 1716, serving as sheriff in 1710–11. The court of aldermen chose to co-opt a whig merchant prince to balance John Cass. On 1 December 1714 Eyles was created one of the first Hanoverian baronets. His wife predeceased him and was buried on 14 February 1716. Eyles himself died on 24 May 1716 and was buried on 5 June in the family vault at St Helen, Bishopsgate, London. Three sons and one daughter predeceased him: Samuel was baptized on 21 October 1688 and buried on 4 September 1689, another son named Samuel, baptized on 7 June 1691, died before reaching adulthood; Edward was buried on 24 July 1697; and Mary, who was born on 21 November 1695, was buried on 5 November 1698.

None the less, Eyles founded a London business dynasty. His first surviving son, John, second baronet, of Gidea Hall, Essex, became a director of the Bank of England and of the East India and South Sea companies; he was also an MP. He cleared up the mess of the South Sea Bubble and became lord mayor of London in 1726–7. Eyles's second surviving son, Joseph (*b. c.*1690), also became an alderman, was knighted by George I, and served as sheriff of London in 1734–5.   RICHARD GRASSBY

Sources J. R. Woodhead, *The rulers of London, 1660–1689* (1965) · G. S. De Krey, *A fractured society: the politics of London in the first age of party, 1688–1715* (1985) · D. W. Jones, *War and economy in the age of William III and Marlborough* (1988) · GEC, *Baronetage* · W. B. Bannerman, ed., *The registers of St Helen's, Bishopsgate, London*, Harleian Society, register section, 31 (1904) · A. B. Beaven, ed., *The aldermen of the City of London, temp. Henry III–[1912]*, 2 vols. (1908–13) · W. A. Shaw, ed., *Calendar of treasury books*, [33 vols. in 64], PRO (1904–69) · CSP col. · CSP dom. · *The manuscripts of the House of Lords*, new ser., 12 vols. (1900–77) · P. Morant, *The history and antiquities of the county of Essex*, 2 vols. (1768) · APC, *1542–1631* · will, PRO, PROB 11/552, sig. 115
Wealth at death over £50,000

Eyles, Sir John (*d.* **1703**), merchant and financier, was the first son of John Eyles (*d.* 1662), a mercer and wool-stapler with a shop in Devizes from 1640 onwards, and his wife, Mary (*d. c.*1666). Eyles chose to pursue a career in London and it has been widely assumed that, like his brother Francis *Eyles, he was a haberdasher. But his name does not appear in the Haberdashers' Company's records and it is doubtful whether he was ever a freeman of London.

An original subscriber of £400 to the Royal Africa Company in 1671, Eyles's principal business from at least 1674 onwards was as a commission agent and broker in the Barbados trade in sugar and slaves. Although he was in business with his brother Francis, as Eyles & Co., John was the senior partner and he alone was listed in the *London Directory* of 1677. The Africa Company's records list 126 bills drawn on him from Barbados. Eyles handled the sugar exported to England by the Barbados planters and purchased their return cargoes. Since the planters usually needed to settle outstanding liabilities and make purchases in advance of receipts from sales, Eyles provided them with credit.

The firm acted for fourteen years as agent for John Hothersall of Barbados who, in his will of 1694, appointed the Eyleses receivers of the product of his estate and guardians of his children. When a ship captain seized some people of the island of Johanna and sold them in Barbados, the East India Company approached Eyles to redeem them at £25 apiece. Two petitions to the Treasury from Eyles, one in May 1686 and the other on 7 July 1689, suggest that he acted as spokesman for Barbados. His West Indies commission business does not, however, appear to have passed to the next generation.

Eyles, who supported the exclusion of the duke of York from the throne, was elected a member for Devizes by popular outcry in October 1679, but the return was challenged by Sir Walter Ernle and George Johnson, who had been elected by the corporation, and he does not seem to have taken his seat in the Commons. Eyles unsuccessfully again contested Devizes in 1681 and 1689. Despite his political stance, he seems to have remained in favour with the government. He was asked by Henry Guy to report on the accounts of the farmers of the Barbados 4½ per cent sugar duty. The thorough and generally favourable report, which was presented on 26 April 1679, pointed out that the wastage on sales was 4 to 5 per cent higher than among private merchants and that the practice of selling to the same buyers probably brought down prices below market levels. After investing £9000 in a lease of the alnage duty with his son-in-law in 1680, he became a principal farmer of the alnage and his allegedly oppressive tactics in that office became the subject of a committee of inquiry.

Although he obtained a pass for the Netherlands on 28 September 1683, Eyles does not seem to have left England for political reasons. When James II turned to the dissenters, Eyles became one of the whig collaborators. After the Anglican aldermen of London were ejected in August 1687, Eyles was made an alderman of Broad Street by royal commission on 12 August 1687 and he sat until September 1688. He was also knighted on 15 August 1687. Although he never served as sheriff, he did serve as temporary lord mayor, when Sir John Shorter died in office, from 8 September until the restoration of the charter on 3 October 1688. He was also recommended as an honest and fit dissenter in his native county and he became deputy lieutenant for Wiltshire from 1687 until October 1688 and a JP from June to October 1688.

During the French wars, Eyles moved into government finance and exploited his contacts on the continent. In July and September 1689 the Treasury books record total advances of £29,000 on the 12*d.* aid. In the 1690s, together with his brother, he remitted funds to the English army in Flanders. The contractors in London made arrangements with bankers in the Netherlands so that the Dutch paymaster of the army could draw bills on the English paymaster-general, the earl of Ranelagh. They supplied Ranelagh with letters or bills of credit drawn in Flemish current money (the unit of pay for the soldiers), payable in sterling in London at an agreed rate. In return for a substantial discount, Eyles assumed the risk of exposure to a fluctuating market rate of exchange, with the additional risk of delays in repayment by the government. On 23 July 1690 Eyles was still owed £13,600 and the forces in Flanders lacked subsistence and were in danger of melting away. In 1694, however, the £20,000 which he provided was repaid the same year and, in 1695, Eyles and his brother remitted a further £33,800 for Schuylenberg to be repaid in tallies.

Eyles married Sarah Cowper (*d.* 1705) of London and they had two sons: the heir, John, married in 1702 Mary, daughter of John Eyles of Chalford, Gloucestershire; the other son, Francis (*c.*1679–1735), became a major figure in the business world of eighteenth-century London. Eyles and his wife also had five daughters, the eldest of whom, Sarah, married Joseph Haskins-Stiles, the nephew of a Dutch tycoon. The second daughter, Mary, married on 22

September 1691 Sir John Smith, bt, of Islewood, son of Sir John Smith, alderman and sheriff of London.

Sir John Bramston in his *Autobiography* (315) repeated rumours that Eyles was an Anabaptist and he was certainly a strict Baptist who, according to Luttrell (1.459, 467), shut the chapel at Guildhall when he was lord mayor. He left bequests to Baptist chapels in London and Devizes and gave the Baptists of Devizes the lease of 22 and 23 The Brittox.

Success in London allowed Eyles to acquire landed property in his native county. In 1683 he purchased 2 acres near Devizes from Edward Hope and ultimately he acquired an estate at South Broome in Wiltshire, which served as a country seat for what became a London whig mercantile dynasty. Eyles was buried in the family vault at St Helen, Bishopsgate, London, on 6 July 1703.

RICHARD GRASSBY

Sources K. G. Davies, 'The origins of the commission system', *TRHS*, 5th ser., 2 (1952), 89–107 • W. A. Shaw, ed., *Calendar of treasury books*, [33 vols. in 64], PRO (1904–69) • *CSP col.*, vols. 9–13 • J. R. Woodhead, *The rulers of London, 1660–1689* (1965), 14–204 • *Wiltshire Notes and Queries*, 1 (1893–5) • *Wiltshire Notes and Queries*, 6–7 (1908–13) • HoP, *Commons* • D. R. Lacey, *Dissent and parliamentary politics in England, 1661–1689* (1969) • W. A. Shaw, *The knights of England*, 2 vols. (1906) • *CSP dom.*, 1683–5; 1689–1702 • N. Luttrell, *A brief historical relation of state affairs from September 1678 to April 1714*, 6 vols. (1857) • G. S. De Krey, *A fractured society: the politics of London in the first age of party, 1688–1715* (1985) • A. B. Beaven, ed., *The aldermen of the City of London, temp. Henry III–[1912]*, 2 vols. (1908–13) • *The autobiography of Sir John Bramston*, ed. [Lord Braybrooke], CS, 32 (1845) • E. B. Sainsbury, ed., *A calendar of the court minutes … of the East India Company*, 11 vols. (1907–38) • W. B. Bannerman, ed., *The registers of St Helen's, Bishopsgate, London*, Harleian Society, register section, 31 (1904) • will, PRO, PROB 11/470, sig. 109

Archives PRO, C 8/242/138 • PRO, C 7/530/76, C 7/405/40 • PRO, T 70/269–77, T/70 282 • PRO, East India Office, papers, court minutes

Wealth at death over £30,000

Eyles [*née* Pitcairn; *other married name* Murray], **(Margaret) Leonora** (1889–1960), novelist and journalist, was born on 1 September 1889 at 5 Eastcott Street, Swindon, the eldest of three children of Thomas Andrew Tennant Pitcairn and his wife, Rosa, *née* Bevan. Her family were Staffordshire china manufacturers whose fortunes declined after her birth. She was brought up at Tunstall, near Stoke-on-Trent, and educated at day school and then a local board school, passing the examination entitling her to stay at school as a pupil teacher at the age of fourteen. After being orphaned she was left in the care of a young stepmother whom she detested. Forbidden to take up a place at a teachers' training college to which her matriculation results had entitled her, Leonora ran away to London where, at the age of eighteen, she scraped together a meagre living by addressing envelopes in a basement office. She sold one or two things left by her mother to raise the passage to work as a domestic servant in Australia. There she married Alfred William Eyles, who left her to bring up their two daughters and son on her own; she eventually obtained a divorce.

Leonora Eyles returned to England and at the age of twenty-four found herself living in a terraced house in Peckham in the East End of London, where she supported her family as best she could through poorly paid jobs including factory garment making and typing. She found more congenial work when, pushing her pram up Peckham Rye where William Blake had once seen a tree of angels, she chanced upon an advertisement for an appeals writer for the Dr Barnardo's group of orphanages, and was the successful candidate from five hundred applicants.

After the outbreak of the First World War, Eyles volunteered to become a munitions worker in the Woolwich arsenal, where she greatly enjoyed the camaraderie of some 2000 women workers. The experience of urban poverty and economic deprivation affected Eyles deeply. Her observations formed the basis of a book, *The Woman in the Little House* (1922), a documentary study of working women's lives, which appeared in serial form in the journal *Time and Tide*. Like Maud Pember Reeves's *Round about a Pound a Week* (1913), *The Woman in the Little House* directed the attention of the reading public to the struggles against poverty and hardship which formed the day-to-day existence of women in the inner-city slum. After the war Eyles was much in demand to address trade union meetings recruiting women workers. She argued that the state should recognize the importance of motherhood and was a strong advocate of the family allowance. Eyles wrote regularly for socialist publications including George Lansbury's *Labour Leader* and the *Daily Herald*, and edited the women's page in *The Miner* before becoming a columnist in *Woman's Own* and the country's best-known 'agony aunt' before the *Daily Mirror*'s Marjorie Proops. She married the journalist David Leslie *Murray (1888–1962), editor of the *Times Literary Supplement* (1938–44) on 21 May 1928, but continued to publish as Leonora Eyles. She and Murray lived on the south coast of England for some of their married life. A pacifist and lifelong socialist, and also a vegetarian, Eyles was converted to theosophy in later life and abandoned her pacifist ideals at the start of the Second World War. *For my Enemy Daughter* (1941) is addressed to her elder daughter, who had married an Italian and was resident in Italy during the Second World War.

The first of Eyles's slum novels contrasting urban deprivation to rural freedom was the best-selling *Margaret Protests* (1919). The subtext of *Margaret Protests*, published shortly after Marie Stopes's *Married Love* (1918) and *Wise Parenthood* (1918), is birth control, a subject about which Eyles had learned from reading Havelock Ellis and Stopes. Faced with a feckless husband and then unexpected widowhood, Margaret Wayre, the central protagonist of *Margaret Protests*, supports herself by trading in abortifacients before realizing the folly of her ways and trekking out to the countryside to begin life anew. Like several of Eyles's novels, *Margaret Protests* is concerned with women's spirituality and depicts with unusual sensitivity and compassion a resourceful and resilient unsupported mother. *Margaret Protests* was followed by *Hidden Lives* (1922), the story of a woman doctor in an inner-city practice, and other novels including *The Hare of Heaven* (1924) and *Captivity* (1922), based on her own marriage. Eyles wrote two novels based on religious themes, *The Shepherd of Israel* (1929) and *Strength of the Spirit* (1930), as well as the successful crime thrillers *They Wanted him Dead* (1936), *Death of a Dog* (1936), and *No Second Best* (1939).

Leonora Eyles became the trusted confidante of hundreds of working women who read her journalism and wrote to her about their problems. Although she lived in comfort in later life, she never lost the insights into poverty and hardship which her years in the East End of London had given her. Her column in the inaugural issue of *Woman's Own* (15 October 1932) introduced her as 'the woman who understands'. She wrote several popular books offering advice on subjects including good housekeeping, sex education, nutrition, and family relationships. *Women's Problems of To-Day* was a best-seller in 1926. Other manuals included *Careers for Women* (1930), *Common Sense about Sex* (1933), and *Eat Well in War-Time* (1940). Her autobiographical fragment is *The Ram Escapes: the Story of a Victorian Childhood* (1953). Leonora Eyles died on 27 July 1960 at her home, 32 Eton Avenue, Hampstead, London, from intestinal problems and diabetes mellitus.

MAROULA JOANNOU

Sources L. Eyles, *The ram escapes: the story of a Victorian childhood* (1953) · L. Eyles, *Women's problems of to-day* (1926) · L. Eyles, *For my enemy daughter* (1941) · L. Eyles, *Margaret protests* (1919) · L. Eyles, *The woman in the little house* (1922) · M. Joannou, 'Ladies please don't smash these windows': women's writing, feminist consciousness and social change, 1918–38 (1995), 54–76 · N. Beauman, *A very great profession: the woman's novel, 1914–1939* (1984), 101–2, 136–9 · b. cert. · m. cert. · d. cert.

Likenesses photograph, repro. in *Woman's Own* (15 Oct 1932)

Eynsham, Adam of (*b. c.*1155, *d.* in or after **1233**), abbot of Eynsham and hagiographer, came from a middle-class Oxford family, and became a monk and then in due course first prior, and then abbot, of the Benedictine monastery at Eynsham. His father, Edmund, was a doctor who owned properties in Oxford (probably in the Osney district), but went to the Holy Land and died there *c.*1187. One of Adam's brothers, William of Oxford, is mentioned as the abbot's brother in Eynsham charters, and a younger brother, also called Edmund, had studied at Oxford and in 1196 experienced a vision of the next world. Adam wrote an account of this, *The Vision of the Monk of Eynsham*, which survives in several manuscripts and printed editions.

Eynsham is a rare English example of an abbey founded by the local bishop (Lincoln), who had the right of patronage. This right deeply affected Adam three times in his life. Hugh (bishop of Lincoln, 1186–1200) successfully claimed it against the king in 1197, and Adam, prior or subprior during the vacancy caused by Abbot Godfrey's death in 1195, probably compiled the Eynsham cartulary for this lawsuit. In 1197 Robert, prior of Dover, became abbot and Hugh shrewdly chose Adam as his chaplain. From then until Hugh's death Adam was his companion and confidant, travelling with him in England, Anjou, and the Dauphiné. This experience enabled Adam to write the life of Hugh, one of the fullest and most trustworthy saints' lives of the middle ages. This work is Adam's principal title to fame. It is mainly through his portrait, although both idealized and selective, that Hugh can be known in such great detail today.

Adam completed this life after Hugh's death. Like many of the English clergy he went abroad during the interdict (1208–13) under King John. He was certainly in Paris for some of this time. Hugh of Wells, bishop of Lincoln (1209–35) returned to England in 1213 and exercised his right to preside over the election at Eynsham of a successor to Abbot Robert, who had died in 1208. Adam, whose research had earlier established the bishop of Lincoln's rights, was elected abbot and ruled for fifteen years.

Eynsham was never a very large monastery, but it was important for the many visitors who stayed there on the way to the west and to Wales, and it was frequently chosen by kings as the place for episcopal elections, which were held there while the king stayed in the palace at Woodstock. Such events were inevitably expensive for the monastery. While Adam was abbot, the monks incurred another expense, that of providing 52*s.*, as well as a meal, for 200 poor (clerical) students each year. This had been imposed on the town of Oxford, in reparation for the townspeople's having killed some student clerics in a riot in 1209, by the papal legate Nicolò of Tusculum. The town, it seems, persuaded Eynsham to provide this annual sum in return for a cash or property payment. Although Eynsham owned considerable estates (including woodlands, which Adam had cut wastefully), the abbey had fallen into debt under Abbot Godfrey, and by 1227 it owed £152 15*s.* to David the Jew of Lincoln. This they managed to repay on 29 June of that year, but in 1228 Adam, now an old man, was deposed by the bishop of Lincoln, Hugh of Wells (again exercising his powers over a 'bishop's monastery'), as a 'manifest dilapidator' of monastic property. This needs to be considered in the context of widespread monastic financial problems at this time, and of the claims of communities to exercise more control over spending, not to mention the interdict and royal exactions. On the other hand, it may be that Adam, although a good scholar in the monastic tradition, was a poor administrator. His abbatial seal survives.

After his retirement he lived in the manor of Little Rollright and witnessed charters. In 1233 he was exempted from doing suit for the manor, and presumably died soon afterwards. From his writings, composed just when Oxford schools were developing into a university, Adam emerges as one well read in the Bible and the fathers who was also a keen and articulate observer of events, people (including three Angevin kings), and even animals (such as the swan of St Hugh of Lincoln), and as one tellingly depicted the weak and the strong aspects of twelfth-century church life.

D. H. FARMER

Sources H. E. Salter, ed., *Eynsham cartulary*, 2 vols., OHS, 49, 51 (1907–8) · Adam of Eynsham, *Magna vita sancti Hugonis / The life of Saint Hugh of Lincoln*, ed. D. L. Douie and D. H. Farmer, 2 vols., OMT (1961–2) · *Ann. mon.*, vol. 1 · D. Knowles, C. N. L. Brooke, and V. C. M. London, eds., *The heads of religious houses, England and Wales, 1: 940–1216* (1972) · D. Knowles, *The monastic order in England* (1940) · [Adam of Eynsham], *Magna vita s. Hugonis episcopi Lincolniensis*, ed. J. F. Dimock, Rolls Series, 37 (1864) · T. D. Hardy, *Descriptive catalogue of* *materials relating to the history of Great Britain and Ireland*, 2, Rolls Series, 26 (1865), 542–5 • D. H. Farmer, *St Hugh of Lincoln* (1985) **Archives** BL • Bodl. Oxf.

Eynsham, Ælfric of. *See* Ælfric of Eynsham (*c*.950–*c*.1010).

Eyre, Adam (1614–1661), parliamentarian army officer, was born on 25 April 1614, the son of Thomas Eyre (*d.* before 1640), yeoman, of Haslehead in Thurleston township, Penistone parish, in the West Riding of Yorkshire, and his wife, Ellen Ramscar (*d.* before 1640). His early life and education are unknown, but in 1640 he married Susanna (*d.* 1668), daughter of Godfrey Mathewman of Eden-tree Head, in the neighbouring parish of Kirkburton.

During the civil war Eyre resided in a strongly parliamentarian locality. He, his brother Joseph Eyre (*d. c.*1647), and his neighbour William Rich of Bullhouse, were all commissioned captains in parliament's army under Ferdinando, Lord Fairfax. Eyre's journal of his wartime service was in 'a little parchment covered book' now lost (Eyre, appx, 352).

Adam Eyre's later 'dyurnall' covering 1647–9 survives and provides a valuable source for social historians. It records his mediation in local quarrels and assistance to needy neighbours. In March 1647 he was a trustee in a petition to remove Penistone's vicar, Christopher Dickinson, for unsatisfactory preaching and alleged inclination to royalism and drunkenness. Apart from meticulously chronicling expenditure, the diurnal reveals Eyre's matrimonial distress. Despite puritan leanings he was prone to tobacco, gambling at bowls, and bouts of heavy drinking, much to his wife's distaste. Certainly the 'inconsistency between his religious beliefs and self-indulgent lifestyle seems also to have demanded resolution' (Wrightson, 97). On 8 June 1647 Eyre wrote:

> This morne my wife began, after her old manner, to braule and revile mee for wishing her only to wear such apparrell as was decent and comly, and accused mee for treading on her sore foote, with curses and othes … at diner I told her I purposed never to com in bed with her til shee tooke more notice of what I formerly had sayd to her. (Eyre, 43)

On 16 August he was possibly considering adultery; after words written in cipher he stated he was subject to 'a great temptation' (Eyre, 55). On 5 October he returned home late at night to find Susanna had locked him out. The couple completed a return journey to London between 6 and 22 September 1647, during which, Eyre's previous allegiance and religious position notwithstanding, his wife 'procured a touch from the King for the evil' (Eyre, 62) in pursuit of a cure for skin problems.

On 1 January 1648, after deliverance from a storm that shook his house, Eyre mended his marriage. He conceded his partial responsibility for their conflicts: 'Now I pray God that both shee and I may leave of all our old and foolish contentions, and joyne together in His service' (Eyre, 84). He experienced a spiritual reawakening and the diurnal becomes thick with religious language. Yet on 15 February he wrote 'This day I abused myselfe with too much drink, God have mercy on mee' (Eyre, 98). On 4 April 1648 he watched a football match between Penistone and Thurleston, and on 25 September he had a clock installed at home. He spent much time reading religious works, purchasing, borrowing, or lending books by Erasmus, John Foxe, John Saltmarsh, William Dell, and William Lilly.

In August 1648 Eyre was appointed a commissioner to receive the pay arrears of 115 reduced officers in parliament's northern army. He incurred further debts riding to York, Leeds, Bradford, Wakefield, and Doncaster vainly pursuing these arrears. His diurnal ends on 26 January 1649 noting he intended to leave for London, perhaps to witness the king's execution.

In 1651 Eyre styled himself gentleman, and purchased enclosed crown lands at Blandesby Park, in Pickering, in the North Riding of Yorkshire, for £5966. This purchase created difficulty as he had borrowed heavily and could not sell the land or borrow more money. He complained of the great losses he had 'susteyned in the late warrs and above 6 yeares Continuall waiting on the late Parliamt for our just due' (BL, Add. MS 21427, fol. 177). His will directed his funeral to be 'without outward pompe or great congregating of people' (Eyre, appx, 353). He died in 1661 and was buried on 6 April, probably at Penistone. His wife died between 25 April and 6 July 1668.   ANDREW J. HOPPER

Sources A. Eyre, 'A dyurnall, or, Catalogue of all my accions and expences from the 1st of January 1646-[7-]', ed. H. J. Morehouse, *Yorkshire diaries and autobiographies*, 1, ed. C. Jackson, SurtS, 65 (1877) • K. Wrightson, *English society, 1580–1680* (1982) • J. N. Dransfield, *History of Penistone* (1906) • J. Lister, ed., *West Riding sessions records: orders, 1611–1642, indictments, 1637–1642*, Yorkshire Archaeological Society, records ser., 53 (1915), vol. 2 • D. Hey, 'The Riches of Bullhouse: a family of Yorkshire dissenters', *Northern History*, 31 (1995), 178–93 • certificates for the sale of crown lands, PRO, E121/5/5 • Baynes correspondence, BL, Add. MS 21427, fol. 177 • PRO, SP 23/1/191; 23/110/342; 23/135/241; 19/123/15 • BL, Egerton MS 1048, fol. 85 • T. Dyson, *The history of Huddersfield and district* (1932) • J. Hunter, *Familiae minorum gentium*, ed. J. W. Clay, 2, Harleian Society, 38 (1895) • *Memoirs of Master John Shawe*, ed. J. R. Boyle (1882) **Archives** BL, diary and will, Add. MS 25463 • BL, Add. MSS 21419, fol. 243; 21420, fol. 176; 21421, fols. 131, 200; 21422, fols. 72, 93; 21423, fols. 72, 142; 21424, fols. 33, 45, 298; 21425, fol. 122; 21426, fol. 118; 21427, fols. 253–4 • W. Yorks. AS, Kirklees, county diary relating to accounts, amusements, daily life, fishing, and religion **Wealth at death** house and lands at Haslehead; land at Grimble Carr; bequests of £40; army arrears up to £688; Haslehead valued at £900 in 1647: Eyre, 'A dyurnall', 354–5

Eyre [*née* Aldersey], **Anne** (1612/13–1681), account keeper, was probably the third of seven children of Samuel Aldersey (*d.* 1633), a London merchant and haberdasher who had traded to Nuremberg, and his wife, Mary (*d.* 1628), daughter of Philip van Oyrle of Nuremberg and Antwerp. Samuel Aldersey's association with the Collectors of St Antholin's, an influential puritan group aiming to control appointments to church livings and lectureships, among whose members was Robert Eyre, a prominent Lincoln's Inn bencher, resulted in a meeting between Anne and Eyre's son, Robert Eyre junior (1609/10–1655). They married at St Antholin's, London, on 22 March 1631, when Anne was eighteen years old. Her portion was £1000, a large sum which reflected the two families' wealth.

The newly married couple went to Salisbury, Wiltshire,

to reside in the house of Anne's father-in-law, The Cheese-cross, a three-storeyed, fourteenth-century, timber-framed building (later 31 Cheesemarket). They attended services in the adjacent parish of St Edmund, led by a puritan rector, Peter Thacher. When in 1637 their own parish of St Thomas objected they and other offenders were summoned to the subdean's court in the cathedral for admonishment.

In August 1638 Robert Eyre senior died and his son, now head of the household, started an accounts book. After six months Anne took over the book and the family's finances. The book survives, a remarkably detailed and interesting statement of the household's expenditure for the years 1638 to 1645. Neatly and conscientiously kept, it provides a possibly unique insight into the lifestyle of an urban family of the middling sort. By this time the household comprised, in addition to Anne and Robert, their four children, including Samuel *Eyre (*bap.* 1638, *d.* 1698), the future judge (a fifth child having died in 1635), and four servants, including Anne Thacher, daughter of the puritan minister. The family's expenditure declined once the civil war started, despite additional spending on such items as cleaning armour and weapons, mending a musket, purchase of ammunition, and barricading the town. Despite these defensive preparations, when nearby Marlborough was looted in December 1642, the Eyres rented accommodation in the comparative safety of the Isle of Wight, where in July 1643 Anne and two of her children survived a smallpox attack. The Eyres had returned to Salisbury by October 1646, though their income, derived from property rents, was depleted.

A surviving letter from Anne to her son, Samuel, in 1660 tactfully advises him to make enquiries before getting engaged: 'when done, not to be undone, and done either happy or unhappy' (Wilts. & Swindon RO, Eyre–Matcham MSS 1369, box 36); Samuel duly made an advantageous marriage. By 1672 Anne was living in Watling Street, London, with her mentally deranged daughter, Margaret Hassell, but she later moved back to Salisbury. In her will dated 1681 she left Samuel her book of Luther's sermons and 'all my surgery and physic books and receipts'; she was evidently living in comfortable circumstances. She was buried at St Thomas's, Salisbury, on 20 October 1681. Industrious and methodical, her life had been dominated by religion and family responsibilities. C. G. LEWIN

Sources account book of Robert and Anne Eyre, 1638–45, priv. coll. [in possession of C. G. Lewin] · marriage settlement, Wilts. & Swindon RO, Eyre–Matcham MS 1369, box 38 [Robert and Anne Eyre] · A. Eyre, letter, 24 May 1660, Wilts. & Swindon RO, Eyre–Matcham MS 1369, box 36 · parish register, St Thomas's, Salisbury, Wilts. & Swindon RO, parish registers 1900 · will, 1681, Wilts. & Swindon RO, sub-dean of Salisbury [Anne Eyre] · Wilts. & Swindon RO, D4/5/1 [sub-dean of Sarum's citations quorum nomina, 1611–1638, for 1636 and 1637] · sub-dean of Sarum's presentments, 1612–39, Wilts. & Swindon RO [presentments for St Thomas's, Sarum, 1636 and 1637] [unnumbered] · M. E. F. Richardson-Eyre, *A history of the Wiltshire family of Eyre* (1897) · I. M. Calder, *Activities of the puritan faction of the Church of England, 1625–33* (1957) · *Calendar of the manuscripts of Major-General Lord Sackville*, 2 vols., HMC, 80 (1940–66), vol. 2, pp. 138–40, 143, 147, 153, 164–5, 181 · C. G. O. Bridgeman, *The family of Aldersley* (1899)

Archives priv. coll., MS account book | Wilts. & Swindon RO, Eyre–Matcham MSS, 1369
Wealth at death fairly wealthy; bequests incl. books, two silver trencher plates, pearl-mother spoon, gilt cup with inscription, set of damask linen, furniture, gold rings, pearl necklace of three rows, gold and silver pieces, etc.: will, Wilts. & Swindon RO

Eyre, Charles (1784–1864), writer, was the son of John Eyre of Sherfield, Hampshire, and was educated at Dr Valpy's school in Reading before proceeding in 1803 to Trinity College, Cambridge, where he proceeded BA in 1807. He afterwards took orders in the Church of England, but finally attached himself to the Unitarians. He took considerable interest in the movement that led to the Reform Bill of 1832, and on that matter published a *Letter Addressed to the Dukes of Norfolk and Grafton* (1831). He was for some time the proprietor of three liberal newspapers printed at Colchester. His religious bent found expression in such publications as *An Illustration of the Epistles of St Paul* (1832) and *The Fall of Adam* (1852), an amended edition of Milton's *Paradise Lost*. In later life he managed a large farm, but agreed to part with it at the solicitation of some members of his family. Before he had signed the transfer, however, he committed suicide by hanging himself at his residence, Upper Park, Dedham, Essex, on 28 September 1864. An inquest ruled that he had been temporarily insane. He left two daughters: Elizabeth, who married George Gretton and went to live in Boulogne, and Mary Anne.

FRANCIS WATT, *rev.* NILANJANA BANERJI

Sources Venn, *Alum. Cant.*, 2/2 · *GM*, 3rd ser., 17 (1864), 662, 797 · *Essex Standard and Eastern Counties Advertiser* (5 Oct 1864)
Wealth at death under £35,000: resworn probate, Aug 1865, CGPLA Eng. & Wales

Eyre, Charles Petre (1817–1902), Roman Catholic archbishop of Glasgow, was born on 7 November 1817 at York, the fifth of nine children and third of five sons of John Lewis Eyre (1789–1880), later a director of the South Western Railway Company, and his wife, Sara Parker (1790/91–1825), daughter of William Parker of Kingston upon Thames. After his mother's death, Eyre's father married Augustine Cecile Pulcherie (*d.* 1876), daughter of Armand Dumesniel, marquis de Sommery, in 1828. The Eyre family had been settled in Derbyshire since the thirteenth century, but had lost most of their lands by confiscation at the Reformation. They maintained their Catholic allegiance, however, and four of the five sons and one grandson of John Lewis Eyre were ordained priest. His two elder brothers having predeceased him, Charles Eyre succeeded to the papal title of count of the Lateran Hall on his father's death on 11 November 1880.

On 28 March 1826 Eyre entered St Cuthbert's College, Ushaw, near Durham, where his great-uncle, Thomas Eyre, had been president. He was made deacon in May 1838, entered the English College, Rome, in December 1839, and was ordained at Rome on 19 March 1842. His working life was spent in almost equal parts between north-east England (twenty-six years), and Glasgow (thirty-three years). He was appointed to Newcastle in

1843; and to Wooler in 1849. Illness between May 1850 and July 1856 compelled him to undertake light work at Haggerstone Castle near Berwick upon Tweed, before returning to Newcastle. In 1868 he was appointed vicar-general of Hexham and Newcastle.

Eyre had already been identified as a future bishop, having been proposed for Hexham, and as coadjutor-archbishop of Sydney, Australia, in 1866. He was not, however, the first candidate proposed for the western district of Scotland in 1869. Indeed, Michael O'Sullivan of Birmingham was all but appointed before Henry Manning, archbishop of Westminster, submitted Eyre's name to Rome. Other candidates included the Redemptorists Robert Coffin and Edward Bridgett, and Bernard O'Reilly (later bishop of Liverpool). Eyre was nominated as delegate-apostolic for Scotland on 29 November 1868, titular archbishop of Anazarbus on 11 December 1868, and consecrated in Rome on 31 January 1869. On 16 April 1869, his appointment as administrator-apostolic of the western district of Scotland was confirmed.

Eyre arrived in Glasgow on 9 March 1869, with the twin task of preparing for the restoration of a diocesan hierarchy in Scotland, and to restore calm to the western district, which was deeply divided by tension between Scots and Irish Catholics. He attended the First Vatican Council in 1869–70, and he embarked on an extensive programme of school and church building. In 1874, he opened a local seminary, St Peter's College. Although his tenure of office as administrator-apostolic was not without an initially unsettled period, he was presented with an address in 1876, from Scots- and Irish-born clergy, commending the progress of the previous seven years.

Eyre developed an ultramontane identity among his people. But he did not share the view of some northern district clergy, who remained unconvinced of the need for a diocesan hierarchy, viewing it as inserting an intermediary into hitherto direct links with Rome through the Congregatio de Propaganda Fide. With the ending in 1878 of the system of districts and vicariates-apostolic, he became archbishop of the restored archdiocese of Glasgow on 15 March of that year. His archdiocese included Motherwell and Paisley which later became dioceses (1948). Archdiocesan synods were held in 1881, 1888, and 1897, at which Eyre continued to promote schemes for the division of missions, which were almost dioceses in themselves. A cathedral chapter was erected in 1884.

The archbishop wrote extensively on historical and religious matters, including his *History of St Cuthbert*, first published in 1849, which reached a revised third edition in 1887. He also wrote *Children of the Bible*, a collection of leaflet lives of Scottish saints, and papers on the medieval cathedral of Glasgow. Eyre sought to have the Catholic community accepted as an integral part of Scottish life, and his efforts were recognized when he was made LLD by the University of Glasgow in 1892. In quite another sphere Eyre (with Michael Davitt) was among the early patrons of Celtic Football Club, founded in 1888. Eyre died at his home, 6 Bowmont Gardens, Glasgow, aged eighty-four, on 27 March 1902; he was buried on 31 March at St Peter's College, Bearsden, but has since been re-buried at St Andrew's Cathedral, Glasgow.   MARY McHUGH

Sources Glasgow Archdiocesan Archive, Eyre MSS · *DNB* · *Catholic Directory for Scotland* (1903) · J. Darragh, *The Catholic hierarchy of Scotland: a biographical list, 1653–1985* (1986) · B. Aspinwall, 'Anyone for Glasgow — the strange nomination of Rt Revd Charles Eyre in 1868' [preview of as yet unpubd article] · *CCI* (1902)
Archives Glasgow Roman Catholic Archdiocesan Archives, corresp., diaries, and papers, incl. sermons
Wealth at death £149,734 6s. 11d.: confirmation, 2 July 1902, *CCI*

Eyre, Edmund John (1767–1816), playwright, was born on 20 May 1767, the son of Ambrose Eyre (1739/40–1796), rector of Leverington and Outwell, Cambridgeshire, and his wife, the sister of the Revd Mr Underwood, rector of East Barnet. Eyre was sent to the Merchant Taylors' School when he was ten years old, and in 1785 he was appointed exhibitioner—first on Parkin's and afterwards on Stuart's foundation—at Pembroke College, Cambridge. He left the university without graduating to join a theatrical company, and on 28 May 1791 his play *The Dreamer Awake* received its second (and last) performance at Covent Garden, with Eyre in the role of Standfast. This was to be his only London role until 1806, when he appeared at Drury Lane. The interim period was spent at theatres in Bath, Bristol, and Edinburgh, where Eyre gained considerable experience as a comedian, although he is said to have been a 'respectable rather than a great actor' (Baker).

Eyre's personal life was complicated and is shrouded in some mystery. He was married to Mrs Elizabeth Bolton on 22 January 1793 in Birmingham; she was an actress with the Bath company, and continued to act as Mrs Eyre up to the 1799–1800 season. Eyre is said to have left her in 1804, when he eloped with another actress, a Miss Smith, whom he is reported to have married in July of that year at Stratford-le-Bow. Genest claims that 'he either gave his name or was married [to Miss Smith], upon the frivolous pretence of some irregularity with which his first marriage was attended' (Genest, *Eng. stage*, 8.202). Whether or not this second marriage was legal, she was presumably the Mrs Henrietta Eyre who performed in Edinburgh from the spring of 1805, and who acted there with Eyre until his death.

As a writer, Eyre was industrious and versatile. He was the author of two poems, 'A Friend to Old England' (1793), and 'The Two Bills' (1796), and of a volume entitled *Observations Made at Paris during the Peace* (1803), but his reputation rests on his dramatic pieces. These include a tragedy, *The Maid of Normandy* (1793); comedies such as *Consequences* (1794) and *High Life in the City* (1810); *The Lady of the Lake* (1811), a dramatization of Sir Walter Scott's poem; and *The Tears of Britain, or, Funeral of Lord Nelson* (1805).

Eyre died in April 1816, leaving his second wife and their numerous children in some financial difficulty. A theatrical benefit held for his family was very successful, and Henrietta Eyre remained a member of the Theatre Royal company at Edinburgh until at least 1820.

M. CLARE LOUGHLIN-CHOW

Sources Genest, *Eng. stage*, vol. 8 · Highfill, Burnim & Langhans, *BDA*, 5.131–3 · C. J. Robinson, ed., *A register of the scholars admitted into Merchant Taylors' School, from AD 1562 to 1874*, 2 (1883), 143 · *IGI* · D. E. Baker, *Biographia dramatica, or, A companion to the playhouse*, rev. I. Reed, new edn, rev. S. Jones, 3 vols. in 4 (1812) · *N&Q*, 2nd ser., 6 (1858), 414 · *DNB*

Eyre, Edward John (1815–1901), explorer and colonial governor, was born at Whipsnade, Bedfordshire, on 5 August 1815, the third son of Anthony William Eyre, curate of Whipsnade and later vicar of Hornsea and Long Riston in Yorkshire, and his wife, Sarah Mapleton, the daughter of a doctor in Bath. The clergy were important in Eyre's background: his grandfather was canon of York and his grandmother was the daughter of another clergyman.

Eyre attended various schools: at Thorparch, near Rotherham, at Grantham and Louth, both in Lincolnshire, and at Sedbergh, Yorkshire. He was not notable as a scholar but was good with his hands, especially at carpentry, and fond of outdoor activities such as fishing and climbing. At the age of sixteen he left Sedbergh grammar school, intent on entering the army. Although the family was relatively poor, it was able to provide the money for a commission. But before the commission came through his father suggested Australia as an alternative; Eyre liked the idea and accepted the offer, which included £400 capital to begin life as a settler. At the age of seventeen he sailed from London.

Australia Once in Australia, Eyre became a farmer and sheep grazer in New South Wales, working initially for an established settler, William Bell. During his year with Bell he received convict labour to assist him with his sheep. He then established his own farm in a partnership which later ran into difficulties; after three years Eyre was obliged to sell his farm and start again. This time he chose overlanding: driving cattle and sheep from New South Wales to the new settlements in South Australia. Despite the hardships of this life, Eyre was able to make a considerable amount of money. Yet, instead of continuing as an overlander and gaining a measure of financial independence, he decided to devote his energies to exploring the north and west of South Australia.

Eyre's first expedition in 1839 lasted six months and gave him a taste for further exploration, especially to the west of South Australia. In 1840 he began a memorable trek from Adelaide to Western Australia, round the head of the Great Australian Bight. No one had previously made this journey through an area characterized by 1000 miles of intense heat and desolation. Having set out with one other white man and a small group of Aborigines, Eyre reached his destination of Albany more than a year later, but accompanied only by one Aborigine. Although he had not made any important discoveries and, indeed, had ruined himself financially, he had displayed enormous courage and endurance. He returned to Adelaide as a hero. Three years later he received the gold medal of the Royal Geographical Society.

During Eyre's period as an overlander and as an explorer, he had considerable contacts with Aborigines, and in his relations with them had shown humanity and

Edward John Eyre (1815–1901), by Julia Margaret Cameron, 1867

tact. Accordingly, but also in response to the colonists' wish that Eyre be found a position, the new governor of South Australia, Sir George Grey, offered him the post of resident magistrate and protector of the Aborigines on the Murray River in South Australia. This was an area which had witnessed serious problems between the settlers and the indigenous population, and Eyre proved a great success in the job. Unlike many of the settlers, he believed that it was possible for Europeans to co-exist with the Aborigines. At the same time he regarded the Aborigines' culture as inferior to that of the Europeans and sought to introduce features of European civilization to them. He described his encounters with Aborigines in his book *Manners and Customs of the Aborigines of Australia* (1845), which also included the journals of his expeditions.

Eyre returned to England in 1845, seeking a position in the colonial service. He brought two Aborigine boys with him to be educated in England, but one died and Eyre had to send the other one back to Australia. While he was applying for posts he visited friends and family, and in the process met his future wife, Adelaide Fanny (Ada) Ormond. The daughter of a captain in the Royal Navy, Ada Ormond was a beautiful girl then in her teens. She was not to become Eyre's wife until four and a half years later; at the time of their meeting he had no job and no certain prospects. However, in November 1846 he was appointed lieutenant-governor of the South Island of New Zealand, under the governorship of Sir George Grey. He sailed for New Zealand at the beginning of 1847.

Early governmental career Eyre ran into difficulties almost immediately on taking up his duties in New Zealand. The settlers in the colony were indignant that they were to be governed by a 'sheep driver' and 'cattle drover'; moreover, Eyre's personality made the situation that much worse. A favourable biographer described him as 'shy, poor, and a solitary in all he had done ... totally unsuited to public life in the social sense' (Dutton, 176). In addition, Eyre was awkward physically. Descriptions of him in his thirties characterize him as being tall, but with a badly proportioned head, a narrow chest, a speech impediment, and an awkward gait. Although he was conscientious and honest, he was regarded by many of the colonists as excessively pious, as well as cold and aloof. Relations with the governor, Sir George Grey, also deteriorated quickly. Grey clearly disliked Eyre and made his life extremely difficult, effectively depriving his lieutenant-governor of any real power. It did not help matters that Grey's wife nearly stymied Eyre's courtship with Ada Ormond, who came out to New Zealand to marry him. They married on 3 April 1850. By the time his term was finished, in 1853, Eyre had two children and was again in need of a job in the colonial service.

In October 1854 Eyre was appointed lieutenant-governor of the island of St Vincent, where he encountered a very different situation from that in Australia or New Zealand. St Vincent had suffered serious economic difficulties in the wake of emancipation and the loss of the protective sugar duties in the British market. In addition, Eyre believed, the political institutions of the island were unwieldy. Instead of the two-chamber legislature consisting of an elected house of assembly and a nominated council, he recommended a single legislative chamber. But he faced some of the same difficulties he had experienced in New Zealand: he failed to make sufficient personal contact with the colonists. His shyness was not helped by his wife, whose health suffered badly in the tropical climate of St Vincent, but who also adopted unduly grand airs for a lieutenant-governor's wife. In 1857, when the couple visited England on leave, his wife remained there and did not return to St Vincent with her husband. During his remaining time alone in St Vincent, Eyre wrote an *Autobiographical Narrative*, published in 1984, about his early years in Australia.

By this time it was already becoming clear that Eyre had a very different perception of African-Caribbeans from that which he had of Aborigines. He had absorbed the increasingly negative racial perceptions of black people in England in the middle of the century and was nervous about the black and coloured population in the West Indies and the possibilities of racial violence. He would have preferred a post in Australia; instead, in 1859, he was appointed temporary governor of the Leeward Islands. Based in Antigua for the year, he proved to be a reasonable administrator but again failed to mix easily with the colonists. He returned to England in 1860 and had to wait eighteen months for his next appointment, in 1862, as temporary lieutenant-governor of Jamaica. By then he was the father of five children.

Governor of Jamaica Eyre arrived in Jamaica in March 1862 and found himself in a difficult situation. As in New Zealand, the colonists complained that they were being governed by a man who was socially insignificant. Moreover, Eyre was a poor man in a rich man's job; the governor's salary had been cut from £10,000 to £5000, and Eyre received only half that amount as a temporary official acting until the governor's return. To make matters worse, Jamaica was facing serious economic and political problems. Its sugar economy had suffered a dramatic decline in the wake of emancipation, and sugar production in the 1860s was less than half what it had been thirty years previously. Many ex-slaves had moved off the plantations to work on their own land; from the planters' perspective, this had created a labour shortage on the island. The Jamaican house of assembly was divided into factions, consisting of representatives of the planters on the one hand and of coloureds, Jews, and more urban interests on the other.

Once in Jamaica, Eyre almost immediately ran into trouble with the most outspoken and radical coloured politician on the island, George William Gordon. Gordon had grown increasingly concerned about the problems of the poor at about the same time that he was shifting his religious affiliation to the Native Baptists. As a magistrate in Morant Bay, he reported to Eyre about the death of an ill and poor man who had been sent to the local gaol, where he had died. Gordon's complaint concerned the illegal imprisonment of the man and the filthy state of the gaol. Eyre rather impulsively censured Gordon and removed him from the magistracy. Although the Colonial Office supported Eyre's actions in this case, it also applauded Gordon's attempt to improve conditions at the gaol and chided Eyre for not carefully examining the evidence.

This case established a pattern for Eyre. He became embroiled in a series of political difficulties, culminating in a motion of no confidence in him passed by one of the factions in the house of assembly. But the motion had the opposite effect from that intended. Faced with a challenge to its prerogative, the Colonial Office promoted Eyre to the governorship of Jamaica in April 1864. It was no coincidence that Eyre was a strong supporter of Colonial Office plans to reduce the powers of the house of assembly and, ultimately, to transform the legislature into a largely nominated body.

The Morant Bay rebellion and its aftermath The following year, 1865, proved to be calamitous for Jamaica and for Eyre. In March he received a letter forwarded by the Colonial Office from Edward Underhill, the secretary of the Baptist Missionary Society in England. In the letter Underhill claimed that the freed population was in a deplorable state and blamed the Jamaican house of assembly for inept and biased legislation. Underhill also pointed to the deteriorating economic conditions in Jamaica and to the effects of the terrible drought which the island was suffering. The Underhill letter led to a series of island-wide meetings, many of which supported the allegations. More importantly, they helped to inflame the political atmosphere in the colony. During the summer Eyre received reports of a possible conspiracy in western Jamaica. He ordered two men-of-war to be sent to the threatened area. But the rebellion instead broke out two months later on the other side of the island.

On 11 October 1865 several hundred black people marched into the town of Morant Bay, the capital of the predominantly sugar-growing parish of St Thomas in the East. They pillaged the police station of its weapons and then confronted the volunteer militia which had been called up to protect the meeting of the vestry, the political body which administered the parish. Fighting broke out between the militia and the crowd, and by the end of the day the crowd had killed eighteen people and wounded thirty-one others. Seven members of the crowd died. In the days which followed the outbreak, bands of people in different parts of the parish killed two planters and threatened the lives of many others. The disturbances spread across the parish of St Thomas in the East, from its western border with St David to its northern boundary with Portland.

On learning of the outbreak, Eyre acted immediately. He dispatched troops to Morant Bay, declared martial law in the eastern part of the island, and travelled to the affected area to supervise operations. For Eyre the whole island was at risk; he believed that the rebellion was aimed at exterminating the white and brown population and that it had to be suppressed forcefully. Making use of the army, Jamaican forces, and the maroons (formerly a community of runaway slaves who were now an irregular but effective army of the colony), the government vigorously put down the rebellion. In the process nearly 500 people were killed and hundreds of others were seriously wounded. Many of these people were killed without trial and others were flogged indiscriminately.

Eyre concluded that his political enemy, George William Gordon, was behind the rebellion. Gordon was a political ally of the leader of the rebellion, Paul Bogle, who was a Native Baptist deacon in St Thomas in the East. Accordingly, Eyre had Gordon arrested in Kingston, which was under civil jurisdiction, and transferred to Morant Bay for court martial. He was found guilty, a sentence which Eyre approved before Gordon was hanged. It was this act which inspired much of the subsequent opposition to Eyre in Britain. Eyre also made use of the rebellion to achieve a long-term aim: he succeeded in convincing the house of assembly to abolish itself and allow the crown to take full responsibility for the colony.

Once news of the rebellion and the nature of its suppression reached England, there were calls for Eyre's removal from office and for an official inquiry. The government established a royal commission under Sir Henry Storks, then governor of Malta, to investigate the outbreak and took evidence in Jamaica on the disturbances for nearly three months. Its conclusions were critical of Governor Eyre and of the severe repression in the wake of the rebellion. Eyre was dismissed. However, when he left Jamaica in the summer of 1866, he had become immensely popular among the white inhabitants of the island.

Eyre's reception in England was violently varied. The Jamaica Committee, headed by John Stuart Mill, sought to have him tried for murder as well as high crimes and misdemeanours. Its counterpart, the Eyre Defence Committee, included Thomas Carlyle and other leading figures who believed that Eyre had saved Jamaica for the empire. In a series of prosecutions the Jamaica Committee failed to have Eyre indicted; similarly, a number of civil suits brought against Eyre by people who had been injured or lost property during the rebellion also failed. The controversy brought colonial matters to the forefront of public debate and is an interesting if somewhat misleading touchstone of attitudes to empire in mid-Victorian Britain.

Despite his acquittal, Eyre was never offered another post in the colonial service. He even had difficulty gaining a pension. In 1872 the government did agree to defray his legal expenses, and a year later it finally granted him a pension. Eyre eventually moved to a remote house, Walreddon Manor, near Tavistock, Devon, where he lived almost anonymously with his family until his death there, on 30 November 1901 at the age of eighty-six. He was buried at Whitchurch, Devon, on 4 December.

GAD HEUMAN

Sources G. Dutton, *The hero as murderer: the life of Edward John Eyre, Australian explorer and governor of Jamaica, 1815–1901* (1967) · C. Hall, 'Imperial man: Edward Eyre in Australasia and the West Indies, 1833–1866', *The expansion of England: essays in the cultural history of race and ethnicity*, ed. B. Schwartz (1996) · G. Heuman, *The killing time: the Morant Bay rebellion in Jamaica* (1994) · G. J. Heuman, *Between black and white: race, politics and the free coloreds in Jamaica, 1792–1865* (1981) · B. Semmel, *The Governor Eyre controversy* (1962) · D. A. Lorrimer, *Colour, class and the Victorians: English attitudes to the negro in the mid-nineteenth century* (1978) · H. Hume, *The life of Edward John Eyre, late governor of Jamaica* (1867) · *DNB*

Archives National Library of Jamaica, MSS · State Library of New South Wales, Sydney, autobiography · State Library of South Australia, Sydney, corresp. and papers | Archives New Zealand, letters to Alfred Domett · Auckland Public Library, letters to Sir George Grey · BL, letters to Sir Roderick Murchison, Add. MS 46126 · PRO, corresp. with Lord Cardwell, PRO 30/48

Likenesses F. Joubert, line engraving, pubd 1865, NPG · J. Brown, stipple, pubd 1867 (after photograph by H. Hering), NPG · J. M. Cameron, photograph, 1867, NPG [*see illus.*] · C. A. Tomkins, mezzotint, pubd 1868 (after C. Mercier), BM, NPG · drawing, repro. in Dutton, *Hero as murderer*, 64 · photograph, repro. in Dutton, *Hero as murderer*, cover and frontispiece · photograph, repro. in Heuman, *The killing time*, xiv · wood-engraving, NPG; repro. in *ILN* (6 April 1867)

Wealth at death £3950 13s. 2d.: probate, 23 Jan 1902, *CGPLA Eng. & Wales*

Eyre, Francis (c.1732–1804), Roman Catholic apologist, was the younger son and one of five surviving children of Thomas Eyre (1684?–1749), a Roman Catholic landowner of Hassop Hall, Derbyshire, and Eastwell, Leicestershire, and his wife, Mary Holman (d. 1759), daughter and coheir of George Holman of Warkworth, Northamptonshire, and his wife, Lady Anastasia Howard. His maternal grandfather, William, Viscount Stafford, was beheaded after the Popish Plot. Eyre was educated at the English College at St Omer in France, and then at the Jesuit academy at Liège (c.1751–1753). He lived principally at Warkworth, Northamptonshire, the estate settled on him by his father in 1746, and he was twice married. His first marriage, on 11 February 1755, was to Lady Mary Radcliffe (1732–1796). Her father, the staunchly Jacobite Charles Radcliffe, who styled himself the fifth earl of Derwentwater (although legally no longer a peer), was executed after the rising of 1745. They had three sons and one daughter. The eldest, Francis (1762–1827), became the sixth earl of Newburgh in 1814 (a title held by his maternal grandmother in her own right). Lady Mary Eyre died on 27 May 1796. Eyre's second marriage, in 1801, was to Sarah Hernon, sister of a Smithfield druggist, Robert Hernon, also a Catholic.

Although Eyre was a country squire for most of his life, his father's bequest in 1749 of all his books to the young Francis suggests strong scholarly interests. His first two published works, in 1778 and 1779, were pamphlets criticizing Edward Gibbon's irreligiosity in his *Decline and Fall of the Roman Empire*. In 1778 Eyre signed the *Humble Address of the Roman Catholic Peers and Commoners* declaring loyalty to the crown. On the death in March 1792 of his childless nephew Thomas Eyre, he inherited the family estate at Hassop in Derbyshire. He first offered this as a refuge to an exiled community of Catholic nuns from Liège, where he had been educated, and then gave it to his eldest son, Francis. This coincided with Eyre's appointment as one of three conciliators, with John Webbe Weston and William Sheldon of Brailes, in the religious disputes between the Catholic Committee, a body predominantly of lay gentry, and the vicars apostolic, representing the Roman Catholic clergy and their supporters. The mediators' report was accepted and printed in May 1792.

In 1795 Eyre published anonymously (as 'a sincere friend of mankind') *A short essay on the Christian religion … the whole proposed as a preservative against the pernicious doctrines which have overwhelmed France with misery and desolation*. In the same year, under his own name, Eyre responded to attacks on Roman Catholicism in *A Letter to the Rev. Ralph Churton MA*. Churton, a scholar and writer, rector of Middleton Cheney, Northamptonshire, since 1792 (and archdeacon of St David's, Wales, from 1805), replied in *A Short Defence of the Church of England* that 'Popery' was a lie from beginning to end. Undeterred, Eyre closed the controversy in his 1798 *Reply to the Rev. Ralph Churton*, remarking on the happy decline of hostility between Anglicans and Roman Catholics.

A representative of traditional English Catholicism through his family connections and active in the internal disputes among co-religionists at the time of the passing of the second Catholic Relief Act in 1791–2, Francis Eyre came to public notice as an impartial arbitrator. He died on 7 October 1804 in London, where he was then living.

MARGARET O'SULLIVAN

Sources R. Meredith, 'The Eyres of Hassop and some of their connections from the Test Act to emancipation [pt 1]', *Recusant History*, 9 (1967–8), 5–52 • R. Meredith, 'The Eyres of Hassop and some of their connections from the Test Act to emancipation [pt 2]', *Recusant History*, 9 (1967–8), 267–87 • R. Meredith, 'A Derbyshire family in the 17th century: the Eyres of Hassop and their forfeited estates', *Recusant History*, 8 (1965–6), 12–77 • Gillow, *Lit. biog. hist.*, vol. 2 • *GM*, 1st ser., 74 (1804), 1072 • GEC, *Peerage*
Archives Northants. RO, abstract of title to Warkworth estate, MS 2A 4207 | BL, Eyre–Caryll letters, Add. MS 28232 • Sheff. Arch., evidence book of Rowland Eyre, MS A.314 [microfilm]

Eyre, Sir Giles (*bap.* 1635, *d.* 1695), judge, was the eldest son of Giles Eyre (*bap.* 1608, *d.* 1685) of Brickworth, Whiteparish, Wiltshire, and Anne (*bap.* 1617), daughter of Sir Richard Norton, first baronet, of Rotherfield, East Tisted, Hampshire. He was baptized on 28 May 1635 at Downton, Wiltshire. Eyre may have attended Winchester College in 1647, and was admitted to Exeter College, Oxford, in 1653. He entered Lincoln's Inn on 19 October 1654 and was called to the bar on 7 November 1661. Meanwhile he had been elected to parliament for Downton in 1660, and proceeded to join the opposition grouping under Lord Wharton. On 2 August he moved to lay aside the debate on the Thirty-Nine Articles and may have been a moderate dissenter in favour of comprehension. After a double return at the general election of 1661 he abandoned his seat. On 18 November 1662 Eyre was licensed to marry Dorothy (*b.* 1644/5), daughter of Sir John Ryves of Ranston, Shroton, Dorset. She died on 15 January 1668, aged twenty-three, having borne three sons. By July 1673 (when their first child was born) Eyre had married Christabella (*b.* 1654/5), daughter of John Wyndham of Tale Payhembury, Devon.

Eyre seems to have collected local offices, serving as recorder of Newport, Isle of Wight, 1675–84 and 1688–95, and Southampton 1681–90. He also held the office of deputy recorder of Salisbury in 1675, and actively exerted himself in procuring a new charter, receiving a tankard worth £10 in recognition of his services. He succeeded as recorder on the death of the incumbent in 1681, but he was in turn replaced when the corporation charter was surrendered in October 1684. James II's agents had high hopes that Eyre, sympathetic to dissent, would be returned to the parliament expected in 1688; in 1687 he was described as 'a lawyer, a strong dissenter; he manages my Lord Arundell of Warders [*sic*] concerns' (Duckett, 208). Arundell was a Roman Catholic peer, which they felt augured well for support for James II's religious policies: he 'hath been very violent, but ambitious of honour, and supposed he will be right to reconcile himself to your majesty' (ibid., 224). When James II restored the corporation in October 1688 Eyre returned to the recordership. He represented Salisbury in the convention of 1689, spoke in favour of retaining the word 'abdicated' in the resolution declaring the throne vacant in the conference with the House of Lords, and supported the bill declaring the convention a regular parliament. He also played a minor role in the committee and debates which led to the Bill of Rights. Indeed, he may have been the author of *Reflections upon the late great revolution: written by a lay-hand in the country for the satisfaction of some neighbours*, which was a defence of the settlement.

Eyre's parliamentary career came to an end upon his appointment as judge of king's bench on 4 May 1689, and its concomitant creation as a serjeant-at-law. He was knighted on 31 October 1689. When called upon to give his opinion to the Lords on the surrender of charters Eyre believed that they could be surrendered if there was agreement within the corporation, and that surrender was possible because 'otherwise it is to set up a perpetuity, which the law always avoids' (Halliday, 274, 276n.). One of his judicial tasks was to preside over the trial of several suspected Jacobites at Manchester in October 1694, at which the defendants were found not guilty. Eyre died on 2 June 1695 at his London home in Red Lion Square, and was buried ten days later with his first wife in Whiteparish church. His widow married, on 27 March 1699 (aged forty-four), Lord Glasfoord, a needy Scottish Catholic, although she apparently abandoned him in the Fleet prison that same year. Her will was proved in February 1711.

STUART HANDLEY

Sources HoP, *Commons, 1660–90*, 1.456–7; 2.287–8 · Sainty, *Judges*, 35 · Baker, *Serjeants*, 450, 510 · G. Duckett, ed., *Penal laws and Test Act*, 1 (1882), 208, 224 · will, PRO, PROB 11/426, sig. 114 · IGI · *Wiltshire Notes and Queries*, 5 (1905–7), 100 · R. C. Hoare and J. G. Nichols, *The history of modern Wiltshire*, 5/2: *Hundred of Frustfield* (1837), 56 · A. W. Hughes Clarke, ed., *Miscellanea Genealogica et Heraldica*, 5th ser., 9 (1935–7), 107, 109 · L. G. Schwoerer, *The declaration of rights, 1689* (1981), 34n., 41 · P. D. Halliday, *Dismembering the body politic: partisan politics in England's towns, 1650–1730* (1998), 274, 276 · *The manuscripts of Lord Kenyon*, HMC, 35 (1894), 309–10, 365, 372, 383 · Foss, *Judges*, 7.314–16 · Pengelly papers, BL, Add. MS 6722, fol. 20v.

Eyre, Sir James (*bap.* 1734, *d.* 1799), judge, was baptized at Wells, Somerset, on 13 September 1734, the son of the Revd Thomas Eyre (1686/7–1753), of Wells, prebendary of Salisbury from 1733 until his death. He was a scholar of Winchester College in 1747, and matriculated from St John's College, Oxford, on 27 October 1749. He entered Lincoln's Inn, without a degree, on 26 November 1753 and moved to Gray's Inn on 8 November 1755. He was called to the bar on 25 November 1755, under the patronage of Sir Thomas Parker, chief baron of the exchequer; he later was a bencher of Gray's Inn.

Eyre began practice as one of the four counsel for the corporation of London, a position that he purchased on 20 January 1755 for £63, practising in the inferior courts of the City for some years. He was appointed deputy recorder on 17 February 1761, on the recommendation of Sir William Moreton, the recorder, and was himself elected recorder by the court of aldermen in April 1763, on the death of Moreton. He now occupied a highly visible post, with large responsibilities and the right to wear silk. On the bench at the Old Bailey he met the chief justices and almost all the other high-court judges, who took turns in that court. As recorder Eyre pronounced the sentence at the end of the sessions and reported in person to the cabinet and the king on Old Bailey convicts being considered for pardons. His other duties involved him in constitutional controversies, including the rights of the chartered

Sir James Eyre (*bap.* 1734, *d.* 1799), by Lemuel Francis Abbott, 1770

City and of the wider metropolitan electorate. In October 1763 the common council unanimously voted an increase in his salary of £280 over the ancient one of £120. He became one of the counsel for John Wilkes, notably in *Wilkes v. Wood*, in December 1763, in which he attracted attention with an impressive speech against general warrants. Four years later the common council again raised his salary, by another £200.

By the end of the decade, however, Eyre was finding favour with the government, a prerequisite to any higher judicial appointment. In 1769, at government request, he issued a warrant to the sheriffs to hang John Doyle and John Valline (condemned for cutting silk in the loom) near Bethnal Green church, part of the government's attempt to repress riots by the Spitalfields weavers. Eyre, as recorder, had sentenced the men to death without mention of the place of execution, and John Sawbridge and James Townsend, the Wilkesite City sheriffs, strongly resisted the change from Tyburn as an unconstitutional innovation, expanding prerogative powers, and raising the danger of secret executions. They condemned as equally unconstitutional the deployment of troops in Spitalfields to ensure that the executions were carried out. Eyre's power to issue such a warrant was upheld (*Re Doyle and Valline*) but an increasingly Wilkesite common council now opposed him. The following year he decisively joined the government side when he refused to present a remonstrance by the corporation to the king respecting Wilkes's exclusion from parliament. The common council voted by a large majority that he 'be no more advised with, retained or employed in any of the affairs of this Corporation, he being deemed by this Court unworthy of their future trust or confidence' (common council journals, vol. 65). He continued to sit as recorder until October 1772.

Eyre was created serjeant-at-law, knighted, and made a baron of the exchequer on 6 November 1772, ultimately becoming chief baron on 26 January 1787. His first wife, of whom nothing further is known, died on 5 July 1787, and a forthcoming second marriage was announced in *The Times* on 7 April 1788. *The Times* reported persistent rumours in 1787–9 that Eyre might be made lord chancellor of Ireland. In 1789 he prevailed on Gray's Inn, where he had been a bencher, to accommodate the court of exchequer out of term-time, an arrangement that continued well into the nineteenth century. Alexander Wedderburn, first Baron Loughborough, having been made lord chancellor, Eyre followed him in the post of chief justice of common pleas, on 11 February 1793. Before this appointment he had served as chief commissioner of the great seal from 15 June 1792 to 21 January 1793. In civil cases he sometimes opposed innovations by William Murray, first earl of Mansfield, lord chief justice of the king's bench. In *Cocksedge* v. *Fanshaw* (1776–7, unreported), a case in which corn factors were opposed to the City, Eyre was the only judge hearing the appeal in exchequer chamber not to agree with the initial judgment of Mansfield, who favoured the merchants. In *Matthews* v. *Lewis and another* (1792) he resisted the trial in common pleas of issues best tried at equity, observing that it was dangerous 'to confound the jurisdictions of the different Courts'. Other judgments include *Nicholson* v. *Chapman* (1793), where inconvenience to the public was a basis for decision; *Waugh* v. *Carver, Carver, and Giesler* (1793), in which he imposed the liabilities of partnership on a profit-sharing arrangement to protect its creditors from fraud; and *Bush* v. *Steinman* (1799, 1 Bosanquet and Puller 404), on the liability of an employer for the torts of a contractor.

On assize Eyre usually went on the Norfolk circuit, or the western, where he had many relatives. Years after his death he was remembered by John Townsend, the Bow Street runner, for inflicting capital punishment with unremitting severity at one assize on the home circuit. The average ratio of executions to death sentences for all the years and places where he sat at assizes is greater than that of most other judges of the period.

Eyre with other judges sought to expand the law of treason at the end of the century. He sat with Chief Baron Archibald Macdonald on the trials of members of the London Corresponding Society in October 1794, having attended the privy council in May when the prisoners were first questioned. The judges' role there has been defended on the narrow ground that it was magisterial not prosecutorial: to advise the law officers on whether the evidence justified committal and on what charge. Eyre, according to the attorney-general, Sir John Scott, expressed the view that the accused were guilty of treason. When the special commission opened at the Old Bailey in October Eyre began by addressing the grand jury on the dangers of 'a traiterous and detestable conspiracy

… formed for subverting the existing laws and constitution, and for producing the system of anarchy and confusion which have so fatally prevailed in France'. Admitting that the law applicable to the case was unclear (and doing little to clarify it) he suggested that 'men who assemble to procure a Reform in Parliament may involve themselves in the guilt of High Treason'. Overawing parliament could destroy constitution and monarchy, 'that glorious fabric, which it has been the work of ages to erect … cemented by the best blood of our ancestors' (*The Times*, 3 Oct 1794). The cases, he said, would establish the reach of the law of treason.

Eyre's charge was printed in several versions, widely circulated, and provoked several replies, including a famous one by William Godwin, whose close friend Thomas Holcroft was among those indicted. *Cursory Strictures on the Charge Delivered by Lord Chief Justice Eyre to the Grand Jury October 2, 1794* appeared in the *Morning Chronicle* and as a pamphlet on 21 October, a few days before the trials began. Godwin castigated Eyre's 'many new and extraordinary doctrines on the subject of treason', his 'contemptible' play on words, and his 'sanguinary' conjectures on the probable guilt of the accused, 'worthy of the judicial ministers of Tiberius or Nero'. He accused Eyre of prejudice and ignorance and of inventing a new offence. A defence of Eyre, attributed to Sir Francis Buller, judge of king's bench, appeared in *The Times* on 25 October, calling for Godwin's prosecution. Daniel Isaac Eaton republished this attack, together with Godwin's *A Reply to an Answer to Cursory Strictures, Supposed to be Wrote by Judge Buller*, of 23 October, which the *Morning Chronicle* refused, fearing prosecution. Eyre reiterated some of his assertions in his summation of the case against Thomas Hardy, and on the whole summed up against him. In the trial of Horne Tooke, however, he allowed the defendant unusual liberties and summed up for an acquittal, although still proposing an expansive definition of treason. In the trials Eyre cautioned Thomas Erskine, counsel for the defence, for (among other issues) asking leading questions during cross-examination, a practice tolerated in king's bench but not in exchequer. Erskine is reported to have challenged the judge to a duel once the trial was over. Hardy, Tooke, and Thelwall were acquitted, and the other charges dropped. Godwin wrote to Eyre privately, praising his conduct of the trials while still objecting to his doctrine of treason, although also apologizing for his own warmth of expression. The only other treason trial that came before Eyre was that of Crossfield in 1796.

After his death, on 6 July 1799, Eyre was celebrated in obituaries principally as a sound judge, not given to citing precedent but learned in the law, and exceptionally astute at instructing juries. He left the proceeds of his estate—which included the lease of a house in Great George Street, Westminster; his seat, Ruscombe House, Berkshire; and the manor and two farms in the parish of Ruscombe, which he had purchased in 1787—as life estates to his wife, Mary, and his two surviving sisters, then to his brother Dr Thomas Eyre (*d.* 1812) BCL, DCL (Oxon.), treasurer and canon residentiary of Wells Cathedral. Eyre was particularly concerned that his trustees should hire a proper person to maintain his timber plantations. He appears to have had no children. He was buried in Ruscombe parish church.   DOUGLAS HAY

Sources *Annual Register* (1799) · Baker, *Serjeants* · J. Barrell, *Imagining the king's death: figurative treason, fantasies of regicide 1793–1796* (2000) · *The correspondence of Edmund Burke*, ed. T. W. Copeland and others, 10 vols. (1958–78), vol. 2, p. 32; vol. 9, p. 400 · F. Cowper, *A prospect of Gray's Inn*, 2nd edn (1985), 89 · W. R. Douthwaite, *Gray's Inn: its history & associations* (1886), 133, 141 · T. Leach, *Cases in crown law determined by the twelve judges, by the court of king's bench and by the commissioners of oyer and terminer and the general gaol delivery* (1789) [168 ER Leach] · A. Anstruther, *Reports of cases argued and determined in the court of exchequer, from approximately 1792 to 1795*, 2nd edn, 3 vols. (1817) [145 ER Anstruther] · H. Blackstone, *Reports of cases argued and determined in the courts of common pleas and the exchequer chamber … from approximately 1788 to 1796*, 4th edn, 2 vols. (1827) [126 ER H Blackstone] · J. S. Bosanquet and C. Puller, *Reports of cases argued and determined in the courts of common pleas and the exchequer chamber, and in the House of Lords, from approximately 1796 to 1804, both inclusive*, 3 vols. (1826) [126–7 ER Bosanquet and Puller] · Foss, *Judges*, 8.282–5 · E. Foss, *Biographia juridica: a biographical dictionary of the judges of England … 1066–1870* (1870), 245–6 · Foster, *Alum. Oxon.*, 1715–1886, 2.441 · T. P. Gallanis, 'Criminal defence counsel and the leading questions doctrine', American Society of Legal History annual conference, Chicago, 10 Nov 2001 [unpublished paper] · *GM*, 1st ser., 69 (1799), 709–11 · W. Godwin, *Cursory strictures on the charge delivered by Lord Chief Justice Eyre to the grand jury October 2, 1794* (1794) · W. Godwin, *A reply to an answer to cursory strictures, supposed to be wrote by Judge Buller* (1794) · Holdsworth, *Eng. law*, 8.479 · T. F. Kirby, *Winchester scholars: a list of the wardens, fellows, and scholars of … Winchester College* (1888), 248 · D. Lemmings, *Professors of the law: barristers and English legal culture in the eighteenth century* (2000) · M. Lobban, *The common law and English jurisprudence, 1760–1850* (1991) · M. Lobban, 'Nineteenth-century frauds in company formation: *Derry v. Peek* in context', *Law Quarterly Review*, 112 (1996) · P. H. Marshall, *William Godwin* (1984), 139 · R. A. Melikan, *John Scott Lord Eldon, 1751–1838* (1999) · *Engraved Brit. ports.*, 2.184 · J. Oldham, *The Mansfield manuscripts and the growth of English law in the eighteenth century*, 2 vols. (1992), 694 · [*Old Bailey*] *Proceedings* (1762–72) · L. Radzinowicz, *History of English criminal law and its administration from 1750*, 1 (1948) · W. P. Baildon, ed., *The records of the Honorable Society of Lincoln's Inn: the black books*, 4 (1902), 320 · Sainty, *Judges* · *Lord Eldon's anecdote book*, ed. A. L. J. Lincoln and R. L. McEwen (1960), 64 · H. Twiss, *The public and private life of Lord Chancellor Eldon*, 1 (1844), 283 · *State trials*, 24.200–1408; 25.1–748; 26.1–224 · *The Times* · W. P. Treloar, *Wilkes and the City* (1917), 93, 97 · *VCH Berkshire*, 3.204 · *Strictures on the lives and characters of the most eminent lawyers of the present day* (1790) · will, PRO, PROB 11/1328, sig. 584 · PRO, ASSI 5 · *DNB* · journals, CLRO, court of common council, vol. 63 (1762–5), fols. 129*v*–130 (26 Oct 1763); vol. 64 (1764–9), fol. 223 (18 Dec 1767); vol. 65 (1769–73), fol. 121*v* (12 Oct 1770)
Archives CLRO, common council journals, vols. 63–5 · PRO, ASSI 5 and other assize records · PRO, will, PCC, 584 Howe [1799], PROB 11/1328, sig. 584, fols. 321*v*–323*r*
Likenesses L. F. Abbott, oils, 1770, Royal Courts of Justice, London [*see illus.*] · two portraits, 1787–93, Gray's Inn, London · V. Green, mezzotint, pubd 1804 (after L. F. Abbott), BM · L. F. Abbott, oils, Gray's Inn, London · V. Green, mezzotint (after L. F. Abbott) · W. Ridley, stipple (after S. Drummond), BM; repro. in *European Magazine* (1800) · engraving, BM · mezzotint (after R. Dighton), NPG
Wealth at death incl. lease on a house in Great George Street, Westminster; Ruscombe House, Berkshire; manor and two farms in the parish of Ruscombe

Eyre, James (1748–1813), philologist, was the son of John Eyre, of Coventry. He was educated at Trinity College, Oxford, obtaining his BA degree in 1775 (his MA degree was incorporated at Gonville and Caius College, Cambridge, in 1802, which has given rise to some confusion over the university of his undergraduate attendance). Eyre was ordained deacon at Oxford on 11 June 1775, and priest at Worcester on 15 September 1776. He embarked upon a life of teaching about 1783, when he became headmaster of Solihull grammar school, a post he was to hold for thirty years. On 9 April 1790 he married Charlotte Harding, and they had six girls and four boys, all of whom were baptized in Solihull. In addition to his teaching duties, Eyre was the vicar of Winterbourne Stoke, Wiltshire, from 1801 to 1813, and vicar also of Nettleton, Wiltshire, from 1802 until his death.

Eyre is best known for his manuscript annotations of Samuel Johnson's *Dictionary of the English Language*. He died at the Solihull schoolhouse on 10 March 1813, however, before his research could be completed or published. His notes mostly consisted of citations from recent publications, and were incorporated by H. J. Todd in his 1818 edition of Johnson's dictionary. Eyre was summed up by one obituarist as having been 'equally distinguished by the solidity of his understanding and the benevolence of his heart' (*GM*).   JOHN D. HAIGH

Sources *GM*, 1st ser., 83/1 (1813), 499 · H. J. Todd, 'Introduction', in S. Johnson, *A dictionary of the English language*, ed. H. J. Todd, 5 vols. (1818), 1.iv · Venn, *Alum. Cant.*, 2/2.448 · Foster, *Alum. Oxon.* · IGI

Eyre, Sir James (1792–1857), surgeon and physician, the eldest son of William Eyre (1753/4–1830), vicar of Padbury and Hillesden, Buckinghamshire, was born on 14 February 1792. In October 1811 he began his medical education at St Bartholomew's Hospital, London, where he was a pupil of John Abernethy. In 1813 seventy-five students subscribed to give a great silver cup with cover to Abernethy, and Eyre was chosen to present the piece.

Eyre became a member of the Royal College of Surgeons in 1814 and in the same year began to practise in Hereford, where he attained some local celebrity. He was elected mayor in 1829, and was knighted by William IV the next year. Drinkwater, mayor of Liverpool, was the only other mayor knighted; referring to these honours, a remark of Abernethy to a patient preserves the correct pronunciation of Eyre's name: 'Go away', said Abernethy, 'and have always in your thoughts the names of the mayors who have just been knighted, Eyre and Drinkwater, and you will soon recover your wind, and your shape too, I promise you'.

Soon after being knighted, Eyre decided to qualify also as a physician. He studied in Paris for a year, and graduated MD at Edinburgh in 1834 with a thesis on pneumonia. In 1836 he became a member of the Royal College of Physicians, in London, where he set up in practice in Lower Brook Street. He was physician accoucheur to St George's and St James's Dispensary from 1834 until 1851, when he was appointed consulting physician. Eyre published several medical works mainly intended for a popular audience. Although never having a very extensive practice, 'He was a cheerful companion and a kind hearted man; fond and proud of his profession' (*The Lancet*, 27 June 1857, 651).

After practising for several years, Eyre retired to nearby Brompton. He died suddenly while visiting a friend at Lauriston House, Clapham, on 19 June 1857, having attended the queen's levee the night before.

NORMAN MOORE, *rev.* PATRICK WALLIS

Sources *Nomina eorum, qui gradum medicinae doctoris in academia Jacobi sexti Scotorum regis, quae Edinburgi est, adepti sunt, ab anno 1705 ad annum 1845*, University of Edinburgh (1846) · *The Lancet* (27 June 1857), 159, 651 · *GM*, 3rd ser., 3 (1857), 227–8 · Boase, *Mod. Eng. biog.* **Archives** Hereford City Library **Likenesses** C. S. Hervé, lithograph (after daguerreotype), BM

Eyre, John (1754–1803), evangelical and Church of England clergyman, was born in January 1754 in Bodmin, Cornwall, the son of John Eyre, who was in business, and his wife, Grace White. He was baptized on 25 February. Eyre was educated in classics by the Revd John Fisher, master of Bodmin grammar school, and in mathematics by the Revd Joseph Thorpe, rector of Forrabury and Trevalga, Cornwall, in his private school at Forrabury. Despite his childhood education, Eyre was apprenticed by his parents to Mr Oliver, a clothier of Tavistock, at the age of fifteen.

While living in Tavistock, the young man engaged in a life of revelling until he experienced a profound religious conversion and began to preach. For two years Eyre and his evangelical associates conducted revival meetings. At the expiration of his term of apprenticeship, his father persuaded him to return to Bodmin to go into business. When not employed, the young man secured the town hall and preached to all who wished to hear. 'The rich and the poor flocked to hear him' (Collison, June 1803, 229). Such activity infuriated his father, who commanded him to give up preaching. Unwilling to comply, Eyre was driven from his father's home.

After taking refuge with a friend in Plymouth, Eyre applied and secured admission to Trevecca College, the countess of Huntingdon's college in south Wales, in 1777. Under the patronage of the countess, he ministered at Tregony and St Agnes, Cornwall, Lincoln, Worcester, and Mulberry Gardens Chapel, London. Eyre's abilities exceeded those of many of his fellow students and he grew frustrated with the countess's decision to take him away from his studies in favour of itinerant preaching in England and Wales. He desired to take orders in the Church of England, and he matriculated at Emmanuel College, Cambridge, in 1778. On 30 May 1779 he was ordained deacon by Dr Robert Lowth, bishop of London; and he received priest's orders from the bishop of Lincoln on 19 December 1779. In the following years he held curacies in Weston, Lewes, Reading, and Chelsea. In November 1785 Eyre married Mary Keene (1757/8–1827), from near Reading, and the following month he was appointed minister of Homerton, or, as it was often called after its founder, Ram's Chapel, and he opened a school at Well Street, Hackney.

Eyre was active in his ministerial duties and particularly committed to the young and the poor of his parish. He sometimes admitted lay preachers to his pulpit, and occasionally shortened the liturgy. His congregation imitated

his 'generous and enlarged views, his humble Christian temper; and, like him, devoted large portions of their property to the cause of Christ' (Morison, 30). Still his most renowned achievements centred on national evangelical institutions. He conceived and initiated the *Evangelical Magazine*, a joint venture of the Church of England and dissenting ministers, the first number of which appeared in July 1793. He edited and contributed largely to its volumes until 1802.

In 1792 Trevecca College moved from its home in the Welsh mountains to a more central location at Cheshunt, Hertfordshire (where it took the name Cheshunt College). Upon this occasion Eyre and the Revd Anthony Crole conducted the service to commemorate the event. The proceedings, including Eyre's sermon, were published as *The Order Observed at the Opening of the Countess of Huntingdon's College*, in 1792. Eyre was one of the founders of the London Missionary Society (1794–5) and the Village Itinerancy Society. He was instrumental in the establishment of Hackney Theological College (1803) and an academy in Idle, Yorkshire (*c*.1800). After a long illness he died at Homerton on 28 or 29 March 1803, and was buried in a vault on the south side of the communion table in Homerton Chapel on 5 April. His funeral sermon was preached by the Revd Rowland Hill. His wife died at Well Street, Hackney, on 20 June 1827, aged sixty-nine, and was buried by her husband's side on 29 June. An extended memoir of Eyre by the Revd George Collison, president of Hackney Theological Seminary, appeared in the *Evangelical Magazine* for June and July 1803.

W. P. COURTNEY, *rev.*
DOROTHY EUGENIA SHERMAN BROWN

Sources G. Collison, 'Memoir of the late Rev. John Eyre [2 pts]', *Evangelical Magazine*, 11 (1803), 225–30, 273–87 · J. Morison, *The fathers and founders of the London Missionary Society*, new edn [1844] · Westminster College, Cambridge, Cheshunt archives · *GM*, 1st ser., 73 (1803), 386 · J. Campbell, *Maritime discovery and Christian missions* (1840) · Boase & Courtney, *Bibl. Corn.* · IGI **Archives** DWL, corresp. relating to Village Itinerancy Association **Likenesses** N. C. Branwhite, stipple, pubd 1803 (after S. Medley), NPG · sketch, repro. in Morison, *Fathers and founders*

Eyre, Margaret Radclyffe-Livingstone- [*née* Lady Margaret Kennedy], **styled countess of Newburgh** (1800–1889), philanthropist, was born on 6 June 1800, the third daughter of the six children of Archibald Kennedy, twelfth earl of Cassillis, later first marquess of Ailsa (1770–1846), and his wife, Margaret (*d.* 1848), second daughter of John Erskine of Dun, Forfarshire. On 14 November 1817, at Culzean Castle, she married Thomas (1790–1833), known as Viscount Kynnaird, son of Francis Radclyffe-Livingstone-Eyre (1762–1827) of Hassop, Derbyshire, claimant to the disputed earldom of Newburgh, and his wife, Dolly Gladwin (*d.* 1838). On his father's death in 1827 Viscount Kynnaird assumed the title of earl of Newburgh. He himself died on 22 May 1833, leaving Lady Newburgh a childless widow.

The Eyres were a long-established Roman Catholic family, and some time before 1850 Lady Newburgh joined the Roman Catholic church. Subsequently she was associated with Cecil Kerr, Lady Lothian (c.1811–1877), and Lady Georgiana Fullerton (1812–1885), fellow converts who became the doyennes of Catholic philanthropy in London. Lady Newburgh's annual subscription to the church in her own parish, Chelsea, exceeded those of other members of the congregation; £40 a month, a third of her income, was devoted to charities. Besides giving pensions to individuals in difficulties, she gave financial support to the Westminster Sisters of Charity for their soup kitchen and their mission in Horseferry Road. With Lady Georgiana she shared in the establishment and maintenance of the Hospital Society, a convalescent home, and the Catholic mission in Seven Dials. She was also an annual subscriber to the Foreign Mission College at Mill Hill and the Altar Society. In Scotland the new Roman Catholic church of Maybole, Ayrshire, near her former home, was built almost entirely from her contributions. Although she was said to have helped every charity in London, her assistance was given 'so quietly and secretly' (*The Tablet*, 462) that few realized the extent of her generosity. It is probable that, like Lady Georgiana Fullerton, she visited the poor as well as supporting charities.

In her last years, Lady Newburgh lost her sight: a photograph of her, as a frail and rather austere woman in a bath chair, shows her in her old age. A close friend, the Jesuit father Peter Gallwey, recalled that she bore her blindness cheerfully, drawing on psalms and prayers committed to memory to occupy her mind during sleepless nights. The frequent visits of relatives and friends—both Catholic and protestant—and handiwork for the poor also filled her time. She died on 3 September 1889 at her home, 35 Wilton Crescent, London.

With Lady Georgiana Fullerton, Lady Lothian, Lady Herbert of Lea, and Emily Bowles, Lady Newburgh was an archetype of the nineteenth-century charitable Catholic lady, who pursued a traditional philanthropic career, centred on alms-giving, visits to the poor, and the support of Catholic charities, missions, and religious orders, coupled with personal devotion and self-denial.

ROSEMARY MITCHELL

Sources *The Tablet* (21 Sept 1889), 462 · GEC, *Peerage*, new edn, vol. 1 · P. Gallwey, *Salvage from the wreck: a few memories of friends departed, preserved in funeral discourses* (1890) · P. M. A. A. Craven, *Lady Georgiana Fullerton: sa vie et ses œuvres* (Paris, 1888), 377
Likenesses photograph (in old age), repro. in Gallwey, *Salvage from the wreck*, facing p. xxxii
Wealth at death £26,620 12s. 7d.: probate, 8 Nov 1889, *CGPLA Eng. & Wales*

Eyre [*married name* Blythe], **Mary** (*b.* before **1603**, *d.* in or after **1633**), commissioner of a tapestry map, was the eldest daughter of Anthony Eyre (c.1576–1643x58) of Laughton-en-le-Morthen, West Riding of Yorkshire, and of Keveton, Derbyshire, and his first wife, Anne (*d.* 1608), daughter of John Markham of Sedgbrook, Lincolnshire. She had two sisters and four brothers, the younger three of whom were baptized between 1603 and 1607. Following her mother's death in 1608, her father married, on 29 August 1609, Mary (*d.* 1632), daughter of Henry Nevile and widow of John Babington of Rampton, Nottinghamshire,

and had another seven children. The large family seems to have lived mainly at Rampton Manor, their landed base in the area probably consolidated on 30 November 1624, when Mary's eldest brother, Gervase, married Elizabeth, daughter and coheir of John Babington.

Mary's mother, Anne, was a distant cousin of Elizabeth Markham (c.1565–1630) of Ollerton, who married Edward Sheldon (*bap.* 1566, *d.* 1643), son of Ralph Sheldon and grandson of William Sheldon (*d.* 1570), founder of the Sheldon tapestry enterprise that in the second half of the sixteenth century produced notable tapestries, including famous tapestry maps, at the manor of Barcheston, in Warwickshire. Mary Eyre's connection with the Sheldon family, and the leisure afforded her by her marrying late, led her to embark on an ambitious project that resulted in a tapestry map of Nottinghamshire. The map is in two parts, representing the northern and the southern parts of the county respectively, that are inscribed:

> at Rampton made wee were
> by Mistress Mary Eyre.

The tapestries are large: each was originally about 9 feet 6 inches square, but the northern part lacks a strip about 2 feet 2 inches wide down most of its left, or western, side. Apart from this, however, the tapestry is in good condition. By 1632, when it was made, the Sheldon tapestry enterprise was moribund, if not defunct, and Mary Eyre probably hired some of the Sheldon weavers, who then, since it must have been made on a large loom, produced the map within Rampton Manor itself.

The tapestry map is of considerable cartographic and topographic interest. Some of its features are clearly drawn from John Speed's map of Nottinghamshire of 1610, included in his *Theatre of the Empire of Great Britaine* (1611), which was itself based on Christopher Saxton's map of the county of 1576, included in his *Atlas* of 1579. However, much topographical and architectural detail has been added to the map by someone with considerable local knowledge. It is not known whether this person was Mary Eyre herself or a surveyor employed by her. While Speed and Saxton, for example, show stylized churches, castles, and manors Mary Eyre's map shows them as they were, distinguishing for instance between churches with towers and churches with steeples. The map thus gives important information about land use (including the extent of Sherwood Forest) and buildings, such as Belvoir Castle, of which it offers the only known seventeenth-century representation.

On 6 June 1633, at Rampton, Mary Eyre married William Blythe. Nothing further is known of her. Her brother Gervase was killed in 1646, defending Newark for the king; her half-brother Anthony (*bap.* 1612) was also a royalist officer during the siege.

ELIZABETH BAIGENT

Sources M. Clayton, 'A tapestry map of Nottinghamshire', *Transactions of the Thoroton Society of Nottinghamshire*, 38 (1934), 65–80 and pl. · private information (2004) [Roger Mason] · Burke, *Gen. GB* (1838); (1846)
Archives U. Nott. L., estate papers, EB 0159 Ey

Eyre, Sir Robert (1666–1735), judge, was the son and heir of Sir Samuel *Eyre (*bap.* 1638, *d.* 1698) of Newhouse, Wiltshire, and Lincoln's Inn, and his wife, Martha, daughter of Francis Lucy, of the family of Charlecote in Warwickshire. Several generations of Eyres had been members of Lincoln's Inn, and both Robert's father and his cousin Sir Giles *Eyre (*d.* 1695) were judges of king's bench. Robert likewise entered Lincoln's Inn in 1683, became a barrister in 1690, and followed the western circuit. The family had considerable interests in Salisbury, where in 1696 he succeeded Sir Giles as recorder. He subsequently served as MP for Salisbury from 1698 to 1710, and was one of the country (or 'whimsical') whigs who sponsored the place clause of the Regency Bill in January 1706; ultimately, however, he became known as one of the moderate whigs associated with the lord treasurer Godolphin. As such he shared in the promotion of the Marlborough–Godolphin faction in government, becoming queen's counsel in May 1707 and solicitor-general in October 1708.

Although he had argued against impeaching Dr Henry Sacheverell, Eyre was a manager of the doctor's trial in 1710, speaking to the Commons' first article (charging Sacheverell with impugning the legitimacy of the revolution by asserting the high-church doctrine of non-resistance) and effectively undermining the defendant's answer. Like his fellow manager Sir Thomas Parker, who was subsequently made lord chief justice, he made a good impression at the trial, and when a second judicial vacancy occurred in the court of queen's bench, the most politically sensitive of the common law courts, the whigs were able to recommend him to it. Having been knighted a week earlier, Eyre replaced Sir Henry Gould as puisne justice on 13 May 1710, in the dying days of the administration, and over the next four years of tory rule he acted with Parker to sustain the whig interest in cases which related to the parliamentary corporations and the press.

This party service was the main foundation of Eyre's future promotion, and at the accession of George I he was reappointed to the bench and made chancellor to the prince of Wales, with a patent allowing him to advise the prince and take fees in spite of his judicial place. But in 1718, when the breach between the prince and the king resulted in legal questions about prerogative power over the education and marriage of the royal children, Eyre was one of two judges who gave opinions in favour of the prince regarding their education. Thereafter doubts about his political reliability rendered him ineligible for the chief justiceship of king's bench, and in 1718 he was passed over in favour of his junior, Pratt. Instead he was made lord chief baron of exchequer, on 21 November 1723, following pressure from the prince: 'a Situation, where by his great skill in the law he might be of great service to the king, and could not possibly do any hurt of any kind' (Newcastle to Townshend, 1 Nov 1723, BL, Add. MS 32686, fols. 385–6). In 1725 he became lord chief justice of common pleas upon Sir Peter King's promotion to the woolsack, and presided for ten years in that court. Despite his acknowledged legal ability, Eyre was not immune

Sir Robert Eyre (1666–1735), by George Vertue (after Jonathan Richardson)

from the charges of corruption which embroiled the Walpole regime, and in 1729–30 he was one of the judges suspected of 'screening' the prison gaolers who were being investigated by the House of Commons committee of inquiry into the state of prisons. Although Eyre was singled out as a primary target, being accused of collusion with Bainbridge, the warden of Newgate, before presiding at his trial, he was defended by the government and ultimately exonerated by the committee. He died on 28 December 1735 and was buried in St Thomas's Church, Salisbury, on 7 January 1736. With his wife, Elizabeth, who was the daughter of Edward Rudge of Warley Place, Essex, and who had died in 1724, he had three sons and a daughter.

DAVID LEMMINGS

Sources E. Foss, *Biographia juridica: a biographical dictionary of the judges of England … 1066–1870* (1870) · *DNB* · BL, Newcastle MSS, Add. MS 32686 [fols. 383–6] · BL, Hardwicke MSS, Add. MS 35588 [fols. 25–6] · Herts. ALS, Panshanger papers, D/EP F149/7, D/EP F147/19 · G. S. Holmes, *British politics in the age of Anne* (1967) · G. Holmes, *The trial of Doctor Sacheverell* (1973) · Sainty, *Judges* · Sainty, *King's counsel* · ER, 92.357, 368 · *State trials*, xiv–xv · N. Luttrell, *A brief historical relation of state affairs from September 1678 to April 1714*, 6 vols. (1857) · *Bishop Burnet's History* · W. P. Baildon, ed., *The records of the Honorable Society of Lincoln's Inn: admissions*, 2 vols. (1896)

Archives BL, papers relating to dispute between George I and prince of Wales, Add. MSS 21497–21499 · Norfolk RO, MSS | BL, Hardwicke MSS · Herts. ALS, Panshanger MSS

Likenesses G. Vertue, engraving (after J. Richardson), NPG [*see illus.*] · oils, Lincoln's Inn, London · oils, Guildhall, Salisbury

Eyre, Ronald (1929–1992), theatre and television director, was born on 13 April 1929 at 1 Longcroft Cottages, Mapplewell, near Barnsley, Yorkshire, the only son of Christopher Eyre (1899–1970), a miner, and his wife, Mabel, *née* Smith (1902–1965). He was baptized at the United Methodist church, Mapplewell, on 12 May 1929. His father, who was poorly educated, was passionately committed to the idea of a good education for his son. This almost visionary determination encouraged Eyre to succeed, first at Mapplewell infants' and junior schools and Queen Elizabeth Grammar School, Wakefield (1940–47), and then, after two years as a wireless mechanic in the Royal Air Force, at University College, Oxford (1949–52). His talents as actor and director were exploited by the Oxford University Dramatic Society (of which he became secretary in 1951), the Experimental Theatre Club, and the Univ Players. He wrote later that

> Acting, as I then understood it, and would probably understand it still if I tried it again, was an exercise in being beside oneself—and raised alarming possibilities and questions. Hiding in public. Backing into the limelight. Directing seemed, for me, less dangerous. (Eyre to Humphrey Carpenter, 11 March 1984, priv. coll.)

After graduating with a second-class degree in English, Eyre became a teacher, first at Queen Elizabeth Grammar School, Blackburn, and then at Bromsgrove School. He was an inspiring master, but the classroom proved a frustrating arena for his talents, and in 1956 he took up a post at the BBC, where he remained until 1964. He was a founding director of BBC Schools Television, and his productions included *Philoctetes*, *The Bacchae*, and *The Caucasian Chalk Circle*, as well as his own play *The Victim*. In Michael Marland's view, 'he was a pioneering and brilliant figure in bringing the study of television as a dramatic art form into the country's classrooms' (*The Times*, 23 April 1992). Graduating to adult drama (although he would not have seen it that way), he wrote scripts for *Z Cars* and twelve plays for radio and television, including a much praised adaptation of Leskov's *A Crack in the Ice*. His television productions included *Condemned to Acquittal*, the first play to be broadcast on BBC2, and the television version of Michael Elliot's acclaimed Royal Shakespeare Company *As You Like It*, with Vanessa Redgrave as Rosalind.

Eyre's first productions in the professional theatre were at the Birmingham Repertory: *Titus Andronicus* and James Saunders's *Next Time I'll Sing to You* in 1963, *The Quare Fellow* in 1964, and *Heartbreak House* in 1965. This production, together with his *Widowers' Houses* at Stratford East (1965), were credited with starting the so-called 'Shaw revival' of the late 1960s. Productions of two plays by John McGrath at the Hampstead Theatre Club—*Events while Guarding the Bofors Gun* (1966) and *Bakke's Night of Fame* (1968)—took Eyre to the front rank of young directors. Interviewed by Montague Haltrecht after the first of these, he described the job of a director as 'putting actors in circumstances where the play works … creating an atmosphere in which people can function', and said that the special requirement of a

director was 'the capacity to be surprised by people'. He disliked the kind of directing that 'showed off' at the expense of the play (*The Scotsman*, 11 June 1966). This perhaps accounted for his immense popularity with those he directed and the consistently high praise his productions received.

1970 was Eyre's *annus mirabilis*. His production of Donald Howarth's *Three Months Gone* at the Royal Court (starring Jill Bennett and Diana Dors) received excellent notices, and transferred to the Duchess. In June of the same year he directed his own reworking of Dion Boucicault's *London Assurance* for the Royal Shakespeare Company, with Donald Sinden as Sir Harcourt Courtly and Judi Dench as Grace Harkaway. Critics were unanimous in their praise. Harold Hobson called the production 'one of the RSC's outstanding successes'. Success followed success in the early 1970s: *Mrs Warren's Profession* at the National Theatre (1970), *Much Ado about Nothing* at the Royal Shakespeare Company (1971), *A Voyage Round my Father*, starring Alec Guinness, in the West End (1971), and Charles Wood's comedy *Veterans* at the Royal Court (1972), with John Mills and John Gielgud as two dyspeptic actors. In 1973 he directed *Habeas corpus*, the first of his two encounters with new work by Alan Bennett (the second being *Enjoy* in 1980).

Eyre's muse was essentially comic. He relished the absurdity of human relationships—the strange postures and pretences men assume in pursuit of dignity or power or money. He keenly observed the world around him, and in rehearsal could cite a dozen incidents to help an actor find the truth of some comic moment. He was also very funny, a gifted clown with a sharp, at times impatient wit. Tragedy sometimes seemed outside his reach. His *Othello* for the Royal Shakespeare Company in 1979 disappointed him, and it was this experience perhaps that made him suspicious of the Bard. He always claimed that the title of his great unwritten lecture was 'Shakespeare: not my friend'.

From 1975 to 1977 Eyre worked on *The Long Search*, a landmark series for BBC2 on world religions. He was the programme's presenter, guide, and author. His research was tireless and exhaustive, his approach questioning but scrupulously non-judgemental. This project at once depended on and developed his interest in man's spiritual life, an interest that drew him to Shaw's *Saint Joan* at the National Theatre in 1984, to Ronald Harwood's *J. J. Farr* in the West End in 1987, and to a series of religious chat shows for television entitled *Not on Sunday* (1990–91).

Eyre directed Berlioz's *Beatrice and Benedict* in 1980 at the Buxton festival. It was his first attempt at opera. One review described it as 'triumphant' (*Financial Times*, 4 Aug 1980), and another was headlined 'Miracle at Buxton' (*Sunday Times*, 10 Aug 1980). Again his instinct for comedy was sure. He edited the text, translated it into witty, accessible verse, set the whole thing *à la* Jane Austen, and—for the spoken sections of the piece—transformed great singers into great actors. In 1982 his production of Verdi's *Falstaff* for the Los Angeles Philharmonic, Covent Garden, and the Teatro Communale in Florence was hindered by a weight of expectation, and the grandness of Carlo Maria Giulini's return to the world of opera. Relieved of this double burden in a revival two years later, 'Ronald Eyre's exquisitely conceived production', according to *The Times*, had 'at last found itself'.

The 1980s found Eyre in many places. There were plays, of course: the brilliant revival of John Osborne's *A Patriot for Me* at Chichester, in the West End, and then in Los Angeles (1983); another collaboration with Alec Guinness in Lee Blessing's *A Walk in the Woods* at the Comedy (1988); and one of his crowning achievements, *When we are Married* at the Whitehall (1986). On television he conducted an unfashionably low-key survey of the generations called *Seven Ages* (1987). And he taught: in California, at master classes in Oxford, and at the Hong Kong Academy of Performing Arts. One of his students at the latter recalled: 'He not only inspired us with regard to acting—but taught us how to look at life, and face failure as well as success' (*Journal of the Hong Kong Academy of Performing Arts*, 1989).

Eyre felt lucky to be able to do so many different things, and believed that each part of his career gained from not being the exclusive occupation of his life. Fastidious in his choice of work, he gave the most scrupulous attention and commitment to those projects where he thought he might be 'useful'. He was never motivated by a maverick ambition. 'It's not a form of modesty', he once said, 'to say that I lack ambition beyond the success of the current job. It's a fact. And in an odd way, I'm aware of the strength that gives me' (*The Times*, 30 Dec 1970). He was both explorer and guide. He wanted to understand things, and—a wise and kind companion—he knew how to share his discoveries with those around him.

Eyre's immensely successful life might be defined by the glittering prizes he turned down. He declined invitations to become head of drama at the BBC, artistic director of the Birmingham Repertory, artistic director of the Royal Court Theatre, and associate director at the Royal Shakespeare Company. He was merrily critical of organizations, and believed that the corporate life of an institution invariably became a drag on the quality of work it produced. He became instead a dedicated and mischievously independent freelance, bringing his wit, intellect, and perception to bear on the directing of plays, on teaching, on comparative religion, on broadcasting, and on the production and presentation of television documentaries.

Eyre died of cancer on 8 April 1992, at his home, Southfield House, Vicarage Street, Painswick, Stroud, Gloucestershire. He was buried in the graveyard of St Mary's, Painswick, on 13 April. His gravestone recorded simply: 'Ron Eyre, 1929–1992. On the long search'. He was unmarried.   MATTHEW FRANCIS

Sources R. Eyre, *Ronald Eyre on the long search* (1979) · *The Times* (10 April 1992) · *The Times* (23 April 1992) · *The Times* (17 Nov 1992) · *The Independent* (13 April 1992) · *WWW*, 1991–5 · private information (2004) · personal knowledge (2004) · b. cert. · d. cert.
Archives priv. coll., papers, manuscripts, playscripts, etc. | BBC WAC | FILM BBC Television Archive · Channel 4 Archive | SOUND BBC Radio Archive

Likenesses photograph, 1963, Hult. Arch. · J. Voos, double portrait, photograph, 1987 (with Ronald Harwood), repro. in *The Independent* · photograph, repro. in *The Times* (10 April 1992)
Wealth at death £708,396: probate, 12 Aug 1992, *CGPLA Eng. & Wales*

Eyre, Sir Samuel (*bap.* 1638, *d.* 1698), judge, was baptized on 16 March 1638 at St Edmund's Church, Salisbury, Wiltshire, the fourth of the five children of Robert Eyre (*c.*1610–1655) and his wife, Anne *Eyre (1612/13–1681), daughter of Samuel Aldersey, merchant and haberdasher of London, and his first wife, Mary, daughter of Philip van Oyrle of Nuremberg and Antwerp. His grandfather was Robert Eyre (1569–1638), a bencher of Lincoln's Inn and prominent puritan. Samuel was brought up in Salisbury by his parents, also puritans. In November 1646 his uncle William Eyre, a bencher of Lincoln's Inn, left him some valuable lands and tenements called Bonhams in South Newton near Salisbury, plus a library of law books provided he took up a legal career when the time came. On 9 December 1653 Eyre matriculated from Wadham College, Oxford. The following June he was admitted to Lincoln's Inn. His father died in March 1655, leaving moveable possessions worth £251 and about thirty properties yielding rental income, including the Blue Boar, Talbot, and Bell inns in Salisbury.

In June 1661 Eyre qualified at Lincoln's Inn as a barrister. On 21 October 1661, at St Martin-in-the-Fields, London, he married Martha, third daughter of Francis Lucy, and received her £1800 portion. The couple lived at Newhouse Redlynch, a few miles from Salisbury, which Eyre had purchased the previous year, and had four sons including Sir Robert *Eyre, judge of the queen's bench, and two daughters. For over thirty years Eyre followed his profession in Lincoln's Inn and Westminster Hall. In 1677 he had access on four occasions to the earl of Shaftesbury, imprisoned in the Tower, to whom he was reputed to be confidential adviser. By 1678 he was legal guardian of his lunatic sister Margaret, widow of Thomas Hassell of London, merchant tailor. He was active in Lincoln's Inn affairs, being called to the bench (1675), keeper of the black book (1685), and treasurer (1688). In 1685 he was asked to consult Sir Christopher Wren about repairing the chapel. As the executor of his aunt Margaret Blechinden, whose will was proved in 1684, Eyre built Blechinden's Almshouses, for six poor widows over the age of fifty, in Winchester Street, Salisbury. At some point after 1683 he was involved in a dispute about lands which he held as trustee on behalf of Whiteparish church, Wiltshire. He can probably be identified with the Samuel Eyre, esquire, who was one of the two candidates elected to represent Salisbury in the convention of 1689 but who was displaced when it was decided that the right to choose representatives lay with the city's mayor and corporation.

Eyre's puritan background and association with Shaftesbury probably precluded his promotion until after the revolution of 1688. He was made a serjeant on 21 April 1692. On 6 February 1694 he was knighted and appointed one of the four judges of the king's bench at a salary of £250 per term. In 1694 Eyre was one of the judges who decided in favour of Charles Knollys, charged with murder, and liberated him because the indictment should have named him as earl of Banbury. During this case Eyre remarked, 'The House of Lords could no more deprive one of a Peerage than they could confer a Peerage' (Salkeld, 510). Eyre's cases were quite often in the news. It was reported in June 1694 that the case between the king and the bankers had been argued in the exchequer court by Eyre and his cousin Sir Giles Eyre, both of whom were of opinion against the king. That this was only four months after his appointment demonstrates his courage and impartiality. In September 1694 it was reported that he and three other judges formed a special commission of oyer and terminer that was visiting Lancashire and Cheshire to try the prisoners of state who were in custody there. Eyre was one of the judges at several trials for high treason, perhaps the most notorious case being the assassination plot of 1696, when Ambrose Rookwood and his fellow conspirators were sentenced to death for plotting the king's death. However, not all of Eyre's cases were so dramatic. He was often on circuit and he was required to report back to Whitehall on cases involving such diverse offences as horse-stealing, Jacobite meetings, housebreaking, disorders, and forgery. Among the places he visited for these trials were Norwich, Oxford, Maidstone, Kingston, Worcester, and Stafford.

In February 1698 the House of Lords asked Eyre and Lord Justice Holt to give reasons for the decision they had made four years earlier in the case of the earl of Banbury; both courageously refused and were threatened with the Tower, but the matter was dropped a few days later. Eyre's speech to the House of Lords committee at this critical juncture included the following: 'The King intrusts me with the administration of justice. I have ever given my opinion upon the greatest consideration and upon my conscience' (*State trials*, 12.1180). We can accept this as a true statement of how he approached his judicial duties, and indeed his whole life, reflecting his early upbringing and his honesty and integrity. Eyre died on circuit at Lancaster of colic on 12 September 1698, and a monument was erected to him there. His body was removed to St Thomas's, Salisbury, and reburied on 2 July 1699. Martha, his 'ever dear and faithful wife' (as his will described her) survived until 1728.   C. G. LEWIN

Sources Wilts. & Swindon RO, Eyre-Matcham papers, 1369, boxes 20, 24, 25, 36, 38 · R. C. Hoare, *The history of modern Wiltshire*, 3 (1834–5), 493, 5 (1837), 22, 56, no. 1 · PRO, C9/133/67; C8/289/112 · marriage settlement (abstract), Norfolk RO [Samuel Eyre and Martha Lucy] · will of William Eyre, PRO, PROB 11/198, sig. 192 · Hants. RO, 37M85 4/00/12 · *CSP dom.*, 1677, p. 267; 1688, p. 405; 1692, p. 225; 1694–8; 1698, pp. 81–91 · W. A. Shaw, ed., *Calendar of treasury books*, 14, PRO (1934), 47, 242 · C. Fleury, '*Time-honoured Lancaster*' … *historic notes on the ancient borough of Lancaster* (1891), 1–7 · E. Foss, *Biographia juridica: a biographical dictionary of the judges of England … 1066–1870* (1870) · W. P. Baildon, ed., *The records of the Honorable Society of Lincoln's Inn: the black books*, 3 (1899) · accounts book of Samuel Eyre's mother, Anne Eyre, priv. coll. [collection of C. G. Lewin] · 'A comon-place booke of severall titles of the Law: it seems Mr. Sam. Eyres', Lincoln's Inn, London, MSS C.5.15 [ref. from *English legal manuscripts*, 2, Inter Documentation Co., Switzerland, 1978, cross-referencing to 'Powle'] · *The fifth and last part of modern reports … court of king's bench at Westminster* (1720) [references on the following pp. relate to 'Justice Eyre' but it is not clear whether these refer to Sir Samuel or his cousin Sir Giles Eyre: 6, 7–9, 11–12, 23. The following clearly relate to Sir Samuel, since Sir Giles had by then died: 64, 85, 143, 378] · W. Salkeld, *Reports of cases adjudg'd in the court of king's bench* (1717), 509–12 · R. Raymond, *Reports of cases … king's bench*, ed. G. Wilson, 2nd edn (1765), 1.31, 49, 56, 264, 271, 272, 303 · *State trials*, 12.1291, 1179; 13.139, 451 · N. Luttrell, *A brief historical relation of state affairs from September 1678 to April 1714*, 2 (1857), 404, 427; 3 (1857), 265, 271, 273, 331, 374, 395, 478–9, 481, 539; 4 (1857), 302, 340, 343–4, 428, 436, 476 · will, PRO, PROB 11/447, sig. 213 · parish register, St Edmund's Church, Salisbury, Wiltshire, 16 March 1638 [baptism] · 'Churchwarden's accounts of S. Edmund and S. Thomas, Sarum, 1443–1702', 1896, Wiltshire Record Society · PRO, 30/24/19/7 [a receipt of Samuel Eyre for £2000, part of a sum of £3200 lent to Lord Shaftesbury]
Archives Wilts. & Swindon RO, Eyre-Matcham archive, incl. letters
Likenesses marble bust, 1698, St Mary's Church, Lancaster · oils, Guildhall, Salisbury
Wealth at death £4000 owed to him by Mr Rudge on the marriage of the latter's daughter to Eyre's eldest son: will, PRO, PROB 11/447, sig. 213

Eyre, Simon (*c*.1395–1458), merchant, mayor of London, and civic benefactor, was the son of John and Amy Eyre of Brandon, Suffolk, where he was born. He was apprenticed in London to the upholder (second-hand clothes dealer) Peter Smert, but transferred to the more prestigious Drapers' Company in 1419, some six years after completing his apprenticeship. Unlike other successful merchants of this period Eyre did not make his money in overseas trade (his name never appears in the London customs accounts), but acted instead as a middleman, buying cloth in the countryside and selling it to the royal wardrobe and to other merchants, above all to Italians. At the same time he bought dyes and spices from Genoese and Venetian merchants, who were excluded by chartered custom from the retail sale of their imported goods in London, and distributed them throughout England. While other merchants bore the risks, Eyre made the profits. Such was his success that he was elected master of the Drapers in 1425–6, only six years after he had joined the company. He was sheriff of London in 1434–5, and master of the Drapers again in the following year. In 1437 he was an elected auditor of the accounts of London Bridge, and a common councilman by 1441. He was active in the latter role, serving on at least eight important joint committees of the common council and court of aldermen; in October 1444 he was elected an alderman of Walbrook ward.

By this date Eyre was already involved in London's complicated negotiations to buy, or lease, land in Cornhill for the rebuilding of the old Leadenhall as the city's granary—perhaps it was this which secured him an aldermanry. He pursued the scheme energetically, and in consequence was elected mayor in 1445, only a year after he joined the aldermanic bench—an unprecedented dash to the top. In spite of a certain timidity on the part of the common council, anxious about the costs of this ambitious project, the work forged ahead. By 1453 the great quadrangle (80 metres x 150 metres), with its chapel projecting to the east, was completed, much of it at Eyre's expense. But after the completion of the Leadenhall, Eyre appears to have lost interest in his civic career; he served on his last committee in 1454, and attended only one further meeting of the court after 1456. Instead he concentrated on his own plans for the new Leadenhall, giving a different turn to a building which the city had intended solely for a granary. The codicils to his will show him as primarily concerned with the chapel and schools which he had lately constructed there. Teachers of Latin grammar, of writing, and of song were already in post, with an establishment of a master, five priests, six clerks, and two choristers to serve the chapel. Eyre left £2000 with which his executors were to establish the schools, maintain the buildings, and pay the salaries, estimated at £113 per annum. The Drapers' Company was to administer this great scholarly enterprise. The project was a remarkable one, comparable, if on a lesser scale, with Henry VI's contemporary foundation at Eton, but unique in providing for the teaching of (presumably vernacular) writing as well as Latin grammar and song. But Eyre's executors were unable to realize his scheme. Perhaps they encountered resistance from the ecclesiastical authorities, perhaps there was simply not enough money. The schools withered away, and Eyre's wealth was used to set up a modest chantry in the church of St Mary Woolnoth, where he was later buried.

Eyre's energy and forcefulness also manifested itself in his dealings with his own family. He married twice, first, by 1419, Katherine, daughter of Thomas Mulling, a London brazier, and second, Alice, who was the mother of his son Thomas and who had died by 1457. In 1446 Eyre secured a well-endowed city orphan, Elizabeth the daughter of the mayor and mercer Robert Large, as his son's bride. Young Thomas may have found it difficult to establish himself in a city where his father was a prominent, and often quarrelsome, presence. Frequently in debt, by 1456 he had spent some time in the Fleet, and had to be bought out by his father. When Eyre drew up his will in December 1457 he tried to protect his estate from his son's profligacy by making his considerable legacy dependent upon Thomas's not vexing the executors and doing nothing contrary to the will. The rest of the will bears equal witness to Eyre's forceful and dominating personality, and in particular to his hopes of establishing a London dynasty and ruling it from beyond the grave. His three surviving grandchildren, Robert, Thomas, and Jane, were to continue to live in their grandfather's house in Lombard Street, under the rule of his executors, until they were twenty-four years old. Thomas and Robert were to receive their stipulated legacies only if they married women of whom the executors approved. And the grandchildren were to live in the dynastic home, ruled by their grandfather's executors, provided with food and clothing and served by their grandfather's servants. But Eyre's plans came to nothing, for within ten years of his own death on 18 September 1458 his son Thomas and all his grandchildren were dead.

Eyre's memory was kept alive among Londoners by a plaque in the north wall of the Leadenhall Chapel, commemorating the 'famous marchant' Simon Eyre as the 'founder' of the great work. But as time passed he came to be seen in a different, and mellower, light. *The Gentle Craft*, published by Thomas Deloney in 1597, provides an amiable account of how Simon Eyre, 'being at first a shoomaker', with the invaluable assistance of his wife and apprentices, became, in the end, mayor of London and builder of Leadenhall. Thomas Dekker recycled Deloney's fanciful tale to form the play *The Shoemaker's Holiday* (1600). But the story did not share the long-term popularity of the comparable success story of Dick Whittington and his cat. Deloney's tale surfaced once more c.1810 in a chapbook pamphlet, but otherwise Simon Eyre has been lost to view.   CAROLINE M. BARRON

Sources A. B. Beaven, ed., *The aldermen of the City of London, temp. Henry III–*[1912], 2 vols. (1908–13) • M. E. Lawless, 'Another look at Simon Eyre's will', *N&Q*, 199 (1954), 13–16 • J. Stow, *A survey of London*, rev. edn (1603); repr. with introduction by C. L. Kingsford as *A survey of London*, 2 vols. (1908); repr. with addns (1971) • M. Samuel, 'The fifteenth-century garner at Leadenhall, London', *Antiquaries Journal*, 69 (1989), 119–53 • C. M. Barron, 'The expansion of education in fifteenth-century London', *The cloister and the world: essays in medieval history in honour of Barbara Harvey*, ed. J. Blair and B. Golding (1996), 219–45 • S. L. Thrupp, *The merchant class of medieval London, 1300–1500*, pbk edn (1962) • J. Weever, *Antient funeral monuments*, ed. W. Tooke (1767) • A. H. Thomas and P. E. Jones, eds., *Calendar of plea and memoranda rolls preserved among the archives of the corporation of the City of London*, 4–5 (1943–54) • R. R. Sharpe, ed., *Calendar of letter-books preserved in the archives of the corporation of the City of London*, [12 vols.] (1899–1912), vols. I, K, L • journals, CLRO, court of common council, vols. 1–6 • Drapers' Company, wardens' accounts, 1415–42 • will, PRO, PROB 11/4, sig. 13 • Chancery and Exchequer records, PRO
Likenesses probably by R. Leigh, portrait, c.1446–1447, GL
Wealth at death approx. £7000: will, PRO, PROB 11/4, fols. 100v–107

Eyre, Thomas (1670–1715), Jesuit, was born on 23 December 1670, the son of Thomas Eyre and his wife, Mary Bedingfield, of Eastwell, Leicestershire. He studied at the English College at St Omer, was admitted into the Society of Jesus in 1687, and was professed of the four vows on 8 March 1706. Ordained priest in 1696, he served for a time as chaplain to the court of James II at St Germain. He was professor of theology at Liège from 1701 to 1704, and in 1712 was socius to the provincial of his order. He died in London on 9 November 1715. According to one authority he was the author or editor of a biography of James II (Kirk, 198).   THOMPSON COOPER, *rev.* ROBERT BROWN

Sources Gillow, *Lit. biog. hist.* • H. Foley, ed., *Records of the English province of the Society of Jesus*, 7 vols. in 8 (1875–83) • G. Oliver, *Collections towards illustrating the biography of the Scotch, English and Irish members of the Society of Jesus* (1835) • G. Holt, *The English Jesuits, 1650–1829: a biographical dictionary*, Catholic RS, 70 (1984) • J. Kirk, *Biographies of English Catholics in the eighteenth century*, ed. J. H. Pollen and E. Burton (1909)

Eyre, Thomas (1748–1810), Roman Catholic priest and college head, was born at Glossop, Derbyshire, the fourth son of Nathaniel Eyre, steward to the duke of Norfolk at Worksop, Nottinghamshire, and his wife, Jane Bromhead. Like his brothers, he went to the preparatory school at Esquerchin, Douai, from 1758 before moving to the parent English College at Douai in 1762. In 1775, some months after his ordination, he accepted an invitation from his kinsman of the same name who had just inherited Stella Hall, near Ryton, co. Durham, to take charge of the mission which covered the area west of Newcastle as far as Hexham. He stayed seventeen years, during which time he translated and published several of the spiritual works of John Gother in addition to *The Instruction of Youth in Christian Piety* (1783), a translation of the work of Charles Gobinet.

Appointed to Pontop Hall, near Consett, in 1794, Eyre was soon asked by Bishop William Gibson to take charge of a small number of student refugees from Douai while a temporary college was being prepared for them at nearby Crook Hall. Inevitably he was called upon to preside over the new college. During the course of 1795 the Revd John Daniel, the president of the Douai college, paid a visit to Crook Hall, and was persuaded by Bishop Gibson to become its president in order to establish a continuity. Within a day or two, Daniel resigned and Eyre was reinstated. Under his direction the infant college surmounted many hurdles and was eventually transferred in 1808 to the much larger building at Ushaw, 4 miles from Durham. There Eyre died on 7 May 1810, and was buried in the adjoining cemetery on 9 May. His memorial rightly described him as 'benefactor munificus', for he left his entire fortune of £8640 to the college. His portrait by Alexander Rossi at Ushaw reveals Eyre as a somewhat 'cribbed and confined' gentleman. A stern disciplinarian, he was notoriously parsimonious, making use of the litter that others dropped and using the correspondence he received to compose his own draft letters. But there can be little doubt that he was the right man for the task given him by his bishop. Invariably at loggerheads with him, his diplomacy prevented a permanent breakdown of their relationship, which would have immeasurably damaged the educational prospects for northern Catholics of the time.

D. MILBURN

Sources D. Milburn, 'Journey to the promised land: from Douai to Durham', *Ushaw Magazine*, 274 (1993–4), 12–26 • D. Milburn, *A history of Ushaw College* (1964) • B. Ward, *The dawn of the Catholic revival in England, 1781–1803*, 2 vols. (1909) • Gillow, *Lit. biog. hist.* • E. Towers, 'Ushaw benefactors', *Ushaw Magazine*, 62 (1952), 164 • Ushaw College, Durham, Ushaw College diary • G. Anstruther, *The seminary priests*, 4 (1977), 99
Archives Ushaw College, Durham, corresp. and collections
Likenesses A. Rossi, oils, Ushaw College, Durham
Wealth at death £8640: Towers, 'Ushaw benefactors'

Eyre, Sir Vincent (1811–1881), army officer in the East India Company, was born at Portsdown, near Portsmouth, on 22 January 1811, the third son of Captain Henry Eyre, of an old family of Derbyshire cavaliers, and Mary, daughter of J. Concannon of Loughrea, co. Galway, Ireland. He was educated at Norwich grammar school under the Revd E. Valpy. Eyre attended Addiscombe College (1827–8), and passed into the Bengal artillery in December 1828. He landed in Calcutta on 21 May 1829. After eight years he was promoted first lieutenant, and appointed to the horse artillery. In 1833 Eyre married Emily, daughter of Colonel Sir James Mouat, bt, Bengal Engineers. They had three sons and a daughter, and his wife died in 1851.

In 1839 Eyre was appointed commissary of ordnance to the Kabul field force. He took to Kabul a large quantity of ordnance stores, arriving in April 1840. On 2 November 1841 the rising took place in which Sir Alexander Burnes was killed. The British–Indian force was soon besieged in the cantonments by the Afghans. They made desperate sallies, in one of which, on 13 November, Eyre was severely wounded. A treaty for evacuation was ratified on 1 January 1842. Eyre, still suffering from his wound, and accompanied by his wife and child, started with the column but they were taken as hostages by Akbar Khan. They spent nearly nine months in captivity, with other British captives, moved to different forts, and suffered many privations. The climate, however, was healthy; the captives held public worship and established a school for their children. Eyre kept a diary and sketched the officers and ladies. The manuscript was smuggled to a friend in India then published in England as *Military Operations at Cabul* (1843). In August the captives were hurried off towards Bamian in the Hindu Kush, under threat of being sold as slaves to the Uzbeks of Turkestan. They were saved by Pottinger, who on 11 September bought over the Afghan commanding their escort.

Eyre was then again posted to the horse artillery. While quartered at Meerut he founded a club for European soldiers, possibly the first such. In December 1844 he was appointed to command the artillery of the newly formed 'Gwalior contingent' and made it efficient, as its mutiny service proved. While at Gwalior he attempted to found a settlement for Goan families left destitute after the defeat of the Maratha armies in 1803–18. He obtained land for this which, at his wish, was called Esapore (the abode of Christians). It failed because of its unhealthy location. Eyre undertook the duties of engineer, architect, and road maker to the station, and erected an attractive little church.

In 1854 Eyre became major, and in May 1855 visited England on furlough. Inventive, he published in 1856 a pamphlet *On Metallic Boats and Floating Waggons for Naval and Military Service*. In February 1857 he returned to India, and was posted to a horse artillery battery in Burma, but was recalled to India at the mutiny. In July he was sent up the Ganges for Allahabad. On 28 July he reached Buxar, where he learned that a force of mutineers was besieging a fortified house at Arrah, 40 miles from Buxar. Eyre took the responsibility of disembarking 160 men of the 5th foot, who were travelling up the Ganges to Allahabad, and with them and his own force relieved Arrah and destroyed the mutineers' stronghold at Jagdispur. This brief campaign, undertaken on his own responsibility, restored British control of the area, secured communications by the Grand Trunk Road, revived British prestige, and drew from Outram the highest praise and recommendation for the Victoria Cross. Eyre now joined at Cawnpore the force advancing under Outram and Sir Henry Havelock to the relief of Lucknow. This reached Lucknow after four days' fighting. Eyre succeeded to the command of the artillery on the death of Brigadier Cooper. He was mentioned in dispatches, and in December 1857 was made lieutenant-colonel and CB. He became brevet colonel in December 1858.

After the suppression of the mutiny Eyre was appointed to superintend the powder works at Ishapore, near Calcutta. There in 1860, he married his cousin, Catherine Mary, daughter of Captain T. Eyre RN; they had no children and she survived him. In 1861 Eyre was selected by Lord Canning as a member of the commission on the amalgamation of the company's and queen's armies, and in 1862 was appointed inspector-general of ordnance in the Bengal army. In April 1863 he was ordered home on sick leave, and retired with the rank of major-general in October 1863. In 1867 he was made KCSI. He happened to be in France on the outbreak of the Franco-Prussian War, and organized an ambulance service under the rules of the English National Red Cross Society. He formed a local committee in August at Boulogne, and for the next eight months he and Lady Eyre were the moving spirits in a most valuable organization. In 1874 he published *Lays of a Knight-Errant in Many Lands*.

Eyre wintered at Rome during his later years. In the summer of 1880 he was attacked by a spinal disease, and died at Villa des Acacias, Aix-les-Bains, Savoie, on 22 September 1881; his remains were buried in London at Kensal Green cemetery. Eyre was a man of noble character. Handsome, courteous, accomplished, daring, and resourceful, he combined literary and artistic talent with his military qualities.   H. G. KEENE, *rev.* JAMES LUNT

Sources The Times · V. Eyre, *The military operations at Cabul, which ended in the retreat and destruction of the British army, January 1842* (1843); repr. with an introduction by J. Lunt as *Journal of an Afghanistan prisoner* (1976) · J. W. Kaye, *History of the war in Afghanistan*, 3rd edn, 3 vols. (1874) · Lord Roberts [F. S. Roberts], *Forty-one years in India*, 2 vols. (1897) · G. Pottinger, *The Afghan connection* (1983) · Lady Sale, *A journal of the disasters in Affghanistan* (1840) · P. Macrory, *Signal catastrophe: the story of a disastrous retreat from Kabul, 1842* (1966) · W. H. Russell, *My Indian mutiny diary*, ed. M. Edwardes (1957) · Lady Inglis [J. S. Inglis], *The siege of Lucknow* (1892) · *Annual Register* (1881)
Archives BL OIOC, history of Anglo-Afghan War, MS Eur. A 42 · BL OIOC, letters | Hunt. L., letters to Grenville family · NRA, Roberts MSS, notes on Kabul massacre · Wellcome L., corresp. with Thomas Longmore
Wealth at death £720 16s. 1d.: probate, 29 Oct 1881, CGPLA Eng. & Wales

Eyre, William (*fl.* 1642–1660). *See under* Eyre, William (*fl.* 1634–1675).

Eyre [Eyres, Ayres], **William** (*fl.* 1634–1675), parliamentarian army officer and Leveller, is of obscure origins; the place and date of his birth and the names of his parents are not known. His rank of captain in a cavalry regiment during the first civil war suggests that he may have come from the rural middling sort. In his *The Serious Representation* (1649), he stated that, 'fifteen years ago, I was forc'd to leave this my Native Land, for opposing the *Service Book*, and other *Traditions of men*, and lived in *New-England* till the sitting of the last Parliament' (Eyre, *Serious Representation*, 1–2).

In 1642 Eyre became a sergeant in Denzil Holles's regiment, and was engaged at Edgehill and at Brentford, where the regiment was destroyed. Eyre joined the army of the eastern association, and was commissioned by Oliver Cromwell quartermaster in his own troop, and soon promoted captain of the sixth troop in Cromwell's cavalry regiment, the Ironsides. Eyre participated in Cromwell's campaign in Lincolnshire until January 1644, when his troop and two others were captured at Sleaford. By his own later account in *The Serious Representation*, written with the hindsight of a Leveller prisoner in Oxford Castle, he fell out with Cromwell and left the regiment in the summer 'for standing to my first Principles'. Cromwell, he added,

> would often (when he was low) stroke me on the head, saying, *The Nation was bound to bless God for me*: But when he saw the Country and Souldiery respect me, he and his Creatures studied how to make me odious in the sight of all honest men.   (Eyre, *Serious Representation*, 3)

In 1647 Eyre married Mary, *née* Leycester, widow successively of Calcott Chambre (or Culvert Chambers) and of Job Ward. Her first husband's father had bought the half-barony of Shillelagh and Carnew Castle in co. Wicklow, and through his marriage Eyre now acquired a right to this property. Henceforth the relief of Ireland was central to his hopes. Parliament authorized a force for that purpose, directing Sir Thomas Fairfax to nominate the officers, and Eyre was named colonel of a foot regiment to be so raised.

Eyre's regiment was not part of the New Model Army. Nevertheless he was at Corkbush Field, near Ware, in Hertfordshire, on 15 November 1647 for the New Model's mutinous rendezvous, inciting the soldiers and urging them to accept the Leveller *Agreement of the People*. Immediately arrested, he was held pending court martial with William Bray, captain-lieutenant of the regiment of Robert Lilburne which had been so prominent in the mutiny. Hailed as a martyr by the Levellers, Eyre (with eight fellow prisoners) submitted an inflammatory petition clearing the Levellers from an unfounded aspersion made by Lieutenant-Colonel Henry Lilburne of a plot to kill the king. The court martial was convened at Windsor on 3 December and ordinary soldiers among the accused were soon sentenced and punished, but Eyre's trial was postponed. He remained in custody until 23 December, when he was among those allowed to return to their regiments without any further punishment upon acknowledgement and submission to military discipline.

Eyre's regiment was then quartered in Worcestershire, where, with several others, it was scheduled for disbandment as a 'supernumerary' force. Eyre was absent while he lobbied for his men's pay and arrears. In January 1648 about eighty officers representing five regiments (including Eyre's) met at Broadway in Gloucestershire to discuss their discontents, following which they planned to seize Gloucester. In February orders were issued for the regiment's immediate disbandment.

In the summer of 1648 Henry Marten, a member of the Berkshire county committee, began to raise local forces in Berkshire, proclaiming Leveller and egalitarian principles. Joined by Eyre these irregulars terrorized the county. The Commons summoned Marten and Eyre and ordered the Berkshire committee to disband their forces. Both Eyre and Marten left Berkshire and sought protection with Cromwell.

Eyre still wished to serve in Ireland. 'I had three troops that were willing to have engaged in that service, and L[ieutenant-]G[eneral] Cromwel gave me orders to quarter them' (Eyre, *Serious Representation*, 3). But in February 1649 Fairfax, the lord general, issued a declaration against taking quarters without his commission. Fairfax ordered Eyre to a council of war for quartering troops without sanction, 'and then L. G. Cromwell did deny that he gave me any order to do it, and likewise tore his own order in peeces' (ibid., 4). The three troops were ordered to be disbanded. Eyre was now a civilian.

In May 1649 Eyre took part in the Leveller-influenced Burford mutiny; his account in *The Serious Representation* agrees generally with the newsbook accounts. Hearing of the regiments that were refusing to take service in Ireland on the terms of compulsion imposed on them by the generals, he searched them out, conferred with Cornet Henry Denne of Scrope's regiment, and accompanied the mutineers to New Bridge on the Thames, where they faced Colonel John Reynolds who kept the bridge. Eyre exhorted the mutineers to attack, but rather than leading a forlorn hope against Reynolds, Eyre reports that the men, 'unwilling to draw their swords against their fellow souldiers, marched over the River a little above the bridg', Eyre himself 'having no Command, nor being under any' (Eyre, *Serious Representation*, 5). At Burford Fairfax's men 'fell upon shooting in at every window where they saw light', and seized Eyre at an inn where he was lodging (ibid.).

Eyre again appeared before Fairfax and Cromwell and justified his presence at Burford. 'I was a Volunteer at the first, and I hoped I might be so still, and till that which we fought for were accomplished, if there were but ten men appeared for it, I would make eleven' (Eyre, *Serious Representation*, 6). Cromwell railed at him and three days later he was brought to Oxford prison.

In July the council of state, fearful of conspiracies hatching in Oxford, directed that Eyre be removed to Warwick Castle, where he spent the next year. Finally his spirit broke, and in a petition to the council he admitted that he had been misguided and mistaken as to the good purpose of others, and begged that he might go with his family to Ireland. The council ordered his release on 1 August 1650.

In Ireland the lord deputy, Henry Ireton, put Eyre in possession of Shillelagh. His victory was short-lived. In 1654 he was back in London and involved in a new Leveller plot, conspiring with old prison companions against the protectorate and complaining, as a witness reported, 'that it was as good living in Turky as here' (Thurloe, 3.35). In January 1655 he was arrested upon landing in Dublin. In his examination he asserted that it was his duty to 'make good' the principles of the army's engagement at Triploe Heath—a reference to the army's espousal of its solemn engagement in the summer of 1647 (ibid.). While he loved and honoured the protector, even the best of men were subject to corruption.

After eleven weeks, 'very much distempered both in body and mind', Eyre begged either to be tried or else permitted to join Robert Venables's expedition, then at Hispaniola. His appeal was fruitless, and he remained in gaol. Meanwhile a number of suits were entered against his claim to Shillelagh. He was released briefly in 1659, but was arrested again in May 1660 as one of a group of 'rebellious spirits' who threatened the peace of the restored monarchy. Imprisoned in Dublin Castle, he was charged with tampering with members of the Irish foot guards garrisoning the castle, employing a soldier to act as his agent in trying to foment mutiny. However, he was not brought to trial because the only witness, the soldier, was unclear as to the treasonable design. The earl of Clarendon advised that if there were 'a morall satisfaction of the truth of the charge', Ormond might secure Eyre in another prison. In Eyre's words, he was 'hurried (from prison to prison) above ten years space' (Eyre, *William Eyres*, 22). His wife died while he was in prison. About December 1669 he was at last released and, accompanied by his daughter, travelled to England to pursue the case for his Irish estates before parliament and the king. In 1675 he published two appeals, *The Case of William Eyres, Esq.* and *A Particular Deduction of the Case of William Eyre*. The former was referred by the House of Lords to its committee of privileges in May 1675 upon the complaint of the second earl of Strafford that its claims had libelled both himself and his father, though what action the committee took is not recorded. Eyre's subsequent history and the date of his death are unknown.

Eyre has sometimes been confused with his namesake **William Eyre** (*fl.* 1642–1660), parliamentarian army officer and politician, of Neston, Wiltshire. He fought during the civil war—in 1659 he claimed to have served through to the battle of Worcester and to have held the ranks from captain of foot to colonel (the latter probably a reference to his rank in the Wiltshire militia). He was returned MP for Chippenham in that county on 29 November 1648, thereby missing Pride's Purge, and was admitted to the Rump Parliament on 15 January 1649. In January 1660 the restored Rump appointed him colonel of the regiment of foot recently commanded by John Lambert though a suspicious George Monck quickly removed him from its command.

PAUL H. HARDACRE

Sources W. Eyre, *The serious representation of Col. William Eyre* (1649) · W. Eyre, *The case of William Eyres, esq. concerning his estate in Ireland* (1675?) · W. Eyre, *A particular deduction of the case of William Eyre* (1675?) · 'Concerning Ireland, regiments thought fitt to be sent thither', proceedings of the committee of general officers, 25 Sept 1647, Worcester College, Oxford, Clarke MS 66, fol. 16*v* · D. M. Wolfe, ed., *Leveller manifestoes of the puritan revolution* (1944), 235–41 · *The Clarke papers*, ed. C. H. Firth, 1, CS, new ser., 49 (1891), 419 · J. Rushworth, *Historical collections*, 5 pts in 8 vols. (1659–1701), 2.943 · *CSP dom.*, 1649, 251, 25; 1650, 263, 505; 1675–6, 101–6 · *Seventh report*, HMC, 6 (1879), 27a · *The manuscripts of Rye and Hereford corporations*, HMC, 31 (1892), 396 · C. Durston, 'Henry Marten and the high shoon of Berkshire: the Levellers in Berkshire in 1648', *Berkshire Archaeological Journal*, 70 (1979–80), 87–95 · council of state, order that Col. Ayres be removed from Oxford, Worcester College, Oxford, Clarke MS 181, box 1 (2) · Thurloe, *State papers*, 3.35, 126 · *CSP Ire.*, 1660–62, 628 · *Calendar of the Clarendon state papers preserved in the Bodleian Library*, 5: 1660–1726, ed. F. J. Routledge (1970), 301 ·

JHL, 12 (1666–75), 679, 681, 688, 708 • G. Aylmer, 'Gentleman levellers?', *Past and Present*, 49 (1970), 120–25 • A. Woolrych, *Soldiers and statesmen: the general council of the army and its debates, 1647–1648* (1987) • *JHC*, 7 (1651–9), 315–16, 799 • C. H. Firth and G. Davies, *The regimental history of Cromwell's army*, 2 vols. (1940)

Eyre, Sir William (1805–1859), army officer, was born at Hatfield on 21 October 1805, the younger son of Vice-Admiral Sir George Eyre (1769–1839) and Georgina, daughter of Sir George Cooke, bt, of Wheatley. He was educated at Rugby School, where he remained from 1817 until commissioned ensign in the 6th regiment on 17 April 1823. He was promoted lieutenant in that regiment on 5 November 1825, and to a half-pay captaincy on 20 November 1827. He remained unemployed until 21 May 1829, when he received a company in the 73rd regiment, with which he continued nearly twenty-five years. The 73rd was stationed in the Mediterranean from 1829 to 1839, in which year Eyre was promoted major, serving in Canada from 1839 to 1841 and at home from 1841 to 1845. On 16 February 1841 he married Georgiana Lucy (1808–1898), fourth daughter of the Hon. John Bridgeman Simpson (son of the first Baron Bradford); they left one son.

After a detour to fight at Montevideo, Eyre and his regiment reached the Cape of Good Hope in July 1846 and fought in the Cape Frontier War of 1847, with Eyre in command; he was promoted lieutenant-colonel on 12 November 1847. Eyre's fitness for irregular warfare in difficult terrain was recognized by the generals under whom he served, Sir Peregrine Maitland, Henry Somerset, and Sir George Berkeley. When the next frontier war broke out in 1851, he was at once ordered to the front, and placed in command of a column, consisting of his own regiment and some light infantry, by Sir Harry Smith. With this force he accomplished many important feats. On 16 April 1851 he defeated the enemy at Quibigui River, and on 10 September at Committees Hill; on 14 March 1852 he commanded the right column in the attack on Macomo's stronghold, and on 7 April he captured over 800 cattle in an independent expedition into the Amatola country.

When Sir George Cathcart succeeded Sir Harry Smith, he maintained Eyre in command of his independent column, and under the new commander-in-chief Eyre co-operated throughout the final operations of the war with the greatest credit. After the war Eyre was selected for the command of the 2nd brigade of the army, which Sir George Cathcart led in person to punish Moshesh, the Basuto chief. At the battle of Berea he commanded on the right, and did much to win the victory. Nevertheless, in private letters, later published, Cathcart blamed Eyre for thinking more of seizing cattle than of his military duties, which the latter denied in a letter to the *Morning Herald* (23 October 1856). In Fortescue's history of the British army Eyre is described as 'a highly accomplished bush-fighter' (Fortescue, *Brit. army*, 12.560). In his public dispatches Cathcart had nothing but praise for his subordinate, and Eyre was made CB and an aide-de-camp to Queen Victoria, and promoted colonel on 28 May 1853.

Eyre shortly afterwards returned to England, and was then given command of the 2nd brigade of the 3rd division under his former chief, Cathcart. At the head of this brigade during the Crimean War he was present at the Alma, and was honourably mentioned for his command of the trenches during Inkerman. After that battle he succeeded to the command of the 3rd division, although he was not promoted major-general until 12 December 1854, in succession to Cathcart. He remained in the Crimea throughout the terrible winter of 1854–5, and it was partly in recognition of this conduct that Lord Raglan gave him the command of the force which was directed to threaten the dockyard creek on 18 June 1855. Eyre was wounded in the face during the operations. He remained in the Crimea until the end of the war, and was made a KCB on 10 July 1855, and a chevalier of the Légion d'honneur and a knight of the Mejidiye in 1856.

In July 1856 Eyre was appointed to command the forces in Canada, but the privations of the Crimean winter had destroyed his health, and he had to resign in June 1859. He retired to Bilton Hall, near Rugby, where he died on 8 September 1859. A window was erected to his memory in Bilton church.   H. M. Stephens, *rev.* James Lunt

Sources Naval and Military Records of Rugbeians, Rugby School • Burke, *Gen. GB* • Burke, *Peerage* • *The royal highland regiment, the black watch, formerly the 42nd and 73rd foot: medal roll, 1801–1911* (1913) • *Correspondence of Lieut.-General the Hon. Sir George Cathcart* (1856) • H. Ward, *Five years in Kaffirland*, 2 vols. (1848) • W. Cope, *The history of the rifle brigade* (1877) • E. H. Nolan, *The illustrated history of the war against Russia*, 2 vols. (1855–7) • A. W. Kinglake, *The invasion of the Crimea*, [new edn], 8 (1888) • Fortescue, *Brit. army*, vol. 12 • J. H. Lehmann, *Remember you are an Englishman: a biography of Sir Harry Smith* (1977) • Boase, *Mod. Eng. biog.* • *Dod's Peerage* (1858) • *CGPLA Eng. & Wales* (1859)

Archives PRO, letter-books, diaries, and papers, PRO 30/46

Wealth at death under £7000: probate, 19 Nov 1859, *CGPLA Eng. & Wales*

Eyres, William (1734–1809), printer, was born on 12 May 1734 in Warrington, Lancashire, the second son of John Eyres and his wife, Anne; John Eyres was probably the son of Henry Eyres (or Eires), also of Warrington. The family had been involved in the book trade since the time of Henry, who published tracts—three of which survive, dated 1704, 1706, and 1712. William's father had a printing and bookbinding business 'next door to the White Bull in the Horse-Market' (now Golden Square), but no publications with his imprint survive (Perkin, 70).

William and his elder brother Thomas (1731–1780) took over their father's business in partnership at some time before 1756 when their first known publication, *Eyres's Weekly Journal, or, The Warrington Advertiser*, appeared. Because of the wording of an advertisement in the *Weekly Journal* for a book 'sold by A. Eyres in Warrington' it is possible, as Perkin suggests, that after the death of John Eyres the business was managed by his widow, Anne, while the brothers continued with the printing and bookbinding. The *Weekly Journal* seems to have been short-lived with copies surviving only for 1756, and by 1761 Thomas had left Warrington for Prescot near Liverpool, leaving William to run the business alone.

There is not much evidence of the Eyres press output

during these early years but two developments were taking place in Warrington which, together with William Eyres's latent ability, brought his work to much greater prominence: the foundation of the Warrington Academy in 1757 and of the circulating library in 1760. Warrington circulating library kept William Eyres in contact with townspeople who were interested in books, and from its first day (1 May 1760) until he retired from business in 1803 he acted as its librarian and secretary; he remained on the committee until he died. Eyres was paid £5 a year and the library stock was kept in his shop. The circulating library has a direct link to the present Warrington Public Library; John Haddock became librarian when Eyres retired, Haddock himself retired in 1848, and the circulating library was incorporated into the Warrington Municipal Library to become the first British library to be supported by local rates.

Warrington Academy had a more significant effect on Eyres's career. The academy was a nonconformist institution which attracted some outstanding members of staff, notably John Aikin and his son John, William Enfield, Joseph Priestley, John Taylor, and Gilbert Wakefield. William Eyres printed work for all these tutors and became official printer to the academy. All the works are scholarly and many required great skill and attention to detail by the printer. The academy and the output of William Eyres came to the attention of scholars outside Warrington, some of whom were so impressed with Eyres's ability that they too offered work for him to publish. The most famous of these was John Howard's *The State of the Prisons* (1777) but Eyres also printed for Thomas Pennant, Thomas Percival, and William Roscoe. John Aikin's daughter, who became Mrs Anna Laetitia Barbauld, continued to send material to Eyres after she had left Warrington.

Besides excellent letterpress many of these books contain plates, with John Watson's *Memoirs of the Ancient Earls of Warren and Surrey* (1782) being the title receiving most approbation. Eyres's work was certainly more than competent and has been compared to that of the finest British printers, such as Foulis or Baskerville, although Gilbert Wakefield was too extravagant in claiming that Watson's *Memoirs* was 'perhaps the most accurate specimen of typography ever produced by any press' (Plomer and others, 87).

Eyres was also in demand as a printer by publishers in London and other major cities, while at the other extreme, alongside his fine printing, he published a series of chapbooks. After his death at Warrington in 1809 the business was acquired by John Haddock. If he was the William Eyres of Warrington who died on 14 September 1809 and whose will, dated 7 March 1806, was proved on 2 March 1810, then he died a wealthy man, leaving legacies of several thousand pounds to his wife, Ann, and his children Lucy and William.   JOHN R. TURNER

Sources M. Perkin, 'William Eyres and the Warrington press', *Aspects of printing from 1600*, ed. R. Myers and M. Harris (1987), 69–89 • A. J. Hawkes, *Lancashire printed books: a bibliography* (1925) • H. R. Plomer and others, *A dictionary of the printers and booksellers who were at work in England, Scotland, and Ireland from 1726 to 1775* (1932); repr. (1968) • P. O'Brien, *Eyres' press, Warrington (1756–1803)* (1993) • will, Lancs. RO, WCW, William Eyres, 1810
Archives NL Wales
Wealth at death probably wealthy: will, 1810, Lancs. RO, WCW

Eysenck, Hans Jurgen (1916–1997), psychologist, only child of Anton Eduard Eysenck (*b.* 1889) of Borgisch-Gladebach in Germany and Ruth, *née* Werner, of Königshütte in Silesia, was born in Berlin on 4 March 1916 and reared by his Roman Catholic maternal grandmother, A. Werner. His father was an actor and cabaret entertainer, his mother a stage and film actress (who as Helga Molander achieved some contemporary stardom in Germany); their marriage ended when he was two, and Eysenck was left in his grandmother's care. His father remarried in 1925 and his mother entered a relationship with the Jewish film director and producer Max Glass; she married him after the death of his wife, who as a Roman Catholic had refused a divorce. Their itinerant lifestyles rendered Eysenck's parental contacts intermittent, though intense.

Education and departure from Germany Eysenck entered the Bismarck Gymnasium in 1925 and moved to the Prinz Heinrich Gymnasium for his secondary education. Despite frequent poverty (which he blamed on parental meanness) he visited England three times before leaving Germany in 1934: a holiday in Folkestone in 1929, followed by terms in a public school on the Isle of Wight in 1930 and at Exeter University in 1932, studying English language, history, and literature. According to his autobiography, when he sought to study physics at Berlin University in 1934 the authorities made his acceptance conditional on his joining the SS, his father having joined the Nazi party in 1933 and being friendly with Goering, who guaranteed entry at officer rank. Eysenck, who openly detested Nazism from the beginning, declined, joining his mother and Glass in Dijon, where they had fled on Hitler's accession to power. After a few months he left for England, which he already knew and found more congenial. He returned to Germany several times to visit his grandmother and father, the last time being in 1937. A law having been introduced during this stay barring German males from leaving the country without permission, he avoided detection only because an SS inspector on the train assumed that he, like the others in the compartment, was English.

Having qualified for admission to the University of London in 1935 Eysenck discovered that the subjects whose examinations he had passed did not permit him to study physics. He thus accepted the advice to study psychology, knowing nothing of it except a few psychoanalytic ideas, and began the course at University College, London, under Cyril Burt, J. C. Flugel, and S. J. F. Philpott, also attending J. B. S. Haldane's and L. S. Penrose's lectures in genetics. He obtained a first-class BSc degree in 1938, and on 16 July that year married a Canadian-born mathematics graduate, Margaret Malcolm Davies (*b.* 1909/10), the daughter of Richard Llewellyn Davies, a railway engineer. Their only child, Michael, also to become an eminent

Hans Jurgen Eysenck (1916–1997), by Anne-Katrin Purkiss, 1991 [right, with his son, Michael William Eysenck]

psychologist, was born in 1945. Eysenck's PhD degree, on experimental aesthetics, was completed in 1940.

Career and popular publications Narrowly escaping internment in 1939 as an 'enemy alien' Eysenck spent six months in the ARP corps in Islington, London, before being invited by the eminent psychiatrist Aubrey Lewis, on Philip Vernon's recommendation, to join him at Mill Hill Emergency Hospital (the site, along with that in Sutton in south London, of the relocated Maudsley Hospital Clinic) as research psychologist. This proved to be the fulcrum of his career as he launched a research programme on personality (or individual differences) which continued ever after, initially studying suggestibility and the reliability of psychiatric diagnosis. Hilde Himmelweit (later professor of social psychology at the London School of Economics) joined him as his first PhD student, followed by others such as Monte Shapiro. In 1945 Aubrey Lewis, who had been grooming Eysenck from the outset to head the clinical psychology division of a planned institute of psychiatry, returned to the Maudsley, inviting Eysenck and his postgraduate students to join him; these soon included Sarah Petrie, Peter Venables, and Irene Martin, all later prominent in British psychology, and Sybil Bianca Guiletta Rostal (b. 1926/7), later to become his second wife, the daughter of violinist Max Rostal and cellist Sela Trau.

In 1947 the Rockefeller Foundation funding on which Eysenck's post depended ceased and his marriage was foundering. However, the Institute of Psychiatry having become a reality, Lewis offered Eysenck the readership in the department of psychiatry's sub-department of psychology. This he accepted, declining the chair of clinical psychology at Duke University, North Carolina, in the USA, and a senior lectureship at the department of educational psychology at Edinburgh University (under Godfrey Thomson). With Sybil he spent an idyllic six months as visiting professor at the University of Pennsylvania, Philadelphia, in 1949–50, which he later described as 'the happiest time of my life'. The couple married on 30 September 1950 and acquired a flat near the Maudsley in London.

Throughout their marriage Sybil remained a valued professional collaborator, publishing in her own right, as well as raising their four children (three sons and a daughter).

From 1947 Eysenck's fortunes continued an unfaltering ascent into the mid-1960s. In 1955 psychology gained departmental status within the institute; Eysenck was professor of psychology and assumed responsibility for experimental research while Shapiro managed the clinical work. But Eysenck was also rapidly acquiring wider fame with a quartet of highly successful Pelican books: *The Uses and Abuses of Psychology* (1953), *Sense and Nonsense in Psychology* (1957), *Know your Own IQ* (1962), and *Fact and Fiction in Psychology* (1965). These provided thousands of readers with their first introduction to modern psychology. Written in lively style they aimed to debunk what Eysenck saw as fallacious theories and ideas and to promote a 'hard' scientific vision of psychology. Many other successful popularizing texts followed, but none achieved quite the best-seller status of this first group (one of the last was *Mindwatching*, in 1981, co-authored with his son Michael). An augury of future controversies came when, in *The Psychology of Politics* (1954), he proposed, on the basis of statistical analysis of political and social attitudes, that there was, in addition to right-wing authoritarianism, an equally irrational left-wing version—an idea that had been gestating in his mind since the early 1940s. This angered many on the left and it transpired that the 'extreme' 'tough-minded' scores he attributed to the allegedly authoritarian left-wing British subjects fell within the normal range in the United States (though Eysenck challenged the comparability of the samples). 1958 saw a collision on the professional front. Addressing the Royal Medico-Psychological Association, Eysenck attacked the effectiveness of psychotherapy, proposing the alternative technique of behaviour modification therapy (see below) as superior on both theoretical and empirical grounds. This elicited fury from the assembled psychiatrists, partly because it was seen as a bid by psychology for psychiatry's medical territory. A breach with Aubrey Lewis ensued, though civilities were maintained, and Eysenck's institutional position remained secure.

Thereafter Eysenck frequently found himself publicly embattled. In 1965 he challenged the evidence on cigarette smoking causing lung cancer (in *Smoking, Health and Personality*), to the wrath of the growing anti-smoking lobby. Also of serious consequence was the fact that while he had always considered himself a moderate socialist, his personal temperament and strongly hereditarian theoretical position clashed with the more radical tone of the 1960s and 1970s. In 1969 he defended the American psychologist Arthur Jensen (who had spent two years under him as post-doctoral researcher) when his views on 'race differences' in intelligence triggered heated controversy at the height of the campaigns for civil rights and black liberation in America—an issue second only to the Vietnam War as the focus of radical anger. Disruptive, sometimes violent, protests accompanied invited appearances at several universities (notably Birmingham, Leicester, Sydney, Melbourne, and, most notoriously, the London School of

Economics). Pilloried as a racist fascist Eysenck seems to have been somewhat bemused. Contempt for his most hostile assailants as beyond the appeal of reason disinclined him from answering them. When animal rights activists daubed his house in 1970 his bafflement and contempt only increased since he had rarely undertaken animal experiments and opposed vivisection except under conditions of greatest medical necessity. (A small animal behaviour laboratory at Bethlem Royal Hospital—a branch of the Maudsley—involved no physical suffering.)

Eysenck's other unpopular or heretical stances included opposition to the introduction of comprehensive schools, giving both astrology and parapsychology sympathetic hearings, and a lifelong, ever intensifying, hostility to psychoanalysis which was first aired in a paper in 1949 and which culminated in *The Decline and Fall of the Freudian Empire* (1985). While his productivity did not decline until his final years, his post-1970 mainstream research consisted mainly of elaborations and applications of the theoretical position he had reached during the 1940s and 1950s.

Other writings His popular books aside, Eysenck's publications fell into two main categories. First: serious scientific work addressing the nature and assessment of individual differences (*Dimensions of Personality*, 1947, being his first book-length contribution), begun at Mill Hill and developed in the context of his ambitions to create a scientifically based clinical psychology at the Institute of Psychiatry. He strove to synthesize the behaviourist and psychometric traditions into a physiologically (and genetically) grounded theory of personality differences as rooted in variations in cortical arousal (low arousal being associated with extraversion) and autonomic nervous system activity determined by the region of the brainstem known as the ascending reticular activating system or ARAS (high variability being linked to neurosis). Behaviourally, extraversion signified low conditionability, Eysenck drawing first on Hullian drive theory and later on the Pavlovian theory of cortical inhibition in formulating this relationship. He soon came to favour the physiologically based character of the Russian school over the American behaviourist learning-theory tradition. The two major dimensions of personality, extraversion (adopted from C. G. Jung's typology) and neuroticism, had first been studied in Eysenck's early psychometric work, which involved applying the statistical technique of factor analysis to questionnaire responses (the method determining how many dimensions or factors are needed to account for the variability of the data). This yielded in 1959 the highly successful Maudsley personality inventory (MPI), which was revised as the Eysenck personality inventory (EPI) in 1963, and again, in conjunction with Sybil Eysenck, as the Eysenck personality questionnaire (EPQ) in 1975, giving extraversion, neuroticism, and, in the EPQ, psychoticism scores (a dimension first postulated in *The Scientific Study of Personality*, 1952). Eysenck believed his work provided a basis for more effective techniques in treating psychological disorders, notably the 'behaviour modification therapy' method pioneered by Joseph Wolpe. He played little

part, however, in its actual clinical development, a task pursued, first (unenthusiastically!) by Shapiro, and then by his successor, Wolpe's ex-student S. Rachman (whose PhD degree Eysenck had supervised), Gwynne Jones, and Victor Meyer. This work established Eysenck's scientific reputation within experimental psychology and supplied the theoretical framework for all his other writings, though from the late 1960s he became additionally involved with theories of intelligence.

Second: monographs on specific topics, often popularly pitched and frequently contributions to current controversies (such as the 'race and IQ' debate). In these Eysenck tackled matters as various as smoking, crime, astrology, and extrasensory perception (ESP), frequently (as in the cases of astrology and ESP) adopting scientifically unorthodox positions on the grounds that statistical analysis of data yielded significant results. Alone or jointly Eysenck wrote or edited more than seventy books and hundreds of journal papers and book chapters. He also edited the international series of Monographs in Experimental Psychology and launched several journals (such as *Behaviour Research and Therapy*).

Eysenck's international prominence and impact, as gauged by citation levels and translations of his books (into all major European and Asian languages), were unmatched among post-Second World War British psychologists, but his relationships with others in the discipline were increasingly chequered after the mid-1960s, reinforcing his self-perception as an outsider and rebel. For non-psychologists, by contrast, he embodied the disciplinary establishment. While by general testimony a congenial social companion, Eysenck was not really a 'team player' beyond his immediate research colleagues and supporters. The publicly visible consequence of this was that, on the more heated issues, he rarely engaged in collaborative or respectful intellectual debate with his critics, viewing opposition as due to ignorance of scientific methods, personal animosity, or 'racial and class-inspired hatreds' (Eysenck). By the 1960s he was sufficiently eminent and professionally invulnerable to be able to operate largely on his own terms. He strongly denied enjoying controversy, but being proudly possessed of a strong theatrical streak he seized the opportunities for rhetorical combat which it offered. It must, however, be conceded that such combats were frequently not of his own choosing.

Race and IQ The 'race and IQ' controversy of the early 1970s requires further comment since it was this damaging issue with which Eysenck became most identified publicly. His handling of the subject partly exacerbated the situation, attracting widespread vilification and, as noted earlier, occasionally violent protest. An interview which, embarrassingly, appeared in the first issue of a neo-Nazi magazine, *Bulldog*, was almost certainly given in ignorance of the interviewer's ideological affiliations, but it confirmed perceptions of Eysenck as at worst fascistic and at best naïve. As late as 1981 he contributed a foreword to a work by an avowed Nazi sympathizer. The later discovery that the right-wing Pioneer Fund had supported his work on race differences (and the American tobacco giant Reynolds his smoking research) made matters no easier. Their methodology being effectively the same as his, and many (such as Richard Lynn and Jensen) being personal friends, he accepted the legitimacy of the work of those researching race differences in intelligence. How far he accepted their conclusions in favour of such differences is not in fact entirely clear since his statements on the matter are less than consistent. For Eysenck it was a purely scientific and 'free speech' issue. A further factor was also involved. The target of Jensen's original paper on the issue was the Head Start programme aimed at raising the educational performance of impoverished children (including African Americans) by special remedial methods. This was a cause with which Eysenck had considerable sympathy, being opposed to the introduction of comprehensive schooling in Britain (on which he contributed to the *Black Paper* series of attacks on this policy). He appeared to have a blind spot regarding the authenticity of the passions the question aroused and a reluctance to engage in depth with serious theoretical critiques of research into race differences. Ironically he saw his attackers as akin to the fanatical Nazi ideologues from whom he had originally fled, left- as opposed to right-wing authoritarians—a view which their own conduct occasionally reinforced. In his autobiography he emerged as genuinely bewildered by the animosity his views elicited and, on this issue especially, ignorance, personal dislike, and bigotry were his preferred explanations. He incredulously dismissed accusations of racism or fascism—noting that his first cohort of research students and colleagues were either Jewish women or communist men—while his own political sympathies were to the left. It is relevant to observe here that, while often tackling social issues, Eysenck rarely invoked explanations of behaviour at a truly social level, generally explaining the social in terms of individuals' genetically determined personalities. Even if this was perhaps due less to his belief in the irrelevance of the social than to his feeling that it was too obvious to need articulating or beyond his professional remit, it exacerbated the hostility of more socially oriented psychologists.

Final years, reputation, and personality In 1996 Eysenck was diagnosed as suffering from brain cancer, from which he died at 51 Lawrie Park Road, Sydenham, London, on 4 September 1997. He was survived by his wife and children. The protracted decline in his condition was particularly distressing for one who had hitherto never really known, or at least admitted, defeat. It is premature to predict Eysenck's long-term reputation. Many working in the fields of individual differences and neuropsychology, such as former colleagues Jeffrey Gray and Tony Gibson, rate his contribution as of the very highest level of importance and argue that subsequent research on brain functioning and behaviour-genetics confirms hypotheses which Eysenck first proposed on the basis of much less sophisticated research. British psychology certainly benefited from his popularizing efforts even if many of those he attracted to the discipline eventually adopted positions

divergent from his own. Internationally Eysenck was one of very few British psychologists of his generation to have a major impact in the United States (eventually earning the distinguished scientist award of the American Psychological Association), and, as previously noted, his more popular books were translated into an exceptionally wide range of languages. Yet despite his breadth of interest and independent-mindedness, his work remained constrained within a somewhat narrow conception of what it was to be scientific in which a fascination with measurement and statistical analysis *per se* left him impatient with broader theoretical and philosophical debates. This was widely construed as signifying indifference or insensitivity to broader social and existential issues.

Eysenck's personality was certainly complex. Early circumstances clearly conspired to instil both a sense of outsidership and autonomous self-confidence, boosted by physical robustness and facility in sports (tennis remaining a lifelong passion). This engendered an enduring ability to meet difficult situations with remarkable *sang froid* but also an unshakeable belief in his own intellectual capacities and rational acuity. The downside was that he could, in print particularly, appear vain and arrogant—which he sensed but did not care to remedy. Another legacy of his childhood and of the later death of his adored grandmother in a Nazi concentration camp was a high level of emotional, and even intellectual, self-protectiveness which he said left him unable to read or watch anything related to the Holocaust. This self-protectiveness may also have underlain his propensity for dismissing as worthless whole swathes of psychological thought and even entire disciplines (such as economics). Many contemporaries were quick to pass judgement on his character, whether condemning him as a racist reactionary or a narrow-minded positivist or exalting him as the greatest psychologist of his age. It is unlikely that posterity's verdict will confirm either assessment. Despite its ostensible frankness, his autobiography, *Rebel with a Cause* (1990), conveys the impression of a seemingly unassailable self-sufficiency and a refusal publicly to engage in profound self-analysis. Eysenck remains, in fact, something of an enigma; and while at heart a romantic rebel, it is still, despite that title, somewhat unclear quite what he was rebelling against.

GRAHAM RICHARDS

Sources H. J. Eysenck, *Rebel with a cause: the autobiography of Hans Eysenck* (1990) · private information (2004) [T. Gibson] · *The Guardian* (8 Sept 1997) · *Daily Telegraph* (10 Sept 1997) · m. certs. · d. cert. **Archives** Bodl. Oxf., Society for Protection of Science and Learning, corresp. file · Schönklinik, Chiemsee, Germany, complete set of his books, memorabilia, and inscribed books · University of Staffordshire, Stoke-on-Trent, Centre for the History of Psychology, memorabilia | SOUND Staffordshire University, Stoke on Trent, Centre for the History of Psychology, two taped interviews with associates **Likenesses** C. Ware, photograph, c.1968, Hult. Arch. · P. Wardle, red chalk and pencil, 1990, NPG · A.-K. Purkiss, photograph, 1991, NPG [*see illus.*] · M. Gerson, photograph, repro. in Eysenck, *Rebel with a cause*, jacket · C. Howes, photograph, repro. in Eysenck, *Rebel with a cause*, jacket · photograph, repro. in *Guardian* · photograph, repro. in *The Times* · photograph, repro. in *Daily Telegraph*

Wealth at death £35,955: probate, 21 Aug 1998, *CGPLA Eng. & Wales*

Eyston, Charles (1667–1721), antiquary, was born on 22 September 1667, the eldest son of George Eyston (1636–1691), landowner, of East Hendred, near Wantage, Berkshire, and Anne (1631–1712), daughter of Robert Dormer of Peterley, Buckinghamshire. His family were ardent Catholics and both his father and brother were educated at Douai and St Omer. Of his own education, possibly abroad, no record is extant. The manor house at East Hendred, owned by the family since the fifteenth century, had a private chapel, where services were resumed after its desecration in 1688. In 1690 Eyston was arrested for alleged Jacobite activities and held in custody for some time. In 1692 he married Winifrid Dorothy Fitzherbert (*d.* 1753), daughter of Basil Fitzherbert, of Swinnerton, Staffordshire, and Norbury, Derbyshire. They had four sons and six daughters. Their sons were educated at Douai and St Omer, and one, Basil, became a Benedictine monk and was a professor at Douai in 1733. Several of their daughters became nuns. Their descendants are still seated at East Hendred.

Eyston became distinguished as an antiquary, and was a great friend of Thomas Hearne, who published some fragments from his collections. To Hearne, 'he was a man of a sweet temper and … an excellent scholar, but so modest that he did not care to have it at any time mentioned' (*Remarks and Collections*, 7.294). In 1716 he completed 'A little monument to the once famous abbey and borough of Glastonbury' (MS Hendred House). It was published anonymously by Hearne in his *History and Antiquities of Glastonbury* (1722) and for some time wrongly attributed to Richard Rawlinson. Richard Warner republished Eyston's essay in 1826. Eyston also composed 'A Poor Little Monument to All the Old Pious Dissolved Foundations of England', which, together with related studies and correspondence, is preserved at Hendred House. Eyston died of diabetes on 5 November 1721 at Hendred House, and was buried on 8 November 1721 in the Eystons' chapel in the parish church of East Hendred. THEODOR HARMSEN

Sources Hendred House, East Hendred, Wantage, Berkshire, Charles Eyston MSS · Bodl. Oxf., MSS Eyston, MSS Top. Berks. d.5, b.2, c.40–43 · will, proved 1722, PRO, PROB 11/583/185 · *Remarks and collections of Thomas Hearne*, ed. C. E. Doble and others, 11 vols., OHS, 2, 7, 13, 34, 42–3, 48, 50, 65, 67, 72 (1885–1921) · A. L. Humphreys, *East Hendred: a Berkshire parish historically treated* (1923) · *Report on the manuscripts of Allan George Finch*, 5 vols., HMC, 71 (1913–2003), vol. 3, pp. 379–80, 387 · T. Hearne, preface and appendix, in C. Eyston, *The history and antiquities of Glastonbury*, ed. T. Hearne (1722), vii–xciii, 237–333 · N. Harpsfield, *A treatise on the pretended divorce between Henry VIII and Catharine of Aragon*, ed. N. Pocock, CS, new ser., 21 (1878) · *Pedigree of the family of Eyston of East Hendred in the county of Berks.* (1875) · R. Warner, *History of the abbey of Glaston and the town of Glastonbury* (1826) · E. E. Estcourt and J. O. Payne, eds., *The English Catholic nonjurors of 1715* (1885), 3, 5, 72 · Gillow, *Lit. biog. hist.* · *Third report*, HMC, 2 (1872), 260–61 · G. Holt, *St Omers and Bruges colleges, 1593–1773: a biographical dictionary*, Catholic RS, 69 (1979) · parish register, East Hendred, 1667, Berks. RO, D/P66/1/1 · parish register, East Hendred, 1721

Archives Bodl. Oxf., notes taken anonymously from his writings, MSS Top. Berks d5; b2; c40–43 · Hendred House, East Hendred, Wantage, Berkshire · priv. coll., journal and accounts of journey to Rome; corresp. with Thomas Hearne and Richard Rawlinson | Bodl. Oxf., letters to Thomas Hearne

Likenesses oils, priv. coll.

Wealth at death manor of East Hendred; farms in Henbury, (Westbury-upon-Trym), Stowick, and Barton Regis; manors of Arches and Catner in Henbury: will, 1722, PRO, PROB 11/583/185; Estcourt and Payne, eds., *English Catholic nonjurors*

Eyston, George Edward Thomas (1897–1979), racing driver, was born at Bampton, Oxfordshire, on 28 June 1897, the elder of the two sons of Edward Robert Joseph Eyston, gentleman, and his wife, Annie Maude Earle. He was educated at Stonyhurst College and Trinity College, Cambridge, a process interrupted by the First World War. Commissioned as second lieutenant in the 3rd battalion, Dorset regiment, he was transferred to the Royal Artillery, where his mathematical and engineering skills could be put to better use. He served in France throughout the war. He was wounded at the battle of Arras, became a staff captain, won the MC, and was twice mentioned in dispatches. After the armistice he resumed his engineering studies at Cambridge which he combined with an interest in rowing: he was captain of the Trinity boat club and spare man to the Cambridge crew of 1919 which won the international eights in Paris.

In 1921 Eyston returned to France to study the language, and it was while holidaying with a French family near Le Mans that he was to discover his true métier: cars and speed. The American ace Ralph de Palma was testing a French Ballot racing car and Eyston decided that this was something he had to try. On returning to England he bought a secondhand Sunbeam grand prix car and in 1922 stripped down and reconditioned a 4.5 litre Vauxhall to get experience of racing machinery. Although he was gaining practical engineering knowledge, it was a meeting with Lionel Martin that really set Eyston on the road to racing and record-breaking success. Martin suggested that he should drive an Aston Martin at the 1923 Brooklands Whitsun meeting. 'The Captain', as he was generally known, won two races and was placed second in two others.

Eyston drove many marques of racing car, including Bugatti (in which he won the 1926 Boulogne grand prix), Monza Alfa Romeo, Maserati (in sports car races), Bentley, and Riley. But his name became linked with MG because of the number of races won and records set with those cars, from the early 1930s onwards. Eyston first achieved fame with his Magic Midget when he exceeded 100 m.p.h. with a 750cc car. He then announced his intention of driving the 750cc Midget for an hour at over 100 m.p.h. at the Montlhéry circuit near Paris. At this period Eyston was spending half as much time in France on speed attempts as he was to spend later in America, and was known as 'Le Recordbreaker'. He achieved the 750cc 100 miles in the hour record, but on the last lap of Montlhéry the engine blew up and the car caught fire. With his clothing in flames, Eyston had to jump for his life and was severely burnt. Undeterred, he started work from his hospital bed on an improved Midget to achieve 120 m.p.h. with a 750cc car. As a by-product, Eyston invented flameproof racing overalls and then, defying doctor's orders, left his bed to break the 120 m.p.h. record.

After having taken so many class records for long and short distances, Eyston realized that world records were also within his grasp, and in 1932 he decided to attach the world hour record using the unlikely Panhard et Levassor 8 litre sleeve valve car. Heavy, old, and difficult to handle, this was by no means the ideal vehicle for the purpose but after a tyre burst Eyston succeeded in averaging 130.73 m.p.h for the hour. The thin tyres of the day were a major hazard in prolonged high-speed running and even Eyston's engineering skill could not overcome the danger. After the record was beaten at the Avus track in Berlin, he took it back in 1934 again with the old Panhard which he persuaded to run for an hour at 133.21 m.p.h. Many other records were achieved by Eyston in a great variety of marques, including Riley, Hotchkiss, Delage, and diesel-engined cars which he designed and built himself. In fact he held more records than any driver before him. A first-class engineer and designer as well as a thoughtful racing driver who achieved results by attention to detailed preparation, Eyston invented the Powerplus super-charger and a rudimentary disc brake. A steward of the Royal Automobile Club, he was also for many years on its technical and engineering committee.

Apart from the Magic Midget, the Eyston car which captured the public imagination was *Speed of the wind*, which had a V-12 Rolls-Royce Kestrel aero-engine. Extremely advanced for the 1930s, the car had automatic transmission, front-wheel drive, and independent suspension. In July 1936 Eyston drove it 162 miles in an hour to take the world hour record. Success with *Speed of the wind* led to the design, in collaboration with Ernest Eldridge, of *Thunderbolt* to attack the world land speed record. A monster with two Rolls aero-engines and a total capacity of 56 litres, it had four front wheels and twin rear tyres. At his first attempt in 1937 Eyston set a new record at 312 m.p.h. His old friend and rival John Cobb then took the record, but Eyston beat him at 345.5 m.p.h. in 1938 and raised the speed later the same year to 357.5 m.p.h. Sadly, neither *Speed of the wind* nor *Thunderbolt* survived for honourable retirement in a motor museum. Both were destroyed, *Speed of the wind* by a flying bomb in Eyston's Kilburn workshop and *Thunderbolt* in a fire during a visit to Australia and New Zealand. However, one of his engines is in the Science Museum in South Kensington.

During the Second World War Eyston was a regional controller for the Ministry of Production. After the war he became a director of Castrol but, feeling himself not fully qualified, he returned to Cambridge in 1950 to read geology. He also still took part in world and American sports car speed and distance records at Utah for both Austin–Healey and MG. A well-built, quiet, bespectacled man, Eyston liked nothing better than to relax during delays in record-breaking attempts with a trout rod by a mountain stream. A devout Roman Catholic and a descendant of Sir Thomas More, he was a member of the board of governors of the Oxford and Cambridge University chaplaincy and a papal chamberlain. In 1937 he was awarded the Segrave

trophy. The following year he became a chevalier of the French Légion d'honneur. In 1948 he was appointed OBE. Modest to a fault, he sought records for his country rather than for himself. He never received the knighthood that many felt was his due.

In 1924 Eyston married Olga Mary, the daughter of Edward Eyre, a banker with W. R. Grace & Co., of New York and London. They had two daughters. His diary still filled with engagements, Eyston died on 11 June 1979 in a railway carriage between Winchester and London.

COLIN DRYDEN, *rev.*

Sources G. Eyston, *Flat out* (1933) · G. Eyston and B. Lyndon, *Motor racing and record breaking* (1935) · G. Eyston and W. F. Bradley, *Speed on salt* (1936) · private information (1986) · CGPLA Eng. & Wales (1979)
Archives FILM BFI NFTVA, '136 mph for two days', British Paramount News, 23 July 1936 · BFI NFTVA, 'Eyston breaks world speed record', Gaumont British News, 25 Aug 1938 · BFI NFTVA, 'The fastest men on earth', Gaumont British News, 29 Aug 1938 · BFI NFTVA, home footage · BFI NFTVA, 'Landspeed record broken again', Gaumont British News, 19 Sept 1938 · BFI NFTVA, news footage
Likenesses Sallon, caricature (in later life) · photographs, Hult. Arch.
Wealth at death £24,729: probate, 29 Oct 1979, CGPLA Eng. & Wales

Eyston [*alias* Elston], **John** [*name in religion* Bernardine of St Francis] (**1627–1709**), Franciscan friar, was a son of Thomas Eyston, esquire (1588–1669), of Finchampstead, Berkshire, a councillor-at-law and representative of an old recusant family settled at East Hendred, Berkshire, and Mary (*d.* 1671), daughter of Thomas Yate of Lyford, Berkshire. He entered the English Franciscan recollects at St Bonaventure's, Douai, was professed in 1644, and was ordained priest in 1651. After studying in the University of Douai he taught there for eighteen years as professor of philosophy and theology, taking his doctorate of divinity in 1668. In 1693 he became prefect of studies at Douai. On a number of occasions he acted as spiritual director and confessor to the English nuns of the third order regular of St Francis at Aire (1668–71, 1683–6, 1691–5, 1700–06) and Princenhoff, near Bruges (1674–7, 1687–91, 1696–7) in the Spanish Netherlands. While at Aire he published in 1684 *The Christian Duty Composed by B. Bernard Francis Student in Divinity*, a commentary on the creed, the virtues, the commandments, and sacraments, of which there were a number of Irish editions at the end of the eighteenth century. It is reputed to have been the first book published in that town. He went as a missionary to England in 1677 but, because of lameness and the persecution occasioned by the Popish Plot, he returned to the continent where he acted as definitor to the general chapter (1680–83, 1686–9), holding the title 'Jubilat doctor'. He retired to Douai in 1708 and died suddenly on 28 May 1709 of an apoplectic fit during mass at St Bonaventure's Friary. He was buried in the south cloister at St Bonaventure's near the door.

GEOFFREY SCOTT

Sources R. Trappes-Lomax, ed., *The English Franciscan nuns, 1619–1821, and the Friars Minor of the same province, 1618–1761*, Catholic RS, 24 (1922) · A. L. Humphreys, *East Hendred: a Berkshire parish historically treated* (1923) · Father Thaddeus [F. Hermans], *The Franciscans in*

England, 1600–1850 (1898) • B. Francis [B. Eyton], *The Christian duty* (1684) • T. H. Clancy, *English Catholic books, 1641–1700: a bibliography*, rev. edn (1996) • F. Blom and others, *English Catholic books, 1701–1800: a bibliography* (1996) • Gillow, *Lit. biog. hist.* • D. A. Bellenger, ed., *English and Welsh priests, 1558–1800* (1984)

Archives Franciscan Friary, Forest Gate, London, MSS • Hendred, MSS

Likenesses oils, Hendred House, Oxfordshire • portrait (after earlier portrait), repro. in Thaddeus, *Franciscans in England*

Eythin. For this title name *see* King, James, Lord Eythin (1589–1652).

Eyton, Robert William (1815–1881), historian, born at Wellington vicarage, Shropshire, on 21 December 1815, was the fourth son, and seventh of ten children, of the Revd John Eyton (1778–1823) and his wife, Anna Maria (1787–1825), only child of Edmund Joseph Plowden (1756–1838), of Plowden, and his wife, also Anna Maria, *née* Burton. The Plowdens were Roman Catholic, but the future Mrs John Eyton was brought up in her mother's faith, that of the Church of England. Eyton thus descended from two of Shropshire's oldest families; his father's family, seated at Eyton upon the Weald Moors by the mid-twelfth century, he considered to be a probable cadet branch of the Norman Pantulfs, barons of Wem.

Orphaned young, Eyton lived at first with his Plowden grandfather (who left his grandchildren very well provided for), probably at Tong Castle in Shropshire and later at Haughton Hall near Shifnal, also in Shropshire; after 1830 he was generally with his great-uncle Robert Burton, of Longner near Shrewsbury. He was entered at his father's school, Rugby, in 1829; the following year, however, he was moved to Bridgnorth grammar school, then flourishing under Thomas Rowley. In 1835 he matriculated from Christ Church, Oxford, where he was a Fell's exhibitioner; having graduated BA (with second-class honours in *literae humaniores*) in 1839, he proceeded MA in 1845. Also in 1839 he was ordained deacon, became curate of Morville and Aston Eyre, Shropshire, with Tickwood House as his residence, and on 26 September married Mary Elizabeth, also known as Eliza (*d.* 1883), daughter of the Revd James Watts, vicar of Ledbury, Herefordshire. Eyton was ordained priest in 1840, and in 1841 he was instituted to Ryton rectory, near Shifnal, a good living in his own patronage. Between 1840 and 1850 he and his wife had three sons and four daughters, and in 1844–5 Eyton built a very large new rectory at Ryton.

Eyton was assisted in his small parish by successive curates; one, appointed in 1852, stayed until about 1861. Those years saw the appearance of his *Antiquities of Shropshire*, issued to subscribers in forty-eight parts between 1853 and 1860 and forming twelve octavo volumes. With Eyton's brother Walter as business manager, the work paid its way. Its quality was quickly recognized. Sir William Hardy placed Eyton far ahead of all county historians, and Chester Waters acknowledged that he stood alone in their company. Among them Eyton was preeminent in the critical use of original records to trace the descent of feudal estates and delineate the genealogies and public lives of their lords. *Antiquities of Shropshire*

remains 'the most important single work ever devoted to the history of Shropshire' (Mason), and Eyton's single-handed completion of it was ensured in part by the practical elimination of topographical and architectural description but mainly by his limitation of the work to the 250-odd years between the conquest and the reign of Edward II, a period of which he 'was peculiarly the master' (*VCH Shropshire*, 1.xxi). Eyton corresponded widely with scholars and others who shared his interests: Hardy and Colonel George Wrottesley may be instanced, and also Sir Thomas Phillipps, whose invitation to Middle Hill he adroitly avoided. In 1857 he wrote disinterestedly—not wishing to do the work himself—to suggest materials for inclusion in the Rolls Series.

Eyton left Ryton in 1863, disposed of the advowson there, and spent his remaining years in the south of England. He had sold his library (which he was later to regret), but he kept his manuscript collections (most of which, after his death, were bought by the British Museum) and soon returned to his favourite studies, which claimed him until a few weeks before his death. Important works appeared, notably the *Itinerary* of Henry II (1878) and Domesday Book studies of Dorset, Somerset, and Staffordshire (1877–81); and there were contributions to the *Transactions of the Shropshire Archaeological Society* (a full list of his works is in volume 10, 1887, 6–7) and the William Salt Archaeological Society's *Collections*. A Lincolnshire Domesday study remained unpublished. In his leisure Eyton bred pheasants; 'his notes', according to his grandson, 'on their pedigrees and performances are as painstaking and meticulous … as any on the fortunes of FitzAlan or Le Strange'. He also produced fine petit point pictures. All his occupations were consistent with frequent moves: after residing at Calehill Park, Ashford, Kent (1863–7), Eyton lived at Ripple Court near Dover (1867–71) and then at Albury House near Guildford, Surrey (1871–3). He lived from 1873 until about 1877 at Iwerne Minster, Dorset, and then until 1879 at Cattistock rectory, Somerset. Thereafter he lived at Winchfield House, near Basingstoke, Hampshire, where he died on 8 September 1881, having suffered from cancer and asthma for some time. He was buried on 13 September at Winchfield parish church.

GEORGE C. BAUGH

Sources Shrops. RRC, Eyton papers, M.I. 6783 [transcripts] • genealogies of the Plowden and Eyton families, Shrops. RRC, 6001/2788, pp. 268–88, esp. 286; 6001/2790, pp. 457–8 and n. • B. M. P. [Plowden], *Records of the Plowden family* (privately printed, 1887), 139–42 • G. C. Baugh, 'Shropshire', *English county histories: a guide*, ed. C. R. J. Currie and C. P. Lewis (1994), 341–2 • J. F. A. Mason, 'The centenary of Eyton's "Antiquities of Shropshire"', *Transactions of the Shropshire Archaeological Society*, 55 (1954–6), 102–4 • details of Eyton's education, Shrops. RRC, 1104/17/15 • *Transactions of the Shropshire Archaeological Society*, 10 (1887), 1–7 • records of church career and curacies, Lichfield RO, B/A/1, B/A/11 • G. A. Solly, ed., *Rugby School register*, 1 (1933), 282 • *VCH Shropshire*, 1.21; 2.143; 9.139–40 • *DNB* • Crockford (1880) • m. cert. • d. cert. • parish register, Winchfield, Hants. RO, 13 Sept 1881 [burial] • T. P. Marshall, 'Shropshire men, cxxxv — Robert William Eyton', *Shrewsbury Chronicle* (3 June 1910), 8

Archives BL, notebooks containing the results on his studies on Domesday and other early records, Add. MSS 31923–31946 • BL, transcripts of MS notes in his own copy of *Antiquities of Shropshire*, Add. MS 33226 · Bodl. Oxf., Shropshire collections, MSS Top. Salop. d. 2–3 · Shrops. RRC, transcripts of the Haughmond Abbey register and extracts from the diocesan register of Lichfield and Hereford, 6001/114 | BL, copy of Edward Lloyd's *Antiquities of Shropshire* with his MS notes · Shrops. RRC, institutions of Shropshire incumbents

Likenesses photograph, repro. in *Transactions of the Shropshire Archaeological Society*, 10 (1887), frontispiece

Wealth at death £77,946 5s. 10d.: resworn probate, March 1882, *CGPLA Eng. & Wales* (1881)

Eyton, Stephen (*fl. c.*1320), Augustinian canon and supposed chronicler, is known only from the writings of John Leland and later antiquaries, who attribute to him a *floruit* in the reign of Edward II. He is described as having been a canon of the Augustinian priory of Warter, a few miles east of York, on the edge of the Yorkshire downs, and it is possible that he took his name from the village of Etton, east of Warter and north-west of Beverley. Leland records Eyton as the author of a history of the reign of Edward II, a copy of which he saw at Fountains Abbey. To this John Bale adds that Eyton's work, of which he claims to have seen a copy in the library of All Souls College, Oxford, had the incipit 'Post mortem mundo deflendam'. However, this incipit is strikingly similar to that of the account of Edward II's reign in Thomas Walsingham's *Historia Anglicana*, which begins with the words 'Post mortem toti mundo deflendam Edwardi primi inclyti regis'. It is therefore possible either that the text Leland saw was in fact that of part of Walsingham's chronicle, and that Eyton was only its later scribe or owner, or that Bale, coming upon the relevant section of Walsingham's chronicle in a version detached from the rest, assumed that this was identical with the account of Edward II's reign noted by Leland at Fountains, and attributed Walsingham's work to Eyton in error. There is nothing inherently improbable about a canon of Warter composing a historical text: the writing of chronicles flourished among the Augustinians in the fourteenth century. But no evidence survives that might now shed light on either the quality or, indeed, the existence of the work attributed to Eyton.

HENRY SUMMERSON

Sources R. Sharpe, *A handlist of the Latin writers of Great Britain and Ireland before 1540* (1997), 527 · Bodl. Oxf., MS Top. Gen. c.4, 247 · *Commentarii de scriptoribus Britannicis, auctore Joanne Lelando*, ed. A. Hall, 2 (1709), 334–5 · Bale, *Cat.*, 1.390 · J. Pits, *Relationum historicarum de rebus Anglicis*, ed. [W. Bishop] (Paris, 1619), 410 · Tanner, *Bibl. Brit.-Hib.*, 257

Eyton, Thomas Campbell (1809–1880), naturalist and agriculturist, was born at Eyton Hall, Wellington, Shropshire, on 10 September 1809, the son of Thomas Eyton (1777–1855), recorder of Wenlock, and later high sheriff of Shropshire, and his wife, Elizabeth (*c.*1780–1817), daughter of Major-General Donald Campbell. Eyton is mainly known as an ornithologist, having become interested in natural history at an early age. Admitted pensioner at St John's College, Cambridge, in 1827, he matriculated the following year, but left without taking a degree. He became the friend and correspondent of Charles Darwin, John Gould, Louis Agassiz, Alfred Russel Wallace, Richard

Owen, and Sir William Jardine, and many other naturalists of the time.

On 13 May 1835 Eyton married Elizabeth Frances (1813?–1870), daughter and coheir of Robert Aglionby Slaney (1792–1862) of Walford and Hatton, MP for Shrewsbury for twenty-three years; they had seven children.

In 1836 Eyton published the first volume of his *History of the Rarer British Birds*, with woodcuts by a local engraver, Mark, which have been compared with Thomas Bewick's for fidelity. In the same year appeared his second volume, *Catalogue of British Birds*; for this he was patron to Edward Lear, employing him for the illustrations. In 1838 Eyton published his elaborate *Monograph of the Anatidae, or Duck Tribe*, which included descriptions of several new ducks to science. On coming into possession of the family estate on the death of his father in 1855, Eyton built a spacious museum at Eyton Hall, in which he formed one of the finest collections of skins and skeletons of birds in Europe. The skeletons were mostly prepared and mounted by his own hands. In 1867 (with supplements in 1869 and 1873–5) Eyton employed Mr Hobson of Wellington as publisher for *Osteologia avium* (1867), a voluminous work on the skeletons of birds, illustrated from the specimens in his own museum. He also compiled *Eyton's Catalogue of Species of Birds in his Possession* (1858), *A Synopsis of the Duck Tribe* (1869), and a catalogue of the skeletons of birds in his museum. His last publication was a final supplement to his fine work *Osteologia avium* in 1878.

Although the contents of his museum were sold after Eyton's death, many of his specimens (both skeletons and cabinet skins) have survived in museums such as the Natural History Museum (Tring), the Liverpool Museum, Cambridge University Museum of Zoology, and the Academy of Natural Sciences in Philadelphia. Many of these specimens are of great importance to zoology and in several cases are the 'types' (or standards) on which that species is based. Eyton named several birds himself, including *Arachnothera flavigaster*, the spectacled spiderhunter from Indo-China, and *Dendrocygna eytoni*, the plumed whistling duck from Australia, which is often alternatively called Eyton's tree duck. Several species of bird were named after Eyton, notably a Brazilian woodcreeper (*Xiphorhynchus guttatus eytoni*) by Philip Lutley Sclater, the first editor of *Ibis*, in 1853.

Eyton spent most of his life on the family estates in Shropshire, and did much to improve the Hereford cattle breed. About 1842 he instituted and conducted the *Herd Book of Hereford Cattle*, and continued its publication to 1860 when Mr T. Duckham became its editor.

Eyton took especial pleasure to help fellow students in natural science, as many of his letters show. A friend of Darwin's since Darwin's Cambridge undergraduate years, Eyton went on to help Darwin prepare the descriptions of the birds collected on the *Beagle* voyage, even though these numbers as part of Darwin's *Zoology* were officially credited to John Gould. Though he was a firm opponent of the Darwinian theory, his friendship with its author continued to his death, but he was much chagrined at finding some of his own observations on the habits of pigeons used by Darwin in support of the hypothesis of natural selection. Eyton's interest in natural history was not confined to birds, and in his own yacht and at his own expense, he conducted an investigation for the government into the oyster fisheries of the British islands, the results of which he published in *A History of the Oyster and the Oyster Fisheries* (1858), which was illustrated by finely drawn lithographs from his own dissections. Eyton also wrote pieces on 'Fishing literature', 'Fox-hunting literature', 'Observations on ozone', and 'Notes on scent' (1870), and made catalogues of the drawings, engravings, and portraits at Eyton Hall.

Eyton was a keen sportsman, and hunted with the Shropshire hounds for several seasons. Throughout his adult life he was an active magistrate; he held a commission in the yeomanry cavalry, and in 1859 was the pioneer of the volunteer movement in Shropshire. Eyton died at the family seat, Eyton Hall, Wellington, Shropshire, on 25 October 1880. He was succeeded by his eldest son, Thomas Slaney Eyton (1843–1899). A daughter, Charlotte Eyton, was author of several works on scientific subjects, including *The Rocks of the Wrekin* (1862) and *By Fell and Flood* (1872).

CLEMENCY THORNE FISHER

Sources *DNB* · Shropshire County Council, Eyton MSS · *The Ibis*, 9th ser., 2 (1908), 79 · *The Ibis*, 4th ser., 5 (1881), 178 · letters from and to other naturalists, NHM · letters from and to other naturalists, American Philosophical Society, Philadelphia · Burke, *Gen. GB* · R. K. Engen, *Dictionary of Victorian wood engravers* (1985) · *CGPLA Eng. & Wales* (1880)

Archives American Philosophical Society, Philadelphia, corresp. · Shropshire County Council, Shrewsbury, family MSS · U. Birm. L., special collections department, corresp. | American Philosophical Society, Philadelphia, letters to T. C. Eyton · National Museums of Scotland Library, Edinburgh, letters to Sir William Jardine · NHM, corresp. with John Gould

Likenesses photograph, repro. in *Ibis* [supplement], 78 · portrait, probably priv. coll.

Wealth at death under £30,000: resworn probate, Dec 1881, *CGPLA Eng. & Wales* (1880)

Ezekiel, Ezekiel Abraham (1757–1806), engraver and printmaker, was born at Exeter, the eldest of the six sons (there were also at least four daughters) of Abraham Ezekiel (*d.* 1799), silversmith and watchmaker, who with his brother Benjamin had come from the Rhineland about 1745, and who founded Exeter synagogue in 1763–4. His mother, whose name is unknown, died in June 1806.

Ezekiel was apprenticed at the age of fifteen to Alexander Jenkins, goldsmith, and published his first engraving, a view of Bideford, in 1779. Portraits, topographical prints, and maps for bookplates formed a considerable part of his output, but in the *Flying Post* of February 1784 he advertised that he executed perspective and ornamental copperplate engraving for various types of stationery, copperplate printing, and jewellery work in general with 'curious devices in hair'; by 1795 he claimed to have studied optical science, and to dispense spectacles, microscopes, and telescopes. He never married, and resided all his adult life with his unmarried siblings Henry, a watchmaker, Kitty, and Amelia at their shop in 179 Fore Street.

By 1805 Ezekiel was too ill with dropsy to be considered for military service in the war with France, and he died on

13 December 1806, leaving an estate of under £600 to be distributed between the synagogue and his family. He was buried in the Magdalen Street cemetery. Ezekiel had many friends in Exeter, within and outside the Jewish community of which he was a staunch member, and his obituarist in the December issue of the *Flying Post* referred to his skills as an engraver, unequalled outside London, and his portraits of several distinguished Exeter characters, admired for their faithful execution. His work survives in Exeter in the Royal Albert Museum and the Devon and Exeter Institution, and in London at the Jewish Museum, British Museum, and Victoria and Albert Museum.

ANITA MCCONNELL

Sources I. Landman and L. Rittenburg, eds., *Universal Jewish encyclopedia*, 10 vols. (New York, 1948) · S. Wininger, *Grosse jüdische National-Biographie*, 2 (1927), 209 · J. Klatzkin, ed., *Encyclopaedia Judaica: das Judentum in Geschichte und Gegenwart*, 10 vols. (Berlin, 1928–34) · G. Werlitz and B. Kirschner, eds., *Jüdisches Lexikon*, 4 vols. (1928), 2 · J. Jacobs and L. Wolf, *Bibliotheca Anglo-Judaica* (1888) · *Engraved Brit. ports.*, 4.295; 6.608 · F. J. Gent, 'Ezekiel Abraham Ezekiel', www.eclipse.co.uk/exeshul/exeshul/ezekiel/ezekiel.htm, 22 Aug 2003 · B. N. Lee, 'The bookplates of Ezekiel Abraham Ezekiel', *Bookplate Journal*, 9/1 (1991), 16–35 · G. Clifton, *Directory of British scientific instrument makers, 1550–1851*, ed. G. L'E. Turner (1995)

Likenesses miniature, exh. 1887, repro. in J. Jacobs and L. Wolf, *Catalogue of the Anglo-Jewish exhibition* (1888), 53

Wealth at death under £600: administration, Jan 1807, archdeaconry court, Exeter

Ezekiel, Solomon (1781–1867), tinsmith and writer on Jewish matters, was born at Newton Abbot, Devon, on 7 June 1781, probably the grandson of Abraham Ezekiel (*d.* 1799), a silversmith who had come from the Rhineland about 1745 and settled in Exeter, where he had founded a synagogue in 1763–4. Ezekiel settled at Penzance, where he advertised as a plumber and tinsmith, living with his wife, Hannah (*b. c.*1776). In January 1820 he published a letter to Sir Rose Price, bt, chairman of a branch of the Society for Promoting Christianity among the Jews, who had asked for a conference with the large and wealthy Hebrew community at Penzance. In consequence of Ezekiel's letter Sir Rose Price made further researches and came to the conclusion that the Jews were not yet prepared to adopt the Christian faith.

A rigid observer of the rites and ceremonies of the Jewish religion, Ezekiel also translated a pamphlet written in Hebrew by the Revd Hart Symons, containing censures of the Authorized Version of the Bible. A reply to this, by John Rogers, canon of Exeter, was published in 1822. Two other works by Ezekiel, *The Life of Abraham* and *The Life of Isaac* (1844–5), were based on a series of lectures on the lives of the patriarchs, which he delivered before the Penzance Hebrew Society for Promoting the Diffusion of Religious Knowledge. His lecture on the Hebrew Festivals, delivered at the Penzance Literary Institute, was also published in 1847. Solomon Ezekiel died at 29 Mount Street, Penzance, on 9 March 1867.

THOMPSON COOPER, *rev.* ROBERT BROWN

Sources Boase & Courtney, *Bibl. Corn.* · J. Jacobs and L. Wolf, *Bibliotheca Anglo-Judaica: a bibliographical guide to Anglo-Jewish history*

(1888) • I. Landman and L. Rittenburg, eds., *Universal Jewish encyclopedia*, 10 vols. (New York, 1948), vol. 4 • *Jewish Chronicle* (22 March 1867) • d. cert.

Fabell, Peter (*fl.* **15th cent.**), supposed magician, was popularly known in the folklore of the sixteenth and seventeenth centuries as the Merry Devil of Edmonton. The earliest known sign of Fabell's legend was a poem in *ottava rima* called *Fabyl's Ghoste*, printed by John Rastell in 1533. Thomas Warton described this poem in 1781, dismissing it as 'of no merit', but it is no longer extant (Warton, 3.81). John Norden briefly notes in his *Speculum Britanniae* (1593) that Fabell is buried in Edmonton's church, and 'is said to have beguiled the Devell by pollicie for money, But the Devell is deceit it selfe, and hardly deceived' (Norden, 18).

Several literary works of the early seventeenth century expand on Norden's description. An anonymous comedy featuring Fabell, *The Merry Devil of Edmonton*, was written before 1604 for the King's Men and became one of the most popular plays of the century. The prologue calls Fabell a 'renowned Scholler' who had studied at Cambridge, and claims that

> In Edmonton yet fresh unto this day,
> Fixt in the wall of that old antient Church,
> His monument remayneth to be seene.
> (*Merry Devil*, sig. A2v)

The play opens with Fabell tricking a demon to whom he has sold his soul, but for the rest of the play he takes a back seat to various comic characters and mismatched lovers. The play was first printed in 1608, with five more editions in the next fifty years.

To capitalize on the play's success, a prose pamphlet called *The Life and Death of the Merry Devil of Edmonton*, by T. B., was written in 1608 and probably printed that year, though the earliest surviving edition dates from 1631. The author states that Peter Fabell was 'a man of good discent' and 'great learning' who was 'very pleasant, kinde, & freehearted', and who was born, lived, and died in Edmonton in the reign of Henry VII (Abrams, 226–7). John Weever cites this pamphlet sceptically in his *Ancient Funerall Monuments* (1631), adding that Fabell 'lieth interred under a seemelie Tombe without Inscription' in Edmonton church (Weever, 534). Thomas Fuller also mentions Fabell sceptically in his *Worthies* (1662), writing that 'some make him a friar, others a lay gentleman, all a conceited person, who with his many devises deceived the devil' (Fuller, *Worthies*, 2.327). Fuller puts Fabell in the reign of Henry VI, rather than Henry VII.

Despite the scepticism of these early accounts, Fabell probably was a real person, though his tricking of the devil is obviously fictional. He may be the 'Favell' who received a BA at Cambridge in 1469–70, given the claims about his education and dates (Venn, *Alum. Cant.*, 2.125). He is less likely to be the Peter Fabell who made his will in Cirencester, Gloucestershire, in 1526, given the distance from Edmonton (Phillimore and Duncan, 205). Alternatively, Bolton suggests that the magician was Peter Favelore, who built a chapel within the Edmonton church before his death in 1360, and who left lands in Edmonton, Enfield, Tottenham, and Kent (Bolton, 131). This man lived a century before the dates given by Fuller and T. B., but would have been entitled to a monument in the church.

DAVID KATHMAN

Sources W. A. Abrams, ed., 'The merry devil of Edmonton', *1608, edited with … a reprint of 'The life and death of the merry devil of Edmonton', 1631* (1942) • J. Weever, *Ancient funerall monuments* (1631) • Fuller, *Worthies* (1662) • J. Norden, *Speculum Britanniae* (1593) • T. Warton, *The history of English poetry*, 4 vols. (1774–81) • Venn, *Alum. Cant.*, 1/2 • D. K. Bolton, 'Edmonton', *A history of Middlesex*, ed. T. F. T. Baker, 5 (1976) • W. P. W. Phillimore and L. L. Duncan, eds., *A calendar of wills proved in the consistory court of Gloucester, 1541–1650* (1895) • *CIPM*, 10, no. 470

Faber, Albert Otto (1612–1684), chemical physician, was born in Lübeck, north Germany, the son of Gallus (or Walter) Faber, a government official. He was educated at the University of Marburg, where he studied jurisprudence and gained a doctorate. Thereafter he practised medicine, at first in Lübeck; he moved to Hamburg in 1641, and later became the personal physician and army physician to the prince of Sultzbach. He then served the king of Denmark in the same capacities and afterwards the king of Sweden; as late as 1663 he continued to refer to himself as 'Royal physician to the Swedish Army' (Faber, *A Relation of some Notable Cures*, 4).

Faber moved to England in early 1661, supposedly at the invitation of Charles II, who gave him £50 on 13 August 1661 'in respect of services and necessities' (*Calendar of Treasury Books, 1660–67*, 276). He was befriended by Samuel Hartlib, who called him an 'excellent Helmontian physician' (*Diary and Correspondence of Dr John Worthington*, 363). By 1662 he was settled in Thames Street, at the bottom of Addle Hill, London, with his wife, Claude, with whom he had two children, Gertrude and Albert Otto.

Faber's first book, *Paradoxon de morbo gallico* (1662), was a curious treatise on syphilis, which traced the origin of the disease to the fall of man, condemned the widespread use of mercury as a cure, and presented his own cure in the disguise of an extravagant metaphorical parable written in a form similar to contemporaneous alchemical allegories. The book was first printed in German (Altona, 1660) and later in English (1662). In 1663 Faber published a four-page *Relation of some Notable Cures*, which, like all his subsequent medical publications, was a privately printed pamphlet advertising remedies he was offering for sale. In April 1666 he acted as a witness to the cures of Valentine Greatrakes, the Stroker, who claimed to cure by his touch.

Shortly after his arrival in England, Faber began an association with the Quakers, possibly at the instigation of his wife and possibly as a 'commercial expediency' to obtain a network through which to vend medicines (Sampson, 484–6). He translated two pamphlets from German, published as *The Twelve Visions of Stephen Melish* (1663) and *England's Warning* (1664), containing prophecies popular in Quaker circles. At a Quaker meeting on 14 August 1664 he was arrested pursuant to the Conventicle Act, fined £5, and imprisoned at Newgate for three months. From prison he wrote *A Remonstrance* (1664), in which he argued that the Conventicle Act did not extend to foreigners such as himself. Faber, described by the lord mayor and lord chancellor as 'a very suspected person, reather of crafty principalls & soe a maker of Quakers' (Penney, 215), was ordered to leave the country. He did not do so and later claimed that he could not obtain a passport. In November 1666 he, his servant, and two Quakers were arrested in Banbury on suspicion of arson. While his co-defendants were quickly acquitted, Faber was sent to Oxford gaol. In a letter to the king dated 30 April 1667, he repudiated Quakerism, stating that he was merely curious about it and claiming regular attendance at the French protestant church of London. He was freed in August and deported (without his wife) to Flanders on 22 August.

In requesting a pass to return to England in 1672, Faber admitted entering England illegally at least once in order to tend to his wife, who was ill. This visit probably occurred in the spring of 1668, during which time his pamphlet *Some Kindling Sparks in Matters of Physick* was published privately in London. He was granted leave to enter the country on 22 April 1672, and took up residence in London near the Old Palace Yard, Westminster. In 1673–4, he corresponded on medical matters with the Galenist physician John Twisden. Copies of their correspondence seem to have been privately circulated: a copy is extant among Isaac Newton's papers.

In 1677 Faber published *De auro potabili medicinali*, on the title page of which he referred to himself as the king's physician-in-ordinary. This brief work described the use and effects of his version of 'potable gold', an esteemed preparation of chemical medicine purportedly made from gold and popularized in the early seventeenth century by one Francis Anthony. Faber's tract compared the successes of his own 'cordial' with those of Anthony, and detailed Faber's administration of the cordial to Sheldon, then archbishop of Canterbury. Faber died on 15 August 1684, in London, and was buried there in St Dunstan-in-the-West, Fleet Street, where in 1685 his daughter, Gertrude, had a marble monument raised to his memory.

LAWRENCE M. PRINCIPE

Sources H. Sampson, 'Dr. Faber and his celebrated cordial', *Isis*, 34 (1942–3), 472–96 · J. L. Nickalls, 'Albertus Otto Faber, the German doctor', *Journal of the Friends' Historical Society*, 32 (1935), 54–7 · A. J. L. Jourdan, ed., *Biographie médicale*, 7 vols. (1820–25), vol. 4, pp. 84–5 · A. O. Faber, *De auro potabili medicinali* (1677) · A. O. Faber, *A relation of some notable cures* (1663) · *The diary and correspondence of Dr John Worthington*, ed. J. Crossley, 1, Chetham Society, 13 (1847), 363 · N. Penney, ed., *Extracts from state papers relating to Friends, 1654–1672* (1913)

Archives CUL, corresp., Keynes MS 50 · RS Friends, Lond., Martin Mason MSS · RS Friends, Lond., Swarthmore MSS, Original III

Faber, Frederick William (1814–1863), Church of England clergyman and Roman Catholic priest, was born on 28 June 1814, the fourth surviving son of Thomas Henry Faber (1779–1833) and his wife, Betty Atkinson (*d.* 1829), daughter of Thomas Atkinson of Bradford, at Calverley

Frederick William Faber (1814–1863), by unknown photographer

vicarage in Yorkshire, the home of his grandfather the Revd Thomas Faber (1729–1821). Faber had a younger sister, Ellen, and there were three other siblings—two older, who died in 1813, and one younger—who died in infancy. These deaths seem to have intensified his mother's love for him. Faber's uncle, George Stanley Faber (1773–1854), was later the master of Sherburn Hospital near Durham and a prolific evangelical theologian. In December 1814 Thomas Henry Faber was appointed secretary to his brother's patron, Shute Barrington, bishop of Durham, and the family moved to Auckland Castle in Bishop Auckland. Frederick Faber was educated briefly at the grammar school in Bishop Auckland and privately by the Revd John Gibson at Kirkby Stephen, where he first learned his love of the upland moors and fells later expressed in his poem *Sir Lancelot* (1844). In 1826 he was sent to Shrewsbury School, but moved in 1827 to Harrow School where, as he afterwards told Lord John Manners, he 'felt always quite wild—wild with power of intellect' (*Selected Letters*, 74), and was considered without intellectual rival. His mother died in 1829, and some of his later Marian hymns show the influence of her early death. He is said to have defied God to strike him dead in a thunderstorm in Harrow churchyard, but his incipient scepticism was arrested by the kindness of his headmaster, Charles Longley (1794–1868), later archbishop of Canterbury, and his faith was given a new turn by John William Cunningham (1780–1861), the evangelical vicar of Harrow and unofficial chaplain to the school.

Faber matriculated at Oxford on 6 July 1832; he failed to win a Balliol scholarship, but came into residence in Balliol in spring 1833. Late in 1834 he was elected a scholar of University College, where he resided from early 1835.

His friends included Roundell Palmer (1812–1895), later Lord Selborne, and the eccentric and gifted scholar John Brande Morris (1812–1880); Faber's letters to Palmer and Morris are important sources for his early life. Faber rejected Newman's influence in 1834 in favour of a position leaning towards evangelical Calvinism, but after Pusey's sermon on Septuagesima Sunday of 1836 he began to embrace Tractarianism, and was thoroughly convinced by what he said he had long wanted: the 'clear and positive statements of Anglican principles' (Bowden, 38) of Newman's *Lectures on the Prophetical Office of the Church* of 1837.

Having postponed his finals in Easter term 1836 until December, Faber graduated in 1836 with a disappointing second-class honours degree and failed to get a fellowship at University College. After a holiday in Germany with his brother Francis (1804–1876), he was elected a fellow of University in 1837 and won the Johnson divinity scholarship. He was made a deacon by Longley, then bishop of Ripon, on 6 August 1837, and ordained as priest by Bishop Bagot of Oxford on 26 May 1839. In summer 1839 he travelled in Belgium and Germany with Richard Church (1815–1890) and Arthur Penrhyn Stanley (1815–1881), but wrote of Romanism that 'it all will not do', expressing his disgust with the 'careless irreverence, the noise, the going in and out, the spitting of the priests on the Altar steps' (Bowden, 65).

Between 1837 and 1842 Faber kept a cottage in the Lake District, and served as a curate in Ambleside. He befriended Wordsworth, the poet Thomas Whytehead (1815–1843), Lord John Manners (1818–1906), the founder of Young England, and George Smythe (1818–1857), later seventh Viscount Strangford. Faber had an intensely romantic if platonic relationship with Smythe in the fashion of its time, but put Smythe from him on scenting moral danger. Faber was a considerable influence on Manners, and figures as the Revd Aubrey St Lys in Disraeli's novel *Sybil*. Faber's productions included *The Cherwell Water-Lily* (1840), which earned him the nickname of Water-Lily Faber, a slur on his facial prettiness and charm of manner. One poem, 'First Love', of 1840, expressed his devotion to Dora Harrison, the twelve- or thirteen-year-old daughter of Benson Harrison of Ambleside, whose son, Matthew, Faber tutored from 1840. From February to August 1841 he travelled with Matthew to Italy, Greece, and Constantinople, returning through eastern Europe, Austria, and Germany, and gathering the materials used in *The Styrian Lake, and other Poems* (1842) and *Sights and Thoughts in Foreign Churches and among Foreign Peoples* (1842), which he dedicated to Wordsworth 'in affectionate remembrance of much personal kindness, and many thoughtful conversations on the rites, prerogatives, and doctrines, of the Holy Church'. The work asked the reader to look on Europe in the spirit of the middle ages, and showed an unsettled attitude to Anglicanism and a fascination with Roman Catholicism.

In 1843 Faber was inducted into the University College living of Elton in Huntingdonshire. On another tour to the continent, also in 1843, he read Gabriello Chiabrera's epitaph at Savona, with its exhortation to choose Mount Calvary rather than Mount Parnassus, henceforward the motto of his life. In Rome he was received in audience by Gregory XVI, and acquired a devotion to St Philip Neri, whose life he translated at Elton, where he turned his household servants into a brotherhood, landscaped his garden on Wordsworthian principles, and opened it to his parishioners for Sunday evening promenades, cricket, and football. He acquired an adoring following among the young, restored the church, replaced the old village orchestra with an organ, fasted to the ruin of his health, and introduced confession. He translated the seven books of St Optatus on the Donatists for The Library of the Fathers, published a poem of nearly 11,000 lines on Sir Lancelot (1844; rev. edn, 1857), and provoked an outcry over his Romanizing 'Life of St Wilfrid' in Newman's *Lives of the English Saints*, for which he also wrote the lives of nine saints of Northumbria.

Only Newman's influence kept Faber from the Roman Catholic church, and Newman's reception on 9 October 1845 removed that obstacle. A Catholic convert benefactor resident in Florence, F. J. Sloane, offered to pay the debts Faber had incurred in his parish, and on 17 November he left Elton, farewelled by weeping parishioners. With Francis Knox and ten other friends and servants, he was received into the Roman Catholic church at Northampton by Bishop William Wareing, vicar apostolic of the eastern district. Two adolescent followers, William and James Pitts, the former later the Brompton Oratory organist, resisted their father's pleas to come home.

Faber leased a house in Birmingham for his new order, the Brothers of the Will of God of the Congregation of St Wilfrid or 'Wilfridians' (mischievously called by Dominic Barberi the Brothers of the Will of Faber). His *Grounds for Remaining in the Anglican Communion* (1846) distressed Newman by its polemics, and was at first banned in Rome by censors misled by its title. On a visit to Florence with a rich young disciple, Antony Hutchison, Faber failed to persuade his benefactor, Sloane, to finance his monastery in Birmingham, but he was received again by the pope. He accepted from the earl of Shrewsbury Cotton Hall, near Cheadle, in Staffordshire, founded schools, built a church designed by A. W. N. Pugin and consecrated to St Wilfrid, and vigorously proselytized in the neighbourhood. He was ordained priest at Oscott on 3 April 1847 by Cardinal Wiseman, his carriage being dragged the last three-quarters of a mile home by local people amid fireworks, gunfire, and a brass band.

But Newman's new Oratory at Birmingham was an irresistible attraction, and on 14 February 1847 Faber joined it with seventeen Wilfridians. Newman found a worshipping but difficult follower. In 1848 Faber had a stormy if comic confrontation at Cotton with Ambrose Phillipps (1809–1878) and Pugin over his own preference for the Italian style in religious architecture and worship over Gothic. He had, in 1846, projected a series of *Lives of the Saints* (42 vols., 1847–56) of the modern era; the 'more than charnel horrors' (Chapman, 194) of the asceticism of St

Rose of Lima provoked a violent attack by the Revd Edward Price in *Dolman's Magazine*. The series was suspended, defended by Newman (against his later judgement), and then restarted under the auspices of the Oratory. Although Newman and Faber came briefly together at Cotton Hall in 1848, Newman's return to Birmingham in January 1849 left Faber at the hall as master of novices, and the temperamental difference between the two men was wisely resolved by the division of the community between London and Birmingham.

In 1849 Faber became rector of the London Oratory in a former assembly room and whisky shop in King William Street off the Strand, and attracted a congregation of wealthy English aristocrats and bug-ridden pauper Irish. On 9 October 1850 Newman released the fathers from their obedience and on 12 October Faber became superior of the independent London Oratory. In the excitement over the 'papal aggression' of the restoration of the Catholic hierarchy in 1850, the black Oratorian habits and broad-brimmed hats made a metropolitan sensation, not least in *Punch*. Faber expounded the character of his institute in *The Spirit and Genius of St Philip Neri* (1850). A ticket system had to be introduced for the chapel, but in 1851 Hutchison opened a ragged school for 1000 poor children in Dunn's Passage, Holborn.

Faber lost his looks in the late 1840s, when he became fat and suffered from periodic ill health. His trip to the Holy Land in 1851 was abandoned at Malta through illness, but he was received in audience on the homeward journey by Pius IX. From 1852 he could recuperate from his ailments at his community's rural retreat at Sydenham. In 1854 the Oratory moved to its permanent home in the Brompton Road. The gap between the London and Birmingham oratories, and between Faber and Newman, was widened by a row in 1855, ostensibly over the London Oratory's wish to hear nuns' confessions. It is difficult to see a higher principle at stake in this unhappy *querelle des moines* between two good men, which was creditable to neither; it was exacerbated by Faber's inability to keep his mouth shut, and sent Newman on a mission of self-defence to Rome. Newman's difficulty in forgiving Faber remains the most signal objection to his canonization.

Faber called the Virgin Mary 'Mamma', and his promotion of devotions to the Madonna, the saints, and the blessed sacrament, more common under skies of Mediterranean blue, also represented a return to the fervour of his early evangelicalism, as did his popular vernacular hymns, which transformed Catholic worship: they include 'Jesus, gentlest Saviour' and 'Hark, hark, my soul'. Despite their failures of taste and style, they represent the best of Victorian Catholic piety in their power to strengthen, to console, to warm, and to delight. Their stress lies on what Faber called the 'wideness in God's mercy', and in their teaching on purificatory suffering they widened the bounds of purgatory.

Faber's eight religious treatises were long premeditated, but were poured out between 1853 and 1860, their manuscripts flowing on in the author's beautiful hand, almost without corrections. They were intended for his 'invalid souls' of the middle class and 'poor Belgravians' on the model of Victorian popular science (Chapman, 296), and are 'not pure theology, nor mere devotion … not explanatory apologetic, but a very individual mixture of the three', written in the light of the 'one large lucid philosophy' of God (Chapman, 292). *All for Jesus, or, The Easy Ways of Divine Love* (1853), the most introductory of them all, was composed for the Confraternity of the Precious Blood, and had sold 100,000 copies by 1869. *Growth in Holiness* (1854) maps out the middle way of the wilderness of 'temptation, struggle, and fatigue' which most religious men occupy, between the delight of spiritual beginnings and 'the beautiful, wooded, watered, yet rocky mountains' of 'the land of high prayer'. *The Blessed Sacrament* (1855) treats its subject as the highest manifestation of God. It is dedicated to Newman, who thought that its argumentative manner would encourage scepticism. *The Creator and the Creature* (1858) is Faber's greatest work in its vision of life as a work of the divine creative love. *The Foot of the Cross* (also 1858) is based on the seven dolours of Mary, *The Precious Blood* (1860) on the doctrine of redemption, and *Bethlehem* (1860) on the infancy of Our Lord. His *Spiritual Conferences* (1859) shows signs of tiredness. These books establish Faber's extraordinary knowledge of the mystical theology, hagiography and history of nineteen centuries, even if his emotive combination of romanticism and evangelicalism is a little strong for modern sensibilities. His *Notes on Doctrinal and Spiritual Subjects* (1866) was edited by his biographer, John Edward Bowden, in 1866. His letters are a more accessible delight, being as racy and unbuttoned as the man.

Criticism among Catholics of Faber's work was muted after Pius IX's award to him of a doctorate of divinity in 1854, and in his *Devotion to the Pope* (1860) he defended the beleaguered papacy, along with Manning and his old Balliol friend William George Ward (1812–1882). Faber died of Bright's disease at the Brompton Oratory aged forty-nine on 26 September 1863 and was buried there on 30 September. More than any other figure, he defined the tone and temper of mid-Victorian ultramontane Catholicism. His legacy is the Brompton Oratory, with its continuing fusion—in music, learning, art, and architecture—of the Catholic faith with the form and spirit of the papal Rome of the high baroque, and of its genius, St Philip Neri.

SHERIDAN GILLEY

Sources R. Chapman, *Father Faber* (1960) · *Faber, poet and priest: selected letters by Frederick William Faber, 1833–1863*, ed. R. Addington (1974) · J. E. Bowden, *The life and letters of Frederick William Faber, DD* (1869) · R. Addington, *The idea of the Oratory* (1966) · S. Gilley, 'Vulgar piety and the Brompton Oratory, 1850–1860', *The Irish in the Victorian city*, ed. R. Swift and S. Gilley (1985), 255–66 · M. Heimann, *Catholic devotion in Victorian England* (1995) · M. Napier and A. Laing, *The London Oratory centenary, 1884–1984* (1984)

Archives BL, letters and poems, Add. MS 58225 · Brompton Oratory, London, corresp. and papers | Arundel Castle, Sussex, corresp. with Henry Fitzalan-Howard, duke of Norfolk · Birmingham Oratory, letters to J. H. Newman · LPL, corresp. with Christopher Wordsworth · Westm. DA, letters to Wiseman

Likenesses J. L. Lomas, oils, exh. 1868, London Oratory · J. Brown, stipple, NPG · photograph, London Oratory [*see illus.*]

Faber, Sir Geoffrey Cust (1889–1961), publisher, was born in College Grounds, Malvern, on 23 August 1889, the second son of the Revd Henry Mitford Faber, a housemaster at Malvern College, and Florence Ellen, daughter of George Nathaniel Colt, barrister. The Faber family, Yorkshire in origin, had long associations with education and the church. Faber's paternal grandfather, a fellow of Magdalen College, Oxford, was a brother of Father F. W. *Faber (1814–1863) and a nephew of G. S. *Faber (1773–1854). Having attended Rugby School, Faber proceeded with a scholarship to Christ Church, Oxford, where he obtained a double first in classical moderations (1910) and *literae humaniores* (1912). Abandoning an idea of life in the Indian Civil Service, he began his publishing career in 1913 when he joined the Oxford University Press at Amen House in London as assistant to the publisher, Humphrey Milford. His experiences during his eighteen-month appointment before the war are recounted in 'Forty years back'. From 1914 to 1919 he was with the London regiment (Post Office Rifles), saw service in France and Belgium, and in 1916 was promoted captain. During the war he published two volumes of verse, *Interflow* (1915) and *In the Valley of Vision* (1918).

In the first post-war election at All Souls College, Oxford, in November 1919, Faber became a prize fellow, an event which, perhaps more directly than any other, shaped the course of his future life (he remained a fellow until he died). In 1923, at the age of thirty-three, Faber succeeded Geoffrey Dawson as estates bursar, an office which he held until 1951. His bursarship was marked by large-scale building activity on the college's Middlesex estates, by expanding and consolidating its rural estates, and by a sharp rise in income. His only failure was his inability to persuade the college to persist with a project close to his heart—the direct farming of some of its own land.

It was some time, however, before the pattern of his career became clearly established. In 1920 he had joined the board of Strong & Co. Ltd, the brewers, of Romsey, a firm with which he had family connections; and, although he never practised as a barrister, he was awarded the Eldon law scholarship and was called to the bar by the Inner Temple in 1921. By 1923, having abandoned both brewing and the bar, Faber was in negotiation with his All Souls colleague Maurice Gwyer, later chief justice of India, whose wife, Lady Alsina Gwyer, had inherited a prosperous but highly specialized publishing firm, the Scientific Press Ltd, from her father, Sir Henry Burdett. Its fortunes were founded on the *Nursing Mirror*, a successful weekly paper for trained nurses, around which had grown up a small but profitable list of medical books designed for the same public. The Gwyers, ambitious to enter the field of general publishing, invited Faber to join them; and he became chairman of a successor company, Faber and Gwyer Ltd, which was established at 24 Russell Square, London, in 1925. Charles Whibley suggested T. S. Eliot as a literary adviser and Faber, who had had in mind only the engagement of a part-time talent scout, was so impressed and

Sir Geoffrey Cust Faber (1889–1961), by Henry Lamb, 1952

charmed by Eliot at their first meeting that shortly afterwards he invited him to become a member of his board. From 1925 to 1929 Faber augmented the staff with Richard de la Mare, Frank Morley, and Morley Kennerley.

After four years of only moderately successful trading the Gwyers were ready to liquidate the business. Faber, determined to continue although the difficulties seemed almost insuperable, found a way out of the impasse. The *Nursing Mirror* was disposed of very advantageously; the Gwyers withdrew their interest; and Faber, with his own capital, transformed the firm into Faber and Faber Ltd in 1929. The second 'Faber' was probably only for effect although it has been suggested that it signified his wife, Enid Eleanor Richards (b. 1900/01), whom he had married on 30 December 1920. She was the daughter of Sir Henry Erle Richards, Chichele professor of international law and diplomacy and a fellow of All Souls. Faber and his wife had two sons and one daughter. The elder son, Richard Stanley Faber, joined the foreign service and the younger, Thomas Erle Faber, a physicist, became a fellow of Corpus Christi College, Cambridge.

During the years which followed, Faber's great driving force, courage, and tenacity were gradually rewarded. While the firm continued to publish scientific titles Faber rapidly expanded the company's literature list, which included some of the most promising young writers, poets in particular, such as W. H. Auden and Stephen Spender, who made their first appearances in the thirties.

Later Faber published Ted Hughes, Sylvia Plath, Thom Gunn, Philip Larkin, and Seamus Heaney. Young artists such as John Piper and Graham Sutherland were commissioned to produce striking book jacket designs.

Faber himself became a prominent figure in the world of publishing. After serving on the joint advisory committee of publishers and booksellers, in 1934 he joined the council of the Publishers' Association; in 1937 he became treasurer; and in 1939 was made president. In this position he had to face a grave crisis which, after the outbreak of war in 1939, threatened the publishing, bookselling, and printing trades—and to some extent the entire literary profession in Britain. In July 1940 Sir Kingsley Wood, chancellor of the exchequer, introduced purchase tax, which was intended to include books. Faber thought this might virtually stifle the nation's literary output during the war and would do irreparable damage not only at home but also abroad. With speed and efficiency he marshalled a large and influential body of supporters to his National Committee for the Defence of Books, which launched an attack on the imposition of 'the tax on knowledge' which finally led the government to exempt books from its operation. Faber continued to chair the Publishers' Association until 1941; and in 1944 he performed his last major service to the book trade by helping to establish the National Book League, of which he became first chairman in the following year. In *A Publisher Speaking* (1934) Faber had outlined measures for reform of the book trade.

During his publishing career Faber continued to produce his own poetry and prose. His prose is more likely to endure than his poetry, yet there is little doubt that the poetry was to him the more important. The title he gave to his collected poems, *The Buried Stream* (1941), is significant. This volume contains all that he wished to preserve of his two earlier collections, together with work written subsequently; and after his death his family published privately *Twelve Years*, a long reflective poem of nearly 400 lines written between 1941 and 1953 and much revised during the remainder of his life. Although his verse seldom attains the force, compression, and inevitability which renders poetry memorable and permanent, it is never meretricious and often very moving—particularly when it deals with deeply felt personal emotions. Moreover, the fact that he was himself a poet was vital in creating and maintaining the Faber poetry list, particularly during the early years when the chairman of an undergraduate society described him as 'the godfather of modern English poetry'.

Faber's minor prose works were *Elnovia* (1925), a light-hearted and eventually rather dated fantasy, and an account of the history of the All Souls bursarships (1950) printed privately. His major works, likely to prove permanent, were *Oxford Apostles* (1933) and *Jowett* (1957). Partly because of his family links with Father Faber, he became fascinated by the great figures of the Oxford Movement, in particular by J. H. Newman. The book which resulted is authoritative. The struggles between the movement and its enemies and within the movement itself are detailed lucidly and with great narrative power. *Jowett*, the result of

many years of research, particularly in the Balliol archives, is a portrait not only of its subject but of the many academic and religious controversies in which he played a central part. One further literary achievement deserves recording—his edition of John Gay in the Oxford Poets series, published by Oxford University Press in 1926. He accepted an invitation to undertake this in 1913, but because of the war and his multifarious activities in the years immediately afterwards it was not completed until 1925. Despite these interruptions and distractions the edition is distinguished and satisfying, marked not only by erudition and industry but also, even when dealing with such matters as punctuation and spelling, by an instinctive sureness which reflects his innate sympathy with Gay's work and temperament.

Faber was knighted in 1954. In 1960 he resigned the chairmanship of Faber and Faber Ltd and was appointed to the newly created post of president, which he held until his death at his home, Minsted House in Minsted Stedham, Midhurst, Sussex, on 31 March 1961. His wife survived him. In his later years Faber's appearance was that of a successful and cultivated man of the world: rubicund, heavily built, bald, with a slight military moustache. Beneath this exterior lay a shy and introspective personality. Although he was justly proud of his achievements, he remained always a little uncertain of himself and in particular of his ability to communicate successfully with other people. To those to whom he had given his confidence and affection he remained unswervingly loyal and dependable: he probably never fully realized how much affection others in return felt for him.

CHARLES MONTEITH, *rev.* CLARE L. TAYLOR

Sources T. S. Eliot, *Geoffrey Faber: a memorial address* (privately printed, 1961) • *The Bookseller* (8 April 1961) • G. Faber, 'Forty years back: a fragment of autobiography', *The Bookseller* (10–17 Jan 1953), 40–42; 94–7 • G. Faber, *A publisher speaking* (1934) • J. Rose and P. J. Anderson, eds., *British literary publishing houses, 1881–1965*, DLitB, 112 (1991) • *The Times* (1 April 1961) • b. cert. • m. cert. • d. cert.
Likenesses H. Lamb, portrait, 1952, priv. coll. • H. Lamb, portrait, 1952, All Souls Oxf. [*see illus.*] • H. Lamb, portrait, 1952, priv. coll. • W. Stoneman, photograph, 1954, NPG
Wealth at death £54,502 10s. 8d.: probate, 18 May 1961, CGPLA Eng. & Wales

Faber, George Stanley (1773–1854), Church of England clergyman and religious writer, the eldest son of the Revd Thomas Faber (1730–1821), vicar of Calverley, Yorkshire, and his wife, Anne, *née* Traviss (*b.* 1745), was born at Calverley parsonage on 25 October 1773. Frederick William Faber, convert to Catholicism and founder of the London Oratory, was his nephew. He was educated at the Hipperholme grammar school, near Halifax, where he remained until he went to university. On 10 June 1789 he matriculated at University College, Oxford, and was elected a scholar of Lincoln College, Oxford, on 25 March 1790, where he was awarded his BA degree and elected a fellow and tutor in 1793. He proceeded MA in 1796 and BD in 1803, and became proctor in 1801. He came to general notice through his *Two sermons before the University of*

Oxford: an attempt to explain by recent events five of the seven vials mentioned in the Revelations (1799). As Bampton lecturer in the same year, he published a paper, *Horae Mosaicae, or, A view of the Mosaical records with respect to their coincidence with profane antiquity and their connection with Christianity*, on the Pentateuch.

On 31 May 1803 Faber married Eliza Sophia Scott-Waring (1776–1851), a philanthropist; they had five children. Since fellows of Oxford colleges were not allowed to marry, he resigned his fellowship and became assistant curate to his father at Calverley. After two years, in 1805, he was made vicar of Stockton-on-Tees. He later served as rector at Redmarshall (1809–11) and at Long Newton (1811–32). He became prebendary at Salisbury Cathedral in 1830, and Bishop van Mildert appointed him master of Sherburn Hospital in 1832. After resigning his post at Long Newton, he spent a good deal of his own income at Sherburn on the successful improvement of the hospital estates.

Faber's brand of Anglicanism was strongly evangelical, and he stressed the protestant doctrines of the necessity of conversion, justification by faith, and the sole authority of scripture as the rule of faith. As a result of his opinions and his writings, he became friendly with Bishop Burgess, Bishop van Mildert, Bishop Barrington, the marquess of Bath, Lord Bexley, and Dr Routh. His writings on *The Origin of Pagan Idolatry* (1816) attempted to demonstrate, mainly through the evidence of the Old Testament, that all pagan nations had worshipped the same gods who, he argued, were in fact men who had been deified by simple people. The origins of their errors stemmed from the Tower of Babel and Noah's three sons. He also gave his Bampton lectures on the so-called 'Arkite Egg', a subject which he also discussed elsewhere. His treatises on Revelation and on the seven vials, prophetic interpretations which included predictions of the restoration of Napoleon in 1815, were old-fashioned approaches in the Church of England of his day. His books on the primitive doctrines of election and justification were noteworthy insofar as they stressed the evangelical view of these doctrines, in opposition to the opinion of contemporary writers of very different schools such as Vicesimus Knox and Joseph Milner. Faber's wife, Eliza, died at their home, Sherburn House, on 28 October 1851, and he died at Sherburn Hospital, near Durham, on 27 January 1854. He was buried in the chapel of the hospital on 1 February.

Faber's less well-known works include *A dissertation on the mysteries of the Cabiri, or, The great gods of Phoenicia, Samothrace, Egypt, Troas, Greece, Italy, and Crete* (2 vols., 1803), *A dissertation on the prophecies relative to the great period of 1200 years, the papal and Mahomedan apostasies, the reign of Antichrist, and the restoration of the Jews* (2 vols., 1807; 5th edn, 1814–18), *A general and connected view of the prophecies relative to the conversion of Judah and Israel, the overthrow of the confederacy in Palestine, and the diffusion of Christianity* (2 vols., 1808), *A practical treatise on the ordinary operations of the Holy Spirit* (1813), and *Remarks on the fifth apocalyptic vial and the restoration of the imperial government of France* (1815). Controversial works included *The difficulties of infidelity* (1824), *The difficulties of Romanism* (1826), *A treatise on the origin of expiatory sacrifice* (1827), *The testimony of antiquity against the peculiarities of the Latin church* (1828), *Letters on Catholic emancipation* (1829), *The apostolicity of trinitarianism: the testimony of history to the antiquity and to the apostolical inculcation of the doctrine of the holy Trinity* (2 vols., 1832), *The primitive doctrine of justification investigated, relatively to the definitions of the Church of Rome and the Church of England* (1837), *Christ's discourse at Capernaum fatal to the doctrine of transubstantiation on the very principle of exposition adopted by the divines of the Roman church* (1840), *Letters on Tractarian secessions to popery* (1846), and *Papal infallibility: a letter to a dignitary of the church of Rome* (1851).   G. C. BOASE, *rev.* SINÉAD AGNEW

Sources F. A. Faber, prefatory memoir, in G. S. Faber, *The many mansions in the house of the Father*, 2nd edn (1854), ix, xi–xvii, lv, lvi • H. Heaviside, *Annals of Stockton-on-Tees* (1865), 101–4 • *Christian Remembrancer*, new ser., 25 (1853), 310–31 • Boase, *Mod. Eng. biog.* • *GM*, 2nd ser., 41 (1854), 537–9 • C. Knight, ed., *The English cyclopaedia: biography*, 2 (1856), 857–8 • Foster, *Alum. Oxon.* • *The Times* (28 Jan 1854), 12 • Allibone, *Dict.* • J. F. Waller, ed., *The imperial dictionary of universal biography*, 3 vols. (1857–63) • S. Maunder, *The biographical treasury*, another edn, rev. W. L. R. Cates, [8 vols.] (1882), 210 • W. D. Adams, *Dictionary of English literature*, rev. edn [1879–80], 213 • T. Cooper, *A new biographical dictionary: containing concise notices of eminent persons of all ages and countries* (1873), 543 • R. Chapman, *Father Faber* (1961), 2–4, 74, 158, 188

Archives Birmingham Oratory, letters to J. H. Newman • LPL, letters to Charles Golightly, MS 1805

Faber, John (*c.*1660–1721), draughtsman and engraver, was born about 1660 at The Hague. He lived in the Netherlands until at least 1696 and established a reputation in Amsterdam as a portrait miniaturist, working with pen and ink on vellum. He then moved to England and settled in London, where his earliest portrait, of Simon Episcopius, was dated 1698. Soon afterwards he started to work with black lead on vellum, in the manner of the celebrated English miniaturists David Loggan and Robert White, and began to experiment with mezzotint engraving. By 1707 he had established a printselling business at the Two Golden Balls, near the Savoy in the Strand, whence he moved about 1716 to the Golden Eagle by the Fountain tavern, near Essex Street. Developing his skill as a mezzotint engraver, Faber published a wide range of portraits between 1707 and 1719, some of them after his own drawings. Many of his subjects were clergy, among them highchurchmen such as Francis Atterbury, Henry Sacheverell, Henry Shute, Andrew Snape, and Philip Stubbs. He also engraved Jacobites, such as James Sheppard and the second duke of Ormond, and produced four portraits of Charles I, one version taken from Van Dyck and three others (1713) after Edward Bower's study made during the king's trial. However, Faber's output was not entirely partisan: he engraved portraits of Oliver Cromwell, George I, dissenting clergy such as Daniel Burgess and Samuel Rosewell, and various 'remarkable' characters, noted for their great age or eccentricity. In addition he produced several sets of portraits: *Twelve Ancient Philosophers* (after Rubens), *Twelve Caesars*, *Twenty-One Reformers*, and *The Four Indian Kings* (1710). In 1711 and 1712 Faber was at Oxford, working with George Vertue to engrave portraits in the picture gallery of the Bodleian Library: these included mezzotints of Geoffrey Chaucer, John Hevelius, Ben Jonson, and Duns Scotus. Between 1712 and 1714 he engraved forty-five portraits of the founders of Oxford and Cambridge colleges, a project that Vertue regarded as his 'most considerable work' (Vertue, *Note books*, 1.73). The plates for these were reworked and republished throughout the eighteenth century.

Faber died at Bristol in May 1721, having for some years worked with his son and pupil John *Faber (*c*.1695–1756), whose prolific achievements eventually eclipsed those of his father.   RICHARD SHARP

Sources J. C. Smith, *British mezzotinto portraits*, 1 (1878), 266–99 · D. B. Brown, 'Faber, John', *The dictionary of art*, ed. J. Turner (1996) · Vertue, *Note books*, 1.73 · T. Clayton, *The English print, 1688–1802* (1997) · *DNB*

Faber, John (*c*.1695–1756), engraver and portrait and miniature painter, the son of John *Faber (*d.* 1721), also an engraver, was born in Amsterdam about 1695. His family settled in England at some time before 1698 and a drawing by his father, dated 1704 and now in the British Museum, shows Faber as a child. He learned drawing and mezzotint engraving from his father and subscribed to the academy in St Martin's Lane founded in 1720 by Louis Cheron and John Vanderbank, where he would have drawn from life and at the same time come to know many of the painters whose work he was to engrave. He also frequented the Rose and Crown Club of artists which met in a Covent Garden tavern on Saturday nights from the beginning of the eighteenth century to 1745.

Until his father's death in 1721 Faber published mezzotints under the name John Faber Junior from addresses in London near the Strand: over against Essex Street, at the Blew Ball in Catherine Street, and at the Two Golden Balls near the Savoy. After 1721 he published at Fountain Court in the Strand (*c*.1721–1725), at the Green Door in the Great Piazza, Covent Garden (late 1720s), at the Green Door in Craven Buildings, Drury Lane (*c*.1731–*c*.1734), and at the Golden Head in Bloomsbury Square, South Side (*c*.1734 onwards). In 1737, while living at the last address, a 'street robber at night attacked him near his own house, as he was going home, and shot him in the breast—of which he was dangerously wounded—but recovered' (Vertue, *Note books*, 3.80).

Faber produced more than 500 mezzotints: a full catalogue of his portraits can be found in John Chaloner Smith's *British Mezzotinto Portraits* (1883). They were mainly portraits after contemporary and seventeenth-century painters. He engraved two important series after Godfrey Kneller—twelve *Hampton Court Beauties* (1727), and forty-seven portraits of members of the Kit-Cat Club (1735)—and he helped to secure the international reputations of Thomas Hudson and Allan Ramsay with, respectively, forty-two and fifteen mezzotints after their portraits. In 1742 Vertue remarked that 'no sooner is a picture painted by any painter of any remarkable person but presently [Faber] has it out in print, also now or lately he has done some plates drawn from the life without the assistance of

a painter' (Vertue, *Note books*, 3.109). Among subjects other than portraits Faber made mezzotints after Philip Mercier's paintings of everyday themes in the manner of Chardin. Larger prints, which sold for the relatively high price of 5*s.*, included an equestrian portrait of Frederick, prince of Wales, after Bartholomew Dandridge (1740), dedicated to the masters and wardens of 'the Antient Society of Free and Accepted Masons … by their faithful Brother … Jno Faber'.

Faber was undoubtedly the leading mezzotint engraver of his day, but his posthumous reputation has been eclipsed by those of James Macardell and other Dublin mezzotint engravers who dominated the medium from the 1750s. Among his apprentices were Andrew Miller and—probably—John Brooks. His wife, whose name is not known, was painted by Thomas Hudson and the portrait was executed in mezzotint by Faber; after Faber's death she married a lawyer named Smith. Faber died, of gout, on 2 May 1756. Fifteen of his plates, including the *Hampton Court Beauties*, were acquired by John Boydell and appeared in Boydell's sale of 2 June 1818.

     SHEILA O'CONNELL

Sources Vertue, *Note books* · J. C. Smith, *British mezzotinto portraits*, 4 vols. in 5 (1878–84) · T. Clayton, *The English print, 1688–1802* (1997) · *DNB*
Likenesses J. Faber, drawing, 1704, BM · H. Hysing, oils, *c*.1729

Faber, Oscar (1886–1956), civil engineer, was born at 56 Dalberg Road, London, on 5 July 1886, the eldest son of Harald Nicolai Faber (1856–1944), chemist and Danish commissioner of agriculture in London, and his wife, Sofie Cecilie, *née* Bentzien. He was educated at St Dunstan's College, Catford, where he excelled at sports and carried off many academic prizes. He won the Clothworkers' scholarship to the Central Technical College (later the City and Guilds College), and qualified two years later in electrical engineering. This gained him an associateship in 1906, and he graduated in civil and mechanical engineering in 1907; he became a fellow of the college in 1929.

Faber worked first as an assistant engineer with the Associated Portland Cement Manufacturers at Gravesend, and in 1909 he took up a similar position with the Indented Bar and Concrete Engineering Company. Among the first to see the possibilities of reinforced concrete, a material then seldom used, for structural work, he undertook many theoretical and experimental investigations into its properties and behaviour, and in 1915 he was awarded the degree of DSc by London University for his original research on the bending and shearing of reinforced concrete beams. In 1912 he was appointed chief engineer of Trollope and Colls, and he was responsible for the structural design of many large London buildings.

On 23 November 1913 Faber married (Helen) Joan (1881–1967), daughter of John Gordon Mainwaring, physician, of London. They had two daughters, Eileen and Barbara, and a son, John, who became one of his partners. During the war his department built factories for war work, and he himself advised the Admiralty on explosive anti-submarine devices made of reinforced concrete with nonferrous reinforcement, for which in 1919 he was appointed OBE.

In 1921, at the height of the depression and with a young family to support, Faber risked his modest capital of £2000 to set up in practice as a consulting engineer. Appreciating the growing importance of the mechanical and electrical services in large buildings, his office dealt almost from the beginning with those services as well as with the foundations and structural design. Faber was responsible for the engineering of numerous large industrial and commercial projects, and he took a lively interest in aesthetic problems. For the new Bank of England, in the heart of the City of London, he burrowed deep beneath Soane's original wall (which was next skilfully underpinned), with the new building rising symbolically and solidly above it. In other fields Faber's office was responsible for such widely differing projects as the installations for the Earls Court exhibition buildings, and the underpinning of Durham Castle—for which, in 1935, he was awarded the honorary degree of DCL by Durham University.

In the course of his work Faber travelled very widely, visiting at different times all five continents and indeed most countries of the world. He lectured in London at the Northern Polytechnic, at University College, and at the City and Guilds College; he continued his researches, particularly into the long-term plastic yield of reinforced concrete under load, the results of which he published in 1936. He took an active part in the affairs of the Institution of Structural Engineers which, as the Concrete Institute, he had joined in 1911 and of which he was president in 1935–6. He was also a member of the institutions of civil, mechanical, and electrical engineers.

With the advent of war in 1939, Faber's office was fully engaged on the design of munitions factories, ordnance depots, and other essential installations, and Faber himself flew to America to advise Winston Churchill on aspects of the Mulberry Harbour project, which he later helped to translate into bold reality. The war was scarcely over when he was appointed consulting engineer for the rebuilding of the House of Commons, destroyed by German bombs in 1940 and ordained by Churchill to be rebuilt in the same style as it was before, but incorporating more accommodation and better facilities. Faber's brief covered the whole of the engineering work including the complicated services, and his approach to the problem of air-conditioning was typical: 'We shall never please six hundred members, so we will do it properly and please ourselves'. At the conclusion of the rebuilding, in 1951, he was appointed CBE.

In 1912 Faber put order and coherence into structural design with his book (with P. G. Bowie) *Reinforced Concrete Design*; and in 1936, with J. R. Kell, he wrote *Heating and Air-Conditioning of Buildings*, which in succeeding editions became the standard work. He was also the author of *Reinforced Concrete Simply Explained* (1922) and *Constructional Steelwork Simply Explained* (1927), and of numerous papers to the engineering institutions, including the Institution

of Heating and Ventilating Engineers, of which he was president during the difficult years of 1944–5.

The post-war period saw the continued expansion of Faber's already large practice. In 1948 he took into partnership five of his senior assistants, but far from taking the opportunity to transfer the burden he continued to extend the range of his travels and to work at full pressure until his death.

Notwithstanding his professional preoccupations Faber found time for relaxation in gardening, music, and painting. He was an excellent watercolour artist, and would seldom return from even the most strenuous business trip abroad without a handful of paintings of great boldness and skill. He was passionately fond of music, and a sympathetic player of the clarinet, the organ, and the piano, for which he composed several delightful works.

Faber was intensely interested in problems of every kind and spared no trouble to arrive at a satisfying and elegant solution. His technical mastery of his subjects was impeccable, and his approach was simple and direct, his clear thinking never obscured by technicalities. To his fellow engineers he was sometimes an enigma and always a challenge. To his staff he was a stimulating if exacting master; impatient of inexact thinking or tardy action; often critical of a proposal, but always willing to spend much time in putting it right. To himself he was unsparing of physical as well as mental effort, and to everything he brought an apparently inexhaustible energy. While properly conscious of his own importance, he scorned the trappings and conventions of importance.

In the midst of the design stage of the Wales Empire Pool in 1956, intended for the forthcoming Commonwealth games, Faber was taken ill while working in his garden. He died at noon at the Luton and Dunstable Hospital, on the following day, 7 May 1956.

J. R. HARRISON, rev. ANITA McCONNELL

Sources 'Induction of president elect', *Journal of the Institution of Heating and Ventilating Engineers*, 12 (1944–5), 7–9 · *Structural Engineer*, 34 (1956), 302–4 · private information (2004) · personal knowledge (1971) · WWW · J. Faber, *Oscar Faber, his work, his firm, and afterwards* (1989) · *The Times* (9 May 1956), 13d · *Register of students of the City and Guilds College, 1884–1934* (1936), 179–80 · d. cert. · m. cert. · b. cert.

Likenesses photograph, 1944, repro. in 'Induction of president elect', 2 · C. Wheeler, bronze bust, Bank of England, London · photograph, repro. in Faber, *Oscar Faber* · print, Oscar Faber & Partners, St Albans, Hertfordshire

Wealth at death £287,778 5s. 1d.: probate, 19 July 1956, CGPLA Eng. & Wales

Fabyan, Robert (d. 1513), chronicler, is said to have been born in London. The son of John and Agnes Fabyan, he had at least one brother, John, who is mentioned in his will. Several other Fabyans are also recorded in London about this time, including John (fl. 1439–1477) and Stephen (fl. 1468–1469), but it is unclear whether any of these were relatives. Robert married Elizabeth Pake, daughter and heir of Johannes Pake, draper, and his wife, Elizabeth Stokker, and through his wife inherited lands in Essex at Theydon Garnon, including a mansion called Halstedys.

With her he had sixteen children, only six of whom survived him.

Robert Fabyan was made free in the Drapers' Company in 1476–7, having been apprenticed to William Holme about 1470, and took up the livery a year later. He was elected renter warden of the company in 1485 and acted as auditor of the city's accounts in 1486 and 1487. Elected sheriff in 1493 on the nomination of the lord mayor, he became alderman of Farringdon Without about December 1494. In 1495–6 he served as master of the Drapers' Company, and held this office again in 1501–2. In 1496 he was assigned to petition the king regarding levies on English cloth exported to Flanders, while in 1497 Fabyan was appointed with John Brooke and John Warner to keep the gates of Ludgate and Newgate against the Cornish rebels, and to accompany the king to Woodstock afterwards. In 1498 he was an assessor of the fifteenth for the Scottish war. In 1503 he resigned from the office of alderman, claiming that he did not have the financial backing to take on the mayoralty—it is recorded that on 'the xx^{th} day of Julii & feest of Seynt mergaret Robert Fabyan aldyrman that long beffore hadd labourid to be dyschargid, at that daye by auctoryte of a Court of aldyrmen was dysmyssid of that Charge' (*Great Chronicle*, 325). Since Fabyan, who was the executor of his father-in-law's will, was then involved in a dispute with another alderman, William Welbeck, over payment of the orphan's portion overdue to Welbeck's wife, it is possible that his retirement was the result of both financial and social embarrassment.

Although clearly a man at the forefront of civic affairs, respected by his peers and the king, Robert Fabyan is best known for the chronicle attributed to him, *The Newe Cronycles of England and Fraunce*, also known as Fabyan's chronicle. In the prologue to the work the author himself calls it the 'Concordance of Storyes', an indication of its uniqueness in presenting parallel histories of England and France. The chronicle exists in manuscript in two volumes, with Holkham Hall, MS 671, covering the period from Brutus to the death of Philip Augustus of France in 1223, and BL, Cotton MS Nero C.xi, continuing from 1223 to 1485. Like all London chronicle manuscripts, Holkham 671 and Cotton Nero C.xi are anonymous. Although these manuscripts are almost certainly not in Fabyan's hand, it is probable that the text was written or continued by Robert Fabyan. Stow states that Fabyan:

> gathered out of divers good Authors, as well Latin as French, a large Chronicle of England and of France, which he published in English, to his great Charges, for the Honour of this City, and common Utility of the whole Realm. (Stow, bk 1, 262)

Fabyan was certainly conversant with French and Latin, and is recorded as borrowing a French chronicle from the Guildhall Library for an extended period of time.

The Newe Cronycles was first printed by Pynson in 1516, but was not attributed to Robert Fabyan until Rastell's edition in 1533, which was entitled *Fabyans Cronycle Newly Prynted*. In the following year, 1534, the court of aldermen agreed that a copy of 'Mr. fabyans cronycles' should be held in the court. It would seem that the continuation to

1509 was also attributed to Fabyan. This is certainly the case in the 1548 Ipswich edition of John Bale's *Illustrium maioris Britanniae scriptorum … summarium* (Bale, 209) where the chronicle and also the continuation are said to be Fabyan's work. John Stow attributes both *The Newe Cronycles* and the great chronicle (London, Guildhall Library, MS 3313) to Robert Fabyan, sometimes confusing the manuscripts. This was easily done as the manuscripts of *The Newe Cronycles* and that of the great chronicle after 1439 are all written largely in the same hand, and contain some similar styles of lettering and decoration. As the writer of the great chronicle records that he was apprenticed to Thomas Coke, there has been some speculation that Robert Fabyan may have been initially apprenticed to Thomas Coke and later changed to William Holme. This is a simple way of supporting the attribution of this manuscript to Fabyan. Because the Drapers' Company registers have been destroyed it is not known when Fabyan's apprenticeship commenced and so this association can be neither confirmed nor denied. However, much internal evidence suggests that the extant manuscripts of both *The Newe Cronycles* and the great chronicle were all copied in the same workshop. Although the similarity of hand does not mean Fabyan wrote the great chronicle, it is evident that all three manuscripts were compiled by individuals with a thorough and personal knowledge of the administration of London. In the case of *The Newe Cronycles* this is consistent with Fabyan's status and interests. It is notable, too, that these texts were perceived by contemporaries as valuable resources.

The Newe Cronycles is written in seven parts, each celebrating a joy of the Virgin Mary. The first six books draw heavily on the *Brut* as the basis of the English history, and also cite numerous medieval sources including Bede, William of Malmesbury, Ranulf Higden, and Henry of Huntingdon. Book 7 begins with the Norman conquest, and at 1189 the English history becomes a London chronicle, dating by mayoral years, and including the names of the mayors and sheriffs of the city of London. This text is clearly related to the London chronicle texts in BL, Cotton MS Vitellius A.xvi, and London, Guildhall Library, MS 3313 (the great chronicle), which, as noted above, has also been attributed, although somewhat dubiously, to Robert Fabyan, and is more distantly related to Bodl. Oxf., MS Gough London 10. *The Newe Cronycles* is particularly important in reflecting a change in the perception of history. It is the first of the London chronicles to cite its sources and to extend a localized history to a more general account of England and France. Furthermore *The Newe Cronycles* is unique in marking a shift from history as a literary representation of the visual (as it was in the earlier London chronicles), to history as a truly literary form. The comparison of different sources throughout the chronicle, and the importance placed on developing historical themes, are further indications of a changed perspective. It is through *The Newe Cronycles* that the London chronicle tradition was transmitted to the later English renaissance writers. John Bale (*d*. 1563) claims that the first edition of *The Newe Cronycles* (1516) was burnt by Cardinal Wolsey, although there is no corroborating evidence for this, save the scarcity of this edition. The second edition, with a continuation, was printed in 1533 after Wolsey's death. Further editions with continuations appeared in 1542 and 1559. The modern edition was edited by Henry Ellis in 1811.

At the time of his death Fabyan had property at Theydon Garnon as well as tenements within the parish of Benet Fink within Warde at Bradstrete, London, and tenements in the parish of St Michael Cornhill. He had other lands and tenements in East Ham, West Ham, and Leyton, and freehold copy in Lambourne, Theydon Bois, Theydon Garnon, Theydon Mount, and Stanford Rivers. He was survived by his wife, two daughters, Joan Haryat and Mary, and four sons, John, Robert, Thomas, and Antony. Also mentioned in his will are his cousin Dorothy and Robert Tate, the latter a mercer and former mayor of London. In his will (which was proved on 12 July 1513) he bequeaths a 'masse bok and a prymer', but does not explicitly bequeath any chronicles. Chronicles are bequeathed in the will of John Fabyan, written in 1541, perhaps a grandson of Robert. Robert Fabyan asked to be buried in Essex, although according to Stow he was buried at St Michael Cornhill. No trace of his monument remained there when Strype's edition of Stow's *Survey* was published in 1720.

M-R. McLaren

Sources R. Fabyan, *The new chronicles of England and France*, ed. H. Ellis, new edn (1811) [incl. copy of Fabyan's will] · BL, Add. Charter 28925 [printed in *EHR*, 3 (1888), 318f.] · A. H. Thomas and I. D. Thornley, eds., *The great chronicle of London* (1938); repr. (1983) · M-R. McLaren, 'The London chronicles of the fifteenth century: the manuscripts, their authors and their aims', PhD diss., University of Melbourne, 1990, 166–73, 334–406 · J. Stow, *A survey of the cities of London and Westminster ... corrected and improved by John Strype* (1720), bk 1, 262; bk 2, 145; bk 4, 113 · Rymer, *Foedera*, 7.648, 654 · W. Herbert, *The history of the twelve great livery companies of London*, 1 (1834); repr. (1968), 389–498 · J. Bale, *Illustrium Maioris Britannie scriptorum ... summarium* (1548), fol. 209 · A. Gransden, *Historical writing in England*, 2 (1982), 245–8 · M-R. McLaren, *The London chronicles of the fifteenth century: a revolution in English writing* (2002)
Archives BL, Cotton MS Nero C.xi · Bodl. Oxf., Pynson's edition of *The newe cronycles*, 1516 · GL, Guildhall MS 3313 · Holkham Hall, Norfolk, Holkham MS 671 | BL, Add. Charter 28925
Wealth at death wealthy; left several properties and other bequests

Faccio, Nicolas. *See* Fatio, Nicolas, of Duillier (1664–1753).

Faceby, John (*d.* in or after 1460), physician, is principally known for his treatment of Henry VI during his insanity and for his involvement in the royal alchemical inquiry of 1456, which was designed to find a cure for the king's ills. Nothing definite is known of Faceby's birth. He was either from Faceby in Yorkshire or, more probably, descended from the Facebys of Caldecote in Cambridgeshire, a minor gentry family. His education is also obscure, though in later life he had an association with Merton College, Oxford. In 1438, styled *magister*, he was established as a medical practitioner in Southwark. He must have made a considerable impact, as he rapidly came to the notice of the crown. On 6 April 1444 he was retained by the king with an annual fee of £100, a large though not exceptional

grant to a physician. A week later his son, John Faceby junior, was appointed one of the king's sergeants-at-arms, at a wage of 12*d.* a day.

During Henry VI's complete mental incapacity, which began in August 1453 and lasted for more than a year, Faceby shared the place of principal physician with another royal doctor, William Hatteclyffe. On 15 March 1454 they were joined by three other physicians and surgeons on a committee appointed by the council to treat Henry with an array of traditional remedies, which ranged from baths, syrups, and unguents to bleeding and the scarification of the skin. The increased prominence which he owed to the king's illness brought financial rewards. Although Faceby's fee was drawn from the petty custom of the port of London (an advantageously secure source of revenue at a time of financial stringency), payments had fallen into arrears. He was now able to make up some of the shortfall. In March 1454 he received payment of money theoretically assigned to him two years earlier. However, in April 1455, following Henry's recovery and the end of the duke of York's first protectorate, a full review was made of payments under the annuity, suggesting that some of the assignments had still not been translated into cash.

Fears that Henry might relapse, and of the political repercussions which would follow, kept Faceby in favour. Following Henry's resumption of power in February 1456, at the end of York's second protectorate, Faceby played an important part in the alchemy commissions of 1456–7, which were partly designed to ensure that no renewed bout of insanity further endangered the dynasty. On 31 May 1456 Faceby and two other doctors, John Kirkeby and John Rayny, jointly described as 'supremely erudite in the natural sciences' (Geoghegan, 15–16), were given a special protection, exempting them from Henry IV's statutes forbidding the investigation and practice of alchemy. No record survives of the proceedings or results of the inquiry. That it was principally aimed at the medical, rather than the financial, benefits of alchemy is revealed by the wording of the licence, which defines the philosophers' stone as a medicine which could prolong life, heal wounds, and sustain virility of body and mind.

Given Edward IV's predilection for doctors and alchemists, and the latitude he showed to former opponents, the fact that Faceby does not appear in his service may indicate that he had died or retired before the change of dynasty. The last record of him occurs in March 1460, in a minor land grant made to him along with his wife, Alice, and son Henry, suggesting that the elder son, John, may have predeceased his father. Two of Faceby's books have been identified, one on surgery (Cambridge, Gonville and Caius College, MS 467/574) and one on astronomy (Cambridge, Pembroke College, MS 227); both were sold to another of Henry VI's doctors, the Cambridge surgeon Roger Marchall.

ANTHONY GROSS

Sources C. H. Talbot and E. A. Hammond, *The medical practitioners in medieval England: a biographical register* (1965), 143 · CPR, 1441–6, 27, 271 · CClR, 1435–41, 183 · exchequer, king's remembrancer, accounts various, PRO, E 101 624/46 · exchequer of receipt, issue rolls, PRO, E 403/796 m.13 /801 m.1 · *VCH Cambridgeshire and the Isle of Ely*, 5.20 · Rymer, *Foedera*, 11.68–9 · Emden, *Oxf.*, 2.663 · L. E. Voigts, 'A doctor and his books: the manuscripts of Roger Marchall', *New science out of old books*, ed. R. Beadle and A. J. Piper (1995), 249–314 · D. Geoghegan, 'A licence of Henry VI to practise alchemy', *Ambix*, 6 (1957–8), 10–17

Archives Gon. & Caius Cam., MS 467/574 · Pembroke Cam., MS 227

Fachiri [*née* D'Arányi], **Adila Adrienne Adalbertina Maria** (1886–1962), violinist, was born in Budapest, Hungary, on 26 February 1886, the eldest of the three daughters of Taksony Arányi de Hunyadvar, chief of police in Budapest, and his wife, Adrienne Nievarovicz de Ligenza, the fourteenth child of a Pole of good family from the Cracow district. Her sister, the third daughter, **Jelly Eva D'Arányi** (1893–1966), also a violinist, was born in Budapest on 30 May 1893. Their mother, Adrienne, was the niece of Joseph Joachim, the celebrated violinist and friend of Brahms. The entire family was musical and both girls began their musical training as children at the piano; Béla Bartók, as a student of twenty-two, was among their teachers and became a lifelong friend. It was as violinists, however, that the two entered the Budapest Academy of Music as children; they became pupils of the great violinist Jenó Hubay.

Adila began to play in public when she was fourteen, winning the approval of Budapest critics and the affection of audiences not only for her playing but also for her charm. In 1906, the year of her début in Vienna, she won the artists' diploma of the Budapest Academy and, although an impresario at once offered her a favourable contract, she went to Berlin to become the only private pupil of her celebrated great-uncle.

Although Joachim died in 1907, not only was Adila's playing profoundly influenced by him, but it also brought her into contact with Joachim's circle, including such musicians as Grieg, Humperdinck, Casals, Ysaÿe, and the distinguished English musicologist Donald Tovey. Her work under Joachim included not only the standard concertos and the violin and piano works of the nineteenth-century masters but also the music of eighteenth-century composers, including the accompanied and unaccompanied violin music of Bach. At the same time she never disdained effective showpieces by composers like Saint-Saëns, Sarasate, and Wieniawski.

Joachim had planned to conduct Adila's début in Berlin, with the Philharmonic Orchestra there, in November 1907, and the concert was given in spite of his death; the impression Adila made opened the doors of many other important concerts for her, and she travelled widely, introducing Jelly as a supporting artist and as her partner in Bach's D minor double concerto. Jelly's formal training thus ended by the time she was fourteen.

Adila's English début took place in 1909. Supported by her great-uncle's English friends and disciples she was a great success. The liveliness, personality, and quite un-English attractiveness of the D'Arányi sisters made them welcome in England, and their associates included Bertrand Russell, as well as Fanny Davies, the pianist pupil of Clara Schumann, and Sir Henry Wood. Kept in Britain by the outbreak of the First World War, they settled down to become a regular part of English musical life, assisted by such friends as Herbert Asquith and A. J. Balfour over any difficulties arising from their nationality. When, after 1919, their international careers could be resumed, England remained their base. Wartime music-making, much of it at private concerts in great houses, turned Adila's attention to chamber music, often with the cellist Guilhermina Suggia.

In November 1915 Adila married Alexander P. Fachiri (*d.* 1939), an American lawyer of Greek descent, and adopted her husband's name for professional purposes. In 1919 Alexander Fachiri, also an accomplished cellist, took British citizenship and practised in international law. They had one daughter. Of a retiring disposition, Fachiri was never entirely happy for his wife to undertake public recitals. However, following his death on 27 March 1939 she was restored to the concert platform. Her broad, powerful style, responsive and high-spirited but essentially classical, remained unimpaired, and her readiness to tackle new music was as great as it had ever been. She was in demand as a teacher, and although after the Second World War she settled near Florence, she returned from Italy from time to time to play in London, where she was last heard in 1957 playing in Bach's double concerto with her sister. She died in Florence after a short illness on 15 December 1962.

It was customary during the lifetime of the two sisters to contrast the classical style of Adila Fachiri with the more impulsively romantic playing of Jelly D'Arányi. The two were, however, such frequently and perfectly matched partners in many works of a variety of styles and periods that to hear them together was to realize that, essentially, they were in complete musical sympathy. Gustav Holst dedicated his double violin concerto to them, and the sisters gave its first performance in 1930.

During the 1920s and 1930s, when Adila Fachiri was heard less frequently in public as a soloist, Jelly D'Arányi combined recitals with concerto performances with major European orchestras and established a reputation in the USA. As well as Bach's unaccompanied violin works she played the concertos of Szymanowski, Respighi, and Vaughan Williams, whose *Concerto accademico* was dedicated to her; she also played his *Lark Ascending* very frequently. Her recital repertory included Ravel's *Tzigane*, perhaps the most important of all the works dedicated to either of the sisters. She played the violin and piano sonatas of Bartók, written for her and her sister, and the sonatas of John Ireland, Eugene Goossens, and Richard Strauss. In addition, Jelly was partly responsible for the rediscovery of Schumann's violin concerto, and she first played it to the public in 1938. This concerto, dismissed as an inferior work by Clara Schumann, the composer's widow, had been allowed to become forgotten. What Jelly apparently called a 'game' with a wine glass on an improvised ouija board put her on to the track of a work she did not even know existed (the violin concerto was not at that time listed in catalogues of Schumann's compositions). It was found in the composer's manuscripts in the Prussian State Library.

Apart from many appearances with her sister Adila, Jelly formed a close friendship and effective musical partnership with the pianist Myra Hess. In 1933 Jelly suggested and began to carry out a series of charity recitals in English cathedrals. She was appointed CBE in 1946. Jelly joined her sister in Florence after the Second World War; she died there, unmarried, on 30 March 1966.

IVOR NEWTON, *rev.* ROBERT BROWN

Sources J. MacLeod, *The sisters D'Aranyi* (1981) · R. Anderson, 'Fachiri, Adila', *New Grove*, 6.357 · *The Times* (1 April 1962) · *The Times* (17 Dec 1962) · *The Times* (1 April 1966) · *CGPLA Eng. & Wales* (1963) · *CGPLA Eng. & Wales* (1966)
Archives SOUND BL NSA, performance recordings
Likenesses Nelson, portrait, *c.*1907 · N. Lytton, portrait, 1919 · W. Rothenstein, drawing, 1920 · P. A. de Laszlo, portrait, 1928 · C. L. G. Dechaume, portrait
Wealth at death £10,605—in England: administration with will, 18 Feb 1963, *CGPLA Eng. & Wales* · £14,144—in England; Jelly Eva d'Arányi: administration with will, 24 Nov 1966, *CGPLA Eng. & Wales*

Fachtna mac Mongaig (*fl.* 6th cent.). *See under* Munster, saints of (*act. c.*450–*c.*700).

Facius, Georg Siegmund (*b. c.*1750, *d.* in or before 1813). *See under* Boydell, John, engravers (*act.* 1760–1804).

Facius, Johann Gottlieb (*b. c.*1750, *d.* in or before 1813). *See under* Boydell, John, engravers (*act.* 1760–1804).

Faden, William (1749–1836), engraver and cartographer, was born in London on 11 July 1749, the younger son and sixth of eight known children of William Faden (1711–1783), formerly Mackfaden, and his wife, Hannah. His father, a well-known printer, then of Salisbury Court, Fleet Street, had abbreviated the family name at the time of the Jacobite rising of 1745.

Faden was apprenticed to the Fleet Street engraver James Wigley on 4 July 1764. At the expiry of his term he became free of the Clothworkers' Company on 7 August 1771. By 1773 he was in partnership with the family of the recently deceased map maker Thomas Jefferys, at Jefferys's premises on the corner of St Martin's Lane. The partnership with the younger Jefferys was dissolved in 1776, the same year in which Faden became an active member of the Society of Civil Engineers (later the Smeatonian Society of Civil Engineers), the influential dining club of John Smeaton and other leading practical men of the day founded in 1771.

In the years of the American wars Faden came to prominence with maps and atlases of considerable historical note, some of the materials for which survive in the Library of Congress. He is glimpsed at this time as the 'very accurate, industrious young man' commended by Thomas Pownall. In 1783 his father's will enabled him to establish full control of the business. That same year he was appointed to 'the place and quality of Geographer in Ordinary to his Majesty'.

Systematic in the acquisition of the best available maps, Faden developed the most competent cartographic service of the period. His was an international concern, in contact with map makers throughout Europe. He supplied government departments and commissioned fresh surveys. A gold medallist of the Society of Arts in 1796, his activities foreshadowed the emergence of national cartographic agencies. He brought out the first published Ordnance Survey map, *An Entirely New & Accurate Survey of the County of Kent* (1801). Some of his plates were likewise adopted as official Admiralty charts. When he moved at this time to larger premises at no. 5 Charing Cross, his maps were reputed the finest being engraved anywhere in the world.

Of Faden's personal life little is known. His sister Hannah married the painter and astronomer John Russell, and there is an excellent Russell pastel (British Library) of Faden, in an attentive and determined pose. The brothers-in-law collaborated on the earliest extant lunar globe.

Faden retired in 1823, the business passing to his former apprentice, James Wyld the elder. He died in Shepperton, where his nephew William Russell was then rector, on 21 March 1836, leaving a considerable fortune. There is an elegant memorial to Faden and his sister Jane (1753–1833) in the parish church, where he was buried.

LAURENCE WORMS, *rev.*

Sources *British Museum catalogue of printed maps, charts and plans*, 16 vols. (1967–78) · Clothworkers' Company archives · J. B. Harley, 'The Society of Arts and the survey of English counties, 1759–1809 [pts 1–4]', *Journal of the Royal Society of Arts*, 112 (1963–4), 43–6, 119–25, 269–75, 538–43 · parish registers and rate-books, St Andrew's, Holborn, St Bride's, Fleet Street, and St Martin-in-the-Fields · W. A. Seymour, ed., *A history of the Ordnance Survey* (1980) · M. S. Pedley, ed., *The map trade in the late eighteenth century: letters to the London map sellers Jefferys and Faden* (2000)
Likenesses J. Russell, pastel, BL

Fadipe, Nathaniel Akinremi (1893–1944), writer and anti-colonialist, was born on 2 October 1893 at Oko-Saje, Abeokuta, Nigeria, the son of the Revd L. O. Fadipe of the Baptist mission at Abeokuta; his mother was a successful market trader. As a child he was educated at church missionary schools. Later, dissatisfied with his poorly paid job as a clerk in the government secretariat, he moved to become personal secretary to the manager of Barclays Bank in Lagos.

In order to further his education Fadipe travelled to Britain. He gained a BA at the London School of Economics (LSE); on graduating in 1929 he was granted a fellowship for two terms at Woodbrooke, an international Quaker residential college in Birmingham. After further study of history and international relations there he was awarded a *testamur* certificate *cum laude*. In 1930, on a two-year fellowship from the Phelps Stokes Fund, he travelled to the United States; he spent a year at Columbia University, New York, and was awarded an MA. His dissertation, 'A Yoruba town: a sociological study of Abeokuta', was the first academic study of a Nigerian city by an African.

The offer of a teaching post at Achimota College, Legon, Gold Coast, drew Fadipe back to West Africa. Achimota, opened in 1926, was the first government-funded educational establishment to offer co-education from kindergarten to lower-level university. Apparently Fadipe met considerable hostility from the European staff, so that his contract was not renewed when it expired in 1934. His name is omitted from the histories of Achimota.

On returning to London, Fadipe enrolled at the LSE in 1934 for postgraduate study under professors Bronislaw Malinowski and Morris Ginsberg. Though in receipt of a fellowship only in his final year, he researched aspects of the political, social, and economic situation in some countries in Africa. It took him five years to gain his PhD. His was the first major sociological study by a Nigerian of the Yoruba; however, *The Sociology of the Yoruba* was not published until 1970.

Fadipe felt that the 'British public [was] most inadequately informed of Africa … [and] of the unjust conditions the Natives laboured under in many parts of Africa' (*West African Pilot*), and his writings, published in a number of British journals, aimed to address this ignorance. These included essays on Abyssinia and a six-part series on traditional and modern education. He also wrote about South Africa, discussed the evolution and effects of indirect rule, and considered plans for white settlement in post-war Africa. In addition he researched and wrote two papers for the West African Students' Union (WASU): a report on Nigerian land tenure (*c*.1939), written for distribution to the members of the unofficial parliamentary committee on west African economic conditions, and a thirty-six-page memorandum, 'Price control and living standards in West Africa' (13 April 1940), which was sent to the government. The Colonial Office sent an amended version to the west African governments as a secret document (PRO, CO 852/341/1). A work on the economic situation in Kenya, which he withdrew from the publishers for unstated reasons, had been commissioned by the Fabian Colonial Bureau.

Involved in anti-imperialist politics in London, Fadipe worked with WASU, the League of Coloured Peoples, and with militants such as George Padmore and Jomo Kenyatta. Naturally, he was also concerned with racism in Britain; his complaints in 1941 about harassment in air raid shelters and racial discrimination in employment exchanges invigorated previous discussions between the Colonial Office and the Ministry of Labour on the issue (PRO, CO 859/80/9; PRO, CO 859/40/15; PRO, CO 859/40/4). He also wrote for, and collaborated with, such white-run political organizations as the National Council for Civil Liberties, and worked with campaigners such as Dr Norman Leys, and Horace Alexander of the peace movement. His work was used by the Independent Labour Party, the Fabian Colonial Bureau, and the Labour Research Department. He was in contact with activists such as the African-American Ralph Bunche (later a Nobel laureate) and Nnamdi Azikiwe, a future president of independent Nigeria.

As there were no university research or teaching posts in London for which an African applicant would have received serious consideration, Fadipe was forced to earn his living as an examiner of students of the Yoruba language, as a marker of school examination papers, as a translator for the Ministry of Information, and as a clerk with Unilever. Inappropriate employment combined with total devotion to the cause of Africa led to gross overwork and resulted in a brain haemorrhage. Fadipe died on 1 June 1944 at St Bartholomew's Hospital, London; he was buried at Hendon Park cemetery.

As the editor of the journal *West Africa* noted, Fadipe was 'one of the ablest and most balanced thinkers Nigeria has produced' (10 June 1944). He was held in 'great admiration for his intellectual powers and the fairness and justice of his opinions'. His 'true place was a responsible one in the administration of his country [but] it is not really an inveterate habit of the Colonial Governments to seek out and prefer men of his independent, critical cast of mind' (ibid.).

MARIKA SHERWOOD

Sources RS Friends, Lond., archives · *The Friend* (18 Aug 1935) [located at Friends House, London] · University of Lagos, Nigeria, Ladipo Solanke, West African Students' Union, papers · Bodl. RH, MS Brit. Emp.s.19 · d. cert. · NYPL, Schomburg Center for Research in Black Culture, Phelps Stokes MSS · NYPL, Schomburg Center for Research in Black Culture, Ralph Bunche MSS · introduction, N. A. Fadipe, *The sociology of the Yoruba* (1970) · 'Colour discrimination – labour exchanges', PRO, CO 859/80/9 · *West African Review* (April–May 1943) · *West African Review* (July 1943) · *West Africa* (10 June 1944) · *West African Pilot* (12 June 1944)
Archives University of Lagos, WASU/Solanke papers, letters
Likenesses photographs, priv. coll.

Faed, James (1821–1911). *See under* Faed, John (1819–1902).

Faed, John (1819–1902), painter, was born on 31 August 1819 at Barley Mill, Girthon, near Gatehouse of Fleet, Kirkcudbrightshire, the eldest of the six children of James Faed (1777–1843), tenant farmer, miller, and engineer, and his wife, Mary McGeoch (1790–1866). Four of his five siblings also displayed great artistic talent. They were James (1821–1911) [*see below*], engraver and painter; Thomas *Faed (1826–1900), whose success as a professional artist surpassed that of John; Susan Bell Faed (1827–1909); and George Faed (1830–1852). The other brother, William Faed (1823–1900), had no interest in art and emigrated to Australia, where he became a farmer.

John Faed displayed prodigious artistic ability which was first noticed when he was eleven, when a book of maps drawn by him was praised in the *Castle Douglas Weekly Visitor*. He left Girthon parish school that year but continued to paint at home, grinding stones to make his colours. His father disapproved of his eldest son's wish to become a professional artist but allowed him to accompany him on his travels around Galloway on business, when he painted miniatures on ivory of the local gentry, including the Galloway poet William Nicholson. In 1839 Faed moved to Edinburgh, where he attended the Board of Trustees' Academy, studying life drawing and painting. He had a portrait of a gentleman accepted by the Royal Scottish Academy a year later, along with four miniatures. Soon after his father's death in 1843 he was joined by his brother Thomas, who also began studying at the Trustees' Academy.

Their brother **James Faed** (1821–1911), who was born on 4 April 1821 at Barley Mill, Girthon, near Gatehouse of Fleet, Kirkcudbrightshire, was a talented young man who made toy pistols and musical instruments, dressed salmon flies, and could also turn his hand to gun making and boat building. On his father's death he also went to Edinburgh, initially to study engineering. He was encouraged by his brothers to take up engraving and through John met the mezzotint engraver John Bonnar. Showing great artistic and technical ability, he abandoned engineering and became a professional engraver, his first plate being his own portrait by his brother Thomas. He subsequently engraved many of his brothers' paintings. He received several commissions from the portraitist Sir John Watson Gordon, and became generally regarded as one of the finest mezzotinters of his time. He exhibited 37 times at the Royal Academy (1855–1904) and engraved at least 133 plates. In 1850 he was invited by Queen Victoria to engrave F. X. Winterhalter's *The Queen and Prince Arthur*, which led to further royal commissions and visits to Balmoral. In 1852 he married Mary, a member of the Cotton tobacco family, and moved from Comely Bank, Edinburgh, to 7 Chalcott Terrace, St John's Wood, London, but returned to Scotland in 1855, and to Comely Bank in 1861. He died in Edinburgh on 23 September 1911. Examples of his work are in the Scottish National Portrait Gallery, Edinburgh; the City of Edinburgh art collection; the Royal Library, Windsor; several Scottish municipal galleries; and the Yale Center for British Art, New Haven, Connecticut.

George, the youngest brother, was brought to Edinburgh to assist James with his engravings, but his early death at the age of twenty-two ended a promising career. As the only daughter in the Faed family, Susan stayed at home to care for her widowed mother. Between the time of her mother's death in 1866 and her own marriage in the late 1870s, however, she had several paintings exhibited at both the Royal Scottish Academy and the Royal Academy.

Having studied both life drawing and painting, John Faed painted fewer miniatures and began painting subject pictures instead. He depicted scenes from Shakespeare and the Bible but came to specialize in Scottish subjects, which had been popularized nationally by the novels of Sir Walter Scott. Scott inspired many of Faed's paintings, such as a scene from his novel *The Abbot, Catherine Seaton and Roland Graeme* (Wolverhampton Art Gallery). Scottish ballads and the writings of Robert Burns were also a great inspiration. Faed illustrated Burns's poems 'The Cotter's Saturday Night', 'Tam o' Shanter', and 'The Soldier's Return', all of which were engraved for the subscribers of the Royal Association for the Promotion of the Fine Arts in Scotland. He also illustrated a book of comical verse entitled *The Legend of St Swithin* (1861) for George Davidson, an Aberdeen poet and bookseller.

John Faed was elected an associate member of the Royal Scottish Academy in 1847 and became a full member in 1851. In 1849 he married Jane Macdonald (1820–1897), youngest child of the Revd Malcolm Macdonald, who had been minister on the Isle of Gigha but had died when Jane was fourteen. They had no children. In Edinburgh Faed took an active part in the artistic life of the city. Along with his younger brother Thomas and also James Archer, John Ballantyne, William Crawford, and the future president of the Royal Scottish Academy, William Fettes Douglas, he helped to found in 1848 a sketching group called the Smashers Club, whose members would meet to sketch chosen subjects together, such as Boyhood, Conspiracy, or Evil, and to discuss artistic theories and styles. The Glasgow Art Gallery and Museum has in its collection some of John and Thomas Faed's quick sketches drawn for the club. Some years later, when several of these artists had moved to London, the club was reconvened there under the name Auld Lang Syne. Several other Scottish artists who were by then resident in London, including John Pettie and W. Q. Orchardson, were invited to join. Faed was also an officer in the no. 1 company (the Artists' company), City of Edinburgh volunteers, which had been founded in August 1859.

In 1857 John Faed travelled for four months in the Middle East, visiting Jerusalem and Cairo and travelling up the Nile. While there he collected armour and costume and, on his return to Scotland, incorporated them into several Eastern and biblical subject paintings, such as *Boaz and Ruth* (1860). His best-known work, *The Wapinshaw* (The National Trust for Scotland), was painted the following year and depicts a shooting party of some forty people. This large painting includes several figure groups, each attending to a different task, and illustrates very clearly his preference for narrative painting. His careful use of minutely detailed and very smooth brushwork is characteristic of his art. *The Wapinshaw* was exhibited at the Royal Scottish Academy in 1863 and subsequently bought by James Baird MP for £1000.

Encouraged by the success of his brother Thomas in London, John Faed moved there in 1864; *The Wapinshaw* was shown at the Royal Academy two years later. However, he decided to return to Scotland in 1869, and built a house, Ardmore, just outside Gatehouse of Fleet, where he continued to paint. His style did not change significantly, in spite of the general movement in Scotland at the time away from precisely painted, anecdotal art. *The Young Duchess* (1870, Art Institute of Chicago), for example, displays the same detailed brushwork as do many of his earlier paintings.

Faed was nominated several times for membership of the Royal Academy but was never elected, though in Galloway he became president of the Kirkcudbright Fine Arts Association. Following his wife's death on 15 November 1897, his widowed sister, Susan Walthew, returned to Galloway and kept house for him. Although in his late seventies, he took on a pupil, John Wilson, who studied with him at Ardmore for four years. After a short illness John Faed died at his home, Ardmore, on 22 October 1902 and was buried beside his wife in Girthon parish churchyard in Kirkcudbrightshire.   JENNIFER MELVILLE

Sources M. McKerrow, *The Faeds: a biography* (1982) · C. B. de Laperriere, ed., *The Royal Scottish Academy exhibitors, 1826–1990*, 4 vols. (1991) · D. Macmillan, *Scottish art, 1460–1990* (1990), 216–17 · J. L. Caw, *Scottish painting past and present, 1620–1908* (1908), 166 · P. J. M. McEwan, *Dictionary of Scottish art and architecture* (1994) · W. D. McKay and F. Rinder, *The Royal Scottish Academy, 1826–1916* (1917) · *CCI* (1902)

Likenesses J. Faed, self-portrait (aged thirteen) · J. Faed, self-portrait, miniature, wash, Carnegie Library, Stranraer · J. Faed, self-portrait, pencil, repro. in McKerrow, *Faeds* · T. Faed, pencil drawing (after bust), Carnegie Library, Stranraer · Schenk & Macfarlane, portrait, Stranraer Public Library; repro. in McKerrow, *Faeds* · S. Shemar, lithograph, repro. in McKerrow, *Faeds* · portrait (after engraving), repro. in McKerrow, *Faeds*

Wealth at death £10,428 8s.: confirmation, 18 Nov 1902, *CCI* · £8875 7s. 3d.—James Faed: confirmation, 2 Nov 1911, *CCI*

Faed, Thomas (1826–1900), genre painter, was born on 8 June 1826 at Barley Mill, Gatehouse of Fleet, Kirkcudbrightshire. He was the fourth of six children of James Faed (1777–1843), engineer and millwright, and Mary McGeoch (1790–1866). Two of his elder brothers, John *Faed (1819–1902) and James *Faed (1821–1911) [*see under* Faed, John], also became painters. Thomas attended Girthon School as a boy and showed early talent as a painter; his first oil painting, *Interior with Figures*, which was executed on a linen apron when he was twelve years old, is now in Glasgow Art Gallery and Museum. In 1842 he became an apprentice draper in the nearby town of Castle Douglas. However, after the death of his father in the following year Faed was invited to join his brother John in Edinburgh. There he assisted in painting miniatures and was admitted to the Trustees' Academy. He studied under Sir William Allan and, more importantly, under Thomas Duncan, who took the colour class. He enjoyed much success and in 1847 he won the life class prize with his oil painting *A Life Study of John Mongo* (1847; 'The Punka-Walla', National Gallery of Scotland, Edinburgh). On completion of these studies he attended the Royal Scottish Academy life school from 1849 to 1852.

Even as a student Thomas Faed was a successful exhibitor at the Royal Scottish Academy annual exhibitions, his first accepted work being a watercolour entitled *Scene from the Old English Baron* (exh. Royal Scottish Academy, 1844). In common with his Scottish contemporaries, many of Faed's early subjects were drawn from literary sources: he painted a series of incidents from Sir Walter Scott's novel *The Heart of Midlothian* in the late 1840s, and in 1849 he produced a major work, an imaginary group portrait entitled *Sir Walter Scott and his Friends at Abbotsford* (Scot. NPG). In recognition of his early success Faed was elected an associate of the Royal Scottish Academy in 1849 at the tender age of twenty-three. In 1851 he sent three works to the Royal Academy in London: all were hung and from then on he was a regular exhibitor there until 1893. The following year his painting of Scottish rural life, *The Patron and Patroness's Visit to the Village School* (1852, exh. RA, 1852; Dundee Museums and Art Galleries), was hung well in the Royal Academy. It demonstrated the popularity of Faed's paintings based on Scottish rural life and drawing heavily on his own childhood memories. At this stage in his career he laid emphasis on narrative, detail, and the fine qualities of light, contrasting with his later Scottish subjects, which were very heavily laden with sentiment, even poignancy.

In 1852, evidently encouraged by early success and following in the footsteps of other ambitious Scottish painters, Faed moved to London, where he was based for the rest of his life. He continued to paint subject pictures on Scottish themes, both individual figure subjects and also themes dealing with wider, serious issues. His painting *The Mitherless Bairn* (1855, exh. RA, 1855; National Gallery of Australia, Melbourne) was a great success in its day. It appealed to Victorian sentiment with its portrayal of an orphan child being taken in by poor cottagers; its depiction of anecdote from Scottish rural life followed in the popular tradition of Sir David Wilkie. During this middle period of Faed's career he also painted a series of works on the theme of Scottish emigration: his *Sunday in the Backwoods* (also called *The Scottish Emigrants' Sunday in the Backwoods*, 1859, exh. RA, 1859; Museum of Fine Arts, Montreal), for example, portrays the emigrants' struggle to honour the sabbath in the wilderness. This series culminated in *The Last of the Clan* of 1865 (exh. RA, 1865; Glasgow Museums and Art Galleries), which portrays the old and infirm remnants of the clan MacAlpine sadly watching all its young members sail away to the New World.

In 1861 Faed became an associate of the Royal Academy. Since moving to London he had resigned his associateship of the Royal Scottish Academy but, in recognition of his success in London, he became an honorary member of the Royal Scottish Academy in 1862. In 1864 he was elevated to the rank of academician in London and deposited a figure subject, *Ere Care Begins*, as his diploma work (1865; RA).

Shortly after his arrival in London Faed married, on 9 November 1852, Frances Mary Rand (b. 1829/30); they had a son and a daughter. There are many portraits of Faed, in which he cuts a dash as a dark, handsome, and well-dressed man; John Ballantyne's 1865 portrait *Thomas Faed in his Studio* (Scot. NPG) catches him *in situ*. As a successful artist Faed enjoyed prosperity not only through the sale of his works but also from the judicious sale of the copyright on many of his most popular paintings; published as prints, they were particularly successful in North America. Towards the end of his life Faed's eyesight deteriorated. He was forced to rely on exhibiting earlier paintings and gradually he ceased to appear at the Royal Academy altogether. He died at 20 Loudoun Road, St John's Wood, London, on 17 August 1900, and was survived by his two children, John Francis and Beatrice. JOANNA SODEN

Sources M. McKerrow, *The Faeds: a biography* (1982) · *Annual Report of the Council of the Royal Scottish Academy of Painting, Sculpture, and Architecture*, 73 (1900), 10–11 · *The Scotsman* (23 Aug 1900) · *The Times* (23 Aug 1900) · J. L. Caw, *Scottish painting past and present, 1620–1908* (1908), 164–6 · D. Irwin and F. Irwin, *Scottish painters at home and abroad, 1700–1900* (1975), 300–03 · C. B. de Laperriere, ed., *The Royal Scottish Academy exhibitors, 1826–1990*, 4 vols. (1991), vol. 2, pp. 29–31 · Graves, *RA exhibitors* · *DNB* · P. J. M. McEwan, *Dictionary of Scottish art and architecture* (1994), 196–7 · W. D. McKay, *The Scottish school of painting* (1906), 343–7 · m. cert. · d. cert. · *CGPLA Eng. & Wales* (1900)

Archives NL Scot., letters · Royal Scot. Acad., letters · U. Edin., letters | U. Nott., letters to Henry Septimus Sutton

Likenesses G. Faed, pencil drawing, 1852, Scot. NPG · H. Watkins, albumen print, 1856–9, NPG · D. Wilkie Wynfield, photograph, c.1860–1869, NPG · J. Ballantyne, oils, 1865, Scot. NPG · J. Pettie, portrait, 1884, Aberdeen Art Gallery, MacDonald collection · W. F. Douglas, oils, Scot. NPG · W. F. Douglas, oils, NPG · E. Edwards, photograph, NPG; repro. in L. Reeve, *Portraits of men of eminence*, 2 (1864) · Elliott & Fry, carte-de-visite, NPG · J. Faed, group portrait, wash, Scot. NPG · J. Faed, watercolour, Scot. NPG · G. Grenville Manton, group portrait, watercolour (*Conversazione at the Royal Academy, 1891*), NPG · Hay, carte-de-visite, NPG · Lock & Whitfield, woodburytype photograph, NPG; repro. in T. Cooper, *Men of mark: a gallery of contemporary portraits* (1880) · Lucas, carte-de-visite, NPG · Maull & Polyblank, carte-de-visite, NPG · J. Pettie, oils, RA · R. W. Robinson, photograph, NPG; repro. in *Members and Associates of the Royal Academy of Arts* (1891) · J. C. Tunny, photograph, Royal Scot. Acad.

Wealth at death £56,199 19s. 7d.: probate, 8 Sept 1900, *CGPLA Eng. & Wales*

Fáelán (*fl. 734*). *See under* Fáelán Amlabar (641/2–724).

Fáelán Amlabar [Fillan the Mute, Fáelchú mac Dorbéni, St Fillan] (641/2–724), abbot of Iona, is one of two saints commemorated under the name of Fillan in Scotland and often confused in the literature of the later middle ages; the epithet Amlabar means 'the Mute'. His seat was at Rotterns in Perthshire and, according to later traditions, he was buried at Strathfillan and his cult is associated with the Scottish king Robert I. Although a later genealogy made this Fáelán the son of the fifth-century Irish prince Óengus, son of Nad Fraích, a more likely identification is with the eighth-century ecclesiastic Fáelchú mac Dorbéni (Fáelán is the diminutive of Fáelchú). Fáelchú was elected abbot of the monastery of Iona on 29 August 716, at the age of seventy-four; he died in 724 and his feast is celebrated on 20 June. The other saint is the Irish cleric **Fáelán** (*fl. 734*) of Cluain Móescna in Meath, whose feast is 9 January and who was buried, according to local tradition, at Kilillin in Kintail. Later traditions make him the son of St *Kentigerna (Caintigern), daughter of the Leinster king Cellach Cualann; she died in 734. Dedications to St Fillan are found throughout Scotland, from Ross to Galloway and from Argyll to Fife. Perthshire has several, especially round Loch Earn, where are found the village of St Fillan's, the hill known as Dunfillan, and the river valley of Strathfillan.

Two precious relics of Fáelán are treasured at Edinburgh in the museum of the Society of Antiquaries of Scotland. They are his crozier and his bell. Of the crozier the earliest existing record is found in an inquiry (of which the original is preserved in the Breadalbane charter room at Taymouth Castle), held before a jury at Glendochart on 2 April 1428, as to the privileges attaching to its possession by the Dewar family. The name by which the crozier was then called was the *coygerach*, or, later, the *quigrich*, a form of the Gaelic *coigrioch* ('stranger, foreigner'). The name demonstrates that the authority of the crozier allowed its holder to travel out of his own district in pursuit of stolen property. It next appears in letters patent of James III, dated 11 July 1487, which testify that it had been in the possession of the same family from the days of Robert I. The Dewar owner emigrated to Canada after 1795, and all trace of the crozier was lost, until in 1859 it was found in the possession of a descendant of the emigrant. He, at the age of eighty-seven, desiring that the relic should be restored to Scotland, sold it on 30 December 1876, to be kept in the museum at Edinburgh. It is of silver gilt and ornamented with filigree work; but upon examination the silver was found to form an outer case enclosing an older staff of bronze or copper.

The second relic is the bell (which weighs 8 lb 14 oz). It was long preserved in an ancient churchyard in Strathfillan in Perthshire, where it was regarded as possessing great curative powers, especially in cases of insanity. It was stolen by an English traveller in 1798 and taken to Hertfordshire, where it remained until 1869, when it was restored to Scotland by Alexander Forbes, bishop of Brechin. Hector Boece (*d. 1536*) has linked the saint with the winning of the battle of Bannockburn by a legend, of which he is the sole narrator: that Robert I (Robert Bruce) was accustomed to carry about with him an arm of St Fillan, set in silver, as an amulet ensuring good fortune; that the chaplain to whose care it was entrusted brought only the empty case to the field, fearing that the fortune of war might lead to the loss of the precious contents; but that the night before the battle the case was suddenly heard to open and close itself, and on examination it was found that the arm had returned to its place. Boece puts in the mouth of the king a reference to this miracle in his speech to his army before the battle. Robert I's veneration for the saint is indicated by his provision, on 26 February 1318, of an Augustinian canon to celebrate divine service in the church of St Fillan at Strathfillan. Later in the same year William, bishop of Dunkeld, promoted the church to a priory, and in 1329, shortly before his death, funds were granted by Robert for building expenses.

W. D. MACRAY, *rev.* BENJAMIN T. HUDSON

Sources A. P. Forbes, *Kalendars of Scottish saints* (1872) · W. J. Watson, *The history of the Celtic place-names of Scotland* (1926) · *Félire Óengusso Céli Dé / The martyrology of Oengus the Culdee*, ed. and trans. W. Stokes, HBS, 29 (1905) · *Ann. Ulster* · D. E. Easson, *Medieval religious houses, Scotland* (1957) · J. Anderson, *Scotland in early Christian times* (1881)

Fáelchú mac Dorbéni (*d. 724*). *See under* Iona, abbots of (*act. 563–927*).

Fagan, James Bernard (1873–1933), actor, theatre manager, and playwright, was born in Belfast on 18 May 1873, the eldest of the five children (three boys and two girls) of Sir John Fagan (1843–1930), consulting surgeon, and his wife, Mary Catherine, *née* Hughes, both of Belfast. He was educated at Clongowes Wood College near Clane, co. Kildare, and at Trinity College, Oxford. Originally intended for holy orders, he studied for the bar, but entered employment for a short time in the Indian Civil Service. He joined the dramatic company of F. R. Benson for two years, making his acting début in October 1895. He was engaged by Sir Herbert Beerbohm Tree for two years (1897–9) at Her Majesty's Theatre, London, appearing in, among others, *Katherine and Petruchio*, *A Man's Shadow*, *Julius Caesar*, *The Musketeers*, and *Carnac Sahib*. He married in 1897 the actress (Susan) Elizabeth Kirby.

Fagan then retired from the stage but embarked on a fruitful career as a dramatist. His first play was *The Rebels* (1899), followed by *The Prayer of the Sword* (1904); *Under which King*, the revue *Shakespeare v. Shaw*, and *Hawthorne, USA* (all 1905; the last filmed in 1919); *Gloria* (1907); *A Merry Devil* and *False Gods*, his translation of Eugène Brieux's *La foi* (1909); *The Dressing Room* (1910); *Bella donna* (1911; adapted from Robert Hitchens's novel and filmed in 1915 and 1923); and *The Happy Island* (1913). It was in 1913 that he returned to the stage, touring as the Rt Hon. Denzil Trevena in his own 1909 play *The Earth*. Divorced from his first wife, Fagan married in 1914 Ada Bevan, daughter of Edward Bevan ap Rees Bryant; she acted under the name Mary Grey. They had a daughter.

In March 1917 Fagan became a producer, débuting at St Martin's Theatre, London, with the controversial Brieux play *Damaged Goods*. After producing *The Wonder Tales* and *The Little Brother* at the Ambassadors', he revived *Damaged Goods* when he took over the management of the Royal Court. Here he sought to establish a permanent home for Shakespeare in the West End:

> His revivals of *Twelfth Night*, *The Merchant of Venice*, *Henry the Fourth (Part one)* [actually *2 Henry IV*] and *A Midsummer Night's Dream* [between 1918 and 1921] were memorable for their freshness, sanity and distinction, and deserve a place in theatrical history. (*The Times*, 25 Feb 1933, 14b)

The Merchant of Venice transferred to the Duke of York's and here Fagan also produced *The Government Inspector* and *Madame Sand* (both 1920).

Meanwhile Fagan had written *The Fourth of August* (1914), *Doctor O'Toole* (1917), and *The Wheel* and *Treasure Island*, adapted from Robert Louis Stevenson's novel (both 1922). The last-named was staged as a Christmas play every year until 1931. In 1923 he opened the Oxford Playhouse, staging many productions there, the repertory including Ibsen, Strindberg, and Shaw. The young company he formed included Flora Robson, John Gielgud, Tyrone Guthrie, and Raymond Massey.

Fagan continued to stage notable productions in London: these included Chekhov's *The Cherry Orchard* at the Lyric, Hammersmith, and O'Casey's *Juno and the Paycock* at the Royalty (both 1925), the former being chiefly responsible for the acceptance of Chekhov on the English stage; O'Casey's *The Plough and the Stars* at the Fortune and his own play *And So to Bed*, 'an adventure with Pepys', at the Queen's (both 1926); and Strindberg's *The Spook Sonata* at the Globe (1927). He wrote *The Greater Love* (1927) and adapted *The Beetle* (1928); earlier that year he was in New York producing *And So to Bed* at the Shubert followed by *The Cherry Orchard* at the Bijou, appearing himself as Leonid Gayev. The following year he became a director of the Festival Theatre in Cambridge.

Fagan was also responsible for many productions of the Irish Players, but was soon again in America, this time in Hollywood, where his play *The Wheel* was being filmed by the Paramount studio as *The Wheel of Life*. In 1932 he supplied the dialogue for MGM's Norma Shearer/Fredric March/Leslie Howard production *Smilin' Through* and he co-scripted Paramount's *Forgotten Commandments*. After his death his play *Bella donna* was again filmed, in 1934, and in 1946 (as *Temptation*). One of his final plays, *The Improper Duchess* (1931), was filmed in Britain in 1936. Away from the theatre he pursued his interest in golf and tennis. Following a severe bout of influenza, Fagan died of a heart attack, at 6665 Emmett Terrace, Hollywood, California, on 17 February 1933. His funeral took place at Monks Horton church, near Hythe in Kent, on 20 March. His wife survived him.   ROBERT SHARP

Sources *The Times* (18 Feb 1933), 12c · W. B. Adams, memoir, *The Times* (25 Feb 1933), 14b · *Who was who in the theatre, 1912–1976*, 4 vols. (1978) · *DNB* · *WWW* · *CGPLA Eng. & Wales* (1933)
Archives BL, corresp. with Society of Authors, Add. MS 56703 | SOUND BL NSA, performance recording
Wealth at death £6016 11s. 5d.: administration with will, 9 Dec 1933, *CGPLA Eng. & Wales*

Fagan, Louis Alexander (1845–1903), etcher and writer, was born on 7 February 1845 in Naples, Italy, the second son in a family of three sons and four daughters of George Fagan (*d.* 1869), a diplomatist, and his wife, Maria, the daughter of Louis Carbone, an officer in the Italian army. Robert *Fagan (1761–1816), diplomat and amateur portrait painter, was his grandfather. His elder brother, Joseph George (*d.* 1908), served in India as a major-general; the younger, Charles Edward, became secretary of the British Museum (Natural History). His father became attaché to the British legation at Naples in 1837 and in this capacity assisted the efforts of Anthony *Panizzi to free political prisoners in 1851; then, after several postings in South and Central America, served as minister and consul-general to Venezuela (1865–9).

Fagan was brought up in Naples until 1860, when he was sent to Leytonstone School in Essex. In England, Anthony Panizzi became his guardian and lifelong friend. As a youth, Fagan carried letters from Panizzi to the revolutionary leaders in the kingdom of the Two Sicilies. On leaving school he entered the Foreign Office, and soon served as attaché, first with Sir James Hudson in Turin, and then in Paris. From 1866 to 1868 he worked under his father as assistant clerk to the British legation in Venezuela, and in 1868 became clerk to the commission for the settlement of British claims against Venezuela.

When his father died of yellow fever at Caracas in 1869 Fagan returned to England, and in October of that year, on Panizzi's recommendation, he obtained a post of assistant in the department of prints and drawings at the British Museum. His sociability and activities as a writer seem to have led to friction with the keeper, George W. Reid, who reported to the trustees in 1882 that 'Mr Fagan's frequent consultations in the print-room with artists, writers, publishers, and printers, whom he employs, caused complete neglect of his duties of supervision' (Reid MSS, British Museum archives). He rose to the position of senior assistant in 1887 but resigned on account of ill health in July 1892. On 8 November 1887 he married Caroline Frances, the daughter of James Purves of Melbourne, Australia.

Fagan published a number of works on art, mostly relating to the collections at the museum, including an introduction to *The Works of Correggio* (1873); *Catalogo dei disegni … di Michelangelo Buonarroti esistenti in Inghilterra*, in volume 2 of *Vita di Michelangelo Buonarroti*, ed. A. Gotti (1875); the almost completely obsolete *Handbook to the Department of Prints and Drawings in the British Museum* (1876); a translation of M. Minghetti's *The Masters of Raffaello* (1882); *Collectors'*

Marks (1883); *The Art of Michel'Angelo Buonarroti … in the British Museum* (1883); *Raffaello Sanzio, his Sonnet in the British Museum* (1884); *Engravings by F. Bartolozzi … in the British Museum* (1885); *The Engraved Works of William Woollett* (1885); *The Engraved Works of William Faithorne* (1888); *Mezzotint Engravings Relating to Ireland or to Irish Artists* (1888); *An Easy Walk through the British Museum* (1891); and a *History of Engraving in England* (1893). Many of the ninety-two entries that Fagan wrote for the *Dictionary of National Biography* were also on artists.

Fagan was an artist in his own right and illustrated many of his own books. Most of his etchings depict Italian scenes and peasants and include *Views and Costumes of Naples* (exh. RA, 1877), *Macaroni Eaters*, and *Salerno* (exh. RA, 1887), which appeared in a volume of twelve etchings called *Souvenirs of Southern Italy* (1873); impressions of each may be found in the British Museum and in the Victoria and Albert Museum. Fagan was made an honorary member of the Société des Artistes Graveurs au Burin de France (before 1884). His known drawings include *Guards' Sergeant* (*c*.1879, British Museum), *Corporal* (1879, British Museum), *Anne Marie Fagan*, and *Self-Portrait* (ex Lieutenant William Lewis Clinton Baker, 1 June 1945). His works are signed 'L. Fagan' or 'Louis Fagan'.

Panizzi died in Fagan's arms in April 1879, having been nursed by his younger companion since an illness of 1868. Fagan received Gladstone's commendation for his *Life of Sir Anthony Panizzi* (1880), which included his etching of Panizzi, after G. F. Watts, as the frontispiece (exh. RA, 1878; impressions in the British Museum and the Victoria and Albert Museum). As literary executor, he edited the *Lettere ad Antonio Panizzi di uomini illustri e di amici italiani, 1823–1870* (1880) and Prosper Mérimée's *Lettres à M. Panizzi* (1881), which he translated into English and Italian.

Always sociable, Fagan was a member of the Arts Club and the Reform Club, and wrote a history of the latter: *1836–1886 the Reform Club: its Founders and Architect* (1887). He travelled widely giving popular lectures on art, including the Lowell lectures at Boston in 1891. While visiting Australia in 1891 he advised the trustees of the National Gallery of Victoria, Melbourne, on the purchasing and arrangement of their collection, his opinions being recorded in a printed report. He was justice of the peace of the county of Middlesex. Panizzi's friend Prosper Mérimée, with whom Fagan stayed in Paris in September 1869, summed up his cosmopolitan nature in this way: 'conservant malgré toutes les nationalités par où il a passé l'air de *l'English boy*' (Fagan, *Panizzi*, 2.275). On his retirement from the museum he returned to live in Italy and built his home, the Villino Francesca, on the viale Principe Eugenio in Florence, where he died suddenly on 5 January 1903.   DANIEL PARKER

Sources DNB · *The Times* (8 Jan 1903) · *Magazine of Art*, 27 (1902–3), 311–12 · L. Fagan, *The life of Sir Anthony Panizzi*, 2 vols. (1880) · L. A. Fagan, preface, *A descriptive catalogue of the engraved works of William Faithorne* (1888) · E. Miller, *Prince of librarians: the life and times of Antonio Panizzi of the British Museum* (1967) · Bénézit, *Dict.*, 3rd edn · Thieme & Becker, *Allgemeines Lexikon*, vol. 11 · Graves, *RA exhibitors*, vol. 3 · A. T. C. Pratt, ed., *People of the period: being a collection of biographies of upwards of six thousand living celebrities*, 2 vols. (1897) ·

Bryan, *Painters* (1903–5), vol. 2 · I. Zdanowicz, 'Prints of fortune: Hubert Herkomer's 1891–92 etching purchases for the National Gallery of Victoria', *Art Bulletin of Victoria*, 33 (1993), 1–17 · L. B. Cox, *The National Gallery of Victoria 1861 to 1968: a search for a collection* (1970), 47–8 · BM, Reid MSS · Gladstone, *Diaries* · CGPLA Eng. & Wales (1903)
Archives BM, works and MSS
Likenesses J. S. Sargent, oils, 1894, Arts Club, London; repro. in *Magazine of Art*, 311
Wealth at death £1533 7s. 3d.: probate, 19 Feb 1903, CGPLA Eng. & Wales

Fagan, Robert (1761–1816), art dealer and portrait painter, the son of Michael Fagan (1728–1783), was born on 5 March 1761. The Fagans were from Cork, but his father had a successful bakery business at Long Acre, London, which was probably Fagan's birthplace. Reputedly a pupil of Bartolozzi, he was admitted to the Royal Academy Schools in 1781, though in the same year, with his fellow student Charles Grignion, he also went to Rome. He returned to London, presumably because of his father's illness, but by 1784 he was back in Rome, where he soon began to deal in pictures and to paint portraits, in the neo-classical style, of fashionable English visitors. On 23 April 1790 he married Anna Maria Aloisa Rosa Ferri (1773–1800), evidently the daughter of an employee of the powerful Cardinal Rezzonico. Some British residents, such as the writer Cornelia Knight and her mother and the sculptor Joseph Nollekens, are reported to have found his social climbing most objectionable. His surviving portraits of that period (now in priv. coll.) include those of Sylvia Cotton (later Lady Mainwaring), Sir Corbet Corbet and his wife, and Elizabeth Webster (later Lady Holland)—which Lord Bristol, bishop of Derry, rather naughtily kept at the foot of his bed. According to the Irish sculptor Christopher Hewetson, Fagan also copied old masters and had commissions for these from 'William Penn of Pennsylvania'. Seventeen of his *trompe-l'œil* grisailles were bought by the second Lord Berwick and are now at Attingham Hall, near Shrewsbury. Fagan's narcissistic self-portrait (*c*.1803, Limerick Museum, Éire), with his bare-breasted and adoring second wife, reveals a handsome man, regular-featured with arched eyebrows and wavy hair, carefully arranged.

In 1792 Fagan was excavating at Gabii with Gavin Hamilton, and by 1794 at Laurentum and Ostia in alliance with Sir Corbet Corbet and Prince Augustus Frederick, later duke of Sussex. There were rich rewards from these diggings; some of them were bought by the prince of Wales, including the *Venus Campo Iemini* (now in the British Museum), while others were destined for the Vatican and Lateran museums. Among other items, Fagan found two important busts—of the fourth-century BC priestess Corinna and of Licinius Sura, one of Trajan's generals; both are now in the Munich Glyptothek. Fagan is also credited with having discovered the first mithraeum at Ostia.

The French invasion of Italy in 1796 and Napoleon's intention of confiscating works of art caused panic among Roman princes. Fagan bought two landscapes by Claude Lorrain at bargain prices from Prince Altieri, and with Charles Grignion smuggled them out of Rome, an exciting Scarlet Pimpernel-type story involving Fagan's temporary imprisonment in Castel Sant'Angelo and a near shipwreck. For a while the pictures were owned by William Beckford; they are now at Anglesey Abbey near Cambridge. Fagan managed to return to Rome, where he set about excavating at Tor Boaccina and elsewhere—only to have many of his treasures (valued at £3000) seized by the French. He fled to Sicily, but was persuaded by Sir William Hamilton to go to Florence, in effect as a spy. After more adventures he returned to Rome, once again making shipments of important princely heirlooms and antiquities: one of these, *Titian's Schoolmaster* by Giovanni Battista Moroni, is now at the National Gallery of Art at Washington. Fagan's much neglected wife died in 1800, and immediately he married Maria Ludovica Francesca Geltrude Flajani, the beautiful fifteen-year-old daughter of a surgeon. From 1800 to 1807 he was mainly in Naples, the pope having forbidden indiscriminate excavations around Rome; here he continued with his portrait painting, and—needless to say—some lucrative excavating at Pompeii. Among the works painted at this time is his fine portrait of a Polish lawyer, Gabriel Taszycki, and his wife (now in the Warsaw National Museum). In 1807 Fagan and his family had to emigrate to Palermo; meanwhile, rich young William Baker, heir to Bayfordbury in Hertfordshire, had fallen in love with Estina, the daughter of Fagan and his first wife.

Having failed to prevent the marriage, Baker's father persuaded the foreign secretary, George Canning, to appoint Fagan consul-general for Sicily and Malta, a post for which he had for long been pestering Nelson and Sir William Hamilton; this was confirmed on 7 June 1809. Sicily by now was occupied by the British and the many political complications appear to have been well handled by Fagan, leading to a reconfirmation of the appointment in 1811. He still found time to excavate at Tyndaris and to make shipments of antiquities to England. He again painted portraits of English aristocrats, including the children of Lord Amherst (National Gallery of Ireland), and Lady Acton and her children (priv. coll.); these works were in a harsher style than hitherto and not so successful. He charmed the unhappy Queen Maria Carolina and became her confidant in her quarrels with the minister-plenipotentiary, Lord William Bentinck (her outpourings in letters to Fagan are in the British Library). Thanks to the queen, he obtained new permits for excavating at Tyndaris and Selinunte.

Baker died in 1813, and in consequence Fagan, in 1814, had permission to return to England. Instead he stopped in Rome, in order to recover property and hoping to become consul there. Social life obviously went to his head, and the pope even asked his advice on political matters. Fagan, however, became seriously ill, but recovered and instead of returning to London went to Naples, again behaving grandly and indiscreetly. He was also in serious financial trouble. Ordered by the British government to return to Sicily, he nevertheless did at last visit London in 1815, but by January was back in Rome, once more ill. On 26 August 1816 he committed suicide, by throwing himself out of a window. He was buried in Rome. His widow

was left in some difficulty, but eventually remarried. In 1817 she sold to the Vatican a colossal mask of Neptune that Fagan had excavated at Hadrian's villa, and in 1818–20 several objects to the archaeological museum in Palermo, all now on view. Their daughter Emilia, Maria Carolina's goddaughter, died young; their son George became a diplomat in Naples and South America. The widowed Estina Baker later married Francis Acton, nephew (and brother-in-law) of Sir John Acton, prime minister of Naples.

RALEIGH TREVELYAN

Sources R. Trevelyan, 'Robert Fagan, an Irish bohemian in Italy', *Apollo*, 96 (1972), 298–311 · R. Trevelyan, 'Robert Fagan, un inglese in Sicilia', *Kalos* [Palermo], anno 5/6 (Nov–Dec 1993), 6–15 · B. de Breffny, 'Robert Fagan, artist', *The Irish Ancestor*, 3/2 (1971), 20–28 · A. Crookshank and the Knight of Glin [D. Fitzgerald], eds., *Irish portraits, 1660–1860* (1969) [exhibition catalogue, Dublin, London, and Belfast, 14 Aug 1969 – 9 March 1970] · N. Figgis, 'Robert Fagan', *A dictionary of British and Irish travellers in Italy, 1701–1800*, ed. J. Ingamells (1997) · R. Trevelyan, *Princes under the volcano* (1972) · Cumberland MSS, BL, MS 36496 · Fagan MSS, BL, Add. MS 36730 · Nelson MSS, BL, Add. MSS 34915, 34930 · Heyterbury MSS, BL, Add. MS 4138 · *Lady Knight's letters from France and Italy*, ed. Lady Elliot-Drake (1905) · church records, Santa Maria del Popolo, Rome, 1789, 1790, 1791 · church records, San Lorenzo, Lucina, Rome, 1797, 1799, 1814 · church records, Santa Maria, via Lata, Rome, 1799, 1806 · W. T. Whitley, *Artists and their friends in England, 1700–1799*, 2 (1928) · J. Zoëga, *Ab Handlungen Herausgegeben* (1817) · A. Michaelis, *Ancient marbles in Great Britain*, trans. C. A. M. Fennell (1882) · A. Salinas, *Memorie*, 4 (1873) · *DNB* · private information (2004)
Archives BL, corresp. and papers relating to Sicily, Add. MS 36730, fols. 1–59 | U. Nott. L., department of manuscripts and special collections, corresp. with Lord William Bentinck
Likenesses R. Fagan, self-portrait, *c*.1803 (with his second wife), Limerick Museum

Fage, Arthur (1890–1977), aerodynamicist, was born on 4 March 1890 at Portsmouth, the youngest in a family of two sons and two daughters born to William John Fage (1859–1947), coppersmith at Portsmouth Dockyard, and his wife, Annie Crook (1862–1943). Educated at Portsmouth secondary school from 1901 to 1904, Fage successfully competed for a shipwright apprenticeship at Portsmouth Dockyard, where he met Ernest Relf (1888–1970), who was to become his lifelong friend and professional colleague. The dockyard apprenticeships, combining practice with study at the Royal Dockyard School, provided a thorough and rigorous training. Fage survived the course, carried off three Admiralty prizes, and spent his fifth year at the Haslar ship tank, with evening classes at Portsmouth Municipal College, where he won prizes for mathematics and theoretical mechanics. In 1909 he won a royal exhibition to the Royal College of Science, South Kensington, where he chose to specialize in mechanics. He enjoyed sports, played football and cricket, and for many years was an enthusiastic long-distance walker, touring in England, Scotland, Germany, and Switzerland.

At the end of three years Fage, who had achieved the highest marks in all subjects and a first class associateship of the Royal College of Science, was offered a research scholarship tenable at the National Physical Laboratory (NPL), Teddington, to work on a topic allied to aeronautics.

Arthur Fage (1890–1977), by Walter Stoneman

Relf had preceded him as a junior assistant in the aeronautics section, and Fage joined for a two-year spell as student assistant, assigned to a variety of projects. He obtained his diploma of Imperial College in 1914 and, as the First World War coincided with the end of his studentship, he was formally appointed to the staff of the NPL.

At this time the science of aerodynamics was ill-defined, its components, such as fluid mechanics, pressure distribution on the ground and on aircraft and airships in flight, and its effect on their structure and component materials, little known. Fage and his colleagues undertook research on many of these aspects. During 1914 he wrote a popular book, *The Aeroplane* (1915), into which he managed to compress the whole of aeronautical engineering, with little mathematics. The book was immediately popular; by 1918 it was in its fifth edition and had also been published in the USA. After the war Fage continued his investigations into the theory and practical engineering of airscrews and published extensively; in 1917–18 he had lectured around Britain. He became ultimately a world authority on this topic. This expertise led to his specialist monograph, *Airscrews in Theory and Experiment* (1920). He married on 1 September 1920 a colleague from the NPL physics department, Winifred Eliza (d. 1951), a botany graduate and daughter of Thomas H. Donnelly, master builder, of Kimberley, Nottinghamshire. It was a most happy marriage.

Their son, John Donnelly Fage (b. 1921), rose to eminence as a professor of African history; their daughter, Christine Mary Fage, later Richards (b. 1924), joined the staff of the University of Durham.

By 1925 Fage had turned to the extremely complex problem of pure fluid mechanics and turbulence. He had already looked at the lift and drag, slipstream effects, and wake turbulence set up by aerofoils; now he concentrated on experimental work associated with these movements, both in free air and within pipes. With H. C. H. Townend he devised the fluid motion microscope, which enabled him to study under high magnification the movement of illuminated ultramicroscopic particles in turbulent water, and to apply the results to similar motions in air. This fruitful research was publicized in numerous papers in the aeronautical and scientific literature, and in his many lectures. It brought Fage, since 1918 a fellow of the Royal Aeronautical Society, the Edward Busk memorial prize (1928), founder membership of the (American) Institute of the Aeronautical Sciences (1933), corresponding membership of the Lilienthal Gesellschaft für Luftfahrtforschung (1937)—he travelled to Berlin in 1936 and Munich in 1937—and, in 1942, election to the Royal Society.

With the outbreak of the Second World War and the arrival of high-speed aircraft, Fage and his colleagues at the NPL were confronted with problems of transonic and supersonic flow. On 1 January 1946 he succeeded Relf as superintendent of the aerodynamics division. New wind tunnels were built to assist with problems of high-speed aerodynamics, in which he took a close interest. However, administrative duties precluded any further personal research, for much of his time was spent on committee work with the Aeronautical Research Council, various government departments, and aircraft companies, and necessarily involved lengthy overseas travel. Following the death of his wife in 1951 Fage lost his zest for work, and he retired from the NPL in June 1953, being then appointed CBE. He continued to travel abroad, and about 1955 moved to Winchelsea, where he took up painting. He returned to Teddington for five years, then gave up his committee work and moved to Yockleton, Shropshire, to be near his daughter. He died at Yockleton Grange on 7 November 1977. An obituarist summed him up as 'one who had led a full life, and had done more than most men. He was widely respected, and held in high esteem and indeed affection by the colleagues of his later years and by others close to him' (Collar, 49). ANITA MCCONNELL

Sources A. R. Collar, *Memoirs FRS*, 24 (1978), 33–53 · A. Fage, 'Early days: memories of people and places', *Journal of the Royal Aeronautical Society*, 70 (1966), 91–2 · *WWW* · *CGPLA Eng. & Wales* (1978) · b. cert. · d. cert.

Likenesses W. Stoneman, photograph, RS [see illus.] · photograph, repro. in Collar, *Memoirs FRS*

Wealth at death £41,385: probate, 10 Jan 1978, *CGPLA Eng. & Wales*

Fage, Mary (*fl.* 1637), poet, has until very recently been known only as the 'wife of Robert Fage the younger, Gentleman', as she is identified on the title-page of *Fames*

Roule (1637), her one published work. It is, however, possible that she was the daughter of Edward Fage (*d.* 1638) of Doddinghurst, Essex, that she married her kinsman Robert Fage, and that this kinsman was the Ro: Fage who published a translation of *Peter Ramus of Vermandois … his Dialectica* (1632): the preliminary matter of this book indicates that the author had Essex connections.

Fames Roule was published in 1637, with a dedicatory poem by Thomas Heywood. It is a collection of over 400 acrostic verses and anagrams, playing on the names and titles of eminent figures at court, and arranged in order of precedence, beginning with Carolus Stuarte: 'Av! Sol's Tru Trace'. Its sheer volume (nearly 300 quarto pages), even for a period that delighted in word play and in which the acrostic and anagram were often overworked, is extraordinary.

Despite the work's familiarity with the court structure, and its tone of support for the embattled Caroline court, it has not been possible to place either Mary or Robert Fage there, and there are occasional gaps and mistaken identifications, which could suggest that the author lived at one remove from her subject. *Fames Roule* might have been an effort to secure patronage through a species of shotgun flattery, although Fage's attempt to wrest meanings from names and titles suggests another context for *Fames Roule*, the genre of prophecy: in this case, the reading of fortunes and secular prophecy that was to appeal to so many women in the latter part of the seventeenth century.

BETTY S. TRAVITSKY

Sources B. S. Travitsky, 'Relations of power, relations to power, and power(ful) relations: Mary Fage, Robert Fage, and *Fames roule*', *Pilgrimage for love: essays in early modern literature, Festschrift in honor of Josephine A. Roberts*, ed. S. King (1999), 95–112 · K. Walker, *Women writers of the English Renaissance* (1996) · W. C. Metcalfe, ed., *The visitations of Essex*, 1, Harleian Society, 13 (1878) · *VCH Essex*, vol. 9 · Harleian Society, register section, 89 vols. (1877–1977) · P. Morant, *The history and antiquities of the county of Essex*, 2 vols. (1768) · G. Rickword, 'Members of parliament for Colchester, 1559–1603', *Essex Review*, 4 (1895), 235–45 · parish register, Doddinghurst, Essex

Fagg, Bernard Evelyn Buller (1915–1987), archaeologist and museum curator, was born on 8 December 1915 in Upper Norwood, London, the son of William Percy Fagg, antiquarian bookseller, and his wife, Lilian (*née* Buller). His brother was William Buller *Fagg. He went to school at Woodford and at Dulwich College, and then entered Downing College, Cambridge, where he read classics in part one of the tripos and archaeology and anthropology in part two (in those days archaeology and anthropology could be read only in part two). He became one of that band of Cambridge undergraduates who 'took archaeology to Africa'.

After taking his degree at Cambridge, Fagg was accepted as a cadet for the colonial administrative service and did his colonial service training course at Oxford. In July 1939 he was posted to the provincial administration of Plateau province in Nigeria, stationed at Jos. On the outbreak of war he enlisted in the 1st field company of the west African engineers, and served in east Africa. He used his army leave there to work with Louis and Mary Leakey. Through them he met Mary Catherine Davidson (*b.* 1915), a teacher, whom he married in 1942. He was recalled in 1943 to Nigeria, where he was assigned to an administrative department in Jos formed to promote the production of tin, which the allies urgently needed following the occupation of the Malayan tin sources by the Japanese.

At Jos, Fagg devoted all his spare time to field research into the prehistoric remains of the area in the form of finds and field monuments, and in this was ably assisted by his wife, who had been trained by working with Mary Leakey in east Africa. His first preliminary excavation was at the Ropp rock shelter, where he discovered a late Stone Age occupation containing microliths.

It was fortunate that Fagg's job kept him closely in touch with tin production, because it was from the diggings for this mineral that a remarkable series of terracotta figurines was being unearthed. As soon as one of these terracotta figurines came to Fagg's notice in 1943, he recognized its importance and uniqueness, and its similarity to one found in 1928 near the village of Nok. Following the archaeological practice of the time, Fagg assigned the name of this first find place to the culture which had produced the figurines. In subsequent years many more figurines in the same style came to light and Fagg was responsible for their preservation. He subsequently wrote more than a dozen articles about them in scientific and art journals, and in 1977 a beautifully illustrated book, *Nok Terracottas*, was published by Ethnographica and the National Museum, Lagos, which enabled the public to appreciate their beauty and significance. Fagg succeeded in dating the Nok figurines to the last centuries BC, which greatly added to their interest. He also discovered and excavated the site of Taruga, where figurine material was associated with iron smelting furnaces. These were dated to the last half of the first millennium BC and were at the time the earliest such known from sub-Saharan Africa.

Soon after the end of the Second World War, Kenneth Murray had persuaded the Nigerian government of the importance of preserving the country's rich heritage of material culture, and he was appointed to the newly created post of surveyor of antiquities. In 1947 Fagg was appointed his number two as assistant surveyor of antiquities. When Murray retired in 1957 Fagg was appointed director of the new department of antiquities, covering the whole of Nigeria. He appreciated the urgent need to house the growing collections of traditional material culture and prehistoric remains, and to provide facilities for their study, conservation, and display. He himself designed, and built with direct labour, the Jos Museum, opened in 1952, only the second public museum in British West Africa. It was soon to be followed by the establishment of the Ife Museum (1954), the Nigerian Museum in Lagos, the Oron Museum, the Gidan Makama Museum in Kano, and the Museum Gallery in Kaduna in 1959. Fagg realized the need for trained staff for museums throughout tropical Africa, and in collaboration with UNESCO and with the support of the federal government of Nigeria he established at Jos a bilingual (English-French) training centre for museum technicians. In 1961 he was elected president of the Museums Association of Tropical Africa, and in 1962 he was made an MBE.

In 1963 Fagg was appointed curator of the Pitt Rivers Museum in Oxford. The university recognized that the museum, although having unique collections, was seriously overcrowded and suffered the constraints of the provisions of its founder. Fagg was chosen to overcome these difficulties and to create a worthy modern museum. He came up with a clever design to reconcile Pitt Rivers's testamentary request for the continuation of his typological principles with the advantages of geographical arrangement. This innovative idea was given effect in Pier Luigi Nervi's design for a new museum to be located on a site on the Banbury Road. Unfortunately the university lacked the necessary money. During this period Fagg spent most of his energies trying to reconcile the dissensions the plan had aroused and to raise the necessary funds, but no wealthy benefactor was found to solve the financial problem within the time limit set by the university. The strain told on Fagg and in May 1968 he suffered a severe stroke which confined him thereafter to a wheelchair. So, sadly, Nervi's plans became a historical relic of a noble plan that failed. Bernard Fagg retired in 1975; he died at his home, 45 Woodstock Road, Oxford, on 14 August 1987 and was cremated at Oxford crematorium. He was survived by his wife.   THURSTAN SHAW

Sources personal knowledge (2004) · private information (2004) [M. Fagg] · *The Independent* (22 Aug 1987) · *The Times* (19 Aug 1987) · *Antiquity*, 61 (1987), 362 · *West Africa* (24 Aug 1987) · *Daily Telegraph* (16 Nov 1987) · *Nigeria Newsletter* (22 Aug 1987) · d. cert.
Archives Jos Museum, Nigeria · priv. coll.
Likenesses photograph, priv. coll.

Fagg, Sir John. *See* Fagge, Sir John, first baronet (1627–1701).

Fagg, William [Bill] **Buller** (1914–1992), ethnologist and art historian, was born on 28 April 1914 at 24 St Aubyn's Road, Upper Norwood, London, the elder son and first of two children of William Percy Fagg (d. 1939), antiquarian bookseller, and his wife, Lilian, *née* Buller. He attended nearby Dulwich College and then went to Magdalene College, Cambridge, where he studied classics (1933–6) and archaeology and anthropology (1936–7), obtaining two BA degrees and prizes for Latin hexameters and epigrams.

In 1938 Fagg started work as an assistant keeper in the ethnography department of the British Museum, which employed him until he retired, save for the wartime years 1940–45, when he monitored corduroy output for the industries and manufactures department of the Board of Trade. At the close of the war, when the British Museum reconstructed its exhibitions, the ethnography department decided that individual curators should take responsibility for the collections from specific continents. Africa was assigned to Fagg, probably because none of his superiors wanted it. As he reviewed the artefacts coming out of storage to choose the best for display, however, he developed a deep love for African art that led to his lifelong immersion in its study. West Africa had produced masterpieces of sculpture, he felt, whose greatness deserved acclaim without qualification. They received from him

the kind of scholarly attention hitherto reserved for European works. One of his first concerns, indeed, was to establish that some of the finest examples were of purely African inspiration and execution. Seized during the British punitive expedition of 1897, the Benin bronzes in the British Museum appeared so sophisticated that European experts had tried to argue that the Edo-speakers who created them must have been influenced by the Portuguese. Fagg devised a chronology of the Benin treasures that represented the first serious attempt to classify African art historically and stylistically.

Fagg led a quiet home life with his widowed mother in the suburb of Barnes, whence he cycled to the museum in Bloomsbury each day. He grew friendly with artists such as Jacob Epstein, Fred Uhlman, and Josef Herman, who shared his admiration for African art, and Leon Underwood taught him the practicalities of lost-wax casting, the process most often used in Africa. While accumulating an encyclopaedic knowledge of tribal pieces in other museums and private collections, he also secured much fresh information from fieldwork. The great majority of African sculptures surviving from past centuries came from Nigeria, so it was there that his endeavours were concentrated—with visits in 1949–50, 1953, 1958–9, 1971, 1974, and 1981—though his research also took him to the Belgian Congo, Mali, and Cameroon. His brother, Bernard *Fagg (1915–1987), a colonial service official, founded the first museums in Nigeria and then headed the federal department of antiquities in Lagos (1957–63). Bill aimed to identify the distinctive artistic styles, not merely of various tribes, but of villages, workshops, and individuals. Among the artists whose output he recorded were Bamgboye of Odo-Owa, Areogun of Osi-Ilorin, and, above all, Olowe of Ise (c.1875–1938), sculptor to the kings of Yorubaland. Where no name could be ascertained, he devised sobriquets which became widely accepted, such as the Master of the Buli or the Master of the Circled Cross.

Promoted to deputy keeper of the ethnographical collections at the British Museum in 1955, Fagg was a longstanding member of the Royal Anthropological Institute, serving as honorary secretary (1939–56) and vice-president (1963–73) as well as meticulously editing its journal *Man* from 1945 until 1965. The controversies that divided British anthropologists did not greatly exercise him, though the separation of physical and social anthropology into discrete disciplines seemed to him undesirable. He judged it the role of scholars to appreciate the achievements of other cultures as well as to analyse them: connoisseurship need never conflict with social science. He sought to place African art within the context of African social history.

Fagg was a portly, bespectacled man with blunt, heavy features. The marked slowness of his utterance concealed his intelligence from strangers (and this had nothing to do with the mild stroke that he suffered in 1967). There was an air of torpor about him which could prove downright exasperating for people of vigorous temperament, along with his habit of whistling classical music. A dull lecturer, he came across best at small gatherings, where he enjoyed sharing his expertise in unhurried conversation. His interests included literature and religion. He was a practising Roman Catholic.

A late riser by preference, Fagg wrote his articles and books at night, slowly and eloquently, making use of his large collection of photographs. *The Sculpture of Africa* (1958), *Afro-Portuguese Ivories* (1959), and *Nigerian Images* (1963) earned him recognition as the principal English-speaking authority on African sculpture. In 1960 he organized an exhibition for the Arts Council to mark Nigerian independence, and his contribution in 1966 to the First World Congress of Negro Arts and Cultures held in Dakar, Senegal, led to his being appointed CMG in 1967. The Museum of Primitive Art in New York (later part of the Metropolitan Museum) engaged him as a consulting fellow (1957–70), and other major museums invited him to weed out fakes and 'tourist art' from their holdings.

Fagg was keeper of the ethnography department of the British Museum from 1969 to 1974. With the help of Bryan Cranstone (1918–1989), his deputy, he oversaw its full relocation to 6 Burlington Gardens, off Piccadilly, where it reopened in 1972 as the Museum of Mankind. There it was possible to present changing exhibitions in specially made 'environments', starting with one of Benin art, set in a partial reconstruction of the Benin palace.

After his retirement in 1974 Fagg acted as a consultant for Christies auction house until 1990. Unlike some museum curators, he had never shown any antagonism towards private collectors. He did insist, though, that catalogues refer to 'tribal art' rather than 'primitive art'. His last major publication was *Africa and the Renaissance: Art in Ivory* (1988), written with Ezio Bassani to accompany a display at the Center for African Art in New York. He died of a cerebral thrombosis at his home, 6 Galata Road, Barnes, London, on 10 July 1992. He was unmarried.

Fagg received some criticism from younger scholars for his adherence to the concept of tribality and his readiness to make 'objective' aesthetic pronouncements. It was natural that the pioneer should be challenged by his successors, but nobody disputed his status as an originator of the systematic study of African art.　　　　　　　　JASON TOMES

Sources *The Guardian* (16 July 1992) · *Daily Telegraph* (15 July 1992) · *The Independent* (14 July 1992) · *The Times* (14 July 1992) · J. Picton, 'A tribute to William Fagg', *African Arts*, 27/3 (1994), 26–9 · 'William Fagg remembered', *African Arts*, 27/3 (1994), 30–33 · M. Adams, 'An evening with William Fagg', *African Arts*, 10/4 (1977), 38–43 · *WW* · b. cert.
Archives Royal Anthropological Institute, London, archive | Bodl. Oxf., corresp. with J. L. Myres
Wealth at death £704,756: probate, 29 Dec 1992, *CGPLA Eng. & Wales*

Fagge, Charles Hilton (1838–1883), physician, son of Charles Fagge, medical practitioner, and nephew of John Hilton, was born at Hythe in Kent on 30 June 1838. Fagge entered Guy's Hospital medical school in October 1856, and in 1859 at his first MB examination at the University of London he gained three scholarships and gold medals, a rare distinction. In 1861 at the final MB examination he gained scholarships and gold medals for medicine and for

physiology, and a gold medal for surgery. In 1863 he graduated MD, and he became a member (1864) and a fellow (1870) of the Royal College of Physicians. After being demonstrator of anatomy from 1862 to 1866, Fagge became medical registrar of Guy's in 1866, assistant physician in 1867, and physician in 1880. He was variously demonstrator of morbid anatomy, lecturer on pathology, and curator of the museum at Guy's. For over five years he was joint editor of *Guy's Hospital Reports*, and at the time of his death he was examiner in medicine to the University of London.

As a consulting physician Fagge had been rapidly rising to the front rank, owing much to his painstaking investigation of cases. His original papers and his *Principles and Practice of Medicine*, published posthumously in 1886, mark out his significant contribution to medicine. The latter was described by *The Lancet* as 'one of the most scientific and philosophical works of its kind, being in truth a mine of clinical and pathological facts' (*The Lancet*, 1, 1886, 20). He was an accomplished clinical physician and pathologist, a patient researcher, and a clear and concise teacher. Fagge was also physician to several insurance companies, and examiner to the Bournemouth Sanatorium. He published widely on a variety of medical topics, and he translated the first volume of Hebra's work on cutaneous diseases into English for the New Sydenham Society. He also classified and catalogued the series of models of skin diseases in the museum of Guy's Hospital.

Fagge and his wife, Emily Mary Christiana, had two daughters. He was quiet and unassuming in manner. He was fond of alpine climbing and in his early years had been a keen mountaineer. For the last year and a half of his life he suffered from an aortic aneurism. Having difficulty breathing, he died at midnight on 18–19 November 1883, at his house in Grosvenor Street, London. His wife survived him.　　　　　　G. T. BETTANY, *rev.* TIM O'NEILL

Sources *The Lancet* (1 Dec 1883), 973–5 · reviews, *The Lancet* (2–9 Jan 1886), 20–22, 69–71 · *BMJ* (24 Nov 1883), 1045–6 · *Medical Times and Gazette* (24 Nov 1883), 614–15 · *Guy's Hospital Reports*, 3rd ser., 27 (1884), xxiii–xxxi · Munk, *Roll*
Likenesses M. Hanart, lithograph, Wellcome L. · photograph, Wellcome L.
Wealth at death £11,149 5s. 10d.: probate, 19 Feb 1884, *CGPLA Eng. & Wales*

Fagge [Fagg], **Sir John**, first baronet (1627–1701), politician, was born on 4 October 1627, the only son of John Fagge (d. 1645) of Rye and his wife, Elizabeth, daughter of Barnaby Hodgson. In 1644 he was (probably) admitted to Emmanuel College, Cambridge, and (certainly, in July) to Gray's Inn, although he did not graduate (r apparently matriculate), nor does he appear to have been called to the bar. Fagge's father was a successful merchant in Rye, and a prominent local puritan who served as the town's mayor, stood unsuccessfully for election to parliament in 1640, and supported the parliamentarians during the civil war. Following his father's death Fagge junior came under the political tutelage of his parliamentarian kinsmen, most obviously Harbert *Morley, who was emerging as a political Independent of growing importance. Morley was

Fagge's guardian and on 19 March 1646 Fagge married Mary Morley (d. 1687), Harbert's sister, the daughter of Robert Morley of Glynde.

In many ways the interest in Fagge's career consists in how it reveals the existence and nature of clientage within the House of Commons, and Fagge's parliamentary career was nothing without Morley. It was Morley's influence which helped to ensure that Fagge was elected to parliament as recruiter MP for Rye in 1645, at the age of only eighteen. The aim was probably to prevent the return of a rival presbyterian candidate, and thereafter Fagge made little impact on the Commons, other than possibly as lobby fodder for Morley and his allies. It was undoubtedly Fagge's association with the increasingly prominent Morley which resulted in his nomination as a commissioner for the trial of Charles I in January 1649. Although he was present at some of the preparatory meetings, Fagge, like Morley, attended little of the trial, and refused to sign the king's death warrant. Similarly, association with Morley probably underlay Fagge's unsuccessful candidature for election to the council of state in November 1652, despite his having played little significant role in the Commons during the preceding years. Fagge probably opposed the dissolution of the Rump, and secured election to Cromwell's parliaments in 1654 and 1656 as an opponent of the protectorate. This was blatantly apparent to the regime, as was Fagge's dependence upon his patron. Major-General William Goffe claimed that Fagge would 'not stir a hair's breadth without Colonel Morley' (Thurloe, *State papers*, 4.161), and both men were excluded from parliament in 1656, although Fagge was subsequently allowed to take his seat.

During 1659, both as knight of the shire for Sussex in Richard Cromwell's parliament and as a member of the restored Rump (May–October), Fagge emerged as a more prominent figure, and as an activist for the civilian republicans and the 'good old cause'. When the army interrupted the sittings of the Rump, Fagge and Morley briefly flirted with the idea of suing for a pardon from Charles II and of working for his restoration. Once George Monck declared in favour of parliament, however, Fagge joined with Morley, Sir Arthur Hesilrige, and Valentine Walton in trying to secure Portsmouth for the Rump, and military support in Sussex. Although Fagge was briefly arrested, their cause was successful, and their efforts contributed to the recall of the Rump once again in December 1659. Fagge was subsequently named to the council of state, although he was prevented from taking his seat for refusing to take an oath abjuring the Stuart dynasty.

Although relatively inactive after the secluded members had been readmitted in February 1660, Fagge was elected to the Convention Parliament for Steyning in Sussex in the following April, indicated his support for Charles II, and secured both a pardon and a baronetcy upon the Restoration. Thereafter Fagge gained election to every parliament during the remainder of the century, almost exclusively representing Steyning. His continued influence at Rye, however, ensured that he was one of the townsmen selected to attend the king's coronation in April 1661, and to carry the royal canopy. Having greatly extended his estate during the 1650s, he remained a substantial gentry figure, whose seat at Wiston was one of the great estates in the region. His abiding friendship with Harbert Morley was evident from his nomination as executor of Morley's will and guardian of his young children.

For the remainder of his life Fagge was reckoned to be a whig sympathizer, but he never again assumed the political prominence he had achieved during the 1650s. However, he did become the focus in 1675 for a famous and acrimonious dispute concerning parliamentary privilege between the Commons and Lords. It was occasioned by a legal dispute over Fagge's estate, and resulted in his being briefly imprisoned in the Tower. The matter twice threatened parliamentary deadlock, and to prevent this sessions had to be prematurely curtailed. In later years he was considered an ally by the earl of Shaftesbury, and a supporter of the exclusion of James II, and the succession of the duke of Monmouth. He was certainly prepared to patronize religious nonconformists. Fagge's first wife, Mary, died on 20 November 1687. His second wife, Anne, daughter of Philip Weston of Newbury in Berkshire and widow of one Thomas Henshaw of Billingshurst in Sussex, lived until 11 May 1694. Fagge died on 18 January 1701 (and was buried the following day), and was succeeded by his son, Sir Robert Fagge, the eldest surviving son of John's and Mary's family of nine sons and five daughters.   J. T. PEACEY

Sources HoP, *Commons, 1640–60* [draft] · *JHC*, 2–7 (1640–59) · *CSP dom.*, 1653–1700 · GEC, *Baronetage* · HoP, *Commons, 1660–90* · W. Sussex RO, Wiston papers · E. Sussex RO, Rye MSS · Thurloe, *State papers* · C. H. Firth and R. S. Rait, eds., *Acts and ordinances of the interregnum, 1642–1660*, 3 vols. (1911) · *Diary of Thomas Burton*, ed. J. T. Rutt, 4 vols. (1828) · Evelyn, *Diary*
Archives W. Sussex RO, Wiston MSS

Fagius, Paul (c.1504–1549), protestant reformer and Hebraist, was born in Rheinzabern in the Rhine Palatinate, son of Peter Büchelin, schoolmaster and city clerk in Rheinzabern, and Margarethe Hirn of Heidelberg. At the age of eleven he went to the Neckarschule in Heidelberg, where he studied under Johann Brentius and Martin Frechtus. In 1521 he matriculated at the University of Heidelberg and graduated MA the following year. In 1522 he moved to Strasbourg to study Hebrew with Wolfgang Capito. He worked as a schoolmaster in Strasbourg from 1522 until 1527, developing a close friendship with Martin Bucer. In 1527 Fagius (the Latinate form of his German surname Büchelin) went to the imperial free city of Isny (in the Allgau, near Lake Constance) as director of the Latin school there, a position he held until his return to Strasbourg during 1536–7 to complete his pastoral training for the ministry. From 1538 until 1543 he was the principal minister in Isny, becoming renowned for his preaching and, crucially, for setting up the first Hebrew printing press in Germany. With the patronage of the Isny magistrate Peter Buffler, Fagius was able to bring the celebrated rabbi Elias Levita from Venice, and the two men published more than twenty Hebrew texts. The press in Isny was invaluable to the growing community of protestant Hebrew scholars.

Fagius left Isny in 1543 to take up the position of minister in Constance following the death of Johannes Zwick. But he remained in Constance for less than two years, as Bucer persuaded Fagius in the summer of 1544 to return to Strasbourg to assume both the position of preacher in St Peter's and the chair of Old Testament. This proved to be another short stay, for in 1546 he moved to Heidelberg at the invitation of the elector palatine, Friedrich II, to serve as an adviser in the establishment of Lutheranism and in the reform of the university. Fagius, who still held his position in Strasbourg, published several works while in Heidelberg. Following the defeat of the Schmalkaldic League by Charles V in 1547, Fagius, like Bucer, refused to accept the compromise settlement embodied in the following year's Interim, and was dismissed from office in Strasbourg by council in March 1549. Archbishop Thomas Cranmer so esteemed these two men that he risked the anger of Charles V by inviting Bucer and Fagius to England with promises of university posts. The two men arrived at Lambeth Palace in April 1549. Troubles within the English government meant that neither man could be offered positions immediately, and Bucer and Fagius lived in the archbishop's house. William Benson, dean of Westminster, who was a friend of Cranmer, made a generous grant to Fagius and Bucer to support them until posts could be obtained.

Cranmer's plans for the Strasbourg refugees centred on a definitive Latin edition of the Bible which would serve as the basis for a new English translation. Fagius was clearly daunted by the task, and the young Edward VI was enlisted to persuade the two scholars to take up this project. Fagius's correspondence from England reflected his concern that the Edwardian Reformation was proceeding too cautiously, and he was outraged by the misuse of church property following the death of Henry VIII. But his contribution to the English Reformation was brief, as he fell ill from plague in the autumn of 1549. He moved to Cambridge in November, having been appointed reader in Hebrew, but he died on 13 November in the arms of Martin Bucer. He was buried in St Michael's Church in Cambridge, but his remains were exhumed during Mary's reign and publicly burnt, a posthumous humiliation likewise inflicted upon Bucer. His honours were restored publicly in July 1560, following Elizabeth's accession. Like Bucer, Fagius was moderate in his theological positions; he was more concerned with scholarship and pastoral care than with doctrinal distinctions. His early death shocked and saddened the protestant world, in which he was regarded as an outstanding Hebrew scholar.

BRUCE GORDON

Sources R. Raubenheimer, *Paul Fagius: sein Leben und Wirken als Reformator und Gelehrter* (1957) · D. MacCulloch, *Thomas Cranmer: a life* (1996)
Likenesses H. Hondius junior, line engraving, BM, NPG; repro. in J. Verheiden, *Effigies* (1602) · woodcut, NPG; repro. in T. Beja, *Icones* (1580)

Fahey, James (1804–1885), watercolour painter, was born on 16 April 1804 at Paddington, near London; he can probably be identified with the James Fahey, son of Patrick and Jane, who was baptized on 19 August 1804 at St Mary's, Marylebone Road, Marylebone, Middlesex. He trained as an engraver with his uncle, John Swaine, before studying watercolour painting with George Scharf the elder. He then went to Paris, where he worked as a surgical draughtsman, making anatomical drawings. He may have been the James Fahey who married Eliza Pepper on 26 August 1831 at St Clement Danes, the Strand, London.

Fahey first exhibited at the Royal Academy in 1825, showing *Portrait of a Young Gentleman*; this was followed in 1827 by drawings of the church of St Jacques in Dieppe and the cathedral of Notre Dame in Paris. Until 1836 he contributed several portraits and watercolour landscapes to the exhibitions of the Royal Academy, the British Institution, and the Society of British Artists, but he later devoted himself entirely to landscape painting, joining the New Watercolour Society in 1834, where he exhibited 127 times. He was secretary from 1838 to 1874, when he resigned because of a financial misdemeanour. Queen Victoria bought some of his watercolours in 1844. He continued to exhibit at the Royal Academy until 1857. He also sometimes painted in oils, and exhibited at the British Institution in 1861 and 1862. From 1856 to 1883 he was drawing-master at the Merchant Taylors' School in London. Fahey died at his home, The Grange, 51 Shepherd's Bush Green, London, on 11 December 1885. One of his sons, Edward Henry Fahey (1844–1907), was also an artist.

ANNE PIMLOTT BAKER

Sources Mallalieu, *Watercolour artists*, vols. 1–2 · *ILN* (26 Dec 1885) · Boase, *Mod. Eng. biog.* · D. Millar, *The Victorian watercolours and drawings in the collection of her majesty the queen*, 2 vols. (1995) · Graves, *RA exhibitors* · J. Johnson, ed., *Works exhibited at the Royal Society of British Artists, 1824–1893, and the New English Art Club, 1888–1917*, 2 vols. (1975) · *IGI* · Bryan, *Painters* (1903–5) · *CGPLA Eng. & Wales* (1886) · *DNB*
Likenesses wood-engraving, repro. in *ILN*, 667
Wealth at death £1064 12s. 4d.: probate, 2 Jan 1886, *CGPLA Eng. & Wales*

Fahie, Sir William Charles (1763–1833), naval officer, came from an Irish family settled at St Kitts, West Indies, where his father was judge of the vice-admiralty court. He entered the navy in 1777, on board the *Seaford*, with Captain Colpoys, and was afterwards in the *Royal George*. In October 1779 he was appointed to the *Sandwich*, bearing the flag of Sir George Rodney, and was present at the defeat of Langara off Cape St Vincent, and in the several actions with De Guichen on 17 April and 15 and 19 May 1780. In August 1780 he was appointed acting lieutenant of the *Russell*, in which he was present in the action off Martinique on 28 April 1781, and at St Kitts on 26 January 1782. On account of his local knowledge he was afterwards sent by Hood to communicate with the garrison of Brimstone Hill, and on the second occasion, being unable to regain his ship, he gave himself up to the French general, but was permitted to depart. He rejoined the *Russell* at St Lucia, and was present in the actions to leeward of Dominica on 9 and 12 April.

In January 1783 Fahie was confirmed in the rank of lieutenant, but he remained with his family at St Kitts until the outbreak of the war with France in 1793, when he was appointed to the sloop *Zebra*, Captain Robert Faulknor, in which he took part in the brilliant assault on Fort Royal. Sir John Jervis consequently appointed him to the flagship, the *Boyne*, and on 5 August 1793 promoted him to be commander of the *Woolwich*. On 2 February 1796 he was posted to command the *Perdrix* (22 guns), in which he continued until she was paid off in August 1799. In 1804 Fahie was again sent out to the West Indies, in command of the *Hyaena*, from which in 1805 he was moved into the frigate *Amelia*, and again in 1806 into the *Ethalion*, in which he assisted at the capture of the Danish West Indian islands by Sir Alexander Cochrane in December 1807. In November 1808 he was appointed to the *Belle Isle* (74 guns), one of the squadron that captured Martinique in February 1809. He afterwards exchanged with Commodore Cockburn into the *Pompée*, another line-of-battle ship, employed in April 1809 in the blockade of three French ships which had anchored in the roadstead of the Saintes. On the night of 14 April they put to sea, closely followed by the sloops *Hazard* and *Recruit* and the *Pompée*, the rest of the squadron being at a considerable distance. The chase continued during the following day. At nightfall the French ships separated; the *Pompée* and the sloops attached themselves to the *Hautpoult*, and, mainly through the persistent gallantry of Captain Charles Napier of the *Recruit*, assisted towards the close by the frigate *Castor*, brought her to action about four o'clock on the morning of the 17th, and captured her after a sharp combat lasting an hour and a half. The following August Fahie was appointed to the *Hautpoult*, which had been commissioned as the *Abercromby*; in November he was ordered to wear a broad pennant, and in February 1810 assisted in the capture of Guadeloupe, from which he was sent by Cochrane to take possession of St Martin's and St Eustatius. In June he sailed for England in charge of a valuable convoy, and after the *Abercromby* had been refitted, in December he joined the flag of Sir George Berkeley at Lisbon. During the three following years he commanded the *Abercromby* in the channel and the Bay of Biscay, and in 1815 was appointed to the *Malta*, which, on the escape of Napoleon from Elba, was sent out to the Mediterranean, where Fahie was employed for some months as senior officer on the coast of Italy, for which the king of the Two Sicilies nominated him a commander of the order of St Ferdinand and Merit. In 1815 he was made a CB.

Fahie attained flag rank on 12 August 1819, and in January 1820 was appointed commander-in-chief on the Leeward Islands station, from which in the following year he was sent to Halifax. With the close of his command, in September 1824, his active career terminated. In October he was nominated a KCB, and on 22 July 1830 he became a vice-admiral. In his intervals of half pay, and on his retirement, he lived almost entirely in the West Indies. He was twice married: first, to Elizabeth Renie Heyliger, daughter of Mr William Heyliger of St Eustatius; and second, to Mary Esther Harvey, daughter of the Hon. Augustus William Harvey, member of council of Bermuda. He died at Bermuda on 11 January 1833. Fahie was an officer with an unusually local career; his ideas on discipline were firm, and his promotions secured by merit.

J. K. LAUGHTON, rev. ANDREW LAMBERT

Sources J. D. Byon, *Crime and punishment in the Royal Navy: discipline on the Leeward Islands station, 1784–1812* (1989) · M. Duffy, *Soldiers, sugar, and sea power: the British expeditions to the West Indies and the war against revolutionary France* (1987) · J. Marshall, *Royal naval biography*, 1 (1823) · J. Ralfe, *The naval biography of Great Britain*, 4 (1828) · *GM*, 1st ser., 103/1 (1833)
Archives NL Scot., corresp. with Sir Alexander Cochrane

Faílbe mac Pípáin (*d.* 679). *See under* Iona, abbots of (*act.* 563–927).

Fairbairn, Andrew Martin (1838–1912), Congregational minister and college head, was born at Inverkeithing, Fife, on 4 November 1838. He came of covenanting stock and received strict religious training. He was the second son of John Fairbairn, a miller, and a leader in the United Secession church, and his wife, Helen, daughter of Andrew Martin, of Blainslie, near Lauder. He had very little regular schooling, and began to earn his own living before he was ten. A voracious reader with a retentive memory, he prepared himself for Edinburgh University, where he afterwards studied, though he took no degree.

Meanwhile Fairbairn had become an adherent of the Evangelical Union founded by James Morison, under whose influence Fairbairn decided to become a minister. He entered the theological college of the union in Glasgow in 1857, and in 1860 was ordained and inducted to the Evangelical Union pastorate in Bathgate. While in that post he visited Germany, where he studied at Berlin from 1865 to 1866 under Dorner, Tholuck, and Hengstenberg, and from that time onwards the advocacy of a freer and broader theology than that prevalent in the Scotland of his day became the passion of Fairbairn's life. He married in 1868 Jane, youngest daughter of John Shields of Byres, Bathgate. They had two sons and two daughters.

Fairbairn wrote, preached, and lectured with untiring persistence, and did not shrink from controversy. He was chairman of the Evangelical Union in 1870. From Bathgate he moved in 1872 to St Paul's Congregational Church, Aberdeen, where he won a great reputation as a preacher and as a lecturer on philosophical and theological subjects. His first book, *Studies in the Philosophy of Religion and History* (1876), at once called attention to him as a forceful religious teacher. In 1877 Fairbairn became principal of Airedale College, Bradford, thus transferring his religious allegiance to English Congregationalism. He soon showed his quality as a religious leader, and while at Airedale became chairman of the Congregational Union of England and Wales in 1883.

During the same period Fairbairn set himself to a task which absorbed him for many years, namely the reform and development of theological education among the free churches. When, therefore, it was proposed in 1886 to establish a Congregational theological college in Oxford, Fairbairn was marked out as the best man to lead the enterprise. He was made principal of the new foundation, Mansfield College, and its early success was largely due to

Andrew Martin Fairbairn (1838–1912), by unknown engraver

his sagacity, industry, and tact. Its standing (and Fairbairn's) was recognized when Gladstone dined there on 5 February 1890. Fairbairn's wide learning and liberal spirit, the rugged eloquence of his style, and his deep insight into human nature made him a most attractive and stimulating teacher; his students responded with loyalty and devotion.

The substance of Fairbairn's teaching was published in 1893 in the volume entitled *Christ in Modern Theology*, which its author described as 'an endeavour, through a Christian doctrine of God, at a sketch of the first lines of a Christian theology'. The book speedily passed through twelve editions. It was followed by *The Philosophy of the Christian Religion* (1902), and the two together gave a fairly complete presentation of a theological position, strongly influenced by Hegelian idealism, which proved both stimulating and constructive at a time of stress and uncertainty. The theology is of a mediating type and, since it expresses the reaction of Fairbairn's own mind to the intellectual conditions of his day, it now seems dated.

Among Fairbairn's other writings are two volumes of sermons—*The City of God* (1882), hailed in its day as a real contribution to apologetics, and *Catholicism, Roman and Anglican* (1899), the substance of which had been the occasion of a sharp controversy with Cardinal Newman—and also a volume of *Studies in Religion and Theology* (1910). He also wrote two chapters, 'Calvin' and 'Tendencies of European thought in the age of the Reformation', for the second volume of the *Cambridge Modern History* (1903). His Gifford lectures on comparative religion were delivered in Aberdeen but, owing to adverse criticism of the sections

on Chinese religion, were not published as they stood, and were never revised.

All this literary work was done in the intervals of an exceedingly busy life. A trusted leader of the free churches, Fairbairn was in demand all over the country as a preacher and lecturer. He paid several visits to America and lectured in many university centres. In 1898 he went as Haskell lecturer to India. Keenly interested in educational questions, he served on a royal commission on education (1894–5); was consulted by the University of Manchester concerning the establishment of its non-sectarian faculty of theology; played a leading part on the Welsh Theological Board, which devised regulations governing the teaching and examining of theology in the fledgeling University of Wales; and participated in the education controversy of 1902.

Fairbairn died at 112 St James's Court, Buckingham Gate, London, on 9 February 1912. He was loved and honoured by a wide circle of friends. He was devoted to his family and never so happy as when in his hospitable home. He was a keen conversationalist, a little dogmatic and assertive in manner; W. B. Glover less deferentially described him as 'a pompous windbag'. But he always had a sense of humour, and a sensitive appreciation of human needs and failings. His wide knowledge of people, books, and affairs made him a most entertaining companion. Above all he was deeply religious. Fairbairn was a DD of Edinburgh, Yale, Wales, Manchester, and Göttingen; a DLitt of Leeds; an LLD of Aberdeen; and a founder and fellow of the British Academy. A collection of *Mansfield College Essays* (1909), which includes a sonnet to him by Edward Shillito and a bibliography of his writings, was presented to him on his seventieth birthday. His monument is the college that he founded, which became a full college of Oxford University in 1995.

W. B. SELBIE, rev. ALAN P. F. SELL

Sources W. B. Selbie, *The life of Andrew Martin Fairbairn* (1914) · A. P. F. Sell, 'An Arminian, a Calvinist and a liberal', *Dissenting thought and the life of the churches: studies in an English tradition* (1990) · A. M. Fairbairn, 'Experience in theology: a chapter of autobiography', *Contemporary Review*, 91 (1907), 554–73 · R. S. Franks, 'The theology of Andrew Martin Fairbairn', *Transactions of the Congregational Historical Society*, 13 (1937–9), 140–50 · J. W. Grant, *Free churchmanship in England, 1870–1940* [1955] · W. B. Glover, *Evangelical nonconformists and higher criticism in the nineteenth century* (1954) · M. D. Johnson, *The dissolution of dissent, 1850–1918* (1987) · E. J. Price, 'Dr Fairbairn and Airedale College: the hour and the man', *Transactions of the Congregational Historical Society*, 13 (1937–9), 131–9 · K. W. Wadsworth, *Yorkshire United Independent College* (1954), 127–32 · H. Escott, *A history of Scottish Congregationalism* (1960) · *Congregational Year Book* (1913), 165–6 · W. D. McNaughton, *The Scottish Congregational ministry, 1794–1993* (1993), 45–6 · R. Tudur Jones, *Congregationalism in England, 1662–1962* (1962) · A. P. F. Sell, *A reformed, evangelical, Catholic theology: the contribution of the World Alliance of Reformed Churches, 1875–1982* (1991) · A. P. F. Sell, *Saints: visible, orderly and Catholic: the Congregational idea of the church* (1986) · A. P. F. Sell, *Theology in turmoil: the roots, course and significance of the conservative-liberal debate in modern theology* (1986) · J. Ross, *A history of Congregational independency in Scotland* (1900) · Gladstone, *Diaries* · E. Kaye, *Mansfield College, Oxford: its origin, history and significance* (1996)

Likenesses G. Reid, portrait, Mansfield College, Oxford · stipple, NPG [*see illus.*] · tablet, Fairbairn Hall, Barking Road, London

Wealth at death £3462 6s. 2d.: probate, 5 June 1912, *CGPLA Eng. & Wales*

Fairbairn, John (1794–1864), newspaper proprietor and politician in Cape Colony, son of James Fairbairn, tenant of Carolside mill, and his wife, Agnes Bruce, was born at Legerwood, near Berwick, Scotland, on 9 April 1794. He attended Edinburgh University in 1812 (studying classics, theology, and medicine), but poverty prevented him graduating. As a schoolmaster in Newcastle upon Tyne, Fairbairn wrote articles in the *Edinburgh Magazine* and *The Star*, both edited by John Pringle, future secretary of the Aborigines' Protection Society. Pringle was the first of Fairbairn's several mentors and, in 1822, persuaded him to emigrate to Cape Town, promising a literary and teaching career in the recently annexed Cape Colony. Fairbairn responded enthusiastically, writing that they could become the 'Franklins of the Kaap' (Pringle, 176–7).

Fairbairn initially taught at the Classical and Commercial Academy in the Keizergracht (Darling Street), which Pringle and he founded but which closed in 1825. He was editor (1824–59) and eventually proprietor (1835–64) of the *South African Commercial Advertiser* (*SACA*). Published in Dutch and English, this first South African newspaper was immediately threatened with government censorship, but Fairbairn's resistance led to an ordinance safeguarding freedom of the press. Fairbairn, whose journalism was coloured by his Ricardian political economy, initially believed that British settlers had a divine and heroic role to play in the Cape. His overly theoretical approach led him to seemingly contradictory policies, causing his contemporary and modern detractors to see only opportunism in his editorials. He grew increasingly pessimistic about a British civilizing mission, since his chosen means, a free press and constitutional reform, required a limit on colonial expansion and cultural homogeneity. He played a major role in establishing the Cape's educational system and in modernizing its financial institutions. His activities in banking and insurance brought him considerable profit.

Criticism of the government's arbitrary powers and its use of patronage led to Fairbairn's call for representative institutions. However, the strategic importance of the colony meant that the British government would not leave it to a legislature certain to be dominated by a more numerous, wealthy, but questionably loyal, Cape Dutch-Afrikaner electorate. Nor, in the era of emancipation, could a slave-holding society be relinquished to settler control.

Initially Fairbairn's relations with this Afrikaner élite were cordial, and he must have hoped for its support over representative government, given his assertion that all who made Africa their home, whether from 'England or Holland' were 'all Africans' (*SACA*, 17 March 1824). Moreover, his attitude to emancipation would have won endorsement. While he claimed to favour the abolition of slavery, he distanced himself from those who advocated 'liberty' on 'moral and religious grounds', arguing for a 'statecraft' determined by the 'principles of Political Science'. 'The Ten commandments', Fairbairn wrote, might

be employed by others, but he was 'content with the Multiplication Table' (*SACA*, 2 March 1831). Slaves could only be freed if compensation was paid.

Yet Fairbairn's conviction that the newly arrived British colonists had a unique role to play in making the Cape a 'fit abode for free men' was resented. His British patriotism led to relations with Afrikaners cooling, bringing serious consequences for his political and financial ambitions. Moreover, despite his tortuous position on abolition, Fairbairn supported Dr John Philip's campaign—parallel with that of the anti-slavery movement in Britain—to extend civil rights to the Cape's Khoi-Khoi (Hottentot) population. Fairbairn distinguished between Khoi-Khoi, held in serf-like bondage, and slaves who, unlike Khoi-Khoi, were property.

Fairbairn's support for 'Hottentot emancipation' not only angered Afrikaner farmers and their commercial and professional kinsmen, but also brought hostility from eastern Cape British settlers intent on maintaining control over Khoi-Khoi labourers with a Vagrancy Act, whose passage the *SACA* successfully opposed. In the 1830s Fairbairn became critical of British settler and government expansionism on the colony's eastern frontier. Settlers were located on seized Xhosa land, where incursions and retaliations continued. Conquest bred insecurity and chauvinism, and Fairbairn's editorials blamed the new colonists for increased conflict. The establishment of two conservative newspapers followed: *De Zuid Afrikaan* for Afrikaners in the western Cape, and the *Grahamstown Journal* for British settlers. Both papers achieved sales at the expense of the *SACA*, and threatened Fairbairn's influence and livelihood.

Fairbairn now saw representative institutions imperilling the newly created Khoi-Khoi civil liberties and the increasing economic freedoms which the colony had won. He did not abandon the hope of an elected government but urged a political campaign to create a non-racial, if British led, alliance which would defeat Afrikaner power.

In the 1830s, the *SACA* led the attack on existing monopolies and government economic intervention. Fairbairn helped transform the banking system and validated joint stock companies. Championing friendly societies and commercial insurance companies, he became a leader in these institutions. He advocated building railways, regulating merchant shipping, bills of exchange, the reform of auctions, limited liability legislation, mechanisms for rehabilitating insolvents, and the modernization of agriculture. He married Elizabeth (1812–1840), second daughter of Dr John *Philip, the South African director of the London Missionary Society, in Cape Town on 24 May 1831.

By 1841 Fairbairn's efforts had contributed significantly to the growth of common interests among new Afrikaner and British capitalists and his editorials announced a 'reconciliation' which removed the 'very appearance of disunion' (*SACA*, 2 Jan 1841). An expanding middle class, resentful of its lack of influence and of privileges given to older commercial rivals, combined in calling for a legislative assembly. When in 1849 the colonial secretary and the governor landed convicts at the Cape, breaking previous promises, a politically astute cabal, including Fairbairn, created an Anti-Convict Association which focused on agitation for self-government. The *SACA* became one of the association's major propagandists, joining the call for a boycott of state institutions until the convicts were deported. Grandiloquently, Fairbairn reminded his readers of the social contract made by 'Englishmen' in 1688, and of the need to 'resist despotism', that 'dry rot of the constitution' (*SACA*, 23 May 1849).

The association's successful boycott, and its almost colony-wide coalition against the government, convinced the administration to redirect the convicts and hastened the government's decision to create an elected assembly. Fairbairn and three other 'popular members' were elected to conclude the government's legislative council business and to act as advisers in drafting the proposed constitution. Fairbairn (who was assaulted in his home by a mob incited almost certainly by government officials) was elected with the support of Cape Town merchants, mission station Khoi-Khoi, and rural Afrikaners, each group with its own agenda. When the governor chose to deal with non-constitutional matters first, Fairbairn and his associates resigned and pursued their campaign in London. Although receiving no immediate help from the colonial secretary, their proposals were subsequently accepted, allowing a substantial number of Afrikaners and a smaller group of Khoi-Khoi and ex-slaves to be enfranchised. With his standing among rural Afrikaners restored, Fairbairn was elected to the first legislative assembly as member for the rural Swellendam constituency (1854–64) and increasingly reflected the opinions of his conservative electors.

More and more pessimistic about the efficacy of the British mission, Fairbairn still hoped, in the 1840s, that its influence would overcome 'the evil genius of Africa'. By the 1850s, he gloomily prophesied that the civilizing power of the colony would be weakened if it moved beyond its coastal base, as 'the repelling genius of Africa becomes stronger' (*SACA*, 13 Dec 1851). He also foresaw that settler expansion would provoke bloody conquest and a 'terrible spirit of war and revenge'. The English settlers, he concurred, were 'more stern and implacable than the Boers', and a new generation was emerging 'full of enterprize and bent on conquest, whom no government will be able to control' (John Fairbairn to James Fairbairn, 28 Aug 1851, University of the Witwatersrand, MS A663/BA).

Fairbairn's wife died on 30 May 1840, nine years after their marriage, leaving two sons and a daughter. The eldest son, John Philip, drowned in the Gamtoos River on 1 July 1845, aged eleven. Personal loss and political foreboding blunted the satisfaction Fairbairn might have felt in his achievements. He died on 5 October 1864 at the Wynberg home of his son-in-law, advocate F. S. Watermeyer, and was buried in the Somerset Road cemetery in Cape Town.　　　　　　　　　　　STANLEY TRAPIDO

Sources *South African Commercial Advertiser* (1824–59) • H. C. Botha, *John Fairbairn in South Africa* (1984) • T. E. Kirk, 'Self-government and self-defence in South Africa: the interrelations between British and Cape politics, 1846–54', DPhil diss., U. Oxf., 1973 • J. L. Meltzer, 'The growth of Cape Town commerce and the role of John Fairbairn's *Advertiser* (1835–1859)', MA diss., University of Cape Town, 1989 • T. Pringle, *Narrative of a residence in South Africa* (1835) • B. A. Le Cordeur, *The politics of eastern Cape separatism, 1820–1854* (1981) • *Herschel at the Cape: diaries and correspondence of Sir John Herschel, 1834–1838*, ed. D. E. Evans and others (1969) • *DSAB*

Archives Library of Parliament, Cape Town, corresp. • National Library of South Africa, Cape Town, family MSS • University of the Witwatersrand, Johannesburg, department of historical papers • University of the Witwatersrand, Johannesburg, department of historical papers, family MSS

Likenesses F. A. V. York, photograph, 1861, Cory Library, Grahamstown, South Africa • W. H. Schroder, portrait, Cape Town chamber of commerce, South Africa

Fairbairn, Sir Nicholas Hardwick (1933–1995), lawyer and politician, was born on 24 December 1933 at 18 Lansdowne Crescent, Edinburgh, the third surviving child and younger son of (William) Ronald Dodds *Fairbairn (1889–1964), psychotherapist and psychoanalyst, and his wife, Mary Ann (d. 1952), daughter of Henry More Gordon of Charleton and Kinnaber, Angus. His father was a psychoanalyst of international repute, but the life of the family became overshadowed by his strained relations with his wife. Fairbairn was educated at Loretto School (1941–51) and the University of Edinburgh (1951–4), where he first followed his father in studying medicine, but switched to classics. He then read for the bar, being admitted in 1957. He early developed interests in conservation and in culture. He founded the Society for the Preservation of Duddingston Village, a picturesque suburb of Edinburgh where his family lived. He began painting and sold his first picture as a student. He overcame the penury of devilling by putting on a one-man exhibition which earned £2000.

Fairbairn's career did not take off until 1960, when he was instructed as junior counsel for the defence in a celebrated trial for the 'Calton murder'; he made a flamboyant appearance which did not quite save his client, and this became a frequent experience. His most famous defence was of Patrick Meehan, wrongly sentenced for murder in 1969 but pardoned in 1976 after a long campaign in which Fairbairn also took a leading role. Exposure to the seamy side of Scotland seemed to be making a social liberal of him. He became an active campaigner for birth-control, a subject still *risqué* in staid Edinburgh. The city's bourgeoisie was also regularly shocked by avant-garde productions in the annual festival of the arts, which Fairbairn loved. One year, after a 'happening' featured a nude young lady being pushed across a stage in a trolley, the procurator fiscal decided to prosecute the offenders, but Fairbairn defended them successfully. On 29 September 1962 he married Elizabeth Mary (b. 1938), daughter of Aeneas Alexander Mackay, thirteenth Lord Reay and chief of the clan Mackay (1905–1963), and his wife, Charlotte Mary, *née* Younger (d. 1963). The Fairbairns bought and restored the ruined castle of Fordell in Fife. They had a son and four daughters, of whom the son and a daughter died in infancy, before the marriage was dissolved in 1979.

Fairbairn became a queen's counsel in 1972, and entered parliament after Sir Alec Douglas-Home stood down from

Sir Nicholas Hardwick Fairbairn (1933–1995), by unknown photographer

his seat of Kinross and West Perthshire at the general election of October 1974. In a traditional Conservative constituency, Fairbairn, known as a maverick dandy, won nomination against the odds. This came during an upsurge of Scottish nationalism, and he held the seat by just fifty-three votes. In later polls he raised his majorities. At Westminster he surprised many by aligning himself with the right. He supported Margaret Thatcher's bid for the Conservative leadership in 1975. His reward came with the post of solicitor-general for Scotland in her first ministry in 1979. But office did not suit him. Now divorced, he was at the centre of a scandal in 1981: there were allegations that he had had an affair with a secretary at the House of Commons and that she was later found trying to hang herself from a lamp-post outside his home in London. Responsible for prosecutions by the crown, in 1982 he exercised his powers not to arraign a gang of men who had raped a woman in Glasgow. This ugly case ended in a successful private prosecution by her, a rarity in Scotland. Fairbairn compounded his misjudgement by announcing to the press, not to parliament, that he had lacked evidence to indict. On 28 January 1982 he was obliged to resign.

On 28 May 1983 Fairbairn married Suzanne Mary MacInnes (b. 1942), daughter of Lieutenant-Colonel Hilary George Wheeler of the Baluch regiment. For the wedding at Fordell Castle, Fairbairn designed clothes for both bride and groom in styles of princely India. This ceremony set the tone for the colourful remainder, which was also the prime, of his life. His ministerial career never resumed and he was hardly, except in his own eyes, taken seriously as a politician. But he found his *métier* as an independent back-bencher. His appearance at Westminster in bizarre, often tartan, costumes signalled his resolve to act and speak in his own way. He did not hesitate to rebel over such matters as saving Scottish regiments, and later over Europe. He also did sterling work in causes close to his heart, as in his chairmanship of the Historic Buildings Council for Scotland from 1988, in which year he was also knighted. He gave a great impression of zest for life, summed up in his entries in *Who's Who*, changed for every edition: 'drawing ships, making quips, confounding Whips, scuttling drips' was the last (*WW*, 1995, 174). He became, in short, a popular eccentric. Much of his humour, as of his acerbity, was unfortunately fuelled by drink. He contracted cirrhosis of the liver and died at Queen Margaret Hospital, Dunfermline, on 19 February 1995. He was buried on 22 February in the crypt of the chapel at Fordell Castle. A memorial service was held at St John's Kirk, Perth, on 3 March, at which Baroness Thatcher read from Kahlil Gibran's *The Prophet*. Fairbairn was survived by both wives and by three daughters of his first marriage.   MICHAEL FRY

Sources N. Fairbairn, *A life is too short* (1987) · *The Times* (20 Feb 1995) · *The Times* (23 Feb 1995) · *The Times* (4 March 1995) · *The Independent* (20 Feb 1995) · *WWW*, 1991–5 · m. cert. · d. cert.
Archives SOUND BBC Scotland, Queen Margaret Drive, Glasgow · BL NSA, performance recordings
Likenesses A. Sutherland, oils, c.1960, priv. coll. · photograph, 1981, Hult. Arch. · photograph, *The Scotsman* archives, Edinburgh · photograph, *The Herald* archives, Glasgow · photograph, News International Syndication, London [*see illus.*] · photograph, repro. in *The Independent*
Wealth at death £408,948.25: confirmation, 30 June 1995, SC/CO 846/119

Fairbairn, Patrick (1805–1874), theologian, was born at Hallyburton in the parish of Greenlaw, Berwickshire, on 28 January 1805, the second of five children of John Fairbairn, farmer, and his wife, Jessie Johnston (d. 1861). He was educated locally before entering Edinburgh University in November 1818, although this proved rather too early and Fairbairn did not reveal the extent of his mental powers at this stage. He proceeded to the study of divinity and was licensed by the presbytery of Duns on 3 October 1826. During his time in Edinburgh Fairbairn was greatly influenced by the preaching of Dr Robert Gordon. In 1827 he became tutor in the family of Captain Balfour of Balfour, a large Orkney proprietor. Balfour's influence was no doubt instrumental in Fairbairn's presentation to the parliamentary chapel on North Ronaldsay, the most northerly of the Orkney Islands, where he was ordained on 28 July 1830. Fairbairn was credited with the spiritual transformation of his congregation, whose bad habits were said to include shipwrecking. However, the tiny and remote island also provided a perfect setting for a programme of study in German and Hebrew, which Fairbairn laid down for himself. It was during this period that he translated the first of many works from German.

On 27 March 1833 Fairbairn married Margaret Pitcairn (d. 1837), with whom he had three children. Her death following childbirth was soon followed by that of their infant daughter and one of their sons. By this time Fairbairn had moved to the church extension charge of Bridgeton, in the east end of Glasgow, to which he was translated on 16 March 1837. On 23 July 1839 he married,

Patrick Fairbairn (1805–1874), by John Cochran

second, Mary Playfair (d. 1852), with whom he had four children. From Bridgeton Fairbairn was translated and admitted to the pleasant East Lothian parish of Saltoun, whose attractions included a ministerial library endowed by Gilbert Burnet, on 25 June 1840. While he had not taken a prominent role in events leading up to the Disruption in the Church of Scotland, Fairbairn was a staunch supporter of the Free Church of Scotland and took most of his congregation with him into the new denomination.

The appearance of his *Typology of Scripture* (1845–7) established Fairbairn's credentials as a scholar. His translation of E. W. Hengstenberg's *Commentary on the Psalms* appeared, in three volumes, between 1844 and 1848, and was followed by *Jonah* (1849) and *Ezekiel, and the Book of his Prophecy* (1851). As the Free Church considered the expansion of its theological training, it became clear that Fairbairn would be at the centre of those plans. In 1852 he was appointed to assist Dr Maclagan at Aberdeen and Fairbairn succeeded to the professorship on Maclagan's death in 1853. In 1854 Glasgow University honoured him with the degree of DD. When the Glasgow theological hall was established in 1856 Fairbairn transferred there as its first professor and, the following year, its first principal. The wisdom of the choice was underlined by the fact that Fairbairn not only had the intellectual weight commensurate with his position, but he was also a very capable administrator.

Following the death of his second wife Fairbairn travelled extensively in the company of John Elliot Wilson. Wilson was with Fairbairn on several continental trips and was in Germany when they had a meeting with Hengstenberg which Fairbairn found rather disappointing. On 21 September 1861 Fairbairn married again; his third wife was Frances (Fanny) Eliza Turnbull (1817/18–1903). They had no children. Fairbairn maintained his published output with *Prophecy* (1856) and his *Hermeneutical Manual*

(1858). A project long in preparation came to fruition under his editorship as the *Imperial Bible Dictionary*, to which he contributed many of the articles himself. In 1864 he was made moderator of the general assembly of the Free Church of Scotland and in 1868 he was Cunningham lecturer, his lectures being published as *The Revelation of Law in Scripture*. In 1867 he was one of a deputation sent to the United States by the Free Church of Scotland. Fairbairn supported the movement towards union with the United Presbyterian church, and he was a natural choice to serve on the committee to revise the Old Testament. His last enthusiasm was for the revivalism of Moody and Sankey and it was at an evangelistic convention in Glasgow in April 1874 that he became unwell. A heart condition was diagnosed and while he appeared to make some recovery, he died shortly after retiring to bed on 6 August 1874 at his home, 13 Elmbank Crescent, Glasgow. He was buried in the Grange cemetery, Edinburgh, on 13 August. His third wife survived him.

Fairbairn was a tall man of good humour, majestic presence, and robust constitution who managed to avoid the controversy and personal animosities that often went with the status of Free Church leader. His knowledge of German scholarship might easily have brought him under the suspicion of colleagues, but while his sympathies were liberal, his orthodoxy was never impugned.

LIONEL ALEXANDER RITCHIE

Sources P. Fairbairn, *Pastoral theology … with a biographical sketch of the author by the Rev. James Dodds, Dunbar* (1875) · J. A. Wylie, *Disruption worthies: a memorial of 1843*, ed. J. B. Gillies, new edn (1881), 242–52 · *Fasti Scot.*, 1.394 · *Free Church of Scotland Monthly Record*, no. 147, new ser. (Oct 1874), 217–18 · *Glasgow Herald* (8 Aug 1874) · *The Scotsman* (8 Aug 1874) · DSCHT · D. M. Lewis, ed., *The Blackwell dictionary of evangelical biography, 1730–1860*, 2 vols. (1995) · S. Mechie, *Trinity College, Glasgow, 1856–1956* (1956) · DNB · personal knowledge (1888) [DNB]

Likenesses J. Cochran, engraving, NPG [*see illus.*] · portrait, repro. in Wylie, *Disruption worthies*, facing p. 245

Fairbairn, Sir Peter (1799–1861), mechanical engineer, youngest son of Andrew Fairbairn, a farmer, and brother of Sir William *Fairbairn, was born at Kelso, Roxburghshire, in September 1799. He left school at eleven to work in the Percy Main colliery near Newcastle upon Tyne. At fourteen he was apprenticed to John Casson, a millwright and engineer, in Newcastle.

After completing his apprenticeship, Fairbairn worked for Henry Houldsworth of Glasgow, a cotton spinner and machine maker, first as foreman, later as traveller. He then spent five years broadening his experience in millwrights' and machine-making firms in England and France, including spells with his brother William in Manchester, and at the works of John Rennie (1761–1821) in London. He returned to Glasgow as a partner of Houldsworth.

Fairbairn's first wife, mother of his only son, Andrew, and two daughters, was Margaret, daughter of Robert Kennedy of Glasgow; she died in 1843. In 1855 he married Rachel Anne, fourth daughter of Robert William Brandling, of Low Gosforth, Newcastle, and widow of Captain Charles Bell RN.

Armed with ideas for improving flax and woollen machinery, Fairbairn moved to Leeds about 1826, where he set up in business in a small rented room. Lack of capital did not long hold him back, for he was assisted by John Marshall, the flax spinner, who had seen potential in Fairbairn's improved and simplified flax machinery. Marshall helped Fairbairn to move to larger premises, and for a time bought as many machines as Fairbairn could produce. Fairbairn's innovations included applying differential motion to the roving frame; introducing a rotary gill which was used widely on tow machinery; developing the screw gill motion into usable form; and increasing flax-spinning frames from forty spindles to eighty, as well as producing machines for preparing and spinning silk waste, and improvements in machinery for making rope yarn.

Fairbairn's designs were praised for their classical neatness, and they revolutionized flax and hemp preparation, enabling spinners to produce a far superior yarn at lower cost. He soon grew independent of Marshall's support, expanding his Wellington foundry to employ 550 men and boys by 1841, 850 a decade later, and 1400 in 1861. Fairbairn had been asked by the government to make special machine tools for armament production at Woolwich and Enfield during the Crimean War, and general engineering tools subsequently made up a large share of his business.

A Liberal of moderate views, Fairbairn served on the town council from 1836 until 1842, and in 1854 was elected an alderman. A Leeds and West Riding magistrate, Fairbairn was mayor of Leeds in 1857–8 and 1858–9. A new town hall was opened by the queen in 1858 and Fairbairn was knighted during the royal visit. Besides the energy, resolution, and business acumen which had brought him commercial success, he was admired for his integrity. He supported educational and religious causes, and had a broad interest in the arts, including music and drama.

Peter Fairbairn died on 4 January 1861, at Woodsley House, Clarendon Road, Leeds, and was buried in Adel churchyard, Leeds, after a public funeral attended by 700 of his workpeople. He was survived by his second wife.

GILLIAN COOKSON

Sources R. V. Taylor, ed., *The biographia Leodiensis, or, Biographical sketches of the worthies of Leeds* (1865), 491–6 · *The Engineer* (11 Jan 1861) · [J. Hogg], ed., *Fortunes made in business: a series of original sketches*, 2 (1884), 252–78 · G. Cookson, 'Early textile engineers in Leeds, 1780–1850', *Publications of the Thoresby Society*, 2nd ser., 4 (1994), 40–61 · *Memoirs of eminent men of Leeds* (1868), 68–70 · *The life of Sir William Fairbairn, bart.*, ed. W. Pold (1970) · *CGPLA Eng. & Wales* (1861) · *DNB*
Archives W. Yorks. AS, Leeds, MSS, Accession 2371
Likenesses photograph, 1858; formerly in possession of Fairbairn, Lawson Ltd · engraving, c.1858–1859 (after portrait), Leeds Central Library · F. Grant, oils, 1859, Leeds Civic Hall · M. Noble, bronze statue, c.1868, Woodhouse Square, Leeds · wood-engraving, NPG; repro. in *ILN* (1858)
Wealth at death £45,000: probate, 15 March 1861, *CGPLA Eng. & Wales*

Fairbairn, Sir Robert Duncan (1910–1988), banker, was born on 25 September 1910 in Longhirst, near Morpeth, Northumberland, the youngest of three sons and fourth of five children of Robert Fairbairn and his wife, Christina Robertson. His father was a borderer who moved to Perth not long after Robert's birth to become head gamekeeper to the Dewar family. His mother, from the highlands and a Gaelic speaker, had been a lady's maid. Fairbairn grew up in the strict but benign atmosphere of a happy, relatively simple, rural home, while mixing on terms of easy familiarity with the family his father served. His natural talent for ball games, and for cricket in particular, was developed in family games on the Dewar estate, where he benefited from tuition by the professional engaged in the summers by the first Baron Forteviot for his son. Fairbairn had many and varied talents, a robust character, and an attractive personality that, allied to his enthusiasm and industry, brought him distinction, and many friends, in widely different fields.

Fairbairn was educated at Perth Academy, where he showed an aptitude for science. His teachers had intended him to develop this interest at St Andrews University, but when he left school in 1927 he secured an apprenticeship in the Perth branch of the Clydesdale Bank. By 1930 he had taken second place in the members' examination of the Institute of Bankers in Scotland and he was in due course transferred to the head office of the bank in Glasgow. While there he studied for the examinations of the English Institute of Bankers, and in the finals of 1934 won the Beckett memorial prize for first place overall, the White-head prize for practice and law of banking, and other distinctions.

In 1920 the Clydesdale had become affiliated with the Midland Bank, then in a period of acquisitive expansion, and in 1934 Fairbairn was invited by the Midland to work in London. He gained experience in London, Liverpool, and Bradford until 1939 when, having earlier joined the Royal Naval Volunteer Reserve in Liverpool, he was mobilized for war service in the Royal Navy. He served for six years, attaining the rank of lieutenant-commander (S) RNVR, and saw service first at Scapa Flow, then in the Admiralty, and finally, until the Second World War ended, in India.

Fairbairn returned to the Midland Bank in 1946 and gained rapid promotion there, but in 1950 he was needed in Scotland to help with the amalgamation of the Clydesdale with another Midland affiliate, the North of Scotland Bank. After a period in Aberdeen on this assignment he was brought back to Glasgow as assistant general manager (1951), and in 1958 he was appointed general manager in succession to Sir John Campbell. In 1967 he was elected to the board and when he retired as general manager in 1971 he was invited to become vice-chairman. He was appointed chairman in 1975 and retired in 1985. It was a rare distinction at that time for a practising Scottish banker to become chairman of the bank in which he had served, and clear evidence of the high esteem in which Fairbairn was held.

Throughout his career Fairbairn made his presence and his opinions powerfully and persuasively felt in many areas, not least in defending the distinctiveness of Scottish banking within the United Kingdom. Among his more notable initiatives at the Clydesdale was the radical review he instigated of the bank's public appearance and image, particularly as influenced by design, leading in the 1960s to the introduction of a fresh, modern, and much admired house style. His academic and practical abilities as a banker, his interest in matters of design, and his concern for the economic development of Scotland brought him many awards and appointments, public and private. He was a director of several major companies including the Midland Bank, Scottish Amicable Life Assurance Society, British National Oil Corporation, and Newarthill Ltd. He held senior offices in many banking and business organizations, and was a distinguished and effective chairman from 1972 until 1981 of the Scottish Industrial Development Advisory Board established under the Industry Act of 1970. In 1975 he was knighted in recognition of his services to economic development in Scotland.

Fairbairn's distinguished business career was matched by the development of his early promise as a sportsman. As a young man he played cricket—for Perthshire, West of Scotland, Cheshire, and eventually for the MCC and Scotland. His involvement in football led to his membership of the Queen's Park Football Club and of the celebrated Corinthian Casuals, for both of whom he played. When he turned to golf he was as competitive and as successful, winning the Silver Boomerang in his first year as a member of the Royal and Ancient and later captaining Royal Troon Golf Club. Fairbairn was 5 feet 10 inches in height, a strongly built, handsome man with a large head, blue-grey eyes, and a winning smile. He never lost his plentiful golden (later silver) hair, nor his robust, competitive, and cheerful athleticism and vitality. He had a quiet Scottish voice and an air of calm authority. In 1939 he married Sylvia Lucinda (d. 2001), daughter of Henry Coulter, a parish minister of the Church of Scotland in Glasgow. Their house in Bridge of Weir, Renfrewshire, bore witness to Fairbairn's interest in the visual arts. It was typical of his energy and zest even in retirement that when he was over seventy-five he and his wife enrolled as students at the Glasgow School of Art, where he was remembered as an assiduous and talented pupil. He died on 26 March 1988 in Guildford, Surrey, at his daughter's home, following a hip replacement operation.   THOMAS RISK, rev.

Sources C. W. Munn, *Clydesdale Bank: the first one hundred and fifty years* (1988) · private information (1996) · personal knowledge (1996) · *CCI* (1988)

Likenesses D. Poole, oils (?), 1981, priv. coll.

Wealth at death £355,222.76: confirmation, 1988, *CCI*

Fairbairn, (William) Ronald Dodds (1889–1964), psychiatrist and psychoanalyst, was born on 11 August 1889 at the Red House, Cluny Gardens, Edinburgh, the only child of Thomas Fairbairn (1854–1925), chartered surveyor and secretary of the Edinburgh Architectural Association, and Cecilia Leefe (1854–1946). Ronald Fairbairn lived in Edinburgh all his life except for periods as a student and while on foreign service during the First World War. His whole school career was passed at Merchiston Castle School in Edinburgh. He wanted to go on to Oxford University but his father forbade this as offering too much opportunity

for wickedness, and thus from 1907 he read mental philosophy at Edinburgh, obtaining his MA in 1911. From 1911 to 1914 he took courses in divinity and Hellenic studies in Manchester, London, Kiel, and Strasbourg and entered theological college in Edinburgh. Fairbairn joined the Royal Garrison Artillery as a territorial in 1915 and was posted abroad in 1916, serving in Egypt and Palestine. He had visited Craiglockhart, near Edinburgh, in 1915, where W. H. R. Rivers was pioneering psychotherapeutic work with shell-shock victims, and by the time that he was demobilized he had decided to become a psychotherapist. At that time most of the senior psychoanalysts were medically qualified, and so Fairbairn began his training by undertaking accelerated medical (1919–23), MB ChB, and then psychiatric (DipPsych) qualifications at Edinburgh University. An essential element in psychoanalytic training involved having a personal analysis, and Fairbairn went into treatment in 1921 with E. H. Connell. After qualification Fairbairn became assistant physician, Royal Edinburgh Hospital For Mental Diseases (1923–4). He had begun an MD on 'The relationship of dissociation and repression, considered from the point of view of medical psychology' immediately after qualification as a doctor but did not submit it until March 1929 when the examiners highly commended it. Between 1926 and 1931 Fairbairn was assistant physician at the Longmore Hospital, Edinburgh.

Fairbairn married Mary Ann More Gordon (1901–1952), daughter of Harry More Gordon, in 1926 and in 1927 became a lecturer in psychology in the department of philosophy at the University of Edinburgh. The first of the Fairbairns' children, Ellinor, was born in 1927 and the following year twins were born who did not survive. Their loss of the twins may have been the trigger for the breakdown in the mental and physical health of Mary Fairbairn, which cast a shadow over the remainder of the Fairbairns' marriage. The birth of their fourth child occurred in 1929, the same year that Fairbairn's ideas on 'The cause of mental disease' appeared in the *British Medical Journal*. Sir Nicholas Hardwick *Fairbairn (1933–1995), barrister and MP, was their fifth child. In 1928 Fairbairn had given a paper to the Scottish branch of the British Psychological Society entitled 'Notes on the religious phantasies of a female patient', which described the madness, invalidism, and, ultimately, the death of one of his patients, and expressed a concern with unsatisfiable longing which was to be a cornerstone of his psychological theory subsequently. Between 1929 and 1934 Fairbairn was medical psychologist to the Jordanburn Nerve Hospital, Edinburgh, and Edinburgh University Psychological Clinic for Children. He was elected to associate membership of the British Psycho-Analytic Society in 1931 and to full membership a few years later. In 1931 and 1932 he was lecturer in psychology at Edinburgh University. Preparing lectures for psychology students, being an active member of interdisciplinary meetings, and his own critical reading of Freud prevented him from becoming too immersed in psychoanalysis. His election to fellow of the Royal Anthropological Institute in 1932 reflected these wider interests.

Fairbairn enjoyed the company of children, and a significant part of his early clinical work was with them. He wrote a number of papers on education and on the effects of childhood sexual abuse. Despite this work becoming well known Fairbairn did not publish it, and these writings did not become widely available until the publication of two volumes of Fairbairn's work in an edition by D. Scharff and Fairbairn's daughter, Ellinor Fairbairn Birtles, in 1994. Fairbairn also had a considerable sympathy for people who cannot engage with others, or commit themselves emotionally. He applied to them the term that had become fashionable in Germany—schizoid—but unlike the German psychiatrists, who considered schizoidia an inborn temperament, Fairbairn thought that it was forced on a person by the conflict between desire for another person (prototypically the mother) and that person's constantly frustrating response to the desire. In 'The libido theory: the theory of the pleasure principle interpreted in terms of appetite', written in 1930 but first published in 1994, Fairbairn drew on the work of the social psychologist James Drever, and William McDougall, and proposed that Freud's assertion that behaviour is motivated by sexual and death instincts should be replaced by appetitive tendencies, which are triggered by needs such as hunger, and reactive tendencies, which are stirred by object-interest. The failure of these tendencies to remove what caused them leads to feelings which are characteristic of the tendency and which themselves function like appetites. A loving tendency, if it does not meet a loving response from its object, becomes an appetitive tendency of frustration or sorrow. Objects are usually important others, but may be animals, things, or institutions: indeed anything which a person might think can provide them with what they need or want. Fairbairn's emphasis on the importance of social relationships involving objects marked a turning point in psychoanalysis. It was, however, Melanie Klein, and not Fairbairn, who developed object-relations theory and Fairbairn's only acknowledged contribution is the inclusion by Klein of 'schizoid' in her characterization of the infant's early relationship to its carer, the 'paranoid-schizoid' position.

Fairbairn's classic papers, 'A revised psychopathology of the psychoses and psychoneuroses' (1940) and 'Endopsychic structure considered in terms of object-relationships' (1941), were both published in the *International Journal of Psychoanalysis*. Although they made his reputation, they also show imprints of Fairbairn's long incubation with Kleinian ideas. Earlier themes recur, but in a more formal, orthodox formulation, lacking the vigour of the earlier unpublished work. Fairbairn became disenchanted by psychoanalysis towards the end of his life. He felt able to reduce his own theory to a single page of principles for the *British Journal of Medical Psychology* in 1963, and his correspondence with up-and-coming psychoanalysts at the end of his career indicates a pessimism about the approach and development of psychoanalysis.

Mary Fairbairn died, after many years of ill health, on 28 September 1952, a year that also saw the publication of Fairbairn's collected papers, *Psychoanalytic Studies of the Personality*. Fairbairn's personal life took on a new dimension when he began a relationship with Marion Frances Mackintosh (1907–1995), daughter of Captain H. E. M. Archer. Fairbairn married Marion, who had become his secretary, in April 1959, but was in failing health and from 1960 had a series of attacks, the first on the day of Melanie Klein's funeral, which were associated with a decline in his mental and physical health. Fairbairn died on 31 December 1964 at 19 Drumsheugh Gardens, Edinburgh. He was buried in Dean cemetery, Edinburgh, after a service in St Mary's Cathedral. He was survived by his second wife.

Since his death Fairbairn's work has found a new relevance, and its influence has been particularly strong on the theory of highly disturbed or 'borderline' patients. Fairbairn would sometimes recall an occasion when, as a young child, he had begged a young girl to come to play but, when she finally acceded to his request, she had been knocked down and killed as she crossed the road to his house. Whether or not Fairbairn was personally preoccupied with the perils of needs and longings, his single most important theoretical contribution is his precise delineation of the allure, the struggles to reject, and the impossibility of giving up the object of desire whose recognition must be bought at a price of guilt, fear, jealousy, or shame. DIGBY TANTAM

Sources private information (2004) · W. R. D. Fairbairn, Autobiographical note, *British Journal of Medical Psychology*, 36 (1963), 107 · J. Sutherland, *Fairbairn's journey into the interior* (1989) · *From instinct to self: selected papers of W. R. D. Fairbairn*, ed. D. Scharff and E. Fairbairn Birtles, 2 vols. (1994) · *WWW* · b. cert. · d. cert.
Archives NL Scot., corresp. and papers · U. Edin. L., MSS
Likenesses photographs, repro. in Fairbairn, Scharff, and Birtles, eds., *From instinct to self*
Wealth at death £43,576 19s. 2d.: confirmation, 5 March 1965, *CCI*

Fairbairn, Stephen (1862–1938), oarsman, was born at Toorak, Melbourne, Australia, on 25 August 1862, the fifth of the six sons of George Fairbairn and his wife, Virginia Charlotte, youngest daughter of George Armytage of Geelong, Victoria, a native of Derbyshire. George Fairbairn, having emigrated from Berwickshire in 1839, owned a large sheep station and in the 1870s started the first canning and meat-freezing works in Australia. The Scottish theologian Patrick Fairbairn was Stephen's uncle, and one of his elder brothers was Sir George Fairbairn, agent-general for Victoria from 1924 to 1927.

Fairbairn was a spirited and somewhat unruly child, and he passed through several schools before settling at Geelong grammar school, under the guiding influence of the headmaster, J. B. Wilson. A tall and handsome youth, he earned distinction in all forms of sport, but also performed well academically, and he followed his brothers to Jesus College, Cambridge, where he read law, graduating in 1884. He was called to the bar by the Inner Temple in 1886 but did not practise. In 1884 he returned to Australia, where, but for two intervals in England, in 1886–7 and 1897–8, he worked at the family's farming interests in Victoria and western Queensland. On 18 November 1891 he married Ellen, daughter of Sydney Sharwood of Aramac,

Queensland; they had two sons. Fairbairn came back to England in 1904 and thereafter devoted himself almost exclusively to coaching various rowing clubs, both in London, where he worked as a director of Dalgety & Co., Australia, merchants, and in Cambridge.

Fairbairn rowed in the losing Cambridge crews of 1882 and 1883 and in the victorious crews of 1886 and 1887, and won many other races besides, including the Grand Challenge Cup, the stewards', and the Wyfold at Henley. However, his claim to fame rests on his methods of coaching and the success of the crews that he coached. In an era of competing rowing styles, with their emphasis on differing body positions during the stroke, some tried to attribute to Fairbairn a new style, 'Fairbairnism'. That, however, came from a complete misunderstanding of the man. Fairbairn created no new style and had no desire to invent one. He wrote: 'There are certain principles underlying rowing, and what is called style is the endeavour to carry them out. Variations are merely failures to carry out the principles. There can be only one true style.' He emphasized above all a powerful leg drive and a relaxed recovery to maximize the boat speed, and he cared little for the aesthetic effect that this produced. He turned the pupil's mind to the oar in the water and to moving the boat, regardless of the angle of the head or the straightness of the back, whereas the orthodox coach would concentrate on positioning the body in order to produce certain results on the oar and the passage of the boat. Fairbairn summed up the debate over style as '"pretty pretty" versus honest hard work' and wrote: 'Never sacrifice work to appearance; but of course style is effect, and honest hard work will give true style eventually' (*The Times*, 1 June 1931; *Fairbairn on Rowing*, 542).

Fairbairn coached always for looseness and ease. A favourite remark was: 'If you can't do it easily, you can't do it at all'. He would never try to correct by condemnation and gave wide licence to individuals to develop their stroke naturally. He was ahead of his time in recognizing the importance of the subconscious mind in the development of technique, and his famous phrase 'Mileage makes champions' resonates still. He set before the performer an ideal after which to strive: if in his striving he did some odd things, never mind; the key was to be positive in coaching and encourage rather than criticize. It was inevitable that some of his crews, which had moved only a little way along the road to perfection, showed ungainly attitudes and exaggerations of ideals which earned bitter condemnation from more orthodox coaches, but what Fairbairn's crews lost in aesthetics they often gained in speed.

Fairbairn was an enthusiast, and was able to impart his enthusiasm to his pupils. He was ever progressive, ever ready to try out some new idea in coaching or some new device such as long slides or swivel rowlocks. He did much to make rowing popular, particularly in the clubs at Putney, and in 1925 he instituted the 'head of the river' race on the Putney to Mortlake course: a bronze bust of Fairbairn, by George Drinkwater, is held each year by the winning crew as the trophy. He coached many successful crews of both the London Rowing Club and the Thames Rowing Club, but his old college, Jesus, always took first place in his affections, and for more than thirty-three years he devoted himself to coaching its crews. It was a small college with a small boat club, but Fairbairn brought it many successes. His crews always raced hard and often won against crews which seemed to be better or more experienced.

Fairbairn was known throughout the rowing world as Steve, and even those who disagreed with his unorthodox ways admitted his genuine love of rowing, his boundless enthusiasm, his kindliness, and his genius for coaching. He cut a tall, portly figure on the river bank, 'in an old blue blazer, with back as straight as when he rowed in '82, chest thrown out, head slightly on one side, and eyes fixed immovably on the crews racing past' (*The Times*, 17 May 1938). His writings include *Rowing Notes* (1926) and an autobiography, *Fairbairn of Jesus* (1931). His collected writings on rowing were published in a single volume in 1990, *Steve Fairbairn on Rowing*, edited by his son Ian. Fairbairn died at his residence, the Mostyn Hotel, Portman Square, London, on 16 May 1938, in which year Jesus College retained the headship of the Cam; his ashes rest beneath the shadow of the college chapel. He is remembered in Cambridge by the Fairbairn cup races, which he inaugurated in the late 1920s as a handicap race between Jesus crews to serve as a form guide towards the end of Michaelmas term. The event later expanded to include other colleges and, in 1976, a women's event as well. And on the Thames in London there is the Steve Fairbairn memorial stone: marking 1 mile from the start of the boat race course at Putney, and 1 mile from the finish of the head of the river race, it aptly commemorates Fairbairn's immense contribution both to varsity and to tideway rowing.

H. B. PLAYFORD, rev. MARK POTTLE

Sources personal knowledge (1949) · private information (1949) · *Steve Fairbairn on rowing*, ed. I. Fairbairn (1990) · *The Times* (1 June 1931) · *The Times* (17 May 1938) · *AusDB* · Venn, *Alum. Cant.* · *CGPLA Eng. & Wales* (1938)
Likenesses J. Quinn, oils, c.1926, Jesus College, Cambridge · G. Drinkwater, bronze bust
Wealth at death £8495 1s. 7d.: probate, 12 July 1938, *CGPLA Eng. & Wales*

Fairbairn, Sir Thomas, second baronet (1823–1891), art administrator and patron, was born on 18 January 1823 at The Polygon, Ardwick, Manchester, the third of the eight surviving children of Sir William *Fairbairn, first baronet (1789–1874), engineer, and his wife, Dorothy (1788/9–1882), daughter of John Mar of Morpeth. He was educated privately, and in 1840 joined his father's firm, William Fairbairn & Co. This entailed sacrificing an intended university career; however, a ten-month tour of Italy in 1841–2 enabled him to consolidate his interest in the arts. His immediate course lay in the metropolis, where he became the partner in charge of the ailing Millwall shipbuilding works. Although by baptism and upbringing a Unitarian (his father was a stalwart of the famous Cross Street Chapel in Manchester), on 23 March 1848 he married

Allison Callaway (1827–1907), the daughter of a London surgeon, in an Anglican church in Greenwich. That year the Millwall concern was sold off at a great loss, but this was absorbed by the Manchester works, which went on to make considerable fortunes for all the partners.

Fairbairn's means enabled him to make a valuable contribution to national life as an art patron, collector, and exhibition organizer. Based in Manchester from 1848, he began buying contemporary works from the exhibitions of the Royal Manchester Institution (where his father was a governor), but seeing the works of William Holman Hunt at the 1853 Royal Academy exhibition was a turning point in the development of his collection. Fairbairn sponsored completion of *The Awakening Conscience* (1853–4; Tate collection), the first of his many Hunt purchases. Friendship between the two men channelled the patron's taste towards the Pre-Raphaelites, leading to commissions from Thomas Woolner of a marble statue of Fairbairn's eldest surviving children entitled *Constance and Arthur, or, Deaf and Dumb* (1857–62; priv. coll.) and a marble bust of James Brooke, raja of Sarawak (1858; priv. coll.). Through Hunt, Fairbairn bought paintings by John Brett and Robert Braithwaite Martineau, and in 1858 and 1862 commissioned three landscapes from Edward Lear, to whom the Pre-Raphaelite described Fairbairn in early 1860 as a patron who 'has really got an immense instinct for what is good in Art which makes him enjoy the right thing when he comes across it' (Bronkhurst, 597).

As chairman of the great Manchester Art Treasures Exhibition of 1857, Fairbairn was responsible for its inclusion of the Soulages collection of decorative art; this had been purchased by the committee for £13,500 and was sold on to the South Kensington Museum (later the V&A) from 1859 to 1865. The chairman was deeply involved in the selection of contemporary pictures, and, by putting Augustus Egg in charge of their hanging, Fairbairn ensured that progressive artists as well as academicians were well represented. For the first time in Britain, Pre-Raphaelite art was widely shown, while the old master exhibits were arranged chronologically, with Italian art hung opposite other paintings of the same date. Having refused the offer of a knighthood for his efforts, in January 1860 Fairbairn launched a campaign to establish a free art gallery and museum in Manchester, as 'a sure means of strengthening the feelings of mutual regard and dependence which, in a free and advancing country, knits the different ranks and interests of society together' (*Manchester Guardian*, 25 Sept 1860, 3). Fairbairn was no stranger to class conflict: his series of letters to *The Times* under the pseudonym Amicus had championed the employers' cause in the Manchester lock-out strike of 1851–2.

The museum project foundered, and Fairbairn channelled his energies into the metropolitan art world, as a member of the Royal Commission for the Exhibition of 1851 (to which he was elected in May 1861), and as commissioner for the International Exhibition of 1862 with responsibility for the fine art department. About this time he acquired Burton Park, near Petworth in Sussex; *The*

Children's Holiday (Torre Abbey, Torquay), the group portrait of his wife and five children commissioned from Holman Hunt in 1864, was probably painted to hang at the head of the staircase there. Furnishing both a London and a country establishment accelerated the pace of his collecting. Records of his acquisitions indicate that his taste was very catholic—an inventory of 1870 lists paintings by Constable, Turner, Richard Wilson, and Zoffany, by contemporary French artists, and by academicians such as Frederick Goodall and Thomas Creswick, as well as those of the British avant-garde.

By July 1866 Fairbairn had moved to Brambridge House, Bishopstoke, near Southampton, and four years later he was appointed high sheriff of Hampshire. The portrait which he commissioned from Holman Hunt in 1873 (priv. coll.) memorably conveys his thickset and imposing appearance. Its backdrop was of the interior of the South Kensington Museum—an apt reflection of his role as commissioner for the international exhibitions of 1851, 1862, 1867, and 1871. After he succeeded to the baronetcy in 1874, the depression in the iron industry led Fairbairn to wind up the Fairbairn Engineering Company. He now employed his administrative abilities as a magistrate and deputy lieutenant for Hampshire. In 1889 he gave up his London home at 42 Wilton Place, Belgravia, and retired to Brambridge House, where he died of a stroke on 12 August 1891; he was buried six days later at Twyford church. Bequests in his will included gifts presented to him by the emperor Napoleon III, the crown prince of Prussia, and the emperor of Austria, in recognition of his role as promoter of the arts. No provision was made for his extensive art collection to remain intact, and some of his pictures were auctioned at Phillips on 3 May 1892. A further sale took place at Christies on 2 March 1895.

JUDITH BRONKHURST

Sources W. Pole, ed., *The life of Sir William Fairbairn, bart.* (1877), 317, 323–4, 325, 330–31, 342, 379, 394, 440–41, 449 · J. Bronkhurst, 'Fruits of a connoisseur's friendship: Sir Thomas Fairbairn and William Holman Hunt', *Burlington Magazine*, 125 (1983), 586–97 · C. Arscott, 'Employer, husband, spectator: Thomas Fairbairn's commission of *The awakening conscience*', *The culture of capital: art, power and the nineteenth-century middle class*, ed. J. Wolff and J. Seed (1988), 159–90 · private information (2004) · Burke, *Peerage* (1949) · d. cert. · *Catalogue of a valuable collection of oil paintings* (1892), lots 80–111 [sale catalogue, Phillips, Son, and Neale, 3 May 1892] · *Catalogue of the valuable collection of modern pictures [including] the property of the late Sir Thomas Fairbairn* (1895), lots 126–35 [sale catalogue, Christie, Manson, and Woods, 2 March 1895] · *Catalogue of a very large assemblage of modern pictures* (1866), lots 261–72 [sale catalogue, Christie, Manson, and Woods, 16–17 March 1866] · *Catalogue [including] three works of W. Holman Hunt, the property of Sir Thomas Fairbairn, Bart.* (1887), lots 141–4 [sale catalogue, Christie, Manson, and Woods, 7 May 1887] · D. S. Macleod, *Art and the Victorian middle class: money and the making of cultural identity* (1996)

Archives Man. CL, Manchester Archives, letters to George Wilson · Man. CL, Manchester Archives, Royal Manchester Institution collection, corresp.

Likenesses L. Haghe, group portrait, watercolour, 1857 (*Sir Thomas Fairbairn Handing over the Address to the Prince Consort in the Art Treasures Exhibition at Manchester in May 1857*), Man. City Gall. · W. H. Hunt, oils, 1873, repro. in Bronkhurst, 'Fruits of a connoisseur's friendship', 589; priv. coll. · lithograph, in or after 1874, priv. coll. ·

D. J. Pound, engraving (after photograph by John & Chas. Watkins), priv. coll. • engraving, repro. in *The Queen* (18 Jan 1862), 397
Wealth at death £72,661 2*s.* 8*d.*: probate, 17 Oct 1891, *CGPLA Eng. & Wales*

Fairbairn, Sir William, first baronet (1789–1874), engineer, was born at Kelso, Roxburghshire, on 19 February 1789. He was the son of Andrew Fairbairn, a farmer. After serving in the navy during the American War of Independence, his father returned to Scotland, and married the daughter of a Jedburgh tradesman, a Miss Henderson, with whom he had five children, another of whom was Peter *Fairbairn (1799–1861), engineer and inventor. Fairbairn learned to read and do arithmetic at a parish school, and began to build boats and little mills. He had further schooling at Mullochy, and studied book-keeping under an uncle who kept a school at Galashiels. In 1799 his father began to farm 300 acres at Dingwall, in the north of Scotland, but moved back to Kelso in 1801, and subsequently to Knaresborough, in Yorkshire. Aged fourteen, Fairbairn got employment on a bridge being built by John Rennie, until he was injured by an accident.

Towards the end of 1803 Fairbairn's father moved to a farm near Newcastle upon Tyne belonging to the Percy Main colliery, and William got a job in the colliery. On 24 March 1804 he was apprenticed to John Robinson, a millwright, but continued his mathematical and other studies. Because of his technical ingenuity he was appointed to look after the engines at the colliery, and became acquainted with George Stephenson.

At the end of his apprenticeship, in March 1811, Fairbairn obtained employment as a millwright at Newcastle. He then sailed for London in December 1811 and secured an introduction to the Society of Arts and to Alexander Tilloch (1795–1825), the founder of the *Philosophical Magazine*, who employed him in the construction of a steam engine for digging. Fairbairn subsequently moved to Manchester and on 16 June 1816 he married Dorothy Mar (1788/9–1882), youngest daughter of John Mar of Morpeth; they had seven sons and two daughters. His heir, Thomas *Fairbairn, became a successful art administrator and patron. In 1817 Fairbairn had a disagreement with his employer about a new Blackfriars Bridge over the River Irwell at Manchester, and this led to his setting up in partnership with an old shopmate, James Lillie. They soon acquired a good reputation by providing the machinery for a cotton mill, and their business rapidly increased. In 1824 Fairbairn went to Zürich to erect two watermills. By an ingenious contrivance he surmounted the difficulties due to the irregular supply of water, and constructed wheels which worked regularly whatever the height of the river. By 1830 Fairbairn and Lillie had cash in hand of £40,000, and were employing three hundred workers.

The firm began to construct light iron steam passenger boats, but Fairbairn and Lillie lost heavily in a cotton mill venture, which crippled their resources as millwrights and led to a dissolution of the partnership in 1832, Lillie setting up in opposition. Fairbairn subsequently devoted his energies to shipbuilding. He first built his ships in sections at Manchester, but in 1835 decided to establish his works at Millwall, on the Thames in east London, in partnership with an old pupil, Andrew Murray. He subsequently found the strain too great and in 1844 abandoned the Millwall establishment, where two thousand men were employed. At Manchester he undertook many engineering schemes, experimented on the properties of iron, and, to meet a strike of his workmen, introduced the riveting machine, which was a great advance in the manufacture of boilers.

In 1839 Fairbairn inspected the government works at Constantinople, and was decorated by the sultan, who also appointed him as 'chief fabricator' of machinery for the Turkish government in England. He was consulted in 1840 on the drainage of the Haarlem Lake. In 1841 he gave advice to the British government on the prevention of accidents by machinery. In 1842 he took out a patent (no. 9409) for improvements in the construction of iron ships, but this proved too troublesome for general application. Fairbairn assisted Robert Stephenson with the design of the tubular bridge over the Menai Strait. The bridge was successfully raised in April 1848, but there was later a controversy over Fairbairn's contribution. In order to put the record straight he published his own version of events, *An account of the construction of the Britannia and Conway tubular bridges, with a complete history of their progress* (1849). He and Stephenson had also in October 1846 jointly taken out a patent for the new principle of wrought-iron girders that had been devised for the bridge.

Fairbairn declined a knighthood in 1861, but accepted a baronetcy in 1869. In 1840 he bought the Polygon, Ardwick, near Manchester, where he lived until his death, and where he received many distinguished visitors. He often spoke at the British Association and similar meetings, and served as juror in the London exhibitions of 1851 and 1862, and at the Paris Exhibition of 1855. Made a member of the Légion d'honneur in 1855, he also became a foreign member of the Institut de France. He received the gold medal of the Royal Society in 1860, and was president of the British Association in 1861. He received the honorary LLD degree of Edinburgh in 1860 and of Cambridge in 1862.

Fairbairn was elected president of the Institution of Mechanical Engineers in 1854, and was president of the Manchester Literary and Philosophical Society from 1855 to 1860. He made numerous contributions to the *Transactions of the Royal Society* as well as to the proceedings of other learned societies. He also made many investigations into the properties of the earth's crust in conjunction with William Hopkins, the Cambridge mathematician, and was an authority upon a wide range of mechanical and engineering problems. He published a number of works, including a handbook for engineers (1856), an examination of the properties of iron (1861), and a treatise on mills (1861–3), all of which went through further editions.

Fairbairn caught a chill, from which he never recovered, at the opening of the new buildings of Owens College in Manchester in 1870. He died of a severe bronchial cold on

18 August 1874 at the house of his son-in-law, a Mr Bateman of Moor Park, near Farnham in Surrey. He was survived by his wife, and was buried at Prestwick, Northumberland. A giant water-wheel, designed by Fairbairn for a mill at Pateley Bridge in Yorkshire, was restored and reintegrated at Quarry Bank Mill at Styal in Cheshire in the 1980s by the National Trust. It is one of the few surviving examples of Fairbairn's contribution to water-wheel technology. JAMES BURNLEY, *rev.* ROBERT BROWN

Sources W. Pole, ed., *The life of Sir William Fairbairn, bart.* (1877) · S. Smiles, *Lives of the engineers*, new edn, 5 (1874); repr. with introduction by E. le Maré as *The lives of George and Robert Stephenson* (1975) · probate · *CGPLA Eng. & Wales* (1874)
Archives Museum of Science and Industry, Manchester, notebook on boiler efficiency, EN 12 | BL, letters to Charles Babbage, Add. MSS 37191–37196 · CUL, letters to T. R. Robinson · CUL, letters to Sir George Stokes · ICL, letters to W. C. Unwin and W. J. Unwin
Likenesses P. Park, marble bust, 1855, RS · B. R. Faulkner, oils, 1872, RS · E. E. Geflowski, marble statue, *c.*1878, Town Hall, Manchester · W. H. Hunt, oils, Institute of Mechanical Engineers, London · P. Westcott, oils, Inst. CE · stipple and line engraving, NPG
Wealth at death under £120,000: probate, 22 Sept 1874, *CGPLA Eng. & Wales*

Fairbank family (*per. c.*1725–1848), surveyors, were of a family settled in Sheffield since the second half of the sixteenth century. The family surveying tradition began with **William [i] Fairbank** (*c.*1688–1759), surveyor and schoolmaster, born in Sheffield about 1688. It was quite common to practise these two professions as both demanded similar skills, although once a surveyor became well established and busy it could prove difficult to remain in the field, surveying for days at a stretch, without jeopardizing the running of a school. The family were Quakers from about the end of the seventeenth century. William married Emma (*d.* 1756), widow of William Broadhead of Sheffield and daughter of John Clark of Swinton, near Rotherham, on 9 December 1725 at the Friends' meeting-house in Sheffield; they had three sons and two daughters. He was a committed Quaker, being appointed representative at a meeting of Friends in 1733 and that year having his goods distrained for non-payment of tithes. He left maps and plans dated 1737 to 1750, but the surviving maps are a tiny proportion of the many plans his daybooks show him to have drawn. He also kept a school in Sheffield, possibly at White House, Bramall Lane, at least from 1753 until his death, which occurred at a roadside inn outside Sheffield on 5 December 1759 as a result of a riding accident the previous day; he was buried in the Quaker burial-ground in Sheffield. His youngest son, **William [ii] Fairbank** (*c.*1730–1801), followed him as both surveyor and schoolmaster. He married Mary, daughter of Josiah Forster, surveyor and schoolmaster, of Tottenham High Cross, Middlesex, at the Tottenham Friends' meeting-house on 11 May 1758. He combined his two professions until demand for his services as a surveyor led him to give up the school in 1774. He did much surveying for the town trustees and for private landowners, as well as laying out and constructing many turnpike roads in and around Sheffield. He also did engineering works on the River Don and other waterways, and laid out and built many public and private buildings. The family surveys of Sheffield were so numerous that he was able to publish a street map of the town in 1771 and revise and extend it in 1801. He died on 9 August 1801 at his home at West Hill, Lee's Croft, Sheffield; he was survived by his wife.

William [ii] Fairbank had three sons and two daughters, and his eldest son, **William [iii] Fairbank** (*c.*1771–1846), and his second son, **Josiah Fairbank** (1777–1844), both of whom had been helping their father in the business, formed a partnership after his death. In 1808 they published a revised map of Sheffield, then growing rapidly. William [iii] was never very active in the family firm and long before he died, unmarried, at Sheffield on 15 July 1846 his brother Josiah took sole control and moved the business to East Parade, Sheffield, from where he valued the whole of Sheffield and Halifax for rating purposes, built roads, and constructed reservoirs, as well as continuing with private estate mapping. He married Sarah Carbutt (1783–1853) of Leeds and they had seven sons and four daughters. Josiah left the Society of Friends shortly before his death on 23 April 1844 in Sheffield. He was buried in Sheffield general cemetery. Three of his sons became surveyors in the business and of these **William Fairbank Fairbank** (1805–1848) became his father's partner. He married Frances Royston Fisher. He inherited much parliamentary work from his father—some road projects, but mainly railway schemes. The pressure of work in the railway mania and its subsequent collapse in 1844–5 led to his suffering a stroke in 1846 after which he worked only from his office, not in the field, and on 29 May 1848 he had a second, fatal, stroke while in his garden at South Street, Sheffield. He was buried at Eccleshall; he was survived by his wife.

The death of William Fairbank Fairbank brought the Sheffield surveying family to a close, although his brothers Josiah Forster Fairbank (*d.* 1899)—who had been in the family firm until the railway collapse of the 1840s—and John Tertius Fairbank, and other descendants, continued surveying outside Sheffield. The several thousand maps, plans, drawings, and elevations in the Fairbank collection are particularly valuable for those involved in legal disputes over rights of way and boundaries, and for students of the geography and history of Sheffield and the surrounding area, since the large-scale plans and their careful annotations provide evidence of local landownership and landholding over a very considerable period. The collection includes the first known maps of many localities and the field and account books also shed light on the daily routine and livelihood of the family as surveyors, schoolmasters, and building contractors.

ELIZABETH BAIGENT

Sources T. W. Hall, *The Fairbanks of Sheffield, 1688–1848* (1932) · B. English, *Yorkshire enclosure awards* (1985) · [Sheffield City Libraries], *A guide to the Fairbank collection* (1936)
Archives Sheffield Central Library, collection
Likenesses silhouettes, repro. in Hall, *Fairbanks*

Fairbank, Alfred John (1895–1982), calligrapher, was born on 12 July 1895 in Grimsby, Lincolnshire, the elder of the two sons of Alfred John Fairbank (1868–1953), engine fitter, and his wife, Emma Greetham (1863–1929), a Salvation Army officer. His parents moved to Gillingham, Kent, when his father became a chargeman of engine fitters in Chatham Dockyard. He was educated at the Wesleyan higher grade school, Gillingham, and at Chatham Dockyard school.

When fifteen Fairbank joined the dockyard as a boy writer. It was a modest beginning to a career culminating in the rank of senior executive officer, but it was a family triumph in 1911. Competition for civil service entry was stiff: success depended on good handwriting. Thus Fairbank developed the interest and skill which led the first Baron Bridges to write of him when seventy 'No man of our time has done more for good handwriting, whether for the individual or the community, than Alfred Fairbank' (Osley, ix). On 2 April 1919 he married Elsie (1893–1987), daughter of George Kneeshaw, master bricklayer. They had one son, John, a chartered civil engineer, and one daughter, who died as an infant in 1922.

A dockyard colleague introduced Fairbank to the arts and crafts movement and calligraphy. William Morris was especially influential through his manuscript books and his copies of italic writing manuals. Transfer to the Admiralty enabled him in 1920 to attend evening classes in writing and illuminating at the Central School of Arts and Crafts, London. He met Edward Johnston who came to regard him highly and whose seminal book, *Writing and Illuminating and Lettering* (1906), stimulated his study of Renaissance handwriting and of palaeography—the inspiration for the italic script and type associated with his name.

In the inter-war years Fairbank established a reputation in both calligraphy and type design. Notable examples were his text in roman script of *Ecclesiasticus* (1929) and his type design, narrow Bembo italic (1928). A founding member of the Society of Scribes and Illuminators (SSI), he became honorary secretary in 1931 and its first president twenty years later. After 1945 his fame as a calligrapher grew, marked by the success of *A Book of Scripts*, the Penguin book of the year in 1949. He was appointed CBE in 1951. During his twelve years as SSI president (1951–63) he completed the best-known of his many calligraphy projects, the design and direction of the RAF book of remembrance at St Clement Danes, London.

Fairbank's contribution to handwriting made him known to a larger public. In 1932 the Dryad Press published *A Handwriting Manual* and also his writing cards for schools. The *Beacon Writing Books*, a collaborative work with Charlotte Stone and Winifred Hooper, followed after the Second World War. The adoption of the italic script by many schools and a wider interest in the reform of handwriting encouraged him to initiate the founding of the Society for Italic Handwriting in 1952, with a director of education, Joseph Compton, as chairman; it soon had more than 500 members. Fairbank's later books included *Renaissance Handwriting: an Anthology of Italic Scripts*, with Berthold Wolpe (1960), *A Roman Script for Schools* (1961), and *The Story of Handwriting* (1970).

Fairbank's personality reflected wide cultural interests

and a gift for friendship. He was an influential figure in the field of calligraphy—tall and spare, exacting and conservative in his craft, but with a sense of humour and a love of beauty which his colleagues and pupils relished. His fame may, however, rest primarily on his own writing and texts as a scholar penman. He described handwriting as a 'dance of the pen': so it was when he himself wrote.

Fairbank retired from the Admiralty to Hove. He died on 14 March 1982 at 4 Preston Park Avenue, Brighton. His remains were cremated on the 18th at Woodvale, Brighton, and his ashes scattered on Ditchling Beacon, Sussex, on 10 April.　　　　　　　　　　PATRICK NAIRNE

Sources A. S. Osley, ed., *Calligraphy and palaeography: essays presented to Alfred Fairbank on his 70th birthday* (1965) • 'In memoriam - A. J. Fairbank', *Journal of the Society for Italic Handwriting*, 107 (1982) • J. Fairbank, 'The work of Alfred Fairbank (1895–1982)', *Letter Arts Review*, 11/4 (1994) • *The story of Kormak, the son of Ogmund, by Wm. Morris and Eirikr Magnusson, including a note on the manuscript work of William Morris by Alfred Fairbank*, William Morris Society (1970) • *CGPLA Eng. & Wales* (1982) • private information (2004)
Archives Bodl. Oxf., MSS, incl. letters • U. Birm. L., special collections department, collection of calligraphic fragments | NL Scot., corresp. with Ruari McLean • NL Wales, letters to James Wardrop of the Gregynog Press
Likenesses photograph, repro. in Osley, ed., *Calligraphy and palaeography*, frontispiece
Wealth at death £53,550: probate, 22 June 1982, *CGPLA Eng. & Wales*

Fairbank, Josiah (1777–1844). *See under* Fairbank family (*per. c.*1725–1848).

Fairbank, William (*c.*1688–1759). *See under* Fairbank family (*per. c.*1725–1848).

Fairbank, William (*c.*1730–1801). *See under* Fairbank family (*per. c.*1725–1848).

Fairbank, William (*c.*1771–1846). *See under* Fairbank family (*per. c.*1725–1848).

Fairbank, William Fairbank (1805–1848). *See under* Fairbank family (*per. c.*1725–1848).

Fairborne, Sir Palmes (1644–1680), colonial administrator, was a son of the royalist Colonel Stafford Fairborne of Newark. In his teens he fought as a mercenary for the Venetians in the defence of Candia (Crete). He returned to England in 1661, when he became a captain in the newly raised Tangier regiment of foot. In January 1662 this was shipped to Tangier, where in 1664 Fairborne was promoted major. He was back in England briefly in the winter of 1665–6 for a recruiting tour of the west country. By this time he had married Margaret or Margery Devereux (*d.* 1694); their eldest son, Stafford *Fairborne, was born about 1666. In March or April 1675, shortly before his return to Tangier after another spell in England, Fairborne was knighted. In May 1676 he became deputy governor in the absence of William O'Brien, earl of Inchiquin, and in January 1677 he was promoted lieutenant-colonel. After two years in effective sole command of Tangier he returned to England, in 1678, and in the same year he served as commissary-general of the army in Flanders. He returned to Tangier on 8 April 1680 and became governor *de facto* in June when Inchiquin went home and his intended successor, Thomas Butler, earl of Ossory, died before he could set out. Only a fortnight before Fairborne's return, the Moors had begun their most ambitious attempt yet to reconquer the colony, the siege continuing through the summer and into the autumn. On 24 October Fairborne rode out to inspect the defences and was hit by a 'chance shot', according to the epitaph, penned partly by John Dryden, erected in Westminster Abbey by Fairborne's widow. He lingered long enough to see the successful counter-attack by his deputy, Colonel Sackville, which raised the siege, and died on the evening of 27 October 1680.

Throughout the 1660s and 1670s Fairborne's own (invariably forthright) letters, and a number of detailed accounts by others, give a vivid picture of his time at Tangier and of the life of the English garrison. Fairborne's hot temper often got him into trouble with his superiors and equals. He fought a number of duels; in 1671 he threw a bucket of water over a Mrs Pope, who had been swearing at his wife; and in 1674 he was sentenced to be shot for insubordination to the governor, the earl of Middleton, and was kept under restraint until eventually pardoned. Much of Fairborne's brashness stemmed from deep financial insecurity. He had a rapidly growing family that was always on 'the verge of poverty', according to the historian of Tangier (Routh, 155), and his career displays ample evidence of concern to obtain as much money as possible from legitimate, and sometimes other, sources. He regularly sent presents to successive secretaries of state Henry Bennet, earl of Arlington, and Sir Joseph Williamson; he was implicated in 1672 in the theft of jewels belonging to the Moorish ruler, Guylan; and he worried in 1680 that as a result of Ossory's appointment over his head, 'the small pittance of £500 per annum allowed him as commander-in-chief might not be taken away ... as things at Tangier are three times as dear as in England, and he had not received a farthing of pay' (Davis, 1.158–60). His willingness to go behind the backs of his superiors by writing directly to England hardly endeared him to them. Nevertheless, Fairborne was far from being entirely selfish and corrupt. In 1676–7 he paid for improvements to the fortifications at his own expense, and he was just as persistent in pressing for payment of the entire garrison's arrears as he was for his own. He saw clearly the link between lack of pay and lack of discipline, but came down hard on the latter: one potential mutiny was stymied when he summarily shot the ringleader.

During his time in the colony Fairborne fought frequent skirmishes against the Moors. In September 1675 he commanded a sortie ordered by Inchiquin, but this was revealed to be a Moorish trap and Fairborne bitterly criticized the governor to the authorities in London. On 7 January 1678 he led out the relief force to forts Henrietta and Kendal, which had been attacked by the Moors on the previous day. In the final attacks in 1680, as throughout his career, Fairborne proved himself to be a competent and cautious tactician, always aware of the limitations imposed on him by a relatively small garrison, an effective organizer, and above all a highly professional soldier of undoubted courage. Only a few days before his death, he reiterated his oft-expressed opinion that Tangier 'could never be made steadable to the king in no fashion' (Halkett, 12): three years after his death, the colony he had fought so hard to defend was evacuated, and its buildings blown up.

Fairborne's death left his widow and their seven children in the poverty he had always feared: the pension of £500 per annum, granted to her by Charles II in 1681, was already £1500 in arrears in 1685. On 1 April 1683 at St Marylebone, Middlesex, she married Jasper Paston, a son of the earl of Yarmouth; she died in 1698. Fairborne's eldest son, Stafford, entered the navy, and became a knight and an admiral. J. D. DAVIES

Sources E. M. G. Routh, *Tangier: England's lost Atlantic outpost, 1661–84* (1912) · J. Childs, *The army of Charles II* (1976) · 1676–80, BL, Add. MS 17021 [Fairborne's letters and papers] · *Tangier at high tide: the journal of John Luke, 1670–73*, ed. H. A. Kaufman (Paris, 1958) · PRO, colonial office MSS, CO 279/1–33 [relating to Tangier] · J. Davis, *The history of the second queen's royal regiment*, 1 (1887) · 'Tangier 1680: the diary of Sir James Halkett', ed. H. M. McCance, *Journal of the Society for Army Historical Research*, 1 (Dec 1922) [whole issue] · BL, Add. MS 19872, fols. 42–52 [Fairborne's letters to Henry Sheres] · H. Cholmley, *An account of Tangier* (1787) · W. A. Shaw, ed., *Calendar of treasury books*, 5–9, PRO (1911–31), 1679–89 · *Le Neve's Pedigrees of the knights*, ed. G. W. Marshall, Harleian Society, 8 (1873), 268–9 · *CSP dom.*, 1673–81 · IGI [registers of St Mary Marylebone, London]
Archives BL, corresp. and papers relating to negotiation of peace between England and Morocco, Add. MS 17021 | BL, letters to Henry Sheres, Add. MSS 19872, fols. 42–52; 38849, fol. 102 · Hunt. L., letters to Lord Bridgewater, MSS 8471–8504 · PRO, CO 279/1–33

Fairborne, Sir Stafford (*c.*1666–1742), naval officer, was the eldest son of Sir Palmes *Fairborne (1644–1680), governor of Tangier, and his wife, Margery, *née* Devereux (*d.* 1694). He received a series of army commissions from 1678 onwards, holding these simultaneously with his naval posts, the first of which was as a 'king's letter boy' in 1681. In June 1685 Fairborne was lieutenant of the *Bonadventure* at Tangier, and during the illness of his captain commanded the ship in a successful encounter with some Salé vessels at Mamora. On 12 July 1686 he was promoted to command the *Half Moon*, a Salé prize, and in August 1688 he was appointed to the *Richmond* fireship, from which, after the revolution, he was moved successively to the *Phoenix* and the *Warspite* (70 guns); he commanded the latter at the battle of Beachy Head on 30 June 1690. At the siege of Cork, in the following September, he served on shore under the duke of Marlborough. Thus far his rapid rise can be attributed largely to the patronage of Arthur Herbert, earl of Torrington, an old friend of his father.

In 1692 Fairborne commanded the *Elizabeth* (70 guns) at the battle of Barfleur, and in 1693 the *Monck* (52 guns) in the fleet under Sir George Rooke, which on 19 June, while escorting the Smyrna convoy, was disastrously scattered by the French off Cape St Vincent. Between 1693 and 1697 he commanded, in quick succession, the *Grafton, Vanguard, London* (twice), *Victory* (twice), *Defiance*, and *Albemarle*, a rate of turnover which gave Fairborne great difficulty when pursuing his arrears of pay. During this period, and indeed throughout his career, he was always jealous of pay and promotion. For many years he regularly pressed his claims to advancement on influential political figures such as the dukes of Ormond and Shrewsbury, the earl of Oxford, and Lord Godolphin, attempting to reclaim the arrears allegedly due on his late mother's pension, and trying to obtain additional employment ashore to supplement his naval income. In May 1699 he was appointed to the *Torbay*, but as she was not ready, he was transferred to the *Suffolk*, which he commanded until the end of the year as senior officer in the Downs or at Spithead. In January 1700 he was appointed to the *Tilbury*, in which he went to Newfoundland with a convoy, and to clear the coast of pirates. He then took the convoy to Cadiz and into the Mediterranean. By March 1701 he was back at Cadiz, and soon after that he returned to England. In June he was promoted rear-admiral of the blue, and on 3 November he was knighted in a ceremony which occurred aboard ship as he carried William III back from the king's last-ever visit to the Netherlands.

In 1702 Fairborne was appointed, with his flag in the *St George*, to a command in the fleet under Rooke, which failed in its attempt on Cadiz, despite Fairborne's adroit handling of the inshore squadron. He had strenuously supported a more immediate attack than the one which took place. During the later victory at Vigo he moved into the *Essex*, a ship of lighter draught. He was afterwards left under Sir Cloudesley Shovell to bring the prizes home, a service which, in spite of exceptionally bad weather, was safely accomplished by 17 November 1702. In February 1703 Fairborne refused to take command of the West Indies squadron, and, believing that in consequence the Admiralty had refused to employ him again, he tried to challenge George Churchill—the first commissioner he happened to meet—to a duel, which was averted only by the arrest of both men. Shortly afterwards, Fairborne returned to favour and was made vice-admiral of the red, flying his flag in the *Association* and joining Shovell in the Mediterranean before returning with him to England in November. From the Downs the squadron was ordered into the Thames, and on the evening of 25 November anchored for the night off the Gunfleet. There the great storm of 1703, which broke out the next day, found them. They were unable to weigh, but in the early morning of 27 November the *Association* was blown violently from her anchors, and, with the wind at WSW, was driven helplessly across the North Sea to the coast of the Netherlands. After many dangers and narrow escapes she reached Göteborg, underwent refitting, and was finally able to return to the Thames.

In 1704 Fairborne hoisted his flag on board the *Shrewsbury*, in the fleet under Shovell at Lisbon, and, when Shovell went to the Mediterranean, he remained in command of the ships in the channel with his flag in the *Exeter*. He accompanied Shovell to the Mediterranean in 1705, and was present at the siege and capture of Barcelona in September and October. In 1706 he was again employed on the home station, commanding the squadrons sent against La Rochelle and Rochfort in May, and at the capture of Ostend in June. Fairborne distinguished himself in both actions by moving to smaller craft to take personal command of dangerous inshore operations; as the historian of Queen Anne's navy said of his cavalier attitude to such operations, and his unwillingness to delegate authority, 'Fairborne courted danger like a mistress' (Owen, 10).

Fairborne was MP for Rochester from 1705 to 1710, usually supporting the whig administration; and in February 1706 he was appointed a member of the council of the lord admiral, a post from which he retired in June 1708. Following Shovell's death in October 1707 he was promoted admiral of the white on 7 January 1708, and on 21 December 1708 he became admiral of the fleet; but the return to office in the Admiralty of his adversary, Edward Russell, earl of Orford, in 1709 effectively ended his prospects of further naval service. In 1713 he declined the position of commissioner for disbanding the marine regiments in the hope of returning to the Admiralty. His long-standing financial concerns were, finally, addressed by the award in 1715 of a pension of £600 p.a. in lieu of half pay.

Fairborne had married first, on 24 June 1694, Dorothy Fane (*d.* 1707), and second, on 20 October 1708, Rebecca, daughter of Colonel Thomas Paston. Fairborne died on 11 November 1742, and was buried in Westminster Abbey. His younger brother, William, who served with him in the *Victory* as a lieutenant, had died on 5 October 1708, in command of the *Centurion* at Leghorn.

J. K. LAUGHTON, *rev.* J. D. DAVIES

Sources HoP, *Commons, 1690–1715* [draft] · J. H. Owen, *War at sea under Queen Anne, 1702–1708* (1938) · W. L. Clowes, *The Royal Navy: a history from the earliest times to the present*, 7 vols. (1897–1903); repr. (1996–7), vol. 2, pp. 335, 349, 358, 377–8, 382, 459, 509–10 · D. Syrett and R. L. DiNardo, *The commissioned sea officers of the Royal Navy, 1660–1815*, rev. edn, Occasional Publications of the Navy RS, 1 (1994), 149 · NMM, Sergison MSS, SER/136 · *Calendar of the manuscripts of the marquess of Ormonde*, new ser., 8 vols., HMC, 36 (1902–20), vol. 8, pp. 70, 110, 147 · *The manuscripts of his grace the duke of Portland*, 10 vols., HMC, 29 (1891–1931), vol. 10, pp. 54, 246 · *CSP dom., 1696*, 175 · PRO, ADM/6/424 · J. Charnock, ed., *Biographia navalis*, 2 (1795), 143–54 · W. A. Shaw, *The knights of England*, 2 (1906), 272
Archives NMM, MSS · PRO, MSS | CAC Cam., corresp. with Thomas Erle · University of Kansas, Lawrence, Kenneth Spencer Research Library, instructions to Captain Mighells, incl. line of battle diagram
Likenesses G. Kneller, oils, *c.*1703–1708, NMM

Fairbridge, Kingsley Ogilvie (1885–1924), founder of farm schools overseas, was born on 5 May 1885 at Grahamstown, Cape Colony, the elder son of Rhys Seymour Fairbridge, surveyor to the government of Cape Colony and later to the British South Africa Company, and his wife, Rosalie Ogilvie. At the age of eight he was sent to St Andrew's preparatory school, Grahamstown. When he was eleven his parents moved to Rhodesia, and that ended his schooling. His father said that he must make himself useful. An old wagon, raised on stones, provided an office, a tent on the top a bedroom. There Kingsley Fairbridge slept and worked, making calculations for his father. Sometimes, for weeks together, he camped on the veld, 'dragging Dad's survey chain' (Fairbridge, 21). He was only twelve, he relates in his autobiography, when he first asked himself, 'Why are there no farms here?', and then said to himself, 'Some day I will bring farmers here' (ibid., 29–30). The idea which thus sprang up in his mind stayed there; it came in time to possess him.

Meanwhile Fairbridge helped his father; he was also, at different times, bank clerk, market gardener, and journalist. He educated himself as best he could, reading, scribbling verses, translating native folk stories. At seventeen he spent a year in England. In London he went to the East End and saw women fight and men beat their wives. He visited other cities, too, noting things. He returned to Rhodesia with a clearer vision of what he would attempt. Not clerks or mill hands should be his emigrants, nor men soiled by life in slums, but children. Caught young, they should be trained under decent and kindly conditions in the new land where they were to spend their lives.

In 1906 Fairbridge was promised a Rhodes scholarship at Oxford if he passed responsions. He sailed for England, passed responsions at the fourth attempt, and entered Exeter College in October 1908. One year later, at a meeting of the Oxford Colonial Club, the Child Emigration Society was founded to forward Fairbridge's idea. He remained at Oxford until 1911, studying forestry, in which he obtained a diploma, entering vigorously into the life of the university, and devoting much time to nursing the infant society.

A grant from the Rhodes trustees enabled Fairbridge to carry on his emigration work after leaving Oxford. In December 1911 he married Ruby Ethel, daughter of Harry Whitmore, of Edenbridge, Kent, and the following March he and his wife sailed for Western Australia—Rhodesia having dropped out of the scheme. They settled on a farm near Pinjarra, in the neighbourhood of Perth, where they opened a school. Early in 1913 twelve children were sent out to them; twenty-two more followed five months later. It was a desperate struggle. In 1915 the home committee instructed Fairbridge to close the school. He protested, and his protest was backed by the Perth committee. The school survived and after the war, on a new site, grew rapidly in numbers. By 1935 it had 365 children, and was the accepted model for similar institutions in other dominions.

Fairbridge died at Perth, Western Australia, on 19 July 1924, worn out at the age of thirty-nine, leaving a widow, two sons, and two daughters. He published a volume of poems, *Veld Verse*, in 1909, and an incomplete but very interesting autobiography appeared posthumously in 1927.   F. J. WYLIE, rev.

Sources *The Times* (23 July 1924) · K. O. Fairbridge, *The autobiography of Kingsley Fairbridge*, ed. V. F. Boyson (1927) · private information (1937) · personal knowledge (1937)
Archives FILM BFI NFTVA, documentary footage
Likenesses A. K. Lawrence, oils (posthumous), Bodl. RH

Fairbrother, Nancy Mary [Nan] (1912–1971), author and environmentalist, was born on 23 December 1912 at 4 Caldecote Road, Coventry, the daughter of Arthur Fairbrother, a stoker at an electric light works, and his wife, Lily Agnes Dickinson. Although born into modest circumstances, which she later referred to as her 'hilarious slum background' (Fairbrother, 83), she inherited from her Yorkshire forebears good health and energy, a serious outlook on life, and a passion for reading. After the First World War the family moved to the Coventry suburbs, where her father ran a grocer's business and she was able to have her own small garden. While she always regarded herself as a city child, her interest in wild flowers and the countryside seemed to come naturally, nurtured on rare outings and by her reading of history and literature, and informed by her treasured volumes of C. A. Johns's *Flowers of the Field* (33rd edn, 1911). Academic success followed at her co-educational state school at Coventry, and she graduated from the University of London with honours in English in 1933. Having found congenial and like-minded friends, she remained in London to work, living in Handel Street in Bloomsbury. She met a young surgeon, William Stewart McKenzie (b. 1908/9), of Halton, near Wendover, Buckinghamshire, and they were married on 14 September 1939 at St Pancras register office, just before his departure for war service in the RAF.

Nan Fairbrother's first book, *Children in the House*, appeared in 1954, published—as all her works were— under her maiden name. It was written at the end of the Second World War in a mood of literary reverie: thankful for her husband's imminent return to civilian life, she contemplated her rural surroundings in a farmhouse in the vale of Aylesbury, where she had spent the war with her two young sons, Dan and Stewart, born in 1942 and 1943 respectively. The book contrasts the street games and 'gangs' of her own childhood with the nature study and gardening she sought to share with her sons, imparting to them (as perhaps to herself) their legacy of the English countryside, a legacy she saw reflected in the works of Beatrix Potter, Shelley, Walter Scott, Wordsworth, Constable, and Turner. *Children in the House* was accepted by the Hogarth Press, who also published her second book, *Men and Gardens* (1956), a less personal but lively history of gardening and landscape design. When William McKenzie resumed his medical career in London after the war the family lived in Weymouth Mews, between Harley Street and Portland Place. Nan's third book, *The Cheerful Day* (1960), depicted their life there, and was followed by *The House* (1965), describing how they built their country home at Wendover. By this time she had perfected her vision of the British landscape, mediated through the urban and rural rhythms of her life, as she travelled out of the city through the suburbs to Wendover or Cambridge (where Dan McKenzie was launched on his career as a physicist and tectonist) and for family holidays in the Lake District or Scottish highlands. She photographed with a photo-journalist's acute perception of the moment and an equal appreciation for a well-designed factory or caravan site as for Wordsworth's Rydal Water. Her view was unique, untrammelled by either nostalgia or any political agenda: she firmly believed that the best landscapes of the past could be incorporated and conserved within a setting suited to a late twentieth-century industrial democracy, and pointed to the landscaping of the British countryside during the century of the industrial revolution as a precursor of this contemporary paradox. Her interests brought her to the Institute of Landscape Architects, where she worked with landscape planning and research committees and contributed a great deal to the 1968 London conference on the theme of landscape planning. Her younger son, Stewart McKenzie, became a landscape architect.

The outcome of this work was Nan Fairbrother's *New Lives, New Landscapes*, published by the Architectural Press (1970) and awarded the W. H. Smith literary prize in 1971: it remains the supreme example of an optimistic and creative outlook on the national environment, rare among so many doomsday scenarios. In it she analysed the social, economic, agricultural, and industrial changes in the landscape, 'since unless we understand their action we cannot use their energy—as we must—to create a new pattern'; a brief history of the landscape followed: 'for without the past the present is merely an incomprehensible point in time not part of a continuous process'. 'But', she warned, though the past may explain the present it is not a mirror of the way ahead, and many of the mistakes 'we blunder into … are because we use it as such a mirror—we are looking backward while moving forward' (p. 8). The substantial third part of the book proposed a planning system based upon the practical recognition of four divisions: wild country, lowland farmland, urban concentrations, and the 'penumbra of disturbed landscape which is the new industrial sub-division of urban' (p. 309). She advocated the restoration of much of Britain's lost tree cover to give a visual pattern to lowland scenery, for urban containment and the provision of recreational space, and for the protection of agricultural land. Her final pages demonstrated the importance of landscape texture from the geological to garden scale, from the wooded scarp that separates clay pasture from corallian limestone cornfields in Wiltshire, from the use of local building materials to the creation of a wildflower-covered bank—as opposed to dead grass—in a London street.

In *New Lives, New Landscapes* Nan Fairbrother knew that she had attempted 'to translate accepted land-use policy into appropriate landscape by simple general principles' (p. 383), because any achievement depended upon the goodwill of thousands of people interested in the environment in one way or another rather than on a few planning theorists. The book's success gave her strong, clear voice the influence she deserved: Frank Fraser Darling hailed her as 'among the first to see the essential link between ecology and landscape design' in his foreword to her final book, *The Nature of Landscape Design* (1974), which developed the last creative chapters of *New Lives, New Landscapes* in greater detail. The writer Jonathan Raban praised *New Lives, New Landscapes* for its 'sweep, excitement and rich allusiveness of prophecy', when he reviewed her last book in the *Sunday Times* of 12 January 1975; he added that Nan Fairbrother's death from cancer four years earlier had been a tragedy. She had worked on *The Nature of Landscape Design* throughout her illness, maintaining her characteristic poise, grace, and humour to the admiration of many; she died in Grosvenor Hospital, Westminster, on 24 November 1971.

In appearance Nan Fairbrother was exceptionally beautiful, with a finely boned face and large dark eyes. Although she was chic and naturally eloquent, she was supremely unselfconscious about the effect she made on others. With hindsight, the loss of her vibrant voice as an inspiration to landscape architects and planners has been disastrous, and these professionals have failed to pursue her vision. As British society on the brink of European integration enters even greater depths of controversy between town and countryside, *New Lives, New Landscapes* remains a voice of reason for those who will hear it.

JANE BROWN

Sources *The Times* (25 Nov 1971) · *The Times* (6 Dec 1971) · *The Times* (11 Dec 1971) · N. Fairbrother, *Children in the house* (1954) · private information (2004) · b. cert. · m. cert. · F. F. Darling, 'Foreword', in N. Fairbrother, *The nature of landscape design* (1974) · J. Raban, 'She came to a city', *Sunday Times* (12 Jan 1975) · d. cert.
Likenesses photograph, repro. in N. Fairbrother, *New lives, new landscapes* (1970), jacket · photograph (during her last years), repro. in Fairbrother, *The nature of landscape design*

Fairburn, Charles Edward (1887–1945), railway engineer, was born in Bradford on 5 September 1887, the only son of Robert Fairburn and his wife, Elizabeth. He was educated at Bradford grammar school, where he gained an open scholarship in mathematics to Brasenose College, Oxford. Brasenose awarded him a senior Hulme exhibition and he obtained first classes in mathematical moderations (1906), mathematics (1908), and engineering science (1910). For the next two years he was a pupil under Henry Fowler, chief mechanical engineer of the Midland Railway at its Derby works. He studied engineering drawing at Derby Technical College and metallurgy at Sheffield University, gaining his MA in 1912.

Fairburn then joined the railway engineering department of Siemens Dynamo Works Ltd in Stafford and from 1913 to 1916 was assistant to the resident engineer for the electrification of the first freight railway in Britain to be operated by electric traction, the Newport (Middlesbrough) to Shildon line of the former North Eastern Railway. In this he was responsible for the design and installation of the overhead contact system and for putting the locomotives into service. In 1914 he married Eleanor, daughter of Dr Cadman of Bradford. They had one son and one daughter.

In 1916 Fairburn joined the Royal Flying Corps as an officer in an experimental squadron developing new flying formation and fighting techniques, and he attained the rank of major in 1918.

Fairburn joined the English Electric Company Ltd in 1919. He established and developed their engineering department for railway electrification in Britain and overseas. In addition, in 1926 he became general manager of their Preston works and, in 1928, of the Stafford works also. In 1931 he became manager and chief engineer of the traction department, which carried out many important railway electrification schemes, including those of the Southern Railway, New Zealand government railways, Great Indian Peninsula Railway, Danish State Railways, and the Post Office electric railway in London.

In 1934 Fairburn joined the London, Midland, and Scottish Railway (LMS) as chief electrical engineer and in 1937 became deputy chief mechanical engineer and electrical engineer under William Stanier. In 1942 the latter was seconded as scientific adviser to the Ministry of Production and Fairburn became acting chief mechanical engineer, an appointment confirmed in 1944.

Fairburn's wide experience, combined with great technical and organizing abilities, enabled him to achieve improved efficiency in the railway workshops, which became all the more necessary when during the war tank, gun, and aircraft production and repair were added to their activities. From 1934 he was responsible for the introduction on the LMS of substantial numbers of diesel-electric locomotives for heavy-duty service in marshalling yards, where they showed great economies over steam and were the forerunners of more than 1400 of this type on British railways. He also had a keen grasp of steam locomotive matters and was responsible for introducing suburban passenger locomotives in 1945, in which year he also made proposals for the first LMS (and British) main-line diesel-electric locomotives, which were finally introduced under his successor, H. G. Ivatt, two years later. He was an outstanding engineer with quick perception of any issue and great powers of concentration.

Fairburn was an active member of the institutions of Civil, Electrical, Mechanical, and Welding Engineers and a vice-president of the Institution of Locomotive Engineers, to which he gave two important papers on diesel-electric shunting locomotives.

Fairburn died at the London Hospital, Whitechapel, London, on 12 October 1945 following a heart attack. He was survived by his wife.

GEORGE W. CARPENTER, rev.

Sources *Institution of Mechanical Engineers: Proceedings*, 154 (1946) · *The Engineer* (19 Oct 1945) · E. S. Cox, *Locomotive panorama*, 1 (1965) · private information (1993) · *Brasenose College register, 1509–1909*, 1 (1909), 738 · *CGPLA Eng. & Wales* (1946)
Wealth at death £47,071 9s. 7d.: probate, 19 Jan 1946, *CGPLA Eng. & Wales*

Fairchild, Thomas (1667–1729), gardener, was born about May 1667, the son of John Fairchild of Alwine, or Allane, Wiltshire, farmer. He was apprenticed to a clothmaker in 1682, but decided to become a gardener, and established himself about 1690 as a nurseryman and florist at Hoxton in the parish of St Leonard, Shoreditch, London. In 1704, as well as receiving the freedom of the Clothworkers' Company, he took up the freedom of the City in the Worshipful Company of Gardeners.

Fairchild's gardens, known as the City Gardens, were said to have extended from the west end of Ivy Lane to the New North Road, and to have been greatly resorted to, as much for their delectable situation as for the curious plants there. The vineyard, one of the last to be cultivated in England, was famous, and Richard Bradley, in his *General Treatise of Husbandry and Gardening* (1726), lists fifty varieties of grape grown there. Fairchild's plants included a number of American plants grown from seeds and plants sent from Virginia, by Mark Catesby, including

tulip trees, which he distributed widely; Fairchild was probably responsible for introducing the catalpa and was also one of the first to grow bananas in England. He corresponded with Linnaeus, and in 1719 he was the first person to produce an artificial hybrid of the Caryophyllaceae family: *Dianthus barbatus*, a cross between a sweet william and a carnation pink, known as 'Fairchild's mule'. He also introduced *Pavia rubra*, *Cornus florida*, and other plants, and grafted the evergreen oak of Virginia on to the common English oak.

In 1722 Fairchild published *The City Gardener*, which described the trees, plants, shrubs, and flowers which would thrive best in London. He stated that pear trees still bore excellent fruit in the Barbican, Aldersgate, and Bishopsgate areas, that in Leicester Fields there was a vine producing good grapes every year, and that figs and mulberries throve very well in the city. He was the first to concern himself with the increase in smoke pollution and the problems caused by this for gardeners in London. He suggested flowers suitable for growing in city squares, courtyards, and balconies, and also listed suitable houseplants. In 1724 Fairchild read a paper to the Royal Society entitled 'Some new experiments relating to the different and sometimes contrary motion of the sap in plants and trees' (*PTRS*, 1724, 33.127).

About 1725 the Society of Gardeners was founded for gardeners residing in the neighbourhood of London, and Fairchild was a founder member. Meeting every month at Newhall's coffee house in Chelsea or some similar place, members compared plants they had grown. After a time they produced the first and only part of *A catalogue of trees and shrubs both exotic and domestic which are propagated for sale in the gardens near London*. This was copiously illustrated by Jacob Van Huysum, but it did not appear until 1730, some months after Fairchild's death.

Fairchild died on 10 October 1729, in Hoxton. At his wish he was buried in Poor's Ground, St Leonard's churchyard, Hackney Road, Shoreditch. He bequeathed £25 to the trustees of the charity school and to the churchwardens of St Leonard's, for the endowment of an annual Whitsun sermon on either the wonderful works of God or the certainty of the creation. From 1873 the administration of the trust was handed over to the Worshipful Company of Gardeners, and the lecturers were appointed by the bishop of London. Fairchild left the bulk of his property to his nephew, John Bacon of Hoxton, who was a member of the Society of Gardeners; but his daughter-in-law, Mary Price, was also a beneficiary. ANNE PIMLOTT BAKER

Sources H. G. Lyons, 'The Fairchild Trust', *Notes and Records of the Royal Society*, 3 (1940), 80–84 · R. P. Brotherston, 'The city gardener', *Gardeners' Chronicle*, 3rd ser., 51 (1912), 65–6 · T. Fairchild, memoir, *Cottage Gardener*, 6 (1851), 143 · A. Coats, 'Notes on some portraits of British botanists and gardeners', *Huntia*, 2 (1965) · A. Amherst, *A history of gardening in England*, 2nd edn (1896) · D. McD., 'A philanthropic horticulturalist', *Gardeners' Magazine* (23 May 1896), 335 · *Gardeners' Chronicle*, new ser., 15 (1881), 48 · 'The Dianthus', *Gardeners' Chronicle*, 3rd ser., 13 (1893), 546 · G. W. Johnson, *A history of English gardening* (1829), 191 · private information (1901) · Desmond, *Botanists*, rev. edn

Likenesses R.? van Bleeck, oils, before 1750, U. Oxf., school of botany; repro. in Coats, 'Notes on some portraits of British botanists and gardeners'

Fairclough, Daniel. *See* Featley, Daniel (1582–1645).

Fairclough, John. *See* Featley, John (1604/5–1667).

Fairclough, Richard (1621?–1682), clergyman and ejected minister, was the eldest son of Samuel *Fairclough (1594–1677), lecturer at Clare, Suffolk, and his first wife, Susan Blackerby (*d*. 1638); Samuel *Fairclough (1625–1691) was his younger brother. Admitted in 1637 to Emmanuel College, Cambridge, he graduated BA in 1641 and proceeded MA and became a fellow in 1644. The year before he had accompanied Benjamin Whichcote, another Emmanuel fellow, to Somerset when the latter was presented to the college living of North Cadbury, and he remained to serve the parish after his friend's recall to Cambridge. About this time, at the request of Sir John Horner, the presbyterian sheriff of Somerset, Fairclough preached an assize sermon which so impressed Horner that he offered the young minister the living of Mells. On 24 September 1647 Fairclough was admitted to the rectory, where he quickly established his reputation as a diligent, loving pastor. Besides Sunday sermons, he regularly preached five weekday lectures. He found time not only to visit the sick, 'but also … all the families within his charge', striving 'to understand the present state of their souls'. His 'almost incredible' labours reportedly transformed 'an obscure country village' into a 'most noted place', and his parishioners into a 'much enlightened … seriously religious people' (Howe, 52, 51). But Mells was no dark corner before Fairclough's arrival. The cloth towns of north-eastern Somerset had emerged during the previous generation as hotbeds of popular puritanism; indeed, at Mells parish élites had vigorously resisted the ceremonial innovations of their Laudian rector, Henry Ancketyll. Fairclough signalled his commitment to presbyterian discipline in 1648 by endorsing the Somerset *Attestation*, and was named an assistant to the county's commission of ejectors in 1654. He also took an active role in Somerset's voluntary clerical association. Despite his partisan sympathies he attempted to steer a moderate course and aligned himself with the most conciliatory godly clergy—men such as William Thomas of Ubley, John Chetwind of Wells, and John Humfrey of nearby Frome.

Unable to accept the terms imposed by the Act of Uniformity, Fairclough was ejected in August 1662. Along with his father, brother Samuel, and two brothers-in-law, Richard Shute and George Jones, who had all lost their livings at the Restoration, he retired to his sister's house in Finchingfield, Essex. This 'little Colledge of Divines' lived together for several years before Richard left for London (Clark, 175). In May 1672 he took out a licence as a presbyterian teacher in Thames Street, and he later served a congregation in Newman Street. Although he had returned west to Bristol by April 1681, he continued to visit his London flock once a fortnight. Like his father Fairclough allegedly refused payment for his preaching after 1662. Along with his own extensive charity, this ultimately left him dependent upon the financial assistance of unnamed London benefactors.

Fairclough's fame certainly does not rest on his published works. To the collection *Suffolk's Tears* (1653), edited by his brother Samuel, he contributed an elegy on the death of his father's patron, Sir Nathaniel Barnardiston. His anonymous *Pastor's Legacy* (1663) is an abridgement, based on the notes of one of the congregation, of fourteen farewell sermons preached at Mells. An exhortation to practical piety, it is a far cry from his ponderously learned sermon in defence of the doctrine of assurance, published in the *Morning-Exercise Against Popery* (1675). He also wrote several passages in the popular *Life and Death of … Joseph Alleine* (1672) and, with John Chetwind, edited William Thomas's posthumous *Scriptures Opened* (1675).

Fairclough was married to a 'most pious, prudent matron', of whom nothing more is known (Howe, 57). She must have died before he made his will in April 1681. The couple had no surviving children. Fairclough died in London on 4 July 1682, probably aged sixty-one, and was buried six days later in Bunhill Fields. Some 500 people, including such prominent conformists as John Tillotson and Edward Stillingfleet, attended his funeral. As this suggests, Fairclough's moderation was celebrated: 'In the substantials of religion, no man was more fervently zealous; about the circumstantials, none more cool and temperate' (ibid., 56). JIM BENEDICT

Sources J. Howe, *A funeral sermon for that faithful and laborious servant of Christ, Mr. Richard Fairclough* (1682) • *Calamy rev.*, 187–8, 562 • E. Calamy, ed., *An abridgement of Mr. Baxter's history of his life and times, with an account of the ministers, &c., who were ejected after the Restauration of King Charles II*, 2nd edn, 2 vols. (1713), vol. 2, p. 589 • E. Calamy, *A continuation of the account of the ministers … who were ejected and silenced after the Restoration in 1660*, 2 vols. (1727), vol. 2, p. 735 • *The nonconformist's memorial … originally written by … Edmund Calamy*, ed. S. Palmer, [3rd edn], 3 (1803), 199–202 • S. Clark [S. Clarke], *The lives of sundry eminent persons in this later age* (1683), 167–92 • T. Alleine, *The life and death of that excellent minister of Christ, Mr Joseph Alleine* (1677) • *The life and times of Anthony Wood*, ed. A. Clark, 3, OHS, 26 (1894), 23–4 • *Calendar of the correspondence of Richard Baxter*, ed. N. H. Keeble and G. F. Nuttall, 2 vols. (1991), vol. 1, p. 169; vol. 2, pp. 30, 184 • *Remarks and collections of Thomas Hearne*, ed. C. E. Doble and others, 4, OHS, 34 (1898), 190 • *CSP dom.*, 1654, 276, 353; 1655, 398 • will, PRO, PROB 11/371, sig. 129 • D. Underdown, *Somerset in the civil war and interregnum* (1973), 129, 144, 177, 194 • D. Underdown, *Revel, riot and rebellion* (1985), 78, 130 • W. A. Shaw, *A history of the English church during the civil wars and under the Commonwealth, 1640–1660*, 2 (1900), 345, 417 • Wood, *Ath. Oxon.*, new edn, 3.730, 822
Wealth at death see will, PRO, PROB 11/371, sig. 129

Fairclough, Samuel (1594–1677), clergyman and ejected minister, was born on 29 April 1594 at Haverhill, Suffolk, the youngest of four sons of Laurence Fairclough (*d*. 1603), vicar of Haverhill, and his wife, Mary, daughter of John Cole, the 'chief lord' of that town (Clark, 153). He was educated by Edmund Robotham, 'the most famous schoolmaster of that age' (ibid., 154), who pronounced him the best scholar he had taught in thirty years. After an episode of pear-stealing with a fellow student, a sermon by Samuel Ward awakened Fairclough to 'the terrours of the Law … sincere repentance … and an effectual faith', and 'he became a true and sincere *Convert*' (ibid., 154–5).

Samuel Fairclough (1594–1677), by Frederick Hendrick van Hove, pubd 1683

Sent to Queens' College, Cambridge, before his fourteenth birthday, Fairclough lived strictly, refusing on principle to take a woman's part in the comedy *Ignoramus*, presented before James I. About 1610, while still an undergraduate, he was appointed sub-tutor to Spencer, Lord Compton, eldest son of the earl of Northampton, taking responsibility for his 'civil' and 'moral' education even before Compton was admitted to the college in 1614. The appointment brought Fairclough £30 a year and potentially valuable connections. Other connections made at Cambridge were less orthodox: he was taken up by leading puritan divines such as John Preston and John Davenant and began to question the value of church ceremonies. Having delayed graduation in order to read more widely, he took his BA in 1615.

Shortly afterwards Fairclough refused with regret Northampton's invitation to travel to France and Italy with Lord Compton, deferring to his mother's fear that, like his brothers who had served as soldiers in the Low Countries, he would die there. He was also offered a living in Suffolk, and although under age to receive priest's orders, occupied it as a curate to the nominal rector with great success. After two years he declined the rectory, choosing instead, after consultation with 'his spiritual *Father*, Mr Ward' (Clark, 159), to pursue his studies with Richard Blackerby of Ashen, Essex, who was famous for his holiness and learning. While there Fairclough concluded that, although naturally inclined to learning, he was called to 'publick *use* and *service*' (ibid., 159).

In 1619 Fairclough accepted, after some hesitation, an offer on good terms of a lectureship at King's Lynn, Norfolk. 'His popularity', relates Edmund Calamy, 'stirred up the envy of the other ministers, and he was openly opposed by the keepers of public houses, &c. whose business declined from the decrease of drunkenness' (*Calamy rev.*, 3.275). He aroused the ire of Bishop Samuel Harsnett of Norwich, who cited him to his court, declaring that Fairclough had 'grown to be a *popular* man, and therefore he must be *nipt in the bud*' (Clark, 160).

Fairclough retired and accepted a similar but less conspicuous position at Clare, Suffolk, where he had often preached while at Ashen. At this time he married Richard Blackerby's eldest daughter Susan (*d.* 1638); they were to be 'a most *happy* couple … *rejoicing* in each others love' (Clark, 161). On 20 June 1623 Sir Nathaniel Barnardiston presented him to the rectory of Barnardiston, which was close enough to his seat at Kedington, Suffolk, for both Barnardiston and his wife to be Fairclough's constant auditors. Although the living was a poor one it came with the promise of better and was the beginning of a partnership, ended only by Barnardiston's death, which wrought a moral and religious transformation in their south-west corner of Suffolk. None the less Fairclough soon met with further opposition. One Sunday he preached in place of a sick minister at Sudbury and repeated his sermon in the house where he lodged. An envious colleague exhibited articles against him in Star Chamber as a factious and seditious man. He was convened before the court of high commission and spent two years in intermittent attendance at the court, so that journeys and fees swallowed up all his income, leaving him in debt. Finally his counsel, Sir Nathaniel Brent, secured the transfer of the case to Norwich, where 'a certain lady' obtained a discharge from Bishop Harsnett (ibid., 162).

Barnardiston afterwards presented Fairclough to the rectory of Kedington, near Haverhill, and obtained his institution on 26 January 1630 'without his personal attendance [upon the bishop], taking the oath of canonical obedience, or subscribing the three exceptionable articles' (*Calamy rev.*, 3.276). Here 'Sholes and Multitudes of People' came as much as 20 miles to hear Fairclough, arriving hours early to secure a place inside the church, while the churchyard was 'barricadoed with [their] horses' (Clark, 187). Fairclough preached four times a week and gave Thursday lectures, 'Conciones ad clerum', similarly well attended by local ministers and Cambridge scholars. He had two levels of preaching, for the learned and for the people (with whom he avoided speculation and controversy), but both, though delivered without notes, were marked by clarity, learning, scriptural knowledge, and plainly delivered 'gospel truths'; unlike those of some of his famous contemporaries, his sermons were not histrionic. As a pastor he catechized, examined before monthly communion, visited and counselled his parishioners, acted as peacemaker, and engaged in practical charity, from regular almsgiving to distribution of large-print bibles to the aged. He was often cited to appear before the archdeacon at Bury for failure to read the Book of Sports or accept innovations in the church, but he managed to evade attendance on the grounds of inability to ride owing to a providential accident.

Fairclough's first wife died in childbirth in 1638, leaving him with seven young children. She was a *non-such* for beauty and character, and his *over-sorrow* provided fuel for hostile criticism (Clark, 171). Three years later he married the widow of a fellow clergyman named Folke or Folkes, the mother of a young daughter who later married one of his sons. This marriage too was happy, although relatively short. On 4 April 1641, on Barnardiston's initiative and at a key point in the proceedings against the earl of Strafford, Fairclough delivered a fast sermon to MPs calling for 'the execution of penall Justice upon publicke offenders' and in particular upon 'this execrable person that fights against our peace, and welfare' (*The Troublers Troubled*, 1641, 2, 8–9). During the civil war, however, he chose to be passive rather than active, deploring warfare between protestants and attributing much to the divisive designs of the Jesuits, and showed little sympathy with the presbyterians or any other doctrinaire reformers. He was nominated to the Westminster assembly but, dismayed by its divisions, excused himself from attending.

In 1645 Fairclough was a member of the commission appointed to try the Suffolk witches. Although in his sermons he accepted the reality of witchcraft, he insisted that the strict letter of the law be followed, thus making conviction more difficult, and condemned those who would convict 'without *plain convincing* evidence' (Clark, 172). He signed the petition of Suffolk ministers in 1646, but refused to take the engagement, 'which his Soul abhorred' (Clark, 173), and also declined the mastership of Trinity College, Cambridge.

On 28 September 1648 Fairclough preached a public thanksgiving sermon at Romford, Essex, celebrating the surrender of Colchester to Fairfax's army and the release of members of the Essex parliamentary committee, who had been prisoners in the town, later published as *The Prisoners' Praises* (1650). This rare intrusion into national affairs was probably the consequence of Barnardiston's active part in the siege and Arthur Barnardiston's presence among the prisoners. Fairclough thoroughly rejected the regicide, and on its first anniversary preached on Hosea 1:4, 'I will avenge the blood of Jezreel upon the house of Jehu, and will cause to cease the kingdom of the house of Israel'. It is clear from his last venture into print, his funeral sermon for Barnardiston, *Hagioi axioi, or, The Saints Worthinesse and the Worlds Worthlesnesse* (1653), that both Barnardiston and Fairclough were deeply disillusioned with the religious, political, and moral state of the kingdom. The latter was resolute in his preference for a private life and although he was appointed a trier to examine ministers' qualifications in 1654 he seldom attended the committee's meetings in London. When he did so he was honoured for his political and religious impartiality.

Although he was overjoyed at the return of Charles II, in 1662 Fairclough refused to conform and was ejected from his Kedington living, while remaining constant to his principle of passive obedience, and refusing to condemn those who had conformed. Although he and his sons lost collectively more than £1000 a year for their nonconformity, his greatest sorrow was that he was forced to leave his spiritual children. He lived for four or five years in Sculpins, the house of a married daughter in Finchingfield, Essex, with his third wife, Mary Brooke, *née* Sorell (*d.* 1669/70), widow of another minister, two of his sons, Richard *Fairclough (1621?–1682) and Samuel *Fairclough (1625–1691), and his two sons-in-law, George Jones and Richard Shute. They formed 'a little Colledge of Divines' and 'a most happy Family' (Clark, 175–6); as the Fairclough and Barnardiston households had apparently always done, in their practices and relationships they represented something close to the puritan domestic ideal. Father and sons preached by turns 'and the neighbours came in' (*Calamy rev.*, 3.278).

Sculpins proved unhealthy, however, and the family dispersed. Fairclough went to live with his youngest son, a conforming minister at Kennett, Cambridgeshire, and then with his daughters, first at Heveningham, Suffolk, and finally, about 1673, at Stowmarket. He kept his full powers, and preached, until he was over eighty, but then began to fail. He died at Stowmarket on 14 December 1677 after a remarkably healthy and happy life and was buried in Stowmarket church. The conforming minister who contributed a eulogy to Samuel Clark's biography of Fairclough regretted that no formula had been sought by which such 'useful and sober-spirited' men could be retained in the Church of England.

BARBARA DONAGAN

Sources S. Clark [S. Clarke], *The lives of sundry eminent persons in this later age* (1683) · *The nonconformist's memorial … originally written by … Edmund Calamy*, ed. S. Palmer, [3rd edn], 1 (1802) · *The nonconformist's memorial … originally written by … Edmund Calamy*, ed. S. Palmer, [3rd edn], 3 (1803) · *Calamy rev.*, 188 · K. W. Shipps, 'Lay patronage of East Anglian puritan clerics in pre-revolutionary England', PhD diss., Yale U., 1971 · Greaves & Zaller, *BDBR*, 264–5 · J. F. Wilson, *Pulpit in parliament: puritanism during the English civil wars, 1640–1648* (1969)
Likenesses F. H. Van Hove, line engraving, BM, NPG, V&A; repro. in Clark, *Lives* [*see illus.*]

Fairclough, Samuel (1625–1691), clergyman and ejected minister, was probably born at Barnardiston, Suffolk, the third son of Samuel *Fairclough (1594–1677), rector of Barnardiston, and his wife, Susan (*d.* 1638), eldest daughter of Richard *Blackerby. Dedicated to the ministry at birth, Fairclough, like all his siblings, 'had the knowledge of … scripture in [him] from the very breasts' (Clark, 179). In May 1643 he followed his brothers, Nathaniel and Richard *Fairclough, to Emmanuel College, Cambridge. After graduating MA in 1650, he held a fellowship at Gonville and Caius College until 1656, when he left Cambridge to take the rectory of Houghton Conquest, Bedfordshire. On 25 October of the previous year he married his stepsister, Frances (*d.* 1670x1681?), the only daughter and heir of William Folkes of Kirtling, Cambridgeshire, whose widow had married the elder Fairclough in 1641. In 1660 Fairclough was ejected to make room for the sequestered incumbent, Edward Martin, president of Queens' College, Cambridge, and retired to his eldest sister's manor at

Finchingfield, Essex. There he joined his father, brother Richard, and brothers-in-law Richard Shute and George Jones, who had all lost livings at the Restoration, though the latter two subsequently conformed. After four or five years Fairclough resumed preaching in London, although it is not clear that he ever undertook a settled pastoral charge. In November 1672 he obtained a licence as a congregationalist teacher in Chippenham, Cambridgeshire, where he planned to lease the house of the vicar, Isaac Archer, before deciding instead to live 'among relations near Norfolk' (Storey, 148). By 1681 he had returned to London and in 1690, at least when in town, was living in Hatton Garden.

Besides editing *Suffolks Tears* (1653), a collection of elegies upon the death of Sir Nathaniel Barnardiston, Fairclough wrote a short account of the exemplary life and death of the young Anne Barnardiston, which was published in 1682 with her funeral sermon by John Shower, and reprinted in Shower's *Mourner's Companion* (1692). He also added a preface to Samuel Hudson's funeral sermon for Richard Shute, *David's Labour and Rest* (1689). Fairclough died in London, aged sixty-six, on 31 December 1691, and was buried in the vault he had built for his wife in the church at Heveningham, Suffolk, where George Jones had ministered since 1670. Fairclough arranged for the annual payment of 20s. to the rector to help ensure that the vault would not 'be broken open or our bones ... disturbed' (PRO, PROB 11/410 fol. 386). Having no children of his own he divided most of his considerable property, in Suffolk and Cambridgeshire, among the children of his brothers, John and Nathaniel. He also made a number of charitable bequests. In addition to conveying his house and lands at Kedington, Suffolk, to the rectors of that parish, and establishing a scholarship at Gonville and Caius College, he left £10 each to five presbyterian divines—Richard Stretton, Richard Mayo, Samuel Stancliffe, Nathaniel Vincent, and Edward Lawrence. Preaching his funeral sermon the rector of Yoxford, Suffolk, echoed what had earlier been said of Fairclough's illustrious father: 'it had been alone worth an act of comprehension, to have included this one so valuable man' within the Church of England (Parkhurst, 23).	JIM BENEDICT

Sources Calamy rev., 188–9, 302, 441 · N. Parkhurst, *The redeemer's friend ... preached at the funeral of ... Mr. Samuel Fairclough* (1692) · E. Calamy, ed., *An abridgement of Mr. Baxter's history of his life and times, with an account of the ministers, &c., who were ejected after the Restauration of King Charles II*, 2nd edn, 2 vols. (1713), vol. 2, p. 91 · E. Calamy, *A continuation of the account of the ministers ... who were ejected and silenced after the Restoration in 1660*, 2 vols. (1727), vol. 2, p. 129 · *The nonconformist's memorial ... originally written by ... Edmund Calamy*, ed. S. Palmer, [3rd edn], 1 (1802), 283 · S. Clark [S. Clarke], *The lives of sundry eminent persons in this later age* (1683), 167–92 · will, PRO, PROB 11/410, fols. 386–8 · A. Gordon, ed., *Freedom after ejection: a review (1690–1692) of presbyterian and congregational nonconformity in England and Wales* (1917), 1 [Fairclough] · T. W. Davids, *Annals of evangelical nonconformity in Essex* (1863), 614–18 · J. Browne, *A history of Congregationalism and memorials of the churches in Norfolk and Suffolk* (1877), 598 · M. Storey, ed., *Two East Anglian diaries, 1641–1729*, Suffolk Records Society, 36 (1994) · G. L. Turner, ed., *Original records of early nonconformity under persecution and indulgence*, 2 (1912), 862 · *Walker rev.*, 84–5 · *VCH Bedfordshire*, 1.342 · Venn, *Alum. Cant.* · will,

PRO, PROB 11/371, fol. 144 [will of Richard Fairclough] · S. Fairclough, ed., *Suffolks tears* (1653) · Wood, *Ath. Oxon.*, new edn, 3.730 · S. Fairclough, *The saints worthiness* (1653) · S. Fairclough, *The troublers troubled* (1641) · will, PRO, PROB 11/410, fols. 386–8
Wealth at death impressive real estate holdings: will, PRO, PROB 11/410, fols. 386–8

Fairey, Sir (Charles) Richard (1887–1956), aircraft manufacturer, was born in Hendon, London, on 5 May 1887, the son of Richard Fairey, mercantile clerk, timber merchant, and failed importer, and his wife, Frances Jackson. His father died in 1898 leaving his family almost penniless. Both his mother and father could trace their histories back to Elizabethan times, and both families were famous as carriage builders in the old coaching days, providing a rich font of historical memories which made a deep impression on Richard Fairey. He was educated at Merchant Taylors' School until his father's death and Finsbury Technical College, where he was trained under the great Silvanus Thompson in electrical engineering and chemistry.

At the age of fifteen Fairey started work as a non-paying premium apprentice with an electric company in Holloway, while still being trained. At eighteen he had passed his examinations and progressed so well with his firm that he was placed in charge of the installing of electric lighting of the docks and warehouses at Heysham harbour in Lancashire. Shortly afterwards he was given a post in the power station of the Finchley council and added to his earnings by lecturing on engineering subjects. From his schooldays he had designed and built aeroplane models, but it was not until 1910 that he was persuaded to enter an aeroplane model competition at the Crystal Palace, which he won easily. He was a great craftsman, skilled with his hands, and won not only the challenge cup, but gold medals for steering, long distance, and stability, and a silver cup for the best model in both 1910 and 1911. Inadvertently he had infringed an early patent of J. W. Dunne, the pioneer of the stable aeroplane, which led to a meeting with Dunne in the following year. They joined forces and Fairey thus entered aviation. In 1913 he moved to Short Brothers, the aircraft pioneers, as chief engineer, and in 1915, at the age of twenty-eight, at the urging of Commodore Murray Sueter RN, he formed his own aircraft company, nominally capitalized at about £15,000. Short Brothers gave him his first contract, to build a dozen of their aeroplanes.

Fairey's ability quickly became known in the stress of war. Orders came in so fast that the firm steadily increased its output from a few hand-built aircraft per year to hundreds. Fairey learned everything from aircraft design and construction to works organization, government contracts, and the business of selling the aircraft he designed. He was then more often than most managing directors in and out of the drawing and production offices, helping and planning. Not at ease as a proprietor, he nevertheless inspired lifelong loyalties.

For more than forty years Fairey played a leading and dominating part in all the affairs of his company. Over a hundred different types of aircraft were produced, largely

Sir (Charles) Richard Fairey (1887–1956), by Cuthbert Julian Orde, c.1930–34

inspired by Fairey, ranging from small single-seaters to twin-engined bombers, from fast helicopters to supersonic aircraft. He played a vital part in negotiating their details of performance and their sales to the air forces of many countries. By 1925 more than half of all British military aircraft were Fairey types and Fairey himself became the leading aircraft designer with the ability to see future developments even before governments could. In 1925 he had submitted an American Curtiss D-12 engined prototype of a day bomber, which was turned down by the Air Ministry. Built at a cost of £20,000 to his company, it was known as the Fairey Fox, the fastest bomber of its time, an aeroplane which will always be associated with his name. Despite the ministry's reaction, when the Fox was demonstrated before the chief of the air staff, Sir Hugh Trenchard, at Northolt, where 41 fighter squadron was stationed, it made a tremendous impression on the watchers and Trenchard immediately said he would order a squadron of the machines. Its aerodynamic design enabled it to fly 50 miles an hour faster than any other aeroplane of its type in the Royal Air Force. It was clear that the Fox had set a new standard and created a new view of official specifications. In 1931 Fairey founded the Avions Fairey Company in Belgium, which sold many aircraft deriving from the Fox on which the Belgian air force was based. In the meantime Fairey developed the series III for both the Fleet Air Arm and the RAF.

In the year 1928 came the first edition of the aeroplane known as the Long Range Monoplane which in 1933 flew the world's long-distance non-stop record of 5309 miles, from Cranwell in England to Walvis Bay in South Africa. Later, in 1934, came the TSR2 Swordfish, which fought throughout the Second World War and helped cripple the Italian fleet at Taranto in 1940.

Fairey had been overworking during those early years and in 1927, warned by his doctors to rest, he turned to yachting. He became a superb yachtsman, improving the design of racing sails and hulls to such an extent that in the years 1931–3 he was top of the 12-metre class. He became the commodore of the Royal London Yacht Club in 1935, served on the council of the Royal Yachting Association, and began to make preparations to challenge in a new J boat the United States for the America's Cup, until it was stopped by the outbreak of war.

Lord Beaverbrook, appointed to the Ministry of Aircraft Production, called in Fairey to help in the organization of the industry to increase the output of aircraft, both at home and abroad. Fairey was asked in 1940 to go to the United States to act as deputy to Sir Henry Self, director of the British air mission. He was the ideal deputy, for he knew the American designers and the leaders of the aircraft industry, and was well aware of the tremendous help they could give. He visited the chief American factories and research centres and entered into technical discussions of vital importance. A powerful and appealing speaker at gatherings of the leaders and to the press, he proved to be a great ambassador for Anglo-American friendship and help. In 1942 he became the director of the British mission and in the same year he was knighted. He did not return to the UK until 1945. Meanwhile the firm was in constant trouble and in danger of being nationalized. Yet between 1934 and 1946 it produced 10,303 aircraft of six different types. In 1930 the company had moved from Northolt to Hayes and Harmondsworth but in 1944 the latter works was requisitioned, and subsequently became part of the expanded Heathrow airport.

As the war came to an end the tremendous responsibility and unceasing work took its toll. In April 1945 Fairey resigned from his mission in America and for the next three months he was in hospital in Boston. In 1947 the American government awarded him the medal of freedom with silver palm for 'exceptional meritorious service in the field of scientific research and development'. On his return to England he encouraged new ideas on research and turned his attention to the development of helicopters. In 1948 the Fairey Gyrodyne gained the international speed record for helicopters at 124 m.p.h. and work went ahead in the design of passenger-carrying helicopters. Fairey also pushed forward on problems of supersonic flight and on 10 March 1956 the Fairey Delta flew at a speed of 1132 m.p.h., the first plane officially to exceed 1000 m.p.h.

In 1922 Fairey was elected chairman of the Society of British Aircraft Constructors, a position he held for two years. He was twice president of the Royal Aeronautical Society (1930–31, 1932–3). In 1931, at the suggestion of Lord Amulree, secretary of state for air, he founded the British gold and silver medals of the Royal Aeronautical Society, for important achievements leading to advancement in aeronautics. Fairey himself was awarded the Wakefield gold medal of the society in 1936 for his design of the variable camber wing. He was a member of many important committees including the Aeronautical Research Committee (1923–6).

Fairey was a large, dapper man of solid English stock, often seen wearing a bowler hat; of singular courage, he was deeply interested in everything from aeronautical research to chess, from sailing to shooting (in both of which he was highly skilled), and from the guidance of men who served him to the service he gave his country. In whatever he did he displayed enthusiasm, concentration, independence, and originality—he was a pioneer to the end of his life. There was nothing he touched which he did not adorn and embellish. Underneath his serious appearance he was basically shy, but he had the charm of the eternal boy.

In 1915 Fairey married Queenie Henrietta Markey. Their son, Richard (1916–1960), also devoted himself to aviation. The marriage was dissolved and in 1934 he married Esther Sarah, daughter of Francis Stephen Whitmey, bank manager; they had a son and a daughter. Fairey died in the London Clinic, following an operation for cancer, on 30 September 1956.   J. L. PRITCHARD, *rev.* ROBIN HIGHAM

Sources *The Times* (1 Oct 1956) · H. A. Taylor, *Fairey aircraft since 1915* (1974) · J. M. Bruce, *British aeroplanes, 1914–18* (1957) · J. Bradbrooke, ed., *The centennial history of the Royal Aeronautical Society* (1966) · *WW* · R. Higham, 'Fairey, Sir Charles Richard', *DBB* · d. cert.
Archives Royal Airforce Museum, Hendon, department of research and information services, papers
Likenesses C. J. Orde, oils, *c.*1930–1934, Royal Aeronautical Society, 4 Hamilton Place, London [*see illus.*] · F. Eastman, oils, 1962, AVRO, Royal Aero Club; on loan to RAF Museum, Hendon · photographs, Flight International, Quadrant House, The Quadrant, Sutton, Surrey
Wealth at death £883,646 13*s.* 2*d.*: probate, 6 March 1957, *CGPLA Eng. & Wales*

Fairfax [*née* Vere], **Anne**, **Lady Fairfax** (1617/18–1665), noblewoman, was the fourth of the five daughters of Horace *Vere, Baron Vere of Tilbury (1565–1635), military commander, and Mary *Vere, Lady Vere (1581–1671), youngest daughter of Sir John Tracy of Toddington, Gloucester. She spent her early life in the Netherlands, but at the age of nineteen on 20 June 1637 she married the future parliamentarian commander Thomas *Fairfax, later third Lord Fairfax of Cameron (1612–1671), at Hackney, Middlesex. Their daughter, Mary, was born in the following year and in 1640 a second daughter, who died in 1642. Edward Hyde, earl of Clarendon, observed of Anne Fairfax that 'having been bred in Holland, [she] had not that reverence for the Church of England as she ought to have had, and so unhappily concurred in her husband's entering into rebellion' (Clarendon, *Hist. rebellion*, 4.486–7). She was widely believed by contemporaries to have had a considerable influence over her husband's actions during the civil wars. This belief was reinforced by her public support for the presbyterian ministry and her tenacity in accompanying her husband on campaign. In 1643 she was briefly taken prisoner by the earl of Newcastle during the

Anne Fairfax, Lady Fairfax (1617/18–1665), after Gerard Soest

chaotic parliamentarian withdrawal from Bradford led by her husband. She was released a few days later and was sent in a coach with a cavalry escort to rejoin Fairfax at Hull. Despite this experience, Lady Fairfax continued to share her husband's quarters and Lucy Hutchinson described how in 1646 she had 'follow'd his camp to the siege of Oxford and layne at his Quarters there all the while he abode there'. Hutchinson also recorded how Lady Fairfax had initially been favourable to her husband's army chaplains, but when the army returned to London after the fall of Oxford, 'the Presbiterian Ministers quite chang'd the lady' so that these Independent chaplains 'could not endure to come into the Generall's presence while she was there, and the Generall had an unquiett, unpleasant life with her, who drove away from him many of those friends in whose conversation he found much sweetenesse'. At Nottingham in early 1647 Lady Fairfax allegedly showed such 'kindnesse' to the presbyterian minister and 'his brethren' that 'they grew impudent to preach up their faction openly in the pulpitt, and to revile the others, and at length would not suffer any of the Army Chaplains to preach in the Towne' (Hutchinson, 168).

In 1647 an Italian newsletter reported that Lady Fairfax was passing information about the deliberations of the army council to the king, although there is no supporting evidence. She certainly shared Fairfax's dislike for the process which led to the king's trial and in January 1649 the presbyterian cleric John Geree addressed both her and her mother, Lady Vere, in the hope that they could persuade Fairfax to save the king and in the assurance that 'both your Ladyships are affectionately serious against these irregular ways that I implead' (Geree, A2). Later that month Lady Fairfax is believed to have attended the first day of the trial of the king, although her husband refused to take his place as one of the judges. Clarendon records that when Fairfax's name was read out, she allegedly called out that 'he had more wit than to be there' and when the charges were read in the name of 'all the good people of England', she declared 'No, nor the hundredth part of them!', at which one of the officers ordered his men to fire 'into that box whence those presumptuous words were uttered'. When Lady Fairfax's identity was discovered she was 'presently persuaded or forced to leave' (Clarendon, *Hist. rebellion*, 4.486–7). After the king's execution she accompanied her husband into retirement from public life on his Yorkshire estate at Nun Appleton. In 1657 their daughter, Mary, married the royalist duke of Buckingham, who was subsequently arrested by the Cromwellian regime. Lady Fairfax then approached Cromwell's wife to plead for his release, while Fairfax had a series of meetings with Cromwell over the matter. Their son-in-law was eventually freed on security of £20,000. Lady Fairfax died at Nun Appleton in 1665.   JACQUELINE EALES

Sources J. Wilson, *Fairfax: a life of Thomas, Lord Fairfax, captain-general* (1985) · G. W. Johnson, ed., *The Fairfax correspondence: memoirs of the reign of Charles the First*, 1 (1848) · Clarendon, *Hist. rebellion*, vol. 4 · L. Hutchinson, *Memoirs of the life of Colonel Hutchinson*, ed. J. Sutherland (1973) · S. R. Gardiner, *History of the great civil war, 1642–1649*, new edn, 3 (1893) · J. Geree, *Might overcoming right* (1649) · A. Collins, *Historical collections of the noble families of Cavendishe, Holles, Vere, Harley and Ogle* (1752) · GEC, *Peerage*
Likenesses portrait (after G. Soest); Christies, 23 Oct 1970, lot 28 [see illus.]

Fairfax, Blackerby (*bap.* **1669**, *d.* in or after **1730**). *See under* Fairfax, Nathaniel (1637–1690).

Fairfax, Brian (1633–1711), scholar and courtier, was born on 6 October 1633 in the rectory at Newton Kyme in the West Riding of Yorkshire, the third and second surviving son of Henry *Fairfax (1588–1665), the rector, and his wife, Mary (*c*.1593–1650), daughter of Sir Henry Cholmley of Whitby and Roxby and his wife, Margaret. He was educated at Coxwold School from about 1644 to 1647 and was admitted to Trinity College, Cambridge, on 8 April 1648. He graduated BA in 1652, proceeded MA in 1655, and was admitted to Gray's Inn on 10 May 1654. He attended the marriage of Mary Fairfax, daughter of his cousin, the third Baron Fairfax, to the duke of Buckingham on 15 September 1657. When Cromwell imprisoned Buckingham in the Tower, Brian accompanied Lord Fairfax to Whitehall to demand his release. Shortly after, Lord Fairfax sent him to France with the earl of Kildare and his return to England the following year was delayed by a scuffle with a privateer in the channel. On 20 December 1659 he went to Nun Appleton to visit Lord Fairfax, who entrusted him with delivering the verbal message to General George Monck in Scotland that Fairfax would appear in arms on 1 January 1660. He started out on 21 December, disguised by Buckingham as a 'young country clown' (Bell, 2.154), and travelled unarmed save for a swordstick supplied by his brother. Having fended off an attack from a moss-trooper,

he reached Monck at Coldstream near midnight on 25 December. He returned to find Fairfax raising the Yorkshire gentry on 1 January. On 6 January he was sent to London with a letter to Speaker Lenthall, and he returned to witness Monck's interview with Fairfax at Nun Appleton. On 18 May 1660 he accompanied the parliamentary commission led by Lord Fairfax to The Hague to invite Charles II's return. Having been called to the bar in 1661, he became Lord Fairfax's private secretary; he warned him of the northern risings conspiracy of 1663 and later attended him in his dying days.

Fairfax served with Buckingham aboard *The Prince* during the Second Anglo-Dutch War and on 21 January 1670 he was appointed equerry to Charles II. He accompanied Buckingham on embassies to the Netherlands and France in 1673, and on 22 April 1675 he married at Westminster Charlotte (*d.* 1709), daughter of Sir Edmund Carey. The couple settled at Westminster, residing in a 'little pritty house in the Mews, as private as a colledg' (Markham, *Life of Robert Fairfax*, 145). Their third son, Charles Brandon *Fairfax became dean of Down. Fairfax was created DCL at Oxford in 1677. With the king's death on 6 February 1685 he resigned his post of equerry, later reflecting: 'I left Whit-hall when the Mass came into it, I saw a new King who would not know me nor did I desire to wayte on him' (ibid.).

With the death of Buckingham two years later, on 16 April 1687, Fairfax also lost his patron, of whom he warned his sons: 'I came to be related to the duke of Buckingham as a servant and kinsman, and I thank God to none of his vices' (Markham, *Life of Robert Fairfax*, 142). In 1689 William III reinstated him as equerry, and in 1692 he became secretary to John Tillotson, archbishop of Canterbury. On Tillotson's death in 1694 he retired to reside at Bishophill, York, and devoted himself to literary pursuits. In 1699 he edited and published Lord Fairfax's *Short Memorials* of the civil wars, omitting some passages for fear of offending royalists. That July he wrote an account of his adventurous ride to General Monck at Coldstream, entitling it 'Iter boreale' (Bell, 2.151–74). He completed a memoir of the duke of Buckingham and translated the life of the Huguenot political philosopher Philippe du Plessis-Mornay. His poems are preserved in the British Library (some are printed in Johnson, ed., *The Fairfax Correspondence*, 1.cxxii–cxxv). He died on 20 September 1711.

Fairfax's eldest son, **Brian Fairfax the younger** (1676–1749), antiquary and scholar, was born in The Mews, Westminster, on 11 April 1676. He was educated at Westminster School and accompanied his father to The Hague in 1688 to visit the prince of Orange. He was admitted on 28 June 1693 to Trinity College, Cambridge, where he became a fellow and graduated BA in 1697 and proceeded MA in 1700. He was employed as commissioner of customs from 1723 to 1749. He lived with his younger brother, Ferdinando, in Panton Square and Savile Street, London, where he collected a large library and gallery of pictures. Sold after his death, it contained some 2343 volumes, including a first edition of the Coverdale Bible and ten early books printed by Caxton. He died, unmarried, on 7 January 1749.

Ferdinando Fairfax (1678–1749), scholar, was born in The Mews on 11 June 1678. He was educated at Westminster School and in 1694 entered Trinity College, Cambridge, where he graduated BA in 1698. He died, unmarried, on 12 February 1749.   ANDREW J. HOPPER

Sources C. R. Markham, *Life of Robert Fairfax of Steeton* (1885) • C. R. Markham, *A life of the great Lord Fairfax* (1870) • G. W. Johnson, ed., *The Fairfax correspondence: memoirs of the reign of Charles the First*, 1 (1848) • R. Bell, ed., *Memorials of the civil war … forming the concluding volumes of the Fairfax correspondence*, 2 (1849) • J. Foster, ed., *Pedigrees of the county families of Yorkshire*, 1, 3 (1874) • Venn, *Alum. Cant.* • A. H. Woolrych, 'Yorkshire and the Restoration', *Yorkshire Archaeological Journal*, 39 (1956–8), 483–507 • *DNB* • C. R. Markham, *The genealogy of the Fairfaxes* (1870) • will, 1749, PRO, PROB 11/767, fols. 68v–69r [Brian Fairfax the younger] • will, 1748, PRO, PROB 11/759, fol. 388r–v [Ferdinando Fairfax]
Archives BL, Add. MS 5144 • BL, Add. MS 22582 • BL, Add. MS 25447 • BL, Add. MS 25708 • BL, Add. MS 39992 • BL, Egerton MSS 2145–2147 • BL, poems, translations, and genealogical collections, Egerton MS 3252 • U. Edin. L., commonplace book • York Minster Library, letter-book and diary, Add. MS 234 [copies]
Likenesses portrait, oil on canvas, Leeds Castle, Kent

Fairfax, Brian, the younger (1676–1749). *See under* Fairfax, Brian (1633–1711).

Fairfax, Sir Charles (d. 1604), soldier, was the fourth son of Sir Thomas Fairfax (1521–1600) of Denton and Nun Appleton, Yorkshire. Like his elder brother Edward *Fairfax he was illegitimate (his mother may have been Dorothy Gale); their inclusion in their father's will was secured by the lobbying of their legitimate eldest brother, Thomas *Fairfax (later first Lord Fairfax of Cameron). He matriculated from Clare College, Cambridge, in Easter term 1584 and probably accompanied his brother Thomas to the Netherlands in 1585. By 1599 he had been promoted captain, in time to fight at the battle of Nieuwpoort (1600), where he rallied the English troops at a critical juncture.

Fairfax's company was then posted to Ostend and he was an important figure in the heroic defence of the town, christened 'the new Troy' for the length and bitterness of the siege. In early 1602 he and Sir John Ogle volunteered to act as hostages in the Spanish camp during capitulation 'negotiations', which they knew were actually designed to win time. When this was done successfully and talks were broken off, both men were returned unharmed, but could easily have been executed. In the massive Spanish attack which followed Fairfax fought bravely defending the breach and, as he informed the earl of Northumberland, 'was badly wounded in the right arm' (Markham, 329–30).

In common with Vere, Ogle, and other English troops Fairfax was withdrawn from Ostend and spent the rest of 1602 in garrison duties in Holland. He was in England in May 1603, when he was knighted. Twelve months later he won a sharp action near Sluys. Doubtless this helped lead to his recall to Ostend as commander of the English regiment there in June 1604. Fairfax helped conduct a vigorous defence but the city was now doomed. He was killed after 14 September (the date of his last dispatch), probably on the following day. Ostend capitulated on 20 September 1604.

Secondary sources have sometimes been uncertain about the date and manner of Fairfax's death, on occasion suggesting a date as late as 1607. It is worth emphasizing, therefore, that Sir Thomas later stated that his brother, Sir Charles Fairfax, 'was slain at the siege of Ostend, and left no estate' (*CSP dom.*, 1611–18, 106), while Dudley Carleton fixed the approximate date, writing on 21 September 1604 that Ostend had surrendered on honourable conditions and that Sir Charles Fairfax had been slain there (ibid., 1603–10, 68). A new captain was commissioned 'as [his] successor' on 12 October 1604 (Japiske and Rijperman, 136), while in April 1605 the states general voted 900 florins in back pay to Fairfax's 'heirs' (Algemeen Rijksarchief, Den Haag, Collectie Aanwinsten 879, fol. 63v). Fairfax had made his will in May 1602, describing himself as 'Charles Fairefax of Brocket in the Countie of York' (PRO, PROB 11/104, fol. 308v). He evidently died a bachelor, dividing his land in Badsworth, Yorkshire, equally between his nephew Henry, his brother Edward, and William Baynton of Hunslet; the rest of his goods were to go to Baynton, who as his executor proved the will on 19 November 1604.

It is quite clear, then, that Fairfax was slain at Ostend, on the eve of the capitulation that would have brought him momentary safety. Given his military record, however, and the death of two of his nephews fighting for the Dutch in 1620, Charles Fairfax was probably unlikely ever to have died in his bed.   D. J. B. TRIM

Sources J. Foster, ed., *The visitation of Yorkshire made in the years 1584/5 … to which is added the subsequent visitation made in 1612* (privately printed, London, 1875) • 'The *Commentaries* of Sir Francis Vere' [1657], *An English garner*, 7: *Stuart tracts, 1603–1693*, ed. E. Arber and C. H. Firth (1903) • J. Tammel and others, eds., *The pilgrims and other people from the British Isles in Leiden, 1576–1640* (1989) • Venn, *Alum. Cant.* • E. Belleroche, 'The Siege of Ostend; or the New Troy: 1601–1604', *Proceedings of the Huguenot Society of London*, 3 (1888–91), 428–539 • C. R. Markham, *The fighting Veres* (1888) • Nationaal Archief, The Hague, Archief van de staten-generall, 8040–8042 • Nationaal Archief, The Hague, Archief van de raad van state, 1226, 1232 • N. Japiske and H. H. P. Rijperman, eds., *Resolutiën der Staten-Generaal van 1576 tot 1609*, 14 vols. (The Hague, 1915–70), vol. 13 • J. L. Motley, *History of the United Netherlands: from the death of William the Silent to the Twelve Years Truce, 1609*, 4 vols. (New York, 1879–80), vol. 4 • W. A. Shaw, *Knights of England*, 3 vols. (1906), vol. 2 • M. Stapleton, ed., *Cambridge guide to English literature* (1983) • *CSP dom.*, 1603–18 • GEC, *Peerage*, 5.229 • N. M. Sutherland, 'Fairfax, Thomas I', HoP, *Commons, 1558–1603* • *Dugdale's visitation of Yorkshire, with additions*, ed. J. W. Clay, 3 vols. (1899–1917) • will, PRO, PROB 11/104, sig. 87, fol. 308v
Archives PRO, state papers, letters
Wealth at death died leaving heavy debts: *CSP dom.*, 1611–18, 106

Fairfax, Charles (1597–1673), antiquary and genealogist, was born at Denton Hall in the parish of Otley in the West Riding of Yorkshire on 5 March 1597, the seventh and third surviving son of Thomas *Fairfax, first Lord Fairfax of Cameron (1560–1640), and his wife, Ellen (d. 1620), daughter of Robert Aske of Aughton, esquire, and his wife, Elizabeth. He entered Trinity College, Cambridge, on 5 October 1611, and on the 27th of the same month was admitted to Lincoln's Inn, from where he was called to the bar on 9 March 1618. His father allegedly commented, 'I sent him to the Inns of Court, and he is a good divine, but nobody at the law' (Markham, *Life of the Great Lord Fairfax*, 149n.). About 1627 he married Mary Breary (*d.* 1657), daughter and sole heir of John Brearey of Scow Hall and Menston. They had fourteen children, including Henry *Fairfax, later dean of Norwich, establishing their residence at Menston Hall, also in the parish of Otley. He became a governor of Otley grammar school in January 1642.

Fairfax was taken prisoner by the royalists during the civil war, but his elder brother, Ferdinando *Fairfax, second Lord Fairfax and parliament's general of the northern counties, negotiated his exchange at Street Houses, near York. Shortly before the battle of Marston Moor, Oliver Cromwell stayed with him at Menston. After the siege of York, he searched through the rubble of St Mary's Tower with his fellow antiquary, Roger Dodsworth, recovering several ancient relics and documents. Appointed a JP in 1645, he led the initiatives of his fellow magistrates to relieve the poor suffering from plague, and was among the most active West Riding JPs of the interregnum. In 1646 Ferdinando appointed him to intervene in a dispute between Lady Pembroke and Lady Cork over the Clifford estates, in which he spent seven weeks examining evidences at Skipton Castle. He wrote to his brother explaining, 'I am the ill instrument of their unhappy differences betwixt the ladies' (Bell, 1.303). Ferdinando later secured for him the stewardships of the courts at Cawood, Otley, and Ripon.

Fairfax celebrated the victories of the New Model Army, commanded by his nephew Sir Thomas Fairfax, reflecting: 'The giving all unto God (of which he has an honourable testimony) is the most thriving way' (Bell, 1.243). He was commissioned as a colonel himself in time for the second civil war, and his regiment fought at the battle of Preston. In 1649 he supported the creation of a radical chapel at Bramhope, in Otley parish, and was among the five trustees who appointed the minister. Between 1652 and 1660 he wrote the 'Analecta Fairfaxiana', containing detailed pedigrees of all branches of the Fairfax family, with about fifty anagrams, epigrams, and elegies in Latin concerning different members of the family. The work was never printed and only two manuscript copies are thought to exist, one of which is held by the Brotherton Library at Leeds. Along with Roger Dodsworth, he was responsible for the collection and preservation of the valuable Dodsworth MSS volumes, which went to the Bodleian Library at Oxford.

During the 1650s Fairfax's regiment served in Scotland under General George Monck; its colours were deep blue and bore the motto 'Fideliter faeliciter' (C. H. Firth, *Cromwell's Army*, 4th edn, 1962, 46). His regiment had been 'a hotbed of sectarian enthusiasm' (Woolrych, 'Yorkshire and the Restoration', 499n.), but he was personally trusted by Monck and he accompanied him into England in January 1660. His regiment was left behind to garrison York and he also became the military governor of Hull on 12 March. Shortly afterwards he resigned this post to Lord Belasyse, and was granted a pension of £100 a year for himself and his heirs by Charles II out of the customs at Hull. After a long retirement, he died at Menston in 1673. His will, which bequeathed to Lincoln's Inn 'Twoe of my Choysest Manuscripts of Law, one beinge the Annalls of kinge Edw[ard] the 2nd' (will), directed that he should be buried 'without needles Ceremony'. He was interred beside his wife in the Fairfax transept in Otley parish church on 22 December 1673.   ANDREW J. HOPPER

Sources R. Bell, ed., *Memorials of the civil war … forming the concluding volumes of the Fairfax correspondence*, 1 (1849) • G. W. Johnson, ed., *The Fairfax correspondence: memoirs of the reign of Charles the First*, 2 vols. (1848) • J. Foster, ed., *Pedigrees of the county families of Yorkshire*, 1 (1874) • Venn, *Alum. Cant.* • C. R. Markham, *A life of the great Lord Fairfax* (1870) • C. R. Markham, *Life of Robert Fairfax of Steeton* (1885) • C. R. Markham, *The genealogy of the Fairfaxes* (1870) • G. C. F. Forster, 'County government in Yorkshire during the interregnum', *Northern History*, 12 (1976), 84–104 • P. N. Farrar, 'John Waite and the plague of 1645', *Transactions of the Halifax Antiquarian Society* (1978), 13–16 • A. H. Woolrych, 'Yorkshire and the Restoration', *Yorkshire Archaeological Journal*, 39 (1956–8), 483–507 • A. Woolrych, 'The civil wars, 1640–1649', *Stuart England*, ed. B. Worden (1986), 93–122 • will, Borth. Inst., probate register 54, fol. 438 [microfilm 973] • W. Brigg, ed., *The parish registers of Otley, co. York*, 1–2, Yorkshire Parish Register Society, 33, 44 (1908–12) • GEC, *Peerage*, new edn • F. Cobley and L. Padgett, eds., *Chronicles of the free grammar school of Prince Henry at Otley* (1923) • DNB • miscellaneous letters, U. Leeds, Brotherton L.

Archives BL, corresp. and papers, Add. MSS 4275; 15552; 18979; 20778; 21417–21419; 21426; 36996; [Egerton MSS 2146, 2551] • Bodl. Oxf., papers and collection, MS top Yorks. c. 43 • U. Leeds, Brotherton L., Analecta Fairfaxiana | BL, letters to Captain Baynes, Add. MSS 21417–21426 • Worcester College, Oxford, letters to George Monck

Likenesses portrait, repro. in Markham, *Life of Robert Fairfax*; known to be at Bilbrough Manor in 1885

Wealth at death £100 p.a. royal pension settled on him and heirs; mansion house at Scow; copyhold messuage at Scow; also six other messuages and tenements; 73 acres of land in forest of Knaresborough; £200 owed to him: will, Borth. Inst., probate register 54, fol. 438 [microfilm 973]

Fairfax, Charles Brandon (1684–1723), dean of Down, was baptized at St Martin-in-the-Fields, Westminster, on 18 September 1684, the third son of Brian *Fairfax (1633–1711), scholar and courtier, and Charlotte Cary (*d.* 1709). Educated at Westminster School, where he was a king's scholar in 1697, he entered Christ Church, Oxford, on 12 June 1702, at the age of seventeen. There he was exposed to the powerful influence of the dean, Henry Aldrich, who persuaded him to undertake a Latin translation of Palladio's *Antichità di Roma*. This was published in Oxford in 1709 and marked out Fairfax as a member of the cultivated set which, under Aldrich's tutelage, interested itself in architecture as in the other arts. Fairfax's translation was evidence of the growing dissatisfaction with the baroque style of architecture associated with Wren, Vanbrugh, and Hawksmoor, and a harbinger of the neo-Palladian revival that would soon gather momentum.

Fairfax graduated BA in 1707 and proceeded MA in 1709. Thereafter, having been ordained, he secured preferments in Suffolk, first at Barnham and then, in 1718, at Euston. The latter incumbency suggested the patronage of the local grandee, the duke of Grafton. The duke's backing explained the unexpected removal of Fairfax to Ireland (of which Grafton was lord lieutenant), as dean of

Down, in 1722. The emoluments of the deanery were estimated variously to be worth £1000 to £1300 annually—more than many Irish bishoprics. This appointment may also have owed something to the intervention of Edward Southwell, the absentee owner of Downpatrick, the location of Fairfax's cathedral. Southwell, an Oxford graduate, retained strong connections with the university and also a lively interest in the arts, including architecture. Fairfax was rumoured still to sympathize with the Jacobites and was also suspected to be part of a clerical combination to embarrass the whig bishop of Down and Connor, Francis Hutchinson.

Although, as dean, Fairfax lacked any permanent residence in the town he attended assiduously to his duties, entertaining the young and poor of the district at Christmas 1722. He may already have been qualified in one regard for the post, being—reputedly—skilled in Old Irish. Less welcome was his treatment of the numerous Presbyterians in the area. He revived the controversy from the 1690s about the validity of marriages performed by Presbyterian ministers when he had some who had been married in this way presented in the ecclesiastical courts for fornication. However, the impact of Fairfax was limited by his premature death, in London, on 27 July 1723. He was unmarried. His short tenure of the deanery also prevented his introducing his architectural tastes into Downpatrick. The building there, shortly afterwards, of almshouses and a court house in a provincial classical style owed more to the Southwells than to the cultivated dean.

TOBY BARNARD

Sources Christ Church Oxf., Wake MSS 14/21, 60, 72, 86, 87, 158 · BL, Add. MS 20131, fol. 54 · Colvin, *Archs.*, 71 · J. B. Leslie and H. B. Swanzy, *Biographical succession lists of the clergy of diocese of Down* (1936) · Foster, *Alum. Oxon.* · *Old Westminsters*, 1.318 · E. McParland, 'Edward Lovett Pearce and the new junta for architecture', *Lord Burlington: architecture, art and life*, ed. T. Barnard and J. Clark (1995), 151–65 · H. Cotton, *Fasti ecclesiae Hibernicae*, 3 (1849), 227 · E. Parkinson, ed., 'The vestry book of the parish of Down', *Ulster Journal of Archaeology*, new ser., 14 (1908) · J. F. Rankin, *Down Cathedral: the church of St. Patrick of Down* (1997) · IGI · DNB

Fairfax, Edward (1568?–1632×5?), translator, was the third of the four sons of Sir Thomas Fairfax (1521–1600), of Denton, Yorkshire. Edward's birth date of 1568 rests on nineteenth-century sources; he was probably born at Denton or Leeds. The records of his birth, baptism, marriages, and burial were presumably destroyed in the 1696 fire in Fewston church. Both he and his younger brother, Charles *Fairfax, are attested as illegitimate in Brian Fairfax's *Analecta Fairfaxiana* (c.1705) and Thoresby's *Ducatus Leodiensis* (1715), but this was too much for some Victorian editors to swallow. We know nothing about his education, but he may be the Edward Fairfax who matriculated at Clare College, Cambridge, in 1581. From 1595 to 1600 he managed the Fairfax property. As his father's favourite son he was left the bulk of his father's estate and his eldest brother, Thomas *Fairfax (1560–1640), received 'divers legacies of good valew' (*Godfrey of Bulloigne*, 5). Edward received a licence to marry Catherine Calverley, a widow from Otley in 1597, but there is no record of the marriage.

Early in January 1600 Thomas, whom his father had banished from the estate, led a gang of armed men into Denton Hall and forced his father to redraw his will. Edward was left only £150 and Newhall at Fewston which the family had acquired in 1597. Edward's attempts to gain legal redress came to nothing. In 1600 came Fairfax's *Godfrey of Bulloigne, or, The Recoverie of Jerusalem*, a translation of Tasso's *Gerusalemme liberata*. Fairfax translated with an eye to Carew's version of the first five cantos (1594), Harington's version of Ariosto, and Spenser's *Faerie Queene*. *Godfrey* is shot through with echoes of Homer and Virgil's *Aeneid*, most of them developed from hints in Tasso. Fairfax's command of the telling phrase and wide-ranging and aptly used scholarship established his reputation. There were several seventeenth-century reprints, that of 1624 being at the order of James I. It is supposed to have been a solace to Charles I during his time in prison. Robert Alott included 50 passages from it in *England's Parnassus* (1600). The poem strongly influenced the development of English poetry from Webster to Dryden. Waller, for instance, 'derived the harmony of his number from "Godfrey of Bulloigne", which was turned into English by Mr Fairfax' (J. Dryden, *Fables Ancient and Modern*, 1700, preface). However Fairfax's Elizabethan verve fell foul of the eighteenth century, and of nineteenth-century critics who admired his style while doubting his fidelity. Also in 1600 he married Dorothy Laycock (d. 1648) of Copmanthorpe, the sister of Walter Laycock, the chief aulnager of the northern counties. Fairfax made peace with his elder brother, assisting him with the education of his children. Between 1600 and 1619 he moved backwards and forwards between Leeds and Newhall. He is recorded as resident in Kirkgate, near St Peter's, Leeds. He was interested in local antiquities and took a hand in parish affairs. In 1618 Fairfax was one of the signatories of a bill of complaint concerning the purchase of the advowson (the rights to assign the benefice) of Leeds parish church. He finally settled at Newhall the next year. There he lived the quiet life of a scholarly country gentleman, assisted his brother-in-law in checking the quality of locally made cloth, and owned the local flour mill. Fairfax also wrote twelve eclogues imitating Virgil and Theocritus. Only three of them have been published. He also wrote 'History of the Black Prince' and an epitaph for James I.

After the death of Fairfax's youngest daughter, Anne, in October 1621, his eldest daughter, Ellen, reported seeing visions, and she, her sister Elizabeth, and a friend finally accused some local women of witchcraft. Edward took the matter to the assizes in August 1622. His case collapsed when the girls' friend confessed that the whole thing had been a hoax devised by her father and agreed to by the Fairfax girls who treated it as a bid for their father's attention. The friend's father was sent to prison, and the judges roundly criticized Fairfax's common sense. Fairfax recorded the whole affair in his *Daemonologia*, which never casts doubt on his daughters' story and ascribes Anne's death to witchcraft. In that account Fairfax describes himself as 'neither a fantastic Puritan nor superstitious Papist, but so settled in conscience that I have sure ground of God's word to warrant all I believe, and the commendable practices of our English Church to approve all I practise' (*Godfrey of Bulloigne*, 4). He corresponded on religious matters with John Dorrel (Darrel), a Roman Catholic priest imprisoned in York Castle. According to the *Analecta Fairfaxiana* Fairfax died 'about 1632'. Morley claims he died in January 1635 and was buried at Fewston on 27 January. His widow was buried at Fewston on 21 January 1648. His eldest son, William, was grammatical tutor to Thomas Stanley, a noted editor of Aeschylus.   L. G. KELLY

Sources *Godfrey of Bulloigne: a critical edition of Edward Fairfax's translation of Tasso's Gerusalemme liberata, together with Fairfax's original poems*, ed. K. M. Lea and T. M. Gang (1981) · C. G. Bell, 'Edward Fairfax, a natural son', *Modern Language Notes*, 62 (1947), 24–7 · T. M. Gang, 'The quarrel between Edward Fairfax and his brother', *N&Q*, 214 (1969), 28–33 · G. W. Johnson, ed., *The Fairfax correspondence: memoirs of the reign of Charles the First*, 2 vols. (1848) · Venn, *Alum. Cant.*

Archives LPL, MS vol. 708, fol. 212 · priv. coll., Analecta Fairfaxiana · PRO, relating to family quarrel, Star Chamber 5/F31/33

Fairfax, Ferdinando, **second Lord Fairfax of Cameron** (1584–1648), parliamentarian army officer, was born on 29 March 1584 at Denton Hall, in the parish of Otley, in the West Riding of Yorkshire, the eldest son of Thomas *Fairfax, first Lord Fairfax of Cameron (1560–1640), and his wife, Ellen (d. 1620), daughter of Robert Aske of Aughton and his wife, Elizabeth. The warlike Thomas had been a soldier in the Low Countries and France, and was to purchase the peerage for £1500 in 1627. He reportedly said that he sent Ferdinando 'into the Netherlands to train him up a soldier, and he makes a tolerable country justice, but is a mere coward at fighting' (Markham, *Lord Fairfax*, 12). Having been admitted to Gray's Inn on 3 May 1602, Ferdinando was knighted at Theobalds on 30 January 1608. One commemoration of his funeral recounted: 'in his younger yeares he was given to the study of Arts and Sciences, that must make him usefull and serviceable to his Countrey, and not to Dogs, Hawkes, &c.' (*A Perfect Narrative*, 4).

In 1607 Fairfax married Mary Sheffield (d. 1619), daughter of Edmund *Sheffield, first earl of Mulgrave, lord president of the council of the north, and his first wife, Ursula. Mary died in childbirth at Steeton in 1619, and Fairfax remained a widower for twenty-seven years. He was MP for Boroughbridge in the parliaments of 1614, 1621, 1624, 1628, and the Short Parliament of 1640. He entered the West Riding's commission of the peace in 1611 and was a particularly active justice, defending the authority of the post against interference from the council of the north. Fairfax was of Calvinist sympathies and by the early 1640s was mildly presbyterian. During the 1629 parliament he reported to his father with evident sympathy the sense of the House of Commons that 'the danger by the growth of Arminianism and countenancing of [its] professors' threatened the very 'subversion of the religion now established' (Johnson, 1.155). During the 1630s he assisted godly ministers in trouble with ecclesiastical

authority, while the influence of Richard Neile, archbishop of York, intruded onto his estates and, as a principal governor of Otley grammar school, he resented Neile's intervention over the choice of headmaster. He came to desire that episcopal power should be limited and sponsored presbyterian preaching in the West Riding. However, in March 1641 he expressed his opposition to altering the liturgy, 'which many shoot at' (ibid., 1.180).

Fairfax remained loyal during the bishops' wars, commanding a regiment of trained bands in the royal army, but on 10 September 1640 he helped organize the petition of Yorkshire gentry calling for a parliament. In October he was returned to the Long Parliament as knight of the shire for Yorkshire, where he joined the opposition to royal policies. He assisted in the trial of the earl of Strafford and was among the committee that presented the grand remonstrance to the king. When the king established himself at York in March 1642 Fairfax was among the five parliamentary commissioners who arrived on 8 May to observe his actions. While in York on 17 June he fell from his horse and broke two ribs; he withdrew to Denton to patronize godly sermons and prepare his neighbourhood for armed resistance. He headed the declaration at Otley on 29 August condemning the king's raising of forces, and on 7 September he wrote to request arms from parliament's governor of Hull, Sir John Hotham. He was proclaimed leader of Yorkshire's parliamentarians at Leeds on 19 September, provoking Hotham's animosity by concluding a treaty of neutrality with leading royalists at Rothwell on 29 September. Parliament condemned the treaty and encouraged Fairfax to abandon it.

On 21 October 1642 Fairfax repelled a royalist attack on his headquarters at Bradford and, joining with forces sent from Hull, blockaded the royalists in York. On 3 December he received his commission as general of parliament's forces in the northern counties, but he was forced to retreat as the earl of Newcastle's larger royalist army marched southwards. On 6 December he successfully defended Tadcaster from that army, but he was forced to retreat that night to establish new headquarters at Selby. In January and February 1643 he engaged in a propaganda battle with the earl of Newcastle, accusing him of invading Yorkshire with an army largely officered by Roman Catholics. On 5 February he was hailed during John Shaw's sermon to his army as 'our new Joshua of the North' (*Yorkshire Diaries and Autobiographies in the Seventeenth and Eighteenth Centuries*, ed. C. Jackson, Surtees Society, 65, 1877, 367). The motto on his standard, the only one in Spanish on either side, read *Viva el rey y muerra el mal govierno* ('Long live the king and death to bad government'; I. Gentles, 'The iconography of revolution: England, 1642–1649', *Soldiers, Writers and Statesmen of the English Revolution: Essays Presented to Austin Woolrych*, ed. I. Gentles, J. Morrill, and B. Worden, 1998, 109).

The defection of Sir Hugh Cholmley and doubts over Hotham's continued allegiance led Fairfax to move his headquarters to Leeds on 30 March, and *en route* his rearguard was defeated at Seacroft Moor. In April he resisted Newcastle's attacks on Leeds, but on 30 June he was severely defeated at Adwalton Moor, near Bradford. He fled through Leeds to Selby and then by boat to Hull where he found that Hotham had just been arrested for conspiracy to betray the town. Fairfax was welcomed and appointed governor on 22 July. Within weeks he raised a new force which provoked Newcastle's army into besieging Hull on 2 September. A decisive sally on 11 October 1643 ended the siege, and he spent the winter regaining control of the East Riding for parliament. On 11 April 1644 his army captured Selby, Fairfax himself leading one of the storming divisions, and so Newcastle's army was forced to return to defend York. Joining forces with the Scots and parliament's eastern association army, Fairfax besieged York. After the siege was broken by Prince Rupert he commanded the infantry on the right of the victorious allied army at Marston Moor on 2 July, where his younger son, Charles, was slain. After the city's surrender on 16 July Fairfax was appointed governor of York, where, along with his elder son, Sir Thomas *Fairfax, he protected the minster from iconoclasm and preserved the library and archives. Sir Thomas had served as his general of horse in the northern campaigns, and despite their early defeats of 1643, the Fairfaxes' tenacity and powers of recovery contributed a great deal to frustrating the royalist war effort.

Fairfax resigned his command when the self-denying ordinance was passed but remained influential on the parliamentary committee at York established to govern the northern counties. On 21 January 1645 Sir Thomas Fairfax was appointed general of parliament's New Model Army. Ferdinando's pay arrears amounted to £13,480, of which he had received only £2,069 by August 1646. At St Giles-in-the-Fields, Middlesex, on 16 October 1646, he married Rhoda Hussey (1616/17–1686), daughter of Thomas Chapman of London and widow of Thomas Hussey of Lincolnshire. Part of Fairfax's pay arrears had been assigned from the composition fine of her late husband's royalist father, Sir Edward Hussey.

Fairfax died at Denton Hall on 13 or 14 March 1648 from a fever caused by a gangrenous foot. He was survived by his second wife, and was succeeded by his son Sir Thomas. His will directed that his funeral should be 'without much pomp or ceremony' (Johnson, 1.xc), and on 15 March he was buried beside his first wife at All Saints' Church, Bolton Percy, where a monumental inscription remains to his memory. His library is now held by York Minster and consists of about 400 volumes, some of which had been owned by Sir John Hotham.   ANDREW J. HOPPER

Sources R. Bell, ed., *Memorials of the civil war … forming the concluding volumes of the Fairfax correspondence*, 1 (1849) • G. W. Johnson, ed., *The Fairfax correspondence: memoirs of the reign of Charles the First*, 2 vols. (1848) • C. R. Markham, *A life of the great Lord Fairfax* (1870) • C. R. Markham, *The genealogy of the Fairfaxes* (1870) • J. Rushworth, *Historical collections*, 2nd edn, 3/2 (1692) • J. T. Cliffe, *The Yorkshire gentry from the Reformation to the civil war* (1969) • Keeler, *Long Parliament* • *A perfect narrative of the late proceedings of the parliament of Scotland in relation to the affaires of England; also the manner of the funeral of the Right Honourable Ferdinando Lord Fairfax* (1648) [Thomason tract E 433(13)] • P. C. D. Brears, ed., *Yorkshire probate inventories, 1542–1689*, Yorkshire Archaeological Society, Records Ser., 134 (1972) • W. J. Sheils, 'Provincial preaching on the eve of the civil war: some West Riding sermons', *Religion, culture and society in early modern Britain: essays in honour of Patrick Collinson*, ed. A. Fletcher and P. Roberts (1994), 291–312 • U. Hull, Brynmor Jones L., Hotham papers, DDHO/1/9 • papers of the Hull corporation relating to the civil wars, City of Hull Archives, BRS/7 • commonwealth exchequer papers, PRO, SP 28/3A/195 • committee for compounding, PRO, SP 23/1/128, 23/3/214 • A. H. Woolrych, 'Yorkshire's treaty of neutrality', *History Today*, 6 (1956), 696–704 • GEC, *Peerage*, new edn, vol. 5 • J. Lister, ed., *West Riding sessions records*, 2, Yorkshire Archaeological Society, 54 (1915) • *Fifth report*, HMC, 4 (1876) [Sutherland MSS] • J. Foster, *The register of admissions to Gray's Inn, 1521–1889, together with the register of marriages in Gray's Inn chapel, 1695–1754* (privately printed, London, 1889) • DNB

Archives BL, letters, Add. MSS 15857, 15858, 18979, 20778, 21506, 29747, 31116, 30305, 34195, 34274; Egerton MSS 1048, 2647, 2648 • Bodl. Oxf., corresp. and papers • Derbys. RO, letters and proclamations • Hull Central Library, BRS/7 • U. Leeds, Brotherton L., corresp. • York Minster Library, personal library of books | U. Hull, Brynmor Jones L., Hotham MSS

Likenesses E. Bower, oils, 1646, City of York Art Gallery; repro. in *Catalogue of paintings, City of York Art Gallery*, 2: *English school, 1500–1850* (1963), pl. 6 • mezzotint, pubd 1811 (after unknown artist), NPG • R. Sawyer, line engraving, BM, NPG; repro. in J. Ricraft, *A survey of England's champions* (1647) • line engraving, BM; repro. in J. Vicars, *England's worthies* (1647) • medals, repro. in Markham, *Life of the great Lord Fairfax* • portrait, repro. in Markham, *Life of the great Lord Fairfax* • silver badges, BM

Wealth at death over £10,350—incl. manors of Otley, Ripon, Bolton Percy, Oulston, and Hartlington; £2000 to daughter; approx. £1050 inventory of personal estate, excl. library; approx. £7000 army pay arrears: Johnson, ed., *Fairfax correspondence*, 1.lxxxix–xciv; Brears, ed; *Yorkshire probate inventories*, 93–4; PRO, SP 23/3/214

Fairfax, Ferdinando (1678–1749). *See under* Fairfax, Brian (1633–1711).

Fairfax, Sir Guy (d. 1495), justice, came of a Yorkshire family, the third son of Richard Fairfax of Walton and his wife, Anastasia, daughter of John Carthorpe. From his father he inherited the manor of Steeton in the West Riding of Yorkshire, where he built a castle. At first he seems to have been occupied with purely local business, and in April 1451 was granted an annual fee by the powerful Percy family. He was a commissioner of array for the West Riding in 1435, a justice of the peace there from 1456, and in 1460 he was commissioned to inquire into lands in that riding possessed by the recently attainted Richard, duke of York (d. 1460). One of his colleagues was Sir William Plumpton (d. 1480), whose counsel he was in 1469, and in 1483 he acted as an arbitrator in the great dispute over the Plumpton inheritance (as he had done earlier for Durham Priory in 1431). Common serjeant of London (1456–9), under-sheriff (1459–60), and counsel to the City (1460), he was retained by the London mercers in 1455–6 and 1457–8, by the goldsmiths in 1468–9 and 1472–3, and by St Augustine's, Canterbury, in 1468–9. During the 1470s he became a member of the northern affinity of Richard, duke of Gloucester, serving him in a legal capacity. He first appears in the yearbooks in Michaelmas term 1463 as a serjeant and member of Gray's Inn. On 28 April 1467 he was appointed king's serjeant and in 1476–7 served as recorder of York. Regularly a justice of assize in the palatinate of Durham from 1457, and a justice of the peace in a number of counties from 1471, he also developed a close association with the duchy of Lancaster—as second justice at Lancaster in 1471, deputy chief steward and a member of duchy council in 1476, and chief justice at Lancaster in 1480. In these capacities he became actively involved in determined efforts to restore law and order in Lancashire.

In 1477 Fairfax was appointed a justice of the king's bench. In this office he won an honourable reputation, and on 8 October 1482 received a grant of 100 marks yearly in addition to his salary. He continued to serve as a justice of the king's bench and chief justice of Lancaster under Edward V, Richard III, and Henry VII. He certainly enjoyed a long and highly successful legal career, whether the reigning monarch was of the house of Lancaster, York, or Tudor, and he firmly established the fortunes of his family. On numerous occasions he served on commissions of oyer and terminer, in counties ranging from Yorkshire to Cornwall, and during his last decade figured particularly as a justice of assize in the midlands. On at least six occasions between 1470 and 1495 he was summoned by writ to attend parliament, while in his native county of Yorkshire he was much in demand as a trustee for, and executor of, the wills of neighbouring landed families. With his wife, Isabel, a daughter of Sir William Ryther, Fairfax had four sons and two daughters. He died in 1495. Two of his sons—William, the eldest, who became a justice of common pleas in 1510, and Thomas, a serjeant in 1521—ensured the family's continuing prominence in the legal profession.

KEITH DOCKRAY

Sources *Chancery records* · Foss, *Judges*, vol. 5 · R. Somerville, *History of the duchy of Lancaster, 1265–1603* (1953) · R. Horrox, *Richard III, a study of service*, Cambridge Studies in Medieval Life and Thought, 4th ser., 11 (1989) · E. W. Ives, *The common lawyers of pre-Reformation England* (1983)

Fairfax, Henry (1588–1665), Church of England clergyman, was born on 14 January 1588 at Denton Hall, in the parish of Otley in the West Riding of Yorkshire; he was the fourth but second surviving son of Thomas Fairfax (1560–1640), later first Baron Fairfax of Cameron, and his wife, Ellen (*d.* 1620), daughter of Robert Aske, esquire, of Aughton and his wife, Elizabeth. Henry's warlike father had been a soldier in the Low Countries and in France, and purchased the peerage for £1500 in 1627. From 1602 Henry was educated at Trinity College, Cambridge. Tutored by a Dr Duckett, he was awarded the degrees of BA and MA and was a fellow of the college from 1608 to 1616. He was a close friend of George Herbert, orator of the university until his death in 1634. Ordained a deacon in 1614 and a priest in 1616, Fairfax served briefly as rector of Newton Kyme in Yorkshire, a living in his father's gift, before Sir George Booth procured his appointment as rector of Ashton under Lyne, Lancashire, in 1619.

On 4 February 1627, at St Helen's in York, Fairfax married Mary (*c.*1593–1650), daughter of Sir Henry Cholmley of Whitby and his wife, Margaret, daughter of Sir William Babthorpe. Noted for her zeal, Mary committed to writing her pious meditations on Matthew 6. The couple returned to Yorkshire in 1633, when Fairfax was reinstated as rector of Newton Kyme. He was active in attempts to establish a

university in the north, either at York or at Manchester. On 20 March 1641 he wrote to his brother Ferdinando, second Baron Fairfax, requesting his aid in the design, enclosing in his letter a petition advocating the choice of Manchester. His son Brian *Fairfax recalled that during the civil wars Fairfax was brought before Prince Rupert at York in 1644 and asked if he had taken the covenant; having replied that he had not he was released and sent home with a note of protection. Brian remarked that his parents' house at Newton Kyme was 'a refuge and sanctuary to their friends and relations on both sides'. He further recalled of his father:

> I have heard say that King James bid my Grandfather make him a Scollar, and he would make him a Bishop: but the storme that fell upon Church and State made him incapable of that dignety, liveing quietly like Lot in Zoar, from whence he saw Sodome all in flames. (Markham, *Life of Robert Fairfax*, 134–5)

Fairfax had inherited estates in nearby Oglethorpe, and in 1646 he was made rector of the larger and more prosperous living at Bolton Percy. He was also a canon of York and prebendary of Fridaythorpe from 1615 to 1665.

Mary Fairfax died of pleurisy on 24 December 1649 and was buried the following day in Bolton Percy church. Fairfax mourned for her so passionately, it was said, that he lost the sight in one of his eyes. His son recalled his religious zeal and how he 'was ever lifting up his eyes and hands to Heaven' (Markham, *Life of Robert Fairfax*, 135–6). Among his parishioners during the 1650s was his nephew the retired general Thomas, third Baron Fairfax. At the Restoration Fairfax resigned as rector in favour of Mr Wickham, and in 1662 he retired to his estate at Oglethorpe. His recreations included the study of antiquities and heraldry, while he spent much time meditating, reading the Bible, and taking notes. His brother, the antiquarian Charles Fairfax, frequently quoted from these notes in compiling his 'Analecta Fairfaxiana', where some of Henry's anagrams and epigrams may be found.

Having enjoyed good health throughout his life Fairfax died 'of a kind of lethargy' at Oglethorpe on 6 April 1665 (Markham, *Life of Robert Fairfax*, 138). He was buried two days later, beside his wife, under a flagstone within the altar rails of Bolton Percy church, where a monumental inscription remains. His eldest surviving son, Henry, succeeded as fourth Baron Fairfax in 1671.

ANDREW J. HOPPER

Sources C. R. Markham, *Life of Robert Fairfax of Steeton* (1885) · J. Foster, ed., *Pedigrees of the county families of Yorkshire*, 1, 3 (1874) · Venn, *Alum. Cant.*, 1/2 · G. W. Johnson, ed., *The Fairfax correspondence: memoirs of the reign of Charles the First*, 2 vols. (1848) · parish register, Bolton Percy, Borth. Inst., microfilm 644 · GEC, *Peerage*, new edn, vol. 5 · *Fasti Angl., 1541–1857*, [York] · *DNB* · C. R. Markham, *The genealogy of the Fairfaxes* (1870) · C. R. Markham, *A life of the great Lord Fairfax* (1870) · E. W. Crossley, ed., *Wills in the York registry, 1660–1665*, Yorkshire Archaeological Society, records series, 49 (1912) · W. Brigg, ed., *The parish registers of Otley, co. York*, 1, Yorkshire Parish Register Society, 33 (1908)

Archives BL, catalogue of his library, Sloane MS 1872, fols. 60–81b · Bodl. Oxf., corresp. and papers · U. Leeds, Brotherton L., notes on Yorkshire wapentakes and their armigerous families; York-shire notes

Fairfax, Henry (1634–1702), dean of Norwich, was born at Menston in the West Riding of Yorkshire, and was baptized on 28 October 1634 at Otley, the sixth son of Charles *Fairfax (1597–1673), antiquary and genealogist, and Mary Breary (*bap.* 1609, *d.* 1657), and a grandson of Thomas, first Lord *Fairfax (1560–1640). He was a cousin of Thomas Fairfax, the parliamentarian general. Fairfax clearly took some pride in his family, as he wrote a panegyrical Latin poem to his cousin (Bodl. Oxf., MS Fairfax 32). He matriculated from Exeter College, Oxford, on 21 July 1653, graduating BA in 1657 and MA in 1659, and in 1659 was elected a fellow of Magdalen College, from where he graduated BD in 1666 and DD in 1681. Within Magdalen, Fairfax took his due share of college duties, acting as bursar, dean of divinity, and vice-president, and in 1683 was presented to the college living of Tubney, Berkshire. He evidently remained a Yorkshireman at heart: Henry Clerke, president of Magdalen (1672–87), once described Fairfax as speaking 'very bluntly (and with too much shew of his northern humour)' (Magd. Oxf., MS 427, fol. 59v).

Fairfax's unexceptional career was transformed by the death of Clerke in March 1687, and the subsequent efforts of James II to impose a president of his choice on the college, when (perhaps mindful of his older cousin's stand against excessive royal authority) Fairfax achieved a national reputation through the leading role he took in the fellows' struggle against the crown to elect their own candidate, John Hough. By now senior fellow of Magdalen, Fairfax showed his courage best on two occasions when he was brought before commissioners sent to investigate Magdalen. At the first of these, held in London on 13 June, Fairfax put his 'northern humour' to good effect when he told the lord chancellor, George Jeffreys, that he did not recognize the commission's jurisdiction. According to one source (Magd. Oxf., MS 432), an infuriated Jeffreys told Fairfax that he should have been 'brought to me in the Chancery, as a Lunatiq', and that 'the room is too light for you, you are mad', and on 22 June Fairfax was suspended from his fellowship. At another commission, held in Oxford in October, he was the only fellow to refuse outright to accept James's candidate as president, and was finally expelled from the college. Most of the other fellows, perhaps emboldened by Fairfax's resistance, eventually also refused to co-operate with the commissioners, who therefore expelled them all and, in December 1687, banned them and Fairfax from receiving any post within the church.

On 25 October 1688, as James's power ebbed, Fairfax and the other fellows were restored to their emoluments. After his courageous behaviour his preferment was only a matter of time, and on 23 September 1689 he was appointed dean of Norwich, a post he held until his death. Fairfax was not a successful dean. Perhaps promoted beyond his ability, he acquired a reputation for being high-handed with the cathedral prebendaries, for excessive drinking, and for taking little or no interest in his duties. He died at

Norwich on 20 May 1702 (thus his memorial; his tombstone says it was 10 May) and was buried in the cathedral, where his nephew and heir, Thomas, erected a memorial to him. Fairfax never married, and no portraits of him are known to survive. He is thought to have written the pamphlet entitled *An Impartial Relation of the Proceedings Against St. Mary Magdalen College in Oxford* (1688; 2nd edn, 1689), which, despite its title, none the less subtly defends the fellows' cause through its judicious selection of documents quoted.   R. H. DARWALL-SMITH

Sources J. R. Bloxam, ed., *Magdalen College and James II, 1686–1688: a series of documents*, OHS, 6 (1886) • W. D. Macray, *A register of the members of St Mary Magdalen College, Oxford*, 8 vols. (1894–1915), vol. 4, pp. 99–102 • L. Brockliss, G. Harriss, and A. Macintyre, *Magdalen College and the crown: essays for the tercentenary of the restoration of the college, 1688* (1988) • C. W. Boase, ed., *Registrum Collegii Exoniensis*, new edn, OHS, 27 (1894) • *The life and times of Anthony Wood*, ed. A. Clark, 3, OHS, 26 (1894) • *Letters of Humphrey Prideaux … to John Ellis*, ed. E. M. Thompson, CS, new ser., 15 (1875), 150, 157, 160–61 • Burke, *Peerage* • R. A. Beddard, 'James II and the Catholic challenge', *Hist. U. Oxf.* 4: *17th-cent. Oxf.*, 907–54 • Bodl. Oxf., MS Fairfax 32 [incl. poem by Fairfax] • notebook of Henry Clerke, Magd. Oxf., MS 427 • papers relating to the expulsion of the fellows, Magd. Oxf., CRC/132, BB/2, CS/36/10/4 • Magd. Oxf., MSS 249, 285, 293, 418, 420–423, 425–426, 429–432, 448, 454, 791, 714–717, 719, 722, 724, 908/26 [several repr. in J. R. Bloxam, *Magdalen College and James II, 1686–1688*, OHS, 6 (1886)] • parish register, Otley, 28 Oct 1634, W. Yorks. AS, Leeds • memorial, Norwich Cathedral • *DNB*

Fairfax, John (1623/4–1700), clergyman and ejected minister, was born in Norfolk, the second son of four sons and six daughters of Benjamin Fairfax (or Fayerfaxe; 1592–1675/6) and his wife, Sarah Gallard (*d.* 1671). Benjamin was the son of John Fairfax, master of the Great Hospital in Norwich, and was from 1626 minister of Rumburgh, near Halesworth, Suffolk. Sarah was the daughter of Roger Gallard, rector of Ashwellthorpe, Norfolk, and his wife, Joane, whose sister Abigail married the sabbatarian writer Theophilus Brabourne. The East Anglian Fairfaxes sprang originally from Yorkshire: both John and the parliamentarian general Sir Thomas Fairfax were seventh-generation descendants of Sir Richard Fairfax, lord chief justice in the time of Henry VI, John in the senior branch.

John Fairfax claimed that his spiritual conversion followed from an incident when he was ten, the apparently sudden death of a baby sister in her cradle, which put him in a great fear and trembling about his own mortality and eternal welfare. At Easter 1640 he was admitted a sizar at Corpus Christi College, Cambridge, where, after graduating BA in January 1645, subscribing to the solemn league and covenant, and undergoing an examination by the Westminster assembly, he was admitted by the earl of Manchester to the fellowship vacated by the ejection of Thomas Briggs. Fairfax proceeded MA in 1647 but was ejected from his fellowship in 1650 for refusing to subscribe to the engagement of loyalty to the republican government. In 1649 he was vicar of Swaffham Bulbeck, Cambridgeshire. By the following year he was rector of Barking with Needham Market in Suffolk, a living worth £140 per annum. He served as an assistant to the Suffolk commission of triers. Fairfax was ejected from Barking for his refusal to conform in 1662. His father, described by

Edmund Calamy as 'a very lively preacher, [who] had great success in converting souls to the love of God and true goodness', was ejected from Rumburgh at the same time (Calamy, *Abridgement*, 2.648).

About 1650 Fairfax had married Elizabeth (*d.* 1695), daughter of William Cowper of Mosborough, Derbyshire, and over a dozen years they had five sons and a short-lived daughter, Elizabeth. A second Elizabeth was born to complete their family in 1668. They continued to live in Barking, in their own house, Spalding Hall, where by mixed livestock and arable farming they helped to support themselves. In addition they had two generous friends. One was Dame Elizabeth, widow of Sir Robert Brooke of Yoxford; although 'separation was grievous to her, and she thought it unreasonable', she 'relieved many sober nonconformists with great bounty, and most earnestly desired to have seen them legally settled in a publick ministry' (Parkhurst, 71–2). John and his father desired the same end quite as much as their benefactress. John *Meadows, ejected from Ousden, near Newmarket, who later moved to Stowmarket and married Fairfax's niece, was the other friend. The Fairfaxes could afford to educate Benjamin (*b.* 1654) and Thomas (*b.* 1656) under Philip Candler at Woodbridge School, whence they entered their father's college at Cambridge, the former studying at Leiden after graduating. The more practical youngest son, Nathaniel, eventually ran the farm, which he inherited on his father's death.

Fairfax continued to take every opportunity to preach, which more than once led him into difficulties with the authorities. In April 1665 the archdeacon of Suffolk reported how he had been informed the previous year that Fairfax was preaching constantly in his old parish; despite being told to desist, Fairfax had repeated the offence. It is a measure both of his standing among nonconformists and of his skill as an orator that he was chosen to preach the memorial sermon at Dedham, Essex, on 16 September 1669 for Matthew Newcomen, the former lecturer there, who had recently died at Leiden. It was reported to Archbishop Sheldon how the large congregation, an 'outragious conventicle', heard Fairfax's 'dangerous words' (Gordon, 261). Two themes were contentious, to judge from the text as it was published ten years later by John Collinges as *The Dead Saint Speaking*, under Fairfax's initials but without his permission. Fairfax dwelt on Newcomen's rejection by the England which had nurtured him and which he had loved. Worse, and given more edge by the time it was published by protestant fears stirred by the Popish Plot, there is the providentialist ring to Fairfax's warning that 'some dreadful Judgement may hang over the head of England, and this righteous man may be taken away from the evil to come' (Fairfax, *Dead Saint Speaking*, 21).

Perhaps the stir created by the preaching of this sermon led to the severe consequences of another apparently harmless affair. On Tuesday 5 July 1670 Fairfax and other ministers attended service at Walsham-le-Willows church. After the liturgy was read by the incumbent, the sermon was delivered by the presbyterian Stephen Scandrett of Haverhill, who held no licence to preach. Six local magistrates arrived and, arresting Scandrett, Fairfax, and four other ministers, committed them to the county gaol at Bury St Edmunds. They were bailed at quarter sessions to appear at the next assizes before Sir Richard Rainsford, a judge noted for his severity to nonconformists. Fairfax was one of those who on 'a general suggestion' of the JPs who had committed them that they were 'persons dangerous to the public peace', were sent to prison until 'they should find sureties for their good behaviour' (Taylor, 131). When Fairfax had spent five months in gaol, during which time he suffered fever and fainting fits, a writ of habeas corpus was applied for. This the judges felt unable to grant, advising instead a petition to the king. The following March, John's sister, Priscilla Fairfax, then in the service of Edward Reynolds, bishop of Norwich, wrote urging her brother, unavailingly, to conform. Fairfax was probably set free at the following assizes, and on the issue of the king's declaration of indulgence (15 Mar 1672) took out a licence as a presbyterian teacher ministering at the house of Margaret, widow of the clothier Simon Rozier, in Needham Market, thus resuming the pastoral care of the nonconformists of his own parish. Here he was assisted by Margaret Rozier's brother, Timothy Wright of Ipswich.

Throughout the 1680s and 1690s Fairfax continued his ministry, preaching 'seven times in a fortnight', besides frequent 'occasional sermons' (Bury, 36). When his energy waned or his health failed him he found preaching the ideal remedy. He prepared his sermons by meditation rather than in writing, but they were always pertinent and well structured. A sermon he delivered on 6 January 1688, in the shadow of James II's Catholicizing policies, had a similar warning tone to that he had preached at Newcomen's funeral. Much of the sermon contained warnings that were at most implicit, but he opened by reminding his hearers that Jeremiah had prophesied 'against the people in Generall as appears throughout all his Prophessys and he Prophesyed in perticuler in the 22d. chapter against the Royall family' (DWL, MS 24.13, fol. 35*r*). Fairfax actively encouraged younger ministers, who were needed to replace the ageing ejected men. When Owen Stockton died in 1680, he preached and published the funeral sermon (*The True Dignity of St Paul's Elder …*), and took on Stockton's congregation in Greyfriars House in Rose Lane, Ipswich, as well as his own at Needham. The family continued to live at Barking, where he buried his wife on 22 November 1695.

The Ipswich Independents formed a separate congregation in 1686, and with the coming of toleration Fairfax hired another building for public presbyterian worship in St Nicholas parish. Swelled by a number of Huguenots sent to Ipswich by Thomas Firmin to staff a linen manufactory, the congregation needed better provision. Timothy Wright joined Fairfax as his assistant in 1698 just as plans were made to build a new meeting-house in the same parish, at the opening of which on 26 April 1700 Fairfax preached *Primititiae synagogae*. Daniel Defoe described the meeting-house in 1724: 'as large and fine a building of that kind as most on this side of England, and the inside the best finished of any I have seen, London not excepted' (Defoe, 64). It is now Unitarian.

Fairfax's preface dedicating the printed *Primititiae synagogae* to his patron Sir Thomas Cuddon, chamberlain of the City of London, is valedictory:

> I have so much satisfaction in what my congregation hath done tho' at their great charge, in building such a convenient and decent Synagogue for the solemn worship of god, that I was willing to leave behind me, now that I am going out of the World being in my 77th year, something that might be a memorial of this building to posterity in the next generations.

He wrote this on 3 June and died at Barking on 11 August 1700, aged seventy-six. Permission was given for his funeral sermon four days later to be preached in the parish church at his burial, by his fellow presbyterian Samuel Bury, who gave another funeral sermon to the Ipswich congregation on 23 August. Fairfax was succeeded at Needham by his great-nephew John Meadows, and at Ipswich by Timothy Wright, who died a year later aged only forty-two.

J. M. BLATCHLY

Sources Venn, *Alum. Cant.* · *Calamy rev.* · A. Gordon, ed., *Freedom after ejection: a review (1690–1692) of presbyterian and congregational nonconformity in England and Wales* (1917) · E. Taylor, *The Suffolk Bartholomeans* (1840) · J. Browne, *A history of Congregationalism and memorials of the churches in Norfolk and Suffolk* (1877) · S. Bury, *The peoples lamentations for the loss of their dead ministers* (1702) · will, Suffolk RO, Ipswich, IC/AA1/131/67 · J. Fairfax, *The dead saint speaking, or, A sermon … on the death of … Mr. Newcombe* (1679) · J. Fairfax, *The true dignity of St Paul's elder* (1681) · J. Fairfax, *Primititiae synagogae: a sermon preached at Ipswich* (1700) · D. Defoe, *Tour through the eastern counties*, ed. R. A. N. Dixon (1924) · N. Parkhurst, *The faithful and diligent Christian described and exemplified* (1684) · sermons by John Fairfax, DWL, MS 24.13, fols. 24r–33r, 35r–46v · E. Calamy, ed., *An abridgement of Mr. Baxter's history of his life and times, with an account of the ministers, &c., who were ejected after the Restauration of King Charles II*, 2nd edn, 2 vols. (1713)
Likenesses lithograph (after portrait by W. Taylor), repro. in Taylor, *Suffolk Bartholomeans*, facing p. 78

Fairfax, John (1804–1877), newspaper proprietor and politician in Australia, was born at Warwick on 25 October 1804, the second son of William Fairfax of Birmingham and his wife, Elizabeth, *née* Jesson. He was reared a Congregationalist. After a short time spent at school he was apprenticed, at the age of twelve, to William Perry, printer and bookseller in Warwick. Having served his time he went to London and from 1825 worked briefly on the *Morning Chronicle*. His next step was to set up as printer and bookseller in Leamington, near his home and friends. On 31 July 1827 he married Sarah, daughter of James Reading of Warwick; they had three sons and one daughter. In 1828 he founded, with James Sharp, the *Leamington Spa Courier* (Sharp soon dropping out). In 1835 he became part owner of the *Leamington Chronicle and Warwickshire Reporter*. In 1836 he successfully defended a libel action, but the costs bankrupted him. He and his family emigrated, arriving at Sydney, New South Wales, in September 1838 with £5.

Fairfax became librarian to the Australian Subscription Library in April 1839 and soon resumed his journalistic activities. In February 1841, with Charles Kemp, he bought the *Sydney Herald* (for which he was already writing), changing its name in 1842 to the *Sydney Morning Herald*. It was soon established as the leading paper of eastern Australia. In 1851 Fairfax visited Britain, paid off his debts, and became something of a celebrity in Warwickshire. He returned to Sydney with the first steam press to be used in Australia. In 1853 he bought out Kemp's interest in the *Herald* and took on his eldest son, Charles Fairfax, as his partner. He broadened his base, developing interests in insurance, banking, and utilities. A deeply religious person, he was president of the Young Men's Christian Association in Sydney, and was a deacon in the Congregational church. He stood unsuccessfully in 1856 for election to the legislative assembly but accepted nomination in 1874 to a seat on the legislative council.

In 1858 Fairfax built Ginahgulla in Bellvue Hill, Port Jackson. He died there on 16 June 1877, and was buried in Rookwood cemetery; his wife predeceased him. His two surviving sons carried on the *Herald*, by then one of the best-known newspapers of the British empire.

ROBERT HARRISON, rev. H. C. G. MATTHEW

Sources 'Fairfax, John', *AusDB*, vol. 4 · *In memoriam: obituary notices and funeral services having reference to the late Hon. J. Fairfax* (privately printed, Sydney, [1877]) · *A century of journalism: the Sydney Morning Herald and its record of Australian life, 1831–1931*, Sydney Morning Herald (1931) · J. F. Fairfax, *The story of John Fairfax* (1941) · *The Argus* [Melbourne] (18 June 1877) · *Sydney Morning Herald* (18 June 1877)
Archives Mitchell L., NSW, MSS | Mitchell L., NSW, Parkes MSS
Likenesses portraits, priv. coll.

Fairfax, Nathaniel (1637–1690), physician and antiquary, was born on 24 July 1637 at the rectory of Rumburgh in Suffolk and baptized in the parish on 30 July, the fourth and youngest son of Benjamin Fayerfaxe (1592–1676), rector of Rumburgh, and his wife, Sarah, daughter of Roger Gallard, rector of Ashwellthorpe, Norfolk, and his wife, Joane. The family were originally from Yorkshire. Nathaniel matriculated at Corpus Christi College, Cambridge, in 1655, graduating BA in 1658 and proceeding MA three years later in 1661. Ordained deacon that year, he was presented to the perpetual curacy of Willisham, Suffolk, but was ejected a year later on refusing to conform. Turning to medicine, he was licensed to practise at Norwich on 10 June 1665, and in 1670 took an MD at Leiden, where he published his inaugural dissertation, *De lumbricis*.

Having moved to Woodbridge in Suffolk, Fairfax established a medical practice where he cared, according to his Latin epitaph, 'equally for the needy and [the wealthy]' (Dallenger, 69). However, this still left time for his many literary, topographical, and heraldic interests. Much in sympathy with the aims of the newly formed Royal Society, although never a fellow, Fairfax corresponded regularly with the secretary, Henry Oldenburg. His contributions to the first volumes of the society's *Philosophical Transactions* included one giving 'instances of peculiarities of nature both in men and brutes' (vol. 2, 1667, p. 549) and others on the size of hailstones, and bodies dead of unusual diseases. They show that he was on familiar terms with Sir Thomas Browne of Norwich, the physician and author. About 1668 he married Elizabeth (*bap.* 1640, *d.*

1680), daughter of Thomas and Elizabeth Blackerby of St Michael's, Cambridge, and widow of Samuel Richardson. They had four sons and four daughters, of whom one son, Blackerby Fairfax [*see below*], and three daughters survived him.

In 1674 Fairfax published *A treatise of the bulk and selvedge of the world. Wherein the greatness, littleness, and lastingness of bodies are freely handled*, notable for its unvarnished expression and freedom from words borrowed from other languages. This was in line with the Royal Society's then current concern to describe scientific observations plainly. In his foreword Fairfax refers to the interregnum as the 'late dayes of Blame, and years of Topsie-turvy'. In the final part of the book, his *Answer to 'Tentamina de Deo', by S[amuel] P[arker], DD*, Fairfax was concerned to refute Henry More's belief in a boundless universe, and Parker's in the coextension of body and soul. He believed in the optimistic faith engendered by contemplation of the natural world, from which there were political as well as religious lessons to be learned.

Having lost his first wife in October 1680, on 3 August 1683 Fairfax married, at St Margaret's Church, Ipswich, Elizabeth (*b. c.*1633, *d.* 1723), widow of Francis Willard, and daughter of Nathaniel Bacon and Susanna Holloway, his second wife; there were no children of the marriage. During the 1680s Fairfax made antiquarian collections for Suffolk, notable for his own observations added to works copied from earlier topographers. In Peter Le Neve's hands they were cut up and pasted, by parish, into Hengrave MSS 2–19 in Cambridge University Library. As his last task, Fairfax gathered a 'Catalogue of Suffolk arms of many authors' in a thick folio volume now in private hands, drawing on the armories of twenty earlier collectors, many of them his friends: Blois, Candler, Leverland, Ryece, Staveley, and Tyllotson. He died at Woodbridge on 12 June 1690, and was buried there two days later on 14 June in the central aisle of the nave of St Mary's Church. There on 21 April 1723 his aged widow finally joined him under a slab which also commemorates and probably covers his first wife, their children, and two sons-in-law.

Nathaniel's son **Blackerby Fairfax** (*bap.* 1669, *d.* in or after 1730), physician and author, was baptized at St Mary's, Woodbridge, on 16 February 1669. He entered Woodbridge School in 1677 and followed his father to Corpus Christi College, Cambridge, in 1686, where he graduated BA in 1690 and proceeded MA in 1693. He left Cambridge to study at Leiden, where he was admitted MD on 18 April 1696. He was then appointed a physician in the navy, retiring in 1717. In 1728 he was created MD *comitiis regiis* at Cambridge. He published works in the fields of history, politics, botany, and medicine including *A Discourse upon the Uniting Scotland with England* (1702) and *In laudem botanices oratio: on the praise of botany, a speech to which is added a prefatory discourse for establishing a lecture on botany* (1717). He also published *A Treatise of the Just Interest of the Kings of England, in their Free Disposing Power* (1703), a tract attributed to Sir Matthew Hale, to which he added 'a prefatory discourse in answer to a discourse on grants and resumptions', and *The letter which Pope Gregory XV wrote to Charles I of England concerning his marriage to the infanta of Spain, and that prince's answer*. This work drew forth some *Observations* (1729) from William Matthews, perpetual curate of St Margaret's, Ipswich. Fairfax is last heard of in his sister Sarah Hall's will dated 27 January 1730.

J. M. BLATCHLY

Sources L. Dow, 'A Suffolk heraldic manuscript', *Proceedings of the Suffolk Institute of Archaeology*, 25 (1949–51), 288–96 · N. Fairfax, *A treatise on the bulk and selvedge of the world* (1674) · N. Fairfax, 'Catalogue of Suffolk arms of many authors', priv. coll., Suffolk · J. Dallenger, ed., *A record of Woodbridge parish church* (1875) · *PTRS*, 1–2 (1666–7) · CUL, Hengrave MSS 2–19 · *Calamy rev.*, 189 · *The Knyvett letters, 1620–1644*, ed. B. Schofield, Norfolk RS, 20 (1949)
Archives CUL, Hengrave MSS 2–19 · priv. coll., 'Catalogue of Suffolk arms of many authors' | RS, letters to Henry Oldenburg

Fairfax, Robert. *See* Fayrfax, Robert (1464–1521).

Fairfax, Robert (1666–1725), naval officer, was born in February 1666, and baptized on the 23rd of that month at Steeton Chapel, the second son of William Fairfax (1630–1673) of Steeton and Newton Kyme in Yorkshire, and his wife, Catherine Stapleton (*d.* 1695). He was a grandson of Sir William *Fairfax, colonel in the parliamentary army, killed at the relief of Montgomery Castle in 1644. Robert first went to sea in 1681, in a merchant ship, the *Mary*, commanded by Captain Bushell, with whom he made two voyages to the Mediterranean. On his return in December 1685 his friends wanted him to enter the Royal Navy, but it was not until January 1688 that he was received as a volunteer on board the *Mary*, the flagship of Sir Roger Strickland. A few weeks after the accession of William and Mary, Fairfax was promoted to be lieutenant of the *Bonaventure*, commanded by Captain Thomas Hopson. In her he was present at the battle in Bantry Bay (1 May 1689) and afterwards at the relief of Londonderry (28 July). In June of the following year Hopson was relieved in the command of the *Bonaventure* by Captain Hubbard, but Fairfax, remaining in her, was present at the battle of Beachy Head on 30 June 1690. On 15 November he was promoted to command the *Conception* prize, and for the next two years was stationed at Boston, Massachusetts, cruising against French privateers. In June 1693 Fairfax was moved into the *Pembroke* (60 guns) and, returning in her to England, was appointed to command the *Ruby* (48 guns) and ordered to cruise on the coast of Ireland for the protection of trade. While on this service he captured, after a hard-fought action, the 44-gun *Entreprenante*, a larger French privateer. In recognition of this service he was promoted, on 24 December 1694, to the command of the *Newark* (80 guns) in which, and afterwards in the *Cornwall*, he was employed in convoy service in the channel, the Bay of Biscay, and on the coast of Portugal, until the peace of Ryswick.

On the death of Fairfax's elder brother (20 January 1694) he had succeeded to the Steeton and Newton Kyme estates, and on 20 November of that year he married Esther (*c.*1655–1735), the sister of Captain Bushell and widow of Charles Tomlinson of Whitby. She was ten years older than Fairfax, but had befriended him in his youth, and he had continued to be deeply attached to her during her first marriage. A register ticket from this time describes Fairfax as a tall and well-set man of fair complexion, an image which corresponds with the first of three portraits painted at the ages of thirty and forty-two, and shortly before his death.

In May 1699 Fairfax commissioned the *Severn*, which in the following year was one of the fleet sent under Sir George Rooke to maintain the treaty of Altona as between Denmark and Holstein. On returning from the Baltic he was appointed to the *Cambridge*, and in January 1702, on the eve of the declaration of war, was transferred to the 70-gun *Restoration*, one of the squadron which sailed under Sir John Munden in May. After failing to intercept the French squadron off Corunna, Munden and his ships returned to Spithead, and in the following autumn Fairfax was sent out to reinforce the Grand Fleet, which he joined at Vigo on 18 October, too late to share in the glory or the treasure, but in time to take part in the labour of refitting the prizes and bringing them to England. The *Restoration* was then paid off and in January 1703 Fairfax was appointed to the *Somerset*, from which in May he was transferred to the *Kent* as flag captain to Rear-Admiral Thomas Dilkes, with whom he served during the summer, most notably in the wholesale capture or destruction of French merchant ships at Granville on 26 July, a service for which Fairfax and the other captains, as well as Dilkes, received a gold medal. Early in 1704 Fairfax commissioned the *Berwick*, a 70-gun ship, in which he sailed in March to join Rooke and the Grand Fleet at Lisbon; remaining with the fleet through the summer. The *Berwick* was one of the six ships which vainly chased a French squadron off Cape Palos on 8 May, a failure for which Fairfax and the other captains were tried by court martial, but fully acquitted; and was one of the division actually engaged under George Byng at the capture of Gibraltar (23 July), for his share in which exploit 'the queen afterwards presented Fairfax with a silver cup and cover bearing a suitable inscription' (Markham, 181). The *Berwick* also fought in the battle of Malaga (13 August), where her masts, rigging, and sails were shattered and torn, and she had sixty-nine men killed and wounded. The fleet afterwards returned to England for the winter, and in the following February the *Berwick* was paid off at Chatham, although Fairfax was immediately appointed to the *Torbay*. In her he again went to the Mediterranean, under the command of Shovell, and participated with the fleet in the capture of Barcelona. After the capture of Monjuich the prisoners were sent on board the *Torbay* which supplied guns to arm the fort, and sailors to haul them up the hill. Her marines were landed for service in the trenches, and Fairfax commanded seven bomb vessels, whose fire cowed the garrison, and enabled the marines' approach. When the town capitulated on 4 October the season was already far advanced, and the fleet at once returned to England.

In March 1706 Fairfax was appointed to the *Barfleur* as commander-in-chief in the Thames and Medway, but in May he was ordered round to Spithead to join Shovell, then preparing to carry over an expeditionary force intended to raid the coast of France. After vainly waiting for a promised Dutch squadron until the summer was past, a westerly gale forced the fleet to take shelter in Torbay, where it was detained for several weeks, and the original idea of a landing in France had to be given up. After a storm the *Berwick* sprang a leak, was found to be unseaworthy, and returned with difficulty to Portsmouth. In December Fairfax, with his ship's company, was turned over to the *Albemarle*, and during the early part of 1707 he was commander-in-chief at Portsmouth. In August, however, he was superseded, Sir John Leake having chosen the *Albemarle* as his flagship.

Following the death of Sir Cloudesley Shovell (22 October 1707), a promotion of flag officers was made on 8 January 1708. Fairfax, by his seniority, was properly included, and a commission as vice-admiral of the blue was made out for him, signed by the lord high admiral, and gazetted. It was then cancelled, and Lord Dursley, who was much his junior, was, by the political interest of his family, made vice-admiral of the blue in his place, with seniority of 10 January. Fairfax, indignant at this treatment, refused all further service. The queen's consort, Prince George, obtained for him a commission as rear-admiral, and half pay equal to that of the rank which he had been deprived of; and on 20 June 1708 had Fairfax nominated a member of the council of the lord high admiral. However, the appointment came to an end with the prince's death (28 October), whereupon Fairfax retired from naval life. At a by-election in 1713 he was returned to parliament for the city of York, but lost his seat in the general election after the accession of George I. He had meantime been elected an alderman of York, and was elected lord mayor in 1715. He spent the rest of his life in these and other local duties, and in the management and development of his property. He died at Newton Kyme on 17 October 1725 and was buried in the church there, where he had been baptized sixty years before. He was survived by his wife, who died aged eighty in 1735, and by two children: a daughter who married Henry Pawson, the son of an alderman of York, and a son, Thomas, whose descendants long held the estates of Steeton, Newton Kyme, and Bilbrough.

Fairfax gained a posthumous reputation arguably out of proportion to his achievements, primarily because of the chance survival of his papers (now in the National Maritime Museum) when those of many more prominent and interesting officers disappeared, and the subsequent decision by Sir Clements Markham to make these the basis of a slight and fanciful biography, published in 1885. Fairfax attracted more mixed opinions from contemporaries. The antiquarian Le Neve damned every line of his monument in Newton Kyme church, saying of Fairfax's alleged 'piety, courage and simplicity, the first two are generally denied, but as to the last *convenit inter omnes*', before condemning him as a parsimonious husband, a false friend, and a dishonourable hypocrite. Rather than investigating the charges, Markham dismissed them as 'garbage' emanating from Le Neve's 'small mind' (Markham, 280–81).

J. K. LAUGHTON, *rev.* J. D. DAVIES

Sources NMM, Fairfax papers, MS 81/116 · C. R. Markham, *Admiral Robert Fairfax* (1885) · PRO, admiralty MSS, esp. ADM 1/5265, 6/424, 51/104

Archives Borth. Inst., log books, order book · NMM, corresp. and papers, MS 81/116 | PRO, Admiralty MSS, especially ADM 1/5265, 6/424, 51/104
Likenesses M. Beale, oils, 1685, Gorhambury, Hertfordshire · three portraits, *c.*1695–1725; formerly in family possession, Bilbrough, 1885
Wealth at death left estates at Steeton and Newton Kyme, Yorkshire, a house in York, and a gift of £50 to the poor of Steeton, Newton Kyme, and Bilbrough: Markham, *Admiral Robert Fairfax*, 277

Fairfax, Thomas, first Lord Fairfax of Cameron (1560–1640), diplomat, soldier, and horse breeder, was born at Bilbrough, near York, the eldest son of Sir Thomas Fairfax (1521–1600) of Denton and Nun Appleton, Yorkshire, and Dorothy (*d.* 1596), daughter of George Gale, goldsmith and lord mayor of York, and widow of John Rokeby of Sandal. In the Easter term of 1577 he matriculated from Queens' College, Cambridge, and on 22 October 1579 was admitted to Lincoln's Inn. In 1582 he married Ellen (*d.* 1620), daughter of Robert Aske of Aughton, and they had nine sons and two daughters. Their seventh son, Charles *Fairfax, became an antiquary and genealogist.

Fairfax's early career was diplomatic. During the 1580s he undertook several government missions to Scotland which earned him a reputation for loyalty and discretion. King James offered him a peerage which he wisely refused, no doubt aware of Queen Elizabeth's disapproval of other people's collars for her dogs. In 1588 he was back in Scotland to help James suppress Maxwell's pro-Spanish rising there. Yet Fairfax seems to have lacked political ambition. Although he sat for Lincoln in 1586–7, for Aldborough in 1589, and for the county of Yorkshire in 1601, he made no mark in the House of Commons. However, he was a JP in Cumberland and Westmorland from about 1583, as well as in the West Riding of Yorkshire from about 1592.

Fairfax's political activity may have been curtailed by his love of soldiering. Probably in 1589 he went to the Netherlands to serve under Sir Francis Vere, and after brave conduct at the siege of Rouen in 1591 he was knighted by the earl of Essex. After the deaths of four of his sons in foreign wars and his disappointment with the others, his hopes of military glory centred on his eldest grandson, the future general, to whom in his will he left his best arms and his best horse. After his father died he built, on the strength of his substantial and increasing income, a fine mansion house at Denton, near Ilkley, in Wharfedale, yet even at home he demanded military discipline from his servants and every event of the day was timetabled precisely. His greatest pleasure was in horses and horsemanship: his stud at Denton was one of the best in the country and among his many treatises was one entitled *Conjectures about Horsemanship* and another on Yorkshire cavalry.

Although from 1599 Fairfax, in succession to his father, had a seat on the council of the north, he seemed content to live in the shadow of other Yorkshiremen. In 1607 Ferdinando *Fairfax, his heir, married Mary, daughter of his friend and patron Lord Sheffield, the council's president. Later, Fairfax associated himself with his younger neighbour Thomas Wentworth, and together they successfully contested with the Saviles for Yorkshire's two seats in the infamous election of 1625. King Charles's need for ready money and his activity in collecting the forced loan of 1627 explain why Fairfax was created Lord Fairfax of Cameron in the Scottish peerage on 4 May of that year on down payment of £1500 in gold. Fairfax died at Denton Hall on 1 May 1640 and was buried the next day in the south transept of All Saints' Church, Otley, Yorkshire, next to his wife, who had died on 23 August 1620.   JACK BINNS

Sources DNB · N. M. Sutherland, 'Fairfax, Thomas I', HoP, *Commons, 1558–1603* · G. W. Johnson, ed., *The Fairfax correspondence: memoirs of the reign of Charles the First*, 2 vols. (1848) · C. R. Markham, *A life of the great Lord Fairfax* (1870) · J. T. Cliffe, *The Yorkshire gentry from the Reformation to the civil war* (1969) · *Dugdale's visitation of Yorkshire, with additions*, ed. J. W. Clay, 2 (1907), 188–9 · CSP Scot., *1585–6*, 10, 90 · F. Collins, ed., *Wills in the York registry from 1636 to 1652*, Yorkshire Archaeological Society Record series, 4 (1888), 67 · A. Gooder, ed., *The parliamentary representation of the county of York, 1258–1832*, 2, Yorkshire Archaeological Society, 96 (1938), 38 · tomb inscription, All Saints' Church, Otley, Yorkshire
Archives BL, corresp.; deeds of the Fairfax family of Denton, Add. MSS 18979, 20778; Add. charters 1790–1791, 1797–1798 · W. Yorks. AS, Leeds, Yorkshire Archaeological Society, MSS
Likenesses effigy, All Saints' Church, Otley, south transept · oils, Aynho Park, Northamptonshire · portrait, Newton Kyme; repro. in E. Hailstone, *Portraits of Yorkshire worthies* (1869), no. 72; copy, Leeds Castle
Wealth at death a rich man; substantial rental income; cash bequeathed to grandchildren and servants; estate entailed to eldest son, and then to eldest grandson: Johnson, ed., *Fairfax correspondence*, vol. 2, pp. 425–7

Fairfax, Thomas, third Lord Fairfax of Cameron (1612–1671), parliamentarian army officer, was born at Denton, Yorkshire, on 17 January 1612, the first son of Ferdinando *Fairfax, second Lord Fairfax of Cameron (1584–1648), and his first wife, Mary Sheffield (*d.* 1619), the daughter of Edmund *Sheffield, first earl of Mulgrave. He matriculated at St John's College, Cambridge, in 1626, and entered Gray's Inn in 1628.

Early military career, 1629–1635 Between 1629 and 1632 Fairfax travelled in France and the Low Countries, where he learned the art of war under Horace Vere, Baron Vere of Tilbury. Present at the siege of Bois-le-Duc in 1629, he then visited France and elsewhere, returning to England in 1632 in the vain hope of obtaining his grandfather's permission to join the Swedish army in Germany. On 20 June 1637 he contracted an arranged (but in the event happy) marriage with Anne Vere (*d.* 1665) [see Fairfax, Anne, Lady Fairfax], the second daughter and coheir of his old commander and his widow, Mary. With her he had two daughters: Mary, born in 1638, and Anne, who was born in 1640 and died two years later.

Military service under Charles I, 1639–1640 Fairfax fought for Charles I in the first bishops' war against the Scots in 1639, commanding a troop of 160 Yorkshire dragoons. He also participated in the second bishops' war, commanding 150 horse under Lord Conway. According to Burnet, after the English defeat at Newburn, Fairfax, as he freely admitted, shared in the general panic of the fleeing army: 'all were put in such great disorder, that the whole army did

Thomas Fairfax, third Lord Fairfax of Cameron (1612–1671), by William Marshall, pubd 1647 (after Edward Bower)

run with so great precipitation, that sir Thomas Fairfax … did not stick to own, that till he passed the Tees his legs trembled under him' (*Bishop Burnet's History*, 1.51). Half a year later, on 28 January 1641, the king knighted him, perhaps in the hope of cementing his allegiance to the crown.

However, the humiliating defeat at the hands of the Scots had completed the undermining of Charles's government, and compelled him to summon parliament once again. When civil war broke out in 1642, Fairfax, in spite of the honour recently bestowed on him, was prominent among the supporters of parliament in Yorkshire. On 3 June the freeholders and farmers of the county assembled at Heworth Moor near York, in obedience to a royal proclamation. Those gentry and freeholders who wanted the king to reconcile himself to parliament had drafted a petition to Charles, which Fairfax was selected to present. At the meeting Fairfax had to force his way past royal courtiers, who attempted to block him, but at last he reached the king's side and placed the petition on the pommel of his saddle. Charles refused to accept it, and pressed his horse forward, nearly trampling Fairfax underfoot.

Military service in parliament's northern army, 1642–1645
Fairfax also signed the protest of the Yorkshire parliamentarians on 29 August 1642, which prompted John Rushworth to write to Ferdinando, 'the House is much contented with Sir Thomas Fairfax's noble carriage of Thursday last' (Bell, 3.18). He was also among the negotiators of the Yorkshire treaty of neutrality of 29 September. When

parliament annulled the treaty, he became second in command to his father, and general of horse. Accompanied by his wife, he distinguished himself in minor battles at Wetherby and Tadcaster at the end of 1642. With scarcely 1000 men in the northern parliamentary army, however, Fairfax and his father were no match for the earl of Newcastle and his well-equipped royalist army of 9000 men. Nevertheless, on 23 January 1643 Fairfax won his first notable victory, driving the royalists out of Leeds, forcing Newcastle to take refuge in York, and leaving the country open between Selby and the west. But two months later (30 March 1643) Lord Goring delivered a severe defeat on Seacroft Moor, as Fairfax was engaged in covering the retreat of his father and the main body of his army from Selby to Leeds. Despite being completely routed, Fairfax did achieve his main objective of enabling his father's larger force to effect its retreat. Writing to Prince Rupert about this episode, Secretary Edward Nicholas termed Fairfax 'the man most beloved and relyed upon by the rebells in the north' (BL, Add. MS 18980, fol. 33*v*).

The position of the northern army was now precarious. With the impetuosity of youth Fairfax conceived the idea of attacking Wakefield, which he believed was occupied by no more than 800 or 900 royalist troops. By the time he found out that they in fact numbered 3000 it was too late, and he had to press ahead, leading the assault on the town from the front. He personally took several prisoners, was himself almost captured, but in the end was completely victorious. Among the 1400 royalist prisoners was General Goring himself. No victory against such heavy odds was won by any other general during the whole civil war.

Fairfax was allowed only a short time to savour his success. The weakness of the northern army meant that he had to abandon Wakefield and rejoin his father at Leeds. Newcastle was now advancing on Bradford with about 12,000 men. On 30 June the Fairfaxes rode out to meet them on Adwalton Moor with a quarter that number. Leading the right wing of cavalry, Sir Thomas initially repulsed the royalist horse, but the left wing was completely overthrown, and in the end the royalists' superior numbers carried the day. Fairfax personally brought off a number of his troops safely into Halifax, returning during the night to take charge of the besieged town of Bradford. Coming under extreme pressure the next day, he cut his way through the besieging army with about fifty horse, and rejoined his father at Leeds.

After the disaster at Adwalton Moor, Leeds could not be defended for long; in the first week of July, therefore, the Fairfaxes retreated to the one remaining parliamentarian garrison in Yorkshire: Hull. Sir Thomas took charge of the rearguard, was shot through the wrist, and suffered a serious loss of blood before he finally reached safety.

While Ferdinando maintained the defence of Hull, Sir Thomas Fairfax took the cavalry, which were of no use in the besieged town, to join Cromwell and Manchester in Lincolnshire. There he contributed to the parliamentary victory at Winceby on 11 October 1643. In the face of a large body of royalist cavalry Fairfax was reported to have cried, 'Come let us fall on; I never prospered better then

when I fought against the enemy three or four to one'
(*Scotish Dove*, 13–20 Oct 1643, 5). In his letter to the House of
Lords Manchester eulogized him as 'a person that exceeds
any expressions as a commendation of his resolution and
valour' (*The Parliamentary or Constitutional History of England*,
12.423).

Fairfax was now beginning to be recognized as one of
parliament's most valuable commanders, and further
exploits were just around the corner. On 20 December, in
the company of Sir John Meldrum, he retook Gainsborough by storm. His great accomplishment in 1643, in combination with his father, was to keep Lord Newcastle and
his army, which had swelled to 12,000 or more, pinned
down in the north, so that they could not march south and
join forces with the king. According to his nineteenth-
century biographer Markham, the most striking quality
of the Fairfaxes was their 'inability to understand that
they had been beaten … no odds [were] too great for the
enterprising spirit of Sir Thomas Fairfax' (Markham, 123).

At the end of 1643 parliament decided that Fairfax's services were required on the other side of the country,
where Nantwich had come under siege. The royalist build-
up in Cheshire was now all the more menacing thanks to
the addition of reinforcements from Ormond's army in
Ireland. Crossing the Pennines in the dead of winter, Fairfax brought to Nantwich a relief force of 2800 horse and
500 dragoons, to which he added 3000 foot from Lancashire and Cheshire recruited on the way. In conjunction
with Sir William Brereton and the governor of Nantwich,
Sir George Booth, he attacked the royalist army under
Lord Byron. The action, on 29 January 1644, was a complete success. All the royalist colonels and 1500 prisoners
were taken. It furnished a tremendous boost to parliamentary morale.

By March Fairfax was back in Yorkshire joining forces
once again with his father. Newcastle by now had his
hands full trying to keep the Scottish army under Lord
Leven at bay in Durham. The parliamentarian plan was for
Sir Thomas and Ferdinando to rendezvous at Selby and
march from there to link up with the Scots in Durham.
When the royalist governor of York, John, Lord Bellasis,
got wind of the plan, he decided to intercept the Fairfaxes
at Selby. The engagement there on 11 April 1644 was a
shining parliamentarian victory, to which the younger
Fairfax's cavalry contributed greatly. Fairfax's stock at
once rose higher at Westminster, and parliament proclaimed a day of public thanksgiving. Clarendon,
unaware of his previous feats, believed that Selby 'was the
first action Sir Thomas Fairfax was taken notice for' (Clarendon, *Hist. rebellion*, 3.310).

Marston Moor Selby led directly to the battle of Marston
Moor and the destruction of royalist power in the north.
When the news of it reached Durham, both Newcastle
and Leven hastened to bring their armies into Yorkshire.
Newcastle occupied York with 6000 troops, while Leven's
Scots and the Fairfaxes' northern parliamentarian army,
together now 20,000 strong, besieged the city. By the
beginning of June the earl of Manchester had arrived with
over 6000 troops from the eastern association, and the

city was completely encircled. Meanwhile Charles I had
sent Prince Rupert on a recruiting expedition in Lancashire, and on 30 June he arrived at York with 14,000 men
intending to raise the siege. The allied parliamentarian
and Scottish forces withdrew to Marston Moor, 7 miles
beyond the city, and prepared for the largest battle ever to
be fought on English soil. On the fateful day (2 July 1644)
Fairfax commanded the horse on the right wing, consisting of fifty-five troops of Yorkshire cavalry, and twenty-
two of Scots—about 4000 men in all. While his own regiment charged successfully, the rest of his division was
routed; it was with difficulty that he made his way,
wounded, at the head of his own regiment, through the
ranks of the enemy to the parliamentarian left, who were
victorious. Although his contribution to the battle itself
was not distinguished, he and his father had laid the
groundwork for the victory by holding out for more than a
year against overwhelming odds, and by their decisive
conquest of Bellasis at Selby, which had triggered the
siege of York, and the ensuing battle beyond its walls.

At the siege of Helmsley Castle the following month
Fairfax was dangerously wounded by a musket ball, which
broke his shoulder. It was not the last of the many wounds
he suffered during a long military career.

The New Model Army While Fairfax was slowly convales-
cing from this wound the political struggle against the
existing parliamentarian commanders in the south was
nearing its climax. In December the Commons passed the
resolution for a self-denying ordinance to exclude the
members of both houses from all commands. Though
rejected by the Lords, the Commons majority proceeded
as if it had been passed. The three existing armies were
amalgamated, and by a Commons vote of 101 to 69 Fairfax
was named commander-in-chief of the new entity, soon to
be known as the New Model. The choice of Fairfax was the
product of several factors. At the age of thirty-two he had
already chalked up an impressive military record. A stranger to political manoeuvre, he had few enemies at Westminster. Perhaps he was already seen as politically malle-
able. At any rate, the men with whom he and his father
corresponded in the early 1640s show that he had important friends in the war party, of which Oliver Cromwell
was an increasingly prominent member. Looking back
later, Fairfax declared that he was overwhelmed by the
burden placed on his shoulders.

> I was so far from desiring it that had not so great an authority
> commanded obedience, being then unseparated from the
> royal interest, besides the persuasions of nearest friends not
> to decline so free and general a call, I should have hid my self
> to have avoyded so great a charge.   ('Short Memoriall', Bodl.
> Oxf., MS Fairfax 36, fol. 3v)

At first the Lords were unwilling to allow Fairfax to
appoint his own officers. At length a compromise was
worked out with the Commons by which the commander-
in-chief was to appoint his officers in the first instance,
but submit their names to parliament for final approval.
In the event the two houses attempted to change a third of
Fairfax's list. Almost all the changes were suggested by the
Lords with the aim of eliminating or demoting radicals

and promoting moderates and presbyterians. In the end the Commons majority browbeat the Lords into accepting, by the narrowest of majorities, the list that Fairfax had submitted. Political wrangling was even more bitter over the wording of his commission. The Lords baulked at the attempt by the Commons war party to exempt Fairfax from the obligation to preserve the king's safety on the battlefield. Only by dint of persistent bullying was Fairfax, unlike his predecessors, relieved of the pretence that he was fighting the king's evil counsellors and not the king himself.

It was not just Charles I who scoffed at the new army and its 'brutish generall' (*The Kings Cabinet Opened*, 1645, 3). Friends as well as foes would shortly be compelled to revise their opinions. In April Fairfax was engaged in reorganizing the New Model. In May he left Reading, under instructions from the committee of both kingdoms to relieve Taunton. But before he could get there, he was redirected to besiege the royalist headquarters at Oxford. Meanwhile the king was in the field recruiting his army. 'I am very sorry', Fairfax wrote to his father, 'we should spend our time unprofitably before a town, whilst the king hath time to strengthen himself, and by terror to force obedience of all places where he comes' (Bell, 3.228).

Naseby When the king's sack of Leicester cruelly exposed the strategic ineptitude of the committee of both kingdoms, Fairfax was finally given the free hand he sought to direct his own field operations. On 14 June, with close to 17,000 soldiers at his command, he met a royalist army of less than 9000 at Naseby. To Cromwell belongs the credit for the battle formation and the successful charge of cavalry on the right wing, but contemporaries were agreed in awarding the laurels for the day's victory to Fairfax. When he saw the rout of the left wing of cavalry, and the distress of the infantry in the middle, he commanded Cromwell to wheel about and divide his forces. The two generals then charged from opposite sides into the royalist infantry, bringing relief to their own beleaguered regiments. Fairfax then re-formed the whole army for a second advance on the royalist lines. This time he was careful to ensure that the horse did not leave the ranks of the foot exposed by too impetuous a charge. Sighting the monolithic approach of the New Model and overawed by its crushing superiority of numbers, the remnant of the king's army now turned tail and fled. The genius that Fairfax revealed at Naseby did not lie in his strategic capability, but in his popularity with his men, his flawless courage, and his ability, reinforced by years of experience, to respond to the unpredictable fluidity, the breathtaking rush of events during the two hours when the outcome of the English civil war was decided.

Langport Once he had recaptured Leicester, Fairfax marched to the south-west to confront Goring, who commanded the only remaining royalist field army of any importance, at Taunton. On Fairfax's approach Goring withdrew from Taunton, and the two armies met at Langport. Staging an audacious charge across a swollen stream

and up a steep hill, Fairfax quickly destroyed Goring's cavalry. This follow-up to Naseby was decisive. There he had struck the king a mortal blow. Then swinging round to face the only other army in the field, he lunged at Goring. The war was effectively over, although the participants were not yet aware of this fact. Ahead lay eleven more months of sieges, pitched battles, cold, hunger, sickness, and anxiety. Bridgwater, Bath, and Sherborne were taken in quick succession. Bristol was a tougher nut to crack. The second port in the realm, protected by 15-foot-thick walls, it was the main distribution point for the king's weaponry, ammunition, and materials. The letter in which Fairfax summoned Prince Rupert to surrender the city contains an interesting exposition of his political creed at that time. He assured the prince that neither he nor parliament harboured any animus against the institution of monarchy. Rather, they were fighting 'to maintain the rights of the crown and kingdom joyntly; a principal part whereof is, that the king … is … to be advised … by his Parliament, the great Counsel of the Kingdom, in whom … he hears all his people as it were at once advising him; and in which multitude of councellours lyes his safety, and his peoples interest' (Sprigge, 98). It was similar to the political philosophy that his father had proclaimed on his own battle flag: 'Long live the king, but death to bad government' (BL, Sloane MS 5247, fol. 20v). After a three-week siege and heavy artillery bombardment which failed to open a breach in the walls, the city was finally overrun on 10 September in a lightning assault. Showing great daring, Fairfax's infantry scaled the walls as withering fire was poured down upon them.

By the time of the winter respite the remaining royalists were mostly bottled up in Devon and Cornwall. It did not take long to reduce Tiverton, Dartmouth, Torrington, Exeter, and the remaining Cornish strongholds. Hopton's small army capitulated on 14 March. At Torrington Fairfax had a narrow escape when eighty barrels of gunpowder were blown up in the royalist magazine. Writing afterwards to his father, he expressed gratitude for 'God's great mercy to me and some others that stood where great webs of lead fell thickest, yet, praised be God, no man hurt'— apart from the 200 royalist prisoners who were killed by the explosion (Bell, 3.285). Fairfax's last task was to invest Oxford. As his 3000 cavalry approached, Charles slipped out of the city in disguise and surrendered himself to the Scots, leaving Sir Thomas Glemham the distasteful task of yielding up the royal headquarters. Wishing to spare Oxford's intellectual and aesthetic treasures, Fairfax granted generous terms, and the city was handed over on 24 June 1646. Aubrey later hailed him as the saviour of the Bodleian for putting a strong guard around the library to stop the thieving and vandalism of books that had been tolerated by the royalists during their occupation.

The fifteen months culminating in the surrender of Oxford were the most glorious period of Fairfax's life. Out of the remnants of three older armies he had welded together a supremely effective fighting force. After his initial stunning success at Naseby he had driven the royalists before him in a long string of victorious battles, sieges, and storms. Under his leadership the New Model Army never lost so much as a skirmish. At all times until the beginning of 1647 he was in control of this army, first of all shaking off the irksome interference of the committee of both kingdoms, and then several times bringing his council of war around to his way of thinking, or on occasion simply overruling it and ordering the implementation of strategies he had decided upon.

Health and illness   In July Fairfax and his wife, both unwell after the rigours of more than a year's intensely active service, fled to Bath to take the waters there and restore their health. All his life Fairfax was a sickly individual, notwithstanding his physical courage and his boundless energy on the battlefield. The 'infirmities' of his body to which Sprigge alludes (Sprigge, 323) were many. In the autumn of 1645 it was rheumatism; by mid-1646 he was afflicted with kidney stone; two years later he was suffering from gout. Yet ill health never seemed to stop him from being present at the scene of military action when he was needed. It did, however, give him a ready-made excuse for absenting himself from the army's councils when awkward political issues were being contested. Thus, in the second civil war he threw himself into the thick of the battle at Maidstone (2 June 1648) despite the pain of a terrible fit of the gout. By contrast, in the spring of 1647, as the army became politically turbulent, Fairfax excused himself, pleading illness. When he went to London in April for medical treatment, Holles angrily accused him of merely pretending to be sick so as to let the army revolt boil out of control. He was said to be sick when the army seized the king, and again throughout the autumn of 1647, when the Leveller challenge was being debated in the general council. He fell sick once more around the time of Pride's Purge in December 1648. On the 20th of that month he was too ill to meet sixteen of the imprisoned members of parliament who had been summoned to his lodging in Whitehall.

The political wars, 1646–1648   Apart from the brief interval of the second civil war, the three years from spring 1646 to winter 1649 were the most painfully embarrassing of Fairfax's life. The logic of events obliged him to tread paths he would sooner have avoided and to implement decisions that had been made by others. In the world of subtle intrigue and political manoeuvre he was out of his depth, and helpless to thwart the efforts of men far more adept than himself. The political crisis burgeoned in the late winter of 1646–7, when the peace party led by Holles persuaded the Commons to send part of Fairfax's army to Ireland and disband most of the rest with only a fraction of their arrears of pay. The soldiers petitioned for all their arrears, and an indemnity act to protect them from prosecution for whatever they had done while in the army. Parliament instructed Fairfax to suppress the petition, and he did so, but ineffectually. When parliament heard that petitioning was continuing, Holles got it to approve a declaration that those who persisted in this illegal activity would be regarded as 'enemies to the state and disturbers of the public peace' (*JHL*, 9, 115). Conscientiously Fairfax

strove to effect a rapprochement between the parliamentary commissioners and the officers, most of whom sympathized with the rank and file. When his efforts failed, he threw up his hands and retreated to London for a month (21 April to 20 May 1647) for medical treatment, though he did take the precaution of ordering all other officers to repair to their commands.

At the end of May parliament issued its final offer and ordered Fairfax back to the army. He communicated the offer to a meeting of officers at Bury St Edmunds, but it fell on deaf ears since the regiments had already begun to organize resistance to disbandment. The officers instead advised their commander to appoint a general rendezvous of the army to discuss the situation. Fairfax wrote back to parliament imploring them to back off. 'I intreat you that there may be ways of love and composure thought upon. I shall do my endeavours, tho' I am forced to yield something out of order, to keep the army from disorder or worse inconveniences' (*The Parliamentary or Constitutional History of England*, 15.390). In the meantime he shifted his headquarters from Saffron Walden to the agitators' meeting place at Bury St Edmunds, but then fell ill once again. The collapse of Fairfax's control at this point was starkly exposed when on 2–3 June, with Cromwell's covert support, Cornet George Joyce seized the king, and later without authority removed him from Holdenby. In his 'Short Memorialls' Fairfax writes that he immediately dispatched Colonel Whalley with two regiments to reverse Joyce's flagrant disobedience. But Charles turned down Fairfax's efforts to get him to return, saying, 'Sir, I have as great an interest in the army as you' (Bodl. Oxf., MS Fairfax 36, fol. 5v). A further rebuff to Fairfax came when the council of war rejected his proposal to punish Joyce. Nevertheless, writing to the House of Lords, he assured them 'as in the presence of God … that [Joyce's] remove of his Majesty from Holdenby was without any design, knowledge, or privity thereof on our parts; and a thing altogether unexpected to us' (*The Parliamentary or Constitutional History of England*, 15.410).

Between June 1647 and the outbreak of the second civil war Fairfax was marginal to the army's political mobilization, its negotiations with the king, and its debates on the future constitution of England. He later disingenuously confessed,

> the power of the army (which I once had) was usurped by the forerunners of confusion and anarchy … the arbitrary and unlimited power of this new counsel would act without a General, and all that I could doe could not prevaile against this streame … For now the officers of the army were placed and displaced by the will of the new agitators who with violence so carried all things as it was above my power to restraine it.

Again,

> I must needs say, from the time they declared their usurped authority at Triplo Heath [5 June 1647] I never gave my free consent to anything they did but (being then undischarged of my place) they set my hand by way of course to all their papers whether I consented or not.   (Bodl. Oxf., MS Fairfax 36, fols. 4, 4v, 6v)

He twice tried to resign his commission but was prevented. He did, however, claim credit for one political achievement. He managed to delay the march on London to purge eleven leading presbyterian MPs long enough to allow those targets of the army's wrath to flee. Thus he 'diverted this humor of the army from being statesmen to their more proper dutye of soldiers', and postponed the purge of parliament by over a year (ibid., fol. 5).

There is, however, other evidence that Fairfax was rather more active in these months than he later acknowledged. At the general rendezvous of the army near Newmarket on 4–5 June he personally visited and addressed each regiment, to the rapturous joy of the soldiers. On 3 August he conducted the speakers of both houses and the MPs who had been forced to flee parliament by counter-revolutionary violence, on a review of the New Model Army, and three days later escorted the MPs back to their seats at the Palace of Westminster. He also vetoed several proposals in September to promote Cornet Joyce, John Wildman, and other radicals (minute book of the committee of general officers, Worcester College, Oxford, MS 66, fols. 6, 12, 15v).

The second civil war: Maidstone and Colchester If ill health prevented Fairfax from playing any part in the Putney debates on the *Agreement of the People*, it did not stand in his way when the time came to return to the battlefield in 1648. While Cromwell rode west to suppress the insurrection in Wales, and Lambert was dispatched to the north to check the march of the Scots, Fairfax, who had recently inherited his father's Scottish baronage of Cameron, took responsibility for the south. At the end of May he led a force of 4000 to attack the royalist stronghold at Maidstone. In agonizing pain from gout he led his men on horseback, his right foot wrapped in a bandage, and was 'one of the first in all this action' (Whitelocke, 2.324). On 13 June he pursued the fleeing royalists to Colchester and settled down to a seventy-five-day siege. While Fairfax was at Colchester, Milton addressed a sonnet to him, summoning him to the 'nobler task' of settling the kingdom and cleansing the land of avarice and rapine.

On 27 August, reduced to starvation and despair, the garrison surrendered, the rank and file to 'quarter', and the superior officers to 'mercy'. The former term implied that their lives would be spared, but the latter meant that they would be at the mercy of the lord-general, who, as he explained ahead of time, would be 'free to put some immediately to the sword, if he see cause' (Rushworth, 7.1247). Using the discretionary power he had thus reserved himself, he tried Sir Charles Lucas and Sir George Lisle by court martial and had them shot to death. Norwich, Capel, and Hastings he turned over to parliament because they were peers. The justifications for the executions were several. First, according to the rules of war, officers who continued to hold an untenable position, thereby causing unnecessary bloodshed, forfeited their right to quarter. Second, an officer taken prisoner and then released broke his parole if he again bore arms

against the enemy who had released him. At the beginning of the siege Fairfax had written to Lucas pointing out that he had broken the parole he had given when released at Marston Moor, and that he would therefore be excepted from mercy. The case against Lucas was clinched when two private soldiers testified that at Stinchcombe, Gloucestershire, he had ordered that over twenty captured prisoners be put to the sword in cold blood. '[I]n this distribution of Justice', explained Fairfax in his 'Short memorials', 'I did nothing but according to my Commission and the trust vested in mee' (T. Fairfax, 'Short memorials', William Andrews Clark Memorial Library, fol. 24v).

The army remonstrance, Pride's Purge, and regicide At about this time Edmund Ludlow came to the camp and urged Fairfax to put a stop to the treaty that parliament was about to negotiate with the king at Newport. Fairfax equivocated, so the republican Ludlow turned to Ireton, who agreed with him but cautioned that they should wait to see what agreement king and parliament came to before moving against them. That autumn one regiment after another petitioned Fairfax against the Newport treaty, and urged that the king be called to account as a man of blood. The remonstrance of the army, framed by Ireton and adopted by the council of officers on 16 November, demanded that the treaty be broken off and the king tried for treason. At the time Fairfax wrote to parliament that the remonstrance had been approved by the officers unanimously, but much later he maintained, and royalist intelligence at the time reported, that he 'absolutely refused to concurre' (Bodl. Oxf., MS Clarendon 31, fol. 312).

Orders were issued in Fairfax's name for securing the king on the Isle of Wight and complaining to parliament for its laying aside of the remonstrance. Fairfax also put his name to a letter to the speaker of the House of Commons declaring that because of his failure to reply, 'we are attending and acting the providence of God, for the gaining of such ends as we have proposed in our aforesaid Remonstrance' (Worcester College, Oxford, MS 114, fol. 115). Nevertheless, it was almost certainly Ireton, not Fairfax, who was directing affairs at this moment. However, Fairfax strains credulity when he writes of Pride's Purge that the other officers planned the forcible exclusion of unfriendly MPs 'with that great secrecy as that I had not the least intimation of it till it was done ... It was so secretly carried on that I should get no notice of it' (Bodl. Oxf., MS Fairfax 36, fol. 6). He did not resign his command after this assault on the liberties of parliament, nor did he stop signing letters on behalf of the army, including a sardonic order to London to pay its assessment arrears, a rebuff of the Commons' demand to release their imprisoned members, and warrants for their confinement.

When it came to the king's trial, Fairfax finally rediscovered his courage, and began to work against his fellow officers. Named to the court of high commission, he attended the first preliminary session, perhaps thinking that the trial might be an instrument for either deposing the king or intimidating him into unconditional surrender. When the truth came home to him that the revolutionaries were in deadly earnest, Fairfax attended no further sessions despite strenuous efforts to secure his presence. On the first day of the trial, when his name was read out, his wife shouted from behind her mask in one of the galleries, 'he had more wit than to be here' (Clarendon, *Hist. rebellion*, 4.486). On the day of sentencing (27 January), when the president of the court, John Bradshaw, declared that they were trying the king in the name of 'the commons and people of England', she intervened a second time, calling out, 'not half, nor a quarter of the people. Oliver Cromwell is a rogue and a traitor' (Hargrave, 1.370). The next day Fairfax hosted a meeting of officers at his house to hear a last-minute appeal from the Dutch ambassadors to save the king's life. On the 29th he summoned a council of war, where he implored his fellow officers to postpone the execution. Afterwards he wrote admitting his ineffectuality, but pleading 'my afflicted and troubled minde for it and my earnest endeavours to prevent it will, I hope, sufficiently testify my abhorrance of the fact' (Bodl. Oxf., MS Fairfax 36, fol. 6). According to his cousin Brian Fairfax, on the eve of the execution, 'when some of his friends proposed to him to attempt the next day to rescue the king, telling him that twenty thousand men were ready to join with him; he said, he was ready to venture his own life, but not the lives of others against the army united against them' (B. Fairfax, 32). On the day itself he continued his efforts right up to the moment of beheading, in prayer or conversation with the officers in Colonel Thomas Harrison's apartment near the long gallery of the Banqueting House. When Bishop Juxon and Thomas Herbert were escorting the king's corpse back through the long gallery, they bumped into Fairfax, who to their amazement enquired 'how the king did', and 'seemed much surprised' to learn that he was already dead (Herbert, 194). The episode was a poignant comment on the commander-in-chief's political irrelevance.

Fairfax later underlined his disapproval of the king's death by the reservations that he made in his engagement to be faithful to the Commonwealth. Like the other peers who became members of the council of state, he declared that he had served the parliament faithfully, and was willing to do so again, since there was no longer any power but that of the House of Commons, but could not sign the engagement because it was retrospective. Besides sitting in the council of state Fairfax was also elected MP for Cirencester (7 February 1649), although he appears not to have taken his seat. He was also reappointed commander-in-chief of all the forces in England and Ireland (30 March 1649).

Suppressing the Levellers and resignation As commander of the army Fairfax was personally involved in suppressing a mutiny in Colonel Whalley's regiment at the end of April 1649. Against Cromwell's plea for clemency, Fairfax insisted that the ringleader, Robert Lockyer, be executed. Lockyer instantly became a Leveller martyr. A little over two weeks later Fairfax had to cope with much more serious Leveller-inspired mutinies against the forthcoming

Irish expedition: at Banbury, Burford, and Northampton. Leading a force of nearly 4000, he swiftly overtook the main body, 900 strong, and crushed their resistance in a late-night surprise attack at Burford. Once again Fairfax showed severity by pronouncing them all liable to the death penalty. In the end three mutineers were executed in Burford churchyard, and were added to the Leveller pantheon.

After this accomplishment Fairfax visited Oxford and was created a DCL on 19 May 1649, while many of his fellow officers were made honorary MAs. He remained in England during Cromwell's expedition to Ireland, but in summer 1650 he was nominated to lead the invasion of Scotland. Willing to oppose the Scots if they invaded England again, he could not in conscience invade their territory. 'Human probabilities are not sufficient grounds to make war upon a neighbour nation, especially our brethren of Scotland, to whom we are engaged in a solemn league and covenant' (Whitelocke, 3.209). A committee of the council of state including Cromwell, Whitelocke, and Harrison tried to change his mind, but he would not budge. In his letter of resignation he cited infirmities of mind and body, but commentators at the time agreed that it was the influence of his wife and the presbyterian clergy that had caused him to baulk at invading Scotland.

Literary and religious pursuits For the rest of the interregnum Fairfax lived quietly at Nun Appleton, Yorkshire, where he nursed his health and devoted himself to literature and religion. Though elected for the West Riding of Yorkshire in the first protectorate parliament of 1654, he seems again not to have taken his seat. His energies were directed to building up a collection of coins and engravings, translating Vegetius from the Latin, and Mercurius Trismegistus from the French, and producing a metrical version of the Psalms, as well as translating the Song of Solomon and other books of the Bible. He was perhaps inspired by Andrew Marvell, the tutor whom he engaged for his daughter in 1651–2, and who is thought to have written much of his best poetry at Nun Appleton. While Fairfax's own poetry has no literary merit, his writing shows a sensuous appreciation of natural beauty that was at war with a puritan estrangement from the attractions of this world. His three volumes of sermon notes which he took during the twenty years before his death provide insight into his deeply religious nature. A non-sectarian puritan, he had a strong, simple belief in the dynamic role of divine providence in his life. At the same time that he had become politically passive he retained a millenarian hope. The 'gravious conflict' of this world was but a preparation for 'a glorious conquest in the next' (Folger Shakespeare Library, MS V.a.14, unfoliated). As a Calvinist he believed in the 'originall corrupcion' of his soul, which could be saved only by 'the meritts of the precious blood of Jesus Christ' (will, fol. 1). For Fairfax there was no contradiction in protecting the Bodleian Library and intervening to save the largest collection of medieval stained glass in England at York Minster on the one hand, while on the other holding that the appetite for material things was one of the devil's snares. During his retirement from public life he also found time to write a treatise on horse breeding and a history of the church up to the Reformation.

Family and property affairs As the heir to the ancestral estates of his family Fairfax was one of the leading gentry of Yorkshire. At the beginning of the civil war he had invested heavily in the war against the king. After 1645 that investment was amply repaid. As commander-in-chief of the New Model Army he was paid £10 a day, and unlike every other officer in the army he was paid promptly and in full. Over the five-year period of his supreme command he garnered a salary of £19,000 (Bodl. Oxf., MS Fairfax 32, fol. 173). As an additional expression of gratitude parliament voted him a jewel worth £800 at the beginning of his generalship, as well as £1000 worth of horses. Near the end of his generalship he was voted York House in the Strand and lands worth £5000 per annum from the estates of the second duke of Buckingham. This was subsequently converted to a cash grant of £10,000 and Buckingham estates to the value of £4000 per annum.

The last thing parliament would have expected was that these very lands would revert to their original owner, as they did on 7 September 1657, when Fairfax married his daughter Mary to Buckingham. The marriage was said to have been arranged by Fairfax's mother-in-law, Lady Vere, and his cousin Major Robert Harley, a prominent presbyterian leader. The government regarded it with suspicion, partly as 'a Presbyterian plott' (Thurloe, 6.617), and partly because Buckingham was still regarded as a cavalier. When Cromwell ordered Buckingham to be arrested and thrown in the Tower, Fairfax at his daughter's behest went to Whitehall to demand his release. Cromwell was unyielding, and upbraided his former comrade-in-arms for not sticking with his old friends and taking their advice. Infuriated, Fairfax terminated the interview, 'turning abruptly from him in the gallery at Whitehall, cocking his hat, and throwing his cloak under his arm, as he used to do when he was angry' (B. Fairfax, 31). Later, after Cromwell died, Fairfax appealed to parliament for Buckingham's release. Several MPs spoke in favour, citing Fairfax's trustworthiness, and Buckingham was freed on 21 February 1659. But Fairfax was affronted by the requirement that he put up £20,000 bail, and was reported to have said in private that

> since the dissolving of the [Long] parliament, which was broke up wrongfully, there was nothing but shifting and a kind of confusion; and that he knew not but he might chuse by his old commission as generall to appear in armes on behalf of the people of these nations.   (Thurloe, 6.706)

The Restoration In Richard Cromwell's parliament Fairfax sat for Yorkshire, and intervened rarely but effectively. He attracted particular admiration for opposing military rule. On one occasion he declared that parliament must not give the militia 'out of our hands to any single person, but that it must be intrusted where it may be serviceable to … the people' (*Diary of Thomas Burton*, 273). He was seen as a man devoid of ambition, who 'sides with republicans and carryes a name above Lambert' (Thurloe, 7.616), and some thought would make an excellent general once

again. A sign of his high reputation was his election to the council of state on 19 May 1659, but he declined to serve.

By summer 1659, with the protectorate having collapsed and the struggle between the army and the Rump having ended in stalemate, the government was in disarray. By September General Monck had issued his call from Scotland for an end to military interference in politics. This was the break for which Fairfax had been waiting. Ever since his resignation as commander-in-chief he had scrupulously abstained from any involvement in royalist intrigue. But after Lambert's expulsion of the Rump in November he opened negotiations with Monck, employing his friend and former New Model Army chaplain the Yorkshire presbyterian Edward Bowles and Monck's brother-in-law Thomas Clarges as intermediaries.

At the same time that he declared his support, Fairfax also signalled his disapproval of Monck's apparent unwillingness to go any farther than recalling the Rump parliament. Monck responded that his hands were tied for the moment by his fear that his army would not support him. This was good enough reassurance for Fairfax, who sent back word that he would raise the county for Monck. By 30 December, so racked by kidney stone and gout that he had to travel to the rendezvous in a carriage, he mustered 450 supporters at Knaresborough. On new year's day the force, now swollen to 1800, besieged York, where Lambert had installed Robert Lilburne to hold the garrison against Monck and Fairfax. But the city was taken without a blow, and the next day Monck crossed the Tweed. Fairfax's raising of Yorkshire to neutralize Lambert's army was the key factor in the timing of Monck's march into England. Thanks to his preparatory work not a single unit of the English army opposed Monck. Fairfax thus deserves much of the credit for the achievement of a restoration without bloodshed. He alone was able 'to embody the moderate parliamentary gentry's revolt against military tyranny without either scandalizing the army or creating a premature breach between Presbyterians and commonwealthsmen' (Woolrych, 505). It was a fitting symbol of Fairfax's role in bringing back the king that the chestnut-brown horse which Charles II rode at his coronation was a gift from Fairfax's own stable.

Fairfax's conduct just prior to Charles's return proved that he was not an unqualified royalist. In April 1660 the cavaliers were startled to hear that he had joined Manchester and the presbyterians in an attempt to impose terms on Charles. But Monck made it clear that he alone would negotiate with the king. Nevertheless, Fairfax was honoured by being selected for the interim council of state on 3 March, by being elected member for Yorkshire in the same month, and by being chosen to head the commissioners of the two houses sent to the king at The Hague.

Final illness and death With Charles back on the throne Fairfax retired again to Nun Appleton. He was upset by the Cavalier Parliament's exclusion of regicides from the Act of Oblivion. If Ludlow can be believed, he candidly acknowledged 'that if any person must be excepted, he knew no man that deserved it more than himself, who being general of the army at that time, and having power sufficient to prevent the proceedings against the King, had not thought fit to make use of it to that end' (*Memoirs of Edmund Ludlow*, 2.268). Illness blighted the remaining years of his life. He filled them with reading, religious duties, and composing autobiographical accounts of his service in the northern army and the New Model.

Lady Fairfax died on 16 October 1665, Fairfax himself on 12 November 1671. Both were buried in Bilbrough parish church, near York. In his will he left his Denton estate for the use of his daughter during her lifetime, with the reversion to his cousin Henry Fairfax after her death. He thereby kept it out of the grasp of his profligate son-in-law. His pious and generous nature was displayed in his bequest of half a year's wages to each of his servants, and £100 to 'twenty poore ministers' (will, fol. 4). Other beneficiaries included a maimed soldier, and his cousin John Rushworth, who had been secretary to the New Model Army.

Conclusion Many contemporaries vouched for the attractiveness of character that is reflected in Fairfax's will. To Joshua Sprigge, historian of the New Model, he was a man of 'the best piety' (Sprigge, 321) who neither played favourites nor let passion govern his acts. Charles I pronounced him 'a man of honour, faithfull to his trust, and one that ever kept his word with him' (*Speech to the Commissioners*, 3). While a correspondent of Clarendon called him 'a slow beast and inconstant' (Bodl. Oxf., MS Clarendon 57, fol. 129v), the royalist secretary Edward Nicholas had to admit that he was 'most beloved' (BL, Add. MS 18980, fol. 33v), and the parliamentary diarist Sir Simonds D'Ewes echoed the opinion of many when he called him 'very gallant' (BL, Harley MS 165, fol. 107v). Fairfax was never noted for fluency of speech, but he was heard attentively when he chose to voice his opinion. Popular with his men, he was at the same time a strict disciplinarian, who did not shrink from imposing the severest punishments when he thought the army's integrity was at stake. He won his men's loyalty by his care for their safety and his carelessness for his own. When it came to political scheming he was like a lamb among wolves. As early as autumn 1645 the perceptive Thomas Juxon commented that Fairfax was 'wax which as often as melted receives impression' (Juxon, 94). Clement Walker later dismissed him as someone 'fitter to follow another man's counsel than his own' (C. Walker, *The Compleat History of Independency*, 4 vols., 1660–61, 1.29). Yet he knew his own mind well enough to present a petition to Charles I in 1642, and later to boycott the king's trial in 1649, the invasion of Scotland in 1650, and several royalist conspiracies prior to 1660.

The life of a warrior was Fairfax's first love. An excellent battlefield commander, he was not a distinguished military strategist. His greatest achievement was to weld the New Model Army into a supremely effective fighting force. The nadir of his life occurred between 1647 and 1649, when he was manipulated by men much shrewder than himself. His autobiographical attempt to excuse the political failings of these years does not command respect. Yet in 1659–60 he chalked up his second most

important achievement when he neutralized Lambert's army in Yorkshire, enabling Monck to march into England unopposed. One of the ironies of English history is that the man who as much as anyone was responsible for the ruin of Charles I was the same man who played an essential part in restoring that king's son to the throne.

IAN J. GENTLES

Sources G. W. Johnson, ed., *The Fairfax correspondence: memoirs of the reign of Charles the First*, 2 vols. (1848) • R. Bell, ed., *Memorials of the civil war … forming the concluding volumes of the Fairfax correspondence*, 2 vols. (1849) • C. R. Markham, *A life of the great Lord Fairfax* (1870) • letters and 'Short memorialls', Bodl. Oxf., MSS Fairfax, 32, 36 • J. Sprigge, *Anglia rediviva* (1647) • I. Gentles, *The New Model Army in England, Ireland, and Scotland, 1645–1653* (1992) • M. A. Gibb, *The lord general: a life of Thomas Fairfax* (1938) • J. Wilson, *Fairfax: a life of Thomas, Lord Fairfax, captain-general* (1985) • B. Whitelocke, *Memorials of English affairs*, new edn, 4 vols. (1853) • HoP, *Commons, 1660–90* • J. Rushworth, *Historical collections*, new edn, 4–7 (1721–2) • A. H. Woolrych, 'Yorkshire and the Restoration', *Yorkshire Archaeological Journal*, 39 (1956–8), 483–507 • D. Underdown, *Pride's Purge: politics in the puritan revolution* (1971) • T. Fairfax, 'Short memorials', BL, Harley MS 2315 • T. Fairfax, 'Short memorials', U. Cal., Los Angeles, William Andrews Clark Memorial Library, MS 95041 • miscellaneous heraldic collections, BL, Harley MS 6832, fol. 75v • autograph letters, 1433–1817, BL, Add. MS 18738, fol. 82 • BL, Add. MS 18980, fol. 33v • T. Fairfax, notes of sermons, BL, Add. MS 4929 • T. Fairfax, notes of sermons, poems, catechism, meditations, BL, Add. MS 11744 • T. Fairfax, notes of sermons, Folger, MS V.a.14–15 • will, Borth. Inst., will 52/145 (proved 8/12/1671) [Thomas Fairfax, third Lord Fairfax of Cameron] • Thurloe, *State papers* • R. Scrope and T. Monkhouse, eds., *State papers collected by Edward, earl of Clarendon*, 3 vols. (1767–86) • B. Fairfax, *A catalogue of the curious collection of pictures of George Villiers, duke of Buckingham … with the life of George Villiers, duke of Buckingham, the celebrated poet* (1758) • T. Herbert, *Memoirs of the two last years of the reign of King Charles I*, another edn (1813) • *Aubrey's Brief lives*, ed. O. L. Dick (1949) • *The journal of Thomas Juxon*, ed. K. Lindley and D. Scott, CS, 5th ser., 13 (1999) • army pay warrants, PRO, SP 28/51, vol. 48, fol. 435; vol. 51, fol. 339 • *The kings majesties speech to the commissioners at Nottingham on Saturday the 13 of February, in the praise of Sir Thomas Fairfax* (1646) • F. Hargrave, ed., *A complete collection of state-trials*, 4th edn, 11 vols. (1776–81), vol. 1 • *The parliamentary or constitutional history of England* [Old parliamentary history], 2nd edn, 24 vols. (1762–3) • Clarendon, *Hist. rebellion* • *Diary of Thomas Burton*, ed. J. T. Rutt, 4 vols. (1828), vol. 3 • F. M. S. McDonald, 'The timing of General George Monck's march into England, 1 January 1660', *EngHR*, 105 (1990), 363–76 • *The memoirs of Edmund Ludlow*, ed. C. H. Firth, 2 vols. (1894)

Archives BL, corresp., Sloane MS 1519 • BL, corresp., family and military MSS, Add. MS 18979 • BL, memorials of the civil war, Add. MS 25708 • BL, Harley MSS, papers • Bodl. Oxf., corresp. • Bodl. Oxf., papers • Devon RO, 'Sir Thomas Fairfax's proceedings about the storming of Exeter' • Harvard U., 'Short memorials' • Sheff. Arch., 'A discourse of the Ld Thomas Fairfax's actions in the last warre. Short memorialls of some things to be cleared during my command of the army' • U. Cal., Los Angeles, William Andrews Clark Memorial Library, 'Short memorials', MS 95041 • Worcester College, Oxford, corresp. • Yale U., 'Short memorialls of some things to be cleared during my command of the army' | BL, letters to James Chaloner, MP, Add. MS 71448 • BL, letters to General George Monck, Egerton MS 2618

Likenesses T. Simon, gold medal, 1645, NPG • lead bust, c.1650, NPG • attrib. E. Bower, oils, Althorp, Northamptonshire • attrib. E. Bower, oils (as a young man), Leeds Castle, Kent • W. R. Faithorne, line engraving (after R. Walker), BM, NPG • W. Marshall, line engraving (after E. Bower), BM, NPG; repro. in Sprigge, *Anglia rediviva* [*see illus.*] • R. Walker, oils (as a general), Leeds Castle, Kent • engraving, repro. in Sprigge, *Anglia rediviva* • engraving, Hunt. L. • medals and badges, BM

Wealth at death £555 in cash bequests; plus manors of Bilbrough, Rigton [Ryton?], and Boulton Percy; lands in Clifford, Steeton, and Sandwath, Yorkshire; books, MSS, and numerous horses: will, proved 8 Dec 1671, Borth. Inst., will 52/145

Fairfax, Thomas (1655/6–1716), Jesuit, was born at Gilling in Yorkshire on 24 October 1655 or 1656 and was almost certainly the son of Nicholas Fairfax (1606–1657) and his wife, Isabella Beckwith. After his education at the English College, St Omer, he entered the noviciate of the Jesuits at Watten on 7 September 1675 and was ordained priest on 18 December 1683. In 1685 he was professing Hebrew at the Jesuit college at Liège and preparing himself to teach philosophy. With the accession of James II it was decided to try to obtain a footing for Catholics in Oxford and it was considered essential by the English Jesuit superior, John Keynes, that some who might lecture in the university should obtain academic degrees. Thus Fairfax was sent with one or two others to Trèves, where they obtained doctorates 'after due examination and much expense' (Archivum Romanum Societatis Iesu, MS Literae Annuae, Anglia 35, fol. 110v).

At Oxford Obadiah Walker had opened a Catholic chapel in University College and Dean Massey another at Christ Church but it was at Magdalen that the king hoped to obtain admission for Catholics and that they would be able to take degrees there. At the king's insistence, despite the opposition of the fellows, of whom twenty-five were expelled, Samuel Parker, bishop of Oxford, was elected president of the college. Fairfax and other Catholics (some of them priests) were by the king's instructions admitted as fellows on 9 January 1688 and Fairfax was nominated dean of arts. It was reported that he was appointed professor of philosophy and was teaching oriental languages. On the death of Bishop Parker in March 1688 Dr Bonaventure Giffard, one of the newly appointed vicars apostolic, was nominated president by royal mandate.

In 1688 there was printed on Obadiah Walker's press at University College Fairfax's *Some reasons tendred to impartial people, why Dr Henry Maurice, chaplain to his grace of Canterbury, ought not to be traduc'd as a licenser of a pamphlet entitled, A plain answer to a popish priest, &c*. It was subjoined to *Twenty-One Questions Further Demonstrating the Schism of the Church of England* and was written in reply to the Revd Abednego Seller's *Plain Answer to a Popish Priest, Questioning the Orders of the Church of England* (1688). To a second edition of this pamphlet Seller annexed *An Answer to the Oxford Animadverter's Reflections* (1688). The revolution brought the controversy to an end.

In July 1688 Fairfax wrote to a correspondent, probably Dr Nathaniel Johnston, of the resistance the expelled fellows had made to the king's demands on the grounds that they were against the statutes of the college. He remarked that in the past the statutes had not been observed in a number of ways. The king, in October, in view of the deterioration of affairs, instructed the bishop of Winchester, the visitor of the college, 'to settle that society regularly and statutably' (Bloxam, 252–3). The expelled fellows were returned at the end of October and Fairfax and his colleagues were removed. Fairfax narrowly escaped being murdered in the streets of Oxford and was imprisoned for about a year. On his release, after visiting his native Yorkshire, he returned to Liège to teach theology. He was professed of the four vows in 1693. For much of the rest of his life he was stationed in London managing the financial business of the English Jesuits. During these years he may have published translations of attacks on Jansenism; certainly his former colleague Bonaventure Giffard was among those who considered him among the first to introduce the controversy to English Catholicism. He may have translated *The Secret Policy of the Jansenists* by Étienne Agard de Champs (or Deschamps), 'one of the most virulent attacks on Jansenism' (Blom, 6), of which an expanded edition was published in 1702, and *A Case of Conscience* (1703). From about 1710 Fairfax was at Wardour Castle in Wiltshire and there, it is believed, he died on 2 March 1716.   GEOFFREY HOLT

Sources CSP dom., 1687–9 · DNB · J. R. Bloxam, ed., *Magdalen College and James II, 1686–1688: a series of documents*, OHS, 6 (1886) · Wood, *Ath. Oxon.*, new edn, 4.563 · G. Holt, 'Two seventeenth-century Hebrew scholars: Thomas Fairfax and Edward Slaughter', *Recusant History*, 22 (1994–5), 482–90 · G. Oliver, *Collections towards illustrating the biography of the Scotch, English and Irish members, SJ* (1838), 72–3 · G. Oliver, *Collections illustrating the history of the Catholic religion in the counties of Cornwall, Devon, Dorset, Somerset, Wilts, and Gloucester* (1857), 299 · H. Foley, ed., *Records of the English province of the Society of Jesus*, 5 (1879), 821–3, 956; 7 (1882–3), 241 · Gillow, *Lit. biog. hist.* · A. de Backer and others, *Bibliothèque de la Compagnie de Jésus*, new edn, 3, ed. C. Sommervogel (Brussels, 1892), 530–31, appx · Literae Annuae Societatis Jesu, Archivum Romanum Societatis Iesu, Rome, Anglia 35, fols. 110v, 111 · H. Aveling, 'The Catholic recusancy of the Yorkshire Fairfaxes [pt 1]', *Biographical Studies*, 3 (1955–6), 69–114 · T. Jones, ed., *A catalogue of the collection of tracts for and against popery*, 1, Chetham Society, 48 (1859), 208–9 · F. Blom and others, *English Catholic books, 1701–1800: a bibliography* (1996) · R. Clark, *Strangers and sojourners at Port Royal* (1932) · catalogues, British Province of the Society of Jesus, 114 Mount Street, London · G. Holt, *The English Jesuits, 1650–1829: a biographical dictionary*, Catholic RS, 70 (1984)

Archives N. Yorks. CRO, family and estate MSS | Archives of the British Province of the Society of Jesus, London

Fairfax, Thomas, sixth Lord Fairfax of Cameron (1693–1781), landowner, was born on 22 October 1693 at Leeds Castle, Kent, the eldest son of Thomas, fifth Lord Fairfax (1657–1710), landowner and politician, and Catherine Culpeper (d. 1719), heir of the great estates of Lord Culpeper, including Leeds Castle and the northern neck between the Rappahannock and Potomac rivers in Virginia. He was educated at Oriel College, Oxford, between 1710 and 1713. In 1710 he became sixth Lord Fairfax on the death of his father, whose legacy brought debts and required the sale of the Yorkshire estates in 1716. Three years later he inherited his mother's estates in Kent and Virginia.

Fairfax was a talented and ambitious man who included Viscount Bolingbroke, Joseph Addison, and Richard Steele among his friends. He was deputy treasurer of the king's household until 1721, when he was dismissed and commissioned in the Horse Guards. He resided at Leeds Castle on retiring from the army, and in 1735 he made his first visit to Virginia, where his cousin William Fairfax acted as proprietary agent and collector of customs.

In the following decade Fairfax was involved in negotiations to implement the recommendations of a survey ordered by the privy council to settle a dispute over territory on the western boundary of the northern neck. In 1745 the privy council upheld the survey's conclusions, enabling Fairfax to more than double his holding to 5 million acres. Two years later he moved permanently to Virginia, and for some time lived at his cousin's house at Belvoir. Here he made the acquaintance of the Washington family.

Fairfax moved to the Shenandoah valley, where he built two properties, Leeds Manor and Greenway Court, near Winchester. George Washington, then a young man of sixteen, was asked to survey and map his property. At Greenway Court Fairfax combined a lifestyle befitting a country gentleman (his passion was for fox-hunting) with an active interest in improving his estate. He also assisted in the development of Winchester and Alexandria, and supported the construction of a Potomac River canal.

Fairfax avoided having to take sides during the American War of Independence and was able to maintain his property intact when other estates were confiscated. At the time of his death he had amassed a considerable fortune (£47,377 3s. 9d. in Virginia currency), which made him one of America's richest men. Despite his wealth, Fairfax favoured a simple life and was known for his generosity. He died at Greenway Court on 9 December 1781, and was buried at the parish church of Winchester, Virginia. On his death he was unmarried and had no children, and the title passed to Robert Fairfax, his only surviving brother.

PHILIP CARTER

Sources S. S. Hughes, 'Fairfax, Thomas', *ANB* · S. E. Brown jun., *Virginia baron: the story of Thomas, sixth Lord Fairfax* (1965) · *DNB*
Archives Bodl. Oxf., MSS · NRA, priv. coll., corresp.
Likenesses portrait, repro. in F. Harrison, *Landmarks of old Prince William*, 2 vols. (1924) · portrait, Masonic Temple, Alexandria, Virginia; repro. in guidebook to Leeds Castle (2000)
Wealth at death £47,377 3s. 9d.: Hughes, 'Fairfax, Thomas'

Fairfax, Sir William (*bap.* 1610, *d.* 1644), parliamentarian army officer, was baptized in Steeton Chapel, Bolton Percy, in the West Riding of Yorkshire, the second son of Sir Philip Fairfax of Steeton (*bap.* 1586, *d.* 1613), and his wife, Frances Sheffield (*d.* 1615), daughter of Edmund, Baron Sheffield and earl of Mulgrave, and his wife, Ursula. Sir Philip's extravagance at court left the estate in debt, and William was raised by his grandmother, Mabel, Lady Fairfax, after the early death of both his parents. He was probably the William Fairfax who matriculated at St John's College, Cambridge, in 1625, graduated BA in 1628, and was created MA in 1633. In 1629 he married Frances Chaloner (1610–1692/3), daughter of Sir Thomas Chaloner of Guisborough in Cleveland, and sister of the regicide Thomas Chaloner. In appearance Fairfax was a very tall man with dark eyes and brown hair.

Fairfax was knighted by Charles I at Whitehall on 1 June 1630. On the death of his elder brother Edmund in 1636 he succeeded to the family estates at Steeton and Newton Kyme, and he settled at Steeton in 1640. In July 1641 he accepted a captaincy in his uncle Ferdinando, second

Baron Fairfax's regiment of trained bands and by October he was serving as a West Riding JP. He accompanied his cousin Sir Thomas Fairfax (later third baron) to confront the king with a parliamentarian petition on Heworth Moor outside York on 3 June 1642.

William Fairfax probably already possessed considerable military experience, for in August 1642 he travelled south to assume command of an infantry regiment in the earl of Essex's parliamentarian army. He fought at Edgehill, where most of his regiment fled 'in despight of the officers' (*Two speeches of the Lord Wharton*). Accompanied by his officers, he joined Lord Fairfax's northern army at Selby in December 1642. Sir William raised a new regiment around Bradford, and commanded the parliamentarian infantry at the capture of Leeds on 23 January 1643. He was briefly governor there, before delivering Lord Fairfax's offer of protection to the queen at Bridlington. On his return his forces occupied Pontefract town, where they blockaded the castle during March 1643. He was among the victorious commanders at Wakefield on 21 May, where the royalist Sir George Goring was captured. Fairfax was in London questioning Goring on 11 August. In November he travelled to King's Lynn to persuade the earl of Manchester to advance against the royalists at Chesterfield, and wrote to his wife from Boston: 'for Thomas's partt and mine we rest neither night nor day, nor will willingly till we have done God some good service against his and our enimyes' (Markham, *Life of Robert Fairfax*, 14). He commanded a wing of cavalry at Nantwich on 25 January 1644, and was subsequently engaged in the siege of Lathom House. In May, recovering from a fever, he joined the allied army before York, and he commanded an infantry brigade on the allied right at Marston Moor on 2 July.

In August 1644 Fairfax was sent into Lancashire with 2000 cavalry and was present at the siege of Liverpool. He was mortally wounded relieving Montgomery Castle on 18 September 1644, and died the following day. Lord Fairfax reflected: 'blessed be God, the victory obtained over our enemies doth abate my sorrow for any particular friends' (*CSP dom., 1644*, 529), while Sir William's widow 'grieved not that he died in the cause, but that he died so soon that he could do no more for it' (Markham, *Life of Robert Fairfax*, 23). In 1647 he appeared as third on a list of slain parliamentarian worthies (J. Ricraft, *A Survey of England's Champions and Truths Faithful Patriots*, 1647, 155). He died without making a will to provide for his children so parliament voted his widow £1500. On 7 September 1655 the council of state voted a further £2000 from his pay arrears.

ANDREW J. HOPPER

Sources C. R. Markham, *Life of Robert Fairfax of Steeton* (1885) · J. Foster, ed., *Pedigrees of the county families of Yorkshire*, 1 (1874) · *DNB* · C. R. Markham, *A life of the great Lord Fairfax* (1870) · G. W. Johnson, ed., *The Fairfax correspondence: memoirs of the reign of Charles the First*, 2 vols. (1848) · R. Bell, ed., *Memorials of the civil war … forming the concluding volumes of the Fairfax correspondence*, 2 vols. (1849) · E. Hailstone, ed., *Portraits of Yorkshire worthies*, 2 vols. (1869), vol. 1 · J. Lister, ed., *West Riding sessions records*, 2, Yorkshire Archaeological Society, 54 (1915) · J. Rushworth, *Historical collections*, new edn, 8 vols. (1721–2) · J. T. Cliffe, *The Yorkshire gentry from the Reformation to the civil war* (1969) · Venn, *Alum. Cant.*, 1/2 · *CSP dom.*, 1644–55 · PRO,

SP 28/1A/36 · *The two speeches of the Lord Wharton spoken in Guild-Hall* (1642) [Thomason tract E 127(27)] · *Certaine Informations from Severall Parts of the Kingdome* (27 March–3 April 1643) [Thomason tract E 94(29)] · *Letters from Sir William Brereton, Sir Thomas Middleton, Sir John Meldrum, of the great victory (by Gods providence) given them, in raising the siege from before Montgomery-castle*, BL, E10/4 · *Kingdomes Weekly Intelligencer*, 73 (17–24 Sept 1644) [Thomason tract E 10(7)] · *The Weekly Account, Containing Certain Speciall and Remarkable Passages*, 56 (18–24 Sept 1644) [Thomason tract E 10(6)] · *The London Post*, no. 5, 24 Sept 1644, BL, E10/5

Archives BL, Add. MSS 18979, 20778, 30305–30306
Likenesses Cooper, miniature · portrait, repro. in Hailstone, ed., *Portraits of Yorkshire worthies*, vol. 1, pl. lxxvii · portrait; formerly priv. coll.
Wealth at death was owed £4677 9s. 0d. pay by army: *CSP dom.*, 1655

Fairfax, Sir William George (1739–1813), naval officer, was born on 8 March 1739, possibly at Windlesham, Bagshot, the son of Joseph Fairfax, an officer of the Horse Guards, of Bagshot, Surrey, and grandson of Joseph Fairfax of Saxton, Yorkshire. Fairfax entered the navy in 1750 in the *Centurion*, under Augustus Keppel, in the Mediterranean and then served in the *Mars* and the *Garland* under Marriot Arbuthnot. He was promoted lieutenant on 20 December 1757 in the *Duke*. From 1758 to 1760 he was in the *Eurus* in North America with Captain John Elphinston in the operations in the St Lawrence. Fairfax had no further employment until June 1766, when he was appointed to the *Greyhound*, and from June 1769 to September 1776 he was again on half pay as a lieutenant. In May 1778 he was promoted to the command of the cutter *Alert*. In the following month, while attached to the Grand Fleet under Keppel, and in company with the *Arethusa*, the *Alert* captured the French lugger *Coureur*, at the same time that the *Arethusa* was beaten off in her celebrated fight with the *Belle Poule*. In August, however, the *Alert* was herself captured by the frigate *Junon* (40 guns), and Fairfax was detained as a prisoner during the greater part of the American War of Independence. In January 1782 he was promoted to post rank, and appointed to the frigate *Tartar* in the West Indies, which he commanded until the peace in 1783. In 1793 he was appointed to the *Sheerness* in which (and in the *Repulse*) he remained until 1796. He was then in the North Sea Fleet, and was appointed flag-captain to Admiral Adam Duncan, the commander-in-chief of the fleet. In the *Venerable* with Duncan he shared in the difficulties of the mutiny of 1797 and the famous victory at Camperdown, where his services were rewarded by his being made a knight banneret. He continued in command of the *Venerable* until 1798. On 7 January 1801 he was promoted to flag rank, but though considered for the third post in the Baltic fleet of 1801, he appears to have offended George, second Earl Spencer, the first lord of the Admiralty, and had no further service. He was advanced to vice-admiral on 13 December 1806. He was twice married: first, in 1767, to Hannah (d. 1770), daughter of the Revd Robert Spears of Burntisland; secondly, in 1772, to Janet Margaret, daughter of Samuel Charters, and cousin of Sir Samuel Greig, an admiral in the Russian service; the couple had four sons and two daughters, several of whom died

young. The fourth and then only surviving son, Henry, was created a baronet in 1836 as a recognition of his father's services, while one of the daughters, Mary [see Somerville, Mary], married first Samuel Greig the younger, and then William Somerville. William George Fairfax, who is generally referred to by both his Christian names, settled in Burntisland, Fife, where he had property, possibly derived from his first wife or her family. He died in Edinburgh on 7 November 1813.

J. K. LAUGHTON, *rev.* A. W. H. PEARSALL

Sources *The private papers of John, earl of Sandwich*, ed. G. R. Barnes and J. H. Owen, 2, Navy RS, 71 (1933), 95; 4, Navy RS, 78 (1938), 111 · *Private papers of George, second Earl Spencer*, ed. J. S. Corbett and H. W. Richmond, 2, Navy RS, 48 (1924), 188, 198–201 · *Letters of … the earl of St Vincent, whilst the first lord of the admiralty, 1801–1804*, ed. D. B. Smith, 2 vols., Navy RS, 55, 61 (1922–7), 1.319–21 · Lord Camperdown [R. A. P. H. Duncan], *Admiral Duncan* (1898) · J. Ralfe, *The naval biography of Great Britain*, 4 vols. (1828) · *GM*, 1st ser., 83/2 (1813), 622 · PRO, ADM 1/1792 · passing certificate, PRO, ADM 107/5, 19 · PRO, ADM 36/560, 5520, 5656, 6293
Archives Bodl. Oxf., corresp. and papers · PRO
Likenesses M. A. Shee, oils, exh. RA 1798, Charlecote Park, Warwickshire · G. Noble and J. Parker, group portrait, line print, pubd 1803 (*Commemoration of 11th Oct 1797*; after J. Smart), BM, NPG · D. Orme, oils, NMM · W. Ridley, stipple, BM, NPG; repro. in *Naval Chronicle* (1801)

Fairfield. For this title name *see* Greer, (Frederick) Arthur, Baron Fairfield (1863–1945).

Fairfield, Charles (*c.*1759–1804), painter, of whose parents nothing is known, is best known as a copyist of the works of the Dutch and Flemish masters of the seventeenth century. These were extremely well done, and were eagerly sought after by dealers, who disposed of them as originals. A copy by him of Teniers's *Le bonnet rouge* was 'of the most striking perfection of finish and tone, capable of deceiving any one could it have but age' (Anderdon).

Fairfield did also produce original works of great merit. His small, brilliantly coloured landscapes have been compared in style to those of George Morland. Yet Fairfield was diffident, modest, and lived a secluded life, never really pursuing the full potential of his own talents. He etched a few plates, including *Cavalier at the Door of an Inn*, after Metsu. He is also known to have been employed painting figures into the landscapes of his contemporaries such as John Rathbone. He died in Brompton, London, in 1804 aged about forty-five. His obituarist noted that he sold his pictures:

> at a very low rate, and never represented them otherwise than as copies by himself. Notwithstanding Mr. Fairfield's great merit, he was never in easy circumstances, and for a great part of his laborious life was under the clutches of the griping and unconscientious picture-dealer, who gathered the fruits of his labours by practising deceits upon the world. (*GM*)

L. H. CUST, *rev.* JILL SPRINGALL

Sources M. H. Grant, *A chronological history of the old English landscape painters*, 1 (1926), 164–4 · *GM*, 1st ser., 75 (1805), 880 · Thieme & Becker, *Allgemeines Lexikon* · Redgrave, *Artists* · J. H. Anderdon,

'Collectanea biographica', BM, department of prints and drawings

Wealth at death never in easy circumstances: *GM*

Fairfield, (Josephine) Letitia Denny (1885–1978), public health physician and campaigner for social reform, was born on 10 March 1885 at 26 Acland Street, St Kilda, Melbourne, Australia, the eldest of three daughters of Charles Fairfield (*c*.1842–1906), journalist, and his wife, Isabella Campbell Mackenzie (*c*.1853–1921), daughter of Alexander Mackenzie and his wife, Jessie Watson Campbell. Her father was of Irish descent and her mother's parents both came from Edinburgh families, but they married in Australia where Charles Fairfield worked as a journalist on the Melbourne *Argus*. Letitia Fairfield's family moved to Britain when she was about three years old, living first in Glasgow and then, later, in various parts, including in and around London. In 1892 her younger sister, Cicily Isabel (1892–1983), was born: the sister who was to become well known as the journalist and novelist Rebecca West [*see* Andrews, Dame Cicily Isabel].

Faced with deteriorating financial circumstances related to Charles Fairfield's frequent changes of job, the family then moved to Richmond, Surrey, where from 1896 Letitia Fairfield attended Richmond High School for Girls. When her father left permanently in 1901, her mother took her three daughters to live in Edinburgh. After a year at George Watson's Ladies' College she entered the Edinburgh Medical College for Women, then an extramural school for the University of Edinburgh; this was a step made possible only by the award of one of the first Carnegie scholarships and the gift of £100 from an aunt.

Fairfield graduated MB ChB from the University of Edinburgh in 1907, with honours in all subjects and with several medals. Over the next four years she gained clinical experience through a series of temporary hospital posts as house officer or equivalent, including seven months at Birmingham City Asylum and, in 1908, nine months at the Manchester Victoria Memorial Jewish Hospital, where she learned enough Yiddish to talk to her patients. Fairfield was awarded her MD degree from the University of Edinburgh in 1911. In that year she returned to London with her mother and her two sisters, and took a house in Hampstead Garden Suburb.

Fairfield now began her work in public health for the London county council (LCC) which was to continue, apart from wartime interruptions, until 1948. After several part-time posts in the LCC's newly reorganized school medical service, she was appointed, in 1912, as a full-time medical assistant in the public health department, the same year that she passed her diploma in public health from the University of London. She was to become the first woman senior medical officer at the LCC. Before the First World War, her main responsibilities there were concerned with the health and welfare of schoolchildren, including the inspection of schools for those with physical or mental handicaps and of teacher training colleges. She retained a particular involvement with the care and education of children with epilepsy throughout her career.

At the outbreak of war in 1914 Fairfield was one of a group of women doctors who offered their services to the War Office, only to be told that the war could be won without them. However, in 1917 she became a medical officer to the new Women's Army Auxiliary Corps, serving as medical controller for southern command. She was then appointed, in June 1918, as chief medical officer to the new Women's Royal Air Force with responsibility for the medical care of 8000 women in military quarters and a further 22,000 living at home. Fairfield was active in the internal battle that medical women in the armed services waged, with only limited success, with the War Office to be appointed on comparable terms to men, including full rather than honorary commissions. In 1919 she was created CBE in recognition of her war service.

In 1920 Fairfield returned to the LCC. Although involved in a broad range of public health activities, her work in relation to children and women's health was to be particularly important. When, following the 1929 Local Government Act, the LCC took responsibility for London's poor-law board hospitals, improving them especially in relation to maternity and obstetric care was one of her major concerns. Medico-legal matters were another professional interest, Fairfield having been called to the bar at the Middle Temple, London, in 1923. She was co-editor of the *Medico-Legal and Criminological Review* for some years, and president of the Medico-Legal Society in 1957 and 1958. In 1940 her administrative expertise was again sought by the War Office, where she became the senior woman doctor (with the now fully commissioned rank of lieutenant-colonel) and assistant director-general for medical services. In 1942, having reached the compulsory retirement age for the army, she returned to the LCC, where she continued to work until the inception of the National Health Service in July 1948. She published a number of professional articles on public health matters, and short books, including one on epilepsy in 1954.

Before, during, and after her distinguished career as a medical administrator, Fairfield was actively involved in many contemporary social controversies. As a medical student and young doctor she threw herself wholeheartedly into the campaign for women's suffrage, including addressing many public meetings. Her blonde good looks caught the attention of her audiences and, with her confident voice, she could dominate the roughest open-air meetings. She joined the militant suffragette Women's Social and Political Union for a time but soon became critical of Christabel Pankhurst's authoritarianism. After moving to London she joined the Fabian Society, and spoke in public and wrote regularly on women's and health issues. She also developed a strong commitment to the cause of Irish independence. In 1922 Fairfield became a Roman Catholic. During the 1920s she was a prominent opponent of birth control, though she later modified her views following a visit to Malta, where problems ensuing from a high birth-rate and poverty were all too apparent. For many years she was a regular contributor to the Catholic press on matters such as medical evidence for miracle cures, the supernatural, and exorcism. In later life she became an expert on witchcraft. In 1965 she was awarded the papal medal, *Pro ecclesia et pontifice*. Before and during the Second World War she helped many refugees from the Nazi regime in Germany settle in Britain.

'A delightful, vigorous, dogmatic, and at times infuriating companion' (*BMJ*, 873), Fairfield was much loved by colleagues and family. Her interest in children was not just professional and she spent much time entertaining her nieces and nephews. As eldest sister and with respect to appearance, she was the model for the character of Cordelia in Rebecca West's loosely autobiographical, best-selling novel *The Fountain Overflows* (1957), but the unsympathetic personality portrayed there was fictional. The relationship between the two sisters, however, was sometimes strained, particularly in later life.

Fairfield died on 1 February 1978 at St Mary Abbots Hospital, London, having been ill for fifteen months following a stroke. M. A. ELSTON

Sources Wellcome L., Fairfield MSS, GC/193 · *BMJ* (11 Feb 1978), 872–3 · L. Fairfield, 'Women doctors in the British forces, 1914–1918 war', *Journal of Medical Women's Federation*, 49/2, 99–102 · V. Glendinning, *Rebecca West: a life* (1987) · b. cert.
Archives IWM, MSS · LMA, public health department, London county council archives, MSS · Wellcome L., MSS |SOUND Wellcome L., some recordings |transcripts in subject's MSS]
Likenesses double portrait, photograph, c.1892 (with her sister Rebecca West; as children), repro. in J. Marcus, ed., *The young Rebecca* (1982) · photographs, c.1904–1970, Wellcome L. · photographs, repro. in Glendinning, *Rebecca West*
Wealth at death £44,757: probate, 6 July 1978, *CGPLA Eng. & Wales*

Fairholm, Adam (c.1722–1764). *See under* Select Society (act. 1754–1764).

Fairholt, Frederick William (bap. 1813, d. 1866), artist and antiquary, was born in London and baptized on 18 July 1813 at St Anne's, Soho, the sixteenth and only surviving child of a Prussian immigrant, whose name, Fahrholz, was Anglicized when he settled in London, and his wife, Sarah, the daughter of a Spitalfields silk weaver of Scottish origin named Dugweel or Dugwell. Initially Fairholt worked in his father's trade as a tobacco manufacturer. He developed an early interest in literature and drama and, from the age of twelve, received regular drawing lessons. Intrigued by woodcuts in books of border ballads and Scottish legends, he contributed his first wood-engraving to *The Mirror*. In 1831 he won the silver Isis medal of the Society of Arts for a watercolour copy of a landscape drawing. He became a drawing teacher, though he also gained employment as an assistant scene-painter. Illness led him to print colouring, for which he earned 10s. a week. John Jackson employed him to copy Hogarth prints for £1 a week. In 1835 he became an assistant to the wood-engraver Stephen Sly (earning £3 to £6 weekly), through whom he began to draw and engrave for Charles Knight's publications, notably the *Penny Magazine* and *London*.

Fairholt's first major commission was for around 200 drawings on wood for J. Jackson and W. A. Chatto's *Treatise on Wood Engraving* (1839). From 1839 he was employed as

artist and writer for the *Art Union* (from 1848 the *Art Journal*), for which he served as an assistant editor under Samuel Carter Hall. His fidelity as a draughtsman and his antiquarian knowledge, particularly of medieval art and customs, were much in demand for the illustration of learned publications. He drew and wrote regularly for the Society of Antiquaries (of which he was elected fellow in 1844), the British Archaeological Association (member), and the Numismatic Society (elected member in 1845). His illustrated antiquarian works include Charles Roach Smith's *The Antiquities of Richborough* (1850), Thomas Wright's *Archaeological Album* (1845), and *Miscellanea graphica* (1854–7) by Lord Londesborough, whom he accompanied to southern France and Rome in 1856 and later to Egypt. Among Fairholt's best-known works as author and illustrator are *The Lord Mayors' Pageants* (1843–4) and *Costume in England* (1846), and, as editor, *A Dictionary of Terms in Art* (1854). His dexterity enabled him to etch, coins especially, direct on the plate without preliminary drawing.

A methodical worker, Fairholt signed his engravings 'F. W. F.' Kind, unassuming, and companionable, he had a wry sense of humour that was reflected in his caricature drawing. Since he strongly disliked the country, he spent his busy life chiefly in London, where he died from tubercular consumption on 3 April 1866, at 22 Montpelier Square, Brompton Road, Kensington. He was buried in Brompton cemetery. He bequeathed his Shakespearian collection to Shakespeare's birthplace in Stratford upon Avon and other material to the Society of Antiquaries and the British Museum. JOANNA SELBORNE

Sources DNB · B. Hunnisett, *An illustrated dictionary of British steel engravers*, new edn (1989) · R. K. Engen, *Dictionary of Victorian engravers, print publishers and their works* (1979) · R. K. Engen, *Dictionary of Victorian wood engravers* (1985) · Redgrave, *Artists*, 2nd edn · Bryan, *Painters* (1903–5) · *Proceedings of the Society of Antiquaries of London*, 2nd ser., 3 (1864–7), 286–7 · *Art Journal*, 28 (1866), 179–80 · S. C. Hall, *Retrospect of a long life: from 1815 to 1883*, 1 (1883), 360–63 · *Encyclopaedia Britannica*, 9th edn (1875–89) · W. A. Chatto, preface, in W. A. Chatto, J. Jackson, and H. G. Bohn, *A treatise on wood engraving*, 2nd edn (1861) · C. R. Smith, *Collectanea antiqua*, 6 (1868), 296–311 · *Transactions of the Society of Arts* (1831) · J. Johnson, ed., *Works exhibited at the Royal Society of British Artists, 1824–1893, and the New English Art Club, 1888–1917*, 2 vols. (1975) · S. Houfe, *The dictionary of 19th century British book illustrators and caricaturists*, rev. edn (1996) · M. H. Grant, *A dictionary of British landscape painters, from the 16th century to the early 20th century* (1952) · Mallalieu, *Watercolour artists*, vol. 1 · Wood, *Vic. painters* · IGI · *CGPLA Eng. & Wales* (1866)
Archives BM, department of prints and drawings · Bodl. Oxf., corresp. · S. Antiquaries, Lond. · Shakespeare Birthplace Trust RO, Stratford upon Avon | GL, corresp. with Thomas Crofton Croker · U. Edin. L., special collections division, corresp. with James Halliwell-Phillipps
Likenesses A. S., etching, 1847, BM, NPG · etching, 1857, NPG
Wealth at death under £6000: probate, 7 May 1866, *CGPLA Eng. & Wales*

Fairland, Thomas (1804–1852), lithographer and engraver, took an interest in drawing at an early age and worked from nature in London's Kensington Gardens; later he studied under Fuseli at the Royal Academy, where he gained a silver medal for a drawing of a cast of Hercules which then stood in the academy's entrance hall. On leaving the academy he became a pupil of the line engraver Charles Warren, but in the late 1820s he was attracted to lithography, which was then challenging engraving in several fields of printmaking. About this time he exhibited a few works at the Suffolk Street Galleries (1828–33). Lithography seems to have suited his talents as a draughtsman, and he soon became one of the best-known reproductive lithographers in Britain, though he had no reputation at all as an original lithographer and therefore hardly figures in the literature of the subject. His reproductive lithography includes work after his British contemporaries, among them A. Cooper, R. Farrier, C. Hancock, and Edwin Landseer, and after major artists such as David, Matsys, and Raphael. A volume of *Comic Sketches* (1844), after W. Hunt, is said to have been particularly popular, and his reproduction of a cartoon of the *Virgin and Child* by Raphael attracted attention. He also lithographed many portraits, pictures of animals, and plates for drawing books. Though his work as a lithographic draughtsman was much admired in its day, it was also criticized. An anonymous contemporary writer referred to the comic pictures he lithographed after Farrier as done 'with great boldness and spirit', but noted that 'He does not succeed, however, in producing clear and brilliant tints and effects, and consequently his style appears heavy when it would otherwise be forcible' (*Library of the Fine Arts*, 210).

With the passing of time Fairland has come to be seen as one of the minor reproductive lithographic draughtsmen of the second quarter of the nineteenth century. In 1829 he lithographed two plates, as did his brother William, for Flaxman's *Lectures on Sculpture*, and by 1830 the two men were listed as working together as lithographic printers in London. From the late 1830s into the 1840s Fairland worked as a lithographic printer on his own account from 45 St John's Square, Clerkenwell, sometimes printing his own lithographs. As a draughtsman he appears to have had no firm allegiance to any one printer and his lithographs were printed by several firms: Hullmandel, Day, Graf, and M. and N. Hanhart. Nevertheless, in 1842 he submitted affidavits (as did William Day and Jeremiah Graf) in support of Charles Hancock in his dispute with Charles Hullmandel over the latter's lithotint patent. He also worked as a portrait painter, undertaking commissions for eminent people, including royalty. Despite a large output of reproductive lithography, he struggled to make a good living from his work; he was not helped by long-term health problems, which led to his premature death on 22 October 1852, at his home, 15 Aberdeen Place, Marylebone.

His younger brother William Fairland (*b.* 1806), also an engraver and lithographer, took up lithography before him; among his earliest lithographs are some fine plates for the second volume of George Simpson's *The Anatomy of the Bones and Muscles* (1825).   Michael Twyman

Sources Bryan, *Painters* (1886–9) · *Library of the Fine Arts*, 1 (1831), 210 · G. Wakeman and G. D. R. Bridson, *A guide to nineteenth century colour printers* (1975), 41 · *Art Union*, 5 (1843), 312 · *Engraved Brit. ports.* · D. H. Boalch, *Prints and paintings of British farm livestock, 1780–*
1910: a record of the Rothamsted collection (1958) · Thieme & Becker, *Allgemeines Lexikon* · Graves, *Artists*, 3rd edn · W. S. Williams, 'On lithography', *Transactions of the Society for the Encouragement of Arts, Manufactures, and Commerce* (1847–8), 234–5, 240 · M. Twyman, *A directory of London lithographic printers, 1800–1850* (1976), 32 · Redgrave, *Artists*, 2nd edn · A. Dyson, *Pictures to print: the nineteenth-century engraving trade* (1984) · d. cert. · *DNB*

Fairless, Michael. *See* Barber, Margaret Fairless (1869–1901).

Fairless, Thomas Kerr (1825–1853), landscape painter, born at Hexham, Northumberland, was one of the sons of Joseph Fairless of Hexham, an antiquary. He showed an early talent for art, which was encouraged by his parents. He was a dedicated student of Thomas Bewick's vignette engravings, and for some time worked under Bewick's pupil, the wood-engraver Isaac Nicholson, in Newcastle upon Tyne. Dissatisfied with his progress, he went to London and devoted himself to landscape painting, executing works in a broad and vigorous manner with a keen eye for colour and the beauties of country scenery. From 1848 to 1853 he exhibited twenty-two paintings at the Royal Academy, the British Institution, and the Society (later Royal Society) of British Artists. He also gave lessons in drawing and painting. As well as landscapes, he painted views of the sea and shipping scenes, and intended to practise his art in Scotland and on the continent. However, his health broke down, and in August 1851 he returned to Hexham, where he died on 14 July 1853, in his twenty-eighth year.

L. H. Cust, rev. Romita Ray

Sources *Art Journal*, 15 (1853), 215 · Redgrave, *Artists* · Bryan, *Painters* (1877) · Graves, *Artists* · private information (1888)

Fairley, Gordon Hamilton- (1930–1975), oncologist, was born on 20 April 1930 at 73 Harley Street, London, the younger son of Sir Neil Hamilton *Fairley (1891–1966), and his second wife, Mary Evelyn Greaves (*b.* 1902). His father, a member of a distinguished Melbourne medical family, was director of medical services in the Australian army in the Second World War and later became the first Wellcome professor of tropical medicine in London. Hamilton-Fairley (the hyphen was adopted later in life) was educated at Geelong grammar school in Victoria, Australia, and, when the family moved to England, at Marlborough College, Wiltshire. He entered Magdalen College, Oxford, where he did his preclinical training; he completed a BA in physiology in 1951. He started his clinical studies at St Bartholomew's Hospital, London, in 1952, and was known to be a lively student with a keen wit and an appreciation of the amusing aspects of a medical student's life. His ebullience of spirit made him a delightful companion but there was also a seriousness of purpose. He was certainly ambitious and able but there must have been some pressure on him from such a distinguished and successful father. He married Daphne Vera Hillier-Holt (*b.* 1931), daughter of Geoffrey Hillier-Holt, a company director, on 28 March 1953, before he qualified, a most unusual practice in those days and one which did not altogether meet with his father's approval. The couple soon showed, however, that it was possible both to be married and to achieve academic success, for in 1954 Hamilton-Fairley won a prestigious undergraduate prize, the Burrows prize in pathology, shortly before qualifying BM, BCh (Oxon). Daphne Hamilton-Fairley became a speech therapist, remedial teacher, and headteacher.

After pre-registration posts at St Bartholomew's Hospital, Hamilton-Fairley went on to be a house physician at the Royal Postgraduate Medical School at Hammersmith Hospital in west London. He was fortunate to succeed to the Hammersmith–Brompton hospital circuit at an early age, an essential step at that time for anyone wishing to specialize. After further experience at Bart's, where he passed the MRCP examination, in 1958 he was awarded the Leverhulme research scholarship at the Royal College of Physicians, tenable in the department of haematology at the Royal Postgraduate Medical School. The subject of his research was the role of immunity in malignant disease. He was jointly supervised by Sir Ronald Bodley Scott and Sir John Dacie. This undoubtedly helped to give him direction and promote his knowledge of malignant disease of the haemopoietic system. This research was the basis for his DM thesis in 1961 on immunity mechanisms in chronic lymphatic leukaemia and other reticuloses. Surgery, radiotherapy, and chemotherapy were then, as later, the chief modalities for treatment of cancer but there were well-founded observations that the body could mount a weak but definite response to cancerous cells. It was the nature of this immunity that fascinated Hamilton-Fairley and led to the work which resulted in his invitation to give the Goulstonian lecture at the Royal College of Physicians in 1969 on the immunity to malignant disease in man. His last major lecture was given at a plenary session of the International Society of Haematology in 1975 (published in the *British Journal of Haematology*, 31, August 1975, suppl. p. 181) and indicated the progress that had been made in less than a decade. Another factor in Hamilton-Fairley's particular interest was the shock of finding that he himself had cancer. A diagnosis of seminoma of the testis, a curable cancer if localized, was made. Perhaps much of his compassion for patients with cancer came from his own experience; he commented that during radiotherapy the only thing tolerable was a large brandy.

Essentially a practical physician like his father and realizing that the use of immunological treatments still lay in the future, Hamilton-Fairley turned to improving current chemotherapy for disseminated Hodgkin's disease. He successfully modified a treatment introduced by Vincent Devita at the National Cancer Institute in the USA, which became standard therapy in Britain for many years (*BMJ*, 4 July 1970, 7), curing many patients and rendering life more tolerable for others. Giving these successful but toxic treatments led to the development of a new discipline: cancer medicine or medical oncology. Hamilton-Fairley's charm and quiet persistence enabled him to overcome entrenched resistance and to introduce the idea of medical oncology as a sub-specialty of general internal medicine. The expansion of medical oncology owed much to his foresight. As the result of an initiative by Sir Eric Scowen, chairman of the Imperial Cancer

Research Fund, a medical oncology unit was founded at St Bartholomew's Hospital. Hamilton-Fairley became in turn director and then professor of medical oncology in the first university chair in the subject in the United Kingdom in 1971. His influence was soon manifest not only in research but also in training. At one time, five of the premier chairs in medical oncology in Britain were occupied by doctors who had worked with him.

Inevitably such a busy professional life must have made demands on Hamilton-Fairley's family. Friends were never aware of this. Their homes in Northumberland Place and later in Campden Hill Square overflowed with warmth and a joy of living that were sensed immediately on entering. Daphne and the four children, Diana, Sarah, Geoffrey, and Fiona, made up a most vivacious household. Diana, the eldest daughter, qualified in medicine and became a consultant obstetrician and gynaecologist at Guy's and St Thomas's hospitals.

Hamilton-Fairley's life ended tragically as the result of a Provisional IRA terrorist bomb in Campden Hill Square on the morning of 23 October 1975. He had risen early to take their terrier Bini for a walk. Bini caused the explosion of a bomb which had been planted under the car of their next-door neighbour, Hugh Fraser MP. Death was instantaneous. This cruel act shattered a family and deprived the country of a leading clinician and cancer researcher—an incalculable loss. This feeling was witnessed by the overwhelming attendance at the service of thanksgiving for his life held at St Paul's Cathedral on 4 December 1975. A plaque to his memory was placed in the crypt.

J. S. MALPAS

Sources personal knowledge (2004) · *BMJ* (1 Nov 1975), 290 · *The Lancet* (1 Nov 1975) · *St Bartholomew's Hospital Journal*, [79] (1975), 148–9 · *The Times* (24 Oct 1975) · *The Guardian* (24 Oct 1975) · Munk, *Roll* · private information (2004) · b. cert. · d. cert. · m. cert.
Wealth at death £105,295: probate, 17 Dec 1975, *CGPLA Eng. & Wales*

Fairley, Sir Neil Hamilton (1891–1966), physician, was born in Inglewood, Victoria, Australia, on 15 July 1891, the third of the six sons of James Fairley, a bank manager of Scottish descent, and his wife, Margaret Louise Jones. From his school, Scotch College, Melbourne, Fairley went on to study medicine in Melbourne University and qualified with first-class honours in 1915. In 1916 he was commissioned in the Australian Army Medical Service and went to Egypt as pathologist to a military hospital, where he developed an interest in research. In 1919 he went to London and spent some months in the Lister Institute. He also obtained his MRCP (London) and DPH (Cambridge). Also in 1919 he married Violet May Phillips; they had one son. The marriage was dissolved in 1924.

Fairley returned to Australia in 1920 as first assistant to the director of the Walter and Eliza Hall Research Institute, Melbourne. In 1922 he was appointed medical research officer of the Bombay Bacteriological Laboratory, where he continued his early work on fluke-borne diseases in humans and domestic animals. He developed a blood test and later a simpler skin test, which were of value in early diagnosis and, in the case of farmyard animals, in the detection of infection, a matter of considerable economic importance. He also studied sprue in India, and devised improved methods of treatment, though he failed to discover the cause of the disease, which he himself contracted. After recuperating in Britain, Fairley returned to the Walter and Eliza Hall Research Institute in Melbourne, where he investigated snake venoms and snake-bite, and showed that the wider 'gape' of the viper's jaw enabled it to inject more venom than other snakes, thus adding to the deadly efficacy of its bite.

In 1925 Fairley married Mary Evelyn, daughter of Herbert R. Greaves, of Bombay. They had two sons, one of whom was Gordon Hamilton-*Fairley (1930–1975) who became a distinguished oncologist. In 1929 the family settled in London, where Fairley filled an appointment in the Hospital for Tropical Diseases and also lectured at the London School of Hygiene and Tropical Medicine. He traced the cause of severe, sometimes fatal, cases of hepatitis, which cropped up at irregular intervals in sewer workers, and showed that it was associated with an infectious and preventable disease, leptospirosis, contracted from sewer rats.

Later, in Cairo in 1941, Fairley showed that sulphaguanidine produced a specific cure for acute bacillary dysentery, a discovery which proved of particular value during the battle with the Japanese for Port Moresby, when a severe outbreak of 'Shiga' dysentery ravaged the Japanese but was successfully controlled in the Australian troops.

In the latter part of his life Fairley's predominant interest was in malaria. Prior to the Second World War he paid several visits to a malaria research unit in Salonika to study blackwater fever, a complication of malaria, and while there he became well acquainted with the malaria problems of Macedonia. This was to stand him in good stead later. After he became consultant in medicine to the Australian troops in the Middle East force in 1940 he discovered that plans had been made to send British and Australian troops to Macedonia in support of the Greek army. He succeeded, after some argument, in persuading General Sir Archibald P. Wavell to change these plans and deploy the troops in a less dangerous locality. As it transpired, this achieved nothing, as the allies were turned out of Greece before the onset of the season of malaria transmission.

When Japan entered the war Fairley left Egypt for the south Pacific and was promoted brigadier and director of medicine in the Australian medical service. Later he was made chairman of the combined advisory committee on tropical medicine, south Pacific area, directly responsible to General Douglas MacArthur. Realizing that the outstanding medical problem in that area was malaria, he went to Java and bought some 120 tons of quinine. None reached Australia, however, and when Fairley reached Australia he faced a desperate situation. The only potent anti-malarial drug other than quinine known at that time was mepacrine (atebrin), hitherto manufactured chiefly in Germany. Fairley visited London and Washington to plead at the highest level for the urgent manufacture of adequate supplies. His mission was successful, but, back in Australia, he was disappointed to find that mepacrine failed to prevent infection with malaria in hyperendemic areas. Determined to discover a drug which would confer complete protection, Fairley directed a massive research project and proved that, unlike quinine and sulphamerazine, mepacrine was effective in suppressing malaria when taken daily with unfailing regularity. Fairley's lucid exposition of his findings convinced senior army officers, and orders were issued making unit commanding officers responsible for ensuring that the troops received and swallowed the daily dose. The result was dramatic. Malaria ceased to be a problem in all commands where this procedure was adopted and followed. This proved of vast importance in the latter days of the war.

After the war Fairley returned to London to resume teaching and to become one of the elder statesmen in the field of tropical medicine. In 1946 he was appointed to the Wellcome chair of tropical medicine in the University of London. The advice he was able to give on the developmental phases of the malaria parasites was of great importance in the discovery of the exoerythrocytic phase of the parasites. Fairley was elected a fellow of the Royal Society in 1942. In 1918 he was appointed OBE, in 1941 CBE, and in 1950 KBE. He was awarded many honorary degrees and medals by universities, colleges, and learned societies. He was honorary secretary of the Royal Society of Tropical Medicine and Hygiene from 1930 to 1951 and its president in 1951–3.

Fairley's health began to fail at a comparatively early age, slowly bringing his professional life to an end. He resigned from his chair in 1949 and died at his home, The Grove, in Sonning, Berkshire, on 19 April 1966.

JOHN BOYD, rev.

Sources *Medical Journal of Australia*, 2 (1969), 991 · personal knowledge (1981) · private information (1981)
Archives RS, MSS
Likenesses W. Dargie, portrait, 1944, priv. coll. · W. Stoneman, photograph, 1946, NPG, RS · probably by C. J. Hackett, two photographs, 1956, RS · W. Stoneman, two photographs, RS
Wealth at death £4706: probate, 9 Aug 1966, *CGPLA Eng. & Wales*

Fairlie, Alison Anna Bowie (1917–1993), scholar of French literature, was born on 23 May 1917 at the manse, Lerwick, Shetland, the eldest daughter of Robert Paul Fairlie, minister of the Church of Scotland, and his wife, Florence Annie Allan, *née* Wilson. She always maintained an intense feeling for her homeland. Scotland was where she spent most of every August, on holiday with her family, up to 1947, and thereafter she returned at every opportunity. She was educated at Ardrossan Academy, Dumfries Academy, and then, between the ages of twelve and seventeen, as a boarder at Penrhos College, Colwyn Bay. As an undergraduate at St Hugh's College, Oxford, she came into contact with the group of scholars who were then laying the foundations for Oxford's outstanding contribution to the development of French studies as a modern university discipline. She remembered with particular pleasure the lectures or tutorials given by Gustave Rudler, Will Moore,

Alison Anna Bowie Fairlie (1917–1993), by unknown photographer

Enid Starkie, E. A. Francis, Cécile Hugon, Rhoda Sutherland, L. A. Bisson, and H. J. Hunt. At Oxford she also joined the Communist Party, at the same time as her exact contemporary Denis Healey and many others of their generation. She joined not because she had deeply studied Marxist doctrine, nor even because she had been persuaded by its principal tenets, but as a way of expressing her indignation and disgust at the rise of fascism in Europe. Her membership probably lapsed at the end of her undergraduate career, but throughout her later life her political views remained steadily of a sceptical left-wing kind.

After taking a first in medieval and modern languages in 1938, Fairlie began work on her DPhil thesis, supervised by Rudler. Initially her research was conducted in Paris, but on the outbreak of war she returned to Britain and undertook voluntary work in billeting and rationing offices. Early in 1940 she was advised by the central employment bureau for universities to complete her research. In accordance with this advice she returned to Paris with the Zaharoff research scholarship that she had been awarded in the summer of 1939, and continued research until the fall of France in June 1940. For Fairlie these were months of intensive and exhilarating scholarly enquiry, during which she accumulated the unruly mass of material on nineteenth-century intellectual history that was eventually published, in a pruned and methodized form, in *Leconte de Lisle's Poems on the Barbarian Races* (1947), the book form of her thesis, for which she was awarded a DPhil in 1943. What emerges from her own modestly worded accounts of this period is the single-mindedness of her devotion to scholarship—part of her fully expected the Bibliothèque Nationale to remain open in defiance of the German armies as they advanced on Paris—and the good-humoured courage with which she faced physical danger. By the time she reached Bordeaux, and a cargo steamer prepared to convey her back to Britain, the local docks and shipping offshore were already under German bombardment.

The years 1940–42 saw Fairlie back in Oxford, finishing her thesis. From September 1942 she served for two years as a temporary administrative officer with the Foreign Office, spending most of her time in naval section 6 at Bletchley Park. Her academic career began in the autumn of 1944, when she was appointed lecturer in French at Girton College, Cambridge. She was elected fellow and director of studies in modern languages in 1946, and university lecturer two years later. The arrival of Odette de Mourgues as a research fellow of Girton in 1948 marked the beginning of a long professional collaboration and a lifelong friendship between the two. In 1967 Fairlie became university reader, and in 1972 the first holder of a personal professorship in the Cambridge French department. Although she repeatedly refused offers of professorships at other universities, new and old, her outlook was in no way parochial. In 1968 and 1969 she was elected president of the Society for French Studies; in 1969 a member of the council of the Association Internationale des Études Françaises, becoming one of its vice-presidents in 1983; and in 1972 a member of the editorial board of *French Studies*. Her election to an honorary fellowship of St Hugh's in 1972 gave her particular pleasure. She was elected a fellow of the British Academy in 1984, and became one of the founding honorary senior research fellows of the Institute of Romance Studies, University of London, in 1989.

Very soon after her arrival in Cambridge Fairlie's name became a byword in the university and outside for her abilities as a college teacher. She had an unusual and not entirely comfortable tutorial style. She considered that the function of the tutorial hour was for students to bring and explore their own ideas: *they* were expected to do the talking, with only occasional incisive comments from her. If they had not done enough work, or if their ideas dried up, she would ask a probing question and then simply wait and wait for the answer, the ash on her cigarette growing ever longer and sometimes finally dropping off on her clothes. The silence would grow until it became unbearable, and would at last be broken either by an admission of ignorance from the student or by a pointed remark from her to the effect that such and such 'needed further thought'. Many Girtonians found this technique terrifying.

Fairlie's most remarkable achievement as a university teacher was the central part she played in relaunching modern languages as a serious intellectual discipline in British universities. Until then the subject had been something of a poor relation to history and classics, and had often had little ambition beyond the efficient inculcation of basic linguistic skills. Fairlie brought to the study of French a keen responsiveness to the grain and texture of literary language, and in her own critical writing skilfully exposed layers of implied meaning in works that others had been content to characterize simply as 'masterpieces' or as 'typical of their time'.

In her criticism Fairlie's manner was often one of questioning and speculation, but the questions she asked and the hypotheses she ventured invariably took their cue from the words on the author's page and, far from clothing the literary text in interpretative fantasies, sought to bring the reader back with clearer sight and a renewed power of enjoyment to its central riches. During a period when criticism of French literature suffered from severe factional narrowness and ill temper, she remained generously plural in her interests and approach. While attending closely to the formal and expressive properties of the individual literary work, she remained scrupulously aware that many things lying beyond that work—manuscripts, variant readings or 'sources', the author's personal relationships or his letters—could prompt the scholar to valuable new kinds of critical perception. Perhaps most important of all, the language she herself used was, in its attunement to the subjects discussed, its economy, and its discreet inventiveness, a lesson to all those critics who sought, by their luxuriant verbal displays, to outwit and outwrite their writers.

The close examination of Leconte de Lisle was an improbable training ground for a scholar who later contributed decisively to the study of Constant, Baudelaire, Flaubert, and Nerval. For although the poet in mid-career was still driven by strong sexual and political passions, he had the ambition of becoming the exemplary literary artist of his age and this involved him in an extensive programme of scholarly and semi-scholarly reading. Fairlie took her reader back from the serried verbal textures of Leconte de Lisle's poems to the bibliographical labyrinth in which they had been conceived. What was more impressive, however, than her willingness to document the poet's reading was her insistence upon historicizing his historical project. The historians of Leconte de Lisle's day, upon whose work he drew so trustingly, were often exceptionally unreliable. Their skewed and imprecise vision of the past was then subject to a variety of further distortions, conscious and unconscious, as the poetic imagination played upon it and turned it into verse. Fairlie proved adept at detecting and teasing out the disparate source materials that lay behind Leconte de Lisle's orotund periods. Her readings of the *Poèmes barbares* were a series of elaborate radiographic portraits, and the book as a whole offered a working model of the acquisitive and integrative literary imagination at work.

This quality of Fairlie's book prepared her extremely well for her later researches. Although she never again devoted such intensive scrutiny to any single body of textual sources, her later work was born of the same fascination with literary texts as complex semantic fields. Constant, Baudelaire, Flaubert, and even Nerval, who was extremely erudite in his own fashion, did not call for the same sort of detective work as had Leconte de Lisle. But in Fairlie's view all four writers did demand to be discussed in terms of the co-present and interactive ideas, images, and verbal motifs that their works contained. Her skill in anatomizing such canonical texts as Constant's *Adolphe*, Baudelaire's *Les fleurs du mal*, or Flaubert's *Madame Bovary*, and her ability to preserve, while doing so, an overall sense of their drama, made her essays and monographs into standard works.

Fairlie's 'retirement' was energetic: during it she was a member of the editorial team responsible for the new *Œuvres complètes* of Benjamin Constant and always available to help and encourage an innumerable company of friends, colleagues, and fellow scholars from around the world. Her appetite for experience persisted even after she had been diagnosed as having inoperable lung cancer. Equally persistent, however, was the wish to share her experience with others, and it was this that made her into a compelling literary critic, an inspiring teacher, and an irreplaceable friend. She died at Papworth Hospital near Cambridge on 21 February 1993; her body was cremated at Cambridge. She was unmarried.   MALCOLM BOWIE

Sources *The Independent* (3 March 1993) · *The Times* (4 March 1993) · *WWW* · personal knowledge (2004) · private information (2004) · b. cert. · d. cert.
Likenesses photograph, repro. in *The Independent* · photograph, repro. in *The Times* [*see illus.*]
Wealth at death £312,293: probate, 7 May 1993, *CGPLA Eng. & Wales*

Fairlie, Henry Jones (1924–1990), political journalist and author, was born on 13 January 1924 in Crouch End, London, the second son and fifth child in the family of three sons and four daughters of James Fairlie, journalist, and his wife, Marguerita Vernon. He was educated at Highgate School and Corpus Christi College, Oxford, where he read modern history, obtaining second-class honours in 1945, and becoming secretary of the union in the Trinity term of 1945. A weak heart disqualified him from any form of military service, both during the Second World War and after it, but an interest in liberal politics led to his being appointed a lobby correspondent for the *Manchester Evening News* at the remarkably early age of twenty-one. He progressed from there to *The Observer* in 1948, and then in 1950 to *The Times*, where he wrote political leaders.

Anonymity, however, did not suit Fairlie, and in 1954 he accepted an invitation to join the staff of *The Spectator*. Building there on the foundations laid by his former colleague, Hugh Massingham of *The Observer*, he perfected the journalistic art form of the modern political column. Irreverent, witty, and seldom anything but well informed, Fairlie's weekly columns (appearing first under the pseudonym of Trimmer and later under his own byline) became required reading for politicians of all parties. This achievement was all the more notable as the time he spent at *The Spectator* was relatively short, barely two years in duration. But it was during this period that Fairlie made perhaps his most lasting contribution to the vocabulary of British politics, putting into circulation the term 'the establishment' to describe those who, while often unelected, controlled the power points of British public life.

In some ways, it was an uncharacteristic notion for Fairlie to have propagated—the phrase had, in fact, first been given its modern usage by A. J. P. Taylor—since by the mid-1950s his own political stance had become that of a romantic, if radical, tory. It was this which gave him his curious affinity with Harold Macmillan, to whom, especially after he started writing for the *Daily Mail*, he enjoyed regular access. Fairlie, however, was often wayward in his political judgements, and it was typical of this flaw in his journalistic make-up that he should have predicted in the *Mail* that Labour under Hugh Gaitskell would defeat Macmillan in the 1959 general election. The *Mail*, after the tories had won a majority of 100, soon dispensed with his services. Thereafter he found an impecunious refuge in the columns of *Time and Tide*, where (as in *Encounter*) some of his more penetrating longer articles appeared in the early 1960s. He also enjoyed a brief Indian summer in another mass-circulation paper, the *Daily Express*, with some notable news scoops in the turbulent political year of 1963. Well before this, however, his personal difficulties had tended to overshadow his professional success, as marked in television and radio as it had originally been in the press. Always hospitable and, when in funds, generous to a fault, Fairlie exercised only the loosest control over the management of his own life. Pursued by debt, hounded by libel writs, and regularly the subject of bankruptcy proceedings (leading on one occasion to his imprisonment in Brixton), he eventually left Britain for the United States in 1965, never to return to his native land.

In America, Fairlie built up a fresh, if equally controversial, journalistic reputation. Moving now steadily to the left, he early on attacked the power of money in American politics, as symbolized by the Kennedys. His assault on the funding of the Kennedy Library in Boston—originally published in the *Sunday Telegraph*—briefly became a *cause célèbre* in American newspapers, making him for a time something of a pariah in a Kennedy-nostalgic Washington. But even when denied his customary access to the power structure, Fairlie could feel that his own fame was secure. His first, and best, book, *The Life of Politics* (published in 1968 but largely written before he left Britain), drew on all his experience of Westminster and remains one of the most vivid defences of the parliamentary system. His subsequent two books—*The Kennedy Promise* (1973) and *The Spoiled Child of the Western World* (1976)—concentrated on critical American themes but were respectfully received on both sides of the Atlantic.

Boyish in looks and capable, when sober, of being captivating in conversation, Fairlie exerted a powerful charm, particularly upon women. He was married in 1949 to Lisette Todd, daughter of Arthur Todd Phillips, architect. They had a son and two daughters. Fairlie's bohemian streak never allowed him to accept the normal constraints of matrimony (although never divorced, he and his wife separated in 1967). The tales of his various *affaires* were legendary but were usually related, even by his romantic victims, with affection mingled with exasperated amusement.

Fairlie's last years were spent working for the *New Republic* in Washington, in whose offices he was eventually afforded the unusual facility of a bedroom in which to sleep. It was a striking testimony of the regard in which he was held by all those who shared his consuming interest in 'the life of politics'. He died in a Washington hospital on 25 February 1990, of heart failure.

ANTHONY HOWARD, *rev.*

Sources *The Times* (27 Feb 1990) · *The Independent* (27 Feb 1990) · personal knowledge (1996) · private information (1996)

Fairlie, Robert Francis (1830–1885), civil and mechanical engineer, was born in Glasgow on 5 April 1830, the son of T. Archibald Fairlie, an engineer, and his wife, Margaret McCall. He gained practical experience of locomotive design and construction at Crewe and Swindon. His first appointment was in 1853 as engineer and general manager of the Londonderry and Coleraine Railway, but he did not stay long in Ireland before accepting a post with the Bombay and Baroda Railway of India.

By the early 1860s Fairlie had returned to Britain and set up in business at 56 Gracechurch Street, London, as a railway consultant. On 5 January 1862 he married Eliza Ann (1844?–1907), daughter of the well-known New Cross builder of small locomotives, George *England. The couple had five children. According to his *Times* obituary, Fairlie had been married once before.

In 1864 and 1865 Fairlie patented his ideas for an articulated locomotive intended to meet the problems of railway operation in mountainous areas, with sharp curves and steep gradients, at the same time reducing the need for heavy expenditure on civil works and permanent way. He was not the first to consider this concept, but earlier experiments in the United States and Belgium had not been successful, and Fairlie led the way in arriving at a practical solution. His first locomotive type consisted of two powered bogies pivoted at each end of a frame, which carried the boiler, together with fuel and water supplies. The boiler had two barrels back-to-back, with a central firebox and cab, and smokeboxes at the outer ends. Thus, the whole of the weight of the fuel and water, as well as that of the locomotive, was used for adhesion, while the pivoting of the bogies afforded a flexibility which a long fixed wheelbase could not provide. Initial difficulties in steaming were resolved by the provision of separate fireboxes, and problems in providing suitable steam and exhaust connections to the cylinders were also overcome.

The first two locomotives built under the patents were for the Neath and Brecon Railway in 1865 and the Anglesey Central Railway in 1866. They were constructed by J. Cross of St Helens, Lancashire, who also built three locomotives for Queensland, Australia, which were, however, rejected because of defective construction and working. After this inauspicious start, the order for a double engine by the Ffestiniog Railway Company, placed with George England in September 1868, marked an important turning point. This was delivered in August 1869 from Hatcham ironworks, which was, by that time, being run by Fairlie and partners as the Fairlie Engine and Steam Carriage Company.

Little Wonder, as the locomotive was called, was designed

to haul slate trains on the 1 ft 11½ in. gauge Ffestiniog Railway in north Wales, a hilly line with tortuous curves. At several sets of trials it demonstrated its capacity to haul much heavier loads than previous locomotives. Its performance demonstrated the practicability of low cost narrow gauge railways to carry substantial loads in difficult country, a principle which was extended to many parts of the then developing world.

Modifications of the original design were introduced in later years, some with single boilers and others featuring one powered and one trailing bogie. Many were built for overseas railways, notably in Australia, Brazil, New Zealand, and Russia. On the Moscow and St Petersburg line 'Fairlie's Railway' was so successful that the tsar had a special gold medal struck in Fairlie's honour. The concept was also taken up in America by the Mason Machine Works of Taunton, Massachusetts, who built some 150 locomotives known as Mason–Fairlies between 1871 and 1889, all except the first being to the single boiler design. Later, construction was carried on by the American Locomotive Company until 1914.

Around the turn of the century attention began to be centred on the Kitson–Meyer and Beyer–Garratt types of articulated locomotive, in which steam for the powered bogies was supplied by a single large boiler; later Fairlie designs, known as 'Modified Fairlies', had many points of resemblance to these. Eventually, some fifty-two railways were to see Fairlie locomotives, which continued to be built into the 1920s, notable examples being three for Mexico, turned out in 1911 and weighing 138 tons.

From 1870 onwards Fairlie secured orders for patent locomotives for railway development all over the world. However, he was more than a locomotive engineer, and offered a comprehensive design and construction package, including rolling stock, generally featuring his type of locomotive. He advocated narrow gauge lines (but of wider gauge than the Ffestiniog Railway) permitting the use of sharp curves and steep gradients. In 1872 he published *Railways or No Railways*, which developed his ideas. By the early 1870s Fairlie's business had become a design agency called the Fairlie Engine and Rolling Stock Company, with its locomotives being built by the Vulcan Foundry, the Avonside Engine Company, and Yorkshire Engine Company to virtually standard designs. Fairlie was a member of the Institution of Mechanical Engineers, 1857–72.

In December 1873 Fairlie was commissioned to undertake a number of railway projects in the republic of Venezuela. He suffered sunstroke soon after landing at Trinidad, and this was followed by jungle fever while surveying the marshes near Puerto Cabello. Fairlie returned to Britain, but his health never fully recovered. However, he continued his business, selling patent locomotives.

Fairlie died at his London home, Woodlands, 13 Church Buildings, Clapham, on 31 July 1885. His business interests were continued by his children, three of whom made their lives in Peru and Chile. One of them, Frank Archibald Fairlie, was locomotive superintendent of the Nitrate Railways (1911–20) and, as such, had the care of locomotives built to his father's designs.

Fairlie's contribution to the development of the steam locomotive lay in the application of basic principles to a novel form of construction. His ideas were later improved upon but, on a number of railways in hilly terrain, his designs lasted until the steam locomotive itself was replaced by diesel or electric traction.

GEOFFREY HUGHES

Sources *The Times* (3 Aug 1885) · R. A. S. Abbott, *The Fairlie locomotive* (1970) · *The Times* (18 Feb 1870) · *The Times* (1 March 1870) · P. J. G. Ransom, *Narrow gauge steam: its origins and world-wide development* (1996) · L. Day and I. McNeil, eds., *Biographical dictionary of the history of technology* (1996) · L. Wiener, *Articulated locomotives* (1930) · P. C. Dewhurst and H. Holcroft, 'The Fairlie locomotive', *Transactions* [Newcomen Society], 34 (1961–2), 105–32; 39 (1966–7), 1–34 · M. Seymour, 'Robert Francis Fairlie, 1831–1885', Ffestiniog Railway Co., Porthmadog, Wales · *DNB* · *CGPLA Eng. & Wales* (1885) · d. cert. · parish register (births and baptisms), 5 April 1830, Glasgow, Lanarkshire

Archives Ffestiniog Railway Co., Porthmadog, Wales

Wealth at death £17,416 1s. 11d.: probate, 12 Nov 1885, *CGPLA Eng. & Wales*

Fairman, William Blennerhasset (*fl.* 1798–1837), army officer and Orangeman, was probably born in south-east England in the mid-1770s, and had family ties with the Netherlands. In July 1798 he unsuccessfully sought a commission in the Cambridgeshire militia, but he was recruited elsewhere and after the resumption of war with France in 1803 was involved in the construction of fortifications on the coast of Kent. He was then appointed to an ensigncy in the reserve, but subsequently placed on half pay and returned to the militia. In early 1807 Fairman was employed as a recruiting officer, in which role he had limited success, but was subsequently commissioned as a lieutenant in the 18th Royal Irish regiment and posted to Curaçao in the West Indies. On the island he assumed the role of quarter- and barrack-master-general and then in August 1808 became aide-de-camp to the governor, an appointment that carried the honorary 'colonial rank' of lieutenant-colonel, which Fairman thereby considered himself entitled to use in later life. By September 1809, however, he was back in London petitioning the commander-in-chief for speedy promotion from his substantive rank of lieutenant on the strength of his zeal for the service. In August 1810 he was commissioned as a captain in the 4th Ceylon regiment, but was placed on half pay in December 1815 and retired from the army in 1826, still in the substantive rank of captain.

In itself Fairman's undistinguished military career did little to mark him out from the hundreds of other junior officers who struggled unsuccessfully for glory and fortune during the Napoleonic wars. It was during this period, however, that he began a pattern of behaviour which was to lead to his ending his active life in a blaze of notoriety. Fairman was clearly convinced that he deserved better from his country, and lobbied the influential, from the prince of Wales and successive prime ministers downwards, with assorted schemes for national salvation coupled with demands for remuneration for previous services rendered. He claimed to have himself first conceived the scheme for the fortification of Kent, and to have been the originator of the expansion of the militia in 1802–3. An 1804 pamphlet, *A letter on the expediency of allowing a drawback on the duties on wines for the consumption of the army*, was followed in 1813 by printed fulminations against the 'tyranny' of President Madison of the USA, and private exhortations to Lord Liverpool to use the militia to launch an immediate amphibious invasion of Normandy. A contemporary dictionary of authors (J. Walkins and F. Jhobert, *Biographical Dictionary of Authors*, 1816) identified him as the editor of 'a short-lived periodical work … the *Military Magazine*'. In 1814 a pamphlet opposing the reduction of the forces was prefaced by a dedication to Lord Palmerston in which the author acknowledged himself 'a disappointed man'.

Fairman was left to nurse his disappointment in obscurity, living a bachelor existence in London coffee houses, making abortive forays into political journalism, and being sued at least once for debt. Like some other discontented former soldiers he had joined the Orange order, in 1814, and during the 1820s rose in its ramshackle ranks to become deputy grand master of London. In 1832, having lost none of his visionary grandiloquence, he succeeded in bringing himself to the attention of George, Lord Kenyon, and the duke of Cumberland, who, desperate to promote tory recovery after the split over Catholic emancipation in 1829, employed him as deputy grand secretary for Great Britain, with a brief to reorganize and expand the movement. Fairman himself, however, had wilder ideas and seemed to be contemplating mobilizing the Orangemen in support of a *coup d'état* to install Cumberland as regent or even king.

Whatever Fairman's intentions, his bubble soon burst. He travelled the country during 1832 and 1833, visiting the small and scattered Orange lodges, boosting morale but not numbers, and raising insufficient subscriptions to cover his own lavish expenses. By the autumn of 1834 he was losing the confidence of his employers and resigned as deputy grand secretary. In the following year he became a focus of parliamentary investigation of Orangeism and was questioned at length by a select committee. When ordered in August 1835 to produce a letter-book dealing with military lodges, he flatly refused and absconded when a warrant was issued for his arrest. Finally, early in 1836, some of Fairman's letters somehow came into the hands of Joseph Hume, who used them in a further devastating attack on the Orange order, which left Cumberland with no option but to dissolve it.

Fairman's slide into the underworld was now final. Late in 1837 he wrote to Sir Robert Peel to ask him to present a petition exposing 'whig delinquincies', but the latter refused, and it is likely, but not certain, that Fairman shortly afterwards died, in a state of reinforced disappointment.   JOHN WOLFFE

Sources BL, Peel, Liverpool and Windham MSS, Add. MS 37889, fol. 37 [esp. memorial by W. B. F. to the commander-in-chief, 11 Sept 1809] · H. Senior, *Orangeism in Ireland and Britain, 1795–1836* (1966) · 'Select committee … into the origin, nature, extent, and tendency of Orange institutions', *Parl. papers* (1835), vol. 17, no. 605 · W. B. Fairman, *The reduction of the forces* (1814) · W. B. Fairman, *A series of letters … on the existing differences between England and America* (1813) · W. B. Fairman, *Ways and means: submitted to, and approved, by the late Mr Perceval* (1815) · J. Wolffe, *The protestant crusade in Great Britain, 1829–1860* (1991) · BL, Add. MS 35670, fol. 222 · Add. MS 40424, fol. 220
Archives BL, Peel, Liverpool, and Windham MSS · NRA, priv. coll., Kenyon MSS

Fairweather [*née* Runciman]**, Margaret** (1901–1944), airwoman, was born at West Denton Hall, near Newcastle upon Tyne, on 23 September 1901, the second in a family of two sons and three daughters of Walter *Runciman, first Viscount Runciman (1870–1949), and his wife, Hilda Stevenson (1869–1956) [*see* Runciman, Hilda]. Margie, as she was always known, was educated initially at home together with her younger brother Steven (later Sir Steven Runciman) by a governess who taught them Greek and Latin at an early age. She then attended a number of educational institutions including The Mount, a Quaker school in York, and Notting Hill high school, from where she went to Girton College, Cambridge. After a year she dropped out of Girton to study singing in Paris, though she never performed professionally. She married Roderick Sydney Nettleton King-Farlow (1900–1988), the son of Sir Sydney Charles Nettleton King-Farlow, at St Margaret's, Westminster, on 15 July 1925. A daughter was born in 1931. The marriage ended in divorce in 1936.

In the autumn of 1936 Margie learned to fly at Newcastle Aero Club and was issued with her aviator's certificate (licence no. 14687) by the Royal Aero Club on 13 January 1937. She was planning to fly solo to Australia but changed her mind when she met a fellow pilot, Douglas Keith Fairweather (1891–1944), son of Sir Walter Fairweather. They were married on 28 March 1938. In that year Lord Runciman was sent on the ill-fated mission to Prague to mediate between the German and Czech governments. Fairweather flew out herself to visit him. During a European tour that same year she and Douglas, under the guise of tourists, photographed unrecorded German airfields. She also sent back letters to her brother Steven which seemingly contained only trivial domestic details. On her return, however, she decoded these to recover intelligence data.

With the threat of war looming, in October 1938 the Civil Air Guard scheme was inaugurated to provide subsidized training of pilots through the civil flying clubs. As experienced pilots, Margie and her husband became instructors at Renfrew. Douglas Fairweather was one of the first to sign contracts with the British Overseas Airways Corporation (BOAC) for service with the Air Transport Auxiliary (ATA) in September 1939.

Many women, qualified flying instructors with considerable flying experience, volunteered to serve with the ATA. However, the pilots enrolled by BOAC under the ATA scheme were employed in RAF ferry pilots' pools and the RAF would not agree to the employment of women in their ferry pools. This problem was solved in December 1939 when Pauline Gower (who became commandant of the women's ATA) was informed that a small pool of eight women based at Hatfield could be formed to ferry Tiger Moths to stored reserves.

With over 1000 flying hours, Margaret Fairweather was one of that select band who signed contracts with the ATA on 1 January 1940. This departure from tradition caused a furore in a world in which professional women were still a novelty. Press and newsreel gave full publicity to the event and the so-called 'ATA girls' were under constant scrutiny. However, ferrying Tiger Moths from Hatfield to storage reserves, some as far away as Kinloss, Perth, and Lossiemouth, and returning by overnight train, often with no sleeper in midwinter, was not the glamorous occupation some imagined. In July 1941 ATA women pilots were cleared to fly operational aircraft and Margaret Fairweather was one of the first four chosen to do practice landings in a Hurricane. These four carried a burden of responsibility as the future of all women pilots in the ATA depended on them.

Meanwhile Douglas Fairweather was joint commanding officer at Prestwick. In 1942 he was posted to no. 1 ferry pool, White Waltham, to take charge of the air movements flight. Margie was then posted to join him. For the rest of her time there she was engaged in communication duties and it was on one such assignment that she met her death—the only one not to survive among the original eight who served from the very beginning.

Gradually more operational types of plane were being flown by women and the progression was made from single engine to twin aircraft to advanced twin, and eventually eleven women pilots were qualified to fly four-engined aircraft. Fairweather was one of the eleven. She was considered by her fellow pilots to be one of the most intelligent and able, though rather quiet and self-effacing. In fact, according to her daughter, her nickname was Mrs Cold Front.

On 3 April 1944 Douglas Fairweather volunteered to go to Prestwick to collect an ambulance case requiring special treatment. In appalling weather, somewhere over the Irish Sea, the Anson came down and both he and the nurse travelling with him were lost. Margie gave birth to their daughter Elizabeth a few days later. Margie returned to flying only to be killed herself four months later. She was piloting a Proctor to Scotland on 4 August 1944 with two passengers on board when the engine failed near Malpas, Cheshire. All three were taken to Chester Royal Infirmary where Fairweather died soon afterwards. Her passengers were her sister, the Hon. Kitty Farrer, adjutant of the ATA, and Louis Kendrick of the Ministry of Aircraft Production. They recovered, escaping with injuries. Douglas Fairweather's body was washed up on the Ayrshire coast. Margaret Fairweather and he were both buried in the small churchyard of Dunure, Ayrshire.   ENID deBois

Sources L. Curtis, *The forgotten pilots: a story of the Air Transport Auxiliary, 1939–45* (1971) · private information (2004) [Sir Steven Runciman, brother; Mrs Ann Shukman, daughter; fellow ATA pilots] · *DNB* · *WW* · *The Times* (5 Aug 1944)
Likenesses photographs, British Women Pilots' Association, Weybridge, Surrey
Wealth at death £57,828 5s. 10d.: probate, 13 April 1945, *CGPLA Eng. & Wales*

Faithfull, Emily (1835–1895), publisher and women's activist, was born on 27 May 1835 at Headley rectory, Surrey, the youngest of five daughters and the last of eight children of Ferdinand Faithfull, rector of Headley, and his wife, Elizabeth Mary Harrison, *née* Timberlake. Little is known of her early life, but she was educated at home and attended a school in Kensington. She was presented at court in 1857.

During the 1850s a movement was growing in support of women's legal, economic, and educational rights. A group of women who had come together under the aegis of Barbara Leigh Smith (later Bodichon), formed the Langham Place circle (named after their meeting place) and produced in 1858 the first number of the *English Woman's Journal* (later the *Englishwoman's Review*) which was to be the organ for the circle's ideas. The young Emily Faithfull joined this well-connected group, which included Bessie Rayner Parkes, Jessie Boucherett, Emily Davies, and Helen Blackburn. The group pressed for legal reform in women's status (including suffrage), explored new areas for women's employment, and campaigned for improved educational opportunities for girls and women. Emily Faithfull was at the heart of this multi-faceted campaign and identified with all three dimensions, although she is best known for her work in women's employment. Her public support of the enfranchisement of women developed later from her investigations and practical campaigns surrounding employment, but from the beginning she was actively involved in the successful movement led by Emily Davies to have the university local examinations opened to women, which began in 1858.

Early on members of the group began to explore new openings for respectable employment for all classes of women, and in 1859 they formed the Society for Promoting the Employment of Women. One possibility considered was that of compositor, a skilled trade almost wholly confined to men, already effectively unionized and jealously guarded against both unskilled machine operators and any incursions by women. Bessie Parkes bought a small printing press, and she and Emily Faithfull employed a compositor, Austin Holyoake (brother of George Jacob Holyoake), to give instruction in composing. On the basis of this experience they concluded that composing could be a suitable occupation for women. To this end, on 25 March 1860, Emily Faithfull opened the Victoria Press at Great Coram Street, London. She invested her own capital in the press and had the financial backing of another committee member of the Society for Promoting the Employment of Women, G. W. Hastings.

The press employed at the outset some semi-experienced female compositors, who existed despite the trade restrictions practised by men, but the venture was to remain an irritant to many compositors and others in the printing trade. It was nevertheless a commercial success, although the women compositors only composed and proof-read, unlike later women printers working for the Women's Printing Society (founded in 1876 by Emma Paterson's Women's Protective and Provident League, with which Emily Faithfull was also associated), who also

Emily Faithfull (1835–1895), by Leonida Caldesi & Co.

carried out both imposition and 'making up' (making up the type into pages and placing them in the iron frame or chase for printing). Initially Emily Faithfull both printed and published, one of her earliest works being *The Victoria Regia* (1861), edited by Adelaide Ann Proctor. The work and the press attracted the approval of Queen Victoria, and in that same year Emily Faithfull was appointed by royal warrant 'Printer and Publisher in Ordinary to Her Majesty'. In 1863 she was the founder editor of the *Victoria Magazine*, a monthly periodical, to which she contributed until it ceased publication in 1880. The press published the *Transactions* of the National Association for the Promotion of Social Science from 1860 to 1864. Emily Faithfull was connected with the association, and remained for the rest of her life actively engaged in promoting women's employment and their right to enjoy educational opportunity and legal status equivalent to that of men. In 1862 the press moved to Farringdon Street, London, where the printing was carried out with steam presses, and in 1867 she handed the management of the press to William Wilfred Head, who bought her out in 1869 and continued to run the press as a vehicle for the employment of women until 1882.

In 1864 Emily Faithfull became caught up in a divorce case when Admiral Henry Codrington sought a divorce from his wife on grounds of adultery. Helen Codrington

counter-claimed, as she was able to do under the 1857 Marriage and Divorce Act, on grounds which included the accusation that in October 1856 he had attempted to rape Emily Faithfull while she was a guest in their house. At first Emily Faithfull agreed to give evidence on behalf of Mrs Codrington but later changed her mind. The reasons for this are not clear, but her own reputation, at risk by virtue of an association with a divorce case, would have been even more vulnerable had she agreed to take the stand. There is also a suggestion that she was threatened with further counter-claims by Admiral Codrington. She exercised discretion and withdrew.

During her continuing association with the Victoria Press and the *Victoria Magazine* Emily Faithfull became a writer as well as an editor. In 1868 she published her only novel, *Change upon Change*, a tragic romance with an underlying theme about the need for women to have access to education, training, and work if they were not to be at risk of being destroyed by their often frivolous and trivial schooling and their dependence upon men. The book was published in America as *A Reed Shaken with the Wind* in 1873, at the time of her first visit to the United States. She became a prolific journalist and author, contributing articles to the *Lady's Pictorial* and the *Pall Mall Gazette*, as well as the *Victoria Magazine*. One of her obituarists described her as a very popular lecturer on both sides of the Atlantic, and her visits to America (the second and third taking place in 1882–3 and 1883–4) were to lecture as well as to investigate women's employment in the USA. She was also associated with educational developments in America and was invited to open a kindergarten in San Francisco which was named after her. Her second book, *Three Visits to America* (1884), was a collection of her writings, lectures, and impressions, and in it she made known her views on employment, education, and women's legal status, including suffrage. Like other members of the Langham Place circle Faithfull did not feel it necessary to refrain from commenting upon votes for women because she was already engaged in promoting women's employment. The fear that suffrage supporters might taint other campaigns, because the issue was the least acceptable or popular, did cause activists to exercise caution but did not prevent them from expressing firm opinions. As early as 1870 Faithfull wrote to *The Times* supporting the enfranchisement of women and in *Three Visits* she called for 'political status' for women, arguing that there was 'an inseparable connection between political power and the redress of social grievances'. Women's suffrage was an 'urgent necessity' not an issue of 'abstract justice'.

Faithfull benefited in her career as a lecturer from the gift of a 'singularly musical voice' (according to her obituarist in the *Illustrated London News*), 'which she used to great effect on the platform, though it was heard to better advantage in private readings'. Emily Faithfull used her musical voice in a two-year period from 1872 in a series of dramatic readings. She had theatrical connections, and in 1881 she founded the International Musical, Dramatic and

Literary Association, an organization to protect the rights of composers and artists.

Emily Faithfull was a prolific author, and a dedicated propagandist and pioneer for women's rights in employment and other spheres. Her contributions were both practical and exhortatory, and she succeeded in carrying out her self-appointed tasks at the same time as appealing to popular audiences and retaining the patronage of Queen Victoria, who was no general supporter of women's rights. In 1886 she received £100 from the royal bounty, in 1888 she was presented with an inscribed engraved portrait of the queen in recognition of her dedicated work over thirty years in the interests of women, and in 1889 she was awarded a civil-list pension of £50.

Faithfull's photograph in late middle age shows an ample woman with a benign expression, dressed in all the accoutrements of Victorian middle-class womanhood. This respectable daughter of an Anglican clergyman had an eclectic and varied career, which included challenging one of the most tightly regulated and jealously guarded of the older trades, and speaking publicly about acutely sensitive issues. She died, aged sixty, on 31 May 1895, at 10 Plymouth Grove, Manchester, lamented by her sister, Mrs John George Fleet of Chiswick. She herself was unmarried, but left a legacy of writings and activity in one of the most controversial issues of her age.   FELICITY HUNT

Sources W. E. Fredeman, 'Emily Faithfull and the Victoria Press: an experiment in sociological bibliography', *The Library*, 5th ser., 29 (1974), 139–64 · J. S. Stone, 'More light on Emily Faithfull and the Victoria Press', *The Library*, 5th ser., 33 (1978), 63–7 · *The Times* (3 June 1895), 4 · *ILN* (15 June 1895), 735 · *Men and women of the time* (1895) · W. W. Head, *The Victoria Press* (1869) · *DNB* · private information (2004) · d. cert.

Archives Boston PL, corresp.

Likenesses L. Caldesi & Co., photograph, NPG [*see illus.*] · photograph, repro. in *ILN*

Wealth at death £1081 10s. 2d.: probate, 30 Aug 1895, *CGPLA Eng. & Wales*

Faithfull, Lilian Mary (1865–1952), headmistress, was born on 12 March 1865 in Hoddesdon, Hertfordshire, daughter of Francis Grantham Faithfull (1832–1892), clerk to the Merchant Taylors' Company, and his wife, Edith, *née* Lloyd. There were eight children (three boys and five girls) in the family. Emily *Faithfull was a cousin. There being few girls' schools then that provided solid teaching in classics and mathematics, her father, recognizing Lilian's ability, sent her to his brother-in-law's prep school, The Grange, in Hoddesdon, where she was the only girl among twenty-five boys. In her memoirs she paid tribute to the thoroughness with which they were taught. After The Grange, she learned at home and through the university extension movement, which had begun to provide lectures in history, literature, archaeology, and economics in provincial centres. In 1883 she went up to Somerville College, Oxford, where she was captain of hockey and obtained a first class in English language and literature in 1887. As Oxford degrees remained closed to women, she could not graduate, though she claimed an *ad eundem* MA from Trinity College, Dublin, in 1905. She acted as secretary to the principal of Somerville, Madeleine Shaw

Lilian Mary Faithfull (1865–1952), by unknown photographer, in or before 1922

Lefevre, during 1887–8, and then taught for a year at Oxford high school.

After holding a post as lecturer in English at the Royal Holloway College (1889–94), Lilian Faithfull was appointed to succeed Cornelia Schmitz as vice-principal of the ladies' department of King's College, London, in Kensington Square, which she described as 'one of the happiest educational posts for women in England' (Faithfull, *House of my Pilgrimage*, 102). This establishment aimed to provide women with the same sort of cultural opportunities as the university extension lectures organized by Oxford and Cambridge, and women of all ages from seventeen to seventy came to Kensington Square to hear lectures by professors from King's College. Lilian Faithfull helped to bring about a change of emphasis from passive lecture attendance to the pursuit of courses of study leading to university examinations, degrees, and diplomas. The serious study of English literature was particularly encouraged. Students holding local authority scholarships while training to be teachers were admitted to read for degrees, and they helped to raise academic standards in the department. She also introduced sporting activities, being president of the All-England Women's Hockey Association. During her thirteen years as vice-principal the numbers doubled, a hall of residence was opened (1897), household science was developed as a serious branch of study, and the debt to King's was cleared.

In 1906, after the death of Dorothea Beale, Lilian Faithfull was persuaded to apply for the post of principal of Cheltenham Ladies' College. She was reluctant; her only experience of girls' schools was the one year she had spent at Oxford high school. The vast Gothic pile which symbolized the lofty ideals of the high-churchwoman Miss Beale daunted her, and she likened entering the room for her interview by the council to entering 'a church full of silent prayer' (Faithfull, *House of my Pilgrimage*, 128). She was never to shake off her awe at having inherited the mantle of Miss Beale—when she received the post 'it seemed to me that I had been appointed to a high and holy office'. But, she said, 'one of the greatest conquests [which] Miss Beale made was the conquest of her successor' (ibid., 131).

Cheltenham Ladies' College, when Lilian Faithfull arrived in 1907, was a community of over 900 which provided education at every stage; there was a kindergarten, a main school of some 600 pupils (more than half of them boarders), a university college with young women studying for external degrees, and three departments for the training of teachers—secondary, elementary, and kindergarten. Lilian Faithfull, though she was to make some innovations, introducing for instance a very successful course in library training, did not try to make changes to Miss Beale's structure. She had, after all, taken over most of her predecessor's staff, and knew how they treasured the Beale inheritance.

What was unusual in Lilian Faithfull's regime, at a time when headmistresses tended to be remote and austere, was her easy manner with her pupils and her concern for their welfare—though in a school of that size it was impossible to know any individual well. Margaret Kennedy, who portrayed her as Miss Helen Butterfield in her novel *The Constant Nymph* (1924), described her as having:

a most beautiful voice … And she saw the girls if anybody had died, or if they'd done anything perfectly dreadful. And she used to give addresses to us on Fortitude and Friendship and things like that. She was very nice looking and had lovely clothes. She very nearly knew our names.

In fact, Lilian Faithfull was to recall how often during the First World War she had to break the news of the death of a father or brother; she provided an intercession room near her own office where girls could pray and find privacy. She also organized a Red Cross hospital in one of the boarding-houses. Her Saturday talks to the senior girls, collected under the title *You and I* (1927), often took the form of acute and amusing criticism of different aspects of schoolgirl behaviour—on emotional friendships, on the sadly limited topics of school conversation, on slang. She encouraged the pupils to respond and printed some of their comments as appendages to her own text.

Lilian Faithfull had always taken an enthusiastic interest in public affairs. As a leading member of the Association of Head Mistresses she was appointed to the departmental committee on the organization of secondary education in Wales (1919). In 1920 she was one of the six Gloucestershire members elected to the newly founded church assembly. In the same year she became a JP for Cheltenham, as one of the first women magistrates to be appointed in England. She took a particular interest in penal reform. Finding these duties hard to combine with her heavy administrative load at Cheltenham, she resigned in 1922 at the early age of fifty-seven, leaving her successor, Beatrice Sparks, with her greater experience of schools, to reshape the college to suit educational needs which had vastly changed since Miss Beale's time. She was awarded an honorary MA degree from Oxford in 1925 and the CBE in 1926.

In retirement Lilian Faithfull spent half the year in Four Winds, the thatched cottage she had built herself in Birdlip on the southern edge of the Cotswolds, and the other half in London, where she was active in working to provide better conditions for the poor of Shoreditch. She founded the Under-Forty Club to interest the prosperous young with her aims, and inaugurated a cookhouse in Marylebone to provide good cheap meals. All this was described in *The Evening Crowns the Day* (1940), the postscript to her memoirs, *In the House of my Pilgrimage* (1924), and 'a record of the miscellaneous activities which have occupied my leisure' in retirement. (Her private interest was in cars and driving.) She continued to be active in educational organizations, as vice-chair of the Conservative Teachers' Advisory Committee, of which she was a founder, the National Council of Education in Canada, which reflected her interest in pupil and teacher exchanges between Britain and the dominions, and the International Federation of University Women. She died on 2 May 1952 at Faithfull House, Cheltenham, a home for elderly people which she had helped found, and was buried in Cheltenham. GILLIAN AVERY

Sources L. M. Faithfull, *In the house of my pilgrimage* (1924) · L. M. Faithfull, *The evening crowns the day* (1940) · *WWW* · A. K. Clarke, *A history of the Cheltenham Ladies' College, 1853–1953* (1953) · *Cheltenham Chronicle* (10 May 1952) · E. Ratcliffe, *The Caxton of her age: the career and family background of Emily Faithfull* (1993) · *Somerville College register, 1879–1971* [1972] · P. Adams, *Somerville for women: an Oxford college, 1879–1993* (1996) · N. Marsh, *The history of Queen Elizabeth College: one hundred years of university education in Kensington* (1986) · *Men and women of the time* (1899) · b. cert.

Archives Cheltenham Ladies' College, MSS

Likenesses Lafayette, photograph, 1907, Cheltenham Ladies' College · photograph, in or before 1922, Cheltenham Ladies' College [*see illus.*] · G. Kelly, oils, *c.*1923, Cheltenham Ladies' College · P. Fripp, photograph, *c.*1924, repro. in Faithfull, *In the house of my pilgrimage*, facing p. 280 · E. O. Hoppé, photograph, 1924, repro. in Faithfull, *In the house of my pilgrimage*, frontispiece

Wealth at death £9468 12s. 0d.: probate, 30 Dec 1952, CGPLA Eng. & Wales

Faithfull, Lucy, Baroness Faithfull (1910–1996), social worker and children's campaigner, was born on 26 October 1910 in South Africa, the only daughter and elder child of Sydney Leigh Faithfull, a lieutenant in the Royal Engineers, and his wife, Elizabeth Adie Algie, a nurse. After her father was killed in action in 1916, the family returned to England where, in straitened circumstances, her mother found residential employment. From the age of seven Faithfull was sent to boarding-school, an unhappy experience which was later to influence strongly her determination to confront childhood suffering in all its manifestations. For many years there was no settled family home,

Lucy Faithfull, Baroness Faithfull (1910–1996), by Roger Scruton

as Faithfull and her brother followed their mother to her successive places of employment. In later life she told few of this early deprivation; indeed, many thought that wider family connections had meant privilege which had eased her way into the House of Lords. After her education at Talbot Heath School, Bournemouth, she attended the Sorbonne in Paris and Birmingham University, graduating with a diploma in social sciences from the latter in 1933. Her subsequent career was largely in the field of child care. She was club leader and sub-warden, Birmingham settlement, from 1932 to 1935; assistant organizer of child care, London county council education department, 1935–40; regional welfare officer (evacuation), Ministry of Health, 1940–48; inspector, children's branch, Home Office, 1948–58; and children's officer (1958–70), and then director of social services (1970–74), Oxford city council. She was made OBE in 1972.

In 1975 Faithfull was created Baroness Faithfull of Wolvercote; it was an ironic commentary on political priorities of the period that it was left to a septuagenarian, and subsequently octogenarian, tory peer to take the lead on so many social policy campaigns between 1980 and 1996. She was the only social worker of her generation to be created a life peer, and there were some who felt at the time that she was a curious choice, Oxford city being one of the smallest local authorities, which had just disappeared in the latest reorganization. She was to prove them wrong, for it was in parliament, and in particular in her last decade, that she really flowered. During most of her time in the Lords, she was almost the only member with direct professional experience of services for children in need and social work. She felt that she had an absolute responsibility to act as the voice in parliament of those who worked with and for children, and to advise and educate her colleague peers. She was proud of voting according to a conscience, rather than the party line, often to the despair of tory whips, to some of whom she became known as Lady Faithless; for them the problem was not

just her vote, but the numbers of her colleagues that she persuaded to follow her into the opposition lobbies.

For much of her time in parliament, Faithfull chaired the all-party group on children; from this base she co-ordinated the cross-party campaign for parliamentary time for the Children Act of 1989. Much of the groundwork which had exposed the need for this act had been done in a succession of select committees with which she had a close direct or indirect association in the late 1970s and early 1980s. As the bill was regarded as politically uncontentious (a strange judgement, since it anticipated many of what were to become the social exclusion policies of the 1997 Labour administration), it was introduced in the Lords, where much of the detailed work was done.

One great cause of Faithfull's was to alleviate the brutality with which the criminal justice system could treat children. She was a passionate advocate of the superior approach of the Scottish system of children's panels, and when the possibility of introducing similar reforms into England presented itself in the bill which was to become the Prosecution of Offences Act of 1985, she lobbied energetically throughout. She met the responsible senior Home Office minister, who was unwise enough to patronize her; he, as a barrister, recognized her case, but said that there was no way that it could be a political priority. The faces of the condescending civil servants sheltering behind their minister looked a little different four days later when they sought to negotiate for terms during the tea break as an alternative to her defeating the government. She had persuaded most of the cross-benchers to support her, law lords, bishops, and all.

Faithfull had other campaigns—in particular for mental health and more effective care in the community. She was also most concerned about the resources for social work training, and once used her direct access to the prime minister to lead a delegation of social workers to meet with her. Theirs was not a popular cause of Mrs Thatcher's, but Faithfull, fearless of the handbag, told her at the start of the allotted hour that she should listen and not interrupt. A few days later a discreet announcement eased the crisis of resources. Her last campaign was against the Conservative government's plans to establish a network of commercially managed secure training centres for young offenders under the age of fifteen. She found the idea of profits being made from these children offensive, and challenged the need for more of these expensive facilities when inefficient use was being made of those that already existed. She also played an active role in many voluntary organizations. She was a vice-president of Barnardos; had been a founder, and for many years president, of the National Children's Bureau; was chair of Council of Caldecott, a therapeutic community for children; and gave her name to the Lucy Faithfull Foundation, which pioneered advanced child protection strategies in its work with abusers.

A small, trim figure, usually moving at a brisk trot from one meeting to another, weighed down with at least two briefcases overflowing with paper, Faithfull was, until the end, a very familiar sight in the House of Lords, and to the host of those whom she invited to the succession of campaigning meetings she convened there. Indeed, on the day before her death she hosted a meeting of nearly a hundred friends and colleagues to discuss how the fiftieth anniversary of the Children Act of 1948, to which they had all contributed so much, should be marked. Taken ill at the end of the meeting, and on her way to hospital, she passed the House's electronic screens announcing the order that would require every local authority to prepare a statutory plan for its children services. This had been a missing component of the Children Act of 1989, which had been a major cause of hers all through the 1980s, and she had campaigned ceaselessly for this later 1996 legislation.

Faithfull's last day in the House of Lords was a vignette of her life and summed up both her continuity and her persistence. She made no claims to intellectual brilliance, and could at times be impatient of detail and see or describe things in a broad-brush way. Often, this apparent vagueness could be deceptive, as many a minister found to his cost. She was remorseless in seeking briefing from those from whom she sought advice—successions of notes in indecipherable handwriting would arrive. She died at St Thomas's Hospital, London, on 13 March 1996, following a stroke, and was cremated in Oxford. She was unmarried.   JOHN REA PRICE

Sources *The Times* (14 March 1996) · *The Independent* (15 March 1996) · *The Guardian* (14 March 1996) · private information (2004) [Baroness Park of Monmouth; Simon Rodway] · personal knowledge (2004) · WWW

Archives St Hilda's College, Oxford, MSS

Likenesses R. Scruton, photograph, News International Syndication, London [*see illus.*] · photograph, repro. in *The Independent* · photograph, repro. in *The Guardian* · photographs, priv. coll.

Wealth at death £535,316: probate, 30 May 1996, *CGPLA Eng. & Wales*

Faithorne, William [*known as* William Faithorne the elder] (*c.*1620–1691), engraver, was apprenticed in the Goldsmiths' Company to the printseller William Peake for ten years from 9 October 1635, and the date of birth given here is deduced from this; the traditional date of about 1616 is derived from Buckeridge's assertion in 'An essay towards the English school' that he died aged near seventy-five. The entry records that his father was Daniel Faithorne of London, a lorimer (bridle maker for horses). Peake was the eldest son of Robert Peake, serjeant-painter to James I, and inherited his printselling and stationery business. He was not himself an engraver, and the statement of Faithorne's early biographer John Bagford that he was trained by John Payne is therefore entirely believable. On William Peake's early death in 1639, Faithorne was turned over to complete his apprenticeship with William's son Robert, who had taken over the business and was not an engraver either. The situation was hardly conventional, because in the early 1640s, while Faithorne was still notionally an apprentice, Peake published no fewer than sixteen portrait engravings signed with Faithorne's name. None gives the name of a designer, and they were evidently drawn by Faithorne himself from life or another picture.

The ancestral connection of the Peake family with the royal court ensured that, when Charles I raised his standard at Nottingham in August 1642, Peake enrolled in the royalist army, and Faithorne went with him as an ensign. The two men served in the garrison of Basing House during its long siege and were both captured when it fell in October 1645. Faithorne was then imprisoned in Petre House in Aldersgate Street, but was evidently allowed to take up engraving again, for four plates were published by Peake's associate Thomas Rowlett. Three were of such arch-royalist subjects as the prince of Wales, Prince Rupert of the Rhine, and Endymion Porter, and were after paintings by William Dobson, who had also been apprenticed to William Peake. In style they imitate the manner of the then fashionable Claude Mellan, using parallel lines rather than cross-hatching to create tone. The fourth plate was of the parliamentary general Thomas Fairfax, a print collector himself, and it may have been through his intercession that Faithorne's imprisonment was commuted to banishment. The date of this is not certain, but was probably in 1647 or 1648.

Faithorne went to France, where Bagford records that he was much helped by another great print collector, the Abbé Marolles, whose first collection was purchased by Louis XIV in 1667 and now serves as the foundation of the *cabinet des estampes* in the Bibliothèque Nationale. During these years Faithorne earned a living by making plates for Parisian publishers, especially Herman Weyen. Under the influence of Robert Nanteuil he began to make his own finished portrait drawings in black chalk, both as objects in their own right and as the basis for engravings. He also altered his manner of engraving, which, as George Vertue noted, now reflected that of Antoine Masson.

Faithorne was still in Paris in February 1651, when he signed a petition with twenty-seven of the leading figures of the French print world against a proposed tax on print production, but was back in London by November 1652, when he was made free of the Goldsmiths' Company, having completed his term of service 'long since'. His close links with the international print trade enabled him to establish his own print shop, first 'at the Sign of the Ship within Temple Bar' (by 1654) and then 'next to the Sign of the Drake without Temple Bar' (by 1662). There he took on the role of the old Peake shop as the main importer of foreign prints. He also dealt in artists' materials, and published in 1662 his own translation, *The Art of Graveing and Etching*, of the *Traité des manières de graver en taille douce* which had been written by Abraham Bosse in 1645; he dedicated it to his old master, Robert Peake. Its publication was linked with the appearance of John Evelyn's *Sculptura* in the same year, and Evelyn abandoned his own translation of Bosse so as not to compete with Faithorne's work.

Faithorne continued to engrave himself, and during the 1650s and 1660s made his finest plates, which are of high quality by any standards. His supremacy in London was challenged only by Pierre Lombard and later by David Loggan. These single-sheet portraits he published himself, but his output of this type was small. Most of his plates were made as frontispieces for booksellers, and their quality was much more ordinary. As a publisher, he expanded his range beyond an exclusive concentration on portraiture. A major undertaking was a twelve-sheet map of London published in 1658, which is now extremely rare. He also published many anonymous plates, often copied from continental originals, which he must have had made by apprentices in his shop.

At the Restoration Faithorne was appointed (on 12 October 1660) engraver in copper to the king, doubtless in reward for his devotion to the Stuart cause. Curiously he made no mention of this on his plates, and the appointment remained unknown to his early biographers. He was elected to the livery of the Goldsmiths' Company in May 1660, and served as second warden in 1683 and 1684. In 1679 he declined the position of touchwarden and, in place of paying a fine, presented the company with a painting of Sir Martin Bowes that still hangs in the court room. A marked decline in his output and quality may be seen in the 1670s, and he must have been severely put out by the arrival of Abraham Blooteling and Gerard Valck in 1673 and of Peter Vandrebanc in 1674. At some point in the 1680s he left his shop and retired to a house in Printing House Yard, Blackfriars. Bagford says that he continued engraving there, but the surviving works from his last years are mostly portrait drawings, usually made in the fashionable medium of coloured crayons.

Samuel Pepys and Robert Hooke record many visits to Faithorne's shop in their diaries. On 7 November 1666, for instance, Pepys went to buy some prints for his wife to copy, and saw there Faithorne's copy in coloured chalks from Peter Lely's painting of a countess, which he was using as the basis for his engraving. Pepys thought it the finest thing he had ever seen in his life and tried to purchase it, but Faithorne would not sell it until he had finished correcting his plate from it.

Soon after his return from Paris, Faithorne married Judith, who was, according to Bagford, the sister of 'the famous Captain Grand' (despite his fame, his identity remains uncertain). She was buried in St Ann Blackfriars on 26 December 1690, and a few months later, on 13 May 1691, Faithorne too was buried there. He made bequests in his will to his two sons, William and Henry, and to a married daughter, Judith Thorpe. The elder son, William *Faithorne (c.1670–1703), entered his father's trade.

Faithorne was the finest native-born engraver working before the eighteenth century, and when the art of line engraving reached its apogee of critical esteem at the end of the eighteenth century this became of great importance. Horace Walpole elevated Faithorne into the English equivalent of Robert Nanteuil and the other great seventeenth-century French engravers, and this fed a collectors' frenzy that ensured that fine proofs of Faithorne's prints fetched extraordinary prices. In the sale of Sir Mark Masterman Sykes's collection in 1824, his Faithorne engravings fetched a total of £1271. These prices proved unsustainable, and in the inevitable reaction Faithorne and his work fell into an equally indefensible critical oblivion.   ANTONY GRIFFITHS

Sources J. Bagford, 'The life of Mr William Ffathorne', BL, Harleian MS 5910, fol. 135 [printed in S. Colvin, *Early engraving and engravers in England, 1545–1695* (1905), 132–3] • [B. Buckeridge], 'An essay towards an English school of painters', in R. de Piles, *The art of painting, with the lives and characters of above 300 of the most eminent painters*, 2nd edn (1744), 354–430, esp. 371–2 • L. Fagan, *A descriptive catalogue of the engraved works of William Faithorne* (1888) • Vertue, *Note books*, 1.140–42 • C. F. Bell and R. L. Poole, 'English seventeenth-century portrait drawings in Oxford collections, pt 2', *Walpole Society*, 14 (1925–6), 49–80, esp. 49–55 • E. Croft-Murray and P. H. Hulton, eds., *Catalogue of British drawings*, 1 (1960), 314–15 • M. Edmond, 'Limners and picturemakers', *Walpole Society*, 47 (1978–80), 60–242, esp. 131–2 • A. Griffiths and R. A. Gerard, *The print in Stuart Britain, 1603–1689* (1998), 125–8, 175–8, 198 [exhibition catalogue, BM, 8 May – 20 Sept 1998] • PRO, LC3/25, 113 • Goldsmiths' Company, London, Goldsmiths' Company Records • will, GL, Guildhall MS 9171/43, fols. 173*v*–174*v*
Archives V&A NAL, catalogue of his works
Likenesses J. Fillian, line print (after W. Faithorne), BM, NPG • R. Walker, portrait, NPG

Faithorne, William [*known as* William Faithorne the younger] (*c.*1670–1703), engraver, was the eldest son of the engraver William *Faithorne (*c.*1620–1691), and his wife, Judith (*d.* 1690), said to be the sister of Captain Grand. He was apprenticed to his father for eight years on 2 January 1683 in the Goldsmiths' Company. He never took up his freedom. As an artist Faithorne the younger is known only as the author of forty-three mezzotint plates. The earliest, datable 1688–9, were published by Grace Beckett, the widow of Isaac Beckett, and by William Beckett, who was probably Isaac Beckett's son.

One further plate from the same years was published by Faithorne's father, who emerged from retirement to do so. This lends support to John Bagford who, in his biography of the father, says in his inimitable spelling that 'the misfortune of his eldest sonne mutch broke his sperits althou of a rabust and stron constitusion' (Colvin, 133). George Vertue noted that the younger Faithorne never published one of his own plates, and comments that 'he was somewhat negligent of his affairs that put him under a necessity of working for them [publishers]' (Vertue, 1.141). It was presumably this same incompetence that prevented his taking over his father's business.

Faithorne was bequeathed two-thirds of his father's estate in 1691, and henceforth most of his plates were published by the leading London printseller Edward Cooper. His last datable plate is of the duke of Ormond, which was made in or shortly after October 1702. As a mezzotint engraver, in Vertue's opinion, Faithorne 'arrived to a considerable perfection' (Vertue, 1.141), but he has never been regarded as a major figure in the history of English mezzotint. Faithorne was buried in St Martin-in-the-Fields on 7 February 1703. Vertue states that he died young, aged about thirty. This would place his birth around 1673, but this is probably a few years too late, given that he was apprenticed in 1683.   ANTONY GRIFFITHS

Sources S. Colvin, *Early engravings and engravers in England, 1545–1695* (1915) • Vertue, *Note books*, 1.141 • C. F. Bell and R. L. Poole, 'English seventeenth-century portrait drawings in Oxford collections, pt 2', *Walpole Society*, 14 (1925–6), 49–80, esp. 52 • parish register (burial), St Martin-in-the-Fields, Westminster Reference Library • J. C. Smith, *British mezzotinto portraits*, 2 (1879), 461–77

Fakenham, Nicholas (d. 1407), Franciscan friar and theologian, was said by Bale to have been a native of Norfolk. By 1395 he was a doctor of divinity of Oxford, and provincial minister of his order. He clearly enjoyed the favour and patronage of the king, for on 5 November that year, probably at his inception, he 'determined' at Oxford on the papal schism, by the king's command. Though a supporter of the Roman obedience, in this lecture he urged that if a settlement could not be agreed by the rival popes, prelates and princes could impose one, because, although canon law provided for the deposition of a pope only on grounds of heresy, equity suggested that, in a case of grave necessity, this provision could be extended to cover pertinacious schism. Fakenham's *Determinatio* on the great schism was published by Bliemetzrieder in *Archivum Franciscanum Historicum*, 1–2 (1908–9), and two further *quaestiones* of his on the same subject were published in the same journal by Harvey in 1977.

Fakenham was absolved from the provincialate about 1402, probably at the general chapter at Assisi. In 1405 he was appointed commissioner by the protector of the order, the cardinal-bishop of Sabina, to examine the charges against John Zouche, then provincial minister, whose arbitrary conduct had produced 'a great and scandalous schism' among the English Minorites. Fakenham and his colleague, one Joannes Mallaert, deposed Zouche, called a chapter at Oxford (3 May 1405), and elected a successor. Zouche was reappointed by the general chapter, at the instance of the protector, and confirmed by the pope in 1406.

In addition to his writings on the schism Fakenham is credited by Bale with the following works: *De suffragiis viatorum*, *De fraternitate Christiana*, *De valore missae*, and *De orationibus* (with incipits given for all except the last, which is clearly conjectured from the incipit of *De valore missae*). Bale, referring to 'a register of the Minorites', says that Fakenham died in 1407. He was buried at Colchester.

RICHARD REX

Sources F. Bliemetzrieder, 'Traktat des Minoritensprovinzials von England Fr. Nikolaus de Fakenham (1395) über das grosse abendländische Schisma', *Archivum Franciscanum Historicum*, 1 (1908), 577–600; 2 (1909), 79–91 · M. Harvey, 'Two *quaestiones* on the Great Schism by Nicholas Fakenham', *Archivum Franciscanum Historicum*, 70 (1977), 97–127 · C. Eubel, ed., *Bullarium Franciscanum Romanorum pontificum*, 7 (Rome, 1904), no. 513, 185–6 · Bale, *Index*, 300–01 · Bale, *Cat.*, 1.530 · J. S. Brewer, ed., *Monumenta Franciscana*, 1, Rolls Series, 4 (1858), 538 · F. S. Haydon, ed., *Eulogium historiarum sive temporis*, 3 vols., Rolls Series, 9 (1858–63), vol. 3, pp. 404–5 · L. Wadding, *Annales minorum*, ed. J. M. Fonseca and others, 2nd edn, 9 (1734), 241, 278, 342 · A. G. Little, *The Grey friars in Oxford*, OHS, 20 (1892), 252–3

Falcke, Isaac (1819–1909), art collector and benefactor, was born in Great Yarmouth, one of some twenty children of Jacob Falcke. His father moved to London soon after Isaac's birth and started a business as an art dealer in Oxford Street; in due course he was joined by his sons David and Isaac. After Jacob Falcke's death, the business, which mainly handled decorative art objects, moved to 92 New Bond Street. Isaac Falcke accumulated a comfortable fortune, allowing him to retire from business some time before 1858, when his brother also retired, liquidating the firm's stock in a major sale at Christies. Subsequently Falcke devoted himself to the study and collecting of art for his own gratification, although he appears to have continued to deal on an occasional basis. However, a sizeable part of his wide-ranging collections, including most of the Wedgwood china, appears to have been assembled before his retirement from business. Portions were lent to the 1862 International Exhibition in South Kensington and the 1868 Leeds Art-Treasures Exhibition and between 1875 and 1877 to the Bethnal Green Museum.

Between 1868 and 1872 Falcke's collection of maiolica was sold to Sir Richard Wallace and later became part of the Wallace Collection. The circumstances of the sale, undertaken through the agency of Falcke's brother-in-law Frederik Davis, another Bond Street dealer, remain unclear. Falcke is thought to have been obliged to sell because of some unfortunate investment, but he later claimed that Davis had sold the collection without his knowledge and against his will, a deed for which he never forgave him. Some two decades later financial losses on the stock market forced Falcke to sell another large portion of his collection, including an important group of Renaissance bronzes, to Wilhelm Bode for the Berlin museums. This sale, too, caused great personal distress and enduring bitterness; Falcke regarded it as 'the great regret of his life' (*The Times*, 29 Dec 1909). However, he retained until his death his collection of oriental porcelain, and he continued to buy bronzes and other objects. With the exception of the Wedgwood, after his death his collection was sold in a series of sales at Christies between April and July 1910, the bronzes fetching notably high prices. Falcke's collection of Wedgwood ware was one of the largest ever assembled in the United Kingdom. Parts of it were exhibited not only in 1862, 1868, and 1875–7, but also at the opening of the Crystal Palace in 1856, and at Burslem in 1895. He appears to have decided at an early date to leave his Wedgwood to the nation; it was presented to the British Museum on 17 June 1909 as a gift from Mr and Mrs Isaac Falcke, 'a thank-offering for having been permitted to attain his great age' (*Jewish Chronicle*, 18 June 1909). The collection—still held in the museum—comprises about 500 pieces, including one of the few original copies of the famous Portland vase.

On 13 May 1847 Falcke had married Mary Ann (1827–1919), daughter of James Reid of Edinburgh; the couple were childless, and it is possible that Falcke viewed the objects in his collection, to which he was passionately attached, as in some sense substitutes for children. In his later years Falcke was dignified and patriarchal in appearance. Although a well-known figure in the London auction rooms, he played no active part in the art world politics of his time, being described as 'a most retiring man' who had 'always declined to belong to any society or club' (*Jewish Chronicle*, 18 June 1909). He was nevertheless generous and helpful to younger people with an interest in the arts, such as the art dealer Alfred Spero. Both Falcke's 'life of exemplary regularity' (*Jewish Chronicle*, 31 Dec 1909) and his long and close marriage helped him to retain his full physical and mental faculties until late in his life. He was a generous philanthropist, not only during his lifetime but also in the varied bequests made in his will. He died at his residence, 104 Gower Street, London, on 23 December 1909, and was buried in the Jewish cemetery at Willesden. JEREMY WARREN

Sources The Times (29 Dec 1909) · Jewish Chronicle (31 Dec 1909) · 'The Falcke collection', Jewish Chronicle (2 July 1909) · J. Warren, 'Bode and the British', Jahrbuch der Berliner Museen, 38 (1996), 121–42 [Beiheft] · A. Dawson, Masterpieces of Wedgwood in the British Museum (1984) · A. V. B. Norman, Pottery, maiolica, faience, stoneware (1976), vol. 1 of Wallace Collection: catalogue of ceramics · 'Wedgwood scrapbook', BM, department of medieval and modern Europe [album of cuttings etc. kept by Falcke] · I. Falcke, 'Catalogue of my art property', BM, department of medieval and modern Europe [MS] · 'Description of the art collection lent by Isaac Falcke to the Bethnal Green Museum, 1875–76–77', BM, department of medieval and modern Europe [printed MS] · Catalogue of the collection of bronzes … objects of art … formed by Isaac Falcke [1910] [sale catalogue, Christies, 19 April 1910] · Catalogue of the magnificent collection of works of art and vertu, formed by Mr. David Falcke (1858) [sale catalogue, Christie and Mason, London, 19 April 1858] · 'Jewish collector's gift to the British Museum', Jewish Chronicle (18 June 1909) · 'High prices for bronzes', The Times (20 April 1910) · DNB
Archives BM, department of medieval and modern Europe, books and MSS
Likenesses photograph, 1890?–1899, BM, department of medieval and modern Europe · double portrait, photograph, before 1891 (with his wife), BM, department of medieval and modern Europe · photograph, c.1909, repro. in Jewish Chronicle (2 July 1909)
Wealth at death £61,612 19s. 7d.: probate, 19 Feb 1910, CGPLA Eng. & Wales

Falcon, Norman Leslie (1904–1996), geologist, was born on 29 May 1904 at Seaview, Braunton, north Devon, the younger son and second of three children of Thomas Adolphus Falcon (1872–c.1942), artist and silversmith, and his wife, Julie Alice Schwabe, of Manchester. He grew up in a thoroughly English environment, which proved to be a strong lifelong influence. From childhood his father introduced him to an outdoor way of life, walking, cycling, and climbing along the north Devon coast or in the Lake District, where the family had ancestral property. His early schooling was at home, followed from 1914 to 1923 by attendance at Exeter School, where he excelled at sports and became head boy, and where he was greatly affected by the death of his elder brother. In 1923 he went to Trinity College, Cambridge, graduating with a first-class degree in geology in 1927.

In 1927 Falcon joined the Anglo-Persian Oil Company and was sent immediately to Persia to work in the oilfields of Khuzestan (south-west Persia). This commenced his lifelong career in the oil industry. He found his first work in Persia somewhat slow and dull, working as a geologist on drilling rigs on various fields that were being developed at the time. In 1930, as he was about to return to England, he met J. V. Harrison at Khorramshahr. He was persuaded to stay on and under Harrison's direction to help to map geologically the whole of the Zagros Mountains from Lurestan in the north-west to the Makran in the south-east, an area of some 90,000 square miles. He remained in Iran (as Persia was renamed in 1935) for a further seven years. He and Harrison made a geological map, at a scale of

4 miles to the inch, of the greater part of the project area, and the maps remain a fundamental data source for the geology of south-west Asia. The work was carried out entirely in the mountainous tribal country, either on foot or horseback, with camels substituting for horses in the Makran, often taking Harrison and Falcon into areas previously unexplored by Western travellers.

After Iran Falcon worked in the United Kingdom and Holland, escaping from there just ahead of the German invasion. On 29 January 1938 he married Dorothy Muriel Freeman (b. 1910), younger daughter of Frederick George Freeman, of HM consular service; they had two sons and a daughter. During the Second World War he served in military intelligence, interpreting aerial photographs, attaining the rank of lieutenant-colonel, and being awarded the United States bronze star for his work in charge of the joint command photographic interpretation unit. Following the end of the war he returned to the, now, Anglo-Iranian Oil Company (AIOC) and, based in London, carried on his work on Iran and developing an exploration programme for the United Kingdom. He was also responsible for gradually building up a small, but expert, head office exploration department and an exploration research unit at Sunbury-on-Thames that would allow AIOC to compete in the post-war international business that was quickly developing.

In 1955 Falcon was made chief geologist of the renamed British Petroleum Company (BP). This appointment followed the company's decision, consequent upon the nationalization of the Iranian oil industry in 1951, to be less dependent upon Iran for its main source of supply of crude oil. Falcon effectively managed and controlled all the technical exploration carried out worldwide by the company. The following decade, until his retirement in 1965, coincided with a period of intense and burgeoning international oil and gas exploration. It was marked by exploration success, adding significantly to the company's oil and gas reserves worldwide but primarily in the Middle East. During this period the foundations were laid for BP's later successes in the North Sea and Alaska. For most of Falcon's working life exploration, both geological and geophysical, had been land-based, but the last few years of his career saw the beginning of change to the offshore as suitable technology developed. The first British offshore commercial gas field was discovered by BP in the North Sea shortly before his retirement. As a measure of his success in direct management of BP's exploration programmes it was estimated that at the time of his retirement BP had title to approximately 22 per cent of the non-communist world's oil reserves, a figure never matched by any other company. This success gave rise to the creation of tremendous wealth for his company and his country, to both of which he was fiercely loyal throughout his life.

Falcon published sparingly on a wide range of geological topics and is best known for the series of geological maps of the Zagros Mountains, with accompanying cross-sections and notes on the stratigraphy of the region. He encouraged his staff to publish their work and took an enlightened attitude for the time that companies stood to gain more from sharing their knowledge than from being secretive. He was always keen to keep abreast of modern ideas and developments in science, although not academically inclined. Early on he had decided not to enter a university career, but he always remained interested in new developments that might be practically applied. A lifelong supporter of the Geological Society, he received a number of awards including the Murchison medal (1963). He was also an enthusiastic member of the Royal Geographical Society, from whom he received the founder's medal (1973). He was elected a fellow of the Royal Society in 1960, serving as a member of numerous committees, and was an honorary member of a number of other professional societies.

Well respected by his staff and regarded as a fair and supportive, if demanding, manager, Falcon was an extremely modest and private man, which made him distant and reserved towards colleagues, although always ready to give credit when due. Typically, he would speak kindly of someone being criticized by others. He died on 31 May 1996 at Witney Community Hospital, and was cremated at Oxford crematorium on 5 June. He had been respected and honoured by his profession but ignored by his country, which he had served well both in peace and war. He was survived by his wife and three children.

A. J. MARTIN

Sources A. J. Martin and P. B. Lapworth, *Memoirs FRS*, 44 (1998), 161–74 · autobiographical notes, RS · 'Norman Leslie Falcon', *American Association of Petroleum Geologists Bulletin*, 82/6 (1996), 1233–6 · A. J. Martin, 'Norman Leslie Falcon', *Annual Report* [Geological Society of London] (1997), 19–20 · private information (2004) [Mrs D. M. Falcon] · WWW

Archives RGS, diaries, papers, and photographs · RS, autobiographical notes

Likenesses C. Vita-Finzi, photographs, c.1975, priv. coll.; repro. in Martin and Lapworth, *Memoirs FRS*, 163 · photograph, 1984, RS; repro. in Martin and Lapworth, *Memoirs FRS*, 160 · photographs, personnel department, British Petroleum Co. Ltd, Warwick

Wealth at death under £180,000: probate, 20 Dec 1996, CGPLA Eng. & Wales

Falconbridge, Alexander (c.1760–1792), doctor and slavery abolitionist, whose family was associated with Bristol, where he grew up, spent twelve months in 1779–80 as a pupil in Bristol Infirmary. Too poor to start his own practice, he became a surgeon on board a slave ship—a potentially lucrative employment since surgeons received, as well as their salary, 1s. a head per slave landed, and the chance of eventually becoming a ship's captain. Between 1780 and 1787 he sailed on four ships which took him along the west coast of Africa, chiefly to the Niger delta, and to the Caribbean. On his first two voyages he served under a captain whom he later described as one of the best in the trade. Then, under a brutal captain named Mactaggart, he became sickened by its conditions. In 1787 he left it in disgust and went back to working as a pupil with a Bristol doctor.

In spring 1787 Thomas Clarkson, one of the founders of the committee for effecting the abolition of the slave trade, went to Bristol to gather evidence. Falconbridge, alone among those he questioned, was courageously ready to testify publicly to the horrors of the traffic in slaves. He accompanied Clarkson to Liverpool to gather more information, and also to act as his bodyguard— Clarkson called him 'an athletic and resolute-looking man' (Clarkson, 1.318)—then to London to report his findings to the committee. He also gave evidence to a privy council committee, and underwent four days of hostile grilling by a House of Commons committee. With the help of Richard Phillips, an abolitionist lawyer, he reduced his voluminous material to a substantial pamphlet, published in 1790 as *An Account of the Slave Trade, on the Coast of Africa*, the first piece of published abolitionist propaganda. He sold the copyright to the abolition committee which printed 6000 copies, and with the proceeds set up as a doctor at Lodway, near Bristol. There on 16 October 1788 he married Anna Maria Horwood (b. 1769) [see Falconbridge, Anna Maria].

In 1790 Clarkson recruited Falconbridge to go out to Sierra Leone on behalf of the St George's Bay (renamed later Sierra Leone) Company, a company that blended commercial profit with abolitionist philanthropy, to refound a colony of free black settlers, established there three years earlier, but dispersed after a quarrel with their Temne neighbours. His wife accompanied him, and in 1794 was to describe their experiences in her *Narrative of Two Voyages*. A passionate abolitionist, he quarrelled with the local slave traders, but managed to reassemble the dispersed settlers, and to persuade Naimbana, the Temne ruler, to let them return. He and his wife then sailed home in a tiny boat, narrowly escaping shipwreck.

The Sierra Leone Company was controlled by its chairman, Henry Thornton, a London banker. Realizing that Falconbridge, with his knowledge of the country, was indispensably necessary to the project, Thornton tempted him to return as commercial agent with a £300 salary, even though he knew he had no commercial experience. Falconbridge accepted, returned with his wife, and got Naimbana to approve the foundation of what was now named Freetown. The company's employees soon began quarrelling and all was in confusion until order was restored by Clarkson's brother John, a naval lieutenant, who arrived from Nova Scotia in 1792 with over a thousand black American loyalist settlers, and was eventually appointed governor.

During the first months many settlers fell ill. Mortality was high and Falconbridge was active as a doctor. But he made no attempt, as commercial agent, to initiate trade with the neighbouring peoples. He had by now taken heavily to drink: even on the voyage out, at Tenerife, he had been noisily and publicly drunk. Thornton saw him as expendable and sent out a new commercial agent to replace him. A few days after the new agent's arrival at Freetown, Falconbridge, now in a state of almost permanent intoxication, died, on 19 December 1792, in Freetown, where he was buried.

Falconbridge's reputation suffered posthumously. Thornton singled him out as a scapegoat in his published report on the colony (1794), making him responsible for its early misfortunes, while his widow presented him in her *Narrative* in a most unfavourable light. Both thus diminished the memory of his courageous pioneer achievements in the campaign against the slave trade.

CHRISTOPHER FYFE

Sources A. M. Falconbridge, *Narrative of two voyages to the River Sierra Leone during the years 1791–1792–1793, and, The journal of Isaac Dubois: with Alexander Falconbridge, An account of the slave trade on the coast of Africa*, ed. C. Fyfe (2000) · T. Clarkson, *The history ... of the abolition of the slave trade*, 2 vols. (1808) · 'Report of the lords of the committee of council ... particularly the trade in slaves', *British Sessional Papers: Accounts and Papers*, 26 (1788–9), no. 646a · *House of Commons Papers*, 71–3 (1790) [Slave trade] · proceedings of the committee for the abolition of the slave trade, 1787–90, BL, Add. MSS 21254–21255 · parish register, Bristol, All Saints' Church, 13 July 1769 [baptism; Anna Maria Horwood]

Archives BL, proceedings of the committee for the abolition of the slave trade, Add. MSS 21254–21255

Falconbridge [*née* Horwood], **Anna Maria** (b. **1769**, d. in or after **1802**?), traveller and writer, was born in All Saints' Lane, Bristol, in July 1769, the daughter of Charles Horwood (d. 1787), a watchmaker and goldsmith, and his wife, Grace Roberts (d. 1774). After her parents' deaths, against her family's wishes, she married on 16 October 1788 Alexander *Falconbridge, formerly a surgeon employed in the slave trade, who had turned violently against it and given crucial help to Thomas Clarkson at the outset of the abolition campaign. Soon after their marriage he left his medical practice at Lodway, near Bristol, to return to the campaign as an employee of the Sierra Leone Company, a commercial company founded by Clarkson and other abolitionists to sponsor a settlement of free black people in Sierra Leone. A previous attempt, sponsored by Granville Sharp in 1787, had ended abruptly when the settlers quarrelled with a neighbouring Temne ruler, who burnt their town. Falconbridge's task was to reassemble the surviving settlers and negotiate with the Temne authorities for a new settlement.

Anna Maria accompanied her husband, and described her experiences in a series of lively, informative letters (witness to her good education) to a friend in Bristol, intended ultimately, she openly declared, for publication. Their port of destination was a slave-trading fort, Bance Island, in the Sierra Leone River, where they were politely received by the employees, whom she, coming from a family associated with the slave trade, found sympathetic. But Falconbridge, passionately opposed to the trade, refused to let her stay there, and forced her to live on board a tiny, filthy, single-masted boat. Protracted negotiations then began with Naimbana, styled king, though in fact regent, of the Koya Temne. Anna Maria accompanied Falconbridge on some of his visits, and recounted her experiences in her letters in a light-hearted way. Eventually it was agreed a new settlement might be founded, the former settlers were gathered, and a site was prepared. Once huts were built she moved in, making light of the difficulties, 'for I now find 'tis necessary to accommodate myself to whatever I meet with' (Falconbridge, 67).

During her stay Anna Maria observed all she could of the country and its people, their customs, religion, and economy, and wrote about what she saw with obvious enjoyment ('there is such a variety here as to afford a continual zest to the sight'; Falconbridge, 72) in a dispassionate, uncensorious way. As the heavy rains approached she and her husband embarked for England on the tiny boat. It took six weeks, through constant storms, to reach the Cape Verde Islands. Then, after nearly being shipwrecked, they were blown to the Azores, and finally reached Penzance in September 1791, seventy-eight days after embarking.

Meanwhile the directors of the Sierra Leone Company were investing heavily in the new settlement, and had sent Clarkson's naval officer brother John to Nova Scotia to recruit settlers among the self-liberated black American loyalists located there. Falconbridge was appointed commercial agent, and in December he and his wife set out again. On arrival they found confusion, with a governing council of eight, appointed by the directors, quarrelling and giving contradictory orders. Clarkson arrived soon after with more than a thousand settlers, who began laying out Freetown. But they had arrived at the start of the rainy season. Living without shelter, hundreds fell ill and died. Anna Maria, who had kept her health, wrote, 'It is quite customary of a morning to ask "how many died last night?"' (Falconbridge, 148). Then she too became ill with a violent fever but recovered. Falconbridge, who knew nothing about commerce and had taken heavily to drink, was dismissed by the directors, fell ill, and died on 19 December 1792. 'I will not be guilty of such meanness as to tell a falsehood on this occasion', wrote Anna Maria, 'by saying I regret his death, no! I really do not' (ibid., 169).

Within a fortnight, on 7 January 1793, Anna Maria had remarried, celebrating with a 'convivial gala ... garnished with comfort and pleasantry' (Falconbridge, 200), with her brother-in-law Captain Morley, the captain of a passing slave ship, present. Her new husband, Isaac DuBois, was one of the company's employees, a ruined and uncompensated white American loyalist from North Carolina. Meanwhile mismanagement and acrimonious party strife, which Anna Maria reported in her letters in entertaining detail, continued. Clarkson went home on leave and was dismissed by the directors, who laid all the blame on him and the late Falconbridge. Anna Maria and DuBois then left for England, travelling via Jamaica on board Morley's slave ship. 'Having heard such a vast deal of the ill treatment of slaves,' she wrote, 'I did not omit to make the nicest observations in my power, and ... I had not the slightest reason to suspect any inhumanity or malpractice was shown towards them' (ibid., 232–3).

Having arrived in London, Anna Maria demanded from the directors money she claimed was due to Falconbridge. Her claims were summarily refused, so she published her letters denouncing the company, in particular the chairman, Henry Thornton. Three editions of her *Narrative of Two Voyages to the River Sierra Leone during the Years 1791–1792–1793* appeared during 1794 and 1795, but the directors remained obdurate. A further edition was issued in 1802 with a new title-page which mentioned the 'improbability' of the total abolition of the slave trade, thus placing it firmly in the anti-abolitionist camp. All appeared under the name Falconbridge: DuBois's name appears nowhere in the book.

In 1807 parliament belatedly awarded DuBois some compensation for his losses as a loyalist. The subsequent careers of him and his wife have not been traced. Anna Maria's book, the first Englishwoman's narrative of a visit to Africa, remains as her memorial.

CHRISTOPHER FYFE

Sources A. M. Falconbridge, Narrative of two voyages to the River Sierra Leone during the years 1791-1792-1793, and, The journal of Isaac Dubois: with Alexander Falconbridge, An account of the slave trade on the coast of Africa, ed. C. Fyfe (2000) · C. Fyfe, A history of Sierra Leone (1962) · A. Mackenzie-Grieve, The great accomplishment (1953) · D. Coleman, ed., Maiden voyages and infant colonies: two women's travel narratives of the 1790s (1998) Archives BL, Clarkson MSS, Add. MSS 41262A, 41263

Falconer, Alexander, Lord Falconer of Halkertoun (1593/4–1671), judge, was the eldest son of Sir Alexander Falconer of Halkertoun (or Halkerton), Kincardineshire (d. 1645/6), and Agnes (d. 1634), daughter of Sir David Carnegie of Colluthie and Kinnaird and his second wife, Euphame Wemyss, and sister of David Carnegie, first earl of Southesk (1574/5–1658). He married, about April 1619, Anne, daughter of John, Lord Lindsay of the Byres (d. 1609), and Anne, daughter of Lawrence Oliphant, master of Oliphant; they had two sons and a daughter. He and his wife separated in 1627 by agreement approved by the privy council.

Falconer was appointed a lord of session on 9 July 1639, at the beginning of a turbulent period in the court's history, taking the judicial title of Lord Halkertoun. According to Fountainhall he gained office by paying his predecessor, Lord Woodhall, 7000 merks to stand down. He was reappointed *ad vitam aut culpam* on 13 November 1641, but was removed from the session in the purge of 1649 for 'malignancy' in supporting the engagement. He was reappointed at the Restoration and remained in office until his death. Falconer was commissioner to the convention of estates in 1643–4, and commissioner to parliament in 1644–6, representing Kincardineshire. He was also a commissioner for the loan and tax in 1643; commissioner of treasury in 1645; on the committee of estates in 1645, 1646, and 1648; and on the committee of war for Kincardineshire in 1643, 1644, 1646, and 1648. He was a commissioner of supply for Kincardineshire in 1656 and 1659. He was created Lord Falconer of Halkertoun on 20 December 1646 and a privy councillor in 1661. Falconer died in Edinburgh on 1 October 1671.

A brother, Sir David Falconer of Glenfarquhar, was also a member of the committee of war, and assented for Kincardineshire to the English parliament's tender of union in 1652, being one of twenty-one deputies elected to treat in London with the parliament. Another brother, Sir John (d. 1670), was master of the (Scottish) mint to Charles I and Charles II.

W. D. H. SELLAR

Sources GEC, Peerage · Scots peerage [Kintore and corrigenda] · M. D. Young, ed., The parliaments of Scotland: burgh and shire commissioners, 2 vols. (1992–3) · Journals of Sir John Lauder, ed. D. Crawford, Scottish History Society, 36 (1900) · Reg. PCS, 2nd ser., vol. 1 · D. Stevenson, 'The covenanters and the court of session', Juridical Review, new ser., 17 (1972), 227–47 · G. Brunton and D. Haig, An historical account of the senators of the college of justice, from its institution in MDXXXII (1832) · APS, 1643–60 Archives BL, letters to Lord Lauderdale and Charles II, Add. MSS 23114–23129

Falconer, Sir David (1638/9–1685), lawyer and judge, was the second son of Sir David Falconer of Glenfarquhar (d. before 1682), one of the commissaries of Edinburgh, and Margaret, daughter of Sir Robert Hepburn of Bearford. His elder brother was Sir Alexander Falconer of Glenfarquhar (d. 1717), who was created a baronet in 1670. Falconer received an MA from Edinburgh University on 26 July 1657, studied law 'under the eye of his father' (Brunton and Haig, 405), and was admitted an advocate on 29 June 1661. He became a commissary of Edinburgh in 1661 and was knighted. Falconer married, probably around this date, Elizabeth (1635–1676), daughter of Robert Nairn of Muckersy, Kincardine, and sister of Robert Nairn, advocate, created Lord Nairn in 1681. They had one son, born on 6 August 1663, who died young. His wife was buried on 20 January 1676.

Falconer was nominated a lord of session on 24 May 1676, and took his seat on 12 June. On 16 February 1678 he married Mary (bap. 1654), daughter of George Norvell, advocate, of Boghall, Linlithgowshire. They had three sons and four daughters, including Catherine, the mother of the philosopher David *Hume. All Falconer's children survived him. On 2 March 1678 he became a lord of justiciary, and on 24 September 1679 he was admitted a burgess of Edinburgh. On 5 June 1682 he became lord president of session. In this capacity 'he introduced regulations tending to enlarge the attendance of judges' (Brunton and Haig, 405), which did not earn him the approbation of his fellow judges. In 1684 he was made a privy councillor of Scotland, and he was reappointed in 1685 following the accession of James VII and II. In the parliament of 1685 he sat for Forfarshire, was chosen a lord of the articles, and was nominated to the commissions on trade, the plantation of kirks and the regulation of inferior jurisdictions.

After four days' illness Falconer died in Edinburgh on 15 December 1685, aged forty-six, and was buried on the 21st in Greyfriars churchyard in Edinburgh, where a monument was erected to his memory. His widow remarried John Hume of Ninewells. Falconer had been assiduous in collecting legal materials until the last day he sat in court. These were published by John Spottiswood in 1705 as *Decisions of the Court of Session November 1681 to December 1685*.

STUART HANDLEY

Sources M. D. Young, ed., The parliaments of Scotland: burgh and shire commissioners, 1 (1992), 235 · Scots peerage, 5.247–8; 6.393 · G. Brunton and D. Haig, An historical account of the senators of the college of justice, from its institution in MDXXXII (1832), 405–6 · H. Paton, ed., Register of interments in the Greyfriars burying-ground, Edinburgh, 1658–1700, Scottish RS, 26 (1902), 212 · H. Paton, ed., The register of marriages for the parish of Edinburgh, 1595–1700, Scottish RS, old ser., 27 (1905), 224 · W. Anderson, The Scottish nation, 2 (1868), 188 ·

C. B. B. Watson, ed., *Roll of Edinburgh burgesses and guild-brethren, 1406–1700*, Scottish RS, 59 (1929), 177 · *IGI*
Archives U. Aberdeen, documents relating to the affairs of Sir David Newton

Falconer, Edmund. *See* O'Rourke, Edmund (*c*.1814–1879).

Falconer, Forbes (1805–1853), orientalist, was born at Aberdeen on 10 September 1805, the second and only surviving son of Gilbert Falconer, schoolmaster of Braeside, Fife, and his wife, Jane, *née* Donald. He was educated at Aberdeen grammar school and at Marischal College, where he obtained prizes in classical studies. His first publications, which appeared anonymously in local journals, were also classical, consisting of metrical translations from the Greek anthology. He began his oriental studies before the age of twenty, by attending the Hebrew classes of Professor Bentley in Aberdeen, and by private study of Arabic and Persian. He then went to Paris where for five years he attended the courses of De Sacy, De Chézy, and, for Hindustani, of Garcin de Tassy.

After short visits to several German universities, Falconer returned to Britain and settled in London as a teacher of oriental languages. For a short time he was professor of oriental languages in University College, London. He was perhaps best known for his works on Saʿdi's *Bustan*, from which he published in 1839 a volume of selections, very neatly lithographed from his own transcript. He also published a translation of part of the same poem, as well as selections from several of the Sufi poets including a poem of Hafiz, signed F. F., and a critical study of the *Sindibad Namah* in the *Asiatic Journal*. Falconer also edited Persian texts of Jami for the Society for the Publication of Oriental Texts. The critical ability demonstrated in these texts is attested by Francis Johnson in the preface to his edition of Richardson's *Persian Dictionary*.

Falconer was a member of the Asiatic societies of London and Paris, and an honorary member of the American Oriental Society. He died of bronchitis on 7 November 1853 at 6 Edwardes Square, London.

CECIL BENDALL, *rev.* PARVIN LOLOI

Sources *Journal of the Royal Asiatic Society of Great Britain and Ireland*, 15 (1855), v–viii · J. T. Zenker, *Bibliotheca orientalis*, [rev. edn] (Leipzig, 1846–61) · Boase, *Mod. Eng. biog.* · C. E. Buckland, *Dictionary of Indian biography* (1906) · d. cert.

Falconer, Hugh (1808–1865), palaeontologist and naturalist, was born at Forres, Moray, on 29 February 1808, one of five sons and two daughters of David Falconer and his wife, Isabel Mcrae. He was educated at the local grammar school and the University of Aberdeen, where he obtained his MA degree. He later attended Edinburgh University, learning botany from Professor Robert Graham and geology from Professor Robert Jameson, and obtained his MD degree there in 1829, his thesis being entitled 'De chorea'. He went to London soon after and there met Nathaniel Wallich and worked with him on his Indian herbarium specimens. He also worked with William Lonsdale, curator at the Geological Society of London museum and worked at the Geological Society on the Ava (Burma) collection of fossil mammals made by John Crawfurd from

the banks of the Irrawaddi. Both these activities were important in directing his later career.

Falconer went to India as surgeon with the East India Company, Bengal establishment, arriving at Calcutta in September 1830, and obtained a position in the museum of the Asiatic Society of Bengal. There he saw fossil material from the Ava collection in the museum of the Asiatic Society of Bengal and this topic was one of his first publications (1831 in *Gleanings in Science*, 3). In the course of duties he met J. Forbes Royal of the Saharanpur/Serempore Botanic Gardens and was made his deputy, and in 1832, superintendent of the gardens. His resourcefulness there in making a mercury barometer for measuring altitude from materials obtainable locally was recorded by a contemporary writer. There too, in 1832, he was shown animal fossils from the Sewalik hills in the Himalayan foothills by P. T. Cautley, which they identified as fossil mammals of Tertiary age. Over the next twenty years and more Cautley and Falconer, with few resources, investigated the Sewalik hills fossil fauna with great skill and vigour. They later discovered and investigated further Tertiary fossiliferous material deposits at the Kalomal Pass. Yet more fossil bones of this formation were found by Lieutenant William Erskine Baker and Lieutenant Henry Durand during work at Markunda, west of Jumma, which came into Falconer's possession.

Falconer demonstrated considerable stratigraphic ability in deducing that the Sewalik fossil material was not of New Red Sandstone age (Triassic) as was supposed, but late Tertiary (it is now known to be predominantly Plio-Pleistocene) and that the deposit was of a similar sedimentary facies to the molasse of Switzerland. The mammalian fauna consisted of mastodons, elephants, rhinoceros, hippopotamus, pig, and giraffe. They also found one of the first fossil monkey skulls, a fact noted by Charles Darwin during his earliest evolutionary musings. There were fossil fishes, and among the reptilian remains of crocodiles and tortoises was a giant tortoise which caught the public imagination. Falconer's work was detailed and he is known to have captured living animals to compare their anatomy with his fossil material. In recognition of their work on vertebrate palaeontology Falconer and Cautley jointly received the Wollaston medal of the Geological Society of London in 1837.

Falconer was sent to the north-west of India in 1837 and made initial investigations of the natural history and geology of the Salt range (in present-day Pakistan), Kashmir, and south-eastern Afghanistan. Here his health began to suffer and he returned to England in 1842 bringing with him 5 tons of fossil bones in their rock matrix. He remained in England until 1846 or 1847. In London he worked on the Indian fossils at the British Museum and also worked at the museum of the East India Company in Leadenhall Street. During this home leave work was begun on the illustrations (lithographs) for what was to become Falconer's best-known publication, his uncompleted *Fauna antiqua Sivalensis* (1846–9). Such of the letterpress and plate description as were ever published appeared in 1868 under Sir Roderick Murchison's editorship. Falconer was elected a fellow of the Royal Society in 1845. In India in the same year he was appointed professor of botany at Calcutta medical college and superintendent of the Royal Botanic Garden, Calcutta (1848) as successor to Wallich. It was from here that Falconer undertook botanical work associated with the introduction of tea and *Cinchona* species, which produce quinine, into cultivation in India. He selected and arranged the Bengal exhibits for the Great Exhibition of 1851. After this he undertook the task of preparing a catalogue of the fossils in the museum of the Asiatic Society of Bengal which appeared in 1859. This was a formidable task, as few records had been kept before his time. In India he continued his palaeontological work in the Sewalik hills as best he could with the resources at his disposal. However, his health was impaired and he returned to London for good in 1855, visiting Palestine, Syria, and the Crimea (during the siege of Sevastopol) on the way. In Europe a second phase of his career began: he worked on many aspects of vertebrate palaeontology and especially Pleistocene cave fossil faunas—elephants and mastodons being a particular interest. He developed a reputation for thorough work and became an active member of the scientific community in London. In a memoir in 1857 he concluded that there had been three species of Pleistocene fossil elephant in southern Britain, disagreeing with Richard Owen in the process, who had considered there to have been only one. He also examined flint artefacts from the Somme valley of northern France in 1858 and the fossil fauna of caves in the Gower peninsula. Falconer in 1858 excavated chipped flints in Brixham cave, and was foremost in arguing that these were tools and therefore proof of mankind's antiquity (then disputed). His discoveries were exploited by Charles Lyell in his *Geological Evidence of the Antiquity of Man* (1863) which led to acrimonious exchanges. At this time Falconer was also one of the committee who commented on the future housing of the botanical collections in the British Museum following the death of the botanist Robert Brown.

For health reasons Falconer spent the winters of 1858–61 in the western Mediterranean, and investigated cave faunas in Malta, Sicily, and Gibraltar. His botanical and palaeobotanical interests continued: in 1860–62 he was able to conclude that the Bovey Tracy (Devon) lignite was of Miocene age and corresponded with the better-known German deposits of the same age. In the early 1860s he visited major British, French, German, and Italian museums and examined their fossil collections. At the time of his death he was vice-president of the Royal Society and foreign secretary of the Geological Society of London. He died at his home, 21 Park Crescent, Marylebone, London, on 31 January 1865 and was buried at Kensal Green cemetery, London, on 4 February.

Regrettably Falconer's large and important Sewalik hills fossil fauna collection was never fully published, partly because of his ill health in later years and partly because some of his lithographic drawings made for the project had been removed from the stones between 1845

and 1855 while he was in India. The failure to complete this work was one of the tragedies of nineteenth-century Anglo-Indian science and Falconer cannot be held entirely responsible. In 1863 Falconer published on an American fossil elephant *Elephas columbi* and it is known that he disagreed with Sir Richard Owen on some aspects of the Pleistocene fossil elephant taxonomy from the Gulf of Mexico and felt that Owen had ignored his prior name in favour of his own name, *Elephas texianus* (Murchison, *Palaeontological Memoir*, 215–16); the belief persists that Owen, the Natural History Museum's first director, may have suppressed the publication of some of this work until after Falconer's death. Certainly it fell to Murchison in 1867–8 to publish much of what survived of Falconer's palaeontological notes and material as *Palaeontological Memoirs and Notes of the Late Hugh Falconer*.

Falconer's botanical collecting was also considerable. His plant material consisted of eighty cases of dried plants and these were passed initially to the museum of the East India Company, London, and after the company's suppression (1858) to the herbarium of the Royal Botanic Gardens, Kew. His botanical notes and coloured drawings were also passed to Kew at this time. He was commemorated in the now obsolete plant genus *Falconeria* J. D. Hooker (Scrophulariaceae), and in *Rhododendron falconeri* (Ericaceae). The Falconer Museum in Forres, Moray, commemorates Hugh and his brother Alexander Falconer (1797–1856).   D. T. MOORE

Sources J. Chaloner, 'Falconer, Hugh (1808–1865)', *DSB*, vol. 4 · *DNB* · R. I. Murchison, *PRS*, 15 (1866–7), xiv-xxiii · R. I. Murchison, *Journal of the Royal Geographical Society*, 35 (1865), cxv-cxviii · R. I. Murchison, ed., *Palaeontological memoirs and notes of the late Hugh Falconer*, 2 vols. (1868) · F. A. Stafleu and R. S. Cowan, *Taxonomic literature: a selective guide*, 2nd edn, 1, Regnum Vegetabile, 94 (1976) · W. T. Stearn, *The Natural History Museum at South Kensington: a history of the British Museum (Natural History), 1753–1980* (1981) · P. J. Boylan, 'The controversy of the Moulin-Quignon jaw: the role of Hugh Falconer', in L. J. Jordanova and R. S. Porter, *Images of the earth* (1979), 171–99 · L. G. Wilson, 'Brixham cave and Sir Charles Lyell's *The Antiquity of Man*: the roots of Hugh Falconer's attack on Lyell', *Archives of Natural History*, 23 (1996), 79–97 · d. cert. · card catalogue, RS · Scottish old parish register

Archives Falconer Museum, Forres, corresp. and MSS · NHM, MSS · NHM, specimens · RBG Kew, drawings and MSS · RCS Eng., MSS | Elgin Museum, Elgin, letters to George Gordon · U. Edin. L., letters to Sir Charles Lyell

Likenesses E. Edwards, photograph, 1865, NPG; repro. in *Portraits of men of eminence*, 3 (1865) · J. Bell, bust, 1867, Madras, India · T. Butler, bust, RS · bust, Asiatic Society of Bengal, Calcutta · photograph, repro. in Murchison, *Palaeontological memoirs* · photograph, NHM, Palaeontology Library

Wealth at death under £16,000: resworn probate, May 1865, *CGPLA Eng. & Wales*

Falconer, Ion Grant Neville Keith- (1856–1887), Arabic scholar, third son of Francis Alexander Keith-Falconer, eighth earl of Kintore (1828–1880), and Louisa Madeleine Hawkins (d, 1916), was born at Edinburgh (probably at 24 Abercromby Place) on 5 July 1856. His family were the representatives of the Keiths, earls Marischal of Scotland. Educated first at home, and then at Cheam, Surrey, under the Revd R. S. Tabor, at the age of thirteen he won a scholarship to Harrow School. After four years he left to be coached in mathematics before entering Trinity College, Cambridge, in October 1874. After his first year he gave up mathematics to read theology, and graduated with first-class honours in January 1878. He was awarded the Hebrew prize. From his schooldays he had taken an interest in evangelistic efforts. At Barnwell, a poor working-class suburb of Cambridge, he involved himself in charitable work. He spent much time and money in similar work in London, especially in connection with the Tower Hamlets Mission at the Great Assembly Hall in the Mile End Road.

Keith-Falconer was specially attracted by the biblical, and pre-eminently the Hebrew, part of his studies. After taking his degree he turned his attention to oriental languages, Hebrew and Syriac, and ultimately Arabic. At these he worked hard, first at Cambridge, where he won the Tyrwhitt University Hebrew scholarship, and obtained a first class in the newly founded Semitic languages tripos in February 1880, and afterwards at Leipzig University, where he spent the winter of 1880–81. In order to improve his knowledge of modern spoken Arabic, he decided to stay the winter months of 1881–2 at Asyut in Upper Egypt, but two attacks of fever forced him to return in late January 1882.

Although never of very robust health, Keith-Falconer was from his schooldays an enthusiastic and outstanding cyclist. His height (6 ft 3 in.) enabled him to ride 'high-wheelers' with a wheel span of 62 inches. He was elected vice-president of the Cambridge University Bicycle Club before he came into residence (June 1874), and was president of the London Bicycle Club from May 1877 until he left England. His cycling successes, from 1874 to 1882, were numerous. At the 2 mile race of 11 May 1878 at Cambridge he defeated the well-known professional champion John Keen by 5 yards, and in the 50 mile bicycle union amateur championship race at the Crystal Palace, on 9 July 1882, accomplished in 2 hrs, 43 min., 55.2 sec., he beat all previous records. In June 1882 he made a then unprecedented bicycle ride, from Land's End to John o' Groat's House, a journey of 994 miles, in 13 days less 45 minutes.

After his return from Egypt Keith-Falconer stayed in Cambridge more often than in the previous two years and devoted much of his time to studying Arabic with the noted orientalist, William Wright. He was already Hebrew lecturer at Clare College, Cambridge, and had been since 1881 engaged upon a translation from the Syriac version, discovered by Professor Wright in the library of Trinity College, Dublin, of the Kalilah and Dimnah, otherwise known as the Fables of Bidpai. This was published early in 1885, with a long introduction on the literary history of the document, and the bibliography of the versions. Its learning and critical acumen were recognized by Professor Nöldeke and other leading oriental scholars. Keith-Falconer also wrote a very full article on shorthand for the ninth edition of the Encyclopaedia Britannica; he had taught himself the Pitman system at school.

On 4 March 1884 Keith-Falconer married Gwendolen (d. 1937), the daughter of Robert *Bevan, managing director of Barclays Bank. They settled in Cambridge, and lived at 5 Salisbury Villas, Station Road. Within a few months, however, he became engrossed with the idea of mission work in a field where his knowledge of Arabic might be directly utilized. After reading a paper by Major-General Haig in The Christian for February 1885 he began to consider Aden as a possible centre for this. With his wife he made a preliminary visit of four months at the end of 1885 to test the climate, and acquired some medical knowledge with a view to founding a hospital, which formed part of his scheme. He decided to station himself not in the town of Aden itself where the Church Missionary Society had recently become active, but at Shaykh 'Uthman, 9½ miles inland but just inside British territory, where schools and a hospital could be built. He made some lengthy excursions inland, and began to study Hindustani and also Somali, as several thousand Somali immigrants had settled in and around Aden.

In April 1886 Keith-Falconer and his wife returned to England, and on 26 May he was formally recognized as a missionary by the general assembly of the Free Church of Scotland, in which his father had been an elder, and in which he himself had been brought up. Early in the following summer he accepted the post of lord almoner's professor of Arabic at Cambridge, which required the delivery of one lecture annually and had a nominal stipend of £50 p.a. He gave a course of three lectures in November entitled 'Pilgrimage to Mecca'. These lectures were not published. On the day after the last lecture he left England, again accompanied by his wife, and arrived at Aden on 8 December 1886. He travelled at his own expense, and took with him, also at his own cost, Dr Stewart Cowen of the Western Infirmary, Glasgow. He had obtained a grant of land at Shaykh 'Uthman, on which he at once began to build a permanent home for the mission, which was to comprise an orphanage, a dispensary, a hospital, and a school. Early in February 1887, however, Keith-Falconer had the first of several attacks of Aden fever. He died on 11 May and was buried that day in the Aden cemetery. His library of over 400 Arabic books was given to the Edinburgh New College, an educational institution founded and supported by the Free Church of Scotland.

ROBERT SINKER, rev. JOHN GURNEY

Sources R. Sinker, *Memorials of the Hon. Ion Keith-Falconer* (1888) · R. Sinker, 'In memoriam: Ion Grant Neville Keith-Falconer', *Cambridge Review* (25 May 1887) · J. McGurn, *On your bicycle: an illustrated history of cycling* (1987) · 'Hon. Ion Grant Neville Keith-Falconer', *Sporting Mirror*, 4/20 (1888), 49–52 · personal knowledge (1891) · private information (1891) [relatives and friends]
Likenesses photograph, 1882, repro. in McGurn, *On your bicycle*, 64 · photograph, c.1885–1886, repro. in Sinker, *Memorials*, repr. 1903, frontispiece · etching?, repro. in 'Hon. Ion Grant Neville Keith-Falconer' · watercolour, priv. coll. · wood-engraving, NPG; repro. in *ILN* (30 Jan 1875)
Wealth at death £1648 15s.: administration, 30 July 1887, *CGPLA Eng. & Wales*

Falconer, John (d. 1560), botanist, was the first English person known to possess a herbarium. His antecedents are unknown: a suggestion (Garrett, 152) that he came from Rutland lacks confirmation. Falconer was tutor in William Lucy's household at Charlecote, Warwickshire, until

1545, when his friend John Foxe succeeded him there. He was at Ferrara, and a fellow student of William Turner at Bologna at some time between 1540 and 1547. Back in England, he was ordained deacon (1550) but fled to Strasbourg in 1554; by the autumn of 1556 he had moved to Frankfurt am Main, with property valued at 500 florins.

Herbaria had appeared, as valuable complements to accurate botanical drawings, at least by 1551, when Luca Ghini of Bologna possessed one. 'Amatus Lusitanus' (João Rodrigues de Castelo Branco), who had received specimens—including *Symphyto petraeo*, common comfrey—from Falconer, referred to the latter's collection of dried plants using 'codici cuidam consitas ac agglutinatas' ('special sheets sewn and glued'; 337): 'maister Falkonners boke' contained an Italian specimen of sea trefoil (sea milkwort) (Turner, *Seconde Parte*, fol. 11v). Falconer had discovered rose parsley (pasqueflower, recorded by 1551) and his collection included *Faba aegypta* (a *Vicia narbonensis*), *Elaphobosco* (both 1554), and a species of *Stachys* (woundwort; 1562).

Seemingly, Falconer never married, and his will, made on 16 April 1558, mentions no relatives. He left to John Hales 'my Avicenna with the index' (presumably an edition of *The Canon of Medicine*, and Palamedes's *Index*); to 'Mr Railton', *Imagines quadrupedum et avium* (perhaps Conrad Gesner's two books of *Icones*); and to 'Mr Dr Turner, my herball [i.e. herbarium]'. Following some small bequests, including one of 40 shillings to John Foxe in Basel, the residue of his goods, 'here on this side the seas and in England' was left to his executrix, Elizabeth Lucy. If she died before he had 'finished this my journey', her brother Thomas was to officiate instead. Falconer was then in Frankfurt, with John Hales and Gregory Railton, staying in Thomas Watts's house.

John Falconer, 'phisicyon' (presumed, perhaps, from his knowledge of simples), was buried in St Stephen's Church, Coleman Street, London, on 11 May 1560; on 22 May, John Jewel wrote to P. M. Vermigli, saying 'Our friend Falconer is dead' (*Zurich Letters* 1.79). Probate was granted to Elizabeth Lucy on 24 May 1560. Falconer's colleagues testified to his learning, and the *Falconera* Salisb. (perhaps *Albuca* in the Hyacinthaceae) was apparently named after him. JOHN BENNELL

Sources will register, GL, Commissary Court of London MS 9171/15, fol. 19v, MS 9172/3C, no. 82 · will, GL · C. H. Garrett, *The Marian exiles: a study in the origins of Elizabethan puritanism* (1938), 148 · Emden, *Oxf.* · C. E. Raven, *English naturalists from Neckam to Ray: a study of the making of the modern world* (1947), 69, 77–8, 82 · A. Arber, *Herbals, their origin and evolution* (1938), 139–40 · L. Amatus [J. R. de Castelo Branco], *In dioscoridis de medica materia libros quinque, enarrationes* (Strasbourg, 1554), 240, 337, 394 · W. Turner, *A new herball* (1551), fols. C.vv, vi · W. Turner, *The seconde parte of William Turners herball* (1562), fol. 1.11v · GL, Commissary Court of London, Probate act book, MS 9168/12, fol. 41 · parish register, London, St Stephen Coleman Street, 1538–98, GL, MS 4448, fol. 36 · H. Robinson, ed. and trans., *The Zurich letters, comprising the correspondence of several English bishops and others with some of the Helvetian reformers, during the early part of the reign of Queen Elizabeth*, 1, Parker Society, 7 (1842), 79, 216, 222 · H. Robinson, ed. and trans., *Original letters relative to the English Reformation*, 1, Parker Society, [26] (1846), 228 ·

E. H. F. Meyer, *Geschichte der Botanik*, 4 (1854–7), 240, 270, 271 · private information (2004)

Falconer, John (1577–1656), Jesuit, was the second son of Henry Falconer (d. 1579) and his wife, Martha Pike (d. c.1579/80), and was born at Litton, Dorset, on 25 March 1577. His father was the second son of an 'ancient and rich family' (Kenny, 70), his mother a wealthy widow from a respectable Cheshire family. Both parents died while Falconer was an infant. He and his four sisters were raised by their uncle John Brook and a cousin Edward Peto. At the age of eleven Falconer was sent to the grammar school of Sherborne, Dorset, for five years. He spent a year in service to his elder brother in Wiltshire before going up to Oxford in February 1595. He studied for nearly a year at St Mary Hall, and another year at Gloucester Hall, 'but visiting his tutor only once a month and avoiding all private and public disputations thus becoming less rather than more learned' (Kenny, 70). He then 'wasted' about two years with his brother in Wiltshire before joining the earl of Essex's expedition against Spain and 'returned to London without booty (thank God)' (Kenny, 70). As a result of the expedition he decided to repent and reform his life. Influenced by Catholics in Henry, Lord Windsor's household, where he served for nearly two and a half years, he converted to Catholicism in 1598. Selling his inheritance to his brother, Falconer left England and was admitted into the English College, Rome, on 27 May 1600 under the assumed name of Dingley. Ordained priest on 20 December 1603, he entered the Society of Jesus in Rome on 18 November 1604. On 28 May 1607 he was sent from Rome to Flanders to prepare to cross into England. Arrested in England some time in 1617 or 1618 he was among the Jesuits banished in 1618. For a year he served as assistant to the master of novices at the English Jesuit noviciate in Liège. Professed of the four vows at Arras on 21 July 1619 he returned to England about 1620. Between 1621 and 1624 he ministered to Catholics in the London area. In 1624 he was transferred to the residence of St Mary, a Jesuit district that comprised Northamptonshire and Oxfordshire. Between 1631 and 1648 he served as confessor, admonitor, and spiritual prefect at English Jesuit houses in Ghent, Liège, and Watten.

Foley assigned Falconer a spirited role in the defence of Wardour Castle against the forces of Sir Edward Hungerford in May 1643 (Foley, 3.525–32). However, according to Jesuit catalogues Falconer was in Ghent at that time. Thus it is more likely that the Falconer involved in the defence was his nephew, a secular priest with the same name.

Falconer's first publication, *A Briefe Refutation of Iohn Traskes Iudaical and Novel Fancyes* (1618), castigated John Traske's insistence that certain Jewish traditions and customs must be practised in Christianity. His *Fasciculus myrrhae* (1633) and *The Mirrour of Created Perfection* (1632) treated two favourite Jesuit themes, the Eucharist and the mother of God. *The Life of S. Catherine* (1634) and his translation of *The Admirable Life of Saint Wenefride* (1635) by Robert, prior of Shrewsbury, were traditional lives of the saints.

The latter was probably written for the use of Catholic pilgrims to the shrine of St Winifred at Holywell, still popular despite the Reformation. In 1648 Falconer returned to London and moved to the residence of St Mary in 1651. There he died on 7 July 1656.　　　THOMAS M. MCCOOG

Sources G. Anstruther, *The seminary priests*, 2 (1975), 99 · T. M. McCoog, ed., *Monumenta Angliae, 2: English and Welsh Jesuits, catalogues, 1630–1640* (1992), 302 · W. Kelly, ed., *Liber ruber venerabilis collegii Anglorum de urbe*, 1, Catholic RS, 37 (1940), 118–19 · H. Foley, ed., *Records of the English province of the Society of Jesus*, 7/1 (1882), 242 · T. M. McCoog, *English and Welsh Jesuits, 1555–1650*, 2 vols., Catholic RS, 74–5 (1994–5) · A. F. Allison and D. M. Rogers, eds., *The contemporary printed literature of the English Counter-Reformation between 1558 and 1640*, 2 vols. (1989–94) · A. Kenny, ed., *The responsa scholarum of the English College, Rome*, 1, Catholic RS, 54 (1962), 67–71 · Foster, *Alum. Oxon., 1500–1714* [John Fawkner]

Archives Archivum Romanum Societatis Iesu, Rome, MSS · Stonyhurst College, Lancashire, MSS

Falconer, Lanoe. *See* Hawker, Mary Elizabeth (1848–1908).

Falconer, Randle Wilbraham (1816–1881), physician, the fourth son of the classical scholar the Revd Thomas *Falconer MD (1771–1839) and his wife, Frances, daughter of Lieutenant-Colonel Robert Raitt, was for many years one of the leading physicians of Bath. His grandfather William *Falconer MD (1744–1824) and his father had also practised there, the latter offering medical assistance to the poor while acting as a clergyman. Randle Wilbraham Falconer began to study medicine at Edinburgh University in 1835, and graduated MD in 1839. Initially he settled at Tenby in Wales, and in 1842 married Maria, daughter of John Wood of Carmarthenshire. She died in 1847, and the same year he moved to Bath, where he lived and practised until his death. In 1850 he married Sophia Harriet Frances, the younger daughter of Major-General Howard-Vyse, formerly MP for Beverley and Honiton.

In addition to his Edinburgh doctorate, Falconer became a fellow of the Royal College of Physicians in 1866, and held the honorary title of doctor from the Queen's University, Ireland, and that of fellow from the King and Queen's College, Dublin. He was also a fellow of the Medico-Chirurgical Society of London and president of the Bath and Bristol section of the British Medical Association in 1864–5. He was physician to the Institute for Idiot Children, Bath, and physician to the Bath General or Mineral Water Hospital between 1856 and 1881. He investigated the curative virtues of the spa, and produced several works on this subject. In *The Baths and Mineral Waters of Bath*, which was first published in 1857 and which reached a fifth edition in 1871, he argued that although drinking from the springs could have unpleasant side effects, they could 'accelerate the pulse, increase temperature of the body, and excite the secretions'—frequently more rapidly and permanently 'than might at first be anticipated' (R. W. Falconer, *Baths and Mineral Waters of Bath*, 1857, 39). His study of patients with rheumatism, sciatica, gouts, and related conditions, which appeared in 1861, was praised by *The Athenaeum* for being 'free from the pretensions and quackery that too often disgrace the literature of mineral waters'.

Falconer had a wide range of interests, and was fond of

Randle Wilbraham Falconer (1816–1881), by unknown photographer

archaeology and botany. Much esteemed by his fellow citizens, he was also elected mayor of Bath on two occasions, served as a respected magistrate, and supported a number of civic initiatives including the successful Bath city lectures; other schemes, for a public abattoir and a public library, were less successful. After his death at his home, 22 Bennett Street, Bath, on 6 May 1881, he was celebrated by the local historian Jerom Murch as a man who, having made the world a better place, would not be quickly forgotten in Bath. Falconer was survived by his second wife.

ANNE BORSAY

Sources J. Murch, *Biographical sketches of Bath celebrities, ancient and modern* (1893), 125–8 · R. Rolls, *The hospital of the nation: the story of spa medicine and the Mineral Water Hospital at Bath* (1988), 125, 158 · *CGPLA Eng. & Wales* (1881) · *London and Provincial Medical Directory* (1867) · *DNB* · R. E. M. Peach, *Historic houses of Bath and their associations*, 2 (1884), 109–10

Archives Bath and North East Somerset RO, Bath General Hospital archives | ICL, letters to Sir Andrew Ramsay

Likenesses J. L. Gardie, bust, 1860, Royal National Hospital for Rheumatic Diseases, Bath · photograph, St John's Hospital, Bath [*see illus.*] · silhouette drawings, Somerset County Library

Wealth at death under £6000: probate, 31 May 1881, *CGPLA Eng. & Wales*

Falconer, Sir Robert Alexander (1867–1943), university principal and biblical scholar in Canada, was born on 10 February 1867 at the manse, Zion Church, Charlottetown, Prince Edward Island, Canada, the eldest of the three children (Robert, James, and Jean) of the Revd Alexander

Sir Robert Alexander Falconer (1867–1943), by unknown photographer, 1908

Falconer (1838–1911), Presbyterian minister and missionary, and his wife, Susan (d. 1887), daughter of the Revd Robert Douglas. They were of Scottish descent and Presbyterian affiliation.

Universally described by contemporaries as cosmopolitan, Falconer spent his most formative years outside Canada. From 1873 to 1876 he studied at MacKay's academy in Dartmouth, Nova Scotia, and then, from 1877 to 1884, at Queen's Royal College, Port of Spain, Trinidad, his father having been appointed missionary pastor to Greyfriars Church in Port of Spain. Excelling at that school's Etonian curriculum, he won the Gilchrist scholarship for the Caribbean and enrolled in the University of Edinburgh in 1885, where he completed a classical honours MA degree (there was no degree of BA) in 1889. He immediately entered the divinity college of the Free Church of Scotland (New College), where he was introduced to the higher criticism and philosophical idealism, chiefly by Andrew Bruce Davidson and Marcus Dods. As he later recalled, however, in *Religion on my Life's Road* (1938), it was only during summer study in Germany under church historian Adolf Harnack that he truly encountered 'the full throb of the modern mind' (Falconer, 61) and found it fully compatible with inherited faith. Thereafter Falconer retained a confident and eclectic cast of mind for life. He spoke or read English, French, German, Latin, Greek, and Hebrew, graduated a bachelor of divinity in April 1892, and returned to Halifax, one of the best-trained and most liberal Canadian biblical scholars of his generation.

Although Falconer never held a pulpit and seldom preached, in 1892 he accepted ordination in order to take up the post of lecturer in New Testament Greek and exegesis at the Presbyterian college (Pine Hill), Halifax. He became principal there in 1904. A dozen or so learned articles in journals such as *The Expositor* (1901–2) led to an Edinburgh DD degree in 1902. On 12 May 1897 he married Sophia, known as Sophie (1870–1968), daughter of the Revd Joseph Gandier of Newburgh, Ontario. Disappointed by two early stillbirths, the couple later had two sons, James Gilbert and Robert Douglas Falconer, a physician and an engineer respectively. At Pine Hill, Falconer befriended a tightly knit group, including Daniel M. Gordon, Walter Murray, Alfred Gandier, and Clarence Mackinnon, who would also become university and college leaders, thus intensifying the already strong maritime and Presbyterian influence on Canadian higher education. With Falconer, several of these men played important parts in the founding of the United Church of Canada in 1925.

In 1907 Falconer was appointed president of the University of Toronto, following major reforms of that institution orchestrated by Conservative premier James Pliny Whitney. Harmonizing diverse theories, Falconer subscribed to an organic idea of the university which combined the pursuit of culture with pure scholarship and practical community service. Thus, while arguing for the centrality of the arts, he also promoted professional education and graduate studies. While the latter were being developed, he tried to offset the pull of American programmes by urging British graduate schools to develop a PhD degree more accessible to Canadians. Throughout his tenure he also exercised great tact in cementing relations among the numerous sectarian colleges which together comprised the federated University of Toronto. That institution expanded substantially from 3545 students in 1907 to over 8000 when Falconer retired in 1932.

Falconer was obsessed with keeping both government and the public at arm's length from the university in a province he deemed to be particularly intolerant. This was especially the case after 1914, when he failed in a bid to save the jobs of three German faculty members. Partly in consequence, his approach to academic freedom was, and would remain, controversial. Remarkably tolerant by contemporary standards concerning classroom expression, he sometimes chided professors who played politics off campus. Ironically, Falconer himself was knighted, being made KCMG in 1917 for his outspoken public sponsorship of wartime recruitment. This went far beyond encouraging student enlistment. Indeed, he chaired the War Lectures Bureau, championed conscription, and addressed patriotic rallies throughout the dominion. Inconsistent on the issue of extramural politicking, he nevertheless personified the strengths and weaknesses of the official mind of Canadian higher academe until he left office in 1932.

Falconer accumulated a score of honorary doctorates. To him, however, the highest honour came when the University of Edinburgh offered him its principalship in 1929.

Failing health ruled out acceptance, but it did not preclude a resumption of serious scholarship, the chief fruit of which was *The Pastoral Epistles* (1937). While this work was, perhaps, his highest achievement as a biblical historian, Falconer was a prolific author throughout his life. Ranging freely over topics as varied as philosophy, religion, history, art, education, and politics, he produced numerous occasional, as well as several more extended, works. Particularly influential were his *The German Tragedy and its Meaning for Canada* (1915) and *Idealism in National Character* (1920), in which he argued that great issues of the war and reconstruction were, at heart, matters pitting materialism against philosophic idealism. The same themes resurface in most of his major writings on public affairs. This extended to his *The United States as a Neighbour* (1926), in which he pictured broad Anglo-Saxon co-operation as the model upon which a true internationalism might be built. In his more purely scholarly works, he displayed a liberal, historical approach to biblical study, largely eschewing eschatological or 'social gospel' interpretations that gained favour in the early part of the twentieth century.

A long-time fellow of the Royal Society of Canada, Falconer was its president for 1931–2. He also championed the League of Nations, even as Canada slipped into isolationism between the wars. On 4 November 1943 he died suddenly at his home, 81 Glengowan Road, Toronto, Ontario, Canada, of heart failure; he was buried in Mount Pleasant cemetery, Toronto, on 8 November. Tall, sturdy, and, until late in life, boyishly handsome, Falconer is well captured in a photographic collection and a portrait by Maurice Greiffenhagen held by the University of Toronto.   JAMES G. GREENLEE

Sources J. G. Greenlee, *Sir Robert Falconer: a biography* (1988) [with full bibliography] • R. A. Falconer, *Religion on my life's road* (1938) • *University of Toronto Quarterly* (Jan 1944) • *Globe and Mail* [Toronto] (5 Nov 1943) • *Toronto Star* (5 Nov 1943) • *Proceedings and Transactions of the Royal Society of Canada*, 3rd ser., 38 (1944) • Emmanuel College, Toronto, United Church of Canada records • *Halifax Herald* (1892–1907) • *Chronicle* (1892–1907) • *WWW* • M. Horn, 'Free speech within the law', *Ontario History*, 72 (1980), 27–48 • J. Moir, '"Mildewed with discretion": Toronto's higher critics and public opinion in the 1920s', *Studies in Religion*, 2 (1982), 173–9 • private information (2004) • C. Mackinnon, *Reminiscences* (1938) • *Presbyterian Witness* (July 1911)
Archives Emmanuel College, Toronto, United Church of Canada archives, biographical files • University of Toronto, official presidential papers | Queen's University, Kingston, Ontario, J. W. Flavelle MSS, archives • University of Saskatchewan, Saskatoon, Walter Murray MSS, archives • University of Toronto, James Mavor MSS • University of Toronto, B. E. Walker MSS, archives | SOUND University of Toronto, oral history project
Likenesses photograph, 1908, University of Toronto, Canada [see illus.] • M. Greiffenhagen, oils, 1932, University of Toronto, Canada • photographs, University of Toronto, Canada

Falconer, Thomas (1736/7–1792), classical scholar, was the son of William Falconer, recorder of Chester, and Elizabeth, daughter of Randle Wilbraham de Townsend. He matriculated from Brasenose College, Oxford, on 12 March 1754, aged seventeen, but left without taking a degree. He was called to the bar at Lincoln's Inn on 20 June

1760. Being prevented by chronic ill health from practising at the bar, he led a studious life at Chester.

His main interest was in classical antiquities but he was also a patron of literature. Anna Seward called him the Maecenas of Chester. In 1771 Foote Gower addressed a letter to him, which was published as *A Sketch of the Materials for a New History of Cheshire*. John Reinhold Forster dedicated to him his translation of Baron Riedesel's *Travels through Sicily, and that Part of Italy Formerly called Magna Graecia* (1773).

A paper Falconer read to the Society of Antiquaries in 1791, on the accuracy of Pliny's description of the temple of Diana at Ephesus, was published in *Archaeologia*, 11. His other published works were *Devotions for the Sacrament of the Lord's Supper, by a Layman* (1786; 2nd edn 1798); *Chronological Tables, Beginning with the Reign of Solomon and Ending with the Death of Alexander the Great* (1796); and an *Ode to Sleep*, the publication date of which is uncertain. He also left material for an edition of Strabo which formed the basis for the work brought out in 1807 by his nephew, the Revd Thomas Falconer. From the evidence of his will, Falconer does not seem to have married; he died on 4 September 1792 and was buried in St Michael's Church, Chester. There is an inscribed monument to his memory in St John's Church, Chester.

J. M. RIGG, *rev.* J. A. MARCHAND

Sources T. Falconer, *A bibliography of works by members of the Falconer family, with genealogical notices* (1866) • Foster, *Alum. Oxon.* • G. Ormerod, *The history of the county palatine and city of Chester*, 1 (1819), 321 • *Letters of Anna Seward: written between the years 1784 and 1807*, ed. A. Constable, 3 (1811), 167 • will, PRO, PROB 11/1223, sig. 510
Archives Essex RO, Colchester, letters to Charles Gray • RBG Kew, corresp. with Sir Joseph Banks • Warks. CRO, letters to Thomas Pennant and David Pennant
Wealth at death brother William main beneficiary: will, PRO, PROB 11/1223, fols. 353r–355v

Falconer, Thomas (1771–1839), classical scholar, was born on 24 December 1771 in Duke Street, Bath, the son of William *Falconer, MD, FRS, of Bath, and Henrietta, daughter of Thomas Edmunds of Worsborough Hall, Yorkshire. He was educated at the cathedral school in Chester, Bath grammar school, Manchester grammar school, the King's School in Chester, and Corpus Christi College, Oxford. He was a precocious boy, and some of his verses were published in *Prulusiones poeticae* (1788). He was elected a scholar of Corpus in 1788, and graduated BA in 1791 and MA in 1795. He was elected a fellow in November 1794, vacating his fellowship after his marriage on 7 December 1797 to Frances, daughter of Lieutenant-Colonel Robert Raitt, with whom he had six sons and five daughters. After taking holy orders he spent some time in Edinburgh studying medicine. He took the degrees of MB and MD in Oxford in 1822, but never practised medicine, nor did he ever do any ordinary clerical duty apart from a short curacy in Bath. His lack of preferment may have been caused by his liking for controversy: he quarrelled with the bishop of Salisbury and turned down at least one living.

Falconer's love of argument and wide but disorganized intellectual interests are evident from his works. Many of his published sermons, including the eight Oxford Bampton lectures entitled *Certain Principles in Evanson's 'Dissonance of the Four Generally Received Evangelists' etc.* (1811), deal critically with the views of others, although his time in Edinburgh made him sympathetic to the ideas of nonconformists.

Falconer's classical work lay chiefly in the field of ancient geography. In 1797 he published *The Voyage of Hanno, Translated and Accompanied with the Greek Text and Dissertations*, and he left a manuscript translation of Strabo which was later completed by his son William *Falconer. With his father he also wrote a *Discourse on the Measure of the Olympic Stadium* (1805) which was appended to his father's translation of Arrian's *Periplus*.

Although Falconer was not a particularly distinguished scholar, he was unlucky that his edition of Strabo became notorious through a review by Payne Knight in the *Edinburgh Review* of July 1809 which formed a famous attack on Oxford and its scholarship. Falconer's elegantly produced two-volume folio edition was published by the Oxford University Press in 1807. It was based on material left by his uncle Thomas Falconer (1738–1792). The first two books had been seen through the press by Dr Parsons, master of Balliol College, and five more had been edited by the Revd Henry Halliwell of Brasenose College, Oxford. The edition was described by Knight as a 'ponderous monument of operose ignorance and vain expense'. His criticisms of Falconer and Oxford learning were answered by a series of lengthy *Replies* by Edward Copleston (later provost of Oriel) which form an important—if at times complacent—apologia for Oxford education. Copleston's vigorous defence produced a personal letter of thanks from the chancellor and the conferring on him of the degree of DD by diploma.

Falconer's edition hardly deserves the vehemence of Payne Knight's attack. Although the text is reprinted from Almeloveen's edition (itself a reprint of Casaubon's), Falconer senior had assembled a wide and valuable array of variant readings which proved very helpful to later editors. His manuscript (preserved in the Bodleian Library) contains collations made by several European scholars of manuscripts of Strabo from foreign libraries, including Paris, Florence, Madrid, and Moscow.

Falconer died at his home in The Circus, Bath, on 19 February 1839. Thomas *Falconer (1805–1882), the county court judge, and Randle Wilbraham *Falconer (1816–1881), the physician, were his sons, and John Arthur Roebuck, the radical politician, was his son-in-law.

RICHARD SMAIL

Sources GM, 2nd ser., 11 (1839), 326–7, 435–6 · J. F. Smith, ed., *The admission register of the Manchester School, with some notes of the more distinguished scholars*, 2, Chetham Society, 73 (1868) · *Hist. U. Oxf.* 5: 18th-cent. Oxf. · M. L. Clarke, *Greek studies in England, 1700–1830* (1945) · A. Diller, *The textual tradition of Strabo's geography* (1975)

Falconer, Thomas (1805–1882), judge, was born on 25 June 1805, the second son of the Revd Thomas *Falconer, MD, (1771–1839), of Bath, and his wife, Frances, daughter of Lieutenant-Colonel Robert Raitt of the 2nd regiment; he was a great-grandson of William Falconer, recorder of Chester. He was admitted a member of Lincoln's Inn on 13 November 1823 and was called to the bar on 8 February 1830. Falconer practised as an equity draftsman and conveyancer, and from 1837 to 1840 held the post of revising barrister for the boroughs of Finsbury, Tower Hamlets, and Marylebone. In the 1830s he was an active committee member of the Society for the Diffusion of Useful Knowledge, playing an important part in choosing manuscripts for publication by the society. Falconer also acted as nominal editor of the *London Review* after its foundation in 1834 by a group of philosophic radicals (including his sister's husband, J. A. Roebuck) who were dissatisfied with the *Westminster Review*. In practice, however, he was only the sub-editor. He resigned his post in 1837, as a result of disagreements with the true editor, John Stuart Mill, who was often exasperated by what he saw as Falconer's inefficiency. Falconer also contributed a tract on *Orange Societies* (1835) to Roebuck's Pamphlets for the People, and wrote an account, published by the English Presbyterian Association in 1834, of the history and legal position of English Presbyterians.

Falconer was a laborious worker, a staunch Liberal, a committed law reformer, and an energetic opponent of abuses. He was highly critical of the policies pursued in Lower Canada regarding political prisoners detained in the aftermath of the rebellion of the *patriotes* in 1837. He subsequently spent more than two years in travelling through North America, returning to England in December 1842. His interest in Canada continued: in 1850 he was appointed by the earl of Elgin, governor-in-chief of British North America, and his council to act as arbitrator on behalf of that province for the purpose of determining the boundaries between Canada and New Brunswick.

On 29 July 1851 he was nominated colonial secretary of Western Australia, but after resigning his appointment he was appointed on 22 December 1851 by the lord chancellor, Lord Truro, to be the judge of the county courts of Glamorgan and Brecknockshire, and of the district of Rhayader. Falconer was an energetic county court judge, who worked tirelessly in this position, travelling twenty-two days and covering 400 miles on circuit every month. Through his dedication, he managed almost to extinguish the civil business of the assizes in Glamorgan. He was also a staunch defender of the county court system against those who doubted its efficiency.

After sitting on the bench for thirty years he retired in December 1881. He died at 18 Royal Crescent, Bath, on 28 August 1882, in the seventy-eighth year of his age. He appears never to have married. He was a member of several learned societies, and was a traveller of much experience. He was an occasional contributor to the *Westminster Review* and the *Colonial Magazine*, and was the author of several books and a very large number of pamphlets.

MICHAEL LOBBAN

Sources *Law Times* (2 Sept 1882), 315–16 · *ILN* (16 Sept 1882) · *Wellesley index* · *The earlier letters of John Stuart Mill, 1812–1848*, ed. F. E. Mineka (1963), vol. 12 of *The Collected Works of John Stuart Mill*, ed. J. M. Robson (1963–91) · T. Falconer, *John Falconer: cryptomenysis*

patefacta (1866) [bibliography of the writings of the Falconer family with biographical notes] · *CGPLA Eng. & Wales* (1882) · d. cert.
Archives Duke U., Perkins L., corresp. · UCL, letters to Society for the Diffusion of Useful Knowledge | BL, letters to Joseph Humber, Add. MS 24868 · UCL, Brougham MSS · Yale U., Beinecke L., Osborn collection, letters to T. J. Pettigrew
Likenesses engraving (after photograph by W. G. Lewis), repro. in *ILN*
Wealth at death £6668 19s. 10d.: probate, 20 Sept 1882, *CGPLA Eng. & Wales*

Falconer, William (*bap.* 1732, *d.* 1770), poet and lexicographer, was baptized in Edinburgh on 11 February 1732, which was possibly also the day of his birth. He was one of three children of William Falconer, wig maker, and Agnes Shand of the Nether Bow, Edinburgh. Nothing is known of Falconer's childhood except that he had some rudimentary schooling under one Webster before he went to sea as an apprentice, probably in the coal trade from Northumberland to London, about which he makes knowledgeable references in his poetry.

Evidence for Falconer's seafaring life is to be adduced from his long poem *The Shipwreck*, which he claims to be autobiographical. If so, by 1749 he had completed his apprenticeship and had joined a British merchant ship in the Levant trade at Alexandria as second mate. The ship, homeward bound via Venice, was driven off course by a furious gale and was wrecked at Sunium in Greece. Falconer was one of three survivors. In 1751 he was in Edinburgh for his first publication, an ode on the death of Frederick, prince of Wales. His life for the next decade is obscure. He was almost certainly at sea in merchant ships, and there is evidence from *The Shipwreck* that he also served in the Royal Navy and may have been in Hawke's fleet at Quiberon Bay (November 1759). A surviving logbook records that in 1760 he was serving as mate on the *Vestal* frigate in the north Atlantic trade.

Falconer's serious literary career began in May 1762, when he was in London for the publication of *The Shipwreck: a Poem, in Three Cantos, by a Sailor*. The poem was favourably reviewed in the *Gentleman's Magazine* on 1 June, and the reviewer's hope that the poem would achieve for its author 'preferment in the service' was fulfilled on Falconer's appointment as midshipman on the *Royal George* on 10 June, though with peace approaching the ship was laid up and the crew paid off in December.

Nothing is known of the following year until Falconer's appointment as purser of the *Glory*, laid up in Chatham Dockyard in Kent. Falconer perhaps gained this post on the recommendation of Edward, duke of York, who had shown the poet some patronage. This began a period of appointments as purser of laid-up vessels (*Medway*, 1767; *Swiftsure*, 1767; *Cumberland*, 1768); these positions can be regarded as sinecures since Falconer was able to employ deputies for his peacetime purser's duties, leaving time for literary pursuits. Clarke records that the captain's cabin on the *Glory* was 'fitted up with a stove, and with every addition of comfort … in order that Falconer might thus be enabled to enjoy his favourite propensity' (Clarke, xxxv).

The first fruit of this change from seafaring was the publication in 1764 of a second edition, extended and much revised, of *The Shipwreck*. That spring Falconer married Jane (1734/5–1796), daughter of William Hicks, surgeon of Sheerness Dockyard. He began to engage in literary and intellectual friendships, for example with Thomas, brother of Jonas Hanway, and with John Murray, whose invitation to enter into his new publishing venture in 1768 Falconer declined. Friendship with George Lewis Scott led to the suggestion in 1764–5 that Falconer compile a nautical dictionary, an undertaking that had its origins in the copious notes of technical explanation he had attached to *The Shipwreck*. Proposals were published in 1767, and *The Universal Dictionary of the Marine* was published in March 1769, by which time Falconer and his wife were living in Somerset House, London.

Falconer's reputation rests on these two major works: the *Dictionary of the Marine* and *The Shipwreck*. The former is a work of extraordinary care and scientific thoroughness, and it became the standard nautical dictionary until the end of sail. The popularity of *The Shipwreck* derives from its unique character as a technically detailed seafaring verse narrative, full of pathos and sublimity, from the pen of a professional sailor. Of the three versions, the first is the most accessible to a modern reader, unembellished by the extensive refinements added later to suit contemporary taste. It was highly praised by later writers, including Byron and Coleridge, and its popularity continued into the mid-nineteenth century. J. S. Clarke's 1804 edition, followed by all subsequent editors, is textually very faulty. Falconer's other poems—short lyrics, a political squib on Pitt, odes, and descriptive pieces—are unremarkable.

In the summer of 1769 Falconer agreed to sail with the East India Company commissioners who were appointed for the restoration of order in India, probably with the promise of a secretaryship on arrival. The frigate *Aurora* sailed on 30 September; contrary to most accounts Falconer was a passenger, not the purser. After his departure a third and again much revised edition of *The Shipwreck* was published in November. The *Aurora* arrived at Cape Town on 6 December 1769, sailing on 22 December. She was reported in Madagascar in April 1770. Nothing was heard of her again, despite searches by the *Morse* Indiaman in 1771. Falconer can be presumed to have died in 1770.　　　　　　　　　　　　WILLIAM R. JONES

Sources W. R. Jones, 'A critical edition of the poetical works of William Falconer', PhD diss., U. Southampton, 1977 · M. K. Joseph, 'William Falconer', *Studies in Philology*, 47 (1950), 72–101 · J. S. Clarke, *The shipwreck, a poem by William Falconer … with a life of the author* (1804) · M. K. Joseph, 'William Falconer', MLitt diss., U. Oxf., 1954 · W. H. D. Adams, 'Life of Falconer', in W. Falconer, *The shipwreck, a poem* (1887) · R. Anderson, *A complete edition of the poets of Great Britain*, 13 vols. (1792–5), vol. 10, pp. 571–610 · bap. reg. Scot., Edinburgh parochial registers, 685 1/19, fol. 259 · *GM*, 1st ser., 41 (1771), 190 · letter from Jane Falconer to William Falconer, 1 Jan 1771, BM, Add. MSS 29.132.402, 404
Archives NMM, journal kept as mate in ships trading with America, MS 58/112
Wealth at death widow left poor, and relied on gifts from Cadell, publisher of *Dictionary of the Marine*

Falconer, William (1744–1824), physician, was born in Chester on 23 February 1744, the younger of two surviving sons of William Falconer of the Inner Temple, recorder of Chester, and his wife and second cousin, Elizabeth, daughter of Randle Wilbraham of Townsend near Nantwich, Cheshire. After graduating MD from Edinburgh in 1766 he attended the lectures of Gaubius and Albinus at Leiden and gained a second MD on 22 May 1767. He had become an extra-licentiate of the Royal College of Physicians on 12 March 1767 and in the same year was appointed physician to the Chester Infirmary. Falconer established a good practice in the town. In January 1770, however, at the suggestion of the Quaker physician John Fothergill, he moved to Bath where he lived briefly in Duke Street and then at 29 The Circus. On 18 March 1773 he was elected a fellow of the Royal Society and on 12 May 1784 he was appointed physician of the Bath General Hospital, a post which he retained until 10 February 1819. Falconer married Henrietta (1739–1803), daughter of Thomas Edmunds of Worsbrough Hall in Yorkshire. Their only child, Thomas *Falconer (1771–1839), took holy orders and gained the degrees of MB and MD; Thomas's fifth son, Randle Wilbraham *Falconer (1816–1881), followed in his grandfather's footsteps by becoming a physician to the general hospital.

Though greatly esteemed, William Falconer was not a popular man. As the nineteenth-century commentator, R. E. M. Peach, observed: 'He was too proud and too independent to stoop to the arts of his profession … [and] had a peculiar *brusqueness* of manner, which has been sometimes referred to as the *Falconer temper*' (Peach, 101). Despite this abrasive personality Falconer ran a successful spa practice, counting among his patients the duke of Portland, Lord Chancellor Thurlowe, William Pitt, and Horatio Nelson. A cultivated man, Falconer engaged in the activities of the Bath and West of England Society and the Manchester Literary and Philosophical Society. He was also a prolific writer who published over forty books as well as numerous papers. These works ranged over topics in the classics, theology, and natural history, but medicine featured most prominently, including studies of plague, influenza, and fever, the antiseptic qualities of fixed air or carbon dioxide, and the implications of climate, diet, and lifestyle for health. *A Dissertation on the Influence of the Passions upon Disorders of the Body* (1788) won the Fothergill gold medal of the Medical Society of London in 1796. However, William Falconer was most famous for his research into the Bath waters and their impact on chronic conditions, notably rheumatism, gout, and ischias, or the hip case. The Medical Society of London awarded its silver medal to him for an essay on this last subject in 1805.

In investigating the efficacy of the spa, William Falconer made an important contribution to later Georgian medical quantification, which contests the view that clinical statistics only emerged at the Paris hospitals after the French Revolution. Building on the mortality and morbidity ratios which James Jurin had constructed to evaluate smallpox inoculation, Falconer was an 'arithmetic observationist clinician' who recognized that numerical analysis had to accompany simple counting if patient records were to yield their full potential (Tröhler, 62–4). His training at the progressive Edinburgh medical school under William Cullen primed him for this role and brought him into contact with a group of students—including Thomas Percival and John Haygarth—who were to become pioneers of a social medicine which used statistical comparisons to tackle problems of urban public health. Like Falconer, Haygarth joined the staff of the Chester Infirmary in the late 1760s, and his subsequent control of its fever wards received widespread acclaim. Falconer, however, applied his Edinburgh education to the evaluation of balneology after his transfer to Bath in 1770.

Falconer was the latest in a line of medical practitioners to subject the springs to scientific enquiry. Election to the Bath Hospital, while not inducing regular attendance at its weekly management committee, did enable him to follow the example of predecessors like William Oliver and Rice Charleton, and use the patient records for research purposes. This was the source for his most sophisticated project, *An Account of the Use, Application and Success of the Bath Waters in Rheumatic Cases* (1795). More than 400 patients with rheumatism, admitted to the hospital between 1785 and 1793, were divided into five categories according to their state of health when discharged. One-third were described as 'cured', almost four out of ten as 'much better', and 15 per cent as 'better'. Therefore, Falconer concluded that the spa was beneficial. Furthermore, by adjusting for the sex ratio, and projecting a success rate for men from the rate achieved by women, he was able to suggest that male patients responded more effectively to treatment.

The roots of Falconer's statistical methodologies in Edinburgh medicine linked him to the religious and political radicalism which informed this intellectual culture. Though pious and an 'earnest reformer', however, he was neither a dissenter nor a committed whig, believing that the party 'cared less for reform than they did for office' (Peach, 102). Support for Edmund Burke's early reaction against the French Revolution encouraged him to respond with what Burke himself praised as a 'temperate, judicious, and reasonable paper' (Peach, 102). Moreover, Falconer joined with his conservative medical colleagues in 1792 to resist a campaign to relocate the general hospital which was articulated through the new language of social medicine.

Falconer died at his house in The Circus on 31 August 1824. He was buried at Weston, outside Bath. A contemporary chronicler compared 'his general manner, and sententious, pithy observations … to the style and address of Dr Samuel Johnson. Science and learning … [were] indebted to his pen' (Mainwaring, 260).

ANNE BORSAY

Sources R. E. M. Peach, *Historic houses of Bath and their associations*, 2 (1884) · U. Tröhler, 'Quantification in British medicine and surgery, 1750–1830', PhD diss., U. Lond., 1978 · F. M. Lobo, 'John Haygarth, smallpox and religious dissent in eighteenth-century England', *The medical Enlightenment of the eighteenth century*, ed. A. Cunningham and R. French (1990), 217–53 · J. Murch, *Biographical sketches of Bath celebrities, ancient and modern* (1893) · R. Mainwaring,

Annals of Bath (1838) · A. Borsay, 'An example of political arithmetic: the evaluation of spa therapy at the Georgian Bath Infirmary, 1742–1830', *Medical History*, 44 (2000) · R. Rolls, *The hospital of the nation: the story of spa medicine and the mineral water hospital at Bath* (1988) · *An address to the governors of the Bath Hospital on the propriety of extending the benefits of that humane and laudable institution* (1792) · *DNB*

Archives Bath Central Library, receipt and notebook | Bath and North East Somerset RO, Bath General Hospital MSS
Likenesses attrib. T. West, coloured etching, 1803 (*Physicians expressing thanks to influenza*), Wellcome L. · Daniel, portrait, repro. in Evans, *Catalogue of engraved portraits*, 2, 148 · J. Fittler, line engraving (after Daniel), NPG, Wellcome L.

Falconer, William (1801–1885), classical scholar, was born on 27 December 1801 at Corston, Somerset, the eldest son of the Revd Thomas *Falconer MD (1771–1839) and Frances, only child of Lieutenant-Colonel Robert Raitt. He was a member of a remarkable family. His paternal grandfather (1744–1824), also named William, was a physician and a writer of some twenty-five miscellaneous tracts. William the younger had two brothers, Thomas *Falconer (1805–1882), jurist and writer largely on legal matters, and Randle Wilbraham *Falconer (1816–1881), physician and writer on medical matters. William Falconer matriculated from Oriel College, Oxford, on 10 December 1819, took a first in mathematics and a third in classics, graduated BA in 1823 and proceeded MA in 1827. On 30 June 1827 he was elected a Petrean fellow of Exeter College where he examined in mathematics in 1832–3 and from 1836 to 1838. In 1839 he opened the Petrean scholarship to natives of Cheshire and on 26 January the same year he was given the rectory of Bushey, Hertfordshire. On 8 August 1839 he married Isabella Jane, daughter of J. Robinson, and widow of W. S. Douglas; she died at St Alessi, near Pistoia, on 7 February 1869.

William's father edited the text of Strabo's *Geography* in 1807, using materials left by his uncle Thomas Falconer (1738–1792). He also left a manuscript translation of that work. Hans Claude Hamilton of the Public Record Office, antiquary and classical scholar, was appointed to translate Strabo for the Bohn Classical Library. It took him three years to finish the first six books, and Falconer, as son of the Oxford editor of Strabo, known to have had a translation of the *Geography* intended for publication, was asked to complete the translation of the remaining eleven books. The 'Notice' prefatory to the first volume of the Bohn edition states that the text used for the translation was that of the edition by the German scholar Gustav Cramer. There is no mention of the two Thomas Falconers. The Bohn translation did not attract much attention, the reviewer of the first volume for the *Gentleman's Magazine* displaying his knowledge of the descent of the text of Strabo, but expressing no opinion of the translation (*GM*, 2nd ser., 43, 1855, 55–6). William Falconer died at Bushey, Hertfordshire, on 9 February 1885.　　ARTHUR SHERBO

Sources *DNB* · m. cert.
Wealth at death £6835 11s. 7d.: probate, 22 July 1885, *CGPLA Eng. & Wales*

Falconer, Pierre-Étienne [Peter] (1741–1791), portrait painter, was born in Paris on 8 October 1741, the son of Étienne-Maurice Falconet (1716–1791), sculptor to Catherine II of Russia. He probably underwent some training in the French Academy of Art, but his father, who was on personal terms with Sir Joshua Reynolds, sent his son to London about 1765 to work under that painter's direction. In 1766 he obtained a premium of 20 guineas for a painting in chiaroscuro, and another of 26 guineas, in 1768, for a historical composition. He was a member of the Incorporated Society of Artists, and contributed forty pictures to their exhibitions from 1767 to 1773. He was elected a fellow of the Society of Antiquaries in 1771 and in 1772 sold a portrait of his wife to Horace Walpole (exh. Society of Artists, 1772; sold Strawberry Hill sale, 1842, day 22, lot 46). He entered the Royal Academy Schools on 14 February 1769 and exhibited at the Royal Academy in 1773.

Falconet is best known for a set of portraits of eminent artists (1768–9). Drawn in profile in blacklead, with a slight tint of colour on the cheeks, they comprise portraits of Sir William Chambers, Francis Cotes, Joshua Kirby, Francis Hayman, Jeremiah Meyer, Ozias Humphry, George Stubbs, Benjamin West, James Paine, the architect, W. W. Ryland, Paul Sandby, and Sir Joshua Reynolds (the likeness is attested by Northcote) among others. Those of Sandby and Chambers are in the British Museum, as are engraved versions by D. P. Pariset and B. Reading. Other portraits by Falconet engraved by Pariset include Horace Walpole; the Revd James Granger (frontispiece to his *Biographical History of England*, 1769–74); and the *Earl of Marchmont* (Scottish National Portrait Gallery, Edinburgh). Others were engraved in mezzotint by Valentine Green, some by J. Hibbert, J. Watson, John Dixon, Gabriel Smith, and J. F. Bause. There is a small engraving, from a design by Falconet, representing the interior of his father's studio. His engraved illustrations to his father's article on sculpture in Diderot's *Encyclopédie* are noted to have been one of his achievements. He also engraved some designs of F. Boucher and decorated a Chinese temple for Lady de Grey at Wrest, Bedfordshire.

In 1773 Falconet travelled to St Petersburg to join his father. He married on 30 January 1777 Marie Anne Collot (1748–1821), his father's assistant, and herself a talented sculptor. Returning to Paris in 1778, he died there on 25 June 1791, having possibly separated from his wife. His daughter, Madame Jankowitz, bequeathed a collection of his works and some plaster busts by his wife, including one of Falconet himself, to the Musée de Nancy. Three of his autograph drawings are in the British Museum.

L. H. CUST, rev. TINA FISKE

Sources Bénézit, *Dict.*, 3rd edn · E. Edwards, *Anecdotes of painters* (1808); facs. edn (1970) · L. Gonse, *Les chefs-d'oeuvre des musées de France* (1904) · B. Stewart and M. Cutten, *The dictionary of portrait painters in Britain up to 1920* (1997) · D. Foskett, *A dictionary of British miniature painters*, 2 vols. (1972) · Graves, *RA exhibitors* · Graves, *Soc. Artists* · S. C. Hutchison, 'The Royal Academy Schools, 1768–1830', *Walpole Society*, 38 (1960–62), 123–91, esp. 133 · H. Smailes, *The concise catalogue of the Scottish National Portrait Gallery* (1990) · L. Binyon, *Catalogue of drawings by British artists and artists of foreign origin working in Great Britain*, 4 vols. (1898–1907) · *Engraved Brit. ports.* · Redgrave, *Artists* · Bryan, *Painters* (1903–5) · J. C. Smith, *British* *mezzotinto portraits*, 4 vols. in 5 (1878–84) · 'Falconet, Etienne-Maurice', *The dictionary of art*, ed. J. Turner (1996)

Likenesses M. Collot, bust, Musée de Nancy, France; repro. in Gonse, *Les chefs-d'oeuvre* · M. Collot, bust, The Hermitage, St Petersburg · P. E. Falconet, self-portrait, drawing, Musée de Nancy, France

Faldo, John (1633/4–1691), nonconformist minister and religious controversialist, is of unknown parentage. He is said to have been educated at Cambridge but does not appear in the records of the university and is first heard of as a chaplain to Colonel John Hewson's regiment during the civil war. He also preached to Robert Lilburne's regiment. By 1669 he was living at East Barnet, Hertfordshire, and preaching in nearby Chipping Barnet in a hired room. He was licensed as a nonconformist preacher at Chipping Barnet on 13 May 1672, although the designation 'presbyterian' may well be a clerical error as he was described as 'congregational' (Gordon, 261), on his application for a licence for preaching in a room at Wood Street, Chipping Barnet, in the same year.

Replying to the Quaker William Penn's *Spirit of Truth* (1672), Faldo published a 370-page anti-Quaker tract, *Quakerism No Christianity* (1672). To this Penn replied in the 254 pages of *Quakerism a New Nick-name for Old Christianity* (1673), for which Faldo offered only the 96-page *Vindication of Quakerism No Christianity* (1673). Penn again replied with *The Invalidity of John Faldo's Vindication* (1673). Faldo then issued a challenge to Penn to have a public debate, but Penn declined. After further publications, a new edition of Faldo's first work in the controversy, *Quakerism No Christianity*, was published in 1675 with an 'epistle' commending it and its author by '21 learned divines', leading London nonconformists of a moderate persuasion, including five Independent or congregational and eleven clearly presbyterian leaders, men such as Thomas Jenkyn, Thomas Manton, Matthew Barker, and George Griffith. The epistle's plea to Quakers, 'honest, well-meaning, ignorant persons' (Faldo, 'epistle', *Quakerism*, 1675 edn, unpag. 7), not to confuse strict morality with theological wisdom strongly suggests the pen of Richard Baxter, who was indeed one of the twenty-one. A rather fierce two-page 'letter to the reader' was also included, written by four ministers from Theobalds and Chipping Barnet representing Faldo's Hertfordshire friends. Penn answered this latest work and the controversy then closed with Faldo's reply, *XXI Divines Cleared* (1675), which added little to the debate.

Faldo's tracts covered many of the issues raised in earlier debates between Quakers and other Christians: the sacramental ordinances; whether 'the word of God' referred primarily to the Bible or to Christ; whether Jesus's resurrection was physical or spiritual; whether the historical Jesus was the source of human salvation or was merely the prototype life in a 'prepared body' of the eternal Christ-spirit who must transform people within; whether the spirit's inspiration could still produce moral perfection and infallible messages. Before they descended to biblical 'Billingsgate', Penn's and Faldo's pamphlet war served a useful purpose in forcing them to authenticate and clarify their doctrinal beliefs.

After the controversy Faldo continued in his ministry. He was fined for preaching in February 1683 and in 1684 was in Newgate for the same offence. He was chosen minister of the congregational church at Plaisterers Hall, Addle Street, Aldermanbury, in 1684, apparently preaching to a congregation of some 2000, and later moved his church to Ropemakers' Alley, Moorfields. In 1687 he published a fine book of sermons, *A Discourse of the Gospel of Peace, and of the Government of our own Spirits*, dedicated to Lady Clinton, and in the same year was among eight Independent ministers who took an address of thanks to James II for his declaration for the liberty of conscience. After the revolution of 1688 and the Act of Toleration in 1689, Faldo and the nine still living from the twenty-one, notably Griffith and Barker, shared in the short-lived 'happy union' of presbyterians and congregationalists and Faldo was one of seven congregational managers of the resulting common fund for the support of ministers.

Faldo's will of 5 February 1691 named his wife, Mary, as executor and left her property in Essex and Hertfordshire, including a house at Rye Hill, Epping. Faldo died from gallstones on 7 February 1691 and was buried in Bunhill Fields, London, in the fifty-seventh year of his age according to his tombstone. John Quick preached his funeral sermon and singled out his reputation as a reconciler of the differences between the sects for praise: 'If the peace-makers are blessed, and shall be called the children of God, then blessed is Mr Faldo; who had an especial hand in the healing of our breaches' (Quick, 30). Mary Faldo died on 5 March 1706. HUGH BARBOUR

Sources *A collection of the works of William Penn*, 2 (1726) · H. Barbour, ed., *William Penn on religion and ethics* (Lewiston, 1991) · *The Quakers ballad* (1674) · J. Quick, *The dead prophet yet speaking, being a funeral sermon preached at Plaisterers Hall, on the decease of their late reverend pastor, Mr John Faldo* (1691) · C. G. Bolam and others, *The English presbyterians: from Elizabethan puritanism to modern Unitarianism* (1968) · K. Cragg, *Puritanism in the period of the Great Persecution, 1660–1688* (1957) · *The nonconformist's memorial … originally written by … Edmund Calamy*, ed. S. Palmer, [3rd edn], 3 (1803) · DNB · R. L. Greaves, *Saints and rebels: seven nonconformists in Stuart England* (1985) · *Calamy rev.* · G. F. Nuttall and O. Chadwick, eds., *From uniformity to unity, 1662–1962* (1962) · J. Smith, *Bibliotheca anti-Quakeriana* (1873) · J. Spurr, *English puritanism, 1603–1689* (New York, 1998) · A. Gordon, ed., *Freedom after ejection: a review (1690–1692) of presbyterian and congregational nonconformity in England and Wales* (1917)

Fale, Thomas (*bap.* 1561, *d.* after 1604), mathematician, was baptized on 20 April 1561 at Redgrave, Suffolk, one of several children born to James Fale, yeoman. He was educated at Botesdale School, and in February 1579 admitted pensioner at Gonville and Caius College, Cambridge. He migrated in 1582 to Corpus Christi College, graduated BA in 1583, and commenced MA in 1586. Ordained deacon in 1585, Fale proceeded BD in 1597, and was appointed curate of Roydon, Essex.

In 1593 Fale published his only known book, *Horologiographia: the Art of Dialling*, in which he described the design and construction of various dials to tell the time by day or night. His declared aim was to instruct students of mathematics and assist architects, surveyors, sailors, and others. A prefatory letter was addressed to his kinsman Thomas Osborne, who had invented and made one of the dials mentioned. This took the form of a semicircle carrying a sighting arm on which was set a small compass. The mathematician Augustus De Morgan considered Fale's table of sines to be probably the earliest such table to be printed in England. Later editions of the book appeared in 1626 and 1652. In 1604 Fale had a licence from the university to practise physic, but nothing is known of his later life or the circumstances of his death.

GORDON GOODWIN, rev. ANITA McCONNELL

Sources E. G. R. Taylor, *The mathematical practitioners of Tudor and Stuart England* (1954); repr. (1970), 187–8 · Cooper, *Ath. Cantab.*, 2.396 · A. De Morgan, *N&Q*, 2nd ser., 4 (1857), 282 · private information (2004) · parish register (baptism), 20/4/1561, Suffolk, Redgrave with Botesdale

Herman Eugene Falk (1820–1898), by unknown photographer, c.1870

Falk, Herman Eugene (1820–1898), salt manufacturer, was born on 20 November 1820 in Danzig, the fourth of five children of David Wilhelm Falk (1773–1848), merchant, and his second wife, Julianne Rickert. His parents were both German, though his grandfather, he claimed, was English. In 1839 Falk emigrated to England where since 1829 his half-brother, Eduard, and brother, Robert, had been separately in business. Robert's partnerships failed in 1836 and 1840 but Herman invested family capital in Robert's new scheme trading from Liverpool in coal, iron, grain, silk, guano, and salt. Both brothers married into Liverpool commerce, their wives being the daughters of John Thompson, glazier, painter, and plumber; Herman married Elizabeth in 1844, his brother her sister. Elizabeth Falk died after giving birth to her first child (1851). In 1854 Falk married his daughter's governess, Anne Hadfield. The couple had two sons and three daughters. In 1841 the Falks invested in salt works at Winsford, Cheshire, where Herman, as resident manager, mined at record depths. Herman also founded the industry's standard information bulletin, *Falk's Salt Circular*.

In 1843 Herman moved to Hull to organize the import of Baltic timber for railway sleepers commissioned by the engineer Robert Stephenson. Business confidence faltered in 1845. Crucial railway contracts were lost. The brothers faced two crippling actions in chancery, one raised by their half-brother. Their partnership, denuded of capital, was dissolved. While Robert maintained businesses in England, Herman in 1846 took up forestry in New Brunswick, Canada. Returning in 1848 he was forced out of Winsford salt works in 1850 through the actions of the salt traders' association, unimpressed by his vacillating attitude to agreements on prices and production. He was arrested for debt, and costly legal actions came eventually into chancery (1850–53). He overcame difficulties, establishing himself at Meadowbank (Winsford) salt works, with Robert as London agent until the latter's bankruptcy in 1856.

Following an economic recession Falk united the major salt proprietors of Cheshire and Worcestershire in a Salt chamber of commerce (1858), whose committee regulated production and prices. In 1860 he successfully advanced the interests of British salt manufacturers at negotiations for the Anglo-French commercial treaty.

Falk claimed that the industry's stability was threatened by the 'proletariat element' of family proprietors reducing prices and expanding production. To outmanoeuvre these firms and destroy the business of independent hauliers, he constructed in his own shipyard, from 1863, the River Weaver's first iron steamboats to tow strings of dumb barges. In 1868 a strike of saltworkers forced proprietors to increase wages and reduce hours. Falk stood firm upon economic grounds, replacing his own workers with Germans, hired for low wages in Liverpool while in transit to America. When the Germans in turn 'conspired with rebellious spirit', Falk recruited 'docile' Poles and Hungarians to his 350-strong workforce. Falk determined to counter the 'gross materialism' of wage demands by providing schooling and housing, though conditions, particularly for foreign workers—criticized by the press and xenophobic locals—were eventually (inconclusively) investigated by the select committee on the emigration and immigration of foreigners (1888).

Falk travelled widely and published papers on the world's salt. He provided evidence to official inquiries of 1873–81 concerning the environmental impact of his salt works, particularly subsidences and noxious acid emissions. He identified labour obstruction and poor coal as factors, reporting that his own model farm at Catsclough in the heart of the salt districts was, through skilful management, flourishing. His authoritative pronouncements delayed compensation legislation until 1891. From 1873 Cheshire's burgeoning chemical industry boosted Falk's business, though competition from Teesside and manufacturing processes independent of salt limited profits. In 1884 Falk devised the first British joint-stock industrial combination, an attempt legitimized by limited liability, to control production and prices. Falk wrote in his annual report for the Salt chamber of commerce (1886–7), 26: 'The tendency of the age is for an amalgamation and co-operation of all manufactures, in order to lay the great bully competition'. In 1888 a syndicate, having purchased the majority of salt works in Britain and Ireland for above their market value, converted itself into a limited company, the Salt Union. Falk, who by now enjoyed the popular title 'Father of the salt trade', refused to serve on the board, though his barrister son did. The inefficient combine tottered through strikes and commercial crises until absorbed into Imperial Chemical Industries in 1937.

Falk retired to his farm, Catsclough, Winsford, Cheshire, where, following the death of his second wife, he married in 1894 an engineer's daughter, Alice Stanley. He died at Catsclough on 19 January 1898, leaving his effects to Alice and directing that his body be cremated without a funeral and that mourning should be limited to six months.　　　　　　　　　　　　　　　　DAVID IREDALE

Sources 'Report on landslips in the salt districts', *Parl. papers* (1873), 53.589, no. 185 · 'Cheshire salt districts compensation bill', *Parl. papers* (1881) · 'Select committee on emigration and immigration', *Parl. papers* (1888), 11.419, no. 305 · 'Royal commission on … vapours and gases', *Parl. papers* (1878), 44.1, C. 2159; 44.43, C. 2159-I [noxious vapours] · *Chester Chronicle* (9 June 1888) · *Liverpool Daily Post* (10 June 1872) · *The Economist* (13 Oct 1888) · *The Economist* (18 Nov 1901) · *Northwich Guardian* (20 Aug 1892) · *Northwich Guardian* (7 Sept 1892) · *Sunday Chronicle* [Manchester] (5 Sept 1886) · *Sunday Chronicle* [Manchester] (12 Sept 1886) · *The Times* (15 Sept 1888) · *The Times* (24 Sept 1888) · *The Times* (20 Jan 1898) · *The Umpire* (3 March 1889) · *The Umpire* (10 March 1889) · T. Ward, *Notes on the Cheshire salt districts compensation bill* (1881) · d. cert. · will, proved Chester, 1898 **Archives** Ches. & Chester ALSS, DCN 13–19 · Ches. & Chester ALSS, salt circular · Ches. & Chester ALSS, Salt Union Ltd archives, DIC/SU 1–14 · JRL, annual reports, Salt Chamber of Commerce · Man. CL, MSS · priv. coll. · PRO, court of bankruptcy proceedings, C 14, C 31, C 33 **Likenesses** photograph, *c.*1870, Salt Museum, Northwich, Cheshire [*see illus.*] · photograph, *c.*1885, priv. coll. **Wealth at death** £16,948 11*s.* 5*d.*: probate, 18 Feb 1898, CGPLA Eng. & Wales

Falk, Oswald Toynbee (1879–1972), stockbroker and economist, was born on 25 May 1879 at 23 Greenhays Road, Toxteth Park, West Derby, Liverpool, the son of Hermann John Falk, then a law student, and his wife, Rachel Russell Everard Toynbee. Falk's grandfather Herman Eugene *Falk (1820–1898) had emigrated from Danzig in Poland about 1839 and become a leader in the important Cheshire salt trade, but left only a modest fortune of £17,000. His maternal grandfather was the distinguished aural surgeon Joseph *Toynbee (1815–1866).

Falk—known to his friends as Foxy—was educated at Rugby School and at Balliol College, Oxford, where his uncle, the social philosopher and economist Arnold Toynbee, had taught. After Oxford, in a decade he likened to the experience of a 'delicious novel by Henry James' (Skidelsky, 2.423), Falk worked as an actuary for the National Mutual Life Assurance Society and became a fellow of the Institute of Actuaries. He married Florence Ethel, daughter of John Michael Hanglar, on 29 March 1906; but nothing else is known about this relationship. In 1914, having left the actuarial profession, he was admitted a member of the London stock exchange; by 1918 he was a partner in the prominent stockbrokers Buckmaster and Moore. Falk soon developed a reputation for intellectual brilliance combined with an 'explosive personality' (Davenport, 44).

Falk first made his mark in 1917 when J. M. Keynes invited him to join his division of the Treasury. He worked there with impressive intellectuals—Geoffrey Fry and Dudley Ward among them—and proved himself a gifted 'practical economist' interested in currency and exchange. In 1919 he joined the Treasury team, under Keynes's leadership, at the Paris peace conference, and in 1920 he was created CBE. By 1924 Falk was married to Diana Guendolen Edith Cecil, daughter of Captain Gerald Stracey; and they had two sons.

At Buckmasters, Falk became senior partner. An early proponent of 'active investment', in 1923 he counselled investors to give advisers 'the widest possible discretion' and not 'to tie their hands by rules of investment which may have worked tolerably well in the comparative calm of the Victorian age but which are utterly useless in the typhoons of this generation' (*The Times*, 15 March 1923). The consequence, according to a later commentator, was that 'the poor victim either made a killing in the market or was wiped out completely' (Davenport, 44). Falk's rules were specialization within portfolios on particular assets—currency and commodities as well as securities—and frequent if not daily switching between them as guided by the predictions of economic analysis. He achieved spectacular gains but also heavy losses, as in mid-1929 when he led his clients into US securities (having eschewed them a year before). His own losses forced him to sell his country home at Codford St Mary, Wiltshire.

In February 1932 Falk resigned from Buckmasters and from the stock exchange, along with four of his partners, including Sir Maurice Bonham Carter, to form O. T. Falk & Partners, investment bankers, initially operating out of Buckmasters' offices. Here Falk employed bright young men such as the economist Thomas Balogh and the physicist Lancelot Law Whyte. The latter recognized the potential of Whittle's jet engine and the firm developed it via a special company, Power Jets Ltd, which was later compulsorily acquired by the wartime government. Despite his natural impatience, Falk had infinite forbearance with the young men he employed, encouraging them to think courageously and to act with intellectual integrity. His relationship with Bonham Carter and his wife, Violet (née Asquith), was especially close; he was rumoured to have had an affair with Violet Bonham Carter, but the exact nature of their relationship is unclear.

Falk was exceptionally close to Keynes, acting as his broker and co-speculator, introducing him to the City, active investment, and the 'psychology of businessmen' (Skidelsky, 694), and sharing with him a love of ballet and pictures. They worked together on the boards of businesses involved in investment, notably the National Mutual Life Assurance Society, and the Independent Investment Trust Ltd, which they promoted in 1924. Their pursuit of active investment had mixed results, most notably the losses incurred by the trust in 1929–30. Falk, who was always 'sharp in his personal relations' (Davenport,

45), had refused to speak to his friend Montagu Norman, governor of the Bank of England, after the return to the gold standard in 1925. Then in 1930 Keynes disagreed with Falk that British industry was finished and that investors should sell their shares and buy into American industry instead. These and other issues resulted in a 'flaming quarrel' (Davenport, 51) between them, after which their friendship waned. Falk was nevertheless the originator of many ideas developed by Keynes. The latter, who reckoned Falk one of 'nature's economists' (Harrod, 220), owed to him 'his superb understanding of the unruly financial mechanism of capitalism—something which distinguishes his work from that of other economists of his age' (Skidelsky, 2.25).

In 1917 Falk had first brought together practical economists interested in finance and currency issues, and in the 1920s he developed the group into the prestigious Tuesday Club, where influential politicians and economists debated over dinner at the Café Royal in an atmosphere of 'intellectual ferment' (Harrod, 220). There he attacked the Treasury view on debt, arguing that borrowing was 'the instrument of progress. … Better a decade of inflation than a cycle of decay' (Davenport, 193).

Falk was 'tall … with a fine head, aquiline features and broad shoulders … prodigiously gifted intellectually, his faults were hauteur and impetuosity' (Skidelsky, 2.25). The financial journalist Nicholas Davenport thought him 'quick, rude and decisive' and referred to his 'intellectual violence' (Davenport, 44). He held extreme views, often on the right, and expressed them forcibly, for example dismissing the Beveridge report as 'the road to the moral ruin of the nation … it is the way tending to weaken still further the spirit of initiative and adventure, the stimulus of competition, courage and self reliance' (*The Times*, 5 Dec 1941).

Falk's unconventional brilliance won him many friends, and he was widely if not universally respected in the City of London. A champion golfer, he lamented the passing of the traditional game, which he regarded as the victim of the 'modern mechanical game with its battery of irons and extravagant expenditure' (*The Times*, 1 Dec 1934). Fond of the arts, he was at ease in that circle and was rumoured to have been Pavlova's lover. He had a notable collection of post-Impressionist pictures and wrote about twentieth-century art with authority.

In retirement Falk lived at Tall Trees, Boars Hill, near Oxford, and he died on 12 November 1972 at Wardington House Nursing Home, Wardington, Oxfordshire.

JUDY SLINN

Sources *The Times* (20 Nov 1972) · *The Times* (22 Nov 1972) · R. J. A. Skidelsky, *The economist as saviour, 1920–1937* (1992), vol. 2 of *John Maynard Keynes* (1983–2000) · *WWW* · N. Davenport, *Memoirs of a City radical* (1974) · R. Boothby, *Recollections of a rebel* (1978) · W. L. Fraser, *All to the good* (1963) · L. E. Jones, *Georgian afternoon* (1958) · D. E. Moggridge, 'Keynes, John Maynard', *DBB* · D. Iredale, 'Falk, Herman Eugene', *DBB* · R. F. Harrod, *The life of John Maynard Keynes* (1951) · E. Street, *The history of the National Mutual Life Assurance Society, 1830–1980* (1980) · M. Keynes, *Essays on John Maynard Keynes* (1975) · O. M. Westall, *The Provincial Insurance Company, 1903–38: family, markets, and competitive growth* (1992) · *CGPLA Eng. & Wales* (1973) ·

b. cert. · m. cert. · d. cert. · *The Times* (15 March 1923) · *The Times* (5 Dec 1941) · *The Times* (1 Dec 1934)
Archives Bodl. Oxf., corresp. with Margot Asquith
Wealth at death £20,748: probate, 24 Jan 1973, *CGPLA Eng. & Wales*

Falk, Samuel Jacob Hayyim (*c.*1710–1782), alchemist, was born in Galicia, possibly in the town of Podhayce. After spending some time in Furth, Falk moved to Westphalia, where he was accused of witchcraft and sentenced to death. He escaped and settled in London in 1742, where he spent the remaining years of his life. He was commonly known as the *Baal-Shem* ('master of the name [of God]') of London.

Falk established his home and private synagogue in Wellclose Square, and a kind of magical-alchemical laboratory on London Bridge, attracting considerable attention from Jews and non-Jews alike. Three Hebrew documents provide the fullest picture of Falk's bizarre life and occult activities: the stinging denunciation of him by the controversial rabbi Jacob Emden, associating him with the much maligned Sabbatean Jewish heresy; the diary of Falk's personal valet, Hirsh Kalish, for the years 1747–51, describing some of his magical activities and his strained relations with members of the London Jewish community; and one of his own cabbalistic notebooks. Kalish mentions Falk's wife but does not give her name. Falk died in London on 17 April 1782, and was buried the next day.

In contrast to the relative silence of Jewish contemporaries in London regarding Falk, he was considered a legend among some Christian freemasons and others fascinated by the occult. He was visited by a steady stream of adventurers, dissenters, and occultists from all over Europe. He was in contact with Baron von Neuhoff, the king of Corsica, the Polish prince Adam Czartotyski, the duke of Orléans, the marquis de la Croix, the Danish count Albrech Rantzau, and others. He maintained a close association with Joseph Balsamo, known as Count Cagliostro, the freemason and radical politician. It has even been suggested that he knew Emanuel Swedenborg during his sojourn in London.

In Emden's discussion of Falk he included a letter of Sussman Shesnowzi, who described a typical magical ceremony performed by Falk, including the lighting of candles, the pronunciation and writing down of holy names, and the holding of the event in a forest or near water. Similar activities were recorded by Hirsh Kalish. His activities often seem to have had an alchemical dimension as well, when, in the case of several visitors, large sums of money seem to have been exchanged. Shesnowzi also pointed out that Falk was a close friend of Moses David of Podhayce, well known for his Sabbatean affiliation, who visited him in London.

One recent interpretation of Falk portrays him as not only an occultist with possible Sabbatean connections but also as a dissenter seeking to promote a new form of Judaeo-Christian freemasonry based on the cabbala. This intriguing reconstruction of Falk's ideological agenda is more suggestive than conclusive, however. Nowhere in his own writings did he refer to Sabbatean beliefs and practices. There is also little evidence in them that he was a serious intellectual or that he had an ideological understanding of either Judaism or of a syncretistic Judaeo-Christianity. He was clearly a practical magician, a performer who was sometimes successful in extorting huge sums of money from his Christian and occasional Jewish supporters. But this hardly suggests a deep student of the cabbala, or of comparative religion, or of radical politics. While his magical aura elevated his stature among Christian 'illuminated' radicals, there is little to suggest he was capable of constructing and articulating an ideology of Jewish–Christian merger fused with radical political activity. Nevertheless, Falk remains an intriguing figure. He dramatically demonstrates how a mere Jewish magician and charlatan could make a greater impression in his time than his more sober and conventional Jewish contemporaries.

No doubt Falk's mystique was enhanced by his well-known portrait commonly (but wrongly) attributed to the American artist John Singelton Copley. The painting captures his wonder-working aura—his mystical gaze, Eastern dress, and scientific measuring instrument. Ironically, not only was the painter misidentified but also his subject was taken to be the *Baal Shem Tov*, the founder of the Hasidic movement in eastern Europe. True to his reputation established in his own lifetime, Falk seemed capable of performing yet another trick long after his death.

DAVID B. RUDERMAN

Sources H. Adler, 'The Baal-Shem of London', *Transactions of the Jewish Historical Society of England*, 5 (1902–5), 148–73 • C. Roth, 'The king and the cabalists', *Essays and portraits in Anglo-Jewish history* (1962), 139–64 • D. S. Katz, *The Jews in the history of England, 1485–1850* (1994), 300–03 • M. Oron, 'Mysticism and magic in London in the eighteenth-century: Samuel Falk the Baal-Shem of London (Hebrew)', *Sefer Yisra'el Levin: Kovez Meḥkarim Be-Sifrut ha-Ivrit Le-Doroteha*, ed. R. Zur and T. Rosen (1995), 7–20 • M. Oron, 'Dr Samuel Falk and the Eibeschuetz–Emden controversy', *Mysticism, magic and kabbala in Ashkenazi Judaism: Fifth International Congress on the History of Jewish Mysticism* [Frankfurt am Main 1991], ed. K. E. Grözinger and J. Dan (1995), 243–56 • M. K. Schuchard, 'Yeats and the "Unknown Superiors": Swedenborg, Falk, and Cagliostro', *Secret texts*, ed. M. Roberts and H. Ormsby-Lennon (1995), 114–67 • R. I. Cohen, *Jewish icons: art and society in modern Europe* (1998), 125–6
Archives Rabbinical Seminary of London, cabbalistic notebook, MS [*Catalogue of Jewish Museum of London*, A. Neubauer, n. 127] | Jewish Theological Society of America, Hirsh Kalish diary, MS, MIC.3599
Likenesses portrait, repro. in Adler, 'The Baal-Shem of London', following p.148

Falkener, Edward [*pseud.* E. F. O. Thurcastle] (1814–1896), architect and archaeologist, was born in London on 28 February 1814, the son of Lyon Falkener (1777–1864), clerk of the ordnance department in the Tower of London, and his wife, Mary, *née* Stowell (1775–1840). He was educated at a private school in Kent, and after declining a nomination for the civil service of the East India Company on the ground of delicate health, he was articled to John Newman (1786–1859), an architect. He became a student of the Royal Academy in 1836, and in 1839 gained its gold medal for a design for a cathedral church. In the latter year he published *Was the Ceiling of the Parthenon Flat or Curved?*

which was described as 'the introduction to a proposed work on Greek sculpture'.

In 1842 Falkener started on a tour through all the countries of Europe except Spain and Portugal, through Asia Minor, Syria, Palestine, and Egypt, and visited some of the Greek islands. He was a skilful draughtsman and made careful studies of the architectural remains in the various places he visited. While in Denmark he made sketches of the palace of Fredericksberg. When it was burnt in 1859 the king of Denmark, desiring to restore it in its original form, obtained Falkener's original drawings. In acknowledgement the king made him a knight of the order of the Dannebrog. In 1847, when he was at Pompeii, Falkener was allowed to excavate, at his own expense, a house named the house of Marcus Lucretius, a plan and description of which is given in the journal he edited, *The Museum of Classical Antiquities* (2 vols., 1851–3). The Greek inscriptions he collected during his travels were edited in 1852 by Dr W. Henzen. During his travels he also acquired many examples of medieval Arab metalwork, pottery, arms, and armour. He was one of the first English collectors of such material and was a major lender to the Manchester exhibition in 1857. Unfortunately, his arms and armour were destroyed in a fire at Crystal Palace in 1858.

On his return to London in 1849, Falkener practised his profession for a few years, building some offices on St Dunstan's Hill, east London, which he occupied, but he devoted most of his time to literary work and making drawings of restorations. His drawings, which were exhibited at the Paris Universal Exhibition (1855), gained him the grand medal of honour, and in 1861 he was presented with another gold medal by the king of Prussia for his works on classical archaeology.

On 11 May 1866 Falkener married Blanche Mary Golding Victoria (1835–1917), daughter of Benjamin Golding. The next few years were spent near St Briavels, north of Chepstow, where he bought some land and built walled gardens and a belvedere of Agra sandstone overlooking the River Wye. In 1875 the couple moved to Glan-y-môr, St Clears, Carmarthenshire, to which he made substantial alterations (such as the addition of Ottoman stained-glass windows).

Falkener had a thorough knowledge of architecture and classical archaeology, and, among other things, wrote on the lighting of museums of sculpture, and the artificial illumination of churches and mosques. He was a firm supporter of the lighting of Greek temples by the hypaethron, in opposition to the views of James Fergusson (1808–1886) and Dr Dörpfeld, and published a treatise *On the Hypaethron of Greek Temples* (1861). Some of the illustrations in Fergusson's *A History of Architecture in All Countries* (2 vols., 1865–7) were furnished by him, and many of his sketches were published in the Architectural Publication Society's *Dictionary of Architecture*, ed. W. Papworth (8 vols., n.d. [1852]–1892). He was a member of the academy of Bologna, and of the architectural institutes of Berlin and Rome, and was elected honorary fellow of the Royal Institute of British Architects on 2 December 1895.

Besides the works mentioned, and *Daedalus, or, The*

Causes and Principles of the Excellence of Greek Sculpture (1860) and *Ephesus and the Temple of Diana* (1862), Falkener frequently contributed to the *Proceedings of the Royal Institute of British Architects*. Under the pseudonym of E. F. O. Thurcastle (Edward Falkener of Thurcastle) he published in 1884 *Does the 'Revised Version' Affect the Doctrine of the New Testament?*

In 1892, at the age of seventy-eight, Falkener published *Games Ancient and Oriental and How to Play Them*, a pioneering (and somewhat misleading) study of board games with suggested reconstructions, four of which were manufactured and advertised for sale in the book. He continued his studies to the end of his life, and was engaged on a treatise on the Greek houses at Pompeii up to the time of his death at Glan-y-môr on 17 December 1896. He was buried two days later at Laugharne church, Carmarthenshire. His wife, son, and three daughters survived him.

GEORGE AITCHISON, rev. RACHEL WARD

Sources *The Times* (23 Dec 1896) · F. C. Penrose, 'The late Edward Falkener', *RIBA Journal*, 4 (1896–7), 149–52 · 'Pedigree of the family of Le Fauconer, Falkener and Fawkener', *The Genealogist*, new ser., 1 (1884), 129–39 · W. G. D. Fletcher, *Leicestershire pedigrees and royal descents* (1887), 45–9 · private information (2004) [family] · I. Finkel, 'Edward Falkener: old board games for new', *Board games in academia*, ed. A. J. de Voogt (1997) · *CGPLA Eng. & Wales* (1897)
Archives priv. coll., diaries, letters, drawings, architectural designs, Arab metalwork collection, oriental games collection · RIBA, MS catalogue of publications | CUL, corresp. with Joseph Bonomi · NL Wales, letters to Johnes family
Likenesses C. C. Vogel, drawing, 1847, Staatliche Kunstsammlungen, Dresden · S. V. von Vogelstein, drawing, 1847, Staatliche Kunstsammlungen, Dresden · photograph, 1855, priv. coll. · photographs, priv. coll. · two photographs (in old age), priv. coll.
Wealth at death £23,145 16s. 8d.: probate, 7 May 1897, *CGPLA Eng. & Wales*

Falkiner, Caesar Litton (1863–1908), writer and historian, was born in Dublin on 20 September 1863, the second son of Sir Frederick Richard *Falkiner (1831–1908), recorder of Dublin, and his first wife, Adelaide Matilda Sadleir (d. 1877). From the Royal School, Armagh, he went to the University of Dublin, where he graduated BA in 1886 and proceeded MA in 1890. At college he wrote an essay on Macaulay as a historian, and in 1885 he was elected president of the college philosophical society. Much interested in politics, he entitled his presidential address 'A new voyage to Utopia', a kind of appeal from the new whigs to the old, which was prompted by the passing of the third Reform Bill.

In 1887 Falkiner was called to the Irish bar, and in 1888 he began to work actively on behalf of the unionist cause. In the 1890s he served as treasurer of the Dublin unionist registration association. At the general election of 1892 he contested, unsuccessfully, South Armagh. On 4 August 1892 he married Henrietta Mary, daughter of Sir Thomas Newenham *Deane, architect, of Dublin. Falkiner was a member of Joseph Plunkett's committee which met in the parliamentary recess of 1895 to press for government support for Irish agriculture. Its report led to the creation of the Irish department of agriculture and technical instruction (1899). Falkiner gave much thought to the Irish land problem, and mastered the intricacies of the many Irish

land acts. In 1898 he was appointed temporary assistant land commissioner, and in 1905 this appointment became permanent. For the first half of his work his duty lay in the western counties, for the latter half in the southern counties.

Meanwhile Falkiner devoted much time to the study of Irish history and literature. He planned a history of 1798, and consulted W. E. H. Lecky about its format and content. In the event he opted for the essay form. His first book, *Studies in Irish History and Biography, Mainly in the Eighteenth Century* (1902), threw new light on the history of Ireland in the last quarter of that century. Increasingly Falkiner turned back to the seventeenth century. Again he at first proposed a complete history, but instead published collections of essays. Some of these, in *Illustrations of Irish History and Topography, Mainly of the Seventeenth Century* (1904), had been read originally as papers before the Royal Irish Academy. He had become a member of the academy in 1896 and, having served on its council, was elected as secretary in 1907. In 1899 he succeeded Sir John Thomas Gilbert as editor of the Ormond papers at Kilkenny for the Historical Manuscripts Commission. Under his editorship five volumes of these seventeenth-century manuscripts were published between 1902 and 1908, in part realizing the design first sketched by Gilbert in 1870. A posthumous book, *Essays Relating to Ireland* (1909), continued his preoccupation with the seventeenth century.

Falkiner's interests extended to literature, and in the *Dictionary of National Biography* and in Chambers's *Cyclopaedia of English Literature* he dealt with writers. In 1903 he edited the poems of Charles Wolfe and selections from the poems of Thomas Moore (in the Golden Treasury series), and shortly before his death he designed editions of Moore's complete poetical works and of Dean Swift's letters.

Falkiner died on 5 August 1908, through an accident on the Alps while on a brief holiday at Chamonix. He was buried in the English churchyard in Chamonix. His wife and their two daughters survived him. A memorial tablet was placed by his friends in St Patrick's Cathedral, Dublin, in 1910.

TOBY BARNARD

Sources DNB · E. Dowden, 'Memoir of the author', in C. L. Falkiner, *Essays relating to Ireland, biographical, historical and topographical*, ed. F. E. Ball (1909) · Royal Irish Acad., Falkiner MSS, 12 F 49–50 · C. L. Falkiner, letters to W. E. H. Lecky, TCD, MSS 1827–1836 · Burke, *Gen. Ire.* (1912) · *CGPLA Eng. & Wales* (1908)
Archives Royal Irish Acad., MSS 12 F 49–50 · TCD, historical collection, MS 3568
Wealth at death £12,122 3s. 10d.: probate, 12 Oct 1908, *CGPLA Ire.* · £1642 12s. 2d.: Irish probate sealed in England, 10 Nov 1908, *CGPLA Eng. & Wales*

Falkiner, Sir Frederick Richard (1831–1908), judge, was born at Mount Falcon, Borrisokane, co. Tipperary, on 19 January 1831, the third son of Richard Miles Falkiner (1778–1833) and his wife, Tempe, *née* Litton (1796–1888). The Falkiner family came to Ireland from Leeds in the time of the protector and were wool manufacturers by trade. Frederick's father held a commission in the 4th Royal Irish Dragoons, and his brother, Travers Hartley, was a well-known engineer (he designed the first railway line from Zürich to Chur and supervised works on the Forth Bridge). Falkiner was educated at Trinity College, Dublin, where he graduated BA in 1852. He was then called to the Irish bar, in the autumn of 1852, and joined the north-east circuit. A hard-working and eloquent man, he soon held briefs in many important cases. On 1 April 1861 he married Adelaide Matilda Sadleir; they had three sons and four daughters before her death in 1877. The second son was the historian Caesar Litton *Falkiner (1863–1908). In 1878 he married Robina Hall M'Intire of Dublin, who also predeceased him, dying in 1895.

After becoming queen's counsel in 1867, Falkiner continued to build up his practice. In 1875 he was appointed law adviser at Dublin Castle, an office afterwards abolished, and in 1876 he was appointed recorder of Dublin, on the death of Sir Frederick Shaw. As the 'poor man's judge' he earned a reputation for compassion, and he was energetic in fulfilling his duties as recorder. He became particularly involved in cases concerning the application of the licensing laws, but he also took a keen interest in the acts of parliament concerning the regulation of labour and compensation claims for working men who had been injured at work. Chamberlain's bill on workmen's compensation (1897) made use of several of Falkiner's recommendations. In 1880 Falkiner was elected a bencher of the King's Inns, and in August 1896 he was knighted. He retired from his office on 22 January 1905, when he was made a privy councillor.

Falkiner was one of the most prominent members of the general synod of the Church of Ireland, and he often spoke in its debates, especially on financial questions. He was chancellor to the bishops of Tuam, Clogher, Kilmore, and Derry and Raphoe. He was also chairman of the board of King's Hospital, previously known as the Blue Coat School; in 1906 he published a history of the school, which included much detail on Dublin between the Restoration and the Victorian period. He also wrote on the subject of Swift's portraits (Swift's *Prose Works*, 1908, vol. 12), and a collection of his *Literary Miscellanies*, edited by M. Falkiner, was published posthumously in 1909. Falkiner died of pneumonia on 22 March 1908 at Funchal, Madeira, where he had gone to improve his health, and was buried there.

R. H. MURRAY, rev. SINÉAD AGNEW

Sources M. Falkiner, preface, in *Literary miscellanies. The Right Honorable Sir F. R. Falkiner*, ed. M. Falkiner (1909) · Burke, *Gen. Ire.* · Burtchaell & Sadleir, *Alum. Dubl.* · D. J. O'Donoghue, *The poets of Ireland: a biographical dictionary with bibliographical particulars*, 1 vol. in 3 pts (1892–3) · F. B. Falkiner, *A pedigree, with personal sketches, of the Falkiners of Mount Falcon* (1894) · *The Times* (24 March 1908)

Likenesses memorial window, c.1909, St Patrick's Cathedral, Dublin, Lady chapel · W. Osborne, portrait, NG Ire.

Wealth at death £56,683 3s. 8d.: probate, 23 April 1908, *CGPLA Ire.* · £23,230 3s. 7d. in England: Irish probate sealed in England, 19 May 1908, *CGPLA Eng. & Wales*

Falkland. For this title name *see* Cary, Henry, first Viscount Falkland (c.1575–1633); Cary, Elizabeth, Viscountess Falkland (1585–1639); Cary, Lucius, second Viscount Falkland (1609/10–1643); Cary, Lettice, Viscountess Falkland (c.1612–

1647); Carey, Anthony, fifth Viscount Falkland (1656–1694).

Falkner [Faulkner; *married names* Donaldson, Lumm], **Anna Maria** (d. 1796/7), singer, was said to have been the niece and adopted daughter of the Dublin publisher George *Faulkner (1703?–1775). On 23 November 1745 she sang Eurydice in the pantomime afterpiece *Orpheus and Eurydice* (music by J. F. Lampe) at Covent Garden, billed as a young gentlewoman who 'never appear'd on any Stage before' (*General Advertiser*, 23 Nov 1745). She sang the role more than thirty times before the middle of May but was not advertised at Covent Garden again for nearly two years. Aided by her striking appearance—she was above average height with large dark eyes and black hair—she established her reputation as a singer at Marylebone Gardens, being an attraction there every summer from 1747 to 1752. Many songs by Thomas Augustine Arne, Willem De Fesch, Joseph Baildon, and others were published as sung by her at the gardens. De Fesch was in charge of the music at Marylebone, and she is holding his 'I sing not of battles' in her portrait by Andreas Van der Mijn.

Miss Falkner returned to Covent Garden on 13 February 1748 with two songs in Italian and Handel's 'O sleep' and ''Tis liberty'. She sang between the acts of plays, took leading roles in musical afterpieces, and played Polly in John Gay's *The Beggar's Opera*. Her name is in Handel's manuscript for incidental music for *Alceste*, never performed but recast as *The Choice of Hercules* and sung with *Alexander's Feast* in March 1751. She may have sung the music then; certainly she sang two arias from *Alexander's Feast* for her benefit that April. 'Amid a croud of exalted admirers and profuse offers, she kept her character unimpeached' (Trusler, 63). On 19 May 1748 she married William George Donaldson (d. 1780). Their son John was baptized in January 1752, and she did not play Polly that season although she still appeared frequently in two pantomime afterpieces.

In autumn 1752 Anna Maria went to Dublin for a season at the Smock Alley Theatre, where she appeared first as Miss Falkner but then as Mrs Donaldson. She opened as Polly and among other parts in a busy season performed Ophelia, Jessica, and Ariel (Shakespearian characters then viewed as essentially singing roles), Sabrina in Arne's *Comus*, and Philidel in the Dryden–Purcell *King Arthur*. She was frequently advertised as singing between the acts and appeared in concerts in March and April. She was not re-engaged by Smock Alley, and in September 1753 advertised a subscription series of concerts in Dublin for the winter, but these do not seem to have been very successful. Her husband, a 'handsome and sprightly man' (Taylor, 1.56), appears to have begun an affair with the actress Mary Ann Graham while in Ireland and to have lived with her in London for two years before her marriage to the actor Richard Yates in 1756. After a season in the theatre at Bath, Mrs Donaldson made a final London appearance on 2 April 1755, singing a cantata by the young Michael Arne and the Irish song 'Ellen a Roon'.

All accounts agree that it was her musical powers that

Anna Maria Falkner (*d.* 1796/7), by Andreas van der Myn

attracted George Montagu *Dunk, second earl of Halifax (1716–1771). Their relationship lasted until his death. He obtained a lucrative government post in Jamaica for Donaldson, and built a house for Anna Maria adjoining Bushy Park, Middlesex, where he was ranger. This was Hampton Court House, with a charming rococo garden and elaborate shell grotto. In 1760 Halifax was in serious financial difficulties and arranged a marriage to an heiress to restore his fortunes; in desperation Anna Maria took their daughter, who was born on 24 July 1759 (in one account also their son, who died young), to plead with him, and he called the marriage off. She was in Ireland while Halifax was lord lieutenant there and behaved discreetly, although she was accused of selling places later. On his death in 1771 he provided fully and carefully for 'my Dearest Friend Anna Maria Donaldson' and for their daughter, Anna Maria Montagu.

William Donaldson, who had been living with a mistress and children at Turnham Green, died in 1780, and on 17 July 1784 his widow married Major Charles Lumm, recently returned from service in North America. Anna Maria Lumm of Gloucester Street, Portman Square, London, made her will on 28 December 1796, dividing her wealth and mementoes of Halifax among her five grandchildren and asking to be buried 'in the Chapel at Horton in Northamptonshire as near the Family vault of the Earl of Halifax as possible'. She was interred at St Margaret's, Westminster, on 16 January 1797.

Olive Baldwin and Thelma Wilson

Sources A. H. Scouten, ed., *The London stage, 1660–1800*, pt 3: 1729–1747 (1961) · G. W. Stone, ed., *The London stage, 1660–1800*, pt 4: 1747–1776 (1962) · B. Boydell, *A Dublin musical calendar, 1700–1760* (Dublin, 1988) · parish register, 1748, St George's Chapel, Mayfair [marriage] · parish register, 1752, St Paul's, Covent Garden [son's baptism] · parish register, 1780, St Nicholas's, Chiswick [burial; William Donaldson] · parish register, 1784, St Mary le Bone [marriage] · parish register, 1759, 1797, St Margaret's, Westminster [daughter's baptism; burial] · L. Baillie and R. Balchin, eds., *The catalogue of printed music in the British Library to 1980*, 62 vols. (1981–7) · *The genuine memoirs of Miss Faulkner* (1770) · 'Histories of the têtes-à-têtes annexed: Dunkaro and Marianne', *Town and Country Magazine*, 1 (1769), 225–7 · E. Harris, 'Villa for a mortal miss: Hampton Court House, Middlesex', *Country Life*, 172 (1982), 392–4 · E. Harris, 'So rare, so elegant: the restored grotto at Hampton Court House', *Country Life*, 180 (1986), 1956–9 · J. Taylor, *Records of my life*, 1 (1832) · J. Trusler, *Memoirs of the life of the Rev. Dr. Trusler* (1806) · Walpole, *Corr.*, vols. 9–10, 35, 38 · *The letters of David Garrick*, ed. D. M. Little and G. M. Kahrl, 3 vols. (1963) · M. Sands, *The eighteenth-century pleasure gardens of Marylebone, 1737–1777* (1987) · S. Rosenfeld, *Strolling players and drama in the provinces, 1660–1765* (1939) · W. Dean, *Handel's dramatic oratorios and masques* (1959) · E. K. Sheldon, *Thomas Sheridan of Smock-Alley: recording his life as actor and theater manager in both Dublin and London* (1967) · wills, earl of Halifax, William Donaldson and Anna Maria Lumm, Family Records Centre, London

Likenesses Mrs D-s-n, double portrait, engraving (with Hurgo Dunkaro), repro. in *Town and Country Magazine* · A. van der Myn, mezzotint (after his portrait), BM, NPG [*see illus.*]

Wealth at death over £18,500; plus plate and jewellery: will

Falkner, Harold (1875–1963), architect, was born on 28 November 1875 at White House, Bramley, Surrey, the son of Charles Falkner and his wife, Mary Watson. He was educated at the high school in Farnham, Surrey, and came to appreciate the quality of the town's eighteenth-century architecture through W. H. Allen, the master of Farnham School of Art, which he later attended. After completing his articles in Reginald Blomfield's office, Falkner designed Strangers Corner in Farnham for Allen, built in 1897. Although Falkner's training versed him in the neo-Georgian style, he was an architect of the arts and crafts movement and from about 1902 to 1906 practised in partnership with Niven and Wigglesworth, prolific domestic architects of the Edwardian period. An accomplished perspectivist, Falkner exhibited regularly at the Royal Academy at this stage of his career.

In practice on his own and later with Maxwell Aylwin, Falkner worked extensively in Farnham. He altered and looked after some of the best eighteenth-century buildings that graced the town and added to them, starting with the public swimming baths (1897), which he designed at the age of twenty-one. From the beginning, however, Falkner liked to work with his own hands, learning from local builders. Designing and building speculatively, first in Great Austins from about 1903 to 1906, he used what would now be termed architectural salvage and here, at Ilona, he carved a stone doorcase to take an old French panelled door. Although the mainstream of his architectural practice continued in the neo-Georgian tradition, his direct involvement in the building process is illustrated by his presence about 1920 as master of the works on site, as well as architect, during the restoration of the old Goat's Head pub in Farnham. His client, in this instance and many others, was Charles Ernest Borelli, a landowner sensitive to the character of the town and instrumental, with Falkner, in the preservation of its Georgian architecture.

Falkner's compulsion to build found another outlet in the construction of nine houses over forty years at nearby Dippenhall, all with his own hands. First he bought Deans Farm, which he extended as Dippenhall Grange and where he turned a cottage in the garden into a half-timbered house. Falkner formed a gatehouse through another cottage, behind which he re-erected the timber frames of a large barn and a stable to form The Barn. Here an emergent expressionism became apparent, which typified the houses that were to follow. The roof swoops low over the entrance, while inside steps descend into a double-height hall. The garden lies beyond and reflects Falkner's association with his godmother, Gertrude Jekyll. On either side of the hall, stairs wind to upper landings and passages at different levels, one of which emerges as a bridge across the back of the drawing-room.

In 1925 Falkner bought land near by from his brother and built Overdeans Court, which was followed by Meads in 1930. Both are barn-frame houses like The Barn: in the former he placed two such frames end to end, cranked in the middle; in the latter he set one as a cross-wing to the other. Halfway House then used up the bits and pieces and was followed in 1937 by Burles, built from two more barn frames, this time from Gloucestershire, on a sloping site. Falkner snaked the drive round the hill and jettied triple gables towards the approaching visitor. Steps lead to the front door, set amid a confusion of roofs sweeping to low eaves, a huge chimney, and varied dormers. The garden side has a long jetty, and the western gable, like Overdeans, contains a tall bay.

Throughout this period Falkner continued his formal architectural work in Farnham and elsewhere. Tancredesford at Tilford (1920) epitomizes the elegance of his neo-Georgian country houses, but in the end it is perhaps Falkner's work in Farnham itself that is his most important contribution. In partnership with Maxwell Aylwin up to about 1934, Falkner built the new town hall (1932), a neo-Georgian structure that replaced an unsympathetic Victorian predecessor. Next door his refronting of the Bailiffs' Hall (1934) is perhaps more inspired. Other good examples of his carefully integrated approach include 40 West Street and his work at the Surrey and Hampshire News office, further down the same street. Products of his sensitive intervention can be found elsewhere throughout the town, often hardly discernible within the Georgian townscape.

In old age Falkner continued to build at Dippenhall and these houses, wilder and more personal than his Farnham work, give an insight into his character. Although Burles was the last of the big barn houses, Burles Lodge, Grovers Farm, and the Black Barn followed. Falkner's loyal helpers Algie Bass and the brothers Alfred and Bert Hack were getting old too, and only Alfred stayed with him after Burles. Increasing bureaucracy frustrated Falkner, and the building control department eventually condemned the Black Barn for non-compliance. During its construction Alfred Hack, ninety years old, fell to his death from the scaffold.

Soon after, following Falkner's own death from pneumonia at 44 Hale Road, Farnham, on 30 November 1963, the Black Barn was pulled down. Although his other Dippenhall houses, all tenanted, fell into disrepair, all have now been rescued, with even the Black Barn being rebuilt in a different form.   MICHAEL DRURY

Sources M. Drury, *Wandering architects: in pursuit of an arts and crafts ideal* (2000) · R. Blomfield, *Memoirs of an architect* (1932) · M. Brandon-Jones, 'Harold Falkner architect', unpublished, 1971, West Surrey College of Art and Design, Farnham · 'Harold Falkner', *Architects' Journal* (23 June 1938), 1055–6 · N. Taylor, 'The private world of Dippenhall', *ArchR*, 143 (1968), 158–60, esp. 159 · C. Blyth, 'Dippenhall', diss., West Surrey College of Art and Design, Farnham · N. Temple, *Farnham buildings and people* (1963) · b. cert. · d. cert.

Wealth at death £114,030: probate, 3 July 1964, *CGPLA Eng. & Wales*

Falkner, John Meade (1858–1932), armaments manufacturer and writer, was born on 8 May 1858, at Manningford Bruce, Vale of Pewsey, Wiltshire, second but eldest surviving of the four sons (there were also two daughters) of Thomas Alexander Falkner (1819–1887), a penurious curate, and his wife, Grace Elizabeth (d. 1871), the daughter of John Mead, ordnance storekeeper, of Weymouth, Dorset; she died from being poisoned by foul water in a domestic accident which nearly killed her children. Falkner attended grammar schools at Dorchester and Weymouth before completing his schooling at Marlborough College. In 1882 he graduated with a third-class degree in modern history from Hertford College, Oxford, where he was later (1927) elected an honorary fellow.

After leaving Oxford, Falkner went to Newcastle upon Tyne in 1883 as tutor to the sons of Andrew Noble, an armaments manufacturer. He became an intimate member of the household and private secretary to Noble when the tuition of the sons ended (1885). About 1888 he was appointed secretary to the board of Sir W. G. Armstrong & Co., in which post he continued after its reconstitution (1896) as a limited liability company (later known as Armstrong Whitworth). Despite finding that all women looked as alike as shelled peas, on 18 October 1899 he married Evelyn Violet (1869–1940), daughter of General Sir John *Adye and sister-in-law of the second Baron Armstrong, and in 1901 he became a director of Armstrongs. Bachelordom was his natural vocation: in his own phrase he regarded women at Oxford University with the repugnance he otherwise reserved for black beetles. He and his wife had no children.

The technology and power of Armstrongs' business thrilled Falkner: 'It is to me hunting, fishing, shooting and everything else all in one' (Rendel MSS, Falkner to Rendel, 21 March 1905). As Armstrongs' chief overseas negotiator in the Edwardian period he relished his opportunities to sell armaments abroad, and he revelled in diplomatic scheming: 'Archané rivalries and personal animosities still prevail in Italy', he reported when trying to achieve a price ring to protect Armstrongs' armour-plate works at Naples (Armstrong Whitworth MSS, Falkner to Rendel, 13 Jan 1907). When the increasingly ineffective Noble refused to retire as chairman, Falkner became his severe critic, correctly predicting that Armstrongs would be defeated and consumed by its chief rival, Vickers. His colleague Lord Rendel declared: 'Falkner's judgement is … his weakest point. He is brilliant, romantic and picturesque, but like Rosebery, not so sagacious as he is clever. He would make us, if loyal, an always invaluable colleague, but … a reckless and ruinous master' (Armstrong Whitworth MSS, Rendel to Henry Whitehead, 1 Sept 1909). But by 1912 Henry Gladstone described Falkner as 'the main strength of the Company: nobody else counts very much' (Armstrong Whitworth MSS, Gladstone to Rendel, 9 Feb 1912). As a result of prolonged intrigues, Falkner became chairman in 1915 at the height of the munitions crisis. He was not a strong leader, and was superseded in 1920, though remaining a director until 1926.

Falkner modelled his exquisite handwriting on that of medieval scribes, studied medieval lore including demonology, had a fine collection of missals, and recited the canonical hours when bored on long business journeys. As an expert in excursions from Oxford he compiled two Murray's handbooks, *Oxfordshire* (1894) and *Berkshire* (1902), which contain close architectural observations on churches and other buildings. He also wrote a successful *History of Oxfordshire* (1899) and a pamphlet history of Bath (1918). His *Poems*, published in a collected edition of 1933, anticipate the themes and charms of John Betjeman. Each of his three novels was written while travelling on trains. *The Lost Stradivarius* (1895) is a Gothic romance about the haunting of a Victorian violin-playing baronet by an eighteenth-century rake with occult tastes; its details sprang from Falkner's antiquarianism and musical scholarship, and its tensions are sustained by inexplicit sexual ambiguities. Loving evocations of Dorset, Oxford, and Naples attest to Falkner's keen sense of place. *Moonfleet* (1898; filmed 1955) is a rattling story set in 1757 about an orphan boy whose guardian leads a smuggling gang, and is set mainly on the Dorset coast, but with an interlude in which the boy is imprisoned by sinister Dutchmen. Falkner did not tarry over subtle characterization: like the adventure stories of Robert Louis Stevenson, *Moonfleet* combines consummate atmospheric effects—such as the boy's horror at inadvertently plucking the beard off Blackbeard's skeleton while hiding in the Mohune vault— with the excitement of a lost diamond, contraband, hot pursuits by excisemen, and the last superb climax of shipwreck and rescue in a storm. *The Nebuly Coat* (1903) was described by Falkner's lifelong acquaintance Thomas Hardy as 'an interesting romance of the oldfashioned sort' (*Collected Letters*, 3.87). Set in the vividly imagined town of Cullerne, it is enhanced by precise architectural and musical scholarship: the plot reflects Falkner's talent for mystification which so successfully served his armaments interests. The story's ostensible villain Lord Blandamer resembles Falkner: widely travelled, with scholarly avocations, evasive and intriguing, making a cynical marriage, yet behaving decently to his bride, ruthless and deliberative in pursuing his interests, yet punctilious in courtesy. Though apparently a murderer, Blandamer achieves a heroic stature surpassing the weakly virtuous men of Cullerne. (In 1905 Falkner was himself granted armorial bearings only slightly different from the fictional arms of Lord Blandamer.)

In 1899 Falkner took a house in the cathedral close at Durham and became devoted to its music, services, and library. After his retirement as Armstrongs' chairman he was appointed honorary librarian to the dean and chapter at Durham (1921), and honorary reader in palaeography to the university (1924). In addition to Japanese and Ottoman decorations he received when he was an arms dealer, a papal medal was bestowed on him for his palaeography. (He filled forty notebooks, all in Latin, on the Vatican manuscripts.)

Falkner by 1905 weighed over 17 stone and had long endured a bowel disorder. He recovered his health by dieting but thereafter was gaunt and stooping, with the intense eyes of an insomniac. He was an incorrigible romancer, who claimed that when young he could see Jupiter's moons with his naked eye; his stories, however, served his preference for the bizarre rather than promoting any sordid self-interest. Falkner was described by H. H. Asquith in 1915 as 'about 6 ft. 6 ins. in height, with a rather melancholy face & voice, and the general air of a transplanted hidalgo' (*Letters to Venetia Stanley*, 560). 'He is a very strange man, and makes his conversation a shrouding veil for his thoughts more successfully than most men whom I know', recorded his Durham neighbour Hensley Henson (Henson, 19 Oct 1915). 'Proclaiming himself a recluse, he enjoyed congenial society; in politics, he was one day a Radical and the next a reactionary; while he affected a cynicism which covered much real kindness of heart' (*The Times*, 25 July 1932). Falkner died of congestion of the lungs and a weak heart, on 22 July 1932, at his residence, the Divinity House, Palace Green, Durham. His ashes were interred on 27 July at Burford. Pope Pius XI received a bequest of £500 in his will.

RICHARD DAVENPORT-HINES

Sources *The Times* (23 July 1932) · *The Times* (25 July 1932) · *The Times* (26 July 1932) · *Durham County Advertiser* (29 July 1932) · *Manchester Guardian* (5 Aug 1932) · *The Spectator* (6 Aug 1932) · *Library Association Record*, 3rd ser., 2 (1932) · *Armstrong Whitworth Record* (autumn 1932) · *The Draconian* [magazine of the Dragon School, Oxford], 135 (Jan 1933) · *Hertford College Magazine*, 21 (1933) · K. Warren, *John Meade Falkner, 1858–1932* (1995) · C. Hawtree, 'Introduction', in J. M. Falkner, *The Nebuly coat* (1988) · E. Wilson, 'Introduction', in J. M. Falkner, *The lost Stradivarius* (1991) · G. M. Young and E. Craster, 'Introduction', in J. M. Falkner, *The Nebuly coat and the lost Stradivarius*, joint edn (1954) · W. Haley, 'John Meade Falkner', *Essays by Divers Hands, being the Transactions of the Royal Society of Literature*, new ser., 30 (1960), 55–67 · V. Pritchett, *Complete essays* (1991), 273–7 · H. Newbolt, *My world as in my time* (1932) · G. Grigson, *The Listener* (10 Jan 1946), 47 · *H. H. Asquith: letters to Venetia Stanley*, ed. M. Brock and E. Brock (1982) · H. H. Henson, *Retrospect of an unimportant life*, 1: *1863–1920* (1942) · *Catalogue of collection of illuminated manuscripts, early service books, etc. formed by J. M. Falkner* (1932) [sale catalogue, Sothebys] · *The collected letters of Thomas Hardy*, ed. R. Purdy and M. Millgate, 3 (1982); 7 (1988) · A. Bell, 'Introduction', in J. M. Falkner, *A midsummer night's marriage* (1977) · Tyne and Wear RO, Rendel MSS · Tyne and Wear RO, Armstrong Whitworth MSS · H. H. Henson, diary, Durham Cath. CL, Henson MSS · A. C. Fox-Davies, ed., *Armorial families: a directory of gentlemen of coat-armour*, 7th edn, 1 (1929), 642 · d. cert.

Archives Bodl. Oxf., notebooks mainly relating to Berkshire churches · Dorset RO, genealogical and antiquarian collections · NL Wales, MSS · PRO, archives | Bodl. Oxf., corresp. with Christopher Wordsworth · Durham Cath. CL, H. H. Henson MSS · priv. coll., Noble MSS · Tyne and Wear Archives Service, Newcastle upon Tyne, Armstrong Whitworth MSS, letters to Lord Rendel **Likenesses** photographs, c.1883–1922, repro. in Warren, *John Meade Falkner* · photograph, c.1915, repro. in K. Warren, *Armstrongs of Elswick* (1989) **Wealth at death** £215,524 7s. 1d.: probate, 28 Nov 1932, CGPLA Eng. & Wales

Falkner, Sir (Donald) Keith (1900–1994), singer and college administrator, was born on 1 March 1900 at Sawston, near Cambridge, the youngest son of John Charles Falkner, a schoolmaster, and his wife, Alice Hannah, *née* Wright. He was educated as a chorister at New College School, Oxford, during the period when Sir Hugh Allen was director of the choir. Later he attended the Perse School, Cambridge, and during the final years of the First World War trained for the Royal Naval Air Service at the Royal Naval College, Greenwich. After demobilization he decided to become a professional singer, and in 1920 he enrolled at the Royal College of Music, where his former mentor, Allen, was now director.

Falkner had developed a fine, firm, and resonant bass-baritone voice, and during his six years at the Royal College of Music he sang in the choir of St Paul's Cathedral (1923–7) and also took the role of the Constable in the first performance of Ralph Vaughan Williams's first opera, *Hugh the Drover*, produced at the college on 7 July 1924, prior to its professional première on 14 July at His Majesty's Theatre. He also studied in London with the great Irish bass-baritone Harry Plunket Greene (whose superb diction he acquired), in Vienna with Theo Lierhammer, in Berlin with Grenzebach, and in Paris with D. Dossert.

Having been launched on a highly successful career as a concert singer and recitalist, Falkner appeared throughout the UK and in Europe and North America. He sang in Hubert Parry's oratorio *Job* at the Three Choirs festival in 1925, and the same year appeared for the first time at the Henry Wood Promenade Concerts; he became a particular favourite with the Prom audiences. At a concert with the Bach Choir in 1927 he took on for the first time the part of Christ in Bach's St Matthew passion, which he sang with the Bach Choir annually until the outbreak of the Second World War, and which became his most famous interpretation. On 2 June 1930 he married, at Christ Church, Chelsea, the pianist Christabel Margaret (1902/3–1990), the only daughter of Thomas Fletcher Fullard, a foreign correspondent; they had two daughters.

In 1931 Falkner made the first of eight annual tours of the USA, singing with orchestras such as the Boston Symphony and the New York Philharmonic and appearing at the Cincinnati music festival (1935 and 1937), then directed by Eugene Goossens, and the Bach festival in Bethlehem, Pennsylvania. He visited Canada, South Africa, and New Zealand, as well as Austria, the Netherlands, France, and other European countries. His repertory included the bass arias from Bach's B minor mass, the title role of Mendelssohn's oratorio *Elijah*, the bass part in Handel's oratorio *Alexander's Feast*, and the bass solo in Beethoven's *Missa solemnis*, which he sang at the Leeds festival in 1937 under the baton of Sir Thomas Beecham.

As a recitalist Falkner excelled in English songs, in which he gave the words and the music equal weight, so that they were perfectly matched. At many of his recitals he was accompanied by his wife. Among his many recordings was a selection of English madrigals by Giles Farnaby, Orlando Gibbons, Thomas Morley, John Wilbye, and Thomas Weelkes, sung alongside the soprano Isobel Baillie and other soloists, about which Edward Sackville-West and Desmond Shawe-Taylor wrote in *The Record Guide* (1951): 'Keith Falkner in particular can be heard drawing a delightfully firm and delicate bass line.'

During the Second World War Falkner served in an administrative capacity with the Royal Air Force, and from 1946 to 1950 he was music organizer for the British Council in Italy, based in Rome. He organized many concerts and recitals of British music, in a number of which he sang himself, though his professional career as a singer was over. In 1950 he became professor of singing at Cornell University in the USA, the first incumbent of the post, which he held very successfully for ten years. After returning to the UK in 1960 he took on the directorship of his alma mater, the Royal College of Music, where, during the fourteen years of his tenure, he was responsible for a great many improvements, both to the building and to the institution and its running.

Falkner introduced masterclasses by distinguished musicians from Britain and abroad. He arranged for the return of the college's collection of manuscripts from the British Library in 1961, and the Parry Library was restored to house the collection. In 1965 a building was erected to contain a recital hall and the first electronic music studio in a British music college, and in 1970 a museum for the Donaldson collection of instruments was opened. Falkner instituted exchange concerts and scholarships with foreign students, many of whom now attended the Royal College. One of the founders of the Association of Heads of European Conservatoires, he later became its president. He was knighted in 1967 and appointed a fellow of the Royal Society of Arts in 1979.

After he left the Royal College of Music in 1974 Falkner did not immediately retire from the music scene. He was artistic director of the King's Lynn festival (1981–3) and vice-president of the Royal College of Music from 1984 until his death. His wife, Christabel, died in 1990, after sixty years of marriage. Falkner himself died of kidney and heart failure, resulting from ischaemic heart disease, on 17 May 1994 at his home, Low Cottages, St Margaret's Road, Ilketshall St Margaret, Suffolk. He was survived by his two daughters. ELIZABETH FORBES

Sources *New Grove* · *The Times* (20 May 1994) · *The Independent* (3 June 1994) · E. Sackville-West and D. Shawe-Taylor, *The record guide* (1951) · J. Day, *Vaughan Williams* (1961) · J. Falkner, *Keith Falkner* (1998) · b. cert. · m. cert. · d. cert. · WWW [forthcoming] · Burke, *Peerage* · CGPLA Eng. & Wales (1994)

Archives FILM BFI NFTVA, films made in London in 1930s | SOUND BL NSA, current affairs recordings · BL NSA, documentary recordings · BL NSA, performance recordings · BL NSA, recorded talk
Likenesses photographs, News Int. RO, *The Times* archive · photographs, repro. in *Royal College of Music Magazine* · photographs, repro. in Falkner, *Keith Falkner*
Wealth at death £280,837: probate, 23 Nov 1994, *CGPLA Eng. & Wales*

Falkner, Thomas (1707–1784), Jesuit and missionary in South America, the son of Thomas Falkner (or Falconer), a Presbyterian apothecary, and his wife, Hannah (*née* Walker), was born at Manchester on 6 October 1707 and baptized at Manchester parish church on 12 October 1707. He was educated at Manchester grammar school. He studied medicine in London under Richard Mead, and physics and mathematics under Isaac Newton, who is said to have considered Falkner his favourite pupil.

After practising as a surgeon at home, Falkner joined a slave ship of the South Sea Company in Guinea, partly to improve his own health by a sea voyage, partly on behalf of the Royal Society, which was interested in the research of Jesuit doctors in American Indian herbal medicine. Having arrived in Buenos Aires on 7 May 1730, he headed for Chile with a caravan of slaves, through Santa Fé, Córdoba, and Mendoza, to Santiago de Chile. He returned to Buenos Aires, dangerously ill, and was treated by the Jesuit Sebastián de San Martín with such kindness that he became a Catholic and sought entry into the Society of Jesus. He became a Jesuit novice of the Paraguay province in May 1732, being ordained in 1739 and professed in 1749. Having published his treatise on Indian medicines for the Royal Society, he was sent to Santiago del Estero, Tucumán, Córdoba, and Santa Fé to further his research, and then joined an expedition to Patagonia.

Although several of his manuscript scientific works are now lost, Falkner made an important contribution to introducing Enlightenment ideas into South America. In Córdoba he introduced experiments in the natural sciences and followed Christian Wolff (1679–1754) in his philosophy lectures, while in Paraguay he was looked upon as a Galenist. He spent thirty-eight years as a missionary, at first around Paraguay and in Tucumán, and then, from 1741 until 1753, working as a missionary and doctor in the southern Pampa, notably in the reduction of Our Lady of Concepción. Here he assisted Father Matias Strobel in his mission to the Patagonian Indians. After an unsuccessful expedition to found a new reduction at Sierra de Volcan (Laguna de los Padres), near Mar del Plata, he returned to Buenos Aires to study Indian dialects. With Father José Cardiel in August 1746 he established the reduction of Our Lady of Pilar. Since he knew the country so well, he was appointed to accompany Strobel in 1748 on an expedition as far as the Rio Negro. The Jesuits realized that his medical skills would give him superiority over native witchdoctors. Like the Indians, Falkner lived on horseflesh, and for a plate used his hat, which became so greasy that it was devoured by wild dogs while he slept. In 1751 he took charge of *estancias* in Santa Fé, but continued

his scientific interests. He moved to the college of Córdoba in 1756, where he converted to Catholicism twenty British survivors from the man-of-war *Lord Clive*. In 1758 he was probably the first to occupy the new chair of mathematics at Córdoba.

In July 1767 the Jesuits were expelled from Córdoba, and Falkner returned to England via Cadiz and Sardinia. He joined the English province of the Society of Jesus about 1771, and after a period in Lancashire acted as chaplain to Robert Berkeley (1713–1804) at Spetchley Park, Worcester. There his vivid memoirs were tamed into the abridgement *A Description of Patagonia* (1774), edited by William Combe with Berkeley's help, which Charles Darwin used while on board *The Beagle*. He then became chaplain to the Beringtons at Winsley, Herefordshire, and the Plowdens at Plowden Hall, Shropshire. He died at Plowden Hall on 30 January 1784 and was buried at Lydbury North, Shropshire. Thomas Pennant, who met him at Spetchley and edited his book *Of the Patagonians* (1788), remarked that his long involvement with the Patagonian Indians had made him lose all European guile and acquire the simplicity and honest impetuosity of that people.

C. W. SUTTON, rev. GEOFFREY SCOTT

Sources G. Furlong, *Tomás Falkner y su 'Acerca de los patagones'* (1788) (Buenos Aires, 1954) · R. F. Doublet, 'An Englishman in Rio de la Plata', *The Month*, new ser., 23 (1960), 216–26 · G. Furlong Cardiff, *Misiones y sus pueblos guaraníes* (1962) · P. Caraman, *The lost paradise* (1975) · D. Mitchell, *The Jesuits: a history* (1980) · H. Jedin and J. Nolan, eds., *History of the church*, 6 (1981) · J. Kirk, *Biographies of English Catholics in the eighteenth century*, ed. J. H. Pollen and E. Burton (1909) · Gillow, *Lit. biog. hist.*, vol. 2 · G. Furlong, *Nacimiento y desarrollo de la filosofiá en el Rió de la Plata* (1952) · G. Oliver, *Collections towards illustrating the biography of the Scotch, English and Irish members, SJ* (1838) · H. Storni, 'Tómas Falkner', *New Catholic encyclopedia* (1967–89) · E. Burton, 'Falkner, Thomas', *Catholic encyclopedia*, 5 (1909)
Archives Archives of the British Province of the Society of Jesus, London, Thorpe MSS

Falkner, William (*d.* 1682), Church of England clergyman, was admitted sizar at St Catharine's College, Cambridge, on 20 December 1648, migrated to Peterhouse on 6 July 1650, and graduated BA in 1652–3. He became a fellow of Peterhouse in 1654 and proceeded MA in 1656. He was ordained deacon in Lincoln on 8 June 1661 and priest two days later. By 1662, when a son, Thomas, was buried, Falkner had married Susan (1639/40–1680), daughter of Thomas Greene, merchant, alderman, and mayor of King's Lynn. They had at least two sons and three daughters who died young and a son, William, who survived his parents. By October 1662 he was described as preacher of St Nicholas Chapel in Lynn.

Falkner published *Libertas ecclesiastica, or, A discourse, vindicating the lawfulness of those things, which are chiefly excepted against in the Church of England, especially in its liturgy and worship* (1674). As its full title suggests this work was an argument for religious uniformity. Falkner was committed to the national vocation of the Church of England. While he held the established church to be legitimated by God's word he also held that it was the role of the church to affirm royal supremacy. The church, therefore, had an

William Falkner (d. 1682), by John Sturt, pubd 1684

important role in legitimating the crown, and he maintained that the church had to discharge this duty in order to secure blessing for the realm. Falkner sincerely desired that the prayer book should be an instrument of national unity through the weekly round of services, and held that nothing could be adduced that could 'hinder pious men from hearty joining therein, or yielding unfeigned assent thereto' (Falkner, *Libertas ecclesiastica*, 55).

Richard Baxter was somewhat dismissive of Anglican claims that Falkner's text was unanswerable. He conceded Falkner to be 'a sober learned man' and 'indeed he speaketh plausibly to many of the nonconformists smallest exceptions'. Nevertheless, on a whole range of weightier matters Baxter found 'his defence is so poor and slight, as is fit to satisfy no judicious man, that is not prepared for error by interest and will' (*Reliquiae Baxterianae*, pt 3, 108).

In 1679 Falkner also published *Christian Loyalty*, a book apparently completed by mid-1678 and prompted by the parliamentary defeat of two bills in the 1677 session. It read as a tory alternative to exclusion, which aimed to impose limitations on the ecclesiastical power of a Catholic monarch, while at the same time enhancing the power and authority of the bishops. The succession would stand, but the church would be protected from the monarch by removing from the civil power all authority in spiritual matters. A popish prince would be expected to practise his religion privately while upholding the protestant church in public. Clearly Falkner's literary efforts

gained the approval of the Anglican hierarchy and in 1679 he was appointed rector of Glemsford, Suffolk. He became a DD in 1680.

Falkner died at King's Lynn on 9 April 1682. Several of his works were published posthumously, including *Two Treatises*, edited by William Sherlock in 1684, to which some sermons were added which detail Falkner's ideal for the Anglican clergy.

STUART HANDLEY and RICHARD J. GINN

Sources DNB · W. Falkner, *Libertas ecclesiastica* (1674) · W. Falkner, *Two treatises … to which are annexed three sermons*, ed. W. Sherlock (1684) · Venn, *Alum. Cant.* · M. Goldie, 'Danby, the bishops and the whigs', *The politics of religion in Restoration England*, ed. T. Harris, P. Seaward, and M. Goldie (1990), 77–105 · *Reliquiae Baxterianae, or, Mr Richard Baxter's narrative of the most memorable passages of his life and times*, ed. M. Sylvester, 1 vol. in 3 pts (1696), pt 3, p. 108 · B. Mackerell, *The history and antiquities of the flourishing corporation of Kings-Lynn in the county of Norfolk* (1738), 124–5 · H. Harrod, *Report on the deeds and records of the borough of King's Lynn* (1874), 147
Likenesses J. Sturt, line engraving, BM, NPG; repro. in W. Falkner, *Two treatises* [see illus.]

Falkus, Hugh Edward Lance (1917–1996), angler and naturalist, was born on 15 May 1917 at Melton, Cornwall Road, Cheam, Surrey, during a zeppelin raid, the son of James Everest Falkus, bank clerk (shortly bank manager), and his wife, Alice Maud, *née* Musgrove. His father retired from the City early and lived on a boat on the Essex marshes and then on another boat in Devon. Falkus, who was educated at the East Anglian School, Bury St Edmunds, Suffolk, caught his first fish when he was four, learned to shoot when he was six, and was an expert helmsman by the age of fifteen. By eighteen he had learned to fly and at twenty he became a pilot in the RAF. On 11 July 1939 he married Doris Marjorie (b. 1915/16), daughter of Harold Walter, garage proprietor. They had two sets of twins (three sons and a daughter). The youngest son died in infancy.

Falkus was a brilliant and headstrong pilot who had many brushes with death, partly because he insisted on performing aerobatics in all types of plane, including bombers. By 1941 he was flying Spitfires. He was scrambled to intercept enemy bombers, ran out of fuel, and crash landed in France. He was wearing only his pyjamas under his flying suit and the Germans took him for a spy. He narrowly avoided summary execution but for the intervention of an English-educated Wehrmacht major-general, who entertained him to champagne and cigars before he was sent on to prison camps in Poland and Germany. He made numerous attempts to escape, working on thirteen tunnels including the famous wooden horse tunnel. However, he refused to participate in the 'Great escape' of March 1944, trying to dissuade others from doing so; fifty of those who escaped were caught and shot. Falkus finally broke out and reached England ten days before the war ended.

Falkus's years as a prisoner of war left deep scars. He resolved that 'no one else is going to give me another order, no one is going to shout at me again' (*Daily Telegraph*). His first marriage had ended in 1947 and by the late 1940s he was making documentary films for cinema and television, including the acclaimed *Drake's Island* (1950).

He also gave broadcasts for the BBC, where he developed friendships with Dylan Thomas, Louis MacNeice, and his second wife, Diana Jane Vaughan (*b.* 1922/3), editor of *Argosy* and daughter of Rowland Vaughan, schoolmaster. They married on 22 December 1950. Five months later, Falkus, with his wife and a crew, was shooting *Shark Island* (1952) off the west coast of Ireland when his boat hit a rock and went down. He and his boatman collected floating objects for his wife and crewmen to hold on to while they swam for help, but only Falkus survived. He went on to finish the film, which again was received with international acclaim, and donated the proceeds of it to the dependants of the lost crew. On 18 July 1952 he married Lady Margaret Frances Anne Muntz (1910–1966), divorced wife of Frederick Alan Irving Muntz and second of four daughters of Charles Stewart Henry Vane-Tempest-Stewart, seventh marquess of Londonderry. The marriage ended in divorce in 1958 and on 15 November that year Falkus (who was now living at Cragg Cottage, Ravenglass, Cumberland, under Ravenscrag in the Esk valley) married Kathleen Armstrong (*b.* 1931/2), daughter of Benjamin Armstrong, farmer, of Cragg Farm, Ravenglass. There were no children of the marriage, which was a happy one.

Falkus made several films for the BBC's natural history unit and narrated many programmes, including all forty episodes of Jacques Cousteau's *The Undersea World of Jacques Cousteau*. In the 1960s he collaborated with Niko Tinbergen, the Nobel prize-winning specialist in animal behaviour, on a series of outstanding wildlife films, including *Signals for Survival* (1969), which won the Italia prize in that year and the American blue ribbon in 1971. *The Gull Watchers*, *The Sign Readers*, *The Beachcombers*, *The Riddle of the Rook* (shown at the Venice Film Festival in 1972), and *The Tender Trap* (awarded a certificate of merit by the British Association for the Advancement of Science in 1975) followed. Two highly personal films, *Salmo the Leaper* (1977) and the semi-autobiographical *Portrait of a Happy Man* (1982) were highly successful. In 1982, Falkus was awarded the Cherry Kearton medal by the Royal Geographical Society for his wildlife work. He was also a highly successful author. He would write all night, aided by copious doses of whisky. *Nature Detective* (1978) was a highly regarded study of animal tracks and signs, and *The Stolen Years* (1965; 2nd edn, 1979)—'the best book I've written' (*Daily Telegraph*)—gave a vivid account of his early life.

Falkus will be best remembered, however, as one of the greatest writers and authorities the world has ever seen on salmon and sea trout fishing. He became fascinated by sea trout which, like salmon, spend part of their lives in rivers and part in the sea. Through years of dedicated study he concluded that sea trout fed mostly at night in the sea, and devised a series of strategies to trigger similar responses in rivers, though, for physiological reasons, they do not feed in fresh water. His book, *Sea Trout Fishing* (1962, 1975) revolutionized sea trout fishing. He also co-authored, with Fred Buller, *Fresh Water Fishing* (1975), a book of immense scholarship and charm, which has become the standard work on the subject and ran through

nine editions by 1987. His *Salmon Fishing* (1984) was regarded from its publication as the authority on the subject. His *Speycasting: a New Technique* (1994) described an advanced method of casting for salmon, and was another best-seller.

Falkus was a restless and iconoclastic figure, with the stature and looks of a *Boy's Own Paper* hero and a life to match. He could be intolerant and generous, egotistical and loyal, outspoken and compassionate. He could inspire fear in some, and complete devotion in others, touched by his deep kindness. Despite his share of tragedy, he insisted that his life had been predominantly happy. Through his lucid prose, dedicated research, and piscatorial wisdom he can be considered as one of the greatest angler–writers of the twentieth century.

In his final years Falkus suffered from cancer. He died of bronchopneumonia at Cragg Cottage on 30 March 1996. He was survived by his fourth wife, Kathleen, by two children from his first marriage—Malcolm, professor of economic history in Australia, and a daughter who became a nun at Stanbrook Abbey. His oldest son Christopher, publisher, died in 1995.   KENNETH ROBSON

Sources H. Falkus, *The stolen years* (1965) · *The Times* (1 April 1996) · *The Independent* (2 April 1996) · *Daily Telegraph* (2 April 1996) · *WWW* · b. cert. · m. certs. · d. cert. · private information (2004) · personal knowledge (2004)
Likenesses photograph, repro. in *The Times* · photograph, repro. in *The Independent* · photograph, repro. in *Daily Telegraph*
Wealth at death under £145,000: administration with will, 5 Aug 1996, *CGPLA Eng. & Wales*

Fall, James (1646/7–1711), university principal and Church of Scotland and Church of England clergyman, was born of unknown parents, who were related to merchants in Leith and Dunbar. He graduated MA at Edinburgh University in 1665. After serving as governor in the family of Sir Thomas Hope of Craighall he accompanied the sons of Sir George Mowat of Ingliston to France in 1672. Later he attended Lord Charles Bruce at Utrecht and Paris. The bishop of London ordained him deacon in 1678 and priest in 1679. From 1680 to 1683 Fall acted as governor to the earl of Queensberry's two eldest sons in France and Italy and left an account of their travels, eventually published as *Memoires of my Lord Drumlangrig's … Travells Abroad* (1931).

Fall's acquaintance with Catholic and protestant scholars and divines in France broadened his theological and ecclesiastical outlook, and reinforced the pietistic influence of Archbishop Robert Leighton. Scottish friends and patrons consulted him about their foreign book purchases. Thanks to Queensberry he became historiographer royal in 1682, but although he translated some Italian histories, he is not known to have written any historical work.

Appointed principal of Glasgow University in June 1684 Fall was created doctor of theology at St Andrews on 6 August. As principal he made a lasting contribution by improvements to the buildings and precincts. Losing the favour of the duke of Perth in 1686 he was replaced as historiographer by Christopher Irvine. In 1689 he was an important agent representing the grievances of the rabbled and deprived episcopal clergy at court. Although a Williamite and generously latitudinarian, he could not conform to the re-established presbyterian system nor subscribe to the confession of faith. When reluctantly depriving Fall of office in September 1690 the commissioners of visitation of the university acknowledged his good management and his improvement of its revenues.

It was owing to the archbishops of Canterbury and York, rather than to his old friend Gilbert Burnet, bishop of Salisbury, that Fall was appointed precentor of York Minster in February 1692. In this refuge he gladly adapted to Anglican ways, leading the daily offices, modulating his accent, and becoming a respected member of the cathedral community and of antiquarian circles. His friend Sir Robert Sibbald described him as 'of great learning, of a penetrating mind, and of a solid judgement, one that knoweth the world, men and business well' (Maidment, 135). As executor of Robert Leighton, Fall edited and published his commentaries and discourses on the Psalms and the first epistle of Peter in 1693 and 1694. He maintained warm friendships across the confessional divide in Scotland, and revisited Scotland to help the trustees of Leighton's library at Dunblane.

Appointed archdeacon of Cleveland in 1700 Fall also enjoyed the wealthy rectory of Londesborough, 1707–8. Having bequeathed his fine French and Italian books to the minster library, he died unmarried at his home in Minster Yard, York, on 12 June 1711, aged sixty-four, and was buried in the lady chapel of the minster.

TRISTRAM CLARKE

Sources J. F. Leishman, 'Principal James Fall of Glasgow (1647–1711)', *Transactions of the Glasgow Archaeological Society*, new ser., 7 (1924), 342–50 · letters to R. Wylie, 1670–1707, NL Scot., Wodrow MS Qto 30, fol. 26 · J. Maidment, ed., *Analecta Scotica: collections illustrative of the civil, ecclesiastical and literary history of Scotland*, 2 vols. (1834–7), vol. 1, p. 135 · C. Innes, ed., *Munimenta alme Universitatis Glasguensis / Records of the University of Glasgow from its foundation till 1727*, 3, Maitland Club, 72 (1854), 589–94 · T. Clarke, 'The Williamite episcopalians and the Glorious Revolution in Scotland', *Records of the Scottish Church History Society*, 24 (1990–92), 33–51 · C. B. L. Barr, 'The minster library', *A history of York minster*, ed. G. E. Aylmer and R. Cant (1977), 509–11 · 'Letters relating to the Leightonian Library, Dunblane, 1703–1710', *The Bannatyne miscellany*, ed. D. Laing, 3, Bannatyne Club, 19b (1855), 265–72 · M. C. T. Simpson, 'Some aspects of book purchasing in Restoration Scotland: two letters from James Fall to the earl of Tweeddale, May 1678', *Edinburgh Bibliographical Society Transactions*, 6/1 (1990–2002), 2–9 · D. Butler, *The life and letters of Robert Leighton* (1903) · J. Fall, *Memoires of my Lord Drumlangrig's and his brother Lord William's travells abroad for the space of three years beginning Septr 13th 1680* (1931) · will, dated 9 May 1711, Borth. Inst., wills, 67, fol. 265
Archives BL, Birch collection, MSS · Bodl. Oxf., MSS Rawl. · Christ Church Oxf., Wake MSS · Glos. RO, Lloyd-Baker-Sharp MSS · NL Scot., Wodrow MSS · NL Scot., Edward Lightmaker MSS, MS 3650 · University of Stirling, Leighton Library, MSS
Wealth at death books left to clergy and York Minster Library; money to relations, servants, and York charity schools; money and household goods to manservant: will, 9 May 1711, Borth. Inst., wills, 67, fol. 265

Falle, Philip (1656–1742), historian and Church of England clergyman, was born in St Saviour, Jersey, the son of

Thomas Falle (1629–1673), farmer, centenier or parish constable of St Saviour from 1658 to 1660, and his wife, Marie Dumaresq (d. before 1670). The eldest of four surviving brothers and half-brothers and two sisters descended from an old Jersey family, Falle was sent to England at an early age, and educated at a school kept by a Transylvanian in Great Queen Street in London and then by a Mr Dalgarno, probably George Dalgarno, in Oxford. Late in 1669 he was entered at Exeter College, Oxford, but he followed his tutor at Exeter, Narcissus Marsh, to St Alban's Hall on Marsh's becoming principal there in 1673. He proceeded MA from St Alban's Hall in 1676, and was ordained deacon by Bishop Ralph Brideoake of Chichester in 1677, and priest by Brideoake's successor, Dr Guy Carleton, in 1679.

In 1681 Falle was presented to Trinity parish in Jersey by the governor, Sir John Lanier. The stipend was about £40 a year. Falle also inherited an estate from his father and served the religious needs of the island's garrison, then without a chaplain. In 1687 Lord Jermyn, Lanier's successor, took Falle back to England with him as tutor for his only son. Falle lived at Rusbrook, Suffolk, Jermyn's country seat, until he returned to Jersey in 1689. In 1690 he received the appointment of St Saviour's.

As a clergyman Falle was a member of the states of Jersey, where he played an active role. A zealous English patriot and francophobe, he was an obvious choice for the delegation sent by the states to beg assistance of William III against French raiders in 1692. He may have drafted the address as well. Falle and Nicholas Durrell, the advocate-general of Jersey, introduced by Jermyn, waited on William at Kensington on 6 February 1693 and also called upon government officials to press their case, succeeding in gaining more military supplies for Jersey. Falle was appointed chaplain-in-ordinary to the king in 1694, and in that capacity preached a sermon on 20 December on Queen Mary's death. He eventually settled in England, and his Jersey parishioners were served by a series of curates. He received a stall at Durham Cathedral in January 1700 and a living at Shenley, near St Albans, in 1709, upon which he resigned his living in Jersey.

During his mission in 1692 and 1693, Falle was struck by the ignorance of Jersey shown by the English people he met at the court and in London. Determining to make the island, and what he considered to be its fierce loyalty to the English crown, better known to public opinion, he wrote his most significant work, *An account of the Isle of Jersey, the greatest of the islands that are now the only remainder of the English dominions in France, with a new and accurate map of that island*. It appeared in two editions during his life, in 1694, dedicated to William, then greatly expanded with a substantial documentary appendix in 1734. It was based on materials collected by Falle's friend and parishioner the Jersey magistrate John Poingdestre and also benefited from contributions by Phillip Dumaresq, including the map. The 1734 edition included a letter from Falle's friend Philip Morant refuting the argument of John Selden's *Mare clausus* (1635) that the Channel Islands had always been an English possession. *An account of the Isle of Jersey* was strongly providentialist, emphasizing how God had defended Jersey from the French and in latter years from Catholicism. Falle also argued that Jersey and the Channel Islands generally were great economic and military assets to England in its struggle with France. Although undistinguished in style and marred by credulity, Falle's work, which included discussion of the island's institutions and natural history, was the first and for a long time the standard work on Jersey, reprinted as late as 1837. Falle contributed an account of the Channel Islands to Edmund Gibson's edition of William Camden's *Britannia* in 1722, and published several sermons, including one in Jersaise, mostly during the reign of William III. He also saw through the press *The History of the Last Campagne in the Spanish Netherlands, anno. Dom. 1693* (1693) by his friend and fellow Jerseyman the Revd Edward Dauvergne, contributing a fulsome letter of dedication to the duke of Ormond.

Falle travelled to France, and to the United Provinces as one of William's chaplains. On the continent he collected many printed music books. His music manuscripts included the only surviving works of Sainte-Colombe the younger, the French violist resident in Britain, of whom he may have been a student. Falle donated his printed music books, 266 items with substantial representation of music published in Antwerp, Amsterdam, and Venice, and his musical manuscripts, together with his catalogue, to the library of the dean and chapter of Durham. His other books he presented to the people of Jersey in 1736 together with money to build a library, although it was not built until 1742. Along with other donations, they have developed into the Jersey Library in St Helier.

Falle never married. His will reveals that he maintained a household in Durham, supervised by 'my agent and steward there … Mrs Elizabeth Robinson, wife of Mr Michael Robinson', who had 'been faithfull and diligent in my Business during many years', but that he lived at Shenley with his niece Judith Aubin (PRO, PROB 11/719, fols. 230r–232r). He died at Shenley on 7 May 1742 and was buried on 12 May at St Botolph's, Shenley.

WILLIAM E. BURNS

Sources E. Durell, 'Sketch of the life of the Reverend Philip Falle', in P. Falle, *An account of the island of Jersey*, [new edn.] (1837) · *DNB* · Wing, *STC* · PRO, PROB 11/719, fols. 230r–232r · J. Dunford, *Sainte-Colombe le fils, 'Tombeau pour Mr de Sainte-Colombe le père: 5 suites pour viole seule'* [CD, Adès 206042 (March 1997); liner notes] · J. Boswell, *The book of Shenley* (1985) · U. Durham L., archives and special collections · private information (2004) · B. Crosby, *A catalogue of Durham Cathedral music manuscripts* (1986), 79

Archives BL, corresp. with Philip Morant, Add. MS 37216

Likenesses portrait, Jersey Library, St Helier

Falleron, James (*fl.* 1439–1463), merchant, was a native of Venice, who settled in London, being first attested in the capital in 1439. During the year from October 1440 to October 1441 he was assigned to the supervision of the English host Richard Quatremains; although no view of his own trade survives, he is known to have brokered the sale of English cloth worth £145 to the Venetian galley patron James Corner by a provincial draper in January 1442. Falleron's career as a merchant reached its peak in the 1450s, although direct evidence for his activity in London

is slim. He exported English cloth worth just over £244 on the Venetian galleys in 1449/50, and imported ginger, mace, and pepper worth almost £40 in 1450, as well as forty butts of sweet wine from a Genoese carrack in February 1457. Originally a householder in Broad Street ward in 1441, he was still resident in the Broad Street and Bishopsgate area in September 1449 and in Bishopsgate in August 1451, being recorded as a Venetian merchant stranger on both the latter occasions. He was granted letters of denization by 27 May 1452, and took the freedom of London by redemption on 27 January 1453 on the surety of four of his fellow drapers. This did not, however, stop the grocer John Payne seizing a consignment of wood and wine belonging to Falleron at Southampton in 1457, as part of a campaign against Italian merchants by the London grocers. By 1463 Falleron was alleged to be in the service of the earl of Warwick (*d.* 1471), captain of Calais and the marches, but his protection on that account was withdrawn because he was still in London.

However, it seems likely that at least some of Falleron's business interests were based outside the capital. For instance, in partnership with the Venetian Francesco de Nicholo and the Londoners Richard Acreman and Robert Glover, he farmed the old shafts of a mine called Higesbale, at Lockridge Hill, Bere Ferrers, in Devon. The site appears to have been just to the north of Plymouth, and north-west of Bere Ferrers, closer in fact to Bere Alston. The mine was one of a group of three royal silver mines at Bere Alston, Bere Ferrers, and Combe Martin which had been pledged to the Frescobaldi in 1299. These mines had a chequered history, having yielded quite well during the period 1290–1340, except apparently during the period when they were held by the Frescobaldi. The indentures drawn up between Falleron and the German clerk Adrian Sprynker, warden of the gold and silver mines of Devon and Cornwall, were dated 20 March 1453, and were to run for twelve years. The lease was taken up from 3 June 1452, which may have been the underlying reason for Falleron's acquisition of denizen status just beforehand. This and his citizenship, some eight months after the date of the indentures, would have helped him greatly in the project, giving him liberty to trade without English supervision and to move goods through the country without payment of toll. According to the usual rules, he and his partners paid the king one-tenth of the ore produced, the slags and deadwork being purified at their own expense. But the venture proved less successful than Falleron might have hoped. In his account of the workings of the mine, prepared for royal officials after four and a half years, he claimed to have spent over £250 on pumping alone as the mine was subject to continual flooding, quite apart from other sums laid out to cover essential works. There was no profit. Falleron's lease was one of several to be granted during the fifteenth century, most of which were unproductive, and the workings were abandoned by 1500.

H. L. BRADLEY

Sources PRO, Exchequer, king's remembrancer, accounts various, E 101/128/33 · PRO, Exchequer, king's remembrancer, accounts various, E 101/512/2 [part of E 101/128/30] · recognisance roll, 21, 27 Jan 1453, CLRO • PRO, E 101/265/18 • P. E. Jones, ed., *Calendar of plea and memoranda rolls preserved among the archives of the corporation of the City of London at the Guildhall*, 5: *1437–1457* (1954), 19/1/1439 • *CPR, 1452–67* • PRO, E 122/73/23, E 122/73/25, E 122/203/4 • PRO, E 179/144/42, E 179/235/23, E 179/144/64 • W. G. Hoskins, *Devon* (1954) • P. Nightingale, *A medieval mercantile community: the Grocers' Company and the politics and trade of London, 1000–1485* (1995), 507

Fallows, Fearon (1788–1831), astronomer, was born in Cockermouth, Cumberland, on 4 July 1788, the son of John Fallows, a hand-loom weaver of sufficient education to act as clerk in the neighbouring parish of Bridekirk. Although he was brought up to his father's trade, he was a keen student of mathematics. With the help of the Revd H. A. Hervey, vicar of Bridekirk, he became assistant to the headmaster of Plumbland School. Supported by an anonymous patron, in October 1809 he entered St John's College, Cambridge, whence he graduated as third wrangler in the mathematics tripos, after John Herschel and George Peacock. He held a mathematical lectureship at Corpus Christi College for two years, and was then elected a fellow of St John's. He was ordained deacon in 1815 and priest in 1819, and was elected to the Royal Society in June 1820. In 1821 he married Mary Anne Hervey, the eldest daughter of the vicar. The fellows of the newly founded Astronomical Society had lobbied extensively in influential quarters for an observatory in the southern hemisphere, and as a result an order in council of George IV was issued on 20 October 1820 directing the establishment of an astronomical observatory at the Cape of Good Hope.

Although his experience of practical astronomy was rather slight, Fallows was appointed astronomer by the board of longitude, largely on an enthusiastic recommendation by Sir John Herschel. Fallows consulted with John Rennie, who, as his last work, had designed the observatory building on the lines of that at Cambridge—that is, two residences with flat roofs for telescope domes joined by a central section devoted to meridian instruments. Fallows and his wife embarked on the 360 ton *Sappho* on 4 May 1821, accompanied by his assistant James Fayrer, the son of a London instrument maker. The ship docked at the naval base at Simonstown, where Fallows to his dismay found no funds available to have his instruments transported to Cape Town. They eventually came round the peninsula by sea at his own expense before being stored in the town granary. From a lodging in town Fallows made positional observations of 273 southern stars, the first such since those of Lacaille seventy years before, which were published by the Royal Society in 1824. After several expeditions to explore the area, Fallows chose for the permanent observatory a site between the Liesbeeck and Black rivers near their confluence, about 3 miles from the town, but there were long delays before construction could commence in 1825.

Meanwhile Fallows's assistant Fayrer had been dismissed for drunkenness, and a replacement, the (Catholic) Revd Patrick Scully, was fired for sexual misconduct. Nevertheless Fallows had happily participated in many aspects of colonial life, including acting as chaplain to the forces. As a fellow of the Royal Society he took an active part in local scientific and intellectual activity, and later arranged to conduct divine service in one of the observatory rooms. He personally supervised excavation of the foundations for a building constructed according to a rather amateurish scheme of his own, but fortunately a professional clerk of works, John Skirrow, arrived in February to build it in local stone. An unexpected cargo of Burmese teak provided material for the roof, shutters, and internal joinery. The roof was finished in lead. A professional assistant, Captain William Ronald, arrived on 19 November 1826; although appointed two years previously, he had been kept in London to inspect the principal meridian instruments of the observatory and to accompany them to South Africa. The instrument cases were somewhat roughly handled during landing at the wharf and damage was feared. Fallows always praised the transit circle used to determine right ascensions, but the mural circle, used for declinations, proved erratic, a failing due not to damage, but, as was found many years later, to a defect of construction. Fallows was an assiduous observer; he constructed necessary features such as meridian pillars for the adjustment of these instruments, provided primitive time signals for ships in Table Bay by the discharge of a pistol on the roof at settled times, and made regular observations of stars, sun, moon, and planets, most of which were published by his successors.

Fallows himself published in 1830 measurements of the local acceleration of gravity from pendulum observations. Ronald took sick leave in October 1830 and left for England, to be replaced by a young clerk, James Robertson, but Fallows had to call on his wife for astronomical assistance. Skirrow departed for a colonial post, but supervised the installation of the roof domes—never to be occupied in Fallows's time. Worn out by overwork and relentless official parsimony, Fallows fell ill with scarlet fever and, in spite of a recuperative visit to Simonstown, died at the observatory on 25 July 1831. He was buried there, in front of the main building, at his own request, 12 feet deep under a slab of Robben Island stone. Mrs Fallows, with whom he had only one son, who died young, returned to England with all his papers and unpublished observations, which she handed over to the Admiralty.

A. M. CLERKE, *rev.* DAVID S. EVANS

Sources D. S. Evans, *Under Capricorn: a history of southern hemisphere astronomy* (1988) • D. Gill, *A history and description of the Royal Observatory, Cape of Good Hope* (1913) • B. Warner, *Royal Observatory, Cape of Good Hope, 1820–1831: the founding of a colonial observatory* (1995) • B. Warner, 'The Age of Fallows', *Monthly Notes, Astronomical Society of Southern Africa*, 56 (1997), 107
Archives CUL, department of manuscripts and university archives, corresp. and papers • RS, corresp.
Likenesses portrait, repro. in Warner, *Royal Observatory*

Falls, Cyril Bentham (1888–1971), military historian and journalist, was born in Dublin on 2 March 1888, the elder son in the family of three children of Sir Charles Fausset Falls (1860–1936), who represented Fermanagh and Tyrone at Westminster from 1924 to 1929, and his wife, Clare, daughter of William Bentham JP of co. Dublin. He was educated in England at Bradfield College and London University, in Ireland at Portora Royal School, Enniskillen, co. Fermanagh, and on the continent; but he remained a loyal Ulsterman throughout his life.

In 1914 Falls joined the 11th battalion of the Royal Inniskilling Fusiliers, which formed part of the 36th (Ulster) division—a remarkable formation which had grown out of the paramilitary Ulster Volunteer Force raised by Sir Edward Carson to defend Ulster against home rule. In 1915 he married Elizabeth, daughter of George Heath, farmer; they had two daughters. Falls went to France with his battalion in that year and served on the western front for the remainder of the war, at regimental duty, on the staff of the 36th and later the 62nd divisions, and finally as liaison officer with the French, with the rank of captain; he was twice mentioned in dispatches and twice cited for the Croix de Guerre.

At the conclusion of the war Falls was employed to write the history of the 36th division, work which brought him into contact with the team writing the official history of the war for the historical section of the committee of imperial defence. He joined that team in 1923 and remained with it until 1939, writing the official volumes on the Egyptian and Palestine campaigns (1928), on the Macedonian campaign (1933), and one volume on the campaign on the western front in 1917 (1940). A fluent and prolific writer and one deeply versed in English and French literature, he also published numerous articles and reviews which made his name familiar to the reading public at large. In 1939 he was the natural choice to succeed Captain B. H. Liddell Hart as the military correspondent of *The Times*, a task he fulfilled throughout the war and until 1953 with great distinction. Falls's deep knowledge of military matters, his good contacts with senior military figures, and his balanced judgement made his comments on the course of the war widely appreciated by both military and civil readers.

After the war Falls was elected to the Chichele chair of the history of war in Oxford (which brought with it a fellowship of All Souls), a post he held from 1946 to 1953 and which enabled him, while lecturing on military history in general, to focus his researches on his first love and to write two works on Irish military history, *Elizabeth's Irish Wars* (1950) and *Mountjoy: Elizabethan General* (1955). After his retirement he continued to produce a stream of books of which perhaps the most notable was *The First World War* (1960), while at the same time writing a weekly commentary on political affairs for the *Illustrated London News*.

Falls was a small, neat man who cultivated an elegant Edwardian moustache and took justifiable pride in his immaculate appearance. A somewhat dry manner concealed a wide range of historical and literary interests, and a deep humanity which found expression in all that he wrote. He attached great importance to conveying the realities of war as they were experienced by the men fighting it, and his *History of the 36th (Ulster) Division* (1922) contains some of the finest descriptions of conditions on the western front to be found anywhere in the literature of the war. But he had no time for those historians who concentrated on the horrors of war to the exclusion of all else, and his critical study *War Books* (1930) set the anti-war literature in a balanced historical context. He never claimed to be making any major contribution to strategic thought, but he did much to improve the general understanding of the nature and problems of war in an age of rapid technological transition; and his historical works are notable for their solid knowledge, their good sense, and the distinction of their prose.

Falls was made a CBE in 1967. He lived in later life at 16 Archery Close, London, and died at Walton-on-Thames, Surrey, on 23 April 1971. MICHAEL HOWARD, *rev.*

Sources *The Times* (24 April 1971) · personal knowledge (1986) · private information (1986) · *CGPLA Eng. & Wales* (1971)
Likenesses H. Coster, photographs, 1940–49, NPG · photograph, All Souls Oxf.
Wealth at death £25,312: probate, 16 Sept 1971, *CGPLA Eng. & Wales*

Falmouth. For this title name *see* Berkeley, Charles, earl of Falmouth (*bap.* 1630, *d.* 1665); Boscawen, Hugh, first Viscount Falmouth (*c.*1680–1734); Boscawen, Edward, first earl of Falmouth (1787–1841).

Fancourt, Samuel (1678–1768), librarian and Presbyterian minister, was born at Oakham, Rutland, one of the four boys and two girls of Richard Fancourt, a prosperous merchant, and Anne Tresham. He was educated at the dissenting academy in Hungerford, Berkshire, under Benjamin Robinson and was ordained minister on 24 May 1709. He had married Martha Clempson on 5 August 1706 in Hungerford and remained there until 1715 or 1716, when he moved to become minister of Wilton, 3 miles west of Salisbury. In 1721 he moved to Salisbury and settled in the Dolphin Chequer, but subsequently moved to Salt Lane, where he lived from 1723 to 1742.

In 1735 Fancourt 'contrived a Circulating Library for the Entertainment of distant as well as home Subscribers' (Fancourt, 4). This was an innovative but over-ambitious venture which aimed to supply a wide range of books and pamphlets for a fee of a half-guinea a year, plus 5s. for delivery, within a 60 miles radius of Salisbury. In late 1741 or early 1742 he issued a catalogue advertising books in English and French of his New Circulary Library at Salisbury, but the library proved uneconomical: 'at Salisbury they would yield nothing', as he later described it (ibid., 5). He and his wife moved their possessions and a 5000 volume circulating library on wagons to London and settled at 6 Crane Court, off Fleet Street, in late 1742. From here he recommenced his business as the First Universal Circulating Library, which was succeeded by the Second Universal Circulating Library (1745–50), and finally the Associated Circulating Library (1750–*c.*1760). From 1746 to 1748 he issued in parts a comprehensive two-volume library catalogue, which listed the books, in English, French, and Latin, alphabetically and included a subject index.

Fancourt's home was adjacent to the Royal Society, and while this proximity was good for business it brought him into direct conflict with the powerful secretary to the society, Dr Cromwell Mortimer. A physician notorious for charging high fees, he had treated Martha Fancourt and published an account of her illness with his *Address to the public: containing narratives of the effects of certain chemical remedies in most diseases* in 1745. This, coupled with Mortimer's interference in Fancourt's library, caused great difficulties in his library until Mortimer's death in 1752. As a fellow Presbyterian, Mortimer was one of several fellows of the Royal Society who were included in the original deed of trust of the library, yet he soon meddled in the library's affairs by criticizing Fancourt's management and by using his considerable influence for negative purposes, which made a business that was of doubtful viability even more precarious. In 1760 Fancourt and his wife retired to Hoxton Square, Shoreditch, London—a pleasant area popular with dissenters and home to a dissenting academy, the Hoxton Independent Academy—and he died there on 8 June 1768. He was buried in Bunhill Fields.

Fancourt was a resolute, innovative librarian who provided 'the link between the Clerical Subscription Libraries of the 17th and 18th centuries and the secular subscription libraries and book clubs of later times' (Kelly, 146). A tenacious theologian and author of eighteen books and pamphlets published between 1720 and 1745, Fancourt debated such complex theological questions as 'the Doctrine of Reprobation', 'Divine Prescience', and the 'Freedom of Will' both within the Presbyterian church and outside. These doctrinal debates were described as 'swelling into so many Volumes that no Head can compass it' and brought him into conflict with Bishop Benjamin Hoadly of Salisbury. It was librarianship, however, that became his primary vocation, and he devised schemes for the delivery of library services both in Salisbury and in London and produced library catalogues that were far ahead of his time and not bettered until the following century.

MONTE LITTLE

Sources S. Fancourt, 'Narrative', DWL, Walter Wilson MS A8 · *VCH Wiltshire*, vol.6 · A. D. McKillop, 'English circulating libraries, 1720–50', *The Library*, 4th ser., 14 (1933–4), 477–85 · *Salisbury Journal* · *Daily Advertiser* [London] · *Lloyds Evening Post* (6–8 June 1768) · T. Kelly, *Early public libraries* (1966) · *GM*, 1st ser., 2 (1732), 863, 953 · *GM*, 1st ser., 54 (1784), 273ff. · I. Parker, *Dissenting academies in England* (1914), 86 · *DNB* · H. de Shortt, *City of Salisbury* (1957) · B. M. Little, 'A study of libraries in Salisbury, 1700–1850', fellowship diss., Library Association, 1973 [copies held by Library Association and Salisbury Reference Library] · *IGI* · 'The tombs in Bunhill Fields', *Transactions of the Congregational Historical Society*, 4 (1909–10), 362 · *VCH Rutland*, 2.185 · W. H. Summers, *History of the Berkshire, south Buckinghamshire and south Oxfordshire congregational churches* (1905) **Archives** DWL, Walter Wilson MSS

PICTURE CREDITS

Elder, Sir (William) Stewart Duke-(1898–1978)—© National Portrait Gallery, London

Elder, Thomas (*bap.* 1737, *d.* 1799)—courtesy of the University of Edinburgh's Collections

Elder, William (*fl.* 1680–1701)—© National Portrait Gallery, London

Eleanor [of Aquitaine], *suo jure* duchess of Aquitaine (*c.*1122–1204)—photograph: AKG London

Eleanor [of Provence] (*c.*1223–1291)—The British Library

Eleanor [of Castile] (1241–1290)—© Dean and Chapter of Westminster

Elen, Ernest Augustus (1862–1940)—© National Portrait Gallery, London

Elgar, Sir Edward William, baronet (1857–1934)—© National Portrait Gallery, London

Elias, John (1774–1841)—by courtesy of the National Library of Wales

Eliot, Edward Craggs-, first Baron Eliot (1727–1804)—private collection / National Portrait Gallery, London

Eliot, Edward Granville, third earl of St Germans (1798–1877)—private collection. Photograph: Photographic Survey, Courtauld Institute of Art, London

Eliot, Grace (1754?–1823)—© The Frick Collection, New York

Eliot, Sir John (1592–1632)—private collection

Eliot, Thomas Stearns (1888–1965)—© Cecil Beaton Archive, Sotheby's; collection National Portrait Gallery, London

Eliott, George Augustus, first Baron Heathfield of Gibraltar (1717–1790)—© The National Gallery, London

Elizabeth (*c.*1437–1492)—The Royal Collection © 2004 HM Queen Elizabeth II

Elizabeth [of York] (1466–1503)—The Royal Collection © 2004 HM Queen Elizabeth II

Elizabeth, Princess (1596–1662)—© The National Gallery, London

Elizabeth, margravine of Brandenburg-Ansbach-Bayreuth (1750–1828)—private collection; photograph © Christie's Images Ltd

Elizabeth I (1533–1603)—© National Portrait Gallery, London

Ellerman, Sir John Reeves, first baronet (1862–1933)—© News International Newspapers Ltd

Ellice, Edward (1783–1863)—© Copyright The British Museum

Ellicott, John (1702/3–1772)—© Copyright The British Museum

Elliot, Jean (1727–1805)—Scottish National Portrait Gallery

Elliotson, John (1791–1868)—by permission of the Royal College of Physicians, London

Elliott, Sir Claude Aurelius (1888–1973)—© reserved; collection Eton College; photograph National Portrait Gallery, London

Elliott, Denholm Mitchell (1922–1992)—© Kenneth Hughes / National Portrait Gallery, London

Elliott, Ebenezer (1781–1849)—Rotherham Libraries Museums and Arts Service

Ellis, Alexander John (1814–1890)—© National Portrait Gallery, London

Ellis, Sir (Bertram) Clough Williams-(1883–1978)—© John Hedgecoe; collection National Portrait Gallery, London

Ellis, (Henry) Havelock (1859–1939)—by permission of the E. O. Hoppé Trust, Curatorial Assistance, Inc., Los Angeles; collection National Portrait Gallery, London

Ellis, Sir Henry (1777–1869)—© National Portrait Gallery, London

Ellis, John (1698–1791)—© National Portrait Gallery, London

Ellis, John (1874–1932)—PA Photos

Ellis, Mary Baxter (1892–1968)—© National Portrait Gallery, London

Ellis, Ruth (1926–1955)—Getty Images – Hulton Archive

Ellis, Welbore, first Baron Mendip (1713–1802)—Christ Church, Oxford

Ellis, William (1794–1872)—© National Portrait Gallery, London

Ellis, Sir William Henry (1860–1945)—© Institution of Civil Engineers; collection National Portrait Gallery, London

Ellis, William Webb (1807–1872)—© National Portrait Gallery, London

Elliston, Robert William (1774–1831)—© National Portrait Gallery, London

Ellmann, Richard David (1918–1987)—© Estate of Seán O'Mordha

Elmes, Harvey Lonsdale (1814–1847)—© National Portrait Gallery, London

Elmes, James (1782–1862)—RIBA Library Photographs Collection

Elmhirst, Dorothy Payne (1887–1968)—The Dartington Hall Trust Archive

Elmhirst, Sir Thomas Walker (1895–1982)—© National Portrait Gallery, London

Elmy, Elizabeth Clarke Wolstenholme (1833–1918)—Mary Evans / The Women's Library

Elphinston, James (1721–1809)—© National Portrait Gallery, London

Elphinstone, George Keith, Viscount Keith (1746–1823)—The Royal Collection © 2004 HM Queen Elizabeth II

Elphinstone, Mountstuart (1779–1859)—Ashmolean Museum, Oxford

Elphinstone, William George Keith (1782–1842)—© National Portrait Gallery, London

Elssler, Fransiska (1810–1884)—© Copyright The British Museum

Elstob, Elizabeth (1683–1756)—© Copyright The British Museum

Elton, Sir Arthur Hallam Rice, tenth baronet (1906–1973)—© Wolfgang Suschitzky / National Portrait Gallery, London

Elton, Charles Sutherland (1900–1991)—© reserved; collection Corpus Christi College, Oxford; photograph

News International Syndication / National Portrait Gallery, London

Elton, (James) Frederic (1840–1877)—© National Portrait Gallery, London

Elton, Sir Geoffrey Rudolph (1921–1994)—© News International Newspapers Ltd

Elton, Godfrey, first Baron Elton (1892–1973)—© National Portrait Gallery, London

Elton, Oliver (1861–1945)—University of Liverpool Art Gallery and Collections

Elvey, Maurice (1887–1967)—© National Portrait Gallery, London

Elwell, Ann Catherine (1922–1996)—© reserved; News International Syndication; photograph National Portrait Gallery, London

Elwes, Henry John (1846–1922)—Royal Horticultural Society, Lindley Library; photograph National Portrait Gallery, London

Elwes, John (1714–1789)—© National Portrait Gallery, London / Country Life Picture Library

Elwin, (Harry) Verrier Holman (1902–1964)—by kind permission of Wycliffe Hall, Oxford

Elwin, Whitwell (1816–1900)—© National Portrait Gallery, London

Elyot, Sir Thomas (*c.*1490–1546)—The Royal Collection © 2004 HM Queen Elizabeth II

Eméleus, Harry Julius (1903–1993)—reproduced courtesy of the Library and Information Centre, Royal Society of Chemistry

Emerson, Peter Henry (1856–1936)—© Copyright The British Museum

Emerson, William (1701–1782)—© National Portrait Gallery, London

Emery, Richard Gilbert (1915–1983)—Camera Press

Emery, Winifred (1861–1924)—© National Portrait Gallery, London

Emlyn, Thomas (1663–1741)—© National Portrait Gallery, London

Emma (*d.* 1052)—The British Library

Emmet, Dorothy Mary (1904–2000)—© National Portrait Gallery, London

Emmet, Robert (1778–1803)—National Gallery of Ireland

Emmet, Thomas Addis (1764–1827)—National Gallery of Ireland

Emmott, Alfred, Baron Emmott (1858–1926)—© National Portrait Gallery, London

Empson, Sir William (1906–1984)—© Estate of Rupert Shephard; collection National Portrait Gallery, London

Engels, Friedrich (1820–1895)—© National Portrait Gallery, London

Englefield, Sir Henry Charles, seventh baronet (*c.*1752–1822)—© National Portrait Gallery, London

Engleheart, George (1750–1829)—© National Portrait Gallery, London

English, Sir David (1930–1998)—© Nikki English

Ennals, David Hedley, Baron Ennals (1922–1995)—PA Photos

Entwistle, William James (1895–1952)—© National Portrait Gallery, London

Epstein, Brian Samuel (1934–1967)—© Robert Whitaker; collection National Portrait Gallery, London

Epstein, Sir Jacob (1880–1959)—© Tate, London, 2004; The Garman Ryan Collection, The New Art Gallery, Walsall

Equiano, Olaudah (*c.*1745–1797)—© National Portrait Gallery, London

Erasmus, Desiderius (*c.*1467–1536)—private collection. Photograph: Photographic Survey, Courtauld Institute of Art, London

Erdélyi, Arthur (1908–1977)—courtesy of D. S. Jones, F.R.S.

Ernest (1830–1904)—The Royal Collection © 2004 HM Queen Elizabeth II

Ernest Augustus (1771–1851)—© National Portrait Gallery, London

Erpingham, Sir Thomas (*c.*1355–1428)—photograph © Norwich Cathedral; photographer Mike Trendell

Errol, Bert (1883–1949)—Getty Images – Hulton Archive

Erskine, David, second Lord Cardross (*bap.* 1627, *d.* 1671)—photograph by kind permission of The National Trust for Scotland

Erskine, David Steuart, eleventh earl of Buchan (1742–1829)—© National Portrait Gallery, London

Erskine, Ebenezer (1680–1754)—Scottish National Portrait Gallery

Erskine, Edward Morris (1817–1883)—© reserved

Erskine, Henry, third Lord Cardross (1650–1693)—Scottish National Portrait Gallery

Erskine, Henry (1746–1817)—Ashmolean Museum, Oxford

Erskine, John, eighteenth or second earl of Mar (*c.*1562–1634)—Scottish National Portrait Gallery

Erskine, John, styled twenty-second or sixth earl of Mar and Jacobite duke of Mar (*bap.* 1675, *d.* 1732)—in the collection of the Earl of Mar and Kellie at Alloa Tower; photograph courtesy the Scottish National Portrait Gallery

Erskine, John (1721–1803)—Scottish National Portrait Gallery

Erskine, Rachel, Lady Grange (*bap.* 1679, *d.* 1745)—in the collection of the Earl of Mar and Kellie; photograph courtesy the Scottish National Portrait Gallery

Erskine, Ralph (1686–1752)—Scottish National Portrait Gallery

Erskine, Thomas, first Baron Erskine (1750–1823)—The Honourable Society of Lincoln's Inn. Photograph: Photographic Survey, Courtauld Institute of Art, London

Erskine, Thomas, of Linlathen (1788–1870)—Scottish National Portrait Gallery

Esau, Abraham (1864–1901)—© reserved / Cambridge University Press

Escoffier, Georges Auguste (1846–1935)—© reserved

Essex, William (1784–1869)—Photography by Stan Speel

Estcourt, James Bucknall Bucknall (1802–1855)—© National Portrait Gallery, London

Esten, Harriet Pye (1761?–1865)—Garrick Club / the art archive

Etty, William (1787–1849)—© Manchester City Art Galleries

Eustace (II), count of Boulogne (d. c.1087)—by special permission of the City of Bayeux

Eustace fitz John (d. 1157)—© Copyright The British Museum

Eustace the Monk (c.1170–1217)—Master and Fellows of Corpus Christi College, Cambridge

Evans, Sir Arthur John (1851–1941)—Ashmolean Museum, Oxford

Evans, Sir (Robert) Charles (1918–1995)—The Royal Geographical Society, London

Evans, Sir Charles Arthur Lovatt (1884–1968)—© National Portrait Gallery, London

Evans, Dame Edith Mary (1888–1976)—Getty Images – Sasha

Evans, Edward Ratcliffe Garth Russell, first Baron Mountevans (1880–1957)—The de László Foundation; Witt Library, Courtauld Institute of Art, London

Evans, Florence Annie [Nancy] (1915–2000)—Getty Images – Bert Hardy

Evans, Sir Frederick John Owen (1815–1885)—© National Maritime Museum, London

Evans, Sir George de Lacy (1787–1870)—© National Portrait Gallery, London

Evans, Sir Geraint Llewellyn (1922–1992)—Arnold Newman / Getty Images; collection National Portrait Gallery, London

Evans, (Benjamin) Ifor, Baron Evans of Hungershall (1899–1982)—© courtesy the Artist's Estate / Bridgeman Art Library; The College Art Collections, University of London

Evans, Sir John (1823–1908)—© National Portrait Gallery, London

Evans, Marguerite Florence Laura (1886/7–1964)—© reserved

Evans, Marian [George Eliot] (1819–1880)—© National Portrait Gallery, London

Evans, Philip [St Philip Evans] (1645–1679)—© National Portrait Gallery, London

Evans, William [of Eton] (1798–1877)—private collection

Evans, Sir William David (1767–1821)—© National Portrait Gallery, London

Evatt, Herbert Vere (1894–1965)—© National Portrait Gallery, London

Evelyn, John (1620–1706)—© National Portrait Gallery, London

Evens, George Bramwell (1884–1943)—© reserved; photograph National Portrait Gallery, London

Everard, John (1584?–1640/41)—© National Portrait Gallery, London

Everest, Sir George (1790–1866)—© National Portrait Gallery, London

Everett, Kenny (1944–1995)—© Lewis Morley, courtesy of The Akehurst Bureau; collection National Portrait Gallery, London

Ewing, Sir (James) Alfred (1855–1935)—© National Portrait Gallery, London

Ewing, Juliana Horatia (1841–1885)—Royal Photographic Society

Eyre, Edward John (1815–1901)—© National Portrait Gallery, London

Eyre, Sir James (bap. 1734, d. 1799)—© Crown copyright in photograph: UK Government Art Collection

Eyre, Sir Robert (1666–1735)—© National Portrait Gallery, London

Eysenck, Hans Jurgen (1916–1997)—© Anne-Katrin Purkiss; collection National Portrait Gallery, London

Faber, Frederick William (1814–1863)—© reserved

Faber, Sir Geoffrey Cust (1889–1961)—Estate of Henry Lamb; All Souls College, Oxford

Fage, Arthur (1890–1977)—Godfrey Argent Studios / Royal Society

Fairbairn, Andrew Martin (1838–1912)—© National Portrait Gallery, London

Fairbairn, Sir Nicholas Hardwick (1933–1995)—© News International Newspapers Ltd

Fairbairn, Patrick (1805–1874)—© National Portrait Gallery, London

Fairclough, Samuel (1594–1677)—© National Portrait Gallery, London

Fairey, Sir (Charles) Richard (1887–1956)—Royal Aeronautical Society Library

Fairfax, Anne, Lady Fairfax (1617/18–1665)—unknown collection / Christie's; photograph National Portrait Gallery, London

Fairfax, Thomas, third Lord Fairfax of Cameron (1612–1671)—© National Portrait Gallery, London

Fairlie, Alison Anna Bowie (1917–1993)—by permission of the Syndics of Cambridge University Library

Faithfull, Emily (1835–1895)—© National Portrait Gallery, London

Faithfull, Lilian Mary (1865–1952)—The Cheltenham Ladies' College

Faithfull, Lucy, Baroness Faithfull (1910–1996)—© News International Newspapers Ltd

Falconer, Randle Wilbraham (1816–1881)—Trustees of St John's Hospital, Bath; photograph National Portrait Gallery, London

Falconer, Sir Robert Alexander (1867–1943)—courtesy University of Toronto Archives B1976-0005/P

Falk, Herman Eugene (1820–1898)—from the Salt Museum, Northwich

Falkner, Anna Maria (d. 1796/7)—© National Portrait Gallery, London

Falkner, William (d. 1682)—© National Portrait Gallery, London